ENCYCLOPAEDIA OF OCCUPATIONAL HEALTH AND SAFETY

ENCYCLOPAEDIA OF OCCUPATIONAL HEALTH AND SAFETY

4TH EDITION

2

Editor-in-Chief
Jeanne Mager Stellman, PhD

Senior Associate Editor
Michael McCann, PhD, CIH

Associate Editors
Leon Warshaw, MD   Carole Brabant, PhD

Senior Editors

John Finklea, MD, Dr PH	Jacqueline Messite, MD
Georges H. Coppée, MD	Steven L. Sauter, PhD
Vilma R. Hunt, BDS, AM	Jerry Spiegel, MA, MSc
Richard S. Kraus, PE, CSP	Colin L. Soskolne, PhD
Wolfgang Laurig, Dr-Ing	Benedetto Terracini, MD

Melvin L. Myers, BS, MPA

Managing Editor
Chantal Dufresne, BA

INTERNATIONAL LABOUR OFFICE
GENEVA

Stellman, Jeanne Mager (ed.)
Encyclopaedia of Occupational Health and Safety. 4th ed.
Geneva, International Labour Office, 1998. 4 V.

/Encyclopaedia/, /Occupational health/, /Occupational safety/. 13.04.2
ISBN 92-2-109203-8 (set)
92-2-109814-1 (V. 1)   92-2-109815-X (V. 2)   92-2-109816-8 (V. 3)   92-2-109817-6 (V. 4)

Contents: V. 1. The Body; Health Care; Management and Policy; Tools and Approaches—V. 2. Hazards—V. 3. Chemicals; Industries and Occupations—V. 4.Indexes

ILO Cataloguing in Publication Data

Cover and production design: Robert Silverman Design
Pagesetting by the International Labour Office, Geneva
Printed in the United States of America

A

Ursula Ackermann-Liebrich, *MD, MSc*
Professor
Department of Social and Preventive
    Medicine
University of Basel
Basel
Switzerland

Elena Adán Liébana, *Chem Eng*
Occupational Health and Safety Technician
National Centre of Working Conditions
National Institute for Occupational Safety
    and Hygiene
Barcelona
Spain

Alfred A. Amendola, *PhD*
Research Associate Professor, Associate Director
Safety Engineering Program
Texas A&M University
College Station, Texas
United States

Yngve Anderberg, *MD, PhD*
Fire Safety Design AB
Lund
Sweden

Ragnar Andersson, *PhD, M Eng*
Injury Program Director
Department of Public Health Sciences
Karolinska Institute
Sundbyberg
Sweden

Diego Andreoni, *Dr Ing*
Former Director-General
Ente Nazionale Prevenzione Infortuni
Rome
Italy

Jean Arteau, *Ing, PhD, MSc*
Researcher
Safety and Engineering
Institute for Occupational Safety and
    Health Research
Montreal, Quebec
Canada

B

Tomas Backström, *PhD*
Researcher
National Institute for Working Life
Solna
Sweden

Gabriele Bammer, *PhD*
National Centre for Epidemiology and
    Population Health
Australian National University
Canberra
Australia

Tamas Banky, *Dr*
Head of Fire Protection Scientific Department
Institute for Quality Control and
    Innovation in Building
Budapest
Hungary

Julian Barling, *PhD*
Professor of Organizational Behavior
School of Business
Queen's University
Kingston, Ontario
Canada

Rosalind C. Barnett, *PhD*
Senior Scholar in Residence
Murray Research Center
Women's Studies Program
Brandeis University
Waltham, Massachusetts
United States

Peter J. Baxter, *MD, MSc*
Institute of Public Health
University of Cambridge
Cambridge
United Kingdom

François Béland, *PhD*
Professor
Groupe de Recherche Interdisciplinaire
    en Santé
University of Montreal
Montreal, Quebec
Canada

Ron Bell, *BSc*
Head
Electrical and Control Systems Unit
Health and Safety Executive
Bootle, Merseyside
United Kingdom

David Bennett, *PhD, MA*
National Director
Workplace Health, Safety and
    Environment
Canadian Labour Congress
Ottawa, Ontario
Canada

Alan J. Benson, *MSc, MB, ChB, FRACS*
Consultant
Royal Air Force School of Aviation
    Medicine
Farnborough, Hants
United Kingdom

María José Berenguer, *M Chem*
Head
Mass Spectrometry Laboratory
National Centre for Working Conditions
National Institute for Occupational Safety
    and Hygiene
Barcelona
Spain

Mats Berg, *MD*
Department of Dermatology
Karolinska Hospital
Stockholm
Sweden

Kenneth I. Berger, *MD*
Instructor of Medicine
Division of Pulmonary and Critical Care
    Medicine
New York University
New York, New York
United States

Ulf Bergqvist, *Dr med sci, MSc Techn*
Research Scientist
Department of Occupational Medicine
National Institute for Working Life
Solna
Sweden

Pier Alberto Bertazzi, *MD, MPH*
Associate Professor
Institute of Occupational Medicine
University of Milan
Milan
Italy

Diane Berthelette, *PhD*
Associate Professor
Department of Administrative Sciences
University of Quebec-Montreal
Montreal, Quebec
Canada

Ronald Bisset, *MA, MSc*
Scott Wilson Resource Consultants
Edinburgh, Scotland
United Kingdom

Jacques H.M. Bittel, *MD, DERBH*
Chief
Human Factors Department
Army Health Service Research
    Centre-Emile Pardé
La Tronche
France

Massimo Bovenzi, *MD*
*Senior Physician, Contract Professor of Industrial
    Hygiene*
Institute of Occupational Medicine
University of Trieste
Trieste
Italy

Carole Brabant, *PhD*
Associate Editor
Encyclopaedia of Occupational Health and Safety
International Labour Office
Geneva
Switzerland

John Brazendale, *BSc, MSc*
Principal Specialist Inspector
Health and Safety Executive
Bootle, Merseyside
United Kingdom

Cecilia Brighi
International Policy Department
CISL National Trade Union
   Confederation
Rome
Italy

Robert Bringer, *PhD*
Staff Vice-President (Retired)
Environmental Technology and Services
3M
St. Paul, Minnesota
United States

Peter Bruckmann, *PhD*
Head of Division
Environmental Monitoring
Landesumweltamt, Nordrhein-Westfalen
Essen
Germany

Françoise Burhenne-Guilmin,
   Dr Law
Head
Environmental Law Centre
International Union for the Conservation
   of Nature
Bonn
Germany

Ronald J. Burke, *PhD*
Professor
Faculty of Administrative Studies
York University
North York, Ontario
Canada

Ahmet Çakir, *Dr-Ing, F Erg S*
Scientific President
Ergonomic Institute for Social and
   Occupational Sciences
Berlin
Germany

Donald M. Campbell, *FFPHM*
Consultant in Public Health Medicine
Scottish Centre for Infection and
   Environmental Health
Glasgow
United Kingdom

Robert D. Caplan, *PhD*
*Professor of Psychology, Psychiatry and Behavioral
   Science*
Department of Psychology
George Washington University
Washington, DC
United States

Pascale Carayon, *PhD*
Visiting Professor
Ecole des Mines de Nancy
Nancy
France
Associate Professor
Department of Industrial Engineering
University of Wisconsin
Madison, Wisconsin
United States

Sue Cartwright, *PhD*
Senior Research Fellow
Manchester School of Management
University of Manchester
Manchester
United Kingdom

Emilio Castejón Vilella, *Ing Ind*
Director
National Centre of Working Conditions
National Institute for Occupational Safety
   and Hygiene
Barcelona
Spain

Weiping Chen, *MD, MSc*
Health Risk Assessment Specialist
Health Strategies and Research Division
Alberta Health
Edmonton, Alberta
Canada

V. I. Chernyuk, *MD, ScD*
Professor, Scientific Director
Institute for Occupational Health
Kiev
Ukraine

Robert N. Cherry Jr., *PhD, MS*
Colonel and Director of Army Radiation Safety
HQDA (DACS-SF)
U.S. Army
Washington, DC
United States

Eric Chivian, *MD*
Director
Center for Health and the Global
   Environment
Harvard Medical School
Boston, Massachusetts
United States

Renzo Comini
Responsable
DSG Unita' Centrale Sicurezza Ed Igiene
   del Lavoro
ENEL SpA
Rome
Italy

Cary L. Cooper, *PhD, MBA, MSc*
Professor of Organizational Psychology
Institute of Science and Technology
University of Manchester
Manchester
United Kingdom

Georges H. Coppée, *MD*
Chief of Medical Section
Occupational Safety and Health Branch
International Labour Office
Geneva
Switzerland

D. Wayne Corneil, *ScD*
Director
Operations Eastern Region
Health Canada
Ottawa, Ontario
Canada

Robert Coyle
Principal Environmental Specialist
European Bank for Reconstruction and
   Development
London
United Kingdom

Derrick Crump, *PhD*
Section Head, Indoor Air Quality
Materials Group
Building Research Establishment
Watford
United Kingdom

Göran Dahlström, *MD*
Commanding Medical Officer, Director
Cold Center
Kiruna
Sweden

J.C. Davies, *PhD, MSc*
Principal Programmer/Analyst
Computing Services Department
University of Liverpool
Liverpool
United Kingdom

Nicole Dedobbeleer, *ScD*
Associate Professor of Research
Department of Social and Preventive
   Medicine
University of Montreal
Montreal
Canada

Edouard I. Denisov, *Cand tech sci*
Senior Researcher
RAMS Institute of Occupational Health
Moscow
Russian Federation

S.K. Dheri
Chief Fire Officer
Headquarters Delhi Fire Service
New Delhi
India

Leonard A. Dobrovolsky, *MD, PhD, D Sci*
Head
Department of Scientific and Medical
 Information
Institute of Occupational Health
Kiev
Ukraine

Alexander E. Donagi, *D Sc, MPH*
Professor
School of Medicine
Tel Aviv University
Director
Information Centre
Institute of Occupational Safety and
 Hygiene
Tel Aviv
Israel

Marianne Döös, *BSc*
Senior Researcher
National Institute for Working Life
Solna
Sweden

Dennis P. Driscoll, *PE, MSc*
President
Associates in Acoustics Inc.
Evergreen, Colorado
United States

Dougal Drysdale, *BSc, PhD*
Reader in Fire and Safety Engineering
Department of Civil and Environmental
 Engineering
University of Edinburgh
Edinburgh, Scotland
United Kingdom

Walter Dümmer, *MPh*
Technical Advisor
Chilean Safety Association
Santiago
Chile

William W. Eaton, *PhD, MS*
Professor
Department of Mental Hygiene
School of Hygiene and Public Health
Johns Hopkins University
Baltimore, Maryland
United States

John Elias, *MPH*
Senior Occupational Hygienist
Occupational and Environmental
 Medicine
Health Sciences Center
Winnipeg, Manitoba
Canada

Zuheir Ibrahim Fakhri, *MBBS, DIH, MSc OM, MD*
Occupational Health Consultant
Ministry of Health
Riyadh
Saudi Arabia

Anne-Marie Feyer, *PhD*
Director
New Zealand Occupational and
 Environmental Health Research Centre
Dunedin
New Zealand

John Finklea, *MD, Dr PH*
Medical Officer
Center to Protect Workers' Rights
Former Director
National Institute for Occupational
 Safety and Health
Washington, DC
United States

Brian Flannigan, *PhD*
Department of Biological Sciences
Heriot-Watt University
Edinburgh, Scotland
United Kingdom

Dominique Folliot, *MD*
Deputy Head of Department
Service Général de Médecine du Travail
Paris
France

Richard Forster
Lighting Consultant
Crowthorne, Berkshire
United Kingdom

Bernard H. Fox, *PhD*
Professor of Psychiatry
School of Medicine
Boston University
Boston, Massachusetts
United States

T.J.R. Francis, *MSc, PhD, MFOM*
Naval Medical Research Laboratory
Naval Submarine Base
Groton, Connecticut
United States

Marianne Frankenhaeuser, *PhD, MA*
Professor Emeritus of Psychology
University of Stockholm
Stockholm
Sweden

David Freestone, *LLB, LLM*
Legal Adviser, Environment
Environmental and International Law Unit
Legal Department
World Bank
Washington, DC
United States

Jean G. French, *Dr PH*
Adjunct Professor
Department of Epidemiology
School of Public Health
University of North Carolina
Chapel Hill, North Carolina
United States

Daniel Ganster, *PhD*
Professor, Chair
Department of Management
University of Arkansas
Fayetteville, Arkansas
United States

Kenneth Gerecke
Assistant Regional Administrator
Occupational Safety and Health
 Administration
US Department of Labor
Philadelphia, Pennsylvania
United States

Adrian Gheorghe, *PhD, MSc*
Professor of Industrial Management
University Polytechnic
Bucharest, Romania
Director of Research
Swiss Federal Institute of Technology
Zurich
Switzerland

Berenice I. Ferrari Goelzer, *CIH, MPH*
Occupational Hygienist
Office of Occupational Health
World Health Organization
Geneva
Switzerland

Des Gorman, *MD, PhD*
Head of Occupational Medicine
School of Medicine
University of Auckland
Auckland
New Zealand

Marilyn K. Gowing, *PhD*
Director
Personnel Resources and Development
  Center
United States Office of Personnel
  Management
Washington, DC
United States

Per-Ola Granberg, *MD, PhD*
Former Professor of Endocrine Surgery
Karolinska Hospital
Stockholm
Sweden

Martino Grandolfo, *PhD*
Director
Department of Physics
Instituto Superiore di Sanità
Rome
Italy

Casey C. Grant, *PE*
Assistant Vice-President
Codes and Standards Administration
National Fire Protection Association
  International
Quincy, Massachusetts
United States

Michael J. Griffin, *PhD*
Professor of Human Factors
Institute of Sound and Vibration Research
University of Southampton
Southampton
United Kingdom

Jop Groeneweg, *PhD*
Senior Researcher
Centre for Safety Research
Leiden University
Leiden
The Netherlands

Carsten Grønberg, *MSc*
Research Engineer
RISØ National Laboratory
Roskilde
Denmark

Xavier Guardino Solá, *PhD*
Chief of Department
National Centre for Working Conditions
National Institute for Occupational Safety
  and Hygiene
Barcelona
Spain

Juan Guasch Farrás
Head of Working Conditions Area
National Centre for Working Conditions
National Institute for Occupational Safety
  and Hygiene
Barcelona
Spain

Tee L. Guidotti, *MD, MPH*
Professor, Director
Occupational Health Program
Faculty of Medicine
University of Alberta
Edmonton, Alberta
Canada

K.C. Gupta, *BE*
Director-General
National Safety Council
Bombay
India

Niels Jørn Hahn, *MSc*
Managing Director
Working Group on Recycling and Waste
  Minimization
ISWA
Copenhagen
Denmark

Kari K. Häkkinen, *PhD*
Development Manager
Workers' Compensation Department
Industrial Insurance Ltd.
Helsinki
Finland

Andrew R. Hale, *PhD*
Professor of Safety Science
Safety Science Group
Delft University of Technology
Delft
The Netherlands

L.D. Hamilton, *MD, PhD*
Professor
Biomedical and Environmental
  Assessment Group
Brookhaven National Laboratory
Upton, New York
United States

Kjell Hansson Mild, *PhD*
Researcher
National Institute for Working Life
Umeå
Sweden

Richard Helmer, *PhD, MA*
Chief
Urban Environmental Health
World Health Organization
Geneva
Switzerland
Visiting Professor
University of Surrey
Guildford
United Kingdom

Ana Hernández Calleja
Occupational Health and Safety Technician
National Centre of Working Conditions
National Institute for Occupational Safety
  and Hygiene
Barcelona
Spain

Ivanildo Hespanhol
Community Water Supply and Sanitation
World Health Organization
Geneva
Switzerland

Raymond Hétu, *PhD* (deceased)
Former Director
Acoustic Group
Medical Faculty
University of Montreal
Montreal, Quebec
Canada

Manh Trung Ho, *Ing civ*
Former Assistant Director
Applications Prevention
National Institute of Safety and Research
Paris
France

Dietrich Hoffmann, *PhD, MS*
Associate Director
Naylor Dana Institute for Disease
  Prevention
American Health Foundation
Valhalla, New York
United States

Ingvar Holmér, *PhD*
Professor
Department of Ergonomics
National Institute for Working Life
Solna
Sweden

Vilma Hunt, *BDS, AM*
Adjunct Professor
Department of Work Environment
University of Massachusetts-Lowell
Lowell, Massachusetts
United States

Joseph J. Hurrell, Jr., *PhD*
Senior Research Epidemiologist
Hazard Evaluation and Technical
  Assistance Branch
National Institute for Occupational Safety
  and Health
Cincinnati, Ohio
United States

Claire Infante-Rivard, *MD,*
PhD, MPH
Professor
Department of Occupational Health
Faculty of Medicine
McGill University
Montreal, Quebec
Canada

John M. Ivancevich, *DBA*
Hugh Roy and Lillie Cranz Cullen Chair,
Professor of Organizational Behavior and
Management
College of Business Administration
University of Houston
Houston, Texas
United States

C. David Jenkins, *PhD, MA*
Adjunct Professor of Psychiatry and Preventive
Medicine and Community Health
University of North Carolina
Chapel Hill, North Carolina
United States

Steve M. Jex, *PhD*
Associate Professor
Department of Psychology
University of Wisconsin-Oshkosh
Oshkosh, Wisconsin
United States

Jeffrey V. Johnson, *PhD*
Associate Professor of Social Science, Medicine
and Occupational Health
Johns Hopkins School of Hygiene and
Public Health
Baltimore, Maryland
United States

Peter F. Johnson, *MSc, Dipl Ed*
Manager
Arup Fire Engineering
Melbourne, Victoria
Australia

B. Juminer, *PhD**
Faculty of Medicine
Meshed
Islamic Republic of Iran

Kirsten Jørgensen, *PhD, MSc*
Head of Department
Analysis and Documentation Office
Danish Work Environment Service
Copenhagen
Denmark

Friedrich Karl Käferstein,
Dr med vet
Director
Programme of Food Safety and Food Aid
World Health Organization
Geneva
Switzerland

Robert Karasek, *PhD*
Professor of Work Environment
University of Massachusetts-Lowell
Lowell, Massachusetts
United States

Waldemar Karwowski, *PhD*
Director, Professor of Industrial Engineering
Center for Industrial Ergonomics
University of Louisville
Louisville, Kentucky
United States

Gwendolyn Puryear Keita, *PhD*
Associate Executive Director
Public Interest Directorate
Director of Women's Programs
American Psychological Association
Washington, DC
United States

W. Larry Kenney, *PhD*
Professor of Physiology and Kinesiology
Laboratory of Human Performance
Research
Pennsylvania State University
University Park, Pennsylvania
United States

Eric P. Kindwall, *MD*
Associate Professor, Director of Hyperbaric
Medicine
Medical College of Wisconsin
Milwaukee, Wisconsin
United States

Urban Kjellén, *PhD*
Professor of Safety Management
Department of Industrial Economics and
Technology Management
Norwegian University of Science and
Technology
Trondheim
Norway

Tord Kjellström, *MD*
Director
Office of Global and Integrated
Environmental Health
World Health Organization
Geneva
Switzerland

Peter Knauth, *Dr-Ing*
Professor, Head
Department of Ergonomics
Institute of Industrial Production
University of Karlsruhe
Karlsruhe
Germany

Bengt Knave, *MD, PhD*
Head of International Secretariat and Committee
National Institute for Working Life
Solna
Sweden

Larry R. Kohler, *PhD*
Focal Point for Environment and Sustainable
Development
Department of Working Conditions and
Environment
International Labour Office
Geneva
Switzerland

Richard S. Kraus, *PE, CSP*
Principal
Petroleum Safety Consultants
Annandale, Virginia
United States

Yuri Kundiev, *MD, Dr med sci*
Director
Institute for Occupational Health
Kiev
Ukraine

Poul Lauridsen, *MSc*
Technical Advisor
Working Group on Recycling and Waste
Minimization
ISWA
Copenhagen
Denmark

Wolfgang Laurig, *Dr-Ing*
Professor, Director
Department of Ergonomics
Institut für Arbeitsphysiologie
University of Dortmund
Germany

Tom B. Leamon, *PhD, MSc*
Vice-President
Liberty Mutual Insurance Group
Director
Liberty Mutual Research Center for
Safety and Health
Hopkinton, Massachusetts
United States

---

* Contributor to the 3rd edition of this **Encyclopaedia.** This biographical information has not been updated.

Mark R. Lehto, *PhD*
Associate Professor
School of Industrial Engineering
Purdue University
West Lafayette, Indiana
United States

Lennart Levi, *MD, PhD*
Professor Emeritus, Former Director
Department of Stress Research
Karolinska Institute
Stockholm
Sweden

Sture Lidén, *MD, PhD*
Professor
Department of Dermatology
Karolinska Institute
Karolinska Hospital
Stockholm
Sweden

Soo-Yee Lim, *PhD*
National Research Council Associate
Applied Psychology and Ergonomics
    Branch
National Institute for Occupational Safety
    and Health
Cincinnati, Ohio
United States

Kari Lindström, *PhD*
Research Professor
Department of Psychology
Finnish Institute of Occupational Health
Helsinki
Finland

Anthony Linehan, *BA, FIOSH*
Former Director of Field Operations
H.M. Chief Inspector of Factories
Health and Safety Executive
Dorset
United Kingdom

Herbert I. Linn, *MS*
Chief of Information Management and
    Dissemination Activity
Division of Safety Research
National Institute for Occupational Safety
    and Health
Morgantown, West Virginia
United States

Gordon M. Lodde, *BS*
Health Physics Consultant
Mount Joy, Pennsylvania
United States

Wouter A. Lotens, *PhD*
Head
Department of Work Environment
TNO Human Factors Research Institute
Soesterberg
The Netherlands

Jacques B. Malchaire, *PhD, MSc*
Professor of Occupational Health
Unit of Hygiene and Work Physiology
Catholic University of Louvain
Brussels
Belgium

Albert Marty, *HTL Mech Eng*
Senior Safety Engineer for Product Certification
Swiss National Accident Insurance
    Organization
Luzern
Switzerland

Christina Maslach, *PhD*
Professor
Department of Psychology
University of California-Berkeley
Berkeley, California
United States

R. Matthes, *Dip-Ing*
Head NIR Dosimetry, Scientific Secretary
Institut für Strahlenhygiene
Oberschleissheim
Germany

Lucien Y. Maystre, *MSc, Dip-Ing*
Director
Institut de Génie de l'Environnement
Ecole Polytechnique Fédérale de Lausanne
Lausanne
Switzerland

Michael McCann, *PhD*
Senior Associate Editor
Encyclopaedia of Occupational Health and Safety
International Labour Office
New York, New York
United States

Neil McManus, *MSc, M Eng*
Consulting Industrial Hygienist
NorthWest Occupational Health and
    Safety
North Vancouver, British Columbia
Canada

Karlheinz Meffert, *Dr-Ing*
Director
Berufsgenossenschaftliches Institut für
    Arbeitssicherheit
Hauptverband der gewerblichen
    Berufsgenossenschaften
Sankt Augustin
Germany

Claude Menguy, *Dip Ing*
Department Manager
Materials and Environmental Stress
Central Laboratory of Electronic Industries
Fontenay aux Roses
France

Jacqueline Messite, *MD*
Clinical Professor
Department of Environmental Medicine
New York University College of Medicine
New York, New York
United States

Jean-Jacques Meyer, *PhD*
Professor of Ergonomics, Head of Laboratory
Vision Ergonomics Laboratory
Institute of Occupational Health Sciences
Lausanne
Switzerland

James M. Miller, *PE, PhD*
Professor
Industrial and Operations Engineering
University of Michigan
Ann Arbor, Michigan
United States

Timothy H. Monk, *PhD*
Professor of Psychiatry
Western Psychiatric Institute and Clinic
University of Pittsburgh
Pittsburgh, Pennsylvania
United States

Michel Monteau
Head of Accidentology
National Institute of Research and Safety
Vandoeuvre
France

Carles Muntaner, *MD, PhD*
Assistant Professor
Institute of Occupational and
    Environmental Health/Prevention
    Research Center
West Virginia University
Morgantown, West Virginia
United States

Lawrence R. Murphy, *PhD*
Research Psychologist
Applied Psychology and Ergonomics
    Branch
National Institute for Occupational Safety
    and Health
Cincinnati, Ohio
United States

Melvin L. Myers, *BS, MPA*
Deputy Director
Office of Extramural Coordination and
    Special Projects
National Institute for Occupational Safety
    and Health
Atlanta, Georgia
United States

N

Debra L. Nelson, *PhD*
Professor
CBA Associates
Oklahoma State University
Stillwater, Oklahoma
United States

Bodil Nielsen, *Dr Phil*
Associate Professor
August Krogh Institute
Copenhagen University
Copenhagen
Denmark

Sarah A. Nunneley, *MS, MD*
Research Physician
Air Force Research Laboratory
Brooks Air Force Base
San Antonio, Texas
United States

O

Tokuo Ogawa, *MD, PhD*
Professor Emeritus
Aichi Medical University
Nagakute
Japan

Kristina Orth-Gomér, *MD, PhD*
Professor
Department of Public Health Sciences
Karolinska Institute
Stockholm
Sweden

Suzanne C. Ouellette, *PhD*
Professor of Psychology
Graduate School and University Center
City University of New York
New York, New York
United States

P

Kenneth C. Parsons, *PhD*
Professor of Environmental Ergonomics
Department of Human Sciences
Loughborough University
Leicester
United Kingdom

Jonathan A. Patz, *MD, MPH*
Assistant Scientist, Director
Department of Environmental Health
  Sciences
Program on Health Effects of Global
  Environmental Change
Johns Hopkins School of Hygiene and
  Public Health
Baltimore, Maryland
United States

Dan Petersen, *Ed D*
Professor
Arizona State University
President
DPA Consulting Inc.
Tempe, Arizona
United States

Hans-Ulrich Pfeffer, *Dr*
Head of Department
Environmental Monitoring
LandesumweltamtNordrhein-
  Westfalen
Essen
Germany

Chaya S. Piotrkowski, *PhD*
Professor
Graduate School of Social Service
Fordham University
New York, New York
United States

Thomas W. Planek, *PhD, CSP*
Director
Research and Statistical Services
National Safety Council
Itasca, Illinois
United States

Gustav Poinstingl, *Dipl-Ing*
Leiter des Verkehrs-Arbeitsinspektorates
Bundesministerium für öffentliche
  Wirtschaft und Verkehr
Vienna
Austria

Tessa M. Pollard, *D Phil*
Lecturer in Biological Anthropology
Department of Anthropology
University of Durham
Durham
United Kingdom

Charles T. Pope
Area Director
Norfolk Area Office
Occupational Safety and Health
  Administration
US Department of Labor
Norfolk, Virginia
United States

Sydney W. Porter Jr., *BS*
Adjunct Professor
Graduate Institute of Environmental
  Studies
Drexel University
Ardmore, Pennsylvania
United States

Herbert C. Preul, *PhD*
Professor Emeritus
Department of Civil and Environmental
  Engineering
University of Cincinnati
Cincinnati, Ohio
United States

Q

James Campbell Quick, *PhD*
Professor of Organizational Behavior
University of Texas
Arlington, Texas
United States

R

Fernando Ramos Pérez, *Ind Eng*
Management Engineer, Risk Prevention Specialist
Labour Accident Prevention Service
Valencia
Spain

A. Raouf, *PhD*
Rector
GIK Institute
Topi, Swabi
Pakistan

John T. Reeves, *MD*
Professor Emeritus
Department of Medicine and Pediatrics
University of Colorado Health Sciences
  Center
Denver, Colorado
United States

Dietmar A.J. Reinert, *Dr rer nat*
Head of Section
Berufsgenossenschaftliches Institut für
  Arbeitssicherheit
Hauptverband der gewerblichen
  Berufsgenossenschaften
Sankt Augustin
Germany

Michael H. Repacholi, *PhD, MSc*
Responsible Officer
Radiation Protection and Global Hazards
  Assessment
World Health Organization
Geneva
Switzerland

Toni Retsch, *Dipl-Ing, ETH*
Bereichsleiter-ALM2
Swiss National Accident Insurance
  Organization
Luzern
Switzerland

Paule Rey, *MD, MPH*
Professor Emeritus
Faculty of Medicine
University of Geneva
Geneva
Switzerland

J. Rioux, *PhD**
Chaire de parasitologie
Faculté de médecine de Montpellier
Montpellier
France

* Contributor to the 3rd edition of this
Encyclopaedia. This biographical information has
not been updated.

Jean-Marc Robert, PhD
Professor
Department of Mathematics and
  Industrial Engineering
École Polytechnique
Montreal, Quebec
Canada

William N. Rom, MD, MPH
Professor of Medicine
Division of Pulmonary and Critical Care
  Medicine
New York University
New York, New York
United States

Isabelle Romieu, MD, ScD, MPH
Medical Epidemiologist
Pan American Center for Human Ecology
  and Health
Mexico City
Mexico

M. Gracia Rosell, Ing TQ
Head of Gas Chromatography Laboratory
National Institute for Occupational Safety
  and Hygiene
Barcelona
Spain

Denise M. Rousseau, PhD
Professor of Organizational Behavior
Carnegie Mellon University
Pittsburgh, Pennsylvania
United States

Julia D. Royster, PhD
Environmental Noise Consultants Inc.
Raleigh, North Carolina
United States

Larry H. Royster
Department of Mechanical Engineering
North Carolina State University
Raleigh, North Carolina
United States

Sven-Olof Ryding, PhD
Assistant Professor
Managing Director
Swedish EMAS Council
Stockholm
Sweden

Jorma Saari, Dr Tech
Professor
Department of Safety
Finnish Institute of Occupational Health
Helsinki
Finland

Gavriel Salvendy, PhD
NEC Professor of Industrial Engineering
School of Industrial Engineering
Purdue University
West Lafayette, Indiana
United States

Steven L. Sauter, PhD
Chief
Applied Psychology and Ergonomics
  Branch
National Institute for Occupational Safety
  and Health
Cincinnati, Ohio
United States

Gustave Savourey, MD, PhD
Research Specialist in Physiology
Thermophysiology Unit
Research Centre, Army Health
  Service-Emile Pardé
La Tronche
France

John M. Schaubroeck, PhD
Associate Professor
College of Business Administration
University of Nebraska
Lincoln, Nebraska
United States

Lawrence M. Schleifer, EdD
Adjunct Professor
Department of Health Education
University of Maryland
Baltimore, Maryland
United States

Guido Schmitter, HTL
Mechanical and Safety Engineer
Swiss National Accident Insurance
  Organization
Luzern
Switzerland

Paul Schreiber, Dr rer nat
Physicist
Federal Institute for Occupational Safety
  and Health
Dortmund
Germany

Dietrich Schwela, PhD
Urban Environment Health
World Health Organization
Geneva
Switzerland

Helmut Seidel, Dr med sci
Head of Research Group
Biological Effects of Vibration and Noise
Bundesanstalt für Arbeitsschütz und
  Arbeitsmedizin
Berlin
Germany

Hansjörg Seiler, PD, Dr jur
Court Secretary
Swiss Federal Court (Bundesgericht)
Lausanne
Switzerland

Harry S. Shannon, PhD, MSc
Professor
Occupational Health Programme
Department of Clinical Epidemiology and
  Biostatistics
McMaster University
Hamilton, Ontario
Senior Scientist
Institute for Work and Health
Toronto, Ontario
Canada

Victor Shantora, MSc
Director General
Toxics Pollution Prevention Directorate
Environment Canada
Ottawa, Ontario
Canada

Richard L. Shell, PhD
*Professor of Industrial Engineering and
  Environmental Health*
Department of Mechanical, Industrial and
  Nuclear Engineering
University of Cincinnati
Cincinnati, Ohio
United States

Arie Shirom
Professor
Faculty of Management
Tel Aviv University
Tel Aviv
Israel

Niu Shiru, PhD
Professor
Institute of Environmental Health and
  Engineering
Chinese Academy of Preventive Medicine
Beijing
China

Marcel Simard, PhD
Assistant Professor
School of Industrial Relations
University of Montreal
Montreal, Quebec
Canada

Reinald Skiba, Dr-Ing
Professor of Technical Safety / Production
Bergische Universitat-Gesamthochschule
Wuppertal
Germany

David H. Sliney, *PhD*
Commander
Laser Hazards Branch
USA-CHPPM
Aberdeen Proving Ground, Maryland
United States

Gordon S. Smith, *MB, MPH*
Associate Professor
Johns Hopkins University School of Public
   Health
Baltimore, Maryland
United States

Ian R. Smith, *MSc*
LAMP Coordinator
Program Development
Ontario Ministry of Environment and
   Energy
Toronto, Ontario
Canada

Michael J. Smith, *PhD*
Professor
Department of Industrial Engineering
University of Wisconsin
Madison, Wisconsin
United States

Mike Smith, *PhD*
Manchester School of Management
Institute of Science and Technology
University of Manchester
Manchester
United Kingdom

N. A. Smith, *PhD*
Lighting Consultant
Doncaster
United Kingdom

Colin L. Soskolne, *PhD*
Professor, Director of Graduate Training
Department of Public Health Services
University of Alberta
Edmonton, Alberta
Canada

Jerry Spiegel, *MA, MSc*
Director
Pollution Prevention
Manitoba Environment
Winnipeg, Manitoba
Canada

Bengt Springfeldt, *PhD*
Department for Social Medicine and
   International Health
Karolinska Institute
Sundbyberg
Sweden

Jeanne M. Stellman, *PhD*
Editor-in-Chief
Encyclopaedia of Occupational Health and Safety
International Labour Office
Geneva
Switzerland

School of Public Health
Columbia University
New York, New York
United States

Terje Sten, *Cand*
Senior Researcher
Division of Safety and Reliability
Foundation for Scientific and Industrial
   Research
Trondheim
Norway

Andrew Steptoe, *DPhil, DSc*
Professor of Psychology
St. George's Hospital Medical School
University of London
London
United Kingdom

Tom F.M. Stewart, *BSc*
Managing Director
System Concepts Ltd.
London
United Kingdom

Daniel Stokols, *PhD*
Professor, Dean
School of Social Ecology
University of California-Irvine
Irvine, California
United States

Jerry Suls, *PhD*
Professor
Department of Psychology
University of Iowa
Iowa City, Iowa
United States

Alice H. Suter, *PhD*
Principal Consultant
Industrial Audiology and Community
   Noise
Alice Suter and Associates
Ashland, Oregon
United States

German A. Suvorov, *Dr*
Professor of Medicine, Deputy Director
RAMS Institute of Occupational Health
Moscow
Russian Federation

Naomi G. Swanson, *PhD*
Chief
Motivation and Stress Research Section
National Institute for Occupational Safety
   and Health
Cincinnati, Ohio
United States

Gary M. Taylor
Taylor-Wagner Inc.
Willowdale, Ontario
Canada

Benedetto Terracini, *MD*
Former Head
Unit of Cancer Epidemiology
University Hospital and University of
   Turin
Turin
Italy

Lois E. Tetrick, *PhD*
Professor
Department of Psychology
University of Houston
Houston, Texas
United States

Töres Theorell, *MD, PhD*
Professor, Director
National Institute for Psychosocial Factors
   and Health
Stockholm
Sweden

Dennis Tolsma, *MPH*
Director, Prevention and Practice Analysis
Kaiser Permanente Medical Care Program
Atlanta, Georgia
United States

Rüdiger M. Trimpop, *PhD*
Professor
Department of Industrial and
   Organizational Psychology
University of Yena
Yena
Germany

René Troxler, *Dipl-Ing, HTL/STV*
Senior Safety Engineer
Swiss National Accident Insurance
   Organization
Luzern
Switzerland

Tom Tseng, *PhD*
Manager
Toxics Prevention Division
Environmental Protection Branch
Environment Canada-Ontario Region
Downsview, Ontario
Canada

U

Arthur C. Upton, *MD*
Clinical Professor
Environmental and Community
    Medicine
UMDNJ-Robert Wood Johnson
    Medical School
Piscataway, New Jersey
United States

Holger Ursin, *MD*
Professor
Department of Biological and Medical
    Psychology
University of Bergen
Bergen
Norway

V

Johan Van de Kerckhove, *Dr soc sci*
Director
HIVA-VORMING
Professor
Katholieke Universiteit Leuven
Pellenberg
Belgium

Mark A. Veazie, *Dr PH*
National Institute for Occupational Safety
    and Health
Morgantown, West Virginia
United States

Pierre Verger, *MD, MSc, MPH*
Project Manager
Laboratory of Epidemiology and Health
    Risk Analysis
Institute of Nuclear Protection and Safety
Fontenay-aux-Roses
France

Amiran D. Vinokur, *PhD*
Research Scientist
Institute for Social Research
University of Michigan
Ann Arbor, Michigan
United States

Jean-Jacques Vogt, *MD*
Former Deputy Director General
Institut National de Recherche et de
    Sécurité
Paris
France

Georg Vondracek, *Dipl-Ing*
Department of Industrial Machines and
    Control Systems
Swiss National Accident Insurance
    Organization
Luzern
Switzerland

W

Peter Warr, *PhD*
Research Professor
Institute of Work Psychology
University of Sheffield
Sheffield
United Kingdom

David A. Warrell, *DM, DSc*
Professor, Director
Centre for Tropical Medicine
University of Oxford
Oxford
United Kingdom

Leon J. Warshaw, *MD*
Clinical Professor
Department of Environmental Medicine
New York University
New York, New York
United States

John V. Weil, *MD*
Director
Cardiovascular-Pulmonary Research
    Laboratory
University of Colorado Health Sciences
    Center
Denver, Colorado
United States

Edmundo Werna, *PhD*
Research Fellow
South Bank University
Univerity of Sao Paolo
Sao Paolo
Brazil

John B. West, *MD, PhD, DSc*
Professor of Medicine and Physiology
Department of Medicine
University of California-San Diego
San Diego, California
United States

Gunnela Westlander, *PhD*
Professor Emeritus
Department of Psychology
University of Stockholm
Stockholm
Sweden

Marion Wichmann-Fiebig, *MSc*
Dezerucutin Schutz der Atmosphäre
Landesumweltamt des Landes
    Nordrhein-Westfalen
Essen
Germany

Gerald J.S. Wilde, *PhD*
Professor of Psychology
Queen's University
Kingston, Ontario
Canada

Ann M. Williamson, *PhD*
School of Psychology
University of New South Wales
Sydney
Australia

Denis Winter
Deputy Head
Accident Studies Division
Institute for Nuclear Safety and Protection
Fontenay-aux-Roses
France

Ernst L. Wynder, *MD*
President
American Health Foundation
New York, New York
United States

Y

Annalee Yassi, *MD, MSc*
Director
Occupational and Environmental
    Medicine
Health Sciences Centre and Unit
University of Manitoba
Winnipeg, Manitoba
Canada

Z

D. Zannini, *PhD**
Institute of Occupational Medicine
Ospedale San Martino
Genoa
Italy

José Luis Zeballos, *MD, MPH*
Pan American Health Organization
Washington, DC
United States

Bernhard M. Zimolong, *PhD*
Professor
Work and Organizational Psychology
Ruhr University
Bochum
Germany

Thomas Zosel, *BS*
Manager
Environmental Initiatives
3M Inc.
St. Paul, Minnesota
United States

Jozef Zurada, *PhD*
Assistant Professor
Computer Information Systems
University of Louisvillle
Louisville, Kentucky
United States

---

* Contributor to the 3rd edition of this *Encyclopaedia.* This biographical information has not been updated.

VOLUME

2

PART V. PSYCHOSOCIAL AND ORGANIZATIONAL FACTORS

34. Psychosocial and Organizational Factors Steven L. Sauter, Lawrence R. Murphy, Joseph J. Hurrell and Lennart Levi, *Chapter Editors*

PART VII. THE ENVIRONMENT

55. Environmental Pollution Control   **Jerry Spiegel**
                                              and Lucien Y. Maystre, *Chapter Editors*

PART VIII. ACCIDENTS AND SAFETY MANAGEMENT

56. Accident Prevention   **Jorma Saari, *Chapter Editor***

57. Audits, Inspections and Investigations   **Jorma Saari, *Chapter Editor***

PSYCHOSOCIAL AND ORGANIZATIONAL FACTORS

34

Chapter Editor
Steven L. Sauter, Lawrence R. Murphy,
Joseph J. Hurrell and Lennart Levi

Contents

• PSYCHOSOCIAL AND ORGANIZATIONAL FACTORS

Steven L. Sauter, Joseph J. Hurrell Jr.,
Lawrence R. Murphy and Lennart Levi

In 1966, long before *job stress* and *psychosocial factors* became household expressions, a special report entitled "Protecting the Health of Eighty Million Workers—A National Goal for Occupational Health" was issued to the Surgeon General of the United States (US Department of Health and Human Services 1966). The report was prepared under the auspices of the National Advisory Environmental Health Committee to provide direction to Federal programmes in occupational health. Among its many observations, the report noted that psychological stress was increasingly apparent in the workplace, presenting "... new and subtle threats to mental health," and possible risk of somatic disorders such as cardiovascular disease. Technological change and the increasing psychological demands of the workplace were listed as contributing factors. The report concluded with a list of two dozen "urgent problems" requiring priority attention, including occupational mental health and contributing workplace factors.

Thirty years later, this report has proven remarkably prophetic. Job stress has become a leading source of worker disability in North America and Europe. In 1990, 13% of all worker disability cases handled by Northwestern National Life, a major US underwriter of worker compensation claims, were due to disorders with a suspected link to job stress (Northwestern National Life 1991). A 1985 study by the National Council on Compensation Insurance found that one type of claim, involving psychological disability due to "gradual mental stress" at work, had grown to 11% of all occupational disease claims (National Council on Compensation Insurance 1985).[1]

These developments are understandable considering the demands of modern work. A 1991 survey of European Union members found that "The proportion of workers who complain from organizational constraints, which are in particular conducive to stress, is higher than the proportion of workers complaining from physical constraints" (European Foundation for the Improvement of Living and Working Conditions 1992). Similarly, a more recent study of the Dutch working population found that one-half of the sample reported a high work pace, three-fourths of the sample reported poor possibilities of promotion, and one-third reported a poor fit between their education and their jobs (Houtman and Kompier 1995). On the American side, data on the prevalence of job stress risk factors in the workplace are less available. However, in a recent survey of several thousand US workers, over 40% of the workers reported excessive workloads and said they were "used up" and "emotionally drained" at the end of the day (Galinsky, Bond and Friedman 1993).

The impact of this problem in terms of lost productivity, disease and reduced quality of life is undoubtedly formidable, although difficult to estimate reliably. However, recent analyses of data from over 28,000 workers by the Saint Paul Fire and Marine Insurance company are of interest and relevance. This study found that time pressure and other emotional and personal problems at work were more strongly associated with reported health problems than any other personal life stressor; more so than even financial or family problems, or death of a loved one (St. Paul Fire and Marine Insurance Company 1992).

Looking to the future, rapid changes in the fabric of work and the workforce pose unknown, and possibly increased, risks of job stress. For example, in many countries the workforce is rapidly ageing at a time when job security is decreasing. In the United States, corporate downsizing continues almost unabated into the last half of the decade at a rate of over 30,000 jobs lost per month (Roy 1995). In the above-cited study by Galinsky, Bond and Friedman (1993) nearly one-fifth of the workers thought it likely they would lose their jobs in the forthcoming year. At the same time the number of contingent workers, who are generally without health benefits and other safety nets, continues to grow and now comprises about 5% of the workforce (USBLS 1995).

The aim of this chapter is to provide an overview of current knowledge on conditions which lead to stress at work and associated health and safety problems. These conditions, which are commonly referred to as *psychosocial factors*, include aspects of the job and work environment such as organizational climate or culture, work roles, interpersonal relationships at work, and the design and content of tasks (e.g., variety, meaning, scope, repetitiveness, etc.). The concept of psychosocial factors extends also to the extra-organizational environment (e.g., domestic demands) and aspects of the individual (e.g., personality and attitudes) which may influence the development of stress at work. Frequently, the expressions *work organization* or *organizational factors* are used interchangeably with *psychosocial factors* in reference to working conditions which may lead to stress.

This section of the *Encyclopaedia* begins with descriptions of several models of job stress which are of current scientific interest, including the job demands-job control model, the person- environment (P-E) fit model, and other theoretical approaches to stress at work. Like all contemporary notions of job stress, these models have a common theme: job stress is conceptualized in terms of the relationship between the job and the person. According to this view, job stress and the potential for ill health develop when job demands are at variance with the needs, expectations or capacities of the worker. This core feature is implicit in figure 34.1, which shows the basic elements of a stress model favoured by researchers at the National Institute for Occupational Safety and Health (NIOSH). In this model, work-related psychosocial factors (termed stressors) result in psychological, behavioural and physical reactions which may ultimately influence health. However, as illustrated in figure 34.1, individual and contextual factors (termed stress moderators) intervene to influence the effects of job stressors on health and well-being. (See Hurrell and Murphy 1992 for a more elaborate description of the NIOSH stress model.)

But putting aside this conceptual similarity, there are also non-trivial theoretical differences among these models. For example, unlike the NIOSH and P-E fit models of job stress, which acknowledge a host of potential psychosocial risk factors in the workplace, the job demands-job control model focuses most intensely on a more limited range of psychosocial dimensions pertaining to psychological workload and opportunity for workers to exercise control (termed decision latitude) over aspects of their jobs. Further, both the demand-control and the NIOSH models can be distinguished from the P-E fit models in terms of the focus placed on the individual. In the P-E fit model, emphasis is placed on individuals' perceptions of the balance between features of the job and individual attributes. This focus on perceptions provides a bridge between P-E fit theory and another variant of stress theory attributed to Lazarus (1966), in which individual differences in appraisal of psychosocial stressors and in coping strategies become critically important in determining stress outcomes. In contrast, while not denying the importance of individual differences, the NIOSH stress model gives primacy to environmental factors in determining stress outcomes as suggested

---

[1] In the United States, occupational disease claims are distinct from injury claims, which tend to greatly outnumber disease claims.

Figure 34.1 • The Job Stress Model of the National Institute for Occupational Safety and Health (NIOSH).

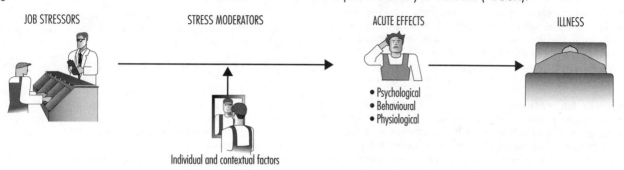

by the geometry of the model illustrated in figure 34.1. In essence, the model suggests that most stressors will be threatening to most of the people most of the time, regardless of circumstances. A similar emphasis can be seen in other models of stress and job stress (e.g., Cooper and Marshall 1976; Kagan and Levi 1971; Matteson and Ivancevich 1987).

These differences have important implications for both guiding job stress research and intervention strategies at the workplace. The NIOSH model, for example, argues for primary prevention of job stress via attention first to psychosocial stressors in the workplace and, in this regard, is consistent with a public health model of prevention. Although a public health approach recognizes the importance of host factors or resistance in the aetiology of disease, the first line of defence in this approach is to eradicate or reduce exposure to environmental pathogens.

The NIOSH stress model illustrated in figure 34.1 provides an organizing framework for the remainder of this section. Following the discussions of job stress models are short articles containing summaries of current knowledge on workplace psychosocial stressors and on stress moderators. These subsections address conditions which have received wide attention in the literature as stressors and stress moderators, as well as topics of emerging interest such as organizational climate and career stage. Prepared by leading authorities in the field, each summary provides a definition and brief overview of relevant literature on the topic. Further, to maximize the utility of these summaries, each contributor has been asked to include information on measurement or assessment methods and on prevention practices.

The final subsection of the chapter reviews current knowledge on a wide range of potential health risks of job stress and underlying mechanisms for these effects. Discussion ranges from traditional concerns, such as psychological and cardiovascular disorders, to emerging topics such as depressed immune function and musculoskeletal disease.

In summary, recent years have witnessed unprecedented changes in the design and demands of work, and the emergence of job stress as a major concern in occupational health. This section of the *Encyclopaedia* tries to promote understanding of psychosocial risks posed by the evolving work environment, and thus better protect the well-being of workers.

THEORIES OF JOB STRESS

PSYCHOSOCIAL FACTORS, STRESS AND HEALTH

Lennart Levi

In the language of engineering, stress is "a force which deforms bodies". In biology and medicine, the term usually refers to a process in the body, to the body's general plan for adapting to all the influences, changes, demands and strains to which it is exposed. This plan swings into action, for example, when a person is assaulted on the street, but also when someone is exposed to toxic substances or to extreme heat or cold. It is not just physical exposures which activate this plan however; mental and social ones do so as well. For instance, if we are insulted by our supervisor, reminded of an unpleasant experience, expected to achieve something of which we do not believe we are capable, or if, with or without cause, we worry about our job or marriage.

There is something common to all these cases in the way the body attempts to adapt. This common denominator—a kind of "revving up" or "stepping on the gas"—is stress. Stress is, then, a stereotype in the body's responses to influences, demands or strains. Some level of stress is always to be found in the body, just as, to draw a rough parallel, a country maintains a certain state of military preparedness, even in peacetime. Occasionally this preparedness is intensified, sometimes with good cause and at other times without.

In this way the stress level affects the rate at which processes of wear and tear on the body take place. The more "gas" given, the higher the rate at which the body's engine is driven, and hence the more quickly the "fuel" is used up and the "engine" wears out. Another metaphor also applies: if you burn a candle with a high flame, at both ends, it will give off brighter light but will also burn down more quickly. A certain amount of fuel is necessary otherwise the engine will stand still, the candle will go out; that is, the organism would be dead. Thus, the problem is not that the body has a stress response, but that the degree of stress—the rate of wear and tear—to which it is subject may be too great. This stress response varies from one minute to another even in one individual, the variation depending in part on the nature and state of the body and in part on the external influences and demands—the stressors—to which the body is exposed. (A stressor is thus something that produces stress.)

Sometimes it is difficult to determine whether stress in a particular situation is good or bad. Take, for instance, the exhausted athlete on the winner's stand, or the newly appointed but stress-racked executive. Both have achieved their goals. In terms of pure accomplishment, one would have to say that their results were well worth the effort. In psychological terms, however, such a conclusion is more doubtful. A good deal of torment may have been necessary to get so far, involving long years of training or never-ending overtime, usually at the expense of family life. From the medical viewpoint such achievers may be considered to have burnt their candles at both ends. The result could be physiological; the athlete may rupture a muscle or two and the executive develop high blood pressure or have a heart attack.

Stress in relation to work

An example may clarify how stress reactions can arise at work and what they might lead to in terms of health and quality of life. Let us imagine the following situation for a hypothetical male worker. Based on economic and technical considerations, management has decided to break up a production process into very simple and primitive elements which are to be performed on an assembly line. Through this decision, a social structure is created and a process set into motion which can constitute the starting point in a stress- and disease-producing sequence of events. The new situation becomes a psychosocial stimulus for the worker, when he first perceives it. These perceptions may be further influenced by the fact that the worker may have previously received extensive training, and thus was consequently expecting a work assignment which required higher qualifications, not reduced skill levels. In addition, past experience of work on an assembly line was strongly negative (that is, earlier environmental experiences will influence the reaction to the new situation). Furthermore, the worker's hereditary factors make him more prone to react to stressors with an increase in blood pressure. Because he is more irritable, perhaps his wife criticizes him for accepting his new assignment and bringing his problems home. As a result of all these factors, the worker reacts to the feelings of distress, perhaps with an increase in alcohol consumption or by experiencing undesirable physiological reactions, such as the elevation in blood pressure. The troubles at work and in the family continue, and his reactions, originally of a transient type, become sustained. Eventually, he may enter a chronic anxiety state or develop alcoholism or chronic hypertensive disease. These problems, in turn, increase his difficulties at work and with his family, and may also increase his physiological vulnerability. A vicious cycle may set in which may end in a stroke, a workplace accident or even suicide. This example illustrates the environmental *programming* involved in the way a worker reacts behaviourally, physiologically and socially, leading to increased vulnerability, impaired health and even death.

Psychosocial conditions in present working life

According to an important International Labour Organization (ILO) (1975) resolution, work should not only respect workers' lives and health and leave them free time for rest and leisure, but also allow them to serve society and achieve self-fulfilment by developing their personal capabilities. These principles were also set down as early as 1963, in a report from the London Tavistock Institute (Document No. T813) which provided the following general guidelines for job design:

1. The job should be reasonably demanding in terms other than sheer endurance and provide at least a minimum of variety.
2. The worker should be able to learn on the job and go on learning.
3. The job should comprise some area of decision-making that the individual can call his or her own.
4. There should be some degree of social support and recognition in the workplace.
5. The worker should be able to relate what he or she does or produces to social life.

6. The worker should feel that the job leads to some sort of desirable future.

The Organization for Economic Cooperation and Development (OECD), however, draws a less hopeful picture of the reality of working life, pointing out that:

- Work has been accepted as a duty and a necessity for most adults.
- Work and workplaces have been designed almost exclusively with reference to criteria of efficiency and cost.
- Technological and capital resources have been accepted as the imperative determinants of the optimum nature of jobs and work systems.
- Changes have been motivated largely by aspirations to unlimited economic growth.
- The judgement of the optimum designs of jobs and choice of work objectives has resided almost wholly with managers and technologists, with only a slight intrusion from collective bargaining and protective legislation.
- Other societal institutions have taken on forms that serve to sustain this type of work system.

In the short run, benefits of the developments which have proceeded according to this OECD list have brought more productivity at lesser cost, as well as an increase in wealth. However, the long-term disadvantages of such developments are often more worker dissatisfaction, alienation and possibly ill health which, when considering society in general, in turn, may affect the economic sphere, although the economic costs of these effects have only recently been taken into consideration (Cooper, Luikkonen and Cartwright 1996; Levi and Lunde-Jensen 1996).

We also tend to forget that, biologically, humankind has not changed much during the last 100,000 years, whereas the environment—and in particular the work environment—has changed dramatically, particularly during the past century and decades. This change has been partly for the better; however, some of these "improvements" have been accompanied by unexpected side effects. For example, data collected by the National Swedish Central Bureau of Statistics during the 1980s showed that:

- 11% of all Swedish employees are continuously exposed to deafening noise.
- 15% have work which makes them very dirty (oil, paint, etc.).
- 17% have inconvenient working hours, i.e., not only daytime work but also early or late night work, shift work or other irregular working hours.
- 9% have gross working hours exceeding 11 per day (this concept includes hours of work, breaks, travelling time, overtime, etc.; in other words, that part of the day which is set aside for work).
- 11% have work that is considered both "hectic" and "monotonous".
- 34% consider their work "mentally exacting".
- 40% consider themselves "without influence on the arrangement of time for breaks".
- 45% consider themselves without "opportunities to learn new things" at their work.
- 26% have an instrumental attitude to their work. They consider "their work to yield nothing except the pay—i.e. no feeling of personal satisfaction". Work is regarded purely as an instrument for acquiring an income.

In its major study of conditions of work in the 12 member States of the European Union at that time (1991/92), the European Foundation (Paoli 1992) found that 30% of the workforce regarded their work to risk their health, 23 million to have night work more than 25% of total hours worked, each third to report highly repetitive, monotonous work, each fifth male and each sixth female to work under "continuous time pressure", and each fourth worker to carry heavy loads or to work in a twisted or painful position more than 50% of his or her working time.

Main psychosocial stressors at work

As already indicated, stress is caused by a bad "person-environment fit", objectively, subjectively, or both, at work or elsewhere and in an interaction with genetic factors. It is like a badly fitting shoe: environmental demands are not matched to individual ability, or environmental opportunities do not measure up to individual needs and expectations. For example, the individual is able to perform a certain amount of work, but much more is required, or on the other hand no work at all is offered. Another example would be that the worker needs to be part of a social network, to experience a sense of belonging, a sense that life has meaning, but there may be no opportunity to meet these needs in the existing environment and the "fit" becomes bad.

Any fit will depend on the "shoe" as well as on the "foot", on situational factors as well as on individual and group characteristics. The most important situational factors that give rise to "misfit" can be categorized as follows:

Quantitative overload. Too much to do, time pressure and repetitive work-flow. This is to a great extent the typical feature of mass production technology and routinized office work.

Qualitative underload. Too narrow and one-sided job content, lack of stimulus variation, no demands on creativity or problem-solving, or low opportunities for social interaction. These jobs seem to become more common with suboptimally designed automation and increased use of computers in both offices and manufacturing even though there may be instances of the opposite.

Role conflicts. Everybody occupies several roles concurrently. We are the superiors of some people and the subordinates of others. We are children, parents, marital partners, friends and members of clubs or trade unions. Conflicts easily arise among our various roles and are often stress evoking, as when, for instance, demands at work clash with those from a sick parent or child or when a supervisor is divided between loyalty to superiors and to fellow workers and subordinates.

Lack of control over one's own situation. When someone else decides what to do, when and how; for example, in relation to work pace and working methods, when the worker has no influence, no control, no say. Or when there is uncertainty or lack of any obvious structure in the work situation.

Lack of social support at home and from your boss or fellow workers.

Physical stressors. Such factors can influence the worker both physically and chemically, for example, direct effects on the brain of organic solvents. Secondary psychosocial effects can also originate from the distress caused by, say, odours, glare, noise, extremes of air temperature or humidity and so on. These effects can also be due to the worker's awareness, suspicion or fear that he is exposed to life-threatening chemical hazards or to accident risks.

Finally, real life conditions at work and outside work usually imply a combination of many exposures. These might become superimposed on each other in an additive or synergistic way. The straw which breaks the camel's back may therefore be a rather trivial environmental factor, but one that comes on top of a very considerable, pre-existing environmental load.

Some of the specific stressors in industry merit special discussion, namely those characteristic of:

- mass production technology
- highly automated work processes
- shift work.

Mass production technology. Over the past century work has become fragmented in many workplaces, changing from a well defined job activity with a distinct and recognized end-product, into numerous narrow and highly specified subunits which bear little apparent relation to the end-product. The growing size of many factory units has tended to result in a long chain of command between management and the individual workers, accentuating remoteness between the two groups. The worker also becomes remote from the consumer, since rapid elaborations for marketing, distribution and selling interpose many steps between the producer and the consumer.

Mass production, thus, normally involves not just a pronounced fragmentation of the work process but also a decrease in worker control of the process. This is partly because work organization, work content and work pace are determined by the machine system. All these factors usually result in monotony, social isolation, lack of freedom and time pressure, with possible long-term effects on health and well-being.

Mass production, moreover, favours the introduction of piece rates. In this regard, it can be assumed that the desire—or necessity—to earn more can, for a time, induce the individual to work harder than is good for the organism and to ignore mental and physical "warnings", such as a feeling of tiredness, nervous problems and functional disturbances in various organs or organ systems. Another possible effect is that the employee, bent on raising output and earnings, infringes safety regulations thereby increasing the risk of occupational disease and of accidents to oneself and others (e.g., lorry drivers on piece rates).

Highly automated work processes. In automated work the repetitive, manual elements are taken over by machines, and the workers are left with mainly supervisory, monitoring and controlling functions. This kind of work is generally rather skilled, not regulated in detail and the worker is free to move about. Accordingly, the introduction of automation eliminates many of the disadvantages of the mass-production technology. However, this holds true mainly for those stages of automation where the operator is indeed assisted by the computer and maintains some control over its services. If, however, operator skills and knowledge are gradually taken over by the computer—a likely development if decision making is left to economists and technologists—a new impoverishment of work may result, with a re-introduction of monotony, social isolation and lack of control.

Monitoring a process usually calls for sustained attention and readiness to act throughout a monotonous term of duty, a requirement that does not match the brain's need for a reasonably varied flow of stimuli in order to maintain optimal alertness. It is well documented that the ability to detect critical signals declines rapidly even during the first half-hour in a monotonous environment. This may add to the strain inherent in the awareness that temporary inattention and even a slight error could have extensive economic and other disastrous consequences.

Other critical aspects of process control are associated with very special demands on mental skill. The operators are concerned with symbols, abstract signals on instrument arrays and are not in touch with the actual product of their work.

Shift work. In the case of shift work, rhythmical biological changes do not necessarily coincide with corresponding environmental demands. Here, the organism may "step on the gas" and activation occurs at a time when the worker needs to sleep (for example, during the day after a night shift), and deactivation correspondingly occurs at night, when the worker may need to work and be alert.

A further complication arises because workers usually live in a social environment which is not designed for the needs of shift workers. Last but not least, shift workers must often adapt to regular or irregular changes in environmental demands, as in the case of rotating shifts.

In summary, the psychosocial demands of the modern workplace are often at variance with the workers' needs and capabilities, leading to stress and ill health. This discussion provides only a snapshot of psychosocial stressors at work, and how these unhealthy conditions can arise in today's workplace. In the sections that follow, psychosocial stressors are analysed in greater detail with respect to their sources in modern work systems and technologies, and with respect to their assessment and control.

● DEMAND/CONTROL MODEL: A SOCIAL, EMOTIONAL, AND PHYSIOLOGICAL APPROACH TO STRESS RISK AND ACTIVE BEHAVIOUR DEVELOPMENT

Robert Karasek

Most previous stress theories were developed to describe reactions to "inevitable" acute stress in situations threatening biological survival (Cannon 1935; Selye 1936). However, the *Demand/Control model* was developed for work environments where "stressors" are chronic, not initially life threatening, and are the product of sophisticated human organizational decision making. Here, the controllability of the stressor is very important, and becomes more important as we develop ever more complex and integrated social organizations, with ever more complex limitations on individual behaviour. The Demand/Control model (Karasek 1976; Karasek 1979; Karasek and Theorell 1990), which is discussed below, is based on psychosocial characteristics of work: the psychological demands of work and a combined measure of task control and skill use (*decision latitude*). The model predicts, first, stress-related illness risk, and, secondly, active/passive behavioural correlates of jobs. It has mainly been used in epidemiological studies of chronic disease, such as coronary heart disease.

Pedagogically, it is a simple model which can help to demonstrate clearly several important issues relevant for social policy discussions of occupational health and safety:

1. that the social organizational characteristics of work, and not just physical hazards, lead to illness and injury
2. that stress-related consequences are related to the social organization of work activity and not just its demands
3. that work's social activity affects stress-related risks, not just person-based characteristics
4. that the possibility of both "positive stress" and "negative stress" can be explained in terms of combinations of demands and control
5. that can provide the simple model—with basic face validity—to begin discussions on personal stress response for shop-floor workers, clerical staff and other lay people for whom this is a sensitive topic.

Beyond the health consequences of work, the model also captures the perspectives of the work's organizers who are concerned with productivity results. The psychological demand dimension relates to "how hard workers work"; the decision latitude dimension reflects work organization issues of who makes decisions and who does what tasks. The model's active learning hypothesis describes the motivation processes of high performance work. The economic logic of extreme labour

specialization, the past conventional wisdom about productive job design is contradicted by adverse health consequences in the Demand/Control model. The model implies alternative, health-promoting perspectives on work organization which emphasize broad skills and participation for workers, and which may also bring economic advantages for innovative manufacturing and in service industries because of the increased possibilities for learning and participation.

Hypotheses of the Demand/Control Model

Psychosocial functioning at the workplace, based on psychological demands and decision latitude

Job strain hypothesis

The first hypothesis is that the most adverse reactions of psychological strain occur (fatigue, anxiety, depression and physical illness) when the psychological demands of the job are high and the worker's decision latitude in the task is low (fig. 34.2, lower right cell). These undesirable stress-like reactions, which result when arousal is combined with restricted opportunities for action or coping with the stressor, are referred to as psychological strain (the term *stress* is not used at this point as it is defined differently by many groups).

For example, the assembly-line worker has almost every behaviour rigidly constrained. In a situation of increased demands ("speed-up"), more than just the constructive response of arousal, the often helpless, long-lasting, and negatively experienced response of residual psychological strain occurs. When the lunch-time rush occurs (Whyte 1948), it is the restaurant worker who does not know how to "control" her customers' behaviour ("get the jump on the customer") who experiences the greatest strain on the job. Kerckhoff and Back (1968) describe garment workers under heavy deadline pressure and the subsequent threat of layoff. They conclude that when the actions normally needed to cope with job pressures cannot be taken, the most severe behavioural symptoms of strain occur (fainting, hysteria, social contagion). It is not only the freedom of action as to how to accomplish the formal work task that relieves strain, it may also be the freedom to engage in the informal "rituals", the coffee break, smoke break or fidgeting, which serve as supplementary "tension release" mechanisms during the work day (Csikszentmihalyi 1975).These are often social activities with other workers—precisely those activities eliminated as "wasted motions" and "soldiering" by Frederick Taylor's methods (1911 (1967)). This implies a needed expansion of the model to include social relations and social support.

In the model, decision latitude refers to the worker's ability to control his or her own activities and skill usage, not to control others. Decision latitude scales have two components: *task authority*—a socially predetermined control over detailed aspects of task performance (also called autonomy); and *skill discretion*— control over use of skills by the individual, also socially determined at work (and often called variety or "substantive complexity" (Hackman and Lawler 1971; Kohn and Schooler 1973)). In modern organizational hierarchies, the highest levels of knowledge legitimate the exercise of the highest levels of authority, and workers with limited-breadth, specialized tasks are coordinated by managers with higher authority levels. Skill discretion and authority over decisions are so closely related theoretically and empirically that they are often combined.

Examples of work's psychological demands—"how hard you work"—include the presence of deadlines, the mental arousal or stimulation necessary to accomplish the task, or coordination burdens. The physical demands of work are not included (although psychological arousal comes with physical exertion).

Figure 34.2 • Psychological demand/decision latitude model.

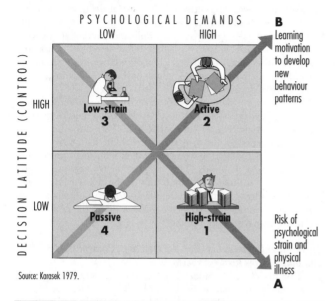

Source: Karasek 1979.

White's "concept of competence" (1959): the psychological state of individuals in challenging circumstances is enhanced by increasing "demands", an environment-based theory of motivation. The model also predicts that the growth and learning stimuli of these settings, when they occur in a job context, are conducive to high productivity.

In the Demand/Control model, learning occurs in situations which require both individual psychological energy expenditure (demands or challenges) and the exercise of decision-making capability. As the individual with decision-making latitude makes a "choice" as to how to best cope with a new stressor, that new behaviour response, if effective, will be incorporated into the individual's repertoire of coping strategies (i.e., it will be "learned"). The potential activity level in the future will be raised because of the expanded range of solutions to environmental challenges, yielding an increase in motivation. Opportunities for constructive reinforcement of behaviour patterns are optimal when the challenges in the situation are matched by the individual's control over alternatives or skill in dealing with those challenges (Csikszentmihalyi 1975). The situation will not be unchallengingly simple (thus, unimportant) nor so demanding that appropriate actions can not be taken because of high anxiety level (the psychological "strain" situation).

The Demand/Control model predicts that situations of low demand and low control (fig. 34.2 opposite end of diagonal B) cause a very "unmotivating" job setting which leads to "negative learning" or gradual loss of previously acquired skills. Evidence shows that disengagement from leisure and political activity outside the job appear to increase over time in such jobs (Karasek and Theorell 1990). These "passive" job, may be the result of "learned helplessness", discussed by Seligman (1975) from a sequence of job situations which reject worker's initiatives.

The fact that environmental demands can thus be conceptualized in both positive and negative terms is congruent with the common understanding that there is both "good" and "bad" stress. Evidence that at least two separable mechanisms must be used to describe "psychological functioning" on the job is one of the primary validations of the multidimensional "Demand/Control" model structure. The "active"-"passive" diagonal B implies that learning mechanisms are independent of (i.e., orthogonal to) psychological strain mechanisms. This yields a parsimonious model with two broad dimensions of work activity and two major psychological mechanisms (the primary reason for calling it an "interaction" model (Southwood 1978)). (Multiplicative interactions for the axes is too restrictive a test for most sample sizes.)

Other components of psychological job demands are stressors arising from personal conflicts. Fear of losing a job or skill obsolescence may obviously be a contributor. Overall, Buck (1972) notes that "task requirements" (workload) are the central component of psychological job demands for most workers in spite of the above diversity. While simple measures of working hours, in moderate ranges, do not seem to strongly predict illness, one such measure, shiftwork—especially rotating shiftwork, is associated with substantial social problems as well as increased illness.

While some level of "demands" is necessary to achieve new learning and effective performance on the job (i.e., interest), too high a level is obviously harmful. This has implied the inverted "U-shaped" curve of "optimal" level of demands in the well known General Adaptation Syndrome of Selye (1936) and related, classic theories by Yerkes and Dodson (1908) and Wundt (1922) on stress and performance.[2] However, our findings show that most work situations have an overload, rather than an underload, problem.

Active learning hypothesis

When control on the job is high, and psychological demands are also high, but not overwhelming (fig. 34.2 upper right cell) learning and growth are the predicted behavioural outcomes (i.e., the active learning hypothesis). Such a job is termed the "active job", since research in both the Swedish and American populations has shown this to be the most active group outside of work in leisure and political activity, in spite of heavy work demands (Karasek and Theorell 1990). Only average psychological strain is predicted for the 'active job' because much of the energy aroused by the job's many stressors ("challenges") are translated into direct action—effective problem solving—with little residual strain to cause disturbance. This hypothesis parallels

Clarifying Demand and Control definitions

The Demand/Control model has sometimes been assumed to be congruent with a model of "demands and resources", allowing a simple fit with currently common "cost/benefit" thinking—where the positive "benefits" of resources are subtracted from the negative "costs" of demands. "Resources" allows inclusion of many factors outside the worker's immediate task experience of obvious importance. However, the logic of the Demand/Control model hypotheses cannot be collapsed into a unidimensional form. The distinction between decision latitude and psychological stressors must be retained because the model predicts both learning and job strain—from two different combinations of demands and control which are not simply mathematically additive. Job "control" is not merely a negative stressor, and "demands and challenges" associated with lack of control are not associated with increased learning. Having decision latitude over the work process will reduce a worker's stress, but increase his learning, while psychological demands would increase both learning and stress. This distinction between demands and control

---

[2] Although Selye's "U-shaped" association between demands and stress purported to be unidimensional along a stressor axis, it probably also included a second dimension of constraint in his animal experiments—and thus was really a composite model of stress-related physiological deterioration—potentially similar to the high demand, low control situation, as other researchers have found (Weiss 1971).

allows understanding of the otherwise unclear prediction of the effects of: (a) "responsibility", which actually combines high demands and high decision latitude; (b) "qualitative job demands", which also measures the possibility of decision making about what skills to employ; and (c) "piece work", where the decision latitude to work faster almost directly brings with it increased demands.

Expanding the Model

Social support hypotheses

The Demand/Control model has been usefully expanded by Johnson by the addition of social support as a third dimension (Johnson 1986; Kristensen 1995). The primary hypothesis, that jobs which are high in demands, low in control—and also low in social support at work (high "iso-strain") carry the highest risks of illness, has been empirically successful in a number of chronic disease studies. The addition clearly acknowledges the need of any theory of job stress to assess social relations at the workplace (Karasek and Theorell 1990; Johnson and Hall 1988). Social support "buffering" of psychological strain may depend on the degree of social and emotion integration and trust between co-workers, supervisors, etc.—"socio-emotional support" (Israel and Antonnuci 1987). Addition of social support also makes the Demand/Control perspective more useful in job redesigning. Changes in social relations between workers (i.e., autonomous work groups) and changes in decision latitude are almost inseparable in job redesign processes, particularly "participatory" processes (House 1981).

However, a full theoretical treatment of the impact of social relations on both job stress and behaviour is a very complex problem which needs further work. The associations with measures of co-worker and supervisor interactions and chronic disease are less consistent than for decision latitude, and social relations can strongly increase, as well as decrease, the nervous system arousal that may be the risk-inducing link between social situation and illness. The dimensions of work experience that reduce job stress would not necessarily be the same dimensions that are relevant for active behaviour in the Demand/Control model. Facilitating collective forms of active behaviour would likely focus on the distribution of and ability to use competences, communication structure and skills, coordination possibilities, "emotional intelligence skills" (Goleman 1995)—as well as the trust important for social support.

Occupation and psychosocial job characteristics

Job characteristics can be displayed in a four quadrant diagram using the average job characteristics of occupations in the US Census occupation codes (Karasek and Theorell 1990). The "active" job quadrant, with high demand and high control, has high-prestige occupations: lawyers, judges, physicians, professors, engineers, nurses and managers of all kinds. The "passive" job quadrant, with low demands and low control, has clerical workers such as stock and billing clerks, transport operatives and low status service personnel such as janitors. The "high strain" quadrant, with high demands and low control, has machine-paced operatives such as assemblers, cutting operatives, inspectors and freight handlers, as well as other low-status service operatives such as waiters or cooks. Female-dominated occupations are frequent (garment stitchers, waitresses, telephone operators and other office automation workers). "Low strain" self-paced occupations, such as repairmen, sales clerks, foresters, linemen and natural scientists, often involve significant training and self-pacing.

Thus, executives and professionals have a moderate level of stress, and not the highest level of stress, as popular belief often holds. While "managerial stress" certainly exists because of the high psychological demands that come with these jobs, it appears that the frequent occasions for decision-making and deciding how to do the job are a significant stress moderator. Of course, at the highest status levels, executive jobs consist of decision-making as the primary psychological demand, and then the Demand/Control model fails. However, the implication here is that executives could reduce their stress if they made fewer decisions, and lower status workers would be better off with more decision opportunities, so that all groups could be better off with a more equal share of decision power.

Men are more likely than women to have high control over their work process at the task level, with a difference as great as wage differentials (Karasek and Theorell 1990). Another major gender difference is the negative correlation between decision latitude and demands for women: women with low control also have higher job demands. This means that women are several times as likely to hold high strain jobs in the full working population. By contrast, men's high demand jobs are generally accompanied by somewhat higher decision latitude ("authority commensurate with responsibility").

Theoretical linkages between the Demand/Control model and other theoretical perspectives

The Demand/Control models arises out of theoretical integration of several disparate scientific directions. Thus, it falls outside the boundaries of a number of established scientific traditions from which it has gained contributions or with which it is often contrasted: mental health epidemiology and sociology, and stress physiology, cognitive psychology and personality psychology. Some of these previous stress theories have focused on a person-based causal explanation, while the Demand/Control model predicts a stress response to social and psychological environments. However, the Demand/Control model has attempted to provide a set of interfacing hypotheses with person-based perspectives. In addition, linkage to macro social organizational and political economic issues, such as social class, have also been proposed. These theoretical integrations and contrasts with other theories are discussed below at several levels. The linkages below provide the background for an extended set of scientific hypotheses.

Contrast between the Demand/Control model and the cognitive psychological model

One area of stress theory grows out of the currently popular field of cognitive psychology. The central tenet of the cognitive model of human psychological functioning is that it is the processes of perception and interpretation of the external world that determine the development of psychological states in the individual. Mental workload is defined as the total information load that the worker is required to perceive and interpret while performing job tasks (Sanders and McCormick 1993; Wickens 1984). "Overload" and stress occur when this human information processing load is too large for the individual's information processing capabilities. This model has enjoyed great currency since modelling human mental functions in the same rough conceptual model as modern computers utilize, and thus fits an engineering conception of work design. This model makes us aware of the importance of information overloads, communication difficulties and memory problems. It does well in the design of some aspects of human/computer interfaces and human monitoring of complex processes. .

However, the cognitive psychological perspective tends to downplay the importance of "objective" workplace stressors, for example, and emphasize instead the importance of the stressed individuals' interpretation of the situation. In the cognitive-based "coping approach", Lazarus and Folkman (1986) advocate that quilibrium state. In general, "lack of control" may represent restriction of the organism's ability to use all of its adaptive mechanisms to maintain physiological equilibrium in the face of demands, leading to increased long-term burdens and disease risk. This is a direction for future Demand/Control physiological research.

One potentially consistent finding is that while the Demand/Control model predicts cardiovascular mortality, no single conventional risk factor or physiological indicator seems to be the primary pathway of this risk. Future research may show whether "systems dynamic failures" are the pathway.

Macro-social implications of Demand/Control model

Models which integrate over several spheres of research allow broader predictions about the health consequences of human social institutions. For example, Henry and Stephens (1977) observe that in the animal world "psychological demands" result from the thoroughly "social" responsibilities of finding family food and shelter, and rearing and defending offspring; situations of enforced demands combined with social isolation would be hard to imagine. However, the human world of work is so organized that demands can occur without any social affiliation at all. Indeed, according to Frederick Taylor's *Principles of Scientific Management* (1911 (1967)), increasing workers' job demands often should be done in isolation, otherwise the workers would revolt against the process—and return to time-wasting socializing! In addition to showing the utility of an integrated model, this example shows the need to expand even further the social understanding of the human stress response (for example, by adding a social support dimension to the Demand/Control model).

An integrated, socially anchored, understanding of human stress response is particularly needed to understand future economic and political development. Less comprehensive models could be misleading. For example, according to the cognitive model which has dominated public dialogues about future social and industrial development (i.e., the direction for worker's skills, life in the information society, etc.), an individual has freedom to interpret—i.e., reprogramme—his perception of real world events as stressful or non-stressful. The social implication is that, literally, we can design for ourselves any social arrangement—and we should take the responsibility for adapting to any stresses it may cause. However, many of the physiological consequences of stress relate to the "emotional brain" in the limbic system, which has a deterministic structure with clear limitations on overall demands. It is definitely not "infinitely" re-programmable, as studies of post traumatic stress syndrome clearly indicate (Goleman 1995). Overlooking the limbic system's limits—and the integration of emotional response and social integration—can lead to a very modern set of basic conflicts for human development. We may be developing social systems on the basis of the extraordinary cognitive capabilities of our brain cortex that place impossible demands on the more basic limbic brain functions in terms of overloads: lost social bonds, lack of internal control possibilities, and restricted ability to see the "whole picture". In short, we appear to be running the risk of developing work organizations for which we are sociobiologically misfit. These results are not just the consequence of scientific incomplete models, they also facilitate the wrong kinds of social process—processes where the interests of some groups with social power are served to the cost of others of previously inexperienced levels of social and personal dysfunction.

Social class and psychosocial job measures

In many cases, individual level stressors can be modelled as the causal outcome of larger-scale social, dynamic and political-economic processes. Thus, theoretical linkages to concepts such as social class are also needed. Assessment of associations between social situation and illness raise the question of the relation between psychosocial Demand/Control factors and broad measures of social circumstance such as social class. Job decision latitude measure is, indeed, clearly correlated with education and other measures of social class. However, social class conventionally measures effects of income and education which operate via different mechanisms than the psychosocial pathways of the Demand/Control model. Importantly, the job strain construct is almost orthogonal to most social class measures in national populations (however, the active/passive dimension is highly correlated with social class among high status workers (only)) (Karasek and Theorell 1990). The low-decision latitude aspects of low status jobs appear to be a more important contributor to psychological strain than the distinction between mental and physical workload, the conventional determinant of white/blue-collar status. Indeed, the physical exertion common in many blue-collar jobs may be protective for psychological strain in some circumstances. While job strain is indeed more common in low status jobs, psychosocial job dimensions define a strain-risk picture which is significantly independent of the conventional social class measures.

Although it has been suggested that the observed Demand/Control job/illness associations merely reflect social class differences (Ganster 1989; Spector 1986), a review of evidence rejects this view (Karasek and Theorell 1990). Most of the Demand/Control research has simultaneously controlled for social class, and Demand/Control associations persist within social class groups. However, blue-collar associations with the model are more consistently confirmed, and the strength of white-collar associations varies (see "Job strain and cardiovascular disease", below) across studies, with white-collar single occupation studies being somewhat less robust. (Of course, for the very highest status managers and professionals decision making may become a significant demand in itself.)

The fact that conventional "social class" measures often find weaker associations with mental distress and illness outcomes than the Demand/Control model actually makes a case for new social class conceptions. Karasek and Theorell (1990) define a new set of psychosocially advantaged and disadvantaged workers, with job stress "losers" in routinized, commercialized and bureaucratized jobs, and "winners" in highly creative learning-focused intellectual work. Such a definition is consistent with a new, skill-based industrial output in the "information society", and a new perspective on class politics.

Methodological Issues

Objectivity of psychosocial job measures

Self-report questionnaires administered to workers have been the most common method of gathering data on psychosocial characteristics of work since they are simple to administer and can be easily designed to tap core concepts in work redesign efforts also (Hackman and Oldham's JDS 1975), Job Content Questionnaire (Karasek 1985), the Swedish Statshalsan questionnaire. While designed to measure the objective job, such questionnaire instruments inevitably measure job characteristics as perceived by the worker. Self-report bias of findings can occur with self-reported dependent variables such as depression, exhaustion and dissatisfaction. One remedy is to aggregate self-report responses by work groups with similar work situations—diluting individual biases (Kristensen 1995). This is the basis of extensively used systems linking psychosocial job characteristics to occupations (Johnson et al. 1996).

There is also evidence assessing the "objective" validity of self-reported psychosocial scales: correlations between self-report and expert observation data are typically 0.70 or higher for decision

the individual "cognitively reinterpret" the situation in a way that makes it appear less threatening, thus reducing experienced stress. However, this approach could be harmful to workers in situations where the environmental stressors are "objectively" real and must be modified. Another variant of the cognitive approach, more consistent with worker empowerment, is Bandura's (1977) "self-efficacy /motivation" theory which emphasizes the increases in self-esteem which occur when individuals: (a) define a goal for a change process; (b) receive feedback on the positive results from the environment; and (c) successfully achieve incremental progress.

Several omissions in the cognitive model are problematic for an occupational health perspective on stress and conflict with the Demand/Control model:

- There is no role for the social and mental "demands" of work that do not translate into information loads (i.e., no role for tasks which require social organizational demands, conflicts and many non-intellectual time deadlines).
- The cognitive model predicts that situations which require taking a lot of decisions are stressful because they can overload the individual's information-processing capacity. This directly contradicts the Demand/Control model which predicts lower strain in demanding situations that allow freedom of decision making. The majority of epidemiological evidence from field studies supports the Demand/Control model, but laboratory tests can generate decision-based cognitive overload effect also.
- The cognitive model also omits physiological drives and primitive emotions, which often dominate cognitive response in challenging situations. There is little discussion of how either negative emotions, nor learning-based behaviour (except for Bandura, above) arise in common adult social situations.

Although overlooked in the cognitive model, emotional response is central to the notion of "stress", since the initial stress problem is often what leads to unpleasant emotional states such as anxiety, fear and depression. "Drives" and emotions are most centrally affected by the limbic regions of the brain—a different and more primitive brain region than the cerebral cortex addressed by most of the processes described by cognitive psychology. Possibly, the failure to develop an integrated perspective on psychological functioning reflects the difficulty of integrating different research specializations focusing on two different neurological systems in the brain. However, recently, evidence has begun to accumulate about the joint effects of emotion and cognition. The conclusion seems to be that emotion is an underlying determinant of strength of behaviour pattern memory and cognition (Damasio 1994; Goleman 1995).

Integrating Sociological and Emotional Stress Perspectives

Development of the Demand/Control model

The goal of the Demand/Control model has been to integrate understanding of the social situation with evidence of emotional response, psychosomatic illness symptoms and active behaviour development in major spheres of adult life activity, particularly in the highly socially structured work situation. However, when the model was being developed, one likely platform for this work, sociological research exploring illness in large population studies, often omitted the detailed level of social or personal response data of stress research, and thus much integrating work was needed to develop the model.

The first Demand/Control integrating idea—for social situation and emotional response—involved stress symptoms, and linked two relatively unidimensional sociological and social psychological research traditions. First, the life stress/illness

tradition (Holmes and Rahe 1967; Dohrenwend and Dohrenwend 1974) predicted that illness was based on social and psychological demands alone, without mention of control over stressors. Second, the importance of control at the workplace had been clearly recognized in the job satisfaction literature (Kornhauser 1965): task autonomy and skill variety were used to predict job satisfaction, absenteeism or productivity, with limited additions reflecting the workers' social relationship to the job—but there was little mention of job workloads. Integrating studies helped bridge the gaps in the area of illness and mental strain. Sundbom (1971) observed symptoms of psychological strain in "mentally heavy work"—which was actually measured by questions relating to both heavy mental pressures and monotonous work (presumably also representing restricted control). The combined insight of these two studies and research traditions was that a two-dimensional model was needed to predict illness: the level of psychological demands determined whether low control could lead to two significantly different types of problem: psychological strain, or passive withdrawal.

The second Demand/Control integration predicted behaviour patterns related to work experience. Behavioural outcomes of work activity also appeared to be affected by the same two broad job characteristics—but in a different combination. Kohn and Schooler (1973) had observed that active orientations to the job were the consequence of both high skill and autonomy levels, plus psychologically demanding work. Social class measures were important correlates here. Meissner (1971) had also found that leisure behaviour was positively associated with opportunities both to take decisions on the job and to perform mentally challenging work. The combined insight of these studies was that "challenge" or mental arousal was necessary, on the one hand, for effective learning and, on the other, could contribute to psychological strain. "Control" was the crucial moderating variable that determined whether environmental demands would lead to "positive" learning consequences, or "negative" strain consequences.

The combination of these two integrating hypotheses, predicting both health and behavioural outcomes, is the basis of the Demand/Control model. "Demand" levels are the contingent factor which determines whether low control leads to either passivity or psychological strain; and "control" levels are the contingent factor which determines whether demands lead to either active learning or psychological strain (Karasek 1976; 1979). The model was then tested on a representative national sample of Swedes (Karasek 1976) to predict both illness symptoms and leisure and political behavioural correlates of psychosocial working conditions. The hypotheses were confirmed in both areas, although many confounding factors obviously share in these results. Shortly after these empirical confirmations, two other conceptual formulations, consistent with the Demand/Control model, appeared, which confirmed the robustness of the general hypotheses. Seligman (1976) observed depression and learned helplessness in conditions of intense demand with restricted control. Simultaneously, Csikszentmihalyi (1975) found that an "active experience" ("flow") resulted from situations which involved both psychological challenges and high levels of competence. Use of this integrated model was able to resolve some paradoxes in job satisfaction and mental strain research (Karasek 1979): for example, that qualitative workloads were often negatively associated with strain (because they also reflected the individual's control over his or her use of skills). The most extensive acceptance of the model by other researchers came in 1979 after the expansion of empirical prediction to coronary heart disease, with the assistance of colleague Tores Theorell, a physician with significant background in cardiovascular epidemiology.

Figure 34.3 • Dynamic associations linking environmental strain and learning to evolution of personality.

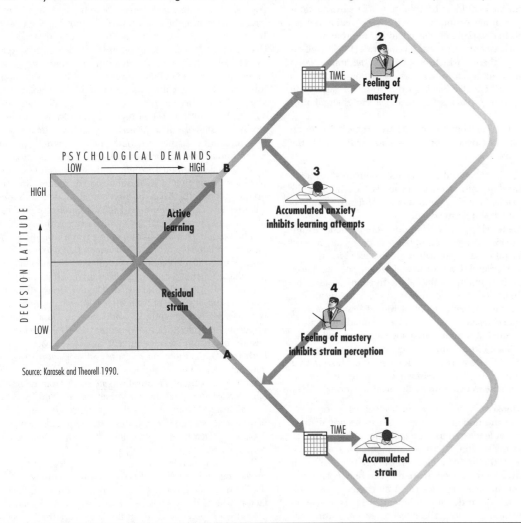

Source: Karasek and Theorell 1990.

A second Demand/Control model integration—physiological response

Additional research has allowed a second level of integration linking the Demand/Control model to physiological response.[3] The main research developments in physiological research had identified two patterns of an organism's adaptation to its environment. Cannon's (1914) fight-flight response is most associated with stimulation of the adrenal medulla—and adrenaline secretion. This pattern, occurring in conjunction with sympathetic arousal of the cardiovascular system, is clearly an active and energetic response mode where the human body is able to use maximum metabolic energy to support both mental and physical exertion necessary to escape major threats to its survival. In the second physiological response pattern, the adrenocortical response is a response to defeat or withdrawal in a situation with

little possibility of victory. Selye's research (1936) on stress dealt with the adrenocortical response to animals in a stressed but passive condition (i.e., his animal subjects were restrained while they were stressed, not a fight-flight situation). Henry and Stephens (1977) describe this behaviour as the defeat or loss of social attachments, which leads to a withdrawal and submissiveness in social interactions.

In the early 1980s, Frankenhaeuser's (1986) research demonstrated the congruence of these two patterns of physiological response with the main hypotheses of the Demand/Control model—allowing linkage to be made between physiological response and social situation, and emotional response patterns. In high-strain situations, cortisol from the adrenal cortex, and adrenaline from the adrenal medulla, secretions are both elevated, whereas in a situation where the subject has a controllable and predictable stressor, adrenaline secretion alone is elevated (Frankenhaeuser, Lundberg and Forsman 1980). This demonstrated a significant differentiation of psychoendocrine response associated with different environmental situations. Frankenhaeuser used a two-dimension model with the same structure as the Demand/Control model, but with dimensions labelling personal emotional response. "Effort" describes adrenal-medullary stimulating activity (demands in the

Demand/Control model) and "distress" describes adrenocortical stimulating activity (lack of decision latitude in the Demand/Control model). Frankenhaeuser's emotional response categories illuminate a clearer link between emotion and physiological response, but in this form the Demand/Control model fails to illuminate the association between work sociology and physiological response, which has been another strength of the model.

Integrating person-based stress theory: The dynamic version of the Demand/Control model

One of the challenges behind the development of the Demand/Control model has been to develop an alternative to the socially conservative explanation that the worker's perception or response orientations are primary responsible for stress—the claim of some person-based stress theories. For example, it is hard to accept the claims, extended by personality-based stress models, that the majority of stress reactions develop because common individual personality types habitually misinterpret real world stresses or are oversensitive to them, and that these types of personality can be identified on the basis of simple tests. Indeed, evidence for such personality effects has been mixed at best with even the most common measures (although a stress denial personality has been identified—alexithymia (Henry and Stephens 1977). The Type A behaviour pattern, for example, was originally interpreted as the individual's proclivity to select stressful activities, but research in this area has now shifted to the "anger-prone" personality (Williams 1987). Of course, anger response could have a significant environment-response component. A more generalized version of the personality approach is found in the "person-environment fit" model (Harrison 1978), which postulates that a good match between the person and the environment is what reduces stress. Here also it has been difficult to specify the specific personality characteristics to be measured. Nevertheless, personal response/personality-based approaches addressed the obvious fact that: (a) person-based perceptions are an important part of the process in which environments affect individuals; and (b) there are long-term differences in personal responses to environments. Thus, a time dynamic, integrated environment and person-based version of the Demand/Control model was developed.

The dynamic version of the Demand/Control model (fig. 34.3) integrates environment effects with person-based phenomena such as self-esteem development and long-term exhaustion. The dynamic version integrates person-based and environmental factors by building two combined hypotheses on the original strain and learning mechanisms: (a) that stress inhibits learning; and (b) that learning, in the long term, can inhibit stress. The first hypothesis is that high-strain levels may inhibit the normal capacity to accept a challenge, and thus inhibit new learning. These high-strain levels may be the result of long-lasting psychological strain accumulated over time—and reflected in person-based measures (fig. 34.3, diagonal arrow B). The second hypothesis is that new learning may lead to feelings of mastery or confidence—a person-based measure. These feelings of mastery, in turn, can lead to reduced perceptions of events as stressful and increased coping success (fig. 34.3, diagonal arrow A). Thus, environmental factors, over the long term, partly determine personality, and later, environmental effects are moderated by these previously developed personality orientations. This broad model could incorporate the following, more specific measures of personal response: feelings of mastery, denial, alexithymia, trait anxiety, trait anger, vital exhaustion, burnout, culmulative life-stressor implications, and possibly Type A behaviour components.

The dynamic model yields the possibility of two long-term dynamic "spirals" of behaviour. The positive behavioural dynamic begins with the active job setting, the increased "feeling of mastery", and the increased ability to cope with inevitable job

stressors. These, in turn, reduce accumulated a
increase the capacity to accept still more lear
—yielding still further positive personality chang
well-being. The undesirable behavioural dynamic
high-strain job, the high accumulated residual
restricted capacity to accept learning challenges.
lead to diminishing self-esteem and increased
tions—yielding still further negative personalit
diminished well-being. Evidence for submechanis
in Karasek and Theorell (1990), although the comp
not been tested. Two promising research directio
easily integrate with Demand/Control resear
exhaustion" research integrated with changing re
demands (Appels 1990), and Bandura's (1977)
methods, which integrate skill development a
development.

The Demand/Control model and the system dyna of physiological stress

One necessary next step for Demand/Control rese
comprehensive specification of the physiological pa
ness causation. Physiological response is increasingly
stood as a complex system response. The physiolo
stress response—to accomplish, for example, a figh
haviour—is a highly integrated combination of char
vascular output, brain-stem regulation, respirator
limbic-system control of the endocrine response, ge
activation and peripheral circulatory system changes.
of "stress" is very possibly most relevant for
tems—which involve multiple, interacting subsyste
plex causality.[4] Accompanying this new perspectiv
dynamic principles in physiology, are definitions of
as disorders of system regulation (Henry and Ste
Weiner 1977), and investigation of the results of tim
multifactoral adjustments to system equilibrium, or
their absence in "chaos".

Interpreting such observations from the persp
"generalized" Demand/Control model, we could sa
refers to a disequilibrium of the system as a whole.
parts of the system are functioning. All organism
control mechanisms to integrate the actions of sepa
tems (i.e., the brain, the heart and the immune system
job strain) would be an overload condition experie
organism's "control system" when it attempts t
integrated functioning in the face of too many en
challenges ("high demands"), and when the system's
integrated control of its submechanisms fails ("high
impose order on its chaotic environment, the individu
physiological control systems must "do the work" of
a coordinated physiological regularity (i.e., a constant
in the face of irregular environmental demands. T
organism's control capacity is exhausted after
"organizing" (a low entropy condition, by analogy fro
dynamics), further demands lead to excess fatigue or
strain. Furthermore, all organisms must periodically r
control systems to the rest-state—sleep or relaxation
state of relaxed disorder or high entropy)—to be
undertaking the next round of coordinating tasks. Th
coordination processes or its relaxation attempts may b
if it cannot follow its own optimal course of action, i.e.,
possibilities to control its situation or find a satisfactor

[3] A major stimulus for the development of the strain hypothesis of the Demand/Control model in 1974 were Dement's observations (1969) that vital relaxation related to REM dreaming was inhibited if sleep-deprived cats were "constrained" by a treadmill (perhaps like an assembly line) after periods of extreme psychological stressor exposure. The combined actions of both environmental stressors and low environmental control were essential elements in producing these effects. The negative impacts, in terms of mental derangement, were catastrophic and led to inability to coordinate the most basic physiological processes.

[4] Instead of a single and unambiguous cause and effect linkag
"hard sciences" (or hard science mythologically), in stress models
ciations are more complex: there may be many causes which "accu
contribute to a single effect; a single cause ("stressor") may have m
or effects which occur only after significant time delays.

latitude, and lower (0.35) correlations for work demands (Frese and Zapf 1988). Also supporting objective validity is the high between-occupation variances of (40 to 45%) of decision latitude scales, which compare favourably with 21% for income and 25% for the physical exertion, which are acknowledged to vary dramatically by occupation (Karasek and Theorell 1990). However, only 7% and 4%, of psychological demands and social support scale variance, respectively, is between occupations, leaving the possibility of a large person-based component of self-reports of these measures.

More objective measurement strategies would be desirable. Some well-known objective assessment methods are congruent with the Demand/Control model (for decision latitude: VERA, Volpert et al. (1983)). However, expert observations have problems also: observations are costly, time consuming, and, in assessment of social interactions, obviously do not generate more accurate measures. There are also theoretical biases involved in the very concept of standard "expert" measures: it is much easier to "measure" the easily observed, repetitive quality of the low status assembly-line worker jobs, than the diverse tasks of high status managers or professionals. Thus, objectivity of the psychosocial measures is inversely related to the decision latitude of the subject.

Some reviews of empirical evidence for the Demand/Control model

Job strain and cardiovascular disease (CVD)
Job strain and heart disease associations represent the broadest base of empirical support for the model. Recent comprehensive reviews have been done by Schnall, Landsbergis and Baker (1994), Landsbergis et al. (1993) and Kristensen (1995). Summarizing Schnall, Landsbergis and Baker(1994) (updated by Landsbergis, personal communication, Fall 1995): 16 of 22 studies have confirmed a job strain association with cardiovascular mortality using a wide range of methodologies, including 7 of 11 cohort studies; 2 of 3 cross-sectional studies; 4 of 4 case control studies; and 3 of 3 studies utilizing disease symptom indicators. Most negative studies have been in older populations (mainly over age 55, some with much post-retirement time) and are mainly based upon aggregated occupation scores which, although they minimize self-report bias, are weak in statistical power. The job strain hypothesis appears to be somewhat more consistent when predicting blue-collar than white-collar CVD (Marmot and Theorell 1988). Conventional CVD risk factors such as serum cholesterol, smoking and even blood pressure, when measured in the conventional manner, have so far only shown inconsistent or weak job-strain effects. However, more sophisticated methods (ambulatory blood pressures) show substantial positive results (Theorell and Karasek 1996).

Job strain and psychological distress/behaviour, absenteeism
Psychological disorder findings are reviewed in Karasek and Theorell (1990). The majority of the studies confirm a job strain association and are from broadly representative or nationally representative populations in a number of countries. The common study limitations are cross-section design and the difficult-to-avoid problem of self-reported job and psychological strain questionnaires, although some studies also include objective observer assessment of work situations and there are also supportive longitudinal studies. While some have claimed that a person-based tendency towards negative affect inflates work-mental strain associations (Brief et al. 1988), this could not be true for several strong findings on absenteeism (North et al. 1996; Vahtera Uutela and Pentii 1996). Associations in some studies are very strong and,

in a number of studies, are based on a linkage system which minimizes potential self-report bias (at the risk of loss of statistical power). These studies confirm associations for a broad range of psychological strain outcomes: moderately severe forms of depression, exhaustion, drug consumption, and life and job dissatisfaction, but findings also differ by outcome. There is also some differentiation of negative affect by Demand/Control model dimensions. Exhaustion, rushed tempo or simply reports of "feeling stressed" are more strongly related to psychological demands—and are higher for managers and professionals. More serious strain symptoms such as depression, loss of self-esteem, and physical illness seem to be more strongly associated with low decision latitude—a larger problem for low status workers.

Job strain and musculoskeletal disorders and other chronic diseases
Evidence of the utility of the Demand/Control model is accumulating in other areas (see Karasek and Theorell 1990). Prediction of occupational musculoskeletal illness is reviewed for 27 studies by Bongers et al. (1993) and other researchers (Leino and Hääninen 1995; Faucett and Rempel 1994). This work supports the predictive utility of the Demand/ Control/support model, particularly for upper extremity disorders. Recent studies of pregnancy disorders (Fenster et al. 1995; Brandt and Nielsen 1992) also show job strain associations.

Summary and Future Directions
The Demand/Control/support model has stimulated much research during recent years. The model has helped to document more specifically the importance of social and psychological factors in the structure of current occupations as a risk factor for industrial society's most burdensome diseases and social conditions. Empirically, the model has been successful: a clear relationship between adverse job conditions (particularly low decision latitude) and coronary heart disease has been established.

However, it is still difficult to be precise about which aspects of psychological demands, or decision latitude, are most important in the model, and for what categories of workers. Answers to these questions require more depth of explanation of the physiological and micro-behavioural effects of psychological demands, decision latitude and social support than the model's original formulation provided, and require simultaneous testing of the dynamic version of the model, including the active/passive hypotheses. Future utility of Demand/Control research could be enhanced by an expanded set of well-structured hypotheses, developed through integration with other intellectual areas, as outlined above (also in Karasek and Theorell 1990). The active/passive hypotheses, in particular, have received too little attention in health outcome research.

Other areas of progress are also needed, particularly new methodological approaches in the psychological demand area. Also, more longitudinal studies are needed, methodological advances are needed to address self-report bias and new physiological monitoring technologies must be introduced. At the macro level, macro social occupational factors, such as worker collective and organizational level decision influence and support, communication limitations and job and income insecurity, need to be more clearly integrated into the model. The linkages to social class concepts need to be further explored, and the strength of the model for women and the structure of work/family linkages need to be further investigated. Population groups in insecure employment arrangements, which have the highest stress levels, must be covered by new types of study designs—especially relevant as the global economy changes the nature of work relationships. As we are more exposed to the strains of the global economy, new measures at macro levels are needed to test the lack of local control and increased intensity of work activity—apparently making the general form of the Demand/Control model relevant in the future.

SOCIAL SUPPORT: AN INTERACTIVE STRESS MODEL

Kristina Orth-Gomér

The stress concept

Various definitions of stress have been formulated since the concept was first named and described by Hans Selye (Selye 1960). Almost invariably these definitions have failed to capture what is perceived as the essence of the concept by a major proportion of stress researchers.

The failure to reach a common and generally acceptable definition may have several explanations; one of them may be that the concept has become so widespread and has been used in so many different situations and settings and by so many researchers, professionals and lay persons that to agree on a common definition is no longer possible. Another explanation is that there really is no empirical basis for a single common definition. The concept may be so diverse that one single process simply does not explain the whole phenomenon. One thing is clear—in order to examine the health effects of stress, the concept needs to include more than one component. Selye's definition was concerned with the physiological fight or flight reaction in response to a threat or a challenge from the environment. Thus his definition involved only the individual physiological response. In the 1960s a strong interest arose in so-called life events, that is, major stressful experiences that occur in an individual's life. The work by Holmes and Rahe (1967) nicely demonstrated that an accumulation of life events was harmful to health. These effects were found mostly in retrospective studies. To confirm the findings prospectively proved to be more difficult (Rahe 1988).

In the 1970s another concept was introduced into the theoretical framework, that of the vulnerability or resistance of the individual who was exposed to stressful stimuli. Cassel (1976) hypothesized that host resistance was a crucial factor in the outcome of stress or the impact of stress on health. The fact that host resistance had not been taken into account in many studies might explain why so many inconsistent and contradictory results had been obtained on the health effect of stress. According to Cassel, two factors were essential in determining the degree of a person's host resistance: his or her capacity for coping and his or her social supports.

Today's definition has come to include considerably more than the physiological "Selye stress" reactions. Both social environmental effects as represented by (for instance) life events and the resistance or vulnerability of the individual exposed to the life events are included.

In the stress-disease model proposed by Kagan and Levi (1971), several distinctions between different components are made (fig. 34.4). These components are:

- stressful factors or stressors in the environment— social or psychological stimuli that evoke certain harmful reactions
- the individual psychobiological programme, predetermined both by genetic factors and early experiences and learning
- individual physiological stress reactions ("Selye Stress" reactions). A combination of these three factors may lead to
- precursors which may eventually provoke the final outcome, namely

- manifest physical illness.

It is important to note, that—contrary to Selye's beliefs—several different physiological pathways have been identified that mediate the effects of stressors on physical health outcomes. These include not only the originally described sympatho-adreno-medullary reaction but also the action of the sympatho-adreno-cortical axis, which may be of equal importance, and the counterbalance provided by parasympathetic gastrointestinal neurohormonal regulation, which has been observed to dampen and buffer the harmful effects of stress. In order for a stressor to evoke such reactions, a harmful influence of the psychobiological programme is required— in other words, an individual propensity to react to stressors has to be present. This individual propensity is both genetically determined and based on early childhood experiences and learning.

If the physiological stress reactions are severe and long-standing enough, they may eventually lead to chronic states, or become precursors of illness. An example of such a precursor is hypertension, which is often stress-related and may lead to manifest somatic disease, such as stroke or heart disease.

Another important feature of the model is that the interaction effects of intervening variables are anticipated at each step, further increasing the complexity of the model. This complexity is illustrated by feed-back loops from all stages and factors in the model to every other stage or factor. Thus the model is complex—but so is nature.

Our empirical knowledge about the accuracy of this model is still insufficient and unclear at this stage, but further insight will be gained by applying the interactive model to stress research. For example, our ability to predict disease may increase if the attempt is made to apply the model.

Empirical evidence on host resistance

In our group of investigators at the Karolinska Institute in Stockholm, recent research has been focused on factors that promote host resistance. We have hypothesized that one such powerful factor is the health-promoting effects of well-functioning social networks and social support.

Our first endeavour to investigate the effects of social networks on health were focused on the entire Swedish population from a "macroscopic" level. In cooperation with the Central Swedish Bureau of Statistics we were able to evaluate the effects of self-assessed social network interactions on health outcome, in this case on survival (Orth-Gomér and Johnson 1987).

Representing a random sample of the adult Swedish population, 17,433 men and women responded to a questionnaire about their social ties and social networks. The questionnaire was included in two of the annual *Surveys of Living Conditions* in Sweden, which were designed to assess and measure the welfare of the nation in material as well as in social and psychological terms. Based on the questionnaire, we created a comprehensive social network interaction index which included the number of members in the network and the frequency of contacts with each member. Seven sources of contacts were identified by means of factor analysis: parents, siblings, nuclear family (spouse and children), close relatives, co-workers, neighbours, distant relatives and friends. The contacts with each source were calculated and added up to a total index score, which ranged from zero to 106.

By linking the *Surveys of Living Conditions* with the national death register, we were able to investigate the impact of the social network interaction index on mortality. Dividing the study population into tertiles according to their index score, we found that those men and women who were in the lower tertile had an invariably higher mortality risk than those who were in the middle and upper tertiles of the index score.

Figure 34.4 • Components of stress in the stress-disease model of Kagan and Levi (1971).

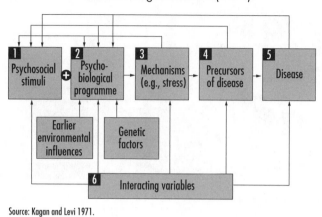

Source: Kagan and Levi 1971.

The risk of dying if one was in the lower tertile was four to five times higher than in the other tertiles, although many other factors might explain this association such as the fact that increasing age is associated with higher risk of dying. Also, as one ages the number of social contacts decrease. If one is sick and disabled, mortality risk increases and it is likely that the extent of the social network decreases. Morbidity and mortality are also higher in lower social classes, and social networks are also smaller and social contacts less abundant. Thus, controlling for these and other mortality risk factors is necessary in any analysis. Even when these factors were taken into account, a statistically significant 40% increase in risk was found to be associated with a sparse social network among those in the lowest third of the population. It is interesting to note that there was no additional health-promoting effect of being in the highest as compared to the middle tertile. Possibly, a great number of contacts can represent a strain on the individual as well as protection against harmful health effects.

Thus, without even knowing anything further about the stressors in the lives of these men and women we were able to confirm a health-promoting effect of social networks.

Social networks alone cannot explain the health effects observed. It is probable that the way in which a social network functions and the basis of support the network members provide are more important than the actual number of people included in the network. In addition, an interactive effect of different stressors is possible. For example the effects of work-related stress have been found to worsen when there is also a lack of social support and social interaction at work (Karasek and Theorell 1990).

In order to explore the issues of interaction, research studies have been carried out using various measures for assessing both qualitative and quantitative aspects of social support. Several interesting results were obtained which are illustrative of the health effects that have been associated with social support. For example, one study of heart disease (myocardial infarct and sudden cardiac death) in a population of 776 fifty-year-old men born in Gothenburg, randomly selected from the general population and found healthy on initial examination, smoking and lack of social support were found to be the strongest predictors of disease (Orth-Gomér, Rosengren and Wilheemsen 1993). Other risk factors included elevated blood pressure, lipids, fibrinogen and a sedentary lifestyle.

In the same study it was shown that only in those men who lacked support, in particular emotional support from a spouse, close relatives or friends, were the effects of stressful life events harmful. Men who both lacked support and had experienced several serious life events had more than five times the mortality of men who enjoyed close and emotional support (Rosengren et al. 1993).

Another example of interactive effects was offered in a study of cardiac patients who were examined for psychosocial factors such as social integration and social isolation, as well as myocardial indicators of an unfavourable prognosis and then followed for a ten-year period. Personality and behaviour type, in particular the Type A behaviour pattern, was also assessed.

The behaviour type in itself had no impact on prognosis in these patients. Of Type A men, 24% died as compared to 22% of Type B men. But when considering the interactive effects with social isolation another picture emerged.

Using a diary of activities during a regular week, men participating in the study were asked to describe anything they would do in the evenings and weekends of a normal week. Activities were then divided into those that involved physical exercise, those that were mainly involved with relaxation and performed at home and those that were performed for recreation together with others. Of these activity types, lack of social recreational activity was the strongest predictor of mortality. Men who never engaged in such activities—called socially isolated in the study—had about three times higher mortality risk than those who were socially active. In addition, Type A men who were socially isolated had an even higher mortality risk than those in any of the other categories (Orth-Gomér, Undén and Edwards 1988).

These studies demonstrate the need to consider several aspects of the psychosocial environment, individual factors as well as of course the physiological stress mechanisms. They also demonstrate that social support is one important factor in stress-related health outcomes.

• PERSON–ENVIRONMENT FIT

Robert D. Caplan

Person–environment fit (PE) theory offers a framework for assessing and predicting how characteristics of the employee and the work environment jointly determine worker well-being and, in the light of this knowledge, how a model for identifying points of preventive intervention may be elaborated. Several PE fit formulations have been proposed, the most widely known ones being those of Dawis and Lofquist (1984); French, Rodgers and Cobb (1974);

Levi (1972); McGrath (1976); and Pervin (1967). The theory of French and colleagues, illustrated in figure 34.5, may be used to discuss the conceptual components of PE fit theory and their implications for research and application.

Poor PE fit can be viewed from the perspectives of the employee's needs (*needs–supplies fit*) as well as the job–environment's demands (*demands–abilities fit*). The term needs–supplies fit refers to the degree to which employee needs, such as the need to use skills and abilities, are met by the work environment's supplies and opportunities to satisfy those needs. Demands–abilities fit refers to the degree to which the job's demands are met by the employee's skills and abilities. These two types of fit can overlap. For

Figure 34.5 • Schematic of French, Rogers and Cobb's theory of person-environment (PE) fit.

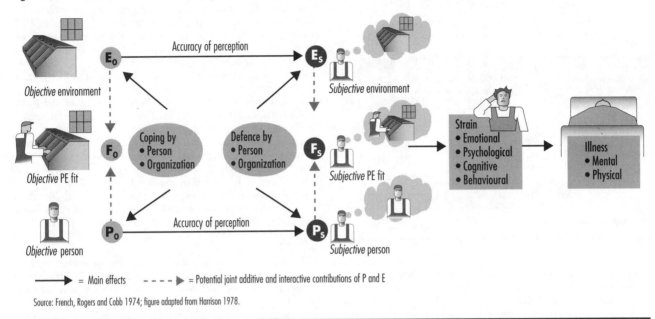

$\longrightarrow$ = Main effects $- - - \rightarrow$ = Potential joint additive and interactive contributions of P and E

Source: French, Rogers and Cobb 1974; figure adapted from Harrison 1978.

example, work overload may leave the employer's demands unmet as well as threaten the employee's need to satisfy others.

Conceptualizing Person (P) and Environment (E)

Characteristics of the person (P) include needs as well as abilities. Characteristics of the environment (E) include supplies and opportunities for meeting the employee's needs as well as demands which are made on the employee's abilities. In order to assess the degree to which P equals (or fits), exceeds, or is less than E, the theory requires that P and E be measured along commensurate dimensions. Ideally, P and E should be measured on equal interval scales with true zero points. For example, one could assess PE fit on workload for a data-entry operator in terms of both the number of data-entry keystrokes per minute demanded by the job (E) and the employee's keystroke speed (P). As a less ideal alternative, investigators often use Likert type scales. For example, one could assess how much the employee wants to control the work pace (P) and how much control is provided by the job's technology (E) by using a rating scale, where a value of 1 corresponds to no control, or almost no control and a value of 5 corresponds to complete control.

Distinguishing Subjective from Objective Fit

Subjective fit (F_S) refers to the employee's perceptions of P and E, whereas objective fit (F_O) refers to assessments that are, in theory, free of subjective bias and error. In practice, there is always measurement error, so that it is impossible to construct truly objective measures. Consequently, many researchers prefer to create a working distinction between subjective and objective fit, referring to measures of objective fit as ones which are relatively, rather than absolutely, immune to sources of bias and error. For example, one can assess objective PE fit on keystroke ability by examining the fit between a count of required keystrokes per minute in the actual workload assigned to the employee (E_O) and the employee's ability as assessed on an objective-type test of keystroke ability (P_O). Subjective PE fit might be assessed by asking the employee to estimate per minute keystroke ability (P_S) and the number of keystrokes per minute demanded by the job (E_S).

Given the challenges of objective measurement, most tests of PE fit theory have used only subjective measures of P and E (for an exception, see Chatman 1991). These measures have tapped a variety of dimensions including fit on responsibility for the work and well-being of other persons, job complexity, quantitative workload and role ambiguity.

Dynamic Properties of the PE Fit Model

Figure 34.5 depicts objective fit influencing subjective fit which, in turn, has direct effects on well-being. Well-being is broken down into responses called strains, which serve as risk factors for

Figure 34.6 • Hypothetical U-shaped relation of person-environment fit to psychological strain.

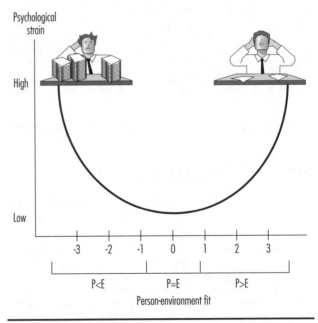

subsequent illness. These strains can involve emotional (e.g., depression, anxiety), physiological (e.g., serum cholesterol, blood pressure), cognitive (e.g., low self-evaluation, attributions of blame to self or others), as well as behavioural responses (e.g., aggression, changes in lifestyle, drug and alcohol use).

According to the model, levels of and changes in objective fit, whether due to planned intervention or otherwise, are not always perceived accurately by the employee, so that discrepancies arise between objective and subjective fit. Thus, employees can perceive good fit as well as poor fit when, objectively, such is not the case.

Inaccurate employee perceptions can arise from two sources. One source is the organization, which, unintentionally or by design (Schlenker 1980), may provide the employee with inadequate information regarding the environment and the employee. The other source is the employee. The employee might fail to access available information or might defensively distort objective information about what the job requires or about his or her abilities and needs — Taylor (1991) cites such an example.

French, Rodgers and Cobb (1974) use the concept of defences to refer to employee processes for distorting the components of subjective fit, P_S and E_S, without changing the commensurate components of objective fit, P_O and E_O. By extension, the organization can also engage in defensive processes—for example, cover-ups, denial or exaggeration—aimed at modifying employee perceptions of subjective fit without concomitantly modifying objective fit.

The concept of coping is, by contrast, reserved for responses and processes that aim to alter and, in particular, improve objective fit. The employee can attempt to cope by improving objective skills (P_O) or by changing objective job demands and resources (E_O) such as through a change of jobs or assigned responsibilities. By extension, the organization can also apply coping strategies to improve objective PE fit. For example, organizations can make changes in selection and promotion strategies, in training and in job design to alter E_O and P_O.

The distinctions between coping and defence on the one hand and objective and subjective fit on the other can lead to an array of practical and scientific questions regarding the consequences of using coping and defence and the methods for distinguishing between effects of coping and effects of defence on PE fit. By derivation from the theory, sound answers to such questions require sound measures of objective as well as subjective PE fit.

Statistical Models

PE fit can have non-linear relations with psychological strain. Figure 34.6 presents a U-shaped curve as an illustration. The lowest level of psychological strain on the curve occurs when employee and job characteristics fit each other (P = E). Strain increases as the employee's abilities or needs respectively fall short of the job's demands or resources (P<E or exceed them (P>E). Caplan and colleagues (1980) report a U-shaped relation between PE fit on job complexity and symptoms of depression in a study of employees from 23 occupations.

Efficacy of the Model

A variety of different approaches to the measurement of PE fit demonstrate the model's potential for predicting well-being and performance. For example, careful statistical modelling found that PE fit explained about 6% more variance in job satisfaction than was explained by measures of P or E alone (Edwards and Harrison 1993). In a series of seven studies of accountants measuring PE fit using a card-sort method, high-performers had higher correlations between P and E (average $r = 0.47$) than low performers (average $r = 0.26$; Caldwell and O'Reilly 1990). P was assessed as the employee's knowledge, skills and abilities (KSAs),

and E was assessed as the commensurate KSAs required by the job. Poor PE fit between the accountant's values and the firm's also served to predict employee turnover (Chatman 1991).

WORKLOAD

Marianne Frankenhaeuser

Workload and Brain Function

Knowledge about human needs, abilities and constraints provides guidelines for shaping psychosocial work conditions so as to reduce stress and improve occupational health (Frankenhaeuser 1989). Brain research and behavioural research have identified the conditions under which people perform well and the conditions under which performance deteriorates. When the total inflow of impressions from the outside world falls below a critical level and work demands are too low, people tend to become inattentive and bored and to lose their initiative. Under conditions of excessive stimulus flow and too high demands, people lose their ability to integrate messages, thought processes become fragmented and judgement is impaired. This inverted U-relationship between workload and brain function is a fundamental biological principle with wide applications in working life. Stated in terms of efficiency at different workloads, it means that the optimal level of mental functioning is located at the midpoint of a scale ranging from very low to very high work demands. Within this middle zone the degree of challenge is "just right", and the human brain functions efficiently. The location of the optimal zone varies among different people, but the crucial point is that large groups spend their lives outside the optimal zone that would provide opportunities for them to develop their full potential. Their abilities are constantly either underutilized or overtaxed.

A distinction should be made between quantitative overload, which means too much work within a given time period, and qualitative underload, which means that tasks are too repetitive, lacking variety and challenge (Levi, Frankenhaeuser and Gardell 1986).

Research has identified criteria for "healthy work" (Frankenhaeuser and Johansson 1986; Karasek and Theorell 1990). These criteria emphasize that workers should be given the opportunity to: (a) influence and control their work; (b) understand their contribution in a wider context; (c) experience a sense of togetherness and belonging at their place of work; and (d) develop their own abilities and vocational skill by continuous learning.

Monitoring Bodily Responses at Work

People are challenged by different work demands whose nature and strength are appraised via the brain. The appraisal process involves a weighing, as it were, of the severity of the demands against one's own coping abilities. Any situation which is perceived as a threat or challenge requiring compensatory effort is accompanied by the transmission of signals from the brain to the adrenal medulla, which responds with an output of the catecholamines epinephrine and norepinephrine. These stress hormones make us mentally alert and physically fit. In the event that the situation induces feelings of uncertainty and helplessness, the brain messages also travel to the adrenal cortex, which secretes cortisol, a hormone which plays an important part in the body's immune defence (Frankenhaeuser 1986).

With the development of biochemical techniques that permit the determination of exceedingly small amounts of hormones in blood, urine and saliva, stress hormones have come to play an increasingly important role in research on working life. In the short term, a rise in stress hormones is often beneficial and seldom a threat to health. But in the longer term, the picture may include damaging effects (Henry and Stephens 1977; Steptoe 1981). Frequent or long-lasting elevations of stress-hormone levels in the course of daily life may result in structural changes in the blood vessels which, in turn, may lead to cardiovascular disease. In other words, consistently high levels of stress hormones should be regarded as warning signals, telling us that the person may be under excessive pressure.

Biomedical recording techniques permit the monitoring of bodily responses at the workplace without interfering with the worker's activities. Using such ambulatory-monitoring techniques, one can find out what makes the blood pressure rise, the heart beat faster, the muscles tense up. These are important pieces of information which, together with stress-hormone assays, have helped in identifying both aversive and protective factors related to job content and work organization. Thus, when searching the work environment for harmful and protective factors, one can use the people themselves as "measuring rods". This is one way in which the study of human stress and coping may contribute to intervention and prevention at the workplace (Frankenhaeuser et al. 1989; Frankenhaeuser 1991).

Personal Control as a "Buffer"

Data from both epidemiological and experimental studies support the notion that personal control and decision latitude are important "buffering" factors which help people to simultaneously work hard, enjoy their jobs and remain healthy (Karasek and Theorell 1990). The chance of exercising control may "buffer" stress in two ways: first, by increasing job satisfaction, thus reducing bodily stress responses, and secondly, by helping people develop an active, participatory work role. A job that allows the worker to use his or her skills to the full will increase self-esteem. Such jobs, while demanding and taxing, may help to develop competencies that aid in coping with heavy workloads.

The pattern of stress hormones varies with the interplay of positive versus negative emotional responses evoked by the situation. When demands are experienced as a positive and manageable challenge, the adrenaline output is typically high, whereas the cortisol-producing system is put to rest. When negative feelings and uncertainty dominate, both cortisol and adrenaline increase. This would imply that the total load on the body, the "cost of achievement", will be lower during demanding, enjoyable work than during less demanding but tedious work, and it would seem that the fact that cortisol tends to be low in controllable situations could account for the positive health effects of personal control. Such a neuroendocrine mechanism could explain the epidemiological data obtained from national surveys in different countries which show that high job demands and work overload have adverse health consequences mainly when combined with low control over job-related decisions (Frankenhaeuser 1991; Karasek and Theorell 1990; Levi, Frankenhaeuser and Gardell 1986).

Total Workload of Women and Men

In order to assess the relative workloads associated with men's and women's different life situations, it is necessary to modify the concept of work so as to include the notion of total workload, that is, the combined load of demands related to paid and unpaid work. This includes all forms of productive activities defined as "all the things that people do that contribute to the goods and services that other people use and value" (Kahn 1991). Thus, a person's total workload includes regular employment and overtime at work as well as housework, child care, care of elderly and sick relatives and work in voluntary organizations and unions. According to this definition, employed women have a higher workload than men at all ages and all occupational levels (Frankenhaeuser 1993a, 1993b and 1996; Kahn 1991).

The fact that the division of labour between spouses in the home has remained the same, while the employment situation of women has changed radically, has led to a heavy workload for women, with little opportunity for them to relax in the evenings (Frankenhaeuser et al. 1989). Until a better insight has been gained into the causal links between workload, stress and health, it will remain necessary to regard prolonged stress responses, displayed in particular by women at the managerial level, as warning signals of possible long-term health risks (Frankenhaeuser, Lundberg and Chesney 1991).

HOURS OF WORK

Timothy H. Monk

Introduction

The patterning and duration of the hours a person works are a very important aspect of his or her experience of the work situation. Most workers feel that they are paid for their time rather than explicitly for their efforts, and thus the transaction between the worker and the employer is one of exchanging time for money. Thus, the quality of the time being exchanged is a very important part of the equation. Time that has high value because of its importance to the worker in terms of allowing sleep, interaction with family and friends and participation in community events may be more highly prized, and thus require extra financial compensation, as compared to normal "day work" time when many of the worker's friends and family members are themselves at work or at school. The balance of the transaction can also be changed by making the time spent at work more congenial to the worker, for example, by improving working conditions. The commute to and from work is unavailable to the worker for recreation, so this time too must be considered as "grey time" (Knauth et al. 1983) and therefore a "cost" to the worker. Thus, measures such as compressed workweeks, which reduce the number of commuting trips taken per week, or flexitime, which reduces the commute time by allowing the worker to avoid the rush hour, are again likely to change the balance.

Background Literature

As Kogi (1991) has remarked, there is a general trend in both manufacturing and service industries towards greater flexibility in the temporal programming of work. There are a number of reasons for this trend, including the high cost of capital equipment, consumer demand for around-the-clock service, legislative pressure to reduce the length of the workweek and (in some societies such as the United States and Australia) taxation pressure on the employer to have as few different employees as possible. For many employees, the conventional "9 to 5" or "8 to 4", Monday through Friday workweek is a thing of the past, either because of new work systems or because of the large amounts of excessive overtime required.

Kogi notes that while the benefits to the employer of such flexibility are quite clear in allowing extended business hours, accommodation of market demand and greater management flexibility, the benefits to the worker may be less certain. Unless the flexible schedule involves elements of choice for workers with respect to their particular hours of work, flexibility can often mean disruptions in their biological clocks and domestic situations. Extended work shifts may also lead to fatigue, compromising safety and productivity, as well as to increased exposure to chemical hazards.

Biological Disruptions due to Abnormal Work Hours

Human biology is specifically oriented towards wakefulness during daylight and sleep at night. Any work schedule which requires late evening or all-night wakefulness as a result of compressed workweeks, mandatory overtime or shiftwork will lead, therefore, to disruptions of the biological clock (Monk and Folkard 1992). These disruptions can be assessed by measuring workers' "circadian rhythms", which comprise regular fluctuations over the 24 hours in vital signs, blood and urine composition, mood and performance efficiency over the 24-hour period (Aschoff 1981). The measure used most often in shiftwork studies has been body temperature, which, under normal conditions, shows a clear rhythm with a peak at about 2000 hours, a trough at about 0500 hours and a difference of about 0.7°C. between the two. After an abrupt change in routine, the amplitude (size) of the rhythm diminishes and the phase (timing) of the rhythm is slow to adjust to the new schedule. Until the adjustment process is complete, sleep is disrupted and daytime mood and performance efficiency are impaired. These symptoms can be regarded as the shiftwork equivalent of jet-lag and can be extremely long lasting (Knauth and Rutenfranz 1976).

Abnormal work hours can also lead to poor health. Although it has proved difficult to precisely quantify the exact size of the effect, it appears that, in addition to sleep disorders, gastrointestinal disorders (including peptic ulcers) and cardiovascular disease can be more frequently found in shift workers (and former shift workers) than in day workers (Scott and LaDou 1990). There is also some preliminary evidence for increased incidence of psychiatric symptoms (Cole, Loving and Kripke 1990).

Social Disruptions due to Abnormal Work Hours

Not only human biology, but also human society, opposes those who work abnormal hours. Unlike the nocturnal sleep of the majority, which is carefully protected by strict taboos against loud noise and telephone use at night, the late wakening, day-sleeping and napping that are required by those working abnormal work hours is only grudgingly tolerated by society. Evening and weekend community events can also be denied to these people, leading to feelings of alienation.

It is with the family, however, that the social disruptions of abnormal work hours may be the most devastating. For the worker, the family roles of parent, caregiver, social companion and sexual partner can all be severely compromised by abnormal work hours, leading to marital disharmony and problems with children (Colligan and Rosa 1990). Moreover, the worker's attempts to rectify, or to avoid, such social problems may result in a decrease in sleep time, thus leading to poor alertness and compromised safety and productivity.

Suggested Solutions

Just as the problems of abnormal work hours are multifaceted, so too must be the solutions to those problems. The primary areas to be addressed should include:

1. selection and education of the worker
2. selection of the most appropriate work schedule or roster
3. improvement of the work environment.

Selection and education of the worker should involve identification and counselling of those persons likely to experience difficulties with abnormal or extended work hours (e.g., older workers and those with high sleep needs, extensive domestic workloads or long commutes). Education in circadian and sleep hygiene principles and family counselling should also be made available (Monk and Folkard 1992). Education is an extremely powerful tool in helping those with abnormal work hours to cope, and in reassuring them about why they may be experiencing

problems. Selection of the most appropriate schedule should begin with a decision as to whether abnormal work hours are actually needed at all. For example, night work may in many cases be done better at a different time of day (Knauth and Rutenfranz 1982). Consideration should be also be given to the schedule best suited to the work situation, bearing in mind the nature of the work and the demographics of the workforce. Improvement of the work environment may involve raising illumination levels and providing adequate canteen facilities at night.

Conclusions

The particular pattern of work hours chosen for an employee can represent a significant challenge to his or her biology, domestic situation and role in the community. Informed decisions should be made, incorporating a study of the demands of the work situation and the demographics of the workforce. Any changes in hours of work should be preceded by detailed investigation and consultation with the employees and followed by evaluation studies.

ENVIRONMENTAL DESIGN

Daniel Stokols

Overview

In this article, the links between the physical features of the workplace and occupational health are examined. Workplace design is concerned with a variety of physical conditions within work environments that can be objectively observed or recorded and modified through architectural, interior design and site planning interventions. For the purposes of this discussion, occupational health is broadly construed to encompass multiple facets of workers' physical, mental and social well-being (World Health Organization 1984). Thus, a broad array of health outcomes is examined, including employee satisfaction and morale, workgroup cohesion, stress reduction, illness and injury prevention, as well as environmental supports for health promotion at the worksite.

Empirical evidence for the links between workplace design and occupational health is reviewed below. This review, highlighting the health effects of specific design features, must be qualified in certain respects. First, from an ecological perspective, worksites function as complex systems comprised of multiple social and physical environmental conditions, which jointly influence employee well-being (Levi 1992; Moos 1986; Stokols 1992). Thus, the health consequences of environmental conditions are often cumulative and sometimes involve complex mediated and moderated relationships among the sociophysical environment, personal resources and dispositions (Oldham and Fried 1987; Smith 1987; Stellman and Henifin 1983). Moreover, enduring qualities of people-environment transaction, such as the degree to which employees perceive their work situation to be controllable, socially supportive and compatible with their particular needs and abilities, may have a more pervasive influence on occupational health than any single facet of workplace design (Caplan 1983; Karasek and Theorell 1990; Parkes 1989; Repetti 1993; Sauter, Hurrell and Cooper 1989). The research findings reviewed should be interpreted in light of these caveats.

Research Findings

The relationships between worksite design and occupational health can be considered at several levels of analysis, including the:

1. physical arrangement of employees' immediate work area
2. ambient environmental qualities of the work area

Table 34.1 • Workplace design resources and potential health benefits.

Levels of environmental design	Environmental design features of the workplace	Emotional, social and physical health outcomes
Immediate work area	Physical enclosure of the work area	Enhanced privacy and job satisfaction
	Adjustable furniture and equipment	Reduced eyestrain and repetitive-strain and lower-back injuries
	Localized controls of acoustics, lighting and ventilation	Enhanced comfort and stress reduction
	Natural elements and personalized decor	Enhanced sense of identity and involvement at the workplace
	Presence of windows in work area	Job satisfaction and stress reduction
Ambient qualities of the work area	Speech privacy and noise control	Lower physiological, emotional stress
	Comfortable levels of social density	Lower physiological, emotional stress
	Good mix of private and team spaces	Improved social climate, cohesion
	Symbols of corporate and team identity	Improved social climate, cohesion
	Natural, task, and lensed indirect lighting	Reduced eyestrain, enhanced satisfaction
	Natural ventilation vs. chilled-air systems	Lower rates of respiratory problems
Building organization	Adjacencies among interacting units	Enhanced coordination and cohesion
	Legible signage and wayfinding aids	Reduced confusion and distress
	Injury-resistant architecture	Lower rates of unintentional injuries
	Attractive lounge and food areas onsite	Enhanced satisfaction with job, worksite
	Availability of worksite child care	Employee convenience, stress reduction
	Physical fitness facilities onsite	Improved health practices, lower stress
Exterior amenities and site planning	Availability of outside recreation areas	Enhanced cohesion, stress reduction
	Access to parking and public transit	Employee convenience, stress reduction
	Proximity to restaurants and stores	Employee convenience, stress reduction
	Good air quality in surrounding area	Improved respiratory health
	Low levels of neighbourhood violence	Reduced rates of intentional injuries

3. physical organization of buildings that comprise a particular workplace
4. exterior amenities and site planning of those facilities.

Previous research has focused primarily on the first and second levels, while giving less attention to the third and fourth levels of workplace design.

Physical features of the immediate work area

The immediate work area extends from the core of an employee's desk or workstation to the physical enclosure or imaginary boundary surrounding his or her work space. Several features of the immediate work area have been found to influence employee well-being. The degree of physical enclosure surrounding one's desk or workstation, for example, has been shown in several studies to be positively related to the employee's perception of privacy, satisfaction with the work environment and overall job satisfaction (Brill, Margulis and Konar 1984; Hedge 1986; Marans and Yan 1989; Oldham 1988; Sundstrom 1986; Wineman 1986). Moreover, "open-plan" (low enclosure) work areas have been linked to more negative social climates in work groups (Moos 1986) and more frequent reports of headaches among employees (Hedge 1986). It is important to note, however, that the potential health effects of workstation enclosure may depend on the type of work being performed (e.g., confidential versus non-confidential, team versus individualized tasks; see Brill, Margulis and Konar 1984), job status (Sundstrom 1986), levels of social density adjacent to one's work

area (Oldham and Fried 1987), and workers' needs for privacy and stimulation screening (Oldham 1988).

A number of studies have shown that the presence of windows in the employees' immediate work areas (especially windows that afford views of natural or landscaped settings), exposure to indoor natural elements (e.g., potted plants, pictures of wilderness settings), and opportunities to personalize the decor of one's office or workstation are associated with higher levels of environmental and job satisfaction and lower levels of stress (Brill, Margulis and Konar 1984; Goodrich 1986; Kaplan and Kaplan 1989; Steele 1986; Sundstrom 1986). Providing employees with localized controls over acoustic, lighting and ventilation conditions within their work areas has been linked to higher levels of environmental satisfaction and lower levels of stress in some studies (Becker 1990; Hedge 1991; Vischer 1989). Finally, several research programmes have documented the health benefits associated with employees' use of adjustable, ergonomically sound furniture and equipment; these benefits include reduced rates of eyestrain and of repetitive motion injuries and lower back pain (Dainoff and Dainoff 1986; Grandjean 1987; Smith 1987).

Ambient environmental qualities of the work area

Ambient environmental conditions originate from outside the worker's immediate work area. These pervasive qualities of the worksite influence the comfort and well-being of employees whose work spaces are located within a common region (e.g., a suite of offices located on one floor of a building). Examples of ambient environmental qualities include levels of noise, speech privacy, social density, illumination and air quality—conditions that are typically present within a particular portion of the work-site. Several studies have documented the adverse health impacts of chronic noise disturbance and low levels of speech privacy in the workplace, including elevated levels of physiological and psychological stress and reduced levels of job satisfaction (Brill, Margulis and Konar 1984; Canter 1983; Klitzman and Stellman 1989; Stellman and Henifin 1983; Sundstrom 1986; Sutton and Rafaeli 1987). High levels of social density in the immediate vicinity of one's work area have also been linked with elevated stress levels and reduced job satisfaction (Oldham 1988; Oldham and Fried 1987; Oldham and Rotchford 1983).

Health consequences of office lighting and ventilation systems have been observed as well. In one study, lensed indirect fluorescent uplighting was associated with higher levels of employee satisfaction and reduced eyestrain, in comparison with traditional fluorescent downlighting (Hedge 1991). Positive effects of natural lighting on employees' satisfaction with the workplace also have been reported (Brill, Margulis and Konar 1984; Goodrich 1986; Vischer and Mees 1991). In another study, office workers exposed to chilled-air ventilation systems evidenced higher rates of upper-respiratory problems and physical symptoms of "sick building syndrome" than those whose buildings were equipped with natural or mechanical (non-chilled, non-humidified) ventilation systems (Burge et al. 1987; Hedge 1991).

Features of the ambient environment that have been found to enhance the social climate and cohesiveness of work groups include the provision of team-oriented spaces adjacent to individualized offices and workstations (Becker 1990; Brill, Margulis and Konar 1984; Steele 1986; Stone and Luchetti 1985) and visible symbols of corporate and team identity displayed within lobbies, corridors, conference rooms, lounges and other collectively used areas of the worksite (Becker 1990; Danko, Eshelman and Hedge 1990; Ornstein 1990; Steele 1986).

Overall organization of buildings and facilities

This level of design encompasses the interior physical features of work facilities that extend throughout an entire building, many of which are not immediately experienced within an employee's own work space or within those adjacent to it. For example, enhancing the structural integrity and fire-resistance of buildings, and designing stairwells, corridors and factories to prevent injuries, are essential strategies for promoting worksite safety and health (Archea and Connell 1986; Danko, Eshelman and Hedge 1990). Building layouts that are consistent with the adjacency needs of closely interacting units within an organization can improve coordination and cohesion among work groups (Becker 1990; Brill, Margulis and Konar 1984; Sundstrom and Altman 1989). The provision of physical fitness facilities at the worksite has been found to be an effective strategy for enhancing employees' health practices and stress management (O'Donnell and Harris 1994). Finally, the presence of legible signs and wayfinding aids, attractive lounge and dining areas, and child-care facilities at the worksite have been identified as design strategies that enhance employees' job satisfaction and stress management (Becker 1990; Brill, Margulis and Konar 1984; Danko, Eshelman and Hedge 1990; Steele 1986; Stellman and Henifin 1983; Vischer 1989).

Exterior amenities and site planning

Exterior environmental conditions adjacent to the worksite may also carry health consequences. One study reported an association between employees' access to landscaped, outdoor recreational areas and reduced levels of job stress (Kaplan and Kaplan 1989). Other researchers have suggested that the geographic location and site planning of the worksite can influence the mental and physical well-being of workers to the extent that they afford greater access to parking and public transit, restaurants and retail services, good regional air quality and the avoidance of violent or otherwise unsafe areas in the surrounding neighbourhood (Danko, Eshelman and Hedge 1990; Michelson 1985; Vischer and Mees 1991). However, the health benefits of these design strategies have not yet been evaluated in empirical studies.

Directions for Future Research

Prior studies of environmental design and occupational health reflect certain limitations and suggest several issues for future investigation. First, earlier research has emphasized the health effects of specific design features (e.g., workstation enclosure, furnishings, lighting systems), while neglecting the joint influence of physical, interpersonal and organizational factors on well-being. Yet the health benefits of improved environmental design may be moderated by the social climate and organizational qualities (as moderated, for example, by a participative versus non-participative structure) of the workplace (Becker 1990; Parkes 1989; Klitzman and Stellman 1989; Sommer 1983; Steele 1986). The interactive links between physical design features, employee characteristics, social conditions at work and occupational health, therefore, warrant greater attention in subsequent studies (Levi 1992; Moos 1986; Stokols 1992). At the same time, an important challenge for future research is to clarify the operational definitions of particular design features (e.g., the "open plan" office), which have varied widely in earlier studies (Brill, Margulis and Konar 1984; Marans and Yan 1989; Wineman 1986).

Secondly, employee characteristics such as job status, gender and dispositional styles have been found to mediate the health consequences of worksite design (Burge et al. 1987; Oldham 1988; Hedge 1986; Sundstrom 1986). Yet, it is often difficult to disentangle the separate effects of environmental features and individual differences (these differences may have to do with, for example, workstation enclosures, comfortable furnishings, and job status) because of ecological correlations among these variables (Klitzman and Stellman 1989). Future studies should incorporate experimental techniques and sampling strategies that permit an assessment of the main and interactive effects of personal and environmental factors on occupational health. Moreover, specialized design and ergonomic criteria to enhance the health of diverse and vulnerable employee groups (e.g., disabled, elderly and single-parent female workers) remain to be developed in future research (Michelson 1985; Ornstein 1990; Steinfeld 1986).

Thirdly, prior research on the health outcomes of worksite design has relied heavily on survey methods to assess employees' perceptions of both their work environments and health status, placing certain constraints (for example, "common method variance") on the interpretation of data (Klitzman and Stellman 1989; Oldham and Rotchford 1983). Furthermore, the majority of these studies have used cross-sectional rather than longitudinal research designs, the latter incorporating comparative assessments of intervention and control groups. Future studies should emphasize both field-experimental research designs and multi-method strategies that combine survey techniques with more objective observations and recordings of environmental conditions, medical exams and physiological measures.

Finally, the health consequences of building organization, exterior amenities and site-planning decisions have received considerably less attention in prior studies than those associated with the more immediate, ambient qualities of employees' work areas. The health relevance of both proximal and remote aspects of workplace design should be examined more closely in future research.

Role of Workplace Design in Illness Prevention and Health Promotion

Several environmental design resources and their potential health benefits are summarized in table 34.1, based on the preceding review of research findings. These resources are grouped according to the four levels of design noted above and emphasize physical features of work settings that have been empirically linked to improved mental, physical and social health outcomes (especially those found at levels 1 and 2), or have been identified as theoretically plausible leverage points for enhancing employee well-being (e.g., several of the features subsumed under levels 3 and 4).

The incorporation of these resources into the design of work environments should, ideally, be combined with organizational and facilities management policies that maximize the health- promoting qualities of the workplace. These corporate policies include:

1. the designation of worksites as "smoke-free" (Fielding and Phenow 1988)
2. the specification and use of non-toxic, ergonomically sound furnishings and equipment (Danko, Eshelman and Hedge 1990)
3. managerial support for employees' personalization of their workspace (Becker 1990; Brill, Margulis and Konar 1984; Sommer 1983; Steele 1986)
4. job designs that prevent health problems linked with computer-based work and repetitive tasks (Hackman and Oldham 1980; Sauter, Hurrell and Cooper 1989; Smith and Sainfort 1989)
5. the provision of employee training programmes in the areas of ergonomics and occupational safety and health (Levy and Wegman 1988)
6. incentive programmes to encourage employees' use of physical fitness facilities and compliance with injury prevention protocols (O'Donnell and Harris 1994)
7. flexitime, telecommuting, job-sharing and ride-sharing programmes to enhance workers' effectiveness in residential and corporate settings (Michelson 1985; Ornstein 1990; Parkes 1989; Stokols and Novaco 1981)
8. the involvement of employees in the planning of worksite relocations, renovations and related organizational developments (Becker 1990; Brill, Margulis and Konar 1984; Danko, Eshelman and Hedge 1990; Miller and Monge 1986; Sommer 1983; Steele 1986; Stokols et al. 1990).

Organizational efforts to enhance employee well-being are likely to be more effective to the extent that they combine complementary strategies of environmental design and facilities management, rather than relying exclusively on either one of these approaches.

● ERGONOMIC FACTORS

Michael J. Smith

The purpose of this article is to afford the reader an understanding of how ergonomic conditions can affect the psychosocial aspects of working, employee satisfaction with the work environment, and employee health and well-being. The major thesis is that, with respect to physical surroundings, job demands and technological factors, improper design of the work environment and job activities can cause adverse employee perceptions, psychological stress and health problems (Smith and Sainfort 1989; Cooper and Marshall 1976).

Industrial ergonomics is the science of fitting the work environment and job activities to the capabilities, dimensions and needs of people. Ergonomics deals with the physical work environment, tools and technology design, workstation design, job demands and physiological and biomechanical loading on the body. Its goal is to increase the degree of fit among the employees, the environments in which they work, their tools and their job demands. When the fit is poor, stress and health problems can occur. The many relationships between the demands of the job and psychological distress are discussed elsewhere in this chapter as well as in Smith and Sainfort (1989), in which a definition is given of the balance theory of job stress and job design. Balance is the use of different aspects of job design to counteract job stressors. The concept of job balance is important in the examination of ergonomic considerations and health. For instance, the discomforts and disorders produced by poor ergonomic conditions can make an individual more susceptible to job stress and psychological disorders, or can intensify the somatic effects of job stress.

As spelled out by Smith and Sainfort (1989), there are various sources of job stress, including

1. job demands such as high workload and work pace
2. poor job content factors that produce boredom and lack of meaningfulness
3. limited job control or decision latitude
4. organizational policies and procedures that alienate the workforce
5. supervisory style affecting participation and socialization
6. environmental contamination
7. technology factors
8. ergonomic conditions.

Smith (1987) and Cooper and Marshall (1976) discuss the characteristics of the workplace that can cause psychological stress. These include improper workload, heavy work pressure, hostile environment, role ambiguity, lack of challenging tasks, cognitive overload, poor supervisory relations, lack of task control or decision-making authority, poor relationship with other employees and lack of social support from supervisors, fellow employees and family.

Adverse ergonomic characteristics of work can cause visual, muscular and psychological disturbances such as visual fatigue, eye strain, sore eyes, headaches, fatigue, muscle soreness, cumulative trauma disorders, back disorders, psychological tension, anxiety and depression. Sometimes these effects are temporary and may disappear when the individual is removed from work or given an opportunity to rest at work, or when the design of the work environment is improved. When exposure to poor ergonomic conditions is chronic, then the effects can become permanent. Visual and muscular disturbances, and aches and pains can induce anxiety in employees. The result may be psychological stress or an exacerbation of the stress effects of other adverse working conditions that cause stress. Visual and musculoskeletal disorders that lead to a loss of function and disability can lead to anxiety, depression, anger and melancholy. There is a synergistic relationship among the disorders caused by ergonomic misfit, so that a circular effect is created in which visual or muscular discomfort generates more psychological stress, which then leads to a greater sensitivity in pain perception in the eyes and muscles, which leads to more stress and so on.

Smith and Sainfort (1989) have defined five elements of the work system that are significant in the design of work that relate to the causes and control of stress. These are: (1) the person; (2) the physical work environment; (3) tasks; (4) technology; and (5) work organization. All but the person are discussed.

Physical Work Environment

The physical work environment produces sensory demands which affect an employee's ability to see, hear and touch properly, and includes such features as air quality, temperature and humidity. In addition, noise is one of the most prominent of the ergonomic conditions that produce stress (Cohen and Spacapan 1983). When physical working conditions produce a "poor fit" with employees' needs and capabilities, generalized fatigue, sensory fatigue and performance frustration are the result. Such conditions can lead to psychological stress (Grandjean 1968).

Technology and Workstation Factors

Various aspects of technology have proved troublesome for employees, including incompatible controls and displays, poor response characteristics of controls, displays with poor sensory sensitivity, difficulty in operating characteristics of the technology, equipment that impairs employee performance and equipment breakdowns (Sanders and McCormick 1993; Smith et al. 1992a). Research has shown that employees with such problems report more physical and psychological stress (Smith and Sainfort 1989; Sauter, Dainoff and Smith 1990).

Tasks

Two very critical ergonomic task factors that have been tied to job stress are heavy workloads and work pressure (Cooper and Smith 1985). Too much or too little work produces stress, as does unwanted overtime work. When employees must work under time pressure, for example, to meet deadlines or when the workload is unrelentingly high, then stress is also high. Other critical task factors that have been tied to stress are machine pacing of the work process, a lack of cognitive content of the job tasks and low task control. From an ergonomic perspective, workloads should be established using scientific methods of time and motion evaluation (ILO 1986), and not be set by other criteria such as economic need to recover capital investment or by the capacity of the technology.

Organizational Factors

Three ergonomic aspects of the management of the work process have been identified as conditions that can lead to employee psychological stress. These are shift work, machine-paced work or assembly-line work, and unwanted overtime (Smith 1987). Shift work has been shown to disrupt biological rhythms and basic physiological functioning (Tepas and Monk 1987; Monk and Tepas 1985). Machine-paced work or assembly-line work that produces short-cycle tasks with little cognitive content and low employee control over the process leads to stress (Sauter, Hurrell and Cooper 1989). Unwanted overtime can lead to employee fatigue and to adverse psychological reactions such as anger and mood disturbances (Smith 1987). Machine-paced work, unwanted overtime and perceived lack of control over work activities have also been linked to mass psychogenic illness (Colligan 1985).

● AUTONOMY AND CONTROL

Daniel Ganster

Autonomy and job control are concepts with a long history in the study of work and health. Autonomy—the extent to which workers can exercise discretion in how they perform their work—is most closely associated with theories that are concerned with the challenge of designing work so that it is intrinsically motivating, satisfying and conducive to physical and mental well-being. In virtually all such theories, the concept of autonomy plays a central role. The term control (defined below) is generally understood to have a broader meaning than autonomy. In fact, one could consider autonomy to be a specialized form of the more general concept of control. Because control is the more inclusive term, it will be used throughout the remainder of this article.

Throughout the 1980s, the concept of control formed the core of perhaps the most influential theory of occupational stress (see, for example, the review of the work stress literature by Ganster and Schaubroeck 1991b). This theory, usually known as the Job Decision Latitude Model (Karasek 1979) stimulated many large-scale epidemiological studies that investigated the joint effects of control in conjunction with a variety of demanding work conditions on worker health. Though there has been some controversy regarding the exact way that control might help determine health outcomes, epidemiologists and organizational psychologists have come to regard control as a critical variable that should be given serious consideration in any investigation of psychosocial work stress conditions. Concern for the possible detrimental effects of low worker control was so high, for example, that in 1987 the National Institute for Occupational Safety and Health (NIOSH) of the United States organized a special workshop of authorities from epidemiology, psychophysiology, and industrial and organizational psychology to critically review the evidence concerning the impact of control on worker health and well-being. This workshop eventually culminated in the comprehensive volume *Job Control and Worker Health* (Sauter, Hurrell and Cooper 1989) that provides a discussion of the global research efforts on control. Such widespread acknowledgement of the role of control in worker well-being also had an impact on governmental policy, with the Swedish Work Environment Act (Ministry of Labour 1987) stating that "the aim must be for work to be arranged in such a way so that the employee himself can influence his work situation". In the remainder of this article I summarize the research evidence on work control with the goal of providing the occupational health and safety specialist with the following:

1. a discussion of aspects of worker control that might be important
2. guidelines about how to assess job control in the worksite
3. ideas on how to intervene so as to reduce the deleterious effects of low worker control.

First, what exactly is meant by the term control? In its broadest sense it refers to workers' ability to actually influence what happens in their work environment. Moreover, this ability to influence the work setting should be considered in light of the worker's goals. The term refers to the ability to influence matters that are relevant to one's personal goals. This emphasis on being able to influence the work environment distinguishes control from the related concept of predictability. The latter refers to one's being able to anticipate what demands will be made on oneself, for example, but does not imply any ability to alter those demands. Lack of predictability constitutes a source of stress in its own right, particularly when it produces a high level of ambiguity about what performance strategies one ought to adopt to perform effectively or if one even has a secure future with the employer. Another distinction that should be made is that between control and the more inclusive concept of job complexity. Early conceptualizations of control considered it together with such aspects of work as skill level and availability of social interaction. Our discussion here discriminates control from these other domains of job complexity.

One can consider mechanisms by which workers can exercise control and the domains over which that control can apply. One way that workers can exercise control is by making decisions as individuals. These decisions can be about what tasks to complete, the order of those tasks, and the standards and processes to follow in completing those tasks, to name but a few. The worker might also have some collective control either through representation or by social action with co-workers. In terms of domains, control might apply to such matters as the work pace, the amount and timing of interaction with others, the physical work environment (lighting, noise and privacy), scheduling of vacations or even matters of policy at the worksite. Finally, one can distinguish between objective and subjective control. One might, for example, have the ability to choose one's work pace but not be aware of it. Similarly, one might believe that one can influence policies in the workplace even though this influence is essentially nil.

How can the occupational health and safety specialist assess the level of control in a work situation? As recorded in the literature, basically two approaches have been taken. One approach has been to make an occupational-level determination of control. In this case every worker in a given occupation would be considered to have the same level of control, as it is assumed to be determined by the nature of the occupation itself. The

disadvantage to this approach, of course, is that one cannot obtain much insight as to how workers are faring in a particular worksite, where their control might have been determined as much by their employer's policies and practices as by their occupational status. The more common approach is to survey workers about their subjective perceptions of control. A number of psychometrically sound measures have been developed for this purpose and are readily available. The NIOSH control scale (McLaney and Hurrell 1988), for example, consists of sixteen questions and provides assessments of control in the domains of task, decision, resources and physical environment. Such scales can easily be incorporated into an assessment of worker safety and health concerns.

Is control a significant determinant of worker safety and health? This question has driven many large-scale research efforts since at least 1985. Since most of these studies have consisted of non-experimental field surveys in which control was not purposely manipulated, the evidence can only show a systematic correlation between control and health and safety outcome variables. The lack of experimental evidence prevents us from making direct

Figure 34.7 • Classification of paced work.

NON-MACHINE-PACED WORK

Truly unpaced	Socially paced	Self-paced	Incentive-paced
No internal or external pacing is imposed. The task is performed at a pace chosen by the operator.	Although no pacing is imposed by management or machinery, there is peer or group pressure to perform to a set pace. There are two classes of socially paced work. One is customer-based: a number of customers queued up for services will affect the pace of work so as to elicit service at an acceptable rate. The other is group pressure to perform to a set pace. Performers in entertainment, lecturers, teachers and sports players are clearly examples in this connection.	Although there is no machine pacing, the work is paced by management objectives. An example is day rate work, where an operator must produce a specified number of items by the end of the workday. Provided that by the end of the day the operators produce the required amount, they may spend different amounts of time on each cycle of the job.	An incentive-paced task consists of two additive parts, namely the "self-paced" component and the operator's financial motivation to produce above the self-paced work. The more the operator produces above this self-paced level, the higher the operator's income will be. Hence, the intensity and severity of the pacing is dictated by how much the operator wants to earn.

MACHINE-PACED WORK

Pacing influenced by length of work cycle	Pacing in a buffer stock system	Pacing influenced by the rate of machine-paced work	Continuous versus discrete pacing
When the cycle length in machine-paced work is extremely long, it approaches the state of the self-paced condition. The shorter the cycle time, the less the operator's performance variability can be tolerated.	Buffer stock system is "an arrangement which makes more than one component or feeding position available to an operative at the same time" (Murrell 1965). Machine-paced work can be carried out with or without buffer stocks. When machine-paced work is designed with a buffer between stations, the effects of stringency associated with machine-paced work may be reduced: the larger the buffer stocks, the smaller the stringency associated with machine-paced work. Extremely large buffer stock between workstations may reduce the effects of machine-paced work to those of self-paced work.	When a fair day's work is defined as 100%, the rate of machine-paced work is frequently performed at rates ranging from 100 to 125. The impact of machine-paced work on the operator may be different, depending at which rate the task is performed.	Both pacing modes are widely utilized in industry. For example, in conveyor operations the conveyor can either move continuously, in which case the operator performs the task in a dynamic visual work environment, or the conveyor can be indexed in a discrete mode. In the latter case, the conveyor is stationary during a fixed job-cycle period when the operator is working on the job. At the end of each work cycle, the conveyor indexes to the next workstation. During this indexing period (which usually takes two to eight seconds), the operator can either be doing preparatory work for the next cycle of operation or be idle.

causal assertions, but the correlational evidence is quite consistent in showing that workers with lower levels of control suffer more from mental and physical health complaints. The evidence is strongly suggestive, then, that increasing worker control constitutes a viable strategy for improving the health and welfare of workers. A more controversial question is whether control interacts with other sources of psychosocial stress to determine health outcomes. That is, will high control levels counteract the deleterious effects of other job demands? This is an intriguing question, for, if true, it suggests that the ill effects of high workloads, for example, can be negated by increasing worker control with no corresponding need to lower workload demands. The evidence is clearly mixed on this question, however. About as many investigators have reported such interaction effects as have not. Thus, control should not be considered a panacea that will cure the problems brought on by other psychosocial stressors.

Work by organizational researchers suggests that increasing worker control can significantly improve health and well-being. Moreover, it is relatively easy to make a diagnosis of low worker control through the use of brief survey measures. How can the health and safety specialist intervene, then, to increase worker control levels? As there are many domains of control, there are many ways to increase workplace control. These range from providing opportunities for workers to participate in decisions that affect them to the fundamental redesign of jobs. What is clearly important is that control domains be targeted that are relevant to the primary goals of the workers and that fit the situational demands. These domains can probably best be determined by involving workers in joint diagnosis and problem-solving sessions. It should be noted, however, that the kinds of changes in the workplace that in many cases are necessary to achieve real gains in control involve fundamental changes in management systems and policies. Increasing control might be as simple as providing a switch that allows machine-paced workers to control their pace, but it is just as likely to involve important changes in the decision-making authority of workers. Thus, organizational decision makers must usually be full and active supporters of control enhancing interventions.

WORK PACING

Gavriel Salvendy

In this article, the reasons machine-pacing is utilized in the workplace are reviewed. Furthermore, a classification of machine-paced work, information on the impact of machine-paced work on well-being and methodologies by which the effects can be alleviated or reduced, are set forth.

Benefits of Machine-Paced Work
The effective utilization of machine-paced work has the following benefits for an organization:

- It increases customer satisfaction: for example, it provides speedier service in drive-in restaurants when a number of stations are assigned to serve the customers sequentially.
- It reduces overhead cost through economic use of high technology, reduction of stock set aside for processing, reduction in factory floor space and reduction in supervisory costs.
- It reduces direct costs through reduced training time, lower hourly wages and high production return per unit of wages.
- It contributes to national productivity through provision of employment for unskilled workers and reduction in the production costs of goods and services.

Table 34.2 • Psychological profiles of operators who prefer self-paced and machine-paced work.

Machine-paced work	Self-paced work
Less intelligent	More intelligent
Humble	Assertive
Practical	Imaginative
Forthright	Shrewd
Group-dependent	Self-sufficient

Classification of Machine-Paced Work
A classification of paced work is provided in figure 34.7.

Effect of Machine-Paced Work on Well-Being
Machine-paced research has been carried out in laboratory settings, in industry (by case studies and controlled experiments) and by epidemiological studies (Salvendy 1981).

An analysis was performed of 85 studies dealing with machine-paced and self-paced work, of which 48% were laboratory studies, 30% industrial, 14% review studies, 4% combined laboratory and industrial, and 4% conceptual studies (Burke and Salvendy 1981). Of the 103 variables used in these studies, 41% were physiological, 32% were performance variables and 27% psychological. From this analysis, the following practical implications were derived for the use of machine-paced versus self-paced work arrangements:

- Tasks with high cognitive or perceptual load should be administered under self-paced as opposed to machine-paced conditions.

Figure 34.8 • Effects of performance feedback on reduction of stress.

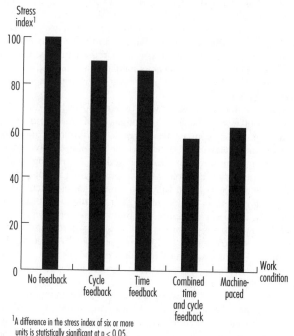

[1]A difference in the stress index of six or more units is statistically significant at p < 0.05.

- To reduce error and low productivity, jobs should be allocated according to the worker's personality and capacities.
- Intelligent, shrewd, creative and self-sufficient operators prefer to work on self-paced rather than machine-paced tasks. (See table 34.2 for more complete psychological profiles.)
- Workers should be encouraged to select a workload capacity which is optimum for them in any given situation.
- To maintain a high activation level (or the required level for performing the task), the work sessions should be interrupted by rest periods or by other types of work. This type of break should be implemented before the onset of deactivation.
- Maximal work speeds are not economical and can result in workers' becoming overstrained when they continue to work excessively fast for a long time. On the other hand, too low a speed may also be detrimental to workers' performance.

In studying industrial workers for an entire year in our experimentally controlled situation, in which over 50 million data points were collected, it was shown that 45% of the labour force prefers self-paced work, 45% prefers machine-paced work, and 10% does not like work of any type (Salvendy1976).

Uncertainty is the most significant contributor to stress and can be effectively managed by performance feedback (see fig. 34.8) (Salvendy and Knight 1983).

● ELECTRONIC WORK MONITORING

Lawrence M. Schleifer

The computerization of work has made possible the development of a new approach to work monitoring called electronic performance monitoring (EPM). EPM has been defined as the "computerized collection, storage, analysis, and reporting of information about employees' activities on a continuous basis" (USOTA 1987). Although banned in many European countries, electronic performance monitoring is increasing throughout the world on account of intense competitive pressures to improve productivity in a global economy.

EPM has changed the psychosocial work environment. This application of computer technology has significant implications for work supervision, workload demands, performance appraisal, performance feedback, rewards, fairness and privacy. As a result, occupational health researchers, worker representatives, government agencies and the public news media have expressed concern about the stress-health effects of electronic performance monitoring (USOTA 1987).

Traditional approaches to work monitoring include direct observation of work behaviours, examination of work samples, review of progress reports and analysis of performance measures (Larson and Callahan 1990). Historically, employers have always attempted to improve on these methods of monitoring worker performance. Considered as part of a continuing monitoring effort across the years, then, EPM is not a new development. What is new, however, is the use of EPM, particularly in office and service work, to capture employee performance on a second-by-second, keystroke-by-keystroke basis so that work management in the form of corrective action, performance feedback, delivery of incentive pay, or disciplinary measures can be taken at any time (Smith 1988). In effect, the human supervisor is being replaced by an electronic supervisor.

EPM is used in office work such as word processing and data entry to monitor keystroke production and error rates. Airline reservation clerks and directory assistance operators are monitored by computers to determine how long it takes to service customers and to measure the time interval between calls. EPM also is used in more traditional economic sectors. Freight haulers, for example, are using computers to monitor driver speed and fuel consumption, and tire manufacturers are electronically monitoring the productivity of rubber workers. In sum, EPM is used to establish performance standards, track employee performance, compare actual performance with predetermined standards and administer incentive pay programmes based on these standards (USOTA 1987).

Advocates of EPM assert that continuous electronic work monitoring is essential to high performance and productivity in the contemporary workplace. It is argued that EPM enables managers and supervisors to organize and control human, material and financial resources. Specifically, EPM provides for:

1. increased control over performance variability
2. increased objectivity and timeliness of performance evaluation and feedback
3. efficient management of large office and customer service operations through the electronic supervision of work, and
4. establishment and enforcement of performance standards (for example, number of forms processed per hour).

Supporters of electronic monitoring also claim that, from the worker's perspective, there are several benefits. Electronic monitoring, for example, can provide regular feedback of work performance, which enables workers to take corrective action when necessary. It also satisfies the worker's need for self-evaluation and reduces performance uncertainty.

Despite the possible benefits of EPM, there is concern that certain monitoring practices are abusive and constitute an invasion of employee privacy (USOTA 1987). Privacy has become an issue particularly when workers do not know when or how often they are being monitored. Since work organizations often do not share performance data with workers, a related privacy issue is whether workers should have access to their own performance records or the right to question possible wrong information.

Workers also have raised objections to the manner in which monitoring systems have been implemented (Smith, Carayon and Miezio 1986; Westin 1986). In some workplaces, monitoring is perceived as an unfair labour practice when it is used to measure individual, as opposed to group, performance. In particular, workers have taken exception to the use of monitoring to enforce compliance with performance standards that impose excessive workload demands. Electronic monitoring also can make the work process more impersonal by replacing a human supervisor with an electronic supervisor. In addition, the overemphasis on increased production may encourage workers to compete instead of cooperate with one another.

Various theoretical paradigms have been postulated to account for the possible stress-health effects of EPM (Amick and Smith 1992; Schleifer and Shell 1992; Smith et al. 1992b). A fundamental assumption made by many of these models is that EPM indirectly influences stress-health outcomes by intensifying workload demands, diminishing job control and reducing social support. In effect, EPM mediates changes in the psychosocial work environment that result in an imbalance between the demands of the job and the worker's resources to adapt.

The impact of EPM on the psychosocial work environment is felt at three levels of the work system: the organization-technology interface, the job-technology interface and the human-technology interface (Amick and Smith 1992). The extent of work system transformation and the subsequent implications for stress outcomes are contingent upon the inherent characteristics of the EPM process; that is, the type of information gathered, the method of gathering the information and the use of the information (Carayon 1993). These EPM characteristics can interact with various job design factors and increase stress-health risks.

An alternative theoretical perspective views EPM as a stressor that directly results in strain independent of other job-design stress factors (Smith et al. 1992b; Carayon 1994). EPM, for example, can generate fear and tension as a result of workers being constantly watched by "Big Brother". EPM also may be perceived by workers as an invasion of privacy that is highly threatening.

With respect to the stress effects of EPM, empirical evidence obtained from controlled laboratory experiments indicates that EPM can produce mood disturbances (Aiello and Shao 1993; Schleifer, Galinsky and Pan 1995) and hyperventilatory stress reactions (Schleifer and Ley 1994). Field studies have also reported that EPM alters job-design stress factors (for example, workload), which, in turn, generate tension or anxiety together with depression (Smith, Carayon and Miezio 1986; Ditecco et al. 1992; Smith et al. 1992b; Carayon 1994). In addition, EPM is associated with symptoms of musculoskeletal discomfort among telecommunication workers and data-entry office workers (Smith et al. 1992b; Sauter et al. 1993; Schleifer, Galinsky and Pan 1995).

The use of EPM to enforce compliance with performance standards is perhaps one of the most stressful aspects of this approach to work monitoring (Schleifer and Shell 1992). Under these conditions, it may be useful to adjust performance standards with a stress allowance (Schleifer and Shell 1992): a stress allowance would be applied to the normal cycle time, as is the case with other more conventional work allowances such as rest breaks and machine delays. Particularly among workers who have difficulty meeting EPM performance standards, a stress allowance would optimize workload demands and promote well-being by balancing the productivity benefits of electronic performance monitoring against the stress effects of this approach to work monitoring.

Beyond the question of how to minimize or prevent the possible stress-health effects of EPM, a more fundamental issue is whether this "Tayloristic" approach to work monitoring has any utility in the modern workplace. Work organizations are increasingly utilizing sociotechnical work-design methods, "total quality management" practices, participative work groups, and organizational, as opposed to individual, measures of performance. As a result, electronic work monitoring of individual workers on a continuous basis may have no place in high-performance work systems. In this regard, it is interesting to note that those countries (for example, Sweden and Germany) that have banned EPM are the same countries which have most readily embraced the principles and practices associated with high-performance work systems.

● ROLE CLARITY AND ROLE OVERLOAD

Steve M. Jex

Roles represent sets of behaviours that are expected of employees. To understand how organizational roles develop, it is particularly informative to see the process through the eyes of a new employee. Starting with the first day on the job, a new employee is presented with considerable information designed to communicate the organization's role expectations. Some of this information is presented formally through a written job description and regular communications with one's supervisor. Hackman (1992), however, states that workers also receive a variety of informal communications (termed *discretionary stimuli*) designed to shape their organizational roles. For example, a junior school faculty member who is too vocal during a departmental meeting may receive looks of disapproval from more senior colleagues. Such

looks are subtle, but communicate much about what is expected of a junior colleague.

Ideally, the process of defining each employee's role should proceed such that each employee is clear about his or her role. Unfortunately, this is often not the case and employees experience a lack of role clarity or, as it is commonly called, role ambiguity. According to Breaugh and Colihan (1994), employees are often unclear about how to do their jobs, when certain tasks should be performed and the criteria by which their performance will be judged. In some cases, it is simply difficult to provide an employee with a crystal-clear picture of his or her role. For example, when a job is relatively new, it is still "evolving" within the organization. Furthermore, in many jobs the individual employee has tremendous flexibility regarding how to get the job done. This is particularly true of highly complex jobs. In many other cases, however, role ambiguity is simply due to poor communication between either supervisors and subordinates or among members of work groups.

Another problem that can arise when role-related information is communicated to employees is role overload. That is, the role consists of too many responsibilities for an employee to handle in a reasonable amount of time. Role overload can occur for a number of reasons. In some occupations, role overload is the norm. For example, physicians in training experience tremendous role overload, largely as preparation for the demands of medical practice. In other cases, it is due to temporary circumstances. For example, if someone leaves an organization, the roles of other employees may need to be temporarily expanded to make up for the missing worker's absence. In other instances, organizations may not anticipate the demands of the roles they create, or the nature of an employee's role may change over time. Finally, it is also possible that an employee may voluntarily take on too many role responsibilities.

What are the consequences to workers in circumstances characterized by either role ambiguity, role overload or role clarity? Years of research on role ambiguity has shown that it is a noxious state which is associated with negative psychological, physical and behavioural outcomes (Jackson and Schuler 1985). That is, workers who perceive role ambiguity in their jobs tend to be dissatisfied with their work, anxious, tense, report high numbers of somatic complaints, tend to be absent from work and may leave their jobs. The most common correlates of role overload tend to be physical and emotional exhaustion. In addition, epidemiological research has shown that overloaded individuals (as measured by work hours) may be at greater risk for coronary heart disease. In considering the effects of both role ambiguity and role overload, it must be kept in mind that most studies are cross-sectional (measuring role stressors and outcomes at one point in time) and have examined self-reported outcomes. Thus, inferences about causality must be somewhat tentative.

Given the negative effects of role ambiguity and role overload, it is important for organizations to minimize, if not eliminate, these stressors. Since role ambiguity, in many cases, is due to poor communication, it is necessary to take steps to communicate role requirements more effectively. French and Bell (1990), in a book entitled *Organization Development*, describe interventions such as responsibility charting, role analysis and role negotiation. (For a recent example of the application of responsibility charting, see Schaubroeck et al. 1993). Each of these is designed to make employees' role requirements explicit and well defined. In addition, these interventions allow employees input into the process of defining their roles.

When role requirements are made explicit, it may also be revealed that role responsibilities are not equitably distributed among employees. Thus, the previously mentioned interventions may also prevent role overload. In addition, organizations should keep up to date regarding individuals' role responsibilities by reviewing job descriptions and carrying out job analyses (Levine 1983). It may also help to encourage employees to be realistic about the number of role responsibilities they can handle. In some cases, employees who are under pressure to take on too much may need to be more assertive when negotiating role responsibilities.

As a final comment, it must be remembered that role ambiguity and role overload are subjective states. Thus, efforts to reduce these stressors must consider individual differences. Some workers may in fact enjoy the challenge of these stressors. Others, however, may find them aversive. If this is the case, organizations have a moral, legal and financial interest in keeping these stressors at manageable levels.

INTERPERSONAL FACTORS

● SEXUAL HARASSMENT

Chaya S. Piotrkowski

Historically, the sexual harassment of female workers has been ignored, denied, made to seem trivial, condoned and even implicitly supported, with women themselves being blamed for it (MacKinnon 1978). Its victims are almost entirely women, and it has been a problem since females first sold their labour outside the home.

Although sexual harassment also exists outside the workplace, here it will be taken to denote harassment in the workplace.

Sexual harassment is not an innocent flirtation nor the mutual expression of attraction between men and women. Rather, sexual harassment is a workplace stressor that poses a threat to a woman's psychological and physical integrity and security, in a context in which she has little control because of the risk of retaliation and the fear of losing her livelihood. Like other workplace stressors, sexual harassment may have adverse health consequences for women that can be serious and, as such, qualifies as a workplace health and safety issue (Bernstein 1994).

In the United States, sexual harassment is viewed primarily as a discrete case of wrongful conduct to which one may appropriately respond with blame and recourse to legal measures for the individual. In the European Community it tends to be viewed rather as a collective health and safety issue (Bernstein 1994).

Because the manifestations of sexual harassment vary, people may not agree on its defining qualities, even where it has been set forth in law. Still, there are some common features of harassment that are generally accepted by those doing work in this area:

1. Sexual harassment may involve verbal or physical sexual behaviours directed at a specific woman (*quid pro quo*), or it may involve more general behaviours that create a "hostile environment" that is degrading, humiliating and intimidating towards women (MacKinnon 1978).
2. It is unwelcome and unwanted.
3. It can vary in severity.

When directed towards a specific woman it can involve sexual comments and seductive behaviours, "propositions" and pressure for dates, touching, sexual coercion through the use of threats or bribery and even physical assault and rape. In the case of a "hostile environment", which is probably the more common state of affairs, it can involve jokes, taunts and other sexually charged comments that are threatening and demeaning to women; pornographic or sexually explicit posters; and crude sexual gestures, and so forth. One can add to these characteristics what is sometimes called "gender harassment", which more involves sexist remarks that demean the dignity of women.

Women themselves may not label unwanted sexual attention or sexual remarks as harassing because they accept it as "normal" on the part of males (Gutek 1985). In general, women (especially if

they have been harassed) are more likely to identify a situation as sexual harassment than men, who tend rather to make light of the situation, to disbelieve the woman in question or to blame her for "causing" the harassment (Fitzgerald and Ormerod 1993). People also are more likely to label incidents involving supervisors as sexually harassing than similar behaviour by peers (Fitzgerald and Ormerod 1993). This tendency reveals the significance of the differential power relationship between the harasser and the female employee (MacKinnon 1978.) As an example, a comment that a male supervisor may believe is complimentary may still be threatening to his female employee, who may fear that it will lead to pressure for sexual favours and that there will be retaliation for a negative response, including the potential loss of her job or negative evaluations.

Even when co-workers are involved, sexual harassment can be difficult for women to control and can be very stressful for them. This situation can occur where there are many more men than women in a work group, a hostile work environment is created and the supervisor is male (Gutek 1985; Fitzgerald and Ormerod 1993).

National data on sexual harassment are not collected, and it is difficult to obtain accurate numbers on its prevalence. In the United States, it has been estimated that 50% of all women will experience some form of sexual harassment during their working lives (Fitzgerald and Ormerod 1993). These numbers are consistent with surveys conducted in Europe (Bustelo 1992), although there is variation from country to country (Kauppinen-Toropainen and Gruber 1993). The extent of sexual harassment is also difficult to determine because women may not label it accurately and because of underreporting. Women may fear that they will be blamed, humiliated and not believed, that nothing will be done and that reporting problems will result in retaliation (Fitzgerald and Ormerod 1993). Instead, they may try to live with the situation or leave their jobs and risk serious financial hardship, a disruption of their work histories and problems with references (Koss et al. 1994).

Sexual harassment reduces job satisfaction and increases turnover, so that it has costs for the employer (Gutek 1985; Fitzgerald and Ormerod 1993; Kauppinen-Toropainen and Gruber 1993). Like other workplace stressors, it also can have negative effects on health that are sometimes quite serious. When the harassment is severe, as with rape or attempted rape, women are seriously traumatized. Even where sexual harassment is less severe, women can have psychological problems: they may become fearful, guilty and ashamed, depressed, nervous and less self-confident. They may have physical symptoms such as stomach-aches, headaches or nausea. They may have behavioural problems such as sleeplessness, over- or undereating, sexual problems and difficulties in their relations with others (Swanson et al. 1997).

Both the formal American and informal European approaches to combating harassment provide illustrative lessons (Bernstein 1994). In Europe, sexual harassment is sometimes dealt with by conflict resolution approaches that bring in third parties to help eliminate the harassment (e.g., England's "challenge technique").

In the United States, sexual harassment is a legal wrong that provides victims with redress through the courts, although success is difficult to achieve. Victims of harassment also need to be supported through counselling, where needed, and helped to understand that they are not to blame for the harassment.

Prevention is the key to combating sexual harassment. Guidelines encouraging prevention have been promulgated through the European Commission Code of Practice (Rubenstein and DeVries 1993). They include the following: clear anti-harassment policies that are effectively communicated; special training and education for managers and supervisors; a designated ombudsperson to deal with complaints; formal grievance procedures and alternatives to them; and disciplinary treatment of those who violate the policies. Bernstein (1994) has suggested that mandated self-regulation may be a viable approach.

Finally, sexual harassment needs to be openly discussed as a workplace issue of legitimate concern to women and men. Trade unions have a critical role to play in helping place this issue on the public agenda. Ultimately, an end to sexual harassment requires that men and women reach social and economic equality and full integration in all occupations and workplaces.

● WORKPLACE VIOLENCE

Julian Barling

The nature, prevalence, predictors and possible consequences of workplace violence have begun to attract the attention of labour and management practitioners, and researchers. The reason for this is the increasing occurrence of highly visible workplace murders. Once the focus is placed on workplace violence, it becomes clear that there are several issues, including the nature (or definition), prevalence, predictors, consequences and ultimately prevention of workplace violence.

Definition and Prevalence of Workplace Violence

The definition and prevalence of workplace violence are integrally related.

Consistent with the relative recency with which workplace violence has attracted attention, there is no uniform definition. This is an important issue for several reasons. First, until a uniform definition exists, any estimates of prevalence remain incomparable across studies and sites. Secondly, the nature of the violence is linked to strategies for prevention and interventions. For example, focusing on all instances of shootings within the workplace includes incidents that reflect the continuation of family conflicts, as well as those that reflect work-related stressors and conflicts. While employees would no doubt be affected in both situations, the control the organization has over the former is more limited, and hence the implications for interventions are different from those situations in which workplace shootings are a direct function of workplace stressors and conflicts.

Some statistics suggest that workplace murders are the fastest growing form of murder in the United States (for example, Anfuso 1994). In some jurisdictions (for example, New York State), murder is the modal cause of death in the workplace. Because of statistics such as these, workplace violence has attracted considerable attention recently. However, early indications suggest that those acts of workplace violence with the highest visibility (for example, murder, shootings) attract the greatest research scrutiny, but also occur with the least frequency. In contrast, verbal and psychological aggression against supervisors, subordinates and co-workers are far more common, but gather less attention. Supporting the notion of a close integration between definitional and prevalence issues, this would suggest that what is being studied in most cases is aggression rather than violence in the workplace.

Predictors of Workplace Violence

A reading of the literature on the predictors of workplace violence would reveal that most of the attention has been focused on the development of a "profile" of the potentially violent or "disgruntled" employee (for example, Mantell and Albrecht 1994; Slora, Joy and Terris 1991), most of which would identify the following as the salient personal characteristics of a disgruntled employee: white, male, aged 20-35, a "loner", probable alcohol problem and a fascination with guns. Aside from the problem of the number of false-positive identifications this would lead to, this strategy is also based on identifying individuals predisposed to the most extreme forms of violence, and ignores the larger group involved in most of the aggressive and less violent workplace incidents.

Going beyond "demographic" characteristics, there are suggestions that some of the personal factors implicated in violence outside of the workplace would extend to the workplace itself. Thus, inappropriate use of alcohol, general history of aggression in one's current life or family of origin, and low self-esteem have been implicated in workplace violence.

A more recent strategy has been to identify the workplace conditions under which workplace violence is most likely to occur: identifying the physical and psychosocial conditions in the workplace. While the research on psychosocial factors is still in its infancy, it would appear as though feelings of job insecurity, perceptions that organizational policies and their implementation are unjust, harsh management and supervision styles, and electronic monitoring are associated with workplace aggression and violence (United States House of Representatives 1992; Fox and Levin 1994).

Cox and Leather (1994) look to the predictors of aggression and violence in general in their attempt to understand the physical factors that predict workplace violence. In this respect, they suggest that workplace violence may be associated with perceived crowding, and extreme heat and noise. However, these suggestions about the causes of workplace violence await empirical scrutiny.

Consequences of workplace violence

The research to date suggests that there are primary and secondary victims of workplace violence, both of which are worthy of research attention. Bank tellers or store clerks who are held up and employees who are assaulted at work by current or former co-workers are the obvious or direct victims of violence at work. However, consistent with the literature showing that much human behaviour is learned from observing others, witnesses to workplace violence are secondary victims. Both groups might be expected to suffer negative effects, and more research is needed to focus on the way in which both aggression and violence at work affect primary and secondary victims.

Prevention of workplace violence

Most of the literature on the prevention of workplace violence focuses at this stage on prior selection, i.e., the prior identification of potentially violent individuals for the purpose of excluding them from employment in the first instance (for example, Mantell and Albrecht 1994). Such strategies are of dubious utility, for ethical and legal reasons. From a scientific perspective, it is equally doubtful whether we could identify potentially violent employees with sufficient precision (e.g., without an unacceptably high number of false-positive identifications). Clearly, we need to focus on workplace issues and job design for a preventive approach. Following Fox and Levin's (1994) reasoning, ensuring that organizational policies and procedures are characterized by perceived justice will probably constitute an effective prevention technique.

Conclusion

Research on workplace violence is in its infancy, but gaining increasing attention. This bodes well for the further understanding, prediction and control of workplace aggression and violence.

JOB SECURITY

● JOB FUTURE AMBIGUITY

John M. Ivancevich

Downsizing, layoffs, re-engineering, reshaping, reduction in force (RIF), mergers, early retirement, and outplacement—the description of these increasingly familiar changes has become a matter of commonplace jargon around the world in the past two decades. As companies have fallen on hard times, workers at all organizational levels have been expended and many remaining jobs have been altered. The job loss count in a single year (1992–93) includes Eastman Kodak, 2,000; Siemens, 13,000; Daimler-Benz, 27,000; Phillips, 40,000; and IBM, 65,000 (*The Economist* 1993, extracted from "Job Future Ambiguity" (John M. Ivancevich)). Job cuts have occurred at companies earning healthy profits as well as at firms faced with the need to cut costs. The trend of cutting jobs and changing the way remaining jobs are performed is expected to continue even after worldwide economic growth returns.

Why has losing and changing jobs become so widespread? There is no simple answer that fits every organization or situation. However, one or more of a number of factors is usually implicated, including lost market share, increasing international and domestic competition, increasing labour costs, obsolete plant and technologies and poor managerial practices. These factors have resulted in managerial decisions to slim down, re-engineer jobs and alter the psychological contract between the employer and the worker.

A work situation in which an employee could count on job security or the opportunity to hold multiple positions via career-enhancing promotions in a single firm has changed drastically. Similarly, the binding power of the traditional employer-worker psychological contract has weakened as millions of managers and non-managers have been let go. Japan was once famous for providing "lifetime" employment to individuals. Today, even in Japan, a growing number of workers, especially in large firms, are not assured of lifetime employment. The Japanese, like their counterparts across the world, are facing what can be referred to as increased job insecurity and an ambiguous picture of what the future holds.

Job Insecurity: An Interpretation

Maslow (1954), Herzberg, Mausner and Snyderman (1959) and Super (1957) have proposed that individuals have a need for safety or security. That is, individual workers sense security when holding a permanent job or when being able to control the tasks performed on the job. Unfortunately, there has been a limited number of empirical studies that have thoroughly examined the job security needs of workers (Kuhnert and Pulmer 1991; Kuhnert, Sims and Lahey 1989).

On the other hand, with the increased attention that is being paid to downsizing, layoffs and mergers, more researchers have begun to investigate the notion of job insecurity. The nature, causes and consequences of job insecurity have been considered by Greenhalgh and Rosenblatt (1984) who offer a definition of job insecurity as "perceived powerlessness to maintain desired continuity in a threatened job situation". In Greenhalgh and Rosenblatt's framework, job insecurity is considered a part of a person's environment. In the stress literature, job insecurity is considered to be a stressor that introduces a threat that is interpreted and responded to by an individual. An individual's interpretation and response could possibly include the decreased effort to perform well, feeling ill or below par, seeking employment elsewhere, increased coping to deal with the threat, or seeking more colleague interaction to buffer the feelings of insecurity.

Lazarus' theory of psychological stress (Lazarus 1966; Lazarus and Folkman 1984) is centred on the concept of cognitive appraisal. Regardless of the actual severity of the danger facing a person, the occurrence of psychological stress depends upon the individual's own evaluation of the threatening situation (here, job insecurity).

Selected Research on Job Insecurity

Unfortunately, like the research on job security, there is a paucity of well-designed studies of job insecurity. Furthermore, the majority of job insecurity studies incorporate unitary measurement methods. Few researchers examining stressors in general or job insecurity specifically have adopted a multiple-level approach to assessment. This is understandable because of the limitations of resources. However, the problems created by unitary assessments of job insecurity have resulted in a limited understanding of the construct. There are available to researchers four basic methods of measuring job insecurity: self-report, performance, psychophysiological and biochemical. It is still debatable whether these four types of measure assess different aspects of the consequences of job insecurity (Baum, Grunberg and Singer 1982). Each type of measure has limitations that must be recognized.

In addition to measurement problems in job insecurity research, it must be noted that there is a predominance of concentration in imminent or actual job loss. As noted by researchers (Greenhalgh and Rosenblatt 1984; Roskies and Louis-Guerin 1990), there should be more attention paid to "concern about a significant deterioration in terms and conditions of employment." The deterioration of working conditions would logically seem to play a role in a person's attitudes and behaviours.

Brenner (1987) has discussed the relationship between a job insecurity factor, unemployment, and mortality. He proposed that uncertainty, or the threat of instability, rather than unemployment itself causes higher mortality. The threat of being unemployed or losing control of one's job activities can be powerful enough to contribute to psychiatric problems.

In a study of 1,291 managers, Roskies and Louis-Guerin (1990) examined the perceptions of workers facing layoffs, as well as those of managerial personnel working in firms that worked in stable, growth-oriented firms. A minority of managers were stressed about imminent job loss. However, a substantial number of managers were more stressed about a deterioration in working conditions and long-term job security.

Roskies, Louis-Guerin and Fournier (1993) proposed in a research study that job insecurity may be a major psychological stressor. In this study of personnel in the airline industry, the researchers determined that personality disposition (positive and negative) plays a role in the impact of job security or the mental health of workers.

Addressing the Problem of Job Insecurity

Organizations have numerous alternatives to downsizing, layoffs and reduction in force. Displaying compassion that clearly shows that management realizes the hardships that job loss and future job ambiguity pose is an important step. Alternatives such as reduced work weeks, across-the-board salary cuts, attractive early retirement packages, retraining existing employees and voluntary layoff programmes can be implemented (Wexley and Silverman 1993).

The global marketplace has increased job demands and job skill requirements. For some people, the effect of increased job demands and job skill requirements will provide career opportunities. For others, these changes could exacerbate the feelings of job insecurity. It is difficult to pinpoint exactly how individual workers will respond. However, managers must be aware of how job insecurity can result in negative consequences. Furthermore, managers need to acknowledge and respond to job insecurity. But possessing a better understanding of the notion of job insecurity and its potential negative impact on the performance, behaviour and attitudes of workers is a step in the right direction for managers.

It will obviously require more rigorous research to better understand the full range of consequences of job insecurity among selected workers. As additional information becomes available, managers need to be open-minded about attempting to help workers cope with job insecurity. Redefining the way work is organized and executed should become a useful alternative to traditional job design methods. Managers have a responsibility:

1. to identify and attempt to alleviate sources of job insecurity among workers
2. to attempt to encourage feelings of being in control and of empowerment in the workforce, and
3. to show compassion when workers express feelings of job insecurity.

Since job insecurity is likely to remain a perceived threat for many, but not all, workers, managers need to develop and implement strategies to address this factor. The institutional costs of ignoring job insecurity are too great for any firm to accept. Whether managers can efficiently deal with workers who feel insecure about their jobs and working conditions is fast becoming a measure of managerial competency.

• UNEMPLOYMENT

Amiran D. Vinokur

The term unemployment describes the situation of individuals who desire to work but are unable to trade their skills and labour for pay. It is used to indicate either an individual's personal experience of failure to find gainful work, or the experience of an aggregate in a community, a geographic region or a country. The collective phenomenon of unemployment is often expressed as the unemployment rate, that is, the number of people who are seeking work divided by the total number of people in the labour force, which in turn consists of both the employed and the unemployed. Individuals who desire to work for pay but have given up

their efforts to find work are termed discouraged workers. These persons are not listed in official reports as members of the group of unemployed workers, for they are no longer considered to be part of the labour force.

The Organization for Economic Cooperation and Development (OECD) provides statistical information on the magnitude of unemployment in 25 countries around the world (OECD 1995). These consist mostly of the economically developed countries of Europe and North America, as well as Japan, New Zealand and Australia. According to the report for the year 1994, the total unemployment rate in these countries was 8.1% (or 34.3 million individuals). In the developed countries of central and western Europe, the unemployment rate was 9.9% (11 million), in the southern European countries 13.7% (9.2 million), and in the United States 6.1% (8 million). Of the 25 countries studied, only six (Austria, Iceland, Japan, Mexico, Luxembourg and Switzerland) had an unemployment rate below 5%. The report projected only a slight overall decrease (less than one-half of 1%) in unemployment for the years 1995 and 1996. These figures suggest that millions of individuals will continue to be vulnerable to the harmful effects of unemployment in the foreseeable future (Reich 1991).

A large number of people become unemployed at various periods during their lives. Depending on the structure of the economy and on its cycles of expansion and contraction, unemployment may strike students who drop out of school; those who have been graduated from a high school, trade school or college but find it difficult to enter the labour market for the first time; women seeking to return to gainful employment after raising their children; veterans of the armed services; and older persons who want to supplement their income after retirement. However, at any given time, the largest segment of the unemployed population, usually between 50 and 65%, consists of displaced workers who have lost their jobs. The problems associated with unemployment are most visible in this segment of the unemployed partly because of its size. Unemployment is also a serious problem for minorities and younger persons. Their unemployment rates are often two to three times higher than that of the general population (USDOL 1995).

The fundamental causes of unemployment are rooted in demographic, economic and technological changes. The restructuring of local and national economies usually gives rise to at least temporary periods of high unemployment rates. The trend towards the globalization of markets, coupled with accelerated technological changes, results in greater economic competition and the transfer of industries and services to new places that supply more advantageous economic conditions in terms of taxation, a cheaper labour force and more accommodating labour and environmental laws. Inevitably, these changes exacerbate the problems of unemployment in areas that are economically depressed.

Most people depend on the income from a job to provide themselves and their families with the necessities of life and to sustain their accustomed standard of living. When they lose a job, they experience a substantial reduction in their income. Mean duration of unemployment, in the United States for example, varies between 16 and 20 weeks, with a median between eight and ten weeks (USDOL 1995). If the period of unemployment that follows the job loss persists so that unemployment benefits are exhausted, the displaced worker faces a financial crisis. That crisis plays itself out as a cascading series of stressful events that may include loss of a car through repossession, foreclosure on a house, loss of medical care, and food shortages. Indeed, an abundance of research in Europe and the United States shows that economic hardship is the most consistent outcome of unemployment (Fryer and Payne 1986), and that economic hardship mediates the adverse impact of unemployment on various other outcomes, in particular, on mental health (Kessler, Turner and House 1988).

There is a great deal of evidence that job loss and unemployment produce significant deterioration in mental health (Fryer and Payne 1986). The most common outcomes of job loss and unemployment are increases in anxiety, somatic symptoms and depression symptomatology (Dooley, Catalano and Wilson 1994; Hamilton et al. 1990; Kessler, House and Turner 1987; Warr, Jackson and Banks 1988). Furthermore, there is some evidence that unemployment increases by over twofold the risk of onset of clinical depression (Dooley, Catalano and Wilson 1994). In addition to the well-documented adverse effects of unemployment on mental health, there is research that implicates unemployment as a contributing factor to other outcomes (see Catalano 1991 for a review). These outcomes include suicide (Brenner 1976), separation and divorce (Stack 1981; Liem and Liem 1988), child neglect and abuse (Steinberg, Catalano and Dooley 1981), alcohol abuse (Dooley, Catalano and Hough 1992; Catalano et al. 1993a), violence in the workplace (Catalano et al. 1993b), criminal behaviour (Allan and Steffensmeier 1989), and highway fatalities (Leigh and Waldon 1991). Finally, there is also some evidence, based primarily on self-report, that unemployment contributes to physical illness (Kessler, House and Turner 1987).

The adverse effects of unemployment on displaced workers are not limited to the period during which they have no jobs. In most instances, when workers become re-employed, their new jobs are significantly worse than the jobs they lost. Even after four years in their new positions, their earnings are substantially lower than those of similar workers who were not laid off (Ruhm 1991).

Because the fundamental causes of job loss and unemployment are rooted in societal and economic processes, remedies for their adverse social effects must be sought in comprehensive economic and social policies (Blinder 1987). At the same time, various community-based programmes can be undertaken to reduce the negative social and psychological impact of unemployment at the local level. There is overwhelming evidence that re-employment reduces distress and depression symptoms and restores psychosocial functioning to pre-unemployment levels (Kessler, Turner and House 1989; Vinokur, Caplan and Williams 1987). Therefore, programmes for displaced workers or others who wish to become employed should be aimed primarily at promoting and facilitating their re-employment or new entry into the labour force. A variety of such programmes have been tried successfully. Among these are special community-based intervention programmes for creating new ventures that in turn generate job opportunities (e.g., Last et al. 1995), and others that focus on retraining (e.g., Wolf et al. 1995).

Of the various programmes that attempt to promote re-employment, the most common are job search programmes organized as job clubs that attempt to intensify job search efforts (Azrin and Beasalel 1982), or workshops that focus more broadly on enhancing job search skills and facilitating transition into re-employment in high-quality jobs (e.g., Caplan et al. 1989). Cost/benefit analyses have demonstrated that these job search programmes are cost effective (Meyer 1995; Vinokur et al. 1991). Furthermore, there is also evidence that they could prevent deterioration in mental health and possibly the onset of clinical depression (Price, van Ryn and Vinokur 1992).

Similarly, in the case of organizational downsizing, industries can reduce the scope of unemployment by devising ways to involve workers in the decision-making process regarding the management of the downsizing programme (Kozlowski et al. 1993; London 1995; Price 1990). Workers may choose to pool their resources and buy out the industry, thus avoiding layoffs; to reduce working hours to spread and even out the reduction in force; to agree to a reduction in wages to minimize layoffs; to retrain and/or relocate to take new jobs; or to participate in outplacement programmes. Employers can facilitate the process by timely implementation of a strategic plan that offers the above-mentioned programmes and services to workers at risk of being laid off. As has been indicated already, unemployment leads to pernicious outcomes at both the personal and societal level. A combination of comprehensive government policies, flexible downsizing strategies by business and industry, and community-based programmes can help to mitigate the adverse consequences of a problem that will continue to affect the lives of millions of people for years to come.

MACRO-ORGANIZATIONAL FACTORS

● TOTAL QUALITY MANAGEMENT

Dennis Tolsma

One of the more remarkable social transformations of this century was the emergence of a powerful Japanese economy from the debris of the Second World War. Fundamental to this climb to global competitiveness were a commitment to quality and a determination to prove false the then-common belief that Japanese goods were shoddy and worthless. Guided by the innovative teachings of Deming (1993), Juran (1988) and others, Japanese managers and engineers adopted practices that have ultimately evolved into a comprehensive management system rooted in the basic concept of quality. Fundamentally, this system represents a shift in thinking. The traditional view was that quality had to be balanced against the cost of attaining it. The view that Deming and Juran urged was that higher quality led to lower total cost and that a systems approach to improving work processes would help in attaining both of these objectives. Japanese managers adopted this management philosophy, engineers learned and practised statistical quality control, workers were trained and involved in process improvement, and the outcome was dramatic (Ishikawa 1985; Imai 1986).

By 1980, alarmed at the erosion of their markets and seeking to broaden their reach in the global economy, European and American managers began to search for ways to regain a competitive position. In the ensuing 15 years, more and more companies came to understand the principles underlying quality management and to apply them, initially in industrial production and later in the service sector as well. While there are a variety of names for this management system, the most commonly used is total quality management or TQM; an exception is the health care sector, which more frequently uses the term continuous quality improvement, or CQI. Recently, the term business process reengineering (BPR) has also come into use, but this tends to mean an emphasis on specific techniques for process improvement rather than on the adoption of a comprehensive management system or philosophy.

TQM is available in many "flavours," but it is important to understand it as a system that includes both a management philosophy and a powerful set of tools for improving the efficiency of work processes. Some of the common elements of TQM include the following (Feigenbaum 1991; Mann 1989; Senge 1991):

- primary emphasis on quality
- focus on meeting customer expectations ("customer satisfaction")
- commitment to employee participation and involvement ("empowerment")
- viewing the organization as a system ("optimization")
- monitoring statistical outputs of processes ("management by fact")
- leadership ("vision")
- strong commitment to training ("becoming a learning organization").

Typically, organizations successfully adopting TQM find they must make changes on three fronts.

One is *transformation*. This involves such actions as defining and communicating a vision of the organization's future, changing the management culture from top-down oversight to one of employee involvement, fostering collaboration instead of competition and refocusing the purpose of all work on meeting customer requirements. Seeing the organization as a system of interrelated processes is at the core of TQM, and is an essential means of securing a totally integrated effort towards improving performance at all levels. All employees must know the vision and the aim of the organization (the system) and understand where their work fits in it, or no amount of training in applying TQM process improvement tools can do much good. However, lack of genuine change of organizational culture, particularly among lower echelons of managers, is frequently the downfall of many nascent TQM efforts; Heilpern (1989) observes, "We have come to the conclusion that the major barriers to quality superiority are not technical, they are behavioural." Unlike earlier, flawed "quality circle" programmes, in which improvement was expected to "convect" upward, TQM demands top management leadership and the firm expectation that middle management will facilitate employee participation (Hill 1991).

A second basis for successful TQM is *strategic planning*. The achievement of an organization's vision and goals is tied to the development and deployment of a strategic quality plan. One corporation defined this as "a customer-driven plan for the application of quality principles to key business objectives and the continuous improvement of work processes" (Yarborough 1994). It is senior management's responsibility—indeed, its obligation to workers, stockholders and beneficiaries alike—to link its quality philosophy to sound and feasible goals that can reasonably be attained. Deming (1993) called this "constancy of purpose" and saw its absence as a source of insecurity for the workforce of the organization. The fundamental intent of strategic planning is to align the activities of all of the people throughout the company or organization so that it can achieve its core goals and can react with agility to a changing environment. It is evident that it both requires and reinforces the need for widespread participation of supervisors and workers at all levels in shaping the goal-directed work of the company (Shiba, Graham and Walden 1994).

Only when these two changes are adequately carried out can one hope for success in the third: the implementation of *continuous quality improvement*. Quality outcomes, and with them customer satisfaction and improved competitive position, ultimately rest on widespread deployment of process improvement skills. Often, TQM programmes accomplish this through increased investments in training and through assignment of workers (frequently volunteers) to teams charged with addressing a problem. A basic concept of TQM is that the person most likely to know how a job can be done better is the person who is doing it at a given

moment. Empowering these workers to make useful changes in their work processes is a part of the cultural transformation underlying TQM; equipping them with knowledge, skills and tools to do so is part of continuous quality improvement.

The collection of statistical data is a typical and basic step taken by workers and teams to understand how to improve work processes. Deming and others adapted their techniques from the seminal work of Shewhart in the 1920s (Schmidt and Finnigan 1992). Among the most useful TQM tools are: (a) the Pareto Chart, a graphical device for identifying the more frequently occurring problems, and hence the ones to be addressed first; (b) the statistical control chart, an analytic tool for ascertaining the degree of variability in the unimproved process; and (c) flow charting, a means to document exactly how the process is carried out at present. Possibly the most ubiquitous and important tool is the Ishikawa Diagram (or "fishbone" diagram), whose invention is credited to Kaoru Ishikawa (1985). This instrument is a simple but effective way by which team members can collaborate on identifying the root causes of the process problem under study, and thus point the path to process improvement.

TQM, effectively implemented may be important to workers and worker health in many w: For example, the adoption of TQM can have an indirect influence. In a very basic sense, an organization that makes a quality transformation has arguably improved its chances of economic survival and success, and hence those of its employees. Moreover, it is likely to be one where respect for people is a basic tenet. Indeed, TQM experts often speak of "shared values", those things that must be exemplified in the behaviour of both management and workers. These are often publicized throughout the organization as formal values statements or aspiration statements, and typically include such emotive language as "trust", "respecting each other", "open communications", and "valuing our diversity" (Howard 1990).

Thus, it is tempting to suppose that quality workplaces will be "worker-friendly"—where worker-improved processes become less hazardous and where the climate is less stressful. The logic of quality is to build quality into a product or service, not to detect failures after the fact. It can be summed up in a word—prevention (Widfeldt and Widfeldt 1992). Such a logic is clearly compatible with the public health logic of emphasizing prevention in occupational health. As Williams (1993) points out in a hypothetical example, "If the quality and design of castings in the foundry industry were improved there would be reduced exposure ... to vibration as less finishing of castings would be needed." Some anecdotal support for this supposition comes from satisfied employers who cite trend data on job health measures, climate surveys that show better employee satisfaction, and more numerous safety and health awards in facilities using TQM. Williams further presents two case studies in UK settings that exemplify such employer reports (Williams 1993).

Unfortunately, virtually no published studies offer firm evidence on the matter. What is lacking is a research base of controlled studies that document health outcomes, consider the possibility of detrimental as well as positive health influences, and link all of this causally to measurable factors of business philosophy and TQM practice. Given the significant prevalence of TQM enterprises in the global economy of the 1990s, this is a research agenda with genuine potential to define whether TQM is in fact a supportive tool in the prevention armamentarium of occupational safety and health.

We are on somewhat firmer ground to suggest that TQM can have a direct influence on worker health when it explicitly focuses quality improvement efforts on safety and health. Obviously, like all other work in an enterprise, occupational and environmental health activity is made up of interrelated processes, and the tools of process improvement are readily applied to them. One of the criteria against which candidates are examined for the Baldridge Award, the most important competitive honour granted to US organizations, is the competitor's improvements in occupational health and safety. Yarborough has described how the occupational and environmental health (OEH) employees of a major corporation were instructed by senior management to adopt TQM with the rest of the company and how OEH was integrated into the company's strategic quality plan (Yarborough 1994). The chief executive of a US utility that was the first non-Japanese company ever to win Japan's coveted Deming Prize notes that safety was accorded a high priority in the TQM effort: "Of all the company's major quality indicators, the only one that addresses the internal customer is employee safety." By defining safety as a process, subjecting it to continuous improvement, and tracking lost-time injuries per 100 employees as a quality indicator, the utility reduced its injury rate by half, reaching the lowest point in the history of the company (Hudiberg 1991).

In summary, TQM is a comprehensive management system grounded in a management philosophy that emphasizes the human dimensions of work. It is supported by a powerful set of technologies that use data derived from work processes to document, analyse and continuously improve these processes.

● MANAGERIAL STYLE

Cary L. Cooper and Mike Smith

Selye (1974) suggested that having to live with other people is one of the most stressful aspects of life. Good relations between members of a work group are considered a central factor in individual and organizational health (Cooper and Payne 1988) particularly in terms of the boss–subordinate relationship. Poor relationships at work are defined as having "low trust, low levels of supportiveness and low interest in problem solving within the organization" (Cooper and Payne 1988). Mistrust is positively correlated with high role ambiguity, which leads to inadequate interpersonal communications between individuals and psychological strain in the form of low job satisfaction, decreased well-being and a feeling of being threatened by one's superior and colleagues (Kahn et al. 1964; French and Caplan 1973).

Supportive social relationships at work are less likely to create the interpersonal pressures associated with rivalry, office politics and unconstructive competition (Cooper and Payne 1991). McLean (1979) suggests that social support in the form of group cohesion, interpersonal trust and liking for a superior is associated with decreased levels of perceived job stress and better health. Inconsiderate behaviour on the part of a supervisor appears to contribute significantly to feelings of job pressure (McLean 1979). Close supervision and rigid performance monitoring also have stressful consequences—in this connection a great deal of research has been carried out which indicates that a managerial style characterized by lack of effective consultation and communication, unjustified restrictions on employee behaviour, and lack of control over one's job is associated with negative psychological moods and behavioural responses (for example, escapist drinking and heavy smoking) (Caplan et al. 1975), increased cardiovascular risk (Karasek 1979) and other stress-related manifestations. On the other hand, offering broader opportunities to employees to participate in decision making at work can result in improved performance, lower staff turnover and improved levels of mental and physical well-being. A participatory style of management should also extend to worker involvement in the improvement of safety in the workplace; this could help to overcome apathy among blue-collar workers, which is acknowledged as a significant

factor in the cause of accidents (Robens 1972; Sutherland and Cooper 1986).

Early work in the relationship between managerial style and stress was carried out by Lewin (for example, in Lewin, Lippitt and White 1939), in which he documented the stressful and unproductive effects of authoritarian management styles. More recently, Karasek's (1979) work highlights the importance of managers' providing workers with greater control at work or a more participative management style. In a six-year prospective study he demonstrated that job control (i.e., the freedom to use one's intellectual discretion) and work schedule freedom were significant predictors of risk of coronary heart disease. Restriction of opportunity for participation and autonomy results in increased depression, exhaustion, illness rates and pill consumption. Feelings of being unable to make changes concerning a job and lack of consultation are commonly reported stressors among blue-collar workers in the steel industry (Kelly and Cooper 1981), oil and gas workers on rigs and platforms in the North Sea (Sutherland and Cooper 1986) and many other blue-collar workers (Cooper and Smith 1985). On the other hand, as Gowler and Legge (1975) indicate, a participatory management style can create its own potentially stressful situations, for example, a mismatch of formal and actual power, resentment of the erosion of formal power, conflicting pressures both to be participative and to meet high production standards, and subordinates' refusal to participate.

Although there has been a substantial research focus on the differences between authoritarian versus participatory management styles on employee performance and health, there have also been other, idiosyncratic approaches to managerial style (Jennings, Cox and Cooper 1994). For example, Levinson (1978) has focused on the impact of the "abrasive" manager. Abrasive managers are usually achievement-oriented, hard-driving and intelligent (similar to the type A personality), but function less well at the emotional level. As Quick and Quick (1984) point out, the need for perfection, the preoccupation with self and the condescending, critical style of the abrasive manager induce feelings of inadequacy among their subordinates. As Levinson suggests, the abrasive personality as a peer is both difficult and stressful to deal with, but as a superior, the consequences are potentially very damaging to interpersonal relationships and highly stressful for subordinates in the organization.

In addition, there are theories and research which suggest that the effect on employee health and safety of managerial style and personality can only be understood in the context of the nature of the task and the power of the manager or leader. For example, Fiedler's (1967) contingency theory suggests that there are eight main group situations based upon combinations of dichotomies: (a) the warmth of the relations between the leader and follower; (b) the level structure imposed by the task; and (c) the power of the leader. The eight combinations could be arranged in a continuum with, at one end (octant one) a leader who has good relations with members, facing a highly structured task and possessing strong power; and, at the other end (octant eight), a leader who has poor relations with members, facing a loosely structured task and having low power. In terms of stress, it could be argued that the octants formed a continuum from low stress to high stress. Fiedler also examined two types of leader: the leader who would value negatively most of the characteristics of the member he liked least (the lower LPC leader) and the leader who would see many positive qualities even in the members whom he disliked (the high LPC leader). Fiedler made specific predictions about the performance of the leader. He suggested that the low LPC leader (who had difficulty in seeing merits in subordinates he disliked) would be most effective in octants one and eight, where there would be very low and very high levels of stress, respectively. On the other hand, a high LPC leader (who is able to see merits even in those he disliked) would be more effective in the middle octants, where moderate stress levels could be expected. In general, subsequent research (for example, Strube and Garcia 1981) has supported Fiedler's ideas.

Additional leadership theories suggest that task-oriented managers or leaders create stress. Seltzer, Numerof and Bass (1989) found that intellectually stimulating leaders increased perceived stress and "burnout" among their subordinates. Misumi (1985) found that production-oriented leaders generated physiological symptoms of stress. Bass (1992) finds that in laboratory experiments, production-oriented leadership causes higher levels of anxiety and hostility. On the other hand, transformational and charismatic leadership theories (Burns 1978) focus upon the effect which those leaders have upon their subordinates who are generally more self-assured and perceive more meaning in their work. It has been found that these types of leader or manager reduce the stress levels of their subordinates.

On balance, therefore, managers who tend to demonstrate "considerate" behaviour, to have a participative management style, to be less production- or task-oriented and to provide subordinates with control over their jobs are likely to reduce the incidence of ill health and accidents at work.

● ORGANIZATIONAL STRUCTURE

Lois E. Tetrick

Most of the articles in this chapter deal with aspects of the work environment that are proximal to the individual employee. The focus of this article, however, is to examine the impact of more distal, macrolevel characteristics of organizations as a whole that may affect employees' health and well-being. That is, are there ways in which organizations structure their internal environments that promote health among the employees of that organization or, conversely, place employees at greater risk of experiencing stress? Most theoretical models of occupational or job stress incorporate organizational structural variables such as organizational size, lack of participation in decision making, and formalization (Beehr and Newman 1978; Kahn and Byosiere 1992).

Organizational structure refers to the formal distribution of work roles and functions within an organization coordinating the various functions or subsystems within the organization to efficiently attain the organization's goals (Porras and Robertson 1992). As such, structure represents a coordinated set of subsystems to facilitate the accomplishment of the organization's goals and mission and defines the division of labour, the authority relationships, formal lines of communication, the roles of each organizational subsystem and the interrelationships among these subsystems. Therefore, organizational structure can be viewed as a system of formal mechanisms to enhance the understandability of events, predictability of events and control over events within the organization which Sutton and Kahn (1987) proposed as the three work-relevant antidotes against the stress-strain effect in organizational life.

One of the earliest organizational characteristics examined as a potential risk factor was organizational size. Contrary to the literature on risk of exposure to hazardous agents in the work environment, which suggests that larger organizations or plants are safer, being less hazardous and better equipped to handle potential hazards (Emmett 1991), larger organizations originally were hypothesized to put employees at greater risk of occupational stress. It was proposed that larger organizations tend to adapt a bureaucratic organizational structure to coordinate the increased complexity. This bureaucratic structure would be characterized by a division of labour based on functional specialization, a well-defined hierarchy of authority, a system of rules covering the rights and duties of job incumbents, impersonal treatment of workers and a system of procedures for dealing with work situations (Bennis 1969). On the surface, it would appear that many of these dimensions of bureaucracy would actually improve or maintain the predictability and understandability of events in the work environment and thus serve to reduce stress within the work environment. However, it also appears that these dimensions can reduce employees' control over events in the work environment through a rigid hierarchy of authority.

Given these characteristics of bureaucratic structure, it is not surprising that organizational size, *per se*, has received no consistent support as a macro-organization risk factor (Kahn and Byosiere 1992). Payne and Pugh's (1976) review, however, provides some evidence that organizational size indirectly increases the risk of stress. They report that larger organizations suffered a reduction in the amount of communication, an increase in the amount of job and task specifications and a decrease in coordination. These effects could lead to less understanding and predictability of events in the work environment as well as a decrease in control over work events, thus increasing experienced stress (Tetrick and LaRocco 1987).

These findings on organizational size have led to the supposition that the two aspects of organizational structure that seem to pose the most risk for employees are formalization and centralization. Formalization refers to the written procedures and rules governing employees' activities, and centralization refers to the extent to which the decision-making power in the organization is narrowly distributed to higher levels in the organization. Pines (1982) pointed out that it is not formalization within a bureaucracy that results in experienced stress or burnout but the unnecessary red tape, paperwork and communication problems that can result from formalization. Rules and regulations can be vague creating ambiguity or contradiction resulting in conflict or lack of understanding concerning appropriate actions to be taken in specific situations. If the rules and regulations are too detailed, employees may feel frustrated in their ability to achieve their goals especially in customer or client-oriented organizations. Inadequate communication can result in employees feeling isolated and alienated based on the lack of predictability and understanding of events in the work environment.

While these aspects of the work environment appear to be accepted as potential risk factors, the empirical literature on formalization and centralization are far from consistent. The lack of consistent evidence may stem from at least two sources. First, in many of the studies, there is an assumption of a single organizational structure having a consistent level of formalization and centralization throughout the entire organization. Hall (1969) concluded that organizations can be meaningfully studied as totalities; however, he demonstrated that the degree of formalization as well as decision-making authority can differ within organizational units. Therefore, if one is looking at an individual level phenomenon such as occupational stress, it may be more meaningful to look at the structure of smaller organizational units than that of the whole organization. Secondly, there is some evidence suggesting that there are individual differences in response to structural variables. For example, Marino and White (1985) found that formalization was positively related to job stress among individuals with an internal locus of control and negatively related to stress among individuals who generally believe that they have little control over their environments. Lack of participation, on the other hand, was not moderated by locus of control and resulted in increased levels of job stress. There also appear to be some cultural differences affecting individual responses to structural variables, which would be important for multinational organizations having to operate across national boundaries (Peterson et al. 1995). These cultural differences also may explain the difficulty in adopting organizational structures and procedures from other nations.

Despite the rather limited empirical evidence implicating structural variables as psychosocial risk factors, it has been recommended that organizations should change their structures to be flatter with fewer levels of hierarchy or number of communication channels, more decentralized with more decision- making authority at lower levels in the organization and more integrated with less job specialization (Newman and Beehr 1979). These recommendations are consistent with organizational theorists who have suggested that traditional bureaucratic structure may not be the most efficient or healthiest form of organizational structure (Bennis 1969). This may be especially true in light of technological advances in production and communication that characterize the postindustrial workplace (Hirschhorn 1991).

The past two decades have seen considerable interest in the redesign of organizations to deal with external environmental threats resulting from increased globalization and international competition in North America and Western Europe (Whitaker 1991). Straw, Sandelands and Dutton (1988) proposed that organizations react to environmental threats by restricting information and constricting control. This can be expected to reduce the predictability, understandability and control of work events thereby increasing the stress experienced by the employees of the organization. Therefore, structural changes that prevent these threat-ridigity effects would appear to be beneficial to both the organization's and employees' health and well-being.

The use of a matrix organizational structure is one approach for organizations to structure their internal environments in response to greater environmental instability. Baber (1983) describes the ideal type of matrix organization as one in which there are two or more intersecting lines of authority, organizational goals are achieved through the use of task-oriented work groups which are cross-functional and temporary, and functional departments continue to exist as mechanisms for routine personnel functions and professional development. Therefore, the matrix organization provides the organization with the needed flexibility to be responsive to environmental instability if the personnel have sufficient flexibility gained from the diversification of their skills and an ability to learn quickly.

While empirical research has yet to establish the effects of this organizational structure, several authors have suggested that the matrix organization may increase the stress experienced by employees. For example, Quick and Quick (1984) point out that the multiple lines of authority (task and functional supervisors) found in matrix organizations increase the potential for role conflict. Also, Hirschhorn (1991) suggests that with postindustrial work organizations, workers frequently face new challenges requiring them to take a learning role. This results in employees having to acknowledge their own temporary incompetencies and loss of control which can lead to increased stress. Therefore, it appears that new organizational structures such as the matrix organization also have potential risk factors associated with them.

Attempts to change or redesign organizations, regardless of the particular structure that an organization chooses to adopt, can have stress-inducing properties by disrupting security and stability, generating uncertainty for people's position, role and status, and exposing conflict which must be confronted and resolved (Golembiewski 1982). These stress-inducing properties can be offset, however, by the stress-reducing properties of organizational development which incorporate greater empowerment and decision making across all levels in the organization, enhanced openness in communication, collaboration and training in team building and conflict resolution (Golembiewski 1982; Porras and Robertson 1992).

Conclusion

While the literature suggests that there are occupational risk factors associated with various organizational structures, the impact of these macrolevel aspects of organizations appear to be indirect. Organizational structure can provide a framework to enhance the predictability, understandability and control of events in the work environment; however, the effect of structure on employees' health and well-being is mediated by more proximal work-environment characteristics such as role characteristics and interpersonal relations. Structuring organizations for healthy employees as well as healthy organizations requires organizational flexibility, worker flexibility and attention to the sociotechnical systems that coordinate the technological demands and the social structure within the organization.

ORGANIZATIONAL CLIMATE AND CULTURE

Denise M. Rousseau

The organizational context in which people work is characterized by numerous features (e.g., leadership, structure, rewards, communication) subsumed under the general concepts of organizational climate and culture. Climate refers to perceptions of organizational practices reported by people who work there (Rousseau 1988). Studies of climate include many of the most central concepts in organizational research. Common features of climate include communication (as describable, say, by openness), conflict (constructive or dysfunctional), leadership (as it involves support or focus) and reward emphasis (i.e., whether an organization is characterized by positive versus negative feedback, or reward- or punishment-orientation). When studied together, we observe that organizational features are highly interrelated (e.g., leadership and rewards). Climate characterizes practices at several levels in organizations (e.g., work unit climate and organizational climate). Studies of climate vary in the activities they focus upon, for example, climates for safety or climates for service. Climate is essentially a description of the work setting by those directly involved with it.

The relationship of climate to employee well-being (e.g., satisfaction, job stress and strain) has been widely studied. Since climate measures subsume the major organizational characteristics workers experience, virtually any study of employee perceptions of their work setting can be thought of as a climate study. Studies link climate features (particularly leadership, communication openness, participative management and conflict resolution) with employee satisfaction and (inversely) stress levels (Schneider 1985). Stressful organizational climates are characterized by limited participation in decisions, use of punishment and negative feedback (rather than rewards and positive feedback), conflict avoidance or confrontation (rather than problem solving), and nonsupportive group and leader relations. Socially supportive climates benefit employee mental health, with lower rates of anxiety and depression in supportive settings (Repetti 1987). When collective climates exist (where members who interact with each other share common perceptions of the organization) research observes that shared perceptions of undesirable organizational features are linked with low morale and instances of psychogenic illness (Colligan, Pennebaker and Murphy 1982). When climate research adopts a specific focus, as in the study of climate for safety in an organization, evidence is provided that lack of openness in communication regarding safety issues, few rewards for reporting occupational hazards, and other negative climate features increase the incidence of work-related accidents and injury (Zohar 1980).

Since climates exist at many levels in organizations and can encompass a variety of practices, assessment of employee risk factors needs to systematically span the relationships (whether in the work unit, the department or the entire organization) and activities (e.g., safety, communication or rewards) in which employees are involved. Climate-based risk factors can differ from one part of the organization to another.

Culture constitutes the values, norms and ways of behaving which organization members share. Researchers identify five basic elements of culture in organizations: fundamental assumptions (unconscious beliefs that shape member's interpretations, e.g., views regarding time, environmental hostility or stability), values (preferences for certain outcomes over others, e.g., service or profit), behavioural norms (beliefs regarding appropriate and inappropriate behaviours, e.g., dress codes and teamwork), patterns of behaviours (observable recurrent practices, e.g., structured performance feedback and upward referral of decisions) and artefacts (symbols and objects used to express cultural messages, e.g., mission statements and logos). Cultural elements which are more subjective (i.e., assumptions, values and norms) reflect the way members think about and interpret their work setting. These subjective features shape the meaning that patterns of behaviours and artefacts take on within the organization. Culture, like climate, can exist at many levels, including:

1. a dominant organizational culture
2. subcultures associated with specific units, and
3. countercultures, found in work units that are poorly integrated with the larger organization.

Cultures can be strong (widely shared by members), weak (not widely shared), or in transition (characterized by gradual replacement of one culture by another).

In contrast with climate, culture is less frequently studied as a contributing factor to employee well-being or occupational risk. The absence of such research is due both to the relatively recent emergence of culture as a concept in organizational studies and to ideological debates regarding the nature of culture, its measurement (quantitative versus qualitative), and the appropriateness of the concept for cross-sectional study (Rousseau 1990). According to quantitative culture research focusing on behavioural norms and values, team-oriented norms are associated with higher member satisfaction and lower strain than are control- or bureaucratically-oriented norms (Rousseau 1989). Furthermore, the extent to which the worker's values are consistent with those of the organization affects stress and satisfaction (O'Reilly and Chatman 1991). Weak cultures and cultures fragmented by role conflict and member disagreement are found to provoke stress reactions and crises in professional identities (Meyerson 1990). The fragmentation or breakdown of organizational cultures due to economic or political upheavals affects the well-being of members psychologically and physically, particular in the wake of downsizings, plant closings and other effects of concurrent organizational restructurings (Hirsch 1987). The appropriateness of particular cultural forms (e.g., hierarchic or militaristic) for modern society has been challenged by several culture studies (e.g., Hirschhorn 1984; Rousseau 1989) concerned with the stress and health-related outcomes of operators (e.g., nuclear power technicians and air traffic controllers) and subsequent risks for the general public.

Assessing risk factors in the light of information about organizational culture requires first attention to the extent to which organization members share or differ in basic beliefs, values and norms. Differences in function, location and education create subcultures

within organizations and mean that culture-based risk factors can vary within the same organization. Since cultures tend to be stable and resistant to change, organizational history can aid assessment of risk factors both in terms of stable and ongoing cultural features as well as recent changes that can create stressors associated with turbulence (Hirsch 1987).

Climate and culture overlap to a certain extent, with perceptions of culture's patterns of behaviour being a large part of what climate research addresses. However, organization members may describe organizational features (climate) in the same way but interpret them differently due to cultural and subcultural influences (Rosen, Greenlagh and Anderson 1981). For example, structured leadership and limited participation in decision making may be viewed as negative and controlling from one perspective or as positive and legitimate from another. Social influence reflecting the organization's culture shapes the interpretation members make of organizational features and activities. Thus, it would seem appropriate to assess both climate and culture simultaneously in investigating the impact of the organization on the well-being of members.

PERFORMANCE MEASURES AND COMPENSATION

Richard L. Shell

There are many forms of compensation used in business and government organizations throughout the world to pay workers for their physical and mental contribution. Compensation provides money for human effort and is necessary for individual and family existence in most societies. Trading work for money is a long-established practice.

The health-stressor aspect of compensation is most closely linked with compensation plans that offer incentives for extra or sustained human effort. Job stress can certainly exist in any work setting where compensation is not based on incentives. However, physical and mental performance levels that are well above normal and that could lead to physical injury or injurious mental stress is more likely to be found in environments with certain kinds of incentive compensation.

Performance Measures and Stress

Performance measurements in one form or another are used by most organizations, and are essential for incentive programmes. Performance measures (standards) can be established for output, quality, throughput time, or any other productivity measure. Lord Kelvin in 1883 had this to say about measurements: "I often say that when you can measure what you are speaking about, and express it in numbers, you know something about it; but when you cannot measure it, when you cannot express it in numbers, your knowledge is a meagre and unsatisfactory kind; it may be the beginning of knowledge, but you have scarcely, in your thoughts, advanced to the stage of science, whatever the matter may be."

Performance measures should be carefully linked to the fundamental goals of the organization. Inappropriate performance measurements have often had little or no effect on goal attainment. Some common criticisms of performance measures include unclear purpose, vagueness, lack of connection (or even opposition, for that matter) to the business strategy, unfairness or inconsistency, and their liability to be used chiefly for "punishing" people. But measurements can serve as indispensable benchmarks: remember the saying, "If you don't know where you are, you can't get to where you want to be". The bottom line is that workers at all levels in an organization demonstrate more of the behaviours that they are measured on and rewarded to evince. What gets measured and rewarded gets done.

Performance measures must be fair and consistent to minimize stress among the workforce. There are several methods utilised to establish performance measures ranging from judgement estimation (guessing) to engineered work measurement techniques. Under the work measurement approach to setting performance measures, 100% performance is defined as a "fair day's work pace". This is the work effort and skill at which an average well-trained employee can work without undue fatigue while producing an acceptable quality of work over the course of a work shift. A 100% performance is not maximum performance; it is the normal or average effort and skill for a group of workers. By way of comparison, the 70% benchmark is generally regarded as the minimum tolerable level of performance, while the 120% benchmark is the incentive effort and skill that the average worker should be able to attain when provided with a bonus of at least 20% above the base rate of pay. While a number of incentive plans have been established using the 120% benchmark, this value varies among plans. The general design criteria recommended for wage incentive plans provide workers the opportunity to earn approximately 20 to 35% above base rate if they are normally skilled and execute high effort continuously.

Despite the inherent appeal of a "fair day's work for a fair day's pay", some possible stress problems exist with a work measurement approach to setting performance measures. Performance measures are fixed in reference to the normal or average performance of a given work group (i.e., work standards based on group as opposed to individual performance). Thus, by definition, a large segment of those working at a task will fall below average (i.e., the 100% performance benchmark) generating a demand–resource imbalance that exceeds physical or mental stress limits. Workers who have difficulty meeting performance measures are likely to experience stress through work overload, negative supervisor feedback, and threat of job loss if they consistently perform below the 100% performance benchmark.

Incentive Programmes

In one form or another, incentives have been used for many years. For example, in the New Testament (II Timothy 2:6) Saint Paul declares, "It is the hard-working farmer who ought to have the first share of the crops". Today, most organizations are striving to improve productivity and quality in order to maintain or improve their position in the business world. Most often workers will not give extra or sustained effort without some form of incentive. Properly designed and implemented financial incentive programmes can help. Before any incentive programme is implemented, some measure of performance must be established. All incentive programmes can be categorized as follows: direct financial, indirect financial, and intangible (non-financial).

Direct financial programmes may be applied to individuals or groups of workers. For individuals, each employee's incentive is governed by his or her performance relative to a standard for a given time period. Group plans are applicable to two or more individuals working as a team on tasks that are usually interdependent. Each employee's group incentive is usually based on his or her base rate and the group performance during the incentive period.

The motivation to sustain higher output levels is usually greater for individual incentives because of the opportunity for the high-performing worker to earn a greater incentive. However, as organizations move toward participative management and empowered work groups and teams, group incentives usually provide the best overall results. The group effort makes overall improvements to the total system as compared to optimizing individual outputs. Gainsharing (a group incentive system that has

teams for continuous improvement and provides a share, usually 50%, of all productivity gains above a benchmark standard) is one form of a direct group incentive programme that is well suited for the continuous improvement organization.

Indirect financial programmes are usually less effective than direct financial programmes because direct financial incentives are stronger motivators. The principal advantage of indirect plans is that they require less detailed and accurate performance measures. Organizational policies that favourably affect morale, result in increased productivity and provide some financial benefit to employees are considered to be indirect incentive programmes. It is important to note that for indirect financial programmes no exact relationship exists between employee output and financial incentives. Examples of indirect incentive programmes include relatively high base rates, generous fringe benefits, awards programmes, year-end bonuses and profit-sharing.

Intangible incentive programmes include rewards that do not have any (or very little) financial impact on employees. These programmes, however, when viewed as desirable by the employees, can improve productivity. Examples of intangible incentive programmes include job enrichment (adding challenge and intrinsic satisfaction to the specific task assignments), job enlargement (adding tasks to complete a "whole" piece or unit of work output), nonfinancial suggestion plans, employee involvement groups and time off without any reduction in pay.

Summary and Conclusions

Incentives in some form are an integral part of many compensation plans. In general, incentive plans should be carefully evaluated to make sure that workers are not exceeding safe ergonomic or mental stress limits. This is particularly important for individual direct financial plans. It is usually a lesser problem in group direct, indirect or intangible plans.

Incentives are desirable because they enhance productivity and provide workers an opportunity to earn extra income or other benefits. Gainsharing is today one of the best forms of incentive compensation for any work group or team organization that wishes to offer bonus earnings and to achieve improvement in the workplace without risking the imposition of negative health-stressors by the incentive plan itself.

STAFFING ISSUES

Marilyn K. Gowing

Contingent Workforce

The nations of the world vary dramatically in both their use and treatment of employees in their contingent workforce. Contingent workers include temporary workers hired through temporary help agencies, temporary workers hired directly, voluntary and "non-voluntary" part-timers (the non-voluntary would prefer full-time work) and the self-employed. International comparisons are difficult due to differences in the definitions of each of these categories of worker.

Overman (1993) stated that the temporary help industry in Western Europe is about 50% larger than it is in the United States, where about 1% of the workforce is made up of temporary workers. Temporary workers are almost non-existent in Italy and Spain.

While the subgroups of contingent workers vary considerably, the majority of part-time workers in all European countries are women at low salary levels. In the United States, contingent workers also tend to be young, female and members of minority groups. Countries vary considerably in the degree to which they protect contingent workers with laws and regulations covering their working conditions, health and other benefits. The United Kingdom, the United States, Korea, Hong Kong, Mexico and Chile are the least regulated, with France, Germany, Argentina and Japan having fairly rigid requirements (Overman 1993). A new emphasis on providing contingent workers with greater benefits through increased legal and regulatory requirements will help to alleviate occupational stress among those workers. However, those increased regulatory requirements may result in employers' hiring fewer workers overall due to increased benefit costs.

Job Sharing

An alternative to contingent work is "job sharing," which can take three forms: two employees share the responsibilities for one full-time job; two employees share one full-time position and divide the responsibilities, usually by project or client group; or two employees perform completely separate and unrelated tasks but are matched for purposes of headcount (Mattis 1990). Research has indicated that most job sharing, like contingent work, is done by women. However, unlike contingent work, job sharing positions are often subject to the protection of wage and hour laws and may involve professional and even managerial responsibilities. Within the European Community, job sharing is best known in Britain, where it was first introduced in the public sector (Lewis, Izraeli and Hootsmans 1992). The United States Federal Government, in the early 1990s, implemented a nationwide job sharing programme for its employees; in contrast, many state governments have been establishing job sharing networks since 1983 (Lee 1983). Job sharing is viewed as one way to balance work and family responsibilities.

Flexiplace and Home Work

Many alternative terms are used to denote flexiplace and home work: telecommuting, the alternative worksite, the electronic cottage, location-independent work, the remote workplace and work-at-home. For our purposes, this category of work includes "work performed at one or more 'predetermined locations' such as the home or a satellite work space away from the conventional office where at least some of the communications maintained with the employer occur through the use of telecommunications equipment such as computers, telephones and fax machines" (Pitt-Catsouphes and Marchetta 1991).

LINK Resources, Inc., a private-sector firm monitoring worldwide telecommuting activity, has estimated that there were 7.6 million telecommuters in 1993 in the United States out of the over 41.1 million work-at-home households. Of these telecommuters 81% worked part-time for employers with less than 100 employees in a wide array of industries across many geographical locations. Fifty-three% were male, in contrast to figures showing a majority of females in contingent and job-sharing work. Research with fifty US companies also showed that the majority of telecommuters were male with successful flexible work arrangements including supervisory positions (both line and staff), client-centred work and jobs that included travel (Mattis 1990). In 1992, 1.5 million Canadian households had at least one person who operated a business from home.

Lewis, Izraeli and Hootsman(1992) reported that, despite earlier predictions, telecommuting has not taken over Europe. They added that it is best established in the United Kingdom and Germany for professional jobs including computer specialists, accountants and insurance agents.

In contrast, some home-based work in both the United States and Europe pays by the piece and involves short deadlines. Typically, while telecommuters tend to be male, homeworkers in low-paid, piece-work jobs with no benefits tend to be female (Hall 1990).

Recent research has concentrated on identifying; (a) the type of person best suited for home work; (b) the type of work best accomplished at home; (c) procedures to ensure successful home work experiences and (d) reasons for organizational support (Hall 1990; Christensen 1992).

Welfare Facilities

The general approach to social welfare issues and programmes varies throughout the world depending upon the culture and values of the nation studied. Some of the differences in welfare facilities in the United States, Canada and Western Europe are documented by Ferber, O'Farrell and Allen (1991).

Recent proposals for welfare reform in the United States suggest overhauling traditional public assistance in order to make recipients work for their benefits. Cost estimates for welfare reform range from US$15 billion to $20 billion over the next five years, with considerable cost savings projected for the long term. Welfare administration costs in the United States for such programmes as food stamps, Medicaid and Aid to Families with Dependent Children have risen 19% from 1987 to 1991, the same percentage as the increase in the number of beneficiaries.

Canada has instituted a "work sharing" programme as an alternative to layoffs and welfare. The Canada Employment and Immigration Commission (CEIC) programme enables employers to face cutbacks by shortening the work week by one to three days and paying reduced wages accordingly. For the days not worked, the CEIC arranges for the workers to draw normal unemployment insurance benefits, an arrangement that helps to compensate them for the lower wages received from their employer and to relieve the hardships of being laid off. The duration of the programme is 26 weeks, with a 12-week extension. Workers can use work-sharing days for training and the federal Canadian government may reimburse the employer for a major portion of the direct training costs through the "Canadian Jobs Strategy".

Child Care

The degree of child-care support is dependent upon the sociological underpinnings of the nation's culture (Scharlach, Lowe and Schneider 1991). Cultures that:

1. support the full participation of women in the workplace
2. view child care as a public responsibility rather than a concern of individual families
3. value child care as an extension of the educational system, and
4. view early childhood experiences as important and formative

will devote greater resources to supporting those programmes. Thus, international comparisons are complicated by these four factors and "high quality care" may be dependent on the needs of children and families in specific cultures.

Within the European Community, France provides the most comprehensive child-care programme. The Netherlands and the United Kingdom were late in addressing this issue. Only 3% of British employers provided some form of child care in 1989. Lamb et al. (1992) present nonparental child-care case studies from Sweden, the Netherlands, Italy, the United Kingdom, the United States, Canada, Israel, Japan, the People's Republic of China, Cameroon, East Africa and Brazil. In the United States, approximately 3,500 private companies of the 17 million firms nationwide offer some type of child-care assistance to their employees. Of those firms, approximately 1,100 offer flexible spending accounts, 1,000 offer information and referral services and fewer than 350 have onsite or near-site child-care centres (Bureau of National Affairs 1991).

In a research study in the United States, 44% of men and 76% of women with children under six missed work in the previous three months for a family-related reason. The researchers estimated that the organizations they studied paid over $4 million in salary and benefits to employees who were absent because of child-care problems (see study by Galinsky and Hughes in Fernandez 1990). A study by the United States General Accounting Office in 1981 showed that American companies lose over $700 million a year because of inadequate parental leave policies.

Elder Care

It will take only 30 years (from the time of this writing, 1994) for the proportion of elderly in Japan to climb from 7% to 14%, while in France it took over 115 years and in Sweden 90 years. Before the end of the century, one out of every four persons in many member States of the Commission of the European Communities will be over 60 years old. Yet, until recently in Japan, there were few institutions for the elderly and the issue of eldercare has found scant attention in Britain and other European countries (Lewis, Izraeli and Hootsmans 1992). In America, there are approximately five million older Americans who require assistance with day-to-day tasks in order to remain in the community, and 30 million who are currently age 65 or older. Family members provide more than 80% of the assistance that these elderly people need (Scharlach, Lowe and Schneider 1991).

Research has shown that those employees who have elder-care responsibilities report significantly greater overall job stress than do other employees (Scharlach, Lowe and Schneider 1991). These caretakers often experience emotional stress and physical and financial strain. Fortunately, global corporations have begun to recognize that difficult family situations can result in absenteeism, decreased productivity and lower morale, and they are beginning to provide an array of "cafeteria benefits" to assist their employees. (The name "cafeteria" is intended to suggest that employees may select the benefits that would be most helpful to them from an array of benefits.) Benefits might include flexible work hours, paid "family illness" hours, referral services for family assistance, or a dependent-care salary-reduction account that allows employees to pay for elder care or day care with pre-tax dollars.

The author wishes to acknowledge the assistance of Charles Anderson of the Personnel Resources and Development Center of the United States Office of Personnel Management, Tony Kiers of the C.A.L.L. Canadian Work and Family Service, and Ellen Bankert and Bradley Googins of the Center on Work and Family of Boston University in acquiring and researching many of the references cited in this article.

CAREER DEVELOPMENT

● SOCIALIZATION

Debra L. Nelson and James Campbell Quick

The process by which outsiders become organizational insiders is known as organizational socialization. While early research on socialization focused on indicators of adjustment such as job satisfaction and performance, recent research has emphasized the links between organizational socialization and work stress.

Socialization as a Moderator of Job Stress

Entering a new organization is an inherently stressful experience. Newcomers encounter a myriad of stressors, including role ambiguity, role conflict, work and home conflicts, politics, time pressure and work overload. These stressors can lead to distress symptoms. Studies in the 1980s, however, suggest that a properly managed socialization process has the potential for moderating the stressor-strain connection.

Two particular themes have emerged in the contemporary research on socialization:

1. the acquisition of information during socialization,
2. supervisory support during socialization.

Information acquired by newcomers during socialization helps alleviate the considerable uncertainty in their efforts to master their new tasks, roles and interpersonal relationships. Often, this information is provided via formal orientation-cum-socialization programmes. In the absence of formal programmes, or (where they exist) in addition to them, socialization occurs informally. Recent studies have indicated that newcomers who proactively seek out information adjust more effectively (Morrison 1993). In addition, newcomers who underestimate the stressors in their new job report higher distress symptoms (Nelson and Sutton 1991).

Supervisory support during the socialization process is of special value. Newcomers who receive support from their supervisors report less stress from unmet expectations (Fisher 1985) and fewer psychological symptoms of distress (Nelson and Quick 1991). Supervisory support can help newcomers cope with stressors in at least three ways. First, supervisors may provide instrumental support (such as flexible work hours) that helps alleviate a particular stressor. Secondly, they may provide emotional support that leads a newcomer to feel more efficacy in coping with a stressor. Thirdly, supervisors play an important role in helping newcomers make sense of their new environment (Louis 1980). For example, they can frame situations for newcomers in a way that helps them appraise situations as threatening or nonthreatening.

In summary, socialization efforts that provide necessary information to newcomers and support from supervisors can prevent the stressful experience from becoming distressful.

Evaluating Organizational Socialization

The organizational socialization process is dynamic, interactive and communicative, and it unfolds over time. In this complexity lies the challenge of evaluating socialization efforts. Two broad approaches to measuring socialization have been proposed. One approach consists of the stage models of socialization (Feldman 1976; Nelson 1987). These models portray socialization as a multi-stage transition process with key variables at each of the stages. Another approach highlights the various socialization tactics that organizations use to help newcomers become insiders (Van Maanen and Schein 1979).

With both approaches, it is contended that there are certain outcomes that mark successful socialization. These outcomes include performance, job satisfaction, organizational commit-ment, job involvement and intent to remain with the organization. If socialization is a stress moderator, then distress symptoms (specifically, low levels of distress symptoms) should be included as an indicator of successful socialization.

Health Outcomes of Socialization

Because the relationship between socialization and stress has only recently received attention, few studies have included health outcomes. The evidence indicates, however, that the socialization process is linked to distress symptoms. Newcomers who found interactions with their supervisors and other newcomers helpful reported lower levels of psychological distress symptoms such as depression and inability to concentrate (Nelson and Quick 1991). Further, newcomers with more accurate expectations of the stressors in their new jobs reported lower levels of both psychological symptoms (e.g., irritability) and physiological symptoms (e.g., nausea and headaches).

Because socialization is a stressful experience, health outcomes are appropriate variables to study. Studies are needed that focus on a broad range of health outcomes and that combine self-reports of distress symptoms with objective health measures.

Organizational Socialization as Stress Intervention

The contemporary research on organizational socialization suggests that it is a stressful process that, if not managed well, can lead to distress symptoms and other health problems. Organizations can take at least three actions to ease the transition by way of intervening to ensure positive outcomes from socialization.

First, organizations should encourage realistic expectations among newcomers of the stressors inherent in the new job. One way of accomplishing this is to provide a realistic job preview that details the most commonly experienced stressors and effective ways of coping (Wanous 1992). Newcomers who have an accurate view of what they will encounter can preplan coping strategies and will experience less reality shock from those stressors about which they have been forewarned.

Secondly, organizations should make numerous sources of accurate information available to newcomers in the form of booklets, interactive information systems or hotlines (or all of these). The uncertainty of the transition into a new organization can be overwhelming, and multiple sources of informational support can aid newcomers in coping with the uncertainty of their new jobs. In addition, newcomers should be encouraged to seek out information during their socialization experiences.

Thirdly, emotional support should be explicitly planned for in designing socialization programmes. The supervisor is a key player in the provision of such support and may be most helpful by being emotionally and psychologically available to newcomers (Hirshhorn 1990). Other avenues for emotional support include mentoring, activities with more senior and experienced co-workers, and contact with other newcomers.

● CAREER STAGES

Kari Lindström

Introduction

The career stage approach is one way to look at career development. The way in which a researcher approaches the issue of career stages is frequently based on Levinson's life stage development model (Levinson 1986). According to this model, people grow through specific stages separated by transition periods. At each stage a new and crucial activity and psychological adjustment may be completed (Ornstein, Cron and Slocum 1989). In this way, defined career stages can be, and usually are, based on chronological age. The age ranges assigned for each stage have varied considerably between empirical studies, but usually the early career stage is considered to range from the ages of 20 to 34 years, the mid-career from 35 to 50 years and the late career from 50 to 65 years.

According to Super's career development model (Super 1957; Ornstein, Cron and Slocum 1989) the four career stages are

based on the qualitatively different psychological task of each stage. They can be based either on age or on organizational, positional or professional tenure. The same people can recycle several times through these stages in their work career. For example, according to the Career Concerns Inventory Adult Form, the actual career stage can be defined at an individual or group level. This instrument assesses an individual's awareness of and concerns with various tasks of career development (Super, Zelkowitz and Thompson 1981). When tenure measures are used, the first two years are seen as a trial period. The establishment period from two to ten years means career advancement and growth. After ten years comes the maintenance period, which means holding on to the accomplishments achieved. The decline stage implies the development of one's self-image independently of one's career.

Because the theoretical bases of the definition of the career stages and the sorts of measure used in practice differ from one study to another, it is apparent that the results concerning the health- and job-relatedness of career development vary, too.

Career Stage as a Moderator of Work-Related Health and Well-Being

Most studies of career stage as a moderator between job characteristics and the health or well-being of employees deal with organizational commitment and its relation to job satisfaction or to behavioural outcomes such as performance, turnover and absenteeism (Cohen 1991). The relationship between job characteristics and strain has also been studied. The moderating effect of career stage means statistically that the average correlation between measures of job characteristics and well-being varies from one career stage to another.

Work commitment usually increases from early career stages to later stages, although among salaried male professionals, job involvement was found to be lowest in the middle stage. In the early career stage, employees had a stronger need to leave the organization and to be relocated (Morrow and McElroy 1987). Among hospital staff, nurses' measures of well-being were most strongly associated with career and affective-organizational commitment (i.e., emotional attachment to the organization). Continuance commitment (this is a function of perceived number of alternatives and degree of sacrifice) and normative commitment (loyalty to organization) increased with career stage (Reilly and Orsak 1991).

A meta-analysis was carried out of 41 samples dealing with the relationship between organizational commitment and outcomes indicating well-being. The samples were divided into different career stage groups according to two measures of career stage: age and tenure. Age as a career stage indicator significantly affected turnover and turnover intentions, while organizational tenure was related to job performance and absenteeism. Low organizational commitment was related to high turnover, especially in the early career stage, whereas low organizational commitment was related to high absenteeism and low job performance in the late career stage (Cohen 1991).

The relationship between work attitudes, for instance job satisfaction and work behaviour, has been found to be moderated by career stage to a considerable degree (e.g., Stumpf and Rabinowitz 1981). Among employees of public agencies, career stage measured with reference to organizational tenure was found to moderate the relationship between job satisfaction and job performance. Their relation was strongest in the first career stage. This was supported also in a study among sales personnel. Among academic teachers, the relationship between satisfaction and performance was found to be negative during the first two years of tenure.

Most studies of career stage have dealt with men. Even many early studies in the 1970s, in which the sex of the respondents was not reported, it is apparent that most of the subjects were men. Ornstein and Lynn (1990) tested how the career stage models of Levinson and Super described differences in the career attitudes and intentions among professional women. The results suggest that career stages based on age were related to organizational commitment, intention to leave the organization and a desire for promotion. These findings were, in general, similar to the ones found among men (Ornstein, Cron and Slocum 1989). However, no support was derived for the predictive value of career stages as defined on a psychological basis.

Studies of stress have generally either ignored age, and consequently career stage, in their study designs or treated it as a confounding factor and controlled its effects. Hurrell, McLaney and Murphy (1990) contrasted the effects of stress in mid-career to its effects in early and late career using age as a basis for their grouping of US postal workers. Perceived ill health was not related to job stressors in mid-career, but work pressure and underutilization of skills predicted it in early and late career. Work pressure was related also to somatic complaints in the early and late career group. Underutilization of abilities was more strongly related to job satisfaction and somatic complaints among mid-career workers. Social support had more influence on mental health than physical health, and this effect is more pronounced in mid-career than in early or late career stages. Because the data were taken from a cross sectional study, the authors mention that cohort explanation of the results might also be possible (Hurrell, McLaney and Murphy 1990).

When adult male and female workers were grouped according to age, the older workers more frequently reported overload and responsibility as stressors at work, whereas the younger workers cited insufficiency (e.g., not challenging work), boundary-spanning roles and physical environment stressors (Osipow, Doty and Spokane 1985). The older workers reported fewer of all kinds of strain symptoms: one reason for this may be that older people used more rational-cognitive, self-care and recreational coping skills, evidently learned during their careers, but selection that is based on symptoms during one's career may also explain these differences. Alternatively it might reflect some self-selection, when people leave jobs that stress them excessively over time.

Among Finnish and US male managers, the relationship between job demands and control on the one hand, and psychosomatic symptoms on the other, was found in the studies to vary according to career stage (defined on the basis of age) (Hurrell and Lindström 1992, Lindström and Hurrell 1992). Among US managers, job demands and control had a significant effect on symptom reporting in the middle career stage, but not in the early and late stage, while among Finnish managers, the long weekly working hours and low job control increased stress symptoms in the early career stage, but not in the later stages. Differences between the two groups might be due to the differences in the two samples studied. The Finnish managers, being in the construction trades, had high workloads already in their early career stage, whereas US managers—these were public sector workers—had the highest workloads in their middle career stage.

To sum up the results of research on the moderating effects of career stage: early career stage means low organizational commitment related to turnover as well as job stressors related to perceived ill health and somatic complaints. In mid-career the results are conflicting: sometimes job satisfaction and performance are positively related, sometimes negatively. In mid-career, job demands and low control are related to frequent symptom reporting among some occupational groups. In late career, organizational commitment is correlated to low absenteeism and good performance. Findings on relations between job stressors and strain are inconsistent for the late career stage. There are some indications that more effective coping decreases work-related strain symptoms in late career.

Interventions

Practical interventions to help people to cope better with the specific demands of each career stage would be beneficial. Vocational counselling at the entry stage of one's work life would be especially useful. Interventions for minimizing the negative impact of career plateauing are suggested because this can be either a time of frustration or an opportunity to face new challenges or to reappraise one's life goals (Weiner, Remer and Remer 1992). Results of age-based health examinations in occupational health services have shown that job-related problems lowering working ability gradually increase and qualitatively change with age. In early and mid-career they are related to coping with work overload, but in later middle and late career they are gradually accompanied by declining psychological condition and physical health, facts that indicate the importance of early institutional intervention at an individual level (Lindström, Kaihilahti and Torstila 1988). Both in research and in practical interventions, mobility and turnover pattern should be taken into account, as well as the role played by one's occupation (and situation within that occupation) in one's career development.

INDIVIDUAL FACTORS

TYPE A/B BEHAVIOUR PATTERN

C. David Jenkins

Definition

The Type A behaviour pattern is an observable set of behaviours or style of living characterized by extremes of hostility, competitiveness, hurry, impatience, restlessness, aggressiveness (sometimes stringently suppressed), explosiveness of speech, and a high state of alertness accompanied by muscular tension. People with strong Type A behaviour struggle against the pressure of time and the challenge of responsibility (Jenkins 1979). Type A is neither an external stressor nor a response of strain or discomfort. It is more like a style of coping. At the other end of this bipolar continuum, Type B persons are more relaxed, cooperative, steady in their pace of activity, and appear more satisfied with their daily lives and the people around them.

The Type A/B behavioural continuum was first conceptualized and labelled in 1959 by the cardiologists Dr. Meyer Friedman and Dr. Ray H. Rosenman. They identified Type A as being typical of their younger male patients with ischaemic heart disease (IHD).

The intensity and frequency of Type A behaviour increases as societies become more industrialized, competitive and hurried. Type A behaviour is more frequent in urban than rural areas, in managerial and sales occupations than among technical workers, skilled craftsmen or artists, and in businesswomen than in housewives.

Areas of Research

Type A behaviour has been studied as part of the fields of personality and social psychology, organizational and industrial psychology, psychophysiology, cardiovascular disease and occupational health.

Research relating to personality and social psychology has yielded considerable understanding of the Type A pattern as an important psychological construct. Persons scoring high on Type A measures behave in ways predicted by Type A theory. They are more impatient and aggressive in social situations and spend more time working and less in leisure. They react more strongly to frustration.

Research that incorporates the Type A concept into organizational and industrial psychology includes comparisons of different occupations as well as employees' responses to job stress. Under conditions of equivalent external stress, Type A employees tend to report more physical and emotional strain than Type B employees. They also tend to move into high-demand jobs (Type A behavior 1990).

Pronounced increases in blood pressure, serum cholesterol and catecholamines in Type A persons were first reported by Rosenman and al. (1975) and have since been confirmed by many other investigators. The tenor of these findings is that Type A and Type B persons are usually quite similar in chronic or baseline levels of these physiological variables, but that environmental demands, challenges or frustrations create far larger reactions in Type A than Type B persons. The literature has been somewhat inconsistent, partly because the same challenge may not physiologically activitate men or women of different backgrounds. A preponderance of positive findings continues to be published (Contrada and Krantz 1988).

The history of Type A/B behaviour as a risk factor for ischeamic heart disease has followed a common historical trajectory: a trickle then a flow of positive findings, a trickle then a flow of negative findings, and now intense controversy (Review Panel on Coronary-Prone Behavior and Coronary Heart Disease 1981). Broad-scope literature searches now reveal a continuing mixture of positive associations and non-associations between Type A behaviour and IHD. The general trend of the findings is that Type A behaviour is more likely to be positively associated with a risk of IHD:

1. in cross-sectional and case-control studies rather than prospective studies
2. in studies of general populations and occupational groups rather than studies limited to persons with cardiovascular disease or who score high on other IHD risk factors
3. in younger study groups (under age 60) rather than older populations
4. in countries still in the process of industrialization or still at the peak of their economic development.

The Type A pattern is not "dead" as an IHD risk factor, but in the future must be studied with the expectation that it may convey greater IHD risk only in certain sub-populations and in selected social settings. Some studies suggest that hostility may be the most damaging component of Type A.

A newer development has been the study of Type A behaviour as a risk factor for injuries and mild and moderate illnesses both in occupational and student groups. It is rational to hypothesize that people who are hurried and aggressive will incur the most accidents at work, in sports and on the highway. This has been found to be empirically true (Elander, West and French 1993). It is less clear theoretically why mild acute illnesses in a full array of physiologic systems should occur more often to Type A than Type B persons, but this has been found in a few studies (e. g. Suls and Sanders 1988). At least in some groups, Type A was found to be associated with a higher risk of future mild episodes of emotional distress. Future research needs to address both the validity of these associations and the physical and psychological reasons behind them.

Methods of Measurement

The Type A/B behaviour pattern was first measured in research settings by the Structured Interview (SI). The SI is a carefully administered clinical interview in which about 25 questions are asked at different rates of speed and with different degrees of challenge or intrusiveness. Special training is necessary for an interviewer to be certified as competent both to administer and interpret the SI. Typically, interviews are tape-recorded to permit subsequent study by other judges to ensure reliability. In comparative studies among several measures of Type A behaviour, the SI seems to have greater validity for cardiovascular and psychophysiological studies than is found for self-report questionnaires, but little is known about its comparative validity in psychological and occupational studies because the SI is used much less frequently in these settings.

Self-Report Measures

The most common self-report instrument is the Jenkins Activity Survey (JAS), a self-report, computer-scored, multiple-choice questionnaire. It has been validated against the SI and against the criteria of current and future IHD, and has accumulated construct validity. Form C, a 52-item version of the JAS published in 1979 by the Psychological Corporation, is the most widely used. It has been translated into most of the languages of Europe and Asia. The JAS contains four scales: a general Type A scale, and factor-analytically derived scales for speed and impatience, job involvement and hard-driving competitiveness. A short form of the Type A scale (13 items) has been used in epidemiological studies by the World Health Organization.

The Framingham Type A Scale (FTAS) is a ten-item questionnaire shown to be a valid predictor of future IHD for both men and women in the Framingham Heart Study (USA). It has also been used internationally both in cardiovascular and psychological research. Factor analysis divides the FTAS into two factors, one of which correlates with other measures of Type A behaviour while the second correlates with measures of neuroticism and irritability.

The Bortner Rating Scale (BRS) is composed of fourteen items, each in the form of an analogue scale. Subsequent studies have performed item-analysis on the BRS and have achieved greater internal consistency or greater predictability by shortening the scale to 7 or 12 items. The BRS has been widely used in international translations. Additional Type A scales have been developed internationally, but these have mostly been used only for specific nationalities in whose language they were written.

Practical Interventions

Systematic efforts have been under way for at least two decades to help persons with intense Type A behaviour patterns to change them to more of a Type B style. Perhaps the largest of these efforts was in the Recurrent Coronary Prevention Project conducted in the San Francisco Bay area in the 1980s. Repeated follow-up over several years documented that changes were achieved in many people and also that the rate of recurrent myocardial infarction was reduced in persons receiving the Type A behaviour reduction efforts as opposed to those receiving only cardiovascular counselling (Thoreson and Powell 1992).

Intervention in the Type A behaviour pattern is difficult to accomplish successfully because this behavioural style has so many rewarding features, particularly in terms of career advancement and material gain. The programme itself must be carefully crafted according to effective psychological principles, and a group process approach appears to be more effective than individual counselling.

● HARDINESS

Suzanne C. Ouellette

The characteristic of hardiness is based in an existential theory of personality and is defined as a person's basic stance towards his or his place in the world that simultaneously expresses commitment, control and readiness to respond to challenge (Kobasa 1979; Kobasa, Maddi and Kahn 1982). Commitment is the tendency to involve oneself in, rather than experience alienation from, whatever one is doing or encounters in life. Committed persons have a generalized sense of purpose that allows them to identify with and find meaningful the persons, events and things of their environment. Control is the tendency to think, feel and act as if one is influential, rather than helpless, in the face of the varied contingencies of life. Persons with control do not naïvely expect to determine all events and outcomes but rather perceive themselves as being able to make a difference in the world through their exercise of imagination, knowledge, skill and choice. Challenge is the tendency to believe that change rather than stability is normal in life and that changes are interesting incentives to growth rather than threats to security. So far from being reckless adventurers, persons with challenge are rather individuals with an openness to new experiences and a tolerance of ambiguity that enables them to be flexible in the face of change.

Conceived of as a reaction and corrective to a pessimistic bias in early stress research that emphasized persons' vulnerability to stress, the basic hardiness hypothesis is that individuals characterized by high levels of the three interrelated orientations of commitment, control and challenge are more likely to remain healthy under stress than those individuals who are low in hardiness. The personality possessing hardiness is marked by a way of perceiving and responding to stressful life events that prevents or minimizes the strain that can follow stress and that, in turn, can lead to mental and physical illness.

The initial evidence for the hardiness construct was provided by retrospective and longitudinal studies of a large group of middle- and upper-level male executives employed by a Midwestern telephone company in the United States during the time of the divestiture of American Telephone and Telegraph (ATT). Executives were monitored through yearly questionnaires over a five-year period for stressful life experiences at work and at home, physical health changes, personality characteristics, a variety of other work factors, social support and health habits. The primary finding was that under conditions of highly stressful life events, executives scoring high on hardiness are significantly less likely to become physically ill than are executives scoring low on hardiness, an outcome that was documented through self-reports of physical symptoms and illnesses and validated by medical records based on yearly physical examinations. The initial work also demonstrated: (a) the effectiveness of hardiness combined with social support and exercise to protect mental as well as physical health; and (b) the independence of hardiness with respect to the frequency and severity of stressful life events, age, education, marital status and job level. Finally, the body of hardiness research initially assembled as a result of the study led to further research that showed the generalizability of the hardiness effect across a number of occupational groups, including non-executive telephone personnel, lawyers and US Army officers (Kobasa 1982).

Since those basic studies, the hardiness construct has been employed by many investigators working in a variety of occupational and other contexts and with a variety of research strategies ranging from controlled experiments to more qualitative field investigations (for reviews, see Maddi 1990; Orr and Westman 1990; Ouellette 1993). The majority of these studies have basically supported and expanded the original hardiness formulation, but there have also been disconfirmations of the moderating effect of hardiness and criticisms of the strategies selected for the measurement of hardiness (Funk and Houston 1987; Hull, Van Treuren and Virnelli 1987).

Emphasizing individuals' ability to do well in the face of serious stressors, researchers have confirmed the positive role of hardiness among many groups including, in samples studied in the United States, bus drivers, military air-disaster workers, nurses working in a variety of settings, teachers, candidates in training for a number of different occupations, persons with chronic illness and Asian immigrants. Elsewhere, studies have been carried out among businessmen in Japan and trainees in the Israeli defence forces. Across these groups, one finds an association between hardiness and lower levels of either physical or mental symptoms, and, less frequently, a significant interaction between stress levels and hardiness that provides support for the buffering role of personality. In addition, results establish the effects of hardiness on non-health outcomes such as work performance and job satisfaction as well as on burnout. Another large body of work, most of it conducted with college-student samples, confirms the hypothesized mechanisms through which hardiness has its health-protective effects. These studies demonstrated the influence of hardiness upon the subjects' appraisal of stress (Wiebe and Williams 1992). Also relevant to construct validity, a smaller number of studies have provided some evidence for the psychophysiological arousal correlates of hardiness and the relationship between hardiness and various preventive health behaviours.

Essentially all of the empirical support for a link between hardiness and health has relied upon data obtained through self-report questionnaires. Appearing most often in publications is the composite questionnaire used in the original prospective test of hardiness and abridged derivatives of that measure. Fitting the broad-based definition of hardiness as defined in the opening words of this article, the composite questionnaire contains items from a number of established personality instruments that include Rotter's *Internal-External Locus of Control Scale* (Rotter, Seeman and Liverant 1962), Hahn's *California Life Goals Evaluation Schedules* (Hahn 1966), Maddi's *Alienation versus Commitment Test* (Maddi, Kobasa and Hoover 1979) and Jackson's *Personality Research Form* (Jackson 1974). More recent efforts at questionnaire development have led to the development of the Personal Views Survey, or what Maddi (1990) calls the "Third Generation Hardiness Test". This new questionnaire addresses many of the criticisms raised with respect to the original measure, such as the preponderance of negative items and the instability of hardiness factor structures. Furthermore, studies of working adults in both the United States and the United Kingdom have yielded promising reports as to the reliability and validity of the hardiness measure. Nonetheless, not all of the problems have been resolved. For example, some reports show low internal reliability for the challenge component of hardiness. Another pushes beyond the measurement issue to raise a conceptual concern about whether hardiness should always be seen as a unitary phenomenon rather than a multidimensional construct made up of separate components that may have relationships with health independently of each other in certain stressful situations. The challenge to future on researchers hardiness is to retain both the conceptual and human richness of the hardiness notion while increasing its empirical precision.

Although Maddi and Kobasa (1984) describe the childhood and family experiences that support the development of personality hardiness, they and many other hardiness researchers are committed to defining interventions to increase adults' stress-resistance. From an existential perspective, personality is seen as something that one is constantly constructing, and a person's social context, including his or her work environment, is seen as either supportive or debilitating as regards the maintenance of hardiness. Maddi (1987, 1990) has provided the most thorough depiction and rationale for hardiness intervention strategies. He outlines a combination of focusing, situational reconstruction, and compensatory self-improvement strategies that he has used successfully in small group sessions to enhance hardiness and decrease the negative physical and mental effects of stress in the workplace.

SELF-ESTEEM

John M. Schaubroeck

Low self-esteem (SE) has long been studied as a determinant of psychological and physiological disorders (Beck 1967; Rosenberg 1965; Scherwitz, Berton and Leventhal 1978). Beginning in the 1980s, organizational researchers have investigated self-esteem's moderating role in relationships between work stressors and individual outcomes. This reflects researchers' growing interest in dispositions that seem either to protect or make a person more vulnerable to stressors.

Self-esteem can be defined as "the favorability of individuals' characteristic self-evaluations" (Brockner 1988). Brockner (1983, 1988) has advanced the hypothesis that persons with low SE (low SEs) are generally more susceptible to environmental events than are high SEs. Brockner (1988) reviewed extensive evidence that this "plasticity hypothesis" explains a number of organizational processes. The most prominent research into this hypothesis has tested self-esteem's moderating role in the relationship between role stressors (role conflict and role ambiguity) and health and affect. Role conflict (disagreement among one's received roles) and role ambiguity (lack of clarity concerning the content of one's role) are generated largely by events that are external to the individual, and therefore, according to the plasticity hypothesis, high SEs would be less vulnerable to them.

In a study of 206 nurses in a large southwestern US hospital, Mossholder, Bedeian and Armenakis (1981) found that self-reports of role ambiguity were negatively related to job satisfaction for low SEs but not for high SEs. Pierce et al. (1993) used an organization-based measure of self-esteem to test the plasticity hypothesis on 186 workers in a US utility company. Role ambiguity and role conflict were negatively related to satisfaction only among low SEs. Similar interactions with organization-based self-esteem were found for role overload, environmental support and supervisory support.

In the studies reviewed above, self-esteem was viewed as a proxy (or alternative measure) for self-appraisals of competence on the job. Ganster and Schaubroeck (1991a) speculated that the moderating role of self-esteem on role stressors' effects was instead caused by low SEs' lack of confidence in influencing their social environment, the result being weaker attempts at coping with these stressors. In a study of 157 US fire-fighters, they found that role conflict was positively related to somatic health complaints only among low SEs. There was no such interaction with role ambiguity.

In a separate analysis of the data on nurses' reported in their earlier study (Mossholder, Bedeian and Armenakis 1981), these authors (1982) found that peer group interaction had a significantly more negative relationship to self-reported tension among low SEs than among high SEs. Likewise, low SEs reporting high peer-group interaction were less likely to wish to leave the organization than were high SEs reporting high peer-group interaction.

Several measures of self-esteem exist in the literature. Possibly the most often used of these is the ten-item instrument developed by Rosenberg (1965). This instrument was used in the Ganster and Schaubroeck (1991a) study. Mossholder and his colleagues (1981, 1982) used the self-confidence scale from Gough and Heilbrun's (1965) *Adjective Check List*. The organization-based measure of self-esteem used by Pierce et al. (1993) was a ten-item instrument developed by Pierce et al. (1989).

The research findings suggest that health reports and satisfaction among low SEs can be improved either by reducing their role stressors or increasing their self-esteem. The organization development intervention of role clarification (dyadic supervisor-subordinate exchanges directed at clarifying the subordinate's role and reconciling incompatible expectations), when combined with responsibility charting (clarifying and negotiating the roles of different departments), proved successful in a randomized field experiment at reducing role conflict and role ambiguity (Schaubroeck et al. 1993). It seems unlikely, however, that many organizations will be able and willing to undertake this rather extensive practice unless role stress is seen as particularly acute.

Brockner (1988) suggested a number of ways organizations can enhance employee self-esteem. Supervision practices are a major area in which organizations can improve. Performance appraisal feedback which focuses on behaviours rather than on traits, providing descriptive information with evaluative summations, and participatively developing plans for continuous improvement, is likely to have fewer adverse effects on employee self-esteem, and it may even enhance the self-esteem of some workers as they discover ways to improve their performance. Positive reinforcement of effective performance events is also critical. Training approaches such as mastery modelling (Wood and Bandura 1989) also ensure that positive efficacy perceptions are developed for each new task; these perceptions are the basis of organization-based self-esteem.

LOCUS OF CONTROL

Lawrence R. Murphy and Joseph J. Hurrell, Jr.

Locus of control (LOC) refers to a personality trait reflecting the generalized belief that either events in life are controlled by one's own actions (an internal LOC) or by outside influences (an external LOC). Those with an internal LOC believe that they can exert control over life events and circumstances, including the associated reinforcements, that is, those outcomes which are perceived to reward one's behaviours and attitudes. In contrast, those with an external LOC believe they have little control over life events and circumstances, and attribute reinforcements to powerful others or to luck.

The construct of locus of control emerged from Rotter's (1954) social learning theory. To measure LOC, Rotter (1966) developed the Internal-External (I-E) scale, which has been the instrument of choice in most research studies. However, research has questioned the unidimensionality of the I-E scale, with some authors suggesting that LOC has two dimensions (e.g., personal control and social system control), and others suggesting that LOC has three dimensions (personal efficacy, control ideology and political control). More recently developed scales to measure LOC are multidimensional, or assess LOC for specific domains, such as health or work (Hurrell and Murphy 1992).

One of the most consistent and widespread findings in the general research literature is the association between an external LOC and poor physical and mental health (Ganster and Fusilier

1989). A number of studies in occupational settings report similar findings: workers with an external LOC tended to report more burnout, job dissatisfaction, stress and lower self-esteem than those with an internal LOC (Kasl 1989). Recent evidence suggests that LOC moderates the relationship between role stressors (role ambiguity and role conflict) and symptoms of distress (Cvetanovski and Jex 1994; Spector and O'Connell 1994).

However, research linking LOC beliefs and ill health is difficult to interpret for several reasons (Kasl 1989). First, there may be conceptual overlap between the measures of health and locus of control scales. Secondly, a dispositional factor, like negative affectivity, may be present which is responsible for the relationship. For example, in the study by Spector and O'Connell (1994), LOC beliefs correlated more strongly with negative affectivity than with perceived autonomy at work, and did not correlate with physical health symptoms. Thirdly, the direction of causality is ambiguous; it is possible that the work experience may alter LOC beliefs. Finally, other studies have not found moderating effects of LOC on job stressors or health outcomes (Hurrell and Murphy 1992).

The question of how LOC moderates job stressor-health relationships has not been well researched. One proposed mechanism involves the use of more effective, problem-focused coping behaviour by those with an internal LOC. Those with an external LOC might use fewer problem-solving coping strategies because they believe that events in their lives are outside their control. There is evidence that people with an internal LOC utilize more task-centred coping behaviours and fewer emotion-centred coping behaviours than those with an external LOC (Hurrell and Murphy 1992). Other evidence indicates that in situations viewed as changeable, those with an internal LOC reported high levels of problem-solving coping and low levels of emotional suppression, whereas those with an external LOC showed the reverse pattern. It is important to bear in mind that many workplace stressors are not under the direct control of the worker, and that attempts to change uncontrollable stressors might actually increase stress symptoms (Hurrell and Murphy 1992).

A second mechanism whereby LOC could influence stressor-health relationships is via social support, another moderating factor of stress and health relationships. Fusilier, Ganster and Mays (1987) found that locus of control and social support jointly determined how workers responded to job stressors and Cummins (1989) found that social support buffered the effects of job stress, but only for those with an internal LOC and only when the support was work-related.

Although the topic of LOC is intriguing and has stimulated a great deal of research, there are serious methodological problems attaching to investigations in this area which need to be addressed. For example, the trait-like (unchanging) nature of LOC beliefs has been questioned by research which showed that people adopt a more external orientation with advancing age and after certain life experiences such as unemployment. Furthermore, LOC may be measuring worker perceptions of job control, instead of an enduring trait of the worker. Still other studies have suggested that LOC scales may not only measure beliefs about control, but also the tendency to use defensive manoeuvres, and to display anxiety or proneness to Type A behaviour (Hurrell and Murphy 1992).

Finally, there has been little research on the influence of LOC on vocational choice, and the reciprocal effects of LOC and job perceptions. Regarding the former, occupational differences in the proportion of "internals" and "externals" may be evidence that LOC influences vocational choice (Hurrell and Murphy 1992). On the other hand, such differences might reflect exposure to the job environment, just as the work environment is thought to be instrumental in the development of the Type A behaviour pattern. A final alternative is that occupational differences in LOC are be due to "drift", that is the movement of workers into or out of certain occupations as a result of job dissatisfaction, health concerns or desire for advancement.

In summary, the research literature does not present a clear picture of the influence of LOC beliefs on job stressor or health relationships. Even where research has produced more or less consistent findings, the meaning of the relationship is obscured by confounding influences (Kasl 1989). Additional research is needed to determine the stability of the LOC construct and to identify the mechanisms or pathways through which LOC influences worker perceptions and mental and physical health. Components of the path should reflect the interaction of LOC with other traits of the worker, and the interaction of LOC beliefs with work environment factors, including reciprocal effects of the work environment and LOC beliefs. Future research should produce less ambiguous results if it incorporates measures of related individual traits (e.g., Type A behaviour or anxiety) and utilizes domain-specific measures of locus of control (e.g., work).

COPING STYLES

Ronald J. Burke

Coping has been defined as "efforts to reduce the negative impacts of stress on individual well-being" (Edwards 1988). Coping, like the experience of work stress itself, is a complex, dynamic process. Coping efforts are triggered by the appraisal of situations as threatening, harmful or anxiety producing (i.e., by the experience of stress). Coping is an individual difference variable that moderates the stress-outcome relationship.

Coping styles encompass trait-like combinations of thoughts, beliefs and behaviours that result from the experience of stress and may be expressed independently of the type of stressor. A coping style is a dispositional variable. Coping styles are fairly stable over time and situations and are influenced by personality traits, but are different from them. The distinction between the two is one of generality or level of abstraction. Examples of such styles, expressed in broad terms, include: monitor-blunter (Miller 1979) and repressor-sensitizer (Houston and Hodges 1970). Individual differences in personality, age, experience, gender, intellectual ability and cognitive style affect the way an individual copes with stress. Coping styles are the result of both prior experience and previous learning.

Shanan (1967) offered an early perspective on what he termed an adaptive coping style. This "response set" was characterized by four ingredients: the availability of energy directly focused on potential sources of the difficulty; a clear distinction between events internal and external to the person; confronting rather than avoiding external difficulties; and balancing external demands with needs of the self. Antonovsky (1987) similarly suggests that, to be effective, the individual person must be motivated to cope, have clarified the nature and dimensions of the problem and the reality in which it exists, and then selected the most appropriate resources for the problem at hand.

The most common typology of coping style (Lazarus and Folkman 1984) includes problem-focused coping (which includes information seeking and problem solving) and emotion-focused coping (which involves expressing emotion and regulating emotions). These two factors are sometimes complemented by a third factor, appraisal-focused coping (whose components include denial, acceptance, social comparison, redefinition and logical analysis).

Moos and Billings (1982) distinguish among the following coping styles:

- *Active-cognitive*. The person tries to manage their appraisal of the stressful situation.
- *Active-behavioural*. This style involves behaviour dealing directly with the stressful situations.
- *Avoidance*. The person avoids confronting the problem.

Greenglass (1993) has recently proposed a coping style termed social coping, which integrates social and interpersonal factors with cognitive factors. Her research showed significant relationships between various kinds of social support and coping forms (e.g., problem-focused and emotion-focused). Women, generally possessing relatively greater interpersonal competence, were found to make greater use of social coping.

In addition, it may be possible to link another approach to coping, termed preventive coping, with a large body of previously separate writing dealing with healthy lifestyles (Roskies 1991). Wong and Reker (1984) suggest that a preventive coping style is aimed at promoting one's well-being and reducing the likelihood of future problems. Preventive coping includes such activities as physical exercise and relaxation, as well as the development of appropriate sleeping and eating habits, and planning, time management and social support skills.

Another coping style, which has been described as a broad aspect of personality (Watson and Clark 1984), involves the concepts of negative affectivity (NA) and positive affectivity (PA). People with high NA accentuate the negative in evaluating themselves, other people and their environment in general and reflect higher levels of distress. Those with high PA focus on the positives in evaluating themselves, other people and their world in general. People with high PA report lower levels of distress.

These two dispositions can affect a person's perceptions of the number and magnitude of potential stressors as well as his or her coping responses (i.e., one's perceptions of the resources that one has available, as well as the actual coping strategies that are used). Thus, those with high NA will report fewer resources available and are more likely to use ineffective (defeatist) strategies (such as releasing emotions, avoidance and disengagement in coping) and less likely to use more effective strategies (such as direct action and cognitive reframing). Individuals with high PA would be more confident in their coping resources and use more productive coping strategies.

Antonovsky's (1979; 1987) sense of coherence (SOC) concept overlaps considerably with PA. He defines SOC as a generalized view of the world as meaningful and comprehensible. This orientation allows the person to first focus on the specific situation and then to act on the problem and the emotions associated with the problem. High SOC individuals have the motivation and the cognitive resources to engage in these sorts of behaviours likely to resolve the problem. In addition, high SOC individuals are more likely to realize the importance of emotions, more likely to experience particular emotions and to regulate them, and more likely to take responsibility for their circumstances instead of blaming others or projecting their perceptions upon them. Considerable research has since supplied support for Antonovsky's thesis.

Coping styles can be described with reference to dimensions of complexity and flexibility (Lazarus and Folkman 1984). People using a variety of strategies exhibit a complex style; those preferring a single strategy exhibit a single style. Those who use the same strategy in all situations exhibit a rigid style; those who use different strategies in the same, or different, situations exhibit a flexible style. A flexible style has been shown to be more effective than a rigid style.

Coping styles are typically measured by using self-reported questionnaires or by asking individuals, in an open-ended way, how they coped with a particular stressor. The questionnaire developed by Lazarus and Folkman (1984), the "Ways of Coping Checklist", is the most widely used measure of problem-focused and emotion-focused coping. Dewe (1989), on the other hand, has frequently used individuals' descriptions of their own coping initiatives in his research on coping styles.

There are a variety of practical interventions that may be implemented with regard to coping styles. Most often, intervention consists of education and training in which individuals are presented with information, sometimes coupled with self-assessment exercises that enable them to examine their own preferred coping style as well as other varieties of coping styles and their potential usefulness. Such information is typically well received by the persons to whom the intervention is directed, but the demonstrated usefulness of such information in helping them cope with real life stressors is lacking. In fact, the few studies that considered individual coping (Shinn et al. 1984; Ganster et al. 1982) have reported limited practical value in such education, particularly when a follow-up has been undertaken (Murphy 1988).

Matteson and Ivancevich (1987) outline a study dealing with coping styles as part of a longer programme of stress management training. Improvements in three coping skills are addressed: cognitive, interpersonal and problem solving. Coping skills are classified as problem-focused or emotion-focused. Problem-focused skills include problem solving, time management, communication and social skills, assertiveness, lifestyle changes and direct actions to change environmental demands. Emotion-focused skills are designed to relieve distress and foster emotion regulation. These include denial, expressing feelings and relaxation.

The preparation of this article was supported in part by the Faculty of Administrative Studies, York University.

SOCIAL SUPPORT

D. Wayne Corneil

During the mid-1970s public health practitioners, and in particular, epidemiologists "discovered" the concept of social support in their studies of causal relationships between stress, mortality and morbidity (Cassel 1974; Cobb 1976). In the past decade there has been an explosion in the literature relating the concept of social support to work-related stressors. By contrast, in psychology, social support as a concept had already been well integrated into clinical practice. Rogers' (1942) client-centred therapy of unconditional positive regard is fundamentally a social support approach. Lindeman's (1944) pioneering work on grief management identified the critical role of support in moderating the crisis of death loss. Caplin's (1964) model of preventive community psychiatry (1964) elaborated on the importance of community and support groups.

Cassel (1976) adapted the concept of social support into public health theory as a way of explaining the differences in diseases that were thought to be stress-related. He was interested in understanding why some individuals appeared to be more resistant to stress than others. The idea of social support as a factor in disease causation was reasonable since, he noted, both people and animals who experienced stress in the company of "significant others" seemed to suffer fewer adverse consequences than those who were isolated. Cassel proposed that social support could act as a protective factor buffering an individual from the effects of stress.

Cobb (1976) expanded on the concept by noting that the mere presence of another person is not social support. He suggested that an exchange of "information" was needed. He established three categories for this exchange:

- information leading the person to the belief that one is loved or cared for (emotional support)
- information leading to the belief that one is esteemed and valued (esteem support)
- information leading to the belief that one belongs to a network of mutual obligations and communication.

Cobb reported that those experiencing severe events without such social support were ten times more likely to come to be depressed and concluded that somehow intimate relations, or social support, was protective of the effects of stress reactions. He also proposed that social support operates throughout one's life span, encompassing various life events such as unemployment, severe illness and bereavement. Cobb pointed out the great diversity of studies, samples, methods and outcomes as convincing evidence that social support is a common factor in modifying stress, but is, in itself, not a panacea for avoiding its effects.

According to Cobb, social support increases coping ability (environmental manipulation) and facilitates adaptation (self-change to improve the person-environment fit). He cautioned, however, that most research was focused on acute stressors and did not permit generalizations of the protective nature of social support for coping with the effects of chronic stressors or traumatic stress.

Over the intervening years since the publication of these seminal works, investigators have moved away from considering social support as a unitary concept, and have attempted to understand the components of social stress and social support.

Hirsh (1980) describes five possible elements of social support:

- *emotional support:* care, comfort, love, affection, sympathy
- *encouragement:* praise, compliments; the extent to which one feels inspired by the supporter to feel courage, hope or to prevail
- *advice:* useful information to solve problems; the extent to which one feels informed
- *companionship:* time spent with supporter; the extent to which one does not feel alone
- *tangible aid:* practical resources, such as money or aid with chores; the extent to which one feels relieved of burdens.

Another framework is used by House (1981), to discuss social support in the context of work-related stress:

- *emotional:* empathy, caring, love, trust, esteem or demons-trations of concern
- *appraisal:* information relevant to self-evaluation, feedback from others useful in self-affirmation
- *informational:* suggestions, advice or information useful in problem-solving
- *instrumental:* direct aid in the form of money, time or labour.

House felt that emotional support was the most important form of social support. In the workplace, the supportiveness of the supervisor was the most important element, followed by co-worker support. The structure and organization of the enterprise, as well as the specific jobs within it, could either enhance or inhibit potential for support. House found that greater task specialization and fragmentation of work leads to more isolated work roles and to decreased opportunities for support.

Pines' (1983) study of burnout, which is a phenomenon discussed separately in this chapter, found that the availability of social support at work is negatively correlated with burnout. He identifies six different relevant aspects of social support which modify the burnout response. These include listening, encouragement, giving advice and, providing companionship and tangible aid.

As one may gather from the foregoing discussion in which the models proposed by several researchers have been described, while the field has attempted to specify the concept of social support, there is no clear consensus on the precise elements of the concept, although considerable overlap between models is evident.

Interaction between Stress and Social Support

Although the literature on stress and social support is quite extensive, there is still considerable debate as to the mechanisms by which stress and social support interact. A long-standing question is whether social support has a direct or indirect effect on health.

Main effect/Direct effect

Social support can have a direct or main effect by serving as a barrier to the effects of the stressor. A social support network may provide needed information or needed feedback in order to overcome the stressor. It may provide a person with the resources he or she needs to minimize the stress. An individual's self-perception may also be influenced by group membership so as to provide self-confidence, a sense of mastery and skill and hence thereby a sense of control over the environment. This is relevant to Bandura's (1986) theories of personal control as the mediator of stress effects. There appears to be a minimum threshold level of social contact required for good health, and increases in social support above the minimum are less important. If one considers social support as having a direct—or main—effect, then one can create an index by which to measure it (Cohen and Syme 1985; Gottlieb 1983).

Cohen and Syme (1985), however, also suggest that an alternative explanation to social support acting as a main effect is that it is the isolation, or lack of social support, which causes the ill health rather than the social support itself promoting better health. This is an unresolved issue. Gottlieb also raises the issue of what happens when the stress results in the loss of the social network itself, such as might occur during disasters, major accidents or loss of work. This effect has not yet been quantified.

Buffering/Indirect effect

The buffering hypothesis is that social support intervenes between the stressor and the stress response to reduce its effects. Buffering could change one's perception of the stressor, thus diminishing its potency, or it could increases one's coping skills. Social support from others may provide tangible aid in a crisis, or it may lead to suggestions that facilitate adaptive responses. Finally, social support may be the stress-modifying effect which calms the neuroendocrine system so that the person may be less reactive to the stressor.

Pines (1983) notes that the relevant aspect of social support may be in the sharing of a social reality. Gottlieb proposes that social support could offset self-recrimination and dispel notions that the individual is him or herself responsible for the problems. Interaction with a social support system can encourage the venting of fears and can assist re-establishing a meaningful social identity.

Additional Theoretical Issues

Research thus far has tended to treat social support as a static, given factor. While the issue of its change over time has been raised, little data exist on the time course of social support (Gottlieb 1983; Cohen and Syme 1985). Social support is, of course, fluid, just as the stressors that it affects. It varies as the individual passes through the stages of life. It can also change over the short-term experience of a particular stressful event (Wilcox 1981).

Such variability probably means that social support fulfils different functions during different developmental stages or during different phases of a crisis. For example at the onset of a crisis, informational support may be more essential than tangible aid. The source of support, its density and the length of time it is operative will also be in flux. The reciprocal relationship between stress and social support must be recognized. Some stressors themselves have a direct impact on available support. Death of a spouse, for example, usually reduces the extent of the network and may have serious consequences for the survivor (Goldberg et al. 1985).

Social support is not a magic bullet that reduces the impact of stress. Under certain conditions it may exacerbate or be the cause of stress. Wilcox (1981) noted that those with a denser kin network had more difficulties adjusting to divorce because their families were less likely to accept divorce as a solution to marital problems. The literature on addiction and family violence also shows possible severe negative effects of social networks. Indeed, as Pines and Aronson (1981) point out, much of professional mental health interventions are devoted to undoing destructive relationships, and to teaching interpersonal skills and to assisting people to recover from social rejection.

There are a large number of studies employing a variety of measures of the functional content of social support. These measures have a wide range of reliability and construct validity. Another methodological problem is that these analyses depend largely on the self-reports of those being studied. The responses will therefore of necessity be subjective and will cause one to wonder whether it is the actual event or level of social support that is important or whether it is the individual's perception of support and outcomes that is more critical. If it is the perception that is critical, then it may be that some other, third variable, such as personality type, is affecting both stress and social support (Turner 1983). For example, a third factor, such as age or socio-economic status, may influence change in both social support and outcome, according to Dooley (1985). Solomon (1986) provides some evidence for this idea with a study of women who have been forced by financial constraints into involuntary interdependence on friends and kin. She found that such women opt out of these relationships as quickly as they are financially able to do so.

Thoits (1982) raises concerns about reverse causation. It may be, she points out, that certain disorders chase away friends and lead to loss of support. Studies by Peters-Golden (1982) and Maher (1982) on cancer victims and social support appear to be consistent with this proposition.

Social Support and Work Stress

Studies on the relationship between social support and work stress indicate that successful coping is related to the effective use of support systems (Cohen and Ahearn 1980). Successful coping activities have emphasized the use of both formal and informal social support in dealing with work stress. Laid-off workers, for example, are advised to actively seek support to provide informational, emotional and tangible support. There have been relatively few evaluations of the effectiveness of such interventions. It appears, however, that formal support is only effective in the short term and informal systems are necessary for longer-term coping. Attempts to provide institutional formal social support can create negative outcomes, since the anger and rage about layoff or bankruptcy, for example, may be displaced to those who provide the social support. Prolonged reliance on social support may create a sense of dependency and lowered self-esteem.

In some occupations, such as seafarers, fire-fighters or staff in remote locations such as on oil rigs, there is a consistent, long-term, highly defined social network which can be compared to a family or kin system. Given the necessity for small work groups and joint efforts, it is natural that a strong sense of social cohesion and support develops among workers. The sometimes hazardous nature of the work requires that workers develop mutual respect, trust and confidence. Strong bonds and interdependence are created when people are dependent on each other for their survival and well-being.

Further research on the nature of social support during routine periods, as well as downsizing or major organizational change, is necessary to further define this factor. For example, when an employee is promoted to a supervisory position, he or she normally must distance him or herself from the other members of the work group. Does this make a difference in the day-to-day levels of social support he or she receives or requires? Does the source of support shift to other supervisors or to the family or somewhere else? Do those in positions of responsibility or authority experience different work stressors? Do these individuals require different types, sources or functions of social support?

If the target of the group-based interventions is also changing the functions of social support or the nature of the network, does this provide a preventive effect in future stressful events?

What will be the effect of growing numbers of women in these occupations? Does their presence change the nature and functions of support for all or does each sex require different levels or types of support?

The workplace presents a unique opportunity to study the intricate web of social support. As a closed subculture, it provides a natural experimental setting for research into the role of social support, social networks and their interrelationships with acute, cumulative and traumatic stress.

GENDER, JOB STRESS AND ILLNESS

Rosalind C. Barnett

Do job stressors affect men and women differently? This question has only recently been addressed in the job stress–illness literature. In fact, the word gender does not even appear in the index of the first edition of the *Handbook of Stress* (Goldberger and Breznitz 1982) nor does it appear in the indices of such major reference books as *Job Stress and Blue Collar Work* (Cooper and Smith 1985) and *Job Control and Worker Health* (Sauter, Hurrell and Cooper 1989). Moreover, in a 1992 review of moderator variables and interaction effects in the occupational stress literature, gender effects were not even mentioned (Holt 1992). One reason for this state of affairs lies in the history of occupational health and safety psychology, which in turn reflects the pervasive gender stereotyping in our culture. With the exception of reproductive health, when researchers have looked at physical health outcomes and physical injuries, they have generally studied men and variations in their work. When researchers have studied mental health outcomes, they have generally studied women and variations in their social roles.

As a result, the "available evidence" on the physical health impact of work has until recently been almost completely limited to men (Hall 1992). For example, attempts to identify correlates of coronary heart disease have been focused exclusively on men and on aspects of their work; researchers did not even inquire into their male subjects' marital or parental roles (Rosenman et al. 1975). Indeed, few studies of the job stress–illness relationship in men include assessments of their marital and parental relationships (Caplan et al. 1975).

In contrast, concern about reproductive health, fertility and pregnancy focused primarily on women. Not surprisingly, "the research on reproductive effects of occupational exposures is far more extensive on females than on males" (Walsh and Kelleher 1987). With respect to psychological distress, attempts to specify the psychosocial correlates, in particular the stressors associated with balancing work and family demands, have centred heavily on women.

By reinforcing the notion of "separate spheres" for men and women, these conceptualizations and the research paradigms they generated prevented any examination of gender effects, thereby effectively controlling for the influence of gender. Extensive sex segregation in the workplace (Bergman 1986; Reskin and Hartman 1986) also acts as a control, precluding the study of gender as a moderator. If all men are employed in "men's jobs" and all women are employed in "women's jobs", it would not be reasonable to ask about the moderating effect of gender on the job stress–illness relationship: job conditions and gender would be confounded. It is only when some women are employed in jobs that men occupy and when some men are employed in jobs that women occupy that the question is meaningful.

Controlling is one of three strategies for treating the effects of gender. The other two are ignoring these effects or analysing them (Hall 1991). Most investigations of health have either ignored or controlled for gender, thereby accounting for the dearth of references to gender as discussed above and for a body of research that reinforces stereotyped views about the role of gender in the job stress–illness relationship. These views portray women as essentially different from men in ways that render them less robust in the workplace, and portray men as comparatively unaffected by non-workplace experiences.

In spite of this beginning, the situation is already changing. Witness the publication in 1987 of *Gender and Stress* (Barnett, Biener and Baruch 1987), the first edited volume focusing specifically on the impact of gender at all points in the stress reaction. And the second edition of the *Handbook of Stress* (Barnett 1992) includes a chapter on gender effects. Indeed, current studies increasingly reflect the third strategy: analysing gender effects. This strategy holds great promise, but also has pitfalls. Operationally, it involves analysing data relating to males and females and estimating both the main and the interaction effects of gender. A significant main effect tells us that after controlling for the other predictors in the model, men and women differ with respect to the level of the outcome variable. Interaction-effects analyses concern differential reactivity, that is, does the relationship between a given stressor and a health outcome differ for women and men?

The main promise of this line of inquiry is to challenge stereotyped views of women and men. The main pitfall is that conclusions about gender difference can still be drawn erroneously. Because gender is confounded with many other variables in our society, these variables have to be taken into account *before* conclusions about gender can be inferred. For example, samples of employed men and women will undoubtedly differ with respect to a host of work and non-work variables that could reasonably affect health outcomes. Most important among these contextual variables are occupational prestige, salary, part-time versus full-time employment, marital status, education, employment status of spouse, overall work burdens and responsibility for care of younger and older dependants. In addition, evidence suggests the existence of gender differences in several personality, cognitive, behavioural and social system variables that are related to health outcomes. These include: sensation seeking; self-efficacy (feelings of competence); external locus of control; emotion-focused versus problem-focused coping strategies; use of social resources and social support; harmful acquired risks, such as smoking and alcohol abuse; protective behaviours, such as exercise, balanced diets and preventive health regimens; early medical intervention; and social power (Walsh, Sorensen and Leonard, in press). The better one can control these contextual variables, the closer one can get to understanding the effect of gender *per se* on the relationships of

interest, and thereby to understanding whether it is gender or other, gender-related variables that are the effective moderators.

To illustrate, in one study (Karasek 1990) job changes among white-collar workers were less likely to be associated with negative health outcomes if the changes resulted in increased job control. This finding was true for men, not women. Further analyses indicated that job control and gender were confounded. For women, one of "the less aggressive [or powerful] groups in the labour market" (Karasek 1990), white-collar job changes often involved reduced control, whereas for men, such job changes often involved increased control. Thus, power, not gender, accounted for this interaction effect. Such analyses lead us to refine the question about moderator effects. Do men and women react differentially to workplace stressors because of their inherent (i.e., biological) nature or because of their different experiences?

Although only a few studies have examined gender interaction effects, most report that when appropriate controls are utilized, the relationship between job conditions and physical or mental health outcomes is not affected by gender. (Lowe and Northcott 1988 describe one such study). In other words, there is no evidence of an inherent difference in reactivity.

Findings from a random sample of full-time employed men and women in dual-earner couples illustrates this conclusion with respect to psychological distress. In a series of cross-sectional and longitudinal analyses, a matched pairs design was used that controlled for such individual-level variables as age, education, occupational prestige and marital-role quality, and for such couple-level variables as parental status, years married and household income (Barnett et al. 1993; Barnett et al. 1995; Barnett, Brennan and Marshall 1994). Positive experiences on the job were associated with low distress; insufficient skill discretion and overload were associated with high distress; experiences in the roles of partner and parent moderated the relationship between job experiences and distress; and change over time in skill discretion and overload were each associated with change over time in psychological distress. In no case was the effect of gender significant. In other words, the magnitude of these relationships was not affected by gender.

One important exception is tokenism (see, for example, Yoder 1991). Whereas "it is clear and undeniable that there is a considerable advantage in being a member of the male minority in any female profession" (Kadushin 1976), the opposite is not true. Women who are in minority in a male work situation experience a considerable disadvantage. Such a difference is readily understandable in the context of men's and women's relative power and status in our culture.

Overall, studies of physical health outcomes also fail to reveal significant gender interaction effects. It appears, for example, that characteristics of work activity are stronger determinants of safety than are attributes of workers, and that women in traditionally male occupations suffer the same types of injury with approximately the same frequency as their male counterparts. Moreover, poorly designed protective equipment, not any inherent incapacity on the part of women in relation to the work, is often to blame when women in male-dominated jobs experience more injuries (Walsh, Sorensen and Leonard, 1995).

Two caveats are in order. First, no one study controls for all the gender-related covariates. Therefore, any conclusions about "gender" effects must be tentative. Secondly, because controls vary from study to study, comparisons between studies are difficult.

As increasing numbers of women enter the labour force and occupy jobs similar to those occupied by men, both the opportunity and the need for analysing the effect of gender on the job stress–illness relationship also increase. In addition, future research needs to refine the conceptualization and measurement of the stress construct to include job stressors important to women; extend interaction effects analyses to studies previously restricted to male or female samples, for example, studies of reproductive health and of stresses due to non-workplace variables; and examine the interaction effects of race and class as well as the joint interaction effects of gender x race and gender x class.

● ETHNICITY

Gwendolyn Puryear Keita

Major changes are taking place within the workforces of many of the world's leading industrial nations, with members of ethnic minority groups making up increasingly larger proportions. However, little of the occupational stress research has focused on ethnic minority populations. The changing demographics of the world's workforce give clear notice that these populations can no longer be ignored. This article briefly addresses some of the major issues of occupational stress in ethnic minority populations with a focus on the United States. However, much of the discussion should be generalizable to other nations of the world.

Much of the occupational stress research either excludes ethnic minorities, includes too few to allow meaningful comparisons or generalizations to be made, or does not report enough information about the sample to determine racial or ethnic participation. Many studies fail to make distinctions among ethnic minorities, treating them as one homogeneous group, thus minimizing the differences in demographic characteristics, culture, language and socio-economic status which have been documented both between and within ethnic minority groups (Olmedo and Parron 1981).

In addition to the failure to address issues of ethnicity, by far the greater part of research does not examine class or gender differences, or class by race and gender interactions. Moreover, little is known about the cross-cultural utility of many of the assessment procedures. Documentation used in such procedures is not adequately translated nor is there demonstrated equivalency between the standardized English and other language versions. Even when the reliabilities appear to indicate equivalence across ethnic or cultural groups, there is uncertainty about which symptoms in the scale are elicited in a reliable fashion, that is, whether the phenomenology of a disorder is similar across groups (Roberts, Vernon and Rhoades 1989).

Many assessment instruments inadequately assess conditions within ethnic minority populations; consequently results are often suspect. For example, many stress scales are based on models of stress as a function of undesirable change or readjustment. However, many minority individuals experience stress in large part as a function of ongoing undesirable situations such as poverty, economic marginality, inadequate housing, unemployment, crime and discrimination. These chronic stressors are not usually reflected in many of the stress scales. Models which conceptualize stress as resulting from the interplay between both chronic and acute stressors, and various internal and external mediating factors, are more appropriate for assessing stress in ethnic minority and poor populations (Watts-Jones 1990).

A major stressor affecting ethnic minorities is the prejudice and discrimination they encounter as a result of their minority status in a given society (Martin 1987; James 1994). It is a well-established fact that minority individuals experience more prejudice and discrimination as a result of their ethnic status than do members of the majority. They also perceive greater discrimi-

nation and fewer opportunities for advancement as compared with whites (Galinsky, Bond and Friedman 1993). Workers who feel discriminated against or who feel that there are fewer chances for advancement for people of their ethnic group are more likely to feel "burned out" in their jobs, care less about working hard and doing their jobs well, feel less loyal to their employers, are less satisfied with their jobs, take less initiative, feel less committed to helping their employers succeed and plan to leave their current employers sooner (Galinsky, Bond and Friedman 1993). Moreover, perceived prejudice and discrimination are positively correlated with self-reported health problems and higher blood pressure levels (James 1994).

An important focus of occupational stress research has been the relationship between social support and stress. However, there has been little attention paid to this variable with respect to ethnic minority populations. The available research tends to show conflicting results. For example, Hispanic workers who reported higher levels of social support had less job-related tension and fewer reported health problems (Gutierres, Saenz and Green 1994); ethnic minority workers with lower levels of emotional support were more likely to experience job burn-out, health symptoms, episodic job stress, chronic job stress and frustration; this relationship was strongest for women and for management as opposed to non-management personnel (Ford 1985). James (1994), however, did not find a significant relationship between social support and health outcomes in a sample of African-American workers.

Most models of job satisfaction have been derived and tested using samples of white workers. When ethnic minority groups have been included, they have tended to be African-Americans, and potential effects due to ethnicity were often masked (Tuch and Martin 1991). Research that is available on African-American employees tends to yield significantly lower scores on overall job satisfaction in comparison to whites (Weaver 1978, 1980; Staines and Quinn 1979; Tuch and Martin 1991). Examining this difference, Tuch and Martin (1991) noted that the factors determining job satisfaction were basically the same but that African-Americans were less likely to have the situations that led to job satisfaction. More specifically, extrinsic rewards increase African-Americans' job satisfaction, but African-Americans are disadvantaged relatively to whites on these variables. On the other hand, blue-collar incumbency and urban residence decrease job satisfaction for African-Americans but African-Americans are overrepresented in these areas. Wright, King and Berg (1985) found that organizational variables (i.e., job authority, qualifications for the position and a sense that advancement within the organization is possible) were the best predictors of job satisfaction in their sample of black female managers in keeping with previous research on primarily white samples.

Ethnic minority workers are more likely than their white counterparts to be in jobs with hazardous work conditions. Bullard and Wright (1986/1987) noted this propensity and indicated that the population differences in injuries are likely to be the result of racial and ethnic disparities in income, education, type of employment and other socio-economic factors correlated with exposure to hazards. One of the most likely reasons, they noted, was that occupational injuries are highly dependent on the job and industry category of the workers and ethnic minorities tend to work in more hazardous occupations.

Foreign workers who have entered the country illegally often experience special work stress and maltreatment. They often endure substandard and unsafe working conditions and accept less than minimum wages because of fear of being reported to the immigration authorities and they have few options for better employment. Most health and safety regulations, guidelines for use, and warnings are in English and many immigrants, illegal or otherwise, may not have a good understanding of written or spoken English (Sanchez 1990).

Some areas of research have almost totally ignored ethnic minority populations. For example, hundreds of studies have examined the relationship between Type A behaviour and occupational stress. White males constitute the most frequently studied groups with ethnic minority men and women almost totally excluded. Available research—e.g., a study by Adams et al. (1986), using a sample of college freshmen, and e.g., Gamble and Matteson (1992), investigating black workers—indicates the same positive relationship between Type A behaviour and self-reported stress as that found for white samples.

Similarly, little research on issues such as job control and work demands is available for ethnic minority workers, although these are central constructs in occupational stress theory. Available research tends to show that these are important constructs for ethnic minority workers as well. For example, African-American licensed practical nurses (LPNs) report significantly less decision authority and more dead-end jobs (and hazard exposures) than do white LPNs and this difference is not a function of educational differences (Marshall and Barnett 1991); the presence of low decision latitude in the face of high demands tends to be the pattern most characteristic of jobs with low socio-economic status, which are more likely to be held by ethnic minority workers (Waitzman and Smith 1994); and middle- and upper-level white men rate their jobs consistently higher than their ethnic minority (and female) peers on six work design factors (Fernandez 1981).

Thus, it appears that many research questions remain regarding ethnic minority populations in the occupational stress and health arena as regards ethnic minority populations. These questions will not be answered until ethnic minority workers are included in study samples and in the development and validation of investigatory instruments.

• SELECTED ACUTE PHYSIOLOGICAL OUTCOMES

Andrew Steptoe and Tessa M. Pollard

The acute physiological adjustments recorded during the performance of problem-solving or psychomotor tasks in the laboratory include: raised heart rate and blood pressure; alterations in cardiac output and peripheral vascular resistance; increased muscle tension and electrodermal (sweat gland) activity; disturbances in breathing pattern; and modifications in gastrointestinal activity and immune function. The best studied neurohormonal responses are those of the catecholamines (adrenaline and noradrenaline) and cortisol. Noradrenaline is the primary transmitter released by the nerves of the sympathetic branch of the autonomic nervous system. Adrenaline is released from the adrenal medulla following stimulation of the sympathetic nervous system, while activation of the pituitary gland by higher centres in the brain results in the release of cortisol from the adrenal cortex. These hormones support autonomic activation during stress and are responsible for other acute changes, such as stimulation of the processes that govern blood clotting, and the release of stored energy supplies from adipose tissue. It is likely that these kinds of response will also be seen during job stress, but studies in which work conditions are simulated, or in which people are tested in their normal jobs, are required to demonstrate such effects.

A variety of methods is available to monitor these responses. Conventional psychophysiological techniques are used to assess autonomic responses to demanding tasks (Cacioppo and Tassinary 1990). Levels of stress hormones can be measured in the blood or urine, or in the case of cortisol, in the saliva. The sympathetic activity associated with challenge has also been documented by measures of noradrenaline spillover from nerve terminals, and by direct recording of sympathetic nervous activity with miniature electrodes. The parasympathetic or vagal branch of the autonomic nervous system typically responds to task performance with reduced activity, and this can, under certain circumstances, be indexed through recording heart rate variability or sinus arrhythmia. In recent years, power spectrum analysis of heart rate and blood pressure signals has revealed wave bands that are characteristically associated with sympathetic and parasympathetic activity. Measures of the power in these wavebands can be used to index autonomic balance, and have shown a shift towards the sympathetic branch at the expense of the parasympathetic branch during task performance.

Few laboratory assessments of acute physiological responses have simulated work conditions directly. However, dimensions of task demand and performance that are relevant to work have been investigated. For example, as the demands of externally paced work increase (through faster pace or more complex problem solving), there is a rise in adrenaline level, heart rate and blood pressure, a reduction in heart rate variability and an increase in muscle tension. In comparison with self-paced tasks performed at the same rate, external pacing results in greater blood pressure and heart rate increases (Steptoe et al. 1993). In general, personal control over potentially stressful stimuli reduces autonomic and neuroendocrine activation in comparison with uncontrollable situations, although the effort of maintaining control over the situation itself has its own physiological costs.

Frankenhaeuser (1991) has suggested that adrenaline levels are raised when a person is mentally aroused or performing a demanding task, and that cortisol levels are raised when an individual is distressed or unhappy. Applying these ideas to job stress, Frankenhaeuser has proposed that job demand is likely to lead to increased effort and thus to raise levels of adrenaline, while lack of job control is one of the main causes of distress at work and is therefore likely to stimulate raised cortisol levels. Studies comparing levels of these hormones in people doing their normal work with levels in the same people at leisure have shown that adrenaline is normally raised when people are at work. Effects for noradrenaline are inconsistent and may depend on the amount of physical activity that people carry out during work and leisure time. It has also been shown that adrenaline levels at work correlate positively with levels of job demand. In contrast, cortisol levels have not been shown typically to be raised in people at work, and it is yet to be demonstrated that cortisol levels vary according to the degree of job control. In the "Air Traffic Controller Health Change Study", only a small proportion of workers produced consistent increases in cortisol as the objective workload became greater (Rose and Fogg 1993).

Thus only adrenaline among the stress hormones has been shown conclusively to rise in people at work, and to do so according to the level of demand they experience. There is evidence that levels of prolactin increase in response to stress while levels of testosterone decrease. However, studies of these hormones in people at work are very limited. Acute changes in the concentration of cholesterol in the blood have also been observed with increased workload, but the results are not consistent (Niaura, Stoney and Herbst 1992).

As far as cardiovascular variables are concerned, it has repeatedly been found that blood pressure is higher in men and women during work than either after work or during equivalent times of day spent at leisure. These effects have been observed both with self-monitored blood pressure and with automated portable (or ambulatory) monitoring instruments. Blood pressure is especially high during periods of increased work demand (Rose and Fogg 1993). It has also been found that blood pressure rises with emotional demands, for example, in studies of paramedics attending the scenes of accidents. However, it is often difficult to determine whether blood pressure fluctuations at work are due to psychological demands or to associated physical activity and changes in posture. The raised blood pressure recorded at work is especially pronounced among people reporting high job strain according to the Demand-Control model (Schnall et al. 1990).

Heart rate has not been shown to be consistently raised during work. Acute elevations of heart rate may nevertheless be elicited by disruption of work, for example with breakdown of equipment. Emergency workers such as fire-fighters exhibit extremely fast heart rates in response to alarm signals at work. On the other hand, high levels of social support at work are associated with reduced heart rates. Abnormalities of cardiac rhythm may also be elicited by stressful working conditions, but the pathological significance of such responses has not been established.

Gastrointestinal problems are commonly reported in studies of job stress (see "Gastrointestinal problems" below). Unfortunately, it is difficult to assess the physiological systems underlying gastrointestinal symptoms in the work setting. Acute mental stress has variable effects on gastric acid secretion, stimulating large increases in some individuals and reduced output in others. Shift workers have a particularly high prevalence of gastrointestinal problems, and it has been suggested that these may arise when diurnal rhythms in the central nervous system's control of gastric acid secretion are disrupted. Anomalies of small bowel motility have been recorded using radiotelemetry in patients diagnosed with irritable bowel syndrome while they go about their everyday lives. Health complaints, including gastrointestinal symptoms, have been shown to co-vary with perceived workload, but it is not clear whether this reflects objective changes in physiological function or patterns of symptom perception and reporting.

BEHAVIOURAL OUTCOMES

Arie Shirom

Researchers may disagree on the meaning of the term stress. However, there is a basic agreement that perceived work-related stress may be implicated in behavioural outcomes such as absenteeism, substance abuse, sleep disturbances, smoking and caffeine use (Kahn and Byosiere 1992). Recent evidence supporting these relationships is reviewed in this chapter. Emphasis is placed upon the aetiological role of work-related stress in each of these outcomes. There are qualitative differences, along several dimensions, among these outcomes. To illustrate, in contrast to the other behavioural outcomes, which are all considered problematic to the health of those engaging in them excessively, absenteeism, while detrimental to the organization, is not necessarily harmful to those employees who are absent from work. There are, however, common problems in the research on these outcomes, as discussed in this section.

The varying definitions of work-related stress have already been mentioned above. By way of illustration, consider the different conceptualizations of stress on the one hand as events and on the other as chronic demands at the workplace. These two approaches to stress measurement have seldom been combined in a single study designed to predict the sorts of behavioural outcome considered here. The same generalization is relevant to the combined use, in the same study, of family-related and work-related stress to predict any of these outcomes. Most of the studies referred to in this chapter were based on a cross-sectional design and employees' self-reports on the behavioural outcome in question. In most of the research that concerned behavioural outcomes of work-related stress, the joint moderating or mediating roles of predisposing personality variables, like the Type A behaviour pattern or hardiness, and situational variables like social support and control, have hardly been investigated. Seldom have antecedent variables, like objectively measured job stress, been included in the research designs of the studies reviewed here. Finally, the research covered in this article employed divergent methodologies. Because of these limitations, a frequently encountered conclusion is that the evidence for work-related stress as a precursor of a behavioural outcome is inconclusive.

Beehr (1995) considered the question of why so few studies have systematically examined the associations between work-related stress and substance abuse. He argued that such neglect may be due in part to the failure of researchers to find these associations. To this failure, one should add the well-known bias of periodicals against publishing research that reports null results. To illustrate the inconclusiveness of the evidence linking stress and substance abuse, consider two large-scale national samples of employees in the United States. The first, by French, Caplan and Van Harrison (1982), failed to find significant correlations between types of work-related stress and either smoking, drug use or on-the-job caffeine ingestion. The second, an earlier research study by Mangione and Quinn (1975), did report such associations.

The study of the behavioural outcomes of stress is further complicated because they frequently appear in pairs or triads. Different combinations of outcomes are the rule rather than the exception. The very close association of stress, smoking and caffeine is alluded to below. Yet another example concerns the comorbidity of post-traumatic stress disorder (PTSD), alcoholism and drug abuse (Kofoed, Friedman and Peck 1993). This is a basic characteristic of several behavioural outcomes considered in this article. It has led to the construction of "dual diagnosis" and "triple diagnosis" schemes and to the development of comprehensive, multifaceted treatment approaches. An example of such an approach is that in which PTSD and substance abuse are treated simultaneously (Kofoed, Friedman and Peck 1993).

The pattern represented by the appearance of several outcomes in a single individual may vary, depending on background characteristics and genetic and environmental factors. The literature on stress outcomes is only beginning to address the complex questions involved in identifying the specific pathophysiological and neurobiological disease models leading to different combinations of outcome entities.

Smoking Behaviour

A large body of epidemiological, clinical and pathological studies relates cigarette smoking to the development of cardiovascular heart disease and other chronic diseases. Consequently, there is a growing interest in the pathway leading from stress, including stress at work, to smoking behaviour. Stress, and the emotional responses associated with it, anxiety and irritability, are known to be attenuated by smoking. However, these effects have been shown to be short-lived (Parrott 1995). Impairments of mood and affective states tend to occur in a repetitive cycle between each cigarette smoked. This cycle provides a clear pathway leading to the addictive use of cigarettes (Parrott 1995). Smokers, therefore, obtain only a short-lived relief from adverse states of anxiety and irritability that follow the experience of stress.

The aetiology of smoking is multifactorial (like most other behavioural outcomes considered here). To illustrate, consider a recent review of smoking among nurses. Nurses, the largest professional group in health care, smoke excessively compared with the adult population (Adriaanse et al. 1991). According to their study, this is true for both male and female nurses, and is explained by work stress, lack of social support and unmet expectations that characterize nurses' professional socialization. Nurses' smoking is considered a special public health problem since nurses often act as role models to patients and their families.

Smokers who express high motivation to smoke have reported, in several studies, above-average stress that they had experienced before smoking, rather than below-average stress after smoking (Parrott 1995). Consequently, stress management and anxiety reduction programmes in the workplace do have the potential of influencing motivation for smoking. However, workplace-based smoking-cessation programmes do bring to the fore the conflict between health and performance. Among aviators, as an example, smoking is a health hazard in the cockpit. However, pilots who are required to abstain from smoking during and before flights may suffer cockpit performance decrements (Sommese and Patterson 1995).

Drug and Alcohol Abuse

A recurrent problem is that often researchers do not distinguish between drinking and problem-drinking behaviour (Sadava 1987). Problem-drinking is associated with adverse health or performance consequences. Its aetiology has been shown to be associated with several factors. Among them, the literature refers to prior incidents of depression, lack of supportive family environment, impulsiveness, being female, other concurrent substance abuse and stress (Sadava 1987). The distinction between the simple act of drinking alcohol and problem drinking is important because of the current controversy on the reported beneficial effects of alcohol on low density lipoprotein (LDL) cholesterol and on the incidence of heart disease. Several studies have shown a J-shaped or U-shaped relationship between alcohol ingestion and the incidence of cardiovascular heart disease (Pohorecky 1991).

The hypothesis that people ingest alcohol even in an incipiently abusive pattern to reduce stress and anxiety is no longer accepted as adequate. Contemporary approaches to alcohol abuse view it as determined by processes set forth in a multifactorial model or models (Gorman 1994). Among risk factors for alcohol abuse, recent reviews refer to the following factors: sociocultural (i.e., whether alcohol is readily available and its use tolerated, condoned or even promoted), socio-economic (i.e., the price of alcohol), environmental (alcohol advertising and licensing laws affect the consumers' motivation to drink), interpersonal influences (such as family drinking habits), and employment-related factors, including stress at work (Gorman 1994). It follows that stress is but one of several factors in a multidimensional model that explains alcohol abuse.

The practical consequence of the multifactorial model view of alcoholism is the decrease in the emphasis on the role of stress in the diagnosis, prevention and treatment of substance abuse in the workplace. As noted by a recent review of this literature (Peyser 1992), in specific job situations, such as those illustrated below, attention to work-related stress is important in formulating preventive policies directed at substance abuse.

Despite considerable research on stress and alcohol, the mechanisms that link them are not entirely understood. The most widely accepted hypothesis is that alcohol disrupts the subject's initial appraisal of stressful information by constraining the spread of activation of associated information previously stored in long-term memory (Petraitis, Flay and Miller 1995).

Work organizations contribute to and may induce drinking behaviour, including problem drinking, by three basic processes documented in the research literature. First, drinking, abusive or not, may be affected by the development of organizational norms with respect to drinking on the job, including the local "official" definition of problem drinking and the mechanisms for its control established by management. Secondly, some stressful working conditions, like sustained overload or machine-paced jobs or the lack of control may produce alcohol abuse as a coping strategy alleviating the stress. Thirdly, work organizations may explicitly or implicitly encourage the development of occupationally based drinking subcultures, such as those that often emerge among professional drivers of heavy vehicles (James and Ames 1993).

In general, stress plays a different role in provoking drinking behaviour in different occupations, age groups, ethnic categories and other social groupings. Thus stress probably plays a predisposing role with respect to alcohol consumption among adolescents, but much less so among women, the elderly and college-age social drinkers (Pohorecky 1991).

The social stress model of substance abuse (Lindenberg, Reiskin and Gendrop 1994) suggests that the likelihood of employees' drug abuse is influenced by the level of environmental stress, social support relevant to the experienced stress, and individual resources, particularly social competence. There are indications that drug abuse among certain minority groups (like Native American youth living on reservations: see Oetting, Edwards and Beauvais 1988) is influenced by the prevalence of acculturation stress among them. However, the same social groups are also exposed to adverse social conditions like poverty, prejudices and impoverished opportunities for economic, social and educational opportunities.

Caffeine Ingestion

Caffeine is the most widely consumed pharmacologically active substance in the world. The evidence bearing upon its possible implications for human health, that is whether it has chronic physiological effects on habitual consumers, is as yet inconclusive (Benowitz 1990). It has long been suspected that repeated exposure to caffeine may produce tolerance to its physiological effects (James 1994). The consumption of caffeine is known to improve physical performance and endurance during prolonged activity at submaximal intensity (Nehlig and Debry 1994). Caffeine's physiological effects are linked to the antagonism of adenosine receptors and to the increased production of plasma catecholamines (Nehlig and Debry 1994).

The study of the relationship of work-related stress on caffeine ingestion is complicated because of the significant inter-dependance of coffee consumption and smoking (Conway et al. 1981). A meta-analysis of six epidemiological studies (Swanson, Lee and Hopp 1994) has shown that about 86% of smokers consumed coffee while only 77% of the non-smokers did so. Three major mechanisms have been suggested to account for this close association: (1) a conditioning effect; (2) reciprocal interaction, that is, caffeine intake increases arousal while nicotine intake decreases it and (3) the joint effect of a third variable on both. Stress, and particularly work-related stress, is a possible third variable influencing both caffeine and nicotine intake (Swanson, Lee and Hopp 1994).

Sleep Disturbances

The modern era of sleep research began in the 1950s, with the discovery that sleep is a highly active state rather than a passive condition of nonresponsiveness. The most prevalent type of sleep disturbance, insomnia, may occur in a transient short-term form or in a chronic form. Stress is probably the most frequent cause of transient insomnia (Gillin and Byerley 1990). Chronic insomnia usually results from an underlying medical or psychiatric disorder. Between one-third and two-thirds of patients with chronic insomnia have a recognizable psychiatric illness (Gillin and Byerley 1990).

One of the mechanisms suggested is that the effect of stress on sleep disturbances is mediated via certain changes in the cerebral system at different levels, and changes in the biochemical body functions that disturb the 24-hour rhythms (Gillin and Byerley 1990). There is some evidence that the above linkages are moderated by personality characteristics, such as the Type A behaviour pattern (Koulack and Nesca 1992). Stress and sleep disturbances may reciprocally influence each other: stress may promote transient insomnia, which in turn causes stress and increases the risk of episodes of depression and anxiety (Partinen 1994).

Chronic stress associated with monotonous, machine-paced jobs coupled with the need for vigilance—jobs frequently found in continuous-processing manufacturing industries—may lead to sleep disturbances, subsequently causing decrements in performance (Krueger 1989). There is some evidence that there are synergetic effects among work-related stress, circadian rhythms and reduced performance (Krueger 1989). The adverse effects of sleep loss, interacting with overload and a high level of arousal, on certain important aspects of job performance have been documented in several studies of sleep deprivation among hospital doctors at the junior level (Spurgeon and Harrington 1989).

The study by Mattiason et al. (1990) provides intriguing evidence linking chronic job stress, sleep disturbances and increases in plasma cholesterol. In this study, 715 male shipyard employees exposed to the stress of unemployment were systematically compared with 261 controls before and after the economic instability stress was made apparent. It was found that among the shipyard employees exposed to job insecurity, but not among the controls, sleep disturbances were positively correlated with increases in total cholesterol. This is a naturalistic field study in which the period of uncertainty preceding actual layoffs was allowed to elapse for about a year after some employees received notices concerning the impending layoffs. Thus the stress studied was real, severe, and could be considered chronic.

Absenteeism

Absence behaviour may be viewed as an employee coping behaviour that reflects the interaction of perceived job demands and control, on the one hand, and self-assessed health and family conditions on the other. Absenteeism has several major dimensions, including duration, spells and reasons for being absent. It was shown in a European sample that about 60% of the hours lost to absenteeism were due to illness (Ilgen 1990). To the extent that work-related stress was implicated in these illnesses, then there should be some relationship between stress on the job and that part of absenteeism classified as sick days. The literature on absenteeism covers primarily blue-collar employees, and few studies have included stress in a systematic way. (McKee, Markham and Scott 1992). Jackson and Schuler's meta-analysis (1985) of the consequences of role stress reported an average correlation of 0.09 between role ambiguity and absence and -0.01 between role conflict and absence. As several meta-analytic studies of the literature on absenteeism show, stress is but one of many variables accounting for these phenomena, so we should not expect work-related stress and absenteeism to be strongly correlated (Beehr 1995).

The literature on absenteeism suggests that the relationship between work-related stress and absenteeism may be mediated by employee-specific characteristics. For example, the literature refers to the propensity to use avoidance coping in response to stress at work, and to being emotionally exhausted or physically fatigued (Saxton, Phillips and Blakeney 1991). To illustrate, Kristensen's (1991) study of several thousand Danish slaughterhouse employees over a one-year period has shown that those who reported high job stress had significantly higher absence rates and that perceived health was closely associated with absenteeism due to illness.

Several studies of the relationships between stress and absenteeism provide evidence that supports the conclusion that they may be occupationally determined (Baba and Harris 1989). To illustrate, work-related stress among managers tends to be associated with the incidence of absenteeism but not with days lost attributed to illness, while this is not so with shop-floor employees (Cooper and Bramwell 1992). Occupational specificity of the stresses predisposing employees to be absent has been regarded as a major explanation of the meagre amount of absence variance explained by work-related stress across many studies (Baba and Harris 1989). Several studies have found that among blue-collar employees who work on jobs considered stressful—that is those that possess a combination of the characteristics of assembly-line type of jobs (namely, a very short cycle of operations and a piece-rate wage system)—job stress is a strong predictor of unexcused absence. (For a recent review of these studies, see McKee, Markham and Scott 1992; note that Baba and Harris 1989 do not support their conclusion that job stress is a strong predictor of unexcused absence).

The literature on stress and absenteeism provides a convincing example of a limitation noted in the introduction. The reference is to the failure of most research on stress-behavioural outcome relations to cover systematically, in the design of this research, both work and non-work stresses. It was noted that in research on absenteeism non-work stress contributed more than work-related stress to the prediction of absence, lending support to the view that absence may be non-work behaviour more than work-related behaviour (Baba and Harris 1989).

WELL-BEING OUTCOMES

Peter Warr

Jobs can have a substantial impact on the affective well-being of job holders. In turn, the quality of workers' well-being on the job influences their behaviour, decision making and interactions with colleagues, and spills over into family and social life as well.

Research in many countries has pointed to the need to define the concept in terms of two separate dimensions that may be viewed as independent of each other (Watson, Clark and Tellegen 1988; Warr 1994). These dimensions may be referred to as "pleasure" and "arousal". As illustrated in figure 34.9, a particular degree of pleasure or displeasure may be accompanied by high or low levels of mental arousal, and mental arousal may be either pleasurable or unpleasurable. This is indicated in terms of the three axes of well-being which are suggested for measurement: displeasure-to-pleasure, anxiety-to-comfort, and depression-to-enthusiasm.

Job-related well-being has often been measured merely along the horizontal axis, extending from "feeling bad" to "feeling good". The measurement is usually made with reference to a scale of job satisfaction, and data are obtained by workers' indicating their agreement or disagreement with a series of statements

Figure 34.9 • Three principal axes for the measurement of affective well-being.

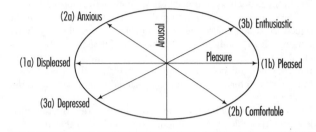

describing their feelings about their jobs. However, job satisfaction scales do not take into account differences in mental arousal, and are to that extent relatively insensitive. Additional forms of measurement are also needed, in terms of the other two axes in the figure.

When low scores on the horizontal axis are accompanied by raised mental arousal *(upper left quadrant)*, low well-being is typically evidenced in the forms of anxiety and tension; however, low pleasure in association with low mental arousal *(lower left)* is observable as depression and associated feelings. Conversely, high job-related pleasure may be accompanied by positive feelings that are characterized either by enthusiasm and energy *(3b)* or by psychological relaxation and comfort *(2b)*. This latter distinction is sometimes described in terms of motivated job satisfaction *(3b)* versus resigned, apathetic job satisfaction *(2b)*.

In studying the impact of organizational and psychosocial factors on employee well-being, it is desirable to examine all three of the axes. Questionnaires are widely used for this purpose. Job satisfaction *(1a to 1b)* may be examined in two forms, sometimes referred to as "facet-free" and "facet-specific" job satisfaction. Facet-free, or overall, job satisfaction is an overarching set of feelings about one's job as a whole, whereas facet-specific satisfactions are feelings about particular aspects of a job. Principal facets include pay, working conditions, one's supervisor and the nature of the work undertaken.

These several forms of job satisfaction are positively intercorrelated, and it is sometimes appropriate merely to measure overall, facet-free satisfaction, rather than to examine separate, facet-specific satisfactions. A widely used general question is "On the whole, how satisfied are you with the work you do?". Commonly used responses are *very dissatisfied, a little dissatisfied, moderately satisfied, very satisfied* and *extremely satisfied,* and are designated by scores from 1 to 5 respectively. In national surveys it is usual to find that about 90% of employees report themselves as satisfied to some degree, and a more sensitive measuring instrument is often desirable to yield more differentiated scores.

A multi-item approach is usually adopted, perhaps covering a range of different facets. For instance, several job satisfaction questionnaires ask about a person's satisfaction with facets of the following kinds: the physical work conditions; the freedom to choose your own method of working; your fellow workers; the recognition you get for good work; your immediate boss; the amount of responsibility you are given; your rate of pay; your opportunity to use your abilities; relations between managers and workers; your workload; your chance of promotion; the equipment you use; the way your firm is managed; your hours of work; the amount of variety in your job; and your job security. An average satisfaction score may be calculated across all the items, responses to each item being scored from 1 to 5, for instance (see the preceding paragraph). Alternatively, separate values can be

computed for "intrinsic satisfaction" items (those dealing with the content of the work itself) and "extrinsic satisfaction" items (those referring to the context of the work, such as colleagues and working conditions).

Self-report scales which measure axes two and three have often covered only one end of the possible distribution. For example, some scales of job-related anxiety ask about a worker's feelings of tension and worry when on the job *(2a)*, but do not in addition test for more positive forms of affect on this axis *(2b)*. Based on studies in several settings (Watson, Clark and Tellegen 1988; Warr 1990), a possible approach is as follows.

Axes 2 and 3 may be examined by putting this question to workers: "Thinking of the past few weeks, how much of the time has your job made you feel each of the following?", with response options of *never, occasionally, some of the time, much of the time, most of the time,* and *all the time* (scored from 1 to 6 respectively). Anxiety-to-comfort ranges across these states: tense, anxious, worried, calm, comfortable and relaxed. Depression-to-enthusiasm covers these states: depressed, gloomy, miserable, motivated, enthusiastic and optimistic. In each case, the first three items should be reverse-scored, so that a high score always reflects high well-being, and the items should be mixed randomly in the questionnaire. A total or average score can be computed for each axis.

More generally, it should be noted that affective well-being is not determined solely by a person's current environment. Although job characteristics can have a substantial effect, well-being is also a function of some aspects of personality; people differ in their baseline well-being as well as in their reactions to particular job characteristics.

Relevant personality differences are usually described in terms of individuals' continuing affective dispositions. The personality trait of positive affectivity (corresponding to the *upper right-quadrant*) is characterized by generally optimistic views of the future, emotions which tend to be positive and behaviours which are relatively extroverted. On the other hand, negative affectivity (corresponding to the *upper left-hand quadrant*) is a disposition to experience negative emotional states. Individuals with high negative affectivity tend in many situations to feel nervous, anxious or upset; this trait is sometimes measured by means of personality scales of neuroticism. Positive and negative affectivities are regarded as traits, that is, they are relatively constant from one situation to another, whereas a person's well-being is viewed as an emotional state which varies in response to current activities and environmental influences.

Measures of well-being necessarily identify both the trait (the affective disposition) and the state (current affect). This fact should be borne in mind in examining people's well-being score on an individual basis, but it is not a substantial problem in studies of the average findings for a group of employees. In longitudinal investigations of group scores, observed changes in well-being can be attributed directly to changes in the environment, since every person's baseline well-being is held constant across the occasions of measurement; and in cross-sectional group studies an average affective disposition is recorded as a background influence in all cases.

Note also that affective well-being may be viewed at two levels. The more focused perspective relates to a specific domain, such as an occupational setting: this may be a question of "job-related" well-being (as discussed here) and is measured through scales which directly concern feelings when a person is at work. However, more wide-ranging, "context-free" or "general," well-being is sometimes of interest, and measurement of that wider construct requires a less specific focus. The same three axes should be examined in both cases, and more general scales are available for life satisfaction or general distress *(axis 1)*, context-free anxiety *(axis 2)* and context-free depression *(axis 3)*.

IMMUNOLOGICAL REACTIONS

Holger Ursin

When a human being or an animal is subjected to a psychological stress situation, there is a general response involving psychological as well as somatic (bodily) responses. This is a general alarm response, or general activation or wake-up call, which affects all physiological responses, including the musculoskeletal system, the vegetative system (the autonomic system), the hormones and also the immune system.

Since the 1960s, we have been learning how the brain, and through it, psychological factors, regulates and influences all physiological processes, whether directly or indirectly. Previously it was held that large and essential parts of our physiology were regulated "unconsciously," or not by brain processes at all. The nerves that regulate the gut, glands and the cardiovascular system were "autonomic", or independent of the central nervous system (CNS); similarly, the hormones and the immune system were beyond central nervous control. However, the autonomic nervous system is regulated by the limbic structures of the brain, and may be brought under direct instrumental control through classical and instrumental learning procedures. The fact that the central nervous system controls endocrinological processes is also well established.

The last development to undercut the view that the CNS was isolated from many physiological processes was the evolution of psychoimmunology. It has now been demonstrated that the interaction of the brain (and psychological processes), may influence immune processes, either via the endocrine system or by direct innervation of lymphoid tissue. The white blood cells themselves may also be influenced directly by signal molecules from nervous tissue. Depressed lymphocyte function has been demonstrated to follow bereavement (Bartrop et al. 1977), and conditioning of the immune-suppressive response in animals (Cohen et al. 1979) and psychological processes were shown to have effects bearing on animal survival (Riley 1981); these discoveries were milestones in the development of psychoimmunology.

It is now well established that psychological stress produces changes in the level of antibodies in the blood, and in the level of many of the white blood cells. A brief stress period of 30 minutes may produce significant increases in lymphocytes and natural killer (NK) cells. Following more long-lasting stress situations, changes are also found in the other components of the immune system. Changes have been reported in the counts of almost all types of white blood cell and in the levels of immunoglobulins and their complements; the changes also affect important elements of the total immune response and the "immune cascade" as well. These changes are complex and seem to be bidirectional. Both increases and decreases have been reported. The changes seem to depend not only on the stress-inducing situation, but on also what type of coping and defence mechanisms the individual is using to handle this situation. This is particularly clear when the effects of real long-lasting stress situations are studied, for instance those associated with the job or with difficult life situations ("life stressors"). Highly specific relationships between coping and defence styles and several subsets of immune cells (number of lympho-, leuko- and monocytes; total T cells and NK cells) have been described (Olff et al. 1993).

The search for immune parameters as markers for long-lasting, sustained stress has not been all that successful. Since the relationships between immunoglobulins and stress factors have been dem-

onstrated to be so complex, there is, understandably, no simple marker available. Such relationships as have been found are sometimes positive, sometimes negative. As far as psycho-logical profiles are concerned, to some extent the correlation matrix with one and the same psychological battery shows different patterns, varying from one occupational group to another (Endresen et al. 1991). Within each group, the patterns seem stable over long periods of time, up to three years. It is not known whether there are genetic factors that influence the highly specific relationships between coping styles and immune responses; if so, the manifestions of these factors must be highly dependent on interaction with life stressors. Also, it is not known whether it is possible to follow an individual's stress level over a long period, given that the individual's coping, defence and immune response style is known. This type of research is being pursued with highly selected personnel, for instance astronauts.

There may be a major flaw in the basic argument that immunoglobulins can be used as valid health risk markers. The original hypothesis was that low levels of circulating immunoglobulins might signal a low resistance and low immune competence. However, low values may not signal low resistance: they may only signal that this particular individual has not been challenged by infectious agents for a while—in fact, they may signal an extraordinary degree of health. The low values sometimes reported from returning astronauts and Antarctic personnel may not be a signal of stress, but only of the low levels of bacterial and viral challenge in the environment they have left.

There are many anecdotes in the clinical literature suggesting that psychological stress or critical life events can have an impact on the course of serious and non-serious illness. In the opinion of some, placebos and "alternative medicine" may exert their effects through psychoimmunological mechanisms. There are claims that reduced (and sometimes increased) immune competence should lead to increased susceptibility to infections in animals and in humans, and to inflammatory states like rheumatoid arthritis as well. It has been demonstrated convincingly that psychological stress affects the immune response to various types of inoculations. Students under examination stress report more symptoms of infectious illness in this period, which coincides with poorer cellular immune control (Glaser et al. 1992). There are also some claims that psychotherapy, in particular cognitive stress-management training, together with physical training, may affect the antibody response to viral infection.

There are also some positive findings with regard to cancer development, but only a few. The controversy over the claimed relationship between personality and cancer susceptibility has not been solved. Replications should be extended to include measures of immune responses to other factors, including lifestyle factors, which may be related to psychology, but the cancer effect may be a direct consequence of the lifestyle.

There is ample evidence that acute stress alters immune functions in human subjects and that chronic stress may also affect these functions. But to what extent are these changes valid and useful indicators of job stress? To what extent are immune changes—if they occur—a real health risk factor? There is no consensus in the field as of the time of this writing (1995).

Sound clinical trials and sound epidemiological research are required to advance in this field. But this type of research requires more funds than are available to the researchers. This work also requires an understanding of the psychology of stress, which is not always available to immunologists, and a profound understanding of how the immune system operates, which is not always available to psychologists.

• CARDIOVASCULAR DISEASES

Töres Theorell and Jeffrey V. Johnson

The scientific evidence suggesting that exposure to job stress increases the risk for cardiovascular disease increased substantially beginning in the mid-1980s (Gardell 1981; Karasek and Theorell 1990; Johnson and Johansson 1991). Cardiovascular disease (CVD) remains the number one cause of death in economically developed societies, and contributes to increasing medical care costs. Diseases of the cardiovascular system include coronary heart disease (CHD), hypertensive disease, cerebrovascular disease and other disorders of the heart and circulatory system.

Most manifestations of coronary heart disease are caused partly by narrowing of the coronary arteries due to atherosclerosis. Coronary atherosclerosis is known to be influenced by a number of individual factors including: family history, dietary intake of saturated fat, high blood pressure, cigarette smoking and physical exercise. Except for heredity, all these factors could be influenced by the work environment. A poor work environment may decrease the willingness to stop smoking and adopt a healthy lifestyle. Thus, an adverse work environment could influence coronary heart disease via its effects on the classical risk factors.

There are also direct effects of stressful work environments on neurohormonal elevations as well as on heart metabolism. A combination of physiological mechanisms, shown to be related to stressful work activities, may increase the risk of myocardial infarction. The elevation of energy-mobilizing hormones, which increase during periods of excessive stress, may make the heart more vulnerable to the actual death of the muscle tissue. Conversely, energy-restoring and repairing hormones which protect the heart muscle from the adverse effects of energy-mobilizing hormones, decrease during periods of stress. During emotional (and physical) stress the heart beats faster and harder over an extended period of time, leading to excessive oxygen consumption in the heart muscle and the increased possibility of a heart attack. Stress may also disturb the cardiac rhythm of the heart. A disturbance associated with a fast heart rhythm is called tachyarrhythmia. When the heart rate is so fast that the heartbeat becomes inefficient a life-threatening ventricular fibrillation may result.

Early epidemiological studies of psychosocial working conditions associated with CVD suggested that high levels of work demands increased CHD risk. For example a prospective study of Belgian bank employees found that those in a privately owned bank had a significantly higher incidence of myocardial infarction than workers in public banks, even after adjustment was made for biomedical risk factors (Komitzer et al. 1982). This study indicated a possible relationship between work demands (which were higher in the private banks) and risk of myocardial infarction. Early studies also indicated a higher incidence of myocardial infarction among lower level employees in large companies (Pell and d'Alonzo 1963). This raised the possibility that psychosocial stress may not primarily be a problem for people with a high degree of responsibility, as had been assumed previously.

Since the early 1980s, many epidemiological studies have examined the specific hypothesis suggested by the Demand/ Control model developed by Karasek and others (Karasek and Theorell 1990; Johnson and Johansson 1991). This model states that job strain results from work organizations that combine high-performance demands with low levels of control over how the work is to be done. According to the model, work control can be understood as "job decision latitude", or the task-related decision-making authority permitted by a given job or work organization. This model predicts that those workers who are exposed to high demand and low control over an extended period of time will have a higher risk of neurohormonal arousal which may result in adverse pathophysiological effects on the CVD system—which could eventually lead to increased risk of atherosclerotic heart disease and myocardial infarction.

Between 1981 and 1993, the majority of the 36 studies that examined the effects of high demands and low control on cardiovascular disease found significant and positive associations. These studies employed a variety of research designs and were performed in Sweden, Japan, the United States, Finland and Australia. A variety of outcomes was examined including CHD morbidity and mortality, as well as CHD risk factors including blood pressure, cigarette smoking, left ventricular mass index and CHD symptoms. Several recent review papers summarize these studies (Kristensen 1989; Baker et al. 1992; Schnall, Landsbergis and Baker 1994; Theorell and Karasek 1996). These reviewers note that the epidemiological quality of these studies is high and, moreover, that the stronger study designs have generally found greater support for the Demand/Control models. In general the adjustment for standard risk factors for cardiovascular disease does not eliminate nor significantly reduce the magnitude of the association between the high demand/low control combination and the risk of cardiovascular disease.

It is important to note, however, that the methodology in these studies varied considerably. The most important distinction is that some studies used the respondent's own descriptions of their work situations, whereas others used an 'average score' method based on aggregating the responses of a nationally representative sample of workers within their respective job title groups. Studies utilizing self-reported work descriptions showed higher relative risks (2.0–4.0 versus 1.3–2.0). Psychological job demands were shown to be relatively more important in studies utilizing self-reported data than in studies utilizing aggregated data. The work control variables were more consistently found to be associated with excess CVD risk regardless of which exposure method was used.

Recently, work-related social support has been added to the demand-control formulation and workers with high demands, low control and low support, have been shown to have over a twofold risk for CVD morbidity and mortality compared to those with low demands, high control and high support (Johnson and Hall 1994). Currently efforts are being made to examine sustained exposure to demands, control and support over the course of the "psychosocial work career". Descriptions of all the occupations during the whole work career are obtained for the participants and occupational scores are used for a calculation of the total lifetime exposure. The "total job control exposure" in relation to cardiovascular mortality incidence in working Swedes was studied and even after adjustment was made for age, smoking habits, exercise, ethnicity, education and social class, low total job control exposure was associated with a nearly twofold risk of dying a cardiovascular death over a 14-year follow-up period (Johnson et al. 1996).

A model similar to the Demand/Control model has been developed and tested by Siegrist and co-workers 1990 that uses "effort" and "social reward" as the crucial dimensions, the hypothesis being that high effort without social reward leads to increasing risk of cardiovascular disease. In a study of industrial workers it was shown that combinations of high effort and lack of reward predicted increased myocardial infarction risk independently of biomedical risk factors.

Other aspects of work organization, such as shift work, have also been shown to be associated with CVD risk. Constant rotation between night and day work has been found to be associated with increased risk of developing a myocardial infarction (Kristensen 1989; Theorell 1992).

Future research in this area particularly needs to focus on specifying the relationship between work stress exposure and CVD risk across different class, gender and ethnic groups.

● GASTROINTESTINAL PROBLEMS

Jerry Suls

For many years, psychological stress has been assumed to contribute to the development of peptic ulcer disease (which involves ulcerating lesions in the stomach or duodenum). Researchers and health care providers have proposed more recently that stress might also be related to other gastrointestinal disorders such as non-ulcer dyspepsia (associated with symptoms of upper abdominal pain, discomfort and nausea persisting in the absence of any identifiable organic cause) and irritable bowel syndrome (defined as altered bowel habits plus abdominal pain in the absence of abnormal physical findings). In this article, the question is examined whether there is strong empirical evidence to suggest that psychological stress is a predisposing factor in the aetiology or exacerbation of these three gastrointestinal disorders.

Gastric and Duodenal Ulcer

There is clear evidence that humans who are exposed to acute stress in the context of severe physical trauma are prone to the development of ulcers. It is less obvious, however, whether life stressors per se (such as job demotion or the death of a close relative) precipitate or exacerbate ulcers. Lay people and health care practitioners alike commonly associate ulcers and stress, perhaps as a consequence of Alexander's (1950) early psychoanalytic perspective on the topic. Alexander proposed that ulcer-prone persons suffered dependency conflicts in their relationships with others; coupled with a constitutional tendency toward chronic hypersecretion of gastric acid, dependency conflicts were believed to lead to ulcer formation. The psychoanalytic perspective has not received strong empirical support. Ulcer patients do not appear to display greater dependency conflicts than comparison groups, though ulcer patients do exhibit higher levels of anxiety, submissiveness and depression (Whitehead and Schuster 1985). The level of neuroticism characterizing some ulcer patients tends to be slight, however, and few could be considered as exhibiting psychopathological signs. In any case, studies of emotional disorder in ulcer patients have generally involved those persons who seek medical attention for their disorder; these individuals may not be representative of all ulcer patients.

The association between stress and ulcers follows from the assumption that certain persons are genetically predisposed to hypersecrete gastric acid, especially during stressful episodes. Indeed, about two thirds of duodenal ulcer patients show elevated pepsinogen levels; elevated levels of pepsinogen are also associated with peptic ulcer disease. Brady and associates' (1958) studies of "executive" monkeys lent initial support to the idea that a stressful lifestyle or vocation may contribute to the pathogenesis of gastrointestinal disease. They found that monkeys required to perform a lever press task to avoid painful electric shocks (the presumed "executives", which controlled the stressor) developed more gastric ulcers than comparison monkeys that passively received the same number and intensity of shocks. The analogy to the hard-driving businessman was very cogent for a time. Unfor-

tunately, their results were confounded with anxiety; anxious monkeys were more likely to be assigned to the "executive" role in Brady's laboratory because they learned the lever press task quickly. Efforts to replicate their results, using random assignment of subjects to conditions, have failed. Indeed, evidence shows that animals who lack control over environmental stressors develop ulcers (Weiss 1971). Human ulcer patients also tend to be shy and inhibited, which runs counter to the stereotype of the ulcer-prone hard-driving businessman. Finally, animal models are of limited utility because they focus on the development of gastric ulcers, while most ulcers in humans occur in the duodenum. Laboratory animals rarely develop duodenal ulcers in response to stress.

Experimental studies of the physiological reactions of ulcer patients versus normal subjects to laboratory stressors do not uniformly show excessive reactions in the patients. The premise that stress leads to increased acid secretion which, in turn, leads to ulceration, is problematic when one realizes that psychological stress usually produces a response from the sympathetic nervous system. The sympathetic nervous system inhibits, rather than enhances, the gastric secretion that is mediated via the splanchnic nerve. Besides hypersecretion other factors in the aetiology of ulcer have been proposed, namely, rapid gastric emptying, inadequate secretion of bicarbonate and mucus, and infection. Stress could potentially affect these processes though evidence is lacking.

Ulcers have been reported to be more common during wartime, but methodological problems in these studies necessitate caution. A study of air traffic controllers is sometimes cited as evidence supporting the role of psychological stress for the development of ulcers (Cobb and Rose 1973). Although air traffic controllers were significantly more likely than a control group of pilots to report symptoms typical of ulcer, the incidence of confirmed ulcer among the air traffic controllers was not elevated above the base rate of ulcer occurrence in the general population.

Studies of acute life events also present a confusing picture of the relationship between stress and ulcer (Piper and Tennant 1993). Many investigations have been conducted, though most of these studies employed small samples and were cross-sectional or retrospective in design. The majority of studies did not find that ulcer patients incurred more acute life events than community controls or patients with conditions in which stress is not implicated, such as gallstones or renal stones. However, ulcer patients reported more chronic stressors involving personal threat or goal frustration prior to the onset or recrudescence of ulcer. In two prospective studies, reports of subjects being under stress or having family problems at baseline levels predicted subsequent development of ulcers. Unfortunately, both prospective studies used single-item scales to measure stress. Other research has shown that slow healing of ulcers or relapse was associated with higher stress levels, but the stress indices used in these studies were unvalidated and may have been confounded with personality factors.

In summary, evidence for the role of stress in ulcer causation and exacerbation is limited. Large-scale population-based prospective studies of the occurrence of life events are needed which use validated measures of acute and chronic stress and objective indicators of ulcer. At this point, evidence for an association between psychological stress and ulcer is weak.

Irritable Bowel Syndrome

Irritable bowel syndrome (IBS) has been considered a stress-related disorder in the past, in part because the physiological mechanism of the syndrome is unknown and because a large proportion of IBS sufferers report that stress caused a change in their bowel habits. As in the ulcer literature, it is difficult to evaluate the value of retrospective accounts of stressors and symptoms among IBS patients. In an effort to explain their discomfort, ill persons may mistakenly associate symptoms with stressful life events. Two recent prospective studies shed more light on the subject, and both found a limited role for stressful events in the occurrence of IBS symptoms. Whitehead et al. (1992) had a sample of community residents suffering from IBS symptoms report life events and IBS symptoms at three-month intervals. Only about 10% of the variance in bowel symptoms among these residents could be attributed to stress. Suls, Wan and Blanchard (1994) had IBS patients keep diary records of stressors and symptoms for 21 successive days. They found no consistent evidence that daily stressors increased the incidence or severity of IBS symptomatology. Life stress appears to have little effect on acute changes in IBS.

Non-Ulcer Dyspepsia

The symptoms of non-ulcer dyspepsia (NUD) include bloating and fullness, belching, borborygmi, nausea and heartburn. In one retrospective study, NUD patients reported more acute life events and more highly threatening chronic difficulties compared to healthy community members, but other investigations failed to find a relationship between life stress and functional dyspepsia. NUD cases also show high levels of psychopathology, notably anxiety disorders. In the absence of prospective studies of life stress, few conclusions can be made (Bass 1986; Whitehead 1992).

Conclusions

Despite considerable empirical attention, no verdict has yet been reached on the relationship between stress and the development of ulcers. Contemporary gastroenterologists have focused mainly on heritable pepsinogen levels, inadequate secretion of bicarbonate and mucus, and *Heliobacter pylori* infection as causes of ulcer. If life stress plays a role in these processes, its contribution is probably weak. Though fewer studies address the role of stress in IBS and NUD, evidence for a connection to stress is also weak here. For all three disorders, there is evidence that anxiety is higher among patients compared to the general population, at least among those persons who refer themselves for medical care (Whitehead 1992). Whether this is a precursor or a consequence of gastrointestinal disease has not been definitively determined, although the latter opinion seems to be more likely to be true. In current practice, ulcer patients receive pharmacological treatment, and psychotherapy is rarely recommended. Anti-anxiety drugs are commonly prescribed to IBS and NUD patients, probably because the physiological origins of these disorders are still unknown. Stress management has been employed with IBS patients with some success (Blanchard et al. 1992) although this patient group also responds to placebo treatments quite readily. Finally, patients experiencing ulcer, IBS or NUD may well be frustrated by assumptions from family members, friends and practitioners alike that their condition was produced by stress.

● CANCER

Bernard H. Fox

Stress, the physical and/or psychological departure from a person's stable equilibrium, can result from a large number of stressors, those stimuli that produce stress. For a good general view of stress and the most common job stressors, Levi's discussion in this chapter of job stress theories is recommended.

In addressing the question of whether job stress can and does affect the epidemiology of cancer, we face limitations: a search of the literature located only one study on actual job stress and cancer in urban bus drivers (Michaels and Zoloth 1991) (and there are only few studies in which the question is considered more generally). We cannot accept the findings of that study, because the authors did not take into account either the effects of high density exhaust fumes or smoking. Further, one cannot carry over the findings from other diseases to cancer because the disease mechanisms are so vastly different.

Nevertheless, it is possible to describe what is known about the connections between more general life stressors and cancer, and further, one might reasonably apply those findings to the job situation. We differentiate relationships of stress to two outcomes: cancer incidence and cancer prognosis. The term *incidence* evidently means the occurrence of cancer. However, incidence is established either by the doctor's clinical diagnosis or at autopsy. Since tumour growth is slow—1 to 20 years may elapse from the malignant mutation of one cell to the detection of the tumour mass—incidence studies include both initiation and growth. The second question, whether stress can affect prognosis, can be answered only in studies of cancer patients after diagnosis.

We distinguish cohort studies from case-control studies. This discussion focuses on cohort studies, where a factor of interest, in this case stress, is measured on a cohort of healthy persons, and cancer incidence or mortality is determined after a number of years. For several reasons, little emphasis is given to case-control studies, those which compare reports of stress, either current or before diagnosis, in cancer patients (cases) and persons without cancer (controls). First, one can never be sure that the control group is well-matched to the case group with respect to other factors that can influence the comparison. Secondly, cancer can and does produce physical, psychological and attitudinal changes, mostly negative, that can bias conclusions. Thirdly, these changes are known to result in an increase in the number of reports of stressful events (or of their severity) compared to reports by controls, thus leading to biased conclusions that patients experienced more, or more severe, stressful events than did controls (Watson and Pennebaker 1989).

Stress and Cancer Incidence

Most studies on stress and cancer incidence have been of the case-control sort, and we find a wild mix of results. Because, in varying degrees, these studies have failed to control contaminating factors, we don't know which ones to trust, and they are ignored here. Among cohort studies, the number of studies showing that persons under greater stress did not experience more cancer than those under lesser stress exceeded by a large margin the number showing the reverse (Fox 1995). The results for several stressed groups are given.

1. *Bereaved spouses.* In a Finnish study of 95,647 widowed persons their cancer death rate differed by only 3% from the rate of an age-equivalent non-widowed population over a period of five years. A study of causes of death during the 12 years following bereavement in 4,032 widowed persons in the state of Maryland showed no more cancer deaths among the widowed than among those still married—in fact, there were slightly fewer deaths than in the married. In England and Wales, the Office of Population Censuses and Surveys showed little evidence of an increase in cancer incidence after death of a spouse, and only a slight, non-significant increase in cancer mortality.

2. *Depressed mood.* One study showed, but four studies did not, an excess of cancer mortality in the years following the measurement of a depressed mood (Fox 1989). This must be distinguished from hospitalizable depression, on which no well-controlled large-scale cohort studies have been done, and which clearly involves pathological depression, not applicable to the healthy working population. Even among this group of

clinically depressed patients, however, most properly analysed smaller studies show no excess of cancer.

3. A group of 2,020 men, aged 35 to 55, working in an electrical products factory in Chicago, was followed for 17 years after being tested. Those whose highest score on a variety of personality scales was reported on the depressed mood scale showed a cancer death rate 2.3 times that of men whose highest score was not referable to depressed mood. The researcher's colleague followed the surviving cohort for another three years; the cancer death rate in the whole high-depressed-mood group had dropped to 1.3 times that of the control group. A second study of 6,801 adults in Alameda County, California, showed no excess cancer mortality among those with depressed mood when followed for 17 years. In a third study of 2,501 people with depressed mood in Washington County, Maryland, non-smokers showed no excess cancer mortality over 13 years compared to non-smoking controls, but there was an excess mortality among smokers. The results for smokers were later shown to be wrong, the error arising from a contaminating factor overlooked by the researchers. A fourth study, of 8,932 women at the Kaiser-Permanente Medical Center in Walnut Creek, California showed no excess of deaths due to breast cancer over 11 to 14 years among women with depressed mood at the time of measurement. A fifth study, done on a randomized national sample of 2,586 people in the National Health and Nutrition Examination Survey in the United States, showed no excess of cancer mortality among those showing depressed mood when measured on either of two independent mood scales. The combined findings of studies on 22,351 persons made up of disparate groups weigh heavily against the contrary findings of the one study on 2,020 persons.

4. *Other stressors.* A study of 4,581 Hawaiian men of Japanese descent found no greater cancer incidence over a period of 10 years among those reporting high levels of stressful life events at the start of the study than those reporting lower levels. A study was carried out on 9,160 soldiers in the US Army who had been prisoners of war in the Pacific and European theatres in the Second World War and in Korea during the Korean conflict. The cancer death rate from 1946 to 1975 was either less than or no different from that found among soldiers matched by combat zone and combat activity who were not prisoners of war. In a study of 9,813 US Army personnel separated from the army during the year 1944 for "psychoneurosis", a prima facie state of chronic stress, their cancer death rate over the period 1946 to 1969 was compared with that of a matched group not so diagnosed. The psychoneurotics' rate was no greater than that of matched controls, and was, in fact, slightly lower, although not significantly so.

5. *Lowered levels of stress.* There is evidence in some studies, but not in others, that higher levels of social support and social connections are associated with less cancer risk in the future. There are so few studies on this topic and the observed differences so unconvincing that the most a prudent reviewer can reasonably do is suggest the possibility of a true relationship. We need more solid evidence than that offered by the contradictory studies that have already been carried out.

Stress and cancer prognosis

This topic is of lesser interest because so few people of working age get cancer. Nevertheless, it ought to be mentioned that while survival differences have been found in some studies with regard to reported pre-diagnosis stress, other studies have shown no differences. One should, in judging these findings, recall the parallel ones showing that not only cancer patients, but also those with

other ills, report more past stressful events than well people to a substantial degree because of the psychological changes brought about by the disease itself and, further, by the knowledge that one has the disease. With respect to prognosis, several studies have shown increased survival among those with good social support as against those with less social support. Perhaps more social support produces less stress, and vice versa. As regards both incidence and prognosis, however, the extant studies are at best only suggestive (Fox 1995).

Animal studies

It might be instructive to see what effects stress has had in experiments with animals. The results among well-conducted studies are much clearer, but not decisive. It was found that stressed animals with viral tumours show faster tumour growth and die earlier than unstressed animals. But the reverse is true of non-viral tumours, that is, those produced in the laboratory by chemical carcinogens. For these, stressed animals have fewer tumours and longer survival after the start of cancer than unstressed animals (Justice 1985). In industrial nations, however, only 3 to 4% of human malignancies are viral. All the rest are due to chemical or physical stimuli—smoking, x rays, industrial chemicals, nuclear radiation (e.g., that due to radon), excessive sunlight and so on. Thus, if one were to extrapolate from the findings for animals, one would conclude that stress is beneficial both to cancer incidence and survival. For a number of reasons one should not draw such an inference (Justice 1985; Fox 1981). Results with animals can be used to generate hypotheses relating to data describing humans, but cannot be the basis for conclusions about them.

Conclusion

In view of the variety of stressors that has been examined in the literature—long-term, short-term, more severe, less severe, of many types—and the preponderance of results suggesting little or no effect on later cancer incidence, it is reasonable to suggest that the same results apply in the work situation. As for cancer prognosis, too few studies have been done to draw any conclusions, even tentative ones, about stressors. It is, however, possible that strong social support may decrease incidence a little, and perhaps increase survival.

MUSCULOSKELETAL DISORDERS

Soo-Yee Lim, Steven L. Sauter and Naomi G. Swanson

There is growing evidence in the occupational health literature that psychosocial work factors may influence the development of musculoskeletal problems, including both low back and upper extremity disorders (Bongers et al. 1993). Psychosocial work factors are defined as aspects of the work environment (such as work roles, work pressure, relationships at work) that can contribute to the experience of stress in individuals (Lim and Carayon 1994; ILO 1986). This paper provides a synopsis of the evidence and underlying mechanisms linking psychosocial work factors and musculoskeletal problems with the emphasis on studies of upper extremity disorders among office workers. Directions for future research are also discussed.

An impressive array of studies from 1985 to 1995 had linked workplace psychosocial factors to upper extremity musculoskeletal problems in the office work environment (see Moon and Sauter 1996 for an extensive review). In the United States, this relationship was first suggested in an exploratory research by the

National Institute for Occupational Safety and Health (NIOSH) (Smith et al. 1981). Results of this research indicated that video display unit (VDU) operators who reported less autonomy and role clarity and greater work pressure and management control over their work processes also reported more musculoskeletal problems than their counterparts who did not work with VDUs (Smith et al. 1981).

Recent studies employing more powerful inferential statistical techniques point more strongly to an effect of psychosocial work factors on upper extremity musculoskeletal disorders among office workers. For example, Lim and Carayon (1994) used structural analysis methods to examine the relationship between psychosocial work factors and upper extremity musculoskeletal discomfort in a sample of 129 office workers. Results showed that psychosocial factors such as work pressure, task control and production quotas were important predictors of upper extremity musculoskeletal discomfort, especially in the neck and shoulder regions. Demographic factors (age, gender, tenure with employer, hours of computer use per day) and other confounding factors (self-reports of medical conditions, hobbies and keyboard use outside work) were controlled for in the study and were not related to any of these problems.

Confirmatory findings were reported by Hales et al. (1994) in a NIOSH study of musculoskeletal disorders in 533 tele-communication workers from 3 different metropolitan cities. Two types of musculoskeletal outcomes were investigated: (1) upper extremity musculoskeletal symptoms determined by questionnaire alone; and (2) potential work-related upper extremity musculoskeletal disorders which were determined by physical examination in addition to the questionnaire. Using regression techniques, the study found that factors such as work pressure and little decision-making opportunity were associated both with intensified musculoskeletal symptoms and also with increased physical evidence of disease. Similar relationships have been observed in the industrial environment, but mainly for back pain (Bongers et al. 1993).

Researchers have suggested a variety of mechanisms underlying the relationship between psychosocial factors and musculoskeletal problems (Sauter and Swanson 1996; Smith and Carayon 1996; Lim 1994; Bongers et al. 1993). These mechanisms can be classified into four categories:

1. psychophysiological
2. behavioural
3. physical
4. perceptual.

Psychophysiological mechanisms

It has been demonstrated that individuals subject to stressful psychosocial working conditions also exhibit increased autonomic arousal (e.g., increased catecholamine secretion, increased heart rate and blood pressure, increased muscle tension etc.) (Frankenhaeuser and Gardell 1976). This is a normal and adaptive psychophysiological response which prepares the individual for action. However, prolonged exposure to stress may have a deleterious effect on musculoskeletal function as well as on health in general. For example, stress-related muscle tension may increase the static loading of muscles, thereby accelerating muscle fatigue and associated discomfort (Westgaard and Bjorklund 1987; Grandjean 1986).

Behavioural mechanisms

Individuals who are under stress may alter their work behaviour in a way that increases musculoskeletal strain. For example, psychological stress may result in greater application of force than necessary during typing or other manual tasks, leading to increased wear and tear on the musculoskeletal system.

Physical mechanisms

Psychosocial factors may influence the physical (ergonomic) demands of the job directly. For example, an increase in time pressure is likely to lead to an increase in work pace (i.e., increased repetition) and increased strain. Alternatively, workers who are given more control over their tasks may be able to adjust their tasks in ways that lead to reduced repetitiveness (Lim and Carayon 1994).

Perceptual mechanisms

Sauter and Swanson (1996) suggest that the relationship between biomechanical stressors (e.g., ergonomic factors) and the development of musculoskeletal problems is mediated by perceptual processes which are influenced by workplace psychosocial factors. For example, symptoms might become more evident in dull, routine jobs than in more engrossing tasks which more fully occupy the attention of the worker (Pennebaker and Hall 1982).

Additional research is needed to assess the relative importance of each of these mechanisms and their possible interactions. Further, our understanding of causal relationships between psychosocial work factors and musculoskeletal disorders would benefit from: (1) increased use of longitudinal study designs; (2) improved methods for assessing and disentangling psychosocial and physical exposures; and (3) improved measurement of musculoskeletal outcomes.

Still, the current evidence linking psychosocial factors and musculoskeletal disorders is impressive and suggests that psychosocial interventions probably play an important role in preventing musculoskeletal problems in the workplace. In this regard, several publications (NIOSH 1988; ILO 1986) provide directions for optimizing the psychosocial environment at work. As suggested by Bongers et al. (1993), special attention should be given to providing a supportive work environment, manageable workloads and increased worker autonomy. Positive effects of such variables were evident in a case study by Westin (1990) of the Federal Express Corporation. According to Westin, a programme of work reorganization to provide an "employee-supportive" work environment, improve communications and reduce work and time pressures was associated with minimal evidence of musculoskeletal health problems.

MENTAL ILLNESS

Carles Muntaner and William W. Eaton

Introduction

Mental illness is one of the chronic outcomes of work stress that inflicts a major social and economic burden on communities (Jenkins and Coney 1992; Miller and Kelman 1992). Two disciplines, psychiatric epidemiology and mental health sociology (Aneshensel, Rutter and Lachenbruch 1991), have studied the effects of psychosocial and organizational factors of work on mental illness. These studies can be classified according to four different theoretical and methodological approaches: (1) studies of only a single occupation; (2) studies of broad occupational categories as indicators of social stratification; (3) comparative studies of occupational categories; and (4) studies of specific psychosocial and organizational risk factors. We review each of these approaches and discuss their implications for research and prevention.

Studies of a Single Occupation

There are numerous studies in which the focus has been a single occupation. Depression has been the focus of interest in recent studies of secretaries (Garrison and Eaton 1992), professionals and managers (Phelan et al. 1991; Bromet et al. 1990), computer workers (Mino et al. 1993), fire-fighters (Guidotti 1992), teachers (Schonfeld 1992), and "maquiladoras" (Guendelman and Silberg 1993). Alcoholism and drug abuse and dependence have been recently related to mortality among bus drivers (Michaels and Zoloth 1991) and to managerial and professional occupations (Bromet et al. 1990). Symptoms of anxiety and depression which are indicative of psychiatric disorder have been found among garment workers, nurses, teachers, social workers, offshore oil industry workers and young physicians (Brisson, Vezina and Vinet 1992; Fith-Cozens 1987; Fletcher 1988; McGrath, Reid and Boore 1989; Parkes 1992). The lack of a comparison group makes it difficult to determine the significance of this type of study.

Studies of Broad Occupational Categories as Indicators of Social Stratification

The use of occupations as indicators of social stratification has a long tradition in mental health research (Liberatos, Link and Kelsey 1988). Workers in unskilled manual jobs and lower-grade civil servants have shown high prevalence rates of minor psychiatric disorders in England (Rodgers 1991; Stansfeld and Marmot 1992). Alcoholism has been found to be prevalent among blue-collar workers in Sweden (Ojesjo 1980) and even more prevalent among managers in Japan (Kawakami et al. 1992). Failure to differentiate conceptually between effects of occupations per se from "lifestyle" factors associated with occupational strata is a serious weakness of this type of study. It is also true that occupation is an indicator of social stratification in a sense different from social class, that is, as the latter implies control over productive assets (Kohn et al. 1990; Muntaner et al. 1994). However, there have not been empirical studies of mental illness using this conceptualization.

Comparative Studies of Occupational Categories

Census categories for occupations constitute a readily available source of information that allows one to explore associations between occupations and mental illness (Eaton et al. 1990). Epidemiological Catchment Area (ECA) study analyses of comprehensive occupational categories have yielded findings of a high prevalence of depression for professional, administrative support and household services occupations (Roberts and Lee 1993). In another major epidemiological study, the Alameda county study, high rates of depression were found among workers in blue-collar occupations (Kaplan et al. 1991). High 12-month prevalence rates of alcohol dependence among workers in the Unites States have been found in craft occupations (15.6%) and labourers (15.2%) among men, and in farming, forestry and fishing occupations (7.5%) and unskilled service occupations (7.2%) among women (Harford et al. 1992). ECA rates of alcohol abuse and dependence yielded high prevalence among transportation, craft and labourer occupations (Roberts and Lee 1993). Workers in the service sector, drivers and unskilled workers showed high rates of alcoholism in a study of the Swedish population (Agren and Romelsjo 1992). Twelve-month prevalence of drug abuse or dependence in the ECA study was higher among farming (6%), craft (4.7%), and operator, transportation and labourer (3.3%) occupations (Roberts and Lee 1993). The ECA analysis of combined prevalence for all psychoactive substance abuse or dependence syndromes (Anthony et al. 1992) yielded higher prevalence rates for construction labourers, carpenters, construction trades as a whole, waiters, waitresses and transportation and moving occupations. In another ECA analysis (Muntaner et al. 1991), as compared to managerial occupations, greater risk of schizophrenia was found among private household workers, while artists and

construction trades were found at higher risk of schizophrenia (delusions and hallucinations), according to criterion A of the Diagnostic and Statistics Manual of Mental Disorders (DSM-III) (APA 1980).

Several ECA studies have been conducted with more specific occupational categories. In addition to specifying occupational environments more closely, they adjust for sociodemographic factors which might have led to spurious results in uncontrolled studies. High 12-month prevalence rates of major depression (above the 3 to 5% found in the general population (Robins and Regier 1990), have been reported for data entry keyers and computer equipment operators (13%) and typists, lawyers, special education teachers and counsellors (10%) (Eaton et al. 1990). After adjustment for sociodemographic factors, lawyers, teachers and counsellors had significantly elevated rates when compared to the employed population (Eaton et al. 1990). In a detailed analysis of 104 occupations, construction labourers, skilled construction trades, heavy truck drivers and material movers showed high rates of alcohol abuse or dependence (Mandell et al. 1992).

Comparative studies of occupational categories suffer from the same flaws as social stratification studies. Thus, a problem with occupational categories is that specific risk factors are bound to be missed. In addition, "lifestyle" factors associated with occupational categories remain a potent explanation for results.

Studies of Specific Psychosocial and Organizational Risk Factors

Most studies of work stress and mental illness have been conducted with scales from Karasek's Demand/Control model (Karasek and Theorell 1990) or with measures derived from the *Dictionary of Occupational Titles* (DOT) (Cain and Treiman 1981). In spite of the methodological and theoretical differences underlying these systems, they measure similar psychosocial dimensions (control, substantive complexity and job demands) (Muntaner et al. 1993). Job demands have been associated with major depressive disorder among male power-plant workers (Bromet 1988). Occupations involving lack of direction, control or planning have been shown to mediate the relation between socioeconomic status and depression (Link et al. 1993). However, in one study the relationship between low control and depression was not found (Guendelman and Silberg 1993). The number of negative work-related effects, lack of intrinsic job rewards and organizational stressors such as role conflict and ambiguity have also been associated with major depression (Phelan et al. 1991). Heavy alcohol drinking and alcohol-related problems have been linked to working overtime and to lack of intrinsic job rewards among men and to job insecurity among women in Japan (Kawakami et al. 1993), and to high demands and low control among males in the United States (Bromet 1988). Also among US males, high psychological or physical demands and low control were predictive of alcohol abuse or dependence (Crum et al. 1995). In another ECA analysis, high physical demands and low skill discretion were predictive of drug dependence (Muntaner et al. 1995). Physical demands and job hazards were predictors of schizophrenia or delusions or hallucinations in three US studies (Muntaner et al. 1991; Link et al. 1986; Muntaner et al. 1993). Physical demands have also been associated with psychiatric disease in the Swedish population (Lundberg 1991). These investigations have the potential for prevention because specific, potentially malleable risk factors are the focus of study.

Implications for Research and Prevention

Future studies might benefit from studying the demographic and sociological characteristics of workers in order to sharpen their focus on the occupations proper (Mandell et al. 1992). When occupation is considered an indicator of social stratification, adjustment for non-work stressors should be attempted. The effects of chronic exposure to lack of democracy in the workplace need to be investigated (Johnson and Johansson 1991). A major initiative for the prevention of work-related psychological disorders has emphasized improving working conditions, services, research and surveillance (Keita and Sauter 1992; Sauter, Murphy and Hurrell 1990).

While some researchers maintain that job redesign can improve both productivity and workers' health (Karasek and Theorell 1990), others have argued that a firm's profit maximization goals and workers' mental health are in conflict (Phelan et al. 1991; Muntaner and O'Campo 1993; Ralph 1983).

● BURNOUT

Christina Maslach

Burnout is a type of prolonged response to chronic emotional and interpersonal stressors on the job. It has been conceptualized as an individual stress experience embedded in a context of complex social relationships, and it involves the person's conception of both self and others. As such, it has been an issue of particular concern for human services occupations where: (a) the relationship between providers and recipients is central to the job; and (b) the provision of service, care, treatment or education can be a highly emotional experience. There are several types of occupations that meet these criteria, including health care, social services, mental health, criminal justice and education. Even though these occupations vary in the nature of the contact between providers and recipients, they are similar in having a structured caregiving relationship centred around the recipient's current problems (psychological, social and/or physical). Not only is the provider's work on these problems likely to be emotionally charged, but solutions may not be easily forthcoming, thus adding to the frustration and ambiguity of the work situation. The person who works continuously with people under such circumstances is at greater risk from burnout.

The operational definition (and the corresponding research measure) that is most widely used in burnout research is a three-component model in which burnout is conceptualized in terms of *emotional exhaustion, depersonalization* and *reduced personal accomplishment* (Maslach 1993; Maslach and Jackson 1981/1986). Emotional exhaustion refers to feelings of being emotionally overextended and depleted of one's emotional resources. Depersonalization refers to a negative, callous or excessively detached response to the people who are usually the recipients of one's service or care. Reduced personal accomplishment refers to a decline in one's feelings of competence and successful achievement in one's work.

This multidimensional model of burnout has important theoretical and practical implications. It provides a more complete understanding of this form of job stress by locating it within its social context and by identifying the variety of psychological reactions that different workers can experience. Such differential responses may not be simply a function of individual factors (such as personality), but may reflect the differential impact of situational factors on the three burnout dimensions. For example, certain job characteristics may influence the sources of emotional stress (and thus emotional exhaustion), or the resources available to handle the job successfully (and thus personal accomplishment). This multidimensional approach also implies that interventions to reduce burnout should be planned and designed in terms of the

particular component of burnout that needs to be addressed. That is, it may be more effective to consider how to reduce the likelihood of emotional exhaustion, or to prevent the tendency to depersonalize, or to enhance one's sense of accomplishment, rather than to use a more unfocused approach.

Consistent with this social framework, the empirical research on burnout has focused primarily on situational and job factors. Thus, studies have included such variables as relationships on the job (clients, colleagues, supervisors) and at home (family), job satisfaction, role conflict and role ambiguity, job withdrawal (turnover, absenteeism), expectations, workload, type of position and job tenure, institutional policy and so forth. The personal factors that have been studied are most often demographic variables (sex, age, marital status, etc.). In addition, some attention has been given to personality variables, personal health, relations with family and friends (social support at home), and personal values and commitment. In general, job factors are more strongly related to burnout than are biographical or personal factors. In terms of antecedents of burnout, the three factors of role conflict, lack of control or autonomy, and lack of social support on the job, seem to be most important. The effects of burnout are seen most consistently in various forms of job withdrawal and dissatisfaction, with the implication of a deterioration in the quality of care or service provided to clients or patients. Burnout seems to be correlated with various self-reported indices of personal dysfunction, including health problems, increased use of alcohol and drugs, and marital and family conflicts. The level of burnout seems fairly stable over time, underscoring the notion that its nature is more chronic than acute (see Kleiber and Enzmann 1990; Schaufeli, Maslach and Marek 1993 for reviews of the field).

An issue for future research concerns possible diagnostic criteria for burnout. Burnout has often been described in terms of dysphoric symptoms such as exhaustion, fatigue, loss of self-esteem and depression. However, depression is considered to be context-free and pervasive across all situations, whereas burnout is regarded as job-related and situation-specific. Other symptoms include problems in concentration, irritability and negativism, as well as a significant decrease in work performance over a period of several months. It is usually assumed that burnout symptoms manifest themselves in "normal" persons who do not suffer from prior psychopathology or an identifiable organic illness. The implication of these ideas about possible distinctive symptoms of burnout is that burnout could be diagnosed and treated at the individual level.

However, given the evidence for the situational aetiology of burnout, more attention has been given to social, rather than personal, interventions. Social support, particularly from one's peers, seems to be effective in reducing the risk of burnout. Adequate job training that includes preparation for difficult and stressful work-related situations helps develop people's sense of self-efficacy and mastery in their work roles. Involvement in a larger community or action-oriented group can also counteract the helplessness and pessimism that are commonly evoked by the absence of long-term solutions to the problems with which the worker is dealing. Accentuating the positive aspects of the job and finding ways to make ordinary tasks more meaningful are additional methods for gaining greater self-efficacy and control.

There is a growing tendency to view burnout as a dynamic process, rather than a static state, and this has important implications for the proposal of developmental models and process measures. The research gains to be expected from this newer perspective should yield · increasingly sophisticated knowledge about the experience of burnout, and will enable both individuals and institutions to deal with this social problem more effectively.

SUMMARY OF GENERIC PREVENTION AND CONTROL STRATEGIES

Cary L. Cooper and Sue Cartwright

Any organization which seeks to establish and maintain the best state of mental, physical and social wellbeing of its employees needs to have policies and procedures which comprehensively address health and safety. These policies will include a mental health policy with procedures to manage stress based on the needs of the organization and its employees. These will be regularly reviewed and evaluated.

There are a number of options to consider in looking at the prevention of stress, which can be termed as primary, secondary and tertiary levels of prevention and address different stages in the stress process (Cooper and Cartwright 1994). *Primary prevention* is concerned with taking action to reduce or eliminate stressors (i.e., sources of stress), and positively promoting a supportive and healthy work environment. *Secondary prevention* is concerned with the prompt detection and management of depression and anxiety by increasing self-awareness and improving stress management skills. *Tertiary prevention* is concerned with the rehabilitation and recovery process of those individuals who have suffered or are suffering from serious ill health as a result of stress.

To develop an effective and comprehensive organizational policy on stress, employers need to integrate these three approaches (Cooper, Liukkonen and Cartwright 1996).

Primary Prevention

First, the most effective way of tackling stress is to eliminate it at its source. This may involve changes in personnel policies, improving communication systems, redesigning jobs, or allowing more decision making and autonomy at lower levels. Obviously, as the type of action required by an organization will vary according to the kinds of stressor operating, any intervention needs to be guided by some *prior diagnosis* or stress *audit* to identify what these stressors are and whom they are affecting.

Stress audits typically take the form of a self-report questionnaire administered to employees on an organization- wide, site or departmental basis. In addition to identifying the sources of stress at work and those individuals most vulnerable to stress, the questionnaire usually measures levels of employee job satisfaction, coping behaviour, and physical and psychological health comparative to similar occupational groups and industries. Stress audits are an extremely effective way of directing organizational resources into areas where they are most needed. Audits also provide a means of regularly monitoring stress levels and employee health over time, and provide a base line whereby subsequent interventions can be evaluated.

Diagnostic instruments, such as the *Occupational Stress Indicator* (Cooper, Sloan and Williams 1988) are increasingly being used by organizations for this purpose. They are usually administered through occupational health and/or personnel/human resource departments in consultation with a psychologist. In smaller companies, there may be the opportunity to hold employee discussion groups or develop checklists which can be administered on a more informal basis. The agenda for such discussions/ checklists should address the following issues:

- job content and work scheduling
- physical working conditions

- employment terms and expectations of different employee groups within the organization
- relationships at work
- communication systems and reporting arrangements.

Another alternative is to ask employees to keep a stress diary for a few weeks in which they record any stressful events they encounter during the course of the day. Pooling this information on a group/departmental basis can be useful in identifying universal and persistent sources of stress.

Creating healthy and supportive networks/environments

Another key factor in primary prevention is the development of the kind of supportive organizational climate in which stress is recognized as a feature of modern industrial life and not interpreted as a sign of weakness or incompetence. Mental ill health is indiscriminate—it can affect anyone irrespective of their age, social status or job function. Therefore, employees should not feel awkward about admitting to any difficulties they encounter.

Organizations need to take explicit steps to remove the stigma often attached to those with emotional problems and maximize the support available to staff (Cooper and Williams 1994). Some of the formal ways in which this can be done include:

- informing employees of existing sources of support and advice within the organization, like occupational health
- specifically incorporating self-development issues within appraisal systems
- extending and improving the "people" skills of managers and supervisors so they that convey a supportive attitude and can more comfortably handle employee problems.

Most importantly, there has to be demonstrable commitment to the issue of stress and mental health at work from both senior management and unions. This may require a move to more open communication and the dismantling of cultural norms within the organization which inherently promote stress among employees (e.g., cultural norms which encourage employees to work excessively long hours and feel guilty about leaving "on time"). Organizations with a supportive organizational climate will also be proactive in anticipating additional or new stressors which may be introduced as a result of proposed changes. For example, restructuring, new technology and take steps to address this, perhaps by training initiatives or greater employee involvement. Regular communication and increased employee involvement and participation play a key role in reducing stress in the context of organizational change.

Secondary Prevention

Initiatives which fall into this category are generally focused on training and education, and involve awareness activities and skill-training programmes.

Stress education and stress management courses serve a useful function in helping individuals to recognize the symptoms of stress in themselves and others and to extend and develop their coping skills and abilities and stress resilience.

The form and content of this kind of training can vary immensely but often includes simple relaxation techniques, lifestyle advice and planning, basic training in time management, assertiveness and problem-solving skills. The aim of these programmes is to help employees to review the psychological effects of stress and to develop a personal stress-control plan (Cooper 1996).

This kind of programme can be beneficial to all levels of staff and is particularly useful in training managers to recognize stress in their subordinates and be aware of their own managerial style and its impact on those they manage. This can be of great benefit if carried out following a stress audit.

Health screening/health enhancement programmes

Organizations, with the cooperation of occupational health personnel, can also introduce initiatives which directly promote positive health behaviours in the workplace. Again, health promotion activities can take a variety of forms. They may include:

- the introduction of regular medical check-ups and health screening
- the design of "healthy" canteen menus
- the provision of on-site fitness facilities and exercise classes
- corporate membership or concessionary rates at local health and fitness clubs
- the introduction of cardiovascular fitness programmes
- advice on alcohol and dietary control (particularly cutting down on cholesterol, salt and sugar)
- smoking-cessation programmes
- advice on lifestyle management, more generally.

For organizations without the facilities of an occupational health department, there are external agencies that can provide a range of health-promotion programmes. Evidence from established health-promotion programmes in the United States have produced some impressive results (Karasek and Theorell 1990). For example, the New York Telephone Company's Wellness Programme, designed to improve cardiovascular fitness, saved the organization $2.7 million in absence and treatment costs in one year alone.

Stress management/lifestyle programmes can be particularly useful in helping individuals to cope with environmental stressors which may have been identified by the organization, but which cannot be changed, e.g., job insecurity.

Tertiary Prevention

An important part of health promotion in the workplace is the detection of mental health problems as soon as they arise and the prompt referral of these problems for specialist treatment. The majority of those who develop mental illness make a complete recovery and are able to return to work. It is usually far more costly to retire a person early on medical grounds and re-recruit and train a successor than it is to spend time easing a person back to work. There are two aspects of tertiary prevention which organizations can consider:

Counselling

Organizations can provide access to confidential professional counselling services for employees who are experiencing problems in the workplace or personal setting (Swanson and Murphy 1991).

Such services can be provided either by in-house counsellors or outside agencies in the form of an Employee Assistance Programme (EAP).

EAPs provide counselling, information and/or referral to appropriate counselling treatment and support services. Such services are confidential and usually provide a 24-hour contact line. Charges are normally made on a per capita basis calculated on the total number of employees and the number of counselling hours provided by the programme.

Counselling is a highly skilled business and requires extensive training. It is important to ensure that counsellors have received recognized counselling skills training and have access to a suitable environment which allows them to conduct this activity in an ethical and confidential manner.

Again, the provision of counselling services is likely to be particularly effective in dealing with stress as a result of stressors operating within the organization which cannot be changed (e.g., job loss) or stress caused by non-work related problems (e.g., bereavement, marital breakdown), but which nevertheless tend to spill over into work life. It is also useful in directing employees to the most appropriate sources of help for their problems.

Facilitating the return to work

For those employees who are absent from work as a result of stress, it has to be recognized that the return to work itself is likely to be a "stressful" experience. It is important that organizations are sympathetic and understanding in these circumstances. A "return to work" interview should be conducted to establish whether the individual concerned is ready and happy to return to all aspects of their job. Negotiations should involve careful liaison between the employee, line manager and doctor. Once the individual has made a partial or complete return to his or her duties, a series of follow-up interviews are likely to be useful to monitor their progress and rehabilitation. Again, the occupational health department can play an important role in the rehabilitation process.

The options outlined above should not be regarded as mutually exclusive but rather as being potentially complimentary. Stress-management training, health-promotion activities and counselling services are useful in extending the physical and psychological resources of the individual to help them to modify their appraisal of a stressful situation and cope better with experienced distress (Berridge, Cooper and Highley 1997). However, there are many potential and persistent sources of stress the individual is likely to perceive him- or herself as lacking the resource or positional power to change (e.g., the structure, management style or culture of the organization). Such stressors require organizational level intervention if their long-term dysfunctional impact on employee health is to be overcome satisfactorily. They can only be identified by a stress audit.

References

Adams, LL, RE LaPorte, KA Matthews, TJ Orchard, and LH Kuller. 1986. Blood pressure determinants in a middle-class black population: The University of Pittsburgh experience. *Prevent Med* 15:232-242.

Adriaanse, H, J vanReek, L Zanbelt, and G Evers. 1991. Nurses' smoking worldwide. A review of 73 surveys of nurses' tobacco consuption in 21 countries in the period of 1959-1988. *Journal of Nursing Studies* 28:361-375.

Agren, G and A Romelsjo. 1992. Mortality and alcohol-related diseases in Sweden during 1971-80 in relation of occupation, marital status and citizenship in 1970. *Scand J Soc Med* 20:134-142.

Aiello, JR and Y Shao. 1993. Electronic performance monitoring and stress: The role of feedback and goal setting. In *Proceedings of the Fifth International Conference On Human-Computer Interaction*, edited by MJ Smith and G Salvendy. New York: Elsevier.

Akselrod, S, D Gordon, JB Madwed, NC Snidman, BC Shannon, and RJ Cohen. 1985. Hemodynamic regulation: Investigation by spectral analysis. *Am J Physiol* 241:H867-H875.

Alexander, F. 1950. *Psychosomatic Medicine: Its Principles and Applications.* New York: WW Norton.

Allan, EA and DJ Steffensmeier. 1989. Youth, underemployment, and property crime: Differential effects of job availability and job quality on juvenile and young arrest rates. *Am Soc Rev* 54:107-123.

Allen, T. 1977. *Managing the Flow of Technology.* Cambridge, Mass: MIT Press.

Amick, BC, III and MJ Smith. 1992. Stress, computer-based work monitoring and measurement systems: A conceptual overview. *Appl Ergon* 23:6-16.

Anderson, EA and AL Mark. 1989. Microneurographic measurement of sympathetic nerve activity in humans. In *Handbook of Cardiovascular Behavioral Medicine*, edited by N Schneiderman, SM Weiss, and PG Kaufmann. New York: Plenum.

Aneshensel, CS, CM Rutter, and PA Lachenbruch. 1991. Social structure, stress and mental health: Competing conceptual and analytic models. *Am Soc Rev* 56:166-178.

Anfuso, D. 1994. Workplace violence. *Pers J* :66-77.

Anthony, JC et al. 1992. Psychoactive drug dependence and abuse: More common in some occupations than others? *J Employ Assist Res* 1:148-186.

Antonovsky, A. 1979. *Health, Stress and Coping: New Perspectives On Mental and Physical Well-Being.* San Francisco: Jossey-Bass.

—. 1987. *Unravelling the Mystery of Health: How People Manage Stress and Stay Well.* San Francisco: Jossey-Bass.

Appels, A. 1990. Mental precursors of myocardial infarction. *Brit J Psychiat* 156:465-471.

Archea, J and BR Connell. 1986. Architecture as an instrument of public health: Mandating practice prior to the conduct of systematic inquiry. In *Proceedings of the Seventeenth Annual Conference of the Environmental Design Research Association*, edited by J Wineman, R Barnes, and C Zimring. Washington, DC: Environmental Design Research Association.

Aschoff, J. 1981. *Handbook of Behavioral Neurobiology.* Vol. 4. New York: Plenum.

Axelrod, J and JD Reisine. 1984. Stress hormones: Their interaction and regulation. *Science* 224:452-459.

Azrin, NH and VB Beasalel. 1982. *Finding a Job.* Berkeley, Calif: Ten Speed Press.

Baba, VV and MJ Harris. 1989. Stress and absence: A cross-cultural perspective. *Research in Personnel and Human Resource Management* Suppl. 1:317-337.

Baker, D, P Schnall, and PA Landsbergis. 1992. Epidemiologic research on the association between occupational stress and cardiovascular disease. In *Behavioral Medicine: An Integrated Approach to Health and Illness*, edited by S Araki. New York: Elsevier Science.

Bandura, A. 1977. Self-efficacy: Toward a unifying theory of behavioral change. *Psychol Rev* 84:191-215.

—. 1986. *Social Foundations of Thought and Action: A Social Cognitive Theory.* Englewood Cliffs: Prentice Hall.

Barnett, BC. 1992. . In *Handbook of Stress*, edited by L Goldberger and S Breznitz. New York: Free Press.

Barnett, RC, L Biener, and GK Baruch. 1987. *Gender and Stress.* New York: Free Press.

Barnett, RC, RT Brennan, and NL Marshall. 1994. Forthcoming. Gender and the relationship between parent-role quality and psychological distress: A study of men and women in dual-earner couples. *J Fam Issues.*

Barnett, RC, NL Marshall, SW Raudenbush, and R Brennan. 1993. Gender and the relationship between job experiences and psychological distress: A study of dual-earner couples. *J Personal Soc Psychol* 65(5):794-806.

Barnett, RC, RT Brennan, SW Raudenbush, and NL Marshall. 1994. Gender, and the relationship between marital role-quality and psychological distress: A study of dual-earner couples. *Psychol Women Q* 18:105-127.

Barnett, RC, SW Raudenbush, RT Brennan, JH Pleck, and NL Marshall. 1995. Change in job and marital experiences and change in psychological distress: A longitudinal study of dual-earner couples. *J Personal Soc Psychol* 69:839-850.

Bartrop, RW, E Luckhurst, L Lazarus, LG Kiloh, and R Penny. 1977. Depressed lymphocyte function after bereavement. *Lancet* 1:834-836.

Bass, BM. 1992. Stress and leadership. In *Decision Making and Leadership*, edited by F Heller. Cambridge: Cambridge Univ. Press.

Bass, C. 1986. Life events and gastrointestinal symptoms. *Gut* 27:123-126.

Baum, A, NE Grunberg, and JE Singer. 1982. The use of psychological and neuroendocrinological measurements in the study of stress. *Health Psychology* (Summer):217-236.

Beck, AT. 1967. *Depression: Clinical, Experimental, and Theoretical Aspects.* New York: Hoeber.

Becker, FD. 1990. *The Total Workplace: Facilities Management and the Elastic Organization.* New York: Van Nostrand Reinhold.

Beehr, TA. 1995. *Psychological Stress in the Workplace.* London, U.K.: Routledge.

Beehr, TA and JE Newman. 1978. Job stress, employee health and organizational effectiveness: A facet analysis, model and literature review. *Pers Psychol* 31:665-669.

Bennis, WG. 1969. Organizational developments and the fate of bureaucracy. In *Readings in Organizational Behavior and Human Performance*, edited by LL Cummings and WEJ Scott. Homewood, Il:Richard D. Irwin, Inc. and The Dorsey Press.

Benowitz, NL. 1990. Clinical pharmacology of caffeine. *Ann Rev Med* 41:277-288.

Bergman, BR. 1986. *The Economic Emergence of Women.* New York: Basic.

Bernstein, A. 1994. Law, culture and harassment. *Univ Penn Law Rev* 142(4):1227-1311.

Berntson, GG, JT Cacioppo, and KS Quigley. 1993. Respiratory sinus arrhythmia: Autonomic origins, physiological mechanisms, and psychophysiological implications. *Psychophysiol* 30:183-196.

Berridge, J, CL Cooper and C Highley. 1997. Employee Assistance Programs and Workplace Counselling. Chisester and New York: Wiley.

Billings, AG and RH Moos. 1981. The role of coping responses and social resources in attenuating the stress of life events. *J Behav Med* 4(2):139-157.

Blanchard, EB, SP Schwarz, J Suls, MA Gerardi, L Scharff, B Green, AE Taylor, C Berreman, and HS Malamood. 1992. Two controlled evaluations of multicomponent psychological treatment of irritable bowel syndrome. *Behav Res Ther* 30:175-189.

Blinder, AS. 1987. *Hard Heads and Soft Hearts: Tough Minded Economics for a Just Society.* Reading, Mass: Addison-Wesley.

Bongers, PM, CR de Winter, MAJ Kompier, and VH Hildebrandt. 1993. Psychosocial factors at work and musculoskeletal disease. *Scand J Work Environ Health* 19:297-312.

Booth-Kewley, S and HS Friedman. 1987. Psychological predictors of heart disease: A quantitative review. *Psychol Bull* 101:343-362.

Brady, JV, RW Porter, DG Conrad, and JW Mason. 1958. Avoidance behavior and the development of gastrointestinal ulcers. *J Exp Anal Behav* 1:69-73.

Brandt, LPA and CV Nielsen. 1992. Job stress and adverse outcome of pregnancy: A causal link or recall bias? *Am J Epidemiol* 135(3).

Breaugh, JA and JP Colihan. 1994. Measuring facets of job ambiguity: Construct validity evidence. *J Appl Psychol* 79:191-202.

Brenner, M. 1976. *Estimating the social costs of economic policy: implications for mental and physical health and criminal aggression.* Report to the Congressional Research Service of the Library of Congress and Joint Economic Committee of Congress. Washington, DC: US GPO.

Brenner, MH. March 1987. Relations of economic change to Swedish health and social well-being, 1950-1980. *Soc Sci Med* :183-195.

Brief, AP, MJ Burke, JM George, BS Robinson, and J Webster. 1988. Should negative affectivity render an unmeasured variable in the study of job stress? *J Appl Psychol* 73:193-198.

Brill, M, S Margulis, and E Konar. 1984. *Using Office Design to Increase Productivity.* Buffalo, NY: Workplace Design and Productivity.

Brisson, C, M Vezina, and A Vinet. 1992. Health problems of women employed in jobs involving psychological and ergonomic stressors: The case of garment workers in Quebec. *Women Health* 18:49-65.

Brockner, J. 1983. Low self-esteem and behavioral plasticity: Some implications. In *Review of Personality and Social Psychology*, edited by L Wheeler and PR Shaver. Beverly Hills, Calif.: Sage.

—. 1988. *Self-Esteem At Work.* Lexington, Mass: Heath.

Bromet, EJ. 1988. Predictive effects of occupational and marital stress on the mental health of a male workforce. *J Organ Behav* 9:1-13.

Bromet, EJ, DK Parkinson, EC Curtis, HC Schulberg, H Blane, LO Dunn, J Phelan, MA Dew, and JE Schwartz. 1990. Epidemiology of depression and alcohol abuse/dependence in a managerial and professional workforce. *J Occup Med* 32(10):989-995.

Buck, V. 1972. *Working Under Pressure.* London: Staples.

Bullard, RD and BH Wright. 1986/1987. Blacks and the environment. *Humboldt J Soc Rel* 14:165-184.

Bureau of National Affairs (BNA). 1991. *Work and Family Today: 100 Key Statistics.* Washington, DC: BNA.

Burge, S, A Hedge, S Wilson, JH Bass, and A Robertson. 1987. Sick building syndrome: A study of 4373 office workers. *Ann Occup Hyg* 31:493-504.

Burke, W and G Salvendy. 1981. *Human Aspects of Working On Repetitive Machine-Paced and Self-Paced Work: A Review and Reappraisal.* West Lafayette, Ind: School of Industrial Engineering, Purdue Univ.

Burns, JM. 1978. *Leadership.* New York: Harper & Row.

Bustelo, C. 1992. The "international sickness" of sexual harassment. *World Press Rev* 39:24.

Cacioppo, JT and LG Tassinary. 1990. *Principles of Psychophysiology*. Cambridge: Cambridge Univ. Press.

Cain, PS and DJ Treiman. 1981. The dictionary of occupational titles as a source of occupational data. *Am Soc Rev* 46:253-278.

Caldwell, DF and CA O'Reilly. 1990. Measuring person-job fit with a profile-comparison process. *J Appl Psychol* 75:648-657.

Caplan, RD, S Cobb, JRPJ French, RV Harrison, and SRJ Pinneau. 1980. *Job Demands and Worker Health*. Ann Arbor, Mich: Institute for Social Research.

Caplan, RD. 1983. Person-environment fit: Past, present, and future. In *Stress Research: Issues for the Eighties*, edited by CL Cooper. New York: Wiley.

Caplan, RD, S Cobb, JRPJ French, R Van Harrison, and R Pinneau. 1975. *Job Demands and Worker Health: Main Effects and Occupational Differences*. Washington, DC: US Department of Health, Education, and Welfare.

Caplan, RD, AD Vinokur, RH Price, and M van Ryn. 1989. Job seeking, reemployment and mental health: A randomized field experiment in coping with job loss. *J Appl Psychol* 74(5):759-769.

Caplin, G. 1969. *Principles of Preventive Psychiatry*. New York: Basic Books.

Cannon, WB. 1914. The emergency function of the adrenal medulla in pain and other emotions. *Am J Physiol* 33:356-372.

—. 1935. Stresses and strains of homeostasis. *Am J Med Sci* 189:1-14.

Canter, D. 1983. The physical context of work. In *The Physical Environment At Work*, edited by DJ Osborne and MM Grunberg. Chichester: Wiley.

Carayon, P. 1993. Effect of electronic performance monitoring on job design and worker stress: A review of the literature and conceptual model. *Hum Factors* 35(3):385-396.

—. 1994. Effects of electronic performance monitoring on job design and worker stress: Results of two studies. *Int J Hum Comput Interact* 6:177-190.

Cassel, JP. 1974. The contribution of the social environment to host resistance. *American Journal of Epidemiology* 104:161-166.

Cassel, J. 1976. The contribution of the social environment to host resistance. *Am J Epidemiol* 104:107-123.

Catalano, R. 1991. The health effects of economic insecurity. *Am J Public Health* 81:1148-1152.

Catalano, R, D Dooley, R Novaco, G Wilson, and R Hough. 1993a-a. Using ECA survey data to examine the effect of job layoffs on violent behavior. *Hosp Community Psychiat* 44:874-879.

Catalano, R, D Dooley, G Wilson, and R Hough. 1993b. Job loss and alcohol abuse: A test using data from the Epidemiologic Catchment Area project. *J Health Soc Behav* 34:215-225.

Chatman, JA. 1991. Matching people and organizations: Selection and socialization in public accounting firms. *Adm Sci Q* 36:459-484.

Christensen, K. 1992. Managing invisible employees: How to meet the telecommuting challenge. *Employ Relat Today* :133-143.

Cobb, S. 1976. Social support as a mediator of life stress. *Psychosocial Medicine* 38:300-314.

Cobb, S and RM Rose. 1973. Hypertension, peptic ulcer, and diabetes in air traffic controllers. *J Am Med Assoc* 224(4):489-492.

Cohen, A. 1991. Career stage as a moderator of the relationships between organizational commitment and its outcomes: A meta-analysis. *J Occup Psychol* 64:253-268.

Cohen, RL and FL Ahearn. 1980. *Handbook for Mental Health Care of Disaster Victims*. Baltimore: The Johns Hopkins University Press.

Cohen, S and SL Syme. 1985. *Social Support and Health*. New York: Academic Books.

Cohen, N, R Ader, N Green, and D Bovbjerg. 1979. Conditioned suppression of thymus-independent antibody response. *Psychosom Med* 41:487-491.

Cohen, S and S Spacapan. 1983. The after effects of anticipating noise exposure. In *Noise As a Public Health Problem*, edited by G Rossi. Milan: Centro Ricerche e Studi Amplifon.

Cole, RJ, RT Loving, and DF Kripke. 1990. Psychiatric aspects of shiftwork. *Occup Med* 5:301-314.

Colligan, MJ. 1985. An apparent case of mass psychogenic illness in an aluminium furniture assembly plant. In *Job Stress and Blue Collar Work*, edited by C Cooper and MJ Smith. London: John Wiley & Sons.

Colligan, MJ, JW Pennebaker, and LR Murphy. 1982. *Mass Psychogenic Illness: A Social Psychological Analysis*. Hillsdale, NJ: Erlbaum.

Colligan, MJ and RR Rosa. 1990. Shiftwork effects on social and family life. *Occup Med* 5:315-322.

Contrada, RJ and DS Krantz. 1988. Stress, reactivity and type A behavior: Current status and future directions. *Ann Behav Med* 10:64-70.

Conway, TL, RR Vickers, HW Ward, and RH Rahe. 1981. Occupational stress and variation in cigarette, coffee and alcohol consumption. *Journal of Health & Social Behaviour* 22:155-165.

Cooper, C. 1996. *Handbook of Stress, Medicine and Health*. Boca Raton, FL: CRC Press.

Cooper, CL and RS Bramwell. 1992. Predictive validity of the strain component of the occupational stress indicator. *Stress Medicine* 8:57-60.

Cooper, C and J Marshall. 1976. Occupational sources of stress: A review of the literature relating to coronary heart disease and mental ill health. *J Occup Psychol* 49:11-28.

Cooper, CL and S Cartwright. 1994. *Mental Health and Stress in the Workplace: A Guide to Employers*. London: HMSO.

Cooper, CL, P Liukkonen, and S Cartwright. 1996. *Stress Prevention in the Workplace: Assessing the Costs and Benefits to Organisations*. Dublin: European Foundation.

Cooper, CL and R Payne. 1988. *Causes, Coping, and Consequences of Stress At Work*. New York: Wiley.

—. 1991. *Personality and Stress: Individual Differences in the Stress Process*. Chichester: Wiley.

Cooper, CL and MJ Smith. 1985. *Job Stress and Blue Collar Work*. New York: Wiley.

Cox, S, T Cox, M Thirlaway, and C MacKay. 1982. Effects of simulated repetitive work on urinary catecholamine excretion. *Ergonomics* 25:1129-1141.

Cox, T and P Leather. 1994. The prevention of violence at work: Application of a cognitive behavioral theory. In *International Review of Industrial and Organizational Psychology*, edited by CL Cooper and IT Robertson. London: Wiley.

Crum, RM, C Mutaner, WW Eaton, and JC Anthony. 1995. Occupational stress and the risk of alcohol abuse and dependence. *Alcohol, Clin Exp Res* 19(3):647-655.

Cummins, R. 1989. Locus of control and social support: Clarifiers of the relationship between job stress and job satisfaction. *J Appl Soc Psychol* 19:772-788.

Cvetanovski, J and SM Jex. 1994. Locus of control of unemployed people and its relationship to psychological and physical health. *Work Stress* 8:60-67.

Csikszentmihalyi, M. 1975. *Beyond Boredom and Anxiety*. San Francisco: Jossey-Bass.

Dainoff, MJ and MH Dainoff. 1986. *People and Productivity*. Toronto: Holt, Reinhart, & Winston of Canada.

Damasio, A. 1994. *Descartes' Error: Emotion, Reason and the Human Brain*. New York: Grosset/Putnam.

Danko, S, P Eshelman, and A Hedge. 1990. A taxonomy of health, safety, and welfare, implications of interior design decisions. *J Interior Des Educ Res* 16:19-30.

Dawis, RV and LH Lofquist. 1984. *A Psychological Theory of Work Adjustment*. Minneapolis, Minnesota: University of Minnesota Press.

The death of corporate loyalty. 1993. *Economist* 3 April, 63-64.

Dement, W. 1969. The biological role of REM sleep. In *Sleep Physiology and Pathology: A Symposium*, edited by A Kales. Philadelphia: JB Lippincott.

Deming, WE. 1993. *The New Economics for Industry, Government, Education*. Cambridge, Mass: MIT Center for Advance Engineering Study.

Dewe, PJ. 1989. Examining the nature of work stress: Individual evaluations of stressful experiences and coping. *Hum Relat* 42:993-1013.

Ditecco, D, G Cwitco, A Arsenault, and M Andre. 1992. Operator stress and monitoring practices. *Appl Ergon* 23(1):29-34.

Dohrenwend, BS and BP Dohrenwend. 1974. *Stressful Life Events: Their Nature and Effects*. New York: Wiley.

Dohrenwend, BS, L Krasnoff, AR Askenasy, and BP Dohrenwend. 1978. Exemplification of a method for scaling life events: The PERI life events scale. *J Health Soc Behav* 19:205-229.

Dooley, D. 1985. Causal inference in the study of social support. In *Social Support and Health*, edited by S Cohen and SL Syme. New York:Academic Books.

Dooley, D, R Catalano, and R Hough. 1992. Unemployment and alcohol disorder in 1910 and 1990: Drift versus social causation. *J Occup Organ Psychol* 65:277-290.

Dooley, D, R Catalano, and G Wilson. 1994. Depression and unemployment: Panel findings from the Epidemiologic Catchment Area study. *Am J Community Psychol* 22:745-765.

Douglas, RB, R Blanks, A Crowther, and G Scott. 1988. A study of stress in West Midlands firemen, using ambulatory electrocardiograms. *Work Stress*: 247-250.

Eaton, WW, JC Anthony, W Mandel, and R Garrison. 1990. Occupations and the prevalence of major depressive disorder. *J Occup Med* 32(11):1079-1087.

Edwards, JR. 1988. The determinants and consequences of coping with stress. In *Causes, Coping and Consequences of Stress At Work*, edited by CL Cooper and R Payne. New York: Wiley.

Edwards, JR and RV Harrison. 1993. Job demands and worker health: A three dimensional reexamination of the relationship between person-environment fit and strain. *J Appl Psychol* 78:628-648.

Elander, J, R West, and D French. 1993. Behavioral correlates of individual differences in road-traffic crash risk: An examination of methods and findings. *Psychol Bull* 113:279-294.

Emmett, EA. 1991. Physical and chemical agents at the workplace. In *Work, Health and Productivity*, edited by GM Green and F Baker. New York:Oxford University Press.

Endresen, IM, B Ellersten, C Endresen, AM Hjelmen, R Matre, and H Ursin. 1991. Stress at work and psychological and immunological parameters in a group of Norwegian female bank employees. *Work Stress* 5:217-227.

Esler, M, G Jennings, and G Lambert. 1989. Measurement of overall and cardiac norepinephrine release into plasma during cognitive challenge. *Psychoneuroendocrinol* 14:477-481.

European Foundation for the Improvement of Living and Working Conditions. 1992. *First European Suvey On the Work Environment 1991-1992*. Luxembourg: Office of the Official Publications of the European Community.

Everly, GS, Jr and RH Feldman. 1985. *Occupational Health Promotion: Health Behavior in the Workplace*. New York: John Wiley & Sons.

Faucett, J and D Rempel. 1994. VDT-related musculoskeletal symptoms: Interactions between work and posture and psychosocial factors. *Am J Ind Med* 26:597-612.

Feigenbaum, AV. 1991. Total quality: An international imperative. In *Maintaining the Total Quality Advantage*, edited by BH Peters and JL Peters. New York: The Conference Board.

Feldman, DC. l976. A contingency theory of socialization. *Adm Sci Q* 21:433-452.

Fenster, L, C Schaefer, A Mathur, RA Hiatt, C Pieper, AE Hubbard, J Von Behren, and S Swan. 1995. Psychological stress in the workplace and spontaneous abortion. *Am J Epidemiol* 142(11).

Ferber, MA, B O'Farrell, and L Allen. 1991. *Work and Family: Policies for a Changing Workforce*. Washington, DC: National Academy Press.

Fernandez, JP. 1981. *Racism and Sexism in Corporate Life*. Lexington, Mass.: Lexington Books.

—. 1990. *The Politics and Reality of Family Care in Corporate America*. Lexington, Mass: Lexington Books.

Fiedler, FE. 1967. *A Theory of Leadership Effectiveness*. New York: McGraw-Hill.

Fielding, JE and KJ Phenow. 1988. Health effects of involuntary smoking. *New Engl J Med* 319:1452-1460.

Fisher, C. l985. Social support and adjustment to work: A longitudinal study. *J Manage* 11:39-53.

Fith-Cozens, J. 1987. Emotional distress in junior house officers. *Brit Med J* 295:533-536.

Fitzgerald, LF and AJ Ormerod. 1993. Breaking silence: The sexual harassment of women in academia and the workplace. In *Psychology of Women*, edited by FL Denmark and MA Paludi. London: Greenwood Press.

Flechter, B. 1988. Occupation, marriage and disease specific mortality concordance. *Soc Sci Med* 27:615-622.

Ford, DL. 1985. Facets of work support and employee work outcomes: An exploratory analysis. *J Manage* 11:5-20.

Fox, AJ and J Levin. 1994. Firing back: The growing threat of workplace homicide. *Ann Am Acad Polit SS* 536:16-30.

Fox, BH. 1995. The role of psychological factors in cancer incidence and prognosis. *Oncology* 9(3):245-253.

—. 1989. Depressive symptoms and risk of cancer. *J Am Med Assoc* 262(9): 1231.

—. 1981. Psychosocial factors and the immune system in human cancer. In *Psychoneuroimmunology*, edited by R Ader. New York: Academic Press.

Frankenhaeuser, M. 1986. A psychobiological framework for research on human stress and coping. In *Dynamics of Stress*, edited by MH Appley and R Trumbull. New York: Plenum.

—. 1989. A biopsychosocial approach to work life issues. *Int J Health Serv* 19:747-758.

—. 1991. The psychophysiology of workload, stress and health: Comparison between the sexes. *Ann Behav Med* 13:197-204.

—. 1993a. Current issues in psychobiological stress research. In *European Views in Psychology - Keynote Lectures*, edited by M Vartiainen. Helsinki: Acta Psychologica Fennica XIII.

—. 1993b. The measurement of the total workload of men and women. In *A Healthier Work Environment - Basic Concepts and Methods of Measurements*, edited by L Levi. Geneva: WHO.

—. 1996. Stress and gender. *Eur Rev, Interdis J Acad Eur* 4.

Frankenhaeuser, M and G Johansson. 1986. Stress at work: Psychobiological and psychosocial aspects. *Int Rev Appl Psychol* 35:287-299.

Frankenhaeuser, M, C Lundberg, and L Forsman. 1980. Dissociation between sympathetic-adrenal and pituitary-adrenal responses to an achievement situation characterized by high controllability: Comparison between Type A and Type B males and females. *Biol Psychol* 10:79-91.

Frankenhaeuser, M, U Lundberg, and MA Chesney. 1991. *Women, Work and Health. Stress and Opportunities*. New York: Plenum.

Frankenhaeuser, M, U Lundberg, M Fredrikson, B Melin, M Tuomisto, A-L Myrsten, M Hedman, B Bergman-Losman, and L Wallin. 1989. Stress on and off the job as related to sex and occupational status in white-collar workers. *J Organ Behav* 10:321-346.

Frankenhaeuser, M and B Gardell. 1976. Underload and overload in working life: Outline of a multidisciplinary approach. *Journal of Human Stress* 2:35-46.

French, JRP and RD Caplan. 1973. Organizational stress and individual strain. In *The Failure of Success*, edited by AJ Marrow. New York: Amacon.

French, JRP, W Rodgers, and S Cobb. 1974. Adjustment as person-environment fit. In *Coping and Adaption*, edited by GV Coelho, DA Hamburg, and JE Adams. New York:Basic Books.

French, WL and CH Bell. 1990. *Organizational Development*. Englewood Cliffs, NJ: Prentice Hall.

French, JRP, RD Caplan, and R van Harrison. 1982. *The Mechanisms of Job Stress and Strain*. New York: Wiley.

Frese, M and D Zapf. 1988. Methodological issues in the study of work stress: Objective vs. subjective measurement of work stress and the question of longitudinal studies. In *Causes, Coping and Consequences of Stress At Work*, edited by CL Cooper and R Payne. New York: Wiley.

Friedman, M, CE Thoresen, JJ Gill, D Ulmer, LII Powell, VA Prince, et al. 1986. Alteration of type A behavior and its effect on cardiac recurrences in post myocardial infarction patients; summary results of the Recurrent Coronary Prevention Project. *Am Heart J* 112:653-665.

Fryer, D and R Payne. 1986. Being unemployed: A review of the literature on the psychological experience of unemployment. In *International Review of Industrial Organizational Psychology*, edited by CL Cooper and I Robertson. Chichester: Wiley.

Funk, SC and BK Houston. 1987. A critical analysis of the hardiness scales' validity and utility. *J Personal Soc Psychol* 53:572-578.

Fusilier, MR, DC Ganster, and BT Mays. 1987. Effects of social support, role stress, and locus of control on health. *J Manage* 13:517-528.

Galinsky, E, JT Bond, and DE Friedman. 1993. *Highlights: The National Study of the Changing Workforce*. New York: Families and Work Institute.

Gamble, GO and MT Matteson. 1992. Type A behavior, job satisfaction, and stress among Black professionals. *Psychol Rep* 70:43-50.

Ganster, DC and MR Fusilier. 1989. Control in the workplace. In *International Review of Industrial and Organizational Psychology*, edited by C Cooper and I Robertson. Chichester, U.K.:Wiley.

Ganster, DC. 1989. Worker control and well-being: A review of research in the workplace. In *Job Control and Worker Health*, edited by SL Sauter, JJ Hurrell, and CL Cooper. New York: Wiley.

Ganster, DC and J Schaubroeck. 1991a. Role stress and worker health: An extension of the plasticity hypothesis of self-esteem. *J Soc Behav Personal* 6:349-360.

—. 1991b. Work stress and employee health. *J Manage* 17:235-271.

Ganster, DC, BT Mayes, WE Sime, and GD Tharp. 1982. Managing occupational stress: A field experiment. *J Appl Psychol* 67:533-542.

Gardell, B. 1981. Psychosocial aspects of industrial production methods. In *Society, Stress and Disease*, edited by L Levi. Oxford: OUP.

Garrison, R and WW Eaton. 1992. Secretaries, depression and absenteeism. *Women Health* 18:53-76.

Gillin, JC and WF Byerley. 1990. The diagnosis and management of insomnia. *New England Journal of Medicine* 322:239-248.

Glaser, R, JK Kiecolt-Glaser, RH Bonneau, W Malarkey, S Kennedy, and J Hughes. 1992. Stress induced modulation of the immune response to recombinant hepatitts B vaccine. *Psychosom Med* 54:22-29.

Goldberg, E et al. 1985. Depressive symptoms, social networks and social support of elderly women. *American Journal of Epidemiology* :448-456.

Goldberger, L and S Breznitz. 1982. *Handbook of Stress*. New York: Free Press.

Goldstein, I, LD Jamner, and D Shapiro. 1992. Ambulatory blood pressure and heart rate in healthy male paramedics during a work day and a non-work day. *Health Psychol* 11:48-54.

Golemblewski, RT. 1982. Organizational development (OD) interventions: Changing interaction, structures, and policies. In *Job Stress and Burnout Research, Theory, and Intervention Perspectives*, edited by WE Paine. Beverly Hills:Sage Publications.

Goleman, D. 1995. *Emotional Intelligence*. New York: Bantam Books.

Goodrich, R. 1986. The perceived office: The office environment as experienced by its users. In *Behavioral Issues in Office Design*, edited by JD Wineman. New York: Van Nostrand Reinhold.

Gorman, DM. 1994. Alcohol misuse and the predisposing environment. *British Medical Bulletin* :36-49.

Gottlieb, BH. 1983. *Social Support Strategies*. Beverly Hills: Sage.

Gough, H and A Heilbrun. 1965. *The Adjective Check List Manual*. Palo Alto, Calif: Consulting Psychologists Press.

Gowler, D and K Legge. 1975. Stress and external relationships: The 'hidden' contract. In *Managerial Stress*, edited by D Gowler and K Legge. London: Gower.

Grandjean, E. 1968. Fatigue: Its physiological and psychological significance. *Ergonomics* 11(5):427-436.

—. 1986. *Fitting the Task to the Man: An Ergonomic Approach*. : Taylor and Francis.

—. 1987. *Ergonomics in Computerized Offices*. London: Taylor & Francis.

Greenglass, ER. 1993. The contribution of social support to coping strategies. *Appl Psychol Intern Rev* 42:323-340.

Greenhalgh, L and Z Rosenblatt. 1984. Job insecurity: Toward conceptual clarity. *Acad Manage Rev* (July):438-448.

Guendelman, S and MJ Silberg. 1993. The health consequences of maquiladora work: Women on the US-Mexican border. *Am J Public Health* 83:37-44.

Guidotti, TL. 1992. Human factors in firefighting: Ergonomic-, cardiopulmonary-, and psychogenic stress- related issues. *Int Arch Occup Environ Health* 64:1-12.

Gutek, B. 1985. *Sex and the Workplace*. San Francisco: Jossey-Bass.

Gutierres, SE, D Saenz, and BL Green. 1994. Job stress and health outcomes among Anglo and Hispanic employees: A test of the person-environment fit model. In *Job Stress in a Changing Workforce*, edited by GP Keita and JJ Hurrell. Washington, DC: American Psychological Association.

Hackman, JR. 1992. Group influences on individuals in organizations. In *Handbook of Industrial and Organizational Psychology*, edited by MD Dunnette and LM Hough. Palo Alto, Calif: Consulting Psychologists' Press.

Hackman, JR and EE Lawler. 1971. Employee reactions to job characteristics. *J Appl Psychol* 55:259-286.

Hackman, JR and GR Oldham. 1975. The job diagnostic survey. *J Appl Psychol* 60:159-170.

—. 1980. *Work Redesign*. Reading, Mass: Addison-Wesley.

Hales, TR, SL Sauter, MR Peterson, LJ Fine, V Putz-Anderson, LR Schleifer, TT Ochs, and BP Bernard. 1994. Musculoskeletal disorders among visual display terminal users in a telecommunication company. *Ergonomics* 37(10):1603-1621.

Hahn, ME. 1966. *California Life Goals Evaluation Schedule*. Palo Alto, CA: Western Psychological Services.

Hall, DT. 1990. *Telecommuting and the Management of Work-Home Boundaries. Working Paper No. 90-05*. Boston: Boston Univ. School of Management.

Hall, E. 1991. Gender, work control and stress: A theoretical discussion and an empirical test. In *The Psychosocial Work Environment: Work Organization; Democratization and Health*, edited by JV Johnson and G Johansson. Amityville, NY: Baywook.

—. 1992. Double exposure: The combined impact of the home and work environments on psychosomatic strain in Swedish men and women. *Int J Health Serv* 22:239-260.

Hall, RB. 1969. Intraorganizational structural variation: Application of the bureaucratic model. In *Readings in Organizational Behavior and Human Performance*, edited by LL Cummings and WEJ Scott. Homewood, Il:Richard D. Irwin, Inc. and the Dorsey Press.

Hamilton, LV, CL Broman, WS Hoffman, and D Brenner. 1990. Hard times and vulnerable people: Initial effects of plant closing on autoworkers' mental health. *J Health Soc Behav* 31:123-140.

Harford, TC, DA Parker, BF Grant, and DA Dawson. 1992. Alcohol use and dependence among employed men and women in the United States in 1988. *Alcohol, Clin Exp Res* 16:146-148.

Harrison, RV. 1978. Person-environment fit and job stress. In *Stress At Work*, edited by CL Cooper and R Payne. New York: Wiley.

Hedge, A. 1986. Open vs. enclosed workspaces: The impact of design on employees' reactions to their offices. In *Behavioral Issues in Office Design*, edited by JD Wineman. New York: Van Nostrand Reinhold.

—. 1991. Design innovations in office environments. In *Design Intervention: Toward a More Humane Architecture*, edited by WFE Presiser, JC Vischer, and ET White. New York: Van Nostrand Reinhold.

Heilpern, J. 1989. Are American companies 'hostile' to quality improvement? *Quality Exec* (November).

Henderson, S, P Duncan-Jones, and G Byrne. 1980. Measuring social relationships. The interview schedule for social interaction. *Psychol Med* 10:723-734.

Henry, JP and PM Stephens. 1977. *Stress, Health, and the Social Environment. A Sociobiologic Approach to Medicine*. New York: Springer-Verlag.

Herzberg, F, B Mausner, and BB Snyderman. 1959. *The Motivation to Work*. New York: Wiley.

Hill, S. 1991. Why quality circles failed but total quality management might succeed. *Br J Ind Relat* (4 December):551-568.

Hirsh, BJ. 1980. Natural support systems and coping with major life changes. *Am J Comm Psych* 8:159-171.

Hirsch, PM. 1987. *Pack Your Own Parachute*. Reading, Mass: Addison-Wesley.

Hirschhorn, L. 1991. Stresses and patterns of adjustment in the postindustrial factory. In *Work, Health and Productivity*, edited by GM Green and F Baker. New York:Oxford University Press.

Hirshhorn, L. 1990. Leaders and followers in the postindustrial age: A psychodynamic view. *J Appl Behav Sci* 26:529-542.

—. 1984. *Beyond Mechanization*. Cambridge, Mass: MIT Press.

Holmes, TH and HR Richard. 1967. The social readjustment rating scale. *J Psychosomat Res* 11:213-218.

Holt, RR. 1992. Occupational stress. In *Handbook of Stress*, edited by L Goldberger and S Breznitz. New York: Free Press.

Holtmann, G, R Kreibel, and MV Singer. 1990. Mental stress and gastric acid secretion: Do personality traits influence the response? *Digest Dis Sci* 35:998-1007.

House, J. 1981. *Work Stress and Social Support*. Reading, Mass.: Addison-Wesley.

Houtman, I and M Kompler. 1995. Risk factors and occupational risk groups for work stress in the Netherlands. In *Organizational Risk Factors for Job Stress*, edited by S Sauter and L Murphy. Washington:American psychological Association.

Houston, B and W Hodges. 1970. Situational denial and performance under stress. *J Personal Soc Psychol* 16:726-730.

Howard, R. 1990. Values make the company. *Harvard Business Rev* (September-October):133-144.

Hudiberg, JJ. 1991. *Winning With Quality - The FPL Story*. White Plains, NY: Quality Resources.

Hull, JG, RR Van Treuren, and S Virnelli. 1987. Hardiness and health: A critique and alternative approach. *J Personal Soc Psychol* 53:518-530.

Hurrell, JJ Jr, MA McLaney, and LR Murphy. 1990. The middle years: Career stage differences. *Prev Hum Serv* 8:179-203.

Hurrell, JJ Jr and LR Murphy. 1992. Locus of control, job demands, and worker health. In *Individual Differences, Personality, and Stress*, edited by CL Cooper and R Payne. Chichester: John Wiley & Sons.

Hurrell JJ Jr and K Lindström. 1992. Comparison of job demands, control and psychosomatic complaints at different career stages of managers in Finland and the United States. *Scand J Work Environ Health* 18 Suppl. 2:11-13.

Ihman, A and G Bohlin. 1989. The role of controllability in cardiovascular activation and cardiovascular disease: Help or hindrance? In *Stress, Personal Control and Health*, edited by A Steptoe and A Appels. Chichester: Wiley.

Ilgen, DR. 1990. Health issues at work. *American Psychologist* 45:273-283.

Imai, M. 1986. *Kaizen: The Key to Japan's Competitive Success*. New York: McGraw-Hill.

International Labour Organization (ILO). 1975. *Making Work More Human. Report of the Director General to the International Labour Conference*. Geneva: ILO.

—. 1986. *Introduction to Work Study*. Geneva: ILO.

Ishikawa, K. 1985. *What Is Total Quality Control? The Japanese Way*. Englewood Cliffs, NJ: Prentice Hall.

Israel, BA and TC Antonucci. 1987. Social network characteristics and psychological well-being: A replication and extension. *Health Educ Q* 14(4):461-481.

Jackson, DN. 1974. *Personality Research Form Manual*. New York: Research Psychologists Press.

Jackson, SE and RS Schuler. 1985. A meta-analysis and conceptual critique of research on role ambiguity and role conflict in work settings. *Organ Behav Hum Decision Proc* 36:16-78.

James, CR and CM Ames. 1993. Recent developments in alcoholism: The workplace. *Recent Develop Alcohol* 11:123-146.

James, K. 1994. Social identity, work stress and minority worker's health. In *Job Stress in a Changing Workforce*, edited by GP Keita and JJ Hurrell. Washington, DC: APA.

Jenkins, CD. 1979. The coronary-prone personality. In *Psychological Aspects of Myocardial Infarction and Coronary Care*, edited by WD Gentry and RB Williams. St.Louis: Mosby.

Jenkins, R and N Coney. 1992. *Prevention of Mental Ill Health At Work. A Conference*. London: HMSO.

Jennings, R, C Cox, and CL Cooper. 1994. *Business Elites: The Psychology of Entrepreneurs and Intrapreneurs*. London: Routledge.

Johansson, G and G Aronsson. 1984. Stress reactions in computerized administrative work. *J Occup Behav* 15:159-181.

Johnson, JV. 1986. *The impact of workplace social support, job demands and work control upon cardiovascular disease in sweden*. PhD Dissertation, Johns Hopkins University.

Johnson, JV and EM Hall. 1988. Job strain, workplace social support and cardiovascular disease: A cross-sectional study of a random sample of Swedish working population. *Am J Public Health* 78:1336-1342.

—. 1994. Social support in the work environment and cardiovascular disease. In *Social Support and Cardiovascular Disease*, edited by S Shumaker and S Czajkowski. New York: Plenum Press.

Johnson, JV and G Johansson. 1991. *The Psychosocial Work Environment: Work Organization, Democratization and Health*. Amityville, NY: Baywood.

Johnson, JV, W Stewart, EM Hall, P Fredlund, and T Theorell. 1996. Long-term psychosocial work environment and cardiovascular mortality among Swedish men. *Am J Public Health* 86(3):324-331.

Juran, JM. 1988. *Juran On Planning for Quality*. New York: Free Press.

Justice, A. 1985. Review of the effects of stress on cancer in laboratory animals: The importance of time of stress application and type of tumor. *Psychol Bull* 98(1):108-138.

Kadushin, A. 1976. Men in a woman's profession. *Social Work* 21:440-447.

Kagan, A and L Levi. 1971. Adaptation of the psychosocial environment to man's abilities and needs. In *Society, Stress and Disease*, edited by L Levi. New York:Oxford University Press.

Kahn, RL. 1991. The forms of women's work. In *Women, Work and Health. Stress and Opportunities*, edited by M Frankenhaeuser, U Lundberg, and MA Chesney. New York: Plenum.

Kahn, RL and P Byosiere. 1992. Stress in organizations. In *Handbook of Industrial and Organizational Psychology*, edited by MD Dunnette and LM Hough. Palo Alto, CA:Consulting Psychology Press.

Kahn, RL, DM Wolfe, RP Quinn, JD Snoek, and RA Rosenthal. 1964. *Organisational Stress: Studies in Role Conflict and Ambiguity*. Chichester: Wiley.

Kaplan, GA et al. 1991. Psychosocial factors and the natural history of physical activity. *Am J Prev Medicine* 7:12-17.

Kaplan, R and S Kaplan. 1989. *The Experience of Nature: A Psychological Perspective*. New York: Cambridge Univ. Press.

Karasek, RA. 1976. The impact of the work environment on life outside the job. Doctoral Dissertation, Massachusetts Institute of Technology, Cambridge, Mass.

—. 1979. Job demands, job decision latitude, and mental strain: Implications for job redesign. *Adm Sci Q* 24:285-308.

—. 1985. *The Job Content Questionnaire (JCQ) and User's Guide*. Lowell, Mass: JCQ Center, Department of Work Environment, Univ. of Massachusetts Lowell.

—. 1990. Lower health risk with increased job control among white collar workers. *J Organ Behav* 11:171-185.

Karasek, R and T Theorell. 1990. *Healthy Work, Stress, Productivity and the Reconstruction of Working Life*. New York: Basic Books.

Kasl, SV. 1989. An epidemiological perspective on the role of control in health. In *Job Control and Worker Health*, edited by SL Sauter, JJ Hurrell Jr, and CL Cooper. Chichester: Wiley.

Kauppinen-Toropainen, K and JE Gruber. 1993. Antecedants and outcomes of woman-unfriendly experiences: A study of Scandanavian, former Soviet and American women. *Psychol Women Q* 17(4):431-456.

Kawakami, N, T Haratani, T Hemmi, and S Araki. 1992. Prevalence and demographic correlates of alcohol-related problems in Japanese employees. *Social Psych Psychiatric Epidemiol* 27:198-202.

—. 1993. Relations of work stress to alcohol use and drinking problems in male and female employees of a computer factory in Japan. *Environ Res* 62:314-324.

Keita, GP and SL Sauter. 1992. *Work and Well Being: An Agenda for the 1990s*. Washington, DC: APA.

Kelly, M and CL Cooper. 1981. Stress among blue collar workers: A case study of the steel industry. *Employee Relations* 3:6-9.

Kerckhoff, A and K Back. 1968. *The June Bug*. New York: Appelton-Century Croft.

Kessler, RC, JS House, and JB Turner. 1987. Unemployment and health in a community sample. *J Health Soc Behav* 28:51-59.

Kessler, RC, JB Turner, and JS House. 1988. The effects of unemployment on health in a community survey: Main, modifying and mediating effects. *J Soc Issues* 44(4):69-86.

—. 1989. Unemployment, reemployment, and emotional functioning in a community sample. *Am Soc Rev* 54:648-657.

Kleiber, D and D Enzmann. 1990. *Burnout: 15 Years of Research: An International Bibliography*. Gottingen: Hogrefe.

Klitzman, S and JM Stellman. 1989. The impact of physical environment on the psychological well-being of office workers. *Soc Sci Med* 29:733-742.

Knauth, P and J Rutenfranz. 1976. Experimental shift work studies of permanent night, and rapidly rotating, shift systems. I. Circadian rhythm of body temperature and re-entrainment at shift change. *Int Arch Occup Environ Health* 37:125-137.

—. 1982. Development of criteria for the design of shiftwork systems. *J Hum Ergol* 11 Shiftwork: Its Practice and Improvement: 337-367.

Knauth, P, E Kiesswetter, W Ottmann, MJ Karvonen, and J Rutenfranz. 1983. Time-budget studies of policemen in weekly or swiftly rotating shift systems. *Appl Ergon* 14(4):247-252.

Kobasa, SC. 1979. Stressful life events, personality and health: An inquiry into hardiness. *J Personal Soc Psychol* 37:1-11.

—. 1982. The hardy personality: Toward a social psychology of stress and health. In *Social Psychology of Health and Illness*, edited by G Sanders and J Suls. Hillsdale, NJ: Erlbaum.

Kobasa, SC, SR Maddi, and S Kahn. 1982. Hardiness and health: A prospective study. *J Personal Soc Psychol* 42:168-177.

Kofoed, L, MJ Friedman, and P Peck. 1993. Alcoholism and drug abuse in patients with PTSD. *Psychiatry* 64:151-171.

Kogi, K. 1991. Job content and working time: The scope for joint change. *Ergonomics* 34(6):757-773.

Kohn, M and C Schooler. 1973. Occupational experience and psychological functioning: An assessment of reciprocal effects. *Am Soc Rev* 38:97-118.

Kohn, ML, A Naoi, V Schoenbach, C Schooler, et al. 1990. Position in the class structure and psychological functioning in the United States, Japan, and Poland. *Am J Sociol* 95(4):964-1008.

Kompier, M and L Levi. 1994. *Stress At Work: Causes, Effects, and Prevention. A Guide for Small and Medium Sized Enterprises*. Dublin: European Foundation.

Kornhauser, A. 1965. *The Mental Health of the Industrial Worker*. New York: Wiley.

Komitzer, M, F Kittel, M Dramaix, and G de Backer. 1982. Job stress and coronary heart disease. *Adv Cardiol* 19:56-61.

Koss, MP, LA Goodman, A Browne, LF Fitzgerald, GP Keita, and NF Russo. 1994. *No Safe Haven*. Washington, DC: APA Press.

Koulack, D and M Nesca. 1992. Sleep parameters of Type A and B scoring college students. *Perceptual and Motor Skills* 74:723-726.

Kozlowski, SWJ, GT Chao, EM Smith, and J Hedlund. 1993. Organizational downsizing: Strategies, interventions, and research implications. In *International Review of Industrial and Organizational Psychology*, edited by CL Cooper and I Robertson. Chichester: Wiley.

Kristensen, TS. 1989. Cardiovascular diseases and the work environment. A critical review of the epidemiologic literature on nonchemical factors. *Scand J Work Environ Health* 15:165-179.

—. 1991. Sickness absence and work strain among Danish slaughterhouse workers. An analysis of absence from work regarded as coping behaviour. *Social Science and Medicine* 32:15-27.

—. 1995. The Demand-Control-Support model: Methodological challenges for future research. *Stress Medicine* 11:17-26.

Krueger, GP. 1989. Sustained work, fatigue, sleep loss and performance: A review of the issues. *Work and Stress* 3:129-141.

Kuhnert, KW. 1991. Job security, health, and the intrinsic and extrinsic characteristics of work. *Group Organ Stud* :178-192.

Kuhnert, KW, RR Sims, and MA Lahey. 1989. The relationship between job security and employee health. *Group Organ Stud* (August):399-410.

Kumar, D and DL Wingate. 1985. The irritable bowel syndrome. *Lancet* ii:973-977.

Lamb, ME, KJ Sternberg, CP Hwang, and AG Broberg. 1992. *Child Care in Context: Cross-Cultural Perspectives*. Hillsdale, NJ: Earlbaum.

Landsbergis, PA, PL Schnall, D Deitz, R Friedman, and T Pickering. 1992. The patterning of psychological attributes and distress by "job strain" and social support in a sample of working men. *J Behav Med* 15(4):379-405.

Landsbergis, PA, SJ Schurman, BA Israel, PL Schnall, MK Hugentobler, J Cahill, and D Baker. 1993. Job stress and heart disease: Evidence and strategies for prevention. *New Solutions* (Summer):42-58.

Larson, JRJ and C Callahan. 1990. Performance monitoring: How does it affect work productivity. *J Appl Psychol* 75:530-538.

Last, LR, RWE Peterson, J Rappaport, and CA Webb. 1995. Creating opportunities for displaced workers: Center for Commercial Competitiveness. In *Employees, Careers, and Job Creation: Developing Growth-Oriented Human Resource Strategies and Programs*, edited by M London. San Francisco: Jossey-Bass.

Laviana, JE. 1985. *Assessing the Impact of Plants in the Simulated Office Environment: A Human Factors Approach*. Manhattan, Kans: Department of Horticulture, Kansas State Univ.

Lazarus, RS. 1966. *Psychological Stress and Coping Process*. New York: McGraw-Hill.

Lazarus, RS and S Folkman. 1984. *Stress, Appraisal, and Coping*. New York: Springer.

Lee, P. 1983. *The Complete Guide to Job Sharing*. New York: Walker & Co.

Leibson, B. 1990. Corporate child care: "Junior Execs" on the job. *Faculty Design Manage* :32-37.

Leigh, JP and HM Waldon. 1991. Unemployment and highway fatalities. *J Health Policy* 16:135-156.

Leino, PI and V Hänninen. 1995. Psychosocial factors at work in relation to back and limb disorders. *Scand J Work Environ Health* 21:134-142.

Levi, L. 1972. *Stress and Distress in Response to Psychosocial Stimuli*. New York: Pergamon Press.

—. 1981. *Society, Stress and Disease*. Vol. 4: Working Life. Oxford: Oxford Univ Press.

—. 1992. Psychosocial, occupational, environmental, and health concepts: Research results and applications. In *Work and Well-Being: An Agenda for the 1990s*, edited by GP Keita and SL Sauter. Washington, DC: APA.

Levi, L, M Frankenhaeuser, and B Gardell. 1986. The characteristics of the workplace and the nature of its social demands. In *Occupational Stress and Performance At Work*, edited by S Wolf and AJ Finestone. Littleton, Mass: PSG.

Levi, L and P Lunde-Jensen. 1996. *Socio-Economic Costs of Work Stress in Two EU Member States. A Model for Assessing the Costs of Stressors At National Level*. Dublin: European Foundation.

Levine, EL. 1983. *Everything You Always Wanted to Know About Job Analysis*. Tampa: Mariner.

Levinson, DJ. 1986. A conception of adult development. *American Psychologist* 41:3-13.

Levinson, H. 1978. The abrasive personality. *Harvard Bus Rev* 56:86-94.

Levy, BS and DH Wegman. 1988. *Occupational Health: Recognizing and Preventing Work-Related Disease*. Boston: Little, Brown & Co.

Lewin, K, R Lippitt, and RK White. 1939. Patterns of aggressive behaviour in experimentally created social climates. *J Soc Psychol* 10:271-299.

Lewis, S, DN Izraeli, and H Hootsmans. 1992. *Dual-Earner Families: International Perspectives*. London: Sage.

Liberatos, P, BG Link, and J Kelsey. 1988. The measurement of social class in epidemiology. *Epidemiol Rev* 10:87-121.

Liem, R and JH Liem. 1988. The psychological effects of unemployment on workers and their families. *J Soc Issues* 44:87-105.

Light, KC, JR Turner, and AL Hinderliter. 1992. Job strain and ambulatory work blood pressure in healthy young men and women. *Hypertension* 20:214-218.

Lim, SY. 1994. *An integrated approach to upper extremity musculoskeletal discomfort in the office work environment: The role of psychosocial work factors, psychological stress, and ergonomic risk factors*. Ph.D. Dissertation, University of Wisconsin-Madison.

Lim, SY and P Carayon. 1994. *Relationship between physical and psychosocial work factors and upper extremity symptoms in a group of office workers*. Proceedings of the 12th Triennial Congress of the International Ergonomic Association. 6:132-134.

Lindeman, E. 1944. Symptomatology and management of acute grief. *American Journal of Psychiatry* 101:141-148.

Lindenberg, CS, HK Reiskin, and SC Gendrop. 1994. The social system model of substance abuse among childbearing age women: A review of the literature. *Journal of Drug Education* 24:253-268.

Lindström, K and JJ Hurrell Jr. 1992. Coping with job stress by managers at different career stages in Finland and the United States. *Scand J Work Environ Health* 18 Suppl. 2:14-17.

Lindström, K, J Kaihilahti and I Torstila. 1988. *Ikäkausittaiset Terveystarkastukset Ja Työn Muutos Vakuutus- Ja Pankkialalla (in Finnish With English Summary)*. Espoo: The Finnish Work Environment Fund.

Link, B et al. 1986. Socio-economic status and schizophrenia: Noisome occupational characteristics as a risk factor. *Am Soc Rev* 51:242-258.

—. 1993. Socioeconomic status and depression: The role of occupations involving direction, control and planning. *Am J Sociol* 6:1351-1387.

Locke, EA and DM Schweiger. 1979. Participation in decision-making: One more look. *Res Organ Behav* 1:265-339.

London, M. 1995. *Employees, Careers, and Job Creation: Developing Growth-Oriented Human Resource Strategies and Programs*. San Francisco: Jossey-Bass.

Louis, MR. 1980. Surprise and sense-making: What newcomers experience in entering unfamiliar organizational settings. *Adm Sci Q* 25:226-251.

Lowe, GS and HC Northcott. 1988. The impact of working conditions, social roles, and personal characteristics on gender differences in distress. *Work Occup* 15:55-77.

Lundberg, O. 1991. Causal explanations for class inequality in health-an empirical analysis. *Soc Sci Med* 32:385-393.

Lundberg, U, M Granqvist, T Hansson, M Magnusson, and L Wallin. 1989. Psychological and phsiological stress responses during repetitive work at an assembly line. *Work Stress* 3:143-153.

Maher, EL. 1982. Anomic aspects of recovery from cancer. *Social Science and Medicine* 16:907-912.

MacKinnon, CA. 1978. *Sexual Harassment of Working Women: A Case of Sex Discrimination.* New Haven, Conn: Yale Univ. Press.

Maddi, SR, SC Kobasa, and MC Hoover. 1979. An alienation test. *Journal of Humanistic Psychology* 19:73-76.

Maddi, SR and SC Kobasa. 1984. *The Hardy Executive: Health Under Stress.* Homewood, Il: Dow-Jones Irwin.

Maddi, SR. 1987. Hardiness training at Illinois Bell Telephone. In *Health Promotion Evaluation,* edited by JP Opatz. Stevens Point, Wisc: National Wellness Insitutue.

—. 1990. Issues and interventions in stress mastery. In *Personality and Disease,* edited by HS Friedman. New York: Wiley.

Mandell, W et al. 1992. Alcoholism and occupations: A review and analysis of 104 occupations. *Alcohol, Clin Exp Res* 16:734-746.

Mangione, TW and RP Quinn. 1975. Job satisfaction, counterproductive behavior, and drug use at work. *Journal of Applied Psychology* 60:114-116.

Mann, N. 1989. *The Keys to Excellence. The Story of Deming Philosophy.* Los Angeles: Prestwick.

Mantell, M and S Albrecht. 1994. *Ticking Bombs: Defusing Violence in the Workplace.* New York: Irwin Professional.

Marans, RW and X Yan. 1989. Lighting quality and environmental satisfaction in open and enclosed offices. *J Architect Plan Res* 6:118-131.

Margolis, B, W Kroes, and R Quinn. 1974. Job stress and unlisted occupational hazard. *J Occup Med* 16:659-661.

Marino, KE and SE White. 1985. Departmental structure, locus of control, and job stress: The effect of a moderator. *Journal of Applied Psychology* 70:782-784.

Marmot, M. 1976. Acculturation and coronary heart disease in Japanese Americans. In *The Contribution of the Social Environment to Host Resistance,* edited by JP Cassel.

Marmot, M and T Theorell. 1988. Social class and cardiovascular disease: The contribution of work. *Int J Health Serv* 18:659-674.

Marshall, NL and RC Barnett. 1991. Race, class and multiple roles strains and gains among women employed in the service sector. *Women Health* 17:1-19.

Martin, DD and RL Shell. 1986. *Management of Professionals.* New York: Marcel Dekker.

Martin, EV. 1987. Worker stress: A practitioner's perspective. In *Stress Management in Work Setting,* edited by LR Murphy and TF Schoenborn. Cincinnati, Ohio: NIOSH.

Maslach, C. 1993. Burnout: A multidimentional perspective. In *Professional Burnout,* edited by WB Schaufeli, C Maslach and T Marek. Washington, DC: Taylor and Francis.

Maslach, C and SE Jackson. 1981/1986. *The Maslach Burnout Inventory.* Palo Alto, Calif: Consulting Psychologists.

Maslow, AH. 1954. *Motivation and Personality.* New York: Harper.

Matteson, MT and JM Ivancevich. 1987. *Controlling Work Stress.* San Francisco: Jossey-Bass.

Mattiason, I, F Lindgarden, JA Nilsson, and T Theorell. 1990. Threat of unemployment and cardiovascular risk factors: Longitudinal study of quality of sleep and serum cholesterol concentrations in men threatened with redundancy. *British Medical Journal* 301:461-466.

Mattis, MC. 1990. New forms of flexible work arrangements for managers and professionals: Myths and realities. *Hum Resour Plan* 13(2):133-146.

McGrath, A, N Reid, and J Boore. 1989. Occupational stress in nursing. *Int J Nursing Stud* 26(4):343-358.

McGrath, JE. 1976. Stress and behavior in organizations. In *Handbook of Industrial and Organizational Psychology,* edited by MD Dunnette. Chicago: Rand McNally.

McKee, GH, SE Markham, and DK Scott. 1992. Job stress and employee withdrawal from work. In *Stress & Well-Being At Work,* edited by JC Quick, LR Murphy, and JJ Hurrel. Washington, D.C.: APA.

McLaney, MA and JJ Hurrell Jr. 1988. Control, stress and job satisfaction. *Work Stress* 2:217-224.

McLean, LA. 1979. *Work Stress.* Boston: Addison-Wesley.

Meisner, M. 1971. The long arm of the job. *Industrial Relations* :239-260.

Meyer, BD. 1995. Lessons from the US unemployment insurance experiments. *J Econ Lit* 33:91-131.

Meyerson, D. 1990. Uncovering socially undesirable emotions: Experience of ambiguity in organizations. *Am Behav Sci* 33:296-307.

Michaels, D and SR Zoloth. 1991. Mortality among urban bus drivers. *Int J Epidemiol* 20(2):399-404.

Michelson, W. 1985. *From Sun to Sun: Maternal Obligations and Community Structure in the Lives of Employed Women and Their Families.* Totowa, NJ: Rowman & Allanheld.

Miller, KI and PR Monge. 1986. Participation, satisfaction, and productivity: A meta-analytic review. *Acad Manage J* 29:727-753.

Miller, LS and S Kelman. 1992. Estimates of the loss of individual productivity from alcohol and drug abuse and from mental illness. In *Economics and Mental Health,* edited by RG Frank and MG Manning. Baltimore: Johns Hopkins Univ. Press.

Miller, S. 1979. Controllability and human stress: Method, evidence and theory. *Behav Res Ther* 17:287-304.

Ministry of Labour. 1987. *The Swedish Work Environment Act (With Amendments) and the Swedish Work Environment Ordinance (With Amendments).* Stockholm: Ministry of Labour.

Mino, Y, T Tsuda, A Babazona, H Aoyama, S Inoue, H Sato, and H Ohara. 1993. Depressive states in workers using computers. *Environmental Research* 63(1):54-59.

Misumi, J. 1985. *The Behavioural Science of Leadership Concept: Third Leadership Symposium.* Carbondale, Ill: Souther Illinois Univ.

Moleski, WH and JT Lang. 1986. Organizational goals and human needs in office planning. In *Behavioral Issues in Office Design,* edited by J Wineman. New York: Van Nostrand Rinehold.

Monk, TH and S Folkard. 1992. *Making Shift Work Tolerable.* London: Taylor & Francis.

Monk, T and D Tepas. 1985. Shift work. In *Job Stress and Blue Collar Work,* edited by C Cooper and MJ Smith. London: John Wiley & Sons.

Moon, S and SL Sauter. 1996. *Psychosocial Factors and Musculoskeletal Disorders in Office Work.* : Taylor and Francis,Ltd.

Moos, RH. 1986. Work as a human context. In *Psychology and Work: Productivity, Change, and Employment,* edited by MS Pallak and R Perloff. Washington, DC: APA.

Moos, R and A Billings. 1982. Conceptualizing and measuring coping resources and process. In *Handbook of*

Stress: Theoretical and Clinical Aspects, edited by L Goldberger and S Breznitz. New York: Free Press.

Morrison, EW. l993. Longitudinal study of the effects of information seeking on newcomer socialization. *J Appl Psychol* 78:173-183.

Morrow, PC and JC McElroy. 1987. Work commitment and job satisfaction over three career stages. *J Vocationl Behav* 30:330-346.

Mossholder, KW, AG Bedeian, and AA Armenakis. 1981. Role perceptions, satisfaction, and performance: Moderating effects of self-esteem and organizational level. *Organ Behav Hum Perform* 28:224-234.

—. 1982. Group process-work outcome relationships: A note on the moderating impact of self-esteem. *Acad Manage J* 25:575-585.

Muntaner, C and P O'Campo. 1993. A critical appraisal of the Demand/Control model of the psychosocial work environment: Epistemological, social, behavioral and class considerations. *Soc Sci Med* 36:1509-1517.

Muntaner, C, A Tien, WW Eaton, and R Garrison. 1991. Occupational characteristics and the occurence of psychotic disorders. *Social Psych Psychiatric Epidemiol* 26:273-280.

Muntaner, C et al. 1993. Dimensions of the psychosocial work environment in five US metropolitan areas. *Work Stress* 7:351-363.

Muntaner, C, P Wolyniec, J McGrath, and A Palver. 1993. Work environment and schizophrenia: An extension of the arousal hypothesis to occupational self-selection. *Social Psych Psychiatric Epidemiol* 28:231-238.

—. 1994. Psychotic inpatients' social class and their first admission to state or private psychiatric hospitals in Baltimore. *Am J Public Health* 84:287-289.

Muntaner, C, JC Anthony, RM Crum, and WW Eaton. 1995. Psychosocial dimensions of work and the risk of drug dependence among adults. *Am J Epidemiol* 142(2):183-190.

Murphy, LR. 1988. Workplace interventions for stress reduction and prevention. In *Causes, Coping and Consequences of Stress At Work,* edited by CL Cooper and R Payne. New York: Wiley.

Murrell, KFH. 1965. A classification of pacing. *Int J Prod Res* 4:69-74.

National Council on Compensation Insurance. 1985. *Emotional Stress in the Workplace. New Legal Rights in the Eighties.* New York: National Council on Compensation Insurance.

Nehling, A and G Debry. 1994. Caffeine and sport activity: A review. *International Journal of Sports Medicine* 15:215-223.

Nelson, DL. l987. Organizational socialization: A stress perspective. *J Occup Behav* 8:3ll-324.

Nelson, DL and JC Quick. 1991. Social support and newcomer adjustment in organization: Attachment theory at work? *J Organ Behav* 12:543-554.

Nelson, DL and CD Sutton. 1991. The relationship between newcomer expectations of job stressors and adjustment to the new job. *Work Stress* 5:241-251.

Newman, JE and TA Beehr. 1979. Personal and organizational strategies for handling job stress: A review of research and opinion. *Personnel Psychology* 32:1-43.

Niaura, R, CM Stoney, and PN Herbst. 1992. *Biol Psychol* 34:1-43.

National Institute for Occupational Safety and Health (NIOSH). 1988. *Prevention of Work-Related Psychological Disorders in Proposed National Strategies for the Prevention of Leading Work-Related Diseases and Injuries.*: NIOSH.

North, FM, SL Syme, A Feeney, M Shipley, and M Marmot. 1996. Psychosocial work environment and sickness absence among British civil servants: The Whitehall II study. *Am J Public Health* 86(3):332.

Northwestern National Life. 1991. Employee burnout: America's newest epidemic. Minneapolis, Mn. Northern National Life.

Nuckolls, KB et al. 1972. Psychosocial assets, life crisis and the prognosis of pregnancy. *American Journal of Epidemiology* 95:431-441.

O'Donnell, MP and JS Harris. 1994. *Health Promotion in the Workplace*. New York: Delmar.

Oetting, ER, RW Edwards, and F Beauvais. 1988. Drugs and native-American youth. *Drugs and Society* 3:1-34.

Öhman, A and G Bohlin. 1989. The role of controllability in cardiovascular activation and cardiovascular disease: Help or hindrance? In *Stress, Personal Control and Health*, edited by A Steptoe and A Appels. Chichester: Wiley.

Ojesjo, L. 1980. The relationship to alcoholism of occupation, class and employment. *J Occup Med* 22:657-666.

Oldham, GR. 1988. Effects of change in workspace partitions and spatial density on employee reactions: A quasi-experiment. *J Appl Psychol* 73:253-258.

Oldham, GR and Y Fried. 1987. Employee reactions to workspace characteristics. *J Appl Psychol* 72:75-80.

Oldham, GR and NL Rotchford. 1983. Relationships between office characteristics and employee reactions: A study of the physical environment. *Adm Sci Q* 28:542-556.

Olff, M, JF Brosschot, RJ Benschop, RE Ballieux, GLR Godaert, CJ Heijnen, and H Ursin. 1995. Modulatory effects of defense and coping on stress-induced changes in endocrine and immune parameters. *Int J Behav Med* 2:85-103.

Olff, M, JF Brosschot, RJ Benchop, RE Ballieux, GLR Godaert, CJ Heijnen, and H Eursin. 1993. Defence and coping in relation to subjective health and immunology.

Olmedo, EL and DL Parron. 1981. Mental health of minority women: Some special issues. *J Prof Psychol* 12:103-111.

O'Reilly, CA and JA Chatman. 1991. People and organizational culture: A profile comparison approach to assessing person-organization fit. *Acad Manage J* 34:487-516.

Organization for Economic Cooperation and Development (OECD). 1995. *OECD Economic Outlook* 57. Paris: OECD.

Ornstein, S. 1990. Linking environmental and industrial/organizational psychology. In *International Review of Industrial and Organizational Psychology*, edited by CL Cooper and IT Robertson. Chichester: Wiley.

Ornstein, S, WL Cron, and JWJ Slocum. 1989. Life stage versus career stage: A comparative test of the theories of Levinson and Super. *J Organ Behav* 10:117-133.

Ornstein, S and I Lynn. 1990. Age vs stage models of career attitudes of women: A partial replication and extension. *Journal of Vocational Behavior* 36:1-19.

Orr, E and M Westman. 1990. Does hardiness moderate stress and how? A review. In *On Coping Skills, Self-Control, and Adoptive Behavior*, edited by M Rosenbaum. New York: Springer.

Orth-Gomér, K and JV Johnson. 1987. Social network interaction and mortality. A six year follow-up study of a random sample of the Swedish population. *J Chron Dis* 40(10):949-957.

Orth-Gomér, K, A Rosengren, and L Wilhelmsen. 1993. Lack of social support and incidence of coronary heart disease in middle-aged Swedish men. *Psychosom Med* 55:37-43.

Orth-Gomér, K and A-L Undén. 1987. The measurement of social support in population surveys. *Soc Sci Med* 24(1):83-94.

—. 1990. Type A behavior, social support and coronary risk. Interaction and significance for mortality in cardiac patients. *Psychosom Med* 52:59-72.

Orth-Gomér, K, A-L Undén, and ME Edwards. 1990. Social isolation and mortality in ischemic heart dis-

ease. A ten year follow-up study of 150 middle-aged men. *Acta Med Scand* 224:205-215.

Osipow, SH, RE Doty, and AR Spokane. 1985. Occupational stress, strain, and coping across the life span. *J Vocat Behav* 27:98-108.

Ouellette, SC. 1993. Inquiries into hardiness. In *Handbook of Stress: Theoretical and Clinical Aspects*, edited by L Goldberger and S Breznitz. New York: Free Press.

Overman, S. 1993. Temporary services go global. *HR Mag* (August):72-74.

Pagani, M, O Rimoldi, P Pizzinelli, R Furlan, W Crivellaro, D Liberati, S Cerutti, and A Malliani. 1991. Assessment of the neural control of the circulation during psychological stress. *J Autonom Nerv Sys* 35:33-42.

Paoli, P. 1992. *First European Survey On the Work Environment 1991-1992*. Dublin: European Foundation.

Parkes, KR. 1989. Personal control in an occupational context. In *Stress, Personal Control, and Health*, edited by A Steptoe and A Appels. Chichester: John Wiley & Sons.

—. 1992. Mental health in the oil industry: A comparative study of onshore and offshore employees. *Psychol Med* 22:997-1009.

Parrot, AC. 1995. Stress modulation over the day in cigarette smokers. *Addiction* 20:233-244.

Partinen, M. 1994. Sleep disorders and stress. *Journal of Psychosomatic Research* 38:89-91.

Payne, R and DS Pugh. 1976. Organizational structure and climate. In *Handbook of Industrial and Organizational Psychology*, edited by MD Dunnette. Chicago:Rand McNally Publishing Company.

Pell, S and CA d'Alonzo. 1963. Acute myocardial infarction in a large employed population: Report of six-year study of 1356 cases, *J Am Med Assoc* 185:831-841.

Pennebaker, JW and G Hall. 1982. *The Psychology of Symptoms*. New York: Springer-Verlag.

Peters-Golden, H. 1982. Breast cancer: Varied perceptions of social support in the illness experience. *Social Science and Medicine* 16:483-491.

Peterson, MF, PB Smith, A Akande, S Ayestaran, S Bochner, V Callan, N Guk Cho, JC Jusuino, M D'Amorim, P Francois, K Hofmann, PL Koopman, K Leung, TK Lim, S Mortazavi, J Munene, M Radford, A Ropo, G Savage, B Setiadi, TN Sinha, R Sorenson, and C Viedge. 1995. Role conflict, abiguity and overload: A 21-nation study. *Academy of Management Journal* 38:429-452.

Pervin, LA. 1967. A twenty-college study of student x college interaction using TAPE (Transactional Analysis of Personality and Environment): Rationale, reliability, and validity. *J Educ Psychol* 58:290-302.

Petraitis, J, BR Flay, and TQ Miller. 1995. Reviewing theories of adolescent substance use: Organizing pieces in the puzzle. *Psychol Bull* 117:76-86.

Peyser, HS. 1992. Stress, ethylalcohol, and alcoholism. In *Handbook of Stress: Theoretical and Clinical Aspects*, edited by L Goldberger and S Breznitz. New York:Free Press.

Phelan, J, JE Schwartz, EJ Bromet, MA Dew, et al. 1991. Work stress and depression in professional and managerial employees. *Psychol Med* 21:999-1012.

Pickering, TG. 1991. *Ambulatory Monitoring and Blood Pressure Variability*. Philadelphia: Science Press.

Pierce, JL, DG Gardner, RB Dunham, and LL Cummings. 1989. Organization-based self esteem: Construct definition, measurement, and validation. *Acad Manage J* 32:622-648.

—. 1993. Moderation by organization-based self-esteem of role condition-employee response relationships. *Acad Manage J* 36:271-288.

Pines, AM. 1982. Changing organizations: Is a work environment without burnout an impossible goal? In *Job Stress and Burnout: Research, Theory, and Intervention*

Perspectives, edited by WS Paine. Beverly Hills:Sage Publications.

—. 1983. Burnout and the buffering effects of social support. In *Stress and Burnout in the Human Service Professions*, edited by BA Farber. New York:Peramon Press.

Pines, AM and E Aronson. 1981. *Burnout: From Tedium to Personal Growth*. New York: MacMillian.

Piper, DW and C Tennant. 1993. Stress and personality in patients with chronic peptic ulcer. *J Clin Gastroenterol* 16:211-214.

Pitt-Catsouphes, M and A Marchetta. 1991. *A Coming of Age : Telework*. Boston: Center on Work and Family, Boston Univ.

Pohorecky, LA. 1991. Stress and alcohol interaction: An update of human research. *Alcoholism Clinical and Experimental Research* 15:438-459.

Pollard, TM, G Ungpakorn, and GA Harrison. 1992. Some determinants of population variation in cortisol levels in a British urban community. *J Biosoc Sci* 24:477-485.

Porras, JI and PJ Robertson. 1992. Organizational development: Theory, practice and research. In *Handbook of Industrial and Organizational Psychology*, edited by MD Dunnette and LM Hough. Palo Alto, CA:Consulting Psychologists Press, Inc.

Price, RH. 1990. Strategies for managing plant closings and downsizings. In *The Human Side of Corporate Competitiveness*, edited by D Fishman and C Cherniss. Beverly Hills: Sage.

Price, RH, M van Ryn, and AD Vinokur. 1992. Impact of preventive job search intervention on the likelihood of depression among the unemployed. *J Health Soc Behav* 33:158-167.

Quick, JC and JD Quick. 1984. *Organisational Stress and Preventive Management*. New York: McGraw-Hill.

Ragland, DR and RJ Brand. 1988. Type A behavior and mortality from coronary heart disease. *N Engl J Med* 318:65-69.

Rahe, RH. 1988. Recent life changes and coronary heart disease: 10 years' research. In *Handbook of Life Stress, Cognition and Health*, edited by S Fisher and J Reason. New York: Wiley.

Ralph, D. 1983. *Work and Madness*. Montreal: Black Rose Books.

Reich, RB. 1991. *The Work of Nations: Preparing Ourselves for 21st Century Capitalism*. New York: A.A. Knopf.

Reilly, NP and CL Orsak. 1991. A career stage analysis of career and organizational commitment in nursing. *J Vocat Behav* 39:311-330.

Repetti, RL. 1987. Individual and common components of the social environment at work and psychological well-being. *J Personal Soc Psychol* 52:710-720.

—. 1993. The effects of workload and the social environment at work on health. In *Handbook of Stress: Theoretical, and Clinical Aspects*, edited by L Goldberger and S Breznitz. New York: Free Press.

Reskin, BF and HT Hartmann. 1986. *Women's Work, Men's Work: Sex Segregation On the Job*. Washington, DC: National Academy Press.

Review Panel on Coronary-Prone Behavior and Coronary Heart Disease. 1981. Coronary-prone behavior and coronary heart disease: A critical review. *Circulation* 63:1199-1215.

Riad-Fahmy, D, GF Read, RF Walker, and K Griffiths. 1982. Steroids in saliva for assessing endocrine functions. *Endocr Rev* 3:367-395.

Riley, V. 1981. Psychoneuroendocrine influences on immune competence and neoplasia. *Science* 212:1100-1109.

The Robens Report: Safety and health at work. 1972. London: HMSO.

Roberts, RE and EU Lee. 1993. Occupation and the prevalence of major depression, alcohol and drug abuse in the United states. *Environ Res* 61:266-278.

Roberts, RR, SW Vernon, and HM Rhoades. 1989. Effects of language and ethnic status on reliability and validity of the Center for Epidemiologic Studies Depression Scale with psychiatric patients. *J Nerv Mental Dis* 117:581-592.

Robins, LN and DA Regier. 1990. *Psychiatric Disorders in America*. New York: Free Press.

Rodgers, B. 1991. Socio-economic status, employment and neurosis. *Soc Psychiatry Psychiat Epidemiol* 26:104-114.

Rogers, CR. 1942. *Counseling and Psychotherapy*. Boston: Houghton-Mifflin.

Rose, RM and LF Fogg. 1993. Definition of a responder: Analysis of behavior, cardiovascular and endocrine responses to varied workload in air traffic controllers. *Psychosom Med* 55:325-338.

Rosen, N, L Greenlagh, and JC Anderson. 1981. The cognitive structure of industrial/labor relationships. *Int Rev Appl Psychol* 30:217-233.

Rosenberg, M. 1965. *Society and Adolescent Self-Image*. Princeton: Princeton Univ. Press.

Rosengren, A, K Orth-Gomér, H Wedel, and L Wilhelmsen. 1993. Stressful life events, social support, and mortality in men born in 1933. *Brit Med J* 307:1102-1105.

Rosenman, RH, RJ Brand, CD Jenkins, M Friedman, R Straus, and M Wurm. 1975. Coronary heart disease in the Western Collaborative Group Study: Final follow-up experience of 8 1/2 years. *J Am Med Assoc* 233:872-877.

Roskies, E. 1991. Individual differences in health behavior. In *Personality and Stress: Individual Differences in the Stress Process*, edited by CL Cooper and R Payne. New York: Wiley.

Roskies, E and C Louis-Guerin. 1990. Job insecurity in managers: Antecedents and consequences. *J Organ Behav* :345-359.

Roskies, E, C Louis-Guerin, and C Fournier. 1993. Coping with job insecurity: How does personality make a difference. *J Organ Behav* (October):617-630.

Rotter, JB. 1954. *Social Learning and Clinical Psychology*. Englewood Cliffs, NJ: Prentice Hall.

—. 1966. Generalized expectancies for internal versus external control of reinforcement. *Psychol Monog* 80:1-28.

Rousseau, DM. 1988. The construction of climate in organizational research. In *International Review of Industrial and Organizational Psychology*, edited by CL Cooper and I Robertson. London: Wiley.

—. 1989. Price of success? *Ind Crisis Q* 3:285-302.

—. 1990. Assessing organizational culture. In *Organizational Climate and Culture*, edited by B Schneider. San Francisco: Jossey-Bass.

Roy, DJ. 1995. Layoffs down, but will continue despite surging economy, analysts say. *BNA Labor Daily* .

Rozanski, A, CN Balcry, DS Krantz, J Friedman, K Resser, M Morell, S Hilton-Chalfen, L Hestrin, J Bietendorf, and DS Berman. 1988. Mental stress and the induction of silent myocardial ischemia in patients with coronary artery disease. *New Engl J Med* 318:1005-1012.

Rubenstein, M and I DeVries. 1993. *How to Combat Sexual Harassment: A Guide to Implementing the European Commission Code of Practice*. Luxembourg: Commision of the European Communities.

Ruhm, CJ. 1991. Are workers permanently scarred by job displacement? *American Economic Review* 81:319-324.

Sadava, SW. 1987. Psychosocial interactionism and substance use. *Drugs Society* 2:7-24.

Salvendy, G. 1981. Classification and characterisitics of paced work. In *Machine Pacing and Occupational Stress*, edited by G Salvendy and MJ Smith. London: Taylor & Francis.

—. 1976. Effects of equitable and inequitable financial compensation on operator's productivity, satisfaction and motivation. *Inter J Prod Res*. 14(2):305-310.

Salvendy, G and JL Knight. 1983. Circulatory tesponses to machine-paced and self-paced work: An industrial study, *Ergonomics*. 26(7): 713-717.

Sanchez, C. 1990. A vulnerable work force. *The Washington Post*, 7 January, D1,D5.

Sanders, M and EJ McCormick. 1993. *Human Factors in Engineering and Design*. New York: McGraw-Hill.

Sauter, SL, JJ Hurrell Jr, and CL Cooper. 1989. *Job Control and Worker Health*. Chichester: John Wiley & Sons.

Sauter, SL, LR Murphy, and JJ Hurrell Jr. 1990. Prevention of work related psychosocial disorders: A national strategy proposed by the National Institute for Occupational Health and Safety (NIOSH). *Am Psychol* 45:1146-1158.

Sauter, SL, T Hales, B Bernard, L Fine, M Petersen, V Putz-Anderson, LM Schleifer, and T Ochs. 1993. Summary of two NIOSH studies of musculoskeletal disorders and VDT work among telecommunications and newspaper workers. In *Work With Display Units '92*, edited by A Luczak, A Cakir, and G Cakir. Amsterdam: North Holland.

Sauter, SL and NG Swanson. 1996. An ecological model of musculoskeletal disorders in office work. In *Psychosocial Factors and Musculoskeletal Disorders in Office Work*, edited by S Moon and SL Sauter. :Taylor and Francis. in press

Sauter, S, M Dainoff, and MJ Smith. 1990. *Promoting Health and Productivity in the Computerized Office: Models of Successful Ergonomic Interventions*. London: Taylor and Francis.

Saxton, MJ, JS Phillips, and RN Blakeney. 1991. Antecedents and consequences of emotional exhaustion in the airline reservations service center. *Human Relations* 44:583-595.

Scharlach, AE, BF Lowe, and EL Schneider. 1991. *Elder Care and Work Force: Blueprint for Action*. Lexington, Mass: Lexington.

Schaubroeck, J, DC Ganster, WE Sime, and D Ditman. 1993. A field experiment testing supervisory role clarification. *Pers Psychol* 46:1-25.

Schaufeli, WB, C Maslach, and T Marek. 1993. *Professional Burnout: Recent Developments in Theory and Research*. Washington, DC: Taylor & Francis.

Scherwitz, L, K Berton, and H Leventhal. 1978. Type A Behavior, self-involvement, and cardiovascular response. *Psychosom Med* 40:593-609.

Schleifer, LM, T Galinsky, and CS Pan. 1995. Mood disturbance and musculoskeletal discomfort effects of electronic performance monitoring in a VDT data-entry task. In *Job Stress 2000: Emergent Issues*, edited by GP Keita and SL Sauter. Washington, DC: APA.

Schleifer, LM and R Ley. 1994. End-tidal PCO2 as an index of psychophysiological activity under high and low data-entry workload demands. Paper presented at the inaugural meeting of the International Society for the Advancement of Respiratory Psychophysiology, Saint Flour, France.

Schleifer, LM and RL Shell. 1992. A review and reappraisal of electronic performance monitoring, performance standards, and stress allowances. *Appl Ergon* 23:49-53.

Schlenker, B. 1980. *Impression Management*. Montery, California: Brooks Cole.

Schmidt, WH and JP Finnigan. 1992. *The Race Without a Finish Line: America's Quest for Total Quality*. San Francisco: Jossey-Bass.

Schnall, PL, PA Landsbergis, and D Baker. 1994. Job strain and cardiovascular disease. *Annu Rev Publ Health* 15:381-411.

Schnall, PL, C Pieper, JE Schwartz, RA Karasek, Y Schlussel, RB Devereux, A Ganau, M Alderman, K Warren, and TG Pickering. 1990. The relationship between "job strain", work place diastolic blood

pressure, and left ventricular mass index. *J Am Med Assoc* 263:1929-1935.

Schneider, B. 1985. Organizational behavior. *Annu Rev Psychol* 36:573-611.

Schonfeld, IS. 1992. Assessing occupational stress in teachers: Depressive symptoms scales and neutral self-reports of the work environment. In *Stress and Well Being At Work: Assessments and Interventions for Occupational Mental Health*, edited by RC Quick, LR Murphy, and JJ Hurrell. Washington, DC: APA.

Schwartz, J, C Pieper, and RA Karasek. 1988. A procedure for linking job characteristics to health surveys. *Am J Public Health* 78:904-909.

Scott, AJ and J LaDou. 1990. Shiftwork: effects on sleep and health with recommendations for medical surveillance and screening. *Occup Med* 5:273-299.

Seligman, MEP. 1975. *Helplessness*. San Francisco: WH Freeman.

Seltzer, J, RE Numerof, and BM Bass. 1989. Transformation leadership: Is it a source of more or less burnout and stress. *J Health Hum Resource Admin* 12:174-185.

Selye, H. 1936. A syndrome produced by diverse noxious agents. *Nature* 138:32.

—. 1960. The concept of stress in experimental physiology. In *Stress and Psychiatric Disorder*, edited by JM Tanner. Oxford: Blackwell.

—. 1974. *Stress Without Distress*. Philadelphia: JB Lippincott.

—. 1976. *The Stress of Life*. New York: McGraw-Hill.

Senge, P. 1991. *The Fifth Discipline: The Art and Practice of the Learning Organization*. New York: Doubleday.

Shanan, J. 1967. Adaptive coping. *Behav Sci* 16:188-196.

Shiba, S, A Graham, and D Walden. 1994. *A New American TQM. Four Practical Revolutions in Management*. Cambridge, Mass: Productivity Press.

Shinn, M, M Rosario, H Morch, and DE Chestnut. 1984. Coping with job stress and burnout in the human services. *J Personal Soc Psychol* 46:864-876.

Siegrist, J, R Peter, A Junge, P Cremer, and D Seidel. 1990. Low status control, high effort at work and ischemic heart disease: Prospective evidence from blue-collar men. *Soc Sci Med* 31:1127-1134.

Slora, KB, DS Joy, and W Terris. 1991. Personnel selection to control employee violence. *J Bus Psychol* 5:417-426.

Smith, MJ. 1984. The physical, mental, and emotional stress of VDT work. *Comput Graph Appl* 4(4):23-27.

—. 1985. Machine-paced work and stress. In *Job Stress and Blue Collar Work*, edited by C Cooper and MJ Smith. London: John Wiley & Sons.

—. 1987. Occupational stress. In *Handbook of Human Factors*, edited by G Salvendy. New York: John Wiley & Sons.

—. 1988. Electronic performance monitoring at the workplace: Part of a new industrial revolution. *Human Factors Society Bulletin* 31:1-3.

Smith, MJ and P Carayon (1996): Work organization, stress, and cumulative trauma disorders. Presented at the conference on Psychosocial Influence in Office Work CTD. Duke university, Nov. 11-12, 1993 In *Psychosocial Factors and Musculoskeletal Disorders in Office Work*. edited by S Moon and S.L. Sauter.

Smith, MJ, P Carayon, and K Miezio. 1986. *Motivational, Behavioral, and Psychological Implications of Electronic Monitoring of Worker Performance*. Washington, DC: NTIS.

Smith, MJ, BGF Cohen, L Stammerjohn, and A Happ. 1981. An investigation of health complaints and job stress in video display operators. *Human Factors* 23:389-400.

Smith, MJ and PC Sainfort. 1989. A balance theory of job design for stress reduction. *Int J Ind Erg* 4:67-79.

Smith, MJ, P Carayon, R Eberts, and G Salvendy. 1992a. Human-computer interaction. In *Handbook of*

Industrial Engineering, edited by G Salvendy. New York: John Wiley & Sons.

Smith, MJ, P Carayon, K Sanders, SY Lim, and D LeGrande. 1992b. Employee stress and health complaints in jobs with and without electronic performance monitoring. *Appl Ergon* 23:17-27.

Solomon, SR. 1986. Mobilizing social support networks in times of disaster. In *Trauma an Its Wake*, edited by CR Figley. New York:Brunner-Mazel.

Sommer, R. 1983. *Social Design: Creating Buildings With People in Mind*. New Jersey: Prentice Hall.

Sommese, T and JC Patterson. 1995. Acute effects of cigarette smoking withdrawal: A review of the literature. *Aviation, Space and Environmental Medicine* 66:164-167.

Southwood, KE. 1978. Substantive theory and statistical interaction: Five models. *Am J Sociol* 83:1154-1203.

Spector, P. 1986. Perceived control by employees: A meta-analysis of studies concerning autonomy and participation at work. *Hum Relat* 39:1005-1016.

Spector, PE and BJ O'Connell. 1994. The contribution of personality trait, negative affectivity, locus of control, and type A to the subsequent reports of job stressors and job strains. *J Occup Organ Psychol* 67:1-11.

Spurgeon, A and JM Harrington. 1989. Work performance and health of junior hospital doctors. A review of the literature. *Work and Stress* 3:117-128.

St. Paul Fire and Marine. 1992. *American Workers Under Pressure Technical Report*. Minneapolis, MN: St. Paul Fire and Marine.

Stack, S. 1981. Divorce and suicide: A time series analysis, 1933-1970. *Journal of Family Issues* 2:77-90.

Staines, G and R Quinn. 1979. American workers evaluate the quality of their jobs. *Monthly Labor Review* 102:2-12.

Stansfeld, SA and MG Marmot. 1992. Social class and minor psychiatric disorder in British civil servants. *Psychol Med* 22:739-749.

Steele, FI. 1986. *Making and Managing High-Quality Workplaces: An Organizational Ecology*. London: Teacher's College Press.

Steinberg, L, R Catalano, and D Dooley. 1981. Economic antecedents of child abuse and neglect. *Child Development* 52(3):975-985.

Steinfeld, E. 1986. A case study in the development of a research-based building accessibility standard. In *Proceedings of the Seventeenth Annual Environmental Design Research Association*, edited by J Wineman, R Barnes, and C Zimring. Washington, DC: Environmental Design Research Association.

Stellman, JM and MS Henifin. 1983. *Office Work Can Be Dangerous to Your Health: A Handbook On Office Health and Safety Hazards and What You Can Do About Them*. New York: Fawcett Crest.

Steptoe, A. 1981. *Psychological Factors in Cardiovascular Disorders*. London: Academic Press.

—. 1990. Psychobiological stress responses. In *Stress and Medical Procedures*, edited by M Johnston and J Wallace. Oxford: OUP.

Steptoe, A, G Fieldman, O Evans, and L Perry. 1993. Control over work pace, job strain, and cardiovascular responses in middle-aged men. *J Hypertension* 11:751-759.

Stokols, D. 1992. Establishing and maintaining healthy environments: Toward a social ecology of health promotion. *Am Psychol* 47:6-22.

Stokols, D and RW Novaco. 1981. Transportation and well-being: An ecological perspective. In *Human Behavior and Environment: Advances in Theory and Research*, edited by J Wohlwill, P Everett, and I Altman. New York: Plenum.

Stokols, D, A Churchman, T Scharf, and S Wright. 1990. Workers' experiences of environmental change and transition at the office. In *On the Move:*

The Psychology of Change and Transition, edited by S Fisher and CL Cooper. Chichester: John Wiley & Sons.

Stone, PJ and R Luchetti. 1985. Your office is where you are. *Harvard Bus Rev* 2:102-177.

Straw, BM, LE Sandelands, and JE Dutton. 1988. Threat-rigidity effects in organizational behavior: A multilevel analysis. In *Readings in Organizational Decline: Frameworks, Research, and Prescriptions*, edited by RI Sutton and DA Whetten. Cambridge, MA: Ballinger Publishing Company.

Strube, MJ and JE Garcia. 1981. A meta-analytic investigation of Fiedler's contingency model of leadership effectiveness. *Psychol Bull* 90:307-321.

Stumpf, SA and S Rabinowitz. 1981. Career stage as a moderator of performance relationships with facets of job satisfaction and role perceptions. *J Vocat Behav* 18:202-218.

Suls, J and GS Sanders. 1988. Type A behavior as a general risk factor for physical disorder. *J Behav Med* 11:201-226.

Suls, J, CK Wan, and EB Blanchard. 1994. A multilevel data-analytic approach for evaluation of relationships between daily life stressors and symptomatology: Patients with irritable bowel syndrome. *Health Psychol* 13:103-113.

Sundborm, L. 1971. *Work Site Conditions for the Working Population (in Swedish)*. Stockholm: Låginkom-stutredningen, Allmänna Förlaget.

Sundstrom, E. 1986. *Workplaces: The Psychology of the Physical Environment in Offices and Factories*. New York: Cambridge Univ. Press.

—. 1987. Work environments: offices and factories. In *Handbook of Environmental Psychology*, edited by D Stokols and I Altman. New York: John Wiley & Sons.

Sundstrom, E and I Altman. 1989. Physical environments and work group effectiveness. In *Research in Organizational Behavior*. Greenwich, Conn: JAI.

Super, DE. 1957. *The Psychology of Careers*. New York: Harper & Brothers.

Super, DE, RS Zelkowitz, and AS Thompson. 1981. *Career Development Inventory: Adult Form 1*. New York: Teachers' College, Columbia University.

Sutherland, VJ and CL Cooper. 1986. *Man and Accidents Offshore: The Costs of Stress Among Workers On Oil and Gas Rigs*. London: Dietsmann International.

Sutton, RI and A Rafaeli. 1987. Characteristics of work stations as potential occupational stressors. *Acad Manage J* 30:260-276.

Sutton, RI and RL Kahn. 1987. Prediction, understanding and control as antidotes to organizational stress. In *Handbook of Organizational Behavior*, edited by JW Lorsch. Englewood Cliffs, NJ:Prentice-Hall.

Swanson, JA, JW Lee, and JW Hopp. 1994. Caffeine and nicotine: A review of their joint use and possible interaction effects in tobacco withdrawal. *Addictive Behaviors* 19:229-256.

Swanson, NG, CS Piotrkowski, GP Keita, and AG Becker. 1997. Occupational stress and women's health. In *Psychosocial and Behavioral Factors in Women's Health Care: A Handbook for Medical Education Practitioners and Psychologists*, edited by S Gallant, GP Keita, and R Royak-Schaler. Washington, DC: APA Press.

Taylor, FW. 1911. *The Principles of Scientific Management*. New York: Norton & Co.

Taylor, SE. 1991. Asymmetrical effects of positive and negative events: The mobilization-minimization hypothesis. *Psychological Bulletin* 110(1):67-85.

Tepas, D and T Monk. 1987. Work schedules. In *Handbook of Human Factors*, edited by G Salvendy. New York: John Wiley & Sons.

Tetrick, LE and JM LaRocco. 1987. Understanding, prediction, and control as moderators of the relationships between perceived stress, satisfaction, and psychological well-being. *Journal of Applied Psychology* 72:538-543.

Theorell, T. 1992. The psychosocial environment, stress, and coronary heart disease. In *Coronary Heart Disease Epidemiology*, edited by M Marmot and P Elliot. Oxford: OUP.

Theorell, T and RA Karasek. 1996. Current issues relating to psychosocial job strain and cardiovascular disease research. *J Occup Health Psychol* 1(1):9-26.

Thoits, PA. 1982. Conceptual, methodological and theoretical problems in studying social support as a buffer against life stress. *Journal of Health & Social Behaviour* 23:145-159.

Thoresen, CE and LH Powell. 1992. Type A behavior pattern: New perspectives on theory, assessment and intervention. *J Consult Clin Psychol* 60:595-604.

Tuch, SA and JK Martin. 1991. Race in the workplace: Black/White differences in the sources of job satisfaction. *Sociol Q* 23:103-116.

Turner, RJ. 1983. Direct, indirect and moderating effects of social support on psychological distress and associated conditions. In Chap. 3 in *Psychosocial Stress: Trends in Theory and Research*, edited by HB Kaplan. New York:Academic Press.

Type A behavior. 1990. *J Soc Behav Personal* 5(1):Special Issue.

Undén, A-L and K Orth-Gomér. 1989. Development of a social support instrument for use in population surveys. *Soc Sci Med* 29(12):1387-1392.

Undén, A-L, K Orth-Gomér, and S Elofsson. 1991. Cardiovascular effects of social support in the work place: Twenty-four hour ECG monitoring of men and women. *Psychosom Med* 53:50-60.

United States Bureau of Labor Statistics (USBLS). 1995. *Contingent and Alternative Employment Arrangements*. Washington, DC:USBLS

United States Department of Health and Human Services (USDHHS). 1966. *Protecting the Health of Eighty Million Americans: A National Goal for Occupational Health*. Washington, DC: USDHHS.

United States Department of Labor. (USDOL) 1995. *Monthly Review* 118(7):98-99.

United States House of Representatives. 1992. *A Post Office Tragedy: The Shooting At Royal Oak*. Washington, DC: US Government Printing Office.(Report of the Committee on Post Office and Civil Service)

United States Office of Technology Assessment (USOTA). 1987. *The Electronic Supervisor: New Technology, New Tensions*. Washington DC: USOTA

Vahtera, J, A Uutela, and J Pentii. 1996. The influence of objective job demands on registered sickness absence spells: Do personal, social and job related resources work as moderators?

Van Maanen, J and EH Schein. l979. Toward a theory of organizational socialization. In *Research in Organizational Behavior*, edited by BM Staw. Greenwich, Conn: JAI.

Vener, KJ, S Szabo, and JG Moore. 1989. The effect of shift work on gastrointestinal (GI) function: A review. *Chronobiologia* 16:421-439.

Vinokur, A, RD Caplan, and CC Williams. 1987. Effects of recent and past stresses on mental health: Coping with unemployment among Vietnam veterans and nonveterans. *Journal of Applied Social Psychology* 17(8):710-730.

Vinokur, A, M van Ryn, EM Gramlich, and RH Price. 1991. Long-term follow-up and benefit-cost analysis of the Jobs Program: A preventive intervention for the unemployed. *Journal of Applied Psychology* 756(2):213-219.

Vischer, JC. 1989. *Environmental Quality in Offices*. New York: Van Nostrand Rinehold.

Vischer, JC and WC Mees. 1991. Organic design in the Netherlands: Case study of an innovative office building. In *Design Intervention: Toward a More Humane Architecture*, edited by WFE Preisser, JC Vischer, and ET White. New York: Van Nostrand Reinhold.

Volpert, W, R Oesterreich, S Gablenz-Kolakovic, T Krogoll, and M Resch. 1983. *Method of Measuring Regulation Demands At Work: Analysis of the Planning and Thinking Process in Industrial Production (in German)*. Cologne: TüV.

Waitzman, NJ and KR Smith. 1994. The effects of occupational class transitions on hypertension: Racial disparities among working-age men. *Am J Public Health* 84:945-950.

Walsh, DC and SE Kelleher. 1987. The "corporate perspective" on the health of women at work. In *Women and Work: An Annual Review*, edited by AH Stromberg, L Larwood, and BA Gutek. Newbury Park, NJ: Sage.

Walsh, DC, G Sorensen, and L Leonard. 1995. A "society and health" perspective on gender and health: Cigarette smoking as an exploratory case study. In *Society and Health: Foundations for a Nation's Health*, edited by BC Amick, S Levine, AR Tarlov, and DC Walsh. New York: Oxford Univ. Press.

Wanous, JP. 1992. *Organizational Entry: Recruitment, Selection, and Socialization of Newcomers*. Reading, Mass: Addison-Wesley.

Warr, PB, P Jackson, and M Banks. 1988. Unemployment and mental health: Some British studies. *Journal of Social Issues* 44:47-68.

Warr, PB. 1990. The measurement of well-being and other aspects of mental health. *J Occup Psychol* 63:193-210.

—. 1994. A conceptual framework for the study of work and mental health. *Work and Stress* 8:84-97.

Watson, D and L Clark. 1984. Negative affectivity: The disposition to experience aversive emotional states. *Psychol Bull* 96:465-490.

Watson, D, LA Clark, and A Tellegen. 1988. Development and validation of brief measures of positive and negative affect: The PANAS scales. *J Personal Soc Psychol* 54:1063-1070.

Watts-Jones, D. 1990. Toward a stress scale for African-American women. *Psychol Women Q* 14:271-275.

Weaver, CN. 1978. Black-White correlates of job satisfaction. *J Appl Psychol* 63:255-258.

—. 1980. Job satisfaction in the United States in the 1970's. *J Appl Psychol* 65:364-367.

Weiner, A, R Remer, and P Remer. 1992. Career plateauing: Implications for career development specialists. *J Career Devel* 19:37-48.

Weiner, H. 1977. *Psychobiology of Human Disease*. New York: Elesvier.

Westgaard.RH and R Bjorklund. 1987. Generation of muscle tension additional to postural muscle load. *Ergonomics* 30(6):911-923.

Weiss, JM. 1971. Effects of coping behavior in different warning signal conditions on stress pathology in rats. *J Comp Physiol Psychol* 77:1-13.

Westin, AF. 1986. *Privacy and Quality-Of-Worklife Issues in Employee Monitoring*. Washington, DC: USOTA.

—. 1990. Organizational culture and VDT policies: A case study of the Federal Express Corporation. In *Promoting Health and Productivity in the Computerized Office*, edited by SL Sauter, M Dianoff, and M Smith. :Taylor and Francis.

Wexley, KN and SB Silverman. 1993. *Working Scared*. San Francisco: Jossey-Bass.

White, R. 1959. Motivation reconsidered: The concept of competence. *Psychol Rev* 66:297-333.

Whitehead, WE. 1992. Behavioral medicine approaches to gastrointestinal disorders. *J Consult Clin Psychol* 60:605-612.

Whitehead, WE and MM Schuster. 1985. *Gastrointestinal Disorders: Behavioral and Physiological Basis for Treatment*. Orlando: Academic Press.

Whitehead, WE, MD Crowell, JC Robinson, BR Heller, and MM Schuster. 1992. Effects of stressful life events on bowel symptoms: Subjects with irittable bowel syndrome compared with subjects without bowel dysfunction. *Gut* 33:825-830.

Whitaker, A. 1992. The transformation in work Post-Fordism. In *Rethinking Organization: New Directions in Organization, Theory and Analysis*, edited by M Reed and M Hughes. Newbury Park, CA:Sage Publishing.

Whyte, WF. 1948. *Human Relations in the Restaurant Industry*. New York: McGraw-Hill.

Wickens, C. 1984. *Engineering Psychology and Human Performance*. Columbus, Ohio: Merrill.

Widfeldt, AK and JR Widfeldt. 1992. Total quality management in American industry. *AAHON Journal* 40(7):311-318.

Wiebe, DJ and PG Williams. 1992. Hardiness and health: A social psychophysiological perspective on stress and adaptation. *J Soc Clin Psychol* 11:238-262.

Wilcox, BL. 1981. Social support, lifestyles and psychological adjustment: A test of the buffering hypothesis. *Am J Comm Psych* 9:371-386.

Williams, NR. 1993. The impact of total quality management on health and safety. *Occup Med* 43(4):173-174.

Williams, RBJ. 1987. Psychological factors in coronary artery disease: Epidemiologic evidence. *Circulation* 76 Suppl. 1:I77-I123.

Wineman, J. 1982. The office environment as a source of stress. In *Environmental Stress*, edited by GW Evans. New York: Cambridge Univ. Press.

—. 1986. *Behavioral Issues in Office Design*. New York: Van Nostrand Rinehold.

Wong, PTP and GT Reker. 1984. Coping behaviors of successful agers. Paper presented at the Thirtieth Annual Meeting of the Canadian Psychological Association, Ottawa.

Wood, R and A Bandura. 1989. Social cognitive theory of organization management. *Acad Manage Rev* 14:361-383.

World Health Organization (WHO). 1984. Health promotion: A discussion document on the concept and principles. *Health Promot* 1:73-76.

Wright, R, SW King, and WE Berg. 1985. Job satisfaction in the workplace: A study of Black females in management positions. *Journal of Social Service Research* 8:65-79.

Wundt, W. 1922. *Introduction to Philosophy (in German)*. Leipzig: Alfred Kroner.

Yarborough, CM. 1994. Strategic quality planning. *J Occup Med* 36(4):414-417.

Yerkes, RM and JD Dodson. 1908. The relation of stimulus to rapidity of habit formation. *J Comp Neurol Psychol* 18:482-495.

Yoder, JD. 1991. Rethinking tokenism: Looking beyond the numbers. *Gender Society* 5:178-192.

Zohar, D. 1980. Safety climate in industrial organizations. Theoretical and applied implications. J Appl Psychol 65:96-102.

Other relevant readings

Bockerstette, JA and RL Shell. 1993. *Time Based Manufacturing*. New York: McGraw-Hill.

Broadhead, WF et al. 1983. The epidemiological evidence for a relationship between social support and health. *American Journal of Epidemiology* 117:521-537.

Bureau of National Affairs (BNA). 1992. *The Work and Family Manager: Evolution of a New Job*. Special Report No. 45. Washington, DC: BNA.

Caplan, RD. 1987. Person-environment fit in organizations: Theories, facts, and values. In *Occupational Stress and Organizational Effectiveness*, edited by AW Riley and SJ Zaccaro. New York: Praeger.

Christensen, K. 1989. *Flexible Staffing and Scheduling in US Corporations*. Research Bulletin No. 240. New York: The Conference Board.

Clark, ID. 1992. Balancing work and family: A study of the Canadian work force. *Optimum* :25-29.

Colquhoun, WP, G Costa, S Folkard, and P Knauth. 1996. *Shiftwork: Problems and Solutions*. Frankfurt: Peter Lang.

Creedon, MA. 1987. *Issues for an Aging America: Employees and Eldercare - A Briefing Book*. Bridgeport: Univ. of Bridgeport Center for the Study of Aging.

Dunnette, MD and L Hough. 1992. *The Handbook of Industrial and Organizational Psychology*. Palo Alto, Calif: Consulting Psychologists Press.

Fein, M. 1986. Improved productivity through worker involvement. In *Work Measurement Principles and Practice*, edited by RL Shell. Norcross, Ga: Industrial Engineering and Management.

Fernandez, JP. 1986. *Childcare and Corporate Productivity: Resolving Family/Work Conflicts*. Lexington, Mass: Health.

Fox, BH. 1988. Psychogenic factors in cancer, especially its incidence. In *Topics in Health Psychology*, edited by S Maes, CD Spielberger, PB Defares, and IG Sarason. Chichester: Wiley.

French, JRP, RD Caplan, and RV Harrison. 1982. *The Mechanism of Job Stress and Strain*. Chichester: Wiley.

Friedman, DE. 1988. *Issues for an Aging America: Elder Care*. New York: The Conference Board.

—. 1991. *Linking Work-Family Issues to the Bottom Line*. New York: The Conference Board.

Friedman, DE and E Galinsky. 1992. Work and family issues: A legitimate business concern. In *Work, Families and Organizations*, edited by S Zedeck. San Francisco: Jossey-Bass.

Galinsky, E, DE Friedman, and CA Hernandez. 1991. *The Corporate Reference Guide to Work-Family Programs*. New York: The Conference Board.

Hagman, N. 1988. *Sexual Harassment On the Job*. Helsinki: Wahlstrom & Widstrand.

Hewitt Associates. 1992. *Work and Family Benefits Provided By Major US Employers in 1992: Based On Practices of 1,026 Employers*. Lincolnshire, Ill: Hewitt Associates.

Hodson, WK. 1992. *Maynard's Industrial Engineering Handbook*. New York: McGraw-Hill.

Johnson, BL. 1983. *Working Whenever You Want: All About Temporary Employment*. Englewood Cliffs, NJ: Prentice Hall.

Karwowski, W and G Salvendy. 1994. *Organization and Management of Advanced Manufacturing*. New York: John Wiley & Sons.

Klitzman, S, JS House, BA Israel, and RP Mero. 1990. Work stress, nonwork stress and health. *J Behav Med* 13(3):221-243.

Landy, FJ. 1989. *The Psychology of Work Behavior*. Homewood, Ill: Irwin.

Lewis, S. 1992. Work and families in the United Kingdom. In *Work, Families and Organizations*, edited by S Zedeck. San Francisco: Jossey-Bass.

Mundel, ME and DL Danner. 1994. *Motion and Time Study: Improving Productivity*. Englewood Cliffs, NJ: Prentice Hall.

Niebel, BW. 1993. *Motion and Time Study*. Homewood, Ill: Irwin.

Nye, D. 1988. *Alternative Staffing Strategies*. Washington, DC: BNA.

Parris, H. 1990. Balancing work and family responsibilities: Canadian employer and employee viewpoints. *Hum Resour Plan* 13(2).

Pervin, LA. 1989. Persons, situations, interactions: The history of a controversy and a discussion of theoretical models. *Acad Manage Rev* 14:350-360.

Richter, J. 1992. Balancing work and family in Israel. In *Work, Families and Organizations*, edited by S Zedeck. San Francisco: Jossey-Bass.

Rubenstein, M. 1987. *The Dignity of Women At Work: A Report On the Problem of Sexual Harassment in the Member States of the European Community*. Geneva: ILO.

Salvendy, G. 1987. *Handbook of Human Factors*. New York: John Wiley & Sons.

—. 1992. *Handbook of Industrial Engineering*. New York: Wiley.

Salvendy, G and W Karwowski. 1994. *Design of Work and Development of Personnel in Advanced Manufacturing*. New York: John Wiley & Sons.

Schneider, B. 1990. *Organizational Climate and Culture*. San Francisco: Jossey-Bass.

Selye, H. 1936. *The Stress of Life*. New York: Crane, Russek.

Spector, PE. 1988. Development of the work locus of control scale. *J Occup Psychol* 61:335-340.

Sweeney, JJ and K Nussbaum. 1989. *Solutions for the New Work Force*. Washington, DC: Seven Locks.

United States General Accounting Office (GAO). 1981. *Productivity Sharing Programs: Can They Contribute to Productivity Improvement?* Gaithersburg, MD: GAO

United States House of Representatives. 1992. *A Report of the Select Committee On Children, Youth and Families*. Washington, DC: United States House of Representatives.

United States Merit Systems Protection Board. 1991. *Balancing Work Responsibilities and Family Needs: The Federal Civil Service Response*. Washington, DC: GPO.

United States Office of Personnel Management. 1992. *A Study of the Work and Family Needs of the Federal Workforce. A Report to Congress By the Office of Personnel Management*. Washington, DC: US Office of Personnel Management.

Vanderkolk, BS and A Armstrong. 1991. *The Work and Family Revolution: How Companies Can Keep Employees Happy and Business Profitable*. New York: Facts on file.

Warr, PB. 1996. Employee well-being. In *Psychology At Work*, edited by PB Warr. London: Penguin.

Watson, D and JW Pennebaker. 1989. Health complaints, stress, and distress: The central role of negative affectivity. *Psychol Rev* 96(2):234-254.

Zedeck, S. 1992. *Work, Families, and Organizations*. San Francisco: Jossey-Bass.

Zimmer, L. 1988. Tokenism and women in the workplace: The limits of gender-neutral theory. *Social Prob* 35:64-77.

ORGANIZATIONS AND HEALTH AND SAFETY

Chapter Editor
Gunnela Westlander

Contents

PSYCHOSOCIAL FACTORS AND ORGANIZATIONAL MANAGEMENT

Gunnela Westlander

The term *organization* is often used in a broad sense, which is not so strange because the phenomenon of an "organization" has many aspects. It can be said that studying organizations makes up an entire problem area of its own, with no natural location within any specific academic discipline. Certainly the concept of organization has obtained a central position within what is called management science—which, in some countries, is a subject in its own right within the field of business studies. But in a number of other subject areas, among them occupational safety and health, there has also been reason to ponder why one is considering organizational theory and to determine which aspects of organization to embrace in research analyses.

The organization is not just of importance to company management, but is also of great significance for each person's work situation, both in health terms and in relation to his or her short- and long-term opportunities for making an effective contribution to work. Thus, it is of key importance for specialists in the field of occupational safety and health to be acquainted with the theorizing, conceptualization and forms of thinking about social reality to which the terms *organization* and *organizational development* or *change* refer.

Organizational arrangements have consequences for social relationships that exist amongst the people who work in the organization. Organizational arrangements are conceived of and intended to achieve certain social relations at work. A multiplicity of studies on psychosocial aspects of working life have affirmed that the form of an organization "breeds" social relations. The choice between alternative organizational structures is governed by a variety of considerations, some of which have their origins in a particular approach to management and organizational coordination. One form can be based on the view that effective organizational management is achieved when specific social interactions between the organization's members are enabled.

Figure 35.1 • Likert's linking pin model.

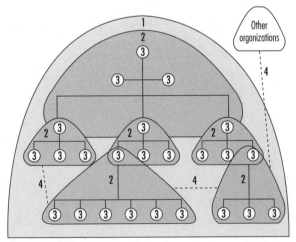

Key to numbers

① Overall organization focus of analysis ③ Individual job or position focus of analysis

② Organizational unit focus of analysis ④ Relations within and between units focus of analysis

The choice of the structural form in an organization is made on the basis of the way in which people are intended to be linked together to establish organizationally effective interdependent relations; or, as theorists of business administration tend to express the idea: "how the growth of critical combinations is facilitated".

One of the prominent members of the "human relations school", Rensis Likert (1961, 1967) has provided an enduring idea on how hierarchical "subsystems" in a complex organizational structure ideally should be linked together. Likert pointed to the importance of unity and solidarity among members of an organization. Here, the job supervisor/manager has a dual task:

1. to maintain unity and create a sense of belonging within a work group, and
2. to represent his or her work group in meetings with superior and parallel managerial staff. In this way the bonds between the hierarchical levels are reinforced.

Likert's "linking pin model" is shown in figure 35.1. Likert employed the analogy of the family to characterize desirable social interaction between different work units, which he conceived as functioning as "organizational families". He was convinced that the provision by management of scope and encouragement for the strengthening of personal relations between workers at different levels was a powerful means for increasing organizational effectiveness and uniting personnel behind the goals of the company. Likert's model is an attempt to achieve "a regularity of practice" of some kind, which would further reinforce the organizational structure laid down by management. From around the beginning of the 1990s his model has acquired increasing relevance. Likert's model may be regarded as an example of a recommended structure.

One way of using the term *organization* is with the focus on the human beings' competence; the organization in that sense is the total combination of competences and, if one wants to go a bit further, their synergetic effects. Another and opposite perspective places its focus on the coordination of people's activities needed to fulfil a set of goals of a business. We can call that the "organizational arrangement" which is decided upon on an agreed basis. In this chapter on organizational theory the presentation has its point of departure in organizational arrangement, and the members or workers participating in this arrangement are looked at from an occupational health perspective.

Structure as a Basic Concept in Organizational Theory

Structure is a common term within organization theory, referring to the form of organizational arrangement intended to bring a goal effectiveness. Business activities in working life can be analysed from a *structural* perspective. The structural approach has for long been the most popular, and has contributed most—quantitatively speaking—to the knowledge we have on organizations. (At the same time, members of a younger generation of organization researchers have expressed a series of misgivings concerning the value of this approach (Alvesson 1989; Morgan 1986)).

When adopting a structural perspective it is taken more or less for granted that there exists an *agreed order* (structure) to the form in which a set of activities is carried out. On the basis of this fundamental assumption, the organizational issue posed becomes one of the specific appearance of this form. In how much detail and in which ways have the tasks of persons in different job positions been described in formally issued, official documents? What rules apply to people in managerial positions? Information on the organizational pattern, the body of regulations and specified relations is available in documents such as instructions for management and job descriptions.

A second issue raised is how activities are organized and patterned *in practice:* what regularities actually exist, and what is the nature of relations between people? Raising this question in itself implies that a complete correspondence between formally decreed and practised forms of activities should not be expected. There are several reasons for this. Naturally, not all phases of work can be covered by a prescribed body of rules. Also, defining operations as they should be carried out will often not be adequate to describe the actual activities of workers and their interaction with each other because:

- The official structure will not necessarily be completely detailed, thus providing different degrees of scope for coordination/cooperation in practice.
- The normative (specified) nature of organizational structure will not match exactly the forms that members of the organization consider to be effective for activities.
- An organization's stated norms or rules provide a greater or lesser degree of motivation.
- The normative structure itself will have varying degrees of visibility within the organization, depending on the access of members of the organization to relevant information.

In practical terms, it is probably impossible for the *scope* of any norms which are developed to describe adequately the normal routines that occur. Defined norms simply cannot encompass the full range of practice and relations between human beings. The adequacy of the norms will be dependent on the level of detail in which the official structure is expressed. It is interesting and important in the assessment of organizations and for any preventive programmes to establish the extent of the correspondence between the norms and the practices of organizational activities.

The extent of the contrast between norms and practices (objective and subjective definitions of organizational structure) is important as is the difference between the organizational structure that is perceived by an "investigator" and the individual organizational member's image or perception of it. Not only is a lack of correspondence between the two of great intellectual interest, it can also constitute a handicap for the individual in the organization in that he or she may have far too inadequate a picture of the organization to be able to protect and/or promote his or her own interests.

Some Basic Structural Dimensions

There has been a long succession of ideas and principles concerning the management of organizations, each in turn striving for something new. Despite this, however, it remains the case that the official organizational structure generally stipulates a form of *hierarchical order* and a *division of responsibilities.* Thus, it specifies major aspects of *vertical integration* and *functional responsibility* or *authorization.*

We encounter the idea of vertical influence most readily in its simplest, *classical original form* (see figure 35.2). The organization comprises one superior and a number of subordinates, a number small enough for the superior to exercise direct control. The *developed classical form* (see figure 35.3) demonstrates how a complex organizational structure can be built up from small hierarchical systems (see figure 35.1). This common, extended form of the classical organization, however, does not necessarily specify the nature of horizontal interaction between people in non-management positions.

An organizational structure mostly consists of managerial layers (i.e., a "triangular" structure, with a few or several layers descending from the apex), and there is almost always a more or less accentuated hierarchically ordered form of organization desired.

Figure 35.2 • The classical original organizational form.

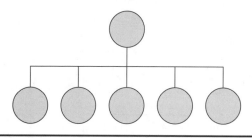

The basic principle is that of "unity of command" (Alvesson 1989): a "scalar" chain of authority is created, and applied more or less strictly according to the nature of the organizational structure selected. There may be long vertical channels of influence, forcing personnel to cope with the inconveniences of lengthy chains of command and indirect paths of communication when they wish to reach a decision-maker. Or, when there are only a few management layers (i.e., the organizational structure is *flat*—see figure 35.4), this indicates a preference on the part of top management to de-emphasize the supervisor-subordinate relationship. The distance between top management and employees is shorter, and lines of contact are more direct. At the same time, however, each manager will have a relatively large number of subordinates—in fact, sometimes so many that he or she cannot usually exercise direct control over personnel. Greater scope is thereby given for horizontal interaction, which becomes a necessity for operational effectiveness.

In a flat organizational structure, the norms for vertical influence are only crudely specified in a simple organizational chart. The chart thus has to be supplemented by instructions for managers and by detailed job instructions.

Hierarchical structures may be viewed as a *normative means of control,* which in turn may be characterized as offering minimum liability to members of the organization. Within this framework there is a more or less generously allocated amount of scope for individual influence and action, depending on what has been decided in relation to the decentralization of decision-making, delegation of tasks, temporary coordinating groups, and the structure of budgetary responsibilities. Where there is less generous scope for influence and action, there will be correspondingly smaller margin for error on the part of the individual. The degree

Figure 35.3 • The extended classical form.

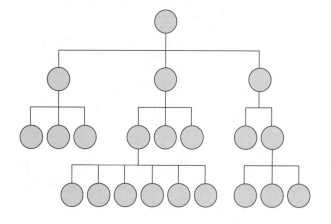

Figure 35.4 • The flat organization.

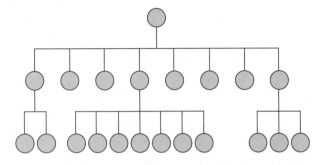

of latitude can usually only be guessed at from the content of the official documents referred to.

In addition to the hierarchical order (vertical influence), the official organizational structure specifies some (normative) form of division of responsibility and thereby *functional authority*. It might be said that the art of leading an organization as a whole is largely a matter of structuring all its activities in such a way that the combination of different functions arrived at has the greatest conceivable external impact. The names of the different parts (the functions) of the structure specify, albeit only as an outline, how management has conceived the breakdown into various sections of activities and how these shall then be combined and accounted for. From this we can also trace the demands placed on managers' functional authority.

Modifying the Organizational Structures

There are many variants on how an organization as a whole can be built up. One of the basic issues is how core activities (the production of goods or services) are to be combined with other necessary operational elements, including personnel management, information, administration, maintenance, marketing and so on. One alternative is to place major departments for administration, personnel, company finances and so on alongside production units (a functional or "staff" organization). Behind such an arrangement lies management's interest in personnel, within their specialized areas, developing a broad range of skills so that they can provide production units with assistance and support, reduce the burden upon them and promote their development.

An alternative to "administration parallel" is to staff production units with people possessing the required specialized administrative skills. In this way cooperation across specialized administrative boundaries can be brought about, thus benefiting the production unit in question. Additional alternative structures are possible, based on ideas concerning functional combinations which would promote cooperative working within organizations. Often organizations are required to respond to change in the operating environment, and hence a change in structure occurs. The transition from one organizational structure to another can involve drastic changes in desired forms of interaction and cooperation. These need not affect everyone in the organization; often they are imperceptible to the occupiers of certain job positions. It is important to take the changes into account in any analysis of organizational structures.

Identifying types of existing structures has become a major research task for many organization theorists in the business administration field (see, for example, Mintzberg 1983; Miller and Mintzberg 1983), the idea being that it would be of benefit if researchers could recognize the nature of organizations and place them in easily identifiable categories. By contrast, other re-

searchers have used empirical data (data based on observations of organizational structures) to demonstrate that limiting description to such strict typologies obscures the nuances of reality (Alvesson 1989). In their view, it is relevant to *learn* from the individual case rather than simply to generalize immediately to an existing typology. A researcher of occupational health should prefer the latter reality-based approach as it contributes to a better, more adequate understanding of the situational conditions in which the individual workers are involved.

Parallel Structures

Alongside its basic organizational structure (which specifies vertical influence and the functional distribution for core activities), an organization may also possess certain ad hoc structures, which may be set up for *either a definite or indefinite time period*. These are often called "parallel structures". They can be instituted for a variety of reasons, such as to further reinforce the competitiveness of the company (primarily serve the company's interests), as is the case with networking, or to strengthen the rights of employees (primarily serve the interests of employees), such as mechanisms for surveillance (e.g., health and safety committees).

As surveillance of the work environment has as its primary function to promote the safety interests of employees, it is frequently organized in a rather more permanent parallel structure. Such structures exist in many countries, often with operational procedures that are laid down by national legislation (see the chapter *Labour Relations and Human Resources Management*).

Networking

In modern corporate management, *network* is a term that has acquired a specialized usage. Creating a network means organizing circles of intermediate-level managers and key personnel from diverse parts of an organization for a specific purpose. The task of the network may be to promote development (e.g., that of secretarial positions throughout the company), provide training (e.g., personnel at all retail outlets), or effect rationalization (e.g., all the company's internal order routines). Typically, a networking task involves improving corporate operations in some concrete respect, such that the entire company is permeated by the improvement.

Compared with Likert's linking pin model, which aims to promote vertical as well as horizontal interaction within and between layers in the hierarchical structure, the point of a network is to tie people together in different constellations than those offered by the base structure (but, note, for no other reason than that of serving the interests of the company).

Networking is initiated by management to counter—but not dismantle—the established hierarchical structure (with its functional divisions) which has emerged as being far too sluggish in

Networking

One example of networking is the recent effort aimed at improving the general level of competence of operators which took place in a Volvo firm. Management initiated a network whose members could work out a system of tasks ordered according to the level of difficulty. A corresponding training programme guaranteed the workers a possibility of following a "career ladder" including a corresponding wage system. The members of the network were selected from among experienced employees from different parts of the plant and at different levels. Because the proposed system was perceived as an innovation, the collaboration in the network became highly motivating and the plan was realized in the shortest possible time.

Figure 35.5 • The organization of occupational safety —a parallel structure.

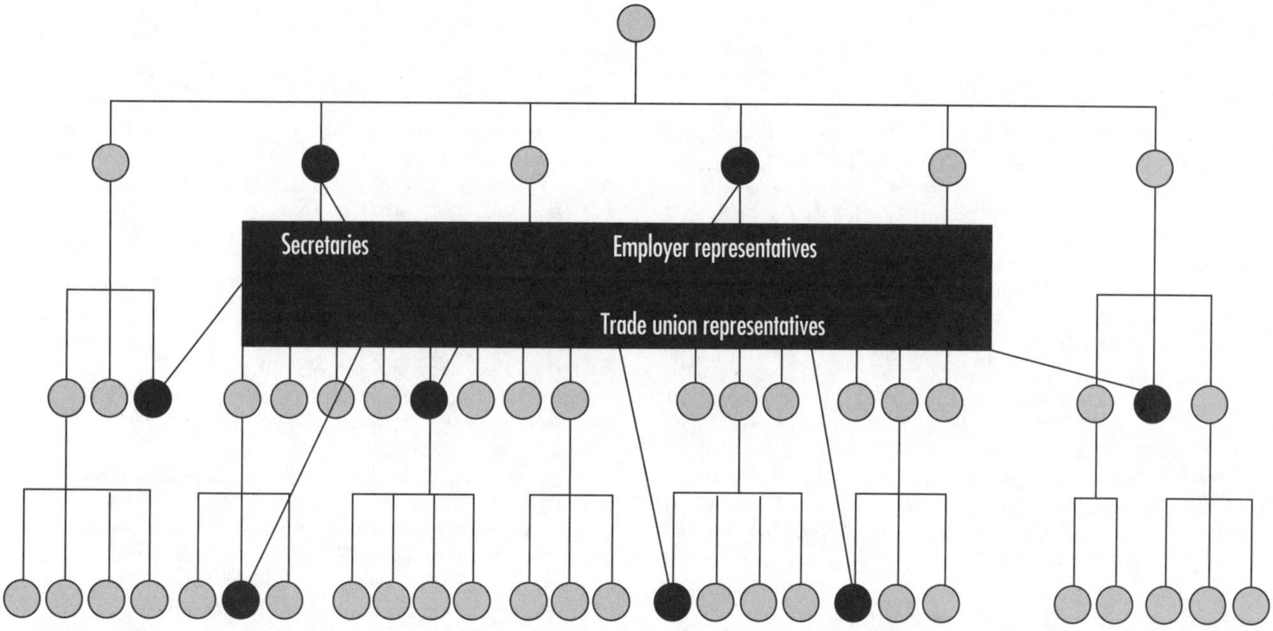

Secretaries

Employer representatives

Trade union representatives

response to new demands from the environment. Creating a network can be a better option than embarking on an arduous process of changing or restructuring the entire organization. According to Charan (1991), the key to effective networking is that top management gets the network working and selects its members (who should be highly motivated, energetic and committed, quick and effective, and with an ability to easily disseminate information to other employees). Top management should also keep a watchful eye on continued activities within the network. In this sense, networking is a "top-down" approach. With the sanction of management and funds at its disposal, a network can become a powerful structure which cuts across the base organization.

Implications for Health and Safety

The occupational health specialist has much to gain by asking how much of the interaction between people in the organization rests on the basic organizational structure and how much on the parallel structures that have been set up. In which does the individual actively take part? What is demanded from the individual in terms of effort and loyalty? How does this affect encounters with and cooperation between colleagues, work mates, managers and other active participants in formal contexts?

To the occupational health specialist concerned with psychosocial issues it is important to be aware that there is always some person(s) (from outside or inside the organization) who has taken on or been allocated the task of designing the set of normative prescriptions for activities. These "organizational creators" do not act alone but are assisted within the organization by loyal supporters of the structure they create. Some of the supporters are active participants in the creative process who use and further develop the principles. Others are the representatives or "mouthpieces" of personnel, either collectively or of specific groups (see figure 35.5). Moreover, there is also a large group of personnel who can be characterized as administrators of the prescribed form of activities but who have no say in its design or the method of its implementation.

Organizational Change

By studying organizational change we adopt a process perspective. The concept *organizational change* covers everything from a change in the total macrostructure of a company to alterations in work allocation—coordination of activity in precisely defined smaller units; it may involve changes in administration or in production. In one or another way the issue is to rearrange the work-based relations between employees.

Organizational changes will have implications for the health and well-being of those in the organization. The most easily observed dimensions of health are in the psychosocial domain. We can state that organizational change is very demanding for many employees. It will be a positive challenge to many individuals, and periods of lassitude, tiredness and irritation are unavoidable. The important thing for those responsible for occupational health is to prevent such feelings of lassitude from becoming permanent and to turn them into something positive. Attention must be paid to the more enduring attitudes to job quality and the feedback one gets in the form of one's own competence and personal development; the social satisfactions (of contacts, collaboration, "belongingness", team spirit, cohesiveness) and finally the emotions (security, anxiety, stress and strain) deriving from these conditions. The success of an organizational change should be assessed by taking into consideration these aspects of job satisfaction.

A common misconception which may hinder the ability to respond positively to organizational change is that normative structures are just formalities which have no relevance to how people really act or how they perceive the state of affairs they encounter. People who are labouring under this misconception believe that what is important is "the order in practice". They concentrate on how people actually act in "reality". Sometimes this point of view may seem convincing, especially in the case of those organizations where structural change has not been implemented for a considerable period of time and where people have got used to the existing organizational system. Employees have become accustomed to an accepted, tried and tested order. In

Organizational Change as the Method—Health at Work as the Main Goal

The following organizational change was studied in one of the major Swedish engineering companies. Here we find a good example of where the main objective was to improve/increase the level of health at work. The locality is a large industry in a rural area where it is impossible for trained secretaries to easily find other jobs. In practice, staff are forced to accept what this major concern can offer if they want to carry on with their special working skills. Some 50 women worked there as secretaries. Most of them were married to men also employed by the company and so were doubly bound to whatever work the area could offer. The common problems for the secretaries were the duties and salary scales. The company offered no opportunities for job development, training or promotion, and the work of the secretaries in the main consisted of simple routine duties, and so some of them were regarded as over-qualified. Management saw secretarial positions as "the end of the line", a staff policy which created great irritation among the secretaries. The work changes which arose out of this discontent went on for four years.

The intention was to obtain professional vocational development within the framework of secretarial employment; the problem was that there was no demand for this either from management or other staff categories. So the 50 secretaries had to carry through their objectives in the face of strong opposition. Here is a summary of how their efforts to bring about change progressed step by step.

The problem was first raised at a local meeting of the white-collar union. One of the secretaries was present. She pointed out that most of her colleagues did work which seemed to fall into other occupational classifications. The matter was noted but no action was taken. Some secretaries then approached the union's local committee and asked the chair to arrange a meeting with a number of their executives. This was done. Salary scales and vocational development for the secretaries was discussed. But interest declined after the meeting.

An internal consultant took over the problem and tried, in vain, to make the union take responsibility for some follow-up. A second internal consultant, an expert in job evaluation, became involved. Together with a firm of consultants, a survey was carried out among the secretaries. The result showed that dissatisfaction was widespread.

At the request of the union and management, the consultants arranged a number of conferences for the secretaries and their immediate superiors.

The intention here was to clarify for management what their working conditions were in practice and what, in more explicit form, their wishes for vocational development were, all within the framework of their secretarial duties. A great deal of hard work was done at these conferences. Prejudices and oppositional attitudes were ventilated. A list of problems was drawn up. A total of 45 managers and 53 secretaries participated. After this problem analysis stage

was completed, the consultants made it clear that their contribution was over.

The secretaries decided to take on the job themselves in the phase which now followed. Among possible solutions, they selected a business-economic strategy—this with the assumption that it would increase managerial interest in the matter. They divided themselves into small, specialist working groups (technology, ergonomy, purchasing and so on). Each group took upon itself to produce proposals to improve secretarial work. They also worked out a cost calculation for each proposal.

During the next few years 22 working groups were formed to solve varied problems. Six working groups were in operation 4 years after the start. From the names of these groups we can see where interest for effectiveness lay: technology in the future, office materials, travel service, copy-saving measures, training, sensitivity training. They were more and more successful in gaining attention for their proposals, many of which were carried through.

A number of rationalization measures arose from the studies made by the groups. Now nobody does any unnecessary work. Manuscripts are accepted as working material. Secretaries perform copy typing only where necessary. An office computer system has been procured. The secretarial group lost 10 staff by attrition (usually by moving to another part of the country.) The secretaries started to be consulted by the company's recruitment department when a vacant secretarial post was to be filled. They were asked to propose reorganizations so that new staff would not be needed. Up to now, 19 secretaries have been promoted to a higher job classification with higher salaries as their work became more skilled. Management is satisfied with the organizational changes which have taken place.

The original idea of the project was to cut out unnecessary and unqualified items from secretarial work and add more qualified duties. This succeeded; at the same time a great deal of expensive duplication of work and long-winded working routines were discovered. After a while, the process could continue in other forms. It was integrated into the work of the staff department under the name RGSD (Reference Group for Secretarial Development).

For some while, this organizational change became known all over the country. A number of group members were invited to committees and conferences around the country to describe the project.

Psychosocial health consequences. These work changes were of immense importance for the secretaries personally. For most, it meant a greater consciousness of their vocational role and of the opportunities which existed to improve the secretarial function in the company. A team spirit grew up when they looked at problems common to them all. As a job collective they saw, step by step, the result of their tenacious work. Their higher qualifications came from their own efforts (Westlander 1991).

---

these situations, they do not reflect upon whether it is normative or just operates in practice, and do not care very much whether their own "image" of the organization corresponds with the official one.

On the other hand, it should also be noted that the normative descriptions may seem to provide a more accurate picture of an organization's reality than is the case. Simply because such descriptions are documented in writing and have received an official stamp does not mean that they are an accurate representation of the organization in practice. Reality can differ greatly, as for example when normative organizational descriptions are so out of date as to have lost current relevance.

To optimize effectiveness in responding to change, one has to sort out carefully the norms and the practices of the organization undergoing change. That formally laid down norms for operations affect and intervene in interactions between people, first becomes apparent to many when they have personally witnessed or been drawn into structural change. Studying such changes requires a *process perspective* on the organization.

A process perspective includes questions of the type:

• How in reality do people interact within an organization that has been structured according to a certain principle or model?

- How do people react to a prescribed formal order for activities and how do they handle this?
- How do people react to a *new order*, proposed or already decided upon, and how do they handle this?

The point is to obtain an overall picture of how it is envisaged that workers shall relate to each other, the ways in which this happens in practice, and the nature of the state of tension between the official order and the order in practice.

The incompatibility between the description of organizations and their reality is one of the indications that there is no organizational model which is always "the best" for describing a reality. The structure selected as a model is an attempt (made with a greater or lesser degree of success) to adapt activities of the problems which management finds it most urgent to solve at a particular point in time when it is clear that an organization must undergo change.

The reason for effecting a transition from one structure to another may be the result of a variety of causes, such as changes in the skills of personnel available, the need for new systems of remuneration, or the requirement that the influence of a particular section of functions of the organization should be expanded—or contracted. One or several strategic motives can lie behind changes in the structure of an organization. Often the driving force behind change is simply that the need is so great, the goal has become one of organizational survival. Sometimes the issue is ease of survival and sometimes survival itself. In some cases of structural change, employees are involved to only a limited extent, sometimes not at all. The consequences of change can be favourable for some, unfavourable for others. One occasionally encounters instances where organizational structures are changed primarily for the purpose of promoting employees' occupational health and safety (Westlander 1991).

The Concept of Work Organization

Until now we have focused on the organization as a whole. We can also restrict our unit of analysis to the job content of the individual worker and the nature of his or her collaboration with colleagues. The most common term we find used for this is *work organization*. This too is a term which is employed in several disciplines and within various research approaches.

First, for example, the concept of work organization is to be found in the *pure ergonomic occupational research tradition* which considers the way in which equipment and people are adapted to each other at work. With respect to human beings, what is central is how they react to and cope with the equipment. In terms of strain and effectiveness, the *amount of time spent at work* is also important. Such time aspects include how long the work should go on, during which periods of the day or night, with what degree of regularity, and which time-related opportunities for recovery are offered in the form of the scheduling of breaks and the availability of lengthier periods of rest or time off. These time conditions must be organized by management. Thus, such conditions should be regarded as organizational factors within the field of ergonomic research—and as very important ones. It may be said that the time devoted to the work task can moderate the relationship between equipment and worker with respect to health effects.

But there are also *wider ergonomic approaches*: analyses are extended to take into account the work situation in which the equipment is employed. Here it is a question of the work situation and the worker being well adapted to each other. In such cases, it is the equipment plus a series of work organizational factors (such as job content, kinds and composition of tasks, responsibilities, forms of cooperation, forms of supervision, time devoted in all its aspects) which make up the complex situation which the worker reacts to, copes with and acts within.

Such work organizational factors are taken account of in broader ergonomic analyses; ergonomics has often included consideration of the type of work psychology which focuses on the job content of the individual (kinds and composition of tasks) plus other related demands. These are regarded as operating in parallel with physical conditions. In this way, it becomes the task of the researcher to adopt a position on whether and how the physical and work organizational conditions with which the individual is regularly confronted contribute to aspects of ill-health (e.g., to stress and strain). To isolate cause and effect is a considerably more difficult undertaking than is the case when a narrow ergonomic approach is adopted.

In addition to the work organizational conditions to which the individual is regularly exposed there are a number of work organizational phenomena (such as recruitment policies, training programmes, salary systems) which may be more peripheral, but still have decisive importance in terms of what is offered to the worker by his or her immediate work situation. This broader spectrum (and one might still wonder whether it has been treated broadly enough) is of interest to the researcher who wishes to understand the relationship between the individual worker and activities as a whole.

Organizational Psychology

Whereas work psychology has its focus on the individual's occupational tasks and connected job demands in relation to the individual's capacity, the subject of organizational psychology refers to individuals as defined by the place they occupy within an organization, as organizational members more or less outwardly visible, more or less active. The point of departure for the organizational approach is the operation of a company or organization and those various parts of it in which individuals are themselves involved.

Carrying out activities requires various organizational arrangements. A unifying organizational structure is required; activities as a whole need to be broken down into identifiable job tasks. A task structure has to be created in accordance with selected job distribution principles. Thus, management systems, technical systems and maintenance routines are all required; and, in many cases, there is a need for special safety systems and occupational health promotion systems in addition to the legally required safety organization.

In addition to the structural requirements for accomplishing tasks, systems for remuneration and control must be implemented. Co-determination systems and systems for skills development and training (not least so that the technical systems can be mastered) must all be in operation. All of these systems can be described as organizational factors. They have the character of formalized activities designed to achieve a specific purpose, and have a parallel existence within the company. As mentioned above, they may be either permanent or instigated for a shorter or longer temporary period, but they all have some sort of influence on the terms on which the individual works. They can be examined from various psychosocial perspectives: as support resources for the worker, as control instruments employed by management, or as success factors for management or employees. The interaction between these various organizational systems is of the greatest interest: their aims are not always compatible; rather, they can be on a collision course. The "bearers" of the systems are human beings.

Organizational Change and its Psychosocial Aspects

To survive as an organization, management must constantly pay attention to what is going on in the world outside, and must be

Applying Organizational Psychology

The official in the company's EDP Department and the claims adjuster in the Occupational Injury Department were involved in intensive collaboration for a period of about six months. They had never previously had the opportunity to work together and did not know each other well. The EDP specialist is the head of his department, which forms a part of the company's central financial administration, positioned immediately below head-office management. The occupational-injury claims adjuster is head of one of the company's business units, the Occupational Injury Department, which is geographically located in another part of the town.

The EDP Department has the duty, on a continuous basis, to rationalize and redesign the forms used by the company, so that the registration of documents and correspondence within the company's various business units is simplified and made as effective as possible.

The Occupational Injury Department has the task of handling the occupational-injury claims of its policyholders (circle of clients) in a scrupulous and accurate manner, so that clients feel that they are correctly treated. The EDP Department has a rationalizing function in the company, whereas the Occupational Injury Department has a client-oriented function in a specialized area of insurance business.

The occupational-injury claims adjuster has daily contacts with other officials in his own work group and also with members of other work groups within the Occupational Injury Department. These contacts are made primarily to discuss matters concerning occupational injuries that will enable the maintenance of an intra-departmental consensus on the guiding principles for claims adjustment. The Occupational Injury Department lives in a world of its own within the company, and has very few direct contacts beyond those with its own circle of clients. Contact with the rest of the company is extremely limited.

The EDP Department is a part of the company's central financial-control system. The head of department has brief but regular contacts with all parts of the company, in fact more with these parts than with the personnel of parallel departments in central finance.

The primary reason why collaboration between the EDP official and the occupational-injury claims adjuster arose is that the EDP Department received instructions from management to so design its rationalization activities that insurance officials in the business units were able to increase their productivity, and thereby provide scope to accommodate a wider circle of clients (in part by offering new kinds of policies/insurance packages). The occupational-injury claims adjuster reacts with great hesitation to the EDP official's proposal when the latter indicates management's motive. The adjuster wants to achieve his own goal and fulfil his own function in the company, namely that of satisfying the needs of policy holders for the scrupulous administration of matters concerned with occupational injuries. He considers that this goal is incompatible with a further increase in productivity.

The interaction between the official from the EDP Department and the occupational-injury claims adjuster is complicated by factors concerned with their different locations within the organization, their different kinds of obligations and their differing "points of view" on activities in general. In other words, the two officials have to approach problems (in this case the problems of profitability) from different perspectives.

What we have discovered is the existence of conflicting goals and forces, which are built into an organizational design for activities, and which make up a platform for interaction between two officials.

constantly ready for change. Sudden changes forced by outside influences—such as a loss of interest by a major customer, changes in demand, sudden appearance of new competitors, demands for information from government authorities or governmental acts which restructure the public sector—must produce immediate but rational reactions from management. The reaction is often to reorganize part or all of the business activity. Most of the time, the situation is hardly one that puts the needs of health of the individual in the foreground, or provides the time required for long-drawn-out participation of employees in negotiations over change. Even if, in the long run, such negotiations would have been constructive, the fact is that management usually places its hope in the obedience and trust of the employees. Those who want to remain employed must accept the situation.

Karasek (1992) in a survey of papers written for the ILO distinguishes between planned organizational changes with regard to the extent to which they are "expert-directed" or "participation-directed". The projects did not display any national differences with regard to the relative weight placed on expert and participation direction. However, it is maintained (Ivancevich et al. 1990) that the role of top management is important in organizational-change projects designed to reduce the presence of occupational stress and improve workers' well-being and health. Such interventions require the collaborative efforts of management/staff and employees, and possibly also of experts.

When structural changes occur, it is inevitable that feelings of uncertainty will arise in all members of the organization. Despite the fact that all will experience uncertainty, the degree and types of uncertainty will vary according to position in the organization. The prerequisites for gaining a true picture of how well or badly the company is proceeding in the changes are completely different at the management and employee levels. At the risk of oversimplifying the situation somewhat, we can speak of two types of feelings of uncertainty:

1. *Knowing about the uncertainty of the organization's continued existence or success*. This type of uncertainty feeling will be found in decision-makers. "Knowing about the uncertainty" means that the person in question can make an evaluation of the relative advantages and disadvantages in coping with the uncertain situation. He or she has the opportunity to deal with the situation actively (e.g., by obtaining more information, trying to influence people and so on). Alternatively, a person can react to the change negatively by trying to avoid the situation in various ways, such as seeking other employment.

2. *Not knowing about the uncertainty of the organization's continued existence or success*. This type of uncertainty will be found in employees in non-decision-making posts. "Not knowing about the uncertainty" means that the individual has difficulty in making a judgement and generally has only the opportunity to react passively (taking a wait-and-see approach, remaining in an unsettled and diffuse state, letting others take action).

Psychologically, especially when trying to prevent environmental effects of work, these differing feelings of uncertainty are very important. One side will feel alienated toward the subjective reality of the other side. The initiative for a change in organization usually comes from high up in the hierarchy, and the primary aim is increased efficiency. Work on organizational change revitalizes a manager's work content since change brings about new conditions which must be dealt with. This can become a positive challenge, often a stimulation. Among non-management employees, a reorganization has a more conditional function: it is a good thing only to the extent that it improves, or leaves unaltered, the employees' current and future work situation.

From a more detached perspective, people in specialist administrative positions or organizational experts may show a third reaction pattern: the reorganization is interesting, whatever the result. It can be looked on as an experiment showing how the employees and the business are affected—knowledge that will be of value in the future to an administrator or organizational expert in the same or another company.

Changes in organization are complicated actions not only because of the practical changes that must be introduced, but also because they often have psychological and psychosocial consequences. The result is that the atmosphere at work reflects differing interests in the proposed changes and various types of psychic stress. Also this complex social reality is difficult to study in a systematic way.

Business economists, sociologists, and psychologists differ in their approach to interpreting the links between organizational change and individual working conditions. The psychology of work and organization directs attention to the employees and to the conditions under which they labour. An effort is made to obtain systematized knowledge about the effects of organizational change on individual health and work opportunities. It is this approach that gives us information on the occupational mental health consequences.

In organizational sociology the individual conditions upon which organizational change has an impact are mostly analysed in order to understand/describe/discover the consequences for the content of intergroup and interorganizational relationships and dependencies. In the business and administrative sciences there may be an interest in psychological aspects, with the aim of understanding certain attitudes and behaviours of the members of the organization (sometimes only those of the key persons in some sense) crucial for the progress of business activities.

Measurement of Organizational Factors

Organizational factors, division of work, decentralization, reward systems are not physical objects! They are intangible. It is not possible to take hold of them, and most of them express themselves in activities and interactions which disappear with greater or lesser rapidity, only to be replaced by new ones. Those work organization dimensions which it is possible to "measure" (in roughly the same way as is the case with physical factors) are, not surprisingly, also the ones that a researcher with a background in the natural sciences finds most manageable and acceptable. Time, for example, can be measured objectively, with a measuring instrument that is independent of the human being. How work is organized in terms of time (the time spent at work and time for breaks and lengthier periods of rest) can scarcely cause major measurement problems for ergonomists. On the other hand, the individual's own perception of aspects of time is psychological, and this is considerably more difficult to measure.

It is also relatively easier for the investigator to come to terms with work *organizational factors* that are given material form. This is what happens when instructions for managers, job descriptions and work procedures are put in writing, and also applies when control systems and forms of personnel coordination are documented. The systematic analysis of the contents of these texts can provide useful information. However, it should be remembered that actual practice can deviate—sometimes significantly—from what is prescribed in writing. In such cases, it is not so easy to obtain a systematic picture of people's activities and attitudes.

Taking the Step from Conceptualization to Empirical Study

Measurement of organizational phenomena is based on a variety of information sources:

- written prescriptions of operational and coordinative procedures
- investigators' systematic observation of work behaviour and social interaction
- employees' self-reports on behaviour, interactions, activities, attitudes, intentions and thoughts
- policy documents, agreements, minutes of conferences, long-term prospects
- views of key persons.

Which kind of information should be given priority has to do partly with the kind of organizational factor to be assessed and with method preferences, and partly with the organization's generosity to let the investigator explore the field in the way he or she prefers.

Measurement in organizational research is seldom an either/or issue, and is most often a "multisource" enterprise.

In measuring *organizational change* it is even more necessary to give attention to the characteristic features. A great deal happens in interpersonal relationships before and at a very early stage after change is initiated. In contrast to laboratory experiments or in meetings where group questionnaires can be taken, the situation (i.e., the process of change) is not under control. Researchers who study organizational change should find this unpredictable process fascinating and not be irritated by it or be impatient. Industrial sociologists ought to have the same feeling. The idea of evaluating final effects should be abandoned. We must realize that preventive work consists of being at hand the whole time and providing adequate support. One should be especially careful with formal superior-subordinate (employee) situations.

Evaluating the research on organizational change from an occupational health perspective leads to the conclusion that there has been a great variation of interest shown in the health of employees, especially their psychosocial health, when organizational changes are taking place. In some cases the matter has been left totally to chance, with a complete lack of interest or consideration by top management and even among members of safety and health committees. In other cases there may be an interest, but no experience to base it on. In some cases, however, one can glimpse a combination of efficiency and health reasons as the motivation for organizational change. The case in which the main objective is to preserve or improve employee psychosocial health is a rarity. However, there is a growing awareness of the importance of considering employee health during all stages of organizational change (Porras and Robertson 1992).

During organizational change, relationships should ideally be marked by a feeling of cooperation, at least at the informal level. Resources for all these activities are available in many present-day companies with their personnel functions, their department charged with organization, company-run occupational health departments and interested union representatives. In some of these companies there is also a more explicit philosophy of prevention directing management on different levels towards an effective use of all these resources and moving the professionals of these various functions towards fruitful cooperation. This visible trend to consider occupational health aspects in the implementation of organizational change may hopefully expand—something which, however, requires more consciousness among occupational health-experts of the importance of being well acquainted with the thinking and theorizing on organizational conditions.

References

Alvesson, M. 1989. A flat pyramid: a symbolic processing of organizational structure. *Int Studies Manag Org* 14(4):5-23.

Charan, R. 1991. How networks reshape organizations—for results. *Harvard Bus Rev* September/October:104-115.

Ivancevich, JM, MT Matteson, SM Freedman, and JS Phillips. 1990. Worksite stress management interventions. *Am Psychol* February:252-261.

Karasek, R. 1992. Stress prevention through work reorganization: a summary of 19 international case studies. *Cond Work Dig* 11(2):23-41.

Likert, R. 1961 and 1967. *The Human Organization*. New York: McGraw Hill.

Miller, D and H Mintzberg. 1983. The case of configuration. In *Beyond Method: Strategies for Social Research*, edited by G Morgan. Beverly Hills,CA: Sage Publications.

Mintzberg, H. 1983. *Structure in Fives: Designing Effective Organizations*. Englewood Cliffs: Prentice-Hall.

Morgan, G. 1986. *Images of Organizations*. Beverly Hills: Sage Publications.

Porras, JI and PJ Robertson. 1992. Organizational development: theory, practice, and research. In Chap. 12 in *Handbook of Industrial and Organizational Psychology*, edited by D Dunnette and LM Hough. Chicago: Rand McNally College Publishing Company.

Westlander, G. 1991. Organizational change and health at work. In *The Psychosocial Work Environment: Work Organization, Democratization and Health*, edited by JV Johnson and G Johansson. New York: Baywood Publishing Company,Inc.

Other relevant readings

Westlander, G. 1997. *People At Work: The Socio-Psychological Context*. In press.

BAROMETRIC PRESSURE, INCREASED

36

Chapter Editor
T.J.R. Francis

Contents

WORKING UNDER INCREASED BAROMETRIC PRESSURE

Eric Kindwall

The atmosphere normally consists of 20.93% oxygen. The human body is naturally adapted to breathe atmospheric oxygen at a pressure of approximately 160 torr at sea level. At this pressure, haemoglobin, the molecule which carries oxygen to the tissue, is approximately 98% saturated. Higher pressures of oxygen cause little important increase in oxyhaemoglobin, since its concentration is virtually 100% to begin with. However, significant amounts of unburnt oxygen may pass into physical solution in the blood plasma as the pressure rises. Fortunately, the body can tolerate a fairly wide range of oxygen pressures without appreciable harm, at least in the short term. Longer term exposures may lead to oxygen toxicity problems.

When a job requires breathing compressed air, as in diving or caisson work, oxygen deficiency (hypoxia) is rarely a problem, as the body will be exposed to an increasing amount of oxygen as the absolute pressure rises. Doubling the pressure will double the number of molecules inhaled per breath while breathing compressed air. Thus the amount of oxygen breathed is effectively equal to 42%. In other words, a worker breathing air at a pressure of 2 atmospheres absolute (ATA), or 10 m beneath the sea, will breathe an amount of oxygen equal to breathing 42% oxygen by mask on the surface.

Oxygen toxicity

On the earth's surface, human beings can safely continuously breathe 100% oxygen for between 24 and 36 hours. After that, pulmonary oxygen toxicity ensues (the Lorrain-Smith effect). The symptoms of lung toxicity consist of substernal chest pain; dry, non-productive cough; a drop in the vital capacity; loss of surfactant production. A condition known as *patchy atelectasis* is seen on x-ray examination, and with continued exposure microhaemorrhages and ultimately production of permanent fibrosis in the lung will develop. All stages of oxygen toxicity through the microhaemorrhage state are reversible, but once fibrosis sets in, the scarring process becomes irreversible. When 100% oxygen is breathed at 2 ATA, (a pressure of 10 m of sea water), the early symptoms of oxygen toxicity become manifest after about six hours. It should be noted that interspersing short, five-minute periods of air breathing every 20 to 25 minutes can double the length of time required for symptoms of oxygen toxicity to appear.

Oxygen can be breathed at pressures below 0.6 ATA without ill effect. For example, a worker can tolerate 0.6 atmosphere oxygen breathed continuously for two weeks without any loss of vital capacity. The measurement of vital capacity appears to be the most sensitive indicator of early oxygen toxicity. Divers working at great depths may breathe gas mixtures containing up to 0.6 atmospheres oxygen with the rest of the breathing medium consisting of helium and/or nitrogen. Six tenths of an atmosphere corresponds to breathing 60% oxygen at 1 ATA or at sea level.

At pressures greater than 2 ATA, pulmonary oxygen toxicity no longer becomes the primary concern, as oxygen can cause seizures secondary to cerebral oxygen toxicity. Neurotoxicity was first described by Paul Bert in 1878 and is known as the Paul Bert effect. If a person were to breathe 100% oxygen at a pressure of 3 ATA for much longer than three continuous hours, he or she will very likely suffer a *grand mal* seizure. Despite over 50 years of active research as to the mechanism of oxygen toxicity of the brain and lung, this response is still not completely understood.

Certain factors are known, however, to enhance toxicity and to lower the seizure threshold. Exercise, CO_2 retention, use of steroids, presence of fever, chilling, ingestion of amphetamines, hyperthyroidism and fear can have an oxygen tolerance effect. An experimental subject lying quietly in a dry chamber at pressure has much greater tolerance than a diver who is working actively in cold water underneath an enemy ship, for example. A military diver may experience cold, hard exercise, probable CO_2 build-up using a closed-circuit oxygen rig, and fear, and may experience a seizure within 10-15 minutes working at a depth of only 12 m, whereas a patient lying quietly in a dry chamber may easily tolerate 90 minutes at a pressure of 20 m without great danger of seizure. Exercising divers may be exposed to partial pressure of oxygen up to 1.6 ATA for short periods up to 30 minutes, which corresponds to breathing 100% oxygen at a depth of 6 m. It is important to note that one should never expose anyone to 100% oxygen at a pressure greater than 3 ATA, nor for a time longer than 90 minutes at that pressure, even with a subject quietly recumbent.

There is considerable individual variation in susceptibility to seizure between individuals and, surprisingly, within the same individual, from day to day. For this reason, "oxygen tolerance" tests are essentially meaningless. Giving seizure-suppressing drugs, such as phenobarbital or phenytoin, will prevent oxygen seizures but do nothing to mitigate permanent brain or spinal cord damage if pressure or time limits are exceeded.

Carbon monoxide

Carbon monoxide can be a serious contaminant of the diver's or caisson worker's breathing air. The most common sources are internal combustion engines, used to power compressors, or other operating machinery in the vicinity of the compressors. Care should be taken to be sure that compressor air intakes are well clear of any sources of engine exhaust. Diesel engines usually produce little carbon monoxide but do produce large quantities of oxides of nitrogen, which can produce serious toxicity to the lung. In the United States, the current federal standard for carbon monoxide levels in inspired air is 35 parts per million (ppm) for an 8-hour working day. For example, at the surface even 50 ppm would not produce detectable harm, but at a depth of 50 m it would be compressed and produce the effect of 300 ppm. This concentration can produce a level of up to 40% carboxyhaemoglobin over a period of time. The actual analysed parts per million must be multiplied by the number of atmospheres at which it is delivered to the worker.

Divers and compressed-air workers should become aware of the early symptoms of carbon monoxide poisoning, which include headache, nausea, dizziness and weakness. It is important to ensure that the compressor intake be always located upwind from the compressor engine exhaust pipe. This relationship must be continually checked as the wind changes or the vessels position shifts.

For many years it was widely assumed that carbon monoxide would combine with the body's haemoglobin to produce carboxyhaemoglobin, causing its lethal effect by blocking transport of oxygen to the tissues. More recent work shows that although this effect does cause tissue hypoxia, it is not in itself fatal. The most serious damage occurs at the cellular level due to direct toxicity of the carbon monoxide molecule. Lipid peroxidation of cell membranes, which can only be terminated by hyperbaric oxygen treatment, appears to be the main cause of death and long-term sequelae.

Carbon dioxide

Carbon dioxide is a normal product of metabolism and is eliminated from the lungs through the normal process of respiration. Various types of breathing apparatus, however, can impair its elimination or cause high levels to build up in the diver's inspired air.

From a practical point of view, carbon dioxide can exert deleterious effects on the body in three ways. First, in very high concentrations (above 3%), it can cause judgmental errors, which at first may amount to inappropriate euphoria, followed by depression if the exposure is prolonged. This, of course, can have serious consequences for a diver under water who wants to maintain good judgement to remain safe. As the concentration climbs, CO_2 will eventually produce unconsciousness when levels rise much above 8%. A second effect of carbon dioxide is to exacerbate or worsen nitrogen narcosis (see below). At partial pressures of above 40 mm Hg, carbon dioxide begins to have this effect (Bennett and Elliot 1993). At high PO_2's, such as one is exposed to in diving, the respiratory drive due to high CO_2 is attenuated and it is possible under certain conditions for divers who tend to retain CO_2 to increase their levels of carbon dioxide sufficient to render them unconscious. The final problem with carbon dioxide under pressure is that, if the subject is breathing 100% oxygen at pressures greater than 2 ATA, the risk for seizures is greatly enhanced as carbon dioxide levels rise. Submarine crews have easily tolerated breathing 1.5% CO_2 for two months at a time with no functional ill effect, a concentration that is thirty times the normal concentration found in atmospheric air. Five thousand ppm, or ten times the level found in normal fresh air, is considered safe for the purposes of industrial limits. However, even 0.5% CO_2 added to 100% oxygen mix will predispose a person to seizures when breathed at increased pressure.

Nitrogen

Nitrogen is an inert gas with regard to normal human metabolism. It does not enter into any form of chemical combination with compounds or chemicals within the body. However, it is responsible for severe impairment in a diver's mental functioning when breathed under high pressure.

Nitrogen behaves as an aliphatic anaesthetic as atmospheric pressure increases, which results in the concentration of nitrogen also increasing. Nitrogen fits well into the Meyer-Overton hypothesis which states that any aliphatic anaesthetic will exhibit anaesthetic potency in direct proportion to its oil-water solubility ratio. Nitrogen, which is five times more soluble in fat than in water, produces an anaesthetic effect precisely at the predicted ratio.

In actual practice, diving to depths of 50 m can be accomplished with compressed-air, although the effects of nitrogen narcosis first become evident between 30 and 50 m. Most divers, however, can function adequately within these parameters. Deeper than 50 m, helium/oxygen mixtures are commonly used to avoid the effects of nitrogen narcosis. Air diving has been done to depths of slightly over 90 m, but at these extreme pressures, the divers were barely able to function and could hardly remember what tasks they had been sent down to accomplish. As noted earlier, any excess CO_2 build-up further worsens the effect of nitrogen. Because ventilatory mechanics are affected by the density of gas at great pressures, there is an automatic CO_2 build-up in the lung because of changes in laminar flow within the bronchioles and the diminution of the respiratory drive. Thus, air diving deeper than 50 m can be extremely dangerous.

Nitrogen exerts its effect by its simple physical presence dissolved in neural tissue. It causes a slight swelling of the neuronal cell membrane, which makes it more permeable to sodium and potassium ions. It is felt that interference with the normal depolarization/repolarization process is responsible for clinical symptoms of nitrogen narcosis.

Decompression

Decompression tables

A decompression table sets out the schedule, based on depth and time of exposure, for decompressing a person who has been exposed to hyperbaric conditions. Some general statements can be made about decompression procedures. No decompression table can be guaranteed to avoid decompression illness (DCI) for everyone, and indeed as described below, many problems have been noted with some tables currently in use. It must be remembered that bubbles are produced during every normal decompression, no matter how slow. For this reason, although it can be stated that the longer the decompression the less the likelihood of DCI, at the extreme of least likelihood, DCI becomes an essentially random event.

Habituation

Habituation, or acclimatization, occurs in divers and compressed-air workers, and renders them less susceptible to DCI after repeated exposures. Acclimatization can be produced after about a week of daily exposure, but it is lost after an absence from work of between 5 days to a week or by a sudden increase in pressure. Unfortunately construction companies have relied on acclimatization to make work possible with what are viewed as grossly inadequate decompression tables. To maximize the utility of acclimatization, new workers are often started at midshift to allow them to habituate without getting DCI. For example, the present Japanese Table 1 for compressed-air workers utilizes the split shift, with a morning and afternoon exposure to compressed air with a surface interval of one hour between exposures. Decompression from the first exposure is about 30% of that required by the US Navy and the decompression from the second exposure is only 4% of that required by the Navy. Nevertheless, habituation makes this departure from physiologic decompression possible. Workers with even ordinary susceptibility to decompression illness self-select themselves out of compressed-air work.

The mechanism of habituation or acclimatization is not understood. However, even if the worker is not experiencing pain, damage to brain, bone, or tissue may be taking place. Up to four times as many changes are visible on MRIs taken of the brains of compressed-air workers compared to age-matched controls that have been studied (Fueredi, Czarnecki and Kindwall 1991). These probably reflect lacunar infarcts.

Diving decompression

Most modern decompression schedules for divers and caisson workers are based on mathematical models akin to those developed originally by J.S. Haldane in 1908 when he made some empirical observations on permissible decompression parameters. Haldane observed that a pressure reduction of one half could be tolerated in goats without producing symptoms. Using this as a starting point, he then, for mathematical convenience, conceived of five different tissues in the body loading and unloading nitrogen at varying rates based on the classical half time equation. His staged decompression tables were then designed to avoid exceeding a 2:1 ratio in any of the tissues. Over the years, Haldane's model has been modified empirically in attempts to make it fit what divers were observed to tolerate. However, all mathematical models for the loading and elimination of gases are flawed, since there are no decompression tables which remain as safe or become safer as time and depth are increased.

Probably the most reliable decompression tables currently available for air diving are those of the Canadian Navy, known as the DCIEM tables (Defence and Civil Institute of Environmental Medicine). These tables were tested thoroughly by non-habituated divers over a wide range of conditions and produce a very low rate of decompression illness. Other decompression schedules which have been well tested in the field are the French National Standards, originally developed by Comex, the French diving company.

The US Navy Air Decompression tables are unreliable, especially when pushed to their limits. In actual use, US Navy Master Divers routinely decompress for a depth 3 m (10 ft) deeper and/or one exposure time segment longer than required for the actual dive to avoid problems. The Exceptional Exposure Air Decompression Tables are particularly unreliable, having produced decompression illness on 17% to 33% of all the test dives. In general, the US Navy's decompression stops are probably too shallow.

Tunnelling and caisson decompression

None of the air decompression tables which call for air breathing during decompression, currently in wide use, appear to be safe for tunnel workers. In the United States, the current federal decompression schedules (US Bureau of Labor Statuties 1971), enforced by the Occupational Safety and Health Administration (OSHA), have been shown to produce DCI in one or more workers on 42% of the working days while being used at pressures between 1.29 and 2.11 bar. At pressures over 2.45 bar, they have been shown to produce a 33% incidence of aseptic necrosis of the bone (dysbaric osteonecrosis). The British Blackpool Tables are also flawed. During the building of the Hong Kong subway, 83% of the workers using these tables complained of symptoms of DCI. They have also been shown to produce an incidence of dysbaric osteonecrosis of up to 8% at relatively modest pressures.

The new German oxygen decompression tables devised by Faesecke in 1992 have been used with good success in a tunnel under the Kiel Canal. The new French oxygen tables also appear to be excellent by inspection but have not yet been used on a large project.

Using a computer which examined 15 years of data from successful and unsuccessful commercial dives, Kindwall and Edel devised compressed-air caisson decompression tables for the US National Institute for Occupational Safety and Health in 1983 (Kindwall, Edel and Melton 1983) using an empirical approach which avoided most of the pitfalls of mathematical modelling. Modelling was used only to interpolate between real data points. The research upon which these tables was based found that when air was breathed during decompression, the schedule in the tables did not produce DCI. However, the times used were prohibitively long and therefore impractical for the construction industry. When an oxygen variant of the table was computed, however, it was found that decompression time could be shortened to times similar to, or even shorter than, the current OSHA-enforced air decompression tables cited above. These new tables were subsequently tested by non-habituated subjects of varying ages at pressures ranging from 0.95 bar to 3.13 bar in 0.13 bar increments. Average work levels were simulated by weight lifting and treadmill walking during exposure. Exposure times were as long as possible, in keeping with the combined work time and decompression time fitting into an eight-hour work day. These are the only schedules which will be used in actual practice for shift work. No DCI was reported during these tests and bone scan and x ray failed to reveal any dysbaric osteonecrosis. To date, these are the only laboratory-tested decompression schedules in existence for compressed-air workers.

Decompression of hyperbaric chamber personnel

US Navy air decompression schedules were designed to produce a DCI incidence of less than 5%. This is satisfactory for operational diving, but much too high to be acceptable for hyperbaric workers who work in clinical settings. Decompression schedules for hyperbaric chamber attendants can be based on naval air decompression schedules, but since exposures are so frequent and thus are usually at the limits of the table, they must be liberally lengthened and oxygen should be substituted for compressed-air breathing during decompression. As a prudent measure, it is recommended that a two-minute stop be made while breathing oxygen, at least three metres deeper than called for by the decompression schedule chosen. For example, while the US Navy requires a three-minute decompression stop at three metres, breathing air, after a 101 minute exposure at 2.5 ATA, an acceptable decompression schedule for a hyperbaric chamber attendant undergoing the same exposure would be a two-minute stop at 6 m breathing oxygen, followed by ten minutes at 3 m breathing oxygen. When these schedules, modified as above, are used in practice, DCI in an inside attendant is an extreme rarity (Kindwall 1994a).

In addition to providing a fivefold larger "oxygen window" for nitrogen elimination, oxygen breathing offers other advantages. Raising the PO_2 in venous blood has been demonstrated to lessen blood sludging, reduce the stickiness of white cells, reduce the no-reflow phenomenon, render red cells more flexible in passing through capillaries and counteract the vast decrease in deformability and filterability of white cells which have been exposed to compressed air.

Needless to say, all workers using oxygen decompression must be thoroughly trained and apprised of the fire danger. The environment of the decompression chamber must be kept free of combustibles and ignition sources, an overboard dump system must be used to convey exhaled oxygen out of the chamber and redundant oxygen monitors with a high oxygen alarm must be provided. The alarm should sound if oxygen in the chamber atmosphere exceeds 23%.

Working with compressed air or treating clinical patients under hyperbaric conditions sometimes can accomplish work or effect remission in disease that would otherwise be impossible. When rules for the safe use of these modalities are observed, workers need not be at significant risk for dysbaric injury.

Caisson Work and Tunnelling

From time to time in the construction industry it is necessary to excavate or tunnel through ground which is either fully saturated with water, lying below the local water table, or following a course completely under water, such as a river or lake bottom. A time-tested method for managing this situation has been to apply compressed air to the working area to force water out of the ground, drying it sufficiently so that it can be mined. This principle has been applied to both caissons used for bridge pier construction and soft ground tunnelling (Kindwall 1994b).

Caissons

A caisson is simply a large, inverted box, made to the dimensions of the bridge foundation, which typically is built in a dry dock and then floated into place, where it is carefully positioned. It is then flooded and lowered until it touches bottom, after which it is driven down further by adding weight as the bridge pier itself is constructed. The purpose of the caisson is to provide a method for cutting through soft ground to land the bridge pier on solid rock or a good geologic weight-bearing stratum. When all sides of the caisson have been embedded in the mud, compressed air is applied to the interior of the caisson and water is forced out, leaving a muck floor which can be excavated by men working within the caisson. The edges of the caisson consist of a wedge-shaped cutting shoe, made of steel, which continues to descend as earth is removed beneath the descending caisson and weight is applied from above as the bridge tower is constructed. When bed rock is reached, the working chamber is filled with concrete, becoming the permanent base for the bridge foundation.

Caissons have been used for nearly 150 years and have been successful in the construction of foundations as deep as 31.4 m below mean high water, as on Bridge Pier No. 3 of the Auckland, New Zealand, Harbour Bridge in 1958.

Design of the caisson usually provides for an access shaft for workers, who can descend either by ladder or by a mechanical lift and a separate shaft for buckets to remove the spoil. The shafts are provided with hermetically sealed hatches at either end which enable the caisson pressure to remain the same while workers or materials exit or enter. The top hatch of the muck shaft is provided with a pressure sealed gland through which the hoist cable for the muck bucket can slide. Before the top hatch is opened, the lower hatch is shut. Hatch interlocks may be necessary for safety, depending on design. Pressure must be equal on both sides of any hatch before it can be opened. Since the walls of the caisson are generally made of steel or concrete, there is little or no leakage from the chamber while under pressure except under the edges. The pressure is raised incrementally to a pressure just slightly greater than is necessary to balance off sea pressure at the edge of the cutting shoe.

People working in the pressurized caisson are exposed to compressed air and may experience many of the same physiologic problems that face deep-sea divers. These include decompression illness, barotrauma of the ears, sinus cavities and lungs and if decompression schedules are inadequate, the long-term risk of aseptic necrosis of the bone (dysbaric osteonecrosis).

It is important that a ventilation rate be established to carry away CO_2 and gases emanating from the muck floor (especially methane) and whatever fumes may be produced from welding or cutting operations in the working chamber. A rule of thumb is that six cubic metres of free air per minute must be provided for each worker in the caisson. Allowance must also be made for air which is lost when the muck lock and man lock are used for the passage of personnel and materials. As the water is forced down to a level exactly even with the cutting shoe, ventilation air is required as the excess bubbles out under the edges. A second air supply, equal in capacity to the first, with an independent power source, should be available for emergency use in case of compressor or power failure. In many areas this is required by law.

Sometimes if the ground being mined is homogeneous and consists of sand, blow pipes can be erected to the surface. The pressure in the caisson will then extract the sand from the working chamber when the end of the blow pipe is located in a sump and the excavated sand is shovelled into the sump. If coarse gravel, rock, or boulders are encountered, these have to be broken up and removed in conventional muck buckets.

If the caisson should fail to sink despite the added weight on top, it may sometimes be necessary to withdraw the workers from the caisson and reduce the air pressure in the working chamber to allow the caisson to fall. Concrete must be placed or water admitted to the wells within the pier structure surrounding the air shafts above the caisson to reduce the stress on the diaphragm at the top of the working chamber. When just beginning a caisson operation, safety cribs or supports should be kept in the working chamber to prevent the caisson from suddenly dropping and crushing the workers. Practical considerations limit the depth to which air-filled caissons can be driven when men are used to hand mine the muck. A pressure of 3.4 kg/cm^2 gauge (3.4 bar or 35 m of fresh water) is about the maximum tolerable limit because of decompression considerations for the workers.

An automated caisson excavating system has been developed by the Japanese wherein a remotely operated hydraulically powered backhoe shovel, which can reach all corners of the caisson, is used for excavation. The backhoe, under television control from the surface, drops the excavated muck into buckets which are hoisted remotely from the caisson. Using this system, the caisson can proceed down to almost unlimited pressures. The only time that workers need enter the working chamber is to repair the excavating machinery or to remove or demolish large obstacles which appear below the cutting shoe of the caisson and which cannot be removed by the remote-controlled backhoe. In such cases, workers enter for short periods much as divers and can breathe either air or mixed gas at higher pressures to avoid nitrogen narcosis.

When people have worked long shifts under compressed-air at pressures greater than 0.8 kg/cm^2 (0.8 bar), they must decompress in stages. This can be accomplished either by attaching a large decompression chamber to the top of the man shaft into the caisson or, if space requirements are such at the top that this is impossible, by attaching "blister locks" to the man shaft. These are small chambers which can accommodate only a few workers at a time in a standing position. Preliminary decompression is taken in these blister locks, where the time spent is relatively short. Then, with considerable excess gas remaining in their bodies, the workers rapidly decompress to the surface and quickly move to a standard decompression chamber, sometimes located on an adjacent barge, where they are repressurized for subsequent slow decompression. In compressed-air work, this process is known as "decanting" and was fairly common in England and elsewhere, but is prohibited in the United States. The object is to return workers to pressure within five minutes, before bubbles can grow sufficiently in size to cause symptoms. However, this is inherently dangerous because of the difficulties of moving a large gang of workers from one chamber to another. If one worker has trouble clearing his ears during repressurization, the whole shift is placed in jeopardy. There is a much safer procedure, called "surface decompression", for divers, where only one or two are decompressed at the same time. Despite every precaution on the Auckland Harbour Bridge project, as many as eight minutes occasionally elapsed before bridge workers could be put back under pressure.

Compressed air tunnelling

Tunnels are becoming increasingly important as the population grows, both for the purposes of sewage disposal and for unobstructed traffic arteries and rail service beneath large urban centres. Often, these tunnels must be driven through soft ground considerably below the local water table. Under rivers and lakes, there may be no other way to ensure the safety of the workers than to put compressed air on the tunnel. This technique, using a hydraulically driven shield at the face with compressed air to hold back the water, is known as the plenum process. Under large buildings in a crowded city, compressed air may be necessary to prevent surface subsidence. When this occurs, large buildings can develop cracks in their foundations, sidewalks and streets may drop and pipes and other utilities can be damaged.

To apply pressure to a tunnel, bulkheads are erected across the tunnel to provide the pressure boundary. On smaller tunnels, less than three metres in diameter, a single or combination lock is used to provide access for workers and materials and removal of the excavated ground. Removable track sections are provided by the doors so that they may be operated without interference from the muck-train rails. Numerous penetrations are provided in these bulkheads for the passage of high-pressure air for the tools, low-pressure air for pressurizing the tunnel, fire mains, pressure gauge lines, communications lines, electrical power lines for lighting and machinery and suction lines for ventilation and removal of water in the invert. These are often termed blow lines or "mop lines". The low-pressure air supply pipe, which is 15-35 cm in diameter, depending on the size of the tunnel, should extend to the working face in order to ensure good ventilation for the workers. A second low-pressure air pipe of equal size should also extend through both bulkheads, terminating just inside the inner bulkhead, to provide air in the event of rupture or break in the primary air supply. These pipes should be fitted with flapper valves which will close automatically to prevent depressurization of the tunnel if the supply pipe is broken. The volume of air required to efficiently ventilate the tunnel and keep CO_2 levels low will vary greatly depending on the porosity of the ground and how close the finished concrete lining has been brought to the shield. Sometimes micro-organisms in the soil produce large amounts of CO_2. Obviously, under such conditions, more air will be required. Another useful property of compressed air is that it tends to force

Table 36.1 • Instructions for compressed-air workers.

- Never "short" yourself on the decompression times prescribed by your employer and the official decompression code in use. The time saved is not worth the risk of decompression illness (DCI), a potentially fatal or crippling disease.

- Do not sit in a cramped position during decompression. To do so allows nitrogen bubbles to gather and concentrate in the joints, thereby contributing to the risk of DCI. Because you are still eliminating nitrogen from your body after you go home, you should refrain from sleeping or resting in a cramped position after work, as well.

- Warm water should be used for showers and baths up to six hours after decompressing; very hot water can actually bring on or aggravate a case of decompression illness.

- Severe fatigue, lack of sleep and heavy drinking the night before can also help bring on decompression illness. Drinking alcohol and taking aspirin should never be used as a "treatment" for pains of decompression illness.

- Fever and illness, such as bad colds, increase the risk of decompression illness. Strains and sprains in muscles and joints are also "favourite" places for DCI to begin.

- When stricken by decompression illness away from the job site, immediately contact the company's physician or one knowledgeable in treating this disease. Wear your identifying bracelet or badge at all times.

- Leave smoking materials in the changing shack. Hydraulic oil is flammable and should a fire start in the closed environment of the tunnel, it could cause extensive damage and a shutdown of the job, which would lay you off work. Also, because the air is thicker in the tunnel due to compression, heat is conducted down cigarettes so that they become too hot to hold as they get shorter.

- Do not bring thermos bottles in your lunch box unless you loosen the stopper during compression; if you do not do this, the stopper will be forced deep into the thermos bottle. During decompression, the stopper must also be loosened so that the bottle does not explode. Very fragile glass thermos bottles might implode when pressure is applied, even if the stopper is loose.

- When the air lock door has been closed and pressure is applied, you will notice that the air in the air lock gets warm. This is called the "heat of compression" and is normal. Once the pressure stops changing, the heat will dissipate and the temperature will return to normal. During compression, the first thing you will notice is a fullness of your ears. Unless you "clear your ears" by swallowing, yawning, or holding your nose and trying to "blow the air out through your ears", you will experience ear pain during compression. If you cannot clear your ears, notify the shift foreman immediately so that compression can be halted. Otherwise you may break your eardrums or develop a severe ear squeeze. Once you have reached maximum pressure, there will be no further problems with your ears for the remainder of the shift.

- Should you experience buzzing in your ears, ringing in your ears, or deafness following compression which persists for more than a few hours, you must report to the compressed-air physician for evaluation. Under extremely severe but rare conditions, a portion of the middle ear structure other than the eardrum may be affected if you have had a great deal of difficulty clearing your ears and in that case this must be surgically corrected within two or three days to avoid permanent difficulty.

- If you have a cold or an attack of hay fever, it is best not to try compressing in the air lock until you are over it. Colds tend to make it difficult or impossible for you to equalize your ears or sinuses.

- Very occasionally, some people experience pain in a filled tooth. This may happen if there is air under a filling and it cannot easily equalize. If you explain this problem to your dentist, he can repair it. Unfilled teeth, even with bad cavities in them, rarely if ever present problems.

- False teeth and soft contact lenses, as well as regular glasses, can be worn with perfect safety in the compressed-air environment.

- Should anybody sustain a severe injury to the chest, back, or rib cage while working at pressure in the tunnel, special care must be exercised before and during decompression. If the victim has a broken rib which has punctured the lung, air can leak out of the lung and collapse the good lung as it expands inside the rib cage during decompression. Anyone suspected of having such an injury should be examined by the compressed-air physician before he is decompressed and should only be decompressed under his supervision.

- During decompression, the air in the man lock will become cold. This is known as the "chilling of decompression", which is entirely normal. Fog may form in the chamber. Again, the temperature will return to normal and the fog will disappear as soon as the pressure stops changing when you reach the surface.

- It is very important that you breathe normally during decompression and not hold your breath for any reason. This is because the air must freely exchange in and out of your lungs to avoid air trapping in the lungs. Should this occur, the lungs will overexpand and theoretically could rupture with the possibility that air could be forced into your bloodstream with very serious consequences to your brain. This kind of disorder is called air embolism. Though experienced by divers, it has never been truly proven to happen in tunnel workers. Nevertheless, you should be aware of its theoretical possibility and its symptoms. These could include unconsciousness, paralysis of one side of the body, or one pupil appearing to be bigger than the other. These symptoms, should they ever appear, would come on immediately (within seconds) after the decompression is completed and there is no possibility of their occurring later. Should anyone ever experience collapse on leaving the chamber, he should be taken immediately to your designated recompression chamber and the compressed-air physician notified.

- If at any time after leaving the decompression lock you experience pain, numbness, weakness or tingling in any part of your body, this may be a sign of decompression illness. If you feel a "pins and needles" sensation in your legs or a clumsiness of your hands, arms, or legs, this should be considered decompression illness with bubbles in the spinal cord until proved otherwise. Other symptoms may be dizziness and nausea ("the staggers") or difficulty breathing ("the chokes"). If any of the above symptoms appear, report immediately to your medical recompression chamber.

- Avoid taking round-faced watches into the working chamber unless they are definitely labelled to be pressure-proof. Sometimes compressed-air can leak into a "water resistant" watch and then during decompression when the air inside the watch expands, the crystal will pop out. Squarefaced watches are usually leaky enough so that this does not happen.

- Avoid flying on commercial or private aeroplanes for at least 24 hours after decompressing from a work shift. Also, avoid scuba diving for 24 hours before or after working in compressed-air.

explosive gases such as methane away from the walls and out of the tunnel. This holds true when mining areas where spilled solvents such as petrol or degreasers have saturated the ground.

A rule of thumb developed by Richardson and Mayo (1960) is that the volume of air required usually can be calculated by multiplying the area of the working face in square metres by six and adding six cubic metres per man. This gives the number of cubic metres of free air required per minute. If this figure is used, it will cover most practical contingencies.

The fire main must also extend through to the face and be provided with hose connections every sixty metres for use in case of fire. Thirty metres of rotproof hose should be attached to the water-filled fire main outlets.

In very large tunnels, over about four metres in diameter, two locks should be provided, one termed the muck lock, for passing muck trains, and the man lock, usually positioned above the muck lock, for the workers. On large projects, the man lock is often made of three compartments so that engineers, electricians and others can lock in and out past a work shift undergoing decompression. These large man locks are usually built external to the main concrete bulkhead so they do not have to resist the external compressive force of the tunnel pressure when open to the outside air.

On very large subaqueous tunnels a safety screen is erected, spanning the upper half of the tunnel, to afford some protection should the tunnel suddenly flood secondary to a blow-out while tunnelling under a river or lake. The safety screen is usually placed as close as practicable to the face, avoiding the excavating machinery. A flying gangway or hanging walkway is used between the screen and the locks, the gangway dropping down to pass at least a metre below the lower edge of the screen. This will allow the workers egress to the man lock in the event of sudden flooding. The safety screen can also be used to trap light gases which may be explosive and a mop line can be attached through the screen and coupled to a suction or blow line. With the valve cracked, this will help to purge any light gases from the working environment. Because the safety screen extends nearly down to the centre of the tunnel, the smallest tunnel it can be employed on is about 3.6 m. It should be noted that workers must be warned to keep clear of the open end of the mop line, as serious accidents can be caused if clothing is sucked into the pipe.

Table 36.1 is a list of instructions which should be given to compressed-air workers before they first enter the compressed-air environment.

It is the responsibility of the retained physician or occupational health professional for the tunnel project to ensure that air purity standards are maintained and that all safety measures are in effect. Adherence to established decompression schedules by periodically examining the pressure recording graphs from the tunnel and man locks must also be carefully monitored.

Hyperbaric chamber workers

Hyperbaric oxygen therapy is becoming more common in all areas of the world, with some 2,100 hyperbaric chamber facilities now functioning. Many of these chambers are multiplace units, which are compressed with compressed air to pressures ranging from 1 to 5 kg/cm^2 gauge. Patients are given 100% oxygen to breathe, at pressures up to 2 kg/cm^2 gauge. At pressures greater than that they may breathe mixed gas for treatment of decompression illness. The chamber attendants, however, typically breathe compressed air and so their exposure in the chamber is similar to that experienced by a diver or compressed-air worker.

Typically the chamber attendant working inside a multiplace chamber is a nurse, respiratory therapist, former diver, or hyperbaric technician. The physical requirements for such workers are similar to those for caisson workers. It is important to

remember, however, that a number of chamber attendants working in the hyperbaric field are female. Women are no more likely to suffer ill effects from compressed-air work than men, with the exception of the question of pregnancy. Nitrogen is carried across the placenta when a pregnant woman is exposed to compressed air and this is transferred to the foetus. Whenever decompression takes place, nitrogen bubbles form in the venous system. These are silent bubbles and, when small, do no harm, as they are removed efficiently by the pulmonary filter. The wisdom, however, of having these bubbles appear in a developing foetus is doubtful. What studies have been done indicate that foetal damage may occur under such circumstances. One survey suggested that birth defects are more common in the children of women who have engaged in scuba diving while pregnant. Exposure of pregnant women to hyperbaric chamber conditions should be avoided and appropriate policies consistent with both medical and legal considerations must be developed. For this reason, female workers should be precautioned about the risks during pregnancy and appropriate personnel job assignment and health education programmes should be instituted in order that pregnant women not be exposed to hyperbaric chamber conditions.

It should be pointed out, however, that patients who are pregnant may be treated in the hyperbaric chamber, as they breathe 100% oxygen and are therefore not subject to nitrogen embolization. Previous concerns that the foetus would be at increased risk for retrolental fibroplasia or retinopathy of the newborn have proven to be unfounded in large clinical trials. Another condition, premature closure of the patent ductus arteriosus, has also not been found to be related to the exposure.

Other Hazards

Physical injuries

Divers

In general, divers are prone to the same types of physical injury that any worker is liable to sustain when working in heavy construction. Breaking cables, failing loads, crush injuries from machines, turning cranes and so on, can be commonplace. However, in the underwater environment, the diver is prone to certain types of unique injury that are not found elsewhere.

Suction/entrapment injury is something especially to be guarded against. Working in or near an opening in a ship's hull, a caisson which has a lower water level on the side opposite the diver, or a dam can be causative of this type of mishap. Divers often refer to this type of situation as being trapped by "heavy water".

To avoid dangerous situations where the diver's arm, leg, or whole body may be sucked into an opening such as a tunnel or pipe, strict precautions must be taken to tag out pipe valves and flood gates on dams so that they cannot be opened while the diver is in the water near them. The same is true of pumps and piping within ships that the diver is working on.

Injury can include oedema and hypoxia of an entrapped limb sufficient to cause muscle necrosis, permanent nerve damage, or even loss of the entire limb, or it may occasion gross crushing of a portion of the body or the whole body so as to cause death from simple massive trauma. Entrapment in cold water for a long period of time may cause the diver to die of exposure. If the diver is using scuba gear, he may run out of air and drown before his release can be effected, unless additional scuba tanks can be provided.

Propeller injuries are straightforward and must be guarded against by tagging out a ship's main propulsion machinery while the diver is in the water. It must be remembered, however, that steam turbine-powered ships, when in port, are continuously turning over their screws very slowly, using their jacking gear to avoid cooling and distortion of the turbine blades. Thus the diver, when working on such a blade (trying to clear it from entangled cables, for example), must be aware that the turning blade must be avoided as it approaches a narrow spot close to the hull.

Whole-body squeeze is a unique injury which can occur to deep sea divers using the classical copper helmet mated to the flexible rubberized suit. If there is no check valve or non-return valve where the air pipe connects to the helmet, cutting the air line at the surface will cause an immediate relative vacuum within the helmet, which can draw the entire body into the helmet. The effects of this can be instant and devastating. For example, at a depth of 10 m, about 12 tons of force is exerted on the soft part of the diver's dress. This force will drive his body into the helmet if pressurization of the helmet is lost. A similar effect may be produced if the diver fails unexpectedly and fails to turn on compensating air. This can produce severe injury or death if it occurs near the surface, as a 10-metre fall from the surface will halve the volume of the dress. A similar fall occurring between 40 and 50 m will change the suit volume only about 17%. These volume changes are in accordance with Boyle's Law.

Caisson and tunnel workers

Tunnel workers are subject to the usual types of accidents seen in heavy construction, with the additional problem of a higher incidence of falls and injuries from cave-ins. It must be stressed that an injured compressed-air worker who may have broken ribs should be suspected of having a pneumothorax until proven otherwise and therefore great care must be taken in decompressing such a patient. If a pneumothorax is present, it must be relieved at pressure in the working chamber before decompression is attempted.

Noise

Noise damage to compressed-air workers may be severe, as air motors, pneumatic hammers and drills are never properly equipped with silencers. Noise levels in caissons and tunnels have been measured at over 125 dB. These levels are physically painful, as well as causative of permanent damage to the inner ear. Echo within the confines of a tunnel or caisson exacerbates the problem.

Many compressed-air workers balk at wearing ear protection, saying that blocking the sound of an approaching muck train would be dangerous. There is little foundation for this belief, as hearing protection at best only attenuates sound but does not eliminate it. Furthermore, not only is a moving muck train not "silent" to a protected worker, but it also gives other cues such as moving shadows and vibration in the ground. A real concern is complete hermetic occlusion of the auditory meatus provided by a tightly fitting ear muff or protector. If air is not admitted to the external auditory canal during compression, external ear squeeze may result as the ear drum is forced outward by air entering the middle ear via the Eustachian tube. The usual sound protective ear muff is usually not completely air tight, however. During compression, which lasts only a tiny fraction of the total shift time, the muff can be slightly loosened should pressure equalization prove a problem. Formed fibre ear plugs which can be moulded to fit in the external canal provide some protection and are not air tight.

The goal is to avoid a time weighted average noise level of higher than 85 dBA. All compressed-air workers should have pre-employment base line audiograms so that auditory losses which may result from the high-noise environment can be monitored.

Hyperbaric chambers and decompression locks can be equipped with efficient silencers on the air supply pipe entering the chamber. It is important that this be insisted on, as otherwise the workers will be considerably bothered by the ventilation noise and may neglect to ventilate the chamber adequately. A continuous vent can be maintained with a silenced air supply producing no more than 75dB, about the noise level in an average office.

Fire

Fire is always of great concern in compressed-air tunnel work and in clinical hyperbaric chamber operations. One can be lulled into a false sense of security when working in a steel-walled caisson which has a steel roof and a floor consisting only of unburnable wet muck. However, even in these circumstances, an electrical fire can burn insulation, which will prove highly toxic and can kill or incapacitate a work crew very quickly. In tunnels which are driven using wooden lagging before the concrete is poured, the danger is even greater. In some tunnels, hydraulic oil and straw used for caulking can furnish additional fuel.

Fire under hyperbaric conditions is always more intense because there is more oxygen available to support combustion. A rise from 21% to 28% in the oxygen percentage will double the burning rate. As the pressure is increased, the amount of oxygen available to burn increases The increase is equal to the percentage of oxygen available multiplied by the number of atmospheres in absolute terms. For example, at a pressure of 4 ATA (equal to 30 m of sea water), the effective oxygen percentage would be 84% in compressed-air. However, it must be remembered that even though burning is very much accelerated under such conditions, it is not the same as the speed of burning in 84% oxygen at one atmosphere. The reason for this is that the nitrogen present in the atmosphere has a certain quenching effect. Acetylene cannot be used at pressures over one bar because of its explosive properties. However, other torch gases and oxygen can be used for cutting steel. This has been done safely at pressures up to 3 bar. Under such circumstances, however, scrupulous care must be exercised and someone must stand by with a fire hose to immediately quench any fire which might start, should an errant spark come in contact with something combustible.

Fire requires three components to be present: fuel, oxygen and an ignition source. If any one of these three factors is absent, fire will not occur. Under hyperbaric conditions, it is almost impossible to remove oxygen unless the piece of equipment in question can be inserted into the environment by filling it or surrounding it with nitrogen. If fuel cannot be removed, an ignition source must be avoided. In clinical hyperbaric work, meticulous care is taken to prevent the oxygen percentage in the multiplace chamber from rising above 23%. In addition, all electrical equipment within the chamber must be intrinsically safe, with no possibility of producing an arc. Personnel in the chamber should wear cotton clothing which has been treated with flame retardant. A water-deluge system must be in place, as well as a hand-held fire hose independently actuated. If a fire occurs in a multiplace clinical hyperbaric chamber, there is no immediate escape and so the fire must be fought with a hand-held hose and with the deluge system.

In monoplace chambers pressurized with 100% oxygen, a fire will be instantly fatal to any occupant. The human body itself supports combustion in 100% oxygen, especially at pressure. For this reason, plain cotton clothing is worn by the patient in the monoplace chamber to avoid static sparks which could be produced by synthetic materials. There is no need to fireproof this clothing, however, as if a fire should occur, the clothing would afford no protection. The only method for avoiding fires in the monoplace oxygen-filled chamber is to completely avoid any source of ignition.

When dealing with high pressure oxygen, at pressures over 10 kg/cm^2 gauge, adiabatic heating must be recognized as a possible source of ignition. If oxygen at a pressure of 150 kg/cm^2 is suddenly admitted to a manifold via a quick-opening ball valve, the oxygen may "diesel" if even a tiny amount of dirt is present. This can produce a violent explosion. Such accidents have occurred and for this reason, quick-opening ball valves should never be used in high pressure oxygen systems.

DECOMPRESSION DISORDERS

Dees F. Gorman

A wide range of workers are subject to decompression (a reduction in ambient pressure) as part of their working routine. These include divers who themselves are drawn from a wide range of occupations, caisson workers, tunnellers, hyperbaric chamber workers (usually nurses), aviators and astronauts. Decompression of these individuals can and does precipitate a variety of decompression disorders. While most of the disorders are well understood, others are not and in some instances, and despite treatment, injured workers can become disabled. The decompression disorders are the subject of active research.

Mechanism of Decompression Injury

Principles of gas uptake and release

Decompression may injure the hyperbaric worker via one of two primary mechanisms. The first is the consequence of inert gas uptake during the hyperbaric exposure and bubble formation in tissues during and after the subsequent decompression. It is generally assumed that the metabolic gases, oxygen and carbon dioxide, do not contribute to bubble formation. This is almost certainly a false assumption, but the consequent error is small and such an assumption will be made here.

During the compression (increase in ambient pressure) of the worker and throughout their time under pressure, inspired and arterial inert gas tensions will be increased relative to those experienced at normal atmospheric pressure—the inert gas(es) will then be taken up into tissues until an equilibrium of inspired, arterial and tissue inert gas tensions is established. Equilibrium times will vary from less than 30 minutes to more than a day depending upon the type of tissue and gas involved, and, in particular, will vary according to:

- the blood supply to the tissue
- the solubility of the inert gas in blood and in the tissue
- the diffusion of the inert gas through blood and into the tissue
- the temperature of the tissue
- the local tissue work-loads
- the local tissue carbon dioxide tension.

The subsequent decompression of the hyperbaric worker to normal atmospheric pressure will clearly reverse this process, gas will be released from tissues and will eventually be expired. The rate of this release is determined by the factors listed above, except, for as yet poorly understood reasons, it appears to be slower than the uptake. Gas elimination will be slower still if bubbles form. The factors that influence the formation of bubbles are well established qualitatively, but not quantitatively. For a bubble to form the bubble energy must be sufficient to overcome ambient pressure, surface tension pressure and elastic tissue pressures. The disparity between theoretical predictions (of surface tension and critical bubble volumes for bubble growth) and actual observation of bubble formation is explained variously by arguing that bubbles form in tissue (blood vessel) surface defects and/or on the basis of small short-lived bubbles (nuclei) that are continually formed in the body (e.g., between tissue planes or in areas of cavitation). The conditions that must exist before gas comes out of solution are also poorly defined—although it is likely that bubbles form whenever tissue gas tensions exceed ambient pressure. Once formed, bubbles provoke injury (see below) and become increasingly stable as a consequence of coalescence and recruitment of surfactants to the bubble surface. It may be possible for bubbles to form without decompression by changing the inert gas that the hyperbaric worker is breathing. This effect is probably small and those workers that have had a sudden onset of a decompression illness after a change in inspired inert gas almost certainly already had "stable" bubbles in their tissues.

It follows that to introduce a safe working practice a decompression programme (schedule) should be employed to avoid bubble formation. This will require modelling of the following:

- the uptake of the inert gas(es) during the compression and the hyperbaric exposure
- the elimination of the inert gas(es) during and after the decompression
- the conditions for bubble formation.

It is reasonable to state that to date no completely satisfactory model of decompression kinetics and dynamics has been produced and that hyperbaric workers now rely on programmes that have been established essentially by trial and error.

Effect of Boyle's Law on barotrauma

The second primary mechanism by which decompression can cause injury is the process of barotrauma. The barotraumata can arise from compression or decompression. In compression barotrauma, the air spaces in the body that are surrounded by soft tissue, and hence are subject to increasing ambient pressure (Pascal's principle), will be reduced in volume (as reasonably predicted by Boyles' law: doubling of ambient pressure will cause gas volumes to be halved). The compressed gas is displaced by fluid in a predictable sequence:

- The elastic tissues move (tympanic membrane, round and oval windows, mask material, clothing, rib cage, diaphragm).
- Blood is pooled in the high compliance vessels (essentially veins).
- Once the limits of compliance of blood vessels are reached, there is an extravasation of fluid (oedema) and then blood (haemorrhage) into the surrounding soft tissues.
- Once the limits of compliance of the surrounding soft tissues are reached, there is a shift of fluid and then blood into the air space itself.

This sequence can be interrupted at any time by an ingress of additional gas into the space (e.g., into the middle ear on performing a valsalva manoeuvre) and will stop when gas volume and tissue pressure are in equilibrium.

The process is reversed during decompression and gas volumes will increase, and if not vented to atmosphere will cause local trauma. In the lung this trauma may arise from either over-distension or from shearing between adjacent areas of lung that have significantly different compliance and hence expand at different rates.

Pathogenesis of Decompression Disorders

The decompression illnesses can be divided into the barotraumata, tissue bubble and intravascular bubble categories.

Barotraumata

During compression, any gas space may become involved in barotrauma and this is especially common in the ears. While damage to the external ear requires occlusion of the external ear canal (by plugs, a hood, or impacted wax), the tympanic membrane and middle ear is frequently damaged. This injury is more likely if the worker has upper respiratory tract pathology that causes eustachian tube dysfunction. The possible consequences are middle ear congestion (as described above) and/or tympanic membrane rupture. Ear pain and a conductive deafness are likely. Vertigo may result from an ingress of cold water into the middle ear through a ruptured tympanic membrane. Such vertigo is transient. More commonly, vertigo (and possibly also a sensorineural deafness) will result from inner ear barotrauma. During compression, inner ear damage often results from a forceful valsalva manoeuvre (that will cause a fluid wave to be transmitted to the inner ear via the cochlea duct). The inner ear damage is usually within the inner ear—round and oval window rupture is less common.

The paranasal sinuses often are similarly involved and usually because of a blocked ostium. In addition to local and referred pain, epistaxis is common and cranial nerves may be "compressed". It is noteworthy that the facial nerve may be likewise affected by middle ear barotrauma in individuals with a perforate auditory nerve canal. Other areas that may be affected by compressive barotrauma, but less commonly, are the lungs, teeth, gut, diving mask, dry-suits and other equipment such as buoyancy compensating devices.

Decompressive barotraumata are less common than compressive barotraumata, but tend to have a more adverse outcome. The two areas primarily affected are the lungs and inner ear. The typical pathological lesion of pulmonary barotrauma has yet to be described. The mechanism has been variously ascribed to the over-inflation of alveoli either to "open up pores" or mechanically to disrupt the alveolus, or as the consequence of shearing of lung tissue due to local differential lung expansion. Maximum stress is likely at the base of alveoli and, given that many underwater workers often breathe with small tidal excursions at or near total lung capacity, the risk of barotrauma is increased in this group as lung compliance is lowest at these volumes. Gas release from damaged lung may track through the interstitium to the hilum of the lungs, mediastinum and perhaps into the subcutaneous tissues of the head and neck. This interstitial gas may cause dyspnoea, substernal pain and coughing which may be productive of a little bloodstained sputum. Gas in the head and neck is self-evident and may occasionally impair phonation. Cardiac compression is extremely rare. Gas from a barotraumatised lung may also escape into the pleural space (to cause a pneumothorax) or into the pulmonary veins (to eventually become arterial gas emboli). In general, such gas most commonly either escapes into the interstitium and pleural space or into the pulmonary veins. Concurrent obvious damage to the lung and arterial gas embolism are (fortunately) uncommon.

Autochthonous tissue bubbles

If, during decompression, a gas phase forms, this is usually, initially, in tissues. These tissue bubbles may induce tissue dysfunction via a variety of mechanisms—some of these are mechanical and others are biochemical.

In poorly compliant tissues, such as long bones, the spinal cord and tendons, bubbles may compress arteries, veins, lymphatics and sensory cells. Elsewhere, tissue bubbles may cause mechanical disruption of cells or, at a microscopic level, of myelin sheaths. The solubility of nitrogen in myelin may explain the frequent involvement of the nervous system in decompression illness amongst workers who have been breathing either air or an oxygen-nitrogen gas mixture. Bubbles in tissues may also induce a biochemical "foreign-body" response. This provokes an inflammatory response and may explain the observation that a common presentation of decompression illness is an influenza-like illness. The significance of the inflammatory response is demonstrated in animals such as rabbits, where inhibition of the response prevents the onset of decompression illness. The major features of the inflammatory response include a coagulopathy (this is particularly important in animals, but less so in humans) and the release of kinins. These chemicals cause pain and also an extravasation of fluid. Haemoconcentration also results from the direct effect of bubbles on blood vessels. The end result is a significant compromise of the microcirculation and, in general, measurement of the haematocrit correlates well with the severity of the illness. Correction of this haemoconcentration has a predictably significant benefit on outcome.

Intravascular bubbles

Venous bubbles may either form *de-novo* as gas comes out of solution or they may be released from tissues. These venous bubbles travel with blood flow to the lungs to be trapped in the pulmonary vasculature. The pulmonary circulation is a highly effective filter of bubbles because of the relatively low pulmonary artery pressure. In contrast, few bubbles are trapped for long periods in the systemic circulation because of the significantly greater systemic arterial pressure. The gas in bubbles trapped in the lung diffuses into the pulmonary air spaces from where it is exhaled. While these bubbles are trapped, however, they may cause adverse effects by either provoking an imbalance of lung perfusion and ventilation or by increasing pulmonary artery pressure and consequently right heart and central venous pressure. The increased right heart pressure can cause "right to left" shunting of blood through pulmonary shunts or intra-cardiac "anatomical defects" such that bubbles bypass the lung "filter" to become arterial gas emboli. Increases in venous pressure will impair venous return from tissues, thereby impairing the clearance of inert gas from the spinal cord; venous haemorrhagic infarction may result. Venous bubbles also react with blood vessels and blood constituents. An effect on blood vessels is to strip the surfactant lining from endothelial cells and hence to increase vascular permeability, which may be further compromised by the physical dislocation of endothelial cells. However, even in the absence of such damage, endothelial cells increase the concentration of glycoprotein receptors for polymorphonuclear leukocytes on their cell surface. This, together with a direct stimulation of white blood cells by bubbles, causes leucocyte binding to endothelial cells (reducing flow) and subsequent infiltration into and through the blood vessels (diapedesis). The infiltrating polymorphonuclear leukocytes cause future tissue injury by release of cytotoxins, oxygen free radicals and phospholipases. In blood, bubbles will not only cause the activation and accumulation of polymorphonuclear leukocytes, but also the activation of platelets, coagulation and complement, and the formation of fat emboli. While these effects have relatively minor importance in the highly compliant venous circulation, similar effects in the arteries can reduce blood flow to ischaemic levels.

Arterial bubbles (gas emboli) can arise from:

- pulmonary barotrauma causing the release of bubbles into the pulmonary veins
- bubbles being "forced" through the pulmonary arterioles (this process is enhanced by oxygen toxicity and by those bronchodilators that are also vasodilators such as aminophylline)

• bubbles bypassing the lung filter through a right to left vascular channel (e.g., patent foramen ovale).

Once in the pulmonary veins, bubbles return to the left atrium, left ventricle, and then are pumped into the aorta. Bubbles in the arterial circulation will distribute according to buoyancy and blood flow in large vessels, but elsewhere with blood flow alone. This explains the predominant embolism of the brain and, in particular, the middle cerebral artery. The majority of bubbles that enter the arterial circulation will pass through into the systemic capillaries and into the veins to return to the right side of the heart (usually to be trapped in the lungs). During this transit these bubbles may cause a temporary interruption of function. If the bubbles remain trapped in the systemic circulation or are not redistributed within five to ten minutes, then this loss of function may persist. If bubbles embolise the brain stem circulation, then the event may be lethal. Fortunately, the majority of bubbles will be redistributed within minutes of first arrival in the brain and a recovery of function is usual. However, during this transit the bubbles will cause the same vascular (blood vessels and blood) reactions as described above in venous blood and veins. Consequently, a significant and progressive decline in cerebral blood flow may occur, which may reach the levels at which normal function cannot be sustained. The hyperbaric worker will, at this time, suffer a relapse or deterioration in function. In general, about two-thirds of hyperbaric workers who suffer cerebral arterial gas embolism will spontaneously recover and about one-third of these will subsequently relapse.

Clinical Presentation of Decompression Disorders

Time of onset

Occasionally, the onset of decompression illness is during the decompression. This is most commonly seen in the barotraumata of ascent, particularly involving the lungs. However, the onset of the majority of decompression illnesses occurs after decompression is complete. Decompression illnesses due to the formation of bubbles in tissues and in blood vessels usually become evident within minutes or hours after decompression. The natural history of many of these decompression illnesses is for the spontaneous resolution of symptoms. However, some will only resolve spontaneously incompletely and there is a need for treatment. There is substantial evidence that the earlier the treatment the better the outcome. The natural history of treated decompression illnesses is variable. In some cases, residual problems are seen to resolve over the following 6-12 months, while in others symptoms appear not to resolve.

Clinical manifestations

A common presentation of decompression illness is an influenza-like condition. Other frequent complaints are various sensory disorders, local pain, particularly in the limbs; and other neurologic manifestations, which may involve higher functions, special senses and motor weariness (less commonly the skin and lymphatic systems may be involved). In some groups of hyperbaric workers, the most common presentation of decompression illness is pain. This may be a discrete pain about a specific joint or joints, back pain or referred pain (when the pain is often located in the same limb as are overt neurologic deficits), or less commonly, in an acute decompression illness, vague migratory aches and pains may be noticed. Indeed, it is reasonable to state that the manifestations of the decompression illnesses are protean. Any illness in a hyperbaric worker that occurs up to 24-48 hours after a decompression should be assumed to be related to that decompression until proven otherwise.

Classification

Until recently, the decompression illnesses were classified into:

• the barotraumata
• cerebral arterial gas embolism
• decompression sickness.

Decompression sickness was further subdivided into Type 1 (pain, itch, swelling and skin rashes), Type 2 (all other manifestations) and Type 3 (manifestations of both cerebral arterial gas embolism and decompression sickness) categories. This classification system arose from an analysis of the outcome of caisson workers using new decompression schedules. However, this system has had to be replaced both because it is neither discriminatory nor prognostic and because there is a low concordance in diagnosis between experienced physicians. The new classification of the decompression illnesses recognises the difficulty in distinguishing between cerebral arterial gas embolism and cerebral decompression sickness and similarly the difficulty in distinguishing Type 1 from Type 2 and Type 3 decompression sickness. All decompression illnesses are now classified as such—decompression illness, as described in table 36.2. This term is prefaced with a description of the nature of the illness, the progression of symptoms and a list of the organ systems in which the symptoms are manifest (no assumptions are made about the underlying pathology). For example, a diver may have acute progressive neurological decompression illness. The complete classification of the decompression illness includes a comment on the presence or absence of barotrauma and the likely inert gas loading. These latter terms are relevant to both treatment and likely fitness to return to work.

First Aid Management

Rescue and resuscitation

Some hyperbaric workers develop a decompression illness and require to be rescued. This is particularly true for divers. This rescue may require their recovery to a stage or diving bell, or a rescue from underwater. Specific rescue techniques must be established and practised if they are to be successful. In general, divers should be rescued from the ocean in a horizontal posture (to avoid possibly lethal falls in cardiac output as the diver is re-subjected to gravity—during any dive there is a progressive loss of blood volume consequent to displacement of blood from the peripheries into the chest) and consequent diuresis and this posture should be maintained until the diver is, if necessary, in a recompression chamber.

The resuscitation of an injured diver should follow the same regimen as used in resuscitations elsewhere. Of specific note is

Table 36 .2 • Revised classification system of the decompression illnesses

Duration	Evolution	Symptoms	
Acute	Progressive	Musculoskeletal	
Chronic	Spontaneously resolving	Cutaneous	Decompression illness + or − Evidence of barotrauma
	Static	Lymphatic	
	Relapsing	Neurological	
		Vestibular	
		Cardiorespiratory	

36. BAROMETRIC PRESSURE, INCREASED

that the resuscitation of a hypothermic individual should continue at least until the individual is rewarmed. There is no convincing evidence that resuscitation of an injured diver in the water is effective. In general, the divers' best interests are usually served by early rescue ashore, or to a diving bell/platform.

Oxygen and fluid resuscitation

A hyperbaric worker with a decompression illness should be laid flat, to minimize the chances of bubbles distributing to the brain, but not placed in a head-down posture which probably adversely affects the outcome. The diver should be given 100% oxygen to breathe; this will require either a demand valve in a conscious diver or a sealing mask, high flow rates of oxygen and a reservoir system. If oxygen administration is to be prolonged, then airbreaks should be given to ameliorate or retard the development of pulmonary oxygen toxicity. Any diver with decompression illness should be re-hydrated. There is probably no place for oral fluids in the acute resuscitation of a severely injured worker. In general, it is difficult to administer oral fluids to someone lying flat. Oral fluids will require the administration of oxygen to be interrupted and then usually have negligible immediate effect on the blood volume. Finally, since subsequent hyperbaric oxygen treatment may cause a convulsion, it is not desirable to have any stomach contents. Ideally then, fluid resuscitation should be by the intravenous route. There is no evidence of any advantage of colloid over crystalloid solutions and the fluid of choice is probably normal saline. Solutions containing lactate should not be given to a cold diver and dextrose solutions should not be given to anyone with a brain injury (as aggravation of the injury is possible). It is essential that an accurate fluid balance be maintained as this is probably the best guide to the successful resuscitation of a hyperbaric worker with decompression illness. Bladder involvement is sufficiently common that early recourse to bladder catheterization is warranted in the absence of urinary output.

There are no drugs that are of proven benefit in the treatment of the decompression illnesses. However, there is growing support for lignocaine and this is under clinical trial. The role of lignocaine is thought to be both as a membrane stabiliser and as an inhibitor of the polymorphonuclear leukocyte accumulation and blood vessel adherence that is provoked by bubbles. It is noteworthy that one of the probable roles of hyperbaric oxygen is also to inhibit the accumulation of and adherence to blood vessels of leucocytes. Finally, there is no evidence that any benefit is derived from the use of platelet inhibitors such as aspirin or other anticoagulants. Indeed, as haemorrhage into the central nervous system is associated with severe neurological decompression illness, such medication may be contra-indicated.

Retrieval

Retrieval of a hyperbaric worker with decompression illness to a therapeutic recompression facility should occur as soon as is possible, but must not involve any further decompression. The maximum altitude to which such a worker should be decompressed during aeromedical evacuation is 300 m above sea level. During this retrieval, the first aid and adjuvant care described above should be provided.

Recompression Treatment

Applications

The definitive treatment of most of the decompression illnesses is recompression in a chamber. The exception to this statement are the barotraumata that do not cause arterial gas embolism. The majority of aural barotrauma victims require serial audiology, nasal decongestants, analgesics and, if inner ear barotrauma is suspected, strict bed rest. It is possible however that hyperbaric oxygen (plus stellate

ganglion blockade) may be an effective treatment of this latter group of patients. The other barotraumata that often require treatment are those of the lung—most of those respond well to 100% oxygen at atmospheric pressure. Occasionally, chest cannulation may be needed for a pneumothorax. For other patients, early recompression is indicated.

Mechanisms

An increase in ambient pressure will make bubbles smaller and hence less stable (by increasing surface tension pressure). These smaller bubbles will also have a greater surface area to volume for resolution by diffusion and their mechanical disruptive and compressive effects on tissue will be reduced. It is also possible that there is a threshold bubble volume that will stimulate a "foreign-body" reaction. By reducing bubble size, this effect may be reduced. Finally, reducing the volume (length) of columns of gas that are trapped in the systemic circulation will promote their redistribution to the veins. The other outcome of most recompressions is an increase in the inspired (P_IO_2) and arterial oxygen tension (P_aO_2). This will relieve hypoxia, lower interstitial fluid pressure, inhibit the activation and accumulation of polymorphonuclear leukocytes that is usually provoked by bubbles, and lower the haematocrit and hence blood viscosity.

Pressure

The ideal pressure at which to treat decompression illness is not established, although the conventional first choice is 2.8 bar absolute (60 fsw; 282 kPa), with further compression to 4 and 6 bar absolute pressure if the response of symptoms and signs is poor. Experiments in animals suggest that 2 bars absolute pressure is as effective a treatment pressure as greater compressions.

Gas(es)

Similarly, the ideal gas to be breathed during the therapeutic recompression of these injured workers is not established. Oxygen-helium mixtures may be more effective in the shrinkage of air bubbles than either air or 100% oxygen and are the subject of ongoing research. The ideal P_IO_2 is thought, from *in vivo* research, to be about 2 bar absolute pressure although it is well established, in head injured patients, that the ideal tension is lower at 1.5 bars absolute. The dose relationship with regard to oxygen and inhibition of bubble-provoked polymorphonuclear leukocyte accumulation has not yet been established.

Adjuvant care

The treatment of an injured hyperbaric worker in a recompression chamber must not be allowed to compromise his/her need for adjuvant care such as ventilation, rehydration and monitoring. To be a definitive treatment facility, a recompression chamber must have a working interface with the equipment routinely used in critical care medical units.

Follow-up treatment and investigations

Persistent and relapsing symptoms and signs of decompression illness are common and most injured workers will require repeated recompressions. These should continue until the injury is and remains corrected or at least until two successive treatments have failed to produce any sustained benefit. The basis of ongoing investigation is careful clinical neurological examination (including mental status), as available imaging or provocative investigative techniques have either an associated excessive false positive rate (EEG, bone radio-isotope scans, SPECT scans) or an associated excessive false negative rate (CT, MRI, PET, evoked response studies). One year after an episode of decompression illness, the worker should be x-rayed to determine if there is any dysbaric osteonecrosis (aseptic necrosis) of their long bones.

Outcome

The outcome after recompression therapy of decompression illness depends entirely upon the group being studied. Most hyperbaric workers (e.g., military and oil-field divers) respond well to treatment and significant residual deficits are uncommon. In contrast, many recreational divers treated for decompression illness have a subsequent poor outcome. The reasons for this difference in outcome are not established. Common sequelae of decompression illness are in order of decreasing frequency: depressed mood; problems in short-term memory; sensory symptoms such as numbness; difficulties with micturition and sexual dysfunction; and vague aches and pains.

Return to hyperbaric work

Fortunately, most hyperbaric workers are able to return to hyperbaric work after an episode of decompression illness. This should be delayed for at least a month (to allow a return to normal of the disordered physiology) and must be discouraged if the worker suffered pulmonary barotrauma or has a history of recurrent or severe inner ear barotrauma. A return to work should also be contingent upon:

- the severity of the decompression illness being commensurate with the extent of the hyperbaric exposure/decompression stress
- a good response to treatment
- no evidence of sequelae.

References

Bennett, P and D Elliot (eds.) 1993. *The Physiology and Medicine of Diving*. London: WB Saunders.

Fueredi, GA, DJ Czarnecki, and EP Kindwall. 1991. MR findings in the brains of compressed-air tunnel workers: Relationship to psychometric results. *Am J Neuroradiol* 12(1):67-70.

Kindwall, EP. 1994a. *Hyperbaric Medicine Practice*. Flagstaff, Ariz: Best Publishers.

—. 1994b. Medical aspects of commercial diving and compressed-air work. In *Occupational Medicine*, edited by C Zenz. St. Louis: Mosby.

Kindwall, EP, PO Edel, and HE Melton. 1983. Safe decompression schedules for caisson workers. Final report, National Institute of Occupational Safety and Health research grant number 5R01-OH0094703, December l.

Richardson, HW and RS Mayo. 1960. *Practical Tunnel Driving*. New York: McGraw-Hill.

US Bureau of Labor Statistics. 1971. Federal Register. Vol. 36, no. 75, part 2, sub-part S, para. 1518.803, 17 April.

Other relevant readings

Dutka, AJ. 1990. Therapy for dysbaric central nervous system ischaemia: Adjuncts to recompression. In *Diving Accident Management*, edited by PB Bennet and RE Moon. Bethesda, Md: Undersea and Hyperbaric Medical Society.

Edmonds, C, C Lowry, and J Pennefather. 1992. *Diving and Subaquatic Medicine*. Oxford: Butterworh-Heinemann.

Francis, TJR and Dr Gorman. 1993. Pathogenesis of the decompression disorders. In *The Physiology and Medicine of Diving*, edited by PB Bennett and DH Elliot. London: WB Saunders.

Francis, TJR and DJ Smith. 1991. *Describing Decompression Illness*. Bethesda, Md: Undersea and Hyperbaric Medical Society.

Moon, RE and DF Gorman. 1993. Treatment of the decompression disorders. In *The Physiology and Medicine of Diving*, edited by PB Bennett and DH Elliot. London: WB Saunders.

Proceedings of the Conference on Engineering and Health in Compressed Air Work, St. Catherine's College, Oxford. 1992. British Health and Safety Executive, Birdcage Walk, London.

36. BAROMETRIC PRESSURE, INCREASED

Chapter Editor
Walter Dümmer

Contents

VENTILATORY ACCLIMATIZATION TO HIGH ALTITUDE

John T. Reeves and John V. Weil

People are increasingly working at high altitudes. Mining operations, recreational facilities, modes of transportation, agricultural pursuits and military campaigns are often at high altitude, and all of these require human physical and mental activity. All such activity involves increased requirements for oxygen. A problem is that as one ascends higher and higher above sea level, both the total air pressure (the barometric pressure, P_B) and the amount of oxygen in the ambient air (that portion of total pressure due to oxygen, PO_2) progressively fall. As a result, the amount of work we can accomplish progressively decreases. These principles affect the workplace. For example, a tunnel in Colorado was found to require 25% more time to complete at an altitude of 11,000 ft than comparable work at sea level, and altitude effects were implicated in the delay. Not only is there increased muscular fatigue, but also, deterioration of mental function. Memory, computation, decision making and judgement all become impaired. Scientists doing calculations at the Mona Loa Observatory at an altitude above 4,000 m on the island of Hawaii have found they require more time to perform their calculations and they make more mistakes than at sea level. Because of the increasing scope, magnitude, variety and distribution of human activities on this planet, more people are working at high altitude, and effects of altitude become an occupational issue.

Fundamentally important to occupational performance at altitude is maintaining the oxygen supply to the tissues. We (and other animals) have defences against low oxygen states (hypoxia). Chief among these is an increase in breathing (ventilation), which begins when the oxygen pressure in the arterial blood (PaO_2) decreases (hypoxemia), is present for all altitudes above sea level, is progressive with altitude and is our most effective defence against low oxygen in the environment. The process whereby breathing increases at high altitude is called *ventilatory acclimatization*. The importance of the process can be seen in figure 37.1, which shows that the oxygen pressure in the arterial blood is higher in acclimatized subjects than in unacclimatized subjects. Further, the importance of acclimatization in maintaining the arterial oxygen pressure increases progressively with increasing altitude. Indeed, the unacclimatized person is unlikely to survive above an altitude of 20,000 ft, whereas acclimatized persons have been able to climb to the summit of Mount Everest (29,029 ft, 8,848 m) without artificial sources of oxygen.

Mechanism

The stimulus for the increase in ventilation at high altitude largely and almost exclusively arises in a tissue which monitors the oxygen pressure in the arterial blood and is contained within an organ called the carotid body, about the size of a pinhead, located at a branch point in each of the two carotid arteries, at the level of the angle of the jaw. When the arterial oxygen pressure falls, nerve-like cells (chemoreceptor cells) in the carotid body sense this decrease and increase their firing rate along the 9th cranial nerve, which carries the impulses directly to the respiratory control centre in the brain stem. When the respiratory centre receives increased numbers of impulses, it stimulates an increase in the frequency and depth of breathing via complex nerve pathways, which activate the diaphragm and the muscles of the chest wall. The result is an increased amount of air ventilated by the lungs, figure 37.2 which in turn acts to restore the arterial oxygen pressure. If a subject breathes oxygen or air enriched with oxygen, the reverse happens. That is, the chemoreceptor cells decrease their firing rate, which decreases the nerve traffic to the respiratory centre, and breathing decreases. These small organs on each side of the neck are very sensitive to small changes in oxygen pressure in the blood. Also, they are almost entirely responsible for maintaining the body's oxygen level, for when both of them are damaged or removed, ventilation no longer increases when blood oxygen levels fall. Thus an important factor controlling breathing is the arterial oxygen pressure; a decrease in oxygen level leads to an increase in breathing, and an increase in oxygen level leads to a

Figure 37.1 • Ventilatory acclimatization.

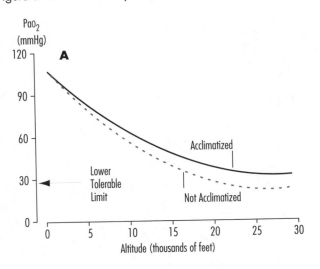

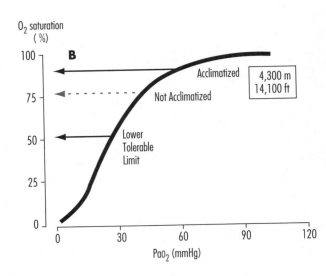

Arterial oxygen pressure (PaO_2) falls with increasing altitude, but the pressures are higher in acclimatized than unacclimatized subjects. (Panel A)

When the PaO_2 falls below 60 mmHg, the ability of haemoglobin to carry oxygen (O_2 per % saturation) falls sharply. Thus, in terms of blood oxygen transport, acclimatization becomes progressively more important the higher the altitude. (Panel B)

Figure 37.2 • Sequence of events in acclimatization.

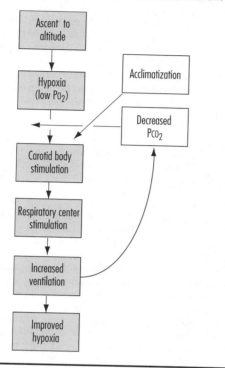

decrease in breathing. In each case the result is, in effect, the body's effort to maintain blood oxygen levels constant.

Time course (factors opposing the increase in ventilation at altitude)

Oxygen is required for the sustained production of energy, and when oxygen supply to tissues is reduced (hypoxia), tissue function may become depressed. Of all organs, the brain is most sensitive to lack of oxygen, and, as noted above, centres within the central nervous system are important in the control of breathing. When we breathe a low-oxygen mixture, the initial response is an increase in ventilation, but after 10 minutes or so the increase is blunted to some extent. While the cause for this blunting is not known, its suggested cause is depression of some central neural function related to the ventilation pathway, and has been called *hypoxic ventilatory depression*. Such depression has been observed shortly after ascent to high altitude. The depression is transient, lasting only a few hours, possibly because there is some tissue adaptation within the central nervous system.

Nevertheless, some increase in ventilation usually begins immediately on going to high altitude, although time is required before maximum ventilation is achieved. On arrival at altitude, increased carotid body activity attempts to increase ventilation, and thereby to raise the arterial oxygen pressure back to the sea level value. However, this presents the body with a dilemma. An increase in breathing causes an increased excretion of carbon dioxide (CO_2) in the exhaled air. When CO_2 is in body tissues, it creates an acid aqueous solution, and when it is lost in exhaled air, the body fluids, including blood, become more alkaline, thus altering the acid-base balance in the body. The dilemma is that ventilation is regulated not only to keep oxygen pressure constant, but also for acid-base balance. CO_2 regulates breathing in the opposite direction from oxygen. Thus when the CO_2 pressure (i.e., the degree of acidity somewhere within the respiratory centre)

rises, ventilation rises, and when it falls, ventilation falls. On arrival at high altitude, any increase in ventilation caused by the low oxygen environment will lead to a fall in CO_2 pressure, which causes alkalosis and acts to oppose the increased ventilation (figure 37.2). Therefore, the dilemma on arrival is that the body cannot maintain constancy in both oxygen pressure and acid-base balance. Human beings require many hours and even days to regain proper balance.

One method for rebalancing is for the kidneys to increase alkaline bicarbonate excretion in the urine, which compensates for the respiratory loss of acidity, thus helping to restore the body's acid-base balance toward the sea-level values. The renal excretion of bicarbonate is a relatively slow process. For example, on going from sea level to 4,300 m (14,110 ft), acclimatization requires from seven to ten days (figure 37.3). This action of the kidneys, which reduces the alkaline inhibition of ventilation, was once thought to be the major reason for the slow increase in ventilation following ascent, but more recent research assigns a dominant role to a progressive increase in the sensitivity of the hypoxic sensing ability of the carotid bodies during the early hours to days following ascent to altitude. This is the interval of *ventilatory acclimatization*. The acclimatization process allows, in effect, ventilation to rise in response to low arterial oxygen pressure even though the CO_2 pressure is falling. As the ventilation rises and CO_2 pressure falls with acclimatization at altitude, there is a resultant and concomitant rise in oxygen pressure within the lung alveoli and the arterial blood.

Because of the possibility of transient hypoxic ventilatory depression at altitude, and because acclimatization is a process which begins only upon entering a low oxygen environment, the minimal arterial oxygen pressure occurs upon arrival at altitude. Thereafter, the arterial oxygen pressure rises relatively rapidly for the initial days and thereafter increases more slowly, as in figure 37.3. Because the hypoxia is worse soon after arrival, the lethargy and symptoms which accompany altitude exposure are also worse during the first hours and days. With acclimatization, a restored sense of well-being usually develops.

The time required for acclimatization increases with increasing altitude, consistent with the concept that greater increase in ventilation and acid-base adjustments require longer intervals for renal compensation to occur. Thus while acclimatization may require three to five days for a sea-level native to acclimatize at 3,000 m, for altitudes above 6,000 to 8,000 m, complete acclimatization, even if it is possible, may require six weeks or more (figure 37.4). When the altitude-acclimatized person returns to sea level, the process reverses. That is, the arterial oxygen pressure now rises to the sea-level value and ventilation falls. Now there is less CO_2 exhaled, and CO_2 pressure rises in the blood and in the respiratory centre. The acid-base balance is altered toward the acid side, and the kidneys must retain bicarbonate to restore balance. Although the time required for the loss of acclimatization is not as well understood, it seems to require approximately as long an interval as the acclimatization process itself. If so, then return from altitude, hypothetically, gives a mirror image of altitude ascent, with one important exception: arterial oxygen pressures immediately become normal on descent.

Variability among individuals

As might be expected, individuals vary with regard to time required for, and magnitude of, ventilatory acclimatization to a given altitude. One very important reason is the large variation between individuals in the ventilatory response to hypoxia. For example, at sea level, if one holds the CO_2 pressure constant, so that it does not confound the ventilatory response to low oxygen, some normal persons show little or no increase in ventilation, while others show a very large (up to fivefold) increase. The

Figure 37.3 • Time course of ventilatory acclimatization for sea level subjects taken to 4,300 m altitude.

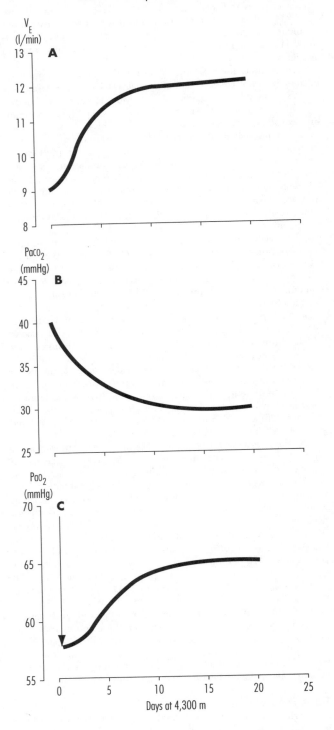

The increase in ventilation (V_E, panel A), the decrease in alveolar P_{CO_2} (P_{aCO_2}, Panel B), and the increase in alveolar P_{O_2} ((P_{aO_2} panel C). (The pressures of O_2 and CO_2 in the lung alveoli are close to those in arterial blood and are often used as non-invasive measurements.)

ventilatory response to breathing low-oxygen mixtures seems to be an inherent characteristic of an individual, because family members behave more alike than do persons who are not related. Those persons who have poor ventilatory responses to low oxygen at sea level, as expected, also seem to have smaller ventilatory responses over time at high altitude. There may be other factors causing inter-individual variability in acclimatization, such as variability in the magnitude of ventilatory depression, in the function of the respiratory centre, in sensitivity to acid-base changes, and in renal handling of bicarbonate, but these have not been evaluated.

Sleep

Poor sleep quality, particularly before there is ventilatory acclimatization, is not only a common complaint, but also a factor that will impair occupational efficiency. Many things interfere with the act of breathing, including emotions, physical activity, eating and the degree of wakefulness. Ventilation decreases during sleep, and the capacity for breathing to be stimulated by low oxygen or high CO_2 also decreases. Respiratory rate and depth of breathing both decrease. Further, at high altitude, where there are fewer oxygen molecules in the air, the amount of oxygen stored in the lung alveoli between breaths is less. Thus if breathing ceases for a few seconds (called apnoea, which is a common event at high altitude), the arterial oxygen pressure falls more rapidly than at sea level, where, in essence, the reservoir for oxygen is greater.

Periodic cessation of breathing is almost universal during the first few nights following ascent to high altitude. This is a reflection of the respiratory dilemma of altitude, described earlier,

Figure 37.4 • For residents of sea level, time required for full ventilatory acclimatization increases with ascent to progressively higher altitudes.

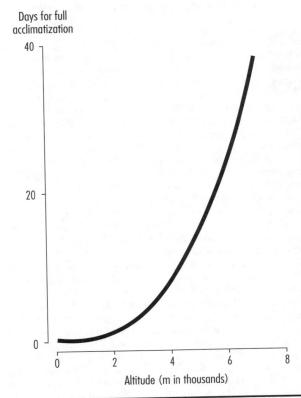

working in cyclic fashion: hypoxic stimulation increases ventilation, which in turn lowers carbon dioxide levels, inhibits breathing, and increases hypoxic stimulation, which again stimulates ventilation. Usually there is an apnoeic period of 15 to 30 seconds, followed by several very large breaths, which often briefly awakens the subject, after which there is another apnoea. The arterial oxygen pressure sometimes falls to alarming levels as a result of the apnoeic periods. There may be frequent awakenings, and even when total sleep time is normal its fragmentation impairs sleep quality such that there is the impression of having had a restless or sleepless night. Giving oxygen eliminates the cycling of hypoxic stimulation, and alkalotic inhibition abolishes the periodic breathing and restores normal sleep.

Middle-aged males in particular also are at risk for another cause of apnoea, namely intermittent obstruction of the upper airway, the common cause of snoring. While intermittent obstruction at the back of the nasal passages usually causes only annoying noise at sea level, at high altitude, where there is a smaller reservoir of oxygen in the lungs, such obstruction may lead to severely low levels of arterial oxygen pressure and poor sleep quality.

Intermittent Exposure

There are work situations, particularly in the Andes of South America, that require a worker to spend several days at altitudes above 3,000 to 4,000 m, and then to spend several days at home, at sea level. The particular work schedules (how many days are to be spent at altitude, say four to 14, and how many days, say three to seven, at sea level) are usually determined by the economics of the workplace more than by health considerations. However, a factor to be considered in the economics is the interval required both for acclimatization and loss of acclimatization to the altitude in question. Particular attention should be placed on the worker's sense of well-being and performance on the job on arrival and the first day or two thereafter, regarding fatigue, time required to perform routine and non-routine functions, and errors made. Also strategies should be considered to minimize the time required for acclimatization at altitude, and to improve function during the waking hours.

PHYSIOLOGICAL EFFECTS OF REDUCED BAROMETRIC PRESSURE

Kenneth I. Berger and William N. Rom

The major effects of high altitude on humans relate to the changes in barometric pressure (P_B) and its consequential changes in the ambient pressure of oxygen (O_2). Barometric pressure decreases with increasing altitude in a logarithmic fashion and can be estimated by the following equation:

$$P_B = 760(e^{-a/7924})$$

where a = altitude, expressed in metres. In addition, the relationship of barometric pressure to altitude is influenced by other factors such as distance from the equator and season. West and Lahiri (1984) found that direct measurements of barometric pressure near the equator and at the summit of Mt. Everest (8,848 m) were greater than predictions based on the International Civil Aviation Organization Standard Atmosphere. Weather and temperature also affect the relationship between barometric pressure and altitude to the extent that a low-pressure weather system can reduce pressure, making sojourners to high altitude "physiologically higher". Since the inspired partial pressure of oxygen (PO_2) remains constant at approximately 20.93% of barometric pressure, the most important determinant of inspired PO_2 at any altitude is the barometric pressure. Thus, inspired oxygen decreases with increasing altitude due to decreased barometric pressure, as shown in figure 37.5.

Temperature and ultraviolet radiation also change at high altitudes. Temperature decreases with increasing altitude at a rate of approximately 6.5 °C per 1,000 m. Ultraviolet radiation increases approximately 4% per 300 m due to decreased cloudiness, dust, and water vapour. In addition, as much as 75% of ultraviolet radiation can be reflected back by snow, further increasing exposure at high altitude. Survival in high altitude environments is dependent on adaptation to and/or protection from each of these elements.

Acclimatization

While rapid ascent to high altitudes often results in death, slow ascent by mountaineers can be successful when accompanied by compensatory physiological adaptation measures. Acclimatization to high altitudes is geared towards maintaining an adequate supply of oxygen to meet metabolic demands despite the decreasing inspired PO_2. In order to achieve this goal, changes occur in all organ systems involved with oxygen uptake into the body, distribution of O_2 to the necessary organs, and O_2 unloading to the tissues.

Discussion of oxygen uptake and distribution requires understanding the determinants of oxygen content in the blood. As air

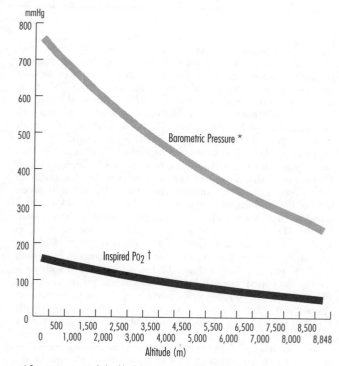

Figure 37.5 • Effects of altitude on barometric pressure and inspired PO_2.

* Barometric pressure calculated by the equation: $P_B = 760(e^{-a/7924})$ where
  P_B = barometric pressure in mmHg,
  e = natural antilog, and
  a = altitude in m.
† Inspired PO_2 calculated by the equation: Inspired $PO_2 = P_B \times .2093$ where
  PO_2 = partial pressure of oxygen in mmHg,
  P_B = barometric pressure in mmHg.

Figure 37.6 • Oxyhaemoglobin dissociation curve.

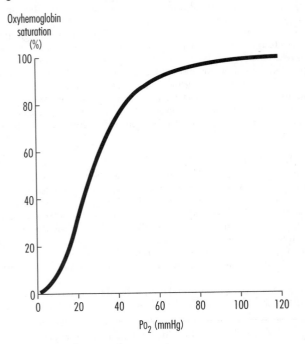

Po₂ = Arterial partial pressure of oxygen.

enters the alveolus, the inspired PO_2 decreases to a new level (called the alveolar PO_2) because of two factors: increased partial pressure of water vapour from humidification of inspired air, and increased partial pressure of carbon dioxide (PCO_2) from CO_2 excretion. From the alveolus, oxygen diffuses across the alveolar capillary membrane into the blood as a result of a gradient between alveolar PO_2 and blood PO_2. The majority of oxygen found in blood is bound to haemoglobin (oxyhaemoglobin). Thus, oxygen content is directly related to both the haemoglobin concentration in the blood and the percentage of O_2 binding sites on haemoglobin that are saturated with oxygen (oxyhaemoglobin saturation). Therefore, understanding the relationship between arterial PO_2 and oxyhaemoglobin saturation is essential for understanding the determinants of oxygen content in the blood. Figure 37.6 illustrates the oxyhaemoglobin dissociation curve. With increasing altitude, inspired PO_2 decreases and, therefore, arterial PO_2 and oxyhaemoglobin saturation decreases. In normal subjects, altitudes greater than 3,000 m are associated with sufficiently decreased arterial PO_2 that oxyhaemoglobin saturation falls below 90%, on the steep portion of the oxyhaemoglobin dissociation curve. Further increases in altitude will predictably result in significant desaturation in the absence of compensatory mechanisms.

The ventilatory adaptations that occur in high-altitude environments protect the arterial partial pressure of oxygen against the effects of decreasing ambient oxygen levels, and can be divided into acute, subacute and chronic changes. Acute ascent to high altitude results in a fall in the inspired PO_2 which in turn leads to a decrease in the arterial PO_2 (hypoxia). In order to minimize the effects of decreased inspired PO_2 on arterial oxyhaemoglobin saturation, the hypoxia that occurs at high altitude triggers an increase in ventilation, mediated through the carotid body (hypoxic ventilatory response–HVR). Hyperventilation increases

carbon dioxide excretion and subsequently the arterial and then the alveolar partial pressure of carbon dioxide (PCO_2) falls. The fall in alveolar PCO_2 allows alveolar PO_2 to rise, and consequently, arterial PO_2 and arterial O_2 content increases. However, the increased carbon dioxide excretion also causes a decrease in blood hydrogen ion concentration ($[H^+]$) leading to the development of alkalosis. The ensuing alkalosis inhibits the hypoxic ventilatory response. Thus, on acute ascent to high altitude there is an abrupt increase in ventilation that is modulated by the development of an alkalosis in the blood.

Over the next several days at high altitude, further changes in ventilation occur, commonly referred to as ventilatory acclimatization. Ventilation continues to increase over the next several weeks. This further increase in ventilation occurs as the kidney compensates for the acute alkalosis by excretion of bicarbonate ions, with a resultant rise in blood $[H^+]$. It was initially believed that renal compensation for the alkalosis removed the inhibitory influence of alkalosis on the hypoxic ventilatory response, thereby allowing the full potential of the HVR to be reached. However, measurements of blood pH revealed that the alkalosis persists despite the increase in ventilation. Other postulated mechanisms include: (1) cerebrospinal fluid (CSF) pH surrounding the respiratory control centre in the medulla may have returned to normal despite the persistent serum alkalosis; (2) increased sensitivity of the carotid body to hypoxia; (3) increased response of the respiratory controller to CO_2. Once ventilatory acclimatization has occurred, both hyperventilation and the increased HVR persist for several days after return to lower altitudes, despite resolution of hypoxia.

Further ventilatory changes occur after several years of living at high altitude. Measurements in high-altitude natives have shown a decreased HVR when compared to values obtained in acclimatized individuals, although not to levels seen in subjects at sea level. The mechanism for the decreased HVR is unknown, but may be related to hypertrophy of the carotid body and/or development of other adaptive mechanisms for preserving tissue oxygenation such as: increased capillary density; increased gas exchange capacity of the tissues; increased number and density of mitochondria; or increased vital capacity.

In addition to its effect on ventilation, hypoxia also induces constriction of the vascular smooth muscle in the pulmonary arteries (hypoxic vasoconstriction). The ensuing increase in pulmonary vascular resistance and pulmonary artery pressure redirects blood flow away from poorly ventilated alveoli with low alveolar PO_2 and towards better ventilated alveoli. In this manner, pulmonary arterial perfusion is matched to lung units that are well ventilated, providing another mechanism for preserving arterial PO_2.

Oxygen delivery to the tissues is further enhanced by adaptations in the cardiovascular and haematological systems. On initial ascent to high altitude, heart rate increases, resulting in an increase in cardiac output. Over several days, cardiac output falls due to decreased plasma volume, caused by an increased water loss that occurs at high altitudes. With more time, increased erythropoietin production leads to increased haemoglobin concentration, providing the blood with increased oxygen-carrying capacity. In addition to increasing levels of haemoglobin, changes in the avidity of oxygen binding to haemoglobin may also help maintain tissue oxygenation. A shift of the oxyhaemoglobin dissociation curve to the right may be expected because it would favour release of oxygen to the tissues. However, data obtained from the summit of Mt. Everest and from hypobaric chamber experiments simulating the summit suggest that the curve is shifted to the left (West and Lahiri 1984; West and Wagner 1980; West et al. 1983). Although a left shift would make oxygen unloading to the tissues more difficult, it may be advantageous at extreme altitudes because it would facilitate oxygen uptake in the lungs despite markedly reduced inspired PO_2 (43 mmHg on the summit of Mt. Everest versus 149 mmHg at sea level).

The last link in the chain of oxygen supply to the tissues is cellular uptake and utilization of O_2. Theoretically, there are two potential adaptations that can occur. First, minimization of the distance that oxygen has to travel on diffusion out of the blood vessel and into the intracellular site responsible for oxidative metabolism, the mitochondria. Second, biochemical alterations can occur that improve mitochondrial function. Minimization of diffusion distance has been suggested by studies that show either increased capillary density or increased mitochondrial density in muscle tissue. It is unclear whether these changes reflect either recruitment or development of capillaries and mitochondria, or are an artefact due to muscle atrophy. In either case, the distance between the capillaries and the mitochondria would be decreased, thereby facilitating oxygen diffusion. Biochemical alterations that may improve mitochondrial function include increased myoglobin levels. Myoglobin is an intracellular protein that binds oxygen at low tissue PO_2 levels and facilitates oxygen diffusion into the mitochondria. Myoglobin concentration increases with training and correlates with muscle cell aerobic capacity. Although these adaptations are theoretically beneficial, conclusive evidence is lacking.

Early accounts of high altitude explorers describe changes in cerebral function. Decreased motor, sensory and cognitive abilities, including decreased ability to learn new tasks and difficulty expressing information verbally, have all been described. These deficits may lead to poor judgement and to irritability, further compounding the problems encountered in high-altitude environments. On return to sea level, these deficits improve with a variable time course; reports have indicated impaired memory and concentration lasting from days to months, and decreased finger-tapping speed for one year (Hornbein et al. 1989). Individuals with greater HVR are more susceptible to long-lasting deficits, possibly because the benefit of hyperventilation on arterial oxyhaemoglobin saturation may be offset by hypocapnia (decreased PCO_2 in the blood), which causes constriction of the cerebral blood vessels leading to decreased cerebral blood flow.

The preceding discussion has been limited to resting conditions; exercise provides an additional stress as oxygen demand and consumption increases. The fall in ambient oxygen at high altitude causes a fall in maximal oxygen uptake and, therefore, maximal exercise. In addition, the decreased inspired PO_2 at high altitudes severely impairs oxygen diffusion into the blood. This is illustrated in figure 37.7, which plots the time course of oxygen diffusion into the alveolar capillaries. At sea level, there is excess time for equilibration of end-capillary PO_2 to alveolar PO_2, whereas at the summit of Mt. Everest, full equilibration is not realized. This difference is due to the decreased ambient oxygen level at high altitudes leading to a decreased diffusion gradient between alveolar and venous PO_2.

Figure 37.7 • The calculated time course of oxygen tension in the alveolar capillary.

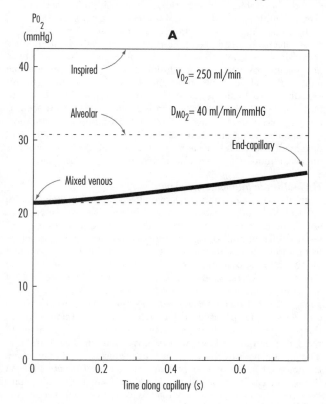 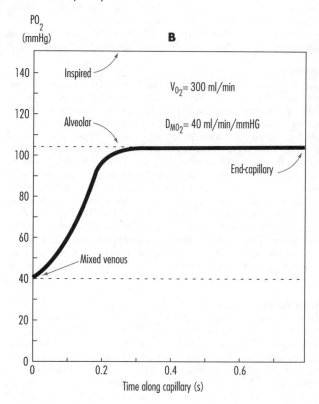

The calculated time course of oxygen tension in the alveolar capillary is illustrated at rest on the summit Mt. Everest (left panel), and at rest at sea level (right panel). At sea level, there is excess time for equilibration of end-capillary PO_2 to alveolar PO_2, whereas at the summit of Mt. Everest, full equilibration is not realized. This difference is due to the decreased ambient oxygen level at high altitudes leading to a decreased diffusion gradient between alveolar and venous PO_2.

With exercise, cardiac output and blood flow increase, thereby reducing transit time of blood cells across the alveolar capillary, further exacerbating the problem. From this discussion, it becomes apparent that the left shift in the O_2 and haemoglobin dissociation curve with altitude is necessary as compensation for the decreased diffusion gradient for oxygen in the alveolus.

Disturbed sleep is common among sojourners at high altitude. Periodic (Cheyne-Stokes) breathing is universal and characterized by periods of rapid respiratory rate (hyperpnoea) alternating with periods of absent respirations (apnoea) leading to hypoxia. Periodic breathing tends to be more pronounced in individuals with the greatest hypoxic ventilatory sensitivity. Accordingly, sojourners with lower HVR have less severe periodic breathing. However, sustained periods of hypoventilation are then seen, corresponding with sustained decreases in oxyhaemoglobin saturation. The mechanism for periodic breathing probably relates to increased HVR causing increased ventilation in response to hypoxia. The increased ventilation leads to increased blood pH (alkalosis), which in turn suppresses ventilation. As acclimatization progresses, periodic breathing improves. Treatment with acetazolamide reduces periodic breathing and improves arterial oxyhaemoglobin saturation during sleep. Caution should be used with medications and alcohol that suppress ventilation, as they may exacerbate the hypoxia seen during sleep.

Pathophysiological Effects of Reduced Barometric Pressure

The complexity of human physiological adaptation to high altitude provides numerous potential maladaptive responses. Although each syndrome will be described separately, there is considerable overlap between them. Illnesses such as acute hypoxia, acute mountain sickness, high-altitude pulmonary oedema, and high-altitude cerebral oedema most likely represent a spectrum of abnormalities that share a similar pathophysiology.

Hypoxia

Hypoxia occurs with ascent to high altitudes because of the decreased barometric pressure and the resultant decrease in ambient oxygen. With rapid ascent, hypoxia occurs acutely, and the body does not have time to adjust. Mountaineers have generally been protected from the effects of acute hypoxia because of the time that elapses, and hence the acclimatization that occurs, during the climb. Acute hypoxia is problematic for both aviators and rescue personnel in high-altitude environments. Acute oxyhaemoglobin desaturation to values less than 40 to 60% leads to loss of consciousness. With less severe desaturation, individuals note headache, confusion, drowsiness and loss of coordination. Hypoxia also induces a state of euphoria which Tissandier, during his balloon flight in 1875, described as experiencing "inner joy". With more severe desaturation, death occurs. Acute hypoxia responds rapidly and completely to either administration of oxygen or descent.

Acute mountain sickness

Acute mountain sickness (AMS) is the most common disorder in high-altitude environments and afflicts up to two-thirds of sojourners. The incidence of acute mountain sickness is dependent on multiple factors, including rate of ascent, length of exposure, degree of activity, and individual susceptibility. Identification of affected individuals is important in order to prevent progression to pulmonary or cerebral oedema. Identification of acute mountain sickness is made through recognition of characteristic signs and symptoms occurring in the appropriate setting. Most often, acute mountain sickness occurs within a few hours of a rapid ascent to altitudes greater than 2,500 m. The most common symptoms include headache that is more pronounced at night, loss of appetite that may be accompanied by nausea and vomiting, disturbed sleep, and fatigue. Individuals with AMS often complain of shortness of breath, cough and neurological symptoms such as memory deficits and auditory or visual disturbances. Findings on physical exam may be lacking, although fluid retention may be an early sign. The pathogenesis of acute mountain illness may relate to relative hypoventilation that would increase cerebral blood flow and intracranial pressure by increasing arterial PCO_2 and decreasing arterial PO_2. This mechanism may explain why persons with greater HVR are less likely to develop acute mountain sickness. The mechanism for fluid retention is not well understood, but may be related to abnormal plasma levels for proteins and/or hormones that regulate renal excretion of water; these regulators may respond to the increased activity of the sympathetic nervous system noted in patients with acute mountain sickness. The accumulation of water may in turn lead to the development of oedema or swelling of the interstitial spaces in the lungs. More severe cases may go on to develop pulmonary or cerebral oedema.

Prevention of acute mountain sickness can be accomplished through slow, graded ascent, allowing adequate time for acclimatization. This may be especially important for those individuals with greater susceptibility or a prior history of acute mountain sickness. In addition, administration of acetazolamide before or during ascent may help prevent and ameliorate symptoms of acute mountain sickness. Acetazolamide inhibits the action of carbonic anhydrase in the kidneys and leads to increased excretion of bicarbonate ions and water, producing an acidosis in the blood. The acidosis stimulates respiration, leading to increased arterial oxyhaemoglobin saturation and decreased periodic breathing during sleep. Through this mechanism, acetazolamide speeds the natural process of acclimatization.

Treatment of acute mountain sickness can be accomplished most effectively by descent. Further ascent to high altitudes is contra-indicated, as the disease may progress. When descent is not possible, oxygen may be administered. Alternatively, portable lightweight fabric hyperbaric chambers may be brought on expeditions to high-altitude environments. Hyperbaric bags are particularly valuable when oxygen is not available and descent is not possible. Several drugs are available that improve symptoms of acute mountain sickness, including acetazolamide and dexamethasone. The mechanism of action of dexamethasone is unclear, although it may act by decreasing oedema formation.

High-altitude pulmonary oedema

High-altitude pulmonary oedema affects approximately 0.5 to 2.0% of individuals who ascend to altitudes greater than 2,700 m and is the most common cause of death due to illnesses encountered at high altitudes. High-altitude pulmonary oedema develops from 6 to 96 hours after ascent. Risk factors for the development of high-altitude pulmonary oedema are similar to those for acute mountain sickness. Common early signs include symptoms of acute mountain sickness accompanied by decreased exercise tolerance, increased recovery time after exercise, shortness of breath on exertion, and persistent dry cough. As the condition worsens, the patient develops shortness of breath at rest, findings of audible congestion in the lungs, and cyanosis of the nail beds and lips. The pathogenesis of this disorder is uncertain but probably relates to increased microvascular pressure or increased permeability of the microvasculature leading to the development of pulmonary oedema. Although pulmonary hypertension may help explain the pathogenesis, elevation in the pulmonary artery pressure due to hypoxia has been observed in all individuals who ascend to high altitude, including those who do not develop pulmonary oedema. Nevertheless, susceptible individuals may possess uneven hypoxic constriction of the pulmonary arteries, leading to over-perfusion of the microvasculature in localized areas where hypoxic vasoconstriction was absent or diminished. The resulting increase in pressure and shear forces may damage the capillary membrane, leading to oedema formation. This mechanism explains the patchy nature of this disease and its appearance on x-ray examination of the lungs. As with acute mountain sickness, individuals with a lower HVR are more likely to develop high-altitude pulmonary oedema as they have lower oxy-haemoglobin saturations and, therefore, greater hypoxic pulmonary vasoconstriction.

Prevention of high-altitude pulmonary oedema is similar to prevention of acute mountain sickness and includes gradual ascent and use of acetazolamide. Recently, use of the smooth-muscle relaxing agent nifedipine has been shown to be of benefit in preventing disease in individuals with a prior history of high-altitude pulmonary oedema. Additionally, avoidance of exercise may have a preventive role, although it is probably limited to those individuals who already posses a subclinical degree of this disease.

Treatment of high-altitude pulmonary oedema is best accomplished by assisted evacuation to a lower altitude, keeping in mind that the victim needs to limit his or her exertion. After descent, improvement is rapid and additional treatment other than bed rest and oxygen are usually not necessary. When descent is not possible, oxygen therapy may be beneficial. Drug treatment has been attempted with multiple agents, most successfully with the diuretic furosemide and with morphine. Caution must be used with these drugs, as they can lead to dehydration, decreased blood pressure, and respiratory depression. Despite the effectiveness of descent as therapy, mortality remains at approximately 11%. This high mortality rate may reflect failure to diagnose the disease early in its course, or inability to descend coupled with lack of availability of other treatments.

High-altitude cerebral oedema

High-altitude cerebral oedema represents an extreme form of acute mountain sickness that has progressed to include generalized cerebral dysfunction. The incidence of cerebral oedema is unclear because it is difficult to differentiate a severe case of acute mountain sickness from a mild case of cerebral oedema. The pathogenesis of high-altitude cerebral oedema is an extension of the pathogenesis of acute mountain sickness; hypoventilation increases cerebral blood flow and intracranial pressure progressing to cerebral oedema. Early symptoms of cerebral oedema are identical to symptoms of acute mountain sickness. As the disease progresses, additional neurological symptoms are noted, including severe irritability and insomnia, ataxia, hallucinations, paralysis, seizures and eventually coma. Examination of the eyes commonly reveals swelling of the optic disc or papilloedema. Retinal haemorrhages are frequently noted. In addition, many cases of cerebral oedema have concurrent pulmonary oedema.

Treatment of high-altitude cerebral oedema is similar to treatment of other high-altitude disorders, with descent being the preferred therapy. Oxygen should be administered to maintain oxyhaemoglobin saturation greater that 90%. Oedema formation may be decreased with use of corticosteroids such as dexamethasone. Diuretic agents have also been utilized to decrease oedema, with uncertain efficacy. Comatose patients may require additional support with airway management. The response to treatment is variable, with neurological deficits and coma persisting for days to weeks after evacuation to lower altitudes. Preventative measures for cerebral oedema are identical to measures for other high-altitude syndromes.

Retinal haemorrhages

Retinal haemorrhages are extremely common, affecting up to 40% of individuals at 3,700 m and 56% at 5,350 m. Retinal haemorrhages are usually asymptomatic. They are most likely caused by increased retinal blood flow and vascular dilatation due to arterial hypoxia. Retinal haemorrhages are more common in individuals with headaches and can be precipitated by strenuous exercise. Unlike other high-altitude syndromes, retinal haemorrhages are not preventable by acetazolamide or furosemide therapy. Spontaneous resolution is usually seen within two weeks.

Chronic mountain sickness

Chronic mountain sickness (CMS) afflicts residents and long-term inhabitants of high altitude. The first description of chronic mountain sickness reflected Monge's observations of Andean natives living at altitudes above 4,000 m. Chronic mountain sickness, or Monge's disease, has since been described in most high-altitude dwellers except Sherpas. Males are more commonly affected than females. Chronic mountain sickness is characterized by plethora, cyanosis and elevated red blood cell mass leading to neurological symptoms that include headache, dizziness, lethargy and impaired memory. Victims of chronic mountain sickness may develop right heart failure, also called *cor pulmonale*, due to pulmonary hypertension and markedly reduced oxyhaemoglobin saturation. The pathogenesis of chronic mountain sickness is unclear. Measurements from affected individuals have revealed a decreased hypoxic ventilatory response, severe hypoxemia that is exacerbated during sleep, increased haemoglobin concentration and increased pulmonary artery pressure. Although a cause-and-effect relationship seems likely, evidence is lacking and often confusing.

Many symptoms of chronic mountain sickness can be ameliorated by descent to sea level. Relocation to sea level removes the hypoxic stimulus for red blood cell production and pulmonary vasoconstriction. Alternate treatments include: phlebotomy to reduce red blood cell mass, and low-flow oxygen during sleep to improve hypoxia. Therapy with medroxyprogesterone, a respiratory stimulant, has also been found to be effective. In one study, ten weeks of medroxyprogesterone therapy was followed by improved ventilation and hypoxia, and decreased red blood cell counts.

Other conditions

Patients with sickle cell disease are more likely to suffer from painful vaso-occlusive crisis at high altitude. Even moderate altitudes of 1,500 m have been known to precipitate crises, and altitudes of 1,925 m are associated with a 60% risk of crises. Patients with sickle cell disease residing at 3,050 m in Saudi Arabia have twice as many crises as patients residing at sea level. In addition, patients with sickle cell trait may develop splenic infarct syndrome on ascent to high altitude. Likely aetiologies for the increased risk of vaso-occlusive crisis include: dehydration, increased red blood cell count, and immobility. Treatment of vaso-occlusive crisis includes descent to sea level, oxygen and intravenous hydration.

Essentially no data exist describing the risk to pregnant patients on ascent to high altitudes. Although patients residing at high altitude have an increased risk of pregnancy-induced hypertension, no reports of increased foetal demise exist. Severe hypoxia may cause abnormalities in foetal heart rate; however, this occurs only at extreme altitudes or in the presence of high-altitude pulmonary oedema. Therefore, the greatest risk to the pregnant patient may relate to the remoteness of the area rather than to altitude-induced complications.

HEALTH CONSIDERATIONS FOR MANAGING WORK AT HIGH ALTITUDES

John B. West

Large numbers of people work at high altitudes, particularly in the cities and villages of the South American Andes and the Tibetan plateau. The majority of these people are highlanders who have lived in the area for many years and perhaps several generations. Much of the work is agricultural in nature—for example, tending domesticated animals.

However, the focus of this article is different. Recently there has been a large increase in commercial activities at altitudes of 3,500 to 6,000 m. Examples include mines in Chile and Peru at altitudes of around 4,500 m. Some of these mines are very large, employing over 1,000 workers. Another example is the telescope facility at Mauna Kea, Hawaii, at an altitude of 4,200 m.

Traditionally, the high mines in the South American Andes, some of which date back to the Spanish colonial period, have been worked by indigenous people who have been at high altitude for generations. Recently however, increasing use is being made of workers from sea level. There are several reasons for this change. One is that there are not enough people in these remote areas to operate the mines. An equally important reason is that as the mines become increasingly automated, skilled people are required to operate large digging machines, loaders and trucks, and local people may not have the necessary skills. A third reason is the economics of developing these mines. Whereas previously whole towns were set up in the vicinity of the mine to accommodate the workers' families, and necessary ancillary facilities such as schools and hospitals, it is now seen to be preferable to have the families live at sea level, and have the workers commute to the mines. This is not purely an economic issue. The quality of life at an altitude of 4,500 m is less than at lower altitudes (e.g., children grow more slowly). Therefore the decision to have the families remain at sea level while the workers commute to high altitude has a sound socio-economic basis.

The situation where a workforce moves from sea level to altitudes of approximately 4,500 m raises many medical issues, many of which are poorly understood at the present time. Certainly most people who travel from sea level to an altitude of 4,500 m develop some symptoms of acute mountain sickness initially. Tolerance to the altitude often improves after the first two or three days. However, the severe hypoxia of these altitudes has a number of deleterious effects on the body. Maximal work capacity is decreased, and people fatigue more rapidly. Mental efficiency is reduced and many people find it is much more difficult to concentrate. Sleep quality is often poor, with frequent arousals and periodic breathing (the breathing waxes and wanes three or four times every minute) with the result that that the arterial PO_2 falls to low levels following the periods of apnoea or reduced breathing.

Tolerance to high altitude varies greatly between individuals, and it is often very difficult to predict who is going to be intolerant of high altitude. A substantial number of people who would like to work at an altitude of 4,500 m find that they are unable to do so, or that the quality life is so poor that they refuse to remain at that altitude. Topics such as the selection of workers who are likely to tolerate high altitude, and the scheduling of their work between high altitude and the period with their families at sea level, are relatively new and not well understood.

Pre-employment Examination

In addition to the usual type of pre-employment examination, special attention should be given to the cardio-pulmonary system, because working at high altitude makes great demands on the respiratory and cardiovascular systems. Medical conditions such as early chronic obstructive pulmonary disease and asthma will be much more disabling at high altitude because of the high levels of ventilation, and should be specifically looked for. A heavy cigarette smoker with symptoms of early bronchitis is likely to have difficulty tolerating high altitude. Forced spirometry should be measured in addition to the usual chest examination including chest radiograph. If possible, an exercise test should be carried out because any exercise intolerance will be exaggerated at high altitude.

The cardiovascular system should be carefully examined, including an exercise electrocardiogram if that is feasible. Blood counts should be made to exclude workers with unusual degrees of anaemia or polycythaemia.

Living at high altitude increases the psychological stress in many people, and a careful history should be taken to exclude prospective workers with previous behavioural problems. Many modern mines at high altitude are dry (no alcohol permitted). Gastro-intestinal symptoms are common in some people at high altitude, and workers who have a history of dyspepsia may do poorly.

Selection of Workers to Tolerate High Altitude

In addition to excluding workers with lung or heart disease who are likely to do poorly at high altitude, it would be very valuable if tests could be carried out to determine who is likely to tolerate altitude well. Unfortunately little is known at the present time about predictors of tolerance to high altitude, though considerable work is being done on this at the present time.

The best predictor of tolerance to high altitude is probably previous experience at high altitude. If someone has been able to work at an altitude of 4,500 m for several weeks without appreciable problems, it is very likely that he or she will be able to do this again. By the same token, somebody who tried to work at high altitude and found that he or she could not tolerate it, is very likely to have the same problem next time. Therefore in selecting workers, a great deal of emphasis should be placed on successful previous employment at high altitude. However, clearly this criterion cannot be used for all workers because otherwise no new people would enter the high-altitude working pool.

Another possible predictor is the magnitude of the ventilatory response to hypoxia. This can be measured at sea level by giving the prospective worker a low concentration of oxygen to breathe and measuring the increase in ventilation. There is some evidence that people who have a relatively weak hypoxic ventilatory response tolerate high altitude poorly. For example, Schoene (1982) showed that 14 high-altitude climbers had significantly higher hypoxic ventilatory responses than ten controls. Further measurements were made on the 1981 American Medical Research Expedition to Everest, where it was shown that the hypoxic ventilatory response measured before and on the Expedition correlated well with performance high on the mountain (Schoene, Lahiri and Hackett 1984). Masuyama, Kimura and Sugita (1986) reported that five climbers who reached 8,000 m in Kanchenjunga had a higher hypoxic ventilatory response than five climbers who did not.

However, this correlation is by no means universal. In a prospective study of 128 climbers going to high altitudes, a measure of hypoxic ventilatory response did not correlate with the height reached, whereas a measurement of maximal oxygen uptake at sea level did correlate (Richalet, Kerome and Bersch 1988). This study also suggested that the heart rate response to acute hypoxia might be a useful predictor of performance at high altitude. There have been other studies showing a poor correlation between hypoxic ventilatory response and performance at extreme altitude (Ward, Milledge and West 1995).

The problem with many of these studies is that the results are chiefly applicable to much higher altitudes than of interest here. Also there are many examples of climbers with moderate values of hypoxic ventilatory response who do well at high altitude. Nevertheless, an abnormally low hypoxic ventilatory response is probably a risk factor for tolerating even medium altitudes such as 4,500 m.

One way of measuring the hypoxic ventilatory response at sea level is to have the subject rebreathe into a bag which is initially filled with 24% oxygen, 7% carbon dioxide, and the balance nitrogen. During rebreathing the PCO_2 is monitored and held constant by means of a variable bypass and carbon dioxide absorber. Rebreathing can be continued until the inspired PO_2 falls to about 40 mmHg (5.3 kPa). The arterial oxygen saturation is measured continually with a pulse oximeter, and the ventilation plotted against the saturation (Rebuck and Campbell 1974). Another way of measuring the hypoxic ventilatory response is to determine the inspiratory pressure during a brief period of airway occlusion while the subject is breathing a low-oxygen mixture (Whitelaw, Derenne and Milic-Emili 1975).

Another possible predictor of tolerance to high altitude is work capacity during acute hypoxia at sea level. The rationale here is that someone who is not able to tolerate acute hypoxia is more likely to be intolerant of chronic hypoxia. There is little evidence for or against this hypothesis. Soviet physiologists used tolerance to acute hypoxia as one of the criteria for selection of climbers for their successful 1982 Everest expedition (Gazenko 1987). On the other hand, the changes that occur with acclimatization are so profound that it would not be surprising if exercise performance during acute hypoxia were poorly correlated with the ability to work during chronic hypoxia.

Another possible predictor is the increase in pulmonary artery pressure during acute hypoxia at sea level. This can be measured non-invasively in many people by Doppler ultrasound. The main rationale for this test is the known correlation between the development of high-altitude pulmonary oedema and the degree of hypoxic pulmonary vasoconstriction (Ward, Milledge and West 1995). However, since high-altitude pulmonary oedema is uncommon in people working at an altitude of 4,500 m, the practical value of this test is questionable.

The only way to determine whether these tests for the selection of workers have practical value is a prospective study where the results of the tests done at sea level are correlated with subsequent assessment of tolerance to high altitude. This raises the question of how high-altitude tolerance will be measured. The usual way of doing this is by questionnaires such as the Lake Louise questionnaire (Hackett and Oelz 1992). However, questionnaires may be unreliable in this population because workers perceive that if they admit to altitude intolerance, they might lose their jobs. It is true that there are objective measures of altitude intolerance such as quitting work, rales in the lungs as indications of subclinical pulmonary oedema, and mild ataxia as an indication of subclinical high-altitude cerebral oedema. However, these features will be seen only in people with severe altitude intolerance, and a prospective study based solely on such measurements would be very insensitive.

It should be emphasized that the value of these possible tests for determining tolerance to working at high altitude has not been established. However, the economic implications of taking on a substantial number of workers who are unable to perform satisfactorily at high altitude are such that it would be very valuable to have useful predictors. Studies are presently underway to determine whether some of these predictors are valuable and feasible. Measurements such as the hypoxic ventilatory response to hypoxia, and work capacity during acute hypoxia at sea level, are not particularly difficult. However, they need to be done by a professional laboratory, and the cost of these investigations can be justified only if the predictive value of the measurements is substantial.

Scheduling between High Altitude and Sea Level

Again, this article is addressed to the specific problems which occur when commercial activities such as mines at altitudes of about 4,500 m employ workers who commute from sea level where their families live. Scheduling is obviously not an issue where people live permanently at high altitude.

Designing the optimal schedule for moving between high altitude and sea level is a challenging problem, and as yet there is little scientific basis for the schedules that have been employed so far. These have been based mainly on social factors such as how long the workers are willing to spend at high altitude before seeing their families again.

The main medical rationale for spending several days at a time at high altitude is the advantage gained from acclimatization. Many people who develop symptoms of acute mountain sickness after going to high altitude feel much better after two to four days. Therefore rapid acclimatization is occurring over this period. In addition it is known that the ventilatory response to hypoxia takes seven to ten days to reach a steady state (Lahiri 1972; Dempsey and Forster 1982). This increase in ventilation is one of the most important features of the acclimatization process, and therefore it is reasonable to recommend that the working period at high altitude be at least ten days.

Other features of high-altitude acclimatization probably take much longer to develop. One example is polycythaemia, which takes several weeks to reach a steady state. However, it should be added that the physiological value of polycythaemia is much less certain than was thought at one time. Indeed, Winslow and Monge (1987) have shown that the severe degrees of polycythaemia which are sometimes seen in permanent dwellers at altitudes of about 4,500 m are counterproductive in that work capacity can sometimes be increased if the haematocrit is lowered by removing blood over several weeks.

Another important issue is the rate of deacclimatization. Ideally the workers should not lose all the acclimatization that they have developed at high altitude during their period with their families at sea level. Unfortunately, there has been little work on the rate of deacclimatization, although some measurements suggest that the rate of change of the ventilatory response during deacclimatization is slower than during acclimatization (Lahiri 1972).

Another practical issue is the time required to move workers from sea level to high altitude and back again. In a new mine at Collahuasi in north Chile, it takes only a few hours to reach the mine by bus from the coastal town of Iquique, where most of the families are expected to live. However, if the worker resides in Santiago, the trip could take over a day. Under these circumstances, a short working period of three or four days at high altitude would clearly be inefficient because of the time wasted in travelling.

Social factors also play a critical role in any scheduling that involves time away from the family. Even if there are medical and physiological reasons why an acclimatization period of 14 days is optimal, the fact that the workers are unwilling to leave their families for more than seven or ten days may be an overriding factor. Experience so far shows that a schedule of seven days at high altitude followed by seven days at sea level, or ten days at high altitude followed by the same period at sea level are probably the most acceptable schedules.

Note that with this type of schedule, the worker never fully acclimatizes to high altitude, nor fully deacclimatizes while at sea level. He therefore spends his time oscillating between the two extremes, never receiving the full benefit of either state. In addition, some workers complain of extreme tiredness when they return to sea level, and spend the first two or three days recovering. Possibly this is related to the poor quality of sleep which is often a feature of living at high altitude. These problems highlight our ignorance of the factors that determine the best schedules, and more work is clearly needed in this area.

Whatever schedule is used, it is highly advantageous if the workers can sleep at a lower altitude than the workplace. Naturally whether this is feasible depends on the topography of the region. A lower altitude for sleeping is not feasible if it takes several hours to reach it because this cuts too much off the working day. However, if there is a location several hundred metres lower which can be reached within, say, one hour, setting up sleeping quarters at this lower altitude will improve sleep quality, workers' comfort and sense of well-being, and productivity.

Oxygen Enrichment of Room Air to Reduce the Hypoxia of High Altitude

The deleterious effects of high altitude are caused by the low partial pressure of oxygen in the air. In turn, this results from the fact that while the oxygen concentration is the same as at sea level, the barometric pressure is low. Unfortunately there is little that can be done at high altitude to counter this "climatic aggression", as it was dubbed by Carlos Monge, the father of high-altitude medicine in Peru (Monge 1948).

One possibility is to increase the barometric pressure in a small area, and this is the principle of the Gamow bag, which is sometimes used for the emergency treatment of mountain sickness. However, pressurizing large spaces such as rooms is difficult from a technical point of view, and there are also medical problems associated with entering and leaving a room with increased pressure. An example is middle ear discomfort if the Eustachian tube is blocked.

The alternative is to raise the oxygen concentration in some parts of the work facility, and this is a relatively new development that shows great promise (West 1995). As pointed out earlier, even after a period of acclimatization of seven to ten days at an altitude of 4,500 m, severe hypoxia continues to reduce work capacity, mental efficiency and sleep quality. It would therefore be highly advantageous to reduce the degree of hypoxia in some parts of the work facility if that were feasible.

This can be done by adding oxygen to the normal air ventilation of some rooms. The value of relatively minor degrees of oxygen enrichment of the room air is remarkable. It has been shown that every 1% increase in oxygen concentration (for example from 21 to 22%) reduces the equivalent altitude by 300 m. The equivalent altitude is that which has the same inspired PO_2 during air breathing as in the oxygen-enriched room. Thus at an altitude of 4,500 m, raising the oxygen concentration of a room from 21 to 26% would reduce the equivalent altitude by 1,500 m. The result would be an equivalent altitude of 3,000 m, which is easily tolerated. The oxygen would be added to the normal room ventilation and therefore would be part of the air conditioning. We all expect that a room will provide a comfortable temperature and humidity. Control of the oxygen concentration can be regarded as a further logical step in humanity's control of our environment.

Oxygen enrichment has become feasible because of the introduction of relatively inexpensive equipment for providing large quantities of nearly pure oxygen. The most promising is the oxygen concentrator that uses a molecular sieve. Such a device preferentially adsorbs nitrogen and thus produces an oxygen-enriched gas from air. It is difficult to produce pure oxygen with this type of concentrator, but large amounts of 90% oxygen in nitrogen are readily available, and these are just as useful for this application. These devices can work continuously. In practice, two molecular sieves are used in an alternating fashion, and one is purged while the other is actively adsorbing nitrogen. The only requirement is electrical power, which is normally in abundant supply at a modern mine. As a rough indication of the cost of oxygen enrichment, a small commercial device can be bought off the shelf, and this produces 300 litres per hour of 90% oxygen. It was developed to produce oxygen for treating patients with lung disease in their homes. The device has a power requirement of 350 watts and the initial cost is about US$2,000. Such a machine is sufficient to raise the oxygen concentration in a room by 3% for one person at a minimal though acceptable level of room ventilation. Very large oxygen concentrators are also available, and they are used in the paper pulp industry. It is also possible that liquid oxygen might be economical under some circumstances.

There are several areas in a mine, for example, where oxygen enrichment might be considered. One would be the director's office or conference room, where important decisions are being made. For example, if there is a crisis in the mine such as a serious accident, such a facility would probably result in clearer thinking than the normal hypoxic environment. There is good evidence that an altitude of 4,500 m impairs brain function (Ward, Milledge and West 1995). Another place where oxygen enrichment would be beneficial is a laboratory where quality control measurements are being carried out. A further possibility is oxygen enrichment of sleeping quarters to improve sleep quality. Double blind trials of the effectiveness of oxygen enrichment at altitudes of about 4,500 m would be easy to design and should be carried out as soon as possible.

Possible complications of oxygen enrichment should be considered. Increased fire hazard is one issue that has been raised. However, increasing the oxygen concentration by 5% at an altitude of 4,500 m produces an atmosphere which has a lower flammability than air at sea level (West 1996). It should be borne in mind that although oxygen enrichment increases the PO_2, this is still much lower than the sea-level value. Flammability of an atmosphere depends on two variables (Roth 1964):

- the partial pressure of oxygen, which is much lower in the enriched air at high altitude than at sea level
- the quenching effect of the inert components (i.e., nitrogen) of the atmosphere.

This quenching is slightly reduced at high altitude, but the net effect is still a lower flammability. Pure or nearly pure oxygen is dangerous, of course, and the normal precautions should be taken in piping the oxygen from the oxygen concentrator to the ventilation ducting.

Loss of acclimatization to high altitude is sometimes cited as a disadvantage of oxygen enrichment. However, there is no basic difference between entering a room with an oxygen-enriched atmosphere, and descending to a lower altitude. Everybody would sleep at a lower altitude if they could, and therefore this is hardly an argument against using oxygen enrichment. It is true that frequent exposure to a lower altitude will result in less acclimatization to the higher altitude, other things being equal. However, the ultimate objective is effective working at the high altitude of the mine, and this can presumably be enhanced using oxygen enrichment.

It is sometimes suggested that altering the atmosphere in this way might increase the legal liability of the facility if some kind of hypoxia-related illness developed. Actually, the opposite view seems more reasonable. It is possible that a worker who develops, say, a myocardial infarction while working at high altitude could claim that the altitude was a contributing factor. Any procedure which reduces the hypoxic stress makes altitude-induced illnesses less likely.

Emergency Treatment

The various types of high-altitude sickness, including acute mountain sickness, high-altitude pulmonary oedema and high-altitude cerebral oedema, were discussed earlier in this chapter. Little needs to be added in the context of work at high altitude.

Anyone who develops a high-altitude illness should be allowed to rest. This may be sufficient for conditions such as acute mountain sickness. Oxygen should be given by mask if this is available. However, if the patient does not improve, or deteriorates, descent is by far the best treatment. Usually this is easily done in a large commercial facility, because transportation is always available. All the high-altitude-related illnesses usually respond rapidly to removal to lower altitude.

There may be a place in a commercial facility for a small pressurized container in which the patient can be placed, and the equivalent altitude reduced by pumping in air. In the field, this is commonly done using a strong bag. One design is known as the Gamow bag, after its inventor. However, the main advantage of the bag is its portability, and since this feature is not really essential in a commercial facility, it would probably be better to use a larger, rigid tank. This should be big enough for an attendant to be inside the facility with the patient. Of course adequate ventilation of such a container is essential. Interestingly, there is anecdotal evidence that raising the atmospheric pressure in this way is sometimes more efficacious in the treatment of high-altitude illness than giving the patient a high concentration of oxygen. It is not clear why this should be so.

Acute mountain sickness

This is usually self-limiting and the patient feels much better after a day or two. The incidence of acute mountain sickness can be reduced by taking acetazolamide (Diamox), one or two 250 mg tablets per day. These can be started before reaching high altitude or can be taken when symptoms develop. Even people with mild symptoms find that half a tablet at night often improves the quality of sleep. Aspirin or paracetamol is useful for headache. Severe acute mountain sickness can be treated with dexamethasone, 8 mg initially, followed by 4 mg every six hours. However, descent is by far the best treatment if the condition is severe.

High-altitude pulmonary oedema

This is a potentially serious complication of mountain sickness and must be treated. Again the best therapy is descent. While awaiting evacuation, or if evacuation is not possible, give oxygen or place in a high-pressure chamber. Nifedipine (a calcium channel blocker) should be given. The dose is 10 mg sublingually followed by 20 mg slow release. This results in a fall in pulmonary artery pressure and is often very effective. However, the patient should be taken down to a lower altitude.

High-altitude cerebral oedema

This is potentially a very serious complication and is an indication for immediate descent. While awaiting evacuation, or if evacuation is not possible, give oxygen or place in an increased pressure environment. Dexamethasone should be given, 8 mg initially, followed by 4 mg every six hours.

As indicated earlier, people who develop severe acute mountain sickness, high-altitude pulmonary oedema or high-altitude cerebral oedema are likely to have a recurrence if they return to high altitude. Therefore if a worker develops any of these conditions, attempts should be made to find employment at a lower altitude.

PREVENTION OF OCCUPATIONAL HAZARDS AT HIGH ALTITUDES

Walter Dümmer

Working at high altitudes induces a variety of biological responses, as described elsewhere in this chapter. The hyperventilatory response to altitude should cause a marked increase in the total dose of hazardous substances which may be inhaled by persons occupationally exposed, as compared to people working under similar conditions at sea level. This implies that 8-hour exposure limits used as the basis of exposure standards should be reduced. In Chile, for example, the observation that silicosis progresses faster in mines at high altitudes, led to the reduction of the permitted exposure level proportional to the barometric pressure at the workplace, when expressed in terms of mg/m^3. While this may be overcorrecting at intermediate altitudes, the error will be in the favour the exposed worker. The threshold limit values (TLVs), expressed in terms of parts per million (ppm), require no adjustment, however, because both the proportion of millimoles of contaminant per mole of oxygen in air and the number of moles of oxygen required by a worker remain approximately constant at different altitudes, even though the air volume containing one mole of oxygen will vary.

In order to assure that this is true, however, the method of measurement used to determine the concentration in ppm must be truly volumetric, as is the case with Orsat's apparatus or the Bacharach Fyrite instruments. Colourimetric tubes that are calibrated to read in ppm are not true volumetric measurements because the markings on the tube are actually caused by a chemical reaction between the air contaminant and some reagent. In all chemical reactions, substances combine in proportion to the number of moles present, not in proportion to volumes. The hand-operated air pump draws a constant volume of air through the tube at any altitude. This volume at a higher altitude will contain a smaller mass of contaminant, giving a reading lower than the actual volumetric concentration in ppm (Leichnitz 1977). Readings should be corrected by multiplying the reading by the barometric pressure at sea level and dividing the result by the barometric pressure at the sampling site, using the same units (such as torr or mbar) for both pressures.

Diffusional samplers: The laws of gas diffusion indicate that the collection efficiency of diffusional samplers is independent of barometric pressure changes. Experimental work by Lindenboom and Palmes (1983) shows that other, as yet undetermined factors influence the collection of NO_2 at reduced pressures. The error is approximately 3.3% at 3,300 m and 8.5% at 5,400 m equivalent altitude. More research is needed on the causes of this variation and the effect of altitude on other gases and vapours.

No information is available on the effect of altitude on portable gas detectors calibrated in ppm, which are equipped with electrochemical diffusion sensors, but it could reasonably be expected that the same correction mentioned under colourimetric tubes would apply. Obviously the best procedure would be to calibrate them at altitude with a test gas of known concentration.

The principles of operation and measurement of electronic instruments should be examined carefully to determine whether they need recalibration when employed at high altitudes.

Sampling pumps: These pumps usually are volumetric—that is, they displace a fixed volume per revolution—but they usually are the last component of the sampling train, and the actual volume of air aspirated is affected by the resistance to flow opposed by the filters, hose, flow meters and orifices that are part of the sampling train. Rotameters will indicate a lower flow rate than that actually flowing through the sampling train.

The best solution of the problem of sampling at high altitudes is to calibrate the sampling system at the sampling site, obviating the problem of corrections. A briefcase sized bubble film calibration laboratory is available from sampling pump manufacturers. This is easily carried to location and permits rapid calibration under actual working conditions. It even includes a printer which provides a permanent record of calibrations made.

TLVs and Work Schedules

TLVs have been specified for a normal 8-hour workday and a 40-hour workweek. The present tendency in work at high altitudes is to work longer hours for a number of days and then commute to the nearest town for an extended rest period, keeping the average time at work within the legal limit, which in Chile is 48 hours per week.

Departures from the normal 8-hour working schedules make it necessary to examine the possible accumulation in the body of toxic substances due to the increase in exposure and reduction of detoxification times.

Chilean occupational health regulations have recently adopted the "Brief and Scala model" described by Paustenbach (1985) for reducing TLVs in the case of extended working hours. At altitude, the correction for barometric pressure should also be used. This usually results in very substantial reductions of permissible exposure limits.

In the case of cumulative hazards not subject to detoxifying mechanisms, such as silica, correction for extended working hours should be directly proportional to the actual hours worked in excess of the usual 2,000 hours per year.

Physical Hazards

Noise: The sound pressure level produced by noise of a given amplitude is in direct relation to air density, as is the amount of energy transmitted. This means that the reading obtained by a sound level meter and the effect on the inner ear are reduced in the same way, so no corrections would be required.

Precautionary note: Air sampling

The monitoring and maintenance of the occupational safety of workers requires special consideration for high altitude environments. High-altitude conditions can be expected to influence the accuracy of sampling and measuring instruments that have been calibrated for use at sea level. For example, active sampling devices rely on pumps to pull a volume of air onto a collection medium. Accurate measurement of the pump flow rate is essential in order to determine the exact volume of air drawn through the sampler and, therefore, the concentration of the contaminant. Flow calibrations are often performed at sea level. However, changes in air density with increasing altitude may alter the calibration, thereby invalidating subsequent measurements made in high altitude environments. Other factors that may influence the accuracy of sampling and measurement instruments at high altitude include changing temperature and relative humidity. An additional factor that should be considered when evaluating worker exposure to inhaled substances is the increased respiratory ventilation that occurs with acclimatization. Since ventilation is markedly increased after ascent to high altitude, workers may be exposed to excessive total doses of inhaled occupational contaminants, even though measured concentrations of the contaminant are below the threshold limit value.

Kenneth I. Berger and William N. Rom

Accidents: Hypoxia has a pronounced influence on the central nervous system, reducing response time and disrupting vision. An increase in the incidence of accidents should be expected. Above 3,000 m, the performance of persons engaged in critical tasks will benefit from supplementary oxygen.

References

Dempsey, JA and HV Forster. 1982. Mediation of ventilatory adaptations. *Physiol Rev* 62:262-346.

Gazenko, OG (ed.) 1987. *Physiology of Man At High Altitudes* (in Russian). Moscow: Nauka.

Hackett, PH and O Oelz. 1992. The Lake Louise consensus on the definition and quantification of altitude illness. In *Hypoxia and Mountain Medicine*, edited by JR Sutton, G Coates, and CS Houston. Burlington: Queen City Printers.

Hornbein, TF, BD Townes, RB Schoene, JR Sutton, and CS Houston. 1989. The cost to the central nervous system of climbing to extremely high altitude. *New Engl J Med* 321:1714-1719.

Lahiri, S. 1972. Dynamic aspects of regulation of ventilation in man during acclimatization to high altitude. *Resp Physiol* 16:245-258.

Leichnitz, K. 1977. Use of detector tubes under extreme conditions (humidity, pressure, temperature). *Am Ind Hyg Assoc J* 38:707.

Lindenboom, RH and ED Palmes. 1983. Effect of reduced atmospheric pressure on a diffusional sampler. *Am Ind Hyg Assoc J* 44:105.

Masuyama, S, H Kimura, and T Sugita. 1986. Control of ventilation in extreme-altitude climbers. *J Appl Physiol* 61:500-506.

Monge, C. 1948. *Acclimatization in the Andes: Historical Confirmations of "Climatic Aggression" in the Development of Andean Man*. Baltimore: Johns Hopkins Univ. Press.

Paustenbach, DJ. 1985. Occupational exposure limits, pharmacokinetics and unusual work schedules. In *Patty's Industrial Hygiene and Toxicology*, edited by LJ Cralley and LV Cralley. New York: Wiley.

Rebuck, AS and EJ Campbell. 1974. A clinical method for assessing the ventilatory response to hypoxia. *Am Rev Respir Dis* 109:345-350.

Richalet, J-P, A Keromes, and B Bersch. 1988. Physiological characteristics of high altitude climbers. *Sci Sport* 3:89-108.

Roth, EM. 1964. *Space Cabin Atmospheres: Part II, Fire and Blast Hazards*. NASA Report SP-48. Washington, DC: NASA.

Schoene, RB. 1982. Control of ventilation in climbers to extreme altitude. *J Appl Physiol* 53:886-890.

Schoene, RB, S Lahiri, and PH Hackett. 1984. Relationship of hypoxic ventilatory response to exercise performance on Mount Everest. *J Appl Physiol* 56:1478-1483.

Ward, MP, JS Milledge, and JB West. 1995. *High Altitude Medicine and Physiology*. London: Chapman & Hall.

West, JB. 1995. Oxygen enrichment of room air to relieve the hypoxia of high altitude. *Resp Physiol* 99:225-232.

—. 1997. Fire hazard in oxygen-enriched atmospheres at low barometric pressures. *Aviat Space Environ Med.* 68: 159-162.

West, JB and S Lahiri. 1984. *High Altitude and Man*. Bethesda, Md: American Physiological Society.

West, JB and PD Wagner. 1980. Predicted gas exchange on the summit of Mount Everest. *Resp Physiol* 42:1-16.

West, JB, SJ Boyer, DJ Graber, PH Hackett, KH Maret, JS Milledge, RM Peters, CJ Pizzo, M Samaja, FH Sarnquist, RB Schoene and RM Winslow. 1983. Maximal exercise at extreme altitudes on Mount Everest. *J Appl Physiol.* 55:688-698.

Whitelaw, WA, JP Derenne, and J Milic-Emili. 1975. Occlusion pressure as a measure of respiratory center output in conscious man. *Resp Physiol* 23:181-199.

Winslow, RM and CC Monge. 1987. *Hypoxia, Polycythemia, and Chronic Mountain Sickness*. Baltimore: Johns Hopkins Univ. Press.

Other relevant readings

Bisgard, GE. 1994. The role of arterial chemoreceptors in ventilatory acclimatization to hypoxia. In *Arterial Chemoreceptors*, edited by RG O'Regan, P Nolan, DS McQueen, and DJ Patterson. New York: Plenum Press.

Hackett, PH and RC Roach. 1995. High-altitude medicine. In *Wilderness Medicine*, edited by PS Auerbach. St. Louis: Mosby.

Reeves, JT, RE McCullough, LG Moore, A Cymerman, and JV Weil. 1993. Sea-level PCO2 relates to ventilatory acclimatization at 4,300m. *J Appl Physiol* 75:1117-1122.

Rom, WN. 1992. High altitude environments. In *Environmental and Occupational Medicine*, edited by WN Rom. Boston: Little, Brown & Co.

Schoene, RB, PH Hackett, and TF Hornbein. 1994. High altitude. In *Textbook of Respiratory Medicine*, edited by JF Murray and JA Nadel. Philadelphia: WB Saunders.

Weil, JV. 1986. Ventilatory control at high altitude. In *Handbook of Physiology, Respiratory System*, edited by NS Cherniack, JG Widdicomb, and AP Fishman. Bethesda, Md: American Physiological Society.

White, DP, K Gleeson, CK Pickett, AM Rannels, A Cymerman, and JV Weil. 1987. Altitude acclimatization: Influence on periodic breathing and chemoresponsiveness during sleep. *J Appl Physiol* 63:401-412.

BIOLOGICAL HAZARDS

38

Chapter Editor
Zuheir Ibrahim Fakhri

Contents

38. BIOLOGICAL HAZARDS

● WORKPLACE BIOHAZARDS

Zuheir I. Fakhri

The assessment of biohazards in the workplace has been concentrated on agricultural workers, health-care workers and laboratory personnel, who are at considerable risk of adverse health effects. A detailed compilation of biohazards by Dutkiewicz et al. (1988) shows how widespread the risks can be to workers in many other occupations as well (table 38.1).

Dutkiewicz et al. (1988) further taxonomically classified the micro-organisms and plants (table 38.2, opposite), as well as animals (table 38.3, p. 4), which might possibly present biohazards in work settings.

Micro-organisms

Micro-organisms are a large and diverse group of organisms that exist as single cells or cell clusters (Brock and Madigan 1988). Microbial cells are thus distinct from the cells of animals and plants, which are unable to live alone in nature but can exist only as parts of multicellular organisms.

Very few areas on the surface of this planet do not support microbial life, because micro-organisms have an astounding range of metabolic and energy-yielding abilities and many can exist under conditions that are lethal to other life forms.

Four broad classes of micro-organisms that can interact with humans are bacteria, fungi, viruses and protozoa. They are hazardous to workers due to their wide distribution in the working environment. The most important micro-organisms of occupational hazard are listed in tables 38.2 and 38.3.

Table 38.1 • Occupational settings with potential exposure of workers to biological agents.

Sector	Examples
Agriculture	Cultivating and harvesting Breeding and tending animals Forestry Fishing
Agricultural products	Abattoirs, food packaging plants Storage facilities: grain silos, tobacco and other processing Processing animal hair and leather Textile plants Wood processing: sawmills, papermills, cork factories
Laboratory animal care	
Health care	Patient care: medical, dental
Pharmaceutical and herbal products	
Personal care	Hairdressing, chiropody
Clinical and research laboratories	
Biotechnology	Production facilities
Day-care centres	
Building maintenance	"Sick" buildings
Sewage and compost facilities	
Industrial waste disposal systems	

Source: Dutkiewicz et al., 1988.

There are three major sources of such microbes:

1. those arising from microbial decomposition of various substrates associated with particular occupations (e.g., mouldy hay leading to hypersensitivity pneumonitis)
2. those associated with certain types of environments (e.g., bacteria in water supplies)
3. those stemming from infective individuals harbouring a particular pathogen (e.g., tuberculosis).

Ambient air may be contaminated with or carry significant levels of a variety of potentially harmful micro-organisms (Burrell 1991). Modern buildings, especially those designed for commercial and administrative purposes, constitute a unique ecological niche with their own biochemical environment, fauna and flora (Sterling et al. 1991). The potential adverse effects on workers are described elsewhere in this *Encyclopaedia*.

Water has been recognized as an important vehicle for extra-intestinal infection. A variety of pathogens are acquired through occupational, recreational and even therapeutic contact with water (Pitlik et al. 1987). The nature of non-enteric water-borne disease is often determined by the ecology of aquatic pathogens. Such infections are of basically two types: superficial, involving damaged or previously intact mucosae and skin; and systemic, often serious infections that may occur in the setting of depressed immunity. A broad spectrum of aquatic organisms, including viruses, bacteria, fungi, algae and parasites may invade the host through such extra-intestinal routes as the conjunctivae, respiratory mucosae, skin and genitalia.

Although zoonotic spread of infectious disease continues to occur in laboratory animals used in biomedical research, reported outbreaks have been minimized with the advent of rigorous veterinary and husbandry procedures, the use of commercially reared animals and the institution of appropriate personnel health programmes (Fox and Lipman 1991). Maintaining animals in modern facilities with appropriate safeguards against the introduction of vermin and biological vectors is also important in preventing zoonotic disease in personnel. Nevertheless, established zoonotic agents, newly discovered micro-organisms or new animal species not previously recognized as carriers of zoonotic micro-organisms are encountered, and the potential for spread of infectious disease from animals to humans still exists.

Active dialogue between veterinarians and physicians regarding the potential of zoonotic disease, the species of animals that are involved, and the methods of diagnosis, is an indispensable component of a successful preventive health programme.

Some Occupational Settings with Biohazards

Medical and laboratory staff and other health-care workers, including related professions, are exposed to infection by micro-organisms if the appropriate preventive measures are not taken. Hospital workers are exposed to many biological hazards, including human immunodeficiency virus (HIV), hepatitis B, herpes viruses, rubella and tuberculosis (Hewitt 1993).

Work in the agricultural sector is associated with a wide variety of occupational hazards. Exposure to organic dust, and to airborne micro-organisms and their toxins, may lead to respiratory disorders (Zejda et al. 1993). These include chronic bronchitis, asthma, hypersensitivity pneumonitis, organic dust toxic syndrome and chronic obstructive pulmonary disease. Dutkiewicz and his colleagues (1988) studied samples of silage for the identification of potential agents causing symptoms of organic and toxic syndrome. Very high levels of total aerobic bacteria and fungi were found. *Aspergillus fumigatus* predominated among the fungi, whereas bacillus and gram-negative organisms (*Pseudomonas, Alcaligenes, Citrobacter* and *Klebsiella* species) and actinomycetes prevailed

Table 38.2 • Viruses, bacteria, fungi and plants: Known biohazards in the workplace.

	Infection	Infection zoo-nosis[1]	Allergic response	Respirable toxin	Toxin	Carcinogenic
Viruses	x	x				
Bacteria						
Rickettsiae		x				
Chlamydiae		x				
Spiral bacteria		x				
Gram-negative bacteria	x	x	x	x(e)[2]		
Gram-positive cocci		x	x			
Spore-forming bacilli		x	x	x		
Non-sporing gram-positive rods and coryne-bacteria		x	x			
Mycobacteria	x	x				
Actinomycetes		x				
Fungi						
Moulds	x		x	x(m)[3]		x
Dermatophytes	x	x	x			
Yeast-like geo philic fungi	x	x				
Endogenous yeasts	x					
Parasites of wheat			x			
Mushrooms			x			
Other lower plants						
Lichens			x			
Liverworts			x			
Ferns			x			
Higher plants						
Pollen			x			
Volatile oils			x		x	
Dusts-processing			x		x	x

[1] Infection-zoonosis: Causes infection or invasion usually contracted from vertebrate animals (zoonosis).

[2] (e) Endotoxin.

[3] (m) Mycotoxin.

Source: Dutkiewicz et al. 1988.

among the bacteria. These results show that contact with aerosolized silage carries the risk of exposure to high concentrations of micro-organisms, of which *A. fumigatus* and endotoxin-producing bacteria are the most probable disease agents.

Short-term exposures to certain wood dusts may result in asthma, conjunctivitis, rhinitis or allergic dermatitis. Some ther-

mophilic micro-organisms found in wood are human pathogens, and inhalation of ascomycete spores from stored wood chips has been implicated in human illnesses (Jacjels 1985).

Examples illustrative of specific working conditions follow:

1. The fungus *Penicillium camemberti* var. *candidum* is used in the production of some types of cheese. The high frequency of precipitating antibodies of this fungus in the workers' blood samples, together with the clinical causes of the airway symptoms, indicate an aetiological relationship between airway symptoms and heavy exposure to this fungus (Dahl et al. 1994).

2. Micro-organisms (bacteria and fungi) and endotoxins are potential agents of occupational hazard in a potato processing plant (Dutkiewicz 1994). The presence of precipitins to microbial antigens was significantly correlated with the occurrence of the work-related respiratory and general symptoms that were found in 45.9% of the examined workers.

3. Museum and library personnel are exposed to moulds (e.g., *Aspergillus, Pencillium*) which, under certain conditions, contaminate books (Kolmodin-Hedman et al. 1986). Symptoms experienced are attacks of fever, chill, nausea and cough.

4. Ocular infections can result from the use of industrial microscope eyepieces on multiple shifts. *Staphylococcus aureus* has been identified among the micro-organism cultures (Olcerst 1987).

Prevention

An understanding of the principles of epidemiology and the spread of infectious disease is essential in the methods used in the control of the causing organism.

Preliminary and periodic medical examinations of workers should be carried out in order to detect biological occupational diseases. There are general principles for conducting medical examinations in order to detect adverse health effects of workplace exposure, including biological hazards. Specific procedures are to be found elsewhere in this *Encyclopaedia*. For example, in Sweden the Farmers' Federation initiated a programme of preventive occupational health services for farmers (Hoglund 1990). The main goal of the Farmers' Preventive Health Service (FPHS) is to prevent work-related injuries and illnesses and to provide clinical services to farmers for occupational medical problems.

For some infectious disease outbreaks, appropriate preventive measures may be difficult to put in place until the disease is identified. Outbreaks of the viral Crimean-Congo haemorrhagic fever (CCHF) which demonstrated this problem were reported among hospital staff in the United Arab Emirates (Dubai), Pakistan and South Africa (Van Eeden et al. 1985).

Vertebrates: Snakes and Lizards

In hot and temperate zones, snakebites may constitute a definite hazard for certain categories of workers: agricultural workers, woodcutters, building and civil engineering workers, fishermen, mushroom gatherers, snake charmers, zoo attendants and laboratory workers employed in the preparation of antivenom serums. The vast majority of snakes are harmless to humans, although a number are capable of inflicting serious injury with their venomous bites; dangerous species are found among both the terrestrial snakes (*Colubridae* and *Viperidae*) and aquatic snakes (*Hydrophiidae*) (Rioux and Juminer 1983).

According to the World Health Organization (WHO 1995), snakebites are estimated to cause 30,000 deaths per year in Asia and about 1,000 deaths each in Africa and South America. More detailed statistics are available from certain countries. Over 63,000 snakebites and scorpion stings with over 300 deaths are reported yearly in Mexico. In Brazil, about 20,000 snakebites and

Table 38.3 • Animals as a source of occupational hazards.

	Infection	Infection[1] Zoonosis	Allergic response	Toxin	Vector[2]
Invertebrates other than arthropods					
Protozoa	X	X			
Sponges				X	
Coelenterates				X	
Flatworms	X	X			
Roundworms	X	X	X		
Bryozoa				X	
Sea-squirts			X		
Arthropods					
Crustaceans			X		
Arachnids					
Spiders				x(B)[3]	
Mites	X		X	x(B)	X
Ticks				x(B)	X
Insects					
Cockroaches			X		
Beetles			X		
Moths			X	X	
Flies				x(B)	X
Bees			X	x(B)	
Vertebrates					
Fish			X	x(B)	
Amphibians			X		
Reptiles				x(B)	
Birds			X		
Mammals			X		

[1] Infection-zoonosis: Causes infection or invasion contracted from vertebrate animals.

[2] Vector of pathogenic viruses, bacteria or parasites.

[3] Toxic B produces toxin or venom transmitted by bite or sting.

Source: Dutkiewicz et al. 1988.

7,000 to 8,000 scorpion stings occur annually, with a case-fatality rate of 1.5% for snake bites and between 0.3% and 1% for scorpion stings. A study in Ouagadougou, Burkina Faso, showed 7.5 snakebites per 100,000 population in peri-urban areas and up to over 69 per 100,000 in more remote areas, where case-fatality rates reached 3%.

Snakebites are a problem also in developed parts of the world. Each year about 45,000 snakebites are reported in the United States, where the availability of health care has reduced the number of deaths to 9–15 per year. In Australia, where some of the world's most venomous snakes exist, the annual number of snakebites is estimated at between 300 and 500, with an average of two deaths.

Environmental changes, particularly deforestation, may have caused the disappearance of many snake species in Brazil. However, the number of reported cases of snakebites did not decrease

as other and sometimes more dangerous species proliferated in some of the deforested areas (WHO 1995).

Sauria (lizards)

There are only two species of venomous lizards, both members of the genus Heloderma: *H. suspectum* (Gila monster) and *H. horridum* (beaded lizard). Venom similar to that of the Viperidae penetrates wounds inflicted by the anterior curved teeth, but bites in humans are uncommon and recovery is generally rapid (Rioux and Juminer 1983).

Prevention

Snakes do not usually attack humans unless they feel menaced, are disturbed or are trodden on. In regions infested with venomous snakes, workers should wear foot and leg protection and be provided with monovalent or polyvalent antivenom serum. It is recommended that persons working in a danger area at a distance of over half-an-hour's travel from the nearest first-aid post should carry an antivenom kit containing a sterilized syringe. However, it should be explained to workers that bites even from the most venomous snakes are seldom fatal, since the amount of venom injected is usually small. Certain snake charmers achieve immunization by repeated injections of venom, but no scientific method of human immunization has yet been developed (Rioux and Juminer 1983).

International Standards and Biological Hazards

Many national occupational standards include biological hazards in their definition of harmful or toxic substances. However, in most regulatory frameworks, biological hazards are chiefly restricted to micro-organisms or infectious agents. Several US Occupational Safety and Health Administration (OSHA) regulations include provisions on biological hazards. The most specific are those concerning hepatitis B vaccine vaccination and blood-borne pathogens; biological hazards are also covered in regulations with a broader scope (e.g., those on hazard communication, the specifications for accident prevention signs and tags, and the regulation on training curriculum guidelines).

Although not the subject of specific regulations, the recognition and avoidance of hazards relating to animal, insect or plant life is addressed in other OSHA regulations concerning specific work settings—for example, the regulation on telecommunications, the one on temporary labour camps and the one on pulpwood logging (the latter including guidelines concerning snake-bite first-aid kits).

One of the most comprehensive standards regulating biological hazards in the workplace is European Directive No. 90/679. It defines biological agents as "micro-organisms, including those which have been genetically modified, cell cultures and human endoparasites, which may be able to provoke any infection, allergy or toxicity," and classifies biological agents into four groups according to their level of risk of infection. The Directive covers the determination and assessment of risks and employers' obligations in terms of the replacement or reduction of risks (through engineering control measures, industrial hygiene, collective and personal protection measures and so on), information (for workers, workers' representatives and the competent authorities), health surveillance, vaccination and record-keeping. The Annexes provide detailed information on containment measures for different "containment levels" according to the nature of the activities, the assessment of risk to workers and the nature of the biological agent concerned.

● AQUATIC ANIMALS

D. Zannini*

Aquatic animals dangerous to humans are to be found among practically all of the divisions (phyla). Workers may come into contact with these animals in the course of various activities including surface and underwater fishing, the installation and handling of equipment in connection with the exploitation of petroleum under the sea, underwater construction, and scientific research, and thus be exposed to health risks. Most of the dangerous species inhabit warm or temperate waters.

Characteristics and Behaviour

Porifera. The common sponge belongs to this phylum. Fishermen who handle sponges, including helmet and scuba divers, and other underwater swimmers, may contract contact dermatitis with skin irritation, vesicles or blisters. The "sponge diver's sickness" of the Mediterranean region is caused by the tentacles of a small coelenterate (*Sagartia rosea*) that is a parasite of the sponge. A form of dermatitis known as "red moss" is found among North American oyster fishers resulting from contact with a scarlet sponge found on the shell of the oysters. Cases of type 4 allergy have been reported. The poison secreted by the sponge *Suberitus ficus* contains histamine and antibiotic substances.

Coelenterata. These are represented by many families of the class known as Hydrozoa, which includes the Millepora or coral (stinging coral, fire coral), the Physalia (*Physalia physalis*, sea wasp, Portuguese man-of-war), the Scyphozoa (jellyfish) and the Actiniaria (stinging anemone), all of which are found in all parts of the ocean. Common to all these animals is their ability to produce an urticaria by the injection of a strong poison that is retained in a special cell (the cnidoblast) containing a hollow thread, which explodes outwards when the tentacle is touched, and penetrates the person's skin. The various substances contained in this structure are responsible for such symptoms as severe itching, congestion of the liver, pain, and depression of the central nervous system; these substances have been identified as thalassium, congestine, equinotoxin (which contains 5-hydroxytryptamine and tetramine) and hypnotoxin, respectively. Effects on the individual depend upon the extent of the contact made with the tentacles and hence on the number of microscopic punctures, which may amount to many thousands, up to the point where they may cause the death of the victim within a few minutes. In view of the fact that these animals are dispersed so widely throughout the world, many incidents of this nature occur but the number of fatalities is relatively small. Effects on the skin are characterized by intense itching and the formation of papules having a bright red, mottled appearance, developing into pustules and ulceration. Intense pain similar to electric shock may be felt. Other symptoms include difficulty in breathing, generalized anxiety and cardiac upset, collapse, nausea and vomiting, loss of consciousness, and primary shock.

Echinoderma. This group includes the starfishes and sea urchins, both of which possess poisonous organs (pedicellariae), but are not dangerous to humans. The spine of the sea urchin can penetrate the skin, leaving a fragment deeply imbedded; this can give rise to a secondary infection followed by pustules and persistent granuloma, which can be very troublesome if the wounds are close to tendons or ligaments. Among the sea urchins, only the *Acanthaster planci* seems to have a poisonous spine, which can give rise to general disturbances such as vomiting, paralysis and numbness.

Mollusca. Among the animals belonging to this phylum are the cone shells, and these can be dangerous. They live on a sandy sea-bottom and appear to have a poisonous structure consisting of a radula with needle-like teeth, which can strike at the victim if the shell is handled incautiously with the bare hand. The poison acts on the neuromuscular and central nervous systems. Penetration of the skin by the point of a tooth is followed by temporary ischaemia, cyanosis, numbness, pain, and paraesthesia as the poison spreads gradually through the body. Subsequent effects include paralysis of the voluntary muscles, lack of coordination, double vision and general confusion. Death can follow as a result of respiratory paralysis and circulatory collapse. Some 30 cases have been reported, of which 8 were fatal.

Platyhelminthes. These include the *Eirythoe complanata* and the *Hermodice caruncolata*, known as "bristle worms". They are covered with numerous bristle-like appendages, or setae, containing a poison (nereistotoxin) with a neurotoxic and local irritant effect.

Polyzoa (Bryozoa). These are made up of a group of animals which form plant-like colonies resembling gelatinous moss, which frequently encrust rocks or shells. One variety, known as Alcyonidium, can cause an urticarious dermatitis on the arms and face of fishermen who have to clean this moss off their nets. It can also give rise to an allergic eczema.

Selachiis (Chondrichthyes). Animals belonging to this phylum include the sharks and sting-rays. The sharks live in fairly shallow water, where they search for prey and may attack people. Many varieties have one or two large, poisonous spines in front of the dorsal fin, which contain a weak poison that has not been identified; these can cause a wound giving rise to immediate and intense pain with reddening of the flesh, swelling and oedema. A far greater danger from these animals is their bite, which, because of several rows of sharp pointed teeth, causes severe laceration and tearing of the flesh leading to immediate shock, acute anaemia and drowning of the victim. The danger that sharks represent is a much-discussed subject, each variety seeming to be particularly aggressive. There seems no doubt that their behaviour is unpredictable, although it is said that they are attracted by movement and by the light colour of a swimmer, as well as by blood and by vibrations resulting from a fish or other prey that has just been caught. Sting-rays have large, flat bodies with a long tail having one or more strong spines or saws, which can be poisonous. The poison contains serotonine, 5-nucleotidase and phosphodiesterase, and can cause generalized vasoconstriction and cardio-respiratory arrest. Sting-rays live in the sandy regions of coastal waters, where they are well hidden, making it easy for bathers to step on one without seeing it. The ray reacts by bringing over its tail with the projecting spine, impaling the spike keep into the flesh of the victim. This may cause piercing wounds in a limb or even penetration of an internal organ such as the peritoneum, lung, heart or liver, particularly in the case of children. The wound can also give rise to great pain, swelling, lymphatic oedema and various general symptoms such as primary shock and cardio-circulatory collapse. Injury to an internal organ may lead to death in a few hours. Sting-ray incidents are among the most frequent, there being some 750 every year in the United States alone. They can also be dangerous for fishermen, who should immediately cut off the tail as soon as the fish is brought aboard. Various species of rays such as the torpedo and the narcine possess electric organs on their back, which, when stimulated by touch alone, can produce electric shocks ranging from 8 up to 220 volts; this may be enough to stun and temporarily disable the victim, but recovery is usually without complications.

Osteichthyes. Many fishes of this phylum have dorsal, pectoral, caudal and anal spines which are connected with a poison system and whose primary purpose is defence. If the fish is disturbed or stepped upon or handled by a fisherman, it will erect the spines,

---

* Adapted from 3rd edition, *Encyclopaedia of Occupational Health and Safety.*

which can pierce the skin and inject the poison. Not infrequently they will attack a diver seeking fish, or if they are disturbed by accidental contact. Numerous incidents of this kind are reported because of the widespread distribution of fish of this phylum, which includes the catfish, which are also found in fresh water (South America, West Africa and the Great Lakes), the scorpion fish (*Scorpaenidae*), the weever fish (*Trachinus*), the toadfish, the surgeon fish and others. Wounds from these fishes are generally painful, particularly in the case of the catfish and the weever fish, causing reddening or pallor, swelling, cyanosis, numbness, lymphatic oedema and haemorrhagic suffusion in the surrounding flesh. There is a possibility of gangrene or phlegmonous infection and peripheral neuritis on the same side as the wound. Other symptoms include faintness, nausea, collapse, primary shock, asthma and loss of consciousness. They all represent a serious danger for underwater workers. A neurotoxic and haemotoxic poison has been identified in the catfish, and in the case of the weever fish a number of substances have been isolated such as 5-hydroxytryptamine, histamine and catecholamine. Some catfishes and stargazers that live in fresh water, as well as the electric eel (Electrophorus), have electric organs (see under Selachii above).

Hydrophiidae. This group (sea snakes) is to be found mostly in the seas around Indonesia and Malaysia; some 50 species have been reported, including *Pelaniis platurus*, *Enhydrina schistosa* and *Hydrus platurus*. The venom of these snakes is very similar to that of the cobra, but is 20 to 50 times as poisonous; it is made up of a basic protein of low molecular weight (erubotoxin) which affects the neuromuscular junction blocking the acetylcholine and provoking myolysis. Fortunately sea snakes are generally docile and bite only when stepped on, squeezed or dealt a hard blow; furthermore, they inject little or no venom from their teeth. Fishermen are among those most exposed to this hazard and account for 90% of all reported incidents, which result either from stepping on the snake on the sea bottom or from encountering them among their catch. Snakes are probably responsible for thousands of the occupational accidents attributed to aquatic animals, but few of these are serious, while only a small percentage of the serious accidents turn out to be fatal. Symptoms are mostly slight and not painful. Effects are usually felt within two hours, starting with muscular pain, difficulty with neck movement, lack of dexterity, and trismus, and sometimes including nausea and vomiting. Within a few hours myoglobinuria (the presence of complex proteins in urine) will be seen. Death can ensue from paralysis of the respiratory muscles, from renal insufficiency due to tubular necrosis, or from cardiac arrest due to hyperkalaemia.

Prevention

Every effort should be made to avoid all contact with the spines of these animals when they are being handled, unless strong gloves are worn, and the greatest care should be taken when wading or walking on a sandy sea bottom. The wet suit worn by skin divers offers protection against the jellyfish and the various Coelenterata as well as against snakebite. The more dangerous and aggressive animals should not be molested, and zones where there are jellyfish should be avoided, as they are difficult to see. If a sea snake is caught on a line, the line should be cut and the snake allowed to go. If sharks are encountered, there are a number of principles that should be observed. People should keep their feet and legs out of the water, and the boat should be gently brought to shore and kept still; a swimmer should not stay in the water with a dying fish or with one that is bleeding; a shark's attention should not be attracted by the use of bright colours, jewellery, or by making a noise or explosion, by showing a bright light, or by waving the hands towards it. A diver should never dive alone.

TERRESTRIAL VENOMOUS ANIMALS

J.A. Rioux and B. Juminer*

Annually millions of scorpion stings and anaphylactic reactions to insect stings may occur worldwide, causing tens of thousands of deaths in humans each year. Between 30,000 and 45,000 cases of scorpion stings are reported annually in Tunisia, causing between 35 and 100 deaths, mostly among children. Envenomation (toxic effects) is an occupational hazard for populations involved in agriculture and forestry in these regions.

Among the animals that can inflict injury on humans by the action of their venom are invertebrates, such as *Arachnida* (spiders, scorpions and sun spiders), *Acarina* (ticks and mites), *Chilopoda* (centipedes) and *Hexapoda* (bees, wasps, butterflies, and midges).

Invertebrates

Arachnida (spiders—Aranea)

All species are venomous, but in practice only a few types produce injury in humans. Spider poisoning may be of two types:

1. Cutaneous poisoning, in which the bite is followed after a few hours by oedema centred around a cyanotic mark, and then by a blister; extensive local necrosis may ensue, and healing may be slow and difficult in cases of bites from spiders of the Lycosa genus (e.g., the tarantula).
2. Nerve poisoning due to the exclusively neurotoxic venom of the mygales (*Latrodectus ctenus*), which produces serious injury, with early onset, tetany, tremors, paralysis of the extremities and, possibly, fatal shock; this type of poisoning is relatively common amongst forestry and agricultural workers and is particularly severe in children: in the Amazonas, the venom of the "black widow" spider (*Latrodectus mactans*) is used for poison arrows.

Prevention. In areas where there is a danger of venomous spiders, sleeping accommodation should be provided with mosquito nets and workers should be equipped with footwear and working clothes that give adequate protection.

Scorpions (Scorpionida)

These arachnids have a sharp poison claw on the end of the abdomen with which they can inflict a painful sting, the seriousness of which varies according to the species, the amount of venom injected and the season (the most dangerous season being at the end of the scorpions' hibernation period). In the Mediterranean region, South America and Mexico, the scorpion is responsible for more deaths than poisonous snakes. Many species are nocturnal and are less aggressive during the day. The most dangerous species (*Buthidae*) are found in arid and tropical regions; their venom is neurotropic and highly toxic. In all cases, the scorpion sting immediately produces intense local signs (acute pain, inflammation) followed by general manifestations such as tendency to fainting, salivation, sneezing, lachrymation and diarrhoea. The course in young children is often fatal. The most dangerous species are found amongst the genera Androctonus (sub-Saharan Africa), Centrurus (Mexico) and Tituus (Brazil). The scorpion will not spontaneously attack humans, and stings only when it considers itself endangered, as when trapped in a dark corner or when boots or clothes in which it has taken refuge are shaken or put on. Scorpions are highly sensitive to halogenated pesticides (e.g., DDT).

*Adapted from 3rd edition, *Encyclopaedia of Occupational Health and Safety*.

Sun spiders (Solpugida)

This order of arachnid is found chiefly in steppe and sub-desert zones such as the Sahara, Andes, Asia Minor, Mexico and Texas, and is non-venomous; nevertheless, sun spiders are extremely aggressive, may be as large as 10 cm across and have a fearsome appearance. In exceptional cases, the wounds they inflict may prove serious due to their multiplicity. Solpugids are nocturnal predators and may attack a sleeping individual.

Ticks and mites (Acarina)

Ticks are blood-sucking arachnids at all stages of their life cycle, and the "saliva" they inject through their feeding organs may have a toxic effect. Poisoning may be severe, although mainly in children (tick paralysis), and may be accompanied by reflex suppression. In exceptional cases death may ensue due to bulbar paralysis (in particular where a tick has attached itself to the scalp). Mites are haematophagic only at the larval stage, and their bite produces pruritic inflammation of the skin. The incidence of mite bites is high in tropical regions.

Treatment. Ticks should be detached after they are anaesthetized with a drop of benzene, ethyl ether or xylene. Prevention is based on the use of organophosphorus pesticide pest repellents.

Centipedes (Chilopoda)

Centipedes differ from millipedes (*Diplopoda*) in that they have only one pair of legs per body segment and that the appendages of the first body segment are poison fangs. The most dangerous species are encountered in the Philippines. Centipede venom has only a localized effect (painful oedema).

Treatment. Bites should be treated with topical applications of dilute ammonia, permanganate or hypochlorite lotions. Antihistamines may also be administered.

Insects (Hexapoda)

Insects may inject venom via the mouthparts (Simuliidae—black flies, Culicidae—mosquitoes, Phlebotomus—sandflies) or via the sting (bees, wasps, hornets, carnivorous ants). They may cause rash with their hairs (caterpillars, butterflies), or they may produce blisters by their haemolymph (Cantharidae—blister flies and Staphylinidae—rove beetles). Black fly bites produce necrotic lesions, sometimes with general disorders; mosquito bites produce diffuse pruriginous lesions. The stings of Hymenoptera (bees, etc.) produce intense local pain with erythema, oedema and, sometimes, necrosis. General accidents may result from sensitization or multiplicity of stings (shivering, nausea, dyspnoea, chilling of the extremities). Stings on the face or the tongue are particularly serious and may cause death by asphyxiation due to glottal oedema. Caterpillars and butterflies may cause generalized pruriginous skin lesions of an urticarial or oedematous type (Quincke's oedema), sometimes accompanied by conjunctivitis. Superimposed infection is not infrequent. The venom from blister flies produces vesicular or bullous skin lesions (Poederus). There is also the danger of visceral complications (toxic nephritis). Certain insects such as Hymenoptera and caterpillars are found in all parts of the world; other suborders are more localized, however. Dangerous butterflies are found mainly in Guyana and the Central African Republic; blister flies are found in Japan, South America and Kenya; black flies live in the intertropical regions and in central Europe; sandflies are found in the Middle East.

Prevention. First level prevention includes mosquito nets and repellent and/or insecticide application. Workers who are severely exposed to insect bites can be desensitized in cases of allergy by the administration of increasingly large doses of insect body extract.

CLINICAL FEATURES OF SNAKEBITE   ●

David A. Warrell*

Clinical Features

A proportion of patients bitten by venomous snakes (between <10% to >60%), depending on the species, will develop minimal or no signs of toxic symptoms (envenoming) despite having puncture marks which indicate that the snake's fangs have penetrated the skin.

Fear and effects of treatment, as well as the snake's venom, contribute to the symptoms and signs. Even patients who are not envenomed may feel flushed, dizzy and breathless, with constriction of the chest, palpitations, sweating and acroparaesthesiae. Tight tourniquets may produce congested and ischaemic limbs; local incisions at the site of the bite may cause bleeding and sensory loss; and herbal medicines often induce vomiting.

The earliest symptoms directly attributable to the bite are local pain and bleeding from the fang punctures, followed by pain, tenderness, swelling and bruising extending up the limb, lymphangitis and tender enlargement of regional lymph nodes. Early syncope, vomiting, colic, diarrhoea, angio-oedema and wheezing may occur in patients bitten by European Vipera, *Daboia russelii*, *Bothrops* sp, Australian Elapids and *Atractaspis engaddensis*. Nausea and vomiting are common symptoms of severe envenoming.

Types of bites

Colubridae (back-fanged snakes such as Dispholidus typus, Thelotornis sp, Rhabdophis sp, Philodryas sp)

There is local swelling, bleeding from the fang marks and sometimes (*Rhabophis tigrinus*) fainting. Later vomiting, colicky abdominal pain and headache, and widespread systemic bleeding with extensive ecchymoses (bruising), incoagulable blood, intravascular haemolysis and kidney failure may develop. Envenoming may develop slowly over several days.

Atractaspididae (burrowing asps, Natal black snake)

Local effects include pain, swelling, blistering, necrosis and tender enlargement of local lymph nodes. Violent gastro-intestinal symptoms (nausea, vomiting and diarrhoea), anaphylaxis (dyspnoea, respiratory failure, shock) and ECG changes (a-v block, ST, T-wave changes) have been described in patients envenomed by *A. engaddensis*.

Elapidae (cobras, kraits, mambas, coral snakes and Australian venomous snakes)

Bites by kraits, mambas, coral snakes and some cobras (e.g., *Naja haje* and *N. nivea*) produce minimal local effects, whereas bites by African spitting cobras (*N. nigricollis*, *N. mossambica*, etc.) and Asian cobras (*N. naja*, *N. kaouthia*, *N. sumatrana*, etc.) cause tender local swelling which may be extensive, blistering and superficial necrosis.

Early symptoms of neurotoxicity before there are objective neurological signs include vomiting, "heaviness" of the eyelids, blurred vision, fasciculations, paraesthesiae around the mouth, hyperacusis, headache, dizziness, vertigo, hypersalivation, congested conjunctivae and "gooseflesh". Paralysis starts as ptosis and external ophthalmoplegia appearing as early as 15 minutes after the bite, but sometimes delayed for ten hours or more. Later the face, palate, jaws, tongue, vocal cords, neck muscles and muscles

* Adapted from *The Oxford Textbook of Medicine*, edited by DJ Weatherall, JGG Ledingham and DA Warrell (2nd edition, 1987), pp. 6.66-6.77. By permission of Oxford University Press.

of deglutition become progressively paralysed. Respiratory failure may be precipitated by upper airway obstruction at this stage, or later after paralysis of intercostal muscles, diaphragm and accessory muscles of respiration. Neurotoxic effects are completely reversible, either acutely in response to antivenom or anticholinesterases (e.g., following bites by Asian cobras, some Latin American coral snakes—*Micrurus,* and Australian death adders—*Acanthophis*) or they may wear off spontaneously in one to seven days.

Envenoming by Australian snakes causes early vomiting, headache and syncopal attacks, neurotoxicity, haemostatic disturbances and, with some species, ECG changes, generalized rhabdomyolysis and kidney failure. Painful enlargement of regional lymph nodes suggests impending systemic envenoming, but local signs are usually absent or mild except after bites by *Pseudechis* sp.

Venom ophthalmia caused by "spitting" elapids

Patients "spat" at by spitting elapids experience intense pain in the eye, conjunctivitis, blepharospasm, palpebral oedema and leucorrhoea. Corneal erosions are detectable in more than half the patients spat at by *N. nigricollis*. Rarely, venom is absorbed into the anterior chamber, causing hypopyon and anterior uveitis. Secondary infection of corneal abrasions may lead to permanent blinding opacities or panophthalmitis.

Viperidae (vipers, adders, rattlesnakes, lance-headed vipers, moccasins and pit vipers)

Local envenoming is relatively severe. Swelling may become detectable within 15 minutes but is sometimes delayed for several hours. It spreads rapidly and may involve the whole limb and adjacent trunk. There is associated pain and tenderness in regional lymph nodes. Bruising, blistering and necrosis may appear during the next few days. Necrosis is particularly frequent and severe following bites by some rattlesnakes, lance-headed vipers (genus *Bothrops*), Asian pit vipers and African vipers (genera *Echis* and *Bitis*). When the envenomed tissue is contained in a tight fascial compartment such as the pulp space of the fingers or toes or the anterior tibial compartment, ischaemia may result. If there is no swelling two hours after a viper bite it is usually safe to assume that there has been no envenoming. However, fatal envenoming by a few species can occur in the absence of local signs (e.g., *Crotalus durissus terrificus, C. scutulatus* and Burmese Russell's viper).

Blood pressure abnormalities are a consistent feature of envenoming by Viperidae. Persistent bleeding from fang puncture wounds, venepuncture or injection sites, other new and partially healed wounds and post partum, suggests that the blood is incoagulable. Spontaneous systemic haemorrhage is most often detected in the gums, but may also be seen as epistaxis, haematemesis, cutaneous ecchymoses, haemoptysis, subconjunctival, retroperitoneal and intracranial haemorrhages. Patients envenomed by the Burmese Russell's viper may bleed into the anterior pituitary gland (Sheehan's syndrome).

Hypotension and shock are common in patients bitten by some of the North American rattlesnakes (e.g., *C. adamanteus, C. atrox* and *C. scutulatus*), *Bothrops, Daboia* and *Vipera* species (e.g., *V. palaestinae* and *V. berus*). The central venous pressure is usually low and the pulse rate rapid, suggesting hypovolaemia, for which the usual cause is extravasation of fluid into the bitten limb. Patients envenomed by Burmese Russell's vipers show evidence of generally increased vascular permeability. Direct involvement of the heart muscle is suggested by an abnormal ECG or cardiac arrhythmia. Patients envenomed by some species of the genera *Vipera* and *Bothrops* may experience transient recurrent fainting attacks associated with features of an autopharmacological or anaphylactic reaction such as vomiting, sweating, colic, diarrhoea,

shock and angio-oedema, appearing as early as five minutes or as late as many hours after the bite.

Renal (kidney) failure is the major cause of death in patients envenomed by Russell's vipers who may become oliguric within a few hours of the bite and have loin pain suggesting renal ischaemia. Renal failure is also a feature of envenoming by *Bothrops* species and *C. d. terrificus*.

Neurotoxicity, resembling that seen in patients bitten by Elapidae, is seen after bites by *C. d. terrificus, Gloydius blomhoffii, Bitis atropos* and Sri Lankan *D. russelii pulchella*. There may be evidence of generalized rhabdomyolysis. Progression to respiratory or generalized paralysis is unusual.

Laboratory Investigations

The peripheral neutrophil count is raised to 20,000 cells per microlitre or more in severely envenomed patients. Initial haemoconcentration, resulting from extravasation of plasma (*Crotalus* species and Burmese *D. russelii*), is followed by anaemia caused by bleeding or, more rarely, haemolysis. Thrombocytopenia is common following bites by pit vipers (e.g., *C. rhodostoma, Crotalus viridis helleri*) and some Viperidae (e.g., *Bitis arietans* and *D. russelii*), but is unusual after bites by *Echis* species. A useful test for venom-induced defibrin(ogen)ation is the simple whole blood clotting test. A few millilitres of venous blood is placed in a new, clean, dry, glass test tube, left undisturbed for 20 minutes at ambient temperature, and then tipped to see if it has clotted or not. Incoagulable blood indicates systemic envenoming and may be diagnostic of a particular species (for example *Echis* species in Africa). Patients with generalized rhabdomyolysis show a steep rise in serum creatine kinase, myoglobin and potassium. Black or brown urine suggests generalized rhabdomyolysis or intravascular haemolysis. Concentrations of serum enzymes such as creatine phosphokinase and aspartate aminotransferase are moderately raised in patients with severe local envenoming, probably because of local muscle damage at the site of the bite. Urine should be examined for blood/haemoglobin, myoglobin and protein and for microscopic haematuria and red cell casts.

Treatment

First aid

Patients should be moved to the nearest medical facility as quickly and comfortably as possible, avoiding movement of the bitten limb, which should be immobilized with a splint or sling.

Most traditional first-aid methods are potentially harmful and should not be used. Local incisions and suction may introduce infection, damage tissues and cause persistent bleeding, and are unlikely to remove much venom from the wound. The vacuum extractor method is of unproven benefit in human patients and could damage soft tissues. Potassium permanganate and cryotherapy potentiate local necrosis. Electric shock is potentially dangerous and has not proved beneficial. Tourniquets and compression bands can cause gangrene, fibrinolysis, peripheral nerve palsies and increased local envenoming in the occluded limb.

The pressure immobilization method involves firm but not tight bandaging of the entire bitten limb with a crepe bandage 4-5 m long by 10 cm wide starting over the site of the bite and incorporating a splint. In animals, this method was effective in preventing systemic uptake of Australian elapid and other venoms, but in humans it has not been subjected to clinical trials. Pressure immobilization is recommended for bites by snakes with neurotoxic venoms (e.g., *Elapidae, Hydrophiidae*) but not when local swelling and necrosis may be a problem (e.g., *Viperidae*).

Pursuing, capturing or killing the snake should not be encouraged, but if the snake has been killed already it should be taken with the patient to hospital. It must not be touched with bare hands, as reflex bites may occur even after the snake is apparently dead.

Patients being transported to hospital should be laid on their side to prevent aspiration of vomit. Persistent vomiting is treated with chlorpromazine by intravenous injection (25 to 50 mg for adults, 1 mg/kg body weight for children). Syncope, shock, angio-oedema and other anaphylactic (autopharmacological) symptoms are treated with 0.1% adrenaline by subcutaneous injection (0.5 ml for adults, 0.01 ml/kg body weight for children), and an antihistamine such as chlorpheniramine maleate is given by slow intravenous injection (10 mg for adults, 0.2 mg/kg body weight for children). Patients with incoagulable blood develop large haematomas after intramuscular and subcutaneous injections; the intravenous route should be used whenever possible. Respiratory distress and cyanosis are treated by establishing an airway, giving oxygen and, if necessary, assisted ventilation. If the patient is unconscious and no femoral or carotid pulses can be detected, cardiopulmonary resuscitation (CPR) should be started immediately.

Hospital treatment

Clinical assessment
In most cases of snakebite there are uncertainties about the species responsible and the quantity and composition of venom injected. Ideally, therefore, patients should be admitted to hospital for at least 24 hours of observation. Local swelling is usually detectable within 15 minutes of significant pit viper envenoming and within two hours of envenoming by most other snakes. Bites by kraits (Bungarus), coral snakes (Micrurus, Micruroides), some other elapids and sea snakes may cause no local envenoming. Fang marks are sometimes invisible. Pain and tender enlargement of lymph nodes draining the bitten area is an early sign of envenoming by Viperidae, some Elapidae and Australasian elapids. All the patient's tooth sockets should be examined meticulously, as this is usually the first site at which spontaneous bleeding can be detected clinically; other common sites are nose, eyes (conjunctivae), skin and gastro-intestinal tract. Bleeding from venipuncture sites and other wounds implies incoagulable blood. Hypotension and shock are important signs of hypovolaemia or cardiotoxicity, seen particularly in patients bitten by North American rattlesnakes and some Viperinae (e.g., V berus, D russelii, V palaestinae). Ptosis (e.g., drooping of the eyelid) is the earliest sign of neurotoxic envenoming. Respiratory muscle power should be assessed objectively—for example, by measuring vital capacity. Trismus, generalized muscle tenderness and brownish-black urine suggests rhabdomyolysis (Hydrophiidae). If a procoagulant venom is suspected, coagulability of whole blood should be checked at the bedside using the 20-minute whole blood clotting test.

Blood pressure, pulse rate, respiratory rate, level of consciousness, presence/absence of ptosis, extent of local swelling and any new symptoms must be recorded at frequent intervals.

Antivenom treatment
The most important decision is whether or not to give antivenom, as this is the only specific antidote. There is now convincing evidence that in patients with severe envenoming, the benefits of this treatment far outweigh the risk of antivenom reactions (see below).

General indications for antivenom
Antivenom is indicated if there are signs of systemic envenoming such as:

1. haemostatic abnormalities such as spontaneous systemic bleeding, incoagulable blood or profound thrombocytopenia ($<50/1 \times 10^{-9}$)

2. neurotoxicity
3. hypotension and shock, abnormal ECG or other evidence of cardiovascular dysfunction
4. impaired consciousness of any cause
5. generalized rhabdomyolysis.

Supporting evidence of severe envenoming is a neutrophil leucocytosis, elevated serum enzymes such as creatine kinase and aminotransferases, haemoconcentration, severe anaemia, myoglobinuria, haemoglobinuria, methaemoglobinuria, hypoxaemia or acidosis.

In the absence of systemic envenoming, local swelling involving more than half the bitten limb, extensive blistering or bruising, bites on digits and rapid progression of swelling are indications for antivenom, especially in patients bitten by species whose venoms are known to cause local necrosis (e.g., Viperidae, Asian cobras and African spitting cobras).

Special indications for antivenom
Some developed countries have the financial and technical resources for a wider range of indications:

United States and Canada: After bites by the most dangerous rattlesnakes (C. atrox, C. adamanteus, C. viridis, C. horridus and C. scutulatus) early antivenom therapy is recommended before systemic envenoming is evident. Rapid spread of local swelling is considered to be an indication for antivenom, as is immediate pain or any other symptom or sign of envenoming after bites by coral snakes (Micruroides euryxanthus and Micrurus fulvius).

Australia: Antivenom is recommended for patients with proved or suspected snakebite if there are tender regional lymph nodes or other evidence of systemic spread of venom, and in anyone effectively bitten by an identified highly venomous species.

Europe: (Adder: Vipera berus and other European Vipera): Antivenom is indicated to prevent morbidity and reduce the length of convalescence in patients with moderately severe envenoming as well as to save the lives of severely envenomed patients. Indications are:

1. fall in blood pressure (systolic to less than 80 mmHg, or by more than 50 mmHg from the normal or admission value) with or without signs of shock
2. other signs of systemic envenoming (see above), including spontaneous bleeding, coagulopathy, pulmonary oedema or haemorrhage (shown by chest radiograph), ECG abnormalities and a definite peripheral leucocytosis (more than 15,000/µl) and elevated serum creatine kinase
3. severe local envenoming—swelling of more than half the bitten limb developing within 48 hours of the bite—even in the absence of systemic envenoming
4. in adults, swelling extending beyond the wrist after bites on the hand or beyond the ankle after bites on the foot within four hours of the bite.

Patients bitten by European Vipera who show any evidence of envenoming should be admitted to hospital for observation for at least 24 hours. Antivenom should be given whenever there is evidence of systemic envenoming—(1) or (2) above—even if its appearance is delayed for several days after the bite.

Prediction of antivenom reactions
It is important to realize that most antivenom reactions are not caused by acquired Type I, IgE-mediated hypersensitivity but by complement activation by IgG aggregates or Fc fragments. Skin and conjunctival tests do not predict early (anaphylactic) or late

38. BIOLOGICAL HAZARDS

(serum sickness type) antivenom reactions but delay treatment and may sensitize the patient. They should not be used.

Contraindications to antivenom

Patients with a history of reactions to equine antiserum suffer an increased incidence and severity of reactions when given equine antivenom. Atopic subjects have no increased risk of reactions, but if they develop a reaction it is likely to be severe. In such cases, reactions may be prevented or ameliorated by pretreatment with subcutaneous adrenaline, antihistamine and hydrocortisone, or by continuous intravenous infusion of adrenaline during antivenom administration. Rapid desensitization is not recommended.

Selection and administration of antivenom

Antivenom should be given only if its stated range of specificity includes the species responsible for the bite. Opaque solutions should be discarded, as precipitation of protein indicates loss of activity and increased risk of reactions. Monospecific (monovalent) antivenom is ideal if the biting species is known. Polyspecific (polyvalent) antivenoms are used in many countries because it is difficult to identify the snake responsible. Polyspecific antivenoms may be just as effective as monospecific ones but contain less specific venom-neutralizing activity per unit weight of immunoglobulin. Apart from the venoms used for immunizing the animal in which the antivenom has been produced, other venoms may be covered by paraspecific neutralization (e.g., Hydrophiidae venoms by tiger snake—*Notechis scutatus*—antivenom).

Antivenom treatment is indicated as long as signs of systemic envenoming persist (i.e., for several days) but ideally it should be given as soon as these signs appear. The intravenous route is the most effective. Infusion of antivenom diluted in approximately 5 ml of isotonic fluid/kg body weight is easier to control than intravenous "push" injection of undiluted antivenom given at the rate of about 4 ml/min, but there is no difference in the incidence or severity of antivenom reactions in patients treated by these two methods.

Dose of antivenom

Manufacturers' recommendations are based on mouse protection tests and may be misleading. Clinical trials are needed to establish appropriate starting doses of major antivenoms. In most countries the dose of antivenom is empirical. Children must be given the same dose as adults.

Response to antivenom

Marked symptomatic improvement may be seen soon after antivenom has been injected. In shocked patients, the blood pressure may rise and consciousness return (*C. rhodostoma, V. berus, Bitis arietans*). Neurotoxic signs may improve within 30 minutes (*Acanthophis* sp, *N. kaouthia*), but this usually takes several hours. Spontaneous systemic bleeding usually stops within 15 to 30 minutes, and blood coagulability is restored within six hours of antivenom, provided that a neutralizing dose has been given. More antivenom should be given if severe signs of envenoming persist after one to two hours or if blood coagulability is not restored within about six hours. Systemic envenoming may recur hours or days after an initially good response to antivenom. This is explained by continuing absorption of venom from the injection site and the clearance of antivenom from the bloodstream. The apparent serum half-lives of equine F(ab′)₂ antivenoms in envenomed patients range from 26 to 95 hours. Envenomed patients should therefore be assessed daily for at least three or four days.

Antivenom reactions

- *Early (anaphylactic) reactions* develop within 10 to 180 minutes of starting antivenom in 3 to 84% of patients. The incidence increases with dose and decreases when more highly refined antivenom is used and administration is by intramuscular rather than intravenous injection. The symptoms are itching, urticaria, cough, nausea, vomiting, other manifestations of autonomic nervous system stimulation, fever, tachycardia, bronchospasm and shock. Very few of these reactions can be attributed to acquired Type I IgE-mediated hypersensitivity.
- *Pyrogenic reactions* result from contamination of the antivenom with endotoxins. Fever, rigors, vasodilatation and a fall in blood pressure develop one to two hours after treatment. In children, febrile convulsions may be precipitated.
- *Late reactions* of serum sickness (immune complex) type may develop 5 to 24 (mean 7) days after antivenom. The incidence of those reactions and the speed of their development increases with the dose of antivenom. Clinical features include fever, itching, urticaria, arthralgia (including the temporomandibular joint), lymphadenopathy, periarticular swellings, mononeuritis multiplex, albuminuria and, rarely, encephalopathy.

Treatment of antivenom reactions

Adrenaline (epinephrine) is the effective treatment for early reactions; 0.5 to 1.0 ml of 0.1% (1 in 1000, 1 mg/ml) is given by subcutaneous injection to adults (children 0.01 ml/kg) at the first signs of a reaction. The dose may be repeated if the reaction is not controlled. An antihistamine H_1 antagonist, such as chlorpheniramine maleate (10 mg for adults, 0.2 mg/kg for children) should be given by intravenous injection to combat the effects of histamine release during the reaction. Pyrogenic reactions are treated by cooling the patient and giving antipyretics (paracetamol). Late reactions respond to an oral antihistamine such as chlorpheniramine (2 mg every six hours for adults, 0.25 mg/kg/day in divided doses for children) or to oral prednisolone (5 mg every six hours for five to seven days for adults, 0.7 mg/kg/day in divided doses for children).

Supportive treatment

Neurotoxic envenoming

Bulbar and respiratory paralysis may lead to death from aspiration, airway obstruction or respiratory failure. A clear airway must be maintained and, if respiratory distress develops, a cuffed endotracheal tube should be inserted or tracheostomy performed. Anticholinesterases have a variable but potentially useful effect in patients with neurotoxic envenoming, especially when post-synaptic neurotoxins are involved. The "Tensilon test" should be done in all cases of severe neurotoxic envenoming as with suspected myasthenia gravis. Atropine sulphate (0.6 mg for adults, 50 μg/kg body weight for children) is given by intravenous injection (to block muscarinic effects of acetylcholine) followed by an intravenous injection of edrophonium chloride (10 mg for adults, 0.25 mg/kg for children). Patients who respond convincingly can be maintained on neostigmine methyl sulphate (50 to 100 μg/kg body weight) and atropine, every four hours or by continuous infusion.

Hypotension and shock

If the jugular or central venous pressure is low or there is other clinical evidence of hypovolaemia or exsanguination, a plasma expander, preferably fresh whole blood or fresh frozen plasma, should be infused. If there is persistent or profound hypotension or evidence of increased capillary permeability (e.g., facial and conjunctival oedema, serous effusions, haemoconcentration, hypoalbuminaemia) a selective vasoconstrictor such as dopamine (starting dose 2.5 to 5 µg/kg body weight/min by infusion into a central vein) should be used.

Oliguria and renal failure

Urine output, serum creatinine, urea and electrolytes should be measured each day in patients with severe envenoming and in those bitten by species known to cause renal failure (e.g., *D. russelii*, *C. d. terrificus*, *Bothrops* species, sea snakes). If urine output drops below 400 ml in 24 hours, urethral and central venous catheters should be inserted. If urine flow fails to increase after cautious rehydration and diuretics (e.g., frusemide up to 1000 mg by intravenous infusion), dopamine (2.5 µg/kg body weight/min by intravenous infusion) should be tried and the patient placed on strict fluid balance. If these measures are ineffective, peritoneal or haemodialysis or haemofiltration are usually required.

Local infection at the site of the bite

Bites by some species (e.g., *Bothrops* sp, *C. rhodostoma*) seem particularly likely to be complicated by local infections caused by bacteria in the snake's venom or on its fangs. These should be prevented with penicillin, chloramphenicol or erythromycin and a booster dose of tetanus toxoid, especially if the wound has been incised or tampered with in any way. An aminoglycoside such as gentamicin and metronidazole should be added if there is evidence of local necrosis.

Management of local envenoming

Bullae can be drained with a fine needle. The bitten limb should be nursed in the most comfortable position. Once definite signs of necrosis have appeared (blackened anaesthetic area with putrid odour or signs of sloughing), surgical debridement, immediate split skin grafting and broad-spectrum antimicrobial cover are indicated. Increased pressure within tight fascial compartments such as the digital pulp spaces and anterior tibial compartment may cause ischaemic damage. This complication is most likely after bites by North American rattlesnakes such as *C. adamanteus*, *Calloselasma rhodostoma*, *Trimeresurus flavoviridis*, *Bothrops* sp and *Bitis arietans*. The signs are excessive pain, weakness of the compartmental muscles and pain when they are passively stretched, hypaesthesia of areas of skin supplied by nerves running through the compartment, and obvious tenseness of the compartment. Detection of arterial pulses (e.g., by Doppler ultrasound) does not exclude intracompartmental ischaemia. Intracompartmental pressures exceeding 45 mm Hg are associated with a high risk of ischaemic necrosis. In these circumstances, fasciotomy may be considered but must not be attempted until blood coagulability and a platelet count of more than 50,000/µl have been restored. Early adequate antivenom treatment will prevent the development of intracompartmental syndromes in most cases.

Haemostatic disturbances

Once specific antivenom has been given to neutralize venom procoagulants, restoration of coagulability and platelet function may be accelerated by giving fresh whole blood, fresh frozen plasma, cryoprecipitates (containing fibrinogen, factor VIII, fibronectin and some factors V and XIII) or platelet concentrates. Heparin must not be used. Corticosteroids have no place in the treatment of envenoming.

Treatment of snake venom ophthalmia

When cobra venom is "spat" into the eyes, first aid consists of irrigation with generous volumes of water or any other bland liquid which is available. Adrenaline drops (0.1 per cent) may relieve the pain. Unless a corneal abrasion can be excluded by fluorescein staining or slit lamp examination, treatment should be the same as for any corneal injury: a topical antimicrobial such as tetracycline or chloramphenicol should be applied. Instillation of diluted antivenom is not currently recommended.

References

Brock, TD and MT Madigan. 1988. *Biology of Microorganisms*. London: Prentice Hall.

Burrell, R. 1991. Microbiological agents as health risks in indoor air. *Environ Health Persp* 95:29-34.

Dahl, S, JT Mortensen, and K Rasmussen. 1994. Cheese-packers' disease: Respiratory complaints at a cheese-packing dairy. *Ugeskrift for Laeger* 156(4):5862-5865.

Dutkiewicz, J.1994. Bacteria, fungi, and endotoxin as potential agents of occupational hazard in a potato processing plant. *Am J Ind Med* 25(1):43-46.

Dutkiewicz, J, L Jablonski, and S-A Olenchock. 1988. Occupational biohazards. A review. *Am J Ind Med* 14:605-623.

Fox, JG and NS Lipman. 1991. Infections transmitted by large and small laboratory animals. *Dis Clin North Am* 5:131-63.

Hewitt, JB, ST Misner, and PF Levin. 1993. Health hazards of nursing; identifying work place hazards and reducing risks. *Health Nurs* 4(2):320-327.

Hoglund, S. 1990. Farmers' health and safety program in Sweden. *Am J Ind Med* 18(4):371-378.

Jacjels, R. 1985. Health hazards of natural and introduced chemical components of boatbuilding woods. *Am J Ind Med* 8(3):241-251.

Kolmodin Hedman, B, G Blomquist, and E Sikstorm. 1986. Mould exposure in museum personnel. *Int Arch Occup Environ Health* 57(4):321-323.

Olcerst, RB. 1987. Microscopes and ocular infections. *Am Ind Hyg Assoc J* 48(5):425-431.

Pitlik, S, SA Berger, and D Huminer. 1987. Nonenteric infections acquired through contact with water. *Rev Infect Dis* 9(1):54-63.

Rioux, AJ and B Juminer. 1983. Animals, venomous. In *Encyclopaedia of Occupational Health and Safety* (3rd ed.), edited by L Parmeggiani. Geneva: ILO.

Sterling, TD, C Collett, and D Rumel. 1991. Epidemiology of sick buildings (in Portuguese). *Rev Sauda Publica* 25(1):56-63.

Van Eeden, PJ, JR Joubert, BW Van De Wal, JB King, A De Kock, and JH Groenewald. 1985. A nosocomial outbreak of Crimean-Congo haemorrhagic fever at Tyberg Hospital: Part 1, Clinical features. *S Afr Med J (SAMJ)* 68(9):711-717.

Weatherall, DJ, JGG Ledingham and DA Warrell (eds.). 1987. *The Oxford Textbook of Medicine*. 2nd edition. Oxford: OUP.

World Health Organization (WHO). 1995. WHO XVII occupational health and safety. In *International Digest of Health Legislation* Geneva: WHO.

Zejda, JE, HH McDuffie, and JA Dosman. 1993. Epidemiology of health and safety risks in agriculture and related industries. Practical applications for rural physicians. *Western J Med* 158(1):56-63.

Other relevant readings

Angelillo, IF, MM D'Erico, M Pavia, E Prospero, and F Romano. 1990. Evaluation of microbial air contamination in dental areas. *Archivio Stomatologoco* 31(3):511-518.

Berardi, BM and E Leoni. 1993. Indoor air climate and microbiological airborne contamination in various hospital areas. *Zentralblatt fuer Hygiene und Umweltmedizin* 194(4):405-418.

Berlin, A, WJ Hunter, and MT Van-der-Venne. 1986. Epidemiology and prevention of occupational health hazards within the European community. *Rev Epidemiol Santé Publ* 34(4-5):261-265.

Bücherl, W, EE Buckley and V Deulofue (eds.). 1968, 1971. *Venomous Animals and their Venoms*. Vols. 1 and 2. New York: Academic Press.

Cardoso, JLC, HW Fan, FOS Franca et al. 1993. Randomized comparative trial of three antivenoms in the treatment of envenoming by lance-headed vipers (*Bothrops jararaca*) in São Paulo, Brazil. *QJ Med.* (in press).

Doumenge, JP, KE Mott, C Cheung, D Villenave, O Chapius, MF Perrin, and G Reaud Thomas. 1987. *Atlas of the Global Distribution of Schistosomiasis*. Talence: PUB.

Dutkiewicz, J. 1978. Exposure to dust-borne bacteria in agriculture. I Environmental studies. *Arch Environ Health* 33(5):250-259.

Dutkiewicz, J, SA Olenchock, WG Sorenson, Gerencser.VF, JJ May, DS Pratt, and VA Robinson. 1989. Levels of bacteria, fungi, and endotoxin in bulk and aerosolized corn silage. *Appl Environ Microbiol* 55(5):1093-1099.

Egalite, ME, ME Kapitonova, SI Karpachevska, TA Farbtukh, and IA Khintsenberg. 1991. Problems of work hygiene and occupational pathology in industrial poultry breeding farms (in Russian). *Gig Truda i Professional'nye Zabolevaniya* (2):3-6.

Eikmann, T, S Schrader, J Pieler, H Bahr, and HJ Einbrodt. 1986. Emission of microorganisms from sewage treatment plants depending upon construction differences of single structural parts (in German). *Zentralblatt fuer Bakteriologie Mikrobiologie und Hygiene B* 182(2):216-236.

Forster, HW, B Crook, BW Platts, J Lacey, and MD Topping. 1989. Investigation of organic aerosols generated during sugar beet slicing. *Am Ind Hyg Assoc J* 50(1):44-50.

Fuerst, R. 1983. Brucellosis and leptospirosis. Chap. 25 in *Frobisher and Fuerst's Microbiology in Health and Disease*. Philadelphia: WB Saunders.

Gans, C and KA Gans (eds.). 1978. *Biology of the Reptilia*. Vol. 8. London: Academic Press.

Garber, N. 1993. Fulfilling record keeping requirements mandated in OSHA regulations. *J Ophthal Nurs Tech* 12(3):129-136.

Gopalakrishnakone, P (ed.). 1994. *Sea Snake Toxinology*. Singapore: National University of Singapore Press.

Gopalakrichnakone, P and LM Chou (eds.). 1990. *Snakes of Medical Importance (Asia-Pacific Region)*. Singapore: National University of Singapore Press.

Harrison, DI. 1991. Control of substances hazardous to health (COSHH) regulations and hospital infection. *J Hosp Infect* 18 Suppl. A:530-534.

Harvey, AL (ed.). 1991. *Snake Toxins. International Encyclopedia of Pharmacology and Therapeutics*. Section 134. New York: Pergamon.

Hoff, JC and FW Akin. 1986. Microbial resistance to disinfectants: Mechanisms and significance. *Environ Health Persp* 69:7-13.

Hu, DJ, MA Kane, and DL Heymann. 1991. Transmissions of HIV, hepatitis B virus, and other bloodborne pathogens in health care settings: A review of risk factors and guidelines for prevention. *Bull WHO* 69(5):623-630.

Hughes, RT and DM O'Berien. 1986. Evaluation of building ventilation systems. *Am Ind Hyg Assoc J* 47(4):207-213.

Junghanss, T and M Bodie. 1995. *Notfal-Handbook Gifttiere. Diagnose-Therapie-Biologie*. Stuttgart: Georg Thieme Verlag.

Karlsson, K and P Malmberg. 1989. Characterization of exposure to molds and actinomycetes in agricultural dusts by scanning electron microscopy, fluorescence microscopy and the culture method. *Scand J Work Environ Health* 15(5):353-359.

Klen, K. 1990. Biological hazards in the activity of organ and tissue banks and in transplantation surgery. *Sbornik Vedeckych Praci Lekarske Fakulty University Karlovy v Hradci Kralove* 33(2):109-114.

Korte, R and KE Mott. 1980. Maintenance of shistosomiasis control—An overview. *Trop Med Parasitol* 40:130-131.

Lanphear, BP. 1994. Trends and patterns in the transmission of bloodborne pathogens to health care workers. *Epidemiol Rev* 16(2):437-450.

Lebedev, SV, VG Aleksandrovskii, and VP Checkhonin. 1988. Humidifier fever (in Russian). *Terapevticheskii Arkhiv* 60(11):90-93.

Lee, CY (ed.). 1979. Snake venoms. *Handbook of Experimental Pharmacology*. Vol. 52. Berlin: Springer-Verlag.

Levy, BA, T Kjellstorm, G Forget, MR Jones, and L Pollier. 1992. Ongoing research in occupational health and environmental epidemiology in developing countries. *Arch Environ Health* 47(3):231-235.

Lund, E. 1982. Waterborne virus diseases. *Ecol Dis* 1(1):27-35.

Maciejewska, A, J Wojtczak, G Bielichowska-Cybula, A Domanska, J Dutkiewicz, and A Molocznik. 1993. Biological effect of wood dust (in Polish). *Medycyna Pracy* 44(3):277-288.

Malasit, P, DA Warrell, P Chanthavanich, C Viravan, J Mongkolsapaya, B Shinghthong and C Supich. 1986. Prediction, prevention and mechanism of early (anaphylactic) antivenom reactions in victims of snake bites. *Br Med J* 292:17-20.

Malmberg, P, A Rask-Anderson, S Hoglund, B Kolmodin-Hedman, and J Read-Guernsey. 1988. Incidence of organic dust toxic syndrome and allergic alveolitis in Swedish farmers. *Int Arch Allergy Imm* 87(1):47-54.

Matte, TD, L Fine, TJ Meinhardt, and EL Baker. 1990. Guidelines for the medical screening in the workplace. *Occup Med* 5(3):439-456.

Meier, J and J White (eds.). 1995. *Clinical Toxicology of Animal Venoms*. Boca Raton: CRC Press.

Mellstrom, G. 1991. Protective gloves of plymeric materials. Experimental permeation testing and clinical study of side effects. *Acta Derm-Venereol Suppl* 163:1-54.

Mel'nikova, EA and VI Murza. 1980. Investigations of the safety of industrial strains of microorganisms and microbial insecticides. *J Hyg Epidemiol Microbiol Immunol* 24(4):425-431.

Myint-Lwin, DA Warrell, RE Phillips, Tin-Nu-Swe, Tun-Pe and Maung-Maung-Lay. 1985. Bites by Russell's viper (*Vipera russelli siamensis*) in Burma: haemostatic, vascular and renal disturbances and response to treatment. *Lancet* ii, 1259-1264.

Reid, HA. 1976. Adder bites in Britain. *Br Med J* 2:153-156.

Reid, HA, PC Thean, KE Chan and AR Baharom. 1963. Clinical effects of bites by Malayan viper (*Ancistrodon rhodostoma*). *Lancet* i, 617-621.

Richardson, JH. 1987. Basic considerations in assessing and preventing occupation infections in personnel working with nonhuman primates. *J Med Primatol* 16(2):83-89.

Rochanachin, M and N Ardsmiti. 1987. A primary study of the number and type of microorganisms in a Thai textile factory. *Am J Ind Med* 12(6):765-766.

Russell, FE. 1980. *Snake Venom Poisoning*. Philadelphia: Lippincott.

Sadecky, E. 1981. Infection of cattle and livestock handlers with coxiella burnetti and chlamydiae in the farm of Bernolakovo (West Slovakia). *J Hyg Epidemiol Microbiol Immunol* 25(1):52-59.

Savchenko, IL, AA Kuchuk, NW Dmitrukha, AY Chudnovetes, NI Savchenko, and GV Prokopets.

1990. On the health status of subjects employed at factories manufacturing enzyme preparations. *J Hyg Epidemiol Microbiol Immunol* 34(3):253-259.

Scarlett-Kranz, JM, JG Babish, D Strickland, and DJ Lisk. 1987. Health among municipal sewage and water treatment workers. *Toxicol Ind Health* 3(3):311-319.

Sherris, JC. 1990. *Medical Microbiology—An Introduction to Infectious Diseases*. London: Prentice Hall.

Simor, AE, JL Brunton, IE Salit, H Vellend, L Ford-Jones, and IP Spence. 1984. Q fever: Hazard from sheep used in research. *Can Med Assoc J* 130(8):1013-1016.

Sutherland, SK. 1983. *Australian Animal Toxins. The Creatures, their Toxins and Care of the Poisoned Patient*. Melbourne: OUP.

Theakston, RDG and DA Warrell. 1991. Antivenoms: a list of hyperimmune sera currently available for the treatment of envenoming by bites and stings. *Toxicon* 29:1419-1470.

Tu, AT (ed.). 1991. *Handbook of Natural Toxins*. Vol. 5. Reptile venoms and toxins. New York: Marcel Dekker Inc.

Van Amerongen, WE and J de Graaff. 1988. Hygiene in dental practice. Part 1: Potential pathogens and possibilities of contamination. *ASDC J Dent Child* 55(1):47-55.

Vesterberg, O and K Holmberg. 1982. Characterization of allergen extracts by two dimensional electrophoretic techniques: Micropolyspora faeni antigens. *Clin Chem* 28(4 part 2):993-997.

Warrell, DA, BM Greenwood, N.McD Davidson et al. 1976. Necrosis, hemorrhage and complement depletion following bites by the spitting cobra (*Naja nigricollis I*). *Q J Med* 45:1-22.

Warrell, DA, N.McD Davidson, BM Greenwood, LD Ormerod, HM Pope, BJ Watkins and CR Prentice. 1977. Poisoning by bites of the saw-scaled of carpet viper (*Echis carinatus*) in Nigeria. *Q J Med* 46:33-62

Warrell, DA. 1990. Treatment of snake bite in the Asia-Pacific region: A personal view. In *Snakes of Medical Importance (Asia-Pacific Region)*. Edited by P Gopalakrishnakone, and LM Chou. Singapore: Singapore University Press.

Warrell, DA. 1996. Venoms, toxins, and poisons of animals and plants. In *Oxford Textbook of Medicine*, 3rd edition, edited by DJ Weatherall, JGG Ledingham and DA Warrell. Oxford: OUP.

Warrell, DA. 1996. Animal toxins. In *Manson's Tropical Diseases*, edited by GC Cook. London: WB Saunders.

Windle-Taylor, E. 1976. The importance of hygienic practices during the collection and bottling of mineral water. *Annali dell'Istituto Superiore di Sanita* 12(2-3):121-128.

Wlodarczak, K, W Bis, A Kaznowski, P Kuzniewski, J Molska, and H Paetz. 1989. Presence of potentially pathogenic bacteria and fungi in the cooling-lubricating emulsion used in the aluminium sheet rolling process. *Medycyna Pracy* 40(1):24-27.

Zugibe, FT, JT Costello, MK Breithaupt, E Zappi, and B Allyn. 1987. The confined space-hypoxia syndrome. *J Forensic Med* 32(2):554-560.

DISASTERS, NATURAL AND TECHNOLOGICAL

39

Chapter Editor
Pier Alberto Bertazzi

Contents

39. DISASTERS, NATURAL AND TECHNOLOGICAL

● DISASTERS AND MAJOR ACCIDENTS

Pier Alberto Bertazzi

Type and Frequency of Disasters

In 1990, the 44th General Assembly of the United Nations launched the decade for the reduction of frequency and impact of natural disasters (*Lancet* 1990). A committee of experts endorsed a definition of disasters as "a disruption of the human ecology that exceeds the capacity of the community to function normally".

Over the past few decades, disaster data on a global level reveal a distinct pattern with two main features—an increase over time of the number of people affected, and a geographical correlation (International Federation of Red Cross and Red Crescent Societies (IFRCRCS) 1993). In figure 39.1, despite the great variation from year to year, a definite rising trend is quite visible. Figure 39.2 shows the countries most severely affected by major disasters in 1991. Disasters affect every country of the world, but it is the poorest countries where people most frequently lose their lives.

Numerous and different definitions and classifications of disasters are available and have been reviewed (Grisham 1986; Lechat 1990; Logue, Melick and Hansen 1981; Weiss and Clarkson 1986). Three of them are mentioned here as examples: The US Centers for Disease Control (CDC 1989) identified three major categories of disasters: geographical events such as earthquakes and volcanic eruptions; weather-related problems, including hurricanes, tornadoes, heat waves, cold environments and floods; and, finally, human-generated problems, which encompass famines, air pollutions, industrial disasters, fires and nuclear reactor incidents. Another classification by cause (Parrish, Falk and Melius 1987) included weather and geological events among natural disasters, whereas human-made causes were defined as non-natural, technological, purposeful events perpetuated by people (e.g., transportation, war, fire/explosion, chemical and radio-

Figure 39.2 • Number of people dead from major disasters in 1991: Top 20 countries.

Top 20 countries* affected by major disasters in 1991

Country	People killed in 1991
Niger	1,439
Malawi	1,644
Papua N. Guinea	1,700
Sudan	2,070
Burma	2,104
Nigeria	2,218
Chad	2,278
Chile	2,401
Sri Lanka	2,537
Soviet Union	2,658
Afghanistan	2,705
India	4,606
Turkey	6,888
Peru	9,664
Philippines	10,326
China, P. Rep.	12,356
Colombia	23,113
Iran	35,148
Iraq	71,720
Bangladesh	556,442

People killed in 1991

* Countries in existence in 1991
Source: IFRCRCS 1993.

active release). A third classification (table 39.1), compiled at the Centre for Research on the Epidemiology of Disaster in Louvain, Belgium, was based on a workshop convened by the UN Disaster Relief Organization in 1991 and was published in the *World Disaster Report 1993* (IFRCRCS 1993).

Figure 39.3 reports the number of events for individual disaster types. The item "Accidents" includes all sudden human-made events, and is second only to "Flood" in frequency. "Storm" is in third place, followed by "Earthquake" and "Fire".

Additional information on type, frequency and consequences of natural and non-natural disasters between 1969 and 1993 has been drawn from data of the IFRCRCS 1993.

Although agencies measure the severity of disasters by the number of people killed, it is becoming increasingly important also to look at the number affected. Across the world, almost a thousand times more people are affected by disaster than are killed and, for many of these people, survival after the disaster is becoming increasingly difficult, leaving them more vulnerable to future shocks. This point is relevant not only for natural disasters (table 39.2) but also human-made disasters (table 39.3, on page 39.4), especially in the case of chemical accidents whose effects on exposed people may become apparent after years or even decades (Bertazzi 1989). Addressing human vulnerability to disaster is at the heart of disaster preparedness and prevention strategies.

Drought, famine and floods continue to affect far more people than any other type of disaster. High winds (cyclones, hurricanes and typhoons) cause proportionally more deaths than famines and floods, in relation to the affected population as a whole; and earthquakes, the most sudden-onset disaster of all, continue to have the greatest ratio of deaths to affected population (table 39.4, on page 39.5). Technological accidents affected more people than fires (table 39.5, on page 39.5).

Figure 39.1 • Number of persons affected worldwide by disasters per year during 1967-91.

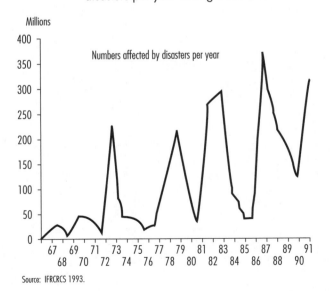

Millions

Numbers affected by disasters per year

Source: IFRCRCS 1993.

Table 39.1 • Definitions of disaster types.

Sudden natural	Long-term natural	Sudden human-made	Long-term human-made
Avalanche	Epidemics	Structural collapse	National (civil strife, civil war)
Cold wave	Drought	Building collapse	International (war-like encounters)
Earthquake	Desertification	Mine collapse or cave-in	Displaced population
Aftershock	Famine	Air disaster	Displaced persons
Floods	Food shortage or crop failure	Land disaster	Refugees
Flash flood		Sea disaster	
Dam collapse		Industrial/technological accident	
Volcanic eruption		Explosions	
Glowing avalanche		Chemical explosions	
Heat wave		Nuclear explosion or thermonuclear explosions	
High wind cyclone		Mine explosions	
Storm		Pollution	
Hail		Acid rain	
Sand storm		Chemical pollution	
Storm surges		Atmosphere pollution	
Thunder storm		Chlorofluoro-carbons (CFCs)	
Tropical storm		Oil pollution	
Tornado		Fires	
Insect infestation		Forest/grassland fire	
Landslide			
Earth flow			
Power shortage			
Tsunami and tidal wave			

Source: IFRCRCS 1993.

Tables 39.6 and 39.7 show the number of grouped disaster types over 25 years, by continent. High winds, accidents (mostly transport accidents) and floods account for the largest number of disaster events, with the largest proportion of events being in Asia. Africa accounts for the vast majority of the world's drought events. While few people are killed by disasters in Europe, the region suffers from disaster events on a scale comparable to that in Asia or Africa, the lower mortality figures reflecting a much lower human vulnerability to crisis. A clear example is the comparison of the human death tolls after the chemical accidents in Seveso (Italy) and in Bhopal (India) (Bertazzi 1989).

Figures for 1994 (tables 39.8 and 39.9 on page 39.6) show that Asia continues to be the most disaster-prone region, with major accidents, floods and high wind disasters being the most common event types. Earthquakes, while causing high death rates per event, are in fact no more common than major technological disasters. The one-year average number of non-natural events, apart from fire, is slightly diminished in comparison with the preceding 25-year period. The average numbers of natural disasters, instead, were higher, with the exception of floods and volcanoes. In 1994, Europe had more human-made disasters than Asia (39 versus 37).

Major Chemical Accidents

In this century, the worst non-natural disasters resulting in human suffering and death have been caused by wars, transport and industrial activities. At first, industrial disasters mainly affected people engaged in specific occupations, but later, particularly after the Second World War with the rapid growth and expansion of the chemical industry and the use of nuclear power, these occurrences led to serious danger even to people outside work areas, and to the general environment. We focus here on major accidents involving chemicals.

The first documented chemical disaster with industrial origins goes back to the 1600s. It was described by Bernardino Ramazzini (Bertazzi 1989). Today's chemical disasters differ in the way they happen and in the type of chemicals involved (ILO 1988). Their potential hazard is a function both of the inherent nature of the chemical and the quantity that is present on site. A common feature is that they usually are uncontrolled events involving fires, explosions or releases of toxic substances that result either in the death and injury of a large number of people inside or outside the plant, extensive property and environmental damage, or both.

Table 39.10 (on page 39.6) gives some examples of typical major chemical accidents due to explosions. Table 39.11 (on page 39.7) lists some major fire disasters. Fires occur in industry more frequently than explosions and toxic releases, although the consequences in terms of loss of life are generally less. Better prevention and preparedness might be the explanation. Table 39.12 (on page 39.7) lists some major industrial accidents involving toxic releases of different chemicals. Chlorine and ammonia are the toxic chemicals most commonly used in major hazard quantities, and both have a history of major accidents. The release of flammable or toxic materials in the atmosphere may also lead to fires.

Table 39.2 • Number of victims of disasters with a natural trigger from 1969 to 1993: 25-year average by region.

	Africa	America	Asia	Europe	Oceania	Total
Killed	76,883	9,027	56,072	2,220	99	144,302
Injured	1,013	14,944	27,023	3,521	100	46,601
Otherwise affected	10,556,984	4,400,232	105,044,476	563,542	95,128	120,660,363
Homeless	172,812	360,964	3,980,608	67,278	31,562	4,613,224

Source: Walker 1995.

Figure 39.3 • 1967-91: Total number of events for each type of disaster.

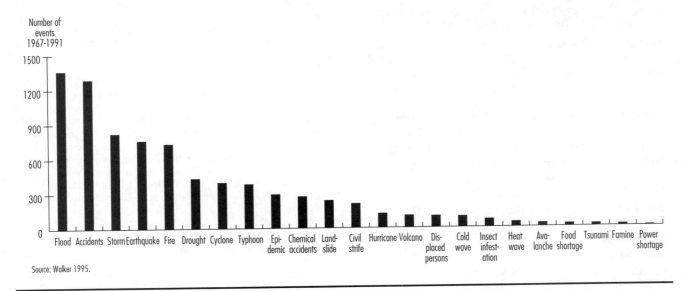

Source: Walker 1995.

A review of the literature concerning major chemical disasters enables us to identify several other common characteristics of today's industrial disasters. We will review them briefly, to provide not only a classification of general value, but also an appreciation of the nature of the problem and the challenges that face us.

Overt Disasters

Overt disasters are environmental releases which leave no ambiguity about their sources and their potential harm. Examples are Seveso, Bhopal and Chernobyl.

Seveso plays the role of prototype for chemical industrial disasters (Homberger et al. 1979; Pocchiari et al. 1983, 1986). The accident took place on 10 July 1976 in the Seveso area, close to Milan, Italy, in a plant where trichlorophenol was produced, and it caused the contamination of several square kilometres of populated countryside by the powerfully toxic 2,3,7,8-tetrachlorodibenzo-p-dioxin (TCDD). More than 700 people were evacuated, and restrictions were applied to another 30,000 inhabitants. The most clearly established health effect was chloracne, but the picture of health consequences possibly linked to this incident has not yet been completed (Bruzzi 1983; Pesatori 1995).

Bhopal represents, probably, the worst chemical industrial disaster ever (Das 1985a, 1985b; Friedrich Naumann Foundation 1987; Tachakra 1987). On the night of 2 December 1984, a gas leak caused a deadly cloud to spread over the city of Bhopal, in central India, leaving thousands dead and hundreds of thousands injured in the space of a few hours. The accident occurred because of a runaway reaction in one of the tanks in which methyl isocyanate (MIC) was stored. The concrete storage tank, containing some 42 tons of this compound, which was used to manufacture pesticides, burst open and vented MIC and other breakdown chemicals into the air. Above and beyond the obvious catastrophic impact of the accident, questions still exist as to the possible long-term consequences for the health of those affected and/or exposed (Andersson et al. 1986; Sainani et al. 1985).

Slow-Onset Disasters

Slow-onset disasters may become apparent only because human targets happen to be on the release path, or because, as time passes, some environmental evidence of a threat from noxious materials crops up.

One of the most impressive and instructive examples of the first type is "Minamata disease". In 1953 unusual neurological disorders began to strike people living in fishing villages along Minamata Bay, Japan. The disease was named *kibyo*, the "mystery illness". After numerous investigations, poisoned fish emerged as the probable culprit, and in 1957 the disease was produced experimentally by feeding cats with fish caught in the bay. The following year, the suggestion was put forward that the clinical picture of *kibyo*, which included polyneuritis, cerebellar ataxia and cortical blindness, was similar to that due to poisoning by alkyl mercury compounds. A source of organic mercury had to be

Table 39.3 • Number of victims of disasters with a non-natural trigger from 1969 to 1993: 25-year average by region.

	Africa	America	Asia	Europe	Oceania	Total
Killed	16,172	3,765	2,204	739	18	22,898
Injured	236	1,030	5,601	483	476	7,826
Affected	3,694	48,825	41,630	7,870	610	102,629
Homeless	2,384	1,722	6,275	7,664	24	18,069

Source: Walker 1995.

Table 39.4 • Number of victims of disasters with a natural trigger from 1969 to 1993: 25-year average by type.

	Earthquake	Drought and famine	Flood	High wind	Landslide	Volcano	Total
Killed	21,668	73,606	12,097	28,555	1,550	1,009	138,486
Injured	30,452	0	7,704	7,891	245	279	46,571
Affected	1,764,724	57,905,676	47,849,065	9,417,442	131,807	94,665	117,163,379
Homeless	224,186	22,720	3,178,267	1,065,928	106,889	12,513	4,610,504

Source: Walker 1995.

Table 39.5 • Number of victims of disasters with a non-natural trigger from 1969 to 1993: 25-year average by type.

	Accident	Technological accident	Fire	Total
Killed	3,419	603	3,300	7,321
Injured	1,596	5,564	699	7,859
Affected	17,153	52,704	32,771	102,629
Homeless	868	8,372	8,829	18,069

Source: Walker 1995.

sought, and it was eventually found in a factory discharging its effluent into Minamata Bay. By July 1961, the disease had occurred in 88 persons, of whom 35 (40%) had died (Hunter 1978).

An example of the second type is Love Canal, an excavation site near Niagara Falls in the United States. The area had been used as a chemical and municipal disposal site over a period of about 30 years, until 1953. Homes were later built next to the landfill. In the late 1960s, there were complaints of chemical odours in home basements, and chemical leaching in areas surrounding the site began to be reported with increasing frequency over time. In the 1970s, residents began to fear that a serious threat to their health could arise, and this shared perception prompted environmental and health investigations to be carried out. None of the published studies could conclusively support a causal link between exposure to chemicals at the disposal site and adverse health effects among the residents. Yet, there is no doubt that serious social and psychological consequences have resulted among the population in the area, particularly those who were evacuated (Holden 1980).

Mass Food Poisonings

Outbreaks of food poisoning can be caused by toxic chemicals released into the environment through the use of chemicals in the handling and processing of food. One of the most serious episodes of this type occurred in Spain (Spurzem and Lockey 1984; WHO 1984; Lancet 1983). In May 1981, an outbreak of a previously unknown syndrome began to appear in the working-class suburbs of Madrid. Over 20,000 persons were ultimately involved.

By June 1982, 315 patients had died (around 16 deaths per 1,000 cases). Initially, the clinical features included interstitial pneumonitis, diverse skin rashes, lymphadenopathies, intense eosinophilia, and gastro-intestinal symptoms. Nearly one-fourth of those who survived the acute phase required later hospitalization for neuromuscular alterations. Schleroderma-like changes of the skin also were observed in this late stage along with pulmonary hypertension and Raynaud's phenomenon.

One month after the occurrence of the first cases, the illness was found to be associated with the consumption of inexpensive denatured rapeseed oil, sold in unlabelled plastic containers and usually acquired from itinerant salesmen. The warning issued by the Spanish government against the consumption of the suspected oil caused a dramatic fall in the number of hospitalizations from toxic pneumonitis (Gilsanz et al. 1984; Kilbourne et al. 1983).

Polychlorinated biphenyls (PCBs) were involved in other widely reported accidental mass food poisonings in Japan (Masuda and Yoshimura 1984) and in Taiwan (Chen et al. 1984).

Table 39.6 • Disasters with a natural trigger from 1969 to 1993: Number of events over 25 years.

	Africa	America	Asia	Europe	Oceania	Total
Earthquake	40	125	225	167	83	640
Drought and famine	277	49	83	15	14	438
Flood	149	357	599	123	138	1,366
Landslide	11	85	93	19	10	218
High wind	75	426	637	210	203	1,551
Volcano	8	27	43	16	4	98
Other*	219	93	186	91	4	593

* Other includes: avalanche, cold wave, heat wave, insect infestation, tsunami.
Source: Walker 1995.

Table 39.7 • Disasters with a non-natural trigger from 1969 to 1993: Number of events over 25 years.

	Africa	America	Asia	Europe	Oceania	Total
Accident	213	321	676	274	18	1,502
Technological accident	24	97	97	88	4	310
Fire	37	115	236	166	29	583

Source: Walker 1995.

Transnational Disasters

Today's human-made disasters do not necessarily respect national political boundaries. An obvious example is Chernobyl, whose contamination reached from the Atlantic Ocean to the Ural Mountains (Nuclear Energy Agency, 1987). Another example comes from Switzerland (Friedrich Naumann Foundation 1987; Salzman 1987). On 1 November 1986, shortly after midnight, a fire developed in a warehouse operated by the multinational pharmaceutical company Sandoz in Schweizerhalle, 10 km southeast of Basel, and some 30 tons of the chemicals stored in the warehouse were drained along with water from the fire-fighting into the nearby River Rhine. Severe ecological damage occurred over a length of about 250 km. Apart from symptoms of irritation reported in the parts of the Basel area reached by gases and vapours produced by the fire, no cases of serious illness were reported. Nonetheless, this accident triggered serious concern in at least four European countries (Switzerland, France, Germany, The Netherlands).

Transnationality applies not only to consequences and harm caused by disasters, but also to their remote causes. Bhopal might serve as an example. In analysing the causes of that disaster, some persons reached the conclusion that "The Bhopal disaster occurred because of specific acts and decisions which were taken in Danbury, Connecticut or elsewhere in the corporate superstructure, but not in Bhopal." (Friedrich Naumann Foundation 1987.)

"Developing" Disasters

The emerging pattern of industrialization as well as modernization of agriculture in developing countries involves the application and use of imported or adopted technology and products,

Table 39.8 • Disasters with a natural trigger: Number by global region and type in 1994.

	Africa	America	Asia	Europe	Oceania	Total
Earthquake	3	3	12	1	1	20
Drought and famine	0	2	1	0	1	4
Flood	15	13	27	13	0	68
Landslide	0	1	3	1	0	5
High wind	6	14	24	5	2	51
Volcano	0	2	5	0	1	8
Other*	2	3	1	2	0	8

* Other includes: avalanche, cold wave, heat wave, insect infestation, tsunami.
Source: Walker 1995.

Table 39.9 • Disasters with a non-natural trigger: Number by global region and type in 1994.

	Africa	America	Asia	Europe	Oceania	Total
Accident	8	12	25	23	2	70
Technological accident	1	5	7	7	0	20
Fire	0	5	5	9	2	21

Source: Walker 1995.

within contexts which are quite different from those in which they were intended to be used. Businesses facing the tightening of regulations in industrial countries may export hazardous industries to world regions where less stringent measures for protection of the environment and public health exist. Industrial activities become concentrated in existing urban settlements and add significantly to the pressure caused by overcrowding and shortages of community services. Such activities are distributed between a small highly organized sector and a large unorganized sector; governmental controls in regard to labour and environmental safety in the latter sector are less stringent (Krishna Murti 1987). An example comes from Pakistan, where among 7,500 field workers in a malaria control programme in 1976, as many as 2,800 experienced some form of toxicity (Baker et al. 1978). It was also estimated that about 500,000 acute pesticide poisonings occur annually, resulting in about 9,000 deaths, and that only about 1% of the deadly cases occur in industrialized countries, although those countries consume about 80% of the total world agrochemical production (Jeyaratnam 1985).

Table 39.10 • Examples of industrial explosions.

Chemical involved	Consequences		Place and date
	Death	Injuries	
Dimethyl ether	245	3,800	Ludwigshafen, Federal Republic of Germany, 1948
Kerosene	32	16	Bitburg, Federal Republic of Germany, 1948
Isobutane	7	13	Lake Charles, Louisiana, United States, 1967
Oil slops	2	85	Pernis, Netherlands, 1968
Propylene	–	230	East Saint Louis, Illinois, United States, 1972
Propane	7	152	Decatur, Illinois, United States, 1974
Cyclohexane	28	89	Flixborough, United Kingdom, 1974
Propylene	14	107	Beek, Netherlands, 1975

Adapted from ILO 1988.

Table 39.11 • Examples of major fires.

Chemical involved	Consequences		Place and date
	Death	Injuries	
Methane	136	77	Cleveland, Ohio, United States, 1944
Liquefied petroleum gas	18	90	Ferzyn, France, 1966
Liquefied natural gas	40	–	Staten Island, New York, United States, 1973
Methane	52	–	Santa Cruz, Mexico, 1978
Liquefied petroleum gas	650	2,500	Mexico City, Mexico, 1985

Adapted from ILO 1988.

It has also been argued that developing societies might actually find themselves carrying a double burden instead of being cleared from the one of underdevelopment. It could be, in fact, that the consequences of improper industrialization are simply being added to those of the countries' underdeveloped states (Krishna Murti 1987). It is clear, thus, that international cooperation ought to be urgently strengthened in three domains: scientific work, public health and industrial siting and safety policies.

Lessons for the Future

Despite the variety of the reviewed industrial disasters, some common lessons have been learned on how to prevent their occurrence, and also on how to mitigate the impact of major chemical disasters on the population. In particular:

- Different experts should be on the scene working in close coordination; they should usually cover the fields related to the environmental fate of the agent, its toxic properties to humans and biota, analytical methods, clinical medicine and pathology, biostatistics and epidemiology.

Table 39.12 • Examples of major toxic releases.

Chemical involved	Consequences		Place and date
	Death	Injuries	
Phosgene	10	–	Poza Rica, Mexico, 1950
Chlorine	7	–	Wilsum, Federal Republic of Germany, 1952
Dioxin/TCDD	–	193	Seveso, Italy, 1976
Ammonia	30	25	Cartagena, Colombia, 1977
Sulphur dioxide	–	100	Baltimore, Maryland, United States, 1978
Hydrogen sulphide	8	29	Chicago, Illinois, United States, 1978
Methyl isocyanate	2,500	200,000	Bhopal, India, 1984

Adapted from ILO 1988.

- Based on pre-existing and/or early available evidence, a comprehensive study plan should be developed as early as possible to identify goals, problems and resource requirements.
- Early phase activities affect the course of any subsequent action. Since long-term effects should be expected after virtually every type of industrial disaster, great care should be devoted to insure availability of requisite information for later studies (e.g., proper identifiers of the exposed for follow-up).
- In planning long-term investigations, feasibility should be given high consideration to facilitate scientific and public health achievements and clarity of communication.
- Overall, for reasons of validity and cost effectiveness, it is advisable to rely on "hard" information, whenever available, either in identifying and enumerating the study population (e.g., residence) or in estimating exposure (e.g., environmental and biological measurements) and choosing the endpoints (e.g., mortality).

Control of Major Hazard Installations for the Prevention of Major Accidents

The objective of this article is to provide guidance for establishing a system to control *major hazard installations*. Two ILO documents and the more recent ILO Convention (see box on page 39.8) form the basis of the first part of this article. The European Directive forms the basis for the second part of this article.

The ILO Perspective

Much of what follows has been extracted from two documents *Prevention of Major Industrial Accidents* (ILO 1991) and *Major Hazard Control: A Practical Manual* (ILO 1988). The document "Convention concerning the Prevention of Major Industrial Accidents" (ILO 1993) (see accompanying box) serves to complement and update material from the earlier two documents. Each of these documents proposes ways to protect workers, the public and the environment against the risk of major accidents by (1) preventing major accidents from occurring at these installations and (2) minimizing the consequences of a major accident onsite and offsite, for example by (a) arranging appropriate separation between major hazard installations and housing and other centres of population nearby, such as hospitals, schools and shops, and (b) appropriate emergency planning.

The 1993 ILO Convention should be referred to for specifics; what follows is more of a narrative overview of the document.

Major hazard installations possess the potential, by virtue of the nature and quantity of hazardous substances present, to cause a *major accident* in one of the following general categories:

- the release of toxic substances in tonnage quantities which are lethal or harmful even at considerable distances from the point of release through contamination of air, water and/or soil
- the release of extremely toxic substances in kilogram quantities, which are lethal or harmful even at considerable distance from the point of release
- the release of flammable liquids or gases in tonnage quantities, which may either burn to produce high levels of thermal radiation or form an explosive vapour cloud
- the explosion of unstable or reactive materials.

Member country obligations

The 1993 Convention expects member countries who are not immediately able to implement all of the preventive and protective measures provided for in the Convention:

- to draw up plans, in consultation with the most representative organizations of employers and workers, and with other interested parties who may be affected, for the progressive implementation of said measures within a fixed time-frame

---

ILO Convention concerning the Prevention of Major Industrial Accidents, 1993 (No. 174)
ILO 80th Session, 2nd June 1993

PART I. SCOPE AND DEFINITIONS

Article 1

1. The purpose of this Convention is the prevention of major accidents involving hazardous substances and the limitation of the consequences of such accidents....

Article 3

For the purposes of this Convention:

(a) the term "hazardous substance" means a substance or mixture of substances which by virtue of chemical, physical or toxicological properties, either singly or in combination, constitutes a hazard;

(b) the term "threshold quantity" means for a given hazardous substance or category of substances that quantity, prescribed in national laws and regulations by reference to specific conditions, which if exceeded identifies a major hazard installation;

(c) the term "major hazard installation" means one which produces, processes, handles, uses, disposes of or stores, either permanently or temporarily, one or more hazardous substances or categories of substances in quantities which exceed the threshold quantity;

(d) the term "major accident" means a sudden occurrence—such as a major emission, fire or explosion—in the course of an activity within a major hazard installation, involving one or more hazardous substances and leading to a serious danger to workers, the public or the environment, whether immediate or delayed;

(e) the term "safety report" means a written presentation of the technical, management and operational information covering the hazards and risks of a major hazard installation and their control and providing justification for the measures taken for the safety of the installation;

(f) the term "near miss" means any sudden event involving one or more hazardous substances which, but for mitigating effects, actions or systems, could have escalated to a major accident.

PART II. GENERAL PRINCIPLES

Article 4

1. In the light of national laws and regulations, conditions and practices, and in consultation with the most representative organizations of employers and workers and with other interested parties who may be affected, each Member shall formulate, implement and periodically review a coherent national policy concerning the protection of workers, the public and the environment against the risk of major accidents.

2. This policy shall be implemented through preventive and protective measures for major hazard installations and, where practicable, shall promote the use of the best available safety technologies.

Article 5

1. The competent authority, or a body approved or recognized by the competent authority, shall, after consulting the most representative organizations of employers and workers and other interested parties who may be affected, establish a system for the identification of major hazard installations as defined in Article 3 (c), based on a list

of hazardous substances or of categories of hazardous substances or of both, together with their respective threshold quantities, in accordance with national laws and regulations or international standards.

2. The system mentioned in paragraph 1 above shall be regularly reviewed and updated.

Article 6

The competent authority, after consulting the representative organizations of employers and workers concerned, shall make special provision to protect confidential information transmitted or made available to it in accordance with Articles 8, 12, 13 or 14, whose disclosure would be liable to cause harm to an employer's business, so long as this provision does not lead to serious risk to the workers, the public or the environment.

PART III. RESPONSIBILITIES OF EMPLOYERS

IDENTIFICATION

Article 7

Employers shall identify any major hazard installation within their control on the basis of the system referred to in Article 5.

NOTIFICATION

Article 8

1. Employers shall notify the competent authority of any major hazard installation which they have identified:
(a) within a fixed time-frame for an existing installation;

(b) before it is put into operation in the case of a new installation.

2. Employers shall also notify the competent authority before any permanent closure of a major hazard installation.

Article 9

In respect of each major hazard installation employers shall establish and maintain a documented system of major hazard control which includes provision for:

(a) the identification and analysis of hazards and the assessment of risks including consideration of possible interactions between substances;

(b) technical measures, including design, safety systems, construction, choice of chemicals, operation, maintenance and systematic inspection of the installation;

(c) organizational measures, including training and instruction of personnel, the provision of equipment in order to ensure their safety, staffing levels, hours of work, definition of responsibilities, and controls on outside contractors and temporary workers on the site of the installation;

(d) emergency plans and procedures, including:

(i) the preparation of effective site emergency plans and procedures, including emergency medical procedures, to be applied in case of major accidents or threat thereof, with periodic testing and evaluation of their effectiveness and revision as necessary;

(ii) the provision of information on potential accidents and site emergency plans to authorities and bodies responsible for the preparation of emergency plans and procedures for the protection of the public and the environment outside the site of the installation;

(iii) any necessary consultation with such authorities and bodies;

(e) measures to limit the consequences of a major accident;

(f) consultation with workers and their representatives;

(g) improvement of the system, including measures for gathering information and analysing accidents and near misses. The lessons so learnt shall be discussed with the workers and their representatives and shall be recorded in accordance with national law and practice....

* * *

PART IV. RESPONSIBILITIES OF COMPETENT AUTHORITIES

OFF-SITE EMERGENCY PREPAREDNESS

Article 15

Taking into account the information provided by the employer, the competent authority shall ensure that emergency plans and procedures containing provisions for the protection of the public and the environment outside the site of each major hazard installation are established, updated at appropriate intervals and coordinated with the relevant authorities and bodies.

Article 16

The competent authority shall ensure that:

(a) information on safety measures and the correct behaviour to adopt in the case of a major accident is disseminated to members of the public liable to be affected by a major accident without their having to request it and that such information is updated and redisseminated at appropriate intervals;

(b) warning is given as soon as possible in the case of a major accident;

(c) where a major accident could have transboundary effects, the information required in (a) and (b) above is provided to the States concerned, to assist in cooperation and coordination arrangements.

Article 17

The competent authority shall establish a comprehensive siting policy arranging for the appropriate separation of proposed major hazard installations from working and residential areas and public facilities, and appropriate measures for existing installations. Such a policy shall reflect the General Principles set out in Part II of the Convention.

INSPECTION

Article 18

1. The competent authority shall have properly qualified and trained staff with the appropriate skills, and sufficient technical and professional support, to inspect, investigate, assess, and advise on the matters dealt with in this Convention and to ensure compliance with national laws and regulations.

2. Representatives of the employer and representatives of the workers of a major hazard installation shall have the opportunity to accompany inspectors supervising the application of the measures prescribed in pursuance of this Convention, unless the inspectors

consider, in the light of the general instructions of the competent authority, that this may be prejudicial to the performance of their duties.

Article 19

The competent authority shall have the right to suspend any operation which poses an imminent threat of a major accident.

PART V. RIGHTS AND DUTIES OF WORKERS AND THEIR REPRESENTATIVES

Article 20

The workers and their representatives at a major hazard installation shall be consulted through appropriate cooperative mechanisms in order to ensure a safe system of work. In particular, the workers and their representatives shall:

(a) be adequately and suitably informed of the hazards associated with the major hazard installation and their likely consequences;

(b) be informed of any orders, instructions or recommendations made by the competent authority;

(c) be consulted in the preparation of, and have access to, the following documents:

(i) the safety report;

(ii) emergency plans and procedures;

(iii) accident reports;

(d) be regularly instructed and trained in the practices and procedures for the prevention of major accidents and the control of developments likely to lead to a major accident and in the emergency procedures to be followed in the event of a major accident;

(e) within the scope of their job, and without being placed at any disadvantage, take corrective action and if necessary interrupt the activity where, on the basis of their training and experience, they have reasonable justification to believe that there is an imminent danger of a major accident, and notify their supervisor or raise the alarm, as appropriate, before or as soon as possible after taking such action;

(f) discuss with the employer any potential hazards they consider capable of generating a major accident and have the right to notify the competent authority of those hazards.

Article 21

Workers employed at the site of a major hazard installation shall:

(a) comply with all practices and procedures relating to the prevention of major accidents and the control of developments likely to lead to a major accident within the major hazard installation;

(b) comply with all emergency procedures should a major accident occur.

PART VI. RESPONSIBILITY OF EXPORTING STATES

Article 22

When, in an exporting member State, the use of hazardous substances, technologies or processes is prohibited as a potential source of a major accident, the information on this prohibition and the reasons for it shall be made available by the exporting member State to any importing country.

Source: Excerpts, Convention No. 174 (ILO 1993).

Table 39.13 • The role of major hazard installations management in hazard control systems.

Actions (depending on local legislation)				Action in the event of a major accident
Provide notification to authorities	Provide information on significant modifications	Prepare an onsite emergency plan	Inform the public about the major hazard	Notify authority about major accident
Prepare and submit safety report	Provide further information on request	Provide information to local authority to enable it to draw up an offsite emergency plan		Provide information on major accident

- to implement and periodically review a coherent national policy concerning the protection of workers, the public and the environment against the risk of major accidents
- to implement the policy through preventive and protective measures for major hazard installations and, where, practicable, promote the use of the best available safety technologies and
- to apply the Convention in accordance with national law and practice.

Table 39.14 • Working methods for hazard assessment.

Method	Purpose	Aim	Working principle
1. Preliminary hazard analysis	1. Identification of hazards	1. Completeness of safety concept	1. Use of "thinking aids"
2. Matrix diagrams of interactions			
3. Use of checklists			
4. Failure effect analysis			2. Use of "searching aids" and schematic documentation
5. Hazard and operability study			
6. Accident sequence analysis (inductive)	2. Assessment of hazard according to occurrence frequency	2. Optimization of reliability and availability of safety systems	3. Graphic description of failure sequences and mathematical calculation of probabilities
7. Fault tree analysis (deductive)			
8. Accident consequence analysis	3. Assessment of accident consequences	3. Mitigation of consequences and development of optimum emergency plans	4. Mathematical modelling of physical and chemical processes

Source: ILO 1988.

Components of a major hazard control system

The variety of major accidents leads to the concept of *major hazard* as an industrial activity requiring controls over and above those applied in normal factory operations, in order to protect both workers and people living and working outside. These controls aim not only at preventing accidents but also at mitigating the consequences of any accidents which could occur.

Controls need to be based on a systematic approach. Basic components of this system are:

- *identification of major hazard installations together with their respective threshold quantities and inventory*. Governmental authorities and employers should require the identification of major hazard installations on a priority basis; these should be regularly reviewed and updated.
- *information about the installation*. Once the major hazard installations have been identified, additional information needs to be collected about their design and operation. The information should be gathered and arranged systematically, and should be accessible to all parties concerned within the industry and outside the industry. In order to achieve a complete description of the hazards, it may be necessary to carry out safety studies and hazard assessments to discover possible process failures and to set priorities during the process of hazard assessment.
- *special provision to protect confidential information*
- *action inside the industrial activity*. Employers have the primary responsibility for operating and maintaining a safe facility. A sound safety policy is required. Technical inspection, maintenance, facility modification, training and selecting of suitable personnel must be carried out according to standard quality control procedures for major hazard installations. In addition to the preparation of the safety report, accidents of any type should be investigated and copies of reports submitted to the competent authority.
- *actions by the government or other competent authorities*. Assessment of the hazards for the purposes of licensing (where appropriate), inspection and enforcement of legislation. Land-use planning can appreciably reduce the potential for a disaster. The training of factory inspectors also is an important role of the government or other competent authority.
- *emergency planning*. This aims at the reduction of the consequences of major accidents. In setting up emergency planning, a distinction is made between onsite and offsite planning.

The responsibilities of employers

Major hazard installations have to be operated at a very high standard of safety. In addition, employers play a key role in the organization and implementation of a major hazard control system. In particular, as outlined in table 39.13, employers have the responsibility to:

- Provide the information required to identify major hazard installations within a fixed time-frame.

- Carry out the hazard assessment.
- Report to the competent authority on the results of the hazard assessment.
- Introduce technical measures, including design, safety systems construction, choice of chemicals, operation, maintenance and systematic inspection of the installation.
- Introduce organizational measures, including, among others, training and instruction of personnel and staffing levels.
- Set up an emergency plan.
- Take measures to improve plant safety and limit the consequences of an accident.
- Consult with workers and their representatives.
- Improve the system by learning from near misses and related information.
- Ensure that quality control procedures are in effect and audit these periodically.
- Notify the competent authority before any permanent closure of a major hazard installation.

First and foremost, employers of installations which can cause a major accident have a duty to control this major hazard. To do this, they must be aware of the nature of the hazard, of the events that cause accidents, and of the potential consequences of such accidents. This means that, in order to control a major hazard successfully, employers must have answers to the following questions:

- Do toxic, explosive or flammable substances in the facility constitute a major hazard?
- Do chemicals or agents exist which, if combined, could become a toxic hazard?
- Which failures or errors can cause abnormal conditions leading to a major accident?
- If a major accident occurs, what are the consequences of a fire, an explosion or a toxic release for the employees, people living outside the facility, the plant or the environment?
- What can management do to prevent these accidents from happening?
- What can be done to mitigate the consequences of an accident?

Hazard assessment

The most appropriate way to answer the above questions is to carry out a hazard assessment, the purpose of which is to understand why accidents occur and how they can be avoided or at least mitigated. Methods which can be used for an assessment are summarized in table 39.14.

Safe operation

A general outline of how the hazards should be controlled will be given.

Plant component design

A component has to withstand the following: static loads, dynamic loads, internal and external pressure, corrosion, loads arising from large differences in temperature, loads arising from external impacts (wind, snow, earthquakes, settling). Design standards are therefore a minimum requirement as far as major hazard installations are concerned.

Operation and control

When an installation is designed to withstand all loads that can occur during normal or foreseen abnormal operating conditions, it is the task of a process control system to keep the plant safely within these limits.

In order to operate such control systems, it is necessary to monitor the process variables and active parts of the plant. Operating personnel should be well trained to be aware of the mode of operation and the importance of the control system. To ensure that the operating personnel do not have to rely solely on the functioning of automatic systems, these systems should be combined with acoustic or optical alarms.

It is most important to realize that any control system will have problems in rare operating conditions such as start-up and shutdown phases. Special attention must be paid to these phases of operation. Quality control procedures will be audited by management periodically.

Safety systems

Any major hazard installation will require some form of safety system. The form and design of the system depend on the hazards present in the plant. The following gives a survey of available safety systems:

- systems preventing deviation from permissible operating conditions
- systems preventing failure of safety-related components
- safety-related utility supplies
- alarm systems
- technical protective measures
- prevention of human and organizational errors.

Maintenance and monitoring

The safety of a plant and the function of a safety-related system can only be as good as the maintenance and monitoring of these systems.

Inspection and repair

It is necessary to establish a plan for onsite inspections, for the operating personnel to follow, which should include a schedule and the operating conditions to be adhered to during inspection work. Strict procedures must be specified for carrying out repair work.

Training

As people can have a negative as well as a positive influence on plant safety, it is important to reduce the negative influences and support the positive ones. Both goals can be achieved by proper selection, training and periodic evaluation/assessment of the personnel.

Mitigation of consequences

Even if a hazard assessment has been carried out and the hazards have been detected and appropriate measures to prevent accidents have been taken, the possibility of an accident cannot be completely ruled out. For this reason, it must be part of the safety concept to plan and provide measures which can mitigate the consequences of an accident.

These measures have to be consistent with the hazards identified in the assessment. Furthermore, they must be accompanied by proper training of plant personnel, the emergency forces and responsible representatives from public services. Only training and rehearsals of accident situations can make emergency plans realistic enough to work in a real emergency.

Safety reporting to the competent authority

Depending on local arrangements in different countries, employers of a major hazard installation shall report to the appropriate competent authority. Reporting may be carried out in three steps. These are:

- identification/notification of major hazard installation (including any future changes that are to be made to the installation)
- the preparation of periodic safety reports (which shall be revised in the light of any modifications made to a facility)

39. DISASTERS, NATURAL AND TECHNOLOGICAL

- immediate reporting of any type of accident, followed by a detailed report.

Rights and duties of workers and their representatives

Workers and their representatives shall be consulted through appropriate cooperative mechanisms in order to ensure a safe system of work. They shall be consulted in the preparation of, and have access to, safety reports, emergency plans and procedures, and accident reports. They shall receive training for preventing major accidents and in emergency procedures to be followed in the event of a major accident. Finally, workers and their representatives should be able to take corrective action where needed within the scope of their duties, if they believe that there is any imminent danger of a major accident. They also have the right to notify the competent authority of any hazard.

Workers shall comply with all practices and procedures for preventing major accidents and for the control of developments likely to lead to a major accident. They shall comply with all emergency procedures should a major accident occur.

Implementation of a major hazard control system

Although the storage and use of large quantities of hazardous materials is widespread across most countries of the world, the present systems for their control will differ substantially from one country to another. This means that the speed of implementation of a major hazard control system will depend on the facilities already existing in each country, particularly with regard to trained and experienced facility inspectors, together with the resources available locally and nationally for the different components of the control system. For all countries, however, implementation will require the setting of priorities for a stage-by-stage programme.

Identification of major hazards

This is the essential starting point for any major hazard control system—the definition of what actually constitutes a major hazard. Although definitions exist in some countries and particularly in the EU, a particular country's definition of a major hazard should reflect local priorities and practices and, in particular, the industrial pattern in that country.

Any definition for identifying major hazards is likely to involve a list of hazardous materials, together with an inventory for each, such that any major hazard installation storing or using any of these in excess quantities is by definition a major hazard installation. The next stage is to identify where the major hazard installation exists for any particular region or country. Where a country wishes to identify major hazard installations before the necessary legislation is in place, considerable progress can be achieved informally, particularly where the cooperation of industry is available. Existing sources such as factory inspectorate records, information from industrial bodies and so on, may enable a provisional list to be obtained which, apart from allowing early inspection priorities to be allocated, will enable an assessment to be made of the resources required for different parts of the control system.

Establishment of a group of experts

For countries considering establishing a major hazard control system for the first time, an important first stage is likely to be setting up a group of experts as a special unit at government level. The group will have to set priorities in deciding on its initial programme of activity. The group may be required to train factory inspectors in the techniques of major hazard inspection, including operational standards for such major hazard installations. They should also be able to provide advice about the siting of new major hazards and the use of land nearby. They will need to establish contacts in other countries in order to keep up to date with major hazard developments.

Onsite emergency preparedness

Emergency plans require that the major hazard installation be assessed for the range of accidents that could take place, together with how they would be tackled in practice. The handling of these potential accidents will require both staff and equipment, and a check should be made to ensure that both are available in sufficient numbers. The plans should include the following elements:

- assessment of the size and nature of the events foreseen and the probability of their occurrence
- formulation of the plan and liaison with outside authorities, including emergency services
- procedures: (a) raising the alarm; (b) communications within the plant and outside the plant
- appointment of key personnel and their duties and responsibilities
- emergency control centre
- action onsite and offsite.

Offsite emergency preparedness

This is an area which has received less attention than onsite emergency planning, and many countries will be faced with considering this for the first time. The offsite emergency plan will have to link the possible accidents identified by the major hazard installation, their expected likelihood of occurrence and the proximity of people living and working nearby. It must have addressed the need for the expeditious warning and evacuation of the public, and how these might be achieved. It should be remembered that conventional housing of solid construction offers substantial protection from toxic gas clouds, whereas a shanty-type house is vulnerable to such accidents.

The emergency plan must identify organizations whose help will be required in the event of an emergency and must ensure that they know what role is expected of them: hospitals and medical staff should, for example, have decided how they would handle large numbers of casualties and in particular what treatment they would provide. The offsite emergency plan will need to be rehearsed with public involvement from time to time.

Where a major accident could have transboundary effects, full information is to be provided to the jurisdictions concerned, as well as assistance in cooperation and coordination arrangements.

Siting

The basis for needing a siting policy for major hazard installations is straightforward: since absolute safety cannot be guaranteed, major hazard installations should be separated from people living and working outside the facility. As a first priority, it may be appropriate to concentrate efforts on proposed new major hazards and to try to prevent the encroachment of housing, particularly shanty houses, which are a common feature in many countries.

Training and facility inspectors

The role of the facility inspectors is likely to be central in many countries in implementing a major hazard control system. Facility inspectors will have the knowledge that will enable early identification of major hazards to take place. Where they have specialist inspectors to call upon, factory inspectors will be assisted in the often highly technical aspects of major hazard inspection.

Inspectors will need appropriate training and qualifications to aid them in this work. Industry itself is likely to be the largest source of technical expertise within many countries, and may be able to provide assistance in facility inspectorate training.

The competent authority shall have the right to suspend any operation which poses an imminent threat of a major accident.

Evaluation of major hazards

This should be carried out by specialists, if possible according to guidelines drawn up, for example, by the group of experts or by specialist inspectors, possibly with assistance from the major hazard installation employer management group. Evaluation involves a systematic study for major accident hazard potential. It will be a similar exercise, although in much less detail, to that carried out by the major hazard installation management in producing its safety report for the facility inspectorate and in establishing an onsite emergency plan.

Evaluation will include a study of all handling operations of hazardous materials, including transport.

An examination of the consequences of process instability or major changes in the process variables will be included.

The evaluation also should consider the positioning of one hazardous material in relation to another.

The consequences of common mode failure will also need to be assessed.

The evaluation will consider the consequences of the identified major accidents in relation to offsite populations; this may determine whether the process or plant can be put into operation.

Information to the public

Experience of major accidents, particularly those involving toxic gas releases, has shown the importance of the public nearby having prior warning of: (a) how to recognize that an emergency is occurring; (b) what action they should take; and (c) what remedial medical treatment would be appropriate for anyone being affected by the gas.

For inhabitants of conventional housing of solid construction, the advice in the event of an emergency usually is to go indoors, close all doors and windows, switch off all ventilation or air conditioning, and switch on the local radio for further instructions.

Where large numbers of shanty-dwellers live close to a major hazard installation, this advice would be inappropriate, and large-scale evacuation might be necessary.

Prerequisites for a major hazard control system

Personnel

A fully developed major hazard control system requires a wide variety of specialized personnel. Apart from industrial staff concerned either directly or indirectly with the safe operation of the major hazard installation, required resources include general factory inspectors, specialist inspectors, risk assessors, emergency planners, quality control officers, local authority land planners, police, medical facilities, river authorities and so on, plus legislators to promulgate new legislation and regulations for major hazard control.

In most countries, human resources for these tasks are likely to be limited, and the setting of realistic priorities is essential.

Equipment

A feature of establishing a major hazard control system is that much can be achieved with very little equipment. Factory inspectors will not need much in addition to their existing safety equipment. What will be required is the acquisition of technical experience and knowledge and the means to relay this from the group of experts to, say, the regional labour institute, the facility inspectorate and the industry. Additional training aids and facilities may be necessary.

Table 39.15 • EC Directive criteria for major hazard installations.

Toxic substances (very toxic and toxic):

Substances showing the following values of acute toxicity and having physical and chemical properties capable of entailing major accident hazards:

	LD_{50} oral. rat mg/kg	LD_{50} cut. rat/rab mg/kg	LC_{50} ihl. 4hr. rat mg/1
1.	$LD_{50} < 5$	$LD < 1$	$LD_{50} < 0.10$
2.	$5 < LD_{50} < 25$	$10 < LD_{50} < 50$	$0.1 < LC_{50} < 0.5$
3.	$25 < LD_{50} < 200$	$50 < LD_{50} < 400$	$0.5 < LC_{50} < 2$

Flammable substances:

1. Flammable gases: substances which in the gaseous state at normal pressure and mixed with air become flammable and the boiling-point of which at normal pressure is 20 °C or below.

2. Highly flammable liquids: substances which have a flashpoint lower than 21 °C and the boiling point of which at normal pressure is above 20 °C.

3. Flammable liquids: substances which have a flashpoint lower than 55 °C and which remain liquid under pressure, where particular processing conditions, such as high pressure and high temperature, may create major accident hazards.

Explosive substances:

Substances which may explode under the effect of flame or which are more sensitive to shocks or friction than dinitrobenzene.

Information

A key element in establishing a major hazard control system is obtaining state-of-the-art information and quickly passing this information on to all those who will need it for their safety work.

The volume of literature covering the various aspects of major hazards work is now considerable, and, used selectively, this could provide an important source of information to a group of experts.

Responsibility of exporting countries

When, in an exporting member country, the use of hazardous substances, technologies or processes is prohibited as a potential source of a major accident, the information on this prohibition and the reasons for it shall be made available by the exporting member country to any importing country.

Certain non-binding recommendations flowed from the Convention. In particular, one had a transnational focus. It recommends that a national or a multinational enterprise with more than one establishment or facility should provide safety measures relating to the prevention of major accidents and the control of developments likely to lead to a major accident, without discrimination, to the workers in all its establishments, regardless of the place or country in which they are situated. (The reader should also refer to the section "Transnational disasters" in this article.)

The European Directive on Major Accident Hazards of Certain Industrial Activities

Following serious incidents in the chemical industry in Europe in the last two decades, specific legislation covering major hazard activities was developed in various countries in Western Europe. A key feature in the legislation was the obligation of the employer of a major hazard industrial activity to submit information about the activity and its hazards based on the results of systematic

Table 39.16 • Priority chemicals used in identifying major hazard installations.

Names of substances	Quantity (>)	EC list serial number
General flammable substances:		
Flammable gases	200 t	124
Highly flammable liquids	50,000 t	125
Specific flammable substances:		
Hydrogen	50 t	24
Ethylene oxide	50 t	25
Specific explosives:		
Ammonium nitrate	2,500 t	146 b
Nitroglycerine	10 t	132
Trinitrotoluene	50 t	145
Specific toxic substances:		
Acrylonitrile	200 t	18
Ammonia	500 t	22
Chlorine	25 t	16
Sulphur dioxide	250 t	148
Hydrogen sulphide	50 t	17
Hydrogen cyanide	20 t	19
Carbon disulphide	200 t	20
Hydrogen fluoride	50 t	94
Hydrogen chloride	250 t	149
Sulphur trioxide	75 t	180
Specific very toxic substances:		
Methyl isocyanate	150 kg	36
Phosgene	750 kg	15

safety studies. After the accident in Seveso (Italy) in 1976, the major hazard regulations in the various countries were put together and integrated in an EC Directive. This Directive, on the major accident hazards of certain industrial activities, has been in force since 1984 and is often referred to as the Seveso Directive (Council of the European Communities 1982, 1987).

For the purpose of identifying major hazard installations, the EC Directive uses criteria based on the toxic, flammable and explosive properties of the chemicals (see table 39.15).

For the selection of specific major hazard industrial activities, a list of substances and threshold limits is provided in annexes to the Directive. An industrial activity is defined by the Directive as the aggregate of all installations within a distance of 500 metres of each other and belonging to the same factory or plant. When the quantity of the substances present exceeds the given threshold limit appearing in the list, the activity is referred to as a major hazard installation. The list of substances consists of 180 chemicals, whereas the threshold limits vary between 1 kg for extremely toxic substances to 50,000 tonnes for highly flammable liquids. For isolated storage of substances, a separate list of a few substances is given.

In addition to flammable gases, liquids and explosives, the list contains chemicals such as ammonia, chlorine, sulphur dioxide and acrylonitrile.

In order to facilitate the application of a major hazard control system and to encourage the authorities and management to apply it, it must be priority oriented, with attention being focused on the more hazardous installations. A suggested list of priorities is given in table 39.16.

With the chemicals shown in the table acting as a guide, a list of installations can be identified. If the list is still too big to be coped with by the authorities, new priorities can be set by means of setting new quantity thresholds. Priority setting also can be used inside the factory to identify the more hazardous parts. In view of the diversity and complexity of industry in general, it is not possible to restrict major hazard installations to certain sectors of industrial activity. Experience, however, indicates that major hazard installations are most commonly associated with the following activities:

- petrochemical works and refineries
- chemical works and chemical production plants
- LPG storage and terminals
- stores and distribution centres for chemicals
- large fertilizer stores
- explosives factories
- works in which chlorine is used in bulk quantities.

DISASTER PREPAREDNESS

Peter J. Baxter

Over the last two decades the emphasis in disaster reduction has switched from mainly improvised relief measures in the post-impact phase to forward planning, or disaster preparedness. For natural disasters this approach has been embraced in the philosophy of the United Nations International Decade for Natural Disaster Reduction (IDNDR) programme. The following four phases are the components of a comprehensive hazard management plan which can be applied to all types of natural and technological disasters:

- pre-disaster planning
- emergency preparedness
- emergency response
- post-impact recovery and reconstruction.

The aim of disaster preparedness is to develop disaster prevention or risk reduction measures in parallel with emergency preparedness and response capabilities. In this process hazard and vulnerability analyses are the scientific activities which provide the basis for the applied tasks of risk reduction and emergency preparedness to be undertaken in collaboration with planners and the emergency services.

Most health professionals would see their role in disaster preparedness as one of planning for the emergency treatment of large numbers of casualties. However, if the impact of disasters is to be drastically reduced in the future, the health sector needs to be involved in the development of preventive measures and in all phases of disaster planning, with scientists, engineers, emergency planners and decision makers. This multidisciplinary approach poses a major challenge to the health sector at the end of the 20th century as natural and human-made calamities become increasingly destructive and costly in terms of lives and property with the expansion of human populations across the globe.

Natural sudden or rapid-onset disasters include extreme weather conditions (floods and high winds), earthquakes, landslides, volcanic eruptions, tsunamis and wild fires, and their impacts have much in common. Famines, drought and desertification, on the other hand, are subject to more long-term processes which at present are only very poorly understood, and their consequences are not so amenable to reduction measures. Presently the most common cause of famine is war or so-called complex disasters (e.g., in Sudan, Somalia or former Yugoslavia).

Large numbers of displaced persons are a common feature of natural and complex disasters, and their nutritional and other health needs require specialized management.

Modern civilization is also becoming accustomed to technological or human-made disasters such as acute air pollution episodes, fires and chemical and nuclear reactor accidents, the last two being the most important today. This article will focus on disaster planning for chemical disasters, as nuclear power accidents are dealt with elsewhere in the *Encyclopaedia*.

Natural Sudden-Onset Disasters

The most important of these in terms of destructiveness are floods, hurricanes, earthquakes and volcanic eruptions. There have already been some well-publicized successes in disaster reduction through early warning systems, hazard mapping and structural engineering measures in seismic zones. Thus satellite monitoring using global weather forecasting, together with a regional system for timely delivery of warnings and effective evacuation planning, was responsible for the comparatively small loss of life (just 14 deaths) when Hurricane Hugo, the strongest hurricane so far recorded in the Caribbean, struck Jamaica and the Cayman Islands in 1988. In 1991 adequate warnings provided by Philippine scientists closely monitoring Mount Pinatubo saved many thousands of lives through timely evacuation in one of the largest eruptions of the century. But the "technological fix" is only one aspect of disaster mitigation. The large human and economic losses wrought by disasters in developing countries highlight the major importance of socio-economic factors, above all poverty, in increasing vulnerability, and the need for disaster preparedness measures to take these into account.

Natural disaster reduction has to compete in all countries with other priorities. Disaster reduction can also be promoted through legislation, education, building practices and so on, as part of a society's general risk reduction programme or safety culture—as an integral part of sustainable development policies and as a quality assurance measure for investment strategies (e.g., in the planning of buildings and infrastructure in new land developments).

Technological Disasters

Clearly, with natural hazards it is impossible to prevent the actual geological or meteorological process from occurring.

However, with technological hazards, major inroads into disaster prevention can be made using risk reduction measures in the design of plants and governments can legislate to establish high standards of industrial safety. The Seveso Directive in EC countries is an example which also includes requirements for the development of onsite and offsite planning for emergency response.

Major chemical accidents comprise large vapour or flammable gas explosions, fires, and toxic releases from fixed hazardous installations or during the transport and distribution of chemicals. Special attention has been given to the storage in large quantities of toxic gases, the most common being chlorine (which, if suddenly released due to the disruption of a storage tank or from a leak in a pipe, can form large denser-than-air clouds which can be blown in toxic concentrations for large distances downwind). Computer models of dispersion of dense gases in sudden releases have been produced for chlorine and other common gases and these are used by planners to devise emergency response measures. These models can also be used to determine the numbers of

casualties in a reasonably foreseeable accidental release, just as models are being pioneered for predicting the numbers and types of casualties in major earthquakes.

Disaster Prevention

A disaster is any disruption of the human ecology that exceeds the capacity of the community to function normally. It is a state which is not merely a quantitative difference in the functioning of the health or emergency services—for example, as caused by a large influx of casualties. It is a qualitative difference in that the demands cannot be adequately met by a society without help from unaffected areas of the same or another country. The word *disaster* is too often used loosely to describe major incidents of a highly publicized or political nature, but when a disaster has actually occurred there may be a total breakdown in normal functioning of a locality. The aim of disaster preparedness is to enable a community and its key services to function in such disorganized circumstances in order to reduce human morbidity and mortality as well as economic losses. Large numbers of acute casualties are not a prerequisite for a disaster, as was shown in the chemical disaster at Seveso in 1976 (when a massive evacuation was mounted because of fears of long-term health risks arising from ground contamination by dioxin). "Near disasters" may be a better description of certain events, and outbreaks of psychological or stress reactions may also be the only manifestation in some events (e.g., at the reactor accident at Three Mile Island, USA, in 1979). Until the terminology becomes established we should recognize Lechat's description of the health objectives of disaster management, which include:

- prevention or reduction of mortality due to the impact, to a delay in rescue and to lack of appropriate care
- provision of care for casualties such as immediate post-impact trauma, burns and psychological problems
- management of adverse climatic and environmental conditions (exposure, lack of food and drinking water)
- prevention of short-term and long-term disaster-related morbidity (e.g., outbreaks of communicable diseases due to disruption of sanitation, living in temporary shelters, overcrowding and communal feeding; epidemics such as malaria due to interruption of control measures; rise of morbidity and mortality due to disruption of the health care system; mental and emotional problems)
- ensuring restoration of normal health by preventing long-term malnutrition due to disruption of food supplies and agriculture.

Disaster prevention cannot take place in a vacuum, and it is essential that a structure exists at the national governmental level of every country (the actual organization of which will vary from country to country), as well as at the regional and community level. In countries with high natural risks, there may be few ministries which can avoid being involved. The responsibility for planning is given to existing bodies such as armed forces or civil defence services in some countries.

Where a national system exists for natural hazards it would be appropriate to build on to it a response system for technological disasters, rather than devise a whole new separate system. The Industry and Environment Programme Activity Centre of the United Nations Environment Programme has developed the Awareness and Preparedness for Emergencies at Local Level (APELL) Programme. Launched in cooperation with industry and government, the programme aims to prevent technological accidents and reduce their impacts in developing countries by raising community awareness of hazardous installations and providing assistance in developing emergency response plans.

Figure 39.4 • Risk is a product of hazard and vulnerability: typical curve shapes.

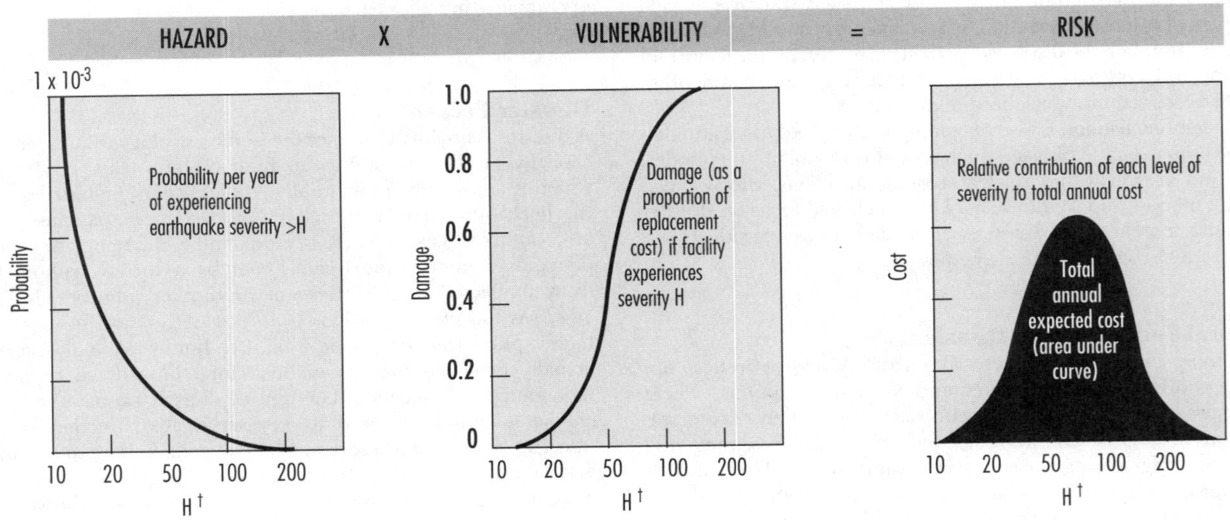

| HAZARD | X | VULNERABILITY | = | RISK |

† Severity of earthquake ground motion, % g @ 0.2s spectral acceleration

Source: Coburn and Spence 1992.

Hazard Assessment

The different types of natural disaster and their impacts need to be assessed in terms of their likelihood in all countries. Some countries such as the UK are at low risk, with wind storms and floods being the main hazards, while in other countries (e.g., the Philippines) there is a wide range of natural phenomena which strike with relentless regularity and can have serious effects on the economy and even the political stability of the country. Each hazard requires a scientific evaluation which will include at least the following aspects:

• its cause or causes
• its geographical distribution, magnitude or severity and probable frequency of occurrence
• the physical mechanisms of destruction
• the elements and activities most vulnerable to destruction
• possible social and economic consequences of a disaster.

Areas at high risk of earthquakes, volcanoes and floods need to have hazard zone maps prepared by experts to predict the locations and nature of the impacts when a major event occurs. Such hazard assessments can then be used by land-use planners for long-term risk reduction, and by emergency planners who have to deal with the pre-disaster response. However, seismic zoning for earthquakes and hazard mapping for volcanoes are still in their infancy in most developing countries, and extending such risk mapping is seen as a crucial need in the IDNDR.

Hazard assessment for natural hazards requires a detailed study of the records of previous disasters in the preceding centuries and exacting geological field work to ascertain major events such as earthquakes and volcanic eruptions in historic or prehistoric times. Learning about the behaviour of major natural phenomena in the past is a good, but far from infallible, guide for hazard assessment for future events. There are standard hydrological methods for flood estimation, and many flood-prone areas can be easily recognized because they coincide with a well-defined natural flood plain. For tropical cyclones, records of impacts around coastlines can be used to determine the probability of a hurricane striking any one part of the coastline in a year, but each hurricane has to be urgently monitored as soon as it has formed in order to actually forecast its path and speed at least 72 hours ahead, before it makes landfall. Associated with earthquakes, volcanoes and heavy rains are landslides which may be triggered by these phenomena. In the last decade it has been increasingly appreciated that many large volcanoes are at risk from slope failure because of the instability of their mass, which has been built up during periods of activity, and devastating landslides may result.

With technological disasters, local communities need to make inventories of the hazardous industrial activities in their midst. There are now ample examples from past major accidents of what these hazards can lead to, should a failure in a process or containment occur. Quite detailed plans now exist for chemical accidents around hazardous installations in many developed countries.

Risk Assessment

After evaluating a hazard and its likely impacts, the next step is to undertake a risk assessment. Hazard may be defined as the possibility of harm, and risk is the probability of lives being lost, persons injured or property damaged due to a given type and magnitude of natural hazard. Risk can be quantitatively defined as:

Risk = value × vulnerability × hazard

where value can represent a potential number of lives or capital value (of buildings, for example) which may be lost in the event. Ascertaining vulnerability is a key part of risk assessment: for buildings it is the measure of the intrinsic susceptibility of structures exposed to potentially damaging natural phenomena. For example, the likelihood of a building collapsing in an earthquake can be determined from its location relative to a fault line and the seismic resistance of its structure. In the above equation the degree of loss resulting from the occurrence of a natural phenomenon of a given magnitude can be expressed on a scale from 0 (no damage) to 1 (total loss), while hazard is the specific risk expressed as a probability of preventable loss per unit time. Vulnerability is therefore the fraction of value that is likely to be lost as a result of an event. The information needed for making a vulnerability analysis can come, for example, from surveys of homes in hazard areas by architects and engineers. Figure 39.4 provides some typical risk curves.

Vulnerability assessments utilizing information on different causes of death and injury according to the different types of impact are much more difficult to undertake at the present time, as the data on which to base them are crude, even for earthquakes, since standardization of injury classifications and even the accurate recording of the number, let alone the causes of deaths, are not yet possible. These serious limitations show the need for much more effort to be put into epidemiological data-gathering in disasters if preventive measures are to develop on a scientific basis.

At present mathematical computation of risk of building collapse in earthquakes and from ash falls in volcanic eruptions can be digitalized onto maps in the form of risk scales, to graphically demonstrate those areas of high risk in a foreseeable event and predict where, therefore, civil defence preparedness measures should be concentrated. Thus risk assessment combined with economic analysis and cost effectiveness will be invaluable in deciding between different options for risk reduction.

In addition to building structures, the other important aspect of vulnerability is infrastructure (lifelines) such as:

- transport
- telecommunications
- water supplies
- sewer systems
- electricity supplies
- health care facilities.

In any natural disaster all of these are at risk of being destroyed or heavily damaged, but as the type of destructive force may differ according to the natural or technological hazard, appropriate protective measures need to be devised in conjunction with the risk assessment. Geographical information systems are modern computer techniques for mapping different data sets to assist in such tasks.

In planning for chemical disasters, quantified risk assessment (QRA) is used as a tool to determine the probability of plant failure and as a guide for decision makers, by providing numerical estimates of risk. Engineering techniques for making this type of analysis are well advanced, as are the means of developing hazard zone maps around hazardous installations. Methods exist for predicting pressure waves and concentrations of radiant heat at different distances from the sites of vapour or flammable gas explosions. Computer models exist for predicting the concentration of denser-than-air gases for kilometres downwind from an accidental release in specified amounts from a vessel or plant under different weather conditions. In these incidents vulnerability mainly has to do with the proximity of housing, schools, hospitals and other key installations. Individual and societal risks need to be computed for the different types of disaster and their significance should be communicated to the local population as part of overall disaster planning.

Risk Reduction

Once vulnerability has been assessed, the feasible measures to reduce vulnerability and overall risk need to be devised.

Thus new buildings should be made seismic resistant if built in a seismic zone, or old buildings can be retrofitted so that they are less likely to collapse. Hospitals may need resiting or "hardening" against hazards such as windstorms, for example. The need for good roads as evacuation routes must never be forgotten in land

developments in areas at risk of windstorms or volcanic eruptions and a host of other civil engineering measures can be enacted depending upon the situation. In the longer term the most important measure is the regulation of land use to prevent the development of settlements in hazardous areas, such as flood plains, the slopes of active volcanoes or around major chemical plants. Overreliance on engineering solutions can bring false reassurance in at-risk areas, or be counterproductive, increasing the risk of rare catastrophic events (e.g., building levees along major rivers prone to severe flooding).

Emergency Preparedness

The planning and organization of emergency preparedness should be a task for a multidisciplinary planning team involved at the community level, and one which should be integrated into hazard assessment, risk reduction and emergency response. In the management of casualties it is now well recognized that medical teams from outside may take at least three days to arrive at the scene in a developing country. As most preventable deaths occur within the first 24 to 48 hours, such assistance will arrive too late. Thus it is at the local level that emergency preparedness should be focused, so that the community itself has the means to begin rescue and relief actions immediately after an event.

Providing adequate information to the public in the planning phase should therefore be a key aspect of emergency preparation.

Information and communication needs

On the basis of the hazard and risk analyses, the means of providing early warning will be essential, together with a system for evacuating people from areas of high risk should an emergency arise. Pre-planning of communications systems between the different emergency services at the local and national levels is necessary and for the effective provision and dissemination of information in a disaster a formal chain of communication will have to be established. Other measures such as stockpiling emergency food and water supplies in households may be included.

A community near a hazardous installation needs to be aware of the warning it may receive in an emergency (e.g., a siren if there is a gas release) and the protective measures people should adopt (e.g., immediately go inside houses and close windows until advised to come out). An essential feature of a chemical disaster is the need to be able to rapidly define the health hazard posed by a toxic release, which means identifying the chemical or chemicals involved, having access to knowledge of their acute or long-term effects and determining who, if anyone, in the general population has been exposed. Establishing lines of communication with poison information and chemical emergency centres is an essential planning measure. Unfortunately it may be difficult or impossible to know the chemicals involved in the event of runaway reactions or chemical fires, and even if it is easy to identify a chemical, knowledge of its toxicology in humans, particularly chronic effects, may be sparse or non-existent, as was found after the release of methyl isocyanate at Bhopal. Yet without information on the hazard, the medical management of casualties and the exposed population, including decisions on the need for evacuation from the contaminated area, will be severely hampered.

A multidisciplinary team to gather information and to undertake rapid health risk assessments and environmental surveys to exclude contamination of ground, water and crops should be pre-planned, recognizing that all available toxicological databases may be inadequate for decision making in a major disaster, or even in small incidents in which a community believes it has suffered serious exposure. The team should have the expertise to confirm the nature of the chemical release and to investigate its likely health and environmental impacts.

39. DISASTERS, NATURAL AND TECHNOLOGICAL

In natural disasters, epidemiology is also important for making an assessment of the health needs in the post-impact phase and for infectious diseases surveillance. Information gathering on the effects of the disaster is a scientific exercise which should also be part of a response plan; a designated team should undertake this work to provide important information for the disaster coordinating team as well as for assisting in the modification and improvement of the disaster plan.

Command and control and emergency communications
The designation of the emergency service in charge, and the constitution of a disaster coordinating team, will vary from country to country and with the type of disaster, but it needs to be pre-planned. At the scene a specific vehicle may be designated as the command and control, or onsite coordinating centre. For example, emergency services cannot rely on telephone communications, as these may become overloaded, and so radio links will be needed.

The hospital major incident plan
The capability of hospitals in terms of staff, physical reserves (theatres, beds and so on) and treatment (medicines and equipment) for dealing with any major incident will need to be assessed. Hospitals should have specific plans for dealing with a sudden large influx of casualties, and there should be provision for a hospital flying squad to go to the scene to work with search and rescue teams in extricating trapped victims or to undertake field triage of large numbers of casualties. Major hospitals may be unable to function because of disaster damage, as happened in the earthquake in Mexico City in 1985. Restoring or supporting devastated health services may therefore be necessary. For chemical incidents, hospitals should have established links with poison information centres. As well as being able to draw on a large fund of health care professionals from inside or outside a disaster area to cope with the injured, planning should also include the means for the rapid sending of emergency medical equipment and drugs.

Emergency equipment
The types of search and rescue equipment needed for a specific disaster should be identified at the planning stage along with where it will be stored, as it will need to be rapidly deployed in the first 24 hours, when the most lives can be saved. Key medicines and medical equipment need to be available for rapid deployment, along with personal protective equipment for emergency crews, including health workers at the disaster scene. Engineers skilled in urgently restoring water, electricity, communications and roads can have a major role in alleviating the worst effects of disasters.

Emergency response plan
The separate emergency services and the health care sector, including public health, occupational health and environmental health practitioners, should each have plans for dealing with disasters, which can be incorporated together as one major disaster plan. In addition to the hospital plans, health planning should include detailed response plans for different types of disaster, and these need to be devised in the light of the hazard and risk assessments produced as part of disaster preparedness. Treatment protocols should be drawn up for the specific types of injury that each disaster may produce. Thus a range of traumas, including crush syndrome, should be anticipated from the collapse of buildings in earthquakes, whereas body burns and inhalational injuries are a feature of volcanic eruptions. In chemical disasters, triage, decontamination procedures, the administration of antidotes where applicable and emergency treatment of acute pulmonary

injury from irritant toxic gases should all be planned for. Forward planning should be flexible enough to cope with transport emergencies involving toxic substances, especially in areas without fixed installations which would normally require the authorities to make intensive local emergency plans. The emergency management of physical and chemical trauma in disasters is a vital area of health care planning and one which requires training of hospital staff in disaster medicine.

The management of evacuees, the location of evacuation centres and the appropriate preventive health measures should be included. The need for emergency stress management to prevent stress disorders in victims and emergency workers should also be considered. Sometimes psychological disorders may be the predominant or even the only health impact, particularly if the response to an incident has been inadequate and engendered undue anxiety in the community. This is also a special problem of chemical and radiation incidents which can be minimized with adequate emergency planning.

Training and education
Medical staff and other health care professionals at the hospital and primary care level are likely to be unfamiliar with working in disasters. Training exercises involving the health sector and the emergency services are a necessary part of emergency preparedness. Table-top exercises are invaluable and should be made as realistic as possible, since large-scale physical exercises are likely to be held very infrequently because of their high cost.

Post-impact recovery
This phase is the returning of the affected area to its pre-disaster state. Pre-planning should include post-emergency social, economic and psychological care and rehabilitation of the environment. For chemical incidents the latter also includes environmental assessments for contaminants of water and crops, and remedial actions, if needed, such as decontamination of soils and buildings and restoration of potable water supplies.

Conclusion
Relatively little international effort has been put into disaster preparedness compared to relief measures in the past; however, although investment in disaster protection is costly, there is now a large body of scientific and technical knowledge available which if applied correctly would make a substantial difference to the health and economic impacts of disasters in all countries.

POST-DISASTER ACTIVITIES

*Benedetto Terracini
and Ursula Ackermann-Liebrich*

Industrial accidents may affect groups of workers exposed in the workplace as well as the population living around the plant where the accident takes place. When pollution caused by accident occurs, the size of the affected population is likely to be orders of magnitude greater than the workforce, posing complex logistic problems. The present article focuses on these problems, and applies to agricultural accidents as well.

Reasons for quantifying health effects of an accident include:

• the need to ensure that all exposed persons have received medical attention (regardless of whether or not treatment was actually needed by each of them). Medical attention may consist of the search for and alleviation of clinically recognizable adverse consequences (if any) as well as implementation of means for preventing possible delayed effects and complications. This is obligatory when an accident occurs within a plant; then all the people working there will be known and full follow-up is feasible

- the need to identify persons deserving of compensation as victims of the accident. This implies that individuals must be characterized as to the severity of disease and the credibility of a causal association between their condition and the disaster.
- the acquisition of new knowledge on disease pathogenesis in humans
- the scientific interest of unravelling mechanisms of toxicity in humans, including those aspects which may help in reassessing, for a given exposure, doses considered to be "safe" in humans.

Characterization of Accidents in Relation to Health Consequences

Environmental accidents include a broad range of events occurring under the most diverse of circumstances. They may be first noticed or suspected because of environmental changes or because of the occurrence of disease. In both situations, the evidence (or suggestion) that "something may have gone wrong" may appear suddenly (e.g., the fire in the Sandoz storehouse in Schweizerhalle, Switzerland, in 1986; the epidemic of the condition later labelled as "toxic oil syndrome" (TOS) in Spain in 1981) or insidiously (e.g., excesses of mesothelioma following environmental—non-occupational—exposure to asbestos in Wittenoom, Australia). In all circumstances, at any given moment, uncertainty and ignorance surround both key questions: "Which health consequences have occurred so far?" and "What can be predicted to occur?"

In assessing the impact of an accident on human health, three types of determinants may interact:

1. the agent(s) being released, its hazardous properties and the risk created by its release
2. the individual disaster experience
3. the response measures (Bertazzi 1991).

The nature and quantity of the release might be difficult to determine, as well as the ability of the material to enter into the different compartments of the human environment, such as the food chain and water supply. Twenty years after the accident, the amount of 2,3,7,8-TCDD released in Seveso on July 10, 1976, remains a matter of dispute. In addition, with the limited knowledge about the toxicity of this compound, in the early days after the accident, any prediction of risk was necessarily questionable.

Individual disaster experience consists of fear, anxiety and distress (Ursano, McCaughey and Fullerton 1994) consequent to the accident, irrespective of the nature of the hazard and of the actual risk. This aspect covers both conscious—not necessarily justified—behavioural changes (e.g., the marked decrease in birth rates in many Western European Countries in 1987, following the Chernobyl accident) and psychogenic conditions (e.g., symptoms of distress in school children and Israeli soldiers following the escape of hydrogen sulphide from a faulty latrine in a school on the West Bank of Jordan in 1981). Attitudes towards the accident are also influenced by subjective factors: in Love Canal, for instance, young parents with little experience of contact with chemicals in the workplace were more prone to evacuate the area than were older people with grown-up children.

Finally, an accident may have an indirect impact on the health of those exposed, either creating additional hazards (e.g., distress associated with evacuation) or, paradoxically, leading to circumstances with some potential for benefit (such as people who stop smoking tobacco as a consequence of contact with the milieu of health workers).

Measuring the Impact of an Accident

There is no doubt that each accident requires an assessment of its measurable or potential consequences on the exposed human population (and animals, domestic and/or wild), and periodic updates of such assessment may be required. In fact, many factors influence the detail, extent and nature of the data which can be collected for such an assessment. The amount of available resources is critical. Accidents of the same severity may be granted different levels of attention in different countries, in relation to the ability to divert resources from other health and social issues. International cooperation may partly mitigate this discrepancy: in fact, it is limited to episodes which are particularly dramatic and/or present unusual scientific interest.

The overall impact of an accident upon health ranges from negligible to severe. Severity depends on the nature of the conditions which are produced by the accident (which may include death), on the size of the exposed population, and on the proportion that develop disease. Negligible effects are more difficult to demonstrate epidemiologically.

Sources of data to be used for evaluating health consequences of an accident include in the first place current statistics which exist already (attention to their potential use should always precede any suggestion of creating new population databases). Additional information can be derived from analytical, hypothesis-centred epidemiological studies for the purpose of which current statistics may or may not be useful. If in an occupational setting no health surveillance of the workers is present, the accident can provide the opportunity to establish a surveillance system which will eventually help to protect workers from other potential health hazards.

For the purposes of clinical surveillance (short or long term) and/or provision of compensation, the exhaustive enumeration of the exposed persons is a *sine qua non*. This is relatively simple in the case of intra-factory accidents. When the affected population can be defined by the place where they live, the list of residents in administrative municipalities (or smaller units, when available) provides a reasonable approach. The construction of a roster may be more problematic under other circumstances, particularly when the need is for a list of people showing symptoms possibly attributable to the accident. In the TOS episode in Spain, the roster of persons to be included in the long-term clinical follow-up was derived from the list of the 20,000 persons applying for financial compensation, subsequently corrected through a revision of the clinical records. Given the publicity of the episode, it is believed that this roster is reasonably complete.

A second requirement is that activities aiming at the measure of the impact of an accident be rational, clear-cut and easy to explain to the affected population. Latency may range between days and years. If some conditions are met, the nature of disease and probability of occurrence can be hypothesized a priori with a precision sufficient for the adequate design of a clinical surveillance programme and ad hoc studies aiming at one or more of the goals mentioned at the beginning of this article. These conditions include the rapid identification of the agent released by the accident, availability of adequate knowledge on its short- and long-term hazardous properties, a quantification of the release, and some information on inter-individual variation in susceptibility to the agent's effects. In fact, these conditions are rarely met; a consequence of the underlying uncertainty and ignorance is that the pressure of public opinion and the media for prevention or definite medical intervention of doubtful usefulness is more difficult to resist.

Finally, as soon as possible after the occurrence of an accident has been established, a multidisciplinary team (including clinicians, chemists, industrial hygienists, epidemiologists, human and experimental toxicologists) needs to be established, which will be responsible to the political authority and the public. In the selection of experts, it must be borne in mind that the range of chemicals and technology which may underlie an accident is very large, so that different types of toxicity involving a variety of biochemical and physiological systems may result.

Measuring the Impact of Accidents through Current Statistics

Current health status indicators (such as mortality, natality, hospital admissions, sickness absence from work and physician visits) have the potential to provide early insight on the consequences of an accident, provided they are stratifiable for the affected region, which often will not be possible because affected areas can be small and not necessarily overlapping with administrative units. Statistical associations between the accident and an excess of early events (occurring within days or weeks) detected through existing health status indicators are likely to be causal, but do not necessarily reflect toxicity (e.g., an excess of physician visits may be caused by fear rather than by actual occurrence of disease). As always, care must be exercised when interpreting any change in health status indicators.

Although not all accidents produce death, mortality is an easily quantifiable endpoint, either by direct count (e.g., Bhopal) or through comparisons between observed and expected number of events (e.g., acute episodes of air pollution in urban areas). Ascertaining that an accident has not been associated with an early excess of mortality may help in assessing the severity of its impact and in addressing attention to non-lethal consequences. Further, the statistics needed in order to calculate expected numbers of deaths are available in most countries and allow for estimates in areas as small as those which are usually affected by an accident. Assessing mortality from specific conditions is more problematic, because of possible bias in certifying causes of death by health officers who are aware of the diseases expected to increase after the accident (diagnostic suspicion bias).

From the foregoing, the interpretation of health status indicators based on existing data sources requires a careful design of ad hoc analyses, including a detailed consideration of possible confounding factors.

On occasions, early after an accident, the question is posed whether the creation of a conventional population-based cancer registry or a registry of malformations is warranted. For these specific conditions, such registries may provide more reliable information than other current statistics (such as mortality or hospital admissions), particularly if newly created registries are run according to internationally acceptable standards. Nevertheless, their implementation requires the diversion of resources. In addition, if a population-based registry of malformations is established *de novo* after an accident, probably within nine months it will hardly be capable of producing data comparable to those produced by other registries and a series of inferential problems (particularly statistical error of the second type) will ensue. In the end, the decision largely relies on the evidence of carcinogenicity, embryotoxicity or teratogenicity of the hazard(s) which have been released, and on possible alternative uses of the available resources.

Ad Hoc Epidemiological Studies

Even in areas covered by the most accurate systems for monitoring the reasons for patients' contacts with physicians and/or hospital admissions, indicators from these areas will not provide all the information needed in order to assess the health impact of an accident and the adequacy of the medical response to it. There are specific conditions or markers of individual response which either do not require contact with the medical establishment or do not correspond to the disease classifications conventionally used in

current statistics (so that their occurrence would hardly be identifiable). There may be the need for counting as "victims" of the accident, subjects whose conditions are borderline between occurrence and non-occurrence of disease. It is often necessary to investigate (and evaluate the efficacy of) the range of therapeutical protocols which are used. The problems noted here are but a sampling and do not cover all those which might create the need for an ad hoc investigation. In any case, procedures should be established in order to receive additional complaints.

Investigations differ from the provision of care in that they are not directly related to the individual's interest as a victim of the accident. An ad hoc investigation should be shaped in order to fulfil its purposes—to provide reliable information and/or demonstrate or disprove a hypothesis. Sampling may be reasonable for research purposes (if accepted by the affected population), but not in the provision of medical care. For instance, in the case of a spill of an agent suspected of damaging bone marrow, there are two totally different scenarios in order to respond to each of the two questions: (1) whether the chemical actually induces leukopenia, and (2) whether all exposed persons have been exhaustively screened for leukopenia. In an occupational setting both questions can be pursued. In a population, the decision also will depend on the possibilities for constructive intervention to treat those affected.

In principle, there is a need to have sufficient epidemiological skill locally to contribute to the decision on whether ad hoc studies ought to be carried out, to design them and to supervise their conduct. However, health authorities, media and/or the population may not consider the epidemiologists of the affected area to be neutral; thus, help from outside may be needed, even at a very early stage. The same epidemiologists should contribute to the interpretation of descriptive data based on the currently available statistics, and to the development of causal hypotheses when needed. If epidemiologists are not available locally, collaboration with other institutions (usually, National Institutes of Health, or WHO) is necessary. Episodes which are unravelled because of the lack of epidemiological skill are regrettable.

If an epidemiological study is believed to be necessary, however, attention should be addressed to some preliminary questions: To what use will predictable results be put? Might the desire for a more refined inference resulting from the planned study unduly delay clean-up procedures or other preventive measures? Must the proposed research programme first be fully documented and evaluated by the multidisciplinary scientific team (and perhaps by other epidemiologists)? Will there be adequate provision of details to the persons to be studied to ensure their fully informed, prior and voluntary consent? If a health effect is found, what treatment is available and how will it be delivered?

Finally, conventional prospective cohort mortality studies ought to be implemented when the accident has been severe and there are reasons to fear later consequences. Feasibility of these studies differs between countries. In Europe, they range between the possibility of nominal "flagging" of persons (e.g., rural populations in Shetland, UK, following the Braer Oil Spill) and the need for systematic contacts with the victims' families in order to identify dying persons (e.g., TOS in Spain).

Screening for Prevalent Conditions

Offering affected people medical attention is a natural reaction to an accident which may have caused them harm. The attempt to identify all those in the exposed population who exhibit conditions related to the accident (and give them medical care if needed) corresponds to the conventional concept of *screening*. Basic principles, potentialities and limitations common to any screening programme (regardless of the population to which it is addressed, the condition to be identified and the tool used as a diagnostic test) are as valid after an environmental accident as in any other circumstance (Morrison 1985).

Estimating participation and understanding reasons for non-response are just as crucial as measuring sensitivity, specificity and predictive value of the diagnostic test(s), designing a protocol for subsequent diagnostic procedures (when needed) and the administration of therapy (if required). If these principles are neglected, short- and/or long-term screening programmes may produce more harm than benefit. Unnecessary medical examinations or laboratory analyses are a waste of resources and a diversion from providing necessary care to the population as a whole. Procedures for ensuring a high level of compliance have to be carefully planned and evaluated.

Emotional reactions and uncertainties surrounding environmental accidents may further complicate things: physicians tend to loose specificity when diagnosing borderline conditions, and some "victims" may consider themselves entitled to receive medical treatment regardless of whether or not it is actually needed or even useful. In spite of the chaos which often follows an environmental accident, some *sine qua non* for any screening programme should be borne in mind:

1. Procedures should be laid down in a written protocol (including second level diagnostic tests and therapy to be provided to those who are found to be affected or sick).
2. One person should be identified as responsible for the programme.
3. There should be a preliminary estimate of specificity and sensitivity of the diagnostic test.
4. There should be coordination between clinicians participating in the programme.
5. Participation rates should be quantified and reviewed at regular intervals.

Some a priori estimates of efficacy of the whole programme would also help in deciding whether or not the programme is worth implementing (e.g., no programme for anticipating the diagnosis of a lung cancer should be encouraged). Also, a procedure should be established in order to recognize additional complaints.

At any stage, screening procedures may have a value of a different type—to estimate the prevalence of conditions, as a basis for an assessment of the consequences of the accident. A major source of bias in these estimates (which becomes more severe with time) is the representativeness of the exposed persons submitting themselves to the diagnostic procedures. Another problem is the identification of adequate control groups for comparing the prevalence estimates which are obtained. Controls drawn from the population may suffer from as much selection bias as the exposed person's sample. Nevertheless, under some circumstances, prevalence studies are of the utmost importance (particularly when the natural history of the disease is not known, such as in TOS), and control groups external to the study, including those assembled elsewhere for other purposes, may be used when the problem is important and/or serious.

Use of Biological Materials for Epidemiological Purposes

For descriptive purposes, the collection of biological materials (urine, blood, tissues) from members of the exposed population can provide markers of internal dose, which by definition are more precise than (but do not replace totally) those obtainable through estimates of the concentration of the pollutant in the relevant compartments of the environment and/or through individual questionnaires. Any evaluation ought to take into account possible bias ensuing from the lack of representativeness of those

members of the community from whom the biological samples were obtained.

Storing biological samples may prove useful, at a later stage, for the purpose of ad hoc epidemiological studies requiring estimates of internal dose (or early effects) at the individual level. Collecting (and properly preserving) the biological samples early after the accident is crucial, and this practice should be encouraged even in the absence of precise hypotheses for their use. The informed consent process must ensure that the patient understands that his or her biological material is to be stored for use in tests hitherto undefined. Here it is helpful to exclude the use of such specimens from certain tests (e.g., identification of personality disorders) to better protect the patient.

Conclusions

The rationale for medical intervention and epidemiological studies in the population affected by an accident ranges between two extremes—*assessing* the impact of agents which are proved to be potential hazards and to which the affected population is (or has been) definitely exposed, and *exploring* the possible effects of agents hypothesized to be potentially hazardous and suspected to be present in the area. Differences between experts (and between people in general) in their perception of the relevance of a problem are inherent to humanity. What matters is that any decision has a recorded rationale and a transparent plan of action, and is supported by the affected community.

WEATHER-RELATED PROBLEMS

Jean French

It was long accepted that weather-related problems were a natural phenomenon and death and injury from such events were inevitable (see table 39.17). It is only in the past two decades that we have begun to look at factors contributing to weather-related death and injury as a means of prevention. Because of the short duration of study in this area, the data are limited, particularly as they pertain to the number and circumstances of weather-related deaths and injuries among workers. The following is an overview of the findings thus far.

Floods, Tidal Waves

Definitions, sources and occurrences

Flooding results from a variety of causes. Within a given climatic region, tremendous variations of flooding occur because of fluctuations within the hydrological cycle and other natural and synthetic conditions (Chagnon, Schict and Semorin 1983). The US National Weather Service has defined *flash floods* as those that follow within a few hours of heavy or excessive rain, a dam or levee failure or a sudden release of water impounded by an ice or log jam. Although most flash floods are the result of intense local thunderstorm activity, some occur in conjunction with tropical cyclones. Forerunners to flash floods usually involve atmospheric conditions that influence the continuation and intensity of rainfall. Other factors that contribute to flash floods include steepness of slopes (mountain terrain), absence of vegetation, lack of infiltration capability of the soil, floating debris and ice jams, rapid snow melt, dam and levee failures, rupture of a glacial lake, and volcanic disturbances (Marrero 1979). *River flooding* can be influenced by factors which cause flash flooding, but more insidious flooding may be caused by stream channel characteristics, character of soil and subsoil, and degree of synthetic modification along its path (Chagnon, Schict and Semorin 1983; Marrero 1979). *Coastal flood-*

39. DISASTERS, NATURAL AND TECHNOLOGICAL

Table 39.17 • Weather-related occupational risks.

Weather event	Type of worker	Biochemical agents	Traumatic injuries	Drowning	Burns/heatstroke	Vehicle accidents	Mental stress
Floods Hurricanes	Police, fire, emergency personnel	*	*	*			
	Transport		*	**			*
	Underground			*			*
	Linemen		*		*		*
	Clean-up	***					*
Tornadoes	Police, fire, emergency personnel	*	*				
	Transportation		***			*	*
	Cleanup	**	*				
Light forest fires	Fire-fighters	**	**		**	***	*

*degree of risk.

ing can result from storm surge, which is the result of a tropical storm or cyclone, or ocean waters driven inland by wind-generated storms. The most devastating type of coastal flooding is the *tsunami*, or tidal wave, which is generated by submarine earthquakes or certain volcanic eruptions. Most recorded tsunamis have occurred in the Pacific and Pacific coast regions. The islands of Hawaii are particularly prone to tsunami damage because of their location in the mid-Pacific (Chagnon, Schict and Semorin 1983; Whitlow 1979).

Factors influencing morbidity and mortality

It has been estimated that floods account for 40% of all the world's disasters, and they do the greatest amount of damage. The most lethal flood in recorded history struck the Yellow River in 1887, when the river overflowed 70-foot-high levees, destroying 11 cities and 300 villages. An estimated 900,000 people were killed. Several hundred thousand may have died in China's Shantung Province in 1969 when storm surges pushed flood tides up the Yellow River Valley. A sudden flood in January 1967 in Rio de Janeiro killed 1,500 people. In 1974 heavy rains flooded Bangladesh and caused 2,500 deaths. In 1963 heavy rains caused an enormous landslide that fell into the lake behind the Vaiont Dam in Northern Italy, sending 100 million tons of water over the dam and causing 2,075 deaths (Frazier 1979). In 1985 an estimated 7 to 15 inches of rain fell in a ten-hour period in Puerto Rico, killing 180 people (French and Holt 1989).

River flooding has been curtailed by engineering controls and increased forestation of watersheds (Frazier 1979). However, flash floods have increased in recent years, and are the number one weather-related killer in the United States. The increased toll from flash floods is attributed to increased and more urbanized populations on sites that are ready targets for flash floods (Mogil, Monro and Groper 1978). Fast-flowing water accompanied by such debris as boulders and fallen trees account for the primary flood-related morbidity and mortality. In the United States studies have shown a high proportion of car-related drownings in floods, due to people driving into low-lying areas or across a flooded bridge. Their cars may stall in high water or be blocked by debris, trapping them in their cars while high levels of fast-flowing water descend upon them (French et al. 1983). Follow-up studies of flood victims show a consistent pattern of psychological problems up to five years after the flood (Melick 1976; Logue 1972). Other studies have shown a significant increase in the incidence of hypertension, cardiovascular disease, lymphoma and leukaemia in flood victims, which some investigators feel are stress related (Logue and Hansen 1980; Janerich et al. 1981; Greene 1954). There is a potential for increased exposure to biological and chemical agents when floods cause disruption of water purification and sewage-disposal systems, rupture of underground storage tanks, overflowing of toxic waste sites, enhancement of vector-breeding conditions and dislodgement of chemicals stored above ground (French and Holt 1989).

Although, in general, workers are exposed to the same flood-related risks as the general population, some occupational groups are at higher risk. Clean-up workers are at high risk of exposure to biological and chemical agents following floods. Underground workers, particularly those in confined places, may be trapped during flash floods. Truck drivers and other transportation workers are at high risk from vehicle-related flood mortality. As in other weather-related disasters, fire-fighters, police and emergency medical personnel are also at high risk.

Prevention and control measures and research needs

Prevention of death and injury from floods can be accomplished by identifying flood-prone areas, making the public aware of these areas and advising them on appropriate prevention actions, conducting dam inspections and issuing dam safety certification, identifying meteorological conditions that will contribute to heavy precipitation and runoff, and issuing early warnings of floods for a specific geographic area within a specific time frame. Morbidity and mortality from secondary exposures can be prevented by assuring that water and food supplies are safe to consume and are not contaminated with biological and chemical agents, and by instituting safe human waste disposal practices. Soil surrounding toxic waste sites and storage lagoons should be inspected to determine if there has been contamination from overflowing storage areas (French and Holt 1989). Although mass vaccination programmes are counterproductive, clean-up and sanitation workers should be properly immunized and instructed in appropriate hygienic practices.

There is a need to improve technology so that early warnings for flash floods can be more specific in terms of time and place. Conditions should be assessed to determine whether evacuation should be by car or on foot. Following a flood a cohort of workers engaged in flood-related activities should be studied to assess the risk of adverse physical and mental health effects.

Hurricanes, Cyclones, Tropical Storms

Definitions, sources and occurrences

A *hurricane* is defined as a rotating wind system that whirls counterclockwise in the northern hemisphere, forms over tropical water, and has sustained wind speeds of at least 74 miles per hour (118.4 km/h). This whirling accumulation of energy is formed when circumstances involving heat and pressure nourish and nudge the winds over a large area of ocean to wrap themselves around an atmospheric low-pressure zone. A *typhoon* is comparable to a hurricane except that it forms over Pacific waters. *Tropical cyclone* is the term for all wind circulations rotating around an atmospheric low over tropical waters. A *tropical storm* is defined as a cyclone with winds from 39 to 73 mph (62.4 to 117.8 km/h), and a *tropical depression* is a cyclone with winds less than 39 mph (62.4 km/h).

It is presently thought that many tropical cyclones originate over Africa, in the region just south of the Sahara. They start as an instability in a narrow east to west jet stream that forms in that area between June and December, as a result of the great temperature contrast between the hot desert and the cooler, more humid region to the south. Studies show that the disturbances generated over Africa have long lifetimes, and many of them cross the Atlantic (Herbert and Taylor 1979). In the 20th century an average of ten tropical cyclones each year whirl out across the Atlantic; six of these become hurricanes. As the hurricane (or typhoon) reaches its peak intensity, air currents formed by the Bermuda or Pacific high-pressure areas shift its course northward. Here the ocean waters are cooler. There is less evaporation, less water vapour and energy to feed the storm. If the storm hits land, the supply of water vapour is cut off entirely. As the hurricane or typhoon continues to move north, its winds begin to diminish. Topographical features such as mountains may also contribute to the breakup of the storm. The geographic areas at greatest risk for hurricanes are the Caribbean, Mexico, and the eastern seaboard and Gulf Coast states of the United States. A typical Pacific typhoon forms in the warm tropical waters east of the Philippines. It may move westward and strike the Chinese mainland or veer to the north and approach Japan. The storm's path is determined as it moves around the western edge of the Pacific high-pressure system (*Understanding Science and Nature: Weather and Climate* 1992).

The destructive power of a hurricane (typhoon) is determined by the way storm surge, wind and other factors are combined. Forecasters have developed a five-category disaster potential scale to make the predicted hazards of approaching hurricanes clearer. Category 1 is a minimum hurricane, category 5 a maximum hurricane. In the period 1900-1982, 136 hurricanes struck the United States directly; 55 of these were of at least category 3 intensity. Florida felt the effects of both the highest number and the most intense of these storms, with Texas, Louisiana and North Carolina following in descending order (Herbert and Taylor 1979).

Factors influencing morbidity and mortality

Although winds do much damage to property, the wind is not the biggest killer in a hurricane. Most victims die from drowning. The flooding that accompanies a hurricane may come from the intense rain or from the storm surges. The US National Weather Service estimates that storm surges cause nine of every ten hurricane-associated fatalities (Herbert and Taylor 1979). The occupational groups most heavily impacted by hurricanes (typhoons) are those related to boating and shipping (which would be affected by the unusually rough seas and high winds); utility line workers who are called into service to repair damaged lines, often while the storm is still raging; fire-fighters and police officers, who are involved in evacuations and protecting the property of evacuees; and emergency medical personnel. Other occupational groups are discussed in the section on floods.

Prevention and control, research needs

The incidence of deaths and injuries associated with hurricanes (typhoons) has dropped dramatically in the past twenty years in those areas where sophisticated advanced warning systems have been put into effect. The principal steps to follow for preventing death and injury are: to identify meteorological precursors of these storms and track their course and potential development into hurricanes, to issue early warnings to provide for timely evacuation when indicated, to enforce stringent land use management practices and building codes in high-risk areas, and to develop emergency contingency plans in high-risk areas to provide for an orderly evacuation and adequate shelter capacity for evacuees.

Because the meteorological factors contributing to hurricanes have been well studied, a good deal of information is available. More information is needed on the variable pattern of incidence and intensity of hurricanes over time. The effectiveness of existing contingency plans should be assessed following each hurricane, and it should be determined if buildings protected from wind speed are also protected from storm surges.

Tornadoes

Formation and patterns of occurrence

Tornadoes are formed when layers of air of different temperature, density and windflow combine to produce powerful updrafts forming huge cumulonimbus clouds which are transformed into rotating tight spirals when strong cross winds blow through the cumulonimbus cloud. This vortex draws even more warm air into the cloud, which makes the air spin faster until a funnel cloud packing explosive force drops out of the cloud (*Understanding Science and Nature: Weather and Climate* 1992). The average tornado has a track approximately 2 miles long and 50 yards wide, affecting about 0.06 square miles and with wind speeds as high as 300 mph. Tornadoes occur in those areas where warm and cold fronts are apt to collide, causing unstable conditions. Although the probability that a tornado will strike any specific location is extremely small (probability 0.0363), some areas, such as the Midwest states in the United States, are particularly vulnerable.

Factors influencing morbidity and mortality

Studies have shown that people in mobile homes and in lightweight cars when tornadoes strike are at particularly high risk. In the Wichita Falls, Texas, Tornado Study, occupants of mobile homes were 40 times more likely to sustain a serious or fatal injury than those in permanent dwellings, and occupants of automobiles were at approximately five times greater risk (Glass, Craven and Bregman 1980). The leading cause of death are craniocerebral trauma, followed by crushing wounds of the head and trunk. Fractures are the most frequent form of non-fatal injury (Mandlebaum, Nahrwold and Boyer 1966; High et al. 1956). Those workers who spend a major part of their working time in lightweight automobiles, or whose offices are in mobile homes, would be at high risk. Other factors relating to clean-up operators discussed in the flood section would apply here.

Prevention and control

The issuing of appropriate warnings, and the need for the population to take appropriate action on the basis of those warnings, are the most important factors in preventing tornado-related death and injury. In the United States, the National Weather Service has acquired sophisticated instrumentation, such as Doppler radar, which permits them to identify conditions conducive to the formation of a tornado and to issue warnings. A tornado *watch* means that conditions are conducive to tornado formation in a given area, and a tornado *warning* means that a tornado has been sighted in a given area and those residing in that area should take appropriate shelter, which entails going to the basement if one exists, going to an inside room or closet, or if outside, going to a ditch or gully.

Research is needed to assess whether warnings are effectively disseminated and the extent to which people heed those warnings. It should also be determined whether the prescribed shelter areas really provide adequate protection from death and injury. Information should be gathered on the number of deaths and injuries to tornado workers.

Lightning and Forest Fires

Definitions, sources and occurrences

When a cumulonimbus cloud grows into a thunderstorm, different sections of the cloud accumulate positive and negative electric charges. When the charges have built up, the negative charges flow toward the positive charges in a lightning flash that travels within the cloud or between the cloud and the ground. Most lightning travels from cloud to cloud, but 20% travels from cloud to ground. A lightning flash between a cloud and the ground can be either positive or negative. Positive lightning is more powerful and is more likely to start forest fires. A lightning strike will not start a fire unless it meets easily ignitable fuel like pine needles, grass and pitch. If the fire hits decaying wood, it can burn unnoticed for a long period of time. Lightning ignites fires more often when it touches the ground and the rain within the thunder cloud evaporates before it reaches the ground. This is called dry lightning (Fuller 1991). It is estimated that in dry, rural areas such as Australia and the western United States, 60% of forest fires are caused by lightning.

Factors causing morbidity and mortality

Most of the fire-fighters who die in a fire die in truck or helicopter accidents or from being hit by falling snags, rather than from the fire itself. However, fighting fire can cause heat stroke, heat exhaustion and dehydration. Heat stroke, caused by the body temperature rising to over 39.4°C, can cause death or brain damage. Carbon monoxide is also a threat, particularly in smouldering fires. In one test, researchers found that the blood of 62 of 293 fire-fighters had carboxyhaemoglobin levels above the maximum allowable level of 5% after eight hours on the fire line (Fuller 1991).

Prevention, control and research needs

Because of the danger and the mental and physical stress associated with fire-fighting, crews should not work for more than 21 days, and must have one day off for every 7 days worked within that time. In addition to wearing appropriate protective gear, fire-fighters must learn safety factors such as planning safety routes, keeping in communication, watching for hazards, keeping track of the weather, making sure of directions and acting before a situation becomes critical. The standard fire-fighting orders emphasize knowing what the fire is doing, posting lookouts and giving clear, understandable instructions (Fuller 1991).

Factors relating to prevention of lightning forest fires include limiting fuels such as dry underbrush or fire-susceptible trees like eucalyptus, preventing building in fire-prone areas and early detection of forest fires. Early detection has been enhanced by the development of new technology such as an infrared system which is mounted on helicopters to check whether lightning strikes reported from aerial lookout and detection systems have actually started fires and to map hot spots for ground crews and helicopter drops (Fuller 1991).

More information is needed on the number and circumstances of deaths and injuries associated with lightning-related forest fires.

AVALANCHES: HAZARDS AND PROTECTIVE MEASURES

Gustav Poinstingl

Ever since people began to settle in mountainous regions, they have been exposed to the specific hazards associated with mountain living. Among the most treacherous hazards are avalanches and landslides, which have taken their toll of victims even up to the present day.

When the mountains are covered with several feet of snow in winter, under certain conditions, a mass of snow lying like a thick blanket on the steep slopes or mountain tops can become detached from the ground underneath and slide downhill under its own weight. This can result in huge quantities of snow hurtling down the most direct route and settling into the valleys below. The kinetic energy thus released produces dangerous avalanches, which sweep away, crush or bury everything in their path.

Avalanches can be divided into two categories according to the type and condition of the snow involved: dry snow or "dust" avalanches, and wet snow or "ground" avalanches. The former are dangerous because of the shock waves they set off, and the latter because of their sheer volume, due to the added moisture in the wet snow, flattening everything as the avalanche rolls downhill, often at high speeds, and sometimes carrying away sections of the subsoil.

Particularly dangerous situations can arise when the snow on large, exposed slopes on the windward side of the mountain is compacted by the wind. Then it often forms a cover, held together only on the surface, like a curtain suspended from above, and resting on a base that can produce the effect of ball-bearings. If a "cut" is made in such a cover (e.g., if a skier leaves a track across the slope), or if for any reason, this very thin cover is torn apart (e.g., by its own weight), then the whole expanse of snow can slide downhill like a board, usually developing into an avalanche as it progresses.

In the interior of the avalanche, enormous pressure can build up, which can carry off, smash or crush locomotives or entire buildings as though they were toys. That human beings have very little chance of surviving in such an inferno is obvious, bearing in mind that anyone who is not crushed to death is likely to die from suffocation or exposure. It is not surprising, therefore, in cases where people have been buried in avalanches, that, even if they are found immediately, about 20% of them are already dead.

The topography and vegetation of the area will cause the masses of snow to follow set routes as they come down to the valley. People living in the region know this from observation and tradition, and therefore keep away from these danger zones in the winter.

In earlier times, the only way to escape such dangers was to avoid exposing oneself to them. Farmhouses and settlements were built in places where topographical conditions were such that avalanches could not occur, or which years of experience had shown to be far removed from any known avalanche paths. People even avoided the mountain areas altogether during the danger period.

Forests on the upper slopes also afford considerable protection against such natural disasters, as they support the masses of snow in the threatened areas and can curb, halt or divert avalanches that have already started, provided they have not built up too much momentum.

Nevertheless, the history of mountainous countries is punctuated by repeated disasters caused by avalanches, which have taken, and still take, a heavy toll of life and property. On the one hand, the speed and momentum of the avalanche is often underestimated. On the other hand, avalanches will sometimes follow paths which, on the basis of centuries of experience, have not previously been considered to be avalanche paths. Certain unfavourable weather conditions, in conjunction with a particular quality of snow and the state of the ground underneath (e.g., damaged vegetation or erosion or loosening of the soil as a result of heavy rains) produce circumstances that can lead to one of those "disasters of the century".

Whether an area is particularly exposed to the threat of an avalanche depends not only on prevailing weather conditions, but to an even greater extent on the stability of the snow cover, and on whether the area in question is situated in one of the usual avalanche paths or outlets. There are special maps showing areas where avalanches are known to have occurred or are likely to occur as a result of topographical features, especially the paths and outlets of frequently occurring avalanches. Building is prohibited in high-risk areas.

However, these precautionary measures are no longer sufficient today, as, despite the prohibition of building in particular areas, and all the information available on the dangers, increasing numbers of people are still attracted to picturesque mountain regions, causing more and more building even in areas known to be dangerous. In addition to this disregard or circumvention of building bans, one of the manifestations of the modern leisure society is that thousands of tourists go to the mountains for sport and recreation in winter, and to the very areas where avalanches are virtually pre-programmed. The ideal ski slope is steep, free of obstacles and should have a sufficiently thick carpet of snow—ideal conditions for the skier, but also for the snow to sweep down into the valley.

If, however, risks cannot be avoided or are to a certain extent consciously accepted as an unwelcome "side-effect" of the enjoyment gained from the sport, then it becomes necessary to develop ways and means of coping with these dangers in another manner.

To improve the chances of survival for people buried in avalanches, it is essential to provide well-organized rescue services, emergency telephones near the localities at risk and up-to-date information for the authorities and for tourists on the prevailing situation in dangerous areas. Early warning systems and excellent organization of rescue services with the best possible equipment can considerably increase chances of survival for people buried in avalanches, as well as reducing the extent of the damage.

Protective Measures

Various methods of protection against avalanches have been developed and tested all over the world, such as cross-frontier warning services, barriers and even the artificial triggering-off of avalanches by blasting or firing guns over the snow fields.

The stability of the snow cover is basically determined by the ratio of mechanical stress to density. This stability can vary considerably according to the type of stress (e.g., pressure, tension, shearing strain) within a geographical region (e.g., that part of the snow field where an avalanche might start). Contours, sunshine, winds, temperature and local disturbances in the structure of the snow cover—resulting from rocks, skiers, snowploughs or other vehicles—can also affect stability. Stability can therefore be reduced by deliberate local intervention such as blasting, or increased by the installation of additional supports or barriers. These measures, which can be of a permanent or temporary nature, are the two main methods used for protection against avalanches.

Permanent measures include effective and durable structures, support barriers in the areas where the avalanche might start, diversionary or braking barriers on the avalanche path, and blocking barriers in the avalanche outlet area. The object of temporary protective measures is to secure and stabilize the areas where an avalanche might start by deliberately triggering off smaller, limited avalanches to remove the dangerous quantities of snow in sections.

Support barriers artificially increase the stability of the snow cover in potential avalanche areas. Drift barriers, which prevent additional snow from being carried by the wind to the avalanche area, can reinforce the effect of support barriers. Diversionary and braking barriers on the avalanche path and blocking barriers in the avalanche outlet area and blocking barriers in the avalanche outlet area can divert or slow down the descending mass of snow and shorten the outflow distance in front of the area to be protected. Support barriers are structures fixed in the ground, more or less perpendicular to the slope, which put up sufficient resistance to the descending mass of snow. They must form supports reaching up to the surface of the snow. Support barriers are usually arranged in several rows and must cover all parts of the terrain from which avalanches could, under various possible weather conditions, threaten the locality to be protected. Years of observation and snow measurement in the area are required in order to establish correct positioning, structure and dimensions. The barriers must have a certain permeability to let minor avalanches and surface landslides flow through a number of barrier rows without getting larger or causing damage. If permeability is not sufficient, there is the danger that the snow will pile up behind the barriers, and subsequent avalanches will slide over them unimpeded, carrying further masses of snow with them.

Temporary measures, unlike the barriers, can also make it possible to reduce the danger for a certain length of time. These measures are based on the idea of setting off avalanches by artificial means. The threatening masses of snow are removed from the potential avalanche area by a number of small avalanches deliberately triggered off under supervision at selected, predetermined times. This considerably increases the stability of the snow cover remaining on the avalanche site, by at least reducing the risk of further and more dangerous avalanches for a limited period of time when the threat of avalanches is acute.

However, the size of these artificially produced avalanches cannot be determined in advance with any great degree of accuracy. Therefore, in order to keep the risk of accidents as low as possible, while these temporary measures are being carried out, the entire area to be affected by the artificial avalanche, from its starting point to where it finally comes to a halt, must be evacuated, closed off and checked beforehand.

The possible applications of the two methods of reducing hazards are fundamentally different. In general, it is better to use permanent methods to protect areas that are impossible or difficult to evacuate or close off, or where settlements or forests could be endangered even by controlled avalanches. On the other hand, roads, ski runs and ski slopes, which are easy to close off for short periods, are typical examples of areas in which temporary protective measures can be applied.

The various methods of artificially setting off avalanches involve a number of operations which also entail certain risks and, above all, require additional protective measures for persons assigned to carry out this work. The essential thing is to cause initial breaks by setting off artificial tremors (blasts). These will sufficiently reduce the stability of the snow cover to produce a snow-slip.

Blasting is especially suitable for releasing avalanches on steep slopes. It is usually possible to detach small sections of snow at intervals and thus avoid major avalanches, which take a long distance to run their course and can be extremely destructive. However, it is essential that the blasting operations be carried out at any time of day and in all types of weather, and this is not always possible. Methods of artificially producing avalanches by blasting differ considerably according to the means used to reach the area where the blasting is to take place.

Areas where avalanches are likely to start can be bombarded with grenades or rockets from safe positions, but this is successful (i.e., produces the avalanche) in only 20 to 30% of cases, as it is virtually impossible to determine and to hit the most effective target point with any accuracy from a distance, and also because the snow cover absorbs the shock of the explosion. Besides, shells may fail to go off.

Blasting with commercial explosives directly into the area where avalanches are likely to start is generally more successful. The most successful methods are those whereby the explosive is carried on stakes or cables over the part of the snow field where the avalanche is to start, and detonated at a height of 1.5 to 3 m above the snow cover.

Apart from the shelling of the slopes, three different methods have been developed for getting the explosive for the artificial production of avalanches to the actual location where the avalanche is to start:

- dynamite cableways
- blasting by hand
- throwing or lowering the explosive charge from helicopters.

The cableway is the surest and at the same time the safest method. With the help of a special small cableway, the dynamite cableway, the explosive charge is carried on a winding rope over the blasting location in the area of snow cover in which the avalanche is to start. With proper rope control and with the help of signals and markings, it is possible to steer accurately towards what are known from experience to be the most effective locations, and to get the charge to explode directly above them. The best results with respect to triggering off avalanches are achieved when the charge is detonated at the correct height above the snow cover. Since the cableway runs at a greater height above the ground, this requires the use of lowering devices. The explosive charge hangs from a string wound around the lowering device. The charge is lowered to the correct height above the site selected for the explosion with the help of a motor which unwinds the string. The use of dynamite cableways makes it possible to carry out the blasting from a safe position, even with poor visibility, by day or night.

Because of the good results obtained and the relatively low production costs, this method of setting off avalanches is used extensively in the entire Alpine region, a licence being required to operate dynamite cableways in most Alpine countries. In 1988, an intensive exchange of experience in this field took place between manufacturers, users and government representatives from the Austrian, Bavarian and Swiss Alpine areas. The information gained from this exchange of experience has been summarized in leaflets and legally binding regulations. These documents basically contain the technical safety standards for equipment and installa-

tions, and instructions on carrying out these operations safely. When preparing the explosive charge and operating the equipment, the blasting crew must be able to move as freely as possible around the various cableway controls and appliances. There must be safe and easily accessible footpaths to enable the crew to leave the site quickly in case of emergency. There must be safe access routes up to cableway supports and stations. In order to avoid failure to explode, two fuses and two detonators must be used for every charge.

In the case of blasting by hand, a second method for artificially producing avalanches, which was frequently done in earlier times, the dynamiter has to climb to the part of the snow cover where the avalanche is to be set off. The explosive charge can be placed on stakes planted in the snow, but more generally thrown down the slope towards a target point known from experience to be particularly effective. It is usually imperative for helpers to secure the dynamiter with a rope throughout the entire operation. Nonetheless, however carefully the blasting team proceeds, the danger of falling or of encountering avalanches on the way to the blasting site cannot be eliminated, as these activities often involve long ascents, sometimes under unfavourable weather conditions. Because of these hazards, this method, which is also subject to safety regulations, is rarely used today.

Using helicopters, a third method, has been practised for many years in the Alpine and other regions for operations to set off avalanches. In view of the dangerous risks for persons on board, this procedure is used in most Alpine and other mountainous countries only when it is urgently needed to avert an acute danger, when other procedures cannot be used or would involve even greater risk. In view of the special legal situation arising from the use of aircraft for such purposes and the risks involved, specific guidelines on setting off avalanches from helicopters have been drawn up in the Alpine countries, with the collaboration of the aviation authorities, the institutions and authorities responsible for occupational health and safety, and experts in the field. These guidelines deal not only with matters concerning the laws and regulations on explosives and safety provisions, but also are concerned with the physical and technical qualifications required of persons entrusted with such operations.

Avalanches are set off from helicopters either by lowering the charge on a rope and detonating it above the snow cover or by dropping a charge with its fuse already lit. The helicopters used must be specially adapted and licensed for such operations. With regard to safely carrying out the operations on board, there must be a strict division of responsibilities between the pilot and the blasting technician. The charge must be correctly prepared and the length of fuse selected according to whether it is to be lowered or dropped. In the interests of safety, two detonators and two fuses must be used, as in the case of the other methods. As a rule, the individual charges contain between 5 and 10 kg of explosive. Several charges can be lowered or dropped one after the other during one operational flight. The detonations must be visually observed in order to check that none has failed to go off.

All these blasting processes require the use of special explosives, effective in cold conditions and not sensitive to mechanical influences. Persons assigned to carry out these operations must be specially qualified and have the relevant experience.

Temporary and permanent protective measures against avalanches were originally designed for distinctly different areas of application. The costly permanent barriers were mainly constructed to protect villages and buildings especially against major avalanches. The temporary protective measures were originally limited almost exclusively to protecting roads, ski resorts and amenities which could be easily closed off. Nowadays, the tendency is to apply a combination of the two methods. To work out the most effective safety programme for a given area, it is necessary to analyse the prevailing situation in detail in order to determine the method that will provide the best possible protection.

TRANSPORTATION OF HAZARDOUS MATERIAL: CHEMICAL AND RADIOACTIVE

Donald M. Campbell

The industries and economies of nations depend, in part, on the large numbers of hazardous materials transported from the supplier to the user and, ultimately, to the waste disposer. Hazardous materials are transported by road, rail, water, air and pipeline. The vast majority reach their destination safely and without incident. The size and scope of the problem is illustrated by the petroleum industry. In the United Kingdom it distributes around 100 million tons of product every year by pipeline, rail, road and water. Approximately 10% of those employed by the UK chemical industry are involved in distribution (i.e., transport and warehousing).

A hazardous material can be defined as "a substance or material determined to be capable of posing an unreasonable risk to health, safety or property when transported". "Unreasonable risk" covers a broad spectrum of health, fire and environmental considerations. These substances include explosives, flammable gases, toxic gases, highly flammable liquids, flammable liquids, flammable solids, substances which become dangerous when wet, oxidizing substances and toxic liquids.

The risks arise directly from a release, ignition, and so on, of the dangerous substance(s) being transported. Road and rail threats are those which could give rise to major accidents "which could affect both employees and members of the public". These dangers can occur when materials are being loaded or unloaded or are en route. The population at risk is people living near the road or railway and the people in other road vehicles or trains who might become involved in a major accident. Areas of risk include temporary stopover points such as railway marshalling yards and lorry parking areas at motorway service points. Marine risks are those linked to ships entering or leaving ports and loading or discharging cargoes there; risks also arise from coastal and straits traffic and inland waterways.

The range of incidents which can occur in association with transport both while in transit and at fixed installations include chemical overheating, spillage, leakage, escape of vapour or gas, fire and explosion. Two of the principal events causing incidents are collision and fire. For road tankers other causes of release may be leaks from valves and from overfilling. Generally, for both road and rail vehicles, non-crash fires are much more frequent than crash fires. These transport-associated incidents can occur in rural, urban industrial and urban residential areas, and can involve both attended and unattended vehicles or trains. Only in the minority of cases is an accident the primary cause of the incident.

Emergency personnel should be aware of the possibility of human exposure and contamination by a hazardous substance in accidents involving railways and rail yards, roads and freight terminals, vessels (both ocean and inland based) and associated waterfront warehouses. Pipelines (both long distance and local utility distribution systems) can be a hazard if damage or leakage occurs, either in isolation or in association with other incidents. Transportation incidents are often more dangerous than those at fixed facilities. The materials involved may be unknown, warning signs may be obscured by rollover, smoke or debris, and knowledgeable operatives may be absent or casualties of the event. The number of people exposed depends on population density, both by day and night, on the proportions indoors and outdoors, and on the proportion who may be considered particularly vulnerable. In addition to the population who are normally in the area, personnel of the emergency services who attend the accident are also at risk. It is not uncommon in an incident involving transport of hazardous materials that a significant proportion of the casualties include such personnel.

In the 20-year period 1971 through 1990, about 15 people were killed on the roads of the United Kingdom because of dangerous chemicals, compared with the annual average of 5,000 persons every year in motor accidents. However, small quantities of dangerous goods can cause significant damage. International examples include:

- A plane crashed near Boston, USA, because of leaking nitric acid.
- Over 200 people were killed when a road tanker of propylene exploded over a campsite in Spain.
- In a rail accident involving 22 rail cars of chemicals in Mississauga, Canada, a tanker containing 90 tonnes of chlorine was ruptured and there was an explosion and a large fire. There were no fatalities, but 250,000 persons were evacuated.
- A rail collision alongside the motorway in Eccles, United Kingdom, resulted in three deaths and 68 injuries from the collision, but none from the resulting serious fire of the petroleum products being transported.
- A petrol tanker went out of control in Herrborn, Germany, burning down a large part of the town.
- In Peterborough, United Kingdom, a vehicle carrying explosives killed one person and almost destroyed an industrial centre.
- A petrol tanker exploded in Bangkok, Thailand, killing a large number of people.

The largest number of serious incidents have arisen with flammable gas or liquids (partially related to the volumes moved), with some incidents from toxic gases and toxic fumes (including products of combustion).

Studies in the UK have shown the following for road transport:

- frequency of accident while conveying hazardous materials: 0.12×10^{-6}/km
- frequency of release while conveying hazardous materials: 0.027×10^{-6}/km
- probability of a release given a traffic accident: 3.3%.

These events are not synonymous with hazardous material incidents involving vehicles, and may constitute only a small proportion of the latter. There is also the individuality of accidents involving the road transport of hazardous materials.

International agreements covering the transport of potentially hazardous materials include:

Regulations for the Safe Transport of Radioactive Material 1985 (as amended 1990): International Atomic Energy Agency, Vienna, 1990 (STI/PUB/866). Their purpose is to establish standards of safety which provide an acceptable level of control of the radiation hazards to persons, property and the environment that are associated with the transport of radioactive material.

The International Convention for the Safety of Life at Sea 1974 (SOLAS 74). This sets basic safety standards for all passenger and cargo ships, including ships carrying hazardous bulk cargoes.

The International Convention for the Prevention of Pollution from Ships 1973, as modified by the Protocol of 1978 (MARPOL 73/78). This provides regulations for the prevention of pollution by oil, noxious liquid substances in bulk, pollutants in packaged form or in freight containers, portable tanks or road and rail wagons, sewage and

Case Study: Transport of Hazardous Materials

An articulated road tanker carrying about 22,000 litres of toluene was travelling on a main arterial road which runs through Cleveland, UK. A car pulled into the path of the vehicle, and, as the truckdriver took evasive action, the tanker overturned. The manlids of all five compartments sprang open and toluene spilled on the roadway and ignited, resulting in a pool fire. Five cars travelling on the opposite carriageway were involved in the fire but all occupants escaped.

The fire brigade arrived within five minutes of being called. Burning liquid had entered the drains, and drain fires were evident approximately 400 m from the main incident. The County Emergency Plan was put into action, with social services and public transport put on alert in case evacuation was needed. Initial action by the fire brigade concentrated on extinguishing car fires and searching for occupants. The next task was identifying an adequate water supply. A member of the chemical company's safety team arrived to coordinate with the police and fire commanders. Also in attendance were staff from the ambulance service and the environmental health and water boards. Following consultation it was decided to permit the leaking toluene to burn rather than extinguish the fire and have the chemical emitting vapours. Police put out warnings over a four-hour period utilizing national and local radio, advising people to stay indoors and close their windows. The road was closed for eight hours. When the toluene fell below the level of the manlids, the fire was extinguished and the remaining toluene removed from the tanker. The incident was concluded approximately 13 hours after the accident.

Potential harm to humans existed from thermal radiation; to the environment, from air, soil and water pollution; and to the economy, from traffic disruption. The company plan which existed for such a transportation incident was activated within 15 minutes, with five persons in attendance. A county offsite plan existed and was instigated with a control centre coming into being involving police and the fire brigade. Concentration measurement but not dispersion prediction was performed. The fire brigade response involved over 50 persons and ten appliances, whose major actions were fire-fighting, washing down and spillage retention. Over 40 police officers were committed in traffic direction, warning the public, security and press control. The health service response encompassed two ambulances and two onsite medical staff. Local government reaction involved environmental health, transport and social services. The public were informed of the incident by loudspeakers, radio and word of mouth. The information focused on what to do, especially on sheltering indoors.

The outcome to humans was two admissions to a single hospital, a member of the public and a company employee, both injured in the crash. There was noticeable air pollution but only slight soil and water contamination. From an economic perspective there was major damage to the road and extensive traffic delays, but no loss of crops, livestock or production. Lessons learned included the value of rapid retrieval of information from the Chemdata system and the presence of a company technical expert enabling correct immediate action to be taken. The importance of joint press statements from responders was highlighted. Consideration needs to be given to the environmental impact of fire-fighting. If the fire had been fought in the initial stages, a considerable amount of contaminated liquid (firewater and toluene) potentially could have entered the drains, water supplies and soil.

garbage. Regulation requirements are amplified in the International Maritime Dangerous Goods Code.

There is a substantial body of international regulation of the transportation of harmful substances by air, rail, road and sea (converted into national legislation in many countries). Most are based on standards sponsored by the United Nations, and cover the principles of identification, labelling, prevention and mitigation. The United Nations Committee of Experts on the Transport of Dangerous Goods has produced *Recommendations on the Transport of Dangerous Goods*. They are addressed to governments and international organizations concerned with the regulation of the transport of dangerous goods. Among other aspects, the recommendations cover principles of classification and definitions of classes, listing of the content of dangerous goods, general packing requirements, testing procedures, making, labelling or placarding, and transport documents. These recommendations—the "Orange Book"—do not have the force of law, but form the basis of all the international regulations. These regulations are generated by various organizations:

- the International Civil Aviation Organization: *Technical Instructions for Safe Transport of Dangerous Goods by Air* (Tis)
- the International Maritime Organization: *International Maritime Dangerous Goods Code* (IMDG Code)
- the European Economic Community: *The European Agreement Concerning the International Carriage of Dangerous Goods by Road* (ADR)
- the Office of International Rail Transport: *Regulations Concerning the International Carriage of Dangerous Goods by Rail* (RID).

The preparation of major emergency plans to deal with and mitigate the effects of a major accident involving dangerous substances is as much needed in the transportation field as for fixed installations. The planning task is made more difficult in that the location of an incident will not be known in advance, thus requiring flexible planning. The substances involved in a transport accident cannot be foreseen. Because of the nature of the incident a number of products may be mixed together at the scene, causing considerable problems to the emergency services. The incident may occur in an area which is highly urbanized, remote and rural, heavily industrialized, or commercialized. An added factor is the transient population who may be unknowingly involved in an event because the accident has caused a backlog of vehicles either on the public highway or where passenger trains are stopped in response to a rail incident.

There is therefore a necessity for the development of local and national plans to respond to such events. These must be simple, flexible and easily understood. As major transport accidents can occur in a multiplicity of locations the plan must be appropriate to all potential scenes. For the plan to work effectively at all times, and in both remote rural and heavily populated urban locales, all organizations contributing to the response must have the ability to maintain flexibility while conforming to the basic principles of the overall strategy.

The initial responders should obtain as much information as possible to try to identify the hazard involved. Whether the incident is a spillage, a fire, a toxic release, or a combination of these will determine responses. The national and international marking systems used to identify vehicles transporting hazardous substances and carrying hazardous packaged goods should be known to the emergency services, who should have access to one of the several national and international databases which can help to identify the hazard and the problems associated with it.

Rapid control of the incident is vital. The chain of command must be identified clearly. This may change during the course of the event from the emergency services through the police to the civil government of the affected area. The plan must be able to recognize the effect on the population, both those working in or resident in the potentially affected area and those who may be transients. Sources of expertise on public health matters should be mobilized to advise on both the immediate management of the incident and on the potential for longer-term direct health effects and indirect ones through the food chain. Contact points for obtaining advice on environmental pollution to water courses and so on, and the effect of weather conditions on the movement of gas clouds must be identified. Plans must identify the possibility of evacuation as one of the response measures. However, the proposals must be flexible, as there may be a range of costs and benefits, both in incident management and in public health terms, which will have to be considered. The arrangements must outline clearly the policy with respect to keeping the media fully informed and the action being taken to mitigate the effects. The information must be accurate and timely, with the spokesperson being knowledgeable as to the overall response and having access to experts to respond to specialized queries. Poor media relations can disrupt the management of the event and lead to unfavourable and sometimes unjustified comments on the overall handling of the episode. Any plan must include adequate mock disaster drills. These enable the responders to and managers of an incident to learn each other's personal and organizational strengths and weaknesses. Both table-top and physical exercises are required.

Although the literature dealing with chemical spills is extensive, only a minor part describes the ecological consequences. Most concern case studies. The descriptions of actual spills have focused on human health and safety problems, with ecological consequences described only in general terms. The chemicals enter the environment predominantly through the liquid phase. In only a few cases did accidents having ecological consequences also affect humans immediately, and the effects on the environment were not caused by identical chemicals or by identical release routes.

Controls to prevent risk to human health and life from the transport of hazardous materials include quantities carried, direction and control of means of transport, routing, as well as authority over interchange and concentration points and developments near such areas. Further research is required into risk criteria, quantification of risk, and risk equivalence. The United Kingdom Health and Safety Executive has developed a Major Incident Data Service (MHIDAS) as a database of major chemical incidents worldwide. It currently holds information on over 6,000 incidents.

RADIATION ACCIDENTS

Pierre Verger and Denis Winter

Description, Sources, Mechanisms
Apart from the transportation of radioactive materials, there are three settings in which radiation accidents can occur:

- use of nuclear reactions to produce energy or arms, or for research purposes
- industrial applications of radiation (gamma radiography, irradiation)
- research and nuclear medicine (diagnosis or therapy).

Radiation accidents may be classified into two groups on the basis of whether or not there is environmental emission or dispersion of radionuclides; each of these types of accident affects different populations.

Table 39.18 • Typical radionuclides, with their radioactive half-lives.

Radionuclide	Symbol	Radiation emitted	Physical half-life*	Biological half-life after incorporation*
Barium-133	Ba-133	γ	10.7 y	65 d
Cerium-144	Ce-144	β,γ	284 d	263 d
Caesium-137	Cs-137	β,γ	30 y	109 d
Cobalt-60	Co-60	β,γ	5.3 y	1.6 y
Iodine-131	I-131	β,γ	8 d	7.5 d
Plutonium-239	Pu-239	α,γ	24,065 y	50 y
Polonium-210	Po-210	α	138 d	27 d
Strontium-90	Sr-90	β	29.1 y	18 y
Tritium	H-3	β	12.3 y	10 d

* y = years; d = days.

The magnitude and duration of the exposure risk for the general population depends on the quantity and the characteristics (half-life, physical and chemical properties) of the radionuclides emitted into the environment (table 39.18). This type of contamination occurs when there is rupture of the containment barriers at nuclear power plants or industrial or medical sites which separate radioactive materials from the environment. In the absence of environmental emissions, only workers present onsite or handling radioactive equipment or materials are exposed.

Exposure to ionizing radiation may occur through three routes, regardless of whether the target population is composed of workers or the general public: external irradiation, internal irradiation, and contamination of skin and wounds.

External irradiation occurs when individuals are exposed to an extracorporeal radiation source, either point (radiotherapy, irradiators) or diffuse (radioactive clouds and fallout from accidents, figure 39.5). Irradiation may be local, involving only a portion of the body, or whole body.

Internal radiation occurs following incorporation of radioactive substances into the body (figure 39.5) through either inhalation of airborne radioactive particles (e.g., caesium-137 and iodine-131,

Figure 39.5 • Exposure pathways to ionizing radiation after an accidental release of radioactivity into the environment.

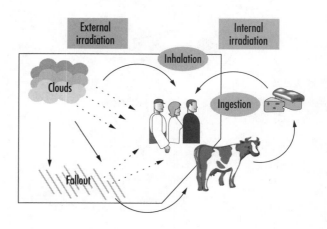

Table 39.19 • Comparison of different nuclear accidents.

Accident	Type of facility	Accident mechanism	Total emitted radioactivity (GBq)	Duration of emission	Main emitted radionuclides	Collective dose (hSv)
Khyshtym 1957	Storage of high-activity fission products	Chemical explosion	740×10^6	Almost instantaneous	Strontium-90	2,500
Windscale 1957	Plutonium-production reactor	Fire	7.4×10^6	Approximately 23 hours	Iodine-131, polonium-210, caesium-137	2,000
Three Mile Island 1979	PWR industrial reactor	Coolant failure	555	?	Iodine-131	16–50
Chernobyl 1986	RBMK industrial reactor	Criticality	$3,700 \times 10^6$	More than 10 days	Iodine-131, iodine-132, caesium-137, caesium-134, strontium-89, strontium-90	600,000

Source: UNSCEAR 1993.

present in the Chernobyl cloud) or ingestion of radioactive materials in the food chain (e.g., iodine-131 in milk). Internal irradiation may affect the whole body or only certain organs, depending on the characteristics of the radionuclides: caesium-137 distributes itself homogeneously throughout the body, while iodine-131 and strontium-90 concentrate in the thyroid and the bones, respectively.

Finally, exposure may also occur through direct contact of radioactive materials with skin and wounds.

Accidents involving nuclear power plants

Sites included in this category include power-generating stations, experimental reactors, facilities for the production and processing or reprocessing of nuclear fuel and research laboratories. Military

Figure 39.6 • Trajectory of emissions from the Chernobyl accident, 26 April–6 May 1986.

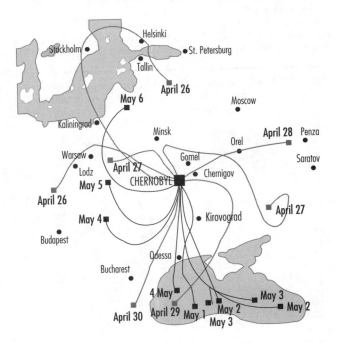

sites include plutonium breeder reactors and reactors located aboard ships and submarines.

Nuclear power plants

The capture of heat energy emitted by atomic fission is the basis for the production of electricity from nuclear energy. Schematically, nuclear power plants can be thought of as comprising: (1) a core, containing the fissile material (for pressurized-water reactors, 80 to 120 tonnes of uranium oxide); (2) heat-transfer equipment incorporating heat-transfer fluids; (3) equipment capable of transforming heat energy into electricity, similar to that found in power plants that are not nuclear.

Strong, sudden power surges capable of causing core meltdown with emission of radioactive products are the primary hazards at these installations. Two accidents involving reactor-core meltdown have occurred: at Three Mile Island (1979, Pennsylvania, United States) and Chernobyl (1986, Ukraine).

The Chernobyl accident was what is known as a *criticality accident*—that is, a sudden (within the space of a few seconds) increase in fission leading to a loss of process control. In this case, the reactor core was completely destroyed and massive amounts of radioactive materials were emitted (table 39.19). The emissions reached a height of 2 km, favouring their dispersion over long distances (for all intents and purposes, the entire Northern hemisphere). The behaviour of the radioactive cloud has proven difficult to analyse, due to meteorological changes during the emission period (figure 39.6) (IAEA 1991).

Contamination maps were drawn up on the basis of environmental measurements of caesium-137, one of the main radioactive emission products (tables 39.18 and 39.19). Areas of Ukraine, Byelorussia (Belarus) and Russia were heavily contaminated, while fallout in the rest of Europe was less significant (figures 39.7 and 39.8 (UNSCEAR 1988). Table 39.20 presents data on the area of the contaminated zones, characteristics of the exposed populations and routes of exposure.

The Three Mile Island accident is classified as a thermal accident with no reactor runaway, and was the result of a reactor-core coolant failure lasting several hours. The containment shell ensured that only a limited quantity of radioactive material was emitted into the environment, despite the partial destruction of the reactor core (table 39.19). Although no evacuation order was issued, 200,000 residents voluntarily evacuated the area.

Finally, an accident involving a plutonium production reactor occurred on the west coast of England in 1957 (Windscale, table 39.19). This accident was caused by a fire in the reactor core

Figure 39.7 • Caesium-137 deposition in Byelorussia, Russia and Ukraine following the Chernobyl accident.

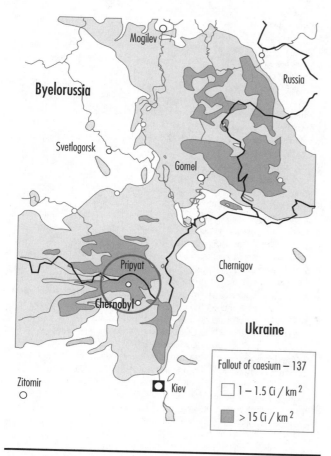

Table 39.20 • Area of contaminated zones, types of populations exposed and modes of exposure in Ukraine, Byelorussia and Russia following the Chernobyl accident.

Type of population	Surface area (km²)	Population size (000)	Main modes of exposure
Occupationally exposed populations:			
Employees onsite at the time of the accident	≈0.44		External irradiation, inhalation, skin contamination from the damaged reactor, fragments of the reactor dispersed throughout the site, radioactive vapours and dusts
Fire-fighters (first-aid)	≈0.12		
Clean-up and relief workers*		600–800	External irradiation, inhalation, skin contamination
General public:			
Evacuated from the prohibited zone in the first few days		115	External irradiation by the cloud, inhalation of radioactive elements present in the cloud
Residents of contaminated** zones (MBq/m²) (Ci/km²)			External radiation from fallout, ingestion of contaminated products
>1.5 (>40)	3,100	33	
0.6–1.5 (15–40)	7,200	216	
0.2–0.6 (5–15)	17,600	584	
0.04–0.2 (1–5)	103,000	3,100	
Residents of other zones <0.04MBq/m²		280,000	External irradiation by fallout, ingestion of contaminated products

* Individuals participating in clean-up within 30 km of the site. These include fire-fighters, military personnel, technicians and engineers who intervened during the first weeks, as well as physicians and researchers active at a later date.
** Caesium-137 contamination.
Source: UNSCEAR 1988; IAEA 1991.

and resulted in environmental emissions from a chimney 120 metres high.

Fuel-processing facilities

Fuel production facilities are located "upstream" from nuclear reactors and are the site of ore extraction and the physical and chemical transformation of uranium into fissile material suitable for use in reactors (figure 39.9). The primary accident hazards present in these facilities are chemical in nature and related to the presence of uranium hexafluoride (UF_6), a gaseous uranium compound which may decompose upon contact with air to produce hydrofluoric acid (HF), a very corrosive gas.

"Downstream" facilities include fuel storage and reprocessing plants. Four criticality accidents have occurred during chemical reprocessing of enriched uranium or plutonium (Rodrigues 1987). In contrast to accidents occurring at nuclear power plants, these accidents involved small quantities of radioactive materials—tens of kilograms at most—and resulted in negligible mechanical effects and no environmental emission of radioactivity. Exposure was limited to very high dose, very short term (of the order of minutes) external gamma ray and neutron irradiation of workers.

In 1957, a tank containing highly radioactive waste exploded at Russia's first military-grade plutonium production facility, located in Khyshtym, in the south Ural Mountains. Over 16,000 km² were contaminated and 740 PBq (20 MCi) were emitted into the atmosphere (tables 39.19 and 39.21).

Research reactors

Hazards at these facilities are similar to those present at nuclear power plants, but are less serious, given the lower power generation. Several criticality accidents involving significant irradiation of personnel have occurred (Rodrigues 1987).

Accidents related to the use of radioactive sources in industry and medicine (excluding nuclear plants) (Zerbib 1993)

The most common accident of this type is the loss of radioactive sources from industrial gamma radiography, used, for example, for the radiographic inspection of joints and welds. However, radioactive sources may also be lost from medical sources (table 39.22). In either case, two scenarios are possible: the source may be picked up and kept by a person for several hours (e.g., in a pocket), then reported and restored, or it may be collected and carried home. While the first scenario causes local burns, the

39. DISASTERS, NATURAL AND TECHNOLOGICAL

Table 39.21 • Surface area of the contaminated zones and size of populations exposed after the Khyshtym accident (Urals 1957), by strontium-90 contamination.

Contamination (kBq/m²)	(Ci/km²)	Area (km²)	Population
≥ 37,000	≥ 1,000	20	1,240
≥ 3,700	≥ 100	120	1,500
≥ 74	≥ 2	1,000	10,000
≥ 3.7	≥ 0.1	15,000	270,000

second may result in long-term irradiation of several members of the general public.

The recovery of radioactive sources from radiotherapy equipment has resulted in several accidents involving the exposure of scrap workers. In two cases—the Juarez and Goiânia accidents—the general public was also exposed (see table 39.22 and box on page 39.32).

The Juarez accident was discovered serendipitously (IAEA 1989b). On 16 January 1984, a truck entering the Los Alamos (New Mexico, United States) scientific laboratory loaded with steel bars triggered a radiation detector. Investigation revealed the presence of cobalt-60 in the bars and traced the cobalt-60 to a Mexican foundry. On January 21, a heavily contaminated scrapyard in Juarez was identified as the source of the radioactive material. Systematic monitoring of roads and highways by detectors resulted in the identification of a heavily contaminated truck. The ultimate radiation source was determined to be a radiotherapy device stored in a medical centre until December 1983, at which time it was disassembled and transported to the scrapyard. At the scrapyard, the protective housing surrounding the cobalt-60 was broken, freeing the cobalt pellets. Some of the

Table 39.22 • Accidents involving the loss of radioactive sources and which resulted in exposure of the general public.

Country (year)	Number of exposed individuals	Number of exposed individuals receiving high doses*	Number of deaths**	Radioactive material involved
Mexico (1962)	?	5	4	Cobalt-60
China (1963)	?	6	2	Cobalt 60
Algeria (1978)	22	5	1	Iridium-192
Morocco (1984)	?	11	8	Iridium-192
Mexico (Juarez, 1984)	≈4,000	5	0	Cobalt-60
Brazil (Goiânia, 1987)	249	50	4	Caesium-137
China (Xinhou, 1992)	≈90	12	3	Cobalt-60
United States (Indiana, 1992)	≈90	1	1	Iridium-192

* Individuals exposed to doses capable of causing acute or long-term effects or death.

** Among individuals receiving high doses.

Source: Nénot 1993.

The Goiânia Accident, 1987

Between 21 September and 28 September 1987, several people suffering from vomiting, diarrhoea, vertigo and skin lesions at various parts of the body were admitted to the hospital specializing in tropical diseases in Goiânia, a city of one million inhabitants in the Brazilian state of Goias. These problems were attributed to a parasitic disease common in Brazil. On 28 September, the physician responsible for health surveillance in the city saw a woman who presented him with a bag containing debris from a device collected from an abandoned clinic, and a powder which emitted, according to the woman "a blue light". Thinking that the device was probably x-ray equipment, the physician contacted his colleagues at the hospital for tropical diseases. The Goias Department of the Environment was notified, and the next day a physicist took measurements in the hygiene department's yard, where the bag was stored overnight. Very high radioactivity levels were found. In subsequent investigations the source of radioactivity was identified as a caesium-137 source (total activity: approximately 50 TBq (1,375 Ci)) which had been contained within radiotherapy equipment used in a clinic abandoned since 1985. The protective housing surrounding the caesium had been disassembled on 10 September 1987 by two scrapyard workers and the caesium source, in powder form, removed. Both the caesium and the fragments of the contaminated housing were gradually dispersed throughout the city. Several people who had transported or handled the material, or who had simply come to see it (including parents, friends and neighbours) were contaminated. In all, over 100,000 people were examined, of whom 129 were very seriously contaminated; 50 were hospitalized (14 for medullary failure), and 4, including a 6-year-old girl, died. The accident had dramatic economic and social consequences for the entire city of Goiânia and the state of Goias: 1/1000 of the city's surface area was contaminated, and the price of agricultural produce, rents, real estate, and land all fell. The inhabitants of the entire state suffered real discrimination.

Source: IAEA 1989a.

---

pellets fell into the truck used to transport scrap, and others were dispersed throughout the scrapyard during subsequent operations, mixing with the other scrap.

Accidents involving the entry of workers into active industrial irradiators (e.g., those used to preserve food, sterilize medical products, or polymerize chemicals) have occurred. In all cases, these have been due to failure to follow safety procedures or to disconnected or defective safety systems and alarms. The dose levels of external irradiation to which workers in these accidents were exposed were high enough to cause death. Doses were received within a few seconds or minutes (table 39.23).

Finally, medical and scientific personnel preparing or handling radioactive sources may be exposed through skin and wound contamination or inhalation or ingestion of radioactive materials. It should be noted that this type of accident is also possible in nuclear power plants.

Public Health Aspects of the Problem

Temporal patterns

The United States Radiation Accident Registry (Oak Ridge, United States) is a worldwide registry of radiation accidents involving humans since 1944. To be included in the registry, an accident must have been the subject of a published report and have resulted in whole-body exposure exceeding 0.25 Sievert (Sv),

Figure 39.8 • Caesium-137 fallout (kBq/km²) in Europe following the Chernobyl accident.

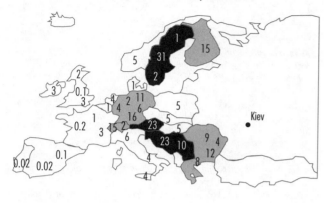

Source: UNSCEAR 1988.

Figure 39.9 • Nuclear fuel processing cycle.

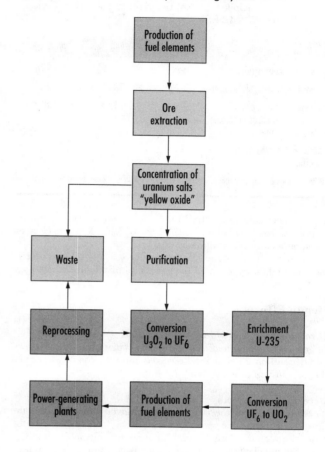

or skin exposure exceeding 6 Sv or exposure of other tissues and organs exceeding 0.75 Sv (see box on page 39.34) for a definition of dose). Accidents that are of interest from the point of view of public health but which resulted in lower exposures are thus excluded (see below for a discussion of the consequences of exposure).

Analysis of the registry data from 1944 to 1988 reveals a clear increase in both the frequency of radiation accidents and the number of exposed individuals starting in 1980 (table 39.24). The increase in the number of exposed individuals is probably accounted for by the Chernobyl accident, particularly the approximately 135,000 individuals initially residing in the prohibited area within 30 km of the accident site. The Goiânia (Brazil) and Juarez (Mexico) accidents also occurred during this period and involved significant exposure of many people (table 39.22).

Potentially exposed populations

From the point of view of exposure to ionizing radiation, there are two populations of interest: occupationally exposed populations

and the general public. United Nations Scientific Committee on the Effects of Atomic Radiation (UNSCEAR 1993) estimates that 4 million workers worldwide were occupationally exposed to ionizing radiation in the period 1985-1989; of these, approximately 20% were employed in the production, use and processing of

Table 39.23 • Main accidents involving industrial irradiators.

Site, date	Equipment*	Number of victims	Exposure level and duration	Affected organs and tissues	Dose received (Gy), site	Medical effects
Forbach, August 1991	EA	2	several deciGy/second	Hands, head, trunk	40, skin	Burns affecting 25–60% of body area
Maryland, December 1991	EA	1	?	Hands	55, hands	Bilateral finger amputation
Viet nam, November 1992	EA	1	1,000 Gy/minute	Hands	1.5, whole body	Amputation of the right hand and a finger of the left hand
Italy, May 1975	CI	1	Several minutes	Head, whole body	8, bone marrow	Death
San Salvador, February 1989	CI	3	?	Whole body, legs, feet	3–8, whole body	2 leg amputations, 1 death
Israel, June 1990	CI	1	1 minute	Head, whole body	10–20	Death
Belarus, October 1991	CI	1	Several minutes	Whole body	10	Death

* EA: electron accelerator CI: cobalt-60 irradiator.
Source: Zerbib 1993; Nénot 1993.

Table 39.24 • Radiation accidents listed in the Oak Ridge (United States) accident registry (worldwide, 1944-88).

	1944–79	1980–88	1944–88
Total number of accidents	98	198	296
Number of individuals involved	562	136,053	136,615
Number of individuals exposed to doses exceeding exposure criteria*	306	24,547	24,853
Number of deaths (acute effects)	16	53	69

* 0.25 Sv for whole-body exposure, 6 Sv for skin exposure, 0.75 Sv for other tissues and organs.

nuclear fuel (table 39.25). IAEA member countries were estimated to possess 760 irradiators in 1992, of which 600 were electron accelerators and 160 gamma irradiators.

The number of nuclear sites per country is a good indicator of the potential for exposure of the general public (figure 39.10, page 39.35).

Health Effects

Direct health effects of ionizing radiation

In general, the health effects of ionizing radiation are well known and depend on the dose level received and the dose rate (received dose per unit of time (see box).

Deterministic effects

These occur when the dose exceeds a given threshold and the dose rate is high. The severity of the effects is proportional to the dose, although the dose threshold is organ specific (table 39.26).

In the accidents such as those discussed above, deterministic effects may be caused by local intense irradiation, such as that caused by external irradiation, direct contact with a source (e.g., a misplaced source picked up and pocketed) or skin contamination. All these result in radiological burns. If the local dose is of the order of 20 to 25 Gy (table 39.23, box 1) tissue necrosis may ensue. A syndrome known as *acute irradiation syndrome*, characterized by digestive disorders (nausea, vomiting, diarrhoea) and bone marrow aplasia of variable severity, may be induced when the average whole-body irradiation dose exceeds 0.5 Gy. It should

Table 39.25 • Temporal pattern of occupational exposure to artificial ionizing radiation worldwide (in thousands).

Activity	1975–79	1980–84	1985–89
Nuclear fuel processing*	560	800	880
Military applications**	310	350	380
Industrial applications	530	690	560
Medical applications	1,280	1,890	2,220
Total	2,680	3,730	4,040

* Production and reprocessing of fuel: 40,000; reactor operation: 430,000.
** including 190,000 shipboard personnel.
Source: UNSCEAR 1993.

What does dose mean?

There are several ways to define a dose of ionizing radiation, each appropriate for different purposes.

Absorbed dose

Absorbed dose resembles pharmacological dose the most closely. While pharmacological dose is the quantity of substance administered to a subject per unit weight or surface, radiological absorbed dose is the amount of energy transmitted by ionizing radiation per unit mass. Absorbed dose is measured in Grays (1 Gray = 1 joule/kg).

When individuals are exposed homogeneously—for example, by external irradiation by cosmic and terrestrial rays or by internal irradiation by potassium-40 present in the body—all organs and tissues receive the same dose. Under these circumstances, it is appropriate to speak of *whole-body* dose. It is, however, possible for exposure to be non-homogenous, in which case some organs and tissues will receive significantly higher doses than others. In this case, it is more relevant to think in terms of *organ dose*. For example, inhalation of radon daughters results in exposure of essentially only the lungs, and incorporation of radioactive iodine results in irradiation of the thyroid gland. In these cases, we may speak of lung dose and thyroid dose.

However, other units of dose that take into account differences in the effects of different types of radiation and the different radiation sensitivities of tissues and organs, have also been developed.

Equivalent dose

The development of biological effects (e.g., inhibition of cell growth, cell death, azoospermia) depends not only on the absorbed dose, but also on the specific type of radiation. Alpha radiation has a greater ionizing potential than beta or gamma radiation. Equivalent dose takes this difference into account by applying radiation-specific weighting factors. The weighting factor for gamma and beta radiation (low ionizing potential), is equal to 1, while that for alpha particles (high ionizing potential) is 20 (ICRP 60). Equivalent dose is measured in Sieverts (Sv).

Effective dose

In cases involving non-homogenous irradiation (e.g., the exposure of various organs to different radionuclides), it may be useful to calculate a global dose that integrates the doses received by all organs and tissues. This requires taking into account the radiation sensitivity of each tissue and organ, calculated from the results of epidemiological studies of radiation-induced cancers. Effective dose is measured in Sieverts (Sv) (ICRP 1991). Effective dose was developed for the purposes of radiation protection (i.e., risk management) and is thus inappropriate for use in epidemiological studies of the effects of ionizing radiation.

Collective dose

Collective dose reflects the exposure of a group or population and not of an individual, and is useful for evaluating the consequences of exposure to ionizing radiation at the population or group level. It is calculated by summing the individual received doses, or by multiplying the average individual dose by the number of exposed individuals in the groups or populations in question. Collective dose is measured in man-Sieverts (man Sv).

Figure 39.10 • Distribution of power-generating reactors and fuel reprocessing plants in the world, 1989-90.

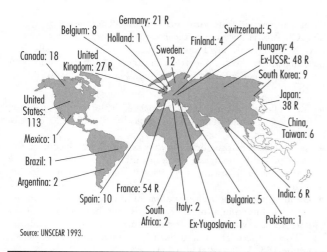

Source: UNSCEAR 1993.

Table 39.26 • Deterministic effects: thresholds for selected organs.

Tissue or effect	Equivalent single dose received at the organ (Sv)
Testicles:	
Temporary sterility	0.15
Permanent sterility	3.5–6.0
Ovaries:	
Sterility	2.5–6.0
Crystalline lens:	
Detectable opacities	0.5–2.0
Impaired vision (cataracts)	5.0
Bone marrow:	
Depression of haemopoiesis	0.5

Source: ICRP 1991.

be recalled that whole-body and local irradiation may occur simultaneously.

Nine of 60 workers exposed during criticality accidents at nuclear fuel processing plants or research reactors died (Rodrigues 1987). Decedents received 3 to 45 Gy, while survivors received 0.1 to 7 Gy. The following effects were observed in survivors: acute irradiation syndrome (gastro-intestinal and haematological effects), bilateral cataracts and necrosis of limbs, requiring amputation.

At Chernobyl, power plant personnel, as well as emergency response personnel not using special protective equipment, suffered high beta and gamma radiation exposure in the initial hours or days following the accident. Five hundred people required hospitalization; 237 individuals who received whole-body irradiation exhibited acute irradiation syndrome, and 28 individuals died despite treatment (table 39.27) (UNSCEAR 1988). Others received local irradiation of the limbs, in some cases affecting over 50% of the body surface and continue to suffer, many years later, multiple skin disorders (Peter, Braun-Falco and Birioukov 1994).

Stochastic effects

These are probabilistic in nature (i.e., their frequency increases with received dose), but their severity is independent of dose. The main stochastic effects are:

- *Mutation.* This has been observed in animal experiments but has been difficult to document in humans.
- *Cancer.* The effect of irradiation on the risk of developing cancer has been studied in patients receiving radiation therapy and in survivors of the Hiroshima and Nagasaki bombings. UNSCEAR (1988, 1994) regularly summarizes the results of these epidemiological studies. The duration of the latency period is typically 5 to 15 years from the date of exposure depending on organ and tissue. Table 39.28 lists the cancers for which an association with ionizing radiation has been established. Significant cancer excesses have been demonstrated among survivors of the Hiroshima and Nagasaki bombings with exposures above 0.2 Sv.
- *Selected benign tumours.* Benign thyroid adenomas.

Two important points concerning the effects of ionizing radiation remain controversial.

Firstly, what are the effects of low-dose irradiation (below 0.2 Sv) and low dose rates? Most epidemiological studies have examined survivors of the Hiroshima and Nagasaki bombings or patients receiving radiation therapy—populations exposed over very short periods to relatively high doses—and estimates of the risk of developing cancer as a result of exposure to low doses and dose rates depends essentially on extrapolations from these populations. Several studies of nuclear power plant workers, exposed to low doses over several years, have reported cancer risks for leukaemia and other cancers that are compatible with extrapolations from high-exposure groups, but these results remain unconfirmed (UNSCEAR 1994; Cardis, Gilbert and Carpenter 1995).

Secondly, is there a threshold dose (i.e., a dose below which there is no effect)? This is currently unknown. Experimental studies have demonstrated that damage to genetic material (DNA) caused by spontaneous errors or environmental factors are constantly repaired. However, this repair is not always effective, and may result in malignant transformation of cells (UNSCEAR 1994).

Other effects

Finally, the possibility of teratogenic effects due to irradiation during pregnancy should be noted. Microcephaly and mental retardation have been observed in children born to female survivors of the Hiroshima and Nagasaki bombings who received

Table 39.27 • Distribution of patients exhibiting acute irradiation syndrome (AIS) after the Chernobyl accident, by severity of condition.

Severity of AIS	Equivalent dose (Gy)	Number of subjects	Number of deaths (%)	Average survival period (days)
I	1–2	140	–	–
II	2–4	55	1 (1.8)	96
III	4–6	21	7 (33.3)	29.7
IV	>6	21	20 (95.2)	26.6

Source: UNSCEAR 1988.

Table 39.28 • Results of epidemiological studies of the effect of high dose rate of external irradiation on cancer.

Cancer site	Hiroshima/Nagasaki		Other studies No. positive/ total No.[1]
	Mortality	Incidence	
Haematopoietic system			
Leukaemia	+*	+*	6/11
Lymphoma (not specified)	+		0/3
Non-Hodgkin lymphoma		+*	1/1
Myeloma	+	+	1/4
Oral cavity	+	+	0/1
Salivary glands		+*	1/3
Digestive system			
Oesophagus	+*	+	2/3
Stomach	+*	+*	2/4
Small intestine			1/2
Colon	+*	+*	0/4
Rectum	+	+	3/4
Liver	+*	+*	0/3
Gall bladder			0/2
Pancreas			3/4
Respiratory system			
Larynx			0/1
Trachea, bronchi, lungs	+*	+*	1/3
Skin			
Not specified			1/3
Melanoma			0/1
Other cancers		+*	0/1
Breast (women)	+*	+*	9/14
Reproductive system			
Uterus (non-specific)	+	+	2/3
Uterine body			1/1
Ovaries	+*	+*	2/3
Other (women)			2/3
Prostate	+	+	2/2
Urinary system			
Bladder	+*	+*	3/4
Kidneys			0/3
Other			0/1
Central nervous system	+	+	2/4
Thyroid		+*	4/7
Bone			2/6
Connective tissue			0/4
All cancers, excluding leukaemias			1/2

+ Cancer sites studied in the Hiroshima and Nagasaki survivors.

* Positive association with ionizing radiation.

[1] Cohort (incidence or mortality) or case-control studies.

Source: UNSCEAR 1994.

irradiation of at least 0.1 Gy during the first trimester (Otake, Schull and Yoshimura 1989; Otake and Schull 1992). It is unknown whether these effects are deterministic or stochastic, although the data do suggest the existence of a threshold.

Effects observed following the Chernobyl accident

The Chernobyl accident is the most serious nuclear accident to have occurred to date. However, even now, ten years after the fact, not all the health effects on the most highly exposed populations have been accurately evaluated. There are several reasons for this:

- Some effects appear only many years after the date of exposure: for example, solid-tissue cancers typically take 10 to 15 years to appear.
- As some time elapsed between the accident and the commencement of epidemiological studies, some effects occurring in the initial period following the accident may not have been detected.
- Useful data for the quantification of the cancer risk were not always gathered in a timely fashion. This is particularly true for data necessary to estimate the exposure of the thyroid gland to radioactive iodides emitted during the incident (tellurium-132, iodine-133) (Williams et al. 1993).
- Finally, many initially exposed individuals subsequently left the contaminated zones and were probably lost for follow-up.

Workers. Currently, comprehensive information is unavailable for all the workers who were strongly irradiated in the first few days following the accident. Studies on the risk to clean-up and relief workers of developing leukaemia and solid-tissue cancers are in progress (see table 39.20). These studies face many obstacles. Regular follow-up of the health status of clean-up and relief workers is greatly hindered by the fact that many of them came from different parts of the ex-USSR and were redispatched after working on the Chernobyl site. Further, received dose must be estimated retrospectively, as there are no reliable data for this period.

General population. The only effect plausibly associated with ionizing radiation in this population to date is an increase, starting in 1989, of the incidence of thyroid cancer in children younger than 15 years. This was detected in Byelorussia (Belarus) in 1989, only three years after the incident, and has been confirmed by several expert groups (Williams et al. 1993). The increase was particularly noteworthy in the most heavily contaminated areas of Belarus, especially the Gomel region. While thyroid cancer was normally rare in children younger than 15 years, (annual incidence rate of 1 to 3 per million), its incidence increased tenfold on a national basis and twentyfold in the Gomel area (table 39.29, figure 39.11), (Stsjazhko et al. 1995). A tenfold increase of the incidence of thyroid cancer was subsequently reported in the five most heavily contaminated areas of Ukraine, and an increase in thyroid cancer was also reported in the Bryansk (Russia) region (table 39.29). An increase among adults is suspected but has not been confirmed. Systematic screening programmes undertaken in the contaminated regions allowed latent cancers present prior to the accident to be detected; ultrasonographic programmes capable of detecting thyroid cancers as small as a few millimetres were particularly helpful in this regard. The magnitude of the increase in incidence in children, taken together with the aggressiveness of the tumours and their rapid development, suggests that the observed increases in thyroid gland cancer are partially due to the accident.

In the most heavily contaminated zones (e.g., the Gomel region), the thyroid doses were high, particularly among children (Williams et al. 1993). This is consistent with the significant iodine emissions associated with the accident and the fact that radioactive iodine will, in the absence of preventive measures, concentrate preferentially in the thyroid gland.

Table 39.29 • Temporal pattern of the incidence* and total number of thyroid cancers in children in Belarus, Ukraine and Russia, 1981-94.

	Incidence (/100,000)		Number of cases	
	1981–85	1991–94	1981–85	1991–94
Belarus				
Entire country	0.3	3.06	3	333
Gomel area	0.5	9.64	1	164
Ukraine				
Entire country	0.05	0.34	25	209
Five most heavily contaminated areas	0.01	1.15	1	118
Russia				
Entire country	?	?	?	?
Bryansk and Kaluga areas	0	1.00	0	20

* Incidence: the ratio of the number of new cases of a disease during a given period to the size of the population studied in the same period.
Source: Stsjazhko et al. 1995.

Exposure to radiation is a well-documented risk factor for thyroid cancer. Clear increases in the incidence of thyroid cancer have been observed in a dozen studies of children receiving radiation therapy to the head and neck. In most cases, the increase was clear ten to 15 years after exposure, but was detectable in some cases within three to seven years. On the other hand, the effects in children of internal irradiation by iodine-131 and by short half-life iodine isotopes are not well established (Shore 1992).

The precise magnitude and pattern of the increase in the coming years of the incidence of thyroid cancer in the most highly exposed populations should be studied. Epidemiological studies currently under way should help to quantify the association between the dose received by the thyroid gland and the risk of developing thyroid cancer, and to identify the role of other genetic and environmental risk factors. It should be noted that iodine deficiency is widespread in the affected regions.

An increase in the incidence of leukaemia, particularly juvenile leukaemia (since children are more sensitive to the effects of ionizing radiation), is to be expected among the most highly exposed members of the population within five to ten years of the accident. Although no such increase has yet been observed, the methodological weaknesses of the studies conducted to date prevent any definitive conclusions from being drawn.

Psychosocial effects

The occurrence of more or less severe chronic psychological problems following psychological trauma is well established and has been studied primarily in populations faced with environmental disasters such as floods, volcanic eruptions and earthquakes. Post-traumatic stress is a severe, long-lasting and crippling condition (APA 1994).

Most of our knowledge on the effect of radiation accidents on psychological problems and stress is drawn from studies conducted in the wake of the Three Mile Island accident. In the year following the accident, immediate psychological effects were observed in the exposed population, and mothers of young children

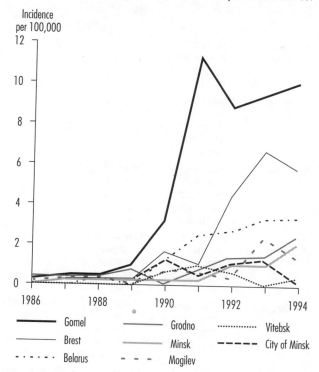

Figure 39.11 • Incidence* of cancer of the thyroid in children younger than 15 years in Belarus.

*Incidence: number of new cases of a disease during a given period, expressed as a fraction of the exposed population.

in particular exhibited increased sensitivity, anxiety and depression (Bromet et al. 1982). Further, an increase in depression and anxiety-related problems was observed in power-plant workers, compared to workers in another power plant (Bromet et al. 1982). In the following years (i.e., after the reopening of the power plant), approximately one-quarter of the surveyed population exhibited relatively significant psychological problems. There was no difference in the frequency of psychological problems in the rest of the survey population, compared to control populations (Dew and Bromet 1993). Psychological problems were more frequent among individuals living close to the power plant who were without a social support network, had a history of psychiatric problems, or who had evacuated their home at the time of the accident (Baum, Cohen and Hall 1993).

Studies are also under way among populations exposed during the Chernobyl accident and for whom stress appears to be an important public health issue (e.g., clean-up and relief workers and individuals living in a contaminated zone). For the moment, however, there are no reliable data on the nature, severity, frequency and distribution of psychological problems in the target populations. The factors that must be taken into account when evaluating the psychological and social consequences of the accident on residents of the contaminated zones include the harsh social and economic situation, the diversity of the available compensation systems, the effects of evacuation and resettlement (approximately 100,000 additional people were resettled in the years following the accident), and the effects of lifestyle limitations (e.g., modification of nutrition).

Table 39.30 • International scale of nuclear incidents.

Level	Offsite	Onsite	Protective structure
7 — Major accident	Major emission, extensive health and environmental effects		
6 — Serious accident	Significant emission, may necessitate the application of all counter-measures.		
5 — Accident	Limited emission, may necessitate the application of some counter-measures.	Serious damage to reactors and protective structures	
4 — Accident	Low emission, public exposure approaching exposure limits	Damage to reactors and protective structures, fatal exposure of workers	
3 — Serious incident	Very low emission, public exposure lower than exposure limits	Serious contamination level, serious effects on workers' heath	Accident barely avoided
2 — Incident		Serious contamination level, over-exposure of workers	Serious failures of safety measures
1 — Abnormality			Abnormality beyond normal functional limits
0 — Disparity	No significance from the point of view of safety		

Principles of Prevention and Guidelines

Safety principles and guidelines

Industrial and medical use of radioactive sources

While it is true that the major radiation accidents reported have all occurred at nuclear power plants, the use of radioactive sources in other settings has nevertheless resulted in accidents with serious consequences for workers or the general public. The prevention of accidents such as these is essential, especially in light of the disappointing prognosis in cases of high-dose exposure. Prevention depends on proper worker training and on the maintenance of a comprehensive life-cycle inventory of radioactive sources which includes information on both the sources' nature and location. The IAEA has established a series of safety guidelines and recommendations for the use of radioactive sources in industry, medicine and research (Safety Series No. 102). The principles in question are similar to those presented below for nuclear power plants.

Safety in nuclear power plants (IAEA Safety Series No. 75, INSAG-3)

The goal here is to protect both humans and the environment from the emission of radioactive materials under any circumstance. To this end, it is necessary to apply a variety of measures throughout the design, construction, operation and decommissioning of nuclear power plants.

The safety of nuclear power plants is fundamentally dependent on the "defence in depth" principle—that is, the redundancy of systems and devices designed to compensate for technical or human errors and deficiencies. Concretely, radioactive materials are separated from the environment by a series of successive barriers. In nuclear power production reactors, the last of these barriers is the *containment structure* (absent on the Chernobyl site but present at Three Mile Island). To avoid the breakdown of these barriers and to limit the consequences of breakdowns, the following three safety measures should be practised throughout the power plant's operational life: control of the nuclear reaction, cooling of fuel, and containment of radioactive material.

Another essential safety principle is "operating experience analysis"—that is, using information gleaned from events, even minor ones, occurring at other sites to increase the safety of an existing site. Thus, analysis of the Three Mile Island and Chernobyl accidents has resulted in the implementation of modifications designed to ensure that similar accidents do not occur elsewhere.

Finally, it should be noted that significant efforts have been expended to promote a culture of safety, that is, a culture that is continually responsive to safety concerns related to the plant's organization, activities and practices, as well as to individual behaviour. To increase the visibility of incidents and accidents involving nuclear power plants, an international scale of nuclear events (INES), identical in principle to scales used to measure the severity of natural phenomena such as earthquakes and wind, has been developed (table 39.30). This scale is not however suitable for the evaluation of a site's safety or for performing international comparisons.

Principles of the protection of the general public from exposure to radiation

In cases involving the potential exposure of the general public, it may be necessary to apply protective measures designed to prevent or limit exposure to ionizing radiation; this is particularly important if deterministic effects are to be avoided. The first measures which should be applied in emergency are evacuation,

Table 39.31 • Examples of generic intervention levels for protective measures for the general population.

Protective measure	Intervention level (averted dose)
Emergency	
Containment	10 mSv
Evacuation	50 mSv
Distribution of stable iodine	100 mGy
Delayed	
Temporary resettlement	30 mSv in 30 days; 10 mSv in the next 30 days
Permanent resettlement	1 Sv lifetime

Source: IAEA 1994.

sheltering and administration of stable iodine. Stable iodine should be distributed to exposed populations, since this will saturate the thyroid and inhibit its uptake of radioactive iodine. To be effective, however, thyroid saturation must occur before or soon after the start of exposure. Finally, temporary or permanent resettlement, decontamination, and control of agriculture and food may eventually be necessary.

Each of these countermeasures has its own "action level" (table 39.31), not to be confused with the ICRP dose limits for workers and the general public, developed to ensure adequate protection in cases of non-accidental exposure (ICRP 1991).

Research Needs and Future Trends

Current safety research concentrates on improving the design of nuclear power-generating reactors—more specifically, on the reduction of the risk and effects of core meltdown.

The experience gained from previous accidents should lead to improvements in the therapeutic management of seriously irradiated individuals. Currently, the use of bone marrow cell growth factors (haematopoietic growth factors) in the treatment of radiation-induced medullary aplasia (developmental failure) is being investigated (Thierry et al. 1995).

The effects of low doses and dose rates of ionizing radiation remains unclear and needs to be clarified, both from a purely scientific point of view and for the purposes of establishing dose limits for the general public and for workers. Biological research is necessary to elucidate the carcinogenic mechanisms involved. The results of large-scale epidemiological studies, especially those currently under way on workers at nuclear power plants, should prove useful in improving the accuracy of cancer risk estimates for populations exposed to low doses or dose rates. Studies on populations which are or have been exposed to ionizing radiation due to accidents should help further our understanding of the effects of higher doses, often delivered at low dose rates.

The infrastructure (organization, equipment and tools) necessary for the timely collection of data essential for the evaluation of the health effects of radiation accidents must be in place well in advance of the accident.

Finally, extensive research is necessary to clarify the psychological and social effects of radiation accidents (e.g., the nature and frequency of, and risk factors for, pathological and non-pathological post-traumatic psychological reactions). This research is essential if the management of both occupationally and non-occupationally exposed populations is to be improved.

OCCUPATIONAL HEALTH AND SAFETY MEASURES IN AGRICULTURAL AREAS CONTAMINATED BY RADIONUCLIDES: THE CHERNOBYL EXPERIENCE

Yuri Kundiev, Leonard Dobrovolsky and V.I. Chernyuk

Massive contamination of agricultural lands by radionuclides occurs, as a rule, due to large accidents at the enterprises of nuclear industry or nuclear power stations. Such accidents occurred at Windscale (England) and South Ural (Russia). The largest accident happened in April 1986 at the Chernobyl nuclear power station. The latter entailed intensive contamination of soils over several thousands of square kilometres.

The major factors contributing to radiation effects in agricultural areas are as follows:

- whether radiation is from a single or a long-term exposure
- total quantity of radioactive substances entering the environment
- ratio of radionuclides in the fallout
- distance from the source of radiation to agricultural lands and settlements
- hydrogeological and soil characteristics of agricultural lands and the purpose of their use
- peculiarities of work of the rural population; diet, water supply
- time since the radiological accident.

As a result of the Chernobyl accident more than 50 million Curies (Ci) of mostly volatile radionuclides entered the environment. At the first stage, which covered 2.5 months (the "iodine period"), iodine-131 produced the greatest biological hazard, with significant doses of high-energy gamma radiation.

Work on agricultural lands during the iodine period should be strictly regulated. Iodine-131 accumulates in the thyroid gland and damages it. After the Chernobyl accident, a zone of very high radiation intensity, where no one was permitted to live or work, was defined by a 30 km radius around the station.

Outside this prohibited zone, four zones with various rates of gamma radiation on the soils were distinguished according to which types of agricultural work could be performed; during the iodine period, the four zones had the following radiation levels measured in roentgen (R):

- zone 1—less than 0.1 mR/h
- zone 2—0.1 to 1 mR/h
- zone 3—1.0 to 5 mR/h
- zone 4—5 mR/h and more.

Actually, due to the "spot" contamination by radionuclides over the iodine period, agricultural work in these zones was performed at levels of gamma irradiation from 0.2 to 25 mR/h. Apart from uneven contamination, variation in gamma radiation levels was caused by different concentrations of radionuclides in different crops. Forage crops in particular are exposed to high levels of gamma emitters during harvesting, transportation, ensilage and when they are used as fodder.

After the decay of iodine-131, the major hazard for agricultural workers is presented by the long-lived nuclides caesium-137 and strontium-90. Caesium-137, a gamma emitter, is a chemical analogue of potassium; its intake by humans or animals results in uniform distribution throughout the body and it is relatively quickly excreted with urine and faeces. Thus, the manure in the contaminated areas is an additional source of radiation and it must be removed as quickly as possible from stock farms and stored in special sites.

Strontium-90, a beta emitter, is a chemical analogue of calcium; it is deposited in bone marrow in humans and animals. Strontium-90 and caesium-137 can enter the human body through contaminated milk, meat or vegetables.

The division of agricultural lands into zones after the decay of short-lived radionuclides is carried out according to a different principle. Here, it is not the level of gamma radiation, but the amount of soil contamination by caesium-137, strontium-90 and plutonium-239 that are taken into account.

In the case of particularly severe contamination, the population is evacuated from such areas and farm work is performed on a 2-week rotation schedule. The criteria for zone demarcation in the contaminated areas are given in table 39.32.

When people work on agricultural lands contaminated by radionuclides, the intake of radionuclides by the body through respiration and contact with soil and vegetable dusts may occur. Here, both beta emitters (strontium-90) and alpha emitters are extremely dangerous.

Table 39.32 • Criteria for contamination zones.

Contamination zones	Soil contamination limits	Dosage limits	Type of action
1. 30 km zone	–	–	Residing of population and agricultural work are prohibited.
2. Unconditional resettlement	15 (Ci)/km² caesium-137 3 Ci/km² strontium-90 0.1 Ci/km² plutonium	0.5 cSv/year	Agricultural work is performed with 2-week rotation schedule under strict radiological control.
3. Voluntary resettlement	5–15 Ci/km² caesium-137 0.15–3.0 Ci/km² strontium-90 0.01–0.1 Ci/km² plutonium	0.01–0.5 cSv/year	Measures are undertaken to reduce contamination of upper soil layer; agricultural work is carried out under strict radiological control.
4. Radio-ecological monitoring	1–5 Ci/km² caesium-137 0.02–0.15 Ci/km² strontium-90 0.05–0.01 Ci/km² plutonium	0.01 cSv/year	Agricultural work is carried out in usual way but under radiological control.

As a result of accidents at nuclear power stations, part of radioactive materials entering the environment are low-dispersed, highly active particles of the reactor fuel—"hot particles".

Considerable amounts of dust containing hot particles are generated during agricultural work and in windy periods. This was confirmed by the results of investigations of tractor air filters taken from machines which were operated on the contaminated lands.

The assessment of dose loads on the lungs of agricultural workers exposed to hot particles revealed that outside the 30 km zone the doses amounted to several millisieverts (Loshchilov et al. 1993).

According to the data of Bruk et al. (1989) the total activity of caesium-137 and caesium-134 in the inspired dust in machine operators amounted to 0.005 to 1.5 nCi/m³. According to their calculations, over the total period of field work the effective dose to lungs ranged from 2 to 70 cSv.

The relation between the amount of soil contamination by caesium-137 and radioactivity of work zone air was established. According to the data of the Kiev Institute for Occupational Health it was found that when the soil contamination by caesium-137 amounted to 7.0 to 30.0 Ci/km² the radioactivity of the breathing zone air reached 13.0 Bq/m³. In the control area, where the density of contamination amounted to 0.23 to 0.61 Ci/km³, the radioactivity of work zone air ranged from 0.1 to 1.0 Bq/m³ (Krasnyuk, Chernyuk and Stezhka 1993).

The medical examinations of agricultural machine operators in the "clear" and contaminated zones revealed an increase in cardiovascular diseases in workers in the contaminated zones, in the form of ischaemic heart disease and neurocirculatory dystonia.

Among other disorders dysplasia of the thyroid gland and an increased level of monocytes in the blood were registered more frequently.

Hygienic Requirements

Work schedules
After large accidents at nuclear power stations, temporary regulations for the population are usually adopted. After the Chernobyl accident temporary regulations for a period of one year were adopted, with the TLV of 10 cSv. It is assumed that workers receive 50% of their dose due to external radiation during work. Here, the threshold of intensity of radiation dose over the eight-hour work day should not exceed 2.1 mR/h.

During agricultural work, the radiation levels at workplaces can fluctuate significantly, depending on the concentrations of radioactive substances in soils and plants; they also fluctuate during technological processing (siloing, preparation of dry fodder and so on). In order to reduce dosages to workers, regulations of time limits for agricultural work are introduced. Figure 39.12 shows regulations which were introduced after the Chernobyl accident.

Agrotechnologies
When carrying out agricultural work in conditions of high contamination of soils and plants, it is necessary to strictly observe measures directed at prevention of dust contamination. The loading and unloading of dry and dusty substances should be mechanized; the neck of the conveyer tube should be covered with fabric. Measures directed at the decrease of dust release must be undertaken for all types of field work.

Figure 39.12 • Time limits for agricultural work depending on intensity of gamma-ray radiation at workplaces.

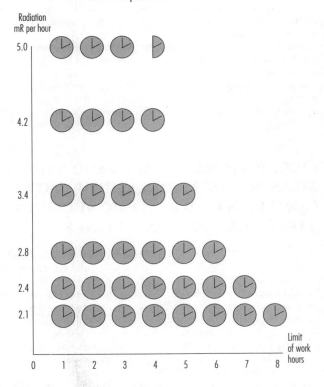

Work using agricultural machinery should be carried out taking due account of cabin pressurization and the choice of the proper direction of operation, with the wind at the side being preferable. If possible it is desirable to first water the areas being cultivated. The wide use of industrial technologies is recommended so as to eliminate manual work on the fields as much as possible.

It is appropriate to apply substances to the soils which can promote absorption and fixation of radionuclides, changing them into insoluble compounds and thus preventing the transfer of radionuclides into plants.

Agricultural machinery

One of the major hazards for the workers is agricultural machinery contaminated by radionuclides. The allowable work time on the machines depends on the intensity of gamma radiation emitted from the cabin surfaces. Not only is the thorough pressurization of cabins required, but due control over ventilation and air conditioning systems as well. After work, wet cleaning of cabins and replacement of filters should be carried out.

When maintaining and repairing the machines after decontamination procedures, the intensity of gamma radiation at the outer surfaces should not exceed 0.3 mR/h.

Buildings

Routine wet cleaning should be done inside and outside buildings. Buildings should be equipped with showers. When preparing fodder which contains dust components, it is necessary to adhere to procedures aimed at prevention of dust intake by the workers, as well as to keep the dust off the floor, equipment and so on.

Pressurization of the equipment should be under control. Workplaces should be equipped with effective general ventilation.

Use of pesticides and mineral fertilizers

The application of dust and granular pesticides and mineral fertilizers, as well as spraying from aeroplanes, should be restricted. Machine spraying and application of granular chemicals as well as liquid mixed fertilizers are preferable. The dust mineral fertilizers should be stored and transported only in tightly closed containers.

Loading and unloading work, preparation of pesticide solutions and other activities should be performed using maximum individual protective equipment (overalls, helmets, goggles, respirators, rubber gauntlets and boots).

Water supply and diet

There should be special closed premises or motor vans without draughts where workers can take their meals. Before taking meals workers should clean their clothes and thoroughly wash their hands and faces with soap and running water. During summer periods field workers should be supplied with drinking water. The water should be kept in closed containers. Dust must not enter containers when filling them with water.

Preventive medical examinations of workers

Periodic medical examinations should be carried out by a physician; laboratory analysis of blood, ECG and tests of respiratory function are compulsory. Where radiation levels do not exceed permissible limits, the frequency of medical examinations should be not less than once every 12 months. Where there are higher levels of ionizing radiation the examinations should be carried out more frequently (after sowing, harvesting and so on) with due account of radiation intensity at workplaces and the total absorbed dose.

Organization of Radiological Control over Agricultural Areas

The major indices characterizing the radiological situation after fallout are gamma radiation intensity in the area, contamination of agricultural lands by the selected radionuclides and content of radionuclides in agricultural products.

The determination of gamma radiation levels in the areas allows the drawing of the borders of severely contaminated areas, estimation of doses of external radiation to people engaged in agricultural work and the establishing of corresponding schedules providing for radiological safety.

The functions of radiological monitoring in agriculture are usually the responsibility of radiological laboratories of the sanitary service as well as veterinary and agrochemical radiological laboratories. The training and education of the personnel engaged in dosimetric control and consultations for the rural population are carried out by these laboratories.

CASE STUDY: THE KADER TOY FACTORY FIRE

Casey Cavanaugh Grant

A tragic industrial fire in Thailand has focused worldwide attention on the need to adopt and enforce state-of-the-art codes and standards in industrial occupancies.

On May 10, 1993, a major fire at the Kader Industrial (Thailand) Co. Ltd. factory located in the Nakhon Pathom Province of Thailand killed 188 workers (Grant and Klem 1994). This disaster stands as the world's worst accidental loss-of-life fire in an industrial building in recent history, a distinction held for 82 years by the Triangle Shirtwaist factory fire that killed 146 workers in New York City (Grant 1993). Despite the years between these two disasters, they share striking similarities.

Various domestic and international agencies have focused on this incident following its occurrence. With respect to fire protection concerns, the National Fire Protection Association (NFPA) cooperated with the International Labour Organization (ILO) and with the Bangkok Police Fire Brigade in documenting this fire.

Questions for a Global Economy

In Thailand, the Kader fire has created a great deal of interest about the country's fire safety measures, particularly its building code design requirements and enforcement policies. Thai Prime Minister Chuan Leekpai, who travelled to the scene on the evening of the fire, has pledged that the government will address fire safety issues. According to the *Wall Street Journal* (1993), Leekpai has called for tough action against those who violate the safety laws. Thai Industry Minister Sanan Kachornprasart is quoted as saying that "Those factories without fire prevention systems will be ordered to install one, or we will shut them down".

The *Wall Street Journal* goes on to state that labour leaders, safety experts and officials say that the Kader fire may help tighten building codes and safety regulations, but they fear that lasting progress is still far off as employers flout rules and governments allow economic growth to take priority over worker safety.

Because the majority of the shares of Kader Industrial (Thailand) Co. Ltd. are owned by foreign interests, the fire has also fuelled international debate about foreign investors' responsibilities for ensuring the safety of the workers in their sponsoring country. Twenty per cent of the Kader shareholders are from Taiwan, and 79.96% are from Hong Kong. A mere 0.04% of Kader is owned by Thai nationals.

Figure 39.13 • Site plan of the Kader toy factory.

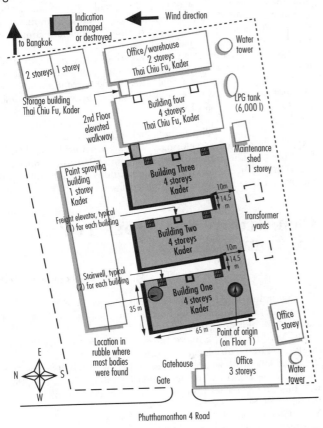

Moving into a global economy implies that products are manufactured at one location and used at other locations throughout the world. Desire for competitiveness in this new market should not lead to compromise in fundamental industrial fire safety provisions. There is a moral obligation to provide workers with an adequate level of fire protection, no matter where they are located.

The Facility

The Kader facility, which manufactured stuffed toys and plastic dolls primarily intended for export to the United States and other developed countries, is located in the Sam Phran District of Nakhon Pathom Province. This is not quite halfway between Bangkok and the nearby city of Kanchanaburi, the site of the infamous Second World War railroad bridge over the River Kwai.

The structures that were destroyed in the blaze were all owned and operated directly by Kader, which owns the site. Kader has two sister companies that also operate at the location on a lease arrangement.

The Kader Industrial (Thailand) Co. Ltd. was first registered on 27 January 1989, but the company's licence was suspended on 21 November 1989, after a fire on 16 August 1989 destroyed the new plant. This fire was attributed to the ignition of polyester fabric used in the manufacture of dolls in a spinning machine. After the plant was rebuilt, the Ministry of Industry allowed it to reopen on 4 July 1990.

Between the time the factory reopened and the May 1993 fire, the facility experienced several other, smaller fires. One of them,

which occurred in February 1993, did considerable damage to Building Three, which was still being repaired at the time of the fire in May 1993. The February fire occurred late at night in a storage area and involved polyester and cotton materials. Several days after this blaze a labour inspector visited the site and issued a warning that pointed out the plant's need for safety officers, safety equipment and an emergency plan.

Initial reports following the May 1993 fire noted that there were four buildings on the Kader site, three of which were destroyed by the fire. In a sense this is true, but the three buildings were actually a single E-shaped structure (see figure 39.13), the three primary portions of which were designated Buildings One, Two and Three. Nearby was a one-storey workshop and another four-storey structure referred to as Building Four.

The E-shaped building was a four-storey structure composed of concrete slabs supported by a structural steel frame. There were windows around the perimeter of each floor and the roof was a gently sloped, peaked arrangement. Each portion of the building had a freight elevator and two stairwells that were each 1.5 metres (3.3 feet) wide. The freight elevators were caged assemblies.

Figure 39.14 • Internal layout of buildings one, two and three.

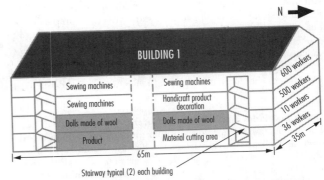

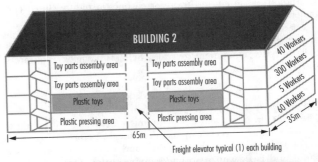

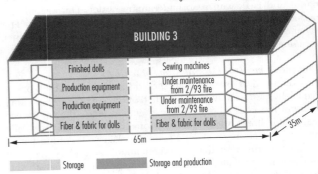

Each building at the plant was equipped with a fire alarm system. None of the buildings had automatic sprinklers, but portable extinguishers and hose stations were installed on outside walls and in the stairwells of each building. None of the structural steel in the building was fireproofed.

There is conflicting information about the total number of workers at the site. The Federation of Thai Industries had pledged to help 2,500 plant employees displaced by the fire, but it is unclear how many employees were at the site at any one time. When the fire occurred, it was reported that there were 1,146 workers in Building One. Thirty-six were on the first floor, 10 were on the second, 500 were on the third, and 600 were on the fourth. There were 405 workers in Building Two. Sixty of them were on the first floor, 5 were on the second, 300 were on the third and 40 were on the fourth. It is not clear how many workers were in Building Three since a portion of it was still being refurbished. Most of the workers at the plant were women.

The Fire

Monday, May 10, was a normal workday at the Kader facility. At approximately 4:00 p.m., as the end of the day shift approached, someone discovered a small fire on the first floor near the south end of Building One. This portion of the building was used to package and store the finished products, so it contained a considerable fuel load (see figure 39.14). Each building at the facility had a fuel load composed of fabric, plastics and materials used for stuffing, as well as other normal workplace materials.

Security guards in the vicinity of the fire tried unsuccessfully to extinguish the flames before they called the local police fire brigade at 4:21 p.m. Authorities received two more calls, at 4:30 p.m. and 4:31 p.m. The Kader facility is just beyond the jurisdictional boundaries of Bangkok, but fire apparatus from Bangkok, as well as apparatus from Nakhon Pathom Province, responded.

As the workers and security guards tried in vain to extinguish the fire, the building began filling with smoke and other products of combustion. Survivors reported that the fire alarm never sounded in Building One, but many workers grew concerned when they saw smoke on the upper floors. Despite the smoke, security guards reportedly told some workers to stay at their stations because it was a small fire that would soon be under control.

The fire spread rapidly throughout Building One, and the upper floors soon became untenable. The blaze blocked the stairwell at the south end of the building, so most of the workers rushed to the north stairwell. This meant that approximately 1,100 people were trying to leave the third and fourth floors through a single stairwell.

The first fire apparatus arrived at 4:40 p.m., their response time having been extended because of the relatively remote location of the facility and the gridlock conditions typical of Bangkok traffic. Arriving fire-fighters found Building One heavily involved in flames and already beginning to collapse, with people jumping from the third and fourth floors.

Despite the fire-fighters' efforts, Building One collapsed completely at approximately 5:14 p.m. Fanned by strong winds blowing toward the north, the blaze spread quickly into Buildings Two and Three before the fire brigade could effectively defend them. Building Two reportedly collapsed at 5:30 p.m., and Building Three at 6:05 p.m. The fire brigade successfully kept the fire from entering Building Four and the smaller, one-storey workshop nearby, and the fire-fighters had the blaze under control by 7:45 p.m. Approximately 50 pieces of fire apparatus were involved in the battle.

The fire alarms in Buildings Two and Three reportedly functioned properly, and all the workers in those two buildings es-

caped. The workers in Building One were not so fortunate. A large number of them jumped from the upper floors. In all, 469 workers were taken to the hospital, where 20 died. The other dead were found during the post-fire search of what had been the north stairwell of the building. Many of them apparently succumbed to lethal products of combustion before or during the building's collapse. According to the latest information available, 188 people, most of them female, have died as a result of this fire.

Even with the help of six large hydraulic cranes that were moved to the site to facilitate the search for victims, it was several days before all the bodies could be removed from the rubble. There were no fatalities among the fire-fighters, although there was one injury.

Traffic in the vicinity, which is normally congested, made transporting the victims to hospitals difficult. Nearly 300 injured workers were taken to the nearby Sriwichai II Hospital, although many of them were transferred to alternate medical facilities when the number of victims exceeded the hospital's capacity to treat them.

The day after the fire, Sriwichai II Hospital reported that it had kept 111 fire victims. The Kasemrat Hospital received 120; Sriwichai Pattanana received 60; Sriwichai I received 50; Ratanathibet I received 36; Siriraj received 22; and Bang Phai received 17. The remaining 53 injured workers were sent to various other medical facilities in the area. In all, 22 hospitals throughout Bangkok and Nakhon Pathom Province participated in treating victims of the disaster.

Sriwichai II Hospital reported that 80% of their 111 victims suffered serious injuries and that 30% required surgery. Half of the patients suffered only from smoke inhalation, while the remainder also suffered burns and fractures that ranged from broken ankles to fractured skulls. At least 10% of the injured Kader workers admitted to Sriwichai II Hospital risk permanent paralysis.

Determining the cause of this fire became a challenge because the portion of the facility in which it began was totally destroyed and the survivors have provided conflicting information. Since the fire started near a large electrical control panel, investigators first thought that problems with the electrical system might have been the cause. They also considered arson. At this time, however, Thai authorities feel that a carelessly discarded cigarette may have been the source of ignition.

Analysing the Fire

For 82 years, the world has recognized the 1911 Triangle Shirtwaist factory fire in New York City as the worst accidental loss-of-life industrial fire in which the fatalities were limited to the building of fire origin. With 188 fatalities, however, the Kader factory fire now replaces the Triangle fire in the record books.

When analysing the Kader fire, a direct comparison with the Triangle fire provides a useful benchmark. The two buildings were similar in a number of ways. The arrangement of the exits was poor, the fixed fire protection systems were insufficient or ineffective, the initial fuel package was readily combustible, and the horizontal and vertical fire separations were inadequate. In addition, neither company had provided its workers with adequate fire safety training. However, there is one distinct difference between these two fires: the Triangle Shirtwaist factory building did not collapse and the Kader buildings did.

Inadequate exit arrangements were perhaps the most significant factor in the high loss of life at both the Kader and the Triangle fires. Had the exiting provisions of NFPA 101, the *Life Safety Code*, which was established as a direct result of the Triangle fire, been applied at the Kader facility, substantially fewer lives would have been lost (NFPA 101, 1994).

39. DISASTERS, NATURAL AND TECHNOLOGICAL

Several fundamental requirements of the *Life Safety Code* pertain directly to the Kader fire. For example, the *Code* requires that every building or structure be constructed, arranged and operated in such a way that its occupants are not placed in any undue danger by fire, smoke, fumes or the panic that may occur during an evacuation or during the time it takes to defend the occupants in place.

The *Code* also requires that every building have enough exits and other safeguards of the proper size and at the proper locations to provide an escape route for every occupant of a building. These exits should be appropriate to the individual building or structure, taking into account the character of the occupancy, the capabilities of the occupants, the number of occupants, the fire protection available, the height and type of building construction and any other factor necessary to provide all the occupants with a reasonable degree of safety. This was obviously not the case in the Kader facility, where the blaze blocked one of Building One's two stairwells, forcing approximately 1,100 people to flee the third and fourth floors through a single stairwell.

In addition, the exits should be arranged and maintained so that they provide free and unobstructed egress from all parts of a building whenever it is occupied. Each of these exits should be clearly visible, or the route to every exit should be marked in such a way that every occupant of the building who is physically and mentally able readily knows the direction of escape from any point.

Every vertical exit or opening between the floors of a building should be enclosed or protected as necessary to keep the occupants reasonably safe while they exit and to prevent fire, smoke and fumes from spreading from floor to floor before the occupants have had a chance to use the exits.

The outcomes of both the Triangle and the Kader fires were significantly affected by the lack of adequate horizontal and vertical fire separations. The two facilities were arranged and built in such a way that a fire on a lower floor could spread rapidly to the upper floors, thus trapping a large number of workers.

Large, open work spaces are typical of industrial facilities, and fire-rated floors and walls must be installed and maintained to slow the spread of fire from one area to another. Fire also must be kept from spreading externally from the windows on one floor to those on another floor, as it did during the Triangle fire.

The most effective way to limit vertical fire spread is to enclose stairwells, elevators, and other vertical openings between floors. Reports of features such as caged freight elevators at the Kader factory raise significant questions about the ability of the buildings' passive fire protection features to prevent vertical spread of fire and smoke.

Fire Safety Training and Other Factors

Another factor that contributed to the large loss of life in both the Triangle and Kader fires was the lack of adequate fire safety training, and the rigid security procedures of both companies.

After the fire at the Kader facility, survivors reported that fire drills and fire safety training were minimal, although the security guards had apparently had some incipient fire training. The Triangle Shirtwaist factory had no evacuation plan, and fire drills were not implemented. Furthermore, post-fire reports from Triangle survivors indicate that they were routinely stopped as they left the building at the end of the work day for security purposes. Various post-fire accusations by Kader survivors also imply that security arrangements slowed their exit, although these accusations are still being investigated. In any case, the lack of a well-understood evacuation plan seems to have been an important factor in the high loss of life sustained in the Kader fire. Chapter 31 of the *Life Safety Code* addresses fire drills and evacuation training.

The absence of fixed automatic fire protection systems also affected the outcome of both the Triangle and the Kader fires. Neither facility was equipped with automatic sprinklers, although the Kader buildings did have a fire alarm system. According to the *Life Safety Code*, fire alarms should be provided in buildings whose size, arrangement or occupancy make it unlikely that the occupants themselves will notice a fire immediately. Unfortunately, the alarms reportedly never operated in Building One, which resulted in a significant delay in evacuation. There were no fatalities in Buildings Two and Three, where the fire alarm system functioned as intended.

Fire alarm systems should be designed, installed and maintained in accordance with documents like NFPA 72, the National Fire Alarm Code (NFPA 72, 1993). Sprinkler systems should be designed and installed in accordance with documents like NFPA 13, *Installation of Sprinkler Systems*, and maintained in accordance with NFPA 25, *Inspection, Testing, and Maintenance of Water-Based Fire Protection Systems* (NFPA 13, 1994; NFPA 25, 1995).

The initial fuel packages in both the Triangle and Kader fires were similar. The Triangle fire started in rag bins and quickly spread to combustible clothing and garments before involving wood furnishings, some of which were impregnated with machine oil. The initial fuel package at the Kader plant consisted of polyester and cotton fabrics, various plastics, and other materials used to manufacture stuffed toys, plastic dolls, and other related products. These are materials that can typically be ignited easily, can contribute to rapid fire growth and spread, and have a high heat release rate.

Industry will probably always handle materials that have challenging fire protection characteristics, but manufacturers should recognize these characteristics and take the necessary precautions to minimize associated hazards.

The Building's Structural Integrity

Probably the most notable difference between the Triangle and Kader fires is the effect they had on the structural integrity of the buildings involved. Even though the Triangle fire gutted the top three floors of the ten-storey factory building, the building remained structurally intact. The Kader buildings, on the other hand, collapsed relatively early in the fire because their structural steel supports lacked the fireproofing that would have allowed them to maintain their strength when exposed to high temperatures. A post-fire review of the debris at the Kader site showed no indication that any of the steel members had been fireproofed.

Obviously, building collapse during a fire presents a great threat to both the building's occupants and to the fire-fighters involved in controlling the blaze. However, it is unclear whether the collapse of the Kader building had any direct effect on the number of fatalities, since the victims may have already succumbed to the effects of heat and products of combustion by the time the building collapsed. If the workers on the upper floors of Building One had been shielded from the products of combustion and heat while they were trying to escape, the building's collapse would have been a more direct factor in the loss of life.

Fire Focused Attention on Fire Protection Principles

Among the fire protection principles on which the Kader fire has focused attention are exit design, occupant fire safety training, automatic detection and suppression systems, fire separations and structural integrity. These lessons are not new. They were first taught more than 80 years ago at the Triangle Shirtwaist fire and again, more recently, in a number of other fatal workplace fires, including those at the chicken-processing plant in Hamlet, North Carolina, USA, that killed 25 workers; at a doll factory in Kuiyong, China, that killed 81 workers; and at the electrical power plant in Newark, New Jersey, USA, that killed all 3 workers in the plant (Grant and Klem 1994; Klem 1992; Klem and Grant 1993).

The fires in North Carolina and New Jersey, in particular, demonstrate that the mere availability of state-of-the-art codes and standards, such as NFPA's *Life Safety Code*, cannot prevent tragic losses. These codes and standards must also be adopted and rigorously enforced if they are to have any effect.

National, state and local public authorities should examine the way they enforce their building and fire codes to determine whether new codes are needed or existing codes need to be updated. This review should also determine whether a building plan review and inspection process is in place to ensure that the appropriate codes are followed. Finally, provisions must be made for periodic follow-up inspections of existing buildings to ensure that the highest levels of fire protection are maintained throughout the life of the building.

Building owners and operators must also be aware that they are responsible for ensuring that their employees' working environment is safe. At the very least, the state-of-the-art fire protection design reflected in fire codes and standards must be in place to minimize the possibility of a catastrophic fire.

Had the Kader buildings been equipped with sprinklers and working fire alarms, the loss of life might not have been so high. Had Building One's exits been better designed, hundreds of people might not have been injured jumping from the third and fourth floors. Had vertical and horizontal separations been in place, the fire might not have spread so quickly throughout the building. Had the buildings' structural steel members been fireproofed, the buildings might not have collapsed.

Philosopher George Santayana has written: "Those who forget the past are condemned to repeat it." The Kader Fire of 1993 was unfortunately, in many ways, a repeat of the Triangle Shirtwaist Fire of 1911. As we look to the future, we need to recognize all that we need to do, as a global society, to prevent history from repeating itself.

• IMPACTS OF DISASTERS: LESSONS FROM A MEDICAL PERSPECTIVE

José Luis Zeballos*

Latin America and the Caribbean have not been spared their share of natural disasters. Almost every year catastrophic events cause deaths, injuries and enormous economic damage. Overall, it is estimated that the major natural disasters of the last two decades in this region caused property losses affecting nearly 8 million people, some 500,000 injuries and 150,000 deaths. These figures rely heavily on official sources. (It is quite difficult to obtain accurate information in sudden-onset disasters, because there are multiple information sources and no standardized information system.) The Economic Commission for Latin America and the Caribbean (ECLAC) estimates that during an average year, disasters in Latin America and the Caribbean cost US$1.5 billion and take 6,000 lives (Jovel 1991).

Table 39.33 lists major natural disasters that struck countries of the region in the 1970-93 period. It should be noted that slow-onset disasters, such as droughts and floods, are not included.

*This article was adapted, with permission, from Zeballos 1993b.

Table 39.33 • Major disasters in Latin America and the Caribbean, 1970-93.

Year	Country	Type of disaster	No. of deaths reported	Est. no. of people affected
1970	Peru	Earthquake	66,679	3,139,000
1972	Nicaragua	Earthquake	10,000	400,000
1976	Guatemala	Earthquake	23,000	1,200,000
1980	Haiti	Hurricane (Allen)	220	330,000
1982	Mexico	Volcanic eruption	3,000	60,000
1985	Mexico	Earthquake	10,000	60,000
1985	Colombia	Volcanic eruption	23,000	200,000
1986	El Salvador	Earthquake	1,100	500,000
1988	Jamaica	Hurricane (Gilbert)	45	500,000
1988	Mexico	Hurricane (Gilbert)	250	200,000
1988	Nicaragua	Hurricane (Joan)	116	185,000
1989	Montserrat, Dominica	Hurricane (Hugo)	56	220,000
1990	Peru	Earthquake	21	130,000
1991	Costa Rica	Earthquake	51	19,700
1992	Nicaragua	Tsunami	116	13,500
1993	Honduras	Tropical storm	103	11,000

Source: PAHO 1989; OFDA (USAID),1989; UNDRO 1990.

Economic Impact

In recent decades, ECLAC has carried out extensive research on the social and economic impacts of disasters. This has clearly demonstrated that disasters have negative repercussions on social and economic development in developing countries. Indeed, the monetary losses caused by a major disaster often exceed the total annual gross income of the affected country. Not surprisingly, such events can paralyze affected countries and foster widespread political and social turmoil.

In essence, disasters have three kinds of economic impacts:

- direct impacts on the affected population's property
- indirect impacts caused by lost economic production and services

Table 39.34 • Losses due to six natural disasters.

Disaster	Location	Year(s)	Total losses (US$ millions)
Earthquake	Mexico	1985	4,337
Earthquake	El Salvador	1986	937
Earthquake	Ecuador	1987	1,001
Volcanic eruption (Nevado del Ruiz)	Colombia	1985	224
Floods, drought ("El Niño")	Peru, Ecuador, Bolivia	1982-83	3,970
Hurricane (Joan)	Nicaragua	1988	870

Source: PAHO 1989; ECLAC.

39. DISASTERS, NATURAL AND TECHNOLOGICAL

Table 39.35 • Number of hospitals and hospital beds damaged or destroyed by three major natural disasters.

Type of disaster	No. of hospitals damaged or destroyed	No. of beds lost
Earthquake, Mexico (Federal District, September 1985)	13	4,387
Earthquake, El Salvador (San Salvador, October 1986)	4	1,860
Hurricane Gilbert (Jamaica, September 1988)	23	5,085
Total	40	11,332

Source: PAHO 1989; OFDA(USAID) 1989; ECLAC.

- secondary impacts that become apparent after the disaster—such as reduced national income, increased inflation, foreign trade problems, heightened financial expenses, a resulting fiscal deficit, decreased monetary reserves and so on (Jovel 1991).

Table 39.34 shows the estimated losses caused by six major natural disasters. While such losses might not seem particularly devastating for developed countries with strong economies, they can have a serious and lasting impact on the weak and vulnerable economies of developing countries (PAHO 1989).

The Health Infrastructure

In any major disaster-related emergency, the first priority is to save lives and provide immediate emergency care for the injured. Among the emergency medical services mobilized for these purposes, hospitals play a key role. Indeed, in countries with a standardized emergency response system (one where the concept of "emergency medical services" encompasses provision of emergency care through the coordination of independent subsystems involving paramedics, fire-fighters and rescue teams) hospitals constitute the major component of that system (PAHO 1989).

Hospitals and other health care facilities are densely occupied. They house patients, personnel and visitors, and they operate 24 hours a day. Patients may be surrounded by special equipment or connected to life-support systems dependent on power supplies. According to project documents available from the Inter-American Development Bank (IDB) (personal communication, Tomas Engler, IDB), the estimated cost of one hospital bed in a specialized hospital varies from country to country, but the average runs

Table 39.36 • Victims in two hospitals collapsed by the 1985 earthquake in Mexico.

	Collapsed hospitals			
	General hospital		Juarez hospital	
	Number	%	Number	%
Fatalities	295	62.6	561	75.8
Rescued	129	27.4	179	24.2
Missing	47	10.0	–	–
Total	471	100.0	740	100.0

Source: PAHO 1987.

Table 39.37 • Hospital beds lost as a result of the March 1985 Chilean earthquake.

Region	No. of existing hospitals	No. of beds	Beds lost in region	
			No.	%
Metropolitan Area (Santiago)	26	11,464	2,373	20.7
Region 5 (Viña del Mar, Valparaíso, San Antonio)	23	4,573	622	13.6
Region 6 (Rancagua)	15	1,413	212	15.0
Region 7 (Ralca, Meula)	15	2,286	64	2.8
Total	79	19,736	3,271	16.6

Source: Wyllie and Durkin 1986.

from US$60,000 to US$80,000 and is greater for highly specialized facilities. In the United States, particularly California, with its extensive experience in seismic-resistant engineering, the cost of one hospital bed can exceed US$110,000. In sum, modern hospitals are highly complex facilities combining the functions of hotels, offices, laboratories and warehouses (Peisert et al. 1984; FEMA 1990).

These health care facilities are highly vulnerable to hurricanes and earthquakes. This has been amply demonstrated by past experience in Latin America and the Caribbean. For example, as table 39.35 shows, just three disasters of the 1980s damaged 39 hospitals and destroyed some 11,332 hospital beds in El Salvador, Jamaica and Mexico. Besides damage to these physical plants at critical times, the loss of human life (including the death of highly qualified local professionals with promising futures) needs to be considered (see tables 39.36 and 39.37).

At present the ability of many Latin American hospitals to survive earthquake disasters is uncertain. Many such hospitals are housed in old structures, some dating from Spanish colonial times; and while many others occupy contemporary buildings of appealing architectural design, lax application of building codes makes their ability to resist earthquakes questionable.

Table 39.38 • Risk factors associated with earthquake damage to hospital infrastructure.

Structural	Non-structural	Behavioural
Design	Medical equipment	Public information
Quality of construction	Laboratory equipment	Motivation
	Office equipment	Plans
Materials	Cabinets, shelves	Educational programmes
Soil conditions	Stoves, refrigerators, heaters	Health care staff training
Seismic characteristics	X-ray machines	
Time of the event	Reactive materials	
Population density		

Risk Factors in Earthquakes

Of the various types of sudden natural disasters, earthquakes are by far the most damaging to hospitals. Of course, each earthquake has its own characteristics relating to its epicentre, type of seismic waves, geological nature of the soil through which the waves travel and so on. Nevertheless, studies have revealed certain common factors that tend to cause death and injuries and certain others that tend to prevent them. These factors include structural characteristics related to building failure, various factors related to human behaviour and certain characteristics of non-structural equipment, furnishings and other items inside buildings.

In recent years, scholars and planners have been paying special attention to identification of risk factors affecting hospitals, in hopes of framing better recommendations and norms to govern the building and organization of hospitals in highly vulnerable zones. A brief listing of relevant risk factors is shown in table 39.38. These risk factors, particularly those related to the structural aspects, were observed to influence patterns of destruction during a December 1988 earthquake in Armenia that killed some 25,000 people, affected 1,100,000 and destroyed or severely damaged 377 schools, 560 health facilities and 324 community and cultural centres (USAID 1989).

Damage on a similar scale occurred in June 1990, when an earthquake in Iran killed about 40,000 people, injured 60,000 others, left 500,000 homeless, and collapsed 60 to 90% of buildings in affected zones (UNDRO 1990).

To address these and like calamities, an international seminar was held in Lima, Peru, in 1989 on the planning, design, repair and management of hospitals in earthquake-prone areas. The seminar, sponsored by PAHO, Peru's National University of Engineering and the Peruvian-Japanese Center for Seismic Research (CISMID), brought together architects, engineers and hospital administrators to study issues related to health facilities located in these areas. The seminar approved a core of technical recommendations and commitments directed at carrying out vulnerability analyses of hospital infrastructures, improving the design of new facilities and establishing safety measures for existing hospitals, with emphasis on those located in high-risk earthquake areas (CISMID 1989)1

Recommendations on Hospital Preparedness

As the foregoing suggests, hospital disaster preparedness constitutes an important component of PAHO's Office of Emergency Preparedness and Disaster Relief. Over the last ten years, member countries have been encouraged to pursue activities directed toward this end, including the following:

- classifying hospitals according to their risk factors and vulnerabilities
- developing internal and external hospital response plans and training personnel
- developing contingency plans and establishing safety measures for the professional and technical hospital staffs

- strengthening lifeline backup systems that help hospitals to function during emergency situations.

More broadly, a principal aim of the current International Decade for Natural Disaster Reduction (IDNDR) is to attract, motivate and commit national health authorities and policy-makers around the world, thereby encouraging them to strengthen the health services directed at coping with disasters and to reduce the vulnerability of those services in the developing world.

Issues Concerning Technological Accidents

During the last two decades, developing countries have entered into intense competition to achieve industrial development. The main reasons for this competition are as follows:

- to attract capital investment and to generate jobs
- to satisfy domestic demand for products at a lower cost and to alleviate dependency on the international market
- to compete with international and subregional markets
- to establish foundations for development.

Unfortunately, efforts made have not always resulted in obtaining the intended objectives. In effect, flexibility in attracting capital investment, lack of sound regulation with respect to industrial safety and environmental protection, negligence in the operation of industrial plants, use of obsolete technology, and other aspects have contributed to increasing the risk of technological accidents in certain areas.

In addition, the lack of regulation regarding the establishment of human settlements near or around industrial plants is an additional risk factor. In major Latin American cities it is common to see human settlements practically surrounding industrial complexes, and the inhabitants of these settlements are ignorant of the potential risks (Zeballos 1993a).

In order to avoid accidents such as those that occurred in Guadalajara (Mexico) in 1992, the following guidelines are suggested for the establishment of chemical industries, to protect industrial workers and the population at large:

- selection of appropriate technology and study of alternatives
- appropriate location of industrial plants
- regulation of human settlements in the neighbourhood of industrial plants
- security considerations for technology transfer
- routine inspection of industrial plants by local authorities
- expertise provided by specialized agencies
- role of workers in compliance with security rules
- rigid legislation
- classification of toxic materials and close supervision of their use
- public education and training of workers
- establishment of response mechanisms in case of emergency
- training of health workers in emergency plans for technological accidents.

References

American Psychiatric Association (APA). 1994. *DSM-IV Diagnostic and Statistical Manual of Mental Disorders.* Washington, DC: APA.

Andersson, N, M Kerr Muir, MK Ajwani, S Mahashabde, A Salmon, and K Vaidyanathan. 1986. Persistent eye watering among Bhopal survivors. *Lancet* 2:1152.

Baker, EL, M Zack, JW Miles, L Alderman, M Warren, RD Dobbin, S Miller, and WR Teeters. 1978. Epidemic malathion poisoning in Pakistan malaria working. *Lancet* 1:31-34.

Baum, A, L Cohen, and M Hall. 1993. Control and intrusive memories as possible determinants of chronic stress. *Psychosom Med* 55:274-286.

Bertazzi, PA. 1989. Industrial disasters and epidemiology. A review of recent experiences. *Scand J Work Environ Health* 15:85-100.

—. 1991. Long-term effects of chemical disasters. Lessons and result from Seveso. *Sci Total Environ* 106:5-20.

Bromet, EJ, DK Parkinson, HC Schulberg, LO Dunn, and PC Condek. 1982. Mental health of residents near the Three Mile Island reactor: A comparative study of selected groups. *J Prev Psychiat* 1(3):225-276.

Bruk, GY, NG Kaduka, and VI Parkhomenko. 1989. Air contamination by radionuclides as a result of the accident at the Chernobyl power station and its contribution to inner irradiation of the population (in Russian). Materials of the First All-Union Radiological Congress, 21-27 August, Moscow. Abstracts (in Russian). *Puschkino,* 1989, vol. II:414-416.

Bruzzi, P. 1983. Health impact of the accidental release of TCDD at Seveso. In *Accidental Exposure to Dioxins. Human Health Aspects,* edited by F Coulston and F Pocchiari. New York: Academic Press.

Cardis, E, ES Gilbert, and L Carpenter. 1995. Effects of low doses and low dose rates of external ionizing radiation: Cancer mortality among nuclear industry workers in three countries. *Rad Res* 142:117-132.

Centers for Disease Control (CDC). 1989. *The Public Health Consequences of Disasters.* Atlanta: CDC.

Centro Peruano-Japones de Investigaciones Sismicas y Mitigacióm de Desastres. Universidad Nacional de Ingeniería (CISMID). 1989. *Seminario Internacional De Planeamiento Diseño, Reparación Y Adminstración De Hospitales En Zonas Sísmicas: Conclusiones Y Recommendaciones.* Lima: CISMID/Univ Nacional de Ingeniería.

Chagnon, SAJR, RJ Schicht, and RJ Semorin. 1983. *A Plan for Research on Floods and their Mitigation in the United States.* Champaign, Ill: Illinois State Water Survey.

Chen, PS, ML Luo, CK Wong, and CJ Chen. 1984. Polychlorinated biphenyls, dibenzofurans, and quaterphenyls in toxic rice-bran oil and PCBs in the blood of patients with PCB poisoning in Taiwan. *Am J Ind Med* 5:133-145.

Coburn, A and R Spence. 1992. *Earthquake Protection.* Chichester: Wiley.

Council of the European Communities (CEC). 1982. Council Directive of 24 June on the major accident hazards of certain industrial activities (82/501/EEC). *Off J Eur Communities* L230:1-17.

—. 1987. Council Directive of 19 March amending Directive 82/501/EEC on the major accident hazards of certain industrial activities (87/216/EEC). *Off J Eur Communities* L85:36-39.

Das, JJ. 1985a. Aftermath of Bhopal tragedy. *J Indian Med Assoc* 83:361-362.

—. 1985b. The Bhopal tragedy. *J Indian Med Assoc* 83:72-75.

Dew, MA and EJ Bromet. 1993. Predictors of temporal patterns of psychiatric distress during ten years following the nuclear accident at Three Mile Island. *Social Psych Psychiatric Epidemiol* 28:49-55.

Federal Emergency Management Agency (FEMA). 1990. *Seismic considerations: Health care facilities.* Earthquake Hazard Reduction Series, No. 35. Washington, DC: FEMA.

Frazier, K. 1979. *The Violent Face of Nature: Severe Phenomena and Natural Disasters. Floods.* New York: William Morrow & Co.

Freidrich Naumann Foundation. 1987. *Industrial Hazards in Transnational Work: Risk, Equity and Empowerment.* New York: Council on International and Public Affairs.

French, J and K Holt. 1989. *Floods: Public Health Consequences of Disasters.* Centers for Disease Control Monograph. Atlanta: CDC.

French, J, R Ing, S Von Allman, and R Wood. 1983. Mortality from flash floods: A review of National Weather Service reports, 1969-1981. *Publ Health Rep* 6(November/December):584-588.

Fuller, M. 1991. *Forest Fires.* New York: John Wiley.

Gilsanz, V, J Lopez Alverez, S Serrano, and J Simon. 1984. Evolution of the alimentary toxic oil syndrome due to ingestion of denatured rapeseed oil. *Arch Int Med* 144:254-256.

Glass, RI, RB Craven, and DJ Bregman. 1980. Injuries from the Wichita Falls tornado: Implications for prevention. *Science* 207:734-738.

Grant, CC. 1993. Triangle fire stirs outrage and reform. *NFPA J* 87(3):72-82.

Grant, CC and TJ Klem. 1994. Toy factory fire in Thailand kills 188 workers. *NFPA J* 88(1):42-49.

Greene, WAJ. 1954. Psychological factors and reticuloendothelial disease: Preliminary observations on a group of males with lymphoma and leukemia. *Psychosom Med*:16-20.

Grisham, JW. 1986. *Health Aspects of the Disposal of Waste Chemicals.* New York: Pergamon Press.

Herbert, P and G Taylor. 1979. Everything you always wanted to know about hurricanes: Part 1. *Weatherwise* (April).

High, D, JT Blodgett, EJ Croce, EO Horne, JW McKoan, and CS Whelan. 1956. Medical aspects of the Worcester tornado disaster. *New Engl J Med* 254:267-271.

Holden, C. 1980. Love Canal residents under stress. *Science* 208:1242-1244.

Homberger, E, G Reggiani, J Sambeth, and HK Wipf. 1979. The Seveso accident: Its nature, extent and consequences. *Ann Occup Hyg* 22:327-370.

Hunter, D. 1978. *The Diseases of Occupations.* London: Hodder & Stoughton.

International Atomic Energy Agency (IAEA). 1988. *Basic Safety Principles for Nuclear Power Plants INSAG-3.* Safety Series, No. 75. Vienna: IAEA.

—. 1989a. *L'accident radiologique de Goiânia.* Vienna: IAEA.

—. 1989b. A large-scale Co-60 contamination case: Mexico 1984. In *Emergency Planning and Preparedness for Accidents Involving Radioactive Materials Used in Medicine, Industry, Research and Teaching.* Vienna: IAEA.

—. 1990. *Recommendations for the Safe Use and Regulation of Radiation Sources in Industry, Medicine, Research and Teaching.* Safety Series, No. 102. Vienna: IAEA.

—. 1991. *The International Chernobyl Project.* Technical report, assessment of radiological consequences and evaluation of protective measures, report by an International Advisory Committee. Vienna: IAEA.

—. 1994. *Intervention Criteria in a Nuclear or Radiation Emergency.* Safety Series, No. 109. Vienna: IAEA.

International Commission on Radiological Protection (ICRP). 1991. *Annals of the ICRP.* ICRP Publication No. 60. Oxford: Pergamon Press.

International Federation of Red Cross and Red Crescent Societies (IFRCRCS). 1993. *The World Disaster Report.* Dordrecht: Martinus Nijhoff.

International Labour Organization (ILO). 1988. *Major Hazard Control. A Practical Manual.* Geneva: ILO.

—. 1991. *Prevention of Major Industrial Accidents.* Geneva: ILO.

—. 1993. Prevention of Major Industrial Accidents Convention, 1993 (No. 174). Geneva: ILO.

Janerich, DT, AD Stark, P Greenwald, WS Bryant, HI Jacobson, and J McCusker. 1981. Increased leukemia, lymphoma and spontaneous abortion in Western New York following a disaster. *Publ Health Rep* 96:350-356.

Jeyaratnam, J. 1985. 1984 and occupational health in developing countries. *Scand J Work Environ Health* 11:229-234.

Jovel, JR. 1991. *Los efectos económicos y sociales de los desastres naturales en América Latina y el Caribe.* Santiago, Chile: Document presented at the First Regional UNDP/UNDRO Disaster Management Training Program in Bogota, Colombia.

Kilbourne, EM, JG Rigau-Perez, J Heath CW, MM Zack, H Falk, M Martin-Marcos, and A De Carlos. 1983. Clinical epidemiology of toxic-oil syndrome. *New Engl J Med* 83:1408-1414.

Klem, TJ. 1992. 25 die in food plant fire. *NFPA J* 86(1):29-35.

Klem, TJ and CC Grant. 1993. *Three Workers Die in Electrical Power Plant Fire. NFPA J* 87(2):44-47.

Krasnyuk, EP, VI Chernyuk, and VA Stezhka. 1993. Work conditions and health status of operators of agricultural machines in areas being under control due to the Chernobyl accident (in Russian). In abstracts Chernobyl and Human Health Conference, 20-22 April.

Krishna Murti, CR. 1987. Prevention and control of chemical accidents: Problems of developing countries. In *Istituto Superiore Sanita', World Health Organization, International Programme On Chemical Safety.* Edinburgh: CEP Consultants.

Lancet. 1983. Toxic oil syndrome. 1:1257-1258.

Lechat, MF. 1990. The epidemiology of health effects of disasters. *Epidemiol Rev* 12:192.

Logue, JN. 1972. Long term effects of a major natural disaster: The Hurricane Agnes flood in the Wyoming Valley of Pennsylvania, June 1972. Ph.D. Dissertation, Columbia Univ. School of Public Health.

Logue, JN and HA Hansen. 1980. A case control study of hypertensive women in a post-disaster community: Wyoming Valley, Pennsylvania. *J Hum Stress* 2:28-34.

Logue, JN, ME Melick, and H Hansen. 1981. Research issues and directions in the epidemiology of health effects of disasters. *Epidemiol Rev* 3:140.

Loshchilov, NA, VA Kashparov, YB Yudin, VP Proshchak, and VI Yushchenko. 1993. Inhalation intake of radionuclides during agricultural works in the areas contaminated by radionuclides due to the Chernobyl accident (in Russian). *Gigiena i sanitarija (Moscow)* 7:115-117.

Mandlebaum, I, D Nahrwold, and DW Boyer. 1966. Management of tornado casualties. *J Trauma* 6:353-361.

Marrero, J. 1979. Danger: Flash floods—the number one killer of the 70's. *Weatherwise* (February):34-37.

Masuda, Y and H Yoshimura. 1984. Polychlorinated biphenyls and dibenzofurans in patients with Yusho and their toxicological significance: A review. *Am J Ind Med* 5:31-44.

Melick, MF. 1976. Social, psychological and medical aspects of stress related illness in the recovery period of a natural disaster. Dissertation, Albany, State Univ. of New York.

Mogil, M, J Monro, and H Groper. 1978. NWS's flash flood warning and disaster preparedness programs. *B Am Meteorol Soc* :59-66.

Morrison, AS. 1985. *Screening in Chronic Disease*. Oxford: OUP.

National Fire Protection Association (NFPA). 1993. *National Fire Alarm Code*. NFPA No. 72. Quincy, Mass: NFPA.

—. 1994. *Standard for the Installation of Sprinkler Systems*. NFPA No. 13. Quincy, Mass: NFPA.

—. 1994. *Life Safety Code*. NFPA No. 101. Quincy, Mass: NFPA.

—. 1995. *Standard for the Inspection, Testing, and Maintenance of Water-Based Fire Protection Systems*. NFPA No. 25. Quincy, Mass: NFPA.

Nénot, JC. 1993. Les surexpositions accidentelles. CEA, Institut de Protection et de Sûreté Nucléaire. Rapport DPHD/93-04.a, 1993, 3-11.

Nuclear Energy Agency. 1987. *The Radiological Impact of the Chernobyl Accident in OECD Countries*. Paris: Nuclear Energy Agency.

Otake, M and WJ Schull. 1992. *Radiation-related Small Head Sizes among Prenatally Exposed Atomic Bomb Survivors*. Technical Report Series, RERF 6-92.

Otake, M, WJ Schull, and H Yoshimura. 1989. *A Review of Radiation-related Damage in the Prenatally Exposed Atomic Bomb Survivors*. Commentary Review Series, RERF CR 4-89.

Pan American Health Organization (PAHO). 1989. *Analysis of PAHO's Emergency Preparedness and Disaster Relief Program*. Executive Committee document SPP12/7. Washington, DC: PAHO.

—. 1987. *Crónicas de desastre: terremoto en México*. Washington, DC: PAHO.

Parrish, RG, H Falk, and JM Melius. 1987. Industrial disasters: Classification, investigation, and prevention. In *Recent Advances in Occupational Health*, edited by JM Harrington. Edinburgh: Churchill Livingstone.

Peisert, M comp, RE Cross, and LM Riggs. 1984. *The Hospital's Role in Emergency Medical Services Systems*. Chicago: American Hospital Publishing.

Pesatori, AC. 1995. Dioxin contamination in Seveso: The social tragedy and the scientific challenge. *Med Lavoro* 86:111-124.

Peter, RU, O Braun-Falco, and A Birioukov. 1994. Chronic cutaneous damage after accidental exposure to ionizing radiation: The Chernobyl experience. *J Am Acad Dermatol* 30:719-723.

Pocchiari, F, A DiDomenico, V Silano, and G Zapponi. 1983. Environmental impact of the accidental release of tetrachlorodibenzo-p-dioxin(TCDD) at Seveso. In *Accidental Exposure to Dioxins: Human Health Aspects*, edited by F Coulston and F Pocchiari. New York: Academic Press.

—. 1986. The Seveso accident and its aftermath. In *Insuring and Managing Hazardous Risks: From Seveso to Bhopal and Beyond*, edited by PR Kleindorfer and HC Kunreuther. Berlin: Springer-Verlag.

Rodrigues de Oliveira, A. 1987. Un répertoire des accidents radiologiques 1945-1985. *Radioprotection* 22(2):89-135.

Sainani, GS, VR Joshi, PJ Mehta, and P Abraham. 1985. Bhopal tragedy -A year later. *J Assoc Phys India* 33:755-756.

Salzmann, JJ. 1987. *"Schweizerhalle" and Its Consequences*. Edinburgh: CEP Consultants.

Shore, RE. 1992. Issues and epidemiological evidences regarding radiation-induced thyroid cancer. *Rad Res* 131:98-111.

Spurzem, JR and JE Lockey. 1984. Toxic oil syndrome. *Arch Int Med* 144:249-250.

Stsjazhko, VA, AF Tsyb, ND Tronko, G Souchkevitch, and KF Baverstock. 1995. Childhood thyroid cancer since accidents at Chernobyl. *Brit Med J* 310:801.

Tachakra, SS. 1987. *The Bhopal Disaster*. Edinburgh: CEP Consultants.

Thierry, D, P Gourmelon, C Parmentier, and JC Nenot. 1995. Hematopoietic growth factors in the treatment of therapeutic and accidental irradiation-induced aplasia. *Int J Rad Biol* (in press).

Understanding Science and Nature: Weather and Climate. 1992. Alexandria, Va: Time-Life.

United Nations Disaster Relief Coordinator Office (UNDRO). 1990. Iran earthquake. *UNDRO News* 4 (September).

United Nations Scientific Committee on the Effects of Atomic Radiation (UNSCEAR). 1988. *Sources, Effects and Risks of Ionizing Radiation*. New York: UNSCEAR.

—. 1993. *Sources and Effects of Ionizing Radiation*. New York: UNSCEAR.

—. 1994. *Sources and Effects of Ionizing Radiation*. New York: UNSCEAR.

Ursano, RJ, BG McCaughey, and CS Fullerton. 1994. *Individual and Community Responses to Trauma and Disaster: The Structure of Human Chaos*. Cambridge: Cambridge Univ. Press.

US Agency for International Development, (USAID). 1989. *Soviet Union: Earthquake*. OFDA/AID Annual Report, FY1989. Arlington, Va: USAID.

Walker, P. 1995. *World Disaster Report*. Geneva: International Federation of Red Cross and Red Crescent Societies.

Wall Street J. 1993 Thailand fire shows region cuts corners on safety to boost profits, 13 May.

Weiss, B and TW Clarkson. 1986. Toxic chemical disaster and the implication of Bhopal for technology transfer. *Milbank Q* 64:216.

Whitlow, J. 1979. *Disasters: The Anatomy of Environmental Hazards*. Athens, Ga: Univ. of Georgia Press.

Williams, D, A Pinchera, A Karaoglou, and KH Chadwick. 1993. *Thyroid Cancer in Children Living Near Chernobyl*. Expert panel report on the consequences of the Chernobyl accident, EUR 15248 EN. Brussels: Commission of the European Communities (CEC).

World Health Organization (WHO). 1984. *Toxic Oil Syndrome. Mass Food Poisoning in Spain*. Copenhagen: WHO Regional office for Europe.

Wyllie, L and M Durkin. 1986. The Chile earthquake of March 3, 1985: Casualties and effects on the health care system. *Earthquake Spec* 2(2):489-495.

Zeballos, JL. 1993a. *Los desastres quimicos, capacidad de respuesta de los paises en vias de desarrollo*. Washington, DC: Pan American Health Organization (PAHO).

—. 1993b. Effects of natural disasters on the health infrastructure: Lessons from a medical perspective. *Bull Pan Am Health Organ* 27: 389-396.

Zerbib, JC. 1993. Les accidents radiologiques survenus lors d'usages industriels de sources radioactives ou de générateurs électirques de rayonnement. In *Sécurité des sources radioactives scellées et des générateurs électriques de rayonnement*. Paris: Société française de radioprotection.

Other relevant readings

Akleyev, AV and ER Lyubchansky. 1994. Environmental and medical effects of nuclear weapon production in the Southern Urals. *Sci Total Environ* 142:1-8.

Baxter, PJ, PC Davies, and V Murray. 1989. Medical planning for toxic releases into the community: The example of chlorine gas. *Brit J Ind Med* 46:277-285.

Bertazzi, PA. 1995. Man-made chemical disasters. In *Environmental Epidemiology: Exposures and Disease*, edited by R Bertollini, MD Lebowitz, R Saracci, and DA Savitz. Boca Raton: Lewis.

Bertazzi, PA and A di Domenico. 1994. Chemical, environment, and health aspects of the Seveso, Italy accident. In *Dioxins and Health*, edited by A Schecter. New York: Plenum.

Bertazzi, PA, C Zocchetti, AC Pesatori, S Guercilena, M Sanarico, and L Radice. 1989. Ten-year mortality study of population involved in the Seveso incident in 1976. *Am J Epidemiol* 129:1187-1200.

Bertazzi, PA, AC Pesatori, D Consonni, A Tironi, MT Landi, and C Zocchetti. 1993. Cancer incidence in a population accidentally exposed to 2,3,7,8-tetrachlorodibenzo-p-dioxin. *Epidemiology* 4:398-406.

Castle, M. 1993. *The Transport of Dangerous Goods: A Short Guide to the International Regulations*. Leatherhead: PIRA International.

Disaster epidemiology. 1990. *Lancet* 336:845.

Doll, R. 1985. Purpose of symposium. In *Interpretation of Negative Epidemiological Evidence for Carcinogenicity*, edited by NJ Wald and R Doll. Lyon: International Agency for Research on Cancer (IARC).

Federal Department of Civil Aviation. 1988. *Weisungen Für Lawinensprengeinsätze Mit Helikoptern*. Switzerland: Federal Department of Civil Aviation.

Federal Ministry for Public Economy and Transport. 1990. *Sicherheitstechnische Richtlinien für das künstliche Auslösen von Lawinen durch Sprengungen von Hubschraubern aus*. Decree of the Federal Ministry for Public Economy and Transport, Austria, Zl. 431,000/31/90, dated 27 June 1990, currently operative version/no copyright.

—. 1993. *Richtlinien für das künstliche Auslösen von Lawinen durch Arbeitnehmer bei Seilbahnunternehmen*. Decree of the Federal Ministry for Public Economy and Transport, Austria,Zl. 443,017/1-IV/52/93, dated January 1993.

Gubler, H. 1988a. Temporäre und permanente Lawinenschutzmaßnahmen für touristische Anlangen. *Int Seilbahnrundschau* 1:22-24.

—. 1988b. Temporäre und permanente Lawinenschutzmaßnahmen für touristische Anlangen. *Int Seilbahnrundschau* 2:18-20.

Health and Safety Commission, AC on DS. 1991. *Major Hazard Aspects of the Transport of Dangerous Substances*. London: HMSO.

Lechat, MF. 1991. The international decade for natural disaster reduction: Background and objectives. *Disasters* 14:1-6.

Meulenbelt, J, GJ Noordergraaf, and TJF Savelkould. 1994. *Health Aspects Chemical Accident*. Den Haag: CIP-Gegevens Koninkluke Bibliotheek.

Murray, V. 1990. *Major Chemical Disasters. Medical Aspects of Management*. London: Royal Society of Medicine Services.

Office of the United Nations Disaster Relief Co-ordinator (UNDRO). 1991. *Mitigating Natural Disasters*. New York: UNDRO.

Organisation for Economic Co-operation and Development (OECD). 1991a. *International Directory of Emergency Response Centres*. OECD Environment Monographs, No. 43. Paris: OECD.

—. 1991b. *Users Guide: Information Systems Useful to Emergency Planners and Responders Available*. Paris: OECD.

—. 1992. *Guiding Principles for Chemical Accident Prevention, Preparedness and Response*. Paris: OECD.

—. 1994. *Health Aspects of Chemical Accidents*. Paris: OECD.

Royal Society of Medicine. 1990. *Major Chemical Disasters: Medical Aspects of Management*, edited by V Murray. London: Royal Society of Medicine.

Technica. 1991. *Lessons Learned from Emergencies After Accidents in the United Kingdom Involving Dangerous Chemical Substances*. London: Technica.

United Nations Environment Programme (UNEP). N.d. *Awareness and Preparedness for Emergencies At Local Level(APPELL) A Process for Responding to Technological Accidents*. Nairobi: UNEP.

WHO-ECEH Working Group. 1995. Assessment of Health Consequences of Major Chemical Incidents. Epidemiological Approach. Bilthoven: European Centre for Environment and Health.

39. DISASTERS, NATURAL AND TECHNOLOGICAL

ELECTRICITY

Chapter Editor
Dominique Folliot

Contents

ELECTRICITY—PHYSIOLOGICAL EFFECTS

Dominique Folliot

The study of the hazards, electrophysiology and prevention of electrical accidents requires an understanding of several technical and medical concepts.

The following definitions of electrobiological terms are taken from chapter 891 of the International Electrotechnical Vocabulary (Electrobiology) (International Electrotechnical Commission) (IEC) (1979).

An *electrical shock* is the physiopathological effect resulting from the direct or indirect passage of an external electrical current through the body. It includes direct and indirect contacts and both unipolar and bipolar currents.

Individuals—living or deceased—having suffered electrical shocks are said to have suffered *electrification*; the term *electrocution* should be reserved for cases in which death ensues. *Lightning strikes* are fatal electrical shocks resulting from lightning (Gourbiere et al. 1994).

International statistics on electrical accidents have been compiled by the International Labour Office (ILO), the European Union (EU), the *Union internationale des producteurs et distributeurs d'énergie électrique* (UNIPEDE), the International Social Security Association (ISSA) and the TC64 Committee of the International Electrotechnical Commission. Interpretation of these statistics is hampered by variations in data collection techniques, insurance policies and definitions of fatal accidents from country to country. Nevertheless, the following estimates of the rate of electrocution are possible (table 40.1).

The number of electrocutions is slowly decreasing, both in absolute terms and, even more strikingly, as a function of the total consumption of electricity. Approximately half of electrical accidents are occupational in origin, with the other half occurring at home and during leisure activities. In France, the average number of fatalities between 1968 and 1991 was 151 deaths per year, according to the *Institut national de la santé et de la recherche médicale* (INSERM).

Physical and Physiopathological Basis of Electrification

Electrical specialists divide electrical contacts into two groups: direct contacts, involving contact with live components, and indirect contacts, involving grounded contacts. Each of these requires fundamentally different preventive measures.

From a medical point of view, the current's path through the body is the key prognostic and therapeutic determinant. For example, bipolar contact of a child's mouth with an extension cord plug causes extremely serious burns to the mouth—but not death if the child is well insulated from the ground.

In occupational settings, where high voltages are common, arcing between an active component carrying a high voltage and workers who approach too closely is also possible. Specific work situations can also affect the consequences of electrical accidents: for example, workers may fall or act inappropriately when surprised by an otherwise relatively harmless electrical shock.

Electrical accidents may be caused by the entire range of voltages present in workplaces. Every industrial sector has its own set of conditions capable of causing direct, indirect, unipolar, bipolar, arcing, or induced contact, and, ultimately, accidents. While it is of course beyond the scope of this article to describe all human activities which involve electricity, it is useful to remind the reader of the following major types of electrical work, which have been the object of international preventive guidelines described in the chapter on prevention:

1. activities involving work on live wires (the application of extremely rigorous protocols has succeeded in reducing the number of electrifications during this type of work)
2. activities involving work on unpowered wires, and
3. activities performed in the vicinity of live wires (these activities require the most attention, as they are often performed by personnel who are not electricians).

Physiopathology

All the variables of Joule's law of direct current—

$$W = V \times I \times t = RI^2 t$$

(the heat produced by an electric current is proportional to the resistance and the square of the current)—are closely interrelated. In the case of alternating current, the effect of frequency must also be taken into account (Folliot 1982).

Living organisms are electrical conductors. Electrification occurs when there is a potential difference between two points in the organism. It is important to emphasize that the danger of electrical accidents arises not from mere contact with a live conductor, but rather from simultaneous contact with a live conductor and another body at a different potential.

The tissues and organs along the current path may undergo functional motor excitation, in some cases irreversible, or may suffer temporary or permanent injury, generally as a result of burns. The extent of these injuries is a function of the energy released or the quantity of electricity passing through them. The transit time of the electric current is therefore critical in determining the degree of injury. (For example, electric eels and rays produce extremely unpleasant discharges, capable of inducing a loss of consciousness. However, despite a voltage of 600 V, a current of approximately 1A and a subject resistance of approximately 600 ohms, these fish are incapable of inducing a lethal shock, since the discharge duration is too brief, of the order of tens of microseconds.) Thus, at high voltages (>1,000 V), death is often due to the extent of the burns. At lower voltages, death is a function of the amount of electricity ($Q = I \times t$), reaching the heart, determined by the type, location and area of the contact points.

The following sections discuss the mechanism of death due to electrical accidents, the most effective immediate therapies and the factors determining the severity of injury—namely, resistance, intensity, voltage, frequency and wave-form.

Table 40.1 • Estimates of the rate of electrocution —1988.

	Electrocutions per million inhabitants	Total deaths
United States[1]	2.9	714
France	2.0	115
Germany	1.6	99
Austria	0.9	11
Japan	0.9	112
Sweden	0.6	13

[1] According to the National Fire Protection Association (Massachusetts, US) these US statistics are more reflective of extensive data collection and legal reporting requirements than of a more dangerous environment. US statistics include deaths from exposure to public utility transmission systems and electrocutions caused by consumer products. In 1988, 290 deaths were caused by consumer products (1.2 deaths per million inhabitants). In 1993, the rate of death by electrocution from all causes dropped to 550 (2.1 deaths per million inhabitants); 38% were consumer product-related (0.8 deaths per million inhabitants).

Causes of Death in Electrical Accidents in Industry

In rare cases, asphyxia may be the cause of death. This may result from prolonged tetanus of the diaphragm, inhibition of the respiratory centres in cases of contact with the head, or very high current densities, for example as a result of lightning strikes (Gourbiere et al. 1994). If care can be provided within three minutes, the victim may be revived with a few puffs of mouth-to-mouth resuscitation.

On the other hand, peripheral circulatory collapse secondary to ventricular fibrillation remains the main cause of death. This invariably develops in the absence of cardiac massage applied simultaneously with mouth-to-mouth resuscitation. These interventions, which should be taught to all electricians, should be maintained until the arrival of emergency medical aid, which almost always takes more than three minutes. A great many electropathologists and engineers around the world have studied the causes of ventricular fibrillation, in order to design better passive or active protective measures (International Electrotechnical Commission 1987; 1994). Random desynchronization of the myocardium requires a sustained electric current of a specific frequency, intensity and transit time. Most importantly, the electrical signal must arrive at the myocardium during the so-called *vulnerable phase of the cardiac cycle*, corresponding to the start of the T-wave of the electrocardiogram.

The International Electrotechnical Commission (1987; 1994) has produced curves describing the effect of current intensity and transit time on the probability (expressed as percentages) of fibrillation and the hand-foot current path in a 70-kg male in good health. These tools are appropriate for industrial currents in the frequency range of 15 to 100 Hz, with higher frequencies currently under study. For transit times of less than 10 ms, the area under the electrical signal curve is a reasonable approximation of the electrical energy.

Role of Various Electrical Parameters

Each of the electrical parameters (current, voltage, resistance, time, frequency) and wave-form are important determinants of injury, both in their own right and by virtue of their interaction.

Current thresholds have been established for alternating current, as well as for other conditions defined above. The current intensity during electrification is unknown, since it is a function of tissue resistance at the moment of contact $(I = V/R)$, but is generally perceptible at levels of approximately 1 mA. Relatively low currents can cause muscular contractions that may prevent a victim from letting go of an energized object. The threshold of this current is a function of condensity, contact area, contact pressure and individual variations. Virtually all men and almost all women and children can let go at currents up to 6 mA. At 10 mA it has been observed that 98.5% of men and 60% of women and 7.5% of children can let go. Only 7.5% of men and no women or children can let go at 20 mA. No one can let go at 30 mA and greater.

Currents of approximately 25 mA may cause tetanus of the diaphragm, the most powerful respiratory muscle. If contact is maintained for three minutes, cardiac arrest may also ensue.

Ventricular fibrillation becomes a danger at levels of approximately 45 mA, with a probability in adults of 5% after a 5-second contact. During heart surgery, admittedly a special condition, a current of 20 to 100×10^{-6} A applied directly to the myocardium is sufficient to induce fibrillation. This myocardial sensitivity is the reason for strict standards applied to electromedical devices.

All other things $(V, R, \text{frequency})$ being equal, current thresholds also depend on the wave-form, animal species, weight, current direction in the heart, ratio of the current transit time to the cardiac cycle, point in the cardiac cycle at which the current arrives, and individual factors.

The voltage involved in accidents is generally known. In cases of direct contact, ventricular fibrillation and the severity of burns are directly proportional to voltage, since

$$V = RI \text{ and } W = V \times I \times t$$

Burns arising from high-voltage electric shock are associated with many complications, only some of which are predictable. Accordingly accident victims must be cared for by knowledgeable specialists. Heat release occurs primarily in the muscles and neurovascular bundles. Plasma leakage following tissue damage causes shock, in some cases rapid and intense. For a given surface area, electrothermic burns—burns caused by an electrical current—are always more severe than other types of burn. Electrothermic burns are both external and internal and, although this may not be initially apparent, can induce vascular damage with serious secondary effects. These include internal stenoses and thrombi which, by virtue of the necrosis they induce, often necessitate amputation.

Tissue destruction is also responsible for the release of chromoproteins such as myoglobin. Such release is also observed in victims of crush injuries, although the extent of release is remarkable in victims of high-voltage burns. Myoglobin precipitation in renal tubules, secondary to acidosis brought on by anoxia and hyperkalaemia, is thought to be the cause of anuria. This theory, experimentally confirmed but not universally accepted, is the basis for recommendations for immediate alkalization therapy. Intravenous alkalization, which also corrects hypovolaemia and acidosis secondary to cell death, is the recommended practice.

In the case of indirect contacts, the contact voltage (V) and conventional voltage limit must also be taken into account.

The contact voltage is the voltage to which a person is subjected on simultaneously touching two conductors between which a voltage differential exists due to defective insulation. The intensity of the resultant current flow depends on the resistances of the human body and the external circuit. This current should not be allowed to rise above safe levels, which is to say that it must conform to safe time-current curves. The highest contact voltage that can be tolerated indefinitely without inducing electropathological effects is termed the *conventional voltage limit* or, more intuitively, the *safety voltage*.

The actual value of the resistance during electrical accidents is unknown. Variations in in-series resistances—for example, clothes and shoes—explain much of the variation observed in the effects of ostensibly similar electrical accidents, but exert little influence on the outcome of accidents involving bipolar contacts and high-voltage electrifications. In cases involving alternating current, the effect of capacitive and inductive phenomena must be added to the standard calculation based on voltage and current $(R = V/I)$.

The resistance of the human body is the sum of the skin resistance (R) at the two points of contact and the body's internal resistance (R). Skin resistance varies with environmental factors and, as noted by Biegelmeir (International Electrotechnical Commission 1987; 1994), is partially a function of the contact voltage. Other factors such as pressure, contact area, the state of the skin at the point of contact, and individual factors also influence resistance. It is thus unrealistic to attempt to base preventive measures on estimates of skin resistance. Prevention should instead be based on the adaptation of equipment and procedures to humans, rather than the reverse. In order to simplify matters, the IEC has defined four types of environment—dry, humid, wet and immersion—and has defined parameters useful for the planning of prevention activities in each case.

The frequency of the electrical signal responsible for electrical accidents is generally known. In Europe, it is almost always 50 Hz and in the Americas, it is generally 60 Hz. In rare cases involving railways in countries such as Germany, Austria and Switzerland, it may be $16^2/_3$ Hz, a frequency which theoretically represents a greater risk of tetanization and of ventricular fibrillation. It should be recalled that fibrillation is not a muscle reaction but is caused by repetitive stimulation, with a maximum sensitivity at approximately 10 Hz. This explains why, for a given voltage, extremely low-frequency alternating current is considered to be three to five times more dangerous than direct current with regard to effects other than burns.

The thresholds described previously are directly proportional to the frequency of the current. Thus, at 10 kHz, the detection threshold is ten times higher. The IEC is studying revised fibrillation hazard curves for frequencies above 1,000 Hz (International Electrotechnical Commission 1994).

Above a certain frequency, the physical laws governing penetration of current into the body change completely. Thermal effects related to the amount of energy released become the main effect, as capacitive and inductive phenomena start to predominate.

The wave-form of the electrical signal responsible for an electrical accident is usually known. It may be an important determinant of injury in accidents involving contact with capacitors or semiconductors.

Clinical Study of Electric Shock

Classically, electrifications have been divided into low- (50 to 1,000 V) and high- (>1,000 V) voltage incidents.

Low voltage is a familiar, indeed omnipresent, hazard, and shocks due to it are encountered in domestic, leisure, agricultural and hospital settings as well as in industry.

In reviewing the range of low-voltage electric shocks, from the most trivial to the most serious, we must start with uncomplicated electrical shock. In these cases, victims are able to remove themselves from harm on their own, retain consciousness and maintain normal ventilation. Cardiac effects are limited to simple sinus tachycardia with or without minor electrocardiographic abnormalities. Despite the relatively minor consequences of such accidents, electrocardiography remains an appropriate medical and medico-legal precaution. Technical investigation of these potentially serious incidents is indicated as a complement to clinical examination (Gilet and Choquet 1990).

Victims of shock involving somewhat stronger and longer-lasting electrical contacts shocks may suffer from perturbations or loss of consciousness, but completely recover more or less rapidly; treatment accelerates recovery. Examination generally reveals neuromuscular hypertonias, hyper-reflective ventilation problems and congestion, the last of which is often secondary to oropharyngeal obstruction. Cardiovascular disorders are secondary to hypoxia or anoxia, or may take the form of tachycardia, hypertension and, in some cases, even infarction. Patients with these conditions require hospital care.

The occasional victims who lose consciousness within a few seconds of contact appear pale or cyanotic, stop breathing, have barely perceptible pulses and exhibit mydriasis indicative of acute cerebral injury. Although usually due to ventricular fibrillation, the precise pathogenesis of this apparent death is, however, irrelevant. The important point is the rapid commencement of well-defined therapy, since it has been known for some time that this clinical state never leads to actual death. The prognosis in these cases of electric shock—from which total recovery is possible—depends on the rapidity and quality of first aid. Statistically, this is most likely to be administered by non-medical personnel, and the training of all electricians in the basic interventions likely to ensure survival is therefore indicated.

In cases of apparent death, emergency treatment must take priority. In other cases, however, attention must be paid to multiple traumas resulting from violent tetanus, falls or the projection of the victim through the air. Once the immediate life-threatening danger has been resolved, trauma and burns, including those caused by low-voltage contacts, should be attended to.

Accidents involving high voltages result in significant burns as well as the effects described for low-voltage accidents. The conversion of electrical energy to heat occurs both internally and externally. In a study of electrical accidents in France made by the medical department of the power utility, EDF-GDF, almost 80% of the victims suffered burns. These can be classified into four groups:

1. arc burns, usually involving exposed skin and complicated in some cases by burns from burning clothing
2. multiple, extensive and deep electrothermic burns, caused by high-voltage contacts
3. classical burns, caused by burning clothing and the projection of burning matter, and
4. mixed burns, caused by arcing, burning and current flow.

Follow-up and complementary examinations are performed as required, depending on the particulars of the accident. The strategy used to establish a prognosis or for medico-legal purposes is of course determined by the nature of observed or expected complications. In high-voltage electrifications (Folliot 1982) and lightning strikes (Gourbiere et al. 1994), enzymology and the analysis of chromoproteins and blood clotting parameters are obligatory.

The course of recovery from electrical trauma may well be compromised by early or late complications, especially those involving the cardiovascular, nervous and renal systems. These complications in their own right are sufficient reason to hospitalize victims of high-voltage electrifications. Some complications may leave functional or cosmetic sequelae.

If the current path is such that significant current reaches the heart, cardiovascular complications will be present. The most frequently observed and most benign of these are functional disorders, in the presence or absence of clinical correlates. Arrhythmias—sinus tachycardia, extrasystole, flutter and atrial fibrillation (in that order)—are the most common electrocardiographic abnormalities, and may leave permanent sequelae. Conduction disorders are rarer, and are difficult to relate to electrical accidents in the absence of a previous electrocardiogram.

More serious disorders such as cardiac failure, valve injury and myocardial burns have also been reported, but are rare, even in victims of high-voltage accidents. Clear-cut cases of angina and even infarction have also been reported.

Peripheral vascular injury may be observed in the week following high-voltage electrification. Several pathogenic mechanisms have been proposed: arterial spasm, the action of electrical current on the media and muscular layers of the vessels and modification of the blood clotting parameters.

A wide variety of neurological complications is possible. The earliest to appear is stroke, regardless of whether the victim initially experienced loss of consciousness. The physiopathology of these complications involves cranial trauma (whose presence should be ascertained), the direct effect of current on the head, or the modification of cerebral blood flow and the induction of a delayed cerebral oedema. In addition, medullary and secondary peripheral complications may be caused by trauma or the direct action of electric current.

Sensory disorders involve the eye and the audiovestibular or cochlear systems. It is important to examine the cornea, crystalline lens and fundus of the eye as soon as possible, and to follow up victims of arcing and direct head contact for delayed effects. Cataracts may develop after an intervening symptom-free period of several months. Vestibular disorders and hearing loss are primarily due to blast effects and, in victims of lightning strike transmitted over telephone lines, to electrical trauma (Gourbiere et al. 1994).

Improvements in mobile emergency practices have greatly reduced the frequency of renal complications, especially oligoanuria, in victims of high-voltage electrifications. Early and careful rehydration and intravenous alkalinization is the treatment of choice in victims of serious burns. A few cases of albuminuria and persistent microscopic haematuria have been reported.

Clinical Portraits and Diagnostic Problems

The clinical portrait of electric shock is complicated by the variety of industrial applications of electricity and the increasing frequency and variety of medical applications of electricity. For a long time, however, electrical accidents were caused solely by lightning strikes (Gourbiere et al. 1994). Lightning strikes may involve quite remarkable quantities of electricity: one out of every three victims of lightning strikes dies. The effects of a lightning strike—burns and apparent death—are comparable to those resulting from industrial electricity and are attributable to electrical shock, the transformation of electrical energy into heat, blast effects and the electrical properties of lightning.

Lightning strikes are three times as prevalent in men as in women. This reflects patterns of work with differing risks for exposure to lightning.

Burns resulting from contact with grounded metallic surfaces of electric scalpels are the most common effects observed in victims of iatrogenic electrification. The magnitude of acceptable leakage currents in electromedical devices varies from one device to another. At the very least, manufacturers' specifications and usage recommendations should be followed.

To conclude this section, we would like to discuss the special case of electric shock involving pregnant women. This may cause the death of the woman, the foetus or both. In one remarkable case, a live foetus was successfully delivered by Caesarian section 15 minutes after its mother had died as a result of electrocution by a 220 V shock (Folliot 1982).

The pathophysiological mechanisms of abortion caused by electric shock requires further study. Is it caused by conduction disorders in the embryonic cardiac tube subjected to a voltage gradient, or by a tearing of the placenta secondary to vasoconstriction?

The occurrence of electrical accidents such as this happily rare one is yet another reason to require notification of all cases of injuries arising from electricity.

Positive and Medico-Legal Diagnosis

The circumstances under which electric shock occurs are generally sufficiently clear to allow unequivocal aetiological diagnosis. However, this is not invariably the case, even in industrial settings.

The diagnosis of circulatory failure following electric shock is extremely important, since it requires bystanders to commence immediate and basic first aid once the current has been shut off. Respiratory arrest in the absence of a pulse is an absolute indication for the commencement of cardiac massage and mouth-to-mouth resuscitation. Previously, these were only performed when mydriasis (dilation of the pupils), a diagnostic sign of acute cerebral injury, was present. Current practice is, however, to begin these interventions as soon as the pulse is no longer detectable.

Since loss of consciousness due to ventricular fibrillation may take a few seconds to develop, victims may be able to distance themselves from the equipment responsible for the accident. This may be of some medico-legal importance—for example, when an accident victim is found several metres from an electrical cabinet or other source of voltage with no traces of electrical injury.

It cannot be overemphasized that the absence of electrical burns does not exclude the possibility of electrocution. If autopsy of subjects found in electrical environments or near equipment capable of developing dangerous voltages reveals no visible Jelinek lesions and no apparent sign of death, electrocution should be considered.

If the body is found outdoors, a diagnosis of lightning strike is arrived at by the process of elimination. Signs of lightning strike should be searched for within a 50-metre radius of the body. The Museum of Electropathology of Vienna offers an arresting exhibition of such signs, including carbonized vegetation and vitrified sand. Metal objects worn by the victim may be melted.

Although suicide by electrical means remains thankfully rare in industry, death due to contributory negligence remains a sad reality. This is particularly true at non-standard sites, especially those involving the installation and operation of provisional electrical facilities under demanding conditions.

Electrical accidents should by all rights no longer occur, given the availability of effective preventive measures described in the article "Prevention and Standards" (below).

STATIC ELECTRICITY

Claude Menguy

All materials differ in the degree to which electric charges can pass through them. *Conductors* allow charges to flow, while *insulators* hinder the motion of charges. Electrostatics is the field devoted to studying charges, or charged bodies at rest. *Static electricity* results when electric charges which do not move are built up on objects. If the charges flow, then a current results and the electricity is no longer static. The current that results from moving charges is commonly referred to by laypeople as electricity, and is discussed in the other articles in this chapter. *Static electrification* is the term used to designate any process resulting in the separation of positive and negative electrical charges. Conduction is measured with a property called *conductance*, while an insulator is characterized by its *resistivity*. Charge separation which leads to electrification can occur as the result of mechanical processes—for example, contact between objects and friction, or the collision of two surfaces. The surfaces can be two solids or a solid and a liquid. The mechanical process can, less commonly, be the rupture or separation of solid or liquid surfaces. This article focuses on contact and friction.

Electrification Processes

The phenomenon of generation of static electricity by friction (triboelectrification) has been known for thousands of years. Contact between two materials is sufficient to induce electrification. Friction is simply a type of interaction which increases the area of contact and generates heat—*friction* is the general term to describe the movement of two objects in contact; the pressure exerted, its shear velocity and the heat generated are the prime determinants of the charge generated by friction. Sometimes friction will lead to the tearing away of solid particles as well.

When the two solids in contact are metals (metal-metal contact), electrons migrate from one to the other. Every metal is characterized by a different initial potential (Fermi potential), and nature always moves towards equilibrium—that is, natural phenomena work to eliminate the differences in potential. This migration of electrons results in the generation of a contact potential. Because the charges in a metal are very mobile (metals are excellent conductors), the charges will even recombine at the last point of contact before the two metals are separated. It is therefore impossible to induce electrification by bringing together two met-

Table 40.2 • Basic relationships in electrostatics—Collection of equations.

Equation 1: Charging by contact of a metal and an insulator

In general, the surface charge density (σ_s) following contact and separation can be expressed by:

$$\sigma_s = eN_E(\phi_m - \phi_i)$$

where
e is the charge of an electron
N_E is the energy state density at the insulator's surface
ϕ_i is the electron affinity of the insulator, and
ϕ_m is the electron affinity of the metal

Equation 2: Charging following contact between two insulators

The following general form of equation 1 applies to the charge transfer between two insulators with different energy states (perfectly clean surfaces only):

$$\sigma_s = e\frac{N_{E1} \cdot N_{E2}}{N_{E1} - N_{E2}}(\phi_1 - \phi_2)$$

where N_{E1} and N_{E2} are the energy state densities at the surface of the two insulators, and ϕ_1 and ϕ_2 are the electron affinities of the two insulators.

Equation 3: Maximum surface charge density

The dielectric strength (E_G) of the surrounding gas imposes an upper limit on the charge it is possible to generate on a flat insulating surface. In air, E_G is approximately 3 MV/m. The maximum surface charge density is given by:

$$\sigma_{smax} = e_0 E_G = 2.66 \times 10^{-5} \text{ C/m}^2 = 2{,}660 \text{ pC/cm}^2$$

Equation 4: Maximum charge on a spherical particle

When nominally spherical particles are charged by the corona effect, the maximum charge which each particle can acquire is given by Pauthenier's limit:

$$q_{max} = 4\pi\varepsilon_0\rho\,E_G a^2$$

where
q_{max} is the maximum charge
a is the particle radius
ε_I is the relative permittivity and

$$\rho = \frac{3\varepsilon_I}{\varepsilon_I + 2}$$

Equation 5: Discharges from conductors

The potential of an insulated conductor carrying charge Q is given by $V = Q/C$ and the stored energy by:

$$W = \frac{1}{2}CV^2 = \frac{1}{2}\frac{Q^2}{C}$$

Equation 6: Time course of potential of charged conductor

In a conductor charged by a constant current (I_G), the time course of the potential is described by:

$$V = R_f I_G \left(1 - e^{\frac{-t}{R_f C}}\right)$$

where
R_f is the conductor's leak resistance

Equation 7: Final potential of charged conductor

For long time course, $t \gg R_f C$, this reduces to:

$$V = R_f I_G$$

and the stored energy is given by:

Equation 8: Stored energy of charged conductor

$$W = \frac{1}{2}CR_f^2 I_G^2$$

als and then separating them; the charges will always flow to eliminate the potential difference.

When a *metal* and an *insulator* come into nearly friction-free contact in a vacuum, the energy level of electrons in the metal approaches that of the insulator. Surface or bulk impurities cause this to occur and also prevent arcing (the discharge of electricity between the two charged bodies—the electrodes) upon separation. The charge transferred to the insulator is proportional to the electron affinity of the metal, and every insulator also has an electron affinity, or attraction for electrons, associated with it. Thus, transfer of positive or negative ions from the insulator to the metal is also possible. The charge on the surface following contact and separation is described by equation 1 in table 40.2.

When two insulators come into contact, charge transfer occurs because of the different states of their surface energy (equation 2, table 40.2). Charges transferred to the surface of an insulator can migrate deeper within the material. Humidity and surface contamination can greatly modify the behaviour of charges. Surface humidity in particular increases surface energy state densities by increasing surface conduction, which favours charge recombination, and facilitates ionic mobility. Most people will recognize this from their daily life experiences by the fact that they tend to be subjected to static electricity during dry conditions. The water content of some polymers (plastics) will change as they are being charged. The increase or decrease in water content may even reverse the direction of the charge flow (its polarity).

The polarity (relative positivity and negativity) of two insulators in contact with each other depends on each material's electron affinity. Insulators can be ranked by their electron affinities, and some illustrative values are listed in table 40.3. The electron affinity of an insulator is an important consideration for prevention programmes, which are discussed later in this article.

Table 40.3 • Electron affinities of selected polymers.[1]

Charge	Material	Electron affinity (EV)
−	PVC (polyvinyl chloride)	4.85
	Polyamide	4.36
	Polycarbonate	4.26
	PTFE (polytetrafluoroethylene)	4.26
	PETP (polyethylene terephthalate)	4.25
	Polystyrene	4.22
+	Polyamide	4.08

[1] A material acquires a positive charge when it comes into contact with a material listed above it, and a negative charge when it comes into contact with a material listed below it. The electron affinity of an insulator is multifactorial, however.

Although there have been attempts to establish a triboelectric series which would rank materials so that those which acquire a positive charge upon contact with materials would appear higher in the series than those that acquire a negative charge upon contact, no universally recognized series has been established.

When a solid and a liquid meet (to form a *solid-liquid interface*), charge transfer occurs due to the migration of ions that are present in the liquid. These ions arise from the dissociation of impurities which may be present or by electrochemical oxidation-reduction reactions. Since, in practice, perfectly pure liquids do not exist, there will always be at least some positive and negative ions in the liquid available to bind to the liquid-solid interface. There are many types of mechanisms by which this binding may occur (e.g., electrostatic adherence to metal surfaces, chemical absorption, electrolytic injection, dissociation of polar groups and, if the vessel wall is insulating, liquid-solid reactions.)

Since substances which dissolve (dissociate) are electrically neutral to begin with, they will generate equal numbers of positive and negative charges. Electrification occurs only if either the positive or the negative charges preferentially adhere to the solid's surface. If this occurs, a very compact layer, known as the Helmholtz layer is formed. Because the Helmholtz layer is charged, it will attract ions of the opposite polarity to it. These ions will cluster into a more diffuse layer, known as the Gouy layer, which rests on top of the surface of the compact Helmholtz layer. The thickness of the Gouy layer increases with the resistivity of the liquid. Conducting liquids form very thin Gouy layers.

This double layer will separate if the liquid flows, with the Helmholtz layer remaining bound to the interface and the Gouy layer becoming entrained by the flowing liquid. The movement of these charged layers produces a difference in potential (the *zeta* potential), and the current induced by the moving charges is known as the *streaming current*. The amount of charge that accumulates in the liquid depends on the rate at which the ions diffuse towards the interface and on the liquid's resistivity (ρ). The streaming current is, however, constant over time.

Neither highly insulating nor conducting liquids will become charged—the first because very few ions are present, and the second because in liquids which conduct electricity very well, the ions will recombine very rapidly. In practice, electrification occurs only in liquids with resistivity greater than $10^7 \, \Omega m$ or less than $10^{11} \, \Omega m$, with the highest values observed for $\rho = 10^9$ to $10^{11} \, \Omega m$.

Flowing liquids will induce charge accumulation in insulating surfaces over which they flow. The extent to which the surface charge density will build up is limited by (1) how quickly the ions in the liquid recombine at the liquid-solid interface, (2) how quickly the ions in the liquid are conducted through the insulator, or (3) whether surface or bulk arcing through the insulator occurs and the charge is thus discharged. Turbulent flow and flow over rough surfaces favour electrification.

When a high voltage—say several kilovolts—is applied to a charged body (an electrode) which has a small radius (e.g., a wire), the electrical field in the immediate vicinity of the charged body is high, but it decreases rapidly with distance. If there is a discharge of the stored charges, the discharge will be limited to the region in which the electrical field is stronger than the dielectric strength of the surrounding atmosphere, a phenomenon known as the corona effect, because the arcing also emits light. (People may actually have seen small sparks formed when they have personally experienced a shock from static electricity.)

The charge density on an insulating surface can also be changed by the moving electrons that are generated by a high-intensity electrical field. These electrons will generate ions from any gas molecules in the atmosphere with which they come into contact. When the electric charge on the body is positive, the charged body will repel any positive ions which have been created. Electrons created by negatively charged objects will lose energy as they recede from the electrode, and they will attach themselves to gas molecules in the atmosphere, thus forming negative ions which continue to recede away from the charge points. These positive and negative ions can come to rest on any insulating surface and will modify the surface's charge density. This type of charge is much easier to control and more uniform than the charges created by friction. There are limits to the extent of the charges it is possible to generate in this way. The limit is described mathematically in equation 3 in table 40.2.

To generate higher charges, the dielectric strength of the environment must be increased, either by creating a vacuum or by metallizing the other surface of the insulating film. The latter stratagem draws the electrical field into the insulator and consequently reduces the field strength in the surrounding gas.

When a conductor in an electrical field *(E)* is grounded (see figure 40.1), charges can be produced by induction. Under these conditions, the electrical field induces polarization—the separation of the centres of gravity of the negative and positive ions of

Figure 40.1 • Mechanism of charging a conductor by induction.

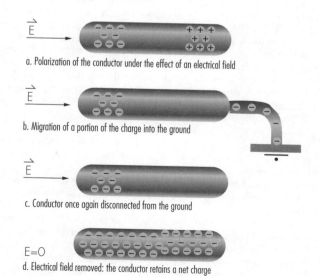

a. Polarization of the conductor under the effect of an electrical field

b. Migration of a portion of the charge into the ground

c. Conductor once again disconnected from the ground

E=O

d. Electrical field removed: the conductor retains a net charge the conductor. A conductor temporarily grounded at only one point will carry a net charge when disconnected from the ground, due to the migration of charges in the vicinity of the point. This explains why conducting particles located in a uniform field oscillate between electrodes, charging and discharging at each contact.

Hazards Associated with Static Electricity

The ill effects caused by the accumulation of static electricity range from the discomfort one experiences when touching a charged object, such as a door handle, to the very serious injuries, even fatalities, which can occur from an explosion induced by static electricity. The physiological effect of electrostatic discharges on humans ranges from uncomfortable prickling to violent reflex actions. These effects are produced by the discharge current and, especially, by the current density on the skin.

In this article we will describe some practical ways in which surfaces and objects can become charged (electrification). When the electrical field induced exceeds the ability of the surrounding environment to withstand the charge (that is, exceeds the dielectric strength of the environment), a discharge occurs. (In air, the dielectric strength is described by Paschen's curve and is a function of the product of the pressure and the distance between the charged bodies.)

Disruptive discharges can take the following forms:

- sparks or arcs which bridge two charged bodies (two metal electrodes)
- partial, or brush, discharges which bridge a metal electrode and an insulator, or even two insulators; these discharges are termed partial because the conducting path does not totally short-circuit two metal electrodes, but is usually multiple and brushlike
- corona discharges, also known as point effects, which arise in the strong electric field around small-radius charged bodies or electrodes.

Insulated conductors have a net capacitance C relative to ground. This relationship between charge and potential is expressed in equation 5 in table 40.2.

A person wearing insulating shoes is a common example of an insulated conductor. The human body is an electrostatic conductor, with a typical capacitance relative to ground of approximately 150 pF and a potential of up to 30 kV. Because people can be insulating conductors, they can experience electrostatic discharges, such as the more or less painful sensation sometimes produced when a hand approaches a door handle or other metal object. When the potential reaches approximately 2 kV, the equivalent to an energy of 0.3 mJ will be experienced, although this threshold varies from person to person. Stronger discharges may cause uncontrollable movements resulting in falls. In the case of workers using tools, the involuntary reflex motions may lead to injuries to the victim and others who may be working nearby. Equations 6 to 8 in table 40.2 describe the time course of the potential.

Actual arcing will occur when the strength of the induced electrical field exceeds the dielectric strength of air. Because of the rapid migration of charges in conductors, essentially all the charges flow to the discharge point, releasing all the stored energy into a spark. This can have serious implications when working with flammable or explosive substances or in flammable conditions.

The approach of a grounded electrode to a charged insulating surface modifies the electric field and induces a charge in the electrode. As the surfaces approach each other, the field strength increases, eventually leading to a partial discharge from the charged insulated surface. Because charges on insulating surfaces are not very mobile, only a small proportion of the surface partici-

Table 40.4 • Typical lower flammability limits.

Discharge	Limit
Some powders	Several joules
Very fine sulphur and aluminium aerosols	Several millijoules
Vapours of hydrocarbons and other organic liquids	200 microjoules
Hydrogen and acetylene	20 microjoules
Explosives	1 microjoule

pates in the discharge, and the energy released by this type of discharge is therefore much lower than in arcs.

The charge and transferred energy appear to be directly proportional to the diameter of the metal electrode, up to approximately 20 mm. The initial polarity of the insulator also influences charge and transferred energy. Partial discharges from positively charged surfaces are less energetic than those from negatively charged ones. It is impossible to determine, *a priori*, the energy transferred by a discharge from an insulating surface, in contrast to the situation involving conducting surfaces. In fact, because the insulating surface is not equipotential, it is not even possible to define the capacitances involved.

Creeping Discharge

We saw in equation 3 (table 40.2) that the surface charge density of an insulating surface in air cannot exceed 2,660 pC/cm^2.

If we consider an insulating plate or a film of thickness a, resting on a metal electrode or having one metal face, it is easy to demonstrate that the electrical field is drawn into the insulator by the induced charge on the electrode as charges are deposited on the non-metallic face. As a result, the electric field in the air is very weak, and lower than it would be if one of the faces were not metal. In this case, the dielectric strength of air does not limit charge accumulation on the insulating surface, and it is possible to reach very high surface charge densities (>2,660 pC/cm^2). This charge accumulation increases the surface conductivity of the insulator.

When an electrode approaches an insulating surface, a creeping discharge involving a large proportion of the charged surface which has become conducting occurs. Because of the large surface areas involved, this type of discharge releases large amounts of energy. In the case of films, the air field is very weak, and the distance between the electrode and the film must be no more than the film thickness for a discharge to occur. A creeping discharge may also occur when a charged insulator is separated from its metallic undercoating. Under these circumstances, the air field increases abruptly and the entire surface of the insulator discharges to re-establish equilibrium.

Electrostatic Discharges and Fire and Explosion Hazards

In explosive atmospheres, violent exothermic oxidation reactions, involving energy transfer to the atmosphere, may be triggered by:

- open flames
- electric sparks
- radio-frequency sparks near a strong radio source
- sparks produced by collisions (e.g., between metal and concrete)
- electrostatic discharges.

We are interested here only in the last case. The flash points (the temperature at which liquid vapours ignite on contact with a

Table 40.5 • Specific charge associated with selected industrial operations.

Operation	Specific charge (q/m) (C/kg)
Screening	10^{-8}–10^{-11}
Silo filling or emptying	10^{-7}–10^{-9}
Transport by worm conveyor	10^{-6}–10^{-8}
Grinding	10^{-6}–10^{-7}
Micronization	10^{-4}–10^{-7}
Pneumatic transport	10^{-4}–10^{-6}

naked flame) of various liquids, and the auto-ignition temperature of various vapours are given in the Chemical Section of this *Encyclopaedia*. The fire hazard associated with electrostatic discharges can be assessed by reference to the lower flammability limit of gases, vapours and solid or liquid aerosols. This limit may vary considerably, as table 40.4 illustrates.

A mixture of air and a flammable gas or vapour can explode only when the concentration of the flammable substance is between its upper and lower explosive limits. Within this range, the minimal ignition energy (MIE)—the energy which an electrostatic discharge must possess to ignite the mixture—is highly concentration dependent. The minimal ignition energy has been consistently shown to depend on the speed of energy release and, by extension, on discharge duration. Electrode radius is also a factor:

- Small-diameter electrodes (of the order of several millimetres) result in corona discharges rather than sparks.
- With larger-diameter electrodes (of the order of several centimetres), the electrode mass serves to cool the sparks.

In general, the lowest MIEs are obtained with electrodes that are just big enough to prevent corona discharges.

The MIE also depends on the interelectrode distance, and is lowest at the quenching distance ("distance de pincement"), the distance at which the energy produced in the reaction zone exceeds the thermal losses at the electrodes. It has been experimentally demonstrated that each flammable substance has a maximum safe distance, corresponding to the minimum interelectrode distance at which an explosion can occur. For hydrocarbons, this is less than 1 mm.

The probability of powder explosions is concentration dependent, with the highest probability associated with concentrations of the order of 200 to 500 g/m^3. The MIE is also dependent on particle size, with finer powders exploding more easily. For both gases and aerosols, the MIE decreases with temperature.

Industrial Examples

Many processes routinely used for handling and transporting chemicals generate electrostatic charges. These include:

- pouring powders from sacks
- screening
- transport in pipework
- liquid agitation, especially in the presence of multiple phases, suspended solids or droplets of non-miscible liquids
- liquid spraying or misting.

The consequences of electrostatic charge generation include mechanical problems, an electrostatic discharge hazard for operators and, if products containing inflammable solvents or vapours are used, even explosion (see table 40.5).

Liquid hydrocarbons, such as oil, kerosene and many common solvents, have two characteristics which render them particularly sensitive to problems of static electricity:

- high resistivity, which allows them to accumulate high levels of charges
- flammable vapours, which increase the risk of low-energy discharges triggering fires and explosions.

Charges may be generated during transport flow (e.g., through pipework, pumps or valves). Passage through fine filters, such as those used during the filling of aeroplane tanks, may result in the generation of charge densities of several hundred microcoulombs per cubic metre. Particle sedimentation and the generation of charged mists or foams during flow-filling of tanks may also generate charges.

Between 1953 and 1971, static electricity was responsible for 35 fires and explosions during or following the filling of kerosene tanks, and even more accidents occurred during the filling of truck tanks. The presence of filters or splashing during filling (due to the generation of foams or mists) were the most commonly identified risk factors. Accidents have also occurred on board oil tankers, especially during tank cleaning.

Principles of Static Electricity Prevention

All problems related to static electricity derive from the:

- generation of electric charges
- accumulation of these charges on insulators or insulated conductors
- electric field produced by these charges, which in turn results in a force or a disruptive discharge.

Preventive measures seek to avoid the accumulation of electrostatic charges, and the strategy of choice is to avoid generating the electric charges in the first place. If this is not possible, measures designed to ground the charges should be implemented. Finally, if discharges are unavoidable, sensitive objects should be protected from the effects of the discharges.

Suppression or reduction of the electrostatic charge generation

This is the first approach to electrostatic prevention that should be undertaken, because it is the only preventive measure that eliminates the problem at its source. However, as discussed earlier, charges are generated whenever two materials, at least one of which is insulating, come into contact and are subsequently separated. In practice, charge generation can occur even on contact and separation of a material with itself. In fact, charge generation involves the surface layers of materials. Because the slightest difference in surface humidity or surface contamination results in the generation of static charges, it is impossible to avoid charge generation completely.

To reduce the quantity of charges generated by surfaces coming into contact:

- Avoid having materials come into contact with one another if they have very different electron affinities—that is, if they are very far apart in the triboelectric series. For example, avoid contact between glass and Teflon (PTFE), or between PVC and polyamide (nylon) (see table 40.3).
- Reduce the rate of flow between materials. This reduces the shear velocity between solid materials. For example, one can reduce the flow rate of the extrusion of plastic films, of the movement of crushed materials on a conveyor, or of liquids in a pipeline.

No definitive safety limits for flow rates have been established. The British standard BS-5958-Part 2 *Code of Practice for Control of Undesirable Static Electricity* recommends that the product of the

Table 40.6 • Examples of equipment sensitive to electrostatic discharges.

Sensitive element	Examples
Source	An operator touching a door handle or the chassis of a car A. Charged electronic component coming into contact with a grounded object
Target	Electronic components or materials touching a charged operator
Environment	An explosive mixture ignited by an electrostatic discharge

velocity (in metres per second) and the pipe diameter (in metres) be less than 0.38 for liquids with conductivities of less than 5 pS/m (in pico-siemens per metre) and less than 0.5 for liquids with conductivities above 5 pS/m. This criterion is valid only for single-phase liquids transported at speeds no greater than 7 m/s.

It should be noted that reducing shear or flow velocity not only reduces charge generation but also helps dissipate any charges that are generated. This is because lower flow velocities result in residence times that are higher than those associated with relaxation zones, where flow rates are reduced by strategies such as increasing pipe diameter. This, in turn, increases grounding.

Grounding of static electricity

The basic rule of electrostatic prevention is to eliminate the potential differences between objects. This can be done by connecting them or by grounding (earthing) them. Insulated conductors, however, can accumulate charges and thus may become charged by induction, a phenomenon which is unique to them. Discharges from conductors may take the form of high-energy—and dangerous—sparks.

This rule is consistent with recommendations regarding the prevention of electric shocks, which also require all accessible metal parts of electrical equipment to be grounded as in the French standard *Low voltage electrical installations* (NFC 15-100). For maximum electrostatic safety, our concern here, this rule should be generalized to all conducting elements. This includes metal table frames, door handles, electronic components, tanks used in the chemical industries, and the chassis of vehicles used to transport hydrocarbons.

From the point of view of electrostatic safety, the ideal world would be one in which everything would be a conductor and would be permanently grounded, thus transferring all charges into the earth. Under these circumstances, everything would be permanently equipotential, and the electric field—and the discharge risk—would consequently be zero. However, it is almost never possible to attain this ideal, for the following reasons:

- Not all products which have to be handled are conductors, and many cannot be made conductive by the use of additives. Agricultural and pharmaceutical products, and high-purity liquids, are examples of these.
- Desirable end-product properties, such as optical transparency or low thermal conductivity, may preclude the use of conductive materials.
- It is impossible to permanently ground mobile equipment such as metal carts, cordless electronic tools, vehicles and even human operators.

Protection against electrostatic discharges

It should be borne in mind that this section is concerned only with the protection of electrostatically sensitive equipment from unavoidable discharges, the reduction of charge generation and the elimination of charges. The ability to protect equipment does not eliminate the fundamental necessity of preventing electrostatic charge accumulation in the first place.

As figure 40.2 illustrates, all electrostatic problems involve a source of electrostatic discharge (the initially charged object), a target which receives the discharge, and the environment through which the discharge travels (dielectric discharge). It should be noted that either the target or the environment can be electrostatically sensitive. Some examples of sensitive elements are listed in table 40.6.

Protection of workers

Workers who have reason to believe that they have become electrically charged (for example, when dismounting from a vehicle in dry weather or walking with certain types of shoes), can apply a number of protective measures, such as the following:

- Reduce the current density at the skin level by touching a grounded conductor with a piece of metal such as a key or tool.
- Reduce the peak value of the current by discharging to a dissipating object, if one is available (a table top or special device such as a protective wrist strap with serial resistance).

Protection in explosive atmospheres

In explosive atmospheres, it is the environment itself that is sensitive to electrostatic discharges, and discharges may result in ignition or explosion. Protection in these cases consists of replacing the air, either with a gas mixture whose oxygen content is less than the lower explosive limit, or with an inert gas, such as nitrogen. Inert gas has been used in silos and in reaction vessels in the chemical and pharmaceutical industries. In this case, adequate precautions to assure that workers receive an adequate air supply are needed.

PREVENTION AND STANDARDS

Renzo Comini

Hazards and Preventive Measures at Electrical Facilities

The many components making up electrical installations exhibit varying degrees of robustness. Regardless of their inherent fragility, however, they must all operate reliably under rigorous conditions. Unfortunately, even under the best circumstances, electrical equipment is subject to failures that may result in human injury or material damage.

Figure 40.2 • Schematic of electrostatic discharge problem

SOURCE

Initially
charged

TARGET

Discharge environment

Safe operation of electrical installations is the result of good initial design, not the mere retrofitting of safety systems. This is a corollary of the fact that while current flows at the speed of light, all electromechanical and electronic systems exhibit reaction latencies, caused primarily by thermal inertia, mechanical inertia and maintenance conditions. These latencies, whatever their origins, are sufficiently lengthy to allow humans to be injured and equipment damaged (Lee, Capelli-Schellpfeffer and Kelly 1994; Lee, Cravalho and Burke 1992; Kane and Sternheim 1978.)

It is essential that equipment be installed and maintained by qualified personnel. Technical measures, it should be emphasized, are necessary both to ensure the safe operation of installations and to protect humans and equipment.

Introduction to electrical hazards
Proper operation of electrical installations requires that machinery, equipment, and electrical circuits and lines be protected from hazards caused by both internal (i.e., arising within the installation) and external factors (Andreoni and Castagna 1983).

Internal causes include:

- overvoltages
- short circuits
- modification of the current's wave-form
- induction
- interference
- overcurrents
- corrosion, leading to electrical current leakages to ground
- heating of conducting and insulating materials, which may result in operator burns, emissions of toxic gases, component fires and, in flammable atmospheres, explosions
- leaks of insulating fluids, such as oil
- generation of hydrogen or other gases which may lead to the formation of explosive mixtures.

Each hazard-equipment combination requires specific protective measures, some of which are mandated by law or internal technical regulations. Manufacturers have a responsibility to be aware of specific technical strategies capable of reducing risks.

External causes include:

- mechanical factors (falls, bumps, vibration)
- physical and chemical factors (natural or artificial radiation, extreme temperatures, oils, corrosive liquids, humidity)
- wind, ice, lightning
- vegetation (trees and roots, both dry and wet)
- animals (in both urban and rural settings); these may damage the power-line insulation, and so cause short circuits or false contacts

and, last but not least,

- adults and children who are careless, reckless or ignorant of risks and operating procedures.

Other external causes include electromagnetic interference by sources such as high-voltage lines, radio receivers, welding machines (capable of generating transient overvoltages) and solenoids.

The most frequently encountered causes of problems arise from malfunctioning or non-standard:

- mechanical, thermal or chemical protective equipment
- ventilation systems, machine cooling systems, equipment, lines or circuits
- coordination of insulators used in different parts of the plant
- coordination of fuses and automatic circuit-breakers.

A single fuse or automatic circuit-breaker is incapable of providing adequate protection against overcurrent on two different circuits. Fuses or automatic circuit breakers can provide protection against phase-neutral failures, but protection against phase-ground failures requires automatic residual-current circuit-breakers.

- use of voltage relays and dischargers to coordinate protective systems
- sensors and mechanical or electrical components in the installation's protective systems
- separation of circuits at different voltages (adequate air gaps must be maintained between conductors; connections should be insulated; transformers should be equipped with grounded shields and suitable protection against overvoltage, and have fully segregated primary and secondary coils)
- colour codes or other suitable provisions to avoid misidentification of wires
- mistaking the active phase for a neutral conductor results in electrification of the equipment's external metallic components
- protective equipment against electromagnetic interference.

These are particularly important for instrumentation and lines used for data transmission or the exchange of protection and/or controlling signals. Adequate gaps must be maintained between lines, or filters and shields used. Fibre-optic cables are sometimes used for the most critical cases.

The risk associated with electrical installations increases when the equipment is subjected to severe operating conditions, most commonly as a result of electrical hazards in humid or wet environments.

The thin liquid conductive layers that form on metallic and insulating surfaces in humid or wet environments create new, irregular and dangerous current pathways. Water infiltration reduces the efficiency of insulation, and, should water penetrate the insulation, it can cause current leakages and short circuits. These effects not only damage electrical installations but greatly increase human risks. This fact justifies the need for special standards for work in harsh environments such as open-air sites, agricultural installations, construction sites, bathrooms, mines and cellars, and some industrial settings.

Equipment providing protection against rain, side-splashes or full immersion is available. Ideally, the equipment should be enclosed, insulated and corrosion proof. Metallic enclosures must be grounded. The mechanism of failure in these wet environments is the same as that observed in humid atmospheres, but the effects may be more severe.

Electrical hazards in dusty atmospheres
Fine dusts that enter machines and electrical equipment cause abrasion, particularly of mobile parts. Conducting dusts may also cause short circuits, while insulating dusts may interrupt current flow and increase contact resistance. Accumulations of fine or coarse dusts around equipment cases are potential humidity and water reservoirs. Dry dust is a thermal insulator, reducing heat dispersion and increasing local temperature; this may damage electrical circuits and cause fires or explosions.

Water- and explosion-proof systems must be installed in industrial or agricultural sites where dusty processes are carried out.

Electrical hazards in explosive atmospheres or at sites containing explosive materials
Explosions, including those of atmospheres containing explosive gases and dusts, may be triggered by opening and closing live electrical circuits, or by any other transient process capable of generating sparks of sufficient energy.

This hazard is present in sites such as:

- mines and underground sites where gases, especially methane, may accumulate
- chemical industries

- lead-battery storage rooms, where hydrogen may accumulate
- the food industry, where natural organic powders may be generated
- the synthetic materials industry
- metallurgy, especially that involving aluminium and magnesium

Where this hazard is present, the number of electrical circuits and equipment should be minimized—for example, by removing electrical motors and transformers or replacing them with pneumatic equipment. Electrical equipment which cannot be removed must be enclosed, to avoid any contact of flammable gases and dusts with sparks, and a positive-pressure inert-gas atmosphere maintained within the enclosure. Explosion-proof enclosures and fireproof electrical cables must be used where there is the possibility of explosion. A full range of explosion-proof equipment has been developed for some high-risk industries (e.g., the oil and chemical industries).

Because of the high cost of explosion-proof equipment, plants are commonly divided into electrical hazard zones. In this approach, special equipment is used in high-risk zones, while a certain amount of risk is accepted in others. Various industry-specific criteria and technical solutions have been developed; these usually involve some combination of grounding, component segregation and the installation of zoning barriers.

Equipotential Bonding

If all the conductors, including the earth, that can be touched simultaneously were at the same potential, there would be no danger to humans. Equipotential bonding systems are an attempt to achieve this ideal condition (Andreoni and Castagna 1983; Lee, Cravalho and Burke 1992).

In equipotential bonding, every exposed conductor of non-transmission electrical equipment and every accessible extraneous conductor in the same site are connected to a protective grounded conductor. It should be recalled that while the conductors of non-transmission equipment are dead during normal operation, they may become live following insulation failure. By decreasing the contact voltage, equipotential bonding prevents metallic components from reaching voltages that are hazardous to both humans and equipment.

In practice, it may prove necessary to connect the same machine to the equipotential bonding grid at more than one point. Areas of poor contact, due, for example, to the presence of insulators such as lubricants and paint, should be carefully identified. Similarly, it is good practice to connect all the local and external service piping (e.g., water, gas and heating) to the equipotential bonding grid.

Grounding

In most cases, it is necessary to minimize the voltage drop between the installation's conductors and the earth. This is accomplished by connecting the conductors to a grounded protective conductor.

There are two types of ground connections:

- functional grounds—for example, grounding the neutral conductor of a three-phase system, or the midpoint of a transformer's secondary coil
- protective grounds—for example, grounding every conductor on a piece of equipment. The object of this type of grounding is to minimize conductor voltages by creating a preferential path for fault currents, especially those currents likely to affect humans.

Under normal operating conditions, no current flows through ground connections. In the event of accidental activation of the circuit, however, the current flow through the low-resistance grounding connection is high enough to melt the fuse or the ungrounded conductors.

The maximum fault voltage in equipotential grids allowed by most standards is 50 V for dry environments, 25 V for wet or humid environments and 12 V for medical laboratories and other high-risk environments. Although these values are only guidelines, the necessity of ensuring adequate grounding in workplaces, public spaces and especially residences, should be emphasized.

The efficiency of grounding depends primarily on the existence of high and stable ground leakage currents, but also on adequate galvanic coupling of the equipotential grid, and the diameter of the conductors leading to the grid. Because of the importance of ground leakage, it must be evaluated with great accuracy.

Ground connections must be as reliable as equipotential grids, and their proper operation must be verified on a regular basis.

As the earth resistance increases, the potential of both the grounding conductor and the earth around the conductor approaches that of the electrical circuit; in the case of the earth around the conductor, the potential generated is inversely proportional to the distance from the conductor. In order to avoid dangerous step voltages, ground conductors must be properly shielded and set in the ground at adequate depths.

As an alternative to equipment grounding, standards allow for the use of double-insulated equipment. This equipment, recommended for use in residential settings, minimizes the chance of insulation failure by providing two separate insulation systems. Double-insulated equipment cannot be relied upon to adequately protect against interface failures such as those associated with loose but live plugs, since some countries' plug and wall-socket standards do not address the use of such plugs.

Circuit-breakers

The surest method of reducing electrical hazards to humans and equipment is to minimize the duration of the fault current and voltage increase, ideally before the electrical energy has even begun to increase. Protective systems in electrical equipment usually incorporate three relays: a residual-current relay to protect against failure towards ground, a magnetic relay and a thermal relay to protect against overloads and short circuits.

In residual-current circuit-breakers, the conductors in the circuit are wound around a ring which detects the vector sum of the currents entering and exiting the equipment to be protected. The vector sum is equal to zero during normal operation, but equals the leakage current in cases of failure. When the leakage current reaches the breaker's threshold, the breaker is tripped. Residual-current circuit-breakers can be tripped by currents as low as 30 mA, with latencies as low as 30 ms.

The maximum current that can be safely carried by a conductor is a function of its cross-sectional area, insulation and installation. Overheating will result if the maximum safe load is exceeded or if heat dissipation is limited. Overcurrent devices such as fuses and magneto-thermal circuit-breakers automatically break the circuit if excessive current flow, ground faults, overloading or short circuits occur. Overcurrent devices should interrupt the current flow when it exceeds the conductor's capacity.

Selection of protective equipment capable of protecting both personnel and equipment is one of the most important issues in the management of electrical installations and must take into account not only the current-carrying capacity of conductors but also the characteristics of the circuits and the equipment connected to them.

Special high-capacity fuses or circuit-breakers must be used on circuits carrying very high current loads.

Figure 40.3 • The framework of international standards and regulations.

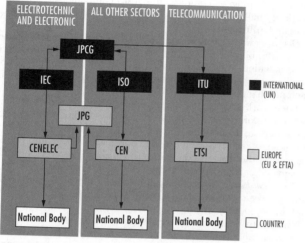

ELECTROTECHNIC AND ELECTRONIC	ALL OTHER SECTORS	TELECOMMUNICATION	
JPCG			■ INTERNATIONAL (UN)
IEC	ISO	ITU	
JPG			
CENELEC	CEN	ETSI	▢ EUROPE (EU & EFTA)
National Body	National Body	National Body	▢ COUNTRY

JPCG = Joint Presidents Coordinating Group
IEC = International Electrotechnical Commission
ISO = International Organization for Standardization
ITU = International Telecommunications Union

JPG = Joint Presidents Group
CENELEC = Comité Européen de Normalisation Electrotechnique
CEN = Comité Européen de Normalisation
ETSI = European Telecommunications Standards Institute

Fuses

Several types of fuse are available, each designed for a specific application. Use of the wrong type of fuse or of a fuse of the wrong capacity may cause injury and damage equipment. Overfusing frequently results in overheated wiring or equipment, which in turn may cause fires.

Before replacing fuses, lock out, tag and test the circuit, to verify that the circuit is dead. Testing can save lives. Next, identify the cause of any short circuits or overloads, and replace blown fuses with fuses of the same type and capacity. Never insert fuses in a live circuit.

Circuit-breakers

Although circuit-breakers have long been used in high-voltage circuits with large current capacities, they are increasingly used in many other kinds of circuits. Many types are available, offering a choice of immediate and delayed onset and manual or automatic operation.

Circuit-breakers fall into two general categories: thermal and magnetic.

Thermal circuit-breakers react solely to a rise of temperature. Variations in the circuit-breaker's ambient temperature will therefore affect the point at which the breaker is tripped.

Magnetic circuit-breakers, on the other hand, react solely to the amount of current passing through the circuit. This type of breaker is preferable where wide temperature fluctuations would require overrating the circuit-breaker, or where the breaker is frequently tripped.

In the case of contact with lines carrying high current loads, protective circuits cannot prevent personal injury or equipment damage, as they are designed only to protect power-lines and systems from excess current flow caused by faults.

Because of the resistance of the contact with the earth, the current passing through an object simultaneously contacting the line and the earth will usually be less than the tripping current. Fault currents flowing through humans may be further reduced by body resistance to the point where they do not trip the breaker,

and are therefore extremely dangerous. It is virtually impossible to design a power system that would prevent injury or damage to any object that faults the power lines while remaining a useful energy transmission system, as the trip thresholds for the relevant circuit protection devices are well above the human hazard level.

Standards and Regulations

The framework of international standards and regulations is illustrated in figure 40.3 (Winckler 1994). The rows correspond to the geographic scope of the standards, either worldwide (international), continental (regional) or national, while the columns correspond to the standards' fields of application. The IEC and the International Organization for Standardization (ISO) both share an umbrella structure, the Joint Presidents Coordinating Group (JPCG); the European equivalent is the Joint Presidents Group (JPG).

Each standardization body holds regular international meetings. The composition of the various bodies reflects the development of standardization.

The *Comité européen de normalisation électrotechnique* (CENELEC) was created by the electrical engineering committees of the countries signing the 1957 Rome Treaty establishing the European Economic Community. The six founding members were later joined by the members of the European Free Trade Association (EFTA), and CENELEC in its present form dates from 13 February, 1972.

In contrast to the International Electrotechnical Commission (IEC), CENELEC focuses on the implementation of international standards in member countries rather than on the creation of new standards. It is particularly important to recall that while the adoption of IEC standards by member countries is voluntary, adoption of CENELEC standards and regulations is obligatory in the European Union. Over 90% of CENELEC standards are derived from IEC standards, and over 70% of them are identical. CENELEC's influence has also attracted the interest of Eastern European countries, most of which became affiliated members in 1991.

The International Association for Testing and Materials, the forerunner of the ISO, as it is known today, was founded in 1886 and was active until The First World War, after which it ceased to function as an international association. Some national organizations, like the American Society for Testing and Materials (ASTM), survived. In 1926, the International Standards Association (ISA) was founded in New York and was active until The Second World War. The ISA was replaced in 1946 by the ISO, which is responsible for all fields except electrical engineering and telecommunications. The *Comité européen de normalisation* (CEN) is the European equivalent of the ISO and has the same function as CENELEC, although only 40% of CEN standards are derived from ISO standards.

The current wave of international economic consolidation creates a need for common technical databases in the field of standardization. This process is presently under way in several parts of the world, and it is likely that new standardization bodies will evolve outside of Europe. CANENA is a regional standardization body created by the North American Free Trade Agreement (NAFTA) countries (Canada, Mexico and the United States). Wiring of premises in the US is governed by the National Electrical Code, ANSI/NFPA 70-1996. This Code is also in use in several other countries in North and South America. It provides installation requirements for premises wiring installations beyond the point of connection to the electric utility system. It covers installation of electric conductors and equipment within or on public and private buildings, including mobil homes, recreational vehicles, and floating buildings, stock yards, carnivals, parking and other lots, and industrial substations. It does not cover installations in ships or watercraft other than floating buildings—railway rolling stop, aircraft, or automotive vehicles. The National Electric Code also does not apply to other areas that are normally regulated by the National Electrical Safety Code, such as installations of communications utility equipment and electric utility installations.

European and American Standards
for the Operation of Electrical Installations

The European Standard EN 50110-1, *Operation of Electrical Installations* (1994a) prepared by CENELEC Task Force 63-3, is the basic document that applies to the operation of and work activities on, with or near electrical installations. The standard sets the minimum requirements for all CENELEC countries; additional national standards are described in separate subparts of the standard (EN 50110-2).

The standard applies to installations designed for the generation, transmission, conversion, distribution and use of electrical power, and operating at commonly encountered voltage levels. Although typical installations operate at low voltages, the standard also applies to extra-low and high-voltage installations. Installations may be either permanent and fixed (e.g., distribution installations in factories or office complexes) or mobile.

Safe operation and maintenance procedures for work on or near electrical installations are set out in the standard. Applicable work activities include non-electrical work such as construction near overhead lines or underground cables, in addition to all types of electrical work. Certain electrical installations, such as those on board aircraft and ships, are not subject to the standard.

The equivalent standard in the United States is the National Electrical Safety Code (NESC), American National Standards Institute (1990). The NESC applies to utility facilities and functions from the point of generation of electricity and communication signals, through the transmission grid, to the point of delivery to a customer's facilities. Certain installations, including those in mines and ships, are not subject to the NESC. NESC guidelines are designed to ensure the safety of workers engaged in the installation, operation or maintenance of electric supply and communication lines and associated equipment. These guidelines constitute the minimum acceptable standard for occupational and public safety under the specified conditions. The code is not intended as a design specification or an instruction manual. Formally, the NESC must be regarded as a national safety code applicable to the United States.

The extensive rules of both the European and American standards provide for the safe performance of work on electrical installations.

The European Standard (1994a)

Definitions

The standard provides definitions only for the most common terms; further information is available in the International Electrotechnical Commission (1979). For the purposes of this standard, electrical installation refers to all equipment involved in the generation, transmission, conversion, distribution and use of electrical energy. This includes all energy sources, including batteries and capacitors (ENEL 1994; EDF-GDF 1991).

Basic principles

Safe operation: The basic principle of safe work on, with or near an electrical installation is the need to assess the electrical risk before commencing work.

Personnel: The best rules and procedures for work on, with or near electrical installations are of no value if workers are not thoroughly conversant with them and do not comply strictly with

them. All personnel involved in work on, with or near an electrical installation shall be instructed in the safety requirements, safety rules and company policies applicable to their work. Where the work is long or complex, this instruction shall be repeated. Workers shall be required to comply with these requirements, rules and instructions.

Organization: Each electrical installation shall be placed under the responsibility of the designated person in control of the electrical installation. In cases of undertakings involving more than one installation, it is essential that the designated persons in control of each installation cooperate with each other.

Each work activity shall be the responsibility of the designated person in control of the work. Where the work comprises subtasks, persons responsible for the safety of each sub-task will be designated, each reporting to the coordinator. The same person can act as the designated person in control of the work and the designated person in control of the electrical installation.

Communication: This includes all means of information transmission between persons, i.e., spoken word (including telephones, radio and speech), writing (including fax) and visual means (including instrument panels, video, signals and lights).

Formal notification of all information necessary for the safe operation of the electrical installation, e.g., network arrangements, switchgear status and the position of safety devices, shall be given.

Worksite: Adequate working space, access and lighting shall be provided at electrical installations on, with or near which any work is to be carried out.

Tools, equipment and procedures: Tools, equipment and procedures shall comply with the requirements of relevant European, national and international standards, where these exist.

Drawings and reports: The installation's drawings and reports shall be up to date and readily available.

Signage: Adequate signage drawing attention to specific hazards shall be displayed as needed when the installation is operating and during any work.

Standard operating procedures

Operating activities: Operating activities are designed to change the electrical state of an electrical installation. There are two types:

- operations intended to modify the electrical state of an electrical installation, e.g., in order to use equipment, connect, disconnect, start or stop an installation or section of an installation to carry out work. These activities may be carried out locally or by remote control.
- disconnecting before or reconnecting after dead-working, to be carried out by qualified or trained workers.

Functional checks: This includes measurement, testing and inspection procedures.

Measurement is defined as the entire range of activities used to collect physical data in electrical installations. Measurement shall be carried out by qualified professionals.

Testing includes all activities designed to verify the operation or electrical, mechanical or thermal condition of an electrical installation. Testing shall be carried out by qualified workers.

Inspection is verification that an electrical installation conforms to applicable specified technical and safety regulations.

Work procedures

General: The designated person in control of the electrical installation and the designated person in control of the work shall both ensure that workers receive specific and detailed instructions before starting the work, and on its completion.

Before the start of work, the designated person in control of the work shall notify the designated person in control of the electrical installation of the nature, site and consequences to the electrical installation of the intended work. This notification shall be given preferably in writing, especially when the work is complex.

Work activities can divided into three categories: dead-working, live-working and work in the vicinity of live installations. Measures designed to protect against electrical shocks, short circuits and arcing have been developed for each type of work.

Induction: The following precautions shall be taken when working on electrical lines subject to current induction:

- grounding at appropriate intervals; this reduces the potential between conductors and earth to a safe level
- equipotential bonding of the worksite; this prevents workers from introducing themselves into the induction loop.

Weather conditions: When lightning is seen or thunder heard, no work shall be started or continued on outdoor installations or on indoor installations directly connected to overhead lines.

Dead-working

The following basic work practices will ensure that the electrical installations at the worksite remain dead for the duration of the work. Unless there are clear contraindications, the practices should be applied in the order listed.

Complete disconnection: The section of the installation in which the work is to be carried out shall be isolated from all sources of current supply, and secured against reconnection.

Securing against reconnection: All circuit-breaking devices used to isolate the electrical installation for the work shall be locked out, preferably by locking the operating mechanism.

Verification that the installation is dead: The absence of current shall be verified at all poles of the electrical installation at or as near as practicable to the worksite.

Grounding and short-circuiting: At all high- and some low-voltage worksites, all parts to be worked on shall be grounded and short-circuited after they have been disconnected. Grounding and short-circuiting systems shall be connected to the earth first; the components to be grounded must be connected to the system only after it has been earthed. As far as practical, the grounding and short-circuiting systems shall be visible from the worksite. Low- and high-voltage installations have their own specific requirements. At these types of installation, all sides of the worksites and all conductors entering the site must be grounded and short-circuited.

Protecting against adjacent live parts: Additional protective measures are necessary if parts of an electrical installation in the vicinity of the worksite cannot be made dead. Workers shall not commence work before receiving permission to do so from the designated person in control of the work, who in turn must receive authorization from the designated person in control of the electrical installation. Once the work has been completed, workers shall leave the worksite, tools and equipment shall be stored, and grounding and short-circuiting systems removed. The designated person in control of the work shall then notify the designated person in control of the electrical installation that the installation is available for reconnection.

Live-working

General: Live-working is work carried out within a zone in which there is current flow. Guidance for the dimensions of the live-working zone can be found in standard EN 50179. Protective measures designed to prevent electric shocks, arcing and short circuits shall be applied.

Training and qualification: Specific training programmes shall be established to develop and maintain the ability of qualified or trained workers to perform live-working. After completing the programme, workers will receive a qualification rating and authorization to perform specific live-work on specific voltages.

Maintenance of qualifications: The ability to carry out live-working shall be maintained by either practice or new training.

Work techniques: Currently, there are three recognized techniques, distinguished by their applicability to different types of live parts and the equipment required to prevent electric shocks, arcing and short circuits:

- hot-stick working
- insulating-glove working
- bare-hand working.

Each technique requires different preparation, equipment and tools, and selection of the most appropriate technique will depend on the characteristics of the work in question.

Tools and equipment: The characteristics, storage, maintenance, transportation and inspection of tools, equipment and systems shall be specified.

Weather conditions: Restrictions apply to live-working in adverse weather conditions, since insulating properties, visibility and worker mobility are all reduced.

Work organization: The work shall be adequately prepared; written preparation shall be submitted in advance for complex work. The installation in general, and the section where the work is to be carried out in particular, shall be maintained in a condition consistent with the preparation required. The designated person in control of the work shall inform the designated person in control of the electrical installation of the nature of the work, the site in the installation at which the work will be performed, and the estimated duration of the work. Before work begins, workers shall have the nature of the work, the relevant safety measures, the role of each worker, and the tools and equipment to be used explained to them.

Specific practices exist for extra-low-voltage, low-voltage, and high-voltage installations.

Work in the vicinity of live parts

General: Work in the vicinity of live parts with nominal voltages above 50 VAC or 120 VDC shall be performed only when safety measures have been applied to ensure that live parts cannot be touched or that the live zone cannot be entered. Screens, barriers, enclosures or insulating coverings may be used for this purpose.

Before the work starts, the designated person in control of the work shall instruct the workers, particularly those unfamiliar with work in the vicinity of live parts, on the safety distances to be observed on the worksite, the principal safety practices to follow, and the need for behaviour that ensures the safety of the entire work crew. Worksite boundaries shall be precisely defined and marked and attention drawn to unusual working conditions. This information shall be repeated as needed, particularly after changes in working conditions.

Workers shall ensure that no part of their body nor any object enters the live zone. Particular care shall be taken when handling long objects, for example, tools, cable ends, pipes and ladders.

Protection by screens, barriers, enclosures or insulating coverings: The selection and installation of these protective devices shall ensure sufficient protection against predictable electrical and mechanical stressors. The equipment shall be suitably maintained and kept secured during the work.

Maintenance

General: The purpose of maintenance is to maintain the electrical installation in the required condition. Maintenance may be preventive (i.e., carried out on a regular basis to prevent breakdowns and keep equipment in working order) or corrective (i.e., carried out to replace defective parts).

Maintenance work can be divided into two risk categories:

- work involving the risk of electrical shock, where procedures applicable to live-working and work in the vicinity of live parts must be followed
- work where equipment design allows some maintenance work to be performed in the absence of full live-working procedures

Personnel: Personnel who are to carry out the work shall be adequately qualified or trained and shall be provided with appropriate measuring and testing tools and devices.

Repair work: Repair work consists of the following steps: fault location; fault rectification and/or replacement of components; recommissioning of the repaired section of the installation. Each of these steps may require specific procedures.

Replacement work: In general, fuse replacement in high-voltage installations shall be performed as dead-work. Fuse replacement shall be performed by qualified workers following appropriate work procedures. The replacement of lamps and removable parts such as starters shall be carried out as dead-work. In high-voltage installations, repair procedures shall also apply to replacement work.

Training of Personnel about Electrical Hazards

Effective work organization and safety training is a key element in every successful organization, prevention programme and occupational health and safety programme. Workers must have proper training to do their jobs safely and efficiently.

The responsibility for implementing employee training rests with management. Management must recognize that employees must perform at a certain level before the organization can achieve its objectives. In order to achieve these levels, worker training policies and, by extension, concrete training programmes must be established. Programmes should include training and qualification phases.

Live-working programmes should include the following elements:

Training: In some countries, programmes and training facilities must be formally approved by a live-working committee or similar body. Programmes are based primarily on practical experience, complemented by technical instruction. Training takes the form of practical work on indoor or outdoor model installations similar to those on which actual work is to be performed.

Qualifications: Live-working procedures are very demanding, and it is essential to use the right person at the right place. This is most easily achieved if qualified personnel of different skill levels are available. The designated person in control of the work should be a qualified worker. Where supervision is necessary, it too should be carried out by a qualified person. Workers should work only on installations whose voltage and complexity corresponds to their level of qualification or training. In some countries, qualification is regulated by national standards.

Finally, workers should be instructed and trained in essential life-saving techniques. The reader is referred to the chapter on first-aid for further information.

References

American National Standards Institute (ANSI). 1990. *National Electrical Safety Code: ANSI C2.* New York: ANSI.

Andreoni, D and R Castagna. 1983. *L'Ingegnere e la Sicurezza.* Vol. 2. Rome: Edizioni Scientifiche.

EDF-GDF. 1991. *Carnet de Prescriptions au Personnel—Prévention du Risque electrique.*

ENEL Spa. 1994. *Disposizioni per la Prevenzione del Rischi Elettrici.*

European Standard (1994a). *Operation of Electrical Installations.* Final draft EN 50110-1.

European Standard (1994b). *Operation of Electrical Installations* (National Annexes.) Final draft EN 50110-2.

European Economic Community (EEC). 1989. *Council Directive of 12 June 1989 on the Introduction of Measures to Encourage Improvements in the Safety and Health of Workers at Work. Document No. 89/391/EEC.* Luxembourg: EEC.

Folliot, D. 1982. *Les accidents d'origine électrique, leur prévention.* Collection monographie de médecine du travail. Paris: Editions Masson.

Gilet, JC and R Choquet. 1990. *La Sécurité électrique: Techniques de prévention.* Grenoble, France: Société alpine de publication.

Gourbiere, E, J Lambrozo, D Folliot, and C Gary. 1994. Complications et séquelles des accidents dus à la foudre. *Rev Gén Electr* 6 (4 June).

International Electrotechnical Commission (IEC). 1979. Electrobiologie. Chap. 891 in *General Index of International Electrotechnical Vocabulary.* Geneva: IEC.

—. 1987. *Effets du Courant Passant par le Corps humain: Deuxième partie.* IEC 479-2. Geneva: IEC.

—. 1994. *Effets du Courant Passant par le Corps humain: Première partie.* Geneva: IEC.

Kane, JW and MM Sternheim. 1980. *Fisica Biomedica.* Rome: EMSI.

Lee, RC, M Capelli-Schellpfeffer, and KM Kelly. 1994. Electrical injury: A multidisciplinary approach to therapy, prevention and rehabilitation. *Ann NY Acad Sci* 720.

Lee, RC, EG Cravalho, and JF Burke. 1992. *Electrical Trauma.* Cambride: Cambridge Univ. Press.

Winckler, R. 1994. *Electrotechnical Standardization in Europe: A Tool for the Internal Market.* Brussels: CENELEC.

Other relevant readings

Association Suisse des Electriciens. 1990. Basic Safety Requirements for Low-Voltage Electric Equipment (Prescriptions de sécurité fondamentales pour matériels électriques à basse tension). Zurich: Association Suisse des Electriciens.

Casini, VJ. 1993. Occupational electrocutions: Investigation and prevention. *Prof Saf* 38(1):34-39.

Donnachie, PE. 1994. Dangers of electricity—An introduction. *Health Safety Data F C:1* (June):1-4.

Fraser, D. 1990. Unit: Safety technology-module: Electrical safety. In *Occupational Health and Safety.* Portsmouth: Portsmouth Polytechnic.

Garside, R. 1990. *Electrical Apparatus and Hazardous Areas.* Aylesbury: Hexagon Technology.

Grube, BJ, DM Heimbach, LH Engrav, and MK Copass. 1990. Neurologic consequences of electrical burns. *J Trauma* 30(3):254-258.

Harvey-Sutton, PL, TR Driscoll, MS Frommer, and JE Harrison. 1992. Work-related electrical fatalities in Australia, 1982-1984. *Scand J Work Environ Health* 18(5):293-297.

Hauptverband der Gewerblichen Berufsgenossenschaften. 1989. *Code of Practice for Preventing Risks of Ignition Due to Electrostatic Charges: Guidelines on Static Electricity* (in German). Cologne: Carl Heymanns Verlag.

Health and Safety Executive. 1993. *Electricity at Work: Safe Working Practices.* London: Her Majesty's Stationery Office.

Institut national de Recherche et de Sécurité. 1993. *Electrical Accidents (Accidents d'origine électrique).* Paris: Institut national de recherche et de sécurité.

International Electrotechnical Commission (IEC). 1990a. *Graphic Symbols for Use on Equipment.* Geneva: IEC.

—. 1990b. *Safety of Transportable Motor-Operated Electric Tools-Part 1: General Requirements.* Geneva: IEC.

—. 1994. *Marking of Electrical Equipment with Ratings Related to Electrical Supply-Safety Requirements.* Geneva: IEC.

Jenkins, BD. 1993. *Touch Voltages in Electrical Installations.* Oxford: Blackwell Scientific Publications.

Kinloch, CD. 1987. *Electrical Installation: Snags and Solutions:* Reed Business Publishing.

Omeish, TM and M Sebastian. 1991. Overcoming electrical risks in hazardous process areas. *Fire Prev* (245) (December):21-26.

Paureau, J and M Rollin. 1990. Antistatic safety footwear: Assessment of the main methods used to determine insulation resistance (in French). Cahiers de notes documentaires—Sécurité et hygiène du travail 2nd quarter(139):405-419.

Pineault, M, M Rossignol, and RG Barr. 1994. Interrater analysis of a classification scheme of occupational fatalities by electrocution. *J Saf Res* 25(2):107-115.

Reilly, JP and H Antoni. 1992. *Electrical Stimulation and Electropathology.* Cambridge: Cambridge Univ. Press.

Suruda, A and L Smith. 1992. Work-related electrocutions involving portable power tools and appliances. *J Occup Med* 34(9):887-892.

Tilley, L. 1992. Electrocution-A shock to the system. *Aust Safety News* 63(11):58-59.

Walker, E. 1992. *Safety Managers Pocket Guide to Electrical Inspection.* Rotherham: Saxton Safety Services.

Yakuboff, KP and HE Kleinert. 1991. Electrical injuries. In *Occupational Hand and Upper Extremity Injuries and Diseases*, edited by ML Kasdan. Philadelphia: Hanley & Belfus.

41

Chapter Editor
Casey C. Grant

Contents

● BASIC CONCEPTS

Dougal Drysdale

The Chemistry and Physics of Fire

Fire is a manifestation of uncontrolled combustion. It involves combustible materials which are found around us in the buildings in which we live, work and play, as well as encountered in industry and commerce. They are commonly carbon-based, and may be referred to collectively as *fuels* in the context of this discussion. Despite the wide variety of these fuels in both their chemical and physical states, in fire they share features that are common to them all. Differences are encountered in the ease with which fire can be initiated (*ignition*), the rate with which fire can develop (*flame spread*), and the power that can be generated (*rate of heat release*), but as our understanding of the science of fire improves, we become better able to quantify and predict fire behaviour and apply our knowledge to fire safety in general. The purpose of this section is to review some of the underlying principles and provide guidance to an understanding of fire processes.

Basic Concepts

Combustible materials are all around us. Given the appropriate circumstances, they can be made to burn by subjecting them to an *ignition source* which is capable of initiating a self-sustaining reaction. In this process, the "fuel" reacts with oxygen from the air to release energy (heat), while being converted to products of combustion, some of which may be harmful. The mechanisms of ignition and burning need to be clearly understood.

Most everyday fires involve solid materials (e.g., wood, wood products and synthetic polymers), although gaseous and liquid fuels are not uncommon. A brief review of the combustion of gases and liquids is desirable before some of the basic concepts are discussed.

Diffusion and premixed flames

A flammable gas (e.g., propane, C_3H_8) can be burned in two ways: a stream or jet of gas from a pipe (cf. the simple Bunsen burner with the air inlet closed) can be ignited and will burn as a *diffusion flame* in which burning occurs in those regions where gaseous fuel and air mix by diffusive processes. Such a flame has a characteristic yellow luminosity, indicating the presence of minute soot particles formed as a result of incomplete combustion. Some of these will burn in the flame, but others will emerge from the flame tip to form *smoke*.

If the gas and air are intimately mixed before ignition, then premixed combustion will occur, provided that the gas/air mixture lies within a range of concentrations bounded by the lower and upper *flammability limits* (see table 41.1). Outside these limits, the mixture is non-flammable. (Note that a *premixed flame* is stabilized at the mouth of a Bunsen burner when the air inlet is open.) If a mixture is flammable, then it can be ignited by a small ignition source, such as an electrical spark. The *stoichiometric* mixture is the most readily ignited, in which the amount of oxygen present is in the correct proportion to burn all the fuel to carbon dioxide and water (see accompanying equation, below, in which nitrogen can be seen to be present in the same proportion as in air but does not take part in the reaction). Propane (C_3H_8) is the combustible material in this reaction:

$$C_3H_8 + 5O_2 + 18.8N_2 = 3CO_2 + 4H_2O + 18.8N_2$$

An electrical discharge as small as 0.3 mJ is sufficient to ignite a stoichiometric propane/air mixture in the reaction illustrated. This represents a barely perceptible static spark, as experienced by someone who has walked across a synthetic carpet and touched a grounded object. Even smaller amounts of energy are required for certain reactive gases such as hydrogen, ethylene and ethyne. In pure oxygen (as in the reaction above, but with no nitrogen present as a diluent), even lower energies are sufficient.

The diffusion flame associated with a flow of gaseous fuel exemplifies the mode of burning that is observed when a liquid or solid fuel is undergoing flaming combustion. However, in this case, the flame is fed by fuel vapours generated at the surface of the condensed phase. The rate of supply of these vapours is coupled to their rate of burning in the diffusion flame. Energy is transferred from the flame to the surface, thus providing the energy necessary to produce the vapours. This is a simple evaporative process for liquid fuels, but for solids, enough energy must be provided to cause chemical decomposition of the fuel, breaking large polymeric molecules into smaller fragments which can vaporize and escape from the surface. This thermal feedback is essential to maintain the flow of vapours, and hence support the diffusion flame (figure 41.1). Flames can be extinguished by interfering with this process in a number of ways (see below).

Heat transfer

An understanding of heat (or energy) transfer is the key to an understanding of fire behaviour and fire processes. The subject deserves careful study. There are many excellent texts to which one may turn (Welty, Wilson and Wicks 1976; DiNenno 1988), but for the present purposes it is necessary only to draw attention to the three mechanisms: conduction, convection and radiation. The basic equations for steady-state heat transfer ($\dot{q}''$) are:

Conduction: $\quad \dot{q}'' = \dfrac{k}{l}(T_1 - T_2) \quad \text{kW/m}^2$

Convection: $\quad \dot{q}'' = h(T_1 - T_2) \quad \text{kW/m}^2$

Radiation: $\quad \dot{q}'' = \varepsilon\sigma(T_1^4 - T_2^4) \quad \text{kW/m}^2$

Conduction is relevant to heat transfer through solids; (k is a material property known as thermal conductivity (kW/mK) and l is the distance (m) over which the temperature falls from T_1 to T_2 (in degrees Kelvin). Convection in this context refers to the transfer of heat from a fluid (in this case, air, flames or fire products) to a surface (solid or liquid); h is the convective heat transfer coefficient kW/m²K) and depends on the configuration of the surface and nature of the flow of fluid past that surface. Radiation is similar to visible light (but with a longer wavelength) and requires no intervening medium (it can traverse a vacuum); ε is the emissivity

Table 41.1 • Lower and upper flammability limits in air.

	Lower flammability limit (% by volume)	Upper flammability limit (% by volume)
Carbon monoxide	12.5	74
Methane	5.0	15
Propane	2.1	9.5
n-Hexane	1.2	7.4
n-Decane	0.75	5.6
Methanol	6.7	36
Ethanol	3.3	19
Acetone	2.6	13
Benzene	1.3	7.9

(efficiency by which a surface can radiate), σ is the Stefan-Boltzman constant $(56.7 \times 10^{-12} \ \text{kW/m}^2\text{K}^4)$. Thermal radiation travels at the speed of light $(3 \times 10^8 \ \text{m/s})$ and an intervening solid object will cast a shadow.

Rate of burning and rate of heat release

Heat transfer from flames to the surface of condensed fuels (liquids and solids) involves a mixture of convection and radiation, although the latter dominates when the effective diameter of the fire exceeds 1 m. The rate of burning ($\dot{m}$, (g/s)) can be expressed by the formula:

$$\dot{m} = \frac{\dot{Q}_F'' - \dot{Q}_L''}{L_v} \cdot A_{fuel} \quad \text{g/s}$$

$\dot{Q}_F''$ is the heat flux from the flame to the surface (kW/m²); $\dot{Q}_L''$ is the heat loss from the surface (e.g., by radiation, and by conduction through the solid) expressed as a flux (kW/m²); A_{fuel} is the surface area of the fuel (m²); and L_v is the heat of gasification (equivalent to the latent heat of evaporation for a liquid) (kJ/g). If a fire develops in a confined space, the hot smoky gases rising from the fire (driven by buoyancy) are deflected beneath the ceiling, heating the upper surfaces. The resulting smoke layer and the hot surfaces radiate down to the lower part of the enclosure, in particular to the fuel surface, thus increasing the rate of burning:

$$\dot{m} = \frac{\dot{Q}_F'' + \dot{Q}_{ext}'' - \dot{Q}_L''}{L_v} \cdot A_{fuel} \quad \text{g/s}$$

where $\dot{Q}_{ext}''$ is the extra heat supplied by radiation from the upper part of the enclosure (kW/m²). This additional feedback leads to greatly enhanced rates of burning and to the phenomenon of flashover in enclosed spaces where there is an adequate supply of air and sufficient fuel to sustain the fire (Drysdale 1985).

The rate of burning is moderated by the magnitude of the value of L_v, the heat of gasification. This tends to be low for liquids and relatively high for solids. Consequently, solids tend to burn much more slowly than liquids.

It has been argued that the most important single parameter which determines the fire behaviour of a material (or assembly of materials) is *the rate of heat release* (RHR) which is coupled to the rate of burning through the equation:

$$\text{RHR} = \dot{m}\Delta H_c \quad \text{kW}$$

where ΔH_c is the effective heat of combustion of the fuel (kJ/g). New techniques are now available for measuring the RHR at different heat fluxes (e.g., the Cone Calorimeter), and it is now possible to measure the RHR of large items, such as upholstered furniture and wall linings in large-scale calorimeters which use oxygen consumption measurements to determine the rate of heat release (Babrauskas and Grayson 1992).

It should be noted that as a fire grows in size, not only does the rate of heat release increase, but the rate of production of "fire products" also increases. These contain toxic and noxious species as well as particulate smoke, the yields of which will increase when a fire developing in a building enclosure becomes underventilated.

Ignition

Ignition of a liquid or solid involves raising the surface temperature until vapours are being evolved at a rate sufficient to support a flame after the vapours have been ignited. Liquid fuels can be classified according to their *flashpoints*, the lowest temperature at which there is a flammable vapour/air mixture at the surface (i.e., the vapour pressure corresponds to the lower flammability limit). These can be measured using a standard apparatus, and typical examples are given in table 41.2. A slightly higher temperature is required to produce a sufficient flow of vapours to support a diffusion flame. This is known as the *firepoint*. For combustible

solids, the same concepts are valid, but higher temperatures are required as chemical decomposition is involved. The firepoint is typically in excess of 300 °C, depending on the fuel. In general, flame-retarded materials have significantly higher firepoints (see table 41.2).

Ease of ignition of a solid material is therefore dependent on the ease with which its surface temperature can be raised to the firepoint, e.g., by exposure to radiant heat or to a flow of hot

Figure 41.1 • Schematic representation of a burning surface showing the heat and mass transfer processes.

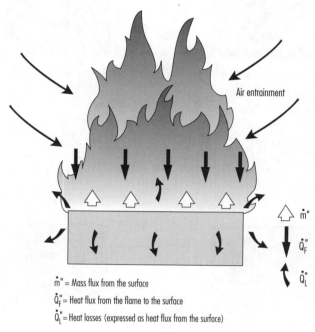

Air entrainment

$\dot{m}''$ = Mass flux from the surface

$\dot{Q}_F''$ = Heat flux from the flame to the surface

$\dot{Q}_L''$ = Heat losses (expressed as heat flux from the surface)

Source: Drysdale 1985.

Table 41.2 • Flashpoints and firepoints of liquid and solid fuels.

	Closed cup flashpoint[1] (°C)	Firepoint[2] (°C)
Gasoline (100 Octane) (l)	−38	−
n-Decane (l)	46	61.5
n-Dodecane (l)	74	103
Polymethylmethacrylate (s)	−	≈310
FR polymethylmethacrylate (s)	−	≈377
Polypropylene (s)	−	≈330
FR polypropylene (s)	−	≈397
Polystyrene (s)	−	≈367
FR polystyrene (s)	−	≈445

l = liquid; s = solid.

[1] By Pensky-Martens closed cup apparatus.

[2] Liquids: by Cleveland open cup apparatus. Solids: Drysdale and Thomson (1994). (Note that the results for the flame-retarded species refer to a heat flux of 37 kW/m².)

Figure 41.2 • The scenario for piloted ignition.

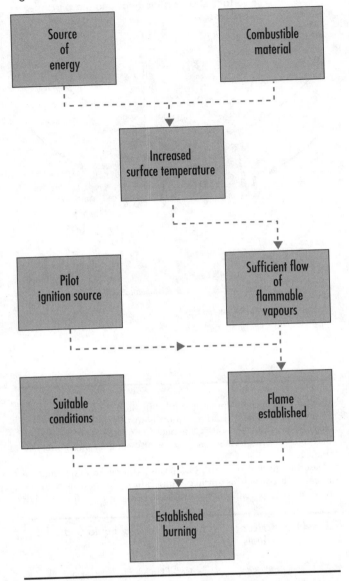

Ignition sources

Ignition is illustrated schematically in figure 41.2 (*piloted ignition*). For successful ignition, an *ignition source* must be capable not only of raising the surface temperature to the firepoint, or above, but it must also cause the vapours to ignite. An impinging flame will act in both capacities, but an imposed radiative flux from a remote source may lead to the evolution of vapours at a temperature above the firepoint, without the vapours igniting. However, if the evolved vapours are hot enough (which requires the surface temperature to be much higher than the firepoint), they may ignite spontaneously as they mix with air. This process is known as *spontaneous ignition*.

A large number of ignition sources can be identified, but they have one thing in common, which is that they are the result of some form of carelessness or inaction. A typical list would include naked flames, "smokers' materials", frictional heating, electrical devices (heaters, irons, cookers, etc.) and so on. An excellent survey may be found in Cote (1991). Some of these are summarized in table 41.3.

It should be noted that smouldering cigarettes cannot initiate flaming combustion directly (even in common gaseous fuels), but can cause *smouldering* in materials which have the propensity to undergo this type of combustion. This is observed only with materials which char on heating. Smouldering involves the surface oxidation of the char, which generates enough heat locally to produce fresh char from adjacent unburnt fuel. It is a very slow process, but may eventually undergo a transition to flaming. Thereafter, the fire will develop very rapidly.

Materials which have the propensity to smoulder can also exhibit the phenomenon of self-heating (Bowes 1984). This arises when such a material is stored in large quantities and in such a way that heat generated by slow surface oxidation cannot escape, leading to a rise in temperature within the mass. If the conditions are right, this can lead to a runaway process ultimately developing into a smouldering reaction at depth within the material.

Flame spread

A major component in the growth of any fire is the rate at which flame will spread over adjacent combustible surfaces. Flame spread can be modelled as an advancing ignition front in which the leading edge of the flame acts as an ignition source for the fuel that is not yet burning. The rate of spread is determined partly by the same material properties that control the ease of ignition and partly by the interaction between the existing flame and the surface ahead of the front. Upward, vertical spread is the

---

gases. This is less dependent on the chemistry of the decomposition process than on the thickness and physical properties of the solid, namely, its *thermal conductivity* (k), *density* (ρ) and *heat capacity* (c). Thin solids, such as wood shavings (and all thin sections), can be ignited very easily because they have a low thermal mass, that is, relatively little heat is required to raise the temperature to the firepoint. However, when heat is transferred to the surface of a thick solid, some will be conducted from the surface into the body of the solid, thus moderating the temperature rise of the surface. It can be shown theoretically that the rate of rise of the surface temperature is determined by the *thermal inertia* of the material, that is, the product $k\rho c$. This is borne out in practice, since thick materials with a high thermal inertia (e.g., oak, solid polyurethane) will take a long time to ignite under a given heat flux, whereas under identical conditions thick materials with a low thermal inertia (e.g., fibre insulating board, polyurethane foam) will ignite quickly (Drysdale 1985).

Table 41.3 • Ignition sources.

	Examples
Electrically powered equipment	Electric heaters, hair dryers, electric blankets, etc.
Open flame source	Match, cigarette lighter, blow torch, etc.
Gas-fuelled equipment	Gas fire, space heater, cooker, etc.
Other fuelled equipment	Wood stove, etc.
Lighted tobacco product	Cigar, pipe, etc.
Hot object	Hot pipes, mechanical sparks, etc.
Exposure to heating	Adjacent fire, etc.
Spontaneous heating	Linseed oil-soaked rags, coal piles, etc.
Chemical reaction	Rare — e.g., potassium permanganate with glycerol

most rapid as buoyancy ensures that the flames flow upwards, exposing the surface above the burning area to direct heat transfer from the flames. This should be contrasted with spread over a horizontal surface when the flames from the burning area rise vertically, away from the surface. Indeed, it is common experience that vertical spread is the most hazardous (e.g., flame spread on curtains and drapes and on loose clothing such as dresses and nightgowns).

The rate of spread is also affected by an imposed radiant heat flux. In the development of a fire in a room, the area of the fire will grow more rapidly under the increasing level of radiation that builds up as the fire progresses. This will contribute to the acceleration of fire growth that is characteristic of flashover.

Theory of Fire Extinguishment

Fire extinction and suppression can be examined in terms of the above outline of the theory of fire. The gas phase combustion processes (i.e., the flame reactions) are very sensitive to chemical inhibitors. Some of the *flame retardants* used to improve the "fire properties" of materials rely on the fact that small amounts of inhibitor released with the fuel vapours will suppress the establishment of flame. The presence of a flame retardant cannot render a combustible material non-combustible, but it can make ignition more difficult—perhaps preventing ignition altogether provided that the ignition source is small. However, if a flame-retarded material becomes involved in an existing fire, it will burn as the high heat fluxes overwhelm the effect of the retardant.

Extinction of a fire may be achieved in a number of ways:

1. stopping the supply of fuel vapours
2. quenching the flame by chemical extinguishers (inhibiting)
3. removing the supply of air (oxygen) to the fire (smothering)
4. "blow-out".

Controlling the flow of fuel vapours

The first method, stopping the supply of fuel vapours, is clearly applicable to a gas-jet fire in which the supply of the fuel can simply be turned off. However, it is also the most common and safest method of extinguishing a fire involving condensed fuels. In the case of a fire involving a solid, this requires the fuel surface to be cooled below the firepoint, when the flow of vapours becomes too small to support a flame. This is achieved most effectively by the application of water, either manually or by means of an automatic system (sprinklers, water spray, etc.). In general, liquid fires cannot be dealt with in this manner: liquid fuels with low firepoints simply cannot be cooled sufficiently, while in the case of a high-firepoint fuel, vigorous vaporization of water when it comes into contact with the hot liquid at the surface can lead to burning fuel being ejected from the container. This can have very serious consequences for those fighting the fire. (There are some special cases in which an automatic high-pressure water-spray system may be designed to deal with the latter type of fire, but this is not common.)

Liquid fires are commonly extinguished by the use of fire-fighting foams (Cote 1991). This is produced by aspirating a foam concentrate into a stream of water which is then directed at the fire through a special nozzle which permits air to be entrained into the flow. This produces a foam which floats on top of the liquid, reducing the rate of supply of fuel vapours by a blockage effect and by shielding the surface from heat transfer from the flames. The foam has to be applied carefully to form a "raft" which gradually increases in size to cover the liquid surface. The flames will decrease in size as the raft grows, and at the same time the foam will gradually break down, releasing water which will aid the cooling of the surface. The mechanism is in fact complex, although the net result is to control the flow of vapours.

There are a number of foam concentrates available, and it is important to choose one that is compatible with the liquids that are to be protected. The original "protein foams" were developed for hydrocarbon liquid fires, but break down rapidly if brought into contact with liquid fuels that are water soluble. A range of "synthetic foams" have been developed to tackle the entire range of liquid fires that may be encountered. One of these, aqueous film-forming foam (AFFF), is an all-purpose foam which also produces a film of water on the surface of the liquid fuel, thus increasing its effectiveness.

Quenching the flame

This method makes use of chemical suppressants to extinguish the flame. The reactions which occur in the flame involve free radicals, a highly reactive species which have only a fleeting existence but are continuously regenerated by a branched chain process that maintains high enough concentrations to allow the overall reaction (e.g., an R1 type reaction) to proceed at a fast rate. Chemical suppressants applied in sufficient quantity will cause a dramatic fall in the concentration of these radicals, effectively quenching the flame. The most common agents that operate in this way are the halons and dry powders.

Halons react in the flame to generate other intermediate species with which the flame radicals react preferentially. Relatively small amounts of the halons are required to extinguish a fire, and for this reason they were traditionally considered highly desirable; extinguishing concentrations are "breathable" (although the products generated while passing through the flame are noxious). Dry powders act in a similar fashion, but under certain circumstances are much more effective. Fine particles are dispersed into the flame and cause termination of the radical chains. It is important that the particles are small and numerous. This is achieved by the manufacturers of many proprietary brands of dry powders by selecting a powder that "decrepitates", that is, the particles fragment into smaller particles when they are exposed to the high temperatures of the flame.

For a person whose clothing has caught fire, a dry powder extinguisher is recognized as the best method to control flames and to protect that individual. Rapid intervention gives rapid "knockdown", thus minimizing injury. However, the flame must be completely extinguished because the particles quickly fall to the ground and any residual flaming will quickly regain hold. Similarly, halons will only remain effective if the local concentrations are maintained. If it is applied out of doors, the halon vapour rapidly disperses, and once again the fire will rapidly re-establish itself if there is any residual flame. More significantly, the loss of the suppressant will be followed by re-ignition of the fuel if the surface temperatures are high enough. Neither halons nor dry powders have any significant cooling effect on the fuel surface.

Removing the supply of air

The following description is an oversimplification of the process. While "removing the supply of air" will certainly cause the fire to extinguish, to do this it is only necessary to reduce the oxygen concentration below a critical level. The well-known "oxygen index test" classifies combustible materials according to the minimum oxygen concentration in an oxygen/nitrogen mixture that will just support flaming. Many common materials will burn at oxygen concentrations down to approximately 14% at ambient temperatures (ca. 20 °C) and in the absence of any imposed heat transfer. The critical concentration is temperature dependent, decreasing as the temperature is increased. Thus, a fire that has been burning for some time will be capable of supporting flames at concentrations perhaps as low as 7%. A fire in a room may be held in check and may even self-extinguish if the supply of oxygen is limited by keeping doors and windows closed. Flaming

Table 41.4 • Comparison of concentrations of different gases required for inerting.

Agent	Minimum concentration (% volume)
Halon 1301	8.0
Halon 1211	8.1
Nitrogen	≈ 58
Carbon dioxide	≈ 35

may cease, but smouldering will continue at very much lower oxygen concentrations. Admission of air by opening a door or breaking a window before the room has cooled sufficiently can lead to a vigorous eruption of the fire, known as *backdraught*, or *backdraft*.

"Removal of air" is difficult to achieve. However, an atmosphere may be rendered "inert" by total flooding by means of a gas which will not support combustion, such as nitrogen, carbon dioxide or gases from a combustion process (e.g., a ship's engines) which are low in oxygen and high in carbon dioxide. This technique can only be used in enclosed spaces as it is necessary to maintain the required concentration of the "inert gas" until either the fire has extinguished completely or fire-fighting operations can begin. Total flooding has special applications, such as for ships' holds and rare book collections in libraries. The required minimum concentrations of the inert gases are shown in table 41.4. These are based on the assumption that the fire is detected at an early stage and that the flooding is carried out before too much heat has accumulated in the space.

"Removal of air" can be effected in the immediate vicinity of a small fire by local application of a suppressant from an extinguisher. Carbon dioxide is the only gas that is used in this way. However, as this gas quickly disperses, it is essential to extinguish all flaming during the attack on the fire; otherwise, flaming will re-establish itself. Re-ignition is also possible because carbon dioxide has little if any cooling effect. It is worth noting that a fine water spray entrained into a flame can cause extinction as the combined result of evaporation of the droplets (which cools the burning zone) and reduction of the oxygen concentration by dilution by water vapour (which acts in the same way as carbon dioxide). Fine water sprays and mists are being considered as possible replacements for halons.

It is appropriate to mention here that it is inadvisable to extinguish a gas flame unless the gas flow can be stopped immediately thereafter. Otherwise, a substantial volume of flammable gas may build up and subsequently ignite, with potentially serious consequences.

Blow-out

This method is included here for completeness. A match flame can easily be blown out by increasing the air velocity above a critical value in the vicinity of the flame. The mechanism operates by destabilizing the flame in the vicinity of the fuel. In principle, larger fires can be controlled in the same way, but explosive charges are normally required to generate sufficient velocities. Oil well fires can be extinguished in this manner.

Finally, a common feature that needs to be emphasized is that the ease with which a fire can be extinguished decreases rapidly as the fire increases in size. Early detection permits extinction with minimal quantities of suppressant, with reduced losses. In choosing a suppressant system, one should take into account the potential rate of fire development and what type of detection system is available.

Explosions

An explosion is characterized by the sudden release of energy, producing a shock wave, or blast wave, that may be capable of causing remote damage. There are two distinct types of sources, namely, the high explosive and the pressure burst. The high explosive is typified by compounds such as trinitrotoluene (TNT) and cyclotrimethylenetrinitramine (RDX). These compounds are highly exothermic species, decomposing to release substantial quantities of energy. Although thermally stable (although some are less so and require desensitization to make them safe to handle), they can be induced to detonate, with decomposition, propagating at the velocity of sound through the solid. If the amount of energy released is high enough, a blast wave will propagate from the source with the potential to do significant damage at a distance.

By assessing remote damage, one can estimate the size of the explosion in terms of "TNT equivalent" (normally in metric tons). This technique relies on the large amount of data that has been gathered on the damage potential of TNT (much of it during wartime), and uses empirical scaling laws which have been developed from studies of the damage caused by known quantities of TNT.

In peacetime, high explosives are used in a variety of activities, including mining, quarrying and major civil engineering works. Their presence on a site represents a particular hazard that requires specific management. However, the other source of "explosions" can be equally devastating, particularly if the hazard has not been recognized. Overpressures leading to pressure bursts can be the result of chemical processes within plants or from purely physical effects, as will occur if a vessel is heated externally, leading to overpressurization. The term *BLEVE* (boiling liquid expanding vapour explosion) has its origins here, referring originally to the failure of steam boilers. It is now also commonly used to describe the event in which a pressure vessel containing a liquefied gas such as LPG (liquified petroleum gas) fails in a fire, releasing the flammable contents, which then ignite to produce a "fireball".

On the other hand, the overpressure may be caused internally by a chemical process. In the process industries, self-heating can lead to a runaway reaction, generating high temperatures and pressures capable of causing a pressure burst. However, the most common type of explosion is caused by the ignition of a flammable gas/air mixture which is confined within an item of a plant or indeed within any confining structure or enclosure. The prerequisite is the formation of a flammable mixture, an occurrence which should be avoided by good design and management. In the event of an accidental release, a flammable atmosphere will exist wherever the concentration of the gas (or vapour) lies between the lower and upper flammability limits (table 41.1). If an ignition source is introduced to one of these regions, a premixed flame will propagate rapidly from the source, converting the fuel/air mixture into combustion products at an elevated temperature. This can be as high as 2,100 K, indicating that in a completely closed system initially at 300 K, an overpressure as high as 7 bars is possible. Only specially designed pressure vessels are capable of containing such overpressures. Ordinary buildings will fall unless protected by pressure relief panels or bursting discs or by an explosion suppression system. Should a flammable mixture form within a building, the subsequent explosion can cause significant structural damage—perhaps total destruction—unless the explosion can vent to the outside through openings (e.g., the failure of windows) created during the early stages of the explosion.

Explosions of this type are also associated with the ignition of dust suspensions in air (Palmer 1973). These are encountered when there is a substantial accumulation of "explosible" dust which is dislodged from shelves, rafters and ledges within a building to form a cloud, which is then exposed to an ignition source (e.g., in flour mills, grain elevators, etc.). The dust must (obviously) be combustible, but not all combustible dusts are explosible at ambient temperatures. Standard tests have been designed to determine whether a dust is explosible. These can also be used to illustrate that explosible dusts exhibit "explosibility limits", similar in concept to the "flammability limits" of gases and vapours. In general, a dust explosion has the potential to do a great deal of damage because the initial event may cause more dust to be dislodged, forming an even greater dust cloud which will inevitably ignite, to produce an even greater explosion.

Explosion venting, or *explosion relief*, will only operate successfully if the rate of development of the explosion is relatively slow, such as associated with the propagation of a premixed flame through a stationary flammable mixture or an explosible dust cloud. Explosion venting is of no use if detonation is involved. The reason for this is that the pressure relief openings have to be created at an early stage of the event when the pressure is still relatively low. If a detonation occurs, the pressure rises too rapidly for relief to be effective, and the enclosing vessel or item of a plant experiences very high internal pressures which will lead to massive destruction. *Detonation of a flammable gas mixture* can occur if the mixture is contained within a long pipe or duct. Under certain conditions, propagation of the premixed flame will push the unburnt gas ahead of the flame front at a rate that will increase turbulence, which in turn will increase the rate of propagation. This provides a feedback loop which will cause the flame to accelerate until a shock wave is formed. This, combined with the combustion process, is a detonation wave which can propagate at velocities well in excess of 1,000 m/s. This may be compared with the *fundamental burning velocity* of a stoichiometric propane/air mixture of 0.45 m/s. (This is the rate at which a flame will propagate through a quiescent (i.e., non-turbulent) propane/air mixture.)

The importance of turbulence on the development of this type of explosion cannot be underestimated. The successful operation of an explosion protection system relies on early venting or early suppression. If the rate of development of the explosion is too fast, then the protection system will not be effective, and unacceptable overpressures can be produced.

An alternative to explosion relief is *explosion suppression*. This type of protection requires that the explosion is detected at a very early stage, as close to ignition as possible. The detector is used to initiate the rapid release of a suppressant into the path of the propagating flame, effectively arresting the explosion before the pressure has increased to an extent at which the integrity of the enclosing boundaries is threatened. The halons have been commonly used for this purpose, but as these are being phased out, attention is now being paid to the use of high-pressure water-spray systems. This type of protection is very expensive and has limited application as it can only be used in relatively small volumes within which the suppressant can be distributed quickly and uniformly (e.g., ducts carrying flammable vapour or explosible dusts).

Information Analysis for Fire Protection

In general terms, fire science has only recently been developed to a stage at which it is capable of providing the knowledge base on which rational decisions regarding engineering design, including safety issues, can be based. Traditionally, fire safety has developed on an *ad hoc* basis, effectively responding to incidents by imposing regulations or other restrictions to ensure that there will be no re-occurrence. Many examples could be quoted. For example, the Great Fire of London in 1666 led in due course to the establishment of the first building regulations (or codes) and the development of fire insurance. More recent incidents, such as the high-rise office block fires in São Paulo, Brazil, in 1972 and 1974,

initiated changes to the building codes, framed in such a way as to prevent similar multiple-fatality fires in the future. Other problems have been addressed in a similar fashion. In California in the United States, the hazard associated with certain types of modern upholstered furniture (particularly those containing standard polyurethane foam) was recognized, and eventually strict regulations were introduced to control its availability.

These are simple cases in which observations of the consequences of fire have led to the imposition of a set of rules intended to improve the safety of the individual and the community in the event of fire. The decision for action on any issue has to be justified on the basis of an analysis of our knowledge of fire incidents. It is necessary to show that the problem is real. In some cases—such as the São Paulo fires—this exercise is academic, but in others, such as "proving" that modern furnishings are a problem, it is necessary to ensure that the associated costs are wisely spent. This requires a reliable database on fire incidents which over a number of years is capable of showing trends in the number of fires, the number of fatalities, the incidence of a particular type of ignition, etc. Statistical techniques can then be used to examine whether a trend, or a change, is significant, and appropriate measures taken.

In a number of countries, the fire brigade is required to submit a report on each fire attended. In the United Kingdom and the United States, the officer in charge completes a report form which is then submitted to a central organization (the Home Office in the United Kingdom, the National Fire Protection Association, NFPA, in the United States) which then codes and processes the data in a prescribed fashion. The data are then available for inspection by government bodies and other interested parties. These databases are invaluable in highlighting (for example) the principal sources of ignition and the items first ignited. An examination of the incidence of fatalities and their relationship to sources of ignition, etc. has shown that the number of people who die in fires started by smokers' materials is significantly out of proportion with the number of fires which originate in this way.

The reliability of these databases depends on the skill with which the fire officers carry out the fire investigation. Fire investigation is not an easy task, and requires considerable ability and knowledge—in particular, a knowledge of fire science. The Fire Service in the United Kingdom has a statutory duty to submit a fire report form for every fire attended, which places a considerable responsibility on the officer in charge. The construction of the form is crucial, as it must elicit the required information in sufficient detail. The "Basic Incident Report Form" recommended by the NFPA is shown in the *Fire Protection Handbook* (Cote 1991).

The data can be used in two ways, either to identify a fire problem or to provide the rational argument necessary to justify a particular course of action that may require public or private expenditure. A long-established database can be used to show the effects of actions taken. The following ten points have been gleaned from NFPA statistics over the period 1980 to 1989 (Cote 1991):

1. Home smoke detectors are widely used and very effective (but significant gaps in the detector strategy remain).
2. Automatic sprinklers produce large reductions in loss of life and property. Increased use of portable and area heating equipment sharply increased home fires involving heating equipment.
3. Incendiary and suspicious fires continued to decline from the 1970's peak, but associated property damage stopped declining.
4. A large share of fire-fighter fatalities are attributed to heart attacks and activities away from the fireground.

5. Rural areas have the highest fire death rates.
6. Smoking materials igniting upholstered furniture, mattresses or bedding produce the most deadly residential fire scenarios.
7. US and Canadian fire death rates are amongst the highest of all the developed countries.
8. The states of the Old South in the United States have the highest fire death rates.
9. Older adults are at particularly high risk of death in fire.

Such conclusions are, of course, country-specific, although there are some common trends. Careful use of such data can provide the means of formulating sound policies regarding fire safety in the community. However, it must be remembered that these are inevitably "reactive", rather than "proactive". Proactive measures can only be introduced following a detailed fire hazard assessment. Such a course of action has been introduced progressively, starting in the nuclear industry and moving into the chemical, petrochemical and offshore industries where the risks are much more easily defined than in other industries. Their application to hotels and public buildings generally is much more difficult and requires the application of fire modelling techniques to predict the course of a fire and how the fire products will spread through the building to affect the occupants. Major advances have been made in this type of modelling, although it must be said that there is a long way to go before these techniques can be used with confidence. Fire safety engineering is still in need of much basic research in fire safety science before reliable fire hazard assessment tools can be made widely available.

SOURCES OF FIRE HAZARDS

Tamás Bánky

Fire and *combustion* have been defined in various ways. For our purposes, the most important statements in connection with combustion, as a phenomenon, are as follows:

- Combustion represents a self-sustaining run of reactions consisting of physical and chemical transformations.
- The materials involved enter into reaction with the oxidizing agent in their surroundings, which in most cases is with the oxygen in the air.
- Ignition requires favourable starting conditions, which are generally a sufficient heating up of the system that covers the initial energy demand of the chain reaction of burning.
- The resultant of the reactions are often exothermic, which means that during burning, heat is released and this phenomenon is often accompanied by visibly observable flaming.

Ignition may be considered the first step of the self-sustaining process of combustion. It may occur as *piloted ignition* (or *forced ignition*) if the phenomenon is caused by any outer ignition source, or it may occur as *auto ignition* (or *self ignition*) if the phenomenon is the result of reactions taking place in the combustible material itself and coupled with heat release.

The inclination to ignition is characterized by an empirical parameter, the *ignition temperature* (i.e., the lowest temperature, to be determined by test, to which the material has to be heated to for ignition). Depending upon whether or not this parameter is determined—with special test methods—by the use of any ignition source, we distinguish between the *piloted ignition temperature* and the *auto ignition temperature*.

In the case of piloted ignition, the energy required for the activation of the materials involved in the burning reaction is supplied by ignition sources. However, there is no direct relationship between the heat quantity needed for ignition and the igni-

tion temperature, because although the chemical composition of the components in the combustible system is an essential parameter of ignition temperature, it is considerably influenced by the sizes and shapes of materials, the pressure of the environment, conditions of air flow, parameters of ignition source, the geometrical features of the testing device, etc. This is the reason for which the data published in literature for autoignition temperature and piloted ignition temperature can be significantly different.

The ignition mechanism of materials in different states may be simply illustrated. This involves examining materials as either solids, liquids or gases.

Most *solid materials* take up energy from any outer ignition source either by conduction, convection or radiation (mostly by their combination), or are heated up as a result of the heat-producing processes taking place internally that start decomposition on their surfaces.

For ignition to occur with *liquids*, these must have the formation of a vapour space above their surface that is capable of burning. The vapours released and the gaseous decomposition products mix with the air above the surface of liquid or solid material.

The turbulent flows that arise in the mixture and/or the diffusion help the oxygen to reach the molecules, atoms and free radicals on and above the surface, which are already suitable for reaction. The particles induced enter into interaction, resulting in the release of heat. The process steadily accelerates, and as the chain reaction starts, the material comes to ignition and burns.

The combustion in the layer under the surface of solid combustible materials is called *smouldering*, and the burning reaction taking place on the interface of solid materials and gas is called *glowing*. Burning with flames (or *flaming*) is the process in the course of which the exothermic reaction of burning runs in the gas phase. This is typical for the combustion of both liquid and solid materials.

Combustible gases burn naturally in the gas phase. It is an important empirical statement that the mixtures of gases and air are capable of ignition in a certain range of concentration only. This is valid also for the vapours of liquids. The lower and upper flammable limits of gases and vapours depend on the temperature and pressure of the mixture, the ignition source and the concentration of the inert gases in the mixture.

Ignition Sources
The phenomena supplying heat energy may be grouped into four fundamental categories as to their origin (Sax 1979):

1. heat energy generated during chemical reactions (heat of oxidation, heat of combustion, heat of solution, spontaneous heating, heat of decomposition, etc.)
2. electrical heat energy (resistance heating, induction heating, heat from arcing, electric sparks, electrostatical discharges, heat generated by lightning stroke, etc.)
3. mechanical heat energy (frictional heat, friction sparks)
4. heat generated by nuclear decomposition.

The following discussion addresses the most frequently encountered sources of ignition.

Open flames
Open flames may be the simplest and most frequently used ignition source. A large number of tools in general use and various types of technological equipment operate with open flames, or enable the formation of open flames. Burners, matches, furnaces, heating equipment, flames of welding torches, broken gas and oil pipes, etc. may practically be considered potential ignition sources. Because with an open flame the primary ignition source itself represents an existing self-sustaining combustion, the igni-

tion mechanism means in essence the spreading of burning to another system. Provided that the ignition source with open flame possesses sufficient energy for initiating ignition, burning will start.

Spontaneous ignition

The chemical reactions generating heat spontaneously imply the risk of ignition and burning as "internal ignition sources". The materials inclined to spontaneous heating and spontaneous ignition may, however, become secondary ignition sources and give rise to ignition of the combustible materials in the surroundings.

Although some gases (e.g., hydrogen phosphide, boron hydride, silicon hydride) and liquids (e.g., metal carbonyls, organometallic compositions) are inclined to spontaneous ignition, most spontaneous ignitions occur as surface reactions of solid materials. Spontaneous ignition, like all ignitions, depends on the chemical structure of the material, but its occurrence is determined by the grade of dispersity. The large specific surface enables the local accumulation of reaction heat and contributes to the increase of temperature of material above spontaneous ignition temperature.

Spontaneous ignition of liquids is also promoted if they come into contact with air on solid materials of large specific surface area. Fats and especially unsaturated oils containing double bonds, when absorbed by fibrous materials and their products, and when impregnated into textiles of plant or animal origin, are inclined to spontaneous ignition under normal atmospheric conditions. Spontaneous ignition of glass-wool and mineral-wool products produced from non-combustible fibres or inorganic materials covering large specific surfaces and contaminated by oil have caused very severe fire accidents.

Spontaneous ignition has been observed mainly with dusts of solid materials. For metals with good heat conductivity, local heat accumulation needed for ignition necessitates very fine crushing of metal. As the particle size decreases, the likelihood of spontaneous ignition increases, and with some metal dusts (for example, iron) pyrophorosity ensues. When storing and handling coal dust, soot of fine distribution, dusts of lacquers and synthetic resins, as well as during the technological operations carried out with them, special attention should be given to the preventive measures against fire to reduce the hazard of spontaneous ignition.

Materials inclined to spontaneous decomposition show special ability to ignite spontaneously. Hydrazine, when set on any material with a large surface area, bursts into flames immediately. The peroxides, which are widely used by the plastics industry, easily decompose spontaneously, and as a consequence of decomposition, they become dangerous ignition sources, occasionally initiating explosive burning.

The violent exothermic reaction that occurs when certain chemicals come into contact with each other may be considered a special case of spontaneous ignition. Examples of such cases are contact of concentrated sulphuric acid with all the organic combustible materials, chlorates with sulphur or ammonium salts or acids, the organic halogen compounds with alkali metals, etc. The feature of these materials to be "unable to bear each other" (incompatible materials) requires special attention particularly when storing and co-storing them and elaborating the regulations of fire-fighting.

It is worth mentioning that such hazardously high spontaneous heating may, in some cases, be due to the wrong technological conditions (insufficient ventilation, low cooling capacity, discrepancies of maintenance and cleaning, overheating of reaction, etc.), or promoted by them.

Certain agricultural products, such as fibrous feedstuffs, oily seeds, germinating cereals, final products of the processing industry (dried beetroot slices, fertilizers, etc.), show an inclination for spontaneous ignition. The spontaneous heating of these materials has a special feature: the dangerous temperature conditions of the systems are exacerbated by some exothermic biological processes that cannot be controlled easily.

Electric ignition sources

Power machines, instruments and heating devices operated by electric energy, as well as the equipment for power transformation and lighting, typically do not present any fire hazard to their surroundings, provided that they have been installed in compliance with the relevant regulations of safety and requirements of standards and that the associated technological instructions have been observed during their operation. Regular maintenance and periodic supervision considerably diminish the probability of fires and explosions. The most frequent causes of fires in electric devices and wiring are *overloading*, *short circuits*, *electric sparks* and *high contact resistances*.

Overloading exists when the wiring and electrical appliances are exposed to higher current than that for which they are designed. The overcurrent passing through the wiring, devices and equipment might lead to such an overheating that the overheated components of the electrical system become damaged or broken, grow old or carbonize, resulting in cord and cable coatings melting down, metal parts glowing and the combustible structural units coming to ignition and, depending on the conditions, also spreading fire to the environment. The most frequent cause of overloading is that the number of consumers connected is higher than permitted or their capacity exceeds the value stipulated.

The working safety of electrical systems is most frequently endangered by short circuits. They are always the consequences of any damage and occur when the parts of the electrical wiring or the equipment at the same potential level or various potential levels, insulated from each other and the earth, come into contact with each other or with the earth. This contact may arise directly as metal-metal contact or indirectly, through electric arc. In cases of short circuits, when some units of the electric system come in contact with each other, the resistance will be considerably lower, and as a consequence, the intensity of current will be extremely high, perhaps several orders of magnitude lower. The heat energy released during overcurrents with large short circuits might result in a fire in the device affected by the short circuit, with the materials and equipment in the surrounding area coming to ignition and with the fire spreading to the building.

Electric sparks are heat energy sources of a small nature, but as shown by experience, act frequently as ignition sources. Under normal working conditions, most electrical appliances do not release sparks, but the operation of certain devices is normally accompanied by sparks.

Sparking introduces a hazard foremost at places where, in the zone of their generation, explosive concentrations of gas, vapour or dust might arise. Consequently, equipment normally releasing sparks during operation is permitted to be set up only at places where the sparks cannot give rise to fire. On its own, the energy content of sparks is insufficient for the ignition of the materials in the environment or to initiate an explosion.

If an electrical system has no perfect metallic contact between the structural units through which the current flows, high contact resistance will occur at this spot. This phenomenon is in most cases due to the faulty construction of joints or to unworkmanlike installations. The disengagement of joints during operation and natural wear may also be cause for high contact resistance. A large portion of the current flowing through places with increased resistance will transform to heat energy. If this energy cannot be dissipated sufficiently (and the reason cannot be eliminated), the extremely large increase of temperature might lead to a fire condition that endangers the surrounding.

If the devices work on the basis of the induction concept (engines, dynamos, transformers, relays, etc.) and are not properly calculated, eddy currents may arise during operation. Due to the eddy currents, the structural units (coils and their iron cores) might warm up, which might lead to the ignition of insulating materials and the burning of the equipment. Eddy currents might arise—with these harmful consequences—also in the metal structural units around high-voltage equipment.

Electrostatic sparks

Electrostatic charging is a process in the course of which any material, originally with electric neutrality (and independent of any electric circuit) becomes charged positively or negatively. This may occur in one of three ways:

1. *charging with separation*, such that charges of subtractive polarity accumulate on two bodies simultaneously
2. *charging with passing*, such that the charges passing away leave charges of opposed polarity signs behind
3. *charging by taking up*, such that the body receives charges from outside.

These three ways of charging may arise from various physical processes, including separation after contact, splitting, cutting, pulverizing, moving, rubbing, flowing of powders and fluids in pipe, hitting, change of pressure, change of state, photoionization, heat ionization, electrostatical distribution or high-voltage discharge.

Electrostatic charging may occur both on conducting bodies and insulating bodies as a result of any of the processes mentioned above, but in most cases the mechanical processes are responsible for the accumulation of the unwanted charges.

From the large number of the harmful effects and risks due to electrostatic charging and the spark discharge resulting from it, two risks can be mentioned in particular: endangering of electronic equipment (for example, computer for process control) and the hazard of fire and explosion.

Electronic equipment is endangered first of all if the discharge energy from the charging is sufficiently high to cause destruction of the input of any semi-conductive part. The development of electronic units in the last decade has been followed by the rapid increase of this risk.

The development of fire or explosion risk necessitates the coincidence in space and time of two conditions: the presence of any combustible medium and the discharge with ability for ignition. This hazard occurs mainly in the chemical industry. It may be estimated on the basis of the so-called *spark sensitivity of hazardous materials* (*minimum ignition energy*) and depends on the extent of charging.

It is an essential task to reduce these risks, namely, the large variety of consequences that extend from technological troubles to catastrophes with fatal accidents. There are two means of protecting against the consequences of electrostatic charging:

1. preventing the initiation of the charging process (it is evident, but usually very difficult to realize)
2. restricting the accumulation of charges to prevent the occurrence of dangerous discharges (or any other risk).

Lightning is an atmospherical electric phenomenon in nature and may be considered an ignition source. The static charging produced in the clouds is equalized towards the earth (*lightning stroke*) and is accompanied by a high-energy discharge. The combustible materials at the place of lightning stroke and its surroundings might ignite and burn off. At some strokes of lightning, very strong impulses are generated, and the energy is equalized in several steps. In other cases, long-lasting currents start to flow, sometimes reaching the order of magnitude of 10 A.

Mechanical heat energy

Technical practice is steadily coupled with friction. During mechanical operation, frictional heat is developed, and if heat loss is restricted to such an extent that heat accumulates in the system, its temperature may increase to a value that is dangerous for the environment, and fire may occur.

Friction sparks normally occur at metal technological operations because of heavy friction (grinding, chipping, cutting, hitting) or because of metal objects or tools dropping or falling on to a hard floor or during grinding operations because of metal contaminations within the material under grinding impact. The temperature of the spark generated is normally higher than the ignition temperature of the conventional combustible materials (such as for sparks from steel, 1,400-1,500 °C; sparks from copper-nickel alloys, 300-400 °C); however, the ignition ability depends on the whole heat content and the lowest ignition energy of the material and substance to be ignited, respectively. It has been proven in practice that friction sparks mean real fire risk in air spaces where combustible gases, vapours and dusts are present in dangerous concentrations. Thus, under these circumstances the use of materials that easily produce sparks, as well as processes with mechanical sparking, should be avoided. In these cases, safety is provided by tools that do not spark, i.e., made from wood, leather or plastic materials, or by using tools of copper and bronze alloys that produce sparks of low energy.

Hot surfaces

In practice, the surfaces of equipment and devices may warm up to a dangerous extent either normally or due to malfunction. Ovens, furnaces, drying devices, waste-gas outlets, vapour pipes, etc. often cause fires in explosive air spaces. Furthermore, their hot surfaces may ignite combustible materials coming close to them or by coming in contact. For prevention, safe distances should be observed, and regular supervision and maintenance will reduce the probability of the occurrence of dangerous overheating.

Fire Hazards of Materials and Products

The presence of combustible material in combustible systems represents an obvious condition of burning. Burning phenomena and the phases of the burning process fundamentally depend on the physical and chemical properties of the material involved. Therefore, it seems reasonable to make a survey of the flammability of the various materials and products with respect to their character and properties. For this section, the ordering principle for the grouping of materials is governed by technical aspects rather than by theoretical conceptions (NFPA 1991).

Wood and wood-based products

Wood is one of the most common materials in the human milieu. Houses, building structures, furniture and consumer goods are made of wood, and it is also widely used for products such as paper as well as in the chemical industry.

Wood and wood products are combustible, and when in contact with high-temperature surfaces and exposed to heat radiation, open flames or any other ignition source, will carbonize, glow, ignite or burn, depending upon the condition of combustion. To widen the field of their application, the improvement of their combustion properties is required. In order to make structural units produced from wood less combustible, they are typically treated with fire-retardant agents (e.g., saturated, impregnated, provided with surface coating).

The most essential characteristic of combustibility of the various kinds of wood is the ignition temperature. Its value strongly depends on some of the properties of wood and the test conditions of determination, namely, the wood sample's density, humidity, size and shape, as well as the ignition source, time of exposure, intensity of exposure and the atmosphere during testing. It is interesting to note that the ignition temperature as determined by various test methods differs. Experience has shown that the inclination of clean and dry wood products to ignition is extremely low, but several fire cases caused by spontaneous ignition have been known to occur from storing dusty and oily waste wood in rooms with imperfect ventilation. It has been proven empirically that higher moisture content increases the ignition temperature and reduces the burning speed of wood. The thermal decomposition of wood is a complicated process, but its phases may clearly be observed as follows:

- The thermal decomposition with mass loss starts already in the range 120-200 °C; moisture content releases and the non-combustible degrades occur in the combustion space.
- At 200-280 °C, mainly endothermic reactions occur while the heat energy of ignition source is taken up.
- At 280-500 °C, the exothermic reactions of decomposition products are steadily accelerating as the primary process, while carbonization phenomena may be observed. In this temperature range, sustaining combustion has already developed. After ignition, burning is not steady in time because of the good heat-insulating ability of its carbonized layers. Consequently, the warming up of the deeper layers is limited and time consuming. When the surfacing of the combustible decomposition products is accelerated, burning will be complete.
- At temperatures exceeding 500 °C, the wood char forms residues. During its additional glowing, ash containing solid, inorganic materials is produced, and the process has come to an end.

Fibres and textiles

The majority of the textiles produced from fibrous materials that are found in the close surrounding of people is combustible. Clothing, furniture and the built environment partly or totally consists of textiles. The hazard which they present exists during their production, processing and storing as well as during their wearing.

The basic materials of textiles are both natural and artificial; synthetic fibres are used either alone or mixed with natural fibres. The chemical composition of the natural fibres of plant origin (cotton, hemp, jute, flax) is cellulose, which is combustible, and these fibres have a relatively high ignition temperature (≈400 °C). It is an advantageous feature of their burning that when brought to high temperature they carbonize but do not melt. This is especially advantageous for the medical treatments of burn casualties.

The fire hazardous properties of fibres of protein base of animal origin (wool, silk, hair) are even more favourable than those of fibres of plant origin, because a higher temperature is required for their ignition (500-600 °C), and under the same conditions, their burning is less intensive.

The plastics industry, utilizing several extremely good mechanical properties of polymer products, has also gained prominence in the textile industry. Among the properties of acrylic, polyester and the thermoplastic synthetic fibres (nylon, polypropylene, polyethylene), those associated with burning are the least advantageous. Most of them, in spite of their high ignition temperature (≈400-600 °C), melt when exposed to heat, easily ignite, burn intensively, drop or melt when burning and release considerably high quantities of smoke and toxic gases. These burning properties may be improved by addition of natural fibres, producing so-called *textiles with mixed fibres*. Further treatment is accomplished with flame-retardant agents. For the manufacture of textiles for industrial purposes and heat-protective clothing, inorganic, non-combustible fibre products (including glass and metal fibres) are already used in large quantities.

The most important fire hazard characteristics of textiles are the properties connected with ignitability, flame spread, heat generation and the toxic combustion products. Special testing methods have been developed for their determination. The test results obtained influence the fields of application for these products (tents and flats, furniture, vehicle upholstery, clothes, carpets, curtains, special protective clothing against heat and weather), as well as the stipulations to restrict the risks in their use. An essential task of industrial researchers is to develop textiles that sustain high temperature, treated with fire-retardant agents, (heavily combustible, with long ignition time, low flame spread rate, low speed of heat release) and produce small amounts of toxic combustion products, as well as to improve the unfavourable effect of fire accidents due to the burning of such materials.

Combustible and flammable liquids

In the presence of ignition sources, combustible and flammable liquids are potential sources of risk. First, the closed or open vapour space above such liquids provides a fire and explosion hazard. Combustion, and more frequently explosion, might occur if the material is present in the vapour-air mixture in suitable concentration. From this it follows that burning and explosion in the zone of combustible and flammable liquids may be prevented if:

- the ignition sources, air, and oxygen are excluded; or
- instead of oxygen, inert gas is present in the surrounding; or
- the liquid is stored in a closed vessel or system (see figure 41.3); or
- by proper ventilation, the development of the dangerous vapour concentration is prevented.

Figure 41.3 • Common types of tanks for storage of flammable and combustible liquids.

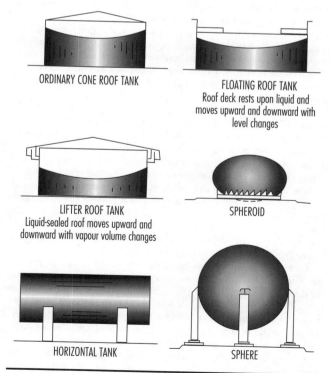

ORDINARY CONE ROOF TANK

FLOATING ROOF TANK
Roof deck rests upon liquid and moves upward and downward with level changes

LIFTER ROOF TANK
Liquid-sealed roof moves upward and downward with vapour volume changes

SPHEROID

HORIZONTAL TANK

SPHERE

In practice, a large number of material characteristics are known in connection with the dangerous nature of combustible and flammable liquids. These are closed-cup and open-cup flash points, boiling point, ignition temperature, rate of evaporation, upper and lower limits of the concentration for combustibility (flammable or explosive limits), the relative density of vapours compared to air and energy required for the ignition of vapours. These factors provide full information about the sensitivity for ignition of various liquids.

Nearly all over the world the flash point, a parameter determined by standard test under atmospherical conditions, is used as the basis to group the liquids (and materials behaving as liquids at relatively low temperatures) into categories of risk. The safety requirements for storage of liquids, their handling, the technological processes, and the electrical equipment to be set up in their zone should be elaborated for each category of flammability and combustibility. The zones of risk around the technological equipment should also to be identified for each category. Experience has shown that fire and explosion might occur—depending on the temperature and pressure of the system—within the range of concentration between the two flammable limits.

Gases

Although all materials—under a specific temperature and pressure—may become gases, the materials considered gaseous in practice are those that are in a gas state at normal temperature (≈ 20 °C) and normal atmospheric pressure (≈ 100 kPa).

In respect to fire and explosion hazards, gases may be ranked in two main groups: *combustible* and *non-combustible gases*. According to the definition accepted in practice, combustible gases are those that burn in air with normal oxygen concentration, provided that the conditions required for burning exist. Ignition only occurs above a certain temperature, with the necessary ignition temperature, and within a given range of concentration.

Non-combustible gases are those that do not burn either in oxygen or in air with any concentration of air. A portion of these gases support combustion (e.g., oxygen), while the other portion inhibit burning. The non-combustible gases not supporting burning are called *inert gases* (nitrogen, noble gases, carbon dioxide, etc.).

In order to achieve economic efficiency, the gases stored and transported in containers or transporting vessels are typically in compressed, liquefied, or cooled-condensated (cryogenic) state. Basically, there are two hazardous situations in connection with gases: when they are in containers and when they are released from their containers.

For compressed gases in storage containers, external heat might considerably increase the pressure within the container, and the extreme overpressure might lead to explosion. Gaseous storage containers will typically include a vapour phase and a liquid phase. Because of changes in pressure and temperature, the extension of the liquid phase gives rise to the further compression of vapour space, while the vapour pressure of the liquid increases in proportion with the increase of temperature. As a result of these processes, critically dangerous pressure may be produced. Storage containers are generally required to contain the application of overpressure relief devices. These are capable of mitigating a hazardous situation due to higher temperatures.

If the storage vessels are insufficiently sealed or damaged, the gas will flow out to the free air space, mix with air and depending on its quantity and the way of its flowing, may cause the formation of a large, explosive air space. The air around a leaking storage vessel can be unsuitable for breathing and may be dangerous for people nearby, partly due to the toxic effect of some gases and partly due to the diluted concentration of oxygen.

Bearing in mind the potential fire hazard due to gases and the need for safe operation, one must get detailed knowledge of the following features of gases either stored or used, especially for industrial consumers: the chemical and physical properties of gases, ignition temperature, the lower and upper limits of concentration for flammability, the hazardous parameters of the gas in the container, the risk factors of the hazardous situation caused by the gases released into the open air, the extent of the necessary safety zones and the special measures to be taken in case of a possible emergency situation connected with fire-fighting.

Chemicals

Knowledge of the hazardous parameters of chemicals is one of the basic conditions of safe working. The preventive measures and requirements for protection against fire may be elaborated only if the physical and chemical properties connected with fire hazard are taken into consideration. Of these properties, the most important ones are the following: combustibility; ignitability; ability to react with other materials, water or air; inclination to corrosion; toxicity; and radioactivity.

Information on the properties of chemicals can be obtained from the technical data sheets issued by manufacturers and from the manuals and handbooks containing the data of hazardous chemicals. These provide users with information not only about the general technical features of materials, but also about the actual values of hazard parameters (decomposition temperature, ignition temperature, limit concentrations of combustion, etc.), their special behaviour, requirements for storage and fire-fighting, as well as recommendations for first aid and medical therapy.

The toxicity of chemicals, as potential fire hazard, may act in two ways. First, the high toxicity of certain chemicals themselves, may be hazardous in a fire. Second, their presence within the fire zone may effectively restrict fire-fighting operations.

The oxidizing agents (nitrates, chlorates, inorganic peroxides, permanganates, etc.), even if they themselves are non-combustible, largely contribute to the ignition of combustible materials and to their intensive, occasionally explosive burning.

The group of unstable materials includes the chemicals (acetaldehyde, ethylene oxide, organic peroxides, hydrogen cyanide, vinyl chloride) which polymerize or decompose in violent exothermic reactions spontaneously or very easily.

The materials sensitive to water and air are extremely dangerous. These materials (oxides, hydroxides, hydrides, anhydrides, alkali metals, phosphorus, etc.) interact with the water and air that are always present in the normal atmosphere, and start reactions accompanied by very high heat generation. If they are combustible materials, they will come to spontaneous ignition. However, the combustible components that initiate the burning may possibly explode and spread to the combustible materials in the surrounding area.

The majority of corrosive materials (inorganic acids—sulphuric acid, nitric acid, perchloric acid, etc.—and halogens—fluorine, chlorine, bromine, iodine) are strong oxidizing agents, but at the same time they have very strong destructive effects on living tissues, and therefore special measures have to be taken for fire-fighting.

The dangerous characteristic of radioactive elements and compounds is increased by the fact that the radiation emitted by them may be harmful in several ways, besides that such materials may be fire hazards themselves. If in a fire the structural containment of the radioactive objects involved becomes damaged, γ-radiating materials might be released. They can have a very strong ionizing effect, and are capable of the fatal destruction of living organisms. Nuclear accidents can be accompanied by fires, the decomposition products of which bind radioactive (α-and β-radiating) contaminants by adsorption. These may cause permanent injuries to the persons taking part in rescue operations if they penetrate into their bodies. Such materials are extremely dangerous, because the persons affected do not perceive any radiation by their sensing organs, and their general state of health does not seem to be any worse. It is obvious that if radioactive materials burn, the radioactivity of the site, the decomposition products and the water used for fire-fighting should be kept under constant observation by means of radioactive signalling devices. The knowledge of these factors has to be taken into account for the strategy of intervention and all additional operations. The buildings for handling and storing radioactive materials as well as for their technological use need to be built of non-combustible materials of high fire resistance. At the same time, high-quality, automatic equipment for detecting, signalling and extinguishing a fire should be provided.

Explosives and blasting agents

Explosive materials are used for many military and industrial purposes. These are chemicals and mixtures which, when affected by strong mechanical force (hitting, shock, friction) or starting ignition, suddenly transform to gases of large volume through an extremely rapid oxidizing reaction (e.g., 1,000-10,000 m/s). The volume of these gases is the multiple of the volume of the explosive material already exploded, and they will exert very high pressure on the surroundings. During an explosion, high temperatures can arise (2,500-4,000 °C) that promote the ignition of the combustible materials in the zone of explosion.

Manufacture, transport and storage of the various explosive materials are governed by rigorous requirements. An example is NFPA 495, Explosive Materials Code.

Besides the explosive materials used for military and industrial purposes, the inductive blasting materials and pyrotechnical products are also treated as hazards. In general, mixtures of explosive materials are often used (picric acid, nitroglycerin, hexogene, etc.), but mixtures of materials capable of explosion are also in use (black powder, dynamite, ammonium nitrate, etc.). In the course of acts of terrorism, plastic materials have become well-known, and are, in essence, mixtures of brisant and plasticizing materials (various waxes, Vaseline, etc.).

For explosive materials, the most effective method of protection against fire is the exclusion of ignition sources from the surroundings. Several explosive materials are sensitive to water or various organic materials with an ability to oxidate. For these materials, the requirements for the conditions of storage and the rules for storing in the same place together with other materials should be carefully considered.

Metals

It is known from practice that nearly all the metals, under certain conditions, are capable of burning in atmospheric air. Steel and aluminium in large structural thickness, on the basis of their behaviour in fire, are clearly evaluated as non-combustible. However, the dusts of aluminium, iron in fine distribution and metal cottons from thin metal fibres can easily be ignited and thus burn intensively. The alkali metals (lithium, sodium, potassium), the alkaline-earth metals (calcium, magnesium, zinc), zirconium, hafnium, titanium, etc. ignite extremely easily in the form of a powder, filings or thin bands. Some metals have such a high sensitivity that they are stored separately from air, in inert gas atmospheres or under a liquid that is neutral for the metals.

The combustible metals and those that are conditioned to burn produce extremely violent burning reactions that are high-speed oxidation processes releasing considerably higher quantities of heat than observed from the burning of combustible and flammable liquids. The burning of metal dust in the case of settled powder, following the preliminary phase of glowing-ignition, might grow to rapid burning. With stirred-up dusts and clouds of dusts that might result, severe explosions can occur. The burning

activity and affinity for oxygen of some metals (such as magnesium) are so high that after being ignited they will continue to burn in certain media (e.g., nitrogen, carbon dioxide, steam atmosphere) that are used for extinguishing fires derived from combustible solid materials and liquids.

Extinguishing metal fires presents a special task for fire-fighters. The choice of the proper extinguishing agent and the process in which it is applied are of great importance.

Fires of metals may be controlled with very early detection, the rapid and appropriate action of fire-fighters using the most effective method and, if possible, removal of metals and any other combustible materials from the zone of burning or at least a reduction of their quantities.

Special attention should be given to the protection against radiation when radioactive metals (plutonium, uranium) burn. Preventive measures have to be taken to avoid the penetration of toxic decomposition products into living organisms. For example, alkali metals, because of their ability to react violently with water may be extinguished with dry fire-extinguishing powders only. Burning of magnesium cannot be extinguished with water, carbon dioxide, halons or nitrogen with good success, and more important, if these agents are used in fire-fighting, the hazardous situation will become even more severe. The only agents that can be applied successfully are the noble gases or in some cases boron trifluoride.

Plastics and rubber

Plastics are macromolecular organic compounds produced synthetically or by modification of natural materials. The structure and shape of these macromolecular materials, produced by polymerizational, polyadditional or polycondensational reactions, will strongly influence their properties. The chain molecules of thermoplastics (polyamides, polycarbonates, polyesters, polystyrene, polyvinyl chloride, polymethyl-metacrylate, etc.) are linear or branched, the elastomers (neoprene, polysulphides, isoprene, etc.) are lightly cross-linked, while thermosetting plastics (duroplastics: polyalkydes, epoxy resins, polyurethanes, etc.) are densely cross-linked.

Natural caoutchouc is used as raw material by the rubber industry, and after being vulcanized, rubber is produced. The artificial caoutchoucs, the structure of which is similar to that of natural chaoutchouc, are polymers and co-polymers of butadiene.

The range of products from plastics and rubber used in nearly all fields of everyday life is steadily widening. Use of the large variety and excellent technical properties of this group of materials results in items such as various building structures, furniture, clothes, commodities, parts for vehicles and machines.

Typically, as organic materials, plastics and rubber also are considered to be combustible materials. For the description of their fire behaviour, a number of parameters are used that can be tested by special methods. With the knowledge of these parameters, one can allocate the fields of their application (determined, pointed out, set), and the fire safety provisions can be elaborated. These parameters are combustibility, ignitability, ability to develop smoke, inclination to produce toxic gases and burning dripping.

In many cases the ignition temperature of plastics is higher than that of wood or any other materials, but in most cases they ignite more easily, and their burning takes place more rapidly and with higher intensity. Fires of plastics are often accompanied by the unpleasant phenomena of large quantities of dense smoke being released that can strongly restrict visibility and develop various toxic gases (hydrochloric acid, phosgene, carbon monoxide, hydrogen cyanide, nitrous gases, etc.). Thermoplastic materials melt during burning, then flow and depending on their location (if mounted in or on a ceiling) produce drops which remain in the burning area and might ignite the combustible materials underneath.

The improvement of burning properties represents a complex problem and a "key issue" of plastics chemistry. Fire-retardant agents inhibit combustibility, ignition will be slower, the rate of combustion will fall, and flame propagation will slow down. At the same time, the quantity and optical density of smoke will be higher and the gas mixture produced will be more toxic.

Dusts

With regard to physical state, dusts belong to the solid materials, but their physical and chemical properties differ from those of those same materials in compact form. It is known that industrial accidents and catastrophes are caused by dust explosions. Materials that are non-combustible in their usual form, such as metals, may initiate an explosion in the form of dust mixed with air when affected by any ignition source, even of low energy. The hazard of an explosion also exists with dusts of combustible materials.

Dust can be an explosion hazard not only when floating in the air, but also when settled. In layers of dust, heat may accumulate, and slow burning may develop in the inside as a result of the increased ability of particles to react and their lower thermal conductivity. Then the dust may be stirred up by flashes, and the possibility of dust explosion will grow.

Floating particles in fine distribution present a more severe hazard. Similar to the explosion properties of combustible gases and vapours, dusts also have a special range of air-dust concentration in which an explosion may occur. The lower and upper limit values of explosion concentration and the width of concentration range depend on the size and distribution of particles. If the dust concentration exceeds the highest concentration leading to an explosion, a portion of the dust is not destroyed by fire and absorbs heat, and as a consequence the explosion pressure developed remains below the maximum. The moisture content of air also influences the occurrence of an explosion. At higher humidity, the ignition temperature of the cloud of dust will increase in proportion with the heat quantity necessary for the evaporation of humidity. If an inert foreign dust is mixed in a cloud of dust, the explosivity of the dust-air mixture will be reduced. The effect will be the same if inert gases are mixed in the mixture of air and dust, because the oxygen concentration necessary for burning will be lower.

Experience has shown that all the ignition sources, even of minimum ignition energy, are capable of igniting dust clouds (open flames, electric arc, mechanical or electrostatic spark, hot surfaces, etc.). According to test results obtained in laboratory, the energy demand for ignition of dust clouds is 20 to 40 times higher than in the case of mixtures of combustible vapour and air.

The factors that influence the explosion hazard for settled dusts are the physical and thermal engineering properties of the dust layer, the glowing temperature of the dust and the ignition properties of the decomposition products released by the dust layer.

● FIRE PREVENTION MEASURES

Peter F. Johnson

History tells us that fires were useful for heating and cooking but caused major damage in many cities. Many houses, major buildings and sometimes whole cities were destroyed by fire.

One of the first fire prevention measures was a requirement to extinguish all fires before nightfall. For example, in 872 in Oxford,

England, authorities ordered a curfew bell to be rung at sunset to remind citizens to extinguish all indoor fires for the night (Bugbee 1978). Indeed, the word curfew is derived from the French *couvre feu* which literally means "cover fire".

The cause of fires is often a result of human action bringing fuel and an ignition source together (e.g., waste paper stored next to heating equipment or volatile flammable liquids being used near open flames).

Fires require fuel, an ignition source and some mechanism to bring the fuel and ignition source together in the presence of air or some other oxidizer. If strategies can be developed to reduce fuel loads, eliminate ignition sources or prevent the fuel/ignition interaction, then fire loss and human death and injury can be reduced.

In recent years, there has been increasing emphasis on fire prevention as one of the most cost-effective measures in dealing with the fire problem. It is often easier (and cheaper) to prevent fires starting than to control or extinguish them once they have started.

This is illustrated in the *Fire Safety Concepts Tree* (NFPA 1991; 1995a) developed by the NFPA in the United States. This systematic approach to fire safety problems shows that objectives, such as reducing fire deaths in the workplace, can be achieved by preventing fire ignition or managing the impact of fire.

Fire prevention inevitably means changing human behaviour. This requires fire safety education, supported by management, using the latest training manuals, standards and other educational materials. In many countries such strategies are reinforced by law, requiring companies to meet legislated fire prevention objectives as part of their occupational health and safety commitment to their workers.

Fire safety education will be discussed in the next section. However, there is now clear evidence in commerce and industry of the important role of fire prevention. Great use is being made internationally of the following sources: Lees, *Loss Prevention in the Process Industries*, Volumes 1 and 2 (1980); *NFPA 1—Fire Prevention Code* (1992); *The Management of Health and Safety at Work Regulations* (ECD 1992); and *Fire Protection Handbook* of the NFPA (Cote 1991). These are supplemented by many regulations, standards and training materials developed by national governments, businesses and insurance companies to minimize losses of life and property.

Fire Safety Education and Practices

For a fire safety education programme to be effective, there must be a major corporate policy commitment to safety and the development of an effective plan that has the following steps: (a) Planning phase—establishment of goals and objectives; (b) Design and implementation phase; and (c) Program evaluation phase—monitoring effectiveness.

Goals and objectives

Gratton (1991), in an important article on fire safety education, defined the differences between goals, objectives and implementation practices or strategies. Goals are general statements of intent that in the workplace may be said "to reduce the number of fires and thus reduce death and injury among workers, and the financial impact on companies".

The people and financial parts of the overall goal are not incompatible. Modern risk management practice has demonstrated that improvements in safety for workers through effective loss control practices can be financially rewarding to the company and have a community benefit.

These goals need to be translated into specific fire safety objectives for particular companies and their workforce. These objectives, which must be measurable, usually include statements such as:

- reduce industrial accidents and resulting fires
- reduce fire deaths and injuries
- reduce company property damage.

For many companies, there may be additional objectives such as reduction in business interruption costs or minimization of legal liability exposure.

The tendency among some companies is to assume that compliance with local building codes and standards is sufficient to ensure that their fire safety objectives are met. However, such codes tend to concentrate on life safety, assuming fires will occur.

Modern fire safety management understands that absolute safety is not a realistic goal but sets measurable performance objectives to:

- minimize fire incidents through effective fire prevention
- provide effective means of limiting the size and consequence of fire incidents through effective emergency equipment and procedures
- use insurance to safeguard against large, unforeseen fires, particularly those arising from natural hazards such as earthquakes and bushfires.

Design and implementation

The design and implementation of fire safety education programmes for fire prevention are critically dependent upon development of well-planned strategies and effective management and motivation of people. There must be strong and absolute corporate support for full implementation of a fire safety programme for it to be successful.

The range of strategies have been identified by Koffel (1993) and in NFPA's *Industrial Fire Hazards Handbook* (Linville 1990). They include:

- promoting the company policy and strategies on fire safety to all company employees
- identifying all potential fire scenarios and implementing appropriate risk reduction actions
- monitoring all local codes and standards that define the standard of care in a particular industry
- operating a loss administration programme to measure all losses for comparison with performance objectives
- training of all employees in proper fire prevention and emergency response techniques.

Some international examples of implementation strategies include:

- courses operated by the Fire Protection Association (FPA) in the United Kingdom that lead to the European Diploma in Fire Prevention (Welch 1993)
- the creation of SweRisk, a subsidiary company of the Swedish Fire Protection Association, to assist companies in undertaking risk assessments and in developing fire prevention programmes (Jernberg 1993)
- massive citizen and worker involvement in fire prevention in Japan to standards developed by the Japan Fire Defence Agency (Hunter 1991)
- fire safety training in the United States through the use of the *Firesafety Educator's Handbook* (NFPA 1983) and the *Public Fire Education Manual* (Osterhoust 1990).

It is critically important to measure the effectiveness of fire safety education programmes. This measurement provides the motivation for further programme financing, development and adjustment where necessary.

The best example of monitoring and success of fire safety education is probably in the United States. The *Learn Not to Burn*® programme, aimed at educating the young people in America on the dangers of fire, has been coordinated by the Public Education Division of the NFPA. Monitoring and analysis in 1990 identified a total of 194 lives saved as a result of proper life safety actions learned in fire safety education programmes. Some 30% of these lives saved can be directly attributed to the *Learn Not to Burn*® programme.

The introduction of residential smoke detectors and fire safety education programmes in the United States have also been suggested as the primary reasons for the reduction in home fire deaths in that country, from 6,015 in 1978 to 4,050 in 1990 (NFPA 1991).

Industrial housekeeping practices

In the industrial field, Lees (1980) is an international authority. He indicated that in many industries today, the potential for very large loss of life, serious injuries or property damage is far greater than in the past. Large fires, explosions and toxic releases can result, particularly in the petrochemical and nuclear industries.

Fire prevention is therefore the key to minimizing fire ignition. Modern industrial plants can achieve good fire safety records through well-managed programmes of:

- housekeeping and safety inspections
- employee fire prevention training
- equipment maintenance and repair
- security and arson prevention (Blye and Bacon 1991).

A useful guide, on the importance of housekeeping for fire prevention in commercial and industrial premises is given by Higgins (1991) in the NFPA's *Fire Protection Handbook*.

The value of good housekeeping in minimizing combustible loads and in preventing exposure of ignition sources is recognized in modern computer tools used for assessing fire risks in industrial premises. The FREM (Fire Risk Evaluation Method) software in Australia identifies housekeeping as a key fire safety factor (Keith 1994).

Heat Utilization Equipment

Heat utilization equipment in commerce and industry includes ovens, furnaces, kilns, dehydrators, dryers and quench tanks.

In the NFPA's *Industrial Fire Hazards Handbook*, Simmons (1990) identified the fire problems with heating equipment to be:

1. the possibility of igniting combustible materials stored nearby
2. fuel hazards resulting from unburned fuel or incomplete combustion
3. overheating leading to equipment failure
4. ignition of combustible solvents, solid materials or other products being processed.

These fire problems can be overcome through a combination of good housekeeping, proper controls and interlocks, operator training and testing, and cleaning and maintenance in an effective fire prevention programme.

Detailed recommendations for the various categories of heat utilization equipment are set out in the NFPA's *Fire Protection Handbook* (Cote 1991). These are summarized below.

Ovens and furnaces

Fires and explosions in ovens and furnaces typically result from the fuel used, from volatile substances provided by the material in the oven or by a combination of both. Many of these ovens or furnaces operate at 500 to 1,000 °C, which is well above the ignition temperature of most materials.

Ovens and furnaces require a range of controls and interlocks to ensure that unburned fuel gases or products of incomplete combustion cannot accumulate and be ignited. Typically, these hazards develop while firing up or during shut-down operations.

41. FIRE

Therefore, special training is required to ensure that operators always follow safety procedures.

Non-combustible building construction, separation of other equipment and combustible materials and some form of automatic fire suppression are usually essential elements of a fire safety system to prevent spread should a fire start.

Kilns

Kilns are used to dry timber (Lataille 1990) and to process or "fire" clay products (Hrbacek 1984).

Again, this high-temperature equipment represents a hazard to its surroundings. Proper separation design and good housekeeping are essential to prevent fire.

Lumber kilns used for drying timber are additionally hazardous because the timber itself is a high fire load and is often heated close to its ignition temperature. It is essential that kilns be cleaned regularly to prevent a build-up of small pieces of wood and sawdust so that this does not come in contact with the heating equipment. Kilns made of fire-resistive construction material, fitted with automatic sprinklers and provided with high-quality ventilation/air circulation systems are preferred.

Dehydrators and dryers

This equipment is used to reduce the moisture content of agricultural products such as milk, eggs, grains, seeds and hay. The dryers may be direct-fired, in which case the productions of combustion contact the material being dried, or they may be indirect-fired. In each case, controls are required to shut off the heat supply in the event of excessive temperature or fire in the dryer, exhaust system or conveyor system or failure of air circulation fans. Again, adequate cleaning to prevent build-up of products that could ignite is required.

Quench tanks

The general principles of fire safety of quench tanks are identified by Ostrowski (1991) and Watts (1990).

The process of quenching, or controlled cooling, occurs when a heated metal item is immersed in a tank of quenching oil. The process is undertaken to harden or temper the material through metallurgical change.

Most quenching oils are mineral oils which are combustible. They must be chosen carefully for each application to ensure that the ignition temperature of the oil is above the operating temperature of the tank as the hot metal pieces are immersed.

It is critical that the oil does not overflow the sides of the tank. Therefore, liquid level controls and appropriate drains are essential.

Partial immersion of hot items is the most common cause of quench tank fires. This can be prevented by appropriate material transfer or conveyor arrangements.

Likewise, appropriate controls must be provided to avoid excessive oil temperatures and entry of water into the tank that can result in boil-over and major fire in and around the tank.

Specific automatic fire extinguishing systems such as carbon dioxide or dry chemical are often used to protect the tank surface. Overhead, automatic sprinkler protection of the building is desirable. In some cases, special protection of operators who need to work close to the tank is also required. Often, water spray systems are provided for exposure protection for workers.

Above all, proper training of workers in emergency response, including use of portable fire extinguishers, is essential.

Chemical Process Equipment

Operations to chemically change the nature of materials have often been the source of major catastrophes, causing severe plant damage and death and injury to workers and surrounding communities. Risks to life and property from incidents in chemical process plants may come from fires, explosions or toxic chemical releases. The energy of destruction often comes from uncontrolled chemical reaction of process materials, combustion of fuels leading to pressure waves or high levels of radiation and flying missiles that can cause damage at large distances.

Plant operations and equipment

The first stage of design is to understand the chemical processes involved and their potential for energy release. Lees (1980) in his *Loss Prevention in the Process Industries* sets out in detail the steps required to be undertaken, which include:

- proper process design
- study of failure mechanisms and reliability
- hazard identification and safety audits
- hazard assessment—cause/consequences.

The assessment of the degrees of hazard must examine:

- potential emission and dispersal of chemicals, particularly toxic and contaminating substances
- effects of fire radiation and dispersal of combustion products
- results of explosions, particularly pressure shock waves that can destroy other plants and buildings.

More details of process hazards and their control are given in *Plant guidelines for technical management of chemical process safety* (AIChE 1993); *Sax's Dangerous Properties of Industrial Materials* (Lewis 1979); and the NFPA's *Industrial Fire Hazards Handbook* (Linville 1990).

Siting and exposure protection

Once the hazards and consequences of fire, explosion and toxic releases have been identified, siting of chemical process plants can be undertaken.

Again, Lees (1980) and Bradford (1991) provided guidelines on plant siting. Plants must be separated from surrounding communities sufficiently to ensure that those communities cannot be affected by an industrial accident. The technique of quantitative risk assessment (QRA) to determine separation distances is widely used and legislated for in the design of chemical process plants.

The disaster in Bhopal, India, in 1984 demonstrated the consequences of locating a chemical plant too close to a community: over 1,000 people were killed by toxic chemicals in an industrial accident.

Provision of separating space around chemical plants also allows ready access for fire-fighting from all sides, regardless of wind direction.

Chemical plants must provide exposure protection in the form of explosion-resistant control rooms, worker refuges and fire-fighting equipment to ensure that workers are protected and that effective fire-fighting can be undertaken after an incident.

Spill control

Spills of flammable or hazardous materials should be kept small by appropriate process design, fail-safe valves and appropriate detection/control equipment. However, if large spills occur, they should be confined to areas surrounded by walls, sometimes of earth, where they can burn harmlessly if ignited.

Fires in drainage systems are common, and special attention must be paid to drains and sewerage systems.

Heat transfer hazards

Equipment that transfers heat from a hot fluid to a cooler one can be a source of fire in chemical plants. Excessive localized temperatures can cause decomposition and burn out of many materials. This may sometimes cause rupture of the heat-transfer equipment and transfer of one fluid into another, causing an unwanted violent reaction.

High levels of inspection and maintenance, including cleaning of heat transfer equipment, is essential to safe operation.

Reactors

Reactors are the vessels in which the desired chemical processes are undertaken. They can be of a continuous or batch type but require special design attention. Vessels must be designed to withstand pressures that might result from explosions or uncontrolled reactions or alternatively must be provided with appropriate pressure-relief devices and sometimes emergency venting.

Safety measures for chemical reactors include:

- appropriate instrumentation and controls to detect potential incidents, including redundant circuitry
- high quality cleaning, inspection and maintenance of the equipment and the safety controls
- adequate training of operators in control and emergency response
- appropriate fire suppression equipment and fire-fighting personnel.

Welding and Cutting

The Factory Mutual Engineering Corporation's (FM) *Loss Prevention Data Sheet* (1977) shows that nearly 10% of losses in industrial properties are due to incidents involving cutting and welding of materials, generally metals. It is clear that the high temperatures required to melt the metals during these operations can start fires, as can the sparks generated in many of these processes.

The FM *Data Sheet* (1977) indicates that the materials most frequently involved in fires due to welding and cutting are flammable liquids, oily deposits, combustible dusts and wood. The types of industrial areas where accidents are most likely are storage areas, building construction sites, facilities undergoing repair or alteration and waste disposal systems.

Sparks from cutting and welding can often travel up to 10 m and lodge in combustible materials where smouldering and later flaming fires can occur.

Electrical processes

Arc welding and arc cutting are examples of processes involving electricity to provide the arc that is the heat source for melting and joining metals. Flashes of sparks are common, and protection of workers from electrocution, spark flashes and intense arc radiation is required.

Oxy-fuel gas processes

This process uses the heat of combustion of the fuel gas and oxygen to generate flames of high temperature that melt the metals being joined or cut. Manz (1991) indicated that acetylene is the most widely used fuel gas because of its high flame temperature of about 3,000 °C.

The presence of a fuel and oxygen at high pressure makes for an increased hazard, as is leakage of these gases from their storage cylinders. It is important to remember that many materials that do not burn, or only burn slowly in air, burn violently in pure oxygen.

Safeguards and precautions

Good safety practices are identified by Manz (1991) in the NFPA *Fire Protection Handbook*.

These safeguards and precautions include:

- proper design, installation and maintenance of welding and cutting equipment, particularly storage and leak testing of fuel and oxygen cylinders

- proper preparation of work areas to remove all chance of accidental ignition of surrounding combustibles
- strict management control over all welding and cutting processes
- training of all operators in safe practices
- proper fire-resistant clothing and eye protection for operators and nearby workers
- adequate ventilation to prevent exposure of operators or nearby workers to noxious gases and fumes.

Special precautions are required when welding or cutting tanks or other vessels that have held flammable materials. A useful guide is the American Welding Society's *Recommended Safe Practices for the Preparation for Welding and Cutting of Containers that have held Hazardous Substances* (1988).

For building works and alterations, a UK publication, the Loss Prevention Council's *Fire Prevention on Construction Sites* (1992) is useful. It contains a sample hot-work permit to control cutting and welding operations. This would be useful for management in any plant or industrial site. A similar sample permit is provided in the FM *Data Sheet* on cutting and welding (1977).

Lightning Protection

Lightning is a frequent cause of fires and deaths of people in many countries in the world. For example, each year some 240 US citizens die as a result of lightning.

Lightning is a form of electrical discharge between charged clouds and the earth. The FM *Data Sheet* (1984) on lightning indicates that lightning strikes may range from 2,000 to 200,000 A as a result of a potential difference of 5 to 50 million V between clouds and the earth.

The frequency of lightning varies between countries and areas depending on the number of thunderstorm-days per year for the locality. The damage that lightning can cause depends very much on the ground condition, with more damage occurring in areas of high earth resistivity.

Protective measures—buildings

The NFPA 780 *Standard for the Installation of Lightning Protection Systems* (1995b) sets out the design requirements for protection of buildings. While the exact theory of lightning discharges is still being investigated, the basic principle of protection is to provide a means by which a lightning discharge may enter or leave the earth without damaging the building being protected.

Lightning systems, therefore, have two functions:

- to intercept the lightning discharge before it strikes the building
- provide a harmless discharge path to earth.

This requires buildings to be fitted with:

- lightning rods or masts
- down conductors
- good ground connections, typically 10 ohms or less.

More details for the design of lightning protection for buildings is provided by Davis (1991) in the NFPA *Fire Protection Handbook* (Cote 1991) and in the British Standards Institute's *Code of Practice* (1992).

Overhead transmission lines, transformers, outdoor substations and other electrical installations can be damaged by direct lightning strikes. Electrical transmission equipment can also pick up induced voltage and current surges that can enter buildings. Fires, damage to equipment and serious interruption to operations may result. Surge arresters are required to divert these voltage peaks to ground through effective earthing.

The increased use of sensitive computer equipment in commerce and industry has made operations more sensitive to transient over-voltages induced in power and communication cables in many buildings. Appropriate transient protection is required and special guidance is provided in the British Standards Institute BS 6651:1992, *The Protection of Structures Against Lightning.*

Maintenance

Proper maintenance of lightning systems is essential for effective protection. Special attention has to be paid to ground connections. If they are not effective, lightning protection systems will be ineffective.

● PASSIVE FIRE PROTECTION MEASURES

Yngve Anderberg

Confining Fires by Compartmentation

Building and site planning

Fire safety engineering work should begin early in the design phase because the fire safety requirements influence the layout and design of the building considerably. In this way, the designer can incorporate fire safety features into the building much better and more economically. The overall approach includes consideration of both interior building functions and layout, as well as exterior site planning. Prescriptive code requirements are more and more replaced by functionally based requirements, which means there is an increased demand for experts in this field. From the beginning of the construction project, the building designer therefore should contact fire experts to elucidate the following actions:

- to describe the fire problem specific to the building
- to describe different alternatives to obtain the required fire safety level
- to analyse system choice regarding technical solutions and economy
- to create presumptions for technical optimized system choices.

The architect must utilize a given site in designing the building and adapt the functional and engineering considerations to the particular site conditions that are present. In a similar manner, the architect should consider site features in arriving at decisions on fire protection. A particular set of site characteristics may significantly influence the type of active and passive protection suggested by the fire consultant. Design features should consider the local fire-fighting resources that are available and the time to reach the building. The fire service cannot and should not be expected to provide complete protection for building occupants and property; it must be assisted by both active and passive building fire defences, to provide reasonable safety from the effects of fire. Briefly, the operations may be broadly grouped as rescue, fire control and property conservation. The first priority of any fire-fighting operation is to ensure that all occupants are out of the building before critical conditions occur.

Structural design based on classification or calculation

A well-established means of codifying fire protection and fire safety requirements for buildings is to classify them by types of construction, based upon the materials used for the structural elements and the degree of fire resistance afforded by each ele-

ment. Classification can be based on furnace tests in accordance with ISO 834 (fire exposure is characterized by the standard temperature-time curve), combination of test and calculation or by calculation. These procedures will identify the standard fire resistance (the ability to fulfil required functions during 30, 60, 90 minutes, etc.) of a structural load-bearing and/or separating member. Classification (especially when based on tests) is a simplified and conservative method and is more and more replaced by functionally based calculation methods taking into account the effect of fully developed natural fires. However, fire tests will always be required, but they can be designed in a more optimal way and be combined with computer simulations. In that procedure, the number of tests can be reduced considerably. Usually, in the fire test procedures, load-bearing structural elements are loaded to 100% of the design load, but in real life the load utilization factor is most often less than that. Acceptance criteria are specific for the construction or element tested. Standard fire resistance is the measured time the member can withstand the fire without failure.

Optimum fire engineering design, balanced against anticipated fire severity, is the objective of structural and fire protection requirements in modern performance-based codes. These have opened the way for fire engineering design by calculation with prediction of the temperature and structural effect due to a complete fire process (heating and subsequent cooling is considered) in a compartment. Calculations based on natural fires mean that the structural elements (important for the stability of the building) and the whole structure are not allowed to collapse during the entire fire process, including cool down.

Comprehensive research has been performed during the past 30 years. Various computer models have been developed. These models utilize basic research on mechanical and thermal properties of materials at elevated temperatures. Some computer models are validated against a vast number of experimental data, and a good prediction of structural behaviour in fire is obtained.

Compartmentation

A fire compartment is a space within a building extending over one or several floors which is enclosed by separating members such that the fire spread beyond the compartment is prevented during the relevant fire exposure. Compartmentation is important in preventing the fire to spread into too large spaces or into the whole building. People and property outside the fire compartment can be protected by the fact that the fire is extinguished or burns out by itself or by the delaying effect of the separating members on the spread of fire and smoke until the occupants are rescued to a place of safety.

The fire resistance required by a compartment depends upon its intended purpose and on the expected fire. Either the separating members enclosing the compartment shall resist the maximum expected fire or contain the fire until occupants are evacuated. The load-bearing elements in the compartment must always resist the complete fire process or be classified to a certain resistance measured in terms of periods of time, which is equal or longer than the requirement of the separating members.

Structural integrity during a fire

The requirement for maintaining structural integrity during a fire is the avoidance of structural collapse and the ability of the separating members to prevent ignition and flame spread into adjacent spaces. There are different approaches to provide the design for fire resistance. They are classifications based on standard fire-resistance test as in ISO 834, combination of test and calculation or solely calculation and the performance-based procedure computer prediction based on real fire exposure.

Interior finish

Interior finish is the material that forms the exposed interior surface of walls, ceilings and floor. There are many types of interior finish materials such as plaster, gypsum, wood and plastics. They serve several functions. Some functions of the interior material are acoustical and insulational, as well as protective against wear and abrasion.

Interior finish is related to fire in four different ways. It can affect the rate of fire build-up to flashover conditions, contribute to fire extension by flame spread, increase the heat release by adding fuel and produce smoke and toxic gases. Materials that exhibit high rates of flame spread, contribute fuel to a fire or produce hazardous quantities of smoke and toxic gases would be undesirable.

Smoke movement

In building fires, smoke often moves to locations remote from the fire space. Stairwells and elevator shafts can become smoke-logged, thereby blocking evacuation and inhibiting fire-fighting. Today, smoke is recognized as the major killer in fire situations (see figure 41.4).

The driving forces of smoke movement include naturally occurring stack effect, buoyancy of combustion gases, the wind effect, fan-powered ventilation systems and the elevator piston effect.

When it is cold outside, there is an upward movement of air within building shafts. Air in the building has a buoyant force because it is warmer and therefore less dense than outside air. The buoyant force causes air to rise within building shafts. This phenomenon is known as the *stack effect*. The pressure difference from the shaft to the outside, which causes smoke movement, is illustrated below:

$$\Delta P_{so} = \frac{g P_{atm}}{R}\left(\frac{1}{T_o} - \frac{1}{T_s}\right)z$$

where

ΔP_{so} = the pressure difference from the shaft to the outside
g = acceleration of gravity
P_{atm} = absolute atmospheric pressure
R = gas constant of air
T_o = absolute temperature of outside air
T_s = absolute temperature of air inside the shaft
z = elevation

High-temperature smoke from a fire has a buoyancy force due to its reduced density. The equation for buoyancy of combustion gases is similar to the equation for the stack effect.

In addition to buoyancy, the energy released by a fire can cause smoke movement due to expansion. Air will flow into the fire compartment, and hot smoke will be distributed in the compartment. Neglecting the added mass of the fuel, the ratio of volumetric flows can simply be expressed as a ratio of absolute temperature.

Wind has a pronounced effect on smoke movement. The elevator piston effect should not be neglected. When an elevator car moves in a shaft, transient pressures are produced.

Heating, ventilating and air conditioning (HVAC) systems transport smoke during building fires. When a fire starts in an unoccupied portion of a building, the HVAC system can transport smoke to another occupied space. The HVAC system should be designed so that either the fans are shut down or the system transfers into a special smoke control mode operation.

Smoke movement can be managed by use of one or more of the following mechanisms: compartmentation, dilution, air flow, pressurization or buoyancy.

Figure 41.4 • The production of smoke from a fire.

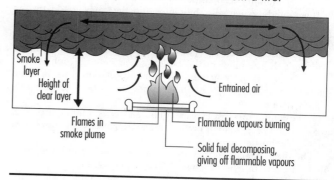

Evacuation of Occupants

Egress design

Egress design should be based upon an evaluation of a building's total fire protection system (see figure 41.5).

People evacuating from a burning building are influenced by a number of impressions during their escape. The occupants have to make several decisions during the escape in order to make the right choices in each situation. These reactions can differ widely,

Figure 41.5 • Principles of exit safety.

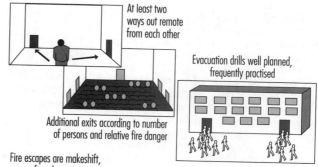

depending upon the physical and mental capabilities and conditions of building occupants.

The building will also influence the decisions made by the occupants by its escape routes, guidance signs and other installed safety systems. The spread of fire and smoke will have the strongest impact on how the occupants make their decisions. The smoke will limit the visibility in the building and create a non-tenable environment to the evacuating persons. Radiation from fire and flames creates large spaces that cannot be used for evacuation, which increases the risk.

In designing means of egress one first needs a familiarity with the reaction of people in fire emergencies. Patterns of movement of people must be understood.

The three stages of evacuation time are notification time, reaction time and time to evacuate. The notification time is related to whether there is a fire alarm system in the building or if the occupant is able to understand the situation or how the building is divided into compartments. The reaction time depends on the occupant's ability to make decisions, the properties of the fire (such as the amount of heat and smoke) and how the building's egress system is planned. Finally, the time to evacuate depends on where in the building crowds are formed and how people move in various situations.

In specific buildings with mobile occupants, for example, studies have shown certain reproducible flow characteristics from persons exiting the buildings. These predictable flow characteristics have fostered computer simulations and modelling to aid the egress design process.

The evacuation travel distances are related to the fire hazard of the contents. The higher the hazard, the shorter the travel distance to an exit.

A safe exit from a building requires a safe path of escape from the fire environment. Hence, there must be a number of properly designed means of egress of adequate capacity. There should be at least one alternative means of egress considering that fire, smoke and the characteristics of occupants and so on may prevent use of one means of egress. The means of egress must be protected against fire, heat and smoke during the egress time. Thus, it is necessary to have building codes that consider the passive protection, according to evacuation and of course to fire protection. A building must manage the critical situations, which are given in the codes concerning evacuation. For example, in the Swedish Building Codes, the smoke layer must not reach below $1.6 + 0.1H$ (H is the total compartment height), maximum radiation 10 kW/m^2 of short duration, and the temperature in the breathing air must not exceed 80 °C.

An effective evacuation can take place if a fire is discovered early and the occupants are alerted promptly with a detection and alarm system. A proper mark of the means of egress surely facilitates the evacuation. There is also a need for organization and drill of evacuation procedures.

Human behaviour during fires

How one reacts during a fire is related to the role assumed, previous experience, education and personality; the perceived threat of the fire situation; the physical characteristics and means of egress available within the structure; and the actions of others who are sharing the experience. Detailed interviews and studies over 30 years have established that instances of non-adaptive, or panic, behaviour are rare events that occur under specific conditions. Most behaviour in fires is determined by information analysis, resulting in cooperative and altruistic actions.

Human behaviour is found to pass through a number of identified stages, with the possibility of various routes from one stage to the next. In summary, the fire is seen as having three general stages:

1. The individual receives initial cues and investigates or misinterprets these initial cues.
2. Once the fire is apparent, the individual will try to obtain further information, contact others or leave.
3. The individual will thereafter deal with the fire, interact with others or escape.

Pre-fire activity is an important factor. If a person is engaged in a well-known activity, for example eating a meal in a restaurant, the implications for subsequent behaviour are considerable.

Cue reception may be a function of pre-fire activity. There is a tendency for gender differences, with females more likely to be recipient of noises and odours, though the effect is only slight. There are role differences in initial responses to the cue. In domestic fires, if the female receives the cue and investigates, the male, when told, is likely to "have a look" and delay further actions. In larger establishments, the cue may be an alarm warning. Information may come from others and has been found to be inadequate for effective behaviour.

Individuals may or may not have realized that there is a fire. An understanding of their behaviour must take account of whether they have defined their situation correctly.

When the fire has been defined, the "prepare" stage occurs. The particular type of occupancy is likely to have a great influence on exactly how this stage develops. The "prepare" stage includes in chronological order "instruct", "explore" and "withdraw".

The "act" stage, which is the final stage, depends upon role, occupancy, and earlier behaviour and experience. It may be possible for early evacuation or effective fire-fighting to occur.

Building transportation systems

Building transportation systems must be considered during the design stage and should be integrated with the whole building's fire protection system. The hazards associated with these systems must be included in any pre-fire planning and fire protection survey.

Building transportation systems, such as elevators and escalators, make high-rise buildings feasible. Elevator shafts can contribute to the spread of smoke and fire. On the other hand, an elevator is a necessary tool for fire-fighting operations in high-rise buildings.

Transportation systems may contribute to dangerous and complicated fire safety problems because an enclosed elevator shaft acts as a chimney or flue because of the stack effect of hot smoke and gases from fire. This generally results in the movement of smoke and combustion products from lower to upper levels of the building.

High-rise buildings present new and different problems to fire-suppression forces, including the use of elevators during emergencies. Elevators are unsafe in a fire for several reasons:

1. Persons may push a corridor button and have to wait for an elevator that may never respond, losing valuable escape time.
2. Elevators do not prioritize car and corridor calls, and one of the calls may be at the fire floor.
3. Elevators cannot start until the lift and shaft doors are closed, and panic could lead to overcrowding of an elevator and the blockage of the doors, which would thus prevent closing.
4. The power can fail during a fire at any time, thus leading to entrapment. (See figure 41.6.)

Fire drills and occupant training

A proper mark of the means of egress facilitates the evacuation, but it does not ensure life safety during fire. Exit drills are necessary to make an orderly escape. They are specially required in schools, board and care facilities and industries with high hazard.

Employee drills are required, for example, in hotel and large business occupancies. Exit drills should be conducted to avoid confusion and ensure the evacuation of all occupants.

All employees should be assigned to check for availability, to count occupants when they are outside the fire area, to search for stragglers and to control re-entry. They should also recognize the evacuation signal and know the exit route they are to follow. Primary and alternative routes should be established, and all employees should be trained to use either route. After each exit drill, a meeting of responsible managers should be held to evaluate the success of the drill and to solve any kind of problem that could have occurred.

● ACTIVE FIRE PROTECTION MEASURES

Gary Taylor

Life Safety and Property Protection

As the primary importance of any fire protection measure is to provide an acceptable degree of life safety to inhabitants of a structure, in most countries legal requirements applying to fire protection are based on life safety concerns. Property protection features are intended to limit physical damage. In many cases these objectives are complementary. Where concern exists with the loss of property, its function or contents, an owner may choose to implement measures beyond the required minimum necessary to address life safety concerns.

Fire Detection and Alarm Systems

A fire detection and alarm system provides a means to detect fire automatically and to warn building occupants of the threat of fire. It is the audible or visual alarm provided by a fire detection system that is the signal to begin the evacuation of the occupants from the premises. This is especially important in large or multi-storey buildings where occupants would be unaware that a fire was underway within the structure and where it would be unlikely or impractical for warning to be provided by another inhabitant.

Basic elements of a fire detection and alarm system

A fire detection and alarm system may include all or some of the following:

1. a system control unit
2. a primary or main electrical power supply
3. a secondary (stand-by) power supply, usually supplied from batteries or an emergency generator
4. alarm-initiating devices such as automatic fire detectors, manual pull stations and/or sprinkler system flow devices, connected to "initiating circuits" of the system control unit
5. alarm-indicating devices, such as bells or lights, connected to "indicating circuits" of the system control unit
6. ancillary controls such as ventilation shut-down functions, connected to output circuits of the system control unit
7. remote alarm indication to an external response location, such as the fire department
8. control circuits to activate a fire protection system or smoke control system.

Smoke Control Systems

To reduce the threat of smoke from entering exit paths during evacuation from a structure, smoke control systems can be used. Generally, mechanical ventilation systems are employed to supply fresh air to the exit path. This method is most often used to

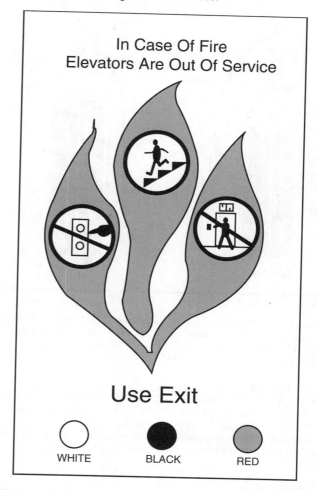

Figure 41.6 • An example of a pictographic warning message for elevator use.

In Case Of Fire
Elevators Are Out Of Service

Use Exit

WHITE   BLACK   RED

pressurize stairways or atrium buildings. This is a feature intended to enhance life safety.

Portable Fire Extinguishers and Hose Reels

Portable fire extinguishers and water hose reels are often provided for use by building occupants to fight small fires (see figure 41.7). Building occupants should not be encouraged to use a portable fire extinguisher or hose reel unless they have been trained in their use. In all cases, operators should be very cautious to avoid placing themselves in a position where safe egress is blocked. For any fire, no matter how small, the first action should always be to notify other building occupants of the threat of fire and summon assistance from the professional fire service.

Water Sprinkler Systems

Water sprinkler systems consist of a water supply, distribution valves and piping connected to automatic sprinkler heads (see figure 41.8). While current sprinkler systems are primarily intended to control the spread of fire, many systems have accomplished complete extinguishment.

A common misconception is that all automatic sprinkler heads open in the event of a fire. In fact, each sprinkler head is designed to open only when sufficient heat is present to indicate a fire.

Figure 41.7 • Portable fire extinguishers.

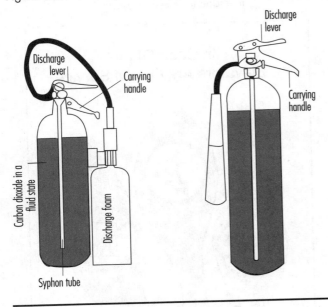

Water then flows only from the sprinkler head(s) that have opened as the result of fire in their immediate vicinity. This design feature provides efficient use of water for fire-fighting and limits water damage.

Water supply

Water for an automatic sprinkler system must be available in sufficient quantity and at sufficient volume and pressure at all times to ensure reliable operation in the event of fire. Where a municipal water supply cannot meet this requirement, a reservoir or pump arrangement must be provided to provide a secure water supply.

Control valves

Control valves should be maintained in the open position at all times. Often, supervision of the control valves can be accomplished by the automatic fire alarm system by provision of valve tamper switches that will initiate a trouble or supervisory signal at

Figure 41.8 • A typical sprinkler installation showing all common water supplies, outdoor hydrants and underground piping.

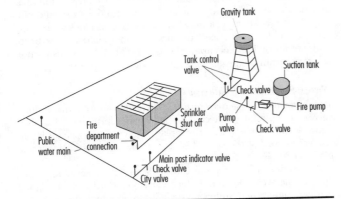

the fire alarm control panel to indicate a closed valve. If this type of monitoring cannot be provided, the valves should be locked in the open position.

Piping

Water flows through a piping network, ordinarily suspended from the ceiling, with the sprinkler heads suspended at intervals along the pipes. Piping used in sprinkler systems should be of a type that can withstand a working pressure of not less than 1,200 kPa. For exposed piping systems, fittings should be of the screwed, flanged, mechanical joint or brazed type.

Sprinkler heads

A sprinkler head consists of an orifice, normally held closed by a temperature-sensitive releasing element, and a spray deflector. The water discharge pattern and spacing requirements for individual sprinkler heads are used by sprinkler designers to ensure complete coverage of the protected risk.

Special Extinguishing Systems

Special extinguishing systems are used in cases where water sprinklers would not provide adequate protection or where the risk of damage from water would be unacceptable. In many cases where water damage is of concern, special extinguishing systems may be used in conjunction with water sprinkler systems, with the special extinguishing system designed to react at an early stage of fire development.

Water and water-additive special extinguishing systems

Water spray systems

Water spray systems increase the effectiveness of water by producing smaller water droplets, and thus a greater surface area of water is exposed to the fire, with a relative increase in heat absorption capability. This type of system is often chosen as a means of keeping large pressure vessels, such as butane spheres, cool when there is a risk of an exposure fire originating in an adjacent area. The system is similar to a sprinkler system; however, all heads are open, and a separate detection system or manual action is used to open control valves. This allows water to flow through the piping network to all spray devices that serve as outlets from the piping system.

Foam systems

In a foam system, a liquid concentrate is injected into the water supply before the control valve. Foam concentrate and air are mixed, either through the mechanical action of discharge or by aspirating air into the discharge device. The air entrained in the foam solution creates an expanded foam. As expanded foam is less dense than most hydrocarbons, the expanded foam forms a blanket on top of the flammable liquid. This foam blanket reduces fuel vapour propagation. Water, which represents as much as 97% of the foam solution, provides a cooling effect to further reduce vapour propagation and to cool hot objects that could serve as a source of re-ignition.

Gaseous extinguishing systems

Carbon dioxide systems

Carbon dioxide systems consist of a supply of carbon dioxide, stored as liquified compressed gas in pressure vessels (see figures 41.9 and 41.10). The carbon dioxide is held in the pressure vessel by means of an automatic valve that is opened upon fire by means of a separate detection system or by manual operation. Once released, the carbon dioxide is delivered to the fire by means of a piping and discharge nozzle arrangement. Carbon

Figure 41.9 • Diagram of a high-pressure carbon dioxide system for total flooding.

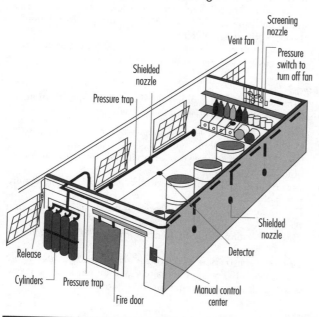

Inert gas systems

Inert gas systems generally use a mixture of nitrogen and argon as an extinguishing medium. In some cases, a small percentage of carbon dioxide is also provided in the gas mixture. The inert gas mixtures extinguish fires by reducing oxygen concentration within a protected volume. They are suitable for use in enclosed spaces only. The unique feature offered by inert gas mixtures is that they reduce the oxygen to a low enough concentration to extinguish many types of fires; however, oxygen levels are not sufficiently lowered to pose an immediate threat to occupants of the protected space. The inert gases are compressed and stored in pressure vessels. System operation is similar to a carbon dioxide system. As the inert gases cannot be liquified by compression, the number of storage vessels required for protection of a given enclosed protected volume is greater than that for carbon dioxide.

Halon systems

Halons 1301, 1211 and 2402 have been identified as ozone-depleting substances. Production of these extinguishing agents ceased in 1994, as required by the Montreal Protocol, an international agreement to protect the earth's ozone layer. Halon 1301 was most often used in fixed fire protection systems. Halon 1301 was stored as liquified, compressed gas in pressure vessels in a similar arrangement to that used for carbon dioxide. The advantage offered by halon 1301 was that storage pressures were lower and that very low concentrations provided effective extinguishing capability. Halon 1301 systems were used successfully for totally enclosed hazards where the extinguishing concentration achieved could be maintained for a sufficient time for extinguishment to occur. For most risks, concentrations used did not pose an immediate threat to occupants. Halon 1301 is still used for several important applications where acceptable alternatives have yet to be developed. Examples include use on-board commercial and military aircraft and for some special cases where inerting concentrations are required to prevent explosions in areas where occupants could be present. The halon in existing halon systems that are no longer required should be made available for use by others with critical applications. This will militate against the need to produce more of these environmentally sensitive extinguishers and help protect the ozone layer.

Halocarbon systems

Halocarbon agents were developed as the result of the environmental concerns associated with halons. These agents differ widely in toxicity, environmental impact, storage weight and volume requirements, cost and availability of approved system hardware. They all can be stored as liquified compressed gases in pressure vessels. System configuration is similar to a carbon dioxide system.

dioxide extinguishes fire by displacing the oxygen available to the fire. Carbon dioxide systems can be designed for use in open areas such as printing presses or enclosed volumes such as ship machinery spaces. Carbon dioxide, at fire-extinguishing concentrations, is toxic to people, and special measures must be employed to ensure that persons in the protected area are evacuated before discharge occurs. Pre-discharge alarms and other safety measures must be carefully incorporated into the design of the system to ensure adequate safety for people working in the protected area. Carbon dioxide is considered to be a clean extinguishant because it does not cause collateral damage and is electrically non-conductive.

Design, Installation and Maintenance of Active Fire Protection Systems

Only those skilled in this work are competent to design, install and maintain this equipment. It may be necessary for many of those charged with purchasing, installing, inspecting, testing, approving and maintaining this equipment to consult with an experienced and competent fire protection specialist to discharge their duties effectively.

Further Information

This section of the *Encyclopaedia* presents a very brief and limited overview of the available choice of active fire protection systems. Readers may often obtain more information by contacting a national fire protection association, their insurer or the fire prevention department of their local fire service.

Figure 41.10 • A total flooding system installed in a room with a raised floor.

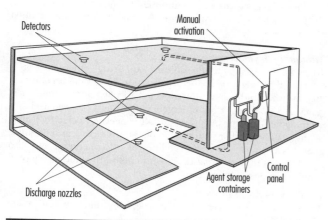

● ORGANIZING FOR FIRE PROTECTION

S. Dheri

Private Emergency Organization

Profit is the main objective of any industry. To achieve this objective, an efficient and alert management and continuity of production are essential. Any interruption in production, for any reason, will adversely affect profits. If the interruption is the result of a fire or explosion, it may be long and may cripple the industry.

Very often, a plea is taken that the property is insured and loss due to fire, if any, will be indemnified by the insurance company. It must be appreciated that insurance is only a device to spread the effect of the destruction brought by fire or explosion on as many people as possible. It cannot make good the national loss. Besides, insurance is no guarantee of continuity of production and elimination or minimization of consequential losses.

What is indicated, therefore, is that the management must gather complete information on the fire and explosion hazard, evaluate the loss potential and implement suitable measures to control the hazard, with a view to eliminating or minimizing the incidence of fire and explosion. This involves the setting up of a private emergency organization.

Emergency Planning

Such an organization must, as far as possible, be considered from the planning stage itself, and implemented progressively from the time of selection of site until production has started, and then continued thereafter.

Success of any emergency organization depends to a large extent on the overall participation of all workers and various echelons of the management. This fact must be borne in mind while planning the emergency organization.

The various aspects of emergency planning are mentioned below. For more details, a reference may be made to the US National Fire Protection Association (NFPA) *Fire Protection Handbook* or any other standard work on the subject (Cote 1991).

Stage 1

Initiate the emergency plan by doing the following:

1. Identify and evaluate fire and explosion hazards associated with the transportation, handling and storage of each raw material, intermediate and finished products and each industrial process, as well as work out detailed preventive measures to counteract the hazards with a view to eliminating or minimizing them.
2. Work out the requirements of fire protection installations and equipment, and determine the stages at which each is to be provided.
3. Prepare specifications for the fire protection installation and equipment.

Stage 2

Determine the following:

1. availability of adequate water supply for fire protection in addition to the requirements for processing and domestic use
2. susceptibility of site and natural hazards, such as floods, earthquakes, heavy rains, etc.
3. environments, i.e., the nature and extent of surrounding property and the exposure hazard involved in the event of a fire or explosion
4. existence of private (works) or public fire brigade(s), the distance at which such fire brigade(s) is (are) located and the suitability of the appliances available with them for the risk to

be protected and whether they can be called upon to assist in an emergency
5. response from the assisting fire brigade(s) with particular reference to impediments, such as railway crossings, ferries, inadequate strength and (or) width of bridges in relation to the fire appliances, difficult traffic, etc.
6. socio-political environment , i.e., incidence of crime, and political activities leading to law-and-order problems.

Stage 3

Prepare the layout and building plans, and the specifications of construction material. Carry out the following tasks:

1. Limit the floor area of each shop, workplace, etc. by providing fire walls, fire doors, etc.
2. Specify the use of fire-resistant materials for construction of building or structure.
3. Ensure that steel columns and other structural members are not exposed.
4. Ensure adequate separation between building, structures and plant.
5. Plan installation of fire hydrants, sprinklers, etc. where necessary.
6. Ensure the provision of adequate access roads in the layout plan to enable fire appliances to reach all parts of the premises and all sources of water for fire-fighting.

Stage 4

During construction, do the following:

1. Acquaint the contractor and his or her employees with the fire risk management policies, and enforce compliance.
2. Thoroughly test all fire protection installations and equipment before acceptance.

Stage 5

If the size of the industry, its hazards or its out-of-the-way location is such that a full-time fire brigade must be available on the premises, then organize, equip and train the required full-time personnel. Also appoint a full-time fire officer.

Stage 6

To ensure full participation of all employees, do the following:

1. Train all personnel in the observance of precautionary measures in their day-to-day work and the action required of them upon an outbreak of fire or explosion. The training must include operation of fire-fighting equipment.
2. Ensure strict observance of fire precautions by all concerned personnel through periodic reviews.
3. Ensure regular inspection and maintenance of all fire protection systems and equipment. All defects must be rectified promptly.

Managing the emergency

To avoid confusion at the time of an actual emergency, it is essential that everyone in the organization knows the precise part that he (she) and others are expected to play during the emergency. A well-thought-out emergency plan must be prepared and promulgated for this purpose, and all concerned personnel must be made fully familiar with it. The plan must clearly and unambiguously lay down the responsibilities of all concerned and also specify a chain of command. As a minimum, the emergency plan should include the following:

1. name of the industry
2. address of the premises, with telephone number and a site plan

3. purpose and objective of the emergency plan and effective date of its coming in force
4. area covered, including a site plan
5. emergency organization, indicating chain of command from the work manager on downwards
6. fire protection systems, mobile appliances and portable equipment, with details
7. details of assistance availability
8. fire alarm and communication facilities
9. action to be taken in an emergency. Include separately and unambiguously the action to be taken by:
   - the person discovering the fire
   - the private fire brigade on the premises
   - head of the section involved in the emergency
   - heads of other sections not actually involved in the emergency
   - the security organization
   - the fire officer, if any
   - the works manager
   - others
10. chain of command at the scene of incident. Consider all possible situations, and indicate clearly who is to assume command in each case, including the circumstances under which another organization is to be called in to assist.
11. action after a fire. Indicate responsibility for:
   - recommissioning or replenishing of all fire protection systems, equipment and water sources
   - investigating the cause of fire or explosion
   - preparation and submission of reports
   - initiating remedial measures to prevent re-occurrence of similar emergency.

When a mutual assistance plan is in operation, copies of emergency plan must be supplied to all participating units in return for similar plans of their respective premises.

Evacuation Protocols

A situation necessitating the execution of the emergency plan may develop as a result of either an explosion or a fire.

Explosion may or may not be followed by fire, but in almost all cases, it produces a shattering effect, which may injure or kill personnel present in the vicinity and/or cause physical damage to property, depending upon the circumstances of each case. It may also cause shock and confusion and may necessitate the immediate shut-down of the manufacturing processes or a portion thereof, along with the sudden movement of a large number of people. If the situation is not controlled and guided in an orderly manner immediately, it may lead to panic and further loss of life and property.

Smoke given out by the burning material in a fire may involve other parts of the property and/or trap persons, necessitating an intensive, large-scale rescue operation/evacuation. In certain cases, large-scale evacuation may have to be undertaken when people are likely to get trapped or affected by fire.

In all cases in which large-scale sudden movement of personnel is involved, traffic problems are also created—particularly if public roads, streets or areas have to be used for this movement. If such problems are not anticipated and suitable action is not preplanned, traffic bottlenecks result, which hamper and retard fire extinguishment and rescue efforts.

Evacuation of a large number of persons—particularly from high-rise buildings—may also present problems. For successful evacuation, it is not only necessary that adequate and suitable means of escape are available, but also that the evacuation be effected speedily. Special attention should be given to the evacuation needs of disabled individuals.

Detailed evacuation procedures must, therefore, be included in the emergency plan. These must be frequently tested in the conduct of fire and evacuation drills, which may also involve traffic problems. All participating and concerned organizations and agencies must also be involved in these drills, at least periodically. After each exercise, a debriefing session must be held, during which all mistakes are pointed out and explained. Action must also be taken to prevent repetition of the same mistakes in future exercises and actual incidents by removing all difficulties and reviewing the emergency plan as necessary.

Proper records must be maintained of all exercises and evacuation drills.

Emergency Medical Services

Casualties in a fire or explosion must receive immediate medical aid or be moved speedily to a hospital after being given first aid.

It is essential that management provide one or more first-aid post(s) and, where necessary because of the size and hazardous nature of the industry, one or more mobile paramedical appliances. All first-aid posts and paramedical appliances must be staffed at all times by fully trained paramedics.

Depending upon the size of the industry and the number of workers, one or more ambulance(s) must also be provided and staffed on the premises for removal of casualties to hospitals. In addition, arrangement must be made to ensure that additional ambulance facilities are available at short notice when needed.

Where the size of the industry or workplace so demands, a full-time medical officer should also be made available at all times for any emergency situation.

Prior arrangements must be made with a designated hospital or hospitals at which priority is given to casualties who are removed after a fire or explosion. Such hospitals must be listed in the emergency plan along with their telephone numbers, and the emergency plan must have suitable provisions to ensure that a responsible person shall alert them to receive casualties as soon as an emergency arises.

Facility Restoration

It is important that all fire protection and emergency facilities are restored to a "ready" mode soon after the emergency is over. For this purpose, responsibility must be assigned to a person or section of the industry, and this must be included in the emergency plan. A system of checks to ensure that this is being done must also be introduced.

Public Fire Department Relations

It is not practicable for any management to foresee and provide for all possible contingencies. It is also not economically feasible to do so. In spite of adopting the most up-to-date method of fire risk management, there are always occasions when the fire protection facilities provided on the premises fall short of actual needs. For such occasions, it is desirable to preplan a mutual assistance programme with the public fire department. Good liaison with that department is necessary so that the management knows what assistance that unit can provide during an emergency on its premises. Also, the public fire department must become familiar with the risk and what it could expect during an emergency. Frequent interaction with the public fire department is necessary for this purpose.

Handling of Hazardous Materials

Hazards of the materials used in industry may not be known to fire-fighters during a spill situation, and accidental discharge and improper use or storage of hazardous materials can lead to dangerous situations that can seriously imperil their health or lead to a serious fire or explosion. It is not possible to remember the hazards of all materials. Means of ready identification of hazards have, therefore, been developed whereby the various substances are identified by distinct labels or markings.

Hazardous materials identification

Each country follows its own rules concerning the labelling of hazardous materials for the purpose of storage, handling and transportation, and various departments may be involved. While compliance with local regulations is essential, it is desirable that an internationally recognized system of identification of hazardous materials be evolved for universal application. In the United States, the NFPA has developed a system for this purpose. In this system, distinct labels are conspicuously attached or affixed to containers of hazardous materials. These labels indicate the nature and degree of hazards in respect of health, flammability and the reactive nature of the material. In addition, special possible hazards to fire-fighters can also be indicated on these labels. For an explanation of the degree of hazard, refer to NFPA 704, *Standard System for the Identification of the Fire Hazards of Materials* (1990a). In this system, the hazards are categorized as *health hazards*, *flammability hazards*, and *reactivity (instability) hazards*.

Health hazards

These include all possibilities of a material causing personal injury from contact with or absorption into the human body. A health hazard may arise out of the inherent properties of the material or from the toxic products of combustion or decomposition of the material. The degree of hazard is assigned on the basis of the greater hazard that may result under fire or other emergency conditions. It indicates to fire-fighters whether they can work safely only with special protective clothing or with suitable respiratory protective equipment or with ordinary clothing.

Degree of health hazard is measured on a scale of 4 to 0, with 4 indicating the most severe hazard and 0 indicating low hazard or no hazard.

Flammability hazards

These indicate the susceptibility of the material to burning. It is recognized that materials behave differently in respect of this property under varying circumstances (e.g., materials that may burn under one set of conditions may not burn if the conditions are altered). The form and inherent properties of the materials influence the degree of hazard, which is assigned on the same basis as for the health hazard.

Reactivity (instability) hazards

Materials capable of releasing energy by itself, (i.e., by self-reaction or polymerization) and substances that can undergo violent eruption or explosive reactions on coming in contact with water, other extinguishing agents or certain other materials are said to possess a reactivity hazard.

The violence of reaction may increase when heat or pressure is applied or when the substance comes in contact with certain other materials to form a fuel-oxidizer combination, or when it comes in contact with incompatible substances, sensitizing contaminants or catalysts.

The degree of reactivity hazard is determined and expressed in terms of the ease, rate and quantity of energy release. Additional information, such as radioactivity hazard or prohibition of water or other extinguishing medium for fire-fighting, can also be given on the same level.

The label warning of a hazardous material is a diagonally placed square with four smaller squares (see figure 41.11).

The top square indicates the health hazard, the one on the left indicates the flammability hazard, the one on the right indicates the reactivity hazard, and the bottom square indicates other special hazards, such as radioactivity or unusual reactivity with water.

To supplement the above mentioned arrangement, a colour code may also be used. The colour is used as background or the numeral indicating the hazard may be in coded colour. The codes are health hazard (blue), flammability hazard (red), reactivity hazard (yellow) and special hazard (white background).

Managing hazardous materials response

Depending on the nature of the hazardous material in the industry, it is necessary to provide protective equipment and special fire-extinguishing agents, including the protective equipment required to dispense the special extinguishing agents.

All workers must be trained in the precautions they must take and the procedures they must adopt to deal with each incident in the handling of the various types of hazardous materials. They must also know the meaning of the various identification signs.

All fire-fighters and other workers must be trained in the correct use of any protective clothing, protective respiratory equipment and special fire-fighting techniques. All concerned personnel must be kept alert and prepared to tackle any situation through frequent drills and exercises, of which proper records should be kept.

To deal with serious medical hazards and the effects of these hazards on fire-fighters, a competent medical officer should be available to take immediate precautions when any individual is exposed to unavoidable dangerous contamination. All affected persons must receive immediate medical attention.

Proper arrangements must also be made to set up a decontamination centre on the premises when necessary, and correct decontamination procedures must be laid down and followed.

Waste control

Considerable waste is generated by industry or because of accidents during handling, transportation and storage of goods. Such

Figure 41.11 • The NFPA 704 diamond.

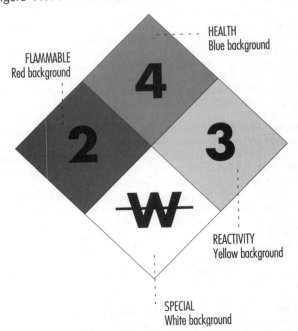

FLAMMABLE
Red background

HEALTH
Blue background

REACTIVITY
Yellow background

SPECIAL
White background

waste may be flammable, toxic, corrosive, pyrophoric, chemically reactive or radioactive, depending upon the industry in which it is generated or the nature of goods involved. In most cases unless proper care is taken in safe disposal of such waste, it may endanger animal and human life, pollute the environment or cause fire and explosions that may endanger property. A thorough knowledge of the physical and chemical properties of the waste materials and of the merits or limitations of the various methods of their disposal is, therefore, necessary to ensure economy and safety.

Properties of industrial waste are briefly summarized below:

1. Most industrial waste is hazardous and can have unexpected significance during and after disposal. The nature and behavioural characteristics of all waste must therefore be carefully examined for their short- and long-term impact and the method of disposal determined accordingly.
2. Mixing of two seemingly innocuous discarded substances may create an unexpected hazard because of their chemical or physical interaction.
3. Where flammable liquids are involved, their hazards can be assessed by taking into consideration their respective flash points, ignition temperature, flammability limits and the ignition energy required to initiate combustion. In the case of solids, particle size is an additional factor that must be considered.
4. Most flammable vapours are heavier than air. Such vapours and heavier-than-air flammable gases that may be accidentally released during collection or disposal or during handling and transportation can travel considerable distances with the wind or towards a lower gradient. On coming in contact with a source of ignition, they flash back to source. Major spills of flammable liquids are particularly hazardous in this respect and may require evacuation to save lives.
5. Pyrophoric materials, such as aluminium alkyls, ignite spontaneously when exposed to air. Special care must therefore be taken in handling, transportation, storage and disposal of such materials, preferably carried out under a nitrogen atmosphere.
6. Certain materials, such as potassium, sodium and aluminium alkyls, react violently with water or moisture and burn fiercely. Bronze powder generates considerable heat in the presence of moisture.
7. The presence of potent oxidants with organic materials can cause rapid combustion or even an explosion. Rags and other materials soaked with vegetable oils or terpenes present a risk of spontaneous combustion due to the oxidation of oils and subsequent build-up of heat to the ignition temperature.
8. Several substances are corrosive and may cause severe damage or burns to skin or other living tissues, or may corrode construction materials, especially metals, thereby weakening the structure in which such materials may have been used.
9. Some substances are toxic and can poison humans or animals by contact with skin, inhalation or contamination of food or water. Their ability to do so may be short lived or may extend over a long period. Such substances, if disposed of by dumping or burning, can contaminate water sources or come into contact with animals or workers.
10. Toxic substances that are spilled during industrial processing, transportation (including accidents), handling or storage, and toxic gases that are released into the atmosphere can affect emergency personnel and others, including the public. The hazard is all the more severe if the spilled substance(s) is vaporized at ambient temperature, because the vapours can be carried over long distances due to wind drift or run-off.
11. Certain substances may emit a strong, pungent or unpleasant odour, either by themselves or when they are burnt in the open. In either case, such substances are a public nuisance, even though they may not be toxic, and they must be disposed of by proper incineration, unless it is possible to collect and recycle them. Just as odorous substances are not necessarily toxic, odourless substances and some substances with a pleasant odour may produce harmful physiological effects.
12. Certain substances, such as explosives, fireworks, organic peroxides and some other chemicals, are sensitive to heat or shock and may explode with devastating effect if not handled carefully or mixed with other substances. Such substances must, therefore, be carefully segregated and destroyed under proper supervision.
13. Waste materials that are contaminated with radioactivity can be as hazardous as the radioactive materials themselves. Their disposal requires specialized knowledge. Proper guidance for disposal of such waste may be obtained from a country's nuclear energy organization.

Some of the methods that may be employed to dispose of industrial and emergency waste are *biodegradation, burial, incineration, landfill, mulching, open burning, pyrolysis* and *disposal through a contractor.* These are briefly explained below.

Biodegradation

Many chemicals are completely destroyed within six to 24 months when they are mixed with the top 15 cm of soil. This phenomenon is known as biodegradation and is due to the action of soil bacteria. Not all substances, however, behave in this way.

Burial

Waste, particularly chemical waste, is often disposed of by burial. This is a dangerous practice in so far as active chemicals are concerned, because, in time, the buried substance may get exposed or leached by rain into water resources. The exposed substance or the contaminated material can have adverse physiological effects when it comes in contact with water that is drunk by humans or animals. Cases are on record in which water was contaminated 40 years after burial of certain harmful chemicals.

Incineration

This is one of the safest and most satisfactory methods of waste disposal if the waste is burned in a properly designed incinerator under controlled conditions. Care must be taken, however, to ensure that the substances contained in the waste are amenable to safe incineration without posing any operating problem or special hazard. Almost all industrial incinerators require the installation of air pollution control equipment, which must be carefully selected and installed after taking into consideration the composition of the stock effluent given out by the incinerator during the burning of industrial waste.

Care must be taken in the operation of the incinerator to ensure that its operative temperature does not rise excessively either because a large amount of volatiles is fed or because of the nature of the waste burned. Structural failure can occur because of excessive temperature, or, over time, because of corrosion. The scrubber must also be periodically inspected for signs of corrosion which can occur because of contact with acids, and the scrubber system must be maintained regularly to ensure proper functioning.

Landfill

Low-lying land or a depression in land is often used as a dump for waste materials until it becomes level with the surrounding land. The waste is then levelled, covered with earth and rolled hard. The land is then used for buildings or other purposes.

For satisfactory landfill operation, the site must be selected with due regard to the proximity of pipelines, sewer lines, power lines, oil and gas wells, mines and other hazards. The waste must then be mixed with earth and evenly spread out in the depression or a wide trench. Each layer must be mechanically compacted before the next layer is added.

A 50 cm layer of earth is typically laid over the waste and compacted, leaving sufficient vents in the soil for the escape of gas that is produced by biological activity in the waste. Attention must also be paid to proper drainage of the landfill area.

Depending on the various constituents of waste material, it may at times ignite within the landfill. Each such area must, therefore, be properly fenced off and continued surveillance maintained until the chances of ignition appear to be remote. Arrangements must also be made for extinguishing any fire that may break out in the waste within the landfill.

Mulching

Some trials have been made for reusing polymers as mulch (loose material for protecting the roots of plants) by chopping the waste into small shreds or granules. When so used, it degrades very slowly. Its effect on the soil is, therefore, purely physical. This method has, however, not been used widely.

Open burning

Open burning of waste causes pollution of the atmosphere and is hazardous in as much as there is a chance of the fire getting out of control and spreading to the surrounding property or areas. Also, there is a chance of explosion from containers, and there is a possibility of harmful physiological effects of radioactive ma-

terials that may be contained in the waste. This method of disposal has been banned in some countries. It is not a desirable method and should be discouraged.

Pyrolysis

Recovery of certain compounds, by distillation of the products given out during pyrolysis (decomposition by heating) of polymers and organic substances, is possible, but not yet widely adopted.

Disposal through contractors

This is probably the most convenient method. It is important that only reliable contractors who are knowledgeable and experienced in the disposal of industrial waste and hazardous materials are selected for the job. Hazardous materials must be carefully segregated and disposed of separately.

Specific classes of materials

Specific examples of the types of hazardous materials that are often found in today's industry include: (1) combustible and reactive metals, such as magnesium, potassium, lithium, sodium, titanium and zirconium; (2) combustible refuse; (3) drying oils; (4) flammable liquids and waste solvents; (5) oxidizing materials (liquids and solids); and (6) radioactive materials. These materials require special handling and precautions that must be carefully studied. For more details on identification of hazardous materials and hazards of industrial materials, the following publications may be consulted: *Fire Protection Handbook* (Cote 1991) and *Sax's Dangerous Properties of Industrial Materials* (Lewis 1979).

References

American Institute of Chemical Engineers (AIChE). 1993. *Plant Guidelines for Technical Management of Chemical Process Safety.* New York: Center for Chemical Process Safety.

American Welding Society (AWS). 1988. *Recommended Safe Practices for the Preparation for Welding and Cutting of Containers that have held Hazardous Substances.* Miami: AWS.

Babrauskas, V and SJ Grayson. 1992. *Heat Release in Fires.* Barking: Elsevier Science.

Blye, P and P Bacon. 1991. Fire prevention practices in commerce and industry. Chap. 2, Section 2 in *Fire Protection Handbook*, 17th ed., edited by AE Cote. Quincy, Mass.: NFPA.

Bowes, PC. 1984. *Self-Heating: Evaluating and Controlling the Hazards.* London: Her Majesty's Stationary Office.

Bradford, WJ. 1991. Chemical processing equipment. Chap. 15, Section 2 in *Fire Protection Handbook*, 17th ed., edited by AE Cote. Quincy, Mass.: NFPA.

British Standards Institute (BSI). 1992. *The Protection of Structures Against Lightning.* British Standard Code of Practice, BS6651. London: BSI.

Bugbee, P. 1978. *Principles of Fire Protection.* Quincy, Mass.: NFPA.

Cote, AE. 1991. *Fire Protection Handbook*, 17th ed. Quincy, Mass.: NFPA.

Davis, NH. 1991. Lightning protection systems. Chap. 32, Section 2 in *Fire Protection Handbook*, 17th ed., edited by AE Cote. Quincy, Mass.: NFPA.

DiNenno, PJ. 1988. *Handbook of Fire Protection Engineering.* Boston: SFPE.

Drysdale, DD. 1985. *Introduction to Fire Dynamics.* Chichester: Wiley.

Drysdale, DD and HE Thomson. 1994. *Fourth International Symposium on Fire Safety Science.* Ottawa: IAFSS.

European Commission Directive (ECD). 1992. The Management of Health and Safety at Work Regulations.

Factory Mutual Engineering Corporation (FM). 1977. Cutting and welding. *Loss Prevention Data Sheets 10-15*, June 1977.

—. 1984. Lightning and surge protection for electrical systems. *Loss Prevention Data Sheets 5-11/14-19*, August 1984.

Gratton, J. 1991. Firesafety education. Chap. 2, Section 1 in *Fire Protection Handbook*, 17th ed., edited by AE Cote. Quincy, Mass.: NFPA.

Higgins, JT. 1991. Housekeeping practices. Chap. 34, Section 2 in *Fire Protection Handbook*, 17th ed., edited by AE Cote. Quincy, Mass.: NFPA.

Hrbacek, EM. 1984. Clay products plants. In *Industrial Fire Hazards Handbook*, edited by J Linville. Quincy, Mass.: NFPA.

Hunter, K. 1991. Technology distinguishes Japan's fire service. *Natl Fire Prev Agen J* (September/October).

Jernberg, LE. 1993. Improving risks in Sweden. *Fire Prev* 257 (March).

Keith, R. 1994. *FREM-Fire Risk Evaluation Method.* Melbourne: R. Keith & Assoc.

Koffel, WE. 1993. Establishing industrial fire safety programs. *Natl Fire Prev Agen J* (March/April).

Lataille, JJ. 1990. Lumber kilns and agricultural dehydrators and dryers. In *Industrial Fire Hazards Handbook*, edited by J Linville. Quincy, Mass.: NFPA.

Lees, FP. 1980. *Loss Prevention in the Process Industries.* Vol. 1, 2. London: Butterworths.

Lewis, RRJ. 1979. *Sax's Dangerous Properties of Industrial Materials.* New York: Van Nostrand Reinhold.

Linville, J (ed.). 1990. *Industrial Fire Hazards Handbook.* Quincy, Mass.: NFPA.

Loss Prevention Council. 1992. *Fire Prevention On Construction Sites.* London: Loss Prevention Council.

Manz, A. 1991. Welding and cutting. Chap. 14, Section 2 in *Fire Protection Handbook*, 17th ed., edited by AE Cote. Quincy, Mass.: NFPA.

National Fire Protection Association (NFPA). 1983. *Firesafety Educator's Handbook: A Comprehensive Guide to*

Planning, Designing, and Implementing Firesafety Programs. FSO-61. Quincy, Mass.: NFPA.

—. 1990a. *Standard System for the Identification of the Fire Hazards of Materials.* NFPA No. 704. Quincy, Mass.: NFPA.

—. 1995a. *Guide to the Fire Safety Concepts Tree.* NFPA No. 550. Quincy, Mass.: NFPA.

—. 1995b. *Standard for the Installation of Lighting Protection Systems.* NFPA No.780. Quincy, Mass.: NFPA.

—. 1992. *Fire Prevention Code.* NFPA No.1. Quincy, Mass.: NFPA.

Osterhout, C. 1990. *Public Fire Education.* IFSTA No. 606. Stillwater, Okla.: International Fire Services Training Association (IFSTA).

Ostrowski, R. 1991. Oil quenching. *Fire Protection Handbook*, 17th ed., edited by AE Cote. Quincy, Mass.: NFPA.

Palmer, KN. 1973. *Dust Explosion and Fires.* London: Chapman & Hall.

Simmons, JM. 1990. Heat processing equipment. In *Industrial Fire Hazards Handbook.* Quincy, Mass.: NFPA.

Welch, J. 1993. The changing face of FPA training: Fire prevention. *Fire Prev* (July/August):261.

Welty, JR, RE Wilson, and CE Wicks. 1976. *Fundamentals of Momentun, Heat and Mass Transfer.* New York: John Wiley & Sons.

Watts, KI. 1990. Oil quenching. In *Industrial Fire Hazards Handbook*, edited by J Linville. Quincy, Mass.: NFPA.

Other relevant readings

Barry, TJ and B Newman. 1976. Some problems of synthetic polymers at elevated temperatures. *Fire Technol* 12(3):186-192.

Berta, I and I Fodor. 1990. Electrostatical ignition sources. In *Fire and Explosion Safety*, edited by T Kompolthy. Budapest: Mûszaki Köyvkiadó.

Boddington, T, JF Griffiths, and K Hasegawa. 1984. Induction times to thermal ignition in systems with distributed temperatures: An experimental test of theoretical interpretations. *Combust Flame* 55(3):297.

Boyle, AR and FJ Llewellyn. 1950. The electrostatic ignitability of dust clouds and powders. *J Appl Chem* 69:173-181.

Bryan, JL. 1991a. Concept of egress design. In *Fire Protection Handbook*, edited by AE Cote. Quincy, MA: NFPA.

—. 1991b. Human behaviour and fire. In *Fire Protection Handbook*, edited by AE Cote. Quincy,MA: NFPA.

—. 1991c. Traffic and exit drill. In *Fire Protection Handbook*, edited by AE Cote. Quincy, MA: NFPA.

Canter, D. 1985. *Studies of Human Behaviour in Fire: Empirical Results and Their Implications for Education and Design.* Herts: Department of Environment, Building Research Establishment, Fire Research Station.

Chamberlain, DL. 1983. *Heat Release Rate Properties of Wood-Based Materials.* NBSIR 82-2597. Washington, DC: National Bureau of Standards.

Coffe, RD. 1971. Evaluation of chemical stability. *Fire Technol* 7(1):37-45.

Dean, JA. 1984. *Lange's Handbook of Chemistry.* Sandusky,OH: Handbook Publishers.

DeHaan, N. 1991. Interior finish. In *Fire Protection Handbook*, edited by AE Cote. Quincy, MA: NFPA.

Donoghue, EA. 1991. Building transportation system. In *Fire Protection Handbook*, edited by AE Cote. Quincy, MA: NFPA.

Eggleston, LA and AJ Pryor. 1967. The limits of dust explosibility. *Fire Technol* 3(2):77-89.

Eurocode 1: Basis of Design and Actions on Structures. Part 2.2: Actions on Structures Exposed to Fire (1991-2-2): CEN, ENV 1991-2-2.

Goodall, DG and R Ingle. 1967. The ignition of flammable liquids by hot surfaces. *Fire Technol* 3(2):115-128.

Gordon, BF. 1981. Flame retardants and textile material. *Fire Safety J* 4:109-123.

Griffith, JF and JR Mullins. 1984. Ignition, self-heating, and the effects of added gases during the thermal decomposition of di-t-butyl peroxide. *Combust Flame* 56(2):135.

Hanson, RJ and A Thomas. 1984. Flame development in swirling flows in closed vessels. *Combust Flame* 55(3):255.

Harley, CS. 1991. Building and site planning for firesafety. In *Fire Protection Handbook*, edited by AE Cote. Quincy, MA: NFPA.

Hilado, CJ. 1982. *Flammability Handbook for Plastics.* Lancaster, PA: Technomic Publishing.

Hilado, CJ and HJ Cumming. 1977. The HC value: A method of estimating the flammability of mixtures of combustible gases. *Fire Technol* 13(3):195.

Hirschler, MM. 1992. Smoke and heat release and ignitability as measures of fire hazard from burning of carpet tiles. *Fire Safety J* 18(4):305.

Hommel, G. 1987. *Handbuch Der Gefährlichen Güter.* Berlin: Springer Verlag.

Ihrig, AM and SL Smith. 1994. The role of alkali and alkaline earth metal ions in cellulosic smoldering. *J Fire Sci* 12(4):357.

Janssens, M. 1991. Piloted ignition of wood: A review. *Fire Mater* 15(4):151.

Karter, MJJ. 1991. Fire loss in the United States during 1990. *NFPA J* September/October:36.

Klote, JH. 1992. *Design of Smoke Management Systems.* Atlanta: .

Martin, JT and B Miller. 1978. The thermal and flammability behaviour of polyester-wool blends. *Textile Res J* 48:97-103.

Mizuno, T and K Kawagoe. 1986. Burning behaviour of upholstered chairs: Part 3, Flame and plume characteristics in fire test. *Fire Sci Technol* 6(12):29.

Nagy, J, HG Dorset, and M Jacobson. 1964. *Preventing Ignition of Dust Dispersions By Inerting.* Pittsburgh, PA: USDI, Bureau of Mines. (RI6543)

Nishimoto, T, M Morita, and H Yajima. 1986. Spontaneous combustion of coal (III) (Isothermal Method). *Fire Sci Technol* 6(1 and 2):1.

Ohlemiller, TJ and FE Rogers. 1978. A survey of several factors influencing smolder combustion in flexible and rigid polymer foams. *J Fire Flamm* 9:489-509.

Ohtani, H. 1990. Theoretical consideration on the ignition of hot iron in high pressure oxygen. *Fire Sci Technol* 10(1 and 2):1.

Pál, K and H Macskásy. 1980. *Plastics and their Combustibility.* Budapest: Mûszaki Könyvkiadó.

Perry, JH and CH Chilton. 1974. *Chemical Engineers' Handbook.* New York: McGraw-Hill.

Purser, DA and WD Woolley. 1983. Biological studies of combustion atmospheres. *J Fire Sci* 1(2):118.

Rasbash, DJ. 1980. Review of explosion and fire hazard of liquified petroleum gas. *Fire Safety J* 2(4):223-236.

SFPE and NFPA. 1988. *The SFPA Handbook of Fire Protection Engineering.* Quincy, MA: SFPE.

Sharma, TP and S Kumar. 1992. Products of combustion of the metal powders. *Fire Sci Technol* 12(2):29.

Sugawa, O and H Yamamoto. 1989. Reduction of Smoke Particles from Fire Retarded Wood. *Fire Sci Technol* 9(1):1.

Tewarson, A. 1975. *Flammability of Polymers and Organic Liquids, Part I, Burning Intensity.* Norwood, MA: Factory Mutual Research Corp.

—. 1994. Flammability parameters of materials: Ignition, combustion, and fire propagation. *Fire Safety J* 12(4):329.

Tewarson, A and DP Macaion. 1993. Polymers and composites—An examination of fire spread and generation of heat and fire products. *J Fire Sci* 11(5):421.

Thorne, PF. 1976. Flashpoints of mixtures of flammable and non-flammable liquids. *Fire Mater* 1:134-140.

White, RH and EV Nordheim. 1992. Charring rate of wood for ASTM E 119 exposure. *Fire Technol* 28(1):5.

41. FIRE

42

Chapter Editor
Jean-Jacques Vogt

Contents

42. HEAT AND COLD

PHYSIOLOGICAL RESPONSES TO THE THERMAL ENVIRONMENT

W. Larry Kenney

Humans live their entire lives within a very small, fiercely protected range of internal body temperatures. The maximal tolerance limits for living cells range from about 0 °C (ice crystal formation) to about 45 °C (thermal coagulation of intracellular proteins); however, humans can tolerate internal temperatures below 35 °C or above 41 °C for only very brief periods of time. To maintain internal temperature within these limits, people have developed very effective and in some instances specialized physiological responses to acute thermal stresses. These responses—designed to facilitate the conservation, production or elimination of body heat—involve the finely controlled coordination of several body systems.

Human Thermal Balance

By far, the largest source of heat imparted to the body results from metabolic heat production *(M)*. Even at peak mechanical efficiency, 75 to 80% of the energy involved in muscular work is liberated as heat. At rest, a metabolic rate of 300 ml O_2 per minute creates a heat load of approximately 100 Watts. During steady-state work at an oxygen consumption of 1 l/min, approximately 350 W of heat are generated—less any energy associated with external work *(W)*. Even at such a mild to moderate work intensity, body core temperature would rise approximately one degree centigrade every 15 min were it not for an efficient means of heat dissipation. In fact, very fit individuals can produce heat in excess of 1,200 W for 1 to 3 hours without heat injury (Gisolfi and Wenger 1984).

Heat can also be gained from the environment via radiation *(R)* and convection *(C)* if the globe temperature (a measure of radiant heat) and air (dry-bulb) temperature, respectively, exceed skin temperature. These avenues of heat gain are typically small relative to *M*, and actually become avenues of heat loss when the skin-to-air thermal gradient is reversed. The final avenue for heat loss—evaporation *(E)*—is also typically the most important, since the latent heat of vaporization of sweat is high—approximately 680 W-h/l of sweat evaporated. These relations are discussed elsewhere in this chapter.

Under cool to thermoneutral conditions, heat gain is balanced by heat loss, no heat is stored, and body temperature equilibrates; that is:

$$M - W \pm R \pm C - E = 0$$

However, in more severe exposure to heat:

$$M - W \pm R \pm C > E$$

and heat is stored. In particular, heavy work (high energy expenditure which increases $M - W$), excessively high air temperatures (which increase $R + C$), high humidity (which limits *E*) and the wearing of thick or relatively impermeable clothing (which creates a barrier to effective evaporation of sweat) create such a scenario. Finally, if exercise is prolonged or hydration inadequate, *E* may be outstripped by the limited ability of the body to secrete sweat (1 to 2 l/h for short periods).

Body Temperature and Its Control

For purposes of describing physiological responses to heat and cold, the body is divided into two components—the "core" and the "shell". Core temperature (T_c) represents internal or deep body temperature, and can be measured orally, rectally or, in laboratory settings, in the oesophagus or on the tympanic membrane (eardrum). The temperature of the shell is represented by mean skin temperature (T_{sk}). The average temperature of the body (T_b) at any time is a weighted balance between these temperatures, that is

$$T_b = k\, T_c + (1-k)\, T_{sk}$$

where the weighting factor *k* varies from about 0.67 to 0.90.

When confronted with challenges to thermal neutrality (heat or cold stresses), the body strives to control T_c through physiological adjustments, and T_c provides the major feedback to the brain to coordinate this control. While the local and mean skin temperature are important for providing sensory input, T_{sk} varies greatly with ambient temperature, averaging about 33 °C at thermoneutrality and reaching 36 to 37 °C under conditions of heavy work in the heat. It can drop considerably during whole-body and local exposure to cold; tactile sensitivity occurs between 15 and 20 °C, whereas the critical temperature for manual dexterity is between 12 and 16 °C. The upper and lower pain threshold values for T_{sk} are approximately 43 °C and 10 °C, respectively.

Precise mapping studies have localized the site of greatest thermoregulatory control in an area of the brain known as the pre-optic/anterior hypothalamus (POAH). In this region are nerve cells which respond to both heating (warm-sensitive neurons) and cooling (cold-sensitive neurons). This area dominates control of body temperature by receiving afferent sensory information about body temperature and sending efferent signals to the skin, the muscles and other organs involved in temperature regulation, via the autonomic nervous system. Other areas of the central nervous system (posterior hypothalamus, reticular formation, pons, medulla and spinal cord) form ascending and descending connections with the POAH, and serve a variety of facilitory functions.

The body's control system is analogous to thermostatic control of temperature in a house with both heating and cooling capabilities. When body temperature rises above some theoretical "set point" temperature, effector responses associated with cooling (sweating, increasing skin blood flow) are turned on. When body temperature falls below the set point, heat gain responses (decreasing skin blood flow, shivering) are initiated. Unlike home heating/cooling systems however, the human thermoregulatory control system does not operate as a simple on-off system, but also has proportional control and rate-of-change control characteristics. It should be appreciated that a "set point temperature" exists in theory only, and thus is useful in visualizing these concepts. Much work is yet to be done toward a full understanding of the mechanisms associated with the thermoregulatory set point.

Whatever its basis, the set point is relatively stable and is unaffected by work or ambient temperature. In fact, the only acute perturbation known to shift the set point is the group of endogenous pyrogens involved in the febrile response. The effector responses employed by the body to maintain thermal balance are initiated and controlled in response to a "load error", that is, a body temperature which is transiently above or below the set point (figure 42.1). A core temperature below the set point creates a negative load error, resulting in heat gain (shivering, vasoconstriction of the skin) being initiated. A core temperature above the set point creates a positive load error, leading to heat loss effectors (skin vasodilatation, sweating) being turned on. In each case, the resultant heat transfer decreases the load error and helps return the body temperature to a steady state.

Temperature Regulation in the Heat

As mentioned above, humans lose heat to the environment primarily through a combination of dry (radiation and convection) and evaporative means. To facilitate this exchange, two primary effector systems are turned on and regulated—skin vasodilatation and sweating. While skin vasodilatation often results in small increases in dry (radiative and convective) heat loss, it functions primarily to transfer heat from the core to the skin (internal heat transfer), while evaporation of sweat provides an extremely effective means of cooling the blood prior to its return to deep body tissues (external heat transfer).

Skin vasodilatation

The amount of heat transferred from the core to the skin is a function of the skin blood flow (SkBF), the temperature gradient between core and skin, and the specific heat of blood (a little less than 4 kJ/°C per litre of blood). At rest in a thermoneutral environment, the skin gets approximately 200 to 500 ml/min of blood flow, representing only 5 to 10% of the total blood pumped by the heart (cardiac output). Because of the 4 °C gradient between T_c (about 37 °C) and T_{sk} (about 33 °C under such conditions), the metabolic heat produced by the body to sustain life is constantly convected to the skin for dissipation. By contrast, under conditions of severe hyperthermia such as high-intensity work in hot conditions, the core-to-skin thermal gradient is smaller, and the necessary heat transfer is accomplished by large increases in SkBF. Under maximal heat stress, SkBF can reach 7 to 8 l/min, about one-third of cardiac output (Rowell 1983). This high blood flow is achieved through a poorly understood mechanism unique to humans which has been called the "active vasodilator system". Active vasodilatation involves sympathetic nerve signals from the hypothalamus to the skin arterioles, but the neurotransmitter has not been determined.

As mentioned above, SkBF is primarily responsive to increases in T_c and, to a lesser extent, T_{sk}. T_c rises as muscular work is initiated and metabolic heat production begins, and once some threshold T_c is reached, SkBF also begins to increase dramatically. This basic thermoregulatory relationship is also acted upon by non-thermal factors. This second level of control is critical in that it modifies SkBF when overall cardiovascular stability is threatened. The veins in the skin are very compliant, and a significant portion of the circulating volume pools in these vessels. This aids in heat exchange by slowing the capillary circulation to increase transit time; however, this pooling, coupled with fluid losses from sweating, may also decrease the rate of blood return to the heart. Among the non-thermal factors which have been shown to influence SkBF during work are upright posture, dehydration and positive-pressure breathing (respirator use). These act through reflexes which are turned on when cardiac filling pressure is decreased and stretch receptors located in the large veins and right atrium are unloaded, and are therefore most evident during prolonged aerobic work in an upright posture. These reflexes function to maintain arterial pressure and, in the case of work, to maintain adequate blood flow to active muscles. Thus, the level of SkBF at any given point in time represents the aggregate effects of thermoregulatory and non-thermoregulatory reflex responses.

The need to increase blood flow to the skin to aid in temperature regulation greatly impacts on the ability of the cardiovascular system to regulate blood pressure. For this reason, a coordinated response of the entire cardiovascular system to heat stress is necessary. What cardiovascular adjustments occur that allow for this increase in cutaneous flow and volume? During work in cool or thermoneutral conditions, the needed increase in cardiac output is well supported by increasing heart rate (HR), since further increases in stroke volume (SV) are minimal beyond exercise intensities of 40% of maximum. In the heat, HR is higher at any given work intensity as compensation for the reduced central blood volume (CBV) and SV. At higher levels of work, maximal heart rate is reached, and this tachycardia is therefore incapable of sustaining the necessary cardiac output. The second way in which the body supplies a high SkBF is by distributing blood flow away

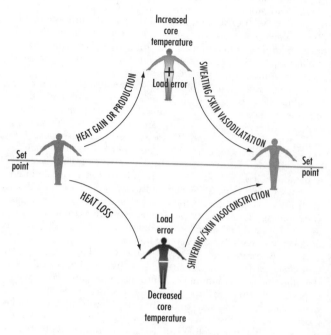

Figure 42.1 • A model of thermoregulation in the human body.

from such areas as the liver, kidneys and intestines (Rowell 1983). This redirection of flow can provide an additional 800 to 1,000 ml of blood flow to the skin, and helps offset the detrimental effects of peripheral pooling of blood.

Sweating

Thermoregulatory sweat in humans is secreted from 2 to 4 million eccrine sweat glands scattered non-uniformly over the body surface. Unlike apocrine sweat glands, which tend to be clustered (on the face and hands and in the axial and genital regions) and which secrete sweat into hair follicles, eccrine glands secrete sweat directly onto the skin surface. This sweat is odourless, colourless and relatively dilute, since it is an ultrafiltrate of plasma. Thus it has a high latent heat of vaporization and is ideally suited for its cooling purpose.

As an example of the effectiveness of this cooling system, a man working at an oxygen cost of 2.3 l/min produces a net metabolic heat ($M - W$) of about 640 W. Without sweating, body temperature would increase at a rate of about 1 °C every 6 to 7 min. With efficient evaporation of about 16 g of sweat per minute (a reasonable rate), the rate of heat loss can match the rate of heat production, and body core temperature can be maintained at a steady state; that is,

$$M - W \pm R \pm C - E = 0$$

Eccrine glands are simple in structure, consisting of a coiled secretory portion, a duct and a skin pore. The volume of sweat produced by each gland is dependent upon both the structure and the function of the gland, and total sweating rate in turn depends on both the recruitment of glands (active sweat gland density) and sweat gland output. The fact that some people sweat more heavily than others is attributable mainly to differences in sweat gland size (Sato and Sato 1983). Heat acclimation is another major determinant of sweat production. With ageing, lower sweating rates are attributable not to fewer activated eccrine glands, but to a decreased sweat output per gland (Kenney and Fowler 1988). This decline probably relates to a combination of structural and functional alterations which accompany the ageing process.

Like vasomotor signals, nerve impulses to the sweat glands originate in the POAH and descend through the brainstem. The fibres which innervate the glands are sympathetic cholinergic fibres, a rare combination in the human body. While acetylcholine is the primary neurotransmitter, adrenergic transmitters (catecholamines) also stimulate eccrine glands.

In many ways, control of sweating is analogous to control of skin blood flow. Both have similar onset characteristics (threshold) and linear relationships to increasing T_c. The back and chest tend to have earlier onsets of sweating, and the slopes for the relationship of local sweat rate to T_c are steepest for these sites. Like SkBF, sweating is modified by non-thermal factors such as hypohydration and hyperosmolality. Also worth noting is a phenomenon called "hidromeiosis", which occurs in very humid environments or on skin areas constantly covered with wet clothing. Such areas of skin, due to their continuously wet state, decrease sweat output. This serves as a protective mechanism against continued dehydration, since sweat which stays on the skin rather than evaporating serves no cooling function.

If sweating rate is adequate, evaporative cooling is determined ultimately by the water vapour pressure gradient between the wet skin and the air surrounding it. Thus, high humidity and heavy or impermeable clothing limit evaporative cooling, while dry air, air movement about the body and minimal, porous clothing facilitate evaporation. On the other hand, if work is heavy and sweating profuse, evaporative cooling can likewise be limited by the body's ability to produce sweat (maximally about 1 to 2 l/h).

Temperature Regulation in the Cold

One important difference in the way humans respond to cold compared to heat is that behaviour plays a much greater role in thermoregulatory response to cold. For example, wearing appropriate clothing and assuming postures which minimize surface area available for heat loss ("huddling") are far more important in cold ambient conditions than in the heat. A second difference is the greater role played by hormones during cold stress, including the increased secretion of catecholamines (norepinephrine and epinephrine) and thyroid hormones.

Skin vasoconstriction

An effective strategy against heat loss from the body through radiation and convection is to increase the effective insulation provided by the shell. In humans this is accomplished by decreasing blood flow to the skin—that is, by skin vasoconstriction. Constriction of the cutaneous vessels is more pronounced in the extremities than on the trunk. Like active vasodilatation, skin vasoconstriction is also controlled by the sympathetic nervous system, and is influenced by T_c, T_{sk} and local temperatures.

The effect of skin cooling on the heart rate and blood pressure response varies with the area of the body which is cooled, and whether the cold is severe enough to cause pain. For example, when the hands are immersed in cold water, HR, systolic blood pressure (SBP) and diastolic blood pressure (DBP) all increase. When the face is cooled, SBP and DBP increase due to the generalized sympathetic response; however, HR goes down due to a parasympathetic reflex (LeBlanc 1975). To further confound the complexity of the overall response to cold, there is a wide range of variability in responses from one person to another. If the cold stress is of sufficient magnitude to decrease body core temperature, HR may either increase (due to sympathetic activation) or decrease (due to the increased central blood volume).

A specific case of interest is termed *cold-induced vasodilatation* (CIVD). When the hands are placed in cold water, SkBF initially

decreases to conserve heat. As tissue temperatures drop, SkBF paradoxically increases, decreases again, and repeats this cyclical pattern. It has been suggested that CIVD is beneficial in preventing tissue damage from freezing, but this is unproven. Mechanistically, the transient dilation probably occurs when the direct effects of the cold are severe enough to decrease nerve transmission, which transiently overrides the effect of the cold on the blood vessel sympathetic receptors (mediating the constrictor effect).

Shivering

As body cooling progresses, the second line of defence is shivering. Shivering is the random involuntary contraction of superficial muscle fibres, which does not limit heat loss but rather increases heat production. Since such contractions do not produce any work, heat is generated. A resting person can increase his or her metabolic heat production about three- to fourfold during intense shivering, and can increase T_c by 0.5 °C. The signals to initiate shivering arise principally from the skin, and, in addition to the POAH region of the brain, the posterior hypothalamus is also involved to a large extent.

Although many individual factors contribute to shivering (and cold tolerance in general), one important factor is body fatness. A man with very little subcutaneous fat (2 to 3 mm thickness) starts shivering after 40 min at 15 °C and 20 min at 10 °C, while a man who has more insulating fat (11 mm) may not shiver at all at 15 °C and after 60 min at 10 °C (LeBlanc 1975).

EFFECTS OF HEAT STRESS AND WORK IN THE HEAT

Bodil Nielsen

When a person is exposed to warm environmental conditions the physiological heat loss mechanisms are activated in order to maintain normal body temperature. Heat fluxes between the body and the environment depend on the temperature difference between:

1. the surrounding air and objects like walls, windows, the sky, and so on
2. the surface temperature of the person

The surface temperature of the person is regulated by physiological mechanisms, such as variations in the blood flow to the skin, and by evaporation of sweat secreted by the sweat glands. Also, the person can change clothing to vary the heat exchange with the environment. The warmer the environmental conditions, the smaller the difference between surrounding temperatures and skin or clothing surface temperature. This means that the "dry heat exchange" by convection and radiation is reduced in warm compared to cool conditions. At environmental temperatures above the surface temperature, heat is gained from the surroundings. In this case this extra heat together with that liberated by the metabolic processes must be lost through evaporation of sweat for the maintenance of body temperature. Thus evaporation of sweat becomes more and more critical with increasing environmental temperature. Given the importance of sweat evaporation it is not surprising that wind velocity and air humidity (water vapour pressure) are critical environmental factors in hot conditions. If the humidity is high, sweat is still produced but evaporation is reduced. Sweat which cannot evaporate has no cooling effect; it drips off and is wasted from a thermoregulatory point of view.

The human body contains approximately 60% water, about 35 to 40 l in an adult person. About one-third of the water in the body, the extracellular fluid, is distributed between the cells and in the vascular system (the blood plasma). The remaining two-thirds of the body water, the intracellular fluid, is located inside the cells. The composition and the volume of the body water compartments is very precisely controlled by hormonal and neural mechanisms. Sweat is secreted from the millions of sweat glands on the skin surface when the thermoregulatory centre is activated by an increase in body temperature. The sweat contains salt (NaCl, sodium chloride) but to a lesser extent than the extracellular fluid. Thus, both water and salt are lost and must be replaced after sweating.

Effects of Sweat Loss

In neutral, comfortable, environmental conditions, small amounts of water are lost by diffusion through the skin. However, during hard work and in hot conditions, large quantities of sweat can be produced by active sweat glands, up to more than 2 l/h for several hours. Even a sweat loss of only 1% of body weight ($\approx$ 600 to 700 ml) has a measurable effect on the ability to perform work. This is seen by a rise in heart rate (HR) (HR increases about five beats per minute for each per cent loss of body water) and a rise in body core temperature. If work is continued there is a gradual increase in body temperature, which can rise to a value around 40 °C; at this temperature, heat illness may result. This is partly due to the loss of fluid from the vascular system (figure 42.2). A loss of water from the blood plasma reduces the amount of blood which fills the central veins and the heart. Each heart beat will therefore pump a smaller stroke volume. As a consequence the cardiac output (the amount of blood which is expelled by the heart per minute) tends to fall, and the heart rate must increase in order to maintain the circulation and the blood pressure.

Figure 42.2 • Calculated distributions of water in the extracellular compartment (ECW) and intracellular compartment (ICW) before and after 2 h of exercise dehydration at 30 °C room temperature.

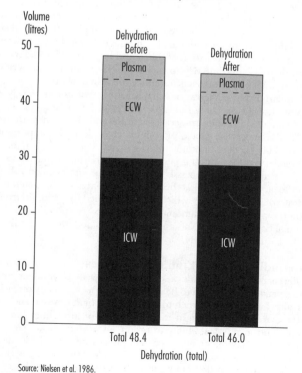

Source: Nielsen et al. 1986.

Table 42.1 • Electrolyte concentration in blood plasma and in sweat.

Electrolytes and other substances	Blood plasma concentrations (g per l)	Sweat concentrations (g per l)
Sodium (Na+)	3.5	0.2–1.5
Potassium (K+)	0.15	0.15
Calcium (Ca++)	0.1	small amounts
Magnesium (Mg++)	0.02	small amounts
Chloride (Cl−)	3.5	0.2–1.5
Bicarbonate (HCO3−)	1.5	small amounts
Proteins	70	0
Fats, glucose, small ions	15–20	small amounts

Adapted from Vellar 1969.

A physiological control system called the baroreceptor reflex system maintains the cardiac output and blood pressure close to normal under all conditions. The reflexes involve receptors, sensors in the heart and in the arterial system (aorta and carotid arteries), which monitor the degree of stretching of the heart and vessels by the blood which fills them. Impulses from these travel through nerves to the central nervous system, from which adjustments, in case of dehydration, cause a constriction in the blood vessels and a reduction in blood flow to splanchnic organs (liver, gut, kidneys) and to the skin. In this way the available blood flow is redistributed to favour circulation to the working muscles and to the brain (Rowell 1986).

Severe dehydration may lead to heat exhaustion and circulatory collapse; in this case the person cannot maintain the blood pressure, and fainting is the consequence. In heat exhaustion, symptoms are physical exhaustion, often together with headache, dizziness and nausea. The main cause of heat exhaustion is the circulatory strain induced by water loss from the vascular system. The decline in blood volume leads to reflexes which reduce circulation to the intestines and the skin. The reduction in skin blood flow aggravates the situation, since heat loss from the surface decreases, so the core temperature increases further. The subject may faint due to a fall in blood pressure and the resulting low blood flow to the brain. The lying position improves the blood supply to the heart and brain, and after cooling and having some water to drink the person regains his or her well-being almost immediately.

If the processes causing the heat exhaustion "run wild", it develops into heat stroke. The gradual reduction in skin circulation makes the temperature rise more and more, and this leads to a reduction, even a stop in sweating and an even faster rise in core temperature, which causes circulatory collapse and may result in death, or irreversible damage to the brain. Changes in the blood (such as high osmolality, low pH, hypoxia, cell adherence of the red blood cells, intravascular coagulation) and damage to the nervous system are findings in heat stroke patients. The reduced blood supply to the gut during heat stress can provoke tissue damage, and substances (endotoxins) may be liberated which induce fever in connection with heat stroke (Hales and Richards 1987). Heat stroke is an acute, life-threatening emergency further discussed in the section on "heat disorders".

Together with water loss, sweating produces a loss of electrolytes, mainly sodium (Na+) and chloride (Cl−), but also to a lesser degree magnesium (Mg++), potassium (K+) and so on (see table 42.1). The sweat contains less salt than the body fluid compartments. This means that they become more salty after sweat loss. The increased saltiness seems to have a specific effect on the circulation via effects on vascular smooth muscle, which controls the degree to which the vessels are open. However, it is shown by several investigators to interfere with the ability to sweat, in such a way that it takes a higher body temperature to stimulate the sweat glands—the sensitivity of the sweat glands becomes reduced (Nielsen 1984). If the sweat loss is replaced only by water, this may lead to a situation where the body contains less sodium chloride than in the normal state (hypo-osmotic). This will cause cramps due to the malfunction of nerves and muscles, a condition known in earlier days as "miner's cramps" or "stoker's cramps". It can be prevented by addition of salt to the diet (drinking beer was a suggested preventive measure in the UK in the 1920s!).

The decreased skin circulation and sweat gland activity both affect thermoregulation and heat loss in such a way that core temperature will increase more than in the fully hydrated state.

In many different trades, workers are exposed to external heat stress—for example, workers in steel plants, glass industries, paper mills, bakeries, mining industries. Also chimney sweeps and firefighters are exposed to external heat. People who work in confined spaces in vehicles, ships and aircraft may also suffer from heat. However, it must be noted that persons working in protective suits or doing hard work in waterproof clothes can be victims of heat exhaustion even in moderate and cool environmental temperature conditions. Adverse effects of heat stress occur in conditions where the core temperature is elevated and the sweat loss is high.

Rehydration

The effects of dehydration due to sweat loss may be reversed by drinking enough to replace the sweat. This will usually take place during recovery after work and exercise. However, during prolonged work in hot environments, performance is improved by drinking during activity. The common advice is thus to drink when thirsty.

But, there are some very important problems in this. One is that the urge to drink is not strong enough to replace the simultaneously occurring water loss; and secondly, the time needed to replace a large water deficit is very long, more than 12 hours. Lastly, there is a limit to the rate at which water can pass from the stomach (where it is stored) to the intestine (gut), where the absorption takes place. This rate is lower than observed sweat rates during exercise in hot conditions.

There have been a large number of studies on various beverages to restore body water, electrolytes and carbohydrate stores of athletes during prolonged exercise. The main findings are as follows:

- The amount of the fluid which can be utilized—that is, transported through the stomach to the intestine—is limited by the "gastric emptying rate", which has a maximum of about 1,000 ml/h.
- If the fluid is "hyperosmotic" (contains ions/molecules in higher concentrations than the blood) the rate is slowed down. On the other hand "iso-osmotic fluids" (containing water and ions/molecules to the same concentration, osmolality, as blood) are passed at the same rate as pure water.
- Addition of small amounts of salt and sugar increases the rate of uptake of water from the gut (Maughan 1991).

With this in mind you can make your own "rehydration fluid" or choose from a large number of commercial products. Normally water and electrolyte balance is regained by drinking in connection with meals. Workers or athletes with large sweat losses should be encouraged to drink more than their urge. Sweat contains about 1 to 3 g of NaCl per litre. This means that sweat losses of above 5 l per day may cause a deficiency in sodium chloride, unless the diet is supplemented.

Workers and athletes are also counselled to control their water balance by weighing themselves regularly—for example, in the morning (at same time and condition)—and try to maintain a constant weight. However, a change in body weight does not necessarily reflect the degree of hypohydration. Water is chemically bound to glycogen, the carbohydrate store in the muscles, and liberated when glycogen is used during exercise. Weight changes of up to about 1 kg may occur, depending on the glycogen content of the body. The body weight "morning to morning" also shows changes due to "biological variations" in water contents—for example, in women in relation to the menstrual cycle up to 1 to 2 kg of water can be retained during the premenstrual phase ("premenstrual tension").

The control of water and electrolytes

The volume of the body water compartments—that is, the extracellular and intracellular fluid volumes—and their concentrations of electrolytes is held very constant through a regulated balance between intake and loss of fluid and substances.

Water is gained from the intake of food and fluid, and some is liberated by metabolic processes, including combustion of fat and carbohydrates from food. The loss of water takes place from the lungs during breathing, where the inspired air takes up water in the lungs from moist surfaces in the airways before it is exhaled. Water also diffuses through the skin in small amount in comfortable conditions during rest. However, during sweating water can be lost at rates of more than 1 to 2 l/h for several hours. The body water content is controlled. Increased water loss by sweating is compensated for by drinking and by a reduction in urine formation, while excess water is excreted by increased urine production.

This control both of intake and output of water is exerted through the autonomic nervous system, and by hormones. Thirst will increase the water intake, and the water loss by the kidneys is regulated; both the volume and electrolyte composition of urine are under control. The sensors in the control mechanism are in the heart, responding to the "fullness" of the vascular system. If the filling of the heart is reduced—for example, after a sweat loss—the receptors will signal this message to the brain centres responsible for the sensation of thirst, and to areas which induce a liberation of anti-diuretic hormone (ADH) from the posterior pituitary. This hormone acts to reduce the urine volume.

Similarly, physiological mechanisms control the electrolyte composition of the body fluids via processes in the kidneys. The food contains nutrients, minerals, vitamins and electrolytes. In the present context, the intake of sodium chloride is the important issue. The dietary sodium intake varies with eating habits, between 10 and 20 to 30 g per day. This is normally much more than is needed, so the excess is excreted by the kidneys, controlled by the action of multiple hormonal mechanisms (angiotensin, aldosterone, ANF, etc.) which are controlled by stimuli from osmoreceptors in the brain and in the kidneys, responding to the osmolality of primarily Na^+ and Cl^- in the blood and in the fluid in the kidneys, respectively.

Interindividual and Ethnic Differences

Differences between male and female as well as younger and older persons in reaction to heat might be expected. They differ in certain characteristics which might influence heat transfer, such as surface area, height/weight ratio, thickness of insulating skin fat layers, and in physical ability to produce work and heat (aerobic capacity ≈ maximal oxygen consumption rate). Available data suggest that heat tolerance is reduced in older persons. They start to sweat later than do young individuals, and older people react with a higher blood flow in their skin during heat exposure.

Comparing the sexes it has been observed that women tolerate humid heat better than men do. In this environment the evaporation of sweat is reduced, so the slightly greater surface/mass area in women could be to their advantage. However, aerobic capacity is an important factor to be considered when comparing individuals exposed to heat. In laboratory conditions the physiological responses to heat are similar, if groups of subjects with the same physical work capacity ("maximal oxygen uptake"—$VO_{2\ max}$) are tested—for instance, younger and older males, or males versus females (Pandolf et al. 1988). In this case a certain work task (exercise on a bicycle ergometer) will result in the same load on the circulatory system—that is, the same heart rate and the same rise in core temperature—independent of age and sex.

The same considerations are valid for comparison between ethnic groups. When differences in size and aerobic capacity are taken into account, no significant differences due to race can be pointed out. But in daily life in general, older persons do have, on average, a lower $VO_{2\ max}$ than younger persons, and females a lower $VO_{2\ max}$ than males in the same age group.

Therefore, when performing a specific task which consists of a certain absolute work rate (measured, e.g., in Watts), the person with a lower aerobic capacity will have a higher heart rate and body temperature and be less able to cope with the extra strain of external heat, than one with a higher $VO_{2\ max}$.

For occupational health and safety purposes a number of heat stress indices have been developed. In these the large interindividual variation in response to heat and work are taken into account, as well as the specific hot environments for which the index is constructed. These are treated elsewhere in this chapter.

Persons exposed repeatedly to heat will tolerate the heat better after even a few days. They become acclimatized. Sweating rate is increased and the resulting increased cooling of the skin leads to a lower core temperature and heart rate during work under the same conditions.

Therefore, artificial acclimation of personnel who are expected to be exposed to extreme heat (firefighters, rescue personnel, military personnel) will probably be of benefit to reduce the strain.

Summing up, the more heat a person produces, the more must be dissipated. In a hot environment the evaporation of sweat is the limiting factor for heat loss. Interindividual differences in the capacity for sweating are considerable. While some persons have no sweat glands at all, in most cases, with physical training and repeated exposure to heat, the amount of sweat produced in a standard heat stress test is increased. Heat stress results in an increase in heart rate and core temperature. Maximal heart rate and/or a core temperature of about 40°C sets the absolute physiological limit for work performance in a hot environment (Nielsen 1994).

HEAT DISORDERS

Tokuo Ogawa

High environmental temperature, high humidity, strenuous exercise or impaired heat dissipation may cause a variety of heat disorders. They include heat syncope, heat oedema, heat cramps, heat exhaustion and heat stroke as systemic disorders, and skin lesions as local disorders.

Systemic Disorders

Heat cramps, heat exhaustion and heat stroke are of clinical importance. The mechanisms underlying the development of these systemic disorders are circulatory insufficiency, water and electrolyte imbalance and/or hyperthermia (high body temperature). The most severe of all is heat stroke, which may lead to death unless promptly and properly treated.

Two distinct populations are at risk of developing heat disorders, excluding infants. The first and the larger population is the elderly, especially the poor and those with chronic conditions, such as diabetes mellitus, obesity, malnutrition, congestive heart failure, chronic alcoholism, dementia and the need to use medications that interfere with thermoregulation. The second population at risk of suffering heat disorders comprises healthy individuals who attempt prolonged physical exertion or are exposed to excessive heat stress. Factors predisposing active young people to heat disorders, other than congenital and acquired sweat gland dysfunction, include poor physical fitness, lack of acclimatization, low work efficiency and a reduced ratio of skin area to body mass.

Heat syncope

Syncope is a transient loss of consciousness resulting from a reduction of cerebral blood flow, preceded frequently by pallor, blurring of vision, dizziness and nausea. It may occur in persons suffering from heat stress. The term *heat collapse* has been used synonymously with *heat syncope*. The symptoms have been attributed to cutaneous vasodilatation, postural pooling of blood with consequently diminished venous return to the heart, and reduced cardiac output. Mild dehydration, which develops in most persons exposed to heat, contributes to the probability of heat syncope. Individuals who suffer from cardiovascular diseases or who are unacclimatized are predisposed to heat collapse. The victims usually recover consciousness rapidly after they are laid supine.

Heat oedema

Mild dependent oedema—that is, swelling of the hands and feet—may develop in unacclimatized individuals exposed to a hot environment. It typically occurs in women and resolves with acclimatization. It subsides in several hours after the patient has been laid in a cooler place.

Heat cramps

Heat cramps may occur after heavy sweating brought about by prolonged physical work. Painful spasms develop in limb and abdominal muscles subjected to intensive work and fatigue, while body temperature hardly rises. These cramps are caused by the salt depletion that results when the loss of water due to prolonged heavy sweating is replenished with plain water containing no supplementary salt and when the sodium concentration in the blood has fallen below a critical level. Heat cramps themselves are a relatively innocuous condition. The attacks are usually seen in physically fit individuals who are capable of sustained physical exertion, and once were called "miner's cramps" or "cane-cutter's cramps" because they would often occur in such labourers.

The treatment of heat cramps consists of cessation of activity, rest in a cool place and replacement of fluid and electrolytes. Heat exposure should be avoided for at least 24 to 48 hours.

Heat exhaustion

Heat exhaustion is the most common heat disorder encountered clinically. It results from severe dehydration after a huge amount of sweat has been lost. It occurs typically in otherwise healthy young individuals who undertake prolonged physical exertion (exertion-induced heat exhaustion), such as marathon runners, outdoor sports players, military recruits, coal miners and construction workers. The basic feature of this disorder is circulatory deficiency due to water and/or salt depletion. It may be considered an incipient stage of heat stroke, and if left untreated, it may eventually progress to heat stroke. It has been conventionally divided into two types: heat exhaustion by water depletion and that by salt depletion; but many cases are a mixture of both types.

Heat exhaustion by water depletion develops as a result of prolonged heavy sweating and insufficient water intake. Since sweat contains sodium ions in a concentration ranging from 30 to 100 milliequivalents per litre, which is lower than that in plasma, a great loss of sweat brings about hypohydration (reduction in body water content) and hypernatraemia (increased sodium concentration in plasma). Heat exhaustion is characterized by thirst, weakness, fatigue, dizziness, anxiety, oliguria (scanty urination), tachycardia (rapid heartbeat) and moderate hyperthermia (39 °C or above). Dehydration also leads to a decline in sweating activity, a rise in skin temperature, and increases in plasma protein and plasma sodium levels and in the haematocrit value (the ratio of blood cell volume to blood volume).

Treatment consists of allowing the victim to rest in a recumbent posture with the knees raised, in a cool environment, wiping the body with a cool towel or sponge and replacing fluid loss by drinking or, if oral ingestion is impossible, by intravenous infusion. The amounts of water and salt replenishment, body temperature and body weight should be monitored carefully. Water ingestion should not be regulated according to the victim's subjective feeling of thirst, especially when fluid loss is replenished with plain water, because dilution of the blood readily induces disappearance of thirst and dilution diuresis, thus delaying the recovery of body fluid balance. This phenomenon of insufficient water ingestion is called voluntary dehydration. Furthermore, a salt-free water supply may complicate heat disorders, as described below. Dehydration of over 3% of body weight should always be treated by water and electrolyte replacement.

Heat exhaustion by salt depletion results from prolonged heavy sweating and replacement of water and insufficient salt. Its occurrence is promoted by incomplete acclimatization, vomiting and diarrhoea, and so on. This type of heat exhaustion usually develops a few days after the development of water depletion. It is most commonly encountered in sedentary elderly individuals exposed to heat who have drunk a large amount of water in order to quench their thirst. Headache, dizziness, weakness, fatigue, nausea, vomiting, diarrhoea, anorexia, muscle spasms and mental confusion are common symptoms. In blood examinations, decrease in plasma volume, increases in the haematocrit and in plasma protein levels, and hypercalcaemia (excess blood calcium) are noted.

Early detection and prompt management are essential, the latter consisting of letting the patient rest in a recumbent posture in a cool room and providing for replacement of water and electrolytes. The osmolarity or specific gravity of the urine should be monitored, as should urea, sodium and chloride levels in the plasma, and body temperature, body weight, and water and salt intake should also be recorded. If the condition is adequately treated, victims generally feel well within a few hours and recover without sequelae. If not, it may readily proceed to heat stroke.

Heat stroke

Heat stroke is a serious medical emergency which may result in death. It is a complex clinical condition in which uncontrollable hyperthermia causes tissue damage. Such an elevation of body temperature is caused initially by severe heat congestion due to excessive heat load, and the resultant hyperthermia induces dysfunction of the central nervous system, including failure of the normal thermoregulatory mechanism, thus accelerating elevation of the body temperature. Heat stroke occurs basically in two forms: classical heat stroke and exertion-induced heat stroke. The former develops in very young, elderly, obese or unfit individuals undertaking normal activities during prolonged exposure to high environmental temperatures, whereas the latter occurs particularly in young, active adults during physical exertion. In addition, there is a mixed form of heat stoke presenting features consistent with both of the above forms.

Elderly individuals, particularly those who have underlying chronic illness, such as cardiovascular diseases, diabetes mellitus and alcoholism, and those taking certain medications, especially psychotropic drugs, are at a high risk of classical heat stroke. During sustained heat waves, for example, the mortality rate for the population older than 60 years has been recorded as more than ten times greater than that for the population aged 60 and under. A similarly high mortality in the elderly population has also been reported among Muslims during the Mecca pilgrimage, where the mixed form of heat stroke has been found to be prevalent. Factors predisposing the elderly to heat stroke, other than chronic diseases as mentioned above, include reduced thermal perception, sluggish vasomotor and sudomotor (sweating reflex) responses to changes in thermal load, and reduced capacity for acclimatization to heat.

Individuals who work or exercise vigorously in hot, humid environments are at a high risk of exertion-induced heat illness, whether heat exhaustion or heat stroke. Athletes undergoing high physical stress can fall victim to hyperthermia by producing metabolic heat at a high rate, even when the environment is not very hot, and have often suffered heat stress illness as a result. Relatively unfit non-athletes are at a lesser risk in this regard as long as they realize their own capacity and limit their exertions accordingly. However, when they play sports for fun and are highly motivated and enthusiastic, they often try to exert themselves at an intensity beyond that for which they have been trained, and may succumb to heat illness (usually heat exhaustion). Poor acclimatization, inadequate hydration, unsuitable dress, alcohol consumption and skin illness causing anhidrosis (reduction in or lack of sweating), notably prickly heat (see below), all aggravate the symptoms.

Children are more susceptible to heat exhaustion or heat stroke than adults. They produce more metabolic heat per unit mass, and are less able to dissipate heat because of a relatively low capacity to produce sweat.

Clinical features of heat stroke

Heat stroke is defined by three criteria:

1. severe hyperthermia with a core (deep body) temperature usually exceeding 42 °C
2. disturbances of the central nervous system
3. hot, dry skin with cessation of sweating.

The diagnosis of heat stroke is easy to establish when this triad of criteria is met. However, it may be missed when one of those criteria is absent, obscure or overlooked. For example, unless core temperature is measured properly and without delay, severe hyperthermia may not be recognized; or, in a very early stage of exertion-induced heat stroke, sweating may still persist or may even be profuse and the skin may be wet.

The onset of heat stroke is usually abrupt and without precursory symptoms, but some patients with impending heat stroke may have symptoms and signs of disturbances of the central nervous system. They include headache, nausea, dizziness, weakness, drowsiness, confusion, anxiety, disorientation, apathy, aggressiveness and irrational behaviour, tremor, twitching and convulsion. Once heat stroke occurs, disturbances of the central nervous system are present in all cases. The level of consciousness is often depressed, deep coma being most common. Seizures occur in the majority of cases, especially in physically fit individuals. Signs of cerebellar dysfunction are prominent and may persist. Pin-pointed pupils are frequently seen. Cerebellar ataxia (lack of muscular co-ordination), hemiplegia (paralysis of one side of the body), aphasia and emotional instability may persist in some of survivors.

Vomiting and diarrhoea often occur. Tachypnoea (rapid breathing) is usually present initially and the pulse may be weak and rapid. Hypotension, one of the most common complications, results from marked dehydration, extensive peripheral vaso-dilatation and eventual depression of cardiac muscle. Acute renal failure may be seen in severe cases, especially in exertion-induced heat stroke.

Haemorrhages occur in all parenchymal organs, in the skin (where they are called petechiae) and in the gastro-intestinal tract in severe cases. Clinical haemorrhagic manifestations include melaena (dark-coloured, tarry faeces), haematemesis (blood vomiting), haematuria (bloody urine), haemoptysis (spitting blood), epistaxis (nosebleed), purpura (purple spots), ecchymosis (black and blue marks) and conjunctival haemorrhage. Intravascular coagulation occurs commonly. Haemorrhagic diathesis (bleeding tendency) is usually associated with disseminated intra-vascular coagulation (DIC). DIC occurs predominantly in exertion-induced heat stroke, where the fibrinolytic (clot-dissolving) activity of plasma is increased. On the other hand, a decrease in platelet count, prolongation of prothrombin time, depletion of coagulation factors and increased level of fibrin degradation products (FDP) are provoked by whole-body hyperthermia. Patients with evidence of DIC and bleeding have higher core temperature, lower blood pressure, lower arterial blood pH and pO$_2$, a higher incidence of oliguria or anuria and of shock, and a higher mortality rate.

Shock is also a common complication. It is attributable to peripheral circulatory failure and is aggravated by DIC, which causes dissemination of clots in the microcirculatory system.

Treatment of heat stroke

Heat stroke is a medical emergency that requires prompt diagnosis and rapid and aggressive treatment to save the patient's life. Proper measurement of core temperature is mandatory: rectal or oesophageal temperature should be measured by using a thermometer which can read up to 45°C. Measurement of oral and axillary temperatures should be avoided because they can vary significantly from real core temperature.

The objective of treatment measures is to lower body temperature by reducing heat load and promoting heat dissipation from the skin. The treatment includes moving the patient to a safe, cool, shady and well-ventilated place, removing unnecessary clothing, and fanning. Cooling the face and head may promote beneficial brain cooling.

The efficiency of some cooling techniques has been questioned. It has been argued that placing cold packs over major blood vessels in the neck, groin and axillae and immersion of the body in cold water or covering it with iced towels may promote shivering and cutaneous vasoconstriction, thus actually impeding cooling efficiency. Traditionally, immersion in an ice-water bath, combined with vigorous skin massage to minimize cutaneous vasoconstriction, has been recommended as the treatment of choice, once the patient is brought to a medical facility. This method of cooling has several disadvantages: there are the nursing difficulties posed by the need to administer oxygen and fluids and to monitor blood pressure and the electrocardiogram continuously, and there are the hygienic problems of contamination of the bath with the vomitus and diarrhoea of comatose patients. An alternative approach is to spray a cool mist over the patient's body while fanning to promote evaporation from the skin. This method of cooling can reduce the core temperature by 0.03 to 0.06 °C/min.

Measures to prevent convulsions, seizures and shivering should also be initiated at once. Continuous cardiac monitoring and determination of serum electrolyte levels and arterial and venous blood-gas analysis are essential, and intravenous infusion of electrolyte solutions at a relatively low temperature of approximately 10 °C, together with controlled oxygen therapy, should be commenced in a timely fashion. Tracheal intubation to protect the airway, insertion of a cardiac catheter to estimate central venous pressure, placement of a gastric tube and insertion of a urinary catheter may also be included among additional recommended measures.

Prevention of heat stroke

For the prevention of heat stroke, a wide variety of human factors should be taken into account, such as acclimatization, age, build, general health, water and salt intake, clothing, peculiarities of religious devotion and ignorance of, or liability to neglect, regulations intended to promote public health.

Prior to physical exertion in a hot environment, workers, athletes or pilgrims should be informed of the work load and the level of heat stress they may encounter, and of the risks of heat stroke. A period of acclimatization is recommended before vigorous physical activity and/or severe exposure is risked. The level of activity should be matched to the ambient temperature, and physical exertion should be avoided or at least minimized during the hottest hours of the day. During physical exertion, free access to water is mandatory. Since electrolytes are lost in sweat and the opportunity for voluntary ingestion of water may be limited, thus delaying restitution from thermal dehydration, electrolytes should also be replaced in case of profuse sweating. Proper clothing is also an important measure. Clothes made of fabrics which are both water-absorbent and permeable to air and water vapour facilitate heat dissipation.

Skin Disorders

Miliaria is the most common skin disorder associated with heat load. It occurs when the delivery of sweat onto the skin surface is prevented due to obstruction of the sweat ducts. Sweat retention syndrome ensues when anhidrosis (inability to release sweat) is widespread over the body surface and predisposes the patient to heat stroke.

Miliaria is commonly induced by physical exertion in a hot, humid environment; by febrile diseases; by the application of wet compresses, bandages, plaster casts or adhesive plaster; and by wearing poorly permeable clothes. Miliaria can be classified into three types, according to the depth of sweat retention: miliaria crystallina, miliaria rubra and miliaria profunda.

Miliaria crystallina is caused by retention of sweat within or just beneath the horny layer of the skin, where tiny, clear, non-inflammatory blisters can be seen. They typically appear in "crops" after severe sunburn or during a febrile illness. This type of miliaria is otherwise symptomless, the least distressing, and heals spontaneously in a few days, when the blisters break out to leave scales.

Miliaria rubra occurs when intense heat load causes prolonged and profuse sweating. It is the most common type of miliaria, in which sweat accumulates in the epidermis. Red papules, vesicles or pustules are formed, accompanied by burning and itching sensations (prickly heat). The sweat duct is plugged at the terminal portion. The production of the plug is attributable to the action of resident aerobic bacteria, notably cocci, which increase in population greatly in the horny layer when it is hydrated with sweat. They secrete a toxin which injures the horny epithelial cells of the sweat duct and provokes an inflammatory reaction, precipitating a cast within the lumen of the sweat duct. Infiltration by leukocytes creates an impaction which completely obstructs the passage of sweat for several weeks.

In miliaria profunda, sweat is retained in the dermis, and produces flat, inflammatory papules, nodules and abscesses, with less itching than in miliaria rubra. The occurrence of this type of miliaria is commonly confined to the tropics. It may develop in a progressive sequence from miliaria rubra after repeated bouts of profuse sweating, as the inflammatory reaction extends downwards from the upper skin layers.

Tropical anhidrotic asthenia. The term achieved currency during the Second World War, when troops deployed to tropical theatres suffered from heat rash and heat intolerance. It is a modality of sweat retention syndrome encountered in hot, humid tropical environments. It is characterized by anhidrosis and miliaria-like rashes, accompanied by symptoms of heat congestion, such as palpitation, rapid pulsation, hyperthermia, headache, weakness and gradually to rapidly progressing inability to tolerate physical activity in the heat. It is usually preceded by widespread miliaria rubra.

Treatment. The initial and essential treatment of miliaria and sweat retention syndrome is to transfer the affected person to a cool environment. Cool showers and gentle drying of the skin and the application of calamine lotion may attenuate the patient's distress. Application of chemical bacteriostats is effective in preventing the expansion of microflora, and is preferable to the use of antibiotics, which may lead these micro-organisms to acquire resistance.

The impactions in the sweat duct slough off after about 3 weeks as a result of epidermal renewal.

● PREVENTION OF HEAT STRESS

Sarah A. Nunneley

Although human beings possess considerable ability to compensate for naturally occurring heat stress, many occupational environments and/or physical activities expose workers to heat loads which are so excessive as to threaten their health and productivity. In this article, a variety of techniques are described which can be used to minimize the incidence of heat disorders and reduce the severity of cases when they do occur. Interventions fall into five categories: maximizing heat tolerance among exposed individuals, assuring timely replacement of lost fluid and electrolytes, altering work practices to reduce exertional heat load, engineering control of climatic conditions, and use of protective clothing.

Factors outside the worksite which may affect thermal tolerance should not be ignored in the evaluation of the extent of exposure and consequently in elaborating preventive strategies. For example, total physiological burden and the potential susceptibility to heat disorders will be much higher if heat stress continues during off-duty hours through work at second jobs, strenuous leisure activities, or living in unremittingly hot quarters. In addition, nutritional status and hydration may reflect patterns of eating and drinking, which may also change with season or religious observances.

Maximizing Individual Heat Tolerance

Candidates for hot trades should be generally healthy and possess suitable physical attributes for the work to be done. Obesity and cardiovascular disease are conditions that add to the risks, and individuals with a history of previous unexplained or repetitive heat illness should not be assigned to tasks involving severe heat stress. Various physical and physiological characteristics which may affect heat tolerance are discussed below and fall into two general categories: inherent characteristics beyond the control of the individual, such as body size, gender, ethnicity and age; and acquired characteristics, which are at least partly subject to control and include physical fitness, heat acclimatization, obesity, medical conditions and self-induced stress.

Workers should be informed of the nature of heat stress and its adverse effects as well as the protective measures provided in the workplace. They should be taught that heat tolerance depends to a large extent upon drinking enough water and eating a balanced diet. In addition, workers should be taught the signs and symptoms of heat disorders, which include dizziness, faintness, breathlessness, palpitations and extreme thirst. They should also learn the basics of first aid and where to call for help when they recognize these signs in themselves or others.

Management should implement a system for reporting heat-related incidents at work. Occurrence of heat disorders in more than one person—or repeatedly in a single individual—is often a warning of serious impending trouble and indicates the need for immediate evaluation of the working environment and review of the adequacy of preventive measures.

Human traits affecting adaptation

Body dimensions. Children and very small adults face two potential disadvantages for work in hot environments. First, externally imposed work represents a greater relative load for a body with a small muscle mass, inducing a greater rise in core body temperature and more rapid onset of fatigue. In addition, the higher surface-to-mass ratio of small people may be a disadvantage under extremely hot conditions. These factors together may explain why men weighing less than 50 kg were found to be at increased risk for heat illness in deep mining activities.

Gender. Early laboratory studies on women seemed to show that they were relatively intolerant to work in heat, compared with men. However, we now recognize that nearly all of the differences can be explained in terms of body size and acquired levels of physical fitness and heat acclimatization. However, there are minor sex differences in heat dissipation mechanisms: higher maximal sweat rates in males may enhance tolerance for extremely hot, dry environments, while females are better able to suppress excess sweating and therefore conserve body water and thus heat in hot, humid environments. Although the menstrual cycle is associated with a shift in basal body temperature and slightly alters thermoregulatory responses in women, these physiological adjustments are too subtle to influence heat tolerance and thermoregulatory efficiency in real work situations.

When allowance is made for individual physique and fitness, men and women are essentially alike in their responses to heat stress and their ability to acclimatize to work under hot conditions. For this reason, selection of workers for hot jobs should be based on individual health and physical capacity, not gender. Very small or sedentary individuals of either sex will show poor tolerance for work in heat.

The effect of pregnancy on women's heat tolerance is not clear, but altered hormone levels and the increased circulatory demands of the foetus on the mother may increase her susceptibility to fainting. Severe maternal hyperthermia (over-heating) due to illness appears to increase the incidence of foetal malformation, but there is no evidence of a similar effect from occupational heat stress.

Ethnicity. Although various ethnic groups have originated in differing climates, there is little evidence of inherent or genetic differences in response to heat stress. All humans appear to function as tropical animals; their ability to live and work in a range of thermal conditions reflects adaptation through complex behaviour and development of technology. Seeming ethnic differences in response to heat stress probably relate to body size, individual life history and nutritional status rather than to inherent traits.

Age. Industrial populations generally show a gradual decline in heat tolerance after age 50. There is some evidence of an obligatory, age-associated reduction in cutaneous vasodilatation (widening of the cavity of blood vessels of the skin) and maximal sweat rate, but most of the change can be attributed to alterations in lifestyle which reduce physical activity and increase the accumulation of body fat. Age does not appear to impair heat tolerance or ability to acclimatize if the individual maintains a high level of aerobic conditioning. However, ageing populations are subject to increasing incidence of cardiovascular disease or other pathologies which may impair individual heat tolerance.

Physical fitness. Maximal aerobic capacity ($VO_{2\ max}$) is probably the strongest single determinant of an individual's ability to carry out sustained physical work under hot conditions. As noted above, early findings of group differences in heat tolerance which were attributed to gender, race or age are now viewed as manifestations of aerobic capacity and heat acclimatization.

Induction and maintenance of high work capacity require repetitive challenges to the body's oxygen transport system through vigorous exercise for at least 30 to 40 min, 3 to 4 days per week. In some cases activity on the job may provide the necessary physical training, but most industrial jobs are less strenuous and require supplementation through a regular exercise programme for optimal fitness.

Loss of aerobic capacity (detraining) is relatively slow, so that weekends or vacations of 1 to 2 weeks cause only minimal changes. Serious declines in aerobic capacity are more likely to occur over weeks to months when injury, chronic illness or other stress causes the individual to change lifestyle.

Heat acclimatization. Acclimatization to work in heat can greatly expand human tolerance for such stress, so that a task which is initially beyond the capability of the unacclimatized person may become easier work after a period of gradual adjustment. Individuals with a high level of physical fitness generally display partial heat acclimatization and are able to complete the process more quickly and with less stress than sedentary persons. Season may also affect the time which must be allowed for acclimatization; workers recruited in summer may already be partly heat acclimatized, while winter hires will require a longer period of adjustment.

In most situations, acclimatization can be induced through gradual introduction of the worker to the hot task. For instance, the new recruit may be assigned to hot work only in the morning or for gradually increasing time periods during the first few days. Such acclimatization on the job should take place under close supervision by experienced personnel; the new worker should have standing permission to withdraw to cooler conditions any time symptoms of intolerance occur. Extreme conditions may warrant a formal protocol of progressive heat exposure such as that used for workers in the South African gold mines.

Maintenance of full heat acclimatization requires exposure to work in heat three to four times per week; lower frequency or passive exposure to heat have a much weaker effect and may allow gradual decay of heat tolerance. However, weekends off work have no measurable effect on acclimatization. Discontinuing exposure for 2 to 3 weeks will cause loss of most acclimatization, although some will be retained in persons exposed to hot weather and/or regular aerobic exercise.

Obesity. High body fat content has little direct effect on thermoregulation, as heat dissipation at the skin involves capillaries and sweat glands which lie closer to the skin surface than the subcutaneous fat layer of skin. However, obese persons are handicapped by their excess body weight because every movement requires greater muscular effort and therefore generates more heat than in a lean person. In addition, obesity often reflects an inactive lifestyle with resulting lower aerobic capacity and absence of heat acclimatization.

Medical conditions and other stresses. A worker's heat tolerance on a given day may be impaired by a variety of conditions. Examples include febrile illness (higher than normal body temperature), recent immunization, or gastroenteritis with associated disturbance of fluid and electrolyte balance. Skin conditions such as sunburn and rashes may limit ability to secrete sweat. In addition, susceptibility to heat illness may be increased by prescription medications, including sympathomimetics, anticholinergics, diuretics, phenothiazines, cyclic antidepressants, and monoamine-oxidase inhibitors.

Alcohol is a common and serious problem among those who work in heat. Alcohol not only impairs intake of food and water, but also acts as a diuretic (increase in urination) as well as disturbing judgement. The adverse effects of alcohol extend many hours beyond the time of intake. Alcoholics who suffer heat stroke have a far higher mortality rate than non-alcoholic patients.

Oral Replacement of Water and Electrolytes

Hydration. Evaporation of sweat is the main path for dissipating body heat and becomes the only possible cooling mechanism when air temperature exceeds body temperature. Water requirements cannot be reduced by training, but only by lowering the heat load on the worker. Human water loss and rehydration have been extensively studied in recent years, and more information is now available.

A human weighing 70 kg can sweat at a rate of 1.5 to 2.0 l/h indefinitely, and it is possible for a worker to lose several litres or up to 10% of body weight during a day in an extremely hot environment. Such loss would be incapacitating unless at least part of the water were replaced during the work shift. However, since water absorption from the gut peaks at about 1.5 l/h during work, higher sweat rates will produce cumulative dehydration through the day.

Drinking to satisfy thirst is not enough to keep a person well hydrated. Most people do not become aware of thirst until they have lost 1 to 2 l of body water, and persons highly motivated to perform hard work may incur losses of 3 to 4 l before clamorous thirst forces them to stop and drink. Paradoxically, dehydration reduces the capacity to absorb water from the gut. Therefore, workers in hot trades must be educated regarding the importance of drinking enough water during work and continuing generous rehydration during off-duty hours. They should also be taught the value of "prehydration"—consuming a large drink of water immediately before the start of severe heat stress—as heat and exercise prevent the body from eliminating excess water in the urine.

Management must provide ready access to water or other appropriate drinks which encourage rehydration. Any physical or procedural obstacle to drinking will encourage "voluntary" dehydration which predisposes to heat illness. The following details are a vital part of any programme for hydration maintenance:

- Safe, palatable water must be located within a few steps of each worker or brought to the worker every hour—more frequently under the most stressful conditions.
- Sanitary drinking cups should be provided, as it is nearly impossible to rehydrate from a water fountain.
- Water containers must be shaded or cooled to 15 to 20 °C (iced drinks are not ideal because they tend to inhibit intake).

Flavourings may be used to improve the acceptance of water. However, drinks that are popular because they "cut" thirst are not recommended, since they inhibit intake before rehydration is complete. For this reason it is better to offer water or dilute, flavoured beverages and to avoid carbonation, caffeine and drinks with heavy concentrations of sugar or salt.

Nutrition. Although sweat is hypotonic (lower salt content) compared to blood serum, high sweat rates involve a continuous loss of sodium chloride and small amounts of potassium, which must be replaced on a daily basis. In addition, work in heat accelerates the turnover of trace elements including magnesium and zinc. All of these essential elements should normally be obtained from food, so workers in hot trades should be encouraged to eat well-balanced meals and avoid substituting candy bars or snack foods, which lack important nutritional components. Some diets in industrialized nations include high levels of sodium chloride, and workers on such diets are unlikely to develop salt deficits; but other, more traditional diets may not contain adequate salt. Under some conditions it may be necessary for the employer to provide salty snacks or other supplementary foods during the work shift.

Industrialized nations are seeing increased availability of "sports drinks" or "thirst quenchers" which contain sodium chloride, potassium and carbohydrates. The vital component of any beverage is water, but electrolyte drinks may be useful in persons who have already developed significant dehydration (water loss) combined with electrolyte depletion (salt loss). These drinks are generally high in salt content and should be mixed with equal or greater volumes of water before consumption. A much more economical mixture for oral rehydration can be made according to the following recipe: to one litre of water, suitable for drinking, add 40 g of sugar (sucrose) and 6 g of salt (sodium chloride). Workers should not be given salt tablets, as they are easily abused, and overdoses lead to gastro-intestinal problems, increased urine output and greater susceptibility to heat illness.

Modified Work Practices

The common goal of modification to work practices is to lower time-averaged heat stress exposure and to bring it within acceptable limits. This can be accomplished by reducing the physical workload imposed on an individual worker or by scheduling appropriate breaks for thermal recovery. In practice, maximum time-averaged metabolic heat production is effectively limited to about 350 W (5 kcal/min) because harder work induces physical fatigue and a need for commensurate rest breaks.

Individual effort levels can be lowered by reducing external work such as lifting, and by limiting required locomotion and static muscle tension such as that associated with awkward posture. These goals may be reached by optimizing task design according to ergonomic principles, providing mechanical aids or dividing the physical effort among more workers.

The simplest form of schedule modification is to allow individual self-pacing. Industrial workers performing a familiar task in a mild climate will pace themselves at a rate which produces a rectal temperature of about 38 °C; imposition of heat stress causes them to voluntarily slow the work rate or take breaks. This ability to voluntarily adjust work rate probably depends on awareness of cardiovascular stress and fatigue. Human beings cannot consciously detect elevations in core body temperature; rather, they rely on skin temperature and skin wettedness to assess thermal discomfort.

An alternative approach to schedule modification is the adoption of prescribed work-rest cycles, where management specifies the duration of each work bout, the length of rest breaks and the number of repetitions expected. Thermal recovery takes much longer than the period required to lower respiratory rate and work-induced heart rate: Lowering core temperature to resting levels requires 30 to 40 min in a cool, dry environment, and takes longer if the person must rest under hot conditions or while wearing protective clothing. If a constant level of production is required, then alternating teams of workers must be assigned sequentially to hot work followed by recovery, the latter involving either rest or sedentary tasks performed in a cool place.

Climate Control

If cost were no object, all heat stress problems could be solved by application of engineering techniques to convert hostile working environments to hospitable ones. A wide variety of techniques may be used depending on the specific conditions of the workplace and available resources. Traditionally, hot industries can be divided into two categories: In hot-dry processes, such as metal smelting and glass production, workers are exposed to very hot air combined with strong radiant heat load, but such processes add little humidity to the air. In contrast, warm-moist industries such as textile mills, paper production and mining involve less extreme heating but create very high humidities due to wet processes and escaped steam.

The most economical techniques of environmental control usually involve reduction of heat transfer from the source to the environment. Hot air may be vented outside the work area and replaced with fresh air. Hot surfaces can be covered with insulation or given reflective coatings to reduce heat emissions, simultaneously conserving heat which is needed for the industrial process. A second line of defence is large-scale ventilation of the work area to provide a strong flow of outside air. The most expensive option is air conditioning to cool and dry the atmosphere in the workplace. Although lowering air temperature does not affect transmission of radiant heat, it does help to reduce the temperature of the walls and other surfaces which may be secondary sources of convective and radiative heating.

When overall environmental control proves impractical or uneconomical, it may be possible to ameliorate thermal conditions in local work areas. Air conditioned enclosures may be provided within the larger work space, or a specific work station may be provided with a flow of cool air ("spot cooling" or "air shower"). Local or even portable reflective shielding may be interposed between the worker and a radiant heat source. Alternatively, modern engineering techniques may allow construction of remote systems to control hot processes so that workers need not suffer routine exposure to highly stressful heat environments.

Where the workplace is ventilated with outside air or there is limited air-conditioning capacity, thermal conditions will reflect climatic changes, and sudden increases in outdoor air temperature and humidity may elevate heat stress to levels which overwhelm workers' heat tolerance. For instance, a spring heat wave can precipitate an epidemic of heat illness among workers who are not yet heat acclimatized as they would be in summer. Management should therefore implement a system for predicting weather-related changes in heat stress so that timely precautions can be taken.

Protective Clothing

Work in extreme thermal conditions may require personal thermal protection in the form of specialized clothing. Passive protection is provided by insulative and reflective garments; insulation alone can buffer the skin from thermal transients. Reflective aprons may be used to protect personnel who work facing a limited radiant source. Fire-fighters who must deal with extremely hot fuel fires wear suits called "bunkers", which combine heavy insulation against hot air with an aluminized surface to reflect radiant heat.

Another form of passive protection is the ice vest, which is loaded with slush or frozen packets of ice (or dry ice) and is worn over an undershirt to prevent uncomfortable chilling of the skin. The phase change of the melting ice absorbs part of the metabolic and environmental heat load from the covered area, but the ice must be replaced at regular intervals; the greater the heat load, the more frequently the ice must be replaced. Ice vests have proven most useful in deep mines, ship engine rooms, and other very hot, humid environments where access to freezers can be arranged.

Active thermal protection is provided by air- or liquid-cooled garments which cover the entire body or some portion of it, usually the torso and sometimes the head.

Air cooling. The simplest systems are ventilated with the surrounding, ambient air or with compressed air cooled by expansion or passage through a vortex device. High volumes of air are required; the minimum ventilation rate for a sealed suit is about 450 l/min. Air cooling can theoretically take place through convection (temperature change) or evaporation of sweat (phase change). However, the effectiveness of convection is limited by the low specific heat of air and the difficulty in delivering it at low temperatures in hot surroundings. Most air-cooled garments therefore operate through evaporative cooling. The worker experiences moderate heat stress and attendant dehydration, but is able to thermoregulate through natural control of the sweat rate. Air cooling also enhances comfort through its tendency to dry the underclothing. Disadvantages include (1) the need to connect the subject to the air source, (2) the bulk of air distribution garments and (3) the difficulty of delivering air to the limbs.

Liquid cooling. These systems circulate a water-antifreeze mixture through a network of channels or small tubes and then return the warmed liquid to a heat sink which removes the heat added during passage over the body. Liquid circulation rates are usually on the order of 1 l/min. The heat sink may dissipate thermal energy to the environment through evaporation, melting, refrigeration or thermoelectric processes. Liquid-cooled garments offer far greater cooling potential than air systems. A full-coverage suit linked to an adequate heat sink can remove all metabolic heat and maintain thermal comfort without the need to sweat; such a system is used by astronauts working outside their spacecraft. However, such a powerful cooling mechanism requires some type of comfort control system which usually involves manual setting of a valve which shunts part of the circulating liquid past the heat sink. Liquid-cooled systems can be configured as a back pack to provide continuous cooling during work.

Any cooling device which adds weight and bulk to the human body, of course, may interfere with the work at hand. For instance, the weight of an ice vest significantly increases the metabolic cost of locomotion, and is therefore most useful for light physical work such as watch-standing in hot compartments. Systems which tether the worker to a heat sink are impractical for many types of work. Intermittent cooling may be useful where workers must wear heavy protective clothing (such as chemical protective suits) and cannot carry a heat sink or be tethered while they work. Removing the suit for each rest break is time consuming and involves possible toxic exposure; under these conditions, it is simpler to have the workers wear a cooling garment which is attached to a heat sink only during rest, allowing thermal recovery under otherwise unacceptable conditions.

THE PHYSICAL BASIS OF WORK IN HEAT

Jacques Malchaire

Thermal Exchanges

The human body exchanges heat with its environment by various pathways: conduction across the surfaces in contact with it, convection and evaporation with the ambient air, and radiation with the neighbouring surfaces.

Conduction

Conduction is the transmission of heat between two solids in contact. Such exchanges are observed between the skin and clothing, footwear, pressure points (seat, handles), tools and so on. In practice, in the mathematical calculation of thermal balance, this heat flow by conduction is approximated indirectly as a quantity

equal to the heat flow by convection and radiation which would take place if these surfaces were not in contact with other materials.

Convection

Convection is the transfer of heat between the skin and the air surrounding it. If the skin temperature, t_{sk}, in units of degrees Celsius (°C), is higher than the air temperature (t_a), the air in contact with the skin is heated and consequently rises. Air circulation, known as natural convection, is thus established at the surface of the body. This exchange becomes greater if the ambient air passes over the skin at a certain speed: the convection becomes forced. The heat flow exchanged by convection, C, in units of watts per square metre (W/m²), can be estimated by:

$$C = h_c F_{clC} (t_{sk} - t_a)$$

where h_c is the coefficient of convection (W/°C m²), which is a function of the difference between t_{sk} and t_a in the case of natural convection, and of the air velocity V_a (in m/s) in forced convection; F_{clC} is the factor by which clothing reduces convection heat exchange.

Radiation

Every body emits electromagnetic radiation, the intensity of which is a function of the fourth power of its absolute temperature T (in degrees Kelvin—K). The skin, whose temperature may be between 30 and 35 °C (303 and 308 K), emits such radiation, which is in the infrared zone. Moreover, it receives the radiation emitted by neighbouring surfaces. The thermal flow exchanged by radiation, R (in W/m²), between the body and its surroundings may be described by the following expression:

$$R = \varepsilon\sigma\left(\frac{A_R}{A_D}\right)F_{clR}\left(T_{sk}^4 - T_r^4\right)$$

where:

σ is the universal constant of radiation ($5.67 \times 10\text{-}8$ W/m² K⁴)

ε is the emissivity of the skin, which, for infrared radiation, is equal to 0.97 and independent of the wavelength, and for solar radiation is about 0.5 for the skin of a White subject and 0.85 for the skin of a Black subject

A_R/A_D is the fraction of the body surface taking part in the exchanges, which is of the order of 0.66, 0.70 or 0.77, depending upon whether the subject is crouching, seated or standing

F_{clR} is the factor by which clothing reduces radiation heat exchange

T_{sk} (in K) is the mean skin temperature

T_r (in K) is the mean radiant temperature of the environment —that is, the uniform temperature of a black mat sphere of large diameter that would surround the subject and would exchange with it the same quantity of heat as the real environment.

This expression may be replaced by a simplified equation of the same type as that for exchanges by convection:

$$R = h_r (A_R/A_D) F_{clR} (t_{sk} - t_r)$$

where h_r is the coefficient of exchange by radiation (W/°C m²).

Evaporation

Every wet surface has on it a layer of air saturated with water vapour. If the atmosphere itself is not saturated, the vapour diffuses from this layer towards the atmosphere. The layer then tends to be regenerated by drawing on the heat of evaporation (0.674 Watt hour per gram of water) at the wet surface, which cools. If the skin is entirely covered with sweat, evaporation is maximal (E_{max}) and depends only on the ambient conditions, according to the following expression:

$$E_{max} = h_e \, F_{pcl} \, (P_{sk,s} - P_a)$$

where:

h_e is the coefficient of exchange by evaporation (W/m²kPa)

$P_{sk,s}$ is the saturated pressure of water vapour at the temperature of the skin (expressed in kPa)

P_a is the ambient partial pressure of water vapour (expressed in kPa)

F_{pcl} is the factor of reduction of exchanges by evaporation due to clothing.

Thermal insulation of clothing

A correction factor operates in the calculation of heat flow by convection, radiation and evaporation so as to take account of clothing. In the case of cotton clothing, the two reduction factors F_{clC} and F_{clR} may be determined by:

$$F_{cl} = 1/(1 + (h_c + h_r)I_{cl})$$

where:

h_c is the coefficient of exchange by convection

h_r is the coefficient of exchange by radiation

I_{cl} is the effective thermal isolation (m²/W) of clothing.

As regards the reduction of heat transfer by evaporation, the correction factor F_{pcl} is given by the following expression:

$$F_{pcl} = 1/(1 + 2.22h_c \, I_{cl})$$

The thermal insulation of the clothing I_{cl} is expressed in m²/W or in clo. An insulation of 1 clo corresponds to 0.155 m²/W and is provided, for example, by normal town wear (shirt, tie, trousers, jacket, etc.).

ISO standard 9920 (1994) gives the thermal insulation provided by different combinations of clothing. In the case of special protective clothing that reflects heat or limits permeability to vapour under conditions of heat exposure, or absorbs and insulates under conditions of cold stress, individual correction factors must be used. To date, however, the problem remains poorly understood and the mathematical predictions remain very approximate.

Evaluation of the Basic Parameters of the Work Situation

As seen above, thermal exchanges by convection, radiation and evaporation are a function of four climatic parameters—the air temperature t_a in °C, the humidity of the air expressed by its partial vapour pressure P_a in kPa, the mean radiant temperature t_r in °C, and the air velocity V_a in m/s. The appliances and methods for measuring these physical parameters of the environment are the subject of ISO standard 7726 (1985), which describes the different types of sensor to use, specifies their range of measurement and their accuracy, and recommends certain measurement procedures. This section summarizes part of the data of that standard, with particular reference to the conditions of use of the most common appliances and apparatus.

Air temperature

The air temperature (t_a) must be measured independent of any thermal radiation; the accuracy of the measurement should be ±0.2 °C within the range of 10 to 30 °C, and ±0.5 °C outside that range.

There are numerous types of thermometers on the market. Mercury thermometers are the most common. Their advantage is accuracy, provided that they have been correctly calibrated originally. Their main disadvantages are their lengthy response time and lack of automatic recording ability. Electronic thermometers, on the other hand, generally have a very short response time (5 s to 1 min) but may have calibration problems.

Whatever the type of thermometer, the sensor must be protected against radiation. This is generally ensured by a hollow cylinder of shiny aluminium surrounding the sensor. Such protection is ensured by the psychrometer, which will be mentioned in the next section.

Partial pressure of water vapour

The humidity of the air may be characterized in four different ways:

1. the *dewpoint temperature*: the temperature to which the air must be cooled to become saturated with humidity (t_d, °C)
2. the *partial pressure of water vapour*: the fraction of atmospheric pressure due to water vapour (P_a, kPa)
3. the *relative humidity (RH)*, which is given by the expression:

$$RH = 100 \cdot P_a / P_{S,ta}$$

where $P_{S,ta}$ is the saturated vapour pressure associated with the air temperature

4. the *wet bulb temperature* (t_w), which is the lowest temperature attained by a wet sleeve protected against radiation and ventilated at more than 2 m/s by the ambient air.

All these values are connected mathematically.

The saturated water vapour pressure $P_{S,t}$ at any temperature t is given by:

$$P_{S,t} = 0.6105 \cdot e^{\left(\frac{17.27 \cdot t}{t+237.3} \right)}$$

while the partial pressure of water vapour is connected to the temperature by:

$$P_a = P_{S,tw} - (t_a - t_w)/15$$

where $P_{S,tw}$ is the saturated vapour pressure at the wet bulb temperature.

The psychrometric diagram (figure 42.3) allows all these values to be combined. It comprises:

- in the y axis, the scale of partial pressure of water vapour P_a, expressed in kPa
- in the x axis, the scale of air temperature
- the curves of constant relative humidity
- the oblique straight lines of constant wet bulb temperature.

Figure 42.3 • Psychrometric diagram.

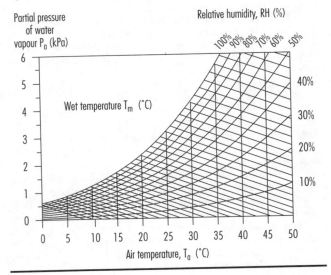

The parameters of humidity most often used in practice are:

- the relative humidity, measured by means of hygrometers or more specialized electronic appliances
- the wet bulb temperature, measured by means of the psychrometer; from this is derived the partial pressure of water vapour, which is the parameter most used in analysing thermal balance

The range of measurement and the accuracy recommended are 0.5 to 6 kPa and ±0.15 kPa. For measurement of the wet bulb temperature, the range extends from 0 to 36 °C, with an accuracy identical with that of the air temperature. As regards hygrometers for measuring relative humidity, the range extends from 0 to 100%, with an accuracy of ±5%.

Mean radiant temperature

The mean radiant temperature (t_r) has been defined previously; it can be determined in three different ways:

1. from the temperature measured by the black sphere thermometer
2. from the plane radiant temperatures measured along three perpendicular axes
3. by calculation, integrating the effects of the different sources of radiation.

Only the first technique will be reviewed here.

The black sphere thermometer consists of a thermal probe, the sensitive element of which is placed at the centre of a completely closed sphere, made of a metal that is a good conductor of heat (copper) and painted matt black so as to have a coefficient of absorption in the infrared zone close to 1.0. The sphere is positioned in the workplace and subjected to exchanges by convection and radiation. The temperature of the globe (t_g) then depends on the mean radiant temperature, the air temperature and the air velocity.

For a standard black globe 15 cm in diameter, the mean temperature of radiation can be calculated from the temperature of the globe on the basis of the following expression:

$$t_r = \sqrt[4]{\left(t_g + 273\right)^4 + 2.5 \times 10^8 \times V_a^{0.6}\left(t_g - t_a\right)} - 273$$

In practice, the need must be stressed to maintain the emissivity of the globe close to 1.0 by carefully repainting it matt black.

The main limitation of this type of globe is its long response time (of the order of 20 to 30 min, depending on the type of globe used and the ambient conditions). The measurement is valid only if the conditions of radiation are constant during this period of time, and this is not always the case in an industrial setting; the measurement is then inaccurate. These response times apply to globes 15 cm in diameter, using ordinary mercury thermometers. They are shorter if sensors of smaller thermal capacity are used or if the diameter of the globe is reduced. The equation above must therefore be modified to take account of this difference in diameter.

The WBGT index makes direct use of the temperature of the black globe. It is then essential to use a globe 15 cm in diameter. On the other hand, other indices make use of the mean radiant temperature. A smaller globe can then be selected to reduce the response time, provided that the equation above is modified to take account of it. ISO standard 7726 (1985) allows for an accuracy of ±2 °C in the measurement of $\bar{t}_r$ between 10 and 40 °C, and ±5 °C outside that range.

Air velocity

The air velocity must be measured disregarding the direction of air flow. Otherwise, the measurement must be undertaken in three perpendicular axes (x, y and z) and the global velocity calculated by vectorial summation:

$$V_a = \sqrt{V_x^2 + V_y^2 + V_z^2}$$

The range of measurements recommended by ISO standard 7726 extends from 0.05 to 2 m/s The accuracy required is 5%. It should be measured as a 1- or 3-min average value.

There are two categories of appliances for measuring air velocity: anemometers with vanes, and thermal anemometers.

Vane anemometers

The measurement is carried out by counting the number of turns made by the vanes during a certain period of time. In this way the mean velocity during that period of time is obtained in a discontinuous manner. These anemometers have two main disadvantages:

1. *They are very directional and have to be oriented strictly in the direction of the air flow.* When this is vague or unknown, measurements have to be taken in three directions at right angles.
2. *The range of measurement extends from about 0.3 m/s to 10 m/s.* This limitation to low velocities is important when, for instance, it is a question of analysing a thermal comfort situation where it is generally recommended that a velocity of 0.25 m/s should not be exceeded. Although the range of measurement can extend beyond 10 m/s, it hardly falls below 0.3 or even 0.5 m/s, which greatly limits the possibilities of use in environments near to comfort, where the maximum permitted velocities are 0.5 or even 0.25 m/s.

Hot-wire anemometers

These appliances are in fact complementary to vane anemometers in the sense that their dynamic range extends essentially from 0 to 1 m/s. They are appliances giving an instantaneous estimate of speed at one point of space: it is therefore necessary to use mean values in time and space. These appliances are also often very directional, and the remarks above also apply. Finally, the measurement is correct only from the moment when the temperature of the appliance has reached that of the environment to be evaluated.

ASSESSMENT OF HEAT STRESS AND HEAT STRESS INDICES

Kenneth C. Parsons

Heat stress occurs when a person's environment (air temperature, radiant temperature, humidity and air velocity), clothing and activity interact to produce a tendency for body temperature to rise. The body's thermoregulatory system then responds in order to increase heat loss. This response can be powerful and effective, but it can also produce a strain on the body which leads to discomfort and eventually to heat illness and even death. It is important therefore to assess hot environments to ensure the health and safety of workers.

Heat stress indices provide tools for assessing hot environments and predicting likely thermal strain on the body. Limit values based upon heat stress indices will indicate when that strain is likely to become unacceptable.

The mechanisms of heat stress are generally understood, and work practices for hot environments are well established. These include knowledge of the warning signs of heat stress, acclimatization programmes and water replacement. There are still many

42. HEAT AND COLD

Figure 42.4 • The variation of three measures of heat strain with increasing heat stress.

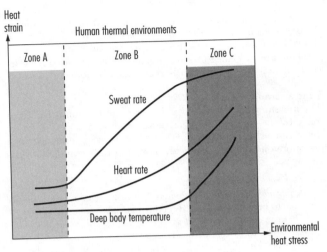

The variation of three measures of heat strain with increasing heat stress. In Zone B, the prescriptive zone (PZ), the deep body temperature is held constant by the increasing sweat rate. In Zone C, the environmentally driven zone (EDZ), sweat rate can no longer increase and the body temperature rises. The transition is termed the upper limit of the prescriptive zone (ULPZ).

Source: WHO 1969.

much can be done if all the requirements for the correct and prompt remedial treatment are available.

Heat Stress Indices

A heat stress index is a single number which integrates the effects of the six basic parameters in any human thermal environment such that its value will vary with the thermal strain experienced by the person exposed to a hot environment. The index value (measured or calculated) can be used in design or in work practice to establish safe limits. Much research has gone into determining the definitive heat stress index, and there is discussion about which is best. For example, Goldman (1988) presents 32 heat stress indices, and there are probably at least double that number used throughout the world. Many indices do not consider all six basic parameters, although all have to take them into consideration in application. The use of indices will depend upon individual contexts, hence the production of so many. Some indices are inadequate theoretically but can be justified for specific applications based on experience in a particular industry.

Kerslake (1972) notes that "It is perhaps self evident that the way in which the environmental factors should be combined must depend on the properties of the subject exposed to them, but none of the heat stress indices in current use make formal allowance for this". The recent surge in standardization (e.g., ISO 7933 (1989b) and ISO 7243 (1989a)) has led to pressure to adopt similar indices worldwide. It will be necessary, however, to gain experience with the use of any new index.

Most heat stress indices consider, directly or indirectly, that the main strain on the body is due to sweating. For example, the more sweating required to maintain heat balance and internal body temperature, the greater the strain on the body. For an index of heat stress to represent the human thermal environment and predict heat strain, a mechanism is required to estimate the capacity of a sweating person to lose heat in the hot environment.

An index related to evaporation of sweat to the environment is useful where persons maintain internal body temperature essentially by sweating. These conditions are generally said to be in the *prescriptive zone* (WHO 1969). Hence deep body temperature remains relatively constant while heart rate and sweat rate rise with heat stress. At the upper limit of the prescriptive zone (ULPZ), thermoregulation is insufficient to maintain heat balance, and body temperature rises. This is termed the *environmentally driven zone* (WHO 1969). In this zone heat storage is related to internal body temperature rise and can be used as an index to determine allowable exposure times (e.g., based on a predicted safety limit for "core" temperature of 38 °C; see figure 42.4).

casualties, however, and these lessons seem to have to be relearned.

In 1964, Leithead and Lind described an extensive survey and concluded that heat disorders occur for one or more of the following three reasons:

1. the existence of factors such as dehydration or lack of acclimatization
2. the lack of proper appreciation of the dangers of heat, either on the part of the supervising authority or of the individuals at risk
3. accidental or unforeseeable circumstances leading to exposure to very high heat stress.

They concluded that many deaths can be attributed to neglect and lack of consideration and that even when disorders do occur,

Table 42.2 • Equations used in the calculation of the Heat Stress Index (HSI) and Allowable Exposure Times (AET).

			Clothed	Unclothed
(1) Radiation loss (R)	$R = k_1(35 - t_r)$ Wm^{-2}	for $k_1 =$	4.4	7.3
(2) Convection loss (C)	$C = k_2.v^{0.6}(35 - t_a)$ Wm^{-2}	for $k_2 =$	4.6	7.6
(3) Maximum evaporative loss (E_{max})	$E_{max} = k_3.v^{0.6}(56 - P_a)$ Wm^{-2} (upper limit of 390 Wm^{-2})	for $k_3 =$	7.0	11.7
(4) Required evaporation loss (E_{req})	$E_{req} = M - R - C$			
(5) Heat stress index (HSI)	$HSI = \dfrac{\left(E_{req}\right)}{\left(E_{max}\right)} \times 100$			
(6) Allowable exposure time (AET)	$AET = \dfrac{2440}{\left(E_{req} - E_{max}\right)}$ mins			

where: M = metabolic power; t_a = air temperature; t_r = radiant temperature; P_a = partial vapour pressure; v = air velocity.

Table 42.3 • Interpretation of Heat Stress Index (HSI) values.

HSI	Effect of eight hour exposure
−20	Mild cold strain (e.g. recovery from heat exposure).
0	No thermal strain
10-30	Mild to moderate heat strain. Little effect on physical work but possible effect on skilled work
40-60	Severe heat strain, involving threat to health unless physically fit. Acclimatization required
70-90	Very severe heat strain. Personnel should be selected by medical examination. Ensure adequate water and salt intake
100	Maximum strain tolerated daily by fit acclimatized young men
Over 100	Exposure time limited by rise in deep body temperature

Heat stress indices can be conveniently categorized as *rational, empirical* or *direct*. Rational indices are based upon calculations involving the heat balance equation; empirical indices are based on establishing equations from the physiological responses of human subjects (e.g., sweat loss); and direct indices are based on the measurement (usually temperature) of instruments used to simulate the response of the human body. The most influential and widely used heat stress indices are described below.

Rational indices

The Heat Stress Index (HSI)
The Heat Stress Index is the ratio of evaporation required to maintain heat balance (E_{req}) to the maximum evaporation that could be achieved in the environment (E_{max}), expressed as a percentage (Belding and Hatch 1955). Equations are provided in table 42.2.

The *HSI* as an index therefore is related to strain, essentially in terms of body sweating, for values between 0 and 100. At *HSI* = 100, evaporation required is the maximum that can be achieved, and thus represents the upper limit of the prescriptive zone. For *HSI* >100, there is body heat storage, and allowable exposure times are calculated based on a 1.8 °C rise in core temperature (heat storage of 264 kJ). For *HSI* <0 there is mild cold strain—for example, when workers recover from heat strain (see table 42.3).

An upper limit of 390 W/m² is assigned to E_{max} (sweat rate of 1 l/h, taken to be the maximum sweat rate maintained over 8 h). Simple assumptions are made about the effects of clothing (long-sleeved shirt and trousers), and the skin temperature is assumed to be constant at 35 °C.

The Index of Thermal Stress (ITS)
Givoni (1963, 1976) provided the Index of Thermal Stress, which was an improved version of the Heat Stress Index. An important improvement is the recognition that not all sweat evaporates. (See "I. Index of thermal stress" in *Heat indices* box on page 42.20.)

Required sweat rate
A further theoretical and practical development of the HSI and ITS was the required sweat rate (SW_{req}) index (Vogt et al. 1981). This index calculated sweating required for heat balance from an improved heat balance equation but, most importantly, also provided a practical method of interpretation of calculations by comparing what is required with what is physiologically possible and acceptable in humans.

Extensive discussions and laboratory and industrial evaluations (CEC 1988) of this index led to it being accepted as International Standard ISO 7933 (1989b). Differences between observed and predicted responses of workers led to the inclusion of cautionary notes concerning methods of assessing dehydration and evaporative heat transfer through clothing in its adoption as a proposed European Standard (prEN-12515). (See "II. Required sweat rate" in *Heat indices* box.)

Interpretation of SW_req
Reference values—in terms of what is acceptable, or what persons can achieve—are used to provide a practical interpretation of calculated values (see table 42.4).

First, a prediction of skin wettedness (W_p), evaporation rate (E_p) and sweat rate (SW_p) are made. Essentially, if what is calculated as required can be achieved, then these are predicted values (e.g., $SW_p = SW_{req}$). If they cannot be achieved, the maximum values can be taken (e.g., $SW_p = SW_{max}$). More detail is given in a decision flow chart (see figure 42.5).

If required sweat rate can be achieved by persons and it will not cause unacceptable water loss, then there is no limit due to heat

Figure 42.5 • Decision flow chart for SW_p (required sweat rate).

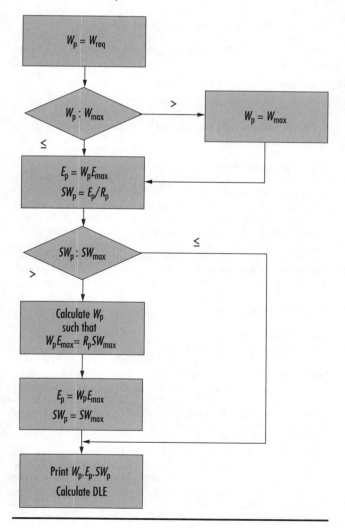

Table 42.4 • Reference values for criteria of thermal stress and strain (ISO 7933, 1989b).

Criteria		Non-acclimatized subjects		Acclimatized subjects	
		Warning	Danger	Warning	Danger
Maximum skin wettedness					
w_{max}		0.85	0.85	1.0	1.0
Maximum sweat rate					
Rest ($M < 65$ Wm^{-2})	SW_{max} Wm^{-2} gh^{-1}	100	150	200	300
		260	390	520	780
Work ($M \geq 65$ Wm^{-2})	SW_{max} Wm^{-2} gh^{-1}	200	250	300	400
		520	650	780	1,040
Maximum heat storage					
Q_{max}	Whm^{-2}	50	60	50	60
Maximum water loss					
D_{max}	Whm^{-2} g	1,000	1,250	1,500	2,000
		2,600	3,250	3,900	5,200

exposure over an 8-hour shift. If not, the duration-limited exposures *(DLE)* are calculated from the following:

When $E_p = E_{req}$ and $SW_p = D_{max}/8$, then $DLE = 480$ mins and SW_{req} can be used as a heat stress index. If the above are not satisfied, then:

$$DLE1 = 60Q_{max}/(E_{req} - E_p)$$

$$DLE2 = 60D_{max}/SW_p$$

DLE is the lower of *DLE*1 and *DLE*2. Fuller details are given in ISO 7933 (1989b).

Other rational indices

The SW_{req} index and ISO 7933 (1989) provide the most sophisticated rational method based on the heat balance equation, and they were major advances. More developments with this approach can be made; however, an alternative approach is to use a thermal model. Essentially, the New Effective Temperature (ET*) and Standard Effective Temperature (SET) provide indices based on the two-node model of human thermoregulation (Nishi and Gagge 1977). Givoni and Goldman (1972, 1973) also provide empirical prediction models for the assessment of heat stress.

Empirical indices

Effective temperature and corrected effective temperature

The Effective Temperature index (Houghton and Yaglou 1923) was originally established to provide a method for determining the relative effects of air temperature and humidity on comfort. Three subjects judged which of two climatic chambers was warmer by walking between the two. Using different combinations of air temperature and humidity (and later other parameters), lines of equal comfort were determined. Immediate impressions were made so the transient response was recorded. This had the effect of over-emphasizing the effect of humidity at low temperatures and underestimating it at high temperatures (when compared with steady-state responses). Although originally a comfort index, the use of the black globe temperature to replace dry bulb temperature in the ET nomograms provided the

Corrected Effective Temperature (CET) (Bedford 1940). Research reported by Macpherson (1960) suggested that the CET predicted physiological effects of increasing mean radiant temperature. ET and CET are now rarely used as comfort indices but have been used as heat stress indices. Bedford (1940) proposed CET as an index of warmth, with upper limits of 34 °C for "reasonable efficiency" and 38.6 °C for tolerance. Further investigation, however, showed that ET had serious disadvantages for use as a heat stress index, which led to the Predicted Four Hour Sweat Rate (P4SR) index.

Predicted Four Hour Sweat Rate

The Predicted Four Hour Sweat Rate (P4SR) index was established in London by McArdle et al. (1947) and evaluated in Singapore in 7 years of work summarized by Macpherson (1960). It is the amount of sweat secreted by fit, acclimatized young men exposed to the environment for 4 hours while loading guns with ammunition during a naval engagement. The single number (index value) which summarizes the effects of the six basic parameters is an amount of sweat from the specific population, but it should be used as an index value and not as an indication of an amount of sweat in an individual group of interest.

Figure 42.6 • Nomogram for the prediction of the "predicted 4-hour sweat rate" (P4SR).

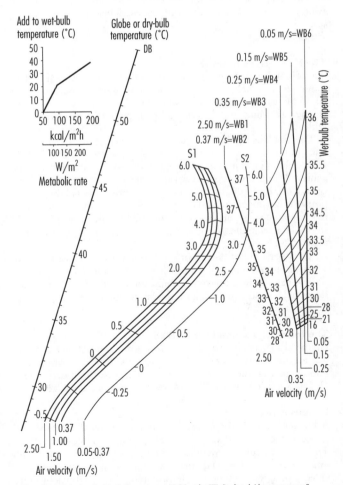

The nomogram is described in the box on page 42.20 under "III. Predicted 4-hour sweat rate".

It was acknowledged that outside of the prescriptive zone (e.g., P4SR>5 l) sweat rate was not a good indicator of strain. The P4SR nomograms (figure 42.6) were adjusted to attempt to account for this. The P4SR appears to have been useful under the conditions for which it was derived; however, the effects of clothing are over-simplified and it is most useful as a heat storage index. McArdle et al. (1947) proposed a P4SR of 4.5 l for a limit where no incapacitation of any fit, acclimatized young men occurred.

Heart rate prediction as an index

Fuller and Brouha (1966) proposed a simple index based on the prediction of heart rate (HR) in beats per minute. The relationship as originally formulated with metabolic rate in BTU/h and partial vapour pressure in mmHg provided a simple prediction of heart rate from $(T + p)$, hence the $T + p$ index.

Givoni and Goldman (1973) also provide equations for changing heart rate with time and also corrections for degree of acclimatization of subjects, which are given in the box on page 42.20 under "IV. Heart rate".

A method of work and recovery heart rate is described by NIOSH (1986) (from Brouha 1960 and Fuller and Smith 1980, 1981). Body temperature and pulse rates are measured during recovery following a work cycle or at specified times during the working day. At the end of a work cycle the worker sits on a stool, oral temperature is taken and the following three pulse rates are recorded:

P_1—pulse rate counted from 30 seconds to 1 minute
P_2—pulse rate counted from 1.5 to 2 minutes
P_3—pulse rate counted from 2.5 to 3 minutes

The ultimate criterion in terms of heat strain is an oral temperature of 37.5 °C.

If $P_3 \le 90$ bpm and $P_3 - P_1 = 10$ bpm, this indicates work level is high but there is little increase in body temperature. If $P_3>90$ bpm and $P_3 - P_1 <10$ bpm, the stress (heat + work) is too high and action is needed to redesign work.

Vogt et al. (1981) and ISO 9886 (1992) provide a model (table 42.5) using heart rate for assessing thermal environments:

The component of thermal strain (possible heat stress index) can be calculated from:

$$HR_t = HR_r - HR_0$$

where HR_r is heart rate after recovery and HR_0 is the resting heart rate in a thermally neutral environment.

Direct Heat Stress Indices

The Wet Bulb Globe Temperature index

The Wet Bulb Globe Temperature (WBGT) index is by far the most widely used throughout the world. It was developed in a US Navy investigation into heat casualties during training (Yaglou and Minard 1957) as an approximation to the more cumbersome Corrected Effective Temperature (CET), modified to account for the solar absorptivity of green military clothing.

WBGT limit values were used to indicate when military recruits could train. It was found that heat casualties and time lost due to cessation of training in the heat were both reduced by using the WBGT index instead of air temperature alone. The WBGT index was adopted by NIOSH (1972), ACGIH (1990) and ISO 7243 (1989a) and is still proposed today. ISO 7243 (1989a), based on the WBGT index, provides a method easily used in a hot environment to provide a "fast" diagnosis. The specification of the measuring instruments is provided in the standard, as are WBGT limit values for acclimatized or non-acclimatized persons (see table 42.6). For example, for a resting

Table 42.5 • Model using heart rate to assess heat stress.

Total heart rate	Activity level
HR_0	Rest (thermal neutrality)
$HR_0 + HR_M$	Work
$HR_0 + HR_S$	Static exertion
$HR_0 + HR_t$	Thermal strain
$HR_0 + HR_N$	Emotion (psychological)
$HR_0 + HR_e$	Residual

Based on Vogt et al. (1981) and ISO 9886 (1992).

acclimatized person in 0.6 clo, the limit value is 33 °C WBGT. The limits provided in ISO 7243 (1989a) and NIOSH 1972 are almost identical. Calculation of the WBGT index is given in section V of the accompanying box.

The simplicity of the index and its use by influential bodies has led to its widespread acceptance. Like all direct indices it has limitations when used to simulate human response, and should be used with caution in practical applications. It is possible to buy portable instruments which determine the WBGT index (e.g., Olesen 1985).

Physiological heat exposure limit (PHEL)

Dasler (1974, 1977) provides WBGT limit values based on a prediction of exceeding any two physiological limits (from experimental data) of impermissible strain. The limits are given by:

$$PHEL = (17.25 \times 10^8 - 12.97M \times 10^6 + 18.61M^2 \times 10^3) \times WBGT^{-5.36}$$

This index therefore uses the WBGT direct index in the environmentally driven zone (see figure 42.4), where heat storage can occur.

Wet globe temperature (WGT) index

The temperature of a wet black globe of appropriate size can be used as an index of heat stress. The principle is that it is affected by both dry and evaporative heat transfer, as is a sweating man, and the temperature can then be used, with experience, as a heat stress index. Olesen (1985) describes WGT as the temperature of a

Table 42.6 • WBGT reference values from ISO 7243 (1989a).

Metabolic rate M (Wm^{-2})	Reference value of WBGT			
	Person acclimatized to heat (°C)		Person not acclimatized to heat (°C)	
0. Resting $M \le 65$	33		32	
1. $65<M\le130$	30		29	
2. $130<M\le200$	28		26	
	No sensible air movement	Sensible air movement	No sensible air movement	Sensible air movement
3. $200<M<260$	25	26	22	23
4. $M>260$	23	25	18	20

Note: The values given have been established allowing for a maximum rectal temperature of 38 °C for the persons concerned.

Heat indices: Formulae and definitions

I. Index of thermal stress (ITS)

The improved *heat balance equation* is:

$$E_{req} = H - (C + R) - R_s$$

where E_{req} is the evaporation required to maintain heat balance, R_s is the solar load, and metabolic heat production H is used instead of metabolic rate to account for external work. An important improvement is the recognition that not all sweat evaporates (e.g., some drips) hence required sweat rate is related to required evaporation rate by:

$$SW = E_{req}/nsc$$

where *nsc* is the efficiency of sweating.

Used indoors, sensible heat transfer is calculated from:

$$R + C = \alpha v^{0.3}(35 - T_g)$$

For outdoor conditions with solar load, T_g is replaced with T_a and allowance made for solar load (R_s) by:

$$R_s = E_s K_{pe} K_{cl} (1 - \alpha(v^{0.2} - 0.88))$$

The equations used are fits to experimental data and are not strictly rational.

Maximum evaporation heat loss is:

$$E_{max} = K_p v^{0.3} (56 - P_a)$$

and efficiency of sweating is given by:

$$nsc = \exp\{-0.6[(E_{req}/E_{max}) - 0.12]\}$$

but

$$nsc = 1 \text{ if } E_{req}/E_{max} < 0.12$$

and

$$nsc = 0.29 \text{ if } E_{req}/E_{max} > 2.15$$

The index of thermal stress *(ITS)* in g/h is given by:

$$ITS = (H - (R + C) - R_s)/(0.37nsc)$$

where $(H - (R + C) - R_s)$ is the required evaporation rate E_{req}, 0.37 converts W/m^2 into g/h and *nsc* is the efficiency of sweating (McIntyre 1980).

II. Required sweat rate

Similar to the other rational indices, SW_{req} is derived from the six basic parameters (air temperature (T_a), radiant temperature (T_r), relative humidity air velocity (v), clothing insulation (I_{cl}), metabolic rate (M) and external work (W)). Effective radiation area values for posture (sitting = 0.72, standing = 0.77) are also required. From this the evaporation required is calculated from:

$$E_{req} = M - W - C_{res} - E_{res} - C - R$$

Equations are provided for each component (see tables 42.10 and 42.9). Mean skin temperature is calculated from a multiple linear regression equation or a value of 36 °C is assumed.

From the required evaporation (E_{req}) and maximum evaporation (E_{max}) and sweating efficiency (r), the following are calculated:

Required skin wettedness $W_{req} = E_{req}/E_{max}$

Required sweat rate $SW_{req} = E_{req}/r$

III. Predicted 4-hour sweat rate (P4SR)

Steps taken to obtain the *P4SR* index value are summarized by McIntyre (1980) as follows:

If $T_g \neq T_a$, increase wet bulb temperature by $0.4 \cdot (T_g - T_a)$ °C.

If the metabolic rate $M > 63$ W/m^2, increase wet bulb temperature by the amount indicated in the chart (see figure 42.6).

If the men are clothed, increase the wet bulb temperature by $1.5 I_{clo}$ (°C).

The modifications are additive.

The (P4SR) is determined from figure 42.6. The *P4SR* is then:

$$P4SR = B4SR + 0.37 I_{clo} + (0.012 + 0.001 I_{clo}) (M - 63)$$

IV. Heart rate

$$HR = 22.4 + 0.18M + 0.25 (5T_a + 2P_a)$$

where M is metabolic rate W/m^2, T_a is air temperature in °C and P_a is vapour pressure in Mb.

Givoni and Goldman (1973) provide equations for predicting heart rate of persons (soldiers) in hot environments. They define an index for heart rate *(IHR)* from a modification of predicted equilibrium rectal temperature,

$$\begin{aligned} T_{ref} = &\ 36.75 + 0.004(M - W_{ex}) \\ &+ (0.025/clo) (T_a - 36) \\ &+ 0.8e^{0.0047} (E_{req} - E_{max}). \end{aligned}$$

IHR is then:

$$IHR = 0.4M + (2.5/clo) (T_a - 36) + 80e^{0.0047} (E_{req} - E_{max})$$

where M = metabolic rate (watts), W_{ex} = mechanical work (watts), clo = thermal insulation of clothing, T_a = air temperature (°C), E_{req} = total metabolic and environmental heat load (watts), E_{max} = evaporative cooling capacity for clothing and environment (watts).

The equilibrium heart rate (HR_f in beats per minute) is then given by:

$$HR_f = 65 + 0.35 (IHR - 25) \text{ for } IHR \leq 225$$

that is, a linear relationship (between rectal temperature and heart rate) for heart rates up to about 150 beats per minute. For IHR >225:

$$HR_f = 65 + (HR_f - 65) (1 - e^{-3t})$$

that is, an exponential relationship as heart rate approaches maximum, where:

HR_f = equilibrium heart rate (bpm),

65 = assumed resting heart rate in comfortable conditions (bpm),

and t = time in hours.

V. Wet bulb globe temperature index (WBGT)

Wet bulb globe temperature is given by:

$$WBGT = 0.7T_{nwb} + 0.2T_g + 0.1T_a$$

for conditions with solar radiation, and:

$$WBGT = 0.7T_{nwb} + 0.3T_g$$

for indoor conditions with no solar radiation, where T_{nwb} = temperature of a naturally ventilated wet bulb thermometer, T_a = air temperature, and T_g = temperature of a 150 mm diameter black globe thermometer.

Table 42.7 • Working practices for hot environments.

A. Engineering controls	Example
1. Reduce heat source	Move away from workers or reduce temperature. Not always practicable.
2. Convective heat control	Modify air temperature and air movements. Spot coolers may be useful.
3. Radiant heat control	Reduce surface temperatures or place reflective shield between radiant source and workers. Change emissivity of surface. Use doors which open only when access required.
4. Evaporative heat control	Increase air movement, decrease water vapour pressure. Use fans or air conditioning. Wet clothing and blow air across person.

B. Work and hygiene practices and administrative controls	Example
1. Limiting exposure time and/or temperature	Perform jobs at cooler times of day and year. Provide cool areas for rest and recovery. Extra personnel, worker freedom to interrupt work, increase water intake.
2. Reduce metabolic heat load	Mechanization. Redesign job. Reduce work time. Increase workforce.
3. Enhance tolerance time	Heat acclimatization programme. Keep workers physically fit. Ensure water loss is replaced and maintain electrolyte balance if necessary.
4. Health and safety training	Supervisors trained in recognizing signs of heat illness and in first aid. Basic instruction to all personnel on personal precautions, use of protective equipment and effects of non-occupational factors (e.g. alcohol). Use of a "buddy" system. Contingency plans for treatment should be in place.
5. Screening for heat intolerance	History of previous heat illness. Physically unfit.

C. Heat alert programme	Example
1. In spring establish heat alert committee (industrial physician or nurse, industrial hygienist, safety engineer, operation engineer, high ranking manager)	Arrange training course. Memos to supervisors to make checks of drinking fountains, etc. Check facilities, practices, readiness, etc.
2. Declare heat alert in predicted hot weather spell	Postpone non-urgent tasks. Increase workers, increase rest. Remind workers to drink. Improve working practices.

D. Auxiliary body cooling and protective clothing
Use if it is not possible to modify worker, work or environment and heat stress is still beyond limits. Individuals should be fully heat acclimatized and well trained in use and practice of wearing the protective clothing. Examples are water-cooled garments, air-cooled garments, ice-packet vests and wetted overgarments.

E. Performance degradation
It must be remembered that wearing protective clothing that is providing protection from toxic agents will increase heat stress. All clothing will interfere with activities and may reduce performance (e.g. reducing the ability to receive sensory information hence impairing hearing and vision for example).

Source: NIOSH 1986.

2.5 inch (63.5 mm) diameter black globe covered with a damp black cloth. The temperature is read when equilibrium is reached after about 10 to 15 minutes of exposure. NIOSH (1986) describe the Botsball (Botsford 1971) as the simplest and most easily read instrument. It is a 3-inch (76.2 mm) copper sphere covered by a black cloth kept at 100% wettedness from a self-feeding water reservoir. The sensing element of a thermometer is located at the centre of the sphere, and the temperature is read on a (colour coded) dial.

A simple equation relating WGT to WBGT is:

$$WBGT = WGT + 2\ °C$$

for conditions of moderate radiant heat and humidity (NIOSH 1986), but of course this relationship cannot hold over a wide range of conditions.

The Oxford Index

Lind (1957) proposed a simple, direct index used for storage-limited heat exposure and based on a weighted summation of aspirated wet bulb temperature (T_{wb}) and dry bulb temperature (T_{db}):

$$WD = 0.85\ T_{wb} + 0.15\ T_{db}$$

Allowable exposure times for mine rescue teams were based on this index. It is widely applicable but is not appropriate where there is significant thermal radiation.

Working Practices for Hot Environments

NIOSH (1986) provides a comprehensive description of working practices for hot environments, including preventive medical practices. A proposal for medical supervision of individuals exposed to hot or cold environments is provided in ISO CD 12894 (1993). It should always be remembered that it is a basic human right, which was affirmed by the 1985 *Declaration of Helsinki*, that, when possible, persons can withdraw from any extreme environment without need of explanation. Where exposure does take place, defined working practices will greatly improve safety.

Table 42.8 • Equations used in the calculation of the SW_{req} index and assessment method of ISO 7933 (1989b).

$$SW_{req} = \frac{E_{req}}{r_{req}}$$

$$E_{req} = M - W - C_{res} - E_{res} - C - R$$

$$C_{res} = 0.0014\, M\, (35 - t_a)$$

$$E_{res} = 0.0173\, M\, (5.624 - P_a)$$

$$C = h_c \cdot F_{cl}\, (\bar{t}_{sk} - \bar{t}_a)$$

$$R = h_r \cdot F_{cl}\, (\bar{t}_{sk} - \bar{t}_r)$$

$$w = E/E_{max}$$

$$r = 1 - w^2/2$$

$$h_c = 2.38\, |\bar{t}_{sk} - t_a|^{0.25} \text{ for natural convection}$$
$$\quad = 3.5 + 5.2\, v_{ar}, \text{ for } v_{ar} < 1ms^{-1}$$
$$\quad = 8.7\, v_{ar}^{0.6}, \text{ for } v_{ar} > 1ms^{-1}$$

$$v_{ar} = v_a + 0.0052(M - 58)$$

$$h_r = (\sigma\, E_{sk} \cdot A_r/A_D)\, \frac{\left[\left(\bar{t}_{sk} + 273\right)^4 - \left(\bar{t}_r + 273\right)^4\right]}{(\bar{t}_{sk} - \bar{t}_r)}$$

$$F_{cl} = \frac{1}{\left[(h_c + h_r)\, I_{cl} + \dfrac{1}{f_{cl}}\right]}$$

$$f_{cl} = 1 + 1.97\, I_{cl}$$

$$E_{max} = \frac{\left(P_{sk,s} - P_a\right)}{R_T}$$

$$R_T = \frac{1}{\left(h_e \cdot F_{pcl}\right)}$$

$$h_e = 16.7\, h_c$$

$$F_{pcl} = \left\{1 + 2.22\, h_c \left[\frac{I_{cl} - \left(1 + \dfrac{1}{f_{cl}}\right)}{h_c - h_r}\right]\right\}^{-1}$$

$$\bar{t}_{sk} = 30.0 + 0.093\, t_a + 0.045\,\bar{t}_r - 0.571 v_a + 0.254 P_a + 0.00128 M - 3.57 I_{cl}$$
or $\bar{t}_{sk} = 36\,°C$, for an approximation or when values are beyond limits for which the equation was derived.

Table 42.9 • Description of terms used in ISO 7933 (1989b).

Symbol	Term	Units
A_r/A_{du}	fraction of skin surface involved in heat exchange by radiation	ND
C	heat exchange on the skin by convection	Wm^{-2}
C_{res}	respiratory heat loss by convection	Wm^{-2}
E	heat flow by evaporation at skin surface	Wm^{-2}
E_{max}	maximum evaporative rate which can be achieved with the skin completely wet	Wm^{-2}
E_{req}	required evaporation for thermal equilibrium	Wm^{-2}
E_{res}	respiratory heat loss by evaporation	Wm^{-2}
E_{sk}	skin emissivity (0.97)	ND
F_{cl}	reduction factor for sensible heat exchange due to clothing	ND
F_{pcl}	reduction factor for latent heat exchange	ND
f_{cl}	ratio of the subject's clothed to unclothed surface area	ND
h_c	convective heat transfer coefficient	$Wm^{-2}K^{-1}$
h_e	evaporative heat transfer coefficient	$Wm^{-2}kPa^{-1}$
h_r	radiative heat transfer coefficient	$Wm^{-2}K^{-1}$
I_{cl}	basic dry thermal insulation of clothing	$m^2\,KW^{-1}$
K	heat exchange on the skin by conduction	Wm^{-2}
M	metabolic power	Wm^{-2}
P_a	partial vapour pressure	kPa
$P_{sk,s}$	saturated vapour pressure at skin temperature	kPa
R	heat exchange on the skin by radiation	Wm^{-2}
R_T	total evaporative resistance of limiting layer of air and clothing	m^2kPaW^{-1}
r_{req}	evaporative efficiency at required sweat rate	ND
SW_{req}	required sweat rate for thermal equilibrium	Wm^{-2}
σ	Stefan-Boltzman constant, 5.67×10^{-8}	$Wm^{-2}K^{-4}$
t_a	air temperature	°C
$\bar{t}_r$	mean radiant temperature	°C
$\bar{t}_{sk}$	mean skin temperature	°C
v_a	air velocity for a stationary subject	ms^{-1}
v_{ar}	relative air velocity	ms^{-1}
W	mechanical power	Wm^{-2}
w	skin wettedness	ND
w_{req}	skin wettedness required	ND

ND = non-dimensional.

Table 42.10 • WBGT values (°C) for four work phases.

Work phase (minutes)	WBGT = $WBGT_{ank} + 2\ WBGT_{obd} + WBGT_{hd}$	WBGT reference
0–60	25	30
60–90	23	33
90–150	23	30
150–180	30	28

It is a reasonable principle in environmental ergonomics and in industrial hygiene that, where possible, the environmental stressor should be reduced at the source. NIOSH (1986) divides control methods into five types. These are presented in table 42.7.

There has been a great deal of military research into so-called NBC (nuclear, biological, chemical) protective clothing. In hot environments it is not possible to remove the clothing, and working practices are very important. A similar problem occurs for workers in nuclear power stations. Methods of cooling workers quickly so that they are able to perform again include sponging the outer surface of the clothing with water and blowing dry air over it. Other techniques include active cooling devices and methods for cooling local areas of the body. The transfer of military clothing technology to industrial situations is a new innovation, but much is known, and appropriate working practices can greatly reduce risk.

Assessment of a Hot Environment Using ISO Standards

The following hypothetical example demonstrates how ISO standards can be used in the assessment of hot environments (Parsons 1993):

Workers in a steel mill perform work in four phases. They don clothing and perform light work for 1 hour in a hot radiant environment. They rest for 1 hour, then perform the same light work for an hour shielded from the radiant heat. They then perform work involving a moderate level of physical activity in a hot radiant environment for 30 minutes.

ISO 7243 provides a simple method for monitoring the environment using the WBGT index. If the calculated WBGT levels are less than the WBGT reference values given in the standard, then no further action is required. If the levels exceed the reference values (table 42.6) then the strain on the workers must be reduced. This can be achieved by engineering controls and working practices. A complementary or alternative action is to conduct an analytical assessment according to ISO 7933.

Table 42.11 • Basic data for the analytical assessment using ISO 7933.

Work phase (minutes)	t_a (°C)	t_r (°C)	P_a (Kpa)	v (ms^{-1})	clo (clo)	Act (Wm^{-2})
0–60	30	50	3	0.15	0.6	100
60–90	30	30	3	0.05	0.6	58
90–150	30	30	3	0.20	0.6	100
150–180	30	60	3	0.30	1.0	150

Table 42.12 • Analytical assessment using ISO 7933.

Work phase (minutes)	Predicted values			Duration limited exposure (minutes)	Reason for limit
	t_{sk} (°C)	w (ND)	SW (gh^{-1})		
0–60	35.5	0.93	553	423	Water loss
60–90	34.6	0.30	83	480	No limit
90–150	34.6	0.57	213	480	No limit
150–180	35.7	1.00	566	45	Body temperature
Overall	—	0.82	382	480	No limit

The WBGT values for the work are presented in table 42.10 and were measured according to the specifications given in ISO 7243 and ISO 7726. The environmental and personal factors relating to the four phases of the work are presented in table 42.11.

It can be seen that for part of the work the WBGT values exceed those of the reference values. It is concluded that a more detailed analysis is required.

The analytical assessment method presented in ISO 7933 was performed using the data presented in table 42.11 and the computer program listed in the annex of the standard. The results for acclimatized workers in terms of alarm level are presented in table 42.12.

An overall assessment therefore predicts that unacclimatized workers suitable for the work could carry out an 8-hour shift without undergoing unacceptable (thermal) physiological strain. If greater accuracy is required, or individual workers are to be assessed, then ISO 8996 and ISO 9920 will provide detailed information concerning metabolic heat production and clothing insulation. ISO 9886 describes methods for measuring physiological strain on workers and can be used to design and assess environments for specific workforces. Mean skin temperature, internal body temperature, heart rate and mass loss will be of interest in this example. ISO CD 12894 provides guidance on medical supervision of an investigation.

HEAT EXCHANGE THROUGH CLOTHING

Wouter A. Lotens

In order to survive and work under colder or hotter conditions, a warm climate at the skin surface must be provided by means of clothing as well as artificial heating or cooling. An understanding of the mechanisms of heat exchange through clothing is necessary to design the most effective clothing ensembles for work at extreme temperatures.

Clothing Heat Transfer Mechanisms

The nature of clothing insulation

Heat transfer through clothing, or conversely the insulation of clothing, depends largely on the air that is trapped in and on the clothing. Clothing consists, as a first approximation, of any sort of material that offers a grip to air layers. This statement is approxi-

Formulae and Definitions

In general there is a square root relationship between thickness d of a static air layer and air velocity v. The exact function depends on the size and shape of the surface, but for the human body a useful approximation is:

$$d = .0031/\sqrt{v}$$

Still air acts as an insulating layer with a conductivity λ (a material constant, regardless of the shape of the material) of .026 W/mK, which has a heat transfer coefficient h (units of W/m^{2}K) (the conductive property of a slab of material) of:

$$h = \lambda \cdot d = 8.3 \sqrt{v} \text{ (Kerslake 1972)}.$$

Radiant heat flow (ϕ_r) between two surfaces is approximately proportional to their temperature difference:

$$\phi_r = 4 \cdot \varepsilon \cdot \sigma \cdot T^3 \Delta T$$

where T is the average absolute temperature (in Kelvin) of the two surfaces, ε is the absorption coefficient and σ is the Stefan-Boltzmann constant (5.67×10^{-8} W/m^{2}K^4). The amount of radiation exchange is inversely related to the number of intercepting layers (n):

$$\phi_r = \phi_{r0}/(1+n)$$

Clothing insulation (I_{cl}) is defined by the following equations:

$$I_{cl} = (T_{sk} - T_{cl})/\phi_{dry}$$

$$I_a = (T_{cl} - T_a) \cdot f_{cl}/\phi_{dry}$$

$$I_t = I_{cl} + I_a/f_{cl}$$

where I_{cl} is intrinsic insulation, I_a is (adjacent) air insulation, I_t is total insulation, T_{sk} is average skin temperature, T_{cl} is the average temperature of the outer surface of the clothing, T_a is air temperature, ϕ_{dry} is the dry heat flow (convective and radiant heat) per unit of skin area

and f_{cl} is the clothing area factor. This coefficient has been underestimated in older studies, but more recent studies converge to the expression $f_{cl} = 1 + 1.9 \cdot I_{cl}$

Often I is expressed in the unit *clo*; one clo equals 0.155 m^{2}K/W. McCullough et al. (1985) deduced a regression equation from data on a mix of clothing ensembles, using thickness of the textile (d_{fabr}, in mm) and percentage covered body area (p_{bc}) as determinants. Their formula for the insulation of single clothing items (I_{cli}) is:

$$I_{cli} = .0012 \cdot p_{bc} + .0002 \cdot p_{bc} \cdot d_{fa\%4br} - .012$$

The evaporative resistance R (units of s/m) can be defined as:

$$R_{cl} = (C_{sk} - C_{cl})/\dot{m}$$

(or sometimes $R_e = (P_{sk} - P_{cl})/\phi_e$, in m^{2}Pa/W)

$$R_{cl} = (d_{ens} + .001 \cdot n + .3 \cdot d_{cl})/D$$

For fabric layers, the air equivalent (d_{eq}) is the thickness of air that provides the same resistance to diffusion as the fabric does. The associated vapour ($\dot{m}$) and latent heat (ϕ_e) flows are:

$$\dot{m} = D \cdot \Delta C/d_{eq} \text{ (in units of g/m}^2\text{s)}$$

$$\phi_e = H_e \cdot \dot{m} \text{ (in units of W/m}^2\text{)}$$

where D is the diffusion coefficient (m^2/s), C the vapour concentration (g/m^3) and H_e the heat of evaporation (2430 J/g).

$$d_{eq} = .001 + 1.3 \cdot d_{fabr}$$

(from Lotens 1993). d_{eq} is related to R by:

$$d_{eq} = R \cdot D$$

where:
D is the diffusion coefficient for water vapour in air, 2.5×10^{-5} m^2/s.

mate because some material properties are still relevant. These relate to the mechanical construction of the fabrics (for instance wind resistance and the ability of fibres to support thick fabrics), and to intrinsic properties of fibres (for instance, absorption and reflection of heat radiation, absorption of water vapour, wicking of sweat). For not too extreme environmental conditions the merits of various fibre types are often overrated.

Air layers and air motion
The notion that it is air, and in particular still air, that provides insulation, suggests that thick air layers are beneficial for insulation. This is true, but the thickness of air layers is physically limited. Air layers are formed by adhesion of gas molecules to any surface, by cohesion of a second layer of molecules to the first, and so on. However, the binding forces between subsequent layers are less and less, with the consequence that the outer molecules are moved by even tiny external motions of air. In quiet air, air layers may have a thickness up to 12 mm, but with vigorous air motion, as in a storm, the thickness decreases to less than 1 mm. In general there is a square-root relationship between thickness and air motion (see "Formulae and Definitions" box). The exact function depends on the size and shape of the surface.

Heat conduction of still and moving air
Still air acts as an insulating layer with a conductivity that is constant, regardless of the shape of the material. Disturbance of air layers leads to loss of effective thickness; this includes disturbances not only due to wind, but also due to the motions of the wearer of the clothing—displacement of the body (a component

of wind) and motions of body parts. Natural convection adds to this effect. For a graph showing the effect of air velocity on the insulating ability of a layer of air, see figure 42.7.

Heat transfer by radiation
Radiation is another important mechanism for heat transfer. Every surface radiates heat, and absorbs heat that is radiated from other surfaces. Radiant heat flow is approximately proportional to the temperature difference between the two exchanging surfaces. A clothing layer between the surfaces will interfere with radiative heat transfer by intercepting the energy flow; the clothing will reach a temperature that is about the average of the temperatures of the two surfaces, cutting the temperature difference between them in two, and therefore the radiant flow is decreased by a factor of two. As the number of intercepting layers is increased, the rate of heat transfer is decreased.

Multiple layers are thus effective in reducing radiant heat transfer. In battings and fibre fleeces radiation is intercepted by distributed fibres, rather than a fabric layer. The density of the fibre material (or rather the total surface of fibre material per volume of fabric) is a critical parameter for radiation transfer inside such fibre fleeces. Fine fibres provide more surface for a given weight than coarse fibres.

Fabric insulation
As a result of the conductivities of enclosed air and radiation transfer, fabric conductivity is effectively a constant for fabrics of various thicknesses and bindings. The heat insulation is therefore proportional to the thickness.

Figure 42.7 • Effect of air velocity on insulating ability of an air layer.

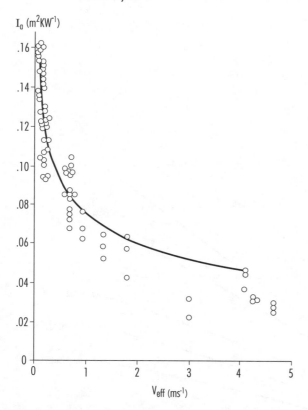

Figure 42.8 • Relationship between thickness and vapour resistance (d_{eq}) for fabrics without coatings.

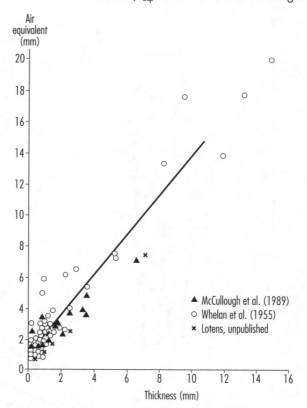

▲ McCullough et al. (1989)
○ Whelan et al. (1955)
✕ Lotens, unpublished

Vapour resistance of air and fabrics

Air layers also create a resistance to the diffusion of evaporated sweat from humid skin to the environment. This resistance is roughly proportional to the thickness of the clothing ensemble. For fabrics, the vapour resistance is dependent on the enclosed air and the density of the construction. In real fabrics, high density and great thickness never go together. Due to this limitation it is possible to estimate the air equivalent of fabrics that do not contain films or coatings (see figure 42.8). Coated fabrics or fabrics laminated to films may have unpredictable vapour resistance, which should be determined by measurement.

From Fabric and Air Layers to Clothing

Multiple layers of fabric

Some important conclusions from the heat transfer mechanisms are that highly insulating clothing is necessarily thick, that high insulation may be obtained by clothing ensembles with multiple thin layers, that a loose fit provides more insulation than a tight fit, and that insulation has a lower limit, set by the air layer that adheres to the skin.

In cold-weather clothing it is often hard to obtain thickness by using thin fabrics only. A solution is to create thick fabrics, by mounting two thin shell fabrics to a batting. The purpose of the batting is to create the air layer and keep the air inside as still as possible. There is also a drawback to thick fabrics: the more the layers are connected, the stiffer the clothing becomes, thereby restricting motion.

Clothing variety

The insulation of a clothing ensemble depends to a large extent on the design of the clothing. Design parameters which affect insulation are number of layers, apertures, fit, distribution of insulation over the body and exposed skin. Some material properties such as air permeability, reflectivity and coatings are important as well. Furthermore, wind and activity change the insulation. Is it possible to give an adequate description of clothing for the purpose of prediction of comfort and tolerance of the wearer? Various attempts have been made, based on different techniques. Most estimates of complete ensemble insulation have been made for static conditions (no motion, no wind) on indoor ensembles, because the available data were obtained from thermal mannequins (McCullough, Jones and Huck 1985). Measurements on human subjects are laborious, and results vary widely. Since the mid-1980s reliable moving mannequins have been developed and used (Olesen et al. 1982; Nielsen, Olesen and Fanger 1985). Also, improved measurement techniques allowed for more accurate human experiments. A problem that still has not been overcome completely is proper inclusion of sweat evaporation in the evaluation. Sweating mannequins are rare, and none of them has a realistic distribution of sweat rate over the body. Humans sweat realistically, but inconsistently.

Definition of clothing insulation

Clothing insulation (I_{cl} in units of m²K/W) for steady state conditions, without radiation sources or condensation in the clothing, is defined in the box. Often I is expressed in the unit clo (not a standard international unit). One clo equals 0.155 m²K/W. The

Figure 42.9 • Intrinsic insulation, as it is influenced by body curvature, bare skin and wind speed.

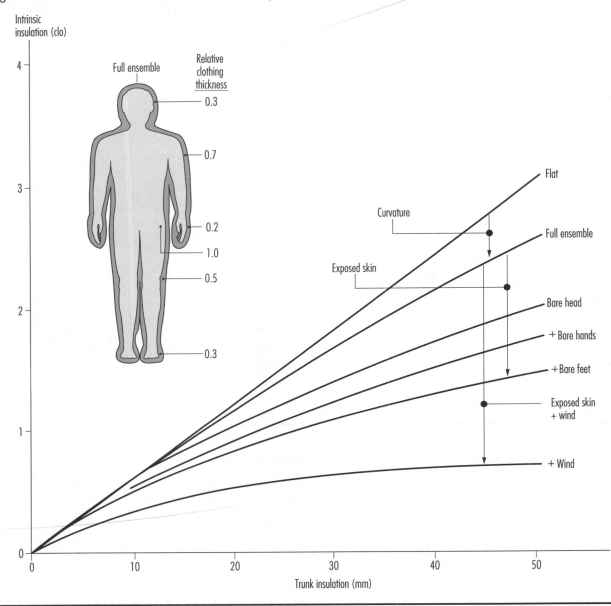

use of the unit clo implicitly means that it relates to the whole body and thus includes heat transfer by exposed body parts.

I is modified by motion and wind, as explained earlier, and after correction the result is called *resultant insulation*. This is a frequently used but not generally accepted term.

Distribution of clothing over the body

Total heat transfer from the body includes heat that is transferred by exposed skin (usually head and hands) and heat passing through the clothing. *Intrinsic insulation* (see box) is calculated over the total skin area, not only the covered part. Exposed skin transfers more heat than covered skin and thus has a profound influence on the intrinsic insulation. This effect is enhanced by increasing wind speed. Figure 42.9 shows how the intrinsic insulation decreases successively due to curvature of body shapes (outer layers less effective than inner), exposed body parts (additional pathway for heat transfer) and increased wind speed (less insulation, in particular for exposed skin) (Lotens 1989). For thick ensembles the reduction in insulation is dramatic.

Typical ensemble thickness and coverage

Apparently both the insulation thickness and the skin coverage are important determinants of heat loss. In real life the two are correlated in the sense that winter clothing is not only thicker, but also covers a larger proportion of the body than summer wear. Figure 42.10 demonstrates how these effects together result in an almost linear relation between clothing thickness (expressed as volume of insulation material per unit of clothing area) and insulation (Lotens 1989). The lower limit is set by the insulation of the adjacent air and the upper limit by usability of the clothing. Uniform distribution may provide the best insulation in the cold, but it is impractical to have much weight and bulk on the limbs.

Therefore the emphasis is often on the trunk, and the sensitivity of local skin to cold is adapted to this practice. Limbs play an important role in controlling human heat balance, and high insulation of the limbs limits the effectiveness of this regulation.

Ventilation of clothing

Trapped air layers in the clothing ensemble are subject to motion and wind, but to a different degree than the adjacent air layer. Wind creates ventilation in the clothing, both as air penetrating the fabric and by passing through apertures, while motion increases internal circulation. Havenith, Heus and Lotens (1990) found that inside clothing, motion is a stronger factor than in the adjacent air layer. This conclusion is dependent on the air permeability of the fabric, however. For highly air-permeable fabrics, ventilation by wind is considerable. Lotens (1993) showed that ventilation can be expressed as a function of effective wind speed and air permeability.

Estimates of Clothing Insulation and Vapour Resistance

Physical estimates of clothing insulation

Thickness of a clothing ensemble provides a first estimate of insulation. Typical conductivity of an ensemble is 0.08 W/mK. At an average thickness of 20 mm, that results in an I_{cl} of 0.25 m²K/W, or 1.6 clo. However, loose-fitting parts, such as trousers or sleeves, have a much higher conductivity, more on the order of 0.15, whereas tightly packed clothing layers have a conductivity of 0.04, the famous 4 clo per inch reported by Burton and Edholm (1955).

Estimates from tables

Other methods use table values for clothing items. These items have been measured previously on a mannequin. An ensemble under investigation has to be separated into its components, and these have to be looked up in the table. Making an incorrect choice of the most similar tabulated clothing item may cause errors. In order to obtain the intrinsic insulation of the ensemble, the single insulation values have to be put in a summation equation (McCullough, Jones and Huck 1985).

Clothing surface area factor

In order to calculate total insulation, f_{cl} has to be estimated (see box, p. 42.24). A practical experimental estimate is to measure the clothing surface area, make corrections for overlapping parts, and divide by total skin area (DuBois and DuBois 1916). Other estimates from various studies show that f_{cl} increases linearly with intrinsic insulation.

Estimate of vapour resistance

For a clothing ensemble, vapour resistance is the sum of resistance of air layers and clothing layers. Usually the number of layers varies over the body, and the best estimate is the area-weighted average, including exposed skin.

Relative vapour resistance

Evaporative resistance is less frequently used than I, because few measurements of C_{cl} (or P_{cl}) are available. Woodcock (1962) avoided this problem by defining the water vapour permeability index i_m as the ratio of I and R, related to the same ratio for a single air layer (this latter ratio is nearly a constant and known as the psychrometric constant S, 0.0165 K/Pa, 2.34 Km³/g or 2.2 K/torr); $i_m = I/(R \cdot S)$. Typical values for i_m for non-coated clothing, determined on mannequins, are 0.3 to 0.4 (McCullough, Jones and Tamura 1989). Values for i_m for fabric composites and their adjacent air can be measured relatively simply on a wet

Figure 42.10 • Total insulation resulting from clothing thickness and distribution over the body.

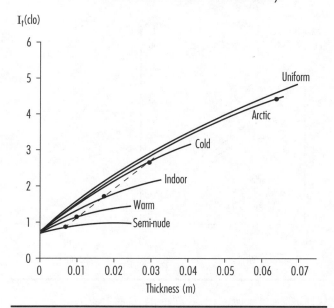

hotplate apparatus, but the value is actually dependent on air flow over the apparatus and the reflectivity of the cabinet in which it is mounted. Extrapolation of the ratio of R and I for clothed humans from measurements on fabrics to clothing ensembles (DIN 7943-2 1992) is sometimes attempted. This is a technically complicated matter. One reason is that R is proportional only to the convective part of I, so that careful corrections have to be made for radiative heat transfer. Another reason is that trapped air between fabric composites and clothing ensembles may be differ-

Figure 42.11 • Articulation of human shape in cyclinders.

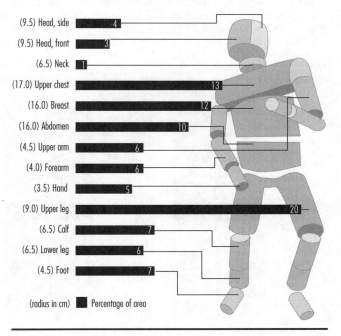

Figure 42.12 • Decrease in vapour resistance with wind and walking for various rainwear.

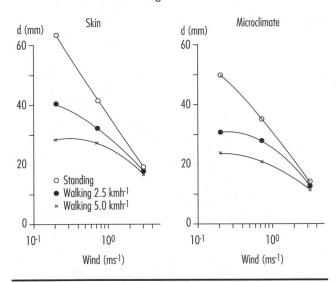

Effect of activity and wind

Lotens and Havenith (1991) also provide modifications, based on literature data, of the insulation and vapour resistance due to activity and wind. Insulation is lower while sitting than standing, and this effect is larger for highly insulating clothing. However, motion decreases insulation more than posture does, depending on the vigour of the movements. During walking both arms and legs move, and the reduction is larger than during cycling, when only the legs move. Also in this case, the reduction is larger for thick clothing ensembles. Wind decreases insulation the most for light clothing and less for heavy clothing. This effect might relate to the air permeability of the shell fabric, which is usually less for cold-weather gear.

Figure 42.12 shows some typical effects of wind and motion on vapour resistance for rainwear. There is no definite agreement in the literature about the magnitude of motion or wind effects. The importance of this subject is stressed by the fact that some standards, such as ISO 7730 (1994), require resultant insulation as an input when applied for active persons, or persons exposed to significant air motion. This requirement is often overlooked.

Moisture Management

Effects of moisture absorption

When fabrics can absorb water vapour, as most natural fibres do, clothing works as a buffer for vapour. This changes the heat transfer during transients from one environment to another. As a person in non-absorbing clothing steps from a dry to a humid environment, the evaporation of sweat decreases abruptly. In hygroscopic clothing the fabric absorbs vapour, and the change in evaporation is only gradual. At the same time the absorption process liberates heat in the fabric, increasing its temperature. This reduces the dry heat transfer from the skin. In first approximation, both effects cancel each other, leaving the total heat transfer unchanged. The difference with non-hygroscopic clothing is the more gradual change in evaporation from the skin, with less risk of sweat accumulation.

ent. In fact, vapour diffusion and heat transfer can be better treated separately.

Estimates by articulated models

More sophisticated models are available to calculate insulation and water vapour resistance than the above-explained methods. These models calculate local insulation on the basis of physical laws for a number of body parts and integrate these to intrinsic insulation for the whole human shape. For this purpose the human shape is approximated by cylinders (figure 42.11). The model by McCullough, Jones and Tamura (1989) requires clothing data for all layers in the ensemble, specified per body segment. The CLOMAN model of Lotens and Havenith (1991) requires fewer input values. These models have similar accuracy, which is better than any of the other methods mentioned, with the exception of experimental determination. Unfortunately and inevitably the models are more complex than would be desirable in a widely accepted standard.

Vapour absorption capacity

Absorption capacity of fabric depends on the fibre type and the fabric mass. Absorbed mass is roughly proportional to the relative humidity, but is higher above 90%. The absorption capacity (called *regain*) is expressed as the amount of water vapour that is

Figure 42.13 • General description of a dynamic thermal model.

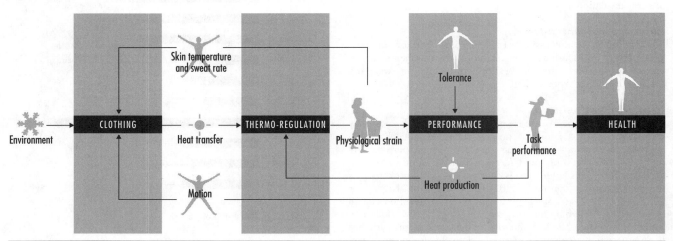

absorbed in 100 g of dry fibre at the relative humidity of 65%. Fabrics can be classified as follows:

- *low absorption*—acrylic, polyester (1 to 2 g per 100 g)
- *intermediate absorption*—nylon, cotton, acetate (6 to 9 g per 100 g)
- *high absorption*—silk, flax, hemp, rayon, jute, wool (11 to 15 g per 100 g).

Water uptake

Water retention in fabrics, often confused with vapour absorption, obeys different rules. Free water is loosely bound to fabric and spreads well sideways along capillaries. This is known as wicking. Transfer of liquid from one layer to another takes place only for wet fabrics and under pressure. Clothing may be wetted by non-evaporated (superfluous) sweat that is taken up from the skin. The liquid content of fabric may be high and its evaporation at a later moment a threat to the heat balance. This typically happens during rest after hard work and is known as *after-chill*. The ability of fabrics to hold liquid is more related to fabric construction than to fibre absorption capacity, and for practical purposes is usually sufficient to take up all the superfluous sweat.

Condensation

Clothing may get wet by condensation of evaporated sweat at a particular layer. Condensation occurs if the humidity is higher than the local temperature allows. In cold weather that will often be the case at the inside of the outer fabric, in extreme cold even in deeper layers. Where condensation takes place, moisture accumulates, but the temperature increases, as it does during absorption. The difference between condensation and absorption, however, is that absorption is a temporary process, whereas condensation may continue for extended times. Latent heat transfer during condensation may contribute very significantly to heat loss, which may or may not be desirable. The accumulation of moisture is mostly a drawback, because of discomfort and risk of after-chill. For profuse condensation, the liquid may be transported back to the skin, to evaporate again. This cycle works as a heat pipe and may strongly reduce the insulation of the underclothing.

Dynamic Simulation

Since the early 1900s many standards and indices have been developed to classify clothing and climates. Almost without exception these have dealt with steady states—conditions in which the climate and work were maintained long enough for a person to develop a constant body temperature. This type of work has become rare, due to improved occupational health and work conditions. The emphasis has shifted to short-duration exposure to harsh circumstances, often related to calamity management in protective clothing.

There is thus a need for dynamic simulations involving clothing heat transfer and thermal strain of the wearer (Gagge, Fobelets and Berglund 1986). Such simulations can be carried out by means of dynamic computer models that run through a specified scenario. Among the most sophisticated models to date with respect to clothing is THDYN (Lotens 1993), which allows for a wide range of clothing specifications and has been updated to include individual characteristics of the simulated person (figure 42.13). More models may be expected. There is a need, however, for extended experimental evaluation, and running such models is the work of experts, rather than the intelligent layperson. Dynamic models based on the physics of heat and mass transfer include all heat transfer mechanisms and their interactions—vapour absorption, heat from radiant sources, condensation, ventilation, moisture accumulation, and so on—for a wide range of clothing ensembles, including civil, work and protective clothing.

COLD ENVIRONMENTS AND COLD WORK

Ingvar Holmér, Per-Ola Granberg and Goran Dahlstrom

A cold environment is defined by conditions that cause greater than normal body heat losses. In this context "normal" refers to what people experience in everyday life under comfortable, often indoor conditions, but this may vary due to social, economic or natural climatic conditions. For the purpose of this article environments with an air temperature below 18 to 20 °C would be considered cold.

Cold work comprises a variety of industrial and occupational activities under different climatic conditions (see table 42.23). In most countries the food industry requires work under cold conditions—normally 2 to 8 °C for fresh food and below –25 °C for frozen food. In such artificial cold environments, conditions are relatively well defined and the exposure is about the same from day to day.

In many countries the seasonal climatic changes imply that outdoor work and work in unheated buildings for shorter or longer periods has to be carried out under cold conditions. The cold exposure may vary considerably between different locations on the earth and type of work (see table 42.23). Cold water presents another hazard, encountered by people engaged in, for example, offshore work. This article deals with responses to cold stress, and preventive measures. Methods for assessment of cold stress and acceptable temperature limits according to recently adopted international standards are dealt with elsewhere in this chapter.

Cold Stress and Work in the Cold

Cold stress may be present in many different forms, affecting the whole-body heat balance as well as the local heat balance of extremities, skin and lungs. The type and nature of cold stress is extensively described elsewhere in this chapter. The natural means of dealing with cold stress is by behavioural action—in particular, change and adjustment of clothing. Sufficient protection prevents cooling. However, protection itself may cause unwanted, adverse effects. The problem is illustrated in figure 42.14.

Cooling of the whole body or parts of the body results in discomfort, impaired sensory and neuro-muscular function and, ultimately, cold injury. Cold discomfort tends to be a strong stimulus to behavioural action, reducing or eliminating the effect. Prevention of cooling by means of donning cold-protective clothing, footwear, gloves and headgear interferes with the mobility and dexterity of the worker. There is a "cost of protection" in the sense that movements and motions become restricted and more exhausting. The continuous need for adjustment of the equipment to maintain a high level of protection requires attention and judgement, and may compromise factors such as vigilance and reaction time. One of the most important objectives of ergonomics research is the improvement of the functionality of clothing while maintaining cold protection.

Accordingly, effects of work in the cold must be divided into:

- effects of tissue cooling
- effects of protective measures ("cost of protection").

On exposure to cold, behavioural measures reduce the cooling effect and, eventually, allow the maintenance of normal thermal balance and comfort. Insufficient measures evoke thermoregulatory, physiologically compensatory reactions (vasoconstriction and shivering). The combined action of behavioural and physiological adjustments determines the resulting effect of a given cold stress.

42. HEAT AND COLD

Figure 42.14 • Examples of cold effects.

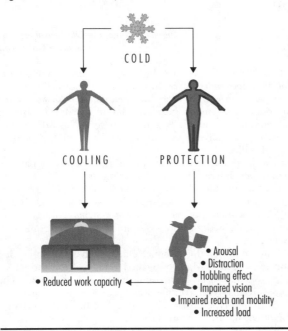

In the following sections these effects will be described. They are divided into acute effects (occurring within minutes or hours), long-term effects (days or even years) and other effects (not directly related to cooling reactions *per se*). Table 42.13 presents examples of reactions associated with the duration of cold exposure. Naturally, types of responses and their magnitude depend largely upon the stress level. However, long exposures (days and longer) hardly involve the extreme levels that can be attained for a short time.

Table 42.13 • Duration of uncompensated cold stress and associated reactions.

Time	Physiological effects	Psychological effect
Seconds	Inspiratory gasp Hyperventilation Heart rate elevation Peripheral vasoconstriction Blood pressure rise	Skin sensation, discomfort
Minutes	Tissue cooling Extremity cooling Neuro-muscular deterioration Shivering Contact and convective frostnip	Performance decrement Pain from local cooling
Hours	Impaired physical work capacity Hypothermia Cold injury	Impaired mental function
Days/months	Non-freezing cold injury Acclimatization	Habituation Reduced discomfort
Years	Chronic tissue effects (?)	

Acute effects of cooling

The most obvious and direct effect of cold stress is the immediate cooling of the skin and the upper airways. Thermal receptors respond and a sequence of thermoregulatory reactions is initiated. The type and magnitude of reaction is determined primarily by the type and severity of cooling. As previously mentioned, peripheral vasoconstriction and shivering are the main defence mechanisms. Both contribute to preserving body heat and core temperature, but compromise cardiovascular and neuro-muscular functions.

However, the psychological effects of cold exposure also modify the physiological reactions in a complex and partly unknown way. The cold environment causes distraction in the sense that it requires increased mental effort to handle the new stress factors (avoid cooling, take protective measures, etc.). On the other hand, the cold also causes arousal, in the sense that the increased stress level increases sympathetic nervous activity and, thereby, preparedness for action. In normal conditions people use only minor portions of their capacity, thereby preserving a large buffer capacity for unexpected or demanding conditions.

Cold perception and thermal comfort

Most humans experience a sensation of thermal neutrality at an operative temperature between 20 and 26 °C when engaged in very light, sedentary work (office work at 70 W/m²) in appropriate clothing (insulation values between 0.6 and 1.0 clo). In this state and in the absence of any local thermal imbalances, like draught, people are in thermal comfort. These conditions are well documented and specified in standards such as ISO 7730 (see the chapter *Controlling the indoor environment* in this *Encyclopaedia*).

Human perception of cooling is closely related to whole-body heat balance as well as local tissue heat balance. Cold thermal discomfort arises when body heat balance cannot be maintained due to inappropriate matching of activity (metabolic heat production) and clothing. For temperatures between +10 and +30 °C, the magnitude of "cold discomfort" in a population can be predicted by Fanger's comfort equation, described in ISO 7730.

A simplified and reasonably accurate formula for computation of the thermoneutral temperature *(t)* for the average person is:

$$t = 33.5 - 3 \cdot I_{cl} - (0.08 + 0.05 \cdot I_{cl}) \cdot M$$

where M is the metabolic heat measured in W/m² and I_{cl} the insulation value of clothing measured in clo.

The required clothing insulation (clo value) is higher at +10°C than that calculated with the IREQ method (calculated required insulation value) (ISO TR 11079, 1993). The reason for this discrepancy is the application of different "comfort" criteria in the two methods. ISO 7730 focuses heavily on thermal comfort and allows for considerable sweating, whereas ISO TR 11079 allows only "control" sweating at minimal levels—a necessity in the cold. Figure 42.15 depicts the relationship between clothing insulation, activity level (heat production) and air temperature according to the equation above and the IREQ method. The filled areas should represent the expected variation in required clothing insulation due to different levels of "comfort".

The information in figure 42.15 is only a guide for establishing optimal indoor thermal conditions. There is considerable individual variation in perception of thermal comfort and discomfort from cold. This variation originates from differences in clothing and activity patterns, but subjective preferences and habituation also contribute.

In particular, people engaged in very light, sedentary activity become increasingly susceptible to local cooling when air temperature drops below 20 to 22 °C. In such conditions air velocity must be kept low (below 0.2 m/s), and additional insulative clothing must be selected to cover sensitive body parts (e.g., head, neck,

Figure 42.15 • Optimal temperature for thermal "comfort" as function of clothing and activity level (W/m²).

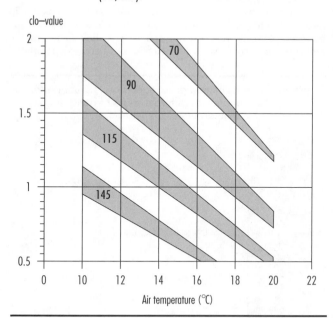

clo–value

Air temperature (°C)

Table 42.14 • Indication of anticipated effects of mild and severe cold exposure.

Performance	Mild cold exposure	Severe cold exposure
Manual performance	0 –	– –
Muscular performance	0	–
Aerobic performance	0	–
Simple reaction time	0	
Choice reaction time	–	– –
Tracking, vigilance	0 –	–
Cognitive, mental tasks	0 –	– –

0 indicates no effect; – indicates impairment; – – indicates strong impairment; 0 – indicates contradictory finding.

Table 42.15 indicates reported relationships between physical performance and temperatures of the body. It is assumed that physical performance is highly dependent on tissue temperature and deteriorates when temperature of vital tissue and organ parts drops. Typically, manual dexterity is critically dependent upon finger and hand temperature, as well as muscle temperature of the forehand. Gross muscular activity is little affected by local surface temperature, but very sensitive to muscle temperature. Since some of these temperatures are related to each other (e.g., core and muscle temperature) it is difficult to determine direct relationships.

The overview of performance effects in tables 42.14 and 42.15 is by necessity very schematic. The information should serve as a signal for action, where action means a detailed assessment of conditions or undertaking of preventive measures.

An important factor contributing to performance decrements is exposure time. The longer the cold exposure, the greater the effect upon the deeper tissues and neuro-muscular function. On the other hand, factors such as habituation and experience modify the detrimental effects and restore some of the performance capacity.

Manual performance

Hand function is very susceptible to cold exposure. Due to their small mass and large surface area, hands and fingers lose much heat while maintaining high tissue temperatures (30 to 35 °C). Accordingly, such high temperatures can be maintained only with

back and ankles). Seated work at temperatures below 20 °C requires insulated seat and backrest to reduce local cooling due to compression of clothing.

When ambient temperature falls below 10 °C, the comfort concept becomes more difficult to apply. Thermal asymmetries become "normal" (e.g., cold face and cold air inhalation). Despite an optimal body heat balance, such asymmetries may be felt to be uncomfortable and require extra heat to eliminate. Thermal comfort in the cold, unlike under normal indoor conditions, is likely to coincide with a slight feeling of warmth. This should be remembered when cold stress is assessed using the IREQ index.

Performance

Cold exposure and the associated behavioural and physiological reactions have an impact on human performance at various levels of complexity. Table 42.14 presents a schematic overview of different types of performance effects that may be anticipated with mild and extreme cold exposure.

Mild exposure in this context implies no or negligible body core cooling and moderate cooling of the skin and extremities. Severe exposure results in negative heat balance, a drop in core temperature and concomitant pronounced lowering of temperature of the extremities.

The physical characteristics of mild and severe cold exposure are very much dependent on the balance between internal body heat production (as a result of physical work) and heat losses. Protective clothing and ambient climatic conditions determine the amount of heat loss.

As previously mentioned, cold exposure causes distraction and cooling (figure 42.14). Both have an impact on performance, although the magnitude of impact varies with the type of task.

Behaviour and mental function are more susceptible to the distraction effect, whereas physical performance is more affected by cooling. The complex interaction of physiological and psychological responses (distraction, arousal) to cold exposure is not fully understood and requires further research work.

Table 42.15 • Importance of body tissue temperature for human physical performance.

Performance	Hand/finger skin temperature	Mean skin temperature	Muscle temperature	Core temperature
Simple manual	–	0	–	0
Complex manual	– –	(–)	– –	–
Muscular	0	0 –	– –	0 –
Aerobic	0	0	–	– –

0 indicates no effect; – indicates impairment with lowered temperature; – – indicates strong impairment; 0 – indicates contradictory findings; (–) indicates possible minor effect.

Figure 42.16 • Relation between finger dexterity and finger skin temperature.

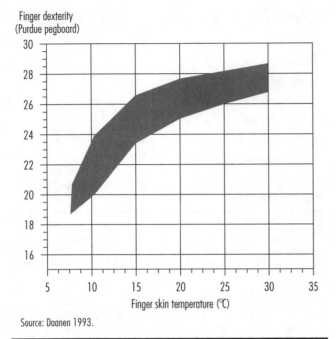

Source: Daanen 1993.

a high level of internal heat production, allowing for sustained high blood flow to the extremities.

Hand heat loss can be reduced in the cold by wearing appropriate handwear. However, good handwear for cold weather means thickness and volume, and, consequently, impaired dexterity and manual function. Hence, manual performance in the cold cannot be preserved by passive measures. At best, the reduction in performance may be limited as the result of a balanced compromise between the choice of functional handwear, work behaviour and exposure scheme.

Hand and finger function is much dependent on local tissue temperatures (figure 42.16). Fine, delicate and fast finger movements deteriorate when tissue temperature drops by a few degrees. With more profound cooling and temperature drop, gross hand functions are also impaired. Significant impairment in hand function is found at hand skin temperatures around 15 °C, and severe impairments occur at skin temperatures about 6 to 8 °C due to blocking of function of sensory and thermal skin receptors. Depending on task requirements, it may be necessary to measure skin temperature at several sites on the hand and fingers. Temperature of the fingertip may be more than ten degrees lower than on the back of the hand under certain exposure conditions. Figure 42.17 indicates critical temperatures for different types of effects on manual function.

Neuro-muscular performance

It is evident from figures 42.16 and 42.17 that there is a pronounced effect of cold on muscular function and performance. Cooling of muscle tissue reduces blood flow and slows down neural processes like transmission of nerve signals and synaptic function. In addition, viscosity of tissues increases, resulting in higher internal friction during motion.

Isometric force output is reduced by 2% per °C of lowered muscle temperature. Dynamic force output is reduced by 2 to 4% per °C of lowered muscle temperature. In other words, cooling

reduces the force output of muscles and has an even greater effect on dynamic contractions.

Physical work capacity

As previously mentioned, muscular performance deteriorates in the cold. With impaired muscle function there is a general impairment of physical work capacity. A contributing factor to the reduction in aerobic work capacity is the increased peripheral

Figure 42.17 • Estimated gross effects on manual performance at different levels of hand/finger temperature.

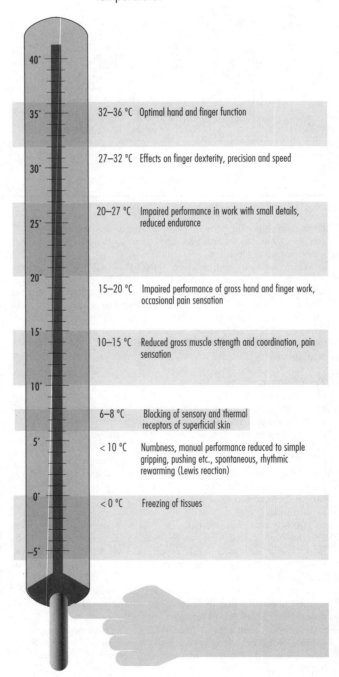

Figure 42.18 • Cold-induced vasodilatation of finger vessels causing cyclic rises in tissue temperature.

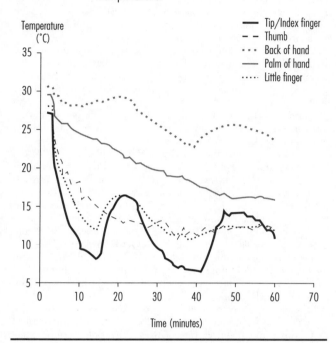

resistance of the systemic circulation. Pronounced vasoconstriction increases central circulation, eventually leading to cold diuresis and elevated blood pressure. Cooling of the core may also have a direct effect on the contractility of the heart muscle.

Work capacity, as measured by maximal aerobic capacity, decreases by 5 to 6% per °C lowered core temperature. Thus endurance may deteriorate rapidly as the practical consequence of the lowered maximal capacity and with an increased energy requirement of muscular work.

Other cold effects

Body temperatures

As the temperature drops, the surface of the body is most affected (and also most tolerant). Skin temperature may fall below 0 °C in a few seconds when the skin is in contact with very cold metal surfaces. Likewise hand and finger temperatures may decrease by several degrees per minute under conditions of vasoconstriction and poor protection. At normal skin temperature the arms and hands are superperfused due to peripheral arterio-venous shunts. This creates warmth and enhances dexterity. Cooling of the skin shuts these shunts and decreases perfusion in hands and feet to one tenth. The extremities constitute 50% of the body surface and 30% of its volume. The return of blood passes via deep veins concomitant to the arteries, thereby reducing heat loss according to the counter-current principle.

Adrenergic vasoconstriction does not occur in the head-neck region, which must be borne in mind in emergency situations to prevent hypothermia. A bareheaded individual may lose 50% or more of his or her resting heat production at subzero temperatures.

A high and sustained rate of whole-body heat loss is required for the development of hypothermia (drop in core temperature)

(Maclean and Emslie-Smith 1977). The balance between heat production and heat loss determines the resultant cooling rate, be it a whole-body cooling or a local cooling of a part of the body. The conditions for heat balance can be analysed and assessed on the basis of the IREQ index. A remarkable response to local cooling of protruding parts of the human body (e.g., fingers, toes and ears) is the hunting phenomenon (Lewis reaction). After an initial drop to a low value, finger temperature increases by several degrees (figure 42.18). This reaction is repeated in a cyclic manner. The response is very local—more pronounced at the tip of the finger than at the base. It is absent in the hand. The response on the palm of the hand most likely reflects the variation in temperature of the blood flow supplying the fingers. The response can be modified by repeated exposures (amplified), but is more or less abolished in association with whole-body cooling.

Progressive cooling of the body results in a number of physiological and mental effects. Table 42.16 indicates some typical responses associated with different levels of core temperature.

Heart and circulation

Cooling of the forehead and head elicit acute elevation of systolic blood pressure and, eventually, elevated heart rate. A similar reaction may be seen when putting bare hands in very cold water. The reaction is of short duration, and normal or slightly elevated values are attained after seconds or minutes.

Table 42.16 • Human responses to cooling: Indicative reactions to different levels of hypothermia.

Phase	Core temperature (°C)	Physiological reactions	Psychological reactions
Normal	37	Normal body temperature	Thermoneutral sensation
	36	Vasoconstriction, cold hands and feet	Discomfort
Mild hypothermia	35	Intense shivering, reduced work capacity	Impaired judgement, disorientation, apathy
	34	Fatigue	Conscious and responsive
	33	Fumbling and stumbling	
Moderate hypothermia	32	Muscle rigidity	Progressive unconsciousness, hallucinations
	31	Faint breathing	Consciousness clouds
	30		Stuporous
	29	No nerve reflexes, heart rate slow and almost unnoticeable	
Severe hypothermia	28	Heart dysrhythmias (atrial and/or ventricular)	
	27	Pupils non reactive to light, deep tendon and superficial reflexes absent	
	25	Death due to ventricular fibrillation or asystole	

Excessive body heat loss causes peripheral vasoconstriction. In particular, during the transient phase the increased peripheral resistance results in an elevation of systolic blood pressure and increased heart rate. Cardiac work is greater than it would be for similar activities at normal temperatures, a phenomenon painfully experienced by persons with angina pectoris.

As previously mentioned, deeper tissue cooling generally slows down the physiological processes of cells and organs. Cooling weakens the innervation process and suppresses heart contractions. Contraction power is reduced and, in addition to the increase in peripheral resistance of the blood vessels, cardiac output is reduced. However, with moderate and severe hypothermia, cardiovascular function declines in relation to the general reduction in metabolism.

Lungs and airways

Inhalation of moderate volumes of cold, dry air presents limited problems in healthy persons. Very cold air may cause discomfort, in particular, with nasal breathing. High ventilation volumes of very cold air may also cause micro-inflammation of the mucosal membrane of the upper airways.

With progression of hypothermia, lung function is depressed contemporaneously with the general reduction in body metabolism.

Functional aspects (work capacity)

A fundamental requirement for function in cold environments is the provision of sufficient protection against cooling. However, protection itself may seriously interfere with conditions for performance. The hobbling effect of clothing is well-known. Headgear and helmets interfere with speech and vision, and handwear impairs manual function. Whereas protection is necessary for preservation of healthy and comfortable working conditions, the consequences in terms of impaired performance must be fully recognized. Tasks take longer to complete and require greater effort.

Protective clothing against cold may easily weigh 3 to 6 kg including boots and headwear. This weight adds to workload, in particular during ambulatory work. Also, friction between layers in multi-layer clothing yields resistance to motion. The weight of boots should be kept low, since added weight on the legs contributes relatively more to workload.

Work organization, workplace and equipment should be adapted to the specific requirements of a cold work task. More time must be allowed for tasks, and frequent breaks for recovery and warming are needed. The workplace must allow for easy movements, despite bulky clothing. Similarly, equipment must be designed so that it can be operated by a gloved hand or insulated in the case of bare hands.

Cold Injuries

Serious injuries by cold air are in most cases preventable and occur only sporadically in civilian life. On the other hand, these injuries are often of major significance in war and in cataclysms. However, many workers run the risk of getting cold injuries in their routine activities. Outdoor work in harsh climate (as in arctic and subarctic areas—for example, fishing, agriculture, construction, gas and oil exploration and reindeer herding) as well as indoor work carried out in cold environments (as in food or warehousing industries) can all involve danger of cold injury.

Cold injuries may be either systemic or localized. The local injuries, which most often precede systemic hypothermia, constitute two clinically different entities: freezing cold injuries (FCI) and non-freezing cold injuries (NFCI).

Freezing cold injuries

Pathophysiology

This type of local injury occurs when heat loss is sufficient to allow a true freezing of the tissue. Besides a direct cryogenic insult to the cells, vascular damage with decreased perfusion and tissue hypoxia are contributing pathogenic mechanisms.

The vasoconstriction of cutaneous vessels is of great importance in the origin of a frostbite. Due to wide arteriovenous shunts, peripheral structures such as hands, feet, nose and ears are superperfused in a warm environment. Only about one-tenth of the blood flow in the hands, for example, is needed for tissue oxygenation. The rest creates warmth, thereby facilitating dexterity. Even in the absence of any decrease in core temperature, local cooling of the skin occludes these shunts.

In order to protect the viability of the peripheral parts of the extremities during cold exposure, an intermittent cold-induced vasodilatation (CIVD) takes place. This vasodilatation is a result of opening of the arteriovenous anastomoses and occurs every 5 to 10 minutes. The phenomenon is a compromise in the human physiological plan to conserve heat and yet intermittently preserve function of hands and feet. The vasodilatation is perceived by the person as periods of prickling heat. CIVD becomes less pronounced as body temperature decreases. Individual variations in the degree of CIVD might explain different susceptibility to local cold injury. People indigenous to a cold climate present a more pronounced CIVD.

In contrast to cryopreservation of living tissue, where ice crystallization occurs both intra- and extracellularly, the clinical FCI, with a much slower rate of freezing, produces only extracellular ice crystals. The process is an exothermic one, liberating heat, and therefore tissue temperature remains at the freezing point until freezing is complete.

As the extracellular ice crystals grow, extracellular solutions are condensed, causing this space to become a hyperosmolar milieu, which leads to passive diffusion of water from the intracellular compartment; that water in turn freezes. This process progresses until all "available" water (not otherwise bound to protein, sugar and other molecules) has been crystallized. Cell dehydration alters protein structures, membrane lipids and cellular pH, leading to destruction incompatible with cell survival. Resistance to FCI varies in different tissues. Skin is more resistant than muscles and nerves, for example, which might be the result of a smaller water content both intra- and intercellularly in the epidermis.

The role of indirect haemorheological factors was earlier interpreted as similar to that found in non-freezing cold injuries. Recent studies in animals have, however, shown that freezing causes lesions in the intima of arterioles, venules and capillaries prior to any evidence of damage to other skin elements. Thus, it is obvious that the rheological part of the pathogenesis of FCI is also a cryobiological effect.

When a frostbite is rewarmed, water begins to rediffuse to the dehydrated cells, leading to intracellular swelling. Thawing induces maximal vascular dilation, creating oedema and blister formation due to the endothelial (internal layer of the skin) cell injury. Disruption of the endothelial cells exposes the basement membrane, which initiates platelet adhesions and starts the coagulation cascade. The following blood stagnation and thrombosis induce anoxia.

As it is the heat loss from the exposed area that determines the risk of getting a frostbite, wind-chill is an important factor in this respect, and this means not only the wind which is blowing but also any movement of air past the body. Running, skiing, skijoring and riding in open vehicles must be considered in this context. However, the exposed flesh will not freeze as long as the ambient temperature is above the freezing point, even at high wind velocities.

Use of alcohol and tobacco products as well as under-nourishment and fatigue are predisposing factors to FCI. A previous cold injury increases the risk of subsequent FCI, due to an abnormal post-traumatic sympathetic response.

Cold metal can rapidly cause a frostbite when grasped with the bare hand. Most people are aware of this, but often don't realize the risk of handling super-cooled liquids. Petrol cooled down to −30 °C will freeze exposed flesh almost instantly as evaporative heat loss is combined with conductive loss. Such rapid freezing causes extra- as well as intracellular crystallization with destruction of cell membranes primarily on a mechanical basis. A similar type of FCI occurs when liquid propane is spilled directly onto the skin.

Clinical picture

Freezing cold injuries are subdivided into superficial and deep frostbites. The superficial injury is limited to the skin and the immediate underlying subcutaneous tissues. In most cases the injury is localized to nose, earlobes, fingers and toes. Stinging, pricking pain is often the first sign. The affected part of the skin turns pale or wax-white. It is numb, and will indent upon pressure, as the underlying tissues are viable and pliable. When the FCI extends into a deep injury, the skin becomes white and marble-like, feels hard, and adheres when touched.

Treatment

A frostbite should be taken care of immediately in order to prevent a superficial injury from turning into a deep one. Try to take the victim indoors; otherwise protect him or her from the wind by shelter of comrades, a wind sack or other similar means. The frost-bitten area should be thawed by passive transmission of heat from a warmer part of the body. Put the warm hand against the face and the cold hand into the armpit or into the groin. As the frostbitten individual is under cold stress with peripheral vaso-constriction, a warm companion is a much better therapist. Massage and rubbing the frostbitten part with snow or woollen muffler is contraindicated. Such mechanical treatment would only aggravate the injury, as the tissue is filled with ice crystals. Nor should thawing in front of a campfire or a camp stove be considered. Such heat does not penetrate to any depth, and as the area is partly anaesthetized the treatment may even result in a burn injury.

The signals of pain in a frostbitten foot disappear before actual freezing takes place, as nerve conductivity is abolished at around +8 °C. The paradox is that the last sensation one feels is that one does not feel anything at all! Under extreme conditions when evacuation requires travel on foot, thawing should be avoided. Walking on frostbitten feet does not seem to increase the risk of tissue loss, whereas refreezing of a frostbite does so in the highest degree.

The best treatment for a frostbite is thawing in warm water at 40 to 42 °C. The thawing procedure should continue at that water temperature until sensation, colour and tissue softness return. This form of thawing often ends up in not a pink, but rather a burgundy hue due to venous stasis.

Under field conditions one must be aware that treatment requires more than local thawing. The whole individual has to be taken care of, as a frostbite is often the first sign of a creeping hypothermia. Put on more clothes and give warm, nourishing beverages. The victim is most often apathetic and has to be forced to cooperate. Urge the victim to do muscular activity such as buffeting arms against sides. Such manoeuvres open peripheral arteriovenous shunts in the extremities.

A deep frostbite is present when thawing with passive warmth transfer for 20 to 30 minutes is without success. If so, the victim should be sent to the nearest hospital. However, if such transpor-tation can take hours, it is preferable to get the person into the nearest housing and thaw his or her injuries in warm water. After complete thawing, the patient should be put to bed with the injured area elevated, and prompt transportation to the nearest hospital should be arranged.

Rapid rewarming gives moderate to severe pain, and the patient will often need an analgesic. The capillary damage causes leakage of serum with local swelling and blister formation during the first 6 to 18 hours. Blisters should be kept intact in order to prevent infection.

Non-freezing cold injuries

Pathophysiology

Prolonged exposure to cold and wet conditions above the freezing point combined with immobilization causing venous stagnation are the prerequisites for NFCI. Dehydration, inadequate food, stress, inter-current illness or injury, and fatigue are contributory factors. NFCI almost exclusively affects legs and feet. Severe injuries of this type occur with great rarity in civilian life, but in wartime and catastrophes it has been and will always be a serious problem, most often caused by an unawareness of the condition due to the slow and indistinct first appearance of symptoms.

NFCI can occur under any conditions where the environmental temperature is lower than body temperature. As in FCI, sympathetic constrictor fibres, together with the cold itself, induce prolonged vasoconstriction. The initial event is rheological in nature and resembles that observed in ischaemic reperfusion injury. In addition to the duration of the low temperature, the susceptibility of the victim seems to be of importance.

The pathological change due to the ischaemic injury affects many tissues. Muscles degenerate, undergoing necrosis, fibrosis and atrophy; bones show early osteoporosis. Of special interest are the effects on the nerves, as nerve damage accounts for the pain, prolonged dysaesthesia and hyperhidrosis often found as a sequel in these injuries.

Clinical picture

In a non-freezing cold injury the victim realizes too late the threatening danger because the initial symptoms are so vague. The feet become cold and swollen. They feel heavy, woody and numb. The feet are presented as cool, painful, tender, often with wrinkled soles. The first ischaemic phase last for hours up to a few days. It is followed by a hyperaemic phase of 2 to 6 weeks, during which the feet are warm, with bounding pulses and increased oedema. Blistering and ulcerations are not uncommon, and in severe cases gangrene can arise.

Treatment

The treatment is above all supportive. On the worksite, the feet should be dried carefully but kept cool. On the other hand, the whole body should be warmed. Plenty of warm beverages should be given. Contrary to the freezing cold injuries, NFCI should never be actively warmed. Warm water treatment in local cold injuries is only allowed when ice-crystals are present in the tissue. The further treatment should as a rule be conservative. However, fever, signs of disseminated intravascular coagulation, and lique-faction of affected tissues requires surgical intervention, occasionally ending in an amputation.

Non-freezing cold injuries can be prevented. Exposure time should be minimized. Adequate foot care with time to dry the feet is of importance, as well as facilities to change into dry socks. Rest with feet elevated as well as administering hot beverages whenever possible may seem ridiculous but often is of crucial importance.

Hypothermia

Hypothermia means subnormal body temperature. However, from a thermal point of view the body consists of two zones—the shell and the core. The former is superficial and its temperature varies considerably according to the external environment. The core consists of deeper tissues (e.g., brain, heart and lungs, and upper abdomen), and the body strives to maintain a core temperature of 37 ± 2 °C. When thermoregulation is impaired and core temperature starts to decline, the individual suffers cold stress, but not until the central temperature reaches 35 °C is the victim considered to be in a hypothermic state. Between 35 and 32 °C, the hypothermia is classified as mild; between 32 and 28 °C it is moderate and below 28 °C, severe (table 42.16).

Physiological effects of lowered core temperature

When core temperature starts to decline, an intense vasoconstriction redirects blood from the shell to the core, thereby preventing heat conduction from the core to the skin. In order to maintain temperature, shivering is induced, often preceded by increased muscular tone. Maximal shivering can increase the metabolic rate four- to sixfold, but as the involuntary contractions oscillate, the net result is often not more than doubled. Heart rate, blood pressure, cardiac output and respiratory rate increase. The centralization of blood volume causes an osmolal diuresis with sodium and chloride as the main constituents.

Atrial irritability in early hypothermia often induces atrial fibrillation. At lower temperatures, ventricular extra systoles are common. Death occurs at or below 28 °C, most often resulting from ventricular fibrillation; asystole may also supervene.

Hypothermia depresses the central nervous system. Lassitude and apathy are early signs of decreasing core temperature. Such effects impair judgement, cause bizarre behaviour and ataxia, and end in lethargy and coma between 30 and 28 °C.

Nerve conduction velocity decreases with lowered temperature. Dysarthria, fumbling and stumbling are clinical manifestations of this phenomena. Cold also affects muscles and joints, impairing manual performance. It slows reaction time and coordination, and increases frequency of mistakes. Muscle rigidity is observed in even mild hypothermia. At a core temperature lower than 30 °C, physical activity is impossible.

Exposure to an abnormally cold environment is the basic prerequisite for hypothermia to occur. Extremes of age are risk factors. Elderly persons with impaired thermoregulatory function, or persons whose muscle mass and insulating fat layer are reduced, run a greater risk of suffering hypothermia.

Classification

From a practical point of view the following subdivision of hypothermia is useful (see also table 42.16):

- accidental hypothermia
- acute immersion hypothermia
- sub-acute exhaustion hypothermia
- hypothermia in trauma
- sub-clinical chronic hypothermia.

Acute immersion hypothermia occurs when a person falls into cold water. Water has a thermal conductivity approximately 25 times that of air. The cold stress becomes so great that the core temperature is forced down despite a maximal heat production of the body. Hypothermia sets in before the victim becomes exhausted.

Sub-acute exhaustion hypothermia may happen to any worker in a cold environment as well as to skiers, climbers and walkers in the mountains. In this form of hypothermia, muscular activity maintains the body temperature as long as energy sources are available. However, then hypoglycaemia ensures the victim is at risk.

Even a relatively mild degree of cold exposure may be sufficient to continue cooling and cause a hazardous situation.

Hypothermia with major trauma is an ominous sign. The injured person is often unable to maintain body temperature, and heat loss may be exacerbated by infusion of cold fluids and by removal of clothing. Patients in shock who become hypothermic have a much higher mortality than normothermic victims.

Sub-clinical chronic hypothermia is often encountered in elderly persons, often in association with malnutrition, inadequate clothing and restricted mobility. Alcoholism, drug abuse and chronic metabolic diseases as well as psychiatric disorders are contributory causes in this type of hypothermia.

Pre-hospital management

The main principle of primary care of a worker suffering from hypothermia is to prevent further heat loss. A conscious victim should be moved indoors, or at least into a shelter. Remove wet clothing and try to insulate the person as much as possible. Keeping the victim in a lying position with the head covered is mandatory.

Patients with acute immersion hypothermia require quite different treatment from that required by those with sub-acute exhaustion hypothermia. The immersion victim is often in a more favourable situation. The decreased core temperature occurs long before the body becomes exhausted, and heat-generating capacity remains unimpaired. Water and electrolyte balance is not deranged. Therefore such an individual may be treated with rapid immersion in a bath. If a tub is not available, put the patient's feet and hands into warm water. The local heat opens the arteriovenous shunts, rapidly increases the blood circulation in the extremities and enhances the warming process.

In exhaustion hypothermia, on the other hand, the victim is in a much more serious situation. The caloric reserves are consumed, the electrolyte balance is deranged and, above all, the person is dehydrated. The cold diuresis starts immediately after cold exposure; the fight against the cold and wind exaggerates sweating, but this is not perceived in the cold and dry environment; and lastly, the victim does not feel thirsty. A patient suffering from exhaustion hypothermia should never be rapidly rewarmed out in the field due to the risk of inducing hypovolemic shock. As a rule it is better not to actively rewarm the patient out in the field or during transportation to hospital. A prolonged state of not progressing hypothermia is far better than enthusiastic efforts to warm the patient under circumstances where supervening complications cannot be managed. It is mandatory to handle the patient gently to minimize the risk of possible ventricular fibrillation.

Even for trained medical personnel it is often difficult to determine whether a hypothermic individual is alive or not. Apparent cardiovascular collapse may actually be only depressed cardiac output. Palpation or auscultation for at least a minute to detect spontaneous pulses is often necessary.

The decision as to whether or not to administer cardiopulmonary resuscitation (CPR) is difficult out in the field. If there is any sign of life at all, CPR is contra-indicated. Prematurely performed chest compressions may induce ventricular fibrillation. CPR should, however, immediately be initiated following a witnessed cardiac arrest and when the situation allows the procedures to be performed reasonably and continuously.

Health and cold

A healthy person with appropriate clothing and equipment and working in an organization suitable for the task is not in a health risk situation, even if it is very cold. Whether or not long-term cold exposure while living in cold climate areas means health risks is controversial. For individuals with health problems the situation is quite different, and cold exposure could be a problem. In a certain situation cold exposure or exposure to cold-related factors or combinations of cold with other risks can produce health risks, especially in an emergency or accident situation. In remote areas, when communication with a supervisor is difficult or does not exist, the employees themselves must be allowed to decide whether a health risk situation is at hand or not. In these situations they must take necessary precautions to make the situation safe or stop work.

In arctic regions, climate and other factors can be so harsh that other considerations must be taken.

Infectious diseases. Infectious diseases are not related to cold. Endemic diseases occur in arctic and subarctic regions. Acute or chronic infectious disease in an individual dictates cessation of exposure to cold and hard work.

The common cold, without fever or general symptoms, does not make work in the cold harmful. However, for individuals with complicating diseases like asthma, bronchitis or cardiovascular problems, the situation is different and indoor work in warm conditions during the cold season is recommended. This is also valid with a cold with fever, deep cough, muscle pain and impaired general condition.

Asthma and bronchitis are more common in cold regions. Exposure to cold air often worsens the symptoms. Change of medication sometimes reduces the symptoms during the cold season. Some individuals can also be helped by using medicinal inhalers.

People with asthmatic or cardiovascular diseases may respond to cold air inhalation with bronchoconstriction and vasospasm. Athletes training several hours at high intensities in cold climates have been shown to develop asthmatic symptoms. Whether or not extensive cooling of the pulmonary tract is the primary explanation is not yet clear. Special, light masks are now on the market that do provide some kind of heat exchanger function, thereby conserving energy and moisture.

An endemic type of chronic disease is "Eskimo lung", typical for Eskimo hunters and trappers exposed to extreme cold and hard work for long periods. A progressive pulmonary hypertension often ends in a right-sided heart failure.

Cardiovascular disorders. Exposure to cold affects the cardiovascular system to a higher degree. The noradrenalin released from the sympathetic nerve terminals raises the cardiac output and heart rate. Chest pain due to angina pectoris often worsens in a cold environment. The risk of getting an infarct increases during cold exposure, especially in combination with hard work. Cold raises blood pressure with an increased risk of cerebral haemorrhage. Individuals at risk should therefore be warned and reduce their exposure to hard work in the cold.

Increased mortality during winter season is a frequent observation. One reason could be the previously mentioned increase in heart work, promoting arrhythmia in sensitive persons. Another observation is that the haematocrit is increased during the cold season, causing increased viscosity of blood and increased resistance to flow. A plausible explanation is that cold weather may expose people to sudden, very heavy work loads, such as snow cleaning, walking in deep snow, slipping and so on.

Metabolic disorders. Diabetes mellitus is also found with a higher frequency in the colder areas of the world. Even an uncomplicated diabetes, especially when treated with insulin, can make cold outdoor work impossible in more remote areas. Early peripheral arteriosclerosis makes these individuals more sensitive to cold and increases the risk of local frostbite.

Individuals with impaired thyroid function can easily develop hypothermia due to lack of the thermogenic hormone, while hyperthyroid persons tolerate cold even when lightly dressed.

Patients with these diagnoses should be given extra attention from health professionals and be informed of their problem.

Musculoskeletal problems. Cold itself is not supposed to cause diseases in the musculoskeletal system, not even rheumatism. On the other hand, work in cold conditions is often very demanding for muscles, tendons, joints and spine because of the high load often involved in these kinds of work. The temperature in the joints decreases faster than the temperature of the muscles. Cold joints are stiff joints, because of increasing resistance to movement due to augmented viscosity of the synovial fluid. Cold decreases the power and duration of muscle contraction. In combination with heavy work or local overload, the risk of injury increases. Furthermore, protective clothing may impair the ability to control movement of body parts, hence contributing to the risk.

Arthritis in the hand is a special problem. It is suspected that frequent cold exposure may cause arthritis, but so far the scientific evidence is poor. An existing arthritis of the hand reduces hand function in the cold and causes pain and discomfort.

Cryopathies. Cryopathies are disorders where the individual is hypersensitive to cold. The symptoms vary, including those involving the vascular system, blood, connective tissue, "allergy" and others.

Some individuals suffer from white fingers. White spots on the skin, a sensation of cold, reduced function and pain are symptoms when fingers are exposed to cold. The problems are more common among women, but above all are found in smokers and workers using vibrating tools or driving snowmobiles. Symptoms can be so troublesome that work during even slight cold exposure is impossible. Certain types of medication can also worsen the symptoms.

Cold urticaria, due to sensitized mast cells, appears as an itching erythema of cold-exposed parts of the skin. If exposure is stopped, the symptoms usually disappear within one hour. Rarely the disease is complicated with general and more threatening symptoms. If so, or if the urticaria itself is very troublesome, the individual should avoid exposure to any kind of cold.

Acrocyanosis is manifested by changes in skin colour towards cyanosis after exposure to cold. Other symptoms could be dysfunction of hand and fingers in the acrocyanotic area. The symptoms are very common, and can often be acceptably reduced by reduced cold exposure (e.g., proper clothing) or reduced nicotine use.

Psychological stress. Cold exposure, especially in combination with cold-related factors and remoteness, stresses the individual, not only physiologically but also psychologically. During work in cold climate conditions, in bad weather, over long distances and perhaps in potentially dangerous situations, the psychological stress can disturb or even deteriorate the individual's psychological function so much that work cannot be safely done.

Smoking and snuffing. The unhealthy long-term effects of smoking and, to some extent, snuffing are well known. Nicotine increases peripheral vasoconstriction, reduces dexterity and raises the risk of cold injury.

Alcohol. Drinking alcohol gives a pleasant feeling of warmth, and it is generally thought that the alcohol inhibits cold-induced vasoconstriction. However, experimental studies on humans during relatively short exposures to cold have shown that alcohol does not interfere with heat balance to any greater extent. However, shivering becomes impaired and, combined with strenuous exercise, the heat loss will become obvious. Alcohol is known to be a dominant cause of death in urban hypothermia. It gives a feeling of bravado and influences judgement, leading to ignoring prophylactic measures.

Pregnancy. During pregnancy women are not more sensitive to cold. To the contrary, they can be less sensitive, due to raised metabolism. Risk factors during pregnancy are combined with the cold-related factors such as accident risks, clumsiness due to clothing, heavy lifting, slipping and extreme working positions.

Table 42.17 • Recommended components of health control programmes for personnel exposed to cold stress and cold-related factors.

Factor	Outdoor work	Cold store work	Arctic and subarctic work
Infectious diseases	**	**	***
Cardio-vascular diseases	***	**	***
Metabolic diseases	**	*	***
Musculoskeletal problems	***	*	***
Cryopathies	**	**	**
Psychological stress	***	**	***
Smoking and snuffing	**	**	**
Alcohol	***	**	***
Pregnancy	**	**	***
Medication	**	*	***

*= routine control, **= important factor to consider, ***= very important factor to consider.

The health care system, the society and the employer should therefore pay extra attention to the pregnant woman in cold work.

Pharmacology and cold

Negative side effects of drugs during cold exposure could be thermoregulatory (general or local), or the effect of the drug can be altered. As long as the worker retains normal body temperature, most prescribed drugs don't interfere with performance. However, tranquilizers (e.g., barbiturates, benzodiazepines, phentothiazides as well as cyclic antidepressants) may disturb vigilance. In a threatening situation the defence mechanisms against hypothermia may be impaired and the awareness of the hazardous situation is reduced.

Beta-blockers induce peripheral vasoconstriction and decrease the tolerance to cold. If an individual needs medication and has cold exposure in his or her working situation, attention should be paid to negative side effects of these drugs.

On the other hand, no drug or anything else drunk, eaten or otherwise administered to the body has been shown to be able to raise normal heat production, for example in an emergency situation when hypothermia or a cold injury threatens.

Health control programme

Health risks connected to cold stress, cold-related factors and accidents or trauma are known only to a limited extent. There is a large individual variation in capacities and health status, and this requires careful consideration. As previously mentioned, special diseases, medication and some other factors may render a person more susceptible to the effects of cold exposure. A health control programme should be part of the employment procedure, as well as a repeated activity for the staff. Table 42.17 specifies factors to control for in different types of cold work.

Prevention of Cold Stress

Human adaptation

With repeated exposures to cold conditions, people perceive less discomfort and learn to adjust to and cope with conditions in an individual and more efficient way, than at the onset of exposure.

This habituation reduces some of the arousal and distraction effect, and improves judgement and precaution.

Behaviour

The most apparent and natural strategy for prevention and control of cold stress is that of precaution and intentional behaviour. Physiological responses are not very powerful in preventing heat losses. Humans are, therefore, extremely dependent on external measures such as clothing, shelter and external heat supply. The continuous improvement and refinement of clothing and equipment provides one basis for successful and safe exposures to cold. However, it is essential that products be adequately tested in accordance with international standards.

Measures for prevention and control of cold exposure are often the responsibility of the employer or the supervisor. However, the efficiency of protective measures relies to a significant degree upon knowledge, experience, motivation and ability of the individual worker to make the necessary adjustments to his or her requirements, needs and preferences. Hence, education, information and training are important elements in health control programmes.

Acclimatization

There is evidence for different types of acclimatization to long-term cold exposure. Improved hand and finger circulation allows for the maintenance of a higher tissue temperature and produces a stronger cold-induced vasodilatation (see figure 42.18). Manual performance is better maintained after repeated cold exposures of the hand.

Repeated whole-body cooling appears to enhance peripheral vasoconstriction, thereby increasing surface tissue insulation. Korean pearl-diving women showed marked increases in skin insulation during the winter season. Recent investigations have revealed that the introduction and use of wet suits reduces the cold stress so much that tissue insulation does not change.

Three types of possible adaptations have been proposed:

- increased tissue insulation (as previously mentioned)
- hypothermic reaction ("controlled" drop in core temperature)
- metabolic reaction (increased metabolism).

The most pronounced adaptations should be found with native people in cold regions. However, modern technology and living habits have reduced most extreme types of cold exposure. Clothing, heated shelters and conscious behaviour allow most people to maintain an almost tropical climate at the skin surface (microclimate), thereby reducing cold stress. The stimuli to physiological adaptation become weaker.

Probably the most cold-exposed groups today belong to polar expeditions and industrial operations in arctic and subarctic regions. There are several indications that any eventual adaptation found with severe cold exposure (air or cold water) is of the insulative type. In other words, higher core temperatures can be kept with a reduced or unchanged heat loss.

Diet and water balance

In many cases cold work is associated with energy-demanding activities. In addition, protection against cold requires clothing and equipment weighing several kilograms. The hobbling effect of clothing increases muscular effort. Hence, given work tasks require more energy (and more time) under cold conditions. The caloric intake through food must compensate for this. An increase of the percentage of calories provided by fat should be recommended to outdoor workers.

Meals provided during cold operations must provide sufficient energy. Enough carbohydrates must be included to ensure stable and safe blood sugar levels for workers engaged in hard work. Recently, food products have been launched on the market with claims that they stimulate and increase body heat production in the cold. Normally, such products consist merely of carbohydrates, and they have so far failed in tests to perform better than similar products (chocolate), or better than expected from their energy content.

Water loss may be significant during cold exposure. First, tissue cooling causes a redistribution of blood volume, inducing "cold diuresis". Tasks and clothing must allow for this, since it may develop rapidly and requires urgent execution. The almost dry air at subzero conditions allows a continuous evaporation from skin and respiratory tract that is not readily perceived. Sweating contributes to water loss, and should be carefully controlled and preferably avoided, due to its detrimental effect on insulation when absorbed by clothing. Water is not always readily available at subzero conditions. Outdoors it must be supplied or produced by melting snow or ice. As there is a depression of thirst it is mandatory that workers in the cold drink water frequently to eliminate the gradual development of dehydration. Water deficit may lead to reduced working capacity and increased risk of getting cold injuries.

Conditioning workers for work in the cold

By far the most effective and appropriate measures for adapting humans to cold work, are by conditioning—education, training and practice. As previously mentioned, much of the success of adjustments to cold exposure depends on behavioural action. Experience and knowledge are important elements of this behavioural process.

Persons engaged in cold work should be given a basic introduction to the specific problems of cold. They must receive information about physiological and subjective reactions, health aspects, risk of accidents, and protective measures, including clothing and first aid. They should be gradually trained for the required tasks. Only after a given time (days to weeks) should they work full hours under the extreme conditions. Table 42.18 provides recommendations as to the contents of conditioning programmes for various types of cold work.

Basic introduction means education and information about the specific cold problems. Registration and analysis of accidents/injuries is the best base for preventive measures. Training in first aid should be given as a basic course for all personnel, and specific groups should get an extended course. Protective measures are natural components of a conditioning programme and are dealt with in the following section. Survival training is important for arctic and subarctic areas, and also for outdoor work in other remote areas.

Technical control

General principles

Due to the many complex factors that influence human heat balance, and the considerable individual variations, it is difficult to define critical temperatures for sustained work. The temperatures given in figure 42.19 must be regarded as action levels for improvement of conditions by various measures. At temperatures below those given in figure 42.19, exposures should be controlled and evaluated. Techniques for assessment of cold stress and recommendations for time-limited exposures are dealt with elsewhere in this chapter. It is assumed that best protection of hands, feet and body (clothing) is available. With inappropriate protection, cooling will be expected at considerably higher temperatures.

Tables 42.19 and 42.20 list different preventive and protective measures that can be applied to most types of cold work. Much effort is saved with careful planning and foresight. Examples given are recommendations. It must be emphasized that the final ad-

Table 42.18 • Components of conditioning programmes for workers exposed to cold.

Element	Outdoor work	Cold store work	Arctic and subarctic work
Health control	***	**	***
Basic introduction	***	**	***
Accident prevention	***	**	***
Basic first aid	***	***	***
Extended first aid	**	*	***
Protective measures	***	**	***
Survival training	see text	*	***

*= routine level, **= important factor to consider, ***= very important factor to consider.

justment of clothing, equipment and work behaviour must be left to the individual. Only with a cautious and intelligent integration of behaviour with the requirements of the real environmental conditions can a safe and efficient exposure be created.

Some recommendations as to the climatic conditions under which certain measures should be taken have been given by the American Conference of Governmental Industrial Hygienists (ACGIH 1992). The fundamental requirements are that:

- workers be provided with sufficient and appropriate protective clothing
- special precautions should be taken for older workers or workers with circulatory problems.

Figure 42.19 • Estimated temperatures at which certain thermal imbalances of the body may develop.*

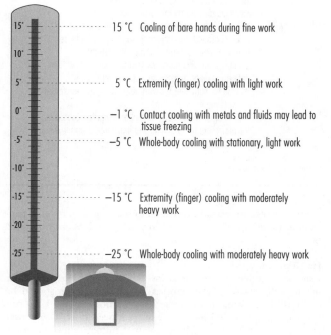

15 °C   Cooling of bare hands during fine work

5 °C   Extremity (finger) cooling with light work

−1 °C   Contact cooling with metals and fluids may lead to tissue freezing

−5 °C   Whole-body cooling with stationary, light work

−15 °C   Extremity (finger) cooling with moderately heavy work

−25 °C   Whole-body cooling with moderately heavy work

* It is assumed that best protective clothing is available.

Table 42.19 • Strategies and measures during various phases of work for prevention and alleviation of cold stress.

Phase/factor	What to do
Planning phase	Schedule work for a warmer season (for outdoor work).
	Check if work can be done indoors (for outdoor work).
	Allow more time per task with cold work and protective clothing.
	Analyse suitability of tools and equipment for work.
	Organize work in suitable work-rest regimens, considering task, load and protection level.
	Provide heated space or heated shelter for recovery.
	Provide training for complex work tasks under normal conditions.
	Check medical records of staff.
	Ascertain appropriate knowledge and competence of staff.
	Provide information about risks, problems, symptoms and preventive actions.
	Separate goods and worker line and keep different temperature zones.
	Care for low velocity, low humidity and low noise level of the air-conditioning system.
	Provide extra personnel to shorten exposure.
	Select adequate protective clothing and other protective equipment.
Before work shift	Check climatic conditions at onset of work.
	Schedule adequate work-rest regimens.
	Allow for individual control of work intensity and clothing.
	Select adequate clothing and other personal equipment.
	Check weather and forecast (outdoors).
	Prepare schedule and control stations (outdoors).
	Organize communication system (outdoors).
During work shift	Provide for break and rest periods in heated shelter.
	Provide for frequent breaks for hot drinks and food.
	Care for flexibility in terms of intensity and duration of work.
	Provide for replacement of clothing items (socks, gloves, etc.).
	Protect from heat loss to cold surfaces.
	Minimize air velocity in work zones.
	Keep workplace clear from water, ice and snow.
	Insulate ground for stationary standing work places.
	Provide access to extra clothing for warmth.
	Monitor subjective reactions (buddy system) (outdoors).
	Report regularly to foreman or base (outdoors).
	Provide for sufficient recovery time after severe exposures (outdoors).
	Protect against wind effects and precipitation (outdoors).
	Monitor climatic conditions and anticipate weather change (outdoors).

Source: Modified from Holmér 1994.

Further recommendations related to the provision of hand protection, to workplace design and to work practices are presented below.

Hand protection
Fine barehanded operations below 16 °C require provision for heating the hands. Metal handles of tools and bars should be covered by insulating materials at temperatures below −1 °C. Anticontact gloves should be worn when surfaces at −7 °C or lower are within reach. At −17 °C insulative mittens must be used. Evaporative liquids at temperatures below 4 °C should be handled so as to avoid splashes to bare or poorly protected skin areas.

Work practices
Below −12 °C Equivalent Chill Temperature, workers should be under constant supervision (buddy system). Many of the measures given in table 42.18 apply. With lowered temperatures it is increasingly important that workers are instructed in safety and health procedures.

Workplace design
Workplaces must be shielded from wind, and air velocities kept below 1 m/s. Wind-protective clothing should be used when appropriate. Eye protection must be supplied for special outdoor conditions with sunshine and snow-covered ground. Medical screening is recommended for persons working routinely in cold below −18 °C. Recommendations as to workplace monitoring include the following:

- Suitable thermometry should be arranged when the temperature is below 16 °C.
- Indoor wind speeds should be monitored at least every 4 hours.
- Outdoor work requires measurement of wind speed and air temperatures below −1 °C.
- The Equivalent Chill Temperature should be determined for combinations of wind and air temperature.

Most of the recommendations in tables 42.19 and 42.20 are pragmatic and straightforward.

Clothing is the most important measure for individual control. The multi-layer approach allows for more flexible solutions than single garments incorporating the function of several layers. In the end, however, the specific needs of the worker should be the ultimate determinant of what would be the most functional system. Clothing protects against cooling. On the other hand overdressing in the cold is a common problem, also reported from the extreme exposures of arctic expeditions. Overdressing may rapidly result in large amounts of sweat, which accumulates in clothing layers. During periods of low activity, the drying of moist clothing increases body heat loss. The obvious preventive measure is to control and reduce sweating by appropriate selection of clothing and early adjustments to changes in work rate and climate conditions. There is no clothing fabric that can absorb large amounts of sweat and also preserve good comfort and insulative properties. Wool remains lofty and apparently dry despite absorption of some water (moisture regain), but large amounts of sweat will condense and cause problems similar to those of other fabrics. The moisture yields some heat liberation and may contribute to the preservation of warmth. However, when the wool garment dries on the body, the process reverses as discussed above, and the person is inevitably cooled.

Modern fibre technology has produced many new materials and fabrics for clothing manufacturing. Garments are now available that combine waterproofness with good water vapour permeability, or high insulation with reduced weight and thickness. It is essential, however, to select garments with guaranteed tested properties and functions. Many products are available that try to mimic the more expensive original products. Some of them represent such poor quality that they may even be hazardous to use.

Protection against cold is determined primarily by the thermal insulation value of the complete clothing ensemble (clo value). However, properties such as air permeability, vapour permeability and waterproofness of the outer layer in particular are essential for cold protection. International standards and test methods are available for measuring and classifying these properties. Similarly, handgear and footwear may be tested for their cold-protective properties using international standards such as European standards EN 511 and EN 344 (CEN 1992, 1993).

Table 42.20 • Strategies and measures related to specific factors and equipment.

Behaviour	Allow for time to adjust clothing. Prevent sweating and chilling effects by making adjustments of clothing in due time before change in work rate and/or exposure. Adjust work rate (keep sweating minimal). Avoid rapid shifts in work intensity. Allow for adequate intake of hot fluid and hot meals. Allow for time to return to protected areas (shelter, warm room) (outdoors). Prevent wetting of clothing from water or snow. Allow for sufficient recovery in protected area (outdoors). Report on progress of work to foreman or base (outdoors). Report major deviations from plan and schedule (outdoors).
Clothing	Select clothing you have previous experience with. With new clothing, select tested garments. Select insulation level on the basis of anticipated climate and activity. Care for flexibility in clothing system to allow for great adjustment of insulation. Clothing must be easy to put on and take off. Reduce internal friction between layers by proper selection of fabrics. Select size of outer layers to make room for inner layers. Use multi-layer system: —inner layer for micro climate control —middle layer for insulation control —outer layer for environmental protection. Inner layer should be non-absorbent to water, if sweating cannot be sufficiently controlled. Inner layer may be absorbent, if sweating is anticipated to be none or low. Inner layer may consist of dual-function fabrics, in the sense that fibre in contact with skin is non-absorbing and fibres next to the middle layer is absorbing water or moisture. Middle layer should provide loft to allow stagnant air layers. Middle layer should be form-stable and resilient. Middle layer may be protected by vapour barrier layers. Garments should provide sufficient overlap in the waist and back region. Outer layer must be selected according to additional protection requirements, such as wind, water, oil, fire, tear or abrasion. Design of outer garment must allow easy and extensive control of openings at neck, sleeves, wrists etc., to regulate ventilation of interior space. Zippers and other fasteners must function also with snow and windy conditions. Buttons should be avoided. Clothing shall allow operation even with cold, clumsy fingers. Design must allow for bent postures without compression of layers and loss of insulation. Avoid unnecessary constrictions. Carry extra wind proof blankets (NOTE! The aluminized "astronaut blanket" does not protect more than expected from being wind proof. A large polyethylene garbage bag has the same effect).
Education Training	Provide education and information on the special problems of cold. Provide information and training in first-aid and treatment of cold injuries.

	Test machinery, tools and equipment in controlled cold conditions. Select tested goods, if available. Train for complex operations under controlled cold conditions. Inform about accidents and accident prevention.
Handwear	Mittens provide the best overall insulation. Mittens should allow fine gloves to be worn underneath. Prolonged exposures requiring fine hand work, must be intercepted by frequent warm-up breaks. Pocket heaters or other external heat sources may prevent or delay hand cooling. Sleeve of clothing must easily accommodate parts of gloves or mittens—underneath or on top. Outer garment must provide easy storage or fixing of handwear when taken off.
Footwear	Boots should provide high insulation to the ground (sole). Sole shall be made of a flexible material and have an anti-slippery pattern. Select size of boot so it can accommodate several layers of socks and an insole. Ventilation of most footwear is poor, so moisture should be controlled by frequent replacement of socks and insole. Control moisture by vapour barrier between inner and outer layer. Allow boots to dry completely between shifts. Legs of clothing must easily accommodate parts of boots—underneath or on top.
Headgear	Flexible headgear comprises an important instrument for control of heat and whole-body heat losses. Headgear should be windproof. Design should allow sufficient protection of ears and neck. Design must accommodate other types of protective equipment (e.g., ear muffs, safety goggles).
Face	Face mask should be windproof and insulative. No metallic details should contact skin. Significant heating and humidification of inspired air can be achieved by special breathing masks or mouth pieces. Use safety goggles outdoors, especially in sleet and snow. Use eye protection against ultra-violet radiation and glare.
Equipment Tools	Select tools and equipment intended and tested for cold conditions. Choose design that allows operation by gloved hands. Prewarm tools and equipment. Store tools and equipment in heated space. Insulate handles of tools and equipment.
Machinery	Select machinery intended for operation in cold environments. Store machinery in protected space. Prewarm machinery before use. Insulate handles and controls. Design handles and controls for operation by gloved hands. Prepare for easy repair and maintenance under adverse conditions.
Workplace	Keep air velocity as low as possible. Use wind-breaking shields or windproof clothing. Provide insulation to ground with prolonged standing, kneeling or lying work. Provide auxiliary heating with light, stationary work.

Source: Modified from Holmér 1994.

42. HEAT AND COLD

Outdoor cold work

Specific problems of outdoor cold work are the aggregate of climatic factors that may result in cold stress. The combination of wind and low air temperature significantly increases the cooling power of the environment, which has to be considered in terms of work organization, workplace shielding and clothing. Precipitation, either in the air as snow or rain, or on the ground, requires adjustments. The variation in weather conditions requires workers to plan for, bring and use additional clothing and equipment.

Much of the problem in outdoor work relates to the sometimes great variations in activity and climate during a work shift. No clothing system is available that can accommodate such large variations. Consequently, clothing must be frequently changed and adjusted. Failure to do so may result in cooling due to insufficient protection, or sweating and overheating caused by too much clothing. In the latter case, most of the sweat condenses or is absorbed by clothing. During periods of rest and low activity, wet clothing represents a potential hazard, since its drying drains the body of heat.

Protective measures for outdoor work include appropriate work-rest regimens with rest pauses taken in heated shelters or cabins. Stationary work tasks can be protected from wind and precipitation by tents with or without additional heating. Spot heating by infrared or gas heaters may be used for certain work tasks. Prefabrication of parts or components may be carried out indoors. Under subzero conditions, workplace conditions including weather should be regularly monitored. Clear rules must exist regarding what procedures to apply when conditions get worse. Temperature levels, eventually corrected for wind (wind chill index), should be agreed upon and linked to an action programme.

Cold storage work

Frozen food requires storage and transportation at low ambient temperatures (<−20 °C). Work in cold stores can be found in most parts of the world. This kind of artificial cold exposure is characterized by a constant, controlled climate. Workers may perform continuous work or, most common, intermittent work, shifting between cold and temperate or warm climates outside the storehouse.

As long as work requires some physical effort, heat balance can be achieved by selecting appropriate protective clothing. The special problems of hand and feet often require regular breaks every 1.5 to 2 hours. The break must be long enough to allow rewarming (20 minutes).

Manual handling of frozen goods requires protective gloves with sufficient insulation (in particular, of the palm of the hand). Requirements and test methods for cold-protective gloves are given in the European standard EN 511, which is described in more detail in the article "Cold indices and standards" in this chapter. Local heaters (e.g., infrared radiator), placed in workplaces with stationary work, improve heat balance.

Much work in cold stores is carried out with fork-lifts. Most of these vehicles are open. Driving creates a relative wind speed, which in combination with the low temperature increases body cooling. In addition, the work itself is rather light and the associated metabolic heat production low. Accordingly, the required clothing insulation is quite high (around 4 clo) and cannot be met with most types of overalls in use. The driver gets cold, starting with feet and hands, and exposure has to be time limited. Depending on available protective clothing, appropriate work schedules should be organized in terms of work in cold and work or rest in normal environments. A simple measure to improve heat balance is to install a heated seat in the truck. This may prolong work time in the cold and prevent local cooling of the seat and back. More sophisticated and expensive solutions include the use of heated cabs.

Special problems arise in hot countries, where the cold store worker, usually the truck driver, is intermittently exposed to cold (−30 °C) and heat (30 °C). Brief exposures (1 to 5 min) to each condition make it difficult to adopt suitable clothing—it may be too warm for the outdoor period and too cold for the cold store work. Truck cabs may be one solution, once the problem of condensation upon windows is solved. Appropriate work-rest regimens must be elaborated and based on work tasks and available protection.

Cool workplaces, found for example in the fresh food industry, comprise climatic conditions with air temperatures of +2 to +16 °C, depending on type. Conditions are sometimes characterized by high relative humidities, inducing condensation of water at cold spots and moist or water-covered floors. The risk of slipping is increased in such workplaces. Problems can be solved by good workplace hygiene and cleaning routines, which contribute to reducing the relative humidity.

The local air velocity of work stations is often too high, resulting in complaints of draught. The problems can often be solved by changing or adjusting the inlets for cold air or by rearranging work stations. Buffers of frozen or cold goods close to work stations may contribute to draught sensation due to the increased radiation heat exchange. Clothing must be selected on the basis of an assessment of the requirements. The IREQ method should be used. In addition clothing should be designed to protect from local draught, moisture and water. Special hygienic requirements for food handling put some restrictions on design and type of clothing (i.e., the outer layer). An appropriate clothing system must integrate underwear, insulating middle layers and the outer layer to form a functional and sufficient protective system. Headgear is often required due to hygienic demands. However, existing headgear for this purpose is often a paper cap, which does not offer any protection against cold. Similarly, footwear often comprises clogs or light shoes, with poor insulation properties. Selection of more suitable headgear and footwear should better preserve warmth of these body parts and contribute to an improved general heat balance.

A special problem in many cool workplaces is the preservation of manual dexterity. Hands and fingers cool rapidly when muscular activity is low or moderate. Gloves improve protection but impair dexterity. A delicate balance between the two demands has to be found. Cutting meat often requires a metal glove. A thin textile glove worn underneath may reduce the cooling effect and improve comfort. Thin gloves may be sufficient for many purposes. Additional measures to prevent hand cooling include the provision of insulated handles of tools and equipment or spot heating using, for example, infrared radiators. Electrically heated gloves are on the market, but often suffer from poor ergonomics and insufficient heating or battery capacity.

Cold-water exposure

During immersion of the body in water the potential for large losses of heat in a short time is great and presents an apparent hazard. The heat conductivity of water is more than 25 times higher than that of air, and in many exposure situations the capacity of surrounding water to absorb heat is effectively infinite.

Thermoneutral water temperature is around 32 to 33 °C, and at lower temperatures the body responds by cold vasoconstriction and shivering. Long exposures in water at temperatures between 25 and 30 °C provoke body cooling and progressive development of hypothermia. Naturally, this response becomes stronger and more serious with the lowering of the water temperature.

Exposure to cold water is common in accidents at sea and in conjunction with water sports of various kinds. However, even in occupational activities, workers run the risk of immersion hypo-

thermia (e.g., diving, fishing, shipping and other ... more operations).

Victims of shipwrecks may ha... heat loss from the head of
protection varies from piece... t of the ship, the efficiency of
Lifejackets are manda... the behaviour of crew and passen-
be equipped with ... ants for the success of the operation
unconsci... sure conditions.

... cold waters. The temperature of most
the... regula... water cold waters, in particular at some depth, is
... mercial diving, in particular at some depth
...s with ...wer than 10°C. Any prolonged exposure in such
low—of... requires thermally insulated diving suits. ... simply a
cold wa... Heat exchange in the water may be seen ... ermal from

Heat loss. Heat exchange in the water ... one ... to the sur-
flow of heat down two temperature gradients—one ... described by:
core to skin, and one external, from the skin s... rounding water. Body surface heat loss can be

$$C_w = h_c \cdot (T_{sk} - T_w) \cdot A$$

where C_w is the *rate of convective heat* ... h_c is the convective
heat transfer coefficient (W/°Cm²... is the average skin temperature (°C), T_w is the water temperature (°C) ... A_D is the body
surface area. The small components of heat lo... from respiration
and from non-immersed parts (e.g., head) ca... neglected (see
the section on diving below... W/°Cm². The

The value of h_c is in the range of 100 to ... ce it caused by
lowest value applies to still water. Turbul... or triples the
swimming movements or flowing water... the unprotected
convection coefficient. It is easily unders... old water—even-
body may suffer a considerable heat los... th heavy exercise.
tually exceeding what can be produc... lls into cold water
In fact, a person (dressed or undress... the water than by
in most cases saves more heat by ... reduced by wearing
swimming.

Heat loss to the water can be... ds of metres below sea
special protective suits. ... s of pressure (one ATA
Diving. Diving operations se... cold air (or a cold gas
level must protect the diver f... he lung tissues of body
or 0.1 MPa/10 m) and c... dy core is large at high
mixture of helium and o... higher than the resting
heat. This direct heat l... It is poorly sensed by the
pressures and can eas... internal temperatures may
metabolic heat produ... f the body surface is warm.
human organism. ... ver to be supplied with extra
develop without a ... thing apparatus, to compen-
Modern offshore ... ses. In deep-sea diving, the
heat to the suit a... r than at sea level: 30 to 32 °C
sate for large ... increasing to 32 to 34 °C up to
comfort zone ...

at 20 to 30 A... sion elicits a strong, acute respi-
50 ATA (5... es include an "inspiratory gasp",
Physiolog... peripheral vasoconstriction and
ratory dilation... apnoea for several seconds is
hyperv... Hence, a person may easily inhale
hyper... the body becomes submersed. The
follo... very cold water, accordingly, are
po... owning may occur. Slow immersion
... he body reduce the reaction and allow
...tion. The reaction gradually fades and
...y achieved within a few minutes.
... loss at the skin surface emphasizes the
... physiological or constitutional) mechan-

isms for reducing the core-to-skin heat flow. Vasoconstriction
reduces extremity blood flow and preserves central heat. Exercise
increases extremity blood flow, and, in conjunction with the increased external convection, it may in fact accelerate heat loss
despite the elevated heat production.

After 5 to 10 min in very cold water, extremity temperature
drops quickly. Neuromuscular function deteriorates and the ability to coordinate and control muscular performance degrades.
Swimming performance may be severely reduced and quickly put
the person at risk in open waters.

Body size is another important factor. A tall person has a larger
body surface area and loses more heat than a small person at
given ambient conditions. However, the relatively larger body
mass compensates for this in two ways. Metabolic heat production
rate increases in relation to the larger surface area, and the heat
content at a given body temperature is greater. The latter factor
comprises a larger buffer to heat losses and a slower rate of core
temperature decrease. Children are at a greater risk than adults.

By far the most important factor is body fat content—in particular, subcutaneous fat thickness. Adipose tissue is more insulating than other tissues and is bypassed by much of the peripheral
circulation. Once vasoconstriction has occurred, the layer of subcutaneous fat acts as an extra layer. The insulative effect is almost
linearly related to the layer thickness. Accordingly, women in
general have more cutaneous fat than men and lose less heat
under the same conditions. In the same way, fat persons are better
off than lean persons.

Personal protection. As previously mentioned, prolonged stay in
cold and temperate waters requires additional external insulation
in the form of diving suits, immersion suits or similar equipment.
The wet suit of foamed neoprene provides insulation by the thickness of the material (closed foam cells) and by the relatively
controlled "leakage" of water to the skin microclimate. The latter
phenomenon results in the warming of this water and the establishment of a higher skin temperature. Suits are available in various thickness, providing more or less insulation. A wet suit
compresses at depth and loses thereby much of its insulation.

The dry suit has become standard at temperatures below 10 °C.
It allows the maintenance of a higher skin temperature, depending
on the amount of extra insulation worn under the suit. It is a fundamental requirement that the suit not leak, as small amounts of
water (0.5 to 1 l) seriously reduce the insulative power. Although
the dry suit also compresses at depth, dry air is automatically or
manually added from the scuba tank to compensate for the reduced volume. Hence, a microclimate air layer of some thickness
can be maintained, providing good insulation.

As previously mentioned, deep-sea diving requires auxiliary
heating. Breathing gas is prewarmed and the suit is heated by the
flushing of warm water from the surface or the diving bell. More
recent warming techniques rely upon electrically heated underwear or closed-circuit tubules filled with warm fluid.

Hands are particularly susceptible to cooling and may require
extra protection in the form of insulative or heated gloves.

Safe exposures. The rapid development of hypothermia and the
imminent danger of death from cold-water exposure necessitates
some sort of prediction of safe and unsafe exposure conditions.
Figure 42.20 depicts predicted survival times for typical North
Sea offshore conditions. The applied criterion is a drop in core
temperature to 34 °C for the tenth percentile of the population.
This level is assumed to be associated with a conscious and manageable person. The proper wearing, use and functioning of a dry
suit doubles the predicted survival time. The lower curve refers to
the unprotected person immersed in normal clothing. As clothing
gets completely soaked with water the effective insulation is very
small, resulting in short survival times (modified from Wissler
1988).

42. HEAT AND COLD

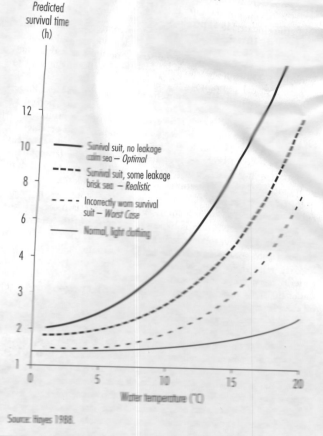

Figure 42.20 • Predicted survival times for typical North Sea offshore scenarios.

Predicted survival time (h)

- Survival suit, no leakage calm sea – *Optimal*
- Survival suit, some leakage brisk sea – *Realistic*
- Incorrectly worn survival suit – *Worst Case*
- Normal, light clothing

Water temperature (°C)

Source: Hayes 1988.

Work in arctic and subarctic regions

Arctic and subarctic regions of the world comprise additional problems to those of normal cold work. The cold season coincides with darkness. Days with sunlight are short. These regions cover vast, unpopulated or sparsely populated areas, such as Northern Canada, Siberia and Northern Scandinavia. In addition nature is harsh. Transportation takes place over large distances and takes a long time. The combination of cold, darkness and remoteness require special consideration in terms of work organization, preparation and equipment. In particular, training in survival and first aid must be provided and the appropriate equipment supplied and made easily available at work.

For the working population in the arctic regions there are many health-threatening hazards, as mentioned elsewhere. The risks of accident and injury are high, drug abuse is common, cultural patterns produce problems, as does the confrontation between local/native culture and modern western industrial demands. Snowmobile driving is an example of multiple-risk exposure in typical arctic conditions (see below). Cold stress is thought to be one of the risk factors that produces higher frequencies of certain diseases. Geographical isolation is another factor producing different types of genetic defects in some native areas. Endemic diseases—for example, certain infectious diseases—are also of local or regional importance. Settlers and guest workers also run a *higher risk for different kinds of psychological stress reactions* secondary to new environment, remoteness, harsh climate conditions, isolation and awareness.

Specific measures for this kind of work must be considered. Work must be carried out in groups of three, so that in case of emergency, care of the victim may offer help while one is left taking care of the victim. Workers must planned accord variation in daylight, for example, climate situations must be available for emergency gency situations.

A specific work problem in these areas such as Since the sixties the snowmobile has developed the snowmobile, low-technology vehicle to one that is fast and developed. It is most frequently used for leisure actually highly for work (10 to 20%). Typical professions using the snowmobile are police, military personnel, reindeer herders, lumberjacks, farmers, tourist trappers and search and rescue teams.

The vibration from a snowmobile means a highly increased risk for exposure to the driver. The driver and the passenger-induced injuries to the driver. The noise produced by the engine are exposed to unpurified exhaust gas, to high speed, main irregularities may induce hearing loss. Due driver and the passengers, the and poor protection for the

The musculoskeletal system is exposed to vibrations and extreme working positions and loads, especially when driving in harsh terrain areas. If you get stuck, handling the heavy engine induces lumbago), and often musculoskeletal problems (e.g., lumbago).

Cold injuries are common among snowmobile workers. The speed of the vehicle on the cold exposure. Typical injured parts of the body are the face (could in extreme cases include cornea), ears, and feet.

Snowmobiles are used in remote areas where climate, terrain and other conditions to the risks.

The snowmobile help developed for the working situation on the snowmobile posure risks produced by the specific exclimate. Clothing must be terrain conditions and activity transients experienced, roof and flexible. The cult to accommodate in one nobile riding are difficonsideration.

Snowmobile traffic in remote and require special tion problem. Work organization a communicasafe communication with the ho should ensure be carried to handle emergency s equipment must for a time long enough for the re protection equipment includes, for example, wi Such aid equipment, snow shovel, repair kit g, first-

PREVENTION OF COLD S EXTREME OUTDOOR CON

Jacques Bittel an ●

The prevention of the physiopathological effect cold must be considered from two points of vie cerns the physiopathological effects observed dur posure to cold (that is, the entire body), and the se those observed during local exposure to cold, mainl extremities (hands and feet). Preventive measures in tion aim to reduce the incidence of the two main ty stress—accidental hypothermia and frostbite of the ext twofold approach is required: physiological meth thermia (e.g., diving, fishing, shipping and oth... ...ore operations).

Victims of shipwrecks may ha... cold water. Their protection varies from piece... at of the ship, the efficiency of Lifejackets are manda... he behaviour of crew and passengers... be equipped wit... ants for the success of the operation ...ure conditions.

unconsc... ter cold waters. The temperature of most ...ercial diving, in particular at some depth, is ... wer than 10°C. Any prolonged exposure in such ...requires thermally insulated diving suits. cold w... loss. Heat exchange in the water may be seen as simply a ... of heat down two temperature gradients—one internal, from core to skin, and one external, from the skin surface to the surrounding water. Body surface heat loss can be simply described by:

$$C_w = h_c \cdot (T_{sk} - T_w) \cdot A$$

where C_w is the *rate of convective heat loss* (W), h_c is the convective heat transfer coefficient (W/°Cm²), T_{sk} is the average skin temperature (°C), T_w is the water temperature (°C) and A is the body surface area. The small components of heat loss from respiration and from non-immersed parts (e.g., head) are neglected (see the section on diving below).

The value of h_c is in the range of 100 to ... W/°Cm². The lowest value applies to still water. Turbulence... doubles or triples the swimming movements or flowing water... the unprotected convection coefficient. It is easily understood... cold water—even body may suffer a considerable heat loss... th heavy exercise. tually exceeding what can be produce... lls into cold water In fact, a person (dressed or undress... the water than by in most cases saves more heat by ... reduced by wearing swimming.

Heat loss to the water can be... s of metres below sea special protective suits. ... of pressure (one ATA

Diving. Diving operations se... cold air (or a cold gas level must protect the diver ... he lung tissues of body or 0.1 MPa/10 m) and c... dy core is large at high mixture of helium and o... higher than the resting heat. This direct heat l... It is poorly sensed by the pressures and can eas... ternal temperatures may metabolic heat produ... f the body surface is warm. human organism. ... wer to be supplied with extra develop without a s... thing apparatus, to compen- Modern offshore ... than at sea level: 30 to 32 °C heat to the suit a... increasing to 32 to 34 °C up to sate for large comfort zone ... ion elicits a strong, acute respi- at 20 to 30 A... s include an "inspiratory gasp",

50 ATA (5... peripheral vasoconstriction and *Physiolog...* apnoea for several seconds is ratory d... ation. The response is almost im- hyperv... Hence, a person may easily inhale hyper... the body becomes submersed. The follo... very cold water, accordingly, are ...wning may occur. Slow immersion po... e body reduce the reaction and allow ...tion. The reaction gradually fades and ... achieved within a few minutes. ... loss at the skin surface emphasizes the ...physiological or constitutional) mechan-

---

isms for reducing the core-to-skin heat flow. Vasoconstriction reduces extremity blood flow and preserves central heat. Exercise increases extremity blood flow, and, in conjunction with the increased external convection, it may in fact accelerate heat loss despite the elevated heat production.

After 5 to 10 min in very cold water, extremity temperature drops quickly. Neuromuscular function deteriorates and the ability to coordinate and control muscular performance degrades. Swimming performance may be severely reduced and quickly put the person at risk in open waters.

Body size is another important factor. A tall person has a larger body surface area and loses more heat than a small person at given ambient conditions. However, the relatively larger body mass compensates for this in two ways. Metabolic heat production rate increases in relation to the larger surface area, and the heat content at a given body temperature is greater. The latter factor comprises a larger buffer to heat losses and a slower rate of core temperature decrease. Children are at a greater risk than adults.

By far the most important factor is body fat content—in particular, subcutaneous fat thickness. Adipose tissue is more insulating than other tissues and is bypassed by much of the peripheral circulation. Once vasoconstriction has occurred, the layer of subcutaneous fat acts as an extra layer. The insulative effect is almost linearly related to the layer thickness. Accordingly, women in general have more cutaneous fat than men and lose less heat under the same conditions. In the same way, fat persons are better off than lean persons.

Personal protection. As previously mentioned, prolonged stay in cold and temperate waters requires additional external insulation in the form of diving suits, immersion suits or similar equipment. The wet suit of foamed neoprene provides insulation by the thickness of the material (closed foam cells) and by the relatively controlled "leakage" of water to the skin microclimate. The latter phenomenon results in the warming of this water and the establishment of a higher skin temperature. Suits are available in various thickness, providing more or less insulation. A wet suit compresses at depth and loses thereby much of its insulation.

The dry suit has become standard at temperatures below 10 °C. It allows the maintenance of a higher skin temperature, depending on the amount of extra insulation worn under the suit. It is a fundamental requirement that the suit not leak, as small amounts of water (0.5 to 1 l) seriously reduce the insulative power. Although the dry suit also compresses at depth, dry air is automatically or manually added from the scuba tank to compensate for the reduced volume. Hence, a microclimate air layer of some thickness can be maintained, providing good insulation.

As previously mentioned, deep-sea diving requires auxiliary heating. Breathing gas is prewarmed and the suit is heated by the flushing of warm water from the surface or the diving bell. More recent warming techniques rely upon electrically heated underwear or closed-circuit tubules filled with warm fluid.

Hands are particularly susceptible to cooling and may require extra protection in the form of insulative or heated gloves.

Safe exposures. The rapid development of hypothermia and the imminent danger of death from cold-water exposure necessitates some sort of prediction of safe and unsafe exposure conditions. Figure 42.20 depicts predicted survival times for typical North Sea offshore conditions. The applied criterion is a drop in core temperature to 34 °C for the tenth percentile of the population. This level is assumed to be associated with a conscious and manageable person. The proper wearing, use and functioning of a dry suit doubles the predicted survival time. The lower curve refers to the unprotected person immersed in normal clothing. As clothing gets completely soaked with water the effective insulation is very small, resulting in short survival times (modified from Wissler 1988).

Figure 42.20 • Predicted survival times for typical North Sea offshore scenarios.

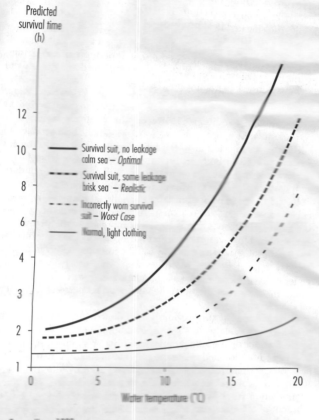

Source: Hayes 1988.

Work in arctic and subarctic regions

Arctic and subarctic regions of the world comprise additional problems to those of normal cold work. The cold season coincides with darkness. Days with sunlight are short. These regions cover vast, unpopulated or sparsely populated areas, such as Northern Canada, Siberia and Northern Scandinavia. In addition nature is harsh. Transportation takes place over large distances and takes a long time. The combination of cold, darkness and remoteness require special consideration in terms of work organization, preparation and equipment. In particular, training in survival and first aid must be provided and the appropriate equipment supplied and made easily available at work.

For the working population in the arctic regions there are many health-threatening hazards, as mentioned elsewhere. The risks of accident and injury are high, drug abuse is common, cultural patterns produce problems, as does the confrontation between local/native culture and modern western industrial demands. Snowmobile driving is an example of multiple-risk exposure in typical arctic conditions (see below). Cold stress is thought to be one of the risk factors that produces higher frequencies of certain diseases. Geographical isolation is another factor producing different types of genetic defects in some native areas. Endemic diseases—for example, certain infectious diseases—are also of local or regional importance. Settlers and guest workers also run a higher risk for different kinds of psychological stress reactions secondary to new environment, remoteness, harsh climate conditions, isolation and awareness.

Specific measures for this kind of work must be considered. Work must be carried out in groups of three, so that in case of emergency, one is left taking care of the victim while one is taking variation in daylight may [...] climate must [...] tasks planned according for [...] problems. If required, climate must [...] situations must be available workers must [...]. The seasonal snowmobiles must carry specific equipment for emergency situations.

A specific work problem in these [...] and work [...] for repair and [...]. Since the sixties the snowmobile has developed the snowmobile low-technology vehicle to one that is fast and [...] a primitive, developed. It is most frequently used for leisure actually highly for work (10 to 20%). Typical professions using the [...] but also are police, military personnel, reindeer herders, lumberjacks, farmers, tourist industry, trappers and search and rescue teams.

The vibration exposure from a snowmobile means a highly increased risk for vibration-induced injuries to the driver. The driver and the passengers are exposed to unpurified exhaust gas. The noise produced by the engine may induce hearing loss. Due to high speed, terrain irregularities and poor protection for the driver and the passengers, the risk of accidents is high.

The musculoskeletal system is exposed to vibrations and extreme working positions and loads, especially when driving in harsh terrain areas [...] slopes. If you get stuck, handling the heavy engine induces [...] action and often musculoskeletal problems (e.g., lumbago).

Cold injuries are [...] among snowmobile workers. The speed of the vehicle [...] the cold exposure. Typical injured parts of the body are [...] the face (could in extreme cases include cornea), ears, feet.

Snowmobiles are used [...] terrain and other conditions.

The snowmobile helm [...] remote areas where climate, situation on the snowmobile [...] to the risks. posture risks produced by [...] developed for the working climate. Clothing must be [...] to the specific exposure risks produced by [...] terrain conditions and activity transients experienced [...] roof and flexible. The cult to accommodate in one [...] mobile riding are difficult consideration.

Snowmobile traffic in remote [...] and require special tion problem. Work organization [...] a communication safe communication with the hon [...] should ensure be carried to handle emergency [...] equipment must for a time long enough for the re [...] protection equipment includes, for example, [...] aid equipment, snow shovel, repair kit [...] on. Such [...] first-

PREVENTION OF COLD S[...] EXTREME OUTDOOR CO[...]

Jacques Bittel an[...]

The prevention of the physiopathological effect [...] cold must be considered from two points of vie [...] cerns the physiopathological *effects observed dur* [...] posure to cold (that is, the entire body), and the se [...] those observed during local exposure to cold, mainly [...] extremities (hands and feet). Preventive measures in [...] tion aim to reduce the incidence of the two main ty [...] stress—accidental hypothermia and frostbite of the ext[...] twofold approach is required: physiological metho[...]

adequate feeding and hydration, development of adaptational mechanisms) and pharmacological ... (... and local levels. (e.g., shelter, clothing). Ultimate... exposed to cold have the crease tolerance to cold ... ing of such injury needed to en- Moreover, it is ess...

information ...

...ethods for Preventing Cold Injury

... in the human being at rest is accompanied by sure eff... vasoconstriction, which limits cutaneous heat loss, and ... ...abolic heat production (essentially by means of the activity shivering), which implies the necessity of food intake. The expenditure of energy required by all physical activity in the cold is increased on account of the difficulty of walking in snow or on ice and the frequent need to deal with heavy equipment. Moreover, water loss may be considerable on account of the sweating associated with this physical activity. If this water loss is not compensated for, dehydration may occur, increasing susceptibility to frostbite. The dehydration is often aggravated not only by voluntary restriction of water intake because of the difficulty of taking in adequate fluid (available water may be frozen, or one may have to melt snow) but also by the tendency to avoid adequately frequent micturition (urination), which requires leaving the shelter. The need for water in the cold is difficult to estimate because it depends on the individual's workload and on the insulation of the clothing. But in any case, fluid intake must be abundant and in the form of hot drinks (5 ... 6 l per day in the case of physical activity). Observation of ... of the course of which must remain clear, gives a good in... ... the colour of the urine, fluid intake.

As regards caloric intake, it may be a...ed that an increase of 25 to 50% in a cold climate, as comp...with temperate or hot climates, is necessary. A formula a... the calculation of the caloric intake (in kcal) essential for ...y equilibrium in the cold per person and per day: kcal/pe...er day = 4,151–28.62T_a, where T_a is the ambient tempe...in °C (1 kcal = 4.18 joule). Thus, for a T_a of –20 °C, a ne...about 4,723 kcal (2.0×10^4 J). must be anticipated. Food ...does not seem to have to be modified qualitatively in o...e cold weather ration (RCW) of diarrhoea type. For exa...ts of 4,568 kcal (1.9×10^4 J), in the United States Arm...per person, and is divided qualitatively as follows: 5...hydrate, 11% protein and 31% fat (Edwards, Robert...tion. dehydrated form, per ...ter 1992). Dehydrated foods have the advantage of be...d easy to prepare, but they have to be rehydrated be...normal amounts. A supplement is provided

As far as ...uits and cereal bars nibbled throughout the breakfast a...ing the caloric intake at dinner. This latter- by hot s...gments diet-induced thermogenesis and helps day, a...asleep. The consumption of alcohol is extremely most ...cold climate because alcohol induces cutaneous the ...(a source of heat loss) and increases diuresis (a in...ter loss), while modifying the sensitivity of the skin ...ng the judgement (which are basic factors involved in ...g the first signs of cold injury). Excessive consumption ...s containing caffeine is also harmful because this sub- ...has a peripheral vasoconstrictor effect (increased risk of ...te) and a diuretic effect.

In addition to adequate food, the development of both general and local adaptational mechanisms can reduce the incidence of cold injury and improve psychological and physical performance by reducing the stress caused by a cold environment. However, it is necessary to define the concepts of *adaptation*, *acclimatization* and *habituation* to cold, the three terms varying in their implications according to the usage of different theorists.

In Eagan's view (1963), the term *adaptation to cold* is a generic term. He groups under the concept of adaptation the concepts of genetic adaptation, acclimatization and habituation. Genetic adaptation refers to physiological changes transmitted genetically that favour survival in a hostile environment. Bligh and Johnson (1973) differentiate between genetic adaptation and phenotypic adaptation, defining the concept of adaptation as "changes which reduce the physiological strain produced by a stressful component of the total environment".

Acclimatization may be defined as functional compensation that is established over a period of several days to several weeks in response either to complex factors of the surroundings such as climatic variations in a natural environment, or to a unique factor in the surroundings, such as in the laboratory (the "artificial acclimatization" or "acclimation" of those writers) (Eagan 1963).

Habituation is the result of a change in physiological responses resulting from a diminution in the responses of the central nervous system to certain stimuli (Eagan 1963). This habituation can be specific or general. Specific habituation is the process involved when a certain part of the body becomes accustomed to a repeated stimulus, while general habituation is that by which the whole body becomes accustomed to a repeated stimulus. Local or general adaptation to cold is generally acquired through habituation.

Both in the laboratory and in natural surroundings, different types of general adaptation to cold have been observed. Hammel (1963) established a classification of these different adaptational types. The metabolic type of adaptation is shown by maintenance of the internal temperature combined with a greater production of metabolic heat, as in the Alacalufs of Tierra del Fuego or the Indians of the Arctic. Adaptation of the insulational type is also shown by maintenance of the internal temperature but with a diminution in the mean cutaneous temperature (aborigines of the tropical coast of Australia). Adaptation of the hypothermal type is shown by a more or less considerable fall in the internal temperature (tribe of the Kalahari Desert, Quechua Indians of Peru). Finally, there is adaptation of mixed isolational and hypothermal type (aborigines of central Australia, Lapps, Amas Korean divers).

In reality, this classification is merely qualitative in character and does not take into account all the components of thermal balance. We have therefore recently proposed a classification that is not only qualitative but also quantitative (see table 42.21). Modification in body temperature alone does not necessarily indi-

Table 42.21 • General adaptational mechanisms to cold studied during a standard cold test carried out before and after a period of acclimatization.

Measure	Use of measure as indicator of adaptation	Change in indicator	Type of adaptation
Rectal temperature t_{re}(°C)	Difference between t_{re} at the end of the cold test and t_{re} at thermal neutrality after acclimatization	+ or = –	normothermal hypothermal
Mean skin temperature $\bar{t}_{sk}$(°C)	$\bar{t}_{sk}$°C after/ $\bar{t}_{sk}$°C before, where $\bar{t}_{sk}$ is the level of at the end of the cold test	<1 =1 >1	insulational iso-insulational hypoinsulational
Mean metabolism $\bar{M}$ (W/m²)	Ratio of $\bar{M}$ after acclimatization to $\bar{M}$ before acclimatization	<1 = >1	metabolic isometabolic hypometabolic

cate the existence of general adaptation to cold. Indeed, a change in the delay in starting to shiver is a good indication of the sensitivity of the thermoregulatory system. Bittel (1987) has also proposed reduction in the thermal debt as an indicator of adaptation to cold. In addition, this author demonstrated the importance of the caloric intake in the development of adaptational mechanisms. We have confirmed this observation in our laboratory: subjects acclimatized to cold in the laboratory at 1 °C for 1 month in a discontinuous manner developed an adaptation of the hypothermal type (Savourey et al. 1994, 1996). The hypothermia is directly related to the reduction in the percentage of the body's fat mass. The level of aerobic physical aptitude ($VO_{2\,max}$) does not seem to be involved in the development of this type of adaptation to cold (Bittel et al. 1988; Savourey, Vallerand and Bittel 1992). Adaptation of the hypothermal type appears to be the most advantageous because it maintains the energy reserves by delaying the onset of shivering but without the hypothermia's being dangerous (Bittel et al. 1989). Recent work in the laboratory has shown that it is possible to induce this type of adaptation by subjecting people to intermittent localized immersion of the lower limbs in iced water. Moreover, this type of acclimatization has developed a "polar tri-iodothyronine syndrome" described by Reed and co-workers in 1990 in subjects who had spent long periods in the polar region. This complex syndrome remains imperfectly understood and is evidenced mainly by a diminution in the pool of total tri-iodothyronine both when the environment is thermally neutral and during acute exposure to cold. The relationship between this syndrome and adaptation of the hypothermal type has yet to be defined, however (Savourey et al. 1996).

Local adaptation of the extremities is well documented (LeBlanc 1975). It has been studied both in native tribes or professional groups naturally exposed to cold in the extremities (Eskimos, Lapps, fishermen on the island of Gaspé, English fish carvers, letter carriers in Quebec) and in subjects artificially adapted in the laboratory. All these studies have shown that this adaptation is evidenced by higher skin temperatures, less pain and earlier paradoxical vasodilatation that occurs at higher skin temperatures, thus permitting the prevention of frostbite. These changes are basically connected with an increase in peripheral skin blood flow and not with local production of heat at the muscular level, as we have recently shown (Savourey, Vallerand and Bittel 1992). Immersion of the extremities several times a day in cold water (5 °C) over several weeks is sufficient to induce the establishment of these local adaptational mechanisms. On the other hand, there are few scientific data on the persistence of these different types of adaptation.

Pharmacological Methods for Preventing Cold Injury

The use of drugs to enhance tolerance to cold has been the subject of a number of studies. General tolerance to cold can be enhanced by favouring thermogenesis with drugs. Indeed, it has been shown in human subjects that the activity of shivering is accompanied notably by an increase in the oxidation of carbohydrates, combined with an increased consumption of muscular glycogen (Martineau and Jacob 1988). Methylxanthinic compounds exert their effects by stimulating the sympathetic system, exactly like cold, thereby increasing the oxidation of carbohydrates. However, Wang, Man and Bel Castro (1987) have shown that theophylline was ineffective in preventing the fall in body temperature in resting human subjects in the cold. On the other hand, the combination of caffeine with ephedrine permits a better maintenance of body temperature under the same conditions (Vallerand, Jacob and Kavanagh 1989), while the ingestion of caffeine alone modifies neither the body temperature nor the metabolic response (Kennet 1990). The pharmacological prevention of the effects of cold is still a matter for research. At the animal level, the experimental model for frostbite, a certain number of drugs is carried out anti-aggregants, corticoids and also various drugs have a protective effect provided that they were administered in the rewarming period. To our knowledge, no study is carried out in humans on this subject.

Technical Methods for Preventing Cold Injury

These methods are a basic element in the prevention of cold injury, and without their use human beings would be incapable of living in cold climatic zones. The construction of shelters, the use of a source of heat and also the use of clothing permit people to live in very cold regions by creating a favourable ambient microclimate. However, the advantages provided by civilization are sometimes not available (in the case of civil and military expeditions, shipwrecked persons, injured persons, vagrants, victims of avalanches, etc.). These groups are therefore particularly liable to cold injury.

Precautions for Work in the Cold

The problem of conditioning for work in the cold relates mainly to people who are not accustomed to work in the cold and/or who come from temperate climatic zones. Information on injury that can be caused by cold is of basic importance, but it is also necessary to acquire information about a certain number of types of behaviour too. Every worker in a cold zone must be familiar with the first signs of injury, especially local injury (skin colour, pain). Behaviour as regards clothing is vital: several layers of clothing permit the wearer to adjust the insulation given by clothing to current levels of energy expenditure and external stress. Wet garments (rain, sweat) must be dried. Every attention must be given to the protection of the hands and feet (no tight bandages, attention to adequate covering, changing of socks—say twice or three times a day—because of sweating). Direct contact with all cold metallic objects must be avoided (risk of immediate frostbite). The clothing must be tested before any exposure to cold. Food should be remembered (with attention to caloric intake and hydration needs). Abuse of alcohol, caffeine and nicotine must be forbidden. Accessory equipment (shelter, tents, sleeping bags) should be checked. Condensation in tents and sleeping bags should be removed in order to avoid ice formation. Workers must not put their gloves to warm them or this will also cause the formation of ice. Finally, recommendations should be made for improving their physical fitness. Indeed, a good level of aerobic physical endurance allows greater thermogenesis in severe cold (Bittel et al.), ensures better physical endurance, a favourable factor which allows the extra energy loss from physical activity in the cold.

Middle-aged persons must be kept under careful surveillance because they are more susceptible to cold injury than younger people on account of their more limited vascular responses. Excessive fatigue and a sedentary occupation increase the risk of cold injury. Persons with certain medical conditions (cold urticaria, Raynaud's syndrome, angina pectoris, prior frostbite) must avoid exposure to intense cold. Certain additional advice may be useful: protect exposed skin against solar radiation, protect the lips with special creams and protect the eyes with sunglasses against ultraviolet radiation.

When a problem does occur, workers in a cold zone must keep calm, must not separate themselves from the group, and must maintain their body heat by digging holes and huddling together.

cate the existence of general adaptation to cold. Indeed, a change in the delay in starting to shiver is a good indication of the sensitivity of the thermoregulatory system. Bittel (1987) has also proposed reduction in the thermal debt as an indicator of adaptation to cold. In addition, this author demonstrated the importance of the caloric intake in the development of adaptational mechanisms. We have confirmed this observation in our laboratory: subjects acclimatized to cold in the laboratory at 1 °C for 1 month in a discontinuous manner developed an adaptation of the hypothermal type (Savourey et al. 1994, 1996). The hypothermia is directly related to the reduction in the percentage of the body's fat mass. The level of aerobic physical aptitude ($VO_{2\,max}$) does not seem to be involved in the development of this type of adaptation to cold (Bittel et al. 1988; Savourey, Vallerand and Bittel 1992). Adaptation of the hypothermal type appears to be the most advantageous because it maintains the energy reserves by delaying the onset of shivering but without the hypothermia's being dangerous (Bittel et al. 1989). Recent work in the laboratory has shown that it is possible to induce this type of adaptation by subjecting people to intermittent localized immersion of the lower limbs in iced water. Moreover, this type of acclimatization has developed a "polar tri-iodothyronine syndrome" described by Reed and co-workers in 1990 in subjects who had spent long periods in the polar region. This complex syndrome remains imperfectly understood and is evidenced mainly by a diminution in the pool of total tri-iodothyronine both when the environment is thermally neutral and during acute exposure to cold. The relationship between this syndrome and adaptation of the hypothermal type has yet to be defined, however (Savourey et al. 1996).

Local adaptation of the extremities is well documented (LeBlanc 1975). It has been studied both in naïve tribes or professional groups naturally exposed to cold in the extremities (Eskimos, Lapps, fishermen on the island of Gaspé, English fish carvers, letter carriers in Quebec) and in subjects artificially adapted in the laboratory. All these studies have shown this adaptation is evidenced by higher skin temperatures, less pain and earlier paradoxical vasodilation that occurs at higher skin temperatures, thus permitting the prevention of frostbite. These changes are basically connected with an increase in peripheral skin blood flow and not with local production of heat at the muscular level, as we have recently shown (Savourey, Vallerand and Bittel 1992). Immersion of the extremities several times a day in cold water (5 °C) over several weeks is sufficient to induce the establishment of these local adaptational mechanisms. On the other hand, there are few scientific data on the persistence of these different types of adaptation.

Pharmacological Methods for Preventing Cold Injury

The use of drugs to enhance tolerance to cold has been the subject of a number of studies. General tolerance to cold can be enhanced by favouring thermogenesis with drugs. Indeed, it has been shown in human subjects that the activity of shivering is accompanied notably by an increase in the oxidation of carbohydrates, combined with an increased consumption of muscular glycogen (Martineau and Jacob 1988). Methylxanthinic compounds exert their effects by stimulating the sympathetic system, exactly like cold, thereby increasing the oxidation of carbohydrates. However, Wang, Man and Bel Castro (1987) have shown that theophylline was ineffective in preventing the fall in body temperature in resting human subjects in the cold. On the other hand, the combination of caffeine with ephedrine permits a better maintenance of body temperature under the same conditions (Vallerand, Jacob and Kavanagh 1989), while the ingestion of caffeine alone modifies neither the body temperature nor the metabolic response (Kenneth et al. 1990). The pharmacological prevention of the effects of cold at the general level is still a matter for research. At the local level, few studies have been carried out on the pharmacological prevention of frostbite. Using an animal model for frostbite, a certain number of drugs were tested. Platelet anti-aggregants, corticoids and also various other substances had a protective effect provided that they were administered before the rewarming period. To our knowledge, no study has been carried out in humans on this subject.

Technical Methods for Preventing Cold Injury

These methods are a basic element in the prevention of cold injury, and without their use human beings would be incapable of living in cold climatic zones. The construction of shelters, the use of a source of heat and also the use of clothing permit people to live in very cold regions by creating a favourable ambient microclimate. However, the advantages provided by civilization are sometimes not available (in the case of civil and military expeditions, shipwrecked persons, injured persons, vagrants, victims of avalanches, etc.). These groups are therefore particularly liable to cold injury.

Precautions for Work in the Cold

The problem of conditioning for work in the cold relates mainly to people who are not accustomed to work in the cold and/or who come from temperate climatic zones. Information on injury that can be caused by cold is of basic importance, but it is also necessary to acquire information about a certain number of types of behaviour too. Every worker in a cold zone must be familiar with the first signs of injury, especially local injury (skin colour, pain). Behaviour as regards clothing is vital: several layers of clothing permit the wearer to adjust the insulation given by clothing to current levels of energy expenditure and external stress. Wet garments (rain, sweat) must be dried. Every attention must be given to the protection of the hands and feet (no tight bandages, attention to adequate covering, timely changing of socks—say twice or three times a day—because of sweating). Direct contact with all cold metallic objects must be avoided (risk of immediate frostbite). The clothing must be guaranteed against cold and tested before any exposure to cold. Feeding rules should be remembered (with attention to caloric intake and hydration needs). Abuse of alcohol, caffeine and nicotine must be forbidden. Accessory equipment (shelter, tents, sleeping bags) must be checked. Condensation in tents and sleeping bags must be removed in order to avoid ice formation. Workers must not blow into their gloves to warm them or this will also cause the formation of ice. Finally, recommendations should be made for improving physical fitness. Indeed, a good level of aerobic physical fitness allows greater thermogenesis in severe cold (Bittel et al. 1988) but also ensures better physical endurance, a favourable factor because of the extra energy loss from physical activity in the cold.

Middle-aged persons must be kept under careful surveillance because they are more susceptible to cold injury than younger people on account of their more limited vascular response. Excessive fatigue and a sedentary occupation increase the risk of injury. Persons with certain medical conditions (cold urticaria, Raynaud's syndrome, angina pectoris, prior frostbite) must avoid exposure to intense cold. Certain additional advice may be useful: protect exposed skin against solar radiation, protect the lips with special creams and protect the eyes with sunglasses against ultraviolet radiation.

When a problem does occur, workers in a cold zone must keep calm, must not separate themselves from the group, and must maintain their body heat by digging holes and huddling together.

adequate feeding and hydration, development of adaptational mechanisms) and pharmacological and technological measures (e.g., shelter, clothing). Ultimately all these methods aim to increase tolerance to cold at both the general and local levels. Moreover, it is essential that workers exposed to cold have the information and the understanding of such injury needed to ensure effective prevention.

Physiological Methods for Preventing Cold Injury

Exposure to cold in the human being at rest is accompanied by peripheral vasoconstriction, which limits cutaneous heat loss, and by metabolic heat production (essentially by means of the activity of shivering), which implies the necessity of food intake. The expenditure of energy required by all physical activity in the cold is increased on account of the difficulty of walking in snow or on ice and the frequent need to deal with heavy equipment. Moreover, water loss may be considerable on account of the sweating associated with this physical activity. If this water loss is not compensated for, dehydration may occur, increasing susceptibility to frostbite. The dehydration is often aggravated not only by voluntary restriction of water intake because of the difficulty of taking in adequate fluid (available water may be frozen, or one may have to melt snow) but also by the tendency to avoid adequately frequent micturition (urination), which requires leaving the shelter. The need for water in the cold is difficult to estimate because it depends on the individual's workload and on the insulation of the clothing. But in any case, fluid intake must be abundant and in the form of hot drinks (5 to 6 l per day in the case of physical activity). Observation of the colour of the urine, which must remain clear, gives a good indication of the course of fluid intake.

As regards caloric intake, it may be assumed that an increase of 25 to 50% in a cold climate, as compared with temperate or hot climates, is necessary. A formula allows the calculation of the caloric intake (in kcal) essential for energy equilibrium in the cold per person and per day: kcal/person per day $= 4{,}151 - 28.62 T_a$, where T_a is the ambient temperature in °C (1 kcal = 4.18 joule). Thus, for a T_a of −20 °C, a need for about 4,723 kcal (2.0×10^4 J) must be anticipated. Food intake does not seem to have to be modified qualitatively in order to avoid digestive troubles of the diarrhoea type. For example, the cold weather ration (RCW) of the United States Army consists of 4,568 kcal (1.9×10^4 J), in dehydrated form, per day and per person, and is divided qualitatively as follows: 58% carbohydrate, 11% protein and 31% fat (Edwards, Roberts and Mutter 1992). Dehydrated foods have the advantage of being light and easy to prepare, but they have to be rehydrated before consumption.

As far as possible, meals must be taken hot and divided into breakfast and lunch in normal amounts. A supplement is provided by hot soups, dry biscuits and cereal bars nibbled throughout the day, and by increasing the caloric intake at dinner. This latter expedient augments diet-induced thermogenesis and helps the subject to fall asleep. The consumption of alcohol is extremely inadvisable in a cold climate because alcohol induces cutaneous vasodilatation (a source of heat loss) and increases cutaneous diuresis (a source of water loss), while modifying the sensitivity of the skin and impairing the judgement (which are basic factors involved in recognizing the first signs of cold injury). Excessive consumption of drinks containing caffeine is also harmful because this substance has a peripheral vasoconstrictor effect (increased risk of frostbite); and a diuretic effect.

In addition to adequate food, the development of both general and local adaptational mechanisms can reduce the incidence of cold injury and improve psychological and physical performance by reducing the stress caused by a cold environment. However, it is necessary to define the concepts of adaptation, acclimatization and habituation to cold, the three terms varying in their implications according to the usage of different theorists.

In Eagan's view (1963), the term *adaptation to cold* is a generic term. He groups under the concept of adaptation the concepts of genetic adaptation, acclimatization and habituation. Genetic adaptation refers to physiological changes transmitted genetically that favour survival in a hostile environment. Bligh and Johnson (1973) differentiate between genetic adaptation and phenotypic adaptation, defining the concept of adaptation as "changes which reduce the physiological strain produced by a stressful component of the total environment."

Acclimatization may be defined as functional compensation that is established over a period of several days to several weeks in response either to complex factors of the surroundings such as climatic variations in a natural environment, or to a unique factor in the surroundings, such as in the laboratory (the "artificial acclimatization" or "acclimation" of those writers) (Eagan 1963).

Habituation is the result of a change in physiological responses resulting from a diminution in the responses of the central nervous system to certain stimuli (Eagan 1963). This habituation can be specific or general. Specific habituation is the process involved when a certain part of the body becomes accustomed to a repeated stimulus, while general habituation is that by which the whole body becomes accustomed to a repeated stimulus. Local or general adaptation to cold is generally acquired through habituation. Both in the laboratory and in natural surroundings, different types of general adaptation to cold have been observed. Hammel (1963) established a classification of these different adaptational types. The metabolic type of adaptation is shown by maintenance of the internal temperature combined with a greater production of metabolic heat, as in the Alacalufs of Tierra del Fuego or the Indians of the Arctic. Adaptation of the insulational type is also shown by maintenance of the internal temperature but with a diminution in the mean cutaneous temperature (aborigines of the tropical coast of Australia). Adaptation of the hypothermal type is shown by a more or less considerable fall in the internal temperature (tribe of the Kalahari Desert, Quechua Indians of Peru). Finally, there is adaptation of mixed isolational and hypothermal type (aborigines of central Australia, Lapps, Amas Korean divers).

In reality, this classification is merely qualitative in character and does not take into account all the components of thermal balance. We have therefore recently proposed a classification that is not only qualitative but also quantitative (see table 42.21). Modification in body temperature alone does not necessarily indi-

Table 42.21 • General adaptational mechanisms to cold studied during a standard cold test carried out before and after a period of acclimatization.

Measure	Use of measure as indicator of adaptation	Change in indicator	Type of adaptation
Rectal temperature t_{re} (°C)	Difference between t_{re} at the end of the cold test and t_{re} at thermal neutrality after acclimatization	+ or =	normothermal
		−	hypothermal
Mean skin temperature $\bar{t}_{sk}$ (°C)	$\bar{t}_{sk}$ °C after / $\bar{t}_{sk}$ °C before, where $\bar{t}_{sk}$ is the level of $\bar{t}_{sk}$ at the end of the cold test	<1	insulational
		=1	iso-insulational
		>1	hypoinsulational
Mean metabolism $\dot{M}$ (W/m²)	Ratio of $\dot{M}$ after acclimatization to $\dot{M}$ before acclimatization	<1	metabolic
		=	isometabolic
		>1	hypometabolic

Work in arctic and subarctic regions

Arctic and subarctic regions of the world comprise additional problems to those of normal cold work. The cold season coincides with darkness. Days with sunlight are short. These regions cover vast, unpopulated or sparsely populated areas, such as Northern Canada, Siberia and Northern Scandinavia. In addition nature is harsh. Transportation takes place over large distances and takes a long time. The combination of cold, darkness and remoteness require special consideration in terms of work organization, preparation and equipment. In particular, training in survival and first aid must be provided and the appropriate equipment supplied and made easily available.

For the working population in the arctic regions there are many health-threatening hazards, as mentioned elsewhere. The risks of accident and injury are high, drug abuse is common, cultural patterns produce problems, as does the confrontation between local/native culture and modern western industrial demands. Snowmobile driving is an example of multiple-risk exposure in typical arctic conditions (see below). Cold stress is thought to be one of the risk factors that produces higher frequencies of certain diseases. Geographical isolation is another factor producing different types of genetic defects in some native areas. Endemic diseases—for example, certain infectious diseases—are also of local or regional importance. Settlers and guest workers also run a higher risk for different kinds of psychological stress reactions secondary to new environment, remoteness, harsh climate conditions, isolation and awareness.

A specific work problem in these regions is the snowmobile. Since the sixties the snowmobile has developed from a primitive, low-technology vehicle to one that is fast and technically highly developed. It is most frequently used for leisure activities, but also for work (10 to 20%). Typical professions using the snowmobile are police, military personnel, reindeer herders, lumberjacks, farmers, tourist industry, trappers and search and rescue teams.

The vibration exposure from a snowmobile means a highly increased risk for vibration-induced injuries to the driver. The driver and the passengers are exposed to unpurified exhaust gas. The noise produced by the engine may induce hearing loss. Due to high speed, terrain irregularities and poor protection for the driver and the passengers, the risk of accidents is high.

The musculoskeletal system is exposed to vibrations and extreme working positions and loads, especially when driving in harsh terrain areas or slopes. If you get stuck, handling the heavy engine induces perspiration and often musculoskeletal problems (e.g., lumbago).

Cold injuries are common among snowmobile workers. The speed of the vehicle aggravates the cold exposure. Typical injured parts of the body are especially the face (could in extreme cases include cornea), ears, hands and feet.

Snowmobiles are usually used in remote areas where climate, terrain and other conditions contribute to the risks.

The snowmobile helmet must be developed for the working situation on the snowmobile with attention to the specific exposure risks produced by the vehicle itself, terrain conditions and climate. Clothing must be warm, windproof and flexible. The activity transients experienced during snowmobile riding are difficult to accommodate in one clothing system and require special consideration.

Snowmobile traffic in remote areas also presents a communication problem. Work organization and equipment should ensure safe communication with the home base. Extra equipment must be carried to handle emergency situations and allow protection for a time long enough for the rescue team to function. Such equipment includes, for example, wind sack, extra clothing, first-aid equipment, snow shovel, repair kit and cooking gear.

Specific measures for this kind of work must be considered. Work must be carried out in groups of three, so that in case of emergency, one person may go for help while one is left taking care of the victim or, for example, an accident. The seasonal variation in daylight and climate must be considered and work tasks planned accordingly. Workers must be checked for health problems. If required, extra equipment for emergency or survival situations must be available. Vehicles such as cars, trucks or snowmobiles must carry special equipment for repair and emergency situations.

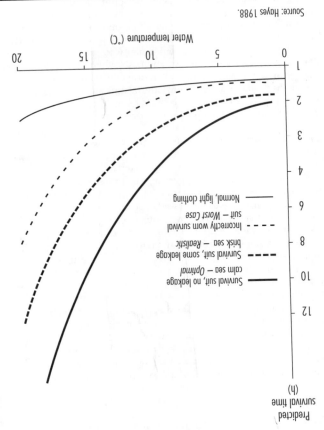

Figure 42.20 • Predicted survival times for typical North Sea offshore scenarios.

Predicted survival time (h)

Survival suit, no leakage — calm sea — *Optimal*
Survival suit, some leakage — brisk sea — *Realistic*
Incorrectly worn survival suit — *Worst case*
Normal, light clothing

Water temperature (°C)

Source: Hayes 1988.

PREVENTION OF COLD STRESS IN EXTREME OUTDOOR CONDITIONS

Jacques Bittel and Gustave Savourey

The prevention of the physiopathological effects of exposure to cold must be considered from two points of view: the first concerns the physiopathological effects observed during general exposure to cold (that is, the entire body), and the second concerns those observed during local exposure to cold, mainly affecting the extremities (hands and feet). Preventive measures in this connection aim to reduce the incidence of the two main types of cold stress—accidental hypothermia and frostbite of the extremities. A twofold approach is required: physiological methods (e.g., thermia (e.g., diving, fishing, shipping and other offshore opera-tions).

Victims of shipwrecks may have to enter cold water. Their protection varies from pieces of thin clothing to immersion suits. Lifejackets are mandatory equipment aboard ships. They should be equipped with a collar to reduce heat loss from the head of unconscious victims. The equipment of the ship, the efficiency of the emergency procedures and the behaviour of crew and passengers are important determinants for the success of the operation and the subsequent exposure conditions.

Divers regularly enter cold waters. The temperature of most waters with commercial diving, in particular at some depth, is low—often lower than 10°C. Any prolonged exposure in such cold water requires thermally insulated diving suits.

Heat loss. Heat exchange in the water may be seen as simply a flow of heat down two temperature gradients—one internal, from core to skin, and one external, from the skin surface to the surrounding water. Body surface heat loss can be simply described by:

$$C_w = h_c \cdot (T_{sk} - T_w) \cdot A_D$$

where C_w is the *rate* of convective heat loss (W), h_c is the convective heat transfer coefficient (W/°Cm²), T_{sk} is the average skin temperature (°C), T_w is the water temperature (°C) and A_D is the body surface area. The small components of heat loss from respiration and from non-immersed parts (e.g., head) can be neglected (see the section on diving below).

The value of h_c is in the range of 100 to 600 W/°Cm². The lowest value applies to still water. Turbulence, be it caused by swimming movements or flowing water, doubles or triples the convection coefficient. It is easily understood that the unprotected body may suffer a considerable heat loss to the cold water—eventually exceeding what can be produced even with heavy exercise. In fact, a person (dressed or undressed) who falls into cold water in most cases saves more heat by lying still in the water than by swimming.

Heat loss to the water can be significantly reduced by wearing special protective suits.

Diving. Diving operations several hundreds of metres below sea level must protect the diver from the effects of pressure (one ATA or 0.1 MPa/10 m) and cold. Breathing cold air (or a cold gas mixture of helium and oxygen) drains the lung tissues of body heat. This direct heat loss from the body core is large at high pressures and can easily achieve values higher than the resting metabolic heat production of the body. It is poorly sensed by the human organism. Dangerously low internal temperatures may develop without a shivering response if the body surface is warm. Modern offshore work requires the diver to be supplied with extra heat to the suit as well as to the breathing apparatus, to compensate for large convective heat losses. In deep-sea diving, the comfort zone is narrow and warmer than at sea level: 30 to 32°C at 20 to 30 ATA (2 to 3 MPa) and increasing to 32 to 34°C up to 50 ATA (5 MPa).

Physiological factors: Cold immersion elicits a strong, acute respiratory drive. The initial responses include an "inspiratory gasp", hyperventilation, tachycardia, peripheral vasoconstriction and hypertension. An inspiratory apnoea for several seconds is followed by an increased ventilation. The response is almost impossible to control voluntarily. Hence, a person may easily inhale water if the sea is rough and the body becomes submersed. The first seconds of exposure to very cold water, accordingly, are dangerous, and sudden drowning may occur. Slow immersion and proper protection of the body reduce the reaction and allow for better control of respiration. The reaction gradually fades and normal breathing is usually achieved within a few minutes.

The rapid rate of heat loss at the skin surface emphasizes the importance of internal (physiological or constitutional) mechan-

isms for reducing the core-to-skin heat flow. Vasoconstriction reduces extremity blood flow and preserves central heat. Exercise increases extremity blood flow, and, in conjunction with the increased external convection, it may in fact accelerate heat loss despite the elevated heat production.

After 5 to 10 min in very cold water, extremity temperature drops quickly. Neuromuscular function deteriorates and the ability to coordinate and control muscular performance degrades. Swimming performance may be severely reduced and quickly put the person at risk in open waters.

Body size is another important factor. A tall person has a larger body surface area and loses more heat than a small person at given ambient conditions. However, the relatively larger body mass compensates for this in two ways. Metabolic heat production rate increases in relation to the larger surface area, and the heat content at a given body temperature is greater. The latter factor comprises a larger buffer to heat losses and a slower rate of core temperature decrease. Children are at a greater risk than adults.

By far the most important factor is body fat content—in particular, subcutaneous fat thickness. Adipose tissue is more insulating than other tissues and is bypassed by much of the peripheral circulation. Once vasoconstriction has occurred, the layer of subcutaneous fat acts as an extra layer. The insulative effect is almost linearly related to the layer thickness. Accordingly, women in general have more cutaneous fat than men and lose less heat under the same conditions. In the same way, fat persons are better off than lean persons.

Personal protection. As previously mentioned, prolonged stay in cold and temperate waters requires additional external insulation in the form of diving suits, immersion suits or similar equipment. The wet suit of foamed neoprene provides insulation by the thickness of the material (closed foam cells) and by the relatively controlled "leakage" of water to the skin microclimate. The latter phenomenon results in the warming of this water and the establishment of a higher skin temperature. Suits are available in various thickness, providing more or less insulation. A wet suit compresses at depth and loses thereby much of its insulation.

The dry suit has become standard at temperatures below 10°C. It allows the maintenance of a higher skin temperature, depending on the amount of extra insulation worn under the suit. It is a fundamental requirement that the suit not leak, as small amounts of water (0.5 to 1 l) seriously reduce the insulative power. Although the dry suit also compresses at depth, dry air is automatically or manually added from the scuba tank to compensate for the reduced volume. Hence, a microclimate air layer of some thickness can be maintained, providing good insulation.

As previously mentioned, deep-sea diving requires auxiliary heating. Breathing gas is prewarmed and the suit is heated by the flushing of warm water from the surface or the diving bell. More recent warming techniques rely upon electrically heated underwear or closed-circuit tubules filled with warm fluid.

Hands are particularly susceptible to cooling and may require extra protection in the form of insulative or heated gloves.

Safe exposures. The rapid development of hypothermia and the imminent danger of death from cold-water exposure necessitates some sort of prediction of safe and unsafe exposure conditions. Figure 42.20 depicts predicted survival times for typical North Sea offshore conditions. The applied criterion is a drop in core temperature to 34°C for the tenth percentile of the population. This level is assumed to be associated with a conscious and manageable person. The proper wearing, use and functioning of a dry suit doubles the predicted survival time. The lower curve refers to the unprotected person immersed in normal clothing. As clothing gets completely soaked with water the effective insulation is very small, resulting in short survival times (modified from Wissler 1988).

Careful attention must be paid to the provision of food and means of calling for help (radio, distress rockets, signal mirrors, etc.). Where there is a risk of immersion in cold water, lifeboats must be provided as well as equipment that is watertight and gives good thermal insulation. In case of shipwreck without a lifeboat, the individual must try to limit heat loss to the maximum by hanging on to floating materials, curling up and swimming in moderation with the chest out of the water if possible, because the convection created by swimming considerably increases heat loss. Drinking sea-water is harmful because of its high salt level.

Modification of Tasks in the Cold

In a cold zone, work tasks are considerably modified. The weight of the clothing, the carrying of loads (tents, food, etc.) and the need to traverse difficult terrain increase the energy expended by physical activity. Moreover, movement, coordination and manual dexterity are hindered by clothing. The field of vision is often reduced by the wearing of sunglasses. Further, perception of the background is altered and reduced to 6 m when the temperature of dry air is below –18 °C or when there is a wind. Visibility may be nil in a snowfall or in fog. The presence of gloves makes difficult certain tasks requiring fine work. Because of condensation, tools are often coated with ice, and grasping them with bare hands carries a certain risk of frostbite. The physical structure of clothing is altered in extreme cold, and the ice that may form as a result of freezing combined with condensation often blocks zip-fasteners. Finally, fuels must be protected against freezing by the use of antifreeze.

Thus, for the optimal performance of tasks in a cold climate there must be several layers of clothing; adequate protection of the extremities; measures against condensation in clothing, on tools and in tents; and regular warming in a heated shelter. Work tasks must be undertaken as a sequence of simple tasks, if possible carried out by two work teams, one working while the other is warming itself. Inactivity in the cold must be avoided, as must solitary work, away from used paths. A competent person may be designated to be responsible for protection and accident prevention.

Table 42.22 • Monthly and annual mean of the number of days when water temperature is below 15 °C.

Month	Western Baltic	German Gulf	Atlantic Ocean (off Brest)	Western Mediterranean
January	31	31	31	31
February	28	28	28	28
March	31	31	31	31
April	30	30	30	26 to 30
May	31	31	31	8
June	25	25	25	sometimes
July	4	6	sometimes	sometimes
August	4	sometimes	sometimes	0
September	19	3	sometimes	sometimes
October	31	22	20	2
November	30	30	30	30
December	31	31	31	31
Total	295	268	257	187

In conclusion, it appears that a good knowledge of cold injury, a knowledge of the surroundings, good preparation (physical fitness, feeding, induction of adaptational mechanisms), appropriate clothing and suitable distribution of tasks can prevent cold injury. Where injury does occur, the worst can be avoided by means of rapid assistance and immediate treatment.

Protective Clothing: Waterproof Garments

Wearing waterproof garments has the object of protecting against the consequences of accidental immersion and therefore concerns not only all workers likely to suffer such accidents (sailors, air pilots) but also those working in cold water (professional divers). Table 42.22, extracted from the *Oceanographic Atlas of the North American Ocean*, shows that even in the western Mediterranean the water temperature rarely exceeds 15 °C. Under conditions of immersion, the survival time for a clothed individual with a lifebelt but without anti-immersion equipment has been estimated at 1.5 hours in the Baltic and 6 hours in the Mediterranean in January, whereas in August it is 12 hours in the Baltic and is limited only by exhaustion in the Mediterranean. Wearing protective equipment is therefore a necessity for workers at sea, particularly those liable to be immersed without immediate assistance.

The difficulties of producing such equipment are complex, because account has to be taken of multiple, often conflicting, requirements. These constraints include: (1) the fact that the thermal protection must be effective in both air and water without impeding evaporation of sweat (2) the need to keep the subject at the surface of the water and (3) the tasks to be carried out. The equipment must furthermore be designed in accordance with the risk involved. This requires exact definition of the anticipated needs: thermal environment (temperature of water, air, wind), time before help arrives, and presence or absence of a lifeboat, for example. The insulation characteristics of the clothing depend on the materials used, the contours of the body, the compressibility of the protective fabric (which determines the thickness of the layer of air imprisoned in the clothing on account of the pressure exerted by the water), and the humidity that may be present in the clothing. The presence of humidity in this type of clothing depends mainly on how watertight it is. Evaluation of such equipment must take into account the effectiveness of the thermal protection provided not only in the water but also in cold air, and involve estimates of both probable survival time in terms of the water and air temperatures, and the anticipated thermal stress and the possible mechanical hindrance of the clothing (Boutelier 1979). Finally, tests of watertightness carried out on a moving subject will allow possible deficiencies in this respect to be detected. Ultimately, anti-immersion equipment must meet three requirements:

- It must provide effective thermal protection in both water and air.
- It must be comfortable.
- It must be neither too restrictive nor too heavy.

To meet these requirements, two principles have been adopted: either to use a material that is not watertight but maintains its insulating properties in the water (as is the case of so-called "wet" suiting) or to ensure total watertightness with materials that are in addition insulating ("dry" suiting). At present, the principle of the wet garment is being applied less and less, especially in aviation. During the last decade, the International Maritime Organization has recommended the use of an anti-immersion or survival suit meeting the criteria of the International Convention for the safety of human life at sea (SOLAS) adopted in 1974. These criteria concern in particular insulation, minimum infiltration of water into the suit, the size of the suit, ergonomics, compatibility with

42. HEAT AND COLD

aids for floating, and testing procedures. However, the application of these criteria poses a certain number of problems (notably, those to do with the definition of the tests to be applied).

Although they have been known for a very long time, since the Eskimos used sealskin or seal intestines sewn together, anti-immersion suits are difficult to perfect and the criteria for standardization will probably be reviewed in future years.

• COLD INDICES AND STANDARDS

Ingvar Holmér

Cold stress is defined as a thermal load on the body under which greater than normal heat losses are anticipated and compensatory thermoregulatory actions are required to maintain the body thermally neutral. Normal heat losses, hence, refer to what people normally experience during indoor living conditions (air temperature 20 to 25 °C).

In contrast to conditions in the heat, clothing and activity are positive factors in the sense that more clothing reduces heat loss and more activity means higher internal heat production and a greater potential for balancing heat loss. Accordingly, assessment methods focus on the determination of required protection (clothing) at given activity levels, required activity levels for given protection or "temperature" values for given combinations of the two (Burton and Edholm 1955; Holmér 1988; Parsons 1993).

It is important to recognize, however, that there are limits as to how much clothing can be worn and how high a level of activity can be sustained for extended time periods. Cold-protective clothing tends to be bulky and hobbling. More space is required for motion and movements. Activity level may be determined by paced work but should, preferably, be controlled by the individual. For each individual there is a certain highest energy production rate, depending on physical work capacity, that can be sustained for prolonged time periods. Thus, high physical work capacity may be advantageous for prolonged, extreme exposures.

Table 42.23 • Air temperatures of various cold occupational environments.

−120 °C	Climatic chamber for human cryotherapy
−90 °C	Lowest temperature at south polar base Vostock
−55 °C	Cold store for fish meat and production of frozen, dried products
−40 °C	"Normal" temperature at polar base
−28 °C	Cold store for deep-frozen products
+2 to +12 °C	Storage, preparation and transportation of fresh, alimentary products
−50 to −20 °C	Average January temperature of northern Canada and Siberia
−20 to −10 °C	Average January temperature of southern Canada, northern Scandinavia, central Russia
−10 to 0 °C	Average January temperature of northern USA, southern Scandinavia, central Europe, parts of middle and far East, central and northern Japan

Source: Modified from Holmér 1993.

Table 42.24 • Schematic classification of cold work.

Temperature	Type of work	Type of cold stress
10 to 20 °C	Sedentary, light work, fine manual work	Whole-body cooling, extremity cooling
0 to 10 °C	Sedentary and stationary, light work	Whole-body cooling, extremity cooling
−10 to 0 °C	Light physical work, handling tools and materials	Whole-body cooling, extremity cooling, contact cooling
−20 to −10 °C	Moderate activity, handling metals and fluids (petrol etc.), windy conditions	Whole-body cooling, extremity cooling, contact cooling, convective cooling
Below −20 °C	All types of work	All types of cold stress

This article deals with methods for assessment and control of cold stress. Problems related to organizational, psychological, medical and ergonomic aspects are dealt with elsewhere.

Cold Work

Cold work encompasses a variety of conditions under natural as well as artificial conditions. The most extreme cold exposure is associated with missions in outer space. However, cold working conditions on the surface of the earth cover a temperature range of more than 100 °C (table 42.23). Naturally, the magnitude and severity of cold stress will be expected to increase with lowered ambient temperature.

It is clear from table 42.23 that large populations of outdoor workers in many countries experience more or less severe cold stress. In addition cold store work occurs in all parts of the world. Surveys in Scandinavian countries reveal that approximately 10% of the total worker population regard cold as a major annoyance factor in the workplace.

Types of Cold Stress

The following types of cold stress can be defined:

- whole-body cooling
- local cooling, including extremity cooling, convective skin cooling (wind chill), conductive skin cooling (contact cooling) and cooling of respiratory tract.

Most likely, several if not all of these may be present at the same time.

The assessment of cold stress involves the ascertainment of a risk of one or more of the mentioned effects. Typically, table 42.24 may be used as a first rough classification. In general cold stress increases, the lower the level of physical activity and the less protection available.

Information given in the table should be interpreted as a signal to action. In other words, the particular type of cold stress should be evaluated and controlled, if required. At moderate temperatures problems associated with discomfort and losses of function due to local cooling prevail. At lower temperatures the imminent risk of a cold injury as a sequel to the other effects is the important factor. For many of the effects discrete relationships between stress level and effect do not yet exist. It cannot be excluded that a particular cold problem may persist also outside the range of temperatures denoted by the table.

Figure 42.21 • Assessment of cold stress in relation to climatic factors and cooling effects.

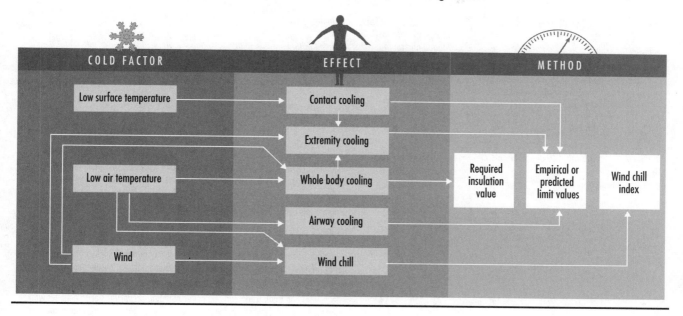

Assessment Methods

Methods for assessment of cold stress are presented in ISO Technical Report 11079 (ISO TR 11079, 1993). Other standards concerning determination of metabolic heat production (ISO 8996, 1988), estimation of clothing thermal characteristics (ISO 9920, 1993), and physiological measurements (ISO DIS 9886, 1989c) provide complementary information useful for the evaluation of cold stress.

Figure 42.21 outlines the relationships between climate factors, anticipated cooling effect and recommended method for assessment. Further details about methods and data collection are given below.

Whole-Body Cooling

The risk of whole-body cooling is determined by analysing the conditions for body heat balance. The clothing insulation level required for heat balance at defined levels of physiological strain, is calculated with a mathematical heat balance equation. The calculated required insulation value, IREQ, can be regarded as a cold stress index. The value indicates a protection level (expressed in clo). The higher the value, the greater the risk of body heat imbalance. The two levels of strain correspond to a low level (neutral or "comfort" sensation) and a high level (slightly cold to cold sensation).

Using IREQ comprises three evaluation steps:

- determination of IREQ for given exposure conditions
- comparison of IREQ with protection level provided by clothing
- determination of exposure time if protection level is of lesser value than IREQ

Figure 42.22 shows IREQ values for low physiological strain (neutral thermal sensation). Values are given for different activity levels.

Methods to estimate activity levels are described in ISO 7243 (table 42.25).

Once IREQ is determined for given conditions, the value is compared with the protection level offered by clothing. Protection level of a clothing ensemble is determined by its resultant insulation value ("clo-value"). This property is measured according to the draft European standard prEN-342 (1992). It can also be derived from basic insulation values provided in tables (ISO 9920).

Table 42.26 provides examples of basic insulation values for typical ensembles. Values must be corrected for presumed reduc-

Figure 42.22 • IREQ values needed to maintain low-level physiological strain (neutral thermal sensation) at varying temperature

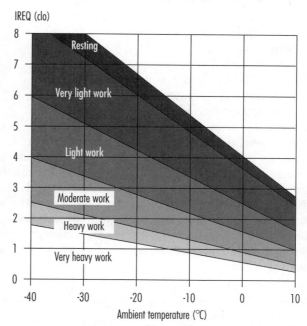

Table 42.25 • Classification of levels of metabolic rate.

Class	Metabolic rate range, M		Value to be used for calculation of mean metabolic rate		Examples
	Related to a unit skin surface area (W/m²)	For a mean skin surface area of 1.8 m² (W)	(W/m²)	(W)	
0 Resting	$M \leq 65$	$M \leq 117$	65	117	Resting
1 Low metabolic rate	$65 < M \leq 130$	$117 < M \leq 234$	100	180	Sitting at ease: light manual work (writing, typing, drawing, sewing, book-keeping); hand and arm work (small bench tools, inspection, assembly or sorting of light material); arm and leg work (driving vehicle in normal conditions, operating foot switch or pedals). Standing: drill (small parts); milling machine (small parts); coil winding; small armature winding; machining with low power tools; casual walking (speed up to 3.5 km/h).
2 Moderate metabolic rate	$130 < M \leq 200$	$234 < M \leq 360$	165	297	Sustained hand and arm work (hammering in nails, filling); arm and leg work (off-road operation of lorries, tractors or construction equipment); arm and trunk work (work with pneumatic hammer, tractor assembly, plastering, intermittent handling of moderately heavy material, weeding, hoeing, picking fruit or vegetables); pushing or pulling light weight carts or wheelbarrows; walking at a speed of 3.5 km/h; forging.
3 High metabolic rate	$200 < M \leq 260$	$360 < M \leq 468$	230	414	Intense arm and trunk work: carrying heavy material; shoveling; sledge hammer work; sawing, planing or chiseling hard wood; hand mowing; digging; walking at a speed of 5.5 km/h to 7 km/h. Pushing or pulling heavily loaded handcarts or wheelbarrows; chipping castings; concrete block laying.
4 Very high metabolic rate	$M > 260$	$M > 468$	290	522	Very intensive activity at fast to maximum pace; working with an axe; intense shoveling or digging; climbing stairs, ramp or ladder; walking quickly with small steps, running, walking at a speed greater than 7 km/h.

Source: ISO 7243 1989a.

Table 42.26 • Examples of basic insulation values (I_{cl}) of clothing.*

Clothing ensemble	I_{cl} (m² °C/W)	I_{cl} (clo)
Briefs, short-sleeve shirt, fitted trousers, calf-length socks, shoes	0.08	0.5
Underpants, shirt, fitted, trousers, socks, shoes	0.10	0.6
Underpants, coverall, socks, shoes	0.11	0.7
Underpants, shirt, coverall, socks, shoes	0.13	0.8
Underpants, shirt, trousers, smock, socks, shoes	0.14	0.9
Briefs, undershirt, underpants, shirt, overalls, calf-length socks, shoes	0.16	1.0
Underpants, undershirt, shirt, trousers, jacket, vest, socks, shoes	0.17	1.1
Underpants, shirt, trousers, jacket, coverall, socks, shoes	0.19	1.3
Undershirt, underpants, insulated trousers, insulated jacket, socks, shoes	0.22	1.4
Briefs, T-shirt, shirt, fitted trousers, insulated coveralls, calf-length socks, shoes	0.23	1.5
Underpants, undershirt, shirt, trousers, jacket, overjacket, hat, gloves, socks, shoes	0.25	1.6
Underpants, undershirt, shirt, trousers, jacket, overjacket, overtrousers, socks, shoes	0.29	1.9
Underpants, undershirt, shirt, trousers, jacket, overjacket, overtrousers, socks, shoes, hat, gloves	0.31	2.0
Undershirt, underpants, insulated trousers, insulated jacket, overtrousers, overjacket, socks, shoes	0.34	2.2
Undershirt, underpants, insulated trousers, insulated jacket, overtrousers, socks, shoes, hat, gloves	0.40	2.6
Undershirt, underpants, insulated trousers, insulated jacket, overtrousers and parka with lining, socks, shoes, hat, mittens	0.40–0.52	2.6–3.4
Arctic clothing systems	0.46–0.70	3–4.5
Sleeping bags	0.46–1.1	3–8

*Nominal protection level applies only to static, windstill conditions (resting). Values must be reduced with increased activity level.

Source: Modified from ISO/TR-11079 1993.

Figure 42.23 • Time limits for light and moderate work with two insulation levels of clothing.

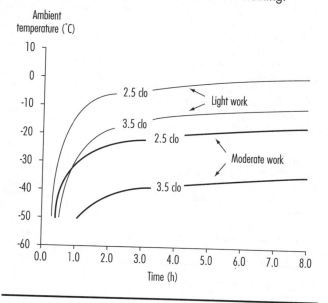

Figure 42.25 • Finger protection.

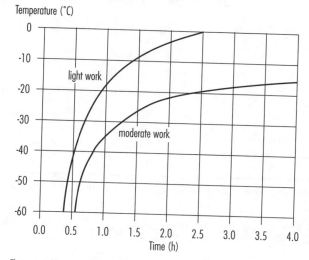

The curves indicate acceptable time and temperature limits for exposure of the fingers to cold under conditions of light and moderate work (data are based on calculations of hand heat exchange and a critical fingertip temperature of 5 °C).

tion caused by body motion and ventilation. Typically, no correction is made for resting level. Values are reduced by 10% for light work and by 20% for higher activity levels.

The protection level offered by the best available clothing systems corresponds to 3 to 4 clo. When the available clothing system does not provide sufficient insulation, a time limit is calculated for the actual conditions. This time limit depends on the difference between required clothing insulation and that of the available clothing. Since, full protection against cooling is no longer achieved, the time limit is calculated on the basis of an anticipated reduction of body heat content. Similarly, a recovery time can be calculated to restore the same amount of heat.

Figure 42.23 shows examples of time limits for light and moderate work with two insulation levels of clothing. Time limits for other combinations may be estimated by interpolation. Figure 42.24 can be used as a guideline for assessment of exposure time, when the best cold protective clothing is available.

Intermittent exposures typically comprise work periods interrupted by warm-up breaks or by work periods in a warmer environment. In most conditions, little or no replacement of clothing takes place (mostly for practical reasons). IREQ may then be determined for the combined exposure as a time-weighted average. Averaging period must not be longer than one to two hours. Time-weighted IREQ values for some types of intermittent exposure are given in figure 42.24.

IREQ values and time limits should be indicative rather than normative. They refer to the average person. The individual variation in terms of characteristics, requirements and preferences is large. Much of this variation must be handled by selecting clothing ensembles with great flexibility in terms of, for example, adjustment of the protection level.

Extremity Cooling

The extremities—in particular, fingers and toes—are susceptible to cooling. Unless sufficient heat input by warm blood can be maintained, tissue temperature progressively falls. Extremity blood flow is determined by energetic (required for muscles activity) as well as thermoregulatory needs. When whole-body thermal balance is challenged, peripheral vasoconstriction helps to reduce core heat losses at the expense of peripheral tissues. With high activity more heat is available and extremity blood flow can more easily be maintained.

The protection offered by handwear and footwear in terms of reducing heat losses is limited. When heat input to the extremity is low (e.g., with resting or low activity), the insulation required to keep hands and feet warm is very large (van Dilla, Day and Siple 1949). The protection offered by gloves and mittens only provides

Figure 42.24 • Time-weighted IREQ values for intermittent and continuous exposure to cold.

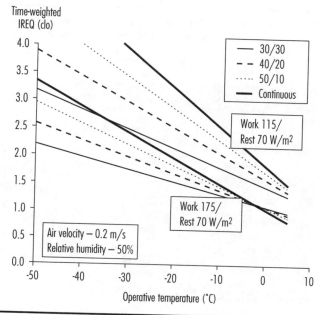

Table 42.27 • Classification of thermal resistance (I) to convective cooling of handwear.

Class	I (m² °C/W)
1	$0.10 \leq I < 0.15$
2	$0.15 \leq I < 0.22$
3	$0.22 \leq I < 0.30$
4	$I \leq 0.30$

Source: Based on EN 511 (1993).

Table 42.28 • Classification of contact thermal resistance of handwear (I).

Class	I (m² °C/W)
1	$0.025 \leq I < 0.05$
2	$0.05 \leq I < 0.10$
3	$0.10 \leq I < 0.15$
4	$I \leq 0.15$

Source: Based on EN 511 (1993).

Table 42.29 • Wind Chill Index (WCI), equivalent cooling temperature (T_{eq}) and freezing time of exposed flesh.

WCI (W/m²)	T_{eq} (°C)	Effect
1,200	−14	Very cold
1,400	−22	Bitterly cold
1,600	−30	Exposed flesh freezes
1,800	−38	within 1 hour
2,000	−45	Exposed flesh freezes
2,200	−53	within 1 minute
2,400	−61	Exposed flesh freezes
2,600	−69	within 30 seconds

retardation of cooling rate and, correspondingly, longer times to reach a critical temperature. With higher activity levels, improved protection allows warm hands and feet at lower ambient temperatures.

No standard method is available for assessment of extremity cooling. However, ISO TR 11079 recommends 24 °C and 15 °C as critical hand temperatures for levels of low and high stress, respectively. Fingertip temperature may easily be 5 to 10 °C lower than the average hand skin temperature or simply the temperature of the back of the hand.

The information given in figure 42.25 is useful when determining acceptable exposure times and required protection. The two curves refer to conditions with and without vasoconstriction (high

and low activity level). Furthermore, it is assumed that finger insulation is high (two clo) and adequate clothing is used.

A similar set of curves should apply to toes. However, more clo may be available for protection of feet, resulting in longer exposure times. Nevertheless, it follows from figures 42.23 and 42.25 that extremity cooling most likely is more critical for exposure time than whole-body-cooling.

Protection provided by handwear is evaluated by using methods described in the European standard EN-511 (1993). Thermal insulation of the whole handwear is measured with an electrically heated hand model. A wind speed of 4 m/s is used to simulate realistic wear conditions. Performance is given in four classes (table 42.27).

Contact Cold

Contact between bare hand and cold surfaces may quickly reduce skin temperature and cause freezing injury. Problems may arise with surface temperatures as high as 15 °C. In particular, metal surfaces provide excellent conductive properties and may quickly cool contacting skin areas.

At present no standard method exists for general assessment of contact cooling. The following recommendations can be given (ACGIH 1990; Chen, Nilsson and Holmér 1994; Enander 1987):

- Prolonged contact with metal surfaces below 15 °C may impair dexterity.
- Prolonged contact with metal surfaces below 7 °C may induce numbness.
- Prolonged contact with metal surfaces below 0 °C may induce frostnip or frostbite.
- Brief contact with metal surfaces below −7 °C may induce frostnip or frostbite.
- Any contact with liquids at subzero temperature must be avoided.

Other materials present a similar sequence of hazards, but temperatures are lower with less conducting material (plastics, wood, foam).

Protection against contact cooling provided by handwear can be determined using the European standard EN 511. Four performance classes are given (table 42.28).

Figure 42.26 • The relationship of expected cold stress risk to required measurement procedures.

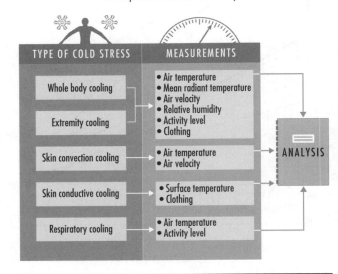

Table 42.30 • Cooling power of wind on exposed flesh expressed as an equivalent cooling temperature under almost calm conditions (wind speed 1.8 m/s).

Wind speed (m/s)	Actual thermometer reading (°C)										
	0	−5	−10	−15	−20	−25	−30	−35	−40	−45	−50
	Equivalent cooling temperature (°C)										
1.8	0	−5	−10	−15	−20	−25	−30	−35	−40	−45	−50
2	−1	−6	−11	−16	−21	−27	−32	−37	−42	−47	−52
3	−4	−10	−15	−21	−27	−32	−38	−44	−49	−55	−60
5	−9	−15	−21	−28	−34	−40	−47	−53	−59	−66	−72
8	−13	−20	−27	−34	−41	−48	−55	−62	−69	−76	−83
11	−16	−23	−31	−38	−46	−53	−60	−68	−75	−83	−90
15	−18	−26	−34	−42	−49	−57	−65	−73	−80	−88	−96
20	−20	−28	−36	−44	−52	−60	−68	−76	−84	−92	−100

Underlined values represent a risk for frostnip or frostbite.

Convective Skin Cooling

The Wind Chill Index (WCI) represents a simple, empirical method for assessment of cooling of unprotected skin (face) (ISO TR 11079). The method predicts tissue heat loss on the basis of air temperature and wind speed.

Responses associated with different values of WCI are denoted in table 42.29.

A frequently used interpretation of WCI is the equivalent cooling temperature. This temperature under calm conditions (1.8 m/s) represents the same WCI value as the actual combination of temperature and wind. Table 42.30 provides equivalent cooling temperatures for combinations of air temperature and wind speed. The table applies to active, well-dressed persons. A risk is present when equivalent temperature drops below −30 °C, and skin may freeze within 1 to 2 min below −60 °C.

Cooling of Respiratory Tract

Inhaling cold, dry air may cause problems for sensitive persons at +10 to 15 °C. Healthy persons performing light to moderate work require no particular protection of the respiratory tract down to −30 °C. Very heavy work during prolonged exposures (e.g., athletic endurance events) should not take place at temperatures below −20 °C.

Similar recommendations apply to cooling of the eye. In practice, the great discomfort and visual impairment associated with eye cooling normally require the use of goggles or other protection long before the exposure becomes hazardous.

Measurements

Depending on type of expected risk, different sets of measurements are required (figure 42.26). Procedures for data collection and accuracy of measurements depend on the purpose of the measurements. Pertinent information must be obtained regarding variation in time of the climatic parameters, as well as of activity level and/or clothing. Simple time-weighting procedures should be adopted (ISO 7726).

Preventive Measures for Alleviation of Cold Stress

Actions and measures for the control and reduction of cold stress imply a number of considerations during the planning and preparatory phases of work shifts, as well as during work, which are dealt with elsewhere in this chapter and this *Encyclopaedia*.

References

ACGIH (American Conference of Governmental Industrial Hygienists). 1990. *Threshold Limit Values and Biological Exposure Indices for 1989–1990.* New York: ACGIH.

—. 1992. Cold stress. In *Threshold Limit Values for Physical Agents in the Work Environment.* New York: ACGIH.

Bedford, T. 1940. Environmental warmth and its measurement. *Medical Research Memorandum No. 17.* London: Her Majesty's Stationery Office.

Belding, HS and TF Hatch. 1955. Index for evaluating heat stress in terms of resulting physiological strain. *Heating Piping Air Condit* 27:129–136.

Bittel, JHM. 1987. Heat debt as an index for cold adaptation in men. *J Appl Physiol* 62(4):1627–1634.

Bittel, JHM, C Nonotte-Varly, GH Livecchi-Gonnot, GLM Savourey and AM Hanniquet. 1988. Physical fitness and thermoregulatory reactions in a cold environment in men. *J Appl Physiol* 65:1984–1989.

Bittel, JHM, GH Livecchi-Gonnot, AM Hanniquet and JL Etienne. 1989. Thermal changes observed before and after J.L. Etienne's journey to the North Pole. *Eur J Appl Physiol* 58:646–651.

Bligh, J and KG Johnson. 1973. Glossary of terms for thermal physiology. *J Appl Physiol* 35(6):941–961.

Botsford, JH. 1971. A wet globe thermometer for environmental heat measurement. *Am Ind Hyg J* 32:1–10.

Boutelier, C. 1979. Survie et protection des équipages en cas d'immersion accidentelle en eau froide. Neuilly-sur-Seine: AGARD A.G. 211.

Brouha, L. 1960. *Physiology in Industry.* New York: Pergamon Press.

Burton, AC and OG Edholm. 1955. *Man in a Cold Environment.* London: Edward Arnold.

Chen, F, H Nilsson and RI Holmér. 1994. Cooling responses of finger pad in contact with an aluminum surface. *Am Ind Hyg Assoc J* 55(3):218–22.

Comité Européen de Normalisation (CEN). 1992. EN 344. *Protective Clothing Against Cold.* Brussels: CEN.

—. 1993. EN 511. *Protective Gloves Against Cold.* Brussels: CEN.

Commission of the European Communities (CEC). 1988. Proceedings of a seminar on heat stress indices. Luxembourg: CEC, Health and Safety Directorate.

Daanen, HAM. 1993. Deterioration of manual performance in cold and windy conditions. AGARD, NATO, CP-540.

Dasler, AR. 1974. Ventilation and thermal stress, ashore and afloat. In Chapter 3, *Manual of Naval Preventive Medicine.* Washington, DC: Navy Department, Bureau of Medicine and Surgery.

—. 1977. Heat stress, work functions and physiological heat exposure limits in man. In *Thermal Analysis—Human Comfort—Indoor Environments*. NBS Special Publication 491. Washington, DC: US Department of Commerce.

Deutsches Institut für Normierung (DIN) 7943-2. 1992. *Schlafsacke, Thermophysiologische Prufung*. Berlin: DIN.

Dubois, D and EF Dubois. 1916. Clinical calorimetry X: A formula to estimate the appropiate surface area if height and weight be known. *Arch Int Med* 17:863–871.

Eagan, CJ. 1963. Introduction and terminology. *Fed Proc* 22:930–933.

Edwards, JSA, DE Roberts, and SH Mutter. 1992. Relations for use in a cold environment. *J Wildlife Med* 3:27–47.

Enander, A. 1987. Sensory reactions and performance in moderate cold. Doctoral thesis. Solna: National Institute of Occupational Health.

Fuller, FH and L Brouha. 1966. New engineering methods for evaluating the job environment. *ASHRAE J* 8(1):39–52.

Fuller, FH and PE Smith. 1980. The effectiveness of preventive work procedures in a hot workshop. In FN Dukes-Dobos and A Henschel (eds.). *Proceedings of a NIOSH Workshop on Recommended Heat Stress Standards*. Washington DC: DHSS (NIOSH) publication No. 81-108.

—. 1981. Evaluation of heat stress in a hot workshop by physiological measurements. *Am Ind Hyg Assoc J* 42:32–37.

Gagge, AP, AP Fobelets and LG Berglund. 1986. A standard predictive index of human response to the thermal environment. *ASHRAE Trans* 92:709–731.

Gisolfi, CV and CB Wenger. 1984. Temperature regulation during exercise: Old concepts, new ideas. *Exercise Sport Sci Rev* 12:339–372.

Givoni, B. 1963. A new method for evaluating industrial heat exposure and maximum permissible work load. Paper submitted to the International Biometeorological Congress in Paris, France, September 1963.

—. 1976. *Man, Climate and Architecture*, 2nd ed. London: Applied Science.

Givoni, B and RF Goldman. 1972. Predicting rectal temperature response to work, environment and clothing. *J Appl Physiol* 2(6):812–822.

—. 1973. Predicting heart rate response to work, environment and clothing. *J Appl Physiol* 34(2):201–204.

Goldman, RF. 1988. Standards for human exposure to heat. In *Environmental Ergonomics*, edited by IB Mekjavic, EW Banister and JB Morrison. London: Taylor & Francis.

Hales, JRS and DAB Richards. 1987. *Heat Stress*. Amsterdam, New York: Oxford Excerpta Medica.

Hammel, HT. 1963. Summary of comparative thermal patterns in man. *Fed Proc* 22:846–847.

Havenith, G, R Heus and WA Lotens. 1990. Clothing ventilation, vapour resistance and permeability index: Changes due to posture, movement and wind. *Ergonomics* 33:989–1005.

Hayes. 1988. In *Environmental Ergonomics*, edited by IB Mekjavic, EW Banister and JB Morrison. London: Taylor & Francis.

Holmér, I. 1988. Assessment of cold stress in terms of required clothing insulation—IREQ. *Int J Ind Erg* 3:159–166.

—. 1993. Work in the cold. Review of methods for assessment of cold stress. *Int Arch Occ Env Health* 65:147–155.

—. 1994. Cold stress: Part 1—Guidelines for the practitioner. *Int J Ind Erg* 14:1–10.

—. 1994. Cold stress: Part 2—The scientific basis (knowledge base) for the guide. *Int J Ind Erg* 14:1–9.

Houghton, FC and CP Yagoglou. 1923. Determining equal comfort lines. *J ASHVE* 29:165–176.

International Organization for Standardization (ISO). 1985. ISO 7726. *Thermal Environments—Instruments and Methods for Measuring Physical Quantities*. Geneva: ISO.

—. 1989a. ISO 7243. *Hot Environments—Estimation of the Heat Stress on Working Man, Based on the WBGT Index (Wet Bulb Globe Temperature)*. Geneva: ISO.

—. 1989b. ISO 7933. *Hot Environments—Analytical Determination and Interpretation of Thermal Stress using Calculation of Required Sweat Rate*. Geneva: ISO.

—. 1989c. ISO DIS 9886. *Ergonomics—Evaluation of Thermal Strain by Physiological Measurements*. Geneva: ISO.

—. 1990. ISO 8996. *Ergonomics—Determination of Metabolic Heat Production*. Geneva: ISO.

—. 1992. ISO 9886. *Evaluation of Thermal Strain by Physiological Measurements*. Geneva: ISO.

—. 1993. *Assessment of the Influence of the Thermal Environment using Subjective Judgement Scales*. Geneva: ISO.

—. 1993. ISO CD 12894. *Ergonomics of the Thermal Environment—Medical Supervision of Individuals Exposed to Hot or Cold Environments*. Geneva: ISO.

—. 1993. ISO TR 11079 *Evaluation of Cold Environments—Determination of Required Clothing Insulation, IREQ*. Geneva: ISO. (Technical Report)

—. 1994. ISO 9920. *Ergonomics—Estimation of the Thermal Characteristics of a Clothing Ensemble*. Geneva: ISO.

—. 1994. ISO 7730. *Moderate Thermal Environments—Determination of the PMV and PPD Indices and Specification of the Conditions for Thermal Comfort*. Geneva: ISO.

—. 1995. ISO DIS 11933. *Ergonomics of the Thermal Environment. Principles and Application of International Standards*. Geneva: ISO.

Kenneth, W, P Sathasivam, AL Vallerand and TB Graham. 1990. Influence of caffeine on metabolic responses of men at rest in 28 and 5 °C. *J Appl Physiol* 68(5):1889–1895.

Kenney, WL and SR Fowler. 1988. Methylcholine-activated eccrine sweat gland density and output as a function of age. *J Appl Physiol* 65:1082–1086.

Kerslake, DMcK. 1972. *The Stress of Hot Environments*. Cambridge: Cambridge University Press.

LeBlanc, J. 1975. *Man in the Cold*. Springfield, IL, US: Charles C Thomas Publ.

Leithead, CA and AR Lind. 1964. *Heat Stress and Head Disorders*. London: Cassell.

Lind, AR. 1957. A physiological criterion for setting thermal environmental limits for everybody's work. *J Appl Physiol* 18:51–56.

Lotens, WA. 1989. The actual insulation of multilayer clothing. *Scand J Work Environ Health* 15 Suppl. 1:66–75.

—. 1993. Heat transfer from humans wearing clothing. Thesis, Technical University. Delft, Netherlands. (ISBN 90-6743-231-8).

Lotens, WA and G Havenith. 1991. Calculation of clothing insulation and vapour resistance. *Ergonomics* 34:233–254.

Maclean, D and D Emslie-Smith. 1977. *Accidental Hypothermia*. Oxford, London, Edinburgh, Melbourne: Blackwell Scientific Publication.

Macpherson, RK. 1960. Physiological responses to hot environments. *Medical Research Council Special Report Series No. 298*. London: HMSO.

Martineau, L and I Jacob. 1988. Muscle glycogen utilization during shivering thermogenesis in humans. *J Appl Physiol* 56:2046–2050.

Maughan, RJ. 1991. Fluid and electrolyte loss and replacement in exercise. *J Sport Sci* 9:117–142.

McArdle, B, W Dunham, HE Halling, WSS Ladell, JW Scalt, ML Thomson and JS Weiner. 1947. The prediction of the physiological effects of warm and hot environments. *Medical Research Council Rep 47/391*. London: RNP.

McCullough, EA, BW Jones and PEJ Huck. 1985. A comprehensive database for estimating clothing insulation. *ASHRAE Trans* 91:29–47.

McCullough, EA, BW Jones and T Tamura. 1989. A database for determining the evaporative resistance of clothing. *ASHRAE Trans* 95:316–328.

McIntyre, DA. 1980. *Indoor Climate*. London: Applied Science Publishers Ltd.

Mekjavic, IB, EW Banister and JB Morrison (eds.). 1988. *Environmental Ergonomics*. Philadelphia: Taylor & Francis.

Nielsen, B. 1984. Dehydration, rehydration and thermoregulation. In E Jokl and M Hebbelinck (eds.). *Medicine and Sports Science*. Basel: S. Karger.

—. 1994. Heat stress and acclimation. *Ergonomics* 37(1):49–58.

Nielsen, R, BW Olesen and P-O Fanger. 1985. Effect of physical activity and air velocity on the thermal insulation of clothing. *Ergonomics* 28:1617–1632.

National Institute for Occupational Safety and Health (NIOSH). 1972. Occupational exposure to hot environments. HSM 72-10269. Washington, DC: US Department of Health Education and Welfare.

—. 1986. Occupational exposure to hot environments. NIOSH Publication No. 86-113. Washington, DC: NIOSH.

Nishi, Y and AP Gagge. 1977. Effective temperature scale used for hypo- and hyperbaric environments. *Aviation Space and Envir Med* 48:97–107.

Olesen, BW. 1985. Heat stress. In *Bruel and Kjaer Technical Review No. 2*. Denmark: Bruel and Kjaer.

Olesen, BW, E Sliwinska, TL Madsen and P-O Fanger. 1982. Effect of body posture and activity on the thermal insulation of clothing: Measurements by a movable thermal manikin. *ASHRAE Trans* 88:791–805.

Pandolf, KB, BS Cadarette, MN Sawka, AJ Young, RP Francesconi and RR Gonzales. 1988. *J Appl Physiol* 65(1):65–71.

Parsons, KC. 1993. *Human Thermal Environments*. Hampshire, UK: Taylor & Francis.

Reed, HL, D Brice, KMM Shakir, KD Burman, MM D'Alesandro and JT O'Brian. 1990. Decreased free fraction of thyroid hormones after prolonged Antarctic residence. *J Appl Physiol* 69:1467–1472.

Rowell, LB. 1983. Cardiovascular aspects of human thermoregulation. *Circ Res* 52:367–379.

—. 1986. *Human Circulation Regulation During Physical Stress*. Oxford: OUP.

Sato, K and F Sato. 1983. Individual variations in structure and function of human eccrine sweat gland. *Am J Physiol* 245:R203–R208.

Savourey, G, AL Vallerand and J Bittel. 1992. General and local adaptation after a ski journey in a severe arctic environment. *Eur J Appl Physiol* 64:99–105.

Savourey, G, JP Caravel, B Barnavol and J Bittel. 1994. Thyroid hormone changes in a cold air environment after local cold acclimation. *J Appl Physiol* 76(5):1963–1967.

Savourey, G, B Barnavol, JP Caravel, C Feuerstein and J Bittel. 1996. Hypothermic general cold adaptation induced by local cold acclimation. *Eur J Appl Physiol* 73:237–244.

Vallerand, AL, I Jacob and MF Kavanagh. 1989. Mechanism of enhanced cold tolerance by an ephedrine/caffeine mixture in humans. *J Appl Physiol* 67:438–444.

van Dilla, MA, R Day and PA Siple. 1949. Special problems of the hands. In *Physiology of Heat Regulation*, edited by R Newburgh. Philadelphia: Saunders.

Vellar, OD. 1969. *Nutrient Losses through Sweating*. Oslo: Universitetsforlaget.

Vogt, JJ, V Candas, JP Libert and F Daull. 1981. Required sweat rate as an index of thermal strain in industry. In *Bioengineering, Thermal Physiology and Comfort*, edited by K Cena and JA Clark. Amsterdam: Elsevier. 99–110.

Wang, LCH, SFP Man and AN Bel Castro. 1987. Metabolic and hormonal responses in theophylline-increased cold resistance in males. *J Appl Physiol* 63:589–596.

World Health Organization (WHO). 1969. Health factors involved in working under conditions of heat stress. *Technical Report 412*. Geneva: WHO.

Wissler, EH. 1988. A review of human thermal models. In *Environmental Ergonomics*, edited by IB Mekjavic, EW Banister and JB Morrison. London: Taylor & Francis.

Woodcock, AH. 1962. Moisture transfer in textile systems. Part I. *Textile Res J* 32:628–633.

Yaglou, CP and D Minard. 1957. Control of heat casualties at military training centers. *Am Med Assoc Arch Ind Health* 16:302–316 and 405.

Other relevant readings

Alm, NO. 1992. Strategies for accident prevention in circumpolar regions. *Arctic Med Res* 50 Suppl. 7:99-101.

Anon. 1993. The support of air operations under extreme hot and cold weather conditions. Neuilly-sur-Seine, France: AGARD/NATO, C10-304.

Bennett, PB and DH Elliot. 1991. *The Physiology and Medicine of Diving*. London: Bailliere Tindall.

Burton, AC and OG Edholm. 1969. *Man in a Cold Environment*. New York: Hafner Publishing Company, Inc.

Clark, RP and OG Edholm. 1985. *Man and his Thermal Environment*. London: Edward Arnold.

Eiken, O, P Kaiser, I Holmér and R Baer. 1989. Physiological effects of a mouth-borne heat exchanger during heavy exercise in a cold environment. *Ergonomics* 32(6):645–653.

Enander, AE. 1990. Working performance in the cold. *Proceedings of Working and Survival in the Cold*. Trondheim, Norway: Sintef Unimed, 69–92.

—. 1987. Effects of moderate cold on performance of psychomotor and cognitive tasks. *Ergonomics* 30(10):1431–1445.

Fanger, P-O. 1970. *Thermal Comfort*. New York: McGraw-Hill Book Co.

Francis, TJR. 1985. Non-freezing cold injuries—The pathogenesis. *J Royal Navies Med Serv* 71:3–8.

Frimodt-Muller, B and H Bay-Nielsen. 1992. Classification of accidents in the Arctic. *Arctic Med Res* 51 Suppl. 7:15–21.

Granberg, PO. 1995. Human endocrine responses to the cold. *Arctic Med Res* 54:91–103.

Granberg, P-O, J Hassi, I Holmér, T Larsen, H Refsum, K Yttrehus and M Knip. 1991. Cold physiology and cold injuries. *Arctic Med Res* 50: Suppl. 6.

Hamlet, MP. 1988. Human cold injuries. In *Human Performance Physiology and Environmental Medicine at Terrestrial Extremes*, edited by KB Pandolf, MN Sawka and RR Gonzalez (eds.). Alexandria, VI: Army Research Institute of Environmental Medicine. 435–466.

Holmér, I (ed.). 1994. *Work in Cold Environments*. Solna, Sweden: National Institute of Occupational Health..

Ingall, TJ. 1993. Hyperthermia and hypothermia. In *Clinical Autonomic Disorders*, edited by PA Low. Boston: Little Brown and Company.

International Organization for Standardization (ISO). 1984. *Thermal Environments—Specifications Relating to Appliances and Methods for Measuring Physical Characteristics of the Environment*. Geneva: ISO.

Khogali, M and JRS Hales. 1983. *Heat Stroke and Temperature Regulation*. Sydney: Academic Press.

Leppäluoto, J (ed.). 1995. Effects of cold on the human organism. *Arctic Med Res* 54: Supp 2.

Litchfield, P. Manual performance in the cold: A review of some of the critical factors. *J Roy Nav Med Serv* 73:173–177.

Lloyd, EL. 1986. *Hypothermia and Cold Stress*. London and Sydney: Croom Helm.

Mekjavic, I and J Bligh. 1987. The pathophysiology of hypothermia. In *International Reviews of Ergonomics*, edited by DJ Oborne. New York:Taylor & Francis. 201–218.

Middaugh, J. 1992. Epidemiology of injuries in northern areas. *Arctic Med Res* 51:5–14.

Mills, WJ. 1991. Cold injury. *Alaska Med* 35:1.

Morton, WE and JWS Hearle. 1975. *Physical Properties of Textile Fibres*. London: Heinemann.

Newburgh, LH (ed.). 1949. *Physiology of Heat Regulation and the Science of Clothing*. New York: Hafner Publishing Co.

Nishi, Y and AP Gagge. 1970. Moisture permeation of clothing—A factor governing thermal equilibrium and comfort. *ASHRAE Trans* 76(1):137–145.

Pandolf, KB, MN Sawka and RR Gonzales. 1988. *Human Performance Physiology and Environmental Medicine at Terrestrial Extremes*. Indianapolis: Benchmark Press.

Parsons, KC, JG Fox and B Metz. 1995. Heat stress indices (special issue). *Ergonomics* Vol. 38, No. 1, January 1995.

Savourey, G, B Barnavol, JP Caravel, G Barbe, and J Bittel. 1993. Induction d'un syndrome polaire de la "tri-iodothyronine" en laboratoire chez l'homme. *CR Acad Sci Paris* 607–610.

Shitzer, A, A Stroschein, WE Santee, RR Gonzales and KB Pandolf. 1991. Quantification of conservative endurance times in thermally insulated cold-stressed digits. *J Appl Physiol* 71(6):2528–2535.

Toner, MM and WD McArdle. 1988. Physiological adjustments of man to the cold. In *Human Performance Physiology and Environmental Medicine at Terrestrial Extremes*, edited by KB Pandolf, MN Sawka and RR Gonzalez. Alexandria, VI: US Army Research Institute of Environmental Medicine.

Whelan, ME, LE MacHattie, AC Goodings and LH Turl. 1955. The diffusion of water vapour through luminae with particular reference to textile fabrics. *Textile Res J* 25(3):197–223.

Young, AJ. 1988. Human adaptation to cold. In *Human Performance Physiology and Environmental Medicine at Terrestrial Extremes*, edited by KB Pandolf, MN Sawka and RR Gonzalez (eds.).. Alexandria, VI: US Army Research Institute of Environmental Medicine.

42. HEAT AND COLD

HOURS OF WORK

43

Chapter Editor
Peter Knauth

Contents

43. HOURS OF WORK

HOURS OF WORK

Peter Knauth

Shiftwork is work scheduled, either permanently or frequently, outside normal daytime working hours. Shiftwork can be e.g., permanent work at night, permanent work during the evening, or work hours can have changing assignment patterns. Each type of shift system has its advantages and disadvantages, and each is associated with differing effects on well-being, health, social life and work performance.

In the traditional slowly rotating shift systems, shifts change weekly; that is, a week of night shifts is followed by a week of evening shifts and then a week of morning shifts. In a quickly rotating shift system only one, two or a maximum of three consecutive days are spent on each shift. In some countries, like the United States, shifts longer than 8 hours, in particular 12 hours, are gaining in popularity (Rosa et al. 1990).

Human beings have evolved as essentially diurnal; that is, the body is mainly "programmed" towards daytime work performance and for night-time recreation and rest. Internal mechanisms (sometimes called the body or biological clock) control the physiology and biochemistry of the body to fit in with a 24-hour environment. These cycles are called *circadian rhythms*. The disruption of circadian variations in physiological function caused by having to be awake and at work at biologically unusual hours, as well as to sleep during the daytime, is one of the major stresses associated with shiftwork.

Despite the widespread assumption that disturbances of the circadian system may result, over the long run, in harmful effects, the actual cause-effect relation has been difficult to establish. Despite this lack of absolute proof, it is widely accepted that it is prudent to adopt shift systems at the workplace that minimize long-lasting disruption of circadian rhythms.

Combined Effects of Workplace Factors

Some shiftworkers are also exposed to other workplace hazards, such as toxic agents, or to jobs with high mental loads or physical demands. Only a few studies, however, have addressed the problems caused by the combination of shiftwork and unfavourable working, organizational and environmental conditions where the negative effects of shiftwork could be caused not only by the phase difference between circadian rhythms and living conditions, but also by the adverse negative working conditions that may be combined with shiftwork.

A variety of workplace hazards, such as noise, unfavourable climatic conditions, unfavourable lighting conditions, vibration and combinations of these, can sometimes occur more often in three-shift systems, irregular systems and night-shift systems than in two-shift systems or daywork.

Intervening Variables

People vary widely in their tolerance of shiftwork, according to Härmä (1993), which may be explained by the influence of many intervening variables. Some individual differences which may modify the strain of shiftworkers are: differences in the phase and amplitude of the circadian cycle, age, gender, pregnancy, physical fitness and flexibility in sleeping habits, and the ability to overcome drowsiness, as illustrated by figure 43.1.

Although some authors found a correlation between a larger amplitude of circadian rhythms and fewer medical complaints (Andlauer et al. 1979; Reinberg et al. 1988; Costa et al. 1989; Knauth and Härmä 1992), others have found that it does not predict adjustment to shiftwork (Costa et al. 1989; Minors and Waterhouse 1981) even after three years of work (Vidacek et al. 1987).

There appear to be two main dimensions of personality related to the circadian phase: "morningness"/"eveningness" and introversion/extroversion (Kerkhof 1985). Morningness/eveningness can be assessed by questionnaire (Horne and Östberg 1976; Folkard et al. 1979; Torsval and Åkerstedt 1980; Moog 1981) or by measuring body temperature (Breithaupt et al. 1978). Morning types, "larks", having an advanced phase position of the circadian body temperature, go to bed earlier and rise earlier than the average population, whereas evening types, "owls," have a delayed circadian phase position and go to bed and rise later. To be a "lark" would appear to be an advantage for morning shifts and an "owl" for night shifts. However, some authors report that a disproportionally large number of those who give up shiftwork were morning types (Åkerstedt and Fröberg 1976; Hauke et al. 1979; Torsvall and Åkerstedt 1979). A relation between morningness and decreased tolerance to shiftwork has been found by Bohle and Tilley (1989) and Vidacek et al. (1987). Other researchers, however, have found opposite results (Costa et al. 1989), and it should be noted that most studies have involved only extreme "larks" and "owls", where each represents only 5% of the population.

In many questionnaire studies, more adverse health effects of shiftwork have been found with increasing *age*, the critical age being 40 to 50 years on average (Foret et al. 1981; Koller 1983; Åkerstedt and Torsvall 1981). With increasing age, sleep during the day becomes progressively more difficult (Åkerstedt and Torsvall 1981). There are also some indications of slower circadian adjustment to shiftwork in middle-aged shiftworkers

Figure 43.1 • Model of stress and strain of shiftworkers.

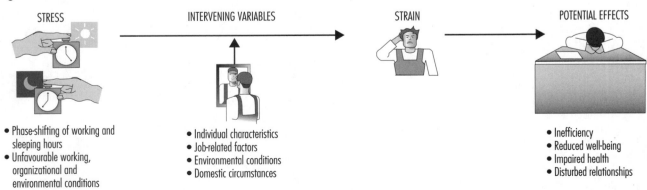

STRESS
• Phase-shifting of working and sleeping hours
• Unfavourable working, organizational and environmental conditions

INTERVENING VARIABLES
• Individual characteristics
• Job-related factors
• Environmental conditions
• Domestic circumstances

STRAIN

POTENTIAL EFFECTS
• Inefficiency
• Reduced well-being
• Impaired health
• Disturbed relationships

Table 43.1 • Time intervals from the beginning of shiftwork to the moment when the three illnesses were diagnosed (mean and standard deviation in years).

Work schedule	Gastroduodenitis	Peptic ulcer	Neurotic disorders
Day work	12.6 ± 10.9	12.2 ± 9.9	9.7 ± 6.8
Two shifts	7.8 ± 6.6	14.4 ± 8.2	9.0 ± 7.5
Three shifts	7.4 ± 6.5	5.0 ± 3.9	6.8 ± 5.2
Night work	4.7 ± 4.3	5.6 ± 2.8	3.6 ± 3.3

Source: Costa et al. 1981

compared to younger ones (Härmä et al. 1990; Matsumoto and Morita 1987).

Gender and *pregnancy* are two intervening variables which have often been discussed but not yet adequately investigated in longitudinal studies. Based on a review of the literature, Rutenfranz et al. (1987) conclude that the circadian rhythms of men and women react in the same way to the phase shifting of work and sleep in connection with night work. However, two aspects—the menstrual cycle and the additional load of child care and household duties—have to be taken into consideration.

Although some authors have found more frequent menstrual problems in groups of women shiftworkers compared to women in day work (Tasto et al. 1978; Uehata and Sasakawa 1982), the comparability of these shift and day-work groups was questionable. Pokorski et al. (1990) studied perception of discomfort among female triple-shift workers during three phases of the menstrual cycle (praemenstruum, menstruation and postmenstruum). Phase-related differences were more pronounced than differences between morning, evening and night shifts.

Child care at home reduced the duration of sleep and of leisure time in female shiftworking nurses. Estryn-Behar questioned 120 women on permanent night shift and found that the average duration of sleep after night shifts was 6 h 31 min for women without children, 5 h 30 min for women with older children, and 4 h 55 min for women with very young children (Estryn-Behar et al. 1978). Nevertheless, a study of policewomen found that those with children were more favourable towards shiftwork than were women without children (Beermann et al. 1990).

Physical fitness appeared to be a factor in increasing tolerance to shiftwork in a study by Härmä et al. (1988a, b). In a follow-up study with matched pair design, the group of participants who exercised regularly on a four-month programme reported a significant decrease in general fatigue, particularly when on the night shift, as well as a decrease in musculoskeletal symptoms and an increase in sleep length.

The *"flexibility of sleeping habits"* and *"ability to overcome drowsiness"*, as assessed by a questionnaire developed by Folkard et al. (1979; 1982) were related, in some studies, to a better tolerance to shiftwork (Wynne et al. 1986; Costa et al. 1989; Vidacek et al. 1987). In other studies, however, this relationship was not confirmed (e.g., Bohle and Tilley 1989).

Other intervening variables that may be important for shiftwork tolerance are the *"commitment to night work"* as the way in which people schedule their lives (Folkard et al. 1979; Minors and Waterhouse 1981) or the *coping style* of shiftworkers (Olsson et al. 1987; Olsson and Kandolin 1990).

Besides individual characteristics, *situational factors* seem to be of importance for explaining the extent of problems reported by

shiftworkers. Küpper et al. (1980) and Knauth (1983) found that shiftworkers who tried to sleep during the day and were often or always disturbed by noise, complained more frequently about nervous and gastrointestinal symptoms than did shiftworkers with undisturbed or rarely disturbed sleep.

Health Effects of Shiftwork

Most of the health complaints of shiftworkers can be related to the quality of the day sleep after night shifts and, to a lesser extent, to the sleep before morning shifts. As circadian rhythms generally function such that the body is programmed for daytime performance and for night-time sleep, after the night shift the body is, in general, not completely adjusted for going to sleep. Other factors may also intervene. Daylight may disturb sleep. Noise during the day is in general louder than during the night. Most nightworkers complain about the noise of children and of traffic. Some nightworkers interrupt their day sleep in order to partake of a joint meal with the family, and some reduce their sleep because of their household duties and child care responsibilities. In one study of shiftworkers, the duration of night sleep was found to be reduced to 6 hours (Knauth 1983). Although there are large interindividual differences in sleep needs, 6 or less hours of sleep per day is inadequate for many human beings (Williams et al. 1974). In particular, after many consecutive night shifts an accumulation of sleep deficits has to be expected, with its accompanying effects in both social life and productivity (Naitoh et al. 1990) as well as the possibility of an increased accident rate. Several electroencephalographic studies have also shown that the quality of day sleep is also lower (Knauth 1983).

Sleep deficits may occur in both a week of night shifts and in a week of morning shifts. The prolonged sleep duration at the weekend after a week of morning shifts seems to indicate that there is an increased need for sleep.

Hak and Kampmann (1981) studied sleep and fatigue in train drivers. The earlier the morning shift started, the shorter was the preceding night-shift sleep and the more fatigued the train drivers during the morning shift. The reduction of sleep in connection with an earlier start of the morning shift has also been confirmed by studies of Moors (1990) as well as Folkard and Barton (1993). Such findings may be partially explained by the social pressure of the family not to go to bed too early, or by the body clock, which according to Lavie (1986) causes a "forbidden zone" for sleep, during which sleep propensity is greatly reduced. The latter explanation means that even if the shiftworkers go to bed earlier—because of the early start of the following morning shift—they might find it difficult to fall asleep.

Gastrointestinal disturbances. Night work leads to a change in the sequence and timing of meals. During the night, the stomach cannot cope with the composition and the quantity of a typical daytime meal. It is then understandable that nightworkers often suffer more from disturbances of appetite than do dayworkers or shiftworkers not on night shift, as Rutenfranz et al. (1981) have concluded from a review of the literature.

In the long run, irregular food intake can lead to gastrointestinal complaints or even to disorders. However, the reasons for the complex gastrointestinal symptoms are surely manifold. An analysis of existing studies, such as that of Costa (1996), is difficult, because of methodological differences. Most results are based on cross-sectional studies—that is, on workers currently engaged in shiftwork. Thus, if individuals have left shiftwork because of problems or diseases, we are left with a more or less self-selected population (the "healthy worker" effect). Therefore the health status of a group of shiftworkers may be better than a group of dayworkers, simply because shiftworkers with poorer health or social problems have changed to day work and those that remain may be better able to cope.

43. HOURS OF WORK

Table 43.2 • Relationship between shiftwork and incidence of cardiovascular disorders.

Reference	Publication years	Conclusion	Methodological comments/ratings
Thiis-Evenson (1949); Aanonsen (1964)	1949-1964	0	2
Taylor and Pocock (1972)	1972	0	? correct choice for controls
Rutenfranz et el. (1977); Carpentier et al. (1977)	1977	0, review articles	
Angersbach et al. (1980); Koller et al. (1983)	1980-1983	+, particularly dropouts; +, with increasing age	2-3
Michel-Briand et al. (1981)	1981	+, in retired workers	1
Alfredsson et al. (1982; 1983; 1985); Knutsson et al. (1986)	1982-1986	+, in men and women; worsens with years on shiftwork	3-4
Åkerstedt et al. (1984)	1984-1986	+, review article	
Orth-Gomer (1985)	1985	+, review article	
Andersen (1985)	1985	+, occupations involving shiftwork	
Frese and Semmer (1986)	1986	+, in dropouts	

Source: Waterhouse et al. 1992. Based on Kristensen 1989. Ratings on conclusions used by Kristensen: +, increased incidence; 0, no difference. Methodological ratings, 1-4 from lowest to highest quality methodology.

In longitudinal studies, which have been almost exclusively retrospective, the problems with self-selection and loss to follow-up are well known. For example, for the sample in the study of Leuliet (1963), the study population was almost halved in size during the study period of 12 years. As with cross-sectional studies, it is often former shiftworkers, who have transferred to day work out of shifts because of medical problems, who show the most serious effects. Thiis-Evensen (1958) found that peptic ulcers were twice as frequent among former shiftworkers as among dayworkers. Aanonsen (1964) and Angersbach et al. (1980) observed, respectively, two and three-and-a-half times as many cases of peptic ulcers among former regular shiftworkers, with a subsequent significant decrease in gastrointestinal disease after the transfer out of the shiftwork pattern.

Costa et al. (1981) computed the time interval between beginning shiftwork and when illnesses were diagnosed (table 43.1). Comparing groups with different working time arrangements, Costa et al. found the shortest mean intervals (4.7 years) for the appearance of gastroduodenitis in permanent nightworkers. In groups with night work (i.e., three-shift workers and permanent nightworkers), within an interval of about 5 years peptic ulcers developed. In his review Costa (1996) concludes that "there is sufficient evidence to consider shiftwork as a risk factor for gastrointestinal disorders and diseases—in particular peptic ulcer" (table 43.1).

Cardiovascular disorders. Kristensen (1989) has analysed the relevant studies on the incidence of cardiovascular disorders in shiftworkers for methodological and analytical factors, as shown in table 43.2. Papers published after 1978 were more likely to report an increase in cardiovascular disorders, particularly among those who transferred away from shiftwork. Waterhouse et al. (1992) conclude that it is not possible simply to dismiss the relationship as had been generally accepted (Harrington 1978).

Neurological disorders. Although there is a lack of standardization of the symptoms and disorders in studies of neurological disorders of shiftworkers (Waterhouse et al. 1992; Costa 1996), according to Waterhouse (1992), however, "there is now evidence for a greater tendency towards general malaise—including anxiety and depression elements—in shiftworkers than in day-working colleagues". Costa (1996) comes to a similar but more cautious conclusion: "there is sufficient evidence to suggest that morbidity for psychoneurotic disorders can be influenced by shiftwork to a greater or lesser extent in relation to other individual and social factors."

Mortality. There is only one very careful epidemiological study on the mortality of shiftworkers. Taylor and Pocock (1972) compared mortality rates in shiftworkers and dayworkers over a 13-year period in a sample of over 8,000 persons. There were no differences in rates between current shiftworkers and dayworkers. However, the standardized mortality ratio for former shiftworkers was 118.9, compared to 101.5 for current shiftworkers, which "might imply a selecting-out of less fit men" (Harrington 1978).

Social Problems of Shiftworkers

Shiftwork may have negative effects on family life, participation in institutional life and social contacts. The extent of problems which may exist is dependent on many factors, such as the type of shift system, gender, age, marital status, composition of family of the shiftworker, as well as how common shiftwork is in a particular region.

During a week of evening shifts, regular contacts between a shiftworker and his or her school-age children, or partner who may work in morning or day shifts, are dramatically reduced. This is an important problem for shiftworkers who work so-called permanent afternoon shifts (Mott et al. 1965). In the traditional discontinuous two-shift system, a week of morning shifts and evening shifts alternates such that every second week the contacts are disturbed. The traditional weekly rotating three-shift system has evening shifts every third week. In quickly rotating shift systems, contacts within the family are never impaired during a whole week. Researchers have obtained contradicting results. Mott et al. (1965) found that many consecutive evening or night shifts could impair the marital happiness of shiftworkers, while Maasen (1981) did not observe this. Shiftwork—in particular when both parents are shiftworkers—may have negative effects on the school performance of children (Maasen 1981; Diekmann et al. 1981).

Studies concerning the subjective value of free time during different hours of the week showed that weekends were rated higher than weekdays, and evenings higher than time off during the day (Wedderburn 1981; Hornberger and Knauth 1993). The contacts with friends, relatives, clubs, political parties, churches

Figure 43.2 • Recommendations for the design of shift systems.

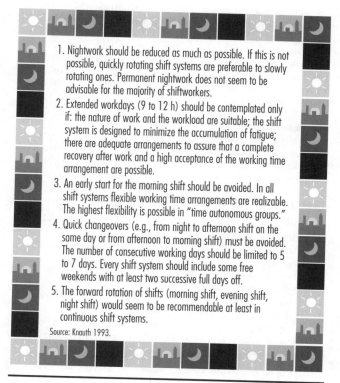

1. Nightwork should be reduced as much as possible. If this is not possible, quickly rotating shift systems are preferable to slowly rotating ones. Permanent nightwork does not seem to be advisable for the majority of shiftworkers.

2. Extended workdays (9 to 12 h) should be contemplated only if: the nature of work and the workload are suitable; the shift system is designed to minimize the accumulation of fatigue; there are adequate arrangements to assure that a complete recovery after work and a high acceptance of the working time arrangement are possible.

3. An early start for the morning shift should be avoided. In all shift systems flexible working time arrangements are realizable. The highest flexibility is possible in "time autonomous groups."

4. Quick changeovers (e.g., from night to afternoon shift on the same day or from afternoon to morning shift) must be avoided. The number of consecutive working days should be limited to 5 to 7 days. Every shift system should include some free weekends with at least two successive full days off.

5. The forward rotation of shifts (morning shift, evening shift, night shift) would seem to be recommendable at least in continuous shift systems.

Source: Knauth 1993.

and so on are mainly impoverished by weekend work, evening shifts and night shifts (Mott et al. 1965), as has been reviewed by Bunnage (1981); Walker (1985); and Colligan and Rosa (1990).

Only with respect to hobbies and activities of a solitary or near-solitary nature are shiftworkers at an advantage compared to dayworkers, since gardening, walking, fishing or "do it yourself" projects are comparatively flexible activities which are possible any time, not only in the evening or on weekends.

Some studies have dealt with the burden of shiftworkers' spouses (Banks 1956; Ulich 1957; Downie 1963; Sergean 1971), who have to alter their lifestyle (for example mealtimes) in order to fit in with the shift system of their mates. They may be forced to postpone noisy household duties and to keep children quiet when the shiftworker is asleep after the night shift. Furthermore, they are alone during evening, night and weekend shifts and have to cope with an irritable spouse. After a change from a weekly to a quickly rotating continuous shift system, 87% of shiftworkers' spouses voted in favour of the new shift system. They argued that in the old shift system the spouse was very tired after the end of the period of night shifts, needed several days to recover and was not in the mood for joint leisure activities. However, in the new shift system with only two or three consecutive night shifts, the worker was less tired and they enjoyed more joint leisure activities.

Women on shiftwork may have more problems with domestic duties and sleep since household responsibility is not equally shared by the marriage partners. Nevertheless some permanent night nurses have specifically chosen to work at night for domestic reasons (Barton et al. 1993). However, as Walker (1985) concludes in his review, "to say that fixed night shifts for mothers is compatible with their child-rearing responsibilities ignores the 'costs'". Constant tiredness because of reduced sleep may be the cost.

Worker Performance

In addition to possible effects of shiftwork on worker health, worker performance can also be affected. Harrington's (1978) generalized conclusions about performance were reached through consideration of productivity and accidents. They are still valid and have been reformulated by Waterhouse et al. (1992):

Errors and general performance often showed rhythmic changes, with the night shift being worst.

- The nocturnal decrement in performance could be lessened or prevented if breaks in the work were feasible, if the work were interesting, or if motivation could be maintained.
- The performance worsened (generally with the night shift being more adversely affected than others) if boring, repetitive tasks were involved, if sleep loss had occurred, or if the amount of time spent on duty were increased.

Differences between individuals were often the largest variable in performance.

One problem in comparing productivity and accidents in morning, afternoon and night shifts is methodological. Working, environmental and organizational conditions at night and in the daytime in general are not completely comparable (Colquhoun 1976; Carter and Corlett 1982; Waterhouse et al. 1992). Therefore it is difficult to control all the variables. It is not astonishing that in a review of 24 studies there were almost as many studies with a higher frequency of accidents at night as studies with a higher frequency of accidents in the daytime (Knauth 1983). In some studies the workload in the daytime and during night-time were comparable and measures were available for all 24 hours. In most of these studies the authors found a degraded night-shift performance (e.g., Browne 1949; Bjerner et al. 1955; Hildebrandt et al. 1974; Harris 1977; Hamelin 1981). However, as Monk (1990) has concluded, it is possible that circadian effects can "show through" only when workers are under pressure. In the absence of pressure, workers may be able to equate day-shift and night-shift performance, because both are considerably suboptimal.

The Design of Shift Systems

The most important recommendations for the design of shift systems are summarized in figure 43.2.

Permanent night work

The night shift is the most disruptive of all shifts in terms of physiological adjustment, sleep and well-being. The circadian physiological rhythms of most shiftworkers may require more than one week for complete adjustment to night work. Any partial adjustment will be lost following days off from night shift. Thus, the body rhythms of permanent nightworkers are constantly in a state of disruption. In one study (Alfredsson et al. 1991) the permanent night security guards had a 2-to-3-times higher occurrence of sleep disturbances and fatigue than the national sample of the working population.

Some authors have suggested various ways in which to match employee tolerance for shiftwork and certain external stimuli for helping workers to adjust. According to Hildebrandt et al. (1987) persons with a late phase position (evening types) are able to adjust to night work. Moog (1988) posited that they should work in very long periods of night shifts—that is, much more than 10 nights in a row. To profit from an adjustment to night work, Folkard (1990) even suggested the creation of a "nocturnal subsociety", which in addition to working permanently at night, would continue to be active at night and to sleep during the day, even when not at work. Although performance at night might in the long run be increased (Wilkinson 1992), such a proposal causes an accumulation of sleep deficits and social isolation, which seems to be unacceptable for most persons (Smith and Folkard 1993).

There are an increasing number of studies dealing with the influence of bright light on re-entrainment of circadian rhythms (some examples are Wever et al. 1983; special session at the IXth International Symposium on Night and Shift Work; Costa et al. 1990a; Rosa et al. 1990; Czeisler et al. 1990). However, "much work is necessary to determine the optimal light-work-sleep schedules for shift workers in terms of their ability to shift circadian rhythms, improve sleep, reduce fatigue, as well as in terms of their social feasibility", according to Eastman (1990).

In comparison with other shift systems, fixed night shifts have more negative effects on families who must adapt their lifestyles to this schedule, on sexual relations and on workers' ability to fulfil familial roles (Stein 1963; Mott et al. 1965; Tasto et al. 1978; Gadbois 1981). However, in some studies of permanent night shift, nurses reported fewer complaints than rotating nurses or dayshift nurses (Verhaegen et al. 1987; Barton et al. 1993). Barton et al. propose that one possible explanation for these results may be that the freedom to choose either day- or night-work may greatly influence the degree to which subsequent problems are experienced. The notion that this represents "freedom" is, however, questionable when many female nurses prefer permanent night work because this represents the only way of better arranging domestic responsibilities and employment outside the home (Gadbois 1981).

Permanent night work also has some advantages. Nightworkers report a greater feeling of independence and less supervision at night (Brown 1990; Hoff and Ebbing 1991). Furthermore, because it is less easy to obtain work relief for night-shift staff, apparently more "team spirit" (*esprit de corps*) develops. However, in most cases night work is chosen because of the increase in income due to the night-shift allowance (Hoff and Ebbing 1991).

Although we have insufficient knowledge about the long-term health effects of permanent night work and about optimal bright-light work-sleep schedules, it is known that the night shift is the most disruptive of all shifts in terms of physiological adjustment, sleep and well-being, and until results from further research are available, we will assume for the moment that permanent night work is not recommended for the majority of shiftworkers.

Quickly rotating versus slowly rotating shift systems

More rapidly rotating schedules are more advantageous compared to weekly shift rotation. A fast rotation keeps the circadian rhythm in a daytime orientation and it is not in a constant state of disruption from partial adjustment to different day and night orientations. Consecutive night shifts may cause an accumulation of sleep deficits—that is, a chronic sleep deprivation (Tepas and Mahan 1989; Folkard et al. 1990). In the long run this could lead to long-term biological "costs" or even medical disorders. However, no well-controlled epidemiological study is available that compares the effects of permanent, slowly and quickly rotating shift systems. In most published studies the groups are not comparable with regard to the age structure, job content, degree of self-selection (e.g., Tasto et al. 1978; Costa et al. 1981) or because the employees working on fixed morning, afternoon and night shifts were combined to form a single category (Jamal and Jamal 1982). In several longitudinal field studies, the effects of a change from weekly to quicker rotating shift systems have been investigated (Williamson and Sanderson 1986; Knauth and Kiesswetter 1987; Knauth and Schönfelder 1990; Hornberger and Knauth 1995; Knauth 1996). In all 27 studied groups of shiftworkers, the majority of the shiftworkers voted in favour of the quicker rotating shifts after a trial period. Summing up, quickly rotating shift systems are preferable to slowly rotating ones. Åkerstedt (1988), however, does not agree, because the maximum sleepiness usually occurs on the first night shift because of extended prior waking. He recommends slow rotation.

Another argument for a quickly rotating shift system is that shiftworkers have free evenings in every week and thus more regular contact with friends and colleagues is possible than with weekly rotating shifts. Based on analyses of the periodic components of work and leisure time, Hedden et al. (1990) conclude that rotations that allow for a shorter but more frequent synchronization of work life with social life result in less impairment than rotations that lead to longer but infrequent synchronization.

Duration of shifts

There are many contradictory results of the effects of extended workdays, and thus a general recommendation for extended workdays cannot be made (Kelly and Schneider 1982; Tepas 1985). An extended workday of 9 to 12 hours should be contemplated only in the following cases (Knauth and Rutenfranz 1982; Wallace 1989; Tsaneva et al. 1990; Ong and Kogi 1990):

1. The nature of work and the workload are suitable for extended working hours.
2. The shift system is designed to minimize the accumulation of fatigue.
3. There are adequate arrangements for cover of absentees.
4. Overtime is not added.
5. Toxic exposure is limited.
6. It is likely that a complete recovery after work and a high acceptance of the working time arrangements are possible (e.g., housing, family problems, commuting, climate, no moonlighting).

Physiological requirements must be taken into account. According to Bonjer (1971), the acceptable oxygen rate consumption during an 8-hour shift should be about 30% or less of the maximum oxygen consumption. During a 12-hour shift it should be about 23% or less of the maximum oxygen consumption. Since the amount of oxygen consumption increases with the physical demands of the job, it would seem that 12-hour shifts are acceptable only for physically light work. However, even in this case, if the mental or emotional stress caused by the job is too high, extended working hours are not advisable. Before the introduction of extended working hours, the stress and strain at the specific workplace must be accurately evaluated by experts.

One of the potential disadvantages of 12-hour shifts, in particular 12-hour night shifts, is increased fatigue. Therefore the shift system should be designed to minimize the accumulation of fatigue—that is, there should not be many 12-hour shifts in a row and the day shift should not start too early. Koller et al. (1991) recommend single night shifts or a maximum of two night shifts. This recommendation is supported by favourable results of studies in shift systems with single 12-hour night shifts (Nachreiner et al. 1975; Nedeltcheva et al. 1990). In a Belgian study, the length of the shift was extended to 9 hours by starting one hour earlier in the morning (Moors 1990). The day shift started at 0630 instead of 0730 and the morning shift in a two-shift system started at 0500 instead of 0600. In a 5-day week these working time arrangements led to an accumulation of sleep deficits and complaints of tiredness. The author recommends that the shifts start as in the old working time arrangements and that the shift be extended by one hour in the evening.

Our knowledge is very limited concerning another problem: toxic exposure and toxic clearance during the time off work in connection with extended working hours (Bolt and Rutenfranz 1988). In general, exposure limits are based on 8 hours exposure, and one cannot simply extrapolate them to cover a 12-hour shift. Some authors have proposed mathematical procedures for

Figure 43.3 • Rotating continuous shift system.

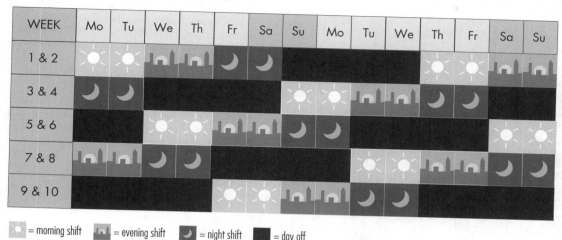

WEEK	Mo	Tu	We	Th	Fr	Sa	Su	Mo	Tu	We	Th	Fr	Sa	Su

Average weekly working hours:
- 33.6 hrs./week without additional shift
- 35.2 hrs./week with 2 additional shifts/10 weeks
- 36.8 hrs./week with 4 additional shifts/10 weeks
- 38.4 hrs./week with 6 additional shifts/10 weeks
- 40.0 hrs./week with 8 additional shifts/10 weeks

= morning shift   = evening shift   = night shift   = day off

adjusting these exposures for working times that deviate from the usual 8-hour shift, but no method has been uniformly adopted (e.g., Hickey and Reist 1977; OSHA 1978; Brief and Scala 1986; Koller et al. 1991).

Designers of shift systems must consider the workload, the working environment and the conditions outside the place of work. Ong and Kogi (1990) report that "the hot, tropical climate and noisy dwelling units of Singapore were not conducive to sound sleep for shiftworkers, who needed to sleep in the daytime". Such circumstances increased fatigue and affected productivity on the 12-hour shift worked the next day. Another concern that relates to workers' well-being is the way shiftworkers use their large blocks of leisure time. In some studies it appears that they may have second jobs (moonlighting), thus increasing their total workload (Angersbach et al. 1980; Wallace 1989; Ong and Kogi 1990). Many other social factors, like commuting, individual differences, social support or events in life must also be considered in the 12-hour shift systems (e.g., Tsaneva et al. 1990).

Timing of shifts

Although there is no optimal solution for the timing of shifts, there is much evidence in the literature that an early start for the morning shift should be avoided. An early start often reduces total sleep because the majority of shiftworkers go to bed at the usual time (Knauth et al. 1980; Åkerstedt et al. 1990; Costa et al. 1990b; Moors 1990; Folkard and Barton 1993). An increase in fatigue during the morning shift has also been observed (Reinberg et. al. 1975; Hak and Kampman 1981; Moors 1990), as well as an increase in the risk of errors and accidents in the morning shift (Wild and Theis 1967; Hildebrandt et al. 1974; Pokorny et al. 1981; Folkard and Totterdell 1991).

Assuming a constant shift length of 8 hours, a late start for the morning shift also means a late start for the night shift (e.g., shift change times at 0700/1500/2300 or 0800/1600/2400). A late start for the night shift means also a late end for the evening shift. In both cases there might be transport problems because buses, trams and trains run less frequently.

The decision in favour of a specific shift change time may also be dependent on the job content. In hospitals, in general, it is the night shift that wakes up, washes and prepares patients (Gadbois 1991).

Arguments in favour of an earlier start have also been made. Some studies have shown that the later the day sleep begins after a night shift, the shorter it will be (Foret and Lantin 1972; Åkerstedt

and Gillberg 1981; Knauth and Rutenfranz 1981). Day sleep may be disturbed and a very early start of sleep after night shifts might avoid these problems. Debry et al. (1967) have proposed shift change times at 0400, 1200 and 2000 in order to facilitate workers having as many meals with the family as possible. According to Gadbois (1991) an early start for the night shift improves the contact between staff and patients in hospitals.

Flexible working time arrangements are also possible even in three-shift systems, where employees can choose their working hours (McEwan 1978; Knauth et al. 1981b; 1984; Knauth and Schönfelder 1988). However, in contrast to flexitime in dayworkers, shiftworkers must make pre-arrangements with co-workers.

Distribution of leisure time within the shift system

The distribution of leisure time between consecutive shifts has important implications for sleep, fatigue and well-being, as well as social and family life and the overall satisfaction of the shiftworker with the shift system. If there are only 8 hours between the end of one shift and the start of the next, there will be a reduction of sleep between the shifts and increased fatigue in the second shift

Figure 43.4 • Rotating discontinuous shift system.

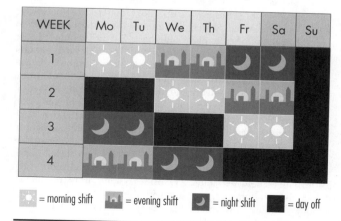

WEEK	Mo	Tu	We	Th	Fr	Sa	Su

= morning shift   = evening shift   = night shift   = day off

Figure 43.5 • Rotating discontinuous shift system with seven teams.

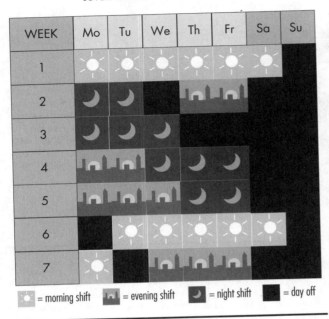

(Knauth and Rutenfranz 1972; Saito and Kogi 1978; Knauth et al. 1983; Totterdell and Folkard 1990).

Too many working days in succession can lead to an accumulation of fatigue and sometimes overexposure to toxic substances (Bolt and Rutenfranz 1988). It is not easy to define a limit for the maximum number of consecutive working days, because the workload, the organization of breaks, and exposure to unfavourable environmental conditions vary. However, Koller et al. (1991) recommend limiting the number of consecutive working days to between 5 and 7.

Free weekends are of particular social importance. Pátkei and Dahlgren (1981) studied satisfaction with different types of rapidly rotating shift systems. The satisfaction with a 7-day shift system with 3 to 5 regular days free was significantly higher than in a system with only 2 free days. The authors concluded that "the length of the break might be an important factor in determining the attractivity of rapidly rotating shifts". On the other hand, free days in the first shift system were counterbalanced by additional periods of holidays during the year.

Direction of rotation. The direction of rotation is another important consideration (Tsaneva et al. 1987; Totterdell and Folkard 1990). A shift system which first moves from morning shift to evening shift, and then to night shift, has a forward rotation (phase delay, clockwise rotation). An anticlockwise, or backward, rotation has a phase advance which moves from night to evening to morning shifts. The forward rotation appears to correspond more closely to the endogenous circadian rhythm, which has a period of more than 24 hours, but only two longitudinal field studies on the effects of different directions of rotation exist (Landen et al. 1981; Czeisler et al. 1982). The majority of the shiftworkers in these studies seem to prefer the forward rotation, but the studies are not definitive. Barton and Folkard (1993) found that an anticlockwise system led to higher levels of fatigue and more sleep disturbances between shifts. "Hybrid" systems were not better. Clockwise rotation was associated with the fewest problems. Turek (1986) proposes, however, that the sleep disturbance of both systems would be comparable.

Shiftworkers on a discontinuous shift system with backward rotation were found to like the long period off work between the end of the last morning shift and the start of the first night shift, in particular if this period includes a weekend.

Although the evidence is limited and further research is needed, forward rotation seems to be recommendable at least in continuous shift systems.

Optimizing shift systems

There is no "optimal" shift system. Each enterprise, its managers and shiftworkers should seek the best compromise between the demands of the enterprise and the needs of the workers. Furthermore, the decision should be founded on scientific recommendations for the design of shift systems. The implementation strategy is of particular importance for the acceptance of a new shift system. Many manuals and guidelines for the implementation of new working time arrangements have been published (ILO 1990). Too often shiftworkers are not sufficiently involved in the analysis, planning and design stage of the shifts.

A continuous shift system that has a rapid forward rotation pattern, with 8 hours of work per shift, some free weekends, at least two successive full days off and no quick changeovers, appears to be the system to be recommended. Such a basic shift system has an average of 33.6 hours per week, which may not be universally acceptable. If additional shifts are required, acceptance is higher when the additional shifts are planned on a long-term basis, such as at the beginning of the year so workers can plan holidays. Some employers do not require older shiftworkers to work additional shifts.

Figures 43.3 and 43.4 show schemes for continuous and discontinuous shift systems which accommodate these rules. Figure 43.5 shows a shift system for a less flexible workplace. It covers 128 operational hours per week, with an average individual workweek of 37 hours. This system has a maximum of three night shifts and two longer free weekends (third week: Thursday to Sunday; fifth/sixth week: Saturday to Monday). It is irregular and does not rotate in a forward direction, which is less optimizing. For shift systems with an operational time of 120 hours per week, gradually rotating shift systems cannot be used, such as from

Figure 43.6 • Discontinuous shift system with a 50% reduced staffing of night shifts.

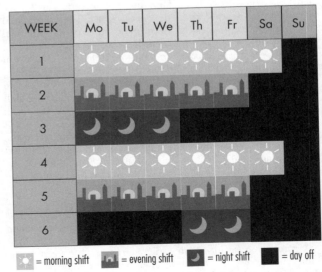

Figure 43.7 • Heart rate during and after heavy physical work with different lengths of work and rest periods but a constant work/rest ratio of 2:3.

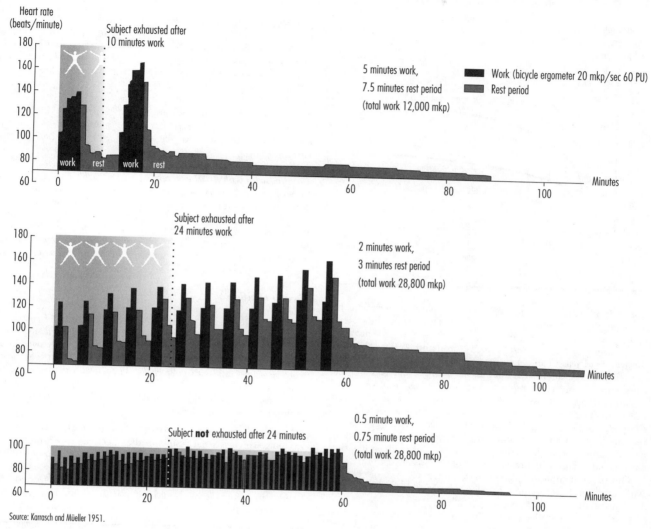

Source: Karrasch and Müeller 1951.

Monday 0600 to Saturday 0600, and an average working time of 40 hours per week.

When the crew can be thinned out during the night, a shift system as shown in figure 43.6 may be possible. From Monday to Friday, each day two subgroups work in morning shifts, two in evening shifts but only one subgroup works in night shifts. Therefore, the number of night shifts per person would be reduced, compared with the traditional three-shift system.

Rest Periods

In connection with the arrangement of hours of work, adequate periods of rest, such as breaks during working hours, breaks for meals, daily or nightly rest and weekly rest are also important for the workers' well-being, health and safety.

There are various reasons for the introduction of rest periods.

Recuperation

When a worker performs heavy physical work, fatigue develops and it is necessary for the worker to stop and rest at intervals. During the breaks the symptoms of reversible functional changes of the organism disappear. When, for instance, heart rate is increased by physical work, it will return to the initial value before work during an adequate rest period. The efficiency of a rest period decreases exponentially with the increasing length of the break. As short breaks have a high efficiency, the rule has been deduced that many short breaks are better than a few long breaks.

Prevention of fatigue

During heavy physical work, many rest periods may not only reduce, but under certain circumstances, also prevent fatigue. This is illustrated by the classic studies of Karrasch and Müller (1951). In the laboratory, subjects had to exercise on bicycle ergonometers (figure 43.7). This heavy physical work (10 mkp/s) was organized in the following way: after each period of work (100%) a longer rest period (150%) followed. The three experiments each had a different arrangement of work and rest periods. In the first experiment the subject worked 5 min, rested for 7.5 min, then worked again for 5 min and broke off the experiment when exhausted. The heart rate reached about 140 beats/minute in the first work period and more than 160 beats/minute in the second

Figure 43.8 • Effect of rest periods on the learning of simple sensumotoric performance.

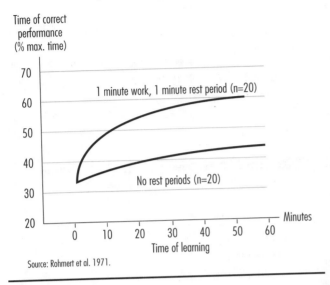

Source: Rohmert et al. 1971.

work period. Even one hour after the end of the experiment the heart rate had not returned to the initial value before the experiment. The second experiment shown in the figure involved shorter work and shorter rest periods (2 min and 3 min). Although the workload was identical to the first experiment, the subject in the second experiment was able to work longer before complete exhaustion set in. An extreme arrangement of 0.5 min work and 0.75 min rest period was set up in the third experiment. The heart rate remained at the steady-state level. The experiment was stopped, not because the subject was exhausted but for technical reasons. This extreme organization of work and of rest periods of course cannot be implemented in industry, but it illustrates that extreme fatigue may be prevented if rest periods are split up.

This phenomenon has also been demonstrated in other studies with other indicators such as blood lactic acid (Åstrand and Rodahl 1970).

In a study on foundry workers, the comparison of an arrangement of 20 min of work followed always by a 10-min break with an arrangement of 10 min of work and a 5-min break showed the superiority of the second approach (Scholz 1963), because the average heart rate over 8 hours was lower in the second case.

The prevention of fatigue has also been demonstrated with help of heart rate measurements in experiments with learning of sensorimotoric performances (Rutenfranz et al. 1971). Moreover, the progress in learning was clearly greater in experiments with regular rest periods compared with experiments without rest periods, as shown in figure 43.8.

Increase in performance

In general, rest periods are considered simply as unproductive interruptions of working time. However, Graf (1922; 1927) showed that rest periods may be, so-to-speak, "rewarding". We know from sports that athletes running 100 metres start at a high speed, whereas athletes running 5,000 metres start at a "throttled down" speed. Analogue findings on mental work have been published by Graf (figure 43.9). Three experimental groups were asked to perform calculations. Wages were dependent on the performance. Without being aware of this fact, group A (having the first rest period after 3 hours) started with a reduced speed compared to group B (expecting the first rest period after 45

minutes of work). The highest initial speed and subsequent performance was found in the group C (with rest periods after each 15 minutes of work).

Maintaining an adequate level of vigilance

In some monotonous monitoring or watchkeeping tasks and in highly simplified tasks with short cycle times, it is difficult to remain alert over longer periods. The reduction of alertness may be overcome by rest periods (or work-structuring measures).

Food intake

The recuperative value of meal breaks is often limited, in particular when the worker has to go a long distance to the canteen, line up for food, eat quickly and hurry back to the working place.

Compensatory physical exercise

If workers, such as visual display unit operators, have to work in constrained postures, it is recommended that they do some compensatory physical exercises during rest periods. Of course the better solution would be to improve the design of the workplace according to ergonomic principles. Physical exercises at the workplace seem to be more accepted in Asian countries than in many other places.

Communication

The social aspect of rest periods, referring to private communication between the workers, should not be neglected. There is a contradiction between the physiologically based recommendation of very short breaks in connection with heavy physical work and the wish of the workers to come together in rest areas and talk with colleagues. Therefore a compromise has to be found.

Hettinger (1993) has published the following rules for the optimal design of rest periods:

- The initial parts of a rest period have the highest recuperative value, which is what results in the effectiveness of short breaks (i.e., many short breaks are more favourable than a few longer breaks with regard to the recuperative value).
- Exceptions to this rule: The cooling-down rest period after work in a hot climate should last at least 10 min in a room with a neutral climate. The warming-up rest period after work in a

Figure 43.9 • Effects of short rest periods on mental performance.

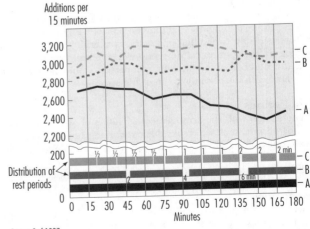

Source: Graf 1927.

cold climate (–15 to –30°C) should last for at least 30 min in a room with a neutral climate. The rest period after working in a very loud working environment should be relatively long in a room with less than 70 dB(A). These rest periods are problematic, if one bears in mind that, if the time of exposure is halved, merely a reduction of about 3 dB(A) is achieved in the noise dose.

- The frequency and duration of the rest period is dependent on the degree of difficulty of the physical or mental work. Concerning physical work, it may be specified that physical work with an energy consumption above the acceptable endurance limit but less than 40 KJ/min permits the rest period to be arranged within the shiftworking time. Physical work with an energy consumption of greater than 40 KJ/min demands a rest period immediately after stopping the heavy work, because of the exponential increase of fatigue.
- The efficiency of a rest period should not be reduced by "pseudo-activities" (disguised breaks). Workers and superiors should be informed accordingly.

Rest periods for food intake should last at least 15 minutes.

For further information concerning rest periods after muscular work, see Laurig (1981); and for rest periods after mental work, see Luczak (1982).

Reduction of Sleep Problems

There are no magic formulae to help shiftworkers fall asleep quickly or sleep well. What works for one person may not work for another.

Some useful proposals, mainly for day sleep following night shifts, include:

- Use individual headphones for TV and radio for the other members of the family, and a silent telephone answering machine. Switch off the door-bell.
- Let one's family know about the work schedule and avoid household noise during sleep times.
- Reduce outside light and noise by using heavy, dark curtains, soundproofed doors and windows, and an air conditioner.
- Ear plugs, a sleeping mask and not drinking any caffeinated drinks within 5 hours of your expected bedtime can also help.
- If the living quarters are noisy, workers should consider moving to quieter living quarters.

Workers should avoid using alcohol to assist in going to sleep and should give themselves time to slow down after work (Community Health Network 1984; Monk 1988; Wedderburn 1991).

For cases where safety is at stake, some authors recommend "maintenance naps" during the night shift as a bridge over the night-time low point in circadian alertness (Andlauer et al. 1982). Many Japanese 24-hour industries allow napping practices on night shifts (Kogi 1981).

Diet

Although there is no evidence that diet assists in coping with night work (Rosa et al. 1990), the following prudent recommendations have been made:

- During night shift, the main meal should be eaten at or before 0100 and should be rich in protein rather than carbohydrates, and have a low fat content.
- Have a snack of fresh fruit or milk products at about 0400–0415.
- Eating meals at the same time each day is recommended.
- A heavy meal just before bedtime should be avoided. Workers should learn to listen to their bodies, to judge stomach comfort and energy levels (Community Health Network 1984; Wedderburn 1991; Knauth et al. 1991).

Occupational Health Measures

Some authors recommend pre-employment screening and medical surveillance of shiftworkers (e.g., Rutenfranz et al. 1985; Scott and LaDou 1990). Workers should be counselled against night work if they have or are:

- a history of digestive tract disorders (e.g., recurrent peptic ulcer disease, irritable bowel syndrome, if symptoms are severe)
- insulin-dependent diabetes mellitus
- thyrotoxicosis
- coronary artery disease, especially if there is unstable angina or a history of myocardial infarction
- narcoleptics and others suffering from chronic sleep disturbances
- epileptics
- severe psychiatric disorders, in particular chronic depression
- asthma requiring medication, especially if the patient is steroid dependent
- active and extensive tuberculosis
- alcoholics and drug addicts
- marked visual impairment or hemeralopia (day blindness) that is too severe for effective correction.

In addition, Scott and LaDou (1990) also mention some "relative contra-indications" most appropriately used for counselling prospective employees, such as extreme "morningness", sleep rigidity. They may wish to consider their age and the extent of their family responsibilities.

Hermann (1982) has proposed the following intervals for regular health checks: there should be a second health check not later than 12 months after starting night work, and regular health checks at least every 2 years for those under 25, every 5 years for those between 25 and 50, every 2 to 3 years for those between 50 and 60, and every 1 to 2 years for those above 60.

Individual Behavioural Techniques

There are only a few studies analysing shiftworkers' ability to cope with stress (Olsson et al. 1987; Olsson and Kandolin 1990; Kandolin 1993, Spelten et al. 1993). An active coping strategy—for example, discussing the problems with others—appears to reduce stress better than passive strategies, such as the use of alcohol (Kandolin 1993). However, longitudinal studies are necessary to study the relationship between coping style or behavioural techniques and stress.

Money Payments

Although many compensation plans exist whereby a worker is compensated more for shiftwork (shift bonus), money payments are not an appropriate trade-off for possible negative health effects and disruption of social life.

The best way, of course, to solve problems is to eliminate or reduce the causes. However, since complete elimination of shiftwork is not possible, an alternative strategy worth considering is such as the following: a reduction of unusual working hours for the individual; reduction of night shifts; reduce the unnecessary part of the night work (sometimes activities may be shifted to the morning or evening shift by reorganization of work); implement mixed shift systems with, for example, at least one month per year without shiftwork; insertion of additional shift crews, such as by changing from a 3-shift system to a 4-shift system or from a 4-shift system to a 5-shift system, or by reduction of overtime. Reduction of working time for shiftworkers is another possibility, with shorter weekly working hours for shiftworkers than for dayworkers, with paid breaks and longer holiday periods. Extra days off and stepwise or early retirement are other possible remedies.

All these proposals have already been implemented in some companies in industry or the services sector (e.g., Knauth et al. 1990).

Other Measures

Many other measures such as physical exercise (Härmä et al. 1988a, b), pharmacological aids (Rosa et al. 1990), family counselling (Rosa et al. 1990), improvement of environmental conditions at work (Knauth et al. 1989), better communication between shiftworkers and unions or shiftworkers and their congressperson (Monk 1988; Knauth et al. 1989), or a "Shift Work Awareness Programme" within the company (Monk 1988) have been proposed to reduce the problems of shiftworkers. As there is not one best way to reduce the problems of shiftworkers many creative solutions should be tried (Colquhoun et al. 1996).

References

Aanonsen, A. 1964. *Shift Work and Health*. Oslo: Universitetsforlaget.

Åkerstedt, T. 1988. Sleepiness as a consequence of shift work. *Sleep* 11:17-34.

Åkerstedt, T and J Fröberg. 1976. Shift work and health-interdisciplinary aspect. In *Shift Work and Health*, edited by PG Rentos and RD Shepard. Washington, DC: Department of Health, Education and Welfare.

Åkerstedt, T and M Gilberg. 1981. Sleep disturbances and shiftwork. In *Night and Shiftwork: Biological and Social Aspects*, edited by A Reinberg, N Vieux, and P Andlauer. Oxford: Pergamon.

Åkerstedt, T and L Torsvall. 1981. Age, sleep and adjustment to shiftwork. In *Sleep 1980*, edited by WP Koella. Basel: Karger.

Åkerstedt, T, A Knutsson, L Alfredsson and T Theorell. 1984. Shiftwork and cardiovascular disease. *Scand J Work Environ Health* 10:409-14.

Åkerstedt, T, L Torsvall, G Kecklund, and A Knutsson. 1990. The shift cycle and clinical indices of insomnia. In *Shiftwork: Health, Sleep and Performance*, edited by G Costa, G Cesana, K Kogi, and A Wedderburn. Frankfurt: Peter Lang.

Alfredsson, L, R Karasek and T Theorell. 1982. Myocardial infarction risk and psychosocial work environment: An analysis of the male Swedish working force. *Soc Sci Med* 16:463-7.

Alfredsson, L and T Theorell. 1983. Job characteristics of occupations and myocardial infarction risk: Effect of possible confounding factors. *Soc Sci Med* 17:1497-1503.

Alfredsson, L, C-L Spetz and T Theorell. 1985. Type of occupation and near-future hospitalization for myocardial infarction and some other diagnoses. *Int J Epidemiol* 14:378-88.

Alfredsson, L, T Åkerstedt, M Mattson, and B Wilborg. 1991. Self-reported health and well-being amongst night security guards: A comparison with the working population. *Ergonomics* 34:525-530.

Andersen, O. 1985. *Dodelight og erhverv 1970-80 [Mortality and occupation 1970-80]*. Statistike Undersogelser nr 41. Copenhagen: Danmarks Statistik.

Andlauer, P, A Reinberg, L Fourré, W Battle, and G Duverneuil. 1979. Amplitude of the oral temperature circadian rhythm and the tolerance to shiftwork. *J Physiol* 75:507-512.

Andlauer, P, J Rutenfranz, K Kogi, H Thierry, N Vieux, and G Duverneuil. 1982. Organization of night shifts in industries where public safety is at stake. *Int Arch Occup Environ Health* 49:353-355.

Angersbach, D, P Knauth, H Loskant, MJ Karvonen, K Undeutsch, and J Rutenfranz. 1980. A retrospective cohort study comparing complaints and diseases in day and shift workers. *Int Arch Occup Environ Health* 45:127-140.

Åstrand, PO and K Rodahl. 1970. *Textbook of Work Physiology*. New York: McGraw-Hill.

Banks, O. 1956. Continuous shift work: The attitudes of wives. *Occup Psychol* 30:69-84.

Barton, J and S Folkard. 1993. Advancing versus delaying shift systems. *Ergonomics* 36:59-64.

Barton, J, L Smith, P Totterdell, E Spelten, and S Folkard. 1993. Does individual choice determine shift system acceptability? *Ergonomics* 36:93-99.

Beermann, B, K-H Schmidt, and J Rutenfranz. 1990. Zur Wirkung verschiedener Schichttypen auf das gesundheitliche Befinden und das Schlaf- und Freizeitverhalten. *Z Arb Wiss* 44:14-17.

Bjerner, B, A Holm, and A Swensson. 1955. Diurnal variation in mental performances. *Br J Ind Med* 12:103-110.

Bohle, P and AJ Tilley. 1989. The impact of night work on psychological well-being. *Ergonomics* 32:1089-1099.

Bolt, HM and J Rutenfranz. 1988. The impact of aspects of time and duration of exposure on toxicokinetics and toxicodynamics of workplace chemicals. In *Health Surveillance of Individual Workers Exposed to Chemical Agents*, edited by WRF Notten, RFM Herber, WJ Hunter, AC Monster, and RL Zielhuis. Berlin: Springer Verlag.

Bonjer, FH. 1971. Temporal factors and physiological load. In *Measurement of Man At Work*, edited by WJ Singleton, JG Fox, and D Whitfield. London: Taylor & Francis.

Breithaupt, H, G Hildebrandt, D Dohr, R Josch, U Sieber, and M Werner. 1978. Tolerance to shift of sleep, as related to the individual circadian phase position. *Ergonomics* 21:767-774.

Brief, RS and RA Scala. 1986. Occupational health aspects of unusual work schedules: A review of Exxon's experiences. *Am Ind Hyg Assoc J* 47:199-202.

Brown, FM. 1990. Sleep-nap behaviors of three permanent shifts of hospital nurses. In *Shiftwork: Health, Sleep and Performance*, edited by G Costa, G Cesana, K Kogi, and A Wedderburn. Frankfurt: Peter Lang.

Browne, RC. 1949. The day and night performance of teleprinter switchboard operators. *Occup Psychol* 23:121-126.

Bunnage, D. 1981. Study on the consequences of shiftwork on social and family life. In *The Effects of Shiftwork On Health, Social and Family Life* Dublin: European Foundation for the Improvement of Living and Working Conditions.

Carpentier, J and P Cazamian. 1977. *Night Work: Its Effects on the Health and Welfare of the Worker*. Geneva: ILO.

Carter, FA and EN Corlett. 1982. *Accidents and Shiftwork*. Dublin: European Foundation for the Improvement of Living and Working Conditions.

Colligan, MJ and RR Rosa. 1990. Shiftwork effects on social and family life. In *Shiftwork*, edited by AJ Scott. Philadelphia: Hanley & Belfus.

Colquhoun, WP. 1976. Accidents, injuries and shift work. In *Shift Work and Health. A Symposium*, edited by PG Rentos and RD Shepard. Washington, DC: Department of Health, Education and Welfare.

Colquhoun, WP, G Costa, S Folkard, and P Knauth. 1996. *Shiftwork: Problems and Solutions*. Frankfurt: Peter Lang.

Community Health Network. 1984. *Shiftwork: How to Cope. Part 1: Sleep. Part 2: Eating. Part 3: The Rest of Your Life*. Claremont, NH: Community Health Network.

Costa, G. 1996. Effects on health and well-being. In *Shiftwork: Problems and Solutions*, edited by WP Colquhoun, S Folkard, G Costa, P Knauth, and P Lang. Frankfurt: Peter Lang.

Costa, G, P Apostoli, F d'Andrea, and E Gaffuri. 1981. Gastrointestinal and neurotic disorders in textile shift workers. In *Night and Shift Work: Biological and Social Aspects*, edited by N Reinberg, N Vieux, and P Andlauer. Oxford: Pergamon Press.

Costa, G, F Lievore, G Casaletti, E Gaffuri, and S Folkard. 1989. Circadian characteristics influencing interindividual differences in tolerance and adjustment to shiftwork. *Ergonomics* 32:373-385.

Costa, G, G Cesana, K Kogi, and A Wedderburn. 1990a. *Shiftwork: Health, Sleep and Performance*. Frankfurt: Peter Lang.

Costa, G, D Olivato, E Peroni, E Mossini, and G Gonella. 1990b. Problems connected to the introduction of night work in a group of female workers of a food industry. In *Shiftwork: Health, Sleep and Performance*, edited by G Costa, G Cesana, K Kogi, and A Wedderburn. Frankfurt: Peter Lang.

Czeisler, CA, MC Moore-Ede, and RM Coleman. 1982. Rotating shift work schedules that disrupt sleep are improved by applying circadian principles. *Science* 217:460-463.

Czeisler, CA, MP Johnson, JF Duffy, EN Brown, JM Ronda, and RE Kronauer. 1990. Exposure to bright light and darkness to treat physiologic maladaptation to night work. *New Engl J Med* 322:1253-1259.

Debry, G, P Girault, J Lefort, and J Thiébault. 1967. Enquête sur les habitudes alimentaires des travailleurs "à feux continus". *B Instit Natl Santé Rech Méd* 22:1169-1202.

Diekmann, A, G Ernst, and F Nachreiner. 1981. Auswirkung der Schichtarbeit des Vaters auf die schulische Entwicklung der Kinder. *Z Arb Wiss* 35:174-178.

Downie, JH. 1963. *Some Social and Industrial Implications of Shift Work. Industrial Welfare Society*. London: Robert Hyde House.

Eastman, CI. 1990. A critical review of the circadian rhythm and bright light literature with recommendations for shift work. *Work Stress* 4:245-260.

Estryn-Behar, M, C Gadbois, and E Vaichere. 1978. Effets du travail de nuit en équipes fixes sur une population féminine. Résultats d'une enquête dans le secteur hospitalier. *Arch Mal Prof* 39:531-535.

Folkard, S. 1990. Circadian performance rhythms: Some practical and theoretical implications. *Phil Trans Royal Soc London* 327:543-553.

Folkard, S and J Barton. 1993. Does the 'forbidden zone' for sleep onset influence morning shift sleep duration? *Ergonomics* 36: 85-91.

Folkard, S, TH Monk, and MC Lobban. 1979. Towards a predictive test of adjustment to shift work. *Ergonomics* 22:79-91.

Folkard, S and P Totterdell. 1991. Circadian variations in performance. Implications for abnormal work hours. Abstracts: International Symposium "Shiftwork and Job Demands". 11-12 July, Paris.

Folkard, S, TH Monk, EK Lewis, and CP Whelpton. 1982. Individual differences and adjustment to shiftwork. In *Shiftwork–Quantity and Quality of Sleep. Individual Differences*. Dublin: European Foundation for the Improvement of Living and working conditions.

Folkard, S, J Arendt, and M Clark. 1990. Sleep and mood on a "weekly" rotating (7-7-7) shift system: Some preliminary results. In *Shiftwork: Health, Sleep and Performance*, edited by G Costa, G Cesana, K Kogi, and A Wedderburn. Frankfurt: Peter Lang.

Foret, J and G Lantin. 1972. The sleep of train drivers: An example of the effects of irregular work schedules on sleep. In *The Sleep of Train Drivers: An Example of the Effects of Aspects of Human Efficiency*, edited by WP Colquhoun. London: English University Press.

Foret, J, G Bensimon, O Benoit, and N Vieux. 1981. Quality of sleep as a function of age and shift work. In *Aspects of Human Efficiency*, edited by A Reinberg, N Vieux, and P Andlauer. London: English University Press.

Frese, M and N Semmer. 1986. Shiftwork, stress, and psychosomatic complaints: A comparison between workers in different shiftwork schedules, non-shiftworkers, and former shiftworkers. *Ergonomics* 29:99-114.

Gadbois, C. 1981. Women on night shift: Interdependence of sleep and off-the-job-activities. In *Night and Shiftwork: Biological and Social Aspects*, edited by A Reinberg, N Vieux, and P Andlauer. Oxford: Pergamon Press.

—. 1991. Round the clock operations in hospitals: Shift scheduling, task demands and work organisation. Abstracts: International Symposium "Shiftwork and Job Demands". Paris 11-12 July.

Graf, O. 1922. Über lohnendste Arbeitspausen bei geistiger Arbeit. *Psychol Arbeiten* 7:548-611.

—. 1927. Die Arbeitspausen in Theorie und Praxis. *Psychol Arbeiten* 9:563-681.

Härmä, MI. 1993. Individual differences in tolerance to shiftwork: A review. *Ergonomics* 36:101-109.

Härmä, MI, J Ilmarinen, P Knauth, J Rutenfranz, and O Hänninen. 1988a. Physical training intervention in female shift workers: I. The effects of intervention on fitness, fatigue, sleep, and psychosomatic symptoms. *Ergonomics* 31:39-50.

—. 1988b. Physical training intervention in female shift workers: II. The effects of intervention on the circadian rythms, short-term memory, and body temperature. *Ergonomics* 31:51-63.

Härmä, MI, P Knauth, J Ilmarinen, and H Ollila. 1990. The relation of age to the adjustment of the circadian rhythms of oral temperature and sleepiness to shift work. *Chronobiol Int* 7:227-233.

Hak, A and R Kampmann. 1981. Working irregular hours: Complaints and state of fitness of railway personnel. In *Night and Shiftwork: Biological and Social Aspects*, edited by A Reinberg, N Vieux, and P Andlauer. Oxford: Pergamon.

Hamelin, P. 1981. Les conditions temporelles de travail des conducteurs routiers et la sécurité routière. *Travail Hum* 44:5-21.

Harrington, JM. 1978. *Shift Work and Health: A Critical Review of the Literature*. London: Her Majesty's Stationery Office.

Harris, W. 1977. Fatigue, circadian rhythm and truck accidents. In *Vigilance, Theory, Operational Performance, and Physiological Correlates*, edited by RR Mackie. New York: Plenum.

Hauke, P, H Kittler, and R Moog. 1979. Inter-individual differences in tolerance to shift-work related to morningness—eveningness. *Chronobiologia* 6:109.

Hedden, I, H Grzech-Sukalo, and F Nachreiner. 1990. Classification of shift rotas on the basis of periodic components. In *Shiftwork, Health, Sleep and Performance*, edited by G Costa, G Cesana, K Kogi, and A Wedderburn. Frankfurt: Peter Lang.

Herrmann, H. 1982. Bedeutung und Bewertung der Nachtarbeit—Gedanken zur Erstellung eines berufsgenossenschaftlichen Grundsatzes. In *Kom-*

binierte Belastungen Am Arbeitsplatz*, edited by TM Fliedner. Stuttgart: Genter Verlag.

Hettinger, T. 1993. Ermüdung und Pausen. In *Kompendium Der Arbeitswissenschaft*, edited by T Hettinger and G Wobbe. Ludwigshafen Rhein: Kiehl.

Hickey, J and P Reist. 1977. Application of occupational exposure limits to unusual working schedules. *Am Ind Hyg Assoc J* 38:613.

Hildebrandt, G, W Rohmert, and J Rutenfranz. 1974. 12 and 24 hour rhythms in error frequency of locomotive drivers and the influence of tiredness. *Int J Chronobiol* 2:175-180.

Hildebrandt, G, P Deitmer, R Moog, and L Poellmann. 1987. Physiological criteria for the optimization of shift work (relations to field studies). In *Contemporary Advances in Shiftwork Research*, edited by A Oginski, J Pokorski, and J Rutenfranz. Krakow: Medical Academy.

Hoff, A and U Ebbing. 1991. *Menschengerechte Umsetzung Von Arbeitszeitverkürzungen*. Dortmund, Forschungsanwendung Fa 25: Bundesanstalt für Arbeitsschutz.

Hornberger, S and P Knauth. 1993. Interindividual differences on the subjective evaluation of leisure time utility. *Ergonomics* 36:255-264.

—. 1995. Effects of various types of change in shift schedules: A controlled longitudinal study. *Work Stress* 9(213):124-133.

Horne, JA and O Östberg. 1976. A self-assessment questionnaire to determine morningness-eveningness in human circadian rhythms. *Int J Chronobiol* 4:97-110.

International Labour Organization (ILO). 1990. The hours we work: New work schedules in policy and practice. *Cond Work Dig* 9. Geneva: ILO.

Jamal, M and SM Jamal. 1982. Work and nonwork experiences of fixed and rotating shifts: An empirical assessment. *J Vocat Behav* 20:282-293.

Kandolin, I. 1993. Burnout of female and male nurses in shiftwork. *Ergonomics* 36:141-147.

Karrasch, K and EA Müller. 1951. Das Verhalten der Pulsfrequenz in der Erholungsperiode nach körperlicher Arbeit. *Arbeitsphysiol* 14:369-382.

Kelly, RJ and MF Schneider. 1982. The twelve-hour shift revisited: Recent trends in the electric power industry. *J Hum Ergol* 11:369-384.

Kerkhof, A. 1985. Inter-individual differences in the human circadian system: A review. *Biol Psychol* 20:83-112.

Knauth, P. 1983. *Ergonomische Beiträge Zu Sicherheitsaspekten Der Arbeitszeitorganisation*. Düsseldorf: Fortschr.-Ber.

—. 1993. The design of shift systems. *Ergonomics* 36:15-28.

—. 1996. Designing better shift systems. *Appl Ergon* 24(1):39-44.

Knauth, P and M Härmä. 1992. The relation of shift work tolerance to the circadian adjustment. *Chronobiol Int* 9:46-54.

Knauth, P and E Kiesswetter. 1987. A change from weekly to quicker shift rotations: A field study of discontinuous three-shift workers. *Ergonomics* 30:1311-1321.

Knauth, P and J Rutenfranz. 1972. Untersuchungen über die Beziehungen zwischen Schichtform und Tagesaufteilung. *Int Arch Arbeitsmed* 30:173-191.

—. 1981. Duration of sleep related to the type of shift work. In *Night and Shiftwork: Biological and Social Aspects*, edited by A Reinberg, N Vieux, and P Andlauer. Oxford: Pergamon Press.

—. 1982. Development of criteria for the design of shiftwork systems. *J Hum Ergol* 11:337-367.

Knauth, P and E Schönfelder. 1988. Systematische Darstellung innovativer. *Arbeitszeitmod Pers* 40:408-412.

—. 1990. Effects of a new shift system on the social life of shiftworkers. In *Shiftwork: Health, Sleep and Perform-*

ance*, edited by G Costa, G Cesana, K Kogi, and A Wedderburn. Frankfurt: Peter Lang.

Knauth, P, K Landau, C Dröge, M Schwitteck, M Widynski, and J Rutenfranz. 1980. Duration of sleep depending on the type of shift work. *Int Arch Occup Environ Health* 46:167-177.

Knauth, E, E Emde, J Rutenfranz, E Kiesswetter, and P Smith. 1981a. Re-entrainment of body temperature in field studies of shiftwork. *Int Arch Occup Environ Health* 49:137-149.

Knauth, P, G Ernst, P Schwarzenau, and J Rutenfranz. 1981b. Möglichkeiten der Kompensation negativer Auswirkungen der Schichtarbeit. *Z Arb Wiss* 35:1-7.

Knauth, P, E Kiesswetter, W Ottmann, MJ Karvonen, and J Rutenfranz. 1983. Time-budget studies of policemen in weekly or swiftly rotating shift systems. *Appl Ergon* 14:247-252.

Knauth, P, E Kiesswetter, and P Schwarzenau. 1984. Erfahrungen mit einer flexiblen Arbeitszeitregelung bei Dreischichtarbeitern. *Z Arb Wiss* 38:96-99.

Knauth, P, S Dovalova, and E Schönfelder. 1989. *Guidelines for Shiftworkers. Bulletin for European Shiftwork Topics (BEST)*. Dublin: European Foundation for the Improvement of Living and Working Conditions.

Knauth, P, E Schönfelder, and S Hornberger. 1991. *Compensation for Shiftwork. Bulletin for European Shiftwork Topics*. Dublin: European Foundation for the Improvement of Living and Working Conditions.

Knutsson, A and KZ de Ancelar. 1982. *Några medicinska och sociala aspekter på skiftarbete vid Ortvikens Pappersbruk [Some medical and social aspects of shift work at Ortviken's Papermill]*. Stressforskingsrapport Nr. 148. Stockholm: Laboratoriet för klinisk stressforskning.

Knutsson, A, A Åkerstedt, BG Jonsson and K Orth-Gomer. 1986. Increased risk of ischaemic heart disease in shift workers. *Lancet* 2:89-92.

Kogi, K. 1981. Comparison of resting conditions between various shift rotation systems for industrial workers. In *Night and Shift Work: Biological and Social Aspects*, edited by A Reinberg, N Vieux, and P Andlauer. Oxford: Pergamon.

Koller, M. 1983. Health risks related to shift work. An example of time-contingent effects of long-term stress. *Int Arch Occup Environ Health* 53:59-75.

Koller, M, M Kundi, and M Haider. 1991. *Neue Herausforderungen menschengerechter Arbeits-Zeitgestaltung*. Vienna: Österreichischer Arbeiterkammertag.

Kristensen, TS. 1989. Cardiovascular diseases and the work environment. A critical review of the epidemiologic literature on nonchemical factors. *Scand J Work Environ Health* 15:165-179.

Küpper, R, J Rutenfranz, P Knauth, R Romahn, K Undeutsch, and I Löwenthal. 1980. Weschelwirkungen zwischen lärmbedingten Störungen des Tagschlafs und der Häufigkeit verschiedener Beschwerden bei Schichtarbeitern. In *Arbeitsbedingte Gesundheitsschäden—Fiktion Oder Wirklichkeit?*, edited by W Brenner, J Rutenfranz, E Baumgartner, and M Haider. Stuttgart: Genter Verlag.

Landen, RO, AO Vikström, and B Öberg. 1981. *Ordningspoliser I Stockholm: Delrapport III: I Intervention—Sociala Och Psykologiska Reactioner På Förändrade Arbetstider*. Stockholm: Laboratoriet för Klinisk Stressforskning Karolinska Institutet.

Laurig, W. 1981. Belastung, Beanspruchung und Erholungszeit bei energetisch-muskulärer Arbeit– Literaturexpertise. In *Forschungsbericht Nr. 272 Der Bundesanstalt Für Arbeitsschutz Und Unfallforschung Dortmund*. Bremerhaven: Wirtschaftsverlag NW.

Lavie, P. 1986. Ultrashort sleep-waking schedule, III. 'Gates' and 'forbidden zones' for sleep. *Electroen Clin Neuro* 63:414-425.

Leuliet, S. 1963. Douze années de travail posté 3 x 8. *Arch Mal Prof* 24:164-171.

Luczak, H. 1982. *Belastung, Beanspruchung Und Erholungszeit Bei Informatorisch-Mentaler Arbeit– Literaturexpertise. Forschungsbericht Der Bundesanstalt Für Arbeitsschutz Und*

Unfallforschung Dortmund. Bremerhaven: Wirtschaftsverlag NW.

Maasen, A. 1981. The family life of shiftworkers and the school career of their children. In *The Effects of Shiftwork On Health, Social and Family Life* Dublin: European Foundation for the Improvement of Living and Working Conditions.

Matsumoto, K and Y Morita. 1987. Effects of nighttime nap and age on sleep patterns of shiftworkers. *Sleep* 10:580-589.

McEwan, YW. 1978. Flexible working arrangements in continuous shift production. *Pers Rev* :12-19.

Michel-Briand, C, JL Chopard, A-Guiot, M Paulmier and G Studer. 1981. The pathological consequences of shift work in retired workers. *Adv Biosci* 30:399-407.

Minors, S and JM Waterhouse. 1981. Anchor sleep as a synchronizer of rhythms on abnormal routines. *Int J Chronobiol* 7:165-188.

Monk, TH. 1988. *How to Make Shift Work Safe and Productive.* Des Plaines, Ill.: American Society of Safety Engineers.

—. 1990. Shiftwork performance. In *Shiftwork*, edited by AJ Scott. Philadelphia: Hanley & Belfus.

Moog, R. 1981. Morning-evening types and shift work. A questionnaire study. *Adv Biosci* 30:481-488.

—. 1988. *Die Individuelle Circadiane Phasenlage-Ein Prädiktor Der Nacht-Und Schicht-Arbeitstoleranz.* Marberg: Thesis.

Moors, SH. 1990. Learning from a system of seasonally-determined flexibility: Beginning work earlier increases tiredness as much as working longer days. In *Shiftwork: Health, Sleep and Performance*, edited by G Costa, G Cesana, K Kogi, and A Wedderburn. Frankfurt: Peter Lang.

Mott, PE, FC Mann, Q McLoughlin, and DP Warwick. 1965. *Shift Work: The Social, Psychological and Physical Consequences.* Ann Arbor, Mich.: The University of Michigan Press.

Nachreiner, F, R Frielingsdorf, R Romahn, P Knauth, W Kuhlmann, F Klimmer, J Rutenfranz, and E Werner. 1975. *Schichtarbeit bei kontinuierlicher Produktion. Arbeitssoziologische, sozialpsychologische, arbeitspsychologische und arbeitsmedizinische Aspekte. Forschungsbericht der Bundesanstalt für Arbeitsschutz Und Unfallforschung Dortmund, Nr 141.* Opladen: Westdeutscher Verlag.

Naitoh, P, TL Kelly, and C Englund. 1990. Health effects of sleep deprivation. In *Shiftwork* Philadelphia: Hanley & Belfus.

Nedeltcheva, K, N Nilolova, A Stoynev, and S Handjiev. 1990. Excretion of catecholamines and glucocorticoids in shift working railwaymen. In *Shiftwork: Health, Sleep and Performance*, edited by G Cesana, K Kogi, and A Wedderburn. Frankfurt: Peter Lang.

Occupational Safety and Health Administration (OSHA). 1978. Modification on PELs for prolonged exposure periods. In *Industrial Hygiene Manual*. Washington, DC: OSHA.

Olsson, K and I Kandolin. 1990. Strains and satisfaction of three-shift workers—an interview method for the occupational health care. In *Shiftwork: Health, Sleep and Performance*, edited by G Costa, G Cesana, K Kogi, and A Wedderburn. Frankfurt: Peter Lang.

Olsson, K, I Kandolin, and K Kauppinen-Toropainen. 1987. Shiftworkers' coping with stress. In *Contemporary Advances in Shiftwork Research*, edited by J Oginski, J Pokorski, and J Rutenfranz. Krakow: Medical Academy.

Ong, CN and K Kogi. 1990. Shiftwork in developing countries: Current issues and trends. In *Shiftwork*, edited by AJ Scott. Philadelphia: Hanley & Belfus.

Orth-Gomer, K. 1985. Cardiovascular disease–factors of importance in shift workers. In *Seventh Swedish-Yugoslavian Symposium on Occupational Health*, edited by B Komodin-Hedman. Stockholm: Arbetarskyddsverket 56-53. (Arbete och hälsa 1985-27.)

Pátkei, P and K Dahlgren. 1981. Satisfaction with different types of rapidly rotating shift systems. In *Night and Shift Work: Biological and Social Aspects*, edited by A Reinberg, N Vieux and P Andlauer. Oxford: Pergamon Press.

Pokorny, MLI, DHJ Blom, and P Van Leeuwen. 1981. Analysis of traffic accident data (from busdrivers) an alternative approach (I). In *Night and Shiftwork: Biological and Social Aspects*. Oxford: Pergamon.

Pokorski, J, I Iskra-Golec, AM Czekaj, and C Noworal. 1990. Menstrual rhythm and shiftwork interference—a subjective retrospective study. In *Shiftwork: Health, Sleep and Performance*, edited by G Costa, G Cesana, K Kogi, and A Wedderburn. Frankfurt: Peter Lang.

Reinberg, A, A-J Chaumont, and A Laporte. 1975. Circadian temporal structure of 20 shift workers (8-hour shift weekly rotation): An autometric field study. In *Experimental Studies of Shiftwork*, edited by P Colquhoun, S Folkard, P Knauth, and J Rutenfranz. Opladen: Westdeutscher Verlag.

Reinberg, A, Y Motohaschi, P Bourdelean, P Andlauer, F Levi, and A Bicakova-Rocher. 1988. Alteration of period and amplitude of circadian rhythms in shiftworkers. *Eur J Appl Physiol* 57:15-25.

Rohmert, W, J Rutenfranz and E Ulich. 1971. *Das Anlernen sensumotorischer Fertigkeiten. Wirtschaftliche und soziale Aspekte des technischen Wandels in der Bundesrepublik Deutschland. Bd. 7.* Frankfurt a.M.: Europäische Verlagsanstalt.

Rosa, RR, MH Bonnet, RR Bootzin, CI Eastman, T Monk, PE Penn, DI Tepas, and JK Walsh. 1990. Intervention factors for promoting adjustment to nightwork and shiftwork. In *Shiftwork*, edited by AJ Scott. Philadelphia: Hanley & Belfus.

Rutenfranz, J, W Rohmert, and A Iskander. 1971. Über das Verhalten der Pulsfrequenz während des Erlernens sensumotorischer Fertigkeiten unter besonderer Berücksichtigung der Pausenwirkung. *Int Zeitschr Angewandte Physiol einsch Arbeitphysiol* 29:101-118.

Rutenfranz, J, WP Colquhoun, P Knauth and JN Ghata. 1977. Biomedical and psychosocial aaspects of shift work: A review. *Scand J Work Environ Health* 3:165-82.

Rutenfranz, J, P Knauth, and D Angersbach. 1981. Shift work research issues. In *Biological Rhythms, Sleep and Shift Work*, edited by LC Johnson, DI Tepas, WP Colquhoun, and MJ Colligan. New York: Spectrum.

Rutenfranz, J, M Haider, and M Koller. 1985. Occupational health measures for nightworkers and shiftworkers. In *Hours of Work: Temporal Factors in Work-Scheduling*, edited by S Folkard and TH Monk. Chichester: Wiley.

Rutenfranz, J, B Beermann, and I Löwenthal. 1987. *Nachtarbeit für Frauen. Überlegungen aus chronophysiologischer und arbeitsmedizinischer Sicht. Schriftenreihe Arbeitsmedizin Sozial-Medizin Präventivmedizin.* Stuttgart: Gentner Verlag.

Saito, Y and K Kogi. 1978. Psychological conditions of working night and subsequent day shifts with short sleep hours between them. *Ergonomics* 21:871.

Scholz, H. 1963. *Die Physische Arbeitsbelastung Der Giessereiarbeiter. Forschungsbericht Des Landes Nordrhein-Westfalen Nr. 1185.* Opladen: Westdeutscher Verlag.

Scott, AJ and J LaDou. 1990. Shiftwork: Effects on sleep and health with recommendations for medical surveillance and screening. In *Shiftwork*, edited by AJ Scott. Philadelphia: Hanley & Belfus.

Seibt, A, G Friedrichsen, A Jakubowski, O Kaugmann, and U Schurig. 1986. Investigations of the effect of work-dependent noise in combination with shift work. In *Night and Shiftwork: Long-Term Effects and Their Prevention*, edited by M Haider, M Koller, and R Cervinka. Frankfurt: Peter Lang.

Sergean, R. 1971. *Managing Shiftwork.* London: Gower Press.

Smith, L and S Folkard. 1993. Is a 'safer' permanent night shift practicable? *Ergonomics* 36:317-318.

Spelten, E, L Smith, P Totterdell, J Barton, S Folkard, and P Bohle. 1993. The relationship between coping strategies and GHQ-scores in nurses. *Ergonomics* 36:227-232.

Stein, A. 1963. *Zur Frage der Belastung berufstätiger Frauen durch Nacht - Und Schichtarbeit.* Munich: Thesis.

Tasto, DL, MJ Colligan, EW Skjei, and SJ Polly. 1978. *Health Consequences of Shift Work, Final Report, SRI Project URU-4426.* Cincinnati: Taft Laboratories, National Institute for Occupational Safety and Health, Behavioral and Motivational Factors Branch.

Taylor, PJ and SJ Pocock. 1972. Mortality of shift and day workers 1956-68. *Br J Ind Med* 29:201-207.

Tepas, DI. 1985. Flexitime, compressed workweeks and other alternative work schedules. In *Hours of Work. Temporal Factors in Work-Scheduling*, edited by S Folkard and T Monk. Chichester: Wiley.

Tepas, DI and RP Mahan. 1989. The many meanings of sleep. *Work Stress* 3:93-102.

Thiis-Evensen, E. 1958. Shiftwork and health. *Ind Med Surgery* 27:493-497. (1949. Originally published in Norwegian.)

Torsvall, L and T Åkerstedt. 1979. Shift work and diurnal type: A questionnaire study. *Chronobiologia* 6:163-164.

—. 1980. A diurnal type scale: Construction, consistency and validation in shift work. *Scand J Work Environ Health* 6:283-290.

Totterdell, P and S Folkard. 1990. The effects of changing from weekly rotating to a rapidly rotating shift schedule. In *Shiftwork: Health, Sleep, and Performance*, edited by G Costa, G Cesana, K Kogi, and A Wedderburn. Frankfurt: Peter Lang.

Tsaneva, N, L Mincheva, M Topalova, and R Beraha. 1987. Holter ECG monitoring of shift workers in modern electronics. In *Contemporary Advances in Shiftwork Research*, edited by A Oginski, J Pokorski, and J Rutenfranz. Krakow: Medical Academy.

Tsaneva, N, R Nicolova, M Topalova, and S Danev. 1990. Changes in the organism of shift workers operating a day and night 12 hour schedule in carbon disulfide production. In *Shiftwork: Health, Sleep, and Performance*, edited by G Costa, G Cesana, K Kogi, and A Wedderburn. Frankfurt: Peter Lang.

Turek, FW. 1986. Circadian principles and design of rotating shift work schedules. *Am J Physiol* 251:R636-R638.

Uehata, T and N Sasakawa. 1982. The fatigue and maternity disturbances of night workwomen. *J Hum Ergol* 11:465-474.

Ulich, E. 1957. Zur Frage der Belastung des arbeitenden Menschen durch Nacht- und Schichtarbeit. *Psychol Rundschau* 8:42-61.

Ulich, E, M Rauterberg, T Moll, T Greutmann, and O Strohm. 1991. Task orientation and user-oriented dialogue design. *Int J Hum Comput Interact* 3:117-144.

Verhaegen, P, R Cober, M De Smedt, J Dirkx, J Kerstens, D Ryvers, and P Van Daele. 1987. The adaptation of night nurses to different work schedules. *Ergonomics* 30:1301-1309.

Vidacek, S, LJ Kaliterna and B Radosevic-Vidacek. 1987. Predictive validity of individual difference measures for health problems in shiftworkers: preliminary results. In *Contemporary Advances in Shiftwork Research*, edited by A Oginski, J. Pokorski and J. Rutenfranz. Krakow: Medical Academy.

Walker, J. 1985. Social problems of shiftwork. In *Hours of Work. Temporal Factors in Work-Scheduling*, edited by S Folkard and T Monk. Chichester: Wiley.

Wallace, M. 1989. The 3 day week: 12 hour shifts. In *Managing Shiftwork*, edited by M Wallace. Bundoora, Australia: La Trobe University, Department of Psychology, Brain-Behaviour Research Institute.

Waterhouse, JM, S Folkard, and DS Minors. 1992. *Shiftwork, Health and Safety. An Overview of the Scientific Literature 1978-1990.* Health and safety executive contract research report No. 3l. London: HMSO.

Wedderburn, AAI. 1981. Is there a pattern in the value of time off work? In *Night and Shiftwork: Biological and Social Aspects,* edited by N Reinberg, N Vieux, and P Andlauer. Oxford: Pergamon.

—. 1991. *Guidelines for Shiftworkers.* Bulletin of European Shiftwork Topics (BEST), no.3. Dublin: European Foundation for the Improvement of Living and Working Conditions.

Wever, RA, J Polasek, and CM Wildgruber. 1983. Bright light effects on human circadian rhythms. *Pflügers Arch* 396:85-87.

Wild, HW and H Theis. 1967. Der Einfluss des Schichtbeginns auf die Unfallhäufigkeit. *Glückauf, Bergmännische Zeitschrift* 103:833-838.

Wilkinson, RT. 1992. How fast should the night shift rotate? *Ergonomics* 35:1425-1446.

Williams, RL, I Karacan, and CI Hursch. 1974. *EEG of Human Sleep: Clinical Application.* New York: Wiley.

Williamson, AM and JW Sanderson. 1986. Changing the speed of shift rotation, a field study. *Ergonomics* 29:1085-1096.

Wynne, RF, GM Ryan, and JH Cullen. 1986. Adjustment to shiftwork and its prediction: Results from a longitudinal study. In *Night and Shiftwork: Long-Term Effects and Their Prevention,* edited by M Haider, M Koller, and R Cervinka. Frankfurt: Peter Lang.

Other relevant readings

Cesana, GC, M Ferrario, R Curti, R Zanettini, A Grieco, R Sega, A Palermo, G Mara, A Libretti, and S Algeri. 1982. Work-stress and urinary catecholamines excretion in shift workers exposed to noise. *Medicina del Lavaro* 2:99-109.

De Haan, EG. 1990. Improving shiftwork schedules in a bus company: Towards more autonomy. In *Shiftwork: Health, Sleep and Performance,* edited by G Costa, G Cesana, K Kogi, and A Wedderburn. Frankfurt: Peter Lang.

Folkard, S and T Åkerstedt. 1992. A three-process model of the regulation of alertness sleepiness. In *Sleep, Arousal and Performance,* edited by RJ Broughton and BD Ogilvie. Boston: Birkhäuser.

Folkard, S and TH Monk. 1985. *Hours of Work: Temporal Factors in Work Scheduling.* Chichester: Wiley.

Folkard, S and P Totterdell. 1993. Circadian variations in performance. *Ergonomics* .

International Labour Organization (ILO). 1989. Part-time work. *Cond Work Dig* 8(1).

Irion, H, R Rossner, and H Lazarus. 1983. *Entwicklung des Hörverlustes in Abhängigkeit von Lärm, Alter und anderen Einflüssen. Bundesanstalt für Arbeitsschutz und Unfallforschung.* Dortmund: Forschungsbericht.

Kiesswetter, E. 1992. The impact of heat stress on adjustment to shift work. *ACES* 4:23-24.

Lehmann, G. 1962. *Praktische Arbeitsphysiologie.* Stuttgart: Georg Thième Verlag.

Monk, TH. 1991. *Sleep, Sleepiness and Performance.* Chichester: Wiley.

Ottmann, W, R Flügge, P Knauth, T Gallwey, A Craig, and J Rutenfranz. 1986. Combined effects of experimental nightwork and heat stress on cognitive performance tasks. In *Night and Shiftwork: Long-Term Effects and Their Prevention,* edited by M Haider, M Koller, and R Cervinka. Frankfurt: Peter Lang.

Pokorski, J, A Oginski, and P Knauth. 1986. Work-physiological field studies concerning effects of combined stress in morning, afternoon and nightshifts. In *Night and Shiftwork: Long-Term Effects and Their Prevention,* edited by M Haider, M Koller, and R Cervinka. Frankfurt: Peter Lang.

Reinberg, A, M Smolensky, G Labrecque, F Levi, and J Cambar. 1986. Biological rhythms and exposure limits to potentially noxious agents. In *Night and Shiftwork: Long-Term Effects and Their Prevention,* edited by M Haider, M Koller, and R Cervinka. Frankfurt: Peter Lang.

Rutenfranz, J, W Ottmann, B Schmitz, R Flügge, and P Knauth. 1986. Circadian rhythms of physiological functions during experimental shift work with additional heat stress. In *Night and Shiftwork: Long-Term Effects and Their Prevention,* edited by M Haider, M Koller, and R Cervinka. Frankfurt: Peter Lang.

Seeber, AE, E Kieswetter, and M Blaszkowicz. 1992. Exposure to mixtures of solvents and shift work: Interrelations concerning neurobehavioral effects. *ACES* 4:20-21.

Seibt, A, C Hilpmann, and G Friedrichsen. 1983. Zur auralen Wirkung des hörschädigenden Lärms bei Schichtarbeit. *Z ges Hyg* 29:206-208.

Smith, AP. 1991. The combined effects of noise, nightwork and meals on mood. *Int Arch Occup Environ Health* 63:105-108.

Smith, A and C Mils. 1986. Acute effects of meals, noise and nightwork. *Brit J Psychol* 77:377-387.

Thierry, H, G Hoolwerf, and PJD Drenth. 1975. Attitudes of permanent day and shift workers towards shiftwork—a field study. In *Experimental Studies of Shiftwork,* edited by P Colquhoun, S Folkard, P Knauth, and J Rutenfranz. Opladen: Westdeutscher Verlag.

Torsvall, L, T Åkerstedt, and M Gillberg. 1981. Age, sleep and irregular workhours: A field study with EEG recording, catecholamine excretion and self-ratings. *Scand J Work Environ Health* 7:196-203.

INDOOR AIR QUALITY

44

Chapter Editor
Xavier Guardino Solá

Contents

44. INDOOR AIR QUALITY

● INDOOR AIR QUALITY: INTRODUCTION

Xavier Guardino Solá

The connection between the use of a building either as a workplace or as a dwelling and the appearance, in certain cases, of discomfort and symptoms that may be the very definition of an illness is a fact that can no longer be disputed. The main culprit is contamination of various kinds within the building, and this contamination is usually referred to as "poor quality of indoor air". The adverse effects due to poor air quality in closed spaces affect a considerable number of people, since it has been shown that urban dwellers spend between 58 and 78% of their time in an indoor environment which is contaminated to a greater or lesser degree. These problems have increased with the construction of buildings that are designed to be more airtight and that recycle air with a smaller proportion of new air from the outside in order to be more energy efficient. The fact that buildings that do not offer natural ventilation present risks of exposure to contaminants is now generally accepted.

The term *indoor air* is usually applied to nonindustrial indoor environments: office buildings, public buildings (schools, hospitals, theatres, restaurants, etc.) and private dwellings. Concentrations of contaminants in the indoor air of these structures are usually of the same order as those commonly found in outdoor air, and are much lower than those found in air in industrial premises, where relatively well-known standards are applied in order to assess air quality. Even so, many building occupants complain of the quality of the air they breathe and there is therefore a need to investigate the situation. Indoor air quality began to be referred to as a problem at the end of the 1960s, although the first studies did not appear until some ten years later.

Although it would seem logical to think that good air quality is based on the presence in the air of the necessary components in suitable proportions, in reality it is the user, through respiration, who is the best judge of its quality. This is because inhaled air is perceived perfectly through the senses, as human beings are sensitive to the olfactory and irritant effects of about half a million chemical compounds. Consequently, if the occupants of a building are as a whole satisfied with the air, it is said to be of high quality; if they are unsatisfied, it is of poor quality. Does this mean that it is possible to predict on the basis of its composition how the air will be perceived? Yes, but only in part. This method works well in industrial environments, where specific chemical compounds related to production are known, and their concentrations in the air are measured and compared with threshold limit values. But in nonindustrial buildings where there may be thousands of chemical substances in the air but in such low concentrations that they are, perhaps, thousands of times less than the limits set for industrial environments, the situation is different. In most of these cases information about the chemical composition of indoor air does not allow us to predict how the air will be perceived, since the combined effect of thousands of these contaminants, together with temperature and humidity, can produce air that is perceived as irritating, foul, or stale—that is, of poor quality. The situation is comparable to what happens with the detailed composition of an item of food and its taste: chemical analysis is inadequate to predict whether the food will taste good or bad. For this reason, when a ventilation system and its regular maintenance are being planned, an exhaustive chemical analysis of indoor air is rarely called for.

Another point of view is that people are considered the only sources of contamination in indoor air. This would certainly be true if we were dealing with building materials, furniture and

Figure 44.1 • Symptoms and illnesses related to the quality of indoor air.

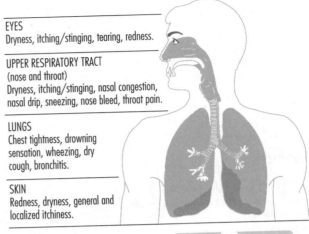

EYES
Dryness, itching/stinging, tearing, redness.

UPPER RESPIRATORY TRACT
(nose and throat)
Dryness, itching/stinging, nasal congestion, nasal drip, sneezing, nose bleed, throat pain.

LUNGS
Chest tightness, drowning sensation, wheezing, dry cough, bronchitis.

SKIN
Redness, dryness, general and localized itchiness.

GENERAL
Headache, weakness, drowsiness/lethargy, difficulty concentrating, irritability, anxiety, nausea, dizziness.

MOST COMMON ILLNESSES:

HYPERSENSITIVITY
Hypersensitivity pneumonitis, humidifier fever, asthma, rhinitis, dermatitis.

INFECTIONS
Legionellosis (Legionnaire's disease), Pontiac fever, tuberculosis, common cold, flu. Of unknown chemical or physical origins, including cancer.

ventilation systems as they were used 50 years ago, when bricks, wood and steel predominated. But with modern materials the situation has changed. All materials contaminate, some a little and others much, and together they contribute to a deterioration in the quality of indoor air.

The changes in a person's health due to poor indoor air quality can show up as a wide array of acute and chronic symptoms and in the form of a number of specific illnesses. These are illustrated in figure 44.1. Although poor indoor air quality results in fully developed illness in only a few cases, it can give rise to malaise, stress, absenteeism and loss of productivity (with concomitant increases in production costs); and allegations about problems related to the building can develop rapidly into conflict between the occupants, their employers and the owners of the buildings.

Normally it is difficult to establish precisely to what extent poor indoor air quality can harm health, since not enough information is available concerning the relationship between exposure and effect at the concentrations in which the contaminants are usually found. Hence, there is a need to take information obtained at high doses—as with exposures in industrial settings—and extrapolate to much lower doses with a corresponding margin of error. In addition, for many contaminants present in the air, the effects of acute exposure are well known, whereas there are considerable gaps in the data regarding both long-term exposures at low concentrations and mixtures of different contaminants. The concepts of no-effect-level (NOEL), harmful effect and tolerable effect, already confusing even in the sphere of industrial toxicology, are here even more difficult to define. There are few conclusive studies on the subject, whether relating to public buildings and offices or private dwellings.

Series of standards for outdoor air quality exist and are relied on to protect the general population. They have been obtained by measuring adverse effects on health resulting from exposure to contaminants in the environment. These standards are therefore useful as general guidelines for an acceptable quality of indoor air, as is the case with those proposed by the World Health Organization. Technical criteria such as the threshold limit value of the American Conference of Governmental Industrial Hygienists (ACGIH) in the United States and the limit values legally established for industrial environments in different countries have been set for the working, adult population and for specific lengths of exposure, and cannot therefore be applied directly to the general population. The American Society of Heating, Refrigeration and Air Conditioning Engineers (ASHRAE) in the United States has developed a series of standards and recommendations that are widely used in assessing indoor air quality.

Another aspect that should be considered as part of the quality of indoor air is its smell, because smell is often the parameter that ends up being the defining factor. The combination of a certain smell with the slight irritating effect of a compound in indoor air can lead us to define its quality as "fresh" and "clean" or as "stale" and "polluted". Smell is therefore very important when defining the quality of indoor air. While odours objectively depend on the presence of compounds in quantities above their olfactory thresholds, they are very often evaluated from a strictly subjective point of view. It should also be kept in mind that the perception of an odour may result from the smells of many different compounds and that temperature and humidity may also affect its characteristics. From the standpoint of perception there are four characteristics that allow us to define and measure odours: intensity, quality, tolerability and threshold. When considering indoor air, however, it is very difficult to "measure" odours from a chemical standpoint. For that reason the tendency is to eliminate odours that are "bad" and to use, in their place, those considered good in order to give air a pleasant quality. The attempt to mask bad odours with good ones usually ends in failure, because odours of very different qualities can be recognized separately and lead to unforeseeable results.

A phenomenon known as *sick building syndrome* occurs when more than 20% of the occupants of a building complain about air quality or have definite symptoms. It is evidenced by a variety of physical and environmental problems associated with non-industrial indoor environments. The most common features seen in cases of sick building syndrome are the following: those affected complain of non-specific symptoms similar to the common cold or respiratory illnesses; the buildings are efficient as regards energy conservation and are of modern design and construction or recently remodelled with new materials; and the occupants cannot control the temperature, humidity and illumination of the workplace. The estimated percentage distribution of the most common causes of sick building syndrome are inadequate ventilation due to lack of maintenance; poor distribution and insufficient intake of fresh air (50 to 52%); contamination generated indoors, including from office machines, tobacco smoke and cleaning products (17 to 19%); contamination from the outside of the building due to inadequate placement of air intake and exhaust vents (11%); microbiological contamination from stagnant water in the ducts of the ventilation system, humidifiers and refrigeration towers (5%); and formaldehyde and other organic compounds emitted by building and decoration materials (3 to 4%). Thus, ventilation is cited as an important contributory factor in the majority of cases.

Another question of a different nature is that of building-related illnesses, which are less frequent, but often more serious, and are accompanied by very definite clinical signs and clear laboratory findings. Examples of building-related illnesses are hypersensitivity pneumonitis, humidifier fever, legionellosis and Pontiac fever. A fairly general opinion among investigators is that these conditions should be considered separately from sick building syndrome.

Studies have been done to ascertain both the causes of air quality problems and their possible solutions. In recent years, knowledge of the contaminants present in indoor air and the factors contributing to a decline in indoor air quality has increased considerably, although there is a long way to go. Studies carried out in the last 20 years have shown that the presence of contaminants in many indoor environments is higher than anticipated, and moreover, different contaminants have been identified from those that exist in outside air. This contradicts the assumption that indoor environments without industrial activity are relatively free of contaminants and that in the worst of cases they may reflect the composition of outside air. Contaminants such as radon and formaldehyde are identified almost exclusively in the indoor environment.

Indoor air quality, including that of dwellings, has become a question of environmental health in the same way as has happened with control of outdoor air quality and exposure at work. Although, as already mentioned, an urban person spends 58 to 78% of his or her time indoors, it should be remembered that the most susceptible persons, namely the elderly, small children and the sick, are the ones who spend most of their time indoors. This subject began to be particularly topical from around 1973 onwards, when, because of the energy crisis, efforts directed at energy conservation concentrated on reducing the entry of outside air into indoor spaces as much as possible in order to minimize the cost of heating and cooling buildings. Although not all the problems relating to indoor air quality are the result of actions aimed at saving energy, it is a fact that as this policy spread, complaints about indoor air quality began to increase, and all the problems appeared.

Another item requiring attention is the presence of micro-organisms in indoor air which can cause problems of both an infectious and an allergic nature. It should not be forgotten that micro-organisms are a normal and essential component of ecosystems. For example, saprophytic bacteria and fungi, which obtain their nutrition from dead organic material in the environment, are found normally in the soil and atmosphere, and their presence can also be detected indoors. In recent years problems of biological contamination in indoor environments have received considerable attention.

The outbreak of Legionnaire's disease in 1976 is the most discussed case of an illness caused by a micro-organism in the indoor environment. Other infectious agents, such as viruses that can cause acute respiratory illness, are detectable in indoor environments, especially if the occupation density is high and much recirculation of air is taking place. In fact, the extent to which micro-organisms or their components are implicated in the outbreak of building-associated conditions is not known. Protocols for demonstrating and analysing many types of microbial agents have been developed only to a limited degree, and in those cases where they are available, the interpretation of the results is sometimes inconsistent.

Aspects of the Ventilation System

Indoor air quality in a building is a function of a series of variables which include the quality of the outdoor air, the design of the ventilation and air-conditioning system, the conditions in which this system operates and is serviced, the compartmentalization of the building and the presence of indoor sources of contaminants and their magnitude. (See figure 44.2.) By way of summary it may be noted that the most common defects are the result of

Figure 44.2 • Diagram of building showing sources of indoor and outdoor pollutants.

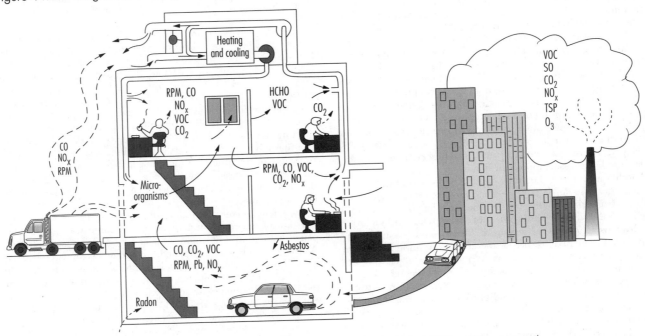

CO = carbon monoxide; CO₂ = carbon dioxide; HCHO = formaldehyde; NOₓ = nitrogen oxides; Pb = lead; RPM = respirable particulate matter; VOC = volatile organic compounds.

inadequate ventilation, contamination generated indoors and contamination coming from outside.

Regarding the first of these problems, causes of inadequate ventilation can include: an insufficient supply of fresh air due to a high level of recirculation of the air or a low volume of intake; incorrect placement and orientation in the building of intake points for outside air; poor distribution and consequently incomplete mixing with the air of the premises, which can produce stratification, unventilated zones, unforeseen pressure differences giving rise to unwanted air currents and continuous changes in the thermohygrometric characteristics noticeable as one moves about the building—and incorrect filtration of the air because of lack of maintenance or inadequate design of the filtering system—a deficiency which is particularly serious where the outdoor air is of poor quality or where there is a high level of recirculation.

Origins of Contaminants

Indoor contamination has different origins: the occupants themselves; inadequate materials or materials with technical defects used in the construction of the building; the work performed within; excessive or improper use of normal products (pesticides, disinfectants, products used for cleaning and polishing); combustion gases (from smoking, kitchens, cafeterias and laboratories); and cross-contamination coming from other poorly ventilated zones which then diffuses towards neighbouring areas and affects them. It should be borne in mind that substances emitted in indoor air have much less opportunity of being diluted than those emitted in outdoor air, given the difference in the volumes of air available. As regards biological contamination, its origin is most frequently due to the presence of stagnant water, materials impregnated with water, exhausts and so on, and to defective maintenance of humidifiers and refrigeration towers.

Finally, contamination coming from outside must also be considered. As regards human activity, three main sources may be

mentioned: combustion in stationary sources (power stations); combustion in moving sources (vehicles); and industrial processes. The five main contaminants emitted by these sources are carbon monoxide, oxides of sulphur, oxides of nitrogen, volatile organic compounds (including hydrocarbons), polycyclic aromatic hydrocarbons and particles. Internal combustion in vehicles is the principal source of carbon monoxide and hydrocarbons and is an important source of oxides of nitrogen. Combustion in stationary sources is the main origin of oxides of sulphur. Industrial processes and stationary sources of combustion generate more than half of the particles emitted into the air by human activity, and industrial processes can be a source of volatile organic compounds. There are also contaminants generated naturally that are propelled through the air, such as particles of volcanic dust, soil and sea salt, and spores and micro-organisms. The composition of outdoor air varies from place to place, depending both on the presence and the nature of the sources of contamination in the vicinity and on the direction of the prevailing wind. If there are no sources generating contaminants, the concentration of certain contaminants that will typically be found in "clean" outdoor air are as follows: carbon dioxide, 320 ppm; ozone, 0.02 ppm: carbon monoxide, 0.12 ppm; nitric oxide, 0.003 ppm; and nitrogen dioxide, 0.001 ppm. However, urban air always contains much higher concentrations of these contaminants.

Apart from the presence of the contaminants originating from outside, it sometimes happens that contaminated air from the building itself is expelled to the exterior and then returns inside again through the intakes of the air-conditioning system. Another possible way by which contaminants may enter from the exterior is by infiltration through the foundations of the building (e.g., radon, fuel vapours, sewer effluvia, fertilizers, insecticides and disinfectants). It has been shown that when the concentration of a contaminant in the outdoor air increases, its concentration in the air inside the building also increases, although more slowly (a corresponding relationship obtains when the concentration decreases); it is therefore said that buildings exert a shielding effect against external contaminants. However, the indoor environment is not, of course, an exact reflection of the conditions outside.

Contaminants present in indoor air are diluted in the outdoor air that enters the building and they accompany it when it leaves. When the concentration of a contaminant is less in the outdoor air than the indoor air, the interchange of indoor and outdoor air will result in a reduction in the concentration of the contaminant in the air inside the building. If a contaminant originates from outside and not inside, this interchange will result in a rise in its indoor concentration, as mentioned above.

Models for the balance of amounts of contaminants in indoor air are based on the calculation of their accumulation, in units of mass versus time, from the difference between the quantity that enters plus what is generated indoors, and what leaves with the air plus what is eliminated by other means. If appropriate values are available for each of the factors in the equation, the indoor concentration can be estimated for a wide range of conditions. Use of this technique makes possible the comparison of different alternatives for controlling an indoor contamination problem.

Buildings with low interchange rates with outdoor air are classified as sealed or energy-efficient. They are energy-efficient because less cold air enters in winter, reducing the energy required to heat the air to the ambient temperature, thus cutting the cost of heating. When the weather is hot, less energy is also used to cool the air. If the building does not have this property, it is ventilated through open doors and windows by a process of natural ventilation. Although they may be closed, differences of pressure, resulting both from the wind and from the thermal gradient existing between the interior and the exterior, force the air to enter through crevices and cracks, window and door joints, chimneys and other apertures, giving rise to what is called ventilation by infiltration.

The ventilation of a building is measured in renewals per hour. One renewal per hour means that a volume of air equal to the volume of the building enters from outside every hour; in the same way, an equal volume of indoor air is expelled to the exterior every hour. If there is no forced ventilation (with a ventilator) this value is difficult to determine, although it is considered to vary between 0.2 and 2.0 renewals per hour. If the other parameters are assumed to be unchanged, the concentration of contaminants generated indoors will be less in buildings with high renewal values, although a high renewal value is not a complete guarantee of indoor air quality. Except in areas with marked atmospheric pollution, buildings that are more open will have a lower concentration of contaminants in the indoor air than those constructed in a more closed manner. However, buildings that are more open are less energy-efficient. The conflict between energy efficiency and air quality is of great importance.

Much action undertaken to reduce energy costs affects indoor air quality to a greater or lesser extent. In addition to reducing the speed with which the air circulates within the building, efforts to increase the insulation and waterproofing of the building involve the installation of materials that may be sources of indoor contamination. Other action, such as supplementing old and frequently inefficient central heating systems with secondary sources that heat or consume the indoor air can also raise contaminant levels in indoor air.

Contaminants whose presence in indoor air is most frequently mentioned, apart from those coming from outside, include metals, asbestos and other fibrous materials, formaldehyde, ozone, pesticides and organic compounds in general, radon, house dust and biological aerosols. Together with these, a wide variety of types of micro-organisms can be found, such as fungi, bacteria, viruses and protozoa. Of these, the saprophytic fungi and bacteria are relatively well known, probably because a technology is available for measuring them in air. The same is not true of agents such as viruses, rickettsiae, chlamydias, protozoa and many pathogenic fungi and bacteria, for the demonstration and counting of which no methodology is as yet available. Among the infectious agents, special mention should be made of: *Legionella pneumophila*, *Mycobacterium avium*, viruses, *Coxiella burnetii* and *Histoplasma capsulatum*; and among the allergens: *Cladosporium*, *Penicillium* and *Cytophaga*.

Investigating Indoor Air Quality

Experience so far suggests that the traditional techniques used in industrial hygiene and heating, ventilation and air-conditioning do not always provide satisfactory results at present for solving the ever more common problems of indoor air quality, although basic knowledge of these techniques permits good approximations for dealing with or reducing problems rapidly and inexpensively. The solution to problems of indoor air quality often requires, in addition to one or more experts in heating, ventilation and air-conditioning and industrial hygiene, specialists in indoor air quality control, analytical chemistry, toxicology, environmental medicine, microbiology, and also epidemiology and psychology.

When a study is carried out on indoor air quality, the objectives set for it will profoundly affect its design and the activities directed at sampling and evaluation, since in some cases procedures giving a rapid response will be required, while in others overall values will be of interest. The duration of the programme will be dictated by the time required to obtain representative samples, and will also depend on the season and on meteorological conditions. If the aim is to carry out an exposure-effect study, in addition to long-term and short-term samples for evaluating peaks, personal samples will be required for ascertaining the direct exposure of individuals.

For some contaminants, well-validated and widely used methods are available, but for the majority this is not the case. Techniques for measuring levels of many contaminants found indoors are normally derived from applications in industrial hygiene but, given that the concentrations of interest in indoor air are usually much lower than those occurring in industrial environments, these methods are frequently inappropriate. As for the measurement methods used in atmospheric contamination, they operate with margins of similar concentrations, but are available for relatively few contaminants and present difficulties in indoor use, such as would arise, for example, with a high-volume sampler for determining particulate matter, which on the one hand would be too noisy and on the other could modify the quality of the indoor air itself.

The determination of contaminants in indoor air is usually carried out by using different procedures: with continuous monitors, whole-time active samplers, whole-time passive samplers, direct sampling and personal samplers. Adequate procedures exist at present for measuring levels of formaldehyde, oxides of carbon and nitrogen, volatile organic compounds and radon, among others. Biological contaminants are measured using techniques of sedimentation on open culture plates or, more frequently nowadays, by using active systems that cause the air to impact on plates containing nutrient, which are subsequently cultured, the quantity of micro-organisms present being expressed in colony-forming units per cubic metre.

When a problem of indoor air quality is being investigated, it is usual to design beforehand a practical strategy consisting of an approximation in phases. This approximation begins with a first phase, the initial investigation, which can be carried out using industrial hygiene techniques. It must be structured so that the investigator does not need to be a specialist in the field of indoor air quality in order to carry out his work. A general inspection of the building is undertaken and its installations are checked, particularly as regards the regulation and adequate functioning of the heating, ventilation and air-conditioning system, according to the standards set at the time of its installation. It is important in this respect to consider whether the persons affected are able to modify the conditions of their surroundings. If the building does not have systems of forced ventilation, the degree of effectiveness of the existing natural ventilation must be studied. If after revision—and adjustment if necessary—the operational conditions of the ventilation systems are adequate for the standards, and if despite this the complaints continue, a technical investigation of a general kind will have to ensue to determine the degree and nature of the problem. This initial investigation should also allow an assessment to be made as to whether the problems can be considered solely from the functional point of view of the building, or whether the intervention of specialists in hygiene, psychology or other disciplines will be necessary.

If the problem is not identified and resolved in this first phase, other phases can follow involving more specialized investigations concentrating on potential problems identified in the first phase. The subsequent investigations may include a more detailed analysis of the heating, ventilation and air-conditioning system of the building, a more extensive evaluation of the presence of materials suspected of emitting gases and particles, a detailed chemical analysis of the ambient air in the building and medical or epidemiological assessments to detect signs of disease.

As regards the heating, ventilation and air-conditioning system, the refrigeration equipment should be checked in order to ensure that there is no microbial growth in them or accumulation of water in their drip trays, the ventilation units must be checked to see that they are functioning correctly, the air intake and return systems must be examined at various points to see that they are watertight, and the interior of a representative number of ducts must be checked to confirm the absence of micro-organisms. This last consideration is particularly important when humidifiers are used. These units require particularly careful programmes of maintenance, operation and inspection in order to prevent the growth of micro-organisms, which can propagate themselves throughout the air-conditioning system.

The options generally considered for improving indoor air quality in a building are the elimination of the source; its insulation or independent ventilation; separating the source from those who may be affected; general cleaning of the building; and increased checking and improvement of the heating, ventilation and air-conditioning system. This may require anything from modifications at particular points to a new design. The process is frequently of a repetitive nature, so that the study has to be started again several times, using more sophisticated techniques on each occasion. A more detailed description of control techniques will be found elsewhere in this *Encyclopaedia*.

Finally, it should be emphasized that, even with the most complete investigations of indoor air quality, it may be impossible to establish a clear relationship between the characteristics and composition of the indoor air and the health and comfort of the occupants of the building under study. Only the accumulation of experience on the one hand, and the rational design of ventilation, occupation and compartmentalization of buildings on the other, are possible guarantees from the outset of obtaining indoor air quality that is adequate for the majority of the occupants of a building.

NATURE AND SOURCES OF INDOOR CHEMICAL CONTAMINANTS

Derrick Crump

Characteristic Chemical Pollutants

Chemical contaminants of the indoor air can occur as gases and vapours (inorganic and organic) and particulates. Their presence in the indoor environment is the result of entry into the building from the outdoor environment or their generation within the building. The relative importance of these indoor and outdoor origins differs for different pollutants and may vary over time.

The major chemical pollutants commonly found in the indoor air are the following:

1. carbon dioxide (CO_2), which is a metabolic product and often used as an indicator of the general level of air pollution related to the presence of humans indoors
2. carbon monoxide (CO), nitrogen oxides (NO_x) and sulphur dioxide (SO_2), which are inorganic combustion gases formed predominantly during the combustion of fuels and ozone (O_3), which is a product of photochemical reactions in polluted atmospheres but may also be released by some indoor sources
3. organic compounds that originate from a variety of indoor sources and outdoors. Hundreds of organic chemicals occur in indoor air although most are present at very low concentrations. These can be grouped according to their boiling points and one widely used classification, shown in table 44.1, identifies four groups of organic compounds: (1) very volatile organic compounds (VVOC); (2) volatile (VOC); (3) semivolatile (SVOC); and (4) organic compounds associated with particulate matter (POM). Particle-phase organics are dissolved in or adsorbed on particulate matter. They may occur in both the vapour and particle phase depending on their volatility. For example, polyaromatic hydrocarbons (PAHs) consisting of two fused benzene rings (e.g., naphthalene) are found principally in the vapour phase and those consisting of five rings (e.g., benz[a]pyrene) are found predominantly in the particle phase.

An important characteristic of indoor air contaminants is that their concentrations vary both spatially and temporally to a greater extent than is common outdoors. This is due to the large

Table 44.1 • Classification of indoor organic pollutants.

Category	Description	Abbreviation	Boiling range (°C)	Sampling methods typically used in field studies
1	Very volatile(gaseous) organic compounds	VVOC	<0 to 50-100	Batch sampling; adsorption on charcoal
2	Volatile organic compounds	VOC	50-100 to 240-260	Adsorption on Tenax, carbon molecular black or charcoal
3	Semivolatile organic compounds	SVOC	240-260 to 380-400	Adsorption on polyurethane foam or XAD-2
4	Organic compounds associated with particulate matter or particulate organic matter	POM	380	Collection filters

variety of sources, the intermittent operation of some of the sources and the various sinks present.

Concentrations of contaminants that arise principally from combustion sources are subject to very large temporal variation and are intermittent. Episodic releases of volatile organic compounds due to human activities such as painting also lead to large variations in emission with time. Other emissions, such as formaldehyde release from wood-based products may vary with temperature and humidity fluctuations in the building, but the emission is continuous. The emission of organic chemicals from other materials may be less dependent upon temperature and humidity conditions but their concentrations in indoor air will be greatly influenced by ventilation conditions.

Spatial variations within a room tend to be less pronounced than temporal variations. Within a building there may be large differences in the case of localized sources, for example, photocopiers in a central office, gas cookers in the restaurant kitchen and tobacco smoking restricted to a designated area.

Sources within the Building

Elevated levels of pollutants generated by combustion, particularly nitrogen dioxide and carbon monoxide in indoor spaces, usually result from unvented, improperly vented or poorly maintained combustion appliances and the smoking of tobacco products. Unvented kerosene and gas space heaters emit significant quantities of CO, CO_2, NO_x, SO_2, particulates and formaldehyde. Gas cooking stoves and ovens also release these products directly into the indoor air. Under normal operating conditions, vented gas-fired forced air heaters and water heaters should not release combustion products into the indoor air. However flue gas spillage and backdrafting can occur with faulty appliances when the room is depressurized by competing exhaust systems and under certain meteorological conditions.

Environmental tobacco smoke

Indoor air contamination from tobacco smoke results from sidestream and exhaled mainstream smoke, usually referred to as environmental tobacco smoke (ETS). Several thousand different constituents have been identified in tobacco smoke and the total quantities of individual components varies depending upon the type of cigarette and the conditions of smoke generation. The main chemicals associated with ETS are nicotine, nitrosamines, PAHs, CO, CO_2, NO_x, acrolein, formaldehyde and hydrogen cyanide.

Building materials and furnishings

The materials which have received greatest attention as sources of indoor air pollution have been wood-based boards containing urea formaldehyde (UF) resin and UF cavity wall insulation (UFFI). Emission of formaldehyde from these products results in elevated levels of formaldehyde in buildings and this has been associated with many complaints of poor indoor air quality in developed countries, particularly during the late 1970s and early 1980s. Table 44.2 gives examples of materials that release formaldehyde in buildings. These show that the highest emission rates may be associated with the wood-based products and UFFI which are products often used extensively in buildings. Particleboard is manufactured from fine (about 1 mm) wood particles which are mixed with UF resins (6 to 8 weight%) and pressed into wood panels. It is widely used for flooring, wall panelling, shelving and components of cabinets and furniture. The plies of hardwood are bonded with UF resin and are commonly used for decorative wall panelling and components of furniture. Medium-density fibreboard (MDF) contains finer wood particles than those used in particleboard and these are also bound with UF resin. MDF is most often used for furniture. The primary source of formalde-

Table 44.2 • Formaldehyde emission rates from a variety of construction material furnishings and consumer products.

	Range of formaldehyde emission rates ($\mu g/m^2/day$)
Medium-density fibreboard	17,600-55,000
Hardwood plywood panelling	1,500-34,000
Particleboard	2,000-25,000
Urea-formaldehyde foam insulation	1,200-19,200
Softwood plywood	240-720
Paper products	260-680
Fibreglass products	400-470
Clothing	35-570
Resilient flooring	<240
Carpeting	0-65
Upholstery fabric	0-7

Table 44.3 • Total volatile organic compound (TVOC) concentrations and emission rates associated with various floor and wall coverings and coatings.

Type of material	Concentrations (mg/m^3)	Emission rate (mg/m^2hr)
Wallpaper		
Vinyl and paper	0.95	0.04
Vinyl and glass fibres	7.18	0.30
Printed paper	0.74	0.03
Wall covering		
Hessian	0.09	0.005
PVC[a]	2.43	0.10
Textile	39.60	1.60
Textile	1.98	0.08
Floor covering		
Linoleum	5.19	0.22
Synthetic fibres	1.62	0.12
Rubber	28.40	1.40
Soft plastic	3.84	0.59
Homogeneous PVC	54.80	2.30
Coatings		
Acrylic latex	2.00	0.43
Varnish, clear epoxy	5.45	1.30
Varnish, polyurethane, two-component	28.90	4.70
Varnish, acid-hardened	3.50	0.83

[a] PVC, polyvinyl chloride.

hyde in all these products is the residual formaldehyde trapped in the resin as a result of its presence in excess needed for the reaction with urea during the manufacture of the resin. Release is therefore highest when the product is new, and declines at a rate dependent upon product thickness, initial emission strength, presence of other formaldehyde sources, local climate and occupant behaviour. The initial decline rate of emissions may be 50% over the first eight to nine months, followed by a much slower rate of decline. Secondary emission can occur due to hydrolysis of the UF resin and hence emission rates increase during periods of elevated temperature and humidity. Considerable efforts by manufacturers have led to the development of lower-emitting materials by use of lower ratios (i.e. closer to 1:1) of urea to formaldehyde for resin production and the use of formaldehyde scavengers. Regulation and consumer demand have resulted in widespread use of these products in some countries.

Building materials and furnishings release a wide range of other VOCs which have been the subject of increasing concern during the 1980s and 1990s. The emission can be a complex mixture of individual compounds, though a few may be dominant. A study of 42 building materials identified 62 different chemical species. These VOCs were primarily aliphatic and aromatic hydrocarbons, their oxygen derivatives and terpenes. The compounds with the highest steady-state emission concentrations, in decreasing order, were toluene, *m*-xylene, terpene, *n*-butylacetate, *n*-butanol, *n*-hexane, *p*-xylene, ethoxyethylacetate, *n*-heptane and *o*-xylene. The complexity of emission has resulted in emissions and concentrations in air often being reported as the total volatile organic compound (TVOC) concentration or release. Table 44.3 gives examples of rates of TVOC emission for a range of building products. These show that significant differences in emissions exist between products, which means that if adequate data were available materials could be selected at the planning stage to minimize the VOC release in newly constructed buildings.

Wood preservatives have been shown to be a source of pentachlorophenol and lindane in the air and in dust within buildings. They are used primarily for timber protection for outdoor exposure and are also used in biocides applied for treatment of dry rot and insect control.

Consumer products and other indoor sources
The variety and number of consumer and household products change constantly, and their chemical emissions depend on use patterns. Products that may contribute to indoor VOC levels include aerosol products, personal hygiene products, solvents, adhesives and paints. Table 44.4 illustrates major chemical components in a range of consumer products.

Other VOCs have been associated with other sources. Chloroform is introduced into the indoor air chiefly as a result of dispensing or heating tap water. Liquid process copiers release isodecanes into the air. Insecticides used to control cockroaches, termites, fleas, flies, ants and mites are widely used as sprays, fogging devices, powders, impregnated strips, bait and pet collars. Compounds include diazinon, paradichlorobenzene, pentachlorophenol, chlordane, malathion, naphthalene and aldrin.

Other sources include occupants (carbon dioxide and odours), office equipment (VOCs and ozone), mould growth (VOCs, ammonia, carbon dioxide), contaminated land (methane, VOCs) and electronic air cleaners and negative ion generators (ozone).

Contribution from the external environment
Table 44.5 shows typical indoor-outdoor ratios for the major types of pollutant that occur in indoor air and average concentrations measured in outdoor air of urban areas in the United Kingdom. Sulphur dioxide in the indoor air is normally of outdoor origin and results from both natural and anthropogenic sources.

Table 44.4 • Components and emissions from consumer products and other sources of volatile organic compounds (VOC).

Source	Compound	Emission rate
Cleaning agents and pesticides	Chloroform	15 µg/m^2.h
	1,2-Dichloroethane	1.2 µg/m^2.h
	1,1,1-Trichloroethane	37 µg/m^2.h
	Carbon tetrachloride	71 µg/m^2.h
	m-Dichlorobenzene	0.6 µg/m^2.h
	p-Dichlorobenzene	0.4 µg/m^2.h
	n-Decane	0.2 µg/m^2.h
	n-Undecane	1.1 µg/m^2.h
Moth cake	*p*-Dichlorobenzene	14,000 µg/m^2.h
Dry-cleaned clothes	Tetrachloroethylene	0.5-1 mg/m^2.h
Liquid floor wax	TVOC (trimethylpentene and dodecane isomers)	96 g/m^2.h
Paste leather wax	TVOC (pinene and 2-methyl-1-propanol)	3.3 g/m^2.h
Detergent	TVOC (limonene, pinene and myrcene)	240 mg/m^2.h
Human emissions	Acetone	50.7 mg/day
	Acetaldehyde	6.2 mg/day
	Acetic acid	19.9 mg/day
	Methyl alcohol	74.4 mg/day
Copy paper	Formaldehyde	0.4 µg/form
Steam humidifier	Diethylaminoethanol, cyclohexylamine	—
Wet copy machine	2,2,4-Trimethylheptane	—
Household solvents	Toluene, ethyl benzene	—
Paint removers	Dichloromethane, methanol	—
Paint removers	Dichloromethane, toluene, propane	—
Fabric protector	1,1,1-Trichloroethane, propane, petroleum distillates	—
Latex paint	2-Propanol, butanone, ethylbenzene, toluene	—
Room freshener	Nonane, decane, ethylheptane, limonene	—
Shower water	Chloroform, trichloroethylene	—

Combustion of fossil fuels containing sulphur and smelting of sulphide ores are major sources of sulphur dioxide in the troposphere. Background levels are very low (1 ppb) but in urban areas maximum hourly concentrations may be 0.1 to 0.5 ppm. Sulphur dioxide can enter a building in air used for ventilation and can infiltrate through small gaps in the building structure. This depends upon the airtightness of the building, meteorological conditions and internal temperatures. Once inside, the incoming air will mix and be diluted by the indoor air. Sulphur dioxide that comes into contact with building and furnishing materials is adsorbed and this can significantly reduce the indoor concentration with respect to the outdoors, particularly when outdoor sulphur dioxide levels are high.

Nitrogen oxides are a product of combustion, and major sources include automobile exhaust, fossil fuel-fired electric generating stations and home space heaters. Nitric oxide (NO) is rela-

Table 44.5 • Major types of chemical indoor air contaminant and their concentrations in the urban United Kingdom.

Substance/group of substances	Ratio of concentrations indoors/outdoors	Typical urban concentrations
Sulphur dioxide	~0.5	10-20 ppb
Nitrogen dioxide	≤5-12 (indoor sources)	10-45 ppb
Ozone	0.1-0.3	15-60 ppb
Carbon dioxide	1-10	350 ppm
Carbon monoxide	≤5-11 (indoor source)	0.2-10 ppm
Formaldehyde	≤10	0.003 mg/m³
Other organic compounds	1-50	
Toluene		5.2 μg/m³
Benzene		6.3 μg/m³
m-and p-xylenes		5.6 μg/m³
Suspended particles	0.5-1 (excluding ETS[a]) 2-10 (including ETS)	50-150 μg/m³

[a] ETS, environmental tobacco smoke.

tively non-toxic but can be oxidized to nitrogen dioxide (NO_2), particularly during episodes of photochemical pollution. Background concentrations of nitrogen dioxide are about 1 ppb but may reach 0.5 ppm in urban areas. The outdoors is the major source of nitrogen dioxide in buildings without unvented fuel appliances. As with sulphur dioxide, adsorption by internal surfaces reduces the concentration indoors compared with that outdoors.

Ozone is produced in the troposphere by photochemical reactions in polluted atmospheres, and its generation is a function of intensity of sunlight and concentration of nitrogen oxides, reactive hydrocarbons and carbon monoxide. At remote sites, background ozone concentrations are 10 to 20 ppb and can exceed 120 ppb in urban areas in summer months. Indoor concentrations are significantly lower due to reaction with indoor surfaces and the lack of strong sources.

Carbon monoxide release as a result of anthropogenic activities is estimated to account for 30% of that present in the atmosphere of the northern hemisphere. Background levels are approximately 0.19 ppm and in urban areas a diurnal pattern of concentrations is related to use of the motor vehicle with peak hourly levels ranging from 3 ppm to 50 or 60 ppm. It is a relatively unreactive substance and so is not depleted by reaction or adsorption on indoor surfaces. Indoor sources such as unvented fuel appliances therefore add to the background level otherwise due to the outdoor air.

The indoor-outdoor relationship of organic compounds is compound-specific and may vary over time. For compounds with strong indoor sources such as formaldehyde, indoor concentrations are usually dominant. For formaldehyde outdoor concentrations are typically below 0.005 mg/m³ and indoor concentrations are ten times higher than outdoor values. Other compounds such as benzene have strong outdoor sources, petrol-driven vehicles being of particular importance. Indoor sources of benzene include ETS and these result in mean concentrations in buildings in the United Kingdom being 1.3 times higher than those outdoors. The indoor environment appears not to be a significant sink for this compound and it is therefore not protective against benzene from outdoors.

Typical Concentrations in Buildings

Carbon monoxide concentrations in indoor environments commonly range from 1 to 5 ppm. Table 44.6 summarizes results reported in 25 studies. Concentrations are higher in the presence of environmental tobacco smoke, though it is exceptional for concentrations to exceed 15 ppm.

Nitrogen dioxide concentrations indoors are typically 29 to 46 ppb. If particular sources such as gas stoves are present, concentrations may be significantly higher, and smoking can have a measurable effect (see table 44.6).

Many VOCs are present in the indoor environment at concentrations ranging from approximately 2 to 20 mg/m³. A US database containing 52,000 records on 71 chemicals in homes, public buildings and offices is summarized in figure 44.3. Environments where heavy smoking and/or poor ventilation create high concentrations of ETS can produce VOC concentrations of 50 to 200 mg/m³. Building materials make a significant contribution to indoor concentrations and new homes are likely to have a greater number of compounds exceeding 100 mg/m³. Renovation and painting contribute to significantly higher VOC levels. Concentrations of compounds such as ethyl acetate, 1,1,1-trichloroethane and limonene can exceed 20 mg/m³ during occupant activities, and during residents' absence the concentration of a range of VOCs may decrease by about 50%. Specific cases of elevated concentrations of contaminants due to materials and furnishings being associated with occupant complaints have been described. These include white spirit from injected damp-proof courses, naphthalene from products containing coal tar, ethylhexanol from vinyl flooring and formaldehyde from wood-based products.

The large number of individual VOCs occurring in buildings makes it difficult to detail concentrations for more than selected compounds. The concept of TVOC has been used as a measure of the mixture of compounds present. There is no widely used definition as to the range of compounds that the TVOC repre-

Table 44.6 • Summary of field measurements of nitrogen oxides (NO_x) and carbon monoxide (CO).

Site	NO_x values (ppb)	CO mean values (ppm)
Offices		
Smoking	42-51	1.0-2.8
Control	—	1.2-2.5
Other workplaces		
Smoking	ND[a]-82	1.4-4.2
Control	27	1.7-3.5
Transportation		
Smoking	150-330	1.6-33
Control	—	0-5.9
Restaurants and cafeterias		
Smoking	5-120	1.2-9.9
Control	4-115	0.5-7.1
Bars and taverns		
Smoking	195	3-17
Control	4-115	~1-9.2

[a] ND = not detected.

44. INDOOR AIR QUALITY

Figure 44.3 • Daily indoor concentrations of selected compounds for indoor sites.

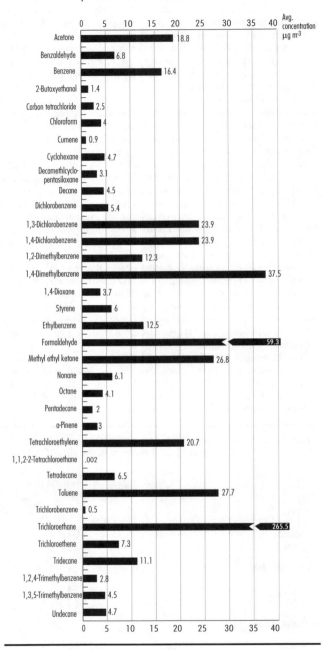

RADON

Mariá José Berenguer

Most of the radiation that a human being will be exposed to during a lifetime comes from natural sources in outer space or from materials present in the earth's crust. Radioactive materials may affect the organism from without or, if inhaled or ingested with food, from within. The dose received may be very variable because it depends, on the one hand, on the amount of radioactive minerals present in the area of the world where the person lives—which is related to the amount of radioactive nuclides in the air and the amount found both in food and especially in drinking water—and, on the other, on the use of certain construction materials and the use of gas or coal for fuel, as well as the type of construction employed and the traditional habits of people in the given locality.

Today, radon is considered the most prevalent source of natural radiation. Together with its "daughters", or radionuclides formed by its disintegration, radon constitutes approximately three fourths of the effective equivalent dose to which humans are exposed due to natural terrestrial sources. The presence of radon is associated with an increase in the occurrence of lung cancer due to the deposition of radioactive substances in the bronchial region.

Radon is a colourless, odourless and tasteless gas seven times as heavy as air. Two isotopes occur most frequently. One is radon-222, a radionuclide present in the radioactive series from the disintegration of uranium-238; its main source in the environment is the rocks and the soil in which its predecessor, radium-226, occurs. The other is radon-220 from the thorium radioactive series, which has a lower incidence than radon-222.

Uranium occurs extensively in the earth's crust. The median concentration of radium in soil is in the order of 25 Bq/kg. A Becquerel (Bq) is the unit of the international system and it represents a unit of radionuclide activity equivalent to one disintegration per second. The average concentration of radon gas in the atmosphere at the surface of the earth is 3 Bq/m^3, with a range of 0.1 (over the oceans) to 10 Bq/m^3. The level depends on the porousness of the soil, the local concentration of radium-226 and the atmospheric pressure. Given that the half-life of radon-222 is 3.823 days, most of the dosage is not caused by the gas but by radon daughters.

Radon is found in existing materials and flows from the earth everywhere. Because of its characteristics it disperses easily outdoors, but it has a tendency to become concentrated in enclosed spaces, notably in caves and buildings, and especially in lower spaces where its elimination is difficult without proper ventilation. In temperate regions, the concentrations of radon indoors are estimated to be in the order of eight times higher than the concentrations outdoors.

Exposure to radon by most of the population, therefore, occurs for the most part within buildings. The median concentrations of radon depend, basically, on the geological characteristics of the soil, on the construction materials used for the building and on the amount of ventilation it receives.

The main source of radon in indoor spaces is the radium present in the soil on which the building rests or the materials employed in its construction. Other significant sources—even though their relative influence is much less—are outside air, water and natural gas. Figure 44.4 shows the contribution that each source makes to the total.

The most common construction materials, such as wood, bricks and cinder blocks, emit relatively little radon, in contrast to granite and pumice-stone. However, the main problems are caused by the use of natural materials such as alum slate in the production

sents, but some investigators have proposed that limiting concentrations to below 300 mg/m^3 should minimize complaints by occupants about indoor air quality.

Pesticides used indoors are of relatively low volatility and concentrations occur in the low microgram-per-cubic-metre range. The volatilized compounds can contaminate dust and all indoor surfaces because of their low vapour pressures and tendency to be adsorbed by indoor materials. PAH concentrations in air are also strongly influenced by their distribution between the gas and aerosol phases. Smoking by occupants can have a strong effect on indoor air concentrations. Concentrations of PAHs range typically range from 0.1 to 99 ng/m^3.

Figure 44.4 • Sources of radon in the indoor environment.

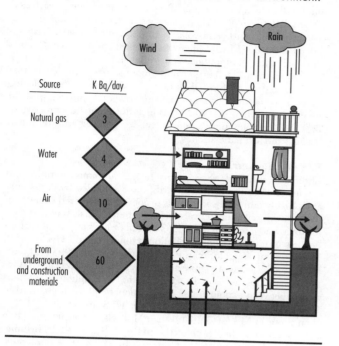

The reference values for radon in indoor spaces, and the remedial recommendations of various organizations are given in "Regulations, recommendations, guidelines and standards" in the chapter.

In conclusion, the main way to prevent exposures to radon is based on avoiding construction in areas that by their nature emit a greater amount of radon into the air. Where that is not possible, floors and walls should be properly sealed, and construction materials should not be used if they contain radioactive matter. Interior spaces, especially basements, should have an adequate amount of ventilation.

TOBACCO SMOKE

Dietrich Hoffmann and Ernst L. Wynder

In 1985 the Surgeon General of the US Public Health Service reviewed the health consequences of smoking with regard to cancer and chronic lung disease in the workplace. It was concluded that for most US workers, cigarette smoking represents a greater cause of death and disability than their workplace environment. However, the control of smoking and a reduction of the exposure to hazardous agents at the workplace are essential, since these factors often act synergistically with smoking in the induction and development of respiratory diseases. Several occupational exposures are known to induce chronic bronchitis in workers. These include exposures to dust from coal, cement and grain, to silica aerosols, to vapours generated during welding, and to sulphur dioxide. Chronic bronchitis among workers in these occupations is often aggravated by cigarette smoking (US Surgeon General 1985).

Epidemiological data have clearly documented that uranium miners and asbestos workers who smoke cigarettes carry significantly higher risks of cancer of the respiratory tract than non-smokers in these occupations. The carcinogenic effect of uranium and asbestos and cigarette smoking is not merely additive, but synergistic in inducing squamous cell carcinoma of the lung (US Surgeon General 1985; Hoffmann and Wynder 1976; Saccomanno, Huth and Auerbach 1988; Hilt et al. 1985). The carcinogenic effects of exposure to nickel, arsenicals, chromate, chloromethyl ethers, and those of cigarette smoking are at least additive (US Surgeon General 1985; Hoffmann and Wynder 1976; IARC 1987a, Pershagen et al. 1981). One would assume that coke-oven workers who smoke have a higher risk of lung and kidney cancer than non-smoking coke-oven workers; however, we lack epidemiological data that substantiate this concept (IARC 1987c).

It is the aim of this overview to evaluate the toxic effects of the exposure of men and women to environmental tobacco smoke (ETS) at the workplace. Certainly, curtailing smoking at the workplace will benefit active smokers by reducing their consumption of cigarettes during the workday, thereby increasing the possibility that they become ex-smokers; but smoking cessation will also be of benefit to those non-smokers who are allergic to tobacco smoke or who have pre-existing lung or heart ailments.

Physico-Chemical Nature of Environmental Tobacco Smoke

Mainstream and sidestream smoke
ETS is defined as the material in indoor air that originates from tobacco smoke. Although pipe and cigar smoking contribute to ETS, cigarette smoke is generally the major source. ETS is a composite aerosol that is emitted primarily from the burning cone of a tobacco product between puffs. This emission is called

of construction materials. Another source of problems has been the use of by-products from the treatment of phosphate minerals, the use of by-products from the production of aluminium, the use of dross or slag from the treatment of iron ore in blast furnaces, and the use of ashes from the combustion of coal. In addition, in some instances, residues derived from uranium mining were also used in construction.

Radon can enter water and natural gas in the subsoil. The water used to supply a building, especially if it is from deep wells, may contain significant amounts of radon. If this water is used for cooking, boiling can free a large part of the radon it contains. If the water is consumed cold, the body eliminates the gas readily, so that drinking this water does not generally pose a significant risk. Burning natural gas in stoves without chimneys, in heaters and in other home appliances can also lead to an increase of radon in indoor spaces, especially dwellings. Sometimes the problem is more acute in bathrooms, because radon in water and in the natural gas used for the water heater accumulates if there is not enough ventilation.

Given that the possible effects of radon on the population at large were unknown just a few years ago, the data available on concentrations found in indoor spaces are limited to those countries which, because of their characteristics or special circumstances, are more sensitized to this problem. What is known for a fact is that it is possible to find concentrations in indoor spaces that are far above the concentrations found outdoors in the same region. In Helsinki (Finland), for instance, concentrations of radon in indoor air have been found that are five thousand times higher than the concentrations normally found outdoors. This may be due in large part to energy-saving measures that can noticeably favour the concentration of radon in indoor spaces, especially if they are heavily insulated. Buildings studied so far in different countries and regions show that the concentrations of radon found within them present a distribution that approximates the normal log. It is worth noting that a small number of the buildings in each region show concentrations ten times above the median.

Table 44.7 • Some toxic and tumorigenic agents in undiluted cigarette sidestream smoke.

Compound	Type of toxicity[a]	Amount in sidestream smoke per cigarette	Ratio of side-stream to main-stream smoke
Vapour phase			
Carbon monoxide	T	26.80-61 mg	2.5-14.9
Carbonyl sulphide	T	2-3 µg	0.03-0.13
1,3-Butadiene	C	200-250 µg	3.8-10.8
Benzene	C	240-490 µg	8-10
Formaldehyde	C	300-1,500 µg	10-50
Acrolein	T	40-100 µg	8-22
3-Vinylpyridine	T	330-450 µg	24-34
Hydrogen cyanide	T	14-110 µg	0.06-0.4
Hydrazine	C	90 ng	3
Nitrogen oxides (NO$_x$)	T	500-2,000 µg	3.7-12.8
N-Nitrosodimethylamine	C	200-1,040 ng	12-440
N-Nitrosodiethylamine	C	ND[b]-1,000 ng	<40
N-Nitrosopyrrolidine	C	7-700 ng	4-120
Particulate phase			
Tar	C	14-30 mg	1.1-15.7
Nicotine	T	2.1-46 mg	1.3-21
Phenol	TP	70-250 µg	1.3-3.0
Catechol	CoC	58-290 µg	0.67-12.8
2-Toluidine	C	2.0-3.9 µg	18-70
β-Naphthylamine	C	19-70 ng	8.0-39
4-Aminobiphenyl	C	3.5-6.9 ng	7.0-30
Benz[a]anthracene	C	40-200 ng	2-4
Benzo[a]pyrene	C	40-70 ng	2.5-20
Quinoline	C	15-20 µg	8-11
NNN[c]	C	0.15-1.7 µg	0.5-5.0
NNK[d]	C	0.2-1.4 µg	1.0-22
N-Nitrosodiethanolamine	C	43 ng	1.2
Cadmium	C	0.72 µg	7.2
Nickel	C	0.2-2.5 µg	13-30
Zinc	T	6.0 ng	6.7
Polonium-210	C	0.5-1.6 pCi	1.06-3.7

[a] C=Carcinogenic; CoC=co-carcinogenic; T=toxic; TP=tumour promoter. [b] ND=not detected.
[c] NNN=N'-nitrosonornicotine. [d] NNK=4-(methylnitrosamino)-1-(3-pyridyl)-1-butanone.

sidestream smoke (SS). To a minor extent, ETS consists also of mainstream smoke (MS) constituents, that is, those that are exhaled by the smoker. Table 44.7 lists the ratios of major toxic and carcinogenic agents in the smoke that is inhaled, the mainstream smoke, and in the sidestream smoke (Hoffmann and Hecht 1990; Brunnemann and Hoffmann 1991; Guerin et al. 1992; Luceri et al. 1993). Under "Type of toxicity", smoke components marked "C" represent animal carcinogens that are recognized by the

International Agency for Research on Cancer (IARC). Among these are benzene, β-naphthylamine, 4-aminobiphenyl and polonium-210, which are also established human carcinogens (IARC 1987a; IARC 1988). When filter cigarettes are being smoked, certain volatile and semi-volatile components are selectively removed from the MS by filter tips (Hoffmann and Hecht 1990). However, these compounds occur in far higher amounts in undiluted SS than in MS. Furthermore, those smoke components that are favoured to be formed during smouldering in the reducing atmosphere of the burning cone, are released into SS to a far greater extent than into MS. This includes groups of carcinogens like the volatile nitrosamines, tobacco-specific nitrosamines (TSNA) and aromatic amines.

ETS in indoor air

Although undiluted SS contains higher amounts of toxic and carcinogenic components than MS, the SS inhaled by non-smokers is highly diluted by air and its properties are altered because of the decay of certain reactive species. Table 44.8 lists reported data for toxic and carcinogenic agents in indoor air samples of various degrees of tobacco smoke pollution (Hoffmann and Hecht 1990; Brunnemann and Hoffmann 1991; Luceri et al. 1993). The air dilution of SS has a significant impact on the physical characteristics of this aerosol. In general, the distribution of various agents between vapour phase and particulate phase is changed in favour of the former. The particles in ETS are smaller (<0.2 µ) than those in MS (~0.3 µ) and the pH levels of SS (pH 6.8 – 8.0) and of ETS are higher than the pH of MS (5.8 – 6.2; Brunnemann and Hoffmann 1974). Consequently, 90 to 95% of nicotine is present in the vapour phase of ETS (Eudy et al. 1986). Similarly, other basic components such as the minor Nicotiana alkaloids, as well as amines and ammonia, are present mostly in the vapour phase of ETS (Hoffmann and Hecht 1990; Guerin et al. 1992).

Biomarkers of the Uptake of ETS by Non-Smokers

Although a significant number of non-smoking workers are exposed to ETS at the workplace, in restaurants, in their own homes or in other indoor places, it is hardly possible to estimate the actual uptake of ETS by an individual. ETS exposure can be more precisely determined by measuring specific smoke constituents or their metabolites in physiological fluids or in exhaled air. Although several parameters have been explored, such as CO in exhaled air, carboxyhaemoglobin in blood, thiocyanate (a metabolite of hydrogen cyanide) in saliva or urine, or hydroxyproline and N-nitrosoproline in urine, only three measures are actually helpful for estimating the uptake of ETS by non-smokers. They allow us to distinguish passive smoke exposure from that of active smokers and from non-smokers who have absolutely no exposure to tobacco smoke.

The most widely used biomarker for ETS exposure of non-smokers is cotinine, a major nicotine metabolite. It is determined by gas chromatography, or by radioimmunoassay in blood or preferably urine, and reflects the absorption of nicotine through the lung and oral cavity. A few millilitres of urine from passive smokers is sufficient to determine cotinine by either of the two methods. In general, a passive smoker has cotinine levels of 5 to 10 ng/ml of urine; however, higher values have occasionally been measured for non-smokers who were exposed to heavy ETS over a longer period. A dose response has been established between duration of ETS exposure and urinary cotinine excretion (table 44.9, Wald et al. 1984). In most field studies, cotinine in the urine of passive smokers amounted to between 0.1 and 0.3% of the mean concentrations found in the urine of smokers; however, upon prolonged exposure to high concentrations of ETS, cotinine levels have corresponded to as much as 1% of the levels measured

Table 44.8 • Some toxic and tumorigenic agents in indoor environments polluted by tobacco smoke.

Pollutant	Location	Concentration/m³
Nitric oxide	Workrooms	50-440 μg
	Restaurants	17-240 μg
	Bars	80-250 μg
	Cafeterias	2.5-48 μg
Nitrogen dioxide	Workrooms	68-410 μg
	Restaurants	40-190 μg
	Bars	2-116 μg
	Cafeterias	67-200 μg
Hydrogen cyanide	Living-rooms	8-122 μg
1,3-Butadiene	Bars	2.7-4.5 μg
Benzene	Public places	20-317 μg
Formaldehyde	Living-rooms	2.3-5.0 μg
	Taverns	89-104 μg
Acrolein	Public places	30-120 μg
Acetone	Coffee houses	910-1,400 μg
Phenols (volatile)	Coffee houses	7.4-11.5 ng
N-Nitrosodimethylamine	Bars, restaurants, offices	<10-240 ng
N-Nitrosodiethylamine	Restaurants	<10-30 ng
Nicotine	Residences	0.5-21 μg
	Offices	1.1-36.6 μg
	Public buildings	1.0-22 μg
2-Toluidine	Offices	3.0-12.8 ng
	Cardroom with smokers	16.9 ng
β-Naphthylamine	Offices	0.27-0.34 ng
	Cardroom with smokers	0.47 ng
4-Aminobiphenyl	Offices	0.1 ng
	Cardroom with smokers	0.11 ng
Benz (a)anthracene	Restaurants	1.8-9.3 ng
Benzo (a)pyrene	Restaurants	2.8-760 μg
	Smokers' rooms	88-214 μg
	Living-rooms	10-20 μg
NNN[a]	Bars	4.3-22.8 ng
	Restaurants	ND[b]-5.7 ng
NNK[c]	Bars	9.6-23.8 ng
	Restaurants	1.4-3.3 ng
	Cars with smokers	29.3 ng

[a] NNN=N'-nitrosonornicotine.
[b] ND=not detected.
[c] NNK=4-(methylnitrosamino)-1-(3-pyridyl)-1-butanone.

Table 44.9 • Urinary cotinine in non-smokers according to the number of reported hours of exposure to other people's tobacco smoke within the previous seven days.

Duration of exposure		Number	Urinary cotinine (mean ± SD) (ng/ml)[a]
Quintile	Limits (hrs)		
1st	0.0-1.5	43	2.8±3.0
2nd	1.5-4.5	47	3.4±2.7
3rd	4.5-8.6	43	5.3±4.3
4th	8.6-20.0	43	14.7±19.5
5th	20.0-80.0	45	29.6±73.7
All	0.0-80.0	221	11.2±35.6

[a] Trend with increasing exposure was significant (p<0.001).
Source: Based on Wald et al. 1984.

in the urine of active smokers (US National Research Council 1986; IARC 1987b; US Environmental Protection Agency 1992). The human bladder carcinogen 4-aminobiphenyl, which transfers from tobacco smoke into ETS, has been detected as a haemoglobin adduct in passive smokers in concentrations up to 10% of the mean adduct level found in smokers (Hammond et al. 1993). Up to 1% of the mean levels of a metabolite of the nicotine-derived carcinogen 4-(methylnitrosamino)-1-(3-pyridyl)-1-butanone (NNK), which occurs in the urine of cigarette smokers, has been measured in the urine of non-smokers who had been exposed to high concentrations of SS in a test laboratory (Hecht et al. 1993). Although the latter biomarker method has not as yet been applied in field studies, it holds promise as a suitable indicator of the exposure of non-smokers to a tobacco-specific lung carcinogen.

Environmental Tobacco Smoke and Human Health

Disorders other than cancer

Prenatal exposure to MS and/or ETS and early postnatal exposure to ETS increase the probability of complications during viral respiratory infections in children during the first year of life.

The scientific literature contains several dozens of clinical reports from various countries, reporting that children of parents who smoke, especially children under the age of two years, show an excess of acute respiratory illness (US Environmental Protection Agency 1992; US Surgeon General 1986; Medina et al. 1988; Riedel et al. 1989). Several studies also described an increase of middle ear infections in children who had exposure to parental cigarette smoke. The increased prevalence of middle ear effusion attributable to ETS led to increased hospitalization of young children for surgical intervention (US Environmental Protection Agency 1992; US Surgeon General 1986).

In recent years, sufficient clinical evidence has led to the conclusion that passive smoking is associated with increased severity of asthma in those children who already have the disease, and that it most likely leads to new cases of asthma in children (US Environmental Protection Agency 1992).

In 1992, the US Environmental Protection Agency (1992) critically reviewed the studies on respiratory symptoms and lung functions in adult non-smokers exposed to ETS, concluding that passive smoking has subtle but statistically significant effects on the respiratory health of non-smoking adults.

A search of the literature on the effect of passive smoking on respiratory or coronary diseases in workers revealed only a few studies. Men and women who were exposed to ETS at the workplace (offices, banks, academic institutions, etc.) for ten or more years had impaired pulmonary function (White and Froeb 1980; Masi et al. 1988).

Lung cancer

In 1985, the International Agency for Research on Cancer (IARC) reviewed the association of passive tobacco smoke exposure with lung cancer in non-smokers. Although in some studies, each non-smoker with lung cancer who had reported ETS exposure was personally interviewed and had supplied detailed information on exposure (US National Research Council 1986; US EPA 1992; US Surgeon General 1986; Kabat and Wynder 1984), the IARC concluded:

The observations on non-smokers that have been made so far, are compatible with either an increased risk from 'passive' smoking, or an absence of risk. Knowledge of the nature of sidestream and mainstream smoke, of the materials absorbed during 'passive' smoking and of the quantitative relationship between dose and effect that are commonly observed from exposure to carcinogens, however, leads to the conclusion that passive smoking gives rise to some risk of cancer (IARC 1986).

Thus, there is an apparent dichotomy between experimental data which support the concept that ETS gives rise to some risk of cancer, and epidemiological data, which are not conclusive with respect to ETS exposure and cancer. Experimental data, including biomarker studies, have further strengthened the concept that ETS is carcinogenic, as was discussed earlier. We will now discuss how far the epidemiological studies that have been completed since the cited IARC report have contributed to a clarification of the ETS lung cancer issue.

According to the earlier epidemiological studies, and in about 30 studies reported after 1985, ETS exposure of non-smokers constituted a risk factor for lung cancer of less than 2.0, relative to the risk of a non-smoker without significant ETS exposure (US Environmental Protection Agency 1992; Kabat and Wynder 1984; IARC 1986; Brownson et al. 1992; Brownson et al. 1993). Few, if any, of these epidemiological studies meet the criteria of causality in the association between an environmental or occupational factor and lung cancer. Criteria that fulfil these requirements are:

1. a well-established degree of association (risk factor ≥3)
2. reproducibility of the observation by a number of studies
3. agreement between duration of exposure and effect
4. biological plausibility.

One of the major uncertainties about the epidemiological data lies in the limited reliability of the answers obtained by questioning cases and/or their next-of-kin with regard to the smoking habits of the cases. It appears that there is generally an accord between parental and spousal smoking histories provided by cases and controls; however, there are low agreement rates for duration and intensity of smoking (Brownson et al. 1993; McLaughlin et al. 1987; McLaughlin et al. 1990). Some investigators have challenged the reliability of the information derived from individuals about their smoking status. This is exemplified by a large-scale investigation carried out in southern Germany. A randomly selected study population consisted of more than 3,000 men and women, ranging in age from 25 to 64 years. These same people were questioned three times in 1984-1985, in 1987-1988 and again in 1989-1990 as to their smoking habits, while each time urine was collected from each proband and was analysed for cotinine. Those volunteers who were found to have more than 20 ng of cotinine per ml of urine were considered to be smokers. Among 800 ex-smokers who claimed to be non-smokers, 6.3%, 6.5% and 5.2% had cotinine levels above 20 ng/ml during the three time periods tested. The self-proclaimed never-smokers, who were identified as actual smokers according to cotinine analyses, constituted 0.5%, 1.0% and 0.9%, respectively (Heller et al. 1993).

The limited reliability of the data obtained by questionnaire, and the relatively limited number of non-smokers with lung cancer who were not exposed to carcinogens at their workplaces, point to the need for a prospective epidemiological study with assessment of biomarkers (e.g., cotinine, metabolites of polynu-

clear aromatic hydrocarbons, and/or metabolites of NNK in urine) to bring about a conclusive evaluation of the question on causality between involuntary smoking and lung cancer. While such prospective studies with biomarkers represent a major task, they are essential in order to answer the questions on exposure which have major public health implications.

Environmental Tobacco Smoke and the Occupational Environment

Although epidemiological studies have thus far not demonstrated a causal association between ETS exposure and lung cancer, it is nevertheless highly desirable to protect workers at the site of employment from exposure to environmental tobacco smoke. This concept is supported by the observation that long-term exposure of non-smokers to ETS at the workplace can lead to reduced pulmonary function. Furthermore, in occupational environments with exposure to carcinogens, involuntary smoking may increase the risk of cancer. In the United States, the Environmental Protection Agency has classified ETS as a Group A (known human) carcinogen; therefore, the law in the United States requires that employees be protected against exposure to ETS.

Several measures can be taken to protect the non-smoker from exposure to ETS: prohibiting smoking at the worksite, or at least separating smokers from non-smokers where possible, and assuring that the smokers' rooms have a separate exhaust system. The most rewarding and by far the most promising approach is to assist employees who are cigarette smokers in cessation efforts.

The worksite can offer excellent opportunities for implementing smoking cessation programmes; in fact, numerous studies have shown that worksite programmes are more successful than clinic-based programmes, because employer-sponsored programmes are more intense in nature and they offer economic and/or other incentives (US Surgeon General 1985). It is also indicated that the elimination of occupationally related chronic lung diseases and cancer frequently cannot proceed without efforts to convert the workers into ex-smokers. Furthermore, worksite interventions, including smoking cessation programmes, can produce lasting changes in reducing some cardiovascular risk factors for the employees (Gomel et al. 1993).

We greatly appreciate the editorial assistance of Ilse Hoffmann and the preparation of this manuscript by Jennifer Johnting. These studies are supported by USPHS Grants CA-29580 and CA-32617 from the National Cancer Institute.

SMOKING REGULATIONS

Xavier Guardino Solá

In regard to taking action to reduce the use of tobacco, governments should keep in mind that while people decide on their own whether they should stop smoking, it is a government's responsibility to take all the necessary measures to encourage them to stop. The steps taken by legislators and governments of many countries have been indecisive, because while the reduction in the use of tobacco is an undisputed improvement in public health—with attendant savings in public health expenditures—there would be a series of economic losses and dislocations in many sectors, at least of a temporary nature. The pressure that international health and environmental organizations and agencies can exert in this regard is very important, because many countries may water down measures against the use of tobacco because of economic problems—especially if tobacco is an important source of income.

This article briefly describes regulatory measures that can be adopted to reduce smoking in a country.

Warnings on Cigarette Packs

One of the first measures adopted in many countries is to require that cigarette packs prominently display the warning that smoking seriously injures the smoker's health. This warning, whose aim is not so much to exert an immediate effect on the smoker, but rather to show that the government is concerned about the problem, is creating a psychological climate that will favour the adoption of later measures that otherwise would be considered aggressive by the smoking population.

Some experts advocate the inclusion of these warnings on cigars and pipe tobacco. But the more general opinion is that those warnings are unnecessary, because people who use that type of tobacco do not normally inhale the smoke, and extending these warnings would lead more likely to a disregard of the messages as a whole. This is why the prevalent opinion is that the warnings should be applied only to cigarette packs. A reference to second-hand smoke has not, for the moment, been considered, but it is not an option that should be discarded.

Smoking Restrictions in Public Spaces

Forbidding smoking in public spaces is one of the most effective regulatory instruments. These prohibitions can significantly reduce the number of people exposed to second-hand smoke and, in addition, can reduce smokers' daily cigarette consumption. The common complaints by owners of public spaces, such as hotels, restaurants, recreational facilities, dance halls, theatres and so forth, are based on the argument that these measures will result in a loss of customers. However, if governments implement these measures across the board, the negative impact of a loss of clientele will occur only in the first phase, because people will eventually adapt to the new situation.

Another possibility is the design of specific spaces for smokers. The separation of smokers from non-smokers should be effective in order to obtain the desired benefits, creating barriers that prevent non-smokers from inhaling tobacco smoke. Separation must thus be physical and, if the air-conditioning system uses recycled air, the air from smoking areas should not be mixed with that from non-smoking areas. Creating spaces for smokers therefore implies construction and compartmentalization expenses, but may be a solution for those who want to serve the smoking public.

Aside from locations where smoking is obviously forbidden for security reasons because of possible explosion or fire, there should also be areas—such as health care and sports facilities, schools and day-care centres—where smoking is not permitted even though there are no safety risks of that kind.

Smoking Restrictions at Work

Smoking restrictions in the workplace may also be considered in light of the above. Governments and business owners, together with trade unions, can establish programmes to reduce the use of tobacco at work. Campaigns to curtail smoking at work are generally successful.

Whenever possible, creating non-smoking areas to establish a policy against tobacco use and to support people who defend the right not to be second-hand smokers is recommended. In case of a conflict between a smoker and a non-smoker, regulations should always allow the non-smoker to prevail, and whenever they cannot be separated, the smoker should be pressured to abstain from smoking at the workstation.

In addition to places where for health or safety reasons smoking should be forbidden, the possibility of synergism between the effects of chemical pollution in the workplace and tobacco smoke should not be ignored in other areas either. The weight of such considerations will result, without a doubt, in a broad extension of smoking restrictions, especially in industrial workplaces.

Greater Economic Pressure against Tobacco

Another regulatory tool governments rely on to curb the use of tobacco is levying higher taxes, chiefly on cigarettes. This policy is intended to lead to lower tobacco consumption, which would justify the inverse relation between the price of tobacco and its consumption and which can be measured when comparing the situation in different countries. It is considered effective where the population is forewarned of the dangers of tobacco use and advised of the need to stop consuming it. An increase in the price of tobacco can be a motivation to quit smoking. This policy, however, has many opponents, who base their criticisms on arguments briefly mentioned below.

In the first place, according to many specialists, the increase in the price of tobacco for fiscal reasons is followed by a temporary reduction in the use of tobacco, followed by a gradual return to the previous consumption levels as the smokers get used to the new price. In other words, smokers assimilate a rise in the price of tobacco much in the same way that people get used to other taxes or to the rise in the cost of living.

In the second place, a shift in the habits of smokers has also been observed. When prices go up they tend to seek out cheaper brands of lower quality that probably also pose a greater risk to their health (because they lack filters or have higher amounts of tar and nicotine). This shift may go so far as to induce smokers to adopt the practice of making home-made cigarettes, which would completely eliminate any possibility of controlling the problem.

In the third place, many experts are of the opinion that measures of this kind tend to bolster the belief that the government accepts tobacco and its consumption as yet another means to collect taxes, leading to the contradictory belief that what the government really wants is that people smoke so that it can collect more money with the special tax on tobacco.

Limiting Publicity

Another weapon used by governments to reduce tobacco consumption is to restrict or simply forbid any publicity for the product. Governments and many international organizations have a policy of forbidding publicity for tobacco in certain spheres, such as sports (at least some sports), health care, the environment, and education. This policy has unquestionable benefits, which are especially effective when it eliminates publicity in those environments that affect young people at a time when they are likely to take up the smoking habit.

Public Programmes that Encourage People to Quit Smoking

The use of anti-smoking campaigns as a normal practice, adequately funded and organized as a rule of conduct in certain spheres, such as the world of work, has been shown to be highly successful.

Campaigns to Educate Smokers

Complementing what was said above, educating smokers so that they will smoke "better" and cut down on their consumption of cigarettes is another avenue available to governments to reduce the adverse health effects of tobacco use on the population. These efforts should be directed at reducing the daily consumption of cigarettes, at inhibiting the inhalation of smoke as much as possible, at not smoking the butts of cigarettes (the toxicity of smoke increases towards the end of the cigarette), at not keeping the cigarette steadily at the lips, and at adopting preferences for brands with lower tar and nicotine.

44. INDOOR AIR QUALITY

Measures of this type evidently do not reduce the number of smokers, but they do reduce how much smokers are harmed by their habit. There are arguments against this type of remedy because it may give the impression that smoking is not intrinsically a bad habit, since smokers are told how best to smoke.

Concluding Remarks

Regulatory and legislative action by different governments is slow and not sufficiently effective, especially given what would be required due to the problems caused by tobacco use. Often this is the case because of legal hurdles against implementing such measures, arguments against unfair competition, or even the protection of the individual's right to smoke. Progress in the use of regulations has been slow but it is nonetheless steady. On the other hand, the difference between active smokers and second-hand or passive smokers should be kept in mind. All the measures that would help someone to stop smoking, or at least to reduce daily consumption effectively, should be directed at the smoker; all the weight of regulations should be brought to bear against this habit. The passive smoker should be given every possible argument to support his or her right not to inhale tobacco smoke, and to defend the right to enjoy the use of smoke-free environments at home, at work and at play.

● MEASURING AND ASSESSING CHEMICAL POLLUTANTS

M. Gracia Rosell Farrás

From the standpoint of pollution, indoor air in non-industrial situations displays several characteristics that differentiate it from outside, or atmospheric, air and from the air in industrial workplaces. Besides contaminants found in atmospheric air, indoor air also includes contaminants generated by building materials and by the activities that take place within the building. The concentrations of contaminants in indoor air tend to be the same or less than concentrations found in outside air, depending on ventilation; contaminants generated by building materials are usually different from those found in outside air and can be found in high concentrations, while those generated by activities inside the building depend on the nature of such activities and may be the same as those found in outside air, as in the case of CO and CO_2.

For this reason, the number of contaminants found in non-industrial inside air is large and varied and the levels of concentration are low (except for instances where there is an important generating source); they vary according to atmospheric/climatologic conditions, the type or characteristics of the building, its ventilation and the activities carried out within it.

Analysis

Much of the methodology used to gauge the quality of indoor air stems from industrial hygiene and from measurements of immission of outdoor air. There are few analytic methods validated specifically for this type of testing, although some organizations, such as the World Health Organization and the Environmental Protection Agency in the United States are conducting research in this field. An additional obstacle is the paucity of information on the exposure-effect relationship when dealing with long-term exposures to low concentrations of pollutants.

The analytical methods used for industrial hygiene are designed to measure high concentrations and have not been defined for many pollutants, while the number of contaminants in indoor air can be large and varied and the levels of concentration can be low, except in certain cases. Most methods used in industrial hygiene are based on the taking of samples and their analysis; many of these methods can be applied to indoor air if several factors are taken into account: adjusting the methods to the typical concentrations; increasing their sensitivity without detriment to precision (for example, increasing the volume of air tested); and validating their specificity.

The analytical methods used to measure concentrations of pollutants in outdoor air are similar to those used for indoor air, and therefore some can be used directly for indoor air while others can be easily adapted. However, it is important to keep in mind that some methods are designed for a direct reading of one sample, while others require bulky and sometimes noisy instrumentation and use large volumes of sampled air which can distort the reading.

Planning the Readings

The traditional procedure in the field of workplace environmental control can be used to improve the quality of indoor air. It consists of identifying and quantifying a problem, proposing corrective measures, making sure that these measures are implemented, and then assessing their effectiveness after a period of time. This common procedure is not always the most adequate because often such an exhaustive evaluation, including the taking of many samples, is not necessary. Exploratory measures, which can range from a visual inspection to assaying of ambient air by direct reading methods, and which can provide an approximate concentration of pollutants, are sufficient for solving many of the existing problems. Once corrective measures have been taken, the results can be evaluated with a second measurement, and only when there is no clear evidence of an improvement a more thorough inspection (with in-depth measurements) or a complete analytical study can be undertaken (Swedish Work Environment Fund 1988).

The main advantages of such an exploratory procedure over the more traditional one are economy, speed and effectiveness. It requires competent and experienced personnel and the use of suitable equipment. Figure 44.5 summarizes the goals of the different stages of this procedure.

Figure 44.5 ● Planning the readings for exploratory evaluation.

TYPE OF MEASUREMENT	GOAL
Exploratory reading 	● Assessment of environmental situation ● Detection of obvious adverse condition ● Corrective action ● Preparation of in-depth readings
In-depth readings 	● Detailing of environmental problems ● Gathering of data as a basis for further action ● Development of new techniques ● Improvements in methodology
Readings for verification 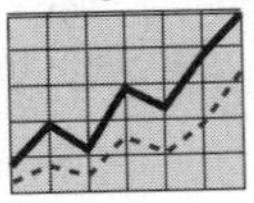	● Evaluation of actions taken ● Fulfillment of the recommended goals

Sampling Strategy

Analytical control of the quality of indoor air should be considered as a last resort only after the exploratory measurement has not given positive results, or if further evaluation or control of the initial tests is needed.

Assuming some previous knowledge of the sources of pollution and of the types of contaminants, the samples, even when limited in number, should be representative of the various spaces studied. Sampling should be planned to answer the questions What? How? Where? and When?

What

The pollutants in question must be identified in advance and, keeping in mind the different types of information that can be obtained, one should decide whether to make *emission* or *immission* measurements.

Emission measurements for indoor air quality can determine the influence of different sources of pollution, of climatic conditions, of the building's characteristics, and of human intervention, which allow us to control or reduce the sources of emissions and improve the quality of indoor air. There are different techniques for taking this type of measurement: placing a collection system adjacent to the source of the emission, defining a limited work area and studying emissions as if they represented general working conditions, or working in simulated conditions applying monitoring systems that rely on head space measures.

Immission measurements allow us to determine the level of indoor air pollution in the different compartmentalized areas of the building, making it possible to produce a map of pollution for the entire structure. Using these measurements and identifying the different areas where people have carried out their activities and calculating the time they have spent at each task, it will be possible to determine the levels of exposure. Another way of doing this is by having individual workers wear monitoring devices while working.

It may be more practical, if the number of pollutants is large and varied, to select a few representative substances so that the reading is representative and not too expensive.

How

Selecting the type of reading to be made will depend on the available method (direct reading or sample-taking and analysis) and on the measuring technique: emission or immission.

Where

The location selected should be the most appropriate and representative for obtaining samples. This requires knowledge of the building being studied: its orientation relative to the sun, the number of hours it receives direct sunlight, the number of floors, the type of compartmentalization, if ventilation is natural or forced air, if its windows can be opened, and so on. Knowing the source of the complaints and the problems is also necessary, for example, whether they occur in the upper or the lower floors, or in the areas close to or far from the windows, or in the areas that have poor ventilation or illumination, among other locations. Selecting the best sites to draw the samples will be based on all of the available information regarding the above-mentioned criteria.

When

Deciding when to take the readings will depend on how concentrations of air pollutants change relative to time. Pollution may be detected first thing in the morning, during the workday or at the end of the day; it may be detected at the beginning or the end of the week; during the winter or the summer; when air-conditioning is on or off; as well as at other times.

To address these questions properly, the dynamics of the given indoor environment must be known. It is also necessary to know the goals of the measurements taken, which will be based on the types of pollutant that are being investigated. The dynamics of indoor environments are influenced by the diversity of the sources of pollution, the physical differences in the spaces involved, the type of compartmentalization, the type of ventilation and climate control used, outside atmospheric conditions (wind, temperature, season, etc.), and the building's characteristics (number of windows, their orientation, etc.).

The goals of the measurements will determine if sampling will be carried out for short or long intervals. If the health effects of the given contaminants are thought to be long-term, it follows that average concentrations should be measured over long periods of time. For substances that have acute but not cumulative effects, measurements over short periods are sufficient. If intense emissions of short duration are suspected, frequent sampling over short periods is called for in order to detect the time of the emission. Not to be overlooked, however, is the fact that in many cases the possible choices in the type of sampling methods used may be determined by the analytical methods available or required.

If after considering all these questions it is not sufficiently clear what the source of the problem is, or when the problem occurs with greatest frequency, the decision as to where and when to take samples must be made at random, calculating the number of samples as a function of the expected reliability and cost.

Measuring techniques

The methods available for taking samples of indoor air and for their analysis can be grouped into two types: methods that involve a direct reading and those that involve taking samples for later analysis.

Methods based on a direct reading are those by which taking the sample and measuring the concentration of pollutants is done simultaneously; they are fast and the measurement is instantaneous, allowing for precise data at a relatively low cost. This group includes *colorimetric tubes* and *specific monitors*.

The use of colorimetric tubes is based on the change in the colour of a specific reactant when it comes in contact with a given pollutant. The most commonly used are tubes that contain a solid reactant and air is drawn through them using a manual pump. Assessing the quality of indoor air with colorimetric tubes is useful only for exploratory measurements and for measuring sporadic emissions since their sensitivity is generally low, except for some pollutants such as CO and CO_2 that can be found at high concentrations in indoor air. It is important to keep in mind that the precision of this method is low and interference from unlooked-for contaminants is often a factor.

In the case of specific monitors, detection of pollutants is based on physical, electric, thermal, electromagnetic and chemoelectromagnetic principles. Most monitors of this type can be used to make measurements of short or long duration and gain a profile of contamination at a given site. Their precision is determined by their respective manufacturers and proper use demands periodic calibrations by means of controlled atmospheres or certified gas mixtures. Monitors are becoming increasingly precise and their sensitivity more refined. Many have built-in memory to store the readings, which can then be downloaded to computers for the creation of databases and the easy organization and retrieval of the results.

Sampling methods and analyses can be classified into *active* (or dynamic) and *passive*, depending on the technique.

Table 44.10 • Methodology for taking samples.

Characteristics	Active	Passive	Direct reading
Timed interval measurements	+		+
Long-term measurements		+	+
Monitoring			+
Concentration of sample	+	+	
Immission measurement	+	+	+
Emission measurement	+	+	+
Immediate response			+

+ Means that the given method is suitable to the method of measurement or desired measurement criteria.

With active systems, this pollution can be collected by forcing air through collecting devices in which the pollutant is captured, concentrating the sample. This is accomplished with filters, adsorbent solids, and absorbent or reactive solutions which are placed in bubblers or are impregnated onto porous material. Air is then forced through and the contaminant, or the products of its reaction, are analysed. For the analysis of air sampled with active systems the requirements are a fixative, a pump to move the air and a system to measure the volume of sampled air, either directly or by using flow and duration data.

The flow and the volume of sampled air are specified in the reference manuals or should be determined by previous tests and will depend on the quantity and type of absorbent or adsorbent used, the pollutants that are being measured, the type of measurement (emission or immission) and the condition of the ambient air during the taking of the sample (humidity, temperature, pressure). The efficacy of the collection increases by reducing the rate of intake or by increasing the amount of fixative used, directly or in tandem.

Another type of active sampling is the direct capture of air in a bag or any other inert and impermeable container. This type of sample gathering is used for some gases (CO, CO_2, H_2S, O_2) and is useful as an exploratory measure when the type of pollutant is unknown. The drawback is that without concentrating the sample there may be insufficient sensitivity and further laboratory processing may be necessary to increase the concentration.

Passive systems capture pollutants by diffusion or permeation onto a base that may be a solid adsorbent, either alone or impregnated with a specific reactant. These systems are more convenient and easy to use than active systems. They do not require pumps to capture the sample nor highly trained personnel. But capturing the sample may take a long time and the results tend to furnish only medium concentration levels. This method cannot be used to measure peak concentrations; in those instances active systems should be used instead. To use passive systems correctly it is important to know the speed at which each pollutant is captured, which will depend on the diffusion coefficient of the gas or vapour and the design of the monitor.

Table 44.11 • Detection methods for gases in indoor air.

Pollutant	Direct reading	Methods — Capture by diffusion	Methods — Capture by concentration	Methods — Direct capture	Analysis
Carbon monoxide	Electrochemical cell Infrared spectroscopy			Bag or inert container	GC[a]
Ozone	Chemiluminescence		Bubbler		UV-Vis[b]
Sulphur dioxide	Electrochemical cell		Bubbler		UV-Vis
Nitrogen dioxide	Chemiluminescence Electrochemical cell	Filter impregnated with a reactant	Bubbler		UV-Vis
Carbon dioxide	Infrared spectroscopy			Bag or inert container	GC
Formaldehyde	—	Filter impregnated with a reactant	Bubbler Adsorbent solids		HPLC[c] Polarography UV-Vis
VOCs	Portable GC	Adsorbent solids	Adsorbent solids	Bag or inert container	GC (ECD[d]-FID[e]-NPD[f]-PID[g]) GC-MS[h]
Pesticides	—		Adsorbent solids Bubbler Filter Combinations		GC (ECD-FPD-NPD) GC-EM
Particulate matter	—	Optical sensor	Filter	Impactor Cyclone	Gravimetry Microscopy

— = Method unsuitable for pollutant.

[a] GC = gas chromatography. [b] UV-Vis = visible ultraviolet spectrophotometry. [c] HPLC = high precision liquid chromatography. [d] CD = electron capture detector. [e] FID = flame, ionization detector. [f] NPD = nitrogen/phosphorous detector. [g] PID = photoionization detector. [h] MS = mass spectrometry.

Table 44.10 shows the salient characteristics of each sampling method and table 44.11 outlines the various methods used to gather and analyse the samples for the most significant indoor air pollutants.

Selecting the method

To select the best sampling method, one should first determine that validated methods for the pollutants being studied exist and see to it that the proper instruments and materials are available to gather and analyse the pollutant. One usually needs to know what their cost will be, and the sensitivity required for the job, as well as things that can interfere with the measurement, given the method chosen.

An estimate of the minimum concentrations of what one hopes to measure is very useful when evaluating the method used to analyse the sample. The minimum concentration required is directly related to the amount of pollutant that can be gathered given the conditions specified by the method used (i.e., the type of system used to capture the pollutant or the duration of sample taking and volume of air sampled). This minimum amount is what determines the sensitivity required of the method used for analysis; it can be calculated from reference data found in the literature for a particular pollutant or group of pollutants, if they were arrived at by a similar method to the one that will be used. For example, if it is found that hydrocarbon concentrations of 30 $(\mu g/m^3)$ are commonly found in the area under study, the analytical method used should allow the measurement of those concentrations easily. If the sample is obtained with a tube of active carbon in four hours and with a flow of 0.5 litres per minute, the amount of hydrocarbons gathered in the sample is calculated by multiplying the flow rate of the substance by the period of time monitored. In the given example this equals:

$$\mu g \text{ of hydrocarbons} \geq \mu g/m^3/10^3 \times 4h \times 60 \text{ min} \times 0.5 \text{ l/min} \geq 3.6 \text{ } \mu g$$

Any method for detecting hydrocarbons that requires the amount in the sample to be under 3.6 μg can be used for this application.

Another estimate could be calculated from the maximum limit established as the allowable limit for indoor air for the pollutant being measured. If these figures don't exist and the usual concentrations found in indoor air are not known, nor the rate at which the pollutant is being discharged into the space, approximations can be used based on the potential levels of the pollutant that can negatively affect health. The method chosen should be capable of measuring 10% of the established limit or of the minimal concentration that could affect health. Even if the method of analysis chosen has an acceptable degree of sensitivity, it is possible to find concentrations of pollutants that are below the lower limit of detection of the chosen method. This should be kept in mind when calculating average concentrations. For example, if out of ten readings taken three are below the detection limit, two averages should be calculated, one assigning these three readings the value of zero and another giving them the lowest detection limit, which renders a minimum average and a maximum average. The true measured average will be found between the two.

Analytical Procedures

The number of indoor air pollutants is great and they are found in small concentrations. The methodology that has been available is based on adapting methods used to monitor the quality of outdoor, atmospheric, air and air found in industrial situations. Adapting these methods for the analysis of indoor air implies changing the range of the concentration sought, when the method allows, using longer sampling times and greater amounts of absorbents or adsorbents. All these changes are appropriate when they do not lead to a loss in reliability or precision. Measuring a mixture of contaminants is usually expensive and the results ob-

Table 44.12 • Methods used for the analysis of chemical pollutants.

Pollutant	Direct-reading monitor[a]	Sampling and analysis
Carbon monoxide	+	+
Carbon dioxide	+	+
Nitrogen dioxide	+	+
Formaldehyde	−	+
Sulphur dioxide	+	+
Ozone	+	+
VOCs	+	+
Pesticides	−	+
Particulates	+	+

[a] ++ = most commonly used; + = less commonly used; − = not applicable.

tained imprecise. In many cases all that will be ascertained will be a pollution profile that will indicate the level of contamination during sampling intervals, compared to clean air, to outside air, or to other indoor spaces. Direct reading monitors are used to monitor the pollution profile and may not be suitable if they are too noisy or too large. Ever smaller and quieter monitors, that afford greater precision and sensitivity, are being designed. Table 44.12 shows in outline the current state of the methods used to measure the different types of contaminants.

Analysis of gases

Active methods are the most common for the analysis of gases, and are carried out using absorbent solutions or adsorbent solids, or by directly taking a sample of air with a bag or some other inert and airtight container. In order to prevent loss of part of the sample and increase the accuracy of the reading, the volume of the sample must be lower and the amount of absorbent or adsorbent used should be more than for other types of pollution. Care should also be taken in transporting and storing the sample (keeping it at low temperature) and minimizing the time before the sample is tested. Direct reading methods are widely used for measuring gases because of the considerable improvement in the capabilities of modern monitors, which are more sensitive and more precise than before. Because of their ease of use and the level and type of information that they furnish, they are increasingly replacing traditional methods of analysis. Table 44.13 shows the minimum detection levels for the various gases studied given the method of sampling and analysis used.

Table 44.13 • Lower detection limits for some gases by monitors used to assess indoor air quality.[a]

Pollutant	Direct-reading monitor	Sample-taking and active/passive analysis
Carbon monoxide	1.0 ppm	0.05 ppm
Nitrogen dioxide	2 ppb	1.5 ppb (1 week)[b]
Ozone	4 ppb	5.0 ppb
Formaldehyde		5.0 ppb (1 week)[b]

[a] Carbon dioxide monitors that use infrared spectroscopy are always sensitive enough. [b] Passive monitors (length of exposure).

44. INDOOR AIR QUALITY

These gases are common pollutants in indoor air. They are measured by using monitors that detect them directly by electro-chemical or infrared means, even though infrared detectors are not very sensitive. They can also be measured by taking air samples directly with inert bags and analysing the sample by gas chromatography with a flame ionization detector, transforming the gases into methane first by means of a catalytic reaction. Thermal conduction detectors are usually sensitive enough to measure normal concentrations of CO_2.

Nitrogen dioxide

Methods have been developed to detect nitrogen dioxide, NO_2, in indoor air by using passive monitors and taking samples for later analysis, but these methods have presented sensitivity problems that will hopefully be overcome in the future. The best known method is the Palmes tube, which has a detection limit of 300 ppb. For non-industrial situations, sampling should be for a minimum of five days in order to obtain a detection limit of 1.5 ppb, which is three times the value of the blank for a one-week exposure. Portable monitors that measure in real time have also been developed based on the chemiluminescence reaction between NO_2 and the reactant luminol, but the results obtained by this method can be affected by temperature and their linearity and sensitivity depend on the characteristics of the solution of luminol used. Monitors that have electrochemical sensors have improved sensitivity but are subject to interference from compounds that contain sulphur (Freixa 1993).

Sulphur dioxide

A spectrophotometric method is used to measure sulphur dioxide, SO_2, in an indoor environment. The air sample is bubbled through a solution of potassium tetrachloromercuriate to form a stable complex which is in turn measured spectrophotometrically after reacting with pararosaniline. Other methods are based on flame photometry and pulsating ultraviolet fluorescence, and there are also methods based on deriving the measurement before the spectroscopic analysis. This type of detection, which has been used for outside air monitors, is not suited for indoor air analysis because of a lack of specificity and because many of these monitors require a venting system to eliminate the gases that they generate. Because emissions of SO_2 have been greatly reduced and it is not considered an important pollutant of indoor air, the development of monitors for its detection have not advanced very much. However, there are portable instruments available on the market that can detect SO_2 based on the detection of pararosaniline (Freixa 1993).

Ozone

Ozone, O_3, can only be found in indoor environments in special situations in which it is generated continuously, since it decays rapidly. It is measured by direct reading methods, by colorimetric tubes and by chemiluminescence methods. It can also be detected by methods used in industrial hygiene that can be easily adapted for indoor air. The sample is obtained with an absorbent solution of potassium iodide in a neutral medium and then subjected to spectrophotometric analysis.

Formaldehyde

Formaldehyde is an important pollutant of indoor air, and because of its chemical and toxic characteristics an individualized evaluation is recommended. There are different methods for detecting formaldehyde in air, all of them based on taking samples for later analysis, with active fixing or by diffusion. The most appropriate capturing method will be determined by the type of sample (emission or immission) used and the sensitivity of the analytical method. The traditional methods are based on obtain-

ing a sample by bubbling air through distilled water or a solution of 1% sodium bisulphate at 5°C, and then analysing it with spectrofluorometric methods. While the sample is stored, it should also be kept at 5°C. SO_2 and the components of tobacco smoke can create interference. Active systems or methods that capture pollutants by diffusion with solid adsorbents are used more and more frequently in indoor air analysis; they all consist of a base that can be a filter or a solid saturated with a reactant, such as sodium bisulphate or 2,4-diphenylhydrazine. Methods that capture the pollutant by diffusion, in addition to general advantages of that method, are more sensitive than active methods because the time required to obtain the sample is longer (Freixa 1993).

Detection of volatile organic compounds (VOCs)

The methods used to measure or monitor organic vapours in indoor air must meet a series of criteria: they should have a sensitivity in the order of parts per billion (ppb) to parts per trillion (ppt), the instruments used to take the sample or make a direct reading must be portable and easy to handle in the field, and the results obtained must be precise and capable of being duplicated. There are a great many methods that meet these criteria, but the ones most frequently used to analyse indoor air are based on sample taking and analysis. Direct detection methods exist that consist of portable gas chromatographs with different detection methods. These instruments are expensive, their handling is sophisticated and they can be operated only by trained personnel. For polar and nonpolar organic compounds that have a boiling point between 0°C and 300°C, the most widely used adsorbent both for active and passive sampling systems has been activated carbon. Porous polymers and polymer resins, such as Tenax GC, XAD-2 and Ambersorb are also used. The most widely used of these is Tenax. The samples obtained with activated carbon are extracted with carbon disulphide and they are analysed by gas chromatography with flame ionization, electron-capture, or mass spectrometry detectors, followed by qualitative and quantitative analysis. Samples obtained with Tenax are usually extracted by thermal desorption with helium and are condensed in a nitrogen cold trap before being fed to the chromatograph. Another common method consists in obtaining samples directly, using bags or inert containers, feeding the air directly to the gas chromatograph, or concentrating the sample first with an adsorbent and a cold trap. The detection limits of these methods depend on the compound analysed, the volume of the sample taken, the background pollution and the detection limits of the instrument used. Because quantifying each and every one of the compounds present is impossible, quantification is normally done by families, by using as a reference compounds that are characteristic of each family of compounds. In detecting VOCs in indoor air, the purity of the solvents used is very important. If thermal desorption is used, the purity of the gases is also important.

Detection of pesticides

To detect pesticides in indoor air, the methods commonly employed consist of taking samples with solid adsorbents, although the use of bubblers and mixed systems is not ruled out. The solid adsorbent most commonly used has been porous polymer Chromosorb 102, although polyurethane foams (PUFs) that can capture a wider number of pesticides are being used more and more. The methods of analysis vary according to the sampling method and the pesticide. Usually they are analysed by using gas chromatography with different specific detectors, from electron capture to mass spectrometry. The potential of the latter for identifying compounds is considerable. The analysis of these compounds presents certain problems, which include the contamination of glass parts in the sample-taking systems with traces of polychlorinated biphenyls (PCBs), phthalates or pesticides.

Detection of environmental dust or particles

For the capture and analysis of particles and fibres in air a great variety of techniques and equipment are available and suited for assessing indoor air quality. Monitors that permit a direct reading of the concentration of particles in the air use diffuse light detectors, and methods that employ sample taking and analysis use weighting and analysis with a microscope. This type of analysis requires a separator, such as a cyclone or an impactor, to sift out larger particles before a filter can be used. Methods that employ a cyclone can handle small volumes, which results in long sessions of sample taking. Passive monitors offer excellent precision, but they are affected by ambient temperature and tend to give readings with higher values when the particles are small.

• BIOLOGICAL CONTAMINATION

Brian Flannigan

Characteristics and Origins of Biological Indoor Air Contamination

Although there is a diverse range of particles of biological origin (bioparticles) in indoor air, in most indoor work environments micro-organisms (microbes) are of the greatest significance for health. As well as micro-organisms, which include viruses, bacteria, fungi and protozoa, indoor air can also contain pollen grains, animal dander and fragments of insects and mites and their excretory products (Wanner et al. 1993). In addition to bioaerosols of these particles, there may also be volatile organic compounds which emanate from living organisms such as indoor plants and micro-organisms.

Pollen

Pollen grains contain substances (allergens) which may cause in susceptible, or atopic, individuals allergic responses usually manifested as "hay fever", or rhinitis. Such allergy is associated primarily with the outdoor environment; in indoor air, pollen concentrations are usually considerably lower than in outdoor air. The difference in pollen concentration between outdoor and indoor air is greatest for buildings where heating, ventilation and air-conditioning (HVAC) systems have efficient filtration at the intake of external air. Window air-conditioning units also give lower indoor pollen levels than those found in naturally ventilated buildings. The air of some indoor work environments may be expected to have high pollen counts, for example, in premises where large numbers of flowering plants are present for aesthetic reasons, or in commercial glasshouses.

Dander

Dander consists of fine skin and hair/feather particles (and associated dried saliva and urine) and is a source of potent allergens which can cause bouts of rhinitis or asthma in susceptible individuals. The main sources of dander in indoor environments are usually cats and dogs, but rats and mice (whether as pets, experimental animals or vermin), hamsters, gerbils (a species of desert-rat), guinea pigs and cage-birds may be additional sources. Dander from these and from farm and recreational animals (e.g., horses) can be brought in on clothes, but in work environments the greatest exposure to dander is likely to be in animal-rearing facilities and laboratories or in vermin-infested buildings.

Insects

These organisms and their excretory products may also cause respiratory and other allergies, but do not appear to contribute significantly to the airborne bioburden in most situations. Particles from cockroaches (especially *Blatella germanica* and *Periplaneta americana*) may be significant in unsanitary, hot and humid work environments. Exposures to particles from cockroaches and other insects, including locusts, weevils, flour beetles and fruit flies, can be the cause of ill health among employees in rearing facilities and laboratories.

Mites

These arachnids are associated particularly with dust, but fragments of these microscopic relatives of spiders and their excretory products (faeces) may be present in indoor air. The house dust mite, *Dermatophagoides pteronyssinus*, is the most important species. With its close relatives, it is a major cause of respiratory allergy. It is associated primarily with homes, being particularly abundant in bedding but also present in upholstered furniture. There is limited evidence indicating that such furniture may provide a niche in offices. Storage mites associated with stored foods and animal feedstuffs, for example, *Acarus*, *Glyciphagus* and *Tyrophagus*, may also contribute allergenic fragments to indoor air. Although they are most likely to affect farmers and workers handling bulk food commodities, like *D. pteronyssinus*, storage mites can exist in dust in buildings, particularly under warm humid conditions.

Viruses

Viruses are very important micro-organisms in terms of the total amount of ill health they cause, but they cannot lead an independent existence outside living cells and tissues. Although there is evidence indicating that some are spread in recirculating air of HVAC systems, the principal means of transmission is by person-to-person contact. Inhalation at short range of aerosols generated by coughing or sneezing, for example, common cold and influenza viruses, is also important. Rates of infection are therefore likely to be higher in crowded premises. There are no obvious changes in building design or management which can alter this state of affairs.

Bacteria

These micro-organisms are divided into two major categories according to their Gram's stain reaction. The most common Gram-positive types originate from the mouth, nose, nasopharynx and skin, namely, *Staphylococcus epidermidis*, *S. aureus* and species of *Aerococcus*, *Micrococcus* and *Streptococcus*. Gram-negative bacteria are generally not abundant, but occasionally *Actinetobacter*, *Aeromonas*, *Flavobacterium* and especially *Pseudomonas* species may be prominent. The cause of Legionnaire's disease, *Legionella pneumophila*, may be present in hot water supplies and air-conditioning humidifiers, as well as in respiratory therapy equipment, jacuzzis, spas and shower stalls. It is spread from such installations in aqueous aerosols, but also may enter buildings in air from nearby cooling towers. The survival time for *L. pneumophila* in indoor air appears to be no greater than 15 minutes.

In addition to the unicellular bacteria mentioned above, there are also filamentous types which produce aerially dispersed spores, that is, the Actinomycetes. They appear to be associated with damp structural materials, and may give off a characteristic earthy odour. Two of these bacteria that are able to grow at 60°C, *Faenia rectivirgula* (formerly *Micropolyspora faeni*) and *Thermoactinomyces vulgaris*, may be found in humidifiers and other HVAC equipment.

Fungi

Fungi comprise two groups: first, the microscopic yeasts and moulds known as microfungi, and, second, plaster and wood-rotting fungi, which are referred to as macrofungi as they produce macroscopic sporing bodies visible to the naked eye. Apart from unicellular yeasts, fungi colonize substrates as a network (mycelium) of filaments (hyphae). These filamentous fungi produce numerous aerially dispersed spores, from microscopic sporing structures in moulds and from large sporing structures in macrofungi.

There are spores of many different moulds in the air of houses and nonindustrial workplaces, but the most common are likely to be species of *Cladosporium*, *Penicillium*, *Aspergillus* and *Eurotium*. Some moulds in indoor air, such as *Cladosporium* spp., are abundant on leaf surfaces and other plant parts outdoors, particularly in summer. However, although spores in indoor air may originate outdoors, *Cladosporium* is also able to grow and produce spores on damp surfaces indoors and thus add to the indoor air bioburden. The various species of *Penicillium* are generally regarded as originating indoors, as are *Aspergillus* and *Eurotium*. Yeasts are found in most indoor air samples, and occasionally may be present in large numbers. The pink yeasts *Rhodotorula* or *Sporobolomyces* are prominent in the airborne flora and can also be isolated from mould-affected surfaces.

Buildings provide a broad range of niches in which the dead organic material which serves as nutriment that can be utilized by most fungi and bacteria for growth and spore production is present. The nutrients are present in materials such as: wood; paper, paint and other surface coatings; soft furnishings such as carpets and upholstered furniture; soil in plant pots; dust; skin scales and secretions of human beings and other animals; and cooked foods and their raw ingredients. Whether any growth occurs or not depends on moisture availability. Bacteria are able to grow only on saturated surfaces, or in water in HVAC drain pans, reservoirs and the like. Some moulds also require conditions of near saturation, but others are less demanding and may proliferate on materials that are damp rather than fully saturated. Dust can be a repository and, also, if it is sufficiently moist, an amplifier for moulds. It is therefore an important source of spores which become airborne when dust is disturbed.

Protozoa
Protozoa such as *Acanthamoeba* and *Naegleri* are microscopic unicellular animals which feed on bacteria and other organic particles in humidifiers, reservoirs and drain pans in HVAC systems. Particles of these protozoa may be aerosolized and have been cited as possible causes of humidifier fever.

Microbial volatile organic compounds
Microbial volatile organic compounds (MVOCs) vary considerably in chemical composition and odour. Some are produced by a wide range of micro-organisms, but others are associated with particular species. The so-called mushroom alcohol, 1-octen-3-ol (which has a smell of fresh mushrooms) is among those produced by many different moulds. Other less common mould volatiles include 3,5-dimethyl-1,2,4-trithiolone (described as "foetid"); geosmin, or 1,10-dimethyl-trans-9-decalol ("earthy"); and 6-pentyl-α-pyrone ("coconut", "musty"). Among bacteria, species of *Pseudomonas* produce pyrazines with a "musty potato" odour. The odour of any individual micro-organism is the product of a complex mixture of MVOCs.

History of Microbiological Indoor Air Quality Problems
Microbiological investigations of air in homes, schools and other buildings have been made for over a century. Early investigations were sometimes concerned with the relative microbiological "purity" of the air in different types of building and any relation it might have to the death rate among occupants. Allied to a long-time interest in the spread of pathogens in hospitals, the development of modern volumetric microbiological air samplers

in the 1940s and 1950s led to systematic investigations of airborne micro-organisms in hospitals, and subsequently of known allergenic moulds in air in homes and public buildings and outdoors. Other work was directed in the 1950s and 1960s to investigation of occupational respiratory diseases like farmer's lung, malt worker's lung and byssinosis (among cotton workers). Although influenza-like humidifier fever in a group of workers was first described in 1959, it was another ten to fifteen years before other cases were reported. However, even now, the specific cause is not known, although micro-organisms have been implicated. They have also been invoked as a possible cause of "sick building syndrome", but as yet the evidence for such a link is very limited.

Although the allergic properties of fungi are well recognized, the first report of ill health due to inhalation of fungal toxins in a non-industrial workplace, a Quebec hospital, did not appear until 1988 (Mainville et al. 1988). Symptoms of extreme fatigue among staff were attributed to trichothecene mycotoxins in spores of *Stachybotrys atra* and *Trichoderma viride*, and since then "chronic fatigue syndrome" caused by exposure to mycotoxic dust has been recorded among teachers and other employees at a college. The first has been the cause of illness in office workers, with some health effects being of an allergic nature and others of a type more often associated with a toxicosis (Johanning et al. 1993). Elsewhere, epidemiologaedia research has indicated that there may be some non-allergic factor or factors associated with fungi affecting respiratory health. Mycotoxins produced by individual species of mould may have an important role here, but there is also the possibility that some more general attribute of inhaled fungi is detrimental to respiratory well-being.

Micro-organisms Associated with Poor Indoor Air Quality and their Health Effects
Although pathogens are relatively uncommon in indoor air, there have been numerous reports linking airborne micro-organisms with a number of allergic conditions, including: (1) atopic allergic dermatitis; (2) rhinitis; (3) asthma; (4) humidifier fever; and (5) extrinsic allergic alveolitis (EAA), also known as hypersensitivity pneumonitis (HP).

Fungi are perceived as being more important than bacteria as components of bioaerosols in indoor air. Because they grow on damp surfaces as obvious mould patches, fungi often give a clear visible indication of moisture problems and potential health hazards in a building. Mould growth contributes both numbers and species to the indoor air mould flora which would otherwise not be present. Like Gram-negative bacteria and Actinomycetales, hydrophilic ("moisture-loving") fungi are indicators of extremely wet sites of amplification (visible or hidden), and therefore of poor indoor air quality. They include *Fusarium*, *Phoma*, *Stachybotrys*, *Trichoderma*, *Ulocladium*, yeasts and more rarely the opportunistic pathogens *Aspergillus fumigatus* and *Exophiala jeanselmei*. High levels of moulds which show varying degrees of xerophily ("love of dryness"), in having a lower requirement for water, can indicate the existence of amplification sites which are less wet, but nevertheless significant for growth. Moulds are also abundant in house dust, so that large numbers can also be a marker of a dusty atmosphere. They range from slightly xerophilic (able to withstand dry conditions) *Cladosporium* species to moderately xerophilic *Aspergillus versicolor*, *Penicillium* (for example, *P. aurantiogriseum* and *P. chrysogenum*) and the extremely xerophilic *Aspergillus penicillioides*, *Eurotium* and *Wallemia*.

Fungal pathogens are rarely abundant in indoor air, but *A. fumigatus* and some other opportunistic aspergilli which can invade human tissue may grow in the soil of potted plants. *Exophiala jeanselmei* is able to grow in drains. Although the spores of these and other opportunistic pathogens such as *Fusarium solani* and

Table 44.14 • Examples of types of fungus in indoor air which can cause rhinitis and/or asthma.

Alternaria	Geotrichum	Serpula
Aspergillus	Mucor	Stachybotrys
Cladosporium	Penicillium	Stemphylium/Ulocladium
Eurotium	Rhizopus	Wallemia
Fusarium	Rhodotorula/Sporobolomyces	

Pseudallescheria boydii are unlikely to be hazardous to the healthy, they may be so to immunologically compromised individuals.

Airborne fungi are much more important than bacteria as causes of allergic disease, although it appears that, at least in Europe, fungal allergens are less important than those of pollen, house dust mites and animal dander. Many types of fungus have been shown to be allergenic. Some of the fungi in indoor air which are most commonly cited as causes of rhinitis and asthma are given in table 44.14. Species of *Eurotium* and other extremely xerophilic moulds in house dust are probably more important as causes of rhinitis and asthma than has been previously recognized. Allergic dermatitis due to fungi is much less common than rhinitis/asthma, with *Alternaria*, *Aspergillus* and *Cladosporium* being implicated. Cases of EAA, which are relatively rare, have been attributed to a range of different fungi, from the yeast *Sporobolomyces* to the wood-rotting macrofungus *Serpula* (table 44.15). It is generally considered that development of symptoms of EAA in an individual requires exposure to at least one million and more, probably one hundred million or so allergen-containing spores per cubic metre of air. Such levels of contamination are only likely to occur where there is profuse fungal growth in a building.

As indicated earlier, inhalation of spores of toxicogenic species presents a potential hazard (Sorenson 1989; Miller 1993). It is not just the spores of *Stachybotrys* which contain high concentrations of mycotoxins. Although the spores of this mould, which grows on wallpaper and other cellulosic substrates in damp buildings and is also allergenic, contain extremely potent mycotoxins, other toxicogenic moulds which are more often present in indoor air include *Aspergillus* (especially *A. versicolor*) and *Penicillium* (for example, *P. aurantiogriseum* and *P. viridicatum*) and *Trichoderma*. Experimental evidence indicates that a range of mycotoxins in the spores of these moulds are immunosuppressive and strongly inhibit scavenging and other functions of the pulmonary macrophage cells essential to respiratory health (Sorenson 1989).

Little is known about the health effects of the MVOCs produced during the growth and sporulation of moulds, or of their bacterial counterparts. Although many MVOCs appear to have relatively low toxicity (Sorenson 1989), anecdotal evidence indicates that they can provoke headache, discomfort and perhaps acute respiratory responses in humans.

Bacteria in indoor air do not generally present a health hazard as the flora is usually dominated by the Gram-positive inhabitants of the skin and upper respiratory passages. However, high counts of these bacteria indicate overcrowding and poor ventilation. The presence of large numbers of Gram-negative types and/or *Actinomycetales* in air indicate that there are very wet surfaces or materials, drains or particularly humidifiers in HVAC systems in which they are proliferating. Some Gram-negative bacteria (or endotoxin extracted from their walls) have been shown to provoke symptoms of humidifier fever. Occasionally, growth in humidifiers has been great enough for aerosols to be generated which contained sufficient allergenic cells to have caused the acute pneumonia-like symptoms of EAA (see table 44.15).

On rare occasions, pathogenic bacteria such as *Mycobacterium tuberculosis* in droplet nuclei from infected individuals can be dispersed by recirculation systems to all parts of an enclosed environment. Although the pathogen, *Legionella pneumophila*, has been isolated from humidifiers and air-conditioners, most outbreaks of Legionellosis have been associated with aerosols from cooling towers or showers.

Table 44.15 • Micro-organisms in indoor air reported as causes of building-related extrinsic allergic alveolitis.

Type	Micro-organism	Source
Bacteria	Bacillus subtilis	Decayed wood
	Faenia rectivirgula	Humidifier
	Pseudomonas aeruginosa	Humidifier
	Thermoactinomyces vulgaris	Air conditioner
Fungi	Aureobasidium pullulans	Sauna; room wall
	Cephalosporium sp.	Basement; humidifier
	Cladosporium sp.	Unventilated bathroom
	Mucor sp.	Pulsed air heating system
	Penicillium sp.	Pulsed air heating system humidifier
	P. casei	Room wall
	P. chrysogenum/P. cyclopium	Flooring
	Serpula lacrimans	Dry rot affected timber
	Sporobolomyces	Room wall; ceiling
	Trichosporon cutaneum	Wood; matting

Influence of Changes in Building Design

Over the years, the increase in the size of buildings concomitantly with the development of air-handling systems which have culminated in modern HVAC systems has resulted in quantitative and qualitative changes in the bioburden of air in indoor work environments. In the last two decades, the move to the design of buildings with minimum energy usage has led to the development of buildings with greatly reduced infiltration and exfiltration of air, which allows a build-up of airborne micro-organisms and other contaminants. In such "tight" buildings, water vapour, which would previously have been vented to the outdoors, condenses on cool surfaces, creating conditions for microbial growth. In addition, HVAC systems designed only for economic efficiency often promote microbial growth and pose a health risk to occupants of large buildings. For example, humidifiers which utilize recirculated water rapidly become contaminated and act as generators of micro-organisms, humidification water-sprays aerosolize micro-organisms, and siting of filters upstream and not downstream of such areas of microbial generation and aerosolization allows onward transmission of microbial aerosols to the workplace. Siting of air intakes close to cooling towers or other sources of micro-organisms, and difficulty of access to the HVAC system for maintenance and cleaning/disinfection, are also among the design, operation and maintenance defects which may endanger health. They do so by exposing occupants to high counts of particular airborne micro-organisms, rather than to the low counts of a mixture of species reflective of outdoor air that should be the norm.

Methods of Evaluating Indoor Air Quality

Air sampling of micro-organisms

In investigating the microbial flora of air in a building, for example, in order to try to establish the cause of ill health among its occupants, the need is to gather objective data which are both detailed and reliable. As the general perception is that the micro-biological status of indoor air should reflect that of outdoor air (ACGIH 1989), organisms must be accurately identified and compared with those in outdoor air at that time.

Air samplers

Sampling methods which allow, directly or indirectly, the culture of viable airborne bacteria and fungi on nutritive agar gel offer the best chance of identification of species, and are therefore most frequently used. The agar medium is incubated until colonies develop from the trapped bioparticles and can be counted and identified, or are subcultured onto other media for further examination. The agar media needed for bacteria are different from those for fungi, and some bacteria, for example, *Legionella pneumophila*, can be isolated only on special selective media. For fungi, the use of two media is recommended: a general-purpose medium as well as a medium that is more selective for isolation of xerophilic fungi. Identification is based on the gross characteristics of the colonies, and/or their microscopical or biochemical characteristics, and requires considerable skill and experience.

The range of sampling methods available has been adequately reviewed (e.g., Flannigan 1992; Wanner et al. 1993), and only the most commonly used systems are mentioned here. It is possible to make a rough-and-ready assessment by passively collecting micro-organisms gravitating out of the air into open Petri dishes containing agar medium. The results obtained using these settlement plates are non-volumetric, are strongly affected by atmospheric turbulence and favour collection of large (heavy) spores or clumps of spores/cells. It is therefore preferable to use a volumetric air sampler. Impaction samplers in which the airborne particles impact on an agar surface are widely used. Air is either drawn through a slit above a rotating agar plate (slit-type impaction sampler) or through a perforated disc above the agar plate (sieve-type impaction sampler). Although single-stage sieve samplers are widely used, the six-stage Andersen sampler is preferred by some investigators. As air cascades through successively finer holes in its six stacked aluminium sections, the particles are sorted out onto different agar plates according to their aerodynamic size. The sampler therefore reveals the size of particles from which colonies develop when the agar plates are subsequently incubated, and indicates where in the respiratory system the different organisms would most likely be deposited. A popular sampler which works on a different principle is the Reuter centrifugal sampler. Centrifugal acceleration of air drawn in by an impeller fan causes particles to impact at high velocity onto agar in a plastic strip lining the sampling cylinder.

Another approach to sampling is to collect micro-organisms on a membrane filter in a filter cassette connected to a low-volume rechargeable pump. The whole assembly can be clipped to a belt or harness and used to collect a personal sample over a normal working day. After sampling, small portions of washings from the filter and dilutions of the washings can then be spread out on a range of agar media, incubated and counts of viable micro-organisms made. An alternative to the filter sampler is the liquid impinger, in which particles in air drawn in through capillary jets impinge on and collect in liquid. Portions of the collection liquid and dilutions prepared from it are treated in the same way as those from filter samplers.

A serious deficiency in these "viable" sampling methods is that what they assess is only organisms which are actually culturable,

and these may only be one or two per cent of the total air spora. However, total counts (viable plus non-viable) can be made using impaction samplers in which particles are collected on the sticky surfaces of rotating rods (rotating-arm impaction sampler) or on the plastic tape or glass microscope slide of different models of slit-type impaction sampler. The counts are made under the microscope, but only relatively few fungi can be identified in this way, namely, those that have distinctive spores. Filtration sampling has been mentioned in relation to the assessment of viable micro-organisms, but it is also a means of obtaining a total count. A portion of the same washings that are plated out on agar medium can be stained and the micro-organisms counted under a microscope. Total counts can be also made in the same way from the collection fluid in liquid impingers.

Choice of air sampler and sampling strategy

Which sampler is used is largely determined by the experience of the investigator, but the choice is important for both quantitative and qualitative reasons. For example, the agar plates of single-stage impaction samplers are much more easily "overloaded" with spores during sampling than those of a six-stage sampler, resulting in overgrowth of the incubated plates and serious quantitative and qualitative errors in assessment of the airborne population. The way in which different samplers operate, their sampling times and the efficiency with which they remove different sizes of particle from the ambient air, extract them from the airstream and collect them on a surface or in liquid all differ considerably. Because of these differences, it is not possible to make valid comparisons between data obtained using one type of sampler in one investigation with those from another type of sampler in a different investigation.

The sampling strategy as well as the choice of sampler, is very important. No general sampling strategy can be set down; each case demands its own approach (Wanner et al. 1993). A major problem is that the distribution of micro-organisms in indoor air is not uniform, either in space or time. It is profoundly affected by the degree of activity in a room, particularly any cleaning or construction work which throws up settled dust. Consequently, there are considerable fluctuations in numbers over relatively short time intervals. Apart from filter samplers and liquid impingers, which are used for several hours, most air samplers are used to obtain a "grab" sample over only a few minutes. Samples should therefore be taken under all conditions of occupation and usage, including both times when HVAC systems are functioning and when not. Although extensive sampling may reveal the range of concentrations of viable spores encountered in an indoor environment, it is not possible to assess satisfactorily the exposure of individuals to micro-organisms in the environment. Even samples taken over a working day with a personal filter sampler do not give an adequate picture, as they give only an average value and do not reveal peak exposures.

In addition to the clearly recognized effects of particular allergens, epidemiological research indicates that there may be some non-allergic factor associated with fungi which affects respiratory health. Mycotoxins produced by individual species of mould may have an important role, but there is also the possibility that some more general factor is involved. In the future, the overall approach to investigating the fungal burden in indoor air is therefore likely to be: (1) to assess which allergenic and toxicogenic species are present by sampling for viable fungi; and (2) to obtain a measure of the total amount of fungal material to which individuals are exposed in a work environment. As noted above, to obtain the latter information, total counts could be taken over a working day. However, in the near future, methods which have recently been developed for the assay of 1,3-β-glucan or ergosterol (Miller 1993) may be more widely adopted. Both substances are structural components of fungi, and therefore give a measure of the amount of fungal material (i.e., its biomass). A link has been reported between levels of 1,3-β-glucan in indoor air and symptoms of sick building syndrome (Miller 1993).

Standards and Guidelines

While some organizations have categorized levels of contamination of indoor air and dust (table 44.16), because of air sampling problems there has been a justifiable reluctance to set numerical standards or guideline values. It has been noted that the airborne microbial load in air-conditioned buildings should be markedly lower than in outdoor air, with the differential between naturally ventilated buildings and outdoor air being less. The ACGIH (1989) recommends that the rank order of fungal species in indoor and outdoor air be used in interpreting air sampling data. The presence or preponderance of some moulds in indoor air, but not outdoors, may identify a problem inside a building. For example, abundance in indoor air of such hydrophilic moulds as *Stachybotrys atra* almost invariably indicates a very damp amplification site within a building.

Although influential bodies such as the ACGIH Bioaerosols Committee have not established numerical guidelines, a Canadian guide on office buildings (Nathanson 1993), based on some five years of investigation of around 50 air-conditioned federal government buildings, includes some guidance on numbers. The following are among the main points made:

1. The "normal" air flora should be quantitatively lower than, but qualitatively similar to, that of outdoor air.
2. The presence of one or more fungal species at significant levels in indoor but not outdoor samples is evidence of an indoor amplifier.
3. Pathogenic fungi such as *Aspergillus fumigatus*, *Histoplasma* and *Cryptococcus* should not be present in significant numbers.
4. The persistence of toxicogenic moulds such as *Stachybotrys atra* and *Aspergillus versicolor* in significant numbers requires investigation and action.
5. More than 50 colony-forming units per cubic metre (CFU/m^3) may be of concern if there is only one species present (other than certain common outdoor leaf-inhabiting fungi); up to 150 CFU/m^3 is acceptable if the species present reflect the flora outdoors; up to 500 CFU/m^3 is acceptable in summer if outdoor leaf-inhabiting fungi are the main components.

These numerical values are based on four-minute air samples collected with a Reuter centrifugal sampler. It must be empha-

sized that they cannot be translated to other sampling procedures, other types of building or other climatic/geographical regions. What is the norm or is acceptable can only be based on extensive investigations of a range of buildings in a particular region using well-defined procedures. No threshold limit values can be set for exposure to moulds in general or to particular species.

Control of Micro-organisms in Indoor Environments

The key determinant of microbial growth and production of cells and spores which can become aerosolized in indoor environments is water, and by reducing moisture availability, rather than by using biocides, control should be achieved. Control involves proper maintenance and repair of a building, including prompt drying and elimination of causes of leakage/flood damage (Morey 1993a). Although maintaining the relative humidity of rooms at a level less than 70% is often cited as a control measure, this is effective only if the temperature of the walls and other surfaces are close to that of the air temperature. At the surface of poorly insulated walls, the temperature may be below the dew point, with the result that condensation develops and hydrophilic fungi, and even bacteria, grow (Flannigan 1993). A similar situation can arise in humid tropical or subtropical climates where the moisture in the air permeating the building envelope of an air-conditioned building condenses at the cooler inner surface (Morey 1993b). In such cases, control lies in the design and correct use of insulation and vapour barriers. In conjunction with rigorous moisture control measures, maintenance and cleaning programmes should ensure removal of dust and other detritus that supply nutrients for growth, and also act as reservoirs of micro-organisms.

In HVAC systems (Nathanson 1993), accumulation of stagnant water should be prevented, for example, in drain pans or under cooling coils. Where sprays, wicks or heated water tanks are integral to humidification in HVAC systems, regular cleaning and disinfection are necessary to limit microbial growth. Humidification by dry steam is likely to reduce greatly the risk of microbial growth. As filters can accumulate dirt and moisture and therefore provide amplification sites for microbial growth, they should be replaced regularly. Micro-organisms can also grow in porous acoustical insulation used to line ducts if it becomes moist. The solution to this problem is to apply such insulation to the exterior rather than the interior; internal surfaces should be smooth and should not provide an environment conducive to growth. Such general control measures will control growth of *Legionella* in HVAC systems, but additional features, such as the installation of a high-efficiency particulate air (HEPA) filter at the intake have been recommended (Feeley 1988). In addition, water systems should ensure that hot water is heated uniformly to 60°C, that there are no areas in which water stagnates and that no fittings contain materials that promote growth of *Legionella*.

Where controls have been inadequate and mould growth occurs, remedial action is necessary. It is essential to remove and discard all porous organic materials, such as carpets and other soft furnishings, ceiling tiles and insulation, on and in which there is growth. Smooth surfaces should be washed down with sodium hypochlorite bleach or suitable disinfectant. Biocides which can be aerosolized should not be used in operating HVAC systems.

During remediation, care must always be taken that micro-organisms on or in contaminated materials are not aerosolized. In cases where large areas of mould growth (ten square metres or more) are being dealt with it may be necessary to contain the potential hazard, maintaining negative pressure in the containment area during remediation and having air locks/decontamination areas between the contained area and the remainder of the building (Morey 1993a, 1993b; New York City Department of Health 1993). Dusts present before or generated during removal of contaminated material into sealed containers should be col-

Table 44.16 • Observed levels of micro-organisms in air and dust of nonindustrial indoor environments.

Category of contamination	CFU[a] per metre of air		Fungi as CFU/g of dust
	Bacteria	Fungi	
Very low	<50	<25	<10,000
Low	<100	<100	<20,000
Intermediate	<500	<500	<50,000
High	<2,000	<2,000	<120,000
Very high	>2,000	>2,000	>120,000

[a] CFU, colony-forming units.
Source: adapted from Wanner et al. 1993.

lected using a vacuum cleaner with a HEPA filter. Throughout operations, the specialist remediation personnel must wear full-face HEPA respiratory protection and disposable protective clothing, footwear and gloves (New York City Department of Health 1993). Where smaller areas of mould growth are being dealt with, regular maintenance staff may be employed after appropriate training. In such cases, containment is not considered necessary, but the staff must wear full respiratory protection and gloves. In all cases, both regular occupants and personnel to be employed in remediation should be made aware of the hazard. The latter should not have pre-existing asthma, allergy or immunosuppressive disorders (New York City Department of Health 1993).

REGULATIONS, RECOMMENDATIONS, GUIDELINES AND STANDARDS

María José Berenguer

Criteria for Establishment

The setting of specific guides and standards for indoor air is the product of proactive policies in this field on the part of the bodies responsible for their establishment and for maintaining the quality of indoor air at acceptable levels. In practice, the tasks are divided and shared among many entities responsible for controlling pollution, maintaining health, ensuring the safety of products, watching over occupational hygiene and regulating building and construction.

The establishment of a regulation is intended to limit or reduce the levels of pollution in indoor air. This goal can be achieved by controlling the existing sources of pollution, diluting indoor air with outside air and checking the quality of available air. This requires the establishment of specific maximum limits for the pollutants found in indoor air.

The concentration of any given pollutant in indoor air follows a model of balanced mass expressed in the following equation:

$$\frac{\mathrm{d}C_i}{\mathrm{d}t} = \frac{Q}{V} + nC_o - aC_i - nC_i$$

where:

C_i = the concentration of the pollutant in indoor air $(\mathrm{mg/m^3})$;
Q = the emission rate $(\mathrm{mg/h})$;
V = the volume of indoor space $(\mathrm{m^3})$;
C_o = the concentration of the pollutant in outdoor air $(\mathrm{mg/m^3})$;
n = the ventilation rate per hour;
a = the pollutant decay rate per hour.

It is generally observed that—in static conditions—the concentration of pollutants present will depend in part on the amount of the compound released into the air from the source of contamination and its concentration in outdoor air, and on the different mechanisms by which the pollutant is removed. The elimination mechanisms include the dilution of the pollutant and its "disappearance" with time. All regulations, recommendations, guidelines and standards that may be set in order to reduce pollution must take stock of these possibilities.

Control of the Sources of Pollution

One of the most effective ways to reduce the levels of concentration of a pollutant in indoor air is to control the sources of contamination within the building. This includes the materials used for construction and decoration, the activities within the building and the occupants themselves.

If it is deemed necessary to regulate emissions that are due to the construction materials used, there are standards that limit

directly the content in these materials of compounds for which harmful effects to health have been demonstrated. Some of these compounds are considered carcinogenic, like formaldehyde, benzene, some pesticides, asbestos, fibreglass and others. Another avenue is to regulate emissions by the establishment of emission standards.

This possibility presents many practical difficulties, chief among them being the lack of agreement on how to go about measuring these emissions, a lack of knowledge about their effects on the health and comfort of the occupants of the building, and the inherent difficulties of identifying and quantifying the hundreds of compounds emitted by the materials in question. One way to go about establishing emission standards is to start out from an acceptable level of concentration of the pollutant and to calculate a rate of emission that takes into account the environmental conditions—temperature, relative humidity, air exchange rate, loading factor and so forth—that are representative of the way in which the product is actually used. The main criticism levelled against this methodology is that more than one product may generate the same polluting compound. Emission standards are obtained from readings taken in controlled atmospheres where conditions are perfectly defined. There are published guides for Europe (COST 613 1989 and 1991) and for the United States (ASTM 1989). The criticisms usually directed against them are based on: (1) the fact that it is difficult to get comparative data and (2) the problems that surface when an indoor space has intermittent sources of pollution.

As for the activities that may take place in a building, the greatest focus is placed on building maintenance. In these activities the control can be established in the form of regulations about the performance of certain duties—like recommendations relating to the application of pesticides or the reduction of exposure to lead or asbestos when a building is being renovated or demolished.

Because tobacco smoke—attributable to the occupants of a building—is so often a cause of indoor air pollution, it deserves separate treatment. Many countries have laws, at the state level, that prohibit smoking in certain types of public space such as restaurants and theatres, but other arrangements are very common whereby smoking is permitted in certain specially designated parts of a given building.

When the use of certain products or materials is prohibited, these prohibitions are made based on their alleged detrimental health effects, which are more or less well documented for levels normally present in indoor air. Another difficulty that arises is that often there is not enough information or knowledge about the properties of the products that could be used in their stead.

Elimination of the Pollutant

There are times when it is not possible to avoid the emissions of certain sources of pollution, as is the case, for example, when the emissions are due to the occupants of the building. These emissions include carbon dioxide and bioeffluents, the presence of materials with properties that are not controlled in any way, or the carrying out of everyday tasks. In these cases one way to reduce the levels of contamination is with ventilation systems and other means used to clean indoor air.

Ventilation is one of the options most heavily relied on to reduce the concentration of pollutants in indoor spaces. However, the need to also save energy requires that the intake of outside air to renew indoor air be as sparing as possible. There are standards in this regard that specify minimum ventilation rates, based on the renewal of the volume of indoor air per hour with outdoor air, or that set a minimum contribution of air per occupant or unit of space, or that take into account the concentration of carbon dioxide considering the differences between spaces with smokers and without smokers. In the case of buildings with natural ventilation, minimum requirements have also been set for different parts of a building, such as windows.

Among the references most often cited by a majority of the existing standards, both national and international—even though it is not legally binding—are the norms published by the American Society of Heating, Refrigerating and Air Conditioning Engineers (ASHRAE). They were formulated to aid air-conditioning professionals in the design of their installations. In ASHRAE Standard 62-1989 (ASHRAE 1989), the minimum amounts of air needed to ventilate a building are specified, as well as the acceptable quality of indoor air required for its occupants in order to prevent adverse health effects. For carbon dioxide (a compound most authors do not consider a pollutant given its human origin, but that is used as an indicator of the quality of indoor air in order to establish the proper functioning of ventilation systems) this standard recommends a limit 1,000 ppm in order to satisfy criteria of comfort (odour). This standard also specifies the quality of outdoor air required for the renewal of indoor air.

In cases where the source of contamination—be it interior or exterior—is not easy to control and where equipment must be used to eliminate it from the environment, there are standards to guarantee their efficacy, such as those that state specific methods to check the performance of a certain type of filter.

Extrapolation from Standards of Occupational Hygiene to Standards of Indoor Air Quality

It is possible to establish different types of reference value that are applicable to indoor air as a function of the type of population that needs to be protected. These values can be based on quality standards for ambient air, on specific values for given pollutants (like carbon dioxide, carbon monoxide, formaldehyde, volatile organic compounds, radon and so on), or they can be based on standards usually employed in occupational hygiene. The latter are values formulated exclusively for applications in industrial environments. They are designed, first of all, to protect workers from the acute effects of pollutants—like irritation of mucous membranes or of the upper respiratory tract—or to prevent poisoning with systemic effects. Because of this possibility, many authors, when they are dealing with indoor environment, use as a reference the limit values of exposure for industrial environments established by the American Conference of Governmental Industrial Hygienists (ACGIH) of the United States. These limits are called *threshold limit values* (TLVs), and they include limit values for workdays of eight hours and work weeks of 40 hours.

Numerical ratios are applied in order to adapt TLVs to the conditions of the indoor environment of a building, and the values are commonly reduced by a factor of two, ten, or even one hundred, depending on the kind of health effects involved and the type of population affected. Reasons given for reducing the values of TLVs when they are applied to exposures of this kind include the fact that in non-industrial environments personnel are exposed simultaneously to low concentrations of several, normally unknown chemical substances which are capable of acting synergistically in a way that cannot be easily controlled. It is generally accepted, on the other hand, that in industrial environments the number of dangerous substances that need to be controlled is known, and is often limited, even though concentrations are usually much higher.

Moreover, in many countries, industrial situations are monitored in order to secure compliance with the established reference values, something that is not done in non-industrial environments. It is therefore possible that in non-industrial environments, the occasional use of some products can produce high concentrations of one or several compounds, without any environmental monitoring and with no way of revealing the levels of exposure that have occurred. On the other hand, the risks inherent in an industrial activity are known or should be known and, therefore, measures for their reduction or monitoring are in place. The affected workers are informed and have the means to reduce the risk and protect themselves. Moreover, workers in industry are usually adults in good health and in acceptable physical condition, while the population of indoor environments presents, in general, a wider range of health statuses. The normal work in an office, for example, may be done by people with physical limitations or people susceptible to allergic reactions who would be unable to work in certain industrial environments. An extreme case of this line of reasoning would apply to the use of a building as a family dwelling. Finally, as noted above, TLVs, just like other occupational standards, are based on exposures of eight hours a day, 40 hours a week. This represents less than one fourth of the time a person would be exposed if he or she remained continually in the same environment or were exposed to some substance for the entire 168 hours of a week. In addition, the reference values are based on studies that include weekly exposures and that take into account times of non-exposure (between exposures) of 16 hours a day and 64 hours on weekends, which makes it is very hard to make extrapolations on the strength of these data.

The conclusion most authors arrive at is that in order to use the standards for industrial hygiene for indoor air, the reference values must include a very ample margin of error. Therefore, the ASHRAE Standard 62-1989 suggests a concentration of one tenth of the TLV value recommended by the ACGIH for industrial environments for those chemical contaminants which do not have their own established reference values.

Regarding biological contaminants, technical criteria for their evaluation which could be applicable to industrial environments or indoor spaces do not exist, as is the case with the TLVs of the ACGIH for chemical contaminants. This could be due to the nature of biological contaminants, which exhibit a wide variability of characteristics that make it difficult to establish criteria for their evaluation that are generalized and validated for any given situation. These characteristics include the reproductive capacity of the organism in question, the fact that the same microbial species may have varying degrees of pathogenicity or the fact that alterations in environmental factors like temperature and humidity may have an effect upon their presence in any given environment. Nonetheless, in spite of these difficulties, the Bioaerosol Committee of the ACGIH has developed guidelines to evaluate these biological agents in indoor environments: *Guidelines for the Assessment of Bioaerosols in the Indoor Environment* (1989). The standard protocols that are recommended in these guidelines set sampling systems and strategies, analytical procedures, data interpretation and recommendations for corrective measures. They can be used when medical or clinical information points to the existence of illnesses like humidifier fever, hypersensitivity pneumonitis or allergies related to biological contaminants. These guidelines can be applied when sampling is needed in order to document the relative contribution of the sources of bioaerosols already identified or to validate a medical hypothesis. Sampling should be done in order to confirm potential sources, but routine sampling of air to detect bioaerosols is not recommended.

Existing Guidelines and Standards

Different international organizations such as the World Health Organization (WHO) and the International Council of Building Research (CIBC), private organizations such as ASHRAE and countries like the United States and Canada, among others, are establishing exposure guidelines and standards. For its part, the European Union (EU) through the European Parliament, has presented a resolution on the quality of air in indoor spaces. This resolution establishes the need for the European Commission to propose, as soon as possible, specific directives that include:

1. a list of substances to be proscribed or regulated, both in the construction and in the maintenance of buildings
2. quality standards that are applicable to the different types of indoor environments
3. prescriptions for the consideration, construction, management and maintenance of air-conditioning and ventilation installations
4. minimum standards for the maintenance of buildings that are open to the public.

Many chemical compounds have odours and irritating qualities at concentrations that, according to current knowledge, are not dangerous to the occupants of a building but that can be perceived by—and therefore annoy—a large number of people. The reference values in use today tend to cover this possibility.

Given the fact that the use of occupational hygiene standards is not recommended for the control of indoor air unless a correction is factored in, in many cases it is better to consult the reference values used as guidelines or standards for the quality of ambient air. The US Environmental Protection Agency (EPA) has set standards for ambient air intended to protect, with an adequate margin of safety, the health of the population in general (primary standards) and even its welfare (secondary standards) against any adverse effects that may be predicted due to a given pollutant. These reference values are, therefore, useful as a general guide to establish an acceptable standard of air quality for a given indoor space, and some standards like ASHRAE-92 use them as quality criteria for the renewal of air in a closed building. Table 44.17 shows the reference values for sulphur dioxide, carbon monoxide, nitrogen dioxide, ozone, lead and particulate matter.

For its part, WHO has established guidelines intended to provide a baseline to protect public health from adverse effects due to air pollution and to eliminate or reduce to a minimum those air pollutants that are known or suspected of being dangerous for human health and welfare (WHO 1987). These

Table 44.17 • Standards of air quality established by the US Environmental Protection Agency.

Pollutant	Average concentration		Time frame for exposures
	µg/m³	ppm	
Sulphur dioxide	80[a]	0.03	1 year (arithmetic mean)
	365[a]	0.14	24 hours[c]
	1,300[b]	0.5	3 hours[c]
Particulate matter	150[a,b]	—	24 hours[d]
	50[a,b]	—	1 year[d] (arithmetic mean)
Carbon monoxide	10,000[a]	9.0	8 hours[c]
	40,000[a]	35.0	1 hour[c]
Ozone	235[a,b]	0.12	1 hour
Nitrogen dioxide	100[a,b]	0.053	1 year (arithmetic mean)
Lead	1.5[a,b]	—	3 months

[a] Primary standard. [b] Secondary standard. [c] Maximum value that should not be exceeded more than once a year. [d] Measured as particles of diameter ≤10 µm.

Source: US Environmental Protection Agency. National Primary and Secondary Ambient Air Quality Standards. Code of Federal Regulations, Title 40, Part 50 (July 1990).

Table 44.18 • WHO guideline values for some substances in air based on known effects on human health other than cancer or odour annoyance.[a]

Pollutant	Guideline value (time-weighted average)	Duration of exposure
Organic compounds		
Carbon disulphide	100 µg/m³	24 hours
1,2-Dichloroethane	0.7 mg/m³	24 hours
Formaldehyde	100 µg/m³	30 minutes
Methylene chloride	3 mg/m³	24 hours
Styrene	800 µg/m³	24 hours
Tetrachloroethylene	5 mg/m³	24 hours
Toluene	8 mg/m³	24 hours
Trichloroethylene	1 mg/m³	24 hours
Inorganic compounds		
Cadmium	1-5 ng/m³	1 year (rural areas)
	10-20 ng/m³	1 year (rural areas)
Carbon monoxide	100 mg/m³ [c]	15 minutes
	60 mg/m³ [c]	30 minutes
	30 mg/m³ [c]	1 hour
	10 mg/m³	8 hours
Hydrogen sulphide	150 µg/m³	24 hours
Lead	0.5-1.0 µg/m³	1 year
Manganese	1 µg/m³	1 hour
Mercury	1 µg/m³ [b]	1 hour
Nitrogen dioxide	400 µg/m³	1 hour
	150 µg/m³	24 hours
Ozone	150-200 µg/m³	1 hour
	10-120 µg/m³	8 hours
Sulphur dioxide	500 µg/m³	10 minutes
	350 µg/m³	1 hour
Vanadium	1 µg/m³	24 hours

[a] Information in this table should be used in conjunction with the rationales provided in the original publication. [b] This value refers to indoor air only. [c] Exposure to this concentration should not exceed the time indicated and should not be repeated within 8 hours.

Source: WHO 1987.

guidelines do not make distinctions as to the type of exposure they are dealing with, and hence they cover exposures due to outdoor air as well as exposures that may occur in indoor spaces. Tables 44.18 and 44.19 show the values proposed by WHO (1987) for non-carcinogenic substances, as well as the differences between those that cause health effects and those that cause sensory discomfort.

For carcinogenic substances, the EPA has established the concept of *units of risk*. These units represent a factor used to calculate the increase in the probability that a human subject will contract cancer due to a lifetime's exposure to a carcinogenic substance in air at a concentration of 1 µg/m³. This concept is applicable to substances that can be present in indoor air, such as metals like arsenic, chrome VI and nickel; organic compounds like benzene, acrylonitrile and polycyclic aromatic hydrocarbons; or particulate matter, including asbestos.

Table 44.19 • WHO guideline values for some non-carcinogenic substances in air, based on sensory effects or annoyance reactions for an average of 30 minutes.

Pollutant	Odour threshold		Guideline value
	Detection	Recognition	
Carbon disulphide	200 µg/m³	—[a]	20 µg/m³ [b]
Hydrogen sulphide	0.2-2.0 µg/m³	0.6-6.0 µg/m³	7 µg/m³
Styrene	70 µg/m³	210-280 µg/m³	70 µg/m³
Tetrachloro-ethylene	8 mg/m³	24-32 mg/m³	8 mg/m³
Toluene	1 mg/m³	10 mg/m³	1 mg/m³

[a] Data not provided. [b] In the manufacture of viscose it is accompanied by other odorous substances such as hydrogen sulphide and carbonyl sulphide.
Source: WHO 1987.

Table 44.20 • Reference values for radon according to three organizations.

Organization	Concentration	Recommendation
Environmental Protection Agency	4-20 pCi/l	Reduce the level in years
	20-200 pCi/l	Reduce the level in months
	≥200 pCi/l	Reduce the level in weeks or evacuate occupants
European Union	>400 Bq/m³ [a,b] (existing buildings)	Reduce the level
	>400 Bq/m³ [a] (new construction)	Reduce the level
World Health Organization	>100 Bq/m³ EER[c]	Reduce the level
	>400 Bq/m³ EER[c]	Take immediate action

[a] Average annual concentration of radon gas. [b] Equivalent to a dose of 20 mSv/year.
[c] Annual average.

In the concrete case of radon, table 44.20 shows the reference values and the recommendations of different organizations. Thus the EPA recommends a series of gradual interventions when the levels in indoor air rise above 4 pCi/l (150 Bq/m³), establishing the time frames for the reduction of those levels. The EU, based on a report submitted in 1987 by a task force of the International Commission on Radiological Protection (ICRP), recommends an average yearly concentration of radon gas, making a distinction between existing buildings and new construction. For its part, WHO makes its recommendations keeping in mind exposure to radon's decay products, expressed as a concentration of equilibrium equivalent of radon (EER) and taking into account an increase in the risk of contracting cancer between 0.7×10^{-4} and 2.1×10^{-4} for a lifetime exposure of 1 Bq/m³ EER.

Finally, it must be remembered that reference values are established, in general, based on the known effects that individual substances have on health. While this may often represent arduous work in the case of assaying indoor air, it does not take into account the possible synergistic effects of certain substances. These include, for example, volatile organic compounds (VOCs). Some authors have suggested the possibility of defining total levels of concentrations of volatile organic compounds (TVOCs) at which the occupants of a building may begin to react. One of the main difficulties is that, from the point of view of analysis, the definition of TVOCs has not yet been resolved to everyone's satisfaction.

In practice, the future establishment of reference values in the relatively new field of indoor air quality will be influenced by the development of policies on the environment. This will depend on the advancements of knowledge of the effects of pollutants and on improvements in the analytical techniques that can help us to determine these values.

References

American Conference of Governmental Industrial Hygienists (ACGIH). 1989. *Guidelines for the Assessment of Bioaerosols in the Indoor Environment*. Cincinnati, Ohio: ACGIH.

American Society for Testing Materials (ASTM). 1989. *Standard Guide for Small-Scale Environmental Determinations of Organic Emissions from Indoor Materials/Products*. Atlanta: ASTM.

American Society of Heating Refrigerating and Air Conditioning Engineers (ASHRAE). 1989. *Ventilation for Acceptable Indoor Air Quality*. Atlanta: ASHRAE.

Brownson, RC, MCR Alavanja, ET Hock, and TS Loy. 1992. Passive smoking and lung cancer in non-smoking women. *Am J Public Health* 82:1525-1530.

Brownson, RC, MCR Alavanja, and ET Hock. 1993. Reliability of passive smoke exposure histories in a case-control study of lung cancer. *Int J Epidemiol* 22:804-808.

Brunnemann, KD and D Hoffmann. 1974. The pH of tobacco smoke. *Food Cosmet Toxicol* 12:115-124.

—. 1991. Analytical studies on N-nitrosamines in tobacco and tobacco smoke. *Rec Adv Tobacco Sci* 17:71-112.

COST 613. 1989. Formaldehyde emissions from wood based materials: Guideline for the determination of steady state concentrations in test chambers. In *Indoor Air Quality & Its Impact On Man*. Luxembourg: EC.

—. 1991. Guideline for the characterization of volatile organic compounds emitted from indoor materials and products using small test chambers. In *Indoor Air Quality & Its Impact On Man*. Luxembourg: EC.

Eudy, LW, FW Thome, DK Heavner, CR Green, and BJ Ingebrethsen. 1986. Studies on the vapour-particulate phase distribution of environmental nicotine by selective trapping and detection methods. In *Proceedings of the Seventy-Ninth Annual Meeting of the Air Pollution Control Association, June 20-27*.

Feeley, JC. 1988. Legionellosis: Risk associated with building design. In *Architectural Design and Indoor Microbial Pollution*, edited by RB Kundsin. Oxford: OUP.

Flannigan, B. 1992. Indoor microbiological pollutants—sources, species, characterisation: An evaluation. In *Chemical, Microbiological, Health and Comfort Aspects of Indoor Air Quality—State of the Art in SBS*, edited by H Knöppel and P Wolkoff. Dordrecht: Kluwer.

—. 1993. Approaches to the assessment of microbial flora of buildings. *Environments for People: IAQ '92*. Atlanta: ASHRAE.

Freixa, A. 1993. *Calidad Del Aire: Gases Presentes a Bajas Concentraciones En Ambientes Cerrados*. Madrid: Instituto Nacional de Seguridad e Higiene en el Trabajo.

Gomel, M, B Oldenburg, JM Simpson, and N Owen. 1993. Work-site cardiovascular risk reduction: A randomized trial of health risk assessment, education, counselling and incentives. *Am J Public Health* 83:1231-1238.

Guerin, MR, RA Jenkins, and BA Tomkins. 1992. *The Chemistry of Environmental Tobacco Smoke*. Chelsea, Mich: Lewis.

Hammond, SK, J Coghlin, PH Gann, M Paul, K Taghizadek, PL Skipper, and SR Tannenbaum. 1993. Relationship between environmental tobacco smoke and carcinogen-hemoglobin adduct levels in non-smokers. *J Natl Cancer Inst* 85:474-478.

Hecht, SS, SG Carmella, SE Murphy, S Akerkar, KD Brunnemann, and D Hoffmann. 1993. A tobacco-specific lung carcinogen in men exposed to cigarette smoke. *New Engl J Med* 329:1543-1546.

Heller, W-D, E Sennewald, J-G Gostomzyk, G Scherer, and F Adlkofer. 1993. Validation of ETS-exposure in a representative population in Southern Germany. *Indoor Air Publ Conf* 3:361-366.

Hilt, B, S Langard, A Anderson, and J Rosenberg. 1985. Asbestos exposure, smoking habits and cancer incidence among production and maintenance workers in an electrical plant. *Am J Ind Med* 8:565-577.

Hoffmann, D and SS Hecht. 1990. Advances in tobacco carcinogenesis. In *Handbook of Experimental Pharmacology*, edited by CS Cooper and PL Grover. New York: Springer.

Hoffmann, D and EL Wynder. 1976. Smoking and occupational cancer. *Prevent Med* 5:245-261.

International Agency for Research on Cancer (IARC). 1986. *Tobacco Smoking*. Vol. 38. Lyon: IARC.

—. 1987a. *Bis(Chloromethyl)Ether and Chloromethyl Methyl Ether*. Vol. 4 (1974), Suppl. 7 (1987). Lyon: IARC.

—. 1987b. *Coke Production*. Vol. 4 (1974), Suppl. 7 (1987). Lyon: IARC.

—. 1987c. *Environmental Carcinogens: Methods of Analysis and Exposure*. Vol. 9. Passive smoking. IARC Scientific Publications, no. 81. Lyon: IARC.

—. 1987d. *Nickel and Nickel Compounds*. Vol. 11 (1976), Suppl. 7 (1987). Lyon: IARC.

—. 1988. *Overall Evaluation of Carcinogenicity: An Updating of IARC Monographs 1 to 42*. Vol. 43. Lyon: IARC.

Johanning, E, PR Morey, and BB Jarvis. 1993. Clinical-epidemiological investigation of health effects caused by *Stachybotrys atra* building contamination. In *Proceedings of Sixth International Conference On Indoor Air Quality and Climate, Helsinki*.

Kabat, GC and EL Wynder. 1984. Lung cancer incidence in non-smokers. *Cancer* 53:1214-1221.

Luceri, G, G Peiraccini, G Moneti, and P Dolara. 1993. Primary aromatic amines from sidestream cigarette smoke are common contaminants of indoor air. *Toxicol Ind Health* 9:405-413.

Mainville, C, PL Auger, W Smorgawiewicz, D Neculcea, J Neculcea, and M Lévesque. 1988. Mycotoxines et syndrome d'extrême fatigue dans un hôpital. In *Healthy Buildings*, edited by B Petterson and T Lindvall. Stockholm: Swedish Council for Building Research.

Masi, MA et al. 1988. Environmental exposure to tobacco smoke and lung function in young adults. *Am Rev Respir Dis* 138:296-299.

McLaughlin, JK, MS Dietz, ES Mehl, and WJ Blot. 1987. Reliability of surrogate information on cigarette smoking by type of informant. *Am J Epidemiol* 126:144-146.

McLaughlin, JK, JS Mandel, ES Mehl, and WJ Blot. 1990. Comparison of next of kin with self-respondents regarding question on cigarette, coffee and alcohol consumption. *Epidemiology* 1(5):408-412.

Medina, E, R Medina, and AM Kaempffer. 1988. Effects of domestic smoking on the frequency of infantile respiratory diseases. *Rev Chilena Pediatrica* 59:60-64.

Miller, JD. 1993. Fungi and the building engineer. *Environments for People: IAQ '92*. Atlanta: ASHRAE.

Morey, PR. 1993a. Microbiological events after a fire in a high-rise building. In *Indoor Air '93*. Helsinki: Indoor Air '93.

—. 1993b. Use of hazard communication standard and general duty clause during remediation of fungal contamination. In *Indoor Air '93*. Helsinki: Indoor Air '93.

Nathanson, T. 1993. *Indoor Air Quality in Office Buildings: A Technical Guide*. Ottawa: Health Canada.

New York City Department of Health. 1993. *Guidelines On Assessment and Remediation of Stachybotrys Atra in Indoor Environments*. New York: New York City Department of Health.

Pershagen, G, S Wall, A Taube, and I Linnman. 1981. On the interaction between occupational arsenic exposure and smoking and its relationship to lung cancer. *Scand J Work Environ Health* 7:302-309.

Riedel, F, C Bretthauer, and CHL Rieger. 1989. Einfluss von paasivem Rauchen auf die bronchiale Reaktivitact bei Schulkindern. *Prax Pneumol* 43:164-168.

Saccomanno, G, GC Huth, and O Auerbach. 1988. Relationship of radioactive radon daughters and cigarette smoking in genesis of lung cancer in uranium miners. *Cancer* 62:402-408.

Sorenson, WG. 1989. Health impact of mycotoxins in the home and workplace: An overview. In *Biodeterioration Research 2*, edited by CE O'Rear and GC Llewellyn. New York: Plenum.

Swedish Work Environment Fund. 1988. *To Measure or to Take Direct Remedial Action? Investigation and Measurement Strategies in the Working Environment*. Stockholm: Arbetsmiljöfonden [Swedish Work Environment Fund].

US Environmental Protection Agency (US EPA). 1992. *Respiratory Health Effects of Passive Smoking: Lung Cancer and Other Disorders*. Washington, DC: US EPA.

US National Research Council. 1986. *Environmental Tobacco Smoke: Measuring Exposures and Assessing Health Effect*. Washington, DC: National Academy of Sciences.

US Surgeon General. 1985. *The Health Consequences of Smoking: Cancer and Chronic Lung Disease in the Workplace*. Washington, DC: DHHS (PHS).

—. 1986. *The Health Consequences of Involuntary Smoking*. Washington, DC: DHHS (CDC).

Wald, NJ, J Borcham, C Bailey, C Ritchie, JE Haddow, and J Knight. 1984. Urinary cotinine as marker of breathing other people's tobacco smoke. *Lancet* 1:230-231.

Wanner, H-U, AP Verhoeff, A Colombi, B Flannigan, S Gravesen, A Mouilleseux, A Nevalainen, J Papadakis, and K Seidel. 1993. *Biological Particles in Indoor Environments. Indoor Air Quality and Its Impact On Man*. Brussels: Commission of the European Communities.

White, JR and HF Froeb. 1980. Small airway dysfunction in non-smokers chronically exposed to tobacco smoke. *New Engl J Med* 302:720-723.

World Health Organization (WHO). 1987. *Air Quality Guidelines for Europe*. European Series, no. 23. Copenhagen: WHO Regional Publications.

Other relevant readings

Berenguer, MJ. 1991. *Sindrome Del Edificio Enfermo: Factores De Reiesgo*. Madrid: Instituto Nacional de Seguridad e Higiene en el Trabajo.

Berenguer, MJ, X Guardino, A Hernández, MC Martí, C Nogareda, and MD Solé. 1994. *El Sindrome Del Edificio Enfermo. Guia Para Su Evalución*. Madrid: Instituto Nacional de Seguridad e Higiene en el Trabajo.

Department of the Environment. 1993. *Urban Air Quality in the United Kingdom*. London: Department of the Environment.

Dudney, CS and ED Copenhaver. 1983. The elements of indoor air quality. In *Indoor Air Quality*, edited by PJ Walsh, CS Dudney, and ED Copenhaver. Boca Raton: CRC Press.

Fanger, PO. 1990. Indoor air quality perceived by human beings. In *The Practitioner's Approach to Indoor Air Quality Investigations: Proceedings, Indoor Air Quality International Symposium*, edited by DM Weekes and RB Gammage. Akron, Ohio: American Industrial Hygiene Association (AIHA).

Godish, T. 1989. *Indoor Air Pollution Control*. Chelsea, Mich: Lewis.

—. 1991. *Air Quality*. Chelsea, Mich: Lewis.

Guardino, X. 1984. *Toma De Muestra De Gases Y Vapores Con Bolsa. Norma General*. Madrid: Instituto Nacional de Seguridad e Higiene en el Trabajo.

International Agency for Research on Cancer (IARC). 1993. *Indoor Air, Environmental Carcinogens. Methods of Analysis and Exposure Measurement*. Vol. 12. Lyon: IARC.

Knoppel, H and P Wolkoff. 1992. *Chemical, Microbiological, Health and Comfort Aspects of Indoor Air Quality—State of the Art in SBS*. Dordrecht: Kluwer Academic.

Lewis, RG and L Wallace. 1989. Workshop: Instrumentation and methods for measurement of indoor air quality and related factors. In *Design and Protocol for Monitoring Indoor Air Quality*, edited by NL Nageda and JP Harper. Philadelphia: American Society for Testing Materials (ASTM).

Morey, PR and JC Feeley. 1990. The landlord, tenant, and investigator: Their needs, concerns, and viewpoints. In *Biological Contaminants in Indoor Environments*, edited by JC Feeley and JA Otten. Philadelphia: American Society for Testing Materials.

Nageda, NL, HE Rector, and MD Koontz. 1987. *Guidelines for Monitoring Indoor Air Quality*. Washington, DC: Hemisphere.

Namiesnik, J, T Gorecki, B Kosdron-Zabiegala, and J Lukasiak. 1992. Indoor air quality, pollutants, their sources and concentration levels. *Build Environ* 27(3):339-356.

Otson, R and P Fellin. 1992. Volatile organics in the indoor environment: Sources and occurrence. In *Gaseous Pollutants: Characterisation and Cycling*, edited by J Nriagu. New York: Wiley.

Rafferty, PJ and PJ Quinlan. 1990. The practitioner's guide to indoor air quality. In *The Practitioner's Approach to Indoor Air Quality Investigations*, edited by DM Weekes and RB Gammage. Akron, Ohio: American Industrial Hygiene Association (AIHA).

Scheff, PA, RA Wadden, and BA Bates. 1990. Indoor air pollution. In *Health and Safety Beyond the Workplace*, edited by LV Cralley, LJ Cralley, and WC Cooper. New York: Willey.

Seifert, J. 1992. *Regulating Indoor Air: Chemical, Microbiological, Health and Comfort Aspects of Indoor Air Quality—State of the Art in SBS*. Brussels: Kluwer Academic.

Turiel, I. 1986. *Indoor Air Quality and Human Health*. Palo Alto, Calif: Stanford Univ. Press.

United Nations. 1985. *Radiation Doses, Effects, Risks*. Nairobi, Kenya: UNEP.

Wadden, RA and PA Scheff. 1983. *Indoor Air Pollution. Characterization, Prediction and Control*. New York: Wiley.

Wolkoff, P. 1992. *Chemical, Microbiological, Health and Comfort Aspects of Indoor Air Quality-State of the Art in SBS*. Brussels: ECSC.

World Health Organization (WHO). 1989. *Indoor Air Quality: Organic Pollutants*. Copenhagen: WHO Regional Office for Europe.

Yocom, JE and SM McCarthy. 1991. *Measuring Indoor Air Quality: A Practical Guide*. Chichester: Wiley.

45

Chapter Editor
Juan Guasch Farrás

Contents

CONTROL OF INDOOR ENVIRONMENTS: GENERAL PRINCIPLES

A. Hernández Calleja

People in urban settings spend between 80 and 90% of their time in indoor spaces while carrying out sedentary activities, both during work and during leisure time. (See figure 45.1).

This fact led to the creation within these indoor spaces of environments that were more comfortable and homogeneous than those found outdoors with their changing climatic conditions. To make this possible, the air within these spaces had to be conditioned, being warmed during the cold season and cooled during the hot season.

For air conditioning to be efficient and cost-effective it was necessary to control the air coming into the buildings from the outside, which could not be expected to have the desired thermal characteristics. The result was increasingly airtight buildings and more stringent control of the amount of ambient air that was used to renew stagnant indoor air.

The energy crisis at the beginning of the 1970s—and the resulting need to save energy—represented another state of affairs often responsible for drastic reductions in the volume of ambient air used for renewal and ventilation. What was commonly done then was to recycle the air inside a building many times over. This was done, of course, with the aim of reducing the cost of air-conditioning. But something else began to happen: the number of complaints, discomfort and/or health problems of the occupants of these buildings increased considerably. This, in turn, increased the social and financial costs due to absenteeism and led specialists to study the origin of complaints that, until then, were thought to be independent of pollution.

It is not a complicated matter to explain what led to the appearance of complaints: buildings are built more and more hermetically, the volume of air supplied for ventilation is reduced, more materials and products are used to insulate buildings thermally, the number of chemical products and synthetic materials used multiplies and diversifies and individual control of the environment is gradually lost. The result is an indoor environment that is increasingly contaminated.

The occupants of buildings with degraded environments then react, for the most part, by expressing complaints about aspects of their environment and by presenting clinical symptoms. The symptoms most commonly heard of are the following sort: irritation of mucous membranes (eyes, nose and throat), headaches, shortness of breath, higher incidence of colds, allergies and so on.

When the time comes to define the possible causes that trigger these complaints, the apparent simplicity of the task gives way in

Table 45.1 • The most common indoor pollutants and their sources.

Site	Sources of emission	Pollutant
Outdoors	**Fixed sources**	
	Industrial sites, energy production	Sulphur dioxide, nitrogen oxides, ozone, particulate matter, carbon monoxide, organic compounds
	Motor vehicles	Carbon monoxide, lead, nitrogen oxides
	Soil	Radon, microorganisms
Indoors	**Construction materials**	
	Stone, concrete	Radon
	Wood composites, veneer	Formaldehyde, organic compounds
	Insulation	Formaldehyde, fiberglass
	Fire retardants	Asbestos
	Paint	Organic compounds, lead
	Equipment and installations	
	Heating systems, kitchens	Carbon monoxide and dioxide, nitrogen oxides, organic compounds, particulate matter
	Photocopiers	Ozone
	Ventilation systems	Fibres, microorganisms
	Occupants	
	Metabolic activity	Carbon dioxide, water vapour, odours
	Biological activity	Microorganisms
	Human activity	
	Smoking	Carbon monoxide, other compounds, particulate matter
	Air fresheners	Fluorocarbons, odours
	Cleaning	Organic compounds, odours
	Leisure, artistic activities	Organic compounds, odours

Figure 45.1 • Urban dwellers spend 80 to 90% of their time indoors.

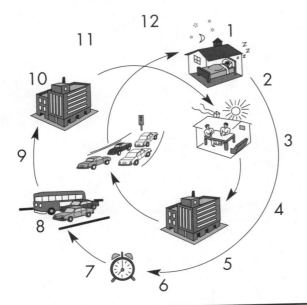

fact to a very complex situation as one attempts to establish the relation of cause and effect. In this case one must look at all the factors (whether environmental or of other origins) that may be implicated in the complaints or the health problems that have appeared.

The conclusion—after many years of studying this problem—is that these problems have multiple origins. The exceptions are those cases where the relationship of cause and effect has been clearly established, as in the case of the outbreak of Legionnaires' disease, for example, or the problems of irritation or of increased sensitivity due to exposure to formaldehyde.

The phenomenon is given the name of *sick building syndrome*, and is defined as those symptoms affecting the occupants of a building where complaints due to malaise are more frequent than might be reasonably expected.

Table 45.1 shows some examples of pollutants and the most common sources of emissions that can be associated with a drop in the quality of indoor air.

In addition to indoor air quality, which is affected by chemical and biological pollutants, sick building syndrome is attributed to many other factors. Some are physical, such as heat, noise and illumination; some are psychosocial, chief among them the way work is organized, labour relations, the pace of work and the workload.

Indoor air plays a very important role in sick building syndrome, and controlling its quality can therefore help, in most cases, to rectify or help improve conditions that lead to the appearance of the syndrome. It should be remembered, however, that air quality is not the only factor that should be considered in evaluating indoor environments.

Measures for the Control of Indoor Environments

Experience shows that most of the problems that occur in indoor environments are the result of decisions made during the design and construction of a building. Although these problems can be solved later by taking corrective measures, it should be pointed out that preventing and correcting deficiencies during the design of the building is more effective and cost-efficient.

The great variety of possible sources of pollution determines the multiplicity of corrective actions that can be taken to bring them under control. The design of a building may involve professionals from various fields, such as architects, engineers, interior designers and others. It is therefore important at this stage to keep in mind the different factors that can contribute to eliminate or minimize the possible future problems that may arise because of poor air quality. The factors that should be considered are

- selection of the site
- architectural design
- selection of materials
- ventilation and air conditioning systems used to control the quality of indoor air.

Selecting a building site

Air pollution may originate at sources that are close to or far from the chosen site. This type of pollution includes, for the most part, organic and inorganic gases that result from combustion—whether from motor vehicles, industrial plants, or electrical plants near the site—and airborne particulate matter of various origins.

Pollution found in the soil includes gaseous compounds from buried organic matter and radon. These contaminants can penetrate into the building through cracks in the building materials that are in contact with the soil or by migration through semi-permeable materials.

When the construction of a building is in the planning stages, the different possible sites should be evaluated. The best site should be chosen, taking these facts and information into consideration:

1. Data that show the levels of environmental pollution in the area, to avoid distant sources of pollution.
2. Analysis of adjacent or nearby sources of pollution, taking into account such factors as the amount of vehicular traffic and possible sources of industrial, commercial or agricultural pollution.
3. The levels of pollution in soil and water, including volatile or semivolatile organic compounds, radon gas and other radioactive compounds that result from the disintegration of radon. This information is useful if a decision must be made to change the site or to take measures to mitigate the presence of these contaminants within the future building. Among the measures that can be taken are the effective sealing of the channels of penetration or the design of general ventilation systems that will insure a positive pressure within the future building.
4. Information on the climate and predominant wind direction in the area, as well as daily and seasonal variations. These conditions are important in order to decide the proper orientation of the building.

On the other hand, local sources of pollution must be controlled using various specific techniques, such as draining or cleaning the soil, depressurizing the soil or using architectural or scenic baffles.

Architectural design

The integrity of a building has been, for centuries, a fundamental injunction at the time of planning and designing a new building. To this end consideration has been given, today as in the past, to the capacities of materials to withstand degradation by humidity, temperature changes, air movement, radiation, the attack of chemical and biological agents or natural disasters.

The fact that the above-mentioned factors should be considered when undertaking any architectural project is not an issue in the current context: in addition, the project must implement the right decisions with regard to the integrity and well-being of the occupants. During this phase of the project decisions must be made about such concerns as the design of interior spaces, the selection of materials, the location of activities that could be potential sources of pollution, the openings of the building to the outside, the windows and the ventilation system.

Building openings

Effective measures of control during the design of the building consist of planning the location and orientation of these openings with an eye to minimizing the amount of contamination that can enter the building from previously detected sources of pollution. The following considerations should be kept in mind:

- Openings should be far from sources of pollution and not in the predominant direction of the wind. When openings are close to sources of smoke or exhaust, the ventilation system should be planned to produce positive air pressure in that area in order to avoid the re-entry of vented air, as shown in figure 45.2 (overleaf).
- Special attention should be given to guarantee drainage and to prevent seepage where the building comes in contact with the soil, into the foundation, in areas that are tiled, where the drainage system and conduits are located, and other sites.

Figure 45.2 • Penetration of pollution from the outside.

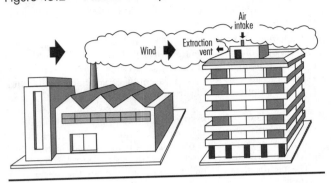

- Access to loading docks and garages should be built far from the normal air intake sites of the building as well as from the main entrances.

Windows

During recent years there has been a reversal of the trend seen in the 1970s and the 1980s, and now there is a tendency to include working windows in new architectural projects. This confers several advantages. One of them is the ability to provide supplementary ventilation in those areas (few in number, it is hoped) that need it, assuming that the ventilation system has sensors in those areas to prevent imbalances. It should be kept in mind that the ability to open a window does not always guarantee that fresh air will enter a building; if the ventilation system is pressurized, opening a window will not provide extra ventilation. Other advantages are of a definitely psychosocial character, allowing the occupants a certain degree of individual control over their surroundings and direct and visual access to the outdoors.

Protection against humidity

The principal means of control consist of reducing humidity in the foundations of the building, where micro-organisms, especially fungi, can frequently spread and develop.

Dehumidifying the area and pressurizing the soil can prevent the appearance of biological agents and can also prevent the penetration of chemical pollutants that may be present in the soil.

Sealing and controlling the enclosed areas of the building most susceptible to humidity in the air is another measure that should be considered, since humidity can damage the materials used to clad the building, with the result that these materials may then become a source of microbiological contamination.

Planning of indoor spaces

It is important to know during the planning stages the use to which the building will be put or the activities that will be carried out within it. It is important above all to know which activities may be a source of contamination; this knowledge can then be used to limit and control these potential sources of pollution. Some examples of activities that may be sources of contamination within a building are the preparation of food, printing and graphic arts, smoking and the use of photocopying machines.

The location of these activities in specific locales, separate and insulated from other activities, should be decided in such a way that occupants of the building are affected as little as possible.

It is advisable that these processes be provided with a localized extraction system and/or general ventilation systems with special characteristics. The first of these measures is intended to control contaminants at the source of emission. The second, applicable when there are numerous sources, when they are dispersed within

a given space, or when the pollutant is extremely dangerous, should comply with the following requirements: it should be capable of providing volumes of new air which are adequate given the established standards for the activity in question, it should not reuse any of the air by mixing it with the general flow of ventilation in the building and it should include supplementary forced-air extraction where needed. In such cases the flow of air in these locales should be carefully planned, to avoid transferring pollutants between contiguous spaces—by creating, for example, negative pressure in a given space.

Sometimes control is achieved by eliminating or reducing the presence of pollutants in the air by filtration or by cleaning the air chemically. In using these control techniques, the physical and chemical characteristics of the pollutants should be kept in mind. Filtration systems, for instance, are adequate for the removal of particulate matter from the air—so long as the efficiency of the filter is matched to the size of the particles that are being filtered—but allow gases and vapours to pass through.

The elimination of the source of pollution is the most effective way to control pollution in indoor spaces. A good example that illustrates the point are the restrictions and prohibitions against smoking in the workplace. Where smoking is permitted, it is generally restricted to special areas that are equipped with special ventilation systems.

Selection of materials

In trying to prevent possible pollution problems within a building, attention should be given to the characteristics of the materials used for construction and decoration, to the furnishings, the normal work activities that will be performed, the way the building will be cleaned and disinfected and the way insects and other pests will be controlled. It is also possible to reduce the levels of volatile organic compounds (VOCs), for example, by considering only materials and furniture that have known rates of emission for these compounds and selecting those with the lowest levels.

Today, even though some laboratories and institutions have carried out studies on emissions of this kind, the information available on the rates of emission of contaminants for construction materials is scarce; this scarcity is moreover aggravated by the vast number of products available and the variability they exhibit over time.

In spite of this difficulty, some producers have begun to study their products and to include, usually at the request of the consumer or the construction professional, information on the research that has been done. Products are more and more frequently labelled *environmentally safe, non-toxic* and so on.

There are still many problems to overcome, however. Examples of these problems include the high cost of the necessary analyses both in time and money; the lack of standards for the methods used to assay the samples; the complicated interpretation of results obtained due to lack of knowledge of the health effects of some contaminants; and the lack of agreement among researchers on whether materials with high levels of emission that emit for a short period of time are preferable to materials with low levels of emission that emit over longer periods of time.

But the fact is that in coming years the market for construction and decoration materials will become more competitive and will come under more legislative pressure. This will result in the elimination of some products or their substitution with other products that have lower rates of emission. Measures of this sort are already being taken with the adhesives used in the production of moquette fabric for upholstery and are further exemplified by the elimination of dangerous compounds such as mercury and pentachlorophenol in the production of paint.

Until more is known and legislative regulation in this field matures, decisions as to the selection of the most appropriate materials and products to use or install in new buildings will be left to the professionals. Outlined here are some considerations that can help them arrive at a decision:

- Information should be available on the chemical composition of the product and the emission rates of any pollutants, as well as any information regarding the health, safety and comfort of occupants exposed to them. This information should be provided by the manufacturer of the product.
- Products should be selected which have the lowest rates of emission possible of any contaminants, giving special attention to the presence of carcinogenic and teratogenic compounds, irritants, systemic toxins, odoriferous compounds and so on. Adhesives or materials that present large emission or absorption surfaces, such as porous materials, textiles, uncoated fibres and the like, should be specified and their use restricted.
- Preventive procedures should be implemented for the handling and installation of these materials and products. During and after the installation of these materials the space should be exhaustively ventilated and the *bake out* process (see below) should be used to cure certain products. The recommended hygienic measures should also be applied.
- One of the procedures recommended to minimize exposure to emissions of new materials during the installation and finishing stages, as well as during the initial occupation of the building, is to ventilate the building for 24 hours with 100 per cent outside air. The elimination of organic compounds by the use of this technique prevents the retention of these compounds in porous materials. These porous materials may act as reservoirs and later sources of pollution as they release the stored compounds into the environment.
- Incrementing ventilation to the maximum possible level before reoccupying a building after it has been closed for a period—during the first hours of the day—and after weekends or vacation shut-downs is also a convenient measure that can be implemented.
- A special procedure, known as *bake out*, has been used in some buildings to "cure" new materials. The *bake out* procedure consists in elevating the temperature of a building for 48 hours or more, keeping air flow at a minimum. The high temperatures favour the emission of volatile organic compounds. The building is then ventilated and its pollution load is thereby reduced. The results obtained so far show that this procedure can be effective in some situations.

Ventilation systems and the control of indoor climates

In enclosed spaces, ventilation is one of the most important methods for the control of air quality. There are so many sources of pollution in these spaces, and the characteristics of these pollutants are so varied, that it is almost impossible to manage them completely in the design stage. The pollution generated by the very occupants of the building—by the activities they engage in and the products they use for personal hygiene—are a case in point; in general, these sources of contamination are beyond the control of the designer.

Ventilation is, therefore, the method of control normally used to dilute and eliminate contaminants from polluted indoor spaces; it may be carried out with clean outdoor air or recycled air that is conveniently purified.

Many different points need to be considered in designing a ventilation system if it is to serve as an adequate pollution control method. Among them are the quality of outside air that will be used; the special requirements of certain pollutants or of their generating source; the preventive maintenance of the ventilation system itself, which should also be considered a possible source of contamination; and the distribution of air inside the building.

Table 45.2 • Basic requirements for a ventilation system by dilution.

System component or function	Requirement
Dilution by outside air	A minimum volume of air by occupant per hour should be guaranteed.
	The aim should be to renew the volume of inside air a minimum number of times per hour.
	The volume of outside air supplied should be increased based on the intensity of the sources of pollution.
	Direct extraction to the outside should be guaranteed for spaces where pollution-generating activities will take place.
Air intake locations	Placing air intakes near plumes of known sources of pollution should be avoided.
	One should avoid areas near stagnant water and the aerosols that emanate from refrigeration towers.
	The entry of any animals should be prevented and birds should be prevented from perching or nesting near intakes.
Location of air extraction vents	Extraction vents should be placed as far as possible from air intake locations and the height of the discharge vent should be increased.
	Orientation of discharge vents should be in the opposite direction from air intake hoods.
Filtration and cleaning	Mechanical and electrical filters for particulate matter should be used.
	One should install a system for the chemical elimination of pollutants.
Microbiological control	Placing any porous materials in direct contact with air currents, including those in the distribution conduits, should be avoided.
	One should avoid the collection of stagnant water where condensation is formed in air-conditioning units.
	A preventive maintenance programme should be established and the periodic cleaning of humidifiers and refrigeration towers should be scheduled.
Air distribution	One should eliminate and prevent the formation of any dead zones (where there is no ventilation) and the stratification of air.
	It is preferable to mix the air where the occupants breathe it.
	Adequate pressures should be maintained in all locales based on the activities that are performed in them.
	Air propulsion and extraction systems should be controlled to maintain equilibrium between them.

Table 45.2 summarizes the main points that should be considered in the design of a ventilation system for the maintenance of quality indoor environments.

In a typical ventilation/air conditioning system, air that has been taken from outside and that has been mixed with a variable

45. INDOOR ENVIRONMENTAL CONTROL

portion of recycled air passes through different air conditioning systems, is usually filtered, is heated or cooled according to the season and is humidified or dehumidified as needed.

Once treated, air is distributed by conduits to every area of the building and is delivered through dispersion gratings. It then mixes throughout the occupied spaces exchanging heat and renewing the indoor atmosphere before it is at last drawn away from each locale by return ducts.

The amount of outside air that should be used to dilute and to eliminate pollutants is the subject of much study and controversy. In recent years there have been changes in the recommended levels of outside air and in the published ventilation standards, in most cases involving increases in the volumes of outside air used. In spite of this, it has been noted that these recommendations are insufficient to control effectively all the sources of pollution. This is because the established standards are based on occupancy and disregard other important sources of pollution, such as the materials employed in construction, the furnishings and the quality of the air taken from the outside.

Therefore, the amount of ventilation required should be based on three fundamental considerations: the quality of air that you wish to obtain, the quality of outside air available and the total load of pollution in the space that will be ventilated. This is the starting point of the studies that have been carried out by professor PO Fanger and his team (Fanger 1988, 1989). These studies are geared to establishing new ventilation standards that meet air quality requirements and that provide an acceptable level of comfort as perceived by the occupants.

One of the factors that affects the quality of air in inside spaces is the quality of outside air available. The characteristics of exterior sources of pollution, like vehicular traffic and industrial or agricultural activities, put their control beyond the reach of the designers, the owners and the occupants of the building. It is in cases of this sort that the environmental authorities must assume the responsibility for establishing environmental protection guidelines and of making sure that they are adhered to. There are, however, many control measures that can be applied and that are useful in the reduction and the elimination of airborne pollution.

As was mentioned above, special care should be given to the location and orientation of air intake and exhaust ducts, in order to avoid drawing pollution back in from the building itself or from its installations (refrigeration towers, kitchen and bathroom vents, etc.), as well as from buildings in the immediate vicinity.

When outside air or recycled air is found to be polluted, the recommended control measures consist of filtering it and cleaning it. The most effective method of removing particulate matter is with electrostatic precipitators and mechanical retention filters. The latter will be most effective the more precisely they are calibrated to the size of the particles to be eliminated.

The use of systems capable of eliminating gases and vapours through chemical absorption and/or adsorption is a technique rarely used in nonindustrial situations; however, it is common to find systems that mask the pollution problem, especially smells for example, by the use of air fresheners.

Other techniques to clean and improve the quality of air consist of using ionizers and ozonizers. Prudence would be the best policy on the use of these systems to achieve improvements in air quality until their real properties and their possible negative health effects are clearly known.

Once air has been treated and cooled or heated it is delivered to indoor spaces. Whether the distribution of air is acceptable or not will depend, in great measure, on the selection, the number and the placement of diffusion grates.

Given the differences of opinion on the effectiveness of the different procedures that should be followed to mix air, some

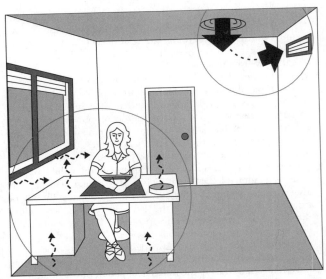

Figure 45.3 • Example of how air distribution can be shortcircuited in indoor spaces.

designers have begun to use, in some situations, air distribution systems that deliver air at floor level or on the walls as an alternative to diffusion grates on the ceiling. In any case, the location of the return registers should be carefully planned to avoid short-circuiting the entry and exit of air, which would prevent it from mixing completely as shown in figure 45.3.

Depending on how compartmentalized workspaces are, air distribution may present a variety of different problems. For example, in open workspaces where diffusion grates are on the ceiling, air in the room may not mix completely. This problem tends to be compounded when the type of ventilation system used can supply variable volumes of air. The distribution conduits of these systems are equipped with terminals that modify the amount of air supplied to the conduits based on the data received from area thermostats.

A difficulty can develop when air flows at a reduced rate through a significant number of these terminals—a situation that arises when the thermostats of different areas reach the desired temperature—and the power to the fans that push the air is automatically reduced. The result is that the total flow of air through the system is less, in some cases much less, or even that the immission of new outside air is interrupted altogether. Placing sensors that control the flow of outside air at the intake of the system can insure that a minimum flow of new air is maintained at all times.

Another problem that regularly emerges is that air flow is blocked due to the placement of partial or total partitions in the workspace. There are many ways to correct this situation. One way is to leave an open space at the lower end of the panels that divide the cubicles. Other ways include the installation of supplementary fans and the placement of the diffusion grilles on the floor. The use of supplementary induction fan coils aid in mixing the air and allow individualized control of the thermal conditions of the given space. Without detracting from the importance of air quality *per se* and the means to control it, it should be kept in mind that a comfortable indoor environment is attained by the equilibrium of the different elements that affect it. Taking any action—even positive action—affecting one of the elements without regard to the rest may affect the equilibrium among them, leading

Table 45.3 • Indoor air quality control measures and their effects on indoor environments.

Action	Effect
Thermal environment	
Increase in volume of fresh air	Increase in draughts
Reduction of relative humidity to check micro-biological agents	Insufficient relative humidity
Acoustic environment	
Intermittent supplying of outside air to conserve energy	Intermittent noise exposure
Visual environment	
Reduction in the use of fluorescent lights to reduce photochemical contamination	Reduction in the effectiveness of the illumination
Psychosocial environment	
Open offices	Loss of intimacy and of a defined workspace

to new complaints from the occupants of the building. Table 45.3 and table 45.4 show how some of these actions, intended to improve the quality of indoor air, lead to the failure of other elements in the equation, so that adjusting the working environment may have repercussions on the quality of indoor air.

Insuring the quality of the overall environment of a building when it is in the design stages depends, to a great extent, on its management, but above all on a positive attitude towards the occupants of that building. The occupants are the best sensors the owners of the building can rely on in order to gauge the proper

Table 45.4 • Adjustments of the working environment and their effects on indoor air quality.

Action	Effect
Thermal environment	
Basing the supply of outside air on thermal considerations	Insufficient volumes of fresh air
The use of humidifiers	Potential microbiological hazard
Acoustic environment	
Increase in the use of insulating materials	Possible release of pollutants
Visual environment	
Systems based solely on artificial illumination	Dissatisfaction, plant mortality, growth of micro-biological agents
Psychosocial environment	
Using equipment in the workspace, such as photocopiers and printer	Increase in the level of pollution

functioning of the installations intended to provide a quality indoor environment.

Control systems based on a "Big Brother" approach, making all the decisions regulating interior environments such as lighting, temperature, ventilation, and so on, tend to have a negative effect on the psychological and sociological well-being of the occupants. Occupants then see their capacity to create environmental conditions that meet their needs diminished or blocked. In addition, control systems of this type are sometimes incapable of changing to meet the different environmental requirements that may arise due to changes in the activities performed in a given space, the number of people working in it or changes in the way space is allocated.

The solution could consist of installing a system of centralized control for the indoor environment, with localized controls regulated by the occupants. This idea, very commonly used in the realm of the visual environment where general illumination is supplemented by more localized illumination, should be expanded to other concerns: general and localized heating and air-conditioning, general and localized supplies of fresh air and so on.

To sum up, it can be said that in each instance a portion of the environmental conditions should be optimized by means of a centralized control based on safety, health and economic considerations, while the different local environmental conditions should be optimized by the users of the space. Different users will have different needs and will react differently to given conditions. A compromise of this sort between the different parts will doubtless lead to greater satisfaction, well-being and productivity.

INDOOR AIR: METHODS FOR CONTROL AND CLEANING

E. Adán Liébana and
A. Hernández Calleja

The quality of air inside a building is due to a series of factors that include the quality of outside air, the design of the ventilation/air-conditioning system, the way that the system works and is maintained and the sources of indoor pollution. In general terms, the level of concentration of any contaminant in an indoor space will be determined by the balance between the generation of the pollutant and the rate of its elimination.

As for the generation of contaminants, the sources of pollution may also be external or internal. The external sources include atmospheric pollution due to industrial combustion processes, vehicular traffic, power plants and so on; pollution emitted near the intake shafts where air is drawn into the building, such as that from refrigeration towers or the exhaust vents of other buildings; and emanations from contaminated soil such as radon gas, leaks from gasoline tanks or pesticides.

Among the sources of internal pollution, it is worth mentioning those associated with the ventilation and air-conditioning systems themselves (chiefly the microbiological contamination of any segment of such systems), the materials used to build and decorate the building, and the occupants of the building. Specific sources of indoor pollution are tobacco smoke, laboratories, photocopiers, photographic labs and printing presses, gyms, beauty parlours, kitchens and cafeterias, bathrooms, parking garages and boiler rooms. All these sources should have a general ventilation system and air extracted from these areas should not be recycled through the building. When the situation warrants it, these areas should also have a localized ventilation system that operates by extraction.

Evaluating the quality of indoor air comprises, among other tasks, the measurement and evaluation of contaminants that may be present in the building. Several indicators are used to ascertain the quality of air inside a building. They include the concentrations of carbon monoxide and carbon dioxide, total volatile organic compounds (TVOC), total suspended particles (TSP) and the rate of ventilation. Various criteria or recommended target values exist for the evaluation of some of the substances found in interior spaces. These are listed in different standards or guidelines, such as the guidelines for the quality of interior air promulgated by the World Health Organization (WHO), or the standards of the American Society of Heating, Refrigerating and Air Conditioning Engineers (ASHRAE).

For many of these substances, however, there are no defined standards. For now the recommended course of action is to apply the values and standards for industrial environments provided by the American Conference of Governmental Industrial Hygienists (ACGIH 1992). Safety or correction factors are then applied on the order of one-half, one-tenth or one-hundredth of the values specified.

The methods of control of indoor air can be divided in two main groups: control of the source of pollution, or control of the environment with ventilation and air cleaning strategies.

Control of the Source of Pollution

The source of pollution can be controlled by various means, including the following:

1. *Elimination.* Eliminating the source of pollution is the ideal method for the control of indoor air quality. This measure is permanent and requires no future maintenance operations. It is applied when the source of pollution is known, as in the case of tobacco smoke, and it requires no substitution for polluting agents.

2. *Substitution.* In some cases, substitution of the product that is the source of contamination is the measure that should be used. Changing the kind of products used (for cleaning, decoration, etc.) with others that provide the same service but are less toxic or present less risk to the people who use them is sometimes possible.

3. *Isolation or spatial confinement.* These measures are designed to reduce exposure by limiting access to the source. The method consists in interposing barriers (partial or total) or containments around the source of pollution to minimize emissions to the surrounding air and to limit the access of people to the area near the source of pollution. These spaces should be equipped with supplementary ventilation systems that can extract air and provide a directed flow of air where needed. Examples of this approach are closed ovens, boiler rooms and photocopying rooms.

4. *Sealing the source.* This method consists of using materials that emit minimal levels of pollution or that emit none at all. This system has been suggested as a way to inhibit the dispersal of loose asbestos fibres from old insulation, as well as to inhibit the emission of formaldehyde from walls treated with resins. In buildings contaminated with radon gas, this technique is used to seal cinder blocks and crevices in basement walls: polymers are used that prevent the immission of radon from the soil. Basement walls may also be treated with epoxy paint and a polymeric sealant of polyethylene or polyamide to prevent contamination that may seep in through walls or from the soil.

5. *Ventilation by localized extraction.* Localized ventilation systems are based on the capture of the pollutant at, or as close as possible to, the source. The capture is accomplished by a bell designed to trap the pollutant in a current of air. The air then

flows by conduits with the help of a fan to be purified. If the extracted air cannot be purified or filtered, then it should be vented outside and should not be recycled back into the building.

Control of the Environment

The indoor environments of nonindustrial buildings usually have many sources of pollution and, in addition, they tend to be scattered. The system most commonly employed to correct or prevent pollution problems indoors, therefore, is ventilation, either general or by dilution. This method consists of moving and directing the flow of air to capture, contain and transport pollutants from their source to the ventilation system. In addition, general ventilation also permits the control of the thermal characteristics of the indoor environment by air conditioning and recirculating air (see "Aims and principles of general and dilution ventilation", elsewhere in this chapter).

In order to dilute internal pollution, increasing the volume of outside air is advisable only when the system is of the proper size and does not cause a lack of ventilation in other parts of the system or when the added volume does not prevent proper air-conditioning. For a ventilation system to be as effective as possible, localized extractors should be installed at the sources of pollution; air mixed with pollution should not be recycled; occupants should be placed near air diffusion vents and sources of pollution near extraction vents; pollutants should be expelled by the shortest possible route; and spaces that have localized sources of pollution should be kept at negative pressure relative to outside atmospheric pressure.

Most ventilation deficiencies seem to be linked to an inadequate amount of outside air. An improper distribution of ventilated air, however, can also result in poor air quality problems. In rooms with very high ceilings, for instance, where warm (less dense) air is supplied from above, air temperature may become stratified and ventilation will then fail to dilute the pollution present in the room. The placement and location of air diffusion vents and air return vents relative to the occupants and the sources of contamination is a consideration that requires special attention when the ventilation system is being designed.

Air Cleaning Techniques

Air cleaning methods should be precisely designed and selected for specific, very concrete types of pollutants. Once installed, regular maintenance will prevent the system from becoming a new source of contamination. The following are descriptions of six methods used to eliminate pollutants from air.

Filtration of particles

Filtration is a useful method to eliminate liquids or solids in suspension, but it should be borne in mind that it does not eliminate gases or vapours. Filters may capture particles by obstruction, impact, interception, diffusion and electrostatic attraction. Filtration of an indoor air conditioning system is necessary for many reasons. One is to prevent the accumulation of dirt that may cause a diminution of its heating or cooling efficiency. The system may also be corroded by certain particles (sulphuric acid and chlorides). Filtration is also necessary to prevent a loss of equilibrium in the ventilation system due to deposits on the fan blades and false information being fed to the controls because of clogged sensors.

Indoor air filtration systems benefit from placing at least two filters in series. The first, a pre-filter or primary filter, retains only the larger particles. This filter should be changed often and will lengthen the life of the next filter. The secondary filter is more efficient than the first, and can filter out fungal spores, synthetic fibres and in general finer dust than that collected by the primary

Table 45.5 • The effectiveness of filters (according to ASHRAE standard 52-76) for particles of 3 μm diameter.

Filter description	ASHRAE 52-76		Efficiency (%)		
	Dust spot (%)	Arrestance (%)	Initial	Final	Median
Medium	25–30	92	1	25	15
Medium	40–45	96	5	55	34
High	60–65	97	19	70	50
High	80–85	98	50	86	68
High	90–95	99	75	99	87
95% HEPA	—	—	95	99.5	99.1
99.97% HEPA	—	—	99.97	99.7	99.97

filter. These filters should be fine enough to eliminate irritants and toxic particles.

A filter is selected based on its effectiveness, its capacity to accumulate dust, its loss of charge and the required level of air purity. A filter's effectiveness is measured according to ASHRAE 52-76 and Eurovent 4/5 standards (ASHRAE 1992; CEN 1979). Their capacity for *retention* measures the mass of dust retained multiplied by the volume of air filtered and is used to characterize filters that retain only large particles (low and medium efficiency filters). To measure its retention capacity, a synthetic aerosol dust of known concentration and granulometry is forced through a filter. the portion retained in the filter is calculated by gravimetry.

The *efficiency* of a filter is expressed by multiplying the number of particles retained by the volume of air filtered. This value is the one used to characterize filters that also retain finer particles. To calculate the efficiency of a filter, a current of atmospheric aerosol is forced through it containing an aerosol of particles with a diameter between 0.5 and 1 μm. The amount of captured particles is measured with an opacitimeter, which measures the opacity caused by the sediment.

The DOP is a value used to characterize very high-efficiency particulate air (HEPA) filters. The DOP of a filter is calculated with an aerosol made by vapourizing and condensing dioctylphthalate, which produces particles 0.3 μm in diameter. This method is based on the light-scattering property of drops of dioctylphthalate: if we put the filter through this test the intensity of scattered light is proportional to the surface concentration of this material and the penetration of the filter can be measured by the relative intensity of scattered light before and after filtering the aerosol. For a filter to earn the HEPA designation it must be better than 99.97 per cent efficient on the basis of this test.

Although there is a direct relationship between them, the results of the three methods are not directly comparable. The efficiency of all filters diminishes as they clog up, and they can then become a source of odours and contamination. The useful life of a high efficiency filter can be greatly extended by using one or several filters of a lower rating in front of the high efficiency filter. Table 45.5 shows the initial, final and mean yields of different filters according to criteria established by ASHRAE 52-76 for particles 0.3 μm in diameter.

Electrostatic precipitation

This method proves useful for controlling particulate matter. Equipment of this sort works by ionizing particles and then elimi-nating them from the air current as they are attracted to and captured by a collecting electrode. Ionization occurs when the contaminated effluent passes through the electrical field generated by a strong voltage applied between the collecting and the discharge electrodes. The voltage is obtained by a direct current generator. The collecting electrode has a large surface and is usually positively charged, while the discharge electrode consists of a negatively charged cable.

The most important factors that affect the ionization of particles are the condition of the effluent, its discharge and the characteristics of the particles (size, concentration, resistance, etc.). The effectiveness of capture increases with humidity, and the size and density of the particles, and decreases with the increased viscosity of the effluent.

The main advantage of these devices is that they are highly effective at collecting solids and liquids, even when particle size is very fine. In addition, these systems may be used for heavy volumes and high temperatures. The loss of pressure is minimal. The drawbacks of these systems are their high initial cost, their large space requirements and the safety risks they pose given the very high voltages involved, especially when they are used for industrial applications.

Electrostatic precipitators are used in a full range, from industrial settings to reduce the emission of particles to domestic settings to improve the quality of indoor air. The latter are smaller devices that operate at voltages in the range of 10,000 to 15,000 volts. They ordinarily have systems with automatic voltage regulators which ensure that enough tension is always applied to produce ionization without causing a discharge between both electrodes.

Generation of negative ions

This method is used to eliminate particles suspended in air and, in the opinion of some authors, to create healthier environments. The efficacy of this method as a way to reduce discomfort or illness is still being studied.

Gas adsorption

This method is used to eliminate polluting gases and vapours like formaldehyde, sulphur dioxide, ozone, nitrogen oxides and organic vapours. Adsorption is a physical phenomena by which gas molecules are trapped by an adsorbent solid. The adsorbent consists of a porous solid with a very large surface area. To clean this kind of pollutant from the air, it is made to flow through a cartridge full of the adsorbent. Activated carbon is the most widely used; it traps a wide range of inorganic gases and organic compounds. Aliphatic, chlorinated and aromatic hydrocarbons, ketones, alcohols and esters are some examples.

Silica gel is also an inorganic adsorbent, and is used to trap more polar compounds such as amines and water. There are also other, organic adsorbents made up of porous polymers. It is important to keep in mind that all adsorbent solids trap only a certain amount of pollutant and then, once saturated, need to be regenerated or replaced. Another method of capture through adsorbent solids is to use a mixture of active alumina and carbon impregnated with specific reactants. Some metallic oxides, for instance, capture mercury vapour, hydrogen sulphide and ethylene. It must be borne in mind that carbon dioxide is not retained by adsorption.

Gas absorption

Eliminating gases and fumes by absorption involves a system that fixes molecules by passing them through an absorbent solution with which they react chemically. This is a very selective method and it uses reagents specific to the pollutant that needs to be captured.

45. INDOOR ENVIRONMENTAL CONTROL

Table 45.6 • Reagents used as absorbents for various contaminents.

Absorbent	Contaminant
Diethylhydroxamine	Hydrogen sulphide
Potassium permangenate	Odiferous gases
Hydrochloric and sulphuric acids	Amines
Sodium sulphide	Aldehydes
Sodium hydroxide	Formaldehyde

The reagent is generally dissolved in water. It also must be replaced or regenerated before it is used up. Because this system is based on transferring the pollutant from the gaseous phase to the liquid phase, the reagent's physical and chemical properties are very important. Its solubility and reactivity are especially important; other aspects that play an important part in this transfer from gaseous to liquid phase are pH, temperature and the area of contact between gas and liquid. Where the pollutant is highly soluble, it is sufficient to bubble it through the solution to fix it to the reagent. Where the pollutant is not as readily soluble the system that must be employed must ensure a greater area of contact between gas and liquid. Some examples of absorbents and the contaminants for which they are especially suited are given in table 45.6.

Ozonization

This method of improving the quality of indoor air is based on the use of ozone gas. Ozone is generated from oxygen gas by ultraviolet radiation or electric discharge, and employed to eliminate contaminants dispersed in air. The great oxidizing power of this gas makes it suitable for use as an antimicrobial agent, a deodorant and a disinfectant and it can help to eliminate noxious gases and fumes. It is also employed to purify spaces with high concentrations of carbon monoxide. In industrial settings it is used to treat the air in kitchens, cafeterias, food and fish processing plants, chemical plants, residual sewage treatment plants, rubber plants, refrigeration plants and so on. In office spaces it is used with air conditioning installations to improve the quality of indoor air.

Ozone is a bluish gas with a characteristic penetrating smell. At high concentrations it is toxic and even fatal to man. Ozone is formed by the action of ultraviolet radiation or an electric discharge on oxygen. The intentional, accidental and natural production of ozone should be differentiated. Ozone is an extremely toxic and irritating gas both at short-term and long-term exposure. Because of the way it reacts in the body, no levels are known for which there are no biological effects. These data are discussed more fully in the chemicals section of this *Encyclopaedia*.

Processes that employ ozone should be carried out in enclosed spaces or have a localized extraction system to capture any release of gas at the source. Ozone cylinders should be stored in refrigerated areas, away from any reducing agents, inflammable materials or products that may catalyze its breakdown. It should be kept in mind that if ozonizers function at negative pressures and have automatic shut-off devices in case of failure, the possibility of leaks is minimized.

Electrical equipment for processes that employ ozone should be perfectly insulated and maintenance on them should be done by experienced personnel. When using ozonizers, conduits and accessory equipment should have devices that shut ozonizers down immediately when a leak is detected; in case of a loss of efficiency

in the ventilation, dehumidifying or refrigeration functions; when there occurs an excess of pressure or a vacuum (depending on the system); or when the output of the system is either excessive or insufficient.

When ozonizers are installed, they should be provided with ozone specific detectors. The sense of smell cannot be trusted because it can become saturated. Ozone leaks can be detected with reactive strips of potassium iodide that turn blue, but this is not a specific method because the test is positive for most oxidants. It is better to monitor for leaks on a continuing basis using electrochemical cells, ultraviolet photometry or chemiluminesence, with the chosen detection device connected directly to an alarm system that acts when certain concentrations are reached.

AIMS AND PRINCIPLES OF GENERAL AND DILUTION VENTILATION

Emilio Castejón

When pollutants generated at a worksite are to be controlled by ventilating the entire locale we speak of *general ventilation*. The use of general ventilation implies accepting the fact that the pollutant will be distributed to some degree through the entire space of the worksite, and could therefore affect workers who are far from the source of contamination. General ventilation is, therefore, a strategy that is the opposite of *localized extraction*. Localized extraction seeks to eliminate the pollutant by intercepting it as closely as possible to the source (see "Indoor air: methods for control and cleaning", elsewhere in this chapter).

One of the basic objectives of any general ventilation system is the control of body odours. This can be achieved by supplying no less than 0.45 cubic metres per minute, m^3/min, of new air per occupant. When smoking is frequent or the work is physically strenuous, the rate of ventilation required is greater, and may surpass 0.9 m^3/min per person.

If the only environmental problems that the ventilation system must overcome are the ones just described, it is a good idea to keep in mind that every space has a certain level of "natural" air renewal by means of so-called "infiltration," which occurs through doors and windows, even when they are closed, and through other sites of wall penetration. Air-conditioning manuals usually provide ample information in this regard, but it can be said that as a minimum the level of ventilation due to infiltration falls between 0.25 and 0.5 renewals per hour. An industrial site will commonly experience between 0.5 and 3 renewals of air per hour.

When used to control chemical pollutants, general ventilation must be limited to only those situations where the amounts of pollutants generated are not very high, where their toxicity is relatively moderate and where workers do not carry out their tasks in the immediate vicinity of the source of contamination. If these injunctions are not respected, it will be difficult to obtain acceptance for adequate control of the work environment because such high renewal rates must be used that the high air speeds will likely create discomfort, and because high renewal rates are expensive to maintain. It is therefore unusual to recommend the use of general ventilation for the control of chemical substances except in the case of solvents which have admissible concentrations of more than 100 parts per million.

When, on the other hand, the goal of general ventilation is to maintain the thermal characteristics of the work environment with a view to legally acceptable limits or technical recommendations such as the International Organization for Standardization (ISO) guidelines, this method has fewer limitations. General ventilation is therefore used more often to control the thermal environment than to limit chemical contamination, but its usefulness as a complement of localized extraction techniques should be clearly recognized.

While for many years the phrases *general ventilation* and *ventilation by dilution* were considered synonymous, today that is no longer the case because of a new general ventilation strategy: *ventilation by displacement*. Even though ventilation by dilution and ventilation by displacement fit within the definition of general ventilation we have outlined above, they both differ widely in the strategy they employ to control contamination.

Ventilation by dilution has the goal of mixing the air that is introduced mechanically as completely as possible with all the air that is already within the space, so that the concentration of a given pollutant will be as uniform as possible throughout (or so that the temperature will be as uniform as possible, if thermal control is the goal desired). To achieve this uniform mixture air is injected from the ceiling as streams at a relatively high speed, and these streams generate a strong circulation of air. The result is a high degree of mixing of the new air with the air already present inside the space.

Ventilation by displacement, in its ideal conceptualization, consists of injecting air into a space in such a way that new air displaces the air previously there without mixing with it. Ventilation by displacement is achieved by injecting new air into a space at a low speed and close to the floor, and extracting air near the ceiling. Using ventilation by displacement to control the thermal environment has the advantage that it profits from the natural movement of air generated by density variations that are themselves due to temperature differences. Even though ventilation by displacement is already widely used in industrial situations, the scientific literature on the subject is still quite limited, and the evaluation of its effectiveness is therefore still difficult.

Ventilation by Dilution

The design of a system of ventilation by dilution is based on the hypothesis that the concentration of the pollutant is the same throughout the space in question. This is the model that chemical engineers often refer to as a stirred tank.

If you assume that the air that is injected into the space is free of the pollutant and that at the initial time the concentration within the space is zero, you will need to know two facts in order to calculate the required rate of ventilation: the amount of the pollutant that is generated in the space and the level of environmental concentration that is sought (which hypothetically would be the same throughout).

Under these conditions, the corresponding calculations yield the following equation:

$$c(t) = \frac{a}{Q}\left(1 - \exp\left(-\frac{Qt}{V}\right)\right)$$

where

$c(t)$ = the concentration of the contaminant in the space at time t
a = the amount of the pollutant generated (mass per unit of time)
Q = the rate at which new air is supplied (volume per unit of time)
V = the volume of the space in question.

The above equation shows that the concentration will tend to a steady state at the value a/Q, and that it will do so faster the smaller the value of Q/V, frequently referred to as "the number of renewals per unit of time". Although occasionally the index of the quality of ventilation is regarded as practically equivalent to that value, the above equation clearly shows that its influence is limited to controlling the *speed of stabilization* of the environmental conditions, but not the level of concentration at which such a steady state will occur. That will depend *only* on the amount of the pollutant that is generated (a), and on the rate of ventilation (Q).

When the air of a given space is contaminated but no new amounts of the pollutant are generated, the speed of diminution of the concentration over a period of time is given by the following expression:

$$c_2 = c_1\exp\left(-\frac{Q\left(t_2 - t_1\right)}{V}\right)$$

where Q and V have the meaning described above, t_1 and t_2 are, respectively, the initial and the final times and c_1 and c_2 are the initial and final concentrations.

Expressions can be found for calculations in instances where the initial concentration is not zero (Constance 1983; ACGIH 1992), where the air injected into the space is not totally devoid of the pollutant (because to reduce heating costs in the winter part of the air is recycled, for example), or where the amounts of the pollutant generated vary as a function of time.

If we disregard the transition stage and assume that the steady state has been achieved, the equation indicates that the rate of ventilation is equivalent to a/c_{lim}, where c_{lim} is the value of the concentration that must be maintained in the given space. This value will be established by regulations or, as an ancillary norm, by technical recommendations such as the threshold limit values (TLV) of the American Conference of Governmental Industrial Hygienists (ACGIH), which recommends that the rate of ventilation be calculated by the formula

$$Q = \frac{a}{c_{lim}} K$$

where a and c_{lim} have the meaning already described and K is a safety factor. A value of K between 1 and 10 must be selected as a function of the efficacy of the air mixture in the given space, of the toxicity of the solvent (the smaller c_{lim} is, the greater the value of K will be), and of any other circumstance deemed relevant by the industrial hygienist. The ACGIH, among others, cites the duration of the process, the cycle of operations and the usual location of the workers with respect to the sources of emission of the pollutant, the number of these sources and their location in the given space, the seasonal changes in the amount of natural ventilation and the anticipated reduction in the functional efficacy of the ventilation equipment as other determining criteria.

In any case, the use of the above formula requires a reasonably exact knowledge of the values of a and K that should be used, and we therefore provide some suggestions in this regard.

The amount of pollutant generated may quite frequently be estimated by the amount of certain materials consumed in the process that generates the pollutant. So, in the case of a solvent, the amount used will be a good indication of the maximum amount that can be found in the environment.

As indicated above, the value of K should be determined as a function of the efficacy of the air mixture in the given space. This value will, therefore, be smaller in direct proportion to how good the estimation is of finding the same concentration of the pollutant at any point within the given space. This, in turn, will depend on how air is distributed within the space being ventilated.

According to these criteria, minimum values of K should be used when air is injected into the space in a distributed fashion (by

Figure 45.4 • Schematic of air circulation in room with two supply openings.

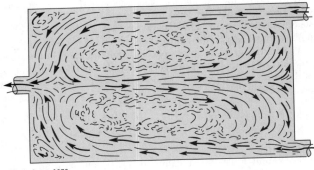

Source: Baturin 1972.

using a plenum, for example), and when the injection and extraction of air are at opposite ends of the given space. On the other hand, higher values for K should be used when air is supplied intermittently and air is extracted at points close to the intake of new air (figure 45.4]).

It should be noted that when air is injected into a given space—especially if it is done at a high speed—the stream of air created will exert a considerable pull on the air surrounding it. This air then mixes with the stream and slows it down, creating measurable turbulence as well. As a consequence, this process results in intense mixing of the air already in the space and the new air that is injected, generating internal air currents. Predicting these currents, even generally, requires a large dose of experience (figure 45.5).

In order to avoid problems that result from workers' being subjected to streams of air at relatively high speeds, air is commonly injected by way of diffusing grates designed in such a way that they facilitate the rapid mixing of new air with the air already present in the space. In this way, the areas where air moves at high speeds are kept as small as possible.

The stream effect just described is not produced near points where air escapes or is extracted through doors, windows, extraction vents or other openings. Air reaches extraction grates from all directions, so even at a relatively short distance from them, air movement is not easily perceived as an air current.

In any case, in dealing with air distribution, it is important to keep in mind the convenience of placing workstations, to the extent possible, in such a way that new air reaches the workers before it reaches the sources of contamination.

When in the given space there are important sources of heat, the movement of air will largely be conditioned by the convection currents that are due to density differences between denser, cold air and lighter, warm air. In spaces of this kind, the designer of air distribution must not fail to keep in mind the existence of these heat sources, or the movement of air may turn out to be very different from the one predicted.

The presence of chemical contamination, on the other hand, does not alter in a measurable way the density of air. While in a pure state the pollutants may have a density that is very different from that of air (usually much greater), given the real, existing concentrations in the workplace, the mix of air and pollutant does not have a density significantly different than the density of pure air.

Furthermore, it should be pointed out that one of the most common mistakes made in applying this type of ventilation is supplying the space only with air extractors, without any fore-

thought given to adequate intakes of air. In these cases, the effectiveness of the extraction ventilators is diminished and, therefore, the actual rates of air extraction are much less than planned. The result is greater ambient concentrations of the pollutant in the given space than those initially calculated.

To avoid this problem some thought should be given to how air will be introduced into the space. The recommended course of action is to use immission ventilators as well as extraction ventilators. Normally, the rate of extraction should be greater than the rate of immission in order to allow for infiltration through windows and other openings. In addition, it is advisable to keep the space under slightly negative pressure to prevent the contamination generated from drifting into areas that are not contaminated.

Ventilation by Displacement

As mentioned above, with ventilation by displacement one seeks to minimize the mixing of new air and the air previously found in the given space, and tries to adjust the system to the model known as plug flow. This is usually accomplished by introducing air at slow speeds and at low elevations in the given space and extracting it near the ceiling; this has two advantages over ventilation by dilution.

In the first place, it makes lower rates of air renewal possible, because pollution concentrates near the ceiling of the space, where there are no workers to breathe it. The *average* concentration in the given space will then be higher than the c_{lim} value we have referred to before, but that does not imply a higher risk for the workers because in the occupied zone of the given space the concentration of the pollutant will be the same or lower than a c_{lim}.

In addition, when the goal of ventilation is the control of the thermal environment, ventilation by displacement makes it possible to introduce warmer air into the given space than would be required by a system of ventilation by dilution. This is because the warm air that is extracted is at a temperature several degrees higher than the temperature in the occupied zone of the space.

The fundamental principles of ventilation by displacement were developed by Sandberg, who in the early 1980s developed a general theory for the analysis of situations where there were nonuniform concentrations of pollutants in enclosed spaces. This allowed us to overcome the theoretical limitations of ventilation by dilution (which presupposes a uniform concentration throughout the given space) and opened the way for practical applications (Sandberg 1981).

Even though ventilation by displacement is widely used in some countries, particularly in Scandinavia, very few studies have been published in which the efficacy of different methods are compared in actual installations. This is no doubt because of the practical difficulties of installing two different ventilation systems in a real factory, and because the experimental analysis of these types of systems require the use of tracers. Tracing is done by adding a tracer gas to the air ventilation current and then measuring the concentrations of the gas at different points within the space and in the extracted air. This sort of examination makes it possible to infer how air is distributed within the space and to then compare the efficacy of different ventilation systems.

The few studies available that have been carried out in actual existing installations are not conclusive, except as regards the fact that systems that employ ventilation by displacement provide better air renewal. In these studies, however, reservations are often expressed about the results in so far as they have not been confirmed by measurements of the ambient level of contamination at the worksites.

Figure 45.5 • Suggested K factors for inlet and exhaust locations.

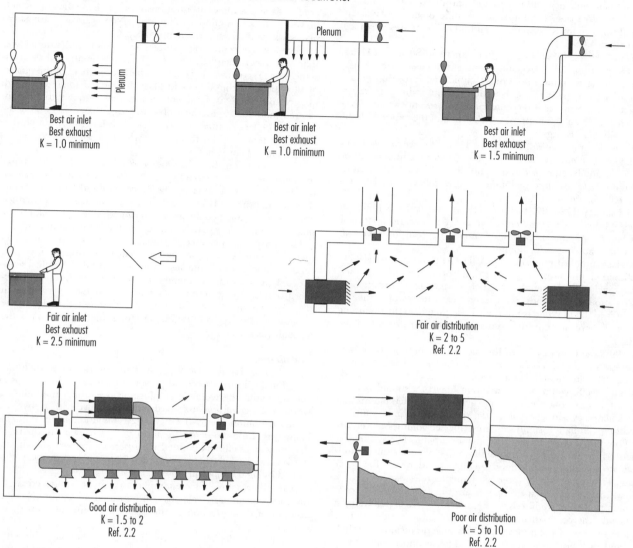

Best air inlet
Best exhaust
K = 1.0 minimum

Best air inlet
Best exhaust
K = 1.0 minimum

Best air inlet
Best exhaust
K = 1.5 minimum

Fair air inlet
Best exhaust
K = 2.5 minimum

Fair air distribution
K = 2 to 5
Ref. 2.2

Good air distribution
K = 1.5 to 2
Ref. 2.2

Poor air distribution
K = 5 to 10
Ref. 2.2

The values of K, a safety factor cited here take only air inlet and air extraction vents into account, and are meant as rough guidelines. The proper value of K to be used for the equation should be determined keeping the following things in mind: a) the number and placement of the workers, b) the source(s) of pollution and c) the toxicity of the contaminant(s). Ref 2.2: Air Force AFOSH Standard 161.2.

Source: ACGIH 1992.

VENTILATION CRITERIA FOR NONINDUSTRIAL BUILDINGS

A. Hernández Calleja

One of the chief functions of a building in which nonindustrial activities are carried out (offices, schools, dwellings, etc.) is to provide the occupants with a healthy and comfortable environment in which to work. The quality of this environment depends, to a large degree, on whether the ventilation and climatization systems of the building are adequately designed and maintained and function properly.

These systems must therefore provide acceptable thermal conditions (temperature and humidity) and an acceptable quality of indoor air. In other words, they should aim for a suitable mix of outside air with indoor air and should employ filtration and cleaning systems capable of eliminating pollutants found in the indoor environment.

The idea that clean outdoor air is necessary for well-being in indoor spaces has been expressed since the eighteenth century. Benjamin Franklin recognized that air in a room is healthier if it is provided with natural ventilation by opening the windows. The idea that providing great quantities of outside air could help reduce the risk of contagion for illnesses like tuberculosis gained currency in the nineteenth century.

Studies carried out during the 1930s showed that, in order to dilute human biological effluvia to concentrations that would not cause discomfort due to odours, the volume of new outside air required for a room is between 17 and 30 cubic metres per hour per occupant.

In standard No. 62 set in 1973, the American Society of Heating, Refrigerating and Air Conditioning Engineers (ASHRAE) recommends a minimum flow of 34 cubic metres of outside air per hour per occupant to control odours. An absolute minimum of 8.5 m^3/hr/occupant is recommended to prevent carbon dioxide from surpassing 2,500 ppm, which is half of the exposure limit set for industrial settings.

This same organization, in standard No. 90, set in 1975—in the middle of an energy crisis—adopted the aforementioned absolute minimum leaving aside, temporarily, the need for greater ventilation flows to dilute pollutants such as tobacco smoke, biological effluvia and so forth.

In its standard No. 62 (1981) ASHRAE rectified this omission and established its recommendation as 34 m^3/hr/occupant for areas where smoking is permitted and 8.5 m^3/hr/occupant in areas where smoking is forbidden.

The last standard published by ASHRAE, also No. 62 (1989), established a minimum of 25.5 m^3/hr/occupant for occupied indoor spaces independently of whether smoking is permitted or not. It also recommends increasing this value when the air brought into the building is not mixed adequately in the breathing zone or if there are unusual sources of pollution present in the building.

In 1992, the Commission of European Communities published its *Guidelines for Ventilation Requirements in Buildings*. In contrast with existing recommendations for ventilation standards, this guide does not specify volumes of ventilation flow that should be provided for a given space; instead, it provides recommendations that are calculated as a function of the desired quality of indoor air.

Existing ventilation standards prescribe set volumes of ventilation flow that should be supplied per occupant. The tendencies evidenced in the new guidelines show that volume calculations alone do not guarantee a good quality of indoor air for every setting. This is the case for three fundamental reasons.

First, they assume that occupants are the only sources of contamination. Recent studies show that other sources of pollution, in addition to the occupants, should be taken into consideration as possible sources of pollution. Examples include furniture, upholstery and the ventilation system itself. The second reason is that these standards recommend the same amount of outside air regardless of the quality of air that is being conveyed into the building. And the third reason is that they do not clearly define the quality of indoor air required for the given space. Therefore, it is proposed that future ventilation standards should be based on the following three premises: the selection of a defined category of air quality for the space to be ventilated, the total load of pollutants in the occupied space and the quality of outside air available.

The Perceived Quality of Air

The quality of indoor air can be defined as the degree to which the demands and requirements of the human being are met. Basically, the occupants of a space demand two things of the air they breathe: to perceive the air they breathe as fresh and not foul, stale or irritating; and to know that the adverse health effects that may result from breathing that air are negligible.

It is common to think that the degree of quality of the air in a space depends more on the components of that air than on the impact of that air on the occupants. It may thus seem easy to evaluate the quality of the air, assuming that by knowing its composition its quality can be ascertained. This method of evaluating air quality works well in industrial settings, where we find

chemical compounds that are implicated in or derived from the production process and where measuring devices and reference criteria to assess the concentrations exist. This method does not, however, work in nonindustrial settings. Nonindustrial settings are places where thousands of chemical substances can be found, but at very low concentrations, sometimes a thousand times lower than the recommended exposure limits; evaluating these substances one by one would result in a false assessment of the quality of that air, and the air would likely be judged to be of a high quality. But there is a missing aspect that remains to be considered, and that is the lack of knowledge that exists about the combined effect of those thousands of substances on human beings, and that may be the reason why that air is perceived as being foul, stale or irritating.

The conclusion that has been reached is that traditional methods used for industrial hygiene are not well-adapted to define the degree of quality that will be perceived by the human beings that breathe the air being evaluated. The alternative to chemical analysis is to use people as measuring devices to quantify air pollution, employing panels of judges to make the evaluations.

Human beings perceive the quality of air by two senses: the olfactory sense, situated in the nasal cavity and sensitive to hundreds of thousands of odorous substances, and the chemical sense, situated in the mucous membranes of the nose and eyes, and sensitive to a similar number of irritating substances present in air. It is the combined response of these two senses that determines how air is perceived and that allows the subject to judge whether its quality is acceptable.

The olf unit

One *olf* (from Latin = *olfactus*) is the emission rate of air pollutants (bioeffluents) from a standard person. One standard person is an average adult who works in an office or in a similar nonindustrial workplace, sedentary and in thermal comfort with a hygienic standard equipment to 0.7 bath/day. Pollution from a human being was chosen to define the term *olf* for two reasons: the first is that biological effluvia emitted by a person are well-known, and the second is that there was much data on the dissatisfaction caused by such biological effluvia.

Any other source of contamination can be expressed as the number of standard persons (olfs) needed to cause the same amount of dissatisfaction as the source of contamination that is being evaluated.

Figure 45.6 depicts a curve that defines an olf. This curve shows how contamination produced by a standard person (1 olf) is

Figure 45.6 • Olf definition curve.

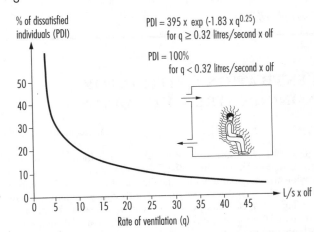

% of dissatisfied individuals (PDI)

$PDI = 395 \times exp\ (-1.83 \times q^{0.25})$
for $q \geq 0.32$ litres/second x olf

$PDI = 100\%$
for $q < 0.32$ litres/second x olf

L/s x olf

Rate of ventilation (q)

Figure 45.7 • Relation between the perceived quality of air expressed as a percentage of dissatisfied individuals and in decipols.

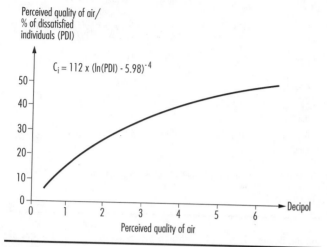

Perceived quality of air/
% of dissatisfied
individuals (PDI)

$C_i = 112 \times (\ln(PDI) - 5.98)^{-4}$

perceived at different rates of ventilation, and allows the calculation of the rate of dissatisfied individuals—in other words, those that will perceive the quality of air to be unacceptable just after they have entered the room. The curve is based on different European studies in which 168 people judged the quality of air polluted by over a thousand people, both men and women, considered to be standard. Similar studies conducted in North America and Japan show a high degree of correlation with the European data.

The decipol unit

The concentration of pollution in air depends on the source of contamination and its dilution as a result of ventilation. Perceived air pollution is defined as the concentration of human biological effluvia that would cause the same discomfort or dissatisfaction as the concentration of polluted air that is being evaluated. One *decipol* (from the Latin *pollutio*) is the contamination caused by a standard person (1 olf) when the rate of ventilation is 10 litres per second of noncontaminated air, so that we may write

1 decipol = 0.1 olf/(litre/second)

Figure 45.7, derived from the same data as the previous figure, shows the relation between the perceived quality of air, expressed as a percentage of dissatisfied individuals and in decipols.

Table 45.7 • Levels of quality of indoor air.

| Category (quality level) | Perceived air quality | | |
	Percentage of dissatisfied individuals	Decipols	Rate of ventilation required[1] litres/second × olf
A	10	0.6	16
B	20	1.4	7
C	30	2.5	4

[1] Assuming that outside air is clean and the efficiency of the ventilation system is equal to one.
Source: CEC 1992.

To determine the rate of ventilation required from the point of view of comfort, selecting the degree of air quality desired in the given space is essential. Three categories or levels of quality are proposed in table 45.7, and they are derived from figure 45.6 and figure 45.7. Each level corresponds to a certain percentage of dissatisfied people. The selection of one or another level will depend, most of all, on what the space will be used for and on economic considerations.

As noted above, the data are the result of experiments carried out with panels of judges, but it is important to keep in mind that some of the substances found in air that can be dangerous (carcinogenic compounds, micro-organisms and radioactive substances, for example) are not recognized by the senses, and that the sensory effects of other contaminants bear no quantitative relationship to their toxicity.

Sources of Contamination

As was indicated earlier, one of the shortcomings of today's ventilation standards is that they take into account only the occupants as the sources of contamination, whereas it is recognized that future standards should take all the possible sources of pollution into account. Aside from the occupants and their activities, including the possibility that they might smoke, there are other sources of pollution that contribute significantly to air pollution. Examples include furniture, upholstery and carpeting, construction materials, products used for decoration, cleaning products and the ventilation system itself.

What determines the load of pollution of air in a given space is the combination of all these sources of contamination. This load can be expressed as chemical contamination or as sensory contamination expressed in olfs. The latter integrates the effect of several chemical substances as they are perceived by human beings.

The chemical load

Contamination that emanates from a given material can be expressed as the rate of emission of each chemical substance. The total load of chemical pollution is calculated by adding all the sources, and is expressed in micrograms per second ($\mu g/s$).

In reality, it may be difficult to calculate the load of pollution because often little data are available on the rates of emission for many commonly used materials.

Sensory load

The load of pollution perceived by the senses is caused by those sources of contamination that have an impact on the perceived quality of air. The given value of this sensory load can be calculated by adding all the olfs of different sources of contamination that exist in a given space. As in the previous case, there is still not much information available on the olfs per square metre ($olfs/m^2$) of many materials. For that reason it turns out to be more practical to estimate the sensory load of the entire building, including the occupants, the furnishings and the ventilation system.

Table 45.8 (overleaf) shows the pollution load in olfs by the occupants of the building as they carry out different types of activities, as a proportion of those who smoke and don't smoke, and the production of various compounds like carbon dioxide (CO_2), carbon monoxide (CO) and water vapour. Table 45.9 (overleaf) shows some examples of the typical occupancy rates in different kinds of spaces. And last, table 45.10 (overleaf) reflects the results of the sensory load—measured in olfs per square metre—found in different buildings.

Quality of Outside Air

Another premise, one that rounds out the inputs needed for creation of ventilation standards for the future, is the quality of

Table 45.8 • Contamination due to the occupants of a building.

	Sensory load olf/occupant	CO_2 [l/(hr × occupant)]	CO^3 [l/(hr × occupant)]	Water vapour[4] [g/(hr × occupant)]
Sedentary, 1-1.2 met[1]				
0% smokers	2	19		50
20% smokers[2]	2	19	11×10^{-3}	50
40% smokers[2]	3	19	21×10^{-3}	50
100% smokers[2]	6	19	53×10^{-3}	50
Physical exertion				
Low, 3 met	4	50		200
Medium, 6 met	10	100		430
High (athletic), 10 met	20	170		750
Children				
Child care centre (3–6 years), 2.7 met	1.2	18		90
School (14–16 years), 1.2 met	1.3	19		50

[1] 1 met is the metabolic rate of a sedentary person at rest (1 met = 58 W/m^2 of skin surface). [2] Average consumption of 1.2 cigarettes/hour per smoker. Average rate of emission, 44 ml of CO per cigarette. [3] From tobacco smoke. [4] Applicable to people close to thermal neutrality.
Source: CEC 1992.

Table 45.9 • Examples of the degree of occupancy of different buildings.

Building	Occupants/m^2
Offices	0.07
Conference rooms	0.5
Theatres, other large gathering places	1.5
Schools (classrooms)	0.5
Child-care centres	0.5
Dwellings	0.05

Source: CEC 1992.

Table 45.10 • Contamination due to the building.

	Sensory load —olf/m^2	
	Average	Interval
Offices[1]	0.3	0.02–0.95
Schools (classrooms)[2]	0.3	0.12–0.54
Child care facilities[3]	0.4	0.20–0.74
Theatres[4]	0.5	0.13–1.32
Low-pollution buildings[5]		0.05–0.1

[1] Data obtained in 24 mechanically ventilated offices. [2] Data obtained in 6 mechanically ventilated schools. [3] Data obtained in 9 mechanically ventilated child-care centres. [4] Data obtained in 5 mechanically ventilated theatres. [5] Goal that should be reached by new buildings.
Source: CEC 1992.

Table 45.11 • Quality levels of outside air.

	Perceived air quality[1]	Environmental pollutants[2]			
	Decipol	CO_2 (mg/m^3)	CO (mg/m^3)	NO_2 ($\mu g/m^3$)	SO_2 ($\mu g/m^3$)
By the sea, in the mountains	0	680	0-0.2	2	1
City, high quality	<0.1	700	1-2	5-20	5-20
City, low quality	>0.5	700-800	4-6	50-80	50-100

[1] The values of perceived air quality are daily average values. [2] The values of pollutants correspond to average yearly concentrations.
Source: CEC 1992.

available outside air. Recommended exposure values for certain substances, both from inside and outside spaces, appear in the publication *Air Quality Guidelines for Europe* by the WHO (1987).

Table 45.11 shows the levels of perceived outside air quality, as well as the concentrations of several typical chemical pollutants found out of doors.

It should be kept in mind that in many cases the quality of outside air can be worse than the levels indicated in the table or in the guidelines of the WHO. In such cases air needs to be cleaned before it is conveyed into occupied spaces.

Efficiency of Ventilation Systems
Another important factor that will affect the calculation of the ventilation requirements for a given space is the efficiency of ventilation (E_v), which is defined as the relation between the concentration of pollutants in extracted air (C_e) and the concentration in the breathing zone (C_b).

$$E_v = C_e / C_b$$

The efficiency of ventilation depends on the distribution of air and the location of the sources of pollution in the given space. If air and the contaminants are mixed completely, the efficiency of ventilation is equal to one; if the quality of air in the breathing zone is better than that of extracted air, then the efficiency is greater than one and the desired quality of air can be attained with lower rates of ventilation. On the other hand, greater rates of ventilation will be needed if the efficiency of ventilation is less than one, or to put it differently, if the quality of air in the breathing zone is inferior to the quality of extracted air.

In calculating the efficiency of ventilation it is useful to divide spaces into two zones, one into which the air is delivered, the other comprising the rest of the room. For ventilation systems that work by the mixing principle, the zone where air is delivered is generally found above the breathing zone, and the best conditions are reached when mixing is so thorough that both zones become one. For ventilation systems that work by the displacement principle, air is supplied in the zone occupied by people and the extraction zone is usually found overhead; here the best conditions are reached when mixing between both zones is minimal.

The efficiency of ventilation, therefore, is a function of the location and characteristics of the elements that supply and extract air and the location and characteristics of the sources of contamination. In addition, it is also a function of the temperature and of the volumes of air supplied. It is possible to calculate the

Figure 45.8 • Effectiveness of ventilation in breathing zone according to different ventilation principles.

Ventilation principle		Temperature differences between air supply and breathing zone $(t_s - t_i)$ in °C	Efficiency of ventilating system
Ventilation by mixing	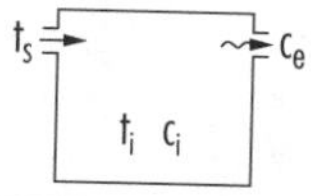 t_s ~c_e t_i c_i	< 0 0 - 2 2 - 5 > 5	0.9 - 1.0 0.9 0.8 0.4 - 0.7
Ventilation by mixing	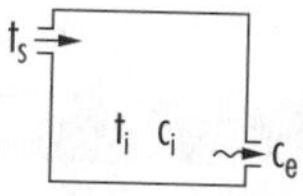 t_s t_i c_i ~c_e	< -5 0 - 5 > 0	0.9 0.9 - 1.0 1.0
Ventilation by displacement	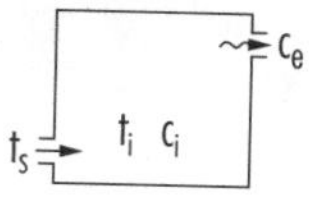 ~c_e t_s t_i c_i	< 2 0 - 2 > 0	0.2 - 0.7 0.7 - 0.9 1.2 - 1.4

efficiency of a ventilation system by numerical simulation or by taking measurements. When data are not available the values in figure 45.8 can be used for different ventilation systems. These reference values take into consideration the impact of air distribution but not the location of sources of pollution, assuming instead that they are uniformly distributed throughout the ventilated space.

Calculating Ventilation Requirements

Figure 45.9 shows the equations used to calculate ventilation requirements from the point of view of comfort as well as that of protecting health.

Ventilation requirements for comfort

The first steps in the calculation of comfort requirements is to decide the level of quality of indoor air that one wishes to obtain for the ventilated space (see table 45.7), and to estimate the quality of outside air available (see table 45.11).

The next step consists in estimating the sensory load, using table 45.8, table 45.9 and table 45.10 to select the loads according

Figure 45.9 • Equations for calculating ventilation requirements.

Comfort	Health
(1) $Q_c = 10 \times \dfrac{G}{C_i - C_o} \times \dfrac{1}{E_v}$	(2) $Q_H = \dfrac{G}{C_v - C_o} \times \dfrac{1}{E_v}$
Q_c = Stream of air required for comfort (litres/second) G = Total sensory load (olf) C_i = Desired quality of indoor air (decipol) C_c = Quality of outside air (intake) (decipol)	Q_c = Stream of air required for health protection (litres/second) G = Concentration of chemical contamination ($\mu g/s$) C_v = Evaluation criteria ($\mu g/l$) C_o = Concentration of the compound (intake) ($\mu g/l$) E_v = Effectiveness of ventilation

to the occupants and their activities, the type of building, and the level of occupancy by square metre of surface. The total value is obtained by adding all the data.

Depending on the operating principle of the ventilation system and using figure 45.9, it is possible to estimate the efficiency of ventilation. Applying equation (1) in figure 45.9 will yield a value for the required amount of ventilation.

Ventilation requirements for health protection

A procedure similar to the one described above, but using equation (2) in figure 45.9, will provide a value for the stream of ventilation required to prevent health problems. To calculate this value it is necessary to identify a substance or group of critical chemical substances which one proposes to control and to estimate their concentrations in air; it is also necessary to allow for different evaluation criteria, taking into account the effects of the contaminant and the sensitivity of the occupants that you wish to protect—children or the elderly, for example.

Unfortunately, it is still difficult to estimate the ventilation requirements for health protection owing to the lack of information on some of the variables that enter into the calculations, such as the rates of emission of the contaminants (G), the evaluation criteria for indoor spaces (C_v) and others.

Studies carried out in the field show that spaces where ventilation is required to achieve comfortable conditions the concentrations of chemical substances is low. Nevertheless, those spaces may contain sources of pollution that are dangerous. The best policy in these cases is to eliminate, to substitute or to control the sources of pollution instead of diluting the contaminants by general ventilation.

HEATING AND AIR-CONDITIONING SYSTEMS

F. Ramos Pérez and J. Guasch Farrás

With regard to heating, a given person's needs will depend on many factors. They can be classified into two main groups, those related to the surroundings and those related to human factors. Among those related to the surroundings one might count geography (latitude and altitude), climate, the type of exposure of the space the person is in, or the barriers that protect the space against the external environment, etc. Among the human factors are the worker's energy consumption, the pace of work or the amount of exertion needed for the job, the clothing or garments used against the cold and personal preferences or tastes.

The need for heating is seasonal in many regions, but this does not mean that heating is dispensable during the cold season. Cold environmental conditions affect health, mental and physical efficiency, precision and occasionally may increase the risk of accidents. The goal of a heating system is to maintain pleasant thermal conditions that will prevent or minimize adverse health effects.

The physiological characteristics of the human body allow it to withstand great variations in thermal conditions. Human beings maintain their thermal balance through the hypothalamus, by means of thermal receptors in the skin; body temperature is kept between 36 and 38°C as shown in figure 45 .10 (overleaf).

Heating systems need to have very precise control mechanisms, especially in cases where workers carry out their tasks in a sitting or a fixed position that does not stimulate blood circulation to their extremities. Where the work performed allows a certain mobility, the control of the system may be somewhat less precise. Finally, where the work performed takes place in abnormally

45. INDOOR ENVIRONMENTAL CONTROL

Figure 45.10 • Thermoregulatory mechanisms in human beings.

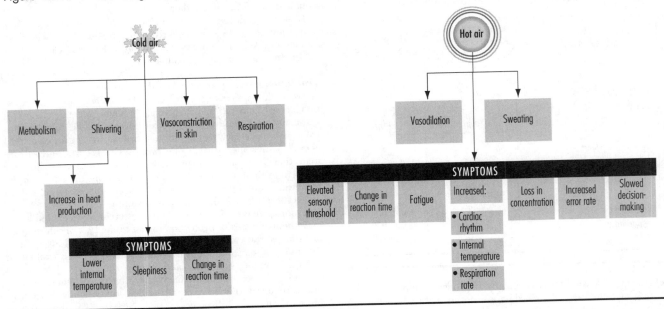

adverse conditions, as in refrigerated chambers or in very cold climatic conditions, support measures may be undertaken to protect special tissues, to regulate the time spent under those conditions or to supply heat by electrical systems incorporated into the worker's garments.

Definition and Description of the Thermal Environment

A requirement that can be demanded of any properly functioning heating or air conditioning system is that it should allow for control of the variables that define the thermal environment, within specified limits, for each season of the year. These variables are

1. air temperature
2. average temperature of the inside surfaces that define the space
3. air humidity
4. speeds and uniformity of speeds of air flow within the space

It has been shown that there is a very simple relation between the temperature of the air and of the wall surfaces of a given space, and the temperatures that provide the same perceived thermal sensation in a different room. This relation can be expressed as

$$T_{eat} = \frac{T_{dbt} + T_{ast}}{2}$$

where

T_{eat} = equivalent air temperature for a given thermal sensation
T_{dbt} = air temperature measured with a dry bulb thermometer
T_{ast} = measured average surface temperature of the walls.

For example, if in a given space the air and the walls are at 20 °C, the equivalent temperature will be 20 °C, and the perceived sensation of heat will be the same as in a room where the average temperature of the walls is 15 °C and the air temperature is 25 °C, because that room would have the same equivalent temperature. From the standpoint of temperature, the perceived sensation of thermal comfort would be the same.

Properties of humid air

In implementing an air-conditioning plan, three things that must be taken into consideration are the thermodynamic state of the air in the given space, of the air outside, and of the air that will be supplied to the room. The selection of a system capable of transforming the thermodynamic properties of the air supplied to the room will then be based on the existing thermal loads of each component. We therefore need to know the thermodynamic properties of humid air. They are as follows:

T_{dbt} = the dry bulb temperature reading, measured with a thermometer insulated from radiated heat
T_{dpt} = the dew point temperature reading. This is the temperature at which nonsaturated dry air reaches the saturation point
W = a humidity relation that ranges from zero for dry air to W_s for saturated air. It is expressed as kg of water vapour by kg of dry air
RH = relative humidity
t^* = thermodynamic temperature with moist bulb
v = specific volume of air and water vapour (expressed in units of m^3/kg). It is the inverse of density
H = enthalpy, kcal/kg of dry air and associated water vapour.

Of the above variables, only three are directly measurable. They are the dry bulb temperature reading, the dew point temperature reading and relative humidity. There is a fourth variable that is experimentally measurable, defined as the wet bulb temperature. The wet bulb temperature is measured with a thermometer whose bulb has been moistened and which is moved, typically with the aid of a sling, through nonsaturated moist air at a moderate speed. This variable differs by an insignificant amount from the thermodynamic temperature with a dry bulb (3 per cent), so they can both be used for calculations without erring too much.

Psychrometric diagram

The properties defined in the previous section are functionally related and can be portrayed in graphic form. This graphic representation is called a psychrometric diagram. It is a simplified graph derived from tables of the American Society of Heating,

Table 45.12 • Proposed norms for environmental factors.

Environmental factor	Proposed norm
Air temperature	21 °C
Average radiant temperature	≥ 21 °C
Relative humidity	30–70%
Speed of air flow	0.05–0.1 metre/second
Temperature gradient (from head to foot)	≤ 2.5 °C

Refrigerating and Air Conditioning Engineers (ASHRAE). Enthalpy and the degree of humidity are shown on the coordinates of the diagram; the lines drawn show dry and humid temperatures, relative humidity and specific volume. With the psychrometric diagram, knowing any two of the aforementioned variables enables you to derive all the properties of humid air.

Conditions for thermal comfort

Thermal comfort is defined as a state of mind that expresses satisfaction with the thermal environment. It is influenced by physical and physiological factors.

It is difficult to prescribe general conditions that should be met for thermal comfort because conditions differ in various work situations; different conditions could even be required for the same work post when it is occupied by different people. A technical norm for thermal conditions required for comfort cannot be applied to all countries because of the different climatic conditions and their different customs governing dress.

Studies have been carried out with workers that do light manual labour, establishing a series of criteria for temperature, speed and humidity that are shown in table 45.12 (Bedford and Chrenko 1974).

The above factors are interrelated, requiring a lower air temperature in cases where there is high thermal radiation and re-

quiring a higher air temperature when the speed of the air flow is also higher.

Generally, the corrections that should be carried out are the following:

The air temperature should be increased:

- if the speed of the air flow is high
- for sedentary work situations
- if clothing used is light
- when people must be acclimatized to high indoor temperatures.

The air temperature should be decreased:

- if the work involves heavy manual labour
- when warm clothing is used.

For a good sensation of thermal comfort the most desirable situation is one where the temperature of the environment is slightly higher than the temperature of the air, and where the flow of radiating thermal energy is the same in all directions and is not excessive overhead. The increase in temperature by height should be minimized, keeping feet warm without creating too much of a thermal load overhead. An important factor that has a bearing on the sensation of thermal comfort is the speed of the air flow. There are diagrams that give recommended air speeds as a function of the activity that is being carried out and the kind of clothing used (figure 45.11).

In some countries there are norms for minimal environmental temperatures, but optimal values have not yet been established. Typically, the maximum value for air temperature is given as 20°C. With recent technical improvements, the complexity of measuring thermal comfort has increased. Many indexes have appeared, including the index of effective temperature (ET) and the index of effective temperature, corrected (CET); the index of caloric overload; the Heat Stress Index (HSI); the wet bulb globe temperature (WBGT); and the Fanger index of median values (IMV), among others. The WBGT index allows us to determine the intervals of rest required as a function of the intensity of the work performed so as to preclude thermal stress under working

Figure 45.11 • Comfort zones based on readings of overall temperatures and speed of air currents.

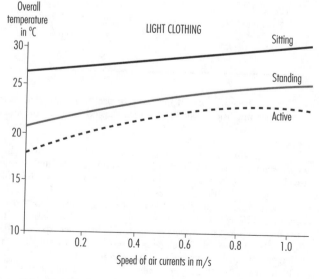

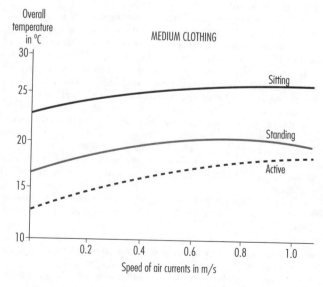

Source: ILO 1983.

conditions. This is discussed more fully in the chapter *Heat and Cold*.

Thermal comfort zone in a psychrometric diagram

The range on the psychrometric diagram corresponding to conditions under which an adult perceives thermal comfort has been carefully studied and has been defined in the ASHRAE norm based on the effective temperature, defined as the temperature measured with a dry bulb thermometer in a uniform room with 50 per cent relative humidity, where people would have the same interchange of heat by radiant energy, convection and evaporation as they would with the level of humidity in the given local environment. The scale of effective temperature is defined by ASHRAE for a level of clothing of 0.6 clo—clo is a unit of insulation; 1 clo corresponds to the insulation provided by a normal set of clothes—that assumes a level of thermal insulation of 0.155 K m²W⁻¹, where K is the exchange of heat by conduction measured in Watts per square metre ($W\,m^{-2}$) for a movement of air of 0.2 m s⁻¹ (at rest), for an exposure of one hour at a chosen sedentary activity of 1 met (unit of metabolic rate = 50 Kcal/m²h). This comfort zone is seen in figure 45.11 and can be used for thermal environments where the measured temperature from radiant heat is approximately the same as the temperature measured by a dry bulb thermometer, and where the speed of air flow is below 0.2 m s⁻¹ for people dressed in light clothing and carrying out sedentary activities.

Comfort formula: The Fanger method

The method developed by PO Fanger is based on a formula that relates variables of ambient temperature, average radiant temperature, relative speed of air flow, pressure of water vapour in ambient air, level of activity and thermal resistance of the clothing worn. An example derived from the comfort formula is shown in table 45.13, which can be used in practical applications for obtaining a comfortable temperature as a function of the clothing worn, the metabolic rate of the activity carried out and the speed of the air flow.

Heating Systems

The design of any heating system should be directly related to the work to be performed and the characteristics of the building where it will be installed. It is hard to find, in the case of industrial buildings, projects where the heating needs of the workers are considered, often because the processes and workstations have yet to be defined. Normally systems are designed with a very free range, considering only the thermal loads that will exist in the building and the amount of heat that needs to be supplied to maintain a given temperature within the building, without regard to heat distribution, the situation of workstations and other similarly less general factors. This leads to deficiencies in the design of certain buildings that translate into shortcomings like cold spots, draughts, an insufficient number of heating elements and other problems.

To end up with a good heating system in planning a building, the following are some of the considerations that should be addressed:

- Consider the proper placement of insulation to save energy and to minimize temperature gradients within the building.
- Reduce as much as possible the infiltration of cold air into the building to minimize temperature variations in the work areas.
- Control air pollution through localized extraction of air and ventilation by displacement or diffusion.

Table 45.13 • Temperatures of thermal comfort (°C), at 50% relative humidity (based on the formula by PO Fanger).

Metabolism (Watts)	105		
Radiating temperature	clo	20 °C	25 °C	30 °C
Clothing (clo) 0.5 V_a /(m.sg⁻¹)	0.2	30.7	27.5	24.3
	0.5	30.5	29.0	27.0
	1.5	30.6	29.5	28.3
Clothing (clo) 0.5 V_a /(m.sg⁻¹)	0.2	26.0	23.0	20.0
	0.5	26.7	24.3	22.7
	1.5	27.0	25.7	24.5

Metabolism (Watts)	157		
Radiating temperature	clo	20 °C	25 °C	30 °C
Clothing (clo) 0.5 V_a /(m.sg⁻¹)	0.2	21.0	17.1	14.0
	0.5	23.0	20.7	18.3
	1.5	23.5	23.3	22.0
Clothing (clo) 0.5 V_a /(m.sg⁻¹)	0.2	13.3	10.0	6.5
	0.5	16.0	14.0	11.5
	1.5	18.3	17.0	15.7

Metabolism (Watts)	210		
Radiating temperature	clo	20 °C	25 °C	30 °C
Clothing (clo) 0.5 V_a /(m.sg⁻¹)	0.2	11.0	8.0	4.0
	0.5	15.0	13.0	7.4
	1.5	18.3	17.0	16.0
Clothing (clo) 0.5 V_a /(m.sg⁻¹)	0.2	−7.0	/	/
	0.5	−1.5	−3.0	/
	1.5	5.0	2.0	1.0

- Control the emissions of heat due to the processes used in the building and their distribution in occupied areas of the building.

When heating is provided by burners without exhaust chimneys, special consideration should be given to the inhalation of the combustible products of combustion. Normally, when the combustible materials are heating oil, gas or coke, they produce sulphur dioxide, nitrogen oxides, carbon monoxide and other combustion products. There exist human exposure limits for these compounds and they should be controlled, especially in closed spaces where the concentration of these gases can increase rapidly and the efficiency of the combustion reaction can decrease.

Planning a heating system always entails balancing various considerations, such as a low initial cost, flexibility of the service, energy efficiency and applicability. Therefore, the use of electricity during off-peak hours when it might be cheaper, for example,

Figure 45.12 • Characteristics of the most common heating systems employed in worksites.

SYSTEM	CHARACTERISTICS											
The heating systems shown here are typical of industrial settings. Floor heating, conventional radiators and air-conditioning systems are more appropriate for sedentary work in offices or situations such as light assembly work.	Positive characteristics (advantages) +			Negative characteristics (disadvantages) −			Neutral characteristics ○			Variable characteristics ?		
	Low initial cost	Low maintenance cost	Frees up floor space	Quick fix	Requires steam or hot water system	Low maintenance	No air currents	Low temperature gradient	Heats zone uniformly	Can move air during the summer	Can heat new incoming air	Can be used for a zone or local area
Radiant heaters												
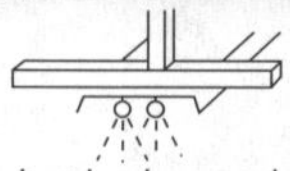 Radiant band mounted on beams or girders	−	+	+	−	+	+	+	+	+	−	−	−
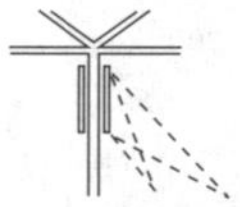 Vertical panel mounted on upright supports	−	+	+	−	+	+	+	+	+	−	−	○
 Gas or electric incandescent heater	+	○	+	+	−	○	+	?	−	−	−	+
Convection heaters (single)												
 Vertical discharge heater mounted at highest point	○	−	+	+	+	○	○	+	+	+	+	○
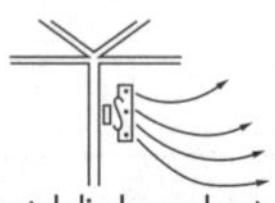 Horizontal discharge heater mounted on beams	○	−	+	+	+	○	−	−	−	+	+	+
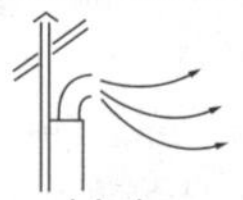 Horizontal discharge floor mounted	+	−	−	+	−	−	−	−	−	+	?	+

Source: ILO 1983.

could make electric heaters cost-effective. The use of chemical systems for heat storage that can then be put to use during peak demand (using sodium sulphide, for example) is another option. It is also possible to study the placement of several different systems together, making them work in such a way that costs can be optimized.

The installation of heaters that are capable of using gas or heating oil is especially interesting. The direct use of electricity means consuming first-class energy that may turn out to be costly in many cases, but that may afford the needed flexibility under certain circumstances. Heat pumps and other cogeneration sys-tems that take advantage of residual heat can afford solutions that may be very advantageous from the financial point of view. The problem with these systems is their high initial cost.

Today the tendency of heating and air conditioning systems is to aim to deliver optimal functioning and energy savings. New systems therefore include sensors and controls distributed throughout the spaces to be heated, obtaining a supply of heat only during the times necessary to obtain thermal comfort. These systems can save up to 30% of the energy costs of heating. Figure 45.12 shows some of the heating systems available, indicat-ing their positive characteristics and their drawbacks.

Figure 45.13 • Simplified schematic of air-conditioning system.

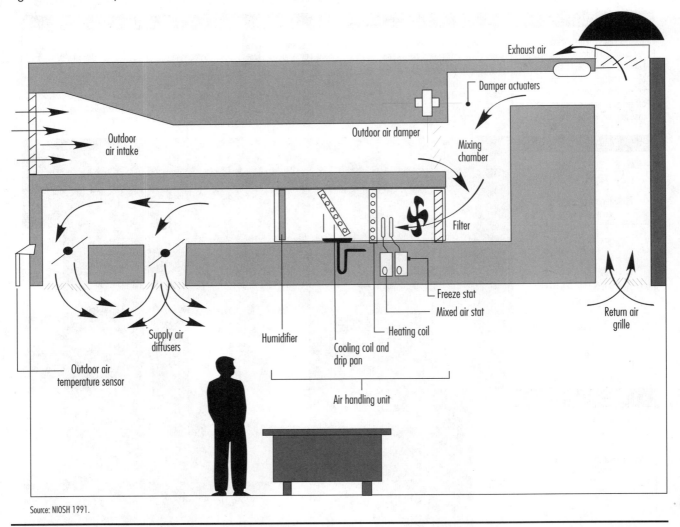

Source: NIOSH 1991.

Air-conditioning systems

Experience shows that industrial environments that are close to the comfort zone during summer months increase productivity, tend to register fewer accidents, have lower absenteeism and, in general, contribute to improved human relations. In the case of retail establishments, hospitals and buildings with large surfaces, air conditioning usually needs to be directed to be able to provide thermal comfort when outside conditions require it.

In certain industrial environments where external conditions are very severe, the goal of heating systems is geared more to providing enough heat to prevent possible adverse health effects than to providing enough heat for a comfortable thermal environment. Factors that should be carefully monitored are the maintenance and proper use of the air-conditioning equipment, especially when equipped with humidifiers, because they can become sources of microbial contamination with the risks that these contaminants may pose to human health.

Today ventilation and climate-control systems tend to cover, jointly and often using the same installation, the needs for heating, refrigerating and conditioning the air of a building. Multiple classifications may be used for refrigerating systems.

Depending on the configuration of the system they may be classified in the following way:

- Hermetically sealed units, with refrigerating fluid installed at the factory, that can be opened and recharged in a repair shop. These are air-conditioning units normally used in offices, dwellings and the like.
- Semi-hermetic units of medium size, factory made, that are of larger size than home units and that can be repaired through openings designed for that purpose.
- Segmented systems for warehouses and large surfaces, which consist of parts and components that are clearly differentiated and physically separate (the compressor and the condenser are physically separate from the evaporator and the expansion valve). They are used for large office buildings, hotels, hospitals, large factories and industrial buildings.

Depending on the coverage they provide, they can be classified in the following way:

- Systems for a single zone: one air treatment unit serves various rooms in the same building and at the same time. The rooms served have similar heating, refrigeration and ventilation needs and they are regulated by a common control (a thermostat or similar device). Systems of this type can end up being unable to supply an adequate level of comfort to each room if the design plan did not take into consideration the different thermal loads between rooms in the same zone. This may happen when there is an increase in the occupancy of a room or when lighting or other heat sources are added, like computers or copying machines, that were unforeseen during the original design of the system. Discomfort may also occur because of seasonal changes in the amount of solar radiation a room receives, or even because of the changes from one room to the next during the day.

- Systems for multiple zones: systems of this type can provide different zones with air at different temperatures and humidities by heating, cooling, humidifying or dehumidifying air in each zone and by varying the flow of air. These systems, even if they generally have a common and centralized air cooling unit (compressor, evaporator, etc.), are equipped with a variety of elements, such as devices that control the flow of air, heating coils and humidifiers. These systems are capable of adjusting the conditions of a room based on specific thermal loads, which they detect by means of sensors distributed in the rooms throughout the area they serve.

Depending on the flow of air that these systems pump into the building they are classified in the following way:

- Constant volume (CV): these systems pump a constant flow of air into each room. Temperature changes are effected by heating or cooling the air. These systems frequently mix a percentage of outside air with recycled indoor air.
- Variable volume (VAV): these systems maintain thermal comfort by varying the amount of heated or cooled air supplied to each space. Even though they function primarily based on this mixing principle, they can also be combined with systems that change the temperature of the air they introduce into the room.

The problems that most frequently plague these types of systems are excess heating or cooling if the system is not adjusted to respond to variations in thermal loads, or a lack of ventilation if the system does not introduce a minimal amount of outside air to renew the circulating indoor air. This creates stale indoor environments in which the quality of air deteriorates.

The basic elements of all air-conditioning systems are (see also figure 45.13):

- Units to retain solid matter, usually bag filters or electrostatic precipitators.
- Air heating or cooling units: heat is exchanged in these units by thermal exchange with cold water or refrigerating liquids, by forced ventilation in the summer and by heating with electrical coils or by combustion in the winter.
- Units to control humidity: in winter humidity can be added by directly injecting water vapour or by direct water evaporation; in the summer it can be removed by refrigerated coils that condense excess humidity in the air, or by a refrigerated water system in which moist air flows through a curtain of drops of water that is colder than the dew point of the moist air.

● INDOOR AIR: IONIZATION

E. Adán Liébana and J. Guasch Farrás

Ionization is one of the techniques used to eliminate particulate matter from air. Ions act as condensation nuclei for small particles which, as they stick together, grow and precipitate.

The concentration of ions in closed indoor spaces is, as a general rule and if there are no additional sources of ions, inferior to that of open spaces. Hence the belief that increasing the concentration of negative ions in indoor air improves air quality.

Some studies based on epidemiological data and on planned experimental research assert that increasing the concentration of negative ions in work environments leads to improved worker efficiency and enhances the mood of employees, while positive ions have an adverse affect. However, parallel studies show that existing data on the effects of negative ionization on workers' productivity are inconsistent and contradictory. Therefore, it seems that it is still not possible to assert unequivocally that the generation of negative ions is really beneficial.

Natural Ionization

Individual gas molecules in the atmosphere can ionize negatively by gaining, or positively by losing, an electron. For this to occur a given molecule must first gain enough energy—usually called the *ionization energy* of that particular molecule. Many sources of energy, both of cosmic and terrestrial origin, occur in nature that are capable of producing this phenomenon: background radiation in the atmosphere; electromagnetic solar waves (especially ultraviolet ones), cosmic rays, atomization of liquids such as the spray caused by waterfalls, the movement of great masses of air over the earth's surface, electrical phenomena such as lightning and storms, the process of combustion and radioactive substances.

The electrical configurations of the ions that are formed this way, while not completely known yet, seems to include the ions of carbonation and H_+, H_3O_+, O_+, N_+, OH^-, H_2O^- and O_2^-. These ionized molecules can aggregate through adsorption on suspended particles (fog, silica and other contaminants). Ions are classified according to their size and their mobility. The latter is defined as a velocity in an electrical field expressed as a unit such as centimetres per second by voltage per centimetre (cm/s/V/cm), or, more compactly,

$$\frac{cm^2}{Vs}$$

Atmospheric ions tend to disappear by recombination. Their half-life depends on their size and is inversely proportional to their mobility. Negative ions are statistically smaller and their half-life is of several minutes, while positive ions are larger and their half-life is about one half hour. The *spatial charge* is the quotient of the concentration of positive ions and the concentration of negative ions. The value of this relation is greater than one and depends on factors such as climate, location and season of the year. In living spaces this coefficient can have values that are lower than one. Characteristics are given in table 45.14.

Table 45.14 • Characteristics of ions of given mobilities and diameter.

Mobility (cm²/Vs)	Diameter (μm)	Characteristics
3.0–0.1	0.001–0.003	Small, high mobility, short life
0.1–0.005	0.003–0.03	Intermediate, slower than small ions
0.005–0.002	>0.03	Slow ions, aggregates on particulate matter (ions of Langevin)

Artificial Ionization

Human activity modifies the natural ionization of air. Artificial ionization can be caused by industrial and nuclear processes and fires. Particulate matter suspended in air favours the formation of Langevin ions (ions aggregated on particulate matter). Electrical radiators increase the concentration of positive ions considerably. Air-conditioners also increase the spatial charge of indoor air.

Workplaces have machinery that produces positive and negative ions simultaneously, as in the case of machines that are important local sources of mechanical energy (presses, spinning and weaving machines), electrical energy (motors, electronic printers, copiers, high-voltage lines and installations), electromagnetic energy (cathode-ray screens, televisions, computer monitors) or radioactive energy (cobalt-42 therapy). These kinds of equipment create environments with higher concentrations of positive ions due to the latter's higher half-life as compared to negative ions.

Environmental Concentrations of Ions

Concentrations of ions vary with environmental and meteorological conditions. In areas with little pollution, such as in forests and mountains, or at great altitudes, the concentration of small ions grows; in areas close to radioactive sources, waterfalls, or river rapids the concentrations can reach thousands of small ions per cubic centimetre. In the proximity of the sea and when the levels of humidity are high, on the other hand, there is an excess of large ions. In general, the average concentration of negative and positive ions in clean air is 500 and 600 ions per cubic centimetre respectively.

Some winds can carry great concentrations of positive ions—the Föhn in Switzerland, the Santa Ana in the United States, the Sirocco in North Africa, the Chinook in the Rocky Mountains and the Sharav in the Middle East.

In workplaces where there are no significant ionizing factors there is often an accumulation of large ions. This is especially true, for example, in places that are hermetically sealed and in mines. The concentration of negative ions decreases significantly in indoor spaces and in contaminated areas or areas that are dusty. There are many reasons why the concentration of negative ions also decreases in indoor spaces that have air-conditioning systems. One reason is that negative ions remain trapped in air ducts and air filters or are attracted to surfaces that are positively charged. Cathode-ray screens and computer monitors, for example, are positively charged, creating in their immediate vicinity a microclimate deficient in negative ions. Air filtration systems designed for "clean rooms" that require that levels of contamination with particulate matter be kept at a very low minimum seem also to eliminate negative ions.

On the other hand, an excess of humidity condenses ions, while a lack of it creates dry environments with large amounts of electrostatic charges. These electrostatic charges accumulate in plastic and synthetic fibres, both in the room and on people.

Ion Generators

Generators ionize air by delivering a large amount of energy. This energy may come from a source of alpha radiation (such as tritium) or from a source of electricity by the application of a high voltage to a sharply pointed electrode. Radioactive sources are forbidden in most countries because of the secondary problems of radioactivity.

Electric generators are made of a pointed electrode surrounded by a crown; the electrode is supplied with a negative voltage of thousands of volts, and the crown is grounded. Negative ions are expelled while positive ions are attracted to the generator. The amount of negative ions generated increases in proportion to the voltage applied and to the number of electrodes that it contains. Generators that have a greater number of electrodes and use a lower voltage are safer, because when voltage exceeds 8,000 to 10,000 volts the generator will produce not only ions, but also ozone and some nitrous oxides. The dissemination of ions is achieved by electrostatic repulsion.

The migration of ions will depend on the alignment of the magnetic field generated between the emission point and the objects that surround it. The concentration of ions surrounding the generators is not homogeneous and diminishes significantly as the distance from them increases. Fans installed in this equipment will increase the ionic dispersion zone. It is important to remember that the active elements of the generators need to be cleaned periodically to insure proper functioning.

The generators may also be based on atomizing water, on thermoelectric effects or on ultraviolet rays. There are many different types and sizes of generators. They may be installed on ceilings and walls or may be placed anywhere if they are the small, portable type.

Measuring Ions

Ion measuring devices are made by placing two conductive plates 0.75 cm apart and applying a variable voltage. Collected ions are measured by a picoamperemeter and the intensity of the current is registered. Variable voltages permit the measurement of concentrations of ions with different mobilities. The concentration of ions (N) is calculated from the intensity of the electrical current generated using the following formula:

$$N = \frac{I}{VqA}$$

where I is the current in amperes, V is the speed of the air flow, q is the charge of a univalent ion (1.6×10^{-19}) in Coulombs and A is the effective area of the collector plates. It is assumed that all ions have a single charge and that they are all retained in the collector. It should be kept in mind that this method has its limitations due to background current and the influence of other factors such as humidity and fields of static electricity.

The Effects of Ions on the Body

Small negative ions are the ones which are supposed to have the greatest biological effect because of their greater mobility. High concentrations of negative ions can kill or block the growth of microscopic pathogens, but no adverse effects on humans have been described.

Some studies suggest that exposure to high concentrations of negative ions produces biochemical and physiological changes in some people that have a relaxing effect, reduce tension and headaches, improve alertness and cut reaction time. These effects could be due to the suppression of the neural hormone serotonin (5-HT) and of histamine in environments loaded with negative ions; these factors could affect a hypersensitive segment of the population. However, other studies reach different conclusions on the effects of negative ions on the body. Therefore, the benefits of negative ionization are still open to debate and further study is needed before the matter is decided.

References

American Conference of Governmental Industrial Hygienists (ACGIH). 1992. *Industrial Ventilation—A Manual of Recommended Practice*. 21st ed. Cincinnati, Ohio: ACGIH.

American Society of Heating, Refrigerating, and Air-Conditioning Engineers (ASHRAE). 1992. *Method of Testing Air Cleaner Devices Used in General Ventilation for Removing Particulate Matter*. Atlanta: ASHRAE.

Baturin, VV. 1972. *Fundamentals of Industrial Ventilation*. New York: Pergamon.

Bedford, T and FA Chrenko. 1974. *Basic Principles of Ventilation and Heating*. London: HK Lewis.

Centre européen de normalisation (CEN). 1979. *Method of Testing Air Filters Used in General Ventilation*. Eurovent 4/5. Antwerp: European Committee of Standards.

Chartered Institution of Building Services. 1978. *Environmental Criteria for Design*. : Chartered Institution of Building Services.

Council of the European Communities (CEC). 1992. *Guidelines for Ventilation Requirements in Buildings*. Luxembourg: EC.

Constance, JD. 1983. *Controlling In-Plant Ariborne Contaminants. System Design and Calculations*. New York: Mercel Dekker.

Fanger, PO. 1988. Introduction of the olf and the decipol units to quantify air pollution perceived by humans indoors and outdoors. *Energy Build* 12:7-19.

—. 1989. The new comfort equation for indoor air quality. *ASHRAE Journal* 10:33-38.

International Labour Organization (ILO). 1983. *Encyclopaedia of Occupational Health and Safety*, edited by L Parmeggiani. 3rd ed. Geneva: ILO.

National Institute for Occupational Safety and Health (NIOSH). 1991. *Building Air Quality: A Guide for Building Owners and Facility Managers*. Cincinnati, Ohio: NIOSH.

Sandberg, M. 1981. What is ventilation efficiency? *Build Environ* 16:123-135.

World Health Organization (WHO). 1987. *Air Quality Guidelines for Europe*. European Series, No. 23. Copenhagen: WHO Regional Publications.

Other relevant readings

Air filters—how effective are they? 1991. *Indoor Air Quality Update* 4(8):1-7.

American Society of Heating, Refrigerating, and Air-Conditioning Engineers (ASHRAE). 1977. *Handbook and Product Directory: Fundamentals*. Atlanta: ASHRAE.

—. 1978. *Handbook and Product Directory: Applications*. Atlanta: ASHRAE.

Berg-Munch, B, G Clausen, and PO Fanger. 1986. Ventilation requirements for the control of body odor in spaces occupied by women. *Environ Int* 12:195-199.

Bethe, RM. 1978. *Air Pollution Control Technology*. New York: Van Nostrand Reinhold.

Billings, CE. 1982. Methods for indoor air quality. *Environ Int* 8:497-504.

Breum, NO. 1991. High versus low momentum ventilation in a machine workshop. *Staub-Reinhaltung der Luft* 51:91-96.

Brunet, R. 1976. Ventilation et chauffage des locaux de travail associés á l'économie et á la récupération d'energie. *Institut National de Recherche et de Securité* 532.

Cain, WS et al. 1983. Ventilation requirements in buildings: Control of occupancy odor and tobacco smoke odor. *Atmos Environ* 17(6):1187-1197.

Central cooling air conditioners: Standard for safety. 1978. Ill.: Underwriters Laboratories,Inc.

Cone, J and MJ Hodgson. 1989. Building-associated illness and problem buildings. *State Art Rev Occup Med* 4(4).

Fanger, PO. 1973. Assessment of man's thermal comfort in practice. *Br J Ind Med* 30:313-324.

Gilet, JC, JC Laforest, P Méreau, and B Vandevyver. 1992. *Ionization négative de l'air*. Cahiers De Notes Documentaires.

Hamilton, M. 1984. *Air Ion Balance in the Workplace*. Vol. 2. Industrial Safety Data File, No. 65. London: United Trade Press.

Hawkins, LH. 1982. Air ions and office health. *Occup Health* 34(3):116-124.

Hawkinson, TE and DE Barber. 1982. The industrial hygiene significance of small air ions. *Am Ind Hyg Assoc J* 42:759-762.

Health and Safety Executive. 1983. *Ozone: Health Hazards and Precautionary Measures*. : Health and Safety Executive.

Hedge, A and MD Collis. 1987. Do negative air ions affect human mood and performance? *Occup Hyg* 31(3):285-290.

Hedge, A and A Eleftherakis. 1982. Air ionization: An evaluation of its physiological and psychological effects. *Occup Hyg* 25(4):409-419.

Heinsohn, RJ. 1991. *Industrial Ventilation. Engineering Principles*. New York: Wiley.

Liu, RT, RR Raber, and HHS Yu. 1991. Filter selection on an engineering basis. *Heating/Piping/Air-Conditioning* 63(5):37-44.

National Institute for Occupational Safety and Health (NIOSH). 1978. *Symposium Proceedings: The Recirculation of Industrial Exhaust Air*. Cincinnati,Ohio: NIOSH.

Rolloos, M. 1993. HVAC systems and indoor air quality. *Indoor Environ* 2:204-212.

Thermal,visual, and acoustic requirements of buildings. 1979. *Building Research Establishment Digest* 226.

Turiel, I. 1986. *Indoor Air Quality and Human Health*. Palo Alto, Calif: Stanford Univ. Press.

Weekes, DM and RB Gammage. 1990. *The Practitioner's Approach to Indoor Air Quality Investigations*. Akron,Ohio: American Industrial Hygiene Association.

45. INDOOR ENVIRONMENTAL CONTROL

LIGHTING

46

Chapter Editor
Juan Guasch Farrás

Contents

TYPES OF LAMPS AND LIGHTING

Richard Forster

A lamp is an energy converter. Although it may carry out secondary functions, its prime purpose is the transformation of electrical energy into visible electromagnetic radiation. There are many ways to create light. The standard method for creating general lighting is the conversion of electrical energy into light.

Types of Light

Incandescence
When solids and liquids are heated, they emit visible radiation at temperatures above 1,000 K; this is known as incandescence.

Such heating is the basis of light generation in filament lamps: an electrical current passes through a thin tungsten wire, whose temperature rises to around 2,500 to 3,200 K, depending upon the type of lamp and its application.

There is a limit to this method, which is described by Planck's Law for the performance of a black body radiator, according to which the spectral distribution of energy radiated increases with temperature. At about 3,600 K and above, there is a marked gain in emission of visible radiation, and the wavelength of maximum power shifts into the visible band. This temperature is close to the melting point of tungsten, which is used for the filament, so the practical temperature limit is around 2,700 K, above which filament evaporation becomes excessive. One result of these spectral shifts is that a large part of the radiation emitted is not given off as light but as heat in the infrared region. Filament lamps can thus be effective heating devices and are used in lamps designed for print drying, food preparation and animal rearing.

Electric discharge
Electrical discharge is a technique used in modern light sources for commerce and industry because of the more efficient production of light. Some lamp types combine the electrical discharge with photoluminescence.

An electric current passed through a gas will excite the atoms and molecules to emit radiation of a spectrum which is characteristic of the elements present. Two metals are commonly used, sodium and mercury, because their characteristics give useful radiations within the visible spectrum. Neither metal emits a continuous spectrum, and discharge lamps have selective spectra. Their colour rendering will never be identical to continuous spectra. Discharge lamps are often classed as high pressure or low pressure, although these terms are only relative, and a high-pressure sodium lamp operates at below one atmosphere.

Types of Luminescence
Photoluminescence occurs when radiation is absorbed by a solid and is then re-emitted at a different wavelength. When the re-emitted radiation is within the visible spectrum the process is called *fluorescence* or *phosphorescence*.

Electroluminescence occurs when light is generated by an electric current passed through certain solids, such as phosphor materials. It is used for self-illuminated signs and instrument panels but has not proved to be a practical light source for the lighting of buildings or exteriors.

Evolution of Electric Lamps
Although technological progress has enabled different lamps to be produced, the main factors influencing their development have been external market forces. For example, the production of filament lamps in use at the start of this century was possible only after the availability of good vacuum pumps and the drawing of

Table 46.1 • Improved light output and wattage requirements of some typical 1,500 mm fluorescent tube lamps.

Rating (W)	Diameter (mm)	Gas fill	Light output (lumens)
80	38	argon	4,800
65	38	argon	4,900
58	25	krypton	5,100
50	25	argon	5,100 (high frequency gear)

tungsten wire. However, it was the large-scale generation and distribution of electricity to meet the demand for electric lighting that determined market growth. Electric lighting offered many advantages over gas- or oil-generated light, such as steady light that requires infrequent maintenance as well as the increased safety of having no exposed flame, and no local by-products of combustion.

During the period of recovery after the Second World War, the emphasis was on productivity. The fluorescent tubular lamp became the dominant light source because it made possible shadow-free and comparatively heat-free lighting of factories and offices, allowing maximum use of the space. The light output and wattage requirements for a typical 1,500 mm fluorescent tubular lamp is given in table 46.1.

By the 1970s oil prices rose and energy costs became a significant part of operating costs. Fluorescent lamps that produce the same amount of light with less electrical consumption were demanded by the market. Lamp design was refined in several ways. As the century closes there is a growing awareness of global environment issues. Better use of declining raw materials, recycling or safe disposal of products and the continuing concern over energy consumption (particularly energy generated from fossil fuels) are impacting on current lamp designs.

Performance Criteria
Performance criteria vary by application. In general, there is no particular hierarchy of importance of these criteria.

Light output: The lumen output of a lamp will determine its suitability in relation to the scale of the installation and the quantity of illumination required.

Colour appearance and colour rendering: Separate scales and numerical values apply to colour appearance and colour rendering. It is important to remember that the figures provide guidance only, and some are only approximations. Whenever possible, assessments of suitability should be made with actual lamps and with the colours or materials that apply to the situation.

Lamp life: Most lamps will require replacement several times during the life of the lighting installation, and designers should minimize the inconvenience to the occupants of odd failures and

Table 46.2 • Typical lamp efficacies.

Lamp efficacies	
100 W filament lamp	14 lumens/watt
58 W fluorescent tube	89 lumens/watt
400 W high-pressure sodium	125 lumens/watt
131 W low-pressure sodium	198 lumens/watt

Table 46.3 • International Lamp Coding System (ILCOS) short form coding system for some lamp types.

Type (code)	Common ratings (watts)	Colour rendering	Colour temperature (K)	Life (hours)
Compact fluorescent lamps (FS)	5–55	good	2,700–5,000	5,000–10,000
High-pressure mercury lamps (QE)	80–750	fair	3,300–3,800	20,000
High-pressure sodium lamps (S-)	50–1,000	poor to good	2,000–2,500	6,000–24,000
Incandescent lamps (I)	5–500	good	2,700	1,000–3,000
Induction lamps (XF)	23–85	good	3,000–4,000	10,000–60,000
Low-pressure sodium lamps (LS)	26–180	monochromatic yellow colour	1,800	16,000
Low-voltage tungsten halogen lamps (HS)	12–100	good	3,000	2,000–5,000
Metal halide lamps (M-)	35–2,000	good to excellent	3,000–5,000	6,000–20,000
Tubular fluorescent lamps (FD)	4–100	fair to good	2,700–6,500	10,000–15,000
Tungsten halogen lamps (HS)	100–2,000	good	3,000	2,000–4,000

maintenance. Lamps are used in a wide variety of applications. The anticipated average life is often a compromise between cost and performance. For example, the lamp for a slide projector will have a life of a few hundred hours because the maximum light output is important to the quality of the image. By contrast, some roadway lighting lamps may be changed every two years, and this represents some 8,000 burning hours.

Further, lamp life is affected by operating conditions, and thus there is no simple figure that will apply in all conditions. Also, the effective lamp life may be determined by different failure modes. Physical failure such as filament or lamp rupture may be preceded by reduction in light output or changes in colour appearance. Lamp life is affected by external environmental conditions such as temperature, vibration, frequency of starting, supply voltage fluctuations, orientation and so on.

It should be noted that the average life quoted for a lamp type is the time for 50% failures from a batch of test lamps. This definition of life is not likely to be applicable to many commercial or industrial installations; thus practical lamp life is usually less than published values, which should be used for comparison only.

Efficiency: As a general rule the efficiency of a given type of lamp improves as the power rating increases, because most lamps have some fixed loss. However, different types of lamps have marked variation in efficiency. Lamps of the highest efficiency should be used, provided that the criteria of size, colour and lifetime are also met. Energy savings should not be at the expense of the visual comfort or the performance ability of the occupants. Some typical efficacies are given in table 46.2.

Main lamp types

Over the years, several nomenclature systems have been developed by national and international standards and registers.

In 1993, the International Electrotechnical Commission (IEC) published a new International Lamp Coding System (ILCOS) intended to replace existing national and regional coding systems. A list of some ILCOS short form codes for various lamps is given in table 46.3.

Incandescent lamps

These lamps use a tungsten filament in an inert gas or vacuum with a glass envelope. The inert gas suppresses tungsten evaporation and lessens the envelope blackening. There is a large variety of lamp shapes, which are largely decorative in appearance. The construction of a typical General Lighting Service (GLS) lamp is given in figure 46.1.

Incandescent lamps are also available with a wide range of colours and finishes. The ILCOS codes and some typical shapes include those shown in table 46.4.

Incandescent lamps are still popular for domestic lighting because of their low cost and compact size. However, for commercial and industrial lighting the low efficacy generates very high operating costs, so discharge lamps are the normal choice. A 100 W lamp has a typical efficacy of 14 lumens/watt compared with 96 lumens/watt for a 36 W fluorescent lamp.

Incandescent lamps are simple to dim by reducing the supply voltage, and are still used where dimming is a desired control feature.

The tungsten filament is a compact light source, easily focused by reflectors or lenses. Incandescent lamps are useful for display lighting where directional control is needed.

Tungsten halogen lamps

These are similar to incandescent lamps and produce light in the same manner from a tungsten filament. However the bulb con-

Figure 46.1 • Construction of a GLS lamp.

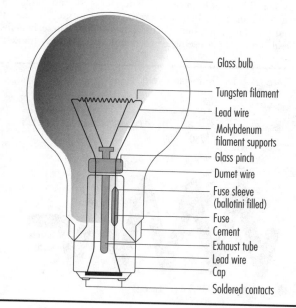

- Glass bulb
- Tungsten filament
- Lead wire
- Molybdenum filament supports
- Glass pinch
- Dumet wire
- Fuse sleeve (ballotini filled)
- Fuse
- Cement
- Exhaust tube
- Lead wire
- Cap
- Soldered contacts

Table 46.4 • Common colours and shapes of incandescent lamps, with their ILCOS codes.

Colour/Shape	Code
Clear	/C
Frosted	/F
White	/W
Red	/R
Blue	/B
Green	/G
Yellow	/Y
Pear shaped (GLS)	IA
Candle	IB
Conical	IC
Globular	IG
Mushroom	IM

tains halogen gas (bromine or iodine) which is active in controlling tungsten evaporation. See figure 46.2.

Fundamental to the halogen cycle is a minimum bulb wall temperature of 250 °C to ensure that the tungsten halide remains in a gaseous state and does not condense on the bulb wall. This temperature means bulbs made from quartz in place of glass. With quartz it is possible to reduce the bulb size.

Most tungsten halogen lamps have an improved life over incandescent equivalents and the filament is at a higher temperature, creating more light and whiter colour.

Tungsten halogen lamps have become popular where small size and high performance are the main requirement. Typical examples are stage lighting, including film and TV, where directional control and dimming are common requirements.

Low-voltage tungsten halogen lamps

These were originally designed for slide and film projectors. At 12 V the filament for the same wattage as 230 V becomes smaller and thicker. This can be more efficiently focused, and the larger filament mass allows a higher operating temperature, increasing light output. The thick filament is more robust. These benefits were realized as being useful for the commercial display market,

Figure 46.2 • The halogen cycle.

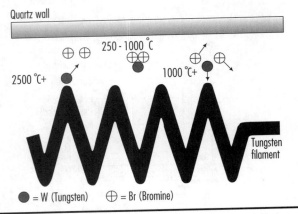

= W (Tungsten)   ⊕ = Br (Bromine)

Figure 46.3 • Low-voltage dichroic reflector lamp.

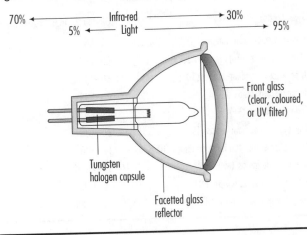

and even though it is necessary to have a step-down transformer, these lamps now dominate shop-window lighting. See figure 46.3.

Although users of film projectors want as much light as possible, too much heat damages the transparency medium. A special type of reflector has been developed, which reflects only the visible radiation, allowing infrared radiation (heat) to pass through the back of lamp. This feature is now part of many low-voltage reflector lamps for display lighting as well as projector equipment.

Voltage sensitivity: All filament lamps are sensitive to voltage variation, and light output and life are affected. The move to "harmonize" the supply voltage throughout Europe at 230 V is being achieved by widening the tolerances to which the generating authorities can operate. The move is towards ±10%, which is a voltage range of 207 to 253 V. Incandescent and tungsten halogen lamps cannot be operated sensibly over this range, so it will be necessary to match actual supply voltage to lamp ratings. See figure 46.4.

Discharge lamps will also be affected by this wide voltage variation, so the correct specification of control gear becomes important.

Figure 46.4 • GLS filament lamps and supply voltage

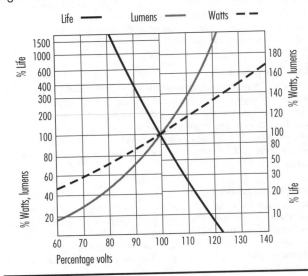

Tubular fluorescent lamps

These are low pressure mercury lamps and are available as "hot cathode" and "cold cathode" versions. The former is the conventional fluorescent tube for offices and factories; "hot cathode" relates to the starting of the lamp by pre-heating the electrodes to create sufficient ionization of the gas and mercury vapour to establish the discharge.

Cold cathode lamps are mainly used for signage and advertising. See figure 46.5.

Fluorescent lamps require external control gear for starting and to control the lamp current. In addition to the small amount of mercury vapour, there is a starting gas (argon or krypton).

The low pressure of mercury generates a discharge of pale blue light. The major part of the radiation is in the UV region at 254 nm, a characteristic radiation frequency for mercury. Inside of the tube wall is a thin phosphor coating, which absorbs the UV and radiates the energy as visible light. The colour quality of the light is determined by the phosphor coating. A range of phosphors are available of varying colour appearance and colour rendering.

During the 1950s phosphors available offered a choice of reasonable efficacy (60 lumens/watt) with light deficient in reds and blues, or improved colour rendering from "deluxe" phosphors of lower efficiency (40 lumens/watt).

By the 1970s new, narrow-band phosphors had been developed. These separately radiated red, blue and green light but, combined, produced white light. Adjusting the proportions gave a range of different colour appearances, all with similar excellent colour rendering. These tri-phosphors are more efficient than the earlier types and represent the best economic lighting solution, even though the lamps are more expensive. Improved efficacy reduces operating and installation costs.

The tri-phosphor principle has been extended by multi-phosphor lamps where critical colour rendering is necessary, such as for art galleries and industrial colour matching.

The modern narrow-band phosphors are more durable, have better lumen maintenance, and increase lamp life.

Compact fluorescent lamps

The fluorescent tube is not a practical replacement for the incandescent lamp because of its linear shape. Small, narrow-bore tubes can be configured to approximately the same size as the incandescent lamp, but this imposes a much higher electrical loading on the phosphor material. The use of tri-phosphors is essential to achieve acceptable lamp life. See figure 46.6.

All compact fluorescent lamps use tri-phosphors, so, when they are used together with linear fluorescent lamps, the latter should also be tri-phosphor to ensure colour consistency.

Some compact lamps include the operating control gear to form retro-fit devices for incandescent lamps. The range is increasing and enables easy upgrading of existing installations to more energy-efficient lighting. These integral units are not suitable for dimming where that was part of the original controls.

High-frequency electronic control gear. If the normal supply frequency of 50 or 60 Hz is increased to 30 kHz, there is a 10% gain in efficacy of fluorescent tubes. Electronic circuits can operate individual lamps at such frequencies. The electronic circuit is designed to provide the same light output as wire-wound control gear, from reduced lamp power. This offers compatibility of lumen package with the advantage that reduced lamp loading will increase lamp life significantly. Electronic control gear is capable of operating over a range of supply voltages.

There is no common standard for electronic control gear, and lamp performance may differ from the published information issued by the lamp makers.

The use of high-frequency electronic gear removes the normal problem of flicker, to which some occupants may be sensitive.

Figure 46.5 • Principle of fluorescent lamp.

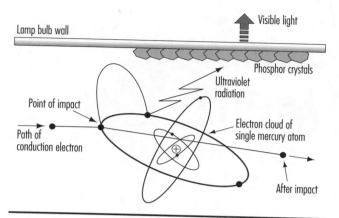

Induction lamps

Lamps using the principle of induction have recently appeared on the market. They are low-pressure mercury lamps with tri-phosphor coating and as light producers are similar to fluorescent lamps. The energy is transferred to the lamp by high-frequency radiation, at approximately 2.5 MHz from an antenna positioned centrally within the lamp. There is no physical connection between the lamp bulb and the coil. Without electrodes or other wire connections the construction of the discharge vessel is simpler and more durable. Lamp life is mainly determined by the reliability of the electronic components and the lumen maintenance of the phosphor coating.

High-pressure mercury lamps

High-pressure discharges are more compact and have higher electrical loads; therefore, they require quartz arc tubes to withstand the pressure and temperature. The arc tube is contained in an outer glass envelope with a nitrogen or argon-nitrogen atmosphere to reduce oxidation and arcing. The bulb effectively filters the UV radiation from the arc tube. See figure 46.7.

At high pressure, the mercury discharge is mainly blue and green radiation. To improve the colour a phosphor coating of the outer bulb adds red light. There are deluxe versions with an

Figure 46.6 • Four-leg compact fluorescent.

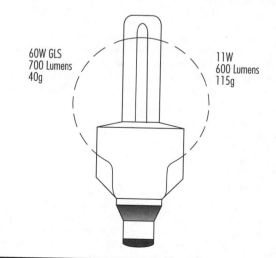

60W GLS
700 Lumens
40g

11W
600 Lumens
115g

Figure 46.7 • Mercury lamp construction.

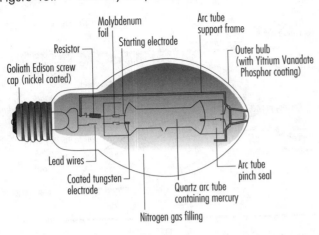

Table 46.5 • Types of high-pressure sodium lamp.

Lamp type (code)	Colour (K)	Efficacy (lumens/watt)	Life (hours)
Standard	2,000	110	24,000
Deluxe	2,200	80	14,000
White (SON)	2,500	50	

increased red content, which give higher light output and improved colour rendering.

All high-pressure discharge lamps take time to reach full output. The initial discharge is via the conducting gas fill, and the metal evaporates as the lamp temperature increases.

At the stable pressure the lamp will not immediately restart without special control gear. There is a delay while the lamp cools sufficiently and the pressure reduces, so that the normal supply voltage or ignitor circuit is adequate to re-establish the arc.

Discharge lamps have a negative resistance characteristic, and so the external control gear is necessary to control the current. There are losses due to these control gear components so the user should consider total watts when considering operating costs and electrical installation. There is an exception for high-pressure mercury lamps, and one type contains a tungsten filament which both acts as the current limiting device and adds warm colours to the blue/green discharge. This enables the direct replacement of incandescent lamps.

Although mercury lamps have a long life of about 20,000 hours, the light output will fall to about 55% of the initial output at the end of this period, and therefore the economic life can be shorter.

Metal halide lamps

The colour and light output of mercury discharge lamps can be improved by adding different metals to the mercury arc. For each lamp the dose is small, and for accurate application it is more convenient to handle the metals in powder form as halides. This breaks down as the lamp warms up and releases the metal.

A metal halide lamp can use a number of different metals, each of which give off a specific characteristic colour. These include:

- dysprosium—broad blue-green
- indium—narrow blue
- lithium—narrow red
- scandium—broad blue-green
- sodium—narrow yellow
- thallium—narrow green
- tin—broad orange-red

There is no standard mixture of metals, so metal halide lamps from different manufacturers may not be compatible in appearance or operating performance. For lamps with the lower wattage ratings, 35 to 150 W, there is closer physical and electrical compatibility with a common standard.

Metal halide lamps require control gear, but the lack of compatibility means that it is necessary to match each combination of lamp and gear to ensure correct starting and running conditions.

Low-pressure sodium lamps

The arc tube is similar in size to the fluorescent tube but is made of special ply glass with an inner sodium resistant coating. The arc tube is formed in a narrow "U" shape and is contained in an outer vacuum jacket to ensure thermal stability. During starting, the lamps have a strong red glow from the neon gas fill.

The characteristic radiation from low-pressure sodium vapour is a monochromatic yellow. This is close to the peak sensitivity of the human eye, and low-pressure sodium lamps are the most efficient lamps available at nearly 200 lumens/watt. However the applications are limited to where colour discrimination is of no visual importance, such as trunk roads and underpasses, and residential streets.

In many situations these lamps are being replaced by high-pressure sodium lamps. Their smaller size offers better optical control, particularly for roadway lighting where there is growing concern over excessive sky glow.

High-pressure sodium lamps

These lamps are similar to high-pressure mercury lamps but offer better efficacy (over 100 lumens/watt) and excellent lumen maintenance. The reactive nature of sodium requires the arc tube to be manufactured from translucent polycrystalline alumina, as glass or quartz are unsuitable. The outer glass bulb contains a vacuum to prevent arcing and oxidation. There is no UV radiation from the sodium discharge so phosphor coatings are of no value. Some bulbs are frosted or coated to diffuse the light source. See figure 46.8.

As the sodium pressure is increased, the radiation becomes a broad band around the yellow peak, and the appearance is golden white. However, as the pressure increases, the efficiency decreases. There are currently three separate types of high-pressure sodium lamps available, as shown in table 46.5.

Figure 46.8 • High-pressure sodium lamp construction.

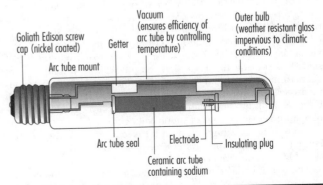

Generally the standard lamps are used for exterior lighting, deluxe lamps for industrial interiors, and White SON for commercial/display applications.

Dimming of Discharge Lamps

The high-pressure lamps cannot be satisfactorily dimmed, as changing the lamp power changes the pressure and thus the fundamental characteristics of the lamp.

Fluorescent lamps can be dimmed using high-frequency supplies generated typically within the electronic control gear. The colour appearance remains very constant. In addition, the light output is approximately proportional to the lamp power, with consequent saving in electrical power when the light output is reduced. By integrating the light output from the lamp with the prevailing level of natural daylight, a near constant level of illuminance can be provided in an interior.

● CONDITIONS REQUIRED FOR VISUAL COMFORT

Fernando Ramos Pérez and Ana Hernández Calleja

Human beings possess an extraordinary capacity to adapt to their environment and to their immediate surroundings. Of all the types of energy that humans can utilize, light is the most important. Light is a key element in our capacity to see, and it is necessary to appreciate the form, the colour and the perspective of the objects that surround us in our daily lives. Most of the information we obtain through our senses we obtain through sight—close to 80%. Very often, and because we are so used to having it available, we take it for granted. We should not fail to keep in mind, however, that aspects of human welfare, like our state of mind or our level of fatigue, are affected by illumination and the colour of the things that surround us. From the point of view of safety at work, visual capacity and visual comfort are extraordinarily important. This is because many accidents are due to, among other reasons, illumination deficiencies or errors made by the worker because he or she finds it hard to identify objects or the risks associated with machinery, conveyances, dangerous containers and so on.

Visual disorders associated with deficiencies in the illumination system are common in the workplace. Due to the ability of sight to adapt to situations with deficient lighting, these aspects are sometimes not considered as seriously as they should be.

The correct design of an illumination system should offer the optimal conditions for visual comfort. For the attainment of this goal an early line of collaboration between architects, lighting designers and those responsible for hygiene at the worksite should be established. This collaboration should precede the beginning of the project, to avoid errors that would be difficult to correct once the project is completed. Among the most important aspects that should be kept in mind are the type of lamp that will be used and the lighting system that will be installed, the distribution of luminance, illumination efficiencies and the spectral composition of light.

The fact that light and colour affect the productivity and the psycho-physiological well-being of the worker should encourage the initiatives of illumination technicians, physiologists and ergonomists, to study and determine the most favourable conditions of light and colour at each work station. The combination of illumination, the contrast of luminances, the colour of light, the reproduction of colour or the selection of colours are the elements that determine colour climate and visual comfort.

Factors that Determine Visual Comfort

The prerequisites that an illumination system must fulfil in order to provide the conditions necessary for visual comfort are the following:

- uniform illumination
- optimal luminance
- no glare
- adequate contrast conditions
- correct colours
- absence of stroboscopic effect or intermittent light.

It is important to consider light in the workplace not only by quantitative criteria, but also by qualitative criteria. The first step is to study the work station, the precision required of the tasks performed, the amount of work, the mobility of the worker and so on. Light should include components both of diffuse and of direct radiation. The result of the combination will produce shadows of greater or lesser intensity that will allow the worker to perceive the form and position of objects at the work station. Annoying reflections, which make it harder to perceive details, should be eliminated, as well as excessive glare or deep shadows.

The periodic maintenance of the lighting installation is very important. The goal is to prevent the ageing of lamps and the accumulation of dust on the luminaries that will result in a constant loss of light. For this reason it is important to select lamps and systems that are easy to maintain. An incandescent light bulb maintains its efficiency until the moments before failure, but this is not the case with fluorescent tubes, which may lower their output down to 75% after a thousand hours of use.

Levels of illumination

Each activity requires a specific level of illumination in the area where the activity takes place. In general, the higher the difficulty for visual perception, the higher the average level of illumination should be as well. Guidelines for minimal levels of illumination associated with different tasks exist in various publications. Concretely, those listed in figure 46.9 have been gleaned from European norms CENTC 169, and are based more on experience than on scientific knowledge.

The level of illumination is measured with a luxometer that converts luminous energy into an electrical signal, which is then amplified and offers an easy reading on a calibrated scale of lux. When selecting a certain level of illumination for a particular work station the following points should be studied:

- the nature of the work
- reflectance of the object and of the immediate surroundings
- differences with natural light and the need for daytime illumination
- the worker's age.

Units and magnitudes of illumination

Several magnitudes are commonly used in the field of illumination. The basic ones are:

Luminous flux: Luminous energy emitted per unit of time by a light source. Unit: lumen (lm).

Luminous intensity: Luminous flux emitted in a given direction by a light that is not equally distributed. Unit: candela (cd).

Level of illumination: Level of illumination of a surface of one square metre when it receives a luminous flux of one lumen. Unit: $lux = lm/m^2$.

Luminance or photometric brilliance: Is defined for a surface in a particular direction, and is the relation between luminous intensity and the surface seen by an observer situated in the same direction (apparent surface). Unit: cd/m^2.

Figure 46.9 • Levels of illumination as a function of tasks performed.

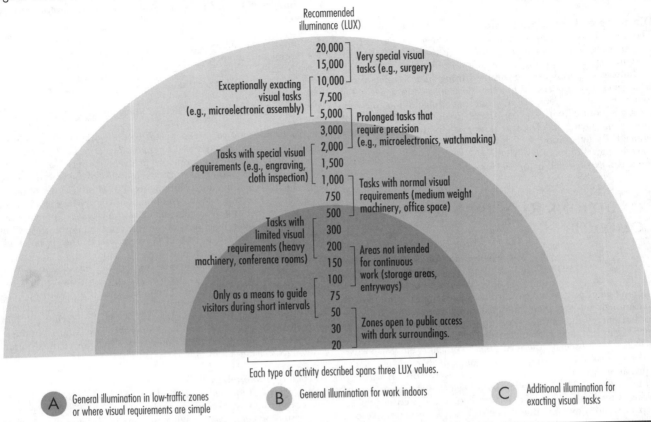

Recommended illuminance (LUX)

	20,000	Very special visual tasks (e.g., surgery)
	15,000	
Exceptionally exacting visual tasks (e.g., microelectronic assembly)	10,000	
	7,500	
	5,000	Prolonged tasks that require precision (e.g., microelectronics, watchmaking)
	3,000	
Tasks with special visual requirements (e.g., engraving, cloth inspection)	2,000	
	1,500	
	1,000	Tasks with normal visual requirements (medium weight machinery, office space)
	750	
	500	
Tasks with limited visual requirements (heavy machinery, conference rooms)	300	
	200	Areas not intended for continuous work (storage areas, entryways)
	150	
	100	
Only as a means to guide visitors during short intervals	75	
	50	
	30	Zones open to public access with dark surroundings.
	20	

Each type of activity described spans three LUX values.

A General illumination in low-traffic zones or where visual requirements are simple

B General illumination for work indoors

C Additional illumination for exacting visual tasks

Contrast: Difference in luminance between an object and its surroundings or between different parts of an object.

Reflectance: Proportion of light that is reflected by a surface. It is a non-dimensional quantity. Its value ranges between 0 and 1.

Factors that affect the visibility of objects

The degree of safety with which a task is executed depends, in large part, on the quality of illumination and on visual capacities. The visibility of an object can be altered in many ways. One of the most important is the contrast of luminances due to reflection factors, to shadows, or to colours of the object itself, and to the reflection factors of colour. What the eye really perceives are the differences of luminance between an object and its surroundings, or between different parts of the same object. Table 46.6 lists the contrasts between colours in descending order.

The luminance of an object, of its surroundings, and of the work area influence the ease with which an object is seen. It is therefore of key importance that the area where the visual task is performed, and its surroundings, be carefully analysed.

The size of the object that must be observed, which may be adequate or not depending on the distance and the angle of vision of the observer, is another factor. These last two factors determine the arrangement of the work station, classifying different zones according to their ease of vision. We can establish five zones in the work area (see figure 46.10).

Another factor is the time frame during which vision occurs. The time of exposure will be greater or smaller depending on whether the object and the observer are static, or whether one or both of them are moving. The adaptive capacity of the eye to

adjust automatically to the different illuminations of objects can also have considerable influence on visibility.

Light distribution; glare

Key factors in the conditions that affect vision are the distribution of light and the contrast of luminances. In so far as the distribution of light is concerned, it is preferable to have good general

Table 46.6 • Colour contrasts.

Colour contrasts in descending order	
Colour of the object	Colour of the background
Black	Yellow
Green	White
Red	White
Blue	White
White	Blue
Black	White
Yellow	Black
White	Red
White	Green
White	Black

Figure 46.10 • Distribution of visual zones in the work-station.

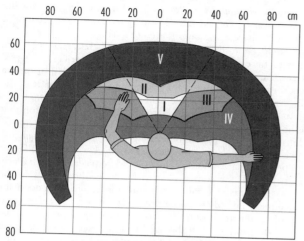

VISUAL ZONES IN THE ORGANIZATION OF THE WORK SPACE

	Work movements	Visual effort
Range I	Frequent movements, imply a lot of time spent	Great visual effort
Range II	Less frequent movements	Frequent visual
Range III	Imply little time	Visual information is not important
Range IV	Even less frequency, little time	No visual effort in particular
Range V	Should be avoided	Should be avoided

illumination instead of localized illumination in order to avoid glare. For this reason, electrical accessories should be distributed as uniformly as possible in order to avoid differences in luminous intensity. Constant shuttling through zones that are not uniformly illuminated causes eye fatigue, and with time this can lead to reduced visual output.

Glare is produced when a brilliant source of light is present in the visual field; the result is a diminution in the capacity to distinguish objects. Workers who suffer the effects of glare constantly and successively can suffer from eye strain as well as from functional disorders, even though in many cases they are not aware of it.

Figure 46.11 • Approximate values of luminance.

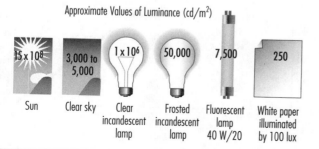

Approximate Values of Luminance (cd/m²)

15 x 10⁸	3,000 to 5,000	1 x 10⁶	50,000	7,500	250
Sun	Clear sky	Clear incandescent lamp	Frosted incandescent lamp	Fluorescent lamp 40 W/20	White paper illuminated by 100 lux

Glare can be direct when its origin is bright sources of light directly in the line of vision, or by reflection when light is reflected on surfaces with high reflectance. The factors involved in glare are:

1. *Luminance of the source of light*: The maximum tolerable luminance by direct observation is 7,500 cd/m². Figure 46.11 shows some of the approximate values of luminance for several sources of light.
2. *Location of the source of light*: This kind of glare occurs when the source of light is within a 45-degree angle of the observer's line of sight, and will be minimized to the degree that the source of light is placed beyond that angle. Ways and methods of avoiding direct and reflective glare can be seen in the following figures (see figure 46.12).
   In general, there is more glare when sources of light are mounted at lower elevations or when installed in large rooms, because sources of light in large rooms or sources of light that are too low can easily fall within the angle of vision that produces glare.
3. Distribution of luminance among different objects and surfaces: The greater the differences in luminance are among the objects within the field of vision, the greater will be the glare created and the greater will be the deterioration in the capacity to see due to the effects on the adaptive processes of sight. The maximum recommended luminance disparities are:
   • visual task—work surface: 3:1
   • visual task—surroundings: 10:1
4. *Time frame of the exposure*: Even light sources with a low luminance can cause glare if the length of the exposure is prolonged too much.

Figure 46.12 • Factors that affect glare.

1. Height of lighting installation

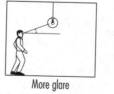

More glare   Less glare

2. Size of room

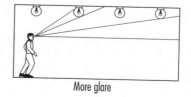 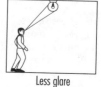

More glare   Less glare

Figure 46.13 • Lighting systems.

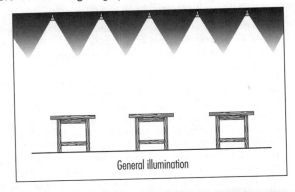

General illumination

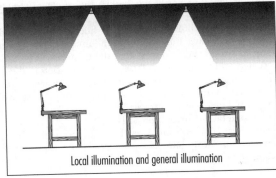

Local illumination and general illumination

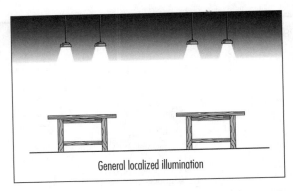

General localized illumination

Avoiding glare is a relatively simple proposition and can be achieved in different ways. One way, for example, is by placing grilles under the sources of illumination, or by using enveloping diffusers or parabolic reflectors that can direct light properly, or by installing the sources of light in such a way that they will not interfere with the angle of vision. When designing the work site, the correct distribution of luminance is as important as the illumination itself, but it is also important to consider that a distribution of luminance that is too uniform makes the three-dimensional and spatial perception of objects more difficult.

Lighting Systems

The interest in natural illumination has increased recently. This is due less to the quality of illumination it affords than to the well-being that it provides. But since the level of illumination from natural sources is not uniform, an artificial lighting system is required.

The most common lighting systems used are the following:

General uniform illumination
In this system light sources are spread out evenly without regard to the location of the work stations. The average level of illumination should be equal to the level of illumination required for the task that will be carried out. These systems are used mainly in workplaces where work stations are not fixed.

It should conform to three fundamental characteristics: The first is to be equipped with anti-glare devices (grilles, diffusers, reflectors and so on). The second is that it should distribute a fraction of the light toward the ceiling and the upper part of the walls. And the third is that the light sources should be installed as high as possible, to minimize glare and achieve illumination that is as homogeneous as possible. (See figure 46.13.)

This system tries to reinforce the general illumination scheme by placing lamps close to the work surfaces. These types of lamps often produce glare, and reflectors should be placed in such a way that they block the source of light from the direct sight of the worker. The use of localized illumination is recommended for those applications where visual demands are very critical, such as levels of illumination of 1,000 lux or greater. Generally, visual capacity deteriorates with the age of the worker, which makes it necessary to increase the level of general illumination or to second it with localized illumination. This phenomenon can be clearly appreciated in figure 46.14.

General localized illumination
This type of illumination consists of ceiling sources distributed with two things in mind—the illumination characteristics of the equipment and the illumination needs of each work station. This type of illumination is indicated for those spaces or work areas that will require a high level of illumination, and it requires knowing the future location of each work station in advance of the design stage.

Colour: Basic Concepts
Selecting an adequate colour for a worksite contributes a great deal to the efficiency, safety and general well-being of the employees. In the same way, the finish of the surfaces and of the equipment found in the work environment contributes to creating pleasant visual conditions and a pleasant work environment.

Ordinary light consists of electromagnetic radiations of different wavelengths that correspond to each of the bands of the visible spectrum. By mixing red, yellow and blue light we can

Figure 46.14 • Loss of visual acuity with age.

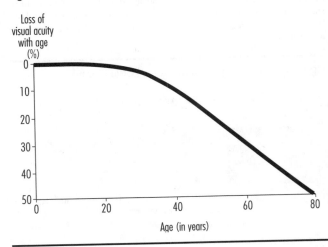

obtain most of the visible colours, including white. Our perception of the colour of an object depends on the colour of the light with which it is illuminated and on the way the object itself reflects light.

Lamps can be classified into three categories depending on the appearance of the light they emit:

- colour with a warm appearance: a white, reddish light recommended for residential use
- colour with intermediate appearance: a white light recommended for worksites
- colour with a cold appearance: a white, bluish light recommended for tasks that require a high level of illumination or for hot climates.

Colours may also be classified as warm or cold according to their tonality (see figure 46.15).

Contrast and temperature of different colours

Colour contrasts are influenced by the colour of the light selected, and for that reason the quality of illumination will depend on the colour of the light chosen for an application. The selection of the colour of light to be used should be made based on the task that will be carried out under it. If the colour is close to white, the rendition of colour and the diffusion of light will be better. The more light approaches the red end of the spectrum the worse the reproduction of colour will be, but the environment will be warmer and more inviting.

The colour appearance of illumination depends not only on the colour of light, but also on the level of luminous intensity. A colour temperature is associated with the different forms of illumination. The sensation of satisfaction with the illumination of a given environment depends on this colour temperature. In this way, for example, a 100 W incandescent filament light bulb has a colour temperature of 2,800 K, a fluorescent tube has a colour temperature of 4,000 K and an overcast sky has a colour temperature of 10,000 K.

Kruithof defined, through empirical observations, a diagram of well-being for different levels of illumination and colour temperatures in a given environment (see figure 46.16). In this way, he demonstrated that it is possible to feel comfortable in certain environments with low levels of illumination if the colour temperature is also low—if the level of illumination is one candle, for example, with a colour temperature of 1,750 K.

The colours of electric lamps can be subdivided into three groups related to their colour temperatures:

- daylight white—around 6,000 K
- neutral white—around 4,000 K
- warm white—around 3,000 K

Combination and selection of colours

The selection of colours is very relevant when we consider it together with those functions where identifying the objects that must be manipulated is important. It is also relevant when delimiting avenues of communication and in those tasks that require sharp contrast.

The selection of tonality is not as important a question as the selection of the proper reflective qualities of a surface. There are several recommendations that apply to this aspect of work surfaces:

Ceilings: The surface of a ceiling should be as white as possible (with a reflection factor of 75%), because light will then reflect from it in a diffuse way, dissipating darkness and reducing the glare from other surfaces. This will also mean a savings in artificial lighting.

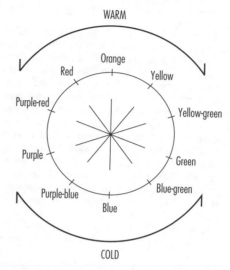

Figure 46.15 • Tonality of "warm" and "cold" colours.

Walls and floors: The surfaces of walls at eye level can produce glare. Pale colours with reflective factors of 50 to 75% tend to be adequate for walls. While glossy paints tend to last longer than matte colours, they are more reflective. Walls should therefore have a matte or semi-gloss finish.

Floors should be finished in slightly darker colours than walls and ceilings to avoid glare. The reflective factor of floors should be between 20 and 25%.

Equipment: Work surfaces, machinery and tables should have reflective factors of between 20 and 40%. Equipment should have a lasting finish of pure colour—light browns or greys—and the material should not be shiny.

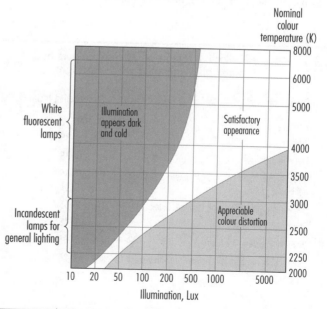

Figure 46.16 • Comfort diagram as a function of illumination and colour temperatures.

The proper use of colours in the work environment facilitates well-being, increases productivity and can have a positive impact on quality. It can also contribute to better organization and the prevention of accidents.

There is a generalized belief that whitening the walls and ceilings and supplying adequate levels of illumination is all that can possibly be done as far as the visual comfort of employees is concerned. But these comfort factors can be improved by combining white with other colours, thus avoiding the fatigue and the boredom that characterize monochromatic environments. Colours also have an effect on a person's level of stimulation; warm colours tend to activate and relax, while cold colours are used to induce the individual to release or liberate his or her energy.

The colour of light, its distribution, and the colours used in a given space are, among others, key factors that influence the sensations a person feels. Given the many colours and comfort factors that exist, it is impossible to set precise guidelines, especially considering that all these factors must be combined according to the characteristics and the requirements of a particular work station. A number of basic and general practical rules can be listed, however, that can help create a liveable environment:

- Bright colours produce comfortable, stimulating and serene feelings, while dark colours tend to have a depressing effect.
- Sources of warm-coloured light help reproduce warm colours well. Warm-coloured objects are more pleasing to the eye in warm light than in cold light.
- Clear and dull colours (like pastels) are very appropriate as background colours, while objects should have rich and saturated colours.
- Warm colours excite the nervous system and give the sensation that temperature is rising.
- Cold colours are preferable for objects. They have a calming effect and can be used to produce the effect of curvature. Cold colours help create the sensation that temperature is dropping.
- The sensation of colour of an object depends on the background colour and on the effect of the light source on its surface.
- Environments that are physically cold or hot can be tempered by using warm or cold lighting, respectively.
- The intensity of a colour will be inversely proportional to the part of the normal visual field that it occupies.

Table 46.7 • Reflection factors of different colours and materials illuminated with white light.

Colour/material	Reflection factor (%)
White	100
White paper	80–85
Ivory, lime-yellow	70–75
Bright yellow, light ochre, light green, pastel blue, light pink, cream	60–65
Lime-green, pale gray, pink, orange, blue-gray	50–55
Blond wood, blue sky	40–45
Oak, dry concrete	30–35
Deep red, leaf-green, olive-green, meadow-green	20–25
Dark blue, purple	10–15
Black	0

- The spatial appearance of a room can be influenced by colour. A room will seem to have a lower ceiling if its walls are painted a bright colour and the floor and ceiling are darker, and it will seem to have a higher ceiling if the walls are darker and the ceiling is bright.

Identifying objects through colour

The selection of colours can influence the effectiveness of lighting systems by influencing the fraction of light that is reflected. But colour also plays a key role when it comes to identifying objects. We can use brilliant and eye-catching colours or colour contrasts to highlight situations or objects that require special attention. Table 46.7 lists some of the factors of reflection for different colours and materials.

In any case, identification by colour should be employed only when it is truly necessary, since identification by colour will work properly only if there are not too many objects that are highlighted by colour. The following are some recommendations for identifying different elements by colour:

- *Fire and safety equipment*: It is advisable to identify this equipment by placing a recognizable graphic on the nearest wall so that it can be found quickly.
- *Machinery*: The colouring of stop or emergency devices with bright colours on all machinery is critical. It is also advisable to mark with colour the areas that need lubrication or periodic maintenance, which can add ease and functionality to these procedures.
- *Tubing and pipes*: If they are important or carry dangerous substances the best advice is to colour them completely. In some cases it may be enough to colour only a line along their length.
- *Stairways*: In order to make descent easier, one band for every step is preferable to several.
- *Risks*: Colour should be used to identify a risk only when the risk cannot be eliminated. Identification will be much more effective if it is carried out according to a predetermined colour code.

GENERAL LIGHTING CONDITIONS

N. Alan Smith

Lighting is provided within interiors in order to satisfy the following requirements:

- to assist in providing a safe working environment
- to assist in the performance of visual tasks
- to develop an appropriate visual environment.

The provision of a safe working environment has to be at the top of the list of priorities, and, in general, safety is increased by making hazards clearly visible. The order of priority of the other two requirements will depend to a large extent upon the use to which the interior is put. Task performance can be improved by ensuring that task detail is easier to see, while appropriate visual environments are developed by varying the lighting emphasis given to objects and surfaces within an interior.

Our general feeling of well-being, including morale and fatigue, is influenced by light and colour. Under low lighting levels, objects would have little or no colour or shape and there would be a loss in perspective. Conversely an excess of light may be just as unwanted as too little light.

In general, people prefer a room with daylight to a room which is windowless. Furthermore, contact with the outside world is considered to aid the feeling of well-being. The introduction of

Figure 46.17 • Lighting systems.

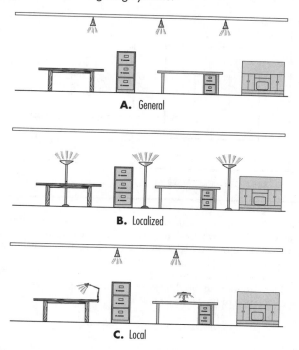

A. General

B. Localized

C. Local

Table 46.8 • Typical recommended levels of maintained illuminance for different locations or visual tasks.

Location/Task	Typical recommended level of maintained illuminance (lux)
General offices	500
Computer workstations	500
Factory assembly areas	
Rough work	300
Medium work	500
Fine work	750
Very fine work	
Instrument assembly	1,000
Jewellery assembly/repairs	1,500
Hospital operating theatres	50,000

automatic lighting controls, together with high-frequency dimming of fluorescent lamps, has made it possible to provide interiors with a controlled combination of daylight and artificial light. This has the added benefit of saving on energy costs.

Perception of the character of an interior is influenced by both the brightness and colour of visible surfaces, both interior and exterior. The general lighting conditions within an interior can be achieved by using daylight or artificial lighting, or more likely by a combination of both.

Evaluation of Lighting

General requirements

Lighting systems used in commercial interiors can be sub-divided into three major categories—general lighting, localized lighting and local lighting.

General lighting installations typically provide an approximately uniform illuminance over the whole of the working plane. Such systems are often based upon the lumen method of design, where an average illuminance is:

Average illuminance (lux) =

$$\frac{Luminous\ flux\ (\text{lumens}) \times Utilization\ factor \times Maintenance\ factor}{Area\ (\text{m}^2)}$$

Localized lighting systems provide illuminance on general work areas with a simultaneous reduced level of illuminance in adjacent areas.

Local lighting systems provide illuminance for relatively small areas incorporating visual tasks. Such systems are normally complemented by a specified level of general lighting. Figure 46.17 illustrates the typical differences between the systems described.

Where visual tasks are to be performed it is essential to achieve a demanded level of illuminance and to consider the circumstances that influence its quality.

The use of daylight to illuminate tasks has both merits and limitations. Windows admitting daylight into an interior provide good three-dimensional modelling, and though the spectral distribution of daylight varies throughout the day, its colour rendering is generally considered to be excellent.

However, a constant illuminance on a task cannot be provided by natural daylight only, due to its wide variability, and if the task is within the same field of view as a bright sky, then disabling glare is likely to occur, thereby impairing task performance. The use of daylight for task illuminance has only partial success, and artificial lighting, over which greater control can be exercised, has a major role to play.

Since the human eye will perceive surfaces and objects only through light which is reflected from them, it follows that surface characteristics and reflectance values together with the quantity and quality of light will influence the appearance of the environment.

When considering the lighting of an interior it is essential to determine the *illuminance* level and to compare it with recommended levels for different tasks (see table 46.8).

Figure 46.18 • Typical relationship between visual acuity and illuminance.

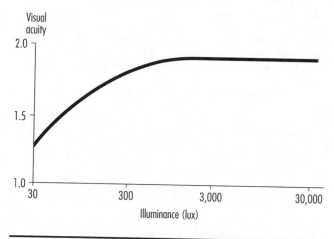

Figure 46.19 • Typical relationship between visual performance and illuminance.

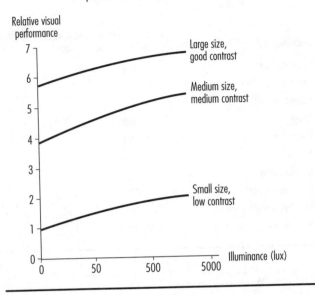

Lighting for visual tasks

The ability of the eye to discern detail—*visual acuity*—is significantly influenced by task size, contrast and the viewer's visual performance. Increase in the quantity and quality of lighting will also significantly improve *visual performance*. The effect of lighting on task performance is influenced by the size of the critical details of the task and upon the contrast between task and surrounding background. Figure 46.18 shows the effects of illuminance upon visual acuity. When considering visual task lighting it is important to consider the ability of the eye to carry out the visual task with both speed and accuracy. This combination is known as *visual performance*. Figure 46.19 gives typical effects of illuminance on the visual performance of a given task.

The prediction of illuminance reaching a working surface is of prime importance in lighting design. However, the human visual system responds to the distribution of luminance within the field of view. The scene within a visual field is interpreted by differentiating between surface colour, reflectance and illumination. Luminance depends upon both the illuminance on, and reflectance of, a surface. Both illuminance and luminance are objective quantities. The response to brightness, however, is subjective.

In order to produce an environment which provides visual satisfaction, comfort and performance, luminances within the field of view need to be balanced. Ideally the luminances surrounding a task should decrease gradually, thereby avoiding harsh contrasts. Suggested variation in luminance across a task is shown in figure 46.20.

The lumen method of lighting design leads to an average horizontal plane illuminance on the working plane, and it is possible to use the method to establish average illuminance values on the walls and ceilings within an interior. It is possible to convert average illuminance values into average luminance values from details of the mean reflectance value of the room surfaces. The equation relating luminance and illuminance is:

$$Luminance \ (\mathrm{cd \cdot m^{-2}}) = \frac{Illuminance \ (\mathrm{lux}) \times Reflectance}{\pi}$$

Figure 46.21 shows a typical office with relative illuminance values (from an overhead general lighting system) on the main

Figure 46.20 • Variation in luminance across a task.

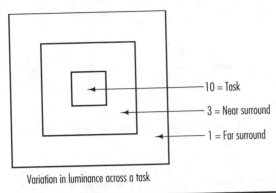

Variation in luminance across a task

room surfaces together with suggested reflectances. The human eye tends to be drawn to that part of the visual scene which is brightest. It follows that higher luminance values usually occur at a visual task area. The eye acknowledges detail within a visual task by discriminating between lighter and darker parts of the task. The variation in brightness of a visual task is determined from calculation of the *luminance contrast*:

$$Luminance \ contrast \ (C) = \frac{|L_t - L_b|}{|L_b|}$$

where
L_t = Luminance of the task
L_b = Luminance of the background
and both luminances are measured in $\mathrm{cd \cdot m^{-2}}$

The vertical lines in this equation signify that all values of luminance contrast are to be considered positive.

The contrast of a visual task will be influenced by the reflectance properties of the task itself. See figure 46.21.

Optical Control of Lighting

If a bare lamp is used in a luminaire, the distribution of light is unlikely to be acceptable and the system will almost certainly be uneconomical. In such situations the bare lamp is likely to be a source of glare to the room occupants, and while some light may eventually reach the working plane, the effectiveness of the installation is likely to be seriously reduced because of the glare.

Figure 46.21 • Typical relative illuminance values together with suggested reflectance values.

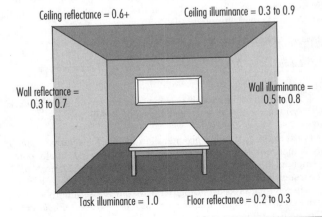

Figure 46.22 • Lighting output control by obstruction.

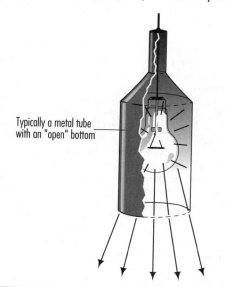

Typically a metal tube with an "open" bottom

It will be evident that some form of light control is required, and the methods most frequently employed are detailed below.

Obstruction

If a lamp is installed within an opaque enclosure with only a single aperture for the light to escape, then the light distribution will be very limited, as shown in figure 46.22.

Reflection

This method uses reflective surfaces, which may vary from a highly matt finish to a highly specular or mirror-like finish. This method of control is more efficient than obstruction, since stray light is collected and redirected to where it is required. The principle involved is shown in figure 46.23.

Diffusion

If a lamp is installed within a translucent material, the apparent size of the light source is increased with a simultaneous reduction in its brightness. Practical diffusers unfortunately absorb some of the emitted light, which consequently reduces the overall effi-

Figure 46.23 • Light output control by reflection.

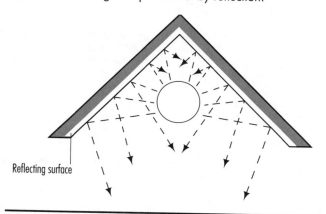

Reflecting surface

Figure 46.24 • Light output control by diffusion.

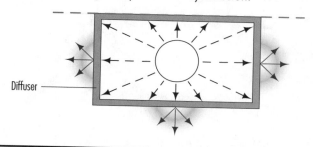

Diffuser

ciency of the luminaire. Figure 46.24 illustrates the principle of diffusion.

Refraction

This method uses the "prism" effect, where typically a prism material of glass or plastic "bends" the rays of light and in so doing redirects the light to where it is required. This method is extremely suitable for general interior lighting. It has the advantage of combining good glare control with an acceptable efficiency. Figure 46.25 shows how refraction assists in optical control.

In many cases a luminaire will use a combination of the methods of optical control described.

Luminance distribution

The light output distribution from a luminaire is significant in determining the visual conditions subsequently experienced. Each of the four methods of optical control described will produce differing light output distribution properties from the luminaire.

Veiling reflections often occur in areas where VDUs are installed. The usual symptoms experienced in such situations are reduced ability to read correctly from the text on a screen due to the appearance of unwanted high-luminance images on the screen itself, typically from overhead luminaires. A situation can develop where veiling reflections also appear on paper on a desk in an interior.

If the luminaires in an interior have a strong vertically downward component of light output, then any paper on a desk beneath such a luminaire will reflect the light source into the eyes of an observer who is reading from or working on the paper. If the paper has a gloss finish, the situation is aggravated.

The solution to the problem is to arrange for the luminaires used to have a light output distribution which is predominantly at an angle to the downward vertical, so that following the basic laws

Figure 46.25 • Light output control by refraction.

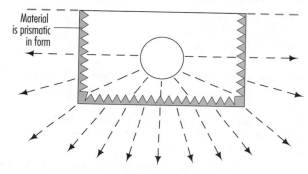

Material is prismatic in form

Figure 46.26 • Veiling reflections.

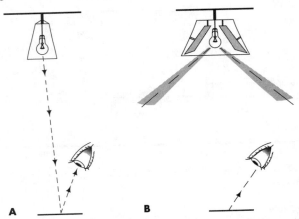

A   B

(a) Veiling reflections caused by fixtures with strong downward component of light output;
(b) Luminaires with batwing distribution in order to overcome veiling reflections on horizontal work surface.

of physics (angle of incidence = angle of reflection) the reflected glare will be minimized. Figure 46.26 shows a typical example of both the problem and the cure. The light output distribution from the luminaire used to overcome the problem is referred to as a *batwing distribution.*

Light distribution from luminaires can also lead to *direct glare,* and in an attempt to overcome this problem, local lighting units should be installed outside the 45-degree "forbidden angle", as shown in figure 46.27.

Optimal Lighting Conditions for Visual Comfort and Performance

It is appropriate when investigating lighting conditions for visual comfort and performance to consider those factors affecting the ability to see detail. These can be sub-divided into two categories—characteristics of the observer and characteristics of the task.

Characteristics of the observer. These include:

- sensitivity of the individual's visual system to size, contrast, exposure time
- transient adaptation characteristics
- susceptibility to glare
- age
- motivational and psychological characteristics.

Characteristics of the task. These include:

- configuration of detail
- contrast of detail/background
- background luminance
- specularity of detail.

With reference to particular tasks, the following questions need to be answered:

- Are the task details easy to see?
- Is the task likely to be undertaken for lengthy periods?
- If errors result from the performance of the task, are the consequences considered to be serious?

In order to produce optimal workplace lighting conditions it is important to consider the requirements placed upon the lighting

installation. Ideally task lighting should reveal colour, size, relief and surface qualities of a task while simultaneously avoiding the creation of potentially dangerous shadows, glare and "harsh" surroundings to the task itself.

Glare. Glare occurs when there is excessive luminance in the field of view. The effects of glare on vision can be divided into two groups, termed *disability glare* and *discomfort glare.*

Consider the example of glare from the headlights of an on-coming vehicle during darkness. The eye cannot adapt simultaneously to the headlights of the vehicle and to the much lower brightness of the road. This is an example of disability glare, since the high luminance light sources produce a disabling effect due to the scattering of light in the optic media. Disability glare is proportional to the intensity of the offending source of light.

Discomfort glare, which is more likely to occur in interiors, can be reduced or even totally eliminated by reducing the contrast between the task and its surroundings. Matt, diffusely reflecting finishes on work surfaces are to be preferred to gloss or specularly reflecting finishes, and the position of any offending light source should be outside the normal field of vision. In general, successful visual performance occurs when the task itself is brighter than its immediate surrounds, but not excessively.

The magnitude of discomfort glare is given a numerical value and compared with reference values in order to predict whether the level of discomfort glare will be acceptable. The method of calculation of glare index values used in the UK and elsewhere is considered under "Measurement".

Measurement

Lighting surveys

One survey technique often used relies upon a grid of measuring points over the whole area under consideration. The basis of this technique is to divide the whole of the interior into a number of equal areas, each ideally square. The illuminance at the centre of each of the areas is measured at desk-top height (typically 0.85 metres above floor level), and an average value of illuminance is calculated. The accuracy of the value of average illuminance is influenced by the number of measuring points used.

Figure 46.27 • Diagrammatic representation of the forbidden angle.

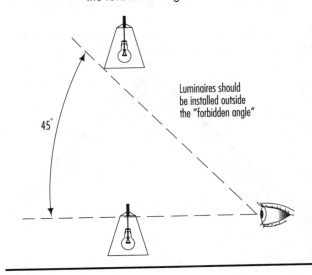

Luminaires should be installed outside the "forbidden angle"

45°

Figure 46.28 • Elevation and plan views of typical interior used in example.

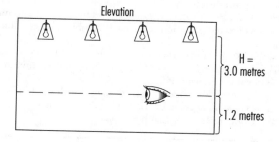
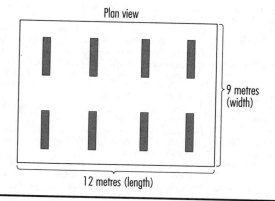

A relationship exists which enables the *minimum* number of measuring points to be calculated from the value of *room index* applicable to the interior under consideration.

$$Room\ index\ (RI) = \frac{Length \times Width}{Mounting\ height \times (Length + Width)}$$

Here, length and width refer to the room dimensions, and mounting height is the vertical distance between the centre of the light source and the working plane.

The relationship referred to is given as:

$$Minimum\ number\ of\ measuring\ points = (x + 2)^2$$

where "*x*" is the value of the room index taken to the next highest whole number, except that for all values of *RI* equal to or greater than 3, *x* is taken as 4. This equation gives the minimum number of measuring points, but conditions often require more than this minimum number of points to be used.

When considering the lighting of a task area and its immediate surround, variance in illuminance or *uniformity* of illuminance must be considered.

$$Uniformity\ of\ illuminance = \frac{Minimum\ illuminance}{Mean\ illuminance}$$

Over any task area and its immediate surround, uniformity should be not less than 0.8.

In many workplaces it is unnecessary to illuminate all areas to the same level. Localized or local lighting may provide some degree of energy saving, but whichever system is used the variance in illuminance across an interior must not be excessive.

The *diversity* of illuminance is expressed as:

$$Diversity\ of\ illuminance = \frac{Maximum\ illuminance}{Minimum\ illuminance}$$

Figure 46.29 • Possible combinations of luminaire orientation and viewing direction within the interior considered in the example.

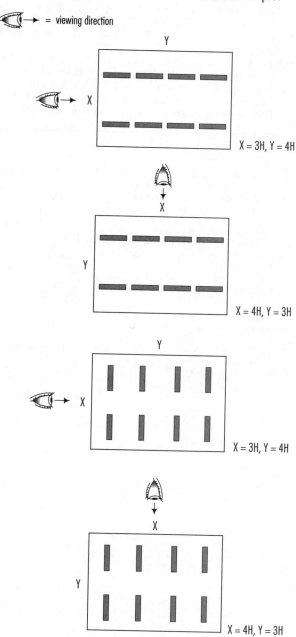

At any point in the major area of the interior, the diversity of illuminance should not exceed 5:1.

Instruments used for measuring illuminance and luminance typically have spectral responses which vary from the response of the human visual system. The responses are corrected, often by the use of filters. When filters are incorporated, the instruments are referred to as *colour corrected*.

Illuminance meters have a further correction applied which compensates for the direction of incident light falling upon the detector cell. Instruments which are capable of accurately measuring illuminance from varying directions of incident light are said to be *cosine corrected*.

Measurement of glare index

The system used frequently in the UK, with variations elsewhere, is essentially a two-stage process. The first stage establishes an *uncorrected glare index* value (UGI). Figure 46.28 provides an example.

The height H is the vertical distance between the centre of the light source and the eye level of a seated observer, which is normally taken as 1.2 metres above floor level. The major dimensions of the room are then converted into multiples of H. Thus, since H = 3.0 metres, then length = 4H and width = 3H. Four

separate calculations of UGI have to be made in order to determine the worst case scenario in accordance with the layouts shown in figure 46.29.

Tables are produced by lighting equipment manufacturers which specify, for given values of fabric reflectance within a room, values of uncorrected glare index for each combination of values of X and Y.

The second stage of the process is to apply correction factors to the UGI values depending upon values of lamp output flux and deviation in value of height (H).

The final glare index value is then compared with the Limiting Glare Index value for specific interiors, given in references such as the CIBSE Code for Interior Lighting (1994).

References

Chartered Institution of Building Services Engineers (CIBSE). 1993. *Lighting Guide*. London: CIBSE.

—. 1994. *Code for Interior Lighting*. London: CIBSE.

Commission Internationale de l'Eclairage (CIE). 1992. *Maintenance of Indoor Electric Lighting Systems*. CIE Technical Report No. 97. Austria: CIE.

International Electrotechnical Commission (IEC). 1993. *International Lamp Coding System*. IEC document no. 123-93. London: IEC.

Lighting Industry Federation. 1994. *Lighting Industry Federation Lamp Guide*. London: Lighting Industry Federation.

Other relevant readings

Association française de normalisation. 1975. Couleurs d'ambiance pour les lieux de travail. Norme française enregistrée NF X 08-004. CIS document No. 76-1288. Paris: Tour Europe.

Bestratén, M, R Chavarria, A Hernandez, P Luna, C Nogareda, S Nogareda, M Oncins, and MG Solé. 1994. *Ergonomía. Centro Nacional De Condiciones De Trabajo*. Barcelona: Instituto Nacional de Seguridad e Higiene en el Trabajo.

Cayless, MA and AM Marsden. 1983. *Lamps and Lighting*. London: E Arnold.

Commission for the European Communities (CEC). 1989. *Framework Directive*. EC Directive No. 89/391/EEC. Brussels: CEC.

De Boer, JB and D Fischer. 1981. *Interior Lighting*. Antwerp: Philips Technical Library.

Department of Productivity. 1979. *Artificial Light at Work*. Occupational Safety and Health Working Environment, No. 6. Canberra: Australian Government Publishing Service.

—. 1980. *Colour at work*. Occupational Safety and Health Working Environment, No. 8. Canberra: Australian Government Publishing Service.

Gardiner, K and JM Harrington. 1995. *Occupational Hygiene*. Oxford: Blackwell Science.

Grandjean, E. 1988. *Fitting the Task to the Man*. London: Taylor & Francis.

Greene, TC and PA Bell. 1980. *Additional Considerations Concerning the Effect of 'Warm' and 'Cool' Wall Colours On Energy Conservation*. London: Ergonomics.

Illuminating Engineers Society of North America. 1979. *American National Standard. Practice of Industrial Lighting*. ANSI/IES RP-7-1979. New York: Illuminating Engineers Society of North America.

—. 1981. *Lighting Handbook*. New York: Illuminating Engineers Society of North America.

International Labour Organization (ILO). N.d. *Artificial Lighting in Factory and Office*. CIS Information Sheet No. 11. Geneva: ILO.

Mandelo, P. 1994. *Fundamentos De Ergonomia*. Barcelona: Universidad Politécnica de Barcelona.

Moon, P. 1961. *Scientific Basis of Illuminating Engineering*. London: Dover Publications.

Walsh, JWT. N.d. *Textbook of Illuminating Engineering*. London: Pitman.

47

Chapter Editor
Alice H. Suter

Contents

THE NATURE AND EFFECTS OF NOISE

Alice H. Suter

The Pervasive Nature of Occupational Noise

Noise is one of the most common of all the occupational hazards. In the United States, for example, more than 9 million workers are exposed to daily average A-weighted noise levels of 85 decibels (abbreviated here as 85 dBA). These noise levels are potentially hazardous to their hearing and can produce other adverse effects as well. There are approximately 5.2 million workers exposed to noise above these levels in manufacturing and utilities, which represents about 35% of the total number of workers in US manufacturing industries.

Hazardous noise levels are easily identified and it is technologically feasible to control excessive noise in the vast majority of cases by applying off-the-shelf technology, by redesigning the equipment or process or by retrofitting noisy machines. But all too often, nothing is done. There are several reasons for this. First, although many noise control solutions are remarkably inexpensive, others can be costly, especially when the aim is to reduce the noise hazard to levels of 85 or 80 dBA.

One very important reason for the absence of noise control and hearing conservation programmes is that, unfortunately, noise is often accepted as a "necessary evil", a part of doing business, an inevitable part of an industrial job. Hazardous noise causes no bloodshed, breaks no bones, produces no strange-looking tissue, and, if workers can manage to get through the first few days or weeks of exposure, they often feel as though they have "got used" to the noise. But what has most likely happened is that they have started to incur a temporary hearing loss which dulls their hearing sensitivity during the work day and often subsides during the night. Thus, the progress of noise-induced hearing loss is insidious in that it creeps up gradually over the months and years, largely unnoticed until it reaches handicapping proportions.

Another important reason why the hazards of noise are not always recognized is that there is a stigma attached to the resulting hearing impairment. As Raymond Hétu has demonstrated so clearly in his article on rehabilitation from noise-induced hearing loss elsewhere in this *Encyclopaedia*, people with hearing impairments are often thought of as elderly, mentally slow and generally incompetent, and those at risk of incurring impairments are reluctant to acknowledge either their impairments or the risk for fear of being stigmatized. This is an unfortunate situation because noise-induced hearing losses become permanent, and, when added to the hearing loss that naturally occurs with ageing, can lead to depression and isolation in one's middle and old age. The time to take preventive steps is before the hearing losses begin.

The Scope of Noise Exposure

As mentioned above, noise is especially prevalent in the manufacturing industries. The US Department of Labor has estimated that 19.3% of the workers in manufacturing and utilities are exposed to daily average noise levels of 90 dBA and above, 34.4% are exposed to levels above 85 dBA, and 53.1% to levels above 80 dBA. These estimates should be fairly typical of the percentage of workers exposed to hazardous levels of noise in other nations. The levels are likely to be somewhat higher in less developed nations, where engineering controls are not used as widely, and somewhat lower in nations with stronger noise control programmes, such as the Scandinavian countries and Germany.

Many workers throughout the world experience some very hazardous exposures, well above 85 or 90 dBA. For example, the US Labor Department has estimated that nearly half a million workers are exposed to daily average noise levels of 100 dBA and above, and more than 800,000 to levels between 95 and 100 dBA in the manufacturing industries alone.

Figure 47.1 ranks the noisiest manufacturing industries in the United States in descending order according to the percentage of workers exposed above 90 dBA and gives estimates of noise-exposed workers by industrial sector.

Figure 47.1 • Occupational noise exposure—the US experience.

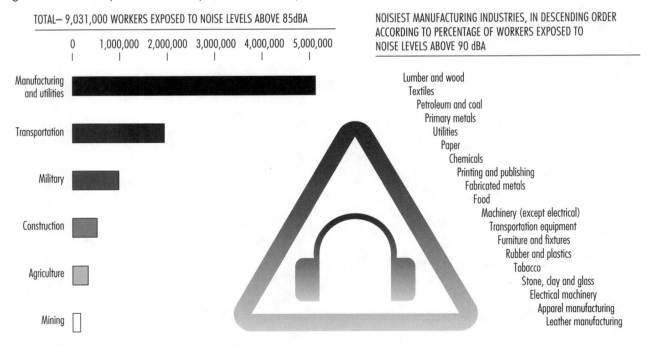

TOTAL— 9,031,000 WORKERS EXPOSED TO NOISE LEVELS ABOVE 85dBA

NOISIEST MANUFACTURING INDUSTRIES, IN DESCENDING ORDER ACCORDING TO PERCENTAGE OF WORKERS EXPOSED TO NOISE LEVELS ABOVE 90 dBA

Manufacturing and utilities
Transportation
Military
Construction
Agriculture
Mining

Lumber and wood
Textiles
Petroleum and coal
Primary metals
Utilities
Paper
Chemicals
Printing and publishing
Fabricated metals
Food
Machinery (except electrical)
Transportation equipment
Furniture and fixtures
Rubber and plastics
Tobacco
Stone, clay and glass
Electrical machinery
Apparel manufacturing
Leather manufacturing

Research Needs

In the following articles of this chapter, it should become clear to the reader that the effects on hearing of most types of noise are well-known. Criteria for the effects of continuous, varying and intermittent noise were developed some 30 years ago and remain essentially the same today. This is not true, however, of impulse noise. At relatively low levels, impulse noise seems to be no more damaging and possibly less so than continuous noise, given equal sound energy. But at high sound levels, impulse noise appears to be more damaging, especially when a critical level (or, more correctly, a critical exposure) is exceeded. Further research needs to be performed to define more exactly the shape of the damage/risk curve.

Another area that needs to be clarified is the adverse effect of noise, both on hearing and on general health, in combination with other agents. Although the combined effects of noise and ototoxic drugs are fairly well known, the combination of noise and industrial chemicals is of growing concern. Solvents and certain other agents appear to be increasingly neurotoxic when experienced in conjunction with high levels of noise.

Around the world, noise-exposed workers in the manufacturing industries and the military receive the major share of attention. There are, however, many workers in mining, construction, agriculture and transportation who are also exposed to hazardous levels of noise, as pointed out in figure 47.1. The unique needs associated with these occupations need to be assessed, and noise control and other aspects of hearing conservation programmes need to be extended to these workers. Unfortunately, the provision of hearing conservation programmes to noise-exposed workers does not guarantee that hearing loss and the other adverse effects of noise will be prevented. Standard methods to evaluate the effectiveness of hearing conservation programmes do exist, but they can be cumbersome and are not widely used. Simple evaluation methods need to be developed that can be used by small as well as large companies, and those with minimal resources.

The technology exists to abate most noise problems, as mentioned above, but there is a large gap between the existing technology and its application. Methods need to be developed by which information on all kinds of noise control solutions can be disseminated to those who need it. Noise control information needs to be computerized and made available not only to users in developing nations but to industrialized nations as well.

Future Trends

In some countries there is a growing trend to place more emphasis on non-occupational noise exposure and its contribution to the burden of noise-induced hearing loss. These kinds of sources and activities include hunting, target shooting, noisy toys and loud music. This focus is beneficial in that it highlights some potentially significant sources of hearing impairment, but it can actually be detrimental if it diverts attention from serious occupational noise problems.

A very dramatic trend is evident among the nations belonging to the European Union, where standardization for noise is progressing at an almost breathless pace. This process includes standards for product noise emissions as well as for noise exposure standards.

The standard-setting process is not moving rapidly at all in North America, especially in the United States, where regulatory efforts are at a standstill and movement toward deregulation is a possibility. Efforts to regulate the noise of new products were abandoned in 1982 when the Noise Office in the US Environmental Protection Agency was closed, and occupational noise standards may not survive the deregulatory climate in the current US Congress.

The developing nations appear to be in the process of adopting and revising noise standards. These standards are tending toward conservatism, in that they are moving toward a permissible exposure limit of 85 dBA, and toward an exchange rate (time/intensity trading relation) of 3 dB. How well these standards are enforced, especially in burgeoning economies, is an open question.

The trend in some of the developing nations is to concentrate on controlling noise by engineering methods rather than to struggle with the intricacies of audiometric testing, hearing protection devices, training and record keeping. This would appear to be a very sensible approach wherever feasible. Supplementation with hearing protectors may be necessary at times to reduce exposures to safe levels.

The Effects of Noise*

Loss of hearing is certainly the most well-known adverse effect of noise, and probably the most serious, but it is not the only one. Other detrimental effects include tinnitus (ringing in the ears), interference with speech communication and with the perception of warning signals, disruption of job performance, annoyance and extra-auditory effects. Under most circumstances, protecting workers' hearing should protect against most other effects. This consideration provides additional support for companies to implement good noise control and hearing conservation programmes.

Hearing impairment

Noise-induced hearing impairment is very common, but it is often underrated because there are no visible effects and, in most cases, no pain. There is only a gradual, progressive loss of communication with family and friends, and a loss of sensitivity to sounds in the environment, such as birdsong and music. Unfortunately, good hearing is usually taken for granted until it is lost.

These losses may be so gradual that individuals do not realize what has happened until the impairment becomes handicapping. The first sign is usually that other people do not seem to speak as clearly as they used to. The hearing-impaired person will have to ask others to repeat themselves, and he or she often becomes annoyed with their apparent lack of consideration. Family and friends will often be told, "Don't shout at me. I can hear you, but I just can't understand what you're saying."

As the hearing loss becomes worse, the individual will begin to withdraw from social situations. Church, civic meetings, social occasions and theatre begin to lose their attraction and the individual will choose to stay at home. The volume of the television becomes a source of contention within the family, and other family members are sometimes driven out of the room because the hearing-impaired person wants it so loud.

Presbycusis, the hearing loss that naturally accompanies the ageing process, adds to the hearing handicap when the person with noise-induced hearing loss becomes older. Eventually, the loss may progress to such a severe stage that the individual can no longer communicate with family or friends without great difficulty, and then he or she is indeed isolated. A hearing aid may help in some cases, but the clarity of natural hearing will never be restored, as the clarity of vision is with eyeglasses.

Occupational hearing impairment

Noise-induced hearing impairment is usually considered an occupational disease or illness, rather than an injury, because its progression is gradual. On rare occasions, an employee may sustain immediate, permanent hearing loss from a very loud event such

* Certain of the materials which follow have been adapted from Suter, AH, "Noise and the conservation of hearing", Chapter 2 in *Hearing Conservation Manual* (3rd ed.), Council for Accreditation in Occupational Hearing Conservation, Milwaukee, WI, USA (1993).

as an explosion or a very noisy process, such as riveting on steel. In these circumstances the hearing loss is sometimes referred to as an injury and is called "acoustic trauma". The usual circumstance, however, is a slow decrease in hearing ability over many years. The amount of impairment will depend on the level of the noise, the duration of the exposure and the susceptibility of the individual worker. Unfortunately, there is no medical treatment for occupational hearing impairment; there is only prevention.

The auditory effects of noise are well documented and there is little controversy over the amount of continuous noise that causes varying degrees of hearing loss (ISO 1990). That intermittent noise causes hearing loss is also uncontested. But periods of noise that are interrupted by periods of quiet can offer the inner ear an opportunity to recover from temporary hearing loss and may therefore be somewhat less hazardous than continuous noise. This is true mainly for outdoor occupations, but not for inside settings such as factories, where the necessary intervals of quiet are rare (Suter 1993).

Impulse noise, such as the noise from gunfire and metal stamping, also damages hearing. There is some evidence that the hazard from impulse noise is more severe than that from other types of noise (Dunn et al. 1991; Thiery and Meyer-Bisch 1988), but this is not always the case. The amount of damage will depend mainly on the level and duration of the impulse, and it may be worse when there is continuous noise in the background. There is also evidence that high-frequency sources of impulse noise are more damaging than those composed of lower frequencies (Hamernik, Ahroon and Hsueh 1991; Price 1983).

Hearing loss due to noise is often temporary at first. During the course of a noisy day, the ear becomes fatigued and the worker will experience a reduction in hearing known as *temporary threshold shift* (TTS). Between the end of one workshift and the beginning of the next the ear usually recovers from much of the TTS, but often, some of the loss remains. After days, months and years of exposure, the TTS leads to permanent effects and new amounts of TTS begin to build onto the now permanent losses. A good audiometric testing programme will attempt to identify these temporary hearing losses and provide for preventive measures before the losses become permanent.

Experimental evidence indicates that several industrial agents are toxic to the nervous system and produce hearing loss in laboratory animals, especially when they occur in combination with noise (Fechter 1989). These agents include (1) heavy metal hazards, such as lead compounds and trimethyltin, (2) organic solvents, such as toluene, xylene and carbon disulphide, and (3) an asphyxiant, carbon monoxide. Recent research on industrial workers (Morata 1989; Morata et al. 1991) suggests that certain of these substances (carbon disulphide and toluene) can increase the damaging potential of noise. There is also evidence that certain drugs which are already toxic to the ear can increase the damaging effects of noise (Boettcher et al. 1987). Examples include certain antibiotics and cancer chemotherapy drugs. Those in charge of hearing conservation programmes should be aware that workers exposed to these chemicals or using these drugs may be more susceptible to hearing loss, especially when exposed to noise in addition.

Non-occupational hearing impairment

It is important to understand that occupational noise is not the only cause of noise-induced hearing loss among workers, but hearing loss can also be caused by sources outside the workplace. These sources of noise produce what is sometimes called "sociocusis", and their effects on hearing are impossible to differentiate from occupational hearing loss. They can only be surmised by asking detailed questions about the worker's recreational and other noisy activities. Examples of sociocusic sources could be

woodworking tools, chain saws, unmuffled motorcycles, loud music and firearms. Frequent shooting with large-calibre guns (without hearing protection) may be a significant contributor to noise-induced hearing loss, whereas occasional hunting with smaller-calibre weapons is more likely to be harmless.

The importance of non-occupational noise exposure and the resulting sociocusis is that this hearing loss adds to the exposure that an individual might receive from occupational sources. For the sake of workers' overall hearing health, they should be counselled to wear adequate hearing protection when they engage in noisy recreational activities.

Tinnitus

Tinnitus is a condition that frequently accompanies both temporary and permanent hearing loss from noise, as well as other types of sensorineural hearing loss. Often referred to as a "ringing in the ears", tinnitus may range from mild in some cases to severe in others. Sometimes individuals report that they are more bothered by their tinnitus than they are by their hearing impairment.

People with tinnitus are likely to notice it the most in quiet conditions, such as when they are trying to go to sleep at night, or when they are sitting in a sound-proof booth taking an audiometric test. It is a sign that the sensory cells in the inner ear have been irritated. It is often a precursor to noise-induced hearing loss and therefore an important warning signal.

Communication interference and safety

The fact that noise can interfere with or "mask" speech communication and warning signals is only common sense. Many industrial processes can be carried out very well with a minimum of communication among workers. Other jobs, however, such as those performed by airline pilots, railroad engineers, tank commanders and many others rely heavily on speech communication. Some of these workers use electronic systems that suppress the noise and amplify the speech. Nowadays, sophisticated communication systems are available, some with devices that cancel unwanted acoustic signals so that communication can take place more easily.

In many cases, workers just have to make do, straining to understand communications above the noise and shouting above it or signalling. Sometimes people may develop hoarseness or even vocal nodules or other abnormalities on the vocal cords from excessive strain. These individuals may need to be referred to for medical care.

People have learned from experience that in noise levels above about 80 dBA they have to speak very loudly, and in levels above 85 dBA they have to shout. In levels much above 95 dBA they have to move close together to communicate at all. Acoustical specialists have developed methods to predict the amount of communication that can take place in industrial situations. The resulting predictions are dependent upon the acoustical characteristics of both the noise and the speech (or other desired signal), as well as the distance between talker and listener.

It is generally known that noise can interfere with safety, but only a few studies have documented this problem (e.g., Moll van Charante and Mulder 1990; Wilkins and Acton 1982). There have been numerous reports, however, of workers who have got clothing or hands caught in machines and have been seriously injured while their co-workers were oblivious to their cries for help. To prevent communication breakdowns in noisy environments, some employers have installed visual warning devices.

Another problem, recognized more by noise-exposed workers themselves than by professionals in hearing conservation and occupational health, is that hearing protection devices may sometimes interfere with the perception of speech and warning signals. This appears to be true mainly when the wearers already have hearing losses and the noise levels fall below 90 dBA (Suter 1992). In these cases, workers have a very legitimate concern about wearing hearing protection. It is important to be attentive to their concerns and either to implement engineering noise controls or to improve the kind of protection offered, such as protectors built into an electronic communication system. In addition, hearing protectors are now available with a flatter, more "high fidelity" frequency response, which may improve workers' abilities to understand speech and warning signals.

Effects on job performance

The effects of noise on job performance have been studied both in the laboratory and in actual working conditions. The results have shown that noise usually has little effect on the performance of repetitive, monotonous work, and in some cases can actually increase job performance when the noise is low or moderate in level. High levels of noise can degrade job performance, especially when the task is complicated or involves doing more than one thing at a time. Intermittent noise tends to be more disruptive than continuous noise, particularly when the periods of noise are unpredictable and uncontrollable. Some research indicates that people are less likely to help each other and more likely to exhibit antisocial behaviour in noisy environments than in quiet ones. (For a detailed review of the effects of noise on job performance see Suter 1992).

Annoyance

Although the term "annoyance" is more often connected with community noise problems, such as airports or race-car tracks, industrial workers may also feel annoyed or irritated by the noise of their workplace. This annoyance may be related to the interference of speech communication and job performance described above, but it may also be due to the fact that many people have an aversion to noise. Sometimes the aversion to noise is so strong that a worker will look for employment elsewhere, but that opportunity is not often feasible. After a period of adjustment, most will not appear to be bothered as much, but they may still complain about fatigue, irritability and sleeplessness. (The adjustment will be more successful if young workers are properly fitted with hearing protectors from the start, before they develop any hearing loss.) Interestingly, this kind of information sometimes surfaces *after* a company starts a noise control and hearing conservation programme because the workers would have become aware of the contrast between earlier and subsequently improved conditions.

Extra-auditory effects

As a biological stressor, noise can influence the entire physiological system. Noise acts in the same way that other stressors do, causing the body to respond in ways that may be harmful in the long run and lead to disorders known as the "stress diseases". When facing danger in primitive times, the body would go through a series of biological changes, preparing either to fight or to run away (the classic "fight or flight" response). There is evidence that these changes still persist with exposure to loud noise, even though a person may feel "adjusted" to the noise.

Most of these effects appear to be transitory, but with continued exposure some adverse effects have been shown to be chronic in laboratory animals. Several studies of industrial workers also point in this direction, while some studies show no significant effects (Rehm 1983; van Dijk 1990). The evidence is probably strongest for cardiovascular effects such as increased blood pressure, or changes in blood chemistry. A significant set of laboratory studies on animals showed chronic elevated blood pressure levels resulting from exposure to noise around 85 to 90 dBA, which did not return to baseline after cessation of the exposure (Peterson et al. 1978, 1981 and 1983).

Studies of blood chemistry show increased levels of the catecholamines epinephrine and norepinephrine due to noise exposure (Rehm 1983), and a series of experiments by German investigators found a connection between noise exposure and magnesium metabolism in humans and animals (Ising and Kruppa 1993). Current thinking holds that the extra-auditory effects of noise are most likely mediated psychologically, through aversion to noise, making it very difficult to obtain dose-response relationships. (For a comprehensive overview of this problem, see Ising and Kruppa 1993.)

Because the extra-auditory effects of noise are mediated by the auditory system, meaning that it is necessary to hear the noise for adverse effects to occur, properly fitted hearing protection should reduce the likelihood of these effects in just the way it does with hearing loss.

NOISE MEASUREMENT AND EXPOSURE EVALUATION

Eduard I. Denisov and German A. Suvorov

For the prevention of adverse effects of noise on workers, attention should be paid to the choice of appropriate instrumentation, measuring methods and procedures for evaluating workers' exposures. It is important to evaluate correctly the different types of noise exposures, such as continuous, intermittent and impulse noise, to distinguish noise environments with differing frequency spectra, as well as to consider the variety of working situations, such as drop-forge hammering shops, rooms housing air compressors, ultrasonic welding processes, and so forth. The main purposes of noise measurement in occupational settings are to (1) identify overexposed workers and quantify their exposures and (2) assess the need both for engineering noise control and the other types of control that are indicated. Other uses of noise measurement are to evaluate the effectiveness of particular noise controls and to determine the background levels in audiometric rooms.

Measuring Instruments

Instruments for noise measurement include sound level meters, noise dosimeters and auxiliary equipment. The basic instrument is the sound level meter, an electronic instrument consisting of a microphone, an amplifier, various filters, a squaring device, an exponential averager and a read-out calibrated in decibels (dB). Sound level meters are categorized by their precision, ranging from the most precise (type 0) to the least (type 3). Type 0 is usually used in the laboratory, type 1 is used for other the precision sound level measurements, type 2 is the general purpose meter, and type 3, the survey meter, is not recommended for industrial use. Figures 47.2 and 47.3, overleaf, illustrate a sound level meter.

Sound level meters also have built-in frequency weighting devices, which are filters that allow most frequencies to pass while discriminating against others. The most commonly used filter is the A-weighting network, which was developed to simulate the response curve of the human ear at moderate listening levels. Sound level meters also offer a choice of meter responses: the "slow" response, with a 1-sec time constant, the "fast" response with a 0.125-sec time constant, and the "impulse" response which has a 35 ms response for the increasing portion of the signal and a 1500 ms time constant for the signal's decay.

Specifications for sound level meters may be found in national and international standards, such as the International Organiza-

Figure 47.2 • Sound level meter—calibration check. Courtesy of Larson Davis.

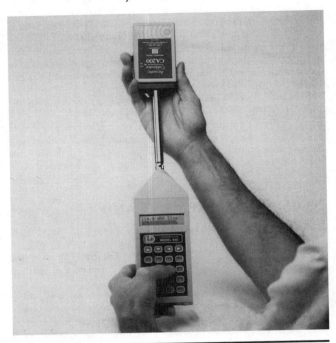

Figure 47.3 • Sound level meter with wind screen. Courtesy of Larson Davis.

tion for Standardization (ISO), the International Electrotechnical Commission (IEC) and the American National Standards Institute (ANSI). The IEC publications IEC 651 (1979) and IEC 804 (1985) pertain to sound level meters of types 0, 1, and 2, with frequency weightings A, B, and C, and "slow," "fast" and "impulse" time constants. ANSI S1.4-1983, as amended by ANSI S1.4A-1985, also provides specifications for sound level meters.

To facilitate more detailed acoustical analysis, full octave-band and 1/3 octave-band filter sets may be attached to or included in modern sound level meters. Nowadays, sound level meters are becoming increasingly small and easy to use, while at the same time their measurement possibilities are expanding.

For measuring non-steady noise exposures, such as those that occur in intermittent or impulse noise environments, an integrating sound level meter is most convenient to use. These meters can simultaneously measure the equivalent, peak and maximum sound levels, and calculate, log and store several values automatically. The noise dose meter or "dosimeter" is a form of integrating sound level meter that can be worn in the shirt pocket or attached to the worker's clothing. Data from the noise dosimeter may be computerized and printed out.

It is important to make sure that noise measuring instruments are always properly calibrated. This means checking the instrument's calibration acoustically before and after each day's use, as well as making electronic assessments at appropriate intervals.

Measurement Methods

The noise measurement methods to be used depend on the measurement objectives, namely, to assess the following:

- the risk of hearing impairment
- the need for and appropriate types of engineering controls
- the "noise load" for compatibility with the type of job to be performed
- the background level necessary for communication and safety.

International standard ISO 2204 gives three types of method for noise measurement: (1) the survey method, (2) the engineering method and (3) the precision method.

The survey method

This method requires the least amount of time and equipment. Noise levels of a working zone are measured with a sound level meter using a limited number of measuring points. Although there is no detailed analysis of the acoustic environment, time factors should be noted, such as whether the noise is constant or intermittent and how long the workers are exposed. The A-weighting network is usually used in the survey method, but when there is a predominant low-frequency component, the C-weighting network or the linear response may be appropriate.

The engineering method

With this method, A-weighted sound level measurements or those using other weighting networks are supplemented with measurements using full octave or 1/3 octave-band filters. The number of measuring points and the frequency ranges are selected according to the measurement objectives. Temporal factors should again be recorded. This method is useful for assessing interference with speech communication by calculating speech interference levels (SILs), as well as for engineering noise abatement programmes and for estimating the auditory and non-auditory effects of noise.

The precision method

This method is required for complex situations, where the most thorough description of the noise problem is needed. Overall measurements of sound level are supplemented with full octave or 1/3 octave-band measurements and time histories are recorded for appropriate time intervals according to the duration and fluctuations of the noise. For example, it may be necessary to measure peak sound levels of impulses using an instrument's "peak hold" setting, or to measure levels of infrasound or ultrasound, requiring special frequency measuring capabilities, microphone directivity, and so forth.

Those who use the precision method should make sure that the instrument's dynamic range is sufficiently great to prevent "overshoot" when measuring impulses and that the frequency response should be broad enough if infrasound or ultrasound is to be measured. The instrument should be capable of making measurements of frequencies as low as 2 Hz for infrasound and up to at least 16 kHz for ultrasound, with microphones that are sufficiently small.

The following "common sense" steps may be useful for the novice noise measurer:

1. Listen for the main characteristics of the noise to be measured (temporal qualities, such as steady-state, intermittent or impulse qualities; frequency characteristics, such as those of wide-band noise, predominant tones, infrasound, ultrasound, etc.). Note the most prominent characteristics.
2. Choose the most suitable instrumentation (type of sound level meter, noise dosimeter, filters, tape recorder, etc.).
3. Check the instrument's calibration and performance (batteries, calibration data, microphone corrections, etc.).
4. Make notes or a sketch (if using a system) of the instrumentation, including model and serial numbers.
5. Make a sketch of the noise environment to be measured, including major noise sources and the size and important characteristics of the room or outdoor setting.
6. Measure the noise and note down the level measured for each weighting network or for each frequency band. Also note the meter response (such as "slow," "fast," "impulse," etc.), and note the extent to which the meter fluctuates (e.g., plus or minus 2 dB).

If measurements are made outdoors, pertinent meteorological data, such as wind, temperature and humidity should be noted if they are considered important. A windscreen should always be used for outdoor measurements, and even for some indoor measurements. The manufacturer's instructions should always be followed to avoid the influence of factors such as wind, moisture, dust and electrical and magnetic fields, which may affect the readings.

Measuring procedures
There are two basic approaches to measuring noise in the workplace:

- The *exposure* of each worker, worker type or worker representative may be measured. The noise dosimeter is the preferable instrument for this purpose.
- Noise *levels* may be measured in various areas, creating a noise map for the determination of risk areas. In this case, a sound level meter would be used to take readings at regular points in a coordinate network

Worker Exposure Evaluation
To assess the risk of hearing loss from specific noise exposures, the reader should consult the international standard, ISO 1999 (1990). The standard contains an example of this risk assessment in its Annex D.

Noise exposures should be measured in the vicinity of the worker's ear and, in assessing the relative hazard of workers' exposures, subtractions should *not* be made for the attenuation provided by hearing protection devices. The reason for this caveat is that there is considerable evidence that the attenuation provided by hearing protectors as they are worn on the job is often less than half the attenuation estimated by the manufacturer. The reason for this is that the manufacturer's data are obtained under laboratory conditions and these devices are not usually fitted and worn so effectively in the field. At the moment, there is no international standard for estimating the attenuation of hearing protectors as they are worn in the field, but a good rule of thumb would be to divide the laboratory values in half.

In some circumstances, especially those involving difficult tasks or jobs requiring concentration, it may be important to minimize the stress or fatigue related to noise exposure by adopting noise control measures. This may be true even for moderate noise levels (below 85 dBA), when there is little risk of hearing impairment, but the noise is annoying or fatiguing. In such cases it may be useful to perform loudness assessments using ISO 532 (1975), *Method for Calculating Loudness Level.*

Interference with speech communication may be estimated according to ISO 2204 (1979) using the "articulation index", or more simply by measuring the sound levels in the octave bands centred at 500, 1,000 and 2,000 Hz, resulting in the "speech interference level".

Exposure criteria
The selection of noise exposure criteria depends on the goal to be attained, such as the prevention of hearing loss or the prevention of stress and fatigue. Maximum permissible exposures in terms of daily average noise levels vary among nations from 80, to 85, to 90 dBA, with trading parameters (exchange rates) of 3, 4, or 5 dBA. In some countries, such as Russia, permissible noise levels are set anywhere from 50 to 80 dBA, according to the type of job performed and taking into account the mental and physical work load. For example, the allowable levels for computer work or the performance of demanding clerical work are 50 to 60 dBA. (For more information on exposure criteria, see the article "Standards and regulations" in this chapter.)

ENGINEERING NOISE CONTROL

Dennis P. Driscoll

Ideally, the most effective means of noise control is to prevent the source of noise from entering into the plant environment in the first place—by establishing an effective "Buy Quiet" programme to furnish the workplace with equipment engineered for low noise output. To carry out such a programme, a clear, well-written statement of specifications for limiting noise characteristics of new plant equipment, facilities and processes must be designed to take the hazard of noise into account. A good programme builds in monitoring and maintenance as well.

Once equipment is installed and excess noise identified through sound level measurements, the problem of controlling noise becomes more complicated. However, there are engineering controls available which can be retrofitted to existing equipment. In addition, there is usually more than one noise control option for each problem. Therefore, it becomes important for the individual managing the noise control programme to determine the most feasible and economical means available for noise reduction in each given situation.

Controlling Noise in Factory and Product Design
The use of written specifications to define the requirements for equipment, its installation, and acceptance are standard practice in today's environment. One of the foremost opportunities in the area of noise control available to the factory designer is to influence the selection, purchase and layout of new equipment. When properly written and administered, implementation of a "Buy

Quiet" programme through purchase specifications can prove to be an effective means of controlling noise.

The most proactive approach towards controlling noise in the facility design and equipment procurement stage exists in Europe. In 1985, the twelve member states of the European Community (EC)—now the European Union (EU)— adopted "New Approach" Directives designed to address a broad class of equipment or machinery, rather than individual standards for each type of equipment. By the end of 1994 there had been three "New Approach" Directives issued that contain requirements on noise. These Directives are:

1. Directive 89/392/EEC, with two amendments 91/368/EEC and 93/44/EEC
2. Directive 89/106/EEC
3. Directive 89/686/EEC, with one amendment 93/95/EEC.

The first item listed above (89/392/EEC) is commonly called the Machinery Directive. This Directive compels equipment manufacturers to include noise control as an essential part of machine safety. The basic aim of these measures is that for machinery or equipment to be sold within the EU, it must satisfy the essential requirements regarding noise. As a result, there has been a major emphasis on the design of low-noise equipment since the late 1980s by manufacturers interested in marketing within the EU.

For companies outside the EU attempting to implement a voluntary "Buy Quiet" programme, the degree of success achieved is largely dependent upon the timing and commitment of the entire management hierarchy. The first step in the programme is to establish acceptable noise criteria for construction of a new plant, expansion of an existing facility and purchase of new equipment. For the programme to be effective, the specified noise limits must be viewed by both the purchaser and vendor as an absolute requirement. When a product does not meet other equipment design parameters, such as size, flow rate, pressure, allowable temperature rise, and so forth, it is deemed unacceptable by company management. This is the same commitment that must be followed regarding noise levels in order to achieve a successful "Buy Quiet" programme.

As regards the timing aspect mentioned above, the earlier in the design process that consideration is given to the noise aspects of a project or equipment purchase, the greater the probability of success. In many situations, the factory designer or equipment buyer will have a choice of equipment types. Knowledge of the noise characteristics of the various alternatives will allow him or her to specify the quieter ones.

Besides selection of the equipment, early involvement in the design of the equipment layout within the plant is essential. Relocating equipment on paper during the design phase of a project is clearly much easier than physically moving the equipment later, especially once the equipment is in operation. A simple rule to follow is to keep machines, processes and work areas of approximately equal noise level together; and separate particularly noisy and particularly quiet areas by buffer zones having intermediate noise levels.

Validation of noise criteria as an absolute requirement requires a cooperative effort between company personnel from departments such as engineering, legal, purchasing, industrial hygiene and environment. For example, the industrial hygiene, safety, and/or personnel departments may determine the desired noise levels for equipment, as well as conduct sound surveys to qualify equipment. Next, company engineers may write the purchase specification, as well as select quiet types of equipment. The purchasing agent will most likely administer the contract and rely upon the law department representatives for assistance with enforcement. Involvement from all these parties should begin with the inception of the project and continue through funding requests, planning, design, bidding, installation and commissioning.

Even the most thorough and concise specification document is of little value unless the onus of compliance is placed on the supplier or manufacturer. Clear contract language must be used to define the means of determining compliance. Company procedures designed to enact guarantees should be consulted and followed. It may be desirable to include penalty clauses for non-compliance. Foremost in one's enforcement strategy is the purchaser's commitment to seeing that the requirements are met. Compromise on the noise criteria in exchange for cost, delivery date, performance, or other concessions should be the exception and not the rule.

Within the United States, ANSI has published the standard ANSI S12.16: *Guidelines for the Specification of Noise of New Machinery* (1992). This standard is a useful guide for writing an internal company noise specification. In addition, this standard provides direction for obtaining sound level data from equipment manufacturers. Once obtained from the manufacturer, the data may then be used by plant designers in planning equipment layouts. Because of the various types of distinctive equipment and tools for which this standard has been prepared, there is no single survey protocol appropriate for the measurement of sound level data. As a result, this standard contains reference information on the appropriate sound measurement procedure for testing a variety of stationary equipment. These survey procedures were prepared by the appropriate trade or professional organization in the United States responsible for a particular type or class of equipment.

Retrofitting Existing Equipment

Before one can decide what needs to be done, it becomes necessary to identify the root cause of noise. Towards this end, it is useful to have an understanding as to how noise is generated. Noise is created for the most part by mechanical impacts, high-velocity air flow, high-velocity fluid flow, vibrating surface areas of a machine, and quite often by the product being manufactured. As regards the lattermost item, it is often the case in manufacturing and process industries such as metal fabrication, glass manufacturing, food processing, mining, and so forth, that the interaction between the product and machines imparts the energy that creates the noise.

Source identification

One of the most challenging aspects of noise control is identification of the actual source. In a typical industrial setting there are usually multiple machines operating simultaneously, which makes it difficult to identify the root cause of noise. This is especially true when a standard sound level meter (SLM) is used to evaluate the acoustical environment. The SLM typically provides a sound pressure level (SPL) at a specific location, which is most likely the result of more than one noise source. Therefore, it becomes incumbent upon the surveyor to employ a systematic approach that will help separate out the individual sources and their relative contribution to the overall SPL. The following survey techniques may be used to help with identifying the origin or source of noise:

- Measure the frequency spectrum and graph the data.
- Measure the sound level, in dBA, as a function of time.
- Compare frequency data from similar equipment or production lines.
- Isolate components with temporary controls, or by turning on and off individual items whenever possible.

One of the most effective methods for locating the source of the noise is to measure its frequency spectrum. Once the data are measured, it is very useful to graph the results so that one can visually observe the characteristics of the source. For most noise

Figure 47.4 • Comparison between 1/1 and 1/3 octave-band data.

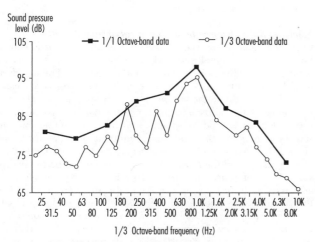

All 1/1 octave-band data are plotted at the centre-band frequency.

Figure 47.5 • Comparison of crossover pipe versus background level.

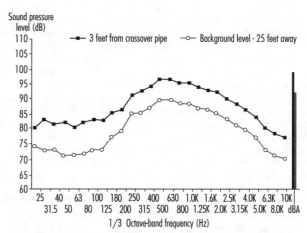

For presentation purposes the overall A-weighted sound level for each measure is depicted on the same figure as the 1/3 octave-band data in the form of separate bars on the right side.

abatement problems, the measurements can be accomplished with either full (1/1) or one-third (1/3) octave-band filters used with the SLM. The advantage of 1/3 octave-band measurement is that it provides more detailed information about what is emanating from a piece of equipment. Figure 47.4 exhibits a comparison between 1/1 and 1/3 octave-band measurements conducted near a nine-piston pump. As depicted in this figure, the 1/3 octave-band data clearly identifies the pumping frequency and many of its harmonics. If one used only 1/1, or full octave-band data, as depicted by the solid line and plotted at each centre-band frequency in figure 47.4, it becomes more difficult to diagnose what is occurring within the pump. With 1/1 octave-band data there are a total of nine data points between 25 Hertz (Hz) and 10,000 Hz, as shown in this figure. However, there are a total of 27 data points in this frequency range with the use of 1/3 octave-band measurements. Clearly, 1/3 octave-band data will provide more useful data towards identifying the root cause of a noise. This information is critical if the objective is to control noise at the source. If the only interest is to treat the path along which sound waves are transmitted, then 1/1 octave-band data will be sufficient for purposes of selecting acoustically appropriate products or materials.

Figure 47.5 shows a comparison between the 1/3 octave-band spectrum measured 3 feet from the crossover pipe of a liquid chiller compressor and the background level measured approximately 25 feet away (please note the approximations given in the footnote). This position represents the general area where employees typically walk through this room. For the most part the compressor room is not routinely occupied by workers. The only exception exists when maintenance workers are repairing or overhauling other equipment in the room. Besides the compressor, there are several other large machines operating in this area. To assist with the identification of the primary noise sources, several frequency spectrums were measured near each of the equipment items. When each spectrum was compared to the data at the background position in the walkway, only the crossover pipe of the compressor unit exhibited a similar spectrum shape. Consequently, it may be concluded this is the primary noise source controlling the level measured at the employee walkway. So as depicted in figure 47.5, through the use of frequency data measured near the equipment and graphically comparing individ-

ual sources to the data recorded at employee workstations or other areas of interest, it is often possible to identify the dominant sources of noises clearly.

When the sound level fluctuates, as with cyclic equipment, it is useful to measure the overall A-weighted sound level versus time. With this procedure it is important to observe and document what events are occurring over time. Figure 47.6 exhibits the sound level measured at the operator's workstation over one full machine cycle. The process depicted in figure 47.6 represents that of a product wrapping machine, which has a cycle time of approximately 95 seconds. As shown in the figure, the maximum noise level of 96.2 dBA occurs during the release of compressed air, 33 seconds into the machine cycle. The other important events are also labelled in the figure, which permits the identification of the source and relative contribution of each activity during the full wrapping cycle.

In industrial settings where there are multiple process lines with the same equipment, it is a worthwhile effort to compare the frequency data for similar equipment to one another.

Figure 47.6 • Workstation for packaging operator.

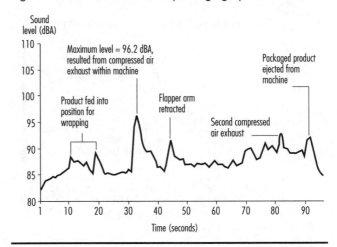

Figure 47.7 depicts this comparison for two similar process lines, both of which manufacture the same product and operate at the same speed. Part of the process involves the use of a pneumatically actuated device that punches a one-half inch hole in the product as a final phase in its production. Inspection of this figure clearly reveals that line #1 has an overall sound level 5 dBA higher than line #2. In addition, the spectrum depicted for line #1 contains a fundamental frequency and many harmonics that do not appear in the spectrum for line #2. Consequently, it is necessary to investigate the cause of these differences. Often significant differences will be an indication of the need for maintenance, such as was the situation for the final punch mechanism of line #2. However, this particular noise problem will require additional control measures since the overall level on line #1 is still relatively high. But the point of this survey technique is to identify the different noise problems that may exist between similar items of equipment and processes that may be easily remedied with effective maintenance or other adjustments.

As mentioned above, an SLM typically provides an SPL that comprises acoustical energy from one or more noise sources. Under optimum measurement conditions, it would be best to measure each item of equipment with all other equipment turned off. Although this situation is ideal, it is rarely practical to shut down the plant to allow isolation of a particular source. In order to circumvent this limitation, it is often effective to use temporary control measures with certain noise sources that will provide some short-term noise reduction so as to allow measurement of another source. Some materials available that can provide a temporary reduction include plywood enclosures, acoustical blankets, silencers and barriers. Often, permanent application of these materials will create long-term problems such as heat build-up, interference with the operator's access or product flow, or costly pressure drops associated with improperly selected silencers. However, for assisting with the isolation of individual components, these materials can be effective as a short-term control.

Another method available for isolating a particular machine or component is to turn different equipment on and off, or sections of a production line. To effectively conduct this type of diagnostic analysis the process must be capable of functioning with the selected item turned off. Next, for this procedure to be legitimate it is critical that the manufacturing process not be affected in any manner. If the process is affected, then it is entirely possible that

the measurement will not be representative of the noise level under normal conditions. Finally, all valid data may then be ranked by magnitude of the overall dBA value to help prioritize equipment for engineering noise control.

Selecting the appropriate noise control options

Once the cause or source of noise is identified and it is known how it radiates to employee work areas, the next step is to decide what the available noise control options may be. The standard model used with respect to the control of almost any health hazard is to examine the various control options as they apply to the source, path and receiver. In some situations, control of one of these elements will be sufficient. However, under other circumstances it may be the case that treatment of more than one element is required to obtain an acceptable noise environment.

The first step in the noise control process should be to attempt some form of source treatment. In effect, source modification addresses the root cause of a noise problem, whereas control of the sound transmission path with barriers and enclosures only treats the symptoms of noise. In those situations where there are multiple sources within a machine and the objective is to treat the source, it will be necessary to address all noise-generating mechanisms on a component-by-component basis.

For excessive noise generated by mechanical impacts, the control options to investigate may include methods to reduce the driving force, reduce the distance between components, balance rotating equipment and install vibration isolation fittings. As regards noise arising from high-velocity air flow or fluid flow, the primary modification is to reduce the velocity of the medium, assuming this is a feasible option. Sometimes the velocity can be reduced by increasing the cross sectional area of the pipeline in question. Obstructions in the pipeline must be eliminated to allow for a streamlined flow, which in turn will reduce pressure variations and turbulence in the medium being transported. Finally, installation of a properly sized silencer or muffler can provide a significant reduction in the overall noise. The silencer manufacturer should be consulted for assistance with selection of the proper device, based on the operating parameters and constraints set forth by the purchaser.

When vibrating surface areas of a machine act as a sounding board for airborne noise, the control options include a reduction in the driving force associated with the noise, creation of smaller sections out of larger surface areas, perforation of the surface, increasing the substrate stiffness or mass, and application of damping material or vibration isolation fittings. As regards the use of vibration isolation and damping materials, the product manufacturer should be consulted for assistance with the selection of the appropriate materials and installation procedures. Finally, in many industries the actual product being manufactured will often be an efficient radiator of airborne sound. In these situations it is important to evaluate ways to tightly secure or better support the product during fabrication. Another noise control measure to investigate would be to reduce the impact force between the machine and product, between parts of the product itself, or between separate product items.

Often process or equipment redesign and source modification may prove to be infeasible. In addition, there may be situations when it is virtually impossible to identify the root cause of the noise. When any of these situations exist, the use of control measures for treatment of the sound transmission path would be an effective means for reducing the overall noise level. The two primary abatement measures for path treatments are acoustical enclosures and barriers.

The development of acoustical enclosures is well advanced in today's marketplace. Both off-the-shelf and custom-made enclosures are available from several manufacturers. In order to pro-

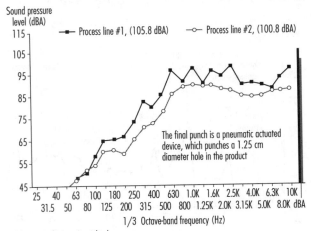

Figure 47.7 • Final punch operation for identical process lines.

All frequency data are A-weighted.

cure the appropriate system it is necessary for the buyer to provide information as to the current overall noise level (and possibly frequency data), the dimensions of the equipment, the noise reduction goal, the need for product flow and employee access, and any other operating constraints. The vendor will then be able to use this information to select a stock item or fabricate a custom enclosure to satisfy the needs of the buyer.

In many situations it may be more economical to design and build an enclosure instead of purchasing a commercial system. In designing enclosures, many factors must be taken into consideration if the enclosure is to prove satisfactory from both an acoustical and a production point of view. Specific guidelines for enclosure design are as follows:

Enclosure dimensions. There is no critical guideline for the size or dimensions of an enclosure. The best rule to follow is *the bigger the better*. It is critical that sufficient clearance be provided to permit the equipment to perform all intended movement without contacting the enclosure.

Enclosure wall. The noise reduction provided by an enclosure is dependent upon the materials used in the construction of the walls and how tightly the enclosure is sealed. Selection of the appropriate materials for the enclosure wall should be determined using the following rules of thumb (Moreland 1979):

- for an enclosure, with no internal absorption:

$$TL_{reqd} = NR + 20 \text{ dBA}$$

- with approximately 50% internal absorption:

$$TL_{reqd} = NR + 15 \text{ dBA}$$

- with 100% internal absorption:

$$TL_{reqd} = NR + 10 \text{ dBA}.$$

In these expressions TL_{reqd} is the transmission loss required of the enclosure wall or panel, and NR is the noise reduction desired to meet the abatement goal.

Seals. For maximum efficiency, all enclosure wall joints must be tight fitting. Openings around pipe penetrations, electrical wiring and so on, should be sealed with non-hardening mastic such as silicon caulk.

Internal absorption. To absorb and dissipate acoustical energy the internal surface area of the enclosure should be lined with acoustically absorptive material. The frequency spectrum of the source should be used to select the appropriate material. The manufacturer's published absorption data provides the basis for matching the material to the source of noise. It is important to match the maximum absorption factors to those frequencies of the source that have the highest sound pressure levels. The product vendor or manufacturer can also assist with selection of the most effective material based on the frequency spectrum of the source.

Enclosure isolation. It is important that the enclosure structure be separated or isolated from the equipment in order to ensure that mechanical vibration is not transmitted to the enclosure itself. When parts of the machine, such as pipe penetrations, do come in contact with the enclosure, it is important to include vibration isolation fittings at the point of contact to short-circuit any potential transmission path. Finally, if the machine causes the floor to vibrate then the base of the enclosure should also be treated with vibration isolation material.

Providing for product flow. As with most production equipment, there will be a need to move product into and out of the enclosure. The use of acoustically lined channels or tunnels can permit product flow and yet provide acoustical absorption. To minimize the leakage of noise, it is recommended that all passageways be three times longer than the inside width of the largest dimension of the tunnel or channel opening.

Providing for worker access. Doors and windows may be installed to provide physical and visual access to the equipment. It is critical that all windows have at least the same transmission loss properties as the enclosure walls. Next, all access doors must tightly seal around all edges. To prevent operation of the equipment with the doors open, it is recommended that an interlocking system be included that permits operation only when the doors are fully closed.

Ventilation of enclosure. In many enclosure applications, there will be excessive heat build-up. To pass cooling air through the enclosure, a blower with a capacity of 650 to 750 cubic feet/metre should be installed on the outlet or discharge duct. Finally, the intake and discharge ducts should be lined with absorptive material.

Protection of absorptive material. To prevent the absorptive material from becoming contaminated, a splash barrier should be applied over the absorptive lining,. This should be of a very light material, such as one-mil plastic film. The absorptive layer should be retained with expanded metal, perforated sheet metal or hardware cloth. The facing material should have at least 25% open area.

An alternative sound transmission path treatment is to use an acoustic barrier to block or shield the receiver (the worker at risk of the noise hazard) from the direct sound path. An acoustic barrier is a high transmission loss material, such as a solid partition or wall, inserted between the noise source and the receiver. By blocking the direct line-of-sight path to the source, the barrier causes the sound waves to reach the receiver by reflection off various surfaces in the room and by diffraction at the edges of the barrier. As a result, the overall noise level is reduced at the receiver's location.

The effectiveness of a barrier is a function of its location relative to the noise source or receivers and of its overall dimensions. To maximize the potential noise reduction, the barrier should be located as closely as practical to either the source or receiver. Next, the barrier should be as tall and wide as possible. To block the sound path effectively, a high-density material, on the order of 4 to 6 lb/ft^3, should be used. Finally, the barrier should not contain any openings or gaps, which can significantly reduce its effectiveness. If it is necessary to include a window for visual access to the equipment, then it is important that the window have a sound transmission rating at least equivalent to that of the barrier material itself.

The final option for reducing worker noise exposure is to treat the space or area where the employee works. This option is most practical for those job activities, such as product inspection or equipment monitoring stations, where employee movement is confined to a relatively small area. In these situations, an acoustical booth or shelter may be installed to isolate the employees and provide relief from excessive noise levels. Daily noise exposures will be reduced as long as a significant portion of the workshift is spent inside the shelter. To construct such a shelter, the previously described guidelines for enclosure design should be consulted.

In conclusion, implementation of an effective "Buy Quiet" programme should be the initial step in a total noise control process. This approach is designed to prevent the purchase or installation of any equipment that might present a noise problem. However, for those situations where excessive noise levels already exist, it is then necessary to evaluate the noise environment systematically in order to develop the most practical engineering control option for each individual noise source. In determining the relative priority and urgency of implementing noise control measures, employee exposures, occupancy of the space, and overall area noise levels should be considered. Obviously, an important aspect of the desired result is to obtain the maximum employee noise exposure reduction for the monetary funds invested and that the greatest degree of employee protection is secured at the same time.

47. NOISE

HEARING CONSERVATION PROGRAMMES

Larry H. Royster and
Julia Doswell Royster*

The primary objective of occupational hearing conservation programmes (HCPs) is to prevent on-the-job noise-induced hearing loss due to hazardous workplace noise exposures (Royster and Royster 1989 and 1990). However, the person—who shall later be characterized as the "key individual"—who is responsible for making the HCP effective should use common sense to modify these practices to fit the local situation in order to achieve the desired goal: protection of workers from harmful occupational noise exposures. A secondary objective of these programmes should be to so educate and motivate individuals that they also elect to protect themselves from harmful non-occupational noise exposures and translate their knowledge about hearing conservation to their families and friends.

Figure 47.8 shows the distributions of over 10,000 noise exposure samples from four sources in two countries, including a variety of industrial, mining and military work environments. The samples are 8-hour time-weighted-average values based on exchange rates of 3, 4 and 5 dB. These data indicate that about 90% of daily equivalent noise exposures are 95 dBA or below, and only 10% exceed 95 dBA.

The importance of the data in figure 47.8, assuming that they apply to most countries and populations, is simply that a vast majority of noise-exposed employees need to achieve only 10 dBA of protection from noise to eliminate the hazard. When hearing protection devices (HPDs) are worn to achieve this protection, those responsible for worker health must take the time to fit each individual with a device that is comfortable, practical for the environment, takes into account the individual's auditory needs (ability to hear warning signals, speech, etc.), and provides an acoustic seal when worn day in and day out in real-world environments.

This article presents a condensed set of good hearing conservation practices, as summarized in the checklist presented in figure 47.9.

Benefits of Hearing Conservation

Prevention of occupational hearing loss benefits the employee by preserving hearing abilities which are critical to good quality of life: interpersonal communication, enjoyment of music, detection of warning sounds, and many more. The HCP provides a health screening benefit, since non-occupational hearing losses and potentially treatable ear diseases are often detected through annual audiograms. Lowering noise exposure also reduces potential stress and fatigue related to noise.

The employer benefits directly by implementing an effective HCP which maintains employees' good hearing, since workers will remain more productive and more versatile if their communication abilities are not impaired. Effective HCPs can reduce accident rates and promote work efficiency.

Phases of an HCP

Refer to the checklist in the figure 47.9 for details of each phase. Different personnel may be responsible for different phases, and these personnel comprise the HCP team.

* The authors thank the North Carolina Department of Labor for permission to re-use materials developed during the writing of an NCDOL industry guide on hearing conservation.

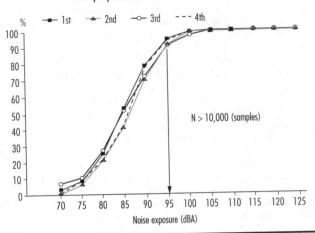

Figure 47.8 • Estimated noise exposure hazard for different populations.

Sound exposure surveys

Sound level meters or personal noise dosimeters are used to measure workplace sound levels and estimate workers' noise exposures to determine if an HCP is needed; if so, the data so gathered will help establish appropriate HCP policies to protect employees (Royster, Berger and Royster 1986). Survey results identify which employees (by department or job) will be included in the HCP, which areas should be posted for required hearing protector use, and which hearing protection devices are adequate. Adequate samples of representative production conditions are needed to classify exposures into ranges (below 85 dBA, 85-89, 90-94, 95-99 dBA, etc.). The measurement of A-weighted sound levels during the general noise survey often identifies dominant noise sources in areas of the plant where follow-up engineering noise control studies may significantly reduce employee exposures.

Engineering and administrative noise controls

Noise controls may reduce employees' noise exposures to a safe level, eliminating the need for a hearing conservation programme. Engineering controls (see "Engineering noise control" in this chapter) involve modifications of the noise source (such as fitting mufflers to air exhaust nozzles), the noise path (such as placing sound-blocking enclosures around equipment) or the receiver (such as constructing an enclosure around the employee's workstation). Worker input is often needed in designing such modifications to ensure that they are practical and will not interfere with his or her tasks. Obviously, hazardous employee noise exposures should be reduced or eliminated by means of engineering noise controls whenever practical and feasible.

Administrative noise controls include replacement of old equipment with quieter new models, adherence to equipment maintenance programmes related to noise control, and changes in employee work schedules to reduce noise doses by limiting exposure time when practical and technically advisable. Planning and designing to achieve non-hazardous noise levels when new production facilities are brought on-line is an administrative control which can also eliminate the need for an HCP.

Education and motivation

HCP team members and employees will not actively participate in hearing conservation unless they understand its purpose, how they will benefit directly from the programme, and that compliance with the company's safety and health requirements is a

Figure 47.9 • Checklist of good HCP practices.

SOUND EXPOSURE SURVEYS

- Representative individual daily noise exposures have been established for all noise-exposed job classifications.
- A noise map of the plant has been posted to show
  1. areas where employees are included in the HCP
  2. areas where HPD utilization is required
- Employees have been told the typical daily noise exposures for their departments.
- HCP team members and department supervisors have summaries of sound survey results.
- Employees' daily noise exposures are listed on their individual audiometric records.

ENGINEERING AND ADMINISTRATIVE NOISE CONTROLS

- An engineering noise control survey has been completed for all areas where individuals have to wear hearing protection devices.
- Dominant production room noise sources have been identified.
- Contributing equipment noise sources within each dominant noise source have been identified.
- Equipment noise purchase specifications exist and are utilized when purchasing new equipment that may contribute to or significantly increase exposures.
- A noise control maintenance programme exists and its continuing implementation is standard practice.
- The HCP education phase includes information with respect to the noise control programme and activities and feedback from the affected individuals is given proper attention.
- New facility planning includes noise control options. Past solutions to noise control problems are documented and discussed during educational programmes.

EDUCATION AND MOTIVATION

- Team members receive education about hearing loss and hearing conservation to enable them to understand the goals and policies of the HCP.
- HCP team members receive training in how to carry out their duties (especially concerning hearing protection fitting and utilization).
- Employees annually attend updated educational programmes which focus on why and how to protect their own hearing on and off the job.
- HCP personnel keep the programme in employees' minds through informal reminders at least quarterly.
- Management backs up the HCP by personal example (wearing hearing protection), policy enforcement and participation in educational programmes.
- Staff are evaluated on their HCP participation during the company's annual personnel

HEARING PROTECTION

- HPD utilization in required areas is strictly and consistently enforced.
- Comfort, practicality, and the achievable level of real-world attenuation are the primary criteria for selecting which hearing protection device will be stocked.
- Each employee is individually fitted with HPDs and trained in their proper use and care.
- Fit is checked for all types of protectors, including earmuffs and single-size earplugs.
- A minimum of two earplugs (one in multiple sizes) and one earmuff are available for selection. It is preferred that three plugs, two earmuffs (one semi-aural) be provided.
- Protectors are replaced on a regular basis.
- Hearing protector reissuers distribute only the type and size of protection that was initially fitted to each employee; to change types or sizes the employee must return to the fitter.
- Each employee's hearing protector is rechecked during the audiometric evaluation for condition, fit, and correct placement.
- Employees are given hearing protection to take home for use during off-the-job noise exposures.

AUDIOMETRIC EVALUATIONS

- Audiometers are in good operating condition.
- Audiometer calibration is not adjusted unless it is out of tolerances, and both pre-adjustment and post-adjustment readings are permanently recorded.
- Audiometric technicians use consistent testing methods under professional supervision.
- Audiometric testing booth in use.
- Technicians instruct employees to listen carefully and respond to the faintest tones they can detect.
- Employees' auditory history information is updated annually and provided to the audiogram reviewer.
- Employees receive immediate feedback from the audiometric technician about audiogram results as related to proper HPD use.
- Employees receive written feedback from the audiogram reviewer about
  1. hearing status compared to normal for age
  2. any hearing change over time
  3. recommendations for better protection on and off the job, or for medical examination or treatment if appropriate
- The audiogram reviewer looks for significant shifts at any audiometric test frequency, not just shift criteria specified in regulations.
- Audiogram reviewers revise employees' reference baseline thresholds for threshold improvement as well as for persistent worsening.
- HCP personnel follow through with counselling and hearing protection retraining for employees exhibiting a significant change in hearing.

PROGRAMME EVALUATION

- There is a key individual overseeing all five phases of the HCP.
- HCP team members check that all tasks are accomplished and documented.
- HPDs are potentially effective in actual use.
- HPD utilization is enforced.
- Active communication is maintained among HCP team members and with all personnel up and down the organization's hierarchy.
- Management holds themselves as well as company personnel responsible for their HCP performance.
- Audiometric database analysis is used to evaluate the HCP's overall effectiveness in preventing on-the-job noise-induced hearing loss.

RECORD KEEPING

- A single source, such as the key individual, is assigned to maintain/oversee all records related to HCP activities.
- Past and present sound survey reports are in order and available for review by all parties involved in the HCP (including employees).
- The representative daily noise exposure is listed on audiograms or is available to the individuals who perform and review audiograms as well as to the fitter and reissuer of hearing protection.
- The contents of educational programmes are documented and attendance records are maintained.
- A summary record of noise control activities is maintained and its educational value utilized during educational and motivational programmes.
- Hearing protection fitting and reissuing procedures are documented.
- All audiometric evaluation related records such as audiometer calibration, testing environment background noise levels, technician training certification and re-training and general procedural guidelines are maintained and available for review.

condition of employment. Without meaningful education to motivate individual actions, the HCP will fail (Royster and Royster 1986). Topics to be covered should include the following: the purpose and benefits of the HCP, sound survey methods and results, using and maintaining engineering noise control treatments to reduce exposures, hazardous off-the-job noise exposures, how noise damages hearing, consequences of hearing loss in daily life, selection and fitting of hearing protection devices and importance of consistent wear, how audiometric testing identifies hearing changes to indicate the need for greater protection and the employer's HCP policies. Ideally, these topics can be explained to small groups of employees in safety meetings, given ample time for questions. In effective HCPs the educational phase is a continuous process—not just an annual presentation—as HCP personnel take daily opportunities to remind others about conserving their hearing.

Hearing protection

The employer provides hearing protection devices (earplugs, earmuffs, and semi-insert devices) for employees to wear as long as hazardous noise levels exist in the workplace. Because feasible engineering noise controls have not been developed for many types of industrial equipment, hearing protectors are the best current option for preventing noise-induced hearing loss in these situations. As indicated earlier, most noise-exposed workers need to achieve only 10 dB of attenuation to be adequately protected from noise. With the large selection of hearing protectors available today, adequate protection can be readily achieved (Royster 1985; Royster and Royster 1986) if devices are individually fitted to each employee to achieve an acoustic seal with acceptable comfort, and if the worker is taught how to wear the device correctly to maintain an acoustic seal, but consistently whenever a noise hazard exists.

Audiometric evaluations

Each exposed individual should receive a baseline hearing check followed by annual rechecks to monitor hearing status and detect any hearing change. An audiometer is used in a sound-attenuating booth to test the employee's hearing thresholds at 0.5, 1, 2, 3, 4, 6 and 8 kHz. If the HCP is effective, employees' audiometric results will not show significant changes associated with on-the-job noise-induced hearing damage. If suspicious hearing changes are found, the audiometric technician and the audiologist or physician who reviews the record can counsel the employee to wear HPDs more carefully, assess whether better-fitting HPDs are needed and motivate the individual to be more careful in protecting his or her hearing both on and off the job. Sometimes non-occupational causes of hearing change may be identified, such as gunfire or hobby noise exposure, or medical ear problems. Audiometric monitoring is useful only if quality control of testing procedures is maintained and if the results are used to trigger follow-up for individuals with significant hearing changes (Royster 1985).

Record Keeping

Requirements for the type of records to be kept and the duration for maintaining them vary among countries. In countries where litigation concerns and worker's compensation are important issues, records should be maintained longer than required by occupational regulations since they are often useful for legal purposes. The goal of record keeping is to document how employees have been protected from noise (Royster and Royster 1989 and 1990). Especially important records include the sound survey procedures and findings, audiometric calibration and results, follow-up actions in response to employees' hearing changes and documentation of hearing protector fitting and training. Records should

include the names of the personnel who carried out the HCP tasks as well as the results.

Programme Evaluation

Characteristics of effective programmes

Successful HCPs share the following characteristics and promote a "safety culture" with respect to all safety programmes (safety eyeglasses, "hard hats", safe lifting behaviour, etc.).

The "key individual"

The most important strategy for making the five phases of the HCP function together effectively is to unite them under the supervision of one individual of central importance (Royster and Royster 1989 and 1990). In smaller companies where one person may actually carry out all facets of the HCP, lack of coordination is not usually a problem. However, as the size of the organization increases, different types of staff become involved in the HCP: safety personnel, medical personnel, engineers, industrial hygienists, tool crib supervisors, production supervisors and others. With personnel from varying disciplines carrying out different aspects of the programme, it becomes very difficult to coordinate their efforts unless one "key individual" is able to oversee the entire HCP. The choice of who this person should be is critical to the success of the programme. One of the primary qualifications for the key individual is genuine interest in the company's HCP.

The key individual is always approachable and is sincerely interested in comments or complaints that can help to improve the HCP. This individual does not take a remote attitude or stay in an office, running the HCP on paper by mandate, but spends time on the production floors or wherever workers are active in order to interact with them and observe how problems can be prevented or solved.

Active communications and roles

The primary HCP team members should meet together regularly to discuss the progress of the programme and ensure that all duties are being carried out. Once people with different tasks understand how their own roles contribute to the overall outcome of the programme, they will cooperate better to prevent hearing loss. The key individual can achieve this active communication and cooperation if management provides him or her with the authority to make HCP decisions and the resource allocations to act on decisions once they are made. The success of the HCP depends on everyone from the top boss to the most recently hired trainee; everyone has an important role. Management's role is largely to support the HCP and enforce its policies as one facet of the company's overall health and safety programme. For middle managers and supervisors the role is more direct: they help carry out the five phases. The role of employees is to participate actively in the programme and be aggressive in making suggestions to improve HCP operation. However, for employee participation to succeed, management and the HCP team must be receptive to comments and actually respond to employee input.

Hearing protectors—effective and enforced

The importance of hearing protection policies to HCP success is underscored by two desired characteristics of effective HCPs: strict enforcement of hearing protector utilization (there must be actual enforcement, not just a paper policy) and the availability of protectors which are potentially effective for use by the wearers in the work environment. Potentially effective devices are practical and comfortable enough for employees to wear consistently, and they provide adequate sound attenuation without impairing communication through overprotection.

Limited external influences on the HCP

If local HCP decisions are limited by policies mandated by corporate headquarters, the key individual may need top management's assistance in obtaining exceptions to the corporate or external rules in order to meet local needs. The key individual also must keep strict control over any services provided by outside consultants, contractors or government officials (such as sound surveys or audiograms). When contractors are used, it is more difficult to integrate their services cohesively into the overall HCP, but it is critical to do so. If in-plant personnel do not follow through by using the information provided by the contractors, then the contracted elements of the programme lose effectiveness. Experience clearly indicates that it is very difficult to establish and maintain an effective HCP which depends predominantly on external contractors.

In contrast to the previous characteristics, the following is a listing of some common causes of HCP ineffectiveness.

- inadequate communication and coordination among HCP personnel
- insufficient or erroneous information used to make decisions
- inadequate training for hearing protector fitters and issuers
- inadequate or inappropriate selection of protectors in stock
- over-reliance on number ratings in choosing devices
- failure to fit and train each HPD wearer individually
- over-reliance on external sources (government or contractors) to provide HCP services
- failure to use audiometric monitoring results to educate and motivate employees
- failure to use audiometric data to evaluate HCP effectiveness.

Objective evaluation of the audiometric data

The audiometric data for the noise-exposed population provide evidence of whether the HCP is preventing occupational hearing loss. Over time, the rate of hearing change for noise-exposed employees should be no greater than that of matched controls without noisy jobs. To give an early indication of HCP effectiveness, procedures for audiometric database analysis have been developed using year-to-year variability in threshold values (Royster and Royster 1986a; ANSI 1991).

• STANDARDS AND REGULATIONS

Alice H. Suter

Terms

In the field of occupational noise, the terms *regulation, standard,* and *legislation* are often used interchangeably, even though technically they may have slightly different meanings. A standard is a codified set of rules or guidelines, much like a regulation, but it can be developed under the auspices of a consensus group, such as the International Organization for Standardization (ISO). Legislation consists of laws prescribed by legislating authorities or by local governing bodies.

Many national standards are called legislation. Some official bodies use the terms standards and regulations as well. The Council of the European Communities (CEC) issues *Directives*. All members of the European Community needed to "harmonize" their noise standards (regulations or legislation) with the 1986 EEC Directive on occupational noise exposure by the year 1990 (CEC 1986). This means that the noise standards and regulations of the member countries had to be at least as protective as the EEC Directive. In the United States, a *regulation* is a rule or order

prescribed by a government authority and is usually more in the nature of a formality than a standard.

Some nations have a *code of practice*, which is somewhat less formal. For example, the Australian national standard for occupational exposure to noise consists of two short paragraphs setting forth mandatory rules, followed by a 35-page code of practice which provides practical guidance on how the standard should be implemented. Codes of practice usually do not have the legal force of regulations or legislation.

Another term that is used occasionally is *recommendation*, which is more like a guideline than a mandatory rule and is not enforceable. In this article, the term *standard* will be used generically to represent noise standards of all degrees of formality.

Consensus Standards

One of the most widely used noise standards is ISO 1999, *Acoustics: Determination of Occupational Noise Exposure and Estimate of Noise-Induced Hearing Impairment* (ISO 1990). This international consensus standard represents a revision of an earlier, less detailed version and it can be used to predict the amount of hearing loss expected to occur in various centiles of the exposed population at various audiometric frequencies as a function of exposure level and duration, age and sex.

The ISO is currently very active in the area of noise standardization. Its technical committee TC43, "Acoustics", is working on a standard to evaluate the effectiveness of hearing conservation programmes. According to von Gierke (1993), TC43's Subcommittee 1 (SC1) has 21 working groups, some of which are considering more than three standards each. TC43/SC1 has issued 58 noise-related standards and 63 additional standards are in a state of revision or preparation (von Gierke 1993).

Damage-Risk Criteria

The term *damage-risk criteria* refers to the risk of hearing impairment from various levels of noise. Many factors enter into the development of these criteria and standards in addition to the data describing the amount of hearing loss resulting from a certain amount of noise exposure. There are both technical and policy considerations.

The following questions are good examples of policy considerations: What proportion of the noise-exposed population should be protected, and how much hearing loss constitutes an acceptable risk? Should we protect even the most sensitive members of the exposed population against any loss of hearing? Or should we protect only against a compensable hearing handicap? It amounts to a question of which hearing loss formula to use, and different governmental bodies have varied widely in their selections.

In earlier years, regulatory decisions were made that allowed substantial amounts of hearing loss as an acceptable risk. The most common definition used to be an average hearing threshold level (or "low fence") of 25 dB or greater at the audiometric frequencies 500, 1,000, and 2,000 Hz. Since that time, the definitions of "hearing impairment" or "hearing handicap" have become more restrictive, with different nations or consensus groups advocating different definitions. For example, certain US government agencies now use 25 dB at 1,000, 2,000, and 3,000 Hz. Other definitions may incorporate a low fence of 20 or 25 dB at 1,000, 2,000, and 4,000 Hz, and may include a broader range of frequencies.

In general, as definitions include higher frequencies and lower "fences" or hearing threshold levels, the acceptable risk becomes more stringent and a higher percentage of the exposed population will appear to be at risk from given levels of noise. If there is to be no risk of any hearing loss from noise exposure, even in the more

Table 47.1 • Permissible exposure limits (PEL), exchange rates, and other requirements for noise exposure according to nation.

Nation, date	PEL $L_{av,}$ 8-hour, dBA[a]	Exchange rate, dBA[b]	L_{max} rms L_{peak} SPL	Level dBA engineering control[c]	Level dBA audiometric test[c]
Argentina	90	3	110 dBA		
Australia,[1] 1993	85	3	140 dB peak	85	85
Brazil, 1992	85	5	115 dBA 140 dB peak	85	
Canada,[2] 1990	87	3		87	84
CEC,[3, 4] 1986	85	3	140 dB peak	90	85
Chile	85	5	115 dBA 140 dB		
China,[5] 1985	70-90	3	115 dBA		
Finland, 1982	85	3		85	
France, 1990	85	3	135 dB peak		85
Germany,[3, 6] 1990	85 55,70	3	140 dB peak	90	85
Hungary	85	3	125 dBA 140 dB peak	90	
India,[7] 1989	90		115 dBA 140 dBA		
Israel, 1984	85	5	115 dBA 140 dB peak		
Italy, 1990	85	3	140 dB peak	90	85
Netherlands,[8] 1987	80	3	140 dB peak	85	
New Zealand,[9] 1981	85	3	115 dBA 140 dB peak		
Norway,[10] 1982	85 55,70	3	110 dBA		80
Spain, 1989	85	3	140 dB peak	90	80
Sweden, 1992	85	3	115 dBA 140 dB C	85	85
United Kingdom, 1989	85	3	140 dB peak	90	85
United States,[11] 1983	90	5	115 dBA 140 dB peak	90	85
Uruguay	90	3	110 dBA		

[a] PEL = Permissible exposure limit. [b] Exchange rate. Sometimes called the doubling rate or time/intensity trading ratio, this is the amount of change in noise level (in dB) allowed for each halving or doubling of exposure duration. [c] Like the PEL, the levels initiating the requirements for engineering controls and audiometric testing also, presumably, are *average* levels.

Sources: Arenas 1995; Gunn; Embleton 1994; ILO 1994. Published standards of various nations have been further consulted.

sensitive members of the exposed population, the permissible exposure limit would have to be as low as 75 dBA. In fact, the EEC Directive has established an equivalent level (L_{eq}) of 75 dBA as the level at which the risk is negligible, and this level has also been put forward as a goal for Swedish production facilities (Kihlman 1992).

Overall, the prevailing thought on this subject is that it is acceptable for a noise-exposed workforce to lose some hearing, but not too much. As for how much is too much, there is no consensus at this time. In all probability, most nations draft standards and regulations in an attempt to keep the risk at a minimum level while taking technical and economic feasibility into account, but without coming to consensus on such matters as the frequencies, fence, or percentage of the population to be protected.

Presenting the Damage-Risk Criteria
Criteria for noise-induced hearing loss may be presented in either of two ways: noise-induced permanent threshold shift (NIPTS) or percentage risk. NIPTS is the amount of permanent threshold shift remaining in a population after subtracting the threshold shift that would occur "normally" from causes other than occupational noise. The percentage risk is the percentage of a popu-

Notes to table 47.1.

[1] Levels for engineering controls, hearing tests, and other elements of the hearing conservation programme are defined in a code of practice.

[2] There is some variation among the individual Canadian provinces: Ontario, Quebec and New Brunswick use 90 dBA with a 5-dB exchange rate; Alberta, Nova Scotia and Newfoundland use 85 dBA with a 5-dB exchange rate; and British Columbia uses 90 dBA with a 3-dB exchange rate. All require engineering controls to the level of the PEL. Manitoba requires certain hearing conservation practices above 80 dBA, hearing protectors and training on request above 85 dBA, and engineering controls above 90 dBA.

[3] The Council of the European Communities (86/188/EEC) and Germany (UVV Larm-1990) state that it is not possible to give a precise limit for the elimination of hearing hazards and the risk of other health impairments from noise. Therefore the employer is obliged to reduce the noise level as far as possible, taking technical progress and the availability of control measures into account. Other EC nations may have adopted this approach as well.

[4] Those countries comprised by the European Community were required to have standards that at least conformed to the EEC Directive by January 1, 1990.

[5] China requires different levels for different activities: e.g., 70 dBA for precision assembly lines, processing workshops and computer rooms; 75 dBA for duty, observation and rest rooms; 85 dBA for new workshops; and 90 dBA for existing workshops.

[6] Germany also has noise standards of 55 dBA for mentally stressful tasks and 70 dBA for mechanized office work.

[7] Recommendation.

[8] The Netherlands' noise legislation requires engineering noise control at 85 dBA "unless this cannot be reasonably demanded". Hearing protection must be provided above 80 dBA and workers are required to wear it at levels above 90 dBA.

[9] New Zealand requires a maximum of 82 dBA for a 16-hour exposure. Ear muffs must be worn in noise levels exceeding 115 dBA.

[10] Norway requires a PEL of 55 dBA for work requiring a large amount of mental concentration, 85 dBA for work requiring verbal communication or great accuracy and attention, and 85 dBA for other noisy work settings. Recommended limits are 10 dB lower. Workers exposed to noise levels greater than 85 dBA should wear hearing protectors.

[11] These levels apply to the OSHA noise standard, covering workers in general industry and the maritime trades. The US military services require standards that are somewhat more stringent. The US Air Force and the US Army both use an 85-dBA PEL and a 3-dB exchange rate.

lation with a certain amount of noise-induced hearing impairment *after* subtracting the percentage of a similar population *not* exposed to occupational noise. This concept is sometimes called *excess risk*. Unfortunately, neither method is without problems.

The trouble with using NIPTS alone is that it is difficult to summarize the effects of noise on hearing. The data are usually set out in a large table showing noise-induced threshold shift for each audiometric frequency as a function of noise level, years of exposure and population centile. The concept of percentage risk is more attractive because it uses single numbers and appears easy to understand. But the trouble with percentage risk is that it can vary enormously depending on a number of factors, particularly the height of the hearing threshold level fence and the frequencies used to define hearing impairment (or handicap).

With both methods, the user needs to be sure that the exposed and non-exposed populations are carefully matched for such factors as age and non-occupational noise exposure.

National Noise Standards

Table 47.1 gives some of the main features of the noise exposure standards of several nations. Most of the information is current as of this publication, but some standards may have been recently revised. Readers are advised to consult the newest versions of the national standards.

Table 47.1 clearly shows the trend of most nations to use a permissible exposure limit (PEL) of 85 dBA, whereas about half of the standards still use 90 dBA for compliance with requirements for engineering controls, as allowed by the EEC Directive. The vast majority of the nations listed above have adopted the 3-dB exchange rate, except for Israel, Brazil and Chile, all of which use the 5-dB rule with an 85-dBA criterion level. The other notable exception is the United States (in the civilian sector), although both the US Army and the US Air Force have adopted the 3-dB rule.

In addition to their requirements to protect workers against hearing loss, several nations include provisions for preventing other adverse effects of noise. Some nations state the need to protect against the extra-auditory effects of noise in their regulations. Both the EEC Directive and the German standard acknowledge that workplace noise involves a risk for the health and safety of workers beyond hearing loss, but that current scientific knowledge of the extra-auditory effects does not enable precise safe levels to be set.

The Norwegian standard includes a requirement that noise levels must not exceed 70 dBA in work settings where speech communication is necessary. The German standard advocates noise reduction for the prevention of accident risks, and both Norway and Germany require a maximum noise level of 55 dBA to enhance concentration and prevent stress during mental tasks.

Some countries have special noise standards for different kinds of workplaces. For example, Finland and the United States have noise standards for motor vehicle cabs, Germany and Japan specify noise levels for offices. Others include noise as one of many regulated hazards in a particular process. Still other standards apply to specific types of equipment or machines, such as air compressors, chain saws and construction equipment.

In addition, some nations have promulgated separate standards for hearing protection devices (such as the EEC Directive, the Netherlands and Norway) and for hearing conservation programmes (such as France, Norway, Spain, Sweden and the United States.)

Some nations use innovative approaches to attack the occupational noise problem. For example, the Netherlands has a separate standard for newly constructed workplaces, and Australia and Norway give information to employers for instructing manufacturers in the provision of quieter equipment.

There is little information about the degree to which these standards and regulations are enforced. Some specify that employers "should" take certain actions (as in codes of practice or guidelines), while most specify that employers "shall". Standards that use "shall" are more apt to be mandatory, but individual nations vary widely in their ability and inclination to secure enforcement. Even within the same nation, enforcement of occupational noise standards may vary considerably with the government in power.

References

American National Standards Institute (ANSI). 1985. *ANSI SI.4-1983, As Amended By ANSI SI.4-1985*. New York: ANSI.

—. 1991. *ANSI SI2.13. Evaluation of Hearing Conservation Programmes*. New York: ANSI.

—. 1992. *ANSI S12.16. Guidelines for the Specification of Noise of New Machinery*. New York: ANSI.

Arenas, JP. 1995. Institute of Acoustics, Universidad Austral de Chile. Paper presented at the 129th meeting of the Acoustical Society of America, Valdivia, Chile.

Boettcher FA, D Henderson, MA Gratton, RW Danielson and CD Byrne. 1987. Synergistic interactions of noise and other ototraumatic agents. *Ear Hear.* 8(4):192-212.

Council of the European Communities (CEC). 1986. Directive of 12 May 1986 on the protection of workers from the risks related to exposure to noise at work (86/188/EEC).

—. 1989a. Directive 89/106/EEC of 21 December 1988 on the approximation of laws, regulations and administrative provisions of the Member States relating to construction products, OJ No. L40, 11 February.

—. 1989b. Directive 89/392/EEC of 14 June 1989 on the approximation of the laws of the Member States relating to machinery, OJ No. L183,29.6.1989.

—. 1989c. Directive 89/686/EEC of 21 December 1989 on the approximation of laws of the Member States relating to personal protective equipment, OJ No. L399, 30.12.1989.

—. 1991. Directive 91/368/EEC of 20 June 1991 amending Directive 89/392/EEC on approximation of the laws of the Member States relating to machinery, OJ No. L198, 22.7.91.

—. 1993a. Directive 93/44/EEC. of 14 June 1993 amending Directive 89/392/EEC on approximation of the laws of the Member States relating to machinery, OJ No. L175, 19.7.92.

—. 1993b. Directive 93/95/EEC of 29 October 1993 amending 89/686/EEC on the approximation of laws of the Member States relating to personal protective equipment(PPE), OJ No. L276, 9.11.93.

Dunn, DE, RR Davis, CJ Merry, and JR Franks. 1991. Hearing loss in the chinchilla from impact and continuous noise exposure. *J Acoust Soc Am* 90:1975-1985.

Embleton, TFW. 1994. Technical assessment of upper limits on noise in the workplace. *Noise/News Intl.* Poughkeepsie, NY: I-INCE.

Fechter, LD. 1989. A mechanistic basis for interactions between noise and chemical exposure. *ACES* 1:23-28.

Gunn, P. N.d. Department of Occupational Health Safety and Welfare, Perth, Western Australia. Personal Comm.

Hamernik, RP, WA Ahroon, and KD Hsueh. 1991. The energy spectrum of an impulse: Its relation to hearing loss. *J Acoust Soc Am* 90:197-204.

International Electrotechnical Commission (IEC). 1979. IEC document No. 651.

—. 1985. IEC document No. 804.

International Labour Organization (ILO). 1994. *Noise Regulations and Standards (Summaries)*. Geneva: ILO.

International Organization for Standardization. (ISO). 1975. *Method for Calculating Loudness Level*. ISO Document No. 532. Geneva:ISO.

—. 1990. *Acoustics: Determination of Occupational Noise Exposure and Estimate of Noise-Induced Hearing Impairment*. ISO Document No. 1999. Geneva: ISO.

Ising, H and B Kruppa. 1993. *Larm und Krankheit [Noise and Disease]*. Stuttgart: Gustav Fischer Verlag.

Kihlman, T. 1992. Sweden's action plan against noise. *Noise/News Intl* 1(4):194-208.

Moll van Charante, AW and PGH Mulder. 1990. Perceptual acuity and the risk of industrial accidents. *Am J Epidemiol* 131:652-663.

Morata, TC. 1989. Study of the effects of simultaneous exposure to noise and carbon disulfide on workers' hearing. *Scand Audiol* 18:53-58.

Morata, TC, DE Dunn, LW Kretchmer, GK Lemasters, and UP Santos. 1991. Effects of simultaneous exposure to noise and toluene on workers' hearing and balance. In *Proceedings of the Fourth International Conference On the Combined Environmental Factors*, edited by LD Fechter. Baltimore: Johns Hopkins Univ.

Moreland, JB. 1979. Noise Control Techniques. In *Handbook of Noise Control*, edited by CM Harris. New York: McGraw-Hill

Peterson, EA, JS Augenstein, and DC Tanis. 1978. Continuing studies of noise and cardiovascular function. *J Sound Vibrat* 59:123.

Peterson, EA, JS Augenstein, D Tanis, and DG Augenstein. 1981. Noise raises blood pressure without impairing auditory sensitivity. *Science* 211:1450-1452.

Peterson, EA, JS Augenstein, DC Tanis, R Warner, and A Heal. 1983. *Proceedings of the Fourth International Congress On Noise As a Public Health Problem*, edited by G Rossi. Milan: Centro Richerche e Studi Amplifon.

Price, GR. 1983. Relative hazard of weapons impulses. *J Acoust Soc Am* 73:556-566.

Rehm, S. 1983. Research on extraaural effects of noise since 1978. In *Proceedings of the Fourth International Congress On Noise As a Public Health Problem*, edited by G Rossi. Milan: Centro Richerche e Studi Amplifon.

Royster, JD. 1985. Audiometric evaluations for industrial hearing conservation. *J Sound Vibrat* 19(5):24-29.

Royster, JD and LH Royster. 1986. Audiometric data base analysis. In *Noise and Hearing Conservation Manual*, edited by EH Berger, WD Ward, JC Morrill, and LH Royster. Akron, Ohio: American Industrial Hygiene Association (AIHA).

—. 1989. *Hearing Conservation. NC-OSHA Industry Guide No. 15*. Raleigh, NC: North Carolina Department of Labor.

—. 1990. *Hearing Conservation Programs: Practical Guidelines for Success*. Chelsea, Mich.: Lewis.

Royster, LH, EH Berger, and JD Royster. 1986. Noise surveys and data analysis. In *Noise and Hearing Conservation Manual*, edited by EH Berger, WH Ward, JC Morill, and LH Royster. Akron, Ohio: American Industrial Hygiene Association (AIHA).

Royster, LH and JD Royster. 1986. Education and motivation. In *Noise & Hearing Conservation Manual*, edited by EH Berger, WH Ward, JC Morill, and LH Royster. Akron, Ohio: American Industrial Hygiene Association (AIHA).

Suter, AH. 1992. *Communication and Job Performance in Noise: A Review*. American Speech-Language Hearing Association Monographs, No.28. Washington, DC: ASHA.

—. 1993. Noise and conservation of hearing. Chap. 2 in *Hearing Conservation Manual* Milwaukee, Wisc: Council for Accreditation in Occupational Hearing Conservation.

Thiery, L and C Meyer-Bisch. 1988. Hearing loss due to partly impulsive industrial noise exposure at levels between 87 and 90 dBA. *J Acoust Soc Am* 84:651-659.

van Dijk, FJH. 1990. Epidemiological research on non-auditory effects of occupational noise exposure since 1983. In *Noise As a Public Health Problem*, edited by B Berglund and T Lindvall. Stockholm: Swedish Council for Building Research.

von Gierke, HE. 1993. Noise regulations and standards: Progress, experiences, and challenges. In *Noise As a Public Health Problem*, edited by M Vallet. France: Institut National de Recherche sur les Transports et leur Securite.

Wilkins, PA and WI Acton. 1982. Noise and accidents: A review. *Ann Occup Hyg* 2:249-260.

Other relevant readings

Berger, EH. 1986. Hearing protection devices. In *Noise and Hearing Conservation Manual*, edited by EH Berger, WH Ward, JC Morill, and LH Royster. Akron, Ohio: American Industrial Hygiene Association (AIHA).

Hassall, A and K Zaveru. 1979. *Acoustic Noise Measurements*. Naerum, Denmark: Bruel & Kjaer.

Royster, LH and JD Royster. 1985. Hearing protection devices. In *Hearing Conservation in Industry*, edited by AS Feldman and CT Grimes. Baltimore: Williams & Wilkins.

Suvorov, GA, LN Shkarinov, and El Denisov. 1984. *Hygienic Assessment of Occupational Noises and Vibration*. Moscow: Meditsina.

48

Chapter Editor
Robert N. Cherry, Jr.

Contents

48. RADIATION, IONIZING

● INTRODUCTION

Robert N. Cherry, Jr.

Ionizing radiation is everywhere. It arrives from outer space as cosmic rays. It is in the air as emissions from radioactive radon and its progeny. Naturally occurring radioactive isotopes enter and remain in all living things. It is inescapable. Indeed, all species on this planet evolved in the presence of ionizing radiation. While humans exposed to small doses of radiation may not immediately show any apparent biological effects, there is no doubt that ionizing radiation, when given in sufficient amounts, can cause harm. These effects are well known both in kind and in degree.

While ionizing radiation can cause harm, it also has many beneficial uses. Radioactive uranium generates electricity in nuclear power plants in many countries. In medicine, x rays produce radiographs for diagnosis of internal injuries and diseases. Nuclear medicine physicians use radioactive material as tracers to form detailed images of internal structures and to study metabolism. Therapeutic radiopharmaceuticals are available to treat disorders such as hyperthyroidism and cancer. Radiotherapy physicians use gamma rays, pion beams, electron beams, neutrons and other types of radiation to treat cancer. Engineers use radioactive material in oil well logging operations and in soil moisture density gauges. Industrial radiographers use x rays in quality control to look at internal structures of manufactured devices. Exit signs in buildings and aircraft contain radioactive tritium to make them glow in the dark in the event of a power failure. Many smoke detectors in homes and commercial buildings contain radioactive americium.

These many uses of ionizing radiation and radioactive materials enhance the quality of life and help society in many ways. The benefits of each use must always be compared with the risks. The risks may be to workers directly involved in applying the radiation or radioactive material, to the public, to future generations and to the environment or to any combination of these. Beyond political and economic considerations, benefits must always outweigh risks when ionizing radiation is involved.

Ionizing Radiation

Ionizing radiation consists of particles, including photons, which cause the separation of electrons from atoms and molecules. However, some types of radiation of relatively low energy, such as ultraviolet light, can also cause ionization under certain circumstances. To distinguish these types of radiation from radiation that always causes ionization, an arbitrary lower energy limit for ionizing radiation usually is set around 10 kiloelectron volts (keV).

Directly ionizing radiation consists of charged particles. Such particles include energetic electrons (sometimes called negatrons), positrons, protons, alpha particles, charged mesons, muons and heavy ions (ionized atoms). This type of ionizing radiation interacts with matter primarily through the Coulomb force, repelling or attracting electrons from atoms and molecules by virtue of their charges.

Indirectly ionizing radiation consists of uncharged particles. The most common kinds of indirectly ionizing radiation are photons above 10 keV (x rays and gamma rays) and all neutrons.

X-ray and gamma-ray photons interact with matter and cause ionization in at least three different ways:

1. Lower-energy photons interact mostly via the photoelectric effect, in which the photon gives all of its energy to an electron, which then leaves the atom or molecule. The photon disappears.

2. Intermediate-energy photons mostly interact through the Compton effect, in which the photon and an electron essentially collide as particles. The photon continues in a new direction with reduced energy while the released electron goes off with the remainder of the incoming energy (less the electron's binding energy to the atom or molecule).

3. Pair production is possible only for photons with energy in excess of 1.02 MeV. (However, near 1.02 MeV, the Compton effect still dominates. Pair production dominates at higher energies.) The photon disappears and an electron-positron pair appears in its place (this occurs only in the vicinity of a nucleus because of conservation of momentum and energy considerations). The total kinetic energy of the electron-positron pair is equal to the energy of the photon less the sum of the rest-mass energies of the electron and positron (1.02 MeV). These energetic electrons and positrons then proceed as directly ionizing radiation. As it loses kinetic energy, a positron will eventually encounter an electron, and the particles will annihilate each other. Two (usually) 0.511 MeV photons are then emitted from the annihilation site at 180 degrees from each other.

For a given photon any of these can occur, except that pair production is possible only for photons with energy greater than 1.022 MeV. The energy of the photon and the material with which it interacts determine which interaction is the most likely to occur.

Figure 48.1 shows the regions in which each type of photon interaction dominates as a function of photon energy and atomic number of absorber.

The most common neutron interactions with matter are inelastic collisions, neutron capture (or activation) and fission. All of these are interactions with nuclei. A nucleus colliding inelastically with a neutron is left at a higher energy level. It can release this energy in the form of a gamma ray or by emitting a beta particle, or both. In neutron capture, an affected nucleus may absorb the neutron and eject energy as gamma or x rays or beta particles, or both. The secondary particles then cause ionization as discussed above. In fission, a heavy nucleus absorbs the neutron and splits into two lighter nuclei that are almost always radioactive.

Quantities, Units and Related Definitions

The International Commission on Radiation Units and Measurements (ICRU) develops internationally accepted formal definitions of quantities and units of radiation and radioactivity. The International Commission on Radiological Protection (ICRP) also

Figure 48.1 • Relative importance of the three principal interactions of photons in matter.

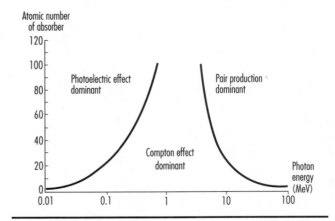

sets standards for definition and use of various quantities and units used in radiation safety. A description of some quantities, units and definitions commonly used in radiation safety follows.

Absorbed dose. This is the fundamental dosimetric quantity for ionizing radiation. Basically, it is the energy ionizing radiation imparts to matter per unit mass. Formally,

$$D = \frac{d\varepsilon}{dm}$$

where D is the absorbed dose, $d\varepsilon$ is the mean energy imparted to matter of mass dm. Absorbed dose has units of joules per kilogram $(J\ kg^{-1})$. The special name for the unit of absorbed dose is the gray (Gy).

Activity. This quantity represents the number of nuclear transformations from a given nuclear energy state per unit time. Formally,

$$A = \frac{dN}{dt}$$

where A is the activity, dN is the expectation value of the number of spontaneous nuclear transitions from the given energy state in the time interval dt. It is related to the number of radioactive nuclei N by:

$$A = \lambda N$$

where λ is the decay constant. Activity has units of inverse seconds (s^{-1}). The special name for the unit of activity is the becquerel (Bq).

Decay constant (λ). This quantity represents the probability per unit time that a nuclear transformation will occur for a given radionuclide. The decay constant has units of inverse seconds (s^{-1}). It is related to the half-life $t_{1/2}$ of a radionuclide by:

$$\lambda = \frac{\ln 2}{t_{1/2}} \approx \frac{0.693}{t_{1/2}}$$

The decay constant λ is related to the mean lifetime, τ, of a radionuclide by:

$$\lambda = \frac{1}{\tau}$$

The time dependence of activity $A(t)$ and of the number of radioactive nuclei $N(t)$ can be expressed by $A(0)e^{-\lambda t}$ and $N(0)e^{-\lambda t}$ respectively.

Deterministic biological effect. This is a biological effect caused by ionizing radiation and whose probability of occurrence is zero at small absorbed doses but will increase steeply to unity (100%) above some level of absorbed dose (the threshold). Cataract induction is an example of a stochastic biological effect.

Effective dose. The effective dose E is the sum of the weighted equivalent doses in all the tissues and organs of the body. It is a radiation safety quantity, so its use is not appropriate for large absorbed doses delivered in a relatively short period of time. It is given by:

$$E = \sum_{T} w_T H_T$$

where w_T is the tissue weighting factor and H_T is the equivalent dose for tissue T. Effective dose has units of $J\ kg^{-1}$. The special name for the unit of effective dose is the sievert (Sv).

Equivalent dose. The equivalent dose H_T is the absorbed dose averaged over a tissue or organ (rather than at a point) and weighted for the radiation quality that is of interest. It is a radiation safety quantity, so its use is not appropriate for large absorbed doses delivered in a relatively short period of time. The equivalent dose is given by:

$$H_T = \sum_{R} w_R D_{T,R}$$

where $D_{T,R}$ is the absorbed dose averaged over the tissue or organ T due to radiation R and w_R is the radiation weighting factor. Equivalent dose has units of $J\ kg^{-1}$. The special name for the unit of equivalent dose is the sievert (Sv).

Half-life. This quantity is the amount of time required for the activity of a radionuclide sample to reduce by a factor of one-half. Equivalently, it is the amount of time required for a given number of nuclei in a given radioactive state to reduce by a factor of one-half. It has fundamental units of seconds (s), but is also commonly expressed in hours, days and years. For a given radionuclide, half-life $t_{1/2}$ is related to the decay constant λ by:

$$t_{1/2} = \frac{\ln 2}{\lambda} \approx \frac{0.693}{\lambda}$$

Linear energy transfer. This quantity is the energy a charged particle imparts to matter per unit length as it traverses the matter. Formally,

$$L = \frac{d\varepsilon}{dl}$$

where L is the linear energy transfer (also called *linear collision stopping power*) and $d\varepsilon$ is the mean energy lost by the particle in traversing a distance dl. Linear energy transfer (LET) has units of $J\ m^{-1}$.

Mean lifetime. This quantity is the average time a nuclear state will survive before it undergoes a transformation to a lower energy state by emitting ionizing radiation. It has fundamental units of seconds (s), but may also be expressed in hours, days or years. It is related to the decay constant by:

$$\tau = \frac{1}{\lambda}$$

where τ is the mean lifetime and λ is the decay constant for a given nuclide in a given energy state.

Radiation weighting factor. This is a number w_R that, for a given type and energy of radiation R, is representative of values of the relative biological effectiveness of that radiation in inducing stochastic effects at low doses. The values of w_R are related to linear energy transfer (LET) and are given in table 48.1. Figure 48.2 (overleaf) shows the relationship between w_R and LET for neutrons.

Table 48.1 • Radiation weighting factors w_R[1].

Type and energy range	w_R
Photons, all energies	1
Electrons and muons, all energies[2]	1
Neutrons, energy <10 keV	5
10 keV to 100 keV	10
>100 keV to 2 MeV	20
>2 MeV to 20 MeV	10
>20 MeV	5
Protons, other than recoil protons, energy >2 MeV	5
Alpha particles, fission fragments, heavy nuclei	20

[1] All values relate to the radiation incident on the body or, for internal sources, emitted from the source.

[2] Excluding Auger electrons emitted from nuclei bound to DNA.

Figure 48.2 • Radiation weighting factors for neutrons (the smooth curve is to be treated as an approximation).

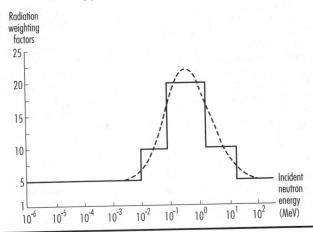

Relative biological effectiveness (RBE). The RBE of one type of radiation compared with another is the inverse ratio of the absorbed doses producing the same degree of a defined biological end point.

Stochastic biological effect. This is a biological effect caused by ionizing radiation whose probability of occurrence increases with increasing absorbed dose, probably with no threshold, but whose severity is independent of absorbed dose. Cancer is an example of a stochastic biological effect.

Table 48.2 • Tissue weighting factors w_T[1].

Tissue or organ	w_T
Gonads	0.20
Bone marrow (red)	0.12
Colon	0.12
Lung	0.12
Stomach	0.12
Bladder	0.05
Breast	0.05
Liver	0.05
Oesophagus	0.05
Thyroid	0.05
Skin	0.01
Bone surface	0.01
Remainder	0.05[2,3]

[1] The values have been developed from a reference population of equal numbers of both sexes and a wide range of ages. In the definition of effective dose they apply to workers, to the whole population, and to either sex.

[2] For purposes of calculation, the remainder is composed of the following additional tissues and organs: adrenals, brain, upper large intestine, small intestine, kidneys, muscle, pancreas, spleen, thymus and uterus. The list includes organs that are likely to be selectively irradiated. Some organs in the list are known to be susceptible to cancer induction.

[3] In those exceptional cases in which a single one of the remainder tissues or organs receives an equivalent dose in excess of the highest dose in any of the twelve organs for which a weighting factor is specified, a weighting factor of 0.025 should be applied to that tissue or organ and a weighting factor of 0.025 to the average dose in the rest of the remainder as defined above.

Tissue weighting factor w_T. This represents the contribution of tissue or organ T to the total detriment due to all of the stochastic effects resulting from uniform irradiation of the whole body. It is used because the probability of stochastic effects due to an equivalent dose depends on the tissue or organ irradiated. A uniform equivalent dose over the whole body should give an effective dose numerically equal to the sum of effective doses for all tissues and organs of the body. Therefore, the sum of all tissue weighting factors is normalized to unity. Table 48.2 gives values for tissue weighting factors.

RADIATION BIOLOGY AND BIOLOGICAL EFFECTS

Arthur C. Upton

After its discovery by Roentgen in 1895, the x ray was introduced so rapidly into the diagnosis and treatment of disease that injuries from excessive radiation exposure began to be encountered almost immediately in pioneer radiation workers, who had yet to become aware of the dangers (Brown 1933). The first such injuries were predominantly skin reactions on the hands of those working with the early radiation equipment, but within a decade many other types of injury also had been reported, including the first cancers attributed to radiation (Stone 1959).

Throughout the century since these early findings, study of the biological effects of ionizing radiation has received continuing impetus from the growing uses of radiation in medicine, science and industry, as well as from the peaceful and military applications of atomic energy. As a result, the biological effects of radiation have been investigated more thoroughly than those of virtually any other environmental agent. The evolving knowledge of radiation effects has been influential in shaping measures for the protection of human health against many other environmental hazards as well as radiation.

Nature and Mechanisms of the Biological Effects of Radiation

Energy deposition. In contrast to other forms of radiation, ionizing radiation is capable of depositing enough localized energy to dislodge electrons from the atoms with which it interacts. Thus, as radiation collides randomly with atoms and molecules in passing through living cells, it gives rise to ions and free radicals which break chemical bonds and cause other molecular changes that injure the affected cells. The spatial distribution of the ionizing events depends on the radiation weighting factor, w_R of the radiation (see table 48.1 and figure 48.3).

Effects on DNA. Any molecule in the cell may be altered by radiation, but DNA is the most critical biological target because of the limited redundancy of the genetic information it contains. An absorbed dose of radiation large enough to kill the average dividing cell—2 gray (Gy)—suffices to cause hundreds of lesions in its DNA molecules (Ward 1988). Most such lesions are reparable, but those produced by a densely ionizing radiation (for example, a proton or an alpha particle) are generally less reparable than those produced by a sparsely ionizing radiation (for example, an x ray or a gamma ray) (Goodhead 1988). Densely ionizing (high LET) radiations, therefore, typically have a higher relative biological effectiveness (RBE) than sparsely ionizing (low LET) radiations for most forms of injury (ICRP 1991).

Effects on genes. Damage to DNA that remains unrepaired or is misrepaired may be expressed in the form of mutations, the frequency of which appears to increase as a linear, non-threshold function of the dose, approximately 10^{-5} to 10^{-6} per locus per Gy

Figure 48.3 • Differences among various types of ionizing radiation in penetrating power in tissue.

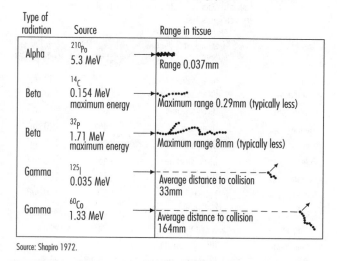

Source: Shapiro 1972.

Figure 48.5 • Mitotic inhibition induced by x rays in rat corneal epithelial cells.

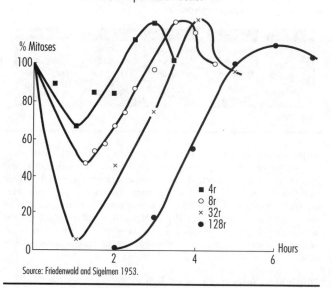

- ■ 4r
- ○ 8r
- × 32r
- ● 128r

Source: Friedenwald and Sigelmen 1953.

(NAS 1990). The fact that the mutation rate appears to be proportional to the dose is interpreted to signify that traversal of the DNA by a single ionizing particle may, in principle, suffice to cause a mutation (NAS 1990). In Chernobyl accident victims, the dose-response relationship for glycophorin mutations in bone marrow cells closely resembles that observed in atomic bomb survivors (Jensen, Langlois and Bigbee 1995).

Effects on chromosomes. Radiation damage to the genetic apparatus may also cause changes in chromosome number and structure, the frequency of which has been observed to increase with the dose in radiation workers, atomic bomb survivors, and others exposed to ionizing radiation. The dose-response relation-

ship for chromosome aberrations in human blood lymphocytes (figure 48.4) has been characterized well enough so that the frequency of aberrations in such cells can serve as a useful biological dosimeter (IAEA 1986).

Effects on cell survival. Among the earliest reactions to irradiation is the inhibition of cell division, which appears promptly after exposure, varying both in degree and duration with the dose (figure 48.5). Although the inhibition of mitosis is characteristically transitory, radiation damage to genes and chromosomes may be lethal to dividing cells, which are highly radiosensitive as a class (ICRP 1984). Measured in terms of proliferative capacity, the survival of dividing cells tends to decrease exponentially with increasing dose, 1 to 2 Gy generally sufficing to reduce the surviving population by about 50% (figure 48.6).

Effects on tissues. Mature, non-dividing cells are relatively radioresistant, but the dividing cells in a tissue are radiosensitive and may be killed in sufficient numbers by intensive irradiation to cause the tissue to become atrophic (figure 48.7, overleaf). The rapidity of such atrophy depends on cell population dynamics

Figure 48.4 • Frequency of dicentric chromosome aberrations in human lymphocytes in relation to dose, dose rate, and quality of irradiation in vitro.

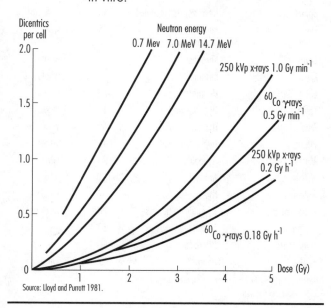

Source: Lloyd and Purrott 1981.

Figure 48.6 • Typical dose-survival curves for mammalian cells exposed to x rays and fast neutrons.

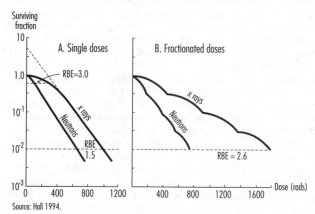

Source: Hall 1994.

Figure 48.7 • Characteristic sequence of events in the pathogenesis of nonstochastic effects of ionizing radiation.

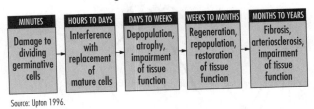

Source: Upton 1996.

within the affected tissue; that is, in organs characterized by slow cell turnover, such as the liver and vascular endothelium, the process is typically much slower than in organs characterized by rapid cell turnover, such as the bone marrow, epidermis and intestinal mucosa (ICRP 1984). It is noteworthy, moreover, that if the volume of tissue irradiated is sufficiently small, or if the dose is accumulated gradually enough, the severity of injury may be greatly reduced by the compensatory proliferation of surviving cells.

Clinical Manifestations of Injury

Types of effects. Radiation effects encompass a wide variety of reactions, varying markedly in their dose-response relationships, clinical manifestations, timing and prognosis (Mettler and Upton 1995). The effects are often subdivided, for convenience, into two broad categories: (1) *heritable* effects, which are expressed in the descendants of exposed individuals, and (2) *somatic* effects, which are expressed in exposed individuals themselves. The latter include acute effects, which occur relatively soon after irradiation, as well as late (or chronic) effects, such as cancer, which may not appear until months, years or decades later.

Acute effects. The acute effects of radiation result predominantly from the depletion of progenitor cells in affected tissues (figure 48.7) and can be elicited only by doses that are large enough to kill many such cells (for example, table 48.3). For this reason, such effects are viewed as *non-stochastic*, or *deterministic*, in nature (ICRP 1984 and 1991), in contradistinction to the mutagenic and carcinogenic effects of radiation, which are viewed as *stochastic* phenomena resulting from random molecular alterations in individual cells that increase as linear-nonthreshold functions of the dose (NAS 1990; ICRP 1991).

Acute injuries of the types that were prevalent in pioneer radiation workers and early radiotherapy patients have been largely eliminated by improvements in safety precautions and treatment methods. Nevertheless, most patients treated with radiation today still experience some injury of the normal tissue that is irradiated. In addition, serious radiation accidents continue to occur. For example, some 285 nuclear reactor accidents (excluding the Chernobyl accident) were reported in various countries between 1945 and 1987, irradiating more than 1,350 persons, 33 of them fatally (Lushbaugh, Fry and Ricks 1987). The Chernobyl accident alone released enough radioactive material to require the evacuation of tens of thousands of people and farm animals from the surrounding area, and it caused radiation sickness and burns in more than 200 emergency personnel and fire-fighters, injuring 31 fatally (UNSCEAR 1988). The long-term health effects of the radioactive material released cannot be predicted with certainty, but estimates of the resulting risks of carcinogenic effects, based on nonthreshold dose-incidence models (discussed below), imply that up to 30,000 additional cancer deaths may occur in the population of the northern hemisphere during the next 70 years as a result of the accident, although the additional cancers in any

Table 48.3 • Approximate threshold doses of conventionally fractionated therapeutic x-radiation for clinically detrimental non-stochastic effects in various tissues.

Organ	Injury at 5 years	Threshold dose (Gy)*	Irradiation field (area)
Skin	Ulcer, severe fibrosis	55	100 cm²
Oral mucosa	Ulcer, severe fibrosis	60	50 cm²
Oesophagus	Ulcer, stricture	60	75 cm²
Stomach	Ulcer, perforation	45	100 cm²
Small intestine	Ulcer, stricture	45	100 cm²
Colon	Ulcer, stricture	45	100 cm²
Rectum	Ulcer, stricture	55	100 cm²
Salivary glands	Xerostomia	50	50 cm²
Liver	Liver failure, ascites	35	whole
Kidney	Nephrosclerosis	23	whole
Urinary bladder	Ulcer, contracture	60	whole
Testes	Permanent sterility	5-15	whole
Ovary	Permanent sterility	2-3	whole
Uterus	Necrosis, perforation	>100	whole
Vagina	Ulcer, fistula	90	5 cm²
Breast, child	Hypoplasia	10	5 cm²
Breast, adult	Atrophy, necrosis	>50	whole
Lung	Pneumonitis, fibrosis	40	lobe
Capillaries	Telangiectasis, fibrosis	50-60	—
Heart	Pericarditis, pancarditis	40	whole
Bone, child	Arrested growth	20	10 cm²
Bone, adult	Necrosis, fracture	60	10 cm²
Cartilage, child	Arrested growth	10	whole
Cartilage, adult	Necrosis	60	whole
Central nervous system (brain)	Necrosis	50	whole
Spinal cord	Necrosis, transection	50	5 cm²
Eye	Panophthalmitis, haemorrhage	55	whole
Cornea	Keratitis	50	whole
Lens	Cataract	5	whole
Ear (inner)	Deafness	>60	whole
Thyroid	Hypothyroidism	45	whole
Adrenal	Hypoadrenalism	>60	whole
Pituitary	Hypopituitarism	45	whole
Muscle, child	Hypoplasia	20-30	whole
Muscle, adult	Atrophy	>100	whole
Bone marrow	Hypoplasia	2	whole
Bone marrow	Hypoplasia, fibrosis	20	localized
Lymph nodes	Atrophy	33-45	—
Lymphatics	Sclerosis	50	—
Foetus	Death	2	whole

* Dose causing effect in 1-5 per cent of exposed persons.
Source: Rubin and Casarett 1972.

Table 48.4 • Major forms and features of the acute radiation syndrome.

Time after irradiation	Cerebral form (>50 Gy)	Gastro-intestinal form (10-20 Gy)	Hemopoietic form (2-10 Gy)	Pulmonary form (>6 Gy to lungs)
First day	nausea vomiting diarrhea headache disorientation ataxia coma convulsions death	nausea vomiting diarrhea	nausea vomiting diarrhea	nausea vomiting
Second week		nausea vomiting diarrhea fever erythema prostration death		
Third to sixth weeks			weakness fatigue anorexia fever haemorrhage epilation recovery (?) death (?)	
Second to eighth months				cough dyspnoea fever chest pain respiratory failure (?)

Source: UNSCEAR 1988.

given country are likely to be too few to be detectable epidemiologically (USDOE 1987).

Less catastrophic, but far more numerous, than reactor accidents have been accidents involving medical and industrial gamma ray sources, which also have caused injuries and loss of life. For example, the improper disposal of a caesium-137 radiotherapy source in Goiânia, Brazil, in 1987, resulted in the irradiation of dozens of unsuspecting victims, four of them fatally (UNSCEAR 1993).

A comprehensive discussion of radiation injuries is beyond the scope of this review, but acute reactions of the more radiosensitive tissues are of widespread interest and are, therefore, described briefly in the following sections.

Skin. Cells in the germinal layer of the epidermis are highly radiosensitive. As a result, rapid exposure of the skin to a dose of 6 Sv or more causes erythema (reddening) in the exposed area, which appears within a day or so, typically lasts a few hours, and is followed two to four weeks later by one or more waves of deeper and more prolonged erythema, as well as by epilation (hair loss). If the dose exceeds 10 to 20 Sv, blistering, necrosis and ulceration may ensue within two to four weeks, followed by fibrosis of the underlying dermis and vasculature, which may lead to

atrophy and a second wave of ulceration months or years later (ICRP 1984).

Bone marrow and lymphoid tissue. Lymphocytes also are highly radiosensitive; a dose of 2 to 3 Sv delivered rapidly to the whole body can kill enough of them to depress the peripheral lymphocyte count and impair the immune response within hours (UNSCEAR 1988). Haemopoietic cells in the bone marrow are similarly radiosensitive and are depleted sufficiently by a comparable dose to cause granulocytopenia and thrombocytopenia to ensue within three to five weeks. Such reductions in granulocyte and platelet counts may be severe enough after a larger dose to result in haemorrhage or fatal infection (table 48.4).

Intestine. Stem cells in the epithelium lining the small bowel also are extremely radiosensitive, acute exposure to 10 Sv depleting their numbers sufficiently to cause the overlying intestinal villi to become denuded within days (ICRP 1984; UNSCEAR 1988). Denudation of a large area of the mucosa can result in a fulminating, rapidly fatal dysentery-like syndrome (table 48.4).

Gonads. Mature spermatozoa can survive large doses (100 Sv), but spermatogonia are so radiosensitive that as little as 0.15 Sv delivered rapidly to both testes suffices to cause oligospermia, and a dose of 2 to 4 Sv can cause permanent sterility. Oocytes, likewise, are radiosensitive, a dose of 1.5 to 2.0 Sv delivered rapidly to both ovaries causing temporary sterility, and a larger dose, permanent sterility, depending on the age of the woman at the time of exposure (ICRP 1984).

Respiratory tract. The lung is not highly radiosensitive, but rapid exposure to a dose of 6 to 10 Sv can cause acute pneumonitis to develop in the exposed area within one to three months. If a large volume of lung tissue is affected, the process may result in respiratory failure within weeks, or may lead to pulmonary fibrosis and cor pulmonale months or years later (ICRP 1984; UNSCEAR 1988).

Lens of the eye. Cells of the anterior epithelium of the lens, which continue to divide throughout life, are relatively radiosensitive. As a result, rapid exposure of the lens to a dose exceeding 1 Sv may lead within months to the formation of a microscopic posterior polar opacity; and 2 to 3 Sv received in a single brief exposure—or 5.5 to 14 Sv accumulated over a period of months—may produce a vision-impairing cataract (ICRP 1984).

Other tissues. In comparison with the tissues mentioned above, other tissues of the body are generally appreciably less radiosensitive (for example, table 48.4); however, the embryo constitutes a notable exception, as discussed below. Noteworthy also is the fact that the radiosensitivity of every tissue is increased when it is in a rapidly growing state (ICRP 1984).

Whole-body radiation injury. Rapid exposure of a major part of the body to a dose in excess of 1 Gy can cause the *acute radiation syndrome.* This syndrome includes: (1) an initial prodromal stage, characterized by malaise, anorexia, nausea and vomiting, (2) an ensuing latent period, (3) a second (main) phase of illness and (4) ultimately, either recovery or death (table 48.4). The main phase of the illness typically takes one of the following forms, depending on the predominant locus of radiation injury: (1) haematological, (2) gastro-intestinal, (3) cerebral or (4) pulmonary (table 48.4).

Localized radiation injury. Unlike the clinical manifestations of acute whole-body radiation injury, which typically are dramatic and prompt, the reaction to sharply localized irradiation, whether from an external radiation source or from an internally deposited radionuclide, tends to evolve slowly and to produce few symptoms or signs unless the volume of tissue irradiated and/or the dose are relatively large (for example, table 48.4).

Effects of radionuclides. Some radionuclides—for example, tritium (^{3}H), carbon-14 (^{14}C) and cesium-137 (^{137}Cs)—tend to be distributed systemically and to irradiate the body as a whole, whereas

48. RADIATION, IONIZING

other radionuclides are characteristically taken up and concentrated in specific organs, producing injuries that are correspondingly localized. Radium and strontium-90 (^{90}Sr), for example, are deposited predominantly in bone and thus injure skeletal tissues primarily, whereas radioactive iodine concentrates in the thyroid gland, the primary site of any resulting injury (Stannard 1988: Mettler and Upton 1995).

Carcinogenic Effects

General features. The carcinogenicity of ionizing radiation, first manifested early in this century by the occurrence of skin cancers and leukaemias in pioneer radiation workers (Upton 1986), has since been documented extensively by dose-dependent excesses of many types of neoplasms in radium-dial painters, underground hardrock miners, atomic bomb survivors, radiotherapy patients and experimentally irradiated laboratory animals (Upton 1986; NAS 1990).

The benign and malignant growths induced by irradiation characteristically take years or decades to appear and exhibit no known features by which they can be distinguished from those produced by other causes. With few exceptions, moreover, their induction has been detectable only after relatively large dose equivalents (0.5 Sv), and it has varied with the type of neoplasm as well as the age and sex of those exposed (NAS 1990).

Mechanisms. The molecular mechanisms of radiation carcinogenesis remain to be elucidated in detail, but in laboratory animals and cultured cells the carcinogenic effects of radiation have been observed to include initiating effects, promoting effects, and effects on the progression of neoplasia, depending on the experimental conditions in question (NAS 1990). The effects also appear to involve the activation of oncogenes and/or the inactivation or loss of tumor-suppressor genes in many, if not all, instances. In addition, the carcinogenic effects of radiation resemble those of chemical carcinogens in being similarly modifiable by hormones, nutritional variables and other modifying factors (NAS 1990). It is noteworthy, moreover, that the effects of radiation may be additive, synergistic or mutually antagonistic with those of chemical carcinogens, depending on the specific chemicals and exposure conditions in question (UNSCEAR 1982 and 1986).

Dose-effect relationship. Existing data do not suffice to describe the dose-incidence relationship unambiguously for any type of neoplasm or to define how long after irradiation the risk of the growth may remain elevated in an exposed population. Any risks attributable to low-level irradiation can, therefore, be estimated only by extrapolation, based on models incorporating assumptions about such parameters (NAS 1990). Of various dose-effect models that have been used to estimate the risks of low-level irradiation, the one that has been judged to provide the best fit to the available data is of the form:

$$R(D) = R_0[1 + f(D) \cdot g(b)]$$

where R_0 denotes the age-specific background risk of death from a specific type of cancer, D the radiation dose, $f(D)$ a function of dose that is linear-quadratic for leukaemia and linear for some other types of cancer, and $g(b)$ is a risk function dependent on other parameters, such as sex, age at exposure and time after exposure (NAS 1990).

Non-threshold models of this type have been applied to epidemiological data from the Japanese atomic-bomb survivors and other irradiated populations to derive estimates of the lifetime risks of different forms of radiation-induced cancer (for example, table 48.5). Such estimates must be interpreted with caution, however, in attempting to predict the risks of cancer attributable to small doses or doses that are accumulated over weeks, months or years, since experiments with laboratory animals have shown the carcinogenic potency of x rays and gamma rays to be reduced by

Table 48.5 • Estimated lifetime risks of cancer attributable to 0.1 Sv rapid irradiation.

Type or site of cancer	Excess cancer deaths per 100,000	
	(No.)	(%)*
Stomach	110	18
Lung	85	3
Colon	85	5
Leukaemia (excluding CLL)	50	10
Urinary bladder	30	5
Oesophagus	30	10
Breast	20	1
Liver	15	8
Gonads	10	2
Thyroid	8	8
Osteosarcoma	5	5
Skin	2	2
Remainder	50	1
Total	500	2

* Percentage increase in "background" expectation for a non-irradiated population.
Source: ICRP 1991.

as much as an order of magnitude when the exposure is greatly prolonged. In fact, as has been emphasized elsewhere (NAS 1990), the available data do not exclude the possibility that there may be a threshold in the millisievert (mSv) dose equivalent range, below which radiation may lack carcinogenicity.

It is also noteworthy that the estimates tabulated are based on population averages and are not necessarily applicable to any given individual; that is, susceptibility to certain types of cancer (for example, cancers of the thyroid and breast) is substantially higher in children than in adults, and susceptibility to certain cancers is also increased in association with some hereditary disorders, such as retinoblastoma and the nevoid basal cell carcinoma syndrome (UNSCEAR 1988, 1994; NAS 1990). Such differences in susceptibility notwithstanding, population-based estimates have been proposed for use in compensation cases as a basis for gauging the probability that a cancer arising in a previously irradiated person may have been caused by the exposure in question (NIH 1985).

Low-dose risk assessment. Epidemiological studies to ascertain whether the risks of cancer from low-level exposure to radiation actually vary with dose in the manner predicted by the above estimates have been inconclusive thus far. Populations residing in areas of elevated natural background radiation levels manifest no definitely attributable increases in cancer rates (NAS 1990; UNSCEAR 1994); conversely, a few studies have even suggested an inverse relationship between background radiation levels and cancer rates, which has been interpreted by some observers as evidence for the existence of beneficial (or hormetic) effects of low-level irradiation, in keeping with the adaptive responses of certain cellular systems (UNSCEAR 1994). The inverse relationship is of questionable significance, however, since it has not persisted after controlling for the effects of confounding variables (NAS 1990). Likewise in today's radiation workers—except for certain cohorts of underground hardrock miners (NAS 1994; Lubin, Boice and Edling 1994)—the rates of cancers other than leukaemia are no longer detectably increased (UNSCEAR 1994), thanks to advances in radiation protection; furthermore, the rates of leukaemia in such workers are consistent with the estimates tabulated above (IARC 1994). In summary, therefore, the data available at present are consistent with the estimates tabulated above (table 48.5), which imply that less than 3% of cancers in the general population are attributable to natural background radiation (NAS 1990; IARC 1994), although up to 10% of lung cancers may be attributable to indoor radon (NAS 1990; Lubin, Boice and Edling 1994).

High levels of radioactive fallout from a thermonuclear weapons test at Bikini in 1954 have been observed to cause a dose-dependent increase in the frequency of thyroid cancer in Marshall Islanders who received large doses to the thyroid gland in childhood (Robbins and Adams 1989). Similarly, children living in areas of Belarus and the Ukraine contaminated by radionuclides released from the Chernobyl accident have been reported to show an increased incidence of thyroid cancer (Prisyazhuik, Pjatak and Buzanov 1991; Kasakov, Demidchik and Astakhova 1992), but the findings are at variance with those of the International Chernobyl Project, which found no excess of benign or malignant thyroid nodules in children living in the more heavily contaminated areas around Chernobyl (Mettler, Williamson and Royal 1992). The basis for the discrepancy, and whether the reported excesses may have resulted from heightened surveillance alone, remain to be determined. In this connection, it is noteworthy that children of south-western Utah and Nevada who were exposed to fallout from nuclear weapons tests in Nevada during the 1950s have shown increase in the frequency of any type of thyroid cancer (Kerber et al. 1993), and the prevalence of acute leukaemia appears to have been elevated in such children dying between 1952 and 1957, the period of greatest exposure to fallout (Stevens et al. 1990).

The possibility that excesses of leukaemia among children residing in the vicinity of nuclear plants in the United Kingdom may have been caused by radioactivity released from the plants has also been suggested. The releases, however, are estimated to have increased the total radiation dose to such children by less than 2%, from which it is inferred that other explanations are more likely (Doll, Evans and Darby 1994). An ineffective aetiology for the observed clusters of leukaemia is implied by the existence of comparable excesses of childhood leukaemia at sites in the UK that lack nuclear facilities but otherwise resemble nuclear sites in having similarly experienced large influxes of population in recent times (Kinlen 1988; Doll, Evans and Darby 1994). Another hypothesis—namely, that the leukaemias in question may have been caused by occupational irradiation of the fathers of the affected children—also has been suggested by the results of a case-control study (Gardner et al. 1990), but this hypothesis is generally discounted for reasons that are discussed in the section to follow.

Heritable Effects

Heritable effects of irradiation, although well documented in other organisms, have yet to be observed in humans. For example, intensive study of more than 76,000 children of the Japanese atomic-bomb survivors, carried out over four decades, has failed to disclose any heritable effects of radiation in this population, as measured by untoward pregnancy outcomes, neonatal deaths, malignancies, balanced chromosomal rearrangements, sex-chromosome aneuploidy, alterations of serum or erythrocyte protein phenotypes, changes in sex ratio or disturbances in growth and development (Neel, Schull and Awa 1990). Consequently, estimates of the risks of heritable effects of radiation must rely heavily on extrapolation from findings in the

Table 48.6 • Estimated frequencies of heritable disorders attributable to natural background ionizing irradiation.

Type of disorder	Natural prevalence (per million live births)	Contribution from natural background radiation[1] (per million live births)[2]	
		First generation	Equilibrium generations[3]
Autosomal dominant	180,000	20-100	300
X-linked	400	<1	<15
Recessive	2,500	<1	very slow increase
Chromosomal	4,400	<20	very slow increase
Congenital defects	20,000-30,000	30	30–300
Other disorders of complex aetiology:			
Heart disease	600,000	not estimated[4]	not estimated[4]
Cancer	300,000	not estimated[4]	not estimated[4]
Selected others	300,000	not estimated[4]	not estimated[4]

[1] Equivalent to ≈1 mSv per year, or ≈30 mSv per generation (30 years).
[2] Values rounded.
[3] After hundreds of generations, the addition of unfavorable radiation-induced mutations eventually becomes balanced by their loss from the population, resulting in a genetic "equilibrium."
[4] Quantitative risk estimates are lacking because of uncertainty about the mutational component of the disease(s) indicated.
Source: National Research Council 1990.

laboratory mouse and other experimental animals (NAS 1990; UNSCEAR 1993).

From the available experimental and epidemiological data, it is inferred that the dose required to double the rate of heritable mutations in human germ cells must be at least 1.0 Sv (NAS 1990; UNSCEAR 1993). On this basis, it is estimated that less than 1% of all genetically determined diseases in the human population can be attributed to natural background irradiation (table 48.6).

The hypothesis that the excess of leukaemia and non-Hodgkin's lymphoma in young people residing in the village of Seascale resulted from heritable oncogenic effects caused by the occupational irradiation of the children's fathers at the Sellafield nuclear installation has been suggested by the results of a case-control study (Gardner et al. 1990), as noted above. Arguments against this hypothesis, however, are:

1. the lack of any comparable excess in larger numbers of children born outside Seascale to fathers who had received similar, or even larger, occupational doses at the same nuclear plant (Wakeford et al. 1994a)
2. the lack of similar excesses in French (Hill and LaPlanche 1990), Canadian (McLaughlin et al. 1993) or Scottish (Kinlen, Clarke and Balkwill 1993) children born to fathers with comparable occupational exposures
3. the lack of excesses in the children of atomic-bomb survivors (Yoshimoto et al. 1990)
4. the lack of excesses in US counties containing nuclear plants (Jablon, Hrubec and Boice 1991)

5. the fact that the frequency of radiation-induced mutations implied by the interpretation is far higher than established rates (Wakeford et al. 1994b).

On balance, therefore, the available data fail to support the paternal gonadal irradiation hypothesis (Doll, Evans and Darby 1994; Little, Charles and Wakeford 1995).

Effects of Prenatal Irradiation

Radiosensitivity is relatively high throughout prenatal life, but the effects of a given dose vary markedly, depending on the developmental stage of the embryo or foetus at the time of exposure (UNSCEAR 1986). During the pre-implantation period,

Table 48.7 • Major developmental abnormalities produced by prenatal irradiation.

Brain		
Anencephaly	Porencephaly	Microcephaly*
Encephalocoele	Mongolism*	Reduced medulla
Cerebral atrophy	Mental retardation*	Neuroblastoma
Narrow aqueduct	Hydrocephalus*	Dilatation of ventricles*
Spinal cord anomalies*	Cranial nerve anomalies	
Eyes		
Anophthalmia	Microphthalmia*	Microcornia*
Coloboma*	Deformed iris	Absence of lens
Absence of retina	Open eyelids	Strabismus*
Nystagmus*	Retinoblastoma	Hypermetropia
Glaucoma	Cataract*	Blindness
Chorioretinitis*	Partial albinism	Ankyloblepharon
Skeleton		
General stunting	Reduced size of skull	Skull deformities*
Head ossification defects*	Vaulted cranium	Narrow head
Cranial blisters	Cleft palate*	Funnel chest
Dislocation of hip	Spina bifida	Deformed tail
Deformed feet	Club foot*	Digital anomalies*
Calcaneo valgus	Odontogenesis imperfecta*	Tibial exostosis
Amelanogenesis*	Scleratomal necrosis	
Miscellaneous		
Situs inversus	Hydronephrosis	Hydroureter
Hydrocoele	Absence of kidney	Gonadal anomalies*
Congenital heart disease	Facial deformities	Pituitary disturbances
Deformities of ears	Motor disturbances	Dermatomal necrosis
Myotomal necrosis	Abnormalities in skin pigmentation	

* These abnormalities have been observed in humans exposed prenatally to large doses of radiation and have, therefore, been tentatively attributed to irradiation.
Source: Brill and Forgotson 1964.

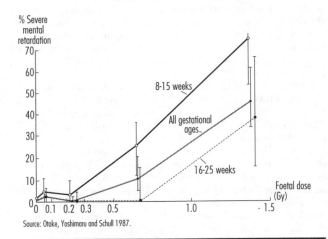

Figure 48.8 • The frequency of severe mental retardation in relation to radiation dose in prenatally irradiated atomic bomb survivors.

Source: Otake, Yoshimaru and Schull 1987.

the embryo is most susceptible to killing by irradiation, while during critical stages in organogenesis it is susceptible to the induction of malformations and other disturbances of development (table 48.7). The latter effects are dramatically exemplified by the dose-dependent increase in the frequency of severe mental retardation (figure 48.8) and the dose-dependent decrease in IQ test scores in atomic-bomb survivors who were exposed between the eighth and fifteenth weeks (and, to a lesser extent, between the sixteenth and twenty-fifth weeks) (UNSCEAR 1986 and 1993).

Susceptibility to the carcinogenic effects of radiation also appears to be relatively high throughout the prenatal period, judging from the association between childhood cancer (including leukaemia) and prenatal exposure to diagnostic x rays reported in case-control studies (NAS 1990). The results of such studies imply that prenatal irradiation may cause a 4,000% per Sv increase in the risk of leukaemia and other childhood cancers (UNSCEAR 1986; NAS 1990), which is a far larger increase than is attributable to postnatal irradiation (UNSCEAR 1988; NAS 1990). Although, paradoxically, no excess of childhood cancer was recorded in A-bomb survivors irradiated prenatally (Yoshimoto et al. 1990), as noted above, there were too few such survivors to exclude an excess of the magnitude in question.

Summary and Conclusions

The adverse effects of ionizing radiation on human health are widely diverse, ranging from rapidly fatal injuries to cancers, birth defects, and hereditary disorders that appear months, years or decades later. The nature, frequency and severity of effects depend on the quality of the radiation in question as well as on the dose and conditions of exposure. Most such effects require relatively high levels of exposure and are, therefore, encountered only in accident victims, radiotherapy patients, or other heavily irradiated persons. The genotoxic and carcinogenic effects of ionizing radiation, by contrast, are presumed to increase in frequency as linear non-threshold functions of the dose; hence, although the existence of thresholds for these effects cannot be excluded, their frequency is assumed to increase with any level of exposure. For most effects of radiation, the sensitivity of exposed cells varies with their rate of proliferation and inversely with their degree of differentiation, the embryo and growing child being especially vulnerable to injury.

SOURCES OF IONIZING RADIATION

Robert N. Cherry, Jr.

Ionizing Radiation Types

Alpha particles

An alpha particle is a tightly bound collection of two protons and two neutrons. It is identical to a helium-4 (^{4}He) nucleus. Indeed, its ultimate fate after it loses most of its kinetic energy is to capture two electrons and become a helium atom.

Alpha-emitting radionuclides are generally relatively massive nuclei. Almost all alpha emitters have atomic numbers greater than or equal to that of lead (^{82}Pb). When a nucleus decays by emitting an alpha particle, both its atomic number (number of protons) and its number of neutrons are reduced by two and its atomic mass number is reduced by four. For example, the alpha decay of uranium-238 (^{238}U) to thorium-234 (^{234}Th) is represented by:

$$^{238}_{92}U_{126} \rightarrow {}^{234}_{90}Th_{124} + \alpha$$

$$\alpha = {}^{4}_{2}He_2$$

The left superscript is the atomic mass number (number of protons plus neutrons), the left subscript is the atomic number (number of protons), and the right subscript is the number of neutrons.

Common alpha emitters emit alpha particles with kinetic energies between about 4 and 5.5 MeV. Such alpha particles have a range in air of no more than about 5 cm (see figure 48.9). Alpha particles with an energy of at least 7.5 MeV are required to penetrate the epidermis (the protective layer of skin, 0.07 mm thick). Alpha emitters generally do not pose an external radiation hazard. They are hazardous only if taken within the body. Because they deposit their energy in a short distance, alpha particles are high linear energy transfer (LET) radiation and have a large radiation weighting factor; typically, $w_R = 20$.

Beta particles

A beta particle is a highly energetic electron or positron. (A positron is the anti-particle of the electron. It has the same mass and most other properties of an electron except for its charge, which is exactly the same magnitude as that of an electron but is positive.) Beta-emitting radionuclides can be of high or low atomic weight.

Radionuclides that have an excess of protons in comparison with stable nuclides of about the same atomic mass number can decay when a proton in the nucleus converts to a neutron. When this occurs, the nucleus emits a positron and an extremely light, very non-interacting particle called a neutrino. (The neutrino and its anti-particle are of no interest in radiation protection.) When it has given up most of its kinetic energy, the positron ultimately collides with an electron and both are annihilated. The annihilation radiation produced is almost always two 0.511 keV (kiloelectron volt) photons travelling in directions 180 degrees apart. A typical positron decay is represented by:

$$^{22}_{11}Na_{11} \rightarrow {}^{22}_{10}Ne_{12} + \beta^+ + \nu$$

where the positron is represented by β^+ and the neutrino by ν. Note that the resulting nuclide has the same atomic mass number as the parent nuclide and an atomic (proton) number larger by one and a neutron number lesser by one than those of the original nuclide.

Electron capture competes with positron decay. In electron capture decay, the nucleus absorbs an orbital electron and emits a neutrino. A typical electron capture decay is given by:

$$^{57}_{27}Co_{30} + {}^{0}_{-1}e_0 \rightarrow {}^{57}_{26}Fe_{31} + \nu$$

Electron capture is always possible when the resulting nucleus has a lower total energy than the initial nucleus. However, positron decay requires that the total energy of the initial *atom* is greater than that of the resulting *atom* by more than 1.02 MeV (twice the rest mass energy of the positron).

Similar to positron and electron capture decay, negatron (β^-) decay occurs for nuclei that have an excess of neutrons compared to stable nuclei of about the same atomic mass number. In this case, the nucleus emits a negatron (energetic electron) and an anti-neutrino. A typical negatron decay is represented by:

$$^{60}_{27}Co_{33} \rightarrow {}^{60}_{28}Ni_{32} + \beta^- + \bar{\nu}$$

where the negatron is represented by β^- and the anti-neutrino by $\bar{\nu}$. Here the resulting nucleus gains one neutron at the expense of one proton but again does not change its atomic mass number.

Alpha decay is a two-body reaction, so alpha particles are emitted with discrete kinetic energies. However, beta decay is a three-body reaction, so beta particles are emitted over a spectrum of energies. The maximum energy in the spectrum depends on the decaying radionuclide. The average beta energy in the spectrum is approximately one-third of the maximum energy (see figure 48.10).

Typical maximum beta energies range from 18.6 keV for tritium (^{3}H) to 1.71 MeV for phosphorus-32 (^{32}P).

The range of beta particles in air is approximately 3.65 m per MeV of kinetic energy. Beta particles of at least 70 keV energy are

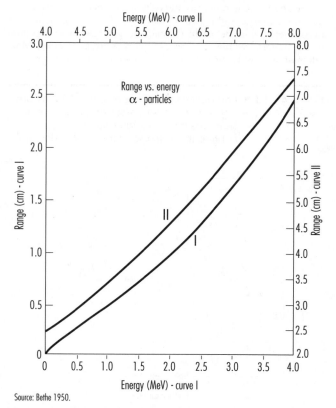

Figure 48.9 • Range-energy relation of slow alpha particles in air at 15 and 760 mm.

Energy (MeV) - curve II

Range vs. energy
α - particles

Range (cm) - curve I

Range (cm) - curve II

Energy (MeV) - curve I

Source: Bethe 1950.

48. RADIATION, IONIZING

Figure 48.10 • Energy spectrum of negatrons emitted from ^{32}P.

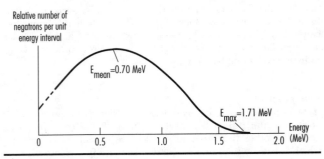

required to penetrate the epidermis. Beta particles are low-LET radiation.

Gamma radiation

Gamma radiation is electromagnetic radiation emitted by a nucleus when it undergoes a transition from a higher to a lower energy state. The number of protons and neutrons in the nucleus does not change in such a transition. The nucleus may have been left in the higher energy state following an earlier alpha or beta decay. That is, gamma rays are often emitted immediately following alpha or beta decays. Gamma rays can also result from neutron capture and inelastic scattering of subatomic particles by nuclei. The most energetic gamma rays have been observed in cosmic rays.

Figure 48.11 is a picture of the decay scheme for cobalt-60 (^{60}Co). It shows a cascade of two gamma rays emitted in nickel-60 (^{60}Ni) with energies of 1.17 MeV and 1.33 MeV following the beta decay of ^{60}Co.

Figure 48.12 is a picture of the decay scheme for molybdenum-99 (^{99}Mo). Note that the resulting technetium-99 (^{99}Tc) nucleus has an excited state that lasts for an exceptionally long time ($t_{1/2} = 6$ h). Such an excited nucleus is called an *isomer*. Most excited nuclear states have half-lives between a few picoseconds (ps) and 1 microsecond (μs).

Figure 48.13 is a picture of the decay scheme for arsenic-74 (^{74}As). It illustrates that some radionuclides decay in more than one way.

Figure 48.12 • Radioactive decay scheme for ^{99}Mo.

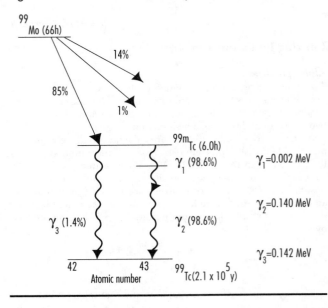

While alpha and beta particles have definite ranges in matter, gamma rays are attenuated exponentially (ignoring build-up that results from scattering within a material) as they pass through matter. When build-up can be ignored the attenuation of gamma rays is given by:

$$I(x) = I(0) \cdot e^{-\mu x}$$

where $I(x)$ is the gamma ray intensity as a function of distance x into the material and μ is the mass attenuation coefficient. The mass attenuation coefficient depends on gamma-ray energy and on the material with which the gamma rays are interacting. Mass attenuation coefficient values are tabulated in many references.

Figure 48.11 • Radioactive decay scheme for ^{60}Co.

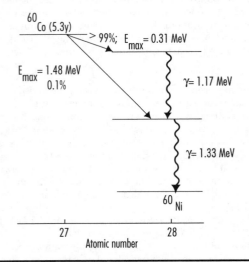

Figure 48.13 • Radioactive decay scheme for ^{74}As, illustrating competing processes of negatron emission, positron emission and electron capture (m_0 is the rest mass of the electron).

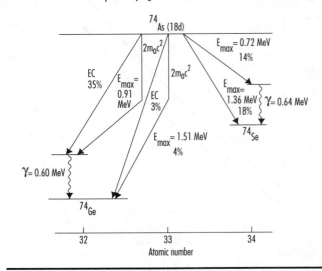

Figure 48.14 • Attenuation of 667 keV gamma rays in Al and Pb under conditions of good geometry (dashed line represents attenuation of a poly-energetic photon beam).

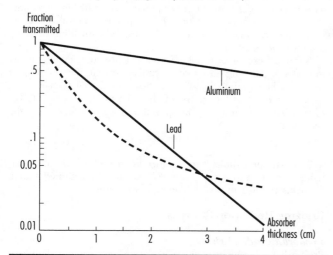

Figure 48.15 • X-ray spectrum illustrating the contribution of characteristic x rays produced as electrons fill holes in the K shell of W (the wavelength of x rays is inversely proportional to their energy).

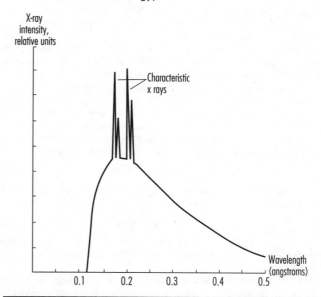

Figure 48.14 shows the absorption of gamma rays in matter in conditions of good geometry (build-up can be ignored).

Build-up occurs when a broad gamma-ray beam interacts with matter. The measured intensity at points within the material is increased relative to the expected "good geometry" (narrow beam) value due to gamma rays scattered from the sides of the direct beam into the measuring device. The degree of build-up depends on the geometry of the beam, on the material and on the energy of the gamma rays.

Internal conversion competes with gamma emission when a nucleus transforms from a higher energy state to a lower one. In internal conversion, an inner orbital electron is ejected from the atom instead of the nucleus emitting a gamma ray. The ejected electron is directly ionizing. As outer orbital electrons drop to lower electronic energy levels to fill the vacancy left by the ejected electron, the atom emits x rays. Internal conversion probability relative to gamma emission probability increases with increasing atomic number.

X rays

X rays are electromagnetic radiation and, as such, are identical to gamma rays. The distinction between x rays and gamma rays is their origin. Whereas gamma rays originate in the atomic nucleus, x rays result from electron interactions. Although x rays often have lower energies than gamma rays, this is not a criterion for differentiating them. It is possible to produce x rays with energies much higher than gamma rays resulting from radioactive decay.

Internal conversion, discussed above, is one method of x ray production. In this case, the resulting x rays have discrete energies equal to the difference in the energy levels between which the orbital electrons transit.

Charged particles emit electromagnetic radiation whenever they are accelerated or decelerated. The amount of radiation emitted is inversely proportional to the fourth power of the particle's mass. As a result, electrons emit much more x radiation than heavier particles such as protons, all other conditions being equal. X-ray systems produce x rays by accelerating electrons across a large electric potential difference of many kV or MV. The electrons are then quickly decelerated in a dense, heat-resistant material, such as tungsten (W).

The x rays emitted from such systems have energies spread over a spectrum ranging from about zero up to the maximum kinetic energy possessed by the electrons before deceleration. Often superimposed on this continuous spectrum are x rays of discrete energy. They are produced when the decelerating electrons ionize the target material. As other orbital electrons move to fill vacancies left after ionization, they emit x rays of discrete energies similar to the way x rays are emitted following internal conversion. They are called *characteristic* x rays because they are characteristic of the target (anode) material. See figure 48.15 for a typical x ray spectrum. Figure 48.16 depicts a typical x ray tube.

X rays interact with matter the same way gamma rays do, but a simple exponential attenuation equation does not adequately describe the attenuation of x rays with a continuous range of energies (see figure 48.14). However, as lower energy x rays are removed more rapidly from the beam than higher energy x rays

Figure 48.16 • A simplified x-ray tube with a stationary anode and a heated filament.

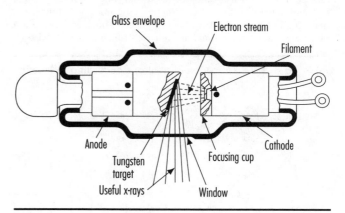

as they pass through material, the description of attenuation approaches an exponential function.

Neutrons

Generally, neutrons are not emitted as a direct result of natural radioactive decay. They are produced during nuclear reactions. Nuclear reactors produce neutrons in the greatest abundance but particle accelerators and special neutron sources, called (α, n) sources, also can yield neutrons.

Nuclear reactors produce neutrons when uranium (U) nuclei in nuclear fuel split, or fission. Indeed, the production of neutrons is essential in maintaining nuclear fission in a reactor.

Particle accelerators produce neutrons by accelerating charged particles, such as protons or electrons, to high energies to bombard stable nuclei in a target. Neutrons are only one of the particles that can result from such nuclear reactions. For example, the following reaction produces neutrons in a cyclotron that is accelerating deuterium ions to bombard a beryllium target:

$$_4^9\text{Be} + _1^2\text{H} \rightarrow _5^{10}\text{B} + _0^1\text{n}$$

Alpha emitters mixed with beryllium are portable sources of neutrons. These (α, n) sources produce neutrons via the reaction:

$$_4^9\text{Be} + _2^4\alpha \rightarrow _6^{12}\text{C} + _0^1\text{n}$$

The source of the alpha particles can be such isotopes as polonium-210 (^{210}Po), plutonium-239 (^{239}Pu) and americium-241 (^{241}Am).

Neutrons are generally classified according to their energy as illustrated in table 48.8. This classification is somewhat arbitrary and may vary in different contexts.

A number of possible modes of neutron interaction with matter exist, but the two main modes for the purposes of radiation safety are elastic scattering and neutron capture.

Elastic scattering is the means by which higher-energy neutrons are reduced to thermal energies. Higher-energy neutrons interact primarily by elastic scattering and generally do not cause fission or produce radioactive material by neutron capture. It is thermal neutrons that are primarily responsible for the latter types of interaction.

Elastic scattering occurs when a neutron interacts with a nucleus and bounces off with reduced energy. The interacting nucleus takes up the kinetic energy the neutron loses. After being excited in this manner, the nucleus soon gives up this energy as gamma radiation.

When the neutron eventually reaches thermal energies (so-called because the neutron is in thermal equilibrium with its environment), it is easily captured by most nuclei. Neutrons, having no charge, are not repelled by the positively charged nucleus as are protons. When a thermal neutron approaches a nucleus and comes within the range of the strong nuclear force, on the order of a few fm (fm = 10^{-15} metres), the nucleus captures the neutron. The result can then be a radioactive nucleus that emits a photon or other particle or, in the case of fissionable nuclei such as ^{235}U and ^{239}Pu, the capturing nucleus can fission into two smaller nuclei and more neutrons.

The laws of kinematics indicate that neutrons will reach thermal energies more rapidly if the elastic scattering medium includes a large number of light nuclei. A neutron rebounding off a light nucleus loses a much larger percentage of its kinetic energy than when it bounces off of a heavy nucleus. For this reason, water and hydrogenous materials are the best shielding material to slow down neutrons.

A monoenergetic beam of neutrons will attenuate exponentially in material, obeying an equation similar to that given above for photons. The probability of a neutron interacting with a given nucleus is described in terms of the quantity *cross section*. Cross section has units of area. The special unit for cross section is the *barn* (b), defined by:

$$1\,\text{b} = 10^{-24}\,\text{cm}^2$$

It is extremely difficult to produce neutrons without accompanying gamma and x rays. It may be generally assumed that if neutrons are present, so are high energy photons.

Ionizing Radiation Sources

Primordial radionuclides

Primordial radionuclides occur in nature because their half-lives are comparable with the age of the earth. Table 48.9 lists the most important primordial radionuclides.

Uranium and thorium isotopes head a long chain of progeny radioisotopes that, as a result, are also naturally occurring. Figure 48.17, A-C, illustrates the decay chains for ^{232}Th, ^{238}U and ^{235}U, respectively. Because alpha decay is common above atomic mass number 205 and an alpha particle's atomic mass number is 4, there are four distinct decay chains for heavy nuclei. One of these chains (see figure 48.17, D), that for ^{237}Np, does not occur in nature. This is because it does not contain a primordial radionuclide (that is, no radionuclide in this chain has a half-life comparable with the age of the earth).

Note that radon (Rn) isotopes occur in each chain (^{219}Rn, ^{220}Rn and ^{222}Rn). Since Rn is a gas, once Rn is produced, it has a chance of escape to the atmosphere from the matrix in which it was formed. However, the half-life of ^{219}Rn is much too short to allow significant amounts of it to reach a breathing zone. The relatively short half-life of ^{220}Rn usually makes it a lesser health hazard concern than ^{222}Rn.

Not including Rn, primordial radionuclides external to the body deliver on the average about 0.3 mSv annual effective dose to the human population. The actual annual effective dose varies widely and is determined primarily by the concentration of uranium and thorium in the local soil. In some parts of the world where monazite sands are common, the annual effective dose to a member of the population is as high as about 20 mSv. In other places such as on coral atolls and near seashores, the value may be as low as 0.03 mSv (see figure 48.17).

Table 48.8 • Classification of neutrons according to kinetic energy.

Type	Energy range
Slow or thermal	0–0.1 keV
Intermediate	0.1–20 keV
Fast	20 keV–10 MeV
High-energy	>10 MeV

Table 48.9 • Primordial radionuclides.

Radioisotope	Half-life (10^9 Y)	Abundance (%)
^{238}U	4.47	99.3
^{232}Th	14.0	100
^{235}U	0.704	0.720
^{40}K	1.25	0.0117
^{87}Rb	48.9	27.9

Figure 48.17 • Decay series (Z = atomic number; N = atomic mass number).

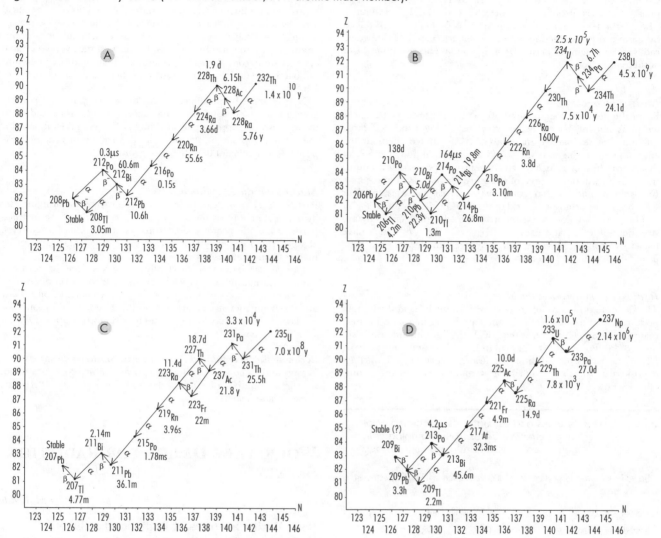

(A): ²³²Th decay series; (B): ²³⁸U decay series; (C): ²³⁵U decay series; (D): ²³⁷Np decay series.

Radon is usually considered separately from other naturally occurring terrestrial radionuclides. It seeps into the air from the soil. Once in the air, Rn further decays to radioactive isotopes of Po, bismuth (Bi) and Pb. These progeny radionuclides attach themselves to dust particles that may be breathed in and trapped in the lungs. Being alpha emitters, they deliver almost all of their radiation energy to the lungs. It is estimated that the average annual lung equivalent dose from such exposure is about 20 mSv. This lung equivalent dose is comparable to a whole body effective dose of about 2 mSv. Clearly, Rn and its progeny radionuclides are the most significant contributors to background radiation effective dose (see figure 48.17).

Cosmic rays

Cosmic radiation includes energetic particles of extraterrestrial origin that strike the atmosphere of the earth (primarily particles and mostly protons). It also includes secondary particles; mostly photons, neutrons and muons, generated by interactions of primary particles with gases in the atmosphere.

By virtue of these interactions, the atmosphere serves as a shield against cosmic radiation, and the thinner this shield, the greater the effective dose rate. Thus, the cosmic-ray effective dose rate increases with altitude. For example, the dose rate at an altitude of 1,800 metres is about double that at sea level.

Because primary cosmic radiation consists mostly of charged particles, it is influenced by the earth's magnetic field. People living in higher latitudes receive greater effective doses of cosmic radiation than those closer to the earth's equator. Variation due to this effect is of the order of 10%.

Finally, the cosmic-ray effective dose rate varies according to modulation of the sun's cosmic-ray output. On the average, cosmic rays contribute about 0.3 mSv to background radiation whole-body effective dose.

Cosmogenic radionuclides

Cosmic rays produce cosmogenic radionuclides in the atmosphere. The most prominent of these are tritium (^{3}H), beryllium-7 (^{7}Be), carbon-14 (^{14}C) and sodium-22 (^{22}Na). They are produced by cosmic rays interacting with atmospheric gases. Cosmogenic radionuclides deliver about 0.01 mSv annual effective dose. Most of this comes from ^{14}C.

Nuclear fallout

From the 1940s through the 1960s, extensive testing of nuclear weapons above ground occurred. This testing produced large quantities of radioactive materials and distributed them to the environment throughout the world as *fallout*. Although much of this debris has since decayed to stable isotopes, small amounts that remain will be a source of exposure for many years to come. In addition, nations that continue to occasionally test nuclear weapons in the atmosphere add to the worldwide inventory.

The primary fallout contributors to effective dose currently are strontium-90 (^{90}Sr) and caesium-137 (^{137}Cs), both of which have half-lives around 30 years. The average annual effective dose from fallout is about 0.05 mSv.

Radioactive material in the body

The deposition of naturally occurring radionuclides in the human body results primarily from the inhalation and ingestion of these materials in air, food and water. Such nuclides include radioisotopes of Pb, Po, Bi, Ra, K (potassium), C, H, U and Th. Of these, ^{40}K is the largest contributor. Naturally occurring radionuclides deposited in the body contribute about 0.3 mSv to the annual effective dose.

Machine-produced radiation

The use of x rays in the healing arts is the largest source of exposure to machine-produced radiation. Millions of medical x ray systems are in use around the world. The average exposure to these medical x ray systems is greatly dependent on a population's access to care. In developed countries, the average annual effective dose from medically prescribed radiation from x rays and radioactive material for diagnosis and therapy is on the order of 1 mSv.

X rays are a by-product of most high-energy physics particle accelerators, especially those that accelerate electrons and positrons. However, appropriate shielding and safety precautions plus the limited population at risk make this source of radiation exposure less significant than the above sources.

Machine-produced radionuclides

Particle accelerators can produce a large variety of radionuclides in varying quantities by way of nuclear reactions. Accelerated particles include protons, deuterons (^{2}H nuclei), alpha particles, charged mesons, heavy ions and so on. Target materials can be made of almost any isotope.

Particle accelerators are virtually the only source for positron-emitting radioisotopes. (Nuclear reactors tend to produce neutron-rich radioisotopes that decay by negatron emission.) They are also being increasingly used to produce short-lived isotopes for medical use, especially for positron-emission tomography (PET).

Technologically enhanced material and consumer products

X rays and radioactive materials appear, wanted and unwanted, in a great number of modern-day operations. Table 48.10 lists these radiation sources.

Table 48.10 • Sources and estimates of associated population effective doses from technologically enhanced material and consumer products.

Group I — Involves large numbers of people and the individual effective dose is very large	
Tobacco products	Combustible fuels
Domestic water supplies	Glass and ceramics
Building materials	Ophthalmic glass
Mining and agricultural products	

Group II — Involves many people but the effective dose is relatively small or is limited to a small portion of the body	
Television receivers	Highway and road construction materials
Radioluminous products	Aircraft transport of radioactive materials
Airport inspection systems	Spark gap irradiators and electron tubes
Gas and aerosol (smoke) detectors	Thorium products — fluorescent lamp starters and gas mantles

Group III — Involves relatively few people and the collective effective dose is small	
Thorium products — tungsten welding rods	

Source: NCRP 1987.

WORKPLACE DESIGN FOR RADIATION SAFETY

Gordon M. Lodde

Basic Design Features of Radiation Facilities

Hazards associated with the handling and use of radiation sources necessitate special features of design and construction that are not required for conventional laboratories or working areas. These special design features are incorporated so that the facility worker is not unduly hampered while ensuring that he or she is not exposed to undue external or internal radiation hazards.

Access to all areas where exposure to radiation sources or radioactive materials could occur must be controlled not only with respect to the facility workers who may be permitted to enter such work areas, but also with respect to the type of clothing or protective equipment that they should wear and the precautions that they should take in controlled areas. In the administration of such control measures, it helps to classify radiation work areas based on the presence of ionizing radiation, on the presence of radioactive contamination or both. The introduction of such work area classification concepts in early planning stages will result in the facility having all the features necessary to make operations with radiation sources less hazardous.

Classification of working areas and laboratory types

The basis for the classification of the work area is the grouping of radionuclides according to their relative radiotoxicities per unit activity. Group I should be classified as very high

Table 48.11 • Radionuclides classified according to relative radiotoxicity per unit activity.

Group I: Very high toxicity

^{210}Pb	^{210}Po	^{223}Ra	^{226}Ra	^{228}Ra	^{227}Ac	^{227}Th	^{228}Th	^{230}Th	^{231}Pa
^{230}U	^{232}U	^{233}U	^{234}U	^{237}Np	^{238}Pu	^{239}Pu	^{240}Pu	^{241}Pu	^{242}Pu
^{241}Am	^{243}Am	^{242}Cm	^{243}Cm	^{244}Cm	^{245}Cm	^{246}Cm	^{249}Cm	^{250}Cf	^{252}Cf

Group II: High toxicity

^{22}Na	^{36}Cl	^{45}Ca	^{46}Sc	^{54}Mn	^{56}Co	^{60}Co	^{89}Sr	^{90}Sr	^{91}Y
^{95}Zr	^{106}Ru	$^{110}Ag^m$	$^{115}Cd^m$	$^{114}In^m$	^{124}Sb	^{125}Sb	$^{127}Te^m$	$^{129}Te^m$	^{124}I
^{126}I	^{131}I	^{133}I	^{134}Cs	^{137}Cs	^{140}Ba	^{144}Ce	^{152}Eu (13 y)	^{154}Eu	^{160}Tb
^{170}Tm	^{181}Hf	^{210}Bi	^{182}Ta	^{192}Ir	^{204}Tl	^{207}Bi	^{230}Pa	^{211}At	^{212}Pb
^{224}Ra	^{228}Ac	^{234}Th	^{236}U	^{249}Bk					

Group III: Moderate toxicity

^{7}Be	^{14}C	^{18}F	^{24}Na	^{38}Cl	^{31}Si	^{32}P	^{35}S	^{41}A	^{42}K
^{43}K	^{47}Sc	^{48}Sc	^{48}V	^{51}Cr	^{52}Mn	^{56}Mn	^{52}Fe	^{55}Fe	^{59}Fe
^{57}Co	^{53}Ni	^{65}Ni	^{64}Cu	^{65}Zn	$^{69}Zn^m$	^{72}Ga	^{73}As	^{74}As	^{76}As
^{77}As	^{82}Br	$^{85}Kr^m$	^{87}Kr	^{86}Rb	^{85}Sr	^{91}Sr	^{90}Y	^{92}Y	^{93}Y
^{97}Zr	^{95}Nb	^{99}Mo	^{96}Tc	$^{97}Tc^m$	^{97}Tc	^{99}Tc	^{97}Ru	^{103}Ru	^{105}Ru
^{105}Rh	^{109}Pd	^{105}Ag	^{111}Ag	^{109}Cd	^{115}Cd	$^{115}In^m$	^{113}Sn	^{125}Sn	^{122}Sb
$^{125}Te^m$	^{129}Te	$^{131}Te^m$	^{132}Te	^{130}I	^{132}I	^{134}I	^{135}I	^{135}Xe	^{131}Cs
^{136}Cs	^{140}La	^{141}Ce	^{143}Ce	^{142}Pr	^{143}Pr	^{147}Nd	^{149}Nd	^{147}Pm	^{149}Pm
^{151}Sm	^{152}Eu (9.2 h)	^{155}Eu	^{153}Gd	^{159}Gd	^{165}Dy	^{166}Dy	^{166}Ho	^{169}Er	^{171}Er
^{171}Tm	^{177}Lu	^{181}W	^{185}W	^{187}W	^{183}Re	^{186}Re	^{188}Re	^{185}Os	^{191}Os
^{193}Os	^{190}Ir	^{195}Ir	^{191}Pt	^{193}Pt	^{197}Pt	^{196}Au	^{198}Au	^{199}Au	^{197}Hg
$^{197}Hg^m$	^{203}Hg	^{200}Tl	^{201}Tl	^{202}Tl	^{203}Pb	^{206}Bi	^{212}Bi	^{220}Rn	^{222}Rn
^{231}Th	^{233}Pa	^{239}Np							

Group IV: Low toxicity

^{3}H	^{15}O	^{37}A	$^{58}Co^m$	^{59}Ni	^{69}Zn	^{71}Ge	^{85}Kr	$^{85}Sr^m$	^{87}Rb
$^{91}Y^m$	^{93}Zr	^{97}Nb	$^{96}Tc^m$	$^{99}Tc^m$	$^{103}Rh^m$	$^{133}In^m$	^{129}I	$^{131}Xe^m$	^{133}Xe
$^{134}Cs^m$	^{135}Cs	^{147}Sm	^{187}Re	$^{191}Os^m$	$^{193}Pt^m$	$^{197}Pt^m$	^{nat}Th	^{232}Th	^{235}U
^{238}U	^{nat}U								

(IAEA 1973)

toxicity radionuclides, Group II as moderate-to-high toxicity radionuclides, Group III as moderate toxicity radionuclides, and Group IV as low toxicity radionuclides. Table 48.11 shows the toxicity group classification of many radionuclides.

Three broad types of laboratories can be envisaged on the basis of radiotoxicity considerations, the amounts or quantities of radioactive materials that will be handled in the work area and the type of operations involved.

Table 48.12 (page 48.18) describes laboratories by type and provides examples for each type. Table 48.13 (page 48.19) shows the types of laboratories along with the work area classification and access control (IAEA 1973).

The hazards involved in working with radioactive material depend not only on the level of radiotoxicity or chemical toxicity and the activity of the radionuclides, but also on the radioactive material's physical and chemical form and on the nature and complexity of the operation or procedure being performed.

Location of a radiation facility in a building

When a radiation facility is part of a large building, the following should be kept in mind when deciding on the location of such a facility:

- The radiation facility should be located in a relatively unfrequented part of the building, so that access to the area can be easily controlled.
- The potential for fires should be minimal in the area chosen.
- The location of the radiation facility and the heating and ventilation provided should be such that possibilities for the spread of both surface and airborne radioactive contamination are minimal.
- The location of the radiation facility should be chosen judiciously, so that with a minimum expenditure for shielding, radiation levels can be effectively maintained within established limits in the immediate vicinity.

Table 48.12 • Classification of working areas.

Type	Definition	Access control	Typical operations
1	Areas in which the external radiation absorbed dose levels or radioactive contamination levels could be high	Access controlled to radiation workers only, under strictly controlled working conditions and with appropriate protective equipment	Hot laboratories, highly contaminated areas
2	Areas in which external radiation levels could exist and in which the possibility of contamination necessitates operating instructions	Access limited to radiation workers with appropriate protective clothing and footwear	Luminizing factories and other equivalent facilities
3	Areas in which the average external radiation level is less than 1 mGy·wk^{-1} and in which the possibility of radioactive contamination necessitates special operating instructions	Access limited to radiation workers, no protective clothing required	Working areas in the immediate vicinity of radiographic operation, for example, control rooms
4	Areas within the confines of a radiation facility where the external radiation levels are less than 0.1 mGy·wk^{-1} and where radioactive contamination is not present	Access uncontrolled	Administration and patient waiting areas

(ICRP 1977, IAEA 1973)

Planning of radiation facilities

Where a gradation of levels of activity is envisioned, the laboratory should be located so that access to areas where high radiation or radioactive contamination levels exist should be gradual; that is, one first enters a non-radiation area, then a low activity area, then a medium activity area and so on.

The need for elaborate control of ventilation in small laboratories can be avoided by the use of hoods or glove boxes for handling unsealed sources of radioactive material. However, the ventilation system should be designed to permit air flow in a direction such that any radioactive material that becomes airborne will flow away from the radiation worker. The air flow should always be from an uncontaminated area toward a contaminated or potentially contaminated area.

For the handling of unsealed sources of low to medium radioactivity, the average air speed through the opening in the hood must be about 0.5 ms^{-1}. For highly radiotoxic or high-level radioactivity, the air velocity through the opening should be raised to an average of 0.6 to 1.0 ms^{-1}. However, excessively high air speeds can draw out radioactive materials from open containers and contaminate the entire hood area.

The placement of the hood in the laboratory is important with respect to cross-drafts. In general, a hood should be located well away from doorways where supply or make-up air must enter. Dual-speed fans will permit operation at a higher air velocity while the hood is in use and a lower velocity when it is closed.

The aim of any ventilating system should be to:

- provide comfortable working conditions
- provide continuous air changes (three to five changes per hour) for the purposes of removing and diluting undesirable air contaminants
- minimize the contamination of other areas of the building and the environment.

In the design of radiation facilities, heavy shielding requirements can be minimized by the adoption of certain simple measures. For example, for radiation therapy, accelerators, neutron generators or panoramic radiation sources, a maze can reduce the need for a heavy lead-lined door. Tapering of the primary protective barrier in areas that are not directly in the useful beam or locating the facility partially or completely underground can significantly reduce the amount of required shielding.

Careful attention must be paid to the proper positioning of viewing windows, underground conduit cables and ventilation system baffles. The viewing window should intercept scattered radiation only. Even better is a closed circuit television, which can also improve efficiency.

Surface finishes within a work area

All raw surfaces, such as plaster, concrete, wood and so on, should be permanently sealed with a suitable material. The choice of material should be made with the following considerations in mind:

- the provision of a smooth, chemically inert surface
- the environmental conditions of temperature, humidity and mechanical wear and tear to which the surfaces may be exposed
- compatibility with radiation fields to which the surface is exposed
- the need for ease of repair in the event of damage.

Ordinary paints, varnishes and lacquers are not recommended for covering wear surfaces. The application of a surfacing material that can be easily removed may be helpful if contamination occurs and decontamination is required. However, the removal of such materials sometimes can be difficult and messy.

Plumbing

Sinks, wash basins and floor drains should be properly marked. Wash basins where contaminated hands may be washed should have knee- or foot-operated faucets. It may be economical to reduce maintenance by using piping which can be easily decontaminated or replaced if required. In some cases it may be advisable to install underground holding or storage tanks to control the disposal of liquid radioactive materials.

Radiation Shielding Design

Shielding is important for reducing radiation exposure of facility workers and members of the general public. Shielding requirements depend on a number of factors, including the time that

Table 48.13 • Classification of laboratories for handling radioactive materials.

Group of radio-nuclides	Type of laboratory required for the activity specified below		
	Type 1	Type 2	Type 3
I	<370 kBq	70 kBq to 37 MBq	>37 MBq
II	<37 MBq	37 MBq to 37 GBq	>37 GBq
III	<37 GBq	37 GBq to 370 GBq	>370 GBq
IV	<370 GBq	370 GBq to 37 TBq	>37 Tbq

Operational factors for laboratory use of radioactive material	Multiplication factors for the activity levels
Simple storage	×100
Simple wet operations (for example, preparation of aliquots of stock solution)	×10
Normal chemical operations (for example, simple chemical preparation and analysis)	×1
Complex wet operations (for example, multiple operations or operations with complex glass ware)	×0.1
Simple dry operations (for example, manipulations of powders of volatile radioactive compounds)	×0.1
Dry and dusty operations (for example, grinding)	×0.01

(ICRP 1977, IAEA 1973)

radiation workers or members of the public are exposed to the radiation sources and the type and energy of the radiation sources and radiation fields.

In the design of radiation shields, the shielding material should be placed near the radiation source if possible. Separate shielding considerations must be made for each type of radiation concerned.

Shielding design can be a complex task. For example, the use of computers to model shielding for accelerators, reactors and other high-level radiation sources is beyond the scope of this article. Qualified experts always should be consulted for complex shielding design.

Gamma source shielding

The attenuation of gamma radiation is qualitatively different from that of either alpha or beta radiation. Both of those types of radiation have a definite range in matter and are completely absorbed. Gamma radiation, on the other hand, can be reduced in intensity by increasingly thicker absorbers but it cannot be completely absorbed. If the attenuation of monoenergetic gamma rays is measured under conditions of good geometry (that is, the radiation is well collimated in a narrow beam) the intensity data, when plotted on a semi-log graph versus absorber thickness, will lie on a straight line with the slope equal to the attenuation coefficient, μ.

The intensity or absorbed dose rate transmitted through an absorber can be calculated as follows:

$$I_{(t)} = I_{(0)}e^{-\mu t}$$

where $I(t)$ is the gamma-ray intensity or absorbed dose rate transmitted through an absorber of thickness t.

The units of μ and t are the reciprocal of each other. If the absorber thickness t is measured in cm, then μ is the linear attenuation coefficient and has units of cm^{-1}. If t has units of areal density (g/cm^2), then μ is the mass attenuation coefficient μ_m and has units of cm^2/g.

As a first-order approximation using areal density, all materials have about the same photon attenuation properties for photons with energies between about 0.75 and 5.0 MeV (mega-electron volts). Within this energy range, gamma shielding properties are approximately proportional to the density of the shielding material. For lower or higher photon energies, absorbers of higher atomic number provide more effective shielding than those of lower atomic number, for a given areal density.

Under conditions of poor geometry (for example, for a broad beam or for a thick shield), the above equation will significantly underestimate the required shield thickness because it assumes that every photon that interacts with the shield will be removed from the beam and not be detected. A significant number of photons may be scattered by the shield into the detector, or photons that had been scattered out of the beam may be scattered back into it after a second interaction.

A shield thickness for conditions of poor geometry may be estimated through the use of the build-up factor B that may be estimated as follows:

$$I_{(t)} = I_{(0)}Be^{-\mu t}$$

The build-up factor is always greater than one, and may be defined as the ratio of the intensity of the photon radiation, including both the primary and scattered radiation, at any point in the beam, to the intensity of the primary beam only at that point. The build-up factor may apply either to radiation flux or to absorbed dose rate.

Build-up factors have been calculated for various photon energies and various absorbers. Many of the graphs or tables give the shield thickness in terms of relaxation lengths. A relaxation length is the thickness of a shield that will attenuate a narrow beam to $1/e$ (about 37%) of its original intensity. One relaxation length, therefore, is numerically equal to the reciprocal of the linear attenuation coefficient (that is, $1/\mu$).

The thickness of an absorber that, when introduced into the primary photon beam, reduces the absorbed dose rate by one-half is called the half-value layer (HVL) or half-value thickness (HVT). The HVL may be calculated as follows:

$$HVL = \frac{\ln 2}{\mu}$$

The required photon shield thickness can be estimated by assuming narrow-beam or good geometry while calculating the required shielding, and then increasing the value thus found by one HVL to account for build-up.

The thickness of an absorber that, when introduced into the primary photon beam, reduces the absorbed dose rate by one-tenth is the tenth-value layer (TVL). One TVL is equal to about 3.32 HVLs, since:

$$\frac{\ln 10}{\ln 2} \approx 3.32$$

Values for both TVLs and HVLs have been tabulated for various photon energies and several common shielding materials (e.g., lead, steel and concrete) (Schaeffer 1973).

The intensity or absorbed dose rate for a point source obeys the inverse square law and may be calculated as follows:

$$\frac{I_1}{I_2} = \left(\frac{d_2}{d_1}\right)^2$$

where I_i is the photon intensity or absorbed dose rate at distance d_i from the source.

Medical and non-medical x-ray equipment shielding

Shielding for x-ray equipment is considered under the two categories, source shielding and structural shielding. Source shielding is usually provided by the manufacturer of the x-ray tube housing.

Safety regulations specify one type of protective tube housing for medical diagnostic x-ray facilities and another type for medical therapeutic x-ray facilities. For non-medical x-ray equipment, the tube housing and other parts of the x-ray apparatus, such as the transformer, are shielded to reduce the leakage x-ray radiation to acceptable levels.

All x-ray machines, both medical and non-medical, have protective tube housings designed to limit the amount of leakage radiation. Leakage radiation, as used in these specifications for tube housings, means all radiation coming from the tube housing except for the useful beam.

Structural shielding for an x-ray facility provides protection from the useful or primary x-ray beam, from leakage radiation and from scatter radiation. It encloses both the x-ray equipment and the object being irradiated.

The amount of scatter radiation depends on the x-ray field size, energy of the useful beam, the effective atomic number of the scattering media and the angle between the incoming useful beam and the direction of scatter.

A key design parameter is the facility workload (W):

$$W = EN_v\mathcal{N}_pk$$

where W is the weekly workload, usually given in mA-min per week; E is the tube current multiplied by the exposure time per view, usually given in mA s; $\mathcal{N}_v$ is the number of views per patient or object irradiated; $\mathcal{N}_p$ is the number of patients or objects per week and k is a conversion factor (1 min divided by 60 s).

Another key design parameter is the use factor U_n for a wall (or floor or ceiling) n. The wall may be protecting any occupied area such as a control room, office or waiting room. The use factor is given by:

$$U_n = \frac{\mathcal{N}_{v,n}}{\mathcal{N}_v}$$

where, $\mathcal{N}_{v,n}$ is the number of views for which the primary x ray beam is directed toward wall n.

The structural shielding requirements for a given x ray facility are determined by the following:

- the maximum tube potential, in kilovolts-peak (kVp), at which the x ray tube is operated
- the maximum beam current, in mA, at which the x ray system is operated
- the workload (W), which is a measure, in suitable units (usually mA-min per week), of the amount of use of the x ray system
- the use factor (U), which is the fraction of the workload during which the useful beam is pointed in the direction of interest
- the occupancy factor (T), which is the factor by which the workload should be multiplied to correct for the degree or type of occupancy of the area to be protected
- the maximum permissible dose equivalent rate (P) to a person for controlled and non-controlled areas (typical absorbed dose

limits are 1 mGy for a controlled area in one week and 0.1 mGy for a non-controlled area in one week)
- type of shielding material (for example, lead or concrete)
- the distance (d) from the source to the location being protected.

With these considerations included, the value of the primary beam ratio or transmission factor K in mGy per mA-min at one metre is given by:

$$K = \frac{Pd^2}{WUT}$$

Shielding of the x-ray facility must be constructed so that protection is not impaired by joints; by openings for ducts, pipes and so on, that pass through the barriers; or by conduits, service boxes and so on, embedded in the barriers. The shielding should cover not only the back of the service boxes, but also the sides, or be extended sufficiently to offer equivalent protection. Conduits that pass through barriers should have sufficient bends to reduce the radiation to the required level. Observation windows must have shielding equivalent to that required for the partition (barrier) or door in which they are located.

Radiation therapy facilities may require door interlocks, warning lights, closed circuit television or means for audible (e.g., voice or buzzer) and visual communication between anyone who may be in the facility and the operator.

Protective barriers are of two types:

1. primary protective barriers, which are sufficient to attenuate the primary (useful) beam to the required level
2. secondary protective barriers, which are sufficient to attenuate leakage, scattered and stray radiation to the required level.

To design the secondary protective barrier, separately calculate the required thickness to protect against each component. If the required thicknesses are about the same, add an additional HVL to the greatest calculated thickness. If the greatest difference between the calculated thicknesses is one TVL or more, the thickest of the calculated values will suffice.

Scattered radiation intensity depends on scattering angle, energy of the useful beam, field size or scattering area, and subject composition.

When designing secondary protective barriers, the following simplifying conservative assumptions are made:

1. When x rays are produced at 500 kV or less, the energy of the scattered radiation is equal to the energy of the useful beam.
2. After being scattered, the x-ray energy spectrum for beams generated at voltages greater than 500 kV are degraded to that of a 500 kV beam, and the absorbed dose rate at 1 m and 90 degrees from the scatterer is 0.1% of that in the useful beam at the point of scattering.

The transmission relationship for scattered radiation is written in terms of the scattering transmission factor ($K_{\mu x}$) with units of mGy·m^2 (mA-min)$^{-1}$:

$$K_{\mu x} = \frac{400\,Pd_{scat}^2 d_{sec}^2}{aWTFf}$$

where P is the maximum weekly absorbed dose rate (in mGy), d_{scat} is the distance from the x ray tube's target and the object (patient), d_{sec} is the distance from the scatterer (object) to the point of interest that the secondary barriers are meant to shield, a is the ratio of scattered radiation to incident radiation, f is the actual scattering field size (in cm^2), and F is a factor accounting for the fact that x ray output increases with voltage. Smaller values of $K_{\mu x}$ require thicker shields.

The leakage attenuation factor B_{LX} for diagnostic x-ray systems is calculated as follows:

$$B_{LX} = \frac{600\,Pd^2I}{WT}\,(diagnostic)$$

where d is the distance from the tube target to the point of interest and I is the tube current in mA.

The barrier attenuation relationship for therapeutic x-ray systems operating at 500 kV or less is given by:

$$B_{LX} = \frac{60\,Pd^2I}{WT}\,(therapeutic\ V \leq 500\ \text{keV})$$

For therapeutic x-ray tubes operating at potentials greater than 500 kV, the leakage is usually limited to 0.1% of the intensity of the useful beam at 1 m. The attenuation factor in this case is:

$$B_{LX} = \frac{1000\,Pd^2}{WT} \cdot \frac{1}{X_n}$$

where X_n is the absorbed dose rate (in mGy/h) at 1 m from a therapeutic x-ray tube operated at a tube current of 1 mA.

The number n of HVLs required to obtain the desired attenuation B_{LX} is obtained from the relationship:

$$B_{LX} = \left(\frac{1}{2}\right)^n$$

or

$$n = -\frac{\ln B_{LX}}{\ln 2}$$

Beta particle shielding

Two factors must be considered when designing a shield for a high-energy beta emitter. They are the beta particles themselves and the *bremsstrahlung* produced by beta particles absorbed in the source and in the shield. *Bremsstrahlung* consists of x-ray photons produced when high-speed charged particles undergo rapid deceleration.

Therefore, a beta shield often consists of a substance of low atomic number (to minimize *bremsstrahlung* production) that is thick enough to stop all the beta particles. This is followed by a material of high atomic number that is thick enough to attenuate *bremsstrahlung* to an acceptable level. (Reversing the order of the shields increases *bremsstrahlung* production in the first shield to a level so high that the second shield may provide inadequate protection.)

For purposes of estimating *bremsstrahlung* hazard, the following relationship may be used:

$$f \approx \frac{6 \times 10^{-4}\,ZE_\beta}{1 + 6 \times 10^{-4}\,ZE_\beta}$$

where f is the fraction of the incident beta energy converted into photons, Z is the atomic number of the absorber, and E_β is the maximum energy of the beta particle spectrum in MeV. To assure adequate protection, it is normally assumed that all *bremsstrahlung* photons are of the maximum energy.

The *bremsstrahlung* flux Φ at a distance d from the beta source can be estimated as follows:

$$\Phi \approx \frac{f\,\overline{E_\beta}}{4\,pd^2E_\beta}$$

$\overline{E_\beta}$ is the average beta particle energy and can be estimated by:

$$\overline{E_\beta} \approx \frac{E_\beta}{3}$$

The range R_β of beta particles in units of areal density (mg/cm^2) may be estimated as follows for beta particles with energies between 0.01 and 2.5 MeV:

$$R_\beta \approx 412 \cdot E_\beta^{\,1.265-0.0954\,\ln E_\beta}$$

where R_β is in mg/cm^2 and E_β is in MeV.

For $E_\beta > 2.5$ MeV, the beta particle range R_β may be estimated as follows:

$$R_\beta \approx 530\,E_\beta - 106$$

where R_β is in mg/cm^2 and E_β is in MeV.

Alpha particle shielding

Alpha particles are the least penetrating type of ionizing radiation. Because of the random nature of its interactions, the range of an individual alpha particle varies between nominal values as indicated in figure 48.18. Range in the case of alpha particles may be expressed in different ways: by minimum, mean, extrapolated, or maximum range. The mean range is the most accurately determinable, corresponds to the range of the "average" alpha particle, and is used most often.

Air is the most commonly used absorbing medium for specifying the range-energy relationship of alpha particles. For alpha energy E_α less than about 4 MeV, R_α in air is approximately given by:

$$R_\alpha \approx 0.56 \cdot E_\alpha$$

where R_α is in cm, E_α in MeV.

For E_α between 4 and 8 MeV, R_α in air is given approximately by:

$$R_\alpha \approx 1.24 \cdot E_\alpha - 2.62$$

where R_α is in cm, E_α in MeV.

The range of alpha particles in any other medium may be estimated from the following relationship:

$$R_\alpha\ (\text{in other medium; mg/cm}^2) \approx 0.56\,A^{1/3}\,R_\alpha\ (\text{in air; cm})$$

where A is the atomic number of the medium.

Neutron shielding

As a general rule of thumb for neutron shielding, neutron energy equilibrium is achieved and then remains constant after one or two relaxation lengths of shielding material. Therefore, for shields thicker than a few relaxation lengths, the dose equivalent outside concrete or iron shielding will be attenuated with relaxation lengths of $120\ \text{g/cm}^2$ or $145\ \text{g/cm}^2$, respectively.

Neutron energy loss by elastic scattering requires a hydrogenous shield to maximize the energy transfer as the neutrons are moderated or slowed down. For neutron energies above 10 MeV, inelastic processes are effective in attenuating neutrons.

Figure 48.18 • Typical range distribution of alpha particles.

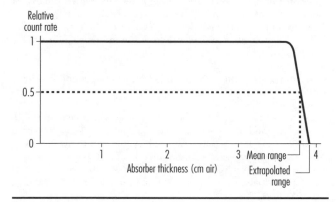

As with nuclear power reactors, high-energy accelerators require heavy shielding to protect workers. Most of the dose equivalents to workers come from exposure to activated radioactive material during maintenance operations. Activation products are produced in the accelerator's components and support systems.

Monitoring of the Workplace Environment

It is necessary to deal separately with the design of routine and of operational monitoring programs for the workplace environment. Special monitoring programs will be designed to achieve specific objectives. It is not desirable to design programs in general terms.

Routine monitoring for external radiation

An important part in the preparation of a program for routine monitoring for external radiation in the workplace is to conduct a comprehensive survey when a new radiation source or a new facility is put into service, or when any substantial changes have been made or may have been made in an existing installation.

The frequency of routine monitoring is determined by consideration of the expected changes in the radiation environment. If changes to the protective equipment or alterations of the processes conducted in the workplace are minimal or non-substantial, then routine radiation monitoring of the workplace is rarely required for review purposes. If the radiation fields are subject to increase rapidly and unpredictably to potentially hazardous levels, then an area radiation monitoring and warning system is required.

Operational monitoring for external radiation

The design of an operational monitoring program depends greatly on whether the operations to be conducted influence the radiation fields or whether the radiation fields will remain substantially constant throughout normal operations. The detailed design of such a survey depends critically on the form of the operation and on the conditions under which it takes place.

Routine monitoring for surface contamination

The conventional method of routine monitoring for surface contamination is to monitor a representative fraction of the surfaces in an area at a frequency dictated by experience. If operations are such that considerable surface contamination is likely and such that workers could carry significant amounts of radioactive material out of the work area in a single event, routine monitoring should be supplemented by the use of portal contamination monitors.

Operational monitoring for surface contamination

One form of operational monitoring is the surveying of items for contamination when they leave a radiologically controlled area. This monitoring must include workers' hands and feet.

The principle objectives of a program of monitoring for surface contamination are:

- to assist in preventing the spread of radioactive contamination
- to detect failures of containment or departures from good operating procedures
- to limit surface contamination to levels at which general standards of good housekeeping are adequate to keep radiation exposures as low as reasonably achievable and to avoid excessive exposures caused by contamination of clothing and skin
- to provide information for the planning of optimized programs for individuals, for air monitoring and for defining operational procedures.

Monitoring for airborne contamination

The monitoring of airborne radioactive materials is important because inhalation is usually the most important route of intake of such material by radiation workers.

The monitoring of the workplace for airborne contamination will be needed on a routine basis in the following circumstances:

- when gaseous or volatile materials are handled in quantity
- when the handling of any radioactive material in such operations results in frequent and substantial contamination of the workplace
- during the processing of moderately to highly toxic radioactive materials
- during the handling of unsealed therapeutic radionuclides in hospitals
- during the use of hot cells, reactors and critical assemblies.

When an air monitoring program is required, it must:

- be able to assess the probable upper limit of the inhalation of radioactive material by radiation workers
- be able to draw attention to unexpected airborne contamination so that radiation workers can be protected and remedial measures instituted
- provide information for planning of programs of individual monitoring for internal contamination.

The most common form of monitoring for airborne contamination is the use of air samplers at a number of selected locations selected to be reasonably representative of the breathing zones of radiation workers. It may be necessary to make samples more accurately represent breathing zones by using personal air or lapel samplers.

Detection and measurement of radiation and radioactive contamination

The monitoring or surveying by wipes and instrument surveys of bench tops, floors, clothing, skin, and other surfaces are at best qualitative procedures. It is difficult to make them highly quantitative. The instruments used are usually detecting types rather than measuring devices. Since the amount of radioactivity involved is often small, the sensitivity of the instruments should be high.

The requirement for portability of contamination detectors depends on their intended uses. If the instrument is for general-purpose monitoring of laboratory surfaces, a portable type of instrument is desirable. If the instrument is for a specific use in which the item to be monitored can be brought to the instrument, then portability is not necessary. Clothing monitors and hand and shoe monitors generally are not portable.

Count-rate instruments and monitors usually incorporate meter readouts and aural outputs or earphone jacks. Table 48.14 identifies instruments that may be used for the detection of radioactive contamination.

Alpha contamination detectors

The sensitivity of an alpha detector is determined by its window area and window thickness. Generally window area is 50 cm^2 or greater with a window areal density of 1 mg/cm^2 or less. Alpha contamination monitors should be insensitive to beta and gamma radiation in order to minimize background interference. This is generally accomplished by pulse height discrimination in the counting circuit.

Portable alpha monitors can be either gas proportional counters or zinc sulphide scintillation counters.

Table 48.14 • Contamination detection instruments.

Instrument	Counting rate range and other characteristics[1]	Typical uses	Remarks
βγ surface monitors[2]			
General			
Portable count rate meter (thin-walled or thin window G-M[3] counter)	0-1,000 cpm 0-10,000 cpm	Surfaces, hands, clothing	Simple, reliable, battery-powered
Thin end-window G-M laboratory monitor	0-1,000 cpm 0-10,000 cpm 0-100,000 cpm	Surfaces, hands, clothing	Line-operated
Personnel			
Hand-and-shoe monitor, G-M or scintillator-type counter	Between 1½ and 2 times natural background	Rapid monitoring for contamination	Automatic operation
Special			
Laundry monitors, floor monitors, doorway monitors, vehicle monitors	Between 1½ and 2 times natural background	Monitoring for contamination	Convenient and rapid
Alpha surface monitors			
General			
Portable air proportional counter with probe	0-100,000 cpm over 100 cm^2	Surfaces, hands, clothing	Not for use in high humidity, battery-powered, fragile window
Portable gas-flow counter with probe	0-100,000 cpm over 100 cm^2	Surfaces, hands, clothing	Battery-powered, fragile window
Portable scintillation counter with probe	0-100,000 cpm over 100 cm^2	Surfaces, hands, clothing	Battery-powered, fragile window
Personal			
Hand-and-shoe proportional counter-type, monitor	0-2,000 cpm over about 300 cm^2	Rapid monitoring of hands and shoes for contamination	Automatic operation
Hand-and-shoe scintillation counter-type, monitor	0-4,000 cpm over about 300 cm^2	Rapid monitoring of hands and shoes for contamination	Rugged
Wound monitors	Low-energy photon detection	Plutonium monitoring	Special design
Air monitors			
Particle samplers			
Filter paper, high-volume	1.1 m^3/min	Quick grab samples	Intermittent use, requires separate counter
Filter paper, low volume	0.2-20 m^3/h	Continuous room air monitoring	Continuous use, requires separate counter
Lapel	0.03 m^3/min	Continuous breathing zone air monitoring	Continuous use, requires separate counter
Electrostatic precipitator	0.09 m^3/min	Continuous monitoring	Sample deposited on cylindrical shell, requires separate counter
Impinger	0.6-1.1 m^3/min	Alpha contamination	Special uses, requires separate counter
Tritium air monitors			
Flow ionization chambers	0-370 kBq/m^3 min	Continuous monitoring	May be sensitive to other ionization sources
Complete air monitoring systems	*Minimum detectable activity*		
Fixed filter paper	$\alpha \gg 0.04$ Bq/m^3; $\beta\gamma \gg 0.04$ Bq/m^3		Background buildup can mask low-level activity, counter included
Moving filter paper	$\alpha \gg 0.04$ Bq/m^3; $\beta\gamma \gg 0.04$ Bq/m^3		Continuous record of air activity, time of measurement can be adjusted from time of collection to any later time.

[1] cpm = counts per minute.
[2] Few surface monitors are suitable for detecting tritium (^{3}H). Wipe tests counted by liquid scintillation devices are appropriate for detecting tritium contamination.
[3] G-M = Geiger-Muller countrate meter.

48. RADIATION, IONIZING

Beta contamination detectors

Portable beta monitors of several types can be used for the detection of beta-particle contamination. Geiger-Mueller (G-M) count-rate meters generally require a thin window (areal density between 1 and 40 mg/cm^2). Scintillation (anthracene or plastic) counters are very sensitive to beta particles and relatively insensitive to photons. Portable beta counters generally cannot be used to monitor for tritium (^{3}H) contamination because tritium beta-particle energy is very low.

All instruments used for beta contamination monitoring also respond to background radiation. This must be taken into account when interpreting instrument readings.

When high background radiation levels exist, portable counters for contamination monitoring are of limited value, since they do not indicate small increases in initially high counting rates. Under these conditions smears or wipe tests are recommended.

Gamma contamination detectors

Since most gamma emitters also emit beta particles, most contamination monitors will detect both beta and gamma radiation. The usual practice is to use a detector that is sensitive to both types of radiation in order to have increased sensitivity, since the detection efficiency is usually greater for beta particles than for gamma rays. Plastic scintillators or sodium iodide (NaI) crystals are more sensitive to photons than are G-M counters, and are therefore recommended for detecting gamma rays.

Air samplers and monitors

Particulates may be sampled by the following methods: sedimentation, filtration, impaction and electrostatic or thermal precipitation. However, particulate contamination in the air is generally monitored by filtration (pumping air through filter media and measuring the radioactivity on the filter). Sampling flow rates generally are greater than 0.03 m^3/min. However, most laboratories' sampling flow rates are no more than 0.3 m^3/min. Specific types of air samplers include "grab" samplers and continuous air monitors (CAM). The CAMs are available with either fixed or moving filter paper. A CAM should include an alarm since its principle function is to warn of changes in airborne contamination.

Because alpha particles have very short range, surface-loading filters (for example, membrane filters) must be used for the measurement of alpha-particle contamination. The sample collected must be thin. The time between collection and measurement must be considered to allow for the decay of radon (Rn) progeny.

Radioiodines such as ^{123}I, ^{125}I and ^{131}I can be detected with filter paper (particularly if the paper is loaded with charcoal or silver nitrate) because some of the iodine will deposit on the filter paper. However, quantitative measurements require activated charcoal or silver zeolite traps or canisters to provide efficient absorption.

Tritiated water and tritium gas are the primary forms of tritium contamination. Although tritiated water has some affinity for most filter papers, filter paper techniques are not very effective for tritiated water sampling. The most sensitive and accurate measurement methods involve the absorption of tritiated water vapour condensate. Tritium in the air (for example, as hydrogen, hydrocarbons or water vapour) can be measured effectively with Kanne chambers (flow-through ionization chambers). Absorption of tritiated water vapour from an air sample can be accomplished by passing the sample through a trap containing a silica-gel molecular sieve or by bubbling the sample through distilled water.

Depending on the operation or process it may be necessary to monitor for radioactive gases. This can be accomplished with Kanne chambers. The most commonly used devices for sampling

by absorption are fretted gas scrubbers and impingers. Many gases may also be collected by cooling the air below the freezing point of the gas and collecting the condensate. This method of collection is most often used for tritium oxide and noble gases.

There are a number of ways to obtain grab samples. The method selected should be appropriate for the gas to be sampled and the required method of analysis or measurement.

Monitoring of effluent

Effluent monitoring refers to the measurement of radioactivity at its point of release to the environment. It is relatively easy to accomplish because of the controlled nature of the sampling location, which is usually in a waste stream that is being discharged through a stack or liquid discharge line.

Continuous monitoring of airborne radioactivity may be necessary. In addition to the sample collection device, usually a filter, a typical sampling arrangement for particulates in air includes an air-moving device, a flowmeter and associated ducting. The air-moving device is located downstream from the sample collector; that is, the air is first passed through the sample collector, then through the remainder of the sampling system. Sampling lines, particularly those ahead of the sample collector system, should be kept as short as possible and free of sharp bends, areas of turbulence, or resistance to the air flow. Constant volume over a suitable range of pressure drops should be used for air sampling. Continuous sampling for radioactive xenon (Xe) or krypton (Kr) isotopes is accomplished by adsorption on activated charcoal or by cryogenic means. The Lucas cell is one of the oldest techniques and still the most popular method for the measurement of Rn concentrations.

Continuous monitoring of liquids and waste lines for radioactive materials is sometimes necessary. Waste lines from hot laboratories, nuclear medicine laboratories and reactor coolant lines are examples. Continuous monitoring can be performed, however, by routine laboratory analysis of a small sample proportional to the effluent flow rate. Samplers that take periodic aliquots or that continuously extract a small amount of liquid are available.

Grab sampling is the usual method used to determine the concentration of radioactive material in a hold-up tank. The sample must be taken after recirculation in order to compare the result of the measurement with allowable discharge rates.

Ideally, results of effluent monitoring and environmental monitoring will be in good agreement, with the latter calculable from the former with the aid of various pathway models. However, it must be recognized and emphasized that effluent monitoring, no matter how good or extensive, cannot substitute for actual measurement of radiological conditions in the environment.

RADIATION SAFETY

Robert N. Cherry, Jr.

This article describes aspects of radiation safety programmes. The objective of radiation safety is to eliminate or minimize harmful effects of ionizing radiation and radioactive material on workers, the public and the environment while allowing their beneficial uses.

Most radiation safety programmes will not have to implement every one of the elements described below. The design of a radiation safety programme depends on the types of ionizing radiation sources involved and how they are used.

Radiation Safety Principles

The International Commission on Radiological Protection (ICRP) has proposed that the following principles should guide the use of ionizing radiation and the application of radiation safety standards:

1. No practice involving exposures to radiation should be adopted unless it produces sufficient benefit to the exposed individuals or to society to offset the radiation detriment it causes (the *justification of a practice*).

2. In relation to any particular source within a practice, the magnitude of individuals doses, the number of people exposed, and the likelihood of incurring exposures where these are not certain to be received should all be kept as low as reasonably achievable (ALARA), economic and social factors being taken into account. This procedure should be constrained by restrictions on the doses to individuals (dose constraints), so as to limit the inequity likely to result from the inherent economic and social judgements (the *optimization of protection*).

3. The exposure of individuals resulting from the combination of all the relevant practices should be subject to dose limits, or to some control of risk in the case of potential exposures. These are aimed at ensuring that no individual is exposed to radiation risks that are judged to be unacceptable from these practices in any normal circumstances. Not all sources are susceptible of control by action at the source and it is necessary to specify the sources to be included as relevant before selecting a dose limit (*individual dose and risk limits*).

Radiation Safety Standards

Standards exist for radiation exposure of workers and the general public and for annual limits on intake (ALI) of radionuclides. Standards for concentrations of radionuclides in air and in water can be derived from the ALIs.

The ICRP has published extensive tabulations of ALIs and derived air and water concentrations. A summary of its recommended dose limits is in table 48.15.

Table 48.15 • Recommended dose limits of the International Commission on Radiological Protection[1].

Application	Dose limit	
	Occupational	Public
Effective dose	20 mSv per year averaged over defined periods of 5 years[2]	1 mSv in a year[3]
Annual equivalent dose in:		
Lens of the eye	150 mSv	15 mSv
Skin[4]	500 mSv	50 mSv
Hands and feet	500 mSv	—

[1] The limits apply to the sum of the relevant doses from external exposure in the specified period and the 50-year committed dose (to age 70 years for children) from intakes in the same period.

[2] With the further provision that the effective dose should not exceed 50 mSv in any single year. Additional restrictions apply to the occupational exposure of pregnant women.

[3] In special circumstances, a higher value of effective dose could be allowed in a single year, provided that the average over 5 years does not exceed 1 mSv per year.

[4] The limitation on the effective dose provides sufficient protection for the skin against stochastic effects. An additional limit is needed for localized exposures in order to prevent deterministic effects.

Dosimetry

Dosimetry is used to indicate dose equivalents that workers receive from *external* radiation fields to which they may be exposed. Dosimeters are characterized by the type of device, the type of radiation they measure and the portion of the body for which the absorbed dose is to be indicated.

Three main types of dosimeters are most commonly employed. They are thermoluminescent dosimeters, film dosimeters and ionization chambers. Other types of dosimeters (not discussed here) include fission foils, track-etch devices and plastic "bubble" dosimeters.

Thermoluminescent dosimeters are the most commonly used type of personnel dosimeter. They take advantage of the principle that when some materials absorb energy from ionizing radiation, they store it such that later it can be recovered in the form of light when the materials are heated. To a high degree, the amount of light released is directly proportional to the energy absorbed from the ionizing radiation and hence to the absorbed dose the material received. This proportionality is valid over a very wide range of ionizing radiation energy and absorbed dose rates.

Special equipment is necessary to process thermoluminescent dosimeters accurately. Reading the thermoluminescent dosimeter destroys the dose information contained in it. However, after appropriate processing, thermoluminescent dosimeters are reusable.

The material used for thermoluminescent dosimeters must be transparent to the light it emits. The most common materials used for thermoluminescent dosimeters are lithium fluoride (LiF) and calcium fluoride (CaF_2). The materials may be doped with other materials or made with a specific isotopic composition for specialized purposes such as neutron dosimetry.

Many dosimeters contain several thermoluminescent chips with different filters in front of them to allow discrimination between energies and types of radiation.

Film was the most popular material for personnel dosimetry before thermoluminescent dosimetry became common. The degree of film darkening depends on the energy absorbed from the ionizing radiation, but the relationship is not linear. Dependence of film response on total absorbed dose, absorbed dose rate and radiation energy is greater than that for thermoluminescent dosimeters and can limit film's range of applicability. However, film has the advantage of providing a permanent record of the absorbed dose to which it was exposed.

Various film formulations and filter arrangements may be used for special purposes, such as neutron dosimetry. As with thermoluminescent dosimeters, special equipment is needed for proper analysis.

Film is generally much more sensitive to ambient humidity and temperature than thermoluminescent materials, and can give falsely high readings under adverse conditions. On the other hand, dose equivalents indicated by thermoluminescent dosimeters may be affected by the shock of dropping them on a hard surface.

Only the largest of organizations operate their own dosimetry services. Most obtain such services from companies specializing in providing them. It is important that such companies be licensed or accredited by appropriate independent authorities so that accurate dosimetry results are assured.

Self-reading, small ionization chambers, also called *pocket chambers*, are used to obtain immediate dosimetry information. Their use is often required when personnel must enter high or very high radiation areas, where personnel could receive a large absorbed dose in a short period of time. Pocket chambers often are calibrated locally, and they are very sensitive to shock. Consequently, they should always be supplemented by thermoluminescent or film dosimeters, which are more accurate and dependable but do not provide immediate results.

Dosimetry is required for a worker when he or she has a reasonable probability of accumulating a certain percentage, usually 5 or 10%, of the maximum permissible dose equivalent for the whole-body or certain parts of the body.

A whole-body dosimeter should be worn somewhere between the shoulders and the waist, at a point where the highest exposure is anticipated. When conditions of exposure warrant, other dosimeters may be worn on fingers or wrists, at the abdomen, on a band or hat at the forehead, or on a collar, to assess localized exposure to extremities, a foetus or embryo, the thyroid or the lenses of the eyes. Refer to appropriate regulatory guidelines about whether dosimeters should be worn inside or outside protective garments such as lead aprons, gloves and collars.

Personnel dosimeters indicate only the radiation to which the *dosimeter* was exposed. Assigning the dosimeter dose equivalent to the person or organs of the person is acceptable for small, trivial doses, but large dosimeter doses, especially those greatly exceeding regulatory standards, should be analysed carefully with respect to dosimeter placement and the actual radiation fields to which the worker was exposed when estimating the dose that the *worker* actually received. A statement should be obtained from the worker as part of the investigation and included in the record. However, much more often than not, very large dosimeter doses are the result of deliberate radiation exposure of the dosimeter while it was not being worn.

Bioassay

Bioassay (also called *radiobioassay*) means the determination of kinds, quantities or concentrations, and, in some cases, the locations of radioactive material in the human body, whether by direct measurement (*in vivo* counting) or by analysis and evaluation of materials excreted or removed from the human body.

Bioassay is usually used to assess worker dose equivalent due to radioactive material taken into the body. It also can provide an indication of the effectiveness of active measures taken to prevent such intake. More rarely it may be used to estimate the dose a worker received from a massive external radiation exposure (for example, by counting white blood cells or chromosomal defects).

Bioassay must be performed when a reasonable possibility exists that a worker may take or has taken into his or her body more than a certain percentage (usually 5 or 10%) of the ALI for a radionuclide. The chemical and physical form of the radionuclide sought in the body determines the type of bioassay necessary to detect it.

Bioassay can consist of analysing samples taken from the body (for example, urine, faeces, blood or hair) for radioactive isotopes. In this case, the amount of radioactivity in the sample can be related to the radioactivity in the person's body and subsequently to the radiation dose that the person's body or certain organs have received or are committed to receive. Urine bioassay for tritium is an example of this type of bioassay.

Whole or partial body scanning can be used to detect radionuclides that emit x or gamma rays of energy reasonably detectable outside the body. Thyroid bioassay for iodine-131 (^{131}I) is an example of this type of bioassay.

Bioassay can be performed in-house or samples or personnel can be sent to a facility or organization that specializes in the bioassay to be performed. In either case, proper calibration of equipment and accreditation of laboratory procedures is essential to ensure accurate, precise, and defensible bioassay results.

Protective Clothing

Protective clothing is supplied by the employer to the worker to reduce the possibility of radioactive contamination of the worker or his or her clothing or to partially shield the worker from beta, x, or gamma radiation. Examples of the former are anti-contamination clothing, gloves, hoods and boots. Examples of the latter are leaded aprons, gloves and eyeglasses.

Respiratory Protection

A respiratory protection device is an apparatus, such as a respirator, used to reduce a worker's intake of airborne radioactive materials.

Employers must use, to the extent practical, process or other engineering controls (for example, containment or ventilation) to limit the concentrations of the radioactive materials in air. When this is not possible for controlling the concentrations of radioactive material in air to values below those that define an airborne radioactivity area, the employer, consistent with maintaining the total effective dose equivalent ALARA, must increase monitoring and limit intakes by one or more of the following means:

- control of access
- limitation of exposure times
- use of respiratory protection equipment
- other controls.

Respiratory protection equipment issued to workers must comply with applicable national standards for such equipment.

The employer must implement and maintain a respiratory protection programme that includes:

- air sampling sufficient to identify the potential hazard, permit proper equipment selection and estimate exposures
- surveys and bioassays, as appropriate, to evaluate actual intakes
- testing of respirators for operability immediately prior to each use
- written procedures regarding selection, fitting, issuance, maintenance and testing of respirators, including testing for operability immediately prior to each use; supervision and training of personnel; monitoring, including air sampling and bioassays; and record-keeping
- determination by a physician prior to the initial fitting of respirators, and periodically at a frequency determined by a physician, that the individual user is medically fit to use the respiratory protection equipment.

The employer must advise each respirator user that the user may leave the work area at any time for relief from respirator use in the event of equipment malfunction, physical or psychological distress, procedural or communication failure, significant deterioration of operating conditions, or any other conditions that might require such relief.

Even though circumstances may not require routine use of respirators, credible emergency conditions may mandate their availability. In such cases, the respirators also must be certified for such use by an appropriate accrediting organization and maintained in a condition ready for use.

Occupational Health Surveillance

Workers exposed to ionizing radiation should receive occupational health services to the same extent as workers exposed to other occupational hazards.

General preplacement examinations assess the overall health of the prospective employee and establish baseline data. Previous medical and exposure history should always be obtained. Specialized examinations, such as of lens of the eye and blood cell counts, may be necessary depending on the nature of the expected radiation exposure. This should be left to the discretion of the attending physician.

Contamination Surveys

A contamination survey is an evaluation of the radiological conditions incident to the production, use, release, disposal or presence of radioactive materials or other sources of radiation. When appropriate, such an evaluation includes a physical survey of the location of radioactive material and measurements or calculations of levels of radiation, or concentrations or quantities of radioactive material present.

Contamination surveys are performed to demonstrate compliance with national regulations and to evaluate the extent of radiation levels, concentrations or quantities of radioactive material, and the potential radiological hazards that could be present.

The frequency of contamination surveys is determined by the degree of potential hazard present. Weekly surveys should be performed in radioactive waste storage areas and in laboratories and clinics where relatively large amounts of unsealed radioactive sources are used. Monthly surveys suffice for laboratories that work with small amounts of radioactive sources, such as laboratories that perform *in vitro* testing using isotopes such as tritium, carbon-14 (^{14}C), and iodine-125 (^{125}I) with activities less than a few kBq.

Radiation safety equipment and survey meters must be appropriate for the types of radioactive material and radiations involved, and must be properly calibrated.

Contamination surveys consist of measurements of ambient radiation levels with a Geiger-Mueller (G-M) counter, ionization chamber or scintillation counter; measurements of possible α or $\beta\gamma$ surface contamination with appropriate thin-window G-M or zinc sulphide (ZnS) scintillation counters; and wipe tests of surfaces to be later counted in a scintillation (sodium iodide (NaI)) well counter, a germanium (Ge) counter or a liquid scintillation counter, as appropriate.

Appropriate action levels must be established for ambient radiation and contamination measurement results. When an action level is exceeded, steps must be taken immediately to mitigate the detected levels, restore them to acceptable conditions and prevent unnecessary personnel exposure to radiation and the uptake and spread of radioactive material.

Environmental Monitoring

Environmental monitoring refers to collecting and measuring environmental samples for radioactive materials and monitoring areas outside the environs of the workplace for radiation levels. Purposes of environmental monitoring include estimating consequences to humans resulting from the release of radionuclides to the biosphere, detecting releases of radioactive material to the environment before they become serious and demonstrating compliance with regulations.

A complete description of environmental monitoring techniques is beyond the scope of this article. However, general principles will be discussed.

Environmental samples must be taken that monitor the most likely pathway for radionuclides from the environment to man. For example, soil, water, grass and milk samples in agricultural regions around a nuclear power plant should be taken routinely and analysed for iodine-131 (^{131}I) and strontium-90 (^{90}Sr) content.

Environmental monitoring can include taking samples of air, ground water, surface water, soil, foliage, fish, milk, game animals and so on. The choices of which samples to take and how often to take them should be based on the purposes of the monitoring, although a small number of random samples may sometimes identify a previously unknown problem.

The first step in designing an environmental monitoring programme is to characterize the radionuclides being released or having the potential for being accidentally released, with respect to type and quantity and physical and chemical form.

The possibility of transport of these radionuclides through the air, ground water and surface water is the next consideration. The objective is to predict the concentrations of radionuclides reaching humans directly through air and water or indirectly through food.

The bioaccumulation of radionuclides resulting from deposition in aquatic and terrestrial environments is the next item of concern. The goal is to predict the concentration of radionuclides once they enter the food chain.

Finally, the rate of human consumption of these potentially contaminated foodstuffs and how this consumption contributes to human radiation dose and resultant health risk are examined. The results of this analysis are used to determine the best approach to environmental sampling and to ensure that the goals of the environmental monitoring programme are met.

Leak Tests of Sealed Sources

A sealed source means radioactive material that is encased in a capsule designed to prevent leakage or escape of the material. Such sources must be tested periodically to verify that the source is not leaking radioactive material.

Each sealed source must be tested for leakage before its first use unless the supplier has provided a certificate indicating that the source was tested within six months (three months for α emitters) before transfer to the present owner. Each sealed source must be tested for leakage at least once every six months (three months for α emitters) or at an interval specified by the regulatory authority.

Generally, leak tests on the following sources are not required:

- sources containing only radioactive material with a half-life of less than 30 days
- sources containing only radioactive material as a gas
- sources containing 4 MBq or less of $\beta\gamma$-emitting material or 0.4 MBq or less of α-emitting material
- sources stored and not being used; however, each such source must be tested for leakage before any use or transfer unless it has been leakage-tested within six months before the date of use or transfer
- seeds of iridium-192 (^{192}Ir) encased in nylon ribbon.

A leak test is performed by taking a wipe sample from the sealed source or from the surfaces of the device in which the sealed source is mounted or stored on which radioactive contamination might be expected to accumulate or by washing the source in a small volume of detergent solution and treating the entire volume as the sample.

The sample should be measured so that the leakage test can detect the presence of at least 200 Bq of radioactive material on the sample.

Sealed radium sources require special leak test procedures to detect leaking radon (Rn) gas. For example, one procedure involves keeping the sealed source in a jar with cotton fibres for at least 24 hours. At the end of the period, the cotton fibres are analysed for the presence of Rn progeny.

A sealed source found to be leaking in excess of allowable limits must be removed from service. If the source is not repairable, it should be handled as radioactive waste. The regulatory authority may require that leaking sources be reported in case the leakage is a result of a manufacturing defect worthy of further investigation.

Inventory

Radiation safety personnel must maintain an up-to-date inventory of all radioactive material and other sources of ionizing radiation for which the employer is responsible. The organization's procedures must ensure that radiation safety personnel are aware of the receipt, use, transfer and disposal of all such material and sources so that the inventory can be kept current. A physical inventory of all sealed sources should be done at least once every three months. The complete inventory of ionizing radiation sources should be verified during the annual audit of the radiation safety programme.

Posting of Areas

Figure 48.19 shows the international standard radiation symbol. This must appear prominently on all signs denoting areas controlled for the purposes of radiation safety and on container labels indicating the presence of radioactive materials.

Areas controlled for the purposes of radiation safety are often designated in terms of increasing dose rate levels. Such areas must be conspicuously posted with a sign or signs bearing the radiation symbol and the words "CAUTION, RADIATION AREA," "CAUTION [or DANGER], HIGH RADIATION AREA," or "GRAVE DANGER, VERY HIGH RADIATION AREA," as appropriate.

1. A radiation area is an area, accessible to personnel, in which radiation levels could result in an individual receiving a dose equivalent in excess of 0.05 mSv in 1 h at 30 cm from the radiation source or from any surface that the radiation penetrates.
2. A high radiation area is an area, accessible to personnel, in which radiation levels could result in an individual receiving a dose equivalent in excess of 1 mSv in 1 h at 30 cm from the radiation source or from any surface that the radiation penetrates.
3. A very high radiation area is an area, accessible to personnel, in which radiation levels could result in an individual receiving an absorbed dose in excess of 5 Gy in 1 h at 1 m from a radiation source or from any surface that the radiation penetrates.

Figure 48.19 • Radiation symbol.

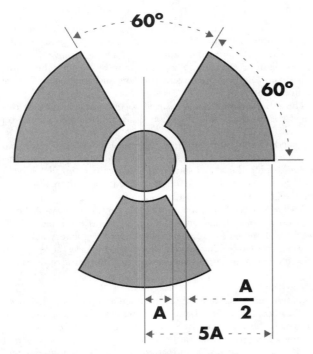

Cross-hatched area is to be magenta or purple. Background is to be yellow.

If an area or room contains a significant amount of radioactive material (as defined by the regulatory authority), the entrance to such area or room must be conspicuously posted with a sign bearing the radiation symbol and the words "CAUTION [or DANGER], RADIOACTIVE MATERIALS".

An airborne radioactivity area is a room or area in which airborne radioactivity exceeds certain levels defined by the regulatory authority. Each airborne radioactivity area must be posted with a conspicuous sign or signs bearing the radiation symbol and the words "CAUTION, AIRBORNE RADIOACTIVITY AREA" or "DANGER, AIRBORNE RADIOACTIVITY AREA".

Exceptions for these posting requirements may be granted for patients' rooms in hospitals where such rooms are otherwise under adequate control. Areas or rooms in which the sources of radiation are to be located for periods of eight hours or less and are otherwise constantly attended under adequate control by qualified personnel need not be posted.

Access Control

The degree to which access to an area must be controlled is determined by the degree of the potential radiation hazard in the area.

Control of access to high radiation areas

Each entrance or access point to a high radiation area must have one or more of the following features:

*   a control device that, upon entry into the area, causes the level of radiation to be reduced below that level at which an individual might receive a dose of 1 mSv in 1 h at 30 cm from the radiation source or from any surface that the radiation penetrates
*   a control device that energizes a conspicuous visible or audible alarm signal so that the individual entering the high radiation area and the supervisor of the activity are made aware of the entry
*   entryways that are locked, except during periods when access to the area is required, with positive control over each individual entry.

In place of the controls required for a high radiation area, continuous direct or electronic surveillance that is capable of preventing unauthorized entry may be substituted.

The controls must be established in a way that does not prevent individuals from leaving the high radiation area.

Control of access to very high radiation areas

In addition to the requirements for a high radiation area, additional measures must be instituted to ensure that an individual is not able to gain unauthorized or inadvertent access to areas in which radiation levels could be encountered at 5 Gy or more in 1 h at 1 m from a radiation source or any surface through which the radiation penetrates.

Markings on Containers and Equipment

Each container of radioactive material above an amount determined by the regulatory authority must bear a durable, clearly visible label bearing the radiation symbol and the words "CAUTION, RADIOACTIVE MATERIAL" or "DANGER, RADIOACTIVE MATERIAL". The label must also provide sufficient information—such as the radionuclide(s) present, an estimate of the quantity of radioactivity, the date for which the activity is estimated, radiation levels, kinds of materials and mass enrichment—to permit individuals handling or using the containers, or working in the vicinity of the containers, to take precautions to avoid or minimize exposures.

Prior to removal or disposal of empty uncontaminated containers to unrestricted areas, the radioactive material label must be removed or defaced, or it must be clearly indicated that the container no longer contains radioactive materials.

Containers need not be labelled if:

1. the containers are attended by an individual who takes the precautions necessary to prevent the exposure of individuals in excess of the regulatory limits
2. containers, when they are in transport, are packaged and labelled in accordance with appropriate transportation regulations
3. containers are accessible only to individuals authorized to handle or use them, or to work in the vicinity of the containers, if the contents are identified to these individuals by a readily available written record (examples of containers of this type are containers in locations such as water-filled canals, storage vaults or hot cells); the record must be retained as long as the containers are in use for the purpose indicated on the record; or
4. the containers are installed in manufacturing or process equipment, such as reactor components, piping and tanks.

Warning Devices and Alarms

High radiation areas and very high radiation areas must be equipped with warning devices and alarms as discussed above. These devices and alarms can be visible or audible or both. Devices and alarms for systems such as particle accelerators should be automatically energized as part of the start-up procedure so that personnel will have time to vacate the area or turn off the system with a "scram" button before radiation is produced. "Scram" buttons (buttons in the controlled area that, when pressed, cause radiation levels to drop immediately to safe levels) must be easily accessible and prominently marked and displayed.

Monitor devices, such as continuous air monitors (CAMs), can be preset to emit audible and visible alarms or to turn off a system when certain action levels are exceeded.

Instrumentation

The employer must make available instrumentation appropriate for the degree and kinds of radiation and radioactive material present in the workplace. This instrumentation may be used to detect, monitor or measure the levels of radiation or radioactivity.

The instrumentation must be calibrated at appropriate intervals using accredited methods and calibration sources. The calibration sources should be as much as possible like the sources to be detected or measured.

Types of instrumentation include hand-held survey instruments, continuous air monitors, hand-and-feet portal monitors, liquid scintillation counters, detectors containing Ge or NaI crystals and so on.

Radioactive Material Transportation

The International Atomic Energy Agency (IAEA) has established regulations for the transportation of radioactive material. Most countries have adopted regulations compatible with IAEA radioactive shipment regulations.

Figures 48.20 through 48.22 are examples of shipping labels that IAEA regulations require on the exterior of packages presented for shipment that contain radioactive materials. The transport index on the labels shown in figures 48.21 and 48.22 refer to the highest effective dose rate at 1 m from any surface of the package in mSv/h multiplied by 100, then rounded up to the nearest tenth. (For example, if the highest effective dose rate at 1 m from any surface of a package is 0.0233 mSv/h, then the transport index is 2.4.)

Figure 48.23 shows an example of a placard that ground vehicles must prominently display when carrying packages containing radioactive materials above certain amounts.

Packaging intended for use in shipping radioactive materials must comply with stringent testing and documentation requirements. The type and quantity of radioactive material being shipped determines what specifications the packaging must meet.

Radioactive material transportation regulations are complicated. Persons who do not routinely ship radioactive materials should always consult experts experienced with such shipments.

Figure 48.20 • Category I—WHITE label.

The label must be diamond-shaped and 10 cm on each side.

Figure 48.21 • Category II—YELLOW label.

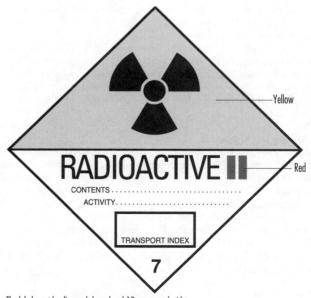

The label must be diamond-shaped and 10 cm on each side.

Figure 48.22 • Category III—YELLOW label.

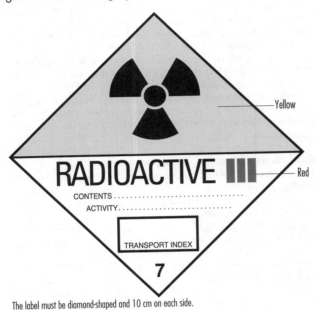

The label must be diamond-shaped and 10 cm on each side.

Figure 48.23 • Vehicle placard.

The overall shape of the placard may be diamond, rectangular or square. The minimum dimension for a side is 15 cm.

Radioactive Waste

Various radioactive waste disposal methods are available, but all are controlled by regulatory authorities. Therefore, an organization must always confer with its regulatory authority to ensure that a disposal method is permissible. Radioactive waste disposal methods include holding the material for radioactive decay and subsequent disposal without regard to radioactivity, incineration, disposal in the sanitary sewerage system, land burial and burial at sea. Burial at sea is often not permitted by national policy or international treaty and will not be discussed further.

Radioactive waste from reactor cores (high-level radioactive waste) presents special problems with regard to disposal. Handling and disposal of such wastes is controlled by national and international regulatory authorities.

Often radioactive waste may have a property other than radioactivity that by itself would make the waste hazardous. Such wastes are called *mixed wastes*. Examples include radioactive waste that is also a biohazard or is toxic. Mixed wastes require special handling. Refer to regulatory authorities for proper disposition of such wastes.

Holding for radioactive decay

If the half-life of the radioactive material is short (generally less than 65 days) and if the organization has enough storage space, the radioactive waste can be held for decay with subsequent disposal without regard to its radioactivity. A holding period of at least ten half-lives usually is sufficient to make radiation levels indistinguishable from background.

The waste must be surveyed before it may be disposed of. The survey should employ instrumentation appropriate for the radiation to be detected and demonstrate that radiation levels are indistinguishable from background.

Incineration

If the regulatory authority allows incineration, then usually it must be demonstrated that such incineration does not cause the con-

centration of radionuclides in air to exceed permissible levels. The ash must be surveyed periodically to verify that it is not radioactive. In some circumstances it may be necessary to monitor the stack to ensure that permissible air concentrations are not being exceeded.

Disposal in the sanitary sewerage system

If the regulatory authority allows such disposal, then usually it must be demonstrated that such disposal does not cause the concentration of radionuclides in water to exceed permissible levels. Material to be disposed of must be soluble or otherwise readily dispersible in water. The regulatory authority often sets specific annual limits to such disposal by radionuclide.

Land burial

Radioactive waste not disposable by any other means will be disposed of by land burial at sites licensed by national or local regulatory authorities. Regulatory authorities control such disposal tightly. Waste generators usually are not allowed to dispose of radioactive waste on their own land. Costs associated with land burial include packaging, shipping and storage expenses. These costs are in addition to the cost of the burial space itself and can often be reduced by compacting the waste. Land burial costs for radioactive waste disposal are rapidly escalating.

Programme Audits

Radiation safety programmes should be audited periodically for effectiveness, completeness and compliance with regulatory authority. The audit should be done at least once a year and be comprehensive. Self-audits are usually permissible but audits by independent outside agencies are desirable. Outside agency audits tend to be more objective and have a more global point of view than local audits. An auditing agency not associated with day-to-day operations of a radiation safety programme often can identify problems not seen by the local operators, who may have become accustomed to overlooking them.

Training

Employers must provide radiation safety training to all workers exposed or potentially exposed to ionizing radiation or radioactive materials. They must provide initial training before a worker begins work and annual refresher training. In addition, each female worker of child-bearing age must be provided special training and information about the effects of ionizing radiation on the unborn child and about appropriate precautions she should take. This special training must be given when she is first employed, at annual refresher training, and if she notifies her employer that she is pregnant.

All individuals working in or frequenting any portion of an area access to which is restricted for the purposes of radiation safety:

- must be kept informed of the storage, transfer or use of radioactive materials or of radiation in such portions of the restricted area
- must be instructed in the health protection problems associated with exposure to such radioactive materials or radiation, in precautions or procedures to minimize exposure, and in the purposes and functions of protective devices employed
- must be instructed in, and instructed to observe, to the extent within the worker's control, the applicable provisions of national and employer regulations for the protection of personnel from exposures to radiation or radioactive materials occurring in such areas
- must be instructed of their responsibility to report promptly to the employer any condition which may lead to or cause a violation of national or employer regulations or unnecessary exposure to radiation or to radioactive material
- must be instructed in the appropriate response to warnings made in the event of any unusual occurrence or malfunction that may involve exposure to radiation or radioactive material
- must be advised as to the radiation exposure reports that workers may request.

The extent of radiation safety instructions must be commensurate with potential radiological health protection problems in the controlled area. Instructions must be extended as appropriate to ancillary personnel, such as nurses who attend radioactive patients in hospitals and fire-fighters and police officers who might respond to emergencies.

Worker Qualifications

Employers must ensure that workers using ionizing radiation are qualified to perform the work for which they are employed. The workers must have the background and experience to perform their jobs safely, particularly with reference to exposure to and use of ionizing radiation and radioactive materials.

Radiation safety personnel must have the appropriate knowledge and qualifications to implement and operate a good radiation safety programme. Their knowledge and qualifications must be at least commensurate with the potential radiological health protection problems that they and the workers are reasonably likely to encounter.

Emergency Planning

All but the smallest operations that use ionizing radiation or radioactive materials must have emergency plans in place. These plans must be kept current and exercised on a periodic basis.

Emergency plans should address all credible emergency situations. The plans for a large nuclear power plant will be much more extensive and involve a much larger area and number of people than the plans for a small radioisotope laboratory.

All hospitals, especially in large metropolitan areas, should have plans for receiving and caring for radioactively contaminated patients. Police and fire-fighting organizations should have

plans for dealing with transportation accidents involving radioactive material.

Record Keeping

The radiation safety activities of an organization must be fully documented and appropriately retained. Such records are essential if the need arises for past radiation exposures or radioactivity releases and for demonstrating compliance with regulatory authority requirements. Consistent, accurate and comprehensive record keeping must receive high priority.

Organizational Considerations

The position of the person primarily responsible for radiation safety must be placed in the organization so that he or she has immediate access to all echelons of workers and management. He or she must have free access to areas to which access is restricted for purposes of radiation safety and the authority to halt unsafe or illegal practices immediately.

PLANNING FOR AND MANAGEMENT OF RADIATION ACCIDENTS

Sydney W. Porter, Jr.

This article describes several significant radiation accidents, their causes and the responses to them. A review of the events leading up to, during and following these accidents can provide planners with information to preclude future occurrences of such accidents and to enhance an appropriate, rapid response in the event a similar accident occurs again.

Acute Radiation Death Resulting from an Accidental Nuclear Critical Excursion on 30 December 1958

This report is noteworthy because it involved the largest accidental dose of radiation received by humans (to date) and because of the extremely professional and thorough work-up of the case. This represents one of the best, if not the best, documented *acute radiation syndrome* descriptions that exists (JOM 1961).

At 4:35 p.m. on 30 December 1958, an accidental critical excursion resulting in fatal radiation injury to an employee (K) took place in the plutonium recovery plant at the Los Alamos National Laboratory (New Mexico, United States).

The time of the accident is important because six other workers had been in the same room with K thirty minutes earlier. The date of the accident is important because the normal flow of fissionable material into the system was interrupted for year-end physical inventory. This interruption caused a routine procedure to become non-routine and led to an accidental "criticality" of the plutonium-rich solids that were accidentally introduced into the system.

Summary of estimates of K's radiation exposure

The best estimate of K's average total-body exposure was between 39 and 49 Gy, of which about 9 Gy was due to fission neutrons. A considerably greater portion of the dose was delivered to the upper half of the body than to the lower half. Table 48.16 (overleaf) shows an estimate of K's radiation exposure.

Clinical course of patient

In retrospect, the clinical course of patient K can be divided into four distinct periods. These periods differed in duration, symptoms and response to supportive therapy.

Table 48.16 • Estimates of K's radiation exposure.

Region and conditions	Fast neutron absorbed dose (Gy)	Gamma absorbed dose (Gy)	Total absorbed dose (Gy)
Head (incident)	26	78	104
Upper abdomen (incident)	30	90	124
Total body (average)	9	30-40	39-49

The first period, lasting from 20 to 30 minutes, was characterized by his immediate physical collapse and mental incapacitation. His condition progressed to semi-consciousness and severe prostration.

The second period lasted about 1.5 hours and began with his arrival by stretcher at the emergency room of the hospital and ended with his transfer from the emergency room to the ward for further supportive therapy. This interval was characterized by such severe cardiovascular shock that death seemed imminent during the whole time. He seemed to be suffering severe abdominal pain.

The third period was about 28 hours long and was characterized by enough subjective improvement to encourage continued attempts to alleviate his anoxia, hypotension and circulatory failure.

The fourth period began with the unheralded onset of rapidly increasing irritability and antagonism, bordering on mania, followed by coma and death in approximately 2 hours. The entire clinical course lasted 35 hours from the time of radiation exposure to death.

The most dramatic clinicopathological changes were observed in the haemopoietic and urinary systems. Lymphocytes were not found in the circulating blood after the eighth hour, and there was virtually complete urinary shutdown despite administration of large amount of fluids.

K's rectal temperature varied between 39.4 and 39.7°C for the first 6 hours and then fell precipitously to normal, where it remained for the duration of his life. This high initial temperature and its maintenance for 6 hours were considered in keeping with his suspected massive dose of radiation. His prognosis was grave.

Of all the various determinations made during the course of the illness, changes in white cell count were found to be the simplest and best prognostic indicator of severe irradiation. The virtual disappearance of lymphocytes from the peripheral circulation within 6 hours of exposure was considered a grave sign.

Sixteen different therapeutic agents were employed in the symptomatic treatment of K over about a 30-hour period. In spite of this and continued oxygen administration, his heart tones became very distant, slow and irregular about 32 hours after irradiation. His heart then became progressively weaker and suddenly stopped 34 hours 45 minutes after irradiation.

Windscale Reactor No. 1 Accident of 9-12 October 1957

Windscale reactor No. 1 was an air-cooled, graphite-moderated natural uranium-fuelled plutonium production reactor. The core was partially ruined by fire on 15 October 1957. This fire resulted in a release of approximately 0.74 PBq (10^{+15} Bq) of iodine-131 (^{131}I) to the downwind environment.

According to a US Atomic Energy Commission accident information report about the Windscale incident, the accident was caused by operator judgement errors concerning thermocouple data and was made worse by faulty handling of the reactor that permitted the graphite temperature to rise too rapidly. Also contributory was the fact that fuel temperature thermocouples were located in the hottest part of the reactor (that is, where the highest dose rates occurred) during normal operations rather than in parts of the reactor which were hottest during an abnormal release. A second equipment deficiency was the reactor power meter, which was calibrated for normal operations and read low during the annealing. As a result of the second heating cycle, the graphite temperature rose on 9 October, especially in the lower front part of the reactor where some cladding had failed because of the earlier rapid temperature rise. Although there were a number of small iodine releases on 9 October, the releases were not recognized until 10 October when the stack activity meter showed a significant increase (which was not regarded as highly significant). Finally, on the afternoon of 10 October, other monitoring (Calder site) indicated the release of radioactivity. Efforts to cool the reactor by forcing air through it not only failed but actually increased the magnitude of the radioactivity released.

The estimated releases from the Windscale accident were 0.74 PBq of ^{131}I, 0.22 PBq of caesium-137 (^{137}Cs), 3.0 TBq (10^{12}Bq) of strontium-89 (^{89}Sr), and 0.33 TBq of strontium-90 (^{90}Sr). The highest offsite gamma absorbed dose rate was about 35 µGy/h due to airborne activity. Air activity readings around the Windscale and Calder plants often were 5 to 10 times the maximum permissible levels, with occasional peaks of 150 times permissible levels. A milk ban extended over a radius of approximately 420 km.

During operations to bring the reactor under control, 14 workers received dose equivalents greater than 30 mSv per calendar quarter, with the maximum dose equivalent at 46 mSv per calendar quarter.

Lessons learned

There were many lessons learned concerning natural uranium reactor design and operation. The inadequacies concerning reactor instrumentation and reactor operator training also bring up points analogous to the Three Mile Island accident (see below).

No guidelines existed for short-term permissible exposure to radioiodine in food. The British Medical Research Council performed a prompt and thorough investigation and analysis. Much ingenuity was used in promptly deriving maximum permissible concentrations for ^{131}I in food. The study Emergency Reference Levels that resulted from this accident serves as a basis for emergency planning guides now used worldwide (Bryant 1969).

A useful correlation was derived for predicting significant radioiodine contamination in milk. It was found that gamma radiation levels in pastures which exceeded 0.3 µGy/h yielded milk which exceeded 3.7 MBq/m³.

Absorbed dose from inhalation of external exposure to radioiodines is negligible compared to that from drinking milk or eating dairy products. In an emergency, rapid gamma spectroscopy is preferable to slower laboratory procedures.

Fifteen two-person teams performed radiation surveys and obtained samples. Twenty persons were used for sample coordination and data reporting. About 150 radiochemists were involved in sampling analysis.

Glass wool stack filters are not satisfactory under accident conditions.

Gulf Oil Accelerator Accident of 4 October 1967

Gulf Oil Company technicians were using a 3 MeV Van de Graaff accelerator for the activation of soil samples on 4 October 1967. The combination of an interlock failure on the power key of the accelerator console and the taping of several of the interlocks on the safety tunnel door and the target room inside door produced serious accidental exposures to three individuals. One individual received approximately 1 Gy whole-body dose equivalent, the second received close to 3 Gy whole-body dose equivalent and the third received approximately 6 Gy whole-body dose equivalent, in addition to approximately 60 Gy to the hands and 30 Gy to the feet.

One of the accident victims reported to the medical department, complaining of nausea, vomiting and generalized muscular aches. His symptoms initially were misdiagnosed as flu symptoms. When the second patient came in with approximately the same symptoms, it was decided that they may possibly have received significant radiation exposures. Film badges verified this. Dr. Niel Wald, University of Pittsburgh Radiological Health Division, supervised the dosimetry tests and also acted as coordinating physician in the work-up and treatment of the patients.

Dr. Wald very quickly had absolute filter units flown in to the western Pennsylvania hospital in Pittsburgh where the three patients had been admitted. He set up these absolute filter/laminar flow filters to clean the patients' environment of all biological contaminants. These "reverse isolation" units were used on the 1 Gy exposure patient for about 16 days, and on the 3 and 6 Gy exposure patients for about a month and half.

Dr. E. Donnal Thomas from the University of Washington arrived to perform a bone marrow transplant on the 6 Gy patient on the eighth day after exposure. The patient's twin brother served as the bone marrow donor. Although this heroic medical treatment saved the 6 Gy patient's life, nothing could be done to save his arms and legs, each of which received tens-of-gray absorbed dose.

Lessons learned

If the simple operating procedure of always using a survey meter when entering the exposure room had been followed, this tragic accident would have been avoided.

At least two interlocks had been taped closed for long periods of time prior to this accident. Defeating of protective interlocks is intolerable.

Regular maintenance checks should have been made on the key-operated power interlocks for the accelerator.

Timely medical attention saved the life of the person with the highest exposure. The heroic procedure of a complete bone marrow transplant together with the use of reverse isolation and quality medical care were all major factors in saving this person's life.

Reverse isolation filters can be obtained in a matter of hours to be set up in any hospital to care for highly exposed patients.

In retrospect, medical authorities involved with these patients would have recommended amputation earlier and at a definitive level within two or three months after the exposure. Earlier amputation decreases the likelihood of infection, gives a shorter period of severe pain, reduces pain medication required for the patient, possibly reduces the patient's hospital stay, and possibly contributes to earlier rehabilitation. Earlier amputation should, of course, be done while correlating dosimetry information with clinical observations.

The SL–1 Prototype Reactor Accident (Idaho, USA, 3 January 1961)

This is the first (and to date the only) fatal accident in the history of US reactor operations. The SL–1 is a prototype of a small Army Package Power Reactor (APPR) designed for air transportation to remote areas for production of electrical power. This reactor was used for fuel testing, and for reactor crew training. It was operated in the remote desert location of the National Reactor Testing Station in Idaho Falls, Idaho, by Combustion Engi-

neering for the US Army. The SL–1 was *not* a commercial power reactor (AEC 1961; American Nuclear Society 1961).

At the time of the accident, the SL–1 was loaded with 40 fuel elements and 5 control rod blades. It could produce a power level of 3 MW (thermal) and was a boiling water–cooled and –moderated reactor.

The accident resulted in the deaths of three military personnel. The accident was caused by the withdrawal of a single control rod for a distance of more than 1 m. This caused the reactor to go into prompt criticality. The reason why a skilled, licensed reactor operator with much refuelling operation experience withdrew the control rod past its normal stop point is unknown.

One of the three accident victims was still alive when initial response personnel first reached the scene of the accident. High activity fission products covered his body and were embedded in his skin. Portions of the victim's skin registered in excess of 4.4 Gy/h at 15 cm and hampered rescue and medical treatment.

Lessons learned

No reactor designed since the SL–1 accident can be brought to "prompt-critical" state with a single control rod.

All reactors must have portable survey meters onsite that have ranges greater than 20 mGy/h. Survey meters of 10 Gy/h maximum range are recommended.

Note: The Three Mile Island accident showed that 100 Gy/h is the required range for both gamma and beta measurements.

Treatment facilities are required where a highly contaminated patient can receive definitive medical treatment with reasonable safeguards for attendant personnel. Since most of these facilities will be in clinics with other ongoing missions, control of airborne and waterborne radioactive contaminants may require special provisions.

X-ray Machines, Industrial and Analytical

Accidental exposures from x-ray systems are numerous and often involve extremely high exposures to small portions of the body. It is not unusual for x-ray diffraction systems to produce absorbed dose rates of 5 Gy/s at 10 cm from the tube focus. At shorter distances, 100 Gy/s rates have often been measured. The beam is usually narrow, but even a few seconds' exposure can result in severe local injury (Lubenau et al. 1967; Lindell 1968; Haynie and Olsher 1981; ANSI 1977).

Because these systems are often used in "non-routine" circumstances, they lend themselves to the production of accidental exposures. X-ray systems commonly used in normal operations appear to be reasonably safe. Equipment failure has not caused severe exposures.

Lessons learned from accidental x-ray exposures

Most accidental exposures occurred during non-routine uses when equipment was partially disassembled or shield covers had been removed.

In most serious exposures, adequate instruction for the staff and maintenance personnel had been lacking.

If simple and fail-safe methods had been used to ensure that x-ray tubes were turned off during repairs and maintenance, many accidental exposures would have been avoided.

Finger or wrist personnel dosimeters should be used for operators and maintenance personnel working with these machines.

If interlocks had been required, many accidental exposures would have been avoided.

Operator error was a contributing cause in most of the accidents. Lack of adequate enclosures or poor shielding design often worsened the situation.

Industrial radiography accidents

From the 1950s through the 1970s, the highest radiation accident rate for a single activity has consistently been for industrial radiographic operations (IAEA 1969, 1977). National regulatory bodies continue to struggle to reduce the rate by a combination of improved regulations, strict training requirements and ever tougher inspection and enforcement policies (USCFR 1990). These regulatory efforts have generally succeeded, but many accidents associated with industrial radiography still occur. Legislation allowing huge monetary fines may be the most effective tool in keeping radiation safety focused in the minds of industrial radiography management (and also, therefore, in workers' minds).

Causes of industrial radiography accidents

Worker training. Industrial radiography probably has lower education and training requirements than any other type of radiation employment. Therefore, existing training requirements must be strictly enforced.

Worker production incentive. For years, major emphasis for industrial radiographers was placed on the amount of successful radiographs produced per day. This practice can lead to unsafe acts as well as to occasional non-use of personnel dosimetry so that exceeding dose equivalent limits would not be detected.

Lack of proper surveys. Thorough surveying of source pigs (storage containers) (figure 48.24) after every exposure is most important. Not performing these surveys is the single most probable cause of unnecessary exposures, many of which are unrecorded, since industrial radiographers rarely use hand or finger dosimeters (figure 48.24).

Equipment problems. Because of heavy use of industrial radiographic cameras, source winding mechanisms can loosen and cause the source to not completely retract into its safe storage position (point A in figure 48.24). There are also many instances of closet-source interlock failures that cause accidental exposures of personnel.

Design of Emergency Plans

Many excellent guidelines, both general and specific, exist for the design of emergency plans. Some references are particularly helpful. These are given in the suggested readings at the end of this chapter.

Figure 48.24 • Industrial radiography camera.

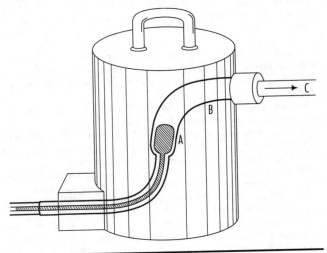

Initial drafting of emergency plan and procedures

First, one must assess the entire radioactive material inventory for the subject facility. Then credible accidents must be analysed so that one can determine the probable maximum source release terms. Next, the plan and its procedures must enable the facility operators to:

1. recognize an accident situation
2. classify the accident according to severity
3. take steps to mitigate the accident
4. make timely notifications
5. call for help efficiently and quickly
6. quantify releases
7. keep track of exposures both on- and offsite, as well as keep emergency exposures ALARA
8. recover the facility as quickly as practical
9. keep accurate and detailed records.

Types of accidents associated with nuclear reactors

A list, from most likely to least likely, of types of accidents associated with nuclear reactors follows. (The non-nuclear reactor, general-industrial type accident is by far the most likely.)

1. Low level unexpected release of radioactive material with little or no external radiation exposure to personnel. Usually occurs during major overhauls or in shipment of spent resin or spent fuel. Coolant system leakage and coolant-sample sink spills are often causes of spread of radioactive contamination.
2. Unexpected external exposure of personnel. This usually occurs during major overhauls or routine maintenance.
3. A combination of contamination spread, contamination of personnel, and low-level personnel external radiation exposure is the next most likely accident. These accidents occur under the same conditions as 1 and 2 above.
4. Gross surface contamination due to a major reactor coolant system leak or a leak of spent fuel coolant.
5. Chips or large particles of activated CRUD (see definition below) in or on skin, ears or eyes.
6. High-level radiation exposure of plant personnel. This is usually caused by carelessness.
7. Release of small but greater than permissible quantities of radioactive wastes to outside the plant boundary. This is usually associated with human failures.
8. Meltdown of reactor. Gross contamination offsite plus high personnel exposure would probably occur.
9. Reactor excursion (SL–1 type of accident).

Radionuclides expected from water-cooled reactor accidents:

- activated corrosion and erosion products (commonly known as *CRUD*) in the coolant; for example, cobalt-60 or -58 (^{60}Co, ^{58}Co), iron-59 (^{59}Fe), manganese-58 (^{58}Mn) and tantalum-183 (^{183}Ta)
- low level fission products usually present in the coolant; for example, iodine-131 (^{131}I) and caesium-137 (^{137}Cs)
- in boiling water reactors, 1 and 2 above plus continuous off-gassing of low levels of tritium (^{3}H) and noble radioactive gases such as xenon-133 and -135 (^{133}Xe, ^{135}Xe), argon-41 (^{41}Ar), and krypton-85 (^{85}Kr)
- tritium (^{3}H) manufactured inside the core at the rate of 1.3×10^{-4} atoms of ^{3}H per fission (only a fraction of this leaves the fuel).

Figure 48.25 • Example of a nuclear power plant emergency plan, table of contents.

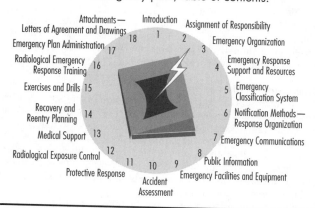

Attachments—Letters of Agreement and Drawings 18
Introduction 1
Assignment of Responsibility 2
Emergency Plan Administration 17
Emergency Organization 3
Radiological Emergency Response Training 16
Emergency Response Support and Resources 4
Exercises and Drills 15
Emergency Classification System 5
Recovery and Reentry Planning 14
Notification Methods—Response Organization 6
Medical Support 13
Emergency Communications 7
Radiological Exposure Control 12
Public Information 8
Protective Response 11
Emergency Facilities and Equipment 9
Accident Assessment 10

Figure 48.26 • Typical power reactor implementation procedures.

1. SENIOR NUCLEAR SHIFT SUPERVISOR/EMERGENCY DUTY OFFICER (SNSS/EDO):
   a. Actions required during an emergency at the unaffected station
   b. Alert—SNSS/EDO
   c. Site area emergency—SNSS/EDO
   d. Protective action recommendations

2. SUPPORT RESPONSE:
   a. Technical support center—integrated engineering team response
   b. Operational support center activation and operation
   c. Technical support center—admin. support/communicator response
   d. Emergency response call-out/personnel recall

3. RADIATION PROTECTION RESPONSE:
   a. Radiation protection technician on-shift response
   b. Technical support center—radiation protection response
   c. Control point—radiation protection/chemistry response
   d. Operational support center—radiation protection response
   e. Stable iodine thyroid blocking
   f. Emergency grab air sampling
   g. Effluent sampling (plant vent/liquid discharge)
   h. Personnel/vehicle survey and decontamination
   i. Dose assessment

Typical Nuclear Power Plant Emergency Plan, Table of Contents

Figure 48.25 is an example of a table of contents for a nuclear power plant emergency plan. Such a plan should include each chapter shown and be tailored to meet local requirements. A list of typical power reactor implementation procedures is given in figure 48.26.

Radiological Environmental Monitoring during Accidents

This task is often called EREMP (Emergency Radiological Environmental Monitoring Programme) at large facilities.

One of the most important lessons learned for the US Nuclear Regulatory Commission and other government agencies from the Three Mile Island accident was that one cannot successfully implement EREMP in one or two days without extensive prior planning. Although the US government spent many millions of dollars monitoring the environment around the Three Mile Island nuclear station during the accident, less then 5% of the total releases were measured. This was due to poor and inadequate prior planning.

Designing Emergency Radiological Environmental Monitoring Programmes

Experience has shown that the only successful EREMP is one that is designed into the routine radiological environmental monitoring programme. During the early days of the Three Mile Island accident, it was learned that an effective EREMP cannot be established successfully in a day or two, no matter how much manpower and money are applied to the programme.

Sampling locations

All routine radiological environmental monitoring programme locations will be used during long-term accident monitoring. In addition, a number of new locations must be set up so that motorized survey teams have pre-determined locations in each portion of each 22½° sector (see figure 48.27). Generally, sampling locations will be in areas with roads. However, exceptions must be made for normally inaccessible but potentially occupied sites such as camp grounds and hiking trails within about 16 km downwind of the accident.

Figure 48.27 • Sector and zone designations for radiological sampling and monitoring points within emergency planning zones.

Sectors N, NNE, NE etc. represent directional sections from the plant in 22½° increments.

Zones ❶ through ❿ represent the distance from plant in 1 mile increments. Zones beyond 10 are in 5 mile increments, called zones 15, 20, 25, etc. through 50.

For example, the area segment in black, between the 7th and 8th miles, in a Northwest direction, from the plant, would be designated NW8.

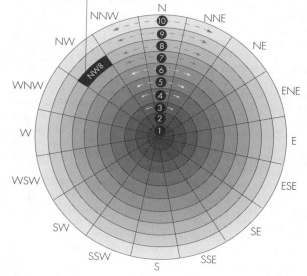

Source: Nuclear Regulatory Commission 1980.

Figure 48.27 shows the sector and zone designation for radiation and environmental monitoring points. One may designate 22½° sectors by cardinal directions (for example, *N*, *NNE*, and *NE*) or by simple letters (for example, *A* through *R*). However, use of letters is not recommended because they are easily confused with directional notation. For example, it is less confusing to use the directional *W* for *west* rather than the letter *N*.

Each designated sample location should be visited during a practice drill so that people responsible for monitoring and sampling will be familiar with the location of each point and will be aware of radio "dead spaces," poor roads, problems with finding the locations in the dark and so on. Since no drill will cover all the pre-designated locations within the 16 km emergency protection zone, drills must be designed so that all sample points will be visited eventually. It is often worthwhile to predetermine the ability of survey team vehicles to communicate with each pre-designated point. The actual locations of the sample points are chosen utilizing the same criteria as in the REMP (NRC 1980); for example, line of site, minimum exclusion area, closest individual, closest community, closest school, hospital, nursing home, milch animal herd, garden, farm and so on.

Radiological monitoring survey team

During an accident involving significant releases of radioactive materials, radiological monitoring teams should be continuously monitoring in the field. They also should continuously monitor onsite if conditions allow. Normally, these teams will monitor for ambient gamma and beta radiation and sample air for the presence of radioactive particulates and halogens.

These teams must be well trained in all monitoring procedures, including monitoring their own exposures, and be able to accurately relay these data to the base station. Details such as survey-meter type, serial number, and open-or closed-window status must be carefully reported on well-designed log sheets.

At the beginning of an emergency, an emergency monitoring team may have to monitor for 12 hours without a break. After the initial period, however, field time for the survey team should be decreased to eight hours with at least one 30 minute break.

Since continuous surveillance may be needed, procedures must be in place to supply the survey teams with food and drink, replacement instruments and batteries, and for back-and-forth transfer of air filters.

Even though survey teams will probably be working 12 hours per shift, three shifts a day are needed to provide continuous surveillance. During the Three Mile Island accident, a minimum of five monitoring teams was deployed at any one time for the first two weeks. The logistics for supporting such an effort must be carefully planned in advance.

Radiological environmental sampling team

The types of environmental samples taken during an accident depend on the type of releases (airborne versus water), direction of the wind and time of year. Soil and drinking water samples must be taken even in winter. Although radio-halogen releases may not be detected, milk samples should be taken because of the large bioaccumulation factor.

Many food and environmental samples must be taken to reassure the public even though technical reasons may not justify the effort. In addition, these data may be invaluable during any subsequent legal proceedings.

Pre-planned log sheets using carefully thought out offsite data procedures are essential for environmental samples. All persons taking environmental samples should have demonstrated a clear understanding of procedures and have documented field training.

If possible, offsite environmental sample data collection should be done by an independent offsite group. It is also preferable that routine environmental samples be taken by the same offsite group, so that the valuable onsite group may be used for other data collection during an accident.

It is notable that during the Three Mile Island accident every single environmental sample that should have been taken was collected, and not one environmental sample was lost. This occurred even though the sampling rate increased by a factor of more than ten over pre-accident sampling rates.

Emergency monitoring equipment

The inventory of emergency monitoring equipment should be at least double that needed at any given time. Lockers should be placed around nuclear complexes in various places so that no one accident will deny access to all of these lockers. To ensure readiness, equipment should be inventoried and its calibration checked at least twice a year and after each drill. Vans and trucks at large nuclear facilities should be completely outfitted for both on and offsite emergency surveillance.

Onsite counting laboratories may be unusable during an emergency. Therefore, prior arrangements must be made for an alternate or a mobile counting laboratory. This is now a requirement for US nuclear power plants (USNRC 1983).

The type and sophistication of environmental monitoring equipment should meet the requirements of attending the nuclear facility's worst credible accident. Following is a list of typical environmental monitoring equipment required for nuclear power plants:

1. Air sampling equipment should include units which are battery operated for short-term sampling and AC operable with strip chart recorders and alarm capabilities for longer-term surveillance.

2. Liquid sampling equipment should contain continuous samplers. The samplers must be operable in the local environment, no matter how harsh it is.

3. Portable gamma survey meters for implant work should have a maximum range of 100 Gy/h, and separate survey equipment should be able to measure beta radiation up to 100 Gy/h.

4. Onsite, personnel dosimetry must include beta measurement capability, as well as finger thermoluminescent dosimeters (TLDs) (figure 48.28). Other extremity dosimetry also may be needed. Extra sets of control dosimeters are always needed in emergencies. A portable TLD reader may be needed to link with the station computer via telephone modem in emergency locations. In-house survey teams, such as rescue and repair teams, should have low- and high-range pocket dosimeters as well as pre-set alarm dosimeters. Careful thought must be given to pre-established dose levels for teams that may be in high radiation areas.

5. Supplies of protective clothing should be supplied in emergency locations and in emergency vehicles. Extra back-up protective clothing should be available in case of accidents lasting for an extended period of time.

6. Respiratory protection equipment should be in all emergency lockers and vehicles. Up-to-date lists of respiratory trained personnel should be kept in each of the major emergency equipment storage areas.

7. Mobile vehicles equipped with radios are essential for emergency radiation monitoring survey teams. The location and availability of back-up vehicles must be known.

8. Environmental survey team equipment should be stored in a convenient place, preferably offsite, so that it is always available.

9. Emergency kits should be placed in the Technical Support Center and the Emergency Offsite Facility so that replace-

Figure 48.28 • An industrial radiographer wearing a TLD badge and a ring thermoluminescent dosimeter (optional in the US).

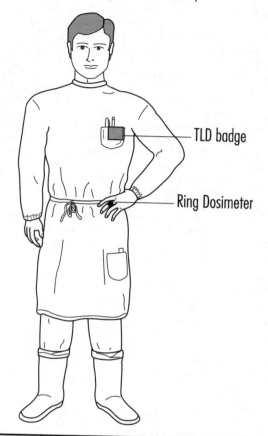

TLD badge

Ring Dosimeter

analysis, report generation, distribution of data to government agencies and power plant owner

- *dose assessment*, including suspected and actual overexposure investigations, skin contamination and internal deposition investigations, significant exposure mock-ups, and dose calculations
- *radiological environmental monitoring programme*, including complete coordination of sample taking, data analysis, report generation and distribution, action-point notifications, expansion of programme for the accident situation and then contraction of the programme for up to one year after the accident
- *special beta dosimetry studies*, including studies of the state of the art in beta personnel monitoring, modelling of the beta dose to skin from radioactive contaminants, inter-comparisons of all commercially available beta-gamma TLD personnel dosimetry systems.

The above list includes examples of activities that the typical utility health physics staff cannot adequately accomplish during a serious accident. The Three Mile Island health physics staff was very experienced, knowledgeable and competent. They worked 15 to 20 hours per day for the first two weeks of the accident without a break. Yet, additional requirements caused by the accident were so numerous that they were unable to perform many important routine tasks that ordinarily would be performed easily.

Lessons learned from the Three Mile Island accident include:

Auxiliary building entry during accident

1. All entries must be on a new radiation work permit reviewed by the senior health physicist onsite and signed by the unit superintendent or designated alternate.
2. The appropriate control room should have absolute control over all Auxiliary and Fuel Handling Building entries. No entries must be allowed unless a health physicist is at the control point during the entry.
3. No entries without a properly operating survey meter of appropriate range should be allowed. A spot check of meter response should be performed immediately prior to entry.
4. Exposure history for all persons prior to their entry into a high radiation area must be obtained.
5. Allowable exposures during entry, no matter how important the task should be designated.

Primary coolant sampling during accident

1. All samples to be taken on a new radiation work permit should be reviewed by the senior health physicist onsite and signed by the unit superintendent or alternate.
2. No coolant samples should be taken unless an extremity dosimeter is worn.
3. No coolant samples should be taken without the availability of shielded gloves and tongs at least 60 cm long in case a sample is more radioactive than expected.
4. No coolant samples should be taken without a leaded-glass personnel shield in place in case a sample is more radioactive than expected.
5. Sample-taking should be discontinued if the exposure to an extremity or to the whole-body is likely to exceed pre-set levels stated on the radiation work permit.
6. Significant exposures should be distributed among a number of workers if possible.
7. All cases of skin contamination in excess of action levels within 24 hours should be reviewed.

Make-up valve room entry

1. Beta and gamma area surveys using remote detectors with appropriate maximum range must be performed.

ment survey teams need not go onsite in order to receive equipment and be deployed.

10. For a severe accident involving the release of radioactive materials into the air, preparations must be in place for the use of helicopters and single-engine airplanes for airborne surveillance.

Data analysis

Environmental data analysis during a serious accident should be shifted as soon as possible to an offsite location such as the Emergency Offsite Facility.

Pre-set guidelines about when environmental sample data are to be reported to management must be established. The method and frequency for transfer of environmental sample data to governmental agencies should be agreed upon early in the accident.

Health Physics and Radiochemistry Lessons Learned from the Three Mile Island Accident

Outside consultants were needed to perform the following activities because plant health physicists were fully occupied by other duties during the early hours of the 28 March 1979 Three Mile Island accident:

- *radioactive effluent release assessment (gaseous and liquid)*, including sample collection, coordination of laboratories for sample counting, quality control of laboratories, data collection, data

2. Initial entry in an area with an absorbed dose rate of more than 20 mGy/h must have prior review to verify that exposure to radiation will be kept as low as reasonably achievable.
3. When water leaks are suspected, possible floor contamination should be detected.
4. A consistent programme for type and placement of personnel dosimetry must be put into operation.
5. With persons entering an area with an absorbed dose rate of more than 20 mGy/h, TLDs must be assessed immediately after exit.
6. It should be verified that all radiation work permit requirements are being carried out prior to entry into an area with an absorbed dose rate of more than 20 mGy/h.
7. Controlled-time entries into hazardous areas must be timed by a health physicist.

Protective actions and offsite environmental surveillance from the local government's perspective

1. Before beginning a sampling protocol, criteria for stopping it should be established.
2. Outside interference should not be allowed.
3. Several confidential telephone lines should be in place. The numbers should be changed after each crisis.
4. The capabilities of aerial measuring systems are better than most people think they are.
5. A tape recorder should be in hand and data recorded regularly.
6. While the acute episode is in progress, the reading of newspapers, watching television and listening to the radio should be abandoned as these activities only add to existing tensions.
7. Food delivery and other comforts such as sleeping facilities should be planned for as it may be impossible to go home for a while.
8. Alternate analytic capabilities should be planned for. Even a small accident can alter laboratory background radiation levels significantly.
9. It should be noted that more energy will be expended in heading off unsound decisions than in dealing with real problems.
10. It should be understood that emergencies cannot be managed from remote locations.
11. It should be noted that protective action recommendations are not amenable to committee vote.
12. All non-essential calls should be put on hold, time-wasters are to be hung up on.

The Goiânia Radiological Accident of 1985

A 51 TBq ^{137}Cs teletherapy unit was stolen from an abandoned clinic in Goiânia, Brazil, on or around 13 September 1985. Two people looking for scrap metal took home the source assembly of the teletherapy unit and attempted to disassemble the parts. The absorbed dose rate from the source assembly was about 46 Gy/h at 1 m. They did not understand the meaning of the three-bladed radiation symbol on the source capsule.

The source capsule ruptured during disassembly. Highly soluble caesium-137 chloride (^{137}CsCl) powder was disbursed throughout a part of this city of 1,000,000 people and caused one of the most serious sealed source accidents in history.

After the disassembly, remnants of the source assembly were sold to a junk dealer. He discovered that the ^{137}CsCl powder glowed in the dark with a blue colour (presumably, this was Cerenkov radiation). He thought that the powder could be a gemstone or even supernatural. Many friends and relatives came to see the "wonderful" glow. Portions of the source were given to

a number of families. This process continued for about five days. By this time a number of people had developed gastro-intestinal syndrome symptoms from radiation exposure.

Patients who went to the hospital with severe gastro-intestinal disorders were misdiagnosed as having allergic reactions to something they ate. A patient who had severe skin effects from handling the source was suspected of having some tropical skin disease and was sent to the Tropical Disease Hospital.

This tragic sequence of events continued undetected by knowledgeable personnel for about two weeks. Many people rubbed the ^{137}CsCl powder on their skins so that they could glow blue. The sequence might have continued much longer except that one of the irradiated persons finally connected the illnesses with the source capsule. She took the remnants of the ^{137}CsCl source on a bus to the Public Health Department in Goiânia where she left it. A visiting medical physicist surveyed the source the next day. He took actions on his own initiative to evacuate two junkyard areas and to inform authorities. The speed and overall size of response of the Brazilian government, once it became aware of the accident, were impressive.

About 249 people were contaminated. Fifty-four were hospitalized. Four people died, one of whom was a six-year-old girl who received an internal dose of about 4 Gy from ingesting about 1 GBq (10^9 Bq) of ^{137}Cs.

Response to the accident

The objectives of the initial response phase were to:

*   identify the main sites of contamination
*   evacuate residences where levels of radioactivity exceeded the intervention levels adopted
*   establish health physics controls around these areas, preventing access where necessary
*   identify persons who had incurred significant doses or were contaminated.

The medical team initially:

*   upon its arrival in Goiânia, took histories and triaged according to acute radiation syndrome symptoms
*   sent all acute radiation patients to Goiânia Hospital (which was set up in advance for contamination and exposure control)
*   transferred by air the next day the six most critical patients to the tertiary care center at a naval hospital in Rio de Janeiro (later eight more patients were transferred to this hospital)
*   made arrangements for cytogenetic radiation dosimetry
*   based medical management on each patient on that patient's clinical course
*   gave informal instruction to clinical laboratory staff to diminish their fears (the Goiânia medical community was reluctant to help).

Health physicists:

*   assisted physicians in radiation dosimetry, bioassay and skin decontamination
*   coordinated and interpreted analysis of 4,000 urine and faecal samples in a four-month period
*   whole-body counted 600 individuals
*   coordinated radio-contamination monitoring of 112,000 individuals (249 were contaminated)
*   performed aerial survey of entire city and suburbs utilizing hastily assembled NaI detectors
*   performed auto-mounted NaI detector surveys of over 2,000 km of roads
*   set up action levels for decontamination of people, buildings, autos, soil and so on
*   coordinated 550 workers employed in decontamination efforts

- coordinated demolition of seven houses and decontamination of 85 houses
- coordinated hauling of 275 truckloads of contaminated waste
- coordinated decontamination of 50 vehicles
- coordinated packaging of 3,500 cubic metres of contaminated waste
- utilized 55 survey meters, 23 contamination monitors and 450 self-reading dosimeters.

Results

Acute radiation syndrome patients
Four patients died as a result of absorbed doses ranging from 4 to 6 Gy. Two patients exhibited severe bone marrow depression, but lived in spite of absorbed doses of 6.2 and 7.1 Gy (cytogenetic estimate). Four patients survived with estimated absorbed doses from 2.5 to 4 Gy.

Radiation-induced skin injury
Nineteen of twenty hospitalized patients had radiation-induced skin injuries, which started with swelling and blistering. These lesions later ruptured and secreted fluid. Ten of the nineteen skin injuries developed deep lesions about four to five weeks after irradiation. These deep lesions were indicative of significant gamma exposure of deeper tissues.

All skin lesions were contaminated with ^{137}Cs, with absorbed dose rates up to 15 mGy/h.

The six-year-old girl who ingested 1 TBq of ^{137}Cs (and who died one month later) had generalized skin contamination that averaged 3 mGy/h.

One patient required an amputation about a month after exposure. Blood-pool imaging was useful in determining the demarcation between injured and normal arterioles.

Internal contamination result
Statistical tests showed no significant differences between body burdens determined by whole body counting as opposed to those determined by urinary excretion data.

Models that related bioassay data with intakes and body burden were validated. These models were also applicable for different age groups.

Prussian Blue was useful in promoting the elimination of ^{137}CsCl from the body (if dosage was greater than 3 Gy/d).

Seventeen patients received diuretics for the elimination of ^{137}CsCl body burdens. These diuretics were ineffective in de-corporating ^{137}Cs and their use was stopped.

Skin decontamination
Skin decontamination using soap and water, acetic acid, and titanium dioxide (TiO_2) was performed on all patients. This decontamination was only partly successful. It was surmised that sweating resulted in recontaminating the skin from the ^{137}Cs body burden.

Contaminated skin lesions are very difficult to decontaminate. Sloughing of necrotic skin significantly reduced contamination levels.

Follow-up study on cytogenetic analysis dose assessment
Frequency of aberrations in lymphocytes at different times after the accident followed three main patterns:

In two cases the frequencies of incidence of aberrations remained constant up to one month after the accident and declined to about 30% of the initial frequency three months later.

In two cases a gradual decrease of about 20% every three months was found.

In two of the cases of highest internal contamination there were increases in the frequency of incidence of aberrations (by about 50% and 100%) over a three-month period.

Follow-up studies on ^{137}Cs body burdens

- Patients' actual committed doses followed by bioassay.
- Effects of Prussian Blue administration followed.
- *In vivo* measurements for 20 people made on blood samples, wounds and organs to look for non-homogenous distribution of ^{137}Cs and its retention in body tissues.
- A woman and her newborn baby studied to look for retention and transfer by nursing.

Action levels for intervention
House evacuation was recommended for absorbed dose rates greater than 10 µGy/h at 1 m height inside the house.

Remedial decontamination of property, clothing, soil and food was based on a person not exceeding 5 mGy in a year. Applying this criterion for different pathways resulted in decontaminating the inside of a house if the absorbed dose could exceed 1 mGy in a year and decontaminating soil if the absorbed dose rate could exceed 4 mGy in a year (3 mGy from external radiation and 1 mGy from internal radiation).

The Chernobyl Nuclear Power Reactor Unit 4 Accident of 1986

General description of the accident
The world's worst nuclear power reactor accident occurred on 26 April 1986 during a very low-powered electrical engineering test. In order to perform this test, a number of safety systems were switched off or blocked.

This unit was a model RBMK-1000, the type of reactor that produced about 65% of all nuclear power generated in the USSR. It was a graphite-moderated, boiling-water reactor that generated 1,000 MW of electricity (MWe). The RBMK-1000 does not have a pressure-tested containment building and is not commonly built in most countries.

The reactor went prompt critical and produced a series of steam explosions. The explosions blew off the entire top of the reactor, destroyed the thin structure covering the reactor, and started a series of fires on the thick asphalt roofs of units 3 and 4. Radioactive releases lasted for ten days, and 31 people died. The USSR delegation to the International Atomic Energy Agency studied the accident. They stated that the Chernobyl Unit 4 RBMK experiments that caused the accident had not received required approval and that the written rules on reactor safety measures were inadequate. The delegation further stated, "The staff involved were not adequately prepared for the tests and were not aware of the possible dangers." This series of tests created the conditions for the emergency situation and led to a reactor accident which most believed could never occur.

Release of Chernobyl Unit 4 accident fission products

Total activity released
Roughly 1,900 PBq of fission products and fuel (which together were labelled *corium* by the Three Mile Island Accident Recovery Team) were released over the ten days that it took to put out all the fires and seal off Unit 4 with a neutron absorbing shielding material. Unit 4 is now a permanently sealed steel and concrete sarcophagus that properly contains the residual corium in and around the remains of the destroyed reactor core.

Twenty-five per cent of the 1,900 PBq was released on the first day of the accident. The rest was released during the next nine days.

The most radiologically significant releases were 270 PBq of ^{131}I, 8.1 PBq of ^{90}Sr and 37 PBq of ^{137}Cs. This can be compared with the Three Mile Island accident, which released 7.4 TBq of ^{131}I and no measurable ^{90}Sr or ^{137}Cs.

Environmental dispersion of radioactive materials

The first releases went in a generally northern direction, but subsequent releases went toward the westerly and southwesterly directions. The first plume arrived in Sweden and Finland on 27 April. Nuclear power plant radiological environmental monitoring programmes immediately discovered the release and alerted the world about the accident. Part of this first plume drifted into Poland and East Germany. Subsequent plumes swept into eastern and central Europe on 29 and 30 April. After this, the United Kingdom saw Chernobyl releases on 2 May, followed by Japan and China on 4 May, India on 5 May and Canada and the US on 5 and 6 May. The southern hemisphere did not report detecting this plume.

The deposition of the plume was governed mostly by precipitation. The fallout pattern of the major radionuclides (^{131}I, ^{137}Cs, ^{134}Cs, and ^{90}Sr) was highly variable, even within the USSR. The major risk came from external irradiation from surface deposition, as well as from ingestion of contaminated food.

Radiological consequences of the Chernobyl Unit 4 accident

General acute health consequences

Two persons died immediately, one during the building collapse and one 5.5 hours later from thermal burns. An additional 28 of the reactor's staff and fire-fighting crew died from radiation injuries. Radiation doses to the offsite population were below levels that can cause immediate radiation effects.

The Chernobyl accident almost doubled the worldwide total of deaths due to radiation accidents through 1986 (from 32 to 61). (It is interesting to note that the three dead from the SL-1 reactor accident in the US are listed as due to a steam explosion and that the first two to die at Chernobyl are also not listed as radiation accident deaths.)

Factors which influenced onsite health consequences of the accident

Personnel dosimetry for the onsite persons at highest risk was not available. The absence of nausea or vomiting for the first six hours after exposure reliably indicated those patients who had received less than potentially fatal absorbed doses. This also was a good indication of patients who did not require immediate medical attention because of radiation exposure. This information together with blood data (decrease in lymphocyte count) was more useful than personnel dosimetry data.

Fire-fighters' heavy protective garments (a porous canvas) allowed high specific activity fission products to contact bare skin. These beta doses caused severe skin burns and were a significant factor in many of the deaths. Fifty-six workers received severe skin burns. The burns were extremely difficult to treat and were a serious complicating element. They made it impossible to decontaminate the patients prior to transport to hospitals.

There were no clinically significant internal radioactive material body burdens at this time. Only two people had high (but not clinically significant) body burdens.

Of the about 1,000 people screened, 115 were hospitalized due to acute radiation syndrome. Eight medical attendants working onsite incurred the acute radiation syndrome.

As expected, there was no evidence of neutron exposure. (The test looks for sodium-24 (^{24}Na) in blood.)

Factors which influenced offsite health consequences of the accident

Public protective actions can be divided into four distinct periods.

1. *The first 24 h*: The downwind public remained indoors with doors and windows shut. Distribution of potassium iodide (KI) began in order to block thyroid uptake of ^{131}I.

2. *One to seven days*: Pripyat was evacuated after safe evacuation routes were established. Decontamination stations were established. The Kiev region was evacuated. The total number of people evacuated was more than 88,000.

3. *One to six weeks*: The total number of evacuated people rose to 115,000. All these were medically examined and resettled. Potassium iodide was administered to 5.4 million Russians, including 1.7 million children. Thyroid doses were reduced by about 80 to 90%. Tens of thousands of cattle were removed from contaminated areas. Local milk and foodstuffs were banned over a large area (as dictated by derived intervention levels).

4. *After 6 weeks*: The 30 km radius circle of evacuation was divided into three sub-zones: (a) a zone of 4 to 5 km where no public re-entry is expected in the foreseeable future, (b) a 5 to 10 km zone where limited public re-entry will be allowed after a specific time and (c) a 10 to 30 km zone where the public will eventually be allowed to return.

A great effort has been expended in decontaminating offsite areas.

International Organizations

International Atomic Energy Agency
P.O. Box 100
A-1400 Vienna
AUSTRIA

International Commission on Radiation Units and Measurements
7910 Woodmont Avenue
Bethesda, Maryland 20814
U.S.A.

International Commission on Radiological Protection
P.O. Box No. 35
Didcot, Oxfordshire
OX11 0RJ
U.K.

International Radiation Protection Association
Eindhoven University of Technology
P.O. Box 662
5600 AR Eindhoven
NETHERLANDS

United Nations Committee on the Effects of Atomic Radiation
BERNAM ASSOCIATES
4611-F Assembly Drive
Lanham, Maryland 20706-4391
U.S.A.

The total radiological dose to the USSR population was reported by the United Nations Scientific Committee on the Effects of Atomic Radiation (UNSCEAR) to be 226,000 person-Sv (72,000 person-Sv committed during the first year). The worldwide estimated collective dose equivalent is on the order of 600,000 person-Sv. Time and further study will refine this estimate (UNSCEAR 1988).

References

American National Standards Institute (ANSI). 1977. *Radiation Safety for X-Ray, Diffraction and Fluorescence Analysis Equipment.* Vol. 43.2. New York: ANSI.

American Nuclear Society. 1961. Special report on SL-1 Accident. *Nuclear News.*

Bethe, HA. 1950. *Revs. Mod. Phys.,* 22, 213.

Brill, AB and EH Forgotson. 1964. Radiation and congenital malformations. *Am J Obstet Gynecol* 90:1149-1168.

Brown, P. 1933. *American Martyrs to Science through the Roentgen Rays.* Springfield, Ill: Charles C Thomas.

Bryant, PM. 1969. Data assessments concerning controlled and accidental releases of I-131 and Cs-137 to the atmosphere. *Health Phys* 17(1).

Doll, R, NJ Evans, and SC Darby. 1994. Paternal exposure not to blame. *Nature* 367:678-680.

Friedenwald, JS and S Sigelmen. 1953. The influence of ionizing radiation on mitotic activity in the rat corneal epithelium. *Exp Cell Res* 4:1-31.

Gardner, MJ, A Hall, MP Snee, S Downes, CA Powell, and JD Terell. 1990. Results of case-control study of leukaemia and lymphoma among young people near Sellafield nuclear plant in West Cumbria. *Brit Med J* 300:423-429.

Goodhead, DJ. 1988. Spatial and temporal distribution of energy. *Health Phys* 55:231-240.

Hall, EJ. 1994. *Radiobiology for the Radiologist.* Philadelphia: JB Lippincott.

Haynie, JS and RH Olsher. 1981. A summary of x-ray machine exposure accidents at the Los Alamos National Laboratory. *LAUP.*

Hill, C and A Laplanche. 1990. Overall mortality and cancer mortality around French nuclear sites. *Nature* 347:755-757.

International Agency for Research on Cancer (IARC). 1994. IARC study group on cancer risk among nuclear industry workers, new estimates of cancer risk due to low doses of ionizing radiation: An international study. *Lancet* 344:1039-1043.

International Atomic Energy Agency (IAEA). 1969. *Symposium on the Handling of Radiation Accidents.* Vienna: IAEA.

—. 1973. *Radiation Protection Procedure.* International Atomic Energy Agency Safety Series, No. 38. Vienna: IAEA.

—. 1977. *Symposium on the Handling of Radiation Accidents.* Vienna: IAEA.

—. 1986. *Biological Dosimetry: Chromosomal Aberration Analysis for Dose Assessment.* Technical report No. 260. Vienna: IAEA.

International Commission on Radiological Protection (ICRP). 1984. Nonstochastic effects of ionizing radiation. *Ann ICRP* 14(3):1-33.

—. 1991. Recommendations of the International Commission on Radiological Protection. *Ann ICRP* 21:1-3.

Jablon, S, Z Hrubec, and JDJ Boice. 1991. Cancer in populations living near nuclear facilities. A survey of mortality nationwide and incidence in two areas. *JAMA* 265:1403-1408.

Jensen, RH, RG Langlois, and WL Bigbee. 1995. Elevated frequency of glycophorin A mutations in erythrocytes from Chernobyl accident victims. *Rad Res* 141:129-135.

Journal of Occupational Medicine (JOM). 1961. Special Supplement. *J Occup Med* 3(3).

Kasakov, VS, EP Demidchik, and LN Astakhova. 1992. Thyroid cancer after Chernobyl. *Nature* 359:21.

Kerber, RA, JE Till, SL Simon, JL Lyon, DC Thomas, S Preston-Martin, ML Rallison, RD Lloyd, and WS Stevens. 1993. A cohort study of thyroid disease in relation to fallout from nuclear weapons testing. *JAMA* 270:2076-2082.

Kinlen, LJ. 1988. Evidence for an infective cause of childhood leukaemia: Comparison of a Scottish New Town with nuclear reprocessing sites in Britain. *Lancet* II:1323-1327.

Kinlen, LJ, K Clarke, and A Balkwill. 1993. Paternal preconceptional radiation exposure in the nuclear industry and leukaemia and non-Hodgkin's lymphoma in young people in Scotland. *Brit Med J* 306:1153-1158.

Lindell, B. 1968. Occupational hazards in x-ray analytical work. *Health Phys* 15:481-486.

Little, MP, MW Charles, and R Wakeford. 1995. A review of the risks of leukemia in relation to parental pre-conception exposure to radiation. *Health Phys* 68:299-310.

Lloyd, DC and RJ Purrott. 1981. Chromosome aberration analysis in radiological protection dosimetry. *Rad Prot Dosimetry* 1:19-28.

Lubenau, JO, J Davis, D McDonald, and T Gerusky. 1967. *Analytical X-Ray Hazards: A Continuing Problem.* Paper presented at the 12th annual meeting of the Health Physics Society. Washington, DC: Health Physics Society.

Lubin, JH, JDJ Boice, and C Edling. 1994. *Radon and Lung Cancer Risk: A Joint Analysis of 11 Underground Miners Studies.* NIH Publication No. 94-3644. Rockville, Md: National Institutes of Health (NIH).

Lushbaugh, CC, SA Fry, and RC Ricks. 1987. Nuclear reactor accidents: Preparedness and consequences. *Brit J Radiol* 60:1159-1183.

McLaughlin, JR, EA Clarke, D Bishri, and TW Anderson. 1993. Childhood leukemia in the vicinity of Canadian nuclear facilities. *Cancer Causes and Control* 4:51-58.

Mettler, FA and AC Upton. 1995. *Medical Effects of Ionizing Radiation.* New York: Grune & Stratton.

Mettler, FA, MR Williamson, and HD Royal. 1992. Thyroid nodules in the population living around Chernobyl. *JAMA* 268:616-619.

National Academy of Sciences (NAS) and National Research Council (NRC). 1990. *Health Effects of Exposure to Low Levels of Ionizing Radiation.* Washington, DC: National Academy Press.

—. 1994. *Health Effects of Exposure to Radon. Time for Reassessment?* Washington, DC: National Academy Press.

National Council on Radiation Protection and Measurements (NCRP). 1987. *Radiation Exposure of the U.S. Population from Consumer Products and Miscellaneous Sources.* Report No. 95, Bethesda, Md: NCRP.

National Institutes of Health (NIH). 1985. *Report of the National Institutes of Health Ad Hoc Working Group to Develop Radioepidemiological Tables.* NIH publication No. 85-2748. Washington, DC: US Government Printing Office.

Neel, JV, W Schull, and A Awa. 1990. The children of parents exposed to atomic bombs: Estimates of the genetic doubling dose of radiation for humans. *Am J Hum Genet* 46:1053-1072.

Nuclear Regulatory Commission (NUREG). 1980. *Criteria for Preparation and Evaluation of Radiological Emergency Response Plans and Preparedness in Support of Nuclear Power Plants.* Document No. NUREG 0654/FEMA-REP-1, Rev. 1. Washington, DC: NUREG.

Otake, M, H Yoshimaru, and WJ Schull. 1987. Severe mental retardation among the prenatally exposed survivors of the atomic bombing of Hiroshima and Nagasaki: A comparison of the old and new dosimetry systems. In *RERF Technical Report.* Hiroshima: Radiation Effects Research Foundation.

Prisyazhiuk, A, OA Pjatak, and VA Buzanov. 1991. Cancer in the Ukraine, post-Chernobyl. *Lancet* 338:1334-1335.

Robbins, J and W Adams. 1989. Radiation effects in the Marshall Islands. In *Radiation and the Thyroid,* edited by S Nagataki. Tokyo: Exerpta Medica.

Rubin, P, and GW Casarett. 1972. A direction for clinical radiation pathology: the tolerance dose. In *Frontiers of Radiation Therapy and Oncology,* edited by J.M.Vaeth. Basel: Karger, and Baltimore: Univ. Park Press.

Schaeffer, NM. 1973. *Reactor Shielding for Nuclear Engineers.* Report No. TID-25951. Springfield, Virginia: National Technical Information Services.

Shapiro, J. 1972. *Radiation Protection: A Guide for Scientists and Physicians.* Cambridge, Mass: Harvard Univ. Press.

Stannard, JN. 1988. *Radioactivity and Health: A History.* U.S. Dept. of Energy Report, DOE/RL/01830-T59. Washington, DC: National Technical Information Services, US. Dept. of Energy.

Stevens, W, JE Till, L Lyon et al. 1990. Leukemia in Utah and radioactive fallout from the Nevada test site. *JAMA.* 264: 585-591.

Stone, RS. 1959. Maximum permissable exposure standards. In: *Protection in Diagnostic Radiology,* edited by BP Sonnenblick. New Brunswick: Rutgers Univ. Press.

United Nations Scientific Committee on the Effects of Atomic Radiation (UNSCEAR). 1982. *Ionizing Radiation: Sources and Biological Effects.* Report to the General Assembly, with Annexes. New York: United Nations.

—. 1986. *Genetic and Somatic Effects of Ionizing Radiation.* Report to the General Assembly, with Annexes. New York: United Nations.

—. 1988. *Sources, Effects, and Risks of Ionizing Radiation.* Report to the General Assembly, with Annexes. New York: United Nations.

—. 1993. *Sources and Effects of Ionizing Radiation.* Report to the General Assembly, with Annexes. New York: United Nations.

—. 1994. *Sources and Effects of Ionizing Radiation.* Report to the General Assembly, with annexes. New York: United Nations.

Upton, AC. 1986. Historical perspectives on radiation carcinogenesis. In *Radiation Carcinogenesis,* edited by AC Upton, RE Albert, FJ Burns, and RE Shore, New York. Elsevier.

Upton, AC. 1996 Radiologic Sciences. In: *The Oxford Textbook of Public Health,* edited by R Detels, W Holland, J McEwen, and GS Omenn. New York. Oxford University Press.

US Atomic Energy Commission (AEC). 1957. The windscale reactor incident. In *Accident Information Bulletin No. 73.* Washington, DC: AEC.

—. 1961. *Investigation Board Report on the Sl-1 Accident.* Washington, DC: US NRC.

US Code of Federal Regulations (USCFR). 1990. *Licenses for Radiography and Radiation Safety Requirements for Radiographic Operations.* Washington, DC: US Government.

US Department of Energy (USDOE). 1987. *Health and Environmental Consequences of the Chernobyl Nuclear Power Plant Accident.* DOE/ER-0332.Washington, DC: US-DOE.

US Nuclear Regulatory Commission (NRC). 1983. Instrumentation for light-water-cooled nuclear power plants to assess plant and environs conditions during and after an accident. In *NRC Regulatory Guide 1.97.* Rev. 3. Washington, DC: NRC.

Wakeford, R, EJ Tawn, DM McElvenny, LE Scott, K Binks, L Parker, H Dickinson, H and J Smith. 1994a. The descriptive statistics and health implications of occupational radiation doses received by men at the Sellafield nuclear installation before the conception of their children. *J. Radiol. Protect.* 14: 3–16.

Wakeford, R., EJ Tawn, DM McElvenny, K Binks, LE Scott and L Parker. 1994b. The Seascale childhood leukaemia cases — the mutation rates implied by paternal preconceptional radiation doses. *J. Radiol. Protect.* 14: 17–24.

Ward, JF. 1988. DNA damage produced by ionizing radiation in mammalian cells: identities, mechanisms of formation, and repairability. *Prog. Nucleic Acid Res. Mol. Biol.* 35: 96–128.

Yoshimoto, Y, JV Neel, WJ Schull, H Kato, M Soda, R Eto, and K Mabuchi. 1990. Malignant tumors during the first two decades of life in the offspring of atomic bomb survivors. *Am. J. Hum. Genet.* 46: 1041–1052.

Other relevant readings

American National Standards Institute (ANSI). 1993. *American National Standards for General Radiation Safety -Installations Using Non-Medical X-Ray and Sealed Gamma-Ray Sources, Energies Up to 10 MeV.* New York: ANSI.

Cember, H. 1996. *Introduction to Health Physics.* New York: McGraw Hill.

Code of Federal Regulations. 1988. *Emergency Planning and Preparedness for Production and Utilization Facilities.*

Title 10, Part 50, Appendix E. Washington, DC: US Government.

Eisenbud, M. 1987. *Environmental Radioactivity.* New York: Academic Press.

Environmental Protection Agency (EPA). 1978. *Protective Action Evaluation, Part 1: The Effectiveness of Sheltering as a Protective Action Against Nuclear Accidents Involving Gaseous Releases.* Washington, DC: EPA.

—. 1991. *Manual of Protective Action Guide and Protective Actions for Nuclear Incidents.* Document No. EPA-400-R-92.001. Washington, DC: EPA.

Goldbud and Jones. 1965. *Radiological Monitoring in the Environment.* New York: Pergamon.

International Atomic Energy Agency (IAEA). 1963. *A Basic Toxicity Classification of Radionuclides.* Technical Report Series, No.15. Vienna: IAEA.

—. 1965. Personnel Dosimetry for Radiation Accidents. *International Atomic Energy Agency Symposium.* Vienna: IAEA.

—. 1973. *Radioactive Contaminants of the Environment.* Vienna: IAEA.

—. 1979. *Radiological Surveillance of Airborne Contaminants in the Working Environment.* International Atomic Energy Agency Safety Series, No. 49. Vienna: IAEA.

—. 1986. *Principles for Limiting Releases of Radioactive Effluent into the Environment.* International Atomic Energy Agency Safety Series, No. 77. Vienna: IAEA.

International Commission of Radiation Units and Measurements (ICRUM). 1971. *Radiation protection instrumentation and its application.* Report No. 20. Vienna: ICRUM.

International Commission on Radiological Protection (ICRP). 1982. *Protection against ionizing radiation from external sources used in medicine. Ann ICRP* 9(1).

—. 1987. Data for use in protection against external radiation. *Ann ICRP* 17(2/3).

Lubin, JH. 1994. Invited commentary: Lung cancer and exposure to residential radon. *Am J Epidemiol* 140:323-332.

National Council on Radiation Protection and Measurements (NCRP). 1964. *Safe handling of radioactive materials.* Report No. 30. Bethesda, Md: NCRP.

—. 1976. *Structural Shielding Design and Evaluation for Medical Use of X Rays and Gamma Rays Up to 10 MeV.* Report No. 49. Bethesda, Md: NCRP.

—. 1978. *Instrumentation and monitoring methods for radiation protection.* Report No. 57. Bethesda, Md: NCRP.

—. 1984. *A handbook of radioactivity measurements procedures.* Report No. 58. 2nd ed. Bethesda, Md: NCRP

Nuclear Regulatory Commission (NUREG). 1970. *Analysis of Techniques for Estimating Evacuation Times for Emergency Planning Zones.* Document No. NUREG/CR-1745. Washington, DC: NUREG.

—. 1978. *Planning Basis for the Development of State and Local Government Radiological Emergency Response Plans in Support of Light Water Nuclear Power Plants.* Document No. 43FR58668. Washington, DC: NUREG.

—. 1978. *Potassium Iodine as a Thyroid-Blocking Agent in a Radiation Emergency.* Document No. 43FR58789. Washington, DC: NUREG.

—. 1979. *Development Plan-Insurance of Protective Action Guides for Airborne Releases of Radioactivity as Federal Guidance.* Document No. 44FR75344. Washington, DC: NUREG

—. 1979. *Radiological Emergency Response Planning, Handbook for Federal Assistance to State and Local Government.* Document No. NUREG-0092. Washington, DC: NUREG.

—. 1980. *Guidance on Off-site Emergency Radiation Measurement Systems. Phase 1: Airborne Releases.* Document No. FEMA-REP-2. Washington, DC: NUREG.

—. 1980a. *Emergency Planning.* Document No. 45FR55402. Washington, DC: NUREG.

—. 1980b. *National Radiological Emergency Preparedness/Response Plan for Commercial Nuclear Power Plant Accident (Master Plan).* Document No. 45FR84910. Washington, DC: NUREG.

—. 1980c. *Nuclear Regulatory Commission Incident Response Plan.* Document No. NUREG-0728. Washington, DC: NUREG.

—. 1981. *Emergency Planning for Nuclear Power Reactors.* Reg. guide 1.101. Washington, DC: NUREG.

—. 1983a. *Emergency Planning for Research and Test Reactors.* Reg. guide 2.6. Washington, DC: NUREG.

—. 1983b. *Instrumentation for Light-Water-Cooled Nuclear Power Plants to Assess Plant and Environs Conditions During and After Accident.* Reg. guide 1.97. Washington, DC: NUREG.

Reinig, WC. 1970. *Environmental Surveillance in the Vicinity of Nuclear Facilities.* HP Symposium Proceedings. Springfield, Ill: Charles C Thomas.

Chapter Editor
Bengt Knave

Contents

● ELECTRIC AND MAGNETIC FIELDS AND HEALTH OUTCOMES

Bengt Knave

In recent years interest has increased in the biological effects and possible health outcomes of weak electric and magnetic fields. Studies have been presented on magnetic fields and cancer, on reproduction and on neurobehavioural reactions. In what follows, a summary is given of what we know, what still needs to be investigated and, particularly, what policy is appropriate—whether it should involve no restrictions of exposure at all, "prudent avoidance" or expensive interventions.

What we Know

Cancer

Epidemiological studies on childhood leukaemia and residential exposure from power lines seem to indicate a slight risk increase, and excess leukaemia and brain tumour risks have been reported in "electrical" occupations. Recent studies with improved techniques for exposure assessment have generally strengthened the evidence of an association. There is, however, still a lack of clarity as to exposure characteristics—for example, magnetic field frequency and exposure intermittence; and not much is known about possible confounding or effect-modifying factors. Furthermore, most of the occupational studies have indicated one special form of leukaemia, acute myeloid leukaemia, while others have found higher incidences for another form, chronic lymphatic leukaemia. The few animal cancer studies reported have not given much help with risk assessment, and in spite of a large number of experimental cell studies, no plausible and understandable mechanism has been presented by which a carcinogenic effect could be explained.

Reproduction, with special reference to pregnancy outcomes

In epidemiological studies, adverse pregnancy outcomes and childhood cancer have been reported after maternal as well as paternal exposure to magnetic fields, the paternal exposure indicating a genotoxic effect. Efforts to replicate positive results by other research teams have not been successful. Epidemiological studies on visual display unit (VDU) operators, who are exposed to the electric and magnetic fields emitted by their screens, have been mainly negative, and animal teratogenic studies with VDU-like fields have been too contradictory to support trustworthy conclusions.

Neurobehavioural reactions

Provocation studies on young volunteers seem to indicate such physiological changes as slowing of heart rate and electroencephalogram (EEG) changes after exposure to relatively weak electric and magnetic fields. The recent phenomenon of hypersensitivity to electricity seems to be multifactorial in origin, and it is not clear whether the fields are involved or not. A great variety of symptoms and discomforts has been reported, mainly of the skin and the nervous system. Most of the patients have diffuse skin complaints in the face, such as flush, rosiness, ruddiness, heat, warmth, pricking sensations, ache and tightness. Symptoms associated with the nervous system are also described, such as headache, dizziness, fatigue and faintness, tingling and pricking sensations in the extremities, shortness of breath, heart palpitations, profuse sweatings, depressions and memory difficulties. No characteristic organic neurological disease symptoms have been presented.

Exposure

Exposure to fields occurs throughout society: in the home, at work, in schools and by the operation of electrically powered means of transport. Wherever there are electric wires, electric motors and electronic equipment, electric and magnetic fields are created. Average workday field strengths of 0.2 to 0.4 µT (microtesla) appear to be the level above which there could be an increased risk, and similar levels have been calculated for annual averages for subjects living under or near power lines.

Many people are similarly exposed above these levels, though for shorter periods, in their homes (via electric radiators, shavers, hair-dryers and other household appliances, or stray currents due to imbalances in the electrical grounding system in a building), at work (in certain industries and offices involving proximity to electric and electronic equipment) or while travelling in trains and other electrically driven conveyances. The importance of such intermittent exposure is not known. There are other uncertainties as to exposure (involving questions relating to the importance of field frequency, to other modifying or confounding factors, or to knowledge of the total exposure day and night) and effect (given the consistency in findings as to type of cancer), and in the epidemiological studies, which make it necessary to evaluate all risk assessments with great caution.

Risk assessments

In Scandinavian residential studies, results indicate a doubled leukaemia risk above 0.2 µT, the exposure levels corresponding to those typically encountered within 50 to 100 metres of an overhead power line. The number of childhood leukaemia cases under power lines are few, however, and the risk is therefore low compared to other environmental hazards in society. It has been calculated that each year in Sweden there are two cases of childhood leukaemia under or near power lines. One of these cases may be attributable to the magnetic field risk, if any.

Occupational exposures to magnetic fields are generally higher than residential exposures, and calculations of leukaemia and brain tumour risks for exposed workers give higher values than for children living close to power lines. From calculations based on the attributable risk discovered in a Swedish study, approximately 20 cases of leukaemia and 20 cases of brain tumours could be attributed to magnetic fields each year. These figures are to be compared with the total number of 40,000 annual cancer cases in Sweden, of which 800 have been calculated to have an occupational origin.

What Still Needs to be Investigated

It is quite clear that more research is needed in order to secure a satisfactory understanding of the epidemiological study results obtained so far. There are additional epidemiological studies in progress in different countries around the world, but the question is whether these will add more to the knowledge we already have. As a matter of fact it is not known which characteristics of the fields are causal to the effects, if any. Thus, we definitely need more studies on possible mechanisms to explain the findings we have assembled.

There are in the literature, however, a vast number of *in vitro* studies devoted to the search for possible mechanisms. Several cancer promotion models have been presented, based on changes in the cell surface and in the cell membrane transport of calcium ions, disruption of cell communication, modulation of cell growth, activation of specific gene sequences by modulated ribonucleic acid (RNA) transcription, depression of pineal melatonin production, modulation of ornithine decarboxylase activity and possible disruption of hormonal and immune-system anti-tumour control mechanisms. Each of these mechanisms has features applicable to explaining reported magnetic field cancer effects; however, none has been free of problems and essential objections.

Melatonin and magnetite

There are two possible mechanisms that may be relevant to cancer promotion and thus deserve special attention. One of these has to do with the reduction of nocturnal melatonin levels induced by magnetic fields and the other is related to the discovery of magnetite crystals in human tissues.

It is known from animal studies that melatonin, via an effect on circulating sex hormone levels, has an indirect oncostatic effect. It has also been indicated in animal studies that magnetic fields suppress pineal melatonin production, a finding that suggests a theoretical mechanism for the reported increase in (for example) breast cancer that may be due to exposure to such fields. Recently, an alternative explanation for the increased cancer risk has been proposed. Melatonin has been found to be a most potent hydroxyl radical scavenger, and consequently the damage to DNA that might be done by free radicals is markedly inhibited by melatonin. If melatonin levels are suppressed, for example by magnetic fields, the DNA is left more vulnerable to oxidative attack. This theory explains how the depression of melatonin by magnetic fields could result in a higher incidence of cancer in any tissue.

But do human melatonin blood levels diminish when individuals are exposed to weak magnetic fields? There exist some indications that this may be so, but further research is needed. For some years it has been known that the ability of birds to orient themselves during seasonal migrations is mediated via magnetite crystals in cells that respond to the earth's magnetic field. Now, as mentioned above, magnetite crystals have also been demonstrated to exist in human cells in a concentration high enough theoretically to respond to weak magnetic fields. Thus the role of magnetite crystals should be considered in any discussions on the possible mechanisms that may be proposed as to the potentially harmful effects of electric and magnetic fields.

The need for knowledge on mechanisms

To summarize, there is a clear need for more studies on such possible mechanisms. Epidemiologists need information as to which characteristics of the electric and magnetic fields they should focus upon in their exposure assessments. In most epidemiological studies, mean or median field strengths (with frequencies of 50 to 60 Hz) have been used; in others, cumulative measures of exposure were studied. In a recent study, fields of higher frequencies were found to be related to risk. In some animal studies, finally, field transients have been found to be important. For epidemiologists the problem is not on the effect side; registers on diseases exist in many countries today. The problem is that epidemiologists do not know the relevant exposure characteristics to consider in their studies.

What Policy is Appropriate

Systems of protection

Generally, there are different systems of protection to be considered with respect to regulations, guidelines and policies. Most often the health-based system is selected, in which a specific adverse health effect can be identified at a certain exposure level, irrespective of exposure type, chemical or physical. A second system could be characterized as an optimization of a known and accepted hazard, which has no threshold below which the risk is absent. An example of an exposure falling within this kind of system is ionizing radiation. A third system covers hazards or risks where causal relationships between exposure and outcome have not been shown with reasonable certainty, but for which there are general concerns about possible risks. This lattermost system of protection has been denoted the *principle of caution*, or more recently *prudent avoidance*, which can be summarized as the future low-cost avoidance of unnecessary exposure in the absence of scientific certainty. Exposure to electric and magnetic fields has been discussed in this way, and systematic strategies have been presented, for instance, on how future power lines should be routed, workplaces arranged and household appliances designed in order to minimize exposure.

It is apparent that the system of optimization is not applicable in connection with restrictions of electric and magnetic fields, simply because they are not known and accepted as risks. The other two systems, however, are both presently under consideration.

Regulations and guidelines for restriction of exposure under the health-based system

In international guidelines limits for restrictions of field exposure are several orders of magnitude above what can be measured from overhead power lines and found in electrical occupations. The International Radiation Protection Association (IRPA) issued *Guidelines on limits of exposure to 50/60 Hz electric and magnetic fields* in 1990, which has been adopted as a basis for many national standards. Since important new studies were published thereafter, an addendum was issued in 1993 by the International Commission on Non-Ionizing Radiation Protection (ICNIRP). Furthermore, in 1993 risk assessments in agreement with that of IRPA were also made in the United Kingdom.

These documents emphasize that the state of scientific knowledge today does not warrant limiting exposure levels for the public and the workforce down to the μT level, and that further data are required to confirm whether or not health hazards are present. The IRPA and ICNIRP guidelines are based on the effects of field-induced currents in the body, corresponding to those normally found in the body (up to about 10 mA/m^2). Occupational exposure to magnetic fields of 50/60 Hz is recommended to be limited to 0.5 mT for all-day exposure and 5 mT for short exposures of up to two hours. It is recommended that exposure to electric fields be limited to 10 and 30 kV/m. The 24-hour limit for the public is set at 5 kV/m and 0.1 mT.

These discussions on the regulation of exposure are based entirely on cancer reports. In studies of other possible health effects related to electric and magnetic fields (for example, reproductive and neurobehavioural disorders), results are generally considered insufficiently clear and consistent to constitute a scientific basis for restricting exposure.

The principle of caution or prudent avoidance

There is no real difference between the two concepts; prudent avoidance has been used more specifically, though, in discussions of electric and magnetic fields. As said above, prudent avoidance can be summarized as the future, low-cost avoidance of unnecessary exposure as long as there is scientific uncertainty about the health effects. It has been adopted in Sweden, but not in other countries.

In Sweden, five government authorities (the Swedish Radiation Protection Institute; the National Electricity Safety Board; the National Board of Health and Welfare; the National Board of Occupational Safety and Health; and the National Board of Housing, Building and Planning) jointly have stated that "the total knowledge now accumulating justifies taking steps to reduce field power". Provided the cost is reasonable, the policy is to protect people from high magnetic exposures of long duration. During the installation of new equipment or new power lines that may cause high magnetic field exposures, solutions giving lower exposures should be chosen provided these solutions do not imply

Figure 49.1 • The electromagnetic spectrum.

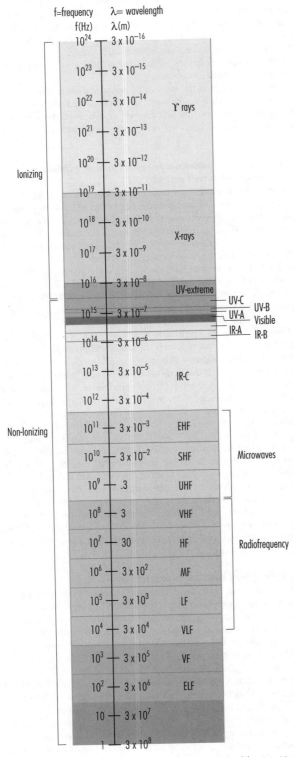

The electromagnetic spectrum is divided into two main regions, the ionizing and the non-ionizing, with further subdivisions as shown. All radiation can be described in terms of its wavelength and frequency. Non-ionizing radiation is that having wavelengths longer than about 100 nm with energies too low to ionize matter.

large inconveniences or costs. Generally, as stated by the Radiation Protection Institute, steps can be taken to reduce the magnetic field in cases where the exposure levels exceed the normally occurring levels by more than a factor of ten, provided such reductions can be done at a reasonable cost. In situations where the exposure levels from existing installations do not exceed the normally occurring levels by a factor of ten, costly rebuilding should be avoided. Needless to say, the present avoidance concept has been criticized by many experts in different countries, such as by experts in the electricity supply industry.

Conclusions

In the present paper a summary has been given of what we know on the possible health effects of electric and magnetic fields, and what still needs to be investigated. No answer has been given to the question of which policy should be adopted, but optional systems of protection have been presented. In this connection, it seems clear that the scientific database at hand is insufficient to develop limits of exposure at the µT level, which means in turn that there are no reasons for expensive interventions at these exposure levels. Whether some form of strategy of caution (e.g., prudent avoidance) should be adopted or not is a matter for decisions by public and occupational health authorities of individual countries. If such a strategy is not adopted it usually means that no restrictions of exposure are imposed because the health-based threshold limits are well above everyday public and occupational exposure. So, if opinions differ today as to regulations, guidelines and policies, there is a general consensus among standard setters that more research is needed to get a solid basis for future actions.

THE ELECTROMAGNETIC SPECTRUM: BASIC PHYSICAL CHARACTERISTICS

Kjell Hansson Mild

The most familiar form of electromagnetic energy is sunlight. The frequency of sunlight (visible light) is the dividing line between the more potent, ionizing radiation (x rays, cosmic rays) at higher frequencies and the more benign, non-ionizing radiation at lower frequencies. There is a spectrum of non-ionizing radiation. Within the context of this chapter, at the high end just below visible light is infrared radiation. Below that is the broad range of radio frequencies, which includes (in descending order) microwaves, cellular radio, television, FM radio and AM radio, short waves used in dielectric and induction heaters and, at the low end, fields with power frequency. The electromagnetic spectrum is illustrated in figure 49.1.

Just as visible light or sound permeates our environment, the space where we live and work, so do the energies of electromagnetic fields. Also, just as most of the sound energy we are exposed to is created by human activity, so too are the electromagnetic energies: from the weak levels emitted from our everyday electrical appliances—those that make our radio and TV sets work—to the high levels that medical practitioners apply for beneficial purposes—for example, diathermy (heat treatments). In general, the strength of such energies decreases rapidly with distance from the source. Natural levels of these fields in the environment are low.

Non-ionizing radiation (NIR) incorporates all radiation and fields of the electromagnetic spectrum that do not have enough energy to produce ionization of matter. That is, NIR is incapable of imparting enough energy to a molecule or atom to disrupt its structure by removing one or more electrons. The borderline between NIR and ionizing radiation is usually set at a wavelength of approximately 100 nanometres.

As with any form of energy, NIR energy has the potential to interact with biological systems, and the outcome may be of no significance, may be harmful in different degrees, or may be beneficial. With radiofrequency (RF) and microwave radiation, the main interaction mechanism is heating, but in the low-frequency part of the spectrum, fields of high intensity may induce currents in the body and thereby be hazardous. The interaction mechanisms for low-level field strengths are, however, unknown.

Quantities and Units

Fields at frequencies below about 300 MHz are quantified in terms of electric field strength (E) and magnetic field strength (H). E is expressed in volts per metre (V/m) and H in amperes per metre (A/m). Both are vector fields—that is, they are characterized by magnitude and direction at each point. For the low-frequency range the magnetic field is often expressed in terms of the flux density, B, with the SI unit tesla (T). When the fields in our daily environment are discussed, the subunit microtesla (μT) is usually the preferred unit. In some literature the flux density is expressed in gauss (G), and the conversion between these units is (for fields in air): $1\ T = 10^4\ G$ or $0.1\ \mu T = 1\ mG$ and $1\ A/m = 1.26\ \mu T$.

Reviews of concepts, quantities, units and terminology for non-ionizing radiation protection, including radiofrequency radiation, are available (NCRP 1981; Polk and Postow 1986; WHO 1993).

The term *radiation* simply means energy transmitted by waves. Electromagnetic waves are waves of electric and magnetic forces, where a wave motion is defined as propagation of disturbances in a physical system. A change in the electric field is accompanied by a change in the magnetic field, and vice versa. These phenomena were described in 1865 by J.C. Maxwell in four equations which have come to be known as Maxwell's Equations.

Electromagnetic waves are characterized by a set of parameters that include frequency (f), wavelength (λ), electric field strength, magnetic field strength, electric polarization (P) (the direction of the E field), velocity of propagation (c) and Poynting vector (S). Figure 49.2 illustrates the propagation of an electromagnetic wave in free space. The frequency is defined as the number of complete changes of the electric or magnetic field at a given point per second, and is expressed in hertz (Hz). The wavelength is the distance between two consecutive crests or troughs of the wave (maxima or minima). The frequency, wavelength and wave velocity (v) are interrelated as follows:

$$v = f\lambda$$

The velocity of an electromagnetic wave in free space is equal to the velocity of light, but the velocity in materials depends on the electrical properties of the material—that is, on its permittivity (ε) and permeability (μ). The permittivity concerns the material interactions with the electric field, and the permeability expresses the interactions with the magnetic field. Biological substances have permittivities that differ vastly from that of free space, being dependant on wavelength (especially in the RF range) and tissue type. The permeability of biological substances, however, is equal to that of free space.

In a plane wave, as illustrated in figure 49.2, the electric field is perpendicular to the magnetic field and the direction of propagation is perpendicular to both the electric and the magnetic fields.

Figure 49.2 • A plane wave propagating with the speed of light in the x-direction.

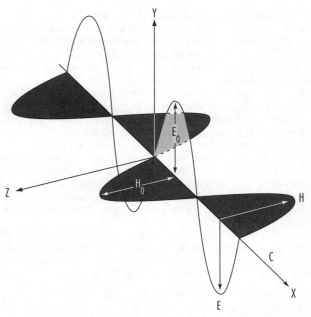

An electromagnetic wave has an electric and a magnetic component. In a plane wave the E and B fields are perpendicular to each other and also perpendicular to the direction of propagation. The E and B fields are related through the relation $E = 377\ H$. In occupational exposure for frequencies below 300 MHz one is in the so called "near field" and both components have to be considered separately.

For a plane wave, the ratio of the value of the electric field strength to the value of the magnetic field strength, which is constant, is known as the characteristic impedance (Z):

$$Z = E/H$$

In free space, $Z = 120\ \pi \approx 377\ \Omega$ but otherwise Z depends on the permittivity and permeability of the material the wave is travelling through.

Energy transfer is described by the Poynting vector, which represents the magnitude and direction of the electromagnetic flux density:

$$S = E \times H$$

For a propagating wave, the integral of S over any surface represents the instantaneous power transmitted through this surface (power density). The magnitude of the Poynting vector is expressed in watts per square metre (W/m²) (in some literature the unit mW/cm² is used—the conversion to SI units is $1\ mW/cm^2 = 10\ W/m^2$) and for plane waves is related to the values of the electric and magnetic field strengths:

$$S = E^2/120\ \pi = E^2/377$$

and

$$S = 120\ \pi\ H^2 = 377\ H^2$$

Not all exposure conditions encountered in practice can be represented by plane waves. At distances close to sources of radiofrequency radiation the relationships characteristic of plane waves are not satisfied. The electromagnetic field radiated by an antenna can be divided into two regions: the near-field zone and the

49. RADIATION, NON-IONIZING

far-field zone. The boundary between these zones is usually put at:

$$r = 2a^2/\lambda$$

where a is the greatest dimension of the antenna.

In the near-field zone, exposure has to be characterized by both the electric and the magnetic fields. In the far-field one of these suffices, as they are interrelated by the above equations involving E and H. In practice, the near-field situation is often realized at frequencies below 300 MHz.

Exposure to RF fields is further complicated by interactions of electromagnetic waves with objects. In general, when electromagnetic waves encounter an object some of the incident energy is reflected, some is absorbed and some is transmitted. The proportions of energy transmitted, absorbed or reflected by the object depend on the frequency and polarization of the field and the electrical properties and shape of the object. A superimposition of the incident and reflected waves results in standing waves and spatially non-uniform field distribution. Since waves are totally reflected from metallic objects, standing waves form close to such objects.

Since the interaction of RF fields with biological systems depends on many different field characteristics and the fields encountered in practice are complex, the following factors should be considered in describing exposures to RF fields:

- whether exposure occurs in the near- or far-field zone
- if near-field, then values for both E and H are needed; if far-field, then either E or H
- spatial variation of the magnitude of the field(s)
- field polarization, that is, the direction of the electric field with respect to the direction of wave propagation.

For exposure to low-frequency magnetic fields it is still not clear whether the field strength or flux density is the only important consideration. It may turn out that other factors are also important, such as the exposure time or the rapidity of the field changes.

The term *electromagnetic field* (EMF), as it is used in the news media and popular press, usually refers to electric and magnetic fields at the low-frequency end of the spectrum, but it can also be used in a much broader sense to include the whole spectrum of electromagnetic radiation. Note that in the low-frequency range the E and B fields are not coupled or interrelated in the same way that they are at higher frequencies, and it is therefore more accurate to refer to them as "electric and magnetic fields" rather than EMFs.

● Ultraviolet Radiation

David H. Sliney

Like light, which is visible, ultraviolet radiation (UVR) is a form of optical radiation with shorter wavelengths and more energetic photons (particles of radiation) than its visible counterpart. Most light sources emit some UVR as well. UVR is present in sunlight and is also emitted from a large number of ultraviolet sources used in industry, science and medicine. Workers may encounter UVR in a wide variety of occupational settings. In some instances, at low ambient light levels, very intense near-ultraviolet ("black light") sources can be seen, but normally UVR is invisible and

must be detected by the glow of materials that fluoresce when illuminated by UVR.

Just as light can be divided into colours which can be seen in a rainbow, UVR is subdivided and its components are commonly denoted as *UVA, UVB* and *UVC*. Wavelengths of light and UVR are generally expressed in nanometres (nm); 1 nm is one-billionth (10^{-9}) of a metre. UVC (very short-wavelength UVR) in sunlight is absorbed by the atmosphere and does not reach the Earth's surface. UVC is available only from artificial sources, such as germicidal lamps, which emit most of their energy at a single wavelength (254 nm) that is very effective in killing bacteria and viruses on a surface or in the air.

UVB is the most biologically damaging UVR to the skin and eye, and although most of this energy (which is a component of sunlight) is absorbed by the atmosphere, it still produces sunburn and other biological effects. Long-wavelength UVR, UVA, is normally found in most lamp sources, and is also the most intense UVR reaching the Earth. Although UVA can penetrate deeply into tissue, it is not as biologically damaging as UVB because the energies of individual photons are less than for UVB or UVC.

Sources of Ultraviolet Radiation

Sunlight
The greatest occupational exposure to UVR is experienced by outdoor workers under sunlight. The energy of solar radiation is greatly attenuated by the earth's ozone layer, limiting terrestrial UVR to wavelengths greater than 290-295 nm. The energy of the more dangerous short-wavelength (UVB) rays in sunlight is a strong function of the atmospheric slant path, and varies with the season and the time of day (Sliney 1986 and 1987; WHO 1994).

Artificial sources
The most significant artificial sources of human exposure include the following:

Industrial arc welding. The most significant source of potential UVR exposure is the radiant energy of arc-welding equipment. The levels of UVR around arc-welding equipment are very high, and acute injury to the eye and the skin can occur within three to ten minutes of exposure at close viewing distances of a few metres. Eye and skin protection is mandatory.

Industrial/workplace UVR lamps. Many industrial and commercial processes, such as photochemical curing of inks, paints and plastics, involve the use of lamps which strongly emit in the UV range. While the likelihood of harmful exposure is low due to shielding, in some cases accidental exposure can occur.

"Black lights". Black lights are specialized lamps that emit predominantly in the UV range, and are generally used for nondestructive testing with fluorescent powders, for the authentication of banknotes and documents, and for special effects in advertising and discotheques. These lamps do not pose any significant exposure hazard to humans (except in certain cases to photosensitized skin).

Medical treatment. UVR lamps are used in medicine for a variety of diagnostic and therapeutic purposes. UVA sources are normally used in diagnostic applications. Exposures to the patient vary considerably according to the type of treatment, and UV lamps used in dermatology require careful use by staff members.

Germicidal UVR lamps. UVR with wavelengths in the range 250–265 nm is the most effective for sterilization and disinfection since it corresponds to a maximum in the DNA absorption spectrum. Low-pressure mercury discharge tubes are often used as the UV source, as more than 90% of the radiated energy lies at the 254 nm line. These lamps are often referred to as "germicidal lamps," "bactericidal lamps" or simply "UVC lamps". Germicidal lamps are used in hospitals to combat tuberculosis infection, and are also used inside microbiological safety cabinets to inactivate airborne and surface microorganisms. Proper installation of the lamps and the use of eye protection is essential.

Cosmetic tanning. Sunbeds are found in enterprises where clients may obtain a tan by special sun-tanning lamps, which emit primarily in the UVA range but also some UVB. Regular use of a sunbed may contribute significantly to a person's annual UV skin exposure; furthermore, the staff working in tanning salons may also be exposed to low levels. The use of eye protection such as goggles or sunglasses should be mandatory for the client, and depending upon the arrangement, even staff members may require eye protectors.

General lighting. Fluorescent lamps are common in the workplace and have been used in the home for a long time now. These lamps emit small amounts of UVR and contribute only a few percent to a person's annual UV exposure. Tungsten-halogen lamps are increasingly used in the home and in the workplace for a variety of lighting and display purposes. Unshielded halogen lamps can emit UVR levels sufficient to cause acute injury at short distances. The fitting of glass filters over these lamps should eliminate this hazard.

Biological Effects

The skin

Erythema

Erythema, or "sunburn", is a reddening of the skin that normally appears in four to eight hours after exposure to UVR and gradually fades after a few days. Severe sunburn can involve blistering and peeling of the skin. UVB and UVC are both about 1,000 times more effective in causing erythema than UVA (Parrish, Jaenicke and Anderson 1982), but erythema produced by the longer UVB wavelengths (295 to 315 nm) is more severe and persists longer (Hausser 1928). The increased severity and time-course of the erythema results from deeper penetration of these wavelengths into the epidermis. Maximum sensitivity of the skin apparently occurs at approximately 295 nm (Luckiesh, Holladay and Taylor 1930; Coblentz, Stair and Hogue 1931) with much less (approximately 0.07) sensitivity occurring at 315 nm and longer wavelengths (McKinlay and Diffey 1987).

The minimal erythemal dose (MED) for 295 nm that has been reported in more recent studies for untanned, lightly pigmented skin ranges from 6 to 30 mJ/cm^2 (Everett, Olsen and Sayer 1965; Freeman, et al. 1966; Berger, Urbach and Davies 1968). The MED at 254 nm varies greatly depending upon the elapsed time after exposure and whether the skin has been exposed much to outdoor sunlight, but is generally of the order of 20 mJ/cm^2, or as high as 0.1 J/cm^2. Skin pigmentation and tanning, and, most importantly, thickening of the stratum corneum, can increase this MED by at least one order of magnitude.

Photosensitization

Occupational health specialists frequently encounter adverse effects from occupational exposure to UVR in photosensitized workers. The use of certain medicines may produce a photosensitizing effect on exposure to UVA, as may the topical application of certain products, including some perfumes, body lotions and so on. Reactions to photosensitizing agents involve both photoallergy (allergic reaction of the skin) and phototoxicity (irritation of the skin) after UVR exposure from sunlight or industrial UVR sources. (Photosensitivity reactions during the use of tanning equipment are also common.) This photosensitization of the skin may be caused by creams or ointments applied to the skin, by medications taken orally or by injection, or by the use of

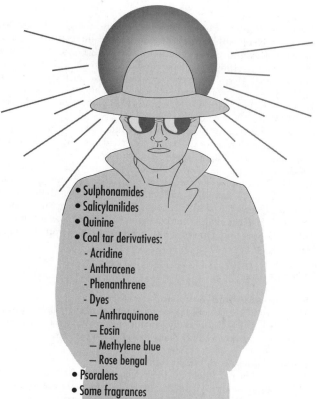

Figure 49.3 • Some photosensitizing substances.

- Sulphonamides
- Salicylanilides
- Quinine
- Coal tar derivatives:
  - Acridine
  - Anthracene
  - Phenanthrene
  - Dyes
    — Anthraquinone
    — Eosin
    — Methylene blue
    — Rose bengal
- Psoralens
- Some fragrances
- Cyclamate (artificial sweetener)
- Nonsteroidal anti-inflammatory drugs (pain reliever, antiarthritics)
- Deodorant and bacteriostatic agents in soaps
- Fluorescent brightening agent for cellulose, nylon or wool fibres
- Phenothiazines (major tranquilizers, antiemetics)
- Sulfonylureas (oral antidiabetics, medication for hypoglycaemia)
- Sunscreen ingredients:
  - 6-Acetoxy-2,4,-dimethly-M-dioxane (preservative)
  - Benzophenones
  - Cinnamates
  - Oxybenzone
  - Para-aminobenzoic acid (PABA)
  - PABA esters
- Tetracyclines (antibiotics, anti-infectives)
- Tricyclic antidepressants

prescription inhalers (see figure 49.3). The physician prescribing a potentially photosensitizing medication should always warn the patient to take appropriate measures to ensure against adverse effects, but the patient frequently is told only to avoid sunlight and not UVR sources (since these are uncommon for the general population).

Delayed effects

Chronic exposure to sunlight—especially the UVB component—accelerates the ageing of the skin and increases the risk of developing skin cancer (Fitzpatrick et al. 1974; Forbes and Davies 1982; Urbach 1969; Passchier and Bosnjakovic 1987). Several epidemiological studies have shown that the incidence of skin cancer is strongly correlated with latitude, altitude and sky cover, which correlate with UVR exposure (Scotto, Fears and Gori 1980; WHO 1993).

Exact quantitative dose-response relationships for human skin carcinogenesis have not yet been established, although fair-skinned individuals, particularly those of Celtic origin, are much more prone to develop skin cancer. Nevertheless, it must be noted that the UVR exposures necessary to elicit skin tumours in animal models may be delivered sufficiently slowly that erythema is not produced, and the relative effectiveness (relative to the peak at 302 nm) reported in those studies varies in the same way as sunburn (Cole, Forbes and Davies 1986; Sterenborg and van der Leun 1987).

The eye

Photokeratitis and photoconjunctivitis

These are acute inflammatory reactions resulting from exposure to UVB and UVC radiation which appear within a few hours of excessive exposure and normally resolved after one to two days.

Retinal injury from bright light

Although thermal injury to the retina from light sources is unlikely, photochemical damage can occur from exposure to sources rich in blue light. This can result in temporary or permanent reduction in vision. However the normal aversion response to bright light should prevent this occurrence unless a conscious effort is made to stare at bright light sources. The contribution of UVR to retinal injury is generally very small because absorption by the lens limits retinal exposure.

Chronic effects

Long-term occupational exposure to UVR over several decades may contribute to cataract and such non-eye-related degenerative effects as skin ageing and skin cancer associated with sun exposure. Chronic exposure to infrared radiation also can increase the risk of cataract, but this is very unlikely, given access to eye protection.

Actinic ultraviolet radiation (UVB and UVC) is strongly absorbed by the cornea and conjunctiva. Overexposure of these tissues causes keratoconjunctivitis, commonly referred to as "welder's flash", "arc-eye" or "snow-blindness". Pitts has reported the action spectrum and time course of photokeratitis in the human, rabbit and monkey cornea (Pitts 1974). The latent period varies inversely with the severity of exposure, ranging from 1.5 to 24 hours, but usually occurs within 6 to 12 hours; discomfort usually disappears within 48 hours. Conjunctivitis follows and may be accompanied by erythema of the facial skin surrounding the eyelids. Of course, UVR exposure rarely results in permanent ocular injury. Pitts and Tredici (1971) reported threshold data for photokeratitis in humans for wavebands 10 nm in width from 220 to 310 nm. The maximum sensitivity of the cornea was found to occur at 270 nm—differing markedly from the maximum for the skin. Presumably, 270 nm radiation is biologically more active because of the lack of a stratum corneum to attenuate the dose to the corneal epithelium tissue at shorter UVR wavelengths. The wavelength response, or action spectrum, did not vary as greatly as did the erythema action spectra, with thresholds varying from 4 to 14 mJ/cm^2 at 270 nm. The threshold reported at 308 nm was approximately 100 mJ/cm^2.

Repeated exposure of the eye to potentially hazardous levels of UVR does not increase the protective capability of the affected tissue (the cornea) as does skin exposure, which leads to tanning and to thickening of the stratum corneum. Ringvold and associates studied the UVR absorption properties of the cornea (Ringvold 1980a) and aqueous humour (Ringvold 1980b), as well as the effects of UVB radiation upon the corneal epithelium (Ringvold 1983), the corneal stroma (Ringvold and Davanger 1985) and the corneal endothelium (Ringvold, Davanger and Olsen 1982; Olsen and Ringvold 1982). Their electron microscopic studies showed that corneal tissue possessed remarkable repair and recovery properties. Although one could readily detect significant damage to all of these layers apparently appearing initially in cell membranes, morphological recovery was complete after a week. Destruction of keratocytes in the stromal layer was apparent, and endothelial recovery was pronounced despite the normal lack of rapid cell turnover in the endothelium. Cullen et al. (1984) studied endothelial damage that was persistent if the UVR exposure was persistent. Riley et al. (1987) also studied the corneal endothelium following UVB exposure and concluded that severe, single insults were not likely to have delayed effects; however, they also concluded that chronic exposure could accelerate changes in the endothelium related to ageing of the cornea.

Wavelengths above 295 nm can be transmitted through the cornea and are almost totally absorbed by the lens. Pitts, Cullen and Hacker (1977b) showed that cataracts can be produced in rabbits by wavelengths in the 295–320 nm band. Thresholds for transient opacities ranged from 0.15 to 12.6 J/cm^2, depending on wavelength, with a minimum threshold at 300 nm. Permanent opacities required greater radiant exposures. No lenticular effects were noted in the wavelength range of 325 to 395 nm even with much higher radiant exposures of 28 to 162 J/cm^2 (Pitts, Cullen and Hacker 1977a; Zuclich and Connolly 1976). These studies clearly illustrate the particular hazard of the 300-315 nm spectral band, as would be expected because photons of these wavelengths penetrate efficiently and have sufficient energy to produce photochemical damage.

Taylor et al. (1988) provided epidemiological evidence that UVB in sunlight was an aetiological factor in senile cataract, but showed no correlation of cataract with UVA exposure. Although once a popular belief because of the strong absorption of UVA by the lens, the hypothesis that UVA can cause cataract has not been supported by either experimental laboratory studies or by epidemiological studies. From the laboratory experimental data which showed that thresholds for photokeratitis were lower than for cataractogenesis, one must conclude that levels lower than those required to produce photokeratitis on a daily basis should be considered hazardous to lens tissue. Even if one were to assume that the cornea is exposed to a level nearly equivalent to the threshold for photokeratitis, one would estimate that the daily UVR dose to the lens at 308 nm would be less than 120 mJ/cm^2 for 12 hours out of doors (Sliney 1987). Indeed, a more realistic average daily exposure would be less than half that value.

Ham et al. (1982) determined the action spectrum for photoretinitis produced by UVR in the 320–400 nm band. They showed that thresholds in the visible spectral band, which were 20 to 30 J/cm^2 at 440 nm, were reduced to approximately 5 J/cm^2 for a 10 nm band centred at 325 nm. The action spectrum was increasing monotonically with decreasing wavelength. We should therefore conclude that levels well below 5 J/cm^2 at 308 nm should produce retinal lesions, although these lesions would not become apparent for 24 to 48 hours after the exposure. There are no published data for retinal injury thresholds below 325 nm, and one can only expect that the pattern for the action spectrum for photochemical injury to the cornea and lens tissues would apply to the retina as well, leading to an injury threshold of the order of $0.1 \, J/cm^2$.

Although UVB radiation has been clearly shown to be mutagenic and carcinogenic to the skin, the extreme rarity of carcinogenesis in the cornea and conjunctiva is quite remarkable. There appears to be no scientific evidence to link UVR exposure with any cancers of the cornea or conjunctiva in humans, although the same is not true of cattle. This would suggest a very effective immune system operating in the human eye, since there are certainly outdoor workers who receive a UVR exposure comparable to that which cattle receive. This conclusion is further supported by the fact that individuals suffering from a defective immune response, as in xeroderma pigmentosum, frequently develop neoplasias of the cornea and conjunctiva (Stenson 1982).

Safety Standards

Occupational exposure limits (EL) for UVR have been developed and include an action spectrum curve which envelops the threshold data for acute effects obtained from studies of minimal erythema and keratoconjunctivitis (Sliney 1972; IRPA 1989). This curve does not differ significantly from the collective threshold data, considering measurement errors and variations in individual response, and is well below the UVB cataractogenic thresholds.

The EL for UVR is lowest at 270 nm ($0.003 \, J/cm^2$ at 270 nm), and, for example, at 308 nm is $0.12 \, J/cm^2$ (ACGIH 1995, IRPA 1988). Regardless of whether the exposure occurs from a few pulsed exposures during the day, a single very brief exposure, or from an 8-hour exposure at a few microwatts per square centimetre, the biological hazard is the same, and the above limits apply to the full workday.

Occupational Protection

Occupational exposure to UVR should be minimized where practical. For artificial sources, wherever possible, priority should be given to engineering measures such as filtration, shielding and enclosure. Administrative controls, such as limitation of access, can reduce the requirements for personal protection.

Outdoor workers such as agricultural workers, labourers, construction workers, fishermen and so on can minimize their risk from solar UV exposure by wearing appropriate tightly woven clothing, and most important, a brimmed hat to reduce face and neck exposure. Sunscreens can be applied to exposed skin to reduce further exposure. Outdoor workers should have access to shade and be provided with all the necessary protective measures mentioned above.

In industry, there are many sources capable of causing acute eye injury within a short exposure time. A variety of eye protection is available with various degrees of protection appropriate to the intended use. Those intended for industrial use include welding helmets (additionally providing protection both from intense visible and infrared radiation as well as face protection), face shields, goggles and UV-absorbing spectacles. In general, protective eyewear provided for industrial use should fit snugly on the face, thus ensuring that there are no gaps through which UVR can directly reach the eye, and they should be well-constructed to prevent physical injury.

The appropriateness and selection of protective eyewear is dependent on the following points:

- the intensity and spectral emission characteristics of the UVR source
- the behavioural patterns of people near UVR sources (distance and exposure time are important)
- the transmission properties of the protective eyewear material

- the design of the frame of the eyewear to prevent peripheral exposure of the eye from direct unabsorbed UVR.

In industrial exposure situations, the degree of ocular hazard can be assessed by measurement and comparison with recommended limits for exposure (Duchene, Lakey and Repacholi 1991).

Measurement

Because of the strong dependence of biological effects on wavelength, the principal measurement of any UVR source is its spectral power or spectral irradiance distribution. This must be measured with a spectroradiometer which consists of suitable input optics, a monochromator and a UVR detector and readout. Such an instrument is not normally used in occupational hygiene.

In many practical situations, a broad-band UVR meter is used to determine safe exposure durations. For safety purposes, the spectral response can be tailored to follow the spectral function used for the exposure guidelines of the ACGIH and the IRPA. If appropriate instruments are not used, serious errors of hazard assessment will result. Personal UVR dosimeters are also available (e.g., polysulphone film), but their application has been largely confined to occupational safety research rather than in hazard evaluation surveys.

Conclusions

Molecular damage of key cellular components arising from UVR exposure occurs constantly, and repair mechanisms exist to deal with the exposure of skin and ocular tissues to ultraviolet radiation. Only when these repair mechanisms are overwhelmed does acute biological injury become apparent (Smith 1988). For these reasons, minimizing occupational UVR exposure continues to remain an important object of concern among occupational health and safety workers.

INFRARED RADIATION

R. Matthes

Infrared radiation is that part of the non-ionizing radiation spectrum located between microwaves and visible light. It is a natural part of the human environment and thus people are exposed to it in small amounts in all areas of daily life—for example, at home or during recreational activities in the sun. Very intense exposure, however, may result from certain technical processes at the workplace.

Many industrial processes involve thermal curing of various kinds of materials. The heat sources used or the heated material itself will usually emit such high levels of infrared radiation that a large number of workers are potentially at risk of being exposed.

Concepts and Quantities

Infrared radiation (IR) has wavelengths ranging from 780 nm to 1 mm. Following the classification by the International Commission on Illumination (CIE), this band is subdivided into IRA (from 780 nm to 1.4 µm), IRB (from 1.4 µm to 3 µm) and IRC (from 3 µm to 1 mm). This subdivision approximately follows the wavelength-dependent absorption characteristics of IR in tissue and the resulting different biological effects.

The amount and the temporal and spatial distribution of infrared radiation are described by different radiometric quantities and units. Due to optical and physiological properties, especially of the eye, a distinction is usually made between small "point" sources and "extended" sources. The criterion for this distinction is the value in radians of the angle (α) measured at the eye that is

Figure 49.4 • Spectral radiance L_λ of a black body radiator at the absolute temperature shown in degrees Kelvin on each curve.

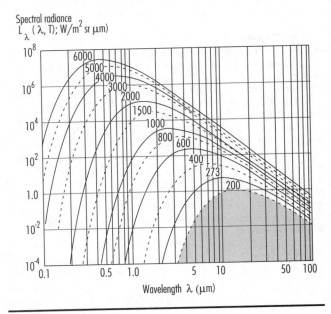

equivalent to the concept of exposure dose rate, and the *radiant exposure* (H, in Jm^{-2}), equivalent to the exposure dose concept.

In some bands of the spectrum, the biological effects due to exposure are strongly dependent on wavelength. Therefore, additional spectroradiometric quantities must be used (e.g., the spectral radiance, L_λ, expressed in $Wm^{-2} sr^{-1} nm^{-1}$) to weigh the physical emission values of the source against the applicable action spectrum related to the biological effect.

Sources and Occupational Exposure

Exposure to IR results from various natural and artificial sources. The spectral emission from these sources may be limited to a single wavelength (laser) or may be distributed over a broad wavelength band.

The different mechanisms for the generation of optical radiation in general are:

- thermal excitation (black-body radiation)
- gas discharge
- light amplification by stimulated emission of radiation (laser), with the mechanism of gas discharge being of lesser importance in the IR band.

The emission from the most important sources used in many industrial processes results from thermal excitation, and can be approximated using the physical laws of black-body radiation if the absolute temperature of the source is known. The total emission (M, in Wm^{-2}) of a black-body radiator (figure 49.4) is described by the Stefan-Boltzmann law:

$$M(T) = 5.67 \times 10^{-8} T^4$$

and depends on the 4th power of the temperature (T, in K) of the radiating body. The spectral distribution of the radiance is described by Planck's radiation law:

$$L_\lambda = \frac{2c^2 h}{\lambda^5 (e^{\frac{hc}{|kT|}} - 1)}$$

c = speed of light

h = Planck's constant

k = Boltzmann's constant

subtended by the source. This angle can be calculated as a quotient, the light source dimension D_L divided by the viewing distance r. Extended sources are those which subtend a viewing angle at the eye greater than α_{min}, which normally is 11 milliradians. For all extended sources there is a viewing distance where α equals α_{min}; at greater viewing distances, the source can be treated like a point source. In optical radiation protection the most important quantities concerning extended sources are the *radiance* (L, expressed in $Wm^{-2}sr^{-1}$) and the *time-integrated radiance* (L_p in $Jm^{-2}sr^{-1}$), which describe the "brightness" of the source. For health risk assessment, the most relevant quantities concerning point sources or exposures at such distances from the source where $\alpha < \alpha_{min}$, are the *irradiance* (E, expressed in Wm^{-2}), which is

Table 49.1 • Different sources of IR, population exposed and approximate exposure levels.

Source	Application or exposed population	Exposure
Sunlight	Outdoor workers, farmers, construction workers, seafarers, general public	$500\ Wm^{-2}$
Tungsten filament lamps	General population and workers General lighting, ink and paint drying	$10^5 - 10^6\ Wm^{-2}sr^{-1}$
Tungsten halogen filament lamps	(See tungsten filament lamps) Copying systems (fixing), general processes (drying, baking, shrinking, softening)	$50 - 200\ Wm^{-2}$ (at 50 cm)
Light emitting diodes (e.g. GaAs diode)	Toys, consumer electronics, data transmission technology, etc.	$10^5\ Wm^{-2}sr^{-1}$
Xenon arc lamps	Projectors, solar simulators, search lights Printing plant camera operators, optical laboratory workers, entertainers	$10^7\ Wm^{-2}sr^{-1}$
Iron melt	Steel furnace, steel mill workers	$10^5\ Wm^{-2}sr^{-1}$
Infrared lamp arrays	Industrial heating and drying	10^3 to $8 \cdot 10^3\ Wm^{-2}$
Infrared lamps in hospitals	Incubators	$100 - 300\ Wm^{-2}$

Figure 49.5 • Spectral absorption of the ocular media.

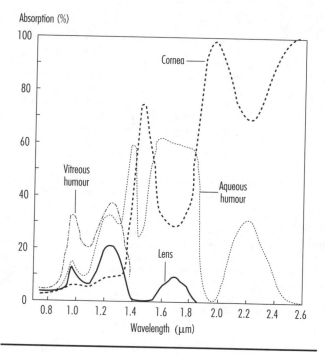

wavelength-dependent optical properties of tissue—for example, the spectral absorption of the ocular media (figure 49.5).

Effects on the eye

In general, the eye is well adapted to protect itself against optical radiation from the natural environment. In addition, the eye is physiologically protected against injury from bright light sources, such as the sun or high intensity lamps, by an aversion response that limits the duration of exposure to a fraction of a second (approximately 0.25 seconds).

IRA affects primarily the retina, because of the transparency of the ocular media. When directly viewing a point source or laser beam, the focusing properties in the IRA region additionally render the retina much more susceptible to damage than any other part of the body. For short exposure periods, heating of the iris from the absorption of visible or near IR is considered to play a role in the development of opacities in the lens.

With increasing wavelength, above approximately 1 μm, the absorption by ocular media increases. Therefore, absorption of IRA radiation by both the lens and the pigmented iris is considered to play a role in the formation of lenticular opacities. Damage to the lens is attributed to wavelengths below 3 μm (IRA and IRB). For infrared radiation of wavelengths longer than 1.4 μm, the aqueous humour and the lens are particularly strongly absorbent.

In the IRB and IRC region of the spectrum, the ocular media become opaque as a result of the strong absorption by their constituent water. Absorption in this region is primarily in the cornea and in the aqueous humour. Beyond 1.9 μm, the cornea is effectively the sole absorber. The absorption of long wavelength infrared radiation by the cornea may lead to increased temperatures in the eye due to thermal conduction. Because of a quick turnover rate of the surface corneal cells, any damage limited to the outer corneal layer can be expected to be temporary. In the IRC band the exposure can cause a burn on the cornea similar to that on the skin. Corneal burns are not very likely to occur, however, because of the aversion reaction triggered by the painful sensation caused by strong exposure.

Effects on the skin

Infrared radiation will not penetrate the skin very deeply. Therefore, exposure of the skin to very strong IR may lead to local thermal effects of different severity, and even serious burns. The

and the wavelength of maximum emission (λ_{max}) is described according to Wien's law by:

$$\lambda_{max} = \frac{2.898 \times 10^{-3}}{T}$$

Many lasers used in industrial and medical processes will emit very high levels of IR. In general, compared with other radiation sources, laser radiation has some unusual features that may influence the risk following an exposure, such as very short pulse duration or extremely high irradiance. Therefore, laser radiation is discussed in detail elsewhere in this chapter.

Many industrial processes require the use of sources emitting high levels of visible and infrared radiation, and thus a large number of workers like bakers, glass blowers, kiln workers, foundry workers, blacksmiths, smelters and fire-fighters are potentially at risk of exposure. In addition to lamps, such sources as flames, gas torches, acetylene torches, pools of molten metal and incandescent metal bars must be considered. These are encountered in foundries, steel mills and in many other heavy industrial plants. Table 49.1 summarizes some examples of IR sources and their applications.

Biological Effects

Optical radiation in general does not penetrate very deeply into biological tissue. Therefore, the primary targets of an IR exposure are the skin and the eye. Under most exposure conditions the main interaction mechanism of IR is thermal. Only the very short pulses that lasers may produce, but which are not considered here, can also lead to mechanothermal effects. Effects from ionization or from the breakage of chemical bonds are not expected to appear with IR radiation because the particle energy, being less than approximately 1.6 eV, is too low to cause such effects. For the same reason, photochemical reactions become significant only at shorter wavelengths in the visual and in the ultraviolet region. The different wavelength-dependent health effects of IR arise mainly from the

Figure 49.6 • Depth of penetration into the skin for different wavelengths.

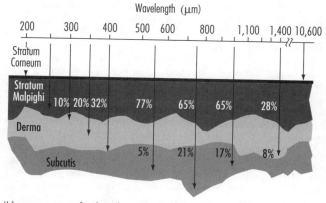

Values are percentages of incident radiation reaching a given layer of the skin.
Source: WHO 1982.

49. RADIATION, NON-IONIZING

Table 49.2 • Retinal thermal hazard function.

Wavelength (nm)	R_λ	Wavelength (nm)	R_λ
400	1.0	460	8.0
405	2.0	465	7.0
410	4.0	470	6.2
415	8.0	475	5.5
420	9.0	480	4.5
425	9.5	485	4.0
430	9.8	490	2.2
435	10.0	495	1.6
440	10.0	500–700	1.0
445	9.7	700–1,050	$10^{((700-\lambda)/500)}$
450	9.4	1,050–1,400	0.2
455	9.0		

Source: ACGIH 1996.

effects on the skin depend on the optical properties of the skin, such as wavelength-dependent depth of penetration (figure 49.6). Especially at longer wavelengths, an extensive exposure may cause a high local temperature rise and burns. The threshold values for these effects are time dependent, because of the physical properties of the thermal transport processes in the skin. An irradiation of 10 kWm^{-2}, for example, may cause a painful sensation within 5 seconds, whereas an exposure of 2 kWm^{-2} will not cause the same reaction within periods shorter than approximately 50 seconds.

If the exposure is extended over very long periods, even at values well below the pain threshold, the burden of heat to the human body may be great. Especially if the exposure covers the whole body as, for example, in front of a steel melt. The result may be an imbalance of the otherwise physiologically well balanced thermoregulation system. The threshold for tolerating such an exposure will depend on different individual and environmental conditions, such as the individual capacity of the thermoregulation system, the actual body metabolism during exposure or the environmental temperature, humidity and air movement (wind speed). Without any physical work, a maximum exposure of 300 Wm^{-2} may be tolerated over eight hours under certain environmental conditions, but this value decreases to approximately 140 Wm^{-2} during heavy physical work.

Exposure Standards

The biological effects of IR exposure which are dependent on wavelength and on the duration of exposure, are intolerable only if certain threshold intensity or dose values are exceeded. To protect against such intolerable exposure conditions, international organizations such as the World Health Organization (WHO), the International Labour Office (ILO), the International Committee for Non-Ionizing Radiation of the International Radiation Protection Association (INIRC/IRPA), and its successor, the International Commission on Non-Ionizing Radiation Protection (ICNIRP) and the American Conference of Governmental Industrial Hygienists (ACGIH) have suggested exposure limits for infrared radiation from both coherent and incoherent optical sources. Most of the national and international suggestions on guidelines for limiting human exposure to infrared radiation are either based on or even identical with the suggested threshold limit values

(TLVs) published by the ACGIH (1993/1994). These limits are widely recognized and are frequently used in occupational situations. They are based on current scientific knowledge and are intended to prevent thermal injury of the retina and cornea and to avoid possible delayed effects on the lens of the eye.

The 1994 revision of the ACGIH exposure limits is as follows:

1. For the protection of the retina from thermal injury in case of exposure to visible light, (for example, in the case of powerful light sources), the spectral radiance L_λ in W/(m^2 sr nm) weighted against the retinal thermal hazard function R_λ (see table 49.2) over the wavelength interval Δ_λ and summed over the range of wavelength 400 to 1400 nm, should not exceed:

$$\sum_{400}^{1400} L_\lambda R_\lambda \Delta_\lambda \leq \frac{5 \times 10^4}{\alpha \cdot t^{1/4}}$$

where t is the viewing duration limited to intervals from 10^{-3} to 10 seconds (that is, for accidental viewing conditions, not fixated viewing), and α is the angular subtense of the source in radians calculated by α = maximum extension of the source/distance to the source R_λ (table 49.2).

2. To protect the retina from the exposure hazards of infrared heat lamps or any near IR source where a strong visual stimulus is absent, the infrared radiance over the wavelength range 770 to 1400 nm as viewed by the eye (based on a 7 mm pupil diameter) for extended duration of viewing conditions should be limited to:

$$\sum_{770}^{1400} L_\lambda \Delta_\lambda \leq \frac{6 \times 10^3}{\alpha}$$

This limit is based on a pupil diameter of 7 mm since, in this case, the aversion response (closing the eye, for example) may not exist due to the absence of visible light.

3. To avoid possible delayed effects on the lens of the eye, such as delayed cataract, and to protect the cornea from overexposure, the infrared radiation at wavelengths greater than 770 nm should be limited to 100 W/m^2 for periods greater than 1,000 s and to:

$$\sum_{770}^{3000} E_\lambda \Delta_\lambda \leq 1.8 \times 10^4 t^{-3/4}$$

or for shorter periods.

4. For aphakic patients, separate weighting functions and resulting TLVs are given for the wavelength range of ultraviolet and visible light (305–700 nm).

Measurement

Reliable radiometric techniques and instruments are available that make it possible to analyse the risk to the skin and the eye from exposure to sources of optical radiation. For characterizing a conventional light source, it is generally very useful to measure the radiance. For defining hazardous exposure conditions from optical sources, the irradiance and the radiant exposure are of greater importance. The evaluation of broad-band sources is more complex than the evaluation of sources that emit at single wavelengths or very narrow bands, since spectral characteristics and source size must be considered. The spectrum of certain lamps consists of both a continuum emission over a wide wavelength band and emission on certain single wavelengths (lines). Significant errors may be introduced into the representation of those spectra if the fraction of energy in each line is not properly added to the continuum.

For health-hazard assessment the exposure values must be measured over a limiting aperture for which the exposure standards are specified. Typically a 1 mm aperture has been considered to be the smallest practical aperture size. Wavelengths greater than 0.1 mm present difficulties because of significant diffraction effects created by a 1 mm aperture. For this wavelength band an aperture of 1 cm² (11 mm diameter) was accepted, because hot spots in this band are larger than at shorter wavelengths. For the evaluation of retinal hazards, the size of the aperture was determined by an average pupil size and therefore an aperture of 7 mm was chosen.

In general, measurements in the optical region are very complex. Measurements taken by untrained personnel may lead to invalid conclusions. A detailed summary of measurement procedures is to be found in Sliney and Wolbarsht (1980).

Protective Measures

The most effective standard protection from exposure to optical radiation is the total enclosure of the source and all of the radiation pathways that may exit from the source. By such measures, compliance with the exposure limits should be easy to achieve in the majority of cases. Where this is not the case, personal protection is applicable. For example, available eye protection in the form of suitable goggles or visors or protective clothing should be used. If the work conditions will not allow for such measures to be applied, administrative control and restricted access to very intense sources may be necessary. In some cases a reduction of either the power of the source or the working time (work pauses to recover from heat stress), or both, might be a possible measure to protect the worker.

Conclusion

In general, infrared radiation from the most common sources such as lamps, or from most industrial applications, will not cause any risk to workers. At some workplaces, however, IR can cause a health risk for the worker. In addition, there is a rapid increase in the application and use of special-purpose lamps and in high temperature processes in industry, science and medicine. If the exposure from those applications is sufficiently high, detrimental effects (mainly in the eye but also on the skin) cannot be excluded. The importance of internationally recognized optical radiation exposure standards is expected to increase. To protect the worker from excessive exposure, protective measures like shielding (eye shields) or protective clothing should be mandatory.

The principal adverse biological effects attributed to infrared radiation are cataracts, known as glass blower's or furnaceman's cataracts. Long-term exposure even at relatively low levels causes heat stress to the human body. At such exposure conditions additional factors such as body temperature and evaporative heat loss as well as environmental factors must be considered.

In order to inform and instruct workers some practical guides were developed in industrial countries. A comprehensive summary can be found in Sliney and Wolbarsht (1980).

● LIGHT AND INFRARED RADIATION

David H. Sliney

Light and infrared (IR) radiant energy are two forms of optical radiation, and together with ultraviolet radiation, they form the optical spectrum. Within the optical spectrum, different wavelengths have considerably different potentials for causing biological effects, and for this reason the optical spectrum may be further subdivided.

The term *light* should be reserved for wavelengths of radiant energy between 400 and 760 nm, which evoke a visual response at

the retina (CIE 1987). Light is the essential component of the output of illuminating lamps, visual displays and a wide variety of illuminators. Aside from the importance of illumination for seeing, some light sources may, however, pose unwanted physiological reactions such as disability and discomfort glare, flicker and other forms of eye stress due to poor ergonomic design of workplace tasks. The emission of intense light is also a potentially hazardous side-effect of some industrial processes, such as arc welding.

Infrared radiation (IRR, wavelengths 760 nm to 1 mm) may also be referred to quite commonly as *thermal radiation* (or *radiant heat*), and is emitted from any warm object (hot engines, molten metals and other foundry sources, heat-treated surfaces, incandescent electric lamps, radiant heating systems, etc.). Infrared radiation is also emitted from a large variety of electrical equipment such as electric motors, generators, transformers and various electronic equipment.

Infrared radiation is a contributory factor in heat stress. High ambient air temperature and humidity and a low degree of air circulation can combine with radiant heat to produce heat stress with the potential for heat injuries. In cooler environments, unwelcome or poorly designed sources of radiant heat can also produce discomfort—an ergonomic consideration.

Biological Effects

Occupational hazards presented to the eye and skin by visible and infrared forms of radiation are limited by the eye's aversion to bright light and the pain sensation in the skin resulting from intense radiant heating. The eye is well-adapted to protect itself against acute optical radiation injury (due to ultraviolet, visible or infrared radiant energy) from ambient sunlight. It is protected by a natural aversion response to viewing bright light sources that normally protects it against injury arising from exposure to sources such as the sun, arc lamps and welding arcs, since this aversion limits the duration of exposure to a fraction (about two-tenths) of a second. However, sources rich in IRR without a strong visual stimulus can be hazardous to the lens of the eye in the case of chronic exposure. One can also force oneself to stare at the sun, a welding arc or a snow field and thereby suffer a temporary (and sometimes a permanent) loss of vision. In an industrial setting in which bright lights appear low in the field of view, the eye's protective mechanisms are less effective, and hazard precautions are particularly important.

There are at least five separate types of hazards to the eye and skin from intense light and IRR sources, and protective measures must be chosen with an understanding of each. In addition to the potential hazards presented by ultraviolet radiation (UVR) from some intense light sources, one should consider the following hazards (Sliney and Wolbarsht 1980; WHO 1982):

1. Thermal injury to the retina, which can occur at wavelengths from 400 nm to 1,400 nm. Normally the danger of this type of injury is posed only by lasers, a very intense xenon-arc source or a nuclear fireball. The local burning of the retina results in a blind spot (scotoma).

2. Blue-light photochemical injury to the retina (a hazard principally associated with blue light of wavelengths from 400 nm to 550 nm) (Ham 1989). The injury is commonly termed "blue light" photoretinitis; a particular form of this injury is named, according to its source, *solar retinitis*. Solar retinitis was once referred to as "eclipse blindness" and associated "retinal burn". Only in recent years has it become clear that photoretinitis results from a photochemical injury mechanism following exposure of the retina to shorter wavelengths in the visible spectrum, namely, violet and blue light. Until the 1970s, it was thought to be the result of a thermal injury mechanism. In contrast to blue light, IRA radiation is very ineffective in

producing retinal injuries. (Ham 1989; Sliney and Wolbarsht 1980).

3. Near-infrared thermal hazards to the lens (associated with wavelengths of approximately 800 nm to 3,000 nm) with potential for industrial heat cataract. The average corneal exposure to infrared radiation in sunlight is of the order of 10 W/m^2. By comparison, glass and steel workers exposed to infrared irradiances of the order of 0.8 to 4 kW/m^2 daily for 10 to 15 years have reportedly developed lenticular opacities (Sliney and Wolbarsht 1980). These spectral bands include IRA and IRB (see figure 49.1). The American Conference of Governmental Industrial Hygienists (ACGIH) guideline for IRA exposure of the anterior of the eye is a time-weighted total irradiance of 100 W/m^2 for exposure durations exceeding 1,000 s (16.7 min) (ACGIH 1992 and 1995).

4. Thermal injury of the cornea and conjunctiva (at wavelengths of approximately 1,400 nm to 1 mm). This type of injury is almost exclusively limited to exposure to laser radiation.

5. Thermal injury of the skin. This is rare from conventional sources but can occur across the entire optical spectrum.

The importance of wavelength and time of exposure

Thermal injuries (1) and (4) above are generally limited to very brief exposure durations, and eye protection is designed to prevent these acute injuries. However, photochemical injuries, such as are mentioned in (2) above, can result from low dose rates spread over the entire workday. The product of the dose rate and the exposure duration always results in the dose (it is the dose that governs the degree of photochemical hazard). As with any photochemical injury mechanism, one must consider the action spectrum which describes the relative effectiveness of different wavelengths in causing a photobiological effect. For example, the action spectrum for photochemical retinal injury peaks at approximately 440 nm (Ham 1989). Most photochemical effects are limited to a very narrow range of wavelengths; whereas a thermal effect can occur at any wavelength in the spectrum. Hence, eye protection for these specific effects need block only a relatively narrow spectral band in order to be effective. Normally, more than one spectral band must be filtered in eye protection for a broad-band source.

Sources of Optical Radiation

Sunlight

The greatest occupational exposure to optical radiation results from exposure of outdoor workers to the sun's rays. The solar spectrum extends from the stratospheric ozone-layer cut-off of about of 290-295 nm in the ultraviolet band to at least 5,000 nm (5 μm) in the infrared band. Solar radiation can attain a level as high as 1 kW/m^2 during the summer months. It can result in heat stress, depending upon ambient air temperature and humidity.

Artificial sources

The most significant artificial sources of human exposure to optical radiation include the following:

1. *Welding and cutting.* Welders and their co-workers are typically exposed not only to intense UV radiation, but also to intense visible and IR radiation emitted from the arc. Under rare instances, these sources have produced acute injury to the retina of the eye. Eye protection is mandatory for these environments.

2. *Metals industries and foundries.* The most significant source of visible and infrared exposure are from molten and hot metal surfaces in the steel and aluminium industries and in foun-

dries. Worker exposure typically ranges from 0.5 to 1.2 kW/m^2.

3. *Arc lamps.* Many industrial and commercial processes, such as those involving photochemical curing lamps, emit intense, short-wave visible (blue) light as well as UV and IR radiation. While the likelihood of harmful exposure is low due to shielding, in some cases accidental exposure can occur.

4. *Infrared lamps.* These lamps emit predominantly in the IRA range and are generally used for heat treatment, paint drying and related applications. These lamps do not pose any significant exposure hazard to humans since the discomfort produced upon exposure will limit exposure to a safe level.

5. *Medical treatment.* Infrared lamps are used in physical medicine for a variety of diagnostic and therapeutic purposes. Exposures to the patient vary considerably according to the type of treatment, and IR lamps require careful use by staff members.

6. *General lighting.* Fluorescent lamps emit very little infrared and are generally not bright enough to pose a potential hazard to the eye. Tungsten and tungsten-halogen incandescent lamps emit a large fraction of their radiant energy in the infrared. Additionally, the blue light emitted by tungsten-halogen lamps can pose a retinal hazard if a person stares at the filament. Fortunately, the eye's aversion response to bright light prevents acute injury even at short distances. Placing glass "heat" filters over these lamps should minimize/eliminate this hazard.

7. *Optical projectors and other devices.* Intense light sources are used in searchlights, film projectors and other light-beam collimating devices. These may pose a retinal hazard with the direct beam at very close distances.

Measurement of Source Properties

The most important characteristic of any optical source is its spectral power distribution. This is measured using a spectroradiometer, which consists of suitable input optics, a monochromator and a photodetector.

In many practical situations, a broad-band optical radiometer is used to select a given spectral region. For both visible illumination and safety purposes, the spectral response of the instrument will be tailored to follow a biological spectral response; for example, lux-meters are geared to the photopic (visual) response of the eye. Normally, aside from UVR hazard meters, the measurement and hazard analysis of intense light sources and infrared sources is too complex for routine occupational health and safety specialists. Progress is being made in standardizations of safety categories of lamps, so that measurements by the user will not be required in order to determine potential hazards.

Human Exposure Limits

From knowledge of the optical parameters of the human eye and the radiance of a light source, it is possible to calculate irradiances (dose rates) at the retina. Exposure of the anterior structures of the human eye to infrared radiation may also be of interest, and it should be further borne in mind that the relative position of the light source and the degree of lid closure can greatly affect the proper calculation of an ocular exposure dose. For ultraviolet and short-wavelength light exposures, the spectral distribution of the light source is also important.

A number of national and international groups have recommended occupational exposure limits (ELs) for optical radiation (ACGIH 1992 and 1994; Sliney 1992). Although most such groups have recommended ELs for UV and laser radiation, only one group has recommended ELs for visible radiation (i.e., light), namely, the ACGIH, an agency well-known in the field of occupational health. The ACGIH refers to its ELs as threshold limit values, or TLVs, and as these are issued yearly, there is an opportunity for a yearly revision (ACGIH 1992 and 1995). They are based in large part on ocular injury data from animal studies and from data from human retinal injuries resulting from viewing the sun and welding arcs. TLVs are furthermore based on the underlying assumption that outdoor environmental exposures to visible radiant energy are normally not hazardous to the eye except in very unusual environments, such as snow fields and deserts, or when one actually fixes the eyes on the sun.

Optical Radiation Safety Evaluation

Since a comprehensive hazard evaluation requires complex measurements of spectral irradiance and radiance of the source, and sometimes very specialized instruments and calculations as well, it is rarely carried out onsite by industrial hygienists and safety engineers. Instead, the eye protective equipment to be deployed is mandated by safety regulations in hazardous environments. Research studies evaluated a wide range of arcs, lasers and thermal sources in order to develop broad recommendations for practical, easier-to-apply safety standards.

Protective Measures

Occupational exposure to visible and IR radiation is seldom hazardous and is usually beneficial. However, some sources emit a considerable amount of visible radiation, and in this case, the natural aversion response is evoked, so there is little chance of accidental overexposure of the eyes. On the other hand, accidental exposure is quite likely in the case of artificial sources emitting only near-IR radiation. Measures which can be taken to minimize the unnecessary exposure of staff to IR radiation include proper engineering design of the optical system in use, wearing appropriate goggles or face visors, limiting access to persons directly concerned with the work, and ensuring that workers are aware of the potential hazards associated with exposure to intense visible and IR radiation sources. Maintainance staff who replace arc lamps must have adequate training so as to preclude hazardous exposure. It is unacceptable for workers to experience either skin erythema or photokeratitis. If these conditions do occur, working practices should be examined and steps taken to ensure that overexposure is made unlikely in the future. Pregnant operators are at no specific risk to optical radiation as regards the integrity of their pregnancy.

Eye protector design and standards

The design of eye protectors for welding and other operations presenting sources of industrial optical radiation (e.g., foundry work, steel and glass manufacture) started at the beginning of this century with the development of Crooke's glass. Eye protector standards which evolved later followed the general principle that since infrared and ultraviolet radiation are not needed for vision, those spectral bands should be blocked as best as possible by currently available glass materials.

The empirical standards for eye protective equipment were tested in the 1970s and were shown to have included large safety factors for infrared and ultraviolet radiation when the transmission factors were tested against current occupational exposure limits, whereas the protection factors for blue light were just sufficient. Some standards requirements were therefore adjusted.

Ultraviolet and infrared radiation protection

A number of specialized UV lamps are used in industry for fluorescence detection and for photocuring of inks, plastic resins, dental polymers and so on. Although UVA sources normally pose little risk, these sources may either contain trace amounts of hazardous UVB or pose a disability glare problem (from fluorescence of the eye's crystalline lens). UV filter lenses, glass or plastic,

with very high attenuation factors are widely available to protect against the entire UV spectrum. A slight yellowish tint may be detectable if protection is afforded to 400 nm. It is of paramount importance for this type of eyewear (and for industrial sunglasses) to provide protection for the peripheral field of vision. Side shields or wraparound designs are important to protect against the focusing of temporal, oblique rays into the nasal equatorial area of the lens, where cortical cataract frequently originates.

Almost all glass and plastic lens materials block ultraviolet radiation below 300 nm and infrared radiation at wavelengths greater than 3,000 nm (3 μm), and for a few lasers and optical sources, ordinary impact-resistant clear safety eyewear will provide good protection (e.g., clear polycarbonate lenses effectively block wavelengths greater than 3 μm). However, absorbers such as metal oxides in glass or organic dyes in plastics must be added to eliminate UV up to about 380–400 nm, and infrared beyond 780 nm to 3 μm. Depending upon the material, this may be either easy or very difficult or expensive, and the stability of the absorber may vary somewhat. Filters that meet the American National Standards Institute's ANSI Z87.1 standard must have the appropriate attenuation factors in each critical spectral band.

Protection in various industries

Fire-fighting

Fire-fighters may be exposed to intense near-infrared radiation, and aside from the crucially important head and face protection, IRR attenuating filters are frequently prescribed. Here, impact protection is also important.

Foundry and glass industry eyewear

Spectacles and goggles designed for ocular protection against infrared radiation generally have a light greenish tint, although the tint may be darker if some comfort against visible radiation is desired. Such eye protectors should not be confused with the blue lenses used with steel and foundry operations, where the objective is to check the temperature of the melt visually; these blue spectacles do not provide protection, and should be worn only briefly.

Welding

Infrared and ultraviolet filtration properties can be readily imparted to glass filters by means of additives such as iron oxide, but the degree of strictly visible attenuation determines the *shade number*, which is a logarithmic expression of attenuation. Normally a shade number of 3 to 4 is used for gas welding (which calls for goggles), and a shade number of 10 to 14 for arc welding and plasma arc operations (here, helmet protection is required). The rule of thumb is that if the welder finds the arc comfortable to view, adequate attenuation is provided against ocular hazards. Supervisors, welder's helpers and other persons in the work area may require filters with a relatively low shade number (e.g., 3 to 4) to protect against photokeratitis ("arc eye" or "welder's flash"). In recent years a new type of welding filter, the autodarkening filter has appeared on the scene. Regardless of the type of filter, it should meet ANSI Z87.1 and Z49.1 standards for fixed welding filters specified for dark shade (Buhr and Sutter 1989; CIE 1987).

Autodarkening welding filters

The autodarkening welding filter, whose shade number increases with the intensity of the optical radiation impinging upon it, represents an important advance in the ability of welders to produce consistently high-quality welds more efficiently and ergonomically. Formerly, the welder had to lower and raise the helmet or filter each time an arc was started and quenched. The welder had to work "blind" just prior to striking the arc. Furthermore, the helmet is commonly lowered and raised with a sharp snap of the neck and head, which can lead to neck strain or more serious injuries. Faced with this uncomfortable and cumbersome procedure, some welders frequently initiate the arc with a conventional helmet in the raised position—leading to photokeratitis. Under normal ambient lighting conditions, a welder wearing a helmet fitted with an autodarkening filter can see well enough with the eye protection in place to perform tasks such as aligning the parts to be welded, precisely positioning the welding equipment and striking the arc. In the most typical helmet designs, light sensors then detect the arc flash virtually as soon as it appears and direct an electronic drive unit to switch a liquid crystal filter from a light shade to a preselected dark shade, eliminating the need for the clumsy and hazardous manoeuvres practised with fixed-shade filters.

The question has frequently been raised whether hidden safety problems may develop with autodarkening filters. For example, can afterimages ("flash blindness") experienced in the workplace result in permanently impaired vision? Do the new types of filter really offer a degree of protection that is equivalent or better than that which conventional fixed filters can provide? Although one can answer the second question in the affirmative, it must be understood that not all autodarkening filters are equivalent. Filter reaction speeds, the values of the light and dark shades achieved under a given intensity of illumination, and the weight of each unit may vary from one pattern of equipment to another. The temperature dependence of the unit's performance, the variation in the degree of shade with electrical battery degradation, the "resting state shade" and other technical factors vary depending upon each manufacturer's design. These considerations are being addressed in new standards.

Since adequate filter attenuation is afforded by all systems, the single most important attribute specified by the manufacturers of autodarkening filters is the speed of filter switching. Current autodarkening filters vary in switching speed from one tenth of a second to faster than 1/10,000th of a second. Buhr and Sutter (1989) have indicated a means of specifying the maximum switching time, but their formulation varies relative to the time-course of switching. Switching speed is crucial, since it gives the best clue to the all-important (but unspecified) measure of how much light will enter the eye when the arc is struck as compared with the light admitted by a fixed filter of the same working shade number. If too much light enters the eye for each switching during the day, the accumulated light-energy dose produces "transient adaptation" and complaints about "eye strain" and other problems. (Transient adaptation is the visual experience caused by sudden changes in one's light environment, which may be characterized by discomfort, a sensation of having been exposed to glare and temporary loss of detailed vision.) Current products with switching speeds of the order of ten milliseconds will better provide adequate protection against photoretinitis. However, the shortest switching time—of the order of 0.1 ms—has the advantage of reducing transient adaptation effects (Eriksen 1985; Sliney 1992).

Simple check tests are available to the welder short of extensive laboratory testing. One might suggest to the welder that he or she simply look at a page of detailed print through a number of autodarkening filters. This will give an indication of each filter's optical quality. Next, the welder may be asked to try striking an arc while observing it through each filter being considered for purchase. Fortunately, one can rely on the fact that light levels which are comfortable for viewing purposes will not be hazardous. The effectiveness of UV and IR filtration should be checked in the manufacturer's specification sheet to make sure that unnecessary bands are filtered out. A few repeated arc strikings should give the welder a sense of whether discomfort will be experienced from transient adaptation, although a one-day trial would be best.

The resting or failure state shade number of an autodarkening filter (a failure state occurs when the battery fails) should provide 100% protection for the welder's eyes for at least one to several seconds. Some manufacturers use a dark state as the "off" position and others use an intermediate shade between the dark and the light shade states. In either case, the resting state transmittance for the filter should be appreciably lower than the light shade transmittance in order to preclude a retinal hazard. In any case, the device should provide a clear and obvious indicator to the user as to when the filter is switched off or when a system failure occurs. This will ensure that the welder is warned in advance in case the filter is not switched on or is not operating properly before welding is begun. Other features, such as battery life or performance under extreme temperature conditions may be of importance to certain users.

Conclusions

Although technical specifications can appear to be somewhat complex for devices that protect the eye from optical radiation sources, safety standards exist which specify shade numbers, and these standards provide a conservative safety factor for the wearer.

LASERS

David H. Sliney

A laser is a device which produces coherent electromagnetic radiant energy within the optical spectrum from the extreme ultraviolet to the far infrared (submillimetre). The term *laser* is actually an acronym for *light amplification by stimulated emission of radiation*. Although the laser process was theoretically predicted by Albert Einstein in 1916, the first successful laser was not demonstrated until 1960. In recent years lasers have found their way from the research laboratory to the industrial, medical and office setting as well as construction sites and even households. In many applications, such as videodisk players and optical fibre communication systems, the laser's radiant energy output is enclosed, the user faces no health risk, and the presence of a laser embedded in the product may not be obvious to the user. However, in some medical, industrial or research applications, the laser's emitted radiant energy is accessible and may pose a potential hazard to the eye and skin.

Because the laser process (sometimes referred to as "lasing") can produce a highly collimated beam of optical radiation (i.e., ultraviolet, visible or infrared radiant energy), a laser can pose a hazard at a considerable distance—quite unlike most hazards encountered in the workplace. Perhaps it is this characteristic more than anything else that has led to special concerns expressed by workers and by occupational health and safety experts. Nevertheless, lasers can be used safely when appropriate hazard controls are applied. Standards for the safe use of lasers exist worldwide, and most are "harmonized" with each other (ANSI 1993; IEC 1993). All of the standards make use of a hazard classification system, which groups laser products into one of four broad hazard classes according to the laser's output power or energy and its ability to cause harm. Safety measures are then applied commensurate to the hazard classification (Cleuet and Mayer 1980; Duchene, Lakey and Repacholi 1991).

Lasers operate at discrete wavelengths, and although most lasers are monochromatic (emitting one wavelength, or single colour), it is not uncommon for a laser to emit several discrete wavelengths. For example, the argon laser emits several different lines within the near ultraviolet and visible spectrum, but is generally designed to emit only one green line (wavelength) at 514.5 nm and/or a blue line at 488 nm. When considering potential health hazards, it is always crucial to establish the output wavelength(s).

All lasers have three fundamental building blocks:

1. an active medium (a solid, liquid or gas) that defines the possible emission wavelengths
2. an energy source (e.g., electric current, pump lamp or chemical reaction)
3. a resonant cavity with output coupler (generally two mirrors).

Most practical laser systems outside of the research laboratory also have a beam delivery system, such as an optical fibre or articulated arm with mirrors to direct the beam to a work station, and focusing lenses to concentrate the beam on a material to be welded, etc. In a laser, identical atoms or molecules are brought to an excited state by energy delivered from the pump lamp. When the atoms or molecules are in an excited state, a photon ("particle" of light energy) can stimulate an excited atom or molecule to emit a second photon of the same energy (wavelength) travelling in phase (coherent) and in the same direction as the stimulating photon. Thus light amplification by a factor of two has taken place. This same process repeated in a cascade causes a light beam to develop that reflects back and forth between the mirrors of the resonant cavity. Since one of the mirrors is partially transparent, some light energy leaves the resonant cavity forming the emitted laser beam. Although in practice, the two parallel mirrors are often curved to produce a more stable resonant condition, the basic principle holds for all lasers.

Although several thousand different laser lines (i.e., discrete laser wavelengths characteristic of different active media) have been demonstrated in the physics laboratory, only 20 or so have been developed commercially to the point where they are routinely applied in everyday technology. Laser safety guidelines and standards have been developed and published which basically cover all wavelengths of the optical spectrum in order to allow for currently known laser lines and future lasers.

Laser Hazard Classification

Current laser safety standards throughout the world follow the practice of categorizing all laser products into hazard classes. Generally, the scheme follows a grouping of four broad hazard classes, 1 through 4. Class 1 lasers cannot emit potentially hazardous laser radiation and pose no health hazard. Classes 2 through 4 pose an increasing hazard to the eye and skin. The classification system is useful since safety measures are prescribed for each class of laser. More stringent safety measures are required for the highest classes.

Class 1 is considered an "eye-safe", no-risk grouping. Most lasers that are totally enclosed (for example, laser compact disc recorders) are Class 1. No safety measures are required for a Class 1 laser.

Class 2 refers to visible lasers that emit a very low power that would not be hazardous even if the entire beam power entered the human eye and was focused on the retina. The eye's natural aversion response to viewing very bright light sources protects the eye against retinal injury if the energy entering the eye is insufficient to damage the retina within the aversion response. The aversion response is composed of the blink reflex (approximately 0.16–0.18 second) and a rotation of the eye and movement of the head when exposed to such bright light. Current safety standards conservatively define the aversion response as lasting 0.25 second. Thus, Class 2 lasers have an output power of 1 milliwatt (mW) or less that corresponds to the permissible exposure limit for 0.25 second. Examples of Class 2 lasers are laser pointers and some alignment lasers.

Some safety standards also incorporate a subcategory of Class 2, referred to as "Class 2A". Class 2A lasers are not hazardous to stare into for up to 1,000 s (16.7 min). Most laser scanners used in point-of-sales (super-market checkout) and inventory scanners are Class 2A.

Class 3 lasers pose a hazard to the eye, since the aversion response is insufficiently fast to limit retinal exposure to a momentarily safe level, and damage to other structures of the eye (e.g., cornea and lens) could also take place. Skin hazards normally do not exist for incidental exposure. Examples of Class 3 lasers are many research lasers and military laser rangefinders.

A special subcategory of Class 3 is termed "Class 3A" (with the remaining Class 3 lasers termed "Class 3B"). Class 3A lasers are those with an output power between one and five times the accessible emission limits (AEL) for the Class 1 or Class 2, but with an output irradiance not exceeding the relevant occupational exposure limit for the lower class. Examples are many laser alignment and surveying instruments.

Class 4 lasers may pose a potential fire hazard, a significant skin hazard or a diffuse-reflection hazard. Virtually all surgical lasers and material processing lasers used for welding and cutting are Class 4 if not enclosed. All lasers with an average power output exceeding 0.5 W are Class 4. If a higher power Class 3 or Class 4 is totally enclosed so that hazardous radiant energy is not accessible, the total laser system could be Class 1. The more hazardous laser inside the enclosure is termed an *embedded laser*.

Occupational Exposure Limits

The International Commission on Non-Ionizing Radiation Protection (ICNIRP 1995) has published guidelines for human exposure limits for laser radiation that are periodically updated. Representative exposure limits (ELs) are provided in table 49.3 for several typical lasers. Virtually all laser beams exceed permissible exposure limits. Thus, in actual practice, the exposure limits are not routinely used to determine safety measures. Instead, the laser classification

Table 49.3 • Exposure limits for typical lasers.

Type of laser	Principal wavelength(s)	Exposure limit
Argon fluoride	193 nm	3.0 mJ/cm² over 8 h
Xenon chloride	308 nm	40 mJ/cm² over 8 h
Argon ion	488, 514.5 nm	3.2 mW/cm² for 0.1 s
Copper vapour	510, 578 nm	2.5 mW/cm² for 0.25 s
Helium-neon	632.8 nm	1.8 mW/cm² for 10 s
Gold vapour	628 nm	1.0 mW/cm² for 10 s
Krypton ion	568, 647 nm	1.0 mW/cm² for 10 s
Neodymium-YAG	1,064 nm 1,334 nm	5.0 μJ/cm² for 1 ns to 50 μs No MPE for t <1 ns, 5 mW/cm² for 10 s
Carbon dioxide	10–6 μm	100 mw/cm² for 10 s
Carbon monoxide	≈5 μm	to 8 h, limited area 10 mW/cm² for >10 s for most of body

All standards/guidelines have MPE's at other wavelengths and exposure durations.

Note: To convert MPE's in mW/cm² to mJ/cm², multiply by exposure time t in seconds. For example, the He-Ne or Argon MPE at 0.1 s is 0.32 mJ/cm².

Source: ANSI Standard Z-136.1(-1993); ACGIH TLVs (1995) and Duchene, Lakey and Repacholi (1991).

scheme—which is based upon the ELs applied under realistic conditions—is really applied to this end.

Laser Safety Standards

Many nations have published laser safety standards, and most are harmonized with the international standard of the International Electrotechnical Commission (IEC). IEC Standard 825-1 (1993) applies to manufacturers; however, it also provides some limited safety guidance for users. The laser hazard classification described above must be labelled on all commercial laser products. A warning label appropriate to the class should appear on all products of Classes 2 through 4.

Safety Measures

The laser safety classification system greatly facilitates the determination of appropriate safety measures. Laser safety standards and codes of practice routinely require the use of increasingly more restrictive control measures for each higher classification.

In practice, it is always more desirable to totally enclose the laser and beam path so that no potentially hazardous laser radiation is accessible. In other words, if only Class 1 laser products are employed in the workplace, safe use is assured. However, in many situations, this is simply not practical, and worker training in safe use and hazard control measures is required.

Other than the obvious rule—not to point a laser at a person's eyes—there are no control measures required for a Class 2 laser product. For lasers of higher classes, safety measures are clearly required.

If total enclosure of a Class 3 or 4 laser is not feasible, the use of beam enclosures (e.g., tubes), baffles and optical covers can virtually eliminate the risk of hazardous ocular exposure in most cases.

When enclosures are not feasible for Class 3 and 4 lasers, a laser controlled area with controlled entry should be established, and the use of laser eye protectors is generally mandated within the nominal hazard zone (NHZ) of the laser beam. Although in most research laboratories where collimated laser beams are used, the NHZ encompasses the entire controlled laboratory area, for focused beam applications, the NHZ may be surprisingly limited and not encompass the entire room.

To assure against misuse and possible dangerous actions on the part of unauthorized laser users, the key control found on all commercially manufactured laser products should be utilized. The key should be secured when the laser is not in use, if people can gain access to the laser.

Special precautions are required during laser alignment and initial set-up, since the potential for serious eye injury is very great then. Laser workers must be trained in safe practices prior to laser set-up and alignment.

Laser-protective eyewear was developed after occupational exposure limits had been established, and specifications were drawn up to provide the optical densities (or ODs, a logarithmic measure of the attenuation factor) that would be needed as a function of wavelength and exposure duration for specific lasers. Although specific standards for laser eye protection exist in Europe, further guidelines are provided in the United States by the American National Standards Institute under the designations ANSI Z136.1 and ANSI Z136.3.

Training

When investigating laser accidents in both laboratory and industrial situations, a common element emerges: lack of adequate training. Laser safety training should be both appropriate and sufficient for the laser operations around which each employee will work. Training should be specific to the type of laser and the task to which the worker is assigned.

Medical Surveillance

Requirements for medical surveillance of laser workers vary from country to country in accordance with local occupational medicine regulations. At one time, when lasers were confined to the research laboratory and little was known about their biological effects, it was quite typical that each laser worker was periodically given a thorough general ophthalmological examination with fundus (retinal) photography to monitor the status of the eye. However, by the early 1970s, this practice was questioned, since the clinical findings were almost always negative, and it became clear that such exams could identify only acute injury which was subjectively detectable. This led the WHO task group on lasers, meeting in Don Leaghreigh, Ireland, in 1975, to recommend against such involved surveillance programmes and to emphasize testing of visual function. Since that time, most national occupational health groups have continuously reduced medical examination requirements. Today, complete ophthalmological examinations are universally required only in the event of a laser eye injury or suspected overexposure, and pre-placement visual screening is generally required. Additional examinations may be required in some countries.

Laser Measurements

Unlike some workplace hazards, there is generally no need to perform measurements for workplace monitoring of hazardous levels of laser radiation. Because of the highly confined beam dimensions of most laser beams, the likelihood of changing beam paths and the difficulty and expense of laser radiometers, current safety standards emphasize control measures based upon hazard class and not workplace measurement (monitoring). Measurements must be performed by the manufacturer to assure compliance with laser safety standards and proper hazard classification. Indeed, one of the original justifications for laser hazard classification related to the great difficulty of performing proper measurements for hazard evaluation.

Conclusions

Although the laser is relatively new to the workplace, it is rapidly becoming ubiquitous, as are programmes concerned with laser safety. The keys to the safe use of lasers are first to enclose the laser radiant energy if at all possible, but if not possible, to set up adequate control measures and to train all personnel working with lasers.

RADIOFREQUENCY FIELDS AND MICROWAVES

Kjell Hansson Mild

Radiofrequency (RF) electromagnetic energy and microwave radiation is used in a variety of applications in industry, commerce, medicine and research, as well as in the home. In the frequency range from 3 to 3×10^8 kHz (that is, 300 GHz) we readily recognize applications such as radio and television broadcasting, communications (long-distance telephone, cellular telephone, radio communication), radar, dielectric heaters, induction heaters, switched power supplies and computer monitors.

High-power RF radiation is a source of thermal energy that carries all of the known implications of heating for biological systems, including burns, temporary and permanent changes in reproduction, cataracts and death. For the broad range of radiofrequencies, cutaneous perception of heat and thermal pain is unreliable for detection, because the thermal receptors are located in the skin and do not readily sense the deep heating of the body caused by these fields. Exposure limits are needed to protect against these adverse health effects of radiofrequency field exposure.

Occupational Exposure

Induction heating
By applying an intense alternating magnetic field a conducting material can be heated by induced *eddy currents*. Such heating is used for forging, annealing, brazing and soldering. Operating frequencies range from 50/60 to several million Hz. Since the dimensions of the coils producing the magnetic fields are often small, the risk of high-level whole-body exposure is small; however, exposure to the hands can be high.

Dielectric heating
Radiofrequency energy from 3 to 50 MHz (primarily at frequencies of 13.56, 27.12 and 40.68 MHz) is used in industry for a variety of heating processes. Applications include plastic sealing and embossing, glue drying, fabric and textile processing, woodworking and the manufacture of such diverse products as tarpaulins, swimming pools, waterbed liners, shoes, travel check folders and so on.

Measurements reported in the literature (Hansson Mild 1980; IEEE COMAR 1990a, 1990b, 1991) show that in many cases, electric and magnetic *leakage fields* are very high near these RF devices. Often the operators are women of child-bearing age (that is, 18 to 40 years). The leakage fields are often extensive in some occupational situations, resulting in whole-body exposure of operators. For many devices, the electric and magnetic field exposure levels exceed all existing RF safety guidelines.

Since these devices may give rise to very high absorption of RF energy, it is of interest to control the leakage fields which emanate from them. Thus, periodic RF monitoring becomes essential to determine whether an exposure problem exists.

Communication systems
Workers in the fields of communication and radar are exposed only to low-level field strengths in most situations. However, the exposure of workers who must climb FM/TV towers can be intense and safety precautions are necessary. Exposure can also be substantial near transmitter cabinets that have their interlocks defeated and doors open.

Medical exposure
One of the earliest applications of RF energy was short-wave diathermy. Unshielded electrodes are usually used for this, leading possibly to high stray fields.

Recently RF fields have been used in conjunction with static magnetic fields in *magnetic resonance imaging* (MRI). Since the RF energy used is low and the field is almost fully contained within the patient enclosure, the exposure to operators is negligible.

Biological Effects
The specific absorption rate (SAR, measured in watts per kilogram) is widely used as a dosimetric quantity, and exposure limits can be derived from SARs. The SAR of a biological body depends upon such exposure parameters as frequency of the radiation, intensity, polarization, configuration of the radiation source and the body, reflection surfaces and body size, shape and electrical properties. Furthermore, the SAR spatial distribution inside the body is highly non-uniform. Non-uniform energy deposition results in non-uniform deep-body heating and may produce internal temperature gradients. At frequencies above 10 GHz, the energy is deposited close to the body surface. The maximum SAR occurs at about 70 MHz for the standard subject, and at about

30 MHz when the person is standing in contact with RF ground. At extreme conditions of temperature and humidity, whole-body SARs of 1 to 4 W/kg at 70 MHz are expected to cause a core temperature rise of about 2 °C in healthy human beings in one hour.

RF heating is an interaction mechanism that has been studied extensively. Thermal effects have been observed at less than 1 W/kg, but temperature thresholds have generally not been determined for these effects. The time-temperature profile must be considered in assessing biological effects.

Biological effects also occur where RF heating is neither an adequate nor a possible mechanism. These effects often involve modulated RF fields and millimetre wavelengths. Various hypotheses have been proposed but have not yet yielded information useful for deriving human exposure limits. There is a need to understand the fundamental mechanisms of interaction, since it is not practical to explore each RF field for its characteristic biophysical and biological interactions.

Human and animal studies indicate that RF fields can cause harmful biological effects because of excessive heating of internal tissues. The body's heat sensors are located in the skin and do not readily sense heating deep within the body. Workers may therefore absorb significant amounts of RF energy without being immediately aware of the presence of leakage fields. There have been reports that personnel exposed to RF fields from radar equipment, RF heaters and sealers, and radio-TV towers have experienced a warming sensation some time after being exposed.

There is little evidence that RF radiation can initiate cancer in humans. Nevertheless, a study has suggested that it may act as a cancer promoter in animals (Szmigielski et al. 1988). Epidemiological studies of personnel exposed to RF fields are few in number and are generally limited in scope (Silverman 1990; NCRP 1986; WHO 1981). Several surveys of occupationally exposed workers have been conducted in the former Soviet Union and Eastern European countries (Roberts and Michaelson 1985). However, these studies are not conclusive with respect to health effects.

Human assessment and epidemiological studies on RF sealer operators in Europe (Kolmodin-Hedman et al. 1988; Bini et al. 1986) report that the following specific problems may arise:

- RF burns or burns from contact with thermally hot surfaces
- numbness (i.e., paresthesia) in hands and fingers; disturbed or altered tactile sensitivity
- eye irritation (possibly due to fumes from vinyl-containing material)
- significant warming and discomfort of the legs of operators (perhaps due to current flow through legs to ground).

Mobile Phones
The use of personal radiotelephones is rapidly increasing and this has led to an increase in the number of base stations. These are often sited in public areas. However, the exposure to the public from these stations is low. The systems usually operate on frequencies near 900 MHz or 1.8 GHz using either analogue or digital technology. The handsets are small, low power radio transmitters that are held in close proximity to the head when in use. Some of the power radiated from the antenna is absorbed by the head. Numerical calculations and measurements in phantom heads show that the SAR values can be of the order of a few W/kg (see further ICNIRP statement, 1996). Public concern about the health hazard of the electromagnetic fields has increased and several research programmes are being devoted to this question (McKinley et al., unpublished report). Several epidemiological studies are ongoing with respect to mobile phone use and brain cancer. So far only one animal study (Repacholi et

Figure 49.7 • IRPA (1988) exposure limits for electric field strength E, magnetic field strength H and power density.

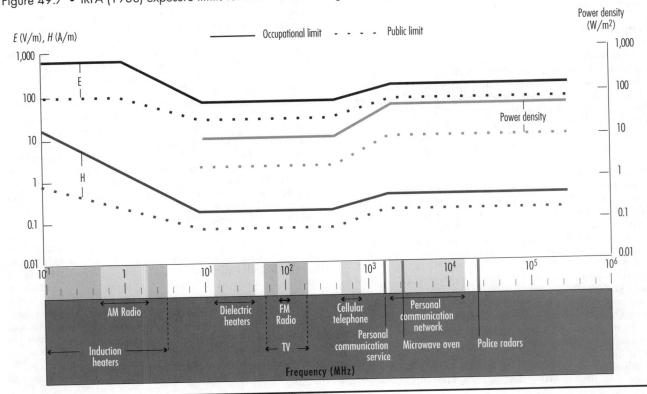

Standards and Guidelines

Several organizations and governments have issued standards and guidelines for protection from excessive exposure to RF fields. A review of worldwide safety standards was given by Grandolfo and Hansson Mild (1989); the discussion here pertains only to the guidelines issued by IRPA (1988) and IEEE standard C 95.1 1991.

The full rationale for RF exposure limits is presented in IRPA (1988). In summary, the IRPA guidelines have adopted a basic limiting SAR value of 4 W/kg, above which there is considered to be an increasing likelihood that adverse health consequences can occur as a result of RF energy absorption. No adverse health effects have been observed due to acute exposures below this level. Incorporating a safety factor of ten to allow for possible consequences of long-term exposure, 0.4 W/kg is used as the basic limit for deriving exposure limits for occupational exposure. A further safety factor of five is incorporated to derive limits for the general public.

Derived exposure limits for the electric field strength (E), the magnetic field strength (H) and the power density specified in V/m, A/m and W/m² respectively, are shown in figure 49.7. The squares of the E and H fields are averaged over six minutes, and it is recommended that the instantaneous exposure not exceed the

al. 1997) with transgenic mice exposed 1 h per day for 18 months to a signal similar to that used in digital mobile communication has been published. By the end of the experiments 43 of 101 exposed animals had lymphomas, compared to 22 of 100 in the sham-exposed group. The increase was statistically significant ($p > 0.001$). These results cannot easily be interpreted with relevance to human health and further research on this is needed.

time-averaged values by more than a factor of 100. Furthermore, the body-to-ground current should not exceed 200 mA.

Standard C95.1, set in 1991, by the IEEE gives limiting values for occupational exposure (controlled environment) of 0.4 W/kg for the average SAR over a person's entire body, and 8 W/kg for the peak SAR delivered to any one gram of tissue for 6 minutes or more. The corresponding values for exposure to the general public (uncontrolled environment) are 0.08 W/kg for whole-body SAR and 1.6 W/kg for peak SAR. The body-to-ground current should not exceed 100 mA in a controlled environment and 45 mA in an uncontrolled environment. (See IEEE 1991 for further details.) The derived limits are shown in figure 49.8.

Further information on radiofrequency fields and microwaves can be found in, for instance, Elder et al. 1989, Greene 1992, and Polk and Postow 1986.

VLF AND ELF ELECTRIC AND MAGNETIC FIELDS

Michael H. Repacholi

Extremely low frequency (ELF) and very low frequency (VLF) electric and magnetic fields encompass the frequency range above static (> 0 Hz) fields up to 30 kHz. For this paper ELF is defined as being in the frequency range > 0 to 300 Hz and VLF in the range > 300 Hz to 30 kHz. In the frequency range > 0 to 30 kHz, the wavelengths vary from ∞ (infinity) to 10 km and so the electric and magnetic fields act essentially independently of each other and must be treated separately. The electric field strength (E) is

Figure 49.8 • IEEE (1991) exposure limits for electric field strength *E*, magnetic field strength *H* and power density.

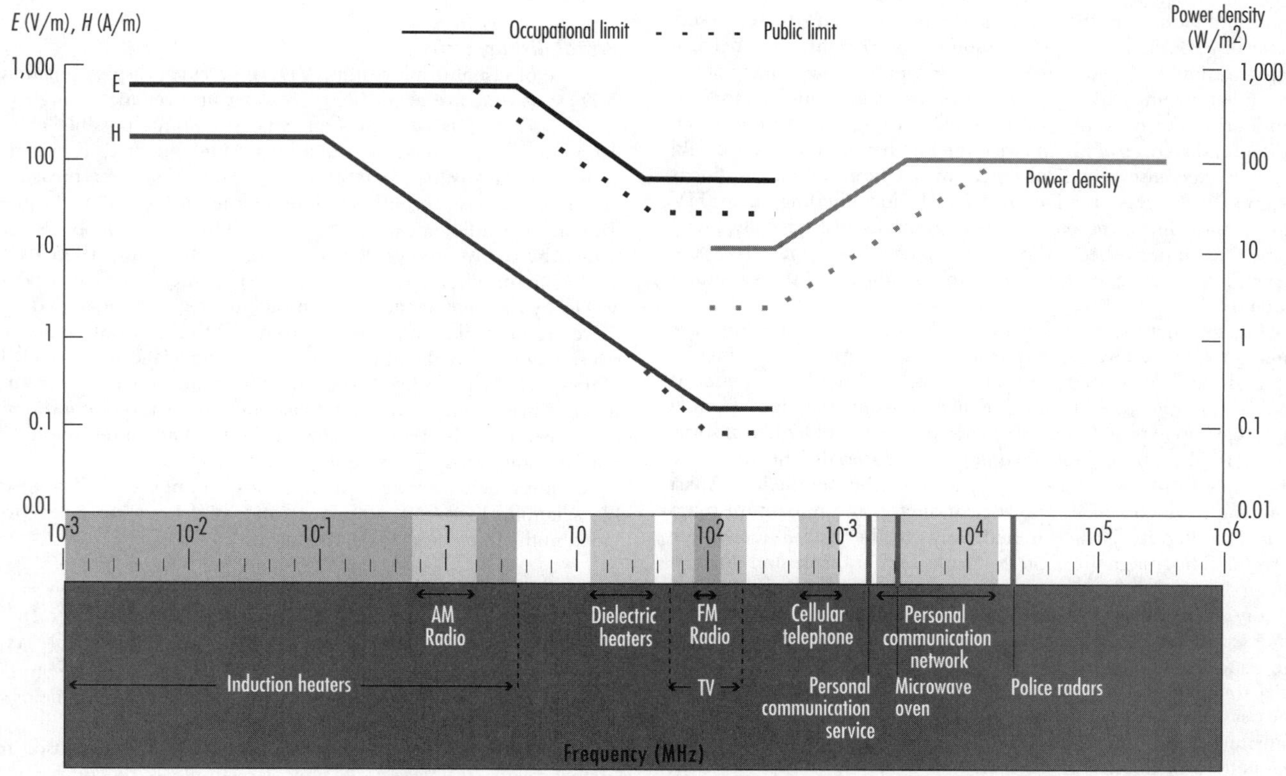

Sources of Occupational Exposure

Levels of occupational exposure vary considerably and are strongly dependent upon the particular application. Table 49.4 gives a summary of typical applications of frequencies in the range > 0 to 30 kHz.

Power generation and distribution

The principal artificial sources of 50/60 Hz electric and magnetic fields are those involved in power generation and distribution, and any equipment using electric current. Most such equipment operates at the power frequencies of 50 Hz in most countries and

measured in volts per metre (V/m), the magnetic field strength (*H*) is measured in amperes per metre (A/m) and the magnetic flux density (*B*) in tesla (T).

Considerable debate about possible adverse health effects has been expressed by workers using equipment that operates in this frequency range. By far the most common frequency is 50/60 Hz, used for the generation, distribution and use of electric power. Concerns that exposure to 50/60 Hz magnetic fields may be associated with an increased cancer incidence have been fuelled by media reports, distribution of misinformation and ongoing scientific debate (Repacholi 1990; NRC 1996).

The purpose of this article is to provide an overview of the following topic areas:

• sources, occupations and applications
• dosimetry and measurement
• interaction mechanisms and biological effects
• human studies and effects on health
• protective measures
• occupational exposure standards.

Summary descriptions are provided to inform workers of the types and strengths of fields from major sources of ELF and VLF, biological effects, possible health consequences and current exposure limits. An outline of safety precautions and protective measures is also given. While many workers use visual display units (VDUs), only brief details are given in this article since they are covered in greater detail elsewhere in the *Encyclopaedia*.

Much of the material contained here can be found in greater detail in a number of recent reviews (WHO 1984, 1987, 1989, 1993; IRPA 1990; ILO 1993; NRPB 1992, 1993; IEEE 1991; Greene 1992; NRC 1996).

Table 49.4 • Applications of equipment operating in the range >0 to 30 kHz.

Frequency	Wavelength(km)	Typical applications
16.67, 50, 60 Hz	18,000–5,000	Power generation, transmissions and use, electrolytic processes, induction heating, arc and ladle furnaces, welding, transportation etc., any industrial, commercial, medical or research use of electric power
0.3–3 kHz	1,000–100	Broadcast modulation, medical applications, electric furnaces, induction heating, hardening, soldering, melting, refining
3–30 kHz	100–10	Very long-range communications, radio navigation, broadcast modulation, medical applications, induction heating, hardening, soldering, melting, refining, VDUs

60 Hz in North America. Some electric train systems operate at 16.67 Hz.

High voltage (HV) transmission lines and substations have associated with them the strongest electric fields to which workers may be routinely exposed. Conductor height, geometrical configuration, lateral distance from the line, and the voltage of the transmission line are by far the most significant factors in considering the maximum electric field strength at ground level. At lateral distances of about twice the line height, the electric field strength decreases with distance in an approximately linear fashion (Zaffanella and Deno 1978). Inside buildings near HV transmission lines, the electric field strengths are typically lower than the unperturbed field by a factor of about 100,000, depending on the configuration of the building and the structural materials.

Magnetic field strengths from overhead transmission lines are usually relatively low compared to industrial applications involving high currents. Electrical utility employees working in substations or on the maintenance of live transmission lines form a special group exposed to larger fields (of 5 mT and higher in some cases). In the absence of ferromagnetic materials, the magnetic field lines form concentric circles around the conductor. Apart from the geometry of the power conductor, the maximum magnetic flux density is determined only by the magnitude of the current. The magnetic field beneath HV transmission lines is directed mainly transverse to the line axis. The maximum flux density at ground level may be under the centre line or under the outer conductors, depending on the phase relationship between the conductors. The maximum magnetic flux density at ground level for a typical double circuit 500 kV overhead transmission lines system is approximately 35 µT per kiloampere of current transmitted (Bernhardt and Matthes 1992). Typical values for the magnetic flux density up to 0.05 mT occur in workplaces near overhead lines, in substations and in power stations operating at frequencies of 16 2/3, 50, or 60 Hz (Krause 1986).

Industrial processes

Occupational exposure to magnetic fields comes predominantly from working near industrial equipment using high currents. Such devices include those used in welding, electroslag refining, heating (furnaces, induction heaters) and stirring.

Surveys on induction heaters used in industry, performed in Canada (Stuchly and Lecuyer 1985), in Poland (Aniolczyk 1981), in Australia (Repacholi, unpublished data) and in Sweden (Lövsund, Oberg and Nilsson 1982), show magnetic flux densities at operator locations ranging from 0.7 µT to 6 mT, depending on the frequency used and the distance from the machine. In their study of magnetic fields from industrial electro-steel and welding equipment, Lövsund, Oberg and Nilsson (1982) found that spot-welding machines (50 Hz, 15 to 106 kA) and ladle furnaces (50 Hz, 13 to 15 kA) produced fields up to 10 mT at distances up to 1 m. In Australia, an induction heating plant operating in the range 50 Hz to 10 kHz was found to give maximum fields of up to 2.5 mT (50 Hz induction furnaces) at positions where operators could stand. In addition maximum fields around induction heaters operating at other frequencies were 130 µT at 1.8 kHz, 25 µT at 2.8 kHz and in excess of 130 µT at 9.8 kHz.

Since the dimensions of coils producing the magnetic fields are often small there is seldom high exposure to the whole body, but rather local exposure mainly to the hands. Magnetic flux density to the hands of the operator may reach 25 mT (Lövsund and Mild 1978; Stuchly and Lecuyer 1985). In most cases the flux density is less than 1 mT. The electric field strength near the induction heater is usually low.

Workers in the electrochemical industry may be exposed to high electric and magnetic field strengths because of electrical furnaces or other devices using high currents. For instance, near induction furnaces and industrial electrolytic cells magnetic flux densities can be measured as high as 50 mT.

Visual display units

The use of visual display units (VDUs) or video display terminals (VDTs) as they are also called, grows at an ever increasing rate. VDT operators have expressed concerns about possible effects from emissions of low-level radiations. Magnetic fields (frequency 15 to 125 kHz) as high as 0.69 A/m (0.9 µT) have been measured under worst-case conditions close to the surface of the screen (Bureau of Radiological Health 1981). This result has been confirmed by many surveys (Roy et al. 1984; Repacholi 1985 IRPA 1988). Comprehensive reviews of measurements and surveys of VDTs by national agencies and individual experts concluded that there are no radiation emissions from VDTs that would have any consequences for health (Repacholi 1985; IRPA 1988; ILO 1993a). There is no need to perform routine radiation measurements since, even under worst-case or failure mode conditions, the emission levels are well below the limits of any international or national standards (IRPA 1988).

A comprehensive review of emissions, summary of the applicable scientific literature, standards and guidelines has been provided in the document (ILO 1993a).

Medical applications

Patients suffering from bone fractures that do not heal well or unite have been treated with pulsed magnetic fields (Bassett, Milchell and Gaston 1982; Mitbreit and Manyachin 1984). Studies are also being conducted on the use of pulsed magnetic fields to enhance wound healing and tissue regeneration.

Various devices generating magnetic field pulses are used for bone growth stimulation. A typical example is the device that generates an average magnetic flux density of about 0.3 mT, a peak strength of about 2.5 mT, and induces peak electric field strengths in the bone in the range of 0.075 to 0.175 V/m (Bassett, Pawluk and Pilla 1974). Near the surface of the exposed limb, the device produces a peak magnetic flux density of the order of 1.0 mT causing peak ionic current densities of about 10 to 100 mA/m² (1 to 10 µA/cm²) in tissue.

Measurement

Prior to the commencement of measurements of ELF or VLF fields, it is important to obtain as much information as possible about the characteristics of the source and the exposure situation. This information is required for the estimation of the expected field strengths and the selection of the most appropriate survey instrumentation (Tell 1983).

Information about the source should include:

- frequencies present, including harmonics
- power transmitted
- polarization (orientation of *E* field)
- modulation characteristics (peak and average values)
- duty cycle, pulse width, and pulse repetition frequency
- antenna characteristics, such as type, gain, beam width and scan rate.

Information about the exposure situation must include:

- distance from the source
- existence of any scattering objects. Scattering by plane surfaces can enhance the *E* field by a factor of 2. Even greater enhancement may result from curved surfaces, e.g., corner reflectors.

Results of surveys conducted in occupational settings are summarized in table 49.5.

Instrumentation

An electric or magnetic field-measuring instrument consists of three basic parts: the probe, the leads and the monitor. To ensure appropriate measurements, the following instrumentation characteristics are required or are desirable:

- The probe must respond only to the E field or the H field and not to both simultaneously.
- The probe must not produce significant perturbation of the field.
- The leads from the probe to the monitor must not disturb the field at the probe significantly, or couple energy from the field.
- The frequency response of the probe must cover the range of frequencies required to be measured.
- If used in the reactive near-field, the dimensions of the probe sensor should preferably be less than a quarter of a wavelength at the highest frequency present.
- The instrument should indicate the root mean square (rms) value of the measured field parameter.
- The response time of the instrument should be known. It is desirable to have a response time of about 1 second or less, so that intermittent fields are easily detected.
- The probe should be responsive to all polarization components of the field. This may be accomplished either by inherent isotropic response, or by physical rotation of the probe through three orthogonal directions.
- Good overload protection, battery operation, portability and rugged construction are other desirable characteristics.
- Instruments provide an indication of one or more of the following parameters: average E field (V/m) or mean square E field (V^2/m^2); average H field (A/m) or mean square H field (A^2/m^2).

Surveys

Surveys are usually conducted to determine whether fields existing in the workplace are below limits set by national standards. Thus the person taking the measurements must be fully familiar with these standards.

All occupied and accessible locations should be surveyed. The operator of the equipment under test and the surveyor should be as far away as practicable from the test area. All objects normally present, which may reflect or absorb energy, must be in position. The surveyor should take precautions against radiofrequency (RF) burns and shock, particularly near high-power, low-frequency systems.

Interaction Mechanisms and Biological Effects

Interaction mechanisms

The only established mechanisms by which ELF and VLF fields interact with biological systems are:

- Electric fields which induce a surface charge on an exposed body which results in currents (measured in mA/m^2) inside the body, the magnitude of which is related to the surface charge density. Depending on the exposure conditions, size, shape and position of the exposed body in the field, the surface charge density can vary greatly, resulting in a variable and non-uniform distribution of currents inside the body.
- Magnetic fields also act on humans by inducing electric fields and currents inside the body.
- Electric charges induced in a conducting object (e.g., an automobile) exposed to ELF or VLF electric fields may cause current to pass through a person in contact with it.
- Magnetic field coupling to a conductor (for example, a wire fence) causes electric currents (of the same frequency as the

Table 49.5 • Occupational sources of exposure to magnetic fields.

Source	Magnetic flux densities (mT)	Distance (m)
VDTs	Up to 2.8×10^{-4}	0.3
HV lines	Up to 0.4	under line
Power stations	Up to 0.27	1
Welding arcs (0–50 Hz)	0.1–5.8	0–0.8
Induction heaters (50–10 kHz)	0.9–65	0.1–1
50 Hz Ladle furnace	0.2–8	0.5–1
50 Hz Arc furnace	Up to 1	2
10 Hz Induction stirrer	0.2–0.3	2
50 Hz Electroslag welding	0.5–1.7	0.2–0.9
Therapeutic equipment	1–16	1

Source: Allen 1991; Bernhardt 1988; Krause 1986; Lövsund, Oberg and Nilsson 1982; Repacholi, unpublished data; Stuchly 1986; Stuchly and Lecuyer 1985, 1989.

exposing field) to pass through the body of a person in contact with it.
- Transient discharges (sparks) can occur when people and metal objects exposed to a strong electric field come into sufficiently close proximity.
- Electric or magnetic fields may interfere with implanted medical devices (e.g., unipolar cardiac pacemakers) and cause malfunction of the device.

The first two interactions listed above are examples of direct coupling between persons and ELF or VLF fields. The last four interactions are examples of indirect coupling mechanisms because they can occur only when the exposed organism is in the vicinity of other bodies. These bodies can include other humans or animals and objects such as automobiles, fences or implanted devices.

While other mechanisms of interaction between biological tissues and ELF or VLF fields have been postulated or there is some evidence to support their existence (WHO 1993; NRPB 1993; NRC 1996), none has been shown to be responsible for any adverse consequence to health.

Health effects

The evidence suggests that most of the established effects of exposure to electric and magnetic fields in the frequency range > 0 to 30 kHz result from acute responses to surface charge and induced current density. People can perceive the effects of the oscillating surface charge induced on their bodies by ELF electric fields (but not by magnetic fields); these effects become annoying if sufficiently intense. A summary of the effects of currents passing through the human body (thresholds for perception, let-go or tetanus) are given in table 49.6.

Human nerve and muscle cells have been stimulated by the currents induced by exposure to magnetic fields of several mT and 1 to 1.5 kHz; threshold current densities are thought to be above 1 A/m^2. Flickering visual sensations can be induced in the human eye by exposure to magnetic fields as low as about 5 to 10 mT (at 20 Hz) or electric currents directly applied to the head. Consideration of these responses and of the results of neurophysiological studies suggests that subtle central nervous system functions, such as reasoning or memory, may be affected by current

Table 49.6 • Effects of currents passing through the human body.

Effect	Subject	Threshold current in mA				
		50 and 60 Hz	300 Hz	1000 Hz	10 kHz	30 kHz
Perception	Men	1.1	1.3	2.2	15	50
	Women	0.7	0.9	1.5	10	35
	Children	0.55	0.65	1.1	9	30
Let-go threshold shock	Men	9	11.7	16.2	55	126
	Women	6	7.8	10.8	37	84
	Children	4.5	5.9	8.1	27	63
Thoracic tetanization; severe shock	Men	23	30	41	94	320
	Women	15	20	27	63	214
	Children	12	15	20.5	47	160

Source: Bernhardt 1988a.

Table 49.8 • Occupational limits of exposure to electric and magnetic fields in the frequency range >0 to 30 kHz (note that f is in Hz).

Country/ Reference	Frequency range	Electric field (V/m)	Magnetic field (A/m)
International (IRPA 1990)	50/60 Hz	10,000	398
USA (IEEE 1991)	3–30 kHz	614	163
USA (ACGIH 1993)	1–100 Hz	25,000	60/f
	100–4,000 Hz	$2.5 \times 10^6/f$	60/f
	4–30 kHz	625	60/f
Germany (1996)	50/60 Hz	10,000	1,600
UK (NRPB 1993)	1–24 Hz	25,000	64,000/f
	24–600 Hz	$6 \times 10^5/f$	64,000/f
	600–1,000 Hz	1,000	64,000/f
	1–30 kHz	1,000	64

densities above 10 mA/m^2 (NRPB 1993). Threshold values are likely to remain constant up to about 1 kHz but rise with increasing frequency thereafter.

Several *in vitro* studies (WHO 1993; NRPB 1993) have reported metabolic changes, such as alterations in enzyme activity and protein metabolism and decreased lymphocyte cytotoxicity, in various cell lines exposed to ELF and VLF electric fields and currents applied directly to the cell culture. Most effects have been reported at current densities between about 10 and 1,000 mA/m^2, although these responses are less clearly defined (Sienkiewicz, Saunder and Kowalczuk 1991). However, it is worth noting that the endogenous current densities generated by the electrical activity of nerves and muscles are typically as high as 1 mA/m^2 and may reach up to 10 mA/m^2 in the heart. These current densities will not adversely affect nerve, muscle and other tissues. Such biological effects will be avoided by restricting the induced current density to less than 10 mA/m^2 at frequencies up to about 1 kHz.

Several possible areas of biological interaction which have many health implications and about which our knowledge is limited include: possible changes in night-time melatonin levels in the pineal gland and alterations in circadian rhythms induced in animals by exposure to ELF electric or magnetic fields, and possible effects of ELF magnetic fields on the processes of development and

Table 49.7 • Approximate current density ranges for various biological effects.

Effect	Current density (mA/m^2)
Direct nerve and muscle stimulation	1,000–10,000
Modulation in central nervous system activity Changes in cell metabolism *in vitro*	100–1,000
Changes in retinal function Probable changes in central nervous system Changes in cell metabolism *in vitro*	10–100
Endogenous current density	1–10

Source: Sienkiewicz et al. 1991.

carcinogenesis. In addition, there is some evidence of biological responses to very weak electric and magnetic fields: these include the altered mobility of calcium ions in brain tissue, changes in neuronal firing patterns, and altered operand behaviour. Both amplitude and frequency "windows" have been reported which challenge the conventional assumption that the magnitude of a response increases with increasing dose. These effects are not well established and do not provide a basis for establishing restrictions on human exposure, although further investigations are warranted (Sienkievicz, Saunder and Kowalczuk 1991; WHO 1993; NRC 1996).

Table 49.7 gives the approximate ranges of induced current densities for various biological effects in humans.

Occupational Exposure Standards

Nearly all standards having limits in the range > 0-30 kHz have, as their rationale, the need to keep induced electric fields and currents to safe levels. Usually the induced current densities are restricted to less than 10 mA/m^2. Table 49.8 gives a summary of some current occupational exposure limits.

Protective Measures

Occupational exposures that occur near high voltage transmission lines depend on the worker's location either on the ground or at the conductor during live-line work at high potential. When working under live-line conditions, protective clothing may be used to reduce the electric field strength and current density in the body to values similar to those that would occur for work on the ground. Protective clothing does not weaken the influence of the magnetic field.

The responsibilities for the protection of workers and the general public against the potentially adverse effects of exposure to ELF or VLF electric and magnetic fields should be clearly assigned. It is recommended that the competent authorities consider the following steps:

- development and adoption of exposure limits and the implementation of a compliance programme
- development of technical standards to reduce the susceptibility to electromagnetic interference, for example, for pacemakers

- development of standards defining zones with limited access around sources of strong electric and magnetic fields because of electromagnetic interference (e.g., for pacemakers and other implanted devices). The use of appropriate warning signs should be considered.
- requirement of specific assignment of a person responsible for the safety of workers and the public at each site with high exposure potentials
- development of standardized measurement procedures and survey techniques
- requirements for the education of workers on the effects of exposure to ELF or VLF electric and magnetic fields and the measures and rules which are designed to protect them
- drafting of guidelines or codes of practice for worker safety in ELF or VLF electric and magnetic fields. ILO (1993) provides excellent guidance for such a code.

STATIC ELECTRIC AND MAGNETIC FIELDS

Martino Grandolfo

Both our natural and our artificial environments generate electric and magnetic forces of various magnitudes—in the outdoors, in offices, in households and in industrial workplaces. This raises two important questions: (1) do these exposures pose any adverse human health effects, and (2) what limits can be set in an attempt to define "safe" limits of such exposures?

This discussion focuses on static electric and magnetic fields. Studies are described on workers in various industries, and also on animals, which fail to demonstrate any clear-cut adverse biological effects at the levels of exposure to electric and magnetic fields usually encountered. Nevertheless, attempts are made to discuss the efforts of a number of international organizations to set guidelines to protect workers and others from any possible dangerous level of exposure.

Definition of Terms

When a voltage or electric current is applied to an object such as an electrical conductor, the conductor becomes charged and forces start to act on other charges in the vicinity. Two types of forces may be distinguished: those arising from stationary electric charges, known as the *electrostatic force*, and those appearing only when charges are moving (as in an electric current in a conductor), known as the *magnetic force*. To describe the existence and spatial distribution of these forces, physicists and mathematicians have created the concept of *field*. One thus speaks of a field of force, or simply, electric and magnetic fields.

The term *static* describes a situation where all charges are fixed in space, or move as a steady flow. As a result, both charges and current densities are constant in time. In the case of fixed charges, we have an electric field whose strength at any point in space depends on the value and geometry of all the charges. In the case of steady current in a circuit, we have both an electric and a magnetic field constant in time (static fields), since the charge density at any point of the circuit does not vary.

Electricity and magnetism are distinct phenomena as long as charges and current are static; any interconnection between electric and magnetic fields disappears in this static situation and thus they can be treated separately (unlike the situation in time-varying fields). Static electric and magnetic fields are clearly characterized by steady, time-independent strengths and correspond to the zero-frequency limit of the extremely low frequency (ELF) band.

Static Electric Fields

Natural and occupational exposure

Static electric fields are produced by electrically charged bodies where an electric charge is induced on the surface of an object within a static electric field. As a consequence, the electric field at the surface of an object, particularly where the radius is small, such as at a point, can be larger than the unperturbed electric field (that is, the field without the object present). The field inside the object may be very small or zero. Electric fields are experienced as a force by electrically charged objects; for example, a force will be exerted on body hair, which may be perceived by the individual.

On the average, the surface charge of the earth is negative while the upper atmosphere carries a positive charge. The resulting static electric field near the earth's surface has a strength of about 130 V/m. This field decreases with height, and its value is about 100 V/m at 100 m elevation, 45 V/m at 1 km, and less than 1 V/m at 20 km. Actual values vary widely, depending upon the local temperature and humidity profile and the presence of ionized contaminants. Beneath thunderclouds, for example, and even as thunderclouds are approaching, large field variations occur at ground level, because normally the lower part of a cloud is negatively charged while the upper part contains a positive charge. In addition, there is a space charge between the cloud and ground. As the cloud approaches, the field at ground level may first increase and then reverse, with the ground becoming positively charged. During this process, fields of 100 V/m to 3 kV/m may be observed even in the absence of local lightning; field reversals may take place very rapidly, within 1 min, and high field strengths may persist for the duration of the storm. Ordinary clouds, as well as thunderclouds, contain electric charges and therefore deeply affect the electric field at ground level. Large deviations from the fair-weather field, up to 200%, are also to be expected in the presence of fog, rain and naturally occurring small and large ions. Electric field changes during the daily cycle can even be expected in completely fair weather: fairly regular changes in local ionization, temperature or humidity and the resulting changes in the atmospheric electrical conductivity near the ground, as well as mechanical charge transfer by local air movements, are probably responsible for these diurnal variations.

Typical levels of man-made electrostatic fields are in the 1 to 20 kV/m range in offices and households; these fields are frequently generated around high-voltage equipment, such as TV sets and video display units (VDUs), or by friction. Direct current (DC) transmission lines generate both static electric and magnetic fields and are an economical means of power distribution where long distances are involved.

Static electric fields are widely used in industries such as chemicals, textile, aviation, paper and rubber, and in transportation.

Biological effects

Experimental studies provide little biological evidence to suggest any adverse effect of static electric fields on human health. The few animal studies that have been carried out also appear to have yielded no data supporting adverse effects on genetics, tumour growth, or on the endocrine or cardiovascular systems. (Table 49.9 summarizes these animal studies.)

No *in vitro* studies have been conducted to evaluate the effect of exposing cells to static electric fields.

Theoretical calculations suggest that a static electric field will induce a charge on the surface of exposed people, which may be perceived if discharged to a grounded object. At a sufficiently high voltage, the air will ionize and become capable of conducting an electric current between, for example, a charged object and a grounded person. The *breakdown voltage* depends on a number of

49. RADIATION, NON-IONIZING

Table 49.9 • Studies on animals exposed to static electric fields.

Biological end-points	Reported effects	Exposure conditions
Haematology and immunology	Changes in the albumin and globulin fractions of serum proteins in rats. Responses not consistent	Continuous exposure to fields between 2.8 and 19.7 kV/m from 22 to 52 days of age
	No significant differences in blood cell counts, blood proteins or blood chemistry in mice	Exposure to 340 kV/m for 22 h/day for a total of 5,000 h
Nervous system	Induction of significant changes observed in the EEGs of rats. However, no clear indication of a consistent response	Exposure to electric field strengths up to 10 kV/m
	No significant changes in the concentrations and utilization rates of various neurotransmitters in brains of male rats	Exposure to a 3 kV/m field for up to 66 h
Behaviour	Recent, well-conducted studies suggesting no effect on rodent behaviour	Exposure to field strengths up to 12 kV/m
	Production of dose-dependent avoidance behaviour in male rats, with no influence of air ions	Exposure to HVD electric fields ranging from 55 to 80 kV/m
Reproduction and development	No significant differences in the total number of offspring nor in the percentage surviving in mice	Exposure to 340 kV/m for 22 h/day before, during and after gestation

factors, including the shape of the charged object and atmospheric conditions. Typical values of corresponding electric field strengths range between 500 and 1,200 kV/m.

Reports from some countries indicate that a number of VDU operators have experienced skin disorders, but the exact relationship of these to VDU work is unclear. Static electric fields at VDU workplaces have been suggested as a possible cause of these skin disorders, and it is possible that the electrostatic charge of the operator may be a relevant factor. However, any relationship between electrostatic fields and skin disorders must still be regarded as hypothetical based on available research evidence.

Measurements, prevention, exposure standards

Static electric field strength measurements may be reduced to measurements of voltages or electric charges. Several electrostatic voltmeters are commercially available which permit accurate measurements of electrostatic or other high-impedance sources without physical contact. Some utilize an electrostatic chopper for low drift, and negative feedback for accuracy and probe-to-surface spacing insensitivity. In some cases the electrostatic electrode "looks" at the surface under measurement through a small hole at the base of the probe assembly. The chopped AC signal induced on this electrode is proportional to the differential voltage between the surface under measurement and the probe assembly. Gradient adapters are also used as accessories to electrostatic voltmeters, and permit their use as electrostatic field strength meters; direct readout in volts per metre of separation between the surface under test and the grounded plate of the adapter is possible.

There are no good data which can serve as guidelines to set base limits of human exposure to static electric fields. In principle, an exposure limit could be derived from the minimum breakdown voltage for air; however, the field strength experienced by a person within a static electric field will vary according to body orientation and shape, and this must be taken into account in attempting to arrive at an appropriate limit.

Threshold limit values (TLVs) have been recommended by the American Conference of Governmental Industrial Hygienists (ACGIH 1995). These TLVs refer to the maximum unprotected workplace static electric field strength, representing conditions under which nearly all workers may be exposed repeatedly without adverse health effects. According to ACGIH, occupational exposures should not exceed a static electric field strength of 25 kV/m. This value should be used as a guide in the control of exposure and, due to individual susceptibility, should not be regarded as a clear line between safe and dangerous levels. (This limit refers to the field strength present in air, away from the surfaces of conductors, where spark discharges and contact currents may pose significant hazards, and is intended for both partial-body and whole-body exposures.) Care should be taken to eliminate ungrounded objects, to ground such objects, or to use insulated gloves when ungrounded objects must be handled. Prudence dictates the use of protective devices (e.g., suits, gloves and insulation) in all fields exceeding 15 kV/m.

According to ACGIH, present information on human responses and possible health effects of static electric fields is insufficient to establish a reliable TLV for time-weighted average exposures. It is recommended that, lacking specific information from the manufacturer on electromagnetic interference, the exposure of wearers of pacemakers and other medical electronic devices should be maintained at or below 1 kV/m.

In Germany, according to a DIN Standard, occupational exposures should not exceed a static electric field strength of 40 kV/m. For short exposures (up to two hours per day) a higher limit of 60 kV/m is permitted.

In 1993, the National Radiological Protection Board (NRPB 1993) provided advice concerning appropriate restrictions on the exposure of people to electromagnetic fields and radiation. This includes both static electric and magnetic fields. In the NRPB document, investigation levels are provided for the purpose of comparing values of measured field quantities in order to determine whether or not compliance with basic restrictions has been achieved. If the field to which a person is exposed exceeds the relevant investigation level, compliance with the basic restrictions must be checked. Factors that might be considered in such an assessment include, for example, the efficiency of the coupling of the person to the field, the spatial distribution of the field across the volume occupied by the person, and the duration of exposure.

According to NRPB it is not possible to recommend basic restrictions for avoiding direct effects of human exposure to static electric fields; guidance is given to avoid annoying effects of direct perception of the surface electric charge and indirect effects such as electric shock. For most people, the annoying perception of surface electric charge, acting directly on the body, will not occur during exposure to static electric field strengths less than about 25 kV/m, that is, the same field strength recommended by ACGIH. To avoid spark discharges (indirect effects) causing stress, NRPB recommends that DC contact currents be restricted to less than 2 mA. Electric shock from low impedance sources can be prevented by following established electrical safety procedures relevant to such equipment.

Static Magnetic Fields

Natural and occupational exposure

The body is relatively transparent to static magnetic fields; such fields will interact directly with magnetically anisotropic materials (exhibiting properties with different values when measured along axes in different directions) and moving charges.

The natural magnetic field is the sum of an internal field due to the earth acting as a permanent magnet and an external field generated in the environment from such factors as solar activity or atmospherics. The internal magnetic field of the earth originates from the electric current flowing in the upper layer of the earth's core. There are significant local differences in the strength of this field, whose average magnitude varies from about 28 A/m at the equator (corresponding to a magnetic flux density of about 35 mT in a non-magnetic material such as air) to about 56 A/m over the geomagnetic poles (corresponding to about 70 mT in air).

Artificial fields are stronger than those of natural origin by many orders of magnitude. Artificial sources of static magnetic fields include all devices containing wires carrying direct current, including many appliances and equipment in industry.

In direct-current power transmission lines, static magnetic fields are produced by moving charges (an electric current) in a two-wire line. For an overhead line, the magnetic flux density at ground level is about 20 mT for a ± 500 kV line. For an underground transmission line buried at 1.4 m and carrying a maximum current of about 1 kA, the maximum magnetic flux density is less than 10 mT at ground level.

Major technologies that involve the use of large static magnetic fields are listed in table 49.10 along with their corresponding exposure levels.

Biological effects

Evidence from experiments with laboratory animals indicates that there are no significant effects on the many developmental, behavioural, and physiological factors evaluated at static magnetic flux densities up to 2 T. Nor have studies on mice demonstrated any harm to the foetus from exposure to magnetic fields up to 1 T.

Theoretically, magnetic effects could retard blood flowing in a strong magnetic field and produce a rise in blood pressure. A flow reduction of at most a few per cent could be expected at 5 T, but none was observed in human subjects at 1.5 T, when investigated.

Some studies on workers involved in the manufacture of permanent magnets have reported various subjective symptoms and functional disturbances: irritability, fatigue, headache, loss of appetite, bradycardia (slow heart beat), tachycardia (rapid heart

Table 49.10 • Major technologies involving the use of large static magnetic fields, and corresponding exposure levels.

Procedures	Exposure levels
Energy technologies	
Thermonuclear fusion reactors	Fringe fields up to 50 mT in areas accessible to personnel. Below 0.1 mT outside the reactor site
Magnetohydrodynamic systems	Approximately 10 mT at about 50 m; 100 mT only at distances greater than 250 m
Superconducting magnet energy storage systems	Fringe fields up to 50 mT at operator-accessible locations
Superconducting generators and transmission lines	Fringe fields projected to be less than 100 mT
Research facilities	
Bubble chambers	During changes of film cassettes, the field is about 0.4–0.5 T at foot level and about 50 mT at the level of the head
Superconducting spectrometers	About 1 T at operator-accessible locations
Particle accelerators	Personnel are seldom exposed because of exclusion from the high radiation zone. Exceptions arise only during maintenance
Isotope separation units	Brief exposures to fields up to 50 mT. Usually field levels are less than 1 mT
Industry	
Aluminium production	Levels up to 100 mT in operator-accessible locations
Electrolytic processes	Mean and maximum field levels of about 10 and 50 mT, respectively
Production of magnets	2–5 mT at worker's hands; in the range of 300 to 500 mT at the level of the chest and head
Medicine	
Nuclear magnetic resonance imaging and spectroscopy	An unshielded 1-T magnet produces about 0.5 mT at 10 m, and an unshielded 2-T magnet produces the same exposure at about 13 m

beat), decreased blood pressure, altered EEG, itching, burning and numbness. However, lack of any statistical analysis or assessment of the impact of physical or chemical hazards in the working environment significantly reduces the validity of these reports and makes them difficult to evaluate. Although the studies are inconclusive, they do suggest that, if long-term effects do in fact occur, they are very subtle; no cumulative gross effects have been reported. Individuals exposed to a 4T magnetic flux density have been reported as experiencing sensory effects associated with motion in the field, such as vertigo (dizziness), feeling of nausea, a metallic taste, and magnetic sensations when moving the eyes or head. However, two epidemiological surveys of general health data in workers chronically exposed to static magnetic fields failed to reveal any significant health effects. Health data of 320 workers were obtained in plants using large electrolytic cells for chemical separation processes where the average static field level in the work environment was 7.6 mT and the maximum field was 14.6 mT. Slight changes in the white blood cell count, but still within the normal range, were detected in the exposed group compared to the 186 controls. None of the observed transient changes in blood pressure or other blood measurements was considered indicative of a significant adverse effect associated with magnetic field exposure. In another study, the prevalence of disease was evaluated among 792 workers who were occupationally exposed to static magnetic fields. The control group consisted of 792 unexposed workers matched for age, race and socio-economic status. The range of magnetic field exposures varied from 0.5 mT for long durations to 2 T for periods of several hours. No statistically significant change in the prevalence of 19 categories of disease was observed in the exposed group compared with the controls. No difference in the prevalence of disease was found between a subgroup of 198 who had experienced exposures of 0.3 T or higher for periods of one hour or longer when compared with the remainder of the exposed population or the matched controls.

A report on workers in the aluminium industry indicated an elevated leukaemia mortality rate. Although this epidemiological study reported an increased cancer risk for persons directly involved in aluminium production where workers are exposed to large static magnetic fields, there is at present no clear evidence to indicate exactly which carcinogenic factors within the work environment are responsible. The process used for aluminium reduction creates coal tar, pitch volatiles, fluoride fumes, sulphur oxides and carbon dioxide, and some of these might be more likely candidates for cancer-causing effects than magnetic field exposure.

In a study on French aluminium workers, cancer mortality and mortality from all causes were found not to differ significantly from that observed for the general male population of France (Mur et al. 1987).

Another negative finding linking magnetic field exposures to possible cancer outcomes comes from a study of a group of workers at a chloroalkali plant where the 100 kA DC currents used for the electrolytic production of chlorine gave rise to static magnetic flux densities, at worker's locations, ranging from 4 to 29 mT. The observed versus expected incidence of cancer among these workers over a 25-year period showed no significant differences.

Measurements, prevention and exposure standards

During the last thirty years, the measurement of magnetic fields has undergone considerable development. Progress in techniques has made it possible to develop new methods of measurement as well as to improve old ones.

The two most popular types of magnetic field probes are a shielded coil and a Hall probe. Most of the commercially available magnetic field meters use one of them. Recently, other semiconductor devices, namely bipolar transistors and FET transistors, have been proposed as magnetic field sensors. They offer some advantages over Hall probes, such as higher sensitivity, greater spatial resolution and broader frequency response.

The principle of the nuclear magnetic resonance (NMR) measurement technique is to determine the resonant frequency of the test specimen in the magnetic field to be measured. It is an absolute measurement that can be made with very great accuracy. The measuring range of this method is from about 10 mT to 10 T, with no definite limits. In field measurements using the proton magnetic resonance method, an accuracy of 10^{-4} is easily obtained with simple apparatus and an accuracy of 10^{-6} can be reached with extensive precautions and refined equipment. The inherent shortcoming of the NMR method is its limitation to a field with a low gradient and the lack of information about the field direction.

Recently, several personal dosimeters suitable for monitoring exposures to static magnetic fields have also been developed.

Protective measures for the industrial and scientific use of magnetic fields can be categorized as engineering design measures, the use of separation distance, and administrative controls. Another general category of hazard-control measures, which include personal protective equipment (e.g., special garments and face masks), does not exist for magnetic fields. However, protective measures against potential hazards from magnetic interference with emergency or medical electronic equipment and for surgical and dental implants are a special area of concern. The mechanical forces imparted to ferromagnetic (iron) implants and loose objects in high-field facilities require that precautions be taken to guard against health and safety hazards.

Techniques to minimize undue exposure to high-intensity magnetic fields around large research and industrial facilities generally fall into four types:

1. distance and time
2. magnetic shielding
3. electromagnetic interference (EMI) and compatibility
4. administrative measures.

The use of warning signs and special-access areas to limit exposure of personnel near large magnet facilities has been of greatest use for controlling exposure. Administrative controls such as these are generally preferable to magnetic shielding, which can be extremely expensive. Loose ferromagnetic and paramagnetic (any magnetizing substances) objects can be converted into dangerous missiles when subjected to intense magnetic field gradients. Avoidance of this hazard can be achieved only by removing loose metallic objects from the area and from personnel. Such items as scissors, nail files, screwdrivers and scalpels should be banned from the immediate vicinity.

The earliest static magnetic field guidelines were developed as an unofficial recommendation in the former Soviet Union. Clinical investigations formed the basis for this standard, which suggested that the static magnetic field strength at the workplace should not exceed 8 kA/m (10 mT).

The American Conference of Governmental Industrial Hygienists issued TLVs of static magnetic flux densities that most workers could be exposed to repeatedly, day after day, without adverse health effects. As for electric fields, these values should be used as guides in the control of exposure to static magnetic fields, but they should not be regarded as a sharp line between safe and dangerous levels. According to ACGIH, routine occupational exposures should not exceed 60 mT averaged over the whole body or 600 mT to the extremities on a daily, time-weighted basis. A flux density of 2 T is recommended as a ceiling value. Safety hazards may exist from the mechanical forces exerted by the magnetic field upon ferromagnetic tools and medical implants.

In 1994, the International Commission on Non-Ionizing Radiation Protection (ICNIRP 1994) finalized and published guidelines on limits of exposure to static magnetic fields. In these guidelines, a distinction is made between exposure limits for workers and the general public. The limits recommended by the ICNIRP for occupational and general public exposures to static magnetic fields are summarized in table 49.11. When magnetic flux densities exceed 3 mT, precautions should be taken to prevent hazards from flying metallic objects. Analogue watches, credit cards, magnetic tapes and computer disks may be adversely affected by exposure to 1 mT, but this is not seen as a safety concern for people.

Occasional access of the public to special facilities where magnetic flux densities exceed 40 mT can be allowed under appropriately controlled conditions, provided that the appropriate occupational exposure limit is not exceeded.

ICNIRP exposure limits have been set for a homogeneous field. For inhomogeneous fields (variations within the field), the average magnetic flux density must be measured over an area of 100 cm^2.

According to a recent NRPB document, the restriction on acute exposure to less than 2 T will avoid acute responses such as vertigo or nausea and adverse health effects resulting from cardiac arrhythmia (irregular heart beat) or impaired mental function. In spite of the relative lack of evidence from studies of exposed populations regarding possible long-term effects of high fields, the Board considers it advisable to restrict long-term, time-weighted exposure over 24 hours to less than 200 mT (one-tenth of that intended to prevent acute responses). These levels are quite similar to those recommended by ICNIRP; ACGIH TLVs are slightly lower.

People with cardiac pacemakers and other electrically activated implanted devices, or with ferromagnetic implants, may not be adequately protected by the limits given here. The majority of

Table 49.11 • Limits of exposure to static magnetic fields recommended by the International Commission on Non-Ionizing Radiation Protection (ICNIRP).

Exposure characteristics	Magnetic flux density
Occupational	
Whole working day (time-weighted average)	200 mT
Ceiling value	2 T
Limbs	5 T
General Public	
Continuous exposure	40 mT

cardiac pacemakers are unlikely to be affected from exposure to fields below 0.5 mT. People with some ferromagnetic implants or electrically activated devices (other than cardiac pacemakers) may be affected by fields above a few mT.

Other sets of guidelines recommending limits of occupational exposure exist: Three of these are enforced in high-energy physics laboratories (Stanford Linear Accelerator Center and Lawrence Livermore National Laboratory in California, CERN accelerator laboratory in Geneva), and an interim guideline at the US Department of Energy (DOE).

In Germany, according to a DIN Standard, occupational exposures should not exceed a static magnetic field strength of 60 kA/m (about 75 mT). When only the extremities are exposed, this limit is set at 600 kA/m; field strength limits up to 150 kA/m are permitted for short, whole-body exposures (up to 5 min per hour).

References

Allen, SG. 1991. Radiofrequency field measurements and hazard assessment. *J Radiol Protect* 11:49-62.

American Conference of Governmental Industrial Hygienists (ACGIH). 1992. *Documentation for the Threshold Limit Values*. Cincinnati, Ohio: ACGIH.

—. 1993. *Threshold Limit Values for Chemical Substances and Physical Agents and Biological Exposure Indices*. Cincinnati, Ohio: ACGIH.

—. 1994a. *Annual Report of ACGIH Physical Agents Threshold Limit Values Committee*. Cincinnati, Ohio: ACGIH.

—. 1994b. *TLV's, Threshold Limit Values and Biological Exposure Indices for 1994-1995*. Cincinnati, Ohio: ACGIH.

—. 1995. *1995-1996 Threshhold Limit Values for Chemical Substances and Physical Agents and Biological Exposure Indices*. Cincinnati, Ohio: ACGIH.

—. 1996. *TLVs© and BEI©. Threshold Limit Values for Chemical Substances and Physical Agents; Biological Exposure Indices*. Cincinnati, Ohio: ACGIH.

American National Standards Institute (ANSI). 1993. *Safe Use of Lasers. Standard No. Z-136.1*. New York: ANSI.

Aniolczyk, R. 1981. Measurements of hygienic evaluation of electromagnetic fields in the environment of diathermy, welders, and induction heaters. *Medycyna Pracy* 32:119-128.

Bassett, CAL, SN Mitchell, and SR Gaston. 1982. Pulsing electromagnetic field treatment in ununited fractures and failed artrodeses. *J Am Med Assoc* 247:623-628.

Bassett, CAL, RJ Pawluk, and AA Pilla. 1974. Augmentation of bone repair by inductively coupled electromagnetic fields. *Science* 184:575-577.

Berger, D, F Urbach, and RE Davies. 1968. The action spectrum of erythema induced by ultraviolet radiation. In *Preliminary Report XIII. Congressus Internationalis Dermatologiae, Munchen*, edited by W Jadassohn and CG Schirren. New York: Springer-Verlag.

Bernhardt, JH. 1988a. The establishment of frequency dependent limits for electric and magnetic fields and evaluation of indirect effects. *Rad Envir Biophys* 27:1.

Bernhardt, JH and R Matthes. 1992. ELF and RF electromagnetic sources. In *Non-Ionizing Radiation Protection*, edited by MW Greene. Vancouver: UBC Press.

Bini, M, A Checcucci, A Ignesti, L Millanta, R Olmi, N Rubino, and R Vanni. 1986. Exposure of workers to intense RF electric fields that leak from plastic sealers. *J Microwave Power* 21:33-40.

Buhr, E, E Sutter, and Dutch Health Council. 1989. Dynamic filters for protective devices. In *Dosimetry of Laser Radiation in Medicine and Biology*, edited by GJ Mueller and DH Sliney. Bellingham, Wash: SPIE.

Bureau of Radiological Health. 1981. *An Evaluation of Radiation Emission from Video Display Terminals*. Rockville, MD: Bureau of Radiological Health.

Cleuet, A and A Mayer. 1980. Risques liés à l'utilisation industrielle des lasers. In *Institut National de Recherche et de Sécurité, Cahiers de Notes Documentaires, No. 99* Paris: Institut National de Recherche et de Sécurité.

Coblentz, WR, R Stair, and JM Hogue. 1931. The spectral erythemic relation of the skin to ultraviolet radiation. In *Proceedings of the National Academy of Sciences of the United States of America* Washington, DC: National Academy of Sciences.

Cole, CA, DF Forbes, and PD Davies. 1986. An action spectrum for UV photocarcinogenesis. *Photochem Photobiol* 43(3):275-284.

Commission International de L'Eclairage (CIE). 1987. *International Lighting Vocabulary*. Vienna: CIE.

Cullen, AP, BR Chou, MG Hall, and SE Jany. 1984. Ultraviolet-B damages corneal endothelium. *Am J Optom Phys Opt* 61(7):473-478.

Duchene, A, J Lakey, and M Repacholi. 1991. *IRPA Guidelines On Protection Against Non-Ionizing Radiation*. New York: Pergamon.

Elder, JA, PA Czerki, K Stuchly, K Hansson Mild, and AR Sheppard. 1989. Radiofrequency radiation. In *Nonionizing Radiation Protection*, edited by MJ Suess and DA Benwell-Morison. Geneva: WHO.

Eriksen, P. 1985. Time resolved optical spectra from MIG welding arc ignition. *Am Ind Hyg Assoc J* 46:101-104.

Everett, MA, RL Olsen, and RM Sayer. 1965. Ultraviolet erythema. *Arch Dermatol* 92:713-719.

Fitzpatrick, TB, MA Pathak, LC Harber, M Seiji, and A Kukita. 1974. *Sunlight and Man, Normal and Abnormal Photobiologic Responses*. Tokyo: Univ. of Tokyo Press.

Forbes, PD and PD Davies. 1982. Factors that influence photocarcinogenesis. Chap. 7 in *Photoimmunol-*

ogy, edited by JAM Parrish, L Kripke, and WL Morison. New York: Plenum.

Freeman, RS, DW Owens, JM Knox, and HT Hudson. 1966. Relative energy requirements for an erythemal response of skin to monochromatic wavelengths of ultraviolet present in the solar spectrum. *J Invest Dermatol* 47:586-592.

Grandolfo, M and K Hansson Mild. 1989. Worldwide public and occupational radiofrequency and microwave protection. In *Electromagnetic Biointeraction. Mechanisms, Safety Standards, Protection Guides*, edited by G Franceschetti, OP Gandhi, and M Grandolfo. New York: Plenum.

Greene, MW. 1992. Non Ionizing Radiation. 2nd International Non Ionizing Radiation Workshop, 10-14 May, Vancouver.

Ham, WTJ. 1989. The photopathology and nature of the blue-light and near-UV retinal lesion produced by lasers and other optic sources. In *Laser Applications in Medicine and Biology*, edited by ML Wolbarsht. New York: Plenum.

Ham, WT, HA Mueller, JJ Ruffolo, D Guerry III, and RK Guerry. 1982. Action spectrum for retinal injury from near ultraviolet radiation in the aphakic monkey. *Am J Ophthalmol* 93(3):299-306.

Hansson Mild, K. 1980. Occupational exposure to radio-frequency electromagnetic fields. *Proc IEEE* 68:12-17.

Hausser, KW. 1928. Influence of wavelength in radiation biology. *Strahlentherapie* 28:25-44.

Institute of Electrical and Electronic Engineers (IEEE). 1990a. *IEEE COMAR Position of RF and Microwaves.* New York: IEEE.

—. 1990b. *IEEE COMAR Position Statement On Health Aspects of Exposure to Electric and Magnetic Fields from RF Sealers and Dielectric Heaters.* New York: IEEE.

—. 1991. *IEEE Standard for Safety Levels With Respect to Human Exposure to Radiofrequency Electromagnetic Fields 3 KHz to 300 GHz.* New York: IEEE.

International Commission on Non-Ionizing Radiation Protection (ICNIRP). 1994. Guidelines on Limits of Exposure to Static Magnetic Fields. *Health Phys* 66:100-106.

—. 1995. *Guidelines for Human Exposure Limits for Laser Radiation.*

ICNIRP statement. 1996. Health issues related to the use of hand-held radiotelephones and base transmitters. *Health Physics*, 70:587-593.

International Electrotechnical Commission (IEC). 1993. *IEC Standard No. 825-1.* Geneva: IEC.

International Labour Office (ILO). 1993a. *Protection from Power Frequency Electric and Magnetic Fields.* Occupational Safety and Health Series, No. 69. Geneva: ILO.

International Radiation Protection Association (IRPA). 1985. Guidelines for limits of human exposure to laser radiation. *Health Phys* 48(2):341-359.

—. 1988a. Change: Recommendations for minor updates to the IRPA 1985 guidelines on limits of exposure to laser radiation. *Health Phys* 54(5):573-573.

—. 1988b. Guidelines on limits of exposure to radiofrequency electromagnetic fields in the frequency range from 100 kHz to 300 GHz. *Health Phys* 54:115-123.

—. 1989. Proposed change to the IRPA 1985 guidelines limits of exposure to ultraviolet radiation. *Health Phys* 56(6):971-972.

International Radiation Protection Association (IRPA) and International Non-Ionizing Radiation Committee. 1990. Interim guidelines on limits of exposure to 50/60 Hz electric and magnetic fields. *Health Phys* 58(1):113-122.

Kolmodin-Hedman, B, K Hansson Mild, E Jönsson, MC Anderson, and A Eriksson. 1988. Health problems among operations of plastic welding machines and exposure to radiofrequency electromagnetic fields. *Int Arch Occup Environ Health* 60:243-247.

Krause, N. 1986. Exposure of people to static and time variable magnetic fields in technology, medicine, research and public life: Dosimetric aspects. In *Biological Effects of Static and ELF-Magnetic Fields*, edited by JH Bernhardt. Munchen: MMV Medizin Verlag.

Lövsund, P and KH Mild. 1978. *Low Frequency Electromagnetic Field Near Some Induction Heaters.* Stockholm: Stockholm Board of Occupational Health and Safety.

Lövsund, P, PA Oberg, and SEG Nilsson. 1982. ELF magnetic fields in electrosteel and welding industries. *Radio Sci* 17(5S):355-385.

Luckiesh, ML, L Holladay, and AH Taylor. 1930. Reaction of untanned human skin to ultraviolet radiation. *J Optic Soc Am* 20:423-432.

McKinlay, AF and B Diffey. 1987. A reference action spectrum for ultraviolet induced erythema in human skin. In *Human Exposure to Ultraviolet Radiation: Risks and Regulations*, edited by WF Passchier and BFM Bosnjakovic. New York: Excerpta medica Division, Elsevier Science Publishers.

McKinlay, A, JB Andersen, JH Bernhardt, M Grandolfo, K-A Hossmann, FE van Leeuwen, K Hansson Mild, AJ Swerdlow, L Verschaeve and B Veyret. Proposal for a research programme by a European Commission Expert Group. Possible health effects related to the use of radiotelephones. Unpublished report.

Mitbriet, IM and VD Manyachin. 1984. Influence of magnetic fields on the repair of bone. Moscow, Nauka, 292-296.

National Council on Radiation Protection and Measurements (NCRP). 1981. *Radiofrequency Electromagnetic Fields. Properties, Quantities and Units, Biophysical Interaction, and Measurements.* Bethesda, MD: NCRP.

—. 1986. *Biological Effects and Exposure Criteria for Radiofrequency Electromagnetic Fields.* Report No. 86. Bethesda, MD: NCRP.

National Radiological Protection Board (NRPB). 1992. *Electromagnetic Fields and the Risk of Cancer.* Vol. 3(1). Chilton, UK: NRPB.

—. 1993. *Restrictions On Human Exposure to Static and Time-Varying Electromagnetic Fields and Radiations.* Didcot, UK: NRPB.

National Research Council (NRC). 1996. *Possible health effects of exposure to residential electric and magnetic fields.* Washington: NAS Press. 314.

Olsen, EG and A Ringvold. 1982. Human corneal endothelium and ultraviolet radiation. *Acta Ophthalmol* 60:54-56.

Parrish, JA, KF Jaenicke, and RR Anderson. 1982. Erythema and melanogenesis: Action spectra of normal human skin. *Photochem Photobiol* 36(2):187-191.

Passchier, WF and BFM Bosnjakovic. 1987. *Human Exposure to Ultraviolet Radiation: Risks and Regulations.* New York: Excerpta Medica Division, Elsevier Science Publishers.

Pitts, DG. 1974. The human ultraviolet action spectrum. *Am J Optom Phys Opt* 51(12):946-960.

Pitts, DG and TJ Tredici. 1971. The effects of ultraviolet on the eye. *Am Ind Hyg Assoc J* 32(4):235-246.

Pitts, DG, AP Cullen, and PD Hacker. 1977a. Ocular effects of ultraviolet radiation from 295 to 365nm. *Invest Ophthalmol Vis Sci* 16(10):932-939.

—. 1977b. *Ultraviolet Effects from 295 to 400nm in the Rabbit Eye.* Cincinnati, Ohio: National Institute for Occupational Safety and Health (NIOSH).

Polk, C and E Postow. 1986. *CRC Handbook of Biological Effects of Electromagnetic Fields.* Boca Raton: CRC Press.

Repacholi, MH. 1985. Video display terminals -should operators be concerned? *Austalas Phys Eng Sci Med* 8(2):51-61.

—. 1990. Cancer from exposure to 50760 Hz electric and magnetic fields: A major scientific debate. *Austalas Phys Eng Sci Med* 13(1):4-17.

Repacholi, M, A Basten, V Gebski, D Noonan, J Finnic and AW Harris. (1997). Lymphomas in E-Pim1 transgenic mice exposed to pulsed 900 MHz electromagnetic fields. *Radiation research*, 147:631-640.

Riley, MV, S Susan, MI Peters, and CA Schwartz. 1987. The effects of UVB irradiation on the corneal endothelium. *Curr Eye Res* 6(8):1021-1033.

Ringvold, A. 1980b. Aqueous humour and ultraviolet radiation. *Acta Ophthalmol* 58:69-82.

—. 1980a. Cornea and ultraviolet radiation. *Acta Ophthalmol* 58:63-68.

—. 1983. Damage of the corneal epithelium caused by ultraviolet radiation. *Acta Ophthalmol* 61:898-907.

Ringvold, A and M Davanger. 1985. Changes in the rabbit corneal stroma caused by UV radiation. *Acta Ophthalmol* 63:601-606.

Ringvold, A, M Davanger, and EG Olsen. 1982. Changes of the corneal endothelium after ultraviolet radiation. *Acta Ophthalmol* 60:41-53.

Roberts, NJ and SM Michaelson. 1985. Epidemiological studies of human exposure to radiofrequency radiation: A critical review. *Int Arch Occup Environ Health* 56:169-178.

Roy, CR, KH Joyner, HP Gies, and MJ Bangay. 1984. Measurement of electromagnetic radiation emitted from visual display terminals (VDTs). *Rad Prot Austral* 2(1):26-30.

Scotto, J, TR Fears, and GB Gori. 1980. *Measurements of Ultraviolet Radiations in the United States and Comparisons With Skin Cancer Data.* Washington, DC: US Government Printing Office.

Sienkiewicz, ZJ, RD Saunder, and CI Kowalczuk. 1991. *Biological Effects of Exposure to Non-Ionizing Electromagnetic Fields and Radiation. 11 Extremely Low Frequency Electric and Magnetic Fields.* Didcot, UK: National Radiation Protection Board.

Silverman, C. 1990. Epidemiological studies of cancer and electromagnetic fields. In Chap. 17 in *Biological Effects and Medical Applications of Electromagnetic Energy*, edited by OP Gandhi. Engelwood Cliffs, NJ: Prentice Hall.

Sliney, DH. 1972. The merits of an envelope action spectrum for ultraviolet radiation exposure criteria. *Am Ind Hyg Assoc J* 33:644-653.

—. 1986. Physical factors in cataractogenesis: Ambient ultraviolet radiation and temperature. *Invest Ophthalmol Vis Sci* 27(5):781-790.

—. 1987. Estimating the solar ultraviolet radiation exposure to an intraocular lens implant. *J Cataract Refract Surg* 13(5):296-301.

—. 1992. A safety manager's guide to the new welding filters. *Welding J* 71(9):45-47.

Sliney, DH and ML Wolbarsht. 1980. *Safety With Lasers and Other Optical Sources.* New York: Plenum.

Stenson, S. 1982. Ocular findings in xeroderma pigmentosum: Report of two cases. *Ann Ophthalmol* 14(6):580-585.

Sterenborg, HJCM and JC van der Leun. 1987. Action spectra for tumourigenesis by ultraviolet radiation. In *Human Exposure to Ultraviolet Radiation: Risks and Regulations*, edited by WF Passchier and BFM Bosnjakovic. New York: Excerpta Medica Division, Elsevier Science Publishers.

Stuchly, MA. 1986. Human exposure to static and time-varying magnetic fields. *Health Phys* 51(2):215-225.

Stuchly, MA and DW Lecuyer. 1985. Induction heating and operator exposure to electromagnetic fields. *Health Phys* 49:693-700.

—. 1989. Exposure to electromagnetic fields in arc welding. *Health Phys* 56:297-302.

Szmigielski, S, M Bielec, S Lipski, and G Sokolska. 1988. Immunologic and cancer related aspects of exposure to low-level microwave and radiofrequency fields. In *Modern Bioelectricity*, edited by AA Mario. New York: Marcel Dekker.

Taylor, HR, SK West, FS Rosenthal, B Munoz, HS Newland, H Abbey, and EA Emmett. 1988. Effect of ultraviolet radiation on cataract formation. *New Engl J Med* 319:1429-1433.

Tell, RA. 1983. Instrumentation for measurement of electromagnetic fields: Equipment, calibrations, and selected applications. In *Biological Effects and Dosimetry of Nonionizing Radiation, Radiofrequency and Microwave Energies*, edited by M Grandolfo, SM Michaelson, and A Rindi. New York: Plenum.

Urbach, F. 1969. *The Biologic Effects of Ultraviolet Radiation*. New York: Pergamon.

World Health Organization (WHO). 1981. *Radiofrequency and microwaves*. Environmental Health Criteria, No.16. Geneva: WHO.

—. 1982. *Lasers and Optical Radiation*. Environmental Health Criteria, No. 23. Geneva: WHO.

—. 1989. *Non-Ionization Radiation Protection*. Copenhagen: WHO Regional Office for Europe.

—. 1994. *Ultraviolet Radiation*. Environmental Health Criteria, No. 160. Geneva: WHO.

—. 1987. *Magnetic Fields*. Environmental Health Criteria, No.69. Geneva: WHO.

—. 1993. *Electromagnetic Fields 300 Hz to 300 GHz*. Environmental Health Criteria, No. 137. Geneva: WHO.

World Health Organization (WHO), United Nations Environmental Programme (UNEP), and International Radiation Protection Association (IRPA). 1984. *Extremely Low Frequency (ELF)*. Environmental Health Criteria, No. 35. Geneva: WHO.

Zaffanella, LE and DW DeNo. 1978. *Electrostatic and Electromagnetic Effects of Ultra-High-Voltage Transmission Lines*. Palo Alto, Calif: Electric Power Research Institute.

Zuclich, JA and JS Connolly. 1976. Ocular damage induced by near-ultraviolet laser radiation. *Invest Ophthalmol Vis Sci* 15(9):760-764.

Other relevant readings

American Conference of Governmental Industrial Hygienists (ACGIH). 1990. *A Guide for Control of Laser Hazards*. Cincinnati, Ohio: ACGIH.

—. 1991. *Threshold Limit Values for Chemical Substances and Physical Agents and Biological Exposure Indices, 1990-1991*. Cincinnati, Ohio: ACGIH.

Avdeev, PS, YD Berezin, YP Gudakovskii, VR Muratov, AG Murzin, and VA Fromzel. 1978. Experimental determination of maximum permissible exposure to laser radiation of 1.54 p wavelength. *Soviet J Quant Electr* 8:137-141.

Bargeron, CB, OJ Deters, RA Farrell, and RL McCally. 1989. Epithelial damage in rabbit corneas exposed to CO_2 laser radiation. *Health Phys* 56:85-95.

Bernhardt, JH. 1988b. Extremely low frequency (ELF) electric fields. In *Non-Ionizing Radiation: Physical Characteristics, Biological Effects and Health Hazard Assessment*, edited by MH Repacholi. Melbourne: International Non-Ionizing Radiation Workshop.

British Standards Organisation (BSO). 1984. *Radiation Safety of Laser Products and Systems*. London: BSO.

Deutsche Electrotechische Kommission. 1996. *Electromagnetic Field Limit*. Berlin: Deutsche Elektrotechische Kommission.

Deutsche Institut für Normung (DIN). 1984. *Radiation Safety of Laser Products*. Berlin: DIN.

Duchene, AR, MA Repacholi, and J Lakey. 1991. *Guidelines for Limits of Human Exposure to Non-Ionizing*

Fankhauser, F. 1977. Physical and biological effects of laser radiation. *Klinische Monatsblatter fur Augenhielkunde* 170(2):219.

Gabel, VP and R Birngruber. 1981. A comparative study of threshold lesions in the retinae of human volunteers and rabbits. *Health Phys* 40(2):238-240.

Geeraets, WJ and ER Berry. 1968. Ocular spectral characteristics as related to hazards from lasers and other light sources. *Am J Ophthalmol* 66:15-20.

Gezonheidsraad (Health Council of the Netherlands). 1979. *Recommendations Concerning Acceptable Levels of Electromagnetic Radiation in the Wavelength Range from 100 nm and Other Optical Radiation Sources*. New York: Plenum.

Grandolfo, M, SM Michaelson, and A Rindi. 1985. *Biological Effects and Dosimetry of Static and ELF Electromagnetic Fields*. New York: Plenum Press.

Grossweiner, LI. 1984. Photochemistry of proteins: A review. *Curr Eye Res* 3(1):137-144.

Harding, JJ and KJ Dilley. 1976. Structural proteins of the mammalian lens: A review with emphasis on changes in development, aging and cataract. *Exp Eye Res* 22(1):1-73.

International Labour Office (ILO). 1993b. *Visual Display Units -Radiation Protection Guidance*. Occupational Safety and Health Series, No. 70. Geneva: ILO.

International Radiation Protection Association (IRPA) and International Commission on Non-Ionizing Radiation Protection (ICNIRP). 1993a. Alleged radiation risks from visual display units. *Health Phys* 54:231-232.

Kowalczuk, CI, ZJ Sienkiewicz, and RD Saunder. 1991. *Biological Effect of Exposure to Non-Ionizing Electromagnetic Fields and Radiation. I-Static Electric and Magnetic Fields*. Chilton, UK: NRPB.

National Radiological Protection Board (NRPB). 1993. *Documents of the National Radiological Protection Board. Board Statement On Restrictions On Human Exposure to Static and Time Varying Electromagnetic Fields and Radiation*. Vol. 4, No.5. Chilton,UK: NRPB.

Parrish, JA, RR Anderson, F Urbach, and D Pitts. 1978. *UVA, Biological Effects of Ultraviolet Radiation With Emphasis On Human Responses to Longwave Radiation*. New York: Plenum.

Pitts, DG and AP Cullen. 1981. Determination of infrared radiation levels for acute ocular cataractogenesis. *Arch Klin Ophthalmol* 217:285-297.

Sliney, DH. 1987. Unintentional exposure to ultraviolet radiation: Risk reduction and exposure limits. In *Human Exposure to Ultraviolet Radiation: Risks and Regulations*, edited by WF Passchier and BFM Bosnjakovic. New York: Excerpta Medica Division, Elsevier Science Publishers.

Sliney, DH and S Trokel. 1992. *Medical Lasers and Their Safe Use*. New York: Springer-Verlag.

Smith, KC. 1988. *The Science of Photobiology*. New York: Plenum.

Stuck, BE, DJ Lund, and ES Beatrice. 1981. Ocular effects of holmium (2.06 um) and erbium (1054 gm) laser radiation. *Health Phys* 40:835-846.

Suess, MJ and DA Benwell-Morison. 1989. *Non-ionizing protection*. WHO Regional Publications European Series, No. 25. Copenhagen: WHO European Office.

Tung, WH, LTJ Chylack, and UP Andley. 1988. Lens hexokinase deactivation by near-UV irradiation. *Curr Eye Res* 7(3):257-263.

Urbach, F and RW Gange. 1986. *The Biological Effects of UVA Radiation*. Westport, Conn: Praeger.

USSR Ministry of Health. 1982. *Sanitary Norms for Designing and Operating Lasers (in Russian)*. Moscow: USSR Ministry of Health.

Willis, I, A Kligman, and J Epstein. 1972. Effects of long ultraviolet rays on human skin: Photoprotective or photoaugmentative. *J Invest Dermatol* 59:416-420.

Yanuzzi, LA, YL Fisher, A Krueger, and J Slater. 1987. Solar retinopathy, a photobiological and geophysical analysis. *Trans Am Ophthalmol Soc* 85:120-158.

Zuclich, JA. 1989. Ultraviolet-induced photochemical damage in ocular tissues. *Health Phys* 56(5):671-682.

49. RADIATION, NON-IONIZING

VIBRATION

Chapter Editor
Michael J. Griffin

50

Contents

50. VIBRATION

• VIBRATION

Michael J. Griffin

Vibration is oscillatory motion. This chapter summarizes human responses to whole-body vibration, hand-transmitted vibration and the causes of motion sickness.

Whole-body vibration occurs when the body is supported on a surface which is vibrating (e.g., when sitting on a seat which vibrates, standing on a vibrating floor or recumbent on a vibrating surface). Whole-body vibration occurs in all forms of transport and when working near some industrial machinery.

Hand-transmitted vibration is the vibration that enters the body through the hands. It is caused by various processes in industry, agriculture, mining and construction where vibrating tools or workpieces are grasped or pushed by the hands or fingers. Exposure to hand-transmitted vibration can lead to the development of several disorders.

Motion sickness can be caused by low frequency oscillation of the body, some types of rotation of the body and movement of displays relative to the body.

Magnitude

Oscillatory displacements of an object involve alternately a velocity in one direction and then a velocity in the opposite direction. This change of velocity means that the object is constantly accelerating, first in one direction and then in the opposite direction. The magnitude of a vibration can be quantified by its displacement, its velocity or its acceleration. For practical convenience, the acceleration is usually measured with accelerometers. The units of acceleration are metres per second per second (m/s^2). The acceleration due to the Earth's gravity is approximately $9.81 m/s^2$.

The magnitude of an oscillation can be expressed as the distance between the extremities reached by the motion (the peak-to-peak value) or the distance from some central point to the maximum deviation (the peak value). Often, the magnitude of vibration is expressed in terms of an average measure of the acceleration of the oscillatory motion, usually the root-mean-square value (m/s^2 r.m.s.). For a single frequency (sinusoidal) motion, the r.m.s. value is the peak value divided by $\sqrt{2}$.

For a sinusoidal motion the acceleration, a (in m/s^2), can be calculated from the frequency, f (in cycles per second), and the displacement, d (in metres):

$$a = (2\pi f)^2 d$$

This expression may be used to convert acceleration measurements to displacements, but it is only accurate when the motion occurs at a single frequency.

Logarithmic scales for quantifying vibration magnitudes in decibels are sometimes used. When using the reference level in International Standard 1683, the acceleration level, L_a, is expressed by $L_a = 20 \log_{10}(a/a_0)$, where a is the measured acceleration (in m/s^2 r.m.s.) and a_0 is the reference level of $10^{-6} m/s^2$. Other reference levels are used in some countries.

Frequency

The frequency of vibration, which is expressed in cycles per second (hertz, Hz), affects the extent to which vibration is transmitted to the body (e.g., to the surface of a seat or the handle of a vibratory tool), the extent to which it is transmitted through the body (e.g., from the seat to the head), and the effect of vibration in the body. The relation between the displacement and the acceleration of a motion are also dependent on the frequency of oscillation: a displacement of one millimetre corresponds to a very low acceleration at low frequencies but a very high acceleration at high frequencies; the vibration displacement visible to the human eye does not provide a good indication of vibration acceleration.

The effects of whole-body vibration are usually greatest at the lower end of the range, from 0.5 to 100 Hz. For hand-transmitted vibration, frequencies as high as 1,000 Hz or more may have detrimental effects. Frequencies below about 0.5 Hz can cause motion sickness.

The frequency content of vibration can be shown in spectra. For many types of whole-body and hand-transmitted vibration the spectra are complex, with some motion occurring at all frequencies. Nevertheless, there are often peaks, which show the frequencies at which most of the vibration occurs.

Since human responses to vibration vary according to the vibration frequency, it is necessary to weight the measured vibration according to how much vibration occurs at each frequency. Frequency weightings reflect the extent to which vibration causes the undesired effect at each frequency. Weightings are required for each axis of vibration. Different frequency weightings are required for whole-body vibration, hand-transmitted vibration and motion sickness.

Direction

Vibration may take place in three translational directions and three rotational directions. For seated persons, the translational axes are designated x-axis (fore-and-aft), y-axis (lateral) and z-axis (vertical). Rotations about the x-, y- and z-axes are designated r_x (roll), r_y (pitch) and r_z (yaw), respectively. Vibration is usually measured at the interfaces between the body and the vibration. The principal coordinate systems for measuring vibration with respect to whole-body and hand-transmitted vibration are illustrated in the next two articles in the chapter.

Duration

Human responses to vibration depend on the total duration of vibration exposure. If the characteristics of vibration do not change with time, the root-mean-square vibration provides a convenient measure of the average vibration magnitude. A stopwatch may then be sufficient to assess the exposure duration. The severity of the average magnitude and total duration can be assessed by reference to the standards in the following articles.

If the vibration characteristics vary, the measured average vibration will depend on the period over which it is measured. Furthermore, root-mean-square acceleration is believed to underestimate the severity of motions which contain shocks, or are otherwise highly intermittent.

Many occupational exposures are intermittent, vary in magnitude from moment to moment or contain occasional shocks. The severity of such complex motions can be accumulated in a manner which gives appropriate weight to, for example, short periods of high magnitude vibration and long periods of low magnitude vibration. Different methods of calculating doses are used (see "Whole-body vibration"; "Hand-transmitted vibration"; and "Motion sickness" in this chapter).

WHOLE-BODY VIBRATION

Helmut Seidel and Michael J. Griffin

Occupational Exposure

Occupational exposures to whole-body vibration mainly occur in transport but also in association with some industrial processes.

Table 50.1 • Activities for which it may be appropriate to warn of the adverse effects of whole-body vibration.

Tractor driving

Armoured fighting vehicles (e.g., tanks) and similar vehicles

Other off-road vehicles:

- Earth-moving machinery—loaders, excavators, bulldozers, graders, scrapers, dumpers, rollers
- Forest machines
- Mine and quarry equipment
- Forklift trucks

Some truck driving (articulated and non-articulated)

Some bus and tram driving

Some helicopter and fixed-wing aircraft flying

Some workers with concrete production machinery

Some railway drivers

Some use of high-speed marine craft

Some motor bicycle riding

Some car and van driving

Some sports activities

Some other industrial equipment

Source: Adapted from Griffin 1990.

Land, sea and air transport can all produce vibration that can cause discomfort, interfere with activities or cause injury. Table 50.1 lists some environments which may be most likely to be associated with a health risk.

The most common exposure to severe vibration and shocks may occur on off-road vehicles, including earth moving machinery, industrial trucks and agricultural tractors.

Biodynamics

Like all mechanical structures, the human body has resonance frequencies where the body exhibits a maximum mechanical response. Human responses to vibration cannot be explained solely in terms of a single resonance frequency. There are many resonances in the body, and the resonance frequencies vary among people and with posture. Two mechanical responses of the body are often used to describe the manner in which vibration causes the body to move: *transmissibility* and *impedance*.

The transmissibility shows the fraction of the vibration which is transmitted from, say, the seat to the head. The transmissibility of the body is highly dependent on vibration frequency, vibration axis and body posture. Vertical vibration on a seat causes vibration in several axes at the head; for vertical head motion, the transmissibility tends to be greatest in the approximate range of 3 to 10 Hz.

The mechanical impedance of the body shows the force that is required to make the body move at each frequency. Although the impedance depends on body mass, the vertical impedance of the human body usually shows a resonance at about 5 Hz. The mechanical impedance of the body, including this resonance, has a large effect on the manner in which vibration is transmitted through seats.

Acute Effects

Discomfort

The discomfort caused by vibration acceleration depends on the vibration frequency, the vibration direction, the point of contact with the body, and the duration of vibration exposure. For vertical vibration of seated persons, the vibration discomfort caused by any frequency increases in proportion to the vibration magnitude: a halving of the vibration will tend to halve the vibration discomfort.

The discomfort produced by vibration may be predicted by the use of appropriate frequency weightings (see below) and described by a semantic scale of discomfort. There are no useful limits for vibration discomfort: the acceptable discomfort varies from one environment to another.

Acceptable magnitudes of vibration in buildings are close to vibration perception thresholds. The effects on humans of vibration in buildings are assumed to depend on the use of the building in addition to the vibration frequency, direction and duration. Guidance on the evaluation of building vibration is given in various standards such as British Standard 6472 (1992) which defines a procedure for the evaluation of both vibration and shock in buildings.

Activity interference

Vibration can impair the acquisition of information (e.g., by the eyes), the output of information (e.g., by hand or foot movements) or the complex central processes that relate input to output (e.g., learning, memory, decision-making). The greatest effects of whole-body vibration are on input processes (mainly vision) and output processes (mainly continuous hand control).

Effects of vibration on vision and manual control are primarily caused by the movement of the affected part of the body (i.e., eye or hand). The effects may be decreased by reducing the transmission of vibration to the eye or to the hand, or by making the task less susceptible to disturbance (e.g., increasing the size of a display or reducing the sensitivity of a control). Often, the effects of vibration on vision and manual control can be much reduced by redesign of the task.

Simple cognitive tasks (e.g., simple reaction time) appear to be unaffected by vibration, other than by changes in arousal or motivation or by direct effects on input and output processes. This may also be true for some complex cognitive tasks. However, the sparsity and diversity of experimental studies does not exclude the possibility of real and significant cognitive effects of vibration. Vibration may influence fatigue, but there is little relevant scientific evidence, and none which supports the complex form of the "fatigue-decreased proficiency limit" offered in International Standard 2631 (ISO 1974, 1985).

Changes in Physiological Functions

Changes in physiological functions occur when subjects are exposed to a novel whole-body vibration environment in laboratory conditions. Changes typical of a "startle response" (e.g., increased heart rate) normalize quickly with continuing exposure, whereas other reactions either proceed or develop gradually. The latter can depend on all characteristics of vibration including the axis, the magnitude of acceleration, and the kind of vibration (sinusoidal or random), as well as on further variables such as circadian rhythm and characteristics of the subjects (see Hasan 1970; Seidel 1975; Dupuis and Zerlett 1986). Changes of physiological functions under field conditions often cannot be related to vibration directly, since vibration is often acting together with other significant factors, such as high mental strain, noise and toxic substances. Physiological changes are frequently less sensitive than psychological reactions (e.g., discomfort). If all available data on persistent physiological changes are summarized with respect to their first significant appearance depending on the magnitude and frequency of whole-body vibration, there is a boundary with a lower border around 0.7 m/s^2 r.m.s. between 1 and 10 Hz, and rising up to 30 m/s^2 r.m.s. at 100 Hz. Many animal studies have been performed, but their relevance to humans is doubtful.

Neuromuscular changes

During active natural motion, motor control mechanisms act as a feed-forward control that is constantly adjusted by additional feedback from sensors in muscles, tendons and joints. Whole-body vibration causes a passive artificial motion of the human body, a condition that is fundamentally different from the self-induced vibration caused by locomotion. The missing feed-forward control during whole-body vibration is the most distinct change of the normal physiological function of the neuromuscular system. The broader frequency range associated with whole-body vibration (between 0.5 and 100 Hz) compared to that for natural motion (between 2 and 8 Hz for voluntary movements, and below 4 Hz for locomotion) is a further difference that helps to explain reactions of the neuromuscular control mechanisms at very low and at high frequencies.

Whole-body vibration and transient acceleration cause an acceleration-related alternating activity in the electromyogram (EMG) of superficial back muscles of seated persons that requires a tonic contraction to be maintained. This activity is supposed to be of a reflex-like nature. It usually disappears completely if the vibrated subjects sit relaxed in a bent position. The timing of muscle activity depends on the frequency and magnitude of acceleration. Electromyographic data suggest that an increased spinal load can occur due to reduced muscular stabilization of the spine at frequencies from 6.5 to 8 Hz and during the initial phase of a sudden upward displacement. In spite of weak EMG activity caused by whole-body vibration, back muscle fatigue during vibration exposure can exceed that observed in normal sitting postures without whole-body vibration.

Tendon reflexes may be diminished or disappear temporarily during exposure to sinusoidal whole-body vibration at frequencies above 10 Hz. Minor changes of postural control after exposure to whole-body vibration are quite variable, and their mechanisms and practical significance are not certain.

Cardiovascular, respiratory, endocrine and metabolic changes

The observed changes persisting during exposure to vibration have been compared to those during moderate physical work (i.e., increases of heart rate, blood pressure and oxygen consumption) even at a vibration magnitude near to the limit of voluntary tolerance. The increased ventilation is partially caused by oscillations of the air in the respiratory system. Respiratory and metabolic changes may not correspond, possibly suggesting a disturbance of the respiration control mechanisms. Various and partially contradictory findings have been reported for changes of the adrenocorticotropic hormones (ACTH) and catecholamines.

Sensory and central nervous changes

Changes of vestibular function due to whole-body vibration have been claimed on the basis of an affected regulation of posture, although posture is controlled by a very complex system in which a disturbed vestibular function can be largely compensated by other mechanisms. Changes of the vestibular function seem to gain significance for exposures with very low frequencies or those near the resonance of the whole body. A sensory mismatch between vestibular, visual and proprioceptive (stimuli received within the tissues) information is supposed to be an important mechanism underlying physiological responses to some artificial motion environments.

Experiments with short-term and prolonged combined exposures to noise and whole-body vibration, seem to suggest that vibration has a minor synergistic effect on hearing. As a tendency, high intensities of whole-body vibration at 4 or 5 Hz were associated with higher additional temporary threshold shifts (TTS). There was no obvious relation between the additional TTS and exposure time. The additional TTS seemed to increase with higher doses of whole-body vibration.

Impulsive vertical and horizontal vibrations evoke brain potentials. Changes of the function of the human central nervous system have also been detected using auditory evoked brain potentials (Seidel et al. 1992). The effects were influenced by other environmental factors (e.g., noise), the difficulty of the task, and by the internal state of the subject (e.g., arousal, degree of attention towards the stimulus).

Long-Term Effects

Spinal health risk

Epidemiological studies have frequently indicated an elevated health risk for the spine in workers exposed for many years to intense whole-body vibration (e.g., work on tractors or earth-moving machines). Critical surveys of the literature have been prepared by Seidel and Heide (1986), Dupuis and Zerlett (1986) and Bongers and Boshuizen (1990). These reviews concluded that intense long-term whole-body vibration can adversely affect the spine and can increase the risk of low-back pain. The latter may be a secondary consequence of a primary degenerative change of the vertebrae and disks. The lumbar part of the vertebral column was found to be the most frequently affected region, followed by the thoracic region. A high rate of impairments of the cervical part, reported by several authors, seems to be caused by a fixed unfavourable posture rather than by vibration, although there is no conclusive evidence for this hypothesis. Only a few studies have considered the function of back muscles and found a muscular insufficiency. Some reports have indicated a significantly higher risk of the dislocation of lumbar disks. In several cross-sectional studies Bongers and Boshuizen (1990) found more low-back pain in drivers and helicopter pilots than in comparable reference workers. They concluded that professional vehicle driving and helicopter flying are important risk factors for low-back pain and back disorder. An increase in disability pensioning and long-term sick leave due to intervertebral disc disorders was observed among crane operators and tractor drivers.

Due to incomplete or missing data on exposure conditions in epidemiological studies, exact exposure-effect relationships have not been obtained. The existing data do not permit the substantiation of a no-adverse-effect level (i.e., safe limit) so as to reliably prevent diseases of the spine. Many years of exposure below or near the exposure limit of the current International Standard 2631 (ISO 1985) are not without risk. Some findings have indicated an increasing health risk with increased duration of exposure, although selection processes have made it difficult to detect a relation in the majority of studies. Thus, a dose-effect relationship cannot currently be established by epidemiological investigations. Theoretical considerations suggest marked detrimental effects of high peak loads acting on the spine during exposures with high transients. The use of an "energy equivalent" method to calculate a vibration dose (as in International Standard 2631 (ISO 1985)) is therefore questionable for exposures to whole-body vibration containing high peak accelerations. Different long-term effects of whole-body vibration depending on the vibration frequency have not been derived from epidemiological studies. Whole-body vibration at 40 to 50 Hz applied to standing workers through the feet was followed by degenerative changes of the bones of the feet.

In general, differences between subjects have been largely neglected, although selection phenomena suggest they may be of major importance. There are no clear data showing whether the effects of whole-body vibration on the spine depend on gender.

The general acceptance of degenerative disorders of the spine as an occupational disease is debated. Specific diagnostic features are not known which would permit a reliable diagnosis of the disorder as an outcome of exposure to whole-body vibration. A high prevalence of degenerative spinal disorders in non-exposed populations hinders the assumption of a predominantly occupational aetiology in individuals exposed to whole-body vibration. Individual constitutional risk factors that might modify vibration-induced strain are unknown. The use of a minimal intensity and/or a minimal duration of whole-body vibration as a prerequisite for the recognition of an occupational disease would not take into account the expected considerable variability in individual susceptibility.

Other health risks

Epidemiological studies suggest that whole-body vibration is one factor within a causative set of factors which contribute to other health risks. Noise, high mental strain and shift work are examples of important concomitant factors which are known to be associated with health disorders. The results of investigations into disorders of other bodily systems have often been divergent or have indicated a paradoxical dependence of the prevalence of pathology on the magnitude of whole-body vibration (i.e., a higher prevalence of adverse effects with a lower intensity). A characteristic complex of symptoms and pathological changes of the central nervous system, the musculo-skeletal system and the circulatory system has been observed in workers standing on machines used for the vibro-compression of concrete and exposed to whole-body vibration beyond the exposure limit of ISO 2631 with frequencies above 40 Hz (Rumjancev 1966). This complex was designated as "vibration disease". Although rejected by many specialists, the same term has sometimes been used to describe a vague clinical picture caused by long-term exposure to low-frequency whole-body vibration which, allegedly, is manifested initially as peripheral and cerebral vegeto-vascular disorders with a non-specific functional character. Based on the available data it can be concluded that different physiological systems react independently of one another and that there are no symptoms which might serve as an indicator of pathology induced by whole-body vibration.

Nervous system, vestibular organ and hearing. Intense whole-body vibration at frequencies higher than 40 Hz can cause damage and disturbances of the central nervous system. Conflicting data have been reported on effects of whole-body vibration at frequencies below 20 Hz. In some studies only, an increase of non-specific complaints such as headache and increased irritability has been found. Disturbances of the electroencephalogram (EEG) after long-term exposure to whole-body vibration have been claimed by one author and denied by others. Some published results are consistent with a decreased vestibular excitability and a higher incidence of other vestibular disturbances, including dizziness. However, it remains doubtful whether there are causal links between whole-body vibration and changes in the central nervous system or vestibular system because paradoxical intensity-effect relationships were detected.

In some studies, an additional increase of the permanent threshold shifts (PTS) of hearing has been observed after a combined long-term exposure to whole-body vibration and noise. Schmidt (1987) studied drivers and technicians in agriculture and compared the permanent threshold shifts after 3 and 25 years on the job. He concluded that whole-body vibration can induce an additional significant threshold shift at 3, 4, 6 and 8 kHz, if the weighted acceleration according to International Standard 2631 (ISO 1985) exceeds 1.2 m/s^2 r.m.s. with a simultaneous exposure to noise at an equivalent level of more than 80 decibels (dBA).

Circulatory and digestive systems. Four main groups of circulatory disturbances have been detected with a higher incidence among workers exposed to whole-body vibration:

1. peripheral disorders, such as the Raynaud-syndrome, near to the site of application of whole-body vibration (i.e., the feet of standing workers or, with a low degree only, the hands of drivers)
2. varicose veins of the legs, haemorrhoids and varicocele
3. ischaemic heart disease and hypertension
4. neurovascular changes.

The morbidity of these circulatory disturbances did not always correlate with the magnitude or duration of vibration exposure. Although a high prevalence of various disorders of the digestive system has often been observed, almost all authors agree that whole-body vibration is but one cause and possibly not the most important.

Female reproductive organs, pregnancy and male urogenital system. Increased risks of abortions, menstrual disturbances and anomalies of positions (e.g., uterine descent) have been assumed to be associated with long-term exposure to whole-body vibration (see Seidel and Heide 1986). A safe exposure limit in order to avoid a higher risk for these health risks cannot be derived from the literature. The individual susceptibility and its temporal changes probably co-determine these biological effects. In the available literature, a harmful direct effect of whole-body vibration on the human foetus has not been reported, although some animal studies suggest that whole-body vibration can affect the foetus. The unknown threshold value for adverse effects on pregnancy suggests a limitation on an occupational exposure to the lowest reasonable extent.

Divergent results have been published for the occurrence of diseases of the male urogenital system. In some studies, a higher incidence of prostatitis was observed. Other studies could not confirm these findings.

Standards

No precise limit can be offered to prevent disorders caused by whole-body vibration, but standards define useful methods of quantifying vibration severity. International Standard 2631 (ISO 1974, 1985) defined exposure limits (see figure 50.1) which were "set at approximately half the level considered to be the threshold of pain (or limit of voluntary tolerance) for healthy human subjects". Also shown in figure 50.1 is a vibration dose value action level for vertical vibration derived from British Standard 6841 (BSI 1987b); this standard is, in part, similar to a draft revision of the International Standard.

The vibration dose value can be considered to be the magnitude of a one-second duration of vibration which will be equally severe to the measured vibration. The vibration dose value uses a fourth-power time dependency to accumulate vibration severity over the exposure period from the shortest possible shock to a full day of vibration (e.g., BSI 6841):

$$\text{Vibration dose value} = \left[\int_{t=0}^{t=\infty} a(t)^4 \, dt \right]^{\frac{1}{4}}$$

The vibration dose value procedure can be used to evaluate the severity of both vibration and repetitive shocks. This fourth-power time dependency is simpler to use than the time dependency in ISO 2631 (see figure 50.2).

Figure 50.1 • Frequency dependencies for human response to whole-body vibration.

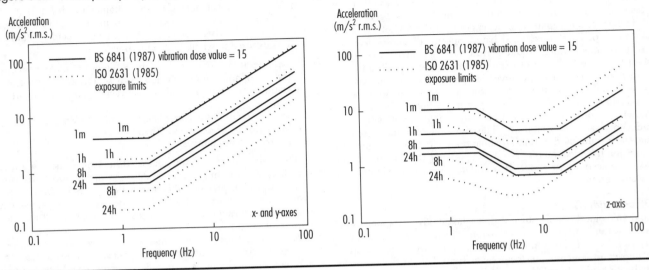

British Standard 6841 offers the following guidance.

High vibration dose values will cause severe discomfort, pain and injury. Vibration dose values also indicate, in a general way, the severity of the vibration exposures which caused them. However there is currently no consensus of opinion on the precise relation between vibration dose values and the risk of injury. It is known that vibration magnitudes and durations which produce vibration dose values in the region of 15 m/s$^{1.75}$ will usually cause severe discomfort. It is reasonable to assume that increased exposure to vibration will be accompanied by increased risk of injury (BSI 1987b).

At high vibration dose values, prior consideration of the fitness of the exposed persons and the design of adequate safety precautions may be required. The need for regular checks on the health of routinely exposed persons may also be considered.

The vibration dose value provides a measure by which highly variable and complex exposures can be compared. Organizations may specify limits or action levels using the vibration dose value. For example, in some countries, a vibration dose value of 15 m/s$^{1.75}$ has been used as a tentative action level, but it may be appropriate to limit vibration or repeated shock exposures to higher or lower values depending on the situation. With current understanding, an action level merely serves to indicate the approximate values that might be excessive. Figure 50.2 illustrates the root-mean-square accelerations corresponding to a vibration dose value of 15 m/s$^{1.75}$ for exposures between one second and 24 hours. Any exposure to continuous vibration, intermittent vibration, or repeated shock may be compared with the action level by calculating the vibration dose value. It would be unwise to exceed an appropriate action level (or the exposure limit in ISO 2631) without consideration of the possible health effects of an exposure to vibration or shock.

The *Machinery Safety Directive* of the European Economic Community states that machinery must be designed and constructed so that hazards resulting from vibration produced by the machinery are reduced to the lowest practicable level, taking into account technical progress and the availability of means of reducing vibration. The *Machinery Safety Directive* (Council of the European Communities 1989) encourages the reduction of vibration by means additional to reduction at source (e.g., good seating).

Measurement and Evaluation of Exposure

Whole-body vibration should be measured at the interfaces between the body and the source of vibration. For seated persons this involves the placement of accelerometers on the seat surface beneath the ischial tuberosities of subjects. Vibration is also sometimes measured at the seat back (between the backrest and the back) and also at the feet and hands (see figure 50.3).

Epidemiological data alone are not sufficient to define how to evaluate whole-body vibration so as to predict the relative risks to health from the different types of vibration exposure. A consideration of epidemiological data in combination with an understanding of biodynamic responses and subjective responses is used to provide current guidance. The manner in which the health effects of oscillatory motions depend upon the frequency, direction and duration of motion is currently assumed to be the same as, or similar to, that for vibration discomfort. However, it is assumed that the total exposure, rather than the average exposure, is important, and so a dose measure is appropriate.

Figure 50.2 • Time dependencies for human response to whole-body vibration.

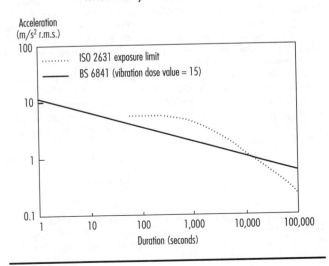

Figure 50.3 • Axes for measuring vibration exposures of seated persons.

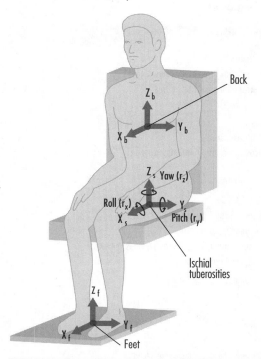

Table 50.2 • Summary of preventive measures to consider when persons are exposed to whole-body vibration.

Group	Action
Management	Seek technical advice
	Seek medical advice
	Warn exposed persons
	Train exposed persons
	Review exposure times
	Have policy on removal from exposure
Machine manufacturers	Measure vibration
	Design to minimize whole-body vibration
	Optimize suspension design
	Optimize seating dynamics
	Use ergonomic design to provide good posture etc.
	Provide guidance on machine maintenance
	Provide guidance on seat maintenance
	Provide warning of dangerous vibration
Technical — at workplace	Measure vibration exposure
	Provide appropriate machines
	Select seats with good attenuation
	Maintain machines
	Inform management
Medical	Pre-employment screening
	Routine medical checks
	Record all signs and reported symptoms
	Warn workers with apparent predisposition
	Advise on consequences of exposure
	Inform management
Exposed persons	Use machine properly
	Avoid unnecessary vibration exposure
	Check seat is properly adjusted
	Adopt good sitting posture
	Check condition of machine
	Inform supervisor of vibration problems
	Seek medical advice if symptoms appear
	Inform employer of relevant disorders

Source: Adapted from Griffin 1990.

In addition to evaluating the measured vibration according to current standards, it is advisable to report the frequency spectra, magnitudes in different axes and other characteristics of the exposure, including the daily and lifetime exposure durations. The presence of other adverse environmental factors, especially sitting posture, should also be considered.

Prevention

Wherever possible, reduction of vibration at the source is to be preferred. This may involve reducing the undulations of the terrain or reducing the speed of travel of vehicles. Other methods of reducing the transmission of vibration to operators require an understanding of the characteristics of the vibration environment and the route for the transmission of vibration to the body. For example, the magnitude of vibration often varies with location: lower magnitudes will be experienced in some areas. Table 50.2 lists some preventive measures that may be considered.

Seats can be designed to attenuate vibration. Most seats exhibit a resonance at low frequencies, which results in higher magnitudes of vertical vibration occurring on the seat than on the floor! At high frequencies there is usually attenuation of vibration. In use, the resonance frequencies of common seats are in the region of 4 Hz. The amplification at resonance is partially determined by the damping in the seat. An increase in the damping of the seat cushioning tends to reduce the amplification at resonance but increase the transmissibility at high frequencies. There are large variations in transmissibility between seats, and these result in significant differences in the vibration experienced by people.

A simple numerical indication of the isolation efficiency of a seat for a specific application is provided by the seat effective amplitude transmissibility (SEAT) (see Griffin 1990). A SEAT value greater than 100% indicates that, overall, the vibration on the seat is worse than the vibration on the floor. Values below 100% indicate that the seat has provided some useful attenuation.

Seats should be designed to have the lowest SEAT value compatible with other constraints.

A separate suspension mechanism is provided beneath the seat pan in suspension seats. These seats, used in some off-road vehicles, trucks and coaches, have low resonance frequencies (around 2 Hz) and so can attenuate vibration at frequencies above about 3 Hz. The transmissibilities of these seats are usually determined by the seat manufacturer, but their isolation efficiencies vary with operating conditions.

HAND-TRANSMITTED VIBRATION

Massimo Bovenzi

Occupational Exposure

Mechanical vibration arising from powered processes or tools and entering the body at the fingers or the palm of the hands is called *hand-transmitted vibration*. Frequent synonyms for hand-transmitted vibration are hand-arm vibration and local or segmental vibration. Powered processes and tools which expose operators' hands to vibration are widespread in several industrial activities. Occupational exposure to hand-transmitted vibration arises from hand-held powered tools used in manufacturing (e.g., percussive metal-working tools, grinders and other rotary tools, impact wrenches), quarrying, mining and construction (e.g., rock-drills, stone-hammers, pick-hammers, vibrocompactors), agriculture and forestry (e.g., chain saws, brush saws, barking machines) and public utilities (e.g., road and concrete breakers, drill-hammers, hand-held grinders). Exposure to hand-transmitted vibration can also occur from vibrating workpieces held in the hands of the operator as in pedestal grinding, and from hand-held vibrating controls as in operating lawn mowers or in controlling vibrating road compactors. It has been reported that the number of persons exposed to hand-transmitted vibration at work exceeds 150,000 in the Netherlands, 0.5 million in Great Britain, and 1.45 million in the United States. Excessive exposure to hand-transmitted vibration can cause disorders in the blood vessels, nerves, muscles, and bones and joints of the upper limbs. It has been estimated that 1.7 to 3.6% of the workers in European countries and the United States are exposed to potentially harmful hand-transmitted vibration (ISSA International Section for Research 1989). The term hand-arm vibration (HAV) syndrome is commonly used to refer to signs and symptoms associated with exposure to hand-transmitted vibration, which include:

- vascular disorders
- peripheral neurological disorders
- bone and joint disorders
- muscle disorders
- other disorders (whole body, central nervous system).

Leisure activities such as motorcycling or using domestic vibrating tools can occasionally expose the hands to vibration of high amplitude, but only long daily exposures may give rise to health problems (Griffin 1990).

The relationship between occupational exposure to hand-transmitted vibration and adverse health effects is far from simple. Table 50.3 lists some of the most important factors which concur to cause injuries in the upper limbs of vibration-exposed workers.

Biodynamics

It may be presumed that factors influencing the transmission of vibration into the finger-hand-arm system play a relevant role in the genesis of vibration injury. The transmission of vibration depends on both the physical characteristics of vibration (magnitude, frequency, direction) and the dynamic response of the hand (Griffin 1990).

Transmissibility and impedance

Experimental results indicate that the mechanical behaviour of the human upper limb is complex, as the impedance of the hand-arm system—that is, its resistance to vibrate—shows pronounced variations with the change in vibration amplitude, frequency and direction, applied forces, and orientation of the hand and arm with respect to the axis of the stimulus. Impedance is also influenced by body constitution and structural differences of the various parts of the upper limb (e.g., the mechanical impedance of the fingers is much lower than that of the palm of the hand). In general, higher vibration levels, as well as tighter hand-grips, result in greater impedance. However, the change in impedance has been found to be highly dependent on the frequency and direction of the vibration stimulus and various sources of both intra- and inter-subject variability. A resonance region for the finger-hand-arm system in the frequency range between 80 and 300 Hz has been reported in several studies.

Table 50.3 • Some factors potentially related to injurious effects during hand-transmitted vibration exposures.

Vibration characteristics
- Magnitude (r.m.s., peak, weighted/unweighted)
- Frequency (spectra, dominant frequencies)
- Direction (x-, y-, z-axes)

Tools or processes
- Tool design (portable, fixed)
- Tool type (percussive, rotary, rotating percussive)
- Condition
- Operation
- Material being worked

Exposure conditions
- Duration (daily, yearly exposures)
- Pattern of exposure (continuous, intermittent, rest periods)
- Cumulative exposure duration

Environmental conditions
- Ambient temperature
- Airflow
- Humidity
- Noise
- Dynamic response of the finger-hand-arm system
- Mechanical impedance
- Vibration transmissibility
- Absorbed energy

Individual characteristics
- Method of working (grip force, push force, hand-arm posture, body position)
- Health
- Training
- Skill
- Use of gloves
- Individual susceptibility to injury

Measurements of the transmission of vibration through the human arm have shown that lower frequency vibration (<50 Hz) is transmitted with little attenuation along the hand and forearm. The attenuation at the elbow is dependent on the arm posture, as the transmission of vibration tends to decrease with the increase of the flexion angle at the elbow joint. For higher frequencies (>50 Hz), the transmission of vibration progressively decreases with increasing frequency, and above 150 to 200 Hz most of the vibrational energy is dissipated in the tissues of the hand and fingers. From transmissibility measurements it has been inferred that in the high-frequency region vibration may be responsible for damage to the soft structures of the fingers and hands, while low-frequency vibration of high amplitude (e.g., from percussive tools) might be associated with injuries to the wrist, elbow and shoulder.

Factors influencing finger and hand dynamics

The adverse effects from vibration exposure may be assumed to be related to the energy dissipated in the upper limbs. Energy absorption is highly dependent on factors affecting the coupling of the finger-hand system to the vibration source. Variations in grip pressure, static force and posture modify the dynamic response of the finger, hand and arm, and, consequently, the amount of energy transmitted and absorbed. For instance, grip pressure has a considerable influence on energy absorption and, in general, the higher the hand grip the greater the force transmitted to the hand-arm system. Dynamic response data can provide relevant information to assess the injury potential of tool vibration and to assist in the development of anti-vibration devices such as hand-grips and gloves.

Acute Effects

Subjective discomfort

Vibration is sensed by various skin mechanoreceptors, which are located in the (epi)dermal and subcutaneous tissues of the smooth and bare (glabrous) skin of the fingers and hands. They are classified into two categories—slow and fast adapting—according to their adaptation and receptive field properties. Merkel discs and Ruffini endings are found in the slow-adapting mechanoreceptive units, which respond to static pressure and slow changes in pressure and are excited at low frequency (<16 Hz). Fast-adapting units have Meissner's corpuscles and Pacinian corpuscles, which respond to rapid changes in stimulus and are responsible for vibratory sensation in the frequency range between 8 and 400 Hz. The subjective response to hand-transmitted vibration has been used in several studies to obtain threshold values, contours of equivalent sensation and unpleasant or tolerance limits for vibratory stimuli at different frequencies (Griffin 1990). Experimental results indicate that human sensitivity to vibration decreases with increasing frequency for both comfort and annoyance vibration levels. Vertical vibration appears to cause more discomfort than vibration in other directions. Subjective discomfort has also been found to be a function of the spectral composition of vibration and the grip force exerted on the vibrating handle.

Activity interference

Acute exposure to hand-transmitted vibration can cause a temporary increase in vibrotactile thresholds due to a depression of the excitability of the skin mechanoreceptors. The magnitude of the temporary threshold shift as well as the time for recovery is influenced by several variables, such as the characteristics of the stimulus (frequency, amplitude, duration), temperature as well as the worker's age and previous exposure to vibration. Exposure to cold aggravates the tactile depression induced by vibration, because low temperature has a vasoconstrictive effect on digital circulation and reduces finger skin temperature. In vibration-exposed workers who often operate in a cold environment, repeated episodes of acute impairment of tactile sensitivity can lead to permanent reduction in sensory perception and loss of manipulative dexterity, which, in turn, can interfere with work activity, increasing the risk for acute injuries due to accidents.

Non-Vascular Effects

Skeletal

Vibration-induced bone and joint injuries are a controversial matter. Various authors consider that disorders of bones and joints in workers using hand-held vibrating tools are not specific in character and similar to those due to the ageing process and to heavy manual work. On the other hand, some investigators have reported that characteristic skeletal changes in the hands, the wrists and the elbows can result from prolonged exposure to hand-transmitted vibration. Early x-ray investigations had revealed a high prevalence of bone vacuoles and cysts in the hands and wrists of vibration-exposed workers, but more recent studies have shown

no significant increase with respect to control groups made up of manual workers. Excess prevalence of wrist osteoarthrosis and elbow arthrosis and osteophytosis has been reported in coal miners, road construction workers and metal-working operators exposed to shocks and low frequency vibration of high amplitude from pneumatic percussive tools. On the contrary, there is little evidence for an increased prevalence of degenerative bone and joint disorders in the upper limbs of workers exposed to mid- or high-frequency vibrations arising from chain saws or grinding machines. Heavy physical effort, forceful gripping and other biomechanical factors can account for the higher occurrence of skeletal injuries found in workers operating percussive tools. Local pain, swelling, and joint stiffness may be associated with radiological findings of bone and joint degeneration. In a few countries (including France, Germany, Italy), bone and joint disorders occurring in workers using hand-held vibrating tools are considered to be an occupational disease, and the affected workers are compensated.

Neurological

Workers handling vibrating tools may experience tingling and numbness in their fingers and hands. If vibration exposure continues, these symptoms tend to worsen and can interfere with work capacity and life activities. Vibration-exposed workers may exhibit increased vibratory, thermal and tactile thresholds in clinical examinations. It has been suggested that continuous vibration exposure can not only depress the excitability of skin receptors but also induce pathological changes in the digital nerves such as perineural oedema, followed by fibrosis and nerve fibre loss. Epidemiological surveys of vibration-exposed workers show that the prevalence of peripheral neurological disorders varies from a few per cent to more than 80 per cent, and that sensory loss affects users of a wide range of tool types. It seems that vibration neuropathy develops independently of other vibration-induced disorders. A scale of the neurological component of the HAV syndrome was proposed at the Stockholm Workshop 86 (1987), consisting of three stages according to the symptoms and the results of clinical examination and objective tests (table 50.4). Careful differential diagnosis is required to distinguish vibration neuropathy from entrapment neuropathies, such as carpal tunnel syndrome (CTS), a disorder due to compression of the median nerve as it passes through an anatomical tunnel in the wrist. CTS seems to be a common disorder in some occupational groups using vibrating tools, such as rock-drillers, platers and forestry workers. It is believed that ergonomic stressors acting on the hand and wrist (repetitive movements, forceful gripping, awkward postures), in addition to vibration, can cause CTS in workers handling vibrating tools. Electroneuromyography measuring sensory and motor nerve velocities has proven to be useful to differentiate CTS from other neurological disorders.

Table 50.4 • Sensorineural stages of the Stockholm Workshop scale for the hand-arm vibration syndrome.

Stage	Signs and symptoms
0SN	Exposed to vibration but no symptoms
1SN	Intermittent numbness, with or without tingling
2SN	Intermittent or persistent numbness, reduced sensory perception
3SN	Intermittent or persistent numbness, reduced tactile discrimination and/or manipulative dexterity

Source: Stockholm Workshop 86 1987.

Muscular

Vibration-exposed workers may complain of muscle weakness and pain in the hands and arms. In some individuals muscle fatigue can cause disability. A decrease in hand-grip strength has been reported in follow-up studies of lumberjacks. Direct mechanical injury or peripheral nerve damage have been suggested as possible aetiological factors for muscle symptoms. Other work-related disorders have been reported in vibration-exposed workers, such as tendinitis and tenosynovitis in the upper limbs, and Dupuytren's contracture, a disease of the fascial tissue of the palm of the hand. These disorders seem to be related to ergonomic stress factors arising from heavy manual work, and the association with hand-transmitted vibration is not conclusive.

Vascular Disorders

Raynaud's phenomenon

Giovanni Loriga, an Italian physician, first reported in 1911 that stone cutters using pneumatic hammers on marble and stone blocks at some yards in Rome suffered from finger blanching attacks, resembling the digital vasospastic response to cold or emotional stress described by Maurice Raynaud in 1862. Similar observations were made by Alice Hamilton (1918) among stone cutters in the United States, and later by several other investigators. In the literature various synonyms have been used to describe vibration-induced vascular disorders: dead or white finger, Raynaud's phenomenon of occupational origin, traumatic vasospastic disease, and, more recently, vibration-induced white finger (VWF). Clinically, VWF is characterized by episodes of white or pale fingers caused by spastic closure of the digital arteries. The attacks are usually triggered by cold and last from 5 to 30 to 40 minutes. A complete loss of tactile sensitivity may be experienced during an attack. In the recovery phase, commonly accelerated by warmth or local massage, redness may appear in the affected fingers as a result of a reactive increase of blood flow in the cutaneous vessels. In the rare advanced cases, repeated and severe digital vasospastic attacks can lead to trophic changes (ulceration or gangrene) in the skin of the fingertips. To explain cold-induced Raynaud's phenomenon in vibration-exposed workers, some researchers invoke an exaggerated central sympathetic vasoconstrictor reflex caused by prolonged exposure to harmful vibration, while others tend to emphasize the role of vibration-induced local changes in the digital vessels (e.g., thickening of the muscular wall, endothelial damage, functional receptor changes). A grading scale for the classification of VWF has been proposed at the Stockholm Workshop 86 (1987), (table 50.5). A numerical system for VWF symptoms developed by Griffin and based on scores for the blanching of different phalanges is also available (Griffin 1990). Several laboratory tests are used to diagnose VWF objectively. Most of these tests are based on cold provocation and the measurement of finger skin temperature or digital blood flow and pressure before and after cooling of fingers and hands. Epidemiological studies have pointed out that the prevalence of VWF is very wide, from less than 1 to 100 per cent. VWF has been found to be associated with the use of percussive metal-working tools, grinders and other rotary tools, percussive hammers and drills used in excavation, vibrating machinery used in the forest, and other powered tools and processes. VWF is recognized as an occupational disease in many countries. Since 1975–80 a decrease in the incidence of new cases of VWF has been reported among forestry workers in both Europe and Japan after the introduction of anti-vibration chain saws and administrative measures curtailing saw usage time. Similar findings are not yet available for tools of other types.

Table 50.5 • The Stockholm Workshop scale for staging cold-induced Raynaud's phenomenon in the hand-arm vibration syndrome.

Stage	Grade	Symptoms
0	—	No attacks
1	Mild	Occasional attacks affecting only the tips of one or more fingers
2	Moderate	Occasional attacks affecting distal and middle (rarely also proximal) phalanges of one or more fingers
3	Severe	Frequent attacks affecting all phalanges of most fingers
4	Very severe	As in stage 3, with trophic skin changes in the finger tips

Source: Stockholm Workshop 86 1987.

Other Disorders

Some studies indicate that in workers affected with VWF hearing loss is greater than that expected on the basis of ageing and noise exposure from the use of vibrating tools. It has been suggested that VWF subjects may have an additional risk of hearing impairment due to vibration-induced reflex sympathetic vasoconstriction of the blood vessels supplying the inner ear. In addition to peripheral disorders, other adverse health effects involving the endocrine and central nervous system of vibration-exposed workers have been reported by some Russian and Japanese schools of occupational medicine (Griffin 1990). The clinical picture, called "vibration disease," includes signs and symptoms related to dysfunction of the autonomic centres of the brain (e.g., persistent fatigue, headache, irritability, sleep disturbances, impotence, electroencephalographic abnormalities). These findings should be interpreted with caution and further carefully designed epidemiological and clinical research work is needed to confirm the hypothesis of an association between disorders of the central nervous system and exposure to hand-transmitted vibration.

Standards

Several countries have adopted standards or guidelines for hand-transmitted vibration exposure. Most of them are based on the International Standard 5349 (ISO 1986). To measure hand-transmitted vibration ISO 5349 recommends the use of a frequency-weighting curve which approximates the frequency-dependent sensitivity of the hand to vibration stimuli. The frequency-weighted acceleration of vibration ($a_{h,w}$) is obtained with an appropriate weighting-filter or by summation of weighted acceleration values measured in octave or one-third octave bands along an orthogonal coordinate system (x_h, y_h, z_h), (figure 50.4). In ISO 5349 the daily exposure to vibration is expressed in terms of energy-equivalent frequency-weighted acceleration for a period of four hours [$(a_{h,w})_{eq(4)}$ in m/s^2 r.m.s], according to the following equation:

$$(a_{h,w})_{eq(4)} = (T/4)^{1/2}(a_{h,w})_{eq(T)}$$

where T is the daily exposure time expressed in hours and $(a_{h,w})_{eq(T)}$ is the energy-equivalent frequency-weighted acceleration for the daily exposure time T. The standard provides guidance to calculate $(a_{h,w})_{eq(T)}$ if a typical work-day is characterized by several exposures of different magnitudes and durations. Annex A to ISO 5349 (which does not form part of the standard) proposes a dose-effect relationship between $(a_{h,w})_{eq(4)}$ and VWF, which can be approximated by the equation:

$$C = [(a_{h,w})_{eq(4)} \, T_F/95]^2 \times 100$$

Figure 50.4 • Basicentric coordinate system for the measurement of hand-transmitted vibration.

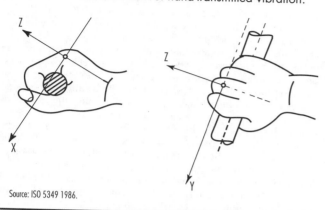

Source: ISO 5349 1986.

Table 50.7 • Proposal of the Council of the European Union for a Council Directive on physical agents: Annex II A. Hand-transmitted vibration (1994).

Levels (ms^{-2})	A(8)*	Definitions
Threshold	1	The exposure value below which continuous and/or repetitive exposure has no adverse effect on health and safety of workers
Action	2.5	The value above which one or more of the measures** specified in the relevant Annexes must be undertaken
Exposure limit value	5	The exposure value above which an unprotected person is exposed to unacceptable risks. Exceeding this level is prohibited and must be prevented through the implementation of the provisions of the Directive***

*A(8) = 8 h energy-equivalent frequency-weighted acceleration.

** Information, training, technical measures, health surveillance.

***Appropriate measures for the protection of health and safety.

where C is the percentile of exposed workers expected to show VWF (in the range 10 to 50%), and T_F is the exposure time before finger blanching among the affected workers (in the range 1 to 25 years). The dominant, single-axis component of vibration directed into the hand is used to calculate $(a_{h,w})_{eq(4)}$, which should not be in excess of 50 m/s^2. According to the ISO dose-effect relationship, VWF may be expected to occur in about 10% of workers with daily vibration exposure to 3 m/s^2 for ten years.

In order to minimize the risk of vibration-induced adverse health effects, action levels and threshold limit values (TLVs) for vibration exposure have been proposed by other committees or organizations. The American Conference of Government Industrial Hygienists (ACGIH) has published TLVs for hand-transmitted vibration measured according to the ISO frequency-weighting procedure (American Conference of Governmental Industrial Hygienists 1992), (table 50.6). According to ACGIH, the proposal TLVs concern vibration exposure to which "nearly all workers may be exposed repeatedly without progressing beyond Stage 1 of the Stockholm Workshop Classification System for VWF". More recently, exposure levels for hand-transmitted vibration have been presented by the Commission of the European Communities within a proposal of a Directive for the protection of workers against the risks arising from physical agents (Council of the European Union 1994), (table 50.7). In the proposed Directive the quantity used for the assessment of vibration hazard is expressed in terms of an eight-hour energy-equivalent frequency-weighted acceleration, $A(8) = (T/8)^{1/2} (a_{h,w})_{eq(T)}$, by using the vector sum of weighted accelerations determined in orthogonal coordi-

nates $a_{sum} = (a_{x,h,w}^2 + a_{y,h,w}^2 + a_{z,h,w}^2)^{1/2}$ on the vibrating tool handle or workpiece. The methods of measurement and assessment of vibration exposure reported in the Directive are basically derived from the British Standard (BS) 6842 (BSI 1987a). The BS standard, however, does not recommend exposure limits, but provides an informative appendix on the state of knowledge of the dose-effect relationship for hand-transmitted vibration. The estimated frequency-weighted acceleration magnitudes liable to cause VWF in 10% of workers exposed to vibration according to the BS standard are reported in table 50.8.

Measurement and Evaluation of Exposure

Vibration measurements are made to provide assistance for the development of new tools, to check vibration of tools at purchase, to verify maintenance conditions, and to assess human exposure to vibration at the workplace. Vibration-measuring equipment generally consists of a transducer (usually an accelerometer), an

Table 50.6 • Threshold limit values for hand-transmitted vibration.

Total daily exposure (hours)	Frequency-weighted r.m.s. acceleration in the dominant direction that should not be exceeded	
	m/s^2	g*
4–8	4	0.40
2–4	6	0.61
1–2	8	0.81
1	12	1.22

* 1 g = 9.81 m/s^2.

Source: According to the American Conference of Government Industrial Hygienists 1992.

Table 50.8 • Frequency-weighted vibration acceleration magnitudes (m/s^2 r.m.s.) which may be expected to produce finger blanching in 10% of persons exposed*.

Daily exposure (hours)	Life-time exposure (years)					
	0.5	1	2	4	8	16
0.25	256.0	128.0	64.0	32.0	16.0	8.0
0.5	179.2	89.6	44.8	22.4	11.2	5.6
1	128.0	64.0	32.0	16.0	8.0	4.0
2	89.6	44.8	22.4	11.2	5.6	2.8
4	64.0	32.0	16.0	8.0	4.0	2.0
8	44.8	22.4	11.2	5.6	2.8	1.4

* With short duration exposure the magnitudes are high and vascular disorders may not be the first adverse symptom to develop.

Source: According to British Standard 6842. 1987, BSI 1987a.

Figure 50.5 • Mean values and range of distribution of frequency-weighted r.m.s. acceleration in the dominant axis measured on the handle(s) of some power tools used in forestry and industry.

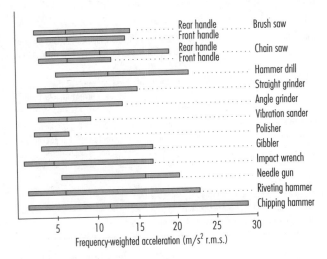

Source: ISSA International Section for Research 1989.

amplifying device, filter (bandpass filter and/or frequency-weighting network), and amplitude or level indicator or recorder. Vibration measurements should be made on the tool handle or workpiece close to the surface of the hand(s) where the vibration enters the body. Careful selection of the accelerometers (e.g., type, mass, sensitivity) and appropriate methods of mounting the accelerometer on the vibrating surface are required to obtain accurate results. Vibration transmitted to the hand should be measured and reported in the appropriate directions of an orthogonal coordinate system (figure 50.4). The measurement should be made over a frequency range of at least 5 to 1,500 Hz, and the acceleration frequency content of vibration in one or more axes can be presented in octave bands with centre frequencies from 8 to 1,000 Hz or in one-third octave bands with centre frequencies from 6.3 to 1,250 Hz. Acceleration can also be expressed as frequency-weighted acceleration by using a weighting network which complies with the characteristics specified in ISO 5349 or BS 6842. Measurements at the workplace show that different vibration magnitudes and frequency spectra can occur on tools of the same type or when the same tool is operated in a different manner. Figure 50.5 reports the mean value and the range of distribution of weighted accelerations measured in the dominant axis of power-driven tools used in forestry and industry (ISSA International Section for Research 1989). In several standards hand-transmitted vibration exposure is assessed in terms of four-hour or eight-hour energy-equivalent frequency-weighted acceleration calculated by means of the equations above. The method for obtaining energy-equivalent acceleration assumes that the daily exposure time required to produce adverse health effects is inversely proportional to the square of frequency-weighted acceleration (e.g., if the vibration magnitude is halved then exposure time may be increased by a factor of four). This time dependency is considered to be reasonable for standardization purposes and is convenient for instrumentation, but it should be noted that it is not fully substantiated by epidemiological data (Griffin 1990).

Prevention

The prevention of injuries or disorders caused by hand-transmitted vibration requires the implementation of administrative, technical and medical procedures (ISO 1986; BSI 1987a). Appropriate advice to the manufacturers and users of vibrating tools should also be given. Administrative measures should include adequate information and training to instruct the operators of vibrating machinery to adopt safe and correct work practices. Since continuous exposure to vibration is believed to increase vibration hazard, work schedules should be arranged to include rest periods. Technical measures should include the choice of tools with the lowest vibration and with appropriate ergonomic design. According to the EC Directive for the safety of machinery (Council of the European Communities 1989), the manufacturer shall make public whether the frequency-weighted acceleration of hand-transmitted vibration exceeds 2.5 m/s^2, as determined by suitable test codes such as indicated in the International Standard ISO 8662/1 and its companion documents for specific tools (ISO 1988). Tool maintenance conditions should be carefully checked by periodic vibration measurements. Pre-employment medical screening and subsequent clinical examinations at regular intervals should be performed on vibration-exposed workers. The aims of medical surveillance are to inform the worker of the potential risk associated with vibration exposure, to assess health status and to diagnose vibration-induced disorders at the early stage. At the first screening examination particular attention should be paid to any condition which may be aggravated by exposure to vibration (e.g., constitutional tendency to white finger, some forms of secondary Raynaud's phenomenon, past injuries to the upper limbs, neurological disorders). Avoidance or reduction of vibration exposure for the affected worker should be decided after considering both the severity of symptoms and the characteristics of the entire working process. The worker should be advised to wear adequate clothing to keep the entire body warm, and to avoid or minimize the smoking of tobacco and the use of some drugs which can affect peripheral circulation. Gloves may be useful to protect the fingers and hands from traumas and to keep them warm. So-called anti-vibration gloves may provide some isolation of the high frequency components of vibration arising from some tools.

MOTION SICKNESS

Alan J. Benson

Motion sickness, or kinetosis, is not a pathological condition, but is a normal response to certain motion stimuli with which the individual is unfamiliar and to which he or she is, therefore, unadapted; only those without a functioning vestibular apparatus of the inner ear are truly immune.

Motions producing sickness

There are many different types of provocative motion that induce the motion sickness syndrome. Most are associated with aids to locomotion—in particular, ships, hovercraft, aircraft, automobiles and trains; less commonly, elephants and camels. The complex accelerations generated by fairground amusements, such as swings, roundabouts (merry-go-rounds), roller-coasters and so on, can be highly provocative. In addition, many astronauts/cosmonauts suffer from motion sickness (space-motion sickness) when they first make head movements in the abnormal force environment (weightlessness) of orbital flight. The motion sickness syndrome is also produced by certain moving visual stimuli, without any physical motion of the observer; the external visual world display of fixed-base simulators (simulator sickness) or a large-screen projection of scenes taken from a moving vehicle (Cinerama or IMAX sickness) are examples.

Aetiology

The essential characteristics of stimuli that induce motion sickness is that they generate discordant information from the sensory systems that provide the brain with information about the spatial orientation and motion of the body. The principal feature of this discord is a mismatch between the signals provided, principally, by the eyes and inner ear, and those that the central nervous system "expects" to receive and to be correlated.

Several categories of mismatch can be identified. Most important is the mismatch of signals from the vestibular apparatus (labyrinth) of the inner ear, in which the semicircular canals (the specialized receptors of angular accelerations) and the otolith organs (the specialized receptors of translational accelerations) do not provide concordant information. For example, when a head movement is made in a car or aircraft which is turning, both the semicircular canals and the otoliths are stimulated in an atypical manner and provide erroneous and incompatible information, information that differs substantially from that generated by the same head movement in a stable, 1-G gravity environment. Likewise, low-frequency (below 0.5 Hz) linear accelerations, such as occur aboard ship in rough seas or in an aircraft during flight through turbulent air, also generate conflicting vestibular signals and, hence, are a potent cause of motion sickness.

The mismatch of visual and vestibular information can also be an important contributory factor. The occupant of a moving vehicle who cannot see out is more likely to suffer from motion sickness than one who has a good external visual reference. The passenger below deck or in an aircraft cabin senses motion of the vehicle by vestibular cues, but he or she receives visual information only of his or her relative movement within the vehicle. The absence of an "expected" and concordant signal in a particular sensory modality is also considered to be the essential feature of visually induced motion sickness, because the visual motion cues are not accompanied by the vestibular signals that the individual "expects" to occur when subjected to the motion indicated by the visual display.

Signs and symptoms

On exposure to provocative motion, the signs and symptoms of motion sickness develop in a definite sequence, the time scale being dependent upon the intensity of the motion stimuli and the susceptibility of the individual. There are, however, considerable differences among individuals not only in susceptibility, but also in the order in which particular signs and symptoms develop, or whether they are experienced at all. Typically, the earliest symptom is epigastric discomfort ("stomach awareness"); this is followed by nausea, pallor and sweating, and is likely to be accompanied by a feeling of bodily warmth, increased salivation and eructation (belching). These symptoms commonly develop relatively slowly, but with continuing exposure to the motion, there is a rapid deterioration in well-being, the nausea increases in severity and culminates in vomiting or retching. Vomiting may bring relief, but this is likely to be short-lived unless the motion ceases.

There are other more variable features of the motion sickness syndrome. Alteration of respiratory rhythm with sighing and yawning may be an early symptom, and hyperventilation may occur, particularly in those who are anxious about the cause or consequence of their disability. Headache, tinnitus and dizziness are reported, while in those with severe malaise, apathy and depression are not uncommon, and may be of such severity that personal safety and survival are neglected. A feeling of lethargy and somnolence may be dominant following the cessation of provocative motion, and these may be the only symptoms in situations where adaptation to unfamiliar motion takes place without malaise.

Adaptation

With continued or repeated exposure to a particular provocative motion, most individuals show a decrease in the severity of symptoms; typically after three or four days of continuous exposure (as aboard ship or in a space vehicle) they have adapted to the motion and can carry out their normal duties without disability. In terms of the "mismatch" model, this adaptation or habituation represents the establishment of a new set of "expectations" in the central nervous system. However, on return to a familiar environment, these will no longer be appropriate and symptoms of motion sickness can recur (mal de débarquement) until readaptation occurs. Individuals differ considerably in the rate at which they adapt, the way they retain adaptation and the degree to which they can generalize protective adaptation from one motion environment to another. Unfortunately, a small proportion of the population (probably about 5%) do not adapt, or adapt so slowly that they continue to experience symptoms throughout the period of exposure to provocative motion.

Incidence

The incidence of sickness in a particular motion environment is governed by a number of factors, notably:

- the physical characteristics of the motion (its intensity, frequency and direction of action)
- the duration of exposure
- the intrinsic susceptibility of the individual
- the task being performed
- other environmental factors (e.g., odour).

Not surprisingly, the occurrence of sickness varies widely in different motion environments. For example: nearly all the occupants of life rafts in rough seas will vomit; 60% of student aircrew members suffer from air sickness at some time during training, which in 15% is sufficiently severe to interfere with training; in contrast, less than 0.5% of passengers in civil transport aircraft are affected, although the incidence is higher in small commuter aircraft flying at low altitude in turbulent air.

Laboratory and field studies have shown that for vertical translational oscillatory motion (appropriately called heave), oscillation at a frequency of about 0.2 Hz is the most provocative (figure 50.6). For a given intensity (peak acceleration) of oscillation, the incidence of sickness falls quite rapidly with an increase in frequency above 0.2 Hz; motion at 1 Hz is less than one-tenth as provocative as that at 0.2 Hz. Likewise, for motion at frequencies below 0.2 Hz, although the relationship between incidence and frequency is not well defined because of a lack of experimental data; certainly, a stable, zero frequency, 1-G environment is not provocative.

Relationships established between the incidence of symptoms of motion sickness and the frequency, magnitude and duration of heave (z-axis) motion have led to the development of simple formulae that can be used to predict incidence when the physical parameters of the motion are known. The concept, embodied in British Standard 6841 (BSI 1987b) and in ISO Draft International Standard 2631-1, is that the incidence of symptoms is proportional to the Motion Sickness Dose Value ($MSDV_z$). The $MSDV_z$ (in $m/s^{1.5}$) is defined:

$$MSDV_z = (a^2 t)^{1/2}$$

where a is the root-mean-square (r.m.s.) value of the frequency-weighted acceleration (in m/s^2) determined by linear integration over the duration, t (in seconds), of exposure to the motion.

Figure 50.6 • Motion sickness incidence as a function of wave frequency and acceleration for 2 hour exposure to vertical sinusoidal motion.

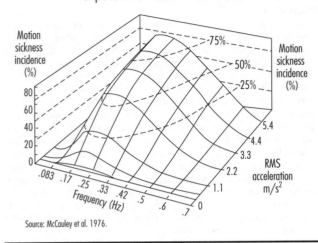

Source: McCauley et al. 1976.

The frequency weighting to be applied to the stimulus acceleration is a filter having a centre frequency and attenuation characteristics similar to those depicted in figure 50.6. The weighting function is defined precisely in the standards.

The percentage of an unadapted adult population (P) who are likely to vomit is given by:

$$P = \tfrac{1}{3}\text{MSDV}_z$$

Furthermore, the MSDV_z may also be used to predict the level of malaise. On a four-point scale of zero (I felt all right) to three (I felt absolutely dreadful) an "illness rating" (I) is given by:

$$I = 0.02\text{MSDV}_z$$

Given the large differences among individuals in their susceptibility to motion sickness, the relationship between MSDV_z and the occurrence of vomiting in laboratory experiments and in sea trials (figure 50.7) is acceptable. It should be noted that the formulae were developed from data acquired on exposures lasting from about 20 minutes to six hours with vomiting occurring in up to 70% of individuals (mostly seated) exposed to vertical, heave, motion.

Knowledge about the effectiveness of translational oscillation acting in other body axes and other than in a vertical direction is fragmentary. There is some evidence from laboratory experiments on small groups of subjects that translational oscillation in a horizontal plane is more provocative, by a factor of about two, than the same intensity and frequency of vertical oscillation for seated subjects, but is less provocative, also by a factor of two, when the subject is supine and the stimulus acts in the longitudinal (z) body axis. Application of formulae and weighting characteristics embodied in standards to the prediction of sickness incidence should, therefore, be made with caution and due concern for the constraints noted above.

The considerable variability between individuals in their response to provocative motion is an important feature of motion sickness. Differences in susceptibility can, in part, be related to constitutional factors. Infants much below the age of about two years are rarely affected, but with maturation, susceptibility increases rapidly to reach a peak between four and ten years. Thereafter, susceptibility falls progressively so that the elderly are less likely to be affected, but are not immune. In any age group, females are more sensitive than males, the incidence data suggest-

Figure 50.7 • Relationship between incidence of vomiting and stimulus dose (MSDV_z), calculated by the procedure described in the text. Data from laboratory experiments involving vertical oscillation (x ■) and sea trials (+).

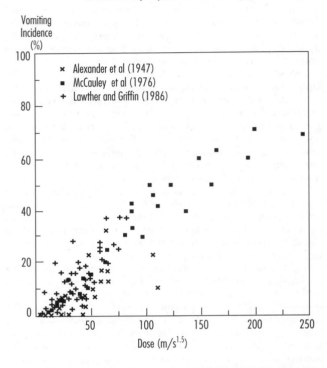

ing a ratio of approximately 1.7:1. Certain dimensions of personality, such as neuroticism, introversion and perceptual style have also been shown to be correlated, albeit weakly, with susceptibility. Motion sickness can also be a conditioned response and a manifestation of phobic anxiety.

Preventive measures

Procedures which minimize the provocative stimulus or increase the tolerance are available. These may prevent sickness in a proportion of the population, but none, other than withdrawal from the motion environment, is 100% effective. In the design of a vehicle, attention to factors which raise the frequency and reduce the magnitude of the oscillations (see figure 50.6) experienced by occupants during normal operation is beneficial. The provision of head support and body restraint to minimize the unnecessary head movements is advantageous, and is further aided if the occupant can assume a reclined or supine position. Sickness is less if the occupant can be given a view of the horizon; for those deprived of an external visual reference, closing the eyes reduces visual/vestibular conflict. Involvement in a task, particularly control of the vehicle, is also helpful. These measures can be of immediate benefit, but in the longer term the development of protective adaptation is of the greatest value. This is achieved by continued and repeated exposure to the motion environment, though it can be facilitated by ground-based exercises in which provocative stimuli are generated by making head movements whilst rotating on a spin table (desensitization therapy).

There are several drugs which increase tolerance, though all have side-effects (in particular, sedation), so that they should not be taken by those in primary control of a vehicle or when optimum performance is mandatory. For short-term (less than four hours) prophylaxis, 0.3 to 0.6 mg hyoscine hydrobromide (scopolamine) is recommended; longer acting are the antihistaminics, promethazine hydrochloride (25 mg), meclozine hydrochloride (50 mg), dimenhydrinate (50 mg) and cinnarizine (30 mg). The combination of either hyoscine or promethazine with 25 mg ephedrine sulphate increases prophylactic potency with some reduction of side-effects. Prophylaxis for up to 48 hours can be achieved using a scopolamine patch, which allows the drug to be slowly absorbed through the skin at a controlled rate. Effective concentrations of the drug in the body are not achieved until six to eight hours after application of the patch, so the need for this type of therapy must be anticipated.

Treatment

Those suffering from established motion sickness with vomiting should, when practicable, be placed in a position where the motion stimulus is minimized, and be given an anti–motion sickness drug, preferably promethazine by injection. Should vomiting be prolonged and repeated, intravenous replacement of fluid and electrolytes may be necessary.

References

Alexander, SJ, M Cotzin, JB Klee, and GR Wendt. 1947. Studies of motion sickness XVI: The effects upon sickness rates of waves and various frequencies but identical acceleration. *J Exp Psy* 37:440-447.

American Conference of Governmental Industrial Hygienists (ACGIH). 1992. Hand-arm (segmental) vibration. In *Threshold Limit Values and Biological Exposures Indices for 1992-1993*. Cincinnati, Ohio: ACGIH.

Bongers, PM and HC Boshuizen. 1990. *Back Disorders and Whole-Body Vibration at Work*. Thesis. Amsterdam: University of Amsterdam.

British Standards Institution (BSI). 1987a. *Measurement and Evaluation of Human Exposure to Vibration Transmitted to the Hand*. BS 6842. London: BSI.

—. 1987b. *Measurement and Evaluation of Human Exposure to Whole-Body Mechanical Vibration and Repeated Shock*. BS 6841. London: BSI.

Council of the European Communities (CEC). 1989. Council Directive of 14 June 1989 on the approximation of the laws of the Member States relating to machinery. *Off J Eur Communities* L 183:9-32.

Council of the European Union. 1994. Amended proposal for a Council Directive on the minimum health and safety requirements regarding the exposure of workers to the risks arising from physical agents. *Off J Eur Communities* C230 (19 August):3-29.

Dupuis, H and G Zerlett. 1986. *The Effects of Whole-Body Vibration*. Berlin: Springer-Verlag.

Griffin, MJ. 1990. *Handbook of Human Vibration*. London: Academic Press.

Hamilton, A. 1918. *A Study of Spastic Anemia in the Hands of Stonecutters*. Industrial Accidents and Hygiene Series no. 19. Bulletin No. 236. Washington, DC: Department of Labor Statistics.

Hasan, J. 1970. Biomedical aspects of low-frequency vibration. *Work Environ Health* 6(1):19-45.

International Organization for Standardization (ISO). 1974. *Guide for the Evaluation of Human Exposure to Whole-Body Vibration*. Geneva: ISO.

—. 1985. *Evaluation of Human Exposure to Whole-Body Vibration. Part 1: General Requirements*. ISO 2631/1. Geneva: ISO.

—. 1986. *Mechanical Vibration-Guidelines for the Measurement and the Assessment of Human Exposure to Hand-Transmitted Vibration*. ISO 5349. Geneva: ISO.

—. 1988. *Hand-Held Portable Power Tools—Measurement of Vibrations at the Handle. Part 1: General*. ISO 8662/1. Geneva: ISO.

ISSA International Section for Research. 1989. *Vibration At Work*. Paris: INRS.

Lawther, A and MJ Griffin. 1986. Prediction of the incidence of motion sickness from the magnitude, frequency and duration of vertical oscillation. *J Acoust Soc Am* 82:957-966.

McCauley, ME, JW Royal, CD Wilie, JF O'Hanlon, and RR Mackie. 1976. *Motion Sickness Incidence: Exploratory Studies of Habituation Pitch and Roll, and the Refinement of a Mathematical Model*. Technical Report No. 1732-2. Golets, Calif: Human Factors Research.

Rumjancev, GI. 1966. Gigiena truda v proizvodstve sbornogo shelezobetona [Occupational hygiene in the production of reinforced concrete]. *Medicina* (Moscow):1-128.

Schmidt, M. 1987. *Die gemeinsame Einwirkung von Lärm und Ganzkörpervibration und deren Auswirkungen auf den Höverlust bei Agrotechnikern*. Dissertation A. Halle, Germany: Landwirtschaftliche Fakultät der Martin-Luther-Universität.

Seidel, H. 1975. Systematische Darstellung physiologischer Reaktionen auf Ganzkörperschwingungen in vertikaler Richtung (Z-Achse) zur Ermittlung von biologischen Bewertungsparametern. *Ergonom Berichte* 15:18-39.

Seidel, H and R Heide. 1986. Long-term effects of whole-body vibration: A critical survey of the literature. *Int Arch Occup Environ Health* 58:1-26.

Seidel, H, R Blüthner, J Martin, G Menzel, R Panuska, and P Ullsperger. 1992. Effects of isolated and combined exposures to whole-body vibration and noise on auditory-event related brain potentials and psychophysical assessment. *Eur J Appl Physiol Occup Phys* 65:376-382.

Stockholm Workshop 86. 1987. Symptomatology and diagnostic methods in the hand-arm vibration syndrome. *Scand J Work Environ Health* 13:271-388.

Other relevant readings

Benson, AJ. 1988. Motion sickness. In *Aviation Medicine*, edited by J Ernsting and P King. London: Butterworths.

Reason, JT and JJ Brand. 1975. *Motion Sickness*. London: Academic Press.

50. VIBRATION

VIOLENCE

51

Chapter Editor
Leon J. Warshaw

Contents

51. VIOLENCE

VIOLENCE IN THE WORKPLACE

Leon J. Warshaw

Violence is pervasive in modern society and appears to be escalating. Entirely apart from repression, wars and terrorist activities, the media daily report in banner headlines on the mayhem inflicted by humans upon each other in "civilized" as well as more primitive communities. Whether there has been a real increase or this simply represents more thorough reporting is arguable. After all, violence has been a feature of human interaction since prehistoric ages. Nevertheless, violence has become one of the leading causes of death in modern industrial societies—in some segments of the community it is *the* leading cause of death—and it is increasingly being recognized as a public health problem.

Inescapably, it finds its way into the workplace. From 1980 to 1989, homicide was the third leading cause of death from injury in North American workplaces, according to data compiled by the National Traumatic Occupational Facilities Surveillance System (NIOSH 1993a). During this period, occupational homicides accounted for 12% of deaths from injury in the workplace; only motor vehicles and machines accounted for more. By 1993, that figure had risen to 17%, a rate of 0.9 per 100,000 workers, now second only to motor vehicle deaths (Toscano and Windau 1994). For women workers, it remained the leading cause of work-related death, although the rate (0.4 deaths per 100,000) was lower than that for men (1.2 deaths per 100,000) (Jenkins 1995).

These deaths, however, represent only the "tip of the iceberg". For example, in 1992, about 22,400 American workers were injured seriously enough in non-fatal assaults in the workplace to require days away from work to recuperate (Toscano and Windau 1994). Reliable and complete data are lacking, but it is estimated that for every death there have been many thousands—perhaps, even hundreds of thousands—of instances of violence in the workplace.

In its newsletter, Unison, the large British union of health care and governmental service workers, has labelled violence as "the most threatening risk faced by members at work. It is the risk which is most likely to lead to injury. It can bring unmanageable levels of occupational stress which damages personal esteem and threatens people's ability to continue on the job" (Unison 1992).

This article will summarize the characteristics of violence in the workplace, the kinds of people involved, its effects on them and their employers, and the steps that may be taken to prevent or control such effects.

Definition of Violence

There is no consensus on the definition of violence. For example, Rosenberg and Mercy (1991) include in the definition both fatal and nonfatal interpersonal violence where physical force or other means is used by one person with the intent of causing harm, injury or death to another. The Panel on the Understanding and Control of Violent Behavior convened by the US National Academy of Sciences adopted the definition of *violence* as: behaviours by individuals that intentionally threaten, attempt or inflict physical harm on others (Reiss and Roth 1993).

These definitions focus on threatening or causing *physical* harm. However, they exclude instances in which verbal abuse, harassment or humiliation and other forms of psychological trauma may be the sole harm to the victim and which may be no less devastating. They also exclude sexual harassment, which may be physical but which is usually entirely non-physical. In the national survey of American workers conducted by the Northwestern National Life Insurance Company, the researchers separated violent acts into: *harassment* (the act of creating a hostile environment through unwelcome words, actions or physical contacts not resulting in physical harm), *threats* (expressions of an intent to cause physical harm), and *physical attacks* (aggression resulting in a physical assault with or without the use of a weapon) (Lawless, 1993).

In the UK, the Health and Safety Executive's working definition of *workplace violence* is: any incident in which an employee is abused, threatened or assaulted by a member of the public in circumstances arising out of the course of his or her employment. Assailants may be patients, clients or co-workers (MSF 1993).

In this article, the term *violence* will be used in its broadest sense to include all forms of aggressive or abusive behaviour that may cause physical or psychological harm or discomfort to its victims, whether they be intentional targets or innocent bystanders involved only impersonally or incidentally. While workplaces may be targets of terrorist attacks or may become involved in riots and mob violence, such instances will not be discussed.

Prevalence of Violence in the Workplace

Accurate information on the prevalence of violence in the workplace is lacking. Most of the literature focuses on cases that are formally reported: homicides which get tallied in the obligatory death registries, cases that get enmeshed in the criminal justice system, or cases involving time off the job that generate workers' compensation claims. Yet, for every one of these, there is an untold number of instances in which workers are victims of aggressive, abusive behaviour. For example, according to a survey conducted by the Bureau of Justice Statistics in the US Department of Justice, over half the victimizations sustained at work were not reported to the police. About 40% of the respondents said they did not report the incident because they considered it to be a minor or a personal matter, while another 27% said they did report it to a manager or a company security officer but, apparently, the report was not relayed to the police (Bachman 1994). In addition to the lack of a consensus on a taxonomy of violence, other reasons for under-reporting include:

- *Cultural acceptance of violence.* There is in many communities a widespread tolerance for violence among or against certain groups (Rosenberg and Mercy 1991). Although frowned upon by many, violence is often rationalized and tolerated as a "normal" response to competition. Violence among minority and ethnic groups is often condoned as a righteous response to discrimination, poverty and lack of access to social or economic equity resulting in low self-esteem and low valuations of human life. As a result, the assault is seen as a consequence of living in a violent society rather than working in an unsafe workplace. Finally, there is the "on-the-job syndrome", in which workers in certain jobs are expected to put up with verbal abuse, threats and, even, physical attacks (SEIU 1995;, Unison 1992).
- *Lack of a reporting system.* Only a small proportion of organizations have articulated an explicit policy on violence or have designed procedures for reporting and investigating instances of alleged violence in the workplace. Even where such a system has been installed, the trouble of obtaining, completing and filing the required report form is a deterrent to reporting all but the most outrageous incidents.
- *Fear of blame or reprisal.* Workers may fear being held responsible when they have been attacked by a client or a patient. Fear of reprisal by the assailant is also a potent deterrent to reporting, especially when that person is the worker's superior and in a position to affect his or her job status.
- *Lack of interest on the part of the employer.* The employer's lack of interest in investigating and reacting to prior incidents will certainly discourage reporting. Also, supervisors, concerned that workplace violence might reflect unfavourably on their

managerial capabilities, may actually discourage or even block the filing of reports by workers in their units.

To determine the prevalence of violence in the workplace in the absence of reliable data, attempts have been made to extrapolate both from available statistics (e.g., death certificates, crime reports and workers' compensation systems) and from specially designed surveys. Thus, the US National Crime Victimization Survey estimated that about 1 million American workers (out of a workforce of 110 million) are assaulted at work each year (Bachman 1994). And, a 1993 telephone survey of a national sample of 600 American full-time workers (excluding self-employed and military personnel) found that one in four said that he or she had been a victim of workplace violence during the study year: 19% were harassed, 7% were threatened, and 3% were attacked physically. The researchers reported further that 68% of the harassment victims, 43% of the threat victims and 24% of the attack victims had not reported the incident (Lawless 1993).

A similar survey of workers in the UK employed by the National Health Service revealed that, during the previous year, 0.5% had required medical treatment following an on-the-job physical assault; 11% had suffered a minor injury requiring only first aid, 4 to 6% had been threatened by persons wielding a deadly weapon, and 17% had received verbal threats. Violence was a special problem for emergency staff in ambulances and accident departments, nurses, and workers involved in the care of psychologically disturbed patients (Health Services Advisory Committee 1987). The risk of health workers being confronted by violence has been labelled a feature of everyday work in primary care and in accident/emergency departments (Shepherd 1994).

Homicide in the Workplace

Although workplace homicides are only a small proportion of all homicides, their substantial contribution to work-related deaths, at least in the United States, their unique features, and the possibility of preventive interventions by employers earn them special attention. For example, while most homicides in the community involve people who know each other, many of them close relatives, and only 13% were reported to have been associated with another felony, these proportions were reversed in the workplace, where more than three-fourths of the homicides were committed in the course of a robbery (NIOSH 1992). Further, while persons aged 65 and older in the general population have the lowest rates of being victims of homicide, this age group has the highest rates of such involvement in workplace homicides (Castillo and Jenkins 1994).

American workplaces with the highest rates of homicide are listed in table 51.1. Over 50% are accounted for by only two industries: retail trade and services. The latter includes taxi driving, which has nearly 40 times the average workplace homicide rate, followed by liquor/convenience stores and gas stations, prime targets for robberies, and by detective/protective services (Castillo and Jenkins 1994).

Table 51.2 lists the occupations with the highest rates of workplace homicides. Again, reflecting the likelihood of involvement in attempted felonies, taxi drivers head the list, followed by law-enforcement personnel, hotel clerks and workers in various types of retail establishments. Commenting on similar data from the UK, Drever (1995) noted that most of the occupations with the highest mortality from homicides had high rates of drug dependence (scaffolders, literary and artistic occupations, painters and decorators) or alcohol abuse (cooks and kitchen porters, publicans, bartenders and caterers).

As noted above, the vast majority of work-related homicides occur during the course of a robbery or other crime committed

Table 51.1 • US workplaces with the highest rates of occupational homicide, 1980–1989.

Workplaces	No. of homicides	Rate[1]
Taxicab establishments	287	26.9
Liquor stores	115	8.0
Gas stations	304	5.6
Detective/protective services	152	5.0
Justice/public order establishments	640	3.4
Grocery stores	806	3.2
Jewellery stores	56	3.2
Hotels/motels	153	3.2
Eating/drinking places	754	1.5

[1] Number per 100,000 workers per year.
Source: NIOSH 1993b.

by a person or persons usually not known to the victim. Risk factors associated with such incidents are listed in table 51.3.

About 4% of workplace homicides occur during confrontations with family members or acquaintances who have followed the victim into the workplace. About 21% arise out of a confrontation related to the workplace: about two-thirds of these are perpetrated by workers or former employees with a grudge against a manager or a co-worker, while angry customers or clients account for the rest (Toscano and Windau 1994). In these cases, the target may be the particular manager or worker whose actions provoked the assault or, where there is a grudge against the organization, the target may be the workplace itself, and any employees and visitors who just happen to be in it at the critical moment. Sometimes, the assailant may be emotionally disturbed, as in the case of Joseph T. Weisbecker, an employee on long-term disability leave from his employer in Louisville, Kentucky, because of mental illness, who killed eight co-workers and injured 12 others before taking his own life (Kuzmits 1990).

Causes of Violence

Current understanding of the causes and risk factors for assaultive violence is very rudimentary (Rosenberg and Mercy 1991). Clearly, it is a multifactorial problem in which each incident is

Table 51.2 • US occupations with the highest rates of occupational homicide, 1980-1989.

Occupations	No. of homicides	Rate[1]
Taxicab drivers/chauffeurs	289	15.1
Law enforcement officers	520	9.3
Hotel clerks	40	5.1
Gas station workers	164	4.5
Security guards	253	3.6
Stock handlers/baggers	260	3.1
Store owners/managers	1,065	2.8
Bartenders	84	2.1

[1] Number per 100,000 workers per year.
Source: NIOSH 1993b.

Table 51.3 • Risk factors for workplace homicides.

Working alone or in small numbers

Exchange of money with the public

Working late night or early morning hours

Working in high crime areas

Guarding valuable property or possessions

Working in community settings (e.g. taxi drivers and police)

Source: NIOSH 1993b.

shaped by the characteristics of the assailant, the characteristics of the victim(s) and the nature of the interplay between them. Reflecting such complexity, a number of theories of causation have been developed. Biological theories, for example, focus on such factors as gender (most of the assailants are male), age (involvement in violence in the community diminishes with age but, as noted above, this is not so in the workplace), and the influence of hormones such as testosterone, neurotransmitters such as serotonin, and other such biological agents. The psychological approach focuses on personality, holding that violence is engendered by deprivation of love during childhood, and childhood abuse, and is learned from role models, reinforced by rewards and punishments in early life. Sociological theories emphasize as breeders of violence such cultural and subcultural factors as poverty, discrimination and lack of economic and social equity. Finally, interactional theories converge on a sequence of actions and reactions that ultimately escalate into violence (Rosenberg and Mercy 1991).

A number of risk factors have been associated with violence. They include:

Mental illness

The vast majority of people who are violent are not mentally ill, and the vast proportion of individuals with mental illness are not violent (American Psychiatric Association 1994). However, mentally disordered individuals are sometimes frightened, irritable, suspicious, excitable, or angry, or a combination of these (Bullard 1994). The resultant behaviour poses a particular risk of violence to the physicians, nurses and staff members involved in their care in ambulances, emergency departments and both inpatient and outpatient psychiatric facilities.

Certain types of mental illness are associated with a greater propensity for violence. Persons with psychopathic personalities tend to have a low threshold for anger and frustration, which often generate violent behaviour (Marks 1992), while individuals with paranoia are suspicious and prone to attack individuals or entire organizations whom they blame when things do not go as they would wish. However, violence may be exhibited by persons with other forms of mental illness. Furthermore, some mentally ill individuals are prone to episodes of acute dementia in which they may inflict violence on themselves as well as on those trying to restrain them.

Alcohol and drug abuse

Alcohol abuse has a strong association with aggressive and violent behaviour. While drunkenness on the part of either assailants or victims, or both, often results in violence, there is disagreement as to whether alcohol is the cause of the violence or merely one of a number of factors involved in its causation (Pernanen 1993).

Fagan (1993) emphasized that while alcohol affects neurobiological functions, perception and cognition, it is the immediate setting in which the drinking takes place that channels the disinhibiting responses to alcohol. This was confirmed by a study in Los Angeles County which found that violent incidents were much more frequent in some bars and relatively uncommon in others where just as much drinking was taking place, and concluded that violent behaviour was not related to the amount of alcohol being consumed but, rather, to the kinds of individuals attracted to a particular drinking establishment and the kinds of unwritten rules in effect there (Scribner, MacKinnon and Dwyer 1995).

Much the same may be said for abuse of illicit drugs. Except perhaps for crack cocaine and the amphetamines, drug use is more likely to be associated with sedation and withdrawal rather than aggressive, violent behaviour. Most of the violence associated with illegal drugs seems to be associated not with the drugs, but with the effort to obtain them or the wherewithal to purchase them, and from involvement in the illegal drug traffic.

Violence in the community

Violence in the community not only spills over into workplaces but is a particular risk factor for workers such as police and firefighters, and for postal workers and other government employees, repair and service personnel, social workers and others whose jobs take them into neighbourhoods in which violence and crime are indigenous. Important factors in the frequency of violence, particularly in the United States, is the prevalence of firearms in the hands of the general public and, especially for young people, the amount of violence depicted in films and on television.

Work-Related Factors Associated with Violence

Instances of violence may occur in any and all workplaces. There are, however, certain jobs and work-related circumstances that are particularly associated with a risk of generating or being subjected to violence. They include:

Criminal activities

Perhaps the least complex of episodes of work-related violence are those associated with criminal violence, the major cause of worksite homicides. These fall into two categories: those involved with attempts at robbery or other felonies, and those related to traffic in illicit drugs. Police, security guards and other personnel with law-enforcement responsibilities face a constant risk of attack by felons attempting to enter the workplace and those resisting detection and arrest. Those working alone and field workers whose duties take them into high-crime neighbourhoods are frequent targets of robbery attempts. Health professionals making home visits to such areas are particularly at risk because they often carry drugs and drug paraphernalia such as hypodermic syringes and needles.

Dealing with the public

Workers in government and private community service agencies, banks and other institutions serving the public are frequently confronted by attacks from individuals who have been kept waiting unduly, have been greeted with disinterest and indifference (whether real or perceived), or were thwarted in obtaining the information or services they desired because of complicated bureaucratic procedures or technicalities that made them ineligible. Clerks in retail establishments receiving items being returned, workers staffing airport ticket counters when flights are overbooked, delayed or cancelled, urban bus or trolley drivers and conductors, and others who must deal with customers or clients whose wants cannot immediately be satisfied are often targets for verbal and sometimes even physical abuse. Then, there are also those who must contend with impatient and unruly crowds, such as police officers, security guards, ticket takers and ushers at popular sporting and entertainment events.

Violent attacks on government workers, particularly those in uniform, and on government buildings and offices in which workers and visitors may be indiscriminately injured or killed, may result from resentment and anger at laws and official policies which the perpetrators will not accept.

Work stress

High levels of work stress may precipitate violent behaviour, while violence in the workplace can, in turn, be a potent stressor. The elements of work stress are well known (see chapter *Psychosocial and Organizational Factors*). Their common denominator is a devaluation of the individual and/or the work he or she performs, resulting in fatigue, frustration and anger directed at managers and co-workers perceived to be inconsiderate, unfair and abusive. Several recent population studies have demonstrated an association between violence and job loss, one of the most potent job-related stressors (Catalano et al. 1993; Yancey et al. 1994).

Interpersonal environment in the workplace

The interpersonal environment in the workplace may be a breeding ground for violence. Discrimination and harassment, forms of violence in themselves as defined in this article, may provoke violent retaliation. For example, MSF, the British union of workers in management, science and finance, calls attention to workplace bullying (defined as persistent offensive, abusive, intimidating, malicious or insulting behaviour, abuse of power or unfair penal sanctions), as a characteristic of the management style in some organizations (MSF 1995).

Sexual harassment has been branded a form of assault on the job (SEIU 1995). It may involve unwelcome touching or patting, physical assault, suggestive remarks or other verbal abuse, staring or leering, requests for sexual favours, compromising invitations, or a work environment made offensive by pornography. It is illegal in the United States, having been declared a form of sexual discrimination under Title VII of the Civil Rights Act of 1964 when the worker feels that his or her job status depends on tolerating the advances or if the harassment creates an intimidating, hostile or offensive workplace environment.

Although women are the usual targets, men have also been sexually harassed, albeit much less frequently. In a 1980 survey of US federal employees, 42% of female respondents and 15% of males said that they had been sexually harassed on the job, and a follow-up survey in 1987 yielded similar results (SEIU 1995). In the United States, extensive media coverage of the harassment of women who had "intruded" into jobs and workplaces traditionally filled by males, and the notoriety given to the involvement of prominent political and public figures in alleged harassment, have resulted in an increase in the number of complaints received by state and federal anti-discrimination agencies and the number of civil law suits filed.

Working in health care and social services

In addition to the attempted robberies as noted above, health care staff are often targets of violence from anxious and disturbed patients, especially in emergency and outpatient departments, where long waits and impersonal procedures are not uncommon and where anxiety and anger may boil over into verbal or physical assaults. They may also be victims of assault by family members or friends of patients who had unfavourable outcomes which they rightly or wrongly attribute to denials, delays or errors in treatment. In such instances they may attack the particular health worker(s) whom they hold responsible, or the violence may be aimed randomly at any staff member(s) of the medical facility.

Effects of Violence on the Victim

The trauma caused by physical assault varies with the nature of the attack and the weapons employed. Bruises and cuts on the hands and forearms are common when the victim has tried to defend himself or herself. Since the face and head are frequent targets, bruises and fractures of the facial bones are common; these can be traumatic psychologically because the swelling and ecchymoses are so visible and may take weeks to disappear (Mezey and Shepherd 1994).

The psychological effects may be more troublesome than the physical trauma, especially when a health worker has been assaulted by a patient. The victims may experience a loss of composure and self-confidence in their professional competence accompanied by a sense of guilt at having provoked the attack or having failed to detect that it was coming. Unfocused or directed anger may persist at the apparent rejection of their well-intended professional efforts, and there may be a persistent loss of confidence in themselves as well as a lack of trust in their co-workers and supervisors that can interfere with work performance. All this may be accompanied by insomnia, nightmares, diminished or increased appetite, increased consumption of tobacco, alcohol and/or drugs, social withdrawal and absenteeism from the job (Mezey and Shepherd 1994).

Post-traumatic stress disorder is a specific psychological syndrome (PTSD) that may develop after major disasters and instances of violent assault, not only in those directly involved in the incident but also in those who have witnessed it. While usually associated with life-threatening or fatal incidents, PTSD may occur after relatively trivial attacks that are perceived as life-threatening (Foa and Rothbaum 1992). The symptoms include: re-experiencing the incident through recurrent and intrusive recollections ("flashbacks") and nightmares, persistent feelings of arousal and anxiety including muscular tension, autonomic hyperactivity, loss of concentration, and exaggerated reactivity. There is often conscious or unconscious avoidance of circumstances that recall the incident. There may be a long period of disability but the symptoms usually respond to supportive psychotherapy. They can often be prevented by a post-incident debriefing conducted as soon as possible after the incident, followed, when needed, by short-term counselling (Foa and Rothbaum 1992).

After the Incident

Interventive measures to be taken immediately after the incident include:

Care of the victim

Appropriate first-aid and medical care should be provided as quickly as possible to all injured individuals. For possible medico-legal purposes (e.g., criminal or civil actions against the assailant) the injuries should be described in detail and, if possible, photographed.

Clean-up of the workplace

Any damage or debris in the workplace should be cleaned up, and any equipment that was involved should be checked to make sure that the safety and cleanliness of the workplace have been fully restored (SEIU 1995).

Post-incident debriefing

As soon as possible, all those involved in or witnessing the incident should participate in a post-incident debriefing or a "trauma-crisis counselling" session conducted by an appropriately qualified staff member or an outside consultant. This will not only provide emotional support and identify those for whom referral for one-on-one counselling may be advisable, but also enable the collection of details of exactly what has happened. Where necessary, the

51. VIOLENCE

counselling may be supplemented by the formation of a peer support group (CAL/OSHA 1995).

Reporting

A standardized report form should be completed and submitted to the proper individual in the organization and, when appropriate, to the police in the community. A number of sample forms that may be adapted to the needs of a particular organization have been designed and published (Unison 1991, MSF 1993, SEIU 1995). Aggregating and analysing incident report forms will provide epidemiological information that may identify risk factors for violence in the particular workplace and point the way to suitable preventive interventions.

Investigating the incident

Each reported incident of alleged violence, however trivial it may seem, should be investigated by a designated properly trained individual. (Assignment for such investigations may be made by the joint labour/management safety and health committee, where one exists.) The investigation should be aimed at identifying the cause(s) of the incident, the person(s) involved, what, if any, disciplinary measures should be invoked, and what may be done to prevent recurrences. Failure to conduct an impartial and effective investigation is a signal of management's disinterest and a lack of concern for employees' health and welfare.

Employer support

Victims and observers of the incident should be assured that they will not be subject to discrimination or any other form of reprisal for reporting it. This is especially important when the alleged assailant is the worker's superior.

Table 51.4 • Guides for programmes to prevent workplace violence.

Date	Title	Source
1991	Violence in the Workplace: NUPE Guidelines	Unison Health Care 1 Marbledon Place London WC1H 9AJ, UK
1993	CAL/OSHA Guidelines for Security and Safety of Health Care and Community Service Workers	Division of Occupational Safety and Health Department of Industrial Relations 45 Fremont Street San Francisco, CA 94105, USA
1993	Prevention of Violence at Work: An MSF Guide with Model Agreement and Violence at Work Questionnaire (MSF Health and Safety Information No. 37)	MSF Health and Safety Office Dane O'Coys Road Bishops Stortford Herts, CM23 2JN, UK
1995	Assault on the Job: We Can Do Something About Workplace Violence (2nd Edition)	Service Employees International Union 1313 L Street, NW Washington, DC 20005, USA
1995	CAL/OSHA: Model Injury and Illness Prevention Program for Workplace Security	Division of Occupational Safety and Health Department of Industrial Relations 45 Fremont Street San Francisco, CA 94105, USA
1996	Guidelines for Preventing Workplace Violence for Health Care and Social Service Workers (OSHA 3148)	OSHA Publications Office P.O. Box 37535 Washington, DC 20013-7535, USA

Depending on the regulations extant in the particular jurisdiction, the nature and extent of any injuries, and the duration of any absence from work, the employee may be eligible for workers' compensation benefits. In such cases, the appropriate claim forms should be filed promptly.

When appropriate, a report should be filed with the local law enforcement agency. When needed, the victim may be provided with legal advice on pressing charges against the assailant, and assistance in dealing with the media.

Union Involvement

A number of unions have been playing a prominent role in dealing with workplace violence, most notably those representing workers in the health care and service industries, such as the Service Employees International Union (SEIU) in the United States, and Management, Science and Finance (MSF) and Unison in the UK. Through the development of guidelines and the publication of fact sheets, bulletins and pamphlets, they have focused on the education of workers, their representatives and their employers about the importance of violence in the workplace, how to deal with it, and how to prevent it. They have acted as advocates for members who have been victims to ensure that their complaints and allegations of violence are given appropriate consideration without threats of reprisal, and that they receive all of the benefits to which they may be entitled. Unions also advocate with employers' and trade associations and government agencies on behalf of policies, rules and regulations intended to reduce the prevalence of violence in the workplace.

Threats of Violence

All threats of violence should be taken seriously, whether aimed at particular individuals or at the organization as a whole. First, steps must be taken to protect the targeted individual(s). Then, where possible, the assailant should be identified. If that person is not in the workforce, the local law enforcement agencies should be notified. If he or she is in the organization, it may be desirable to consult a qualified mental health professional to guide the handling of the situation and/or deal directly with the assailant.

Preventive Strategies

Preventing violence in the workplace is fundamentally the employer's responsibility. Ideally, a formal policy and programme will have been developed and implemented before victimization occurs. This is a process that should involve not only the appropriate individuals in human resources/personnel, security, legal affairs, and employee health and safety departments, but also line managers and shop stewards or other employee representatives. A number of guides for such an exercise have been published (see table 51.4). They are generic and are intended to be tailored to the circumstances of a particular workplace or industry. Their common denominators include:

Establishing a policy

A policy explicitly outlawing discriminatory and abusive behaviour and the use of violence for dispute resolution, accompanied by specified disciplinary measures for infractions (up to and including dismissal), should be formulated and published.

Risk assessment

An inspection of the workplace, supplemented by analysis of prior incidents and/or information from employee surveys, will enable an expert to assess risk factors for violence and suggest preventive interventions. Examination of the prevailing style of management and supervision and the organization of work may disclose high levels of work stress that may precipitate violence. Study of interactions with clients, customers or patients may reveal features that may generate needless anxiety, frustration and anger, and precipitate violent reactions.

Workplace modifications to reduce crime

Guidance from police or private security experts may suggest changes in work procedures and in the layout and furnishing of the workplace that will make it a less attractive target for robbery attempts. In the United States, the Virginia Department of Criminal Justice has been using Crime Prevention Through Environmental Design (CPTED), a model approach developed by a consortium of the schools of architecture in the state that includes: changes in interior and exterior lighting and landscaping with particular attention to parking areas, stairwells and restrooms; making sales and waiting areas visible from the street; use of drop safes or time-release safes to hold cash; alarm systems, television monitors and other security equipment (Malcan 1993). CPTED has been successfully applied in convenience stores, banks (particularly in relation to automatic teller machines which may be accessed around the clock), schools and universities, and in the Washington, DC, Metro subway system.

In New York City, where robbery and killing of taxi drivers is relatively frequent compared to other large cities, the Taxi and Limousine Commission issued regulations that mandated the insertion of a transparent, bullet-resistant partition between the driver and passengers in the rear seat, a bullet-proof plate in the back of the driver's seat, and an external distress signal light that could be turned on by the driver while remaining invisible to those inside the cab (NYC/TLC 1994). (There has been a spate of head and facial injuries among rear seat passengers who were not wearing seat belts and were thrown forward against the partition when the cab stopped suddenly.)

Where work involves interaction with customers or patients, employee safety may be enhanced by interposing barriers such as counters, desks or tables, transparent, shatter-proof partitions, and locked doors with shatter-proof windows (CAL/OSHA 1993). Furniture and equipment can be arranged to avoid entrapment of the employee and, where privacy is important, it should not be maintained at the expense of isolating the employee with a potentially aggressive or violent individual in a closed or secluded area.

Security systems

Every workplace should have a well-designed security system. Intrusion of strangers may be reduced by limiting entry to a designated reception area where visitors may have an identity check and receive ID badges indicating the areas to be visited. In some situations, it may be advisable to use metal detectors to identify visitors carrying concealed weapons.

Electronic alarm systems triggered by strategically located "panic buttons" can provide audible and/or visual signals that can alert co-workers to danger and summon help from a nearby security station. Such alarm systems may also be rigged to summon local police. However, they are of little use if guards and co-workers have not been trained to respond promptly and properly. Television monitors can not only provide protective surveillance but also record any incidents as they occur, and may help identify the perpetrator. Needless to say, such electronic systems are of little use unless they are maintained properly and tested at frequent intervals to ensure that they are in working order.

Two-way radios and cellular telephones can provide a measure of security for field personnel and those who are working alone. They also provide a means of reporting their location and, when necessary, summoning medical and other forms of assistance.

Work practice controls

Work practices should be reviewed periodically and modified to minimize the build-up of work stress. This involves attention to work schedules, work load, job content, and monitoring of work performance. Adequate staffing levels should be maintained in high-risk work areas both to discourage violent behaviour and to deal with it when it occurs. Adjustment of staffing levels to cope with peak flows of clients or patients will help to minimize irritating delays and crowding of work areas.

Staff training

Workers and supervisors should be trained to recognize rising tension and anger and in non-violent methods of defusing them. Training involving role-playing exercises will help employees to cope with overly aggressive or abusive individuals without being confrontational. In some situations, training employees in self-defence may be indicated, but there is the danger that this will breed a level of self-confidence that will lead them to delay or entirely neglect calling for available help.

Security guards, staff in psychiatric or penal institutions, and others likely to be involved with physically violent individuals should be trained to subdue and restrain them with minimal risk of injury to others or to themselves (SEIU 1995). However, according to Unison (1991), training can never be a substitute for good work organization and the provision of adequate security.

Employee assistance programmes

Employee assistance programmes (EAPs—also known as member assistance programmes, or MAPs, when provided by a union) can be particularly helpful in crisis situations by providing counselling and support to victims and witnesses of violent incidents, referring them to outside mental health professionals when needed, monitoring their progress and overseeing any protective arrangements intended to facilitate their return to work.

EAPs can also counsel employees whose frustration and anger might culminate in violent behaviour because they are overburdened by work-related problems or those arising from life in the family and/or in the community, whose frustration and anger might culminate in violent behaviour. When they have several such clients from a particular area of the workplace, they can (without breaching the confidentiality of personal information essential to their operation) guide managers to making desirable work modifications that will defuse the potential "powder keg" before violence erupts.

Research

Because of the seriousness and complexity of the problem and the paucity of reliable information, research is needed in the epidemiology, causation, prevention and control of violence in society in general and in the workplace. This requires a multidisciplinary effort involving (in addition to experts in occupational safety and health), mental health professionals, social workers, architects and engineers, experts in management science, lawyers, judges and experts in the criminal justice system, authorities on public policy, and others. Urgently needed are expanded and improved systems for the collection and analysis of the relevant data and the development of a consensus on a taxonomy of violence so that information and ideas can be more easily transposed from one discipline to others.

Conclusion

Violence is endemic in the workplace. Homicides are a major cause of work-related deaths, but their impact and cost are considerably outweighed by the prevalence of near misses, non-fatal physical assaults, threats, harassment, aggressive behaviour and abuse, much of which remains undocumented and unreported.

Although most of the homicides and many of the assaults occur in conjunction with criminal activities, workplace violence is not just a criminal justice problem. Nor is it solely a problem for mental health professionals and specialists in addictions, although much of it is associated with mental illness, alcoholism and drug abuse. It requires a coordinated effort by experts in a broad variety of disciplines, led by occupational health and safety professionals, and aimed at developing, validating and implementing a coherent set of strategies for intervention and prevention, keeping in mind that the diversity in workers, jobs and industries dictates an ability to tailor them to the unique characteristics of a particular workforce and the organization that employs it.

References

American Psychiatric Association (APA). 1994. *APA Fact Sheet: Violence and Mental Illness*. Washington, DC: APA.

Bachman, R. 1994. *Crime Victimization Survey: Violence and Theft in the Workplace*. Washington, DC: US Department of Justice.

Bullard, H. 1994. Management of violent patients. In *Violence in Health Care: A Practical Guide to Coping With Violence and Caring for Victims*, edited by J Shepherd. Oxford: OUP.

CAL/OSHA. 1993. *Guidelines for the Security and Safety of Health Care and Community Service Workers*. Los Angeles: California Department of Industrial Relations.

CAL/OSHA Consultation Service. 1995. *Model Injury and Illness Prevention Program for Workplace Security*. Los Angeles: California Department of Industrial Relations.

Castillo, DN and EL Jenkins. 1994. Industries and occupations at high risk for work-related homicide. *J Occup Med* 36:125-132.

Catalano, R, D Dooley, RW Novaco, G Wilson, and R Hough. 1993. Using ECA survey data to examine the effect of job layoffs on violent behaviour. *Hospital and Community Psychiatry* 44:874-879.

Drever, F. 1995. *Occupational Health Decennial Supplement: Office of Population Censuses and Survey*. Health and Safety Executive Series D5, no.10. London: HMSO.

Fagan, J. 1993. Set and setting revisited: Influences of alcohol and illicit drugs on the social context of violent events. In *Alcohol and Interpersonal Violence: Fostering Multidisciplinary Perspectives*, edited by SF Martin. Rockville, Md.: National Institute on Alcohol Abuse and Alcoholism.

Foa, EB and BO Rothbaum. 1992. Post-traumatic stress disorder: Clinical features and treatment. In *Aggression and Violence Throughout the Lifespan*, edited by RD Peters, RJ McMahon, and VI Quinsey. Newbury Park, Calif: Sage.

Health Services Advisory Committee. 1987. *Violence to Staff in the Health Services*. London: Health and Safety Commission, HMSO.

Kuzmits, FE. 1990. When employees kill other employees: The case of Joseph T. Weisbecker. *J Occup Med* 32:1014-1020.

Lawless, P. 1993. *Fear and Violence in the Workplace: A Survey Documenting the Experience of American Workers*. Minneapolis, Minn: Northwestern National Life Insurance.

Malcan, JW. 1993. *Report of Virginia Crime Prevention Center on Violent Crimes in Convenience Stores: Analysis of Crimes, Criminals and Costs*. House doc. No. 30. Richmond, Va.; Virginia Department of Criminal Justice.

Marks, B. 1992. Psychopathic and violent patients. *Practitioner* 236:715-719.

Mezey, G and J Shepherd. 1994. Effects of assault on health-care professionals. In *Violence in Health Care: Practical Guide to Coping With Violence and Caring for Victims*, edited by J Shepherd. Oxford: OUP

MSF (Management, Science and Finance). 1993. *Prevention of Violence At Work, and MSF Guide With Model Agreement and Violence At Work Questionnaire*. MSF Health and Safety Information, no.37. Herts, UK: MSF Health and Safety Office.

—. 1995. *Bullying At Work and How to Tackle It: A Guide for MSF Members and Representatives*. Herts, UK: MSF Health and Safety Office.

National Institute of Occupational Safety and Health (NIOSH). 1992. *Homicide in US Workplaces: A Strategy for Prevention and Research*. Cincinnati, Ohio: US Department of Health and Human Resources, NIOSH.

—. 1993a. *Alert: Request for Assistance in Preventing Homicide in the Workplace*. Cincinnati, Ohio: NIOSH.

—. 1993b. *Fatal Injuries to Workers in the United States, 1980-1989: A Decade of Surveillance: National Profile*. Cincinnati, Ohio: US Department of Health and Human Resources, NIOSH.

—. 1993c. *NIOSH Alert: Request*. Cincinnati, Ohio: NIOSH.

New York City and Taxi and Limousine Commission (TLC). 1994. Notice Regarding Mandatory Installation of Partition and Trouble Lights. Industry Notice 94-2.

Pernanen, K. 1993. Alcohol-related violence: Conceptual models and methodological issues. In *Alcohol and Interpersonal Violence: Fostering Multidisciplinary Perspectives*, edited by SE Martin. Rockville, Md.: National Institute of Alcohol Abuse and Alcoholism.

Reiss, AJ and JA Roth. 1993. *Understanding and Preventing Violence*. Washington, DC: National Academy Press.

Rosenberg, MI and JA Mercy. 1991. Assaultive violence. In *Violence in America: A Public Health Approach*, edited by MI Rosenberg and MA Fenley. New York: Oxford Univ. Press.

Scribner, RA, DP MacKinnon, and JH Dwyer. 1995. The risk of assaultive violence and alcohol availability in Los Angeles County. *Am J Public Health* 85(3):335-340.

Service Employees International Union (SEIU), AFL-CIO, and CLC. 1995. *Assault On the Job: We Can Do Something About Workplace Violence*. Washington, DC: SEIU.

Shepherd, J. 1994. *Violence in Health Care: A Practical Guide to Coping With Violence and Caring for Victims*. Oxford: OUP.

Toscano, G and J Windau. 1994. The changing character of fatal work injuries. *Monthly Labor Review* 117(10):17-28.

Unison. 1991. *Violence in the NHS: NUPE Guidelines*. London: Unison.

—. 1992. Violence at work: A preventative strategy. *Unison Work Health Safe* (July):1.

Yancey, AH, KS Gabel-Hughes, S Ezell, and DL Zalkind. 1994. The relationship between violent trauma and nonemployment. *J Natl Med Assoc* 86:661-666.

Other relevant readings

MSF. *Working Alone: Guidance for MSF Members and Safety Representatives*.

VISUAL DISPLAY UNITS

52

Chapter Editor
Diane Berthelette

Contents

• OVERVIEW

Diane Berthelette

New information technologies are being introduced in all industrial sectors, albeit to varying extents. In some cases, the costs of computerizing production processes may constitute an impediment to innovation, particularly in small and medium-sized companies and in developing countries. Computers make possible the rapid collection, storage, processing and dissemination of large quantities of information. Their utility is further enhanced by their integration into computer networks, which allow resources to be shared (Young 1993).

Computerization exerts significant effects on the nature of employment and on working conditions. Beginning about the mid-1980s, it was recognized that workplace computerization may lead to changes in task structure and work organization, and by extension to work requirements, career planning and stress suffered by production and management personnel. Computerization may exert positive or negative effects on occupational health and safety. In some cases, the introduction of computers has rendered work more interesting and resulted in improvements in the work environment and reductions of workload. In others, however, the result of technological innovation has been an increase in the repetitive nature and intensity of tasks, a reduction of the margin for individual initiative and the isolation of the worker. Furthermore, several companies have been reported to increase the number of work shifts in an attempt to extract the largest possible economic benefit from their financial investment (ILO 1984).

As far as we have been able to determine, as of 1994 statistics on the worldwide use of computers are available from one source only—*The Computer Industry Almanac* (Juliussen and Petska-Juliussen 1994). In addition to statistics on the current international distribution of computer use, this publication also reports the results of retrospective and prospective analyses. The figures reported in the latest edition indicate that the number of computers is increasing exponentially, with the increase becoming particularly marked at the beginning of the 1980s, the point at which personal computers began to attain great popularity. Since 1987, total computer processing power, measured in terms of the number of million instructions per second executed (MIPS) has increased 14-fold, thanks to the development of new microprocessors (transistor components of microcomputers which perform arithmetical and logical calculations). By the end of 1993, total computing power attained 357 million MIPS.

Unfortunately, available statistics do not differentiate between computers used for work and personal purposes, and statistics are unavailable for some industrial sectors. These knowledge gaps are most likely due to methodological problems related to the collection of valid and reliable data. However, reports of the International Labour Organization's tripartite sectoral committees contain relevant and comprehensive information on the nature and extent of the penetration of new technologies in various industrial sectors.

In 1986, 66 million computers were in use throughout the world. Three years later, there were more than 100 million, and by 1997, it is estimated that 275–300 million computers will be in use, with this number reaching 400 million by 2000. These predictions assume the widespread adoption of multimedia, information highway, voice recognition and virtual reality technologies. The *Almanac*'s authors consider that most televisions will be equipped with personal computers within ten years of publication, in order to simplify access to the information highway.

According to the *Almanac*, in 1993 the overall computer:population ratio in 43 countries in 5 continents was 3.1 per 100. It

should however be noted that South Africa was the only African country reporting and that Mexico was the only Central American country reporting. As the statistics indicate, there is a very wide international variation in the extent of computerization, the computer:population ratio ranging from 0.07 per 100 to 28.7 per 100.

The computer:population ratio of less than 1 per 100 in developing countries reflects the generally low level of computerization prevailing there (table 52.1) (Juliussen and Petska-Juliussen 1994). Not only do these countries produce few computers and little software, but lack of financial resources may in some cases prevent them from importing these products. Moreover, their often rudimentary telephone and electrical utilities are often barriers to more widespread computer use. Finally, little linguistically and culturally appropriate software is available, and training in computer-related fields is often problematic (Young 1993).

Computerization has significantly increased in the countries of the former Soviet Union since the end of the Cold War. The Russian Federation, for example, is estimated to have increased its stock of computers from 0.3 million in 1989 to 1.2 million in 1993.

The largest concentration of computers is found in the industrialized countries, especially in North America, Australia, Scandinavia and Great Britain (Juliussen and Petska-Juliussen 1994). It was principally in these countries that the first reports of visual display unit (VDU) operators' fears regarding health risks appeared and the initial research aimed at determining the prevalence of health effects and identifying risk factors undertaken. The health problems studied fall into the following categories: visual and ocular problems, musculoskeletal problems, skin problems, reproductive problems, and stress.

It soon became evident that the health effects observed among VDU operators were dependent not only on screen characteristics and workstation layout, but also on the nature and structure of tasks, organization of work and manner in which the technology was introduced (ILO 1989). Several studies have reported a higher prevalence of symptoms among female VDU operators than among male operators. According to recent studies, this difference is more reflective of the fact that female operators typically have less control over their work than do their male counterparts than of true biological differences. This lack of control is thought to result in higher stress levels, which in turn result in increased symptom prevalence in female VDU operators.

VDUs were first introduced on a widespread basis in the tertiary sector, where they were used essentially for office work, more specifically data entry and word processing. We should not therefore be surprised that most studies of VDUs have focused on office workers. In industrialized countries, however, computerization has spread to the primary and secondary sectors. In addition, although VDUs were used almost exclusively by production workers, they have now penetrated to all organizational levels. In recent years, researchers have therefore begun to study a wider range of VDU users, in an attempt to overcome the lack of adequate scientific information on these situations.

Most computerized workstations are equipped with a VDU and a keyboard or mouse with which to transmit information and instructions to the computer. Software mediates information exchange between the operator and the computer and defines the format with which information is displayed on the screen. In order to establish the potential hazards associated with VDU use, it is first necessary to understand not only the characteristics of the VDU but also those of the other components of the work environment. In 1979, Çakir, Hart and Stewart published the first comprehensive analysis in this field.

It is useful to visualize the hardware used by VDU operators as nested components that interact with each other (IRSST 1984). These components include the terminal itself, the workstation

Table 52.1 • Distribution of computers in various regions of the world.

Region	Computers per 100 people	Region	Computers per 100 people
NORTH AMERICA		**EASTERN EUROPE**	
United States	28.7	Czech Republic	2.2
Canada	8.8	Hungary	2.7
		Poland	1.7
CENTRAL AMERICA		Russian Federation	0.78
Mexico	1.7	Ukraine	0.2
SOUTH AMERICA		**OCEANIA**	
Argentina	1.3	Australia	19.2
Brazil	0.6	New Zealand	14.7
Chile	2.6		
Venezuela	1.9	**AFRICA**	
		South Africa	1
WESTERN EUROPE			
Austria	9.5	**ASIA**	
Belgium	11.7	China	0.09
Denmark	16.8	India	0.07
Finland	16.7	Indonesia	0.17
France	12.9	Israel	8.3
Germany	12.8	Japan	9.7
Greece	2.3	Korea Republic of	3.7
Ireland	13.8	Phillipines	0.4
Italy	7.4	Saudi Arabia	2.4
Netherlands	13.6	Singapore	12.5
Norway	17.3	Taiwan	7.4
Portugal	4.4	Thailand	0.9
Spain	7.9	Turkey	0.8
Sweden	15		
Switzerland	14		
United Kingdom	16.2		

Less than 1 ☐   1-5 ▨   6-10 ▨   11-15 ▨   16-20 ▨   21-30 ■

Source: Juliussen and Petska-Juliussen 1994.

(including work tools and furniture), the room in which the work is carried out, and the lighting. The second article in this chapter reviews the main characteristics of workstations and their lighting. Several recommendations aimed at optimizing working conditions while taking into account individual variations and variations in tasks and work organization are offered. Appropriate emphasis is placed on the importance of choosing equipment and furniture which allow flexible layouts. This flexibility is extremely important in light of international competition and rapidly evolving technological development that are constantly driving companies to introduce innovations and while simultaneously forcing them to adapt to the changes these innovations bring.

The next six articles discuss health problems studied in response to fears expressed by VDU operators. The relevant scientific literature is reviewed and the value and limitations of research results highlighted. Research in this field draws upon numerous disciplines, including epidemiology, ergonomics, medicine, engineering, psychology, physics and sociology. Given the complexity of the problems and more specifically their multifactorial nature, the necessary research has often been conducted by multidisciplinary research teams. Since the 1980s, these research efforts have been comple-

mented by regularly organized international congresses such as *Human-Computer Interaction* and *Work with Display Units*, which provide an opportunity to disseminate research results and promote the exchange of information between researchers, VDU designers, VDU producers and VDU users.

The eighth article discusses human-computer interaction specifically. The principles and methods underlying the development and evaluation of interface tools are presented. This article will prove useful not only to production personnel but also those interested in the criteria used to select interface tools.

Finally, the ninth article reviews international ergonomic standards as of 1995, related to the design and layout of computerized workstations. These standards have been produced in order to eliminate the hazards to which VDU operators can be exposed in the course of their work. The standards provide guidelines to companies producing VDU components, employers responsible for the purchase and layout of workstations, and employees with decision-making responsibilities. They may also prove useful as tools with which to evaluate existing workstations and identify modifications required in order to optimize operators' working conditions.

CHARACTERISTICS OF VISUAL DISPLAY WORKSTATIONS

Ahmet Çakir

Workstation Design

On workstations with visual display units

Visual displays with electronically generated images (visual display units or VDUs) represent the most characteristic element of computerized work equipment both in the workplace and in private life. A workstation may be designed to accommodate just a VDU and an input device (normally a keyboard), as a minimum; however, it can also provide room for diverse technical equipment including numerous screens, input and output devices, etc. As recently as the early 1980s, data entry was the most typical task for computer users. In many industrialized countries, however, this type of work is now performed by a relatively small number of users. More and more, journalists, managers and even executives have become "VDU users".

Most VDU workstations are designed for sedentary work, but working in standing postures may offer some benefits for the users. Thus, there is some need for generic design guidelines applicable to simple and complex workstations used both while sitting and standing. Such guidelines will be formulated below and then applied to some typical workplaces.

Design guidelines

Workplace design and equipment selection should consider not only the needs of the actual user for a given task and the variability of users' tasks during the relatively long life cycle of furniture (lasting 15 years or longer), but also factors related to maintenance or change of equipment. ISO Standard 9241, part 5, introduces four guiding principles to be applied to workstation design:

Guideline 1: Versatility and flexibility. A workstation should enable its user to perform a range of tasks comfortably and efficiently. This guideline takes into account the fact that users' tasks may vary often; thus, the chance of a universal adoption of guidelines for the workplace will be small.

Guideline 2: Fit. The design of a workstation and its components should ensure a "fit" to be achieved for a variety of users and a range of task requirements. The concept of fit concerns the extent to which furniture and equipment can accommodate an individual user's various needs, that is, to remain comfortable, free from visual discomfort and postural strain. If not designed for a specific user population, e.g., male European control room operators younger than 40 years of age, the workstation concept should ensure fit for the entire working population including users with special needs, e.g., handicapped persons. Most existing standards for furniture or the design of workplaces take only parts of the working population into consideration (e.g., "healthy" workers between the 5th and 95th percentile, aged between 16 and 60, as in German standard DIN 33 402), neglecting those who may need more attention. Moreover, though some design practices are still based on the idea of an "average" user, an emphasis on individual fit is needed. With regard to workstation furniture, the fit required may be achieved by providing adjustability, designing a range of sizes, or even by custom-made equipment. Ensuring a good fit is crucial for the health and safety of the individual user, since musculoskeletal problems associated with the use of VDUs are common and significant.

Guideline 3: Postural change. The design of the workstation should encourage movement, since static muscular load leads to fatigue and discomfort and may induce chronic musculoskeletal problems. A chair that allows easy movement of the upper half of the body, and provision of sufficient space to place and use paper documents as well as keyboards at varying positions during the day, are typical strategies for facilitating body movement while working with a VDU.

Guideline 4: Maintainability—adaptability. The design of the workstation should take into consideration factors such as maintenance, accessibility, and the ability of the workplace to adapt to changing requirements, such as the ability to move the work equipment if a different task is to be performed. The objectives of this guideline have not received much attention in the ergonomics literature, because problems related to them are assumed to have been solved before users start to work at a workstation. In reality, however, a workstation is an ever-changing environment, and cluttered workspaces, partly or fully unsuitable for the tasks at hand, are very often not the result of their initial design process but are the outcome of later changes.

Figure 52.2 • Flexible workstation layout.

Figure 52.1 • Layout of a flexible workstation that can be adapted to fit the needs of users with different tasks.

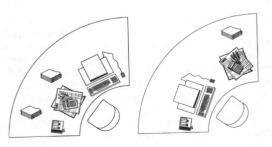

Applying the guidelines

Task analysis. Workplace design should be preceded by a task analysis, which provides information about the primary tasks to be performed at the workstation and the equipment needed for them. In such an analysis, the priority given to information sources (e.g., paper-based documents, VDUs, input devices), the frequency of their use and possible restrictions (e.g., limited space) should be determined. The analysis should include major tasks and their relationships in space and time, visual attention areas (how many visual objects are to be used?) and the position and use of the hands (writing, typing, pointing?).

General design recommendations

Height of the work surfaces. If fixed-height work surfaces are to be used, the minimum clearance between the floor and the surface should be greater than the sum of the *popliteal height* (the distance between the floor and the back of the knee) and thigh clearance height (sitting), plus allowance for footwear (25 mm for male users and 45 mm for female users). If the workstation is designed for general use, the popliteal height and thigh clearance height should be selected for the 95th percentile male population. The resulting height for the clearance under the desk surface is 690 mm for the population of Northern Europe and for North American users of European origin. For other populations, the minimum clearance needed is to be determined according to the anthropometric characteristics of the specific population.

If the legroom height is selected this way, the top of the work surfaces will be too high for a large proportion of intended users, and at least 30 per cent of them will need a footrest.

If work surfaces are adjustable in height, the required range for adjustment can be calculated from the anthropometric dimensions of female users (5th or 2.5th percentile for minimum height) and male users (95th or 97.5th percentile for maximum height). A workstation with these dimensions will in general be able to accommodate a large proportion of persons with little or no change. The result of such a calculation yields a range between 600 mm to 800 mm for countries with an ethnically varied user population. Since the technical realization of this range may cause some mechanical problems, best fit can also be achieved, for example, by combining adjustability with different size equipment.

The minimum acceptable thickness of the work surface depends on the mechanical properties of the material. From a technical point of view, a thickness between 14 mm (durable plastic or metal) and 30 mm (wood) is achievable.

Size and form of the work surface. The size and the form of a work surface are mainly determined by the tasks to be performed and the equipment needed for those tasks.

For data entry tasks, a rectangular surface of 800 mm by 1200 mm provides sufficient space to place the equipment (VDU, keyboard, source documents and copy holder) properly and to rearrange the layout according to personal needs. More complex tasks may require additional space. Therefore, the size of the work surface should exceed 800 mm by 1,600 mm. The depth of the surface should allow placing the VDU within the surface, which means that VDUs with cathode ray tubes may require a depth of up to 1,000 mm.

In principle, the layout displayed in figure 52.1 gives maximum flexibility for organizing the workspace for various tasks. However, workstations with this layout are not easy to construct. Thus, the best approximation of the ideal layout is as displayed in

Table 52.2 • Frequency and importance of elements of equipment for a given task.

ELEMENT	USE			
	TOUCH		SEE	
	Frequency	Importance	Frequency	Importance
KEYBOARD	●	●	●	·
VDU	·		●	●
MOUSE	●	●		
DOCUMENTS	·	●	●	●

● Greater degree of importance or frequency   · Lesser degree of importance or frequency

● Moderate degree of importance or frequency

figure 52.2. This layout allows arrangements with one or two VDUs, additional input devices and so on. The minimum area of the work surface should be larger than 1.3 m^2.

Arranging the workspace. The spatial distribution of equipment in the workspace should be planned after a task analysis determining the importance and use frequency of each element has been conducted (table 52.2). The most frequently used visual display should be located within the central visual space, which is the shaded area of figure 52.3, while the most important and frequently used controls (such as the keyboard) should be located within optimum reach. In the workplace represented by the task analysis (table 52.2), the keyboard and the mouse are by far the most frequently handled pieces of equipment. Therefore, they should be given the highest priority within the reach area. Documents which are frequently consulted but do not need much handling should be assigned priority according to their importance (e.g., handwritten corrections). Placing them on the right-hand side of the keyboard would solve the problem, but this would create a conflict with the frequent use of the mouse which is also to be located to the right of the keyboard. Since the VDU may not need adjustment frequently, it can be placed to the right or left of the central field of vision, allowing the documents to be set on a flat document holder behind the keyboard. This is one possible, though not perfect, "optimized" solution.

Figure 52.3 • Visual workspace range.

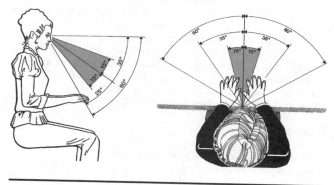

Since many elements of the equipment possess dimensions comparable to corresponding parts of the human body, using various elements within one task will always be associated with some problems. It also may require some movements between parts of the workstation; hence a layout like that shown in figure 52.1 is important for various tasks.

In the course of the last two decades, computer power that would have needed a ballroom at the beginning was successfully miniaturized and condensed into a simple box. However, contrary to the hopes of many practitioners that miniaturization of equipment would solve most problems associated with workplace layout, VDUs have continued to grow: in 1975, the most common screen size was 15″; in 1995 people bought 17″ to 21″ monitors, and no keyboard has become much smaller than those designed in 1973. Carefully performed task analyses for designing complex workstations are still of growing importance. Moreover, although new input devices have emerged, they have not replaced the keyboard, and require even more space on the work surface, sometimes of substantial dimensions, e.g, graphic tablets in an A3-format.

Efficient space management within the limits of a workstation, as well as within work rooms, may help in developing acceptable workstations from an ergonomic point of view, thus preventing the emergence of various health and safety problems.

Efficient space management does not mean saving space at the expense of the usability of input devices and especially vision. Using extra furniture, such as a desk return, or a special monitor-holder clamped to the desk, may appear to be a good way to save desk space; however, it may be detrimental to posture (raised arms) and vision (raising the line of vision upwards from the relaxed position). Space-saving strategies should ensure that an adequate visual distance (approximately 600 mm to 800 mm) is maintained, as well as an optimum line-of-vision, obtained from an inclination of approximately 35° from the horizontal (20° head and 15° eyes).

New furniture concepts. Traditionally, office furniture was adapted to the needs of businesses, supposedly reflecting the hierarchy of such organizations: large desks for executives working in "ceremonial" offices at one end of the scale, and small typists furniture for "functional" offices at the other. The basic design of office furniture did not change for decades. The situation changed substantially with the introduction of information technology, and a completely new furniture concept has emerged: that of systems furniture.

Systems furniture was developed when people realized that changes in working equipment and work organization could not be matched by the limited capabilities of existing furniture to adapt to new needs. Furniture today offers a tool-box that enables the user organizations to create workspace as needed, from a minimal space for just a VDU and a keyboard up to complex workstations that can accommodate various elements of equipment and possibly also groups of users. Such furniture is designed for change and incorporates efficient and flexible cable management facilities. While the first generation of systems furniture did not do much more than add an auxiliary desk for the VDU to an existing desk, the third generation has completely broken its ties to the traditional office. This new approach offers great flexibility in designing workspaces, limited only by the available space and the abilities of organizations to use this flexibility.

Radiation

Radiation in the context of VDU applications

Radiation is the emission or transfer of radiant energy. The emission of radiant energy in the form of light as the intended

purpose for the use of VDUs may be accompanied by various unwanted by-products such as heat, sound, infrared and ultraviolet radiation, radio waves or x rays, to name a few. While some forms of radiation, like visible light, may affect humans in a positive way, some emissions of energy can have negative or even destructive biological effects, especially when the intensity is high and the duration of exposure is long. Some decades ago exposure limits for different forms of radiation were introduced to protect people. However, some of these exposure limits are questioned today, and, for low frequency alternating magnetic fields, no exposure limit can be given based on levels of natural background radiation.

Radiofrequency and microwave radiation from VDUs

Electromagnetic radiation with a frequency range from a few kHz to 10^9 Hertz (the so-called radiofrequency, or RF, band, with wavelengths ranging from some km to 30 cm) can be emitted by VDUs; however, the total energy emitted depends on the characteristics of the circuitry. In practice, however, the field strength of this type of radiation is likely to be small and confined to the immediate vicinity of the source. A comparison of the strength of alternating electric fields in the range of 20 Hz to 400 kHz indicates that VDUs using cathode ray tube (CRT) technology emit, in general, higher levels than other displays.

"Microwave" radiation covers the region between 3×10^8 Hz to 3×10^{11} Hz (wavelengths 100 cm to 1 mm). There are no sources of microwave radiation in VDUs that emit a detectable amount of energy within this band.

Magnetic fields

Magnetic fields from a VDU originate from the same sources as alternating electric fields. Although magnetic fields are not "radiation", alternating electric and magnetic fields cannot be separated in practice, since one induces the other. One reason why magnetic fields are discussed separately is that they are suspected to have teratogenic effects (see discussion later in this chapter).

Although the fields induced by VDUs are weaker than those induced by some other sources, such as high-voltage power lines, power plants, electrical locomotives, steel ovens and welding equipment, the total exposure produced by VDUs may be similar since people may work eight or more hours in the vicinity of a VDU but seldom near power lines or electric motors. The question of the relationship between electromagnetic fields and cancer, however, is still a matter for debate.

Optical radiation

"Optical" radiation covers visible radiation (i.e., light) with wavelengths from 380 nm (blue) to 780 nm (red), and the neighbouring bands in the electromagnetic spectrum (infrared from 3×10^{11} Hz to 4×10^{14} Hz, wavelengths from 780 nm to 1 mm; ultraviolet from 8×10^{14} Hz to 3×10^{17} Hz). Visible radiation is emitted at moderate levels of intensity comparable with that emitted by room surfaces (≈ 100 cd/m^2). However, ultraviolet radiation is trapped by the glass of the tube face (CRTs) or not emitted at all (other display technologies). Levels of ultraviolet radiation, if detectable at all, stay well below occupational exposure standards, as do those of infrared radiation.

X rays

CRTs are well-known sources of x rays, while other technologies like liquid crystal displays (LCDs) do not emit any. The physical processes behind emissions of this type of radiation are well understood, and tubes and circuitry are designed to keep the emitted levels far below the occupational exposure limits, if not below detectable levels. Radiation emitted by a source can only be detected if its level exceeds the background level. In the case of x rays, as for other ionizing radiation, the background level is provided by cosmic radiation and by radiation from radioactive materials in the ground and in buildings. In normal operation, a VDU does not emit x rays exceeding the background level of radiation (50 nGy/h).

Radiation recommendations

In Sweden, the former MPR (Statens Mät och Provråd, the National Council for Metrology and Testing) organization, now SWEDAC, has worked out recommendations for evaluating VDUs. One of their main objectives was to limit any unwanted by-product to levels that can be achieved by reasonable technical means. This approach goes beyond the classical approach of limiting hazardous exposures to levels where the likelihood of an impairment of health and safety seems to be acceptably low.

At the beginning, some recommendations of MPR led to the unwanted effect of reducing the optical quality of CRT displays. However, at present, only very few products with extremely high resolution may suffer any degradation if the manufacturer attempts to comply with the MPR (now MPR-II). The recommendations include limits for static electricity, magnetic and electric alternating fields, visual parameters, etc.

Image Quality

Definitions for image quality

The term *quality* describes the fit of distinguishing attributes of an object for a defined purpose. Thus, the image quality of a display includes all properties of the optical representation regarding the perceptibility of symbols in general, and the legibility or readability of alphanumeric symbols. In this sense, optical terms used by tube manufacturers, like resolution or minimum spot size, describe basic quality criteria concerning the abilities of a given device for displaying thin lines or small characters. Such quality criteria are comparable with the thickness of a pencil or brush for a given task in writing or painting.

Some of the quality criteria used by ergonomists describe optical properties that are relevant for legibility, e.g., contrast, while others, like character size or stroke width, refer more to typographical features. In addition, some technology-dependent features like the flicker of images, the persistence of images, or the *uniformity* of contrast within a given display are also considered in ergonomics (see figure 52.4).

Typography is the art of composing "type", which is not only shaping the fonts, but also selecting and setting of type. Here, the term typography is used in the first meaning.

Basic characteristics

Resolution. Resolution is defined as the smallest discernible or measurable detail in a visual presentation. For example, the resolution of a CRT display can be expressed by the maximum number of lines that can be displayed in a given space, as usually done with the resolution of photographic films. One can also describe the minimum spot size that a device can display at a given luminance (brightness). The smaller the minimum spot, the better the device. Thus, the number of dots of minimum size (picture elements—also known as pixels) per inch (dpi) represents the quality of the device, e.g., a 72 dpi device is inferior to a 200 dpi display.

In general, the resolution of most computer displays is well below 100 dpi: some graphic displays may achieve 150 dpi, however, only with limited brightness. This means, if a high contrast is required, the resolution will be lower. Compared with the resolution of print, e.g., 300 dpi or 600 dpi for laser printers, the quality

Figure 52.4 • Criteria for image evaluation.

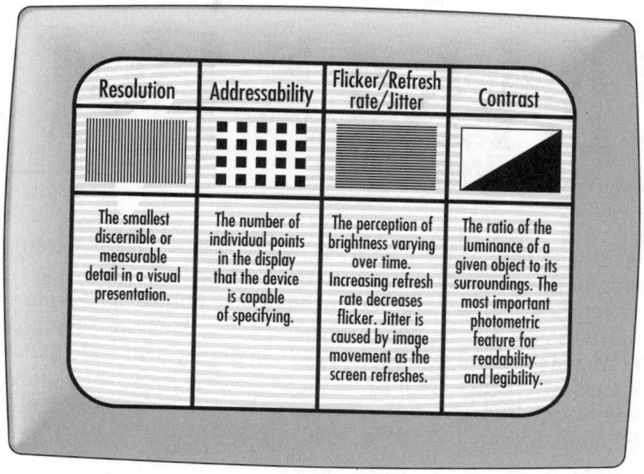

of VDUs is inferior. (An image with 300 dpi has 9 times more elements in the same space than a 100 dpi image.)

Addressability. Addressability describes the number of individual points in the field that the device is capable of specifying. Addressability, which is very often confused with resolution (sometimes deliberately), is one specification given for devices: "800 x 600" means that the graphic board can address 800 points on every one of 600 horizontal lines. Since one needs at least 15 elements in the vertical direction to write numbers, letters and other characters with ascenders and descenders, such a screen can display a maximum of 40 lines of text. Today, the best available screens can address 1,600 x 1,200 points; however, most displays used in industry address 800 x 600 points or even less.

On displays of the so-called "character-oriented" devices, it is not dots (points) of the screen that are addressed but character boxes. In most such devices, there are 25 lines with 80 character positions each in the display. On these screens, each symbol occupies the same space regardless of its width. In industry the lowest number of pixels in a box is 5 wide by 7 high. This box allows both upper and lower case characters, although the descenders in "p", "q" and "g", and the ascenders above "Ä" or "Á" cannot be displayed. Considerably better quality is provided with the 7 x 9 box, which has been "standard" since the mid-1980s. To achieve good legibility and reasonably good character shapes, the character box size should be at least 12 x 16.

Flicker and refresh rate. The images on CRTs and on some other types of VDU are not persistent images, as on paper. They only appear to be steady by taking advantage of an artefact of the eye. This, however, is not without penalty, since the screen tends to flicker if the image is not refreshed constantly. Flicker can influence both performance and comfort of the user and should always be avoided.

Flicker is the perception of brightness varying over time. The severity of flicker depends on various factors such as the characteristics of the phosphor, size and brightness of the flickering image, etc. Recent research shows that refresh rates up to 90 Hz may be needed to satisfy 99 per cent of users, while in earlier research, refresh rates well below 50 Hz were thought to be satisfactory. Depending on various features of the display, a flicker-free image may be achieved by refresh rates between 70 Hz and

Figure 52.5 • Appearance of a letter at various screen resolutions and on paper (right).

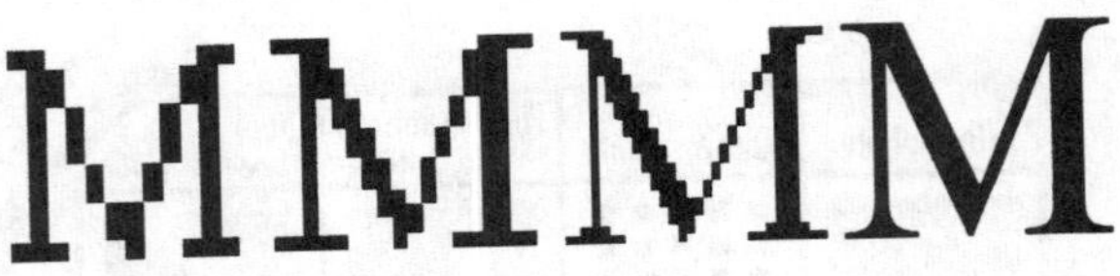

MMMM

90 Hz; displays with a light background (positive polarity) need a minimum of 80 Hz to be perceived as flicker-free.

Some modern devices offer an adjustable refresh rate; unfortunately, higher refresh rates are coupled with lower resolution or addressability. The ability of a device to display high "resolution" images with high refresh rates can be assessed by its video bandwidth. For displays with high quality, the maximum video bandwidth lies above 150 MHz, while some displays offer less than 40 MHz.

To achieve a flicker-free image and a high resolution with devices with lower video bandwidth, the manufacturers apply a trick that stems from commercial TV: the interlace mode. In this case, every second line on the display is refreshed with a given frequency. The result, however, is not satisfactory if static images, such as text and graphics, are displayed and the refresh rate is below 2 x 45 Hz. Unfortunately, the attempt to suppress the disturbing effect of flicker may induce some other negative effects.

Jitter. Jitter is the result of spatial instability of the image; a given picture element is not displayed at the same location on the screen after each refresh process. The perception of jitter cannot be separated from the perception of flicker.

Jitter may have its cause in the VDU itself, but it can also be induced by interaction with other equipment at the workplace, such as a printer or other VDUs or devices that generate magnetic fields.

Contrast. Brightness contrast, the ratio of the luminance of a given object to its surroundings, represents the most important photometric feature for readability and legibility. While most standards require a minimum ratio of 3:1 (bright characters on dark background) or 1:3 (dark characters on bright background), optimum contrast is actually about 10:1, and devices of good quality achieve higher values even in bright environments.

The contrast of "active" displays is impaired when the ambient light is increased, while "passive" displays (e.g., LCDs) lose contrast in dark environments. Passive displays with background lighting may offer good visibility in all environments under which people may work.

Sharpness. Sharpness of an image is a well-known, but still ill-defined feature. Hence, there is no agreed-upon method to measure sharpness as a relevant feature for legibility and readability.

Typographical features

Legibility and readability. Readability refers to whether a text is understandable as a series of connected images, while legibility refers to the perception of single or grouped characters. Thus, good legibility is, in general, a precondition for readability.

Legibility of text depends on several factors: some have been investigated thoroughly, while other relevant factors like character

shapes are yet to be classified. One of the reasons for this is that the human eye represents a very powerful and robust instrument, and the measures used for performance and error rates often do not help to distinguish between different fonts. Thus, to some extent, typography still remains an art rather than a science.

Fonts and readability. A font is a family of characters, designed to yield either optimum readability on a given medium, e.g., paper, electronic display or projection display, or some desired aesthetic quality, or both. While the number of available fonts exceeds ten thousand, only a few fonts, numbered in tens, are believed to be "readable". Since legibility and readability of a font are also affected by the experience of the reader—some "legible" fonts are believed to have become so because of decades or even centuries of use without changing their shape—the same font may be less legible on a screen than on paper, merely because its characters look "new". This, however, is not the main reason for the poor legibility of screens.

In general, the design of screen fonts is restricted by shortcomings in technology. Some technologies impose very narrow limits on the design of characters, e.g., LEDs or other rastered screens with limited numbers of dots per display. Even the best CRT displays can seldom compete with print (figure 52.5). In the last years, research has shown that speed and accuracy of reading on screens is about 30% lower than on paper, but whether this is due to features of the display or to other factors is not yet known.

Characteristics with measurable effects. The effects of some characteristics of alphanumeric representations are measurable, e.g., apparent size of the characters, height/width ratio, stroke width/size ratio, line, word and character spacing.

The apparent size of the characters, measured in minutes of arc, shows an optimum by 20′ to 22′; this corresponds to about 3 mm to 3.3 mm in height under normal viewing conditions in offices. Smaller characters may lead to increased errors, visual strain, and also to more postural strain due to restricted viewing distance. Thus, text should not be represented in an apparent size of less than 16′.

However, graphical representations may require text of smaller size to be displayed. To avoid errors, on the one hand, and a high visual load for the user on the other, parts of the text to be edited should be displayed in a separate window to assure good readability. Characters with an apparent size of less than 12′ should not be displayed as readable text, but replaced by a rectangular grey block. Good programs allow the user to select the minimum actual size of characters that are to be displayed as alphanumerics.

The optimum height/width ratio of characters is about 1:0.8; legibility is impaired if the ratio is above 1:0.5. For good legible print and also for CRT screens, the ratio of character height to stroke width is about 10:1. However, this is only a rule of thumb; legible characters of high aesthetical value often show different stroke widths (see figure 52.5).

Optimal line spacing is very important for readability, but also for space saving, if a given amount of information is to be displayed in limited space. The best example for this is the daily newspaper, where an enormous amount of information is displayed within a page, but is still readable. The optimum line spacing is about 20% of character height between the descenders of a line and the ascenders of the next; this is a distance of about 100% of the character height between the baseline of a line of text and the ascenders of the next. If the length of the line is reduced, the space between the lines may be reduced, too, without losing readability.

Character spacing is invariable on character-oriented screens, making them inferior in readability and aesthetic quality to displays with variable space. Proportional spacing depending on the shape and width of the characters is preferable. However, a typographical quality comparable to well-designed printed fonts is achievable only on few displays and when using specific programs.

Ambient Lighting

The specific problems of VDU workstations

During the last 90 years of industrial history, the theories about the lighting of our workplaces have been governed by the notion that more light will improve vision, reduce stress and fatigue, as well as enhance performance. "More light", correctly speaking "more sunlight", was the slogan of people in Hamburg, Germany, more than 60 years ago when they took to the streets to fight for better and healthier homes. In some countries like Denmark or Germany, workers today are entitled to have some daylight at their workplaces. The advent of information technology, with the emergence of the first VDUs in working areas, was presumably the first event ever when workers and scientists began to complain about *too much light* in working areas. The discussion was fuelled by the easily detectable fact that most VDUs were equipped with CRTs, which have curved glass surfaces prone to veiling reflections. Such devices, sometimes called "active displays", lose contrast when the level of ambient lighting becomes higher. Redesigning lighting to reduce the visual impairments caused by these effects, however, is complicated by the fact that most users also use paper-based information sources, which generally require increased levels of ambient light for good visibility.

The role of ambient light

Ambient light found in the vicinity of VDU workstations serves two different purposes. First, it illuminates the workspace and working materials like paper, telephones, etc. (primary effect). Secondly, it illuminates the room, giving it its visible shape and giving the users the impression of a light surrounding (secondary effect). Since most lighting installations are planned according to the concept of general lighting, the same lighting sources serve both purposes. The primary effect, illuminating passive visual objects to make them visible or legible, became questionable when people started to use active screens that do not need ambient light to be visible. The remaining benefit of the room lighting was reduced to the secondary effect, if the VDU is the major source of information.

The function of VDUs, both of CRTs (active displays) and of LCDs (passive displays), is impaired by the ambient light in specific ways:

CRTs:

- The curved glass surface reflects bright objects in the environment, and forms a kind of visual "noise".
- Depending on the intensity of ambient illumination, the contrast of displayed objects is reduced to a degree that readability or legibility of the objects is impaired.
- Images on colour CRTs suffer a twofold degradation: First, the brightness contrast of all displayed objects is reduced, as on monochrome CRTs. Secondly, the colours are changed so that colour contrast is also reduced. In addition, the number of distinguishable colours is reduced.

LCDs (and other passive displays):

- The reflections on LCDs cause less concern than those on CRT surfaces, since these displays have flat surfaces.

- In contrast to active displays, LCDs (without backlight) lose contrast under low levels of ambient illumination.
- Due to poor directional characteristics of some display technologies, visibility or legibility of displayed objects is substantially reduced if the main direction of light incidence is unfavourable.

The extent to which such impairments exert a stress on users or lead to a substantial reduction of visibility/readability/legibility of visual objects in real working environments varies greatly. For example, the contrast of alphanumeric characters on monochrome (CRT) displays is reduced in principle, but, if the illuminance on the screen is ten times higher than in normal working environments, many screens will still have a contrast sufficient to read alphanumeric characters. On the other hand, colour displays of computer-aided design (CAD) systems decrease substantially in visibility so that most users prefer to dim the artificial lighting or even to switch it off, and, in addition, to keep the daylight out of their working area.

Possible remedies

Changing illuminance levels. Since 1974, numerous studies have been performed which led to recommendations for reducing illuminance at the workplace. However, these recommendations were mostly based on studies with unsatisfactory screens. The recommended levels were between 100 lux and 1,000 lx, and generally, levels well below the recommendations of the existing standards for office lighting (e.g., 200 lx or 300 to 500 lx) have been discussed.

When positive screens with a luminance of approximately 100 cd/m^2 brightness and some kind of efficient anti-glare treatment are used, the utilization of a VDU does not limit the acceptable illuminance level, since users find illuminance levels up to 1,500 lx acceptable, a value which is very rare in working areas.

If the relevant characteristics of the VDUs do not allow comfortable working under normal office lighting, as can occur when working with storage tubes, microimage readers, colour screens etc., the visual conditions can be improved substantially by introducing two-component lighting. Two-component lighting is a combination of indirect room lighting (secondary effect) and direct task lighting. Both components should be controllable by the users.

Controlling glare on screens. Controlling glare on screens is a difficult task since almost all remedies that improve the visual conditions are likely to impair some other important characteristic of the display. Some remedies, proposed for many years, such as mesh filters, remove reflections from the displays but they also impair the legibility of the display. Low luminance luminaires cause less reflected glare on screens, but the quality of such lighting generally is judged by users to be worse than that of any other type of lighting.

For this reason, any measures (see figure 52.6) should be applied cautiously, and only after analysing the real cause of the annoyance or disturbance. Three possible ways of controlling glare on screens are: selection of the correct location of the screen with respect to glare sources; selection of suitable equipment or addition of elements to it; and use of lighting. The costs of the measures to be taken are of the same order: it costs almost nothing to place screens in such a way as to eliminate reflected glare. However, this may not be possible in all cases; thus, equipment-related measures will be more expensive but may be necessary in various working environments. Glare control by lighting is often recommended by lighting specialists; however, this method is

Figure 52.6 • Strategies for controlling glare on screens.

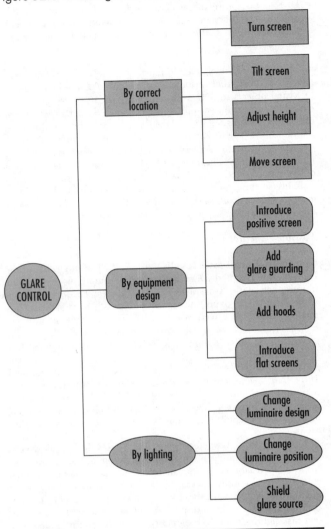

OCULAR AND VISUAL PROBLEMS

Paule Rey and Jean-Jacques Meyer

There have been a comparatively large number of studies devoted to visual discomfort in visual display unit (VDU) workers, many of which have yielded contradictory results. From one survey to another, there are discrepancies in reported prevalence of disorders ranging from practically 0 per cent to 80 per cent or more (Dainoff 1982). Such differences should not be considered too surprising because they reflect the large number of variables which can influence complaints of eye discomfort or disability.

Correct epidemiological studies of visual discomfort must take into account several population variables, such as sex, age, eye deficiencies, or use of lenses, as well as socio-economic status. The nature of the job being carried out with the VDU and the characteristics of the workstation layout and of the work organization are also important and many of these variables are interrelated.

Most often, questionnaires have been used to assess the eye discomfort of VDU operators. The prevalence of visual discomfort differs thus with the content of questionnaires and their statistical analysis. Appropriate questions for surveys concern the extent of symptoms of distress asthenopia suffered by VDU operators. Symptoms of this condition are well known and can include itching, redness, burning and tearing of the eyes. These symptoms are related to the fatigue of the accommodative function in the eye. Sometimes this eye symptoms are accompanied by a headache, with the pain located in the front portion of the head. There may also be disturbances in eye function, with symptoms such as double vision and reduced accommodative power. Visual acuity, itself, however, is rarely depressed, provided the conditions of measurement are carried out with a constant pupil size.

If a survey includes general questions, such as "Do you feel well at the end of the working day?" or "Have you ever had visual problems when working with VDUs?" the prevalence of positive responses may be higher than when single symptoms related to asthenopia are evaluated.

Other symptoms may also be strongly associated to asthenopia. Pains in the neck, shoulders and arms are frequently found. There are two main reasons that these symptoms may occur together with eye symptoms. The muscles of the neck participate in keeping a steady distance between eye and screen in VDU work and VDU work has two main components: screen and keyboard, which means that the shoulders and arms and the eyes are all working at the same time and thus may be subject to similar work-related strains.

User Variables Related to Visual Comfort

Sex and Age

In the majority of surveys, women report more eye discomfort than men. In one French study, for example, 35.6% of women complained of eye discomfort, against 21.8% of men (p ≤ 05 significance level) (Dorard 1988). In another study (Sjödren and Elfstrom 1990) it was observed that while the difference in the degree of discomfort between women (41%) and men (24%) was great, it "was more pronounced for those working 5-8 hours a day than for those working 1-4 hours a day". Such differences are not necessarily sex-related, however, since women and men seldom share similar tasks. For example, in one computer plant studied, when women and men were both occupied in a traditional "woman's job", both sexes displayed the same amount of visual discomfort. Furthermore when women worked in traditional "men's jobs", they did not report more discomfort than men. In

the most expensive but not the most successful way of controlling glare.

The most promising measure at present is the introduction of positive screens (displays with bright background) with an additional anti-glare treatment for the glass surface. Even more successful than this will be the introduction of flat screens with a nearly matt surface and bright background; such screens, however, are not available for general use today.

Adding hoods to displays is the *ultima ratio* of the ergonomists for difficult work environments like production areas, towers of airports or operator cabins of cranes, etc. If hoods are really needed, it is likely that there will be more severe problems with lighting than just reflected glare on visual displays.

Changing luminaire design is mainly accomplished in two ways: first, by reducing the luminance (corresponds to apparent brightness) of parts of the light fittings (so called "VDU lighting"), and secondly, by introducing indirect light instead of direct light. The results of current research show that introducing indirect light yields substantial improvements for users, reduces visual load, and is well accepted by users.

general, regardless of sex, the number of visual complaints among skilled workers who use VDUs on their jobs is much lower than the number of complaints from workers in unskilled, hectic jobs, such as data entry or word processing (Rey and Bousquet 1989). Some of these data are given in table 52.3.

The highest number of visual complaints usually arise in the 40–50-year-old group, probably because this is the time when changes in accommodation ability of the eye are occurring rapidly. However, although older operators are perceived as having more visual complaints than younger workers, and, as a consequence, presbyopia (vision impairment due to ageing) is often cited as the main visual defect associated with visual discomfort at VDU workstations, it is important to consider that there is also a strong association between having acquired advanced skills in VDU work and age. There is usually a higher proportion of older women among unskilled female VDU operators, and younger male workers tend to more often be employed in skilled jobs. Thus before broad generalizations about age and visual problems associated with VDU can be made, the figures should be adjusted to take into account the comparative nature and skill level of the work being done at the VDU.

Eye defects and corrective lenses

In general, about half of all VDU operators display some kind of eye deficiency and most of these people use prescriptive lenses of one type or another. Often VDU user populations do not differ from the working population as far as eye defects and eye correction are concerned. For example, one survey (Rubino 1990) conducted among Italian VDU operators revealed that roughly 46% had normal vision and 38% were nearsighted (myopic), which is consistent with figures observed among Swiss and French VDU operators (Meyer and Bousquet 1990). Estimates of the prevalence of eye defects will vary according to the assessment technique used (Çakir 1981).

Most experts believe that presbyopia itself does not appear to have a significant influence on the incidence of asthenopia (persistent tiredness of the eyes). Rather, the use of unsuitable lenses appears to be likely to induce eye fatigue and discomfort. There is some disagreement about the effects in shortsighted young persons. Rubino has observed no effect while, according to Meyer and Bousquet (1990), myopic operators readily complain of undercorrection for the distance between eye and screen (usually 70 cm). Rubino also has proposed that people who suffer from a deficiency in eye coordination may be more likely to suffer from visual complaints in VDU work.

One interesting observation that resulted from a French study involving a thorough eye examination by ophthalmologists of 275 VDU operators and 65 controls was that 32% of those examined could have their vision improved by good correction. In this study 68% had normal vision, 24% were shortsighted and 8% farsighted (Boissin et al., 1991). Thus, although industrialized countries are, in general, well equipped to provide excellent eye care, eye correction is probably either completely neglected or inappropriate for those working at a VDU. An interesting finding in this study was that more cases of conjunctivitis were found in the VDU operators (48%) than in the controls. Since conjunctivitis and poor eyesight are correlated, this implies that better eye correction is needed.

Physical and Organizational Factors Affecting Visual Comfort

It is clear that in order to assess, correct and prevent visual discomfort in VDU work an approach which takes into account the many different factors described here and elsewhere in this chapter is essential. Fatigue and eye discomfort can be the result of individual physiological difficulties in normal accommodation

and convergence in the eye, from conjunctivitis, or from wearing glasses that are poorly corrected for distance. Visual discomfort can be related to the workstation itself and can also be linked to work organization factors such as monotony and time spent on the job with and without a break. Inadequate lighting, reflections on screen, flicker and too much luminance of characters can also increase the risk of eye discomfort. Figure 52.7 illustrates some of these points.

Many of the appropriate characteristics of workstation layout are described more fully earlier in the chapter.

The best viewing distance for visual comfort which still leaves enough space for the keyboard appears to be about 65 cm. However, according to many experts, such as Akabri and Konz (1991), ideally, "it would be best to determine an individual's dark focus so workstations could be adjusted to specific individuals rather than population means". As far as the characters themselves go, in general, a good rule of thumb is "bigger is better". Usually, letter size increases with the size of the screen, and a compromise is always struck between the readability of letters and the number

Table 52.3 • Prevalence of ocular symptoms in 196 VDU operators according to 4 categories.

Categories	Percentage of symptoms (%)
Females in "female" jobs	81
Males in "female" jobs	75
Males in "male" jobs	68
Females in "male" jobs	65

Source: From Dorard 1988 and Rey and Bousquet 1989.

Figure 52.7 • Factors that increase the risk of eye fatigue among VDU workers.

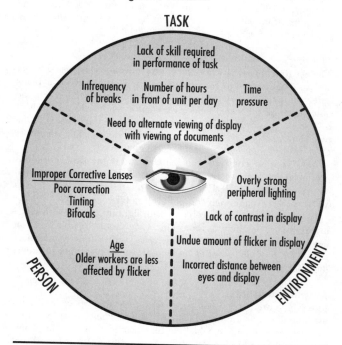

of words and sentences that can be displayed on the screen at one time. The VDU itself should be selected according to the task requirements and should try to maximize user comfort.

In addition to the design of the workstation and the VDU itself is the need to allow the eyes to rest. This is particularly important in unskilled jobs, in which the freedom of "moving around" is generally much lower than in skilled jobs. Data entry work or other activities of the same type are usually performed under time pressure, sometimes even accompanied by electronic supervision, which times operator output very precisely. In other interactive VDU jobs which involve using databases, operators are obliged to wait for a response from the computer and thus must remain at their posts.

Flicker and eye discomfort

Flicker is the change in brightness of the characters on the screen over time and is more fully described above. When characters do not refresh themselves frequently enough, some operators are able to perceive flicker. Younger workers may be more affected since their flicker fusion frequency is higher than that of older people (Grandjean 1987). The rate of flicker increases with increase in brightness, which is one reason why many VDU operators do not commonly make use of the whole range of brightness of the screen that are available. In general a VDU with a refresh rate of at least 70 Hz should "fit" the visual needs of a large proportion of VDU operators.

The sensitivity of the eyes to flicker is enhanced by increased brightness and contrast between the fluctuating area and the surrounding area. The size of the fluctuating area also affects sensitivity because the larger the area to be viewed, the larger the area of the retina that is stimulated. The angle at which the light from the fluctuating area strikes the eye and the amplitude of modulation of the fluctuating area are other important variables.

The older the VDU user, the less sensitive the eye because older eyes are less transparent and the retina is less excitable. This is also true in sick people. Laboratory findings such as these help to explain the observations made in the field. For example, it has been found that operators are disturbed by flicker from the screen when reading paper documents (Isensee and Bennett as quoted in Grandjean 1987), and the combination of fluctuation from the screen and fluctuation of fluorescent light has been found to be particularly disturbing.

Lighting

The eye functions best when the contrast between the visual target and its background is maximum, as for example, with a black letter on white paper. Efficiency is further enhanced when the outer edge of the visual field is exposed to slightly lower levels of brightness. Unfortunately, with a VDU the situation is just the reverse of this, which is one reason that so many VDU operators try to protect their eyes against excess light.

Inappropriate contrasts in brightness and unpleasant reflections produced by fluorescent light, for example, can lead to visual complaints among VDU operators. In one study, 40% of 409 VDU workers made such complaints (Läubli et al., 1989).

In order to minimize problems with lighting, just as with viewing distances, flexibility is important. One should be able to adapt light sources to the visual sensitivity of individuals. Workplaces should be provided to offer individuals the opportunity to adjust their lighting.

Job characteristics

Jobs which are carried out under time pressure, especially if they are unskilled and monotonous, are often accompanied by sensations of general fatigue, which, in turn, can give rise to complaints of visual discomfort. In the authors' laboratory, it was found that visual discomfort increased with the number of accommodative changes the eyes needed to make to carry out the task. This occurred more often in data entry or word processing than in tasks which involved dialogues with the computer. Jobs which are sedentary and provide little opportunity for moving around also provide less opportunity for muscular recovery and hence enhance the likelihood of visual discomfort.

Job organization

Eye discomfort is just one aspect of the physical and mental problems that can be associated with many jobs, as described more fully elsewhere in this chapter. It is not surprising, therefore, to find a high correlation between the level of eye discomfort and job satisfaction. Although night work is still not widely practised in office work, its effects on eye discomfort in VDU work may well be unexpected. This is because, although there are few data as yet available to confirm this, on the one hand, eye capacity during the night shift may be somehow depressed and thus more vulnerable to VDU effects, while on the other hand, the lighting environment is easier to adjust without disturbance from natural lighting, provided that the reflections from fluorescent lamps on dark windows are eliminated.

Individuals who use VDUs to work at home should ensure that they provide themselves with the appropriate equipment and lighting conditions to avoid the adverse environmental factors found in many formal workplaces.

Medical Surveillance

No single, particular hazardous agent has been identified as a visual risk. Asthenopia among VDU operators appears rather to be an acute phenomenon, although there is some belief that sustained strain of accommodation may occur. Unlike many other chronic diseases, misadjustment to VDU work is usually noticed very soon by the "patient", who may be more likely to seek medical care than will workers in other workplace situations. After such visits, spectacles are often prescribed, but unfortunately they are sometimes ill adapted to needs of the workplace which have been described here. It is essential that practitioners be specially trained to care for patients who work with VDUs. A special course, for example, has been created at the Swiss Federal Institute of Technology in Zurich just for this purpose.

The following factors must be taken into consideration in caring for VDU workers. In comparison to traditional office work, the distance between the eye and the visual target, the screen, is usually of 50 to 70 cm and cannot be changed. Therefore, lenses should be prescribed which take this steady viewing distance into account. Bifocal lenses are inappropriate because they will require a painful extension of the neck in order for the user to read the screen. Multifocal lenses are better, but as they limit rapid eye movements, their use can lead to more head movements, producing additional strain.

Eye correction should be as precise as possible, taking into account the slightest visual defects (e.g., astigmatism) and also the viewing distance of the VDU. Tinted glasses which reduce the illumination level in the centre of the visual field should not be prescribed. Partially tinted spectacles are not useful, since eyes at the workplace are always moving in all directions. Offering special spectacles to employees, however, should not mean that further complaints of visual discomfort from workers may be ignored since the complaints could be justified by poor ergonomic design of the workstation and equipment.

It should be said, finally, that the operators who suffer the most discomfort are those who need raised illumination levels for detail work and who, at the same time, have a higher glare sensitivity. Operators with undercorrected eyes will thus display a tendency to get closer to the screen for more light and will be in this way more exposed to flicker.

Screening and secondary prevention

The usual principles of secondary prevention in public health are applicable to the working environment. Screening therefore should be targeted towards known hazards and is most useful for diseases with long latency periods. Screening should take place prior to any evidence of preventable disease and only tests with high sensitivity, high specificity and high predictive power are useful. The results of screening examinations can be used to assess the extent of exposure both of individuals and of groups.

Since no severe adverse effects on the eye have ever been identified in VDU work, and since no hazardous level of radiations associated with visual problems have been detected, it has been agreed that there is no indication that work with VDUs "will cause disease or damage to the eye" (WHO 1987). The ocular fatigue and eye discomfort that have been reported to occur in VDU operators are not the kinds of health effect which generally form the basis for medical surveillance in a secondary prevention programme.

However, pre-employment visual medical examinations of VDU operators are widespread in most member countries of the International Labour Organization, a requirement supported by trade unions and employers (ILO 1986). In many European countries (including France, the Netherlands and the United Kingdom), medical surveillance for VDU operators, including ocular tests, has also been instituted subsequent to the issuing of Directive 90/270/EEC on work with display screen equipment.

If a programme for the medical surveillance of VDU operators is to be set up, the following issues must be addressed in addition to deciding on the contents of the screening programme and the appropriate testing procedures:

- What is the meaning of the surveillance and how should its results be interpreted?
- Are all VDU operators in need of the surveillance?
- Are any ocular effects which are observed appropriate for a secondary prevention programme?

Most routine visual screening tests available to the occupational physician have poor sensitivity and predictive power for eye discomfort associated with VDU work (Rey and Bousquet 1990). Snellen visual testing charts are particularly inappropriate for the measurement of visual acuity of VDU operators and for predicting their eye discomfort. In Snellen charts the visual targets are dark, precise letters on a clear, well illuminated background, not at all like typical VDU viewing conditions. Indeed, because of the inapplicability of other methods, a testing procedure has been developed by the authors (the C45 device) which simulates the reading and lighting conditions of a VDU workplace. Unfortunately, this remains for the time being a laboratory set-up. It is important to realise, however, that screening examinations are not a substitute for a well-designed workplace and good work organization.

Ergonomic Strategies to Reduce Visual Discomfort

Although systematic ocular screening and systematic visits to the eye specialist have not been shown to be effective in reducing visual symptomatology, they have been widely incorporated into occupational health programmes for VDU workers. A more cost-effective strategy could include an intensive ergonomic analysis of both the job and the workplace. Workers with known ocular diseases should try to avoid intensive VDU work as much as possible. Poorly corrected vision is another potential cause of operator complaints and should be investigated if such complaints occur. The improvement of the ergonomics of the workplace,

which could include providing for a low reading angle to avoid a decreased blinking rate and neck extension, and providing the opportunity to rest and to move about on the job, are other effective strategies. New devices, with separate keyboards, allow distances to be adjusted. The VDU may also be made to be moveable, such as by placing it on a mobile arm. Eye strain will thus be reduced by permitting changes in viewing distance which match the corrections to the eye. Often the steps taken to reduce muscular pain in the arms, shoulders and back will at the same time also allow the ergonomist to reduce visual strain. In addition to the design of equipment, the quality of the air can affect the eye. Dry air leads to dry eyes, so that appropriate humidification is needed.

In general the following physical variables should be addressed:

- the distance between the screen and the eye
- the reading angle, which determines the position of the head and the neck
- the distance to walls and windows
- the quality of paper documents (often very poor)
- luminances of screen and surroundings (for artificial and natural lighting)
- flicker effects
- glare sources and reflections
- the humidity level.

Among the organizational variables that should be addressed in improving visual working conditions are:

- content of the task, responsibility level
- time schedules, night work, duration of work
- freedom to "move around"
- full time or part time jobs, etc.

REPRODUCTIVE HAZARDS— EXPERIMENTAL DATA

Ulf Bergqvist

The purpose of the experimental studies described here, using animal models is, in part, to answer the question as to whether extremely low frequency (ELF) magnetic field exposures at levels similar to those around VDU workstations can be shown to affect reproductive functions in animals in a manner that can be equated to a human health risk.

The studies considered here are limited to *in vivo* studies (those performed on live animals) of reproduction in mammals exposed to very low frequency (VLF) magnetic fields with appropriate frequencies, excluding, therefore, studies on the biological effects in general of VLF or ELF magnetic fields. These studies on experimental animals fail to demonstrate unequivocally that magnetic fields, such as are found around VDUs, affect reproduction. Moreover, as can be seen from considering the experimental studies described in some detail below, the animal data do not shed a clear light on possible mechanisms for human reproductive effects of VDU use. These data complement the relative absence of indications of a measurable effect of VDU use on reproductive outcomes from human population studies.

Studies of Reproductive Effects of VLF Magnetic Fields in Rodents

VLF magnetic fields similar to those around VDUs have been used in five teratological studies, three with mice and two with rats. The results of these studies are summarized in table 52.4.

Figure 52.8 • The percentage of female mice with placental resorptions in relation to exposure.

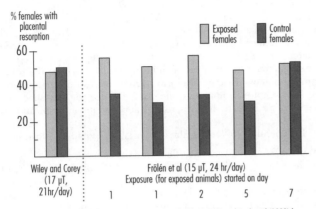

In the study by Wiley and Corey (1992), exposure started at day 1. Frölén and Svedenstål (1993) began at day 1 in two experimental series, and at varying days in the remaining three.

Only one study (Tribukait and Cekan 1987), found an increased number of foetuses with external malformations. Stuchly et al. (1988) and Huuskonen, Juutilainen and Komulainen (1993) both reported a significant increase in the number of foetuses with skeletal abnormalities, but only when the analysis was based on the foetus as a unit. The study by Wiley and Corey (1992) did not demonstrate any effect of magnetic field exposures on placental resorption, or other pregnancy outcomes. Placental resorptions roughly correspond to spontaneous abortions in humans. Finally, Frölén and Svedenstål (1993) performed a series of five experiments. In each experiment, the exposure occurred on a different day. Among the first four experimental subgroups (start day 1–start day 5), there were significant increases in the number of placental resorptions among exposed females. No such effects were seen in the experiment where exposure started on day 7 and which is illustrated in figure 52.8.

The interpretations given by the researchers to their findings include the following. Stuchly and co-workers reported that the abnormalities they observed were not unusual and ascribed the result to "common noise that appears in every teratological evaluation". Huuskonen et al., whose findings were similar to Stuchly et al., were less negative in their appraisal and considered their result to be more indicative of a real effect, but they too remarked in their report that the abnormalities were "subtle and would probably not impair the later development of the foetuses". In discussing their findings in which effects were observed in the early onset exposures but not the later ones, Frölén and Svedenstål suggest that the effects observed could be related to early effects on reproduction, before the fertilized egg is implanted in the uterus.

In addition to the reproductive outcomes, a decrease in white and red blood cells were noted in the highest exposure group in the study by Stuchly and co-workers. (Blood cell counts were not analysed in the other studies.) The authors, while suggesting that this could indicate a mild effect of the fields, also noted that the variations in blood cell counts were "within the normal range". The absence of histological data and the absence of any effects on bone marrow cells made it difficult to evaluate these latter findings.

Interpretation and comparison of studies

Few of the results described here are consistent with one another. As stated by Frölén and Svedenstål, "qualitative conclusions with regard to corresponding effects in human beings and test animals may not be drawn". Let us examine some of the reasoning that could lead to such a conclusion.

The Tribukait findings are generally not considered to be conclusive for two reasons. First, the experiment only yielded positive effects when the foetus was used as the unit of observation for statistical analysis, whereas the data themselves actually indicated a litter-specific effect. Second, there is a discrepancy in the study between the findings in the first and the second part, which implies that the positive findings may be the result of random variations and/or uncontrolled factors in the experiment.

Epidemiological studies investigating specific malformations have not observed an increase in skeletal malformations among children born of mothers working with VDUs—and thus exposed to VLF magnetic fields. For these reasons (foetus-based statistical analysis, abnormalities probably not health-related, and lack of concordance with epidemiological findings), the results—on minor skeletal malformations—are not such as to provide a firm indication of a health risk for humans.

Wiley and Corey (1992) did not observe a placental resorption effect similar to that seen by Frölén and Svedenstål. One reason put forward for this discrepancy is that different strains of mice were used, and the effect could be specific for the strain used by Frölén and Svedenstål. Apart from such a speculated species effect, it is also noteworthy that both females exposed to 17 µT fields and controls in the Wiley study had resorption frequencies similar to those in exposed females in the corresponding Frölén series, whereas most non-exposed groups in the Frölén study had much lower frequencies (see figure 52.8). One hypothetical explanation could be that a higher stress level among the mice in the Wiley study resulted from the handling of animals during the three hour period without exposure. If this is the case, an effect of the magnetic field could perhaps have been "drowned" by a stress effect. While it is difficult to definitely dismiss such a theory from the data provided, it does appear somewhat far-fetched. Furthermore, a "real" effect attributable to the magnetic field would be expected to be observable above such a constant stress effect as the magnetic field exposure increased. No such trend was observed in the Wiley study data.

The Wiley study reports on environmental monitoring and on rotation of cages to eliminate the effects of uncontrolled factors which might vary within the room environment itself, as magnetic fields can, while the Frölén study does not. Thus, control of "other factors" is at least better documented in the Wiley study. Hypothetically, uncontrolled factors that were not randomized

Technical background

Units of observation

When statistically evaluating studies on mammals, consideration must be given to at least one aspect of the (often unknown) mechanism. If the exposure affects the mother—which in turn affects the foetuses in the litter, it is the status of the litter as a whole which should be used as the unit of observation (the effect which is being observed and measured), since the individual outcomes among litter-mates are not independent. If, on the other hand, it is hypothesized that the exposure acts directly and independently on the individual foetuses within the litter, then one can appropriately use the foetus as a unit for statistical evaluation. The usual practice is to count the litter as the unit of observation, unless evidence is available that the effect of the exposure on one foetus is independent of the effect on the other foetuses in the litter.

Table 52.4 • Teratological studies with rats or mice exposed to 18-20 kHz saw-tooth formed magnetic fields.

Study	Subject[1]	Magnetic field exposure			Results[4]
		Frequency	Amplitude[2]	Duration[3]	
Tribukait and Cekan (1987)	76 litters of mice (C3H)	20 kHz	1 μT, 15 μT	Exposed to day 14 of pregnancy	Significant increase in external malformation; *only if foetus is used as the unit of observation; and only in the first half of the experiment;* no difference as to resorption or foetal death.
Stuchly et al. (1988)	20 litters of rats (SD)	18 kHz	5.7μT, 23 μT, 66μT	Exposed throughout pregnancy	Significant increase in minor skeletal malformations; *only if foetus is used as the unit of observation;* some decrease in blood cell concentrations no difference as to resorption, nor as to other types of malformations
Wiley and Corey (1992)	144 litters of mice (CD-1)	20 kHz	3.6 μT, 17μT, 200 μT	Exposed throughout pregnancy	No difference as to any observed outcome (malformation, resorption, etc.).
Frölén and Svedenstål (1993)	In total 707 litters of mice (CBA/S)	20 kHz	15 μT	Beginning on various days of pregnancy in different subexperiments	Significant increase in resorption; *only if exposure starts on day 1 to day 5;* no difference as to malformations
Huuskonen, Juutilainen and Komulainen (1993)	72 litters of rats (Wistar)	20 kHz	15 μT	Exposed to day 12 of pregnancy	Significant increase in minor skeletal malformations; *only if foetus is used as the unit of observation;* no difference as to resorption, nor as to other types of malformations.

[1] Total number of litters in the maximum exposure category.
[2] Peak-to-peak amplitude.
[3] Exposure varied from 7 to 24 hours/day in different experiments.
[4] "Difference" refers to statistical comparisons between exposed and unexposed animals, "increase" refers to a comparison of the highest exposed group vs. the unexposed group.

could conceivably offer some explanations. It is also interesting to note that the lack of effect observed in the day 7 series of the Frölén study appears to be due not to a decrease in the exposed groups, but to an increase in the control group. Thus variations in the control group are probably important to consider while comparing the disparate results of the two studies.

Studies of Reproductive Effects of ELF Magnetic Fields in Rodents

Several studies have been performed, mostly on rodents, with 50–80 Hz fields. Details on six of these studies are shown in table 52.5. While other studies of ELF have been carried out, their results have not appeared in the published scientific literature and are generally available only as abstracts from conferences. In general the findings are of "random effects", "no differences observed" and so on. One study, however, found a reduced number of external abnormalities in CD–1 mice exposed to a 20 mT, 50 Hz field but the authors suggested that this might reflect a selection problem. A few studies have been reported on species other than rodents (rhesus monkeys and cows), again apparently without observations of adverse exposure effects.

As can be seen from table 52.5, a wide range of results were obtained. These studies are more difficult to summarize because there are so many variations in exposure regimens, the endpoints under study as well as other factors. The foetus (or the surviving, "culled" pup) was the unit used in most studies. Overall, it is clear that these studies do not show any gross teratogenic effect of magnetic field exposure during pregnancy. As remarked above, "minor skeletal anomalies" do not appear to be of importance when evaluating human risks. The behavioural study results of Salzinger and Freimark (1990) and McGivern and Sokol (1990) are intriguing, but they do not form a basis for indications of

human health risks at a VDU workstation, either from the standpoint of procedures (use of the foetus, and, for McGivern, a different frequency) or of effects.

Summary of specific studies

Behavioural retardation 3–4 months after birth was observed in the offspring of exposed females by Salzinger and McGivern. These studies appear to have used individual offspring as the statistical unit, which may be questionable if the stipulated effect is due to an effect on the mother. The Salzinger study also exposed the pups during the first 8 days after birth, so that this study involved more than reproductive hazards. A limited number of litters was used in both studies. Furthermore, these studies cannot be considered to confirm each other's findings since the exposures varied greatly between them, as can be seen in table 52.5.

Apart from a behavioural change in the exposed animals, the McGivern study noted an increased weight of some male sex organs: the prostate, the seminal vesicles and the epididymis (all parts of the male reproductive system). The authors speculate as to whether this could be linked to stimulation of some enzyme levels in the prostate since magnetic field effects on some enzymes present in the prostate have been observed for 60 Hz.

Huuskonen and co-workers (1993) noted an increase in the number of foetuses per litter (10.4 foetuses/litter in the 50 Hz exposed group vs. 9 foetuses/litter in the control group). The authors, who had not observed similar trends in other studies, downplayed the importance of this finding by noting that it "may be incidental rather than an actual effect of the magnetic field". In 1985 Rivas and Rius reported a different finding with a slightly lower number of live births per litter among exposed versus nonexposed groups. The difference was not statistically signifi-

Table 52.5 • Teratological studies with rats or mice exposed to 15-60 Hz sinusoidal or square pulsed magnetic fields.

Study	Subject[1]	Magnetic field exposure				Results
		Frequency	Amplitude	Description	Exposure duration	
Rivas and Rius (1985)	25 Swiss mice	50 Hz	83 µT, 2.3 mT	Pulsed, 5 ms pulse duration	Before and during pregnancy and offspring growth; total 120 days	No significant differences at birth in any measured parameter; decreased male body weight when adult
Zecca et al. (1985)	10 SD rats	50 Hz	5.8 mT		Day 6-15 of pregnancy, 3 h/day	No significant differences
Tribukait and Cekan (1987)	35 C3H mice	50 Hz	1 µT, 15 µT (peak)	Square wave-forms, 0.5 ms duration	Day 0-14 of pregnancy, 24 h/day	No significant differences
Salzinger and Freimark (1990)	41 off-spring of SD rats. Only male pups used	60 Hz	100 µT (rms). Also electric field exposure.	Uniform circular polarized	Day 0-22 of pregnancy and 8 days after birth, 20 h/day	Lower increase in operant response during training commencing at 90 days of age
McGivern and Sokol (1990)	11 offspring of SD rats. Only male pups used.	15 Hz	800 µT (peak)	Square wave-forms, 0.3 ms duration	Day 15-20 of pregnancy, 2x15 min/day	Territorial scent marking behaviour reduced at 120 days of age. Some organ weight increased.
Huuskonen et al. (1993)	72 Wistar rats	50 Hz	12.6µT (rms)	Sinusoidal	Day 0-12 of pregnancy, 24 h/day	More foetuses/litter. Minor skeletal malformations

[1] Number of animals (mothers) in the highest exposure category given unless otherwise noted.

cant. They carried out the other aspects of their analyses on both a "per foetus" and "per litter" basis. The noted increase in minor skeletal malformations was only seen with the analysis using the foetus as the unit of observation.

Recommendations and Summary
Despite the relative lack of positive, consistent data demonstrating either human or animal reproductive effects, attempts at replications of the results of some studies are still warranted. These studies should attempt to reduce the variations in exposures, methods of analysis and strains of animals used.

In general, the experimental studies performed with 20 kHz magnetic fields have provided somewhat varied results. If adhering strictly to the litter analysis procedure and statistical hypothesis testing, no effects have been shown in rats (although similar nonsignificant findings were made in both studies). In mice, the results have been varied, and no single coherent interpretation of them appears possible at present. For 50 Hz magnetic fields, the situation is somewhat different. Epidemiological studies which are relevant to this frequency are scarce, and one study did indicate a possible risk of miscarriage. By contrast, the experimental animal studies have not produced results with similar outcomes. Overall, the results do not establish an effect of extremely low frequency magnetic fields from VDUs on the outcome of pregnancies. The totality of results fails thus to suggest an effect of VLF or ELF magnetic fields from VDUs on reproduction.

• REPRODUCTIVE EFFECTS— HUMAN EVIDENCE

Claire Infante-Rivard

The safety of visual display units (VDUs) in terms of reproductive outcomes has been questioned since the widespread introduction of VDUs in the work environment during the 1970s. Concern for adverse pregnancy outcomes was first raised as a result of numer-

ous reports of apparent clusters of spontaneous abortion or congenital malformations among pregnant VDU operators (Blackwell and Chang 1988). While these reported clusters were determined to be no more than what could be expected by chance, given the widespread use of VDUs in the modern workplace (Bergqvist 1986), epidemiologic studies were undertaken to explore this question further.

From the published studies reviewed here, a safe conclusion would be that, in general, working with VDUs does not appear to be associated with an excess risk of adverse pregnancy outcomes. However, this generalized conclusion applies to VDUs as they are typically found and used in offices by female workers. If, however, for some technical reason, there existed a small proportion of VDUs which did induce a strong magnetic field, then this general conclusion of safety could not be applied to that special situation since it is unlikely that the published studies would have had the statistical ability to detect such an effect. In order to be able to have generalizable statements of safety, it is essential that future studies be carried out on the risk of adverse pregnancy outcomes associated with VDUs using more refined exposure measures.

The most frequently studied reproductive outcomes have been:

- Spontaneous abortion (10 studies): usually defined as a hospitalized unintentional cessation of pregnancy occurring before 20 weeks of gestation.
- Congenital malformation (8 studies): many different types were assessed, but in general, they were diagnosed at birth.
- Other outcomes (8 studies) such as low birthweight (under 2,500 g), very low birthweight (under 1,500 g), and fecundability (time to pregnancy from cessation of birth control use) have also been assessed. See table 52.6.

Discussion
Evaluations of reported clusters of adverse pregnancy outcomes and VDU use have concluded that there was a high probability that these clusters occurred by chance (Bergqvist 1986). In addition, the results of the few epidemiologic studies which have assessed the relation between VDU use and adverse pregnancy

A Summary of Studies of Reproductive Outcomes

In a case-control study looking at environmental and occupational factors for congenital malformations (Kurppa et al. 1986), 1,475 cases were identified from the Finnish Register of Congenital Malformations during the period between 1976 and 1982 (see table 52.6). A mother whose delivery immediately preceded a case, and was in the same district, served as a control for that case. Exposure to visual display units (VDUs) during the first trimester of pregnancy was assessed using face-to-face interviews conducted either at the clinic during a post-natal visit, or at home. The classification of probable or obvious VDU use was determined by occupational hygienists, blind to the pregnancy outcomes, using job titles and the responses to open-ended questions asking to describe the ordinary work day. There was no evidence of increased risk either among women who reported exposure to VDUs (OR 0.9; 95% CI 0.6 – 1.2), or among women whose job titles indicated possible exposure to VDUs (235 cases/255 controls).

A cohort of Swedish women from three occupational groups was identified through a linkage of occupational census and the Medical Birth Registry during 1980–1981 (Ericson and Källén 1986). A case-base study was conducted within that cohort: cases were 412 women hospitalized for spontaneous abortion and an additional 110 with other outcomes (such as perinatal death, congenital malformations and birthweight below 1500 g). Controls were 1,032 women of similar age who had infants without any of these characteristics, chosen from the same registry. Using crude odds ratios, there was an exposure–response relation between VDU exposure in estimated hours per week (divided into five-hour categories) and pregnancy outcomes (excluding spontaneous abortion). After controlling for smoking and stress, the effect of VDU use on all adverse pregnancy outcomes was not significant.

Focusing on one of three occupational groups identified from a previous study by Ericson a cohort study was conducted using 4,117 pregnancies among social security clerks in Sweden (Westerholm and Ericson 1986). Rates of hospitalized spontaneous abortion, low birthweight, perinatal mortality and congenital malformations in this cohort were compared to rates in the general population. The cohort was divided into five exposure groups defined by trade union and employer representatives. No excesses were found for any of the studied outcomes. The overall relative risk for spontaneous abortion, standardized for mothers' age was 1.1 (95% CI 0.8 – 1.4).

A cohort study involving 1,820 births was conducted among women having ever worked at the Norwegian Postal Giro Centre between 1967–1984 (Bjerkedal and Egenaes 1986) The rates of stillbirth, first-week death, perinatal death, low and very low birthweight, preterm birth, multiple births and congenital malformations were estimated for pregnancies occurring during employment at the centre (990 pregnancies), and pregnancies occurring before or after employment at the centre (830 pregnancies). Rates of adverse pregnancy outcomes were also estimated for three six-year periods, (1967–1972), (1973–1978) and (1979–1984). Introduction of VDUs began in 1972, and were extensively used by 1980. The study concluded that there was no indication that introduction of VDUs in the centre had led to any increase in the rate of adverse pregnancy outcomes.

A cohort of 9,564 pregnancies was identified through logs of urine pregnancy tests from three California clinics in 1981–1982 (Goldhaber, Polen and Hiatt. 1988). Coverage by a Northern California medical plan was a requirement to be eligible for the study. Pregnancy outcomes were found for all but 391 identified pregnancies. From this cohort, 460 of 556 spontaneous abortion cases (<28 weeks), 137 of

156 congenital abnormality cases and 986 of 1,123 controls (corresponding to every fifth normal birth in the original cohort), responded to a retrospective postal questionnaire on chemical environmental exposures including pesticides and VDU use during pregnancy. Odds ratios for women with first trimester VDU use over 20 hours per week, adjusted for eleven variables including age, previous miscarriage or birth defect, smoking and alcohol, were 1.8 (95% CI 1.2 – 2.8) for spontaneous abortion and 1.4 (95% CI 0.7 – 2.9) for birth defects, when compared to working women who did not report using VDUs.

In a study conducted in 11 hospital maternity units in the Montreal area over a two-year period (1982–1984), 56,012 women were interviewed on occupational, personal and social factors after delivery (51,855) or treatment for spontaneous abortion (4,127) (McDonald et al. 1988). These women also provided information on 48,637 previous pregnancies. Adverse pregnancy outcomes (spontaneous abortion, stillbirth, congenital malformations and low birthweight) were recorded for both current and previous pregnancies. Ratios of observed to expected rates were calculated by employment group for current pregnancies and previous pregnancies. Expected rates for each employment group were based on the outcome in the whole sample, and adjusted for eight variables, including age, smoking and alcohol. No increase in risk was found among women exposed to VDUs.

A cohort study comparing rates of threatened abortion, length of gestation, birthweight, placental weight and pregnancy-induced hypertension between women who used VDUs and women who did not use VDUs was carried out among 1,475 women (Nurminen and Kurppa 1988). The cohort was defined as all non-cases from a previous case-control study of congenital malformations. Information about risk factors was collected using face-to-face interviews. The crude and adjusted rate ratios for the outcomes studied did not show statistically significant effects for working with VDUs.

A case-control study involving 344 cases of hospitalized spontaneous abortion occurring at three hospitals in Calgary, Canada, was conducted in 1984–1985 (Bryant and Love 1989). Up to two controls (314 prenatal and 333 postpartum) were chosen among women having delivered or susceptible of delivering at the study hospitals. The controls were matched to each case on the basis of age at last menstrual period, parity, and intended hospital of delivery. VDU use at home and at work, before and during pregnancy, was determined through interviews at the hospitals for postnatal controls and spontaneous abortion, and at home, work, or the study office for prenatal controls. The study controlled for socioeconomic and obstetric variables. VDU use was similar between the cases and both the prenatal controls (OR=1.14; p=0.47) and postnatal controls (OR=0.80; p=0.2).

A case-control study of 628 women with spontaneous abortion, identified through pathology specimen submissions, whose last menstrual period occurred in 1986, and 1,308 controls who had live births, was carried out in one county in California (Windham et al. 1990). The controls were randomly selected, in a two-to-one ratio, among women matched for date of last menstrual period and hospital. Activities during the first 20 weeks of pregnancy were identified through telephone interviews. The participants were also asked about VDU use at work during this period. Crude odds ratios for spontaneous abortion and VDU use less than 20 hours per week (1.2; 95% CI 0.88 – 1.6), and at least 20 hours per week (1.3; 95% CI 0.87 – 1.5), showed little change when adjusted for variables including employment group, maternal age, prior foetal loss, alcohol consumption and smoking. In a further analysis among

Continued on next page.

the women in the control group, risks for low birthweight and intrauterine growth retardation were not significantly elevated.

A case-control study was conducted within a study base of 24,352 pregnancies occurring between 1982 and 1985 among 214,108 commercial and clerical employees in Denmark (Brandt and Nielsen 1990). The cases, 421 respondents among the 661 women who gave birth to children with congenital abnormalities and who were working at the time of pregnancy, were compared to 1,365 respondents among the 2,252 randomly selected pregnancies among working women. Pregnancies, and their outcomes, and employment were determined through a linkage of three databases. Information on VDU use (yes/no/hours per week), and job-related and personal factors such as stress, exposure to solvents, life-style and ergonomic factors were determined through a postal questionnaire. In this study, the use of VDUs during pregnancy was not associated with an increased risk of congenital abnormalities.

Using the same study base as in the previous study on congenital abnormalities (Brandt and Nielsen 1990) 1,371 of 2,248 women whose pregnancies ended in a hospitalized spontaneous abortion were compared to 1,699 randomly selected pregnancies (Nielsen and Brandt 1990). While the study was carried out among commercial and clerical workers, not all of the pregnancies corresponded to times when the women were gainfully employed as commercial or clerical workers. The measure of association used in the study was the ratio of the rate of VDU use among women with a spontaneous abortion to the rate of VDU use among the sample population (representing all pregnancies including those ending in spontaneous abortion). The adjusted rate ratio for any exposure to VDU and spontaneous abortion was 0.94 (95% CI 0.77 – 1.14).

A case-control study was carried out among 573 women who gave birth to children with cardiovascular malformations between 1982 and 1984 (Tikkanen and Heinonen 1991). The cases were identified through the Finnish register of congenital malformations. The control group consisted of 1,055 women, randomly selected among all hospital deliveries during the same time period. VDU use, recorded as never, regular or occasional, was assessed through an interview conducted 3 months after the delivery. No statistically significant association was found between VDU use, at work or at home, and cardiovascular malformations.

A cohort study was carried out among 730 married women who reported pregnancies between 1983 and 1986 (Schnorr et al. 1991). These women were employed as either directory assistance operators or as general telephone operators at two telephone companies in eight southeastern states in the United States. Only the directory assistance operators used VDUs at work. VDU use was determined through company records. Spontaneous abortion cases (foetal loss at 28 weeks' of gestation or earlier) were identified through a telephone interview; birth certificates were later used to compare women's reporting with pregnancy outcomes and when possible, physicians were consulted. Strengths of electric and magnetic fields were measured at very low and extremely low frequencies for a sample of the workstations. The VDU workstations showed higher field strengths than those not using VDUs. No excess risk was found for women who used VDUs during the first trimester of pregnancy (OR 0.93; 95% CI 0.63 – 1.38), and there was no apparent exposure–response relation when looking at time of VDU use per week.

A cohort of 1,365 Danish commercial and clerical workers who were gainfully employed at the time of pregnancy, and identified through a previous study (Brandt and Nielsen 1990; Nielsen and Brandt 1990), was used to study fecundability rates, in relation to VDU use (Brandt and Nielsen 1992). Fecundability was measured as time from stopping birth control use to time of conception, and was determined through a postal questionnaire. This study showed an increased relative risk for prolonged waiting to pregnancy for the subgroup with at least 21 weekly hours of VDU use. (RR 1.61; 95% CI 1.09 – 2.38).

A cohort of 1,699 Danish commercial and clerical workers, consisting of women employed and unemployed at the time of pregnancy, identified through the study reported on in the previous paragraph, was used to study low birthweight (434 cases), preterm birth (443 cases), small for gestational age (749 cases), and infant mortality (160 cases), in relation to VDU use patterns (Nielsen and Brandt 1992). The study failed to show any increased risk for these adverse pregnancy outcomes among women with VDU use.

In a case-control study, 150 nulliparous women with clinically diagnosed spontaneous abortion and 297 nulliparous working women attending a hospital in Reading, England for antenatal care between 1987 and 1989 were interviewed (Roman et al. 1992). The interviews were conducted face to face at the time of their first antenatal visit for the controls, and three weeks after the abortion for women with spontaneous abortion. For women who mentioned VDU use, estimates of time of exposure in hours per week, and calendar time of first exposure were assessed. Other factors such as overtime, physical activity at work, stress and physical comfort at work, age, alcohol consumption and previous miscarriage were also assessed. Women who worked with VDUs had an odds ratio for spontaneous abortion of 0.9 (95% CI 0.6 – 1.4), and there was no relation with the amount of time spent using VDUs. Adjusting for other factors such as maternal age, smoking, alcohol and previous spontaneous abortion did not alter the results.

From a study base of bank clerks and clerical workers in three companies in Finland, 191 cases of hospitalized spontaneous abortion and 394 controls (live births) were identified from Finnish medical registers for 1975 to 1985 (Lindbohm et al. 1992). Use of VDUs was defined using workers' reports and company information. Magnetic field strengths were retrospectively assessed in a laboratory setting using a sample of the VDUs which had been used in the companies. The odds ratio for spontaneous abortion and working with VDUs was 1.1 (95% CI 0.7 – 1.6). When VDU users were separated in groups according to the field strengths for their VDU models, the odds ratio was 3.4 (95% CI 1.4 – 8.6) for workers who had used VDUs with a high magnetic field strength in the extremely low frequency bandwidth (0.9 μT), compared to those working with VDUs with field strength levels below the detection limits (0.4 μT). This odds ratio changed only slightly when adjusted for ergonomic and mental work-load factors. When comparing workers exposed to high magnetic field strengths to workers not exposed to VDUs, the odds ratio was no longer significant.

A study, looking at adverse pregnancy outcomes and fertility, was carried out among female civil servants working for the British Government tax offices (Bramwell and Davidson 1994). Of the 7,819 questionnaires mailed in the first stage of the study, 3,711 were returned. VDU use was determined through this first questionnaire. Exposure was assessed as hours per week of VDU use during pregnancy. One year later, a second questionnaire was sent out to assess the incidence of adverse pregnancy outcomes among these women; 2,022 of the original participants responded. Possible confounders included pregnancy history, ergonomic factors, job stressors, caffeine, alcohol, cigarette and tranquillizer consumption. There was no relationship between exposure as assessed one year previously and the incidence of adverse pregnancy outcomes.

Table 52.6 • VDU use as a factor in adverse pregnancy outcomes.

Objectives		Methods				Results	
Study	Outcome	Design	Cases	Controls	Exposure	OR/RR (95% CI)	Conclusion
Kurppa et al. (1986)	Congenital malformation	Case-control	1, 475	1, 475 same age, same delivery date	Job titles, face-to-face interviews	235 cases, 255 controls, 0.9 (0.6-1.2)	No evidence of increased risk among women who reported exposure to VDU or among women whose job titles indicated possible exposure
Ericson and Källén (1986)	Spontaneous abortion, infant died, malformation, very low birthweight	Case-base	412 22 62 26	1, 032 similar age and from same registry	Job titles	1.2 (0.6-2.3) (applies to pooled outcome)	The effect of VDU use was not statistically significant
Westerholm and Ericson (1986)	Stillbirth, low birthweight, prenatal mortality, malformations	Cohort	7 — 13 43	4, 117	Job titles	1.1 (0.8-1.4) NR(NS) NR(NS) 1.9 (0.9-3.8)	No excesses were found for any of the studied outcomes.
Bjerkedal and Egenaes (1986)	Stillbirth, first week death, prenatal death, low birthweight, very low birthweight, preterm, multiple birth, malformations	Cohort	17 8 25 46 10 97 16 71	1, 820	Employment records	NR(NS) NR(NS) NR(NS) NR(NS) NR(NS) NR(NS) NR(NS) NR(NS)	The study concluded that there was no indication that introduction of VDUs in the centre has led to any increase in the rate of adverse pregnancy outcomes.
Goldhaber, Polen and Hiatt (1988)	Spontaneous abortion, malformations	Case-control	460 137	1, 123 20% of all normal births, same region, same time	Postal questionnaire	1.8 (1.2-2.8) 1.4 (0.7-2.9)	Statistically increased risk for spontaneous abortions for VDU exposure. No excess risk for congenital malformations associated with VDU exposure.
McDonald et al. (1988)	Spontaneous abortion, stillbirth, malformations, low birthweight	Cohort	776 25 158 228		Face-to-face interviews	1.19 (1.09-1.38) current/0.97 previous 0.82 current/0.71 previous 0.94 current/1, 12 (89-1, 43) previous 1.10	No increase in risk was found among women exposed to VDUs.
Nurminen and Kurppa (1988)	Threatened abortion, gestation < 40 weeks, low birthweight, placental weight, hypertension	Cohort	239 96 57 NR NR		Face-to-face interviews	0.9 VDU:30.5%, non: 43.8% VDU:25.4%, non: 23.6% other comparisons (NR)	The crude and adjusted rate ratios did not show statistically significant effects for working with VDUs.
Bryant and Love (1989)	Spontaneous abortion	Case-control	344	647 Same hospital, age, last menstrual period, parity	Face-to-face interviews	1.14 (p = 0.47) prenatal 0.80 (p = 0.2) postnatal	VDU use was similar between the cases and both the prenatal controls and postnatal controls.
Windham et al. (1990)	Spontaneous abortion, low birth weight, intra-uterine growth retardation	Case-control	626 64 68	1,308 same age, same last menstrual period	Telephone interviews	1.2 (0.88-1.6) 1.4 (0.75-2.5) 1.6 (0.92-2.9)	Crude odds ratios for spontaneous abortion and VDU use less than 20 hours per week were 1.2; 95% CI 0.88-1.6, minimum of 20 hours per week were 1.3; 95% CI 0.87-1.5. Risks for low birthweight and intra-uterine growth retardation were not significantly elevated.

Continues on next page.

Table 52.6 • VDU use as a factor in adverse pregnancy outcomes.
Continued

| Objectives | | Methods | | | | Results | |
Study	Outcome	Design	Cases	Controls	Exposure	OR/RR (95% CI)	Conclusion
Brandt and Nielsen (1990)	Congenital malformation	Case-control	421	1,365; 9.2% of all pregnancies, same registry	Postal questionnaire	0.96 (0.76-1.20)	Use of VDUs during pregnancy was not associated with a risk of congenital malformations.
Nielsen and Brandt (1990)	Spontaneous abortion	Case-control	1,371	1,699 9.2% of all pregnancies, same registry	Postal questionnaire	0.94 (0.77-1.14)	No statistically significant risk for spontaneous abortion with VDU exposure.
Tikkanen and Heinonen (1991)	Cardiovascular malformations	Case-control	573	1,055 same time, hospital delivery	Face-to-face interviews	Cases 6.0%, controls 5.0%	No statistically significant association between VDU use and cardiovascular malformation
Schnorr et al. (1991)	Spontaneous abortion	Cohort	136	746	Company records measurement of magnetic field	0.93 (0.63-1.38)	No excess risk for women who used VDUs during first trimester of pregnancy and no apparent exposure — response relation for time of VDU use per week.
Brandt and Nielsen (1992)	Time to pregnancy	Cohort			Postal questionnaire	1.61 (1.09-2.38)	For a time to pregnancy of greater than 13 months, there was an increased relative risk for the group with at least 21 hours of weekly VDU use.
Nielsen and Brandt (1992)	Low birthweight, preterm birth, small for gestational age, infant mortality	Cohort	434 443 749 160		Postal questionnaire	0.88 (0.67-1.66) 1.11 (0.87-1.47) 0.99 (0.62-1.94) NR(NS)	No increase in risk was found among women exposed to VDUs.
Roman et al. (1992)	Spontaneous abortion	Case-control	150	297 nulliparous hospital	Face-to-face interviews	0.9 (0.6-1.4)	No relation to time spent using VDUs.
Lindbohm et al. (1992)	Spontaneous abortion	Case-control	191	394 medical registers	Employment records field measurement	1.1 (0.7-1.6), 3.4 (1.4-8.6)	Comparing workers with exposure to high magnetic field strengths to those with undetectable levels the ratio was 3.4 (95% CI 1.4-8.6)
Bramwell and Davidson (1994)	Spontaneous abortion, fecundability	Cohort	26	–	Postal questionnaire	NR(NS)	No relationship found between VDU use and adverse pregnancy outcomes.

OR = Odds ratio.   CI = Confidence Interval.   RR = Relative risk.   NR = Value not reported.   NS = Not statistically significant.

outcomes have, on the whole, not shown a statistically significant increased risk.

In this review, out of ten studies of spontaneous abortion, only two found a statistically significant increased risk for VDU exposure (Goldhaber, Polen and Hiatt 1988; Lindbohm et al. 1992). None of the eight studies on congenital malformations showed an excess risk associated with VDU exposure. Of the eight studies which looked at other adverse pregnancy outcomes, one has found a statistically significant association between waiting time to pregnancy and VDU use (Brandt and Nielsen 1992).

Although there are no major differences between the three studies with positive findings and those with negative ones, improvements in exposure assessment may have increased the chances of finding a significant risk. Though not exclusive to the positive studies, these three studies attempted to divide the workers into different levels of exposure. If there is a factor inherent in

VDU use which predisposes a woman to adverse pregnancy outcomes, the dose received by the worker may influence the outcome. In addition, the results of the studies by Lindbohm et al. (1992) and Schnorr et al. (1991) suggest that only a small proportion of the VDUs may be responsible for increasing the risk of spontaneous abortion among users. If this is the case, failure to identify these VDUs will introduce a bias that could lead to underestimating the risk of spontaneous abortion among VDU users.

Other factors associated with work on VDUs, such as stress and ergonomic constraints, have been suggested as possible risk factors for adverse pregnancy outcomes (McDonald et al. 1988; Brandt and Nielsen 1992). Failure of many studies to control for these possible confounders may have lead to unreliable results.

While it may be biologically plausible that exposure to high levels of extremely low frequency magnetic fields through some

VDUs carries an increased risk for adverse pregnancy outcomes (Bergqvist 1986), only two studies have attempted to measure these (Schnorr et al. 1991; Lindbohm et al. 1992). Extremely low frequency magnetic fields are present in any environment where electricity is used. A contribution of these fields to adverse pregnancy outcomes could only be detected if there was a variation, in time or in space, of these fields. While VDUs contribute to the overall levels of magnetic fields in the workplace, only a small percentage of the VDUs are thought to have a strong influence on the magnetic fields measured in the working environment (Lindbohm et al. 1992). Only a fraction of the women working with VDUs are thought to be exposed to levels of magnetic radiation above that which is normally encountered in the working environment (Lindbohm et al. 1992). The lack of precision in exposure assessment encountered in counting all VDU users as "exposed" weakens the ability of a study to detect the influence of magnetic fields from VDUs on adverse pregnancy outcomes.

In some studies, women who are not gainfully employed represented a large proportion of the comparison groups for women exposed to VDUs. In this comparison, certain selective processes may have affected the results (Infante-Rivard et al. 1993); for instance, women with severe diseases are selected out of the workforce, leaving healthier women more likely to have favourable reproductive outcomes in the workforce. On the other hand, an "unhealthy pregnant worker effect" is also possible, since women who have children may stop work, whereas those without children and who experience pregnancy loss may continue working. A suggested strategy to estimate the magnitude of this bias is to do separate analyses with and without women not gainfully employed.

● Musculoskeletal Disorders

Gabriele Bammer

Introduction

VDU operators commonly report musculoskeletal problems in the neck, shoulders and upper limbs. These problems are not unique to VDU operators and are also reported by other workers performing tasks which are repetitive or which involve holding the body in a fixed posture (static load). Tasks which involve force are also commonly associated with musculoskeletal problems, but such tasks are not generally an important health and safety consideration for VDU operators.

Among clerical workers, whose jobs are generally sedentary and not commonly associated with physical stress, the introduction into workplaces of VDUs caused work-related musculoskeletal problems to gain in recognition and prominence. Indeed, an epidemic-like increase in reporting of problems in Australia in the mid 1980s and, to a lesser extent, in the United States and the United Kingdom in the early 1990s, has led to a debate about whether or not the symptoms have a physiological basis and whether or not they are work-related.

Those who dispute that musculoskeletal problems associated with VDU (and other) work have a physiological basis generally put forward one of four alternative views: workers are malingering; workers are unconsciously motivated by various possible secondary gains, such as workers' compensation payments or the psychological benefits of being sick, known as compensation neurosis; workers are converting unresolved psychological conflict or emotional disturbance into physical symptoms, that is, conversion disorders; and finally, that normal fatigue is being blown out of proportion by a social process which labels such fatigue as a problem, termed social iatrogenesis. Rigorous examination of the

evidence for these alternative explanations shows that they are not as well supported as explanations which posit a physiological basis for these disorders (Bammer and Martin 1988). Despite the growing evidence that there is a physiological basis for musculoskeletal complaints, the exact nature of the complaints is not well understood (Quintner and Elvey 1990; Cohen et al. 1992; Fry 1992; Helme, LeVasseur and Gibson 1992).

Symptom Prevalence

A large number of studies have documented the prevalence of musculoskeletal problems among VDU operators and these have been predominantly conducted in western industrialized countries. There is also growing interest in these problems in the rapidly industrializing nations of Asia and Latin America. There is considerable inter-country variation in how musculoskeletal disorders are described and in the types of studies carried out. Most studies have relied on symptoms reported by workers, rather than on the results of medical examinations. The studies can be usefully divided into three groups: those which have examined what can be called composite problems, those which have looked at specific disorders and those which have concentrated on problems in a single area or small group of areas.

Composite problems

Composite problems are a mixture of problems, which can include pain, loss of strength and sensory disturbance, in various parts of the upper body. They are treated as a single entity, which in Australia and the United Kingdom is referred to as repetitive strain injuries (RSI), in the United States as cumulative trauma disorders (CTD) and in Japan as occupational cervicobrachial disorders (OCD). A 1990 review (Bammer 1990) of problems among office workers (75% of the studies were of office workers who used VDUs) found that 70 studies had examined composite problems and 25 had found them to occur in a frequency range of between 10 and 29% of the workers studied. At the extremes, three studies had found no problems, while three found that 80% of workers suffer from musculoskeletal complaints. Half of the studies also reported on severe or frequent problems, with 19 finding a prevalence between 10 and 19%. One study found no problems and one found problems in 59%. The highest prevalences were found in Australia and Japan.

Specific disorders

Specific disorders cover relatively well-defined problems such as epicondylitis and carpal tunnel syndrome. Specific disorders have been less frequently studied and found to occur less frequently. Of 43 studies, 20 found them to occur in between 0.2 and 4% of workers. Five studies found no evidence of specific disorders and one found them in between 40–49% of workers.

Particular body parts

Other studies focus on particular areas of the body, such as the neck or the wrists. Neck problems are the most common and have been examined in 72 studies, with 15 finding them to occur in between 40 and 49% of workers. Three studies found them to occur in between 5 and 9% of workers and one found them in more than 80% of workers. Just under half the studies examined severe problems and they were commonly found in frequencies that ranged between 5% and 39%. Such high levels of neck problems have been found internationally, including Australia, Finland, France, Germany, Japan, Norway, Singapore, Sweden, Switzerland, the United Kingdom and the United States. In contrast, only 18 studies examined wrist problems, and seven found them to occur in between 10% and 19% of workers. One found them to occur in between 0.5 and 4% of workers and one in between 40% and 49%.

Table 52.7 • Summary of empirical fieldwork studies which have used multivariate analyses to study the causes of musculoskeletal problems among office workers.

Reference	No./% VDU users	Factors		
		Non-work	Bio-mechanical	Work organisation
Blignault (1985)	146/90%	○	○	●
South Australian Health Commission Epidemiology Branch (1984)	456/81%	●	●	●
Ryan, Mullerworth and Pimble (1984)	52/100%	●	●	●
Ryan and Bampton (1988)	143			
Ellinger et al. (1982)	280	●	●	●
Pot, Padmos and Bowers (1987)	222/100%	not studied	●	●
Sauter et al. (1983b)	251/74%	○	●	●
Stellman et al. (1987a)	1, 032/ 42%	not studied	●	●

○ = non-factor   ● = factor.
Source: Adapted from Bammer 1990.

Causes

It is generally agreed that the introduction of VDUs is often associated with increased repetitive movements and increased static load through increased keystroke rates and (compared with typewriting) reduction in non-keying tasks such as changing paper, waiting for the carriage return and use of correction tape or fluid. The need to watch a screen can also lead to increased static load, and poor placement of the screen, keyboard or function keys can lead to postures which may contribute to problems. There is also evidence that the introduction of VDUs can be associated with reductions in staff numbers and increased workloads. It can also lead to changes in the psychosocial aspects of work, including social and power relationships, workers' responsibilities, career prospects and mental workload. In some workplaces such changes have been in directions which are beneficial to workers. In other workplaces they have led to reduced worker control over the job, lack of social support on the job, "de-skilling", lack of career opportunities, role ambiguity, mental stress and electronic monitoring (see review by Bammer 1987b and also WHO 1989 for a report on a World Health Organization meeting). The association between some of these psychosocial changes and musculoskeletal problems is outlined below. It also seems that the introduction of VDUs helped stimulate a social movement in Australia which led to the recognition and prominence of these problems (Bammer and Martin 1992).

Causes can therefore be examined at individual, workplace and social levels. At the individual level, the possible causes of these disorders can be divided into three categories: factors not related to work, biomechanical factors and work organization factors (see table 52.7). Various approaches have been used to study causes but the overall results are similar to those obtained in empirical field studies which have used multivariate analyses (Bammer 1990). The results of these studies are summarized in tables 52.7 and 52.8. More recent studies also support these general findings.

Factors not related to work

There is very little evidence that factors not related to work are important causes of these disorders, although there is some evidence that people with a previous injury to the relevant area or with problems in another part of the body may be more likely to develop problems. There is no clear evidence for involvement of age and the one study which examined neuroticism found that it was not related.

Biomechanical factors

There is some evidence that working with certain joints of the body at extreme angles is associated with musculoskeletal problems. The effects of other biomechanical factors are less clear-cut, with some studies finding them to be important and others not. These factors are: assessment of the adequacy of the furniture and/or equipment by the investigators; assessment of the adequacy of the furniture and/or equipment by the workers; visual factors in the workplace, such as glare; personal visual factors, such as the use of spectacles; and years on the job or as an office worker (table 52.8).

Organizational factors

A number of factors related to work organization are clearly associated with musculoskeletal problems and are discussed more fully elsewhere is this chapter. Factors include: high work pressure, low autonomy (i.e., low levels of control over work), low peer cohesion (i.e., low levels of support from other workers) which may mean that other workers cannot or do not help out in times of pressure, and low task variety.

The only factor which was studied for which results were mixed was hours using a keyboard (table 52.8). Overall it can be seen that the causes of musculoskeletal problems on the individual level are multifactorial. Work-related factors, particularly work organization, but also biomechanical factors, have a clear role. The specific factors of importance may vary from workplace to workplace and person to person, depending on individual circumstances. For example, the large-scale introduction of wrist rests into a workplace when high pressure and low task variety are hallmarks is unlikely to be a successful strategy. Alternatively, a worker with satisfactory delineation and variety of tasks may still develop problems if the VDU screen is placed at an awkward angle.

The Australian experience, where there was a decline in prevalence of reporting of musculoskeletal problems in the late 1980s, is instructive in indicating how the causes of these problems can be dealt with. Although this has not been documented or researched in detail, it is likely that a number of factors were associated with the decline in prevalence. One is the widespread introduction into workplaces of "ergonomically" designed furniture and equipment. There were also improved work practices including multiskilling and restructuring to reduce pressure and increase autonomy and variety. These often occurred in conjunction with the implementation of equal employment opportunity and industrial democracy strategies. There was also widespread implementation of prevention and early intervention strategies. Less positively, some workplaces seem to have increased their reliance on casual contract workers for repetitive keyboard work. This means that any problems would not be linked to the employer, but would be solely the worker's responsibility. In addition, the intensity of the controversy surrounding these problems led to their stigmatization, so that many workers have become more reluctant to report and claim compensation when they develop symptoms. This was further exacerbated when workers lost cases brought against employers in well-publicized legal proceedings. A decrease in research funding, cessation in publication of incidence

Table 52.8 • Summary of studies showing involvement of factors thought to cause musculoskeletal problems among office workers.

Country[1]	No./% VDU users	Non-work			Biomechanical						Work organization				
		Age	Biol. predisp.	Neuro-ticism	Joint angles	Furn. Equip. Obj.	Furn. Equip. Subj.	Visual work	Visual self	Years in job	Pressure	Auto-nomy	Peer cohesion	Variety	Key-board-ing
Australia	146/ 90%	Ø		Ø		Ø				Ø	○	●	●	●	Ø
Australia	456/ 81%	●	○			■				Ø	○			●	○
Australia	52/143/ 100%	▲			■	■				○	○			●	○
Germany	280	○	○			■	Ø	■		○	○	●		●	○
Netherlands	222/ 100%				■	■		Ø	Ø		○		●	(Ø)	○
United States	251/ 74%	Ø			Ø	■			■		○	●		(Ø)	●
United States	1,032/ 42%				Ø	■	■				○	●		●	

○ = positive association, statistically significant. ● = negative association, statistically significant. ■ = statistically significant association, non-directional. Ø = no statistically significant association.
(Ø) = no variability in the factor in this study. ▲ = the youngest and the oldest had more symptoms.
Empty box implies that the factor was not included in this study.
[1] Matches references in table 52.7.
Source: Adapted from Bammer 1990.

and prevalence statistics and of research papers about these disorders, as well as greatly reduced media attention to the problem all helped shape a perception that the problem had gone away.

Conclusion

Work-related musculoskeletal problems are a significant problem throughout the world. They represent enormous costs at the individual and social levels. There are no internationally accepted criteria for these disorders and there is a need for an international system of classification. There needs to be an emphasis on prevention and early intervention and this needs to be multifactorial. Ergonomics should be taught at all levels from elementary school to university and there need to be guidelines and laws based on minimum requirements. Implementation requires commitment from employers and active participation from employees (Hagberg et al. 1993).

Despite the many recorded cases of people with severe and chronic problems, there is little available evidence of successful treatments. There is also little evidence of how rehabilitation back into the workforce of workers with these disorders can be most successfully undertaken. This highlights that prevention and early intervention strategies are paramount to the control of work-related musculoskeletal problems.

● SKIN PROBLEMS

Mats Berg and Sture Lidén

The first reports of skin complaints among people working with or near VDUs came from Norway as early as 1981. A few cases have also been reported from the United Kingdom, the United States and Japan. Sweden, however, has provided many case reports and public discussion on the health effects of exposure to VDUs was intensified when one case of skin disease in a VDU worker was accepted as an occupational disease by the Swedish National Insurance Board in late 1985. The acceptance of this case for compensation coincided with a marked increase in the number of cases of skin disease that were suspected to be related to work with VDUs. At the Department of Occupational Dermatology at Karolinska Hospital, Stockholm, the caseload increased from seven cases referred between 1979 and 1985, to 100 new referrals from November 1985 to May 1986.

Despite the relatively large number of people who sought medical treatment for what they believed to be VDU-related skin problems, no conclusive evidence is available which shows that the VDUs themselves lead to the development of occupational skin disease. The occurrence of skin disease in VDU-exposed people appears to be coincidental or possibly related to other workplace factors. Evidence for this conclusion is strengthened by the observation that the increased incidence of skin complaints made by Swedish VDU workers has not been observed in other countries, where the mass media debate on the issue has not been as intense. Further, scientific data collected from *provocation studies*, in which patients have been purposely exposed to VDU-related electromagnetic fields to determine whether a skin effect could be induced, have not produced any meaningful data demonstrating a possible mechanism for development of skin problems which could be related to the fields surrounding a VDU.

It is, however, possible that work-related stress could be an important factor that can explain VDU-associated skin complaints. For example, follow-up studies in the office environment of a subgroup of the VDU-exposed office employees being studied for skin problems showed that significantly more people in the group with skin symptoms experienced extreme occupational stress than people without the skin symptoms. A correlation between levels of the stress-sensitive hormones testosterone, pro-

Case Studies: Skin Problems and VDUs

Sweden: 450 patients were referred and examined for skin problems which they attributed to work at VDUs. Only common facial dermatoses were found and no patients had specific dermatoses that could be related to work with VDUs. While most patients felt that they had pronounced symptoms, their visible skin lesions were, in fact, mild according to standard medical definitions and most of the patients reported improvement without drug therapy even though they continued to work with VDUs . Many of the patients were suffering from identifiable contact allergies, which explained their skin symptoms . Epidemiological studies comparing the VDU-work patients to a non-exposed control population with a similar skin status showed no relationship between skin status and VDU work. Finally, a provocation study did not yield any relation between the patient symptoms and electrostatic or magnetic fields from the VDUs (Wahlberg and Lidén 1988; Berg 1988; Lidén 1990; Berg, Hedblad and Erhardt 1990; Swanbeck and Bleeker 1989).In contrast to a few early nonconclusive epidemiological studies (Murray et al. 1981; Frank 1983; Lidén and Wahlberg 1985), a large-scale epidemiological study (Berg, Lidén, and Axelson 1990; Berg 1989) of 3,745 randomly selected office employees, of whom 809 persons were medically examined, showed that while the VDU-exposed employees reported significantly more skin problems than a nonexposed control population of office employees, upon examination, they were not actually found to have no more visible signs or more skin disease.

Wales [UK]: A questionnaire study found no difference between reports of skin problems in VDU workers and a control population (Carmichael and Roberts 1992).

Singapore: A control population of teachers reported significantly more skin complaints than did the VDU users (Koh et al. 1991).

lactin and thyroxin and skin symptoms were observed during work, but not during days off. Thus, one possible explanation for VDU-associated facial skin sensations could be the effects of thyroxin, which causes the blood vessels to dilate (Berg et al. 1992).

● PSYCHOSOCIAL ASPECTS OF VDU WORK

Michael J. Smith and Pascale Carayon

Introduction
Computers provide efficiency, competitive advantages and the ability to carry out work processes that would not be possible without their use. Areas such as manufacturing process control, inventory management, records management, complex systems control and office automation have all benefited from automation. Computerization requires substantial infrastructure support in order to function properly. In addition to architectural and electrical changes needed to accommodate the machines themselves, the introduction of computerization requires changes in employee knowledge and skills, and application of new methods of managing work. The demands placed on jobs which use computers can be very different from those of traditional jobs. Often computerized jobs are more sedentary and may require more thinking and mental attention to tasks, while at the same time require less physical energy expenditure. Production demands can be high, with constant work pressure and little room for decision-making.

The economic advantages of computers at work have overshadowed associated potential health, safety and social problems for workers, such as job loss, cumulative trauma disorders and increased mental stress. The transition from more traditional forms of work to computerization has been difficult in many workplaces, and has resulted in significant psychosocial and sociotechnical problems for the workforce.

Psychosocial Problems Specific to VDUs
Research studies (for example, Bradley 1983 and 1989; Bikson 1987; Westlander 1989; Westlander and Aberg 1992; Johansson and Aronsson 1984; Stellman et al. 1987b; Smith et al. 1981 and 1992a) have documented how the introduction of computers into the workplace has brought substantial changes in the process of work, in social relationships, in management style and in the nature and content of job tasks. In the 1980s, the implementation of the technological changeover to computerization was most often a "top-down" process in which employees had no input into the decisions regarding the new technology or the new work structures. As a result, many industrial relations, physical and mental health problems arose.

Experts disagree on the success of changes that are occurring in offices, with some arguing that computer technology improves the quality of work and enhances productivity (Strassmann 1985), while others compare computers to earlier forms of technology, such as assembly-line production that also make working conditions worse and increase job stress (Moshowitz 1986; Zuboff 1988). We believe that visual display unit (VDU) technology does affect work in various ways, but technology is only one element of a larger work system that includes the individual, tasks, environment and organizational factors.

Conceptualizing Computerized Job Design
Many working conditions jointly influence the VDU user. The authors have proposed a comprehensive job design model which illustrates the various facets of working conditions which can interact and accumulate to produce stress (Smith and Carayon-Sainfort 1989). Figure 52.9 illustrates this conceptual model for the various elements of a work system that can exert loads on workers and may result in stress. At the centre of this model is the individual with his/her unique physical characteristics, perceptions, personality and behaviour. The individual uses technologies to perform specific job tasks. The nature of the technologies, to a

Figure 52.9 • Model of working conditions and their impact on the individual.

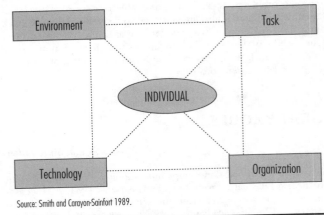

Source: Smith and Carayon-Sainfort 1989.

large extent, determines performance and the skills and knowledge needed by the worker to use the technology effectively. The requirements of the task also affect the required skill and knowledge levels needed. Both the tasks and technologies affect the job content and the mental and physical demands. The model also shows that the tasks and technologies are placed within the context of a work setting that comprises the physical and the social environment. The overall environment itself can affect comfort, psychological moods and attitudes. Finally, the organizational structure of work defines the nature and level of individual involvement, worker interactions, and levels of control. Supervision and standards of performance are all affected by the nature of the organization.

This model helps to explain relationships between job requirements, psychological and physical loads and resulting health strains. It represents a systems concept in which any one element can influence any other element, and in which all elements interact to determine the way in which work is accomplished and the effectiveness of the work in achieving individual and organizational needs and goals. The application of the model to the VDU workplace is described below.

Environment

Physical environmental factors have been implicated as job stressors in the office and elsewhere. General air quality and house-keeping contribute, for example, to sick building syndrome and other stress responses (Stellman et al. 1985; Hedge, Erickson and Rubin 1992.) Noise is a well-known environmental stressor which can cause increases in arousal, blood pressure, and negative psychological mood (Cohen and Weinstein 1981). Environmental conditions that produce sensory disruption and make it more difficult to carry out tasks increase the level of worker stress and emotional irritation are other examples (Smith et al. 1981; Sauter et al. 1983b).

Task

With the introduction of computer technology, *expectations* regarding performance increase. Additional pressure on workers is created because they are expected to perform at a higher level all the time. *Excessive workload* and work pressure are significant stressors for computer users (Smith et al. 1981; Piotrkowski, Cohen and Coray 1992; Sainfort 1990). New types of work demands are appearing with the increasing use of computers. For instance, cognitive demands are likely to be sources of increased stress for VDU users (Frese 1987). These are all facets of job demands.

Positive aspects also exist since computers are able to do many of the simple, repetitive tasks that were previously done manually, which can reduce the repetitiveness of the job, increase the content of the job and make it more meaningful. This is not univer-

Electronic Monitoring of Employee Performance

The use of electronic methods to monitor employee work performance has increased substantially with the widespread use of personal computers which make such monitoring quick and easy. Monitoring provides information which can be used by employers to better manage technological and human resources. With electronic monitoring it is possible to pinpoint bottlenecks, production delays and below average (or below standard) performance of employees in real time. New electronic communication technologies have the capability of tracking the performance of individual elements of a communication system and of pinpointing individual worker inputs. Such work elements as data entry into computer terminals, telephone conversations, and electronic mail messages can all be examined through the use of electronic surveillance.

Electronic monitoring increases management control over the workforce, and may lead to organisational management approaches that are stressful. This raises important issues about the accuracy of the monitoring system and how well it represents worker contributions to the employer's success, the invasion of worker privacy, worker versus technology control over job tasks, and the implications of management styles that use monitored information to direct worker behaviour on the job (Smith and Amick 1989; Amick and Smith 1992; Carayon 1993b). Monitoring can bring about increased production, but it may also produce job stress, absences from work, turnover in the workforce and sabotage. When electronic monitoring is combined with incentive systems for increased production, work-related stress can also be increased (OTA 1987; Smith et al. 1992a). In addition, such electronic performance monitoring raises issues of worker privacy (ILO 1991) and several countries have banned the use of individual performance monitoring.

A basic requirement of electronic monitoring is that work tasks be broken up into activities that can easily be quantified and measured, which usually results in a job design approach that reduces the content of the tasks by removing complexity and thinking, which are replaced by repetitive action. The underlying philosophy is similar to a basic principle of "Scientific Management" (Taylor 1911) that calls for work "simplification."

In one company, for example, a telephone monitoring capability was included with a new telephone system for customer service operators. The monitoring system distributed incoming telephone calls from customers, timed the calls and allowed for supervisor eavesdropping on employee telephone conversations. This system was instituted under the guise of a work flow scheduling tool for determining the peak periods for telephone calls to determine when extra operators would be needed. Instead of using the monitoring system solely for that purpose, management also used the data to establish work performance standards, (seconds per transaction) and to bring disciplinary action against employees with "below average performance." This electronic monitoring system introduced a pressure to perform above average because of fear of reprimand. Research has shown that such work pressure is not conducive to good performance but rather can bring about adverse health consequences (Cooper and Marshall 1976; Smith 1987). In fact, the monitoring system described was found to have increased employee stress and lowered the quality of production (Smith et al. 1992a).

Electronic monitoring can influence worker self-image and feelings of self-worth. In some cases, monitoring could enhance feelings of self-worth if the worker gets positive feedback. The fact that management has taken an interest in the worker as a valuable resource is another possible positive outcome. However, both effects may be perceived differently by workers, particularly if poor performance leads to punishment or reprimand. Fear of negative evaluation can produce anxiety and may damage self-esteem and self-image. Indeed electronic monitoring can create known adverse working conditions, such as paced work, lack of worker involvement, reduced task variety and task clarity, reduced peer social support, reduced supervisory support, fear of job loss, or routine work activities, and lack of control over tasks (Amick and Smith 1992; Carayon 1993).

Michael J. Smith

Figure 52.10 • Keys to reducing isolation and stress.

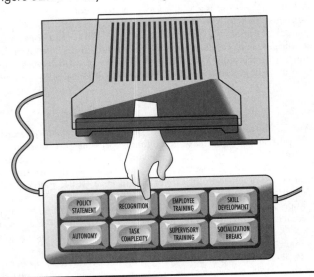

POLICY STATEMENT • RECOGNITION • EMPLOYEE TRAINING • SKILL DEVELOPMENT
AUTONOMY • TASK COMPLEXITY • SUPERVISORY TRAINING • SOCIALIZATION BREAKS

sally true, however, since many new computer jobs, such as data entry, are still repetitive and boring. Computers can also provide performance feedback that is not available with other technologies (Kalimo and Leppanen 1985), which can *reduce ambiguity*.

Some aspects of computerized work have been linked to *decreased control*, which has been identified as a major source of stress for clerical computer users. Uncertainty regarding the duration of computer-related problems, such as breakdown and slowdown, can be a source of stress (Johansson and Aronsson 1984; Carayon-Sainfort 1992). Computer-related problems can be particularly stressful if workers, such as airline reservation clerks, are highly dependent on the technology to perform their job.

Technology

The technology being used by the worker often defines his or her ability to accomplish tasks and the extent of physiological and psychological load. If the technology produces either too much or too little workload, increased stress and adverse physical health outcomes can occur (Smith et al. 1981; Johansson and Aronsson 1984; Ostberg and Nilsson 1985). Technology is changing at a rapid pace, forcing workers to adjust their skills and knowledge continuously to keep up. In addition, today's skills can quickly become obsolete. Technological obsolescence may be due to job de-skilling and impoverished job content or to inadequate skills and training. Workers who do not have the time or resources to keep up with the technology may feel threatened by the technology and may worry about losing their job. Thus, workers' fears of having inadequate skills to use the new technology are one of the main adverse influences of technology, which training, of course, can help to offset. Another effect of the introduction of technology is the fear of job loss due to increased efficiency of technology (Ostberg and Nilsson 1985; Smith, Carayon and Miezio 1987).

Intensive, repetitive, long sessions at the VDU can also contribute to increased ergonomic stress and strain (Stammerjohn, Smith and Cohen 1981; Sauter et al. 1983b; Smith et al. 1992b) and can create visual or musculoskeletal discomfort and disorders, as described elsewhere in the chapter.

Organizational factors

The organizational context of work can influence worker stress and health. When technology requires new skills, the way in

which workers are introduced to the new technology and the organizational support they receive, such as appropriate training and time to acclimatize, has been related to the levels of stress and emotional disturbances experienced (Smith, Carayon and Miezio 1987). The opportunity for growth and promotion in a job (career development) is also related to stress (Smith et al. 1981). Job future uncertainty is a major source of stress for computer users (Sauter et al. 1983b; Carayon 1993a) and the possibility of job loss also creates stress (Smith et al. 1981; Kasl 1978).

Work scheduling, such as shift work and overtime, have been shown to have negative mental and physical health consequences (Monk and Tepas 1985; Breslow and Buell 1960). Shift work is increasingly used by companies that want or need to keep computers running continuously. Overtime is often needed to ensure that workers keep up with the workload, especially when work remains incomplete as a result of delays due to computer breakdown or misfunction.

Computers provide management with the capability to continuously monitor employee performance electronically, which has the potential to create stressful working conditions, such as by increasing work pressure (see the box "Electronic Monitoring"). Negative employee-supervisor relationships and feelings of lack of control can increase in electronically supervised workplaces.

The introduction of VDU technology has affected social relationships at work. Social isolation has been identified as a major source of stress for computer users (Lindström 1991; Yang and Carayon 1993) since the increased time spent working on computers reduces the time that workers have to socialize and receive or give social support. The need for supportive supervisors and co-workers has been well documented (House 1981). Social support can moderate the impact of other stressors on worker stress. Thus, support from colleagues, supervisor or computer staff becomes important for the worker who is experiencing computer-related problems but the computer work environment may, ironically, reduce the level of such social support available.

The individual

A number of personal factors such as personality, physical health status, skills and abilities, physical conditioning, prior experiences and learning, motives, goals and needs determine the physical and psychological effects just described (Levi 1972).

Improving the Psychosocial Characteristics of VDU Work

The first step in making VDU work less stressful is to identify work organization and job design features that can promote psychosocial problems so that they can be modified, always bearing in mind that VDU problems which can lead to job stress are seldom the result of single aspects of the organization or of job design, but rather, are a combination of many aspects of improper work design. Thus, solutions for reducing or eliminating job stress must be comprehensive and deal with many improper work design factors simultaneously. Solutions that focus on only one or two factors will not succeed. (See figure 52.10.)

Improvements in job design should start with the work organization providing a supportive environment for employees. Such an environment enhances employee motivation to work and feelings of security, and it reduces feelings of stress (House 1981). A policy statement that defines the importance of employees within an organization and is explicit on how the organization will provide a supportive environment is a good first step. One very effective means for providing support to employees is to provide supervisors and managers with specific training in methods for being supportive. Supportive supervisors can serve as buffers that "protect" employees from unnecessary organizational or technological stresses.

The content of job tasks has long been recognized as important for employee motivation and productivity (Herzberg 1974; Hackman and Oldham 1976). More recently the relationship between job content and job stress reactions has been elucidated (Cooper and Marshall 1976; Smith 1987). Three main aspects of job content that are of specific relevance to VDU work are task complexity, employee skills and career opportunities. In some respects, these are all related to the concept of developing the motivational climate for employee job satisfaction and psychological growth, which deals with the improvement of employees' intellectual capabilities and skills, increased ego enhancement or self-image and increased social group recognition of individual achievement.

The primary means for enhancing job content is to increase the skill level for performing job tasks, which typically means enlarging the scope of job tasks, as well as enriching the elements of each specific task (Herzberg 1974). Enlarging the number of tasks increases the repertoire of skills needed for successful task performance, and also increases the number of employee decisions made while defining task sequences and activities. An increase in the skill level of the job content promotes employee self-image of personal worth and of value to the organization. It also enhances the positive image of the individual in his or her social work group within the organization.

Increasing the complexity of the tasks, which means increasing the amount of thinking and decision-making involved, is a logical next step that can be achieved by combining simple tasks into sets of related activities that have to be coordinated, or by adding mental tasks that require additional knowledge and computational skills. Specifically, when computerized technology is introduced, new tasks in general will have requirements that exceed the current knowledge and skills of the employees who are to perform them. Thus there is a need to train employees in the new aspects of the tasks so that they will have the skills to perform the tasks adequately. Such training has more than one benefit, since it not only may improve employee knowledge and skills, and thus enhance performance, but may also enhance employee self-esteem and confidence. Providing training also shows the employee that the employer is willing to invest in his or her skill enhancement, and thus promotes confidence in employment stability and job future.

The amount of control that an employee has over the job has a powerful psychosocial influence (Karasek et al. 1981; Sauter, Cooper and Hurrell 1989). Important aspects of control can be defined by the answers to the questions, "What, how and when?" The nature of the tasks to be undertaken, the need for coordination among employees, the methods to be used to carry out the tasks and the scheduling of the tasks can all be defined by answers to these questions. Control can be designed into jobs at the levels of the task, the work unit and the organization (Sainfort 1991; Gardell 1971). At the task level, the employee can be given autonomy in the methods and procedures used in completing the task. At the work-unit level, groups of employees can self-manage several interrelated tasks and the group itself can decide on who will perform particular tasks, the scheduling of tasks, coordination of tasks and production standards to meet organizational goals. At the organization level, employees can participate in structured activities that provide input to management about employee opinions or quality improvement suggestions. When the levels of control available are limited, it is better to introduce autonomy at the task level and then work up the organizational structure, insofar as possible (Gardell 1971).

One natural result of computer automation appears to be an increased workload, since the purpose of the automation is to enhance the quantity and quality of work output. Many organizations believe that such an increase is necessary in order to pay for the investment in the automation. However, establishing the appropriate workload is problematic. Scientific methods have been developed by industrial engineers for determining appropriate work methods and workloads (the performance requirements of jobs). Such methods have been used successfully in manufacturing industries for decades, but have had little application in office settings, even after office computerization. The use of scientific means, such as those described by Kanawaty (1979) and Salvendy (1992), to establish workloads for VDU operators, should be a high priority for every organization, since such methods set reasonable production standards or work output requirements, help to protect employees from excessive workloads, as well as help to ensure the quality of products.

The demand that is associated with the high levels of concentration required for computerized tasks can diminish the amount of social interaction during work, leading to social isolation of employees. To counter this effect, opportunities for socialization for employees not engaged in computerized tasks, and for employees who are on rest breaks, should be provided. Non-computerized tasks which do not require extensive concentration could be organized in such a way that employees can work in close proximity to one another and thus have the opportunity to talk among themselves. Such socialization provides social support, which is known to be an essential modifying factor in reducing adverse mental health effects and physical disorders such as cardiovascular diseases (House 1981). Socialization naturally also reduces social isolation and thus promotes improved mental health.

Since poor ergonomic conditions can also lead to psychosocial problems for VDU users, proper ergonomic conditions are an essential element of complete job design. This is covered in some detail in other articles in this chapter and elsewhere in the *Encyclopaedia*.

Finding Balance

Since there are no "perfect" jobs or "perfect" workplaces free from all psychosocial and ergonomic stressors, we must often compromise when making improvements at the workplace. Redesigning processes generally involves "trade-offs" between excellent working conditions and the need to have acceptable productivity. This requires us to think about how to achieve the best "balance" between positive benefits for employee health and productivity. Unfortunately, since so many factors can produce adverse psychosocial conditions that lead to stress, and since these factors are interrelated, modifications in one factor may not be beneficial if concomitant changes are not made in other related factors. In general, two aspects of balance should be addressed: the balance of the total system and compensatory balance.

System balance is based on the idea that a workplace or process or job is more than the sum of the individual components of the system. The interplay among the various components produces results that are greater (or less) than the sum of the individual parts and determines the potential for the system to produce positive results. Thus, job improvements must take account of and accommodate the entire work system. If an organization concentrates solely on the technological component of the system, there will be an imbalance because personal and psychosocial factors will have been neglected. The model given in figure 52.9 of the work system can be used to identify and understand the relationships between job demands, job design factors, and stress which must be balanced.

Since it is seldom possible to eliminate all psychosocial factors that cause stress, either because of financial considerations, or because it is impossible to change inherent aspects of job tasks, compensatory balance techniques are employed. Compensatory balance seeks to reduce psychological stress by changing aspects of work that can be altered in a positive direction to compensate for those aspects that cannot be changed. Five elements of the work system—physical loads, work cycles, job content, control, and socialization—function in concert to provide the resources for achieving individual and organizational goals through compensatory balance. While we have described some of the potential negative attributes of these elements in terms of job stress, each also has positive aspects that can counteract the negative influences. For instance, inadequate skill to use new technology can be offset by employee training. Low job content that creates repetition and boredom can be balanced by an organizational supervisory structure that promotes employee involvement and control over tasks, and job enlargement that introduces task variety. The social conditions of VDU work could be improved by balancing the loads that are potentially stressful and by considering all of the work elements and their potential for promoting or reducing stress. The organizational structure itself could be adapted to accommodate enriched jobs in order to provide support to the individual. Increased staffing levels, increasing the levels of shared responsibilities or increasing the financial resources put toward worker well-being are other possible solutions.

● ERGONOMIC ASPECTS OF HUMAN-COMPUTER INTERACTION

Jean-Marc Robert

Introduction

The development of effective interfaces to computer systems is the fundamental objective of research on human-computer interactions.

An interface can be defined as the sum of the hardware and software components through which a system is operated and users informed of its status. The hardware components include data entry and pointing devices (e.g., keyboards, mice), information-presentation devices (e.g., screens, loudspeakers), and user manuals and documentation. The software components include menu commands, icons, windows, information feedback, navigation systems and messages and so on. An interface's hardware and software components may be so closely linked as to be inseparable (e.g., function keys on keyboards). The interface includes everything the user perceives, understands and manipulates while interacting with the computer (Moran 1981). It is therefore a crucial determinant of the human-machine relation.

Research on interfaces aims at improving interface utility, accessibility, performance and safety, and usability. For these purposes, utility is defined with reference to the task to be performed. A useful system contains the necessary functions for the completion of tasks users are asked to perform (e.g., writing, drawing, calculations, programming). Accessibility is a measure of an interface's ability to allow several categories of users—particularly individuals with handicaps, and those working in geographically isolated areas, in constant movement or having both hands occupied—to use the system to perform their activities. Performance, considered here from a human rather than a technical viewpoint, is a measure of the degree to which a system improves the efficiency with which users perform their work. This includes the effect of macros, menu short-cuts and intelligent software agents. The safety of a system is defined by the extent to which an interface allows users to perform their work free from the risk of human, equipment, data, or environmental accidents or losses. Finally, usability is defined as the ease with which a system is learned and used. By extension, it also includes system utility and performance, defined above.

Elements of Interface Design

Since the invention of shared-time operating systems in 1963, and especially since the arrival of the microcomputer in 1978, the development of human-computer interfaces has been explosive (see Gaines and Shaw 1986 for a history). The stimulus for this development has been essentially driven by three factors acting simultaneously:

First, the very rapid evolution of computer technology, a result of advances in electrical engineering, physics and computer science, has been a major determinant of user interface development. It has resulted in the appearance of computers of ever-increasing power and speed, with high memory capacities, high-resolution graphics screens, and more natural pointing devices allowing direct manipulation (e.g., mice, trackballs). These technologies were also responsible for the emergence of microcomputing. They were the basis for the character-based interfaces of the 1960s and 1970s, graphical interfaces of the late 1970s, and multi- and hyper-media interfaces appearing since the mid-1980s based on virtual environments or using a variety of alternate-input recognition technologies (e.g., voice-, handwriting-, and movement-detection). Considerable research and development has been conducted in recent years in these areas (Waterworth and Chignel 1989; Rheingold 1991). Concomitant with these advances was the development of more advanced software tools for interface design (e.g., windowing systems, graphical object libraries, prototyping systems) that greatly reduce the time required to develop interfaces.

Second, users of computer systems play a large role in the development of effective interfaces. There are three reasons for this. First, current users are not engineers or scientists, in contrast to users of the first computers. They therefore demand systems that can be easily learned and used. Second, the age, sex, language, culture, training, experience, skill, motivation and interest of individual users is quite varied. Interfaces must therefore be more flexible and better able to adapt to a range of needs and expectations. Finally, users are employed in a variety of economic sectors and perform a quite diverse spectrum of tasks. Interface developers must therefore constantly reassess the quality of their interfaces.

Lastly, intense market competition and increased safety expectations favour the development of better interfaces. These preoccupations are driven by two sets of partners: on the one hand, software producers who strive to reduce their costs while maintaining product distinctiveness that furthers their marketing goals, and on the other, users for whom the software is a means of offering competitive products and services to clients. For both groups, effective interfaces offer a number of advantages:

For software producers:

- better product image
- increased demand for products
- shorter training times
- lower after-sales service requirements
- solid base upon which to develop a product line
- reduction of the risk of errors and accidents
- reduction of documentation.

For users:

- shorter learning phase
- increased general applicability of skills
- improved use of the system
- increased autonomy using the system
- reduction of the time needed to execute a task
- reduction in the number of errors
- increased satisfaction.

Effective interfaces can significantly improve the health and productivity of users at the same time as they improve the quality and reduce the cost of their training. This, however, requires basing interface design and evaluation on ergonomic principles and practice standards, be they guidelines, corporate standards of major system manufacturers or international standards. Over the years, an impressive body of ergonomic principles and guidelines related to interface design has accumulated (Scapin 1986; Smith and Mosier 1986; Marshall, Nelson and Gardiner 1987; Brown 1988). This multidisciplinary corpus covers all aspects of character-mode and graphical interfaces, as well as interface evaluation criteria. Although its concrete application occasionally poses some problems—for example, imprecise terminology, inadequate information on usage conditions, inappropriate presentation—it remains a valuable resource for interface design and evaluation.

In addition, the major software manufacturers have developed their own guidelines and internal standards for interface design. These guidelines are available in the following documents:

- *Apple Human Interface Guidelines* (1987)
- *Open Look* (Sun 1990)
- *OSF/Motif Style Guide* (1990)
- *IBM Common User Access guide to user interface design* (1991)
- *IBM Advanced Interface Design Reference* (1991)
- *The Windows interface: An application design guide* (Microsoft 1992)

These guidelines attempt to simplify interface development by mandating a minimal level of uniformity and consistency between interfaces used on the same computer platform. They are precise, detailed, and quite comprehensive in several respects, and offer the additional advantages of being well-known, accessible and widely used. They are the *de facto* design standards used by developers, and are, for this reason, indispensable.

Furthermore, the International Organization for Standardization (ISO) standards are also very valuable sources of information about interface design and evaluation. These standards are primarily concerned with ensuring uniformity across interfaces, regardless of platforms and applications. They have been developed in collaboration with national standardization agencies, and after extensive discussion with researchers, developers and manufacturers. The main ISO interface design standard is ISO 9241, which describes ergonomic requirements for visual display units. It is comprised of 17 parts. For example, parts 14, 15, 16 and 17 discuss four types of human-computer dialogue—menus, command languages, direct manipulation, and forms. ISO standards should take priority over other design principles and guidelines. The following sections discuss the principles which should condition interface design.

A Design Philosophy Focused on the User

Gould and Lewis (1983) have proposed a design philosophy focused on the video display unit user. Its four principles are:

1. Immediate and continuous attention to users. Direct contact with users is maintained, in order to better understand their characteristics and tasks.
2. Integrated design. All aspects of usability (e.g., interface, manuals, help systems) are developed in parallel and placed under centralized control.
3. Immediate and continuous evaluation by users. Users test the interfaces or prototypes early on in the design phase, under simulated work conditions. Performance and reactions are measured quantitatively and qualitatively.
4. Iterative design. The system is modified on the basis of the results of the evaluation, and the evaluation cycle started again.

These principles are explained in further detail in Gould (1988). Very relevant when they were first published in 1985, fifteen years later they remain so, due to the inability to predict the effectiveness of interfaces in the absence of user testing. These principles constitute the heart of user-based development cycles proposed by several authors in recent years (Gould 1988; Mantei and Teorey 1989; Mayhew 1992; Nielsen 1992; Robert and Fiset 1992).

The rest of this article will analyse five stages in the development cycle that appear to determine the effectiveness of the final interface.

Task Analysis

Ergonomic task analysis is one of the pillars of interface design. Essentially, it is the process by which user responsibilities and activities are elucidated. This in turn allows interfaces compatible with the characteristics of users' tasks to be designed. There are two facets to any given task:

1. The *nominal task*, corresponding to the organization's formal definition of the task. This includes objectives, procedures, quality control, standards and tools.
2. The *real task*, corresponding to the users' decisions and behaviours necessary for the execution of the nominal task.

The gap between nominal and real tasks is inevitable and results from the failure of nominal tasks to take into account variations and unforeseen circumstances in the work flow, and differences in users' mental representations of their work. Analysis of the nominal task is insufficient for a full understanding of users' activities.

Activity analysis examines elements such as work objectives, the type of operations performed, their temporal organization (sequential, parallel) and frequency, the operational modes relied upon, decisions, sources of difficulty, errors and recovery modes. This analysis reveals the different operations performed to accomplish the task (detection, searching, reading, comparing, evaluating, deciding, estimating, anticipating), the entities manipulated (e.g., in process control, temperature, pressure, flow-rate, volume) and the relation between operators and entities. The context in which the task is executed conditions these relations. These data are essential for the definition and organization of the future system's features.

At its most basic, task analysis is composed of data collection, compilation and analysis. It may be performed before, during or after computerization of the task. In all cases, it provides essential guidelines for interface design and evaluation. Task analysis is always concerned with the real task, although it may also study future tasks through simulation or prototype testing. When performed prior to computerization, it studies "external tasks" (i.e., tasks external to the computer) performed with the existing work tools (Moran 1983). This type of analysis is useful even when computerization is expected to result in major modification of the task, since it elucidates the nature and logic of the task, work procedures, terminology, operators and tasks, work tools and sources of difficulty. In so doing, it provides the data necessary for task optimization and computerization.

Task analysis performed during task computerization focuses on "internal tasks", as performed and represented by the computer system. System prototypes are used to collect data at this stage. The focus is on the same points examined in the previous stage, but from the point of view of the computerization process.

Following task computerization, task analysis also studies internal tasks, but analysis now focuses on the final computer system. This type of analysis is often performed to evaluate existing interfaces or as part of the design of new ones.

Hierarchical task analysis is a common method in cognitive ergonomics that has proven very useful in a wide variety of fields, including interface design (Shepherd 1989). It consists of the division of tasks (or main objectives) into sub-tasks, each of which can be further subdivided, until the required level of detail is attained. If data is collected directly from users (e.g., through interviews, vocalization), hierarchical division can provide a portrait of users' mental mapping of a task. The results of the analysis can be represented by a tree diagram or table, each format having its advantages and disadvantages.

User Analysis

The other pillar of interface design is the analysis of *user characteristics*. The characteristics of interest may relate to user age, sex, language, culture, training, technical or computer-related knowledge, skills or motivation. Variations in these individual factors are responsible for differences within and between groups of users. One of the key tenets of interface design is therefore that there is no such thing as the average user. Instead, different groups of users should be identified and their characteristics understood. Representatives of each group should be encouraged to participate in the interface design and evaluation processes.

On the other hand, techniques from psychology, ergonomics and cognitive engineering can be used to reveal information on user characteristics related to perception, memory, cognitive mapping, decision-making and learning (Wickens 1992). It is clear that the only way to develop interfaces that are truly compatible with users is to take into account the effect of differences in these factors on user capacities, limits and ways of operating.

Ergonomic studies of interfaces have focused almost exclusively on users' perceptual, cognitive and motor skills, rather than on affective, social or attitudinal factors, although work in the latter fields has become more popular in recent years. (For an integrated view of humans as information-processing systems see Rasmussen 1986; for a review of user-related factors to consider when designing interfaces see Thimbleby 1990 and Mayhew 1992). The following paragraphs review the four main user-related characteristics that should be taken into account during interface design.

Mental representation

The mental models users construct of the systems they use reflect the manner in which they receive and understand these systems. These models therefore vary as a function of users' knowledge and experience (Hutchins 1989). In order to minimize the learning curve and facilitate system use, the conceptual model upon which a system is based should be similar to users' mental representation of it. It should be recognized however that these two models are never identical. The mental model is characterized by the very fact that it is personal (Rich 1983), incomplete, variable from one part of the system to another, possibly in error on some points and in constant evolution. It plays a minor role in routine tasks but a major one in non-routine ones and during diagnosis of problems (Young 1981). In the latter cases, users will perform poorly in the absence of an adequate mental model. The challenge for interface designers is to design systems whose interaction with users will induce the latter to form mental models similar to the system's conceptual model.

Learning

Analogy plays a large role in user learning (Rumelhart and Norman 1983). For this reason, the use of appropriate analogies or metaphors in the interface facilitates learning, by maximizing the transfer of knowledge from known situations or systems. Analogies and metaphors play a role in many parts of the interface, including the names of commands and menus, symbols, icons, codes (e.g., shape, colour) and messages. When pertinent, they greatly contribute to rendering interfaces natural and more transparent to users. On the other hand, when they are irrelevant, they can hinder users (Halasz and Moran 1982). To date, the two metaphors used in graphical interfaces are the *desktop* and, to a lesser extent, the *room*.

Users generally prefer to learn new software by using it immediately rather than by reading or taking a course—they prefer action-based learning in which they are cognitively active. This type of learning does, however, present a few problems for users (Carroll and Rosson 1988; Robert 1989). It demands an interface structure which is compatible, transparent, consistent, flexible, natural-appearing and fault tolerant, and a feature set which ensures usability, feedback, help systems, navigational aides and error handling (in this context, "errors" refer to actions that users wish to undo). Effective interfaces give users some autonomy during exploration.

Developing knowledge

User knowledge develops with increasing experience, but tends to plateau rapidly. This means that interfaces must be flexible and capable of responding simultaneously to the needs of users with different levels of knowledge. Ideally, they should also be context sensitive and provide personalized help. The EdCoach system, developed by Desmarais, Giroux and Larochelle (1993) is such an interface. Classification of users into beginner, intermediate and expert categories is inadequate for the purpose of interface design, since these definitions are too static and do not account for individual variations. Information technology capable of responding to the needs of different types of users is now available, albeit at the research, rather than commercial, level (Egan 1988). The current rage for performance-support systems suggests intense development of these systems in coming years.

Unavoidable errors

Finally, it should be recognized that users make mistakes when using systems, regardless of their skill level or the quality of the system. A recent German study by Broadbeck et al. (1993) revealed that at least 10% of the time spent by white-collar workers working on computers is related to error management. One of the causes of errors is users' reliance on correction rather than prevention strategies (Reed 1982). Users prefer acting rapidly and incurring errors that they must subsequently correct, to working more slowly and avoiding errors. It is essential that these considerations be taken into account when designing human-computer interfaces. In addition, systems should be fault tolerant and should incorporate effective error management (Lewis and Norman 1986).

Needs Analysis

Needs analysis is an explicit part of Robert and Fiset's development cycle (1992), it corresponds to Nielsen's functional analysis and is integrated into other stages (task, user or needs analysis) described by other authors. It consists of the identification, analysis and organization of all the needs that the computer system can satisfy. Identification of features to be added to the system occurs during this process. Task and user analysis, presented above, should help define many of the needs, but may prove inadequate for the definition of new needs resulting from the introduction of new technologies or new regulations (e.g., safety). Needs analysis fills this void.

Needs analysis is performed in the same way as functional analysis of products. It requires the participation of a group of people interested by the product and possessing complementary training, occupations or work experience. This can include future users of the system, supervisors, domain experts and, as required, specialists in training, work organization and safety. Review of the scientific and technical literature in the relevant field of application may also be performed, in order to establish the current state of the art. Competitive systems used in similar or related fields can also be studied. The different needs identified by this analysis are then classified, weighted and presented in a format appropriate for use throughout the development cycle.

Prototyping

Prototyping is part of the development cycle of most interfaces and consists of the production of a preliminary paper or electronic model (or prototype) of the interface. Several books on the role of prototyping in human-computer interaction are available (Wilson and Rosenberg 1988; Hartson and Smith 1991; Preece et al. 1994).

Prototyping is almost indispensable because:

1. Users have difficulty evaluating interfaces on the basis of functional specifications—the description of the interface is too distant from the real interface, and evaluation too abstract. Prototypes are useful because they allow users to see and use the interface and directly evaluate its usefulness and usability.

2. It is practically impossible to construct an adequate interface on the first try. Interfaces must be tested by users and modified, often repeatedly. To overcome this problem, paper or interactive prototypes that can be tested, modified or rejected are produced and refined until a satisfactory version is obtained. This process is considerably less expensive than working on real interfaces.

From the point of view of the development team, prototyping has several advantages. Prototypes allow the integration and visualization of interface elements early on in the design cycle, rapid identification of detailed problems, production of a concrete and common object of discussion in the development team and during discussions with clients, and simple illustration of alternative solutions for the purposes of comparison and internal evaluation of the interface. The most important advantage is, however, the possibility of having users evaluate prototypes.

Inexpensive and very powerful software tools for the production of prototypes are commercially available for a variety of platforms, including microcomputers (e.g., Visual Basic and Visual C++ (™Microsoft Corp.), UIM/X (™Visual Edge Software), HyperCard (™Apple Computer), SVT (™SVT Soft Inc.)). Readily available and relatively easy to learn, they are becoming widespread among system developers and evaluators.

The integration of prototyping completely changed the interface development process. Given the rapidity and flexibility with which prototypes can be produced, developers now tend to reduce their initial analyses of task, users and needs, and compensate for these analytical deficiencies by adopting longer evaluation cycles. This assumes that usability testing will identify problems and that it is more economical to prolong evaluation than to spend time on preliminary analysis.

Evaluation of Interfaces

User evaluation of interfaces is an indispensable and effective way to improve interfaces' usefulness and usability (Nielsen 1993). The interface is almost always evaluated in electronic form, although paper prototypes may also be tested. Evaluation is an iterative process and is part of the prototype evaluation-modification cycle which continues until the interface is judged acceptable. Several cycles of evaluation may be necessary. Evaluation may be performed in the workplace or in usability laboratories (see the special edition of *Behaviour and Information Technology* (1994) for a description of several usability laboratories).

Some interface evaluation methods do not involve users; they may be used as a complement to user evaluation (Karat 1988;

Nielsen 1993; Nielsen and Mack 1994). A relatively common example of such methods consists of the use of criteria such as compatibility, consistency, visual clarity, explicit control, flexibility, mental workload, quality of feedback, quality of help and error handling systems. For a detailed definition of these criteria, see Bastien and Scapin (1993); they also form the basis of an ergonomic questionnaire on interfaces (Shneiderman 1987; Ravden and Johnson 1989).

Following evaluation, solutions must be found to problems that have been identified, modifications discussed and implemented, and decisions made concerning whether a new prototype is necessary.

Conclusion

This discussion of interface development has highlighted the major stakes and broad trends in the field of human-computer interaction. In summary, (a) task, user, and needs analysis play an essential role in understanding system requirements and, by extension, necessary interface features; and (b) prototyping and user evaluation are indispensable for the determination of interface usability. An impressive body of knowledge, composed of principles, guidelines and design standards, exists on human-computer interactions. Nevertheless, it is currently impossible to produce an adequate interface on the first try. This constitutes a major challenge for the coming years. More explicit, direct and formal links must be established between analysis (task, users, needs, context) and interface design. Means must also be developed to apply current ergonomic knowledge more directly and more simply to the design of interfaces.

ERGONOMICS STANDARDS

Introduction

Ergonomics standards can take many forms, such as regulations which are promulgated on a national level, or guidelines and standards instituted by international organizations. They play an important role in improving the usability of systems. Design and performance standards give managers confidence that the systems they buy will be capable of being used productively, efficiently, safely and comfortably. They also provide users with a benchmark by which to judge their own working conditions. In this article we focus on the International Organization for Standardization (ISO) ergonomics standard 9241 (ISO 1992) because it provides important, internationally recognized, criteria for selecting or designing VDU equipment and systems. ISO carries out its work through a series of technical committees, one of which is ISO TC 159 SC4 Ergonomics of Human System Interaction Committee, which is responsible for ergonomics standards for situations in which human beings and technological systems interact. Its members are representatives of the national standards bodies of member countries and meetings involve national delegations in discussing and voting on resolutions and technical documents. The primary technical work of the committee takes place in eight Working Groups (WGs), each of which has responsibility for different work items listed in figure 52.11. This sub-committee has developed ISO 9241.

The work of the ISO has major international importance. Leading manufacturers pay great heed to ISO specifications. Most producers of VDUs are international corporations. It is obvious that the best and most effective solutions to workplace

Case Study: Display Screen Equipment Directive (90/270/EEC)

The Display Screen Directive is one in a series of "daughter" directives dealing with specific aspects of health and safety. The directives form part of the European Union's programme for promoting health and safety in the single market. The "parent" or "Framework" Directive (89/391/EEC) sets out the general principles of the Community's approach to Health and Safety. These common principles include the avoidance of risk, where possible, by eliminating the source of the risk and the encouragement of collective protective measures instead of individual protective measures.

Where risk is unavoidable, it must be properly evaluated by people with the relevant skills and measures must be taken which are appropriate to the extent of the risk. Thus if the assessment shows that the level of risk is slight, informal measures may be entirely adequate. However, where significant risk is identified, then stringent measures must be taken. The Directive itself only placed obligations on Member States of the EU, not on individual employers or manufacturers. The Directive required Member States to transpose the obligations into appropriate national laws, regulations and administrative provisions. These in turn place obligations on employers to ensure a minimum level of health and safety for display screen users.

The main obligations are for employers to:

- Assess the risks arising from the use of display screen workstations and take steps to reduce any risks identified.
- Ensure that new workstations ("first put into service after 1st January 1993") meet the minimum ergonomics requirements set out in an Annex to the Directive. Existing workstations have a further four years to meet the minimum requirements, provided that they are not posing a risk to their users.
- Inform users about the results of the assessments, the actions the employer is taking and their entitlements under the Directive.
- Plan display screen work to provide regular breaks or changes of activity.
- Offer eye tests before display screen use, at regular intervals and if they are experiencing visual problems. If the tests show that they are necessary and normal glasses cannot be used, then special glasses must be provided.
- Provide appropriate health and safety training for users before display screen use or whenever the workstation is "substantially modified".

The intention behind the Display Screen Directive is to specify how workstations should be used rather than how products should be designed. The obligations therefore fall on employers, not on manufacturers of workstations. However, many employers will ask their suppliers to reassure them that their products "conform". In practice, this means little since there are only a few, relatively simple design requirements in the Directive. These are contained in the Annex [not given here] and concern the size and reflectance of the work surface, the adjustability of the chair, the separation of the keyboard and the clarity of the displayed image.

design problems from the international manufacturers' point of view should be agreed upon internationally. Many regional authorities, such as the European Standardization Organization (CEN) have adopted ISO standards wherever appropriate. The Vienna Agreement, signed by the ISO and CEN, is the official instrument which ensures effective collaboration between the two organizations. As different parts of ISO 9241 are approved and published as international standards, they are adopted as Euro-pean standards and become part of EN 29241. Since CEN standards replace national standards in the European Union (EU) and the European Free Trade Agreement (EFTA) Member States, the significance of ISO standards in Europe has grown, and, in turn, has also increased pressure on the ISO to efficiently produce standards and guidelines for VDUs.

User performance standards

An alternative to product standards is to develop user performance standards. Thus, rather than specify a product feature such as character height which it is believed will result in a legible display, standards makers develop procedures for testing directly such characteristics as legibility. The standard is then stated in terms of the user performance required from the equipment and not in terms of how that is achieved. The performance measure is a composite including speed and accuracy and the avoidance of discomfort.

User performance standards have a number of advantages; they are

- relevant to the real problems experienced by users
- tolerant of developments in the technology
- flexible enough to cope with interactions between factors.

However, user performance standards can also suffer a number of disadvantages. They cannot be totally complete and scientifically valid in all cases, but do represent reasonable compromises, which require significant time to obtain the agreement of all the parties involved in standards-setting.

Coverage and Use of ISO 9241

The VDU ergonomics requirements standard, ISO 9241, provides detail on ergonomic aspects of products, and on assessing the ergonomic properties of a system. All references to ISO 9241 also apply to EN 29241. Some parts provide general guidance to be considered in the design of equipment, software and tasks. Other parts include more specific design guidance and requirements relevant to current technology, since such guidance is useful to designers. In addition to product specifications, ISO 9241 emphasizes the need to specify factors affecting user performance, including how to assess user performance in order to judge whether or not a system is appropriate to the context in which it will be used.

ISO 9241 has been developed with office-based tasks and environments in mind. This means that in other specialized environments some acceptable deviation from the standard may be needed. In many cases, this adaptation of the office standard will achieve a more satisfactory result than the "blind" specification or testing of an isolated standard specific to a given situation. Indeed, one of the problems with VDU ergonomics standards is that the technology is developing faster than standards makers can work. Thus it is quite possible that a new device may fail to meet the strict requirements in an existing standard because it approaches the need in question in a way radically different from any that were foreseen when the original standard was written. For example, early standards for character quality on a display assumed a simple dot matrix construction. Newer more legible fonts would have failed to meet the original requirement because they would not have the specified number of dots separating them, a notion inconsistent with their design.

Unless standards are specified in terms of the performance to be achieved, the users of ergonomics standards must allow suppliers to meet the requirement by demonstrating that their solution provides equivalent or superior performance to achieve the same objective.

Figure 52.11 • Technical Working Groups of the Ergonomics of Human System Interaction Technical Committee (ISO TC 159 SC4). ISO 9241: Five working groups broke down the "parts" of the standard to those listed below. This illustration shows the correspondence between the parts of the standard and the various aspects of the workstation with which they are concerned.

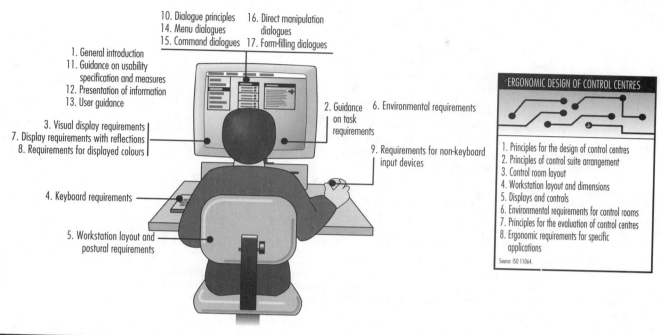

The use of the ISO 9241 standard in the specification and procurement process places display screen ergonomics issues firmly on management's agenda and helps to ensure proper consideration of these issues by both procurer and supplier. The standard is therefore a useful part of the responsible employer's strategy for protecting the health, safety and productivity of display screen users.

General issues

ISO 9241 Part 1 General introduction explains the principles underlying the multipart standard. It describes the user performance approach and provides guidance on how to use the standard and on how conformance to parts of ISO 9241 should be reported.

ISO 9241 Part 2 Guidance on task requirements provides guidance on job and task design for those responsible for planning VDU work in order to enhance the efficiency and the well-being of individual users by applying practical ergonomic knowledge to the design of office VDU tasks. Objectives and characteristics of task design are also discussed (see figure 52.12) and the standard describes how task requirements may be identified and specified within individual organizations and can be incorporated into the organization's system design and implementation process.

Hardware and environmental ergonomics issues

Display screen

ISO 9241 (EN 29241) Part 3 Visual display requirements specifies the ergonomic requirements for display screens which ensure that they can be read comfortably, safely and efficiently to perform office tasks. Although it deals specifically with displays used in offices, the guidance is appropriate to specify for most applications

which require general purpose displays. A user performance test which, once approved, can serve as the basis for performance testing and will become an alternate route to compliance for VDUs.

ISO 9241 Part 7 Display requirements with reflections. The purpose of this part is to specify methods of measurement of glare and reflections from the surface of display screens, including those with surface treatments. It is aimed at display manufacturers who wish to ensure that anti-reflection treatments do not detract from image quality.

ISO 9241 Part 8 Requirements for displayed colours. The purpose of this part is to deal with the requirements for multicolour displays

Figure 52.12 • Guidance and task requirements.

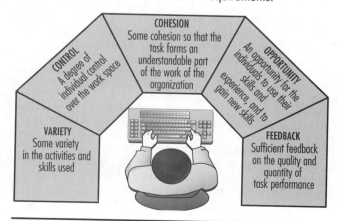

which are largely in addition to the monochrome requirements in *Part 3*, requirements for visual display in general.

Keyboard and other input devices

ISO 9241 Part 4 Keyboard requirements requires that the keyboard should be tiltable, separate from the display and easy to use without causing fatigue in the arms or hands. This standard also specifies the ergonomic design characteristics of an alphanumeric keyboard which may be used comfortably, safely and efficiently to perform office tasks. Again, although *Part 4* is a standard to be used for office tasks, it is appropriate to most applications which require general purpose alphanumeric keyboards. Design specifications and an alternative performance test method of compliance are included.

ISO 9241 Part 9 Requirements for non-keyboard input devices specifies the ergonomic requirements from such devices as the mouse and other pointing devices which may be used in conjunction with a visual display unit. It also includes a performance test.

Workstations

ISO 9241 Part 5 Workstation layout and postural requirements facilitates efficient operation of the VDU and encourages the user to adopt a comfortable and healthy working posture. The requirements for a healthy, comfortable posture are discussed. These include:

- the location of frequently used equipment controls, displays and work surfaces within easy reach
- the opportunity to change position frequently
- the avoidance of excessive, frequent and repetitive movements with extreme extension or rotation of the limbs or trunk
- support for the back allowing an angle of 90 degrees to 110 degrees between back and thighs.

The characteristics of the workplace which promote a healthy and comfortable posture are identified and design guidelines given.

Working environments

ISO 9241 Part 6 Environmental requirements specifies the ergonomic requirements for the visual display unit working environment which will provide the user with comfortable, safe and productive working conditions. It covers the visual, acoustic and thermal environments. The objective is to provide a working environment which should facilitate efficient operation of the VDU and provide the user with comfortable working conditions.

The characteristics of the working environment which influence efficient operation and user comfort are identified, and design guidelines presented. Even when it is possible to control the working environment within strict limits, individuals will differ in their judgements of its acceptability, partly because individuals vary in their preferences and partly because different tasks may require quite different environments. For example, users who sit at VDUs for prolonged periods are far more sensitive to draughts than users whose work involves moving about an office and only working at the VDU intermittently.

VDU work often restricts the opportunities that individuals have for moving about in an office and so some individual control over the environment is highly desirable. Care must be taken in common work areas to protect the majority of users from extreme environments which may be preferred by some individuals.

Software ergonomics and dialogue design

ISO 9241 Part 10 Dialogue principles presents ergonomic principles which apply to the design of dialogues between humans and information systems, as follows:

- suitability for the task
- self-descriptiveness
- controllability
- conformity with user expectations
- error tolerance
- suitability for individualization
- suitability for learning.

The principles are supported by a number of scenarios which indicate the relative priorities and importance of the different principles in practical applications. The starting point for this work was the *German DIN 66234 Part 8 Principles of Ergonomic Dialogue Design for Workplaces with Visual Display Units*.

ISO 9241 Part 11 Guidance on usability specification and measures helps those involved in specifying or measuring usability by providing a consistent and agreed framework of the key issues and parameters involved. This framework can be used as part of an ergonomic requirements specification and it includes descriptions of the context of use, the evaluation procedures to be carried out and the criterion measures to be satisfied when the usability of the system is to be evaluated.

ISO 9241 Part 12 Presentation of information provides guidance on the specific ergonomics issues involved in representing and presenting information in a visual form. It includes guidance on ways of representing complex information, screen layout and design and the use of windows. It is a useful summary of the relevant materials available among the substantial body of guidelines and recommendations which already exist. The information is presented as guidelines without any need for formal conformance testing.

ISO 9241 Part 13 User guidance provides manufacturers with, in effect, guidelines on how to provide guidelines to users. These include documentation, help screens, error handling systems and other aids that are found in many software systems. In assessing the usability of a product in practice, real users should take into account the documentation and guidance provided by the supplier in the form of manuals, training and so on, as well as the specific characteristics of the product itself.

ISO 9241 Part 14 Menu dialogues provides guidance on the design of menu-based systems. It applies to text-based menus as well as to pull-down or pop-up menus in graphical systems. The standard contains a large number of guidelines developed from the published literature and from other relevant research. In order to deal with the extreme variety and complexity of menu-based systems, the standard employs a form of "conditional compliance". For each guideline, there are criteria to help establish whether or not it is applicable to the system in question. If it is determined that the guidelines are applicable, criteria to establish whether or not the system meets those requirements are provided.

ISO 9241 Part 15 Command dialogues provides guidance for the design of text-based command dialogues. Dialogues are the familiar boxes which come onto the screen and query the VDU user, such as in a search command. The software creates a "dialogue" in which the user must supply the term to be found, and any other relevant specifications about the term, such as its case or format.

ISO 9241 Part 16 Direct manipulation dialogues deals with the design of direct manipulation dialogues and WYSIWYG (What You See Is What You Get) dialogue techniques, whether provided as the sole means of dialogue or combined with some other dialogue technique. It is envisaged that the conditional compliance developed for *Part 14* may be appropriate for this mode of interaction also.

ISO 9241 Part 17 Form-filling dialogues is in the very early stages of development.

GENERAL HAZARDS

52. VISUAL DISPLAY UNITS

References

Akabri, M and S Konz. 1991. Viewing distance for VDT work. In *Designing For Everyone*, edited by Y Quinnec and F Daniellou. London: Taylor & Francis.

Apple Computer Co. 1987. *Apple Human Interface Guidelines. The Apple Desktop Interface*. Waltham, Mass.: Addison-Wesley.

Amick, BC and MJ Smith. 1992. Stress, computer-based work monitoring and measuring systems: A conceptual overview. *Appl Ergon* 23(1):6-16.

Bammer, G. 1987. How technologic change can increase the risk of repetitive motions injuries. *Seminars Occup Med* 2:25-30.

—. 1990. Review of current knowledge -Musculoskeletal problems. In *Work With Display Units 89: Selected Papers from the Work with Display Units Conference, September 1989, Montreal*, edited by L Berlinguet and D Berthelette. Amsterdam: North Holland.

Bammer, G and B Martin. 1988. The arguments about RSI: An examination. *Community Health Stud* 12:348-358.

—. 1992. Repetition strain injury in Australia: Medical knowledge, social movement and de facto partisanship. *Social Prob* 39:301-319.

Bastien, JMC and DL Scapin. 1993. *Ergonomic criteria for the evaluation of human-computer interfaces*. Technical Report no. 156, Programme 3 Artificial Intelligence, cognitive systems, and man-machine interaction. France: INRIA.

Berg, M. 1988. Skin problems in workers using visual display terminals: A study of 201 patients. *Contact Dermat* 19:335-341.

—. 1989. Facial skin complaints and work at visual display units. Epidemiological, clinical and histopathological studies. *Acta Derm-Venereol* Suppl. 150:1-40.

Berg, M, MA Hedblad, and K Erkhardt. 1990. Facial skin complaints and work at visual display units: A histopathological study. *Acta Derm-Venereol* 70:216-220.

Berg, M, S Lidén, and O Axelson. 1990. Skin complaints and work at visual display units: An epidemiological study of office employees. *J Am Acad Dermatol* 22:621-625.

Berg, M, BB Arnetz, S Lidén, P Eneroth, and A Kallner. 1992. Techno-stress, a psychophysiological study of employees with VDU-associated skin complaints. *J Occup Med* 34:698-701.

Bergqvist, U. 1986. Pregnancy and VDT work -An evaluation of the state of the art. In *Work With Display Units 86: Selected Papers from the International Scientific Conference On Work With Display Units, May 1986, Stockholm*, edited by B Knave and PG Widebäck. Amsterdam: North Holland.

Bikson, TK. 1987. Understanding the implementation of office technology. In *Technology and the Transformation of White-Collar Work*, edited by RE Kraut. Hillsdale, NJ: Erlbaum Associates.

Bjerkedal, T and J Egenaes. 1986. Video display terminals and birth defects. A study of pregnancy outcomes of employees of the Postal-Giro-Center, Oslo, Norway. In *Work With Display Units 86: Selected Papers from the International Scientific Conference On Work With Display Units, May 1986, Stockholm*, edited by B Knave and PG Widebäck. Amsterdam: North Holland.

Blackwell, R and A Chang. 1988. Video display terminals and pregnancy. A review. *Brit J Obstet Gynaec* 95:446-453.

Blignault, I. 1985. Psychosocial aspects of occupational overuse disorders. Master of Clinical Psychology Thesis, Department of Psychology, The Australian National University, Canberra ACT.

Boissin, JP, J Mur, JL Richard, and J Tanguy. 1991. Study of fatigue factors when working on a VDU. In

Designing for Everyone, edited by Y Quinnec and F Daniellou. London: Taylor & Francis.

Bradley, G. 1983. Effects of computerization on work environment and health: From a perspective of equality between sexes. *Occup Health Nursing*:35-39.

—. 1989. *Computers and the Psychological Environment*. London: Taylor & Francis.

Bramwell, RS and MJ Davidson. 1994. Visual display units and pregnancy outcome: A prospective study. *J Psychosom Obstet Gynecol* 14(3):197-210.

Brandt, LPA and CV Nielsen. 1990. Congenital malformations among children of women working with video display terminals. *Scand J Work Environ Health* 16:329-333.

—. 1992. Fecundity and the use of video display terminals. *Scand J Work Environ Health* 18:298-301.

Breslow, L and P Buell. 1960. Mortality and coronary heart disease and physical activity on work in California. *J Chron Dis* 11:615-626.

Broadbeck, FC, D Zapf, J Prumper, and M Frese. 1993. Error handling in office work with computers: A field study. *J Occup Organ Psychol* 66:303-317.

Brown, CML. 1988. *Human-Computer Interface Guidelines*. Norwood, NJ: Ablex.

Bryant, HE and EJ Love. 1989. Video display terminal use and spontaneous abortion risk. *Int J Epidemiol* 18:132-138.

Çakir, A. 1981. Belastung und Beanspruchung bei Biuldschirmtätigkeiten. In *Schriften zur Arbeitspsychologie*, edited by M Frese. Bern: Huber.

Çakir, A, D Hart, and TFM Stewart. 1979. *The VDT Manual*. Darmstadt: Inca-Fiej Research Association.

Carayon, P. 1993a. Job design and job stress in office workers. *Ergonomics* 36:463-477.

—. 1993b. Effect of electronic performance monitoring on job design and worker stress: A review of the literature and conceptual model. *Hum Factors* 35(3):385-396.

Carayon-Sainfort, P. 1992. The use of computers in offices: Impact on task characteristics and worker stress. *Int J Hum Comput Interact* 4:245-261.

Carmichael, AJ and DL Roberts. 1992. Visual display units and facial rashes. *Contact Dermat* 26:63-64.

Carroll, JM and MB Rosson. 1988. Paradox of the active user. In *Interfacing Thought. Cognitive Aspects of Human-Computer Interaction*, edited by JM Carroll. Cambridge: Bradford.

Cohen, ML, JF Arroyo, GD Champion, and CD Browne. 1992. In search of the pathogenesis of refractory cervicobrachial pain syndrome. A deconstruction of the RSI phenomenon. *Med J Austral* 156:432-436.

Cohen, S and N Weinstein. 1981. Nonauditory effects of noise on behavior and health. *J Soc Issues* 37:36-70.

Cooper, CL and J Marshall. 1976. Occupational sources of stress: A review of the literature relating to coronary heart disease and mental ill health. *J Occup Psychol* 49:11-28.

Dainoff, MG. 1982. *Occupational Stress Factors in VDT Operation: A Review of Empirical Research in Behavior and Information Technology*. London: Taylor & Francis.

Desmarais, MC, L Giroux, and L Larochelle. 1993. An advice-giving interface based on plan-recognition and user-knowledge assessment. *Int J Man Mach Stud* 39:901-924.

Dorard, G. 1988. *Place et validité des tests ophthalmologiques dans l'étude de la fatigue visuelle engendrée par le travail sur écran*. Grenoble: Faculté de médecine, Univ. de Grenoble.

Egan, DE. 1988. Individual differences in human-computer interaction. In *Handbook of Human-Computer Interaction*, edited by M Helander. Amsterdam: Elsevier.

Ellinger, S, W Karmaus, H Kaupen-Haas, KH Schäfer, G Schienstock, and E Sonn. 1982. *1982 Arbeitsbedingungen, gesundheitsverhalten und rheumatische Erkrankungen*. Hamburg: Medizinische Soziologie, Univ. Hamburg.

Ericson, A and B Källén. 1986. An epidemiological study of work with video screens and pregnancy outcome: II. A case-control study. *Am J Ind Med* 9:459-475.

Frank, AL. 1983. *Effects of Health Following Occupational Exposure to Video Display Terminals*. Lexington, Ky: Department of Preventive Medicine and Environmental Health.

Frese, M. 1987. Human-computer interaction in the office. In *International Review of Industrial and Organizational Psychology*, edited by CL Cooper. New York: Wiley.

Frölén, H and N-M Svedenstål. 1993. Effects of pulsed magnetic fields on the developing mouse embryo. *Bioelectromagnetics* 14:197-204.

Fry, HJH. 1992. Overuse syndrome and the Overuse concept. *Discussion Papers On the Pathology of Work-Related Neck and Upper Limb Disorders and the Implications for Treatment*, edited by G Bammer. Working paper No. 32. Canberra: NCEPH, Australian National Univ.

Gaines, BR and MLG Shaw. 1986. From timesharing to the sixth generation: The development of human-computer interaction. Part I. *Int J Man Mach Stud* 24:1-27.

Gardell, B. 1971. Alienation and mental health in the modern industrial environment. In *Society, Stress, and Disease*, edited by L Levi. Oxford: OUP.

Goldhaber, MK, MR Polen, and RA Hiatt. 1988. The risk of miscarriage and birth defects among women who use visual display terminals during pregnancy. *Am J Ind Med* 13:695-706.

Gould, JD. 1988. How to design usable systems. In *Handbook of Human Computer Interaction*, edited by M Helander. Amsterdam: Elsevier.

Gould, JD and C Lewis. 1983. Designing for usability—Key principles and what designers think. In *Proceedings of the 1983 CHI Conference On Human Factors in Computing Systems, 12 December, Boston*. New York: ACM.

Grandjean, E. 1987. *Ergonomics in Computerized Offices*. London: Taylor & Francis.

Hackman, JR and GR Oldham. 1976. Motivation through the design of work: Test of a theory. *Organ Behav Hum Perform* 16:250-279.

Hagberg, M, Å Kilbom, P Buckle, L Fine, T Itani, T Laubli, H Riihimaki, B Silverstein, G Sjøgaard, S Snook, and E Viikari-Juntura. 1993. Strategies for prevention of work-related musculo-skeletal disorders. *Appl Ergon* 24:64-67.

Halasz, F and TP Moran. 1982. Analogy considered harmful. In *Proceedings of the Conference On Human Factors in Computing Systems*. Gaithersburg, Md.: ACM Press.

Hartson, HR and EC Smith. 1991. Rapid prototyping in human-computer interface development. *Interact Comput* 3(1):51-91.

Hedge, A, WA Erickson, and G Rubin. 1992. Effects of personal and occupational factors on sick building syndrome reports in air-conditioned offices. In *Stress and Well-Being At Work-Assessments and Interventions for Occupational Mental Health*, edited by JC Quick, LR Murphy, and JJ Hurrell Jr. Washington, DC: American Psychological Association.

Helme, RD, SA LeVasseur, and SJ Gibson. 1992. RSI revisited: Evidence for psychological and physiological differences from an age, sex and occupation matched control group. *Aust NZ J Med* 22:23-29.

Herzberg, F. 1974. The wise old Turk. *Harvard Bus Rev* (Sept./Oct.):70-80.

ENCYCLOPAEDIA OF OCCUPATIONAL HEALTH AND SAFETY

REFERENCES   52.35

House, J. 1981. *Work Stress and Social Support*. Reading, Mass.: Addison-Wesley.

Hutchins, EL. 1989. Metaphors for interactive systems. In *The Structure of Multimodal Dialogue*, edited by DG Bouwhuis, MM Taylor, and F Néel. Amsterdam: North Holland.

Huuskonen, H, J Juutilainen, and H Komulainen. 1993. Effects of low-frequency magnetic fields on fetal development in rats. *Bioelectromagnetics* 14(3):205-213.

Infante-Rivard, C, M David, R Gauthier, and GE Rivard. 1993. Pregnancy loss and work schedule during pregnancy. *Epidemiology* 4:73-75.

Institut de recherche en santé et en sécurité du travail (IRSST). 1984. *Rapport du groupe de travail sur les terminaux è écran de visualisation*. Montréal: IRSST.

International Business Machines Corp. (IBM). 1991a. *Systems Application Architecture. Common User Access Guide-Advanced Interface Design Reference*. White Plains, NY.: IBM.

—. 1991b. *Systems Application Architecture. Common User Access Guide to User Interface Design*. White Plains, NY.: IBM.

International Labour Organization (ILO). 1984. *Automation, Work Organisation and Occupational Stress*. Geneva: ILO.

—. 1986. Special issue on visual display units. *Cond Work Dig* .

—. 1989. *Working with Visual Display Units*. Occupational Safety and Health Series, No. 61. Geneva: ILO.

—. 1991. Worker's privacy. Part I: Protection of personal data. *Cond Work Dig* 10:2.

International Organization for Standardization (ISO). 1992. *Ergonomic Requirements for Office Work With Visual Display Terminals (VDTs)*. ISO Standard 9241.Geneva: ISO.

Johansson, G and G Aronsson. 1984. Stress reactions in computerized administrative work. *J Occup Behav* 5:159-181.

Juliussen, E and K Petska-Juliussen. 1994. *The Seventh Annual Computer Industry 1994-1995 Almanac*. Dallas: Computer Industry Almanac.

Kalimo, R and A Leppanen. 1985. Feedback from video display terminals, performance control and stress in text preparation in the printing industry. *J Occup Psychol* 58:27-38.

Kanawaty, G. 1979. *Introduction to Work Study*. Geneva: ILO.

Karasek, RA, D Baker, F Marxer, A Ahlbom, and R Theorell. 1981. Job decision latitude, job demands, and cardiovascular disease. In *Machine-Pacing and Occupational Stress*, edited by G Salvendy and MJ Smith. London: Taylor & Francis.

Karat, J. 1988. Software evaluation methodologies. In *Handbook of Human-Computer Interaction*, edited by M Helander. Amsterdam: Elsevier.

Kasl, SV. 1978. Epidemiological contributions to the study of work stress. In *Stress At Work*, edited by CL Cooper and R Payne. New York: Wiley.

Koh, D, CL Goh, J Jeyaratnam, WC Kee, and CN Ong. 1991. Dermatologic complaints among visual display unit operators and office workers. *Am J Contact Dermatol* 2:136-137.

Kurppa, K, PC Holmberg, K Rantala, T Nurminen, L Saxén, and S Hernberg. 1986. Birth defects, course of pregnancy, and work with video display units. A Finnish case-referent study. In *Work With Display Units 86: Selected Papers from the International Scientific Conference On Work With Display Units, May 1986, Stockholm*, edited by B Knave and PG Widebäck. Amsterdam: North Holland.

Läubli, T, H Nibel, C Thomas, U Schwanninger, and H Krueger. 1989. Merits of periodic visual screening tests in VDU operators. In *Work With Computers*, edited by MJ Smith and G Salvendy. Amsterdam: Elsevier Science.

Levi, L. 1972. *Stress and Distress in Response to Psychosocial Stimuli*. New York: Pergamon Press.

Lewis, C and DA Norman. 1986. Designing for error. In *User Centered System: New Perspectives On Human-Computer Interation*, edited by DA Norman and SW Draper. Hillsdale, NJ.: Erlbaum Associates.

Lidén, C. 1990. Contact allergy: A cause of facial dermatitis among visual display unit operators. *Am J Contact Dermatol* 1:171-176.

Lidén, C and JE Wahlberg. 1985. Work with video display terminals among office employees. *Scand J Work Environ Health* 11:489-493.

Lindbohm, M-L, M Hietanen, P Kygornen, M Sallmen, P von Nandelstadh, H Taskinen, M Pekkarinen, M Ylikoski, and K Hemminki. 1992. Magnetic fields of video display terminals and spontaneous abortion. *Am J Epidemiol* 136:1041-1051.

Lindström, K. 1991. Well-being and computer-mediated work of various occupational groups in banking and insurance. *Int J Hum Comput Interact* 3:339-361.

Mantei, MM and TJ Teorey. 1989. Incorporating behavioral techniques into the systems development life cycle. *MIS Q* September:257-274.

Marshall, C, C Nelson, and MM Gardiner. 1987. Design guidelines. In *Applying Cognitive Psychology to User-Interface Design*, edited by MM Gardiner and B Christie. Chichester, UK: Wiley.

Mayhew, DJ. 1992. *Principles and Guidelines in Software User Interface Design*. Englewood Cliffs, NJ.: Prentice Hall.

McDonald, AD, JC McDonald, B Armstrong, N Cherry, AD Nolin, and D Robert. 1988. Work with visual display units in pregnancy. *Brit J Ind Med* 45:509-515.

McGivern, RF and RZ Sokol. 1990. Prenatal exposure to a low-frequency electromagnetic field demasculinizes adult scent marking behavior and increases accessory sex organ weights in rats. *Teratology* 41:1-8.

Meyer, J-J and A Bousquet. 1990. Discomfort and disability glare in VDT operators. In *Work With Display Units 89*, edited by L Berlinguet and D Berthelette. Amsterdam: Elsevier Science.

Microsoft Corp. 1992. *The Windows Interface: An Application Design Guide*. Redmond, Wash.: Microsoft Corp.

Monk, TH and DI Tepas. 1985. Shift work. In *Job Stress and Blue Collar Work*, edited by CL Cooper and MJ Smith. New York: Wiley.

Moran, TP. 1981. The command language grammar: A representation for the user interface of interaction computer systems. *Int J Man Mach Stud* 15:3-50.

—. 1983. Getting into a system: External-internal task mapping analysis. In *Proceedings of the 1983 CHI Conference On Human Factors in Computing Systems, 12-15 December, Boston*. New York: ACM.

Moshowitz, A. 1986. Social dimensions of office automation. *Adv Comput* 25:335-404.

Murray, WE, CE Moss, WH Parr, C Cox, MJ Smith, BFG Cohen, LW Stammerjohn, and A Happ. 1981. *Potential Health Hazards of Video Display Terminals*. NIOSH Research Report 81-129. Cincinnati, Ohio: National Institute for Occupational Safety and Health (NIOSH).

Nielsen, CV and LPA Brandt. 1990. Spontaneous abortion among women using video display terminals. *Scand J Work Environ Health* 16:323-328.

—. 1992. Fetal growth, preterm birth and infant mortality in relation to work with video display terminals during pregnancy. *Scand J Work Environ Health* 18:346-350.

Nielsen, J. 1992. The usability engineering life cycle. *Computer* (Mar.):12-22.

—. 1993. Iterative user-interface design. *Computer* (Nov.):32-41.

Nielsen, J and RL Mack. 1994. *Usability Inspection Methods*. New York: Wiley.

Numéro spécial sur les laboratoires d'utilisabilité. 1994. . *Behav Inf Technol* .

Nurminen, T and K Kurppa. 1988. Office employment, work with video display terminals, and course of pregnancy. Reference mothers' experience from a Finnish case-referent study of birth defects. *Scand J Work Environ Health* 14:293-298.

Office of Technology Assessment (OTA). 1987. *The Electronic Supervisor: New Technology, New Tensions*. Washington, DC: US Government Printing Office.

Open Software Foundation. 1990. *OSF/Motif Style Guide*. Englewood Cliffs, NJ: Prentice Hall.

Ostberg, O and C Nilsson. 1985. Emerging technology and stress. In *Job Stress and Blue Collar Work*, edited by CL Cooper and MJ Smith. New York: Wiley.

Piotrkowski, CS, BFG Cohen, and KE Coray. 1992. Working conditions and well-being among women office workers. *Int J Hum Comput Interact* 4:263-282.

Pot, F, P Padmos, and A Brouwers. 1987. Determinants of the VDU operator's well-being. In *Work With Display Units 86. Selected Papers from the International Scientific Conference On Work With Display Units, May 1986, Stockholm*, edited by B Knave and PG Widebäck. Amsterdam: North Holland.

Preece, J, Y Rogers, H Sharp, D Benyon, S Holland, and T Carey. 1994. *Human Computer Interaction*. Reading, Mass.: Addison-Wesley.

Quinter, J and R Elvey. 1990. The neurogenic hypothesis of RSI. *Discussion Papers On the Pathology of Work-Related Neck and Upper Limb Disorders and the Implications for Treatment*, edited by G Bammer. Working paper No. 24. Canberra: NCEPH, Australian National Univ.

Rasmussen, J. 1986. *Information Processing and Man-Machine Interaction. An Approach to Cognitive Engineering*. New York: North Holland.

Ravden, SJ and GI Johnson. 1989. *Evaluating Usability of Human-Computer Interfaces: A Practical Approach*. West Sussex, UK: E Horwood.

—. 1992. *Systems Application Architecture: Common Communications Support*. Englewood Cliffs, NJ: Prentice Hall.

Reed, AV. 1982. Error correcting strategies and human interaction with computer systems. In *Proceedings of the Conference On Human Factors in Computing Systems Gaithersburg, Md.: ACM.

Rey, P and A Bousquet. 1989. Visual strain of VDT operators: The right and the wrong. In *Work With Computers*, edited by G Salvendy and MJ Smith. Amsterdam: Elsevier Science.

—. 1990. Medical eye examination strategies for VDT operators. In *Work With Display Units 89*, edited by L Berlinguet and D Berthelette. Amsterdam: Elsevier Science.

Rheingold, HR. 1991. *Virtual Reality*. New York: Touchstone.

Rich, E. 1983. Users are individuals: Individualizing user models. *Int J Man Mach Stud* 18:199-214.

Rivas, L and C Rius. 1985. Effects of chronic exposure to weak electromagnetic fields in mice. *IRCS Med Sci* 13:661-662.

Robert, J-M. 1989. Learning a computer system by unassisted exploration. An example: The Macintosh. In *MACINTER II Man-Computer Interaction Research*, edited by F Klix, N Streitz, Y Warren, and H Wandke. Amsterdam: Elsevier.

Robert, J-M and J-Y Fiset. 1992. Conception et évaluation ergonomiques d'une interface pour un logiciel d'aide au diagnostic: Une étude de cas. *ICO* printemps-été:1-7.

Roman, E, V Beral, M Pelerin, and C Hermon. 1992. Spontaneous abortion and work with visual display units. *Brit J Ind Med* 49:507-512.

Rubino, GF. 1990. Epidemiologic survey of ocular disorders: The Italian multicentric research. In *Work With Display Units 89*, edited by L Berlinguet and D Berthelette. Amsterdam: Elsevier Science.

Rumelhart, DE and DA Norman. 1983. Analogical processes in learning. In *Cognitive Skills and Their Acquisition*, edited by JR Anderson. Hillsdale, NJ: Lawrence Erlbaum.

Ryan, GA and M Bampton. 1988. Comparison of data process operators with and without upper limb symptoms. *Community Health Stud* 12:63-68.

Ryan, GA, JH Mullerworth, and J Pimble. 1984. The prevalence of repetition strain injury in data process operators. In *Proceedings of the 21st Annual Conference of the Ergonomics Society of Australia and New Zealand*. Sydney.

Sainfort, PC. 1990. Job design predictors of stress in automated offices. *Behav Inf Technol* 9:3-16.

—. 1991. Stress, job control and other job elements: A study of office workers. *Int J Ind Erg* 7:11-23.

Salvendy, G. 1992. *Handbook of Industrial Engineering*. New York: Wiley.

Salzinger, K and S Freimark. 1990. Altered operant behavior of adult rats after perinatal exposure to a 60-Hz electromagnetic field. *Bioelectromagnetics* 11:105-116.

Sauter, SL, CL Cooper, and JJ Hurrell. 1989. *Job Control and Worker Health*. New York: Wiley.

Sauter, SL, MS Gottlieb, KC Jones, NV Dodson, and KM Rohrer. 1983a. Job and health implications of VDT use: Initial results of the Wisconsin-NIOSH study. *Commun ACM* 26:284-294.

Sauter, SL, MS Gottlieb, KM Rohrer, and NV Dodson. 1983b. *The Well-Being of Video Display Terminal Users. An Exploratory Study*. Cincinnati, Ohio: NIOSH.

Scapin, DL. 1986. *Guide ergonomique de conception des interfaces homme-machine*. Rapport de recherche no. 77. Le Chesnay, France: INRIA.

Schnorr, TM, BA Grajewski, RW Hornung, MJ Thun, GM Egeland, WE Murray, DL Conover, and WE Halperin. 1991. Video display terminals and the risk of spontaneous abortion. *New Engl J Med* 324:727-733.

Shepherd, A. 1989. Analysis and training in information technology tasks. In *Task Analysis for Human-Computer Interaction*, edited by D Diaper. Chichester: E Horwood.

Shneiderman, B. 1987. *Designing the User Interface: Strategies for Effective Human-Computer Interaction*. Reading, Mass.: Addison-Wesley.

Sjödren, S and A Elfstrom. 1990. Eye discomfort among 4000 VDU users. In *Work With Display Units 89*, edited by L Berlinguet and D Berthelette. Amsterdam: Elsevier Science.

Smith, MJ. 1987. Occupational stress. In *Handbook of Ergonomics/Human Factors*, edited by G Salvendy. New York: Wiley.

Smith, MJ and BC Amick. 1989. Electronic monitoring at the workplace: Implications for employee control and job stress. In *Job Control and Worker Health*, edited by S Sauter, J Hurrel, and C Cooper. New York: Wiley.

Smith, MJ, P Carayon, and K Miezio. 1987. VDT technology: Psychosocial and stress concerns. In *Work With Display Units*, edited by B Knave and PG Widebäck. Amsterdam: Elsevier Science.

Smith, MJ and P Carayon-Sainfort. 1989. A balance theory of job design for stress reduction. *Int J Ind Erg* 4:67-79.

Smith, MJ, BFG Cohen, LW Stammerjohn, and A Happ. 1981. An investigation of health complaints and job stress in video display operations. *Hum Factors* 23:387-400.

Smith, MJ, P Carayon, KH Sanders, S-Y Lim, and D LeGrande. 1992a. Electronic performance monitoring, job design and worker stress. *Appl Ergon* 23:17-27.

Smith, MJ, G Salvendy, P Carayon-Sainfort, and R Eberts. 1992b. Human-computer interaction. In *Handbook of Industrial Engineering*, edited by G Salvendy. New York: Wiley.

Smith, SL and SL Mosier. 1986. *Guidelines for Designing User Interface Software*. Report ESD-TR-278. Bedford, Mass.: MITRE.

South Australian Health Commission Epidemiology Branch. 1984. *Repetition Strain Symptoms and Working Conditions Among Keyboard Workers Engaged in Data Entry or Word Processing in the South Australian Public Service*. Adelaide: South Australian Health Commission.

Stammerjohn, LW, MJ Smith, and BFG Cohen. 1981. Evaluation of work station design factors in VDT operations. *Hum Factors* 23:401-412.

Stellman, JM, S Klitzman, GC Gordon, and BR Snow. 1985. Air quality and ergonomics in the office: Survey results and methodologic issues. *Am Ind Hyg Assoc J* 46:286-293.

—. 1987a. Comparison of well-being among non-machine interactive clerical workers and full-time and part-time VDT users and typists. In *Work With Display Units 86. Selected Papers from the International Scientific Conference On Work With Display Units, May 1986, Stockholm*, edited by B Knave and PG Widebäck. Amsterdam: North Holland.

—. 1987b. Work environment and the well-being of clerical and VDT workers. *J Occup Behav* 8:95-114.

Strassman, PA. 1985. *Information Payoff: The Transformation of Work in the Electronic Age*. New York: Free Press.

Stuchly, M, AJ Ruddick, et al. 1988. Teratological assessment of exposure to time-varying magnetic fields. *Teratology* 38:461-466.

Sun Microsystems Inc. 1990. *Open Look. Graphical User Interface Application Style Guidelines*. Reading, Mass.: Addison-Wesley.

Swanbeck, G and T Bleeker. 1989. Skin problems from visual display units: Provocation of skin symptoms under experimental conditions. *Acta Derm-Venereol* 69:46-51.

Taylor, FW. 1911. *The Principles of Scientific Management*. New York: Norton & Co.

Thimbleby, H. 1990. *User Interface Design*. Chichester: ACM.

Tikkanen, J and OP Heinonen. 1991. Maternal exposure to chemical and physical factors during pregnancy and cardiovascular malformations in the offspring. *Teratology* 43:591-600.

Tribukait, B and E Cekan. 1987. Effects of pulsed magnetic fields on embryonic development in mice. In *Work With Display Units 86: Selected Papers from the International Scientific Conference On Work With Display Units, May 1986, Stockholm*, edited by B Knave and PG Widebäck. Amsterdam: North Holland.

Wahlberg, JE and C Lidén. 1988. Is the skin affected by work at visual display terminals? *Dermatol Clin* 6:81-85.

Waterworth, JA and MH Chignell. 1989. A manifesto for hypermedia usability research. *Hypermedia* 1:205-234.

Westerholm, P and A Ericson. 1986. Pregnancy outcome and VDU work in a cohort of insurance clerks. In *Work With Display Units 86. Selected Papers from the International Scientific Conference On Work With Display Units, May 1986, Stockholm*, edited by B Knave and PG Widebäck. Amsterdam: North Holland.

Westlander, G. 1989. Use and non-use of VDTs—Organization of terminal work. In *Work With Computers: Organizational, Management, Stress and Health Aspects*, edited by MJ Smith and G Salvendy. Amsterdam: Elsevier Science.

Westlander, G and E Aberg. 1992. Variety in VDT work: An issue for assessment in work environment research. *Int J Hum Comput Interact* 4:283-302.

Wickens, C. 1992. *Engineering Psychology and Human Performance*. New York: Harper Collins.

Wiley, MJ and P Corey. 1992. The effects of continuous exposure to 20-khz sawtooth magnetic fields on the litters of CD-1 mice. *Teratology* 46:391-398.

Wilson, J and D Rosenberg. 1988. Rapid prototyping for user interface design. In *Handbook of Human-Computer Interaction*, edited by M Helander. Amsterdam: Elsevier.

Windham, GC, L Fenster, SH Swan, and RR Neutra. 1990. Use of video display terminals during pregnancy and the risk of spontaneous abortion, low birthweight, or intrauterine growth retardation. *Am J Ind Med* 18:675-688.

World Health Organization (WHO). 1987. *Visual Display Terminals and Workers' Health*. Geneva: WHO.

—. 1989. Work with visual display terminals: Psychosocial aspects and health. *J Occup Med* 31:957-968.

Yang, C-L and P Carayon. 1993. Effects of job demands and job support on worker stress: A study of VDT users. *Behav Inf Technol*.

Young, JE. 1993. *Global Network. Computers in a Sustainable Society*. Washington, DC: Worldwatch Paper 115.

Young, RM. 1981. The machine inside the machine: Users' models of pocket calculators. *Int J Man Mach Stud* 15:51-85.

Zecca, L, P Ferrario, and G Dal Conte. 1985. Toxicological and teratological studies in rats after exposure to pulsed magnetic fields. *Bioelectrochem Bioenerget* 14:63-69.

Zuboff, S. 1988. *In the Age of the Smart Machine: The Future of Work and Power*. New York: Basic Books.

Other relevant readings

Berlinguet, L and D Berthelette. 1990. *Work With Display Units 89*. Amsterdam: Elsevier Science.

Berthelette, D. 1995. Les changements technologiques et la gestion de la santé et de la sécurité du travail. In *Changement technologique et gestion des ressources humaines: Fondement et pratiques*, edited by J Réal and J Ducharme. Montréal: Gaëtan Morin.

Card, SK, TP Moran, and A Newell. 1983. *The Psychology of Human-Computer Interactions*. Hillsdale, NJ: Lawrence Erlbaum.

Cordingley, ES. 1989. Knowledge elicitation techniques for knowledge-based systems. In *Knowledge Elicitation. Principles, Techniques and Applications*, edited by D Diaper. Chichester: E Horwood.

Diaper, D. 1989. *Task Analysis for Human-Computer Interaction*. Chichester: E Horwood.

DiTecco, D, G Cwitco, A Arsenault, and M Andre. 1992. Operator stress and monitoring practices. *Appl Ergon* 23(1):29-34.

Handcock, PA and MH Chignell. 1989. *Intelligent Interfaces. Theory, Research and Design*. Amsterdam: Elsevier.

Hocking, B. 1987. Epidemiological aspects of "repetition strain injury". *Med J Austral* 147:218-222.

Johnson, P. 1985. Towards a task model of messaging: an example of the application of T.A.K.D. to user interface design. In *People and Computers: Designing the Interface*, edited by P Johnson and S Cook. Cambridge: CUP.

Johnson, P and H Johnson. 1989. Integrating task analysis into system design: Surveying designers' needs. *Ergonomics* 32(11):1451-1467.

Johnson, P, S Wilson, P Markopoulos, and J Pycock. 1993. Adept-Advanced Design Environment for Prototyping With Task Models. In *Proceedings of INTERCHI'93: Conference On Human Factors in Computing Systems, 24-29 April, Amsterdam* Reading, Mass.: Addison-Wesley.

Knave, B and PG Widebäck. 1987. *Work With Display Units 86*. Amsterdam: Elsevier Science.

Krueger, H. 1992. Exigences visuelles au poste d tavail: Diagnostic et traitement. *Cahiers médico-sociaux* 36:171-181.

Mayer, RE. 1988. From novice to expert. In *Handbook of Human-Computer Interaction*, edited by M Helander. Amsterdam: Elsevier.

Meyer, J-J, D Francioli, and P Rey. 1993. Observed variations of lighting conditions versus feelings of visual discomfort in VDT operators: Application of a new model. In *Lux Europa 1993*. Edinburgh: Heriot-Watt Univ.

Rey, P. 1991. *Précis de médecine du travail*. Geneva: Medicine et Hygiène.

Robert, J-M. 1993. Interfaces personne-système et élaboration de normes internationales. In *Francophonie et génie linguistique. Grands enjeux et solutions à Privilégier*. Montréal: UREF.

Scalet, EA, TFM Stewart, and KP McGee. 1987. *VDT Health and Safety*. Issues and Solution. Lawrence, Kans: Ergosyst.

Scapin, DL and C Pierret-Golbreich. 1989. *Mad: Méthode analytique de description des tâches*. Antipolis: Sophia.

Sébillotte, S and DL Scapin. 1992. From User's Task Knowledge to High Level Interface Specification. Communication presented at the Third International Conference on WWDU, 1-4 September, Berlin, Germany.

Wilson, MD, PJ Barnard, and A MacLean. 1986. *Task Analyses in Human-Computer Interaction*. Hursley Human Factors Laboratory HF122.

ENVIRONMENTAL HEALTH HAZARDS

53

Chapter Editors
Annalee Yassi and Tord Kjellström

Contents

LINKAGES BETWEEN ENVIRONMENTAL AND OCCUPATIONAL HEALTH

Annalee Yassi and Tord Kjellström

Development, and industrialization in particular, have made immense positive contributions to health, including greater personal and social wealth, as well as vastly improved health and education services, transportation and communication. Unquestionably, on the global scale, people are living longer and are healthier than they were centuries and even decades ago. However, industrialization has also had adverse health consequences not only for workforces, but for the general population as well. These effects have been caused either directly by exposure to safety hazards and harmful agents, or indirectly through environmental degradation locally and globally (see "Industrial pollution in developing countries" in this chapter).

This article outlines the nature of environmental health hazards and the reasons for linking environmental health with occupational health.

Environmental health hazards, like occupational health hazards, may be biological, chemical, physical, biomechanical or psychosocial in nature. Environmental health hazards include traditional hazards of poor sanitation and shelter, as well as agricultural and industrial contamination of air, water, food and land. These hazards have resulted in a host of health impacts, ranging from catastrophic direct effects (e.g., the recent cholera epidemic in Latin America and the chemical poisoning outbreak in Bhopal, India), to chronic effects (e.g., in Minamata, Japan), to subtle, indirect, and even disputed effects (e.g., in Love Canal, USA). Table 53.1 summarizes some of the major notorious disasters in the last half century that have caused "environmental disease" outbreaks. There are undeniably countless other examples of

environmental disease outbreaks, some of which are not easily detectable on the macrostatistical level. Meanwhile, over a billion people in the world lack access to safe drinking water (WHO 1992b) and over 600 million are exposed to ambient levels of sulphur dioxide that well exceed recommended levels. Moreover the pressure on agriculture and food production as both population and per capita demand increase, will likely lead to a greater burden on the environment (see "Food and agriculture" in this chapter). Environmental health impacts thus include the indirect effects of industrial disruption of adequate food and housing, as well as the degradation of the global systems on which the health of the planet depends.

In many countries large-scale agriculture and the concomitant active use of toxic pesticides is a major health hazard both for workers and for their households. Pollution by fertilizers or biological waste from the food industry, paper industry and so on can also have harmful effects on waterways, reducing fishing and food supplies. The fishermen and gatherers of other seafood may have to travel much further to get their daily catch, with increased risks of drowning accidents and other mishaps. The spread of tropical disease by the environmental changes associated with developments such as the building of dams, roads and so on constitutes another type of environmental health risk. The new dam may create breeding grounds for schistosomiasis, a debilitating disease affecting rice farmers who have to walk in water. The new road may create fast communication between an area with endemic malaria and another area hitherto spared from this disease.

It should be pointed out that the major basis for a harmful environment in the workplace or in the general environment is poverty. The traditional health threats in developing countries or in poor sections of any country include poor sanitation, water and food which spreads communicable diseases, poor housing with high exposures to cooking smoke and high fire risks, as well as high injury risks in small-scale agriculture or cottage industries. Reduction of poverty and improved living and working conditions is a fundamental priority for improved occupational and environ-

Table 53.1 • Selected major "environmental disease" outbreaks.

Location and year	Environmental hazard	Type of disease	Number affected
London, UK 1952	Severe air-pollution with sulphur dioxide and suspended particulate matter (SPM)	Increase in heart and lung disease manifestations	3,000 deaths, many others ill
Toyama, Japan 1950s	Cadmium in rice	Kidney and bone disease ("Itai-itai disease")	200 with severe disease, many more with slight effects
South-east Turkey 1955-61	Hexachlorobenzene in seed grains	Porphyria; neurological disease	3,000
Minamata, Japan 1956	Methylmercury in fish	Neurological disease ("Minamata disease")	200 with severe disease, 2,000 suspected
USA cities 1960s-70s	Lead in paint	Anaemia, behavioural and mental effects	Many thousands
Fukuoka, Japan 1968	Polychlorinated biphenyls (PCBs) in food oil	Skin disease, general weakness	Several thousands
Iraq 1972	Methylmercury in seed grains	Neurological disease	500 deaths, 6,500 hospitalized
Madrid, Spain 1981	Aniline or other toxin in food oil	Various symptoms	340 deaths, 20,000 cases
Bhopal, India 1985	Methylisocyanate	Acute lung disease	2,000 deaths, 200,000 poisoned
California, USA 1985	Carbamate pesticide in watermelons	Gastrointestinal, skeletal, muscle, autonomic and central nervous system effects (Carbamate illness)	1,376 reported cases of illness resulting from consumption, 17 severely ill
Chernobyl, USSR 1986	Iodine-134, Caesium-134 and -137 from a reactor explosion	Radiation illness (including increases in cancer and thyroid diseases in children)	300 injured, 28 died within 3 months, more than 600 cases of thyroid cancer
Goiánia, Brazil 1987	Caesium-137 from an abandoned cancer therapy machine	Radiation illness (follow-up of *in utero* exposures continuing)	Some 240 people were contaminated and 2 died
Peru 1991	Cholera epidemic	Cholera	139 deaths, many thousand ill

mental health for billions of people. Despite efforts for energy conservation and sustainable development, failure to address the underlying inequities in wealth distribution threatens the global ecosystem. Forests, for example, which represent the culmination of ecological successional processes, are being destroyed at an alarming rate, due to commercial logging and clearance by impoverished peoples for agriculture and firewood. The effects of forest depletion include soil erosion, which, if extreme, can lead to desertification. Loss of biodiversity is an important consequence (see "Species extinction, biodiversity loss and human health" in this chapter). It is estimated that one-third of all carbon dioxide emissions are from the burning of tropical forests (the importance of carbon dioxide in creating global warming is discussed in "Global climate change and ozone depletion" in this chapter). Thus, addressing poverty is imperative with respect to global environmental health as well as individual, community and regional well-being.

Reasons for Linking Environmental and Occupational Health

The main link between the workplace and the general environment is that the source of the hazard is usually the same, whether it is an agricultural activity or an industrial activity. In order to control the health hazard, a common approach may work effectively in both settings. This is particularly so when it comes to the choice of chemical technologies for production. If an acceptable result or product can be produced with a less toxic chemical, the choice of such a chemical can reduce or even eliminate the health risk. One example is the use of safer water-based paints instead of paints made with toxic organic solvents. Another example is the choice of non-chemical pest-control methods whenever this is possible. In fact, in many cases, particularly in the developing world, there is no separation between the home and the workplace; thus the setting is truly the same.

It is now well recognized that the scientific knowledge and training required to assess and control environmental health hazards are, for the most part, the same skills and knowledge required to address health hazards within the workplace. Toxicology, epidemiology, occupational hygiene, ergonomics, safety engineering—in fact, the very disciplines included in this *Encyclopaedia*—are the basic tools of environmental science. The process of risk assessment and risk management is also the same: identify the hazards, categorize the risks, assess the exposure and estimate risk. This is followed by evaluating control options, controlling the exposure, communicating the risk to the public and establishing an on-going exposure- and risk-monitoring programme. Thus occupational and environmental health are strongly linked by common methodologies, particularly in health assessment and exposure control.

The identification of environmental health hazards has often come from observations of adverse health outcomes among workers; and unquestionably it is in the workplace that the impact of industrial exposures is best understood. Documentation of health effects generally comes from one of three sources: animal or other laboratory experiments (both non-human and controlled human), accidental high-level exposures or the epidemiological studies that usually follow such exposures. To conduct an epidemiological study it is necessary to be able to define both the exposed population and the nature and level of the exposure, as well as to ascertain the negative health effect. It is generally easier to define the members of a workforce than to determine the membership of a community, particularly in a community that is transient; the nature and level of exposure to various members of the cohort are generally more clear-cut in a workplace population than in a community; and the outcomes of high levels of exposure are almost always easier to delineate than more subtle changes attrib-

utable to low-level exposure. While there are some examples of exposure outside factory gates approaching the worst occupational exposures (e.g., cadmium exposure from mining in China and Japan; lead and cadmium emissions from smelters in Upper Silesia, Poland), the levels of exposure are generally much higher to a workforce than to the surrounding community (WHO 1992b).

Since adverse health outcomes are more apparent in workers, information on occupational health effects of many toxic exposures (including heavy metals such as lead, mercury, arsenic and nickel, as well as such well-known carcinogens as asbestos) has been used to calculate the health risk to the wider community. With respect to cadmium, for example, as early as 1942 reports began to appear of cases of osteomalacia with multiple fractures among workers in a French factory producing alkaline batteries. During the 1950s and 1960s cadmium intoxication was considered to be strictly an occupational disease. However, the knowledge gained from the workplace helped achieve the recognition that osteomalacia and kidney disease that was occurring in Japan at this time, "Itai-itai" disease, was indeed due to contamination of rice from irrigation of soil with water contaminated with cadmium from industrial sources (Kjellström 1986). Thus occupational epidemiology has been able to make a substantive contribution to knowledge of the effects of environmental exposure, constituting another reason for linking the two fields.

On an individual level, occupational disease affects well-being in the home and the community; and, universally, an individual who is ill from inadequacies in the home and the community cannot be productive in the workplace.

Strictly from a scientific viewpoint, there is a need to consider total (environmental plus occupational) exposures in order to truly assess health impact and establish dose-response relationships. Pesticide exposure is a classic example wherein occupational exposure may be supplemented by considerable environmental exposure, through food and water-source contamination, and through non-occupational airborne exposure. From outbreaks in which over 100 poisonings occurred from contaminated food alone, over 15,000 cases and 1,500 deaths due to pesticide poisoning have been documented by the WHO (1990e). In one study of Central American cotton growers using pesticides, not only did very few of the workers have access to protective clothing, but virtually all of the workers lived within 100 metres of the cotton fields, many in temporary housing with no walls for protection from aerial pesticide spraying. The workers also often washed in irrigation channels containing pesticide residues, resulting in increased exposures (Michaels, Barrera and Gacharna 1985). To understand the relationship between pesticide exposure and any health effects reported, all sources of exposure should be taken into consideration. Thus ensuring that occupational and environmental exposures are evaluated together improves the accuracy of exposure assessment in both areas.

The health problems caused by occupational and environmental hazards are particularly acute in developing countries, where well established methods of hazard control are less likely to be applied because of limited awareness of the hazards, low political priority of health and environment matters, limited resources or lack of appropriate occupational and environmental health management systems. A major impediment to environmental health hazard control in many parts of the world is the lack of people with appropriate training. It has been documented that developing countries suffer from a severe shortage of expert staff in occupational health (Noweir 1986). In 1985 a WHO expert committee also concluded that there is an urgent need for staff trained in environmental health matters; indeed Agenda 21, the internationally agreed upon strategy taken by the United Nations Conference on Environment and Development

(UN 1993), identifies training (national "capacity building") as a key element of promoting human health through sustainable development. Where resources are limited, it is not feasible to train one group of people to look after health concerns within the workplace, and another group to attend to hazards outside the factory gate.

Even in developed countries, there is a strong trend to make most efficient use of resources by training and employing "occupational and environmental health" professionals. Today, businesses must find ways to manage their affairs logically and efficiently within the societal framework of duty, law and financial policy. Combining occupational and environment health under one roof is one way of achieving this goal.

Broad environmental concerns must be taken into consideration in designing workplaces and deciding on industrial hygiene control strategies. Substituting for one substance another one that is less acutely toxic may make good occupational health sense; however, if the new substance is not biodegradable, or damages the ozone layer, it would not be an appropriate exposure control solution—it would only move the problem elsewhere. The use of chlorofluorocarbons, now widely used as a refrigerant instead of the more acutely dangerous substance ammonia, is the classic example of what is now known to have been an environmentally inappropriate substitution. Thus linking occupational and environmental health minimizes unwise exposure control decisions.

While understanding of the health effects of various deleterious exposures has usually come from the workplace, the public health impact of environmental exposures to these same agents has often been a major force in stimulating clean-up efforts both inside the workplace and in the surrounding community. For example, discovery of high lead levels in workers' blood by an industrial hygienist in a lead foundry in Bahia, Brazil, led to investigations of lead in the blood of children in nearby residential areas. The finding that the children had high lead levels was a major impetus in the company taking action to reduce occupational exposures as well as lead emissions from the factory (Nogueira 1987), although occupational exposures still remain substantially higher than would be tolerated by the general community.

In fact, environmental health standards are usually much stricter than occupational health standards. The WHO's recommended guideline values for selected chemicals provide an example. The rationale for the difference is generally that the community consists of sensitive populations including the very old, the ill, young children and pregnant women, whereas the workforce is at least healthy enough to work. Also, it is often argued that risk is more "acceptable" to a workforce, as these people are benefiting by having a job, and are therefore more willing to accept the risk. Many political, ethical, as well as scientific, debates rage around the question of standards. Linking occupational and environmental health can be a positive contribution to sorting out these controversies. In this regard, tightening the connection between occupational and environmental health may facilitate greater consistency in approaches to standard setting.

Likely inspired at least in part by the active debate about the environment and sustainable development brought to the forefront by Agenda 21, many occupational health professional organizations have changed their names to "occupational and environmental" organizations in acknowledgement that their members are increasingly devoting their attention to environmental health hazards both inside and outside the workplace. Further, as noted in the chapter on ethics, the International Code of Ethics for Occupational Health Professionals states that the duty to protect the environment is part and parcel of the ethical obligations of occupational health professionals.

In summary, occupational and environmental health are strongly linked by:

- the very fact that the source of the health threat is usually the same
- common methodologies, particularly in health assessment and exposure control
- the contribution that occupational epidemiology makes to knowledge of the effects of environmental exposure
- the effects that occupational disease has on well-being in the home and the community, and conversely the effect of environmental pathology on worker productivity
- the scientific need to consider total exposures in order to determine dose-response relationships
- the efficiency in human resource development and utilization gained by such a linkage
- improvements in exposure control decisions stemming from the broader view
- greater consistency in standard setting facilitated by the link
- the fact that linking environmental and occupational health enhances the incentive for rectification of hazards to both the workforce and the community.

The desirability of bringing together occupational and environmental health notwithstanding, each has a unique and specific orientation that should not be lost. Occupational health must continue to focus on workers' health, and environmental health must continue to concern itself with the health of the general public. None the less, even where it is desirable for professionals to operate strictly in only one of these fields, having a good appreciation of the other enhances the credibility, knowledge base and effectiveness of the overall endeavour. It is in this spirit that this chapter is presented.

FOOD AND AGRICULTURE[1]

Friedrich K. Käferstein

Production Needs in the Face of Population Pressure and Other Forces

Rapid population growth continues in some regions of the world. As compared with the situation in 1990, by the year 2010 there will be an extra 1,900 million people to be fed, a rise of 36% from 5,300 to 7,200 million people.

Ninety per cent of the entire projected growth over the next 20 years is expected to take place in the countries which are currently classified as developing nations. Progressive urbanization of society is taking place. The urban population of the world will reach 3,600 million, a rise of 62% from the 2,200 million city dwellers in 1990. Moreover the urban population of developing countries will increase by 92% (from 1,400 million to 2,600 million) in the twenty years from 1990, a fourfold increase since 1970. Even if family planning receives the urgent attention that it desperately requires from all rapidly growing populations, population growth and urbanization will continue to dominate the scene for the next two decades.

A 36% increase in food, other agricultural products and potable water will be required over the next twenty years simply to match the rise in population; the need for half a billion people to

---

[1] This article has been prepared by Dr F. Käferstein, Chief, Food Safety, World Health Organization. It is entirely based on the report of a WHO Panel on Food and Agriculture which had supported the WHO Commission on Health and Environment to prepare a report for the United Nations Conference on Environment and Development (UNCED), Rio de Janeiro, 1992. Both reports are available from the WHO.

Figure 53.1 • Foodborne diseases in Venezuela.

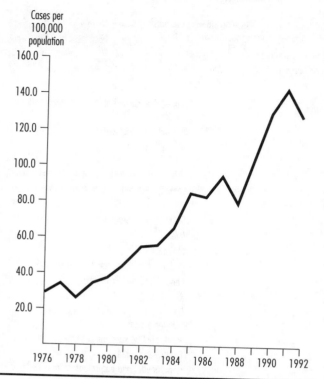

The continuing long-term need for industrial development to produce goods, services and employment will lead to more intensive food production, which will itself become more industrialized. Consequently, and especially because of urbanization, the demand for, and the resources employed in, packaging, processing, storage and distribution of food will increase in volume and importance.

The public is becoming much more aware of the need to produce, protect and market food in ways which minimize adverse change in our environment, and is more demanding in this respect. The emergence of revolutionary scientific tools (e.g., biotechnological advances) offers the possibility of significantly increasing food production, reducing waste and enhancing safety.

The principal challenge is to meet the increasing demands for food, other agricultural products and water in ways that foster long-term improvements in health, and which are also sustainable, economical and competitive.

Despite the fact that globally there is at present sufficient food for all, great difficulties have to be overcome to ensure the availability and equitable distribution of safe, nutritious and affordable food supplies to meet health needs in many parts of the world, and notably in areas of rapid population growth.

There is often a failure to take the possible health consequences fully into account in the design and implementation of agricultural and fisheries policies and programmes. An example is the production of tobacco, which has very serious and negative impacts on human health and on scarce land and fuelwood resources. Moreover, the lack of an integrated approach to development of the agriculture and forestry sectors results in failure to recognize the important relationship of both sectors to the protection of wildlife habitats, biological diversity and genetic resources.

If timely and appropriate action is not taken to mitigate the environmental impacts of agriculture, fisheries, food production and water use, then the following situations will prevail:

- As the urban population increases, the difficulty of maintaining and extending an efficient food distribution system will become greater. This may increase the prevalence of household food insecurity, associated malnutrition and health risks among the growing masses of urban poor.
- Microbial, viral and parasitic diseases from contaminated food and water will continue to be serious health problems. New agents of public health importance will continue to emerge. The diarrhoeal diseases related to food and water, causing high infant mortality and universal morbidity, will increase.
- Vector-borne diseases from irrigation, other water resource developments, and uncontrolled wastewater will increase substantially. Malaria, schistosomiasis, filariasis and arbovirus fevers will continue to be major problems.
- The problems outlined above will be reflected in static or rising levels of infant and young child malnutrition and mortality, as well as morbidity at all ages, but predominantly among the poor, the very young, the aged and the sick.
- Chronic diseases linked to inappropriate life-styles, smoking and diet (for example, obesity, diabetes or coronary heart disease), which are characteristic of the more affluent countries, are now emerging and becoming significant problems also in developing countries. The increasing urbanization will accelerate this trend.
- As the intensity of food production increases, the risk of occupational diseases and accidents among those working in this and related sectors will increase substantially unless sufficient efforts for safety and prevention are made.

be properly fed instead of remaining undernourished, and the greater demand from populations with a rising income, will all lead to a vast increase in total food production. An excessive demand for food of animal origin will continue to characterize people in the higher income groups, leading to increases in animal feed production.

The pressure on agriculture and food production, as both population and per capita demand increase, will lead to a greater burden on the environment. This burden will be unevenly generated and have uneven environmental effects. Globally, these will be adverse and will require concerted action.

This increased demand will fall on resources of land and water which are finite, where the most productive areas have already been used, and where the cost of bringing marginal land into production, and of using less readily available water, will be high. Much of this marginal land may have only temporary fertility unless specific measures are taken to maintain it, while the productivity of natural fisheries is also sharply limited. The area of arable land will decrease due to soil erosion from over-grazing; laterization of clearfelled areas; soil salinization and other types of land degradation; and the expansion of urban, industrial and other developments.

Water availability and quality, already totally inadequate in much of the world, will remain major problems for rural areas of developing countries and also for many urban populations, who may face the additional problem of high utilization charges. Needs for water will increase greatly, and for several large cities the meeting of water demands will become increasingly costly as supplies will have to be brought from far away. Re-use of water implies more stringent standards for treatment. The increasing production of wastewater and sewage will require more extensive treatment facilities, as well as large outlays of capital.

Health Consequences of Biological Contamination and Chemicals in Food

Despite progress in science and technology, contaminated food and water remain to this day major public health problems.

53. ENVIRONMENTAL HEALTH HAZARDS

Table 53.2 • Some agents of important foodborne diseases and salient epidemiological features.

Agents	Important reservoir/carrier	Transmission[a] by			Multiplication in food	Examples of some incriminated foods
		Water	Food	Person to person		
Bacteria						
Baccillus cereus	Soil	−	+	−	+	Cooked rice, cooked meats, vegetables, starchy puddings
Brucella species	Cattle, goats, sheep	−	+	−	+	Raw milk, dairy products
Campylobacter jejuni	Chickens, dogs, cats, cattle, pigs, wild birds	+	+	+	−[b]	Raw milk, poultry
Clostridium botulinum	Soil, mammals, birds, fish	−	+	−	+	Fish, meat, vegetables (home preserved), honey
Clostridium perfringens	Soil, animals, humans	−	+	−	+	Cooked meat and poultry, gravy, beans
Escherichia coli						
Enterotoxigenic	Humans	+	+	+	+	Salad, raw vegetables
Enteropathogenic	Humans	+	+	+	+	Milk
Enteroinvasive	Humans	+	+	0	+	Cheese
Enterohaemorrhagic	Cattle, poultry, sheep	+	+	+	+	Undercooked meat, raw milk, cheese
Listeria monocytogenes	Environment	+	+	−[c]	+	Cheese, raw milk, coleslaw
Mycobacterium bovis	Cattle	−	+	−	−	Raw milk
Salmonella typhi and paratyphi	Humans	+	+	±	+	Dairy products, meat products, shellfish, vegetable salads
Salmonella (non-typhi)	Humans and animals	±	+	±	+	Meat, poultry, eggs, dairy products, chocolate
Shigella spp.	Humans	+	+	+	+	Potato/egg salads
Staphylococcus aureus (enterotoxins)		−	+	−	+	Ham, poultry and egg salads, cream-filled bakery products, ice cream, cheese
Vibrio cholerae, 01	Humans, marine life	+	+	±	+	Salad, shellfish
Vibrio cholerae, non-01	Humans, marine life	+	+	±	+	Shellfish
Vibrio parahaemolyticus	Sea water, marine life	−	+	−	+	Raw fish, crabs, and other shellfish
Vibrio vulnificus	Sea water, marine life	+	+	−	+	Shellfish
Yersinia enterocolitica	Water, wild animals, pigs, dogs, poultry	+	+	−	+	Milk, pork, and poultry
Viruses						
Hepatitis A virus	Humans	+	+	+	−	Shellfish, raw fruit and vegetables
Norwalk agents	Humans	+	+	−	−	Shellfish, salad
Rotavirus	Humans	+	+	+	−	0
Protozoa		+	+	+	+	Raw milk, raw sausage (non-fermented)
Cryptosporidium parvum	Humans, animals	+	+	+	−	Vegetables and fruits
Entamoeba histolytica	Humans	+	+	+	−	Vegetables and fruits
Giardia lamblia	Humans, animals	+	±	+	−	Undercooked meat, raw vegetables
Toxoplasma gondii	Cats, pigs	0	+	−	−	
Helminths						
Ascaris lumbricoides	Humans	+	+	−	−	Soil-contaminated food
Clonorchis sinensis	Freshwater fish	−	+	−	−	Undercooked/raw fish
Fasciola hepatica	Cattle, goats	±	+	−	−	Watercress
Opisthorclis viverrini/felinus	Freshwater fish	−	+	−	−	Undercooked/raw fish
Paragonimus sp.	Freshwater crabs	−	+	−	−	Undercooked/raw crabs
Taenia saginata and T. solium	Cattle, swine	−	+	−	−	Undercooked meat
Trichinella spiralis	Swine, carnivora	−	+	−	−	Undercooked meat
Trichuris trichiura	Humans	0	+	−	−	Soil-contaminated food

[a] Almost all acute enteric infections show increased transmission during the summer and/or wet months, except infections due to Rotavirus and *Yersinia enterocolitica*, which show increased transmission in cooler months. [b] Under certain circumstances, some multiplication has been observed. The epidemiological significance of this observation is not clear. [c] Vertical transmission from pregnant woman to foetus occurs frequently.

+ = Yes; ± = Rare; − = No; 0 = No information.

Adapted from WHO/FAO 1984.

Foodborne diseases are perhaps the most widespread health problems in the contemporary world and important causes of reduced economic productivity (WHO/FAO 1984). They are caused by a wide range of agents, and cover all degrees of severity, from mild indispositions to life-threatening illnesses. However, only a small proportion of cases comes to the notice of health services and even fewer are investigated. As a result, it is believed that in industrialized countries only approximately 10% of the cases are reported, whilst in developing countries reported cases probably account for not more than 1% of the total.

Despite these limitations, the data that are available indicate that foodborne diseases are increasing all over the world, both in developing and industrialized countries. Experience in Venezuela illustrates this trend (PAHO/WHO 1989) (figure 53.1).

Biological contamination

Developing countries

Available information clearly indicates that biological contaminants (bacteria, viruses and parasites) are the major causes of foodborne diseases (table 53.2).

In the developing countries, they are responsible for a wide range of foodborne diseases (e.g., cholera, salmonellosis, shigellosis, typhoid and paratyphoid fevers, brucellosis, poliomyelitis and amoebiasis). Diarrhoeal diseases, especially infant diarrhoea, are the dominant problem and indeed one of massive proportions. Annually, some 1,500 million children under the age of five suffer from diarrhoea and of these over three million die as a result. Formerly it was thought that contaminated water supplies were the main direct source of pathogens causing diarrhoea, but now it has been shown that up to 70% of diarrhoeal episodes may be due to foodborne pathogens (WHO 1990c). However, the contamination of the food may in many cases originate from contaminated water that is used for irrigation and similar purposes.

Industrialized countries

Although the situation regarding foodborne diseases is very serious in developing countries, the problem is not limited to these countries, and in recent years, industrialized countries have experienced a succession of major epidemics. In the United States it is estimated there are 6.5 million cases per year, with 9,000 fatalities, but according to the US Food and Drug Administration this figure is an underestimate and may be as high as 80 million cases (Cohen 1987; Archer and Kvenberg 1985; Young 1987). The estimate for former West Germany was one million cases in 1989 (Grossklaus 1990). A study in the Netherlands found that as many as 10% of the population may be affected by foodborne or waterborne diseases (Hoogenboom-Vergedaal et al. 1990).

With today's improvements in standards of personal hygiene, development of basic sanitation, safe water supplies, effective infrastructure and the increasing application of technologies such as pasteurization, many foodborne diseases have been either eliminated or considerably reduced in certain industrialized countries (e.g., milkborne salmonellosis). Nevertheless, most countries are now experiencing an important increase in several other foodborne diseases. The situation in former West Germany (1946-1991) illustrates this phenomenon (figure 53.2) (Statistisches Bundesamt 1994).

Salmonellosis, specifically, has increased tremendously on both sides of the Atlantic over the past few years (Rodrigue 1990). In many cases it is due to *Salmonella enteritidis*. Figure 53.3 shows the increase of this micro-organism in relation to other *Salmonella* strains in Switzerland. In many countries, poultry meat, eggs and foods containing eggs have been identified as the predominant sources of this pathogen. In certain countries, 60 to 100% of

Figure 53.2 • Infectious enteritis, typhoid fever and paratyphoid fever (A, B and C), Germany.

poultry meat is contaminated with *Salmonella* spp., and meat, frogs' legs, chocolate and milk have also been implicated (Notermans 1984; Roberts 1990). In 1985, some 170,000 to 200,000 persons were involved in an outbreak of salmonellosis in Chicago which was caused by contaminated pasteurized milk (Ryzan 1987).

Chemicals and toxicants in food

Considerable efforts have been undertaken at the national and international levels to ensure the chemical safety of food supplies.

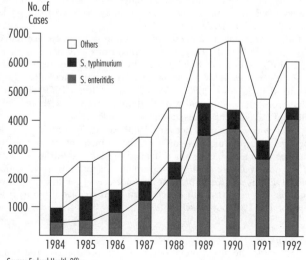

Figure 53.3 • Serotypes of *Salmonella* in Switzerland.

Source: Federal Health Office.

Two joint FAO/WHO committees have, over a period of three decades, evaluated a large number of food chemicals. The Joint FAO/WHO Expert Committee on Food Additives (JECFA) evaluates food additives, contaminants and veterinary drug residues, and the Joint FAO/WHO Meeting on Pesticide Residues (JMPR) evaluates pesticide residues. Recommendations are made on the acceptable daily intake (ADI), on maximum residue levels (MRLs) and maximum levels (MLs). Based on these recommendations, the Codex Alimentarius Commission and governments establish food standards and safe levels for these substances in foodstuffs. Moreover, the Joint UNEP/FAO/WHO Food Contamination Monitoring Programme (GEMS/Food) provides information on the levels of contaminants in food and on time trends of contamination, enabling preventive and control measures.

While information from most of the developing countries is scarce, surveys made in the industrialized countries suggest that the food supply is largely safe from the chemical viewpoint owing to the extensive food safety infrastructure (i.e., legislation, enforcement mechanisms, surveillance and monitoring systems) and the general level of responsibility of the food industry. However, accidental contamination or adulteration does occur, in which case the health consequences may be grave. For example, in Spain in 1981-82, adulterated cooking oil killed some 600 people and disabled—temporarily or permanently—another 20,000 (WHO 1984). The agent responsible for this mass poisoning has not yet been identified in spite of intensive investigations.

Environmental chemicals

A number of chemical substances may occur in the food supply as a result of environmental contamination. Their effects on health may be extremely serious and have caused great concern in recent years.

Serious consequences have been reported when foods contaminated with heavy metals such as lead, cadmium or mercury have been ingested over extended periods of time.

The Chernobyl accident provoked great concern over the health risks to people exposed to accidental radionuclide emissions. People living in the vicinity of the accident were exposed, and this exposure included radioactive contaminants in food and water. In other parts of Europe and elsewhere, at some distance from the accident, this concern focused on contaminated foods as a source of exposure. In most countries, the estimated average dose acquired from eating contaminated foods amounted to only a very small fraction of the dose normally received from background radiation (IAEA 1991).

Other environmental chemicals of interest are polychlorinated biphenyls (PCBs). PCBs are used in various industrial applications. Information on the effects of PCBs on human health were originally noted following from two large-scale incidents which occurred in Japan (1968) and in Taiwan, China (1979). Experience from these outbreaks showed that as well as their acute effects, PCBs may also have carcinogenic effects.

DDT was widely used between 1940 and 1960 as an insecticide for agricultural purposes and for the control of vector-borne diseases. It is now banned or restricted in many countries because of its potential risk to the environment. In many tropical countries, DDT is still an important chemical, used for the control of malaria. No confirmed ill effects have been reported due to residues of DDT in food (UNEP 1988).

Mycotoxins

Mycotoxins, the toxic metabolites of certain microscopic fungi (moulds), may cause serious adverse effects in humans, as well as in animals. Animal studies have shown that besides acute intoxica-tion, mycotoxins are capable of causing carcinogenic, mutagenic and teratogenic effects.

Biotoxins

Intoxication by marine biotoxin (also known as "fish poisoning") is another problem of concern. Examples of such intoxications are ciguatera and various kinds of shellfish poisoning.

Plant toxicants

Toxicants in edible plants and poisonous plants which resemble them (mushrooms, certain wild green plants) are important causes of ill health in many areas of the world and present a troublesome problem for food safety (WHO 1990b).

INDUSTRIAL POLLUTION IN DEVELOPING COUNTRIES

Niu Shiru

While industrialization is an essential feature of economic growth in developing countries, industrial practices may also produce adverse environmental health consequences through the release of air and water pollutants and the disposal of hazardous wastes. This is often the case in developing countries, where less attention is paid to environmental protection, environmental standards are often inappropriate or not effectively implemented, and pollution control techniques are not yet fully developed. With rapid economic development, many developing countries, like China and other Asian countries, face some additional environmental problems. One is the environmental pollution from hazardous industries or technologies transferred from developed countries, which are no longer acceptable for occupational and environmental health reasons in developed countries, but still allowable in developing countries due to looser environmental legislation. Another problem is the rapid proliferation of informal small-scale enterprises in townships as well as in rural areas, which often create serious air and water pollution because of lack of sufficient knowledge and funds.

Air Pollution

Air pollution in developing countries is derived not only from stack emission of pollutants from relatively large industries, like iron and steel, non-ferrous metals and petroleum products industries, but also from fugitive emission of pollutants from small-scale factories, such as cement mills, lead refineries, chemical fertilizer and pesticide factories and so on, where inadequate pollution control measures exist and pollutants are allowed to escape to the atmosphere.

Since industrial activities always involve energy generation, the combustion of fossil fuels is a main source of air pollution in the developing countries, where coal is widely used not only for industrial, but also for domestic consumption. For instance, in China, more than 70% of total energy consumption relies on direct coal combustion, from which large amounts of pollutants (suspended particulates, sulphur dioxide, etc.) are emitted under incomplete combustion and inadequate emission controls.

The kinds of air pollutants emitted vary from industry to industry. The concentrations of different pollutants in the atmosphere also vary widely from process to process, and from place to place with different geographic and climatic conditions. It is difficult to estimate specific exposure levels of various pollutants from different industries to the general population in developing countries, as elsewhere. In general, the workplace exposure levels are much higher than that of the general population, because the emissions are rapidly diluted and dispersed by the wind. But the exposure duration of the general population is much longer than that of workers.

The exposure levels of the general population in developing countries are usually higher than that in developed countries, where air pollution is more strictly controlled and resident areas are usually far from industries. As discussed further on in this chapter, a large number of epidemiological studies have already showed the close association of reduction in pulmonary function and increased incidence of chronic respiratory diseases among residents with long-term exposure to the common air pollutants.

A case study of air pollution effects on the health of 480 primary school children in Cubatao, Brazil, where large quantities of mixed pollutants were emitted from 23 industries (steel mill, chemical industries, cement factory, fertilizer plants, etc.), showed that 55.3% of the children had decreases in pulmonary function. Another example of health effects of air pollution appeared in the Ulsan/Onsan special industrial zone, Republic of Korea, where many large-scale plants (mainly petrochemical plants and metal refineries) are concentrated. Local residents complained of a variety of health problems, particularly of the nervous system disorder called "Onsan Disease".

Accidental releases of toxic substances into the atmosphere resulting in serious health risks are usually more common in developing countries. The reasons include inadequate safety planning, lack of skilled technical personnel to maintain proper facilities, and difficulties in obtaining spare parts and so on. One of the worst of such accidents occurred in Bhopal, India, in 1984, where leaking methyl isocyanide killed 2,000 people.

Water and Soil Pollution

Inappropriate and often careless disposal of industrial wastes—uncontrolled discharge into watercourses and uncontrolled disposal on the land, which often causes water and soil pollution—is another crucial environmental health problem, in addition to industrial air pollution, in developing countries, particularly with numerous small-scale township enterprises, like those in China. Some small-scale factories, such as textile dyeing, pulp and paper, leather tanning, electroplating, fluorescent lamp, lead battery and metal smelting, always produce a large amount of wastes, containing toxic or hazardous substances like chromium, mercury, lead, cyanide and so on, which may pollute the rivers, streams and lakes, and soil as well, when they are untreated. The soil pollution in turn may contaminate groundwater resources.

In Karachi, the Lyan river, which runs through the city, has become an open drain of sewage and untreated industrial effluent from some 300 large and small industries. There is a similar case in Shanghai. Some 3.4 million cubic metres of industrial and domestic waste pour into Suzhou creek and Huangpu river, which flow through the heart of the city. Because of serious pollution, the river and creek have essentially become devoid of life and often produce smells and sights that are unpleasant and offensive to the public living in the surrounding area.

A further problem of water and soil pollution in developing countries is the transfer of toxic or hazardous wastes from developed to developing countries. The cost of transporting these wastes to simple storage sites in developing countries is a mere fraction of the cost required for safely storing or incinerating them in their countries of origin in compliance with the applicable government regulations there. This has occurred in Thailand, Nigeria, Guinea-Bissau and so on. The toxic wastes inside the barrels can leak and pollute the air, water and soil, posing a potential health risk to the people living in the vicinity.

Thus the environmental health problems discussed in this chapter tend to apply to an even greater extent to developing countries.

DEVELOPING COUNTRIES AND POLLUTION

Tee L. Guidotti

Industrial pollution is a more complicated problem in developing countries than in developed economies. There are greater structural obstacles to preventing and cleaning up pollution. These obstacles are largely economic, because developing countries do not have the resources to control pollution to the extent that developed countries can. On the other hand, the effects of pollution may be very costly to a developing society, in terms of health, waste, environmental degradation, reduced quality of life and clean-up costs in the future. An extreme example is concern for the future of children exposed to lead in some megacities in countries where leaded gasoline is still used, or in the vicinity of smelters. Some of these children have been found to have blood lead levels high enough to impair intelligence and cognition.

Industry in developing countries usually operates short of capital compared to industry in developed countries, and those investment funds that are available are first put into the equipment and resources necessary for production. Capital that is applied toward control of pollution is considered "unproductive" by economists because such investment does not lead to increased production and financial return. However, the reality is more complicated. Investment in control of pollution may not bring an obvious direct return on investment to the company or industry, but that does not mean that there is no return on investment. In many cases, as in an oil refinery, control of pollution also reduces the amount of wastage and increases the efficiency of the operation so that the company does benefit directly. Where public opinion carries weight and it is to the advantage of a company to maintain good public relations, industry may make an effort to control pollution in its own interest. Unfortunately, the social structure in many developing countries does not favour this because the people most negatively affected by pollution tend to be those who are impoverished and marginalized in society.

Pollution may damage the environment and society as a whole, but these are "externalized dis-economies" that do not substantially hurt the company itself, at least not economically. Instead, the costs of pollution tend to be carried by society as a whole, and the company is spared the costs. This is particularly true in situations where the industry is critical to the local economy or national priorities, and there is a high tolerance for the damage it causes. One solution would be to "internalize" the external dis-economies by incorporating the costs of clean-up or the estimated costs of environmental damage into the operating costs of the company as a tax. This would give the company a financial incentive to control its costs by reducing its pollution. Virtually no government in any developing country is in a position to do this and to enforce the tax, however.

In practice, capital is rarely available to invest in equipment to control pollution unless there is pressure from government regulation. However, governments are rarely motivated to regulate industry unless there are compelling reasons to do so, and pressure from their citizens. In most developed countries, people are reasonably secure in their health and their lives, and expect a higher quality of life, which they associate with a cleaner environment. Because there is more economic security, these citizens are more willing to accept an apparent economic sacrifice in order to achieve a cleaner environment. However, in order to be competitive in world markets, many developing countries are very reluctant to impose regulation on their industries. Instead, they hope that industrial growth today will lead to a society rich enough tomorrow to clean up the pollution. Unfortunately, the cost of clean-up increases as fast as, or faster than, the costs associated with industrial development. At an early stage of industrial development, a developing country would in theory have very low costs associated with the prevention of pollution, but hardly ever do such countries have the capital resources they need to do so. Later, when such a country does have the resources, the costs are often staggeringly high and the damage has already been done.

Industry in developing countries tends to be less efficient than in developed countries. This lack of efficiency is a chronic problem in developing economies, reflecting untrained human resources, the cost of importing equipment and technology, and the inevitable wastage that occurs when some parts of the economy are more developed than others.

This inefficiency is also based in part on the need to rely on outdated technologies which are freely available, do not require an expensive licence or that do not cost as much to use. These technologies are often more polluting than the state-of-the-art technologies available to industry in developed countries. An example is the refrigeration industry, where the use of chlorofluorocarbons (CFCs) as refrigerant chemicals is much cheaper than the alternatives, despite the serious effects of these chemicals in depleting ozone from the upper atmosphere and thereby reducing the earth's shield from ultraviolet radiation; some countries had been very reluctant to agree to prohibit the use of CFCs because it would then be economically impossible for them to manufacture and purchase refrigerators. Technology transfer is the obvious solution, but companies in developed countries who developed or hold the licence for such technologies are understandably reluctant to share them. They are reluctant because they spent their own resources developing the technology, wish to retain the advantage they have in their own markets by controlling such technology, and may make their money from using or selling the technology only during the limited term of the patent.

Another problem faced by developing countries is lack of expertise in and awareness of the effects of pollution, monitoring methods and the technology of pollution control. There are relatively few experts in the field in developing countries, in part because there are fewer jobs and a smaller market for their services even though the need may actually be greater. Because the market for pollution control equipment and services may be small, this expertise and technology may have to be imported, adding to the costs. General recognition of the problem by managers and supervisors in industry may be lacking or very low. Even when an engineer, manager or supervisor in industry realizes that an operation is polluting, it may be difficult to persuade others in the company, their bosses or the owners that there is a problem that must be solved.

Industry in most developing countries competes at the low end of international markets, meaning that it produces products that are competitive on the basis of price and not quality or special features. Few developing countries specialize in making very fine grades of steel for surgical instruments and sophisticated machinery, for example. They manufacture lesser grades of steel for construction and manufacturing because the market is much larger, the technical expertise required to produce it is less, and they can compete on the basis of price as long as the quality is good enough to be acceptable. Pollution control reduces the price advantage by increasing the apparent costs of production without increasing output or sales. The central problem in developing countries is how to balance this economic reality against the need to protect their citizens, the integrity of their environment, and

their future, realizing that after development the costs will be even higher and the damage may be permanent.

AIR POLLUTION

Isabelle Romieu

The problem of air pollution has grown steadily since the Industrial Revolution began 300 years ago. Four major factors have exacerbated air pollution: growing industrialization; increasing traffic; rapid economic development; and higher levels of energy consumption. The available information shows that the WHO guidelines for the major air pollutants are regularly exceeded in many major urban centres. Although progress has been made in controlling air pollution problems in many industrialized countries over the last two decades, air quality—particularly in the larger cities in the developing world—is worsening. Of major concern are the adverse health effects of ambient air pollutants in many urban areas, where levels are sufficiently high to contribute to increased mortality and morbidity, deficits in pulmonary function and cardiovascular and neurobehavioural effects (Romieu, Weizenfeld and Finkelman 1990; WHO/UNEP 1992). Indoor air pollution due to domestic combustion products is also a major issue in developing countries (WHO 1992b), but it is not part of this review, which considers only the sources, dispersion and health effects of outdoor air pollution, and includes a case study of the situation in Mexico.

Source of Air Pollutants

The most common air pollutants in urban environments include sulphur dioxide (SO_2), suspended particulate matter (SPM), the nitrogen oxides (NO and NO_2, collectively termed NO_X), ozone (O_3), carbon monoxide (CO) and lead (Pb). Combustion of fossil fuels in stationary sources leads to the production of SO_2, NO_X and particulates, including sulphate and nitrate aerosols formed in the atmosphere following gas to particle conversion. Petrol-fuelled motor vehicles are the principal sources of NO_X, CO and Pb, whereas diesel-fuelled engines emit significant quantities of particulates, SO_2 and NO_X. Ozone, a photochemical oxidant and the main constituent of photochemical smog, is not emitted directly from combustion sources but is formed in the lower atmosphere from NO_X and volatile organic compounds (VOCs) in the presence of sunlight (UNEP 1991b). Table 53.3 presents the major sources of outdoor air pollutants.

Table 53.3 • Major sources of outdoor air pollutants.

Pollutants	Sources
Sulphur oxides	Coal and oil combustion, smelters
Suspended particulate matter	Combustion products (fuel, biomass), tobacco smoke
Nitrogen oxides	Fuel and gas combustion
Carbon monoxide	Incomplete petrol and gas combustion
Ozone	Photochemical reaction
Lead	Petrol combustion, coal combustion, producing batteries, cables, solder, paint
Organic substances	Petrochemical solvents, vaporization of unburnt fuels

Source: Adapted from UNEP 1991b.

Table 53.4 • Summary of short-term exposure-response relationship of PM$_{10}$ with different health effects indicators.

Health effect	% changes for each 10 μg/m^3 increase in PM$_{10}$	
	Mean	Range
Mortality		
Total	1.0	0.5–1.5
Cardiovascular	1.4	0.8–1.8
Respiratory	3.4	1.5–3.7
Morbidity		
Hospital admission for respiratory condition	1.1	0.8–3.4
Emergency visits for respiratory conditions	1.0	0.5–4
Symptom exacerbations among asthmatics	3.0	1.1–11.5
Changes in peak expiratory flow	0.08	0.04–0.25

Dispersion and Transport of Air Pollutants

The two major influences on the dispersion and transport of air pollutant emissions are the meteorology (including microclimate effects such as "heat islands") and the topography in relation to the population distribution. Many cities are surrounded by hills which may act as a downwind barrier, trapping pollution. Thermal inversions contribute to a particulate problem in temperate and cold climates. Under normal dispersion conditions, hot pollutant gases rise as they come into contact with colder air masses with increasing altitude. However, under certain circumstances the temperature may increase with altitude, and an inversion layer forms, trapping pollutants close to the emission source and delaying their diffusion. Long-range transport of air pollution from large urban areas may have national and regional impacts. Oxides of nitrogen and sulphur may contribute to acid deposition at

Table 53.5 • Health outcomes associated with changes in peak daily ambient ozone concentration in epidemiological studies.

Health outcome	Changes in 1-h O$_3$ (μg/m^3)	Changes in 8-h O$_3$ (μg/m^3)
Symptom exacerbations among healthy children and adults or asthmatics-normal activity		
25% increase	200	100
50% increase	400	200
100% increase	800	300
Hospital admissions for respiratory conditions[a]		
5%	30	25
10%	60	50
20%	120	100

[a] Given the high degree of correlation between the 1-h and 8-h O$_3$ concentrations in field studies, an improvement in health risk associated with decreasing 1- or 8-h O$_3$ levels should be almost identical.
Source: WHO 1995.

great distances from the emission source. Ozone concentrations are often elevated downwind of urban areas due to the time lag involved in photochemical processes (UNEP 1991b).

Health Effects of Air Pollutants

Pollutants and their derivatives can cause adverse effects by interacting with and impairing molecules crucial to the biochemical or physiological processes of the human body. Three factors influence the risk of toxic injury related to these substances: their chemical and physical properties, the dose of the material that reaches the critical tissue sites and the responsiveness of these sites to the substance. The adverse health effects of air pollutants may also vary across population groups; in particular, the young and the elderly may be especially susceptible to deleterious effects. Persons with asthma or other pre-existing respiratory or cardiac diseases may experience aggravated symptoms upon exposure (WHO 1987).

Sulphur Dioxide and Particulate Matter

During the first half of the twentieth century, episodes of marked air stagnation resulted in excess mortality in areas where fossil-fuel combustion produced very high levels of SO$_2$ and SMP. Studies of long-term health effects have also related the annual mean concentrations of SO$_2$ and SMP to mortality and morbidity. Recent epidemiological studies have suggested an adverse effect of inhalable particulate levels (PM$_{10}$) at relatively low concentrations (not exceeding the standard guidelines) and have shown a dose-response relationship between exposure to PM$_{10}$ and respiratory mortality and morbidity (Dockery and Pope 1994; Pope, Bates and Razienne 1995; Bascom et al. 1996) as shown in table 53.4.

Nitrogen Oxides

Some epidemiological studies have reported adverse health effects of NO$_2$ including increased incidence and severity of respiratory infections and increase in respiratory symptoms, especially with long-term exposure. Worsening of the clinical status of persons with asthma, chronic obstructive pulmonary disease and other chronic respiratory conditions has also been described. However, in other studies, investigators have not observed adverse effects of NO$_2$ on respiratory functions (WHO/ECOTOX 1992; Bascom et al. 1996).

Photochemical Oxidants and Ozone

The health effects of photochemical oxidants exposure cannot be attributed only to oxidants, because photochemical smog typically consists of O$_3$, NO$_2$, acid and sulphate and other reactive agents. These pollutants may have additive or synergistic effects on human health, but O$_3$ appears to be the most biologically active. Health effects of ozone exposure include decreased pulmonary function (including increased airway resistance, reduced air flow, decreased lung volume) due to airway constriction, respiratory symptoms (cough, wheezing, shortness of breath, chest pains), eye, nose and throat irritation, and disruption of activities (such as athletic performance) due to less oxygen availability (WHO/ECOTOX 1992). Table 53.5 summarizes the major acute health effects of ozone (WHO 1990a, 1995). Epidemiological studies have suggested a dose-response relationship between exposure to increasing ozone levels and the severity of respiratory symptoms and the decrement in respiratory functions (Bascom et al. 1996).

Carbon Monoxide

The main effect of CO is to decrease oxygen transport to the tissues through the formation of carboxyhaemoglobin (COHb). With increasing levels of COHb in blood, the following health

Case study: Air pollution in Mexico City

The metropolitan area of Mexico City (MAMC) is situated in the Mexican Basin at a mean altitude of 2,240 metres. The basin covers 2,500 square kilometres and is surrounded by mountains, two of which are over 5,000 metres high. The total population was estimated at 17 million in 1990. Due to the particular geographic characteristics and the light winds, ventilation is poor with a high frequency of thermic inversions, especially during the winter. More than 30,000 industries in the MAMC and the three million motor vehicles circulating daily are responsible for 44% of the total energy consumption. Since 1986, air pollution has been monitored, including SO_2, NO_x, CO, O_3, particulate matter and non-methane hydrocarbon (HCNM). The main air pollutant problems are related to ozone, especially in the southwest part of the city (Romieu et al. 1991). In 1992 the Mexican norm for ozone (110 ppb one-hour maximum) was exceeded in the southwest part more than 1,000 hours and reached a maximum of 400 ppb. Particulate levels are high in the northeast section of the city, close to the industrial park. In 1992, the annual average of inhalable particulate (PM_{10}) was 140 µg/m³. Since 1990, important control measures have been taken by the government to decrease air pollution, including a programme that prohibits use of cars one day a week depending on their terminating licence plate number, the closure of one of the most polluting refineries located in Mexico City, and the introduction of unleaded fuel. These measures have led to a decrease in various air pollutants, mainly SO_2, particulate matter, NO_2, CO and lead. However the ozone level remains a major problem (see figures 53.4, 53.5 and 53.6).

Figure 53.5 • Particulates (PM_{10}) in two zones of Mexico City, 1988-1993.

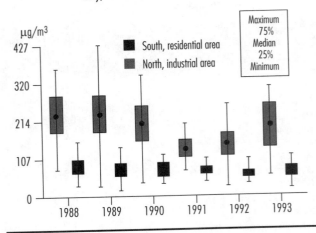

effects can be observed: cardiovascular effects in subjects with previous angina pectoris (3 to 5%); impairment of vigilance tasks (>5%); headache and dizziness (≥10%); fibrinolysis and death (WHO 1987).

Lead

Lead exposure principally affects haem biosynthesis, but also may act on the nervous system and other systems such as the cardiovascular system (blood pressure). Infants and young children less than five years old are particularly sensitive to lead exposure because of its effect on neurological development at blood lead levels close to 10 µg/dl (CDC 1991).

Several epidemiological studies have investigated the effect of air pollution, especially ozone exposure, on the health of the population of Mexico City. Ecological studies have shown an increase in mortality with respect to exposure to fine particulates (Borja-Arburto et al. 1995) and an increase in emergency visits for asthma among children (Romieu et al. 1994). Studies of the adverse effect of ozone exposure conducted among healthy children have shown an increase in school absenteeism due to respiratory illnesses (Romieu et al. 1992), and a decrease in lung function after both acute and subacute exposure (Castillejos et al. 1992, 1995). Studies conducted among asthmatic children have shown an increase in respiratory symptoms and a decrease in peak expiratory flow rate after exposure to ozone (Romieu et al. 1994) and to fine particulate levels (Romieu et al. in press). Although, it seems clear that acute exposure to ozone and particulates is associated with adverse health effects in the population of Mexico City, there is a need to evaluate the chronic effect of such exposure, in particular given the high levels of photo-oxidants observed in Mexico City and the ineffectiveness of control measures.

Figure 53.4 • Ozone levels in two zones of Mexico City. One-hour daily maximum by month, 1994.

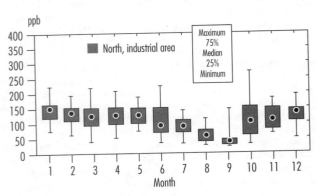

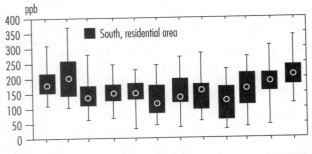

LAND POLLUTION

Tee L. Guidotti and Chen Weiping

The amount of waste produced by human society is increasing. Commercial and domestic solid waste is a great practical problem for many local governments. Industrial wastes are usually much smaller in volume but are more likely to contain hazardous materials, such as toxic chemicals, flammable liquids and asbestos. Although the total amount is less, the disposal of hazardous

Figure 53.6 • Air lead levels in two zones of Mexico City, 1988-1994.

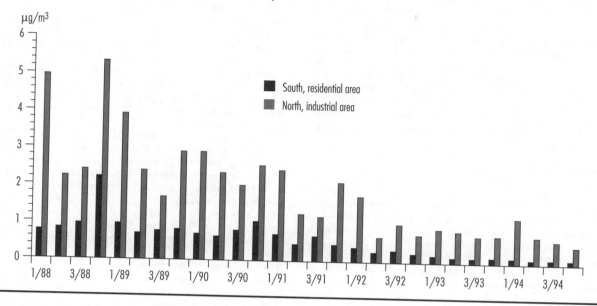

industrial waste has been a greater concern than of domestic waste because of the perceived hazard to health and the risk of environmental contamination.

The generation of hazardous waste has become a major problem worldwide. The root cause of the problem is industrial production and distribution. Land pollution occurs when hazardous wastes contaminate soil and groundwater due to inadequate or irresponsible disposal measures. Abandoned or neglected waste disposal sites are a particularly difficult and expensive problem for society. Sometimes, hazardous waste is disposed of illegally and in an even more dangerous manner because the owner cannot find a cheap way to get rid of it. One of the major unresolved issues in managing hazardous waste is to find methods of disposal that are both safe and inexpensive. Public concern over hazardous waste focuses on the potential health effects of exposure to toxic chemicals, and particularly the risk of cancer.

The Basel Convention passed in 1989 is an international agreement to control the transboundary movement of hazardous waste and to prevent dangerous wastes from being shipped for disposal to countries that do not have the facilities to process them safely. The Basel Convention requires that the generation of hazardous wastes and transboundary movement of the wastes be kept to a minimum. Traffic in hazardous wastes is subject to the informed permission and laws of the receiving country. Transboundary movement of hazardous wastes is subject to good environmental practices and assurance that the receiving country is able to handle them safely. All other traffic in hazardous wastes is considered illegal and therefore criminal in intent, subject to national laws and penalties. This international convention provides an essential framework for controlling the problem at an international level.

Hazardous Properties of Chemicals

Hazardous substances are compounds and mixtures that pose a threat to health and property because of their toxicity, flammability, explosive potential, radiation or other dangerous properties. Public attention tends to focus on carcinogens, industrial wastes, pesticides and radiation hazards. However, innumerable compounds that do not fall into these categories can pose a threat to the public's safety and health.

Hazardous chemicals may present physical hazards, although this is more common in transportation and industrial incidents. Hydrocarbons may catch fire and even explode. Fires and explosions may generate their own toxic hazards depending on the chemicals that were initially present. Fires involving pesticide storage areas are a particularly dangerous situation, as the pesticides may be converted into even more highly toxic combustion products (such as paraoxons in the case of organophosphates) and substantial amounts of environmentally damaging dioxins and furans may be generated from combustion in the presence of chlorine compounds.

Toxicity, however, is the principal concern of most people with respect to hazardous waste. Chemicals may be toxic to human beings and they may also be damaging to the environment through toxicity to animal and plant species. Those that do not readily degrade in the environment (a characteristic called *biopersistence*) or that accumulate in the environment (a characteristic called *bioaccumulation*) are of particular concern.

The number and hazardous nature of toxic substances in common use has changed dramatically. In the last generation, research and development in organic chemistry and chemical engineering have introduced thousands of new compounds into widespread commercial use, including persistent compounds such as the polychlorinated biphenyls (PCBs), more potent pesticides, accelerators and plasticizers with unusual and poorly understood effects. The production of chemicals has risen dramatically. In 1941 production of all synthetic organic compounds in the United States alone, for example, was less than one billion kilograms. Today it is much greater than 80 billion kilograms. Many compounds in common use today underwent little testing and are not well understood.

Toxic chemicals are also much more intrusive in daily life than in the past. Many chemical plants or disposal sites which were once isolated or on the edge of town have become incorporated into urban areas by suburban growth. Communities now lie in closer proximity to the problem than they have in the past. Some communities are built directly over old disposal sites. Although incidents involving hazardous substances take many forms and may be highly individual, the great majority seem to involve a relatively narrow range of hazardous substances, which include:

solvents, paints and coatings, metal solutions, polychlorinated biphenyls (PCBs), pesticides, and acids and alkalis. In studies conducted in the United States, the ten most common hazardous substances found in disposal sites requiring government intervention were lead, arsenic, mercury, vinyl chloride, benzene, cadmium, PCBs, chloroform, benzo(a)pyrene and trichloroethylene. However, chromium, tetrachloroethylene, toluene and di-2-ethylhexylphthalate were also prominent among those substances that could be shown to migrate or for which there was an opportunity for human exposure. The origin of these chemical wastes varies greatly and depends on the local situation, but typically elecroplating solutions, discarded chemicals, manufacturing by-products and waste solvents contribute to the waste stream.

Groundwater Contamination

Figure 53.7 presents a cross-section of a hypothetical hazardous waste site to illustrate problems that may be encountered. (In practice, such a site should never be placed near a body of water or over a gravel bed.) In well-designed hazardous waste disposal (containment) facilities, there is an effectively impermeable seal to prevent hazardous chemicals from migrating out of the site and into the underlying soil. Such a site also has facilities to treat those chemicals that can be neutralized or transformed and to reduce the volume of waste that goes into the site; those chemicals that cannot be so treated are contained in impermeable containers. (Permeability, however, is relative, as described below.)

Chemicals may escape by leaking if the container is compromised, leaching if water gets in or spilling during handling or after the site is disturbed. Once they permeate the liner of a site, or if the liner is broken or if there is no liner, they enter the ground and migrate downward due to gravity. This migration is much more rapid through porous soil and is slow through clay and bedrock. Even underground, water flows downhill and will take the path of least resistance, and so the groundwater level will fall slightly in the direction of flow and the flow will be much faster through sand or gravel. If there is a water table under the ground, the chemicals will eventually reach it. Lighter chemicals tend to float on the groundwater and form an upper layer. Heavier chemicals and water-soluble compounds tend to dissolve or be carried along by the groundwater as it flows slowly underground through porous rock or gravel. The region of contamination, called the *plume*, can be mapped by drilling test wells, or bore holes. The plume slowly expands and moves in the direction of groundwater movement.

Surface water contamination may occur by runoff from the site, if the top layer of soil is contaminated, or by groundwater. When the groundwater feeds into a local body of water, such as a river or lake, the contamination is carried into this body of water. Some chemicals tend to deposit in the bottom sediment and others are carried along by the flow.

Groundwater contamination may take centuries to clear by itself. If shallow wells are used as a water source by local residents, there is a possibility of exposure by ingestion and by skin contact.

Human Health Concerns

People come into contact with toxic substances in many ways. Exposure to a toxic substance may occur at several points in the use cycle of the substance. People work in a plant where the substances arise as waste from an industrial process and do not change clothes or wash before coming home. They may reside near hazardous waste disposal sites which are illegal or poorly designed or managed, with opportunities for exposure as a result of accidents or careless handling or lack of containment of the substance, or lack of fencing to keep children off the site. Ex-

Figure 53.7 • Cross-section or a hypothetical hazardous waste site.

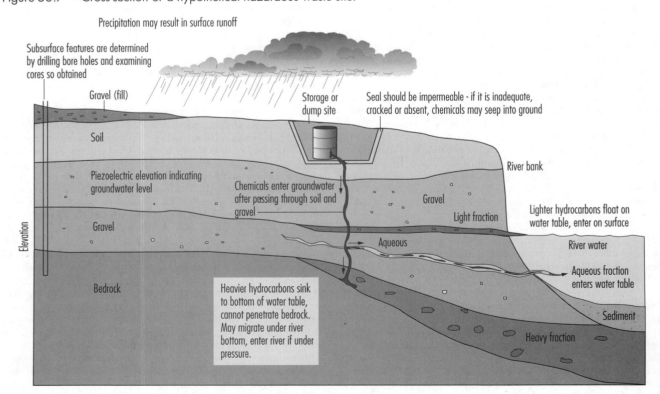

posure may occur in the home as the result of consumer products that are mislabelled, poorly stored and not child-proof.

Three routes of exposure are by far the most important in considering the implications for toxicity of hazardous waste: inhalation, ingestion and absorption through the skin. Once absorbed, and depending on the route of exposure, there are many ways in which people can be affected by toxic chemicals. Obviously, the list of possible toxic effects associated with hazardous waste is very long. However, public concern and scientific studies have tended to concentrate on the risk of cancer and reproductive effects. In general, this has reflected the profile of chemical hazards at these sites.

There have been many studies of residents who live around or near such sites. With a few exceptions, these studies have shown remarkably little in the way of verifiable, clinically significant health problems. The exceptions have tended to be situations where the contamination is exceptionally severe and there has been a clear pathway of exposure of residents immediately adjacent to the site or who drink well water drawing on groundwater contaminated by the site. There are several likely reasons for this surprising absence of documentable health effects. One is that unlike air pollution and surface water pollution, the chemicals in land pollution are not easily available to people. People may live in areas highly contaminated by chemicals, but unless they actually come in contact with the chemicals by one of the routes of exposure mentioned above, no toxicity will result. Another reason may be that the chronic effects of exposure to these toxic chemicals take a long time to develop and are very difficult to study. Yet another reason may be that these chemicals are less potent in causing chronic health effects in humans than is usually supposed.

Notwithstanding the human health effects, the damage of land pollution to ecosystems may be very great. Plant and animal species, soil bacteria (which contribute to agricultural productivity) and other ecosystem constituents may be irreversibly damaged by degrees of pollution that are not associated with any visible human health effect.

Control of the Problem

Because of population distributions, land use restrictions, transportation costs and concern from society over environmental effects, there is intense pressure to find a solution to the problem of economical disposal of hazardous waste. This has led to increased interest in methods such as source reduction, recycling, chemical neutralization and secure hazardous waste disposal (containment) sites. The first two reduce the amount of waste that is produced. Chemical neutralization reduces the toxicity of the waste and may convert it into a more easily handled solid. Whenever possible, it is preferred that this be done at the site of production of the waste to reduce the amount of waste that must be moved. Well-designed hazardous waste disposal facilities, using the best available technologies of chemical processing and containment, are needed for the residual waste.

Secure hazardous waste containment sites are relatively expensive to build. The site needs to be selected carefully to ensure that pollution of surface water and major aquifers (groundwater) will not readily occur. The site must be designed and built with impermeable barriers to prevent contamination of soil and groundwater. These barriers are typically heavy plastic liners and layers of tamped clay fill under the holding areas. In reality, the barrier acts to delay breakthrough and to slow the permeation that eventually does occur to an acceptable rate, one that will not result in accumulation or significant pollution of groundwater. Permeability is a property of the material, described in terms of the resistance of the material to a liquid or gas penetrating it under given conditions of pressure and temperature. Even the least permeable barrier, such as plastic liners or packed clay, will eventually allow the passage of some liquid chemical through the barrier, although it may take years and even centuries, and once breakthrough occurs the flow becomes continuous, although it may occur at a very low rate. This means that groundwater immediately below a hazardous waste disposal site is always at some risk of contamination, even if it is very small. Once groundwater is contaminated, it is very difficult and often impossible to decontaminate.

Many hazardous waste disposal sites are regularly monitored with collection systems and by testing nearby wells to ensure that pollution is not spreading. The more advanced are built with recycling and processing facilities on-site or nearby to further reduce the waste that goes into the disposal site.

Hazardous waste containment sites are not a perfect solution to the problem of land pollution. They require expensive expertise to design, are expensive to build, and may require monitoring, which creates an ongoing cost. They do not guarantee that groundwater contamination will not occur in the future, although they are effective in minimizing this. A major disadvantage is that someone, inevitably, must live near one. Communities where hazardous waste sites are located or proposed to be located usually oppose them strongly and make it difficult for governments to grant approval. This is called the "not in my back yard" (NIMBY) syndrome and is a common response to the siting of facilities considered undesirable. In the case of hazardous waste sites, the NIMBY syndrome tends to be especially strong.

Unfortunately, without hazardous waste containment sites, society may lose control of the situation entirely. When no hazardous waste site is available, or when it is too expensive to use one, hazardous waste is often disposed of illegally. Such practices include pouring liquid waste on the ground in remote areas, dumping the waste into drains that go into local waterways and shipping the waste to jurisdictions that have more lax laws governing the handling of hazardous waste. This may create an even more dangerous situation than a poorly managed disposal site would create.

There are several technologies that can be used to dispose of the remaining waste. High-temperature incineration is one of the cleanest and most effective means of disposing of hazardous waste, but the cost of these facilities is very high. One of the more promising approaches has been to incinerate liquid toxic waste in cement kilns, which operate at the necessary high temperatures and are found throughout the developing as well as the developed world. Injection into deep wells, below the water table, is one option for chemicals that cannot be disposed of in any other way. However, groundwater migration can be tricky and sometimes unusual pressure situations underground or leaks in the well lead to groundwater contamination anyway. Dehalogenation is a chemical technology that strips the chlorine and bromine atoms from halogenated hydrocarbons, such as PCBs, so that they can be easily disposed of by incineration.

A major unresolved issue in municipal solid waste handling is contamination by hazardous waste discarded by accident or intent. This can be minimized by diverting disposal into a separate waste stream. Most municipal solid waste systems divert chemical and other hazardous wastes so that they do not contaminate the solid waste stream. The separate waste stream should, ideally, be diverted to a secure hazardous waste disposal site.

There is a pressing need for facilities to collect and properly dispose of small quantities of hazardous waste, at minimal cost. Individuals who find themselves in possession of a bottle or can of solvents, pesticides or some unknown powder or fluid usually cannot afford the high cost of proper disposal and do not understand the risk. Some system for collecting such hazardous waste from consumers is needed before it is poured on the ground, flushed down the toilet or burned and released into the air. A number of municipalities sponsor "toxic roundup" days, when residents bring small quantities of toxic materials to a central location for safe disposal. Decentralized systems have been introduced in some urban areas, involving home or local pick-up of small quantities of toxic substances to be discarded. In the United States, experience has shown that people are willing to drive up to five miles to dispose of household toxic wastes safely. Consumer education to promote awareness of the potential toxicity of common products is urgently needed. Pesticides in aerosol cans, bleaches, household cleaners and cleaning fluids are potentially dangerous, especially to children.

Abandoned Hazardous Waste Disposal Sites

Abandoned or insecure hazardous waste sites are a common problem worldwide. Hazardous waste sites that need to be cleaned up are great liabilities to society. The ability of countries and local jurisdictions to clean up major hazardous waste sites varies greatly. Ideally, the owner of the site or the person who created the site should pay for its clean-up. In practice, such sites have often changed hands and the past owners have often gone out of business, the current owners may not have the financial resources to clean up, and the clean-up effort tends to be delayed for very long periods by expensive technical studies followed by legal battles. Smaller and less affluent countries have little leverage in negotiating clean-ups with the current site owners or the responsible parties, and no substantial resources to clean up the site.

The traditional approaches to cleaning up hazardous waste sites are very slow and expensive. It requires highly specialized expertise that is often in short supply. A hazardous waste site is first evaluated to determine how serious the land pollution is and whether the groundwater is contaminated. The likelihood of residents coming into contact with hazardous substances is determined and, in some cases, an estimate of the risk to health that this poses is calculated. Acceptable clean-up levels must be decided upon, the extent to which exposure must ultimately be reduced to protect human health and the environment. Most governments makes decisions about clean-up levels by applying various applicable environmental laws, air pollution standards, drinking water standards, and based on a hazards assessment of health risks posed by the particular site. Clean-up levels are therefore set to reflect both health and environmental concerns. A decision must be made on how the site is to be remediated, or how best to achieve this reduction in exposure. Remediation is a technical problem of achieving these clean-up levels by engineering and other methods. Some of the techniques that are used include incineration, solidification, chemical treatment, evaporation, repeated flushing of soil, biodegradation, containment, removal of soil off-site and pumping out groundwater. These engineering options are too complex and specific to the circumstances to describe in detail. Solutions must fit the particular situation and the funds available to achieve control. In some cases, remediation is not feasible. A decision then has to be made on what land use will be permitted on the site.

● WATER POLLUTION

Ivanildo Hespanhol and Richard Helmer

For at least two millennia natural water quality has deteriorated progressively and reached contamination levels where water uses are severely limited or the water can be harmful to humans. This deterioration is related to the socio-economic development within a river basin, but long-range atmospheric transport of contaminants has now changed this picture: even remote areas can be indirectly polluted (Meybeck and Helmer 1989).

Medieval reports and complaints about inadequate excreta disposal, foul and stinking water courses within overcrowded cities and other similar problems were an early manifestation of urban water pollution. The first time that a clear causal linkage between bad water quality and human health effects was established was in 1854, when John Snow traced back the outbreak of cholera epidemics in London to a particular drinking water source.

Since the middle of the twentieth century, and concurrent with the onset of accelerated industrial growth, various types of water pollution problems have occurred in rapid succession. Figure 53.8 illustrates the types of problems as they became apparent in European freshwaters.

In summarizing the European situation it can be stated that: (1) the challenges of the past (pathogens, oxygen balance, eutrophication, heavy metals) have been recognized, researched and the necessary controls identified and more or less implemented and (2) the challenges of today are of a different nature—on the one hand, "traditional" point and non-point pollution sources (nitrates) and ubiquitous environmental contamination problems (synthetic organics), and, on the other hand, "third generation" problems interfering with global cycles (acidification, climate change).

In the past, water pollution in the developing countries resulted mainly from the discharge of untreated wastewater. Today it is more complex as a result of the production of hazardous wastes from industries and the rapidly increasing use of pesticides in agriculture. In fact, water pollution today in some developing countries, at least in the newly industrializing ones, is worse than in industrialized countries (Arceivala 1989). Unfortunately, developing countries, on the whole, are badly lagging behind in getting control over their major pollution sources. As a consequence, their environmental quality is gradually deteriorating (WHO/UNEP 1991).

Types and Sources of Pollution

There are a large number of microbial agents, elements and compounds which may cause water pollution. They can be classified as: microbiological organisms, biodegradable organic compounds, suspended matter, nitrates, salts, heavy metals, nutrients and organic micropollutants.

Microbiological organisms

Microbiological organisms are common in freshwater bodies polluted particularly by discharges of untreated domestic wastewater. These microbial agents include pathogenic bacteria, viruses, helminths, protozoa and several more complex multicellular organisms that can cause gastro-intestinal illness. Other organisms are more opportunistic in nature, infecting susceptible individuals through body contact with contaminated water or by inhalation of poor quality water droplets in aerosols of various origins.

Biodegradable organic compounds

Organic substances of either natural origin (allochthonous terrestrial detritus or autochthonous debris of aquatic plants) or from anthropogenic sources (domestic, agricultural and some industrial wastes) are decomposed by aerobic microbes as the river continues its course. The consequence is a lowering of the oxygen level downstream of the wastewater discharge, impairing the quality of the water and the survival of the aquatic biota, particularly of high-quality fish.

Particulate matter

Particulate matter is a major carrier of organic and inorganic pollutants. Most toxic heavy metals, organic pollutants, pathogens and nutrients, such as phosphorus, are found in suspended matter. An appreciable amount of the biodegradable organic material responsible for consumption of dissolved oxygen from rivers is also found in suspended particles. Particulate matter comes from

Figure 53.8 • Types of water pollution problems.

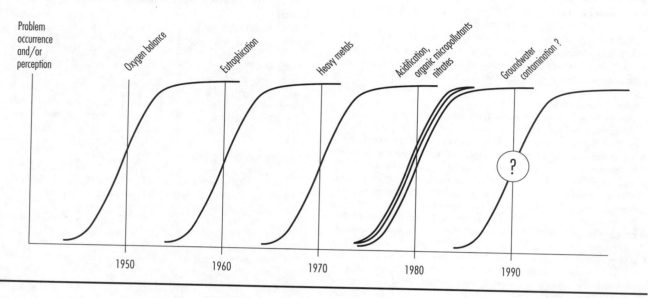

urbanization and road construction, deforestation, mining operations, dredging operations in rivers, natural sources which are linked to continental erosion, or natural catastrophic events. Coarser particles are deposited on river beds, in reservoirs, in the flood plain and in wetlands and lakes

Nitrates

The concentration of nitrates in unpolluted surface waters ranges from less than 0.1 to one milligrams per litre (expressed as nitrogen), so nitrate levels in excess of 1 mg/l indicate anthropogenic influences such as discharge of municipal wastes and urban and agricultural run-off. Atmospheric precipitation is also an important source of nitrate and ammonia to river basins, particularly in areas not affected by direct pollution sources—for example, some tropical regions. High concentrations of nitrate in drinking water may lead to acute toxicity in bottle-fed infants during their first months of life, or in the elderly, a phenomenon called methaemoglobinaemia.

Salts

Water salinization may be caused by natural conditions, such as geochemical interaction of waters with salty soils or by anthropogenic activities, including irrigated agriculture, sea water intrusion due to excessive pumping of groundwaters in islands and coastal areas, disposal of industrial wastes and of oilfield brines, highway de-icing, landfill leachates and leaking sewers.

While hampering beneficial uses, particularly for irrigation of sensitive crops or for drinking, salinity in itself may not, at even quite high levels, be directly harmful to health, but the indirect effects can be dramatic. The loss of fertile agricultural land and reduced crop yields caused by waterlogging and soil salinization of irrigated areas destroy the livelihood of whole communities and cause hardships in the form of food shortages.

Heavy metals

Heavy metals such as lead, cadmium and mercury are micro-pollutants and of special interest as they have health and environmental significance due to their persistence, high toxicity and bio-accumulation characteristics.

There are basically five sources of heavy metals contributing to water pollution: geological weathering, which provides the background level; industrial processing of ores and metals; the use of metal and metal compounds, such as chromium salts in tanneries, copper compounds in agriculture, and tetraethyl lead as an anti-knock agent in gasoline; leaching of heavy metals from domestic wastes and solid waste dumps; and heavy metals in human and animal excretions, particularly zinc. Metals released to the air from automobiles, fuel burning and industrial process emissions may settle on land and ultimately run off to surface waters.

Nutrients

Eutrophication is defined as the enrichment of waters with plant nutrients, primarily phosphorus and nitrogen, leading to enhanced plant growth (both algae and macrophytes) which results in visible algae blooms, floating algal or macrophyte mats, benthic algae and submerged macrophyte agglomerations. When decaying, this plant material leads to the depletion of the oxygen reserves of water bodies, which, in turn, causes an array of secondary problems such as fish mortality and liberation of corrosive gases and other undesirable substances, such as carbonic gas, methane, hydrogen sulphide, organoleptic substances (causing taste and odour), toxins and so on.

The source of phosphorus and nitrogen compounds is primarily untreated domestic wastewater, but other sources such as drainage of artificially fertilized agricultural land, surface run-off from intensive livestock farming and some industrial wastewaters can also substantially increase the trophic level of lakes and reservoirs, particularly in tropical developing countries.

The main problems associated with eutrophication of lakes, reservoirs and impoundments are: oxygen depletion of the bottom layer of lakes and reservoirs; water quality impairment, leading to treatment difficulties, particularly for the removal of taste- and odour-causing substances; recreational impairment, increased health hazards to bathers and unsightliness; fisheries impairment due to fish mortality and the development of undesirable and low-quality fish stocks; ageing and reducing the holding capacity of lakes and reservoirs by silting; and increase of corrosion problems in pipes and other structures.

Organic micropollutants

Organic micropollutants can be classified in groups of chemical products on the basis of how they are used and consequently how they are dispersed in the environment:

- *Pesticides* are substances, generally synthetic, that are deliberately introduced into the environment to protect crops or control disease vectors. They are found in various distinct families, such as organochloride insecticides, organophosphate insecticides, herbicides of the plant hormone type, triazines, substituted ureas and others.
- *Materials for widespread household and industrial use* comprise volatile organic substances used as extraction solvents, solvents for degreasing metals and dry-cleaning clothes, and propellants for use in aerosol containers. This group also includes halogenated derivatives of methane, ethane and ethylene. As they are widely used their rates of dispersion in the environment, compared with the amounts produced, are generally high. The group also contains the polycyclic aromatic hydrocarbons, whose presence in the environment results from the extraction, transport and refining of petroleum products and the dispersion of combustion products resulting from their use (petrol and heating oil).
- *Materials used essentially in industry* include substances which are direct or intermediate agents of chemical synthesis, such as carbon tetrachloride for synthesizing freons; vinyl chloride for polymerizing PVC; and chlorinated derivates of benzene, naphthalene, phenol and aniline for manufacturing dyestuffs. The group also contains finished products used in closed systems, such as heat-exchange fluids and dielectrics.

Organic micropollutants are generated from point and diffuse sources, either urban or rural. The largest part originates in major industrial activities such as petrol refining, coal mining, organic synthesis and the manufacture of synthetic products, the iron and steel industries, the textile industry and the wood and pulp industry. Effluents from pesticides factories may contain considerable quantities of these manufactured products. A significant proportion of organic pollutants are discharged into the aquatic environment as run-off from urban surfaces; and in agricultural areas, pesticides applied to crops may reach surface waters through rainwater run-off and artificial or natural drainage. Also, accidental discharges have led to severe ecological damage and temporary closure of water supplies.

Urban Pollution

Owing to this continuously expanding, aggressive and multi-faceted pollution scenario, the problem of maintaining the quality of water resources has become acute, particularly in the more urbanized areas of the developing world. Maintaining water quality is hampered by two factors: failure to enforce pollution control at the main sources, especially industries, and inadequacy of sanitation systems and of garbage collection and disposal (WHO 1992b). A sidebar gives some examples of water pollution in different cities in developing countries.

Health Impacts of Microbial Pollution

Diseases arising from the ingestion of pathogens in contaminated water have the greatest impact worldwide. "An estimated 80% of all diseases, and over one-third of deaths in developing countries are caused by the consumption of contaminated water, and on average as much as one-tenth of each person's productive time is sacrificed to water-related diseases" (UNCED 1992). Water-borne diseases are the largest single category of communicable diseases contributing to infant mortality in developing countries and second only to tuberculosis in contributing to adult mortality, with one million deaths per year.

Examples of water pollution in selected cities

Karachi (Pakistan)

The Lyari river, which runs through Karachi, Pakistan's largest industrial city, is an open drain from both the chemical and the microbiological point of view, a mixture of raw sewage and untreated industrial effluents. Most industrial effluents come from an industrial estate with some 300 major industries and almost three times as many small units. Three-fifths of the units are textile mills. Most other industries in Karachi also discharge untreated effluents into the nearest water body.

Alexandria (Egypt)

Industries in Alexandria account for around 40% of all Egypt's industrial output, and most discharge untreated liquid wastes into the sea or into Lake Maryut. In the past decade, fish production in Lake Maryut declined by some 80% because of the direct discharge of industrial and domestic effluents. The lake has also ceased to be a prime recreational site because of its poor condition. Similar environmental degradation is taking place along the seafront as a result of the discharge of untreated wastewater from poorly located outfalls.

Shanghai (China)

Some 3.4 million cubic metres of industrial and domestic waste pour mostly into the Suzhou Creek and the Huangpu River, which flows through the heart of the city. These have become the main (open) sewers for the city. Most of the waste is industrial, since few houses possess flush toilets. The Huangpu has essentially been dead since 1980. In all, less than 5% of the city's wastewater is treated. The normally high water table also means that a variety of toxins from industrial plants and local rivers find their way into groundwater and contaminate wells, which also contribute to the city water supply.

São Paulo (Brazil)

The Tiete River, as it passes through Greater São Paulo, one of the world's largest urban agglomerations, receives 300 tonnes of effluents each day from 1,200 industries located in the region. Lead, cadmium and other heavy metals are among the main pollutants. It also receives 900 tonnes of sewage each day, of which only 12.5% is treated by the five sewage treatment stations located in the area.

Source: Based on Hardoy and Satterthwaite 1989.

The total annual number of cholera cases reported to the WHO by its member states has reached levels unprecedented during the seventh pandemic, with a peak of 595,000 cases in 1991 (WHO 1993). Table 53.6 shows the global morbidity and mortality rates of the major water-related diseases. These figures are, in many cases, grossly underestimated, since reporting of disease cases is done quite erratically by many countries.

Health Impacts of Chemical Pollution

The health problems associated with chemical substances dissolved in water arise primarily from their ability to cause adverse effects after prolonged periods of exposure; of particular concern are contaminants that have cumulative toxic properties such as heavy metals and some organic micropollutants, substances that are carcinogenic and substances that may cause reproductive and developmental effects. Other dissolved substances in water are essential ingredients of dietary intake and yet others are neutral with regards to human needs. Chemicals in water, particularly in drinking water, may be classified into three typical categories for the purpose of health impact (Galal-Gorchev 1986):

- *Substances exerting an acute or chronic toxicity upon consumption.* The severity of the health impairment increases with the increase of their concentration in drinking water. On the other hand, below a certain threshold concentration no health effects can be observed—that is, the human metabolism can handle this exposure without measurable long-term effects. Various metals, nitrates, cyanides and so on fall within this category.
- *Genotoxic substances,* which cause health effects such as carcinogenicity, mutagenicity and birth-defects. According to present scientific thinking there is no threshold level which could be considered safe, since any amount of the substance ingested contributes to an increase in cancer and similar risks. Complex mathematical extrapolation models are used to determine such risks, since very little epidemiological evidence exists. Synthetic organics, many chlorinated organic micropollutants, some pesticides and arsenic fall within this category.
- For some elements, such as fluoride, iodine and selenium, the contribution made by drinking water is crucial and, if deficient, causes more or less severe health effects. At high concentrations, however, these same substances cause equally severe health effects, but of a different nature.

Environmental Impacts

The impacts of environmental pollution on freshwater quality are numerous and have existed for a long time. Industrial development, the advent of intensive agriculture, the exponential development of human populations and the production and use of tens of thousands of synthetic chemicals are among the main causes of water quality deterioration at local, national and global scales. The major issue of water pollution is the interference with actual or planned water uses.

One of the most severe and ubiquitous causes of environmental degradation is the discharge of organic wastes into watercourses (see "Biodegradable organic compounds" above). This pollution is mainly of concern in the aquatic environment where many organisms, for example fish, require high oxygen levels. A serious side effect of water anoxia is the release of toxic substances from particulates and bottom sediments in rivers and lakes. Other pollution effects from domestic sewage discharges into watercourses and aquifers include the build-up of nitrate levels in rivers and groundwaters, and the eutrophication of lakes and reservoirs (see above, "Nitrates" and "Salts"). In both cases,

the pollution is a synergistic effect of sewage effluents and agricultural run-off or infiltration.

Economic Impacts

The economic consequences of water pollution can be rather severe due to detrimental effects on human health or on the environment. Impaired health often lowers human productivity, and environmental degradation reduces the productivity of water resources used directly by people.

The economic disease burden can be expressed not only in costs of treatment, but also in quantifying the loss of productivity. This is particularly true for primarily disabling diseases, such as diarrhoea or Guinea Worm. In India, for example, there are about 73 million workdays per year estimated to be lost due to water-related diseases (Arceivala 1989).

Deficiencies in sanitation and the resulting epidemics can also lead to severe economic penalties. This became most apparent during the recent cholera epidemic in Latin America. During the cholera epidemic in Peru, losses from reduced agricultural exports and tourism were estimated at one billion US dollars. This is more than three times the amount that the country had invested in water supply and sanitation services during the 1980s (World Bank 1992).

Water resources affected by pollution become less suitable as sources of water for municipal supply. As a consequence, expensive treatment has to be installed or clean water from far away has to be piped to the city at much higher costs.

In the developing countries of Asia and the Pacific, environmental damage was estimated by Economic and Social Commission for Asia and the Pacific (ESCAP) in 1985 to cost about 3% of the GNP, amounting to US$250 billion, while the cost of repairing such damage would range around 1%.

Table 53.6 • Global morbidity and mortality rates of main diseases related to water.

Disease	Number/Year or Reporting Period	
	Cases	Deaths
Cholera—1993	297,000	4,971
Typhoid	500,000	25,000
Giardiasis	500,000	Low
Amoebiasis	48,000,000	110,000
Diarrhoeal disease (under 5 years)	1,600,000,000	3,200,000
Dracunculiasis (Guinea Worm)	2,600,000	–
Schistosomiasis	200,000,000	200,000

Source: Galal-Gorchev 1994.

ENERGY AND HEALTH

L.D. Hamilton

The WHO Commission on Health and Environment (1992a) Panel on Energy considered four energy-related issues to be of the highest immediate and/or future concern for environmental health:

1. exposure to noxious agents in the course of domestic utilization of biomass and coal
2. exposure resulting from urban air pollution in numerous large cities of the world
3. the possible health-related impacts of climate change
4. serious accidents with environmental impacts on the health of the general public.

Quantitative assessment of the health risks from different energy systems requires system-wide evaluation of *all* steps in a fuel cycle, starting with extraction of raw resources, and concluding with the final consumption of energy. For valid intertechnology comparisons to be made, methods, data and end-use demands must be similar and specified. In quantifying the effects of end-use demands, differences in conversion efficiencies of energy- and fuel-specific devices to useful energy must be evaluated.

Comparative assessment is built around the idea of the Reference Energy System (RES), which depicts fuel cycles step-by-step, from extraction through processing to combustion and ultimate disposal of wastes. The RES provides a common, simple framework for defining flows of energy and related data used for risk assessment. An RES (figure 53.9) is a network representation of the main components of an energy system for a given year, specifying resource consumption, fuel transportation, conversion processes and end uses, thereby compactly incorporating the salient features of the energy system while providing a framework for assessment of major resource, environmental, health and economic effects that can result from new technologies or policies.

Based on their health risks, energy technologies can be classified into three groups:

1. The *fuels group* is characterized by use of large amounts of fossil fuels or biomass—coal, oil, natural gas, wood and so on—the collection, processing and transport of which have high accident rates that dominate occupational risks and the burning of which produces large amounts of air pollution and solid waste that dominate public risks.

2. The *renewable group* is characterized by use of diffuse renewable resources with low energy density—sun, wind, water—which are available in enormous quantities at no cost, but the capturing of which requires large areas and construction of expensive facilities capable of "concentrating" them into useful forms. Occupational risks are high and dominated by construction of the facilities. Public risks are low, mostly confined to low-probability accidents, such as dam failures, equipment failures and fires.

3. The *nuclear group* includes nuclear fission technologies, distinguished by extremely high energy densities in the processed fuel, with corresponding low quantities of fuel and wastes to process, but with low concentrations in the earth's crust, necessitating a large mining or collection effort. Occupational risks are, therefore, relatively high and dominated by mining and processing accidents. Public risks are small and domi-

Figure 53.9 • Reference energy system, year 1979.

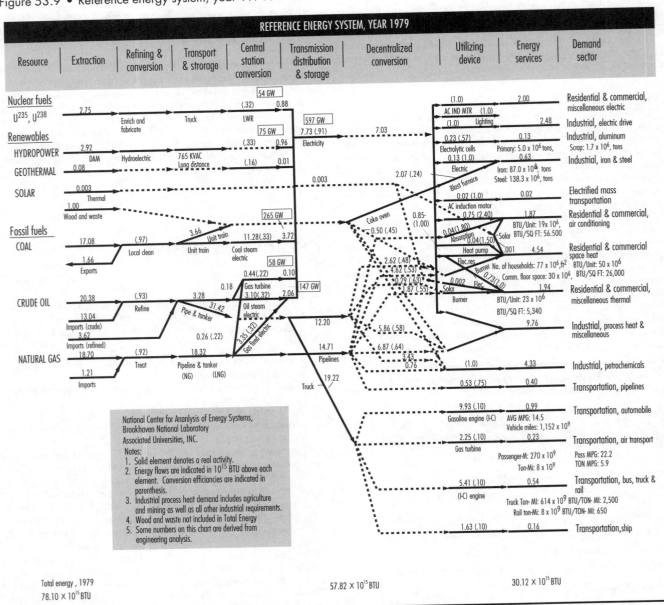

nated by routine operations of reactors. Special attention must be given to public fears of risks from exposure to radiation from nuclear technologies—fears which are relatively large per unit risk to health.

The significant health effects of technologies for generating electricity are shown in tables 53.7, 53.8 and 53.9.

Studies of health effects of wood burning in the United States, like analyses of other energy sources, were based on the health effects of supplying a unit amount of energy, that is, that needed to heat one million dwelling years. This is 6×10^7 GJ heat, or 8.8×10^7 GJ wood input at 69% efficiency. Health effects were estimated in gathering, transport and combustion stages. Oil and coal alternatives were scaled from earlier work (see figure 53.10). The uncertainties in gathering are ± a factor of ~2, those in home fires ± a factor of ~3, and those in air pollution ± a factor greater than 10. If the hazards of nuclear electric were plotted on the same scale, the total risk would be approximately one-half that of mining for coal mining.

A convenient way to help understand the risk is to scale it to a single person supplying one dwelling with wood over 40 years (figure 53.11). This results in a total risk of fatality of $\sim 1.6 \times 10^{-3}$ (i.e., ~0.2%). This can be compared with the risk of death in an automobile accident in the United States during the same time, $\sim 9.3 \times 10^{-3}$ (i.e., ~1%), which is five times greater. Wood burning presents risks which are of the same order as more conventional heating technologies. Both are well below the overall risk of other common activities, and many aspects of the risk are clearly amenable to preventive measures.

The following comparisons for health risks can be made:

- *Acute occupational risk.* For the coal cycle, occupational risk is distinctly higher than that associated with oil and gas; it is about the same as that associated with renewable energy systems, when their construction is included in the assessment, and it is about 8-10 times higher than the corresponding risks for nuclear. Future technological advances in renewable solar and wind energy sources may result in a significant reduction in the acute occupational risk associated with these systems. Hydro-electricity generation entails comparatively high acute occupational risk.
- *Late occupational risk.* Late fatalities arise mainly in coal and uranium mining, and are roughly of the same size. Underground coal mining, however, appears to be more dangerous than underground uranium mining (calculation from the basis of a normalized unit of electricity generated). Use of surface-mined coal, on the other hand, leads in total to fewer late fatalities than does use of nuclear energy.
- *Acute public risk.* These risks, mostly due to transportation accidents, are highly dependent on distance travelled and mode of transport. The risk of nuclear is 10-100 times lower than those of all the other options, mainly because of the relatively low quantity of materials to be transported. The coal cycle has the highest acute public risk because of the large material transport using the same reasoning.
- *Late public risk.* There are great uncertainties associated with late public risks associated with all the energy sources. Late public risks for nuclear and natural gas are about equal and are, at least ten times lower than associated with coal and oil. Future developments are expected to result in significant decreases in late public risks for renewables.

Clearly, health effects of different energy sources depend on the quantity and type of energy use. These vary greatly geographically. Fuelwood is the fourth largest contribution to world energy supply, after petroleum, coal and natural gas. Close to half the world population, especially those living in the rural and urban

areas of developing countries, depend on it for cooking and heating (either wood or its derivative, charcoal, or, in the absence of either of these, on agricultural residues or dung). Fuelwood constitutes more than half the world's consumption of wood, rising to 86% in developing countries and 91% in Africa.

In considering new and renewable sources of energy such as solar energy, wind power, and alcohol fuels, the idea of a "fuel

Table 53.7 • Significant health effects of technologies for generating electricity—fuels group.

Technology	Occupational	Public health effects
Coal	Black lung disease Trauma from mining accidents Trauma from transport accidents	Air pollution health effects Trauma from transport accidents
Oil	Trauma from drilling accidents Cancer from exposure to refinery organics	Air pollution health effects Trauma from explosions and fires
Oil shale	Brown lung disease Cancer from exposure to retorting emissions Trauma from mining accidents	Cancer from exposure to retorting emissions Air pollution health effects
Natural gas	Trauma from drilling accidents Cancer from exposure to refinery emissions	Air pollution health effects Trauma from explosions and fires
Tar sands	Trauma from mining accidents	Air pollution health effects Trauma from explosions and fires
Biomass*	Trauma from accidents during gathering and processing Exposure to hazardous chemicals and biological agents from processing and conversion	Air pollution health effects Diseases from exposure to pathogens Trauma from house fires

* As an energy source, usually considered as renewable.

Table 53.8 • Significant health effects of technologies for generating electricity—renewable group.

Technology	Occupational	Public health effects
Geothermal	Exposure to toxic gases— routine and accidental Stress from noise Trauma from drilling accidents	Disease from exposure to toxic brines and hydrogen sulphide Cancer from exposure to radon
Hydropower, conventional and low-head	Trauma from construction accidents	Trauma from dam failures Disease from exposure to pathogens
Photovoltaics	Exposure to toxic materials during fabrication — routine and accidental	Exposure to toxic materials during fabrication and disposal — routine and accidental
Wind	Trauma from accidents during construction and operation	
Solar thermal	Trauma from accidents during fabrication Exposure to toxic chemicals during operation	

Table 53.9 • Significant health effects of technologies for generating electricity—nuclear group.

Technology	Occupational	Public health effects
Fission	Cancer from exposure to radiation during uranium mining, ore/fuel processing, power plant operation and waste management Trauma from accidents during mining, processing, power plant construction and operation, and waste management	Cancer from exposure to radiation during all stages of the fuel cycle—routine and accidental Trauma from industrial transport accidents

cycle" must encompass industries such as solar photovoltaics, where virtually no risk attaches to the operation of the device but a substantial amount—often ignored—may be involved in its manufacture.

Attempts were made to deal with this difficulty by expanding the fuel cycle concept to include all stages in developing an energy system—including, for example, the concrete that goes into the plant that manufactures the glass for the solar collector. The issue of completeness has been addressed by noting that the backward analysis of manufacturing steps is equivalent to a set of simultaneous equations whose solution—if linear—is expressible as a matrix of values. Such an approach is familiar to economists as input-output analysis; and the appropriate numbers, showing how much each economic activity draws on the others, have already

Figure 53.10 • Health effects per unit amount of energy.

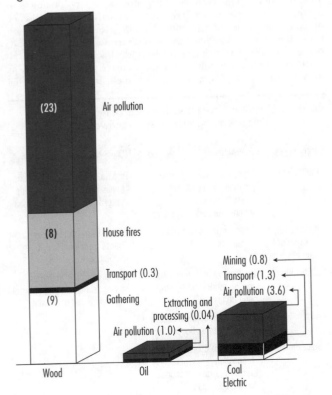

Figure 53.11 • Risk, to a single person, of fatality due to supplying one dwelling with wood fuel for 40 years.

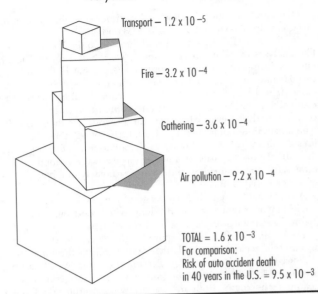

been derived—although for aggregate categories that may not exactly match the manufacturing steps one wishes to scrutinize for measuring health damage.

No single method of comparative risk analysis in the energy industry is fully satisfactory by itself. Each has advantages and limitations; each provides a different kind of information. Given the level of uncertainty of health risk analyses, results from all methods should be examined to provide as detailed a picture as possible, and fuller understanding of the magnitudes of associated uncertainties.

URBANIZATION

Edmundo Werna

Urbanization is a major feature of the contemporary world. At the beginning of the nineteenth century there were some 50 million people living in urban areas. By 1975 there were 1.6 billion, and by the year 2000 there will be 3.1 billion (Harpham, Lusty and Vaugham 1988). Such figures outstrip by far the growth of rural population.

However, the process of urbanization has often had hazardous impacts on the health of those who work and live in cities and towns. To a greater or lesser extent, the production of adequate housing, the provision of urban infrastructure and the control of traffic has not kept pace with the growth of urban population. This has generated a myriad of health problems.

Housing

Housing conditions throughout the world are far from adequate. For example, by the mid-1980s, 40 to 50% of the population in many cities in developing countries were living in substandard accommodations (WHO Commission on Health and Environment 1992b). Such figures have increased ever since. Although the situation in industrialized countries is less critical, housing prob-

Table 53.10 • Housing and health.

Housing problems	Health hazards
Poor control of temperature	Heat stress, hypothermia
Poor control of ventilation (when there is smoke from indoor fires)	Acute and chronic respiratory diseases
Poor control of dust	Asthma
Overcrowding	Household accidents, easier spread of communicable diseases (e.g., tuberculosis, influenza, meningitis)
Poor control of open fires, poor protection against kerosene or bottled gas	Burns
Poor finishing of walls, floors or roofs (allowing the access of vectors)	Chagas' disease, plague, typhus, shigellosis, hepatitis, poliomyelitis, legionnaire's disease, relapsing fever, house dust allergy
Siting of house (close to vector breeding areas)	Malaria, schistosomiasis, filariasis, trypanosomiasis
Siting of house (in area prone to disasters such as landslides or floodings)	Accidents
Construction defects	Accidents

Source: Hardoy et al. 1990; Harpham et al. 1988; WHO Commission on Health and Environment 1992b.

lems such as decay, overcrowding and even homelessness are frequent.

The major aspects of the residential environment which influence health, and their associated hazards, are presented in table 53.10. The health of a worker is likely to be affected if his or her residence is deficient in one or more of these aspects. In developing countries, for instance, some 600 million urban dwellers live in health- and life-threatening homes and neighbourhoods (Hardoy, Cairncross and Satterthwaite 1990; WHO 1992b).

Housing problems may also have a direct effect on occupational health, in the case of those who work in residential environments. Those include domestic servants and also a growing number of small-scale producers in a variety of cottage industries. These producers may be further affected when their production processes generate some form of pollution. Selected studies in these types of industries have detected hazardous wastes with consequences such as cardiovascular diseases, skin cancer, neurological disorders, bronchial cancer, photophobia and infant methaemoglobinaemia (Hamza 1991).

Prevention of home-related problems includes action in different stages of housing provision:

1. location (e.g., safe and vector-free sites)
2. house design (e.g., spaces with adequate size and climatic protection, use of non-perishable building materials, adequate protection for equipment)
3. construction (prevention of construction defects)
4. maintenance (e.g., proper control of equipment, proper screening).

The insertion of industrial activities in the residential environment may require special measures of protection, according to the particular process of production.

The specific housing solutions may vary widely from place to place, depending on the social, economic, technical and cultural circumstances. A great number of cities and towns do have local planning and building legislation that includes measures to prevent health hazards. However, such legislation is often not enforced due to ignorance, lack of legal control or, in most cases, lack of financial resources to build proper housing. Therefore, it is important not only to design (and update) adequate codes, but also to create the conditions for their implementation.

Urban Infrastructure: The Provision of Environmental Health Services

Housing may also affect health when it is not properly supplied with environmental health services such as garbage collection, water, sanitation and drainage. The inadequate provision of these services, however, extend beyond the housing realm, and may cause hazards for the city or town as a whole. Standards of provision of these services are still critical in a large number of places. For example, 30 to 50% of solid waste generated within urban centres is left uncollected. In 1985 there were 100 million more people without water service than in 1975. More than two billion people still have no sanitary means to dispose of human waste (Hardoy, Cairncross and Satterthwaite 1990; WHO Commission on Health and Environment 1992b). And the media have frequently shown cases of floods and other accidents connected to inadequate urban drainage.

Hazards derived from deficient provision of environmental health services are presented in table 53.11. Cross-service hazards are also common—e.g., contamination of water supply due to lack of sanitation, dissemination of refuse through non-drained water. To give one illustration of the extent of infrastructural problems, among many, a child is killed worldwide every 20 seconds due to diarrhoea—which is a major outcome of deficient environmental health services.

Those labourers whose immediate or wider working environment is not adequately supplied with such services are exposed to a profusion of occupational health risks. Those who work in the provision or maintenance of services, such as garbage pickers, sweepers and scavengers, are further exposed.

There exist indeed technical solutions capable of ameliorating the provision of environmental health services. They encompass,

Table 53.11 • Urban infrastructure and health.

Problems in the provision of environmental health services	Health hazards
Uncollected garbage	Pathogens in the refuse, disease vectors (mainly flies and rats) which breed or feed in the refuse, fire hazards, pollution of water flows
Deficiency in quantity and/or quality of water	Diarrhoea, trachoma, infectious skin diseases, infections carried out by body lice, other diseases originated by consumption of non-washed food
Lack of sanitation	Faeco-oral infections (e.g., diarrhoea, cholera, typhoid fever), intestinal parasites, filariasis
Lack of drainage	Accidents (from floods, landslides, collapsing houses), faeco-oral infections, schistosomiasis, mosquito-borne diseases (e.g., malaria, dengue, yellow fever), Bancroftian filariasis

Source: Hardoy et al. 1990; WHO Commission on Health and Environment 1992b.

among many others, garbage recycling schemes (including support to scavengers), use of different kinds of garbage collection vehicles to reach different types of roads (including those of informal settlements), water-saving fittings, tighter control of water leakages and low-cost sanitation schemes such as ventilated pit latrines, septic tanks or small-bore sewers.

However, the success of each solution will depend on its appropriateness to the local circumstances and on the local resources and capacity to implement it. Political willingness is fundamental, but not enough. Governments have frequently found it difficult to provide urban services adequately by themselves. Success stories of good supply have often included cooperation between the public, private and/or voluntary sectors. A thorough involvement and support of the local communities is important. This often requires official recognition of the large number of illegal and semi-legal settlements (especially but not only in developing countries), which bear a heavy part of the environmental health problems. Workers directly involved in services such as garbage collection or recycling and sewerage maintenance need special equipment for protection, such as gloves, overalls and masks.

Traffic

Cities and towns have depended heavily on ground transport for the movement of people and goods. Thus, the increase in urbanization throughout the world has been accompanied by a sharp growth in urban traffic. However, such a situation has generated a large number of accidents. Some 500,000 people are killed in traffic accidents each year, two-thirds of which occur in urban or peri-urban areas. In addition, according to many studies in different countries, for every death there are ten to twenty persons injured. Many cases suffer permanent or prolonged loss of productivity (Urban Edge 1990a; WHO Commission on Health and Environment 1992a). A large share of such data relates to people on their way to or from work—and such a type of traffic accident has lately been considered an occupational hazard.

According to World Bank studies, the main causes of urban traffic accidents include: poor condition of vehicles; deteriorated streets; different types of traffic—from pedestrians and animals to trucks—sharing the same streets or lanes; non-existent foot-paths; and reckless road behaviour (both from drivers and pedestrians) (Urban Edge 1990a, 1990b).

A further hazard generated by the expansion of urban traffic is air and noise pollution. Health problems include acute and chronic respiratory diseases, malignancies and hearing deficiencies (pollution is also dealt with in other articles in this *Encyclopaedia*).

Technical solutions to ameliorate road and car safety (as well as pollution) abound. The major challenge seems to be changing of the attitudes of drivers, pedestrians and public officials. Road safety education—from elementary school teaching to campaigns throughout the media—has often been recommended as a policy to target drivers and/or pedestrians (and such programmes have often had some degree of success when implemented). Public officials have the responsibility to design and enforce traffic legislation, inspect vehicles and design and implement engineering safety measures. However, according to the aforementioned studies, these officials seldom perceive traffic accidents (or pollution) as a top priority, or have the means to act dutifully (Urban Edge 1990a, 1990b). Therefore, they have to be targeted by educational campaigns, and supported in their work.

The Urban Fabric

In addition to the specific issues already noted (housing, services, traffic), the overall growth of the urban fabric also has had an impact on health. Firstly, urban areas are usually dense, a fact which facilitates the spread of communicable diseases. Secondly,

such areas concentrate a large number of industries, and their associated pollution. Thirdly, through the process of urban growth, natural foci of disease vectors may get entrapped within new urban areas, and new niches for disease vectors may be established. Vectors may adapt to new (urban) habitats—for example, those responsible for urban malaria, dengue and yellow fever. Fourthly, urbanization has often had psychosocial consequences such as stress, alienation, instability and insecurity; which, in their turn, have led to problems such as depression and alcohol and drug abuse (Harpham, Lusty and Vaugham 1988; WHO Commission on Health and Environment 1992a).

Past experiences have demonstrated the possibility (and the need) to tackle health problems via improvements in urbanization. For instance, "... the remarkable decline in mortality rates and improvements in health in Europe and North America at the turn of the last century owe more to improved nutrition and improvements in water supply, sanitation and other aspects of housing and living conditions than to medical establishments" (Hardoy, Cairncross and Satterthwaite 1990).

Solutions for the mounting problems of urbanization need sound integration between (often separated) urban planning and management, and the participation of the different public, private and voluntary actors which operate in the urban arena. Urbanization affects a wide range of workers. Contrary to other sources or types of health problems (which might affect specific categories of workers), occupational hazards derived from urbanization cannot be dealt with through single trade union action or pressure. They require inter-profession action, or, even more broadly, action from the urban community in general.

GLOBAL CLIMATE CHANGE AND OZONE DEPLETION

Jonathan A. Patz

Climate Change

The major greenhouse gases (GHGs) consist of carbon dioxide, methane, nitrous oxide, water vapour and chlorofluorocarbons (CFCs). These gases allow sunlight to penetrate to the earth's surface, yet prevent infrared radiant heat from escaping. The Intergovernmental Panel on Climate Change (IPCC) of the United Nations has concluded that emissions, primarily from industry, and destruction of greenhouse gas sinks, via poor land use management, especially deforestation, have substantially increased the concentrations of GHGs beyond natural processes. Without major policy shifts, pre-industrial carbon dioxide levels are expected to increase, yielding a 1.0-3.5 °C rise in average global temperature by the year 2100 (IPCC in press).

The two primary components of climate change include (1) temperature elevation with concomitant weather instability and extremes and (2) rising sea-level due to thermoexpansion. These changes may result in an increased frequency of heat waves and hazardous air pollution episodes, reduced soil moisture, higher incidence of disruptive weather events, and coastal inundation (IPCC 1992). Subsequent health effects may include an increase in (1) heat-related mortality and morbidity; (2) infectious diseases, particularly those that are insect borne; (3) malnutrition from food supply shortages; and (4) public health infrastructural crises from weather disasters and sea-level rise, coupled with climate-related human migration (see figure 53.12).

Humans have an enormous capacity to adapt to climatic and environmental conditions. However, the rate of predicted climatic and potential ecological change is of great concern to medical and earth scientists alike. Many of the health effects will be mediated through ecological responses to altered climate conditions. For example, spread of vector-borne diseases will depend on shifts in vegetation and availability of reservoir or intermediate hosts, in conjunction with the direct effects of temperature and humidity on parasites and their vectors (Patz et al. 1996). Understanding the hazards of climate change will, therefore, require an integrated ecological risk assessment which demands new and complex approaches compared to conventional single-agent cause-and-effect risk analysis from empirical data (McMichael 1993).

Stratospheric Ozone Depletion

Stratospheric ozone depletion is occurring primarily from reactions with halogen free radicals from chlorofluorocarbons (CFCs), along with other halocarbons and methyl bromide (Molina and Rowland 1974). Ozone specifically blocks the penetration of ultravioletB radiation (UVB), which contains the most biologically destructive wavelengths (290-320 nanometres). UVB levels are expected to rise disproportionately in temperate and arctic zones, since a clear relationship has been established between higher latitudes and the extent of ozone thinning (Stolarski et al. 1992).

For the period 1979-91, average ozone loss has been estimated at 2.7% per decade, correcting for solar cycle and other factors (Gleason et al. 1993). In 1993, researchers using a sensitive new spectroradiometer in Toronto, Canada, discovered that current ozone depletion has caused local increases in ambient UVB radiation of 35% in winter and 7% in summer, relative to 1989 levels (Kerr and McElroy 1993). Earlier estimates by the UN Environment Programme (UNEP) predicted a 1.4% rise in UVB per 1% drop in stratospheric ozone (UNEP 1991a).

The direct health impacts from stratospheric ozone depletion, which leads to increased ambient UVB radiation, include (1) skin cancer (2) ocular diseases and (3) immunosuppression. Indirect effects to health may occur from crop damage by ultraviolet radiation.

Health Effects of Temperature and Precipitation Change

Heat-related morbidity and mortality

Physiologically, humans have a great capacity for thermoregulation up to a threshold temperature. Weather conditions exceeding threshold temperatures and persisting for several consecutive days cause increased mortality in the population. In large cities, poor housing combined with the urban "heat island" effect further exacerbate conditions. In Shanghai, for instance, this effect can be as high as 6.5 °C on a windless evening during winter (IPCC 1990). Most heat-related fatalities occur in the elderly population and are attributed to cardiovascular and respiratory disorders (Kilbourne 1989). Key meteorological variables contribute to heat-related mortality, the most significant being high night-time readings; the greenhouse effect is predicted to especially elevate these minimum temperatures (Kalkstein and Smoyer 1993).

Temperate and polar regions are expected to warm disproportionately more than tropical and subtropical zones (IPCC 1990). Based on predictions by the US National Aeronautics and Space Administration (NASA), average summer temperatures in New York and St. Louis, for example, would rise by 3.1 and 3.9 °C, respectively, if ambient CO_2 doubles. Even with adjustment for physiological acclimatization, annual summer mortality in temperate cities such as these could rise over fourfold (Kalkstein and Smoyer 1993).

Atmospheric chemistry is an important contributing factor in the formation of urban photochemical smog, whereby photodecomposition of NO_2 in the presence of volatile organic com-

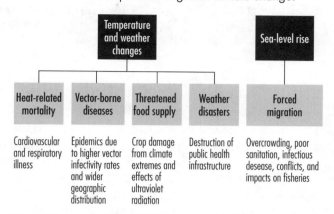

Figure 53.12 • Public health effects from the major components of global climate change.

pounds results in the production of tropospheric (ground-level) ozone. Both increased ambient UV radiation and warmer temperatures would further drive these reactions. Adverse health effects from air pollution are well known, and continued fossil fuel use will extend acute and chronic health impacts. (see "Air pollution" in this chapter).

Infectious diseases and climate/ecosystem change

Coupled atmosphere-ocean general circulation models predict that high latitudes in the northern hemisphere will experience the largest surface temperature elevation based on current IPCC scenarios (IPCC 1992). Minimum winter temperatures are expected to be disproportionately more affected, allowing for certain viruses and parasites to extend into regions where they previously could not live. In addition to direct climate effects on vectors, transformation of ecosystems could have marked implications for diseases whereby the geographic range of vector and/or reservoir host species is defined by these ecosystems.

Vector-borne diseases may spread to temperate regions in both hemispheres and intensify in endemic areas. Temperature determines vector infectivity by affecting pathogen replication, maturation and the period of infectivity (Longstreth and Wiseman 1989). Elevated temperature and humidity also intensify the biting behaviour of several mosquito species. Extreme heat, on the other hand, can shorten insect survival time.

Infectious diseases which incorporate a cold-blooded species (invertebrate) within their life cycles, are most susceptible to subtle climate variations (Sharp 1994). Diseases whose infectious agents, vectors or hosts are affected by climate change include malaria, schistosomiasis, filariasis, leishmaniasis, onchocerciasis (river blindness), trypanosomiasis (Chagas' and African sleeping sickness), dengue, yellow fever and arboviral encephalitis. Current figures of the number of people at risk of these diseases are listed in table 53.12 (WHO 1990d).

Worldwide, malaria is the most prevalent vector-borne disease and causes one to two million deaths annually. An estimated one million additional annual fatalities may arise from climate change by the middle of the next century, according to Martens et al. (1995). The Anopheline mosquito which carries malaria can extend to the 16 °C winter isotherm, since parasite development does not occur below this temperature (Gilles and Warrell 1993). Epidemics occurring at higher altitudes generally coincide with above average temperatures (Loevinsohn 1994). Deforestation also affects malaria, since cleared areas provide an abundance of freshwater pools in which Anopheline larvae can develop (see

Table 53.12 • Global status of major vector-borne diseases.

No.[a]	Disease	Population at risk (millions)[b]	Prevalence of infection (millions)	Present distribution	Possible change of distribution as a result of climatic change
1.	Malaria	2,100	270	Tropics/subtropics	++
2.	Lymphatic filariases	900	90.2	Tropics/subtropics	+
3.	Onchocerciasis	90	17.8	Africa/L. America	+
4.	Schistosomiasis	600	200	Tropics/subtropics	++
5.	African trypanosomiasis	50	(25,000 new cases/year)	Tropical Africa	+
6.	Leishmaniases	350	12 million infected + 400,000 new cases/year	Asia/S. Europe/Africa/S. America	?
7.	Dracunculiasis	63	1	Tropics (Africa/Asia)	0
Arboviral diseases					
8.	Dengue	1,500		Tropics/subtropics	++
9.	Yellow fever	+++		Africa/L. America	+
10.	Japanese encephalitis	+++		E/S.E. Asia	+
11.	Other arboviral diseases	+++			+

[a] The numbers refer to explanations in the text. [b] Based on a world population estimated at 4.8 billion (1989). 0 = unlikely; + = likely; ++ = very likely; +++ = no estimate available; ? = not known.

"Species extinction, biodiversity loss and human health" in this chapter).

Over the past two decades, efforts to control malaria have made only marginal gains. Treatment has not improved as drug-resistance has become a major problem for the most virulent strain, Plasmodium falciparum, and antimalarial vaccines have shown only limited efficacy (Institute of Medicine 1991). Great capacity for antigenic variation of protozoans has thus far prevented acquisition of effective vaccines for malaria and sleeping sickness, leaving little optimism for readily available new pharmaceutical agents against these diseases. Diseases which involve intermediate reservoir hosts (e.g., deer and rodents in the case of Lyme disease) make human herd immunity from vaccination programmes essentially unattainable, representing another hurdle to preventive medical intervention.

As climate change alters habitat, causing a potential reduction of biodiversity, insect vectors will be forced to find new hosts (see "Species extinction, biodiversity loss and human health"). In Honduras, for example, blood-seeking insects such as the assassin beetle, which carries incurable Chagas' disease (or American Trypanosomiasis), has been forced to seek human hosts as biodiversity decreases from deforestation. Of 10,601 Hondurans studied in endemic regions, 23.5% are now seropositive for Chagas' disease (Sharp 1994). Zoonotic diseases are frequently the source of human infections, and generally affect man after an environmental change or alteration of human activity (Institute of Medicine 1992). Many "newly emerging" diseases in humans are actually long-standing zoonoses of animal host species. For example, *Hantavirus*, recently found to be the cause of human fatalities in the southwest United States, has long been established in rodents and the recent outbreak was felt to be related to climatic/ecological conditions (Wenzel 1994).

Marine effects

Climate change may further impact public health through effects on harmful marine phytoplankton (or algae) blooms. Increases in phytoplankton globally has been a consequence of poor erosion control management, liberal agricultural application of fertilizers, and coastal sewage release, all resulting in effluents rich in nutrients which promote algae growth. Conditions that favour this growth could be augmented by warmer sea surface temperatures expected with global warming. Overharvesting of fish and shellfish (algae consumers) coupled with widespread pesticide use toxic to fish, further contribute to plankton overgrowth (Epstein 1995).

Red tides causing diarrhoeal and paralytic diseases and amnesic shellfish poisoning are prime examples of diseases stemming from algal overgrowth. Vibrio cholera has been found to be harboured by marine phytoplankton; thus blooms could represent an expanded reservoir from which cholera epidemics may initiate (Huq et al. 1990).

Food supply and human nutrition

Malnutrition is a major cause of infant mortality and childhood morbidity due to immunosuppression (see "Food and agriculture"). Climate change could adversely affect agriculture both by long-term changes, such as reducing soil moisture through evapotranspiration, and, more immediately, by extreme weather events such as droughts, flooding (and erosion) and tropical storms. Plants may initially benefit from "CO_2 fertilization", which can enhance photosynthesis (IPCC 1990). Even accounting for this, agriculture in developing countries will suffer most, and it is estimated that in these nations, 40-300 million additional people will be at risk from hunger due to climate change (Sharp 1994).

Indirect ecological changes affecting crops will need to be considered as well, since agricultural pests may change in distribution (IPCC 1992) (see "Food and agriculture"). Considering complex ecosystem dynamics, complete assessment will need to extend beyond the direct impacts of changing atmospheric and/or soil conditions.

Health Effects of Weather Disasters and Sea Level Rise

Thermal expansion of oceans may cause sea level to rise at a relatively rapid rate of two to four centimetres per decade, and projected extremes of the hydrologic cycle are expected to produce more severe weather patterns and storms. Such events would directly disrupt dwellings and public health infrastructures, such as sanitation systems and stormwater drainage (IPCC 1992). Vulnerable populations in low-lying coastal areas and small islands would be forced to migrate to safer locations. Resulting overcrowding and poor sanitation among these environmental refugees could amplify the spread of infectious diseases such as cholera, and vector-borne disease transmission rates would escalate due to crowding and potential influxes of infected individuals (WHO 1990d). Flooded drainage systems may further exacerbate the situation, and psychological impacts must also be considered from post-traumatic stress syndrome following major storms.

Fresh water supply would diminish due to saline intrusion of coastal aquifers and coastal farmland lost to salination or outright inundation. For example, a sea-level rise of one metre would destroy 15% and 20% of agriculture in Egypt and Bangladesh respectively (IPCC 1990). As for droughts, adaptive irrigation methods could affect arthropod and invertebrate breeding sites of vectors (e.g., similar to schistosomiasis in Egypt), but cost/benefit evaluation of such impacts will be difficult.

Health Effects of Stratospheric Ozone Depletion

Direct health effects of ultravioletB radiation

Ozone specifically blocks the penetration of ultravioletB radiation, which contains the most biologically destructive wavelengths of 290-320 nanometres. UVB induces the formation of pyrimidine dimers within DNA molecules, which if unrepaired can evolve to cancer (IARC 1992). Non-melanoma skin cancer (squamous and basal cell carcinoma) and superficial spreading melanoma are correlated with sunlight exposure. In Western populations, melanoma incidence has increased by 20 to 50% every five years over the past two decades (Coleman et al. 1993). While there is no direct relationship between cumulative ultraviolet exposure and melanoma, excessive UV exposure during childhood is associated with incidence. For a sustained 10% decline in the stratospheric ozone layer, non-melanoma skin cancer cases could rise by 26%, or 300,000 globally per year; melanoma could increase by 20%, or 4,500 more cases annually (UNEP 1991a).

Eye cataract formation causes half of the world's blindness (17 million cases annually) and is associated with UVB radiation in a dose-response relationship (Taylor 1990). Amino acids and membrane transport systems in the lens of the eye are especially prone to photo oxidation by oxygen radicals generated by UVB irradiation (IARC 1992). A doubling of UVB exposure could cause a 60% increase in cortical cataracts over current levels (Taylor et al. 1988). UNEP estimates that a 10% sustained loss of stratospheric ozone would result in nearly 1.75 million extra cataracts annually (UNEP 1991a). Other ocular effects of UVB exposure include photokeratitis, photokerato-conjunctivitis, pinguecula and pterygium (or overgrowth of the conjunctival epithelium) and climatic droplet keratopathy (IARC 1992).

The ability of the immune system to function effectively depends on "local" antigen processing and presentation to T-cells, as well as augmentation of the "systemic" response via lymphokine (biochemical messenger) production and resultant T-helper/T-suppressor cell ratios. UVB causes immunosuppression at both levels. UVB in animal studies can affect the course of infectious skin diseases, such as onchocerciasis, leishmaniasis and dermatophytosis, and impair immunosurveillance of transformed, precancerous epidermal cells. Preliminary studies further show an influence on vaccine efficacy (Kripke and Morison 1986; IARC 1992).

Indirect public health effects of UVB

Historically, terrestrial plants became established only after the formation of the shielding ozone layer, since UVB inhibits photosynthesis (UNEP 1991a). Weakening of food crops susceptible to UVB damage could further extend the impacts on agriculture due to climate changes and sea-level rise.

Phytoplankton are at the foundation of the marine food chain and also serve as an important carbon dioxide "sink". UV damage to these algae in polar regions, therefore, would detrimentally affect the marine food chain and exacerbate the greenhouse effect. UNEP estimates that a 10% loss of marine phytoplankton would limit the oceans' annual CO_2 uptake by five gigatonnes, which equals the yearly anthropogenic emissions from fossil fuel combustion (UNEP 1991a).

Occupational Hazards and Control Strategies

Occupational hazards

With regard to reduction in GHG emissions from fossil fuels, alternate renewable energy sources will need to be expanded. The public and occupational hazards of nuclear energy are well known, and safeguarding plants, workers and spent fuel will be necessary. Methanol may serve to replace much gasoline usage; however, formaldehyde emission from these sources will present a new environmental hazard. Superconducting materials for energy efficient electricity transfer are mostly ceramics comprised of calcium, strontium, barium, bismuth, thallium and yttrium (WHO in press).

Less is known about the occupational safety in the manufacturing units for solar energy capture. Silicon, gallium, indium, thallium, arsenic and antimony are the primary elements used to build photovoltaic cells (WHO in press). Silicon and arsenic adversely affect the lungs; gallium is concentrated in the kidney, liver, and bone; and ionic forms of indium are nephrotoxic.

The destructive effects of CFCs on the stratospheric ozone layer were recognized in the 1970s, and the US EPA banned these inert propellants in aerosols in 1978. By 1985, widespread concern erupted when an Antarctic-based British team discovered the "hole" in the ozone layer (Farman, Gardiner and Shanklin 1985). Subsequent passage of the Montreal Protocol in 1987, with amendments in 1990 and 1992, has already mandated sharp cuts in CFC production.

The replacement chemicals for CFCs are the hydrochlorofluorocarbons (HCFCs) and the hydrofluorocarbons (HFCs). The presence of the hydrogen atom may more readily subject these compounds to degradation by hydroxyl radicals (OH^-) in the troposphere, thus reducing potential stratospheric ozone depletion. These CFC replacement chemicals are, however, more biologically reactive than CFCs. The nature of a C-H bond makes these chemicals prone to oxidation via the cytochrome P-450 system (WHO in press).

Mitigation and adaptation

Meeting the public health challenges presented by global climate change will require (1) an integrated ecological approach; (2) reduction of greenhouse gases through industrial emission control, land use policies to maximize the extent of CO_2 "sinks" and population policies to achieve both; (3) monitoring of biological indicators on both regional and global scales; (4) adaptive public health strategies to minimize the impacts from unavoidable climate change; and (5) cooperation between developed and developing nations. In short, increased integration of environmental and public health policies must be promoted.

Climate change and ozone depletion present a vast number of health risks at multiple levels and underscore the important relationship between ecosystem dynamics and sustained human

Case Study: Mosquito-borne viruses

Mosquito-borne encephalitis and dengue fever are prime examples of vector-borne diseases whose distributions are limited by climate. Epidemics of St. Louis encephalitis (SLE), the most common arboviral encephalitis in the United States, generally occur south of the 22°C June isotherm, but northerly outbreaks have occurred during unseasonably warm years. Human outbreaks are highly correlated with several-day periods when temperature exceeds 27°C (Shope 1990).

Field studies on SLE indicate that a 1°C increase in temperature significantly shortens the elapsed time between a mosquito bloodmeal and viral replication to the point of infectivity within the vector, or the extrinsic incubation period. Adjusting for reduced adult mosquito survival at elevated temperatures, a 3 to 5 °C temperature increase is predicted to cause a significant northern shift of SLE outbreaks (Reeves et al. 1994).

The range of the primary mosquito vector of dengue (and yellow fever), Aedes aegypti, extends to 35° latitude because freezing temperatures kill both larvae and adults. Dengue is widespread in the Caribbean, tropical America, Oceania, Asia, Africa and Australia. Over the past 15 years, dengue epidemics have increased in both numbers and severity, especially in tropical urban centres. Dengue haemorrhagic fever now ranks as one of the leading causes for hospitalization and mortality of children in Southeast Asia (Institute of Medicine 1992). The same increasing pattern observed in Asia 20 years ago is now occurring in the Americas.

Climate change can potentially alter dengue transmission. In Mexico in 1986, the most important predictor of dengue transmission was found to be the median temperature during the rainy season, with an adjusted fourfold risk observed between 17 °C and 30 °C (Koopman et al. 1991). Lab studies support these field data. In vitro, the extrinsic incubation period for dengue type-2 virus was 12 days at 30 °C and only seven days at 32 to 35 °C (Watts et al. 1987). This temperature effect of shortening the incubation period by five days translates to a potentially threefold higher transmission rate of disease (Koopman et al. 1991). Finally, warmer temperatures result in the hatching of smaller adults, which must bite more frequently to develop an egg batch. In summary, increased temperatures can lead to more infectious mosquitoes that bite more frequently (Focks et al. 1995).

health. Preventive measures must therefore be systems based, and must anticipate significant ecological responses to climate change as well as the direct physical hazards predicted. Some key elements to consider in an ecological risk assessment will include spatial and temporal variations, feedback mechanisms and use of lower level organisms as early biological indicators.

Reduction of greenhouse gases by diverting from fossil fuels to renewable energy resources represents primary prevention of climate change. Similarly, strategic land use planning and stabilization of population stress on the environment will preserve important natural greenhouse gas sinks.

Because some climate change may be unavoidable, secondary prevention through early detection by monitoring of health parameters will require unprecedented coordination. For the first time in history, attempts are being made to monitor the earth system in its entirety. The Global Climate Observing System incorporates the World Weather Watch and Global Atmosphere Watch of the World Meteorological Organization (WMO) with parts of UNEP's Global Environmental Monitoring System. The Global Ocean Observing System is a new joint endeavour by the Intergovernmental Oceanographic Commission of UN Educa-

tional, Scientific and Cultural Organization (UNESCO), WMO and the International Council of Scientific Unions (ICSU). Both satellite and underwater measurements will be utilized to monitor changes in marine systems. The Global Terrestrial Observing System is a new system sponsored by UNEP, UNESCO, WMO, ICSU and the Food and Agricultural Organization (FAO), and will provide the terrestrial component of the Global Climate Observing System (WMO 1992).

Adaptive options to reduce unavoidable health consequences include disaster preparedness programmes; urban planning to reduce the "heat island" effect and improve housing; land use planning to minimize erosion, flash flooding and unnecessary deforestation (e.g., halting the creation of rangeland for meat exportation); personal adaptive behaviours, such as avoiding sun exposure; and vector-control and expanded vaccination efforts. Unintended costs of adaptive control measures of, for example, increased pesticide use will require consideration. Over-dependence on pesticides not only leads to insect resistance but also eliminates natural, beneficial, predatory organisms. The adverse effect on public health and the environment due to current pesticide use is estimated to be between US$100 billion and US$200 billion annually (Institute of Medicine 1991).

Developing countries will suffer disproportionately more from the consequences of climate change, though industrialized nations are presently more responsible for GHGs in the atmosphere. In the future poorer countries will influence the course of global warming significantly more, both through the technologies they choose to adopt as their development accelerates, and by land use practices. Developed nations will need to embrace more environmentally sound energy policies and promptly transfer new (and affordable) technology to developing countries.

SPECIES EXTINCTION, BIODIVERSITY LOSS AND HUMAN HEALTH[1]

Eric Chivian

Human activity is causing the extinction of animal, plant and microbial species at rates that are a thousand times greater than those which would have occurred naturally (Wilson 1992), approximating the largest extinctions in geological history. When *homo sapiens* evolved, some 100 thousand years ago, the number of species that existed was the largest ever to inhabit the Earth (Wilson 1989). Current rates of species loss are reducing these levels to the lowest since the end of the Age of Dinosaurs, 65 million years ago, with estimates that one-fourth of all species will become extinct in the next 50 years (Ehrlich and Wilson 1991).

In addition to the ethical issues involved—that we have no right to kill off countless other organisms, many of which came into being tens of millions of years prior to our arrival— this behaviour is ultimately self-destructive, upsetting the delicate ecological balance on which all life depends, including our own, and destroying the biological diversity that makes soils fertile, creates the air we breathe and provides food and other life-sustaining natural products, most of which remain to be discovered.

The exponential growth in human population coupled with an even greater rise in the consumption of resources and in the

[1] This article is adapted with permission from Chivian, E. 1993. Species Extinction and Biodiversity Loss: The Implications for Human Health. In *Critical Condition: Human Health and the Environment*, edited by E Chivian, M McCally, H Hu and A Haines. Cambridge, Mass. and London, England: MIT Press. With thanks to EO Wilson, Richard Schultes, Stephen Morse, Andrew Spielman, Paul Epstein, David Potter, Nan Vance, Rodney Fujita, Michael Balick, Suzan Strobel and Edson Albuquerque.

production of wastes, are the main factors endangering the survival of other species. Global warming, acid rain, the depletion of stratospheric ozone and the discharge of toxic chemicals into the air, soil and fresh- and salt-water ecosystems—all these ultimately lead to a loss of biodiversity. But it is habitat destruction by human activities, particularly deforestation, that is the greatest destroyer.

This is especially the case for tropical rainforests. Less than 50% of the area originally covered by prehistoric tropical rainforests remains, but they are still being cut and burned at a rate of approximately 142,000 square kilometres each year, equal in area to the countries of Switzerland and the Netherlands combined; this is a loss of forest cover each second the size of a football field (Wilson 1992). It is this destruction which is primarily responsible for the mass extinction of the world's species.

It has been estimated that there are somewhere between 10 million and 100 million different species on Earth. Even if a conservative estimate of 20 million total world species is used, then 10 million species would be found in tropical rainforests, and at current rates of tropical deforestation, this would mean 27,000 species would be lost in tropical rainforests alone each year, or more than seventy-four per day, three each hour (Wilson 1992).

This article examines the human health implications resulting from this widespread loss of biological diversity. It is the author's belief that if people fully comprehended the effect these massive species extinctions will have—in foreclosing the possibility of understanding and treating many incurable diseases, and ultimately, perhaps, in threatening human survival—then they would recognize that the current rates of biodiversity loss represent nothing less than a slowly evolving medical emergency and would demand that efforts to preserve species and ecosystems be given the highest priority.

The Loss of Medical Models

Three groups of endangered animals, far apart in the animal kingdom—dart-poison frogs, bears and sharks—offer striking examples of how important models for biomedical science are in danger of being squandered by humans.

Dart-poison frogs

The entire family of dart-poison frogs, the Dendrobatidae, found in the American tropics, is threatened by destruction of its habitats—the lowland tropical rainforests of Central and South America (Brody 1990). These brightly coloured frogs, which include more than 100 species, are particularly sensitive to deforestation, as they often live only in very specific areas of the forest and cannot live naturally anywhere else. Scientists have come to understand that the toxins they produce, used for centuries to poison arrows and blowgun darts by Central and South American Indians, are among the deadliest natural substances known. They are also enormously useful to medicine. The active ingredients of the toxins are alkaloids, nitrogen-containing ring compounds almost exclusively found in plants (morphine, caffeine, nicotine and cocaine are examples). The alkaloids bind selectively to specific ion channels and pumps in nerve and muscle membranes. Without them, knowledge of these basic units of membrane function, found throughout the animal kingdom, would be very incomplete.

In addition to their value in basic neurophysiological research, dart-poison frogs also offer valuable biochemical clues for the production of new and potent analgesics that have a mechanism of action different from that of morphine, of new medicines for cardiac arrhythmias and of new treatments for the alleviation of some neurological diseases such as Alzheimer's disease, myasthenia gravis and amyotrophic lateral sclerosis (Brody 1990). If rainforest destruction continues at its present rate in Central and South America, these extremely valuable frogs will be lost.

Bears

The growing black market trade in Asia for bear parts, with bear gallbladders being sold for their reputed medicinal value (worth 18 times their weight in gold), and paws for gourmet food (Montgomery 1992), coupled with continued hunting and the destruction of habitats, has imperilled bear populations in many parts of the world. If some species of bears become extinct, we will all be the poorer, not only because they are beautiful, fascinating creatures that fill important ecological niches, but also because some species possess several unique physiological processes that may provide important clues for treating various human disorders. "Hibernating" (or, more accurately, "denning") black bears, for example, are immobile for up to five months in the winter, yet do not lose bone mass (Rosenthal 1993). (True hibernators, like the marmot, woodchuck and ground squirrel, show a marked lowering of body temperature during hibernation and are not easily aroused. Black bears, by contrast, "hibernate" at near normal body temperatures and can be fully responsive to defend themselves instantly.) In contrast to humans, who would lose almost one-fourth of their bone mass during a similar period of immobility (or lack of weight bearing), bears continue to lay down new bone, making use of circulating calcium in their blood (Floyd, Nelson and Wynne 1990). Understanding the mechanisms of how they accomplish this feat may lead to effective ways of preventing and treating osteoporosis in the elderly (an enormous problem leading to fractures, pain and disability), in those confined to bedrest for long periods and in astronauts subject to prolonged states of weightlessness.

In addition, "hibernating" bears do not urinate for months. Humans who cannot excrete their waste products in urine for several days build up high levels of urea in their blood and die from its toxicity. Somehow bears recycle their urea to make new proteins, including those in muscle (Nelson 1973). If we could determine the mechanism of this process, it might lead to successful, long-term treatments for those with kidney failure, who must now rely on regular detoxification by kidney dialysis machines, or on transplantation.

Sharks

Like bears, many species of sharks are being decimated because of the demand for shark meat, especially in Asia, where shark fins for soup command prices as high as $100 a pound (Stevens 1992). Because sharks produce few offspring, grow slowly and take years to mature, they are highly vulnerable to overfishing.

Sharks have been around for almost 400 million years and have evolved highly specialized organs and physiological functions that have protected them against virtually all threats, except slaughter by humans. The wiping out of populations and extinction of some of the 350 species may become a major disaster for human beings.

The immune systems of sharks (and of their relatives, skates and rays) seem to have evolved so that the animals are almost invulnerable to developing cancers and infections. While tumours are often seen in other fish and molluscs (Tucker 1985), they are rare in sharks. Preliminary investigations have supported this finding. It has proved impossible, for example, to produce tumour growth in Nurse Sharks with repeated injections of known potent carcinogenic substances (Stevens 1992). And researchers at the Massachusetts Institute of Technology have isolated a substance, present in large amounts, from Basking Shark cartilage (Lee and Langer 1983) that strongly inhibits the growth of new blood vessels towards solid tumours, and thereby prevents tumour growth.

Sharks may also provide valuable models for developing new types of medications to treat infections, especially important at the present time when infectious agents are developing increasing resistance to currently available antibiotics.

Other models

Countless other examples could be mentioned of unique plants, animals and micro-organisms holding the secrets of billions of evolutionary experiments that are increasingly threatened by human activity and in danger of being lost forever to medical science.

The Loss of New Medicines

Plant, animal and microbial species are themselves the sources for some of today's most important medicines and make up a significant proportion of the total pharmacopoeia. Farnsworth (1990), for example, has found that 25% of all prescriptions dispensed from community pharmacies in the United States from 1959 to 1980 contained active ingredients extracted from higher plants. A much higher percentage is found in the developing world. As many as 80% of all people living in developing countries, or roughly two thirds of the world's population, rely almost exclusively on traditional medicines using natural substances, mostly derived from plants.

The knowledge held by traditional healers, often passed down orally over centuries, has led to the discovery of many medicines that are widely used today—quinine, physostigmine, d-tubocurarine, pilocarpine and ephedrine, to name a few (Farnsworth et al. 1985). But that knowledge is fast disappearing, particularly in the Amazon, as native healers die out and are replaced by more modern medical practitioners. Botanists and pharmacologists are racing to learn these ancient practices, which, like the forest plants they employ, are also endangered (Farnsworth 1990; Schultes 1991; Balick 1990).

Scientists have analysed the chemistry of less than 1% of known rainforest plants for biologically active substances (Gottlieb and Mors 1980)—as well as a similar proportion of temperate plants (Schultes 1992) and even smaller percentages of known animals, fungi and microbes. But there may be tens of millions of species as yet undiscovered in the forests, in soils, and in lakes and oceans. With the massive extinctions currently in progress, we may be destroying new cures for incurable cancers, for AIDS, for arteriosclerotic heart disease and for other illnesses that cause enormous human suffering.

Disturbing Ecosystem Equilibria

Finally, the loss of species and the destruction of habitats may upset delicate equilibria among ecosystems on which all life depends, including our own.

Food supplies

Food supplies, for one, may be seriously threatened. Deforestation, for example, can result in significantly reduced rainfall in adjacent agricultural areas and even in regions at some distance (Wilson 1988; Shulka, Nobre and Sellers 1990), compromising crop productivity. The loss of topsoil from erosion, another consequence of deforestation, can have an irreversible negative impact on crops in forested regions, particularly in areas of hilly terrain, such as in regions of Nepal, Madagascar and the Philippines.

Bats and birds, among the major predators of insects that infest or eat crops, are being lost in record numbers (Brody 1991; Terborgh 1980), with untold consequences for agriculture.

Infectious diseases

Recently in Brazil, malaria has reached epidemic proportions as a consequence of massive settlement and environmental disruption of the Amazon basin. Largely under control in Brazil during the 1960s, malaria has exploded 20 years later, with 560,000 cases reported in 1988, 500,000 in Amazonia alone (Kingman 1989). In large part, this epidemic was a consequence of the influx of huge numbers of people who had little or no immunity to malaria, who lived in make-shift shelters and wore little protective clothing. But it was also an outgrowth of their disturbing the environment of the rainforest, creating in their wake stagnant pools of water everywhere—from road construction, from silt runoff secondary to land clearing, and from open mining—pools where Anopheles darlingi, the most important malaria vector in the area, could multiply unchecked (Kingman 1989).

The story of "emerging" viral illnesses may hold valuable clues for understanding the effects of habitat destruction on human beings. Argentine haemorrhagic fever, for example, a painful viral disease having a mortality of between 3 and 15% (Sanford 1991) has occurred in epidemic proportions since 1958 as a result of the widespread clearing of the pampas of central Argentina and the planting of corn (Kingman 1989).

The emerging viral illness which has had the greatest impact on human health, and which may be a harbinger of future viral outbreaks, is AIDS, caused by the human immunodeficiency virus—types 1 (HIV-1) and 2 (HIV-2). There is general agreement that the current AIDS epidemic originated from non-human primates in Africa, which have acted as natural, asymptomatic hosts and reservoirs for a family of immunodeficiency viruses (Allan 1992). Good genetic evidence exists for the links of HIV-1 to a simian immunodeficiency virus in African chimpanzees (Huet and Cheynier 1990) and of HIV-2 to another simian virus in African sooty mangabeys (Hirsch and Olmsted 1989; Gao and Yue 1992). Are these cross-species viral transmissions from primates to humans the result of human encroachment into degraded forest environments? If this is the case, we may be witnessing with AIDS the beginning of a series of viral epidemics originating from tropical rainforests where there may be thousands of viruses that could infect humans, some of which may be as lethal as AIDS (approaching 100%) but spread more easily, for instance by airborne droplets. These potential viral diseases could become the most serious public health consequence from environmental disruption of the rainforests.

Other effects

But it may be the disruption of other interrelationships among organisms, ecosystems and the global environment, about which almost nothing is known, that may prove the most catastrophic of all for human beings. What will happen to global climate and to the concentration of atmospheric gases, for example, when some critical threshold of deforestation has been reached? Forests play crucial roles in the maintenance of global precipitation patterns and in the stability of atmospheric gases.

What will be the effects on marine life if increased ultraviolet radiation causes massive ocean phytoplankton kills, particularly in the rich seas beneath the Antarctic ozone "hole"? These organisms, which are at the base of the entire marine food chain and which produce a significant portion of the world's oxygen and consume a significant portion of its carbon dioxide, are highly vulnerable to ultraviolet damage (Schneider 1991; Roberts 1989; Bridigare 1989).

What will be the consequences for plant growth if acid rain and toxic chemicals poison soil fungi and bacteria essential for soil fertility? There has already been a 40-50% loss in species of fungi in Western Europe during the past 60 years, including many symbiotic mycorhizal fungi (Wilson 1992), crucial to the absorption of nutrients by plants. No one understands what the effects of this loss will be.

Scientists do not know the answers to these and other critically important questions. But there are worrisome biological signals which suggest that major damage to global ecosystems has already occurred. The rapid simultaneous drop in populations of many species of frogs worldwide, even in pristine environments far from people, indicates that they may be dying as a consequence of some global environmental change (Blakeslee 1990). Recent studies (Blaustein 1994) suggest that increased ultraviolet-B radiation from thinning of the ozone layer may be the cause in some of these cases.

Closer to humans, marine mammals such as striped dolphins in the Mediterranean, European harbour seals off the coast of Scandinavia and of northern Ireland, and Beluga whales in the Saint Lawrence River are also dying in record numbers. In the case of the dolphins and the seals, some of the deaths seem to be due to infections by morbilli viruses (the family of viruses including measles and canine distemper virus) causing pneumonias and encephalitides (Domingo and Ferrer 1990; Kennedy and Smyth 1988), perhaps also the consequence of compromised immune systems. In the case of the whales, chemical pollutants such as DDT, the insecticide Mirex, PCBs, lead and mercury seem to be involved, suppressing the Belugas' fertility and causing their deaths ultimately by a variety of tumours and pneumonias (Dold 1992). The Beluga carcasses were often so filled with these pollutants that they could be classified as hazardous waste.

Are these "indicator species", like canaries that die in coal mines containing poisonous gases, warning us that we are upsetting fragile ecosystem balances that support all life, including our own? The 50% drop in sperm counts in healthy men worldwide during the period 1938-1990 (Carlsen et al. 1992), the marked increases in the rate of congenital malformations of the external genitalia in males in England and Wales from 1964 to 1983 (Matlai and Beral 1985), the dramatic rise in some cancer incidence rates for white children from 1973 to 1988 (Angier 1991) and for white adults from 1973 to 1987 (Davis, Dinse and Hoel 1994) in the United States, and the steady growth in the mortality rates for several cancers worldwide for the last three to four decades (Kurihara, Aoki and Tominaga 1984; Davis and Hoel 1990a, 1990b; Hoel 1992) all suggest that environmental degradation may be starting to compromise not only the survival of frogs, marine mammals and other animal, plant and microbial species, but that of the human species as well.

Summary

Human activity is causing the extinction of animal, plant and microbial organisms at rates that may well eliminate one-fourth of all species on Earth within the next 50 years. There are incalculable human health consequences from this destruction:

- the loss of medical models to understand human physiology and disease
- the loss of new medicines that may successfully treat incurable cancers, AIDS, arteriosclerosis and other diseases that cause great human suffering.

References

Allan, JS. 1992. Viral evolution and AIDS. *J Natl Inst Health Res* 4:51-54.

Angier, N. 1991. Study finds mysterious rise in childhood cancer rate. *New York Times* (26 June):D22.

Arceivala, SJ. 1989. Water quality and pollution control: Planning and management. In *Criteria for and Approaches for Water Quality Management in Developing Countries.* New York: United Nations.

Archer, DL and JE Kvenberg. 1985. Incidence and cost of foodborne diarrhoea disease in the United States. *J Food Prod* 48(10):887-894.

Balick, MJ. 1990. Ethnobotany and the identification of therapeutic agents from the rainforest. *CIBA F Symp* 154:22-39.

Bascom, R et al. 1996. Health effects of outdoor air pollution. State of the Art. *Am J Resp Crit Care Med* 153:3-50.

Blakeslee, S. 1990. Scientists confront an alarming mystery: The vanishing frog. *New York Times.* 20 February:B7.

Blaustein, AR.1994. UL repair and resistance to solar UV-B in amphibian eggs: A link to population declines. *Proc Natl Acad Sci USA* 91:1791-1795.

Borja-Arburto, VH, DP Loomis, C Shy, and S Bangdiwala. 1995. Air pollution and daily mortality in Mexico City. *Epidemiology* S64:231.

Bridigare, RR. 1989. Potential effects of UVB on marine organisms of the Southern Ocean: Distribution of phytoplankton and krill during Austral Spring. *Photochem Photobiol* 50:469-478.

Brody, JE. 1990. Using the toxin from tiny frogs, researchers seek clues to disease. *New York Times.* 23 January.

Brody, JE. 1991. Far from fearsome, bats lose ground to ignorance and greed. *New York Times.* 29 October:Cl,C10.

Carlsen, E and A Gimmercman. 1992. Evidence for decreasing quality of semen during the past 50 years. *Br Med J* 305:609-613.

Castillejos, M, D Gold, D Dockery, T Tosteson, T Baum, and FE Speizer. 1992. Effects of ambient ozone on respiratory functions and symptoms in school children in Mexico City. *Am Rev Respir Dis* 145:276-282.

Castillejos, M, D Gold, A Damokosh, P Serrano, G Allen, WF McDonnell, D Dockery, S Ruiz-Velasco, M Hernandez, and C Hayes. 1995. Acute effects of ozone on the pulmonary function of exercising schoolchildren from Mexico City. *Am J Resp Crit Care Med* 152:1501-1507.

Centers for Disease Control (CDC). 1991. *Preventing Lead Poisoning in Young Children.* Washington, DC: US Department of Health and Human Services.

Cohen, ML. 1987. Prepared statement in "Hearing before the Committee of Agriculture, Nutrition and Forestry". US Senate, 100th Congress, First Session. (US Government Printing Office, Washington, DC).

Coleman, MP, J Esteve, P Damiecki, A Arslan, and H Renard. 1993. *Trends in Cancer Incidence and Mortality.* IARC Scientific Publications, No.121. Lyon: IARC.

Davis, DL, GE Dinse, and DG Hoel. 1994. Decreasing cardiovascular disease and increasing cancer among whites in the United States from 1973-1987. *JAMA* 271(6):431-437.

Davis, DL and D Hoel. 1990a. International trends in cancer mortality in France, West Germany, Italy, Japan, England and Wales and the USA. *Lancet* 336 (25 August):474-481.

—. 1990b. *Trends in Cancer Mortality in Industrial Countries.* Annals of the New York Academy of Sciences, No. 609.

Dockery, DW and CA Pope. 1994. Acute respiratory effects of particulate air pollution. *Ann Rev Publ Health* 15:107-132.

Dold, C. 1992. Toxic agents found to be killing off whales. *New York Times.* 16 June:C4.

Domingo, M and L Ferrer. 1990. Morbillivirus in dolphins. *Nature* 348:21.

Ehrlich, PR and EO Wilson. 1991. Biodiversity studies: Science and policy. *Science* 253(5021):758-762.

Epstein, PR. 1995. Emerging diseases and ecosystem instability. *Am J Public Health* 85:168-172.

Farman, JC, H Gardiner, and JD Shanklin. 1985. Large losses of total ozone in Antarctica reveal seasonal ClOx/NOx interaction. *Nature* 315:207-211.

Farnsworth, NR. 1990. The role of ethnopharmacology in drug development. *CIBA F Symp* 154:2-21.

Farnsworth, NR, O Akerele, et al. 1985. Medicinal plants in therapy. *Bull WHO* 63(6):965-981.

Federal Health Office (Switzerland). 1990. Bulletin of Federal Health Office. 29 October.

Floyd, T, RA Nelson, and GF Wynne. 1990. Calcium and bone metabolic homeostasis in active and denning black bears. *Clin Orthop Relat R* 255 (June):301-309.

Focks, DA, E Daniels, DG Haile, and JE Keesling. 1995. A simulation model of the epidemiology of urban dengue fever: literature analysis, model development, preliminary validation, and samples of simulation results. *Am J Trop Med Hyg* 53:489-506.

Galal-Gorchev, H. 1986. *Drinking-Water Quality and Health.* Geneva:WHO, unpublished.

—. 1994. *WHO Guidelines for Drinking Water Quality.* Geneva:WHO, unpublished.

Gao, F and L Yue. 1992. Human infection by genetically diverse SIVsm-related HIV-2 in West Africa. *Nature* 358:495.

Gilles, HM and DA Warrell. 1993. *Bruce-Chwatt's Essential Malaniology.* London: Edward Arnold Press.

Gleason, JF, PK Bhartia, JR Herman, R McPeters, et al. 1993. Record low global ozone in 1992. *Science* 260:523-526.

Gottlieb, OR and WB Mors. 1980. Potential utilization of Brazilian wood extractives. *J Agricul Food Chem* 28(2): 196-215.

Grossklaus, D. 1990. Gesundheitliche Fragen im EG-Binnemarkt. *Arch Lebensmittelhyg* 41(5):99-102.

Hamza, A. 1991. *Impacts of Industrial and Small-Scale Manufacturing Wastes On Urban Environment in Developing Countries.* Nairobi: United Nations Centre for Human Settlements.

Hardoy, JE, S Cairncross, and D Satterthwaite. 1990. *The Poor Die Young: Housing and Health in Third World Cities.* London: Earthscan Publications.

Hardoy, JE and F Satterthwaite. 1989. *Squatter Citizen: Life in the Urban Third World.* London: Earthscan Publications.

Harpham, T, T Lusty, and P Vaugham. 1988. *In the Shadow of the City—Community Health and the Urban Poor.* Oxford: OUP.

Hirsch, VM and M Olmsted. 1989. An African primate lentivirus (SIVsm) closely related to HIV-s. *Nature* 339:389.

Hoel, DG. 1992. Trends in cancer mortality in 15 industrialized countries, 1969-1986. *J Natl Cancer Inst* 84(5):313-320.

Hoogenboom-Vergedaal, AMM et al. 1990. *Epdemiologisch En Microbiologisch Onderzoek Met Betrekking Tot Gastro-Enteritis Bij De Mens in De Regio's Amsterdam En Helmond in 1987 En 1988.* Netherlands: National Institute of Public Health and Environmental Protection.

Huet, T and A Cheynier. 1990. Genetic organization of a chimpanzee lentivirus related to HIV-1. *Nature* 345:356.

Huq, A, RR Colwell, R Rahman, A Ali, MA Chowdhury, S Parveen, DA Sack, and E Russek-Cohen. 1990. Detection of Vibrio cholerae 01 in the aquatic environment by fluorescent-monoclonal antibody and culture methods. *Appl Environ Microbiol* 56:2370-2373.

Institute of Medicine. 1991. *Malaria: Obstacles and Opportunities.* Washington, DC: National Academy Press.

—. 1992. *Emerging Infections: Microbial Threats to Health in the United States.* Washington, DC: National Academy Press.

Intergovernmental Panel on Climate Change (IPCC). 1990. *Climate Change: The IPCC Impacts Assessment.* Canberra: Australian Government Publishing Service.

—. 1992. *Climate Change 1992: The Supplementary Report to the IPCC Impacts Assessment.* Canberra: Australian Government Publishing Service.

International Agency for Research on Cancer (IARC). 1992. *Solar and Ultraviolet Radiation.* IARC Monographs On the Evaluation of Carcinogenic Risks to Humans Lyon: IARC.

International Atomic Energy Agency (IAEA). 1991. *International Chernobyl Project Assessment of Radiological Consequences and Evaluation of Protective Measures.* Vienna: IAEA.

Kalkstein, LS and KE Smoyer. 1993. The impact of climate change on human health: Some international implications. *Experiencia* 49:469-479.

Kennedy, S and JA Smyth. 1988. Confirmation of cause of recent seal deaths. *Nature* 335:404.

Kerr, JB and CT McElroy. 1993. Evidence for large upward trends of ultraviolet-B radiation linked to ozone depletion. *Science* 262 (November):1032-1034.

Kilbourne EM. 1989. Heat waves. In *The public health consequences of disasters. 1989,* edited by MB Gregg. Atlanta: Centers for Disease Control.

Kingman, S. 1989. Malaria runs riot on Brazil's wild frontier. *New Scientist* 123:24-25.

Kjellström, T. 1986. Itai-itai disease. In *Cadmium and Health,* edited by L Friberg et al. Boca Raton: CRC Press.

Koopman, JS, DR Prevots, MA Vaca-Marin, H Gomez-Dantes, ML Zarate-Aquino, IM Longini Jr, and J Sepulveda-Amor. 1991. Determinants and predictors of dengue infection in Mexico. *Am J Epidemiol* 133:1168-1178.

Kripke, ML and WL Morison. 1986. Studies on the mechanism of systemic suppression of contact hypersensitivity by UVB radiation. II: Differences in the suppression of delayed and contact hypersensitivity in mice. *J Invest Dermatol* 86:543-549.

Kurihara, M, K Aoki, and S Tominaga. 1984. *Cancer Mortality Statistics in the World.* Nagoya, Japan: The University of Nagoya Press.

Lee, A and R Langer. 1983. Shark cartilage contains inhibitors of tumor angiogenesis. *Science* 221:1185-1187.

Loevinsohn, M. 1994. Climatic warming and increased malaria incidence in Rwanda. *Lancet* 343:714-718.

Longstreth, J and J Wiseman. 1989. The potential impact of climate change on patterns of infectious disease in the United States. In *The Potential Effects of Global Climate Change in the United States,* edited by JB Smith and DA Tirpak. Washington, DC: US Environmental Protection Agency.

Martens, WM, LW Niessen, J Rotmans, TH Jetten, and AJ McMichael. 1995. Potential impact of global climate change on malaria risk. *Environ Health Persp* 103:458-464.

Matlai, P and V Beral. 1985. Trends in congenital malformations of external genitalia. *Lancet* 1 (12 January):108.

McMichael, AJ. 1993. *Planetary Overload: Global Environmental Change and the Health of the Human Species.* London: Cambridge University Press.

Meybeck, M, D Chapman, and R Helmer. 1989. *Global Freshwater Quality: A First Assessment.* Geneva: Global Environmental Monitoring System (GEMS/-WATER).

Meybeck, M and R Helmer. 1989. The quality of rivers: From pristine stage to global pollution. *Paleogeogr Paleoclimatol Paleoecol* 75:283-309.

Michaels, D, C Barrera, and MG Gacharna. 1985. Economic development and occupational health in Latin America: New directions for public health in less developed countries. *Am J Public Health* 75(5):536-542.

Molina, MJ and FS Rowland. 1974. Stratospheric sink for chloro-fluoro-methanes: Chlorine atom-catalyzed destruction of ozone. *Nature* 249:810-814.

Montgomery, S. 1992. Grisly trade imperils world's bears. *The Boston Globe.* March 2:23-24.

Nelson, RA. 1973. Winter sleep in the black bear. *Mayo Clin Proc* 48:733-737.

Nimmannitya, S. 1996. Dengue and dengue haemorrhagic fever. In *Manson's Tropical Diseases,* edited by GC Cook. London: WB Saunders.

Nogueira, DP. 1987. Prevention of accidents and injuries in Brazil. *Ergonomics* 30(2):387-393.

Notermans, S. 1984. Beurteilung des bakteriologischen Status frischen Geflügels in Läden und auf Märkten. *Fleischwirtschaft* 61(1):131-134.

Noweir, MH. 1986. Occupational health in developing countries, with special reference to Egypt. *Am J Ind Med* 9:125-141.

Pan American Health Organization (PAHO) and World Health Organization (WHO). 1989. Final Report of the Working Group on Epidemiological Surveillance and Foodborne Diseases. Unpublished document HPV/FOS/89-005.

Patz, JA, PR Epstein, TA Burke, and JM Balbus. 1996. Global climate change and emerging infections diseases. *JAMA* 275:217-223.

Pope, CA, DV Bates, and ME Razienne. 1995. Health effects of particulate air pollution: Time for reassessment? *Environ Health Persp* 103:472-480.

Reeves, WC, JL Hardy, WK Reisen, and MM Milky. 1994. The potential effect of global warming on mosquitoborne arboviruses. *J Med Entomol* 31(3):323-332.

Roberts, D. 1990. Sources of infection: Food. *Lancet* 336:859-861.

Roberts, L. 1989. Does the ozone hole threaten antarctic life. *Science* 244:288-289.

Rodrigue, DG. 1990. International increase in Salmonella enteritidis. A new pandemic? *Epidemiol Inf* 105:21-21.

Romieu, I, H Weizenfeld, and J Finkelman. 1990. Urban air pollution in Latin America and the Caribbean: Health perspectives. *World Health Stat Q* 43:153-167.

—. 1991. Urban air pollution in Latin America and the Caribbean. *J Air Waste Manage Assoc* 41:1166-1170.

Romieu, I, M Cortés, S Ruíz, S Sánchez, F Meneses, and M Hernándes-Avila. 1992. Air pollution and school absenteeism among children in Mexico City. *Am J Epidemiol* 136:1524-1531.

Romieu, I, F Meneses, J Sienra, J Huerta, S Ruiz, M White, R Etzel, and M Hernandez-Avila. 1994. Effects of ambient air pollution on respiratory health of Mexican children with mild asthma. *Am J Resp Crit Care Med* 129:A659.

Romieu, I, F Meneses, S Ruíz, JJ Sierra, J Huerta, M White, R Etzel, and M Hernández. 1995. Effects of urban air pollution on emergency visits for childhood asthma in Mexico City. *Am J Epidemiol* 141(6):546-553.

Romieu, I, F Meneses, S Ruiz, J Sienra, J Huerta, M White, and R Etzel. 1996. Effects of air pollution on respiratory health of children with mild asthma living in Mexico City. *Am J Resp Crit Care Med* 154:300-307.

Rosenthal, E. 1993. Hibernating bears emerge with hints about human ills. *New York Times* 21 April:C1,C9.

Ryzan, CA. 1987. Massive outbreak of antimicrobial-resistant salmonellosis traced to pasteurized milk. *JAMA* 258(22):3269-3274.

Sanford, JP. 1991. Arenavirus infections. In Chap. 149 in *Harrison's Principles of Internal Medicine,* edited by JD Wilson, E Braunwald, KJ Isselbacher, RG Petersdorf, JB Martin, AS Fauci, and RK Root.

Schneider, K. 1991. Ozone depletion harming sea life. *New York Times* 16 November:6.

Schultes, RE 1992: Personal communication. 24 January 1992.

—.1991. Dwindling forest medicinal plants of the Amazon. *Harvard Med Alum Bull* (Summer):32-36.

Sharp, D. (ed.). 1994. *Health and Climate Change.* London: The Lancet Ltd.

Shope, RE. 1990. Infectious diseases and atmospheric change. In *Global Atmospheric Change and Public Health: Proceedings of the Center for Environmental Information,* edited by JC White. New York: Elsevier.

Shulka, J, C Nobre, and P Sellers. 1990. Amazon deforestation and climate change. *Science* 247:1325.

Statistisches Bundesamt. 1994. *Gesundheitswesen: Meldepflichtige Krankheiten.* Wiesbaden: Statistisches Bundesamt.

Stevens, WK. 1992. Terror of the deep faces harsher predator. *New York Times.* 8 December:Cl,C12.

Stolarski, R, R Bojkov, L Bishop, C Zerefos, et al. 1992. Measured trends in stratospheric ozone. *Science* 256:342-349.

Taylor, HR. 1990. Cataracts and ultraviolet light. In *Global Atmospheric Change and Public Health: Proceedings of the Center for Environmental Information,* edited by JC White. New York: Elsevier.

Taylor, HR, SK West, FS Rosenthal, B Munoz, HS Newland, H Abbey, EA Emmett. 1988. Effects of ultraviolet radiation on cataract formation. *N Engl J Med* 319:1429-33.

Terborgh, J. 1980. *Where Have All the Birds Gone?* Princeton, NJ: Princeton University Press.

Tucker, JB. 1985. Drugs from the sea spark renewed interest. *Bioscience* 35(9):541-545.

United Nations (UN). 1993. *Agenda 21.* New York: UN.

United Nations Conference on Environment and Development (UNCED). 1992. Protection for the quality and supply of freshwater resources. In Chap. 18 in *Application of Integrated Approaches to the Development, Management and Use of Water Resources.* Rio de Janeiro: UNCED.

United Nations Environment Programme (UNEP). 1988. *Assessment of Chemical Contaminants in Food.* Nairobi: UNEP/FAO/WHO.

—. 1991a. *Environmental Effects of Ozone Depletion: 1991 Update.* Nairobi: UNEP.

THE ENVIRONMENT

—. 1991b. *Urban Air Pollution*. Environment Library, No. 4. Nairobi: UNEP.

Urban Edge. 1990a. Reducing accidents: Lessons learned. *Urban Edge* 14(5):4-6.

—. 1990b. Road safety a lethal problem in third world. *Urban Edge* 14(5):1-3.

Watts, DM, DS Burke, BA Harrison, RE Whitmire, A Nisalak. 1987. Effect of temperature on the vector efficiency of *Aedes aegypti* for dengue 2 virus. *Am J Trop Med Hyg* 36:143-152.

Wenzel, RP. 1994. A new hantavirus infection in North America. *New Engl J Med* 330(14):1004-1005.

Wilson, EO. 1988. The current state of biological diversity. In *Biodiversity*, edited by EO Wilson. Washington, DC: National Academy Press.

—. 1989. Threats to biodiversity. *Sci Am* 261:108-116.

—. 1992. *The Diversity of Life*. Cambridge, Mass.: Harvard University Press.

World Bank. 1992. *Development and the Environment*. Oxford: OUP.

World Health Organization (WHO). 1984. *Toxic Oil Syndrome: Mass Food Poisoning in Spain*. Copenhagen: WHO Regional Office for Europe.

—. 1987. *Air Quality Guidelines for Europe*. European Series, No. 23. Copenhagen: WHO Regional Office for Europe.

—. 1990a. *Acute Effects On Health of Smog Episodes*. WHO Regional Publications European Series, No. 3. Copenhagen: WHO Regional Office for Europe.

—. 1990b. *Diet, Nutrition and Prevention of Chronic Diseases*. WHO Technical Report Series, No. 797. Copenhagen: WHO Regional Office for Europe.

—. 1990c. *Global Estimates for Health Situation, Assessment and Projections*. WHO Technical Report Series, No. 797. Geneva: WHO.

—. 1990d. *Potential Health Effects of Climatic Change*. Geneva: WHO.

—. 1990e. Public health impact of pesticides used in agriculture. *World Health Statistics Quarterly* 43:118-187.

—. 1992a. *Indoor Air Pollution from Biomass Fuel*. Geneva: WHO.

—. 1992b. *Our Planet, Our Health*. Geneva: WHO.

—. 1993. *Weekly Epidemiol Rec* 3(69):13-20.

—. 1994. *Ultraviolet Radiation*. Environmental Health Criteria, No. 160. Geneva: WHO.

—. 1995. *Update and Revision of the Air Quality Guidelines for Europe*. Copenhagen: WHO Regional Office for Europe.

—. in press. *Potential Health Effects of Global Climate Change: Update*. Geneva: WHO.

World Health Organization (WHO) and ECOTOX. 1992. *Motor Vehicle Air Pollution. Public Health Impact and Control Measures*. Geneva: WHO.

World Health Organization (WHO) and FAO. 1984. *The Role of Food Safety in Health and Development*. WHO Technical Report Series, No. 705. Geneva: WHO.

World Health Organization (WHO) and UNEP. 1991. *Progress in the Implementation of the Mar Del Plata Action Plan and a Strategy for the 1990s*. Geneva: WHO.

—. 1992. *Urban Air Pollution in Megacities of the World*. Blackwells, UK: WHO.

World Health Organization (WHO) Commission on Health and Environment. 1992a. *Report of the Panel On Urbanization*. Geneva: WHO.

—. 1992b. *Report of the Panel On Energy*. Geneva: WHO.

World Meteorological Organization (WMO). 1992. *GCOS: Responding to the Need for Climate Observations*. Geneva: WMO.

Young, FE. 1987. Food safety and FDA's action plan phase II. *Food Technol* 41:116-123.

Other relevant readings

Andrews, JSJ, H Frumkin, BL Johnson, MA Mehlman, C Xintaras, and HA Bucsela. 1994. *Hazardous Waste and Public Health: International Congress On the Health Effects of Hazardous Waste*. Princeton, NJ: Princeton Scientific Publishing.

Batstone, R et al. 1989. *The Safe Disposal of Hazardous Wastes. The Special Needs and Problems of Developing Countries. World Bank Technical Paper No. 93*. Vol. I-III. Washington, DC: World Bank.

Gentner, NE and P Unrau. 1979. *Proceedings of the First International Conference On Health Effects of Energy Production*. Chalk River, Ontario, Canada: Atomic Energy of Canada.

International Atomic Energy Agency (IAEA). 1982. *Proceedings of International Symposium, Health Impacts of Different Sources of Energy*. Vienna: IAEA.

—. 1984. *Proceedings of Symposium Risks and Benefits of Energy Systems*. Vienna:IAEA.

—. 1991. *Senior Expert Symposium On Electricity and the Environment*. Vienna:IAEA.

Kjellstrom, T. 1988. Health hazards of the environment. Measuring the harm. *World Health* :2-5.

National Research Council. 1991. Public Health and Hazardous Wastes. *Environmental Epidemiology*, No. V 1. Washington, DC: National Academy Press.

Societé française d'énergie nucléaire. 1980. *Colloquium On the Risks of Different Energy Sources, Paris, 24-26 Jan. 1980*. Paris: Gedim.

Upton, AC, T Kneip, and P Toniolo. 1989. Public health aspects of toxic chemical disposal sites. *Ann Rev Publ Health* 10:1-25.

53. ENVIRONMENTAL HEALTH HAZARDS

ENCYCLOPAEDIA OF OCCUPATIONAL HEALTH AND SAFETY

REFERENCES 53.33

ENVIRONMENTAL POLICY

54

Chapter Editor
Larry R. Kohler

Contents

OVERVIEW: OCCUPATIONAL SAFETY AND HEALTH AND THE ENVIRONMENT—TWO SIDES OF THE SAME COIN

Larry R. Kohler

This is the first edition of the *Encyclopaedia of Occupational Health and Safety* to explicitly integrate relevant environmental issues within its scope. This chapter highlights a number of basic environmental policy issues which are increasingly linked to occupational safety and health. Other specialized environmental chapters include *Environmental Health Hazards* and *Environmental Pollution Control*. In addition, a special effort has been made to include sections concerning environment within each of the chapters on key industrial sectors. When first considering whether such a strategy to integrate environmental issues was indeed warranted in the *Encyclopaedia*, we began with the very limited perspective of including only a single chapter which would serve as a useful "cross-reference" demonstrating how occupational safety and health issues and the working environment have become increasingly linked to environmental issues. As the ILO has been stating for the past twenty-plus years: the working environment and the general environment represent "two sides of the same coin".

It is also blatantly clear, however, that the magnitude and scope of the challenges this "two-sided coin" represents for the workers of this world are grossly underestimated and under-targeted for action. The meritable successes which receive legitimate attention and praise in this *Encyclopaedia* risk leading us towards a dangerous and false sense of security and confidence as regards the present state of the art in occupational safety and health and the environment. The very best of our technologies, management practices and tools have indeed made impressive strides towards remediating and preventing problems in a number of key sectors, particularly in industrialized countries. But it is also true that the global reach of these technologies, management practices and tools is indeed insufficient and limited, especially in developing countries and in transition economies.

This chapter describes a few of the most useful tools and practices available to deal with occupational health and safety and environmental problems and challenges, although it would be misleading to suggest that these are already in fact widely applied throughout the world. It is important, however, that occupational health and safety practitioners all over the world learn more about these tools and practices as a step towards their greater application and practical adaptation to different economic and social conditions.

The first article in this chapter provides a brief review of inter-relationships between occupational safety and health and the working environment, policies and issues related to the general environment and the concept of "sustainable development". This concept became the guiding principle for Agenda 21, the action plan for the 21st century adopted at the United Nations Conference on Environment and Development (UNCED) in Rio de Janeiro in June 1992. The past comfortable—and yet seriously misleading—view that it was not only possible but essential to differentiate problems and responses between those that deal with action at the workplace and those that deal with what occurs outside the gates of the enterprise has become blurred. In fact, today both workers and employers and their organizations have begun to recognize explicitly that the enterprise gate is far from impermeable to the effects of policies and problems encountered on both sides of that gate.

Given the growing recognition that occupational safety and health issues may have been treated in too isolated a manner in the past, this chapter provides a series of brief descriptions of a number of environmental policy issues which occupational safety and health practitioners may find particularly relevant to their own activities and concerns. The chapter contains two articles on environmental law and regulations which describe the present state of the art as regards the rapid expansion of international and national legal responses to existing and potential future environmental problems and concerns.

The chapter contains four articles describing some of the most important environmental policy tools being used today to improve environmental performance not only in industry, but also in all other sectors of our economy and throughout our societies. The articles focus upon environmental impact assessments, life-cycle analysis, risk assessment and communication and environmental auditing. The final section of this chapter provides two perspectives on pollution prevention and control: one focusing on making pollution prevention a corporate priority and the other providing a trade union perspective of pollution prevention and cleaner production technologies.

The overall objective of this chapter is to enable the reader to better perceive and understand the growing inter-relationships between occupational safety and health and the working environment, and the broader environmental issues beyond the workplace. A greater recognition of these linkages will hopefully also lead to more extensive and effective exchanges of experience and information between occupational health and safety and environmental specialists, with a view to enhancing our capacity to respond to challenges in the working environment and beyond.

ENVIRONMENT AND THE WORLD OF WORK: AN INTEGRATED APPROACH TO SUSTAINABLE DEVELOPMENT, ENVIRONMENT AND THE WORKING ENVIRONMENT

Larry R. Kohler

It should come as no surprise to occupational health and safety practitioners that if one traces back from most of our present major environmental problems—one arrives at a workplace! Likewise, the serious occupational health and safety consequences of some chemicals and substances have become an early warning system of potential environmental health consequences far beyond the workplace.

Despite the obvious inter-relationship between the working environment and the environment, many governments, employers and workers continue to respond to the causes and consequences of both working environment and environment issues in very disparate and isolated ways. (Given the importance of distinguishing between the working environment and those broader environmental perspectives represented by such adjectives as *physical, general* or *external,* this article will use the term *working environment* to encompass all occupational health, safety and environment issues within the workplace and the term *environment* to encompass those environmental issues beyond the workplace.) The goal of this article is to draw attention to the significant advantages which may arise from responding to the environment—within and outside the workplace—in a more integrated and strategic fashion. This is true not only for industrialized countries, which have made significant progress regarding both occupational safety and health and environment, but as well in transition economies and developing countries, which have a much broader and overwhelming challenge yet before them.

As this article has been specifically prepared for the Fourth Edition of the *Encyclopaedia of Occupational Health and Safety* it does not attempt to review the full range of occupational health and safety (OHS) issues related to the environment, many of which are reflected in other chapters of the *Encyclopaedia*. In fact, occupational health and safety is an integral part of every enterprise's "environmental" performance. This is not to suggest that OHS and environmental protection are always totally compatible and mutually reinforcing; occasionally they may also be antagonistic. Nevertheless, the objective should be to find ways to protect both workers' health and safety and the broader environment, and to avoid options which suggest that one needs to choose one *or* the other. The identification of environmental problems and response strategies has too often led to the creation of false dichotomies—environmental protection versus worker safety or environmental protection versus job security. While such conflicts may indeed exist in very specific and special circumstances, the majority of situations require a series of trade-offs and careful longer-term approaches for meeting *both* environmental and worker protection and employment objectives. This leads to a corollary thesis that worker-employer collaboration is a critical factor necessary for improved performance regarding both OHS and environment.

This perspective on environment and the world of work is especially evident if one assumes that OHS performance at the workplace should be driven by a focus on prevention rather than simply on control and remediation. The concept of prevention is fundamental to future improvements in OHS and the environment. Early in the 20th century in industrialized countries, OHS was often driven by a simplistic focus on control—the protection of workers from exposure to health and safety risks. Special emphasis was given to engineering solutions to limit accidents by improving machinery—for example, by introducing protective devices. As our knowledge of the health consequences related to the exposure of workers to certain chemicals and substances expanded, the "logical" response strategy was often first to protect the worker from exposure by improving ventilation systems or the wearing of protective devices. While important early exceptions exist, particularly in industrialized countries, it is a relatively recent phenomenon of the past few decades that so much public attention is being increasingly devoted in a number of key industrial sectors to eliminating or replacing the dangerous or toxic chemicals/substances with those which are significantly less harmful. It is interesting to note that this growing emphasis on prevention of the emission itself, or the use of specific chemicals, has grown at the same time as the public has become increasingly aware of and actively involved in environmental challenges. This new environmental awareness has stressed both the immediate and longer-term consequences of environmental degradation for our societies and our economies. Such public interest in the environment appears to have also supported workers' ongoing efforts to collaborate with employers to improve occupational safety and health. Nevertheless, it is blatantly clear that serious action to date regarding OHS and environment represents only a tip of the proverbial iceberg of OHS and environmental problems evident on our planet, and even more dramatically evident in developing countries and transition economies.

Environmental priorities and policies in industrialized countries have travelled a very similar path from control to prevention strategies, albeit in a much shorter time span than that of OHS. Concern for the environment in its early stages was in fact limited to a concern about "pollution". Attention was focused primarily on emissions to air, water and soils generated by the production process. Therefore, response strategies similarly often focused on "end-of-pipe" strategies to deal with the problem of local emissions. Citing just one rather simple example, this narrow approach led to solutions such as taller chimneys, which unfortunately did not eliminate the pollution but rather dispersed it far beyond the enterprise gate and the local community. While this often satisfied the local community and the workers who lived and worked there, new environmental problems were created—long-distance and even transboundary air pollution, which in some cases leads to what has been called "acid rain". Once the secondary effects of this end-of-pipe solution became evident, there followed considerable delay before some of the relevant stakeholders accepted that there were indeed other serious negative consequences created by the tall-chimney solution. The next innovative step in this process was to add on a sophisticated filtering system to trap the problem emissions before they left the chimney. As this example demonstrates, the focus of policy-makers was not on the prevention of the emissions but rather on various actions to control those emissions. Today, increasing efforts are being made to prevent the emissions by changing fuels and improving combustion technologies, as well as changing the production process itself through the introduction of so-called cleaner production technologies.

This preventive approach—which also requires a more holistic approach—has at least four significant advantages for the world of work and the environment:

- Unlike end-of-pipe technologies, which create additional costs for the production process without usually providing improvements in productivity or economic return, cleaner production technologies often lead to improvements in productivity and in measurable economic returns. In other words, end-of-pipe technologies clean up the environment but usually do not help the balance sheet. Cleaner production technologies prevent environmental degradation while also creating viable economic benefits.
- Cleaner production technologies often lead to significant improvements in the efficient use of natural resources and energy (i.e., use less natural resources to achieve comparable outputs) and also often lead to decreases in the amount of—and the toxicity of—the wastes generated.
- Efforts to introduce cleaner production technologies can and *should* explicitly identify measures to also improve OHS performance within the enterprise.
- Worker involvement concerning the protection of health, safety and environment as part of the cleaner technology process will lead to improvements in worker morale, understanding and job performance—all of which are well-documented factors in achieving good quality production.

Environmental policies, legislation and regulation have evolved and are leading—or at least are trying to keep up with—this process of transition from control-based approaches to prevention-centred strategies.

Both end-of-pipe and cleaner production strategies, however, have direct consequences for employment protection and creation. It is clear that in many parts of the world, particularly in industrialized countries and transition economies, there are major opportunities for job creation related to clean-up and remediation activities. At the same time, cleaner production technologies also represent a vibrant new industry which will lead to the creation of new job opportunities and, of course, will require new efforts to meet skill and training requirements. This is particularly evident in the dire need to ensure that those workers involved in meeting the challenge of environmental remediation receive effective

OHS and environmental training. While much attention is being given to the potential negative impact on employment of increased regulations and controls, in the field of environment, regulation and controls, if properly developed, can lead to the creation of new jobs and promote improved environmental and OHS performance.

Another critical change in perspective towards the environment has occurred since the 1960s: a shift from an exclusive focus on production processes to give attention also to the environmental consequences of the products themselves. The most obvious example is the automobile, where considerable efforts have been made to improve its environmental "efficiency", although much animated debate remains over whether a more efficient car should be complemented by an efficient public transport system. But clearly, all products have some environmental implications—if not in their production or use, most certainly in their eventual disposal. This shift in emphasis has led to an increasing number of environmental laws and regulations concerning the use and disposal of products, even the restriction or elimination of certain products. It also has led to new analytical techniques such as environmental impact assessments, life-cycle analysis, risk assessment and environmental auditing (see the articles later in this chapter). These new, broader perspectives on environment have implications as well for the world of work—for example, upon conditions of work for those involved in the safe disposal of products and on future employment prospects for those involved in the manufacture, sale and servicing of prohibited and restricted products.

Another driving force for environmental policy has been the rather dramatic number and scope of major industrial accidents, particularly since the Bhopal disaster in 1984. Bhopal and other major accidents like Chernobyl and the *Exxon Valdez*, demonstrated to the world—the public, politicians, employers and workers—that the traditional view that what happened within the gates of the workplace could not or would not affect the external environment, the general public or the health and livelihood of surrounding communities, is false. While major accidents had occurred before, the global, visual coverage of *these* events shocked wide segments of the public in developed and developing countries and transitional economies into a new awareness and support for environmental protection which would also protect workers and the public. It should be noted, however, that this provides another similarity to the history of action to improve occupational health and safety laws and regulations, which was also significantly promoted, for example, following early major factory fires and mining disasters.

One of the most obvious examples of the effects of these environmental driving forces, and particularly recent major "environmental" accidents, may be seen within the ILO itself, as reflected in recent decisions by its tripartite constituents. For example, the ILO has significantly enhanced its activities related to environment and the world of work. Most importantly, since 1990 three major sets of ILO working environment Conventions and Recommendations have been adopted:

- Convention No. 170 and Recommendation No. 177 concerning Safety in the Use of Chemicals at Work (1990)
- Convention No. 174 and Recommendation No. 181 concerning the Prevention of Major Industrial Accidents (1992)
- Convention No. 176 and Recommendation No. 183 concerning Safety and Health in Mines (1995).

These standards reflect an explicit extension of the traditional ILO scope from that of an exclusive focus on worker protection to also include a more holistic approach to these matters by references in the preambular or operative paragraphs to relevant aspects of the protection of the public and the environment. For example, Article 3 of Convention No. 174 states that the term *major accident* means "a sudden occurrence leading to a serious danger to workers, the public or environment, whether immediate or delayed", and Article 4 states: "each Member shall formulate, implement and periodically review a coherent national policy concerning the protection of workers, the public and the environment against risk of major accidents." The ILO's wide range of Conventions and Recommendations related to the working environment provides a very useful source of guidance for countries working to improve their OHS and environmental performance. In this regard, it may also be useful to note that the ILO provides advisory assistance and support to its tripartite constituents with a view to helping them to ratify and implement relevant ILO standards.

In addition to these driving forces, however, there is a wide range of other factors which significantly influence the relationship between the working environment and the general environment. Clearly one of the most obvious is that despite many common concerns and issues (e.g., chemicals, accidents, health) the OHS and environmental aspects are often governed by different government ministries, different legislation, regulations and standards, and different enforcement and inspection mechanisms. These differences lead to considerable confusion, possibly additional costs as a result of duplication and, most disconcerting, to the existence of possible gaps which may lead to serious omissions concerning the protection of workers, the public and the environment. For example, recent reviews of a number of national inspectorates have drawn attention to potential problems of duplication, gaps and inconsistencies in the responsibilities assigned to factory, labour and environmental inspectorates. These reviews have also cited examples of situations in which labour inspectorates have been assigned new environmental inspection responsibilities without receiving adequate new staff and financial resources or specialized training. This has tended to deflect existing staff away from fully meeting their OHS inspection responsibilities. In addition, in many countries these legislative and inspectorate responsibilities still remain extremely limited and are not receiving adequate political and financial support. More emphasis will need to be given to developing a more integrated approach to the monitoring, enforcement and dispute settlement mechanisms related to OHS and environment regulations and standards.

While inspectorates will be essential components in any OHS and environmental protection system, by themselves they can never be sufficient. Workplace health and safety and the link between environment and the world of work will need to remain largely the responsibility of those at the enterprise level. The best way to ensure optimal performance is to ensure optimum confidence and collaboration between the workforce and management. This will need to be supported by effective training of workers and management as well as efficient joint mechanisms to support collaboration. These efforts at the enterprise level will be all the more successful if they are supported by good relations with, and access to, an adequately financed, well-trained and independent inspectorate.

The present wave of support for deregulation and structural adjustment, particularly within the public sector, if properly designed and implemented could lead to the more effective and efficient management of occupational safety and health and environmental protection. However, there are very troubling signs that suggest that this process may also lead to a deterioration of both OHS and environmental performance if governments, employers, workers and the public do not give adequate priority to these issues. All too often, OHS and environment are seen as issues which can be dealt with "later", once more immediate economic requirements have been met. Experience suggests, however, that today's short-term savings may lead to expensive remediation activities in the future to rectify the problems which could have been prevented at lower costs today. OHS and environment should not simply be seen as end-of-pipe and unproductive costs but rather as critical and productive social, environmental and economic investments.

Collaborative action between employers and workers at the workplace to deal with OHS issues has a long history and has clearly demonstrated its value. It is interesting to note that initially OHS issues were considered the exclusive prerogative of employers. Nevertheless, today, following very extensive efforts by the social partners, OHS issues are now seen as a matter of bipartite and/or tripartite collaboration in most countries throughout the world. In fact, many countries have established legislation requiring the creation of joint occupational health and safety committees at the workplace.

Here again, however, similar paths of development between OHS and environment are evident. When workers and their trade unions first raised issues of occupational health and safety as issues of direct concern to them, they were often dismissed as not having the knowledge and technical competence to understand or to deal with these issues. It has taken decades of dedicated effort for workers and their unions to demonstrate their fundamental role in understanding and effectively responding to these issues at the enterprise level. Workers had to insist that it was their health and safety and that they had a right to be involved in the process leading to decisions, and a positive contribution to make. Similarly, many employers and their organizations have come to recognize the benefits which have come from this collaborative process. Today, workers and their trade unions are often confronted with similar dismissive attitudes by some employers as regards their capacity and right to contribute to environmental protection. It should also be noted, however, that it is again the far-sighted and responsible employers in a limited number of high-profile sectors who are in the forefront of recognizing the talent, experience and practical common sense approach which workers can provide to improving environmental performance, and who support a well-trained, well-motivated, fully informed and fully involved workforce.

Nevertheless, some employers still argue that environment is an exclusive management responsibility and have opposed the establishment of joint safety, health and environment committees or separate joint environmental committees. Others have recognized the very critical and practical contribution that collaborative employer/worker action can make to ensuring that enterprises set and meet appropriate environmental performance standards. Such standards are no longer restricted to simply meeting mandatory legal requirements, but also include voluntary action to respond to the needs of local communities, global competitiveness, green marketing and so on. Voluntary environmental performance policies and programmes within individual enterprises or through sectoral associations (e.g., the chemical industries Responsible Care programme) often explicitly integrate both OHS and environmental considerations. Similarly, specialized and often voluntary standards prepared by organizations such as the International Organization for Standardization (ISO) also have had an increasing influence on both OHS and environmental protection.

The positive experience with collaboration between employers' and workers' organizations has also led to new collaborative partnerships and alliances which go beyond the workplace to ensure that all the stakeholders concerned with safety, health and environment are able to constructively participate in the process. Within the ILO we have called this new effort to expand collaborative links beyond the workplace to local community

groups, environmental NGOs and other institutions involved in helping to make improvements in the world of work, "tripartite-plus" collaboration.

Several emerging issues are on the horizon which may lead to special challenges and opportunities for more effective linkages between OHS and environment. Two sectors which have been particularly difficult to reach as regards both OHS and environmental performance are small- and medium-sized enterprises (SMEs) and the urban informal sector. This is especially relevant as regards the awesome implications of one of the most critical environmental and developmental challenges of the 21st century: clean water and sanitation. New participatory approaches will need to be developed in order to better communicate the significant risks for workers and the environment related to many existing activities. Beyond the risks, however, there are also new opportunities to make improvements in productivity and to increase incomes from traditional activities, as well as the prospect of the creation of new income-generating activities directly related to the environment. Given the many direct and indirect linkages between the formal sector and SMEs and the urban informal sector, innovative approaches need to be designed which will facilitate the sharing of experiences on ways to improve OHS and environmental performance. Employers' and workers' organizations could play a very positive and practical role in this process.

Another emerging issue area is that of indoor air pollution. In the past we have tended to see large industrial establishments as the primary target to correct unhealthy working conditions. Today, however, there is growing recognition that many offices and commercial premises may also be encountering new occupational health problems due to indoor air pollution. This pollution is related to the increased use of chemicals and electronic equipment, intake of contaminated ambient air, the use of closed air recirculation and air conditioning systems, and the possible increased sensitivity of workers as a result of changing health patterns—for example, the growing number of cases of allergies and asthma. It may be expected that action to respond to indoor air pollution concerns will require a more integrated approach to both OHS and environmental factors than has been the case in the past.

Links to Sustainable Development

This article has so far briefly and superficially highlighted some of the past and potential future inter-relationships between OHS and the environment. This, however, already should be seen as a rather narrow perspective compared to the more holistic and integrated approach represented by the concept of sustainable development. This concept was the key—if not the "magic formula"—underlying the preparatory process to negotiate and endorse Agenda 21, the action plan for the 21st century adopted at the United Nations Conference on Environment and Development (UNCED) in Rio de Janeiro in June 1992 (see Robinson 1993). The concept of sustainable development is and will continue to be the subject of great discussion, debate and dispute. Much of this debate has been focused on semantics. For the purpose of this article, sustainable development represents both a goal and a process. As a goal, sustainable development implies development which equitably meets the needs of today's and future generations. As a process, it means setting policies in such a way that they take into account not only economic factors but environmental and social factors as well.

If such a holistic concept is to be successfully operationalized, then the approach to all these factors will require new analysis and responses. It is essential that OHS issues become a fundamental factor in evaluating future investment and development decisions at all levels from the workplace to the negotiation of international standards. The protection of workers will need to be assessed not simply as one of the costs of doing business, but as a critical factor necessary to the achievement of economic, environmental and social objectives which are an integral part of sustainable development. This means that the protection of workers should be seen and calculated as an investment with a potentially positive rate of return within projects aimed at the achievement of environmental, social and economic objectives. The protection of workers as well cannot simply be seen as protecting them at their workplace, but should take into account the inter-relationship between their work, general health, living conditions (water, sanitation, housing), transport, culture and so on. It also implies that action to improve OHS is a prerequisite for meeting the basic economic and social development perspectives in developing countries, and not simply a luxury to be reserved for the rich countries.

As the Director-General of the ILO, Michel Hansenne, stated in his Report to the International Labour Conference in 1990:

[T]here is in fact one central issue which pervades almost every environmental policy discussion—how to share equitably the costs and benefits of environmental action. "Who will pay for environmental improvements?" is a question which will need to be discussed and resolved at all levels, from the perspective of consumers, workers, employers, as well as from that of local, national, regional and international institutions.

For the ILO, the social and human implications of how these potential environmental costs and benefits are shared within society and between countries may be as important as the environmental actions themselves. An inequitable sharing of the social, economic and environmental costs and benefits of development, within and between countries, cannot lead to global sustainable development. Rather, it could accentuate poverty, injustice and division (ILO 1990).

In the past, and too frequently still today, workers have been called upon to pay an inequitable part of the costs of economic development through deplorable safety and health conditions (e.g., the tragic fire at the Kader Industrial Toy Company in Thailand, which took the lives of 188 workers), inadequate wages (insufficient income to meet basic family needs of food, shelter, education), lack of freedom of association and even the loss of human dignity (e.g., the use of bonded child labour). Similarly, workers and their local communities also have assumed much of the direct costs of day-to-day environmental degradation or decisions to close plants for environmental reasons. It also should be remembered that while most attention in industrialized countries has been focused on ways to avoid the potential loss of jobs as a result of environmental legislation and regulations, millions of people have already lost or have had their traditional livelihoods severely reduced as a result of ongoing desertification, deforestation, flooding and soil erosion.

Sustainable development implies that these environmental and social costs which have been "externalized" by industry and society in the past must now be internalized and reflected in the market costs of products and services. This internalization process is being encouraged by market forces and consumer groups, new laws and regulations including so-called economic instruments, as well as by decisions taken by the enterprises themselves. Nevertheless, to be successful this process of integrating the actual social and environmental costs of production and consumption will require new approaches to collaboration, communication and participation in decision-making processes. Workers' and employers' organizations have a critical stake in this process. They should also have a say in its design, implementation and monitoring.

In this context it may be useful to draw attention to the major diplomatic effort under way as part of the follow-up process of the UNCED Conference to facilitate an examination of the current imbalances in the global patterns of production and consumption. Chapter 4 of *Agenda 21*, entitled "Changing Consumption Patterns", indicates that action is needed to meet the following objectives:

(a) to promote patterns of consumption and production that reduce environmental stress and will meet the basic needs of humanity

(b) to develop a better understanding of the role of consumption and how to bring about more sustainable consumption patterns.

It also clearly encompasses the concept of the need for greatly expanding the basic consumption of millions of people in many parts of our world currently confronted with dire poverty and hardship. Ongoing negotiations and discussions within the framework of the Commission on Sustainable Development (CSD) may be expected to be very slow and complex. Nevertheless they could lead to significant changes in present production and consumption patterns, particularly in some of the most critical industrial sectors of our economies, including chemicals, energy and transport. They also will have significant repercussions on international trade and commerce. Such changes will no doubt also have important implications for OHS and environment practices in developed and developing countries and for many other areas of the world of work, especially employment, incomes and training.

Although these issues currently are being discussed primarily at the global level, it is obvious that it is at each workplace where they will need to be implemented. Therefore, it is essential that this global negotiation process reflect reality, that is, the constraints and opportunities at the workplace level all across our planet. With the globalization of our economies, and the rapid changes in the organization and structures of our workplaces (e.g., sub-contracting, part-time work, homeworkers, teleworking), and indeed changes in our perception of work, livelihoods and employment itself in the 21st century, this will be no easy task. If this process is to be successful, however, it will require the support of a tripartite collaborative process between governments and employers' and workers' organizations at all stages. Clearly such a bottom-up approach will play a vital role in guiding the national and global CSD process to achieve more sustainable production and consumption patterns in the future.

Conclusion

Articles in this chapter focus on action at the national and international levels as well as on practical policy tools to improve environmental performance. It is clear, however, that the most important environmental policies of the future will not be set at the national or international level or even by local communities—although each of these has an essential role to play. The real changes must and will come at the enterprise and workplace level. From the chief executive officer of large multinational corporations to the managers of small family businesses to rural farmers and independent workers in the informal sector will come the true impetus and commitment to follow through to achieve sustainable development. Change will be possible only through the growing awareness and joint action by employers and workers within enterprises and other relevant sectors (e.g., local communities, non-governmental organizations, etc.) to integrate OHS and environmental objectives within the overall objectives and priorities of the enterprise. Despite the magnitude of the challenge, one can foresee the range of formal and informal safety, health and environmental policies at the enterprise level developed, implemented and monitored by a collaborative process between management and workers and other stakeholders.

Occupational health and safety clearly has a significant impact on the achievement of our overall economic, environmental and social objectives. Therefore, OHS must be seen as a critical element to be included within the complex integration process to achieve sustainable development. Following the UNCED Conference, all national governments have been called upon to develop their own national Agenda 21 strategies and plans for sustainable development. Environmental objectives already are seen as an integral part of that process. Much work remains, however, before OHS and employment and social objectives and targets will become an explicit and intrinsic part of that process and the economic and political support necessary for the achievement of those objectives is mobilized.

The preparation of this article has been greatly facilitated by the technical support, useful advice and comments and regular encouragement from colleagues, governments, employers and workers from around the world who are keenly committed and competent in this field, but particularly key representatives from the International Federation of Chemical, Energy and General Workers' Unions (ICEF); Canadian Labour Congress; the Communications, Energy and Paper Workers' Unions of Canada; and the Labourers' International Union of North America, who have stressed the urgent need for action in this field.

● LAWS AND REGULATIONS

Françoise Burhenne-Guilmin

The relationship between human health and the human environment has been recognized from time immemorial. This tenet of medicine can be traced back to Hippocrates, who taught his pupils to "attend to the airs, waters, and places" if they sought to understand the sources of health and diseases in their patients (Lloyd 1983).

This ancient view of the link between human health and the environment has persisted. The degree of a society's acceptance of this link has been influenced by three factors: development of a scientific understanding of the human body; increased capacity to cure individual illnesses; and the evolution of parallel scientific, religious and cultural concepts.

Environmental factors as a cause of health or diseases of entire classes of people were given increased attention during the Industrial Revolution. The trend has continued to this day, assisted by the development of the environmental sciences and of techniques for determining causality and assessing risks.

It was in the workplace that causal links between health and the environment were first clearly established. It was also in the workplace that the consequences of the increase in the amount and variety of contaminants resulting from the diversification of industrial processes were first felt. Yet these contaminants cannot be confined to the occupational environment. Once released, their pathway may become difficult to follow or trace, but it inevitably ends in nature: environmental toxins are present in the soil, water and air of even the most remote environments. Human health, in turn, is affected by the pollution of the natural environment, whether of local, national or transboundary origin. Along with other types of environmental degradation, which cause worldwide depletion of natural resources, this accords a planetary dimension to the interaction between environmental conditions and public health.

The conclusion is inescapable that the quality of the work environment and of the natural environment are inextricably linked. Lasting solutions to either of these problems can be successful only if both are tackled in tandem.

Environmental Law: A Means to an End

The formulation of policies to maintain and improve both the natural and the work environment is a prerequisite to successful environmental management. Policies, however, remain a dead letter unless they are implemented. Such implementation is only achievable through the translation of policy principles into rules of law. From this perspective, law is at the service of policy, giving it concreteness and a degree of permanency through appropriate legislation.

Legislation, in turn, is a framework structure which is useful only if implemented and enforced. Implementation and enforcement are dependent on the political and social contexts in which they take place; if they are not backed by the public, they are likely to remain inefficient.

Therefore, enactment, implementation and enforcement of environmental legislation are, to a large extent, dependent on understanding and acceptance of the rules established by those to whom these rules are addressed—hence the importance of disseminating environmental information and knowledge to the public at large, as well as to specific target groups.

The Role of Environmental Law: Prevention and Cure

The role of law in the environmental field, as in many other fields, is twofold: first, to create rules and conditions which are conducive to the control or prevention of damage to the environment or human health; and, second, to offer remedies for situations where damage has occurred in spite of these rules and conditions.

Prevention through command techniques

Land use controls

The regulation of land use is a major element of environmental law, and a prerequisite to the control and guidance of land development and the utilization of natural resources. The issue is usually whether a particular environment may be put to another use, it being understood that non-use is also a type of land use.

Land use controls allow siting human activities where they are best located (or least damaging), and also subject contemplated activities to restrictions. These two goals are usually achieved by establishing a requirement for prior authorization.

Prior authorization

Prior authorization is a generic term for any form of permission (e.g., licence, permit) which must be obtained from a regulatory authority before certain activities may be undertaken.

The first step is to determine by law those private and public sector activities which are subject to prior authorization. Several approaches are possible and are not mutually exclusive:

Controls of sources. When a category of sources of environmental harm is clearly identifiable, it is usually subject to prior authorization as such (e.g., all classes of industrial facilities and motor vehicles).

Controls of substances. When a particular substance or class of substances is identified as potentially harmful to the environment, the use or release of these substances may be made subject to prior authorization.

Media-oriented controls, and integrated pollution control. Media-oriented controls are those which are directed at protecting a specific component of the environment (air, water, soil). Such controls may lead to shifting environmental harm from one medium to another, and thus fail to reduce (or may even increase) the overall degree of environmental harm. This has led to the development of coordinated prior authorization systems, whereby all pollution from one source and all recipient media are considered before one single, all-embracing authorization is granted.

Environmental standards

Environmental standards are maximum permissible limits which may be imposed directly by a law, or indirectly as conditions to obtain an authorization. These limits may be related either to the effects or the causes of environmental harm:

- Effect-related standards are those which take the target as a baseline. They include: (1) biological standards, (2) exposure standards and (3) environmental quality standards.
- Cause-related standards are those which take the cause of the possible environmental harm as a baseline. They include: (1) emission standards, (2) product standards and (3) process or operating standards.

A variety of factors, including the nature of the pollutant, the recipient media and the state of the art, determine which type of standard is most appropriate. Other considerations also play an important role: standard-setting provides a means to achieve a balance between what is environmentally desirable in a particular place at a particular point in time, and the socioeconomic feasibility of achieving a specific environmental goal.

It goes without saying that the stricter the standards are, the higher production costs become. Therefore, differing standards in different locations within a state or between states play an important role in determining competitive market advantages or disadvantages, and may constitute non-tariff barriers to trade—hence the desirability of seeking harmonization at the regional or global level.

Prevention through incentives and disincentives

Controls voluntarily submitted to may be used as flanking measures or as alternatives to command techniques. They usually consist of setting recommended (rather than compulsory) values, and of providing economic incentives or disincentives to achieve them.

The purpose of an incentive (e.g., accelerated depreciation allowance, tax benefit, subsidy) is to reward and, therefore, to generate, a specific environmentally friendly conduct or activity. Thus, instead of trying to achieve a certain emission level by the stick, the carrot of economic benefit is offered.

The purpose of a disincentive (e.g., fees, such as effluent or emission charge, tax or levy) is to induce environmentally friendly conduct so as to avoid paying the fee in question.

There are also other ways of inducing adherence to recommended values, for instance, through the creation of eco-label award schemes, or providing marketing advantages where consumers are sensitized to environmental concerns.

These so-called voluntary approaches are often referred to as alternatives to "legal" controls, forgetting that incentives and disincentives also have to be established by law!

Cure through sanctions or remedies

Sanctions imposed by the regulatory agency

In cases where environmental management measures may be prescribed by the regulatory agency (e.g., through a prior authorization mechanism), legal regimes usually also provide the agency with enforcement powers. A variety of techniques are available, ranging from the imposition of monetary sanctions (e.g., per day) until compliance with the requirement, to execution of the measures required (e.g., building filters) at the cost of the addressee, and finally to closure of the facility for non-compliance with administrative requirements, etc.

Each legal system provides for ways in which these measures may be challenged by those to whom they are applied. Equally important is to provide the possibility for other interested parties (e.g., NGOs representing the public interest) to challenge the decisions of the regulatory agency. In the latter case, it is not only the action of the administration which should be eligible for challenge, but also its *inaction*.

Penal sanctions

Legislation prescribing a certain environmental norm or conduct usually indicates that disregarding the established rules, whether intentionally or not, constitutes an offence, and determines the type of penal sanctions which are to be applied to each case. Penal sanctions may be monetary (fines) or, in serious cases, may entail incarceration, or a combination of both. Penal sanctions for environmental offences depend upon the penal system of each country. Thus, sanctions are often imposed in reference to the main body of criminal law in a particular country (e.g., a penal code), which may also include a chapter on environmental offences. Penal sanctions can be triggered by the administration or by an aggrieved party.

The legislation of many countries has been criticized for failing to declare certain environmental misconducts as penal offences, or for providing overly mild penalties for environmental offences. It has often been observed that if the quantum of the sanctions is less than the cost of internalizing environmental management measures, the culprits are likely to deliberately prefer the risk of a penal sanction, especially if this sanction may be only a fine. This is especially true when there is an enforcement deficit—that is, when the enforcement of environmental norms is lax or lenient, as is often the case.

Liability for damages

Each legal system's rules applying to liability for damage naturally also apply to health and environmental damage. This usually means that compensation is due either in kind or specie only when the damage proves to have been caused directly by the fault of one or more originators.

In the environmental field, the difficulties in applying these principles are numerous, and have led to the enactment of *sui generis* environmental liability laws in an increasing number of countries. This has made it possible to provide for liability without fault, and, therefore, to allow for compensation independently of the circumstances which caused the damage. In such cases, however, a certain monetary ceiling is usually set with a view to permitting eligibility for insurance coverage, which may also be made compulsory by law.

These special regimes also attempt to better provide redress in cases of damage to the environment *per se* (ecological damage as opposed to economic damage), usually requiring the restoration of the environment to the status quo ante whenever the nature of the damage permits. In such a scenario, monetary damages are in order only if restoration is impossible.

Access to remedies

Not everyone may take action to generate sanctions or obtain remedies. These may traditionally be triggered only by the administration, or a physical or legal person directly affected by a certain situation. In cases where it is the environment that is affected, this is usually insufficient, since much environmental damage is not directly linked to individual human interests. Therefore, it is important for legal systems to grant "representatives" of the public interest the right to sue the administration for failure to act or for insufficient action, or to sue individuals or enterprises for breaking the law or causing damage to the environment. There are various ways in which this can be achieved: designated non-governmental organizations may be given this right; the legal system may provide for class action or citizens' suits, etc. The right to sue in defence of the public interest, rather than only to defend a proprietary interest, is one of the most important elements of modern environmental legislation.

Conclusion

Good environmental legislation is a prerequisite to achieve and maintain the desired levels of quality in the natural, as well as in the work environment.

What "good" environmental legislation is, might be difficult to define. Some wish to see a decline in command and control methods, and their replacement by softer incitation techniques but, in practice, there is no standard formula to decide what the ingredients of the law should be. What is important, however, is to make legislation relevant to the particular situation of the country concerned, adapting available principles, methods and techniques to the needs, capacities and legal traditions of each country.

This is all the more true at a time when large numbers of developing nations and nations with economies in transition seek to equip themselves with "good" environmental legislation, or to retrofit legislation already in place. In striving towards this goal, however, legislation which is successful in a particular legal, economic and social context, frequently that of an industrialized country, is still too often imported as a model in countries and legal systems for which it is totally inappropriate.

"Particularizing" legislation is, therefore, perhaps the most important element in achieving the goal of effective environmental legislation.

• INTERNATIONAL ENVIRONMENTAL CONVENTIONS

David Freestone

The publicity surrounding the UN Conference on Environment and Development (UNCED), which took place in Rio de Janeiro in June 1992, confirmed the central place that global environmental concerns over issues such as global warming and loss of biological diversity have on the world political agenda. In fact, in the twenty years between the 1972 Stockholm Conference on the Human Environment and the 1992 UNCED there has been not only a major increase in awareness of the threats to the environment from human activities on both a local and global scale, but also a massive increase in the number of international legal instruments governing environmental issues. (There are large numbers of collections of environmental treaties: see, e.g., Burhenne 1974a, 1974b,1974c; Hohmann 1992; Molitor 1991. For a contemporary qualitative assessment see Sand 1992.)

It will be recalled that the two main sources of international law (as defined by the 1945 Statute of the International Court of Justice) are international conventions and international customary law (Article 38(1) of the Statute). International customary law derives from state practice repeated over time in the belief that it represents legal obligation. Although it is possible for new rules of custom to emerge relatively swiftly, the speed with which awareness of global environmental problems has reached the international political agenda has meant that customary law has tended to take second place to treaty or conventional law in the evolution of legal norms. Although certain basic principles, such as the equitable utilization of shared resources (Lac Lanoux Arbitration 1957) or the obligation not to allow activities which

damage the environment of neighbouring states (Trail Smelter Arbitration 1939, 1941) can be attributed to judicial decisions derived from customary law, treaties have without doubt been the main method by which the international community has responded to the need to regulate activities which threaten the environment. Another important aspect of international environmental regulation is the development of "soft law": non-binding instruments which lay down guidelines or desiderata for future action, or through which states commit themselves politically to meeting certain objectives. These soft law instruments sometimes develop into formal legal instruments or become linked to binding instruments as, for example, through decisions of the parties to a Convention. (On the significance of soft law in relation to international environmental law see Freestone 1994.) Many of the collections of international environmental law documents cited above include soft law instruments.

This article will give a brief overview of the main international environmental conventions. Although such a review inevitably concentrates on the main global conventions, the significant and growing web of regional and bilateral agreements should also be borne in mind. (For a systematic exposition of the whole body of international environmental law, see Kiss and Shelton 1991; Birnie and Boyle 1992. See also Churchill and Freestone 1991.)

Pre-Stockholm

Prior to the 1972 Stockholm Conference the majority of environmental conventions related to the conservation of wildlife. Of historical interest only are the very early bird protection conventions (e.g., the 1902 Convention for the Protection of Birds Useful to Agriculture; see further Lyster 1985). More significant in the longer term are the general nature conservation conventions, although the 1946 Washington Convention for the Regulation of Whaling (and its 1956 Protocol) is particularly noteworthy in this period—over time it has of course changed its focus from exploitation to conservation. A pioneering convention in conservation terms was the 1968 African Convention on Conservation of Nature and Natural Resources, Algiers, which despite its comprehensive and innovative approach to conservation made the mistake of many other conventions in not establishing an administrative structure to oversee its supervision. Also notable and considerably more successful is the 1971 Ramsar Convention on Wetlands of International Importance, especially as Waterfowl Habitat, which establishes a network of protected wetland areas in the territories of member states.

Other noteworthy developments in this period are the first global Oil Pollution Conventions. The 1954 International Convention for the Prevention of Pollution of the Sea by Oil (OILPOL) (amended 1962 and 1969) broke new ground by developing a regulatory framework for the carriage of oil by sea, but the first conventions to provide for emergency action and for compensation for oil pollution damage were developed directly in response to the world's first major oil-tanker casualty—the wreck of the Liberian oil tanker *Torrey Canyon* off the coast of southwest England in 1967. The 1969 International Convention relating to Intervention on the High Seas in cases of Oil Pollution Damage authorized emergency action by coastal states outside territorial waters, and its fellows, the 1969 International Convention on Civil Liability for Oil Pollution Damage and the 1971 International Convention on the Establishment of an International Fund for Compensation for Oil Pollution Damage of Brussels, provided a basis for compensation claims against the owners and operators of oil tankers supplemented by an international compensation fund. (Note also the significant industry voluntary compensation schemes such as TOVALOP and CRISTAL; see further Abecassis and Jarashow 1985.)

From Stockholm to Rio

The years 1972 to 1992 witnessed an astonishing increase in the number and variety of international environmental law instruments. Much of this activity is directly attributable to the Stockholm Conference. Not only did the famous Conference Declaration (Declaration of the United Nations Conference on the Human Environment 1972) lay down certain principles, the majority of which were *de lege ferenda* (i.e., they stated what the law ought to be rather than what it was), but it also developed a 109-point Environmental Action Plan and a Resolution recommending institutional and financial implementation by the UN. The result of these recommendations was the establishment of the United Nations Environment Programme (UNEP), established by UN General Assembly Resolution (UNGA 1972) and based eventually in Nairobi. UNEP was directly responsible for the sponsoring of a number of key global environmental treaties and for the development of the important Regional Seas Programme, which has resulted in a network of some eight regional framework conventions protecting the marine environment, each with protocols developed to meet the special requirements of the region. A number of new regional programmes are still in the pipeline.

In order to provide an overview of the large number of environmental conventions developed during this period, they are divided into a number of groups: nature conservation; protection of the marine environment; and regulation of transboundary environmental impacts.

Conservation of nature and natural resources

This period saw the conclusion of a number of nature conservation treaties both at a global and regional level. At the global level, particularly noteworthy are the 1972 UNESCO Convention Concerning the Protection of the World Cultural and Natural Heritage, the 1973 Washington Convention on International Trade in Endangered Species (CITES) and the 1979 Bonn Convention on the Conservation of Migratory Species of Wild Animals. At a regional level the large number of treaties include the 1974 Nordic Convention on the Protection of the Environment, the 1976 Convention on Conservation of Nature in the South Pacific (Apia Convention, in Burhenne 1974a) and the 1979 Berne Convention on the Conservation of European Wildlife and Natural Habitats (European Treaty Series). Note also the 1979 EC Directive 79/409 on the conservation of wild birds (OJ 1979), now amended and supplemented by Directive 92/43 on the conservation of natural habitats and of wild flora and fauna (OJ 1992), the 1979 Convention for the Conservation and Management of the Vicuna and the 1985 ASEAN Agreement on the Conservation of Nature and Natural Resources (reproduced in Kiss and Shelton 1991). (Also of note are the treaties relating to the Antarctic—an area of global commons outside the jurisdiction of any state: the 1980 Canberra Convention on the Conservation of Antarctic Marine Living Resources, the 1988 Wellington Convention on the Regulation of Antarctic Mineral Resource Activities and the 1991 Protocol to the Antarctic Treaty on Environmental Protection, signed in Madrid.)

Protection of the marine environment

In 1973 the negotiations began of the Third UN Conference on the Law of the Sea (UNCLOS III). The nine years of UNCLOS negotiations culminated in the 1982 Montego Bay Convention on the Law of the Sea (LOSC), which included in its Part XII a general framework for the regulation of marine environmental issues including vessel and land-based sources of pollution and dumping, as well as laying down certain general duties regarding protection of the marine environment.

At a more detailed level, the International Maritime Organization (IMO) was responsible for the development of two major global conventions: the 1972 London Convention on the Prevention of Marine Pollution by Dumping of Wastes and Other Matter and the 1973 International Convention for the Prevention of Pollution from Ships, as amended in 1978 (MARPOL 1973/78), and a third relating to oil spills entitled the International Convention on Oil Pollution Preparedness, Response and Cooperation in 1990, establishes a global legal framework for collaboration and assistance in response to major oil spills. (Other Maritime Conventions which are not primarily environmental but are of relevance include the 1972 Convention on the International Regulations for Preventing Collisions at Sea (COLREG); the 1974 International Convention for the Safety of Life at Sea (SOLAS); the 1976 ILO Merchant Shipping (Minimum Standards) Convention (No. 147) and the 1978 Convention on Standards of Training, Certification and Watch Keeping for Sea Farers).

The 1972 London Convention adopted what has now become a common approach by listing substances (Annex I) which could not be dumped in the ocean; Annex II listed substances which could be dumped only with a permit. The regulatory structure, which requires signatory states to enforce these obligations against any vessels loading in their ports or their flag vessels anywhere in the world, has progressively tightened its regime to the extent that parties have now effectively ended the ocean dumping of industrial waste. The 1973/78 MARPOL Convention replaces the 1954 OILPOL Convention (above) and provides the main regulatory regime for pollution from vessels of all sorts, including oil tankers. MARPOL requires flag states to impose controls on the "operational discharges" of all controlled substances. The MARPOL regime was amended in 1978 so that it would progressively extend its regime over different forms of vessel sources pollution contained in the five Annexes. All the Annexes are now in force covering oil (Annex I), noxious liquid substances (Annex II), packaged waste (Annex III), sewage (Annex IV) and garbage (Annex V). Stricter standards are enforced within Special Areas agreed by the Parties.

At a regional level, the UNEP Regional Seas Programme provides a wide, although not comprehensive, network of marine protection treaties covering: the Mediterranean (Convention for the Protection of the Mediterranean Sea against Pollution, Barcelona, 16 February, 1976; protocols in 1976 (2), 1980 and 1982); Gulf (Kuwait Regional Convention for Co-operation on the Protection of the Marine Environment from Pollution, Kuwait, 24 April 1978; protocols in 1978, 1989 and 1990); West Africa (Convention for Co-operation in the Protection and Development of the Marine and Coastal Environment of the West and Central African Region (Abidjan, 23 March 1981), with a 1981 protocol); South East Pacific (Convention for the Protection of the Marine Environment and Coastal Areas of the South-East Pacific (Lima, 12 November 1981); protocols in 1981, 1983 (2) and 1989); Red Sea (Regional Convention for the Conservation of the Red Sea and Gulf of Aden Environment (Jeddah, 14 February 1982); protocol in 1982); Caribbean (Convention for the Protection and Development of the Marine Environment of the Wider Caribbean Region, (Cartagena des Indias, 24 March 1983); protocols in 1983 and 1990); East Africa (Convention for the Protection, Management and Development of the Marine and Coastal Environment of the East African Region (Nairobi, 21 June 1985); 2 protocols in 1985); and the South Pacific (Convention for the Protection of the Natural Resources and Environment of the South Pacific Region, (Noumea, 24 November 1986); 2 protocols in 1986)—with another six or so in various stages of planning. (For texts of all the above Conventions and their protocols, as well as details of developing programmes, see Sand 1987.) These treaties are supplemented by protocols covering a wide range of issues including regulation of land-based sources of pollution, ocean dumping, pollution from (and decommissioning of) off-shore oil rigs, specially protected areas and protection of wildlife.

Other regional regimes have been developed outside the UNEP framework, notably in the North East Atlantic, where a highly comprehensive network of regional instruments covers regulation of ocean dumping (1972 Oslo Convention for the Prevention of Marine Pollution by Dumping from Ships and Aircraft; protocols in 1983 and 1989), land-based sources of pollution (1974 Paris Convention for the Prevention of Marine Pollution from Land Based Sources; protocol in 1986), oil pollution monitoring and cooperation (1983 Bonn Agreement for Co-operation in Dealing with Pollution of the North Sea by Oil and other Harmful Substances: Amending Decision 1989), inspection of vessels for safety and protection of the marine environment (1982 Paris Memorandum of Understanding on Port State Control in Implementing Agreements on Maritime Safety and Protection of the Marine Environment, as well as nature conservation and fisheries. (See generally Freestone and IJlstra 1991. Note also the new 1992 Paris Convention for the Protection of the Marine Environment of the North-East Atlantic, which will replace the Oslo and Paris Conventions; text and analysis in Hey, IJlstra and Nollkaemper 1993.) In the Baltic the 1974 Helsinki Convention on the Protection of the Marine Environment of the Baltic Sea Area has recently been revised (for text and analysis of 1992 Convention see Ehlers 1993)), and a new Convention developed for the Black Sea Region (1992 Bucharest Convention on the Protection of the Black Sea; see also 1993 Odessa Ministerial Declaration on the Protection of the Black Sea.)

Transboundary impacts

Principle 21 of the Stockholm Declaration provided that States had "the responsibility to ensure that activities under their jurisdiction and control do not cause damage to the environment of other States or of areas beyond national jurisdiction". Although this principle is now widely regarded as having become part of customary international law, the principle *grosso modo* requires considerable fine tuning to provide the basis for regulation of such activities. Addressing these issues, and largely in response to well publicized crises, international conventions have been developed to address issues such as long-range transboundary air pollution, protection of the ozone layer, notification and cooperation in response to nuclear accidents, transboundary movement of hazardous waste and global climate change.

Long-range transboundary air pollution

Long-range air pollution in Europe was first addressed by the 1979 Geneva Convention (Convention on Long-Range Transboundary Air Pollution). This, however, was a framework convention whose modestly expressed aims were "to limit and, as far as possible, gradually to reduce and prevent air pollution including long range transboundary pollution". Substantive progress in regulating emissions of specific substances was made only with the development of the protocols, of which there are now four: the 1984 Geneva Protocol (Geneva Protocol on Long-term Financing of the Co-operative Programme for Monitoring and Evaluation of the Long-Range Transmission of Air Pollution in Europe) established a network of air quality monitoring stations; the 1985 Helsinki Protocol (on the Reduction of Sulphur Emissions) aimed to reduce sulphur emissions by 30% by 1993; the 1988 Sofia Protocol (Concerning the Control of Emissions of Nitrogen Oxides or their Transboundary Fluxes), now replaced by the Second Sulphur Protocol, Oslo, 1994, provided for a freeze on national emissions of nitrogen oxides at 1987 levels by 1994; and the 1991 Geneva Protocol (Concerning the Control of Emissions of Volatile Organic Compounds or their Transboundary Fluxes) provided a range of options for emission abatement of volatile organic compounds and fluxes.

Transboundary implications of nuclear accidents

World attention had been brought to the transboundary implications of nuclear accidents after the 1986 Chernobyl accident, but even prior to that, previous conventions had addressed a number of the issues relating to the risks from nuclear devices, including the 1961 Convention on Third Party Liability in the Field of Nuclear Energy (1960), and the Vienna Convention on Civil Liability for Nuclear Damage (1963). Note also the 1963 Treaty Banning Nuclear Weapon Tests in the Atmosphere, in Outer Space and Under Water. The 1980 Vienna Convention on the Physical Protection of Nuclear Material had attempted to establish standards for the protection of nuclear material from a number of threats, including terrorism. In the wake of Chernobyl two further conventions were agreed upon in 1986, on early notification of accidents (Vienna Convention on the Early Notification of a Nuclear Accident) and international cooperation in the event of such accidents (Vienna Convention on Assistance in the Case of a Nuclear Accident or Radiological Emergency).

Protection of the ozone layer

The 1985 Vienna Convention for the Protection of the Ozone Layer imposes general obligations on each party "in accordance with the means at their disposal and their capabilities" to:

(a) cooperate by means of systematic observation, research and information exchange in order to better understand and assess the effects of human activities on the ozone layer and the effects on human health and the environment from modification of the ozone layer; (b) adopt appropriate legislative or administrative measures and cooperate in harmonizing appropriate policies to control, limit, reduce or prevent human activities under their jurisdiction or control should it be found that these activities have or are likely to have adverse effects resulting from modification or likely modification of the ozone layer; (c) cooperate in the formulation of agreed measures, procedures and standards for the implementation of the Convention, with a view to the adoption of protocols and annexes; (d) cooperate with competent international bodies to implement effectively the Convention and protocols to which they are party.

The Vienna Convention was supplemented by the 1987 Montreal Protocol on Substances that Deplete the Ozone Layer, itself adjusted and amended by the London Meeting of 1990 and most recently by the Copenhagen Meeting of November 1992. Article 2 of the Protocol requires parties to impose controls on ozone-depleting chemicals, namely CFCs, halons, other fully halogenated CFCs, carbon tetrachloride and 1,1,1-tri-chloroethane (methyl chloroform).

Article 5 provides an exemption from emissions restrictions for certain developing countries, "to meet [their] basic domestic needs" for up to ten years, subject to certain provisos set out in Article 5(2) (3). The Protocol also provides for technical and financial cooperation for developing country parties claiming exemption under Article 5. A Multilateral Fund was agreed upon to assist such parties to research and meet their obligations (Article 10). In Copenhagen in November 1992, in the light of the 1991 Scientific Assessment of Ozone Depletion, which found that there was new evidence of ozone decreases in both hemispheres at middle and high latitudes, a number of new measures were agreed upon, subject of course to the general regime outlined above; delays under Article 5 are still possible for developing states. All parties were required to cease using halons by 1994, and CFCs, HBFCs, carbon tetrachloride and methyl chloroform by 1996. The use of HCFCs should be frozen by 1996, reduced 90% by 2015 and eliminated by 2030. Methyl bromide, still used as a fruit and grain preservative, was subjected to voluntary controls. Contracting parties agreed to "make every effort" to freeze its use by 1995 at 1991 levels. The overall aim was to stabilize atmospheric chlorine loading by the year 2000 and then reduce it to below critical levels by about 2060.

Transboundary movement of hazardous wastes

Following a series of notorious incidents in which shipments of hazardous waste from developed countries were found in uncontrolled and hazardous conditions in developing countries, the transboundary movement of hazardous wastes was made the subject of international regulation by the 1989 Basel Convention on the Control of Transboundary Movement of Hazardous Wastes and their Disposal (see also Kummer 1992). This Convention is premised upon the principle of prior informed consent on a state to state basis before the movement of such waste can take place. The Organization of African Unity has however gone further than this with its 1991 Bamako Convention on the Ban of the Import into Africa and the Control of Transboundary Movement and Management of Hazardous Wastes within Africa, which seeks to ban entirely the import of hazardous waste into Africa.

Environmental impact assessment (EIA) in a transboundary context

The 1991 Espoo Convention on Environmental Impact Assessment in a Transboundary Context sets out a framework for neighbourly relations. It extends the EIA concept, developed to date exclusively in the context of national planning laws and procedures, to the transboundary impacts of development projects and related procedures and decisions.

1992 and Post-Rio Conventions

The Rio UNCED prompted, or coincided with, a large number of new global and regional environment conventions, as well as a major declaration of principles for the future in the Rio Declaration on Environment and Development. In addition to the two conventions concluded at Rio—the Framework Convention on Climate Change and the Convention on Biological Diver-sity—new environmental conventions signed in 1992 included those regulating the use of international watercourses as well as the transboundary effects of industrial accidents. At a regional level 1992 saw the Helsinki Convention on the Protection and Use of the Baltic Sea Area (text and analysis in Ehlers 1993) and the Bucharest Convention on the Protection of the Black Sea against Pollution. Note also the 1993 Ministerial Declaration on the Protection of the Black Sea, which advocates a precautionary and holistic approach, and the Paris Convention for the Protection of the Marine Environment of the North East Atlantic (text and analysis in Hey, IJlstra and Nollkaemper 1993).

The United Nations Framework Convention on Climate Change (UNFCCC)

The UNFCCC, signed at Rio de Janeiro in June 1992 by some 155 states, is loosely modelled on the 1985 Vienna Convention. As its name suggests, it provides a framework within which more detailed obligations will be negotiated by the means of detailed protocols. The basic objective of the Convention is to achieve

stabilization of greenhouse gas concentrations in the atmos-phere at a level that will prevent dangerous anthropogenic interference with the climate system … within a time-frame

sufficient to allow ecosystems to adapt naturally to climate change, to ensure food production is not threatened and to enable economic development to proceed in a sustainable manner. (Article 2)

Two primary duties are imposed on all Parties by Article 4: (a) to develop, periodically update, publish and make available a national inventory of anthropogenic emissions by sources and removals by sinks of all greenhouse gases using comparable (and yet to be agreed upon) methodologies; and (b) to formulate, implement, publish and regularly update national and regional programmes of measures to mitigate climate change by addressing anthropogenic emissions by sources and removals by sinks of all greenhouse gases and measures to facilitate adequate adaptation to climate change. In addition developed country parties agree to a number of general obligations which will be made specific by more detailed protocols. For example, to undertake to promote, and cooperate in, the development of technologies; to control, prevent or reduce anthropogenic emissions of greenhouse gases; to promote sustainable development and the conservation and enhancement of sinks and reservoirs including biomass, forests, oceans and other terrestrial, coastal and marine ecosystems; to cooperate in adaptation to impacts of climate change, by elaboration of plans for integrated coastal zone management, water resources and agriculture and for protection and rehabilitation of areas affected by, inter alia, floods; to promote and cooperate in the exchange of scientific, technological, socioeconomic and legal information relevant to climate, climate change and response strategies; and to promote and cooperate in relevant education, training and public awareness.

The Biological Diversity Convention

The objectives of the Convention on Biological Diversity, also approved at the 1992 UNCED in Rio de Janeiro, are to conserve biological diversity, the sustainable use of its components and the fair and equitable sharing of the benefits arising out of the utilization of genetic resources (Article 1) (for a useful critique, see Boyle 1993). Like the UNFCCC this convention too will be supplemented by protocols, but it establishes general obligations regarding conservation and sustainable use of natural resources, for identification and monitoring of biological diversity, for in situ and ex situ conservation, research and training as well as public education and awareness and EIA of activities likely to affect biodiversity. There are also general provisions relating to access to genetic resources and access to, and transfer of, relevant technology, including biotechnology, as well as international exchange of information and cooperation.

Regulation of the use of international watercourses

The 1992 Helsinki Convention on the Protection and Use of Transboundary Watercourses and International Lakes seeks to establish cooperative frameworks for joint monitoring and assessment, common research and development and information exchange between riparian states. It imposes basic duties on such states to prevent control and reduce transboundary impacts on such shared resources, particularly regarding water pollution, through proper management techniques, including EIA and contingency planning as well as through the adoption of low- or non-waste technology and reduction of pollution from point and diffuse sources.

The transboundary effects of industrial accidents

The Convention on the Transboundary Effects of Industrial Accidents, also signed in Helsinki in March 1992, covers the prevention of, preparedness for and response to industrial accidents capable of having a transboundary effect. The primary obligations are to cooperate and exchange information with other parties. The detailed system of thirteen annexes establishes systems to identify hazardous activities with transboundary implications, for the development of EIA with a transboundary dimension (in accordance with the 1991 Espoo Convention, above) for decisions on siting of potentially hazardous activities. It also provides for emergency preparedness and for access to information for the public as well as the other parties.

Conclusion

As this brief review should have demonstrated, over the last two decades there has been a major change in the attitude of the world community to environmental conservation and management. Part of that change has been a substantial increase in the numbers and the scope of international instruments addressing environmental concerns. The sheer number of instruments has been matched by new principles and institutions. The polluter pays principle, the precautionary principle (Churchill and Freestone 1991; Freestone and Hey 1996) and concern for the rights of future generations (Kiss, in Freestone and Hey 1996) are all reflected in the international conventions reviewed above. The role of the UN Environment Programme and the treaty secretariats established to service and monitor the burgeoning number of treaty regimes lead commentators to suggest that international environmental law, like, for example, the international law of human rights, has emerged as a new discrete branch of international law (Freestone 1994). UNCED played an important role in this, it has established a major agenda—much of which remains unfinished. Detailed protocols are still needed to add substance to the framework of the Climate Change Convention and, arguably, also to the Convention on Biological Diversity. Concern with the environmental impact of fishing in high seas areas led to the conclusion of the UN Agreement on Straddling Fish Stocks and Highly Migratory Fish Stocks was in 1995. Also held in 1995 was another UN Conference on Land Based Sources of Marine Pollution—now agreed to be the cause of more than 70% of all pollution of the oceans. The environmental dimensions of world trade as well as deforestation and desertification are also issues to be addressed for the future at a global level while progress continues to enhance our awareness of impacts of human activities on world eco-systems. The challenge for this emerging international environmental law is not simply to respond with an increase in the numbers of environmental instruments, but also to enhance their impact and effectiveness.

● ENVIRONMENTAL IMPACT ASSESSMENTS

Ron Bisset

The term used as the title of this article, environmental impact assessments, has now been increasingly, but not universally, replaced with the term environmental assessments. A quick review of the reason for this change of name will help us define the essential nature of the activity described by these names, and one of the important factors behind opposition or reluctance to using the word impact.

In 1970, the National Environmental Policy Act (NEPA) became law in the United States, establishing environmental policy goals for the federal government, focusing on the need to take environmental factors into account in decision-making. It is, of course, easy to state a policy objective, but it is more difficult to achieve it. To ensure that the Act had "teeth", legislators incorporated a provision requiring that the Federal government prepare an "Environmental Impact Statement" (EIS) for any

proposed action "likely to significantly affect the quality of the human environment". The content of this document was to be considered before a decision was made on whether the proposed action should be initiated. The work done to prepare the EIS became known as environmental impact assessment (EIA), because it involved the identification, prediction and evaluation of the impacts of the proposed federal action.

The word "impact", in English, unfortunately is not a positive term. An impact is thought to be harmful (almost by definition). Therefore, as the practice of EIA spread beyond the United States to Canada, Europe, Southeast Asia and Australasia, many governments and their advisers wanted to move away from the negative aspects of impact, and so the term environmental assessment (EA) was born. EIA and EA are identical (except in the United States and those few countries which have adopted the US system, where EIA and EA have precise and different meanings). In this article only EIA will be referred to, although it should be remembered that all comments apply equally to EA, and both terms are in use internationally.

In addition to the use of the word impact, the context in which EIA was applied (particularly in the United States and Canada) was also influential on the perceptions of EIA which were (and in some cases still are) common amongst politicians, senior governmental officials and private and public-sector "developers". In both the United States and Canada, land-use planning was weak and preparation of EISs or EIA reports were often "hijacked" by interested parties and almost became plan-making activities. This encouraged the production of large, multi-volume documents which were time-consuming and expensive to produce and, of course, virtually impossible to read and act upon! Sometimes projects were delayed while all this activity was in progress, causing irritation and financial costs to proponents and investors.

Also, in the first five to six years of its operation, NEPA gave rise to many court cases in which project opponents were able to challenge the adequacy of EISs on technical and sometimes procedural grounds. Again, this caused many delays to projects. However, as experience was gained and guidance was issued that was more clear and strict, the number of cases going to court declined significantly.

Unfortunately, the combined effect of these experiences was to give the distinct impression to many external observers that EIA was a well-intentioned activity which, unfortunately, had gone wrong and ended by being more of an obstacle than a help to development. To many people, it seemed an appropriate, if not entirely necessary, activity for self-indulgent developed countries, but for industrializing nations it was an expensive luxury they could not really afford.

Despite the adverse reaction in some places, globally the spread of EIA has proved irresistible. Starting in 1970 in the United States, EIA extended to Canada, Australia and to Europe. A number of developing countries—for example, the Philippines, Indonesia and Thailand—introduced EIA procedures before many Western European countries. Interestingly, the various development banks, such as the World Bank, were amongst the slowest organizations to introduce EIA into their decision-making systems. Indeed, it was only by the late 1980s and early 1990s that the banks and the bilateral aid agencies could be said to have caught up with the rest of the world. There is no sign that the rate at which EIA laws and regulations are being introduced into national decision-making systems is becoming slower. In fact, following the "Earth Summit" held in Rio de Janeiro in 1992, EIA has been used increasingly as international agencies and national governments attempt to meet the recommendations made in Rio regarding the need for sustainable development.

What is EIA?

How can we explain the ever-increasing popularity of EIA? What can it do for governments, private and public sector developers, workers, their families and the communities in which they live?

Before EIA, development projects such as highways, hydro-power dams, ports and industrial installations were assessed on technical, economic and, of course, political bases. Such projects have certain economic and social objectives to achieve, and decision-makers involved in issuing permits, licences or other types of authorization were interested in knowing whether the projects would achieve them (putting to one side those projects conceived and built for political purposes such as prestige). This required an economic study (usually cost-benefit analysis) and technical investigations. Unfortunately, these studies did not take account of environmental effects and, as time passed, more and more people became aware of the increasing damage caused to the environment by such development projects. In many cases, the unintended environmental and social impacts led to economic costs; for example, the Kariba Dam in Africa (on the border between Zambia and Zimbabwe) resulted in the resettlement of many villages into areas which were not suitable for the traditional agriculture practised by the people. In the resettled areas food became scarce and the government had to initiate emergency food supply operations. Other examples of unexpected "add-on" costs as well as environmental damage led to a growing realization that the traditional project appraisal techniques needed an additional dimension to reduce the chances of unexpected and unwelcome impacts.

The increasing awareness amongst governments, non-governmental organizations (NGOs) and members of the public of the unexpected economic penalties that could arise from major development projects coincided with a parallel growth in global understanding of the importance of the environment. In particular, concern focused on the implications of increasing population growth and the accompanying expansion in economic activities, and whether there might be environmental constraints to such growth. The importance of global biogeochemical and other processes for the maintenance of clean air and water as well as renewable resources such as food and timber were recognized increasingly. As a result, many were convinced that the environment could no longer be seen as a passive and never-ending deliverer of goods and a receiver of human wastes. It had to be seen as an active part of the development process which, if treated badly, could reduce the chances of achieving development objectives. This realization has led to the development and implementation of a number of procedures or practices to incorporate the environment into the development process by considering the extent to which it might be harmed or improved. One such procedure is EIA. The overall aim is to reduce the risk—for homo sapiens in general, and local groups in particular—that environmental damage will result in life-threatening consequences such as famines and floods.

Basically, EIA is a means of identifying, predicting and evaluating the environmental impacts of a proposed development action, and its alternatives, before a decision is made to implement it. The aim is to integrate EIA into the standard, pre-feasibility, feasibility, appraisal and design activities which are carried out to test whether a proposal will meet its objectives. By undertaking EIA work in parallel with these studies it should be possible to identify, early, the significant adverse impacts (and those which are beneficial) and to "design out", as far as possible, the harmful impacts. Additionally, benefits can be enhanced. The outcome of any EIA should be a proposal which, in its location, design and method of construction or operation, is "environmentally friendly" in so far as its environmental implications are acceptable and any environmental deterioration is unlikely to cause difficulties. EIA is, therefore, a preventive tool, and medicine provides an appropriate analogy. In the field of community medicine it is better, and economically cheaper, to prevent illness rather than cure it. In the development process it is better to minimize environmental damage (while still achieving economic objectives) than to fund expensive clean-up or rehabilitation actions after damage has occurred.

Application of EIA

To what types of development activities does EIA apply? There is no standard or correct answer. Each country decides on the type and scale of activities to be subject to EIA; for example, a proposed 10 km road in a small tropical island may cause significant impacts, but a similar road in a large, semi-arid country with a low population density probably would be environmentally neutral. In all countries, EIA is applied to "physical" development projects according to national criteria; in some countries EIA is applied also to development plans, programmes and policies (such as sector development programmes for energy supply and national development plans) which might cause significant environmental impacts. Amongst the countries which apply EIA to these kinds of actions are the United States, the Netherlands and China. However, such countries are the exception to normal practice. Most EIAs are prepared for physical development projects, although there is no doubt that "strategic" EIAs will increase in importance in the future.

What kinds of impacts are analysed in EIAs? Again this varies from country to country, but to a lesser extent than in the case of the types of proposed activities subject to EIA. The usual answer given is "environmental" impacts, to which the inevitable response is likely to be, "Yes, but what is 'environmental'?" Generally, most EIAs focus on the biophysical environment—that is, impacts on such factors as:

- water quality and quantity
- air quality
- ecosystems and ecological processes
- noise levels.

In some cases no other impacts are considered. However, the limitations of restricting EIA to biophysical impacts have been questioned and, increasingly, more and more EIAs are based on a broad concept of the environment and include, when appropriate, impacts on:

- local communities ("social" impacts)
- local economies
- health and safety
- landscapes
- cultural resources (archaeological or historical sites, environmental features with spiritual significance for local communities, etc.).

There are two reasons which help explain this wider definition of "environmental" impacts. First, it has been found to be socially and politically unacceptable to consider the impacts of a proposal on the biophysical environment and, at the same time, ignore the social, health and economic effects on local communities and inhabitants. This issue has been dominant in developed countries, especially those which have weak land-use planning systems into which social and economic objectives are incorporated.

In developing countries, this factor also exists and is joined by an additional, complementary explanation. The majority of the population in developing countries has a closer and, in many ways, more complex set of direct relationships with their environment than is the case in developed countries. This means that the way that local communities and their members interact with their environment can be changed by environmental, social and economic impacts. For example, in poor localities a major, new project such as a 2,400 MW power station will introduce a source of new labour opportunities and social infrastructure (schools, clinics) to provide for the large workforce needed. Basically, the income injected into the local economy makes the power station locality an island of prosperity in a sea of poverty. This attracts poor people to the area to try to improve their standard of living by trying to obtain a job and to use the new facilities. Not all will be successful. The unsuccessful will try to offer services to those employed, for example, by supplying firewood or charcoal. This will cause environmental stress, often at locations distant from the power station. Such impacts will occur in addition to the impacts caused by the influx of workers and their families who are directly employed at the station site. Thus, the main induced social effect of a project—in-migration—causes environmental impacts. If these socioeconomic implications were not analysed, then EISs would be in danger of failing to achieve one of their main objectives—that is, to identify, predict, evaluate and mitigate biophysical environmental impacts.

Virtually all project-related EIAs focus on the external environment, that is, the environment outside the site boundary. This reflects the history of EIA. As noted above it had its origins in the developed world. In these countries there is a strong legal framework for occupational health protection and it was inappropriate for EIA to focus on the internal, working environment as well as the external environment, as this would be a duplication of effort and misuse of scarce resources.

In many developing countries the opposite situation is often the reality. In such a context, it would seem appropriate for EIAs, particularly for industrial facilities, to consider the impacts on the internal environment. The main focus of considering such impacts as changes in internal air quality and noise levels is the health of workers. There are two other aspects which are important here. First, in poor countries the loss of a breadwinner through illness, injury or death can force the other members of a family to exploit natural resources to maintain income levels. If a number of families are affected then the cumulative impacts may be locally significant. Secondly, the health of family members can be affected, directly, by chemicals brought into the home on the clothes of workers. So there is a direct link between the internal and external environments. The inclusion of the internal environment in EIA has received little attention in the EIA literature and is conspicuous by its absence from EIA laws, regulations and guidelines. However, there is no logical or practical reason why, if local circumstances are appropriate, EIAs should not deal with the important issues of workers' health and the possible external implications of a deterioration in the physical and mental well-being of workers.

Costs and Benefits of EIAs

Perhaps the most frequent issue raised by those who are either opposed to EIA or are neutral towards it concerns the cost. Preparation of EISs takes time and resources, and, in the end, this means money. It is important, therefore, to consider the economic aspects of EIA.

The main costs of introducing EIA procedures into a country fall on project investors or proponents, and central or local government (depending on the nature of the procedures). In virtually all countries, project investors or proponents pay for preparation of EIAs for their projects. Similarly, initiators (usually government agencies) of sectoral investment strategies and regional development plans pay for their EIAs. Evidence from developed and developing countries indicates that the cost of preparing EISs ranges from 0.1% to 1% of the capital cost of a project. This proportion can increase when mitigating measures recommended in the EISs are taken into account. The cost depends on the type of mitigation recommended. Obviously,

resettling 5,000 families in such a way that their standard of living is maintained is a relatively costly exercise. In such cases the costs of the EIS and mitigation measures can rise to 15 to 20% of capital cost. In other cases it may be between 1 and 5%. Such figures may seem to be excessive and to indicate that EIA is a financial burden. There is no doubt that EIA costs money, but in the experience of the author no major projects have been halted because of the costs of EIA preparation, and in only a few cases have projects been made uneconomical because of the costs of necessary mitigating measures.

EIA procedures also impose costs to central or local governments which arise from the staff and other resources which need to be directed to managing the system and processing and reviewing the EISs. Again, the cost depends on the nature of the procedure and how many EISs are produced per year. The author is not aware of any calculations which attempt to provide an average figure for this cost.

To return to our medical analogy, prevention of illness requires a significant up-front investment to ensure future and possibly long-term dispersed benefits in terms of the health of the population, and EIA is no different. The financial benefits can be examined from the perspectives of the proponent as well as those of the government and the wider society. The proponent can benefit in a number of ways:

- prevention of delays in obtaining authorizations
- identification of mitigation measures involving recycling and recovery of components of waste streams
- creation of cleaner working environments
- identification of cheaper alternatives.

Not all of these will operate in all cases, but it is useful to consider the ways in which savings can accrue to the proponent.

In all countries various permits, permissions and authorizations are needed before a project can be implemented and operated. The authorization procedures take time, and this can be extended if there is opposition to a project and no formal mechanism exists by which concerns may be identified, considered and investigated. There seems little doubt that the days of passive populations welcoming all development as signs of inevitable economic and social progress are nearly over. All projects are subject to increasing local, national and international scrutiny—for example, the continuing opposition in India to the Sardar Sarovar (Narmada) complex of dams.

In this context, EIA provides a mechanism for public concerns to be addressed, if not eliminated. Studies in developed countries (such as the UK) have shown the potential for EIA to reduce the likelihood of delays in obtaining authorizations—and time is money! Indeed, a study by British Gas in the late 1970s showed that the average time taken to obtain authorization was shorter with EIA than for similar projects without EIA.

The add-on costs of mitigation have been mentioned, but it is worth considering the opposite situation. For facilities which produce one or more waste streams, the EIA may identify mitigation measures which reduce the waste load by use of recovery or recycling processes. In the former case recovery of a component from a waste stream might enable the proponent to sell it (if a market is available) and cover the costs of the recovery process or even make a profit. Recycling of an element such as water can reduce consumption, thus lowering expenditure on raw material inputs.

If an EIA has focused on the internal environment, then the working conditions should be better than would have been the case without the EIA. A cleaner, safer workplace reduces worker discontent, illness and absences. The overall effect is likely to be a more productive workforce, which again is a financial benefit to the proponent or operator.

Finally, the favoured option selected using solely technical and economic criteria may, in fact, not be the best alternative. In Botswana, a site had been selected for water to be stored before it was transported to Gaborone (the capital). An EIA was implemented and it was found, early in the EIA work, that the environmental impacts would be significantly adverse. During survey work, the EIA team identified an alternative site which they were given permission to include in the EIA. The alternative site comparison showed that the environmental impacts of the second option were much less severe. Technical and economic studies showed that the site met technical and economic criteria. In fact it was found that the second site could meet the original development objectives with less environmental damage and cost 50% less to build (IUCN and Government of the Republic of Botswana, undated). Unsurprisingly, the second option has been implemented, to the benefit not only to the proponent (a parastatal organization) but to the entire tax-paying population of Botswana. Such examples are likely to be uncommon, but do indicate the opportunity provided by EIA work to "test" various development options.

The main benefits of EIA procedures are dispersed amongst the component parts of society, such as government, communities and individuals. By preventing unacceptable environmental deterioration EIA helps to maintain the essential "life processes" upon which all human life and activities depend. This is a long-term and dispersed benefit. In specific instances, EIA can avoid localized environmental damage which would necessitate remedial measures (usually expensive) at a later date. The cost of remedial measures usually falls on local or central government and not the proponent or operator of the installation which caused the damage.

Recent events, especially since the Rio "Earth Summit", are slowly changing the objectives of development activities. Until recently the objectives of development were to improve economic and social conditions in a specified area. Increasingly, the achievement of "sustainability" criteria or objectives is occupying a central place in the traditional hierarchy of objectives (which still remain relevant). The introduction of sustainability as an important, if not yet primary, objective in the development process will have a profound influence on the future existence of the sterile debate of "jobs versus environment" from which EIA has suffered. This debate had some meaning when environment was on the outside of the development process and looking in. Now the environment is becoming central and the debate is centred on mechanisms of having both jobs and a healthy environment linked in a sustainable manner. EIA still has a crucial and expanding contribution to make as one of the important mechanisms for moving towards, and achieving, sustainability.

● LIFE-CYCLE ASSESSMENT (CRADLE-TO-GRAVE)

Sven-Olof Ryding

The need to safeguard the environment for future generations makes it necessary not only to discuss the emerging environmental problems, but to make progress in identifying strategies that are cost-effective and environmentally sound to solve them and to take actions to enforce the measures that result from such discussion. There is ample evidence that enhancing the state of the environment as well as establishing policies to sustain the environment must take on greater priority within this generation and those that follow. While this belief is commonly held by governments, environmental groups, industry, academics and the

general public, there is considerable debate on how to achieve improved environmental conditions without sacrificing current economic benefits. Furthermore, environmental protection has become an issue of great political importance, and ensuring ecological stability has been pushed to the top of many political agendas.

Past and present efforts to protect the environment are to a large extent characterized as single-issue approaches. Each problem has been dealt with on a case-by-case basis. With regard to problems caused by point-source pollution from easily identified emissions, this was an effective way of reducing environmental impacts. Today, the situation is more complex. Much pollution now originates from a large number of non-point sources easily transported from one country to another. Furthermore, each of us contributes to this total environmental pollution load through our daily patterns of living. The different non-point sources are difficult to identify, and the way in which they interact in impacting the environment is not well known.

The increasing environmental problems of more complex and global character will most likely entail great implications for several sectors of society in enforcing remedial actions. To be able to play a role in environmental protection, sound and universal policies must be applied jointly as an additional, multi-issue approach by all those actors taking part in the process—the scientists, trade unions, non-governmental organizations, companies and agencies of authority at the national and governmental levels, as well as the media. Therefore, it is important that all areas of sectoral interest be coordinated in their environmental ambitions, in order to get necessary interactions and responses to proposed solutions. It is likely that there may be a unanimous view with regard to the ultimate objectives of better environmental quality. However, it is equally likely that there may be disagreement about the pace, means and time required to achieve them.

Environmental protection has become a strategic issue of increasing importance for industry and the business sector, both in the siting of plants and in the technical performance of processes and products. Industrialists are increasingly becoming interested in being able to look holistically at the environmental consequences of their operations. Legislation is no longer the sole dimensioning factor following the growing importance of product-related environmental issues. The concepts of environmentally sound product development and environmentally friendly or "green" products are assuming wider acceptance among producers and consumers.

Indeed, this is a great challenge for industry; yet environmental criteria are often not considered at the beginning of the design of a product, when it may be easiest to avoid adverse impacts. Until recently, most environmental impacts were reduced through end-of-pipe controls and process design rather than product design. As a result, many companies spend too much time fixing problems instead of preventing them. A great deal of work, however, is needed to develop a suitable and accepted approach to incorporate environmental impacts into the various production stages and industrial activities—from raw material acquisition and manufacture to product use and final disposal.

The only known concept to deal with all these new complex issues seems to be a life-cycle approach to the problem. Life-cycle assessments (LCAs) have been widely recognized as an environmental management tool for the future, as product-related issues assume a more central role in the public debate. Although LCAs promise to be a valuable tool for programmes on cleaner production strategies and design for the environment, the concept is relatively new and will require future refinement to be accepted as a general tool for environmentally sound process and product development.

Figure 54.1 • Outline of consecutive steps for setting priorities in decisions on environmental protection measures in industry.

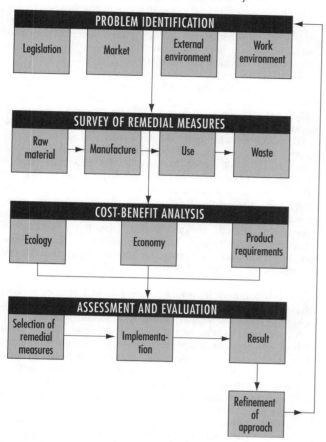

The assessment and evaluation phase should be regarded as an integral part of the procedure of setting priorities to give the necessary input for the final judgement of the efficiency of the suggested remedial measures. The continuous exercise of assessment and evaluation following any measure that is implemented or enforced will give additional feedback for optimization of a general decision model for environmental priority strategies for product decision. The strategic value of such a model will likely increase in industry when it becomes gradually apparent that environmental priorities might be an equally important part of the future planning procedure for new processes or products. As LCA is a tool for identifying the environmental releases and evaluating the associated impacts caused by a process, product or activity, it will likely serve as the major vehicle for industry in their search for practical and user-friendly decision-making models for environmentally sound product development.

technical solutions should be described, if possible, giving their expected value both in reducing resource use and pollution loads as well as in monetary terms. The cost/benefit analysis aims at producing a priority list by comparing the different identified approaches of remedial measures from the perspectives of product specifications and requirements to be met, economic feasibility and ecological efficiency. However, experience has shown that great difficulties often arise when seeking to express environmental assets in monetary terms.

Concept of Life-Cycle Assessment

The concept of LCA is to evaluate the environmental effects associated with any given activity from the initial gathering of raw material from the earth until the point at which all residuals are returned to the earth. Therefore, the concept is often referred to as a "cradle-to-grave" assessment. While the practice of conducting life-cycle studies has existed since the early 1970s, there have been few comprehensive attempts to describe the full procedure in a manner that would facilitate understanding of the overall process, the underlying data requirements, the inherent assumptions and possibilities to make practical use of the methodology. However, since 1992 a number of reports have been published focusing on describing the various parts of a LCA from a theoretical viewpoint (Heijungs 1992; Vigon et al. 1992; Keoleian and Menerey 1993; Canadian Standards Association 1993; Society of Environmental Toxicology and Chemistry 1993). A few practical guides and handbooks have been published taking on the specific perspectives of product designers in making practical use of a complete LCA in environmentally sound product development (Ryding 1996).

LCA has been defined as an objective process to evaluate the environmental burdens associated with a process, product, activity or service system by identifying and quantifying energy and materials used and released to the environment in order to assess the impact of those energy and material uses and releases to the environment, and to evaluate and implement opportunities to effect environmental improvements. The assessment includes the entire life cycle of the process, product, activity or service system, encompassing extracting and processing raw materials, manu-facturing, transportation and distribution, use, reuse, maint-enance, recycling and final disposal.

The prime objectives of carrying out LCA are to provide as complete a picture as possible of the interactions of an activity with the environment, to contribute to the understanding of the overall and interdependent nature of environmental consequences of human activities and to provide decision-makers with information which identifies opportunities for environmental improvements.

The Business Framework for Life-Cycle Assessment

The necessary new approach to environmental protection in the business sector, to look at products and services in their totality, must be linked to development of a common, systematic and structured approach which enables relevant decisions to be made and priorities to be set. Such an approach must be flexible and expandable to cover various decision-making situations in industry as well as new input as science and technology progress. However, it should rest upon some basic principles and issues, for example: problem identification, survey of remedial measures, cost/benefit analysis and final assessment and evaluation (figure 54.1).

The problem identification ought to highlight different types of environmental problems and their causes. These judgements are multidimensional, taking into account various background conditions. There is indeed a close relationship between the work environment and the external environment. The ambition to safeguard the environment should therefore include two dimensions: to minimize the burden on the external environment following all kinds of human activities, and to promote the welfare of employees in terms of a well-planned and safe work environment.

A survey of potential remedial measures should include all the available practical alternatives for minimizing both pollutant emissions and the use of non-renewable natural resources. The

54. ENVIRONMENTAL POLICY

Figure 54.2 • Purposes and completeness of life-cycle assessment.

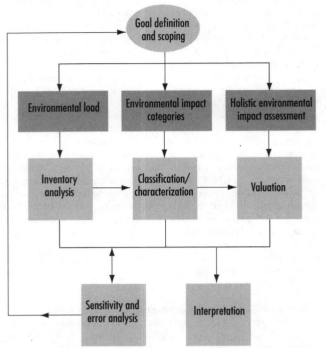

An illustration of the relationship between various purposes of life-cycle assessment studies and the resultant completeness of carrying out the various life-cycle assessment components.

The LCA methodological framework is a stepwise calculation exercise comprising four components: goal definition and scoping, inventory analysis, impact assessment and interpretation. As one component of a broader methodology, none of these components alone can be described as an LCA. LCA ought to include all four. In many cases life-cycle studies focus on the inventory analysis and are usually referred to as LCI (life-cycle inventory).

Goal definition and scoping consists of a definition of the purpose and the system of the study—its scope, definition of the functional unit (the measure of performance which the system delivers), and the establishment of a procedure for quality assurance of the results.

When initiating an LCA study, it is of vital importance to clearly define the goal of the study, preferably in terms of a clear and unambiguous statement of the reason for carrying out the LCA, and the intended use of the results. A key consideration is to decide whether the results should be used for in-company applications to improve the environmental performance of an industrial process or a product, or whether the results should be used externally, for example, to influence public policy or consumer purchase choices.

Without setting a clear goal and purpose for the LCA study in advance, the inventory analysis and the impact assessment may be overdone, and the final results may not be properly used for practical decisions. Defining whether the results should focus on environmental loads, a specific environmental problem or a holistic environmental impact assessment will directly clarify whether to conduct an inventory analysis, classification/characterization or a valuation (figure 54.2). It is important to make all consecutive LCA components "visible" in order to make it easier for any user to choose the level of complexity they wish to use.

In many general programmes for cleaner production strategies, design for the environment or environmentally sound product development, the principal objective is often to lower the overall environmental impact during a product's life cycle. To meet these demands it is sometimes necessary to arrive at a highly aggregated form of the environmental impact assessment which in turn emphasizes the need for identifying a general accepted valuation approach for a scoring system to weigh the different environmental effects against each other.

The scope of an LCA defines the system, boundaries, data requirements, assumptions and limitations. The scope should be defined well enough to ensure that the breadth and depth of analysis are compatible with and sufficient to address the stated purpose and all boundaries, and that assumptions are clearly stated, comprehensible and visible. However, as an LCA is an iterative process, it may be advisable in some cases not to permanently fix all aspects included in the scope. The use of sensitivity and error analysis is recommended to make possible the successive testing and validation of the purpose and scope of the LCA study versus the results obtained, in order to make corrections and set new assumptions.

Inventory analysis is an objective, data-based process of quantifying energy and raw material requirements, air emissions, waterborne effluents, solid waste and other environmental releases throughout the life cycle of a process, product, activity or service system (figure 54.3).

The calculation of inputs and outputs in the inventory analysis refers to the system defined. In many cases, processing operations yield more than one output, and it is important to break down such a complex system into a series of separate sub-processes, each of which produces a single product. During the production of a construction material, pollutant emissions occur in each sub-process, from raw material acquisition to the final product. The total production process may be illustrated by a "process tree" where the stem may be seen as the main chain of flow of materials and energy, whereas the branches may illustrate sub-processes and the leaves the specific figures on pollutant emissions and so on. When added together, these sub-processes have the total characteristics of the original single system of co-products.

To estimate the accuracy of the data gained in the inventory analysis, a sensitivity and error analysis is recommended. All data used should therefore be "labelled" with relevant information not only as to reliability but also source, origin and so on, to facilitate future updating and refinement of the data (so-called meta-data). The use of a sensitivity and error analysis will identify the key data of great importance for the outcome of the LCA study that may need further efforts to increase its reliability.

Impact assessment is a technical, qualitative and/or quantitative process to characterize and assess the effects of the environmental loading identified in the inventory component. The assessment should address both ecological and human health considerations, as well as other effects such as habitat modifications and noise pollution. The impact assessment component could be characterized as three consecutive steps—classification, characterization and valuation—all of which interpret the effects of environmental burdens identified in the inventory analysis, on different aggregated levels (figure 54.4). Classification is the step in which the inventory analyses are grouped together into a number of impact categories; characterization is the step in which analysis and quantification takes place, and, where possible, aggregation of the impacts within the given impact categories is carried out; valuation is the step in which the data of the different specific impact categories are weighted so that they can be compared amongst themselves to arrive at a further interpretation and aggregation of the data of the impact assessment.

Figure 54.3 • Stepwise elements in a life-cycle inventory analysis.

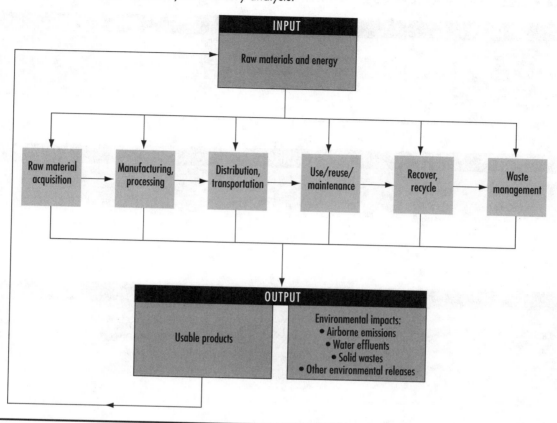

In the classification step, the impacts may be grouped in the general protection areas of resource depletion, ecological health and human health. These areas may be further divided into specific impact categories, preferably focusing on the environ-mental process involved, to allow a perspective consistent with current scientific knowledge about these processes.

There are various approaches to characterization—to relate data to no-observable-effect concentrations or to environmental standards, to model both exposure and effects and apply these models in a site-specific way, or to use equivalency factors for the different impact categories. A further approach is to normalize the aggregated data for each impact category to the actual magnitude of the impacts in some given area, to increase the comparability of the data from the different impact categories.

Valuation, with the aim of further aggregating the data of the impact assessment, is the LCA component that has probably generated the most heated debates. Some approaches, often referred to as decision theory techniques, are claimed to have the potential to make the valuation a rational, explicit method. Valuation principles may rest on scientific, political or societal judgements, and there are currently approaches available that cover all three perspectives. Of special importance is the use of sensitivity and error analysis. The sensitivity analysis enables the identification of those selected valuation criteria that may change the resultant priority between two process or product alternatives because of the uncertainties in the data. The error analysis may be used to indicate the likelihood of one alternative product being more environmentally benign than a competitor product.

Many are of the opinion that valuations have to be based largely on information about social values and preferences.

However, no one has yet defined the specific requirements that a reliable and generally accepted valuation method should meet. Figure 54.5 lists some such specific requirements of potential value. However, it should be clearly emphasized that any valuation system for assessing the "seriousness" of environmental impacts of any human activity must be largely based on subjective value judgements. For such valuations it is probably not possible to establish criteria which are tenable in all situations worldwide.

Interpretation of the results is a systematic evaluation of the needs and opportunities to reduce the environmental burden associated with energy and raw materials use and waste emissions throughout the whole life cycle of a product, process or activity. This assessment may include both quantitative and qualitative measures of improvements, such as changes in product design, raw material use, industrial processing, consumer demands and waste management.

Interpretation of the results is the component of an LCA in which options for reducing the environmental impacts or burdens of the processes or products under study are identified and evaluated. It deals with the identification, evaluation and selection of options for improvements in processes and product design, that is, technical redesign of a process or product to minimize the associated environmental burden while fulfilling the intended function and performance characteristics. It is important to guide the decision-maker regarding the effects of the existing uncertainties in the background data and the criteria used in achieving the results, to decrease the risk of making false conclusions regarding the processes and products under study. Again, a sensitivity and error analysis is needed to gain credibility for the LCA methodology as it provides the decision-maker with

Figure 54.4 • Conceptual framework for the successive level of data aggregation in the impact assessment component.

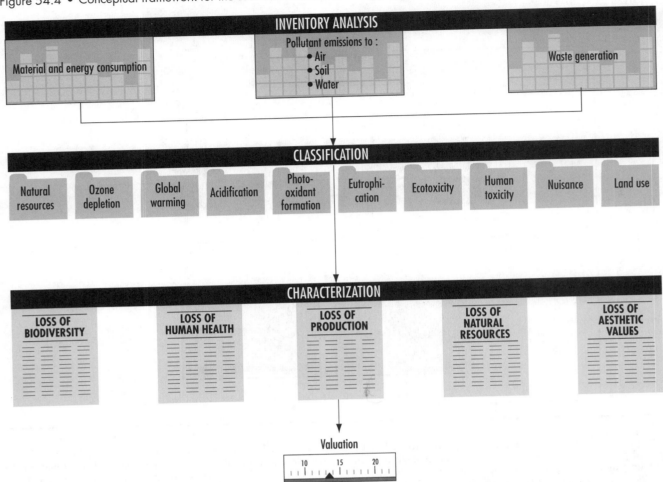

information on (1) key parameters and assumptions, which may need to be further considered and refined to strengthen the conclusions, and (2) the statistical significance of the calculated difference in total environmental burden between the process or product alternatives.

The interpretation component has been identified as the part of an LCA that is least documented. However, preliminary results from some large LCA studies carried out as comprehensive efforts by people from academia, consultancy firms and many companies all indicated that, from a general perspective, significant environmental burdens from products seem to be linked to the product use (figure 54.6). Hence, the potential seems to exist for industry-motivated initiatives to minimize environmental impacts through product development.

A study on international experiences of environmentally sound product development based on LCA (Ryding 1994) indicated that promising general applications of LCA seem to be (1) for internal use by corporations to form the basis for providing guidance in long-term strategic planning concerning product design, but also (2) to some extent for use by regulatory agencies and authorities to suit general purposes of societal planning and decision-making. By developing and using LCA information regarding environmental effects that are both "upstream" and "downstream" of the particular activity under scrutiny, a new paradigm may be created

for basing decisions in both corporate management and regulatory policy-making.

Conclusion

Knowledge about human threats to the environment seems to grow faster than our ability to solve them. Therefore, decisions in the environmental arena must often be taken with greater uncertainties present than those in other areas. Furthermore, very small safety margins usually exist. Present ecological and technical knowledge is not always sufficient to offer a complete, fool-proof strategy to safeguard the environment. It is not possible to gain full understanding of all ecological responses to environmental stress before taking action. However, the absence of complete, irrefutable scientific evidence should not discourage making decisions about and implementation of pollution abatement programmes. It is not possible to wait until all ecological questions are scientifically substantiated before taking action—the damage that may result through such delays could be irreversible. Hence, the meaning and scope of most problems is already known to a sufficient extent to justify action, and there is, in many cases, sufficient knowledge at hand to initiate effective remedial measures for most environmental problems.

Life-cycle assessment offers a new concept to deal with the future complex environmental issues. However, there are no

Figure 54.5 • List of suggested requirements to be met for a LCA valuation method.

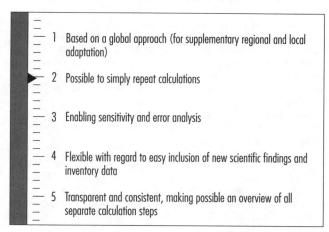

1 Based on a global approach (for supplementary regional and local adaptation)

2 Possible to simply repeat calculations

3 Enabling sensitivity and error analysis

4 Flexible with regard to easy inclusion of new scientific findings and inventory data

5 Transparent and consistent, making possible an overview of all separate calculation steps

shortcuts or simple answers to all questions posed. The rapidly emerging adoption of a holistic approach to combat environmental problems will most likely identify a lot of gaps in our knowledge about new aspects that need to be dealt with. Also, available data that may be used are in many cases intended for other purposes. Despite all difficulties, there is no argument for waiting to use LCA until it gets better. It is by no means hard to find difficulties and uncertainties in the present LCA concept, if one wants to use such arguments to justify an unwillingness to conduct an LCA. One has to decide whether it is worthwhile to seek a holistic life-cycle approach to environmental aspects despite

Figure 54.6 • Outline of some general experiences of where in the life-cycles of products the major environmental burdens occur.

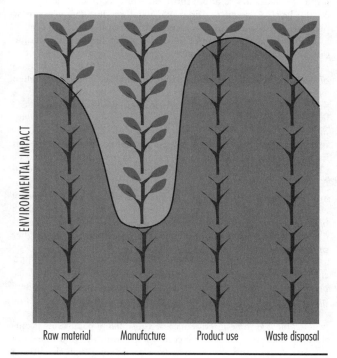

ENVIRONMENTAL IMPACT

Raw material   Manufacture   Product use   Waste disposal

all difficulties. The more LCA is used, the more knowledge will be gained about its structure, function and applicability, which will be the best guarantee for a feedback to ensure its successive improvement.

To make use of LCA today may be more a question of will and ambition than of undisputed knowledge. The whole idea of LCA ought to be to make the best use of present scientific and technical knowledge and to make use of the result in an intelligent and humble way. Such an approach will most likely gain credibility.

RISK ASSESSMENT AND COMMUNICATION

Adrian V. Gheorghe and Hansjörg Seiler

Government, industry and the community recognize the need to identify, assess and control the industrial risks (occupational and public) to people and the environment. Awareness of hazards and of the accidents that may result in significant loss of life and property have led to the development and application of systematic approaches, methods and tools for risk assessment and communication.

The risk assessment process involves: system description, the identification of hazards and the development of accident scenarios and outcomes for events associated with a process operation or a storage facility; the estimation of the effects or consequences of such hazardous events on people, property and the environment; the estimation of the probability or likelihood of such hazardous events occurring in practice and of their effects, accounting for the different operational and organizational hazard controls and practices; the quantification of ensuing risk levels outside the plant boundaries, in terms of both consequences and probabilities; and the assessment of such risk levels by reference to quantified risk criteria.

The process of quantified risk assessment is probabilistic in nature. Because major accidents may or may not occur over the entire life of a plant or a process, it is not appropriate to base the assessment process on the consequences of accidents in isolation. The likelihood or probability of such accidents actually occurring should be taken into account. Such probabilities and resultant risk levels should reflect the level of design, operational and organizational controls available at the plant. There are a number of uncertainties associated with the quantification of risk (e.g., mathematical models for consequence estimation, setting of probabilities for different accident scenarios, probability effects of such accidents). The risk assessment process should, in all cases, expose and recognize such uncertainties.

The main value of the quantified risk assessment process should not rest with the numerical value of the results (in isolation). The assessment process itself provides significant opportunities for the systematic identification of hazards and evaluation of risk. The risk assessment process provides for the identification and recognition of hazards and enables the allocation of relevant and appropriate resources to the hazards control process.

The objectives and uses of the hazard identification process (HIP) will determine in turn the scope of the analysis, the appropriate procedures and methods, and the personnel, expertise, funding and time required for the analysis, as well as the associated documentation necessary. Hazard identification is an efficient and necessary procedure to assist risk analysts and decision making for risk assessment and management of occupational safety and health. A number of major objectives may be identified:

54. ENVIRONMENTAL POLICY

- to establish what dangerous situations exist within a plant or a process operation
- to establish how these dangerous situations may come about
- to assist in the assessment of the safety of a hazardous installation.

The first general objective aims at extending the general understanding of the important issues and situations that might affect the risk analysis process for individual plants and processes; the synergy of individual hazards to the area study level has its special significance. Design and operational problems can be identified and a hazard classification scheme can be considered.

The second objective contains elements of risk assessment and deals with accident scenario development and interpretation of results. Consequence evaluation of various accidents and their impact propagation in time and space has special significance in the hazard identification phase.

The third objective aims at providing information that can later assist further steps in risk assessment and plant operations safety management. This may be in the form of improving the scenario specifications for risk analysis or identifying appropriate safety measures to comply with given risk criteria (e.g., individual or societal), or advice for emergency preparedness and accident management.

After defining objectives, the definition of the scope of the HIP study is the second most relevant element in the management, organization and implementation of the HIP. The scope of the HIP in a complex risk assessment study can be described mainly in terms of the following parameters: (1) potential sources of hazards (e.g., radioactive releases, toxic substances, fire, explosions); (2) plant or process damage states; (3) initiating events; (4) potential consequences; and (5) prioritization of hazards. The relevant factors that determine the extent to which these parameters are included in the HIP are: (a) the objectives and intended uses of the HIP; (b) the availability of appropriate information and data; and (c) the available resources and expertise. Hazard identification requires the consideration of all relevant information regarding the facility (e.g., plant, process). This might typically include: site and plant layout; detailed process information in the form of engineering diagrams and operating and maintenance conditions; the nature and quantities of materials being handled; operational, organizational and physical safeguards; and design standards.

In dealing with the external consequences of an accident, a number of such consequences may result (e.g., number of fatalities, number of people being hospitalized, various types of damage to the ecosystem, financial losses, etc.). The external consequences from an accident caused by the substance i for an identified activity j, can be calculated from the relationship: $C_{ij} = A a\ f_a\ f_m$, where: C_{ij} = number of fatalities per accident caused by the substance i for an identified activity j; A = affected area [ha]; a = population density in populated areas within the affected zone [persons/ha]; f_a and f_m are correction factors.

The consequences of (major) accidents to the environment are more difficult to estimate due to the variety of substances that can be involved, as well as the number of environmental impact indicators relevant in a given accident situation. Usually, a utility scale is associated with various environmental consequences; the relevant utility scale could include events related to incidents, accidents or catastrophic outcomes.

Evaluating monetary consequences of (potential) accidents requires a detailed estimate of possible consequences and their associated costs. A monetary value for special classes of consequences (e.g., loss of life or special biological habitats) is not always accepted a priori. The monetary evaluation of consequences should also include external costs, which are very often difficult to assess.

The procedures for identifying hazardous situations which may arise in process plants and equipment are generally considered to be the most developed and well established element in the assessment process of hazardous installations. It must be recognized that (1) the procedures and techniques vary in terms of comprehensiveness and level of detail, from comparative checklists to detailed structured logic diagrams, and (2) the procedures may apply at various stages of project formulation and implementation (from the early decision-making process to determine the location of a plant, through to its design, construction and operation).

Techniques for hazard identification essentially fall into three categories. The following indicates the most commonly used techniques within each category.

- Category 1: Comparative Methods: Process or System Checklist; Safety Audit Review; Relative Ranking (Dow and Mond Hazard Indices); Preliminary Hazard Analysis
- Category 2: Fundamental Methods: Hazard Operability Studies (HAZOP); "What If" Analysis; Failure Mode and Effect Analysis (FMEA)
- Category 3: Logic Diagrams Methods: Fault Tree Analysis; Event Tree Analysis.

Cause Consequence Analysis; Human Reliability Analysis

The appropriateness and relevancy of any one particular technique of hazard identification largely depend on the purpose for which the risk assessment is being undertaken. When further technical details are available one can combine them in the overall process for risk assessment of various hazards. Expert and engineering judgements can often be employed for further evaluation of risk for installations or processes. The primary principle is to first examine the plant or operations from the broadest viewpoint possible and systematically identify possible hazards. Elaborate techniques as a primary tool may cause problems and result in missing some obvious hazards. Sometimes it may be necessary to adopt more than one technique, depending on the level of detail required and whether the facility is a new proposed installation or an existing operation.

Probabilistic safety criteria (PSC) are associated with a rational decision-making process which requires the establishment of a consistent framework with standards to express the desired level of safety. Societal or group risks should be considered when assessing the acceptability of any hazardous industrial facility. A number of factors should be borne in mind when developing PSC based on societal risk, including public aversion to accidents with high consequences (i.e., the risk level chosen should decrease as the consequence increases). Whilst individual fatality risk levels include all components of risk (i.e., fires, explosions and toxicity), there may be uncertainties in correlating toxic concentrations with fatality risk levels. The interpretation of "fatal" should not rely on any one dose-effect relationship, but should involve a review of available data. The concept of societal risk implies that risk of higher consequences, with smaller frequency, are perceived as more important than those of smaller consequences with higher probabilities.

Irrespective of the numerical value of any risk criteria level for risk assessment purposes, it is essential that certain qualitative principles be adopted as yardsticks for risk assessment and safety management: (1) all "avoidable" risks should be avoided; (2) the risk from a major hazard should be reduced whenever practicable; (3) the consequences of more likely hazardous events should, wherever possible, be contained within the boundaries of the installation; and (4) where there is an existing high risk from a hazardous installation, additional hazardous developments should not be allowed if they add significantly to that existing risk.

In the 1990s an increasing importance has been given to risk communication, which has become a separate branch of risk science.

The main tasks in risk communication are:

- identifying controversial aspects of perceived risks
- presenting and explaining risk information
- influencing risk-related behaviour of individuals
- developing information strategies for emergency cases
- evolving cooperative/participative conflict resolution.

The scope and objectives of risk communication can differ, depending on the actors involved in the communication process as well as the functions and expectations they attribute to the communication process and its environment.

Individual and corporate actors in risk communication use manifold communicative means and channels. The main issues are health and environmental protection, safety improvement and risk acceptability.

According to general communication theory, communication can have the following functions:

- presentation of information
- appeal
- self-presentation
- definition of a relationship or decision path.

For the risk communication process in particular it can be helpful to distinguish between these functions. Depending on the function, different conditions for a successful communication process should be considered.

Risk communication can sometimes play the role of a simple presentation of facts. Information is a general need in a modern society. In environmental matters in particular there exist laws which, on the one hand, give the authorities the duty to inform the public and, on the other hand, give the public the right to know about the environmental and risk situation (e.g., the so-called Seveso Directive of the European Community and "Community Right-to-Know" legislation in the United States). Information can also be determined for a special public segment; for example, the employees in a factory must be informed about the risks they face within their workplace. In this sense risk communication must be:

- as neutral and objective as possible
- complete
- comprehensible for those who should get the information.

Appeals tend to incite someone to do something. In risk-related matters the following appeal functions can be distinguished:

- appeal to the general public or to a special segment of the public about risk prevention measures which could or should be taken (e.g., appeal to employees in a factory to take safety measures at work)
- appeal to the general public or to a special segment of the public about preventive measures for emergency cases
- appeal to the general public or to a special segment of the public about measures to be taken in case of an emergency situation (crisis management).

Appeal communication must be:

- as simple and comprehensible as possible, and as complete as necessary
- reliable; having confidence in the persons, authorities or other bodies which make the appeal is essential for the success of the appeal.

Self-presentation does not impart neutral information, but is mainly part of a persuasion or marketing strategy in order to improve the public image of an individual or to achieve public acceptance for a certain activity or to get public support for some kind of position. The criterion for the success of the communication is whether the public believes in the presentation. In a normative view, although the self-presentation aims at convincing someone, it should be honest and sincere.

These forms of communication are mainly of a one-way type. Communication aimed at reaching a decision or agreement is of a two-way or many-way type: there is not only one side which gives information—various actors are involved in a risk communication process and communicate with each other. This is the usual situation in a democratic society. Especially in risk- and environment-related matters communication is considered as an alternative regulatory instrument in complex situations, where easy solutions are not possible or accessible. Therefore the risky decisions with a relevant political importance have to be taken in a communicative atmosphere. Risk communication, in this sense, may include, among others, communication about highly politicized risk topics, but it may also mean, for example, the communication between an operator, the employees and the emergency services in order that the operator be best prepared in case of accident. Thus, depending on the scope and objective of the risk communication, different actors can participate in the communication process. The potential main actors in a risk communication environment are:

- the operator of a risky facility
- the potential victims of an undesired event (e.g., employees, neighbours)
- the regulatory authorities and appropriate political bodies
- the emergency services and general public
- interest groups
- the media
- insurers
- scientists and experts.

In a systems-theory approach all these categories of actors correspond to a certain social system and therefore have different codes of communication, different values and interests to be communicated. Very often it is not easy to find a common basis for a risk dialogue. Structures must be found in order to combine these different views and to achieve a practical result. Topics for such types of risk communication are, for example, a consensus decision about siting or not siting a hazardous plant in a certain region.

In all societies there exist legal and political procedures in order to deal with risk-related issues (e.g., parliamentary legislation, government or administrative decisions, legal procedures before a court, etc.). In many cases these existing procedures do not result in solutions that are entirely satisfactory for the peaceful settlement of risk disputes. Proposals reached by integrating elements of risk communication into the existing procedures have been found to improve the political decision process.

Two main issues have to be discussed when proposing risk communication procedures:

- the formal organization and legal significance of the process and of its results
- the structure of the communication process itself.

For the formal organization of risk communication there are various possibilities:

- The communication can take place inside or between existing bodies (e.g., between an agency of the central government, a local authority and existing interest groups).

- New bodies can be established specifically for the process of risk communications; various models have been developed (e.g., citizen juries, citizen panels, negotiation and mediation structures, mixed commissions consisting of operators, authorities and citizens). Most of these models are based on the idea of organizing a structured discourse in small groups. Significant differences of opinion exist about whether these groups should consist of experts, laymen, representatives of the political system, etc.

In any case the relationship between these communication structures and the existing legal and political decision-making bodies has to be clarified. Usually the result of a risk communication process has the effect of a non-binding recommendation to the deciding bodies.

Concerning the structure of the communication process, under the general rules of practical discourse, any argument is allowed if it fulfils the following conditions:

- adequate logical consistency
- sincerity (This means: The discourse should not be influenced by strategic or tactical thinking.)
- that the one who promotes an argument must be ready to accept the consequences of that argument also against himself or herself.

In the risk communication process various special rules and proposals have been developed in order to concretize these rules. Among these, the following rules are worth mentioning:

In the risk communication process a distinction must be made between:

- communicative claims
- cognitive claims
- normative claims
- expressive claims.

Correspondingly, differences of opinion can have various reasons, namely:

- differences in information
- differences in the understanding of facts
- differences in normative values.

It may be helpful to make clear through the risk communication process the level of differences and their significance. Various structural proposals have been made for improving the conditions for such a discourse and, at the same time, to help decision-makers to find fair and competent solutions—for example:

- For a fair discourse the result must be open-ended; if the aim is just to achieve acceptance for a decision that has already been made, it would not be sincere to open a discourse.
- If some solutions are simply not possible for factual, political or legal reasons, this must be clarified from the beginning.
- It may be helpful first to discuss not the alternatives, but the criteria which should be applied in evaluating the alternatives.

Effectiveness of risk communication can be defined as the degree to which an initial (undesired) situation is changed toward an intended state, as defined by initial goals. Procedural aspects are to be included in the evaluation of risk communication programmes. Such criteria include practicability (e.g., flexibility, adaptability, implementability) and costs (in terms of money, personnel and time) of the programme.

ENVIRONMENTAL AUDITING— DEFINITION AND METHODOLOGY

Robert Coyle

Origins of Environmental Auditing

Environmental safety and health auditing developed in the early 1970s, largely among companies operating in environmentally intensive sectors such as oils and chemicals. Since then environmental auditing has spread rapidly with a corresponding development of the approaches and techniques adopted. Several factors have influenced this growth.

- *Industrial accidents.* Major incidents such as the Bhopal, Chernobyl and *Exxon-Valdez* disasters have reminded companies that it is not sufficient to set corporate policies and standards on environmental health and safety matters without ensuring that they are being implemented. Audits can help reduce the risk of unpleasant surprises.
- *Regulatory developments.* Since the early 1970s regulations on environmental topics have increased substantially. This has made it steadily more difficult for a company to ascertain whether a specific plant in a particular country is complying with all of the relevant legislation.
- *Public awareness.* The public has become increasingly aware of, and vocal about, environmental and safety issues. Companies have had to demonstrate to the public that they are managing environmental risks effectively.
- *Litigation.* The growth of legislation has led to a corresponding explosion of litigation and liability claims, particularly in the United States. In Europe and elsewhere, there is growing emphasis on the responsibilities of individual directors and on making information available to the public.

What is an Environmental Audit?

It is important to draw the distinction between auditing and techniques such as environmental impact assessment (EIA). The latter assesses the potential environmental effects of a proposed facility. The essential purpose of an environmental audit is the systematic scrutiny of environmental performance throughout a company's existing operations. At best, an audit is a comprehensive examination of management systems and facilities; at worst, it is a superficial review.

The term environmental audit means different things to different people. Terms such as assessment, survey and review are used to describe the same type of activity. Furthermore, some organizations consider that an "environmental audit" addresses only environmental matters, whereas others use the term to mean an audit of health, safety and environmental matters. Although there is no universal definition, auditing, as practised by many leading companies, follows the same basic philosophy and approach summarized by the broad definition adopted by the International Chambers of Commerce (ICC) in its publication *Environmental Auditing* (1989). The ICC defines environmental auditing as:

a management tool comprising a systematic, documented periodic and objective evaluation of how well environmental organization, management and equipment are performing, with the aim of helping safeguard the environment by:

(i) facilitating management control of environmental practices and

(ii) assessing compliance with company policies which would include meeting regulatory requirements.

Table 54.1 • Scope of an environmental audit.

Environmental	Safety	Occupational Health	Product Safety

Site history
Process/materials
Storage of materials
  above ground
  below ground
Air emissions
Water discharges
Liquid/hazardous wastes
Asbestos
Waste disposal
  onsite
  offsite
Oil/chemical spill prevention
Permits/licenses
	Safety policy/procedures
	Accident reporting
	Accident recording
	Accident investigation
	Permit to work systems
	Special procedures for confined space
	  entry, work on electrical equipment,
	  breaking into pipelines, etc.
	Emergency response
	Fire fighting
	Job safety analysis
	Safety training
	Safety communication/promotion
	Housekeeping
	Regulatory compliance
		Employee exposure to air contaminants
		Exposure to physical agents, e.g., noise,
		  radiation, heat
		Measurements of employee exposure
		Exposure records
		Ventilation/engineering controls
		Personal protective equipment
		Information and training on health
		  hazards
		Medical surveillance programme
		Hearing conservation
		First aid
		Regulatory requirements
			Product safety programme
			Product quality control
			Product packaging, storage and shipping
			Product recall/withdrawal procedures
			Customer information on product
			  handling and quality
			Regulatory compliance
			Labelling
			Specifications for purchased
			  materials/products/packaging
			Materials safety data
			Vendor qualification programme
			QA testing and inspections
			Record keeping
			Product literature
			Process control

The European Commission in its proposed regulation on environmental auditing also adopts the ICC definition of environmental audit.

Objectives of Environmental Auditing

The overall objective of environmental auditing is to help safeguard the environment and minimize risks to human health. Clearly, auditing alone will not achieve this goal (hence the use of the word help); it is a management tool. The key objectives of an environmental audit therefore are to:

- determine how well the environmental management systems and equipment are performing
- verify compliance with the relevant national, local or other laws and regulations
- minimize human exposure to risks from environmental, health and safety problems.

Scope of the Audit

As the prime objective of audits is to test the adequacy of existing management systems, they fulfil a fundamentally different role from the monitoring of environmental performance. Audits can address one topic, or a whole range of issues. The greater the scope of the audit, the greater will be the size of the audit team, the time spent onsite and the depth of investigation. Where international audits need to be carried out by a central team, there can be good reasons for covering more than one area while onsite to minimize costs.

In addition, the scope of an audit can vary from simple compliance testing to a more rigorous examination, depending on the perceived needs of the management. The technique is applied not only to operational environmental, health and safety management, but increasingly also to product safety and product quality management, and to areas such as loss prevention. If the intention of auditing is to help ensure that these broad areas are managed properly, then all of these individual topics must be reviewed. Items which may be addressed in audits, including environment, health, safety and product safety are shown in table 54.1.

Although some companies have a regular (often annual) audit cycle, audits are primarily determined by need and priority. Thus not all facilities or aspects of a company will be assessed at the same frequency or to the same extent.

The Typical Audit Process

An audit is usually conducted by a team of people who will assemble factual information prior to and during a site visit, analyse the facts and compare them with the criteria for the audit, draw conclusions and report their findings. These steps are usually conducted within some kind of formal structure (an audit protocol), such that the process can be repeated reliably at other facilities and quality can be maintained. To ensure that an audit is effective, a number of key steps must be included. These are summarized and explained in table 54.2.

Basic Steps in Environmental Auditing

Criteria—what do you audit against?

An essential step in establishing an audit programme is to decide the criteria against which the audit will be conducted and to ensure that management throughout the organization knows what these criteria are. Typically criteria used for audits are:

- company policies and procedures on environmental matters
- applicable legislation and regulations
- good environmental management practice.

Pre-audit steps

Pre-audit steps include the administrative issues associated with planning the audit, selecting the personnel for the audit team (often from different parts of the company or from a specialized unit), preparing the audit protocol used by the organization and obtaining background information about the facility.

If auditing is new, the need for education of those involved in the audit process (the auditors or those being audited) should not be underestimated. This also applies to a multinational company extending an audit programme in its home country to subsidiaries abroad. In these situations, the time spent on explanation and education will pay dividends by ensuring that the audits are approached in a spirit of cooperation and are not seen as a threat by the local management.

When one major US company proposed extending its auditing programme to its operations in Europe, it was particularly concerned to ensure that the plants were properly briefed, that audit protocols were appropriate for European operations and that audit teams understood the relevant regulations. Pilot audits were conducted at selected plants. In addition, the audit process

Table 54.2 • Basic steps in environmental auditing.

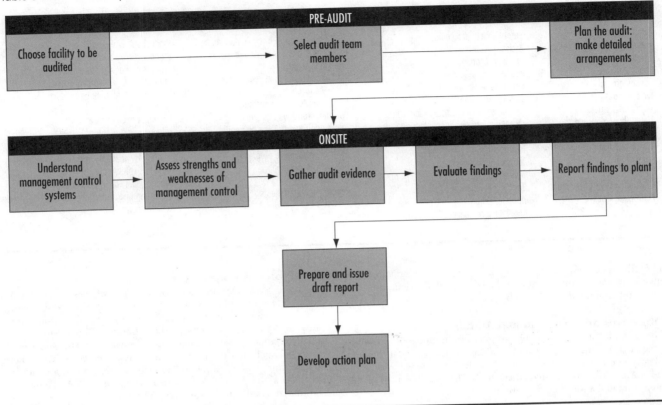

was introduced in a way that stressed the benefits of a cooperative rather than a "policing" approach.

Obtaining background information about a site and its processes can help to minimize the time spent onsite by the audit team and to focus its activities, thus saving resources.

The composition of the audit team will depend on the approach adopted by a particular organization. Where there is a lack of internal expertise, or where resources cannot be devoted to the audit activity, companies frequently use independent consultants to conduct the audits for them. Other companies employ a mix of in-house staff and external consultants on each team to ensure an "independent" view. Some large companies use only in-house staff for audits, and have environmental audit groups for this specific function. Many major companies have their own dedicated audit staff, but also include an independent consultant on many of the audits they carry out.

Onsite steps

- *Understanding the internal controls.* As a first step, it is necessary to develop an understanding of the controls that are in place or are thought to be in place. These will include assessing formal procedures and practices; record keeping and monitoring; inspection and maintenance programmes and physical controls for containing spills. The audit team gathers information on the various controls by observation, interviewing staff and the use of detailed questionnaires.
- *Assessing strengths and weaknesses of internal controls.* Evaluating the strengths and weaknesses of internal controls provides the rationale for conducting subsequent audit steps. Auditors will look for indicators such as clearly defined responsibilities,

competence of personnel, appropriate documentation and records and systems of authorization. It is more important to determine whether the system is effective than whether it is sophisticated.

- *Gathering audit evidence.* The audit team attempts to verify that the steps and controls work as intended. Evidence may be collected through inquiry (e.g., asking a plant operator what he or she would do if there were a major chemical spill), observation (e.g., watching specific activities and operations in progress) and testing (checking records to confirm compliance with regulations).
- *Recording audit findings.* All the information obtained is recorded (usually on the audit protocol document and as working papers), and a comprehensive record of the audit and the state of the facility at the time is thus produced. Where a deficiency is found, it is noted as an audit "finding".
- *Evaluating the audit findings.* The audit team integrates and evaluates the findings of the individual team members. There may also be common findings. For some observations, an informal discussion with the plant manager may be sufficient; for others, inclusion in the formal report will be appropriate.
- *Reporting the audit findings.* This usually is done at a meeting with the plant management at the end of the team's visit. Each finding and its significance can be discussed with the plant personnel. Prior to leaving the site, the audit team will often provide a written summary of findings for the plant management, to ensure that there are no surprises in the final report.

Post-audit steps

Following the onsite work, the next step is to prepare a draft report, which is reviewed by the plant management to confirm its accuracy. It is then distributed to senior management according to the requirements of the company.

The other key step is to develop an action plan to address the deficiencies. Some companies ask for recommendations for corrective action to be included in the formal audit report. The plant will then base its plan on implementing these recommendations. Other companies require the audit report to state the facts and the deficiencies, with no reference to how they should be corrected. It is then the responsibility of the plant management to devise the means of remedying the failings.

Once an audit programme is in place, future audits will include past reports—and progress in the implementation of any recommendations made therein—as part of their evidence.

Extending the Audit Process—Other Types of Audit

Although the most widespread use of environmental auditing is to assess the environmental performance of a company's operations, there are variations on the theme. Other types of audit used in particular circumstances include the following:

- *Pre-acquisition audits.* Concern about potential liabilities has promoted the dramatic increase in environmental auditing prior to acquisition. Pre-acquisition audits are a means of identifying actual or potential problems, and taking these into account in the final negotiations of the deal. Time scales are often very short. However, the information obtained on past operations (perhaps before the present owner), current activities, past incidents and so on can be invaluable.
- *Pre-sale audits.* Less common than pre-acquisition audits, but becoming more popular, are audits conducted by the owner prior to selling a plant or a subsidiary company. A growing number of major organizations, such as the Dutch chemical company DSM and the Finnish conglomerate Neste, undertake pre-sale audits as part of corporate policy. The rationale is that the company will then know the status of environmental issues before the plant is sold, and can take action to remedy any problems if it feels that is appropriate. Equally important, it can present the results of an independent audit to a potential purchaser as confirmation of the situation. Should any environmental problems arise after the sale, a baseline has been established against which issues of liability can be decided.
- *Issues audits.* Some organizations apply the audit technique to a specific issue that may have implications for the whole company, such as waste. The UK-based oil multinational BP has carried out audits examining the impact of ozone depletion and the implications of public concern about tropical deforestation.

Benefits of Environmental Auditing

If environmental auditing is implemented in a constructive way there are many benefits to be derived from the process. The auditing approach described in this paper will help to:

- safeguard the environment
- verify compliance with local and national laws
- indicate current or potential future problems that need to be addressed
- assess training programmes and provide data to assist in training
- enable companies to build on good environmental performance, give credit where appropriate and highlight deficiencies
- identify potential cost savings, such as from waste minimization
- assist the exchange and comparison of information between different plants or subsidiary companies
- demonstrate company commitment to environmental protection to employees, the public and the authorities.

ENVIRONMENTAL MANAGEMENT STRATEGIES AND WORKERS' PROTECTION

Cecilia Brighi

The Evolution of Environmental Response Strategies

In the past thirty years there has been a dramatic increase in environmental problems due to many different factors: demographic expansion (this pace is continuing, with an estimated 8 billion people by the year 2030), poverty, dominant economic models based on growth and quantity rather than quality, high consumption of natural resources driven particularly by industrial expansion, reduction of biological diversity especially as a result of increased agricultural production through monoculture, soil erosion, climate change, the unsustainable use of natural resources and the pollution of air, soils and water resources. However, the negative effects of human activity upon the environment have also accelerated the awareness and social perception of people in many countries, leading to changes in traditional approaches and response models.

Response strategies have been evolving: from no recognition of the problem, to ignoring the problem, to diluting and controlling pollution through a top-down approach—that is, the so-called end-of-pipe strategies. The 1970s marked the first widely relevant local environmental crises and the development of new awareness of environmental pollution. This led to the adoption of the first major series of national legislation, regulations and international conventions aimed at the control and regulation of pollution. This end-of-pipe strategy soon showed its failure, for it was directed in an authoritarian way to interventions related to the symptoms and not the causes of environmental problems. At the same time, industrial pollution also drew attention to the growing contradictions in philosophy between employers, workers and environmental groups.

The 1980s was the period of global environmental issues such as the Chernobyl disaster, acid rain, ozone depletion and the ozone hole, the greenhouse effect and climate change, and the growth in toxic wastes and their export. These events and the resulting problems enhanced public awareness and helped to generate support for new approaches and solutions focusing on environmental management tools and cleaner production strategies. Organizations such as UNEP, OECD, the European Union and many national institutions started to define the issue and work together within a more global framework based on principles of prevention, innovation, information, education and the participation of relevant stakeholders. As we entered the 1990s there was another dramatic increase in awareness that the environmental crisis was deepening, particularly in the developing world and in Central and Eastern Europe. This reached a critical threshold at the United Nations Conference on Environment and Development (UNCED) in Rio de Janeiro in 1992.

Today, the precautionary approach has become one of the most important factors necessary to take into account when assessing environmental policies and solutions. The precautionary approach suggests that even when there is scientific uncertainty or controversy on environmental problems and policies, decisions should reflect the need to take precautions to avoid future negative implications whenever economically, socially and technically feasible. The precautionary approach should be pursued when developing policies and regulations, and when planning and implementing projects and programmes.

In effect, both the preventive and precautionary approaches seek a more integrated approach to environmental action, shifting from an almost exclusive focus on the production process to the development of environmental management tools and techniques applicable to all forms of human economic activity and decision-making processes. Unlike pollution control, which implied a limited, react-and-retreat approach, the environmental management and cleaner production approach is aimed at the integration of a precautionary approach within broader strategies to create a process that will be assessed, monitored and continuously improved. To be effective, however, environmental management and cleaner production strategies need to be carefully implemented through the involvement of all stakeholders and at all levels of intervention.

These new approaches must not be considered as simply technical instruments related to the environment, but rather should be seen as holistic integrating approaches which will help to define new models of an environmentally and socially sound market economy. To be fully effective, these new approaches will also require a regulatory framework, incentive instruments and social consensus defined through the involvement of institutions, social partners and interested environmental and consumer organizations. If the scope of environmental management and cleaner production strategies is to lead to more sustainable socio-economic development scenarios, various factors will need to be taken into consideration in policy-setting, in the development and enforcement of standards and regulations, and in collective agreements and action plans, not only at the company or enterprise level, but at the local, national and international levels as well. Given the wide disparities in economic and social conditions around the world, the opportunities for success also will depend on local political, economic and social conditions.

Globalization, the liberalization of markets and structural adjustment policies, will also create new challenges to our capacity to analyse in an integrated fashion the economic, social and environmental implications of these complex changes within our societies, not the least of which will be the risk that these changes may lead to quite different power relationships and responsibilities, perhaps even ownership and control. Attention will need to be given to ensuring that these changes do not lead to the risk of powerlessness and paralysis in the development of environmental management and cleaner production technologies. On the other hand, this changing situation, in addition to its risks, also offers new opportunities to promote improvements in our present social, economic, cultural, political and environmental conditions. Such positive changes, however, will require a collaborative, participatory and flexible approach to managing change within our societies and within our enterprises. To avoid paralysis, we will need to take measures which will build confidence and emphasize a step-by-step, partial and gradual approach which will generate growing support and capacity aimed at facilitating more substantial changes in our conditions of life and work in future.

Main International Implications

As mentioned above, the new international situation is characterized by the liberalization of markets, the elimination of trade barriers, new information technologies, rapid and enormous daily capital transfers and the globalization of production, especially through multinational enterprises. Deregulation and competitiveness are the dominant criteria for investment strategies. These changes also, however, facilitate the delocalization of plants, the fragmentation of production processes and the establishment of special Export Processing Zones, which exempt industries from labour and environmental regulations and other obligations. Such effects may promote excessively low labour costs and consequently higher profits for industry, but this is frequently accompanied by situations of deplorable human and environmental exploitation. In addition, in the absence of regulations and controls, obsolete plants, technologies and equipment are being exported just as dangerous chemicals and substances which have been banned, withdrawn or severely restricted in one country for environmental or safety reasons are also being exported, particularly to developing countries.

In order to respond to these issues, it is of particular importance that the new World Trade Organization (WTO) rules are defined so as to promote socially and environmentally acceptable trade. This means that WTO, in order to ensure fair competition, should require all countries to fulfil basic international labour standards (e.g., basic ILO Conventions) and environmental conventions and regulations. Moreover, guidelines such as those prepared by OECD on technology transfer and regulations should be effectively implemented in order to avoid the export of highly polluting and unsafe production systems.

International factors to be considered include:

- international trade in equipment and plants
- financial mechanisms and technical assistance
- WTO regulations
- raw material pricing
- tax systems
- transfer of technology and know-how
- transboundary migration of pollution
- multinational companies' production strategies
- development and implementation of international conventions, agreements, guidelines and regulations
- involvement of international organizations of employers, workers and relevant environmental groups.

Developing and other countries in need of assistance should be given special financial assistance, reduction in taxes, incentives and technical assistance to help them implement the above-mentioned basic labour and environmental regulations and to introduce cleaner production technologies and products. An innovative approach which deserves further attention in the future is the development of codes of conduct negotiated by certain companies and their trade unions with a view to promoting the respect of basic social rights and environmental rules. A unique role in the assessment of the process at the international level is being played by the ILO, given its tripartite structure, and in strict coordination with other United Nations agencies and international financial institutions responsible for international aid and financial assistance.

Main National and Local Implications

An appropriate general regulatory framework also has to be defined at both the national and local level in order to develop appropriate environmental management procedures. This will require a decision-making process which links budgetary, fiscal, industrial, economic, labour and environmental policies, and also provides for the full consultation and participation of the social actors most concerned (i.e., employers, trade union organizations, environmental and consumer groups). Such a systematic approach would include linkages between different programmes and policies, for example:

- The taxation system should provide incentives which will encourage the penetration of environmentally sound goods and raw materials into the market and penalize those products, economic activities and collective or individual behaviour which are environmentally unsound.
- Adequate policies and resources should be available to promote research and development of environmentally and socially sound technologies, production processes and infrastructure.

Table 54.3 • Actors involved in voluntary agreements relevant to the environment.

Country	Employer/State	Employer/Union/State	Employer/Union	Employer/Works council
Netherlands	X		X	X
Belgium			X	X
Denmark	X	X	X	X
Austria			X	
Germany	X		X	X
United Kingdom			X	X
Italy	X	X	X	X
France			X	X
Spain			X	X
Greece		X	X	

Source: Hildebrandt and Schmidt 1994.

- Advisory, information and training centres for cleaner production technologies should be established to assist enterprises, especially small- and medium-sized enterprises, to procure, adapt and use the technologies safely and effectively.

National and local industrial policies should be designed and implemented in full consultation with trade union organizations so that business policies and labour policies can match social and environmental needs. Direct negotiations and consultations at the national level with trade unions can help to prevent potential conflicts arising from safety, health and environmental implications of new industrial policies. Such negotiations at the national level, however, should be matched by negotiations and consultations at the level of individual companies and enterprises so as to ensure that adequate controls, incentives and assistance are also available at the workplace.

In summary, national and local factors to be considered include:

- national and local regulations, guidelines, agreements and policies

Table 54.4 • Scope of application of voluntary agreements on environment-protection measures between parties to collective agreements.

Country	National	Branch (regional)	Plant
Netherlands	X	X	X
Belgium	X		X
Denmark	X	X	X
Austria		X	
Germany		X	X
United Kingdom			X
Italy	X	X	X
France			
Spain		X	X
Greece	X		

Source: Hildebrandt and Schmidt 1994.

- industrial relations procedures
- involvement of social partners (trade unions and employers' organizations), environmental NGOs and consumer organizations in all decision-making processes
- industrial policies
- raw material pricing policies
- trade policies
- tax systems
- incentives for research and development
- incentives for introduction of innovative environmental management initiatives
- integration of health and safety procedures/standards
- establishment of advisory, information and training centres for the dissemination of cleaner production technologies
- assistance for overcoming obstacles (conceptual, organizational, technical, skills and financial) to the introduction of new technologies, policies, regulations.

Environmental Management at Company Level

Environmental management within a given company, enterprise or other economic structure requires an ongoing assessment and consideration of environmental effects—at the workplace (i.e., the working environment) and outside the plant gates (i.e., the external environment)—as regards the full range of activities and decisions related to operations. It implies, as well, the consequent modification of the organization of work and production processes to respond efficiently and effectively to those environmental effects.

It is necessary for enterprises to foresee potential environmental consequences of a given activity, process or product from the earliest planning stages in order to ensure the implementation of adequate, timely and participatory response strategies. The objective is to make industry and other economic sectors economically, socially and environmentally sustainable. Most certainly, in many cases there still will need to be a transition period which will require pollution control and remediation activities. Therefore, environmental management should be seen as a composite process of prevention and control that aims to bring company strategies in line with environmental sustainability. To do this, companies will need to develop and implement procedures within their overall management strategy to assess cleaner production processes and to audit environmental performance.

Table 54.5 • Nature of agreements on environment-protection measures between parties to collective agreements.

Country	Joint declarations, recommendations, agreements	Branch-level collective agreements	Agreements on plant level
Netherlands	X	X	X
Belgium	X		X
Denmark	X	X	X
Austria		X	
Germany	X	X	X
United Kingdom		X	
Italy	X	X	X
France		X	X
Spain		X	
Greece	X		

Source: Hildebrandt and Schmidt 1994.

Environmental management and cleaner production will lead to a range of benefits that will not only effect environmental performance but may also lead to improvements in:

- health and safety of workers
- rates of absenteeism
- preventing and resolving conflict with workers and communities
- promoting a cooperative climate within the company
- the company public image
- the market penetration of new green products
- efficient use of energy and raw materials
- waste management, including the safe disposal of wastes
- the productivity and quality of products.

Companies should not simply focus on evaluating company conformity with existing legislation and regulations but should define possible environmental targets to be reached through a time-bound, step-by-step process which would include:

- the definition of company environmental objectives and policy
- the definition of short-, medium- and long-term strategies
- the adoption of a cradle-to-grave approach
- the allocation of appropriate budget resources
- the integration of health and safety within environmental audit procedures
- the participation of workers and trade union representatives in the analysis and decision-making process
- the establishment of an environmental audit team with worker representatives.

There are many different approaches to assessing activities, and the following are important potential components of any such programme:

- definition of flow diagrams for each operational unit
- monitoring of process inputs by operational unit—for example, water, energy, raw materials used, number of workers involved, health, safety and environmental risk assessment, organization of work
- monitoring of process outputs by operational unit—for example, quantification of products/byproducts, waste water, gaseous emissions, solid wastes for disposal on and off site

- adoption of company targets
- feasibility analysis of potential barriers (economic, technical, environmental, social) and adoption of consequent programmes
- adoption and implementation of an information strategy
- adoption and implementation of training strategy to promote worker awareness and full participation
- monitoring and evaluation of performance/results.

Industrial Relations and Environmental Management

While in some countries basic trade union rights are still not recognized and workers are prevented from protecting their health and safety and working conditions and improving environmental performance, in various other countries the participatory approach to company environmental sustainability has been tried with good results. In the last ten years, the traditional approach of industrial relations has shifted more and more to include not only health and safety issues and programmes reflecting national and international regulations in this area, but also has begun to integrate environmental issues into the industrial relations mechanisms. Partnerships between employers and trade union representatives at company, sector and national level have been defined, according to different situations, through collective agreements and sometimes also have been covered in regulations and consultation procedures set up by local or national authorities to manage environmental conflicts. See tables 54.3, 54.4 and 54.5.

Pollution Remediation: Cleaning Up

Cleaning up contaminated sites is a procedure which has become increasingly evident and costly since the 1970s, when awareness was enhanced about the serious cases of soil and water contamination from accumulated chemical wastes, abandoned industrial sites and so on. These contaminated sites have been generated from such activities as the following:

- waste disposal sites (industrial and public)
- abandoned industrial sites (e.g., chemical, metal processing)
- mining activities
- agricultural sites
- major accidents
- incinerator sites
- industrial water discharges
- small and medium enterprise zones.

The design of a remediation/clean-up plan requires complex technical activities and procedures which must be accompanied by the definition of clear management responsibilities and consequent liability. Such initiatives should be carried out in the context of harmonized national legislation, and provide for the participation of interested populations, for the definition of clear conflict resolution procedures and for the avoidance of possible socio-environmental dumping effects. Such regulations, agreements and plans should clearly encompass not only natural biotic and abiotic resources such as water, air, soil or flora and fauna but should also include cultural heritage, other visual aspects of landscapes and damage to physical persons and properties. A restrictive definition of environment will consequently reduce the definition of environmental damage and therefore limit actual remediation of sites. At the same time, it should also be possible not only for the subjects directly affected by damages to be granted certain rights and protection, but it also should be possible for collective group action to be taken to protect collective interests in order to ensure the restoration of previous conditions.

Conclusion

Significant action will be required to respond to our rapidly changing environmental situation. The focus of this article has been on the need for action to be taken to improve the environmental performance of industry and other economic activities. To do this efficiently and effectively, workers and their trade unions must play an active role not only at the enterprise level, but as well within their local communities and at the national level. Workers must be seen and actively mobilized as key partners in meeting future environment and sustainable development objectives. The ability of workers and their trade unions to contribute as partners in this process of environmental management is not dependent simply on their own capacity and awareness—although efforts are indeed needed and underway to increase their capacity—but it will also depend on the commitment of management and communities to create an enabling environment which promotes the development of new forms of collaboration and participation in the future.

ENVIRONMENTAL POLLUTION CONTROL: MAKING POLLUTION PREVENTION A CORPORATE PRIORITY

Robert P. Bringer and Tom Zosel

Seeing the possibilities and making them happen is what pollution prevention is all about. It is a commitment to products and processes that have a minimal impact on the environment.

Pollution prevention is not a new idea. It is the manifestation of an environmental ethic that was practised by the original inhabitants of many cultures, including Native Americans. They lived in harmony with their environment. It was the source of their shelter, their food and the very foundation of their religion. Although their environment was exceedingly harsh, it was treated with honour and respect.

As nations developed and the Industrial Revolution advanced, a very different attitude toward the environment emerged. Society came to view the environment as an endless source of raw materials and a convenient dumping ground for wastes.

Early Efforts to Reduce Waste

Even so, some industries have practised a type of pollution prevention since the first chemical processes were developed. Initially, industry focused on efficiency or increasing process yield through waste reduction, rather than specifically preventing pollution by keeping wastes from entering the environment. However, the end result of both activities is the same—less material waste is released to the environment.

An early example of pollution prevention under another guise was practised in a German sulphuric acid production facility during the 1800s. Process improvements at the plant reduced the amount of sulphur dioxide emitted per pound of product produced. These actions were most likely labelled as efficiency or quality improvements. Only recently has the concept of pollution prevention been directly associated with this type of process change.

Pollution prevention as we know it today began to emerge in the mid-1970s in response to the growing volume and complexity of environmental requirements. The US Environmental Protection Agency (EPA) was created then. The first efforts at pollution reduction were mostly installations of end-of-pipe or costly add-on pollution control equipment. Eliminating the source of a pollution problem was not a priority. When it occurred, it was more a matter of profit or efficiency than an organized effort to protect the environment.

Only recently have businesses adopted a more specific environmental point of view and kept track of progress. However, the processes by which businesses approach pollution prevention can differ significantly.

Prevention versus Control

In time, the focus began to change from pollution control to pollution prevention. It became apparent that the scientists who invent the products, engineers who design the equipment, process experts who operate the manufacturing facilities, marketers who work with customers to improve product environmental performance, sales representatives who bring environmental concerns from customers back to the laboratory for solutions and office employees who work to reduce paper usage all can help reduce the environmental impact of operations or activities under their control.

Developing effective pollution prevention programmes

In state-of-the-art pollution prevention, pollution prevention programmes as well as specific pollution prevention technologies must be examined. Both the overall pollution prevention programme and the individual pollution prevention technologies are equally important in achieving environmental benefit. While the development of technologies is an absolute requirement, without the organizational structure to support and implement those technologies, the environmental benefits will never be fully achieved.

The challenge is to obtain total corporate participation in pollution prevention. Some companies have implemented pollution prevention at every level of their organization through well organized, detailed programmes. Perhaps the three most widely recognized of these in the United States are 3M's Pollution Prevention Pays (3P) programme, Chevron's Save Money and Reduce Toxics (SMART) and Dow Chemical's Waste Reduction Always Pays (WRAP).

The goal of such programmes is to reduce waste as much as technologically possible. But relying on source reduction alone is not always technically feasible. Recycling and reuse also must be part of the pollution prevention effort, as they are in the above programmes. When every employee is asked not only to make processes as efficient as possible, but also to find a productive use for every by-product or residual stream, pollution prevention becomes an integral part of the corporate culture.

In late 1993, The Business Roundtable in the US released the results of a pollution prevention benchmark study of successful efforts. The study identified best-in-class facility pollution prevention programmes and highlighted elements necessary to fully integrate pollution prevention into company operations. Included were facilities from Proctor & Gamble (P&G), Intel, DuPont, Monsanto, Martin Marietta and 3M.

Pollution prevention initiatives

The study found that successful pollution prevention programmes in these companies shared the following elements:

- top management support
- involvement of all employees
- recognition of accomplishments
- facilities had freedom to choose the best method to reach corporate goals
- transfer of information between facilities
- measurement of results

- all included recycling and reuse of waste.

In addition, the study found that each of the facilities had advanced from concentrating on pollution prevention in the manufacturing process to integrating pollution prevention in pre-manufacturing decisions. Pollution prevention had become a core corporate value.

Top management support is a necessity for a fully operational pollution prevention programme. Top officials at both the corporate and facility levels must send a strong message to all employees that pollution prevention is an integral part of their jobs. This must begin at the chief executive officer (CEO) level because that person sets the tone for all corporate activities. Speaking out publicly and within the company gets the message heard.

The second reason for success is employee involvement. Technical and manufacturing people are most involved in develop-ing new processes or product formulations. But employees in every position can be involved in waste reduction through reuse, reclamation and recycling as part of pollution prevention. Employees know the possibilities in their area of responsibility much better than environmental professionals. In order to spur employee involvement, the company must educate employees about the challenge the company faces. For example, articles on environmental issues in the corporate newsletter can increase employee awareness.

Recognition of accomplishments can be done in many ways. The CEO of 3M presents a special environmental leadership award not only to employees who contribute to the company's goals, but also to those who contribute to community environmental efforts. In addition, environmental achievements are recognized in annual performance reviews.

Measuring results is extremely important because that is the driving force for employee action. Some facilities and corporate programmes measure all wastes, while others focus on Toxic Release Inventory (TRI) emissions or on other measurements which best fit within their corporate culture and their specific pollution prevention programmes.

Environmental Programme Examples

Over the course of 20 years, pollution prevention has become imbedded in 3M's culture. 3M management pledged to go beyond government regulations, in part by developing environmental management plans that merge environmental goals with business strategy. The 3P programme focused on preventing pollution, not control.

The idea is to stop pollution before it starts, and seek out prevention opportunities at all stages of a product's life, not just at the end. Successful companies recognize that prevention is more environmentally effective, more technically sound and less costly than conventional control procedures, which do not eliminate the problem. Pollution prevention is economical, because if pollution is avoided in the first place, it does not have to be dealt with later.

3M employees have developed and implemented more than 4,200 pollution prevention projects since the inception of the 3P programme. Over the past 20 years, these projects have resulted in the elimination of more than 1.3 billion pounds of pollutants and saved the company $750 million.

Between 1975 and 1993, 3M reduced the amount of energy needed per unit of production by 3,900 BTUs, or 58%. The annual energy savings for 3M in the United States alone totals 22 trillion BTUs each year. This is enough energy to heat, cool and light more than 200,000 homes in the United States and eliminates more than 2 million tons of carbon dioxide. And in 1993, 3M facilities in the United Sates recovered and recycled more solid waste (199 million pounds) than they sent to landfills (198 million pounds).

Pollution Prevention Technologies

The concept of designing for the environment is becoming important, but technologies used for pollution prevention are as diverse as the companies themselves. In general, this concept can be realized through technical innovation in four areas:

- product reformulation—developing nonpolluting or less-polluting products or processes by using different raw materials
- process modification—changing manufacturing processes so they become nonpolluting or less polluting
- equipment redesign—modifying equipment to perform better under specific operating conditions or to make use of available resources
- resource recovery—recycling by-products for sale or for use by other companies or for use in the company's other products or processes.

Concentrated efforts in each of these areas can mean new and safer products, cost savings and greater customer satisfaction.

Product reformulation can be the most difficult. Many of the attributes which make materials ideal for their intended uses may also contribute to problems for the environment. One example of product reformulation led a team of scientists to eliminate the ozone-depleting chemical methyl chloroform from a fabric protector product. This new water-based product greatly reduces the use of solvents and gives the company a competitive edge in the marketplace.

In making medication tablets for the pharmaceutical industry, employees developed a new water-based coating solution for the solvent-based coating solution that had been used to coat the tablets. The change cost $60,000, but eliminated the need to spend $180,000 for pollution control equipment, saves $150,000 in material cost and prevents 24 tons a year of air pollution.

An example of process modification resulted in a move away from hazardous chemicals to thoroughly clean copper sheeting prior to using it to make electric products. In the past, the sheeting was cleaned by a spray with ammonium persulphate, phosphoric acid and sulphuric acid—all hazardous chemicals. This procedure has been replaced by one that employs a light citric acid solution, a nonhazardous chemical. The process change eliminated the generation of 40,000 pounds of hazardous waste per year and saves the company about $15,000 per year in raw material and disposal costs.

Redesigning equipment also reduces waste. In the resin product area, a company regularly sampled a particular liquid phenolic resin by using a tap on the process flow line. Some of the product was wasted before and after the sample was collected. By installing a simple funnel under the sample tape and a pipe leading back to the process, the company now takes samples without any loss of product. This prevents about 9 tons of waste per year, saves about $22,000, increases the yield and decreases the disposal cost, all for a capital cost of about $1,000.

Resource recovery, the productive use of waste material, is extremely important in pollution prevention. One brand of wool soap pads is now made entirely of post-consumer recycled plastic soda bottles. In the first two years of this new product, the company used in excess of a million pounds of this recycled material to make soap pads. This is the equivalent of more than 10 million two-litre soda bottles. Also, waste rubber trimmed from floor mats in Brazil is used to make sandals. In 1994 alone, the plant recovered about 30 tons of material, enough to make more than 120,000 pairs of sandals.

In another example, Post-it® Recycled Paper Notes use 100% recycled paper. One ton of recycled paper alone saves 3 cubic yards of landfill space, 17 trees, 7,000 gallons of water and 4,100 kilowatt hours of energy, enough to heat the average home for six months.

Life-Cycle Analysis

Life-Cycle Analysis or a similar process is in place at every successful company. This means that each phase of a product's life cycle from development through manufacturing, use and disposal offers opportunities for environmental improvement. The response to such environmental challenges has led to products with strong environmental claims throughout industry.

For example, P&G was the first commercial-goods manufacturer to develop concentrated detergents which require 50 to 60% smaller packaging than the previous formula. P&G also manufacturers refills for more than 57 brands in 22 countries. Refills typically cost less and save up to 70% in solid waste.

Dow has developed a new highly effective herbicide that is non-toxic. It is less risky for people and animals and is applied in ounces rather than pounds per acre. Using biotechnology, Monsanto developed a potato plant that is resistant to insects, so it reduced the need for chemical insecticides. Another herbicide from Monsanto helps restore the natural habitat of wetlands by controlling weeds in a safer way.

Commitment to a Cleaner Environment

It is critical that we approach pollution prevention on a comprehensive scale, including commitment to both programmatic and technological improvements. Increasing efficiency or process yield and reducing waste production has long been a practice of the manufacturing industry. However, only within the last decade have these activities focused more directly on pollution prevention. Substantial efforts are now aimed at improving source reduction as well as tailoring processes to separate, recycle and reuse by-products. All these are proven pollution prevention tools.

References

Abecassis and Jarashow. 1985. *Oil Pollution from Ships.* London: Sweet & Maxwell.

African Convention on Conservation of Nature and Natural Resources, Algiers. 1968. United Nations Treaty Series. Geneva: United Nations.

ASEAN. 1985. *ASEAN Agreement On the Conservation of Nature and Natural Resources.* Kuala Lumpur: ASEAN.

Bamako Convention on the Ban of the Import into Africa and the Control of Transboundary Movement and Management of Hazardous Wastes within Africa. 1991. *Int Legal Mater* 30:775.

Basel Convention on the Control of Transboundary Movement of Hazardous Wastes and their Disposal. 1989.

Berne Convention on the Conservation of European Wildlife and Natural Habitats. 1979. European Treaty Series (ETS) No. 104.

Birnie, PW. 1985. *The International Regulation of Whaling.* 2 vols. New York: Oceana.

Birnie, P and A Boyle. 1992. *International Law and the Environment.* Oxford: OUP.

Bonn Agreement for Co-operation in Dealing with Pollution of the North Sea by Oil and Other Harmful Substances: Amending Decision. 1989. In Freestone and IJlstra 1991.

Bonn Convention on the Conservation of Migratory Species of Wild Animals, 1979. 1980. *Int Legal Mater* 19:15.

Boyle, AE. 1993. The convention on biodiversity. In *The Environment After Rio,* edited by L Campiglio, L Pineschi, and C Siniscalco. Dordrecht: Martinus Nijhoff.

Bucharest Convention on the Protection of the Black Sea. 1992. *Int J Marine Coast Law* 9:76-100.

Burhenne, W. 1974a. Convention on Conservation of Nature in the South Pacific, Apia Convention. In *International Environmental Law: Multilateral Treaties.* Berlin: E Schmidt.

—. 1974b. *International Environmental Law: Multilateral Treaties.* Berlin: E Schmidt.

—. 1994c. *Selected Multilateral Treaties in the Field of the Environment.* Berlin: E Schmit.

Canadian Standards Association. 1993. *Life-Cycle Assessment Guideline.* Rexdale, Ontario: CSA.

Canberra Convention on the Conservation of Antarctic Marine Living Resources. 1980. *Int Legal Mater* 19:837.

Churchill, R and D Freestone. 1991. *International Law and Global Climate Change.* London: Graham & Trotman.

Code permanent environment et nuisances. N.d. Vol. 1 & 2. Montrouge, France: Editions législatives et administratives.

Convention for Co-operation in the Protection and Development of the Marine and Coastal Environment of the West and Central African Region, 23 March, Abidjan. 1981. *Int Legal Mater* 20:746.

Convention for the Protection of Birds Useful to Agriculture. 1902. British and Foreign State Papers (BFSP), No. 969.

Convention for the Protection of the Mediterranean Sea against Pollution, Barcelona, 16 February. 1976. *Int Legal Mater* 15:290.

Convention for the Conservation and Management of the Vicuna. 1979. In *International Environmental Law: Multilateral Treaties,* edited by W Burhenne. Berlin: E Schmidt.

Convention for the Protection and Development of the Marine Environment of the Wider Caribbean Region, 24 March, Cartagena des Indias. 1983. *Int Legal Mater* 22:221.

Convention for the Protection, Management and Development of the Marine and Coastal Environment of the East African Region, 21 June, Nairobi. 1985. In Sand 1987.

Convention for the Protection of the Marine Environment and Coastal Areas of the South-East Pacific, 12 November, Lima. In Sand 1987.

Convention for the Protection of the Natural Resources and Environment of the South Pacific Region, 24 November 1986, Noumea. *Int Legal Mater* 26:38.

Convention on Biological Diversity. 1992. *Int Legal Mater* 31:818.

Convention on Conservation of Nature in the South Pacific. 1976. In *International Environmental Law: Multilateral Treaties,* edited by W Burhenne. Berlin: E. Schmidt.

Convention on Long-Range Transboundary Air Pollution. 1979. *Int Legal Mater* 18:1442.

Convention on the Transboundary Effects of Industrial Accidents. 1992. *Int Legal Mater* 31:1330.

Convention on Third Party Liability in the Field of Nuclear Energy. 1961. *Am J Int Law* 55:1082.

Ehlers, P. 1993. Helsinki Convention on the Protection and Use of the Baltic Sea Area. *Int J Marine Coast Law* 8:191-276.

Espoo Convention on Environmental Impact Assessment in a Transboundary Context. 1991. *Int Legal Mater* 30:802.

Framework Convention on Climate Change. 1992. *Int Legal Mater* 31:848.

Freestone, D. 1994. The Road from Rio: International Environmental Law after the Earth Summit. *J Environ Law* 6:193-218.

Freestone, D. and E Hey (eds.). 1996. *The Precautionary Principle in International Law: The Challenge of Implementation.* The Hague: Kluwer Law International.

Freestone, D and T IJlstra. 1991. *The North Sea: Basic Legal Documents On Regional Environmental Co-operation.* Dordrecht: Graham & Trotman.

Geneva Protocol Concerning the Control of Emissions of Volatile Organic Compounds or their Transboundary Fluxes. 1991. *Int Legal Mater* 31:568.

Geneva Protocol on Long-term Financing of the Co-operative Programme for Monitoring and Evaluation of the Long-Range Transmission of Air Pollution in Europe. 1984. *Int Legal Mater* 24:484.

Heijungs, R. 1992. *Environmental Life Cycle Assessment of Products- National Reuse of Waste Research Programme.* Novem & Rivm.

Helsinki Convention on the Protection of the Marine Environment of the Baltic Sea Area. 1974. *Int Legal Mater* 13:546.

Helsinki Convention on the Protection and Use of Transboundary Watercourses and International Lakes. 1992. *Int Legal Mater* 31:1312.

Helsinki Protocol on the Reduction of Sulphur Emissions. 1988. *Int Legal Mater* 27:64.

Hey, E, T IJlstra, and A Nollkaemper. 1993. *Int J Marine Coast Law* 8:76.

Hildebrandt, E and E Schmidt. 1994. *Industrial Relations and Environmental Protection in Europe.* Dublin: European Foundation for the Improvement of Living and Working Conditions.

Hohmann, H. 1992. *Basic Documents of International Environmental Law.* London: Graham & Trotman.

International Chambers of Commerce. 1989. *Environmental Auditing.* Paris: ICC.

International Convention for the Prevention of Pollution of the Sea by Oil. 1954. United Nations Treaties Series (UNTS), No. 327. Geneva: United Nations.

International Convention for the Prevention of Pollution from Ships (1973), as amended in 1978. *Int Legal Mater* 17:546.

International Convention on Civil Liability for Oil Pollution Damage. 1969. *Int Legal Mater* 16:617.

International Convention on the Establishment of an International Fund for Compensation for Oil Pollution Damage, Brussels, 1971. Amended 1976, Protocols in 1984 and 1992. 1972. *Int Legal Mater* 11:284.

International Convention on Oil Pollution Preparedness, Response and Cooperation. 1991. *Int Legal Mater* 30:735.

International Convention relating to Intervention on the High Seas in cases of Oil Pollution Damage, 1969. 1970. *Int Legal Mater* 9:25.

International Labour Organization (ILO). 1990. *Environment and the World of Work.* Report of the Director-General to the International Labour Conference, 77th Session. Geneva: ILO.

54. ENVIRONMENTAL POLICY

IUCN and Government of the Republic of Botswana. N.d. *Environmental Impact Assessment: Manual for In-Service Training*. Gland, Switzerland: IUCN.

Keoleian, GA and D Menerey. 1993. *Life Cycle Design Guidance Manual*. Washington, DC: Environmental Protection Agency.

Kiss, A and D Shelton. 1991. *International Environmental Law*. New York: Transnational.

Kummer, K. 1992. The Basel Convention. *Int Comp Law Q* 41:530.

Kuwait Regional Convention for Co-operation on the Protection of the Marine Environment from Pollution, 24 April, Kuwait. 1978. *Int Legal Mater* 17:511.

Lac Lanoux Arbitration. 1957. In *24 International Law Reports*, 101.

Lloyd, GER. 1983. *Hippocratic Writings*. London: Penguin Books.

London Convention on the Prevention of Marine Pollution by Dumping of Wastes and Other Matter. 1972. *Int Legal Mater* 11:1294.

Lyster, S. 1985. *International Wildlife Law*. Cambridge: Grotius.

Ministerial Declaration on the Protection of the Black Sea. 1993. *Int J Marine Coast Law* 9:72-75.

Molitor, MR. 1991. *International Environmental Law: Primary Materials*. Deventer: Kluwer Law & Taxation.

Montego Bay Convention on the Law of the Sea (LOSC). 1982. *Int Legal Mater* 21:1261.

Nordic Convention on the Protection of the Environment. 1974. *Int Legal Mater* 13:511.

Odessa Ministerial Declaration on the Protection of the Black Sea, 1993. 1994. *Int J Marine Coast Law* 9:72-75.

QJ L103/1, 24 April 1979, and QJ L206/7, 22 July 1992. 1991. In Freestone and IJlstra 1991.

Oslo Convention for the Prevention of Marine Pollution by Dumping from Ships and Aircraft. 1972. In Freestone and IJlstra 1991.

Paris Convention for the Prevention of Marine Pollution from Land Based Sources. 1974. *Int Legal Mater* 13:352.

Paris Convention for the Protection of the Marine Environment of the North East Atlantic. 1993. *Int J Marine Coast Law* 8:1-76.

Paris Memorandum of Understanding on Port State Control in Implementing Agreements on Maritime Safety and Protection of the Marine Environment. 1982. *Int Legal Mater* 21:1.

Protocol to the Antarctic Treaty on Environmental Protection. 1991. *Int Legal Mater* 30:1461.

Ramsar Convention on Wetlands of International Importance, especially as Waterfowl Habitat. 1971. *Int Legal Mater* 11:963.

Regional Convention for the Conservation of the Red Sea and Gulf of Aden Environment, 14 February, Jeddah. 1982. In Sand 1987.

Rio Declaration on Environment and Development. 1992. *Int Legal Mater* 31:814.

Robinson, NA (ed.). 1993. *Agenda 21: Earths's Action Plan*. New York: Oceana.

Ryding, S-O. 1994. *International Experiences of Environmentally-Sound Product Development Based On Life-Cycle Assessments*. Stockholm: Swedish Waste Research Council.

—. 1996. *Sustainable Product Development*. Geneva: IOS.

Sand, PH (ed.). 1987. *Marine Environmental Law in the United Nations Environment Programme: An Emergent Eco-Regime*. London: Tycooly.

—. 1992. *The Effectiveness of International Environmental Agreements: A Survey of Existing Legal Instruments*. Cambridge: Grotius.

Society of Environmental Toxicology and Chemistry (SETAC). 1993. *Guidelines for Life-Cycle Assessment: A "Code of Practice"*. Boca Raton:Lewis.

Sofia Protocol Concerning the Control of Emissions of Nitrogen Oxides or their Transboundary Fluxes. 1988. *Int Legal Mater* 27:698.

Statute of the International Court of Justice. 1945.

Trail Smelter Arbitration. 1939. *Am J Int Law* 33:182.

—. 1941. *Am J Int Law* 35:684.

Treaty Banning Nuclear Weapon Tests in the Atmosphere, in Outer Space and Under Water. 1963. *Am J Int Law* 57:1026.

UNESCO Convention Concerning the Protection of the World Cultural and Natural Heritage, 1972. *Int Legal Mater* 11:1358.

UNGA Resolution 2997, XXVII. 15 December 1972.

United Nations. N.d. *Declaration of the United Nations Conference On the Human Environment (Stockholm)*. Geneva: United Nations.

Vienna Convention on Civil Liability for Nuclear Damage. 1963. *Int Legal Mater* 2:727.

Vienna Convention on the Physical Protection of Nuclear Material. 1980. *Int Legal Mater* 18:1419.

Vienna Convention on Assistance in the Case of a Nuclear Accident or Radiological Emergency. 1986a. *Int Legal Mater* 25:1377.

Vienna Convention on the Early Notification of a Nuclear Accident. 1986b. *Int Legal Mater* 25:1370.

Vigon, BW et al. 1992. *Life-Cycle Assessment: Inventory Guidelines and Principles*. Boca Raton: Lewis.

Washington Convention for the Regulation of Whaling. 1946. League of Nations Treaty Series (LNTS), No. 155.

Washington Convention on International Trade in Endangered Species (CITES). 1973. *Int Legal Mater* 12:1085.

Wellington Convention on the Regulation of Antarctic Mineral Resource Activities, 1988. *Int Legal Mater* 27:868.

Other relevant readings

Bennett, D. 1991. Pesticide reduction, a case study from Canada. *New Solutions* (Fall).

Blanpain, R. 1991. *International Encyclopedia of Laws: Environmental Law*. Vol. 1-3. Deventer: Kluwer Law & Taxation.

Bonyhady, T. 1992. *Environmental Protection and Legal Change*. Annandale, Australia: Federation Press.

Canadian Labour Congress. 1992. *A Critique of the Ontario Hazard Assessment System*. Ottawa: Canadian Labour Congress.

de Casadevante Romani, CF. 1992. *La Proteccion del Medio Ambiente en Derecho Internacional, Derecho Comunitario Europeo y Derecho Español*. Vitoria-Gasteiz: Publicaciones del Gobierno Vasco.

Center for Chemical Process Safety of the American Institute of Chemical Engineers (AICE). 1989. *Guidelines for Chemical Process Quantitative Risk Analysis*. New York : AICE.

Chance, C. 1992. *European Environmental Law Guide*. London: Environment Group.

Commoner, B. 1990. *Making Peace With the Planet*. New York: Pantheon Books.

Covello, V et al. 1989. *Effective Risk Communication*. New York: Plenum Press.

Environment Canada. 1993. *Pollution Prevention Legislative Task Force, Final Report*. Ottawa: Environment Canada.

European Commission. 1993. *Compendium of EC Environmental Law*. Luxembourg: European Commission Office of Official Publications.

Foran, J and B Glenn. 1993. *Criteria to Identify Chemical Candidates for Sunsetting in the Great Lakes Basin*. Washington, DC: George Washington Univ.

Geiser, K. 1990. Toxics use reduction and pollution prevention. *New Solutions* (Spring).

Great Lakes Scientific Advisory Board. 1991. Report to the International Joint Commission. Revised edition, December 1991.

Hawke, N. 1995. *Environmental Health Law*. London: Sweet & Maxwell.

Kiss, AC. 1983. *Selected Multilateral Treaties in the Field of the Environment*. Nairobi: United Nations Environment Programme (UNEP).

LeBlansch, K, E Hildebrandt, and D Pearson. 1992. *Industrial Relations and the Environment: Case Studies*. Dublin: European Foundation for the Improvement of Living and Working Conditions.

Marco Berg et al. 1994. *Was ist ein Schaden?* Zürich: Verlag der Fachvereine.

OECD. 1991. *Climate Change: Evaluating the Socio-Economic Impact*. Paris: OECD.

Ontario Ministry of the Environment (OME). 1990. *Scoring System for Assessing Environmental Contaminants*. Toronto: OME.

—. 1993. *Candidate Substances List for Bans and Phase-Outs*. Toronto: OME.

Plater, ZJB, RH Abrams, and W Goldfarb. 1992. *Environmental Law and Policy: Nature, Law and Society*. St. Paul, Minn: West Publishing.

Rossi, M, M Ellenbecker, and K Geiser. 1991. Techniques in toxics use reduction: From concept to action. *New Solutions* (Fall).

Rummel-Bulska, I and S Osafo. 1991. *Selected Multilateral Treaties in the Field of the Environment*. Cambridge: Grotius.

Ruster, B and B Simma. 1975. *International Protection of the Environment: Treaties and Related Documents*. Dobbs Ferry, NY: Oceana.

Schrecker, T. 1993. *Sustainable Development: Getting There From Here, A Handbook for Union Environment Committees and Joint Labour-Management Environment Committees*. Ottawa: CLC/NRTEE.

Storm, P-C. 1992. *Einführung in das Umweltrecht*. Berlin: E Schmidt.

United Nations. 1995. *World Summit on Social Development: Action Programme*. Copenhagen: United Nations.

US Office of Technology Assessment. 1986. *Serious Reduction of Hazardous Waste for Pollution Prevention and Industrial Efficiency*. Washington, DC: US Office of Technology Assessment.

Viscusi, WK. 1987. *Learning About Risk*. Cambridge, Mass.: Harvard Univ. Press.

World Bank. N.d. *Environmental Assessment Sourcebook*. Technical Paper, No. 140. Washington,DC: World Bank.

World Commission on Environment and Development (WCED). 1987. *Our Common Future*. Oxford: OUP.

ENVIRONMENTAL POLLUTION CONTROL

55

Chapter Editors
Jerry Spiegel and Lucien Y. Maystre

Contents

55. ENVIRONMENTAL POLLUTION CONTROL

ENVIRONMENTAL POLLUTION CONTROL AND PREVENTION

Jerry Spiegel and Lucien Y. Maystre

Over the course of the twentieth century, growing recognition of the environmental and public health impacts associated with anthropogenic activities (discussed in the chapter *Environmental Health Hazards*) has prompted the development and application of methods and technologies to reduce the effects of pollution. In this context, governments have adopted regulatory and other policy measures (discussed in the chapter *Environmental Policy*) to minimize negative effects and ensure that environmental quality standards are achieved.

The objective of this chapter is to provide an orientation to the methods that are applied to control and prevent environmental pollution. The basic principles followed for eliminating negative impacts on the quality of water, air or land will be introduced; the shifting emphasis from control to prevention will be considered; and the limitations of building solutions for individual environmental media will be examined. It is not enough, for example, to protect air by removing trace metals from a flue gas only to transfer these contaminants to land through improper solid waste management practices. Integrated multimedia solutions are required.

The Pollution Control Approach

The environmental consequences of rapid industrialization have resulted in countless incidents of land, air and water resources sites being contaminated with toxic materials and other pollutants, threatening humans and ecosystems with serious health risks. More extensive and intensive use of materials and energy has created cumulative pressures on the quality of local, regional and global ecosystems.

Before there was a concerted effort to restrict the impact of pollution, environmental management extended little beyond laissez-faire tolerance, tempered by disposal of wastes to avoid disruptive local nuisance conceived of in a short-term perspective. The need for remediation was recognized, by exception, in instances where damage was determined to be unacceptable. As the pace of industrial activity intensified and the understanding of cumulative effects grew, a *pollution control* paradigm became the dominant approach to environmental management.

Two specific concepts served as the basis for the control approach:

- the *assimilative capacity* concept, which asserts the existence of a specified level of emissions into the environment which does not lead to unacceptable environmental or human health effects
- the *principle of control* concept, which assumes that environmental damage can be avoided by controlling the manner, time and rate at which pollutants enter the environment

Under the pollution control approach, attempts to protect the environment have especially relied on isolating contaminants from the environment and using end-of-pipe filters and scrubbers. These solutions have tended to focus on media-specific environmental quality objectives or emission limits, and have been primarily directed at point source discharges into specific environmental media (air, water, soil).

Applying Pollution Control Technologies

Application of pollution control methods has demonstrated considerable effectiveness in controlling pollution problems—particularly those of a local character. Application of appropriate technologies is based on a systematic analysis of the source and nature of the emission or discharge in question, of its interaction with the ecosystem and the ambient pollution problem to be addressed, and the development of appropriate technologies to mitigate and monitor pollution impacts.

In their article on air pollution control, Dietrich Schwela and Berenice Goelzer explain the importance and implications of taking a comprehensive approach to assessment and control of point sources and non-point sources of air pollution. They also highlight the challenges—and opportunities—that are being addressed in countries that are undergoing rapid industrialization without having had a strong pollution control component accompanying earlier development.

Marion Wichman-Fiebig explains the methods that are applied to model air pollutant dispersion to determine and characterize the nature of pollution problems. This forms the basis for understanding the controls that are to be put into effect and for evaluating their effectiveness. As the understanding of potential impacts has deepened, appreciation of effects has expanded from the local to the regional to the global scale.

Hans-Ulrich Pfeffer and Peter Bruckmann provide an introduction to the equipment and methods that are used to monitor air quality so that potential pollution problems can be assessed and the effectiveness of control and prevention interventions can be evaluated.

John Elias provides an overview of the types of air pollution controls that can be applied and the issues that must be addressed in selecting appropriate pollution control management options.

The challenge of water pollution control is addressed by Herbert Preul in an article which explains the basis whereby the earth's natural waters may become polluted from point, non-point and intermittent sources; the basis for regulating water pollution; and the different criteria that can be applied in determining control programmes. Preul explains the manner in which discharges are received in water bodies, and may be analysed and evaluated to assess and manage risks. Finally, an overview is provided of the techniques that are applied for large-scale wastewater treatment and water pollution control.

A case study provides a vivid example of how wastewater can be reused—a topic of considerable significance in the search for ways that environmental resources can be used effectively, especially in circumstances of scarcity. Alexander Donagi provides a summary of the approach that has been pursued for the treatment and groundwater recharge of municipal wastewater for a population of 1.5 million in Israel.

Comprehensive Waste Management

Under the pollution control perspective, waste is regarded as an undesirable by-product of the production process which is to be contained so as to ensure that soil, water and air resources are not contaminated beyond levels deemed to be acceptable. Lucien Maystre provides an overview of the issues that must be addressed in managing waste, providing a conceptual link to the increasingly important roles of recycling and pollution prevention.

In response to extensive evidence of the serious contamination associated with unrestricted management of waste, governments have established standards for acceptable practices for collection, handling and disposal to ensure environmental protection. Particular attention has been paid to the criteria for environmentally safe disposal through sanitary landfills, incineration and hazardous-waste treatment.

To avoid the potential environmental burden and costs associated with the disposal of waste and promote a more thorough stewardship of scarce resources, waste minimization and recycling have received growing attention. Niels Hahn and Poul Lauridsen provide a summary of the issues that are addressed in pursuing recycling as a preferred waste management strategy, and consider the potential worker exposure implications of this.

Shifting Emphasis to Pollution Prevention

End-of-pipe abatement risks transferring pollution from one medium to another, where it may either cause equally serious environmental problems, or even end up as an indirect source of pollution to the same medium. While not as expensive as remediation, end-of-pipe abatement can contribute significantly to the costs of production processes without contributing any value. It also typically is associated with regulatory regimes which add other sets of costs associated with enforcing compliance.

While the pollution control approach has achieved considerable success in producing short-term improvements for local pollution problems, it has been less effective in addressing cumulative problems that are increasingly recognized on regional (e.g., acid rain) or global (e.g., ozone depletion) levels.

The aim of a health-oriented environmental pollution control programme is to promote a better quality of life by reducing pollution to the lowest level possible. Environmental pollution control programmes and policies, whose implications and priorities vary from country to country, cover all aspects of pollution (air, water, land and so on) and involve coordination among areas such as industrial development, city planning, water resources development and transportation policies.

Thomas Tseng, Victor Shantora and Ian Smith provide a case study example of the multimedia impact that pollution has had on a vulnerable ecosystem subjected to many stresses—the North American Great Lakes. The limited effectiveness of the pollution control model in dealing with persistent toxins that dissipate through the environment is particularly examined. By focusing on the approach being pursued in one country and the implications that this has for international action, the implications for actions that address prevention as well as control are illustrated.

As environmental pollution control technologies have become more sophisticated and more expensive, there has been a growing interest in ways to incorporate prevention in the design of industrial processes—with the objective of eliminating harmful environmental effects while promoting the competitiveness of industries. Among the benefits of pollution prevention approaches, clean technologies and toxic use reduction is the potential for eliminating worker exposure to health risks.

David Bennett provides an overview of why pollution prevention is emerging as a preferred strategy and how it relates to other environmental management methods. This approach is central to implementing the shift to sustainable development which has been widely endorsed since the release of the United Nations Commission on Trade and Development in 1987 and reiterated at the Rio United Nations Conference on Environment and Development (UNCED) Conference in 1992.

The pollution prevention approach focuses directly on the use of processes, practices, materials and energy that avoid or minimize the creation of pollutants and wastes at source, and not on "add-on" abatement measures. While corporate commitment plays a critical role in the decision to pursue pollution prevention (see Bringer and Zoesel in *Environmental policy*), Bennett draws attention to the societal benefits in reducing risks to ecosystem and human health—and the health of workers in particular. He identifies principles that can be usefully applied in assessing opportunities for pursuing this approach.

AIR POLLUTION MANAGEMENT

Dietrich Schwela and Berenice Goelzer

Air pollution management aims at the elimination, or reduction to acceptable levels, of airborne gaseous pollutants, suspended particulate matter and physical and, to a certain extent, biological agents whose presence in the atmosphere can cause adverse effects on human health (e.g., irritation, increase of incidence or prevalence of respiratory diseases, morbidity, cancer, excess mortality) or welfare (e.g., sensory effects, reduction of visibility), deleterious effects on animal or plant life, damage to materials of economic value to society and damage to the environment (e.g., climatic modifications). The serious hazards associated with radioactive pollutants, as well as the special procedures required for their control and disposal, also deserve careful attention.

The importance of efficient management of outdoor and indoor air pollution cannot be overemphasized. Unless there is adequate control, the multiplication of pollution sources in the modern world may lead to irreparable damage to the environment and mankind.

The objective of this article is to give a general overview of the possible approaches to the management of ambient air pollution from motor vehicle and industrial sources. However, it is to be emphasized from the very beginning that indoor air pollution (in particular, in developing countries) might play an even larger role than outdoor air pollution due to the observation that indoor air pollutant concentrations are often substantially higher than outdoor concentrations.

Beyond considerations of emissions from fixed or mobile sources, air pollution management involves consideration of additional factors (such as topography and meteorology, and community and government participation, among many others) all of which must be integrated into a comprehensive programme. For example, meteorological conditions can greatly affect the ground-level concentrations resulting from the same pollutant emission. Air pollution sources may be scattered over a community or a region and their effects may be felt by, or their control may involve, more than one administration. Furthermore, air pollution does not respect any boundaries, and emissions from one region may induce effects in another region by long-distance transport.

Air pollution management, therefore, requires a multidisciplinary approach as well as a joint effort by private and governmental entities.

Sources of Air Pollution

The sources of man-made air pollution (or emission sources) are of basically two types:

- *stationary,* which can be subdivided into area sources such as agricultural production, mining and quarrying, industrial, point and area sources such as manufacturing of chemicals, non-metallic mineral products, basic metal industries, power generation and community sources (e.g., heating of homes and buildings, municipal waste and sewage sludge incinerators, fireplaces, cooking facilities, laundry services and cleaning plants)
- *mobile,* comprising any form of combustion-engine vehicles (e.g., light-duty gasoline powered cars, light- and heavy-duty diesel powered vehicles, motorcycles, aircraft, including line sources with emissions of gases and particulate matter from vehicle traffic).

In addition, there are also natural sources of pollution (e.g., eroded areas, volcanoes, certain plants which release great amounts of pollen, sources of bacteria, spores and viruses). Natural sources are not discussed in this article.

55. ENVIRONMENTAL POLLUTION CONTROL

Types of Air Pollutants

Air pollutants are usually classified into suspended particulate matter (dusts, fumes, mists, smokes), gaseous pollutants (gases and vapours) and odours. Some examples of usual pollutants are presented below:

Suspended particulate matter (SPM, PM-10) includes diesel exhaust, coal fly-ash, mineral dusts (e.g., coal, asbestos, limestone, cement), metal dusts and fumes (e.g., zinc, copper, iron, lead) and acid mists (e.g., sulphuric acid), fluorides, paint pigments, pesticide mists, carbon black and oil smoke. Suspended particulate pollutants, besides their effects of provoking respiratory diseases, cancers, corrosion, destruction of plant life and so on, can also constitute a nuisance (e.g., accumulation of dirt), interfere with sunlight (e.g., formation of smog and haze due to light scattering) and act as catalytic surfaces for reaction of adsorbed chemicals.

Gaseous pollutants include sulphur compounds (e.g., sulphur dioxide (SO_2) and sulphur trioxide (SO_3)), carbon monoxide, nitrogen compounds (e.g., nitric oxide (NO), nitrogen dioxide (NO_2), ammonia), organic compounds (e.g., hydrocarbons (HC), volatile organic compounds (VOC), polycyclic aromatic hydrocarbons (PAH), aldehydes), halogen compounds and halogen derivatives (e.g., HF and HCl), hydrogen sulphide, carbon disulphide and mercaptans (odours).

Secondary pollutants may be formed by thermal, chemical or photochemical reactions. For example, by thermal action sulphur dioxide can oxidize to sulphur trioxide which, dissolved in water, gives rise to the formation of sulphuric acid mist (catalysed by manganese and iron oxides). Photochemical reactions between nitrogen oxides and reactive hydrocarbons can produce ozone (O_3), formaldehyde and peroxyacetyl nitrate (PAN); reactions between HCl and formaldehyde can form bis-chloromethyl ether.

While some *odours* are known to be caused by specific chemical agents such as hydrogen sulphide (H_2S), carbon disulphide (CS_2) and mercaptans (R-SH or R1-S-R2) others are difficult to define chemically.

Examples of the main pollutants associated with some industrial air pollution sources are presented in table 55.1 (Economopoulos 1993).

Clean Air Implementation Plans

Air quality management aims at the preservation of environmental quality by prescribing the tolerated degree of pollution, leaving it to the local authorities and polluters to devise and implement actions to ensure that this degree of pollution will not be exceeded. An example of legislation within this approach is the adoption of ambient air quality standards based, very often, on air quality guidelines (WHO 1987) for different pollutants; these are accepted maximum levels of pollutants (or indicators) in the target area (e.g., at ground level at a specified point in a community) and can be either primary or secondary standards. Primary standards (WHO 1980) are the maximum levels consistent with an adequate safety margin and with the preservation of public health, and must be complied with within a specific time limit; secondary standards are those judged to be necessary for protection against known or anticipated adverse effects other than health hazards (mainly on vegetation) and must be complied "within a reasonable time". Air quality standards are short-, medium- or long-term values valid for 24 hours per day, 7 days per week, and for monthly, seasonal or annual exposure of all living subjects (including sensitive subgroups such as children, the elderly and the sick) as well as non-living objects; this is in contrast to maximum permissible levels for occupational exposure, which are for a partial weekly exposure (e.g., 8 hours per day, 5 days per week) of adult and supposedly healthy workers.

Table 55.1 • Common atmospheric pollutants and their sources.

Category	Source	Emitted pollutants
Agriculture	Open burning	SPM, CO, VOC
Mining and quarrying	Coal mining	SPM, SO_2, NO_x, VOC
	Crude petroleum and natural gas production	SO_2
	Non-ferrous ore mining	SPM, Pb
	Stone quarrying	SPM
Manufacturing	Food, beverages and tobacco	SPM, CO, VOC, H_2S
	Textiles and leather industries	SPM, VOC
	Wood products	SPM, VOC
	Paper products, printing	SPM, SO_2, CO, VOC, H_2S, R-SH
Manufacture of chemicals	Phthalic anhydride	SPM, SO_2, CO, VOC
	Chlor-alkali	Cl_2
	Hydrochloric acid	HCl
	Hydrofluoric acid	HF, SiF_4
	Sulphuric acid	SO_2, SO_3
	Nitric acid	NO_x
	Phosphoric acid	SPM, F_2
	Lead oxide and pigments	SPM, Pb
	Ammonia	SPM, SO_2, NO_x, CO, VOC, NH_3
	Sodium carbonate	SPM, NH_3
	Calcium carbide	SPM
	Adipic acid	SPM, NO_x, CO, VOC
	Alkyl lead	Pb
	Maleic anhydride and terephthalic acid	CO, VOC
	Fertilizer and pesticide production	SPM, NH_3
	Ammonium nitrate	SPM, NH_3, HNO_3
	Ammonium sulphate	VOC
	Synthetic resins, plastic materials, fibres	SPM, VOC, H_2S, CS_2
	Paints, varnishes, lacquers	SPM, VOC
	Soap	SPM
	Carbon black and printing ink	SPM, SO_2, NO_x, CO, VOC, H_2S
	Trinitrotoluene	SPM, SO_2, NO_x, SO_3, HNO_3
Petroleum refineries	Miscellaneous products of petroleum and coal	SPM, SO_2, NO_x, CO, VOC
Non-metallic mineral products manufacture	Glass products	SPM, SO_2, NO_x, CO, VOC, F
	Structural clay products	SPM, SO_2, NO_x, CO, VOC, F_2
	Cement, lime and plaster	SPM, SO_2, NO_x, CO
Basic metal industries	Iron and steel	SPM, SO_2, NO_x, CO, VOC, Pb
	Non-ferrous industries	SPM, SO_2, F, Pb
Power generation	Electricity, gas and steam	SPM, SO_2, NO_x, CO, VOC, SO_3, Pb
Wholesale and retail trade	Fuel storage, filling operations	VOC
Transport		SPM, SO_2, NO_x, CO, VOC, Pb
Community services	Municipal incinerators	SPM, SO_2, NO_x, CO, VOC, Pb

Source: Economopoulos 1993.

Typical measures in air quality management are control measures at the source, for example, enforcement of the use of catalytic converters in vehicles or of emission standards in incinerators, land-use planning and shut-down of factories or reduction of traffic during unfavourable weather conditions. The best air quality management stresses that the air pollutant emissions should be kept to a minimum; this is basically defined through emission standards for single sources of air pollution and could be achieved for industrial sources, for example, through closed systems and high-efficiency collectors. An emission standard is a limit on the amount or concentration of a pollutant emitted from a source. This type of legislation requires a decision, for each industry, on the best means of controlling its emissions (i.e., fixing emission standards).

The basic aim of air pollution management is to derive a clean air implementation plan (or air pollution abatement plan) (Schwela and Köth-Jahr 1994) which consists of the following elements:

- description of area with respect to topography, meteorology and socioeconomy
- emissions inventory
- comparison with emission standards
- air pollutant concentrations inventory
- simulated air pollutant concentrations
- comparison with air quality standards
- inventory of effects on public health and the environment
- causal analysis
- control measures
- cost of control measures
- cost of public health and environmental effects
- cost-benefit analysis (costs of control vs. costs of efforts)
- transportation and land-use planning
- enforcement plan; resource commitment
- projections for the future on population, traffic, industries and fuel consumption
- strategies for follow-up.

Some of these issues will be described below.

Emissions Inventory; Comparison with Emission Standards

The emissions inventory is a most complete listing of sources in a given area and of their individual emissions, estimated as accurately as possible from all emitting point, line and area (diffuse) sources. When these emissions are compared with emission standards set for a particular source, first hints on possible control measures are given if emission standards are not complied with. The emissions inventory also serves to assess a priority list of important sources according to the amount of pollutants emitted, and indicates the relative influence of different sources—for example, traffic as compared to industrial or residential sources. The emissions inventory also allows an estimate of air pollutant concentrations for those pollutants for which ambient concentration measurements are difficult or too expensive to perform.

Air Pollutant Concentrations Inventory; Comparison with Air Quality Standards

The air pollutant concentrations inventory summarizes the results of the monitoring of ambient air pollutants in terms of annual means, percentiles and trends of these quantities. Compounds measured for such an inventory include the following:

- sulphur dioxide
- nitrogen oxides
- suspended particulate matter
- carbon monoxide
- ozone
- heavy metals (Pb, Cd, Ni, Cu, Fe, As, Be)
- polycyclic aromatic hydrocarbons: benzo[a]pyrene, benzo[e]pyrene, benzo[a]anthracene, dibenzo[a,h]anthracene, benzo[ghi]perylene, coronen
- volatile organic compounds: n-hexane, benzene, 3-methylhexane, n-heptane, toluene, octane, ethyl-benzene xylene (o-,m-,p-), n-nonane, isopropylbenzene, propylbenezene, n-2-/3-/4-ethyltoluene, 1,2,4-/1,3,5-trimethylbenzene, trichloromethane, 1,1,1 trichloroethane, tetrachloromethane, tri-/tetrachloroethene.

Comparison of air pollutant concentrations with air quality standards or guidelines, if they exist, indicates problem areas for which a causal analysis has to be performed in order to find out which sources are responsible for the non-compliance. Dispersion modelling has to be used in performing this causal analysis (see "Air pollution: Modelling of air pollutant dispersion"). Devices and procedures used in today's ambient air pollution monitoring are described in "Air quality monitoring".

Simulated Air Pollutant Concentrations; Comparison with Air Quality Standards

Starting from the emissions inventory, with its thousands of compounds which cannot all be monitored in the ambient air for economy reasons, use of dispersion modelling can help to estimate the concentrations of more "exotic" compounds. Using appropriate meteorology parameters in a suitable dispersion model, annual averages and percentiles can be estimated and compared to air quality standards or guidelines, if they exist.

Inventory of Effects on Public Health and the Environment; Causal Analysis

Another important source of information is the effects inventory (Ministerium für Umwelt 1993), which consists of results of epidemiological studies in the given area and of effects of air pollution observed in biological and material receptors such as, for example, plants, animals and construction metals and building stones. Observed effects attributed to air pollution have to be causally analysed with respect to the component responsible for a particular effect—for example, increased prevalence of chronic bronchitis in a polluted area. If the compound or compounds have been fixed in a causal analysis (compound-causal analysis), a second analysis has to be performed to find out the responsible sources (source-causal analysis).

Control Measures; Cost of Control Measures

Control measures for industrial facilities include adequate, well-designed, well-installed, efficiently operated and maintained air cleaning devices, also called separators or collectors. A separator or collector can be defined as an "apparatus for separating any one or more of the following from a gaseous medium in which they are suspended or mixed: solid particles (filter and dust separators), liquid particles (filter and droplet separator) and gases (gas purifier)". The basic types of air pollution control equipment (discussed further in "Air pollution control") are the following:

- for particulate matter: inertial separators (e.g., cyclones); fabric filters (baghouses); electrostatic precipitators; wet collectors (scrubbers)
- for gaseous pollutants: wet collectors (scrubbers); adsorption units (e.g., adsorption beds); afterburners, which can be direct-fired (thermal incineration) or catalytic (catalytic combustion).

Wet collectors (scrubbers) can be used to collect, at the same time, gaseous pollutants and particulate matter. Also, certain types of combustion devices can burn combustible gases and vapours as well as certain combustible aerosols. Depending on the type of effluent, one or a combination of more than one collector can be used.

The control of odours that are chemically identifiable relies on the control of the chemical agent(s) from which they emanate (e.g., by absorption, by incineration). However, when an odour is not defined chemically or the producing agent is found at extremely low levels, other techniques may be used, such as masking (by a stronger, more agreeable and harmless agent) or counteraction (by an additive which counteracts or partially neutralizes the offensive odour).

It should be kept in mind that adequate operation and maintenance are indispensable to ensure the expected efficiency from a collector. This should be ensured at the planning stage, both from the know-how and financial points of view. Energy requirements must not be overlooked. Whenever selecting an air cleaning device, not only the initial cost but also operational and maintenance costs should be considered. Whenever dealing with high-toxicity pollutants, high efficiency should be ensured, as well as special procedures for maintenance and disposal of waste materials.

The fundamental control measures in industrial facilities are the following:

Substitution of materials. Examples: substitution of less toxic solvents for highly toxic ones used in certain industrial processes; use of fuels with lower sulphur content (e.g., washed coal), therefore giving rise to less sulphur compounds and so on.

Modification or change of the industrial process or equipment. Examples: in the steel industry, a change from raw ore to pelleted sintered ore (to reduce the dust released during ore handling); use of closed systems instead of open ones; change of fuel heating systems to steam, hot water or electrical systems; use of catalysers at the exhaust air outlets (combustion processes) and so on.

Modifications in processes, as well as in plant layout, may also facilitate and/or improve the conditions for dispersion and collection of pollutants. For example, a different plant layout may facilitate the installation of a local exhaust system; the performance of a process at a lower rate may allow the use of a certain collector (with volume limitations but otherwise adequate). Process modifications that concentrate different effluent sources are closely related to the volume of effluent handled, and the efficiency of some air-cleaning equipment increases with the concentration of pollutants in the effluent. Both the substitution of materials and the modification of processes may have technical and/or economic limitations, and these should be considered.

Adequate housekeeping and storage. Examples: strict sanitation in food and animal product processing; avoidance of open storage of chemicals (e.g., sulphur piles) or dusty materials (e.g., sand), or, failing this, spraying of the piles of loose particulate with water (if possible) or application of surface coatings (e.g., wetting agents, plastic) to piles of materials likely to give off pollutants.

Adequate disposal of wastes. Examples: avoidance of simply piling up chemical wastes (such as scraps from polymerization reactors), as well as of dumping pollutant materials (solid or liquid) in water streams. The latter practice not only causes water pollution but can also create a secondary source of air pollution, as in the case of liquid wastes from sulphite process pulp mills, which release offensive odorous gaseous pollutants.

Maintenance. Example: well maintained and well-tuned internal combustion engines produce less carbon monoxide and hydrocarbons.

Work practices. Example: taking into account meteorological conditions, particularly winds, when spraying pesticides.

By analogy with adequate practices at the workplace, good practices at the community level can contribute to air pollution control—for example, changes in the use of motor vehicles (more collective transportation, small cars and so on) and control of heating facilities (better insulation of buildings in order to require less heating, better fuels and so on).

Control measures in vehicle emissions are adequate and efficient mandatory inspection and maintenance programmes which are enforced for the existing car fleet, programmes of enforcement of the use of catalytic converters in new cars, aggressive substitution of solar/battery-powered cars for fuel-powered ones, regulation of road traffic, and transportation and land use planning concepts.

Motor vehicle emissions are controlled by controlling emissions per vehicle mile travelled (VMT) and by controlling VMT itself (Walsh 1992). Emissions per VMT can be reduced by controlling vehicle performance—hardware, maintenance—for both new and in-use cars. Fuel composition of leaded gasoline may be controlled by reducing lead or sulphur content, which also has a beneficial effect on decreasing HC emissions from vehicles. Lowering the levels of sulphur in diesel fuel as a means to lower diesel particulate emission has the additional beneficial effect of increasing the potential for catalytic control of diesel particulate and organic HC emissions.

Another important management tool for reducing vehicle evaporative and refuelling emissions is the control of gasoline volatility. Control of fuel volatility can greatly lower vehicle evaporative HC emissions. Use of oxygenated additives in gasoline lowers HC and CO exhaust as long as fuel volatility is not increased.

Reduction of VMT is an additional means of controlling vehicle emissions by control strategies such as

- use of more efficient transportation modes
- increasing the average number of passengers per car
- spreading congested peak traffic loads
- reducing travel demand.

While such approaches promote fuel conservation, they are not yet accepted by the general population, and governments have not seriously tried to implement them.

All these technological and political solutions to the motor vehicle problem except substitution of electrical cars are increasingly offset by growth in the vehicle population. The vehicle problem can be solved only if the growth problem is addressed in an appropriate way.

Cost of Public Health and Environmental Effects; Cost-Benefit Analysis

The estimation of the costs of public health and environmental effects is the most difficult part of a clean air implementation plan, as it is very difficult to estimate the value of lifetime reduction of disabling illnesses, hospital admission rates and hours of work lost. However, this estimation and a comparison with the cost of control measures is absolutely necessary in order to balance the costs of control measures versus the costs of no such measure undertaken, in terms of public health and environmental effects.

Transportation and Land-Use Planning

The pollution problem is intimately connected to land-use and transportation, including issues such as community planning, road design, traffic control and mass transportation; to concerns of demography, topography and economy; and to social concerns (Venzia 1977). In general, the rapidly growing urban aggregations have severe pollution problems due to poor land-use and transportation practices. Transportation planning for air pollution control includes transportation controls, transportation policies, mass transit and highway congestion costs. Transportation controls have an important impact on the general public in terms of equity, repressiveness and social and economic disruption—in particular, direct transportation controls such as motor vehicle constraints, gasoline limitations and motor vehicle emission reductions. Emission reductions due to direct controls can be reliably estimated and verified. Indirect transportation controls such as reduction of vehicle miles travelled by improvement of mass transit systems, traffic flow improvement regulations, regulations on parking lots, road and gasoline taxes, car-use permissions and incentives for voluntary approaches are mostly based on past trial-and-error experience, and include many uncertainties when trying to develop a viable transportation plan.

National action plans incurring indirect transportation controls can affect transportation and land-use planning with regard to highways, parking lots and shopping centres. Long-term planning for the transportation system and the area influenced by it will prevent significant deterioration of air quality and provide for compliance with air quality standards. Mass transit is consistently considered as a potential solution for urban air pollution problems. Selection of a mass transit system to serve an area and different modal splits between highway use and bus or rail service will ultimately alter land-use patterns. There is an optimum split that will minimize air pollution; however, this may not be acceptable when non-environmental factors are considered.

The automobile has been called the greatest generator of economic externalities ever known. Some of these, such as jobs and mobility, are positive, but the negative ones, such as air pollution, accidents resulting in death and injury, property damage, noise, loss of time, and aggravation, lead to the conclusion that transportation is not a decreasing cost industry in urbanized areas. Highway congestion costs are another externality; lost time and congestion costs, however, are difficult to determine. A true evaluation of competing transportation modes, such as mass transportation, cannot be obtained if travel costs for work trips do not include congestion costs.

Land-use planning for air pollution control includes zoning codes and performance standards, land-use controls, housing and land development, and land-use planning policies. Land-use zoning was the initial attempt to accomplish protection of the people, their property and their economic opportunity. However, the ubiquitous nature of air pollutants required more than physical separation of industries and residential areas to protect the individual. For this reason, performance standards based initially on aesthetics or qualitative decisions were introduced into some zoning codes in an attempt to quantify criteria for identifying potential problems.

The limitations of the assimilative capacity of the environment must be identified for long-term land-use planning. Then, land-use controls can be developed that will prorate the capacity equitably among desired local activities. Land-use controls include permit systems for review of new stationary sources, zoning regulation between industrial and residential areas, restriction by easement or purchase of land, receptor location control, emission-density zoning and emission allocation regulations.

Housing policies aimed at making home ownership available to many who could otherwise not afford it (such as tax incentives and mortgage policies) stimulate urban sprawl and indirectly discourage higher-density residential development. These policies have now proven to be environmentally disastrous, as no consideration was given to the simultaneous development of efficient transportation systems to serve the needs of the multitude of new communities being developed. The lesson learnt from this development is that programmes impacting on the environment should be coordinated, and comprehensive planning undertaken at the level where the problem occurs and on a scale large enough to include the entire system.

Land-use planning must be examined at national, provincial or state, regional and local levels to adequately ensure long-term protection of the environment. Governmental programmes usually start with power plant siting, mineral extraction sites, coastal zoning and desert, mountain or other recreational development. As the multiplicity of local governments in a given region cannot adequately deal with regional environmental problems, regional governments or agencies should coordinate land development and density patterns by supervising the spatial arrangement and location of new construction and use, and transportation facilities. Land-use and transportation planning must be interrelated with enforcement of regulations to maintain the desired air quality. Ideally, air pollution control should be planned for by the same regional agency that does land-use planning because of the overlapping externalities associated with both issues.

Enforcement Plan, Resource Commitment

The clean air implementation plan should always contain an enforcement plan which indicates how the control measures can be enforced. This implies also a resource commitment which, according to a polluter pays principle, will state what the polluter has to implement and how the government will help the polluter in fulfilling the commitment.

Projections for the Future

In the sense of a precautionary plan, the clean air implementation plan should also include estimates of the trends in population, traffic, industries and fuel consumption in order to assess responses to future problems. This will avoid future stresses by enforcing measures well in advance of imagined problems.

Strategies for Follow-up

A strategy for follow-up of air quality management consists of plans and policies on how to implement future clean air implementation plans.

Role of Environmental Impact Assessment

Environmental impact assessment (EIA) is the process of providing a detailed statement by the responsible agency on the environmental impact of a proposed action significantly affecting the quality of the human environment (Lee 1993). EIA is an instrument of prevention aiming at consideration of the human environment at an early stage of the development of a programme or project.

EIA is particularly important for countries which develop projects in the framework of economic reorientation and restructuring. EIA has become legislation in many developed countries and is now increasingly applied in developing countries and economies in transition.

EIA is integrative in the sense of comprehensive environmental planning and management considering the interactions between different environmental media. On the other hand, EIA integrates the estimation of environmental consequences into the planning process and thereby becomes an instrument of sustainable development. EIA also combines technical and participative properties as it collects, analyses and applies scientific and technical data with consideration of quality control and quality assurance, and stresses the importance of consultations prior to licensing procedures between environmental agencies and the public which could be affected by particular projects. A clean air implementation plan can be considered as a part of the EIA procedure with reference to the air.

55. ENVIRONMENTAL POLLUTION CONTROL

AIR POLLUTION: MODELLING OF AIR POLLUTANT DISPERSION

Marion Wichmann-Fiebig

The aim of air pollution modelling is the estimation of outdoor pollutant concentrations caused, for instance, by industrial production processes, accidental releases or traffic. Air pollution modelling is used to ascertain the total concentration of a pollutant, as well as to find the cause of extraordinary high levels. For

International Monitoring Programmes

International agencies such as the World Health Organization (WHO), the World Meteorological Organization (WMO) and the United Nations Environment Programme (UNEP) have instituted monitoring and research projects in order to clarify the issues involved in air pollution and to promote measures to prevent further deterioration of public health and environmental and climatic conditions.

The Global Environmental Monitoring System GEMS/Air (WHO/ UNEP 1993) is organized and sponsored by WHO and UNEP and has developed a comprehensive programme for providing the instruments of rational air pollution management (see figure 55.1. The kernel of this programme is a global database of urban air pollutant concentrations of sulphur dioxides, suspended particulate matter, lead, nitrogen oxides, carbon monoxide and ozone. As important as this database, however, is the provision of management tools such as guides for rapid emission inventories, programmes for dispersion modelling, population exposure estimates, control measures, and cost-benefit analysis. In this respect, GEMS/Air provides methodology review handbooks (WHO/UNEP 1994, 1995), conducts global assessments of air quality, facilitates review and validation of assessments, acts as a data/information broker, produces technical documents in support of all aspects of air quality management, facilitates the establishment of monitoring, conducts and widely distributes annual reviews, and establishes or identifies regional collaboration centres and/or experts to coordinate and support activities according to the needs of the regions. (WHO/UNEP 1992, 1993, 1995)

The Global Atmospheric Watch (GAW) programme (Miller and Soudine 1994) provides data and other information on the chemical composition and related physical characteristics of the atmosphere, and their trends, with the objective of understanding the relationship between changing atmospheric composition and changes of global and regional climate, the long-range atmospheric transport and deposition of potentially harmful substances over terrestrial, fresh-water and marine ecosystems, and the natural cycling of chemical elements in the global atmosphere/ocean/biosphere system, and anthropogenic impacts thereon. The GAW programme consists of four activity areas: the Global Ozone Observing System (GO3OS), global monitoring of background atmospheric composition, including the Background Air Pollution Monitoring Network (BAPMoN); dispersion, transport, chemical transformation and deposition of atmospheric pollutants over land and sea on different time and space scales; exchange of pollutants between the atmosphere and other environmental compartments; and integrated monitoring. One of the most important aspects of the GAW is the establishment of Quality Assurance Science Activity Centres to oversee the quality of the data produced under GAW.

projects in the planning stage, the additional contribution to the existing burden can be estimated in advance, and emission conditions may be optimized.

Depending on the air quality standards defined for the pollutant in question, annual mean values or short-time peak concentrations are of interest. Usually concentrations have to be determined where people are active—that is, near the surface at a height of about two metres above the ground.

Parameters Influencing Pollutant Dispersion

Two types of parameters influence pollutant dispersion: source parameters and meteorological parameters. For source parameters, concentrations are proportional to the amount of pollutant which is emitted. If dust is concerned, the particle diameter has to be known to determine sedimentation and deposition of the material (VDI 1992). As surface concentrations are lower with greater stack height, this parameter also has to be known. In addition, concentrations depend on the total amount of the exhaust gas, as well as on its temperature and velocity. If the temperature of the exhaust gas exceeds the temperature of the surrounding air, the gas will be subject to thermal buoyancy. Its exhaust velocity, which can be calculated from the inner stack diameter and the exhaust gas volume, will cause a dynamic momentum buoyancy. Empirical formulae may be used to describe these features (VDI 1985; Venkatram and Wyngaard 1988). It has to be stressed that it is not the mass of the pollutant in question but that of the total gas that is responsible for the thermal and dynamic momentum buoyancy.

Meteorological parameters which influence pollutant dispersion are wind speed and direction, as well as vertical thermal stratification. The pollutant concentration is proportional to the reciprocal of wind speed. This is mainly due to the accelerated transport. Moreover, turbulent mixing increases with growing wind speed. As so-called inversions (i.e., situations where temperature is increasing with height) hinder turbulent mixing, maximum surface concentrations are observed during highly stable stratification. On the contrary, convective situations intensify vertical mixing and therefore show the lowest concentration values.

Air quality standards—for example, annual mean values or 98 percentiles—are usually based on statistics. Hence, time series data for the relevant meteorological parameters are needed. Ideally, statistics should be based on ten years of observation. If only shorter time series are available, it should be ascertained that they are representative for a longer period. This can be done, for example, by analysis of longer time series from other observations sites.

The meteorological time series used also has to be representative of the site considered—that is, it must reflect the local characteristics. This is specially important concerning air quality standards based on peak fractions of the distribution, like 98 percentiles. If no such time series is at hand, a meteorological flow model may be used to calculate one from other data, as will be described below.

Concepts of Air Pollution Modelling

As mentioned above, dispersion of pollutants is dependent on emission conditions, transport and turbulent mixing. Using the full equation which describes these features is called Eulerian dispersion modelling (Pielke 1984). By this approach, gains and losses of the pollutant in question have to be determined at every point on an imaginary spatial grid and in distinct time steps. As this method is very complex and computer time consuming, it usually cannot be handled routinely. However, for many applications, it may be simplified using the following assumptions:

Figure 55.1 • Global Environmental Monitoring System/Air pollution management.

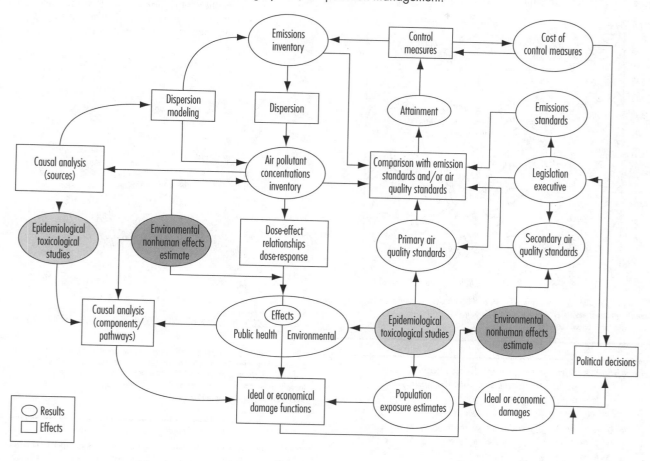

- no change of emission conditions with time
- no change of meteorological conditions during transport
- wind speeds above 1 m/s.

In this case, the equation mentioned above can be solved analytically. The resulting formula describes a plume with Gaussian concentration distribution, the so called Gaussian plume model (VDI 1992). The distribution parameters depend on meteorological conditions and downwind distance as well as on stack height. They have to be determined empirically (Venkatram and Wyngaard 1988). Situations where emissions and/or meteorological parameters vary by a considerable amount in time and/or space may be described by the Gaussian puff model (VDI 1994). Under this approach, distinct puffs are emitted in fixed time steps, each following its own path according to the current meteorological conditions. On its way, each puff grows according to turbulent mixing. Parameters describing this growth, again, have to be determined from empirical data (Venkatram and Wyngaard 1988). It has to be stressed, however, that to achieve this objective, input parameters must be available with the necessary resolution in time and/or space.

Concerning accidental releases or single case studies, a Lagrangian or particle model (*VDI Guideline 3945*, Part 3) is recommended. The concept thereby is to calculate the paths of many particles, each of which represents a fixed amount of the pollutant

in question. The individual paths are composed of transport by the mean wind and of stochastic disturbances. Due to the stochastic part, the paths do not fully agree, but depict the mixture by turbulence. In principle, Lagrangian models are capable of considering complex meteorological conditions—in particular, wind and turbulence; fields calculated by flow models described below can be used for Lagrangian dispersion modelling.

Dispersion Modelling in Complex Terrain

If pollutant concentrations have to be determined in structured terrain, it may be necessary to include topographic effects on pollutant dispersion in modelling. Such effects are, for example, transport following the topographic structure, or thermal wind systems like sea breezes or mountain winds, which change wind direction in the course of the day.

If such effects take place on a scale much larger than the model area, the influence may be considered by using meteorological data which reflect the local characteristics. If no such data are available, the three-dimensional structure impressed on the flow by topography can be obtained by using a corresponding flow model. Based on these data, dispersion modelling itself may be carried out assuming horizontal homogeneity as described above in the case of the Gaussian plume model. However, in situations where wind conditions change significantly inside the model area, dispersion modelling itself has to consider the three-dimensional

Figure 55.2 • Topographic structure of a model region.

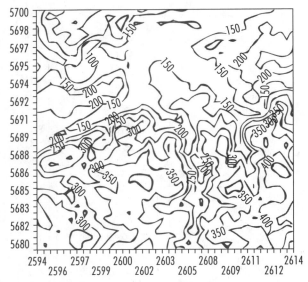

Topography of a model 20x20 km² region, with a source of 8760 kg/year assumed to exist at Gauss-Kruger coordinates 2607/5687 at a height of 20 m above ground.
Source: Wichmann-Fiebig and Brüchner 1997.

Figure 55.3 • Surface frequency distributions as determined from geostrophic frequency distribution.

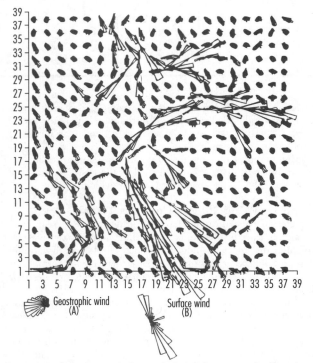

(A) and (B) represent the geostrophic frequency distribution at the source site and resultant surface frequency distribution. Surface frequency distributions for the whole model area mirror the topographical structure of the area.

Source: Wichmann-Fiebig and Brüchner 1997.

Figure 55.4 • Annual mean pollutant concentrations for a hypothetical region calculated from the geostrophic frequency distribution for heterogeneous wind fields.

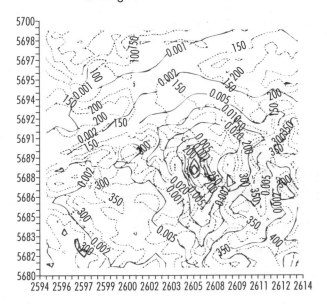

Topographic isopleths are represented by broken lines; pollutant concentration isopleths are represented by solid lines. Preference for transport along the valley axes is demonstrated, leading to a north-south orientation of the concentration distribution in the vicinity of the source. Outside the valley to the north, a more homogeneous distribution is observed.
Source: Wichmann-Fiebig and Brüchner 1997.

flow affected by the topographic structure. As mentioned above, this may be done by using a Gaussian puff or a Lagrangian model. Another way is to perform the more complex Eulerian modelling.

To determine wind direction in accord with the topographically structured terrain, mass consistent or diagnostic flow modelling may be used (Pielke 1984). Using this approach, the flow is fitted to topography by varying the initial values as little as possible and by keeping its mass consistent. As this is an approach which leads to quick results, it may also be used to calculate wind statistics for a certain site if no observations are available. To do this, geostrophic wind statistics (i.e., upper air data from rawinsondes) are used.

If, however, thermal wind systems have to be considered in more detail, so called prognostic models have to be used. Depending on the scale and the steepness of the model area, a hydrostatic, or the even more complex non-hydrostatic, approach is suitable (VDI 1981). Models of this type need much computer power, as well as much experience in application. Determination of concentrations based on annual means, in general, are not possible with these models. Instead, worst case studies can be performed by considering only one wind direction and those wind speed and stratification parameters which result in the highest surface concentration values. If those worst case values do not exceed air quality standards, more detailed studies are not necessary.

Figures 55.2, 55.3 and 55.4 demonstrate how the transport and dispension of pollutants can be presented in relation to the influence of terrain and wind climatologies derived from consideration of surface and geostrophic wind frequencies.

Dispersion Modelling in Case of Low Sources

Considering air pollution caused by low sources (i.e., stack heights on the order of building height or emissions of road traffic) the influence of the surrounding buildings has to be considered. Road traffic emissions will be trapped to a certain amount in street canyons. Empirical formulations have been found to describe this (Yamartino and Wiegand 1986).

Pollutants emitted from a low stack situated on a building will be captured in the circulation on the lee side of the building. The extent of this lee circulation depends on the height and width of the building, as well as on wind speed. Therefore, simplified approaches to describe pollutant dispersion in such a case, based solely on the height of a building, are not generally valid. The vertical and horizontal extent of the lee circulation has been obtained from wind tunnel studies (Hosker 1985) and can be implemented in mass consistent diagnostic models. As soon as the flow field has been determined, it can be used to calculate the transport and turbulent mixing of the pollutant emitted. This can be done by Lagrangian or Eulerian dispersion modelling.

More detailed studies—concerning accidental releases, for instance—can be performed only by using non-hydrostatic flow and dispersion models instead of a diagnostic approach. As this, in general, demands high computer power, a worst case approach as described above is recommended in advance of a complete statistical modelling.

● AIR QUALITY MONITORING

Hans-Ulrich Pfeffer and Peter Bruckmann

Air quality monitoring means the systematic measurement of ambient air pollutants in order to be able to assess the exposure of vulnerable receptors (e.g., people, animals, plants and art works) on the basis of standards and guidelines derived from observed effects, and/or to establish the source of the air pollution (causal analysis).

Ambient air pollutant concentrations are influenced by the spatial or time variance of emissions of hazardous substances and the dynamics of their dispersion in the air. As a consequence, marked daily and annual variations of concentrations occur. It is practically impossible to determine in a unified way all these different variations of air quality (in statistical language, the population of air quality states). Thus, ambient air pollutant concentrations measurements always have the character of random spatial or time samples.

Measurement Planning

The first step in measurement planning is to formulate the purpose of the measurement as precisely as possible. Important questions and fields of operation for air quality monitoring include:

Area measurement:

- representative determination of exposure in one area (general air monitoring)
- representative measurement of pre-existing pollution in the area of a planned facility (permit, TA Luft [Technical instruction, air])
- smog warning (winter smog, high ozone concentrations)
- measurements in hot spots of air pollution to estimate maximum exposure of receptors (EU-NO_2 guideline, measurements in street canyons, in accordance with the German Federal Immission Control Act)
- checking the results of pollution abatement measures and trends over time
- screening measurements

Table 55.2 • Parameters for measurement planning in measuring ambient air pollution concentrations (with example of application).

Parameter	Example of application: Licensing procedure for industrial facilities in Germany
Statement of the question	Measurement of prior pollution in the licensing procedure; representative random probe measurement
Area of measurement	Circle around location with radius 30 times actual chimney height (simplified)
Assessment standards (place and time dependent): characteristic values to be obtained from measurement data	Threshold limits IW1 (arithmetic mean) and IW2 (98th percentile) of TA Luft [Technical instruction, air]; calculation of I1 (arithmetic mean) and I2 (98th percentile) from measurements taken for 1 km^2 (assessment surface) to be compared with IW1 and IW2
Ordering, choice and density of measurement sites	Regular scan of 1km^2, resulting in "random" choice of measurement sites
Measurement time period	1 year, at least 6 months
Measurement height	1.5 to 4 metres above ground
Measurement frequency	52 (104) measurements per assessment area for gaseous pollutants, depending on the height of the pollution
Duration of each measurement	1/2 hour for gaseous pollutants, 24 hours for suspended dust, 1 month for dust precipitation
Measurement time	Random choice
Measured object	Air pollution emitted from the planned facility
Measurement procedure	National standard measurement procedure (VDI guidelines)
Necessary certainty of measurement results	High
Quality requirements, quality control, calibration, maintenance	VDI guidelines
Recording of measurement data, validation, archiving, assessment	Calculation of quantity of data I1V and I2V for every assessment area
Costs	Depend on measurement area and objectives

- scientific investigations—for example, the transport of air pollution, chemical conversions, calibrating dispersion calculations.

Facility measurement:

- measurements in response to complaints
- ascertaining sources of emissions, causal analysis
- measurements in cases of fires and accidental releases
- checking success of reduction measures
- monitoring factory fugitive emissions.

The goal of measurement planning is to use adequate measurement and assessment procedures to answer specific questions with sufficient certainty and at minimum possible expense.

55. ENVIRONMENTAL POLLUTION CONTROL

An example of the parameters that should be used for measurement planning is presented in table 55.2, in relation to an assessment of air pollution in the area of a planned industrial facility. Recognizing that formal requirements vary by jurisdiction, it should be noted that specific reference here is made to German licensing procedures for industrial facilities.

The example in table 55.2 shows the case of a measurement network that is supposed to monitor the air quality in a specific area as representatively as possible, to compare with designated air quality limits. The idea behind this approach is that a random choice of measurement sites is made in order to cover equally locations in an area with varying air quality (e.g., living areas, streets, industrial zones, parks, city centres, suburbs). This approach may be very costly in large areas due to the number of measurement sites necessary.

Another conception for a measurement network therefore starts with measurement sites that are representatively selected. If measurements of differing air quality are conducted in the most important locations, and the length of time that the protected objects remain in these "microenvironments" is known, then the exposure can be determined. This approach can be extended to other microenvironments (e.g., interior rooms, cars) in order to estimate the total exposure. Diffusion modelling or screening measurements can help in choosing the right measurement sites.

A third approach is to measure at the points of presumed highest exposure (e.g., for NO_2 and benzene in street canyons). If assessment standards are met at this site, there is sufficient probability that this will also be the case for all other sites. This approach, by focusing on critical points, requires relatively few measurement sites, but these must be chosen with particular care. This particular method risks overestimating real exposure.

The parameters of measurement time period, assessment of the measurement data and measurement frequency are essentially given in the definition of the assessment standards (limits) and the desired level of certainty of the results. Threshold limits and the peripheral conditions to be considered in measurement planning are related. By using continuous measurement procedures, a resolution that is temporally almost seamless can be achieved. But this is necessary only in monitoring peak values and/or for smog warnings; for monitoring annual mean values, for example, discontinuous measurements are adequate.

The following section is dedicated to describing the capabilities of measurement procedures and quality control as a further parameter important to measurement planning.

Quality Assurance

Measurements of ambient air pollutant concentrations can be costly to conduct, and results can affect significant decisions with serious economic or ecological implications. Therefore, quality assurance measures are an integral part of the measurement process. Two areas should be distinguished here.

Procedure-oriented measures

Every complete measurement procedure consists of several steps: sampling, sample preparation and clean-up; separation, detection (final analytical step); and data collection and assessment. In some cases, especially with continuous measurement of inorganic gases, some steps of the procedure can be left out (e.g., separation). Comprehensive adherence to procedures should be strived for in conducting measurements. Procedures that are standardized and thus comprehensively documented should be followed, in the form of DIN/ISO standards, CEN standards or VDI guidelines.

User-oriented measures

Using standardized and proven equipment and procedures for ambient air pollutant concentration measurement cannot alone ensure acceptable quality if the user does not employ adequate methods of quality control. The standards series DIN/EN/ISO 9000 (Quality Management and Quality Assurance Standards), EN 45000 (which defines the requirements for testing laboratories) and ISO Guide 25 (General Requirements for the Competence of Calibration and Testing Laboratories) are important for user-oriented measures to ensure quality.

Important aspects of user quality control measures include:

- acceptance and practice of the content of the measures in the sense of good laboratory practice (GLP)
- correct maintenance of measurement equipment, qualified measures to eliminate disruptions and ensure repairs
- carrying out calibrations and regular checking to ensure proper functioning
- carrying out interlaboratory testing.

Measurement Procedures

Measurement procedures for inorganic gases

A wealth of measurement procedures exists for the broad range of inorganic gases. We will differentiate between manual and automatic methods.

Manual procedures

In the case of manual measurement procedures for inorganic gases, the substance to be measured is normally adsorbed during the sampling in a solution or solid material. In most cases a photometric determination is made after an appropriate colour reaction. Several manual measurement procedures have special significance as reference procedures. Because of the relatively high personnel cost, these manual procedures are conducted only rarely for field measurements today, when alternative automatic procedures are available. The most important procedures are briefly sketched in table 55.3.

A special sampling variant, used primarily in connection with manual measurement procedures, is the diffusion separation tube (denuder). The denuder technique is aimed at separating the gas and particle phases by using their different diffusion rates. Thus, it is often used on difficult separation problems (e.g., ammonia and ammonium compounds; nitrogen oxides, nitric acid and nitrates; sulphur oxides, sulphuric acid and sulphates or hydrogen halides/halides). In the classic denuder technique, the test air is sucked through a glass tube with a special coating, depending on the material(s) to be collected. The denuder technique has been further developed in many variations and also partially automated. It has greatly expanded the possibilities of differentiated sampling, but, depending on the variant, it can be very laborious, and proper utilization requires a great deal of experience.

Automated procedures

There are numerous different continuous measuring monitors on the market for sulphur dioxide, nitrogen oxides, carbon monoxide and ozone. For the most part they are used particularly in measurement networks. The most important features of the individual methods are collected in table 55.4.

It should be emphasized here that all automatic measurement procedures based on chemical-physical principles must be calibrated using (manual) reference procedures. Since automatic equipment in measurement networks often runs for extended periods of time (e.g., several weeks) without direct human supervision, it is indispensable that their correct functioning is regularly and automatically checked. This generally is done using zero and test gases that can be produced by several methods (preparation of ambient air; pressurized gas cylinders; permeation; diffusion; static and dynamic dilution).

Table 55.3 • Manual measurement procedures for inorganic gases.

Material	Procedure	Execution	Comments
SO_2	TCM procedure	Absorption in tetrachloromercurate solution (wash bottle); reaction with formaldehyde and pararosaniline to red-violet sulphonic acid; photometric determination	EU-reference measurement procedure; DL = 0.2 µg SO_2; s = 0.03 mg/m^3 at 0.5 mg/m^3
SO_2	Silica gel procedure	Removal of interfering substances by concentrated H_3PO_4; adsorption on silica gel; thermal desorption in H_2-stream and reduction to H_2S; reaction to molybdenum-blue; photometric determination	DL = 0.3 µg SO_2; s = 0.03 mg/m^3 at 0.5 mg/m^3
NO_2	Saltzman procedure	Absorption in reaction solution while forming a red azo dye (wash bottle); photometric determination	Calibration with sodium nitrite; DL = 3 µg/m^3
O_3	Potassium iodide procedure	Formation of iodine from aqueous potassium iodide solution (wash bottle); photometric determination	DL = 20 µg/m^3; rel. s = ± 3.5% at 390 µg/m^3
F^-	Silver bead procedure; variant 1	Sampling with dust preseparator; enrichment of F^- on sodium carbonate-coated silver beads; elution and measurement with ion-sensitive lanthanum fluoride-electrode chain	Inclusion of an undetermined portion of particulate fluoride immissions
F^-	Silver bead procedure; variant 2	Sampling with heated membrane filter; enrichment of F^- on sodium carbonate-coated silver beads; determination by electrochemical (variant 1) or photometric (alizarin-complexone) procedure	Danger of lower findings due to partial sorption of gaseous fluoride immissions on membrane filter; DL = 0.5 µg/m^3
Cl^-	Mercury rhodanide procedure	Absorption in 0.1 N sodium hydroxide solution (wash bottle); reaction with mercury rhodanide and Fe(III) ions to iron thiocyanato complex; photometric determination	DL = 9 µg/m^3
Cl_2	Methyl-orange procedure	Bleaching reaction with methyl-orange solution (wash bottle); photometric determination	DL = 0.015 mg/m^3
NH_3	Indophenol procedure	Absorption in dilute H_2SO_4 (Impinger/wash bottle); conversion with phenol and hypochlorite to indophenol dye; photometric determination	DL = 3 µg/m^3 (impinger); partial inclusion of NH_4^+ – compounds and amines
NH_3	Nessler procedure	Absorption in dilute H_2SO_4 (Impinger/wash bottle); distillation and reaction with Nessler's reagent, photometric determination	DL = 2.5 µg/m^3 (impinger); partial inclusion of NH_4^+ – compounds and amines
H_2S	Molybdenum-blue procedure	Absorption as silver sulphide on glass beads treated with silver sulphate and potassium hydrogen sulphate (sorption tube); released as hydrogen sulphide and conversion to molybdenum blue; photometric determination	DL = 0.4 µg/m^3
H_2S	Methylene blue procedure	Absorption in cadmium hydroxide suspension while forming CdS; conversion to methylene blue; photometric determination	DL = 0.3 µg/m^3

DL = detection limit; s = standard deviation; rel. s = relative s.

Measurement procedures for dust-forming air pollutants and its composition

Among particulate air pollutants, dustfall and suspended particulate matter (SPM) are differentiated. Dustfall consists of larger particles, which sink to the ground because of their size and thickness. SPM includes the particle fraction that is dispersed in the atmosphere in a quasi-stable and quasi-homogenous manner and therefore remains suspended for a certain time.

Measurement of suspended particulate matter and metallic compounds in SPM

As is the case with measurements of gaseous air pollutants, continuous and discontinuous measurement procedures for SPM can be differentiated. As a rule, SPM is first separated on glass fibre or membrane filters. It follows a gravimetric or radiometric determination. Depending on the sampling, a distinction can be made between a procedure to measure the total SPM without fractionation according to the size of the particles and a fractionation procedure to measure the fine dust.

The advantages and disadvantages of fractionated suspended dust measurements are disputed internationally. In Germany, for example, all threshold limits and assessment standards are based on total suspended particulates. This means that, for the most part, only total SPM measurements are performed. In the United States, on the contrary, the so-called PM-10 procedure (particulate matter ≤ 10 µm) is very common. In this procedure, only particles with an aerodynamic diameter up to 10 µm are included (50 per cent inclusion portion), which are inhalable and can enter the lungs. The plan is to introduce the PM-10 procedure into the European Union as a reference procedure. The cost for fractionated SPM measurements is considerably higher than for measuring total suspended dust, because the measuring devices must be fitted with special, expensively constructed sampling heads that require costly maintenance. Table 55.5 contains details on the most important SPM measurement procedures.

Recently, automatic filter changers have also been developed that hold a larger number of filters and supply them to the sampler, one after another, at timed intervals. The exposed filters are stored in a magazine. The detection limits for filter procedures lie between 5 and 10 µg/m^3 of dust, as a rule.

Finally, the black smoke procedure for SPM measurements has to be mentioned. Coming from Britain, it has been incorporated

55. ENVIRONMENTAL POLLUTION CONTROL

Table 55.4 • Automated measurement procedures for inorganic gases.

Material	Measuring principle	Comments
SO_2	Conductometry reaction of SO_2 with H_2O_2 in dilute H_2SO_4; measurement of increased conductivity	Exclusion of interferences with selective filter ($KHSO_4/AgNO_3$)
SO_2	UV fluorescence; excitation of SO_2 molecules with UV radiation (190–230 nm); measurement of fluorescence radiation	Interferences, e.g., by hydrocarbons, must be eliminated with appropriate filter systems
NO/NO_2	Chemiluminescence; reaction of NO with O_3 to NO_2; detection of chemiluminescence radiation with photomultiplier	NO_2 only indirectly measurable; use of converters for reduction of NO_2 to NO; measurement of NO and NO_x ($=NO+NO_2$) in separate channels
CO	Non-dispersive infrared absorption; measurement of IR absorption with specific detector against reference cell	Reference: (a) cell with N_2; (b) ambient air after removal of CO; (c) optical removal of CO absorption (gas filter correlation)
O_3	UV absorption; low-pressure Hg lamp as radiation source (253.7 nm); registration of UV absorption in accordance with Lambert-Beer's law; detector: vacuum photodiode, photosensitive valve	Reference: ambient air after removal of ozone (e.g., Cu/MnO_2)
O_3	Chemiluminescence; reaction of O_3 with ethene to formaldehyde; detection of chemiluminescence radiation with photomultiplier	Good selectivity; ethylene necessary as reagent gas

into EU guidelines for SO_2 and suspended dust. In this procedure, the blackening of the coated filter is measured with a reflex photometer after the sampling. The black smoke values that are thus photometrically obtained are converted into gravimetric units ($\mu g/m^3$) with the help of a calibration curve. Since this calibration function depends to a high degree on the composition of the dust, especially its soot content, the conversion into gravimetric units is problematic.

Today, metal compounds are often routinely determined in suspended dust immission samples. In general, the collection of the suspended dust on filters is followed by a chemical dissolution of the separated dusts, since the most common final analytical steps presuppose converting the metallic and metalloid compounds in an aqueous solution. In practice, the most important methods by far are atom absorption spectroscopy (AAS) and spectroscopy with plasma excitation (ICP-OES). Other procedures for determining metallic compounds in suspended dust are x-ray fluorescence analysis, polarography and neutron activation analysis. Although metallic compounds have been measured for more than a decade now as a component of SPM in outside air at certain measurement sites, important unanswered questions remain. Thus the conventional sampling by separating the sus-

pended dust on filters assumes that the separation of the heavy metal compounds on the filter is complete. However, earlier indications have been found in the literature questioning this. The results are very heterogeneous.

A further problem lies in the fact that different compound forms, or single compounds of the respective elements, cannot be distinguished in the analysis of metallic compounds in suspended dust using the conventional measurement procedures. While in many cases adequate total determinations can be made, a more thorough differentiation would be desirable with certain especially carcinogenic metals (As, Cd, Cr, Ni, Co, Be). There are often big

Table 55.5 • Measurement procedures for suspended particulate matter (SPM).

Procedure	Measuring principle	Comments
Small filter device	Non-fractionated sampling; air flow rate 2.7–2.8 m^3/h; filter diameter 50 mm; gravimetric analysis	Easy handling; control clock; device operable with PM-10 preseparator
LIB device	Non-fractionated sampling; air flow rate 15-16 m^3/h; filter diameter 120 mm; gravimetric analysis	Separation of large dust quantities; advantageous for analysis of dust components; control clock
High-Volume-Sampler	Inclusion of particles up to approx. 30 μm diameter; air flow rate approx. 100 m^3/h; filter diameter 257 mm; gravimetric analysis	Separation of large dust quantities, advantageous for analysis of dust components; relatively high noise level
FH 62 I	Continuous, radiometric dust measuring device; non-fractionating sampling; air flow rate 1 or 3 m^3/h; registration of dust mass separated on a filter band by measuring attenuation of β-radiation (krypton 85) in passage through exposed filter (ionization chamber)	Gravimetric calibration by dusting of single filters; device also operable with PM-10 preseparator
BETA dust meter F 703	Continuous, radiometric dust measuring device; non-fractionated sampling; air flow rate 3 m^3/h; registration of dust mass separated on a filter band by measuring attenuation of β-radiation (carbon 14) in passage through exposed filter (Geiger Müller counter tube)	Gravimetric calibration by dusting of single filters; device also operable with PM-10 preseparator
TEOM 1400	Continuous dust measuring device; non-fractionated sampling; air flow rate 1 m^3/h; dust collected on a filter, which is part of a self-resonating, vibrating system, in side stream (3 l/min); registration of the frequency lowering by increased dust load on the filter	Relationship between frequency lowering and dust mass must be established through calibration

differences in the carcinogenic effects of elements and their individual compounds (e.g., chromium compounds in oxidation levels III and VI—only those in level VI are carcinogenic). In such cases a specific measurement of the individual compounds (species analysis) would be desirable. Despite the significance of this problem, only first attempts at species analysis are being made in measurement technique.

Measurement of dustfall and metallic compounds in dustfall

Two fundamentally different methods are used to collect dustfall:

- sampling in collecting vessels
- sampling on adhesive surfaces.

A popular procedure for measuring dustfall (deposited dust) is the so-called Bergerhoff procedure. In this procedure the entire atmospheric precipitation (dry and wet depositions) is collected over 30 ± 2 days in vessels about 1.5 to 2.0 metres above the ground (bulk deposition). Then the collecting vessels are taken to the lab and prepared (filtered, water evaporated, dried, weighed). The result is calculated on the basis of the surface area of the collecting vessel and exposure time in grams per square meter and day (g/m^2d). The relative detection limit is $0.035\ g/m^2d$.

Additional procedures for collecting dustfall include the Liesegang-Löbner device and methods which collect the deposited dust on adhesive foils.

All measurement results for dustfall are relative values that depend on the apparatus used, as the dust separation is influenced by the flow conditions at the device and other parameters. The differences in the measurement values obtained with the different procedures can reach 50 per cent.

Also important is the composition of the deposited dust, such as the content of lead, cadmium and other metallic compounds. The analytical procedures used for this are basically the same as those used for suspended dust.

Measuring special materials in dust form

Special materials in dust form include asbestos and soot. Collecting fibres as air pollutants is important since asbestos has been classified as a confirmed carcinogenic material. Fibres with a diameter of $D \leq 3\mu m$ and a length of $L \geq 5\mu m$, where $L:D \geq 3$, are considered carcinogenic. Measurement procedures for fibrous materials consist of counting, under the microscope, fibres that have been separated on filters. Only electron microscopic procedures can be considered for outside air measurements. The fibres are separated on gold-coated porous filters. Prior to assessment in an electron scan microscope, the sample is freed of organic substances through plasma incineration right on the filter. The fibres are counted on part of the filter surface, randomly chosen and classified by geometry and type of fibre. With the help of energy dispersive x-ray analysis (EDXA), asbestos fibres, calcium sulphate fibres and other inorganic fibres can be differentiated on the basis of elemental composition. The entire procedure is extremely expensive and requires the greatest care to achieve reliable results.

Soot in the form of particles emitted by diesel motors has become relevant since diesel soot was also classified as carcinogenic. Because of its changing and complex composition and because of the fact that various constituents are also emitted from other sources, there is no measurement procedure specific to diesel soot. Nevertheless, in order to say something concrete about the concentrations in ambient air, soot is conventionally defined as elemental carbon, as a part of total carbon. It is measured after sampling and an extraction step and/or thermal desorption. Determination of the carbon content ensues through burning in an oxygen stream and coulometric titration or

Table 55.6 • Long-distance measurement procedures.

Procedure	Application	Advantages, disadvantages
Fourier transform infrared spectroscopy (FTIR)	IR range (approx. 700–3,000 cm^{-1}), several hundred metres light path. Monitors diffuse surface sources (optical fence), measures individual organic compounds	+ Multi-component system + dl a few ppb − Expensive
Differential optical absorption spectrometry (DOAS)	Light path to several km; measures SO_2, NO_2, benzene, HNO_3; monitors linear and surface sources, used in measuring networks	+ Easy to handle + Successful performance test + Multi-component system − High dl under conditions of poor visibility (e.g., fog)
Long-distance laser absorption spectroscopy (TDLAS)	Research area, in low-pressure cuvettes for OH$^-$	+ High sensitivity (to ppt) + Measures unstable trace compounds − High cost − Difficult to handle
Differential Absorption LIDAR (DIAL)	Monitors surface sources, large surface immission measurements	+ Measurements of spatial distribution + Measures inaccessible places (e.g., smoke gas trails) − Expensive − Limited component spectrum (SO_2, O_3, NO_2)

LIDAR = Light detection and ranging; DIAL = differential absorption LIDAR.

non-dispersive IR detection of the carbon dioxide formed in the process.

The so-called aethalometer and the photoelectric aerosol sensor are also used for measuring soot, in principle.

Measuring Wet Depositions

Together with dry deposition, wet deposition in rain, snow, fog and dew constitute the most important means by which harmful materials enter the ground, water or plant surfaces from the air.

In order to clearly distinguish the wet deposition in rain and snow (fog and dew present special problems) from the measurement of total deposition (bulk deposition, see section "Measurement of dustfall and metallic compounds" above) and dry deposition, rain catchers, whose collection opening is covered when there is no rain (wet-only sampler), are used for sampling. With rain sensors, which mostly work on the principle of conductivity changes, the cover is opened when it starts to rain and closed again when the rain stops.

The samples are transferred through a funnel (open area approx. 500 cm^2 and more) into a darkened and if possible insulated collection container (of glass or polyethylene for inorganic components only).

In general, analysing the collected water for inorganic components can be done without sample preparation. The water should be centrifuged or filtered if it is visibly cloudy. The conductivity, pH value and important anions (NO_3^-, SO_4^{2-}, Cl^-) and cations (Ca^{2+}, K^+, Mg^{2+}, Na^+, NH_4^+ and so on) are routinely measured. Unstable trace compounds and intermediate states like H_2O_2 or HSO_3^- are also measured for research purposes.

55. ENVIRONMENTAL POLLUTION CONTROL

For analysis, procedures are used that are generally available for aqueous solutions such as conductometry for conductivity, electrodes for pH values, atom adsorption spectroscopy for cations (see section "Measuring special materials in dust form", above) and, increasingly, ion exchange chromatography with conductivity detection for anions.

Organic compounds are extracted from rain water with, for example, dichloromethane, or blown out with argon and adsorbed with Tenax tubes (only highly volatile materials). The materials are then subjected to a gas chromatographic analysis (see "Measurement procedures for organic air pollutants", below).

Dry deposition correlates directly with ambient air concentrations. The concentration differences of airborne harmful materials in rain, however, are relatively small, so that for measuring wet deposition, wide-mesh measuring networks are adequate. Examples include the European EMEP measurement network, in which the entry of sulphate and nitrate ions, certain cations and precipitation pH values are collected in approximately 90 stations. There are also extensive measurement networks in North America.

Optical Long-Distance Measurement Procedures

Whereas the procedures described up to now catch air pollution at one point, optical long-distance measuring procedures measure in an integrated manner over light paths of several kilometres or they determine the spatial distribution. They use the absorption characteristics of gases in the atmosphere in the UV, visible or IR spectral range and are based on the Lambert-Beer law, according to which the product of light path and concentration are proportional to the measured extinction. If the sender and receiver of the measuring installation change the wavelength, several components can be measured in parallel or sequentially with one device.

In practice, the measurement systems identified in table 55.6 play the biggest role.

Measurement Procedures for Organic Air Pollutants

The measurement of air pollution containing organic components is complicated primarily by the range of materials in this class of compounds. Several hundred individual components with very different toxicological, chemical and physical characteristics are covered under the general title "organic air pollutants" in the emissions registers and air quality plans of congested areas.

Especially due to the great differences in potential impact, collecting relevant individual components has more and more taken the place of previously used summation procedures (e.g., Flame Ionization Detector, total carbon procedure), the results of which cannot be assessed toxicologically. The FID method, however, has retained a certain significance in connection with a short separation column to separate out methane, which is photochemically not very reactive, and for collecting the precursor volatile organic compounds (VOC) for the formation of photo-oxidants.

The frequent necessity of separating the complex mixtures of the organic compounds into relevant individual components makes measuring it virtually an exercise in applied chromatography. Chromatographic procedures are the methods of choice when the organic compounds are sufficiently stable, thermally and chemically. For organic materials with reactive functional groups, separate procedures that use the functional groups' physical characteristics or chemical reactions for detection continue to hold their ground.

Examples include using amines to convert aldehydes to hydrazones, with subsequent photometric measurement; derivatization with 2,4-dinitrophenylhydrazine and separation of the 2,4-hydrazone that is formed; or forming azo-dyes with *p*-nitroaniline for detecting phenols and cresols.

Among chromatographic procedures, gas chromatography (GC) and high-pressure liquid chromatography (HPLC) are most frequently employed for separating the often complex mixtures. For gas chromatography, separation columns with very narrow diameters (approx. 0.2 to 0.3 mm, and approx. 30 to 100 m long), so-called high-resolution capillary columns (HRGC), are almost exclusively utilized today. A series of detectors are available for finding the individual components after the separation column, such as the above-mentioned FID, the ECD (electron capture detector, specifically for electrophilic substitutes such as halogen), the PID (photo-ionization detector, which is especially sensitive to aromatic hydrocarbons and other π-electron systems), and the NPD (thermo-ionic detector specifically for nitrogen and phosphorus compounds). The HPLC uses special through-flow detectors which, for example, are designed as the through-flow cuvette of a UV spectrometer.

Especially effective, but also especially expensive, is the use of a mass spectrometer as a detector. Really certain identification, especially with unknown mixtures of compounds, is often possible only through the mass spectrum of the organic compound. The qualitative information of the so-called retention time (time the material remains in the column) that is contained in the chromatogram with conventional detectors is supplemented with the specific detection of the individual components by mass fragmentograms with high detection sensitivity.

Sampling must be considered before the actual analysis. The choice of sampling method is determined primarily by volatility, but also by expected concentration range, polarity and chemical stability. Furthermore, with non-volatile compounds, a choice must be made between concentration and deposition measurements.

Table 55.7 provides an overview of common procedures in air monitoring for active enrichment and chromatographic analysis of organic compounds, with examples of applications.

Deposition measurements of organic compounds with low volatility (e.g., dibenzodioxins and dibenzofurans (PCDD/PCDF), polycyclic aromatic hydrocarbons (PAH)) are gaining in importance from the perspective of environmental impact. Since food is the main source of human intake, airborne material transferred onto food plants is of great significance. There is, however, evidence that material transfer by way of particulate deposition is less important than dry deposition of quasi-gaseous compounds.

For measuring total deposition, standardized devices for dust precipitation are used (e.g., Bergerhoff procedure), which have been slightly modified by darkening as a protection against the entry of strong light. Important technical measurement problems, such as the resuspension of already separated particles, evaporation or possible photolytic decomposition, are now being systematically researched in order to improve the less-than-optimal sampling procedures for organic compounds.

Olfactometric Investigations

Olfactometric immission investigations are used in monitoring to quantify odour complaints and to determine baseline pollution in licensing procedures. They serve primarily to assess whether existing or anticipated odours should be classified as significant.

In principle, three methodological approaches can be differentiated:

- measurement of the emission concentration (number of odour units) with an olfactometer and subsequent dispersion modelling
- measurement of individual components (e.g., NH_3) or mixtures of compounds (e.g, gas chromatography of gases from landfills), if these adequately characterize the odour
- odour determinations by means of inspections.

Table 55.7 • Overview of common chromatographic air quality measurement procedures of organic compounds (with examples of applications).

Material group	Concentration range	Sampling, preparation	Final analytical step
Hydrocarbons C_1–C_9	$\mu g/m^3$	Gas mice (rapid sampling), gas-tight syringe, cold trapping in front of capillary column (focusing), thermal desorption	GC/FID
Low-boiling hydrocarbons, highly volatile halogenated hydrocarbons	ng/m^3–$\mu g/m^3$	Evacuated, passivated high-grade steel cylinder (also for clean air measurements) Sampling dispatch through gas loops, cold trapping, thermal desorption	GC/FID/ECD/PID
Organic compounds in boiling point range C_6-C_{30} (60–350 °C)	$\mu g/m^3$	Adsorption on activated carbon, (a) desorption with CS_2 (b) desorption with solvents (c) headspace analysis	Capillary GC/FID
Organic compounds in boiling point range 20–300 °C	ng/m^3–$\mu g/m^3$	Adsorption on organic polymers (e.g., Tenax) or molecular carbon sieve (carbopack), thermal desorption with cold trapping in front of capillary column (focusing) or solvent extraction	Capillary GC/FID/ECD/MS
Modification for low-boiling compounds (from −120 °C)	ng/m^3–$\mu g/m^3$	Adsorption on cooled polymers (e.g. thermogradient tube), cooled to −120 °C, use of carbopack	Capillary GC/FID/ECD/MS
High boiling organic compounds partially attached to particles (esp. PAH, PCB, PCDD/PCDF), high sampling volume	fg/m^3–ng/m^3	Sampling on filters (e.g., small filter device or high volume sampler) with subsequent polyurethane cartridges for gaseous portion, solvent desorption of filter and polyurethane, various purification and preparatory steps, for PAH also sublimation	Capillary GC-GCMS (PCDD/PCDF), capillary GC-FID or MS (PAH), HPLC fluorescence detector (PAH)
High boiling organic compounds, esp. PCDD, PCDF, PBDD, PBDF, low sampling volume	fg/m^3–ng/m^3	Adsorption on organic polymers (e.g., polyurethane foam cylinder) with prior filters (e.g., glass fibre) or inorg. adsorp. (e.g., silica gel), extraction with solvents, various purification and preparatory steps, (including multicolumn chromatography), derivatizing for chlorophenols	HRGC/ECD
High boiling organic compounds bound to particles, e.g., components of organic aerosols, deposition samples	ng/m^3 ng–$\mu g/g$ aerosol pg–ng/m^2 day	Separation of aerosols on glass fibre filters (e.g., high or low volume sampler) or dust collection on standardized surfaces, extraction with solvents (for deposition also of remaining filtered water), various purification and preparation steps	HRGC/MS HPLC (for PAHs)

GC = gas chromatography;
FID = flame ionization detector;
ECD = electron capture detector;
PID = photo-ionization detector.

GCMS = GC/mass spectroscopy;
HRGC/ECD = high resolution GC/ECD;
HPLC = high performance liquid chromatography.

The first possibility combines emission measurement with modelling and, strictly speaking, cannot be classified under the term air quality monitoring. In the third method, the human nose is used as the detector with significantly reduced precision as compared to physical-chemical methods.

Details of inspections, measurement plans and assessing the results are contained, for example, in the environmental protection regulations of some German states.

Screening Measurement Procedures

Simplified measurement procedures are sometimes used for preparatory studies (screening). Examples include passive samplers, test tubes and biological procedures. With passive (diffusive) samplers, the material to be tested is collected with freely flowing processes such as diffusion, permeation or adsorption in simple forms of collectors (tubes, plaques) and enriched in impregnated filters, meshes or other adsorption media. So-called active sampling (sucking the sample air through a pump) thus does not occur. The enriched quantity of material, analytically determined according to definite exposure time, is converted into concentration units on the basis of physical laws (e.g., of diffusion) with the

help of collection time and the collector's geometric parameters. The methodology stems from the field of occupational health (personal sampling) and indoor air measurement, but it is increasingly being used for ambient air pollutant concentration measurements. An overview can be found in Brown 1993.

Detector tubes are often used for sampling and quick preparatory analysis of gases. A certain test air volume is sucked through a glass tube that is filled with an adsorptive reagent that corresponds with the test objective. The contents of the tube change colour depending on the concentration of the material to be determined that is present in the test air. Small testing tubes are often used in the field of workplace monitoring or as a quick procedure in cases of accidents, such as fires. They are not used for routine ambient air pollutant concentration measurements due to the generally too high detection limits and too limited selectivity. Detector testing tubes are available for numerous materials in various concentration ranges.

Among the biological procedures, two methods have become accepted in routine monitoring. With the standardized lichen exposure procedure, the mortality rate of the lichen is determined over the exposure time of 300 days. In another procedure, French pasture grass is exposed for 14±1 days. Then the amount of growth is determined. Both procedures serve as summary determinations of air pollutant concentration effects.

Air Quality Monitoring Networks

Around the world, the most varied types of air quality networks are utilized. A distinction should be drawn between measurement networks, consisting of automatic, computer-controlled measuring stations (measurement containers), and virtual measurement networks, which only define the measurement locations for various types of air pollutant concentration measurements in the form of a preset grid. Tasks and conceptions of measurement networks were discussed above.

Continuous monitoring networks

Continuously operating measurement networks are based on automatic measuring stations, and serve primarily for air quality monitoring of urban areas. Measured are air pollutants such as sulphur dioxide (SO_2), dust, nitrogen monoxide (NO), nitrogen dioxide (NO_2), carbon monoxide (CO), ozone (O_3), and to an extent also the sum of the hydrocarbons (free methane, C_nH_m) or individual organic components (e.g., benzene, toluene, xylenes). In addition, depending on need, meteorological parameters such as wind direction, wind speed, air temperature, relative humidity, precipitation, global radiation or radiation balance are included.

The measuring equipment operated in measurement stations generally consists of an analyser, a calibration unit, and control and steering electronics, which monitors the whole measuring equipment and contains a standardized interface for data collection. In addition to the measurement values, the measuring equipment supplies so-called status signals on errors and the operating status. The calibration of the devices is automatically checked by computer at regular intervals.

As a rule, the measurement stations are connected with fixed data lines, dial connections or other data transfer systems to a computer (process computer, workstation or PC, depending on the scope of the system) in which the measurement results are entered, processed and displayed. The measurement network computers and, if necessary, specially trained personnel monitor continuously whether various threshold limits are exceeded. In

this manner critical air quality situations can be recognized at any time. This is very important, especially for monitoring critical smog situations in winter and summer (photo-oxidants) and for current public information.

Measurement networks for random sample measurements

Beyond the telemetric measurement network, other measuring systems for monitoring air quality are used to varying extents. Examples include (occasionally partially automated) measurement networks to determine:

- dust deposition and its components
- suspended dust (SPM) and its components
- hydrocarbons and chlorinated hydrocarbons
- low volatile organic materials (dioxins, furans, polychlorinated biphenyls).

A series of substances measured in this manner have been classified as carcinogens, such as cadmium compounds, PAHs or benzene. Monitoring them is therefore particularly important.

To provide an example of a comprehensive programme, table 55.8 summarizes the air quality monitoring that is systematically conducted in North Rhine-Westphalia, which with 18 million inhabitants is the most populous state in Germany.

AIR POLLUTION CONTROL

John Elias

Management of Air Pollution

The objective of a manager of an air pollution control system is to ensure that excessive concentrations of air pollutants do not reach a susceptible target. Targets could include people, plants, animals and materials. In all cases we should be concerned with the most sensitive of each of these groups. Air pollutants could include gases, vapours, aerosols and, in some cases, biohazardous materials. A well designed system will prevent a target from receiving a harmful concentration of a pollutant.

Most air pollution control systems involve a combination of several control techniques, usually a combination of technological controls and administrative controls, and in larger or more complex sources there may be more than one type of technological control.

Ideally, the selection of the appropriate controls will be made in the context of the problem to be solved.

- What is emitted, in what concentration?
- What are the targets? What is the most susceptible target?
- What are acceptable short-term exposure levels?
- What are acceptable long-term exposure levels?
- What combination of controls must be selected to ensure that the short-term and long-term exposure levels are not exceeded?

Table 55.9 describes the steps in this process.

Some jurisdictions have done some of the work by setting standards based on the maximum concentration of a contaminant that a susceptible target can receive. With this type of standard, the manager does not have to carry out Steps 2 and 3, since the regulating agency has already done this. Under this system, the manager must establish only the uncontrolled emission standards for each pollutant (Step 1), and then determine what controls are necessary to meet the standard (Step 4).

By having air quality standards, regulators can measure individual exposures and thus determine whether anyone is exposed to potentially harmful levels. It is assumed that the standards set under these conditions are low enough to protect the most suscep-

Table 55.8 • Systematic air quality monitoring in North-Rhine-Westphalia (Germany).

Continuous measuring system	Partially automated measuring system	Discontinuous measuring system/Multi-component measurements
Sulphur dioxide	SPM composition:	Benzene and other
Nitrogen monoxide	Lead	hydrocarbons
Nitrogen dioxide	Cadmium	Halogenated
Carbon monoxide	Nickel	hydrocarbons
Suspended particulate	Copper	Dust deposition and
matter (SPM)	Iron	material composition
Ozone	Arsenic	Soot
Hydrocarbons	Beryllium	Polychlorinated
Wind direction	Benzo[a]pyrene	biphenyls
Wind speed	Benzo[e]pyrene	Polyhalogenated
Air temperature	Benzo[a]anthracene	dibenzodioxins and
Air pressure	Dibenzo[a,h]anthracene	dibenzofurans
Relative humidity	Benzo[ghi]perylene	(PCDD/PCDF)
Radiation balance	Coronene	
Precipitation		

Table 55.9 • Steps in selecting pollution controls.

Step 1: Define emissions.	The first part is to determine what will be released from the stack. All potentially harmful emissions must be listed. The second part is to estimate how much of each material will be released. Without this information, the manager cannot begin to design a control programme.
Step 2: Define target groups.	All susceptible targets should be identified. This includes people, animals, plants and materials. In each case, the most susceptible member of each group must be identified. For example, asthmatics near a plant that emits isocyanates.
Step 3: Determine acceptable exposure levels.*	An acceptable level of exposure for the most sensitive target group must be established. If the pollutant is a material that has cumulative effects, such as a carcinogen, then long-term exposure levels (annual) must be set. If the pollutant has short-term effects, such as an irritant or a sensitizer, a short-term or perhaps peak exposure level must be set.**
Step 4: Select controls.	Step 1 identifies the emissions, and Step 3 determines the acceptable exposure levels. In this step, each pollutant is checked to ensure that it does not exceed the acceptable level. If it exceeds the acceptable level, additional controls must be added, and the exposure levels checked again. This process continues until all exposures are at or below the acceptable level. Dispersion modelling can be used to estimate exposures for new plants or to test alternative solutions for existing facilities.

* When setting exposure levels in Step 3, it must be remembered that these exposures are total exposures, not just those from the plant. Once the acceptable level has been established, background levels, and contributions from other plants must be subtracted to determine the maximum amount that the plant can emit without exceeding the acceptable exposure level. If this is not done, and three plants are allowed to emit at the maximum amount, the target groups will be exposed to three times the acceptable level.

** Some materials such as carcinogens do not have a threshold below which no harmful effects will occur. Therefore, as long as some of the material is allowed to escape to the environment, there will be some risk to the target populations. In this case a no effect level cannot be set (other than zero). Instead, an acceptable level of risk must be established. Usually this is set in the range of 1 adverse outcome in 100,000 to 1,000,000 exposed persons.

tible target group. This is not always a safe assumption. As shown in table 55.10, there can be a wide variation in common air quality standards. Air quality standards for sulphur dioxide range from 30 to 140 $\mu g/m^3$. For less commonly regulated materials this variation can be even larger (1.2 to 1,718 $\mu g/m^3$), as shown in table 55.11 for benzene. This is not surprising given that economics can play as large a role in standard setting as does toxicology. If a standard is not set low enough to protect susceptible populations, no one is well served. Exposed populations have a feeling of false confidence, and can unknowingly be put at risk. The emitter may at first feel that they have benefited from a lenient standard, but if effects in the community require the company to redesign their controls, or install new controls, costs could be higher than doing it correctly the first time.

Sometimes this stepwise approach to selecting air pollution controls is short circuited, and the regulators and designers go directly to a "universal solution". One such method is best available control technology (BACT). It is assumed that by using the best combination of scrubbers, filters and good work practices on an emission source, a level of emissions low enough to protect the most susceptible target group would be achieved. Frequently, the resulting emission level will be below the minimum required to protect the most susceptible targets. This way all unnecessary

Table 55.10 • Range of air quality standards for a commonly controlled air contaminant (sulphur dioxide).

Countries and territories	Long-term sulphur dioxide air quality standards ($\mu g/m^3$)
Australia	50
Canada	30
Finland	40
Germany	140
Hungary	70
Taiwan	133

exposures should be eliminated. Examples of BACT are shown in table 55.12.

BACT by itself does not ensure adequate control levels. Although this is the best control system based on gas cleaning controls and good operating practices, BACT may not be good enough if the source is a large plant, or if it is located next to a sensitive target. Best available control technology should be tested to ensure that it is indeed good enough. The resulting emission standards should be checked to determine whether or not they may still be harmful even with the best gas cleaning controls. If emission standards are still harmful, other basic controls, such as selecting safer processes or materials, or relocating in a less sensitive area, may have to be considered.

Another "universal solution" that bypasses some of the steps is source performance standards. Many jurisdictions establish emission standards that cannot be exceeded. Emission standards are based on emissions at the source. Usually this works well, but like

Table 55.11 • Range of air quality standards for a less commonly controlled air contaminant (benzene).

City/State	24-hour air quality standard for benzene ($\mu g/m^3$)
Connecticut	53.4
Massachusetts	1.2
Michigan	2.4
North Carolina	2.1
Nevada	254
New York	1,718
Philadelphia	1,327
Virginia	300

The levels were standardized to an averaging time of 24 hours to assist in the comparisons. (Adapted from Calabrese and Kenyon 1991.)

55. ENVIRONMENTAL POLLUTION CONTROL

Table 55.12 • Selected examples of best available control technology (BACT) showing the control method used and estimated efficiency.

Process	Pollutant	Control method	Estimated efficiency
Soil remediation	Hydrocarbons	Thermal oxidizer	99
Kraft pulp mill recovery boiler	Particulates	Electrostatic precipitator	99.68
Production of fumed silica	Carbon monoxide	Good practice	50
Automobile painting	Hydrocarbons	Oven afterburner	90
Electric arc furnace	Particulates	Baghouse	100
Petroleum refinery, catalytic cracking	Respirable particulates	Cyclone + Venturi scrubber	93
Medical incinerator	Hydrogen chloride	Wet scrubber + dry scrubber	97.5
Coal-fired boiler	Sulphur dioxide	Spray dryer + absorber	90
Waste disposal by dehydration and in-cineration	Particulates	Cyclone + condenser + Venturi scrubber + wet scrubber	95
Asphalt plant	Hydrocarbons	Thermal oxidizer	99

BACT they can be unreliable. The levels should be low enough to maintain the maximum emissions low enough to protect susceptible target populations from typical emissions. However, as with best available control technology, this may not be good enough to protect everyone where there are large emission sources or nearby susceptible populations. If this is the case, other procedures must be used to ensure the safety of all target groups.

Both BACT and emission standards have a basic fault. They assume that if certain criteria are met at the plant, the target groups will be automatically protected. This is not necessarily so, but once such a system is passed into law, effects on the target become secondary to compliance with the law.

BACT and source emission standards or design criteria should be used as minimum criteria for controls. If BACT or emission criteria will protect the susceptible targets, then they can be used as intended, otherwise other administrative controls must be used.

Control Measures

Controls can be divided into two basic types of controls—technological and administrative. Technological controls are defined here as the hardware put on an emission source to reduce contaminants in the gas stream to a level that is acceptable to the community and that will protect the most sensitive target. Administrative controls are defined here as other control measures.

Technological controls

Gas cleaning systems are placed at the source, before the stack, to remove contaminants from the gas stream before releasing it to the environment. Table 55.13 shows a brief summary of the different classes of gas cleaning system.

The gas cleaner is part of a complex system consisting of hoods, ductwork, fans, cleaners and stacks. The design, performance and maintenance of each part affects the performance of all other parts, and the system as a whole.

It should be noted that system efficiency varies widely for each type of cleaner, depending on its design, energy input and the characteristics of the gas stream and the contaminant. As a result, the sample efficiencies in table 55.13 are only approximations. The variation in efficiencies is demonstrated with wet scrubbers in table 55.13. Wet scrubber collection efficiency goes from 98.5 per cent for 5 μm particles to 45 per cent for 1 μm particles at the same pressure drop across the scrubber (6.8 in. water gauge (w.g.)). For the same size particle, 1 μm, efficiency goes from 45 per cent efficiency at 6.8 w.g. to 99.95 at 50 w.g. As a result, gas cleaners must be matched to the specific gas stream in question. The use of generic devices is not recommended.

Waste disposal

When selecting and designing gas cleaning systems, careful consideration must be given to the safe disposal of the collected material. As shown in table 55.14, some processes produce large amounts of contaminants. If most of the contaminants are collected by the gas cleaning equipment there can be a hazardous waste disposal problem.

In some cases the wastes may contain valuable products that can be recycled, such as heavy metals from a smelter, or solvent from a painting line. The wastes can be used as a raw material for another industrial process—for example, sulphur dioxide collected as sulphuric acid can be used in the manufacture of fertilizers.

Where the wastes cannot be recycled or reused, disposal may not be simple. Not only can the volume be a problem, but they may be hazardous themselves. For example, if the sulphuric acid captured from a boiler or smelter cannot be reused, it will have to be further treated to neutralize it before disposal.

Dispersion

Dispersion can reduce the concentration of a pollutant at a target. However, it must be remembered that dispersion does not reduce the total amount of material leaving a plant. A tall stack only allows the plume to spread out and be diluted before it reaches ground level, where susceptible targets are likely to exist. If the pollutant is primarily a nuisance, such as an odour, dispersion may be acceptable. However if the material is persistent or cumulative, such as heavy metals, dilution may not be an answer to an air pollution problem.

Dispersion should be used with caution. Local meteorological and ground surface conditions must be taken into consideration. For example, in colder climates, particularly with snow cover, there can be frequent temperature inversions that can trap pollutants close to the ground, resulting in unexpectedly high exposures. Similarly, if a plant is located in a valley, the plumes may move up and down the valley, or be blocked by surrounding hills so that they do not spread out and disperse as expected.

Administrative controls

In addition to the technological systems, there is another group of controls that must be considered in the overall design of an air pollution control system. For the large part, they come from the basic tools of industrial hygiene.

Substitution

One of the preferred occupational hygiene methods for controlling environmental hazards in the workplace is to substitute a safer material or process. If a safer process or material can be used, and harmful emissions avoided, the type or efficacy of

Table 55.13 • Gas cleaning methods for removing harmful gases, vapours and particulates from industrial process emissions.

Control method Gases/Vapours	Examples	Description	Efficiency
Condensation	Contact condensers Surface condensers	The vapour is cooled and condensed to a liquid. This is inefficient and is used as a preconditioner to other methods	80+% when concentration >2,000 ppm
Absorption	Wet scrubbers (packed or plate absorbers)	The gas or vapour is collected in a liquid.	82–95% when concentration <100 ppm 95–99% when concentration >100 ppm
Adsorption	Carbon Alumina Silica gel Molecular sieve	The gas or vapour is collected on a solid.	90+% when concentration <1,000 ppm 95+% when concentration >1,000 ppm
Incineration	Flares Incinerator Catalytic incinerator	An organic gas or vapour is oxidized by heating it to a high temperature and holding it at that temperature for a sufficient time period.	Not recommended when concentration <2,000 ppm 80+% when concentration >2,000 ppm
Particulates			
Inertial separators	Cyclones	Particle-laden gases are forced to change direction. The inertia of the particle causes them to separate from the gas stream. This is inefficient and is used as a preconditioner to other methods.	70–90%
Wet scrubbers	Venturi Wetted filter Tray or sieve scrubber	Liquid droplets (water) collect the particles by impaction, interception and diffusion. The droplets and their particles are then separated from the gas stream.	For 5 μm particles, 98.5% at 6.8 w.g.; 99.99+% at 50 w.g. For 1 μm particles, 45% at 6.8 w.g.; 99.95 at 50 w.g.
Electrostatic precipitators	Plate-wire Flat-plate Tubular Wet	Electrical forces are used to move the particles out of the gas stream onto collection plates	95–99.5% for 0.2 μm particles 99.25–99.9+% for 10 μm particles
Filters	Baghouse	A porous fabric removes particulates from the gas stream. The porous dust cake that forms on the fabric then actually does the filtration.	99.9% for 0.2 μm particles 99.5% for 10 μm particles

controls becomes academic. It is better to avoid the problem than it is to try to correct a bad first decision. Examples of substitution include the use of cleaner fuels, covers for bulk storage and reduced temperatures in dryers.

This applies to minor purchases as well as the major design criteria for the plant. If only environmentally safe products or processes are purchased, there will be no risk to the environment, indoors or out. If the wrong purchase is made, the remainder of the programme consists of trying to compensate for that first decision. If a low-cost but hazardous product or process is purchased it may need special handling procedures and equipment, and special disposal methods. As a result, the low-cost item may have only a low purchase price, but a high price to use and dispose of it. Perhaps a safer but more expensive material or process would have been less costly in the long run.

Local ventilation

Controls are required for all the identified problems that cannot be avoided by substituting safer materials or methods. Emissions start at the individual worksite, not the stack. A ventilation system that captures and controls emissions at the source will help protect the community if it is properly designed. The hoods and ducts of the ventilation system are part of the total air pollution control system.

A local ventilation system is preferred. It does not dilute the contaminants, and provides a concentrated gas stream that is easier to clean before release to the environment. Gas cleaning equipment is more efficient when cleaning air with higher concentrations of contaminants. For example, a capture hood over the pouring spout of a metal furnace will prevent contaminants from getting into the environment, and deliver the fumes to the gas cleaning system. In table 55.13 it can be seen that cleaning efficiencies for absorption and adsorption cleaners increase with the concentration of the contaminant, and condensation cleaners are not recommended for low levels (<2,000 ppm) of contaminants.

If pollutants are not caught at the source and are allowed to escape through windows and ventilation openings, they become uncontrolled fugitive emissions. In some cases, these uncontrolled fugitive emissions can have a significant impact on the immediate neighbourhood.

Isolation

Isolation—locating the plant away from susceptible targets—can be a major control method when engineering controls are inadequate by themselves. This may be the only means of achieving

55. ENVIRONMENTAL POLLUTION CONTROL

Table 55.14 • Sample uncontrolled emission rates for selected industrial processes.

Industrial source	Emission rate
100 ton electric furnace	257 tons/year particulates
1,500 MM BTU/hr oil/gas turbine	444 lb/hr SO_2
41.7 ton/hr incinerator	208 lb/hr NO_x
100 trucks/day clear coat	3,795 lb/week organics

an acceptable level of control when best available control technology (BACT) must be relied on. If, after applying the best available controls, a target group is still at risk, consideration must be given to finding an alternate site where sensitive populations are not present.

Isolation, as presented above, is a means of separating an individual plant from susceptible targets. Another isolation system is where local authorities use zoning to separate classes of industries from susceptible targets. Once industries have been separated from target populations, the population should not be allowed to relocate next to the facility. Although this seems like common sense, it isn't employed as often as it should be.

Work procedures

Work procedures must be developed to ensure that equipment is used properly and safely, without risk to workers or the environment. Complex air pollution systems must be properly maintained and operated if they are to do their job as intended. An important factor in this is staff training. Staff must be trained in how to use and maintain the equipment to reduce or eliminate the amount of hazardous materials emitted to the workplace or the community. In some cases BACT relies on good practice to ensure acceptable results.

Real time monitoring

A system based on real time monitoring is not popular, and is not commonly used. In this case, continuous emission and meteorological monitoring can be combined with dispersion modelling to predict downwind exposures. When the predicted exposures approach the acceptable levels, the information is used to reduce production rates and emissions. This is an inefficient method, but may be an acceptable interim control method for an existing facility.

The converse of this to announce warnings to the public when conditions are such that excessive concentrations of contaminants may exist, so that the public can take appropriate action. For example, if a warning is sent out that atmospheric conditions are such that sulphur dioxide levels downwind of a smelter are excessive, susceptible populations such as asthmatics would know not to go outside. Again, this may be an acceptable interim control until permanent controls are installed.

Real time atmospheric and meteorological monitoring is sometimes used to avoid or reduce major air pollution events where multiple sources may exist. When it becomes evident that excessive air pollution levels are likely, the personal use of cars may be restricted and major emitting industries shut down.

Maintenance/housekeeping

In all cases the effectiveness of the controls depends on proper maintenance; the equipment has to operate as intended. Not only must the air pollution controls be maintained and used as intended, but the processes generating potential emissions must be maintained and operated properly. An example of an industrial process is a wood chip dryer with a failing temperature controller; if the dryer is operated at too high a temperature, it will emit more materials, and perhaps a different type of material, from the drying wood. An example of gas cleaner maintenance affecting emissions would be a poorly maintained baghouse with broken bags, which would allow particulates to pass through the filter.

Housekeeping also plays an important part in controlling total emissions. Dusts that are not quickly cleaned up inside the plant can become re-entrained and present a hazard to staff. If the dusts are carried outside of the plant, they are a community hazard. Poor housekeeping in the plant yard could present a significant risk to the community. Uncovered bulk materials, plant wastes or vehicle-raised dusts can result in pollutants being carried on the winds into the community. Keeping the yard clean, using proper containers or storage sites, is important in reducing total emissions. A system must be not only designed properly, but used properly as well if the community is to be protected.

A worst case example of poor maintenance and housekeeping would be the lead recovery plant with a broken lead dust conveyor. The dust was allowed to escape from the conveyor until the pile was so high the dust could slide down the pile and out a broken window. Local winds then carried the dust around the neighbourhood.

Equipment for Emission Sampling

Source sampling can be carried out for several reasons:

- *To characterize the emissions.* To design an air pollution control system, one must know what is being emitted. Not only the volume of gas, but the amount, identity and, in the case of particulates, size distribution of the material being emitted must be known. The same information is necessary to catalogue total emissions in a neighbourhood.
- *To test equipment efficiency.* After an air pollution control system has been purchased, it should be tested to ensure that it is doing the intended job.
- *As part of a control system.* When emissions are continuously monitored, the data can be used to fine tune the air pollution control system, or the plant operation itself.
- *To determine compliance.* When regulatory standards include emission limits, emission sampling can be used to determine compliance or non-compliance with the standards.

The type of sampling system used will depend on the reason for taking the samples, costs, availability of technology, and training of staff.

Visible emissions

Where there is a desire to reduce the soiling power of the air, improve visibility or prevent the introduction of aerosols into the atmosphere, standards may be based on visible emissions.

Visible emissions are composed of small particles or coloured gases. The more opaque a plume is, the more material is being emitted. This characteristic is evident to the sight, and trained observers can be used to assess emission levels. There are several advantages to using this method of assessing emission standards:

- No expensive equipment is required.
- One person can make many observations in a day.
- Plant operators can quickly assess the effects of process changes at low cost.
- Violators can be cited without time-consuming source testing.
- Questionable emissions can be located and the actual emissions then determined by source testing as described in the following sections.

Figure 55.5 • A diagram of an isokinetic sampling train for sulphur dioxide.

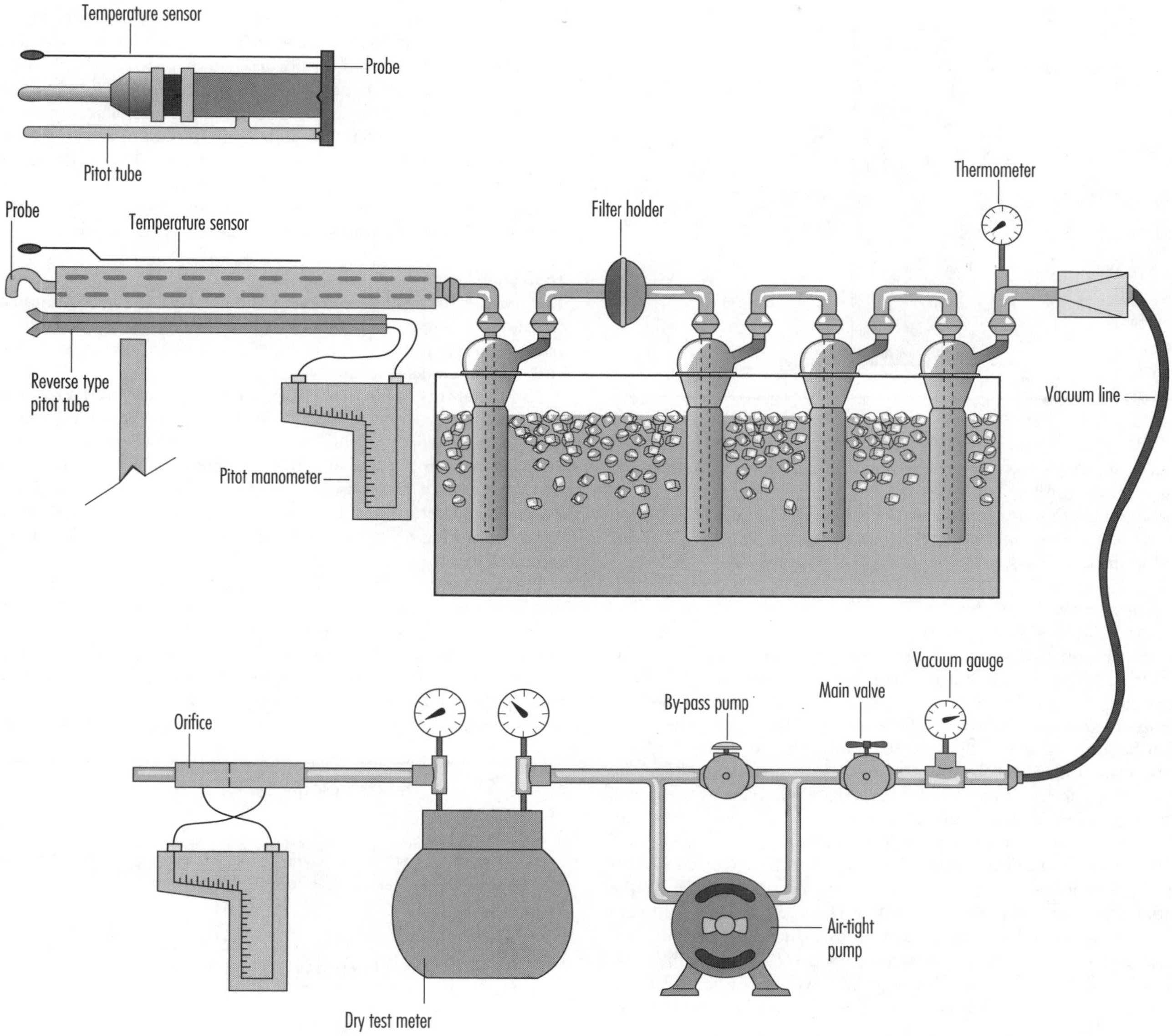

Extractive sampling

A much more rigorous sampling method calls for a sample of the gas stream to be removed from the stack and analysed. Although this sounds simple, it does not translate into a simple sampling method.

The sample should be collected isokinetically, especially when particulates are being collected. Isokinetic sampling is defined as sampling by drawing the sample into the sampling probe at the same velocity that the material is moving in the stack or duct. This is done by measuring the velocity of the gas stream with a pitot tube and then adjusting the sampling rate so that the sample enters the probe at the same velocity. This is essential when sampling for particulates, since larger, heavier particles will not follow a change in direction or velocity. As a result the concentration of larger particles in the sample will not be representative of the gas stream and the sample will be inaccurate.

A sample train for sulphur dioxide is shown in figure 55.5. It is not simple, and a trained operator is required to ensure that a sample is collected properly. If something other than sulphur dioxide is to be sampled, the impingers and ice bath can be removed and the appropriate collection device inserted.

Extractive sampling, particularly isokinetic sampling, can be very accurate and versatile, and has several uses:

• It is a recognized sampling method with adequate quality controls, and thus can be used to determine compliance with standards.
• The potential accuracy of the method makes it suitable for performance testing of new control equipment.
• Since samples can be collected and analysed under controlled laboratory conditions for many components, it is useful for characterizing the gas stream.

Figure 55.6 • A simple transmissometer to measure particulates in a stack.

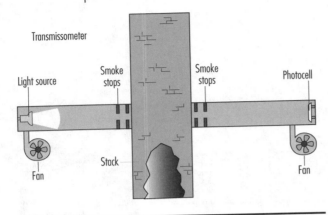

A simplified and automated sampling system can be connected to a continuous gas (electrochemical, ultraviolet-photometric or flame ionization sensors) or particulate (nephelometer) analyzer to continuously monitor emissions. This can provide documentation of the emissions, and instantaneous operating status of the air pollution control system.

In situ sampling

Emissions can also be sampled in the stack. Figure 55.6 is a representation of a simple transmissometer used to measure materials in the gas stream. In this example, a beam of light is projected across the stack to a photocell. The particulates or coloured gas will absorb or block some of the light. The more material, the less light will get to the photocell. (See figure 55.6.)

By using different light sources and detectors such as ultraviolet light (UV), gases transparent to visible light can be detected. These devices can be tuned to specific gases, and thus can measure gas concentration in the waste stream.

An *in situ* monitoring system has an advantage over an extractive system in that it can measure the concentration across the entire stack or duct, whereas the extractive method measures concentrations only at the point from which the sample was extracted. This can result in significant error if the sample gas stream is not well mixed. However, the extractive method offers more methods of analysis, and thus perhaps can be used in more applications.

Since the *in situ* system provides a continuous readout, it can be used to document emissions, or to fine tune the operating system.

● WATER POLLUTION CONTROL

Herbert C. Preul

This article is intended to provide the reader with an understanding of currently available technology for approaching water pollution control, building on the discussion of trends and occurrence provided by Hespanhol and Helmer in the chapter *Environmental Health Hazards*. The following sections address the control of water pollution problems, first under the heading "Surface Water Pollution Control" and then under the heading "Groundwater Pollution Control".

Surface Water Pollution Control

Definition of water pollution

Water pollution refers to the qualitative state of impurity or uncleanliness in hydrologic waters of a certain region, such as a watershed. It results from an occurrence or process which causes a reduction in the utility of the earth's waters, especially as related to human health and environmental effects. The pollution process stresses the loss of purity through contamination, which further implies intrusion by or contact with an outside source as the cause. The term tainted is applied to extremely low levels of water pollution, as in their initial corruption and decay. Defilement is the result of pollution and suggests violation or desecration.

Hydrologic waters

The earth's natural waters may be viewed as a continuously circulating system as shown in figure 55.7, which provides a graphic illustration of waters in the hydrologic cycle, including both surface and subsurface waters.

As a reference for water quality, distilled waters (H_2O) represent the highest state of purity. Waters in the hydrologic cycle may be viewed as natural, but are not pure. They become polluted from both natural and human activities. Natural degradation effects may result from a myriad of sources—from fauna, flora, volcano eruptions, lightning strikes causing fires and so on, which on a long-term basis are considered to be prevailing background levels for scientific purposes.

Human-made pollution disrupts the natural balance by superimposing waste materials discharged from various sources. Pollutants may be introduced into the waters of the hydrologic cycle at any point. For example: atmospheric precipitation (rainfall) may become contaminated by air pollutants; surface waters may become polluted in the runoff process from watersheds; sewage may be discharged into streams and rivers; and groundwaters may

Figure 55.7 • The hydrologic cycle.

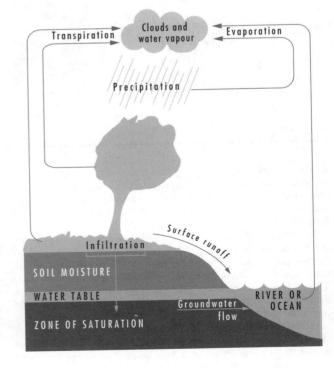

Figure 55.8 • Distribution of precipitation.

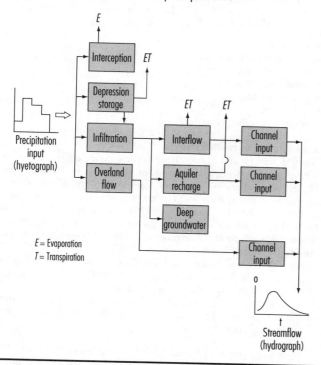

E = Evaporation
T = Transpiration

Figure 55.9 • Regional hydrologic cycle.

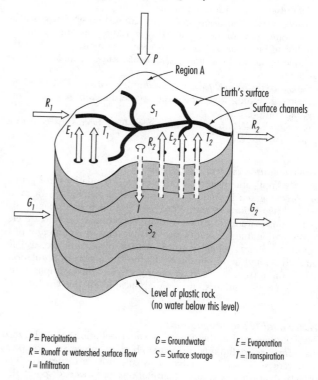

P = Precipitation
R = Runoff or watershed surface flow
I = Infiltration

G = Groundwater
S = Surface storage

E = Evaporation
T = Transpiration

become polluted through infiltration and underground contamination.

Figure 55.8 shows a distribution of hydrologic waters. Pollution is then superimposed on these waters and may therefore be viewed as an unnatural or unbalanced environmental condition. The process of pollution may occur in waters of any part of the hydrologic cycle, and is more obvious on the earth's surface in the form of runoff from watersheds into streams and rivers. However groundwater pollution is also of major environmental impact and is discussed following the section on surface water pollution.

Watershed sources of water pollution

Watersheds are the originating domain of surface water pollution. A watershed is defined as an area of the earth's surface on which hydrologic waters fall, accumulate, are used, disposed of, and eventually are discharged into streams, rivers or other bodies of water. It is comprised of a drainage system with ultimate runoff or collection in a stream or river. Large river watersheds are usually referred to as drainage basins. Figure 55.9 is a representation of the hydrologic cycle on a regional watershed. For a region, the disposition of the various waters can be written as a simple equation, which is the basic equation of hydrology as written by Viessman, Lewis and Knapp (1989); typical units are mm/year:

$$P - R - G - E - T = \pm S$$

where:

P = precipitation (i.e., rainfall, snowfall, hail)
R = runoff or watershed surface flow
G = groundwater
E = evaporation
T = transpiration
S = surface storage

Precipitation is viewed as the initiating form in the above hydrologic budget. The term runoff is synonymous with stream flow. Storage refers to reservoirs or detention systems which collect

waters; for example, a human-made dam (barrage) on a river creates a reservoir for purposes of water storage. Groundwater collects as a storage system and may flow from one location to another; it may be influent or effluent in relation to surface streams. Evaporation is a water surface phenomenon, and transpiration is associated with transmission from biota.

Although watersheds may vary greatly in size, certain drainage systems for water pollution designation are classified as urban or non-urban (agricultural, rural, undeveloped) in character. Pollution occurring within these drainage systems originates from the following sources:

Point sources: waste discharges into a receiving water body at a specific location, at a point such as a sewer pipe or some type of concentrated system outlet.

Non-point (dispersed) sources: pollution entering a receiving water body from dispersed sources in the watershed; uncollected rainfall runoff water drainage into a stream is typical. Non-point sources are also sometimes referred to as "diffuse" waters; however, the term dispersed is seen as more descriptive.

Intermittent sources: from a point or source which discharges under certain circumstances, such as with overloaded conditions; combined sewer overflows during heavy rainfall runoff periods are typical.

Water pollutants in streams and rivers

When deleterious waste materials from the above sources are discharged into streams or other bodies of water, they become pollutants which have been classified and described in a previous section. Pollutants or contaminants which enter a body of water can be further divided into:

• *degradable (non-conservative) pollutants:* impurities which eventually decompose into harmless substances or which may be removed by treatment methods; that is, certain organic materials and chemicals, domestic sewage, heat, plant nutrients, most bacteria and viruses, certain sediments

- *non-degradable (conservative) pollutants*: impurities which persist in the water environment and do not reduce in concentration unless diluted or removed through treatment; that is, certain organic and inorganic chemicals, salts, colloidal suspensions
- *hazardous waterborne pollutants*: complex forms of deleterious wastes including toxic trace metals, certain inorganic and organic compounds
- *radionuclide pollutants*: materials which have been subjected to a radioactive source.

Water pollution control regulations

Broadly applicable water pollution control regulations are generally promulgated by national governmental agencies, with more detailed regulations by states, provinces, municipalities, water districts, conservation districts, sanitation commissions and others. At the national and state (or province) levels, environmental protection agencies (EPAs) and ministries of health are usually charged with this responsibility. In the discussion of regulations below, the format and certain portions follow the example of the water quality standards currently applicable for the US State of Ohio.

Water quality use designations

The ultimate goal in the control of water pollution would be zero discharge of pollutants to water bodies; however, complete achievement of this objective is usually not cost effective. The preferred approach is to set limitations on waste disposal discharges for the reasonable protection of human health and the environment. Although these standards may vary widely in different jurisdictions, use designations for specific bodies of water are commonly the basis, as briefly addressed below.

Water supplies include:

- *public water supply*: waters which with conventional treatment will be suitable for human consumption
- *agricultural supply*: waters suitable for irrigation and livestock watering without treatment
- *industrial/commercial supply*: waters suitable for industrial and commercial uses with or without treatment.

Recreational activities include:

- *bathing waters*: waters which during certain seasons are suitable for swimming as approved for water quality along with protective conditions and facilities
- *primary contact*: waters which during certain seasons are suitable for full body contact recreation such as swimming, canoeing and underwater diving with minimal threat to public health as a result of water quality
- *secondary contact*: waters which during certain seasons are suitable for partial body contact recreation such as, but not limited to, wading, with minimal threat to public health as a result of water quality.

Public water resources are categorized as water bodies which lie within park systems, wetland, wildlife areas, wild, scenic and recreational rivers and publicly owned lakes, and waters of exceptional recreational or ecological significance.

Aquatic life habitats

Typical designations will vary according to climates, but relate to conditions in water bodies for supporting and maintaining certain aquatic organisms, especially various species of fish. For example, use designations in a temperate climate as subdivided in regulations for the State of Ohio Environmental Protection Agency (EPA) are listed below without detailed descriptions:

- warmwater
- limited warmwater
- exceptional warmwater
- modified warmwater
- seasonal salmonid
- coldwater
- limited resource water.

Water pollution control criteria

Natural waters and wastewaters are characterized in terms of their physical, chemical and biological composition. The principal physical properties and the chemical and biological constituents of wastewater and their sources are a lengthy list, reported in a textbook by Metcalf and Eddy (1991). Analytical methods for these determinations are given in a widely used manual entitled *Standard Methods for the Examination of Water and Waste Water* by the American Public Health Association (1995).

Each designated water body should be controlled according to regulations which may be comprised of both basic and more detailed numerical criteria as briefly discussed below.

Basic freedom from pollution. To the extent practical and possible, all bodies of water should attain the basic criteria of the "Five Freedoms from Pollution":

1. free from suspended solids or other substances that enter the waters as a result of human activity and that will settle to form putrid or otherwise objectionable sludge deposits, or that will adversely affect aquatic life
2. free from floating debris, oil, scum and other floating materials entering the waters as a result of human activity in amounts sufficient to be unsightly or cause degradation
3. free from materials entering the waters as a result of human activity, producing colour, odour or other conditions in such degree as to create a nuisance
4. free from substances entering the waters as a result of human activity, in concentrations that are toxic or harmful to human, animal or aquatic life and/or are rapidly lethal in the mixing zone
5. free from nutrients entering the waters as a result of human activity, in concentrations that create nuisance growths of aquatic weeds and algae.

Water quality criteria are numerical limitations and guidelines for the control of chemical, biological and toxic constituents in bodies of water.

With over 70,000-plus chemical compounds in use today it is impractical to specify the control of each. However, criteria for chemicals can be established on the basis of limitations as they first of all relate to three major classes of consumption and exposure:

Class 1: Chemical criteria for protection of human health are of first major concern and should be set according to recommendations from governmental health agencies, the WHO and recognized health research organizations.

Class 2: Chemical criteria for control of agricultural water supply should be based on recognized scientific studies and recommendations which will protect against adverse effects on crops and livestock as a result of crop irrigation and livestock watering.

Class 3: Chemical criteria for protection of aquatic life should be based on recognized scientific studies regarding the sensitivity of these species to specific chemicals and also as related to human consumption of fish and sea foods.

Wastewater effluent criteria relate to limitations on pollutant constituents present in wastewater effluents and are a further method of control. They may be set as related to the water use designations of bodies of water and as they relate to the above classes for chemical criteria.

Biological criteria are based on water body habitat conditions which are needed to support aquatic life.

Organic content of wastewaters and natural waters

The gross content of organic matter is most important in characterizing the pollutional strength of both wastewater and natural waters. Three laboratory tests are commonly used for this purpose:

Biochemical oxygen demand (BOD): five-day BOD (BOD5) is the most widely used parameter; this test measures the dissolved oxygen used by micro-organisms in the biochemical oxidation of organic matter over this period.

Chemical oxygen demand (COD): this test is to measure the organic matter in municipal and industrial wastes that contain compounds that are toxic to biological life; it is a measure of the oxygen equivalent of the organic matter that can be oxidized.

Total organic carbon (TOC): this test is especially applicable to small concentrations of organic matter in water; it is a measure of the organic matter that is oxidized to carbon dioxide.

Antidegradation policy regulations

Antidegradation policy regulations are a further approach for preventing the spread of water pollution beyond certain prevailing conditions. As an example, the Ohio Environmental Protection Agency Water Quality Standards antidegradation policy consists of three tiers of protection:

Tier 1: Existing uses must be maintained and protected. No further water quality degradation is allowed that would interfere with existing designated uses.

Tier 2: Next, water quality better than that needed to protect uses must be maintained unless it is shown that a lower water quality is necessary for important economic or social development, as determined by the EPA Director.

Tier 3: Finally, the quality of water resource waters must be maintained and protected. Their existing ambient water quality is not to be degraded by any substances determined to be toxic or to interfere with any designated use. Increased pollutant loads are allowed to be discharged into water bodies if they do not result in lowering existing water quality.

Water pollution discharge mixing zones and waste load allocation modelling

Mixing zones are areas in a body of water which allow for treated or untreated wastewater discharges to attain stabilized conditions, as illustrated in figure 55.10 for a flowing stream. The discharge is initially in a transitory state which becomes progressively diluted from the source concentration to the receiving water conditions. It is not to be considered as a treatment entity and may be delineated with specific restrictions. Typically, mixing zones must not:

- interfere with migration, survival, reproduction or growth of aquatic species
- include spawning or nursery areas
- include public water supply intakes
- include bathing areas
- constitute more than 1/2 the width of a stream
- constitute more than 1/2 the cross-sectional area of a stream mouth
- extend downstream for a distance more than five times the stream width.

Figure 55.10 • Mixing zones.

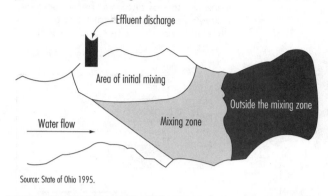

Source: State of Ohio 1995.

Waste load allocation studies have become important because of the high cost of nutrient control of wastewater discharges to avoid instream eutrophication (defined below). These studies generally employ the use of computer models for simulation of water quality conditions in a stream, particularly with regard to nutrients such as forms of nitrogen and phosphorous, which affect the dissolved oxygen dynamics. Traditional water quality models of this type are represented by the US EPA model QUAL2E, which has been described by Brown and Barnwell (1987). A more recent model proposed by Taylor (1995) is the Omni Diurnal Model (ODM), which includes a simulation of the impact of rooted vegetation on instream nutrient and dissolved oxygen dynamics.

Variance provisions

All water pollution control regulations are limited in perfection and therefore should include provisions which allow for judgemental variance based on certain conditions which may prevent immediate or complete compliance.

Risk assessment and management as related to water pollution

The above water pollution control regulations are typical of worldwide governmental approaches for achieving compliance with water quality standards and wastewater effluent discharge limits. Generally these regulations have been set on the basis of health factors and scientific research; where some uncertainty exists as to possible effects, safety factors often are applied. Implementation of certain of these regulations may be unreasonable and exceedingly costly for the public at large as well as for private enterprise. Therefore there is a growing concern for more efficient allocation of resources in achieving goals for water quality improvement. As previously pointed out in the discussion of hydrologic waters, pristine purity does not exist even in naturally occurring waters.

A growing technological approach encourages assessment and management of ecological risks in the setting of water pollution regulations. The concept is based on an analysis of the ecological benefits and costs in meeting standards or limits. Parkhurst (1995) has proposed the application of aquatic ecological risk assessment as an aid in setting water pollution control limits, particularly as applicable for the protection of aquatic life. Such risk assessment methods may be applied to estimate the ecological effects of chemical concentrations for a broad range of surface water pollution conditions including:

- point source pollution
- non-point source pollution

Figure 55.11 • Methods for conducting risk assessment for successive tiers of analysis. Tier 1: Screening level; Tier 2: Quantification of potentially significant risks ; Tier 3: Site-specific risk quantification.

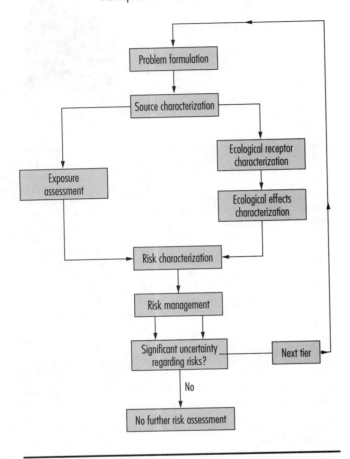

• existing contaminated sediments in stream channels
• hazardous wastes sites as related to water bodies
• analysis of existing water pollution control criteria.

The proposed method consists of three tiers; as shown in figure 55.11 which illustrates the approach.

Water pollution in lakes and reservoirs

Lakes and reservoirs provide for the volumetric storage of watershed inflow and may have long flushing time periods as compared with the rapid inflow and outflow for a reach in a flowing stream. Therefore they are of special concern with regard to the retention of certain constituents, especially nutrients including forms of nitrogen and phosphorous which promote eutrophication. Eutrophication is a natural ageing process in which the water content becomes organically enriched, leading to the domination of undesirable aquatic growth, such as algae, water hyacinth and so on. The eutrophic process tends to decrease aquatic life and has detrimental dissolved oxygen effects. Both natural and cultural sources of nutrients may promote the process, as illustrated by Preul (1974) in figure 55.12, showing a schematic listing of nutrient sources and sinks for Lake Sunapee, in the US State of New Hampshire.

Lakes and reservoirs, of course, can be sampled and analysed to determine their trophic status. Analytical studies usually start with a basic nutrient balance such as the following:

$$\text{(lake influent nutrients)} = \text{(lake effluent nutrients)} + \text{(nutrient retention in lake)}$$

This basic balance can be further expanded to include the various sources shown in figure 55.12.

Flushing time is an indication of the relative retention aspects of a lake system. Shallow lakes, such as Lake Erie, have relatively short flushing times and are associated with advanced eutrophication because shallow lakes often are more conducive to aquatic plant growth. Deep lakes such as Lake Tahoe and Lake Superior have very long flushing periods, which are usually associated with lakes with minimal eutrophication because up to the present time, they have not been overloaded and also because their extreme depths are not conducive to extensive aquatic plant growth except in the epilimnion (upper zone). Lakes in this category are generally classified as oligotrophic, on the basis that they are relatively low in nutrients and support minimal aquatic growth such as algae.

Figure 55.12 • Schematic listing of nutrient (nitrogen and phosphorus) sources and sinks for Lake Sunapee, New Hampshire (US).

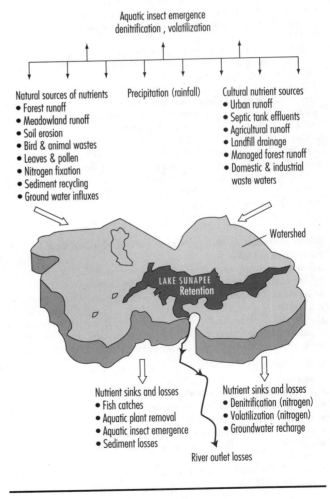

It is of interest to compare the flushing times of some major US lakes as reported by Pecor (1973) using the following calculation basis:

lake flushing time [LFT] = (lake storage volume)/(lake outflow)

Some examples are: Lake Wabesa (Michigan), LFT = 0.30 years; Houghton Lake (Michigan), 1.4 years; Lake Erie, 2.6 years; Lake Superior, 191 years; Lake Tahoe, 700 years.

Although the relationship between the process of eutrophication and nutrient content is complex, phosphorous is typically recognized as the limiting nutrient. Based on fully mixed conditions, Sawyer (1947) reported that algal blooms tend to occur if nitrogen values exceed 0.3 mg/l and phosphorous exceeds 0.01 mg/l. In stratified lakes and reservoirs, low dissolved oxygen levels in the hypoliminion are early signs of eutrophication. Vollenweider (1968, 1969) has developed critical loading levels of total phosphorous and total nitrogen for a number of lakes based on nutrient loadings, mean depths and trophic states. For a comparison of work on this subject, Dillon (1974) has published a critical review of Vollenweider's nutrient budget model and other related models. More recent computer models are also available for simulating nitrogen/phosphorous cycles with temperature variations.

Water pollution in estuaries

An estuary is an intermediate passageway of water between the mouth of a river and a sea coast. This passageway is comprised of a river mouth channel reach with river inflow (fresh water) from upstream and outflow discharge on the downstream side into a constantly changing tailwater level of sea water (salt water). Estuaries are continuously affected by tidal fluctuations and are among the most complex bodies of water encountered in water pollution control. The dominant features of an estuary are variable salinity, a salt wedge or interface between salt and fresh water, and often large areas of shallow, turbid water overlying mud flats and salt marshes. Nutrients are largely supplied to an estuary from the inflowing river and combine with the sea water habitat to provide prolific production of biota and sea life. Especially desired are seafoods harvested from estuaries.

From a water pollution standpoint, estuaries are individually complex and generally require special investigations employing extensive field studies and computer modelling. For a further basic understanding, the reader is referred to Reish 1979, on marine and estuarine pollution; and to Reid and Wood 1976, on the ecology of inland waters and estuaries.

Water pollution in marine environments

Oceans may be viewed as the ultimate receiving water or sink, since wastes carried by rivers finally discharge into this marine environment. Although oceans are vast bodies of salt water with seemingly unlimited assimilation capacity, pollution tends to blight coastlines and further affects marine life.

Sources of marine pollutants include many of those encountered in land-based wastewater environments plus more as related to marine operations. A limited list is given below:

- domestic sewage and sludge, industrial wastes, solid wastes, shipboard wastes
- fishery wastes, sediments and nutrients from rivers and land runoff
- oil spills, offshore oil exploration and production wastes, dredge operations
- heat, radioactive wastes, waste chemicals, pesticides and herbicides.

Table 55.15 • General classification of wastewater treatment operations and processes.

Physical Operations	Chemical Processes	Biological Processes
Flow measurement	Precipitation	Aerobic action
Screening/grit removal	Neutralization	Anaerobic action
Mixing	Adsorption	Aerobic-anaerobic
Flocculation	Disinfection	combinations
Sedimentation	Chemical oxidation	
Flotation	Chemical reduction	
Filtration	Incineration	
Drying	Ion exchange	
Distillation	Electrodialysis	
Centrifuging		
Freezing		
Reverse osmosis		

Each of the above requires special handling and methods of control. The discharge of domestic sewage and sewage sludges through ocean outfalls is perhaps the major source of marine pollution.

For current technology on this subject, the reader is referred to the book on marine pollution and its control by Bishop (1983).

Techniques for reducing pollution in wastewater discharges

Large-scale wastewater treatment is typically carried out by municipalities, sanitary districts, industries, commercial enterprises and various pollution control commissions. The purpose here is to describe contemporary methods of municipal wastewater treatment and then to provide some insights regarding treatment of industrial wastes and more advanced methods.

In general, all processes of wastewater treatment may be grouped into physical, chemical or biological types, and one or more of these may be employed to achieve a desired effluent product. This classification grouping is most appropriate in the understanding of wastewater treatment approaches and is tabulated in table 55.15.

Contemporary methods of wastewater treatment

The coverage here is limited and is intended to provide a conceptual overview of current wastewater treatment practices around the world rather than detailed design data. For the latter, the reader is referred to Metcalf and Eddy 1991.

Municipal wastewaters along with some intermingling of industrial/commercial wastes are treated in systems commonly employing primary, secondary and tertiary treatment as follows:

Primary treatment system: Pre-treat → Primary settling → Disinfection (chlorination) → Effluent

Secondary treatment system: Pre-treat → Primary settling → Biological unit → Second settling → Disinfection (chlorination) → Effluent to stream

Tertiary treatment system: Pre-treat → Primary settling → Biological unit → Second settling → Tertiary unit → Disinfection (chlorination) → Effluent to stream

Figure 55.13 further shows a schematic diagram of a conventional wastewater treatment system. Overview descriptions of the above processes follow.

Primary treatment

The basic objective of primary treatment for municipal wastewaters, including domestic sewage intermingled with some indus-

Figure 55.13 • Schematic diagram of conventional wastewater treatment.

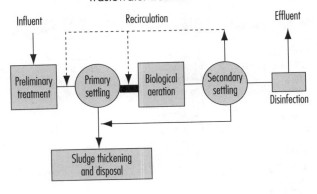

trial/commercial wastes, is to remove suspended solids and clarify the wastewater, to make it suitable for biological treatment. After some pre-treatment handling such as screening, grit removal and comminution, the main process of primary sedimentation is the settling of the raw wastewater in large settling tanks for periods up to several hours. This process removes from 50 to 75% of the total suspended solids, which are drawn off as an underflow sludge collected for separate treatment. The overflow effluent from the process then is directed for secondary treatment. In certain cases, chemicals may be employed to improve the degree of primary treatment.

Secondary treatment

The portion of the organic content of the wastewater which is finely suspended or dissolved and not removed in the primary process, is treated by secondary treatment. The generally accepted forms of secondary treatment in common use include trickling filters, biological contactors such as rotating discs, activated sludge, waste stabilization ponds, aerated pond systems and land application methods, including wetland systems. All of these systems will be recognized as employing biological processes of some form or another. The most common of these processes are briefly discussed below.

Biological contactor systems. Trickling filters are one of the earliest forms of this method for secondary treatment and are still widely used with some improved methods of application. In this treatment, the effluent from the primary tanks is applied uniformly onto a bed of media, such as rock or synthetic plastic media. Uniform distribution is accomplished typically by trickling the liquid from perforated piping rotated over the bed intermittently or continuously according to the desired process. Depending on the rate of organic and hydraulic loadings, trickling filters can remove up to 95% of the organic content, usually analysed as biochemical oxygen demand (BOD). There are numerous other more recent biological contactor systems in use which can provide treatment removals in the same range; some of these methods offer special advantages, particularly applicable in certain limiting conditions such as space, climate and so on. It is to be noted that a following secondary settling tank is considered to be a necessary part of completing the process. In secondary settling, some so-called humus sludge is drawn off as an underflow, and the overflow is discharged as a secondary effluent.

Activated sludge. In the most common form of this biological process, primary treated effluent flows into an activated sludge unit tank containing a previously existing biological suspension called activated sludge. This mixture is referred to as mixed liquor suspended solids (MLSS) and is provided a contact period typically ranging from several hours up to 24 hours or more, depending on the desired results. During this period the mixture is highly aerated and agitated to promote aerobic biological activity. As the process finalizes, a portion of the mixture (MLSS) is drawn off and returned to the influent for continuation of the biological activation process. Secondary settling is provided following the activated sludge unit for the purpose of settling out the activated sludge suspension and discharging a clarified overflow as an effluent. The process is capable of removing up to about 95% of the influent BOD.

Tertiary treatment

A third level of treatment may be provided where a higher degree of pollutant removal is required. This form of treatment may typically include sand filtration, stabilization ponds, land disposal methods, wetlands and other systems which further stabilize the secondary effluent.

Disinfection of effluents

Disinfection is commonly required to reduce bacteria and pathogens to acceptable levels. Chlorination, chlorine dioxide, ozone and ultraviolet light are the most commonly used processes.

Overall wastewater treatment plant efficiency

Wastewaters include a broad range of constituents which generally are classified as suspended and dissolved solids, inorganic constituents and organic constituents.

The efficiency of a treatment system can be measured in terms of the percentage removal of these constituents. Common parameters of measurement are:

- *BOD*: biochemical oxygen demand, measured in mg/l
- *COD*: chemical oxygen demand, measured in mg/l
- *TSS*: total suspended solids, measured in mg/l
- *TDS*: total dissolved solids, measured in mg/l
- *nitrogen forms*: including nitrate and ammonia, measured in mg/l (nitrate is of particular concern as a nutrient in eutrophication)
- *phosphate*: measured in mg/l (also of particular concern as a nutrient in eutrophication)
- *pH*: degree of acidity, measured as a number from 1 (most acid) to 14 (most alkaline)
- *coliform bacteria counts*: measured as most probable number per 100 ml (*Escherichia* and fecal coliform bacteria are most common indicators).

Industrial wastewater treatment

Types of industrial wastes

Industrial (non-domestic) wastes are numerous and vary greatly in composition; they may be highly acidic or alkaline, and often require a detailed laboratory analysis. Specialized treatment may be necessary to render them innocuous before discharge. Toxicity is of great concern in the disposal of industrial wastewaters.

Representative industrial wastes include: pulp and paper, slaughterhouse, brewery, tannery, food processing, cannery, chemical, petroleum, textile, sugar, laundry, meat and poultry, hog feeding, rendering and many others. The initial step in treatment design development is an industrial waste survey, which provides data on variations in flow and waste characteristics. Undesirable waste characteristics as listed by Eckenfelder (1989) can be summarized as follows:

- soluble organics causing depletion of dissolved oxygen
- suspended solids
- trace organics
- heavy metals, cyanide and toxic organics

- colour and turbidity
- nitrogen and phosphorus
- refractory substances resistant to biodegradation
- oil and floating material
- volatile materials.

The US EPA has further defined a list of toxic organic and inorganic chemicals with specific limitations in granting discharge permits. The list includes more than 100 compounds and is too long to reprint here, but may be requested from the EPA.

Treatment methods
The handling of industrial wastes is more specialized than the treatment of domestic wastes; however, where amenable to biological reduction, they are usually treated using methods similar to those previously described (secondary/tertiary biological treatment approaches) for municipal systems.

Waste stabilization ponds are a common method of organic wastewater treatment where sufficient land area is available. Flow-through ponds are generally classified according to their bacterial activity as aerobic, facultative or anaerobic. Aerated ponds are supplied with oxygen by diffused or mechanical aeration systems.

Figures 55.14 and 55.15 show sketches of waste stabilization ponds.

Pollution prevention and waste minimization
When industrial waste in-plant operations and processes are analysed at their source, they often can be controlled so as to prevent significant polluting discharges.

Recirculation techniques are important approaches in pollution prevention programmes. A case study example is a recycling plan for a leather tannery wastewater effluent published by Preul (1981), which included chrome recovery/reuse along with the

Figure 55.14 • Two-cell stabilization pond: cross sectional diagram.

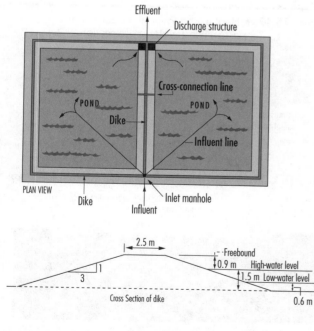

Figure 55.15 • Aerated lagoon types: schematic diagram.

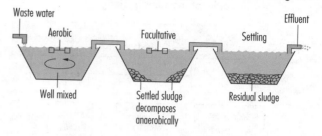

complete recirculation of all tannery wastewaters with no effluent to any stream except in emergencies. The flow diagram for this system is shown in figure 55.16.

For more recent innovations in this technology, the reader is referred to a publication on pollution prevention and waste minimization by the Water Environment Federation (1995).

Advanced methods of wastewater treatment
A number of advanced methods are available for higher degrees of removal of pollution constituents as may be required. A general listing includes:

   filtration (sand and multimedia)
   chemical precipitation
   carbon adsorption
   electrodialysis
   distillation
   nitrification
   algae harvesting
   reclamation of effluents
   micro-straining
   ammonia stripping
   reverse osmosis
   ion exchange
   land application
   denitrification
   wetlands.

The most appropriate process for any situation must be determined on the basis of the quality and quantity of the raw wastewater, the receiving water requirements and, of course, costs. For further reference, see Metcalf and Eddy 1991, which includes a chapter on advanced wastewater treatment.

Advanced wastewater treatment case study
The case study of the Dan Region Sewage Reclamation Project discussed elsewhere in this chapter provides an excellent example of innovative methods for wastewater treatment and reclamation.

Thermal pollution
Thermal pollution is a form of industrial waste, defined as deleterious increases or reductions in normal water temperatures of receiving waters caused by the disposal of heat from human-made facilities. The industries producing major waste heat are fossil fuel (oil, gas and coal) and nuclear power generating plants, steel mills, petroleum refineries, chemical plants, pulp and paper mills, distilleries and laundries. Of particular concern is the electric power generating industry which supplies energy for many countries (e.g., about 80% in the US).

Figure 55.16 • Flow diagram for tannery wastewater effluent recycling system.

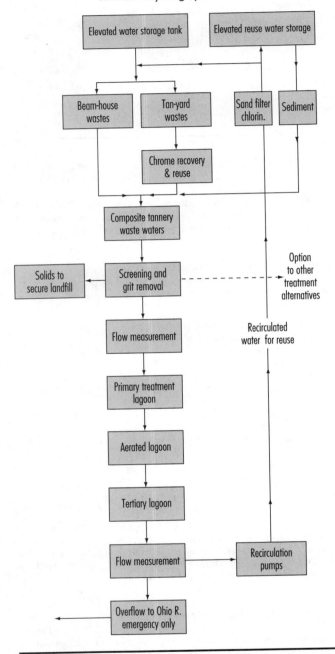

Impact of waste heat on receiving waters

Influence on waste assimilation capacity

- Heat increases biological oxidation.
- Heat decreases oxygen saturation content of water and decreases rate of natural reoxygenation.
- The net effect of heat is generally detrimental during warm months of year.
- Winter effect may be beneficial in colder climates, where ice conditions are broken up and surface aeration is provided for fish and aquatic life.

Influence on aquatic life

Many species have temperature tolerance limits and need protection, particularly in heat affected reaches of a stream or body of water. For example, cold water streams usually have the highest type of sport fish such as trout and salmon, whereas warm waters generally support coarse fish populations, with certain species such as pike and bass fish in intermediate temperature waters.

Thermal analysis in receiving waters

Figure 55.17 illustrates the various forms of natural heat exchange at the boundaries of a receiving water. When heat is discharged to a receiving water such as a river, it is important to analyse the river capacity for thermal additions. The temperature profile of a river can be calculated by solving a heat balance similar to that used in calculating dissolved oxygen sag curves. The principal factors of the heat balance are illustrated in figure 55.18 for a river reach between points A and B. Each factor requires an individual calculation dependent on certain heat variables. As with a dissolved oxygen balance, the temperature balance is simply a summation of temperature assets and liabilities for a given section. Other more sophisticated analytical approaches are available in the literature on this subject. The results from the heat balance calculations can be used in establishing heat discharge limitations and possibly certain use constraints for a body of water.

Thermal pollution control

The main approaches for the control of thermal pollution are:

- improved power plant operation efficiencies
- cooling towers
- isolated cooling ponds
- consideration of alternative methods of power generation such as hydro-power.

Where physical conditions are favourable within certain environmental limits, hydro-electric power should be considered as an alternative to fossil-fuel or nuclear power generation. In hydro-electric power generation, there is no disposal of heat and there is no discharge of waste waters causing water pollution.

Figure 55.17 • Heat exchange at the boundaries of a receiving water cross section.

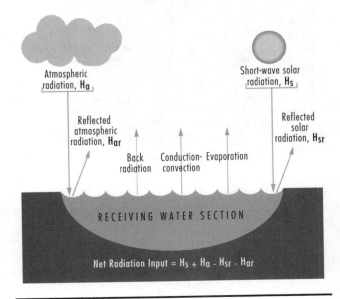

Figure 55.18 • River capacity for thermal additions.

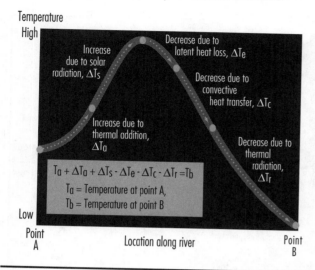

Groundwater Pollution Control

Importance of groundwater

Since the world's water supplies are widely extracted from aquifers, it is most important that these sources of supply be protected. It is estimated that more than 95% of the earth's available fresh water supply is underground; in the United States approximately 50% of the drinking water comes from wells, according to the 1984 US Geological Survey. Because underground water pollution and movement are of subtle and unseen nature, less attention sometimes is given to the analysis and control of this form of water degradation than to surface water pollution, which is far more obvious.

Sources of underground pollution

Figure 55.19 shows the hydrologic cycle with superimposed sources of groundwater contamination. A complete listing of the potential sources of underground pollution is extensive; however, for illustration the most obvious sources include:

- industrial waste discharges
- polluted streams in contact with aquifers
- mining operations
- solid and hazardous waste disposal
- underground storage tanks such as for petroleum
- irrigation systems
- artificial recharge
- sea water encroachment
- spills
- polluted ponds with permeable bottoms
- disposal wells
- septic tank tile fields and leaching pits
- improper well drilling
- agricultural operations
- roadway de-icing salts.

Specific pollutants in underground contamination are further categorized as:

- undesirable chemical constituents (typical, not complete list)—organic and inorganic (e.g., chloride, sulphate, iron, manganese, sodium, potassium)

- total hardness and total dissolved solids
- toxic constituents (typical, not complete list)—nitrate, arsenic, chromium, lead, cyanide, copper, phenols, dissolved mercury
- undesirable physical characteristics—taste, colour and odour
- pesticides and herbicides—chlorinated hydrocarbons and others
- radioactive materials—various forms of radioactivity
- biological—bacteria, viruses, parasites and so on
- acid (low pH) or caustic (high pH).

Of the above, nitrates are of special concern in both ground waters and surface waters. In groundwater supplies, nitrates can cause the disease methaemoglobinaemia (infant cyanosis). They further cause detrimental eutrophication effects in surface waters and occur in a wide range of water resources, as reported by Preul (1991). Preul (1964, 1967, 1972) and Preul and Schroepfer (1968) have also reported on the underground movement of nitrogen and other pollutants.

Pollution travel in underground domain

Groundwater movement is exceedingly slow and subtle as compared with the travel of surface waters in the hydrologic cycle. For a simple understanding of the travel of ordinary groundwater under ideal steady flow conditions, Darcy's Law is the basic approach for the evaluation of groundwater movement at low Reynolds numbers (R):

$$V = K(dh/dl)$$

where:

V = velocity of groundwater in aquifer, m/day
K = coefficient of permeability of aquifer
(dh/dl) = hydraulic gradient which represents the driving force for movement.

In pollutant travel underground, ordinary groundwater (H_2O) is generally the carrying fluid and can be calculated to move at a rate according to the parameters in Darcy's Law. However, the rate of travel or velocity of a pollutant, such as an organic or inorganic chemical, may be different due to advection and hydrodynamic dispersion processes. Certain ions move slower or faster than the general rate of groundwater flow as a result of reactions within the aquifer media, so that they can be categorized as "reacting" or "non-reacting". Reactions are generally of the following forms:

- physical reactions between the pollutant and the aquifer and/or the transporting liquid
- chemical reactions between the pollutant and the aquifer and/or the transporting liquid
- biological actions on the pollutant.

The following are typical of reacting and non-reacting underground pollutants:

- reacting pollutants—chromium, ammonium ion, calcium, sodium, iron and so on; cations in general; biological constituents; radioactive constituents
- non-reacting pollutants—chloride, nitrate, sulphate and so on; certain anions; certain pesticide and herbicide chemicals.

At first, it might seem that reacting pollutants are the worst type, but this may not always be the case because the reactions detain or retard pollutant travel concentrations whereas non-reacting pollutant travel may be largely uninhibited. Certain "soft" domestic and agricultural products are now available which biologically degrade after a period of time and therefore avoid the possibility of groundwater contamination.

Figure 55.19 • Hydrologic cycle and sources of groundwater contamination.

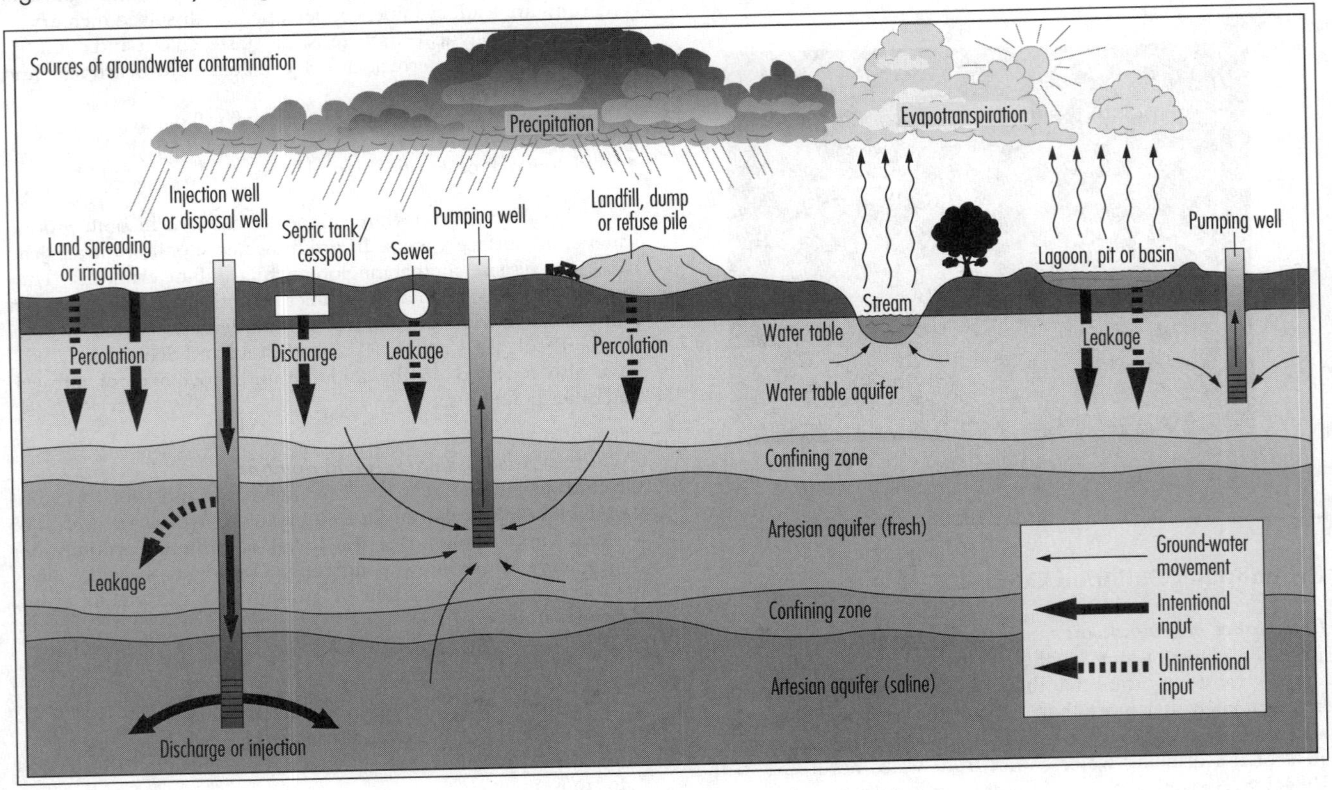

Aquifer remediation

Prevention of underground pollution is obviously the best approach; however, uncontrolled existence of polluted groundwater conditions usually is made known after its occurrence, such as by complaints from water well users in the area. Unfortunately, by the time the problem is recognized, severe damage may have occurred and remediation is necessary. Remediation may require extensive hydro-geological field investigations with laboratory analyses of water samples in order to establish the extent of pollutant concentrations and travel plumes. Often existing wells can be used in initial sampling, but severe cases may require extensive borings and water samplings. These data can then be analysed to establish current conditions and to make future condition predictions. The analysis of groundwater contamination travel is a specialized field often requiring the use of computer models to better understand the groundwater dynamics and to make predictions under various constraints. A number of two- and three-dimensional computer models are available in the literature for this purpose. For more detailed analytical approaches, the reader is referred to the book by Freeze and Cherry (1987).

Pollution prevention

The preferred approach for the protection of groundwater resources is pollution prevention. Although drinking water standards generally apply to the use of groundwater supplies, the raw water supplies require protection from contamination. Governmental entities such as ministries of health, natural resources agencies, and environmental protection agencies are generally responsible for such activities. Groundwater pollution control ef-

forts are largely directed at protection of aquifers and the prevention of pollution.

Pollution prevention requires land-use controls in the form of zoning and certain regulations. Laws may apply to the prevention of specific functions as particularly applicable to point sources or actions which potentially may cause pollution. Control by land-use zoning is a groundwater protection tool which is most effective at the municipal or county level of government. Aquifer and wellhead protection programmes as discussed below are leading examples of pollution prevention.

An aquifer protection programme requires establishing the boundaries of the aquifer and its recharge areas. Aquifers may be of an unconfined or confined type, and therefore need to be analysed by a hydrologist to make this determination. Most major aquifers are generally well known in developed countries, but other areas may require field investigations and hydrogeologic analysis. The key element of the programme in the protection of the aquifer from water quality degradation is control of land use over the aquifer and its recharge areas.

Wellhead protection is a more definitive and limited approach which applies to the recharge area contributing to a particular well. The US federal government by amendments passed in 1986 to the Safe Drinking Water Act (SDWA) (1984) now requires that specific wellhead protection areas be established for public supply wells. The wellhead protection area (WHPA) is defined in the SDWA as "the surface and subsurface area surrounding a water well or well field, supplying a public water supply system, through which contaminants are reasonably likely to move toward and reach such water well or well field." The main objective in the WHPA programme, as outlined by the US EPA (1987), is the delineation of well protection areas based on selected criteria, well operation and hydrogeologic considerations.

DAN REGION SEWAGE RECLAMATION PROJECT: A CASE STUDY

Alexander Donagi

Conception and Design

The Dan Region Reclamation Project of municipal wastewater is the biggest project of its kind in the world. It consists of facilities for treatment and groundwater recharge of municipal wastewater from the Dan Region Metropolitan Area—an eight-city conglomerate centred around Tel Aviv, Israel, with a combined population of about 1.5 million inhabitants. The project was created for the purpose of collection, treatment and disposal of municipal wastewater. The reclaimed effluent, after a relatively long detention period in the underground aquifer, is pumped for unrestricted agricultural use, irrigating the arid Negev (the southern part of Israel). A general scheme of the project is given in figure 55.20. The project was established in the 1960s, and has been growing continuously. At present, the system collects and treats about $110{\times}10^6$ m³ per year. Within a few years, at its final stage, the system will handle 150 to $170{\times}10^6$ m³ per year.

Sewage treatment plants are known to create a multitude of environmental and occupational health problems. The Dan Region project is a unique system of national importance that combines national benefit together with considerable saving of water resources, high treatment efficiency and production of inexpensive water, without creating excessive occupational hazards.

Throughout the design, installation and routine operation of the system, careful consideration has been given to water sanitation and occupational hygiene concerns. All necessary precautions have been taken to ensure that the reclaimed wastewater will be practically as safe as regular drinking water, in the event that people accidentally drink or swallow it. Similarly, appropriate attention has been given to the issue of reducing to the minimum any potential exposure to accidents or other biological, chemical or physical hazards that may affect either the workers at the wastewater treatment plant proper or other workers engaged in the disposal and agricultural use of reclaimed water.

At Stage One of the project, the wastewater was biologically treated by a system of facultative oxidation ponds with recirculation and additional chemical treatment by a lime-magnesium process, followed by detention of the high-pH effluent in "polishing ponds". The partially treated effluent was recharged to the regional groundwater aquifer by means of the Soreq spreading basins.

At Stage Two, the wastewater conveyed to the treatment plant undergoes mechanical-biological treatment by means of an activated-sludge process with nitrification-denitrification. The secondary effluent is recharged to the groundwater by means of the spreading basins Yavneh 1 and Yavneh 2.

The complete system consists of a number of different elements complementing each other:

- a wastewater treatment plant system, comprised of an activated-sludge plant (the biomechanical plant), which treats most of the wastes, and of a system of oxidation and polishing ponds used mostly for treatment of excess sewage flows
- a groundwater recharge system for the treated effluent, which consists of spreading basins, at two different sites (Yavneh and Soreq), that are intermittently flooded; the absorbed effluent passes through the soil's unsaturated zone and through a por-

Figure 55.20 • Dan Region Sewage Reclamation Plant: layout.

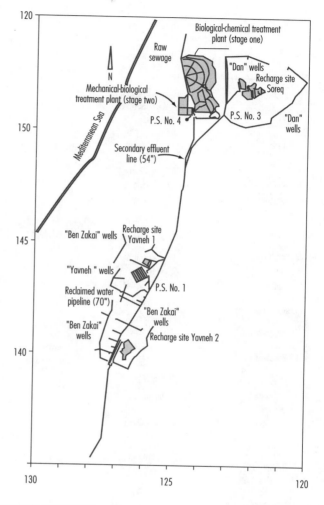

tion of the aquifer, and creates a special zone that is dedicated to complementary effluent treatment and seasonal storage, which is called SAT (soil-aquifer-treatment)
- networks of observation wells (53 wells all together) which surround the recharge basins and allow the monitoring of the efficiency of the treatment process
- networks of recovery wells (a total of 74 active wells in 1993) which surround the recharge sites
- a special and separate reclaimed water conveyance main for unrestricted irrigation of agricultural areas in the Negev; this main is called "The Third Negev Line", and it complements the water supply system to the Negev, which includes another two major fresh water supply main lines
- a setup for chlorination of the effluent, which consists, at present, of three chlorination sites (two more to be added in the future)
- six operational reservoirs along the conveyance system, which regulate the amounts of water pumped and consumed along the system
- an effluent distribution system, composed of 13 major pressure zones, along the effluent main, that supply the treated water to the consumers

Figure 55.21 • Flow diagram of Dan Region Project.

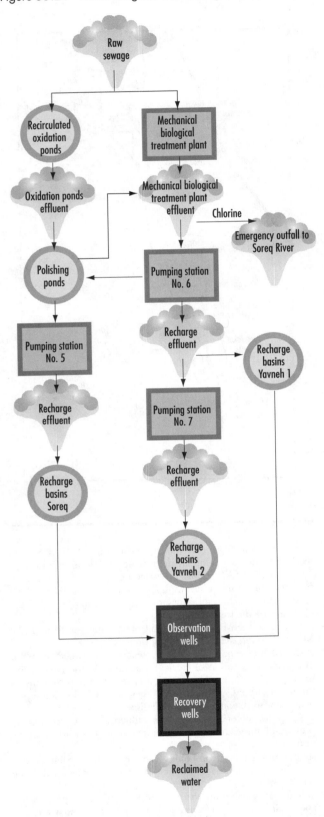

• a comprehensive monitoring system which supervises and controls the complete operation of the project.

Description of the Reclamation System

The general scheme of the reclamation system is presented in figure 55.20 and the flow diagram in figure 55.21. The system consists of the following segments: wastewater treatment plant, water recharge fields, recovery wells, conveyance and distribution system, chlorination setup and a comprehensive monitoring system.

The wastewater treatment plant

The wastewater treatment plant of the Dan Region Metropolitan Area receives the domestic wastes of the eight cities in the region, and also handles part of their industrial wastes. The plant is located within the Rishon-Lezion sand dunes and is based mostly on secondary treatment of the wastes by the activated-sludge method. Some of the wastes, mostly during peak-flow discharges, are treated in another, older system of oxidation ponds occupying an area of 300 acres. The two systems together can handle, at present, about $110 \times 10^6 \, \text{m}^3$ per year.

The recharge fields

The treatment plant effluents are pumped into three different sites located within the regional sand dunes, where they are spread on the sand and percolate downward into the underground aquifer for temporary storage and for additional time-dependent treatment. Two of the spreading basins are used for recharge of the mechanical-biological treatment-plant effluent. These are Yavneh 1 (60 acres, located 7 km to the south of the plant) and Yavneh 2 (45 acres, 10 km south of the plant); the third basin is used for recharge of a mixture of the oxidation ponds effluent and a certain fraction from the biomechanical treatment plant that is required in order to improve the quality of the effluent to the necessary level. This is the Soreq site, which has an area of about 60 acres and is located to the east of the ponds.

The recovery wells

Around the recharge sites there are networks of observation wells through which the recharged water is re-pumped. Not all of the 74 wells in operation in 1993 were active during the whole project. In 1993 a total of about 95 million cubic metres of water were recovered from the system's wells and pumped into the Third Negev Line.

The conveyance and distribution systems

The water pumped from the various recovery wells is collected into the conveyance and distribution system of the Third Line. The conveyance system is composed of three sections, having a combined length of 87 km and a diameter ranging from 48 to 70 inches. Along the conveyance system six different operational reservoirs, "floating" on the main line, were constructed, in order to regulate the water flow of the system. The operational volume of these reservoirs ranges from 10,000 m³ to 100,000 m³.

The water flowing in the Third Line system was supplied to the customers in 1993 through a system of 13 major pressure zones. Numerous water consumers, mostly farms, are connected to these pressure zones.

The chlorination system

The purpose of the chlorination that is carried out in the Third Line is "breakage of the human connection", which means elimination of any possibility for existence of micro-organisms of human origin in Third Line water. Throughout the course of monitoring it was found that there is a considerable increase of

Table 55.16 • List of investigated parameters.

Ag	Silver	µg/l		Mg	Magnesium	mg/l
Al	Aluminium	µg/l		Mn	Manganese	µg/l
ALG	Algae	No./100 ml		Mo	Molybdenum	µg/l
ALKM	Alkalinity as $CaCO_3$	mg/l		Na	Sodium	mg/l
As	Arsenic	µg/l		NH_4^+	Ammonia as NH_4^+	mg/l
B	Boron	mg/l		Ni	Nickel	µg/l
Ba	Barium	µg/l		NKJT	Kjeldahl nitrogen total	mg/l
BOD	Biochemical oxygen demand	mg/l		NO_2	Nitrite as NO_2^-	mg/l
Br	Bromide	mg/l		NO_3	Nitrate as NO_3^-	mg/l
Ca	Calcium	mg/l		ODOR	Odour-threshold odour number	
Cd	Cadmium	µg/l		OG	Oil and grease	µg/l
Cl	Chloride	mg/l		Pb	Lead	µg/l
CLDE	Chlorine demand	mg/l		PHEN	Phenols	µg/l
CLRL	Chlorophile	µg/l		PHFD	pH measured at field	
CN	Cyanides	µg/l		PO_4	Phosphate as PO_4^{-2}	mg/l
Co	Cobalt	µg/l		PTOT	Total phosphorus as P	mg/l
COLR	Colour (platinum cobalt)			RSCL	Residual free chlorine	mg/l
COD	Chemical oxygen demand	mg/l		SAR	Sodium adsorption ratio	
Cr	Chromium	µg/l		Se	Selenium	µg/l
Cu	Copper	µg/l		Si	Silica as H_2SiO_3	mg/l
DO	Dissolved oxygen as O_2	mg/l		Sn	Tin	µg/l
DOC	Dissolved organic carbon	mg/l		SO_4	Sulphate	mg/l
DS_{10}	Dissolved solids at 105 °C	mg/l		Sr	Strontium	µg/l
DS_{55}	Dissolved solids at 550 °C	mg/l		SS_{10}	Suspended solids at 100 °C	mg/l
EC	Electrical conductivity	µmhos/cm		SS_{55}	Suspended solids at 550 °C	mg/l
ENTR	Enterococcus	No./100 ml		STRP	Streptococcus	No./100 ml
F^-	Fluoride	mg/l		T	Temperature	°C
FCOL	Faecal coliforms	No./100 ml		TCOL	Total coliforms	No./100 ml
Fe	Iron	µg/l		TOTB	Total bacteria	No./100 ml
HARD	Hardness as $CaCO_3$	mg/l		TS_{10}	Total solids at 105 °C	mg/l
HCO_3^-	Bicarbonate as HCO_3^-	mg/l		TS_{55}	Total solids at 550 °C	mg/l
Hg	Mercury	µg/l		TURB	Turbidity	NTU
K	Potassium	mg/l		UV	UV (absorb. at 254 nm) (/cm x 10)	
Li	Lithium	µg/l		Zn	Zinc	µg/l
MBAS	Detergents	µg/l				

fecal micro-organisms during the stay of the reclaimed water in the water reservoirs. Therefore it was decided to add more chlorination points along the line, and by 1993 three separate chlorination points were routinely operating. Two more chlorination points are to be added to the system in the near future. The residual chlorine ranges between 0.4 and 1.0 mg/l of free chlorine. This method, whereby low concentrations of free chlorine are maintained at various points along the system rather than a single massive dose at the beginning of the line, secures the breakage of the human connection, and at the same time enables fish to live in the reservoirs. In addition, this chlorination method will disinfect the water in the downstream sections of the conveyance and distribution system, in the event that pollutants entered the system at a point downstream from the initial chlorination point.

The monitoring system

Operation of the reclamation system of the Third Negev Line is dependent upon routine functioning of a monitoring setup which is supervised and controlled by a professional and independent scientific entity. This body is the Research and Development Institute of the Technion—Israel Institute of Technology, in Haifa, Israel.

The establishment of an independent monitoring system has been a mandatory requirement of the Israeli Ministry of Health, the local legal authority according to the Israeli Public Health Ordinance. The need for establishing this monitoring setup stems from the facts that:

1. This wastewater reclamation project is the biggest one in the world.
2. It comprises some non-routine elements that have not as yet been experimented with.
3. The reclaimed water is to be used for unlimited irrigation of agricultural crops.

The major role of the monitoring system is therefore to secure the chemical and sanitary quality of the water supplied by the

55. ENVIRONMENTAL POLLUTION CONTROL

Table 55.17 • The various parameters investigated at the recovery wells.

Group A	Group B	Group C
Indicator parameters	Characteristic Parameters	Complete-Test Parameters
1. Chlorides 2. Electrical conductivity 3. Detergents 4. UV absorption 5. Dissolved oxygen	Group A and: 6. Temperature 7. pH 8. Turbidity 9. Dissolved solids 10. Dissolved organic carbon 11. Alkalinity 12. Hardness 13. Calcium 14. Magnesium 15. Sodium 16. Potassium 17. Nitrates 18. Nitrites 19. Ammonia 20. Kjeldahl total nitrogen 21. Total phosphorus 22. Sulphate 23. Boron	Groups A+B and: 24. Suspended solids 25. Enteric viruses 26. Total bacterial count 27. Coliform 28. Faecal coli 29. Faecal streptococcus 30. Zinc 31. Aluminium 32. Arsenic 33. Iron 34. Barium 35. Silver 36. Mercury 37. Chromium 38. Lithium 39. Molybdenum 40. Manganese 41. Copper 42. Nickel 43. Selenium 44. Strontium 45. Lead 46. Fluoride 47. Cyanides 48. Cadmium 49. Cobalt 50. Phenols 51. Mineral oil 52. TOC 53. Odour 54. Colour

system and to issue warnings regarding any change in the water quality. In addition, the monitoring setup is conducting a follow-up of the complete Dan Region reclamation project, also investigating certain aspects, such as the routine operation of the plant and the chemico-biological quality of its water. This is necessary in order to determine the adaptability of the Third Line water for unlimited irrigation, not only from the sanitary aspect but also from the agricultural viewpoint.

The preliminary monitoring layout was designed and prepared by the Mekoroth Water Co., the major Israeli water supplier and the operator of the Dan Region project. A specially appointed steering committee has been reviewing the monitoring programme on a periodic basis, and has been modifying it according to the accumulated experience gained through the routine operation. The monitoring programme dealt with the various sampling points along the Third Line system, the various investigated parameters and the sampling frequency. The preliminary programme referred to various segments of the system, namely the recovery wells, conveyance line, reservoirs, a limited number of consumer connections, as well as the presence of potable water wells in the vicinity of the plant. The list of parameters included

within the monitoring schedule of the Third Line is given in table 55.16.

Recovery wells monitoring

The sampling programme of the recovery wells is based upon a bi-monthly or tri-monthly measurement of a few "indicator-parameters" (table 55.17). When the chlorides concentration at the sampled well exceeds by more than 15% the initial chlorides level of the well, it is interpreted as a "significant" increase of the share of the recovered effluent within the underground aquifer water, and the well is transferred into the next category of sampling. Here, 23 "characteristic-parameters" are determined, once every three months. In some of the wells, once a year, a complete water investigation, including 54 various parameters, is carried out.

Conveyance system monitoring

The conveyance system, the length of which is 87 km, is monitored at seven central points along the wastewater line. At these points 16 different parameters are sampled once per month. These are: PHFD, DO, T, EC, SS_{10}, SS_{55}, UV, TURB, NO_3^+, PTOT, ALKM, DOC, TOTB, TCOL, FCOL and ENTR. Parameters which are not expected to change along the system are measured at two sampling points only—at the beginning and at the end of the conveyance line. These are: Cl, K, Na, Ca, Mg, HARD, B, DS, SO_4^{-2}, NH_4^+, NO_2^- and MBAS. At those two sampling points, once a year, various heavy metals are sampled (Zn, Sr, Sn, Se, Pb, Ni, Mo, Mn, Li, Hg, Fe, Cu, Cr, Co, Cd, Ba, As, Al, Ag).

Reservoirs monitoring

The monitoring setup of the Third Line reservoirs is based mostly on examination of a limited number of parameters which serve as indicators of biological development in the reservoirs, and for pinpointing the entry of external pollutants. Five reservoirs are sampled, once per month, for: PHFD, T, DO, Total SS, Volatile SS, DOC, CLRL, RSCL, TCOL, FCOL, STRP and ALG. At these five reservoirs Si is also sampled, once per two months. All these parameters are also sampled at another reservoir, Zohar B, at a frequency of six times per year.

Summary

The Dan Region Reclamation Project supplies high-quality reclaimed water for unrestricted irrigation of the Israeli Negev.

Stage One of this project is in partial operation since 1970 and in full operation since 1977. From 1970 to 1993, a total raw sewage amount of 373 million cubic metres (MCM) was conveyed to the facultative oxidation ponds, and a total water amount of 243 MCM was pumped from the aquifer in the period 1974–1993 and supplied to the South of the country. Part of the water was lost, mostly due to evaporation and seepage from the ponds. In 1993 these losses amounted to about 6.9% of the raw sewage conveyed to the Stage One plant (Kanarek 1994).

The mechanical-biological treatment plant, Stage Two of the project, has been in operation since 1987. During the 1987-1993 period of operation a total raw sewage amount of 478 MCM was conveyed to the mechanical-biological treatment plant. In 1993 about 103 MCM of water (95 MCM reclaimed water plus 8 MCM potable water) were conveyed through the system, and used for unlimited irrigation of the Negev.

The recovery-wells water represents the underground aquifer water quality. The aquifer water quality is changing all the time as a result of the percolation of effluent into it. The aquifer water quality approaches that of the effluent for those parameters that are not influenced by the Soil-Aquifer Treatment (SAT) processes, while parameters that are affected by the passage through the soil layers (e.g., turbidity, suspended solids, ammonia, dissolved organic carbon and so on) show considerably lower values. Noteworthy is the chloride content of the aquifer water, which increased within a recent four-year period by 15 to 26%, as evidenced by the changing water quality in the recovery wells. This change indicates the continuous replacement of aquifer water by effluent having a considerably higher chloride content.

The quality of the water in the six reservoirs of the Third Line system is influenced by biological and chemical changes that occur within the open reservoirs. The oxygen content is increased, as a result of photosynthesis of algae and due to dissolution of atmospheric oxygen. Concentrations of various types of bacteria are also increased as a result of random pollution by various water fauna residing near the reservoirs.

The quality of the water supplied to the customers along the system is dependent upon the quality of water from the recovery wells and the reservoirs. Mandatory chlorination of the system's water constitutes an additional safeguard against erroneous use of the water as potable water. Comparison of the Third Line water data with the requirements of the Israeli Ministry of Health regarding quality of wastewater to be used for unlimited agricultural use shows that most of the time the water quality fully satisfies the requirements.

In conclusion it might be said that the Third Line wastewater recovery and utilization system has been a successful environmental and national Israeli project. It has solved the problem of sanitary disposal of the Dan Region sewage and at the same time it has increased the national water balance by a factor of about 5%. In an arid country such as Israel, where water supply, especially for agricultural use, is quite limited, this is a real contribution.

The costs of the recharge operation and maintenance of the reclaimed water, in 1993, was about 3 US cents per m^3 (0.093 NIS/m^3).

The system has been operating since the late 1960s under strict surveillance of the Israeli Ministry of Health and of Mekoroth's occupational safety and hygiene department. There have been no reports of any occupational disease resulting from the operation of this intricate and comprehensive system.

• PRINCIPLES OF WASTE MANAGEMENT

Lucien Y. Maystre

Environmental awareness is leading to a rapid transformation of waste management practices. Interpretation of this change is necessary before examining in more detail the methods that are applied to waste management and to the handling of residues.

Modern principles of waste management are based on the paradigm of a geared connection between the biosphere and the anthroposphere. A global model (figure 55.22) relating these two spheres is based on the assumption that all materials drawn out of the environment end up as waste either directly (from the production sector) or indirectly (from the recycling sector), bearing in mind that all consumption waste flows back to this recycling sector either for recycling and/or for disposal.

From this perspective, recycling must be defined broadly: from the recycling of whole objects (returnables), to the recycling of objects for some of their spare parts (e.g., cars, computers), to the production of new materials (e.g., paper and cardboard, tin cans) or the production of similar objects (recycling, downcycling and so on). Over the long term, this model can be visualized as a steady-state system wherein goods end up as waste after a few days or often a few years.

Deductions from the Model

Some major deductions can be made from this model, provided the various flows are clearly defined. For purposes of this model:

- P_o = *the annual input of materials drawn from the environment (bio-, hydro- or lithospheres). In a steady state, this input is equal to the annual final disposal of waste.*
- P = *the annual production of goods from P_o.*
- C = *the annual flow of goods in the anthroposphere.*
- R = *the annual flow of waste converted to goods through recycling. (In a steady state: $C = R + P$)*
- p = *the effectiveness of production, measured as the ratio of P/P_o.*
- *If r = the effectiveness of recycling, measured as the ratio of R/C, then the relationship is:*
  $C/P_o = p(1-r)$.
- *If $C/P_o = C^*$; then C^* is the ratio of goods to the materials drawn out of nature.*

In other words, C^* is a measure of the meshing of the connection between environment and anthroposphere. It is related to the efficiency of the production and of the recycling sectors. The relationship between C^*, p and r, which is a utility function, can be charted as in figure 55.23, which shows the explicit trade-off between p and r, for a selected value of C^*.

In the past, industry has developed along the line of an increase of the efficiency of production, p. Currently, in the late 1990s, the price of waste disposal through dispersion into the atmosphere, into bodies of water or into soils (uncontrolled tipping), or the burial of waste in confined deposit sites has increased very rapidly, as a result of increasingly stringent environmental protection standards. Under these conditions, it has become economically attractive to increase the effectiveness of recycling (in other words, to increase r). This trend will persist through the coming decades.

One important condition has to be met in order to improve the effectiveness of recycling: the waste to be recycled (in other words the raw materials of the second generation) must be as "pure" as

Figure 55.22 • A global model of the principles of waste management.

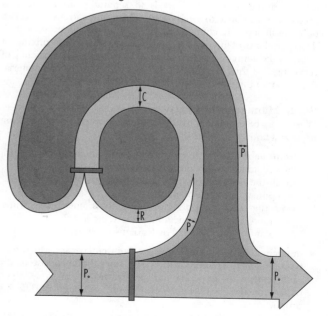

Figure 55.23 • A utility function illustrating production recycling trade-offs.

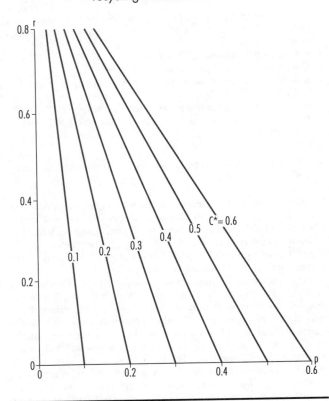

• waste subject to special legislation (e.g., hazardous, infectious, radioactive).

Management of municipal and ordinary commercial waste: Collected by trucks, these wastes can be transported (directly or by road-to-road, road-to-rail or road-to-waterway transfer stations and long-distance transportation means) to a landfill, or to a treatment plant for material recovery (mechanical sorting, composting, biomethanization), or for energy recovery (grid or kiln incinerator, pyrolysis).

Treatment plants produce proportionally small quantities of residues which may be more hazardous for the environment than the original waste. For example, incinerators produce fly ashes with very high heavy metal and complex chemical content. These residues are often classified by legislation as hazardous waste and require appropriate management. Treatment plants differ from landfills because they are "open systems" with inputs and outputs, whereas landfills are essentially "sinks" (if one neglects the small quantity of leachate which deserves further treatment and the production of biogas, which may be an exploited source of energy on very large landfills).

Industrial and domestic equipment: The present trend, which also has commercial contributions, is for the producers of the waste sectors (e.g., cars, computers, machines) to be responsible for the recycling. Residues are then either hazardous waste or are similar to ordinary waste from enterprises.

Construction and demolition waste: The increasing prices of landfills is an incentive for a better sorting of such waste. Separation of the hazardous and burnable waste from the large quantity of inert materials allows the latter to be disposed of at a far lower rate than mixed waste.

Special waste: Chemically hazardous waste must be treated through neutralization, mineralization, insolubilization or be made inert before it can be deposited in special landfills. Infectious waste is best burnt in special incinerators. Radioactive waste is subject to very strict legislation.

Management of Residues

Production and consumption waste which cannot be recycled, down-cycled, reused or incinerated to produce energy must eventually be disposed of. The toxicity for the environment of these residues should be reduced according to the principle of "best available technology at an acceptable price." After this treatment, the residues should be deposited in sites where they will not contaminate the water and the ecosystem and spread into the atmosphere, into the sea or into lakes and streams.

Deposits of waste are usually dated by the combination of multilayer isolation (using clay, geotextiles, plastic foils and so on), the diversion of all exogenous water, and waterproof cover layers. Permanent deposits need to be monitored for decades. Restrictions on land use of a deposit site must also be controlled for long periods of time. Controlled drainage systems for leachates or gases are necessary in most cases.

More biochemically stable and chemically inert residues from waste treatment require less stringent conditions for their final disposal, making it less difficult to find a deposit site for them within the region of production of the waste. Export of wastes or their residues, which always awakens NIMBY (Not In My Back Yard) reactions, might thus be avoided.

possible (i.e., free of unwanted elements which would preclude the recycling). This will be achieved only through the implementation of a generalized policy of "non-mixing" of domestic, commercial and industrial waste at the source. This is often incorrectly termed sorting at the source. To sort is to separate; but the idea is precisely not to have to separate by storing the various categories of waste in separate containers or places until they are collected. The paradigm of modern waste management is non-mixing of waste at the source so as to enable an increase in the efficiency of recycling and thus to achieve a better ratio of goods per material drawn out of the environment.

Waste Management Practices

Waste may be grouped into three major categories, depending on its production:

1. from the primary sector of production (mining, forestry, agriculture, animal breeding, fishery)
2. from the production and transformation industry (foods, equipment, products of all types)
3. from the consumption sector (households, enterprises, transportation, trade, construction, services, etc.).

Waste can be also classified by legislative decree:

• municipal waste and mixed waste from enterprises which may be aggregated as municipal waste, since both consist of the same categories of waste and are of small size (vegetables, paper, metals, glass, plastics and so on), although in differing proportions.
• bulky urban waste (furniture, equipment, vehicles, construction and demolition waste other than inert material)

SOLID WASTE MANAGEMENT AND RECYCLING

Niels Jorn Hahn and Poul S. Lauridsen

Solid wastes are traditionally described as residual products, which represent a cost when one has to resort to disposal.

Management of waste encompasses a complex set of potential impacts on human health and safety, and the environment. The impacts, although the type of hazards may be similar, should be distinguished for three distinct types of operation:

- handling and storage at the waste producer
- collection and transportation
- sorting, processing and disposal.

One should bear in mind that health and safety hazards will arise where the waste is produced in the first place—in the factory or with the consumer. Hence, waste storage at the waste generator—and especially when waste is separated at source—may cause harmful impact on the nearby surroundings. This article will focus on a framework for understanding solid waste management practices and situating the occupational health and safety risks associated with the waste collection, transportation, processing and disposal industries.

Why Solid Waste Management?

Solid waste management becomes necessary and relevant when the structure of the society changes from agricultural with low-density and widespread population to urban, high-density population. Furthermore, industrialization has introduced a large number of products which nature cannot, or can only very slowly, decompose or digest. Hence, certain industrial products contain substances which, due to low degradability or even toxic characteristics, may build up in nature to levels representing a threat to humanity's future use of the natural resources—that is, drinking water, agricultural soil, air and so on.

The objective of solid waste management is to prevent pollution of the natural environment.

A solid waste management system should be based on technical studies and overall planning procedures including:

- studies and estimates on waste composition and amounts
- studies on collection techniques
- studies on processing and disposal facilities
- studies on prevention of pollution of the natural environment
- studies on occupational health and safety standards
- feasibility studies.

The studies must include protection of the natural environment and occupational health and safety aspects, taking the possibilities of sustainable development into consideration. As it seldom is possible to solve all problems at one time, it is important at the planning stage to note that it is helpful to set up a list of priorities. The first step in solving environmental and occupational hazards is to recognize the existence of the hazards.

Principles of Waste Management

Waste management involves a complex and wide range of occupational health and safety relations. Waste management represents a "reverse" production process; the "product" is removal of surplus materials. The original aim was simply to collect the materials, reuse the valuable part of the materials and dispose of

what remained at the nearest sites not used for agriculture purposes, buildings and so on. This is still the case in many countries.

Sources of waste can be described by the different functions in a modern society (see table 55.18).

Each type of waste is characterized by its origin or what type of product it was before it became waste. Hence, basically its health and safety hazards should be laid down upon the restriction of handling the product by the waste producer. In any case, storage of the waste may create new and stronger elements of hazards (chemical and/or biological activity in the storage period).

Solid waste management can be distinguished by the following stages:

- separation at source into specific waste fraction depending on material characteristics
- temporary storage at the waste producer in bins, sacks, containers or in bulk
- collection and transportation by vehicle:
  - manual, horse team, motorized and so on
  - open platform, closed truck body, compacting unit and so on
- transfer station: compaction and reloading to larger transport units
- recycling and/or waste processing facilities
- waste processing:
  - manual or mechanical sorting out into different material fractions for recycling
  - processing of presorted waste fractions to secondary raw materials
  - processing for new (raw) materials
  - incineration for volume reduction and/or energy recovery
  - anaerobic digestion of organics for production of soil conditioner, fertilizer and energy (biogas)
  - composting of organics for production of soil conditioner and fertilizer
- waste disposal:
  - landfill, which should be designed and located to prevent migration of polluted water (landfill leachate), especially into drinking water resources (groundwater resources, wells and rivers).

Recycling of waste can take place at any stage of the waste system, and at each stage of the waste system, special occupational health and safety hazards may arise.

In low-income societies and non-industrial countries, recycling of solid waste is a basic income for the waste collectors. Typically, no questions are put on the health and safety hazards in these areas.

In the intensely industrialized countries, there is a clear trend for putting increased focus on recycling of the huge amounts of waste produced. Important reasons go beyond the direct market value of the waste, and include the lack of proper disposal facilities and the growing public awareness of the imbalance between consumption and protection of the natural environment. Thus, waste collection and scavenging have been renamed recycling to upgrade the activity in the mind of the public, resulting in a steeply growing awareness of the working conditions in the waste business.

Today, the occupational health and safety authorities in the industrialized countries are focusing on working conditions which, a few years ago, passed off unnoticed with unspoken acceptance, such as:

- improper heavy lifting and excessive amount of materials handled per working day

Table 55.18 • Sources of waste.

Activity	Waste description
Industry	Product residues Default products
Wholesale	Default products
Retail	Transport packaging Default products Organics (from food processing) Food waste
Consumer	Transport packaging Retail packaging (paper, glass, metal, plastics, etc.) Kitchen waste (organics) Hazardous waste (chemicals, oil) Bulky waste (used furniture) etc. Garden waste
Construction and demolition	Concrete, bricks, iron, soil, etc.
Infrastructure activities	Park waste Street cleaning waste Clinkers, ashes and flue gas from energy production Sewage sludge Hospital waste
Waste processing	Rejects from sorting facilities Clinkers, ashes and flue gas cleaning products from incineration

- inappropriate exposure to dust of unknown composition
- unnoticed impact by micro-organisms (bacteria, fungi) and endotoxins
- unnoticed exposure to toxic chemicals.

Recycling

Recycling or salvaging is the word covering both reuse (use for the same purpose) and reclamation/recovery of materials or energy.

The reasons for implementing recycling may change depending on national and local conditions, and the key ideas in the arguments for recycling may be:

- detoxification of hazardous waste when high environmental standards are set by the authorities
- resource recovery in low income areas
- reduction of volume in areas where landfilling is predominant
- energy recovery in areas where conversion of waste to energy can replace fossil fuel (coal, natural gas, crude oil and so on) for energy production.

As previously mentioned, recycling can occur at any stage in the waste system, but recycling can be designed to prevent waste from being "born". That is the case when products are designed for recycling and a system for repurchasing after end-use, for instance by putting a deposit on beverage containers (glass bottles and so on).

Hence, recycling may go further than mere implementation of reclamation or recovery of materials from the waste stream.

Recycling of materials implies, in most situations, separation or sorting of the waste materials into fractions with a minimum degree of fineness as a prerequisite to the use of the waste as a substitute for virgin or primary raw materials.

The sorting may be performed by waste producers (source separation), or after collection, meaning separation at a central sorting plant.

Source Separation

Source separation will, by today's technology, result in fractions of waste which are "designed" for processing. A certain degree of source separation is inevitable, as some mixtures of waste fractions can be separated into usable material fractions again only by great (economic) effort. The design of source separation must always take the final type of recycling into consideration.

The goal of the source sorting system should be to avoid a mixing or pollution of the different waste fractions, which could be an obstacle to easy recycling.

The collection of source-sorted waste fractions will often result in more distinct occupational health and safety hazards than does collection in bulk. This is due to concentration of specific waste fractions—for instance, toxic substances. Sorting out of easily degradable organics may result in producing high levels of exposure to hazardous fungi, bacteria, endotoxins and so on, when the materials are handled or reloaded.

Central Sorting

Central sorting may be done by mechanical or manual methods.

It is the general opinion that mechanical sorting without prior source separation by today's known technology should be used only for production of refuse derived fuel (RDF). Prerequisites for acceptable working conditions are total casing of the mechanical equipment and use of personal "space suits" when service and maintenance have to be carried out.

Mechanical central sorting with prior source separation has, with today's technology, not been successful due to difficulties in reaching proper sorting efficiency. When the characteristics of the sorted out waste fractions become more clearly defined, and when these characteristics become valid on a national or international basis, then it can be expected that new proper and efficient techniques will be developed. The success of these new techniques will be closely linked to prudent consideration to obtaining acceptable working conditions.

Manual central sorting should imply prior source separation to avoid occupational health and safety hazards (dust, bacteria, toxic substances and so on). The manual sorting should be limited to only a limited number of waste fraction "qualities" to avoid foreseeable sorting mistakes at the source, and to facilitate easy control facilities at the plant's reception area. As the waste fractions become more clearly defined, it will be possible to develop more and more devices for automatic sorting procedures to minimize direct human exposure to noxious substances.

Why Recycling?

It is important to note that recycling is not a waste processing method that should be seen independently of other waste management practices. In order to supplement recycling, it is necessary to have access to a properly managed landfill and perhaps to more traditional waste processing facilities such as incineration plants and composting facilities.

Recycling should be evaluated in connection with

- local supply of raw materials and energy
- what is substituted—renewable (i.e., paper/tree) resources or non-renewable (i.e., oil) resources.

As long as oil and coal are used as energy resources, for example, incineration of waste and refuse-derived fuel with energy recovery will constitute a viable waste management option based on energy recovery. Minimization of waste quantities by this method, however, must end in final deposits subject to extremely strict environmental standards, which may be very expensive.

CASE STUDY: CANADIAN MULTIMEDIA POLLUTION CONTROL AND PREVENTION ON THE GREAT LAKES

Thomas Tseng, Victor Shantora and Ian R. Smith

The Challenge

The Great Lakes are a shared resource between Canada and the United States (see figure 55.24). The five large lakes contain over 18% of the world's surface water. The basin is home to one in every three Canadians (approximately 8.5 million) and one in every nine Americans (27.5 million). The basin is the industrial heartland of both countries—one-fifth of the US industrial base and one-half of Canada's. Economic activities around the Great Lakes basin generate an estimated 1 trillion dollars of wealth each year. Over time, increasing population and industrial activities created a variety of stresses on the lakes until the need for concerted action to protect the Great Lakes by the two countries was recognized in mid-century.

The Response

Since the 1950s, both countries have put in place domestic and bilateral programmes to address gross pollution problems and also to respond to more subtle water quality concerns. As a result of these actions, Great Lakes waters are visibly cleaner than they were at mid-century, loadings of heavy metals and organic chemicals have decreased and contaminant levels in fish and aquatic birds have gone down significantly. The successes of Canada–United States actions to restore and protect the Great Lakes provide a model for bilateral cooperation on resource management, but challenges remain.

The Case Study in Perspective

The threats posed by persistent toxic substances, however, are long term in nature and their management requires a multimedia, comprehensive at-source approach. To achieve a long-term goal of virtual elimination of persistent toxic substances from the Great Lakes, environmental authorities, industries and other stakeholders in the basin were challenged to develop new approaches and programmes. The purpose of this case study report is to provide a brief summary of Canadian pollution control programmes and the progress achieved by 1995, and to outline initiatives for managing persistent toxics in the Great Lakes. Similar US initiatives and programmes are not discussed herein. Interested readers should contact the Great Lakes National Program Office of the US Environmental Protection Agency in Chicago for information on federal and state programmes for protecting the Great Lakes.

1970s–1980s

A significant problem acknowledged to be affecting Lake Erie in the 1960s was nutrient enrichment or eutrophication. The identified need for bilateral actions prompted Canada and the United States to sign the first Great Lakes Water Quality Agreement (GLWQA) in 1972. The Agreement outlined abatement goals for reducing phosphorus loadings primarily from laundry detergents and municipal sewage effluent. In response to this commitment Canada and Ontario enacted legislation and programmes for controlling point sources. Between 1972 and 1987, Canada and Ontario invested more than 2 billion dollars in sewage treatment plant construction and upgrading in the Great Lakes basin.

Figure 55.24 • Great Lakes drainage basin: St. Lawrence River.

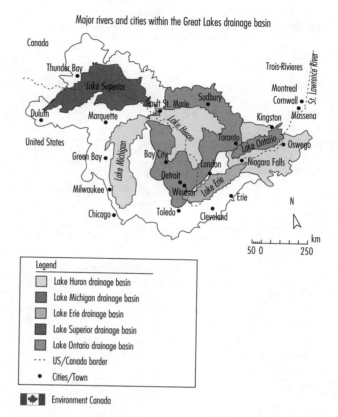

Major rivers and cities within the Great Lakes drainage basin

Legend
- Lake Huron drainage basin
- Lake Michigan drainage basin
- Lake Erie drainage basin
- Lake Superior drainage basin
- Lake Ontario drainage basin
- - - - US/Canada border
- • Cities/Town

Environment Canada

The 1972 GLWQA also identified the need to reduce releases of toxic chemicals into the lakes from industries and other sources such as spills. In Canada, the promulgation of federal effluent (end of pipe) regulations in the 1970s for conventional pollutants from major industrial sectors (pulp and paper, metal mining, petroleum refining and so on) provided a national baseline standard, while Ontario established similar effluent guidelines tailored for local needs including the Great Lakes. Actions by industries and municipalities to meet these federal and Ontario effluent requirements produced impressive results; for example, phosphorus loadings from point sources to Lake Erie were reduced by 70% between 1975 and 1989, and discharges of conventional pollutants from the seven Ontario petroleum refineries were cut by 90% since the early 1970s. Figure 55.25 shows similar loading reduction trends for the pulp and paper and the iron and steel sectors.

By the mid-1970s evidence of elevated concentrations of toxic chemicals in Great Lakes fish and wildlife, reproductive abnormalities in some fish-eating birds and population decline in a number of species implicated persistent bioaccumulative toxic substances, which became the new focus for the binational protection effort. Canada and the United States signed a second Great Lakes Water Quality Agreement in 1978, in which the two countries pledged to "restore and maintain the chemical, physical and biological integrity of the waters of the Great Lakes Ecosystem". A key challenge was the policy "that the discharge of toxic substances in toxic amounts be prohibited and the discharge of any or all persistent toxic substances be virtually eliminated". The call for virtual elimination was necessary, as persistent toxic chemicals

Figure 55.25 • Progress on industrial abatement.

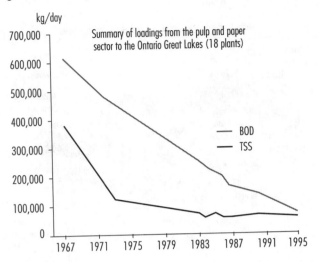

kg/day

Summary of loadings from the pulp and paper sector to the Ontario Great Lakes (18 plants)

BOD
TSS

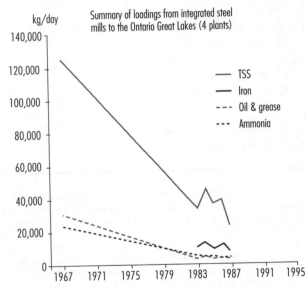

kg/day

Summary of loadings from integrated steel mills to the Ontario Great Lakes (4 plants)

TSS
Iron
Oil & grease
Ammonia

may concentrate and accumulate in the food chain, causing severe and irreversible damages to the ecosystem, whereas chemicals which are not persistent needed to be kept below levels which cause immediate harm.

In addition to tighter controls on point sources, Canada and Ontario developed and/or strengthened controls on pesticides, commercial chemicals, hazardous wastes and non-point sources of pollution such as dump sites and incinerators. Government initiatives became more multimedia oriented, and the concept of "cradle to grave" or "responsible care" for chemicals became the new environmental management philosophy for government and industries alike. A number of persistent toxic pesticides were banned under the federal Pest Control Products Act (DDT, Aldrin, Mirex, Toxaphene, Chlordane) and the Environmental Contaminants Act was used to (1) prohibit commercial, manufacturing and processing uses of persistent toxics (CFC, PPB, PCB, PPT, Mirex, lead) and (2) to limit chemical releases from specific industrial operations (mercury, vinyl chloride, asbestos).

By the early 1980s, results from these programmes and measures and similar American efforts started producing evidence of a rebound. Contaminant levels in Great Lakes sediments, fish and wildlife were on the decline, and noted environmental improvements included the return of bald eagles to the Canadian shore of Lake Erie, a 200-fold increase in cormorant population, a resurgence in osprey on Georgian Bay and the re-establishment in the Toronto Harbour area of common terns—all have been affected by levels of persistent toxic substances in the past, and their recovery illustrates the success of this approach to date.

The trend toward reduced concentrations for some of the persistent toxic substances in fish, wildlife and sediments levelled off by the mid-1980s (see Mirex in herring gull eggs in figure 55.26). It was concluded by scientists that:

1. While the water pollution and contaminants control programmes in place were helpful, they were not enough to bring about further reductions in contaminant concentrations.
2. Additional measures were required for non-point sources of persistent toxics including contaminated sediments, long range atmospheric input of pollutants, abandoned dump sites and so on.
3. Some pollutants can persist in the ecosystem at minute concentrations and can bioaccumulate in the food chain for a long time.
4. The most efficient and effective approach for dealing with persistent toxics is to prevent or eliminate their generation at source rather than virtually eliminate their release.

It was generally agreed that achieving virtual elimination in the environment through the application of zero-discharge philosophy to sources and the ecosystem approach to Great Lakes water quality management needed to be further strengthened and promoted.

To reaffirm their commitment to the virtual elimination goal for persistent toxic substances, Canada and the United States amended the 1978 Agreement through a protocol in November

Figure 55.26 • Mirex in herring gull eggs.

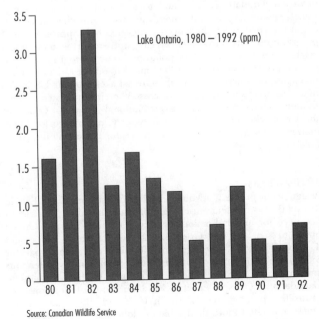

Lake Ontario, 1980 – 1992 (ppm)

Source: Canadian Wildlife Service

1987 (United States and Canada 1987). The protocol designated areas of concern where beneficial uses have been impaired around the Great Lakes, and required the development and implementation of remedial action plans (RAPs) for both point and non-point sources in the designated areas. The protocol also stipulated lakewide management plans (LAMPs) to be used as the main framework for resolving whole-lake impairment of beneficial uses and for coordinating control of persistent toxic substances impacting each of the Great Lakes. Furthermore, the protocol included new annexes for establishing programmes and measures for airborne sources, contaminated sediments and dump sites, spills and control of exotic species.

1990s

Following the signing of the 1987 protocol, the goal of virtual elimination was strongly promoted by environmental interest groups on both sides of the Great Lakes as concerns about the threat of persistent toxics increased. The International Joint Commission (IJC), the binational advisory body created under the 1909 Boundary Waters Treaty, also strongly advocated the virtual elimination approach. An IJC binational task force recommended a strategy for Virtual Elimination in 1993 (see figure 55.27). By the mid-1990s, the IJC and the parties are attempting to define a process for implementing this strategy, including considerations for socioeconomic impacts.

The governments of Canada and Ontario responded in a number of ways to control or reduce the release of persistent toxics. The important programmes and initiatives are briefly summarized below.

Canadian Environmental Protection Act (CEPA)

In 1989, Environment Canada consolidated and streamlined its legal mandates into a single statute. CEPA provides the federal government with comprehensive powers (e.g., information gathering, regulations making, enforcement) over the entire life cycle of chemicals. Under CEPA, the New Substances Notification Regulations establish screening procedures for new chemicals so that persistent toxics that cannot be adequately controlled will be prohibited from being imported, manufactured or used in Canada. The first phase of the Priority Substances List (PSL I) assessment programme was completed in 1994; 25 of the 44 substances assessed were found to be toxic under the definition of CEPA, and the development of management strategies for these toxic chemicals was initiated under a Strategic Options Process (SOP); an additional 56 priority substances will be nominated and assessed in phase II of the PSL programme by the year 2000. The National Pollutant Release Inventory (NPRI) was implemented in 1994 to mandate industrial and other facilities that meet the reporting criteria to annually report their releases to air, water and land, and their transfers in waste, of 178 specified substances. The inventory, modelled on the Toxic Release Inventory (TRI) in the United States, provides an important database for prioritizing pollution prevention and abatement programmes.

Canada-Ontario Agreement (COA)

In 1994, Canada and Ontario set out a strategic framework for coordinated action to restore, protect and conserve the Great Lakes ecosystem with a key focus on reducing the use, generation or release of 13 Tier I persistent toxic substances by the year 2000 (Canada and Ontario 1994). COA also targets an additional list of 26 priority toxics (Tier II) for significant reductions. Specifically for Tier I substances, COA will: (1) confirm zero discharge of five banned pesticides (Aldrin, DDT, Chlordane, Mirex, Toxaphene); (2) seek to decommission 90% of high-level PCBs, destroy 50% now in storage and accelerate destruction of low-level PCBs in storage; and (3) seek 90% reduction in the release of the remain-

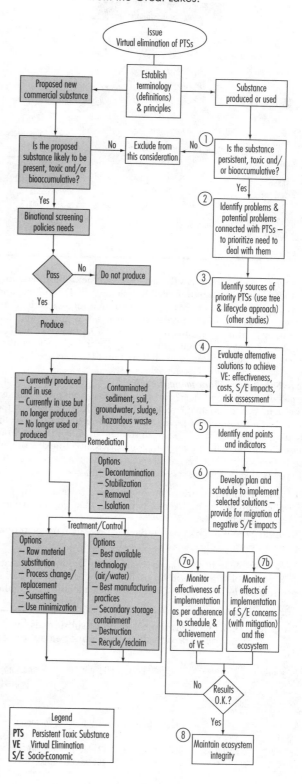

Figure 55.27 • Decision-making process for virtual elimination of persistent toxic substances from the Great Lakes.

55. ENVIRONMENTAL POLLUTION CONTROL

Figure 55.28 • Selection of management objectives under the Toxic Substances Management Policy.

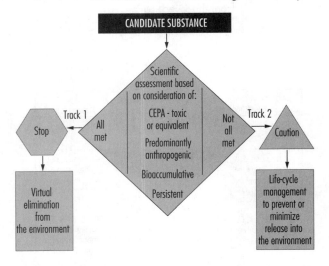

ing seven Tier I substances (benzo(a)pyrene, hexachlorobenzene, alkyl-lead, octachlorostyrene, PCDD (dioxins) PCDF (furans) and mercury). The COA approach is to seek quantitative reductions wherever feasible, and sources are challenged to apply pollution prevention and other means to meet the COA targets. Fourteen projects have already been launched by federal Ontario staff to achieve reduction/elimination of Tiers I and II substances.

Toxic Substances Management Policy

In recognition of the need for a preventive and precautionary approach, Environment Canada announced in June 1995 a national Toxic Substances Management Policy as the framework for efficient management of toxic substances in Canada (Environment Canada 1995a). The policy adopts a two-track approach (see figure 55.28) that recognizes management actions must be tailored to the characteristics of chemicals; that is:

• to virtually eliminate from the environment substances that are predominantly anthropogenic, persistent, bioaccumulative and toxic (Track I)
• to implement full life cycle (cradle-to-grave) management of all other substances of concern (Track II).

A set of scientifically based criteria (Environment Canada 1995b) (see table 55.19) will be used to categorize substances of concern into the two tracks. If a substance identified for either

Table 55.19 • Criteria for the selection of substances for Track 1 toxic substances management policy.

Persistence		Bioaccumulation	Toxicity	Predominantly Anthropogenic
Medium	Half-life			
Air	≥ 2 days	BAF≥ 5,000	CEPA-toxic	Concentration
Water	≥ 182 days	or	or	in environment
Sediment	≥ 365 days	BCP≥ 5,000	CEPA-toxic	largely resulting
Soil	≥ 182 days	or	equivalent	from human
		$\log K_{ow} \geq 5.0$		activity

track is not adequately controlled under existing programmes, additional measures will be identified under the multi-stakeholder Strategic Options Process. The policy is consistent with the Great Lakes Water Quality Agreement and will direct and frame a number of domestic programmes by defining their ultimate environmental objective, but the means and pace of achieving the ultimate objective will vary by chemical and source. Further, Canada's position on persistent toxics will also be framed by this policy in international discussions.

Chlorine Action Plan

A comprehensive approach to managing chlorinated substances within the context of the Toxic Substances Management Policy was announced in October 1994 by Environment Canada (Environment Canada 1994). The approach will be to prune the chlorine-use tree with a five-part action plan that will (1) target action on critical uses and products, (2) improve scientific understanding of chlorine and its impact on health and the environment, (3) detail socioeconomic implications, (4) improve public access to information and (5) promote international actions on chlorinated substances. Chlorine use has already decreased in Canada in recent years, for example by 45% in the pulp and paper sector since 1988. Implementation of the Chlorine Action Plan will accelerate this reduction trend.

Great Lakes Pollution Prevention Initiative

A strong pollution prevention programme has been put in place for the Great Lakes basin. Since March 1991, Environment Canada and the Ontario Ministry of the Environment and Energy have been working together with industries and other stakeholders to develop and implement pollution prevention projects, in contrast to waste treatment or reducing pollution after its generation. In 1995/96, more than 50 projects will cover commercial chemicals, hazardous waste management, federal facilities, industries, municipalities and the Lake Superior basin. Figure 55.29 provides an overview of these projects, which fall into two main categories: programme integration or voluntary agreements. The figure also shows programme linkages with other programmes discussed earlier (NPRI, RAP, LAMP) and a number of institutions that work with Environment Canada closely on green technologies and clean processes, as well as on training, information and communications. Pollution prevention projects can produce impressive results, as evidenced by the Automotive Manufacturers, who have undertaken 15 pilot projects recently, thereby reducing or eliminating 2.24 million kilograms of targeted substances from the manufacture of automobiles at the Ontario facilities of Chrysler, Ford and General Motors.

Accelerated Reduction/Elimination of Toxics (ARET)

ARET is a cooperative multi-stakeholder initiative launched in 1994 that seeks the eventual elimination of 14 priority toxics with an interim target (by the year 2000) of a 90% reduction/elimination and reduced emission (50%) of 87 less harmful toxic substances (ARET Secretariat 1995). As of 1995, more than 200 companies and government agencies are participating in this voluntary initiative. Together, they reduced emissions by 10,300 tonnes in comparison with the 1988 base year and are committed to an additional 8,500 tonnes reduction by the year 2000.

Binational and international strategies

In addition to the above domestic initiatives, Canada and the United States are currently developing a binational strategy to coordinate agency action and to establish shared goals for persistent toxics in the Great Lakes basin. Goals and objectives similar to the Canada-Ontario Agreement for the Tiers I and II substances and a similar US list will be adopted. Joint projects will be

Figure 55.29 • Great Lakes pollution prevention.

		Great Lakes Pollution Prevention Initiative				
PROGRAM INTEGRATION/P2 AGREEMENTS					**LIAISON/LINKAGES**	
Pollution prevention for commercial chemical and hazardous wastes	Pollution prevention at federal facilities	Municipal pollution prevention initiatives	Industrial pollution prevention initiatives	Lake Superior pollution prevention initiatives	Clean process/ Green technology	Training/ Communications/ Information
Collection of alkaline and Ni/Cd batteries EPO	Information/education • Fact sheets EPO • Seminars • Brochures/Literature • Demonstration projects	Hamilton/Wentworth comprehensive pollution prevention planning IIM	Automobile manufacturers IIM	Thunder Bay • Comprehensive pollution prevention planning DIM	Wastewater Technology Center P	GLPPC • Training (full cost accounting, pollution prevention training, TQM)
Mercury and silver from dental offices EPO		Dry cleaning association IIM	Auto parts IIM	• Pollution control planning study EC	Industry Canada P	• Information transfer • Conferences • Stakeholders consultation
Hazardous waste minimization EPO	Agreements with major federal facilities CFB Trenton (8 wing) DIM	Green clean depot EC	Metal finishing IIM	Pollution prevention workshop/training EC	Demonstration projects: (Domtar-Red rock, water-based paints, etc.) EC	
Port Hope community action plan DIM		Pollution prevention assistance to small business (Sarnia) EC	Printing and graphics IIM	Shipping and ports activities DIM		NPRI/ARET
	Federal facility linkages in areas of concern DIM		International automakers (Honda and Toyota) DIM	Metal mining DIM	Environmental industry strategy P	RAPs/LAMPS (Collingwood, Sarnia, Lake Superior)
Refrigerant/Halon/ Sterilant/Solvent Management and conservation DIM		University laboratories Green practices EC		Bombardier DIM		
CFC management plan-Oshawa DIM	ODS/PTS management, hazardous waste minimization and spill prevention EPO	Conservation Council of Ontariao (Toxics campaign, 4 green business guides) EC	Greenhouses and nurseries DIM	Rural hazardous waste awareness DIM	Technical assistance program for metal finishers EPO	Environmental Citizenship Program
Management of CEPA priority substances assessed as "Toxic" EPO		Collingwood green community DIM	Metal mining DIM	Lake Superior Binational Forum P	OWMC/OCETA P	National Office of Pollution Prevention
				Nordic week championship EC		U.S. Great Lakes Pollution Prevention Roundtable

Anagram key				Program key	
ARET	= Accelerated Reduction/Elimination of Toxics	OCETA	= Ontario Centre for Environmental Technology Advancement	IIM	= Pollution prevention project initiated by industries/municipalities
CEPA	= Canadian Environmental Protection Act	ODS	= Ozone Depleting Substances	DIM	= Pollution prevention being developed with industries/municipalities
CFC	= Cholorofluorocarbons	OWMC	= Ontario Waste Management Corporation	EC	= Project funded by Environment Canada
GLPPC	= Great Lakes Pollution Prevention Centre	PTS	= Persistent Toxic Substances	EPO	= Project implemented by Environmental Protection - Ontario Region
LAMPs	= Lakewide Management Plans	RAPs	= Remedial Action Plans	P	= Partners
NPRI	= National Pollutant Release Inventory	TQM	= Total Quality Management		

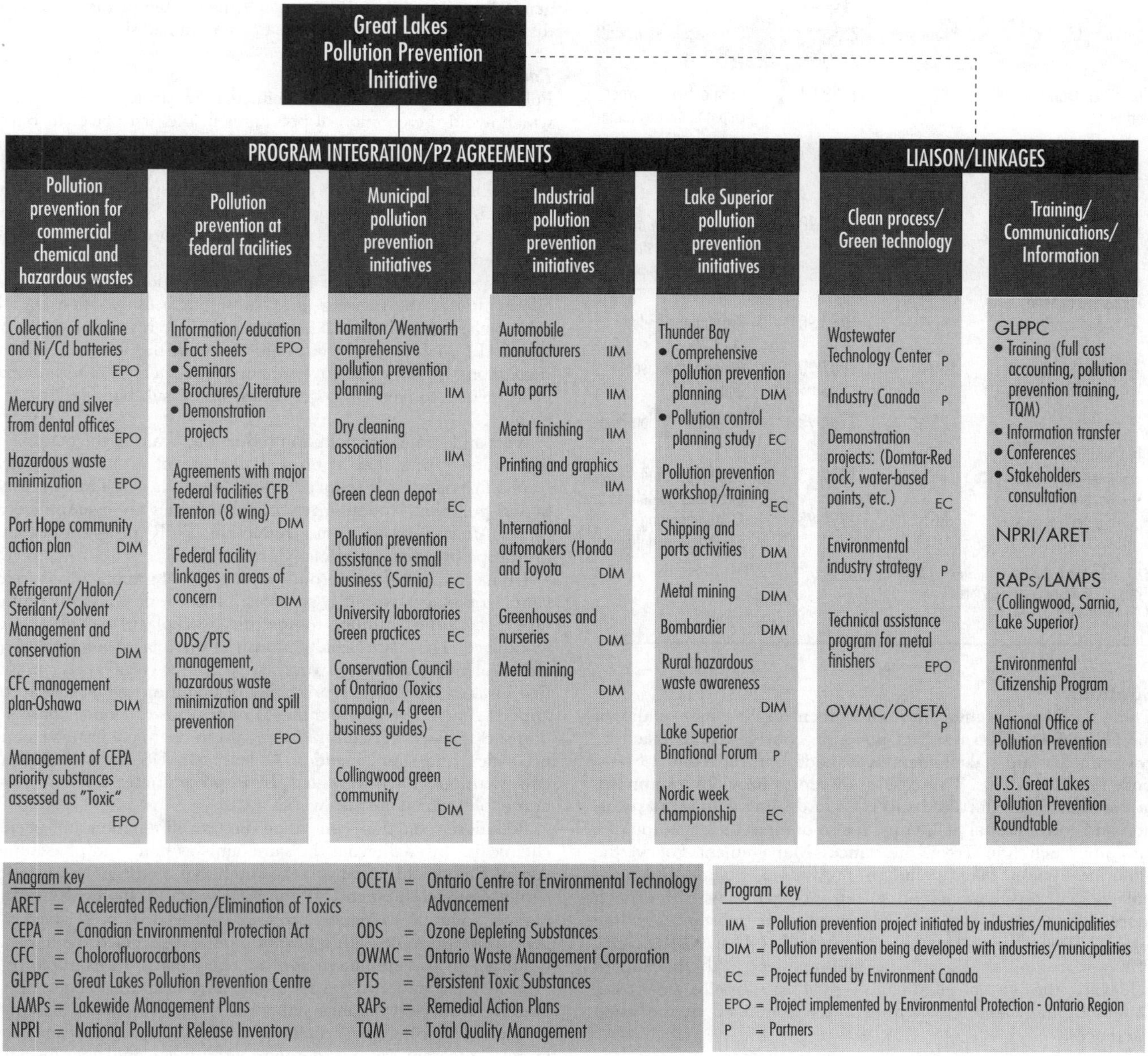

developed and implemented to facilitate information exchange and agency action on priority chemicals such as PCBs and mercury. By taking an aggressive approach to virtual elimination as outlined above, Canada will be able to assume a leadership role in promoting international action on persistent toxics. Canada hosted a United Nations conference in June 1995 in Vancouver to focus global dialogue on persistent organic pollutants (POP) and to explore pollution prevention approaches to reducing their emissions around the world. Canada also co-chairs the United Nations Economic Commission for Europe (UNECE) workgroup to develop a protocol for persistent organic pollutants under the Convention on Long Range Transboundary Air Pollution.

An Example—Dioxins and Furans

For more than a decade, polychlorinated dibenzo-dioxins and furans have been recognized as a group of persistent toxics of concern to the Canadian environment and the Great Lakes. Table 55.20 summarizes federal actions and the reductions in releases achieved to date, illustrating the mix of programmes and initiatives which has resulted in significant reductions of these toxics. In spite of these impressive results, dioxins and furans will remain priorities under the Toxic Substances Management Policy, the Chlorine Action Plan, the Canada Ontario Agreement and the binational strategy outlined above, because virtual elimination requires further reductions.

Table 55.20 • Summary of reductions in releases of dioxin and furan in Canada.

Sources of Emissions	Reductions	Reporting Period	Canadian Government Initiatives
Bleached kraft pulpmill effluents	82%	1989-94	CEPA defoamer, wood chip and dioxin/furan regulations
2,4,5-T—pesticide	100%	1985	Banned from use under PCPA
2,4-D—pesticide	100%	1987-90	Dioxin content and use heavily restricted under PCPA
Pentachlorophenol			
— wood preservation	6.7%	1987-90	Regulations under PCPA
— wood protectant	100%	1987-90	Banned from use under PCPA
PCBs	23%	1984-93	CCME PCB Action Plan
Incineration			
— municipal solid waste	80%	1989-93	CCME operating/ emissions guidelines
— hazardous + biomedical waste	80%	1990-95	CCME operating/ emissions guidelines

CCME: Canadian Council of Environmental Ministers;
CEPA: Canadian Environmental Protection Act;
PCPA: Pest Control Products Act.

Summary

There has been a significant improvement in the water quality of the Great Lakes as a result of pollution control actions taken by governments and stakeholders in Canada and the United States since the early 1970s. This case study report provides a summary of the Canadian effort and successes in dealing with gross pollution and conventional pollutants. It also outlines the evolution of a new approach (the Toxic Substances Management Policy, the Chlorine Action Plan, pollution prevention, voluntary action, stakeholder consultations and so on) for dealing with the much more difficult problems with persistent toxic substances in the Great Lakes. Comprehensive programmes (COA, NPRI, SOP, PSL and so on) that are being put in place with the aim of achieving the virtual elimination goal are briefly described. Details of the Canadian approach are contained in the listed references.

• CLEANER PRODUCTION TECHNOLOGIES

David Bennett

Prevention, Control and Remediation

Conventionally, there are three ways of addressing pollution: prevention, control and remediation. These form a hierarchy, in which the first priority or option is prevention, followed by control measures, with remediation as a poor third. Pollution abatement can refer to any means that lessens pollution, or a mitigation of pollution; in practice, it usually means control. Though the hierarchy of the three ideas is in terms of preference or priority, this is not always so in practice: there may be regulatory pressures to choose one path rather than another; one strategy may be less expensive than another, or remediation may be the most urgent—for example, in the event of a major spill or the hazardous dissemination of pollutants from a contaminated site.

Pollution prevention

Pollution prevention can be defined as a strategy or strategies which avoid the creation of pollutants in the first place. In Barry Commoner's phrase, "If it's not there, it can't pollute." Thus, if a chemical whose use results in pollution is eliminated, there will be "zero discharge" (or "zero emission") of the pollutant. Zero discharge is more convincing if the chemical is not replaced by another chemical—an alternative or substitute—which results in a different pollutant.

One central strategy of pollution prevention is the banning, elimination or the phasing out ("sunsetting") of specified chemicals or classes of chemical. (Alternatively, use-restrictions may be specified.) Such strategies are laid down in the form of laws or regulations by national governments, less often by international instruments (conventions or treaties) or by sub-national governments.

A second strategy is pollution reduction, again in the context of prevention rather than control. If the use of a chemical which results in pollution is reduced, then the result will almost always be less pollution. Pollution reduction strategies are exemplified in North America by toxics use reduction (TUR) programmes and in Europe by "clean technology programmes".

Unlike bans and phase-outs, which usually apply to all (relevant) workplaces within a political jurisdiction, pollution reduction programmes apply to specific workplaces or classes of workplace. These are usually industrial manufacturing (including chemical manufacturing) workplaces over a certain size, in the first instance, though the principles of pollution reduction can be applied generally—for example, to mines, power plants, construction sites, offices, agriculture (in regard to chemical fertilizers and pesticides) and municipalities. At least two US states (Michigan and Vermont) have legislated TUR programmes for individual households which are also workplaces.

Pollution reduction can result in the elimination of specific chemicals, thus achieving the same aims as bans and phase-outs. Again, this would result in zero discharge of the pollutant concerned, but requirements to eliminate specific chemicals are not part of pollution reduction programmes; what is prescribed is a general programme with a flexible range of specified methods. A requirement to eliminate a specific chemical is an example of a "specification standard". A requirement to institute a general programme is a "performance standard" because it allows flexibility in the mode of implementation, though a specific mandatory target (outcome) for a general programme would (confusingly) count as a specification standard. When they have to choose, businesses usually prefer performance to specification standards.

Pollution control

Pollution control measures cannot eliminate pollution; all they can do is to mitigate its effects on the environment. Control measures are instituted "at the end of the (waste) pipe". The usefulness of control measures will depend on the pollutant and the industrial circumstance. The main methods of pollution control, in no particular order, are:

- the capture and subsequent storage of pollutants
- filtration, whereby airborne or waterborne pollutants are removed from the waste stream by physical methods such as meshes, filters and other permeable barriers (such as coke)

- precipitation, whereby the pollutant is chemically precipitated and then captured in its transformed state or captured by physical methods such as an electrostatic charge
- destruction—for example, incineration, or neutralization, whereby pollutants are transformed chemically or biologically into substances which are less harmful
- dilution, whereby the pollutant is diluted or flushed in order to lessen its effects on any one organism or on an ecosystem; or concentration to lessen the effect of disposal
- evaporation or dissolution—for example, dissolving a gas in water
- utilization—for example, transforming a pollutant into a potentially useful (though not necessarily less toxic) product (such as sulphur dioxide into sulphuric acid or using solid waste as hard core or road bed)
- out-of-process recycling (where the recycling is not an integral part of the production process)
- media-shift, whereby a waste-stream is diverted from one medium, such as air, soil or water, to another, on the rationale that the medium-shift makes the pollutant less harmful
- state-changes—a change to the solid, liquid or gaseous state on the rationale that the new state is less harmful.

Pollution remediation

Remediation is needed to the extent that pollution prevention and control fail. It is also very expensive, with the costs not always accruing to the polluter. The modes of remediation are:

The clean-up of contaminated sites

Clean-up has a common sense meaning, as when an employer is required to "clean up his act", which can mean a large number of different things. Within environmental protection, clean-up is a technical term meaning a branch or a mode of remediation. Even within this restricted use of the term, clean-up can mean (1) the removal of pollutants from a contaminated site or (2) the rehabilitation of a site so that it is restored to its full use-potential. Again, clean-up sometimes refers to nothing more than the containment of pollutants within a site, area or body of water—for example, by capping, sealing or the construction of an impermeable floor.

To be successful, clean-up has to be 100% effective, with full protection for workers, bystanders and the general public. A further consideration is whether the clean-up materials, methods and technology do not create further hazards. Though it is desirable to use engineering controls to protect clean-up workers, there will almost always be a need for appropriate personal protective equipment. Normally, workers engaged in remediation are classified as hazardous-waste workers, though aspects of such work are undertaken by fire fighters and municipal workers, among others.

A large number of physical, chemical, biological and biotechnological agents and methods are used in the clean-up of contaminated sites.

Hazardous-waste treatment

Most treatment of hazardous (or toxic) waste now takes place in purpose-built facilities by hazardous-waste workers. From an environmental point of view, the test of effectiveness of a hazardous-waste facility is that it produces no outputs which are not inert or virtually inert, such as silica, insoluble inorganic compounds, insoluble and non-corrosive slags, gaseous nitrogen or carbon dioxide—though carbon dioxide is a "greenhouse gas" which causes climate change and is, thus, a further environmental detriment.

A further test is that the facility be energy efficient—that is, energy is not wasted—and as energy non-intensive as possible (i.e., the ratio of energy use to the volume of waste treated be as low as possible). A general rule of thumb (it is fortunately not a universal law) is that the more effective the pollution (or waste)

abatement strategy, the more energy is consumed, which by sustainable development criteria is another detriment.

Even when the workers are properly protected, it is easy to see the drawbacks of hazardous-waste treatment as a mode of addressing pollution. Pollution prevention methods can be applied to the operation of the treatment process but they cannot be applied to the principal "input"—the waste to be treated. Hazardous-waste treatment facilities will usually require at least as much energy to treat the waste as was expended in its creation, and there will always be further waste as an output, however inert or non-toxic.

Spills and leaks

The same considerations will apply to chemical spills and leaks as to the clean-up of contaminated sites, with the further hazards caused by the urgency of the clean-up. Workers cleaning up spills and leaks are almost always emergency workers. Depending on the scale and the nature of the pollutant, leaks and spills can become major industrial accidents.

The Modes of Pollution Prevention

Definition and philosophy

The definition of pollution prevention may seem to be a trivial matter, but it is important because advocates of pollution prevention want, as a principle of policy, to see a single-minded and aggressive prevention strategy at the expense of control methods, and to avoid remediation. The more strictly pollution prevention is defined, they say, the more likely it is to succeed as a practical strategy. Conversely, the more widely employers are allowed to define the term, the more likely their activities are to result in a mix of the same old (failed) strategies. Employers sometimes reply that even toxic waste can have a market value, and control methods have their place, so pollution is really only potential pollution. Besides, zero discharge is impossible and leads only to false expectations and misguided strategies. Proponents of pollution prevention respond that unless we have zero discharge as an aim or practical ideal, pollution prevention will not succeed and environmental protection will not improve.

Most of the strict definitions of pollution prevention have, as a sole or central element, the avoidance of the use of chemicals which result in pollutants so that pollution is not created in the first place. Some of the most important definitional controversies concern recycling, which is dealt with in the context of pollution prevention below.

Objectives

One possible objective of pollution prevention is zero discharge of pollutants. This is sometimes referred to as "virtual elimination", since even zero discharge cannot solve the problem of contaminants already in the environment. Zero discharge of pollutants is possible using pollution prevention methods (while control methods cannot achieve zero in theory and are even less effective in practice, usually owing to lax enforcement). For instance, we can envisage automobile production in which there is zero discharge of pollutants from the plant; other waste is recycled and the product (the car) consists of parts which are reusable or recyclable. Certainly, zero discharge of specific pollutants has been achieved—for example, by modifying the production process in wood pulp mills so that no dioxins or furans are discharged in the effluent. The aim of zero discharge has also been written into environmental laws and into the policies of bodies commissioned to abate pollution.

In practice, zero discharge often gives way to target reductions—for example, a 50% reduction in pollution emissions by

55. ENVIRONMENTAL POLLUTION CONTROL

such-and-such a year. These targets or interim targets are usually in the form of "challenges" or aims by which to measure the success of the pollution prevention programme. They are rarely the product of a feasibility analysis or calculation, and there are invariably no penalties attached to failure to attain the target. Nor are they measured with any precision.

Reductions would have to be measured (as opposed to estimated) by variations on the formula:

$$\text{Pollution } (P) = \text{Toxicity of the pollutant } (T) \times \text{Volume } (V)$$
$$\text{of the discharges}$$

or:

$$P = T \times V \times E \text{ (exposure potential)}.$$

This is very difficult in theory and expensive in practice, though it could be done in principle by utilizing hazard assessment techniques (see below). The whole issue suggests that resources would be better allocated elsewhere—for example, in ensuring that proper pollution prevention plans are produced.

In regard to chemical pesticides, the objective of use-reduction can be achieved by the methods of integrated pest management (IPM), though this term, too, is capable of a wide or a strict definition.

Methods

The main methods of pollution prevention are:

- The elimination or phasing out of specific hazardous chemicals
- Input substitution—replacing a toxic or hazardous substance with a non-toxic or less hazardous substance or with a non-toxic process. Examples are the substitution of water-based for synthetic organic dyes in the printing industry; water- or citrus-based solvents for organic solvents; and, in some applications, the substitution of vegetable for mineral oils. Examples of non-chemical substitution include the substitution of pellet blasting technology for the use of fluid chemical paint strippers; the use of high-pressure hot water systems instead of caustic cleaning; and the substitution of kiln-drying for the use of pentachlophenols (PCPs) in the lumber industry.

  In all cases, it is necessary to perform a substitution analysis to ensure that substitutes are genuinely less hazardous than what they replace. This is at least a matter of organized common sense, and at best the application of hazard assessment techniques (see below) to the chemical and its proposed substitute.
- Product reformulation—substituting for an existing end-product an end-product which is non-toxic or less toxic upon use, release or disposal

  Whereas input substitution refers to the raw materials and adjuncts at the "front end" of the production process, product reformulation approaches the issue from the final product end of the production cycle.

  General programmes to produce products which are more environmentally benign are examples of "economic conversion". Examples of particular measures in the area of product reformulation include the production of rechargeable batteries instead of throw-away types and the use of water-based product coatings instead of those based on organic solvents and the like.

  Again, substitution analysis will be necessary to ensure that the net environmental benefit is greater for the reformulated products that it is for the originals.
- Production unit redesign modernization or modification, which results in less chemical use or in the use of less toxic substances.
- Improved operation and maintenance of the production unit and production methods, including better housekeeping, more efficient production quality control, and process inspections.

Examples are spill prevention measures; the use of spill-proof containers; leak prevention; and floating lids for solvent tanks.

- Using less and reusing more. For instance, some degreasing operations take place too frequently on a single item. In other cases, chemicals can be used more sparingly in each operation. De-icing fluids can sometimes be reused, a case of "extended use".
- Closed-loop methods and in-process recycling. Strictly speaking, a closed-loop process is one in which there are no emissions into the workplace or into the outside environment, not even waste water into surface water or carbon dioxide into the atmosphere. There are only inputs, finished products, and inert or non-toxic wastes. In practice, closed-loop methods eliminate some, but not all, hazardous releases. To the extent that this is achieved, it will count as a case of in-process recycling (see below).

Recycling

Any definition of pollution prevention is likely to result in a number of "grey areas" in which it is not easy to distinguish prevention measures from emission controls. For instance, to qualify as a prevention method, a phase of a production process may have to be "an integral part of the production unit", but how far away the phase has to be from the periphery of the production process in order to qualify as a prevention measure is not always clear. Some processes may be so remote from the heart of an operation that they look more like an "add on" process and, thus, more like an "end of pipe" control measure than a prevention method. Again, there are unclear cases like a waste pipe that provides the feedstock for a neighbouring plant: taken together, the two plants provide a kind of closed loop; but the "upstream" plant still produces effluent and, thus, fails the prevention test.

Similarly with recycling. Conventionally, there are three types of recycling:

- in-process recycling—for example, when dry-cleaning solvent is filtered, cleaned and dried, then reused within a single process
- out-of-process but on-site, as when pesticide production waste is cleaned and then reused as the so-called inert base in a new production run
- out-of-process and off-site.

Of these, the third is usually ruled out as not qualifying as pollution prevention: the more remote the recycling site, the less of a guarantee that the recycled product is actually reused. There are also hazards in the transporting of waste to be recycled, and the financial uncertainty that the waste will have a continuous market value. Similar, though less acute, considerations apply to out-of-process but on-site recycling: there is always a possibility that the waste will not actually be recycled or, if recycled, not actually reused.

In the initial pollution prevention strategies of the 1980s, on-site but out-of-process recycling was ruled out as not being a genuine pollution prevention measure. There was a fear that an effective pollution prevention programme would be compromised or diluted by too great an emphasis on recycling. In the mid-1990s, some policy-makers are prepared to entertain on-site, out-of-process recycling as a legitimate pollution prevention method. One reason is that there are genuine "grey areas" between prevention and control. Another reason is that some on-site recycling really does do what it is supposed to do, even though it may not technically qualify as pollution prevention. A third reason is business pressure: employers see no reason why techniques should be ruled out it they serve the purposes of a pollution prevention programme.

Pollution prevention planning

Planning is an essential part of pollution prevention methodology, not least because the gains in both industrial efficiency and environmental protection are likely to be in the longer term (not immediate), reflecting the sort of planning that goes into product design and marketing. The production of periodic pollution prevention plans is the most usual way of realizing pollution prevention planning. There is no single model for such plans. One proposal envisages:

- aims and objectives
- chemical inventories and estimates of discharges into the environment
- pollution prevention methods used and methods proposed
- responsibilities and action in the event of the plan not being fulfilled or realized.

Another proposal envisages:

- a review of production processes
- identification of pollution prevention opportunities
- a ranking of the opportunities and a schedule for the implementation of the selected options
- measures of the success of the plan after the implementation period.

The status of such plans varies widely. Some are voluntary, though they can be spelled out in law as a (voluntary) code of practice. Others are mandatory in that they are required (1) to be kept on-site for inspection or (2) submitted to a regulatory authority on completion or (3) submitted to a regulatory authority for some form of scrutiny or approval. There are also variations, such as requiring a plan in the event that a "voluntary" plan is, in some way, inadequate or ineffective.

The degree to which mandatory plans are prescriptive also varies—for example, in regard to penalties and sanctions. Few authorities have the power to require specific changes in the content of pollution prevention plans; almost all have the power to require changes in the plan in the event that the formal requirements have not been met—for example, if some plan headings have not been addressed. There are virtually no examples of penalties or sanctions in the event that the substantive requirements of a plan have not been met. In other words, legal requirements for pollution prevention planning are far from traditional.

Issues surrounding the production of pollution prevention plans concern the degree of confidentiality of the plans: in some cases, only a summary becomes public, while in other cases, plans are released only when the producer fails in some way to comply with the law. In almost no cases do the requirements for pollution prevention planning override existing provisions regarding the trade secrecy or the business confidentiality of inputs, processes or the ingredients of products. In a few cases, community environmental groups have access to the planning process, but there are virtually no cases of this being required by law, nor are the legal rights of workers to participate in the production of plans widespread.

Legislation

In the Canadian provinces of British Columbia and Ontario, pollution prevention measures are "voluntary"; their effectiveness depends on "moral suasion" on the part of governments and environmentalists. In the United States, about half (26) of the states have some form of legislation, while in Europe, several northern countries have legislated clean technology programmes. There is quite a wide variety in both the content and the effectiveness of such legislation. Some laws define pollution prevention strictly; others define it widely or loosely and cover a wide variety

of environmental protection activities concerning pollution and waste, not just pollution prevention. The New Jersey law is highly prescriptive; those of the Commonwealth of Massachusetts and the States of Minnesota and Oregon involve a high degree of government scrutiny and assistance; that of Alaska is little more than a statement of the government's intentions.

Health, safety and employment

Pollution prevention is of central concern to occupational health: if the use of toxic substances decreases, there will almost always be a corresponding decrease in worker exposure to toxic substances and, thus, in industrial diseases. This is a prime case of prevention "at the source" of the hazard and, in many cases, the elimination of hazards by "engineering controls" (i.e., methods), the first and best line of defence against chemical hazards. However, such preventive measures are different from one traditional strategy, which is the "total isolation" or the "total enclosure" of a chemical process. While total enclosure is highly useful and highly desirable, it does not count as a pollution prevention method since it controls, rather that reduces intrinsically, an existing hazard.

The pollutants which pose hazards to workers, communities and the physical environment alike, have usually been addressed primarily because of their impact on human communities (environmental health). Though the greatest exposures are often received by workers within a workplace (workplace pollution), this has not, so far, been the prime focus of pollution prevention measures. The Massachusetts legislation, for instance, aims to reduce the risks to the health of workers, consumers and the environment without shifting the risks between workers, consumers and parts of the environment (New Jersey is similar). But there was no attempt to focus on workplace pollution as a major detriment, nor was there a requirement to accord a primacy to the chief human exposures to hazards—often the workers. Nor is there any requirement to train workers in the discipline of pollution prevention.

There are several reasons for this. The first is that pollution prevention is a new discipline in the context of a general, traditional failure to see environmental protection as a function of processes utilized and adopted within workplaces. A second reason is that worker-management co-determination in the area of environmental protection is not well advanced. Workers in many countries have legal rights, for instance, to joint workplace health and safety committees; to refuse unsafe or unhealthy work; to health and safety information; and to training in health and safety issues and procedures. But there are few legal rights in the parallel and often overlapping area of environmental protection, such as the right to joint union-management environment committees; the right of employees to "blow the whistle" (go public) on an employer's anti-environmental practices; the right to refuse to pollute or to degrade the outside environment; the right to environmental information; and the right to participate in workplace environmental audits (see below).

The impacts of pollution prevention planning on employment are hard to gauge. The explicit aim of pollution prevention initiatives is often to increase industrial efficiency and environmental protection at the same time and by the same set of measures. When this happens, the usual effect is to decrease overall employment within any given workplace (because of technological innovation) but to increase the skills required and then to increase job security (because there is planning for a longer-term future). To the extent that the use of raw materials and adjuncts is reduced, there will be decreased chemical manufacturing employment, though this is likely to be offset by the implied transition of feedstock to speciality chemicals and by the development of alternatives and substitutes.

55. ENVIRONMENTAL POLLUTION CONTROL

There is one aspect of employment which pollution prevention planning cannot address. Pollution emissions from a single facility may decrease but to the extent that there is an industrial strategy to create wealth and value-added employment, an increase in the number of production facilities (however "clean") will tend to nullify the environmental protection gains already achieved. The most notorious failing in environmental protection measures—that pollution emission reductions and controls are nullified by an increase in the number of sources—applies, unfortunately, to pollution prevention as well as to any other form of intervention. Ecosystems, according to one respected theory, have a "carrying capacity", and that limit can be reached equally by a small number of highly polluting or "dirty" sources or by a correspondingly large number of clean ones.

Workplace environmental audits

Pollution prevention planning can form part of or be accommodated in a workplace environmental audit. Though there are many versions of such audits, they are likely to be in the form of a "site audit" or "production audit", in which the whole production cycle is subjected to both an environmental and a financial analysis.

There are roughly three areas of sustainable development and environmental protection which can be covered in a workplace audit:

- the conservation of natural resource inputs—for example, minerals, water and wood products
- energy use, which may also include consideration of energy sources, energy efficiency, energy intensiveness and energy conservation
- pollution prevention, control and remediation.

To the extent that pollution prevention is successful, there will be a corresponding decrease in the importance of control and remediation measures; pollution prevention measures can form a major part of a workplace environmental audit.

Traditionally, businesses were able to "externalize" environmental detriments through such means as the profligate use of water or unloading their wastes onto the outside community and the environment. This has led to demands for taxes on the "front end" such as water use or on "outputs" such as environmentally unfriendly products or on wastes ("pollution taxes").

In this way, costs to business are "internalized". However, it has proved difficult to put the right price on the inputs and on the detriments—for example, the cost to communities and the environment of wastes. Nor is it clear that pollution taxes reduce pollution in proportion to the amounts levied; taxes may well "internalize" costs, but they otherwise only add to the cost of doing business.

The advantage of environmental auditing is that the audit can make economic sense without having to "cost" externalities. For instance, the "value" of waste can be calculated in terms of resource input loss and energy "non-utilization" (inefficiency)—in other words, of the difference in value between resources and energy on one side and the value of the product on the other. Unfortunately, the financial side of pollution prevention planning and its part in workplace environmental audits is not well advanced.

Hazard assessment

Some pollution prevention schemes work without any hazard evaluation—that is, without criteria to decide whether a plant or facility is more or less environmentally benign as a result of pollution prevention measures. Such schemes may rely on a list of chemicals which are objects of concern or which define the scope of the pollution prevention programme. But the list does not grade chemicals as to their relative hazardousness, nor is there a guarantee that a chemical substitute not on the list is, in fact, less hazardous than a listed chemical. Common sense, not scientific analysis, tells us how to go about implementing a pollution prevention programme.

Other schemes rest on criteria for assessing hazardousness, that is, on hazard assessment systems. They work, essentially, by laying down a number of environmental parameters, such as persistence and bioaccumulation in the environment, and a number of human health parameters which serve as measures of toxicity—for example, acute toxicity, carcinogenicity, mutagenicity, reproductive toxicity and so on.

There is then a weighted scoring system and a decision procedure for scoring those parameters on which there is inadequate information on the chemicals to be scored. Relevant chemicals are then scored and ranked, then (often) assembled in groups in descending order of hazardousness.

Though such schemes are sometimes devised with a specific purpose in mind—for example, for assessing priorities for control measures or for elimination (banning)—their essential use is as an abstract scheme which can be used for a large variety of environmental protection measures, including pollution prevention. For instance, the top group of scored chemicals could be the prime candidates for a mandatory pollution prevention programme, or they could be candidates for phasing-out or substitution. In other words, such schemes do not tell us how much we should reduce environmental health hazards; they tell us only that any measures we take should be informed by the hazard assessment scheme.

For instance, if we have to make decisions about substituting a less hazardous chemical for a more dangerous one, we can use the scheme to tell us whether, prima facie, the substitution decision is a good one: we run both chemicals through the scheme to determine whether there is a wide or merely a narrow gap between them regarding their hazardousness.

There are two sorts of considerations which rarely fall within the scope of hazard assessment schemes. The first is exposure data, or the potential for human exposure to the chemical. The latter is difficult to calculate, and, arguably, it distorts the "intrinsic hazard" of the chemicals concerned. For instance, a chemical could be accorded an artificially low priority on the grounds that its exposure potential is low; though it may, in fact, be highly toxic and relatively easy to deal with.

The second sort of consideration is the socioeconomic impact of eliminating or reducing the use of the chemical concerned. While we can start to make substitution decisions on the basis of the hazard analysis, we would have to make a further and distinct socioeconomic analysis and consider, for example, the social utility of the product associated with the chemical use (which may, e.g., be a useful drug), and we would also have to consider the impact on workers and their communities. The reason for keeping such analysis separate is that it is impossible to score the results of a socioeconomic analysis in the same way that the intrinsic hazards of chemicals are scored. There are two entirely distinct sets of values with different rationales.

However, hazard assessment schemes are crucial in assessing the success of pollution prevention programmes. (They are also relatively new, both in their impact and their utility.) For instance, it is possible to apply them without reference to risk assessments, risk analysis and (with reservations) without reference to cost-benefit analysis. An earlier approach to pollution was to first do a risk assessment and only then decide what sort of action, and how much, was necessary to reduce the risk to an "acceptable" level. The results were rarely dramatic. Hazard assessment, on the other hand, can be utilized very quickly and in such a way that it does not delay or compromise the effectiveness of a pollution prevention programme. Pollution prevention is, above all, a pragmatic programme capable of constantly and speedily addressing pollution issues as they arise and before they arise. It is arguable that traditional control measures have reached their limit and only the implementation of comprehensive pollution prevention programmes will be capable of addressing the next phase of environmental protection in a practical and effective way.

References

American Public Health Association (APHA). 1995. *Standard Methods for the Examination of Water and Waste-water*. Alexandria, Va: Water Environment Federation.

ARET Secretariat. 1995. *Environmental Leaders 1, Voluntary Commitments to Action On Toxics Through ARET*. Hull, Quebec: Environment Canada's Public Enquiry Office.

Bishop, PL. 1983. *Marine Pollution and Its Control*. New York: McGraw-Hill.

Brown, LC and TO Barnwell. 1987. *Enhanced Stream Water Quality Models QUAL2E and QUAL2E-UNCAS: Documentation and User Manual*. Athens, Ga: US EPA, Environmental Research Lab.

Brown, RH. 1993. *Pure Appl Chem* 65(8):1859-1874.

Calabrese, EJ and EM Kenyon. 1991. *Air Toxics and Risk Assessment*. Chelsea, Mich:Lewis.

Canada and Ontario. 1994. *The Canada-Ontario Agreement Respecting the Great Lakes Ecosystem*. Hull, Quebec: Environment Canada's Public Enquiry Office.

Dillon, PJ. 1974. A critical review of Vollenweider's nutrient budget model and other related models. *Water Resour Bull* 10(5):969-989.

Eckenfelder, WW. 1989. *Industrial Water Pollution Control*. New York: McGraw-Hill.

Economopoulos, AP. 1993. *Assessment of Sources of Air Water and Land Pollution. A Guide to Rapid Source Inventory Techniques and Their Use in Formulating Environmental Control Strategies. Part One: Rapid Inventory Techniques in Environmental Pollution. Part Two: Approaches for Consideration in Formulating Environmental Control Strategies.* (Unpublished document WHO/YEP/93.1.) Geneva: WHO.

Environmental Protection Agency (EPA). 1987. *Guidelines for Delineation of Wellhead Protection Areas*. Englewood Cliffs, NJ: EPA.

Environment Canada. 1995a. *Pollution Prevention - A Federal Strategy for Action*. Ottawa: Environment Canada.

—. 1995b. *Pollution Prevention - A Federal Strategy for Action*. Ottawa: Environment Canada.

Freeze, RA and JA Cherry. 1987. *Groundwater*. Englewood Cliffs, NJ: Prentice Hall.

Global Environmental Monitoring System (GEMS/Air). 1993. *A Global Programme for Urban Air Quality Monitoring and Assessment*. Geneva: UNEP.

Hosker, RP. 1985. Flow around isolated structures and building clusters, a review. *ASHRAE Trans* 91.

International Joint Commission (IJC). 1993. *A Strategy for Virtual Elimination of Persistent Toxic Substances*. Vol. 1, 2, Windsor, Ont.: IJC.

Kanarek, A. 1994. *Groundwater Recharge With Municipal Effluent, Recharge Basins Soreq, Yavneh 1 & Yavneh 2*. Israel: Mekoroth Water Co.

Lee, N. 1993. Overview of EIA in Europe and its application in the New Bundeslander. In *UVP Leitfaden*, edited by V Kleinschmidt. Dortmund .

Metcalf and Eddy, I. 1991. *Wastewater Engineering Treatment, Disposal, and Reuse*. New York: McGraw-Hill.

Miller, JM and A Soudine. 1994. The WMO global atmospheric watch system. *Hrvatski meteorolski casopsis* 29:81-84.

Ministerium für Umwelt. 1993. *Raumordnung Und Landwirtschaft Des Landes Nordrhein-Westfalen, Luftreinhalteplan Ruhrgebiet West [Clean Air Implementation Plan West-Ruhr Area]*.

Parkhurst, B. 1995. *Risk Management Methods, Water Environment and Technology*. Washington, DC: Water Environment Federation.

Pecor, CH. 1973. *Houghton Lake Annual Nitrogen and Phosphorous Budgets*. Lansing, Mich.: Department of Natural Resources.

Pielke, RA. 1984. *Mesoscale Meteorological Modeling*. Orlando: Academic Press.

Preul, HC. 1964. Travel of nitrogen compounds in soils. Ph.D. Dissertation, University of Minnesota, Minneapolis, Minn.

—. 1967. *Underground Movement of Nitrogen*. Vol. 1. London: International Association on Water Quality.

—. 1972. Underground pollution analysis and control. Water Research. *J Int Assoc Water Quality* (October):1141-1154.

—. 1974. Subsurface waste disposal effects in the Lake Sunapee watershed. Study and report for Lake Sunapee Protective Association, State of New Hampshire, unpublished.

—. 1981. *Recycling Plan for Leather Tannery Wastewater Effluent*. International Water Resources Association.

—. 1991. *Nitrates in Water Resources in the USA.* : Water Resources Association.

Preul, HC and GJ Schroepfer. 1968. Travel of nitrogen compounds in soils. *J Water Pollut Contr Fed* (April).

Reid, G and R Wood. 1976. *Ecology of Inland Waters and Estuaries*. New York: Van Nostrand.

Reish, D. 1979. Marine and estuarine pollution. *J Water Pollut Contr Fed* 51(6):1477-1517.

Sawyer, CN. 1947. Fertilization of lakes by agricultural and urban drainage. *J New Engl Waterworks Assoc* 51:109-127.

Schwela, DH and I Köth-Jahr. 1994. Leitfaden für die Aufstellung von Luftreinhalteplänen [Guidelines for the implementation of clean air implementation plans]. Landesumweltamt des Landes Nordrhein Westfalen.

State of Ohio. 1995. Water quality standards. In Chap. 3745-1 in *Administrative Code*. Columbus, Ohio: Ohio EPA.

Taylor, ST. 1995. Simulating the impact of rooted vegetation on instream nutrient and dissolved oxygen dynamics using the OMNI diurnal model. In *Proceedings of the WEF Annual Conference*. Alexandria, Va: Water Environment Federation.

United States and Canada. 1987. *Revised Great Lakes Water Quality Agreement of 1978 As Amended By Protocol Signed November 18, 1987*. Hull, Quebec: Environmental Canada's Public Enquiry Office.

Venkatram, A and J Wyngaard. 1988. *Lectures On Air Pollution Modeling*. Boston, Mass: American Meteorological Society.

Venzia, RA. 1977. Land use and transportation planning. In *Air Pollution*, edited by AC Stern. New York: Academic Press.

Verein Deutscher Ingenieure (VDI) 1981. Guideline 3783, Part 6: Regional dispersion of pollutants over complex train. Simulation of the wind field. Dusseldorf: VDI.

—. 1985. Guideline 3781, Part 3: Determination of plume rise. Dusseldorf: VDI.

—. 1992. Guideline 3782, Part 1: Gaussian dispersion model for air quality management. Dusseldorf: VDI.

—. 1994. Guideline 3945, Part 1 (draft): Gaussian puff model. Dusseldorf: VDI.

—. n.d. Guideline 3945, Part 3 (in preparation): Particle models. Dusseldorf: VDI.

Viessman, W, GL Lewis, and JW Knapp. 1989. *Introduction to Hydrology*. New York: Harper & Row.

Vollenweider, RA. 1968. *Scientific Fundamentals of the Eutrophication of Lakes and Flowing Waters, With Particular Reference to Nitrogen and Phosphorous Factors in Eutrophication*. Paris: OECD.

—. 1969. Möglichkeiten und Grenzen elementarer Modelle der Stoffbilanz von Seen. *Arch Hydrobiol* 66:1-36.

Walsh, MP. 1992. Review of motor vehicle emission control measures and their effectiveness. In *Motor Vehicle Air Pollution, Public Health Impact and Control Measures*, edited by D Mage and O Zali. Republic and Canton of Geneva: WHO-Ecotoxicology Service, Department of Public Health.

Water Environment Federation. 1995. *Pollution Prevention and Waste Minimization Digest*. Alexandria, Va: Water Environment Federation.

World Health Organization (WHO). 1980. *Glossary On Air Pollution*. European Series, No. 9. Copenhagen: WHO Regional Publications.

—. 1987. *Air Quality Guidelines for Europe*. European Series, No. 23. Copenhagen: WHO Regional Publications.

World Health Organization (WHO) and United Nations Environmental Programme (UNEP). 1994. *GEMS/AIR Methodology Reviews Handbook Series*. Vol. 1-4. Quality Insurance in Urban Air Quality Monitoring, Geneva: WHO.

—. 1995a. *City Air Quality Trends*. Vol. 1-3. Geneva: WHO.

—. 1995b. *GEMS/AIR Methodology Reviews Handbook Series*. Vol. 5. Guidelines for GEMS/AIR Collaborative Reviews. Geneva: WHO.

Yamartino, RJ and G Wiegand. 1986. Development and evaluation of simple models for the flow, turbulence and pollutant concentration fields within an urban street canyon. *Atmos Environ* 20(11):S2137-S2156.

Other relevant readings

Analytische Chemie [Analytical Chemistry]. 1991. Nachr. Chem. Tech. Lab. 40, 146-154.

Atkins, DHF and I Quirino. 1992. *A Survey of Nitrogen Dioxide in Paris*. Brussels: Commission of the European Communities.

Bartels, U and J Block. 1985. *Plant Nutr Soil Sci* 148:689-693.

Beier, R, M Buck, and H-U Pfeffer. n.d. *Proceedings of the 8th World Clean Air Congress*. Amsterdam: Elsevier Science.

Beier, R, PL Gonzales, G Mc Innes, E Mullye, K Stevenson, and K-H Zierrock. 1987. *A Study of Network Design and Measurement Methods in the Member States for the EC Air Quality Directive for Nitrogen Dioxide*. Brussels: Commission of the European Communities.

Bennett, D. 1991. Pesticide reduction, a case study from Canada. *New Solutions* (Fall).

Both, R, K Otterbeck, and B Prinz. 1993. Odorous emissions guidelines (in German). *Staub-Reinhalt* 53:407-412.

Bruckmann, P and H-U Pfeffer. 1991. VDI-Berichte [VDI reports] Report 888. Dusseldorf: VDI.

Buck, M. 1989. *Staub-Reinhaltung der Luft* 49:337-342.

Buck, M and H-U Pfeffer. 1988. *Clean Air* 22:7-12.

55. ENVIRONMENTAL POLLUTION CONTROL

Canadian Labour Congress. 1992. *A Critique of the Ontario Hazard Assessment System*. Ottawa: Canadian Labour Congress.

Clement, RE and CJ Koester. 1993. *Anal chem* 65:85R-116R.

Commoner, B. 1990. *Making Peace With the Planet*. New York: Pantheon Books.

Elbers, G and S Lutz. 1993. VDI-Berichte [VDI report]. Report 1059: 337-356. Dusseldorf: VDI.

Ellermann, K, A Borowiak, and H-U Pfeffer. 1993. *LIMES-Jahresbericht*. LIMES- Annual Report 1993, No. Series B. North-Rhine-Westphalia: State Environmental Office.

Environment Canada. 1993a. *Pollution Prevention Legislative Task Force, Final Report*. Ottawa: Environment Canada.

—. 1993b. *Pollution Prevention Legislative Task Force, Final Report*. Ottawa: Environment Canada.

Erste Allgemeine Verwaltungsvorschrift zum Bundes-Immissionsschutzgesetz (TA Luft) vom [First General administrative Regulations on Federal Immissions Protective Law (TA Air)] of 27 Feb. 1986, GMBI 95-143.

Foran, J and B Glenn. 1993. *Criteria to Identify Chemical Candidates for Sunsetting in the Great Lakes Basin*. Washington, DC: George Washington Univ.

Fox, DL. 1993. Air pollution. *Anal chem* 65:156R-170R.

Geiser, K. 1990. Toxics use reduction and pollution prevention. *New Solutions* (Spring).

Grant, WB, RH Kagann, and WA McClenny. 1992. *J Air Waste Manage Assoc* 42:18-30.

Great Lakes Scientific Advisory Board (1991): Report to the International Joint Commission. Revised edition, December 1991.

Grefen, K. 1991. *Staub-Reinhaltung der Luft* 51:199-205.

Klockow, D and Z Fresenius. 1987. *Anal chem* 326:5-24.

Lahmann, E. 1990. *Luftverunreinigung-Luftreinhaltung* [Polluting the Air and Keeping It Clean]. Berlin: Verlag Paul Parey.

—. 1992. *Determination and Evaluation of Ambient Air Quality-Manual of Ambient Air Quality Control in Germany*. Berlin: Federal Minister for the Environment, Nature Conservation and Nuclear Safety.

—. 1993. *Feststellung Und Bewertung Von Immissionen—Leitfaden Zur Immissionsüberwachung in Deutschland* [Ascertaining and Assessing Immissions: Guidelines for Immission Monitoring in Germany]. Berlin: Federal Environmental Office.

Lodge, JPJ. 1989. *Methods of Air Sampling and Analysis*. Chelsea, Mich.: Lewis.

McClenny, W, J Pleil, G Evans, K Oliver, M Holdren, and W Weinbery. 1991. VDI-Richtlinie 3482 Bl. 3-6 Gaschromatographische Bestimmung organischer Verbindungen [Gas chromatographic determination of organic compounds]. *J Air Waste Manage Assoc* 41:1308-1318.

Medrow, W. 1990. *Geruche, Schriftenreihe Der VDI-Kommission Reinhaltung Luft, Band 12*. Düsseldorf: VDI.

Ministerium für Umwelt, R und L Nordrhein-W. 1992. *Krebsrisiko Durch Luftverunreinigungen, Studie Des Länderausschusses Für Immissionsschutz* [Cancer Risk from Air Pollutants, Study of the State Committee for Environment Protection]. Düsseldorf: North Rhine-Westphalian Ministry for Environment, Regional Planning and Agriculture.

Mohnen, V, J Wilson, and J Kadlecek. 1982. In *Chemistry of the Unpolluted and Polluted Troposphere*, edited by HW Georgii and W Jaeschke. Boston: D. Reichel Publishing Co.

Ontario Ministry of the Environment (OME). 1990a. *Scoring System for Assessing Environmental Contaminants*. Toronto: OME.

—. 1990b. *Scoring System for Assessing Environmental Contaminants*. Toronto: OME.

—. 1992. *Candidate Substances List for Bans and Phase-Outs*. Toronto: OME.

—. 1993. *Candidate Substances List for Bans and Phase-Outs*. Toronto: OME.

Petzold, A and R Niessner. 1993. VDI-Berichte [VDI reports]. Report 1059. Düsseldorf: VDI.

Pfeffer, H-U. 1982. *Staub-Reinhaltung der Luft* 42:233-236.

Pfeffer, H-U and M Buck. 1988. Proceedings of the 11th Triennial World Congress of the International Measurement Confederation (IMEKO), Houston, Texas (USA). *Acta Imeko* 4:527-536.

Pott, F. 1991. *VDI-Berichte [VDI reports]*. Report 888. Düsseldorf: VDI.

Rabano, ES, NT Castillo, KJ Torre, and PA Solomon. 1989. *J Air Pollut Contr Assoc* 39:76-80.

Rossi, M, M Ellenbecker, and K Geiser. 1991. Techniques in toxics use reduction: From concept to action. *New Solutions* (Fall).

Schrecker, T. 1993. *Sustainable Development: Getting There From Here, A Handbook for Union Environment Committees and Joint Labour-Management Environment Committees*. Ottawa: CLC/NRTEE.

Shelef, G and Y Azov. 1994. *Monitoring of the Third-Line* (in Hebrew). Haifa: Technion Research Center for Environmental Engineering and Water Resources.

Slanina, J, GP Wyers, and J Fresenius. 1994. *Anal chem* 350:467-473.

US Office of Technology Assessment. 1986. *Serious Reduction of Hazardous Waste for Pollution Prevention and Industrial Efficiency*. Washington, DC: US Office of Technology Assessment.

Vereine Deutscher Ingenieure (VDI). 1993 Verwaltungsvorschrift des Sächsischen Staatsministeriums für Umwelt und Landesentwicklung zur Feststellung und Beurteilung von Geruchsimmissionen-Geruchsimmions-Richtlinie vom 16.03.93. Sächs. Amtsblatt Nr. 17 vom 22.04.1993. [Administrative regulations of the Saxon state ministry for environment and state development on detecting and assessing odorous immissions-Odorous immissions—guidelines of March 16, 1993.] Düsseldorf: VDI.

—. 1995a. VDI 4280 Blatt 1 (E). Planung von Immissonsmessungen. Allgemeine Regeln (Ausgabe 5 1995). [VDI issue 1 (E). Planning immission measurements. General rules (5th edition, 1995).]

—. 1995b. VDI-Richtlinie 2465 Blatt 1 (Entwurf), März 1995, Messen von Ruß [Measuring soot].

—. n.d. *VDI-Handbuch Reinhaltung Der Luft*. Düsseldorf: VDI.

Weber, K, V Klein, and W Diehl. 1990. Optische Fernmeßverfahren zur Bestimmung gasförmiger Luftschadstoffe in der Troposphäre [Optical long-distance measurement procedures for determining gaseous air pollutants in the troposphere]. In *VDI Berichte [VDI Reports]* Düsseldorf: VDI.

Wight, G. 1994. *Fundamentals of Air Sampling*. Boca Raton: Lewis.

Winkler, P. 1985. *Staub-Reinhaltung der Luft*. 45:256-260.

56

Chapter Editor
Jorma Saari

Contents

56. ACCIDENT PREVENTION

INTRODUCTION

Jorma Saari

According to International Labour Office statistics, 120 million occupational accidents occur annually at workplaces worldwide. Of these, 210,000 are fatal accidents. Every day, more than 500 men or women do not come home because they were killed by accidents at work. These are dramatic numbers which draw fairly little public attention. Considering the fact that accidents take a considerable economic toll from nations, companies and individuals, accidents do not get much publicity.

Fortunately there are people working with a sense of purpose, often behind the scenes, towards understanding and managing safety and accident prevention better, and their efforts have not been wasted. Our understanding of accident prevention and safety is on a far higher level than ever before. Many world-class researchers and safety practitioners share this new knowledge with us through their articles in this *Encyclopaedia*. During the past twenty decades, knowledge about accidents has evolved considerably. We have left behind the simplistic model of dividing behaviour and conditions into two categories: *safe* or *unsafe*. The rigid belief that any activity can be placed into either category has been put aside as more sophisticated systemic models have been developed and proven effective in managing safety.

The important observation is that two safe conditions which by themselves are safe, may not be safe together. Workers are the connecting link, as their behaviour changes according to the environment and their physical surroundings. As an example, power saws caused many accidents when they came into use in the 1960s due to a hazard known as "kickback", which takes the operator by surprise when the chain-saw blades hit a branch, knot or harder point in wood. Kickback killed and injured hundreds of people before a guard was invented to protect the operator. When Sweden implemented regulations requiring the kickback guard, the number of power saw injuries went down from 2,600 in 1971 to 1,700 in 1972. This was a major breakthrough in power saw accident prevention.

Every user of power saws knows from personal experience that this noisy, vibrating and obviously sharp cutting tool appears to be very dangerous to use, and the beginner operator is very cautious. However, after hours of experience operators lose their sense of any hazard and start handling the saw less carefully. The kickback guard may produce a similar effect. Operators who know kickback is possible try to avoid it. When operators know that there is a mechanical device preventing the saw from hurting them in event of kickback, they become less cautious. In another forestry industry chain-saw example, studies have shown that leg protection makes workers less careful and they expose themselves more often to kickbacks, because they believe they are protected.

Despite the fact that kickback protection has helped prevent injuries, the mechanism is not straightforward. Even if these protective arrangements have been successful, in the final analysis their effects do not have a linear relationship with safety. Two safe conditions, kickback guard and leg protection, do not double the safety. The normal arithmetic of one plus one equals two $(1 + 1 = 2)$, does not apply in this case, as one plus one makes less than two. Fortunately, one plus one $(1 + 1)$ makes more than zero in some cases. In other cases, however, the sum may even be negative.

These are phenomena which safety practitioners have started to understand better than before. The simple division of behaviours and conditions into safe and unsafe does not lead very far toward prevention. The credit for progress has to be given to systems management. After understanding that humans, their tasks, their equipment and the environment make up a dynamic system, we have made considerable progress towards more effective accident prevention. The following examples demonstrate the dynamic nature of people and work. If one component is changed, the others do not remain the same, and the ultimate safety effect is hard to estimate in advance.

In aviation and in other highly engineered and automated systems, we have seen that increased automation may not necessarily result in improved safety. For example, operators may not get enough practice to maintain their skills in a highly automated system. When they then are required to intervene, they may not have the necessary competence or ability.

Some paper manufacturers have indicated that younger employees do not understand the functions of a paper machine as well as the older employees. The older employees have operated non-automated machines, and they have seen how these work. The new automated machines are operated from control rooms through computer keyboards and screens. The operators do not know the exact location of each component of the machines they operate. Therefore they may bring a component into a state which, for example, causes a hazard to the maintenance people in the vicinity. A technical improvement in the machinery or controls without simultaneous improvement in operators' skills, knowledge and values may not result in improved safety.

Accident prevention has been traditionally based on learning from accidents and near accidents (near misses). By investigating every incident, we learn about causes and can take actions towards mitigating or removing the causes. The problem is that we have not been able to develop, in the absence of sufficiently good theories, investigation methods which would bring up all the relevant factors for prevention. An investigation may give a fairly good picture about the causes. However, this picture is usually relevant only for the specific case investigated. There may be conditions and factors which contributed to the accident whose connections the investigators do not recognize or understand. Generalizing from one accident to other situations bears a degree of risk.

The good news is that we have made considerable progress in the area of predictive safety management. A number of techniques have been developed and have become routine for industrial safety and risk analysis. These techniques allow us to study industrial production plants systematically for the identification of potential hazards and to institute appropriate action before anything happens.

The chemical and petrochemical industries have shown leadership in this area worldwide. As a result of major catastrophes, such as Bhopal and Chernobyl, the use of the new predictive techniques has increased. Remarkable progress has been made since the mid-1970s in the area of safety. Many governments have also been leaders in making safety analysis mandatory. Sweden, Finland, Japan and the Federal Republic of Germany have all reduced fatal occupational accidents by 60 to 70% during this time. Many other countries show similar progress. Now, the challenge is to transfer our knowledge from research into practical applications and further improve our preventive efforts.

One of the new steps in safety management is the notion of safety culture. It may be a difficult concept, since culture is not a visible entity. It is an abstract concept prevailing within an organization or society. There are no direct ways of adjusting it. Safety culture is, however, a crucial concept for understanding the possibilities of prevention. One of the goals of this edition is to explore this new concept.

This new edition of the *Encyclopaedia* provides a comprehensive review of accident prevention theories and models in order to develop better design and more effective preventive strategies. It is possible to prevent occupational accidents. We do not need to tolerate this unnecessary toll to our well-being and economy.

• CONCEPTS OF ACCIDENT ANALYSIS

Kirsten Jørgensen

The purpose of this article is to provide a guide for calculating the magnitude of the accident problem; it is not a description of the magnitude itself. In dealing with occupational accidents, the magnitude of the problem can be estimated in different ways, depending on one's need to estimate how big the problem has been or how big it will be in the future. (Some people may say that this distinction is an unnecessary one, since knowledge of the current extent of the problem will serve to indicate what is to be expected in the future.) The magnitude of the problem as well as its types differs from country to country, from industry to industry and from workplace to workplace.

An accident may be described as a result of a chain of events in which something has gone wrong, resulting in an undesired conclusion. It has been shown that human intervention may prevent the injury or damage to which such a chain of events would otherwise lead. However, given the fact of human intervention, the potential exists for far more dangerous possible chains of events than those actually leading to injury or damage. These possibilities must be considered in assessing the full extent of workplace risk. Assuming that events that might lead to injury or damage occur because of factors in the workplace, one is led to conclude that the magnitude of the problem has to be determined on the basis of the existence and frequency of such factors.

When dealing with accidents in the workplace, one can estimate the magnitude of the problem retrospectively by comparing the number of accidents (incidence rate) with the severity of the accidents (lost work days). However, if one wants to estimate the magnitude of the problem prospectively, it is done by evaluating the presence of risk factors in the workplace—that is, factors that might lead to accidents.

A sufficiently complete and accurate view of the state of affairs with respect to workplace accidents can be gained by means of a comprehensive reporting and record-keeping system. Analyses of well-prepared accident reports can give a picture of the basic relationships essential to understanding the causes of the accidents. In order to estimate the magnitude of the problem in detail, a determination of risk factors is essential. Knowledge of the relevant risk factors can be obtained by analysing the detailed information provided with each accident record as to where workers and operators were located when the accident occurred, what they were doing or handling, by what means, what damages or injuries occurred and other particulars surrounding the accident.

Risk

Risk measurement must be made on the basis of information regarding the number and seriousness of injuries that have occurred in the past, yielding a retrospective measurement. The risk of injury to individuals may be described by two types of data:

- *Measurement of risk* provides a calculated frequency of injuries and a measurement of the seriousness of the injury. This could be described as the number of lost work day cases (or fatalities) per number of workers (e.g., in Denmark, the risk of dying in an occupational accident is 3 fatalities per 100,000 employees).
- *Type of risk or element of danger assessment* provides not only an indication of the exposure sources and other harmful factors which may cause an accident, but also an indication of the circumstances leading to injury or damage. Work performed at a height, for example, will involve a risk of falling, with serious injury as a possible result. Similarly, work with cutting tools involves a risk of cuts from contact with sharp components, and

work with noisy machines for a long period of time may result in hearing damage.

There exists a good deal of common-sense knowledge on many types of risks. For example, if you work at a height, you may fall; if it is slippery underfoot, then you may slip; and if there are sharp objects nearby, you may cut yourself. Many types of risk, not apparent to common sense, may be overlooked. With regard to these, the worker must be informed of the risk (e.g., that noise causes hearing damage, that some solvents cause brain damage and that certain chemicals cause acute poisoning by inhalation). Our knowledge of types of risk, from the most to the least conspicuous, whether gained through everyday experience or through research efforts, is based on past events. However, it is one thing to know what has happened, and another to assess what will happen in the future. It should be noted that the very knowledge of the exposure sources and other potentially harmful factors which may cause damage or injury in connection with tasks of various sorts, as well as knowledge of the factors that can either heighten or reduce those risk factors that influence risk measurement, can provide a basis for recognition of the risk.

Factors Determining Risk

The factors which are of greatest relevance in determining risk are:

- factors which determine the presence or absence (or potential) of risks of any sort
- factors which either increase or minimize the probability of these risks resulting in accidents or injuries
- factors affecting the seriousness of accidents associated with these risks.

To clarify the first point, it is necessary to identify the causes of the accident—namely, exposure sources and other harmful factors; the two latter points constitute the factors which influence the measurement of risk.

The primary factors in the working environment which are the direct causes of harm, either by way of occupational diseases or occupational accidents, are as follows:

Exposure sources and occupational disorders

The concept of injuries due to exposure sources is often linked to the concept of disease (or disorder) because a disease can be viewed as caused by exposure to one or several agents over a short (acute exposure) or long (chronic exposure) period of time. Chronic exposure agents are usually not directly harmful, but take effect rather after a relatively constant and extended period of exposure, whereas acute exposures are almost instantaneously harmful. The intensity, harmfulness and period of action is of importance to the development of the injury, which may often be a matter of a combination of the effects of several different agents. This fact makes it difficult to point out and determine the exposure sources because (among other reasons) monocausal correlations between specific disorders and specific exposure sources are almost never found.

Examples of exposure sources which may result in an injury in the form of a disease-like condition are:

- chemical exposures (solvents, cleaning agents, degreasing agents, etc.)
- physical exposures (noise, radiation, heat, cold, inadequate lighting, lack of oxygen, etc.)
- physiological exposures (heavy loads, bad work postures or repetitive work)
- biological exposures (viruses, bacteria, flour, animal blood or leather, etc.)

- psychological exposures (work in isolation, threat of violence, changing working hours, unusual job demands, etc.).

Harmful factors and occupational accidents

The concept of harmful factors (not including exposure sources) is linked to occupational accidents, because this is where damages occur and workers are exposed to the type of actions that cause instant injury. This type of action is easily identified because the damage or injury is recognized immediately when it occurs. The difficulty attached to this type of injury is the unexpected contact with the harmful factor.

Examples of harmful factors which may result in persons being injured by an accident are often linked to different energy forms, sources or activity, such as the following:

- energy that involves cutting, dividing or planing, usually in connection with such types of sharp objects as knives, saws and edged tools
- energy that involves pressing and compressing, usually in connection with different shaping means such as presses and clamping tools
- the conversion of kinetic energy into potential energy—for example, when something hits or falls against a worker
- the conversion of potential energy in a person into kinetic energy, such as occurs in falls from one level to another
- heat and cold, electricity, sound, light, radiation and vibration
- toxic and corrosive substances
- energy exposing the body to excessive stress in such actions, for example, as the moving of heavy loads or twisting of the body
- mental and psychological stresses such as the threat of violence.

Controlling Exposures

Exposure sources or other harmful factors are to a great extent governed by the nature of the processes, technologies, products and equipment to be found in the workplace, but may also be governed by the way in which the work is organized. From the point of view of measurable risk, it should be recognized that control of the probability of exposures and the seriousness of injuries to workers often depends on the following three factors:

- *Elimination/substitution safety measures.* Workplace hazards in the form of exposure sources or other harmful factors may be *eliminated* or mitigated by *substitution* (e.g., a less harmful chemical may replace a toxic chemical in a process). It should be noted that this is not totally possible, as exposure sources and other harmful factors will always be present in human surroundings (not least with respect to human working conditions).
- *Technical safety measures.* These measures, often called *engineering controls*, consist of separating persons from harmful factors by encapsulating the harmful elements, or installing barriers between workers and the factors which may cause injury. Examples of these measures include, but are not limited to, automation, remote control, use of ancillary equipment and machine protection (guarding).
- *Organizational safety measures.* Organizational safety measures, also known as *administrative controls,* include separating persons from harmful factors either by means of special working methods or by separation in time or space. Examples of these controls include, but are not limited to, reduced exposure time, preventive maintenance programmes, encapsulating the individual workers with personal protective equipment, and expedient organization of work.

Controlling Human Conduct

It is often not possible to isolate all hazards using the above control measures. It is commonly supposed that accident prevention analysis ends here because it is believed that the workers will then be able to take care of themselves by acting "according to the rules". This means that safety and risk will at some point depend on factors which control human conduct—namely, whether the individual person has the knowledge, the skills, the opportunity and the will to act so as to ensure safety in the workplace. The following illustrates the role of these factors.

- *Knowledge.* Workers must first be aware of the types of risk, potential hazards and elements of danger that may be found in the workplace. This usually requires education, training and job experience. The risks also need to be identified, analysed, recorded and described in a readily understandable manner so that workers know when they are in a specific risk situation and what consequences are liable to follow from their actions.
- *The opportunity to act.* It must be possible for the workers to act safely. It is necessary for workers to be able to make use of the available technical and organizational—as well as physical and psychological—opportunities for action. Positive support of the safety programme must be forthcoming from management, supervisors and the surroundings, including concern about risk taking, designing and following working methods with safety in view, safe use of the proper tools, clearly defining tasks, establishing and following safe procedures, and providing clear instructions on how equipment and materials are to be safely handled.
- *The will to act safely.* Technical and organizational factors are important with respect to workers' readiness to behave in ways that will ensure workplace safety, but social and cultural factors are at least equally important. Risks will arise if, for example, safe conduct is difficult or time-consuming, or if it is not desired by management or colleagues, or is not appreciated by them. Management must be clearly interested in safety, taking steps to prioritize it and displaying a positive attitude towards the need for safe conduct.

Information on the causes of accidents serves the following purposes:

- It can demonstrate where something is wrong and what needs to be changed.
- It indicates the types of harmful factors that cause accidents (or near accidents) and also describes the situations that result in damage and injuries.
- It identifies and describes the underlying circumstances that determine the presence of potential hazards and risky situations and that will result in optimum safety by their being altered or eliminated.

Information of a general sort can be obtained by a thorough analysis of the damage or injuries and the circumstances under which they occurred. Information obtained from other similar accidents may point out more general factors of importance, thus disclosing less immediately visible causal relationships. However, as very detailed and specific information can be obtained by analysing an individual accident, this information may help uncover the specific circumstances which should be addressed. Often, analysis of the individual accident will provide information which it is not possible to obtain from the general analysis, whereas the general analysis may point out factors which the specific analysis does not elucidate. Data from both of these kinds of analyses are important to help disclose obvious and direct causal relations at the individual level.

Analysis of Individual Accidents

Analysis of individual accidents has two primary purposes:

First, it can be used to determine the cause of an accident and the specific work factors that contributed to it. Following analysis, one can assess the extent to which the risk has been recognized.

One may also decide upon technical and organizational safety measures and the degree to which more job experience might have diminished the risk. Furthermore, a clearer view is gained of the possible actions that might have been taken to avoid the risk, and the motivation that a worker must have to take these actions.

Second, one can gain knowledge which may be used for analyses of many similar accidents at both the enterprise level and at more comprehensive (e.g., organization-wide or national) levels. In this connection, it is important to assemble information such as the following:

- the identity of the workplace and the work itself (that is, information relating to the sector or the trade in which the workplace is positioned), and the work processes and the technology that characterize the work
- the nature and the seriousness of the accident
- factors causing the accident, such as exposure sources, the way in which the accident occurred and the specific working situation causing the accident
- general conditions at the workplace and the working situation (comprising the factors mentioned in the foregoing paragraph).

Types of Analyses

There are five primary types of analyses of accidents, each having a distinct purpose:

- *Analyses and identification of where and which types of accidents occur.* The goal is to determine the incidence of the injuries, as associated, for example, with sectors, trade groups, enterprises, work processes and types of technology.
- *Analyses with respect to monitoring developments in the incidence of accidents.* The purpose is to be warned of changes, both positive and negative. Measuring the effect of preventive initiatives may be the result of such analyses, and increases in new types of accidents within a specified area will constitute warning of new risk elements.
- *Analyses to prioritize initiatives that call for high degrees of risk measurement, which in turn involve calculating the frequency and seriousness of accidents.* The goal is to establish a basis for prioritization to determine where it is more important to carry out preventive measures than elsewhere.
- *Analyses to determine how the accidents occurred and, especially, to establish both direct and underlying causes.* This information is then applied to the selection, elaboration and implementation of concrete corrective action and preventive initiatives.
- *Analyses for elucidation of special areas which have otherwise attracted attention (a sort of rediscovery or control analyses).* Examples include analyses of incidences of a special injury risk or the discovery of a hitherto unrecognized risk identified in the course of examining an already known risk.

These types of analyses can be carried out at several different levels, ranging from the individual enterprise to the national level. Analyses at several levels will be necessary for preventive measures. Analyses involving general accident incident rates, monitoring, warning and prioritization will be carried out chiefly at higher levels, whereas analyses describing direct and underlying accident causes will be conducted at lower levels. The results of the analyses will accordingly be more specific at the individual level and more general at the higher level.

Phases of the Analysis

Irrespective of the level from which an analysis starts, it will usually have the following phases:

- identification of where the accidents occur at the general level selected

- specification of where the accidents occur at a more specific level within the general level
- determination of goals in view of the incidence (or frequency) and seriousness of the accidents
- description of exposure sources or other harmful factors—that is, the direct causes of damage and injury
- examination of the underlying causal relation and causal development.

Examples of different levels of analysis are given in figure 56.1.

Summary

Identification of accidents nationwide may provide knowledge of the sectors, trade groups, technologies and working processes within which damages and injuries occur. The goal is solely to identify where the accidents occurred. Measurement of accidents by frequency and seriousness partly establishes where something is wrong in particular and partly indicates where the risk has changed.

The *type* of workplace risk is established by descriptions of the types of accidents that take place and the way in which they arise within the individual workplace areas. In this way, knowledge is obtained of the exposure sources and other harmful factors present in the workplace in the event that preventive measures—attention to safety conditions, awareness of risk, providing opportunity for action and the appeal to the workers' will—have proved insufficient to avert the accident.

Identification, measurement and description of accidents together provide the basis for what is to be done and who is to do it in order to reduce the risk. If, for example, specific exposure sources can be linked to specific technologies, it will help determine what special safety measures are necessary to control the risk. This information may also be used to influence manufacturers and suppliers associated with the technology in question. If it can be demonstrated that frequent and very serious accidents occur in connection with specific processes, the attempt may be made to adjust the nature of the equipment, machinery, operations or work procedures that are associated with these processes.

Figure 56.1 • Different levels of accident analysis.

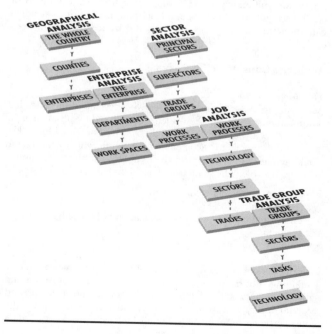

Unfortunately, a typical feature of such initiatives and adjustments is that an almost unambiguous monocausal correlation between accidents and causes is required, and this is available for only a few cases.

Analyses of accidents within an enterprise may also be carried out from a general to a more specific level. However, the problem often is to assemble a sufficiently extensive database. If accident injury data covering a number of years are gathered at an enterprise (including information regarding minor injuries and near accidents), it will be possible to establish a useful database even at this level. The overall analysis of the enterprise will show whether there are special problems in specific sections of the enterprise, or in connection with specific tasks or with the use of specific types of technology. The detailed analysis will then show what is wrong and thus lead to an evaluation of preventive measures.

If workers' conduct within a sector, trade group or enterprise, or the conduct of an individual is to be influenced, knowledge regarding many accidents is required in order to increase workers' awareness. At the same time, information must be made available about the factors which increase the probability of accidents and about known possibilities of action that may minimize the risk of damage or injury. At this point, safety becomes a matter of motivating those responsible for people's conduct at the level of a given sector, an industrial organization, a trade organization, the employer or the employee.

THEORY OF ACCIDENT CAUSES

Abdul Raouf

Accidents are defined as unplanned occurrences which result in injuries, fatalities, loss of production or damage to property and assets. Preventing accidents is extremely difficult in the absence of an understanding of the causes of accidents. Many attempts have been made to develop a prediction theory of accident causation, but so far none has been universally accepted. Researchers from different fields of science and engineering have been trying to develop a theory of accident causation which will help to identify, isolate and ultimately remove the factors that contribute to or cause accidents. In this article, a brief outline of various accident causation theories is presented, followed by a structure of accidents.

Accident Causation Theories

The domino theory

According to W.H. Heinrich (1931), who developed the so-called domino theory, 88% of all accidents are caused by unsafe acts of people, 10% by unsafe actions and 2% by "acts of God". He proposed a "five-factor accident sequence" in which each factor would actuate the next step in the manner of toppling dominoes lined up in a row. The sequence of accident factors is as follows:

1. ancestry and social environment
2. worker fault
3. unsafe act together with mechanical and physical hazard
4. accident
5. damage or injury.

In the same way that the removal of a single domino in the row would interrupt the sequence of toppling, Heinrich suggested that removal of one of the factors would prevent the accident and resultant injury; with the key domino to be removed from the sequence being number 3. Although Heinrich provided no data

for his theory, it nonetheless represents a useful point to start discussion and a foundation for future research.

Multiple causation theory

Multiple causation theory is an outgrowth of the domino theory, but it postulates that for a single accident there may be many contributory factors, causes and sub-causes, and that certain combinations of these give rise to accidents. According to this theory, the contributory factors can be grouped into the following two categories:

Behavioural. This category includes factors pertaining to the worker, such as improper attitude, lack of knowledge, lack of skills and inadequate physical and mental condition.

Environmental. This category includes improper guarding of other hazardous work elements and degradation of equipment through use and unsafe procedures.

The major contribution of this theory is to bring out the fact that rarely, if ever, is an accident the result of a single cause or act.

The pure chance theory

According to the pure chance theory, every one of any given set of workers has an equal chance of being involved in an accident. It further implies that there is no single discernible pattern of events that leads to an accident. In this theory, all accidents are treated as corresponding to Heinrich's acts of God, and it is held that there exist no interventions to prevent them.

Biased liability theory

Biased liability theory is based on the view that once a worker is involved in an accident, the chances of the same worker becoming involved in future accidents are either increased or decreased as compared to the rest of workers. This theory contributes very little, if anything at all, towards developing preventive actions for avoiding accidents.

Accident proneness theory

Accident proneness theory maintains that within a given set of workers, there exists a subset of workers who are more liable to be involved in accidents. Researchers have not been able to prove this theory conclusively because most of the research work has been poorly conducted and most of the findings are contradictory and inconclusive. This theory is not generally accepted. It is felt that if indeed this theory is supported by any empirical evidence at all, it probably accounts for only a very low proportion of accidents without any statistical significance.

The energy transfer theory

Those who accept the energy transfer theory put forward the claim that a worker incurs injury or equipment suffers damage through a change of energy, and that for every change of energy there is a source, a path and a receiver. This theory is useful for determining injury causation and evaluating energy hazards and control methodology. Strategies can be developed which are either preventive, limiting or ameliorating with respect to the energy transfer.

Control of energy transfer at the source can be achieved by the following means:

- elimination of the source
- changes made to the design or specification of elements of the work station
- preventive maintenance.

Figure 56.2 • Structure of accidents.

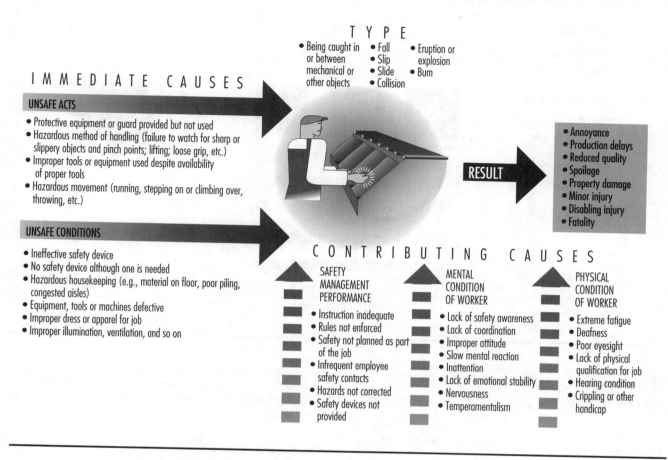

The path of energy transfer can be modified by:

- enclosure of the path
- installation of barriers
- installation of absorbers
- positioning of isolators.

The receiver of energy transfer can be assisted by adopting the following measures:

- limitation of exposure
- use of personal protective equipment.

The "symptoms versus causes" theory

The "symptoms versus causes" theory is not so much a theory as an admonition to be heeded if accident causation is to be understood. Usually, when investigating accidents, we tend to fasten upon the obvious causes of the accident to the neglect of the root causes. Unsafe acts and unsafe conditions are the symptoms—the proximate causes—and not the root causes of the accident.

Structure of Accidents

The belief that accidents are caused and can be prevented makes it imperative for us to study those factors which are likely to favour the occurrence of accidents. By studying such factors, the root causes of accidents can be isolated and necessary steps can be taken to prevent the recurrence of the accidents. These root causes of accidents can be grouped as "immediate" and "contributing". The immediate causes are unsafe acts of the worker and unsafe working conditions. The contributing causes could be management-related factors, the environment and the physical and mental condition of the worker. A combination of causes must converge in order to result in an accident.

Figure 56.2 shows the structure of accidents, including the details of immediate causes, contributing causes, types of accidents and results of accidents. This accounting is not exhaustive by any means. However, an understanding of the "cause and effect" relation of the accident-causing factors is required before continuous improvement of safety processes can be undertaken.

Summary

Accident causation is very complex and must be understood adequately in order to improve accident prevention. Since safety lacks a theoretical base, it cannot be regarded as being a science yet. This fact should not discourage us, as most of the scientific disciplines—mathematics, statistics and so on—passed through a similarly tentative phase at one time or the other. Accident causation study holds great promise for those who are interested in developing the pertinent theory. At present, theories of accident causation are conceptual in nature and, as such, are of limited use in preventing and controlling accidents. With such a diversity of theories, it will not be difficult to understand that there does not exist one single theory that is considered right or correct and is universally accepted. These theories are nonetheless necessary, but not sufficient, for developing a frame of reference for understanding accident occurrences.

Figure 56.3 • Model of accident causation.

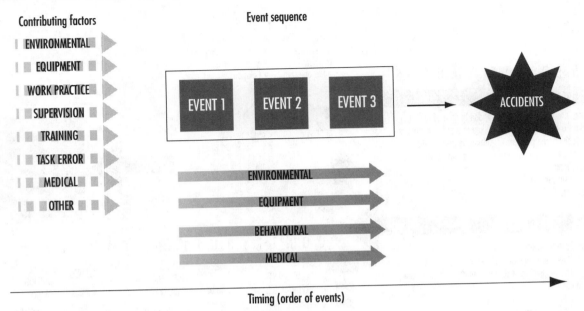

● HUMAN FACTORS IN ACCIDENT MODELLING

Anne-Marie Feyer and Ann M. Williamson

Human factors are a major component of the causes of accidents in the workplace. Estimates of the actual extent of the involvement vary markedly, but a study in the early 1980s of the causes of all work-related fatalities occurring in Australia over three years revealed that behavioural factors were involved in more than 90% of fatal accidents. In view of data like these, it is important to have an understanding of the role of human factors in accidents. Traditional models of accident causation placed superficial emphasis on human factors. Where human factors were included, they were depicted as linked to error occurring in the *immediate sequence* of events leading to the accident. A better understanding of how, why and when human factors become involved in accidents enhances our ability to make predictions about the role of human factors and helps to prevent accidents. A number of models have been put forward that attempt to describe the part that human factors play in accidents.

Accident Causation Models

Recent models have extended the role of human factors beyond the immediate causal events leading to the accident. Models now tend to include additional factors in the wider circumstances of the accident. Figure 56.3 shows details of such an approach: For example, human factors, such as work practices and supervision, can be included both as error in the event sequence leading immediately to the accident and as pre-existing human factors contributing to the accident event sequence. The two main components (contributing factors and event sequences) of this human factors model should be envisaged as occurring on a notional time line on which the order—contributing factors followed by a sequence of errors—is fixed, but the time base on which they occur is not. Both of these components are essential parts of accident causation.

The Nature of Error

An essential component of accident prevention, therefore, is gaining an understanding of the nature, timing and causes of error. One of the important and unique characteristics of error, distinguishing it from other factors involved in accidents, is that error is a normal part of behaviour. Error plays a fundamental role in learning new skills and behaviours and in maintaining those behaviours. Through testing the boundaries of interactions with the environment, and consequently making errors, humans learn just what the boundaries are. This is essential not only for learning a new skill but also for updating and maintaining ones they have already learned. The degree to which humans test the boundaries of their skills is related to the level of risk that they are prepared to accept.

It seems that errors are a constant feature of all behaviour. Studies show also that they occur in the causes of approximately two-thirds of work-related fatal accidents. It is essential therefore to develop some ideas about the form they are likely to take, and when and why they might occur. While there are many aspects of human error that are not yet understood, our current level of understanding allows some predictions to be made about error types. Knowledge of these types of error will, it is to be hoped, guide our efforts to prevent error or at least to modify the adverse consequences of error.

One of the most important features of the nature of error is that it is not a unitary phenomenon. Even though traditional accident analysis often treats error as if it were a singular entity which cannot be dissected further, there are a number of ways that errors can occur. Errors differ depending on the information-processing function being challenged. For example, errors can take the form of false sensations due to poor or degraded stimulation of the sensory organs, attentional failures due to the demands of prolonged or very complex stimulation from the environment, various types of memory lapses, errors of judgement and reasoning errors. All of these types of errors are distinguishable in terms of the context or task characteristics in which they occur. They signify breakdown in different information-processing functions and consequently would require different approaches to overcoming each of them.

Different types of error can also be distinguished with respect to skilled and unskilled behaviour. Training is often said to be a solution to problems of human error since skilled behaviour means that the required sequence of actions can be performed without conscious, constant attention and feedback, requiring only intermittent conscious checking to ensure that the behaviour is on track. The advantages of skilled behaviour are that once triggered, it requires little effort from the operator. It allows other activities to be undertaken at the same time (for instance, one can drive an automobile and talk at the same time) and allows the operator to plan for future aspects of the task. Furthermore, skilled behaviour is usually predictable. Unfortunately, while greater skill reduces the likelihood of many types of error, it increases the likelihood of others. Errors during skilled behaviour occur as absent-minded or unintended actions or lapses and are distinct from the mistakes which occur during unskilled behaviour. Skill-based errors tend to be associated with switching in the nature of attentional control of the task. They can occur during the conscious checking mode or they may be due to conclusion of similar patterns of skilled behaviour.

A second characteristic of errors is that they are not novel or random. Error forms are limited. They take similar forms in all types of functions. For example, "place losing" errors occur in speech and perceptual tasks as well as in knowledge-related or problem-solving tasks. Similarly, the timing and location of error in the accident causation sequence does not appear to be random. An important characteristic of information processing is that it is expressed in the same way regardless of the setting. This means that the error forms that occur in everyday life in the kitchen, for example, occur in the same manner in the most high-risk industries. The consequences of these errors, however, are very different and are determined by the setting in which the error occurs, rather than by the nature of the error itself.

Models of Human Error

In the categorization of error and the development of models of human error, it is important to take all aspects of error into account to the extent possible. The resulting categorization, however, needs to be usable in practice. This is possibly the biggest constraint. What can be done in developing a theory of accident causation can be very difficult to apply in practice. In attempting to analyse the causes of an accident, or to predict the role of human factors in a process, it is not possible to understand all aspects of human information processing which contributed or might contribute. It may never be possible, for example, to know the role of intention before an accident occurred. Even afterwards, the very fact that the accident had occurred can change a person's recall of the events surrounding it. The error categorizations that have been most successful to date therefore focus on the nature of the behaviour that was performed at the time the error occurred. This allows error analysis to be relatively objective and as reproducible as possible.

These categorizations of error distinguish between those occurring during skilled behaviour (slips, lapses or unintended acts) and those occurring during unskilled or problem-solving behaviour (mistakes).

Slips or *skill-based errors* are defined as unintended errors occurring when the behaviour is a highly practised routine or automatic in nature.

Mistakes have been further categorized into two types:
- *rule-based errors*, which occur when the behaviour requires the application of rules
- *knowledge-based errors*, which occur during problem solving when the person has no skill or rule to apply.

This means that knowledge-based errors occur through lack of expertise, rule-based errors through the failure to apply the expertise appropriately, and skill-based errors through a disruption of the execution of the programme of actions, usually due to changes in attentional level (Rasmussen 1982).

Application of these categories in a population study of work-related fatal accidents showed that they could be used reliably. The results showed that skill-based errors occurred most frequently overall and that occurrences of the three error types were distributed differently across the event sequence. Skill-based errors, for example, occurred most commonly as the last event immediately before the accident (79% of fatalities). Since, at this point, there is little time for recovery, their consequences may be more severe. Mistakes, on the other hand, appear to be distributed earlier in the accident sequence.

Human Factors in the Wider Circumstances of Accidents

Elaboration of the involvement of human factors other than human error in the circumstances immediately surrounding the accident represents a major advance in understanding accident genesis. While there is no question that error is present in most accident sequences, human factors are also involved in a broader sense, taking the form, for example, of standard operating work procedures and the influences that determine the nature and acceptability of work procedures, including the earliest decisions of management. Clearly, flawed work procedures and decisions are related to error since they involve errors of judgement and reasoning. However, flawed work procedures are distinguished by the characteristic that the errors of judgement and reasoning have been permitted to become standard ways of operating, since, having no immediate consequences, they do not make their presence urgently felt. They are, nevertheless, recognizable as unsafe work systems with fundamental vulnerabilities that provide the circumstances which may later, unintentionally, interact with human action and lead directly to accidents.

In this context, the term *human factors* covers a wide range of elements involved in the interaction between individuals and their working environment. Some of these are direct and observable aspects of the ways in which work systems function that do not have immediate adverse consequences. Design, use and maintenance of equipment, the provision, use and maintenance of personal protective and other safety equipment and standard operating procedures originating from management or workers, or both, are all examples of such ongoing practices.

These observable aspects of human factors in system functioning are to a large extent manifestations of the overall organizational setting, a human element even more removed from direct involvement in accidents. Characteristics of organizations have been collectively termed *organizational culture* or *climate*. These terms have been used to refer to the set of goals and beliefs an individual holds and the impact of the organization's goals and beliefs on those of the individual. Ultimately, the collective or norm values, reflecting the characteristics of the organization, are likely to be influential determinants of attitude and motivation for safe behaviour at all levels. The level of risk tolerated in a work setting, for example, is determined by such values. Thus, the culture of any organization, clearly reflected in its work system and the standard operating procedures of its workers, is a crucial aspect of the role of human factors in accident causation.

The conventional view of accidents as a number of things suddenly going wrong at the time and the place of the accident, concentrates attention on the overt measurable event at the time of the accident. In fact, errors occur in a context which itself may allow the unsafe act or error to have its consequences. In order to reveal accident causes that originate in pre-existing conditions in work systems, we need to take into account all of the various ways in which the human element can contribute to accidents. This is perhaps the most important consequence of taking a broad view of the role of human factors in accident causation. Flawed decisions and practices in work systems, while not having an immediate impact, act to create the setting conducive to operator error—or to the error's having consequences—at the time of the accident.

Traditionally, organizational aspects of accidents have been the most neglected aspect of accident analysis design and data collection. Because of their distant relationship in time from the occurrence of the accident, the causal link between accidents and organizational factors has often not been obvious. Recent conceptualizations have specifically structured analysis and data collection systems in such a way as to incorporate the organizational components of accidents. According to Feyer and Williamson (1991), who used one of the first systems designed to specifically include the organizational contribution to accidents, a considerable proportion of all occupational fatalities in Australia (42.0%) involved pre-existing and ongoing unsafe work practices as a causal factor. Waganaar, Hudson and Reason (1990), using a similar theoretical framework in which the organizational contribution to accidents was recognized, argued that organizational and managerial factors constitute latent failures in work systems that are analogous to resident pathogens in biological systems. Organizational flaws interact with triggering events and circumstances in the immediate circumstances surrounding accidents much as resident pathogens in the body combine with triggering agents such as toxic factors to bring about disease.

The central notion in these frameworks is that organizational and managerial flaws are present long before the onset of the accident sequence. That is, they are factors which have a latent or delayed-action effect. Thus, to understand how accidents occur, how people contribute to them and why they behave the way that they do, it is necessary to ensure that analysis does not begin and end with the circumstances that most directly and immediately lead to harm.

The Role of Human Factors in Accidents and Accident Prevention

In acknowledging the potential aetiological significance of the wider circumstances surrounding the accident, the model best describing accident causation has to take into account the relative timing of elements and how they relate to each other.

First, causal factors vary in terms of their causal importance, and also in terms of their temporal importance. Furthermore, these two dimensions can vary independently; that is, causes can be important because they occur very close in time to the accident and therefore they reveal something about the time of the accident, or they can be important because they are a prime cause underlying the accident, or both. By examining both the temporal and causal importance of factors involved in the wider circumstances as well as the immediate circumstances of the accident,

analysis focuses on why the accident happened, rather than just describing how it happened.

Second, accidents are generally agreed to be multicausal. Human, technical and environmental components in the work system can interact in critical ways. Traditionally, accident analysis frameworks have been limited in terms of the range of categories defined. This, in turn, limits the nature of the information obtained and so limits the range of options highlighted for preventive action. When the wider circumstances of the accident are taken into consideration, the model has to deal with an even more extensive range of factors. Human factors are likely to interact with other human factors and also with non-human factors. The patterns of occurrences, co-occurrences and inter-relationships of the wide range of possible different elements within the causal network provides the most complete and therefore most informative picture of accident genesis.

Third, these two considerations, the nature of the event and the nature of its contribution to the accident, interact. Although multiple causes are always present, they are not equivalent in role. Accurate knowledge of the role of factors is the essential key to understanding why an accident happens and how to prevent it from recurring. For example, immediate environmental causes of accidents may have their impact because of earlier behavioural factors in the form of standard operating procedures. Similarly, pre-existing aspects of work systems may provide the context in which routine errors committed during skill-based behaviour can precipitate an accident with harmful consequences. Normally these routine errors would have benign consequences. Effective prevention would be best served if it were targeted towards the latent underlying causes, rather than the immediately precipitating factors. This level of understanding of the causal network and how it influences outcome is possible only if all types of factors are included for consideration, their relative timing is examined and their relative importance is determined.

Despite the potential for an almost infinite variety in the ways that human action can directly contribute to accidents, relatively few patterns of causal pathways account for the majority of accident causation. In particular, the range of underlying latent conditions which set the scene for later human and other factors to have their effect are limited predominantly to a small number of aspects of work systems. Feyer and Williamson (1991) reported that only four patterns of factors accounted for the causes of approximately two-thirds of all occupational fatalities in Australia over a 3-year period. Not surprisingly, almost all of these involved human factors at some point.

Summary

The nature of human involvement varies as to type and timing and as to its importance in terms of causing the accident (Williamson and Feyer 1990). Most commonly, human factors in the form of a limited range of pre-existing, flawed work systems create the underlying prime causes of the fatal accidents. These combine with later lapses during skilled performance or with hazards in environmental conditions to precipitate the accident. These patterns illustrate the layered role typical of the involvement of human factors in accident genesis. To be of use in preventive strategy formulation, however, the challenge is not to simply describe the various ways in which the human element is involved but rather to identify where and how it may be possible to intervene most effectively. This is possible only if the model used has the capacity to describe accurately and comprehensively the complex network of interrelated factors involved in accident causation, including the nature of the factors, their relative timing and their relative importance.

ACCIDENT MODELS: RISK HOMEOSTASIS

Gerald J.S. Wilde

Give me a ladder that is twice as stable, and I will climb it twice as high. But give me a cause for caution, and I'll be twice as shy. Consider the following scenario: A cigarette is invented that causes half the frequency of smoking-related deaths per cigarette smoked as compared to present-day cigarettes, but in all other ways it is indistinguishable. Does this constitute progress? When the new cigarette replaces the current one, given that there is no change in people's desire to be healthy (and that this is the only factor inhibiting smoking), smokers will respond by smoking twice as much. Thus, although the death rate per cigarette smoked is cut in half, the death risk due to smoking remains the same per smoker. But this is not the only repercussion: the availability of the "safer" cigarette leads fewer people to stop smoking than presently is the case and seduces more current non-smokers to yield to the temptation to smoke. As a consequence, the smoking-related death rate in the population increases. However, as people are willing to take no more risks with their health and lives than they see fit in exchange for the satisfaction of other desires, they will cut down on other, less appealing, unsafe or unhealthy habits. The end result is that the lifestyle-dependent death rate remains essentially the same.

The above scenario illustrates the following basic premises of risk homeostasis theory (RHT) (Wilde 1988; 1994):

The first is the notion that people have a *target level of risk*—that is, the level of risk they accept, tolerate, prefer, desire or choose. The target level of risk depends on perceived benefits and disadvantages of safe and unsafe behaviour alternatives, and it determines the degree to which they will expose themselves to safety and health hazards.

The second premise is that the actual frequency of lifestyle-dependent death, disease and injury is maintained over time through a closed-loop, self-regulating control process. Thus, fluctuations in the degree of caution people apply in their behaviour determine the ups and downs in the loss to their health and safety. Moreover, the ups and downs in the amount of actual lifestyle-dependent loss determine the fluctuations in the amount of caution people exercise in their behaviour.

Finally, the third premise holds that the level of loss to life and health, in so far as this is due to human behaviour, can be decreased through interventions that are effective in reducing the level of risk people are willing to take—that is, *not* through measures of the "safe cigarette" variety or other such efforts towards a "technological fix" of the problem, but by means of programmes that enhance people's desire to be alive and healthy.

The Risk Homeostasis Theory of Accident Causation and Prevention

Among the many psychological contributions to the literature on occupational accidents and disease, traffic accidents and lifestyle-dependent ill health, only a relatively few deal with *motivational* factors in the causation and the prevention of these problems. Most of the publications deal with variables such as permanent or semi-permanent traits (e.g., gender, personality or experience), transient states (fatigue, blood-alcohol level), information overload or underload (stress or boredom), training and skills, environmental factors and workstation ergonomics. It may be reasoned, however, that all variables other than motivational ones (i.e., those impinging upon the target level of risk) merely have a marginal influence upon the frequency of accidents per operator-hour of task execution. Some, though, may well have a favourable effect upon the accident rate per unit of productivity or per unit distance of mobility.

When applied, for instance, to road traffic, RHT posits that the traffic accident rate per time unit of road-user exposure is the output of a closed-loop control process in which the target level of risk operates as the unique controlling variable. Thus, in contrast with temporary fluctuations, time-averaged accident risk is viewed as *independent* of factors such as the physical features of the vehicle and road environment and of operator skills. Instead, it ultimately depends on the level of accident risk accepted by the road-user population in exchange for the perceived benefits received from motor-vehicle mobility in general (like driving a lot), and from specific risky acts associated with that mobility in particular (like driving well in excess of the average speed).

Thus, it is reasoned that at any moment of time, vehicle operators, equipped with their perceptual skills, perceive a certain level of accident risk and they compare this with the amount of accident risk they are willing to accept. The level of the latter is determined by the pattern of trade-offs between expected costs and benefits associated with the available alternatives for action. Thus, the target level of risk is that level of risk at which the overall utility of manner and amount of mobility is thought to maximize. The expected costs and benefits are a function of economic, cultural and person-related variables, and their long-term, short-term and momentary fluctuations. These control the target level of risk at any specific moment of time.

Whenever road users perceive a discrepancy between target risk and experienced risk in one direction or the other, they will attempt to restore the balance through some behavioural adjustment. Whether the balance is achieved or not depends upon the individual's decision-making and psychomotor skills. However, any action taken carries a certain likelihood of accident risk. The sum total of all actions taken by the road users in a jurisdiction in a given time period (like 1 year), produce the frequency and severity of the traffic accidents in that jurisdiction. It is hypothesized that this accident rate has an influence (through feedback) upon the level of accident risk perceived by the survivors and thus upon their subsequent actions and subsequent accidents, and so forth. Thus, as long as the target level of risk remains unchanged, accident toll and behavioural caution determine each other in a circular causal chain.

The Risk Homeostatic Process

This homeostatic process, in which the accident rate is both consequence and cause of changes in operator behaviour, is modelled in figure 56.4. The self-correcting nature of the homeostatic mechanism can be recognized in the closed loop that runs from box *e* to box *b*, to box *c*, to box *d*, and then back to box *e*. It may take some time for people to become aware of a change in the accident rate (the feedback may be delayed, and this is symbolized by *f*). Note that box *a* is located outside the closed loop, meaning that interventions that lower that target level of risk can bring about a lasting reduction in the accident rate (box *e*).

The process described herein can be further and quite clearly explained by another example of homeostatic regulation: the thermostatic control of the temperature in a house. The set temperature (comparable to box *a*) on the thermostat is at any point in time being compared with the actual temperature (box *b*). Whenever there is a difference between the two, there is a need for adjustment (box *c*), which triggers an adjustment action (i.e., the provision of colder or warmer air, box *d*). As a result, the air that is distributed through the house becomes colder (via air conditioning) or warmer (via heating—box *e*), as desired. After some time (symbolized by *f*) the air at the new temperature reaches the point set on the thermostat and gives rise to a new

56. ACCIDENT PREVENTION

Figure 56.4 • Homeostatic model relating changes in accident loss to changes in operator behaviour and vice versa, with the target level of risk as the controlling variable.

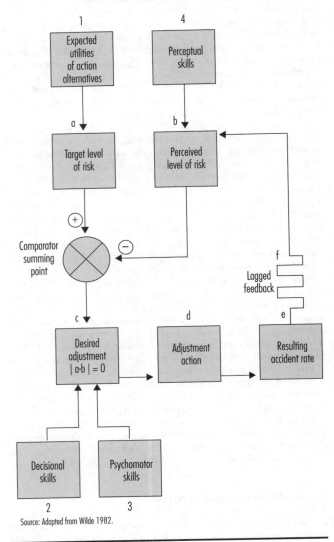

Source: Adapted from Wilde 1982.

under-estimation of risk, just as a thermometer that produces a temperature reading that is consistently too high or too low will cause real temperature to deviate systematically from target temperature.

Evidence in Support of the Model

It may be deduced from the model described above that the introduction of any accident countermeasure that does not alter the target level of risk is followed by road users making an estimate of its *intrinsic effect* upon safety—that is, the change in accident rate that would occur if operator behaviour did not change in response to the new countermeasure. This estimate will enter into the comparison between perceived and accepted level of risk and thus influence subsequent adjustment behaviour. If the initial estimates are incorrect on average, a disturbance in the accident rate will occur, but only temporarily, because of the correcting effect due to the feedback process.

This phenomenon has been discussed in an OECD report. The greater opportunity for safety and the increased level of skill may not be utilized for greater safety, but instead for improved performance: "Behavioural adaptations of road users which may occur following the introduction of safety measures in the transport system are of particular concern to road authorities, regulatory bodies and motor vehicle manufacturers particularly in cases where such adaptations may decrease the expected safety benefit" (OECD 1990). This report mentions numerous examples, as follows:

Taxicabs in Germany equipped with anti-lock brake systems were not involved in fewer accidents than taxis without these brakes, and they were driven in a more careless manner. Increases in lane width of two-lane highways in New South Wales in Australia have been found to be associated with higher driving speeds: a speed increase by 3.2 km/h for every 30 cm additional lane width. This was found for passenger cars, while truck speed increased by about 2 km/h for every 30 cm in lane width. A US study dealing with the effects of lane-width reduction found that drivers familiar with the road reduced their speed by 4.6 km/h and those unfamiliar by 6.7 km/h. In Ontario it was found that speeds decreased by about 1.7 km/h for each 30 cm of reduction in lane width. Roads in Texas with paved shoulders as compared to unpaved shoulders were driven at speeds at least 10% higher. Drivers have generally been found to move at a higher speed when driving at night on roads with clearly painted edge markings.

Recently, a Finnish study investigated the effect of installing reflector posts along highways with an 80 km/h speed limit. Randomly selected road sections which totalled 548 km were equipped with these posts and compared with 586 km that were not. The installation of reflector posts increased speed in darkness. There was not even the slightest indication that it reduced the accident rate per km driven on these roads; if anything, the opposite happened (Kallberg 1992).

Numerous other examples could be mentioned. Seat-belt-wearing legislation has not been seen to reduce traffic fatality rates (Adams 1985). Habitual non-users of seat-belts who were made to buckle up, increased their moving speed and decreased their following distance (Janssen 1994). Following the change-over from left- to right-hand traffic in Sweden and Iceland, there were initially major reductions in the occurrence of serious accidents, but their rates returned to the pre-existing trend when road users found out that the roads had not become as dangerous as they thought at first (Wilde 1982). There have been major reductions in the accident rate per km driven in the course of this century, but the traffic accident rate per head of population has not shown a downward trend (when account is taken of periods of high

temperature reading, which is compared with the set-point temperature (box *a*), and so on.

The house temperature will show major fluctuations if the thermometer is not very sensitive. The same thing will happen when the adjustment action is slow to set in, either due to inertia of the switching mechanism or to a limited capacity of the heating/cooling system. Note, however, that these deficiencies will not alter the *time-averaged* temperature in the house. Note too that the desired temperature (analogous to box *a* in figure 56.4) is the only factor outside the closed loop. Resetting the thermostat to a new target temperature will produce durable changes in the time-averaged temperature. Just as a person chooses a target level of risk on the basis of the perceived benefits and costs of safe and risky behaviour alternatives, so is the target temperature selected in consideration of the pattern of expected costs and benefits of higher or lower temperatures (e.g., energy expenditures and physical comfort). A *lasting* discrepancy between target risk and actual risk can occur only in the case of consistent over- or unemployment in which the target level of accident risk is reduced; Wilde 1991).

Motivation for Accident Prevention

Interestingly, most of the evidence for the phenomena that are postulated by RHT comes from the area of road traffic, while the prospects this theory holds for accident prevention have largely been confirmed in occupational settings. In principle, there are four ways in which workers and drivers may be motivated to lower their target level of risk:

- Reduce the expected *benefits* of risky behaviour alternatives.
- Increase the expected *costs* of risky behaviour alternatives.
- Increase the expected *benefits* of safe behaviour alternatives.
- Decrease the expected *costs* of safe behaviour alternatives.

While some of these approaches have been found to be more effective than others, the notion that safety may be enhanced by acting upon motivation has a long history, as is obvious from the universal presence of punitive law.

Punishment

Although enforcement of punitive law is one of society's traditional attempts at motivating people towards safety, the evidence for its effectiveness has not been forthcoming. It suffers from several other problems as well, some of which have been identified in the context of organizational psychology (Arnold 1989).

First is the "self-fulfilling prophecy" effect of attribution. For example, labelling people with undesirable characteristics may stimulate individuals to behave as if they had these characteristics. Treat people as if they were irresponsible and eventually some will behave as if they were.

Second, the emphasis is on process controls; i.e., on specific behaviours such as using a piece of safety equipment or obeying the speed limit, instead of focusing on the end result, which is safety. Process controls are cumbersome to design and implement, and they can never totally encompass all undesirable specific behaviours of all people at all times.

Third, punishment brings negative side-effects. Punishment creates a dysfunctional organizational climate, marked by resentment, uncooperativeness, antagonism and even sabotage. As a result, the very behaviour that was to be prevented may in fact be stimulated.

Encouragement

In contrast to punishment, incentive programmes have the effect for which they are intended, as well as the positive side-effect of creating a favourable social climate (Steers and Porter 1991). The effectiveness of incentives and recognition programmes in enhancing safety has been clearly established. In a recent review of over 120 published evaluations of different types of occupational accident prevention, incentives and recognition were generally found more effective towards safety than engineering improvements, personnel selection and other types of intervention which included disciplinary action, special licensing, and exercise and stress-reduction programmes (Guastello 1991).

Behavioural Adaptation

According to risk homeostasis theory, the accident rate per person-hour of task performance or the annual accident rate per head of population do not primarily depend upon a person's *ability* to be safe, nor upon the *opportunity* to be safe, but instead upon that person's *desire* to be safe. Thus, it is reasoned that, although education and engineering may provide the ability or the opportunity for greater safety, these approaches to accident prevention will fail to reduce the accident rate per hour, because they do not reduce the amount of risk people are willing to take.

The response to these interventions, therefore, will usually take the form of some behavioural adjustment in which the potential safety advantage is in fact consumed as an addition to performance in terms of greater productivity, more mobility and/or higher speed of mobility.

This can be explained as the consequence of a homeostatic control process in which the degree of behavioural caution determines the accident rate and the accident rate determines the extent of caution in operator behaviour. In this closed-loop process, the *target level of risk* is the only independent variable that ultimately explains the accident rate. The target level of risk depends on the person's perception of the advantages and disadvantages of various action alternatives. To maintain that safety is its own reward is to ignore the fact that people knowingly take risks for various contingencies that are open to modification.

Therefore, of all accident countermeasures that are currently available, those that enhance people's motivation towards safety seem to be the most promising. Furthermore, of all countermeasures that affect people's motivation towards safety, those that reward people for accident-free performance seem to be the most effective. According to McAfee and Winn's literature review: "The major finding was that every study, without exception, found that incentives or feedback enhanced safety and/or reduced accidents in the workplace, at least in the short term. Few literature reviews find such consistent results" (1989).

Summary

Of all possible schemes that reward people for accident-free performance, some promise better results than others because they contain the elements that appear to enhance motivation towards safety. Examples of empirical evidence for the risk-homeostatic process have been selected from the larger information base (Wilde 1994), while the ingredients for effective incentive programming have been discussed in greater detail in Chapter 60.16. The under-reporting of accidents has been mentioned as the only identified negative side-effect of incentive schemes. This phenomenon, however, is limited to minor accidents. It may be possible to conceal a broken finger; it is more difficult to hide a corpse.

ACCIDENT MODELLING

Andrew R. Hale

Humans play important roles in most of the processes leading up to accidents and in the majority of measures aimed at accident prevention. Therefore, it is vital that models of the accident process should provide clear guidance about the links between human actions and accidents. Only then will it be possible to carry out systematic accident investigation in order to understand these links and to make predictions about the effect of changes in the design and layout of workplaces, in the training, selection and motivation of workers and managers, and in the organization of work and management safety systems.

Early Modelling

Up until the 1960s, modelling human and organizational factors in accidents had been rather unsophisticated. These models had not differentiated human elements relevant to accidents beyond rough subdivisions such as skills, personality factors, motivational factors and fatigue. Accidents were seen as undifferentiated problems for which undifferentiated solutions were sought (as doctors two centuries ago sought to cure many then undifferentiated diseases by bleeding the patient).

Figure 56.5 • Individual problem solving in the face of danger.

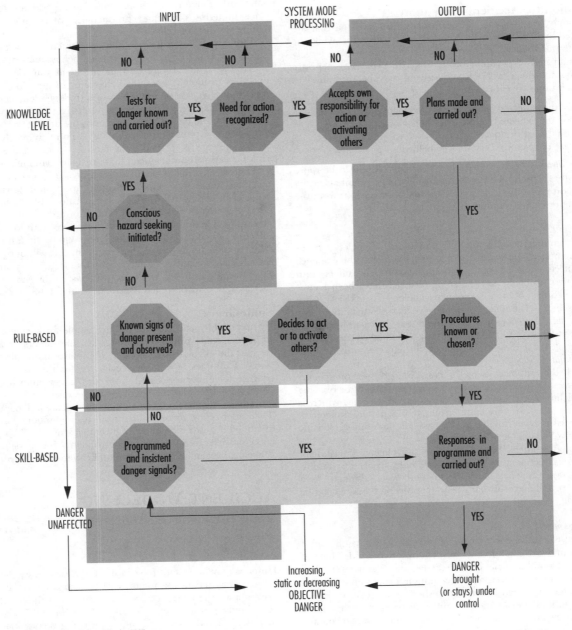

Source: Adapted from Hale and Glendon 1987.

Reviews of accident research literature that were published by Surry (1969) and by Hale and Hale (1972) were among the first attempts to go deeper and offer a basis for classifying accidents into types reflecting differentiated aetiologies, which were themselves linked to failures in different aspects of the man-technology-environment relationships. In both of these reviews, the authors drew upon the accumulating insights of cognitive psychology in order to develop models presenting people as information processors, responding to their environment and its hazards by trying to perceive and control the risks that are present. Accidents were considered in these models as failures of different parts of this process of control that occur when one or more of the control

steps does not perform satisfactorily. The emphasis was also shifted in these models away from blaming the individual for failures or errors, and towards focusing on the mismatch between the behavioural demands of the task or system and the possibilities inherent in the way behaviour is generated and organized.

Human Behaviour

Later developments of these models by Hale and Glendon (1987) linked them to the work of Rasmussen and Reason (Reason 1990), which classified human behaviour into three levels of processing:

Figure 56.6 • Problem-solving cycle.

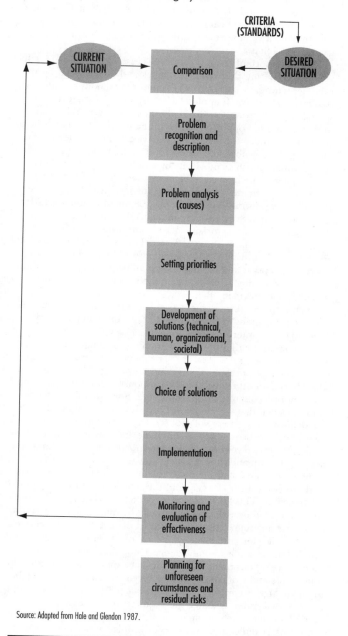

Source: Adapted from Hale and Glendon 1987.

Figure 56.7 • Behaviour in the face of danger.

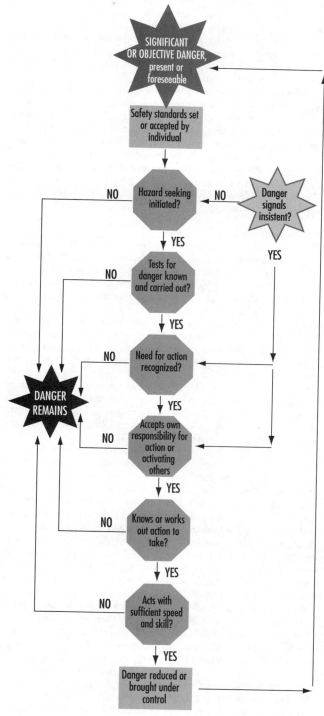

- automatic, largely unconscious responses to routine situations (skill-based behaviour)
- matching learned rules to a correct diagnosis of the prevailing situation (rule-based behaviour)
- conscious and time-consuming problem solving in novel situations (knowledge-based behaviour).

The typical failures of control differ from one level of behaviour to another, as do the types of accidents and the appropriate safety measures used to control them. The Hale and Glendon model, updated with more recent insights, is depicted in figure 56.5. It is made up of a number of building blocks which will be explained successively in order to arrive at the full model.

Link to deviation models

The starting point of the Hale and Glendon model is the way in which danger evolves in any workplace or system. Danger is considered to be always present, but kept under control by a large number of accident-prevention measures linked to hardware (e.g.,

56. ACCIDENT PREVENTION

the design of equipment and safeguards), people (e.g., skilled operators), procedures (e.g., preventive maintenance) and organization (e.g., allocation of responsibility for critical safety tasks). Provided that all relevant dangers and potential hazards have been foreseen and the preventive measures for them have been properly designed and chosen, no damage will occur. Only if a deviation from this desired, normal state takes place can the accident process start. (These deviation models are dealt with in detail in "Accident deviation models".)

The task of the people in the system is to assure proper functioning of the accident-prevention measures so as to avert deviations, by using the correct procedures for each eventuality, handling safety equipment with care, and undertaking the necessary checks and adjustments. People also have the task of detecting and correcting many of the deviations which may occur and of adapting the system and its preventive measures to new demands, new dangers and new insights. All these actions are modelled in the Hale and Glendon model as detection and control tasks related to a danger.

Problem solving

The Hale and Glendon model conceptualizes the role of human action in controlling danger as a problem-solving task. The steps in such a task can be described generically as in figure 56.6.

This task is a goal-seeking process, driven by the standards set in step one in figure 56.6. These are the standards of safety which workers set for themselves, or which are set by employers, manufacturers or legislators. The model has the advantage that it can be applied not only to individual workers faced with imminent or future danger, but also to groups of workers, departments or organizations aiming to control both existing danger from a process or industry and future danger from new technology or products at the design stage. Hence safety management systems can be modelled in a consistent way with human behaviour, allowing the designer or evaluator of safety management to take an appropriately focused or a wide view of the interlocking tasks of different levels of an organization (Hale et al. 1994).

Applying these steps to individual behaviour in the face of danger we obtain figure 56.7. Some examples of each step can clarify the task of the individual. Some degree of danger, as stated above, is assumed to be present all the time in all situations. The question is whether an individual worker responds to that danger. This will depend partly on how insistent the danger signals are and partly on the worker's own consciousness of danger and standards of acceptable level of risk. When a piece of machinery unexpectedly glows red hot, or a fork-lift truck approaches at high speed, or smoke starts seeping from under the door, individual workers skip immediately to considering the need for action, or even to deciding what they or someone else can do.

These situations of imminent danger are rare in most industries, and it is normally desirable to activate workers to control danger when it is much less imminent. For example, workers should recognize slight wear on the machine guard and report it, and realize that a certain noise level will make them deaf if they are continuously exposed to it for some years. Designers should anticipate that a novice worker could be liable to use their proposed new product in a way that could be dangerous.

To do this, all persons responsible for safety must first consider the possibility that danger is or will be present. Consideration of danger is partly a matter of personality and partly of experience. It can also be encouraged by training and guaranteed by making it an explicit part of tasks and procedures at the design and execution phases of a process, where it may be confirmed and encouraged by colleagues and superiors. Secondly, workers and supervisors must know how to anticipate and recognize the signs of danger. To ensure the appropriate quality of alertness, they

must accustom themselves to recognize potential accident scenarios—that is, indications and sets of indications that could lead to loss of control and so to damage. This is partly a question of understanding webs of cause and effect, such as how a process can get out of control, how noise damages hearing or how and when a trench can collapse.

Just as important is an attitude of creative mistrust. This involves considering that tools, machines and systems can be misused, go wrong, or show properties and interactions outside their designers' intentions. It applies "Murphy's Law" (whatever can go wrong will go wrong) creatively, by anticipating possible failures and affording the opportunity of eliminating or controlling them. Such an attitude, together with knowledge and understanding, also helps at the next step—that is, in really believing that some sort of danger is sufficiently likely or serious to warrant action.

Labelling something as dangerous enough to need action is again partly a matter of personality; for instance, it may have to do with how pessimistic a person may be about technology. More importantly, it is very strongly influenced by the kind of experience that will prompt workers to ask themselves such questions as, "Has it gone wrong in the past?" or "Has it worked for years with the same level of risk with no accidents?" The results of research on risk perception and on attempts to influence it by risk communication or feedback on accident and incident experience are given in more detail in other articles.

Even if the need for some action is realized, workers may take no action for many reasons: they do not, for example, think it is their place to interfere with someone else's work; they do not know what to do; they see the situation as unchangeable ("it is just part of working in this industry"); or they fear reprisal for reporting a potential problem. Beliefs and knowledge about cause and effect and about the attribution of responsibility for accidents and accident prevention are important here. For example, supervisors who consider that accidents are largely caused by careless and accident-prone workers will not see any need for action on their own part, except perhaps to eliminate those workers from their section. Effective communications to mobilize and coordinate the people who can and should take action are also vital at this step.

The remaining steps are concerned with the knowledge of what to do to control the danger, and the skills needed to take appropriate action. This knowledge is acquired by training and experience, but good design can help greatly by making it obvious how to achieve a certain result so as to avert danger or to protect one's self from it—for instance, by means of an emergency stop or shutdown, or an avoiding action. Good information resources such as operations manuals or computer support systems can help supervisors and workers to gain access to knowledge not available to them in the course of day-to-day activity. Finally, skill and practice determine whether the required response action can be carried out accurately enough and with the right timing to make it successful. A difficult paradox arises in this connection: the more alert and prepared that people are, and the more reliable the hardware is, the less frequently the emergency procedures will be needed and the harder it will be to sustain the level of skill needed to carry them out when they are called upon.

Links with behaviour based on skill, rules and knowledge

The final element in the Hale and Glendon model, which turns figure 56.7 into figure 56.5, is the addition of the link to the work of Reason and Rasmussen. This work emphasized that behaviour can be evinced at three different levels of conscious control—skill-based, rule-based and knowledge-based—which implicate different aspects of human functioning and are subject to different types and degrees of disturbance or error on account of external signals or internal processing failures.

Skill-based. The skill-based level is highly reliable, but subject to lapses and slips when disturbed, or when another, similar routine captures control. This level is particularly relevant to the kind of routine behaviour that involves automatic responses to known signals indicating danger, either imminent or more remote. The responses are known and practised routines, such as keeping our fingers clear of a grinding wheel while sharpening a chisel, steering a car to keep it on the road, or ducking to avoid a flying object coming at us. The responses are so automatic that workers may not even be aware that they are actively controlling danger with them.

Rule-based. The rule-based level is concerned with choosing from a range of known routines or rules the one which is appropriate to the situation—for example, choosing which sequence to initiate in order to close down a reactor which would otherwise become overpressurized, selecting the correct safety goggles to work with acids (as opposed to those for working with dusts), or deciding, as a manager, to carry out a full safety review for a new plant rather than a short informal check. Errors here are often related to insufficient time spent matching the choice to the real situation, to relying on expectation rather than observation to understand the situation, or to being misled by outside information into making a wrong diagnosis. In the Hale and Glendon model, behaviour at this level is particularly relevant to detecting hazards and choosing correct procedures in familiar situations.

Knowledge-based. The knowledge-based level is engaged only when no pre-existing plans or procedures exist for coping with a developing situation. This is particularly true of the recognition of new hazards at the design stage, of detecting unsuspected problems during safety inspections or of coping with unforeseen emergencies. This level is predominant in the steps at the top of figure 56.5. It is the least predictable and least reliable mode of operation, but also the mode where no machine or computer can replace a human in detecting potential danger and in recovering from deviations.

Putting all the elements together results in figure 56.5, which provides a framework for both classifying where failures occurred in human behaviour in a past accident and analysing what can be done to optimize human behaviour in controlling danger in a given situation or task in advance of any accidents.

● ACCIDENT SEQUENCE MODELS

Ragnar Andersson

This article covers a group of accident models that all share the same basic design. The interplay between human, machine and environment, and the development of this interplay into potential hazards, dangers, damages and injuries, is envisaged by means of a sequence of questions derived and listed in a logical order. This sequence is then applied in a similar manner at different levels of analysis through the use of models. The first of these models was presented by Surry (1969). A few years later, a modified version was presented by the Swedish Work Environment Fund (1983) and received the fund's sobriquet, WEF. A Swedish research team then evaluated the WEF model and suggested some further developments resulting in a third model.

These models are herein described one by one, with comments on the reasons for the changes and developments undertaken. Finally, a tentative synthesis of the three models is proposed. Thus, a total of four models, with considerable similarities, are presented and discussed. Although this may seem confusing, it illustrates the fact that there is no model that is universally accepted as "The Model". Among other things, there is an obvious

conflict between simplicity and completeness with regard to accident models.

Surry's Model

In 1969, Jean Surry published the book *Industrial Accident Research—A Human Engineering Appraisal.* This book contains a review of models and approaches predominantly applied in accident research. Surry grouped the theoretical and conceptual frameworks she identified into five different categories: (1) chain-of-multiple-events models, (2) epidemiological models, (3) energy-exchange models, (4) behaviour models, and (5) systems models. She concluded that none of these models is incompatible with any of the others; each simply stresses different aspects. This inspired her to combine the various frameworks into one comprehensive and general model. She made it clear, though, that her model should be regarded as provisional, without any pretensions of finality.

In Surry's view, an accident can be described by a series of questions, forming a sequential hierarchy of levels, where the answers to each question determine whether an event turns out as an accident or not. Surry's model (see figure 56.8) reflects the principles of human information processing, and is based upon

Figure 56.8 • Surry's model.

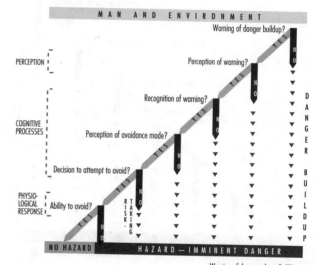

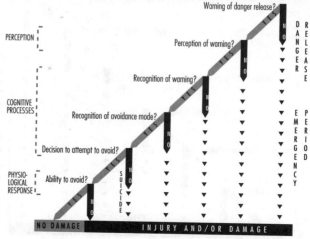

Source: Surry 1969.

the notion of an accident as a deviation from an intended process. It has three principal stages, linked by two similar cycles.

The first stage views human beings in their total environment, including all relevant environmental and human parameters. The potential injury agent is also described at this stage. It is assumed that, through the actions (or non-actions) of the individual, dangers grow out of such an environment. For the purpose of analysis a "danger-build-up" cycle is constituted by the first sequence of questions. If there are negative responses to any of these questions, the danger in question will become imminent.

The second sequence of questions, the "danger-release cycle", links the level of danger to possible alternative outcomes when the danger is triggered. It should be noted that by following different routes through the model, it is possible to distinguish between deliberate (or consciously accepted) dangers and unintentional negative outcomes. The differences between "accident-like" unsafe acts, mishaps (and so on) and completed accidents are also clarified by the model.

Figure 56.9 • The WEF model.

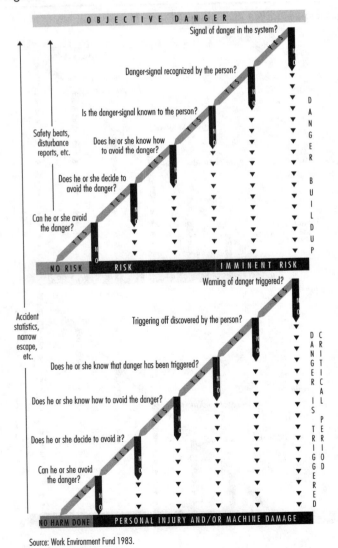

Source: Work Environment Fund 1983.

The WEF Model

In 1973, a committee set up by the Swedish Work Environment Fund to review the state of occupational accident research in Sweden launched a "new" model and promoted it as a universal tool that should be employed for all research in this field. It was announced as a synthesis of existing behavioural, epidemiological and systems models, and was also said to encompass all relevant aspects of prevention. Reference was made to Surry, among others, but without mention of the fact that the proposed model was almost identical to hers. Only a few changes had been made, all for the purpose of improvement.

As often occurs when scientific models and perspectives are recommended by central agencies and authorities, the model is subsequently adopted in only a few projects. Nevertheless, the report issued by the WEF contributed to a rapidly rising interest in modelling and theory development among Swedish and Scandinavian accident researchers, and several new accident models emerged within a short period.

The point of departure in the WEF model (in contrast to Surry's "man and environment" level) lies in the concept of danger, here limited to "objective danger" as opposed to the subjective perception of danger. Objective danger is defined as an integral part of a given system, and is basically determined by the amount of resources available for investment in safety. Increasing a system's tolerance to human variability is mentioned as a way of reducing danger.

When an individual comes into contact with a certain system and its dangers, a process begins. Due to system features and individual behaviour, a risk situation may arise. What is most important (as regards the properties of systems) according to the authors, is how dangers are indicated through various kinds of signals. Risk imminence is determined depending on the individual's perception, understanding and actions in relation to these signals.

The next sequence in the process, which is in principle identical to Surry's, is directly related to the event and whether it will lead to injury or not. If the danger is released, can it be, in fact, observed? Is it perceived by the individual in question and is he or she able to avoid injury or damage? Answers to such questions explain the kind and degree of harmful outcomes that emanate from the critical period.

The WEF model (figure 56.9) was seen as having four advantages:

- It makes clear that safe working conditions presuppose the taking of action at the earliest possible stage.
- It illustrates the importance of working with disturbances and near-accidents, as well as those accidents that lead to damage or injury. Actual outcome is of less importance in a preventive perspective.
- It describes the principles of human information processing.
- It provides for self-correcting safety systems by means of the feedback of results from studied incidents.

Evaluation and Further Development

By the time the WEF report was issued, an epidemiological study on occupational accidents was under way in the city of Malmö, Sweden. The study was based on a modified version of the so-called Haddon Matrix, which cross-tabulates variables along two dimensions: time in terms of pre-accident, accident and post-accident phases; and the epidemiological trichotomy of host, agent (or vehicle/vector) and environment. Although such a model provides a good basis for data collection, it was found by the research team to be insufficient to understand and explain the causal mechanisms underlying accident and injury phenomena. The

WEF model appeared to represent a new approach, and was therefore received with great interest. It was decided to conduct an immediate evaluation of the model by testing it on a random selection of 60 actual cases of occupational accidents that had been previously thoroughly investigated and documented by the Malmö group as a part of its ongoing study.

The results of the evaluation were summarized in four points:

- The model is not the comprehensive tool it was expected to be. Instead, it should be regarded primarily as a behavioural model. The "danger" is given, and the analysis focuses on the individual's behaviour in relation to that danger. Consequently, preventive options derived from such analysis are oriented to human factors rather than to equipment or environment. The "danger" as such is hardly questioned within the framework of the model.

- The model does not take due consideration of technical or organizational constraints in the work process. It creates an illusion of free choice between dangerous and safe alternatives. Some dangers were actually found to be unavoidable by the individual worker, although they were clearly avoidable by management. Hence, it becomes irrelevant and misleading to ask whether people know how to avoid (and choose to avoid) something which is not really avoidable unless they decide to quit their job.

- The model provides no insight into the important issue of why the dangerous activity was necessary to begin with, and why it was performed by the specific individual. Sometimes dangerous tasks can be made unnecessary; and sometimes they can be performed by other, more appropriate persons with greater skills.

- The analysis is restricted to a single person, but many accidents occur in interaction between two or more persons. However, it was suggested that this deficiency could be overcome by combining the results of parallel analyses, each made from the perspective of one of the different individuals involved.

Based on these remarks, the model was further developed by the research group in Malmö. The most important innovation was the addition of a third sequence of questions to complement the other two. This sequence was designed to analyse and explain the existence and nature of "danger" as an inherent feature of a human-machine system. General principles from systems theory and control technology were applied.

Moreover, the work process, thus understood in terms of human-machine-environment interaction, should also be seen in the light of its organizational and structural contexts at both company and societal levels. The need to take personal characteristics and motives for the actual activity into consideration, as well as for the individual to carry out that activity, was also indicated. (See figure 56.10.)

Summary

In reconsidering these early models today, more than twenty years later, against the background of progress made concerning theories and models in accident research, they still seem surprisingly up-to-date and competitive.

The basic underlying assumption of the models—that accidents, as well as their causes, should be seen as deviations from intended processes—is still a dominant perspective (see, inter alia, Benner 1975; Kjellén and Larsson 1981).

The models make a clear distinction between the concept of injury as a health outcome and the concept of accident as a preceding occurrence. Moreover, they demonstrate that an accident is not just an "event", but rather a process which can be analysed as a series of steps (Andersson 1991).

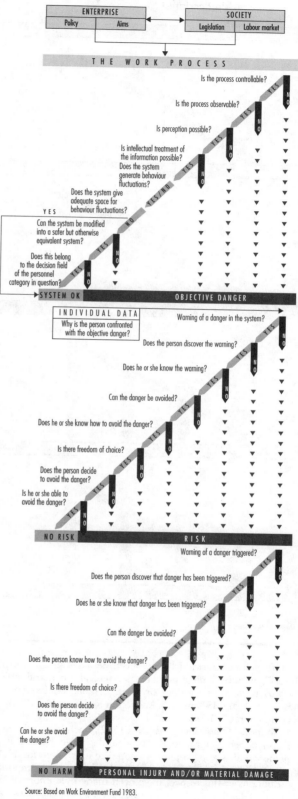

Figure 56.10 • The WEF model developed by introduction of a new first sequence.

Source: Based on Work Environment Fund 1983.

56. ACCIDENT PREVENTION

Figure 56.11 • Tentative comprehensive model on accident causation (based on Surry 1969 and descendants).

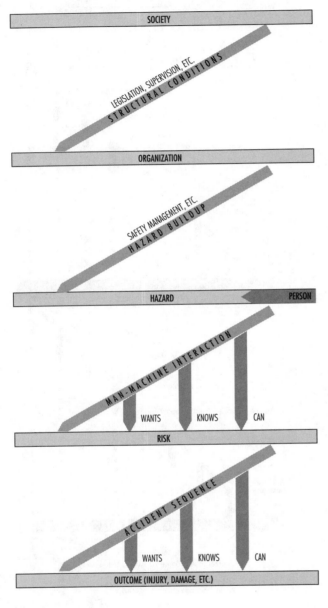

Source: Based on Surry 1969.

Many subsequent models have been designed as a number of "boxes", organized in temporal or hierarchical order, and indicating various temporal phases or levels of analysis. Examples of these include the ISA model (Andersson and Lagerlöf 1983), the deviation model (Kjellén and Larsson 1981) and the so-called Finnish model (Tuominen and Saari 1982). Such levels of analysis are also clearly central to the models described here. But the sequence models also propose a theoretical instrument for analysing the mechanisms which link these levels together. Important contributions in this respect have been made by authors such as Hale and Glendon (1987) from a human factors perspective, and Benner (1975) from a systems point of view.

As clearly emerges when comparing these models, Surry did not give a key position to the concept of danger, as is done in the WEF model. Her starting point was the human-environment interaction, reflecting a broader approach similar to that suggested by the Malmö group. On the other hand, like the WEF committee, she did not refer to any further levels of analysis beyond the worker and environment, such as organizational or societal levels. Further, the comments from the Malmö study cited here in relation to the WEF model also seem relevant to Surry's model.

A modern synthesis of the three models presented above might include fewer details on human information processing and more information on "upstream" conditions (further back in the casual "flow") at organizational and societal levels. Key elements in a sequence of questions designed to address the relationship between the organizational and human-machine levels might be derived from modern principles of safety management, involving quality assurance methodologies (internal control and so on). Similarly, a sequence of questions for the connection between societal and organizational levels might involve modern principles of systems-oriented supervision and auditing. A tentative comprehensive model, based on Surry's original design and including these additional elements, is outlined in figure 56.11.

ACCIDENT DEVIATION MODELS

Urban Kjellén

An occupational accident may be regarded as an abnormal or unwanted effect of the processes in an industrial system, or something which does not work as planned. Unwanted effects other than personal injury are also possible, such as material damage, accidental release of pollution to the environment, time delay or reduced product quality. The *deviation model* is rooted in systems theory. When applying the deviation model, accidents are analysed in terms of *deviations*.

Deviations

The definition of *deviations* in relation to specified requirements coincides with the definition of nonconformities in the International Organization for Standardization's ISO 9000 series of standards on quality management (ISO 1994). The value of a systems variable is classified as a deviation when it falls outside a norm. Systems variables are measurable characteristics of a system, and they can assume different values.

Norms

There are four different types of norms. These relate to: (1) specified requirements, (2) what has been planned, (3) what is normal or usual and (4) what is accepted. Each type of norm is characterized by the way it has been established and its degree of formalization.

Safety regulations, rules and procedures are examples of specified requirements. A typical example of a deviation from a specified requirement is a "human error", which is defined as a transgression of a rule. The norms that relate to what is "normal or usual" and what is "accepted" are less formalized. They are typically applied in industrial settings, where the planning is oriented to outcome and the execution of the work is left to the discretion of the operators. An example of a deviation from an "accepted" norm is an "incidental factor", which is an unusual event that may (or may not) result in an accident (Leplat 1978). A further example is an "unsafe act", which traditionally was defined as a personal action violating a commonly accepted safe procedure (ANSI 1962).

Figure 56.12 • Analysis of an accident at a construction site on the basis of the OARU model.

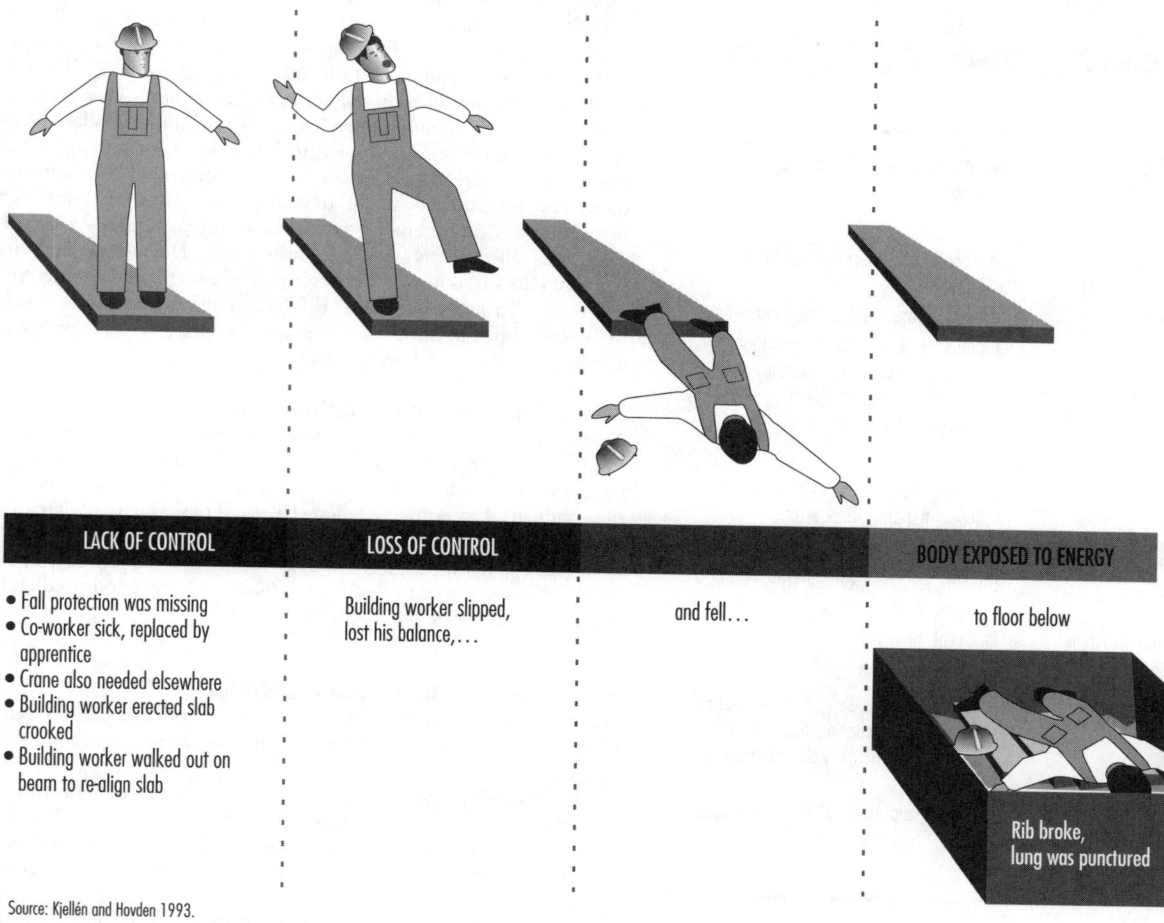

LACK OF CONTROL	LOSS OF CONTROL		BODY EXPOSED TO ENERGY
• Fall protection was missing • Co-worker sick, replaced by apprentice • Crane also needed elsewhere • Building worker erected slab crooked • Building worker walked out on beam to re-align slab	Building worker slipped, lost his balance,...	and fell...	to floor below Rib broke, lung was punctured

Source: Kjellén and Hovden 1993.

Systems Variables

In the application of the deviation model, the set or range of values of systems variables is divided into two classes, namely, normal and deviation. The distinction between normal and deviation may be problematic. Differences of opinion about what is normal may arise, for example, among workers, supervisors, management and systems designers. Another problem relates to the lack of norms in work situations which have not been encountered before (Rasmussen, Duncan and Leplat 1987). These differences of opinion and the lack of norms may in themselves contribute to an increased risk.

The Time Dimension

Time is a basic dimension in the deviation model. An accident is analysed as a process rather than as a single event or a chain of causal factors. The process develops through consecutive phases, so that there is a transition from normal conditions in the industrial system to abnormal conditions or a state of *lack of control*. Subsequently, a *loss of control* of energies in the system occurs and the damage or injury develops. Figure 56.12 shows an example of the analysis of an accident based on a model developed by the Occupational Accident Research Unit (OARU) in Stockholm, in relation to these transitions.

Focus on Accident Control

Each accident model has a unique focus, which is linked to an accident-prevention strategy. The deviation model puts the focus on the initial phase of the accident sequence, which is characterized by the state of abnormal conditions or lack of control. Accident prevention is accomplished through feedback where established information systems for production planning and control and safety management are used. The aim is to conduct a smooth operation with as few disturbances and improvisations as possible, so as to not increase the risk of accidents.

A distinction is made between corrective and preventive actions. Correction of deviations coincides with the first order of feedback in Van Court Hare's hierarchy of feedback, and does not result in any organizational learning from the accident experiences (Hare 1967). Preventive actions are accomplished through higher orders of feedback that involve learning. An example of a preventive action is the development of new work instructions based on commonly shared norms about safe work routines. In general, there are three different aims of preventive actions: (1) to reduce the probability of deviations, (2) to reduce the consequences of deviations and (3) to reduce the time from the occurrence of deviations to their identification and correction.

To illustrate the characteristics of the deviation model, a comparison is made with the *energy model* (Haddon 1980) which directs

56. ACCIDENT PREVENTION

Table 56.1 • Examples of taxonomies for the classification of deviations.

Theory or model and variable	Classes
Process model	
Duration	Event/act, condition
Phase of the accident sequence	Initial phase, concluding phase, injury phase
Systems theory	
Subject-object	(Act of) person, mechanical/physical condition
Systems ergonomics	Individual, task, equipment, environment
Industrial engineering	Materials, labour power, information, technical, human, intersecting/parallel activities, stationary guards, personal protective equipment
Human errors	
Human actions	Omission, commission, extraneous act, sequential error, time error
Energy model	
Type of energy	Thermal, radiation, mechanical, electrical, chemical
Type of energy control system	Technical, human
Consequences	
Type of loss	No significant time loss, degraded output quality, equipment damage, material loss, environmental pollution, personal injury
Extent of loss	Negligible, marginal, critical, catastrophic

Source: Kjellén 1984.

the focus of accident prevention on the later phases of the accident process—that is, the loss of control of energies and subsequent harm. Accident prevention is typically accomplished through limitation or control of energies in the system or by interposing barriers between the energies and the victim.

Taxonomies of Deviations

There are different taxonomies for the classification of deviations. These have been developed to simplify the collection, processing and feedback of data on deviations. Table 56.1 presents an overview.

A classical taxonomy of deviations is the distinction between "unsafe act of persons" and "unsafe mechanical/physical conditions" (ANSI 1962). This taxonomy combines a classification with respect to duration and the subject-object split. The OARU model is based on an industrial engineering systems view (Kjellén and Hovden 1993) wherein each class of deviations is related to a typical system for production control. It follows, for example, that deviations related to work materials are controlled through material control, and technical deviations are controlled through inspection and maintenance routines. Stationary guards are typically controlled through safety inspections. Deviations that describe the loss of control of energies are characterized by the type of energy involved (Haddon 1980). A distinction is also made between failures in human and technical systems for the control of energies (Kjellén and Hovden 1993).

The Validity of the Deviation Concept

No general relationships exist between deviations and the risk of injury. Research results suggest, however, that some types of deviations are associated with an increased risk of accidents in certain industrial systems (Kjellén 1984). These include defective equipment, production disturbances, irregular workload and tools used for unusual purposes. The type and amount of energy that is involved in the uncontrolled energy flow are fairly good predictors of the consequences.

Application of the Deviation Model

Data on deviations are collected in safety inspections, safety sampling, near-accident reporting and accident investigations. (See figure 56.13.)

For example, *Safety sampling* is a method for the control of deviations from safety rules through performance feedback to the workers. Positive effects of safety sampling on safe performance, as measured by the risk of accidents, have been reported (Saari 1992).

The deviation model has been applied in the development of tools for use in accident investigations. In the *incidental factors analysis* method, deviations of the accident sequence are identified and arranged in a logical tree structure (Leplat 1978). The OARU model has been the basis for the design of accident investigation forms and checklists and for the structuring of the accident investigation procedure. Evaluation research shows that these methods support a comprehensive and reliable charting and evaluation of deviations (see Kjellén and Hovden 1993 for a review). The deviation model has also inspired the development of methods for risk analysis.

Figure 56.13 • The coverage of different tools for use in safety practice.

SAFETY INSPECTIONS

SAFETY SAMPLING

NEAR ACCIDENT REPORTING

ACCIDENT INVESTIGATIONS

Deviation analysis is a risk analysis method and encompasses three steps: (1) the summarizing of systems functions and operator activities and their division into subsections, (2) the examination of each activity to identify possible deviations and to assess the potential consequences of each deviation and (3) the development of remedies (Harms-Ringdahl 1993). The accident process is modelled as illustrated by figure 56.12, and the risk analysis covers all three phases. Checklists similar to those applied in accident investigations are used. It is possible to integrate this method with design tasks; it is further effective in identifying needs for remedial actions.

Summary

Deviation models focus on the early part of the accident process, where there are disturbances in the operation. Prevention is accomplished through feedback control in order to achieve a smooth operation with few disturbances and improvisations that may result in accidents.

● MAIM: THE MERSEYSIDE ACCIDENT INFORMATION MODEL

Harry S. Shannon and John Davies

Generally speaking, the term *accident* is used to denote events resulting in undesired or unplanned physical injury or damage; an accident model is a conceptual scheme applied to the analysis of such events. (Some models may explicitly declare that "near accidents"—sometimes known as "near misses"—are covered by the model; however, the distinction is not important to this article.) Models of accidents can serve different purposes. First, they may provide a conceptual understanding of how accidents occur. Second, models may be used to record and store information on accidents. Third, they may provide a mechanism for investigating accidents. These three aims are not entirely distinct, but form a useful means of categorization.

This article describes MAIM, the Merseyside Accident Information Model, which is most naturally adapted to the second purpose—recording and storing accident information. Following an outline of the rationale for MAIM, some early studies evaluating the model are described. The article ends with recent progress with MAIM, including the use of "intelligent software" to collect and analyse information on injury accidents.

Early Accident Modelling

In Heinrich's model (1931), the causal sequence leading to an accident was likened to a sequence of five falling dominoes, each of the first four being necessary before the final event could occur. In a precursor to MAIM, Manning (1971) concluded that "the basic requirements of an accidental injury are the presence of a host [a worker, for example] and an environmental object which contributes to the accident. The host or the object or both move in relation to each other." Kjellén and Larsson (1981) developed their own model, which posited two levels: the accident sequence and the underlying, determining factors. In a later paper, Kjellén and Hovden (1993) described subsequent progress in the context of other literature and noted the need for "efficient use of existing information from routine accident and near accident reports by means of a powerful information retrieval system". This has been achieved for MAIM.

Rationale for MAIM

There appears to be a substantial consensus that useful information on accidents should not merely concentrate on the immediate circumstances of the damage or injury, but should also include an understanding of the preceding chain of events and factors causing the accident sequence to occur. Some early classification systems failed to achieve this. Understanding objects, movements (of people or objects) and events were commonly mixed and successive events were not distinguished.

A simple example illustrates the problem. A worker slips on a patch of oil, falls and strikes his or her head on a machine and suffers a concussion. We can easily distinguish the (immediate) cause of the accident (slipping on oil) and the cause of the injury (hitting the head on the machine). Some classification systems, however, include the categories "falls of persons" and "striking against objects". The accident could be allocated to either of these, although neither describes even the immediate cause of the accident (slipping on oil) or causal factors (such as how did the oil get on the floor).

Essentially, the problem is that just one factor is considered in a multifactorial situation. An accident does not always consist of a single event; there may be many. These points formed the basis for the development of MAIM by Derek Manning, an occupational physician.

Description of MAIM

The centrepiece of the accident is the *first unforeseen (undesired or unplanned) event* involving the damaged equipment or injured person (figure 56.14). This will not always be the first event in the accident process described as a *preceding event*. In the example above, the slip counts as the first unforeseen event of the accident. (Given the presence of oil patches on the floor, it is not unforeseen that someone will slip on one and fall, but the person walking does not foresee this.)

Figure 56.14 • The MAIM Accident Model.

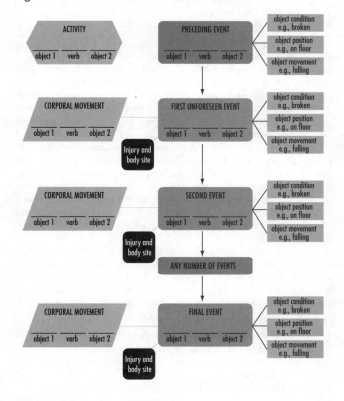

Source: Based on Davies and Manning 1994b.

The behaviour of the equipment or person is described by the general *activity* at the time and a more specific description of the type of *corporal movement* when the first event occurred. Objects involved are described, and for those related to events, characteristics of objects include *position, movement* and *condition.* On occasion, a second object which inter-relates with the first object may be involved (for example, striking a chisel with a hammer).

As noted above, there may be more than one event and the *second event* may also have an object (perhaps different) involved in it. Additionally, the equipment or person may make an additional corporal movement, such as throwing out a hand to prevent or break a fall. These can be included in the model. A third fourth or later event may occur before the sequence finally leads to an injury. The model can be expanded in all directions by recording factors related to each component. For example, branches from activities and corporal movements would record psychological factors, medications or physical limitations of a worker.

In general, separate events may be easily distinguished intuitively, but a stricter definition is useful: an event is *an unexpected change, or lack of change, in the energy state of the situation.* (The term *energy* includes both kinetic and potential energy.) The first event is always unexpected. Subsequent events may be expected, even inevitable, after the first event, but are always unexpected before the accident. An example of unexpected lack of change of energy is when a hammer being swung misses the nail at which it is aimed. The example of a worker who slips on a patch of oil, falls and hits his or her head provides an illustration. The first event is "foot slipped"—instead of remaining still, the foot acquires kinetic energy. The second event is "fell", when further kinetic energy is acquired. This energy is absorbed by the collision of the worker's head with the machine when the injury occurs and the sequence ends. This can be "plotted" onto the model as follows:

1. 1st event: foot slipped on oil.
2. 2nd event: person fell.
3. 3rd event: head struck against machine.

Experience with MAIM

An earlier version of the MAIM model was used in a study of all 2,428 reported accidents in 1973 in a gearbox manufacturing plant on the grounds of an automobile company. (See Shannon 1978 for further details.) The operations included cutting and grinding of gears, heat treatment and gearbox assembly. The cutting process produced sharp metal splinters and shavings, and oil was used as a coolant. Purpose-designed forms were used to collect information. Each accident was plotted independently onto the model by two people and discrepancies were resolved by discussion. For each accident, the components were given numerical codes, so the data could be stored on a computer and analyses performed. The following outlines some basic results and presents an examination made what was learned specifically from the use of the model.

The accident rate was substantially reduced (by nearly 40%), apparently as a result of the study being conducted. The researchers learned that because of the additional questioning that the study called for (and the consequent time involved) many employees "could not be bothered" to report minor injuries. Several items of evidence confirmed this:

1. The rate rose again in 1975 after the study ended.
2. The rate of lost-time injuries was unaffected.
3. Visits to the medical centre for non-industrial complaints were unaffected.
4. Accident rates on the rest of the grounds were unaffected.

Thus the reduced rate did indeed appear to be an artefact of reporting.

Another interesting finding was that there were 217 injuries (8%) for which the workers involved could not be certain how or when they occurred. This was discovered because workers were explicitly asked if they were sure of what happened. Typically, the injuries involved were cuts or splinters, relatively common given the nature of work at this plant.

Of the remaining accidents, nearly half (1,102) consisted of just one event. Two- and three-event accidents were successively less common, and 58 accidents involved four or more events. There was a marked increase in the proportion of accidents resulting in lost time with an increase in the number of events. One possible explanation is that there was an increase in kinetic energy with each event, so that with more events, there was more energy to dissipate when the worker and the object involved collided.

Further examination of differences between lost-time and non-lost-time accidents found very marked differences in the distributions for separate components of the model. For example, when the first event was "person slipped", nearly a quarter of the accidents resulted in lost time; but for "body punctured by", only 1% did so. For combinations of components, such differences were accentuated. For example, with respect to the final events and related objects, none of the 132 accidents in which the casualty was "punctured by" or "splintered" resulted in lost time, but when the final event was "strained/sprained" with "no object involved", 40% of the injuries caused lost time.

These results contradicted the view that the severity of injury is largely a matter of luck and prevention of all types of accidents would lead to a reduction of serious injuries. This means that analysing all accidents and attempting to prevent the most common types would not necessarily have an effect on those causing serious injuries.

A sub-study was conducted to assess the usefulness of information in the model. Several potential uses of accident data were identified:

-   to measure safety performance—the extent to which accidents in a plant, or area of a plant, continue to occur over time
-   to identify causes
-   to identify errors (in the broadest meaning of the term)
-   to check on control—that is, to see whether safety measures taken to prevent some type(s) of accident are indeed effective
-   to provide a basis of expertise, as knowledge of a wide range of accident situations and circumstances might help provide accident prevention advice.

Three safety officers (practitioners) rated the usefulness of the verbal descriptions and the plotted models for a series of accidents. Each rated at least 75 accidents on a scale from 0 (no useful information) to 5 (perfectly adequate for use). For the majority of accidents, the ratings were identical—that is, no information was lost in the transfer from the written descriptions to the model. Where there was a loss of information it was mostly just one point on the 0 to 5 scale—that is, only a small loss.

The information available, though, was rarely "perfectly adequate". This was partly because the safety officers were used to conducting detailed on-the-spot investigations, something not done in this study because all reported accidents, both minor and more serious ones, were included. It should be remembered, however, that the information plotted onto the models was taken directly from written descriptions. Since relatively little information was lost, this suggested the possibility of excluding the intermediate step. The more widespread use of personal computers and availability of improved software make automated data collection possible—and allow checklists to be used by way of insuring that all relevant information is obtained. A program has been written for this purpose and has undergone some initial testing.

Figure 56.15 • Accident summary as recorded by patient interview.

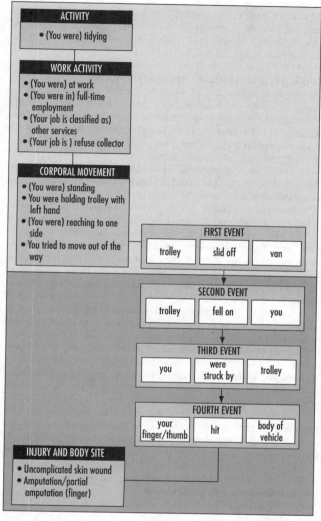

ACTIVITY
- (You were) tidying

WORK ACTIVITY
- (You were) at work
- (You were in) full-time employment
- (Your job is classified as) other services
- (Your job is) refuse collector

CORPORAL MOVEMENT
- (You were) standing
- You were holding trolley with left hand
- (You were) reaching to one side
- You tried to move out of the way

FIRST EVENT

| trolley | slid off | van |

SECOND EVENT

| trolley | fell on | you |

THIRD EVENT

| you | were struck by | trolley |

FOURTH EVENT

| your finger/thumb | hit | body of vehicle |

INJURY AND BODY SITE
- Uncomplicated skin wound
- Amputation/partial amputation (finger)

Source: Based on Davies and Manning 1994b.

MAIM Intelligent Software

The MAIM model was used by Troup, Davies and Manning (1988) to investigate accidents causing back injuries. A database was created on an IBM PC by coding results from patient interviews conducted by an interviewer who was experienced with the MAIM model. The analysis of interviews to obtain the MAIM description (figure 56.14) was done by the interviewer and it was only at this stage that the data were entered into the database. While the method was quite satisfactory, there were potential problems in making the method generally accessible. In particular, two areas of expertise were required—interviewing skills and the familiarity with the analysis needed to form the MAIM description of the accident.

Software was developed by Davies and Manning (1994a) to conduct a patient interview and produce a database of accidents using the MAIM model. The purpose of the software was to provide two areas of expertise—the interview and the analysis to form the MAIM event structure. The MAIM software is, in effect, an intelligent "front end" to a database, and by 1991 it was

sufficiently developed to be tested in a clinical environment. The MAIM software was designed to interact with the patient by means of "menus"—the patient selects options from lists which require only the use of cursor keys and the "Enter" key. The choice of an item from the list of options affected to some extent the path through the interview and also had the effect of recording information at the appropriate part of the MAIM description of the accident. This method of data collection eliminated the need for spelling and typing skills and also gave a repeatable and consistent interview.

The event structure of the MAIM model uses verbs and objects to form simple sentences. Verbs in events can be associated with different accident scenarios, and this property of the model forms the basis for the construction of a set of linked questions that form an interview. Questions are presented in such a way that at any stage only simple choices are needed, effectively breaking the complex account of the accident into a set of simple descriptions. Once an event verb has been identified, associated nouns can be found by locating the objects to form a sentence giving the full detail of the description of the particular event. It is clear that this strategy requires the use of an extensive dictionary of objects which can be searched quickly and efficiently.

The Home Accident Surveillance System (HASS) (Department of Trade and Industry 1987) monitors objects involved in accidents, and the list of objects used by HASS was used as the basis of an object dictionary for the MAIM software and was extended to include objects found in the workplace. Objects can be grouped into classes, and with this structure a hierarchical menu system can be defined—classes of objects form layers that correspond to menu lists. Thus a linked list of associated objects can be used to locate individual items. As an example, the object *hammer* could be found by selecting, in order: (1) tools, (2) hand tools and (3) hammer from three successive menu lists. A given object could potentially be classified into several different groups—for example, a knife could be associated with kitchen items, tools or sharp objects. This observation was used to create redundant links in the object dictionary, allowing many different paths to find the required object. The object dictionary currently has a vocabulary of about 2,000 entries covering work and leisure environments.

The MAIM interview also collects information on activities at the time of the accident, corporal movements, the location of the accident, contributory factors, injuries and disability. All of these elements can occur more than once in an accident, and this is reflected in the structure of the underlying relational database which was used to record the accident.

At the end of the interview, several sentences describing events in the accident will have been recorded and the patient is asked to put them in the correct order. In addition, the patient is asked to link injuries with the recorded events. A summary of the information collected is then presented on the screen of the computer for information.

An example of an accident summary as seen by the patient is shown in figure 56.15. This accident has been superimposed on the MAIM diagram in figure 56.15. Details relating to factors and the location of the accident have been omitted.

The first unforeseen or unintended event (first event) involving the injured person is usually the first event in the accident sequence. For example, when a person slips and falls, the slip is normally the first event in the accident sequence. If, on the other hand, a person is injured by a machine because another person operates the machine before the victim is standing clear, the first event involving the victim is "trapped by machine" but the first event in the accident sequence is "other person operated machine prematurely". In the MAIM software, the first event in the accident sequence is recorded and it may arise either from the first event involving the injured person or as a preceding event (figure 56.14). Theoretically, this way of viewing matters may be unsatisfactory, but from the accident prevention point of view, it identifies the beginning of the accident sequence, which can then be targeted to prevent similar accidents in the future. (The term *action of deviation* is used by some authorities to describe the beginning of the accident sequence, but it is not yet clear if this is always synonymous with the first event in the accident.)

When the MAIM software was first used in a clinical setting it was clear that there were problems in correctly appraising some types of "underfoot" accidents. The MAIM model identifies the first unforeseen event as the starting point of the accident sequence. Consider two similar accidents, one in which a worker *intentionally* steps onto an object which then breaks, and a second accident in which a worker *unintentionally* steps onto an object which breaks. In the first accident stepping on the object is a body movement and the first unforeseen event is the object breaking. In the second accident stepping on the object is the first unforeseen event in the accident. The resolution of these two scenarios is to ask, "Did you accidentally step on something?" This demonstrates how important the correct design of the interview is in obtaining accurate data. The analysis of these two accidents allows recommendations on accident prevention as follows; the first accident could have been prevented by making the patient aware that the object would break. The second accident could have been prevented by making the patient aware that the object was an underfoot hazard.

The MAIM software has been tested successfully in three clinical settings, including a 1-year project in the Accident and Emergency Department of the Royal Liverpool University Hospital. Patient interviews took between 5 and 15 minutes, and on average two patients were interviewed per hour. In all, 2,500 accidents were recorded. Work on publications based on these data is in progress.

● PRINCIPLES OF PREVENTION: THE PUBLIC HEALTH APPROACH TO REDUCING INJURIES IN THE WORKPLACE

Gordon S. Smith and Mark A. Veazie

A public health approach to occupational injury prevention is based on the assumption that injury is a health problem, and as such can either be prevented or its consequences mitigated (Occupational Injury Prevention Panel 1992; Smith and Falk 1987; Waller 1985). When a worker falls from a scaffold, the tissue damage, internal haemorrhage, shock and death that follow are, by definition, a disease process—and also by definition a concern for public health professionals. Just as malaria is defined as a disease whose causal agent is a specific protozoan, injuries are a family of diseases caused by exposure to a particular form of energy (kinetic, electrical, thermal, radiation or chemical) (National Committee for Injury Prevention and Control 1989). Drowning, asphyxiation and poisoning are also considered injuries because they represent a relatively rapid departure from the body's structural or functional norm, as does acute trauma.

As a health problem, injuries are the leading cause of premature death (i.e., before age 65) in most countries (Smith and Falk 1987; Baker et al. 1992; Smith and Barss 1991). In the United States, for example, injury is the third leading cause of death following cardiovascular disease and cancer, the leading cause of hospitalization under the age of 45, and an imposed economic burden of 158 billion dollars in direct and indirect costs in 1985 (Rice et al. 1989). One out of three nonfatal injuries and one out of six fatal injuries to working-aged persons in the United States occur on the job (Baker et al. 1992). Similar patterns apply in most of the developed world (Smith and Barss 1991). In middle- and low-income countries, a rapid and relatively unregulated pace of industrialization may result in a nearly global pandemic of occupational injuries.

Public Health Models for Injury Control

The traditional practice of workplace safety usually focuses on minimizing risks and losses within a single company. Public health practitioners engaged in occupational injury control are interested not only in individual worksites but also in improving the health status of populations in geographic areas that may be exposed to the hazards associated with multiple industries and occupations. Some events such as workplace fatalities may be rare at individual plants, but by studying all fatalities in a community, risk patterns and prevention policy may become evident.

Most models of public health practice are based on three elements: (1) assessment, (2) development of prevention strategies, and (3) evaluation. Public health practice is usually multidisciplinary and founded on the applied science of epidemiology. Epidemiology is the study of the distribution and determinants of diseases and injuries in a population. The three main applications of epidemiology are surveillance, aetiological research and evaluation.

Surveillance is "the ongoing and systematic collection, analysis and interpretation of health data in the process of describing and monitoring a health event. This information is used for planning, implementing and evaluating public health interventions and programs" (CDC 1988).

Aetiological research tests hypotheses regarding the determinants of disease and injuries through the use of controlled, usually observational, studies.

Evaluation in both applied social sciences and epidemiology is "a process that attempts to determine as systematically and objectively as possible the relevance, effectiveness and impact of activities in light of their objectives" (Last 1988). Epidemiological evaluation usually entails the use of controlled study designs to measure the effects of an intervention on the occurrence of health-related events in a population.

The basic model of public health practice is described by a cycle of epidemiological surveillance, research on causes, interventions (targeted to high-risk populations and specific to severe health conditions), and epidemiological evaluation. Important modifications of this model include community-oriented primary care (Tollman 1991), community-based health education and health promotion (Green and Kreuter 1991), community health development (Steckler et al. 1993), participatory action research (Hugentobler, Israel and Schurman 1992) and other forms of community-oriented public health practice that rely on greater participation of communities and labour—as opposed to government officials and industrial management—to define problems, develop solutions and evaluate their effectiveness. Family farming, fishing and hunting, self-employed work, many small business operations and work in the informal economy are all primarily influenced by family and community systems and occur outside the context of an industrial management system. Community-oriented public health practice is a particularly viable approach to occupational injury prevention in these populations.

Outcomes of Interest

The public health approach to workplace safety moves from the concept of accident prevention to a broader approach to injury control where the primary outcomes of interest are both the occurrence and severity of injury. Injury is by definition physical damage due to the transfer of energy. A transfer of mechanical energy can cause trauma, as in the case of a fall or automobile crash. Thermal, chemical, electrical or radiation energy can cause burns and other injuries (Robertson 1992). Not only is the occurrence of injury of interest to public health practitioners, but so is the severity and long-term outcome of injury. Injury severity can be measured in several dimensions, including anatomical (the amount and nature of tissue damage in various regions of the body), physiological (how close to death the patient is, based on vital signs), disability, impairment of quality of life, and indirect and direct costs. Of considerable importance to injury epidemiologists is anatomical severity, often measured by the Abbreviated Injury Score and the Injury Severity Scale (MacKenzie, Steinwachs and Shankar 1989). These measures can predict survival and are a useful indicator of the energy transferred in severe events, but are not sensitive enough to discriminate between severity levels among the relatively less severe, but much more frequent occupational injuries such as sprains and strains.

Among the least useful, but most common measures of severity is days lost from work following injury. From an epidemiological point of view, lost work days are often difficult to interpret because they are a function of some unknown combination of disability, demands of the job, availability of alternative light work, workplace policies such as sick leave, disability qualification criteria and individual differences in pain tolerance, the propensity to work with pain, and possibly the same factors that motivate attendance. More work is needed to develop and validate more interpretable occupational injury severity measures, particularly anatomical scales, disability scales and measures of impairment in the various dimensions of quality of life.

Unlike traditional safety practice, the public health community is not restricted to an interest in unintentional ("accidental") injuries and the events that cause them. Through looking at the individual causes of fatalities in the workplace, it was found, for example, that in the United States, homicide (an intentional injury) is the leading cause of death at work among women and the third leading cause among men (Baker et al. 1992; Jenkins et al. 1993). Such fatalities are very rare events in individual workplaces and thus their importance is often overlooked, as is the fact that motor vehicle injuries are the single leading cause of fatal injuries on the job (figure 56.16). Based on these surveillance data, injuries and death due to violence in the workplace and to motor vehicle crashes are priorities in the public health approach to occupational injury prevention in the United States.

Assessment in Public Health

Assessment in public health is a multidisciplinary effort which involves surveillance, aetiological research, and community and organizational needs assessment. The purpose of injury surveillance is to identify high-risk populations, to identify injuries with significant public health impact, to detect and monitor trends and to generate hypotheses. Surveillance programmes can collect data on injury fatalities, non-fatal injuries, incidents with injury potential, and exposure to hazards. Data sources for occupational injury surveillance include health care providers (hospitals and physicians), death certificates, medical examiner/coroner reports, employer-based reporting to departments of labour or health, workers' compensation agencies, periodic surveys of employers or households, and individual corporate records. Many of these reports and records are required by law but often offer incomplete information due to a lack of coverage of all workers, incentives to under-report, and a poor level of specificity in injury details.

In-depth investigations of individual incidents employ a variety of approaches which permit the use of expert judgement to draw conclusions about what caused the event and how it could have

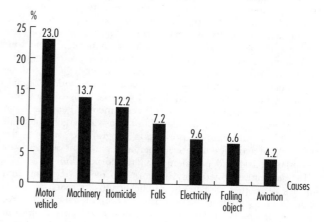

Figure 56.16 • Leading causes of occupational injury death, United States 1980–1989.

Source: Jenkins et al. 1993.

been prevented (Ferry 1988). Preventive action is often taken based on the findings from a single incident. Rate-based surveillance, on the other hand, has a broader significance than the individual incident. Indeed, some information from traditional accident investigations can have little epidemiological interpretation when aggregated into statistics. Accident investigation in the tradition of Heinrich (1959), for example, often produces statistics indicating that in excess of 80% of industrial injuries are caused solely by unsafe acts. From an epidemiological point of view, such statistics are difficult to interpret except as a survey of value judgements, and are rarely included in rate-based surveillance. Many other risk factors such as shift work, work stress, poorly designed work environments and so on, are often not included in investigation forms and thus are not considered in examining statistics on injury causes.

One of the primary purposes of surveillance is to identify high-risk groups in order to target further investigation and prevention. Injuries, like infectious and chronic diseases, have distinct patterns of risk that vary by age, sex, race, geographic region, industry and occupation (Baker et al. 1992). In the United States during the 1980s, for example, surveillance by the National Institute for Occupational Safety and Health (NIOSH) revealed the following high-risk groups for occupational injury fatality: males; elderly workers; blacks; workers in rural Western states; transportation and materials moving occupations; farming, forestry and fishing occupations; and labourers (Jenkins et al. 1993). Another important aspect of surveillance is to identify the types of injury that occur with the greatest frequency and severity, such as the leading external causes of work-related injury fatality in the United States (see figure 56.16). At an individual company level, problems such as homicide and motor vehicle fatalities are rare events and thus are seldom addressed by many traditional safety programmes. However, national surveillance data identified these among the three leading causes of occupational injury fatalities. Assessing the impact of non-fatal injuries requires the use of severity measures in order to make meaningful interpretations. For example, back injuries are a common cause of lost days of work, but an infrequent cause of hospitalization for work-related injuries.

Surveillance data alone do not represent a complete assessment in the public health tradition. Particularly in community-oriented public health practice, needs assessment and community diagnosis using surveys, focus groups and other techniques are important steps to assess what problems workers or communities perceive are important, what are the prevalent attitudes, intentions and barriers regarding the adoption of prevention measures, and how an organization or community really functions. A community-based agricultural safety programme, for example, might need to identify whether or not farmers perceive that tractor rollovers are a critical problem, what barriers such as financial or time constraints may prevent the installation of rollover protective structures, and through whom an intervention strategy should be implemented (e.g., trade association, youth organization, organization of farm wives). In addition to a diagnosis of the community, organizational needs assessment identifies an organization's capacity, workload and constraints to implement fully any already existing prevention programmes such as the enforcement activities of a governmental department of labour (or health) or the safety department of a large corporation.

Investigating the aetiology or causation of loss incidents and injuries is another step in the public health approach to occupational injury control. Such studies of occupational disease have been the mainstay of developing disease-control programmes in the workplace. Aetiological research involves the application of epidemiology to identify risk factors for injury. It also involves applied social sciences to identify the determinants of organizational and individual behaviours that lead to unsafe conditions. Epidemiological research seeks to identify modifiable risk factors through the use of controlled, usually observational study designs such as the case-control study, the cohort study, the panel study and the cross-sectional study. As with epidemiological studies of other acute health events (e.g., asthma attacks, sudden cardiac arrests), aetiological research on injuries is challenged by the need to study either rare or recurrent events that are highly influenced by situational exposures that occur immediately before the event (e.g., distraction by impact noise) and by social and behavioural constructs that are difficult to measure (e.g., safety climate, job strain) (Veazie et al. 1994). Only recently have epidemiological and statistical methods been developed to accommodate the study of these types of health events.

Epidemiological studies that focus on the occurrence of injury are expensive and are not always needed. It does not require a controlled epidemiological study to document the impact of a lack of machine guarding on amputations due to a particular machine; a series of case investigations would suffice. Similarly, if an easily measurable individual behaviour such as failing to use a seat-belt is already a known risk factor, then studies focusing on the determinants of the behaviour and how to improve usage rates, are more useful than studying the injury. However, controlled epidemiological studies of injury and injury severity are needed to provide an understanding of a variety of causal mechanisms that are responsible for decrements in the performance of humans or technology that are difficult to measure. The effect of noise exposure or shift work, for example, on the risk and severity of injury is unlikely to be quantified by case investigations or by studies of easy-to-measure behaviours.

A recent review of studies on risk factors of occupational injuries revealed that age, job title, physical attributes or impairments and experience in the job or task were the most commonly studied human variables (Veazie et al. 1994). Shift work and scheduling were the most commonly studied job content variables. The work environment was the least studied. Most environment factors related to design features or recognized material hazards. Some studies examined factors in the organization and social environment. A few studies evaluated physical stressors such as heat and noise exposure as risk factors for injury. Many of these studies were of poor methodological quality, and few were replicated in different populations. Thus, little is known about risk factors for injury at work, except for the most obvious immediate

causes. Future research may benefit by examining the impact on injury rates of risk factors predicted by theory in human factors, ergonomics, occupational stress and organizational behaviour. These may include design and scheduling of tasks and jobs, psychosocial factors (e.g., worker control, social support, psychological demands), and organizational structure and change (e.g., continuous quality improvement and management commitment to safety).

The public health approach also integrates injury epidemiology with the applied behavioural sciences (particularly health promotion, health behaviour and health policy research) to identify the modifiable, environmental reasons for unsafe worker behaviour and, most important, for behaviours on the part of employers and managers that lead to the creation and persistence of hazards. In the large organizational setting, this effort must involve research in organizational behaviour and industrial psychology. Thus, the assessment phase in the public health approach involves epidemiological surveillance, in-depth investigations, community and organizational needs assessment, and aetiological research based on the application of epidemiology and applied behavioural sciences.

Prevention Strategies

A number of principles guide the selection and implementation of prevention measures in a public health approach to injury control. These include:

(1) *The importance of basing prevention measures on prior assessment and evaluation.* The first principle acknowledges the importance of selecting interventions that are targeted to have a high impact on community health status and are likely to be successfully implemented. Thus, interventions selected on the basis of a thorough assessment phase, rather than merely common sense, are more likely to be effective. Interventions that have been demonstrated as effective in the past are even more promising. Unfortunately, very few occupational injury interventions have been scientifically evaluated (Goldenhar and Schulte 1994).

(2) *The relative importance of control measures that automatically protect the worker.* The second principle emphasizes the continuum between active and passive protection. Active protection is that which requires constant repetitive individual action; passive protection offers relatively automatic protection. For example, seat-belts require individual action to initiate protection each time someone gets into a vehicle. An air bag, on the other hand, bestows protection on a vehicle occupant without any initiating action—it automatically protects that person. Active interventions require modifying and sustaining individual behaviour change, which has been the least successful of injury prevention strategies to date. This principle is similar to the traditional hierarchy of controls in occupational safety which emphasizes the importance of engineering controls over administrative controls, personal protective equipment and training.

(3) *The importance of behaviour modification rather than education.* The third principle recognizes the importance of behaviour modification and that not all hazards can be engineered out of the environment at the manufacturing stage. Modification of the behaviour of employers, managers and employees is central, not only to the installation and maintenance of passive protection, but to most other occupational injury control strategies as well. Another important aspect of this principle is that classroom instruction, posters, pamphlets and other forms of education that merely seek to increase knowledge, usually have little effect on behaviour when used alone. Most health behaviour theories applied in health promotion focus on a variety of factors that motivate behaviour change other than awareness of a physical hazard or safe behaviour. The Health Belief Model, for example, emphasizes that self-protective behaviour is most influenced by the perception

of risk, the perception of severity and the perception of the benefits and barriers associated with taking protective action (Green and Kreuter 1991).

While credible educational messages may alter some of these perceptions, sometimes the best way to alter these perceptions is to change the physical and social environment. A potentially effective approach to behaviour modification is to redesign equipment and the physical environment to make safe behaviour easier, quicker, and more comfortable or socially desirable than unsafe behaviour. If the layout of machine shop equipment is designed to make walking through hazardous zones difficult and unnecessary, then this unsafe behaviour will be reduced. Similarly, if hard hats are designed to be comfortable and to enhance the social image of the construction worker, they may be used more often.

The social environment can also be modified to change behaviour. For example, legislation and enforcement is another far-reaching strategy in injury prevention that changes behaviour and extends beyond education alone. Seat-belt laws and laws requiring the use of infant safety seats, for example, have dramatically reduced motor vehicle fatalities in the United States. The effect of legislation and enforcement on occupational safety, however, is less well-described. One notable exception is the documented clear, dramatic decline in US mine fatalities that followed the implementation of the Federal Coal Mine Health and Safety Act of 1969 (figure 56.17). The resources and administrative authority devoted to mine safety enforcement is, however, much greater than that available to most other agencies (Weeks 1991).

Well-designed occupational safety training often involves modifying the social environment by including a role modelling process, incentives, and feedback on safety performance (Johnston, Cattledge and Collins 1994). Another form of training, labour education, represents an altered social environment (Wallerstein and Baker 1994). It empowers workers to recognize hazards and to modify the behaviour of their employers so as to reduce those hazards. While education alone is not usually sufficient, it is usually a necessary component of any injury prevention programme (Gielen 1992). Educating employers and employees is a necessary part of the implementation of a specific injury prevention programme. Educating legislators, policy makers, health care providers and others is also important to initiating and sustaining community-wide injury prevention efforts. Indeed, interventions most likely to succeed in the field use a multifaceted approach which combines environmental modifications with policy changes and education (National Committee for Injury Prevention and Control 1989).

(4) *Systematic consideration of all available options, including those that reduce not only injury occurrence but the severity and long-term consequences of injuries.* The fourth principle is that the process of choosing interventions should systematically consider a wide range of options. The choice of countermeasures should not be determined by the relative importance of the causal factors or by their earliness in the sequence of events; rather priority must be given to those which most effectively reduce injury. A useful scheme for systematically considering injury control options was proposed by Haddon (1972). The Haddon Matrix reveals that interventions targeted at humans, the vehicles which can transfer damaging energy (e.g., cars, machinery), or the physical or psychosocial environment may operate to control injury in the pre-event, event or post-event phases. Table 56.2 shows the application of the Haddon Matrix to the problem of preventing motor vehicle injuries, which are the leading cause of occupational injury fatalities in many countries.

Traditional occupational safety interventions most often operate in the pre-event phase to prevent the initiation of an incident with potential to cause injury (i.e., an accident). Event phase interventions such as building cars to be more crashworthy or

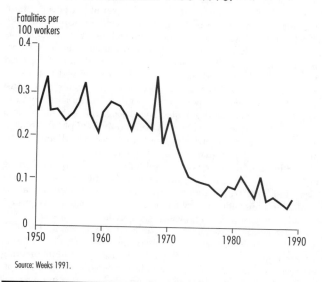

Figure 56.17 • The effects of coal mining regulations on underground coal mining mortality rates, United States 1950–1990.

Source: Weeks 1991.

using safety lanyards while working at elevations, do not prevent accidents, but minimize the probability and severity of injury. After the event is over—the cars in a crash have stopped moving or the worker has stopped falling—post-event interventions such as first aid and prompt transport to appropriate surgical care seek to minimize the health consequences of injury (i.e., the probability of death or long-term disability).

In the public health approach, it is important to avoid getting locked into one phase of the matrix. Just as injury is multifactorial in causation, prevention strategies should address as many phases and aspects of injury as possible (but not necessarily all). The Haddon Matrix, for example, emphasizes that injury control is not limited to preventing accidents. In fact, many of our most

Table 56.2 • The Haddon Matrix applied to motor vehicle injuries.

Phases	Factors		
	Human	Vehicles and equipment	Environment
Pre-event	Educate public in the use of seat-belts and child restraints	Safe brakes and tires	Improved road design; restrict alcohol advertising and availability at gas stations
Event	Prevention of osteoporosis to decrease likelihood of fracture	Air bags and a crashworthy vehicle design	Breakaway utility poles and crash barriers
Post-event	Treatment of haemophilia and other conditions that result in impaired healing	Safe design of fuel tank to prevent rupture and fire	Adequate emergency medical care and rehabilitation

Source: National Committee for Injury Prevention and Control 1989.

56. ACCIDENT PREVENTION

effective control strategies do not prevent accidents or even injuries, but can considerably reduce their severity. Seat-belts and air bags in cars, safety helmets, fall protection in construction, roll-over protective structures in agriculture, and emergency eyewash fountains in the laboratory are but a few examples of event-phase strategies that do nothing to prevent an accident from occurring. Instead, they reduce the severity of injury after the accident has been initiated. Even after the anatomical damage has been done, much can be done to reduce the risk of death and long-term disability. In the United States, it has been estimated that many major trauma deaths could be prevented by systems that minimize the time delay between injury and definitive surgical care. This broader framework is called *injury control* and goes far beyond traditional accident prevention. A commonly used phrase to illustrate this point is "Injuries are not an accident". They can be predicted and their impact on society controlled.

Another useful scheme often used for systematically considering injury control options is Haddon's Ten Countermeasure Strategies (Haddon 1973). Table 56.3 shows how these strategies can be applied to controlling injury from falls in construction. As shown, not all strategies will be applicable for specific problems.

(5) *Involvement of the community, workers and management.* The fifth principle is the importance of involving the target population (communities, workers, managers) in choosing and implementing intervention strategies. Cost, feasibility, convenience and acceptability can all be barriers to developing effective prevention strategies (Schelp 1988).

Evaluation in Public Health

Evaluation in both applied social sciences and epidemiology is "a process that attempts to determine as systematically and objectively as possible the relevance, effectiveness and impact of activities in light of their objectives" (Last 1988). Evaluation is an essential component of public health practice. It occurs at two levels. The first level relies on surveillance systems to determine whether or not entire communities have met their disease and injury reduction objectives, without attempting to determine what caused the observed changes. Federal, state and local government agencies in the United States, for example, have set objectives for the year 2000. One of these objectives is to reduce work-related injuries resulting in medical treatment, lost time from work, or restricted work activity to no more than 6 cases per 100 full-time workers per year. Progress in meeting these objectives will be monitored with the national surveillance systems in place.

The second level of evaluation focuses on determining the effectiveness of policies, programmes and specific interventions. Ideally, this requires the application of controlled experimental or quasi-experimental study designs. Mohr and Clemmer (1989), for example, conducted a time series study of injury rates in those mobile off-shore oil rigs that opted to implement a new technology to assist workers in connecting drill pipes, compared with rates in those rigs that did not have the new technology. Although injury rates were going down over the period of the installation of the new equipment, the authors were able to attribute a decrease of 6 injuries per 100 workers per year to the new safety equipment and to demonstrate that the savings from injury prevention resulted in a full recovery of the initial capital and installation costs within 5.7 years. Unfortunately, this type of scientific evaluation of programmes and interventions in occupational health and safety is rare and often methodologically flawed (Goldenhar and Schulte 1994).

Summary

The above-mentioned programme demonstrates well the various components in the public health approach to reducing injuries in the workplace. Assessing the injury problem and establishing an ongoing surveillance system was an essential part of this and earlier studies of injuries on oil rigs that were conducted by these authors. The subsequent development of a simple engineering prevention strategy was then followed by a rigorous evaluation strategy which included an evaluation of cost savings. Such studies have been the mainstay of the public health approach to the prevention of other occupational diseases. In the future, the integration of occupational injury prevention into the assessment, intervention and evaluation phases of public health practice has the potential to be an important step toward more effective protection and promotion of health in communities.

Table 56.3 • Haddon's Ten Countermeasure Strategies applied to injuries due to falls in construction.

Countermeasure	Intervention (and relevant notes)
Prevent the creation of the hazard.	Do not construct buildings — generally not a practical option, to be sure.
Reduce the amount of the hazard brought into being.	Lower the height of construction project to below fatal levels — usually not practical, but may be possible in some work zones.
Prevent the release of the hazard.	Install non-slip walking surfaces on roofs and other heights.
Modify the rate of release of the hazard from its sources.	Use safety lanyards. Use safety nets.
Separate the hazard from the worker by time and space.	Do not schedule unnecessary foot traffic near fall hazards until the hazards are abated.
Separate the hazard from the worker by physical barriers.	Install guardrails on elevated surfaces.
Modify basic qualities of the hazard.	Remove sharp or protruding projections on the ground surface where workers can fall — practical only for very low heights.
Make worker as injury resistant as possible.	Require, e.g., safety helmets.
Begin to counter damage done by the hazard.	Apply first aid.
Stabilize, treat and rehabilitate worker.	Develop a regionalized trauma system; provide for effective rehabilitation and retraining.

THEORETICAL PRINCIPLES OF JOB SAFETY

Reinald Skiba

This presentation covers the theoretical principles of job safety and the general principles for accident prevention. The presentation does not cover work-related illnesses, which, although related, are different in many respects.

Theory of Job Safety

Job safety involves the interrelationship between people and work; materials, equipment and machinery; the environment; and economic considerations such as productivity. Ideally, work should be healthful, not harmful and not unreasonably difficult. For economic reasons, as high a level of productivity as possible must be achieved.

Job safety should start in the planning stage and continue through the various phases of production. Accordingly, requirements for job safety must be asserted before work begins and be implemented throughout the work cycle, so that the results can be appraised for purposes of feedback, among other reasons. The responsibility of supervision toward maintaining the health and safety of those employed in the production process should also be considered during planning. In the manufacturing process, people and objects interact. (The term *object* is used in the broader sense as expressed in the customary designation "people-(machine)-environment system". This includes not only technical instruments of work, machines and materials, but all surrounding items such as floors, stairs, electrical current, gas, dusts, atmosphere and so on.)

Worker-Job Relationships

The following three possible relationships within the manufacturing process indicate how personal injury incidents (especially accidents) and harmful working conditions are unintended effects of combining people and the objective working environment for the purpose of production.

1. *The relationship between the worker and the objective working environment is optimal.* This means well-being, job safety and labour-saving methods for the employees as well as the reliability of the objective parts of the system, like machines. It also means no defects, accidents, incidents, near misses (potential incidents) or injuries. The result is improved productivity.
2. *The worker and the objective working environment are incompatible.* This may be because the person is unqualified, equipment or materials are not correct for the job or the operation is poorly organized. Accordingly, the worker is unintentionally overworked or underutilized. Objective parts of the system, like machines, may become unreliable. This creates unsafe conditions and hazards with the potential for near misses (near accidents) and minor incidents resulting in delays in production flow and declining output.
3. *The relationship between the worker and the objective working environment is completely interrupted and a disruption results, causing damage, personal injury or both, thereby preventing output.* This relationship is specifically concerned with the question of job safety in the sense of avoiding accidents.

Principles of Workplace Safety

Because it is apparent that questions of accident prevention can be solved not in isolation, but only in the context of their relationship with production and the working environment, the following principles for accident prevention can be derived:

1. Accident prevention must be built into production planning with the goal of avoiding disruptions.
2. The ultimate goal is to achieve a production flow that is as unhindered as possible. This results not only in reliability and the elimination of defects, but also in the workers' well-being, labour-saving methods and job safety.

Some of the practices commonly used in the workplace to achieve job safety and which are necessary for disruption-free production include, but are not limited to the following:

- Workers and supervisors must be informed and aware of the dangers and potential hazards (e.g., through education).
- Workers must be motivated to function safely (behaviour modification).
- Workers must be able to function safely. This is accomplished through certification procedures, training and education.
- The personal working environment should be safe and healthy through the use of administrative or engineering controls, sub-

stitution of less hazardous materials or conditions, or by the use of personal protective equipment.
- Equipment, machinery and objects must function safely for their intended use, with operating controls designed to human capabilities.
- Provisions should be made for appropriate emergency response in order to limit the consequences of accidents, incidents and injuries.

The following principles are important in understanding how accident prevention concepts relate to disruption-free production:

1. Accident prevention is sometimes considered a social burden instead of a major part of disruption prevention. Disruption prevention is a better motivator than accident prevention, because improved production is expected to result from disruption prevention.
2. Measures to ensure workplace safety must be integrated into the measures used to ensure disruption-free production. For example, the instructions on hazards must be an integral part of the general directions governing the flow of production at the workplace.

Accident Theory

An accident (including those that entail injuries) is a sudden and unwanted event, caused by an outside influence, that causes harm to people and results from the interaction of people and objects.

Often the use of the term *accident* in the workplace is linked with personal injury. Damage to a machine is often referred to as a disruption or damage, but not an accident. Damage to the environment is often called an incident. Accidents, incidents and disruptions which do not result in injury or damage are known as "near accidents" or "near misses". So while it may be considered appropriate to refer to accidents as cases of injury to workers and to define the terms *incident, disruption* and *damage* separately as they apply to objects and the environment, in the context of this article they will all be referred to as accidents.

The conceptual model for the term *accident* indicates that workplace accidents occur from workers and objects interacting with each other through the release of energy. The cause of an accident can lie in the characteristics of the injured worker (e.g., not capable of performing the work safely) or of the object (e.g., unsafe or unsuitable equipment). The cause can also be another worker (providing erroneous information), supervisor (receiving incomplete job instructions) or trainer (receiving incomplete or incorrect training). The following can be derived for accident prevention:

Assuming that workers as well as their objective environments can be carriers of hazards or dangers, accident prevention would basically consist of eliminating the hazards or dangers, or impeding the consequences by keeping the carriers apart or by minimizing the effects of the energy.

Potential Hazards and Risks

Although a hazard or danger may exist in an object, if the worker and the object are so separate from one another that they cannot come into contact, no accident is possible. For example, if the object has a potential hazard (e.g., a suspended load is moved by a crane), this potential hazard cannot cause an injury so long as there are no people in the effective area of the suspended load. It is only when a worker comes into the area of the crane's suspended load that an actual hazard or danger to this worker is posed, because an interaction between the worker and the object is possible. It should be noted that objects can also endanger other objects, such as vehicles parked under the crane's load. *Risk,* defined as a means of quantifying the hazard, is the product of the anticipated frequency of the damage and the anticipated scope of

56. ACCIDENT PREVENTION

the damage. *Accident risk* is correspondingly the product of the anticipated frequency of accidents (relative accident frequency) and anticipated accident severity. *Relative accident frequency* is the number of accidents per risk-time (accidents per 1 million hours or injuries per work year). The seriousness of the accident can be shown quantitatively with the lost time (e.g., lost work days), class of injury (minor accident or first aid case, reportable injury, lost-time compensation case and fatal accident), type of injury, and cost of injury. This risk data should be recorded empirically and in terms of a theoretical prognosis.

The risks of accidents are different in various workplaces, under various conditions. For example, the risks involved in drilling for oil, using the same workers and identical equipment, differ widely depending on the geography (drilling on land or off shore) and the climate (Arctic exploration or deserts). The level of accident risk depends on:

- the anticipated frequency of error of the worker and the technology (number per 1 million hours, etc.)
- the probability of the errors resulting in accidents (accident: error = 1:x)
- the probability of the seriousness level of the accident.

The acceptance of accident risks also varies widely. High accident risk appears to be acceptable in road traffic whereas a zero base tolerance is expected in the field of nuclear energy. For purposes of accident prevention, it therefore follows that the driving force is the smallest possible acceptance of accident risk.

Causes of Accidents

The occurrence of an accident requires classification on a scale from cause to effect. Three levels must be differentiated:

- the level of the causes of possible and actual accidents
- the level of the accident's origins
- the level of the accident's consequences in the form of personal and material damages.

Cause is the reason for the accident. Almost every accident has multiple causes such as hazardous conditions, combinations of factors, courses of events, omissions and so on. For example, causes of an accident involving a burst boiler may include one or a combination of the following reasons: faulty materials in the boiler wall, inadequate training to ensure safe operation, failure of a pressure relief device, or violation of an operating procedure such as overheating. Without one or more of these deficiencies, an accident may not have happened. Other conditions, which are not causal to the accident, should be separated. In the case of the burst boiler, these would include conditions such as information about the time, the ambient temperature and the size of the boiler room.

It is important to differentiate the factors associated with the production process from the accident causes linked to workers (conduct of the immediate operator), the organization (safe work procedures or policies) and technical accident causes (environmental changes and object failures). However, in the final analysis, every accident results from faulty conduct of people, because people are always at the end of the causal chain. For example, if faulty material is determined to be the cause of a boiler bursting, then improper conduct existed either on the part of the builder, manufacturer, tester, installer or owner (e.g., corrosion due to inadequate maintenance). Strictly speaking, there is no such thing as a "technical failure" or technical accident cause. The technology is only the intermediate link to the consequences of the improper conduct. Nevertheless, the normal division of causes into behavioural, technical and organizational is useful, because this points toward which group of people behaved improperly and also helps select the appropriate corrective measures.

As previously stated, most accidents are the result of a combination of causes.

For example, a person slips on an oil spot in a dark, unlighted passageway and hits the sharp edge of a replacement part that is lying there, resulting in a head injury. The immediate causes of the accident are inadequate lighting in the passageway, unsafe floor (oil spot), inadequately skid-free shoe soles, not wearing head protection, and the replacement part not in its proper place. The accident could not have happened if the combination of causes had been eliminated or the causal chain had been broken. Successful accident prevention therefore consists of recognizing the causal chain that leads to an accident and breaking it, so that the accident can no longer occur.

Effect of Strains and Demands

Mechanization and automation of production processes have advanced considerably in recent years. It may appear that the causes of many accidents have shifted from human error to those related to the maintenance of and interface with automated processes. However, these positive consequences of technology are counterposed to other, negative ones, particularly the increase in psychological strains and corresponding ergonomic physical demands on workers in automated plants due to the increased attention and responsibility required for overseeing the automated operations process, impersonal working environment and monotony of work. These strains and corresponding demands increase the occurrence of accidents and can be harmful to health.

1. *Strains* are effects on workers which originate in the workplace, such as environmental strains (temperature, heat, humidity, light, noise and air pollution), or they can be static or dynamic strains originating directly from the work process (lifting, climbing, chemical exposure and so on). Strain levels can be physically measured (noise, force, atmospheric exposures and so on), whereas strain factors are physically unmeasurable influences (fatigue, mental stress, plant worker/management relationships and so on).
2. *Demands* on workers are dependent on the type and degree of the strain as well as differing individual capability to withstand the strain. Effects of demands show up physically and psychologically in the human body. The effects of the demands can be desirable or undesirable, depending on the type and degree. Undesirable effects, such as physical and psychological exhaustion, work aggravations, illness, lack of coordination and concentration, and unsafe behaviour cause increased risk of accident.

For purposes of accident prevention, it follows that workers, based on their individual competencies, capabilities and willingness, should be able to physically and psychologically work safely provided that there are no outside factors such as unsuitable equipment, poor environment or unsatisfactory work conditions. Safety may be improved by organizing the work process to include appropriate stimuli such as planned job changes, expansion of work and tasks, and work enrichment.

Near Accidents (Near Misses)

A large part of production loss results from disruptions in the form of near misses (near accidents), which are the basis of occurrences of accidents. Not every disruption affects work safety. Near accidents (near misses) are those occurrences or incidents in which no injury or damage resulted, but if injury or damage had occurred, they would be classified as accidents. For example, a machine that unexpectedly stops running without damage to the equipment or work is considered to be a near accident. Additionally, the disruption may cause another near accident if the machine suddenly starts up again while a worker is inside trying to determine the cause of the stoppage, but the worker is not injured.

Accident Pyramid

Accidents are relatively rare occurrences, and usually the more serious the accident, the more rare the occurrence. Near accidents form the bottom, or base, of the accident pyramid, whereas fatal accidents stand at the top. If lost time is used as a criterion for the seriousness of accidents, we find a relatively high degree of correspondence with the accident pyramid. (There may be a slight deviation as a result of the reporting requirements of different countries, companies and jurisdictions.)

The accident pyramid can be very different for individual types or classifications of accidents. For example, accidents involving electricity are disproportionately serious. When accidents are classified by occupation, we see that certain types of work activities suffer disproportionately more serious accidents. In both cases the accident pyramid is top-heavy due to the relatively high proportion of serious and fatal accidents.

From the accident pyramid, it follows for purposes of accident prevention that:

1. Accident prevention begins with avoiding near accidents (near misses).
2. Eliminating minor accidents usually has a positive effect on eliminating serious accidents.

Accident Prevention

The different paths of accident prevention for ensuring workplace safety are as follows:

1. Eliminate the hazard or danger so that injury or damage is no longer possible.
2. Provide for separation between the worker (or equipment) and the hazard (equal to elimination of the hazard). The danger remains, but an injury (or damage) is not possible since we make sure that the natural zones of influence of workers (equipment) and object (hazard or danger) do not intersect.
3. Provide shielding, such as fireproofing, protective clothing and respirators to minimize the hazard. The hazard still exists, but the possibility of an injury or damage is reduced by minimizing the chances of the hazard having an effect by shielding the danger.
4. Adapt to the hazard by providing measures such as warning systems, monitoring equipment, information about dangers, motivation for safe behaviour, training and education.

Summary

In 1914, Max Planck (German physicist, 1858–1947) said: "In every science the highest watchword is the task of seeking order and continuity from the abundance of individual experiences and individual facts, in order, by filling the gaps, to integrate them into a coherent view." This principle also applies to the complex scientific and practical questions of job safety because they not only interface with many different disciplines, but also are themselves multifaceted. While it is difficult, for this reason, to systematize the many problems involved with job safety, it is necessary to properly organize the individual questions according to significance and context, and to pose effective options for improving job safety.

PRINCIPLES OF PREVENTION: SAFETY INFORMATION

Mark R. Lehto and James M. Miller

Sources of Safety Information

Manufacturers and employers throughout the world provide a vast amount of safety information to workers, both to encourage safe behaviour and to discourage unsafe behaviour. These sources of safety information include, among others, regulations, codes and standards, industry practices, training courses, Material Safety Data Sheets (MSDSs), written procedures, safety signs, product labels and instruction manuals. Information provided by each of these sources varies in its behavioural objectives, intended audience, content, level of detail, format and mode of presentation. Each source may also design its information so as to be relevant to the different stages of task performance within a potential accident sequence.

Four Stages of the Accident Sequence

The behavioural objectives of particular sources of safety information correspond or "map" naturally to the four different stages of the accident sequence (table 56.4).

First stage. At the first stage in the accident sequence, sources of information provided prior to the task, such as safety training materials, hazard communication programmes and various forms of safety programme materials (including safety posters and campaigns) are used to educate workers about risks and persuade them to behave safely. Methods of education and persuasion (behaviour modification) attempt not only to reduce errors by improving worker knowledge and skills but also to reduce intentional violations of safety rules by changing unsafe attitudes. Inexperienced workers are often the target audience at this stage, and therefore the safety information is much more detailed in content than at the other stages. It must be emphasized that a well-trained and motivated workforce is a prerequisite for safety information to be effective at the three following stages of the accident sequence.

Second stage. At the second stage in the accident sequence, sources such as written procedures, checklists, instructions, warning signs and product labels can provide critical safety information during routine task performance. This information usually consists of brief statements which either instruct less skilled workers or remind skilled workers to take necessary precautions. Following this approach can help prevent workers from omitting either precautions or other critical steps in a task. Statements providing such information are often embedded at the appropriate stage within step-by-step instructions describing how to perform a task. Warning signs at appropriate locations can play a similar role: for example, a warning sign located at the entrance to a workplace might state that safety hard hats must be worn inside.

Third stage. At the third stage in the accident sequence, highly conspicuous and easily perceived sources of safety information alert workers of abnormal or unusually hazardous conditions. Examples include warning signals, safety markings, tags, signs, barriers or lock-outs. Warning signals can be visual (flashing lights, movements, etc.), auditory (buzzers, horns, tones, etc.), olfactory (odours), tactile (vibrations) or kinaesthetic. Certain warning signals are inherent to products when they are in hazardous states (e.g., the odour released upon opening a container of acetone). Others are designed into machinery or work environments (e.g., the back-up signal on a fork-lift truck). Safety markings refer to methods of non-verbally identifying or highlighting potentially hazardous elements of the environment (e.g., by painting step edges yellow or emergency stops red). Safety tags, barri-

Table 56.4 • Objectives and example sources of safety information mapped to the accident sequence.

| | Task stage in accident sequence | | | |
	Prior to task	Routine task performance	Abnormal task conditions	Accident conditions
Objectives (Behavioural)	Educate and persuade worker of the nature and level of risk, precautions, remedial measures and emergency procedures.	Instruct or remind worker to follow safe procedures or take precautions.	Alert worker of abnormal conditions. Specify needed actions.	Indicate locations of safety and first aid equipment, exits and emergency procedures. Specify remedial and emergency procedures.
Example sources	Training manuals, videos or programmes, hazard communication programmes, material safety data sheets, safety propaganda, safety feedback	Instruction manuals, job performance aids, checklists, written procedures, warning signs and labels	Warning signals: visual, auditory, or olfactory. Temporary tags, signs, barriers or lock-outs	Safety information signs, labels, and markings, material safety data sheets

ers, signs or lock-outs are placed at points of hazard and are often used to prevent workers from entering areas or activating equipment during maintenance, repair or other abnormal conditions.

Fourth stage. At the fourth stage in the accident sequence, the focus is on expediting worker performance of emergency procedures at the time an accident is occurring, or on the performance of remedial measures shortly after the accident. Safety information signs and markings conspicuously indicate facts critical to adequate performance of emergency procedures (e.g., the locations of exits, fire extinguishers, first aid stations, emergency showers, eyewash stations or emergency releases). Product safety labels and MSDSs may specify remedial and emergency procedures to be followed.

However, if safety information is to be effective at any stage in the accident sequence, it must first be noticed and understood, and if the information has been previously learned, it must also be remembered. Then the worker must both decide to comply with the provided message and be physically able to do so. Successfully attaining each of these steps for effectiveness can be difficult; however, guidelines describing how to design safety information are of some assistance.

Design Guidelines and Requirements

Standards-making organizations, regulatory agencies and the courts through their decisions have traditionally both instituted guidelines and imposed requirements regarding when and how safety information is to be provided. More recently, there has been a trend towards developing guidelines based on scientific research concerning the factors which influence the effectiveness of safety information.

Legal requirements

In most industrialized countries, government regulations require that certain forms of safety information be provided to workers. For example, in the United States, the Environmental Protection Agency (EPA) has developed several labelling requirements for toxic chemicals. The Department of Transportation (DOT) makes specific provisions regarding the labelling of hazardous materials in transport. The Occupational Safety and Health Administration (OSHA) has promulgated a hazard communication standard that applies to workplaces where toxic or hazardous materials are in use, which requires training, container labelling, MSDSs and other forms of warnings.

In the United States, the failure to warn also can be grounds for litigation holding manufacturers, employers and others liable for injuries incurred by workers. In establishing liability, the Theory of Negligence takes into consideration whether the failure to provide adequate warning is judged to be unreasonable conduct based on (1) the foreseeability of the danger by the manufacturer, (2) the reasonableness of the assumption that a user would realize the danger and (3) the degree of care that the manufacturer took to inform the user of the danger. The Theory of Strict Liability requires only that the failure to warn caused the injury or loss.

Voluntary standards

A large set of existing standards provide voluntary recommendations regarding the use and design of safety information. These standards have been developed by multilateral groups and agencies, such as the United Nations, the European Economic Community (EEC's EURONORM), the International Organization for Standardization (ISO) and the International Electrotechnical Commission (IEC); and by national groups, such as the American National Standards Institute (ANSI), the British Standards Institute, the Canadian Standards Association, the German Institute for Normalization (DIN) and the Japanese Industrial Standards Committee.

Among consensus standards, those developed by ANSI in the United States are of special significance. Since the mid-1980s, five new ANSI standards focusing on safety signs and labels have been developed and one significant standard has been revised. The new standards are: (1) ANSI Z535.1, *Safety Color Code*, (2) ANSI Z535.2, *Environmental and Facility Safety Signs*, (3) ANSI Z535.3, *Criteria for Safety Symbols*, (4) ANSI Z535.4, *Product Safety Signs and Labels*, and (5) ANSI Z535.5, *Accident Prevention Tags*. The recently revised standard is ANSI Z129.1–1988, *Hazardous Industrial Chemicals—Precautionary Labeling*. Furthermore, ANSI has published the *Guide for Developing Product Information*.

Design specifications

Design specifications can be found in consensus and governmental safety standards specifying how to design the following:

1. *Material Safety Data Sheets (MSDSs)*. The OSHA hazard communication standard specifies that employers must have a MSDS in the workplace for each hazardous chemical used. The standard requires that each sheet be written in English, list its date of preparation and provide the scientific and common names of the hazardous chemical mentioned. It also requires the MSDS to describe (1) physical and chemical characteristics of the hazardous chemical, (2) physical hazards, including potential for fire, explosion and reactivity, (3) health hazards, including signs and symptoms of exposure, and health conditions potentially aggravated by the chemical, (4) the primary route of entry, (5) the OSHA permissible exposure limit, the ACGIH threshold limit value or other recommended limits, (6) carcinogenic properties, (7) generally applicable precautions, (8) generally applicable control meas-

ures, (9) emergency and first aid procedures and (10) the name, address and telephone number of a party able to provide, if necessary, additional information on the hazardous chemical and emergency procedures.

2. *Instructional labels and manuals.* Few consensus standards currently specify how to design instructional labels and manuals. This situation is, however, quickly changing. The ANSI *Guide for Developing User Product Information* was published in 1990, and several other consensus organizations are working on draft documents. Without an overly scientific foundation, the ANSI Consumer Interest Council, which is responsible for the above guidelines, has provided a reasonable outline to manufacturers regarding what to consider in producing instruction/operator manuals. They have included sections entitled: "Organizational Elements", "Illustrations", "Instructions", "Warnings", "Standards", "How to Use Language", and "An Instructions Development Checklist". While the guideline is brief, the document represents a useful initial effort in this area.

3. *Safety symbols.* Numerous standards throughout the world contain provisions regarding safety symbols. Among such standards, the ANSI Z535.3 standard, *Criteria for Safety Symbols*, is particularly relevant for industrial users. The standard presents a significant set of selected symbols shown in previous studies to be well understood by workers in the United States. Perhaps more importantly, the standard also specifies methods for designing and evaluating safety symbols. Important provisions include the requirement that (1) new symbols must be correctly identified during testing by at least 85% of 50 or more representative subjects, (2) symbols which don't meet the above criteria should be used only when equivalent printed verbal messages are also provided and (3) employers and product manufacturers should train workers and users regarding the intended meaning of the symbols. The standard also makes new symbols developed under these guidelines eligible to be considered for inclusion in future revisions of the standard.

4. *Warning signs, labels and tags.* ANSI and other standards provide very specific recommendations regarding the design of warning signs, labels and tags. These include, among other factors, particular signal words and text, colour coding schemes, typography, symbols, arrangement and hazard identification (table 56.5). Among the most popular signal words recommended are: *DANGER*, to indicate the highest level of hazard; *WARNING*, to represent an intermediate hazard; and *CAUTION*, to indicate the lowest level of hazard. Colour coding methods are to be used to consistently associate colours with particular levels of hazard. For example, red is used in all of the standards in table 56.5 to represent *DANGER*, the highest level of hazard. Explicit recommendations regarding typography are given in nearly all the systems. The most general commonality between the systems is the recommended use of sans-serif typefaces. Varied recommendations are given regarding the use of symbols and pictographs. The FMC and the Westinghouse systems advocate the use of symbols to define the hazard and to convey the level of hazard (FMC 1985; Westinghouse 1981). Other standards recommend symbols only as a supplement to words. Another area of substantial variation, shown in table 56.4, pertains to the recommended label arrangements. The proposed arrangements generally include elements discussed above and specify the image (graphic content or colour), the background (shape, colour); the enclosure (shape, colour) and the surround (shape, colour). Many of the systems also precisely describe the arrangement of the written text and provide guidance regarding methods of hazard identification.

Certain standards may also specify the content and wording of warning signs or labels in some detail. For example, ANSI Z129.1 specifies that chemical warning labels must include (1) identification of the chemical product or its hazardous component(s), (2) a signal word, (3) a statement of hazard(s), (4) precautionary measures, (5) instructions in case of contact or exposure, (6) antidotes, (7) notes to physicians, (8) instructions in case of fire and spill or leak and (9) instructions for container handling and storage. This standard also specifies a general format for chemical labels that incorporate these items. The standard also provides extensive and specific recommended wordings for particular messages.

Cognitive guidelines

Design specifications, such as those discussed above, can be useful to developers of safety information. However, many products and situations are not directly addressed by standards or regulations. Certain design specifications may not be scientifically proven, and, in extreme cases, conforming with standards and regulations may actually reduce the effectiveness of safety information. To ensure effectiveness, developers of safety information consequently may need to go beyond safety standards. Recognizing this issue, the International Ergonomics Association (IEA) and International Foundation for Industrial Ergonomics and Safety Research (IFIESR) recently supported an effort to develop guidelines for warning signs and labels (Lehto 1992) which reflect published and unpublished studies on effectiveness and have implications regarding the design of nearly all forms of safety information. Six of these guidelines, presented in slightly modified form, are as follows.

1. *Match sources of safety information to the level of performance at which critical errors occur for a given population.* In specifying what and how safety information is to be provided, this guideline emphasizes the need to focus attention on (1) critical errors that can cause significant damage and (2) the level of worker performance at the time the error is made. This objective often can be attained if sources of safety information are matched to behavioural objectives consistently with the mapping shown in table 56.4 and discussed earlier.

2. *Integrate safety information into the task and hazard-related context.* Safety information should be provided in a way that makes it likely to be noticed at the time it is most relevant, which almost always is the moment when action needs to be taken. Recent research has confirmed that this principle is true for both the placement of safety messages within instructions and the placement of safety information sources (such as warning signs) in the physical environment. One study showed that people were much more likely to notice and comply with safety precautions when they were included as a step within instructions, rather than separated from instructional text as a separate warning section. It is interesting to observe that many safety standards conversely recommend or require that precautionary and warning information be placed in a separate section.

3. *Be selective.* Providing excessive amounts of safety information increases the time and effort required to find what is relevant to the emergent need. Sources of safety information should consequently focus on providing relevant information which does not exceed what is needed for the immediate purpose. Training programmes should provide the most detailed information. Instruction manuals, MSDSs and other reference sources should be more detailed than warning signs, labels or signals.

4. *Keep the cost of compliance within a reasonable level.* A substantial number of studies have indicated that people become less

Table 56.5 • Summary of recommendations within selected warning systems.

System	Signal words	Colour coding	Typography	Symbols	Arrangement
ANSI Z129.1 Hazardous Industrial Chemicals: Precautionary Labeling (1988)	Danger Warning Caution Poison optional words for "delayed" hazards	Not specified	Not specified	Skull-and-crossbones as supplement to words. Acceptable symbols for 3 other hazards types.	Label arrangement not specified; examples given
ANSI Z535.2 Environmental and Facility Safety Signs (1993)	Danger Warning Caution Notice [general safety] [arrows]	Red Orange Yellow Blue Green as above; black and white otherwise per ANSI Z535.1	Sans serif, upper case, acceptable typefaces, letter heights	Symbols and pictographs per ANSI Z535.3	Defines signal word, word message, symbol panels in 1 to 3 panel designs. 4 shapes for special use. Can use ANSI Z535.4 for uniformity.
ANSI Z535.4 Product Safety Signs and Labels (1993)	Danger Warning Caution	Red Orange Yellow per ANSI Z535.1	Sans serif, upper case, suggested typefaces, letter heights	Symbols and pictographs per ANSI Z535.3; also SAE J284 safety alert symbol	Defines signal word, message, pictorial panels in order of general to specific. Can use ANSI Z535.2 for uniformity. Use ANSI Z129.1 for chemical hazards.
NEMA Guidelines: NEMA 260 (1982)	Danger Warning	Red Red	Not specified	Electric shock symbol	Defines signal word, hazard, consequences, instructions, symbol. Does not specify order.
SAE J115 Safety Signs (1979)	Danger Warning Caution	Red Yellow Yellow	Sans serif typeface, upper case	Layout to accommodate symbols; specific symbols/ pictographs not prescribed	Defines 3 areas: signal word panel, pictorial panel, message panel. Arrange in order of general to specific.
ISO Standard: ISO R557 (1967); ISO 3864 (1984)	None. 3 kinds of labels: Stop/prohibition Mandatory action Warning	Red Blue Yellow	Message panel is added below if necessary	Symbols and pictographs	Pictograph or symbol is placed inside appropriate shape with message panel below if necessary
OSHA 1910.145 Specification for Accident Prevention Signs and Tags (1985)	Danger Warning (tags only) Caution Biological Hazard, BIOHAZARD, or symbol [safety instruction] [slow-moving vehicle]	Red Yellow Yellow Fluorescent Orange/orange-red Green Fluorescent yellow-orange and dark red per ANSI Z535.1	Readable at 5 feet or as required by task	Biological hazard symbol. Major message can be supplied by pictograph (tags only). Slow-moving vehicle (SAE J943)	Signal word and major message (tags only)
OSHA 1910.1200 [Chemical] Hazard Communication (1985)	Per applicable requirements of EPA, FDA, BATF, and CPSC; not otherwise specified.		In English		Only as Material Safety Data Sheet
Westinghouse Handbook (1981); FMC Guidelines (1985)	Danger Warning Caution Notice	Red Orange Yellow Blue	Helvetica bold and regular weights, upper/lower case	Symbols and pictographs	Recommends 5 components: signal word, symbol/pictograph, hazard, result of ignoring warning, avoiding hazard

Source: Adapted from Lehto and Miller 1986; Lehto and Clark 1990.

likely to follow safety precautions when doing so is perceived to involve a significant "cost of compliance". Safety information should therefore be provided in a way that minimizes the difficulty of complying with its message. Occasionally this goal can be attained by providing the information at a time and location when complying is convenient.

5. *Make symbols and text as concrete as possible.* Research has shown that people are better able to understand concrete, rather than abstract, words and symbols used within safety information. Skill and experience, however, play a major role in determining the value of concreteness. It is not unusual for highly skilled workers to both prefer and better understand abstract terminology.

6. *Simplify the syntax and grammar of text and combinations of symbols.* Writing text that poor readers, or even adequate readers, can comprehend is not an easy task. Numerous guidelines have been developed in attempts to alleviate such problems. Some basic principles are (1) use words and symbols understood by the target audience, (2) use consistent terminology, (3) use short, simple sentences constructed in the standard subject-verb-object form, (4) avoid negations and complex conditional sentences, (5) use the active rather than passive voice, (6) avoid using complex pictographs to describe actions and (7) avoid combining multiple meanings in a single figure.

Satisfying these guidelines requires consideration of a substantial number of detailed issues as addressed in the next section.

Developing Safety Information

The development of safety information meant to accompany products, such as safety warnings, labels and instructions, often requires extensive investigations and development activities involving considerable resources and time. Ideally, such activities (1) coordinate the development of product information with design of the product itself, (2) analyse product features which affect user expectations and behaviours, (3) identify the hazards associated with use and likely misuse of the product, (4) research user perceptions and expectations regarding product function and hazard characteristics and (5) evaluate product information using methods and criteria consistent with the goals of each component of product information. Activities accomplishing these objectives can be grouped into several levels. While in-house product designers are able to accomplish many of the tasks designated, some of these tasks involve the application of methodologies most familiar to professionals with backgrounds in human factors engineering, safety engineering, document design and the communication sciences. Tasks falling within these levels are summarized as follows and are shown in figure 56.18:

Level 0: Product design status

Level 0 is both the starting point for initiating a product information project, and the point at which feedback regarding design alternatives will be received and new iterations at the basic model level will be forwarded. At the initiation of a product information project, the researcher begins with a particular design. The design can be in the concept or prototype stage or as currently being sold and used. A major reason for designating a Level 0 is the recognition that the development of product information must be managed. Such projects require formal budgets, resources, planning, and accountability. The largest benefits to be gained from a systematic product information design are achieved when the product is in the pre-production concept or prototype state. However, applying the methodology to existing products and product information is quite appropriate and extremely valuable.

Level 1: Product type investigations

At least seven tasks should be performed at this stage: (1) document characteristics of the existing product (e.g., parts, operation, assembly and packaging), (2) investigate the design features and accompanying information for similar or competitive products, (3) collect data on accidents for both this product and similar or competitive products, (4) identify human factors and safety research addressing this type of product, (5) identify applicable standards and regulations, (6) analyse government and commercial media attention to this type of product (including recall information) and (7) research the litigation history for this and similar products.

Level 2: Product use and user group research

At least seven tasks should be performed at this stage: (1) determine appropriate methods for use of product (including assembly, installation, use and maintenance), (2) identify existing and potential product user groups, (3) research consumer use, misuse, and knowledge of product or similar products, (4) research user perceptions of product hazards, (5) identify hazards associated with intended use(s) and foreseeable misuse(s) of product, (6) analyse cognitive and behavioural demands during product use and (7) identify likely user errors, their consequences and potential remedies.

After completing the analyses in Levels 1 and 2, product design changes should be considered before proceeding further. In the traditional safety engineering sense, this could be called "engineering the hazard out of the product". Some modifications may be for the health of the consumer, and some for the benefit of the company as it attempts to produce a marketing success.

Level 3: Information design criteria and prototypes

In Level 3 at least nine tasks are performed: (1) determine from the standards and requirements applying to the particular product which if any of those requirements impose design or performance criteria on this part of the information design, (2) determine those types of tasks for which information is to be provided to users (e.g., operation, assembly, maintenance and disposal), (3) for each type of task information, determine messages to be conveyed to user, (4) determine the mode of communication appropriate for each message (e.g., text, symbols, signals or product features), (5) determine temporal and spatial location of individual messages, (6) develop desired features of information based on messages, modes and placements developed in previous steps, (7) develop prototypes of individual components of product information system (e.g., manuals, labels, warnings, tags, advertisements, packaging and signs), (8) verify that there is consistency across the various types of information (e.g., manuals, advertisements, tags and packaging) and (9) verify that products with other brand names or similar existing products from the same company have consistent information.

After having proceeded through Levels 1, 2 and 3, the researcher will have developed the format and content of information expected to be appropriate. At this point, the researcher may want to provide initial recommendations regarding the redesign of any existing product information before moving on to Level 4.

Level 4: Evaluation and revision

In Level 4 at least six tasks are performed: (1) define evaluation parameters for each prototype component of the product information system, (2) develop an evaluation plan for each prototype component of the product information system, (3) select representative users, installers and so on, to participate in evaluation, (4) execute the evaluation plan, (5) modify product information

56. ACCIDENT PREVENTION

Figure 56.18 • A model for designing and evaluating product information.

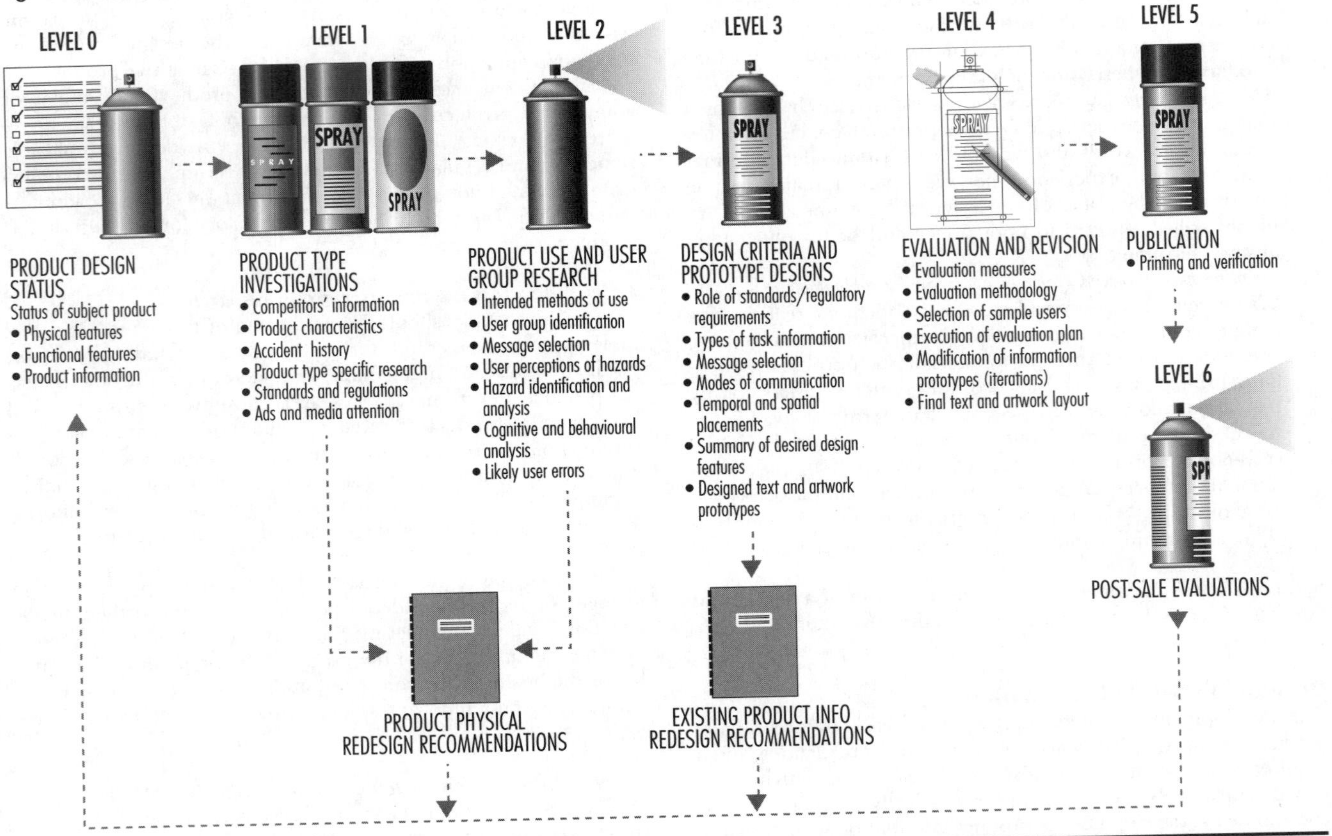

prototypes and/or the design of the product based on the results obtained during evaluation (several iterations are likely to be necessary) and (6) specify the final text and artwork layout.

Level 5: Publication

Level 5, the actual publication of the information, is reviewed, approved and accomplished as specified. The purpose at this level is to confirm that specifications for designs, including designated logical groupings of material, location and quality of illustrations, and special communication features have been precisely followed, and have not been unintentionally modified by the printer. While the publication activity is usually not under the control of the person developing the information designs, we have found it necessary to verify that such designs are precisely followed, the reason being that printers have been known to take great liberties in manipulating design layout.

Level 6: Post-sale evaluations

The last level of the model deals with the post-sale evaluations, a final check to ensure that the information is indeed fulfilling the goals it was designed to achieve. The information designer as well as the manufacturer gains an opportunity for valuable and educational feedback from this process. Examples of post-sale evaluations include (1) feedback from customer satisfaction programmes, (2) potential summarization of data from warranty fulfilments and warranty response cards, (3) gathering of information from accident investigations involving the same or similar products, (4) monitoring of consensus standards and regulatory

activities and (5) monitoring of safety recalls and media attention to similar products.

WORK-RELATED ACCIDENT COSTS

Diego Andreoni

Workers who are the victims of work-related accidents suffer from material consequences, which include expenses and loss of earnings, and from intangible consequences, including pain and suffering, both of which may be of short or long duration. These consequences include:

- doctor's fees, cost of ambulance or other transport, hospital charges or fees for home nursing, payments made to persons who gave assistance, cost of artificial limbs and so on
- the immediate loss of earnings during absence from work (unless insured or compensated)
- loss of future earnings if the injury is permanently disabling, long term or precludes the victim's normal advancement in his or her career or occupation
- permanent afflictions resulting from the accident, such as mutilation, lameness, loss of vision, ugly scars or disfigurement, mental changes and so on, which may reduce life expectancy and give rise to physical or psychological suffering, or to further expenses arising from the victim's need to find a new occupation or interests

- subsequent economic difficulties with the family budget if other members of the family have to either go to work to replace lost income or give up their employment in order to look after the victim. There may also be additional loss of income if the victim was engaged in private work outside normal working hours and is no longer able to perform it.
- anxiety for the rest of the family and detriment to their future, especially in the case of children.

Workers who become victims of accidents frequently receive compensation or allowances both in cash and in kind. Although these do not affect the intangible consequences of the accident (except in exceptional circumstances), they constitute a more or less important part of the material consequences, inasmuch as they affect the income which will take the place of the salary. There is no doubt that part of the overall costs of an accident must, except in very favourable circumstances, be borne directly by the victims.

Considering the national economy as a whole, it must be admitted that the interdependence of all its members is such that the consequences of an accident affecting one individual will have an adverse effect on the general standard of living, and may include the following:

- an increase in the price of manufactured products, since the direct and indirect expenses and losses resulting from an accident may result in an increase in the cost of making the product
- a decrease in the gross national product as a result of the adverse effects of accidents on people, equipment, facilities and materials; these effects will vary according to the availability in each country of workers, capital and material resources
- additional expenses incurred to cover the cost of compensating accident victims and pay increased insurance premiums, and the amount necessary to provide safety measures required to prevent similar occurrences.

One of the functions of society is that it must protect the health and income of its members. It meets these obligations through the creation of social security institutions, health programmes (some governments provide free or low-cost medical care to their constituents), injury compensation insurance and safety systems (including legislation, inspection, assistance, research and so on), the administrative costs of which are a charge on society.

The level of compensation benefits and the amount of resources devoted to accident prevention by governments are limited for two reasons: because they depend (1) on the value placed on human life and suffering, which varies from one country to another and from one era to another; and (2) on the funds available and the priorities allocated for other services provided for the protection of the public.

As a result of all this, a considerable amount of capital is no longer available for productive investment. Nevertheless, the money devoted to preventive action does provide considerable economic benefits, to the extent that there is a reduction in the total number of accidents and their cost. Much of the effort devoted to the prevention of accidents, such as the incorporation of higher safety standards into machinery and equipment and the general education of the population before working age, are equally useful both inside and outside the workplace. This is of increasing importance because the number and cost of accidents occurring at home, on the road and in other non-work-related activities of modern life continues to grow. The total cost of accidents may be said to be the sum of the cost of prevention and the cost of the resultant changes. It would not seem unreasonable to recognize that the cost to society of the changes which could result from the implementation of a preventive measure may exceed the actual cost of the measure many times over. The

necessary financial resources are drawn from the economically active section of the population, such as workers, employers and other taxpayers through systems which work either on the basis of contributions to the institutions that provide the benefits, or through taxes collected by the state and other public authorities, or by both systems. At the level of the undertaking the cost of accidents includes expenses and losses, which are made up of the following:

- expenses incurred while setting up the system of work and the related equipment and machinery with a view to ensuring safety in the production process. Estimation of these expenses is difficult because it is not possible to draw a line between the safety of the process itself and that of the workers. Major sums are involved which are entirely expended before production commences and are included in general or special costs to be amortized over a period of years.
- expenses incurred during production, which in turn include: (1) fixed charges related to accident prevention, notably for medical, safety and educational services and for arrangements for the workers' participation in the safety programme; (2) fixed charges for accident insurance, plus variable charges in schemes where premiums are based on the number of accidents; (3) varying charges for activities related to accident prevention (these depend largely on accident frequency and severity, and include the cost of training and information activities, safety campaigns, safety programmes and research, and workers' participation in these activities); (4) costs arising from personal injuries (These include the cost of medical care, transport, grants to accident victims and their families, administrative and legal consequences of accidents, salaries paid to injured persons during their absence from work and to other workers during interruptions to work after an accident and during subsequent inquiries and investigations, and so on.); (5) costs arising from material damage and loss which need not be accompanied by personal injury. In fact, the most typical and expensive material damage in certain branches of industry arises in circumstances other than those which result in personal injury; attention should be concentrated upon the few points in common between the techniques of material damage control and those required for the prevention of personal injury.
- losses arising out of a fall in production or from the costs of introducing special counter-measures, both of which may be very expensive.

In addition to affecting the place where the accident occurred, successive losses may occur at other points in the plant or in associated plants; apart from economic losses which result from work stoppages due to accidents or injuries, account must be taken of the losses resulting when the workers stop work or come out on strike during industrial disputes concerning serious, collective or repeated accidents.

The total value of these costs and losses are by no means the same for every undertaking. The most obvious differences depend on the particular hazards associated with each branch of industry or type of occupation and on the extent to which appropriate safety precautions are applied. Rather than trying to place a value on the initial costs incurred while incorporating accident prevention measures into the system at the earliest stages, many authors have tried to work out the consequential costs. Among these may be cited: Heinrich, who proposed that costs be divided into "direct costs" (particularly insurance) and "indirect costs" (expenses incurred by the manufacturer); Simonds, who proposed dividing the costs into insured costs and non-insured costs; Wallach, who proposed a division under the different headings used for analysing production costs, viz. labour, machinery, mainte-

56. ACCIDENT PREVENTION

nance and time expenses; and Compes, who defined the costs as either general costs or individual costs. In all of these examples (with the exception of Wallach), two groups of costs are described which, although differently defined, have many points in common.

In view of the difficulty of estimating overall costs, attempts have been made to arrive at a suitable value for this figure by expressing the indirect cost (uninsured or individual costs) as a multiple of the direct cost (insured or general costs). Heinrich was the first to attempt to obtain a value for this figure and proposed that the indirect costs amounted to four times the direct costs—that is, that the total cost amounts to five times the direct cost. This estimation is valid for the group of undertakings studied by Heinrich, but is not valid for other groups and is even less valid when applied to individual factories. In a number of industries in various industrialized countries this value has been found to be of the order of 1 to 7 (4 ±75%) but individual studies have shown that this figure can be considerably higher (up to 20 times) and may even vary over a period of time for the same undertaking.

There is no doubt that money spent incorporating accident prevention measures into the system during the initial stages of a manufacturing project will be offset by the reduction of losses and expenses that would otherwise have been incurred. This saving is not, however, subject to any particular law or fixed proportion, and will vary from case to case. It may be found that a small expenditure results in very substantial savings, whereas in another case a much greater expenditure results in very little apparent gain. In making calculations of this kind, allowance should always be made for the time factor, which works in two ways: current expenses may be reduced by amortizing the initial cost over

several years, and the probability of an accident occurring, however rare it may be, will increase with the passage of time.

In any given industry, where permitted by societal factors, there may be no financial incentive to reduce accidents in view of the fact that their cost is added to the production cost and is thus passed on to the consumer. This is a different matter, however, when considered from the point of view of an individual undertaking. There may be a great incentive for an undertaking to take steps to avoid the serious economic effects of accidents involving key personnel or essential equipment. This is particularly so in the case of small plants which do not have a reserve of qualified staff, or those engaged in certain specialized activities, as well as in large, complex facilities, such as in the process industry, where the costs of replacement could surpass the capacity to raise capital. There may also be cases where a larger undertaking can be more competitive and thus increase its profits by taking steps to reduce accidents. Furthermore, no undertaking can afford to overlook the financial advantages that stem from maintaining good relations with workers and their trade unions.

As a final point, when passing from the abstract concept of an undertaking to the concrete reality of those who occupy senior positions in the business (i.e., the employer or the senior management), there is a personal incentive which is not only financial and which stems from the desire or the need to further their own career and to avoid the penalties, legal and otherwise, which may befall them in the case of certain types of accident. The cost of occupational accidents, therefore, has repercussions on both the national economy and that of each individual member of the population: there is thus an overall and an individual incentive for everybody to play a part in reducing this cost.

References

Adams, JGU. 1985. *Risk and Freedom; The Record of Read Safety Regulation*. London: Transport Publishing Projects.

American National Standards Institute (ANSI). 1962. *Method of Recording and Measuring Work Injury Experience*. ANSI Z-16.2. New York: ANSI.

—. 1978. *American National Standard Manual on Uniform Traffic Control Devices for Streets and Highways*. ANSI D6.1. New York: ANSI.

—. 1988. *Hazardous Industrial Chemicals—Precautionary Labeling*. ANSI Z129.1. New York: ANSI.

—. 1993. *Safety Color Code*. ANSI Z535.1. New York: ANSI.

—. 1993. *Environmental and Facility Safety Signs*. ANSI Z535.2. New York: ANSI.

—. 1993. *Criteria for Safety Symbols*. ANSI Z535.3. New York: ANSI.

—. 1993. *Product Safety Signs and Labels*. ANSI Z535.4. New York: ANSI.

—. 1993. *Accident Prevention Tags*. ANSI Z535.5. New York: ANSI.

Andersson, R. 1991. The role of accidentology in occupational accident research. *Arbete och halsa*. 1991. Solna, Sweden. Thesis.

Andersson, R and E Lagerlöf. 1983. Accident data in the new Swedish information system on occupational injuries. *Ergonomics* 26.

Arnold, HJ. 1989. Sanctions and rewards: Organizational perspectives. In *Sanctions and Rewards in the Legal System: A Multidisciplinary Approach*. Toronto: University of Toronto Press.

Baker, SP, B O'Neil, MJ Ginsburg, and G Li. 1992. *Injury Fact Book*. New York: Oxford University Press.

Benner, L. 1975. Accident investigations—multilinear sequencing methods. *J Saf Res* 7.

Centers for Disease Control and Prevention (CDC). 1988. Guidelines for evaluating surveillance systems. *Morb Mortal Weekly Rep* 37(S-5):1–18.

Davies, JC and DP Manning. 1994a. MAIM: the concept and construction of intelligent software. *Saf Sci* 17:207–218.

—. 1994b. Data collected by MAIM intelligent software: The first fifty accidents. *Saf Sci* 17:219-226.

Department of Trade and Industry. 1987. *Leisure Accident Surveillance System (LASS): Home and Leisure Accident Research 1986 Data*. 11th Annual Report of the Home Accident Surveillance System. London: Department of Trade and Industry.

Ferry, TS. 1988. *Modern Accident Investigation and Analysis*. New York: Wiley.

Feyer, A-M and AM Williamson. 1991. An accident classification system for use in preventive strategies. *Scand J Work Environ Health* 17:302–311.

FMC. 1985. *Product Safety Sign and Label System*. Santa Clara, California: FMC Corporation.

Gielen, AC. 1992. Health education and injury control: Integrating approaches. *Health Educ Q* 19(2):203–218.

Goldenhar, LM and PA Schulte. 1994. Intervention research in occupational health and safety. *J Occup Med* 36(7):763–775.

Green, LW and MW Kreuter. 1991. *Health Promotion Planning: An Educational and Environmental Approach*. Mountainview,CA: Mayfield Publishing Company.

Guastello, SJ. 1991. *The Comparative Effectiveness of Occupational Accident Reduction Programs*. Paper presented at the International Symposium Alcohol Related Accidents and Injuries. Yverdon-les-Bains, Switzerland, Dec. 2-5.

Haddon, WJ. 1972. A logical framework for categorizing highway safety phenomena and activity. *J Trauma* 12:193–207.

—. 1973. Energy damage and the 10 countermeasure strategies. *J Trauma* 13:321–331.

—. 1980. The basic strategies for reducing damage from hazards of all kinds. *Hazard Prevention* September/October:8–12.

Hale, AR and AI Glendon. 1987. *Individual Behaviour in the Face of Danger*. Amsterdam: Elsevier.

Hale, AR and M Hale. 1972. *Review of the Industrial Accident Research Literature*. Research paper No. 1, Committee on Safety & Health. London: HMSO.

Hale, AR, B Heming, J Carthey and B Kirwan. 1994. *Extension of the Model of Behaviour in the Control of Danger*. Vol. 3: *Extended Model Description*. Sheffield: Health and Safety Executive project HF/GNSR/28.

Hare, VC. 1967. *System Analysis: A Diagnostic Approach*. New York: Harcourt Brace World.

Harms-Ringdahl, L. 1993. *Safety Analysis. Principles and Practice in Occupational Safety*. Vol. 289. Amsterdam: Elsevier.

Heinrich, HW. 1931. *Industrial Accident Prevention*. New York: McGraw-Hill.

—. 1959. *Industrial Accident Prevention: A Scientific Approach*. New York: McGraw-Hill Book Company.

Hugentobler, MK, BA Israel, and SJ Schurman. 1992. An action research approach to workplace health: Intergrating methods. *Health Educ Q* 19(1):55–76.

International Organization for Standardization (ISO). 1967. *Symbols, Dimensions, and Layout for Safety Signs*. ISO R557. Geneva: ISO.

—. 1984. *Safety Signs and Colors*. ISO 3864. Geneva: ISO.

—. 1991. *Industrial Automation Systems—Safety of Integrated Manufacturing Systems—Basic Requirements (CD 11161)*. TC 184/WG 4. Geneva: ISO.

—. 1994. *Quality Management and Quality Assurance Vocabulary*. ISO/DIS 8402. Paris: Association française de normalisation.

Janssen, W. 1994. Seat-belt wearing and driving behavior: An instrumented-vehicle study. *Accident analysis and prevention. Accident Anal. Prev.* 26: 249-261.

Jenkins, EL, SM Kisner, D Fosbroke, LA Layne, MA Stout, DN Castillo, PM Cutlip, and R Cianfrocco. 1993. *Fatal Injuries to Workers in the United States, 1980–1989: A Decade of Surveillance.* Cincinnati, OH: NIOSH.

Johnston, JJ, GTH Cattledge, and JW Collins. 1994. The efficacy of training for occupational injury control. *Occup Med: State Art Rev* 9(2):147–158.

Kallberg, VP. 1992. *The Effects of Reflector Posts on Driving Behaviour and Accidents on Two-lane Rural Roads in Finland.* Report 59/1992. Helsinki: The Finnish National Road Administration Technical Development Center.

Kjellén, U. 1984. The deviation concept in occupational accident control. Part I: Definition and classification; Part II: Data collection and assesment of significance. *Accident Anal Prev* 16:289–323.

Kjellén, U and J Hovden. 1993. Reducing risks by deviation control—a retrospection into a research strategy. *Saf Sci* 16:417–438.

Kjellén, U and TJ Larsson. 1981. Investigating accidents and reducing risks—a dynamic approach. *J Occup Acc* 3:129–140.

Last, JM. 1988. *A Dictionary of Epidemiology.* New York: Oxford University Press.

Lehto, MR. 1992. Designing warning signs and warning labels: Part I—Guidelines for the practitioner. *Int J Ind Erg* 10:105–113.

Lehto, MR and D Clark. 1990. Warning signs and labels in the workplace. In *Workspace, Equipment and Tool Design,* edited by A Mital and W Karwowski. Amsterdam: Elsevier.

Lehto, MR and JM Miller. 1986. *Warnings: Volume I: Fundamentals, Design, and Evaluation Methodologies.* Ann Arbor, MI: Fuller Technical Publications.

Leplat, J. 1978. Accident analyses and work analyses. *J Occup Acc* 1:331–340.

MacKenzie, EJ, DM Steinwachs, and BS Shankar. 1989. Classifying severity of trauma based on hospital discharge diagnoses: Validation of an ICD-9CM to AIS-85 conversion table. *Med Care* 27:412–422.

Manning, DP. 1971. Industrial accident-type classifications—A study of the theory and practice of accident prevention based on a computer analysis of industrial injury records. M.D. Thesis, University of Liverpool.

McAfee, RB and AR Winn. 1989. The use of incentives/feedback to enhance work place safety: A critique of the literature. *J Saf Res* 20:7-19.

Mohr, DL and D Clemmer. 1989. Evaluation of an occupational injury intervention in the petroleum industry. *Accident Anal Prev* 21(3):263–271.

National Committee for Injury Prevention and Control. 1989. *Injury Prevention: Meeting the Challenge.* New York: Oxford University Press.

National Electronic Manufacturers Association (NEMA). 1982. *Safety Labels for Padmounted Switch Gear and Transformers Sited in Public Areas.* NEMA 260. Rosslyn, VA: NEMA.

Occupational Health and Safety Administration (OSHA). 1985. *Specification for Accident Prevention Signs and Tags.* CFR 1910.145. Washington DC: OSHA.

—. 1985. *[Chemical] Hazard Communication.* CFR 1910.1200. Washington DC: OSHA.

Occupational Injury Prevention Panel. 1992. Occupational injury prevention. In *Centers for Disease Control. Position Papers from the Third National Injury Control Conference: Setting the National Agenda for Injury Control in the 1990s.* Atlanta, GA: CDC.

Organization for Economic Cooperation and Development (OECD). 1990. *Behavioural Adaptation to Changes in the Road Transport System.* Paris: OECD.

Rasmussen, J. 1982. Human errors. A taxonomy for describing human malfunction in industrial installations. *J Occup Acc* 4:311–333.

Rasmussen, J, K Duncan and J Leplat. 1987. *New Technology and Human Error.* Chichester: Wiley.

Reason, JT. 1990. *Human Error.* Cambridge: CUP.

Rice, DP, EJ MacKenzie and associates. 1989. *Cost of Injury in the United States: A Report to Congress.* San Francisco: Institute for Health and Aging, University of California; and Baltimore: Injury Prevention Center, The Johns Hopkins University.

Robertson, LS. 1992. *Injury Epidemiology.* New York: Oxford University Press.

Saari, J. 1992. Successful implementation of occupational health and safety programs in manufacturing for the 1990s. *J Hum Factors Manufac* 2:55–66.

Schelp, L. 1988. The role of organizations in community participation—prevention of accidental injuries in a rural Swedish municipality. *Soc Sci Med* 26(11):1087–1093.

Shannon, HS. 1978. A statistical study of 2,500 consecutive reported accidents in an automobile factory. Ph.D. thesis, University of London.

Smith, GS and H Falk. 1987. Unintentional injuries. *Am J Prev Medicine* 5, sup.:143–163.

Smith, GS and PG Barss. 1991. Unintentional injuries in developing countries: The epidemiology of a neglected problem. *Epidemiological Reviews* :228–266.

Society of Automotive Engineers (SAE). 1979. *Safety Signs.* SAE J115: SAE.

Steckler, AB, L Dawson, BA Israel, and E Eng. 1993. Community health development: An overview of the works of Guy W. Stewart. *Health Educ Q* Sup. 1: S3-S20.

Steers, RM and LW Porter. 1991. *Motivation and Work Behavior* (5th ed). New York: McGraw-Hill.

Surry, J. 1969. *Industrial Accident Research: A Human Engineering Appraisal.* Canada: University of Toronto.

Tollman, S. 1991. Community-oriented primary care: Origins, evolutions, applications. *Soc Sci Med* 32(6):633-642.

Troup, JDG, J Davies, and DP Manning. 1988. A model for the investigation of back injuries and manual handling problems at work. *J Soc Occup Med* 10:107–119.

Tuominen, R and J Saari. 1982. A model for analysis of accidents and its applications. *J Occup Acc* 4.

Veazie, MA, DD Landen, TR Bender and HE Amandus. 1994. Epidemiologic research on the etiology of injuries at work. *Ann Rev Pub Health* 15:203–21.

Wagenaar, WA, PT Hudson and JT Reason. 1990. Cognitive failures and accidents. *Appl Cogn Psychol* 4:273–294.

Waller, JA. 1985. *Injury Control: A Guide to the Causes and Prevention of Trauma.* Lexington, MA: Lexington Books.

Wallerstein, N and R Baker. 1994. Labor education programs in health and safety. *Occup Med State Art Rev* 9(2):305-320.

Weeks, JL. 1991. Occupational health and safety regulation in the coal mining industry: Public health at the workplace. *Annu Rev Publ Health* 12:195–207.

Westinghouse Electric Corporation. 1981. *Product Safety Label Handbook.* Trafford, Pa: Westinghouse Printing Division.

Wilde, GJS. 1982. The theory of risk homeostasis: Implications for safety and health. *Risk Anal* 2:209-225.

—. 1991. Economics and accidents: A commentary. *J Appl Behav Sci* 24:81-84.

—. 1988. Risk homeostasis theory and traffic accidents: propositions, deductions and discussion of dissemsion in recent reactions. *Ergonomics* 31:441-468.

—. 1994. *Target Risk.* Toronto: PDE Publications.

Williamson, AM and A-M Feyer. 1990. Behavioural epidemiology as a tool for accident research. *J Occup Acc* 12:207–222.

Work Environment Fund [Arbetarskyddsfonden]. 1983. *Olycksfall i arbetsmiljön—Kartläggning och analys av forskningsbehov [Accidents in the work environment—survey and analysis].* Solna: Arbetarskyddsfonden

Other relevant readings

Andersson, R, B Johansson, K Lindén, and L Svanström. 1978. Development of a model for research on occupational accidents. *J Occup Acc* 1.

Apple, J. 1972. *Materials Handling Systems Design.* New York: The Ronald Press.

Bainbridge, L. 1983. Ironies of automation. *Automatica* 19:775-779.

Bamber, L. 1979. Accident costing in industry. *Health and Safety at Work* (Croyden) 2/4:32–34.

Barnett, R and D Brickman. 1986. Safety hierarchy. *J Saf Res* 17:49–55.

Booth, R. 1979. Making factories safe for forklift truck drivers. *Occup Health* 4:193–197.

Collinson, IL. 1980. Safety—the cost of accidents and their prevention. *The Mining Engineer* (London), 561–571.

Corbett, JM. 1988. Ergonomics in the development of human-centred AMT. *Appl Ergon* 19:35-39.

Diekershoff, K, W Hamacher, and G Kliemt. 1986. Gefährdungen und Belastungen beim innerbetrieblichen Transport und Verkehr. *Die Berufsgenossenschaft* 7:378–384.

Franke, A and S Joki. 1975. Die volkswirtschaftlichen Kosten der Arbeitsunfälle [The economic costs of occupational accidents]. *Bundesanstalt für Arbeitsschutz und Unfallforschung.* Forschungsbericht Nr. 148. Dortmund: Marten.

Goodstein, LP, HB Anderson, and SE Olsen. 1988. *Tasks, Errors and Mental Models.* London: Taylor & Francis.

Häkkinen, K. 1992. Failures in materials handling systems with the framework of EN 292. In *Proceedings of the Fourth International Conference on Structural Failure, Product Liability and Technical Insurance, Technical University Vienna July 6–9, 1992,* edited by HP Rossmanith. Amsterdam: Elsevier.

—. 1991. Accidents and technological change in materials handling. In *XIIth World Congress on Occupational Safety and Health, Hamburg 6–11 May 1990, proceedings.* Sankt Augustin: ILO.

Hale, AR and M Hale. 1970. Accidents in perspective. *Occup Psychol* 44:115–122.

Health and Safety Executive. 1992. *Road Transport in Factories and Similiar Workplaces.* Guidance Note GS9(R). London: HMSO.

—. 1982. *Transport Kills. A Study of Fatal Accidents in Industry 1978–1980.* London: HMSO.

Hollnagel, E and D Woods. 1983. Cognitive systems engineering: New wine in new bottles. *Int J Man Mach Stud* 18:593-600.

Kidd, P. 1994. Skill-based automated manufacturing. In *Organization and Management of Advanced Manufacturing Systems,* edited by W Karwowski and G Salvendy. New York: Wiley.

Kuivanen, R. 1990. The impact on safety of disturbances in flexible manufacturing systems. In *Ergonomics of Hybrid Automated Systems II,* edited by W Karwowski and M Rahimi. Amsterdam:Elsevier.

LeNet, M. 1978. Le prix de la vie humaine [The cost of a human life]. *Notes et études documentaires.* No. 4455. Paris: La Documentation française.

Miller, JM, MR Lehto, and JP Frantz. 1994. *Warnings and Safety Instructions: Annotated and Indexed.* Ann Arbor, MI: Fuller Technical Publications.

Rasmussen, J. 1983. Skills, rules, and knowledge: signals, signs, and symbols, and other distinctions in

56. ACCIDENT PREVENTION

human performance models. *IEEE T Syst Man Cyb* 13(3):257–266.

Sinclair, TC. 1972. *A Cost-effectiveness Approach to Industrial Safety*. London: HMSO.

—. 1975. *Safety Alert Symbol for Agricultural, Construction, and Industrial Equipment*. SAE J284: SAE.

—. 1983. *Slow Moving Vehicle Identification Emblem*. SAE J943: SAE.

Sugimoto, N. 1987. Subjects and problems of robot safety technology. In *Occupational Safety and Health in Automation and Robotics*, edited by K Noro. London:Taylor & Francis.

57

Chapter Editor
Jorma Saari

Contents

SAFETY AUDITS AND MANAGEMENT AUDITS

Johan Van de Kerckhove

During the 1990s, the organizational factors in safety policy are becoming increasingly important. At the same time, the views of organizations regarding safety have dramatically changed. Safety experts, most of whom have a technical training background, are thus confronted with a dual task. On the one hand, they have to learn to understand the organizational aspects and take them into account in constructing safety programmes. On the other hand, it is important that they be aware of the fact that the view of organizations is moving further and further away from the machine concept and placing a clear emphasis on less tangible and measurable factors such as organizational culture, behaviour modification, responsibility-raising or commitment. The first part of this article briefly covers developments in opinions relating to organizations, management, quality and safety. The second part of the article defines the implications of these developments for audit systems. This is then very briefly placed in a tangible context using the example of an actual safety audit system based on the International Organization for Standardization (ISO) 9001 standards.

New Opinions Concerning Organization and Safety

Changes in social-economic circumstances

The economic crisis that started to impact upon the Western world in 1973 has had a significant influence on thought and action in the field of management, quality and work safety. In the past, the accent in economic development was placed on expansion of the market, increasing exports and improving productivity. However, the emphasis gradually shifted to the reduction of losses and the improvement of quality. In order to retain and acquire customers, a more direct response was provided to their requirements and expectations. This resulted in a need for greater product differentiation, with the direct consequence of greater flexibility within organizations in order to always be able to respond to market fluctuations on a "just in time" basis. Emphasis was placed on the commitment and creativity of employees as the major competitive advantage in the economic competitive struggle. Besides increasing quality, limiting loss-making activities became an important means of improving operating results.

Safety experts enlisted in this strategy by developing and instituting "total loss control" programmes. Not only are the direct costs of accidents or the increased insurance premiums significant in these programmes, but so also are all direct or indirect unnecessary costs and losses. A study of how much production should be increased in real terms to compensate for these losses immediately reveals that reducing costs is today often more efficient and profitable than increasing production.

In this context of improved productivity, reference was recently made to the major benefits of reducing absenteeism due to sickness and stimulating employee motivation. Against the background of these developments, safety policy is increasingly and clearly taking on a new form with different accents. In the past, most corporate leaders considered work safety as merely a legal obligation, as a burden they would quickly delegate to technical specialists. Today, safety policy is more and more distinctly being viewed as a way of achieving the two aims of reducing losses and optimizing corporate policy. Safety policy is therefore increasingly evolving into a reliable barometer of the soundness of the corporation's success with respect to these aims. In order to measure progress, increased attention is being devoted to management and safety audits.

Organizational Theory

It is not only economic circumstances that have given company heads new insights. New visions relating to management, organizational theory, total quality care and, in the same vein, safety care, are resulting in significant changes. An important turning point in views on the organization was elaborated in the renowned work published by Peters and Waterman (1982), *In Search of Excellence*. This work was already espousing the ideas which Pascale and Athos (1980) discovered in Japan and described in *The Art of Japanese Management*. This new development can be symbolized in a sense by McKinsey's "7-S" Framework (in Peters and Waterman 1982). In addition to three traditional management aspects (Strategy, Structure and Systems), corporations now also emphasize three additional aspects (Staff, Skills and Style). All six of these interact to provide the input to the 7th "S", Superordinate goals (figure 57.1). With this approach, a very clear accent is placed on the human-oriented aspects of the organization.

The fundamental shifts can best be demonstrated on the basis of the model presented by Scott (1978), which was also used by Peters and Waterman (1982). This model uses two approaches:

1. The closed-system approaches deny the influence of developments from outside the organization. With the mechanistic closed approaches, the objectives of an organization are clearly defined and can be logically and rationally determined.

2. Open-system approaches take outside influences fully into account, and the objectives are more the result of diverse processes, in which clearly irrational factors contribute to decision making. These organically open approaches more truly reflect the evolution of an organization, which is not

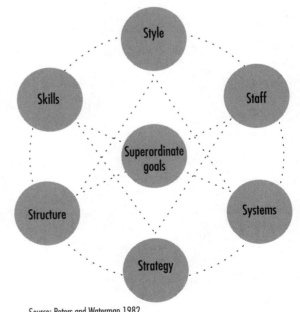

Figure 57.1 • The values, mission and organizational culture of a corporation according to McKinsey's 7-S Framework.

Source: Peters and Waterman 1982.

Figure 57.2 • Organizational theories.

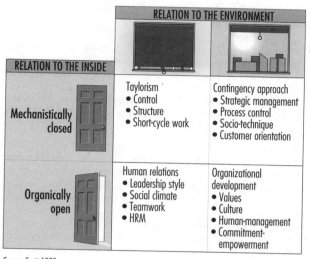

Source: Scott 1978.

determined mathematically or on the basis of deductive logic, but grows organically on the basis of real people and their interactions and values (figure 57.2).

Four fields are thus created in figure 57.2. Two of these (Taylorism and contingency approach) are mechanically closed, and the other two (human relations and organizational development) are organically open. There has been enormous development in management theory, moving from the traditional rational and authoritarian machine model (Taylorism) to the human-oriented organic model of human resources management (HRM).

Organizational effectiveness and efficiency are being more clearly linked to optimal strategic management, a flat organizational structure and sound quality systems. Furthermore, attention is now given to superordinate goals and significant values that have a bonding effect within the organization, such as skills (on the basis of which the organization stands out from its competitors) and a staff that is motivated to maximum creativity and flexibility by placing the emphasis on commitment and empowerment. With these open approaches, a management audit cannot limit itself to a number of formal or structural characteristics of the organization. The audit must also include a search for methods to map out less tangible and measurable cultural aspects.

From product control to total quality management
In the 1950s, quality was limited to a post-factum end product control, total quality control (TQC). In the 1970s, partly stimulated by NATO and the automotive giant Ford, the accent shifted to the achievement of the goal of total quality assurance (TQA) during the production process. It was only during the 1980s that, stimulated by Japanese techniques, attention shifted towards the quality of the total management system and total quality management (TQM) was born. This fundamental change in the quality care system has taken place cumulatively in the sense that each foregoing stage was integrated into the next. It is also clear that while product control and safety inspection are facets more closely related to a Tayloristic organizational concept, quality assurance is more associated with a socio-technical system approach where the aim is not to betray the trust of the (external) customer. TQM, finally, relates to an HRM approach by the organization as it is

no longer solely the improvement of the product that is involved, but continuous improvement of the organizational aspects in which explicit attention is also devoted to the employees.

In the total quality leadership (TQL) approach of the European Foundation for Quality Management (EFQM), the emphasis is very strongly placed on the equal impact of the organization on the customer, the employees and the overall society, with the environment as the key point of attention. These objectives can be realized by including concepts such as "leadership" and "people management".

It is clear that there is also a very important difference in emphasis between quality assurance as described in the ISO standards and the TQL approach of the EFQM. ISO quality assurance is an extended and improved form of quality inspection, focusing not only on the products and internal customers, but also on the efficiency of the technical processes. The objective of the inspection is to investigate the conformity with the procedures set out in ISO. TQM, on the other hand, endeavours to meet the expectations of all internal and external customers as well as all processes within the organization, including the more soft and human-oriented ones. The involvement, the commitment and the creativity of the employees are clearly important aspects of TQM.

From Human Error to Integrated Safety
Safety policy has evolved in a similar manner to quality care. Attention has shifted from post-factum accident analysis, with emphasis on the prevention of injuries, to a more global approach. Safety is seen more in the context of "total loss control"—a policy aimed at the avoidance of losses through management of safety involving the interaction of people, processes, materials, equipment, installations and the environment. Safety therefore focuses on the management of the processes that could lead to losses. In the initial development period of safety policy the emphasis was placed on a *human error* approach. Consequently, employees were given a heavy responsibility for the prevention of industrial accidents. Following a Tayloristic philosophy, conditions and procedures were drawn up and a control system was established to maintain the prescribed standards of behaviour. This philosophy may filter through into modern safety policy via the ISO 9000 concepts resulting in the imposition of a sort of implicit and indirect feeling of guilt upon the employees, with all the adverse consequences this entails for the corporate culture—for instance, a tendency may develop that performance will be impeded rather than enhanced.

At a later stage in the evolution of safety policy, it was recognized that employees carry out their work in a particular environment with well-defined working resources. Industrial accidents were considered as a multicausal event in a human/machine/environment system in which the emphasis shifted in a *technical-system approach*. Here again we find the analogy with quality assurance, where the accent is placed on controlling technical processes through means such as statistical process control.

Only recently, and partly stimulated by the TQM philosophy, has the emphasis in safety policy systems shifted into a *social-system approach*, which is a logical step in the improvement of the prevention system. In order to optimize the human/machine/environment system it is not sufficient to ensure safe machines and tools by means of a well-developed prevention policy, but there is also the need for a preventive maintenance system and the assurance of security among all technical processes. Moreover, it is of crucial importance that employees be sufficiently trained, skilled and motivated with regard to health and safety objectives. In today's society, the latter objective can no longer be achieved through the authoritarian Tayloristic approach, as positive feedback is much more stimulating than a repressive control system that often has only negative effects. Modern management entails an open, motivating corporate culture, in which there is a common commitment to achieving key corporate objectives in a participatory, team-based approach. In the *safety-culture approach*, safety is an integral part of the objectives of the organizations and therefore an essential part of everyone's task, starting with top management and passing along the entire hierarchical line down to employees on the shop floor.

Integrated safety

The concept of integrated safety immediately presents a number of central factors in an integrated safety system, the most important of which can be summarized as follows:

A clearly visible commitment from the top management. This commitment is not only given on paper, but is translated right down to the shop floor in practical achievements.

Active involvement of the hierarchical line and the central support departments. Care for safety, health and welfare is not only an integral part of everyone's task in the production process, but is also integrated into the personnel policy, into preventive maintenance, into the design stage and into working with third parties.

Full participation of the employees. Employees are full discussion partners with whom open and constructive communication is possible, with their contribution being given full weight. Indeed, participation is of crucial importance for carrying through corporate and safety policy in an efficient and motivating way.

A suitable profile for a safety expert. The safety expert is no longer the technician or jack of all trades, but is a qualified adviser to the top management, with particular attention being devoted to optimizing the policy processes and the safety system. He or she is therefore not someone who is only technically trained, but also a person who, as a good organizer, can deal with people in an inspiring manner and collaborate in a synergetic way with other prevention experts.

A pro-active safety culture. The key aspect of an integrated safety policy is a pro-active safety culture, which includes, among other things, the following:

- Safety, health and welfare are the key ingredients of an organization's value system and of the objectives it seeks to attain.
- An atmosphere of openness prevails, based on mutual trust and respect.
- There is a high level of cooperation with a smooth flow of information and an appropriate level of coordination.
- A pro-active policy is implemented with a dynamic system of constant improvement perfectly matching the prevention concept.
- The promotion of safety, health and welfare is a key component of all decision-making, consultations and teamwork.
- When industrial accidents occur, suitable preventive measures are sought, not a scapegoat.
- Members of staff are encouraged to act on their own initiative so that they possess the greatest possible authority, knowledge and experience, enabling them to intervene in an appropriate manner in unexpected situations.
- Processes are set in motion with a view to promoting individual and collective training to the maximum extent possible.
- Discussions concerning challenging and attainable health, safety and welfare objectives are held on a regular basis.

Safety and Management Audits

General description

Safety audits are a form of risk analysis and evaluation in which a systematic investigation is carried out in order to determine the extent to which the conditions are present that provide for the development and implementation of an effective and efficient safety policy. Each audit therefore simultaneously envisions the

objectives that must be realized and the best organizational circumstances to put these into practice.

Each audit system should, in principle, determine the following:

- What is management seeking to achieve, by what means and by what strategy?
- What are the necessary provisions in terms of resources, structures, processes, standards and procedures that are required to achieve the proposed objectives, and what has been provided? What minimum programme can be put forward?
- What are the operational and measurable criteria that must be met by the chosen items to allow the system to function optimally?

The information is then thoroughly analysed to examine to what extent the current situation and the degree of achievement meet the desired criteria, followed by a report with positive feedback that emphasizes the strong points, and corrective feedback that refers to aspects requiring further improvement.

Auditing and strategies for change

Each audit system explicitly or implicitly contains a vision both of an ideal organization's design and conceptualization, and of the best way of implementing improvements.

Bennis, Benne and Chin (1985) distinguish *three strategies* for planned changes, each based on a different vision of people and of the means of influencing behaviour:

- *Power-force strategies* are based on the idea that the behaviour of employees can be changed by exercising sanctions.
- *Rational-empirical strategies* are based on the axiom that people make rational choices depending on maximizing their own benefits.
- *Normative-re-educative strategies* are based on the premise that people are irrational, emotional beings and in order to realize a real change, attention must also be devoted to their perception of values, culture, attitudes and social skills.

Which influencing strategy is most appropriate in a specific situation not only depends on the starting vision, but also on the actual situation and the existing organizational culture. In this respect it is very important to know which sort of behaviour to influence. The famous model devised by Danish risk specialist Rasmussen (1988) distinguishes among the following three sorts of behaviour:

- Routine actions (*skill-based behaviour*) automatically follow the associated signal. Such actions are carried out without one's consciously devoting attention to them—for example, touch-typing or manually changing gears when driving.
- Actions in accordance with instructions (*rule-based*) require more conscious attention because no automatic response to the signal is present and a choice must be made between different possible instructions and rules. These are often actions which can be placed in an "if...then" sequence, as in "If the meter rises to 50 then this valve must be closed".
- Actions based on knowledge and insight (*knowledge-based*) are carried out after a conscious interpretation and evaluation of the different problem signals and the possible alternative solutions. These actions therefore presuppose a fairly high degree of knowledge of and insight into the process concerned, and the ability to interpret unusual signals.

Strata in behavioural and cultural change

Based on the above, most audit systems (including those based on the ISO series of standards) implicitly depart from power-force strategies or rational-empirical strategies, with their emphasis on routine or procedural behaviour. This means that insufficient

Table 57.1 • Strata in quality and safety policy.

Strategies	Skills	Behaviour Rules	Knowledge
Power-force	Human error approach Taylorism TQC		
Rational-empirical		Technical system approach PAS TQA ISO 9000	
Normative-re-educative		Social system approach TQM	Safety culture approach PAS EFQM

attention is paid in these audit systems to "knowledge-based behaviour" that can be influenced mainly via normative–re-educative strategies. In the typology used by Schein (1989), attention is devoted only to the tangible and conscious surface phenomena of the organizational culture and not to the deeper invisible and subconscious strata that refer more to values and fundamental presuppositions.

Many audit systems limit themselves to the question of whether a particular provision or procedure is present. It is therefore implicitly assumed that the sheer existence of this provision or procedure is a sufficient guarantee for the good functioning of the system. Besides the existence of certain measures, there are always different other "strata" (or levels of probable response) that must be addressed in an audit system to provide sufficient information and guarantees for the optimum functioning of the system.

In more concrete terms, the following example concerns response to a fire emergency:

- A given provision, instruction or procedure is present ("sound the alarm and use the extinguisher").
- A given instruction or procedure is also familiarly known to the parties concerned (workers know where alarms and extinguishers are located and how to activate and use them).
- The parties concerned also know as much as possible as to the "why and wherefore" of a particular measure (employees have been trained or educated in extinguisher use and typical types of fires).
- The employee is also motivated to apply needful measures (self preservation, save the job, etc.).
- There is sufficient motivation, competence and ability to act in unforeseen circumstances (employees know what to do in the event fire gets out of hand, requiring professional fire-fighting response).
- There are good human relations and an atmosphere of open communication (supervisors, managers and employees have discussed and agreed upon fire emergency response procedures).
- Spontaneous creative processes originate in a learning organization (changes in procedures are implemented following "lessons learned" in actual fire situations).

Table 57.1 lays out some strata in quality audio safety policy.

The Pellenberg Audit System

The name *Pellenberg Audit System* (PAS) derives from the place where the designers gathered many times to develop the system (the Maurissens Château in Pellenberg, a building of the Catholic University of Leuven). PAS is the result of intense collaboration by an interdisciplinary team of experts with years of practical experience, both in the area of quality management and in the area of safety and environmental problems, in which a variety of approaches and experiences were brought together. The team also received support from the university science and research departments, and thus benefited from the most recent insights in the fields of management and organizational culture.

PAS encompasses an entire set of criteria that a superior company prevention system ought to meet (see table 57.2). These criteria are classified in accordance with the ISO standard system (quality assurance in design, development, production, installation and servicing). However, PAS is not a simple translation of the ISO system into safety, health and welfare. *A new philosophy* is developed, departing from the specific product that is achieved in safety policy: meaningful and safe jobs. The contract of the ISO system is replaced by the provisions of the law and by the evolving expectations that exist among the parties involved in the social field with regard to health, safety and welfare. The creation of safe and meaningful jobs is seen as an essential objective of each organization within the framework of its social responsibility. The enterprise is the supplier and the customers are the employees.

Several other systems are integrated in the PAS system:

- *At a strategic level*, the insights and requirements of ISO are of particular importance. As far as possible, these are complemented by the management vision as this was originally developed by the European Foundation for Quality Management.
- *At a tactical level*, the systematics of the "Management's Oversight and Risk Tree" encourages people to seek out what are the necessary and sufficient conditions in order to achieve the desired safety result.
- *At an operational level* a multitude of sources could be drawn upon, including existing legislation, regulations and other criteria such as the International Safety Rating System (ISRS), in which the emphasis is placed on certain concrete conditions that should guarantee the safety result.

The PAS constantly refers to the broader corporate policy within which the safety policy is embedded. After all, an optimum safety policy is at the same time a product and a producer of a pro-active company policy. Assuming that a safe company is at the same time an effective and efficient organization and vice versa, special attention is therefore devoted to the integration of safety policy in the overall policy. Essential ingredients of a future-oriented corporate policy include a strong corporate culture, a far-reaching commitment, the participation of the employees, a special emphasis on the quality of the work, and a dynamic system of continual improvement. Although these insights also partly form the background of the PAS, they are not always very easy to reconcile with the more formal and procedural approach of the ISO philosophy.

Formal procedures and directly identifiable results are indisputably important in safety policy. However, it is not enough to base the safety system on this approach alone. The future results of a safety policy are dependent on the present policy, on the systematic efforts, on the constant search for improvements, and particularly on the fundamental optimizing of processes that ensure durable results. This vision is incorporated in the PAS system, with strong emphasis among other things on a systematic improvement of the safety culture.

One of the main advantages of the PAS is the opportunity for synergy. By departing from the systematics of ISO, the diverse lines of approach become immediately recognizable for all those concerned with total quality management. There are clearly several opportunities for synergy between these various policy areas because in all these fields the improvement of the management processes is the key aspect. A careful purchasing policy, a

Table 57.2 • PAS safety audit elements.

PAS safety audit elements		Correspondence with ISO 9001
1.	Management responsibility	
1.1.	Safety policy	4.1.1.
1.2.	Organization	
1.2.1.	Responsibility and authority	4.1.2.1.
1.2.2.	Verification resources and personnel	4.1.2.2.
1.2.3.	Health and safety service	4.1.2.3.
1.3.	Safety management system review	4.1.3.
2.	Safety management system	4.2.
3.	Obligations	4.3.
4.	Design control	
4.1.	General	4.4.1.
4.2.	Design and development planning	4.4.2.
4.3.	Design input	4.4.3.
4.4.	Design output	4.4.4.
4.5.	Design verification	4.4.5.
4.6.	Design changes	4.4.6.
5.	Document control	
5.1.	Document approval and issue	4.5.1.
5.2.	Document changes/modifications	4.5.2.
6.	Purchasing and contracting	
6.1.	General	4.6.1.
6.2.	Assessment of suppliers and contractors	4.6.2.
6.3.	Purchasing data	4.6.3.
6.4.	Third party's products	4.7.
7.	Identification	4.8.
8.	Process control	
8.1.	General	4.9.1.
8.2.	Process safety control	4.11.
9.	Inspection	
9.1.	Receiving and pre-start-up inspection	4.10.1. 4.10.3.
9.2.	Periodic inspections	4.10.2.
9.3.	Inspection records	4.10.4.
9.4.	Inspection equipment	4.11.
9.5.	Inspection status	4.12.
10.	Accidents and incidents	4.13.
11.	Corrective and preventive action	4.13. 4.14.
12.	Safety records	4.16.
13.	Internal safety audits	4.17.
14.	Training	4.18.
15.	Maintenance	4.19.
16.	Statistical techniques	4.20.

sound system of preventive maintenance, good housekeeping, participatory management and the stimulation of an enterprising approach by employees are of paramount importance for all these policy areas.

The various care systems are organized in an analogous manner, based on principles such as the commitment of top management, the involvement of the hierarchical line, the active participation of employees, and a valorized contribution from the specific experts. The different systems also contain analogous policy instruments such as the policy statement, annual action plans, measuring and control systems, internal and external audits and so on. The PAS system therefore clearly invites the pursuance of an effective, cost-saving, synergetic cooperation between all these care systems.

The PAS does not offer the easiest road to achievement in the short term. Few company managers allow themselves to be seduced by a system that promises great benefits in the short term with little effort. Every sound policy requires an *in-depth approach*, with strong foundations being laid for future policy. More important than results in the short term is the guarantee that a system is being built up that will generate sustainable results in the future, not only in the field of safety, but also at the level of a generally effective and efficient corporate policy. In this respect working towards health, safety and welfare also means working towards safe and meaningful jobs, motivated employees, satisfied customers and an optimum operating result. All this takes place in a dynamic, pro-active atmosphere.

Summary

Continual improvement is an essential precondition for each safety audit system that seeks to reap lasting success in today's rapidly evolving society. The best guarantee for a dynamic system of continual improvement and constant flexibility is the full commitment of competent employees who grow with the overall organization because their efforts are systematically valorized and because they are given the opportunities to develop and regularly update their skills. Within the safety audit process, the best guarantee of lasting results is the development of a learning organization in which both the employees and the organization continue to learn and evolve.

HAZARD ANALYSIS: THE ACCIDENT CAUSATION MODEL

Jop Groeneweg

This article examines the role of human factors in the accident causation process and reviews the various preventive measures (and their effectiveness) by which human error may be controlled, and their application to the accident causation model. Human error is an important contributing cause in at least 90% of all industrial accidents. While purely technical errors and uncontrollable physical circumstances may also contribute to accident causation, human error is the paramount source of failure. The increased sophistication and reliability of machinery means that the proportion of causes of accidents attributed to human error increases as the absolute number of accidents decreases. Human error is also the cause of many of those incidents that, although not resulting in injury or death, nevertheless result in considerable economic damage to a company. As such, it represents a major target for prevention, and it will become increasingly important. For effective safety management systems and risk identification programmes it is important to be able to identify the human component effectively through the use of general failure type analysis.

The Nature of Human Error

Human error can be viewed as the failure to reach a goal in the way that was planned, either from a local or wider perspective, due to unintentional or intentional behaviour. Those planned actions may fail to achieve the desired outcomes for the following four reasons:

1. Unintentional behaviour:
   - The actions did not go as planned (slips).
   - The action was not executed (lapses).
2. Intentional behaviour:
   - The plan itself was inadequate (mistakes).
   - There were deviations from the original plan (violations).

Deviations can be divided in three classes: skill-, rule- and knowledge-based errors.

1. At the skill-based level, behaviour is guided by pre-programmed action schemes. The tasks are routine and continuous, and feedback is usually lacking.
2. At the rule-based level, behaviour is guided by general rules. They are simple and can be applied many times in specific situations. The tasks consist of relatively frequent action sequences that start after a choice is made among rules or procedures. The user has a choice: the rules are not automatically activated, but are actively chosen.
3. Knowledge-based behaviour is shown in completely new situations where no rules are available and where creative and analytical thinking is required.

In some situations, the term *human limitation* would be more appropriate than *human error*. There also are limits to the ability to foresee the future behaviour of complex systems (Gleick 1987; Casti 1990).

Reason and Embrey's model, the Generic Error Modelling System (GEMS) (Reason 1990), takes into account the error-correcting mechanisms on the skill-, rule- and knowledge-based levels. A basic assumption of GEMS is that day-to-day behaviour implies routine behaviour. Routine behaviour is checked regularly, but between these feedback loops, behaviour is completely automatic. Since the behaviour is skill-based, the errors are slips. When the feedback shows a deviation from the desired goal, rule-based correction is applied. The problem is diagnosed on the basis of available symptoms, and a correction rule is automatically applied when the situation is diagnosed. When the wrong rule is applied there is a mistake.

When the situation is completely unknown, knowledge-based rules are applied. The symptoms are examined in the light of knowledge about the system and its components. This analysis can lead to a possible solution the implementation of which constitutes a case of knowledge-based behaviour. (It is also possible that the problem cannot be solved in a given way and that further knowledge-based rules have to be applied.) All errors on this level are mistakes. Violations are committed when a certain rule is applied that is known to be inappropriate: the thinking of the worker may be that application of an alternative rule will be less time-consuming or is possibly more suitable for the present, probably exceptional, situation. The more malevolent class of violations involves sabotage, a subject that is not within the scope of this article. When organizations are attempting to eliminate human error, they should take into account whether the errors are on the skill-, rule- or knowledge-based level, as each level requires its own techniques (Groeneweg 1996).

Influencing Human Behaviour: An Overview

A comment often made with regard to a particular accident is, "Maybe the person did not realize it at the time, but if he or she had not acted in a certain way, the accident would not have happened." Much of accident prevention is aimed at influencing the crucial bit of human behaviour alluded to in this remark. In many safety management systems, the solutions and policies suggested are aimed at directly influencing human behaviour. However, it is very uncommon that organizations assess how effective such methods really are. Psychologists have devoted much thought to how human behaviour can best be influenced. In this respect, the following six ways of exercising control over human error will be set forth, and an evaluation will be performed of the relative effectiveness of these methods in controlling human behaviour on a long-term basis (Wagenaar 1992). (See table 57.3.)

Do not attempt to induce safe behaviour, but make the system "foolproof"

The first option is to do nothing to influence the behaviour of people but to design the workplace in such a way that whatever the employee does, it will not result in any kind of undesirable outcome. It must be acknowledged that, thanks to the influence of robotics and ergonomics, designers have considerably improved on the user-friendliness of workplace equipment. However, it is almost impossible to anticipate all the different kinds of behaviour that people may evince. Besides, workers often regard so-called foolproof designs as a challenge to "beat the system". Finally, as designers are human themselves, even very carefully foolproof-designed equipment can have flaws (e.g., Petroski 1992). The additional benefit of this approach relative to existing hazard levels is marginal, and in any event initial design and installation costs may increase exponentially.

Tell those involved what to do

Another option is to instruct all workers about every single activity in order to bring their behaviour fully under the control of management. This will require an extensive and not very practical task inventory and instruction control system. As all behaviour is de-automated it will to a large extent eliminate slips and lapses until the instructions become part of the routine and the effect fades away.

It does not help very much to tell people that what they do is dangerous—most people know that very well—because they will make their own choices concerning risk regardless of attempts to

Table 57.3 • Six ways to induce safe behaviour and assessment of their cost-effectiveness.

No.	Way of influencing	Cost	Long-term effect	Assessment
1	Don't induce safe behaviour, but make the system "foolproof".	High	Low	Poor
2	Tell those involved what to do.	Low	Low	Medium
3	Reward and punish.	Medium	Medium	Medium
4	Increase motivation and awareness.	Medium	Low	Poor
5	Select trained personnel.	High	Medium	Medium
6	Change the environment.	High	High	Good

Figure 57.3 • A safety information system.

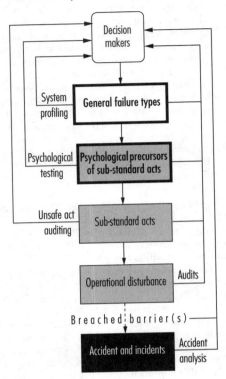

Source: Adapted from Reason et al. 1989.

persuade them otherwise. Their motivation to do so will be to make their work easier, to save time, to challenge authority and perhaps to enhance their own career prospects or claim some financial reward. Instructing people is relatively cheap, and most organizations have instruction sessions before the start of a job. But beyond such an instruction system the effectiveness of this approach is assessed to be low.

Reward and punish

Although reward and punishment schedules are powerful and very popular means for controlling human behaviour, they are not without problems. Reward works best only if the recipient perceives the reward to be of value at the time of receipt. Punishing behaviour that is beyond an employee's control (a slip) will not be effective. For example, it is more cost-effective to improve traffic safety by changing the conditions underlying traffic behaviour than by public campaigns or punishment and reward programmes. Even an increase in the chances of being "caught" will not necessarily change a person's behaviour, as the opportunities for violating a rule are still there, as is the challenge of successful violation. If the situations in which people work invite this kind of violation, people will automatically choose the undesired behaviour no matter how they are punished or rewarded. The effectiveness of this approach is rated as of medium quality, as it usually is of short-term effectiveness.

Increase motivation and awareness

Sometimes it is believed that people cause accidents because they lack motivation or are unaware of danger. This assumption is false, as studies have shown (e.g., Wagenaar and Groeneweg 1987). Furthermore, even if workers are capable of judging danger accurately, they do not necessarily act accordingly (Kruysse

1993). Accidents happen even to people with the best motivation and the highest degree of safety awareness. There are effective methods for improving motivation and awareness which are discussed below under "Change the environment". This option is a delicate one: in contrast with the difficulty to further motivate people it is almost too easy to de-motivate employees to the extent that even sabotage is considered.

The effects of motivation enhancement programmes are positive only when coupled with behaviour modification techniques such as employee involvement.

Select trained personnel

The first reaction to an accident is often that those involved must have been incompetent. With hindsight, the accident scenarios appear straightforward and easily preventable to someone sufficiently intelligent and properly trained, but this appearance is a deceptive one: in actual fact the employees involved could not possibly have foreseen the accident. Therefore, better training and selection will not have the desirable effect. A base level of training is however a prerequisite for safe operations. The tendency in some industries to replace experienced personnel with inexperienced and inadequately trained people is to be discouraged, as increasingly complex situations call for rule- and knowledge-based thinking that requires a level of experience that such lower-cost personnel often do not possess.

A negative side-effect of instructing people very well and selecting only the highest-classified people is that behaviour can become automatic and slips occur. Selection is expensive, while the effect is not more than medium.

Change the environment

Most behaviour occurs as a reaction to factors in the working environment: work schedules, plans, and management expectations and demands. A change in the environment results in different behaviour. Before the working environment can be effectively changed, several problems must be solved. First, the environmental factors that cause the unwanted behaviour must be identified. Second, these factors must be controlled. Third, management must allow discussion about their role in creating the adverse working environment.

It is more practical to influence behaviour through creating the proper working environment. The problems that should be solved before this solution can be put into practice are (1) that it must be known which environmental factors cause the unwanted behaviour, (2) that these factors must be controlled and (3) that previous management decisions must be considered (Wagenaar 1992; Groeneweg 1996). All these conditions can indeed be met, as will be argued in the remainder of this article. The effectiveness of behaviour modification can be high, even though a change of environment may be quite costly.

The Accident Causation Model

In order to get more insight into the controllable parts of the accident causation process, an understanding of the possible feedback loops in a safety information system is necessary. In figure 57.3, the complete structure of a safety information system is presented that can form the basis of managerial control of human error. It is an adapted version of the system presented by Reason et al. (1989).

Accident investigation

When accidents are investigated, substantial reports are produced and decision-makers receive information about the human error component of the accident. Fortunately, this is becoming more and more obsolete in many companies. It is more effective to analyse the "operational disturbances" that precede the accidents

Table 57.4 • General failure types and their definitions.

General failures	Definitions
1. Design (DE)	Failures due to poor design of a whole plant as well as individual items of equipment
2. Hardware (HW)	Failures due to poor state or unavailability of equipment and tools
3. Procedures (PR)	Failures due to poor quality of the operating procedures with respect to utility, availability and comprehensiveness
4. Error enforcing conditions (EC)	Failures due to poor quality of the working environment, with respect to circumstances that increase the probability of mistakes
5. Housekeeping (HK)	Failures due to poor housekeeping
6. Training (TR)	Failures due to inadequate training or insufficient experience
7. Incompatible goals (IG)	Failures due to the poor way safety and internal welfare are defended against a variety of other goals like time pressure and a limited budget
8. Communication (CO)	Failures due to poor quality or absence of lines of communication between the various divisions, departments or employees
9. Organization (OR)	Failures due to the way the project is managed and the company is operated
10. Maintenance management (MM)	Failures due to poor quality of the maintenance procedures regarding quality, utility, availability and comprehensiveness
11. Defences (DF)	Failures due to the poor quality of the protection against hazardous situations

and incidents. If an accident is described as an operational disturbance followed by its consequences, then sliding from the road is an operational disturbance and getting killed because the driver did not wear a safety belt is an accident. Barriers may have been placed between the operational disturbance and the accident, but they failed or were breached or circumvented.

Unsafe act auditing

A wrong act committed by an employee is called a "substandard act" and not an "unsafe act" in this article: the notion of "unsafe" seems to limit the applicability of the term to safety, whereas it can also be applied, for example, to environmental problems. Substandard acts are sometimes recorded, but detailed information as to which slips, mistakes and violations were performed and why they were performed is hardly ever fed back to higher management levels.

Investigating the employee's state of mind

Before a substandard act is committed, the person involved was in a certain state of mind. If these psychological precursors, like being in a state of haste or feeling sad, could be adequately controlled, people would not find themselves in a state of mind in which they would commit a substandard act. Since these states of mind cannot be effectively controlled, such precursors are regarded as "black box" material (figure 57.3).

General failure types

The GFT (general failure type) box in figure 57.3 represents the generating mechanisms of an accident—the causes of substandard

acts and situations. Because these substandard acts cannot be controlled directly, it is necessary to change the working environment. The working environment is determined by 11 such mechanisms (table 57.4). (In the Netherlands the abbreviation GFT already exists in a completely different context, and has to do with ecologically sound waste disposal, and to avoid confusion another term is used: *basic risk factors* (BRFs) (Roggeveen 1994).)

The GFT box is preceded by a "decision-maker's" box, as these people determine to a large extent how well a GFT is managed. It is management's task to control the working environment by managing the 11 GFTs, thereby indirectly controlling the occurrence of human error.

All these GFTs can contribute to accidents in subtle ways by allowing undesirable combinations of situations and actions to come together, by increasing the chance that certain persons will commit substandard acts and by failing to provide the means to interrupt accident sequences already in progress.

There are two GFTs that require some further explanation: maintenance management and defences.

Maintenance management (MM)

Since maintenance management is a combination of factors that can be found in other GFTs, it is not, strictly speaking, a separate GFT: this type of management is not fundamentally different from other management functions. It may be treated as a separate issue because maintenance plays an important role in so many accident scenarios and because most organizations have a separate maintenance function.

Defences (DF)

The category of defences is also not a true GFT, as it is not related to the accident causation process itself. This GFT is related to what happens *after* an operational disturbance. It does not generate either psychological states of mind or substandard acts by itself. It is a reaction that follows a failure due to the action of one or more GFTs. While it is indeed true that a safety management system should focus on the controllable parts of the accident causation chain *before* and not *after* the unwanted incident, nevertheless the notion of defences can be used to describe the perceived effectiveness of safety barriers after a disturbance has occurred and to show how they failed to prevent the actual accident.

Managers need a structure that will enable them to relate identified problems to preventive actions. Measures taken at the levels of safety barriers or substandard acts are still necessary, although these measures can never be completely successful. To trust "last line" barriers is to trust factors that are to a large extent out of management control. Management should not attempt to manage such uncontrollable external devices, but instead must try to make their organizations inherently safer at every level.

Measuring the Level of Control over Human Error

Ascertaining the presence of the GFTs in an organization will enable accident investigators to identify the weak and strong points in the organization. Given such knowledge, one can analyse accidents and eliminate or mitigate their causes and identify the structural weaknesses within a company and fix them before they in fact contribute to an accident.

Accident investigation

The task of an accident analyst is to identify contributing factors and to categorize them. The number of times a contributing factor is identified and categorized in terms of a GFT indicates the extent to which this GFT is present. This is often done by means of a checklist or computer analysis program.

Figure 57.4 • Profile of an accident type.

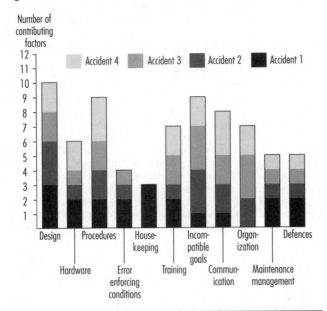

It is possible and desirable to combine profiles from different but similar types of accidents. Conclusions based upon an accumulation of accident investigations in a relatively short time are far more reliable than those drawn from a study in which the accident profile is based upon a single event. An example of such a combined profile is presented in figure 57.4, which shows data relating to four occurrences of one type of accident.

Some of the GFTs—design, procedures and incompatible goals—score consistently high in all four particular accidents. This means that in each accident, factors have been identified that were related to these GFTs. With respect to the profile of accident 1, design is a problem. Housekeeping, although a major problem area in accident 1, is only a minor problem if more than the first accident is analysed. It is suggested that about ten similar types of accidents be investigated and combined in a profile before far-reaching and possibly expensive corrective measures are taken. This way, the identification of the contributing factors and subsequent categorization of these factors can be done in a very reliable way (Van der Schrier, Groeneweg and van Amerongen 1994).

Identifying the GFTs within an organization pro-actively

It is possible to quantify the presence of GFTs pro-actively, regardless of the occurrence of accidents or incidents. This is done by looking for indicators of the presence of that GFT. The indicator used for this purpose is the answer to a straightforward yes or no question. If answered in the undesired way, it is an indication that something is not functioning properly. An example of an indicator question is: "In the past three months, did you go to a meeting that turned out to be cancelled?" If the employee answers the question in the affirmative, it does not necessarily signify danger, but it is indicative of a deficiency in one of the GFTs—communication. However, if enough questions that test for a given GFT are answered in a way that indicates an undesirable trend, it is a signal to management that it does not have sufficient control of that GFT.

To construct a system safety profile (SSP), 20 questions for each of the 11 GFTs have to be answered. Each GFT is assigned a

score ranging from 0 (low level of control) to 100 (high level of control). The score is calculated relative to the industry average in a certain geographical area. An example of this scoring procedure is presented in the box.

The indicators are pseudo-randomly drawn from a database with a few hundred questions. No two subsequent checklists have questions in common, and questions are drawn in such a way that each aspect of the GFT is covered. Failing hardware could, for instance, be the result of either absent equipment or defective equipment. Both aspects should be covered in the checklist. The answering distributions of all questions are known, and checklists are balanced for equal difficulty.

It is possible to compare scores obtained with different checklists, as well as those obtained for different organizations or departments or the same units over a period of time. Extensive validation tests have been done to ensure that all questions in the database have validity and that they are all indicative of the GFT to be measured. Higher scores indicate a higher level of control—that is, more questions have been answered in the "desired" way. A score of 70 indicates that this organization is ranked among the best 30% (i.e., 100 minus 70) of comparable organizations in this kind of industry. Although a score of 100 does not necessarily mean that this organization has total control over a GFT, it does means that with regard to this GFT the organization is the best in the industry.

An example of an SSP is shown in figure 57.5. The weak areas of Organization 1, as exemplified by the bars in the chart, are procedures, incompatible goals, and error enforcing conditions, as they score below the industry average as shown by the dark grey area. The scores on housekeeping, hardware and defences are very good in Organization 1. On the surface, this well-equipped and tidy organization with all safety devices in place appears to be a safe place to work. Organization 2 scores exactly at the industry average. There are no major deficiencies, and although the scores

Figure 57.5 • Example of a system safety profile.

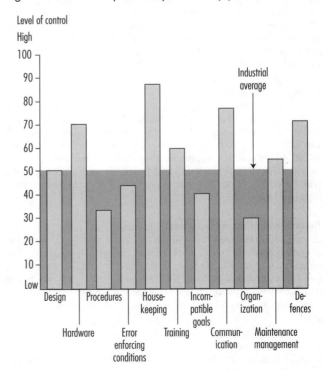

An indication of the level of control your organization has over the GFT "Communication"

In this box a list of 20 questions is presented. The questions in this list have been answered by employees of more than 250 organizations in Western Europe. These organizations were operating in different fields, ranging from chemical companies to refineries and construction companies. Normally, these questions would be tailor-made for each branch. This list serves as an example only to show how the tool works for one of the GFTs. Only those questions have been selected that have proved to be so "general" that they are applicable in at least 80 % of the industries.

In "real life" employees would not only have to answer the questions (anonymously), they would also have to motivate their answers. It is not sufficient to answer "Yes" on, for example, the indicator *"Did you have to work in the past 4 weeks with an outdated procedure?"* The employee would have to indicate which procedure it was and under which conditions it had to be applied. This motivation serves two goals: it increases the reliability of the answers and it provides management with information it can act upon.

Caution is also necessary when interpreting the percentile score: in a real measurement, each organization would be matched against a representative sample of branch-related organizations for each of the 11 GFTs. The distribution of percentiles is from May 1995, and this distribution does change slightly over time.

How to measure the "level of control"

Answer all 20 indicators with your own situation in mind and beware of the time limits in the questions. Some of the questions might not be applicable for your situation; answer them with "n.a." It might be impossible for you to answer some questions; answer them with a question mark "?".

After you have answered all questions, compare your answers with the reference answers. You get a point for each "correctly" answered question.

Add the number of points together. Calculate the percentage of correctly answered questions by dividing the number of points by the number of questions you have answered with either "Yes" or "No". The "n.a." and "?" answers are not taken into account. The result is a percentage between 0 and 100.

The measurement can be made more reliable by having more people answering the questions and by averaging their scores over the levels or functions in the organization or comparable departments.

Twenty questions about the GFT "Communication"

Possible answers to the questions: Y = Yes; N = No; n.a. = not applicable; ? = don't know.

1. In the past 4 weeks has the telephone directory provided you with incorrect or insufficient information?
2. In the past 2 weeks has your telephone conversation been interrupted due to a malfunctioning of the telephone system?
3. Have you received mail in the past week that was not relevant to you?
4. Has there been an internal or external audit in the past 9 months of your office paper trail?
5. Was more than 20 % of the information you received in the past 4 weeks labelled "urgent"?
6. Did you have to work in the past 4 weeks with a procedure that was difficult to read (e.g., phrasing or language problems)?
7. Have you gone to a meeting in the past 4 weeks that turned out not to be held at all?
8. Has there been a day in the past 4 weeks that you had five or more meetings?
9. Is there a "suggestion box" in your organization?
10. Have you been asked to discuss a matter in the past 3 months that later turned out to be already decided upon?
11. Have you sent any information in the past 4 weeks that was never received?
12. Have you received information in the past 6 months about changes in policies or procedures more than a month after it had been put into effect?
13. Have the minutes of the last three safety meetings been sent to your management?
14. Has "office" management stayed at least 4 hours at the location when making the last site visit?
15. Did you have to work in the past 4 weeks with procedures with conflicting information?
16. Have you received within 3 days feedback on requests for information in the past 4 weeks?
17. Do people in your organization speak different languages or dialects (different mother tongue)?
18. Was more than 80% of the feedback you received (or gave) from management in the past 6 months of a "negative nature"?
19. Are there parts of the location/workplace where it is difficult to understand each other due to extreme noise levels?
20. In the past 4 weeks, have tools and/or equipment been delivered that not had been ordered?

Reference answers:

1 = N; 2 = N; 3 = N; 4 = Y; 5 = N; 6 = N; 7 = N; 8 = N; 9 = N; 10 = N; 11 = N; 12 = N; 13 = Y; 14 = N; 15 = N; 16 = Y; 17 = N; 18 = N; 19 = Y; 20 = N.

Scoring GFT "Communication"

Percent score = $(a/b) \times 100$

where a = no. of questions answered correctly
b = no. of questions answered "Y" or "N".

Your score %	Percentile	%	Equal or better
0-10	0-1	100	99
11-20	2-6	98	94
21-30	7-14	93	86
31-40	15-22	85	78
41-50	23-50	79	50
51-60	51-69	49	31
61-70	70-85	30	15
71-80	86-97	14	3
81-90	98-99	2	1
91-100	99-100		

57. AUDITS, INSPECTIONS AND INVESTIGATIONS

on hardware, housekeeping and defences are lower, this company manages (on the average) the human error component in accidents better than Organization 1. According to the accident causation model, Organization 2 is safer than Organization 1, although this would not necessarily be apparent in comparing the organizations in "traditional" audits.

If these organizations had to decide where to allocate their limited resources, the four areas with below average GFTs would have priority. However, one cannot conclude that, since the other GFT scores are so favourable, resources may be safely withdrawn from their upkeep, since these resources are what have most probably kept them at so high a level in the first place.

Conclusions

This article has touched upon the subject of human error and accident prevention. The overview of the literature regarding control of the human error component in accidents yielded a set of six ways by which one can try to influence behaviour. Only one, restructuring the environment or modifying behaviour in order to reduce the number of situations in which people are liable to commit an error, has a reasonably favourable effect in a well-developed industrial organization where many other attempts have already been made. It will take courage on the part of management to recognize that these adverse situations exist and to mobilize the resources that are needed to effect a change in the company. The other five options do not represent helpful alternatives, as they will have little or no effect and will be quite costly.

"Controlling the controllable" is the key principle supporting the approach presented in this article. The GFTs must be discovered, attacked and eliminated. The 11 GFTs are mechanisms that have proven to be part of the accident causation process. Ten of them are aimed at preventing operational disturbances and one (defences) is aimed at the prevention of the operational disturbance's turning into an accident. Eliminating the impact of the GFTs has a direct bearing upon the abatement of contributing causes of accidents. The questions in the checklists are aimed at measuring the "health state" of a given GFT, from both a general and a safety point of view. Safety is viewed as an integrated part of normal operations: doing the job the way it should be done. This view is in accordance with the recent "quality oriented" management approaches. The availability of policies, procedures and management tools is not the chief concern of safety management: the question is rather whether these methods are actually used, understood and adhered to.

The approach described in this article concentrates upon systemic factors and the way in which management decisions can be translated into unsafe conditions at the workplace, in contrast to the conventional belief that attention should be directed towards the individual workers who perform unsafe acts, their attitudes, motivations and perceptions of risk.

● Hardware Hazards

Carsten D. Groenberg

This article addresses "machine" hazards, those which are specific to the appurtenances and hardware used in the industrial processes associated with pressure vessels, processing equipment, powerful machines and other intrinsically risky operations. This article does not address worker hazards, which implicate the actions and behaviour of individuals, such as slipping on working surfaces, falling from elevations and hazards from using ordinary tools. This article focuses on machine hazards, which are charac-

teristic of an industrial job environment. Since these hazards threaten anyone present and may even be a threat to neighbours and the external environment, the analysis methods and the means for prevention and control are similar to the methods used to deal with risks to the environment from industrial activities.

Machine Hazards

Good quality hardware is very reliable, and most failures are caused by secondary effects like fire, corrosion, misuse and so on. Nevertheless, hardware may be highlighted in certain accidents, because a failing hardware component is often the most conspicuous or visibly prominent link of the chain of events. Although the term *hardware* is used in a broad sense, illustrative examples of hardware failures and their immediate "surroundings" in accident causation have been taken from industrial workplaces. Typical candidates for investigation of "machine" hazards include but are not limited to the following:

- pressure vessels and pipes
- motors, engines, turbines and other rotating machines
- chemical and nuclear reactors
- scaffolding, bridges, etc.
- lasers and other energy radiators
- cutting and drilling machinery, etc.
- welding equipment.

Effects of Energy

Hardware hazards can include wrong use, construction errors or frequent overload, and accordingly their analysis and mitigation or prevention can follow rather different directions. However, physical and chemical energy forms that elude human control often exist at the heart of hardware hazards. Therefore, one very general method to identify hardware hazards is to look for the energies that are normally controlled with the actual piece of equipment or machinery, such as a pressure vessel containing ammonia or chlorine. Other methods use the purpose or intended function of the actual hardware as a starting point and then look for the probable effects of malfunctions and failures. For example, a bridge failing to fulfil its primary function will expose subjects on the bridge to the risk of falling down; other effects of the collapse of a bridge will be the secondary ones of falling items, either structural parts of the bridge or objects situated on the bridge. Further down the chain of consequences, there may be derived effects related to functions in other parts of the system that were dependent on the bridge performing its function properly, such as the interruption of emergency response vehicular traffic to another incident.

Besides the concepts of "controlled energy" and "intended function", dangerous substances must be addressed by asking questions such as, "How could agent X be released from vessels, tanks or pipe systems and how could agent Y be produced?" (either or both may be hazardous). Agent X might be a pressurized gas or a solvent, and agent Y might be an extremely toxic dioxin whose formation is favoured by the "right" temperatures in some chemical processes, or it could be produced by rapid oxidation, as the result of a fire. However, the possible hazards add up to much more than just the risks of dangerous substances. Conditions or influences might exist which allow the presence of a particular item of hardware to lead to harmful consequences to humans.

Industrial Work Environment

Machine hazards also involve load or stress factors that may be dangerous in the long run, such as the following:

- extreme working temperatures
- high intensities of light, noise or other stimuli

- inferior air quality
- extreme job demands or workloads.

These hazards can be recognized and precautions taken because the dangerous conditions are already there. They do not depend on some structural change in the hardware to come about and work a harmful result, or on some special event to effect damage or injury. Long-term hazards also have specific sources in the working environment, but they must be identified and evaluated through observing workers and the jobs, instead of just analysing hardware construction and functions.

Dangerous hardware or machine hazards are usually exceptional and rather seldom found in a sound working environment, but cannot be avoided completely. Several types of uncontrolled energy, such as the following risk agents, can be the immediate consequence of hardware malfunction:

- harmful releases of dangerous gas, liquids, dusts or other substances
- fire and explosion
- high voltages
- falling objects, missiles, etc.
- electric and magnetic fields
- cutting, trapping, etc.
- displacement of oxygen
- nuclear radiation, x rays and laser light
- flooding or drowning
- jets of hot liquid or steam.

Risk Agents

Moving objects. Falling and flying objects, liquid flows and jets of liquid or steam, such as listed, are often the first external consequences of hardware or equipment failure, and they account for a large proportion of accidents.

Chemical substances. Chemical hazards also contribute to worker accidents as well as affecting the environment and the public. The Seveso and Bhopal accidents involved chemical releases which affected numerous members of the public, and many industrial fires and explosions release chemicals and fumes to the atmosphere. Traffic accidents involving gasoline or chemical delivery trucks or other dangerous goods transports, unite two risk agents—moving objects and chemical substances.

Electromagnetic energy. Electric and magnetic fields, x rays and gamma rays are all manifestations of electromagnetism, but are often treated separately as they are encountered under rather different circumstances. However, the dangers of electromagnetism have some general traits: fields and radiation penetrate human bodies instead of just making contact on the application area, and they cannot be sensed directly, although very large intensities cause heating of the affected body parts. Magnetic fields are created by the flow of electric current, and intense magnetic fields are to be found in the vicinity of large electric motors, electric arc welding equipment, electrolysis apparatus, metal works and so forth. Electric fields accompany electric tension, and even the ordinary mains voltages of 200 to 300 volts cause the accumulation of dirt over several years, the visible sign of the field's existence, an effect also known in connection with high-tension electrical lines, TV picture tubes, computer monitors and so on.

Electromagnetic fields are mostly found rather close to their sources, but electromagnetic *radiation* is a long-distance traveller, as radar and radio waves exemplify. Electromagnetic radiation is scattered, reflected and damped as it passes through space and meets intervening objects, surfaces, different substances and atmospheres, and the like; its intensity is therefore reduced in several ways.

The general character of the electromagnetic (EM) hazard sources are:

- Instruments are needed to detect the presence of EM fields or EM radiation.
- EM does not leave primary traces in the form of "contamination".
- Dangerous effects are usually delayed or long-term, but immediate burns are caused in severe cases.
- X rays and gamma rays are damped, but not stopped, by lead and other heavy elements.
- Magnetic fields and x rays are stopped immediately when the source is de-energized or the equipment turned off.
- Electric fields can survive for long periods after turning the generating systems off.
- Gamma rays come from nuclear processes, and these radiation sources cannot be turned off as can many EM sources.

Nuclear radiation. The hazards associated with nuclear radiation are of special concern to workers in nuclear power plants and in plants working with nuclear materials such as fuel manufacturing and the reprocessing, transport and storage of radioactive matter. Nuclear radiation sources are also used in medicine and by some industries for measurement and control. One most common usage is in fire alarms/smoke detectors, which use an alpha-particle emitter like americium to monitor the atmosphere.

Nuclear hazards are principally centred around five factors:

- gamma rays
- neutrons
- beta particles (electrons)
- alpha particles (helium nuclei)
- contamination.

The hazards arise from the *radioactive* processes in nuclear fission and the decaying of radioactive materials. This sort of radiation is emitted from reactor processes, reactor fuel, reactor moderator material, from the gaseous fission products that may be developed, and from certain construction materials that become activated by exposure to radioactive emissions arising from reactor operation.

Other risk agents. Other classes of risk agents that release or emit energy include:

- UV radiance and laser light
- infrasound
- high-intensity sound
- vibration.

Triggering the Hardware Hazards

Both *sudden* and *gradual* shifts from the controlled—or "safe"—condition to one with increased danger can come about through the following circumstances, which can be controlled through appropriate organizational means such as user experience, education, skills, surveillance and equipment testing:

- wear and overloads
- external impact (fire or impact)
- ageing and failure
- wrong supply (energy, raw materials)
- insufficient maintenance and repair
- control or process error
- misuse or misapplication
- hardware breakdown
- barrier malfunction.

Since proper operations cannot reliably compensate for improper design and installation, it is important to consider the entire process, from selection and design through installation, use, maintenance and testing, in order to evaluate the actual state and conditions of the hardware item.

Hazard Case: The Pressurized Gas Tank

Gas can be contained in suitable vessels for storage or transport, like the gas and oxygen cylinders used by welders. Often, gas is handled at high pressure, affording a great increase in the storing capacity, but with higher accident risk. The key accidental phenomenon in pressurized gas storage is the sudden creation of a hole in the tank, with these results:

- the confinement function of the tank ceases
- the confined gas gets immediate access to the surrounding atmosphere.

The development of such an accident depends on these factors:

- the type and amount of gas in the tank
- the situation of the hole in relation to the tank's contents
- the initial size and subsequent growth rate of the hole
- the temperature and pressure of the gas and the equipment
- the conditions in the immediate environment (sources of ignition, people, etc.).

The tank contents can be released almost immediately or over a period of time, and result in different scenarios, from the burst of free gas from a ruptured tank, to moderate and rather slow releases from small punctures.

The behaviour of various gases in the case of leakage

When developing release calculation models, it is most important to determine the following conditions affecting the system's potential behaviour:

- the gas phase behind the hole (gaseous or liquid?)
- temperature and wind conditions
- the possible entry of other substances into the system or their possible presence in its surroundings
- barriers and other obstacles.

The exact calculations pertaining to a release process where liquefied gas escapes from a hole as a jet and then evaporates (or alternatively, first becomes a mist of droplets) are difficult. The specification of the later dispersion of the resultant clouds is also a difficult problem. Consideration must be given to the movements and dispersion of gas releases, whether the gas forms visible or invisible clouds and whether the gas rises or stays at ground level.

While hydrogen is a light gas compared to any atmosphere, ammonia gas (NH_3, with a molecular weight of 17.0) will rise in an ordinary air-like, oxygen-nitrogen atmosphere at the same temperature and pressure. Chlorine (Cl_2, with a molecular weight of 70.9) and butane (C_4H_{10}, mol. wt.58) are examples of chemicals whose gas phases are denser than air, even at ambient temperature. Acetylene (C_2H_2, mol. wt. 26.0) has a density of about 0.90g/l, approaching that of air (1.0g/l), which means that in a working environment, leaking welding gas will not have a pronounced tendency to float upwards or to sink downwards; therefore it can mix easily with the atmosphere.

But ammonia released from a pressure vessel as a liquid will at first cool as a consequence of its evaporation, and may then escape via several steps:

- Pressurized, liquid ammonia emanates from the hole in tank as jet or cloud.
- Seas of liquid ammonia can be formed on the nearest surfaces.
- The ammonia evaporates, thereby cooling itself and the near environment.
- Ammonia gas gradually exchanges heat with surroundings and equilibrates with ambient temperatures.

Even a cloud of light gas may not rise immediately from a liquid gas release; it may first form a fog—a cloud of droplets—and stay near the ground. The gas cloud's movement and gradual mixing/dilution with the surrounding atmosphere depends on weather parameters and on the surrounding environment—enclosed area, open area, houses, traffic, presence of the public, workers and so on.

Tank Failure

Consequences of tank breakdown may involve fire and explosion, asphyxiation, poisoning and choking, as experience shows with gas production and gas handling systems (propane, methane, nitrogen, hydrogen, etc.), with ammonia or chlorine tanks, and with gas welding (using acetylene and oxygen). What actually initiates the formation of a hole in a tank has a strong influence on the hole "behaviour"—which in its turn influences the outflow of gas—and is crucial for the effectiveness of prevention efforts. A pressure vessel is designed and built to withstand certain conditions of use and environmental impact, and for handling a certain gas, or perhaps a choice of gases. The actual capabilities of a tank depend on its shape, materials, welding, protection, use and climate; therefore, evaluation of its adequacy as a container for dangerous gas must consider designer's specifications, the tank's history, inspections and tests. Critical areas include the welding seams used on most pressure vessels; the points where appurtenances such as inlets, outlets, supports and instruments are connected to the vessel; the flat ends of cylindrical tanks like railway tanks; and other aspects of even less optimal geometric shapes. Welding seams are investigated visually, by x rays or by destructive test of samples, as these may reveal local defects, say, in the form of reduced strength that might endanger the overall strength of the vessel, or even be a triggering point for acute tank failure.

Tank strength is affected by the history of tank use—first of all by the normal wearing processes and the scratches and corrosion attacks typical of the particular industry and of the application. Other historical parameters of particular interest include:

- casual overpressure
- extreme heating or cooling (internal or external)
- mechanical impacts
- vibrations and stress
- substances that have been stored in or have passed through the tank
- substances used during cleansing, maintenance and repair.

The construction material—steel plate, aluminium plate, concrete for non-pressurized applications, and so on—can undergo deterioration from these influences in ways that are not always possible to check without overloading or destroying the equipment during testing.

Accident Case: Flixborough

The explosion of a large cloud of cyclohexane in Flixborough (UK) in 1974, which killed 28 persons and caused extensive plant damage, serves as a very instructive case. The triggering event was the breakdown of a temporary pipe serving as a substitute in a reactor unit. The accident was "caused" by a piece of hardware breaking down, but on closer investigation it was revealed that the breakdown followed from overload, and that the temporary construction was in fact inadequate for its intended use. After two months' service, the pipe was exposed to bending forces due to a slight pressure rise of the 10-bar (10^6 Pa) cyclohexane content at about 150 °C. The two bellows between the pipe and the nearby reactors broke and 30 to 50 tonnes of cyclohexane was released and soon ignited, probably by a furnace some distance from the

Figure 57.6 • Temporary connection between tanks at Flixborough.

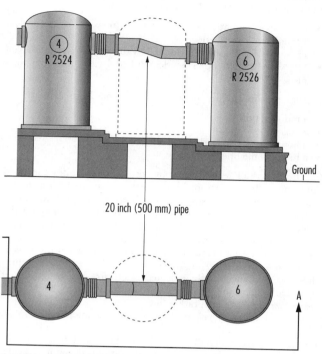

20 inch (500 mm) pipe

Source: Advisory Committee on Major Hazards 1984.

leak. (See figure 57.6.) A very readable account of the case is found in Kletz (1988).

Hazard Analysis

The methods that have been developed to find the risks that may be relevant to a piece of equipment, to a chemical process or to a certain operation are referred to as "hazard analysis". These methods ask questions such as: "What may possibly go wrong?" "Could it be serious?" and "What can be done about it?" Different methods of conducting the analyses are often combined to achieve a reasonable coverage, but no such set can do more than guide or assist a clever team of analysts in their determinations. The main difficulties with hazard analysis are as follows:

- availability of relevant data
- limitations of models and calculations
- new and unfamiliar materials, constructions and processes
- system complexity
- limitations on human imagination
- limitations on practical tests.

To produce usable risk evaluations under these circumstances it is important to stringently define the scope and the level of "ambitiousness" appropriate to the analysis at hand; for example, it is clear that one does not need the same sort of information for insurance purposes as for design purposes, or for the planning of protection schemes and the construction of emergency arrangements. Generally speaking, the risk picture must be filled in by mixing empirical techniques (i.e., statistics) with deductive reasoning and a creative imagination.

Different risk evaluation tools—even computer programs for risk analysis—can be very helpful. The hazard and operability study (HAZOP) and the failure mode and effect analysis (FMEA)

are commonly used methods for investigating hazards, especially in the chemical industry. The point of departure for the HAZOP method is the tracing of possible risk scenarios based on a set of guide words; for each scenario one has to identify probable causes and consequences. In the second stage, one tries to find means for reducing the probabilities or mitigating the consequences of those scenarios judged to be unacceptable. A review of the HAZOP method can be found in Charsley (1995). The FMEA method asks a series of "what if" questions for every possible risk component in order to thoroughly determine whatever failure modes may exist and then to identify the effects that they may have on system performance; such an analysis will be illustrated in the demonstration example (for a gas system) presented later in this article.

Fault trees and event trees and the modes of logical analysis proper to accident causation structures and probability reasoning are in no way specific to the analysis of hardware hazards, as they are general tools for system risk evaluations.

Tracing hardware hazards in an industrial plant

To identify possible hazards, information on construction and function can be sought from:

- actual equipment and plant
- substitutes and models
- drawings, electrical diagrams, piping and instrumentation (P/I) diagrams, etc.
- process descriptions
- control schemes
- operation modes and phases
- work orders, change orders, maintenance reports, etc.

By selecting and digesting such information, analysts form a picture of the risk object itself, its functions and its actual use. Where things are not yet constructed—or unavailable for inspection—important observations cannot be made and the evaluation must be based entirely on descriptions, intentions and plans. Such evaluation might seem rather poor, but in fact, most practical risk evaluations are made this way, either in order to seek authoritative approval for applications to undertake new construction, or to compare the relative safety of alternative design solutions. Real life processes will be consulted for the information not shown on the formal diagrams or described verbally by interview, and to verify that the information gathered from these sources is factual and represents actual conditions. These include the following:

- actual practice and culture
- additional failure mechanisms/construction details
- "sneak paths" (see below)
- common error causes
- risks from external sources/missiles
- particular exposures or consequences
- past incidents, accidents and near accidents.

Most of this additional information, especially sneak paths, is detectable only by creative, skilled observers with considerable experience, and some of the information would be almost impossible to trace with maps and diagrams. *Sneak paths* denote unintended and unforeseen interactions between systems, where the operation of one system affects the condition or operation of another system through other ways than the functional ones. This typically happens where functionally different parts are situated near each other, or (for example) a leaking substance drips on equipment beneath and causes a failure. Another mode of a sneak path's action may involve the introduction of wrong substances or parts into a system by means of instruments or tools during operation or maintenance: the intended structures and their intended functions are changed through the sneak paths. By

57. AUDITS, INSPECTIONS AND INVESTIGATIONS

Figure 57.7 • Transmission line for delivery of liquid gas from ship to storage tank.

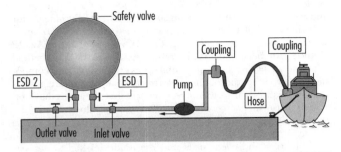

common-mode failures one means that certain conditions—like flooding, lightning or power failure—can disturb several systems at once, perhaps leading to unexpectedly large blackouts or accidents. Generally, one tries to avoid sneak-path effects and common-mode failures through proper layouts and introducing distance, insulation and diversity in working operations.

A Hazards Analysis Case: Gas Delivery from a Ship to a Tank

Figure 57.7 shows a system for delivery of gas from a transport ship to a storage tank. A leak could appear anywhere in this system: ship, transmission line, tank or output line; given the two tank reservoirs, a leak somewhere on the line could remain active for hours.

The most critical components of the system are the following:

- the storage tank
- the pipeline or hose between the tank and the ship
- other hoses, lines, valves and connections
- the safety valve on the storage tank
- the emergency shut-down valves ESD 1 and 2.

A storage tank with a large inventory of liquid gas is put at the top of this list, because it is difficult to stop a leak from a tank on short notice. The second item on the list—the connection to the ship—is critical because leaks in the pipe or hose and loose connections or couplings with worn gaskets, and variations among different ships, could release product. Flexible parts like hoses and bellows are more critical than rigid parts, and require regular maintenance and inspection. Safety devices like the pressure release valve on the top of the tank and the two emergency shut-down valves are critical, since they must be relied upon to reveal latent or developing failures.

Up to this point, the ranking of system components as to their importance with respect to reliability has been of a general nature only. Now, for analytical purposes, attention will be drawn to the particular functions of the system, the chief one of course being the movement of liquefied gas from the ship to the storage tank until the connected ship tank is empty. The overriding hazard is a gas leak, the possible contributory mechanisms being one or more of the following:

- leaking couplings or valves
- tank rupture
- rupture of pipe or hose
- tank breakdown.

Application of the FMEA method

The central idea of the FMEA approach, or "what if" analysis, is to record explicitly, for each component of the system, its failure modes, and for every failure to find the possible consequences to the system and to the environment. For standard components like a tank, pipe, valve, pump, flowmeter and so on, the failure modes follow general patterns. In the case of a valve, for instance, failure modes could include the following conditions:

- The valve cannot close on demand (there is reduced flow through an "open" valve).
- The valve leaks (there is residual flow through a "closed" valve).
- The valve cannot open on demand (the valve position oscillates).

For a pipeline, failure modes would consider items such as:

- a reduced flow
- a leak
- a flow stopped due to blockage
- a break in the line.

The effects of leaks seem obvious, but sometimes the most important effects may not be the first effects: what happens for example, if a valve is stuck in a half-open position? An on-off valve in the delivery line that does not open completely on demand will delay the tank filling process, a non-dangerous consequence. But if the "stuck half-open" condition arises at the same time that a closing demand is made, at a time when the tank is almost full, overfilling might result (unless the emergency shut-down valve is successfully activated). In a properly designed and operated system, the probability of both these valves being stuck *simultaneously* will be kept rather low.

Plainly a safety valve's not operating on demand could mean disaster; in fact, one might justifiably state that latent failures are constantly threatening all safety devices. Pressure relief valves, for instance, can be defective due to corrosion, dirt or paint (typically due to bad maintenance), and in the case of liquid gas, such defects in combination with the temperature decrease at a gas leak could produce ice and thereby reduce or perhaps stop the flow of material through a safety valve. If a pressure relief valve does not operate on demand, pressure may build up in a tank or in connected systems of tanks, eventually causing other leaks or tank rupture.

For simplicity, instruments are not shown on figure 57.7; there will of course be instruments related to pressure, flow and temperature, which are essential parameters for monitoring the system state, relevant signals being transmitted to operator consoles or to a control room for control and monitoring purposes. Furthermore, there will be supply lines other than those intended for materials transport—for electricity, hydraulics and so forth—and extra safety devices. A comprehensive analysis must go through these systems as well and look for the failure modes and effects of these components also. In particular, the detective work on common-mode effects and sneak paths requires one to construct the integral picture of main system components, controls, instruments, supplies, operators, working schedules, maintenance and so on.

Examples of common-mode effects to consider in connection with gas systems are addressed by such questions as these:

- Are activation signals for delivery valves and emergency shut-down valves transmitted on a common line (cable, cabling channels)?
- Do two given valves share the same power line?
- Is maintenance performed by the same person according to a given schedule?

Even an excellently designed system with redundancy and independent power lines can suffer from inferior maintenance, where, for example, a valve and its back-up valve (the emergency shut-down valve in our case) have been left in a wrong state after a test. A prominent common-mode effect with an ammonia-handling system is the leak situation itself: a moderate leak can make all manual operations on plant components rather awkward—and delayed—due to the deployment of the required emergency protection.

Summary

The hardware components are very seldom the guilty parts in accident development; rather, there are *root causes* to be found in other links of the chain: wrong concepts, bad designs, maintenance errors, operator errors, management errors and so on. Several examples of the specific conditions and acts that may lead to failure development have already been given; a broad collection of such agents would take account of the following:

- collision
- corrosion, etching
- excessive loads
- failing support and aged or worn-out parts
- low-quality welding jobs
- missiles
- missing parts
- overheating or chilling
- vibration
- wrong construction material used.

Controlling the hardware hazards in a working environment requires the review of all possible causes and respect for the conditions that are found to be critical with the actual systems. The implications of this for the organization of risk management programmes are dealt with in other articles, but, as the foregoing list clearly indicates, the monitoring and control of hardware conditions can be necessary all the way back to the choice of concepts and designs for the selected systems and processes.

HAZARD ANALYSIS: ORGANIZATIONAL FACTORS—MORT

Urban Kjellén

Through industrialization, workers became organized in factories as the utilization of energy sources such as the steam engine became possible. As compared to traditional handicraft, mechanized production, with sources of higher energy at its disposal, presented new risks of accidents. As the amount of energy increased, workers were removed from the direct control of these energies. Decisions that affected safety were often made at the management level rather than by those directly exposed to these risks. At this stage of industrialization, the need for safety management became evident.

In the late 1920s, Heinrich formulated the first comprehensive theoretical framework for safety management, which was that safety should be sought through management decisions based on identification and analysis of accident causes. At this point in the development of safety management, accidents were attributed to failures at the worker-machine system level—that is, to unsafe acts and unsafe conditions.

Subsequently, various methodologies were developed for the identification and assessment of accident risks. With MORT (Management Oversight and Risk Tree), the focus shifted to the higher orders of control of accident risks—that is, to the control of conditions at the management level. The initiative to develop MORT was taken in the late 1960s by the US Energy Research and Development Administration, which wanted to improve their safety programmes in order to reduce their losses due to accidents.

The MORT Diagram and Underlying Principles

The intent of MORT was to formulate an ideal safety management system based on a synthesis of the best safety programme elements and safety management techniques then available. As the principles underlying the MORT initiative were applied to the contemporary state of the art in safety management, the largely unstructured safety literature and expertise took on the form of an analytical tree. The first version of the tree was published in 1971. Figure 57.8 shows the basic elements of the version of the tree that was published by Johnson in 1980. The tree also appears in a modified form in later publications on the subject of the MORT concept (see, for example, Knox and Eicher 1992).

The MORT Diagram

MORT is used as a practical tool in accident investigations and in evaluations of existing safety programmes. The top event of the tree in figure 57.8 (Johnson 1980) represents the losses (experienced or potential) due to an accident. Below this top event are three main branches: specific oversights and omissions (S), management oversights and omissions (M) and assumed risks (R). The *R-branch* consists of assumed risks, which are events and conditions that are known to management and that have been evaluated and accepted at the proper management level. Other events and conditions that are revealed through the evaluations following the S- and M-branches are denoted "less than adequate" (LTA).

The *S-branch* focuses on the events and conditions of the actual or potential occurrence. (In general, time is shown as one reads from left to right, and the sequence of causes is shown as one reads from bottom to top.) Haddon's strategies (1980) for the prevention of accidents are key elements in this branch. An event is denoted an accident when a target (a person or object) is exposed to an uncontrolled transfer of energy and sustains damage. In the S-branch of MORT, accidents are prevented through barriers. There are three basic types of barriers: (1) barriers that surround and confine the energy source (the hazard), (2) barriers that protect the target and (3) barriers that separate the hazard and the target physically or in time or space. These different types of barriers are found in the development of the branches below the accidental event. Amelioration relates to the actions taken after the accident to limit the losses. At the next level of the S-branch, factors are recognized which relate to the different phases of the life cycle of an industrial system. These are the project phase (design and plan), start up (operational readiness) and operation (supervision and maintenance).

The *M-branch* supports a process in which specific findings from an accident investigation or safety programme evaluation are made more general. Events and conditions of the S-branch thus often have their counterparts in the M-branch. When engaged with the system at the M-branch, the analyst's thinking is expanded to the total management system. Thus, any recommendations will affect many other possible accident scenarios as well. The most important safety management functions can be found in the M-branch: the setting of policy, implementation and follow-up. These are the same basic elements that we find in the quality assurance principles of the ISO 9000 series published by the International Organization for Standardization (ISO).

When the branches of the MORT diagram are elaborated in detail, there are elements from such different fields as risk analysis, human factors analysis, safety information systems and organizational analysis. In total, about 1,500 basic events are covered by the MORT diagram.

Figure 57.8 • A version of the MORT analytical tree.

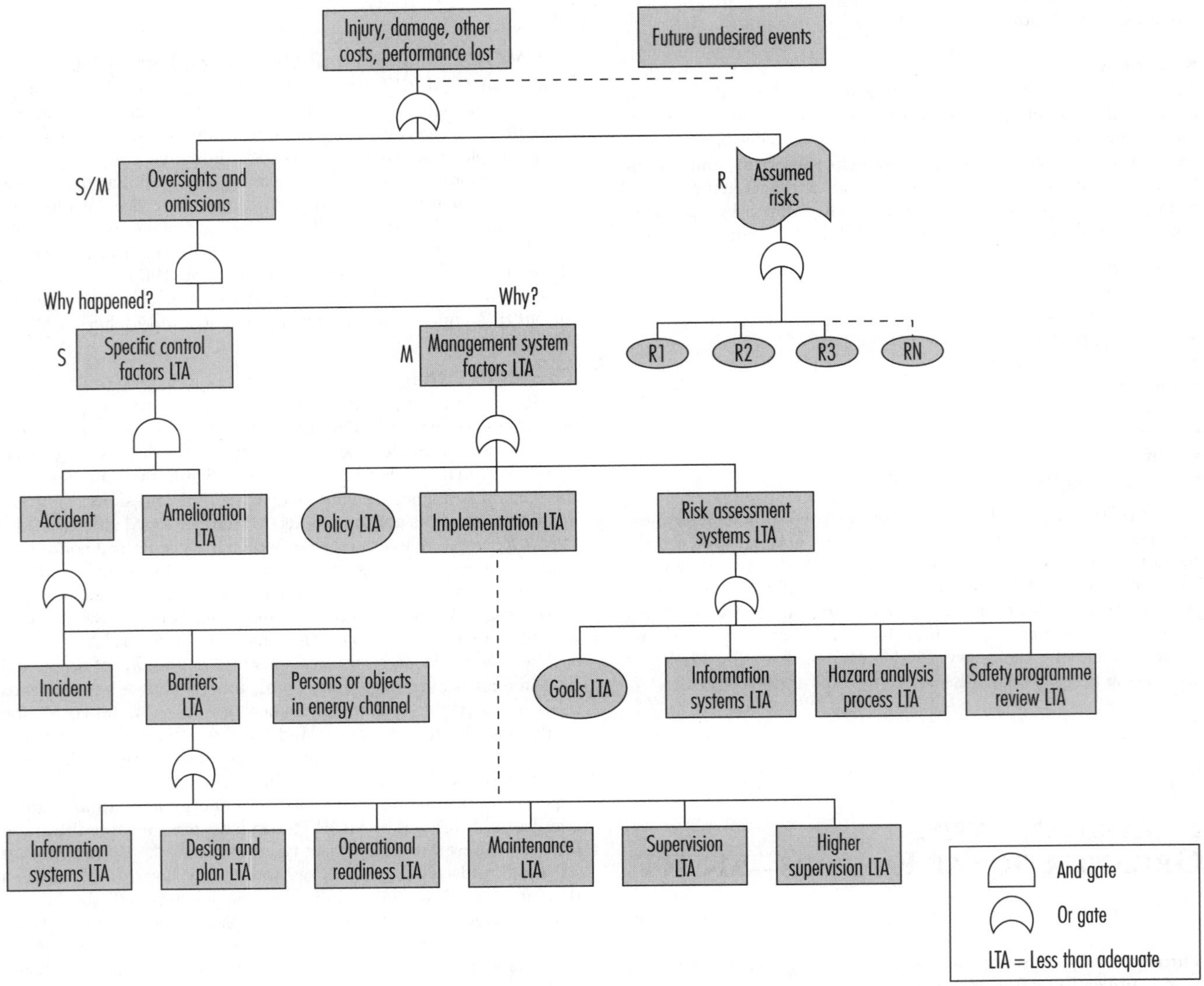

Application of the MORT Diagram

As indicated, the MORT diagram has two immediate uses (Knox and Eicher 1992): (1) to analyse management and organizational factors relative to an accident that has happened and (2) to evaluate or audit a safety programme in relation to a significant accident that has the potential of occurring. The MORT diagram functions as a screening tool in planning the analyses and evaluations. It is also used as a checklist for comparison of actual conditions with the idealized system. In this application, MORT facilitates checking the completeness of the analysis and avoiding personal biases.

At bottom, MORT is made up of a collection of questions. Criteria that guide judgements as to whether specific events and conditions are satisfactory or less than adequate are derived from these questions. In spite of the directive design of the questions, the judgements made by the analyst are partly subjective. It has thus become important to ensure an adequate quality and degree of intersubjectivity among MORT analyses made by different analysts. For example, in the United States, a training programme is available for certification of MORT analysts.

Experiences with MORT

The literature on evaluations of MORT is sparse. Johnson reports significant improvements in the comprehensiveness of accident investigations after the introduction of MORT (Johnson 1980). Deficiencies at the supervisory and management levels were revealed more systematically. Experience has also been gained from evaluations of MORT applications within Finnish industry (Ruuhilehto 1993). Some limitations have been identified in the Finnish studies. MORT does not support the identification of immediate risks due to failures and disturbances. Furthermore, no capability for setting priorities is built into the MORT concept. Consequently, the results of MORT analyses need further evaluation to translate them into remedial actions. Finally, experience shows that MORT is time-consuming and requires expert participation.

Aside from its ability to focus on organizational and management factors, MORT has the further advantage of connecting safety with normal production activities and general management. The application of MORT will thus support general planning and control, and help reduce the frequency of production disturbances as well.

Associated Safety Management Methods and Techniques

With the introduction of the MORT concept in the early 1970s, a development programme started in the United States. The focal point for this programme has been the System Safety Development Center in Idaho Falls. Different MORT-associated methods and techniques in such areas as human factors analysis, safety information systems and safety analysis have resulted from this programme. An early example of a method arising from the MORT development programme is the Operational Readiness Program (Nertney 1975). This programme is introduced during the development of new industrial systems and modifications of existing ones. The aim is to ensure that, from the safety management point of view, the new or modified system is ready at the time of start-up. A condition of operational readiness presupposes that the necessary barriers and controls have been installed in the new system's hardware, personnel and procedures. Another example of a MORT programme element is the MORT-based root cause analysis (Cornelison 1989). It is used to identify the basic safety management problems of an organization. This is done by relating the specific findings of the MORT analyses to 27 different generic safety management problems.

Although MORT is not intended for use directly in the collection of information during accident investigations and safety audits, in Scandinavia, the MORT questions have served as a basis for the development of a diagnostic tool used for this purpose. It is called the Safety Management and Organization Review Technique, or SMORT (Kjellén and Tinmannsvik 1989). A SMORT analysis advances backwards in steps, starting from the specific situation and ending at the general management level. The starting point (level 1) is an accident sequence or a risk situation. At level 2, the organization, system planning and technical factors related to daily operation are scrutinized. The subsequent levels include design of new systems (level 3) and higher management functions (level 4). Findings on one level are extended to the levels above. For example, results related to the accident sequence and to daily operations are used in the analysis of the company's organization and routines for project work (level 3). Results at level 3 will not affect safety in existing operations but may be applied to the planning of new systems and modifications. SMORT also differs from MORT in the way findings are identified. At level 1, these are observable events and conditions that deviate from generally accepted norms. When organizational and management factors are brought into the analysis at levels 2 to 4, the findings are identified through value judgements made by an analysis group and verified through a quality control procedure. The aim is to ensure a mutually shared understanding of the organizational problems.

Summary

MORT has been instrumental in developments within safety management since the 1970s. It is possible to track the influence of MORT to such areas as safety research literature, literature on safety management and audit tools, and legislation on self-regulation and internal control. In spite of this impact, its limitations must be carefully considered. MORT and associated methods are normative in the sense that they prescribe how safety management programmes should be organized and executed. The ideal is a well-structured organization with clear and realistic goals and well-defined lines of responsibility and authority. MORT is thus best suited for large and bureaucratic organizations.

WORKPLACE INSPECTION AND REGULATORY ENFORCEMENT

Anthony Linehan

Inspection Systems

Auditing has been defined as "the structured process of collecting independent information on the efficiency, effectiveness and reliability of the total safety management system and drawing up plans for corrective action" (Successful Health & Safety Management 1991).

The workplace inspection therefore is not only the final stage in setting up a safety management programme but is also a continuing process in its maintenance. It can be conducted only where a properly devised management system for safety has been established. Such a system first envisages a formal policy statement from management setting out its principles for creating a healthy and safe working environment and then establishing the mechanisms and the structures within the organization whereby these principles will be effectively implemented. Management must furthermore be committed to providing adequate resources, both human and financial, to support the system's mechanisms and structures. Thereafter, there must be detailed planning for safety and health, and the defining of measurable goals. Systems must be devised to ensure that safety and health performance in practice can be measured against established norms and against previous achievements. Only when this structure is in place and is operating can an effective management audit system be applied.

Complete safety and health management systems can be devised, produced and implemented from within the resources of larger enterprises. Additionally, there are a number of safety management control systems which are available from consultants, insurance companies, government agencies, associations and specialist companies. It is a matter for the enterprise to decide whether it should produce its own system or obtain outside services. Both alternatives are capable of producing excellent results if there is a genuine commitment by management to apply them diligently and to make them work. But for their success, they do depend heavily on the quality of the audit system.

Management Inspections

The inspection procedure must be as painstaking and objective as the company's financial inspection. The inspection must first determine whether the company's statement of policy on safety and health is properly reflected in the structures and mechanisms created to implement it; if not, then the inspection may recommend that the fundamental policy be reappraised or suggest adjustments or alterations to the existing structures and mechanisms. A similar process must be applied to safety and health planning, to the validity of the goal-setting norms, and to the measurement of performance. The results of any inspection must be considered by the top management of the enterprise, and any correctives must be endorsed and implemented through that authority.

In practice it is undesirable, and often impractical, to undertake a complete inspection of all of a system's features and their application throughout every department of the enterprise at one time. More usually, the inspection procedure concentrates on one feature of the total safety management system throughout the plant, or alternatively on the application of all the features in one department or even subdepartment. But the objective is to cover all the features in all departments over an agreed period in order to validate the results.

To this extent management inspection should be regarded as a continuous process of vigilance. The need for objectivity is clearly of considerable importance. If inspections are conducted in-house then there must be a standardized inspection procedure; inspections should be undertaken by staff who have been properly trained for this purpose; and those selected as inspectors must not assess the departments in which they normally work, nor should they assess any other work in which they have a personal involvement. Where reliance is placed on consultants this problem is minimized.

Many major companies have adopted this type of system, either devised internally or obtained as a proprietary scheme. When the systems have been carefully followed through from policy statement to inspection, feedback and corrective actions, a substantial reduction in accident rates, which is the prime justification for the procedure, and increased profitability, which is a welcome secondary outcome, should result.

Inspections by Inspectorates

The legal framework which is designed to afford protection to people at work must be properly administered and effectively applied if the purpose of the regulatory legislation is to be achieved. Most countries have therefore adopted the broad model of an inspection service which has the duty of ensuring that safety and health legislation is enforced. Many countries see safety and health issues as part of a complete labour relations package covering industrial relations, wages and holiday agreements, and social benefits. In this model, safety and health inspections are one element of the labour inspector's duties. A different model also exists in which the state inspectorate is exclusively concerned with safety and health legislation, so that workplace inspections concentrate solely on this aspect. Further variations are evident in the division of the inspection functions between either a national inspectorate or a regional/provincial inspectorate, or indeed, as in Italy and the United Kingdom, for example, as a working combination of both national and regional inspectorates. But whichever model is adopted, the essential function of the inspectorate is to determine compliance with the legislation by a programme of planned inspections and investigations at the workplace.

There can be no effective inspection system unless those who undertake this work are given adequate powers to carry it out. There is much common ground among inspectorates as regards the powers given to them by their legislators. There must always be the right of entry to premises, which is clearly fundamental for inspection. Thereafter there is the legal right to examine relevant documents, registers and reports, to interview members of the workforce either individually or collectively, to have unrestricted access to trade union representatives at the workplace, to take samples of substances or materials at use in the workplace, to take photographs and, if appropriate, to take written statements from people working at the premises.

Additional powers are often provided to enable inspectors to rectify conditions which might be an immediate source of danger or ill health to the workforce. Again there is a wide variety of practices. Where standards are so poor that there is an imminent risk of danger to the workforce, then an inspector may be authorized to serve a legal document on the spot prohibiting the use of the machinery or plant, or stopping the process until the risk has been effectively controlled. For a lower order of risk, inspectors can issue a legal notice formally requiring that measures be taken within a given time to improve standards. These are effective ways of rapidly improving working conditions, and are often a form of enforcement preferable to formal court proceedings, which may be cumbersome and slow in securing remediation.

Legal proceedings have an important place in the hierarchy of enforcement. There is an argument that because court proceedings are simply punitive and do not necessarily result in changing attitudes to safety and health at work, they should therefore be invoked only as a last resort when all other attempts at securing improvements have failed. But this view has to be set against the fact that where legal requirements have been ignored or disregarded, and where people's safety and health have been significantly put at risk, then the law must be enforced and the courts must decide the issue. There is the further argument that those enterprises which disregard safety and health legislation may thereby enjoy an economic advantage over their competitors, who provide adequate resources to comply with their legal duties. Prosecution of those who persistently disregard their duties is therefore a deterrent to the unscrupulous, and an encouragement to those who try to observe the law.

Every inspection service has to determine the proper balance between providing advice and enforcing the law in the course of inspection work. A special difficulty emerges in connection with the inspection of small enterprises. Local economies, and indeed national economies, are often underpinned by industrial premises each employing fewer than 20 people; in the case of agriculture, the employment figure per unit is very much less. The function of the inspectorate in these cases is to use the workplace inspection to provide information and advice not only on legal requirements, but on practical standards and effective ways of meeting those standards. The technique must be to encourage and stimulate, rather than to immediately enforce the law by punitive action. But even here the balance is a difficult one. People at work are entitled to safety and health standards irrespective of the size of the enterprise, and it would therefore be wholly misguided for an inspection service to ignore or minimize risks and to curtail or even forgo enforcement simply to nurture the existence of the economically fragile small enterprise.

Consistency of Inspections

In the view of the complex nature of their work—with its combined needs for legal, prudential, technical and scientific skills, inspectors do not—indeed should not—adopt a mechanistic approach to inspection. This constraint, combined with a difficult balance between the advisory and enforcement functions, creates yet another concern, that of the consistency of inspection services. Industrialists and trade unions have a right to expect a consistent application of standards, whether technical or legal, by inspectors across the country. In practice this is not always easy to achieve, but it is something for which the enforcing authorities must always strive.

There are ways of achieving an acceptable consistency. First, the inspectorate should be as open as possible in publishing its technical standards and in publicly setting out its enforcement policies. Second, through training, the application of peer review exercises, and internal instructions, it should be able both to recognize a problem and to provide systems to deal with it. Finally, it should ensure that there are procedures for industry, the workforce, the public and the social partners to secure redress if they have a legitimate grievance over inconsistency or other forms of maladministration associated with inspection.

Frequency of Inspections

How frequently should the inspectorates undertake inspections of the workplace? Again there is considerable variation in the way this question may be answered. The International Labour Organization (ILO) holds the view that the minimum requirement should be that every workplace should receive an inspection from the enforcing authorities at least once each year. In practice, few countries manage to produce a programme of work inspection which meets this objective. Indeed, since the major economic depression in the late 1980s some governments have been curtailing inspection services by budget limitations that result in cutbacks in the number of inspectors, or by restrictions on recruiting new staff to replace those who retire.

There are different approaches to determine how frequently inspections should be made. One approach has been purely cyclical. Resources are deployed to provide inspection of all premises on a 2-yearly, or more likely a 4-yearly, basis. But this approach, though possibly having the appearance of equity, treats all premises as the same regardless of size or risk. Yet enterprises are manifestly diverse as regards safety and health conditions, and to the extent that they differ, this system may be regarded as mechanistic and flawed.

A different approach, adopted by some inspectorates, has been to attempt to draw up a programme of work based on hazard; the greater the hazard either to safety or health, the more frequent the inspection. Hence resources are applied by the inspectorate to those places where the potential for harm to the workforce is the greatest. Although this approach has merits, there are still considerable problems associated with it. First, there are difficulties in accurately and objectively assessing hazard and risk. Second, it extends very considerably the intervals between inspections of those premises where hazards and risks are considered to be low. Therefore, extended periods may elapse during which many of the workforce may have to forgo that sense of security and assurance which inspection can provide. Furthermore, the system tends to presume that hazards and risks, once assessed, do not radically change. This is far from being the case, and there is the danger that a low-rated enterprise may change or develop its production in such a way as to increase hazards and risk without the inspectorate's being aware of the development.

Other approaches include inspections based on facility injury rates which are higher than the national averages for the particular industry, or immediately following a fatal injury or major catastrophe. There are no short and easy answers to the problem of determining the frequency of inspection, but what seems to be happening is that inspection services in many countries are too often significantly under-resourced, with the result that the real protection to the workforce afforded by the service is being progressively eroded.

Inspection Goals

Inspection techniques in the workplace vary according to the size and complexity of the enterprise. In smaller companies, the inspection will be comprehensive and will assess all hazards and the extent to which the risks arising from the hazards have been minimized. The inspection will therefore ensure that the employer is fully aware of safety and health problems and is given practical guidance on how they may be addressed. But even in the smallest enterprise the inspectorate should not give the impression that fault-finding and the application of suitable remedies are the function of the inspectorate and not of the employer. Employers must be encouraged by inspection to control and effectively manage safety and health problems, and they must not abdicate their responsibilities by awaiting an inspection from the enforcement authorities before taking needed action.

In larger companies, the emphasis of inspection is rather different. These companies have the technical and financial resources to deal with safety and health problems. They should devise both effective management systems to resolve the problems, as well as management procedures to check that the systems are working. In these circumstances, the inspection emphasis should therefore be on checking and validating the management control systems found at the workplace. The inspection should therefore not be an exhaustive examination of all items of plant and equipment to determine their safety, but rather to use selected examples to test the effectiveness or otherwise of the management systems for ensuring safety and health at work.

Worker Involvement in Inspections

Whatever the premises, a critical element in any type of inspection is contact with the workforce. In many smaller premises, there may be no formal trade union structure or indeed any workforce organization at all. However, to ensure the objectivity and acceptance of the inspection service, contact with individual workers should be an integral part of the inspection. In larger enterprises, contact should always be made with trade union or other recognized worker representatives. Legislation in some countries (Sweden and the United Kingdom, for example) gives official recognition and powers to trade union safety representatives, including the right to make workplace inspections, to investigate accidents and dangerous occurrences and in some countries (though this is exceptional) to stop plant machinery or the production process if it is imminently dangerous. Much useful information can be gained from these contacts with the workers, which should feature in every inspection, and certainly whenever the inspectorate is conducting an inspection as the result of an accident or a complaint.

Inspection Findings

The final element in an inspection is to review the inspection findings with the most senior member of management on the site. Management has the prime responsibility to comply with legal requirements on safety and health, and therefore no inspection should be complete without management's being fully aware of the extent to which it has met those duties, and what needs to be done to secure and maintain proper standards. Certainly if any legal notices are issued as a result of an inspection, or if legal proceedings are likely, then senior management must be aware of this state of affairs at the earliest possible stage.

Company Inspections

Company inspections are an important ingredient in maintaining sound standards of safety and health at work. They are appropriate to all enterprises and, in larger companies, may be an element in the management inspection procedure. For smaller companies, it is essential to adopt some form of regular company inspection. Reliance should not be placed on the inspection services provided by the inspectorates of the enforcing authorities. These are usually far too infrequent, and should serve largely as a stimulus to improve or maintain standards, rather than be the primary source for evaluating standards. Company inspections can be undertaken by consultants or by companies who specialize in this work, but the current discussion will concentrate on inspection by the enterprise's own personnel.

How frequently should company inspections be made? To some degree the answer is dependent on the hazards associated with the work and the complexity of the plant. But even in low-risk premises there should be some form of inspection on a regular (monthly, quarterly, etc.) basis. If the company employs a safety professional, then clearly the organization and the conduct of the inspection must be an important part of this function. The inspection should usually be a team effort involving the safety professional, the departmental manager or foreman, and either a trade union representative or a qualified worker, such as a safety committee member. The inspection should be comprehensive; that is to say, a close examination should be made both of the safety software (for example, systems, procedures and work permits) and the hardware (for example, machinery guarding, firefighting equipment, exhaust ventilation and personal protective equipment). Particular attention should be paid to "near misses"—those incidents which do not result in damages or personal injury but which have the imminent potential for serious accidental injuries. There is an expectation that after an accident resulting in absence from work, the inspection team would immediately convene to investigate the circumstances, as a matter outside the normal cycle of inspection. But even during routine workshop inspection the team should also consider the extent of minor accidental injuries which have occurred in the department since the previous inspection.

It is important that company inspections should not seem to be consistently negative. Where faults exist it is important that they be identified and rectified, but it is equally important to commend the maintenance of good standards, to comment positively on tidiness and good housekeeping, and to reinforce by encouragement those who use personal protective equipment provided for their safety. To complete the inspection a formal written report should be made of the significant deficiencies found. Particular attention should be drawn to any shortcomings which have been identified in previous inspections but have not yet been corrected. Where there exists a works safety council, or a joint management-worker safety committee, the inspection report should be featured as a standing item on the council's agenda. The report on the inspection must be sent to and discussed with the senior management of the enterprise, who should then determine whether action is required and, if so, authorize and support such action.

Even the smallest companies, where there is no safety professional, and where trade unions may not exist, should consider company inspections. Many inspectorates have produced very simple guidelines illustrating the basic concepts of safety and health, their application to a range of industries, and practical ways in which they can be applied in even the smallest enterprises. Many safety associations specifically target small businesses with publications (often free) which provide the basic information to establish safe and healthy working conditions. Armed with this sort of information and with the expenditure of very little time, the proprietor of a small business can establish reasonable standards, and can thus perhaps obviate the sort of accidents which can happen to the workforce in even the smallest business.

ANALYSIS AND REPORTING: ACCIDENT INVESTIGATION

M. Monteau

It is a paradox that the prevention of work-related accidents did not emerge very early as an absolute necessity, since health and safety is fundamental to work itself. In fact it was not until the beginning of the twentieth century that accidents at work ceased to be considered inevitable and their causation became a subject to be investigated and used as a basis for prevention. However, accident investigation long remained cursory and empirical. Historically, accidents were first conceived of as simple phenomena—that is, as resulting from a single (or principal) cause and a small number of subsidiary causes. It is now recognized that accident investigation, which is aimed at identifying the causes of the phenomenon so as to avert its reoccurrence, depends both on the concept underlying the process of investigation and on the complexity of the situation to which it is applied.

Causes of Accidents

It is indeed true that in the most precarious situations, accidents are often the result of a fairly simple sequence of a few causes that can be rapidly traced to basic technical problems that even a summary analysis can reveal (equipment badly designed, working methods undefined, etc.). On the other hand, the more closely that the material elements of work (machines, installations, the

---

Table 57.5 • Principal concepts of the accident phenomenon, their characteristics and the implications for prevention.

Concept or "accident phenomenon"	Significant elements (objectives, procedures, limits, etc.)	Main consequences for prevention
Basic concept (accident as phenomenon with few causes or even one cause	The objective is to identify "the" single or main cause No particular method Little time devoted to the investigation Role of chance and fate often referred to	Simple prevention measures concerning the immediate antecedent of the injury (individual protection, instructions about taking care, protection of dangerous machines)
Concept focused on regulatory measures	Focus on looking for who is responsible; the "enquiry" essentially identifies infringements and faults Rarely concerned about the conditions generating the situations examined	Prevention usually limited to reminders about existing regulatory requirements or formal instructions
Linear (or quasi-linear) concept ("domino" model)	Identification of a chronological succession of "dangerous conditions" and "dangerous acts" Frequent use of checklists The investigation depends very much on the investigator's experience Weak preventive component (dangerous nature of acts determined *a posteriori*)	Conclusions generally concerned with the dangerous acts
Multifactorial concept	Exhaustive research to gather the facts (circumstances, causes, factors, etc.) Focus placed on the contingent character of each accident situation No criteria of relevance in the facts gathered Need for complex statistical treatment	Concept not conducive to the search for solutions case by case (clinical analysis) and better adapted to the identification of statistical aspects (trends, tables, graphs, etc.)
Systematic concept (tree of causes, STEP)	Identification of the network of factors of each accident Use of logical relationships Need for training of investigators	Methods centred on clinical analysis (carried out in participatory manner) Possibility of use for all undesired events (incidents, breakdowns)

Figure 57.9 • Logical links used in the "tree of causes" method.

	SEQUENCE	SEPARATION	CONJUNCTION
Definition	An antecedent (Y) has a single direct origin (X)	Two or several antecedents (Y_1, Y_2) have a single and identical direct origin (X)	An antecedent (Y) has several direct origins (X_1, X_2).
Representation (example)	X → Y. X: Working method difficult for single operative. Y: Forearm under engine	X → Y_1 (Co-worker available), X → Y_2 (Working method more difficult). X: Working alone	X_1 (Co-worker absent), X_2 (Urgent work) → Y (Working alone)
Characteristics	X was necessary and sufficient for Y to be produced.	X was necessary for Y_1 and Y_2 to be produced.	Each of the antecedents X_1 and X_2 was necessary for Y to be produced, but neither was sufficient by itself: together they constitute a sufficient cause.

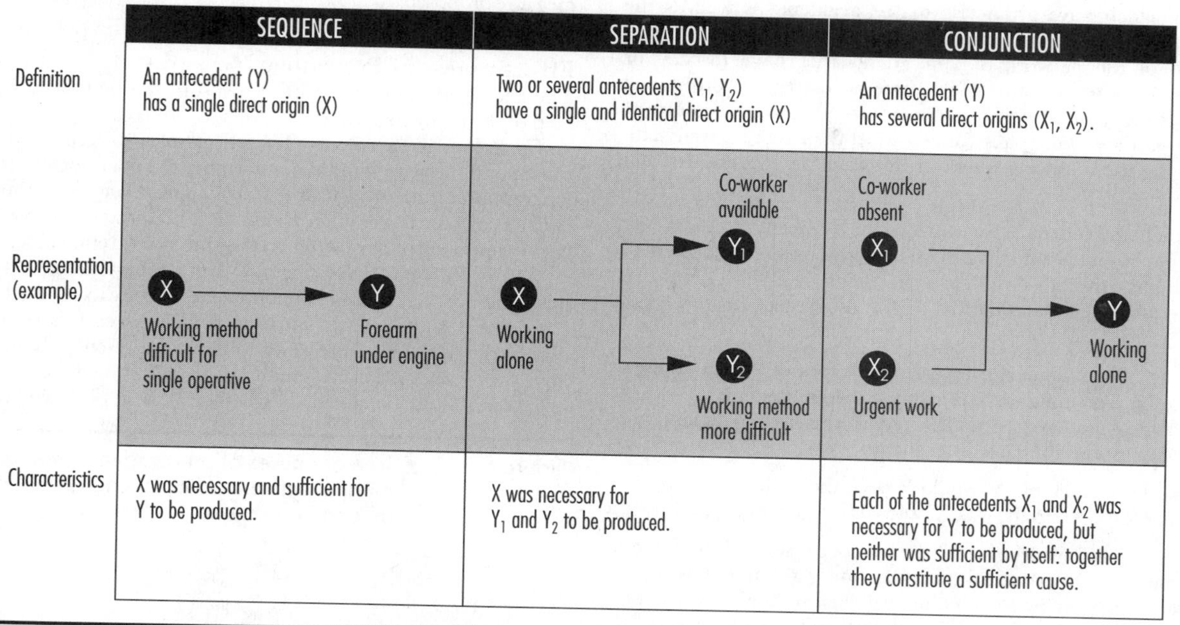

arrangement of the workplace, etc.) conform with the requirements of safe work procedures, standards and regulations, the safer the work situation becomes. The result is that an accident can then occur only when a group of exceptional conditions are present simultaneously—conditions that are becoming ever more numerous. In such cases, the injury or damage appears as the final result of a frequently complex network of causes. This complexity is actually evidence of progress in prevention, and requires appropriate methods of investigation. Table 57.5 lists the principal concepts of the accident phenomenon, their characteristics and implications for prevention.

Nowadays, a work accident is generally viewed as an index (or symptom) of dysfunction in a system consisting of a single production unit, such as a factory, workshop, team or work position. It is the nature of a system that its analysis requires the investigator to examine not only the elements that make up the system but also their relationships with one another and with the work environment. Within the framework of a system, the accident investigation seeks to trace to its origins the sequence of basic dysfunctions that have resulted in the accident and, more generally, the network of antecedents of the undesired event (accident, near accident or incident).

The application of methods of this kind, such as the STEP method (sequentially timed events plotting procedures) and the "tree of causes" method (similar to fault or event trees analyses), allows the accident process to be visualized in the form of an adjusted graph that illustrates the multicausality of the phenomenon. Because these two methods are so similar, it would represent a duplication of effort to describe them both; accordingly, this article concentrates on the tree of causes method and, where applicable, notes its main differences from the STEP method.

Information Useful for the Investigation

The initial phase of the investigation, the gathering of information, must allow the course of the accident to be described in concrete, precise and objective terms. The investigation therefore sets out to ascertain the tangible facts, taking care not to interpret them or to express an opinion about them. These are the antecedents of the accident, of which there are two types:

1. those of an unusual nature (changes or variations) in relation to the "normal" or expected course of the work
2. those of a permanent nature that have played an active part in the occurrence of the accident through the medium of or in combination with the unusual antecedents.

For example, insufficient protection of a machine (a permanent antecedent) can turn out to be a factor in an accident if it allows the operator to take up a position in a dangerous area in order to deal with a particular incident (unusual antecedent).

The information gathering is carried out at the location of the accident itself as soon as possible after its occurrence. It is preferably carried out by persons who know the operation or process and who try to obtain a precise description of the work without limiting themselves to the immediate circumstances of the damage or injury. The investigation is initially effected mainly by means of interviews, if possible with the worker or operator, victims and eyewitnesses, other members of the work team, and the hierarchical supervisors. If appropriate it is completed by means of a technical investigation and the use of outside expertise.

The investigation seeks to identify, in order of priority, the unusual antecedents, and to determine their logical connections. An effort is made at the same time to reveal the permanent antecedents that have allowed the accident to occur. In this way the investigation is able to go back to a stage more remote than the immediate antecedents of the accident. These more remote antecedents may concern individuals, their tasks, the equipment that they use, the environment in which they function and the safety culture. By proceeding in the way just described, it is generally possible to draw up a lengthy list of antecedents, but it will usually be difficult to make immediate use of the data. The interpretation of the data is made possible thanks to a graphic representation of all the antecedents involved in the genesis of the accident—that is, a tree of causes.

Constructing a Tree of Causes

The tree of causes presents all the antecedents that have been gathered which have given rise to the accident, as well as the logical and chronological links that connect them; it is a representation of the network of antecedents that have directly or indirectly caused the injury. The tree of causes is constructed starting from the end-point of the event—that is, the injury or damage—and working backwards toward the cause by systematically asking the following questions for each antecedent that has been gathered:

- By which antecedent X was antecedent Y directly caused?
- Was antecedent X sufficient in itself to give rise to antecedent Y?
- If not, have there been other antecedents (X1, X2 … Xn) that were equally necessary in order to give rise directly to antecedent Y?

This set of questions can reveal three types of logical connection, summarized in figure 57.9, among the antecedents.

The logical coherence of the tree is checked by asking the following questions for each antecedent:

- If X had not taken place, would Y nevertheless have occurred?
- In order for Y to occur, was X, and only X, necessary?

Moreover, the construction of the tree of causes in itself induces the investigators to pursue the information-gathering, and therefore the investigation, to a point well before the accident occurred. When completed, the tree represents the network of antecedents that have given rise to the injury—they are in fact the accident factors. As an example, the accident summarized below produced the tree of causes shown in figure 57.10.

Accident Summary Report: An apprentice mechanic, recently recruited, had to work alone in an emergency. A worn sling was being used to suspend an engine that had to be remounted, and during this operation the sling broke and the engine fell and injured the mechanic's arm.

Analysis by the STEP Method

According to the STEP method (figure 57.11), each event is set out graphically so as to show the chronological order of its appearance, keeping one line per "agent" concerned (an agent is the person or thing that determines the course of events constituting the accident process). Each event is described precisely by indicating its beginning, duration, starting and ending place and so on. When there are several plausible hypotheses, the investigator can show them in the network of events by using the logical relationship "or".

Analysis by the Tree of Causes Method

Making use of the tree of causes for the purposes of accident analysis has two objectives:

- making the reoccurrence of the same accident impossible
- averting the occurrence of more or less similar accidents—that is, accidents whose investigation would reveal common factors with the accidents that have already occurred.

Given the logical structure of the tree, the absence of a single antecedent would have prevented the occurrence of the accident. One judicious prevention measure would therefore suffice, in principle, to satisfy the first objective by preventing the reoccurrence of the same accident. The second objective would require that all the factors discovered should be eliminated, but in practice the antecedents are not all of equal importance for the purposes of prevention. It is therefore necessary to draw up a list of antecedents requiring reasonable and realistic preventive action. If this list is long, a choice has to be made. This choice has more chance of being appropriate if it is made within the framework of a debate between the partners concerned in the accident. Moreover, the debate will gain in clarity to the extent that it is possible to assess the cost-effectiveness of each measure proposed.

Effectiveness of Preventive Measures

The effectiveness of a preventive measure can be judged with the help of the following criteria:

The stability of the measure. The effects of a preventive measure must not disappear with time: informing the operators (in particular, reminding them of instructions) is not a very stable measure because its effects are often transient. The same is moreover true of some protective devices when they are easily removable.

The possibility of integrating safety. When a safety measure is added on—that is, when it does not contribute directly to production—it is said that safety is not integrated. Whenever this is so, it is observed that the measure tends to disappear. Generally speaking, any preventive measure entailing an additional cost for the operator should be avoided, whether it is a physiological cost

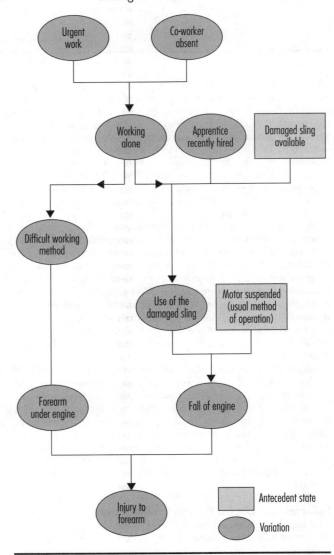

Figure 57.10 • Tree of causes of an accident suffered by an apprentice mechanic when remounting an engine in a car.

Figure 57.11 • Example of representation possible by the STEP method.

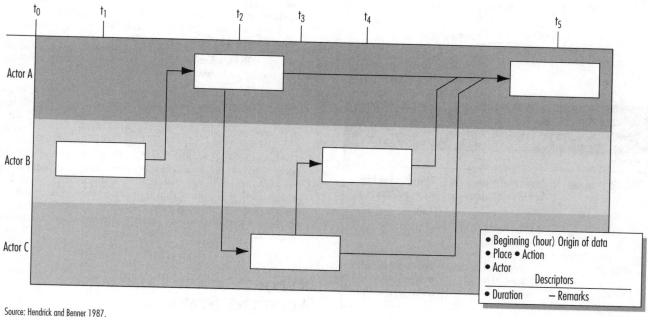

Source: Hendrick and Benner 1987.

(increasing the physical or nervous load), a psychological cost, a financial cost (in the case of salary or output) or even a simple loss of time.

The non-displacement of the risk. Some preventive measures may have indirect effects that are detrimental to safety. It is therefore always necessary to foresee the possible repercussions of a preventive measure on the system (job, team or workshop) in which it is inserted.

The possibility of general application (the notion of potential accident factor). This criterion reflects the concern that the same preventive action may be applicable to other jobs than the one affected by the accident under investigation. Whenever possible, an effort should be made to go beyond the particular case that has given rise to the investigation, an effort that often requires a reformulation of the problems discovered. The information obtained from an accident may thus lead to preventive action relating to factors that are unknown but present in other work situations where they have not yet given rise to accidents. For this reason they are called "potential accident factors". This notion opens the way to the early detection of risks, mentioned later.

The effect on root "causes". As a general rule, the prevention of accident factors near to the point of injury eliminates certain effects of dangerous situations, while prevention acting well upstream of the injury tends to eliminate the dangerous situations themselves. An in-depth investigation of accidents is justified to the extent that the preventive action is equally concerned with the upstream factors.

The time taken for application. The need to act as rapidly as possible after the occurrence of an accident so as to avoid its reoccurrence is often reflected in the application of a simple preventive measure (an instruction, for example), but this does not eliminate the need for other more lasting and more effective action. Every accident must therefore give rise to a series of proposals whose implementation is the subject of follow-up.

The above criteria are intended to give a better appreciation of the quality of preventive action proposed after each accident

investigation. However, the final choice is not made solely on this basis, as other considerations, such as economic, cultural or social ones, must also be taken into account. Finally, the measures decided upon must obviously respect the regulations in force.

Accident Factors

The lessons drawn from each accident analysis deserve to be recorded systematically so as to facilitate passing from knowledge to action. Thus figure 57.12 consists of three columns. In the left-hand column are noted the accident factors requiring preventive measures. Possible preventive action is described in the middle column for each factor decided upon. After the discussion mentioned above, the action selected is recorded in this part of the document.

The right-hand column covers the potential accident factors suggested by the factors listed in the left-hand column: it is considered that each accident factor discovered is often only a particular case of a more general factor known as a potential accident factor. The passage from the particular case to the more general case is often made spontaneously. However, each time that an accident factor is expressed in such a fashion that it is not possible to encounter it elsewhere than in the situation in which it has appeared, a more general formulation must be considered. In doing this, it is necessary to avoid two opposite pitfalls so as to utilize the notion of potential accident factor effectively in the early detection of risks arising later. A formulation that is too circumscribed does not permit systematic detection of the factors, whereas one that is too wide makes the notion unworkable and is of no further practical interest. The detection of potential accident factors thus presupposes their being well formulated. This detection can then be carried out in two ways, which are moreover complementary:

1. either by looking for the possible presence of potential factors already known at the level of a job or a wider area (workshop, service)

57. AUDITS, INSPECTIONS AND INVESTIGATIONS

Figure 57.12 • Lessons drawn from accidents and the use of these lessons.

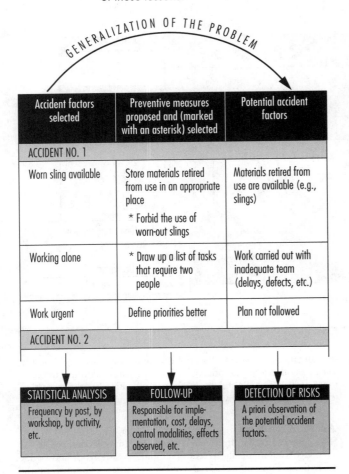

2. training of the investigators
3. management, supervisors and workers fully informed concerning the aims of the investigation, its principles, the requirements of the method and the results expected
4. real improvements in safety conditions that will encourage those involved in future investigations.

Limitations. Even when carried out very well, accident investigation suffers from a double limitation:

• It remains a procedure for investigating risks *a posteriori* (in the manner of systems analysis), with the aim of correcting existing situations. It does not therefore dispense with the need for *a priori* (prospective) investigations, such as the ergonomic investigation of jobs or, for complex systems, safety investigations.
• The usefulness of accident investigations also varies with the safety level of the establishment where they are applied. In particular, when the safety level is high (the accident rate is low or very low), it is evident that serious accidents result from the conjunction of numerous independent random factors that are relatively harmless from the safety viewpoint when considered outside the context under investigation.

REPORTING AND COMPILING ACCIDENT STATISTICS

Kirsten Jorgensen

The Need for Reporting and Compiling Accident Data

The primary purpose of assembling and analysing occupational accident data is to provide knowledge for use in the prevention of occupational injuries, fatalities and other forms of harm such as toxic exposures with long-term effects. These data are also useful in assessing needs for compensating victims for injuries previously incurred. Additional, more specific purposes for the compilation of accident statistics include the following:

• to estimate the causes and magnitude of accident problems
• to identify and prioritize the need for preventive measures
• to evaluate the effectiveness of preventive measures
• to monitor risks, issue warnings and conduct awareness campaigns
• to provide feedback for those involved in prevention.

Often, an overview of the number of accidents occurring on an annual basis is desired. A frequency is often used for this purpose, comparing the number of accidents to a measure relating to the risk group and expressed, for example, in terms of accidents per 100,000 workers or per 100,000 working hours. Such annual counts serve the purpose of revealing variations in an accident rate from one year to another. However, while they may indicate the sorts of accidents that require the most urgent preventive action, by themselves they do not furnish guidance as to the form that this action should take.

The need for accident information pertains to the following three levels of function that make use of it:

• At the workplace level within the individual enterprise, accident data are used in local safety activities. The best opportunities for tackling specific risk factors are to be found immediately at the workplace itself.
• At the level of authority responsible for legislation, accident data are used to regulate the working environment and to promote safety at the workplace. It is possible not only to exert control over the workplace at this level but also to carry out general statistical analyses for use in overall preventive work.

2. or by looking for jobs where a factor already determined may be observed.

Usefulness, Effectiveness and Limitations of Accident Investigation

Usefulness. As compared to non-systematic investigations, methods of accident investigation based on a systematic concept have numerous advantages, which include the following:

• They allow the causal network of each accident to be defined collectively, from which it is easier to devise new preventive measures and foresee their impact without being limited to the direct causes of the injury.
• They provide those involved in the analysis with a richer and more realistic mental representation of the "accident phenomenon" that permits a global understanding of work situations.
• In-depth accident investigations (especially when they are extended to cover incidents and undesired events) can become a means and appropriate occasion for dialogue between management and operators.

Effectiveness. In order to be effective, accident investigation requires that four conditions are satisfied concurrently:

1. an evident commitment on the part of the top management of the establishment, who must be able to ensure the systematic implementation of such procedures

- At the level of authority responsible for payments of compensation to accident victims, accident data are used to help determine rates.

The Role of the Organization in Compiling Accident Information

In many countries it is a legal requirement that enterprises keep statistics of occupational accidents which result in injury, fatality or toxic exposure to a worker. The purpose of this is usually to call attention to risks that have actually led to these types of accidents, with safety activities focusing chiefly on the particular accident and the study of the event itself. However, it is more common for accident information to be collected and recorded systematically, a function that is ordinarily carried out at a higher level.

Since the actual circumstances of most accidents are special, wholly identical accidents seldom occur, and prevention based on the analysis of the individual accident very readily tends to become a highly specific matter. By systematically compiling accident information it is possible to obtain a broader view of those areas where specific risks are to be found, and to uncover the less obvious factors instrumental in the causation of the accident. Specific work processes, specific work teams or work with specific machinery can give rise to highly circumstantial accidents. However, a close study of the types of accidents associated with a given class of uniform work can disclose such factors as inexpedient work processes, incorrect use of materials, difficult working conditions, or lack of adequate worker instruction. An analysis of numerous recurring accidents will reveal the fundamental factors to be dealt with when preventive action is taken.

Reporting Accident Information to Safety Authorities

Legislation requiring the reporting of occupational accidents varies widely from country to country, with the differences chiefly relating to the classes of employers and others to whom the laws apply. Countries that place significant emphasis on safety at the workplace usually mandate that accident data be reported to the authority responsible for supervising compliance with safety legislation. (In some cases, legislation requires reporting of occupational accidents that result in absence from work, the duration of such absence varying from 1 to 3 days in addition to the day of the accident.) Common to most legislation is the fact that reporting is linked with some sort of penalty or compensation for the consequences of accidents.

For the purpose of supplying a sound foundation for the prevention of occupational accidents, it is necessary to secure accident information pertaining to all sectors and to all types of trades. A basis of comparison should be provided at the national level in order to allow prevention action to be prioritized and in order that knowledge of risks associated with tasks across different sectors may be turned to good account in preventive work. It is therefore recommended that the duty of compiling occupational accident information at the national level apply to all occupational accidents of a designated seriousness, no matter whether they concern employees of firms or the self-employed, persons working at temporary jobs or regular salary earners, or workers in the public or private sectors.

While employers, generally speaking, have a duty to report accidents, it is a duty carried out with varying degrees of enthusiasm. The extent of compliance with the obligation to report accidents depends on the incentives driving the employer to do so. Some countries have a rule, for instance, according to which employers will be compensated for an accident victim's lost-time pay, an arrangement that gives them good reason to report occupational injuries. Other countries penalize employers who are found to be not reporting accidents. Where these sorts of incentives do not exist, the merely legal obligation binding upon the employer is not always observed. It is moreover recommended that occupational accident information intended for preventive applications be given to the authority responsible for preventive activities, and be kept separate from the compensating authority.

What Information is to be Compiled?

There are three basic classes of information obtainable by means of accident recording:

- Information identifying *where* the accidents occur—that is, sectors, trades, work processes and so on. This knowledge can be used to determine *where* preventive action is needed.
- Information showing *how* the accidents occur, the situations in which they occur and the ways in which the injuries come about. This knowledge can be used to determine the *type* of preventive action needed.
- Information relating to *the nature and seriousness* of the injuries, describing, for example, the parts of the body affected and the health consequences of the injuries. Such knowledge is to be used for *prioritizing* preventive action in order to ensure that action is taken where the risk is highest.

It is necessary to compile a certain basic complement of data to properly document when and where an accident occurs and to analyse how it occurs. At the enterprise level, the data that are collected are more detailed than those assembled at the national level, but reports generated at the local level will contain items of information valuable at all levels. Table 57.6 illustrates particular sorts of information that might be recorded by way of describing an individual accident. The items especially relevant to the task of preparing statistics relating to the accident are described more fully below.

Accident identification number. All occupational accidents must be assigned a unique identifying number. It is especially advantageous to use a numerical identifier for the purpose of computerized filing and subsequent processing.

Personal identification number and date. Registration of the victim is an essential part of accident identification. The number can be the worker's birthday, employment number, social security number or some other unique identifier. Recording both a personal identification number and the date of the accident will prevent duplicated registration of the same accident event, and also enables a check to be made as to whether the accident has

Table 57.6 • Informational variables characterizing an accident.

Actions	
Step 1	
Activity of the victim: e.g., operating a machine, performing maintenance, driving, walking, etc.	*Component related to the activity of the victim:* e.g., power press, tool, vehicle, floor, etc.
Step 2	
Deviant action: e.g., explosion, structural failure, trip, lost control of, etc.	*Component related to deviant action:* e.g., pressure vessel, wall, cable, vehicle, machine, tool, etc.
Step 3	
Action leading to injury: e.g., struck by, crushed, trapped, in contact with, bitten by, etc.	*Agent of injury:* e.g., brick, ground, machine, etc.

57. AUDITS, INSPECTIONS AND INVESTIGATIONS

been reported. The link between information contained in the accident report with the personal identification number can be protected for the purpose of security.

Nationality. The nationality of the victim may be an especially important item of information in countries with a significantly large foreign labour force. A double-digit code number can be selected from among those listed in the DS/ISO Standard 3166.

Occupation. An occupation registration number can be chosen from the list of four-digit international occupation codes supplied by the International Standard Classification of Occupations (ISCO).

Enterprise. The name, address and identification number of the enterprise are used in the recording of accidents at the national level (although the name and address cannot be used for computer recording). The production sector of the enterprise will usually have been registered with its industrial injury insurance carrier or recorded in connection with the registration of its workforce. A numerical sector identifier can be assigned according to the five-digit NACE international classification system.

The work process. A vital component of information relating to occupational accidents is a description of the work process carried out at the time the accident occurred. Identification of the work process is a prerequisite for accurately targeted prevention. It should be noted that the work process is the actual work function which the victim was performing at the time of the accident and may not necessarily be identical to the work process that caused the injury, fatality or exposure.

The accident event. An accident event normally comprises a chain of events. There is often a tendency on the part of investigators to focus on the part of the event cycle in which the injury actually occurred. From the point of view of prevention, however, a description of that part of the event cycle in which something went wrong, and of what the victim was doing when the event occurred, is just as important.

The consequences of the accident. After the injured part of the body is specified and the type of injury described (this is done partly by coding from a checklist and partly from the description in the event cycle), information is recorded describing the seriousness of the injury, whether it resulted in absence from work (and for how long), or whether it was fatal or involved invalidity. Detailed information in terms of longer-duration absence from work, hospitalization, or disablement is normally available from compensation offices and the social security system.

For recording purposes, the examination of accident events is therefore divided into the following three information components:

- *The activity* associated with an accident is that which was being carried out by the victim at the time of the accident. It is recorded by means of an action code and a technology code. In this connection, the concept of technology is a broad one, covering such instrumentalities as machines, materials, building components and even animals. At present, there exists no international classification for technology, although Denmark has developed a classification scheme for this purpose.
- *The injury event* is the deviant event which led to the accident. This is recorded by means of a code for the deviation and by one or two codes for the technology which formed part of the deviation.
- *The mode of injury* is recorded by using a code for the manner in which the victim came into contact with the injury-causing factor and another code for the technology which caused the injury.

The following examples illustrate the application of these categories of analysis:

1. In the event that a worker trips over a hose-pipe while walking and falls, striking his or her head against a table, the activity is walking, the injury event is tripping over the hose-pipe, and the mode of injury is striking the head against the table.
2. While a worker is standing near a wall, a tank explodes, causing the wall to collapse on the victim. The activity is merely standing near the wall, the injury event is the explosion of the tank, and the mode of injury is the impact of the wall upon the victim.

Reporting Accident Information

The information to be obtained for each accident can be recorded in a report form similar to that shown in figure 57.13.

The information from the report form can be recorded on a computer by using classification keys. (Where international classification systems can be recommended, these are mentioned in the description of the individual information variables, given above.) Classifications for the other variables used to record occupational injuries have been developed by the Danish Working Environment Service, and principles to be used in establishing a harmonized recording system form part of a proposal drafted by the European Union.

The Use of Accident Statistics

Accident statistics form a valuable instrument in a wide range of contexts: mapping, monitoring and warning, prioritization of areas for prevention, specific prevention measures, and information retrieval and research. One area may overlap with another, but the principles of application vary.

Mapping

Mapping of occupational accident data involves the extraction of predetermined sorts of information from an accumulation of registered data and the analysis of the interrelationships among them. The following examples will illustrate the utility of the mapping applications.

- *Mapping of industrial sectors.* Data relating to industrial sectors may be mapped by extracting an appropriate selection of the reports contained in a data register and carrying out the desired analysis. If a trade such as the building industry is of particular interest, reports registered with the International Standard Industrial Classification (ISIC) and coded from 50,000 to 50,199 (building and construction) can be selected. Reports for this trade can then be mapped to show, for example, the geographical location of the enterprises, and the age, sex and occupation of each accident victim.
- *Mapping of injuries.* If selection is based on a specific category of injuries, the reports can be extracted and mapped to show, for example, the trades in which these accidents occur, the occupational categories involved, the age groups affected, the activities in which the accidents occurred and the kind of technology most often involved.
- *Mapping of enterprises.* An evaluation on the enterprise level of accident trends (and thus of the internal work environment of the enterprise) can be carried out by mapping the notified occupational accidents that have occurred over a given time period. In addition, the enterprise will be able to compare its individual position with regard to technology, composition of personnel and other areas of concern with the trade as a whole, and thus determine whether its status in these respects is typical of the trade. Furthermore, if a trade proves to contain a number of typical work environment problems, it will be advisable to investigate whether these problems exist within the individual enterprise.

Figure 57.13 • Sample report form.

Serial no.

		Year	Month	Day
	State date of resumption of work			

Name of injured person

Date of birth

Address of injured person

Postal code

Please send to the address overleaf

✂ -

OCCUPATIONAL ACCIDENT REPORT

Serial no.
Injured Person

Name	Date of birth	
Address	Postal code	Nationality
Occupation	Time of accident Year Month Day Hour	☐ Self-employed ☐ Trainee ☐ Family Member

Employer Information

Name of business	Company registration No.
Address	Postal code Number of staff
Economic Activity	Length of service Years Months
If the accident did not occur at the enterprise address state where	Address Postal code

Type of work and work environment

What type of work was the injured person doing at the time of the accident? (e.g. iron founding, harvesting, slaughtering)

Where was the injured person at the time of the accident? (Inside buildings, underground, etc.)

Circumstances of the accident

Describe what the injured person was doing at the time of the accident and what item (tool, machine, etc.) was associated with the activity

Describe the action of deviation from normal including the item (tool, machine, etc.) associated with the deviation

Describe the action leading to injury including the agent (tool, machine, etc.) that caused the injury

Consequences of the accident

Type of injury

☐ Contrusion, bruise
☐ Concussion and internal injuries
☐ Open wound
☐ Amputation
☐ Open fracture
☐ Closed fracture
☐ Luxation, dislocation
☐ Distortion, sprain, torn ligaments

☐ Asphyxiation, gassing, drowning
☐ Poisoning
☐ Heat injury or frostbite
☐ Chemical burns
☐ Effect of radiation
☐ Electric shock
☐ Injury not ascertained
☐ Other

Injured part of the body

☐ Head except eyes
☐ Eyes
☐ Neck
☐ Back, spine
☐ Chest
☐ Abdomen
☐ Shoulder, upper arm, elbow
☐ Lower arm, wrist

☐ Hand
☐ Fingers, one or more
☐ Hip joint, thigh, knee cap
☐ Knee joint, lower leg, anide area
☐ Foot
☐ Toes, one or more
☐ Large parts of the body
☐ Other injury

Describe fully the nature of the injury and the injured part of the body

Consequences of the accident

☐ No absence/absence less than 1 day   ☐ Absence 1-3 days   ☐ Absence 4-14 days   ☐ Absence expected to exceed 14 days   ☐ Permanent disability   ☐ Death

_____   _____
Date   Signature of person reporting the claim

57. AUDITS, INSPECTIONS AND INVESTIGATIONS

Monitoring and warning

Monitoring is an ongoing surveillance process accompanied by *warning* of major risks, and particularly of changes in such risks. Changes observed in incoming accident reports either may be indicative of changes in the pattern of reporting, or, more seriously, may reflect genuine changes in risk factors. Major risks may be said to exist where there is a high frequency of injuries, where many serious injuries occur and where there is a large human exposure group.

Establishment of priorities

Establishment of priorities is the selection of the most important risk areas or work-environment problems for preventive action. Through the results of mapping surveys and monitoring and warning activities, a register of occupational accidents can be built which can contribute to this establishment of priorities, the elements of which might include the following:

- risks involving serious consequences
- risks which carry a high probability of injury to a large proportion of the exposure group
- risks to which large groups of people are exposed.

Data drawn from a register of occupational accidents can be used in the establishment of priorities on several levels, perhaps at the overall national level or at the more particular enterprise level. Whatever the level, the analyses and assessments can be made on the basis of the same principles.

Prevention

Analyses and documentation which are used for preventive purposes are generally highly specific and concentrated in limited areas which are, however, treated in great depth. An example of such an analysis is the campaign against fatal accidents conducted by the Danish National Labour Inspection Service. Preliminary mapping surveys identified the trades and work functions in which fatal accidents occurred. Farm tractors were selected as a focal area for analysis. The purpose of the analysis was then to determine what it was that made tractors so dangerous. Questions were investigated as to who drove them, where they were operated, when the accidents occurred and, in particular, what types of situations and events led to the accidents. The analysis produced a description of seven typical situations which most frequently led to accidents. Based on this analysis a preventive programme was formulated.

The number of occupational accidents in a single enterprise is often too small to yield workable statistics for preventive analysis. An analysis of the pattern of accidents may be able to be used to prevent repetition of specific injuries, but can hardly be successful in preventing the occurrence of accidents which in one way or another differ from earlier instances. Unless the focus of investigation is quite a large enterprise, such analyses are therefore best performed on a group of enterprises of very similar nature or on a group of production processes of the same type. For example, an analysis of the lumber industry shows that accidents occurring with cutting machines principally involve finger injuries. Transport accidents predominantly consist of foot and leg injuries, and brain damage and eczema are the most common hazards in the surface-treatment trade. A more detailed analysis of the relevant work processes within the industry can reveal which situations typically cause accidents. Based on this information, experts in the relevant industry can then pinpoint when such situations are likely to arise, and the possibilities for prevention.

Information retrieval and research

One of the most common uses of such information systems as filing and library systems is the retrieval of information of a specific and well-defined nature for the purpose of safety research. For instance, in a study whose aim was to formulate regulations concerning work on roofs, the doubt was raised whether any particular risk was attached to such work. The prevailing belief was that people were very seldom injured by falling from roofs while working. However, in this instance, a register of occupational accidents was used to retrieve all reports in which people had been injured by falling from roofs, and a considerable number of cases were indeed discovered, confirming the importance of continuing to formulate regulations in this area.

References

Advisory Committee on Major Hazards. 1976, 1979, 1984. *First, Second and Third Reports.* London: HMSO.

Bennis WG, KD Benne, and R Chin (eds.). 1985. *The Planning of Change.* New York: Holt, Rinehart and Winston.

Casti, JL. 1990. *Searching for Certainty: What Scientists Can Know About the Future.* New York: William Morrow.

Charsley, P. 1995. HAZOP and risk assessment (DNV London). *Loss Prev Bull* 124:16-19.

Cornelison, JD. 1989. *MORT Based Root Cause Analysis.* Working Paper No. 27. Idaho Falls, US: System Safety Development Center.

Gleick, J. 1987. *Chaos: Making a New Science.* New York: Viking Penguin.

Groeneweg, J. 1996. *Controlling the Controllable: The Management of Safety.* 3rd revised edition. The Netherlands: DSWO Press, Leiden University.

Haddon, W. 1980. The basic strategies for reducing damage from hazards of all kinds. *Hazard Prev* September/October:8-12.

Hendrick K and L Benner. 1987. *Investigating Accidents with STEP.* New York: Dekker.

Johnson, WG. 1980. *MORT Safety Assurance Systems.* New York: Marcel Dekker.

Kjellén, U and RK Tinmannsvik. 1989. *SMORT— Säkerhetsanalys av industriell organisation.* Stockholm: Arbetarskyddsnämnden.

Kletz, T. 1988. *Learning from Accidents in Industry.* London: Butterworth.

Knox, NW and RW Eicher. 1992. *MORT User's Manual.* Report No. SSDC-4, Rev. 3. Idaho Falls, US: System Safety Development Center.

Kruysse, HW. 1993. Conditions for safe traffic behaviour. Doctoral thesis, Faculty of Social Sciences, Leiden University, the Netherlands.

Nertney, RJ. 1975. *Occupancy-use Readiness Manual —Safety Considerations.* Report No. SSDC-1. Idaho Falls, US: System Safety Development Center.

Pascale, RTA, and AG Athos. 1980. *The Art of Japanese Management.* London: Penguin.

Peters, TJ and RH Waterman. 1982. *In Search of Excellence. Lessons from America's Best-run Companies.* New York: Haysen & Row.

Petroski, H. 1992. *To Engineer is Human: The Role of Failure in Successful Design.* New York: Vintage.

Rasmussen, J. 1988. *Information Processing and Human-machine Interaction, and Approach to Cognitive Engineering.* Amsterdam: Elsevier.

Reason, JT. 1990. *Human Error.* Cambridge: CUP.

Reason, JT, R Shotton, WA Wagenaar, and PTW Hudson. 1989. *TRIPOD, A Principled Basis for Safer Operations.* Report prepared for Shell Internationale Petroleum Maatschappij, Exploration and Production.

Roggeveen, V. 1994. Care Structuur in Arbeidsomstandighedenzorg. Reader of the Post Hoger Onderwijs Hogere Veiligheids course, Amsterdam.

Ruuhilehto, K. 1993. The management oversight and risk tree (MORT). In *Quality Management of Safety and Risk Analysis,* edited by J Suokas and V Rouhiainen. Amsterdam:Elsevier.

Schein, EH. 1989. *Organizational Culture and Leadership.* Oxford: Jossey-Bass.

Scott, WR. 1978. Theoretical perspectives. In *Environments and Organizations,* edited by MW Meyer. San Francisco:Jossey-Bass.

Successful Health & Safety Management: Appl.1. 1991. London: HMSO.

Van der Schrier, JH, J Groeneweg, and VR van Amerongen. 1994. Accident analysis using the TRIPOD top-down method. Masters thesis, Centre for Safety Research, Leiden University, The Netherlands.

Waganaar, WA. 1992. Influencing human behavior. Toward a practical approach for E&P. *J Petrol Tech* 11:1261-1281.

Wagenaar, WA and J Groeneweg. 1987. Accidents at sea: Multiple causes and impossible consequences. *International Journal of Man-Machine Studies* 27:587-598.

Other relevant readings

Heselmans, M, J Roels, J Stijnen, J Van de Kerckhove, and E Van Gils. 1994. *The Pellenberg Audit System, PAS* (in Dutch). Leuven, Belgium: Garant.

Van Gils, E. 1993. Safety management system elements. A point of view of the Belgian Labour Inspectorate based on ISO 9001, Industry Proceedings CEC Seminar, Ravello.

57. AUDITS, INSPECTIONS AND INVESTIGATIONS

58

Chapter Editors
Kenneth Gerecke and
Charles T. Pope

Contents

● SYSTEMS ANALYSIS

Manh Trung Ho

A *system* can be defined as a set of interdependent components combined in such a way as to perform a given function under specified conditions. A machine is a tangible and particularly clear-cut example of a system in this sense, but there are other systems, involving men and women on a team or in a workshop or factory, which are far more complex and not so easy to define. *Safety* suggests the absence of danger or risk of accident or harm. In order to avoid ambiguity, the general concept of an *unwanted occurrence* will be employed. Absolute safety, in the sense of the impossibility of a more or less unfortunate incident occurring, is not attainable; realistically one must aim for a very low, rather than a zero probability of unwanted occurrences.

A given system may be looked upon as safe or unsafe only with respect to the performance that is actually expected from it. With this in mind, the safety level of a system can be defined as follows: "For any given set of unwanted occurrences, the level of safety (or unsafeness) of a system is determined by the probability of these occurrences taking place over a given period of time". Examples of unwanted occurrences that would be of interest in the present connection include: multiple fatalities, death of one or several persons, serious injury, slight injury, damage to the environment, harmful effects on living beings, destruction of plants or buildings, and major or limited material or equipment damage.

Purpose of the System Safety Analysis

The object of a system safety analysis is to ascertain the factors which have a bearing on the probability of the unwanted occurrences, to study the way in which these occurrences take place and, ultimately, to develop preventive measures to reduce their probability.

The analytic phase of the problem can be divided into two main aspects:

1. identification and description of the *types* of dysfunction or maladjustment
2. identification of the *sequences* of dysfunctions that combine one with another (or with more "normal" occurrences) to lead ultimately to the unwanted occurrence itself, and the assessment of their likelihood.

Once the various dysfunctions and their consequences have been studied, the system safety analysts can direct their attention to preventive measures. Research in this area will be based directly on earlier findings. This investigation of preventive means follows the two main aspects of the system safety analysis.

Methods of Analysis

System safety analysis may be conducted before or after the event (a priori or a posteriori); in both instances, the method used may be either direct or reverse. An a priori analysis takes place before the unwanted occurrence. The analyst takes a certain number of such occurrences and sets out to discover the various stages that may lead up to them. By contrast, an a posteriori analysis is carried out after the unwanted occurrence has taken place. Its purpose is to provide guidance for the future and, specifically, to draw any conclusions that may be useful for any subsequent a priori analyses.

Although it may seem that an a priori analysis would be very much more valuable than an a posteriori analysis, since it precedes the incident, the two are in fact complementary. Which method is used depends on the complexity of the system involved

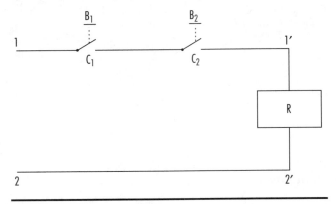

Figure 58.1 ● Two-button control circuit.

and on what is already known about the subject. In the case of tangible systems such as machines or industrial facilities, previous experience can usually serve in preparing a fairly detailed a priori analysis. However, even then the analysis is not necessarily infallible and is sure to benefit from a subsequent a posteriori analysis based essentially on a study of the incidents that occur in the course of operation. As to more complex systems involving persons, such as work shifts, workshops or factories, a posteriori analysis is even more important. In such cases, past experience is not always sufficient to permit detailed and reliable a priori analysis.

An a posteriori analysis may develop into an a priori analysis as the analyst goes beyond the single process that led up to the incident in question and starts to look into the various occurrences that could reasonably lead to such an incident or similar incidents.

Another way in which an a posteriori analysis can become an a priori analysis is when the emphasis is placed not on the occurrence (whose prevention is the main purpose of the current analysis) but on less serious incidents. These incidents, such as technical hitches, material damage and potential or minor accidents, of relatively little significance in themselves, can be identified as warning signs of more serious occurrences. In such cases, although carried out after the occurrence of minor incidents, the analysis will be an a priori analysis as regards more serious occurrences that have not yet taken place.

There are two possible methods of studying the mechanism or logic behind the sequence of two or more events:

1. The *direct*, or *inductive*, method starts with the causes in order to predict their effects.
2. The *reverse*, or *deductive*, method looks at the effects and works backwards to the causes.

Figure 58.1 is a diagram of a control circuit requiring two buttons (B_1 and B_2) to be pressed simultaneously in order to activate the relay coil (R) and start the machine. This example may be used to illustrate, in practical terms, the *direct* and *reverse* methods used in system safety analysis.

Direct method

In the *direct method*, the analyst begins by (1) listing faults, dysfunctions and maladjustments, (2) studying their effects and (3) determining whether or not those effects are a threat to safety. In the case of figure 58.1, the following faults may occur:

* a break in the wire between 2 and 2′
* unintentional contact at C_1 (or C_2) as a result of mechanical blocking

Table 58.1 • Possible dysfunctions of a two-button control circuit and their consequences.

Faults	Consequences
Break in the wire between 2 and 2′	Impossible to start the machine*
Accidental closing of B_1 (or B_2)	No immediate consequence
Contact at C_1 (or C_2) as a result of mechanical blocking	No immediate consequence but possibility of the machine being started simply by pressure on button B_2 (or B_1)**
Short circuit between 1 and 1′	Activation of relay coil R — accidental starting of the machine***

* Occurrence with a direct influence on the reliability of the system.

** Occurrence responsible for a serious reduction in the safety level of the system.

*** Dangerous occurrence to be avoided.

See text and figure 58.1.

- accidental closing of B_1 (or B_2)
- short circuit between 1 and 1′.

The analyst can then deduce the consequences of these faults, and the findings can be set out in tabular form (table 58.1).

In table 58.1 consequences which are dangerous or liable to seriously reduce the safety level of the system can be designated by conventional signs such as ***.

Note: In table 58.1 a break in the wire between 2 and 2′ (shown in figure 58.1) results in an occurrence that is not considered dangerous. It has no direct effect on the safety of the system; however, the probability of such an incident occurring has a direct bearing on the reliability of the system.

The direct method is particularly appropriate for simulation. Figure 58.2 shows an analog simulator designed for studying the safety of press-control circuits. The simulation of the control circuit makes it possible to verify that, so long as there is no fault, the circuit is actually capable of ensuring the required function without infringing the safety criteria. In addition, the simulator can allow the analyst to introduce faults in the various components of the circuit, observe their consequences and thus distinguish those circuits that are properly designed (with few or no

Figure 58.2 • Simulator for the study of press-control circuits.

dangerous faults) from those which are poorly designed. This type of safety analysis may also be performed using a computer.

Reverse method

In the *reverse method*, the analyst works backwards from the undesirable occurrence, incident or accident, towards the various previous events to determine which may be capable of resulting in the occurrences to be avoided. In figure 58.1, the ultimate occurrence to be avoided would be the unintentional starting of the machine.

- The starting of the machine may be caused by an uncontrolled activation of the relay coil (R).
- The activation of the coil may, in turn, result from a short circuit between 1 and 1′ or from an unintentional and simultaneous closing of switches C_1 and C_2.
- Unintentional closing of C_1 may be the consequence of a mechanical blocking of C_1 or of the accidental pressing of B_1. Similar reasoning applies to C_2.

The findings of this analysis can be represented in a diagram which resembles a tree (for this reason the reverse method is known as "fault tree analysis"), such as depicted in figure 58.3.

The diagram follows logical operations, the most important of which are the "OR" and "AND" operations. The "OR" operation signifies that $[X_1]$ will occur if either [A] or [B] (or both) take place. The "AND" operation signifies that before $[X_2]$ can occur, both [C] and [D] must have taken place (see figure 58.4).

The reverse method is very often used in a priori analysis of tangible systems, especially in the chemical, aeronautical, space and nuclear industries. It has also been found extremely useful as a method to investigate industrial accidents.

Although they are very different, the direct and reverse methods are complementary. The direct method is based on a set of faults or dysfunctions, and the value of such an analysis therefore largely depends on the relevance of the various dysfunctions taken into account at the start. Seen in this light, the reverse method seems to be more systematic. Given knowledge of what types of accidents or incidents may happen, the analyst can in theory apply this method to work back towards all the dysfunctions or combinations of dysfunctions capable of bringing them about. However, because all the dangerous behaviours of a system are not necessarily known in advance, they can be discovered by the direct method, applied by simulation, for example. Once these have been discovered, the hazards can be analysed in greater detail by the reverse method.

Problems of System Safety Analysis

The analytical methods described above are not just mechanical processes which need only to be applied automatically in order to reach useful conclusions for improving system safety. On the contrary, analysts encounter a number of problems in the course of their work, and the usefulness of their analyses will depend largely on how they set about solving them. Some of the typical problems that may arise are described below.

Understanding the system to be studied and its operating conditions

The fundamental problems in any system safety analysis are the definition of the system to be studied, its limitations and the conditions under which it is supposed to operate throughout its existence.

If the analyst takes into account a subsystem that is too limited, the result may be the adoption of a series of random preventive measures (a situation in which everything is geared to preventing certain particular types of occurrence, while equally serious hazards are ignored or underestimated). If, on the other hand, the

Figure 58.3 • Possible chain of events.

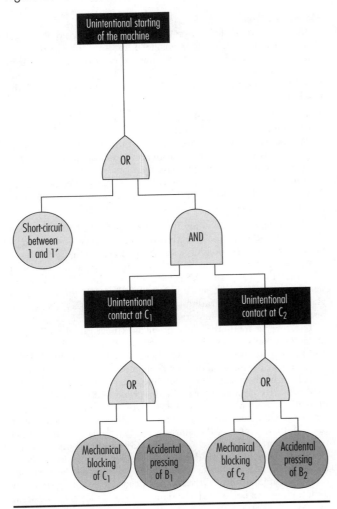

Figure 58.4 • Representation of two logical operations.

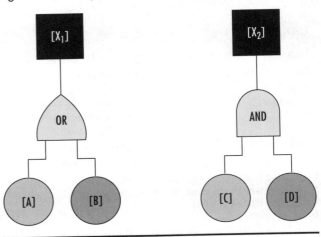

is being considered, the possible types of dysfunction—and the relevant preventive measures—are quite different. A good prevention policy must make allowance for the dysfunctions that may occur at various levels.

The operating conditions of the system may be defined in terms of the way in which the system is supposed to function, and the environmental conditions to which it may be subject. This definition must be realistic enough to allow for the actual conditions in which the system is likely to operate. A system that is very safe only in a very restricted operating range may not be so safe if the user is unable to keep within the theoretical operating range prescribed. A safe system must thus be robust enough to withstand reasonable variations in the conditions in which it functions, and must tolerate certain simple but foreseeable errors on the part of the operators.

System modelling

It is often necessary to develop a model in order to analyse the safety of a system. This may raise certain problems which are worth examining.

For a concise and relatively simple system such as a conventional machine, the model is almost directly derivable from the descriptions of the material components and their functions (motors, transmission, etc.) and the way in which these components are interrelated. The number of possible component failure modes is similarly limited.

Modern machines such as computers and robots, which contain complex components like microprocessors and electronic circuits with very large-scale integration, pose a special problem. This problem has not been fully resolved in terms either of modelling or of predicting the different possible failure modes, because there are so many elementary transistors in each chip and because of the use of diverse kinds of software.

When the system to be analysed is a human organization, an interesting problem encountered in modelling lies in the choice and definition of certain non-material or not fully material components. A particular workstation may be represented, for example, by a system comprising workers, software, tasks, machines, materials and environment. (The "task" component may prove difficult to define, for it is not the prescribed task that counts but the task as it is actually performed).

When modelling human organizations, the analyst may opt to break down the system under consideration into an information subsystem and one or more action subsystems. Analysis of failures

system considered is too comprehensive or general in relation to a given problem, it may result in excessive vagueness of concept and responsibilities, and the analysis may not lead to the adoption of appropriate preventive measures.

A typical example which illustrates the problem of defining the system to be studied is the safety of industrial machines or plant. In this kind of situation, the analyst may be tempted to consider only the actual equipment, overlooking the fact that it has to be operated or controlled by one or more persons. Simplification of this kind is sometimes valid. However, what has to be analysed is not just the machine subsystem but the entire worker-plus-machine system in the various stages of the life of the equipment (including, for example, transport and handling, assembly, testing and adjusting, normal operation, maintenance, disassembly and, in some cases, destruction). At each stage the machine is part of a specific system whose purpose and modes of functioning and malfunctioning are totally different from those of the system at other stages. It must therefore be designed and manufactured in such a way as to permit the performance of the required function under good safety conditions at each of the stages.

More generally, as regards safety studies in firms, there are several system levels: the machine, workstation, shift, department, factory and the firm as a whole. Depending on which system level at different stages of the information subsystem (information acquisition, transmission, processing and use) can be highly instructive.

Problems associated with multiple levels of analysis

Problems associated with multiple levels of analysis often develop because starting from an unwanted occurrence, the analyst may work back towards incidents that are more and more remote in time. Depending on the level of analysis considered, the nature of the dysfunctions that occur varies; the same applies to the preventive measures. It is important to be able to decide at what level analysis should be stopped and at what level preventive action should be taken. An example is the simple case of an accident resulting from a mechanical failure caused by the repeated utilization of a machine under abnormal conditions. This may have been caused by a lack of operator training or from poor organization of work. Depending on the level of analysis considered, the preventive action required may be the replacement of the machine by another machine capable of withstanding more severe conditions of use, the use of the machine only under normal conditions, changes in personnel training, or a reorganization of work.

The effectiveness and scope of a preventive measure depend on the level at which it is introduced. Preventive action in the immediate vicinity of the unwanted occurrence is more likely to have a direct and rapid impact, but its effects may be limited; on the other hand, by working backwards to a reasonable extent in the analysis of events, it should be possible to find types of dysfunction that are common to numerous accidents. Any preventive action taken at this level will be much wider in scope, but its effectiveness may be less direct.

Bearing in mind that there are several levels of analysis, there may also be numerous patterns of preventive action, each of which carries its own share of the work of prevention. This is an extremely important point, and one need only return to the example of the accident presently under consideration to appreciate the fact. Proposing that the machine be replaced by another machine capable of withstanding more severe conditions of use places the onus of prevention on the machine. Deciding that the machine should be used only under normal conditions means placing the onus on the user. In the same way, the onus may be placed on personnel training, organization of work or simultaneously on the machine, the user, the training function and the organization function.

For any given level of analysis, an accident often appears to be the consequence of the combination of several dysfunctions or maladjustments. Depending on whether action is taken on one dysfunction or another, or on several simultaneously, the pattern of preventive action adopted will vary.

HAND AND PORTABLE POWER TOOL SAFETY

US Department of Labor—Occupational Safety and Health Administration; edited by Kenneth Gerecke

Tools are such a common part of our lives that it is sometimes difficult to remember that they may pose hazards. All tools are manufactured with safety in mind, but occasionally an accident may occur before tool-related hazards are recognized. Workers must learn to recognize the hazards associated with the different types of tools and the safety precautions required to prevent those

hazards. Appropriate personal protective equipment, such as safety goggles or gloves, should be worn for protection from potential hazards that may be encountered while using portable power tools and hand tools.

Hand Tools

Hand tools are non-powered and include everything from axes to wrenches. The greatest hazards posed by hand tools result from misuse, use of the wrong tool for the job, and improper maintenance. Some of the hazards associated with the use of hand tools include but are not limited to the following:

- Using a screwdriver as a chisel may cause the tip of the screwdriver to break off and fly, hitting the user or other employees.
- If a wooden handle on a tool such as a hammer or an axe is loose, splintered or cracked, the head of the tool may fly off and strike the user or another worker.
- A wrench must not be used if its jaws are sprung, because it might slip.
- Impact tools such as chisels, wedges or drift pins are unsafe if they have mushroomed heads which might shatter on impact, sending sharp fragments flying.

The employer is responsible for the safe condition of tools and equipment provided to employees, but the employees have the responsibility to use and maintain the tools properly. Workers should direct saw blades, knives or other tools away from aisle areas and other employees working in close proximity. Knives and scissors must be kept sharp, as dull tools can be more hazardous than sharp ones. (See figure 58.5.)

Safety requires that floors be kept as clean and dry as possible to prevent accidental slips when working with or around dangerous hand tools. Although sparks produced by iron and steel hand tools are not normally hot enough to be sources of ignition, when working with or around flammable materials, spark-resistant tools made from brass, plastic, aluminium or wood may be used to prevent spark formation.

Power Tools

Power tools are hazardous when improperly used. There are several types of power tools, usually categorized according to the power source (electric, pneumatic, liquid fuel, hydraulic, steam and explosive powder actuated). Employees should be qualified or trained in the use of all power tools used in their work. They should understand the potential hazards associated with the use of power tools, and observe the following general safety precautions to prevent those hazards from occurring:

- Never carry a tool by the cord or hose.
- Never yank the cord or the hose to disconnect it from the receptacle.
- Keep cords and hoses away from heat, oil and sharp edges.
- Disconnect tools when they are not in use, before servicing, and when changing accessories such as blades, bits and cutters.
- All observers should stay a safe distance away from the work area.
- Secure work with clamps or a vise, freeing both hands to operate the tool.
- Avoid accidental starting. The worker should not hold a finger on the switch button while carrying a plugged-in tool. Tools

Figure 58.5 • A screwdriver.

which have lock-on controls should be disengaged when power is interrupted so that they do not start up automatically upon restoration of power.

- Tools should be maintained with care and kept sharp and clean for best performance. Instructions in the user's manual should be followed for lubrication and changing accessories.
- Workers should assure they have good footing and balance when using power tools. Appropriate apparel should be worn, as loose clothing, ties or jewellery can become caught in moving parts.
- All portable electric tools that are damaged shall be removed from use and tagged "Do Not Use" to prevent electrical shock.

Protective Guards

Hazardous moving parts of power tools need to be safeguarded. For example, belts, gears, shafts, pulleys, sprockets, spindles, drums, flywheels, chains or other reciprocating, rotating or moving parts of equipment must be guarded if such parts are exposed to contact by workers. Where necessary, guards should be provided to protect the operator and others with respect to hazards associated with:

- the point of operation
- in-running nip points
- rotating and reciprocating parts
- flying chips and sparks, and mist or spray from metal-working fluids.

Safety guards must never be removed when a tool is being used. For example, portable circular saws must be equipped with guards. An upper guard must cover the entire blade of the saw. A retractable lower guard must cover the teeth of the saw, except when it makes contact with the work material. The lower guard must automatically return to the covering position when the tool is withdrawn from the work. Note the blade guards in the illustration of a power saw (figure 58.6).

Safety Switches and Controls

The following are examples of hand-held power tools which must be equipped with a momentary contact "on-off" control switch:

- drills, tappers and fastener drivers
- horizontal, vertical and angle grinders with wheels larger than 2 inches (5.1 cm) in diameter
- disc and belt sanders

Figure 58.6 • A circular saw with guard.

- reciprocating and sabre saws.

These tools also may be equipped with a lock-on control, provided that turnoff can be accomplished by a single motion of the same finger or fingers that turn it on.

The following hand-held power tools may be equipped with only a positive "on-off" control switch:

- platen sanders
- disc sanders with discs 2 inches (5.1 cm) or less in diameter
- grinders with wheels 2 inches (5.1 cm) or less in diameter
- routers and planers
- laminate trimmers, nibblers and shears
- scroll saws and jigsaws with blade shanks ¼ inch (0.64 cm) wide or less.

Other hand-held power tools which must be equipped with a constant pressure switch that will shut off the power when the pressure is released include:

- circular saws having a blade diameter greater than 2 inches (5.1 cm)
- chain-saws
- percussion tools without positive accessory-holding means.

Electric Tools

Workers using electric tools must be aware of several dangers. The most serious of these is the possibility of electrocution, followed by burns and slight shocks. Under certain conditions, even a small amount of current can result in fibrillation of the heart which may result in death. A shock also may cause a worker to fall off a ladder or other elevated work surfaces.

To reduce the potential of injury to workers from shock, tools must be protected by at least one of the following means:

- *Grounded* by a three-wire cord (with a ground wire). Three-wire cords contain two current-carrying conductors and a grounding conductor. One end of the grounding conductor connects to the tool's metal housing. The other end is grounded through a prong on the plug. Any time an adapter is used to accommodate a two-hole receptacle, the adapter wire must be attached to a known ground. The third prong should never be removed from the plug. (See figure 58.7.)
- *Double insulated.* The worker and the tools are protected in two ways: (1) by normal insulation on the wires inside, and (2) by a housing that cannot conduct electricity to the operator in the event of a malfunction.
- *Powered by a low-voltage isolation transformer.*
- *Connected through ground fault circuit interrupters.* These are permanent and portable devices which instantaneously disconnect a circuit when it seeks ground through a worker's body or through grounded objects.

Figure 58.7 • An electric drill.

These general safety practices should be followed in using electric tools:

- Electric tools should be operated within their design limitations.
- Gloves and safety footwear are recommended during use of electric tools.
- When not in use, tools should be stored in a dry place.
- Tools should not be used if wires or connectors are frayed, bent or damaged.
- Electric tools should not be used in damp or wet locations.
- Work areas should be well lighted.

Powered Abrasive Wheels

Powered abrasive grinding, cutting, polishing and wire buffing wheels create special safety problems because the wheels may disintegrate and throw off flying fragments.

Before abrasive wheels are mounted, they should be inspected closely and sound (or ring) tested by tapping gently with a light non-metallic instrument to be sure that they are free from cracks or defects. If wheels are cracked or sound dead, they could fly apart in operation and must not be used. A sound and undamaged wheel will give a clear metallic tone or "ring".

To prevent the wheel from cracking, the user should be sure it fits freely on the spindle. The spindle nut must be tightened enough to hold the wheel in place without distorting the flange. Follow the manufacturer's recommendations. Care must be taken to assure that the spindle wheel will not exceed the abrasive wheel specifications. Due to the possibility of a wheel disintegrating (exploding) during start-up, the worker should never stand directly in front of the wheel as it accelerates to full operating speed. Portable grinding tools need to be equipped with safety guards to protect workers not only from the moving wheel surface, but also from flying fragments in case of breakage. In addition, when using a powered grinder, these precautions should be observed:

- Always use eye protection.
- Turn off the power when tool is not in use.
- Never clamp a hand-held grinder in a vise.

Pneumatic Tools

Pneumatic tools are powered by compressed air and include chippers, drills, hammers and sanders. Although there are several potential dangers encountered in the use of pneumatic tools, the main one is the danger of getting hit by one of the tool's attachments or by some kind of fastener the worker is using with the tool. Eye protection is required and face protection is recommended when working with pneumatic tools. Noise is another hazard. Working with noisy tools such as jackhammers requires proper, effective use of appropriate hearing protection.

When using a pneumatic tool, the worker must check to assure that it is fastened securely to the hose to prevent a disconnection. A short wire or positive locking device attaching the air hose to the tool will serve as an added safeguard. If an air hose is more than ½ inch (1.27 cm) in diameter, a safety excess flow valve should be installed at the source of the air supply to shut off the air automatically in case the hose breaks. In general, the same precautions should be taken with an air hose that are recommended for electric cords, because the hose is subject to the same kind of damage or accidental striking, and it also presents a tripping hazard.

Compressed-air guns should never be pointed toward anyone. Workers should never "dead-end" the nozzle against themselves or anyone else. A safety clip or retainer should be installed to prevent attachments, such as a chisel on a chipping hammer, from being unintentionally shot from the barrel. Screens should be set up to protect nearby workers from being struck by flying frag-

ments around chippers, riveting guns, air hammers, staplers or air drills.

Airless spray guns that atomize paints and fluids at high pressures (1,000 pounds or more per square inch) must be equipped with automatic or manual visual safety devices that will prevent activation until the safety device is manually released. Heavy jackhammers can cause fatigue and strains which may be reduced by the use of heavy rubber grips that provide a secure handhold. A worker operating a jackhammer must wear safety glasses and safety shoes to protect against injury if the hammer slips or falls. A face shield also should be used.

Fuel-Powered Tools

Fuel-powered tools are usually operated using small gasoline-powered internal combustion motors. The most serious potential dangers associated with the use of fuel-powered tools comes from hazardous fuel vapours that can burn or explode and give off dangerous exhaust fumes. The worker must be careful to handle, transport and store the gasoline or fuel only in approved flammable liquid containers, according to proper procedures for flammable liquids. Before the tank for a fuel-powered tool is refilled, the user must shut down the engine and allow it to cool to prevent accidental ignition of hazardous vapours. If a fuel-powered tool is used inside a closed area, effective ventilation and/or protective equipment is necessary to prevent exposure to carbon monoxide. Fire extinguishers must be available in the area.

Explosive Powder-Actuated Tools

Explosive powder-actuated tools operate like a loaded gun and should be treated with the same respect and precautions. In fact, they are so dangerous that they must be operated only by specially trained or qualified employees. Suitable ear, eye and face protection are essential when using a powder-actuated tool. All powder-actuated tools should be designed for varying powder charges so that the user can select a powder level necessary to do the work without excessive force.

The muzzle end of the tool should have a protective shield or guard centred perpendicularly on the barrel to protect the user from any flying fragments or particles that might create a hazard when the tool is fired. The tool must be designed so that it will not fire unless it has this kind of safety device. To prevent the tool from firing accidentally, two separate motions are required for firing: one to bring the tool into position, and another to pull the trigger. The tools must not be able to operate until they are pressed against the work surface with a force at least 5 pounds greater than the total weight of the tool.

If a powder-actuated tool misfires, the user should wait at least 30 seconds before trying to fire it again. If it still will not fire, the user should wait at least another 30 seconds so that the faulty cartridge is less likely to explode, then carefully remove the load. The bad cartridge should be put in water or otherwise safely disposed of in accordance with employer's procedures.

If a powder-actuated tool develops a defect during use, it should be tagged and taken out of service immediately until it is properly repaired. Precautions for the safe use and handling of powder-actuated tools include the following:

- Powder-actuated tools should not be used in explosive or flammable atmospheres except upon issuance of a hot-work permit by an authorized person.
- Before using the tool, the worker should inspect it to determine that it is clean, that all moving parts operate freely and that the barrel is free from obstructions.
- The tool should never be pointed at anybody.

- The tool should not be loaded unless it is to be used immediately. A loaded tool should not be left unattended, especially where it may be available to unauthorized persons.
- Hands should be kept clear of the barrel end.

In using powder-actuated tools to apply fasteners, the following safety precautions should be considered:

- Do not fire fasteners into material that would let them pass through to the other side.
- Do not drive fasteners into materials like brick or concrete any closer than 3 inches (7.6 cm) to an edge or corner, or into steel any closer than ½ inch (1.27 cm) to a corner or edge.
- Do not drive fasteners into very hard or brittle material that might chip, shatter or make the fasteners ricochet.
- Use an alignment guide when shooting fasteners into existing holes. Do not drive fasteners into a spalled area caused by an unsatisfactory fastening.

Hydraulic Power Tools

The fluid used in hydraulic power tools must be approved for the expected use and must retain its operating characteristics at the most extreme temperatures to which it will be exposed. The manufacturer's recommended safe operating pressure for hoses, valves, pipes, filters and other fittings must not be exceeded. Where there is a potential for a leak under high pressure in an area where sources of ignition, such as open flames or hot surfaces, may be present, the use of fire-resistant fluids as the hydraulic medium should be considered.

Jacks

All jacks—lever and ratchet jacks, screw jacks and hydraulic jacks—must have a device that stops them from jacking up too high. The manufacturer's load limit must be permanently marked in a prominent place on the jack and should not be exceeded. Use wooden blocking under the base if necessary to make the jack level and secure. If the lift surface is metal, place a 1-inch-thick (2.54 cm) hardwood block or equivalent between the underside of the surface and the metal jack head to reduce the danger of slippage. A jack should never be used to support a lifted load. Once the load has been lifted, it should immediately be supported by blocks.

To set up a jack, make certain of the following conditions:

1. The base rests on a firm level surface.
2. The jack is correctly centred.
3. The jack head bears against a level surface.
4. The lift force is applied evenly.

Proper maintenance of jacks is essential for safety. All jacks must be inspected before each use and lubricated regularly. If a jack is subjected to an abnormal load or shock, it should be thoroughly examined to make sure it has not been damaged. Hydraulic jacks exposed to freezing temperatures must be filled with an adequate antifreeze liquid.

Summary

Workers who use hand and power tools and who are exposed to the hazards of falling, flying, abrasive and splashing objects and materials, or to hazards of harmful dusts, fumes, mists, vapours or gases, must be provided with the appropriate personal equipment necessary to protect them from the hazard. All hazards involved in the use of power tools can be prevented by workers following five basic safety rules:

1. Keep all tools in good condition with regular maintenance.
2. Use the right tool for the job.
3. Examine each tool for damage before use.

4. Operate tools according to the manufacturer's instructions.
5. Select and use appropriate protective equipment.

Employees and employers have a responsibility to work together to maintain established safe work practices. If a an unsafe tool or hazardous situation is encountered, it should be brought to the attention of the proper individual immediately.

MOVING PARTS OF MACHINES

Tomas Bäckström and Marianne Döös

This article discusses situations and chains of events leading to accidents attributable to contact with the moving part of machines. People who operate and maintain machinery run the risk of being involved in serious accidents. US statistics suggest that 18,000 amputations and over 800 fatalities in the United States each year are assignable to such causes. According to the US National Institute for Occupational Safety and Health (NIOSH), the "caught in, under, or between" category of injuries in their classification ranked highest among the most important kinds of occupational injuries in 1979. Such injuries generally involved machines (Etherton and Myers 1990). "Contact with moving machine part" has been reported as the principal injury event in just over 10% of occupational accidents ever since this category was introduced into Swedish occupational-injury statistics in 1979.

Most machines have moving parts that can cause injury. Such moving parts may be found at the point of operation where work is performed on the material, such as where cutting, shaping, boring or deforming takes place. They may be found in the apparatus which transmits energy to the parts of the machine carrying out the work, such as flywheels, pulleys, connecting rods, couplers, cams, spindles, chains, cranks and gears. They may be found in other moving parts of the machine such as wheels on mobile equipment, gear motors, pumps, compressors and so forth. Hazardous machine movements can also be found among other sorts of machinery, especially in the auxiliary pieces of equipment which handle and transport such loads as work pieces, materials, waste or tools.

All parts of a machine that move in the course of the performance of work may contribute to accidents causing injury and damages. Both rotating and linear machine movements, as well as their sources of power, can be dangerous:

Rotating motion. Even smooth rotating shafts can grip an item of clothing and, for example, draw a person's arm into a hazardous position. The danger in a rotating shaft increases if it has projecting parts or uneven or sharp surfaces, such as adjusting screws, bolts, slits, notches or cutting edges. Rotating machine parts give rise to "nip points" in three different ways:

1. There are the points between two rotating parts that rotate in opposite directions and have parallel axes, such as gears or cog-wheels, carriage rollers or mangles.
2. There are the points of contact between rotating parts and parts in linear movement, such as found between a power-transmission belt and its pulley, a chain and a sprocket, or a rack and pinion.
3. Rotating machine movements can give rise to the risk of cuts and crushing injuries when they take place in close proximity to stationary objects—this sort of condition exists between a worm conveyor and its housing, between the spokes of a wheel and the machine bed, or between a grinding wheel and a tool jig.

Figure 58.8 • Examples of mechanical movements that can injure a person.

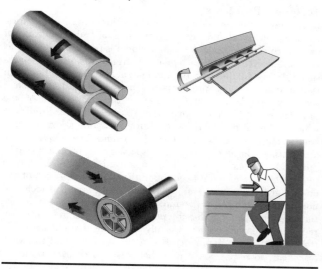

Linear movements. Vertical, horizontal and reciprocating motion can cause injury in several ways: a person may receive a shove or blow from a machine part, and may be caught between the machine part and some other object, or may be cut by a sharp edge, or sustain a nip injury by being trapped between the moving part and another object (figure 58.8).

Power sources. Frequently, external sources of power are employed to run a machine which may involve considerable quantities of energy. These include electric, steam, hydraulic, pneumatic and mechanical power systems, all of which, if released or uncontrolled, can give rise to serious injuries or damage. A study of accidents that occurred over one year (1987 to 1988) among farmers in nine villages in northern India showed that fodder-cutting machines, all otherwise of the same design, are more dangerous when powered by a motor or tractor. The relative frequency of accidents involving more than a minor injury (per machine) was 5.1 per thousand for manual cutters and 8.6 per thousand for powered cutters (Mohan and Patel 1992).

Injuries Associated with Machine Movements

Since the forces associated with machine movements are often quite large, it can be presumed that the injuries to which they give rise will be serious. This presumption is confirmed by several sources. "Contact with moving machinery or material being machined" accounted for only 5% of all occupational accidents but for as much as 10% of fatal and major accidents (fractures, amputations and so on) according to British statistics (HSE 1989). Studies of two vehicle-manufacturing workplaces in Sweden point in the same direction. Accidents caused by machine movements gave rise to twice the number of days of sick leave, as measured by median values, compared to non-machine-related accidents. Machine-related accidents also differed from other accidents with regard to part of the body injured: The results indicated that 80% of the injuries sustained in "machine" accidents were to the hands and fingers, while the corresponding proportion for "other" accidents was 40% (Backström and Döös 1995).

The risk situation at automated installations has turned out to be both different (in terms of type of accident, sequence of events and degree of injury severity) and more complicated (both in technical terms and with regard to the need for specialized skills)

than at installations where conventional machinery is used. The term *automated* is herein meant to refer to equipment which, without the direct intervention of a human being, can either initiate a machine movement or change its direction or function. Such equipment requires sensor devices (e.g., position sensors or microswitches) and/or some form of sequential controls (e.g., a computer program) to direct and monitor their activities. Over recent decades, a *programmable logic controller* (PLC) has been increasingly employed as the control unit in production systems. Small computers are now the most common means used for controlling production equipment in the industrialized world, while other means of control, such as electro-mechanical units, are becoming less and less common. In the Swedish manufacturing industry, the use of numerically controlled (NC) machines increased by 11 to 12% per year over the 1980s (Hörte and Lindberg 1989). In modern industrial production, being injured by "moving parts of machines" is increasingly becoming equivalent to being injured by "computer-controlled machine movements".

Automated installations are found in more and more sectors of industry, and they have an increasing number of functions. Stores management, materials handling, processing, assembly and packaging are all being automated. Series production has come to resemble process production. If the feeding, machining and ejection of work pieces are mechanized, the operator no longer needs to be in the risk zone during the course of regular, undisturbed production. Research studies of automated manufacturing have shown that accidents occur primarily in the handling of disturbances affecting production. However, people can also get in the way of machine movements in performing other tasks, such as cleaning, adjusting, resetting, controlling and repairing.

When production is automated and the process is no longer under the direct control of the human being, the risk of unexpected machine movements increases. Most operators who work with groups or lines of inter-linked machines have experienced such unexpected machine movements. Many *automation accidents* occur as a result of just such movements. An automation accident is an accident in which the automatic equipment controlled (or should have controlled) the energy giving rise to the injury. This means that the force which injures the person comes from the machine itself (e.g., the energy of a machine movement). In a study of 177 automation accidents in Sweden, it was found that injury was caused by the "unexpected start" of a part of a machine in 84% of cases (Backström and Harms-Ringdahl 1984). A typical example of an injury caused by a computer-controlled machine movement is shown in figure 58.9.

One of the studies referred to above (Backström and Döös 1995) showed that automatically controlled machine movements were causally linked to longer periods of sick leave than injuries due to other kinds of machine movements, the median value being four times higher at one of the workplaces. The injury pattern of automation accidents was similar to that for other machine accidents (mainly involving hands and fingers), but the tendency was for the former kind of injuries to be more serious (amputations, crushes and fractures).

Computer control, like manual, has weaknesses from the perspective of reliability. There is no guarantee that a computer program will operate without error. The electronics, with their low signal levels, may be sensitive to interference if not properly protected, and the consequences of resultant failures are not always possible to predict. Furthermore, programming changes are often left undocumented. One method used to compensate for this weakness is, for example, by operating "double" systems in which there are two independent chains of functional components and a method for monitoring such that both chains display the same value. If the systems display different values, this indicates a

Figure 58.9 • A typical example of an injury caused by a computer-controlled machine movement.

An engine block is transported in on a conveyor with turntables at two levels. The block is held by fixtures on the upper level, and the fixtures are returned, empty, on the lower. The conveyor stops suddenly. An assembler sees that one of the return fixtures has become stuck in the turntable again. When he stretches out his hand and pulls on the engine block, a sensor is activated. The turntable starts to turn and traps his hand. (Illustrator: Tomas Karlsson.)

failure in one of them. But there is a possibility that both chains of components may suffer from the same fault and that they both can be put out of order by the same disturbance, thereby giving a false positive reading (as both systems agree). However, in only a few of the cases investigated has it been possible to trace an accident to computer failure (see below), despite the fact that it is common for a single computer to control all the functions of an installation (even the stopping of a machine as a result of the activation of a safety device). As an alternate, consideration may

Figure 58.10 • Types of technical problems involved in automation accidents (number of accidents =127).

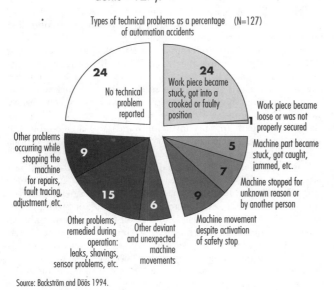

Types of technical problems as a percentage (N=127) of automation accidents

24 — No technical problem reported

24 — Work piece became stuck, got into a crooked or faulty position

1 — Work piece became loose or was not properly secured

5 — Machine part became stuck, got caught, jammed, etc.

7 — Machine stopped for unknown reason or by another person

9 — Machine movement despite activation of safety stop

6 — Other deviant and unexpected machine movements

15 — Other problems, remedied during operation: leaks, shavings, sensor problems, etc.

9 — Other problems occurring while stopping the machine for repairs, fault tracing, adjustment, etc.

Source: Backström and Döös 1994.

be given to providing a tried-and-tested system with electro-mechanical components for safety functions.

Technical Problems

In general, it can be said that a single accident has many causes, including technical, individual, environmental and organizational ones. For preventive purposes, an accident is best looked at not as an isolated event, but as a *sequence* of events or a process (Backström 1996). In the case of automation accidents, it has been shown that technical problems are frequently part of such a sequence and occur either at one of the early stages of the process or close to the injury event of the accident. Studies in which technical problems involved in automation accidents have been examined suggest that these lie behind 75 to 85% of the accidents. At the same time, in any specific case, there are usually other causes, such as those of an organizational nature. Only in one-tenth of cases has it been found that the direct source of the energy giving rise to an injury could be attributed to technical failure—for example, a machine movement taking place despite the machine's being in the stop position. Similar figures have been reported in other studies. Usually, a technical problem led to trouble with the equipment, so that the operator had to switch tasks (e.g., to re-position a part that was in a crooked position). The accident then occurred during the implementation of the task, prompted by the technical failure. A quarter of the automation accidents were preceded by a disturbance in the materials flow such as a part becoming stuck or getting into a crooked or otherwise faulty position (see figure 58.10).

In a study of 127 accidents involving automation, 28 of these accidents, described in figure 58.10, were further investigated to determine the types of technical problems which were involved as causal factors (Backström and Döös, in press). The problems specified in the accident investigations were most frequently caused by jammed, defective or worn-out components. In two cases, a problem was caused by a computer-program error, and in one by electromagnetic interference. In more than half of the cases (17 out of 28), faults had been present for some time but not remedied. Only in 5 of the 28 cases where a technical failure or deviation was referred to, had the defect *not* manifested itself previously. Some faults had been repaired only to reappear later. Certain defects had been present right from the time of installation, while others resulted from wear and the impact of the environment.

The proportion of automation accidents occurring in the course of the correction of a disturbance to production comes to between one-third and two-thirds of all cases, according to most studies. In other words, there is general agreement that handling production disturbances is a hazardous occupational task. The variation in the extent to which such accidents occur has many explanations, among them those related to the type of production and to how occupational tasks are classified. In some studies of disturbances, only problems and machine stops in the course of regular production have been considered; in others, a wider range of problems have been treated—for example, those involved in the setting up of work.

A very important measure in the prevention of automation accidents is to prepare procedures for removing the causes of production disturbances so that they are not repeated. In a specialized study of production disturbances at time of accident (Döös and Backström 1994), it was found that the most common task to which disturbances gave rise was the freeing or the correcting of the position of a work piece that had become stuck or wrongly placed. This type of problem initiated one of two rather similar sequences of events: (1) the part was freed and came into its correct position, the machine received an automatic signal to start, and the person was injured by the machine movement

Figure 58.11 • Type of disturbance handling at time of accident (number of accidents =76).

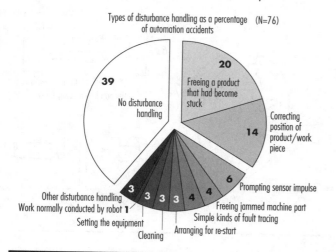

Types of disturbance handling as a percentage (N=76) of automation accidents

initiated, (2) there was not time for the part to be freed or repositioned before the person was injured by a machine movement that came unexpectedly, more quickly or was of greater force than the operator expected. Other disturbance-handling involved prompting a sensor impulse, freeing a jammed machine part, carrying out simple kinds of fault tracing, and arranging for restart (see figure 58.11).

Worker Safety

The categories of personnel which tend to be injured in automation accidents depend on how work is organized—that is, on which occupational group performs the hazardous tasks. In practice, this is a matter of which person at the workplace is assigned to deal with problems and disturbances on a routine basis. In modern Swedish industry, active interventions are usually demanded from the persons operating the machine. This is why, in the previously mentioned vehicle-manufacturing workplace study in Sweden (Backström and Döös, accepted for publication), it was found that 82% of the people who sustained injuries from automated machines were production workers or operators. Operators also had a higher relative accident frequency (15 automation accidents per 1,000 operators per year) than maintenance workers (6 per 1,000). The findings of studies which indicate that maintenance workers are more affected are at least partly to be explained by the fact that operators are not allowed to enter machining areas in some companies. In organizations with a different type of task distribution, other categories of personnel—setters, for example—may be given the task of solving any production problems that arise.

The most common corrective measure taken in this connection in order to raise the level of personal safety is to protect the person from hazardous machine movements by using some kind of safety device, such as machine guarding. The main principle here is that of "passive" safety—that is, the provision of protection that does not require action on the part of the worker. It is, however, impossible to judge the effectiveness of protective devices without very good acquaintance with the actual work requirements at the machine in question, a form of knowledge which is normally possessed only by machine operators themselves.

There are many factors that can put even what is apparently good machine protection out of action. In order to perform their

work, operators may need to disengage or circumvent a safety device. In one study (Döös and Backström 1993), it was found that such disengagement or circumvention had taken place in 12 out of 75 of the automation accidents covered. It is often a matter of the operator's being ambitious, and no longer willing to accept either production problems or the delay to the production process involved in correcting disturbances in accordance with instructions. One way of avoiding this problem is to make the protective device imperceptible, so that it does not affect the pace of production, product quality or task performance. But this is not always possible; and where there are repeated disturbances to production, even minor inconveniences can prompt people not to utilize safety devices. Again, routines should be made available to remove the causes of production disturbances so that these are not repeated. A lack of a means of confirming that safety devices really function according to specifications is a further significant risk factor. Faulty connections, start signals that remain in the system and later give rise to unexpected starts, build-up in air pressure, and sensors that have come loose may all cause failure of protective equipment.

Summary

As has been shown, technical solutions to problems may give rise to new problems. Although injuries are caused by machine movements, which are essentially technical by nature, this does not automatically mean that the potential for their eradication lies in purely technical factors. Technical systems will continue to malfunction, and people will fail to handle the situations to which these malfunctions give rise. The risks will continue to exist, and can be held in check only by a wide variety of means. Legislation and control, organizational measures at individual companies (in the form of training, safety rounds, risk analysis and the reporting of disturbances and near accidents), and an emphasis on steady, ongoing improvements are all needed as complements to purely technical development.

MACHINE SAFEGUARDING

US Department of Labor—Occupational Safety and Health Administration; edited by Kenneth Gerecke

There seem to be as many potential hazards created by moving machine parts as there are different types of machines. Safeguards are essential to protect workers from needless and preventable machinery-related injuries. Therefore, any machine part, function or process which may cause injury should be safeguarded. Where the operation of a machine or accidental contact with it can injure the operator or others in the vicinity, the hazard must be either controlled or eliminated.

Mechanical Motions and Actions

Mechanical hazards typically involve dangerous moving parts in the following three basic areas:

- *the point of operation,* that point where work is performed on the material, such as cutting, shaping, punching, stamping, boring or forming of stock
- *power transmission apparatus,* any components of the mechanical system which transmit energy to the parts of the machine performing the work. These components include flywheels, pulleys, belts, connecting rods, couplings, cams, spindles, chains, cranks and gears

• *other moving parts,* all parts of the machine which move while the machine is working, such as reciprocating, rotating and transversely moving parts, as well as feed mechanisms and auxiliary parts of the machine.

A wide variety of mechanical motions and actions which may present hazards to workers include the movement of rotating members, reciprocating arms, moving belts, meshing gears, cutting teeth and any parts that impact or shear. These different types of mechanical motions and actions are basic to nearly all machines, and recognizing them is the first step toward protecting workers from the hazards they may present.

Motions

There are three basic types of motion: rotating, reciprocating and transverse.

Rotating motion can be dangerous; even smooth, slowly rotating shafts can grip clothing and force an arm or hand into a dangerous position. Injuries due to contact with rotating parts can be severe (see figure 58.12).

Collars, couplings, cams, clutches, flywheels, shaft ends, spindles and horizontal or vertical shafting are some examples of common rotating mechanisms which may be hazardous. There is added danger when bolts, nicks, abrasions and projecting keys or set screws are exposed on rotating parts on machinery, as shown in figure 58.13.

In-running nip points are created by rotating parts on machinery. There are three main types of in-running nip points:

1. Parts with parallel axes can rotate in opposite directions. These parts may be in contact (thereby producing a nip point) or in close proximity to each other, in which case the stock fed between the rolls produces the nip points. This danger is

Figure 58.12 • Mechanical punch press.

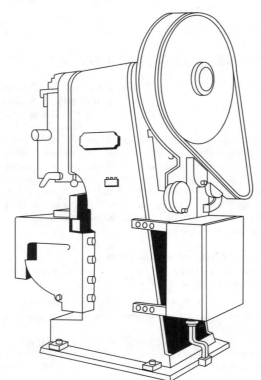

Figure 58.13 • Examples of hazardous projections on rotating parts.

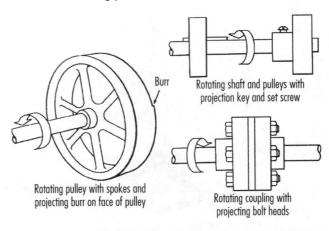

common on machinery with intermeshing gears, rolling mills and calenders, as shown in figure 58.14.
2. Another type of nip point is created between rotating and tangentially moving parts, such as the point of contact between a power transmission belt and its pulley, a chain and a sprocket, or a rack and pinion, as shown in figure 58.15.
3. Nip points can also occur between rotating and fixed parts which create a shearing, crushing or abrading action. Examples include handwheels or flywheels with spokes, screw conveyors or the periphery of an abrasive wheel and an incorrectly adjusted work rest, as shown in figure 58.16.

Reciprocating motions may be hazardous because during the back-and-forth or up-and-down motion, a worker may be struck by or caught between a moving part and a stationary part. An example is shown in figure 58.17.

Transverse motion (movement in a straight, continuous line) creates a hazard because a worker may be struck or caught in a pinch or shear point by a moving part. An example of transverse motion is shown in figure 58.18.

Actions

There are four basic types of action: cutting, punching, shearing and bending.

Cutting action involves rotating, reciprocating or transverse motion. Cutting action creates hazards at the point of operation where finger, head and arm injuries can occur and where flying chips or scrap material can strike the eyes or face. Typical exam-

Figure 58.14 • Common nip points on rotating parts.

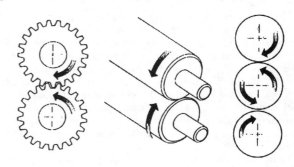

Figure 58.15 • Nip points between rotating elements and parts with longitudinal motions.

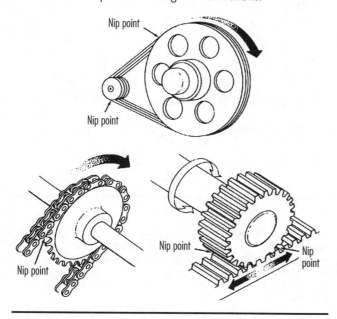

Figure 58.17 • Hazardous reciprocating motion.

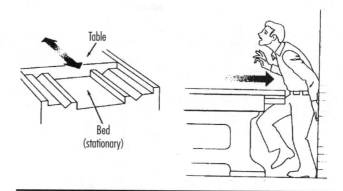

withdrawn. Typical examples of machinery used for shearing operations are mechanically, hydraulically or pneumatically powered shears. (See figure 58.21.)

Bending action results when power is applied to a slide in order to shape, draw or stamp metal or other materials. The hazard occurs at the point of operation where stock is inserted, held and withdrawn. Equipment that uses bending action includes power presses, press brakes and tubing benders. (See figure 58.22.)

Requirements for Safeguards

Safeguards must meet the following minimum general requirements to protect workers against mechanical hazards:

Prevent contact. The safeguard must prevent hands, arms or any part of a worker's body or clothing from making contact with dangerous moving parts by eliminating the possibility of the operators or other workers placing parts of their bodies near hazardous moving parts.

Provide security. Workers should not be able to easily remove or tamper with the safeguard. Guards and safety devices should be made of durable material that will withstand the conditions of normal use and that are firmly secured to the machine.

Protect from falling objects. The safeguard should ensure that no objects can fall into moving parts and damage the equipment or become a projectile that could strike and injure someone.

Not create new hazards. A safeguard defeats its purpose if it creates a hazard of its own, such as a shear point, a jagged edge or an unfinished surface. The edges of guards, for example, should be rolled or bolted in such a way that they eliminate sharp edges.

Not create interference. Safeguards which impede workers from performing their jobs might soon be overridden or disregarded. If

ples of machines with cutting hazards include band saws, circular saws, boring or drilling machines, turning machines (lathes) and milling machines. (See figure 58.19.)

Punching action results when power is applied to a slide (ram) for the purpose of blanking, drawing or stamping metal or other materials. The danger of this type of action occurs at the point of operation where stock is inserted, held and withdrawn by hand. Typical machines which use punching action are power presses and iron workers. (See figure 58.20.)

Shearing action involves applying power to a slide or knife in order to trim or shear metal or other materials. A hazard occurs at the point of operation where stock is actually inserted, held and

Figure 58.16 • Nip points between rotating machine components.

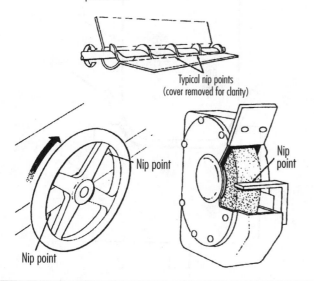

Figure 58.18 • Example of transverse motion.

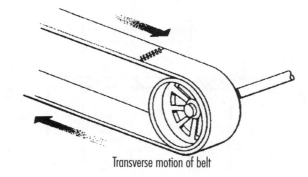

Figure 58.19 • Examples of cutting hazards.

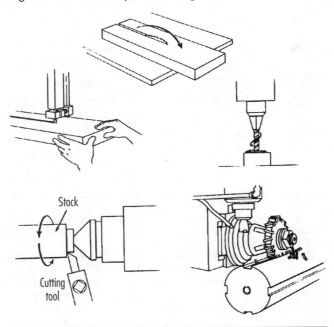

Figure 58.21 • Shearing operation.

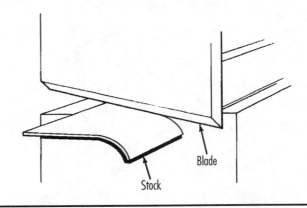

possible, workers should be able to lubricate machines without disengaging or removing safeguards. For example, locating oil reservoirs outside the guard, with a line leading to the lubrication point, will reduce the need to enter the hazardous area.

Safeguard Training

Even the most elaborate safeguarding system cannot offer effective protection unless workers know how to use it and why. Specific and detailed training is an important part of any effort to implement safeguarding against machine-related hazards. Proper safeguarding may improve productivity and enhance efficiency

since it may relieve workers' apprehensions about injury. Safeguard training is necessary for new operators and maintenance or set-up personnel, when any new or altered safeguards are put in service, or when workers are assigned to a new machine or operation; it should involve instruction or hands-on training in the following:

- a description and identification of the hazards associated with particular machines and the specific safeguards against each hazard
- how the safeguards provide protection; how to use the safeguards and why
- how and under what circumstances safeguards can be removed, and by whom (in most cases, repair or maintenance personnel only)
- what to do (e.g., contact the supervisor) if a safeguard is damaged, missing or unable to provide adequate protection.

Figure 58.20 • Typical punching operation.

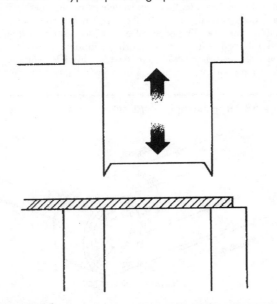

Figure 58.22 • Bending operation.

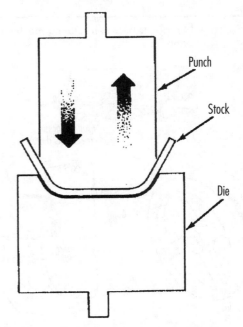

Figure 58.23 • Fixed guard on power press.

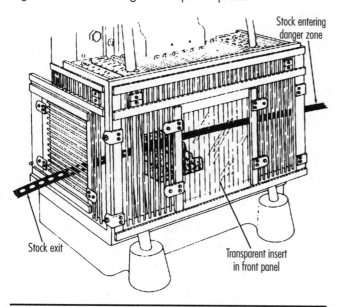

Figure 58.24 • Fixed guard enclosing belts and pulleys.

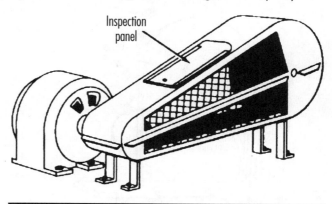

Methods of Machine Safeguarding

There are many ways to safeguard machinery. The type of operation, the size or shape of stock, the method of handling, the physical layout of the work area, the type of material and production requirements or limitations will help to determine the appropriate safeguarding method for the individual machine. The machine designer or safety professional must choose the most effective and practical safeguard available.

Safeguards may be categorized under five general classifications: (1) guards, (2) devices, (3) separation, (4) operations and (5) other.

Safeguarding with guards

There are four general types of guards (barriers which prevent access to danger areas), as follows:

Fixed guards. A fixed guard is a permanent part of the machine and is not dependent upon moving parts to perform its intended function. It may be constructed of sheet metal, screen, wire cloth, bars, plastic or any other material that is substantial enough to withstand whatever impact it may receive and to endure prolonged use. Fixed guards are usually preferable to all other types because of their relative simplicity and permanence (see table 58.2).

In figure 58.23, a fixed guard on a power press completely encloses the point of operation. The stock is fed through the side of the guard into the die area, with the scrap stock exiting on the opposite side.

Figure 58.24 depicts a fixed enclosure guard which shields the belt and pulley of a power transmission unit. An inspection panel is provided on top to minimize the need for removing the guard.

Table 58.2 • Machine guards.

Method	Safeguarding action	Advantages	Limitations
Fixed	• Provides a barrier	• Suits many specific applications • In-plant construction is often possible • Provides maximum protection • Usually requires minimum maintenance • Suitable to high production, repetitive operations	• May interfere with visibility • Limited to specific operations • Machine adjustment and repair often require its removal, thereby necessitating other means of protection for maintenance personnel
Interlocked	• Shuts off or disengages power and prevents starting of machine when guard is open; should require the machine to be stopped before the worker can reach into the danger area	• Provides maximum protection • Allows access to machine for removing jams without time-consuming removal of fixed guards	• Requires careful adjustment and maintenance • May be easy to disengage or bypass
Adjustable	• Provides a barrier which may be adjusted to facilitate a variety of production operations	• Can be constructed to suit many specific applications • Can be adjusted to admit varying sizes of stock	• Operator may enter danger area: protection may not be complete at all times • May require frequent maintenance and/or adjustment • May be made ineffective by the operator • May interfere with visibility
Self-adjusting	• Provides a barrier which moves according to the size of the stock entering danger area	• Off-the-shelf guards are commercially available	• Does not always provide maximum protection • May interfere with visibility • May require frequent maintenance and adjustment

Figure 58.25 • Fixed guards on band-saw.

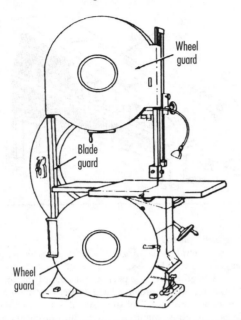

Figure 58.27 • Adjustable guard on band-saw.

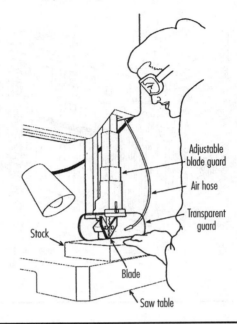

In figure 58.25, fixed enclosure guards are shown on a band-saw. These guards protect operators from the turning wheels and moving saw blade. Normally, the only time the guards would be opened or removed would be for a blade change or for maintenance. It is very important that they be securely fastened while the saw is in use.

Interlocked guards. When interlocked guards are opened or removed, the tripping mechanism and/or power automatically shuts off or disengages, and the machine cannot cycle or be started until the interlock guard is back in place. However, replacing the interlock guard should not automatically restart the machine. Interlocked guards may use electrical, mechanical, hydraulic or pneumatic power, or any combination of these. In-

terlocks should not prevent "inching" (i.e., gradual progressive movements) by remote control, if required.

An example of an interlocking guard is shown in figure 58.26. In this figure, the beater mechanism of a picker machine (used in the textile industry) is covered by an interlocked barrier guard. This guard cannot be raised while the machine is running, nor can the machine be restarted with the guard in the raised position.

Adjustable guards. Adjustable guards allow flexibility in accommodating various sizes of stock. Figure 58.27 shows an adjustable enclosure guard on a band-saw.

Self-adjusting guards. The openings of self-adjusting guards are determined by the movement of the stock. As the operator moves the stock into the danger area, the guard is pushed away, providing an opening which is large enough to admit only the stock.

Figure 58.26 • Interlocked guard on picker machine.

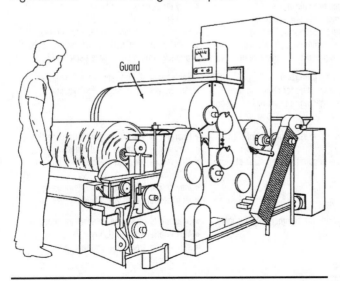

Figure 58.28 • Self-adjusting guard on radial-arm saw.

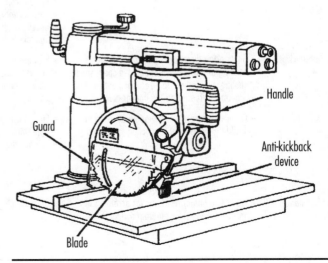

Figure 58.29 • Photoelectric presence-sensing device on press brake.

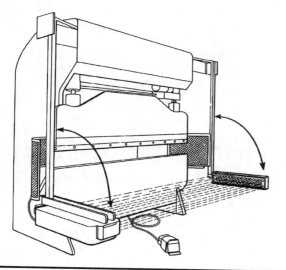

Figure 58.31 • Electromechanical sensing device on eye-letter machine.

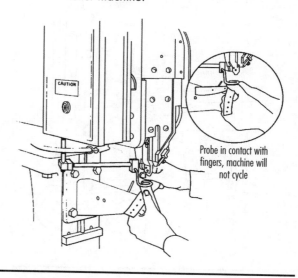

Probe in contact with fingers, machine will not cycle

After the stock is removed, the guard returns to the rest position. This guard protects the operator by placing a barrier between the danger area and the operator. The guards may be constructed of plastic, metal or other substantial material. Self-adjusting guards offer different degrees of protection.

Figure 58.28 shows a radial-arm saw with a self-adjusting guard. As the blade is pulled across the stock, the guard moves up, staying in contact with the stock.

Safeguarding with devices

Safety devices may stop the machine if a hand or any part of the body is inadvertently placed in the danger area, may restrain or withdraw the operator's hands from the danger area during operation, may require the operator to use both hands on machine

controls simultaneously (thus keeping both hands and body out of danger) or may provide a barrier which is synchronized with the operating cycle of the machine in order to prevent entry to the danger area during the hazardous part of the cycle. There are five basic types of safety devices, as follows:

Presence-sensing devices

Three types of sensing devices which stop the machine or interrupt the work cycle or operation if a worker is within the danger zone are described below:

Figure 58.30 • Radio-frequency presence-sensing device on power saw.

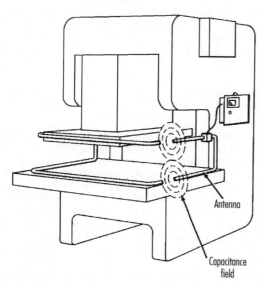

Antenna

Capacitance field

Figure 58.32 • Pullback device on power press.

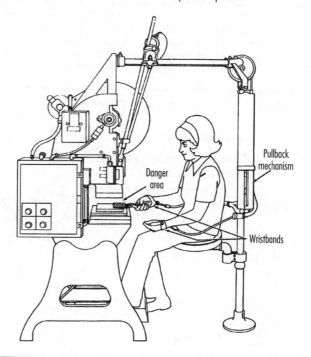

Danger area

Pullback mechanism

Wristbands

Figure 58.33 • Pressure-sensitive body bar on rubber mill.

Bar

Figure 58.35 • Safety tripwire cable on calender.

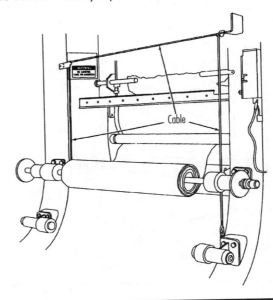

Cable

The *photoelectric (optical) presence-sensing device* uses a system of light sources and controls which can interrupt the machine's operating cycle. If the light field is broken, the machine stops and will not cycle. This device should be used only on machines which can be stopped before the worker reaches the danger area. Figure 58.29 shows a photoelectric presence-sensing device used with a press brake. The device may be swung up or down to accommodate different production requirements.

The *radio-frequency (capacitance) presence-sensing device* uses a radio beam that is part of the control circuit. When the capacitance field is broken, the machine will stop or will not activate. This device should be used only on machines which can be stopped before the worker can reach the danger area. This requires the machine to have a friction clutch or other reliable means for stopping. Figure 58.30 shows a radio-frequency presence-sensing device mounted on a part-revolution power press.

The *electro-mechanical sensing device* has a probe or contact bar which descends to a predetermined distance when the operator initiates the machine cycle. If there is an obstruction preventing it

Figure 58.34 • Safety trip-rod on rubber mill.

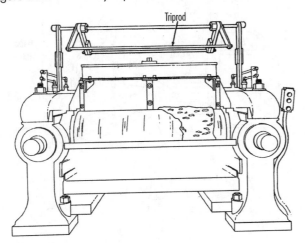

Triprod

from descending its full predetermined distance, the control circuit does not actuate the machine cycle. Figure 58.31 shows an electro-mechanical sensing device on an eyeletter. The sensing probe in contact with the operator's finger is also shown.

Pullback devices

Pullback devices utilize a series of cables attached to the operator's hands, wrists and/or arms and are primarily used on machines with stroking action. When the slide/ram is up, the operator is allowed access to the point of operation. When the slide/ram begins to descend, a mechanical linkage automatically assures withdrawal of the hands from the point of operation. Figure 58.32 shows a pullback device on a small press.

Restraint devices

Restraint devices, which utilize cables or straps that are attached between a fixed point and the operator's hands, have been used in some countries. These devices are not generally considered to be acceptable safeguards because they are easily bypassed by the operator, thus allowing hands to be placed into the danger zone. (See table 58.3.)

Safety control devices

All of these safety control devices are activated manually and must be manually reset to restart the machine:

- *Safety trip controls* such as pressure bars, trip rods and tripwires are manual controls which provide a quick means for deactivating the machine in an emergency situation.
- *Pressure-sensitive body bars*, when depressed, will deactivate the machine if the operator or anyone trips, loses balance or is drawn toward the machine. The positioning of the bar is critical, as it must stop the machine before a part of the body reaches the danger area. Figure 58.33 shows a pressure-sensitive body bar located on the front of a rubber mill.
- *Safety trip-rod devices* deactivate the machine when pressed by hand. Because they have to be actuated by the operator during an emergency situation, their proper position is critical. Figure 58.34 shows a trip-rod located above the rubber mill.

Table 58.3 • Devices.

Method	Safeguarding action	Advantages	Limitations
Photoelectric (optical)	• Machine will not start cycling when the light field is interrupted • When the light field is broken by any part of the operator's body during the cycling process, immediate machine braking is activated	• Can allow freer movement for operator	• Does not protect against mechanical failure • May require frequent alignment and calibration • Excessive vibration may cause lamp filament damage and premature burnout • Limited to machines that can be stopped without completing cycle
Radio frequency (capacitance)	• Machine cycling will not start when the capacitance field is interrupted • When the capacitance field is disturbed by any part of the operator's body during the cycling process, immediate machine braking is activated	• Can allow freer movement for operator	• Does not protect against mechanical failure • Antenna sensitivity must be properly adjusted • Limited to machines that can be stopped without completing cycle
Electro-mechanical	• Contact bar or probe travels a predetermined distance between the operator and the danger area • Interruption of this movement prevents the starting of machine cycle	• Can allow access at the point of operation	• Contact bar or probe must be properly adjusted for each application; this adjustment must be maintained properly
Pullback	• As the machine begins to cycle, the operator's hands are pulled out of the danger area	• Eliminates the need for auxiliary barriers or other interference at the danger area	• Limits movement of operator • May obstruct workspace around operator • Adjustments must be made for specific operations and for each individual • Requires frequent inspections and regular maintenance • Requires close supervision of the operator's use of the equipment
Safety trip controls: • Pressure-sensitive body bar • Safety trip-rod • Safety tripwire	• Stops machine when tripped	• Simplicity of use	• All controls must be manually activated • May be difficult to activate controls because of their location • Protects only the operator • May require special fixtures to hold work • May require a machine brake
Two-hand control	• Concurrent use of both hands is required, preventing the operator from entering the danger area	• Operator's hands are at a predetermined location away from danger area • Operator's hands are free to pick up a new part after first half of cycle is completed	• Requires a partial cycle machine with a brake • Some two-hand controls can be rendered unsafe by holding with arm or blocking, thereby permitting one-hand operation • Protects only the operator
Two-hand trip	• Concurrent use of two hands on separate controls prevent hands from being in danger area when machine cycle starts	• Operator's hands are away from danger area • Can be adapted to multiple operations • No obstruction to hand feeding • Does not require adjustment for each operation	• Operator may try to reach into danger area after tripping machine • Some trips can be rendered unsafe by holding with arm or blocking, thereby permitting one-hand operation • Protects only the operator • May require special fixtures
Gate	• Provides a barrier between danger area and operator or other personnel	• Can prevent reaching into or walking into the danger area	• May require frequent inspection and regular maintenance • May interfere with operator's ability to see the work

- *Safety tripwire cables* are located around the perimeter of, or near the danger area. The operator must be able to reach the cable with either hand to stop the machine. Figure 58.35 shows a calender equipped with this type of control.
- *Two-hand controls* require constant, concurrent pressure for the operator to activate the machine. When installed on power presses, these controls use a part-revolution clutch and a brake monitor, as shown in figure 58.36. With this type of device, the operator's hands are required to be at a safe location (on control buttons) and at a safe distance from the danger area while the machine completes its closing cycle.
- *Two-hand trip*. The two-hand trip shown in figure 58.37 is usually used with machines equipped with full-revolution clutches. It requires concurrent application of both of the operator's control buttons to activate the machine cycle, after which the hands are free. The trips must be placed far enough from the point of operation to make it impossible for operators to move their hands from the trip buttons or handles into the point of

Figure 58.36 • Two-hand control buttons on part-revolution clutch power press.

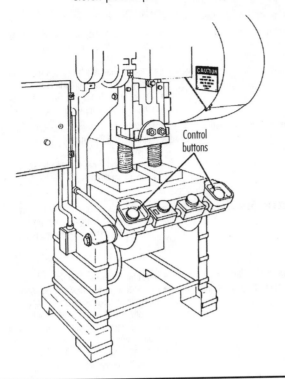

Figure 58.37 • Two-hand control buttons on full-revolution clutch power press.

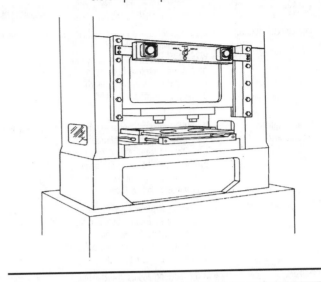

Figure 58.38 • Power press with gate.

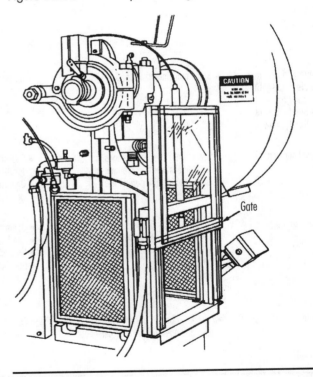

operation before the first half of the cycle is completed. The operator's hands are kept far enough away to prevent them from being accidentally placed in the danger area before the slide/ram or blade reaches the full down position.

- *Gates* are safety control devices which provide a movable barrier that protects the operator at the point of operation before the machine cycle can be started. Gates are often designed to be operated with each machine cycle. Figure 58.38 shows a gate on a power press. If the gate is not permitted to descend to the fully closed position, the press will not function. Another application of gates is their use as a component of a perimeter safeguarding system, where the gates provide protection to the operators and to pedestrian traffic.

Safeguarding by location or distance

To safeguard a machine by location, the machine or its dangerous moving parts must be so positioned that hazardous areas are not accessible or do not present a hazard to a worker during the normal operation of the machine. This may be accomplished with enclosure walls or fences that restrict access to machines, or by locating a machine so that a plant design feature, such as a wall, protects the worker and other personnel. Another possibility is to have dangerous parts located high enough to be out of the normal reach of any worker. A thorough hazard analysis of each machine and particular situation is essential before attempting this safeguarding technique. The examples mentioned below are a few of the numerous applications of the principle of safeguarding by location/distance.

Feeding process. The feeding process can be safeguarded by location if a safe distance can be maintained to protect the worker's hands. The dimensions of the stock being worked on may provide adequate safety. For example, when operating a single-end

punching machine, if the stock is several feet long and only one end of the stock is being worked on, the operator may be able to hold the opposite end while the work is being performed. However, depending upon the machine, protection might still be required for other personnel.

Positioning controls. The positioning of the operator's control station provides a potential approach to safeguarding by location. Operator controls may be located at a safe distance from the machine if there is no reason for the operator to be in attendance at the machine.

Table 58.4 • Feeding and ejection methods.

Method	Safeguarding action	Advantages	Limitations
Automatic feed	• Stock is fed from rolls, indexed by machine mechanism, etc.	• Eliminates the need for operator involvement in the danger area	• Other guards are also required for operator protection—usually fixed barrier guards • Requires frequent maintainance • May not be adaptable to stock variation
Semi-automatic feed	• Stock is fed by chutes, movable dies, dial feed, plungers, or sliding bolster	• Eliminates the need for operator involvement in the danger area	• Other guards are also required for operator protection—usually fixed barrier guards • Requires frequent maintainance • May not be adaptable to stock variation
Automatic ejection	• Work pieces are ejected by air or mechanical means	• Eliminates the need for operator involvement in the danger area	• May create a hazard of blowing chips or debris • Size of stock limits the use of this method • Air ejection may present a noise hazard
Semi-automatic ejection	• Work pieces are ejected by mechanical means which are initiated by the operator	• Operator does not have to enter danger area to remove finished work	• Other guards are required for operator protection • May not be adaptable to stock variation
Robots	• They perform work usually done by operator	• Operator does not have to enter danger area • Are suitable for operations where high stress factors are present, such as heat and noise	• Can create hazards themselves • Require maximum maintenance • Are suitable only to specific operations

Feeding and ejection safeguarding methods

Many feeding and ejection methods do not require the operators to place their hands in the danger area. In some cases, no operator involvement is necessary after the machine is set up, whereas in other situations, operators can manually feed the stock with the assistance of a feeding mechanism. Furthermore, ejection methods may be designed which do not require any operator involvement after the machine starts to function. Some feeding and ejection methods may even create hazards themselves, such as a robot which may eliminate the need for an operator to be near the machine but may create a new hazard by the movement of its arm. (See table 58.4.)

Using one of the following five feeding and ejection methods to safeguard machines does not eliminate the need for guards and other devices, which must be used as necessary to provide protection from exposure to hazards.

Automatic feed. Automatic feeds reduce the operator exposure during the work process, and often do not require any effort by the operator after the machine is set up and running. The power press in figure 58.39 has an automatic feeding mechanism with a transparent fixed enclosure guard at the danger area.

Semi-automatic feed. With semi-automatic feeding, as in the case of a power press, the operator uses a mechanism to place the piece being processed under the ram at each stroke. The operator does not need to reach into the danger area, and the danger area is completely enclosed. Figure 58.40 shows a chute feed into which each piece is placed by hand. Using a chute feed on an

Figure 58.39 • Power press with automatic feed.

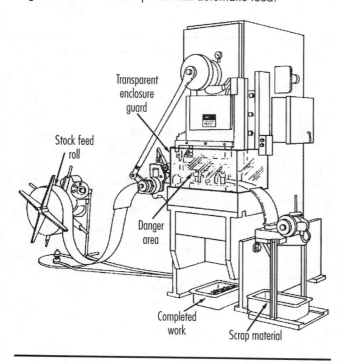

Figure 58.40 • Power press with chute feed.

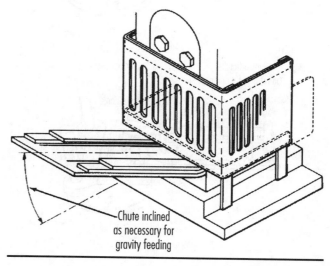

Figure 58.41 • Shuttle ejection system.

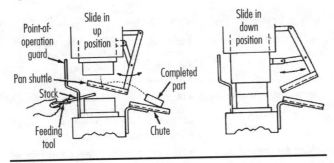

Figure 58.43 • Using barrier guards to protect robot envelope.

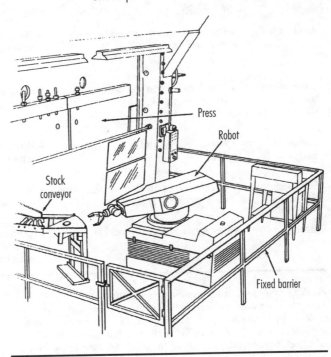

inclined press not only helps centre the piece as it slides into the die, but may also simplify the problem of ejection.

Automatic ejection. Automatic ejection may employ either air pressure or a mechanical apparatus to remove the completed part from a press, and may be interlocked with the operating controls to prevent operation until part ejection is completed. The pan shuttle mechanism shown in figure 58.41 moves under the finished part as the slide moves toward the up position. The shuttle then catches the part stripped from the slide by the knockout pins and deflects it into a chute. When the ram moves down toward the next blank, the pan shuttle moves away from the die area.

Semi-automatic ejection. Figure 58.42 shows a semi-automatic ejection mechanism used on a power press. When the plunger is withdrawn from the die area, the ejector leg, which is mechanically coupled to the plunger, kicks the completed work out.

Figure 58.42 • Semi-automatic ejection mechanism.

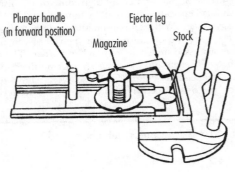

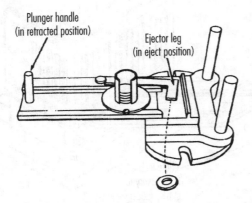

Robots. Robots are complex devices that load and unload stock, assemble parts, transfer objects or perform work otherwise done by an operator, thereby eliminating operator exposure to hazards. They are best used in high-production processes requiring repeated routines, where they can guard against other hazards to employees. Robots may create hazards, and appropriate guards must be used. Figure 58.43 shows an example of a robot feeding a press.

Figure 58.44 • Rear view of power shearing square.

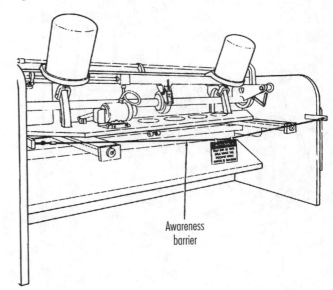

Figure 58.45 • Applications of shields.

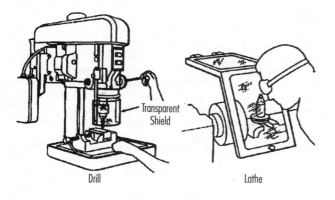

Drill   Lathe

Miscellaneous safeguarding aids

Although miscellaneous safeguarding aids do not give complete protection from machine hazards, they may provide operators with an extra margin of safety. Sound judgement is needed in their application and use.

Awareness barriers. Awareness barriers do not provide physical protection, but serve only to remind operators that they are approaching the danger area. Generally, awareness barriers are not considered adequate when continual exposure to the hazard exists. Figure 58.44 shows a rope used as an awareness barrier on the rear of a power squaring shear. Barriers do not physically prevent persons from entering danger areas, but only provide awareness of the hazard.

Figure 58.46 • Holding tools.

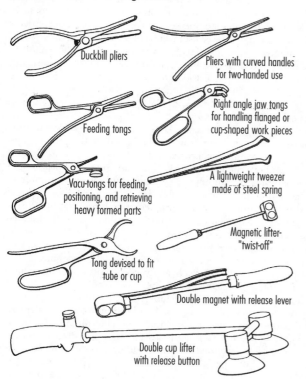

Duckbill pliers

Pliers with curved handles for two-handed use

Feeding tongs

Right angle jaw tongs for handling flanged or cup-shaped work pieces

Vacu-tongs for feeding, positioning, and retrieving heavy formed parts

A lightweight tweezer made of steel spring

Magnetic lifter-"twist-off"

Tong devised to fit tube or cup

Double magnet with release lever

Double cup lifter with release button

Figure 58.47 • Use of push stick or push block.

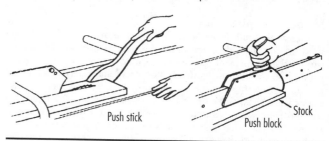

Push stick   Push block   Stock

Shields. Shields may be used to provide protection from flying particles, splashing metal-working fluids or coolants. Figure 58.45 shows two potential applications.

Holding tools. Holding tools place and remove stock. A typical use would be for reaching into the danger area of a press or press brake. Figure 58.46 shows an assortment of tools for this purpose. Holding tools should not be used *instead* of other machine safeguards; they are merely a supplement to the protection that other guards provide.

Push sticks or blocks, such as shown in figure 58.47, may be used when feeding stock into a machine, such as a saw blade. When it becomes necessary for hands to be in close proximity to the blade, the push stick or block may provide a margin of safety and prevent injury.

PRESENCE DETECTORS

Paul Schreiber

General developments in microelectronics and in the technology of sensors give reason to hope that an improvement in occupational safety can be achieved through the availability of reliable, hardy, low-maintenance and inexpensive presence and approach detectors. This article will describe sensor technology, the different detection procedures, the conditions and restrictions applicable to the use of sensor systems, and some completed studies and standardization work in Germany.

Presence Detector Criteria

The development and practical testing of presence detectors is one of the greatest future challenges to technical efforts in improving occupational safety and to the protection of personnel in general. *Presence detectors* are sensors that reliably and with certainty signal the *near presence or approach of a person*. In addition, this warning must occur rapidly so that evasive action, braking or the shutting off of a stationary machine can take place before the predicted contact occurs. Whether the people are big or small, whatever their posture, or how they are clothed should have no effect on the reliability of the sensor. In addition, the sensor must possess certainty of functioning and be sturdy and inexpensive, so that it can be used under the most demanding conditions, such as on construction sites and for mobile applications, with minimal maintenance. Sensors must be like an airbag in that they are maintenance-free and always ready. Given some users' reluctance to maintain what they may regard as nonessential equipment, sensors may be left unserviced for years. Another feature of presence detectors, one that is much more likely to be requested, is that they also detect obstacles other than human beings and alert the operator in time to take defensive action, thus reducing costs of repair and material damage. This is a reason for installing presence detectors that should not be under-appreciated.

Detector Applications

Innumerable fatal accidents and serious injuries which look like unavoidable, individual acts of fate, may be avoided or minimized provided that presence detectors become more accepted as a prevention measure in the field of occupational safety. The newspapers report these accidents all too often: here a person was struck by a backwards-moving loader, there the operator did not see someone who was run over by the front wheel of a power shovel. Trucks moving backwards on streets, company premises and construction sites are the cause of many accidents to people. Today's thoroughly rationalized companies no longer provide co-drivers or other persons to act as guides for the driver who is backing up a truck. These examples of moving accidents can be easily extended to other mobile equipment, such as fork-lift trucks. However, the use of sensors is urgently needed to prevent accidents involving semi-mobile and purely stationary equipment. An example is the rear areas of large loading machines, which have been identified by safety personnel as potentially hazardous areas which could be improved through the use of inexpensive sensors. Many variations of presence detectors can be adapted innovatively to other vehicles and large mobile equipment to protect against the types of accidents discussed in this article, which generally cause extensive damage and serious, if not fatal, injuries.

The tendency of innovative solutions to become more widespread would seem to promise that presence detectors will become the standard safety technology in other applications; however, this is not the case anywhere. The breakthrough, motivated by accidents and high material damages, is expected in monitoring behind delivery vans and heavy trucks and for the most innovative areas of the "new technologies"—the mobile robot machines of the future.

The variation of the fields of application for presence detectors and the variability of the tasks—for example, tolerating objects (even moving objects, under certain conditions) that belong to a detection field and that should not trigger a signal—require sensors in which "intelligent" assessment technology supports the mechanisms of sensor function. This technology, which is a matter for future development, can be elaborated from methods drawing upon the field of artificial intelligence (Schreiber and Kuhn 1995). To date, a limited universality has severely restricted current uses of sensors. There are light curtains; light bars; contact mats; passive infrared sensors; ultrasound and radar motion detectors that use the Doppler effect; sensors that make elapsed time measurements of ultrasound, radar and light impulses; and laser scanners. Normal television cameras connected to monitors are not included in this list because they are not presence detectors. However, those cameras which do activate automatically upon sensing the presence of a person, are included.

Sensor Technology

Today the main sensor issues are (1) optimizing the use of the physical effects (infrared, light, ultrasound, radar, etc.) and (2) self-monitoring. Laser scanners are being intensively developed for use as navigational instruments for mobile robots. For this, two tasks, partially different in principle, must be solved: the navigation of the robot and the protection of persons (and material or equipment) present so that they are not struck, run over or grabbed (Freund, Dierks and Rossman 1993). Future mobile robots cannot retain the same safety philosophy of "spatial separation of robot and person" which is strictly applied to today's stationary industrial robots. This means putting a high premium on the reliable functioning of the presence detector to be used.

The use of "new technology" is often linked to problems of acceptance, and it can be assumed that the general use of mobile robots that can move and grasp, among people in plants, in public traffic areas, or even in homes or recreational areas, will be accepted only if they are equipped with very highly developed, sophisticated and reliable presence detectors. Spectacular accidents must be avoided at all costs in order to avoid exacerbating a possible acceptance problem. The current level of expenditure for the development of this type of occupational protective sensors does not come close to taking this consideration into account. To save a lot of costs, presence detectors should be developed and tested simultaneously with the mobile robots and the navigational systems, not afterwards.

With respect to motor vehicles, safety questions have gained increasing significance. Innovative passenger safety in automobiles includes three-point seat belts, child seats, airbags and the anti-lock brake system verified by serial crash tests. These safety measures represent a relatively increasing portion of production costs. The side airbag and radar sensor systems to measure the distance to the car ahead are evolutionary developments in passenger protection.

External motor vehicle safety—that is, the protection of third parties—is receiving increased attention. Recently, side protection has been required, primarily for trucks, to prevent motorcyclists, bicyclists and pedestrians from the danger of falling under the rear wheels. A next logical step would be monitoring the area behind large vehicles with presence detectors and installing rear area warning equipment. This would have the positive side effect of providing the funding required to develop, test and make available maximum performance, self-monitoring, maintenance-free and reliably functioning, inexpensive sensors for occupational safety purposes. The trial process that would go with the broad implementation of sensors or sensor systems would considerably facilitate innovation in other areas, such as power shovels, heavy loaders and other large mobile machines that back up as much as half the time during their operation. The evolutionary process from stationary robots to mobile robots is an additional path of development for presence detectors. For example, improvements could be made to the sensors currently used on mobile robot material movers or "driverless factory floor tractors", which follow fixed paths and therefore have relatively low safety requirements. The use of presence detectors is the next logical step in improving safety in the area of material and passenger transport.

Detection Procedures

Various physical principles, available in connection with electronic measuring and self-monitoring methods and, to an extent, high-performance computing procedures, may be used to assess and solve the above-mentioned tasks. The apparently effortless and sure operation of automated machines (robots) so common in science-fiction films, will possibly be accomplished in the real world through the use of imaging techniques and high-performance pattern recognition algorithms in combination with distance measurement methods analogous to those employed by laser scanners. The paradoxical situation that everything that seems simple for people is difficult for automatons, must be recognized. For example, a difficult task such as excellent chess playing (which calls for forebrain activity) can be more easily simulated and carried out by automated machines than a simple task such as walking upright or carrying out hand-eye and other movement coordination (mediated by the mid- and hindbrain). A few of these principles, methods and procedures applicable to sensor applications are described below. In addition to these, there are a large number of special procedures for very special tasks that work in part with a combination of various types of physical effects.

Light barrier curtains and bars. Among the first presence detectors were light barrier curtains and bars. They have a flat monitoring geometry; that is, one who has passed the barrier will no longer be detected. An operator's hand, or the presence of tools or parts held in an operator's hand, for instance, can be quickly and reliably detected with these devices. They offer an important contribution to occupational safety for machines (like presses and punching machines) that require that material be put in by hand. The reliability has to be extremely high statistically, because when the hand reaches in only two to three times per minute, about one million operations are performed in just a few years. The mutual self-monitoring of sender and receiver components has been developed to such a very high technical level that it represents a standard for all other presence detection procedures.

Contact mats (switch mats). There are both passive and active (pump) types of electric and pneumatic contact mats and floors, which were initially used in large numbers in service functions (door openers), until they were replaced by motion detectors. Further development evolves with the use of presence detectors in all sorts of danger zones. For example, the development of automated manufacturing with a change in the function of the worker—from operating the machine to strictly monitoring its function—produced a corresponding demand for appropriate detectors. Standardization of this use is well advanced (DIN 1995a), and special limitations (layout, size, maximum allowed "dead" zones) necessitated the development of expertise for installation in this area of usage.

Interesting possible uses of contact mats arise in conjunction with computer-controlled multiple robot systems. An operator switches one or two elements so that the presence detector would pick up his or her exact position and inform the computer, which manages robot control systems with a built-in collision-avoidance system. In one test advanced by the German federal safety institute (BAU), a contact-mat floor, consisting of small electrical switch mats, was built under the robot arm's work area for this purpose (Freund, Dierks and Rossman 1993). This presence detector had the form of a chessboard. The respectively activated mat field told the computer the operator's position (figure 58.48) and when the operator approached too close to the robot, it moved away. Without the presence detector the robot system would not be able to ascertain the operator's position, and the operator then could not be protected.

Reflectors (motion sensors and presence detectors). However meritorious the sensors discussed up to now may be, they are not presence detectors in the broader sense. Their suitability—primarily for reasons of occupational safety—for large vehicles and large mobile equipment presupposes two important characteristics: (1) the ability to monitor an area from one position, and (2) error-free functioning without the need for additional measures on the part of—for example, the use of reflector devices. Detecting the presence of a person entering the monitored area and remaining stopped until this person has gone also implies the need for detecting a person standing absolutely still. This distinguishes so-called motion sensors from presence detectors, at least in connection with mobile equipment; motion sensors are almost always triggered when the vehicle is put into motion.

Motion sensors. The two basic types of motion sensors are: (1) "passive infrared sensors" (PIRS), which react to the smallest change in the infrared beam in the monitored area (the smallest detectable beam is approximately 10^{-9} W with a wavelength range of approximately 7 to 20 μm); and (2) ultrasound and microwave sensors using the Doppler principle, which determines the characteristics of an object's motion according to the frequency changes. For example, the Doppler effect increases the frequency of a locomotive's horn for an observer when it is approaching, and reduces the frequency when the locomotive is moving away. The

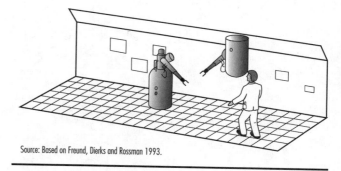

Figure 58.48 • A person (right) and two robots in computed wrapper bodies.

Source: Based on Freund, Dierks and Rossman 1993.

Doppler effect makes possible the building of relatively simple approach sensors, as the receiver needs only to monitor the signal frequency of neighbouring frequency bands for the appearance of the Doppler frequency.

In the mid-1970s the use of motion detectors became prevalent in service function applications such as door openers, theft security and object protection. For stationary use, the detection of an approaching person toward a danger spot was adequate to give a timely warning or to turn off a machine. This was the basis for studying the suitability of motion detectors for their use in occupational safety, especially by means of PIRS (Mester et al. 1980). Because a clothed person generally has a higher temperature than the surrounding area (head 34°C, hands 31°C), detecting an approaching person is somewhat easier than detecting inanimate objects. To a limited extent, machine parts can move about in the monitored area without triggering the detector.

The passive method (without transmitter) has advantages and disadvantages. The advantage is that a PIRS does not add to noise and electrical smog problems. For theft security and object protection, it is particularly important that the detector not be easy to find. A sensor that is purely a receiver, however, can hardly monitor its own effectiveness, which is essential for occupational safety. One method for overcoming this drawback was to test small modulated (5 to 20 Hz) infrared emitters that were installed in the monitored area and that did not trigger the sensor, but whose beams were registered with a fixed electronic amplification set to the modulation frequency. This modification turned it from a "passive" sensor to an "active" sensor. In this way it was also possible to check the geometric accuracy of the monitored area. Mirrors can have blind spots, and a passive sensor's direction can be thrown off by the rough activity in a plant. Figure 58.49 shows a test layout with a PIRS with a monitored geometry in the form of a pyramid mantle. Because of their great reach, passive infrared sensors are installed, for example, in the passageways of shelf storage areas.

Overall, tests showed that motion detectors are not suited to occupational safety. A night-time museum floor cannot be compared to danger zones in a workplace.

Ultra-sound, radar and light-impulse detectors. Sensors that use the pulse/echo principle—that is, elapsed time measurements of ultrasound, radar or light impulses—have great potential as presence detectors. With laser scanners, light impulses can sweep in rapid succession (usually in a rotatory fashion), for example, horizontally, and with the help of a computer one can obtain a distance profile of the objects on a plane that reflect light. If, for example, not only a single line is wanted, but the entirety of what lies before the mobile robot in the area up to a height of 2 metres, then great quantities of data must be processed to depict the

Figure 58.49 • Passive infrared sensor as approach detector in a danger area.

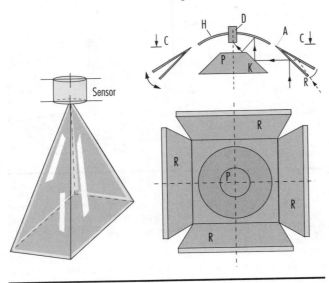

surrounding area. A future "ideal" presence detector will consist of a combination of the following two processes:

1. A pattern-recognition process will be employed, consisting of a camera and a computer. The latter can also be a "neuronal net".
2. A laser scanning process is further required to measure distances; this takes a bearing in a three-dimensional space over from a number of individual points selected by the pattern-recognition process, established to obtain the distance and motion by speed and direction.

Figure 58.50 shows, from the previously cited BAU project (Freund, Dierks and Rossman 1993), the use of a laser scanner on a mobile robot that also assumes navigational tasks (via a direction-sensing beam) and collision protection for objects in the immediate vicinity (via a ground measurement beam for presence detection). Given these features, the mobile robot has the capability of *active automated free driving* (i.e., the ability to drive around obstacles). Technically, this is achieved by utilizing the 45° angle of the scanner rotation toward the rear on both sides (to port and starboard of the robot) in addition to the 180° angle toward the front. These beams are connected with a special mirror which acts as a light curtain on the floor in front of the mobile robot (providing a ground vision line). If a laser reflection comes from there, the robot stops. While laser and light scanners certified for occupational safety use are on the market, these presence detectors have great potential for further development.

Figure 58.50 • Mobile robot with laser scanner for navigation and presence detection use.

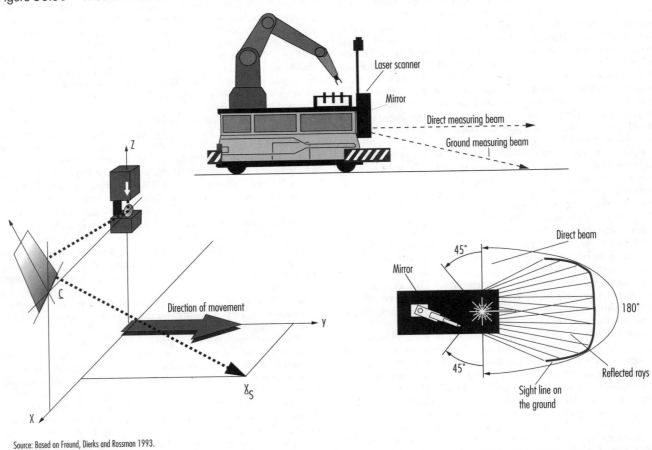

Source: Based on Freund, Dierks and Rossman 1993.

Figure 58.51 • Disposition of measuring head and area monitored on the rear side of a truck.

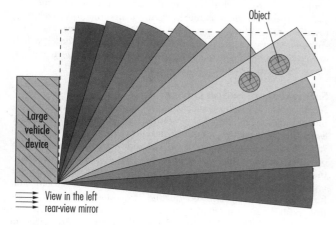

Object

Large vehicle device

⇉ View in the left rear-view mirror

Source: Based on Langer and Kurfürst 1995.

Ultrasound and radar sensors, which use the elapsed time from signal to response to determine distance, are less demanding from a technical perspective and thus can be produced more cheaply. The sensor area is club-shaped and has one or more smaller side clubs, which are symmetrically arranged. The speed of the signal's spread (sound: 330 m/s; electromagnetic wave: 300,000 km/s) determines the requisite speed of the electronics utilized.

Rear-area warning devices. At the 1985 Hanover Exposition, BAU showed the results of an initial project on the use of ultrasound sensors for securing the area behind large vehicles (Langer and Kurfürst 1985). A full-sized model of a sensor head made of Polaroid™ sensors was set up on the back wall of a supply truck. Figure 58.51 shows its functioning schematically. The large diameter of this sensor produces relatively small-angled (approximately 18°), long-range club-shaped measured areas, arranged next to each other and set to different maximum signal ranges. In practice it allows one to set any desired monitored geometry, which is scanned by the sensors approximately four times per second for the presence or entrance of persons. Other demonstrated rear-area warning systems had several parallel individual arrayed sensors.

This vivid demonstration was a great success at the exhibition. It showed that securing the rear area of large vehicles and equipment is being studied in many places—for example, by specialized committees of the industrial trade associations *(Berufsgenossenschaften)*, the municipal accident insurers (who are responsible for municipal vehicles), the state industry oversight officials, and the producers of sensors, who had been thinking more in terms of automobiles as service vehicles (in the sense of focusing on parking systems to protect against auto body damage). An ad hoc committee drawn from the groups to promote rear-area warning devices was formed spontaneously and took as a first task the preparation of a list of requirements from the perspective of occupational safety. Ten years have passed during which time much has been worked out in rear-area monitoring—possibly the most important task of presence detectors; but the big breakthrough is still missing.

Many projects have been conducted with ultrasound sensors—for example, on round-wood sorting cranes, hydraulic shovels, special municipal vehicles, and other utility vehicles, as well as on fork-lift trucks and loaders (Schreiber 1990). Rear-area

warning devices are especially important for large machinery that backs up much of the time. Ultrasound presence detectors are used, for example, for the protection of specialized driverless vehicles such as robot material-handling machines. As compared to rubber bumpers, these sensors have a greater detection area which provides for braking before contact is made between the machine and an object. Corresponding sensors for automobiles are appropriate developments and involve considerably less stringent requirements.

In the meantime, the Transportation System Technical Standards Committee of DIN worked up Standard 75031, "Obstacle detection devices during reversing" (DIN 1995b). The requirements and tests were set for two ranges: 1.8 m for supply trucks and 3.0 m—an additional warning area—for larger trucks. The monitored area is set through the recognition of cylindrical test bodies. The 3-m range is also about the limit of what is presently technically possible, as ultrasound sensors must have closed metal membranes, given their rough working conditions. The requirements for the sensor system's self-monitoring are being set, as the required monitored geometry can be accomplished only with a system of three or more sensors. Figure 58.52 shows a rear-area warning device consisting of three ultrasound sensors (Microsonic GmbH 1996). The same applies for the notification device in the driver's cab and the type of warning signal. The contents of DIN Standard 75031 are also laid out in the international technical ISO Report TR 12155, "Commercial vehicles—Obstacle detection device during reversing" (ISO 1994). Various sensor producers have developed prototypes in accordance with this standard.

Conclusion

Since the early 1970s, several institutions and sensor manufacturers have worked to develop and establish "presence detectors". In the special application of "rear-area warning devices" there are DIN Standard 75031 and ISO Report TR 12155. At present Deutsche Post AG is conducting a major test. Several sensor manufacturers have each equipped five mid-size trucks with such devices. A positive outcome of this test is very much in the interests of occupational safety. As was emphasized at the outset, presence detectors in the required numbers are a big challenge for safety technology in the many areas of application mentioned. They must therefore be realizable at low cost if damages to equipment, machinery and materials, and, above all, injuries to people, often very serious, are to be relegated to the past.

Figure 58.52 • Mid-sized truck equipped with a rear-area warning device (Microsonic photo).

DEVICES FOR CONTROLLING, ISOLATING AND SWITCHING ENERGY

René Troxler

Control devices and devices used for isolating and switching must always be discussed in relation to *technical systems*, a term used in this article to include machines, installations and equipment. Every technical system fulfils a specific and assigned practical task. Appropriate safety control and switching devices are required if this practical task is to be workable or even possible under safe conditions. Such devices are used in order to initiate control, interrupt or retard the current and/or the impulses of electric, hydraulic, pneumatic and also potential energies.

Isolation and Energy Reduction

Isolating devices are used to isolate energy by disconnecting the supply line between the energy source and the technical system. The isolating device must normally yield an unequivocally determinable actual disconnection of the energy supply. Disconnection of the energy supply should also always be combined with the reduction of energy stored in all parts of the technical system. If the technical system is fed by several energy sources, all these supply lines must be capable of being reliably isolated. Persons trained to handle the relevant type of energy and who work at the energy end of the technical system, use isolation devices to shield themselves from the hazards of the energy. For safety reasons, these persons will always check to assure that no potentially hazardous energy remains in the technical system—for instance, by ascertaining the absence of electrical potential in the case of electric energy. Risk-free handling of certain isolating devices is possible only for trained specialists; in such cases, the isolating device must be made inaccessible to unauthorized persons. (See figure 58.53.)

The Master Switch

A master-switch device disconnects the technical system from the energy supply. Unlike the isolating device, it can be operated without danger even by "non-energy specialists". The master-switch device is used to disconnect technical systems not in use at a given moment should, say, their operation be obstructed by unauthorized third persons. It is also used to effect a disconnection for such purposes as maintenance, repair of malfunctions, cleaning, resetting and refitting, provided that such work can be done without energy in the system. Naturally, when a master-switch device also possesses the characteristics of an isolating device, it can also take on and/or share its function. (See figure 58.54.)

Safety-disconnection Device

A safety-disconnection device does not disconnect the entire technical system from the energy source; rather, it removes energy from the parts of the system critical to a particular operational subsystem. Interventions of short duration can be designated for operational subsystems—for instance, for the set-up or resetting/refitting of the system, for the repair of malfunctions, for regular cleaning, and for essential and designated movements and function sequences required during the course of set-up, resetting/refitting or test runs. Complex production equipment and plants cannot simply be shut off with a master-switch device in these cases, as the entire technical system could not start up again where it left off after a malfunction has been repaired. Furthermore, the master-switch device is rarely located, in the more extensive technical systems, at the place where the intervention must be made. Thus the safety disconnection device is obliged to fulfil a number of requirements, such as the following:

- It interrupts the energy flow reliably and in such a way that dangerous movements or processes are not triggered by control signals which are either erroneously entered or erroneously generated.
- It is installed precisely where interruptions must be made in danger areas of operational subsystems of the technical system. If necessary, installation can be in several places (for instance, on various floors, in various rooms, or at various access points on machinery or equipment).
- Its control device has a clearly marked "off" position which registers only once after the flow of energy has been reliably cut off.

Figure 58.53 • Principles of electric and pneumatic isolating devices.

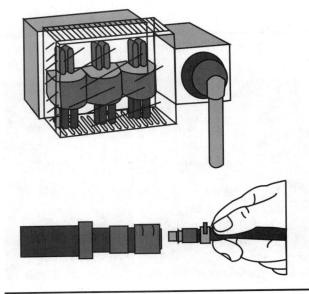

Figure 58.54 • Sample illustration of electric and pneumatic master-switch devices.

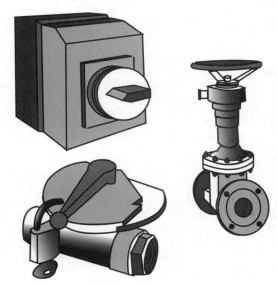

Figure 58.55 • Illustration of elementary principles of a safety disconnection device.

Figure 58.56 • Actuating devices in the control gears for movable and stationary operational subsystems.

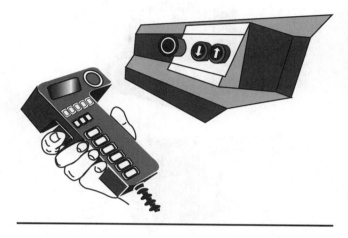

- Once in the "off" position its control device can be secured against being restarted without authorization (a) if the danger areas in question cannot be reliably overseen from the control area and (b) if persons located in the danger area cannot themselves see the control device readily and constantly, or (c) if lock-out/tag-out is required by regulation or organization procedures.
- It should disconnect only a single functional unit of an extended technical system, if other functional units are able to continue to work on their own without danger to the person intervening.

Where the master-switch device used in a given technical system is able to fulfil all the requirements of a safety-disconnection device, it can also take on this function. But that will of course be a reliable expedient only in very simple technical systems. (See figure 58.55.)

Control Gears for Operational Subsystems

Control gears permit movements and functional sequences required for operational subsystems of the technical system to be implemented and controlled safely. Control gears for operational subsystems may be required for set-up (when test runs are to be executed); for regulation (when malfunctions in the operation of the system are to be repaired or when blockages must be cleared); or training purposes (demonstrating operations). In such cases, the normal operation of the system cannot simply be restarted, as the intervening person would be endangered by movements and processes triggered by control signals either erroneously entered or erroneously generated. A control gear for operational subsystems must conform to the following requirements:

- It should permit the safe execution of movements and processes required for operational subsystems of the technical system. For example, certain movements will be executed at reduced speeds, gradually or at lower levels of power (depending on what is appropriate), and processes interrupted immediately, as a rule, if the control panel is no longer attended.

- Its control panels are to be located in areas where their operation does not endanger the operator, and from which the processes controlled are fully visible.
- If several control panels controlling various processes are present at a single location, then these must be clearly marked and arranged in a distinct and understandable manner.
- The control gear for operational subsystems should become effective only when normal operation has been reliably disengaged; that is, it must be guaranteed that no control command can issue effectively from normal operation and over-ride the control gear.
- Unauthorized use of the control gear for operational subsystems should be preventable, for instance, by requiring the use of a special key or code to release the function in question. (See figure 58.56.)

The Emergency Switch

Emergency switches are necessary where the normal operation of technical systems could result in hazards which neither appropriate system design nor the taking of appropriate safety precautions are able to prevent. In operational subsystems, the emergency switch is frequently part of the operational subsystem control gear. When operated in case of danger, the emergency switch implements processes which return the technical system to a safe operating state as quickly as possible. With regard to safety priorities, the protection of persons is of primary concern; prevention of damage to material is secondary, unless the latter is liable to endanger persons as well. The emergency switch must fulfil the following requirements:

- It must bring about a safe operating condition of the technical system as quickly as possible.
- Its control panel must be easily recognizable and placed and designed in such a way that it can be operated without difficulty by the endangered persons and can also be reached by others responding to the emergency.
- The emergency processes it triggers must not bring about new hazards; for example, they must not release clamping devices or disconnect magnetic holding fixtures or block safety devices.
- After an emergency switch process has been triggered, the technical system must not be able to be restarted automatically

Figure 58.57 • Illustration of the principles of control panels in emergency switches.

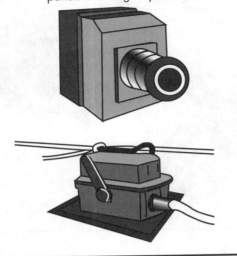

by the resetting of the emergency switch control panel. Rather, the conscious entry of a new function control command must be required. (See figure 58.57.)

Function-switch Control Device

Function-switch control devices are used to switch on the technical system for normal operation and to initiate, implement and interrupt the movements and processes designated for normal operation. The function-switch control device is used exclusively in the course of the normal operation of the technical system—that is, during the undisturbed execution of all assigned functions. It is used accordingly by the persons running the technical system. The function-switch control devices must meet the following requirements:

- Their control panels must be accessible and easy to use without danger.
- Their control panels must be clearly and rationally arranged; for example, control knobs should operate "rationally" with regard to controlled movements up and down, right and left.

Figure 58.58 • Schematic representation of an operations control panel.

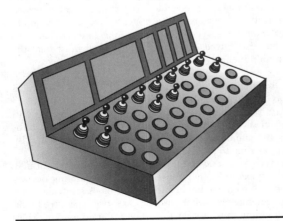

("Rational" control movements and corresponding effects may be subject to local variation and are sometimes defined by stipulation.)
- Their control panels are to be clearly and intelligibly labelled, with symbols which are easily understood.
- Processes which require the complete attention of the user for their safe execution must not be able to be triggered either by control signals generated in error or by inadvertent operation of the control devices governing them. Control panel signal processing must be appropriately reliable, and involuntary operation must be prevented by appropriate design of the control device. (See figure 58.58).

Monitoring Switches

Monitoring switches prevent the starting of the technical system as long as the monitored safety conditions are not fulfilled, and they interrupt operation as soon as a safety condition is no longer being fulfilled. They are used, for example, to monitor doors in protective compartments, to check for the correct position of safety guards or to assure that speed or path limits are not exceeded. Monitoring switches must accordingly fulfil the following safety and reliability requirements:

- The switching gear used for monitoring purposes must emit the protective signal in a particularly reliable fashion; for instance, a mechanical monitoring switch might be designed to interrupt the signal flow automatically and with particular reliability.
- The switching tool used for monitoring purposes is to be operated in a particularly reliable fashion when the safety condition is not fulfilled (e.g., when the plunger of a monitoring switch with automatic interruption is forced mechanically and automatically into the interrupt position).
- The monitoring switch must not be able to be improperly turned off, at least not unintentionally and not without some effort; this condition may be fulfilled, for instance, by a mechanical, automatically controlled switch with automatic interruption, when the switch and the operating element are securely mounted. (See figure 58.59).

Safety Control Circuits

Several of the safety switching devices described above do not execute the safety function directly, but rather by emitting a signal which is then transmitted and processed by a safety control circuit and finally reaches those parts of the technical system which exercise the actual safety function. The safety-disconnection device, for example, frequently causes the disconnection of energy at critical points indirectly, whereas a main switch usually directly disconnects the supply of current to the technical system.

Because safety control circuits must transmit safety signals reliably, the following principles must therefore be taken into consideration:

- Safety should be guaranteed even when outside energy is lacking or insufficient, for example, during disconnects or leaks.
- Protective signals function more reliably by interruption of the signal flow; for example, safety switches with opener contact or an open relay contact.
- The protective function of amplifiers, transformers and the like may be achieved more reliably without outside energy; such mechanisms include, for example, electromagnetic switching devices or vents that are closed when at rest.
- Connections effected in error and leaks in the safety-control circuit must not be allowed to lead to false starts or hindrances to stoppage; particularly in the cases of a short circuit between in- and out-conduits, earth leakage, or grounding.

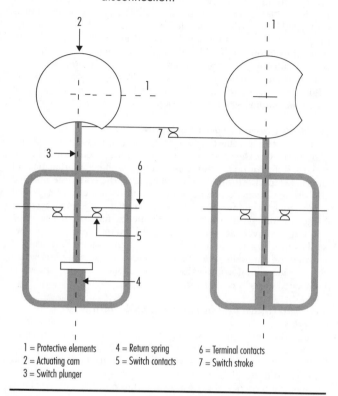

Figure 58.59 • Diagram of a switch with a positive mechanical operation and positive disconnection.

1 = Protective elements 4 = Return spring   6 = Terminal contacts
2 = Actuating cam   5 = Switch contacts   7 = Switch stroke
3 = Switch plunger

- Outside influences affecting the system in a measure not exceeding the expectations of the user should not interfere with the safety function of the safety-control circuit.

The components used in safety-control circuits must execute the safety function in an especially reliable way. The functions of components which do not meet this requirement are to be implemented by arranging for as diversified a redundancy as possible and are to be kept under surveillance.

SAFETY-RELATED APPLICATIONS

Dietmar Reinert and Karlheinz Meffert

In the last few years microprocessors have played an ever-increasing role in the field of safety technology. Because entire computers (i.e., central processing unit, memory and peripheral components) are now available in a single component as "single-chip computers", microprocessor technology is being employed not only in complex machine control, but also in safeguards of relatively simple design (e.g., light grids, two-hand control devices and safety edges). The software controlling these systems comprises between one thousand and several tens of thousands of single commands and usually consists of several hundred program branches. The programs operate in real time and are mostly written in the programmers' assembly language.

The introduction of computer-controlled systems in the sphere of safety technology has been accompanied in all large-scale technical equipment not only by expensive research and development

projects but also by significant restrictions designed to enhance safety. (Aerospace technology, military technology and atomic power technology may here be cited as examples of large-scale applications.) The collective field of industrial mass production has up to now been treated only in a very limited fashion. This is partly for the reason that the rapid cycles of innovation characteristic of industrial machine design make it difficult to carry over, in any but a very restricted manner, such knowledge as may be derived from research projects concerned with the final testing of large-scale safety devices. This makes the development of rapid and low-cost assessment procedures a desideratum (Reinert and Reuss 1991).

This article first examines machines and facilities in which computer systems presently perform safety tasks, using examples of accidents occurring preponderantly in the area of machine safeguards to depict the particular role which computers play in safety technology. These accidents give some indication as to which precautions must be taken so that the computer-controlled safety equipment currently coming into increasingly wide use will not lead to a rise in the number of accidents. The final section of the article sketches out a procedure which will enable even small computer systems to be brought to an appropriate level of technical safety at justifiable expense and within an acceptable period of time. The principles indicated in this final part are currently being introduced into international standardization procedures and will have implications for all areas of safety technology in which computers find application.

Examples of the Use of Software and Computers in the Field of Machine Safeguards

The following four examples make it clear that software and computers are currently entering more and more into safety-related applications in the commercial domain.

Personal-emergency signal installations consist, as a rule, of a central receiving station and a number of personal emergency signalling devices. The devices are carried by persons working onsite by themselves. If any of these persons working alone find themselves in an emergency situation, they can use the device to trip an alarm by radio signal in the central receiving station. Such a will-dependent alarm trigger may also be supplemented by a will-independent triggering mechanism activated by sensors built into the personal emergency devices. Both the individual devices and the central receiving station are frequently controlled by microcomputers. It is conceivable that failure of specific single functions of the built-in computer could lead, in an emergency situation, to a failure to trip the alarm. Precautions must therefore be taken to perceive and to repair such loss of function in time.

Printing presses used today to print magazines are large machines. The paper webs are normally prepared by a separate machine in such a way as to enable a seamless transition to a new paper roll. The printed pages are folded by a folding machine and subsequently worked through a chain of further machines. This results in pallets loaded with fully sewn magazines. Although such plants are automated, there are two points at which manual interventions must be made: (1) in the threading of the paper paths, and (2) in clearing obstructions caused by paper tears at danger spots on the rotating rollers. For this reason, a reduced speed of operation or a path- or time-limited jogging mode must be ensured by the control technology while the presses are being adjusted. On account of the complex steering procedures involved, every single printing station must be equipped with its own programmable logic controller. Any failure occurring in the control of a printing plant while guard grids are open must be kept from leading either to the unexpected start-up of a stopped machine or to operation in excess of appropriately reduced speeds.

In large factories and warehouses, driverless, automated guided robot vehicles move about on specially marked tracks. These tracks can be walked upon at any time by persons, or materials and equipment may be inadvertently left on the tracks, since they are not separated structurally from other lines of traffic. For this reason, some sort of collision-prevention equipment must be used to ensure that the vehicle will be brought to a halt before any dangerous collision with a person or object occurs. In more recent applications, collision prevention is effected by means of ultrasonic or laser light scanners used in combination with a safety bumper. Since these systems work under computer control, it is possible to configure several permanent detection zones so that a vehicle can modify its reaction depending on the specific detection zone in which a person is located. Failures in the protective device must not lead to a dangerous collision with a person.

Paper-cutting control device guillotines are used to press and then cut thick stacks of paper. They are triggered by a two-hand control device. The user must reach into the danger zone of the machine after each cut is made. An immaterial safeguard, usually a light grid, is used in conjunction with both the two-hand control device and a safe machine-control system to prevent injuries when paper is fed during the cutting operation. Nearly all the larger, more modern guillotines in use today are controlled by multichannel microcomputer systems. Both the two-hand operation and the light grid must also be guaranteed to function safely.

Accidents with Computer-Controlled Systems

In nearly all fields of industrial application, accidents with software and computers are reported (Neumann 1994). In most cases, computer failures do not lead to injury to persons. Such failures are in any case made public only when they are of general public interest. This means that the instances of malfunction or accident related to computers and software in which injury to persons is involved make up a relatively high proportion of all publicized cases. Unfortunately, accidents which do not cause much of a public sensation are not investigated as to their causes with quite the same intensity as are more prominent accidents, typically in large-scale plants. For this reason, the examples which follow refer to four descriptions of malfunctions or accidents typical of computer-controlled systems outside the field of machine safeguards, which are used to suggest what has to be taken into account when judgements concerning safety technology are made.

Accidents caused by random failures in hardware

The following mishap was caused by a concentration of random failures in the hardware combined with programming failure: A reactor overheated in a chemical plant, whereupon relief valves were opened, allowing the contents of the reactor to be discharged into the atmosphere. This mishap occurred a short time after a warning had been given that the oil level in a gearbox was too low. Careful investigation of the mishap showed that shortly after the catalyst had initiated the reaction in the reactor—in consequence of which the reactor would have required more cooling—the computer, on the basis of the report of low oil levels in the gearbox, froze all magnitudes under its control at a fixed value. This kept the cold water flow at too low a level and the reactor overheated as a result. Further investigation showed that the indication of low oil levels had been signalled by a faulty component. The software had responded according to the specification with the tripping of an alarm and the fixing of all operative variables. This was a consequence of the HAZOP (hazards and operability analysis) study (Knowlton 1986) done prior to the event, which required that all controlled variables not be modified in the event of a failure. Since the programmer was not acquainted with the procedure in detail, this requirement was interpreted to mean that the controlled actuators (control valves

in this case) were not to be modified; no attention was paid to the possibility of a rise in temperature. The programmer did not take into consideration that after having received an erroneous signal the system might find itself in a dynamic situation of a type requiring the active intervention of the computer to prevent a mishap. The situation which led to the mishap was so unlikely, moreover, that it had not been analysed in detail in the HAZOP study (Levenson 1986). This example provides a transition to a second category of causes of software and computer accidents. These are the systematic failures which are in the system from the beginning, but which manifest themselves only in certain very specific situations which the developer has not taken into account.

Accidents caused by operating failures

In field testing during the final inspection of robots, one technician borrowed the cassette of a neighbouring robot and substituted a different one without informing his colleague that he had done so. Upon returning to his workplace, the colleague inserted the wrong cassette. Since he stood next to the robot and expected a particular sequence of movements from it—a sequence which came out differently on account of the exchanged program—a collision occurred between robot and human. This accident describes the classical example of an operating failure. The role of such failures in malfunctions and accidents is currently increasing due to increasing complexity in the application of computer-controlled safety mechanisms.

Accidents caused by systematic failures in hardware or software

A torpedo with a warhead was to have been fired for training purposes, from a warship on the high seas. On account of a defect in the drive apparatus the torpedo remained in the torpedo tube. The captain decided to return to the home port in order to salvage the torpedo. Shortly after the ship had begun to make its way back home, the torpedo exploded. An analysis of the accident revealed that the torpedo's developers had been obliged to build into the torpedo a mechanism designed to prevent its returning to the launching pad after having been fired and thus destroying the ship that had launched it. The mechanism chosen for this was as follows: After the firing of the torpedo a check was made, using the inertial navigation system, to see whether its course had altered by 180°. As soon as the torpedo sensed that it had turned 180°, the torpedo detonated immediately, supposedly at a safe distance from the launching pad. This detection mechanism was actuated in the case of the torpedo which had not been properly launched, with the result that the torpedo exploded after the ship had changed its course by 180°. This is a typical example of an accident occurring on account of a failure in specifications. The requirement in the specifications that the torpedo should not destroy its own ship should its course change was not formulated precisely enough; the precaution was thus programmed erroneously. The error became apparent only in a particular situation, one which the programmer had not taken into account as a possibility.

On 14 September 1993, a Lufthansa Airbus A 320 crashed while landing in Warsaw (figure 58.60). A careful investigation of the accident showed that modifications in the landing logic of the on-board computer made after an accident with a Lauda Air Boeing 767 in 1991 were partly responsible for this crash landing. What had happened in the 1991 accident was that the thrust deflection, which diverts some part of the motor gases so as to brake the airplane during landing, had engaged while still in the air, thus forcing the machine into an uncontrollable nose-dive. For this reason, an electronic locking of the thrust deflection had been built into the Airbus machines. This mechanism permitted thrust deflection to come into effect only after sensors on both sets of landing gear had signalled the compression of the shock absorbers under the pressure of the wheels touching down. On the basis of incorrect information, the pilots of the plane in Warsaw anticipated a strong side wind. For this reason they brought the machine in at a slight tilt and the Airbus touched down with the right wheel only, leaving the left bearing less than full weight. On account of the electronic locking of the thrust deflection, the on-board computer denied to the pilot for the space of nine seconds such manoeuvers as would have allowed the airplane to land safely despite adverse circumstances. This accident demonstrates very clearly that modifications in computer systems can lead to new and hazardous situations if the range of their possible consequences is not considered in advance.

The following example of a malfunction also demonstrates the disastrous effects which the modification of one single command can have in computer systems. The alcohol content of blood is determined, in chemical tests, using clear blood serum from which the blood corpuscles have been centrifuged out in advance. The alcohol content of serum is therefore higher (by a factor of 1.2) than that of the thicker whole blood. For this reason the alcohol values in serum must be divided by a factor of 1.2 in order to establish the legally and medically critical parts-per-thousand figures. In the inter-laboratory test held in 1984, the blood alcohol values ascertained in identical tests performed at different research institutions using serum were to have been compared with each other. Since it was a question of comparison only, the command to divide by 1.2 was moreover erased from the program at one of the institutions for the duration of the experiment. After the inter-laboratory test had come to an end, a command to multiply by 1.2 was erroneously introduced into the program at this spot. Roughly 1,500 incorrect parts-per-thousand values were calculated between August 1984 and March 1985 as a result. This error was critical for the professional careers of truck drivers with blood alcohol levels between 1.0 and 1.3 per thousand, since a legal penalty entailing confiscation of a driver's licence for a prolonged period is the consequence of a 1.3 per thousand value.

Accidents caused by influences from operating stresses or from environmental stresses

As a consequence of a disturbance caused by collection of waste in the effective area of a CNC (computer numeric control) punching and nibbling machine, the user put into effect the "programmed stop". As he was trying to remove the waste with his hands, the push rod of the machine started moving in spite of the programmed stop and severely injured the user. An analysis of the accident revealed that it had not been a question of an error in the program. The unexpected start-up could not be reproduced. Similar irregularities had been observed in the past on other machines of the same type. It seems plausible to deduce from these that the accident must have been caused by electromagnetic interference. Similar accidents with industrial robots are reported from Japan (Neumann 1987).

A malfunction in the Voyager 2 space probe on January 18, 1986, makes even more clear the influence of environmental stresses on computer-controlled systems. Six days before the closest approach to Uranus, large fields of black-and-white lines covered over the pictures from Voyager 2. A precise analysis showed that a single bit in a command word of the flight data subsystem had caused the failure, observed as the pictures were compressed in the probe. This bit had most likely been knocked out of place within the program memory by the impact of a cosmic particle. Error-free transmission of the compressed photographs from the probe was effected only two days later, using a replacement program capable of bypassing the failed memory point (Laeser, McLaughlin and Wolff 1987).

Summary of the accidents presented

The accidents analysed show that certain risks that might be neglected under conditions using simple, electro-mechanical technology, gain in significance when computers are used. Computers permit the processing of complex and situation-specific safety functions. An unambiguous, error-free, complete and testable specification of all safety functions becomes for this reason especially important. Errors in specifications are difficult to discover and are frequently the cause of accidents in complex systems. Freely programmable controls are usually introduced with the intention of being able to react flexibly and quickly to the changing market. Modifications, however—particularly in complex systems—have side effects which are difficult to foresee. All modifications must therefore be subjected to a strictly formal management of change procedure in which a clear separation of safety functions from partial systems not relevant to safety will help keep the consequences of modifications for safety technology easy to survey.

Computers work with low levels of electricity. They are therefore susceptible to interference from external radiation sources. Since the modification of a single signal among millions can lead to a malfunction, it is worth paying special attention to the theme of electromagnetic compatibility in connection with computers.

The servicing of computer-controlled systems is currently becoming more and more complex and thus more unclear. The software ergonomics of user and configuration software is therefore becoming more interesting from the point of view of safety technology.

No computer system is 100% testable. A simple control mechanism with 32 binary input ports and 1,000 different software paths requires 4.3×10^{12} tests for a complete check. At a rate of 100 tests per second executed and evaluated, a complete test would take 1,362 years.

Procedures and Measures for the Improvement of Computer-Controlled Safety Devices

Procedures have been developed within the last 10 years which permit mastery of specific safety-related challenges in connection with computers. These procedures address themselves to the computer failures described in this section. The examples described of software and computers in machine safeguards and the accidents analysed, show that the extent of damage and thus also the risk involved in various applications are extremely variable. It is there-

Figure 58.60 • Lufthansa Airbus after accident in Warsaw 1993.

Figure 58.61 • Qualitative procedure for risk determination.

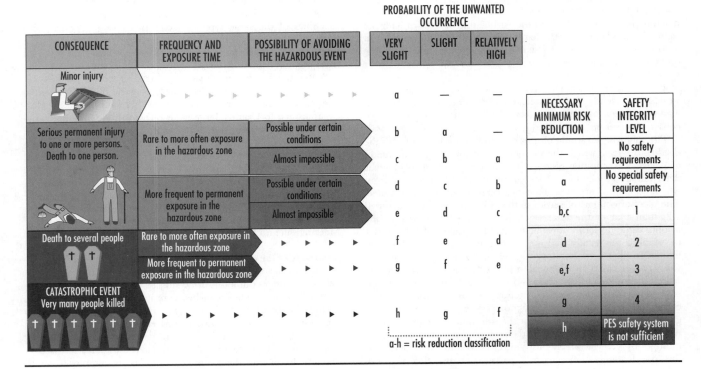

Figure 58.62 • Effectiveness of precautions taken against errors independently of risk.

FAILURE CAUSES	REQUIRED EFFECTIVENESS OF MEASURES TO CONTROL OR AVOID FAILURES FOR EACH SAFETY INTEGRITY LEVEL			
Hardware Integrity: single faults	Measures to control failures; achieved by configuration and/or component measures			
	1	2	3	4
Hardware Integrity: multiple faults by accumulation	Measures to control failures; achieved by configuration and/or component and/or technical measures			
	1	2	3	4
Systematic Integrity: systematic hardware and software	Measures to avoid failures			
	1	2	3	4
	Measures to control failures			
	1	2	3	4
Systematic Integrity: environment	Measures to avoid failures			
	1	2	3	4
	Measures to control failures			
	1	2	3	4
Systematic Integrity: operation	Measures to avoid failures			
	1	2	3	4
	Measures to control failures			
	1	2	3	4

Effectiveness of measures: basic low medium high

fore clear that the requisite precautions for the improvement of computers and software used in safety technology should be established in relation to the risk.

Figure 58.61 shows a qualitative procedure whereby the necessary risk reduction obtainable using safety systems can be determined independently of the extent to which and the frequency with which damage occurs (Bell and Reinert 1992). The types of failures in computer systems analysed in the section "Accidents with computer-controlled systems" (above) may be brought into relation with the so-called Safety Integrity Levels—that is, the technical facilities for risk reduction.

Figure 58.62 makes it clear that the effectiveness of measures taken, in any given case, to reduce error in software and computers needs to grow with increasing risk (DIN 1994; IEC 1993).

The analysis of the accidents sketched above shows that the failure of computer-controlled safeguards is caused not only by random component faults, but also by particular operating conditions which the programmer has failed to take into account. The not immediately obvious consequences of program modifications made in the course of system maintenance constitute a further source of error. It follows that there can be failures in safety systems controlled by microprocessors which, though made during the development of the system, can lead to a dangerous situation only during operation. Precautions against such failures must therefore be taken while safety-related systems are in the development stage. These so-called failure-avoidance measures must be taken not only during the concept phase, but also in the process of development, installation and modification. Certain failures can be avoided if they are discovered and corrected during this process (DIN 1990).

As the last mishap described makes clear, the breakdown of a single transistor can lead to the technical failure of highly complex automated equipment. Since each single circuit is composed of many thousands of transistors and other components, numerous

Figure 58.63 • Examples of precautions taken to control and avoid errors in computer systems.

FAILURES IN PES	MEASURES TO AVOID FAILURES
Before startup, e.g.: • Failure in the specification • Failure in the dimensioning • Programming error • Failure during implementation	• Use of development tools • Structured design • Check of EMC • Simulation • Program analysis • Type-testing • Different design teams
After startup, e.g.: • Failure in RAM/ROM • Failure in CPU • Failure in I/O • Wrong program sequence caused by EMI • Failure caused by modification	**MEASURES TO CONTROL FAILURES** • Redundant hardware • Redundant software • RAM/ROM test • On-line test (single channel) • I/O test • CPU test • Monitored outputs

failure-avoidance measures must be taken to recognize such failures as turn up in operation and to initiate an appropriate reaction in the computer system. Figure 58.63 describes types of failures in programmable electronic systems as well as examples of precautions which may be taken to avoid and control failures in computer systems (DIN 1990; IEC 1992).

Possibilities and Prospects of Programmable Electronic Systems in Safety Technology

Modern machines and plants are becoming increasingly complex and must achieve ever more comprehensive tasks in ever shorter periods of time. For this reason, computer systems have taken over nearly all areas of industry since the mid-1970s. This increase in complexity alone has contributed significantly to the rising costs involved in improving safety technology in such systems. Although software and computers pose a great challenge to safety in the workplace, they also make possible the implementation of new error-friendly systems in the field of safety technology.

A droll but instructive verse by Ernst Jandl will help to explain what is meant by the concept *error-friendly*. "Lichtung: Manche meinen lechts und rinks kann man nicht velwechsern, werch ein Illtum". ("Dilection: Many berieve light and reft cannot be interchanged, what an ellor".) Despite the exchange of the letters *r* and *l*, this phrase is easily understood by a normal adult human. Even someone with low fluency in the English language can translate it into English. The task is, however, nearly impossible for a translating computer on its own.

This example shows that a human being can react in a much more error-friendly fashion than a language computer can. This means that humans, like all other living creatures, can tolerate failures by referring them to experience. If one looks at the machines in use today, one can see that the majority of machines penalize user failures not with an accident, but with a decrease in production. This property leads to the manipulation or evasion of safeguards. Modern computer technology places systems at the disposal of work safety which can react intelligently—that is, in a modified way. Such systems thus make possible an error-friendly mode of behaviour in novel machines. They warn users during a wrong operation first of all and shut the machine off only when this is the only way to avoid an accident. The analysis of accidents shows that there exists in this area a considerable potential for reducing accidents (Reinert and Reuss 1991).

SOFTWARE AND COMPUTERS: HYBRID AUTOMATED SYSTEMS

Waldemar Karwowski and Jozef Zurada

A hybrid automated system (HAS) aims to integrate the capabilities of artificially intelligent machines (based on computer technology) with the capacities of the people who interact with these machines in the course of their work activities. The principal concerns of HAS utilization relate to how the human and machine subsystems should be designed in order to make the best use of the knowledge and skills of both parts of the hybrid system, and how the human operators and machine components should interact with each other to assure their functions complement one another. Many hybrid automated systems have evolved as the products of applications of modern information- and control-based methodologies to automate and integrate different functions of often complex technological systems. HAS was originally identified with the introduction of computer-based systems used in the design and operation of real-time control systems for nuclear power reactors, for chemical processing plants and for discrete parts-manufacturing technology. HAS can now also be found in many service industries, such as air traffic control and aircraft navigation procedures in the civil aviation area, and in the design and use of intelligent vehicle and highway navigation systems in road transportation.

With continuing progress in computer-based automation, the nature of human tasks in modern technological systems shifts from those that require perceptual-motor skills to those calling for cognitive activities, which are needed for problem solving, for decision making in system monitoring, and for supervisory control tasks. For example, the human operators in computer-integrated manufacturing systems primarily act as system monitors, problem solvers and decision makers. The cognitive activities of the human supervisor in any HAS environment are (1) planning what should be done for a given period of time, (2) devising procedures (or steps) to achieve the set of planned goals, (3) monitoring the progress of (technological) processes, (4) "teaching" the system through a human-interactive computer, (5) intervening if the system behaves abnormally or if the control priorities change and (6) learning through feedback from the system about the impact of supervisory actions (Sheridan 1987).

Hybrid System Design

The human-machine interactions in a HAS involve utilization of dynamic communication loops between the human operators and intelligent machines—a process that includes information sensing and processing and the initiation and execution of control tasks and decision making—within a given structure of function allocation between humans and machines. At a minimum, the interactions between people and automation should reflect the high complexity of hybrid automated systems, as well as relevant characteristics of the human operators and task requirements. Therefore, the hybrid automated system can be formally defined as a quintuple in the following formula:

$$HAS = (T, U, C, E, I)$$

where T = task requirements (physical and cognitive); U = user characteristics (physical and cognitive); C = the automation characteristics (hardware and software, including computer interfaces); E = the system's environment; I = a set of interactions among the above elements

The set of interactions I embodies all possible interactions between T, U and C in E regardless of their nature or strength of association. For example, one of the possible interactions might involve the relation of the data stored in the computer memory to the corresponding knowledge, if any, of the human operator. The interactions I can be elemental (i.e., limited to a one-to-one association), or complex, such as would involve interactions between the human operator, the particular software used to achieve the desired task, and the available physical interface with the computer.

Designers of many hybrid automated systems focus primarily on the computer-aided integration of sophisticated machines and other equipment as parts of computer-based technology, rarely paying much attention to the paramount need for effective human integration within such systems. Therefore, at present, many of the computer-integrated (technological) systems are not fully compatible with the inherent capabilities of the human operators as expressed by the skills and knowledge necessary for the effective control and monitoring of these systems. Such incompatibility arises at all levels of human, machine and human-machine functioning, and can be defined within a framework of the individual and the entire organization or facility. For example, the problems of integrating people and technology in advanced manufacturing enterprises occur early in the HAS design stage. These problems can be conceptualized using the following system integration model of the complexity of interactions, I, between the system designers, D, human operators, H, or potential system users and technology, T:

$$I(H, T) = F[I(H, D), I(D, T)]$$

where I stands for relevant interactions taking place in a given HAS's structure, while F indicates functional relationships between designers, human operators and technology.

The above system integration model highlights the fact that the interactions between the users and technology are determined by the outcome of the integration of the two earlier interactions—namely, (1) those between HAS designers and potential users and (2) those between the designers and the HAS technology (at the level of machines and their integration). It should be noted that even though strong interactions typically exist between the designers and technology, only very few examples of equally strong interrelationships between designers and human operators can be found.

It can be argued that even in the most automated systems, the human role remains critical to successful system performance at the operational level. Bainbridge (1983) identified a set of problems relevant to the operation of the HAS which are due to the nature of automation itself, as follows:

1. *Operators "out of the control loop"*. The human operators are present in the system to exercise control when needed, but by being "out of the control loop" they fail to maintain the manual skills and long-term system knowledge that are often required in case of an emergency.
2. *Outdated "mental picture"*. The human operators may not be able to respond quickly to changes in the system behaviour if they have not been following the events of its operation very closely. Furthermore, the operators' knowledge or mental picture of the system functioning may be inadequate to initiate or exercise required responses.
3. *Disappearing generations of skills*. New operators may not be able to acquire sufficient knowledge about the computerized system achieved through experience and, therefore, will be unable to exercise effective control when needed.
4. *Authority of automatics*. If the computerized system has been implemented because it can perform the required tasks better than the human operator, the question arises, "On what basis

should the operator decide that correct or incorrect decisions are being made by the automated systems?"
5. *Emergence of the new types of "human errors" due to automation*. Automated systems lead to new types of errors and, consequently, accidents which cannot be analysed within the framework of traditional techniques of analysis.

Task Allocation

One of the important issues for HAS design is to determine how many and which functions or responsibilities should be allocated to the human operators, and which and how many to the computers. Generally, there are three basic classes of task allocation problems that should be considered: (1) the human supervisor–computer task allocation, (2) the human–human task allocation and (3) the supervisory computer–computer task allocation. Ideally, the allocation decisions should be made through some structured allocation procedure before the basic system design is begun. Unfortunately such a systematic process is seldom possible, as the functions to be allocated may either need further examination or must be carried out interactively between the human and machine system components—that is, through application of the supervisory control paradigm. Task allocation in hybrid automated systems should focus on the extent of the human and computer supervisory responsibilities, and should consider the nature of interactions between the human operator and computerized decision support systems. The means of information transfer between machines and the human input-output interfaces and the compatibility of software with human cognitive problem-solving abilities should also be considered.

In traditional approaches to the design and management of hybrid automated systems, workers were considered as deterministic input-output systems, and there was a tendency to disregard the teleological nature of human behaviour—that is, the goal-oriented behaviour relying on the acquisition of relevant information and the selection of goals (Goodstein et al. 1988). To be successful, the design and management of advanced hybrid automated systems must be based on a description of the human mental functions needed for a specific task. The "cognitive engineering" approach (described further below) proposes that human-machine (hybrid) systems need to be conceived, designed, analysed and evaluated in terms of human mental processes (i.e., the operator's mental model of the adaptive systems is taken into account). The following are the requirements of the human-centred approach to HAS design and operation as formulated by Corbett (1988):

1. *Compatibility*. System operation should not require skills unrelated to existing skills, but should allow existing skills to evolve. The human operator should input and receive information which is compatible with conventional practice in order that the interface conform to the user's prior knowledge and skill.
2. *Transparency*. One cannot control a system without understanding it. Therefore, the human operator must be able to "see" the internal processes of the system's control software if learning is to be facilitated. A transparent system makes it easy for users to build up an internal model of the decision-making and control functions that the system can perform.
3. *Minimum shock*. The system should not do anything which operators find unexpected in the light of the information available to them, detailing the present state of the system.
4. *Disturbance control*. Uncertain tasks (as defined by the choice structure analysis) should be under human operator control with computer decision-making support.
5. *Fallibility*. The implicit skills and knowledge of the human operators should not be designed out of the system. The

operators should never be put in a position where they help-lessly watch the software direct an incorrect operation.

6. *Error reversibility.* Software should supply sufficient feedforward of information to inform the human operator of the likely consequences of a particular operation or strategy.

7. *Operating flexibility.* The system should offer human operators the freedom to trade off requirements and resource limits by shifting operating strategies without losing the control software support.

Cognitive Human Factors Engineering

Cognitive human factors engineering focuses on how human operators make decisions at the workplace, solve problems, formulate plans and learn new skills (Hollnagel and Woods 1983). The roles of the human operators functioning in any HAS can be classified using Rasmussen's scheme (1983) into three major categories:

1. *Skill-based behaviour* is the sensory-motor performance executed during acts or activities which take place without conscious control as smooth, automated and highly integrated patterns of behaviour. Human activities that fall under this category are considered to be a sequence of skilled acts composed for a given situation. Skill-based behaviour is thus the expression of more or less stored patterns of behaviours or pre-programmed instructions in a space-time domain.

2. *Rule-based behaviour* is a goal-oriented category of performance structured by feedforward control through a stored rule or procedure—that is, an ordered performance allowing a sequence of subroutines in a familiar work situation to be composed. The rule is typically selected from previous experiences and reflects the functional properties which constrain the behaviour of the environment. Rule-based performance is based on explicit know-how as regards employing the relevant rules. The decision data set consists of references for recognition and identification of states, events or situations.

3. *Knowledge-based behaviour* is a category of goal-controlled performance, in which the goal is explicitly formulated based on knowledge of the environment and the aims of the person. The internal structure of the system is represented by a "mental model". This kind of behaviour allows the development and testing of different plans under unfamiliar and, therefore, uncertain control conditions, and is needed when skills or rules are either unavailable or inadequate so that problem solving and planning must be called upon instead.

In the design and management of a HAS, one should consider the cognitive characteristics of the workers in order to assure the compatibility of system operation with the worker's internal model that describes its functions. Consequently, the system's description level should be shifted from the skill-based to the rule-based and knowledge-based aspects of human functioning, and appropriate methods of cognitive task analysis should be used to identify the operator's model of a system. A related issue in the development of a HAS is the design of means of information transmission between the human operator and automated system components, at both the physical and the cognitive levels. Such information transfer should be compatible with the modes of information utilized at different levels of system operation—that is, visual, verbal, tactile or hybrid. This informational compatibility ensures that different forms of information transfer will require minimal incompatibility between the medium and the nature of the information. For example, a visual display is best for transmission of spatial information, while auditory input may be used to convey textual information.

Quite often the human operator develops an internal model that describes the operation and function of the system according to his or her experience, training and instructions in connection with the given type of human-machine interface. In light of this reality, the designers of a HAS should attempt to build into the machines (or other artificial systems) a model of the human operator's physical and cognitive characteristics—that is, the system's image of the operator (Hollnagel and Woods 1983). The designers of a HAS must also take into consideration the level of abstraction in the system description as well as various relevant categories of the human operator's behaviour. These levels of abstraction for modelling human functioning in the working environment are as follows (Rasmussen 1983): (1) physical form (anatomical structure), (2) physical functions (physiological functions), (3) generalized functions (psychological mechanisms and cognitive and affective processes), (4) abstract functions (information processing) and (5) functional purpose (value structures, myths, religions, human interactions). These five levels must be considered simultaneously by the designers in order to ensure effective HAS performance.

System Software Design

Since the computer software is a primary component of any HAS environment, software development, including design, testing, operation and modification, and software reliability issues must also be considered at the early stages of HAS development. By this means, one should be able to lower the cost of software error detection and elimination. It is difficult, however, to estimate the reliability of the human components of a HAS, on account of limitations in our ability to model human task performance, the related workload and potential errors. Excessive or insufficient mental workload may lead to information overload and boredom, respectively, and may result in degraded human performance, leading to errors and the increasing probability of accidents. The designers of a HAS should employ adaptive interfaces, which utilize artificial intelligence techniques, to solve these problems. In addition to human-machine compatibility, the issue of human-machine adaptability to each other must be considered in order to reduce the stress levels that come about when human capabilities may be exceeded.

Due to the high level of complexity of many hybrid automated systems, identification of any potential hazards related to the hardware, software, operational procedures and human-machine interactions of these systems becomes critical to the success of efforts aimed at reduction of injuries and equipment damage. Safety and health hazards associated with complex hybrid automated systems, such as computer-integrated manufacturing technology (CIM), is clearly one of the most critical aspects of system design and operation.

System Safety Issues

Hybrid automated environments, with their significant potential for erratic behaviour of the control software under system disturbance conditions, create a new generation of accident risks. As hybrid automated systems become more versatile and complex, system disturbances, including start-up and shut-down problems and deviations in system control, can significantly increase the possibility of serious danger to the human operators. Ironically, in many abnormal situations, operators usually rely on the proper functioning of the automated safety subsystems, a practice which may increase the risk of severe injury. For example, a study of accidents related to malfunctions of technical control systems showed that about one-third of the accident sequences included human intervention in the control loop of the disturbed system.

Since traditional safety measures cannot be easily adapted to the needs of HAS environments, injury control and accident prevention strategies need to be reconsidered in view of the inherent characteristics of these systems. For example, in the area of advanced manufacturing technology, many processes are characterized by the existence of substantial amounts of energy flows which cannot be easily anticipated by the human operators. Furthermore, safety problems typically emerge at the interfaces between subsystems, or when system disturbances progress from one subsystem to another. According to the International Organization for Standardization (ISO 1991), the risks associated with hazards due to industrial automation vary with the types of industrial machines incorporated into the specific manufacturing system and with the ways in which the system is installed, programmed, operated, maintained and repaired. For example, a comparison of robot-related accidents in Sweden to other types of accidents showed that robots may be the most hazardous industrial machines used in advanced manufacturing industry. The estimated accident rate for industrial robots was one serious accident per 45 robot-years, a higher rate than that for industrial presses, which was reported to be one accident per 50 machine-years. It should be noted here that industrial presses in the United States accounted for about 23% of all metalworking machine-related fatalities for the 1980–1985 period, with power presses ranked first with respect to the severity-frequency product for non-fatal injuries.

In the domain of advanced manufacturing technology, there are many moving parts which are hazardous to workers as they change their position in a complex manner outside the visual field of the human operators. Rapid technological developments in computer-integrated manufacturing created a critical need to study the effects of advanced manufacturing technology on the workers. In order to identify the hazards caused by various components of such a HAS environment, past accidents need to be carefully analysed. Unfortunately, accidents involving robot use are difficult to isolate from reports of human operated machine-related accidents, and, therefore, there may be a high percentage of unrecorded accidents. The occupational health and safety rules of Japan state that "industrial robots do not at present have reliable means of safety and workers cannot be protected from them unless their use is regulated". For example, the results of the survey conducted by the Labour Ministry of Japan (Sugimoto 1987) of accidents related to industrial robots across the 190 factories surveyed (with 4,341 working robots) showed that there were 300 robot-related disturbances, of which 37 cases of unsafe acts resulted in some near accidents, 9 were injury-producing accidents, and 2 were fatal accidents. The results of other studies indicate that computer-based automation does not necessarily increase the overall level of safety, as the system hardware cannot be made fail-safe by safety functions in the computer software alone, and system controllers are not always highly reliable. Furthermore, in a complex HAS, one cannot depend exclusively on safety-sensing devices to detect hazardous conditions and undertake appropriate hazard-avoidance strategies.

Effects of Automation on Human Health

As discussed above, worker activities in many HAS environments are basically those of supervisory control, monitoring, system support and maintenance. These activities may also be classified into four basic groups as follows: (1) programming tasks i.e., encoding the information that guides and directs machinery operation, (2) monitoring of HAS production and control components, (3) maintenance of HAS components to prevent or alleviate machinery malfunctions, and (4) performing a variety of support tasks, etc. Many recent reviews of the impact of the HAS on worker well-being concluded that although the utilization of a HAS in the manufacturing area may eliminate heavy and dangerous tasks, working in a HAS environment may be dissatisfying and stressful for the workers. Sources of stress included the constant monitoring required in many HAS applications, the limited

scope of the allocated activities, the low level of worker interaction permitted by the system design, and safety hazards associated with the unpredictable and uncontrollable nature of the equipment. Even though some workers who are involved in programming and maintenance activities feel the elements of challenge, which may have positive effects on their well-being, these effects are often offset by the complex and demanding nature of these activities, as well as by the pressure exerted by management to complete these activities quickly.

Although in some HAS environments the human operators are removed from traditional energy sources (the flow of work and movement of the machine) during normal operating conditions, many tasks in automated systems still need to be carried out in direct contact with other energy sources. Since the number of different HAS components is continually increasing, special emphasis must be placed on workers' comfort and safety and on the development of effective injury control provisions, especially in view of the fact that the workers are no longer able to keep up with the sophistication and complexity of such systems.

In order to meet the current needs for injury control and worker safety in computer integrated manufacturing systems, the ISO Committee on Industrial Automation Systems has proposed a new safety standard entitled "Safety of Integrated Manufacturing Systems" (1991). This new international standard, which was developed in recognition of the particular hazards which exist in integrated manufacturing systems incorporating industrial machines and associated equipment, aims to minimize the possibilities of injuries to personnel while working on or adjacent to an integrated manufacturing system. The main sources of potential hazards to the human operators in CIM identified by this standard are shown in figure 58.64.

Human and System Errors

In general, hazards in a HAS can arise from the system itself, from its association with other equipment present in the physical environment, or from interactions of human personnel with the system. An accident is only one of the several outcomes of human-machine interactions that may emerge under hazardous conditions; near accidents and damage incidents are much more common (Zimolong and Duda 1992). The occurrence of an error can lead to one of these consequences: (1) the error remains unnoticed, (2) the system can compensate for the error, (3) the error leads to a machine breakdown and/or system stoppage or (4) the error leads to an accident.

Since not every human error that results in a critical incident will cause an actual accident, it is appropriate to distinguish further among outcome categories as follows: (1) an unsafe incident (i.e., any unintentional occurrence regardless whether it results in injury, damage or loss), (2) an accident (i.e., an unsafe event resulting in injury, damage or loss), (3) a damage incident (i.e., an unsafe event which results only in some kind of material damage), (4) a near accident or "near miss" (i.e., an unsafe event in which injury, damage or loss was fortuitously avoided by a narrow margin) and (5) the existence of accident potential (i.e., unsafe events which could have resulted in injury, damage, or loss, but, owing to circumstances, did not result in even a near accident).

One can distinguish three basic types of human error in a HAS:

1. skill-based slips and lapses
2. rule-based mistakes
3. knowledge-based mistakes.

This taxonomy, devised by Reason (1990), is based on a modification of Rasmussen's skill-rule-knowledge classification of human performance as described above. At the skill-based level, human performance is governed by stored patterns of pre-programmed instructions represented as analogue structures in a space-time domain. The rule-based level is applicable to tackling familiar problems in which solutions are governed by stored rules (called "productions", since they are accessed, or produced, at need). These rules require certain diagnoses (or judgements) to be made, or certain remedial actions to be taken, given that certain conditions have arisen that demand an appropriate response. At this level, human errors are typically associated with the misclassification of situations, leading either to the application of the wrong rule or to the incorrect recall of consequent judgements or procedures. Knowledge-based errors occur in novel situations for which actions must be planned "on-line" (at a given moment), using conscious analytical processes and stored knowledge. Errors at this level arise from resource limitations and incomplete or incorrect knowledge.

Figure 58.64 • Main source of hazards in computer-integrated manufacturing (CIM) (after ISO 1991).

Moving mechanical components:
• In normal operation either individually or in conjunction with other elements of the system or related equipment in the hazard zone
• An abnormal operation (e.g., falling, tripping)

Interferences:
• Electrical: for example, sources of electromagnetic radiation, electrostatic discharge (ESD) or radio frequency interference (RFI)
• Mechanical (e.g., vibration or shock)

Hazardous atmospheres or materials:
• Explosive or combustible materials
• Corrosive agents
• Radiation (e.g., ionizing or thermal)

Stored energy

Power sources

Failure or fault of the following functions or equipment:
• Protective provisions (as caused by workers' removing, disassembling or defeating them
• Various components, devices or circuits
• Power sources or means of power distribution as caused by fluctuations or disturbances
• Information transmission

Human error in the following areas:
• Design, construction or modification
• Operating systems, application software and programming
• Application and implementation
• Set-up, including work handling/holding and tooling
• Operation or use
• Maintenance and repair
• Documentation and training/instruction

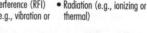

Ergonomic considerations:
• Lighting
• Vibrations
• Noise
• Climatic conditions
• Operator control stations, design and layout

Source: ISO 1991.

The generic error-modelling systems (GEMS) proposed by Reason (1990), which attempts to locate the origins of the basic human error types, can be used to derive the overall taxonomy of human behaviour in a HAS. GEMS seeks to integrate two distinct areas of error research: (1) slips and lapses, in which actions deviate from current intention due to execution failures and/or storage failures and (2) mistakes, in which the actions may run according to plan, but the plan is inadequate to achieve its desired outcome.

Risk Assessment and Prevention in CIM

According to the ISO (1991), risk assessment in CIM should be performed so as to minimize all risks and to serve as a basis for determining safety objectives and measures in the development of programmes or plans both to create a safe working environment and to ensure the safety and health of personnel as well. For example, work hazards in manufacturing-based HAS environments can be characterized as follows: (1) the human operator may need to enter the danger zone during disturbance recovery, service and maintenance tasks, (2) the danger zone is difficult to determine, to perceive and to control, (3) the work may be monotonous and (4) the accidents occurring within computer-integrated manufacturing systems are often serious. Each identified hazard should be assessed for its risk, and appropriate safety measures should be determined and implemented to minimize that risk. Hazards should also be ascertained with respect to all of the following aspects of any given process: the single unit itself; the interaction between single units; the operating sections of the system; and the operation of the complete system for all intended operating modes and conditions, including conditions under which normal safeguarding means are suspended for such operations as programming, verification, troubleshooting, maintenance or repair.

The design phase of the ISO (1991) safety strategy for CIM includes:

• specification of the limits of system parameters
• application of a safety strategy
• identification of hazards
• assessment of the associated risks
• removal of the hazards or diminution of the risks as much as practicable.

The system safety specification should include:

• a description of system functions
• a system layout and/or model
• the results of a survey undertaken to investigate the interaction of different working processes and manual activities
• an analysis of process sequences, including manual interaction
• a description of the interfaces with conveyor or transport lines
• process flow charts
• foundation plans
• plans for supply and disposal devices
• determination of the space required for supply and disposal of material
• available accident records.

In accordance with the ISO (1991), all necessary requirements for ensuring a safe CIM system operation need to be considered in the design of systematic safety-planning procedures. This includes all protective measures to effectively reduce hazards and requires:

• integration of the human-machine interface
• early definition of the position of those working on the system (in time and space)

- early consideration of ways of cutting down on isolated work
- consideration of environmental aspects.

The safety planning procedure should address, among others, the following safety issues of CIM:

- *Selection of the operating modes of the system.* The control equipment should have provisions for at least the following operating modes:(1) normal or production mode (i.e., with all normal safeguards connected and operating), (2) operation with some of the normal safeguards suspended and (3) operation in which system or remote manual initiation of hazardous situations is prevented (e.g., in the case of local operation or of isolation of power to or mechanical blockage of hazardous conditions).
- *Training, installation, commissioning and functional testing.* When personnel are required to be in the hazard zone, the following safety measures should be provided in the control system: (1) hold to run, (2) enabling device, (3) reduced speed, (4) reduced power and (5) moveable emergency stop.
- *Safety in system programming, maintenance and repair.* During programming, only the programmer should be allowed in the safeguarded space. The system should have inspection and maintenance procedures in place to ensure continued intended operation of the system. The inspection and maintenance programme should take into account the recommendations of the system supplier and those of suppliers of various elements of the systems. It scarcely needs mentioning that personnel who perform maintenance or repairs on the system should be trained in the procedures necessary to perform the required tasks.
- *Fault elimination.* Where fault elimination is necessary from inside the safeguarded space, it should be performed after safe disconnection (or, if possible, after a lockout mechanism has been actuated). Additional measures against erroneous initiation of hazardous situations should be taken. Where hazards can occur during fault elimination at sections of the system or at the machines of adjoining systems or machines, these should also be taken out of operation and protected against unexpected starting. By means of instruction and warning signs, attention should be drawn to fault elimination in system components which cannot be observed completely.

System Disturbance Control

In many HAS installations utilized in the computer-integrated manufacturing area, human operators are typically needed for the purpose of controlling, programming, maintaining, pre-setting, servicing or troubleshooting tasks. Disturbances in the system lead to situations that make it necessary for workers to enter the hazardous areas. In this respect, it can be assumed that disturbances remain the most important reason for human interference in CIM, because the systems will more often than not be programmed from outside the restricted areas. One of the most important issues for CIM safety is to prevent disturbances, since most risks occur in the troubleshooting phase of the system. The avoidance of disturbances is the common aim as regards both safety and cost-effectiveness.

A disturbance in a CIM system is a state or function of a system that deviates from the planned or desired state. In addition to productivity, disturbances during the operation of a CIM have a direct effect on the safety of the people involved in operating the system. A Finnish study (Kuivanen 1990) showed that about one-half of the disturbances in automated manufacturing decrease the safety of the workers. The main causes for disturbances were errors in system design (34%), system component failures (31%), human error (20%) and external factors (15%). Most machine failures were caused by the control system, and, in the control system, most failures occurred in sensors. An effective way to increase the level of safety of CIM installations is to reduce the

number of disturbances. Although human actions in disturbed systems prevent the occurrence of accidents in the HAS environment, they also contribute to them. For example, a study of accidents related to malfunctions of technical control systems showed that about one-third of the accident sequences included human intervention in the control loop of the disturbed system.

The main research issues in CIM disturbance prevention concern (1) major causes of disturbances, (2) unreliable components and functions, (3) the impact of disturbances on safety, (4) the impact of disturbances on the function of the system, (5) material damage and (6) repairs. The safety of HAS should be planned early at the system design stage, with due consideration of technology, people and organization, and be an integral part of the overall HAS technical planning process.

HAS Design: Future Challenges

To assure the fullest benefit of hybrid automated systems as discussed above, a much broader vision of system development, one which is based on integration of people, organization and technology, is needed. Three main types of system integration should be applied here:

1. *integration of people*, by assuring effective communication between them
2. *human-computer integration*, by designing suitable interfaces and interaction between people and computers
3. *technological integration*, by assuring effective interfacing and interactions between machines.

The minimum design requirements for hybrid automated systems should include the following: (1) flexibility, (2) dynamic adaptation, (3) improved responsiveness, and (4) the need to motivate people and make better use of their skills, judgement and experience. The above also requires that HAS organizational structures, work practices and technologies be developed to allow people at all levels of the system to adapt their work strategies to the variety of systems control situations. Therefore, the organizations, work practices and technologies of HAS will have to be designed and developed as open systems (Kidd 1994).

An open hybrid automated system (OHAS) is a system that receives inputs from and sends outputs to its environment. The idea of an open system can be applied not only to system architectures and organizational structures, but also to work practices, human-computer interfaces, and the relationship between people and technologies: one may mention, for example, scheduling systems, control systems and decision support systems. An open system is also an adaptive one when it allows people a large degree of freedom to define the mode of operating the system. For example, in the area of advanced manufacturing, the requirements of an open hybrid automated system can be realized through the concept of *human and computer-integrated manufacturing* (HCIM). In this view, the design of technology should address the overall HCIM system architecture, including the following: (1) considerations of the network of groups, (2) the structure of each group, (3) the interaction between groups, (4) the nature of the supporting software and (5) technical communication and integration needs between supporting software modules.

The adaptive hybrid automated system, as opposed to the closed system, does not restrict what the human operators can do. The role of the designer of a HAS is to create a system that will satisfy the user's personal preferences and allow its users to work in a way that they find most appropriate. A prerequisite for permitting user input is the development of an adaptive design methodology—that is, an OHAS that allows enabling, computer-supported technology for its implementation in the design process. The need to develop a methodology for adaptive design is one of the immediate requirements to realize the OHAS concept in practice. A new level of adaptive human supervisory control technology needs also to be developed. Such technology should allow the human operator to "see through" the otherwise invisible control system of HAS functioning—for example, by application of an interactive, high-speed video system at each point of system control and operation. Finally, a methodology for development of an intelligent and highly adaptive, computer-based support of human roles and human functioning in the hybrid automated systems is also very much needed.

PRINCIPLES FOR THE DESIGN OF SAFE CONTROL SYSTEMS

Georg Vondracek

It is generally agreed that control systems must be safe during use. With this in mind, most modern control systems are designed as shown in figure 58.65.

The simplest way to make a control system safe is to construct an impenetrable wall around it so as to prevent human access or interference into the danger zone. Such a system would be very safe, albeit impractical, since it would be impossible to gain access in order to perform most testing, repair and adjustment work. Because access to danger zones must be permitted under certain conditions, protective measures other than just walls, fences and the like are required to facilitate production, installation, servicing and maintenance.

Some of these protective measures can be partly or fully integrated into control systems, as follows:

- Movement can be stopped immediately should anybody enter the danger zone, by means of emergency stop (ES) buttons.
- Push-button controls permit movement only when the push-button is activated.
- Double-hand controls (DHC) permit movement only when both hands are engaged in depressing the two control elements (thus ensuring that hands are kept away from the danger zones).

These types of protective measures are activated by operators. However, because human beings often represent a weak point in applications, many functions, such as the following, are performed automatically:

- Movements of robot arms during the servicing or "teach-in" are very slow. Nonetheless, speed is continuously monitored. If, because of a control system failure, the speed of automatic robot arms were to increase unexpectedly during either the servicing or teach-in period, the monitoring system would activate and immediately terminate movement.
- A light barrier is provided to prevent access into a danger zone. If the light beam is interrupted, the machine will stop automatically.

Normal function of control systems is the most important precondition for production. If a production function is interrupted due to a control failure, it is at most inconvenient but not hazardous. If a safety-relevant function is not performed, it could result in lost production, equipment damage, injury or even death. Therefore, safety-relevant control system functions must be more reliable and safer than normal control system functions. According to European Council Directive 89/392/EEC (Machine Guidelines), control systems must be designed and constructed so that they are safe and reliable.

Controls consist of a number of components connected together so as to perform one or more functions. Controls are subdivided into channels. A channel is the part of a control that

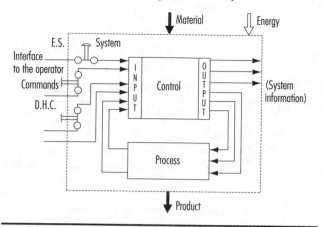

Figure 58.65 • General design of control systems.

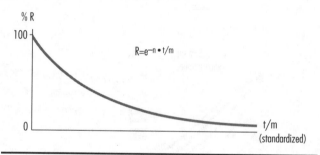

Figure 58.66 • Reliability formula.

$$R = e^{-n \cdot t/m}$$

performs a specific function (e.g., start, stop, emergency stop). Physically, the channel is created by a string of components (transistors, diodes, relays, gates, etc.) through which, from one component to the next, (mostly electrical) information representing that function is transferred from input to output.

In designing control channels for safety-relevant functions (those functions which involve humans), the following requirements must be fulfilled:

- Components used in control channels with safety-relevant functions must be able to withstand the rigours of normal use. Generally, *they must be sufficiently reliable.*
- Errors in the logic must not cause dangerous situations. Generally, *the safety-relevant channel is to be sufficiently failure proof.*
- External influences (factors) should not lead to temporary or permanent failures in safety-relevant channels.

Reliability

Reliability is the ability of a control channel or component to perform a required function under specified conditions for a given period of time *without failing.* (Probability for specific components or control channels can be calculated using suitable methods.) Reliability must always be specified for a specific time value. Generally, reliability can be expressed by the formula in figure 58.66.

Reliability of complex systems

Systems are built from components. If the reliabilities of the components are known, the reliability of the system as a whole can be calculated. In such cases, the following apply:

Figure 58.67 • Reliability graph of serially connected components.

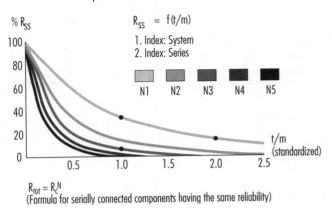

$$R_{tot} = R_c^N$$
(Formula for serially connected components having the same reliability)

Figure 58.68 • Reliability graph of parallel connected components.

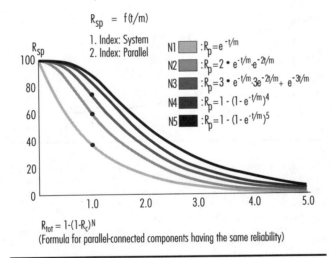

$$R_{tot} = 1-(1-R_c)^N$$
(Formula for parallel-connected components having the same reliability)

Figure 58.69 • Practical example of figure 58.68.

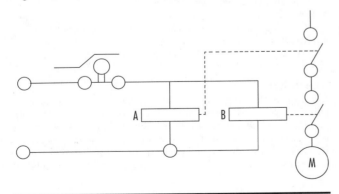

Serial systems

The total reliability R_{tot} of a serial system consisting of N components of the same reliability R_C is calculated as in figure 58.67.

The total reliability is lower than the reliability of the least reliable component. As the number of serially connected components increases, the total reliability of the chain falls significantly.

Parallel systems

The total reliability R_{tot} of a parallel system consisting of N components of the same reliability R_C is calculated as in figure 58.68.

Total reliability can be improved significantly through the parallel connection of two or more components.

Figure 58.69 illustrates a practical example. Note that the circuitry will switch off the motor more reliably. Even if relay A or B fails to open its contact, the motor will still be switched off.

To calculate the total reliability of a channel is simple if all necessary component reliabilities are known and available. In the case of complex components (integrated circuits, microprocessors, etc.) the calculation of the total reliability is difficult or impossible if the necessary information is not published by the manufacturer.

Safety

When professionals speak about safety and call for safe machines, they mean the safety of the entire machine or system. This safety is, however, too general, and not precisely enough defined for the designer of controls. The following definition of *safety* may be practical and usable to designers of control circuitry: Safety is the ability of a control system to perform the required function within prescribed limits, for a given duration, even when anticipated fault(s) occur. Consequently, it must be clarified during the design how "safe" the safety-related channel must be. (The designer can develop a channel that is safe against first failure, against any one failure, against two failures, etc.) Furthermore, a channel that performs a function which is used to prevent accidents may be essentially reliable, but it does not have to be inevitably safe against failures. This may be best explained by the following examples:

Example 1

The example illustrated in figure 58.70 is a safety-relevant control channel performing the required safety function. The first component may be a switch that monitors, for example, the position of an access door to a dangerous area. The last component is a motor which drives moving mechanical parts within the danger area.

The required safety function in this case is a dual one: If the door is closed, the motor may run. If the door is open, the motor must be switched off. Knowing reliabilities R_1 to R_6, it is possible to calculate reliability R_{tot}. Designers should use reliable components in order to maintain sufficiently high reliability of the whole control system (i.e., the probability that this function may still be performed in, say, even 20 years should be accounted for in the design). As a result, designers must fulfil two tasks: (1) the circuitry must perform the required function, and (2) the reliability of the components and of the whole control channel must be adequate.

The following question should now be asked: Will the aforementioned channel perform the required safety functions even if a failure occurs in the system (e.g., if a relay contact sticks or a component malfunctions)? The answer is "No". The reason is that a single control channel consisting only of serially connected components and working with static signals is not safe against one failure. The channel can have only a certain reliability, which guarantees the probability that the function will be carried out. In such situations, safety is always meant as *failure related.*

Example 2

If a control channel is to be both reliable and safe, the design must be modified as in figure 58.71. The example illustrated is a safety-relevant control channel consisting of two fully separated subchannels.

This design is safe against the first failure (and possible further failures in the same subchannel), but is not safe against two failures which may occur in two different subchannels (simultaneously or at different times) because there is no failure detection circuit. Consequently, initially both subchannels work with a high reliability (see parallel system), but after the first failure only one subchannel will work, and reliability decreases. Should a second failure occur in the subchannel still working, both will have then failed, and the safety function will no longer be performed.

Example 3

The example illustrated in figure 58.72 is a safety-relevant control channel consisting of two fully separate subchannels which monitor each other.

Such a design is failure safe because after any failure, only one subchannel will be non-functional, while the other subchannel remains available and will perform the safety function. Moreover, the design has a failure detection circuit. If, due to a failure, both subchannels fail to work in the same way, this condition will be detected by "exclusive or" circuitry, with the result that the machine will be automatically switched off. This is one of the best ways of designing machine controls—designing safety-relevant subchannels. They are safe against one failure and at the same time provide enough reliability so that the chances that two failures will occur simultaneously is minuscule.

Redundancy

It is apparent that there are various methods by which a designer may improve reliability and/or safety (against failure). The previous examples illustrate how a function (i.e., door closed, motor may run; door opened, motor must be stopped) can be realized by various solutions. Some methods are very simple (one subchannel) and others more complicated (two subchannels with mutual supervising). (See figure 58.73.)

There is a certain redundancy in the complex circuitry and/or components in comparison with the simple ones. *Redundancy* can be defined as follows: (1) Redundancy is the presence of more means (components, channels, higher safety factors, additional tests and so on) than are really necessary for the simple fulfilling of the desired function; (2) redundancy obviously does not "improve" the function, which is performed anyway. Redundancy only improves reliability and/or safety.

Some safety professionals believe that redundancy is only the doubling or tripling, and so on, of the system. This is a very limited interpretation, as redundancy may be interpreted much more broadly and flexibly. Redundancy may be not only included in the hardware; it may be included in the software too. Improving the safety factor (e.g., a stronger rope instead of a weaker rope) may also be considered as a form of redundancy.

Entropy

Entropy, a term found mostly in thermodynamics and astronomy, may be defined as follows: Everything tends towards decay. Therefore, it is absolutely certain that all components, subsystems or systems, independently of the technology in use, will fail sometime. This means that there are no 100% reliable and/or safe systems, subsystems or components. All of them are merely more or less reliable and safe, depending on the structure's complexity. The failures which inevitably occur earlier or later demonstrate the action of entropy.

The only means available to designers to counter entropy is redundancy, which is achieved by (a) introducing more reliability into the components and (b) providing more safety throughout the circuit architecture. Only by sufficiently raising the probability

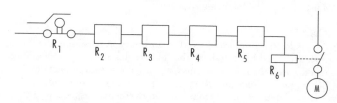

Figure 58.70 • A safety-relevant control channel performing the required safety function.

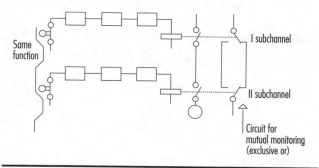

Figure 58.71 • A safety-relevant control channel with two fully separate subchannels.

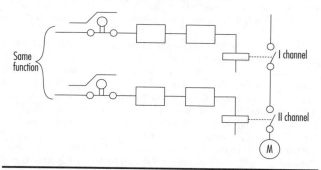

Figure 58.72 • A safety-relevant control channel with two fully separate subchannels which monitor each other.

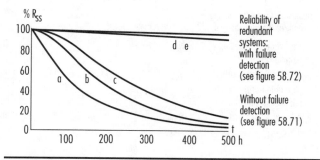

Figure 58.73 • Reliability of redundant systems with or without failure detection.

that the required function will be performed for the required period of time, can designers in some degree defend against entropy.

Risk Assessment

The greater the potential risk, the higher the reliability and/or safety (against failures) that is required (and vice versa). This is illustrated by the following two cases:

Case 1

Access to the mould tool fixed in an injection moulding machine is safeguarded by a door. If the door is closed, the machine may work, and if the door is opened, all dangerous movements have to be stopped. Under no circumstances (even in case of failure in the safety-related channel) may any movements, especially those which operate the tool, occur.

Case 2

Access to an automatically controlled assembly line that assembles small plastic components under pneumatic pressure is guarded by a door. If this door is opened, the line will have to be stopped.

In Case 1, if the door-supervising control system should fail, a serious injury may occur if the tool is closed unexpectedly. In Case 2, only slight injury or insignificant harm may result if the door-supervising control system fails.

It is obvious that in the first case much more redundancy must be introduced to attain the reliability and/or safety (against failure) required to protect against extreme high risk. In fact, according to European Standard EN 201, the supervising control system of the injection moulding machine door has to have three channels; two of which are electrical and mutually supervised and one of which is mostly equipped with hydraulics and testing circuits. All these three supervising functions relate to the same door.

Conversely, in applications like that described in Case 2, a single channel activated by a switch with positive action is appropriate to the risk.

Control Categories

Because all of the above considerations are generally based on information theory and consequently are valid for all technologies, it does not matter whether the control system is based on electronic, electro-mechanical, mechanical, hydraulic or pneumatic components (or a mixture of them), or on some other technology. The inventiveness of the designer on the one hand and economic questions on the other hand are the primary factors affecting a nearly endless number of solutions as to how to realize safety-relevant channels.

To prevent confusion, it is practical to set certain sorting criteria. The most typical channel structures used in machine controls for performing safety-related functions are categorized according to:

- reliability
- behaviour in case of failure
- failure-disclosing time.

Their combinations (not all possible combinations are shown) are illustrated in table 58.5.

The category applicable for a specific machine and its safety-related control system is mostly specified in the new European standards (EN), unless the national authority, the user and the manufacturer mutually agree that another category should be applied. The designer then develops a control system which fulfils the requirements. For example, considerations governing the design of a control channel may include the following:

Table 58.5 • Some possible combinations of circuit structures in machine controls for safety-related functions.

Criteria (Questions)	Basic strategy					
	By raising the reliability (is the occurrence of failure shifted to the possibly far future?)			By suitable circuit structure (architecture) failure will be at least detected (Cat. 2) or failure effect on the channel will be eliminated (Cat. 3) or failure will be disclosed immediately (Cat. 4).		
	Categories					
	This solution is basically wrong.	B	1	2	3	4
Can the circuit components withstand the expected influences; are they constructed according to state of the art?	No	Yes	Yes	Yes	Yes	Yes
Have well tried components and/or methods been used?	No	No	Yes	Yes	Yes	Yes
Can a failure be detected automatically?	No	No	No	Yes	Yes	Yes
Does a failure prevent the performing of the safety-related function?	Yes	Yes	Yes	Yes	No	No
When will the failure be detected?	Never	Never	Never	Early (latest at the end of interval that is not longer than one machine cycle)		Immediately (when the signal loses dynamic character)
		In consumer products	To be used in machines			

- The components have to withstand the expected influences. (YES/NO)
- Their construction should be according to state-of-the-art standards. (YES/NO)
- Well-tried components and methods are used. (YES/NO)
- Failure *must be detected*. (YES/NO)
- Will the safety function be performed even in case of failure? (YES/NO)
- When will the failure be detected? (NEVER, EARLY, IMMEDIATELY)

This process is reversible. Using the same questions, one can decided which category an existing, previously developed control channel belongs to.

Category examples

Category B

The control channel components primarily used in consumer wares have to withstand the expected influences and be designed according to state of the art. A well-designed switch may serve as an example.

Category 1

The use of well-tried components and methods is typical for Category 1. A Category 1 example is a switch with positive action (i.e., requires forced opening of contacts). This switch is designed with robust parts and is activated by relatively high forces, thus reaching extremely high reliability only in contact opening. In spite of sticking or even welded contacts, these switches will open. (Note: Components such as transistors and diodes are not considered as being well-tried components.) Figure 58.74 will serve as an illustration of a Category 1 control.

This channel uses switch S with positive action. The contactor K is supervised by the light L. The operator is advised that the normally open (NO) contacts stick by means of indication light L. The contactor K has forced guided contacts. (Note: Relays or contactors with forced guidance of contacts have, in comparison with usual relays or contactors, a special cage made from insulating material so that if normally closed (NC) contacts are closed, all NO contacts have to be opened, and vice versa. This means that by use of NC contacts a check may be made to determine that the working contacts are not sticking or welded together.)

Category 2

Category 2 provides for automatic detection of failures. Automatic failure detection has to be generated before each dangerous movement. Only if the test is positive may the movement be performed; otherwise the machine will be stopped. Automatic failure detection systems are used for light barriers to prove that they are still working. The principle is illustrated in figure 58.75.

This control system is tested regularly (or occasionally) by injecting an impulse to the input. In a properly working system this impulse will then be transferred to the output and compared to an impulse from a test generator. When both impulses are present, the system obviously works. Otherwise, if there is no output impulse, the system has failed.

Category 3

Circuitry has been previously described under Example 3 in the Safety section of this article, figure 58.72.

The requirement—that is, automatic failure detection and the ability to perform the safety function even if one failure has occurred anywhere—can be fulfilled by two-channel control structures and by mutual supervising of the two channels.

Figure 58.74 • A switch with a positive action.

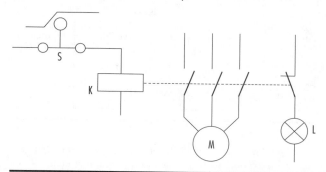

For machine controls only, the dangerous failures have to be investigated. It should be noted that there are two kinds of failure:

- *Non-dangerous* failures are those that, after their occurrence, cause a "safe state" of the machine by providing for switching off the motor.
- *Dangerous* failures are those that, after their occurrence, cause an "unsafe state" of the machine, as the motor cannot be switched off or the motor starts to move unexpectedly.

Category 4

Category 4 typically provides for the application of a dynamic, continuously changing signal on the input. The presence of a dynamic signal on the output means *running* ("1"), and the absence of a dynamic signal means *stop* ("0").

For such circuitry it is typical that after failure of any component the dynamic signal will no longer be available on the output. (Note: The static potential on the output is irrelevant.) Such circuits may be called "fail-safe". All failures will be disclosed immediately, not after the first change (as in Category 3 circuits).

Further comments on control categories

Table 58.5 has been developed for usual machine controls and shows the basic circuit structures only; according to the machine directive it should be calculated on the assumption that only one failure will occur in one machine cycle. This is why the safety function does not have to be performed in the case of two coincident failures. It is assumed that a failure will be detected within one machine cycle. The machine will be stopped and then repaired. The control system then starts again, fully operable, without failures.

The first intent of the designer should be not to permit "standing" failures, which would not be detected during one cycle as

Figure 58.75 • Circuit including a failure detector.

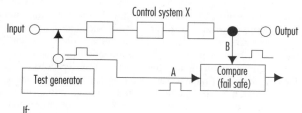

If:
A=B....no failure in the control system X
A≠B....a failure in the control system X

Figure 58.76 • A PES system circuit.

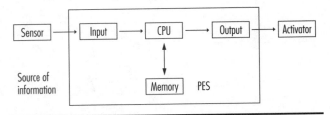

they might later be combined with newly occurring failure(s) (failure cumulation). Such combinations (a standing failure and a new failure) can cause a malfunction of even Category 3 circuitry.

In spite of these tactics, it is possible that two independent failures will occur at the same time within the same machine cycle. It is only very improbable, especially if highly reliable components have been used. For very high-risk applications, three or more subchannels should be used. This philosophy is based on the fact that the mean time between failures is much longer than the machine cycle.

This does not mean, however, that the table cannot be further expanded. Table 58.5 is basically and structurally very similar to the Table 2 used in EN 954-1. However, it does not try to include too many sorting criteria. The requirements are defined according to the rigorous laws of logic, so that only clear answers (YES or NO) can be expected. This allows a more exact assessment, sorting and classification of submitted circuitry (safety-related channels) and, last but not least, significant improvement of assessment reproducibility.

It would be ideal if risks could be classified in various risk levels and then a definite link established between risk levels and categories, with this all independent of the technology in use. However, this is not fully possible. Early after creating categories it became clear that even given the same technology, various questions were not sufficiently answered. Which is better: a very reliable and well-designed component of Category 1, or a system fulfilling the requirements of Category 3 with poor reliability?

To explain this dilemma one must differentiate between two qualities: reliability and safety (against failures). They are not comparable, as both these qualities have different features:

- The component with highest reliability has the unpleasant feature that in the event of failure (even if highly improbable) the function will cease to perform.
- Category 3 systems, where even in case of one failure the function will be performed, are not safe against two failures at the same time (what may be important is whether sufficiently reliable components have been used).

Considering the above, it may be that the best solution (from the high-risk point of view) is to use highly reliable components and configure them so that the circuitry is safe against at least one failure (preferably more). It is clear that such a solution is not the most economical. In practice, the optimization process is mostly the consequence of all these influences and considerations.

Experience with practical use of the categories shows that it is rarely possible to design a control system that can utilize only one category throughout. Combination of two or even three parts, each of a different category, is typical, as illustrated in the following example:

Many safety light barriers are designed in Category 4, wherein one channel works with a dynamic signal. At the end of this

system there usually are two mutually supervised subchannels which work with static signals. (This fulfils the requirements for Category 3.)

According to EN 50100, such light barriers are classified as *Type 4 electro-sensitive protective devices*, although they are composed of two parts. Unfortunately, there is no agreement how to denominate control systems consisting of two or more parts, each part of another category.

Programmable Electronic Systems (PESs)

The principles used to create table 58.5 can, with certain restrictions of course, be generally applied to PESs too.

PES-only system

In using PESs for control, the information is transferred from the sensor to the activator through a large number of components. Beyond that, it even passes "through" software. (See figure 58.76).

Although modern PESs are very reliable, the reliability is not as high as may be required for processing safety functions. Beyond that, the usual PES systems are not safe enough, since they will not perform the safety-related function in case of a failure. Therefore, using PESs for processing of safety functions without any additional measures is not permitted.

Very low-risk applications: Systems with one PES and additional measures

When using a single PES for control, the system consists of the following primary parts:

Input part

The reliability of a sensor and input of a PES can be improved by doubling them. Such a double-system input configuration can be further supervised by software to check if both subsystems are delivering the same information. Thus the failures in the input part can be detected. This is nearly the same philosophy as required for Category 3. However, because the supervising is done by software and only once, this may be denominated as 3- (or not as reliable as 3).

Middle part

Although this part cannot be well doubled, it can be tested. Upon switching on (or during operation), a check of the entire instruction set can be performed. At the same intervals, the memory can also be checked by suitable bit patterns. If such checks are conducted without failure, both parts, CPU and memory, are obviously working properly. The middle part has certain features typical of Category 4 (dynamic signal) and others typical of Category 2 (testing performed regularly at suitable intervals). The problem is that these tests, in spite of their extensiveness, cannot be really complete, as the one-PES system inherently does not allow them.

Output part

Similar to an input, the output (including activators) can also be doubled. Both subsystems can be supervised with respect to the same result. Failures will be detected and the safety function will be performed. However, there are the same weak points as in the input part. Consequently, Category 3 is chosen in this case.

In figure 58.77 the same function is brought to relays *A* and *B*. The control contacts *a* and *b*, then informs two input systems whether both relays are doing the same work (unless a failure in one of the channels has occurred). Supervising is done again by software.

Figure 58.77 • A PES circuit with a failure-detection system.

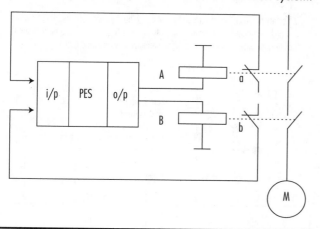

The whole system can be described as Category 3-/4/2/3- if properly and extensively done. Nevertheless, the weak points of such systems as above described cannot be fully eliminated. In fact, improved one PESs are actually used for safety-related func-

tions only where the risks are rather low (Hölscher and Rader 1984).

Low- and medium-risk applications with one PES

Today almost every machine is equipped with a PES control unit. To solve the problem of insufficient reliability and usually insufficient safety against failure, the following design methods are commonly used:

- In relatively simple machines such as lifts, the functions are divided into two groups: (1) the functions that are not related to safety are processed by the PES; (2) the safety-related functions are combined in one chain (safety circuit) and processed outside of the PES (see figure 58.78).
- The method given above is not suitable for more complex machines. One reason is that such solutions usually are not safe enough. For medium-risk applications, solutions should fulfil the requirements for category 3. General ideas of how such designs may look are presented in figures 58.79 and 58.80.

Figure 58.78 • State of the art for stop category 0.

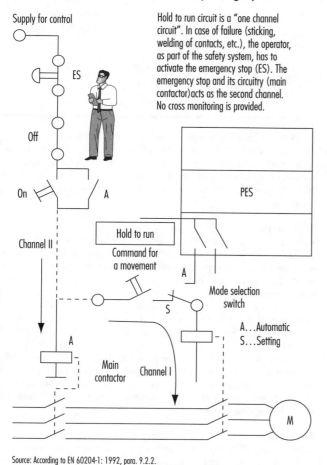

Supply for control

Hold to run circuit is a "one channel circuit". In case of failure (sticking, welding of contacts, etc.), the operator, as part of the safety system, has to activate the emergency stop (ES). The emergency stop and its circuitry (main contactor) acts as the second channel. No cross monitoring is provided.

ES

Off

On   A

Channel II

PES

Hold to run
Command for a movement   A

Mode selection switch

A...Automatic
S...Setting

A

Main contactor   Channel I

M

Source: According to EN 60204-1: 1992, para. 9.2.2.

Figure 58.79 • State of the art for stop category 1.

To move the drive, the enabling push button and the command button (e.g., axis movement) are to be actuated simultaneously. A failure in channel I is not automatically detected. However, for most failures in channel I, the machine will not operate properly; thus, the operator will note the failure. A failure in channel II will be detected by the PES (see monitoring loop X). The stopping of the movement (S) is safe, as the energy is interrupted twice. Cross monitoring may be considered as nearly complete.

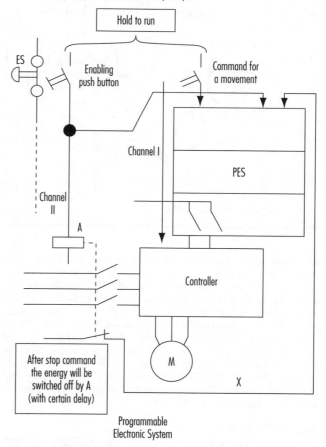

Hold to run

ES   Enabling push button   Command for a movement

Channel I

PES

Channel II

A

Controller

After stop command the energy will be switched off by A (with certain delay)

M   X

Programmable Electronic System

Source: According to EN 60204-1: 1992, para. 9.2.2.

Figure 58.80 • State of the art for stop category 2.

The command for running or stopping is performed by the operating system alone, which is by itself not safe enough. Consequently, an additional "safe speed monitoring system" for "no movement" and "slow speed movement" has to be provided. In case of failure in the operating system (PES, control/drive unit), the additional speed monitoring system will detect the unsafe state and will bring the machine to a safe stop.

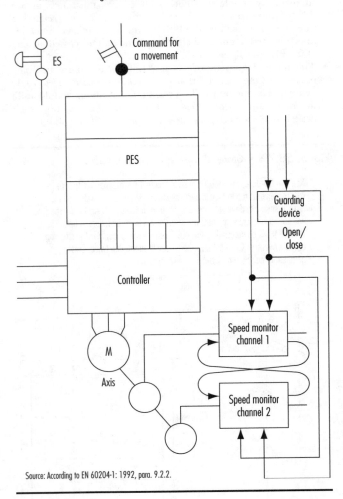

Source: According to EN 60204-1: 1992, para. 9.2.2.

Figure 58.81 • Sophisticated system with two PESs.

All safety functions are electronically processed, but by two independent PESs with full and permanent cross monitoring. Note that this figure describes a basic system architecture only. A wide range of improvements may be introduced.

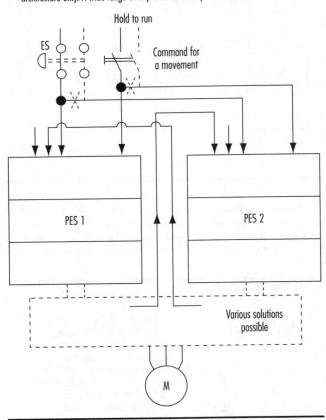

High-risk applications: systems with two (or more) PESs

Aside from complexity and expense, there are no other factors that would prevent designers from using fully doubled PES systems such as Siemens Simatic S5-115F, 3B6 Typ CAR-MIL and so on. These typically include two identical PESs with homogenous software, and assume the use of "well-tried" PESs and "well-tried" compilers (a well-tried PES or compiler can be considered one that in many practical applications over 3 or more years has shown that systematic failures have been obviously eliminated). Although these doubled PES systems do not have the weak points of single-PES systems, it does not mean that doubled PES systems solve all problems. (See figure 58.81.)

Systematic Failures

Systematic failures may result from errors in specifications, design and other causes, and may be present in hardware as well as in software. Double-PES systems are suitable for use in safety-related applications. Such configurations allow the detection of random hardware failures. By means of hardware diversity such as the use of two different types, or products of two different manufacturers, systematic hardware failures could be disclosed (it is highly unlikely that an identical hardware systematic failure would occur in both PES).

Software

Software is a new element in safety considerations. Software is either correct or incorrect (with respect to failures). Once correct, software cannot become instantly incorrect (as compared to hardware). The aims are to eradicate all errors in the software or to at least identify them.

There are various ways of achieving this goal. One is the *verification* of the program (a second person attempts to discover the errors in a subsequent test). Another possibility is *diversity* of the software, wherein two different programs, written by two programmers, address the same problem. If the results are identical (within certain limits), it can be assumed that both program sections are correct. If the results are different, it is presumed that errors are present. (N.B., The *architecture* of the hardware naturally must also be considered.)

Summary

When using PESs, generally the same following basic considerations are to be taken in account (as described in the previous sections).

- One control system without any redundancy may be allocated to Category B. One control system with additional measures may be Category 1 or even higher, but not higher than 2.
- A two-part control system with mutual comparison of results may be allocated to Category 3. A two-part control system with mutual comparison of results and more or less diversity may be allocated to Category 3 and is suitable for higher-risk applications.

A new factor is that for the system with a PES, even software should be evaluated from the correctness point of view. Software, if correct, is 100% reliable. At this stage of technological development, the best possible and known technical solutions will probably not be used, since the limiting factors are still economic. Furthermore, various groups of experts are continuing to develop the standards for safety applications of PESs (e.g., EC, EWICS). Although there are various standards already available (VDE0801, IEC65A and so on), this matter is so broad and complex that none of them may be considered as final.

SAFETY PRINCIPLES FOR CNC MACHINE TOOLS

Toni Retsch, Guido Schmitter and Albert Marty

Whenever simple and conventional production equipment, such as machine tools, is automated, the result is complex technical systems as well as new hazards. This automation is achieved through the use of computer numeric control (CNC) systems on machine tools, called *CNC machine tools* (e.g., milling machines, machining centres, drills and grinders). In order to be able to identify the potential hazards inherent in automatic tools, the various operating modes of each system should be analysed. Previously conducted analyses indicate that a differentiation should be made between two types of operation: normal operation and special operation.

It is often impossible to prescribe the safety requirements for CNC machine tools in the shape of specific measures. This may be because there are too few regulations and standards specific to the equipment which provide concrete solutions. Safety requirements can be determined only if the possible hazards are identified systematically by conducting a hazard analysis, particularly if these complex technical systems are fitted with freely programmable control systems (as with CNC machine tools).

In the case of newly developed CNC machine tools, the manufacturer is obliged to carry out a hazard analysis on the equipment in order to identify whatever dangers may be present and to show by means of constructive solutions that all dangers to persons, in all of the different operating modes, are eliminated. All the hazards identified must be subjected to a risk assessment wherein each risk of an event is dependent on the scope of damage and the frequency with which it may occur. The hazard to be assessed is also given a risk category (minimized, normal, increased). Wherever the risk cannot be accepted on the basis of the risk assessment, solutions (safety measures) must be found. The purpose of these solutions is to reduce the frequency of occurrence and the scope of damage of an unplanned and potentially hazardous incident (an "event").

The approaches to solutions for normal and increased risks are to be found in indirect and direct safety technology; for minimized risks, they are to be found in referral safety technology:

- *Direct safety technology*. Care is taken at the design stage to eliminate any hazards (e.g., the elimination of shearing and trapping points).
- *Indirect safety technology*. The hazard remains. However, the addition of technical arrangements prevents the hazard from turning into an event (e.g., such arrangements may include the prevention of access to dangerous moving parts by means of physical safety hoods, the provision of safety devices which turn power off, shielding from flying parts using safety guards, etc.).
- *Referral safety technology*. This applies only to residual hazards and minimized risks—that is, hazards which can lead to an event as a result of human factors. The occurrence of such an event can be prevented by appropriate behaviour on the part of the person concerned (e.g., instructions on behaviour in the operating and maintenance manuals, personnel training, etc.).

International Safety Requirements

The EC Machinery Directive (89/392/EEC; see box) of 1989 lays down the principal safety and health requirements for machines. (According to the Machinery Directive, a machine is considered to be the sum total of interlinked parts or devices, of which at least one can move and correspondingly has a function.) In addition, individual standards are created by international standardization bodies to illustrate possible solutions (e.g., by attending to fundamental safety aspects, or by examining electrical equipment fitted to industrial machinery). The aim of these standards is to specify protection goals. These international safety requirements give manufacturers the necessary legal basis to specify these requirements in the above-mentioned hazard analyses and risk assessments.

Operating Modes

When using machine tools, a differentiation is made between normal operation and special operation. Statistics and investigations indicate that the majority of incidents and accidents do not take place in normal operation (i.e., during the automatic fulfilment of the assignment concerned). With these types of machines and installations, there is an emphasis on special modes of operations such as commissioning, setting up, programming, test runs, checks, troubleshooting or maintenance. In these operating modes, persons are usually in a danger zone. The safety concept must protect personnel from harmful events in these types of situations.

Normal operation

The following applies to automatic machines when carrying out normal operation: (1) the machine fulfils the assignment for which it was designed and constructed without any further intervention by the operator, and (2) applied to a simple turning machine, this means that a workpiece is turned to the correct shape and chips are produced. If the workpiece is changed manually, changing the workpiece is a special mode of operation.

Special modes of operation

Special modes of operation are working processes which allow normal operation. Under this heading, for example, one would include workpiece or tool changes, rectifying a fault in a production process, rectifying a machine fault, setting up, programming, test runs, cleaning and maintenance. In normal operation, automatic systems fulfil their assignments independently. From the viewpoint of working safety, however, automatic normal operation becomes critical when the operator has to intervene working processes. Under no circumstances may the persons intervening in such processes be exposed to hazards.

Personnel

Consideration must be given to the persons working in the various modes of operation as well as to third parties when safeguarding machine tools. Third parties also include those indirectly concerned with the machine, such as supervisors, inspectors, assistants for transporting material and dismantling work, visitors and others.

Demands and Safety Measures for Machine Accessories

Interventions for jobs in special operation modes mean that special accessories have to be used to assure work can be conducted safely. The *first type* of accessories include equipment and items used to intervene in the automatic process without the operator's having to access a hazardous zone. This type of accessory includes (1) chip hooks and tongs which have been so designed that chips in the machining area can be removed or pulled away through the apertures provided in the safety guards, and (2) workpiece clamping devices with which the production material can be manually inserted into or removed from an automatic cycle

Various special modes of operation—for example, remedial work or maintenance work—make it necessary for personnel to intervene in a system. In these cases, too, there is a whole range of machine accessories designed to increase working safety—for example, devices to handle heavy grinding wheels when the latter are changed on grinders, as well as special crane slings for dismantling or erecting heavy components when machines are overhauled. These devices are the *second type* of machine accessory for increasing safety during work in special operations. Special operation control systems can also be considered to represent a second type of machine accessory. Particular activities can be carried out safely with such accessories—for example, a device can be set up in the machine axes when feed movements are necessary with the safety guards open.

These special operation control systems must satisfy particular safety requirements. For example, they must ensure that only the movement requested is carried out in the way requested and only for as long as requested. The special operation control system must therefore be designed in such a way as to prevent any faulty action from turning into hazardous movements or states.

Equipment which increases the degree of automation of an installation can be considered to be a *third type* of machine accessory for increasing working safety. Actions which were previously carried out manually are done automatically by the machine in normal operation, such as equipment including portal loaders, which change the workpieces on machine tools automatically. The safeguarding of automatic normal operation causes few problems because the intervention of an operator in the course of events is unnecessary and because possible interventions can be prevented by safety devices.

Requirements and Safety Measures for the Automation of Machine Tools

Unfortunately, automation has not led to the elimination of accidents in production plants. Investigations simply show a shift in the occurrence of accidents from normal to special operation, primarily due to the automation of normal operation so that interventions in the course of production are no longer necessary and personnel are thus no longer exposed to danger. On the other hand, highly automatic machines are complex systems which are difficult to assess when faults occur. Even the specialists employed to rectify faults are not always able to do so without incurring accidents. The amount of software needed to operate increasingly complex machines is growing in volume and complexity, with the result that an increasing number of electrical and commissioning engineers suffer accidents. There is no such thing as flawless software, and changes in software often lead to changes elsewhere which were neither expected nor wanted. In order to prevent safety from being affected, hazardous faulty behaviour caused by external influence and component failures must not be possible. This condition can be fulfilled only if the safety circuit is designed as simply as possible and is separate from the rest of the controls. The elements or sub-assemblies used in the safety circuit must also be fail-safe.

It is the task of the designer to develop designs that satisfy safety requirements. The designer cannot avoid having to consider the necessary working procedures, including the special modes of operation, with great care. Analyses must be made to determine which safe work procedures are necessary, and the operating personnel must become familiar with them. In the majority of cases, a control system for special operation will be necessary. The control system usually observes or regulates a movement, while at the same time, no other movement must be initiated (as no other movement is needed for this work, and thus none is expected by the operator). The control system does not necessarily have to carry out the same assignments in the various modes of special operation.

Requirements and Safety Measures in Normal and Special Modes of Operation

Normal operation

The specification of safety goals should not impede technical progress because adapted solutions can be selected. The use of CNC machine tools makes maximum demands on hazard analysis, risk assessment and safety concepts. The following describes several safety goals and possible solutions in greater detail.

Safety goal
- Manual or physical access to hazardous areas during automatic movements must be prevented.

Possible solutions
- Prevent manual or physical access into danger zones by means of mechanical barriers.
- Provide safety devices that respond when approached (light barriers, safety mats) and switch off machinery safely during interventions or entry.
- Allow manual or physical access to machinery (or its vicinity) only when the entire system is in a safe state (e.g., by using interlocking devices with closure mechanisms on the access doors).

Safety goal
- The possibility of any persons being injured as a result of the release of energy (flying parts or beams of energy) should be eliminated.

Possible solution
- Prevent the release of energy from the danger zone—for example, by a correspondingly dimensioned safety hood.

Special operation

The interfaces between normal operation and special operation (e.g., door interlocking devices, light barriers, safety mats) are necessary to enable the safety control system to recognize automatically the presence of personnel. The following describes certain special operation modes (e.g., setting up, programming) on CNC machine tools which require movements that must be assessed directly at the site of operation.

Main Features of the EEC Machinery Directive

The Council Directive of 14 June 1989 on the approximation of the laws of the Member States relating machinery (89/392/EEC) applies to each individual state.

- Each individual state must integrate the directive in its legislation.
- Valid from 1 January 1993.
- Requires that all manufacturers adhere to the state of the art.
- The manufacturer must produce a technical construction file which contains full information on all fundamental aspects of safety and health care.
- The manufacturer must issue the declaration of conformity and the CE marking of the machines.
- Failure to place a complete technical documentation at the disposal of a state supervisory centre is considered to represent the non-fulfilment of the machine guidelines. A pan-EEC sales prohibition may be the consequence.

Safety Goals for the Construction and Use of CNC Machine Tools

1. Lathes

1.1 Normal mode of operation

1.1.1   The work area is to be safeguarded so that it is impossible to reach or step into the danger zones of automatic movements, either intentionally or unintentionally.

1.1.2   The tool magazine is to be safeguarded so that it is impossible to reach or step into the danger zones of automatic movements, either intentionally or unintentionally.

1.1.3   The workpiece magazine is to be safeguarded so that it is impossible to reach or step into the danger zones of automatic movements, either intentionally or unintentionally.

1.1.4   Chip removal must not result in personal injury due to the chips or moving parts of the machine.

1.1.5   Personal injuries resulting from reaching into drive systems must be prevented.

1.1.6   The possibility of reaching into the danger zones of moving chip conveyors must be prevented.

1.1.7   No personal injury to operators or third persons must result from flying workpieces or parts thereof.
For example, this can occur
- due to insufficient clamping
- due to inadmissible cutting force
- due to inadmissible rotation speed
- due to collision with the tool or machine parts
- due to workpiece breakage
- due to defective clamping fixtures
- due to power failure

1.1.8   No personal injury must result from flying workpiece clamping fixtures.

1.1.9   No personal injury must result from flying chips.

1.1.10 No personal injury must result from flying tools or parts thereof.
For example, this can occur
- due to material defects
- due to inadmissible cutting force
- due to a collision with the workpiece or a machine part
- due to inadequate clamping or tightening

1.2 Special modes of operation

1.2.1   Workpiece changing.

1.2.1.1 Workpiece clamping must be done in such a way that no parts of the body can become trapped between closing clamping fixtures and workpiece or between the advancing sleeve tip and workpiece.

1.2.1.2 The starting of a drive (spindles, axes, sleeves, turret heads or chip conveyors) as a consequence of a defective command or invalid command must be prevented.

1.2.1.3 It must be possible to manipulate the workpiece manually or with tools without danger.

1.2.2   Tool changing in tool holder or tool turret head.

1.2.2.1 Danger resulting from the defective behaviour of the system or due to entering an invalid command must be prevented.

1.2.3   Tool changing in the tool magazine.

1.2.3.1 Movements in the tool magazine resulting from a defective or invalid command must be prevented during tool changing.

1.2.3.2 It must not be possible to reach into other moving machine parts from the tool loading station.

1.2.3.3 It must not be possible to reach into danger zones on the further movement of the tool magazine or during the search. If taking place with the guards for normal operation mode removed, these movements may only be of the designated kind and only be carried out during the period of time ordered and only when it can be ensured that no parts of the body are in these danger zones.

1.2.4   Measurement check.

1.2.4.1 Reaching into the work area must only be possible after all movements have been brought to a standstill.

1.2.4.2 The starting of a drive resulting from a defective command or invalid command input must be prevented.

1.2.5   Setup.

1.2.5.1 If movements are executed during setup with the guards for normal mode of operation removed, then the operator must be safeguarded by another means.

1.2.5.2 No dangerous movements or changes of movements must be initiated as a result of a defective command or invalid command input.

1.2.6 Programming.

1.2.6.1 No movements may be initiated during programming which endanger a person in the work area.

1.2.7 Production fault.

1.2.7.1 The starting of a drive resulting from a defective command on invalid command input setpoint must be prevented.

1.2.7.2 No dangerous movements or situations are to be initiated by the movement or removal of the workpiece or waste.

1.2.7.3 Where movements have to take place with the guards for the normal mode of operation removed, these movements may only be of the kind designated and only executed for the period of time ordered and only when it can be ensured that no parts of the body are in these danger zones.

1.2.8 Troubleshooting.

1.2.8.1 Reaching into the danger zones of automatic movements must be prevented.

1.2.8.2 The starting of a drive as a result of a defective command or invalid command input must be prevented.

1.2.8.3 A movement of the machine on manipulation of the defective part must be prevented.

1.2.8.4 Personal injury resulting from a machine part splintering off or dropping must be prevented.

1.2.8.5 If, during troubleshooting, movements have to take place with the guards for the normal mode of operation removed, these movements may only be of the kind designated and only executed for the period of time ordered and only when it can be ensured that no parts of the body are in these danger zones.

1.2.9 Machine malfunction and repair.

1.2.9.1 The machine must be prevented from starting.

1.2.9.2 Manipulation of the different parts of the machine must be possible either manually or with tools without any danger.

1.2.9.3 It must not be possible to touch live parts of the machine.

1.2.9.4 Personal injury must not result from the issue of fluid or gaseous media.

2. Milling machines

2.1 Normal mode of operation

2.1.1 The work area is to be safeguarded so that it is impossible to reach or step into the danger zones of automatic movements, either intentionally or unintentionally.

2.1.2 Chip removal must not result in personal injury due to the chips or moving parts of the machine.

2.1.3 Personal injuries resulting from reaching into drive systems must be prevented.

No personal injury to operators or third persons must result from flying workpieces or parts thereof.

For example, this can occur

- due to insufficient clamping
- due to inadmissible cutting force
- due to collision with the tool or machine parts
- due to workpiece breakage
- due to defective clamping fixtures
- due to power failure

2.1.4 No personal injury must result from flying workpiece clamping fixtures.

2.1.5 No personal injury must result from flying chips.

2.1.6 No personal injury must result from flying tools or parts thereof.

For example, this can occur

- due to material defects
- due to inadmissible speed of rotation
- due to inadmissible cutting force
- due to collision with workpiece or machine part
- due to inadequate clamping or tightening
- due to power failure

2.2 Special modes of operation

2.2.1 Workpiece changing.

2.2.1.1 Where power-operated clamping fixtures are used, it must not be possible for parts of the body to become trapped between the closing parts of the clamping fixture and the workpiece.

2.2.1.2 The starting of a drive (spindle, axis) resulting from a defective command or invalid command input must be prevented.

2.2.1.3 The manipulation of the workpiece must be possible manually or with tools without any danger.

2.2.2 Tool changing.

2.2.2.1 The starting of a drive resulting from a defective command or invalid command input must be prevented.

2.2.2.2 It must not be possible for fingers to become trapped when putting in tools.

2.2.3 Measurement check.

2.2.3.1 Reaching into the work area must only be possible after all movements have been brought to a standstill.

2.2.3.2 The starting of a drive resulting from a defective command or invalid command input must be prevented.

2.2.4 Set-up.

2.2.4.1 If movements are executed during set-up with guards for normal mode of operation removed, the operator must be safeguarded by another means.

2.2.4.2 No dangerous movements or changes of movements must be initiated as a result of a defective command or invalid command input.

2.2.5   Programming.

2.2.5.1 No movements must be initiated during programming which endanger a person in the work area.

2.2.6   Production fault.

2.2.6.1 The starting of drive resulting from a defective command or invalid command input must be prevented.

2.2.6.2 No dangerous movements or situations must be initiated by the movement or removal of the workpiece or waste.

2.2.6.3 Where movements have to take place with the guards for the normal mode of operation removed, these movements may only be of the kind designated and only executed for the period of time ordered and only when it can be ensured that no parts of the body are in these danger zones.

2.2.7   Troubleshooting.

2.2.7.1 Reaching into the danger zones of automatic movements must be prevented.

2.2.7.2 The starting of a drive as a result of a defective command or invalid command input must be prevented.

2.2.7.3 Any movement of the machine on manipulation of the defective part must be prevented.

2.2.7.4 Personal injury resulting from a machine part splintering off or dropping must be prevented.

2.2.7.5 If, during troubleshooting, movements have to take place with the guards for the normal mode of operation removed, these movements may only be of the kind designated and only executed for the period of time ordered and only when it can be ensured that no parts of the body are in these danger zones.

2.2.8   Machine malfunction and repair.

2.2.8.1 Starting the machine must be prevented.

2.2.8.2 Manipulation of the different parts of the machine must be possible manually or with tools without any danger.

2.2.8.3 It must not be possible to touch live parts of the machine.

2.2.8.4 Personal injury must not result from the issue of fluid or gaseous media.

3. Machining centres

3.1 Normal mode of operation

3.1.1   The work area must be safeguarded so that is impossible to reach or step into the danger zones of automatic movements, either intentionally or unintentionally.

3.1.2   The tool magazine must be safeguarded so that it is impossible to reach or step into the danger zones of automatic movements.

3.1.3   The workpiece magazine must be safeguarded so that it is impossible to reach or step into the danger zones of automatic movements.

3.1.4   Chip removal must not result in personal injury due to the chips or moving parts of the machine.

3.1.5   Personal injuries resulting from reaching into drive systems must be prevented.

3.1.6   The possibility of reaching into danger zones of moving chip conveyors (screw conveyors, etc.) must be prevented.

3.1.7   No personal injury to operators or third persons must result from flying workpieces or parts thereof.
For example, this can occur
- due to insufficient clamping
- due to inadmissible cutting force
- due to collision with the tool or machine parts
- due to workpiece breakage
- due to defective clamping fixtures
- due to changing to the wrong workpiece
- due to power failure

3.1.8   No personal injury must result from flying workpiece clamping fixtures.

3.1.9   No personal injury must result from flying chips.

3.1.10   No personal injury must result from flying tools or parts thereof.
For example, this can occur
- due to material defects
- due to inadmissible speed of rotation
- due to inadmissible cutting force
- due to collision with workpiece or machine part
- due to inadequate clamping or tightening
- due to the tool flying out of the tool changer
- due to selecting the wrong tool
- due to power failure

3.2 Special modes of operation

3.2.1   Workpiece changing.

3.2.1.1 Where power-operated clamping fixtures are used, it must not be possible for parts of the body to become trapped between the closing parts of the clamping fixture and the workpiece.

3.2.1.2 The starting of a drive resulting from a defective command or invalid command input must be prevented.

3.2.1.3 It must be possible to manipulate the workpiece manually or with tools without any danger.

3.2.1.4 Where workpieces are changed in a clamping station, it must not be possible from this location to reach or step into automatic movement sequences of the machine or workpiece magazine. No movements must be initiated by the control while a person is present in the clamping zone.

The automatic insertion of the clamped workpiece into the machine or workpiece magazine is only to take place when the clamping station is also safeguarded with a protective system corresponding to that for normal mode of operation.

3.2.2   Tool changing in the spindle.

3.2.2.1 The starting of a drive resulting from a defective command or invalid command input must be prevented.

3.2.2.2 It must not be possible for fingers to become trapped when putting in tools.

3.2.3   Tool changing in tool magazine.

3.2.3.1 Movements in the tool magazine resulting from defective commands or invalid command input must be prevented during tool changing.

3.2.3.2 It must not be possible to reach into other moving machine parts from the tool loading station.

3.2.3.3 It must not be possible to reach into danger zones on the further movement of the tool magazine or during the search. If taking place with the guards for the normal mode of operation removed, these movements may only be of the kind designated and only executed for the period of time ordered and only when it can be ensured that no parts of the body are in these danger zones.

3.2.4   Measurement check.

3.2.4.1 Reaching into the work area must only be possible after all movements have been brought to a standstill.

3.2.4.2 The starting of a drive resulting from a defective command or invalid command input must be prevented.

3.2.5   Set-up.

3.2.5.1 If movements are executed during set-up with the guards for normal mode of operation removed, then the operator must be safeguarded by another means.

3.2.5.2 No dangerous movements or changes of movement must be initiated as a result of a defective command or invalid command input.

3.2.6   Programming.

3.2.6.1 No movements must be initiated during programming which endanger a person in the work area.

3.2.7   Production fault.

3.2.7.1 The starting of a drive resulting from a defective command or invalid command input must be prevented.

3.2.7.2 No dangerous movements or situations must be initiated by the movement or removal of the workpiece or waste.

3.2.7.3 Where movements have to take place with the guards for the normal mode of operation removed, these movements may only be of the kind designated and only executed for the period of time ordered and only when it can be ensured that no parts of the body are in these danger zones.

3.2.8   Troubleshooting.

3.2.8.1 Reaching into the danger zones of automatic movements must be prevented.

3.2.8.2 The starting of a drive as a result of a defective command or invalid command input must be prevented.

3.2.8.3 Any movement of the machine on manipulation of the defective part must be prevented.

3.2.8.4 Personal injury resulting from a machine part splintering off or dropping must be prevented.

3.2.8.5 If, during troubleshooting, movements have to take place with the guards for the normal mode of operation removed, these movements may only be of the kind designated and only executed for the period of time ordered and only when it can be ensured that no parts of the body are in these danger zones.

3.2.9   Machine malfunction and repair.

3.2.9.1 Starting the machine must be prevented.

3.2.9.2 Manipulation of the different parts of the machine must be possible manually or with tools without any danger.

3.2.9.3 It must not be possible to touch live parts of the machine.

3.2.9.4 Personal injury must not result from the issue of fluid or gaseous media.

4. Grinding machines

4.1 Normal mode of operation

4.1.1   The work area is to be safeguarded so that it is impossible to reach or step into the danger zones of automatic movements, either intentionally or unintentionally.

4.1.2   Personal injuries resulting from reaching into drive systems must be prevented.

4.1.3   No personal injury to operators or third persons must result from flying workpieces or parts thereof.
For example, this can occur
- due to insufficient clamping
- due to inadmissible cutting force
- due to inadmissible rotation speed
- due to collision with the tool or machine parts
- due to workpiece breakage
- due to defective clamping fixtures
- due to power failure

4.1.4   No personal injury must result from flying workpiece clamping fixtures.

4.1.5   No personal injury or fires must result from sparking.

4.1.6   No personal injury must result from flying parts of grinding wheels.
For example, this can occur
- due to inadmissible rotation speed
- due to inadmissible cutting force
- due to material defects
- due to collision with workpiece or machine part

- due to inadequate clamping (flanges)
- due to using incorrect grinding wheel

4.2 Special modes of operation

4.2.1   Workpiece changing.

4.2.1.1 Where power-operated clamping fixtures are used, it must not be possible for parts of the body to become trapped between the closing parts of the clamping fixture and the workpiece.

4.2.1.2 The starting of a feed drive resulting from a defective command or invalid command input must be prevented.

4.2.1.3 Personal injury caused by the rotating grinding wheel must be prevented when manipulating the workpiece.

4.2.1.4 Personal injury resulting from a bursting grinding wheel must not be possible.

4.2.1.5 The manipulation of the workpiece must be possible manually or with tools without any danger.

4.2.2   Tool changing (grinding wheel changing)

4.2.2.1 The starting of a feed drive resulting from .a defective command or invalid command input must be prevented.

4.2.2.2 Personal injury caused by the rotating grinding wheel must not be possible during measuring procedures.

4.2.2.3 Personal injury resulting from a bursting grinding wheel must not be possible.

4.2.3   Measurement check.

4.2.3.1 The starting of a feed drive resulting from a defective command or invalid command input must be prevented.

4.2.3.2 Personal injury caused by the rotating grinding wheel must not be possible during measuring procedures.

4.2.3.3 Personal injury resulting from a bursting grinding wheel must not be possible.

4.2.4.   Set-up.

4.2.4.1 If movements are executed during set-up with the guards for normal mode of operation removed, then the operator must be safeguarded by another means.

4.2.4.2 No dangerous movements or changes of movement must be initiated as a result of a defective command or invalid command input.

4.2.5   Programming.

4.2.5.1 No movements must be initiated during programming which endanger a person in the work area.

4.2.6   Production fault.

4.2.6.1 The starting of a feed drive resulting from a defective command or invalid command input must be prevented.

4.2.6.2 No dangerous movements or situations must be initiated by the movement or removal of the workpiece or waste.

4.2.6.3 Where movements have to take place with the guards for the normal mode of operation removed, these movements may only be of the kind designated and only executed for the period of time ordered and only when it can be ensured that no parts of the body are in these danger zones.

4.2.6.4 Personal injury caused by the rotating grinding wheel must be prevented.

4.2.6.5 Personal injury resulting from a bursting grinding wheel must not be possible.

4.2.7   Troubleshooting.

4.2.7.1 Reaching into the danger zones of automatic movements must be prevented.

4.2.7.2 The starting of a drive as a result of a defective command or invalid command input must be prevented.

4.2.7.3 Any movement of the machine on manipulation of the defective part must be prevented.

4.2.7.4 Personal injury resulting from a machine part splintering off or dropping must be prevented.

4.2.7.5 Personal injury caused the operator's contacting or by the bursting of the rotating grinding wheel must be prevented.

4.2.7.6 If, during troubleshooting, movements have to take place with the guards for the normal mode of operation removed, these movements may only be of the kind designated and only executed for the period of time ordered and only when it can be ensured that no parts of the body are in these danger zones.

4.2.8   Machine malfunction and repair.

4.2.8.1 Starting the machine must be prevented.

4.2.8.2 Manipulation of the different parts of the machine must be possible manually or with tools without any danger.

4.2.8.3 It must not be possible to touch live parts of the machine.

4.2.8.4 Personal injury must not result from the issue of fluid or gaseous media.

Safety goals

- Movements must take place only in such a way that they cannot be a hazard for the persons concerned. Such movements must be executed only in the scheduled style and speed and continued only as long as instructed.
- They are to be attempted only if it can be guaranteed that no parts of the human body are in the danger zone.

Possible solution

- Install special operating control systems which permit only controllable and manageable movements using finger-tip control via "acknowledge-type" push buttons. The speed of movements is thus safely reduced (provided that energy has been reduced by means of an isolation transformer or similar monitoring equipment).

Demands on Safety Control Systems

One of the features of a safety control system must be that the safety function is guaranteed to work whenever any faults arise so as to direct processes from a hazardous state to a safe state.

Safety goals

- A fault in the safety control system must not trigger off a dangerous state.
- A fault in the safety control system must be identified (immediately or at intervals).

Possible solutions

- Put in place a redundant and diverse layout of electro-mechanical control systems, including test circuits.

- Put in place a redundant and diverse set-up of microprocessor control systems developed by different teams. This approach is considered to be state of the art, for example, in the case of safety light barriers.

Conclusion

It is apparent that the increasing trend in accidents in normal and special modes of operation cannot be halted without a clear and unmistakable safety concept. This fact must be taken into account in the preparation of safety regulations and guidelines. New guidelines in the shape of safety goals are necessary in order to allow advanced solutions. This objective enables designers to choose the optimum solution for a specific case while at the same time demonstrating the safety features of their machines in a fairly simple way by describing a solution to each safety goal. This solution can then be compared with other existing and accepted solutions, and if it is better or at least of equal value, a new solution can then be chosen. In this way, progress is not hampered by narrowly formulated regulations.

● SAFETY PRINCIPLES FOR INDUSTRIAL ROBOTS

Toni Retsch, Guido Schmitter and Albert Marty

Industrial robots are found throughout industry wherever high productivity demands must be met. The use of robots, however, requires design, application and implementation of the appropriate safety controls in order to avoid creating hazards to production personnel, programmers, maintenance specialists and system engineers.

Why Are Industrial Robots Dangerous?

One definition of robots is "moving automatic machines that are freely programmable and are able to operate with little or no human interface". These types of machines are currently used in a wide variety of applications throughout industry and medicine, including training. Industrial robots are being increasingly used for key functions, such as new manufacturing strategies (CIM, JIT, lean production and so on) in complex installations. Their number and breadth of applications and the complexity of the equipment and installations result in hazards such as the following:

- movements and sequences of movements that are almost impossible to follow, as the robot's high-speed movements within its radius of action often overlap with those of other machines and equipment
- release of energy caused by flying parts or beams of energy such as those emitted by lasers or by water jets
- free programmability in terms of direction and speed
- susceptibility to influence by external errors (e.g., electromagnetic compatibility)
- human factors.

Investigations in Japan indicate that more than 50% of working accidents with robots can be attributed to faults in the electronic circuits of the control system. In the same investigations, "human error" was responsible for less than 20%. The logical conclusion of this finding is that hazards which are caused by system faults cannot be avoided by behavioural measures taken by human beings. Designers and operators therefore need to provide and implement technical safety measures (see figure 58.82).

Accidents and Operating Modes

Fatal accidents involving industrial robots began to occur in the early 1980s. Statistics and investigations indicate that the majority of incidents and accidents do not take place in normal operation (automatic fulfilment of the assignment concerned). When working with industrial robot machines and installations, there is an emphasis on special operation modes such as commissioning, setting up, programming, test runs, checks, troubleshooting or maintenance. In these operating modes, persons are usually in a danger zone. The safety concept must protect personnel from negative events in these types of situations.

International Safety Requirements

The 1989 EEC Machinery Directive (89/392/EEC (see the article "Safety principles for CNC machine tools" in this chapter and elsewhere in this *Encyclopaedia*)) establishes the principal safety and health requirements for machines. A machine is considered to be the sum total of interlinked parts or devices, of which at least one part or device can move and correspondingly has a function. Where industrial robots are concerned, it must be noted that the entire system, not just one single piece of equipment on the machine, must meet the safety requirements and be fitted with the appropriate safety devices. Hazard analysis and risk assessment are suitable methods of determining whether these requirements have been satisfied (see figure 58.83).

Requirements and Safety Measures in Normal Operation

The use of robot technology places maximum demands on hazard analysis, risk assessment and safety concepts. For this reason, the following examples and suggestions can serve only as guidelines:

1. Given the safety goal that manual or physical access to hazardous areas involving automatic movements must be prevented, suggested solutions include the following:
   - Prevent manual or physical access into danger zones by means of mechanical barriers.
   - Use safety devices of the sort which respond when approached (light barriers, safety mats), and take care to switch off machinery safely when accessed or entered.
   - Permit manual or physical access only when the entire system is in a safe state. For example, this can be achieved by the use of interlocking devices with closure mechanisms on the access doors.

Figure 58.82 • Special operating control system for the setting up of a mobile welding robot.

Figure 58.83 • Block diagram for a personnel security system.

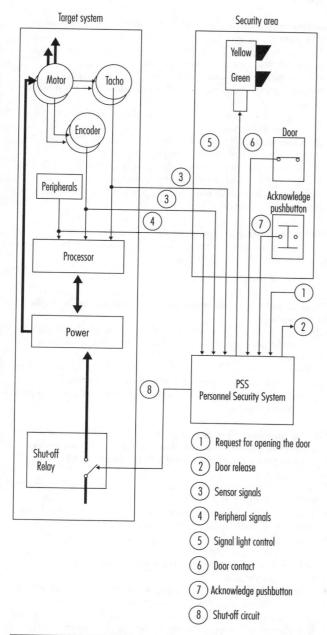

① Request for opening the door

② Door release

③ Sensor signals

④ Peripheral signals

⑤ Signal light control

⑥ Door contact

⑦ Acknowledge pushbutton

⑧ Shut-off circuit

2. Given the safety goal that no person may be injured as a result of the release of energy (flying parts or beams of energy), suggested solutions include:
   • Design should prevent any release of energy (e.g., correspondingly dimensioned connections, passive gripper interlocking devices for gripper change mechanisms, etc.).
   • Prevent the release of energy from the danger zone, for example, by a correspondingly dimensioned safety hood.

3. The interfaces between normal operation and special operation (e.g., door interlocking devices, light barriers, safety mats) are necessary to enable the safety control system to automatically recognize the presence of personnel.

Demands and Safety Measures in Special Operation Modes

Certain special operation modes (e.g., setting up, programming) on an industrial robot require movements which must be assessed directly at the site of operation. The relevant safety goal is that no movements may endanger the persons involved. The movements should be

• only of the scheduled style and speed
• prolonged only as long as instructed
• those which may be performed only if it can be guaranteed that no parts of the human body are in the danger zone.

A suggested solution to this goal could involve the use of special operating control systems which permit only controllable and manageable movements using acknowledgeable controls. The speed of movements is thus safely reduced (energy reduction by the connection of an isolation transformer or the use of fail-safe state monitoring equipment) and the safe condition is acknowledged before the control is allowed to activate (see figure 58.84).

Demands on Safety Control Systems

One of the features of a safety control system must be that the required safety function is guaranteed to work whenever any faults arise. Industrial robot machines should be almost instantaneously directed from a hazardous state to a safe state. Safety control measures needed to achieve this include the following safety goals:

• A fault in the safety control system may not trigger off a hazardous state.
• A fault in the safety control system must be identified (immediately or at intervals).

Suggested solutions to providing reliable safety control systems would be:

• redundant and diverse layout of electro-mechanical control systems including test circuits
• redundant and diverse set-up of microprocessor control systems developed by different teams. This modern approach is considered to be state-of-the-art; for example, those complete with safety light barriers.

Figure 58.84 • Six-axis industrial robot in a safety cage with material gates.

Safety Goals for the Construction and Use of Industrial Robots.

When industrial robots are built and used, both manufacturers as well as users are required to install state-of-the-art safety controls. Apart from the aspect of legal responsibility, there may also be a moral obligation to ensure that robot technology is also a safe technology.

Normal operation mode

The following safety conditions should be provided when robot machines are operating in the normal mode:

- The field of movement of the robot and the processing areas used by peripheral equipment must be secured in such a way as to prevent manual or physical access by persons to areas which are hazardous as a result of automatic movements.
- Protection should be provided so that flying workpieces or tools are not allowed to cause damage.
- No persons must be injured by parts, tools or workpieces ejected by the robot or by the release of energy, due to faulty gripper(s), gripper power failure, inadmissible speed, collision(s) or faulty workpiece(s).
- No persons may be injured by the release of energy or by parts ejected by peripheral equipment.
- Feed and removal apertures must be designed to prevent manual or physical access to areas which are hazardous as a result of automatic movements. This condition must also be fulfilled when production material is removed. If production material is fed to the robot automatically, no hazardous areas may be created by feed and removal apertures and the moving production material.

Special operation modes

The following safety conditions should be provided when robot machines are operating in special modes:

The following must be prevented during rectification of a breakdown in the production process:

- manual or physical access to areas which are hazardous due to automatic movements by the robot or by peripheral equipment
- hazards which arise from faulty behaviour on the part of the system or from inadmissible command input if persons or parts of the body are in the area exposed to hazardous movements
- hazardous movements or conditions initiated by the movement or removal of production material or waste products
- injuries caused by peripheral equipment
- movements that have to be carried out with the safety guard(s) for normal operation removed, to be carried out only within the operational scope and speed, and only as long as instructed. Additionally, no person(s) or parts of the body may be present in the area at risk.

The following safe conditions should be assured during set up:

No hazardous movements may be initiated as a result of a faulty command or incorrect command input.

- The replacement of robot machine or peripheral parts must not initiate any hazardous movements or conditions.
- If movements have to be carried out with the safety guard(s) for normal operation removed when conducting setting-up operations, such movements may be carried out only within the directed scope and speed and only as long as instructed. Additionally, no person(s) or parts of the body may be present in the area at risk.

- During setting-up operations, the peripheral equipment must not make any hazardous movements or initiate any hazardous conditions.

During programming, the following safety conditions are applicable:

- Manual or physical access to areas which are hazardous due to automatic movements must be prevented.
- If movements are carried out with the safety guard(s) for normal operation removed, the following conditions must be fulfilled:
  (a) Only the command to move may be carried out, and only for as long as it is issued.
  (b) Only controllable movements may be carried out (i.e., they must be clearly visible, low-speed movements).
  (c) Movements may be initiated only if they do not constitute a hazard to the programmer or other persons.
- Peripheral equipment must not represent a hazard to the programmer or other persons.

Safe test operations require the following precautions:

Prevent manual or physical access to areas which are hazardous due to automatic movements.

- Peripheral equipment must not be a source of danger.

When inspecting robot machines, safe procedures include the following:

- If it is necessary to enter the robot's field of movement for inspection purposes, this is permissible only if the system is in a safe state.
- Hazards caused by faulty behaviour on the part of the system or by inadmissible command input must be prevented.
- Peripheral equipment must not be a source of danger to inspection personnel.

Troubleshooting often requires starting the robot machine while it is in a potentially hazardous condition, and special safe work procedures such as the following should be implemented:

- Access to areas which are hazardous as a result of automatic movements must be prevented.
- The starting up of a drive unit as a result of a faulty command or false command input must be prevented.
- In handling a defective part, all movements on the part of the robot must be prevented.
- Injuries caused by machine parts which are ejected or fall off must be prevented.
- If, during troubleshooting, movements have to be carried out with the safety guard(s) for normal operation removed, such movements may be carried out only within the scope and speed laid down and only as long as instructed. Additionally, no person(s) or parts of the body may be present in the area at risk.
- Injuries caused by peripheral equipment must be prevented.

Remedying a fault and maintenance work also may require start-up while the machine is in an unsafe condition, and therefore require the following precautions:

- The robot must not be able to start up.
- The handling of various machine parts, either manually or with ancillary equipment, must be possible without risk of exposure to hazards.
- It must not be possible to touch parts that are "live".
- Injuries caused by the escape of liquid or gaseous media must be prevented.
- Injuries caused by peripheral equipment must be prevented.

ELECTRICAL, ELECTRONIC AND PROGRAMMABLE ELECTRONIC SAFETY-RELATED CONTROL SYSTEMS

Ron Bell

This article discusses the design and implementation of safety-related control systems which deal with all types of electrical, electronic and programmable-electronic systems (including computer-based systems). The overall approach is in accordance with proposed International Electrotechnical Commission (IEC) Standard 1508 (*Functional Safety: Safety-Related Systems*) (IEC 1993).

Background

During the 1980s, computer-based systems—generically referred to as programmable electronic systems (PESs)—were increasingly being used to carry out safety functions. The primary driving forces behind this trend were (1) improved functionality and economic benefits (particularly considering the total life cycle of the device or system) and (2) the particular benefit of certain designs, which could be realized only when computer technology was used. During the early introduction of computer-based systems a number of findings were made:

- The introduction of computer control was poorly thought out and planned.
- Inadequate safety requirements were specified.
- Inadequate procedures were developed with respect to the validation of software.
- Evidence of poor workmanship was disclosed with respect to the standard of plant installation.
- Inadequate documentation was generated and not adequately validated with respect to what was actually in the plant (as distinct from what was thought to be in the plant).
- Less than fully effective operation and maintenance procedures had been established.
- There was evidently justified concern about the competence of persons to perform the duties required of them.

In order to solve these problems, several bodies published or began developing guidelines to enable the safe exploitation of PES technology. In the United Kingdom, the Health and Safety Executive (HSE) developed guidelines for programmable electronic systems used for safety-related applications, and in Germany, a draft standard (DIN 1990) was published. Within the European Community, an important element in the work on harmonized European Standards concerned with safety-related control systems (including those employing PESs) was started in connection with the requirements of the Machinery Directive. In the United States, the Instrument Society of America (ISA) has produced a standard on PESs for use in the process industries, and the Center for Chemical Process Safety (CCPS), a directorate of the American Institute of Chemical Engineers, has produced guidelines for the chemical process sector.

A major standards initiative is currently taking place within the IEC to develop a generically based international standard for electrical, electronic and programmable electronic (E/E/PES) safety-related systems that could be used by the many applications sectors, including the process, medical, transport and machinery sectors. The proposed IEC international standard comprises seven Parts under the general title *IEC 1508. Functional safety of electrical/electronic/programmable electronic safety-related systems.* The various Parts are as follows:

- Part 1. General requirements
- Part 2. Requirements for electrical, electronic and programmable electronic systems
- Part 3. Software requirements
- Part 4. Definitions
- Part 5. Examples of methods for the determination of safety integrity levels
- Part 6. Guidelines on the application of Parts 2 and 3
- Part 7. Overview of techniques and measures.

When finalized, this generically based International Standard will constitute an IEC basic safety publication covering functional safety for electrical, electronic and programmable electronic safety-related systems and will have implications for all IEC standards, covering all application sectors as regards the future design and use of electrical/electronic/programmable electronic safety-related systems. A major objective of the proposed standard is to facilitate the development of standards for the various sectors (see figure 58.85).

PES Benefits and Problems

The adoption of PESs for safety purposes had many potential advantages, but it was recognized that these would be achieved only if appropriate design and assessment methodologies were used, because: (1) many of the features of PESs do not enable the safety integrity (that is, the safety performance of the systems carrying out the required safety functions) to be predicted with the same degree of confidence that has traditionally been available for less complex hardware-based ("hardwired") systems; (2) it was recognized that while testing was necessary for complex systems, it was not sufficient on its own. This meant that even if the PES was implementing relatively simple safety functions, the level of complexity of the programmable electronics was significantly greater than that of the hardwired systems they were replacing; and (3) this rise in complexity meant that the design and assessment methodologies had to be given much more consideration than previously, and that the level of personal competence required to achieve adequate levels of performance of the safety-related systems was subsequently greater.

The benefits of computer-based PESs include the following:

- the ability to perform on-line diagnostic proof checks on critical components at a frequency significantly higher than would otherwise be the case

Figure 58.85 • Generic and application sector standards.

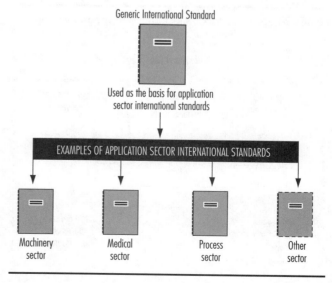

Generic International Standard

Used as the basis for application sector international standards

EXAMPLES OF APPLICATION SECTOR INTERNATIONAL STANDARDS

Machinery sector

Medical sector

Process sector

Other sector

- the potential to provide sophisticated safety interlocks
- the ability to provide diagnostic functions and condition monitoring which can be used to analyse and report on the performance of plant and machinery in real time
- the capability of comparing actual conditions of the plant with "ideal" model conditions
- the potential to provide better information to operators and hence to improve decision-making affecting safety
- the use of advanced control strategies to enable human operators to be located remotely from hazardous or hostile environments
- the ability to diagnose the control system from a remote location.

The use of computer-based systems in safety-related applications creates a number of problems which need to be adequately addressed, such as the following:

- The failure modes are complex and not always predictable.
- Testing the computer is necessary but is not sufficient in itself to establish that the safety functions will be performed with the degree of certainty required for the application.
- Microprocessors may have subtle variations between different batches, and therefore different batches may display different behaviour.
- Unprotected computer-based systems are particularly susceptible to electrical interference (radiated interference; electrical "spikes" in the mains supplies, electrostatic discharges, etc.).
- It is difficult and often impossible to quantify the probability of failure of complex safety-related systems incorporating software. Because no method of quantification has been widely accepted, software assurance has been based on procedures and standards which describe the methods to be used in the design, implementation and maintenance of the software.

Safety Systems under Consideration

The types of safety-related systems under consideration are electrical, electronic and programmable electronic systems (E/E/PESs). The system includes all elements, particularly signals extending from sensors or from other input devices on the equipment under control, and transmitted via data highways or other communication paths to the actuators or other output devices (see figure 58.86).

The term *electrical, electronic and programmable electronic device* has been used to encompass a wide variety of devices and covers the following three chief classes:

Figure 58.86 • Electrical, electronic and programmable electronic system (E/E/PES).

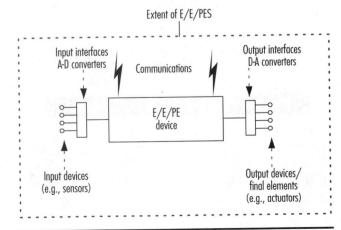

Figure 58.87 • Key features of safety-related systems.

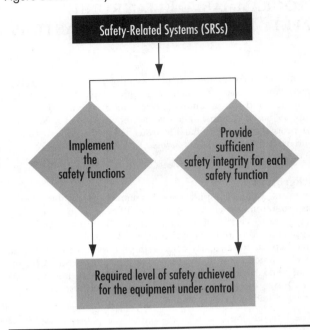

1. electrical devices such as electro-mechanical relays
2. electronic devices such as solid state electronic instruments and logic systems
3. programmable electronic devices, which includes a wide variety of computer-based systems such as the following:
   - microprocessors
   - micro-controllers
   - programmable controllers (PCs)
   - application-specific integrated circuits (ASICs)
   - programmable logic controllers (PLCs)
   - other computer-based devices (e.g., "smart" sensors, transmitters and actuators).

By definition, a safety-related system serves two purposes:

1. It implements the required safety functions necessary to achieve a safe state for the equipment under control or maintains a safe state for the equipment under control. The safety-related system must perform those safety functions that are specified in the safety functions requirements specification for the system. For example, the safety functions requirements specification may state that when the temperature reaches a certain value x, valve y shall open to allow water to enter the vessel.
2. It achieves, on its own or with other safety-related systems, the necessary level of safety integrity for the implementation of the required safety functions. The safety functions must be performed by the safety-related systems with the degree of confidence appropriate to the application in order to achieve the required level of safety for the equipment under control.

This concept is illustrated in figure 58.87.

System Failures

In order to ensure safe operation of E/E/PES safety-related systems, it is necessary to recognize the various possible causes of safety-related system failure and to ensure that adequate precau-

Figure 58.88 • Failure categories.

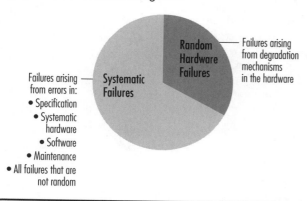

Figure 58.89 • Safety performance terms.

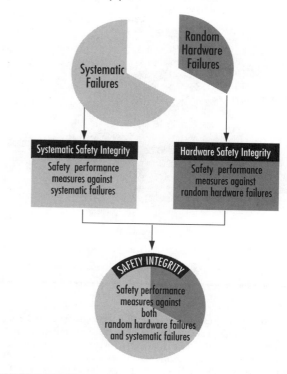

tions are taken against each. Failures are classified into two categories, as illustrated in figure 58.88.

1. Random hardware failures are those failures which result from a variety of normal degradation mechanisms in the hardware. There are many such mechanisms occurring at different rates in different components, and since manufacturing tolerances cause components to fail on account of these mechanisms after different times in operation, failures of a total item of equipment comprising many components occur at unpredictable (random) times. Measures of system reliability, such as the mean time between failures (MTBF), are valuable but are usually concerned only with random hardware failures and do not include systematic failures.

2. Systematic failures arise from errors in the design, construction or use of a system which cause it to fail under some particular combination of inputs or under some particular environmental condition. If a system failure occurs when a particular set of circumstances arises, then whenever those circumstances arise in the future there will always be a system failure. Any failure of a safety-related system which does not arise from a random hardware failure is, by definition, a systematic failure. Systematic failures, in the context of E/E/PES safety-related systems, include:

   - systematic failures due to errors or omissions in the safety functions requirements specification
   - systematic failures due to errors in the design, manufacture, installation or operation of the hardware. These would include failures arising from environmental causes and human (e.g., operator) error
   - systematic failures due to faults in the software
   - systematic failures due to maintenance and modification errors.

Protection of Safety-Related Systems

The terms that are used to indicate the precautionary measures required by a safety-related system to protect against random hardware failures and systematic failures are *hardware safety integrity measures* and *systematic safety integrity measures* respectively. Precautionary measures that a safety-related system can bring to bear against both random hardware failures and systematic failures are termed *safety integrity*. These concepts are illustrated in figure 58.89.

Within the proposed international standard IEC 1508 there are four levels of safety integrity, denoted Safety Integrity Levels 1, 2, 3 and 4. Safety Integrity Level 1 is the lowest safety integrity level

and Safety Integrity Level 4 is the highest. The Safety Integrity Level (whether 1, 2, 3 or 4) for the safety-related system will depend upon the importance of the role the safety-related system is playing in achieving the required level of safety for the equipment under control. Several safety-related systems may be necessary—some of which may be based on pneumatic or hydraulic technology.

Design of Safety-Related Systems

A recent analysis of 34 incidents involving control systems (HSE) found that 60% of all cases of failure had been "built in" before the safety-related control system had been put into use (figure 58.90). Consideration of all the safety life cycle phases is necessary if adequate safety-related systems are to be produced.

Functional safety of safety-related systems depends not only on ensuring that the technical requirements are properly specified but also in ensuring that the technical requirements are effectively implemented and that the initial design integrity is maintained throughout the life of the equipment. This can be realized only if an effective safety management system is in place and the people involved in any activity are competent with respect to the duties they have to perform. Particularly when complex safety-related systems are involved, it is essential that an adequate safety management system is in place. This leads to a strategy that ensures the following:

- An effective safety management system is in place.
- The technical requirements that are specified for the E/E/PES safety-related systems are sufficient to deal with both random hardware and systematic failure causes.
- The competence of the people involved is adequate for the duties they have to perform.

Figure 58.90 • Primary cause (by phase) of control system failure.

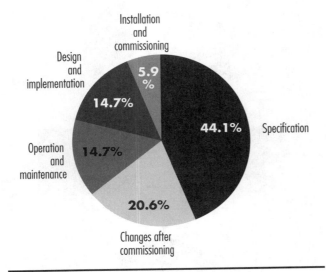

Figure 58.91 • Role of the Safety Lifecycle in achieving functional safety.

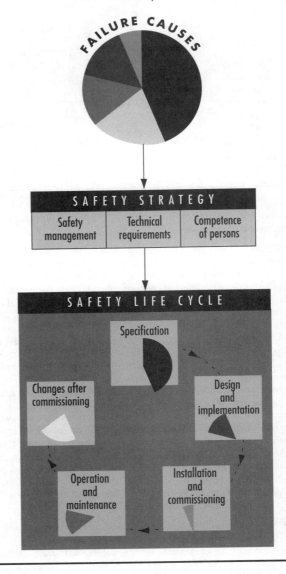

In order to address all the relevant technical requirements of functional safety in a systematic manner, the concept of the Safety Lifecycle has been developed. A simplified version of the Safety Lifecycle in the emerging international standard IEC 1508 is shown in figure 58.91. The key phases of the Safety Lifecycle are:

- specification
- design and implementation
- installation and commissioning
- operation and maintenance
- changes after commissioning.

Level of Safety

The design strategy for the achievement of adequate levels of safety integrity for the safety-related systems is illustrated in figures 58.92 and 58.93. A safety integrity level is based on the role the safety-related system is playing in the achievement of the overall level of safety for the equipment under control. The safety integrity level specifies the precautions that need to be taken into account in the design against both random hardware and systematic failures.

The concept of safety and level of safety applies to the equipment under control. The concept of functional safety applies to the safety-related systems. Functional safety for the safety-related systems has to be achieved if an adequate level of safety is to be achieved for the equipment that is giving rise to the hazard. The specified level of safety for a specific situation is a key factor in the safety integrity requirements specification for the safety-related systems.

The required level of safety will depend upon many factors—for example, the severity of injury, the number of people exposed to danger, the frequency with which people are exposed to danger and the duration of the exposure. Important factors will be the perception and views of those exposed to the hazardous event. In arriving at what constitutes an appropriate level of safety for a specific application, a number of inputs are considered, which include the following:

- legal requirements relevant to the specific application

- guidelines from the appropriate safety regulatory authority
- discussions and agreements with the different parties involved in the application
- industry standards
- national and international standards
- the best independent industrial, expert and scientific advice.

Summary

When designing and using safety-related systems, it must be remembered that it is the equipment under control that creates the potential hazard. The safety-related systems are designed to reduce the frequency (or probability) of the hazardous event and/or the consequences of the hazardous event. Once the level of safety has been set for the equipment, the safety integrity level for the safety-related system can be determined, and it is the safety integrity level that allows the designer to specify the precautions that need to be built into the design to be deployed against both random hardware and systematic failures.

58. SAFETY APPLICATIONS

Figure 58.92 • Role of safety integrity levels in the design process.

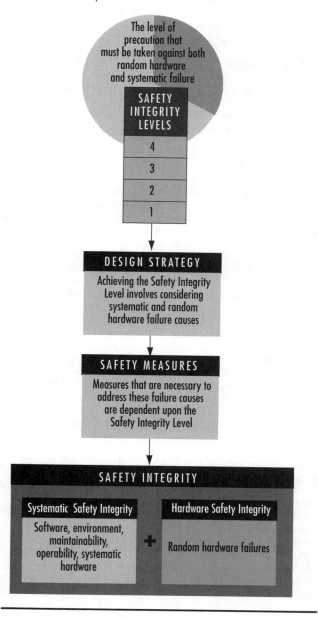

Figure 58.93 • Role of the Safety Lifecycle in the specification and design process.

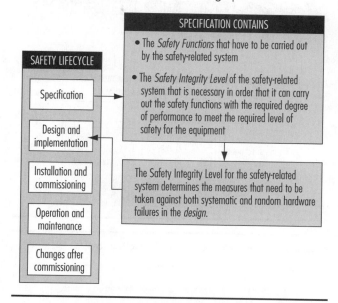

failures of electro-mechanical, electronic and programmable electronic (E/E/PE) devices used in the design of their control or safety systems. These failures can arise either from physical faults in the device (e.g., from wear and tear occurring randomly in time (random hardware failures)); or from systematic faults (e.g., errors made in the specification and design of a system that cause it to fail due to (1) some particular combination of inputs, (2) some environmental condition (3) incorrect or incomplete inputs from sensors, (4) incomplete or erroneous data entry by operators, and (5) potential systematic faults due to poor interface design).

Safety-Related Systems Failures

This article covers the functional safety of safety-related control systems, and considers the hardware and software technical requirements necessary to achieve the required safety integrity. The overall approach is in accordance with the proposed International Electrotechnical Commission Standard IEC 1508, Parts 2 and 3 (IEC 1993). The overall goal of draft international standard IEC 1508, *Functional Safety: Safety-Related Systems*, is to ensure that plant and equipment can be safety automated. A key objective in the development of the proposed international standard is to prevent or minimize the frequency of:

- failures of control systems triggering other events which in turn could lead to danger (e.g., control system fails, control is lost, process goes out of control resulting in a fire, release of toxic materials, etc.)
- failures in alarm and monitoring systems so that operators are not given information in a form that can be quickly identified and understood in order to carry out the necessary emergency actions
- undetected failures in protection systems, making them unavailable when needed for a safety action (e.g., a failed input card in an emergency shut-down system).

The article "Electrical, electronic and programmable electronic safety-related systems" sets out the general safety management approach embodied within Part 1 of IEC 1508 for assuring the safety of control and protection systems that are important to

● **TECHNICAL REQUIREMENTS FOR SAFETY-RELATED SYSTEMS BASED ON ELECTRICAL, ELECTRONIC AND PROGRAMMABLE ELECTRONIC DEVICES**

John Brazendale and Ron Bell

Machinery, process plants and other equipment can, if they malfunction, present risks from hazardous events such as fires, explosions, radiation overdoses and moving parts. One of the ways such plants, equipment and machinery can malfunction is from

Figure 58.94 • Risk reduction: General concepts.

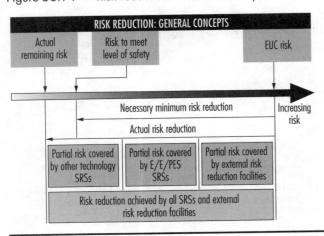

Figure 58.95 • Overall model: Protection layers.

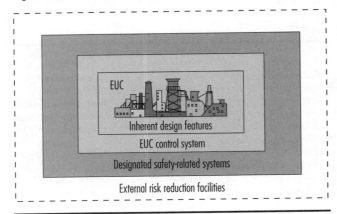

Figure 58.96 • Typical protection system.

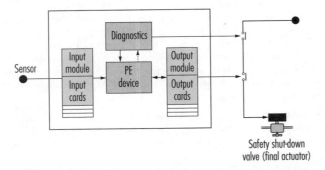

safety. This article describes the overall conceptual engineering design that is needed to reduce the risk of an accident to an acceptable level, including the role of any control or protection systems based on E/E/PE technology.

In figure 58.94, the risk from the equipment, process plant or machine (generally referred to as *equipment under control* (EUC) without protective devices) is marked at one end of the EUC Risk Scale, and the target level of risk that is needed to meet the required level of safety is at the other end. In between is shown the combination of safety-related systems and external risk reduction facilities needed to make up the required risk reduction. These can be of various types—mechanical (e.g., pressure relief valves), hydraulic, pneumatic, physical, as well as E/E/PE systems. Figure 58.95 emphasizes the role of each safety layer in protecting the EUC as the accident progresses.

Provided that a hazard and risk analysis has been performed on the EUC as required in Part 1 of IEC 1508, the overall conceptual design for safety has been established and therefore the required functions and Safety Integrity Level (SIL) target for any E/E/PE control or protection system have been defined. The Safety Integrity Level target is defined with respect to a Target Failure Measure (see table 58.6).

Protection Systems

This paper outlines the technical requirements that the designer of an E/E/PE safety-related system should consider to satisfy the required Safety Integrity Level target. The focus is on a typical protection system utilizing programmable electronics in order to allow for a more in-depth discussion of the key issues with little loss in generality. A typical protection system is shown in figure 58.96, which depicts a single channel safety system with a secondary switch-off activated via a diagnostic device. In normal operation the unsafe condition of the EUC (e.g., overspeed in a machine, high temperature in a chemical plant) will be detected by the sensor and transmitted to the programmable electronics, which will command the actuators (via the output relays) to put the system into a safe state (e.g., removing power to electric motor of the machine, opening a valve to relieve pressure).

But what if there are failures in the protection system components? This is the function of the secondary switch-off, which is activated by the diagnostic (self-checking) feature of this design. However, the system is not completely fail-safe, as the design has only a certain probability of being available when being asked to carry out its safety function (it has a certain probability of failure on demand or a certain Safety Integrity Level). For example, the above design might be able to detect and tolerate certain types of output card failure, but it would not be able to withstand a failure of the input card. Therefore, its safety integrity will be much lower than that of a design with a higher-reliability input card, or improved diagnostics, or some combination of these.

There are other possible causes of card failures, including "traditional" physical faults in the hardware, systematic faults including errors in the requirements specification, implementation faults in the software and inadequate protection against environmental conditions (e.g., humidity). The diagnostics in this single-channel design may not cover all these types of faults, and therefore this will limit the Safety Integrity Level achieved in practice. (Coverage is a measure of the percentage of faults that a design can detect and handle safely.)

Table 58.6 • Safety Integrity Levels for protection systems: Target Failure Measures.

Safety Integrity Level	Demand mode of operation (Probability of failure to perform its design function on demand)
4	$10^{-5} \leq \times < 10^{-4}$
3	$10^{-4} \leq \times < 10^{-3}$
2	$10^{-3} \leq \times < 10^{-2}$
1	$10^{-2} \leq \times < 10^{-1}$

Technical Requirements

Parts 2 and 3 of draft IEC 1508 provide a framework for identifying the various potential causes of failure in hardware and software and for selecting design features that overcome those potential causes of failure appropriate to the required Safety Integrity Level of the safety-related system. For example, the overall technical approach for the protection system in figure 58.96 is shown in figure 58.97. The figure indicates the two basic strategies for overcoming faults and failures: (1) *fault avoidance*, where care is taken in to prevent faults being created; and (2) *fault tolerance*, where the design is created specifically to tolerate specified faults. The single-channel system mentioned above is an example of a (limited) fault tolerant design where diagnostics are used to detect certain faults and put the system into a safe state before a dangerous failure can occur.

Fault avoidance

Fault avoidance attempts to prevent faults being introduced into a system. The main approach is to use a systematic method of managing the project so that safety is treated as a definable and manageable quality of a system, during design and then subsequently during operation and maintenance. The approach, which is similar to quality assurance, is based on the concept of feedback and involves: (1) *planning* (defining safety objectives, identifying the ways and means to achieve the objectives); (2) *measuring* achievement against the plan during implementation and (3) applying *feedback* to correct for any deviations. Design reviews are a good example of a fault avoidance technique. In IEC 1508 this "quality" approach to fault avoidance is facilitated by the requirements to use a safety lifecycle and employ safety management procedures for both hardware and software. For the latter, these often manifest themselves as software quality assurance procedures such as those described in ISO 9000-3 (1990).

In addition, Parts 2 and 3 of IEC 1508 (concerning hardware and software, respectively) grade certain techniques or measures that are considered useful for fault avoidance during the various

Table 58.7 • Software design and development.

Technique/measure	SIL 1	SIL 2	SIL 3	SIL 4
1. Formal methods including, for example, CCS, CSP, HOL, LOTOS	—	R	R	HR
2. Semi-formal methods	HR	HR	HR	HR
3. Structured. Methodology including, for example, JSD, MASCOT, SADT, SSADM and YOURDON	HR	HR	HR	HR
4. Modular approach	HR	HR	HR	HR
5. Design and coding standards	R	HR	HR	HR

HR = highly recommended; R = recommended; NR = not recommended; — = neutral: the technique/measure is neither for or against the SIL. Note: a numbered technique/measure shall be selected according to the safety integrity level.

safety lifecycle phases. Table 58.7 gives an example from Part 3 for the design and development phase of software. The designer would use the table to assist in the selection of fault avoidance techniques, depending on the required Safety Integrity Level. With each technique or measure in the tables there is a recommendation for each Safety Integrity Level, 1 to 4. The range of recommendations covers Highly Recommended (HR), Recommended (R), Neutral—neither for or against (—) and Not Recommended (NR).

Fault tolerance

IEC 1508 requires increasing levels of fault tolerance as the safety integrity target increases. The standard recognizes, however, that fault tolerance is more important when systems (and the components that make up those systems) are complex (designated as Type B in IEC 1508). For less complex, "well proven" systems, the degree of fault tolerance can be relaxed.

Figure 58.97 • Design specification: Design solution.

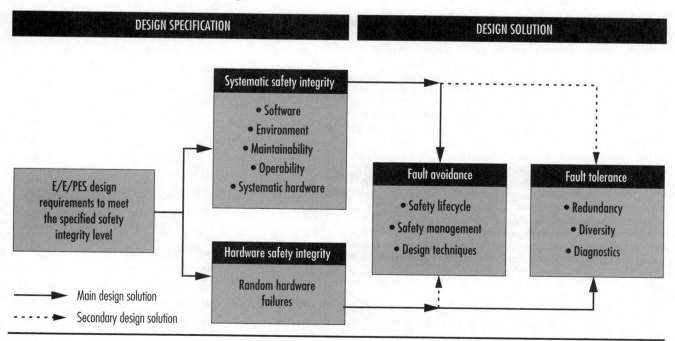

Table 58.8 • Safety Integrity Level—Fault requirements for Type B components.[1]

1 Safety-related undetected faults shall be detected by the proof check.
2 For components without on-line medium diagnostic coverage, the system shall be able to perform the safety function in the presence of a single fault. Safety-related undetected faults shall be detected by the proof check.
3 For components with on-line high diagnostic coverage, the system shall be able to perform the safety function in the presence of a single fault. For components without on-line high diagnostic coverage, the system shall be able to perform the safety function in the presence of two faults. Safety-related undetected faults shall be detected by the proof check.
4 The components shall be able to perform the safety function in the presence of two faults. Faults shall be detected with on-line high diagnostic coverage. Safety-related undetected faults shall be detected by the proof check. Quantitative hardware analysis shall be based on worst-case assumptions.

[1] Components whose failure modes are not well defined or testable, or for which there are poor failure data from field experience (e.g., programmable electronic components).

Tolerance against random hardware faults

Table 58.8 shows the requirements for fault tolerance against random hardware failures in complex hardware components (e.g., microprocessors) when used in a protection system such as is shown in figure 58.96. The designer may need to consider an appropriate combination of diagnostics, fault tolerance and manual proof checks to overcome this class of fault, depending on the required Safety Integrity Level.

IEC 1508 aids the designer by providing design specification tables (see table 58.9) with design parameters indexed against the Safety Integrity Level for a number of commonly used protection system architectures.

The first column of the table represents architectures with varying degrees of fault tolerance. In general, architectures placed near the bottom of the table have a higher degree of fault tolerance than those near the top. A 1oo2 (one out of two) system is able to withstand any one fault, as can 2oo3.

The second column describes the percentage coverage of any internal diagnostics. The higher the level of the diagnostics, the more faults will be trapped. In a protection system this is important because, provided the faulty component (e.g., an input card) is repaired within a reasonable time (often 8 hours), there is little loss in functional safety. (Note: this would not be the case for a continuous control system, because any fault is likely to cause an immediate unsafe condition and the potential for an incident.)

The third column shows the interval between proof tests. These are special tests that are required to be carried out to thoroughly exercise the protection system to ensure that there are no latent faults. Typically these are carried out by the equipment vendor during plant shutdown periods.

The fourth column shows the spurious trip rate. A spurious trip is one that causes the plant or equipment to shut down when there is no process deviation. The price for safety is often a higher spurious trip rate. A simple redundant protection system—1oo2—has, with all other design factors unchanged, a higher Safety Integrity Level but also a higher spurious trip rate than a single-channel (1oo1) system.

If one of the architectures in the table is not being used or if the designer wants to carry out a more fundamental analysis, then IEC 1508 allows this alternative. Reliability engineering techniques such as Markov modelling can then be used to calculate the hardware element of the Safety Integrity Level (Johnson 1989; Goble 1992).

Tolerance against systematic and common cause failures

This class of failure is very important in safety systems and is the limiting factor on the achievement of safety integrity. In a redundant system a component or subsystem, or even the whole system, is duplicated to achieve a high reliability from lower-reliability parts. Reliability improvement occurs because, statistically, the chance of two systems failing simultaneously by random faults will be the product of the reliabilities of the individual systems, and hence much lower. On the other hand, systematic and common cause faults cause redundant systems to fail coincidentally when, for example, a specification error in the software leads the duplicated parts to fail at the same time. Another example would be the failure of a common power supply to a redundant system.

IEC 1508 provides tables of engineering techniques ranked against the Safety Integrity Level considered effective in providing protection against systematic and common cause failures.

Examples of techniques providing defences against systematic failures are diversity and analytical redundancy. The basis of diversity is that if a designer implements a second channel in a redundant system using a different technology or software language, then faults in the redundant channels can be regarded as independent (i.e., a low probability of coincidental failure). However, particularly in the area of software-based systems, there is some suggestion that this technique may not be effective, as most mistakes are in the specification. Analytical redundancy attempts to exploit redundant information in the plant or machine to identify faults. For the other causes of systematic failure—for example, external stresses—the standard provides tables giving advice on good engineering practices (e.g., separation of signal and power cables) indexed against Safety Integrity Level.

Table 58.9 • Requirements for Safety Integrity Level 2— Programmable electronic system architectures for protection systems.

PE system configuration	Diagnostic coverage per channel	Off-line proof test Interval (TI)	Mean time to spurious trip
Single PE, Single I/O, Ext. WD	High	6 months	1.6 years
Dual PE, Single I/O	High	6 months	10 years
Dual PE, Dual I/O, 2oo2	High	3 months	1,281 years
Dual PE, Dual I/O, 1oo2	None	2 months	1.4 years
Dual PE, Dual I/O, 1oo2	Low	5 months	1.0 years
Dual PE, Dual I/O, 1oo2	Medium	18 months	0.8 years
Dual PE, Dual I/O, 1oo2	High	36 months	0.8 years
Dual PE, Dual I/O, 1oo2D	None	2 months	1.9 years
Dual PE, Dual I/O, 1oo2D	Low	4 months	4.7 years
Dual PE, Dual I/O, 1oo2D	Medium	18 months	18 years
Dual PE, Dual I/O, 1oo2D	High	48+ months	168 years
Triple PE, Triple I/O, IPC, 2oo3	None	1 month	20 years
Triple PE, Triple I/O, IPC, 2oo3	Low	3 months	25 years
Triple PE, Triple I/O, IPC, 2oo3	Medium	12 months	30 years
Triple PE, Triple I/O, IPC, 2oo3	High	48+ months	168 years

Conclusions

Computer-based systems offer many advantages—not only economic, but also the potential for improving safety. However, the attention to detail required to realize this potential is significantly greater than is the case using conventional system components. This article has outlined the main technical requirements that a designer needs to take into account to successfully exploit this technology.

● ROLLOVER

Bengt Springfeldt

Tractors and other mobile machinery in agricultural, forestry, construction and mining work, as well as materials handling, can give rise to serious hazards when the vehicles roll over sideways, tip over forwards or rear over backwards. The risks are heightened in the case of wheeled tractors with high centres of gravity. Other vehicles that present a hazard of rollover are crawler tractors, loaders, cranes, fruit-pickers, dozers, dumpers, scrapers and graders. These accidents usually happen too fast for drivers and passengers to get clear of the equipment, and they can become trapped under the vehicle. For example, tractors with high centres of gravity have considerable likelihood of rollover (and narrow tractors have even less stability than wide ones). A mercury engine cut-off switch to shut off power upon sensing lateral movement was introduced on tractors but was proven too slow to cope with the dynamic forces generated in the rollover movement (Springfeldt 1993). Therefore the safety device was abandoned.

The fact that such equipment often is used on sloping or uneven ground or on soft earth, and sometimes in close proximity to ditches, trenches or excavations, is an important contributing cause to rollover. If auxiliary equipment is attached high up on a tractor, the probability of rearing over backwards in climbing a slope (or tipping over forwards when descending) increases. Furthermore, a tractor can roll over because of the loss of control due to the pressure exerted by tractor-drawn equipment (e.g., when the carriage moves downwards on a slope and the attached equipment is not braked and over-runs the tractor). Special hazards arise when tractors are used as tow vehicles, particularly if the tow hook on the tractor is placed on a higher level than the wheel axle.

History

Notice of the rollover problem was taken on the national level in certain countries where many fatal rollovers occurred. In Sweden and New Zealand, development and testing of rollover protective structures (ROPS) on tractors (figure 58.98) already were in progress in the 1950s, but this work was followed up by regulations only on the part of the Swedish authorities; these regulations were effective from the year 1959 (Springfeldt 1993).

Proposed regulations prescribing ROPS for tractors were met by resistance in the agricultural sector in several countries. Strong opposition was mounted against plans requiring employers to install ROPS on existing tractors, and even against the proposal that only new tractors be equipped by the manufacturers with ROPS. Eventually many countries successfully mandated ROPS for new tractors, and later on some countries were able to require ROPS be retrofitted on old tractors as well. International standards concerning tractors and earth-moving machinery, including testing standards for ROPS, contributed to more reliable designs. Tractors were designed and manufactured with lower centres of gravity and lower-placed tow hooks. Four-wheel drive has reduced the risk of rollover. But the proportion of tractors with

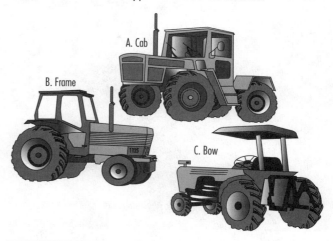

Figure 58.98 • Usual types of ROPS on tractors.

A. Cab

B. Frame

C. Bow

ROPS in countries with many old tractors and without mandates for retrofitting of ROPS is still rather low.

Investigations

Rollover accidents, particularly those involving tractors, have been studied by researchers in many countries. However, there are no centralized international statistics with respect to the number of accidents caused by the types of mobile machinery reviewed in this article. Available statistics at the national level nevertheless show that the number is high, especially in agriculture. According to a Scottish report of tractor rollover accidents in the period 1968–1976, 85% of the tractors involved had equipment attached at the time of the accident, and of these, half had trailed equipment and half had mounted equipment. Two-thirds of the tractor rollover accidents in the Scottish report occurred on slopes (Springfeldt 1993). It was later proved that the number of accidents would be reduced after the introduction of training for driving on slopes as well as the application of an instrument for measuring slope steepness combined with an indicator of safe slope limits.

In other investigations, New Zealand researchers observed that half of their fatal rollover accidents occurred on flat ground or on slight slopes, and only one-tenth occurred on steep slopes. On flat ground tractor drivers may be less attentive to rollover hazards, and they can misjudge the risk posed by ditches and uneven ground. Of the rollover fatalities in tractors in New Zealand in the period 1949–1980, 80% occurred in wheel tractors, and 20% with crawler tractors (Springfeldt 1993). Studies in Sweden and New Zealand showed that about 80% of the tractor rollover fatalities occurred when tractors rolled over sideways. Half of the tractors involved in the New Zealand fatalities had rolled 180°.

Studies of the correlation between rollover fatalities in West Germany and the model year of farm tractors (Springfeldt 1993) showed that 1 of 10,000 old, unprotected tractors manufactured before 1957 was involved in a rollover fatality. Of tractors with prescribed ROPS, manufactured in 1970 and later, 1 of 25,000 tractors was involved in a rollover fatality. Of fatal tractor rollovers in West Germany in the period 1980–1985, two-thirds of the victims were thrown from their protected area and then run over or hit by the tractor (Springfeldt 1993). Of nonfatal rollovers, one-quarter of the drivers were thrown from the driver's seat but not run over. It is evident that the fatality risk increases if the driver is thrown out of the protected area (similar to automobile accidents). Most of the tractors involved had a two-pillar bow

Figure 58.99 • Injuries by rollovers per 100,000 tractors in Sweden between 1957 and 1990.

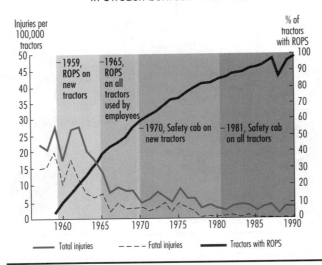

(figure 58.98 C) that does not prevent the driver from being thrown out. In a few cases the ROPS had been subject to breakage or strong deformation.

The relative frequencies of injuries per 100,000 tractors in different periods in some countries and the reduction of the fatality rate was calculated by Springfeldt (1993). The effectiveness of ROPS in diminishing injury in tractor rollover accidents has been proven in Sweden, where the number of fatalities per 100,000 tractors was reduced from approximately 17 to 0.3 over the period of three decades (1960–1990) (figure 58.99). At the end of the period it was estimated that about 98% of the tractors were fitted with ROPS, mainly in the form of a crushproof cab (figure 58.98 A). In Norway, fatalities were reduced from about 24 to 4 per 100,000 tractors during a similar period. However, worse results were achieved in Finland and New Zealand.

Prevention of Injuries by Rollovers

The risk of rollover is greatest in the case of tractors; however, in agricultural and forest work there is little that can be done to prevent tractors from rolling over. By mounting ROPS on tractors and those types of earth-moving machinery with potential rollover hazards, the risk of personal injuries can be reduced, provided that the drivers remain on their seats during rollover events (Springfeldt 1993). The frequency of rollover fatalities depends largely on the proportion of protected machines in use and the types of ROPS used. A bow (figure 58.98 C) gives much less protection than a cab or a frame (Springfeldt 1993). The most effective structure is a crushproof cab, which allows the driver to stay inside, protected, during a rollover. (Another reason for choosing a cab is that it affords weather protection.) The most effective means of keeping the driver within the protection of the ROPS during a rollover is a seat-belt, provided that the driver uses the belt while operating the equipment. In some countries, there are information plates at the driver's seat advising that the steering wheel be gripped in a rollover event. An additional safety measure is to design the driver's cab or interior environment and the ROPS so as to prevent exposure to hazards such as sharp edges or protuberances.

In all countries, rollovers of mobile machinery, mainly tractors, are causing serious injures. There are, however, considerable differences among countries concerning technical specifications re-

lating to machinery design, as well as administrative procedures for examinations, testing, inspections and marketing. The international diversity that characterizes safety efforts in this connection may be explained by considerations such as the following:

- whether there exist mandatory requirements for ROPS (in the form of regulations or legislation), or recommendations only, or no rules at all
- the need for rules for new machinery and rules applicable to older equipment
- the availability of inspection carried out by authorities and the existence of social pressure and cultural climate favourable to observance of safety rules; in many countries, the obedience to safety guidelines is not checked by inspection in agricultural work
- pressure from trade unions; however, it should be borne in mind that workers' organizations have less influence on working conditions in agriculture than in other sectors, because there are many family farms in agriculture
- the type of ROPS used in the country
- information and understanding of the risks to which tractor drivers are exposed; practical problems often stand in the way of reaching farmers and forest workers for the purposes of information and education
- the geography of the country, especially where agricultural, forestry and road work is carried out.

Safety Regulations

The nature of rules governing requirements for ROPS and the degree of implementation of the rules in a country, has a strong influence on rollover accidents, especially fatal ones. With this in mind, the development of safer machinery has been abetted by directives, codes and standards issued by international and national organizations. Additionally, many countries have adopted rigorous prescriptions for ROPS which have resulted in a great reduction of rollover injuries.

European Economic Community

Beginning in 1974 the European Economic Community (EEC) issued directives concerning type-approval of wheeled agricultural and forestry tractors, and in 1977 issued further, special directives concerning ROPS, including their attachment to tractors (Springfeldt 1993; EEC 1974, 1977, 1979, 1982, 1987). The directives prescribe a procedure for type-approval and certification by manufacture of tractors, and ROPS must be reviewed by an EEC Type Approval Examination. The directives have won acceptance by all the member countries.

Some EEC directives concerning ROPS on tractors were repealed as of 31 December 1995 and replaced by the general machinery directive which applies to those sorts of machinery presenting hazards due to their mobility (EEC 1991). Wheeled tractors, as well as some earth-moving machinery with a capacity exceeding 15 kW (namely crawlers and wheel loaders, backhoe loaders, crawler tractors, scrapers, graders and articulated dumpers) must be fitted with a ROPS. In case of a rollover, the ROPS must offer the driver and operators an adequate deflection-limiting volume (i.e., space allowing movement of occupants' bodies before contacting interior elements during an accident). It is the responsibility of the manufacturers or their authorized representatives to perform appropriate tests.

Organization for Economic Cooperation and Development

In 1973 and 1987 the Organization for Economic Cooperation and Development (OECD) approved standard codes for testing of tractors (Springfeldt 1993; OECD 1987). They give results of tests of tractors and describe the testing equipment and test conditions.

The codes require testing of many machinery parts and functions, for instance the strength of ROPS. The OECD Tractor Codes describe a static and a dynamic method of testing ROPS on certain types of tractors. A ROPS may be designed solely to protect the driver in the event of tractor rollover. It must be retested for each model of tractor to which the ROPS is to be fitted. The Codes also require that it be possible to mount a weather protection for the driver onto the structure, of a more or less temporary nature. The Tractor Codes have been accepted by all OECD member bodies from 1988, but in practice the United States and Japan also accept ROPS that do not comply with the code requirements if safety belts are provided (Springfeldt 1993).

International Labour Organization

In 1965, the International Labour Organization (ILO) in its manual, *Safety and Health in Agricultural Work*, required that a cab or a frame of sufficient strength be adequately fixed to tractors in order to provide satisfactory protection for the driver and passengers inside the cab in case of tractor rollover (Springfeldt 1993; ILO 1965). According to ILO Codes of Practice, agricultural and forestry tractors should be provided with ROPS to protect the operator and any passenger in case of rollover, falling objects or displaced loads (ILO 1976).

The fitting of ROPS should not adversely affect

- access between the ground and driver's position
- access to the tractor's main controls
- the manoeuvrability of the tractor in cramped surroundings
- the attachment or use of any equipment that may be connected to the tractor
- the control and adjustment of associated equipment.

International and national standards

In 1981 the International Organization for Standardization (ISO) issued a standard for tractors and machinery for agriculture and forestry (ISO 1981). The standard describes a static test method for ROPS and sets forth acceptance conditions. The standard has been approved by the member bodies in 22 countries; however, Canada and the United States have expressed disapproval of the document on technical grounds. A Standard and Recommended Practice issued in 1974 by the Society of Automotive Engineers (SAE) in North America contains performance requirements for ROPS on wheeled agricultural tractors and industrial tractors used in construction, rubber-tired scrapers, front-end loaders, dozers, crawler loaders, and motor graders (SAE 1974 and 1975). The contents of the standard have been adopted as regulations in the United States and in the Canadian provinces of Alberta and British Columbia.

Rules and Compliance

OECD Codes and International Standards concern the design and construction of ROPS as well as the control of their strength, but lack the authority to require that this sort of protection be put into practice (OECD 1987; ISO 1981). The European Economic Community also proposed that tractors and earth-moving machinery be equipped with protection (EEC 1974-1987). The aim of the EEC directives is to achieve uniformity among national entities concerning the safety of new machinery at the manufacturing stage. The member countries are obliged to follow the directives and issue corresponding prescriptions. Starting in 1996, the member countries of the EEC intend to issue regulations requiring that new tractors and earth-moving machinery be fitted with ROPS.

In 1959, Sweden became the first country to require ROPS for new tractors (Springfeldt 1993). Corresponding requirements came into effect in Denmark and Finland ten years later. Later on, in the 1970s and 1980s, mandatory requirements for ROPS on new tractors became effective in Great Britain, West Germany, New Zealand, the United States, Spain, Norway, Switzerland and other countries. In all these countries except the United States, the rules were extended to old tractors some years later, but these rules were not always mandatory. In Sweden, all tractors must be equipped with a protective cab, a rule that in Great Britain applies only to all tractors used by agricultural workers (Springfeldt 1993). In Denmark, Norway and Finland, all tractors must be provided with at least a frame, while in the United States and the Australian states, bows are accepted. In the United States tractors must have seat-belts.

In the United States, materials-handling machinery that was manufactured before 1972 and is used in construction work must be equipped with ROPS which meet minimum performance standards (US Bureau of National Affairs 1975). The machines covered by the requirement include some scrapers, front-end loaders, dozers, crawler tractors, loaders, and motor graders. Retrofitting was carried out of ROPS on machines manufactured about three years earlier.

Summary

In countries with mandatory requirements for ROPS for new tractors and retrofitting of ROPS on old tractors, there has been a decrease of rollover injuries, especially fatal ones. It is evident that a crushproof cab is the most effective type of ROPS. A bow gives poor protection in case of rollover. Many countries have prescribed effective ROPS at least on new tractors and as of 1996 on earth-moving machines. In spite of this fact some authorities seem to accept types of ROPS that do not comply with such requirements as have been promulgated by the OECD and the ISO. It is expected that a more general harmonization of the rules governing ROPS will be accomplished gradually all over the world, including the developing countries.

FALLS FROM ELEVATIONS

Jean Arteau

Falls from elevations are severe accidents that occur in many industries and occupations. Falls from elevations result in injuries which are produced by contact between the falling person and the source of injury, under the following circumstances:

- The motion of the person and the force of impact are generated by gravity.
- The point of contact with the source of injury is lower than the surface supporting the person at the start of the fall.

From this definition, it may be surmised that falls are unavoidable because gravity is always present. Falls are accidents, somehow predictable, occurring in all industrial sectors and occupations and having a high severity. Strategies to reduce the number of falls, or at least reduce the severity of the injuries if falls occur, are discussed in this article.

The Height of the Fall

The severity of injuries caused by falls is intrinsically related to the height of fall. But this is only partly true: the free-fall energy is the product of the falling mass times the height of the fall, and the severity of the injuries is directly proportional to the energy transferred during the impact. Statistics of fall accidents confirm this strong relationship, but show also that falls from a height of less than 3 m can be fatal. A detailed study of fatal falls in construction shows that 10% of the fatalities caused by falls occurred from

Figure 58.100 • Fatalities caused by falls and the height of fall in the US construction industry, 1985–1993.

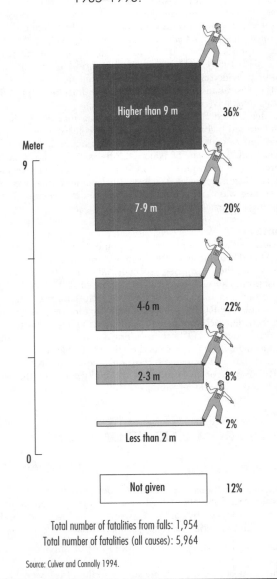

Total number of fatalities from falls: 1,954
Total number of fatalities (all causes): 5,964

Source: Culver and Connolly 1994.

Where Falls Occur

Falls from elevations are frequently associated with the construction industry because they account for a high percentage of all fatalities. For example, in the United States, 33% of all fatalities in construction are caused by falls from elevations; in the UK, the figure is 52%. Falls from elevations also occur in other industrial sectors. Mining and the manufacturing of transportation equipment have a high rate of falls from elevations. In Quebec, where many mines are steep, narrow-vein, underground mines, 20% of all accidents are falls from elevations. The manufacture, use and maintenance of transportation equipment such as airplanes, trucks and railroad cars are activities with a high rate of fall accidents (table 58.10). The ratio will vary from country to country depending on the level of industrialization, the climate, and so on; but falls from elevations do occur in all sectors with similar consequences.

Having taken into consideration the height of fall, the next important issue is how the fall is arrested. Falling into hot liquids, electrified rails or into a rock crusher could be fatal even if the height of fall is less than 3 m.

Causes of Falls

So far it has been shown that falls occur in all economic sectors, even if the height is less than 3 m. But why *do* humans fall? There are many human factors which can be involved in falling. A broad grouping of factors is both conceptually simple and useful in practice:

Opportunities to fall are determined by environmental factors and result in the most common type of fall, namely the tripping or slipping that result in falls from grade level. Other falling opportunities are related to activities above grade.

Liabilities to fall are one or more of the many acute and chronic diseases. The specific diseases associated with falling usually affect the nervous system, the circulatory system, the musculoskeletal system or a combination of these systems.

Tendencies to fall arise from the universal, intrinsic deteriorative changes that characterize normal ageing or senescence. In falling, the ability to maintain upright posture or postural stability is the function that fails as a result of combined tendencies, liabilities and opportunities.

Postural Stability

Falls are caused by the failure of postural stability to maintain a person in an upright position. Postural stability is a system consisting of many rapid adjustments to external, perturbing forces, especially gravity. These adjustments are largely reflex actions, subserved by a large number of reflex arcs, each with its sensory input, internal integrative connections, and motor output. Sensory inputs are: vision, the inner ear mechanisms that detect position in space, the somatosensory apparatus that detects pressure stimuli on the skin, and the position of the weight-bearing joints. It appears that visual perception plays a particularly important role. Very little is known about the normal, integrative structures and functions of the spinal cord or the brain. The motor output component of the reflex arc is muscular reaction.

a height less than 3 m (see figure 58.100). Two questions are to be discussed: the 3-m legal limit, and where and how a given fall was arrested.

In many countries, regulations make fall protection mandatory when the worker is exposed to a fall of more than 3 m. The simplistic interpretation is that falls of less than 3 m are not dangerous. The 3-m limit is in fact the result of a social, political and practical consensus which says it is not mandatory to be protected against falls while working at the height of a single floor. Even if the 3-m legal limit for mandatory fall protection exists, fall protection should always be considered. The height of fall is not the sole factor explaining the severity of fall accidents and the fatalities due to falls; where and how the person falling came to rest must also be considered. This leads to analysis of the industrial sectors with higher incidence of falls from elevations.

Table 58.10 • Falls from elevations: Quebec 1982–1987.

	Falls from elevations per 1,000 workers	Falls from elevations in all accidents
Construction	14.9	10.1%
Heavy industry	7.1	3.6%

Vision

The most important sensory input is vision. Two visual functions are related to postural stability and control of gait:

- the perception of what is vertical and what is horizontal is basic to spatial orientation
- the ability to detect and discriminate objects in cluttered environments.

Two other visual functions are important:

- the ability to stabilize the direction in which the eyes are pointed so as to stabilize the surrounding world while we are moving and immobilize a visual reference point
- the ability to fixate and pursue definite objects within the large field ("keep an eye on"); this function requires considerable attention and results in deterioration in the performance of any other simultaneous, attention-demanding tasks.

Causes of postural instability

The three sensory inputs are interactive and interrelated. The absence of one input—and/or the existence of false inputs—results in postural instability and even in falls. What could cause instability?

Vision

- the absence of vertical and horizontal references—for example, the connector at the top of a building
- the absence of stable visual references—for example, moving water under a bridge and moving clouds are not stable references
- the fixing a definite object for work purposes, which diminishes other visual functions, such as the ability to detect and discriminate objects that can cause tripping in a cluttered environment
- a moving object in a moving background or reference—for example, a structural steel component moved by a crane, with moving clouds as background and visual reference.

Inner ear

- having the person's head upside down while the level equilibrium system is at its optimum performance horizontally
- travelling in pressurized aircraft
- very fast movement, as, for example, in a roller-coaster
- diseases.

Somatosensory apparatus (pressure stimuli on the skin and position of weight-bearing joints)

- standing on one foot

- numbed limbs from staying in a fixed position for a long period of time—for example, kneeling down
- stiff boots
- very cold limbs.

Motor output

- numbed limbs
- tired muscles
- diseases, injuries
- ageing, permanent or temporary disabilities
- bulky clothing.

Postural stability and gait control are very complex reflexes of the human being. Any perturbations of the inputs may cause falls. All perturbations described in this section are common in the workplace. Therefore, falling is somehow natural and prevention must therefore prevail.

Strategy for Fall Protection

As previously noted, the risks of falls are identifiable. Therefore, falls are preventable. Figure 58.101 shows a very common situation where a gauge must be read. The first illustration shows a traditional situation: a manometer is installed at the top of a tank without means of access In the second, the worker improvises a means of access by climbing on several boxes: a hazardous situation. In the third, the worker uses a ladder; this is an improvement. However, the ladder is not permanently fixed to the tank; it is therefore probable that the ladder may be in use elsewhere in the plant when a reading is required. A situation such as this is possible, with fall arrest equipment added to the ladder or the tank and with the worker wearing a full body harness and using a lanyard attached to an anchor. The fall-from-elevation hazard still exists.

In the fourth illustration, an improved means of access is provided using a stairway, a platform and guardrails; the benefits are a reduction in the risk of falling and an increase in the ease of reading (comfort), thus reducing the duration of each reading and providing a stable work posture allowing for a more precise reading.

The correct solution is illustrated in the last illustration. During the design stage of the facilities, maintenance and operation activities were recognized. The gauge was installed so that it could be read at ground level. No falls from elevations are possible: therefore, the hazard is eliminated.

This strategy puts the emphasis on the prevention of falls by using the proper means of access (e.g., scaffolds, ladders,

Figure 58.101 • Installations for reading a gauge.

Figure 58.102 • Fall prevention strategy.

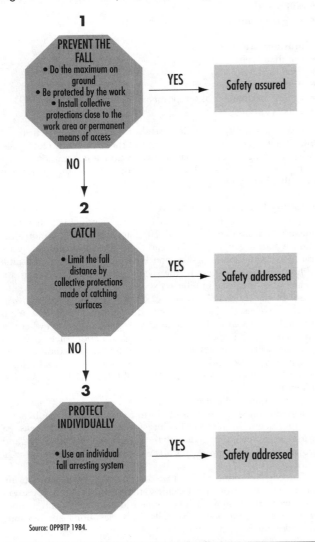

Source: OPPBTP 1984.

Table 58.11 • Typical fall prevention and fall arrest systems.

	Fall prevention systems	Fall arrest systems
Collective protection	Guardrails Railings	Safety net
Individual protection	Travel restricting system (TRS)	Harness, lanyard, energy absorber, anchorage, etc.

Table 58.12 • Differences between fall prevention and fall arrest.

	Prevention	Arrest
Fall occurrence	No	Yes
Typical equipment	Guardrails	Harness, lanyard, energy absorber and anchorage (fall arrest system)
Design load (force)	1 to 1.5 kN applied horizontally and 0.45 kN applied vertically—both at any point on the upper rail	Minimum breaking strength of the anchorage point 18 to 22 kN
Loading	Static	Dynamic

fall does not occur, so the risk of injury does not exist. With fall arrest, the fall does occur and even if arrested, a residual risk of injury exists.

CONFINED SPACES

Neil McManus

Confined spaces are ubiquitous throughout industry as recurring sites of both fatal and nonfatal accidents. The term *confined space* traditionally has been used to label particular structures, such as tanks, vessels, pits, sewers, hoppers and so on. However, a definition based on description in this manner is overly restrictive and defies ready extrapolation to structures in which accidents have occurred. Potentially any structure in which people work could be or could become a confined space. Confined spaces can be very large or they can be very small. What the term actually describes is an environment in which a broad range of hazardous conditions can occur. These condition include personal confinement, as well as structural, process, mechanical, bulk or liquid material, atmospheric, physical, chemical, biological, safety and ergonomic hazards. Many of the conditions produced by these hazards are not unique to confined spaces but are exacerbated by involvement of the boundary surfaces of the confined space.

Confined spaces are considerably more hazardous than normal workspaces. Seemingly minor alterations in conditions can immediately change the status of these workspaces from innocuous to life-threatening. These conditions may be transient and subtle, and therefore are difficult to recognize and to address. Work involving confined spaces generally occurs during construction, inspection, maintenance, modification and rehabilitation. This work is nonroutine, short in duration, nonrepetitive and unpredictable (often occurring during off-shift hours or when the unit is out of service).

stairways) (Bouchard 1991). If the fall cannot be prevented, fall arrest systems must be used (figure 58.102). To be effective, fall arrest systems must be planned. The anchorage point is a key factor and must be pre-engineered. Fall arrest systems must be efficient, reliable and comfortable; two examples are given in Arteau, Lan and Corbeil (to be published) and Lan, Arteau and Corbeil (to be published). Examples of typical fall prevention and fall arrest systems are given in table 58.11. Fall arrest systems and components are detailed in Sulowski 1991.

The emphasis on prevention is not an ideological choice, but rather a practical choice. Table 58.12 shows the differences between fall prevention and fall arrest, the traditional PPE solution.

For the employer and the designer, it is easier to build fall prevention systems because their minimum breaking strength requirements are 10 to 20 times less than those of fall arrest systems. For example, the minimum breaking strength requirement of a guard rail is around 1 kN, the weight of a large man, and the minimum breaking strength requirement of the anchorage point of an individual fall arrest system could be 20 kN, the weight of two small cars or 1 cubic metre of concrete. With prevention, the

Confined Space Accidents

Accidents involving confined spaces differ from accidents that occur in normal workspaces. A seemingly minor error or oversight in preparation of the space, selection or maintenance of equipment or work activity can precipitate an accident. This is because the tolerance for error in these situations is smaller than for normal workplace activity.

The occupations of victims of confined space accidents span the occupational spectrum. While most are workers, as might be expected, victims also include engineering and technical people, supervisors and managers, and emergency response personnel. Safety and industrial hygiene personnel also have been involved in confined space accidents. The only data on accidents in confined spaces are available from the United States, and these cover only fatal accidents (NIOSH 1994). Worldwide, these accidents claim about 200 victims per year in industry, agriculture and the home (Reese and Mills 1986). This is at best a guess based on incomplete data, but it appears to be applicable today. About two-thirds of the accidents resulted from hazardous atmospheric conditions in the confined space. In about 70% of these the hazardous condition existed prior to entry and the start of work. Sometimes these accidents cause multiple fatalities, some of which are the result of the original incident and a subsequent attempt at rescue. The highly stressful conditions under which the rescue attempt occurs often subject the would-be rescuers to considerably greater risk than the initial victim.

The causes and outcomes of accidents involving work external to structures that confine hazardous atmospheres are similar to those occurring inside confined spaces. Explosion or fire involving a confined atmosphere caused about half of the fatal welding and cutting accidents in the United States. About 16% of these accidents involved "empty" 205 l (45 gal UK, 55 gal US) drums or containers (OSHA 1988).

Identification of Confined Spaces

A review of fatal accidents in confined spaces indicates that the best defences against unnecessary encounters are an informed and trained workforce and a programme for hazard recognition and management. Development of skills to enable supervisors and workers to recognize potentially hazardous conditions is also essential. One contributor to this programme is an accurate, up-to-date inventory of confined spaces. This includes type of space, location, characteristics, contents, hazardous conditions and so on. Confined spaces in many circumstances defy being inventoried because their number and type are constantly changing. On the other hand, confined spaces in process operations are readily identifiable, yet remain closed and inaccessible almost all of the time. Under certain conditions, a space may be considered a confined space one day and would not be considered a confined space the next.

A benefit from identifying confined spaces is the opportunity to label them. A label can enable workers to relate the term *confined space* to equipment and structures at their work location. The downside to the labelling process includes: (1) the label could disappear into a landscape filled with other warning labels; (2) organizations that have many confined spaces could experience great difficulty in labelling them; (3) labelling would produce little benefit in circumstances where the population of confined spaces is dynamic; and (4) reliance on labels for identification causes dependence. Confined spaces could be overlooked.

Hazard Assessment

The most complex and difficult aspect in the confined space process is hazard assessment. Hazard assessment identifies both hazardous and potentially hazardous conditions and assesses the level and acceptability of risk. The difficulty with hazard assess-

Table 58.13 • Sample form for assessment of hazardous conditions.

Hazardous condition	Real or potential consequence		
	Low	Moderate	High
Hot work			
Atmospheric hazards			
oxygen deficiency			
oxygen enrichment			
chemical			
biological			
fire/explosion			
Ingestion/skin contact			
Physical agents			
noise/vibration			
heat/cold stress			
non/ionizing radiation			
laser			
Personal confinement			
Mechanical hazard			
Process hazard			
Safety hazards			
structural			
engulfment/immersion			
entanglement			
electrical			
fall			
slip/trip			
visibility/light level			
explosive/implosive			
hot/cold surfaces			

NA = not applicable.
The meanings of certain terms such as *toxic substance, oxygen deficiency, oxygen enrichment, mechanical hazard*, and so on, require further specification according to standards that exist in a particular jurisdiction.

ment occurs because many of the hazardous conditions can produce acute or traumatic injury, are difficult to recognize and assess, and often change with changing conditions. Hazard elimination or mitigation during preparation of the space for entry, therefore, is essential for minimizing the risk during work.

Hazard assessment can provide a qualitative estimate of the level of concern attached to a particular situation at a particular moment (table 58.13). The breadth of concern within each

Table 58.14 • A sample entry permit.

ABC COMPANY
CONFINED SPACE — ENTRY PERMIT

1. DESCRIPTIVE INFORMATION

Department:	
Location:	
Building/Shop:	
Equipment/Space:	
Part:	
Date:	Assessor:
Duration:	Qualification:

2. ADJACENT SPACES

Space:

Description:

Contents:

Process:

3. PRE-WORK CONDITIONS

Atmospheric Hazards

Oxygen Deficiency	❑Yes	❑No	❑Controlled
Concentration:	(Acceptable minimum:		%)
Oxygen Enrichment	❑Yes	❑No	❑Controlled
Concentration:	(Acceptable maximum:		%)
Chemical	❑Yes	❑No	❑Controlled
Substance Concentration	(Acceptable standard:		)
Biological	❑Yes	❑No	❑Controlled
Substance Concentration	(Acceptable standard:		)
Fire/Explosion	❑Yes	❑No	❑Controlled
Substance Concentration	(Acceptable maximum:		% LFL)
Ingestion/Skin Contact Hazard	❑Yes	❑No	❑Controlled

Physical Agents

Noise/Vibration	❑Yes	❑No	❑Controlled
Level:	(Acceptable maximum:		dBA)
Heat/Cold Stress	❑Yes	❑No	❑Controlled
Temperature:	(Acceptable range:		)
Non/Ionizing Radiation	❑Yes	❑No	❑Controlled
Type Level	(Acceptable maximum:		)
Laser	❑Yes	❑No	❑Controlled
Type Level	(Acceptable maximum:		)
Personal Confinement (Refer to corrective action.)	❑Yes	❑No	❑Controlled
Mechanical Hazard (Refer to procedure.)	❑Yes	❑No	❑Controlled
Process Hazard (Refer to procedure.)	❑Yes	❑No	❑Controlled

Continues on next page.

Table 58.14 • A sample entry permit.
Continued.

ABC COMPANY			
CONFINED SPACE — ENTRY PERMIT			
Safety Hazards			
Structural Hazard (Refer to corrective action.)	❑Yes	❑No	❑Controlled
Engulfment/Immersion (Refer to corrective action.)	❑Yes	❑No	❑Controlled
Entanglement (Refer to corrective action.)	❑Yes	❑No	❑Controlled
Electrical (Refer to procedure.)	❑Yes	❑No	❑Controlled
Fall (Refer to corrective action.)	❑Yes	❑No	❑Controlled
Slip/Trip (Refer to corrective action.)	❑Yes	❑No	❑Controlled
Visibility/light level	❑Yes	❑No	❑Controlled
Level:	(Acceptable range:		lux)
Explosive/Implosive (Refer to corrective action.)	❑Yes	❑No	❑Controlled
Hot/Cold Surfaces (Refer to corrective action.)	❑Yes	❑No	❑Controlled

For entries in highlighted boxes, Yes or Controlled, provide additional detail and refer to protective measures. For hazards for which tests can be made, refer to testing requirements. Provide date of most recent calibration. Acceptable maximum, minimum, range or standard depends on the jurisdiction.

4. Work Procedure			
Description:			
Hot Work (Refer to protective measures.)	❑Yes	❑No	❑Possible
Atmospheric Hazard			
Oxygen Deficiency (Refer to requirement for additional testing. Record results. Refer to requirement for protective measures.)	❑Yes	❑No	❑Possible
Concentration:	(Acceptable minimum:		%)
Oxygen Enrichment (Refer to requirement for additional testing. Record results. Refer to requirement for protective measures.)	❑Yes	❑No	❑Possible
Concentration:	(Acceptable maximum:		%)
Chemical (Refer to requirement for additional testing. Record results. Refer to requirement for protective measures.)	❑Yes	❑No	❑Possible
Substance Concentration	(Acceptable standard:		)
Biological (Refer to requirement for additional testing. Record results. Refer to requirement for protective measures.)	❑Yes	❑No	❑Possible
Substance Concentration	(Acceptable standard:		)
Fire/Explosion (Refer to requirement for additional testing. Record results. Refer to requirement for protective measures.)	❑Yes	❑No	❑Possible
Substance Concentration	(Acceptable standard:		)
Ingestion/Skin Contact Hazard (Refer to requirement for protective measures.)	❑Yes	❑No	❑Possible
Physical Agents			
Noise/Vibration (Refer to requirement for protective measures. Refer to requirement for additional testing. Record results.)	❑Yes	❑No	❑Possible
Level:	(Acceptable maximum:		dBA)
Heat/Cold Stress (Refer to requirement for protective measures. Refer to requirement for additional testing. Record results.)	❑Yes	❑No	❑Possible
Temperature:	(Acceptable range:		)
Non/Ionizing Radiation (Refer to requirement for protective measures. Refer to requirement for additional testing. Record results.)	❑Yes	❑No	❑Possible
Type Level	(Acceptable maximum:		)
Laser (Refer to requirement for protective measures.)	❑Yes	❑No	❑Possible

Continues on next page.

Table 58.14 • A sample entry permit.
Continued.

ABC COMPANY			
CONFINED SPACE—ENTRY PERMIT			
Mechanical Hazard (Refer to requirement for protective measures.)	❏Yes	❏No	❏Possible
Process Hazard (Refer to requirement for protective measures.)	❏Yes	❏No	❏Possible
Safety Hazards			
Structural Hazard (Refer to requirement for protective measures.)	❏Yes	❏No	❏Possible
Engulfment/Immersion (Refer to requirement for protective measures.)	❏Yes	❏No	❏Possible
Entanglement (Refer to requirement for protective measures.)	❏Yes	❏No	❏Possible
Electrical (Refer to requirement for protective measures.)	❏Yes	❏No	❏Possible
Fall (Refer to requirement for protective measures.)	❏Yes	❏No	❏Possible
Slip/Trip (Refer to requirement for protective measures.)	❏Yes	❏No	❏Possible
Visibility/light level (Refer to requirement for protective measures.)	❏Yes	❏No	❏Possible
Explosive/Implosive (Refer to requirement for protective measures.)	❏Yes	❏No	❏Possible
Hot/Cold Surfaces (Refer to requirement for protective measures.)	❏Yes	❏No	❏Possible
For entries in highlighted boxes, Yes or Possible, provide additional detail and refer to protective measures. For hazards for which tests can be made, refer to testing requirements. Provide date of most recent calibration.			
Protective Measures			
Personal protective equipment (specify)			
Communications equipment and procedure (specify)			
Alarm systems (specify)			
Rescue Equipment (specify)			
Ventilation (specify)			
Lighting (specify)			
Other (specify)			
Testing Requirements			
Specify testing requirements and frequency			
Personnel			
Entry Supervisor			
Originating Supervisor			
Authorized Entrants			
Testing Personnel			
Attendants			

category ranges from minimal to some maximum. Comparison between categories is not appropriate, since the maximum level of concern can differ considerably.

Each entry in table 58.13 can be expanded to provide detail about hazardous conditions where concern exists. Detail also can be provided to eliminate categories from further consideration where concern is non-existent.

Fundamental to the success of hazard recognition and assessment is the *Qualified Person*. The Qualified Person is deemed capable by experience, education and/or specialized training, of anticipating, recognizing and evaluating exposures to hazardous substances or other unsafe conditions and specifying control measures and/or protective actions. That is, the Qualified Person is expected to know what is required in the context of a particular situation involving work within a confined space.

A hazard assessment should be performed for each of the following segments in the operating cycle of the confined space (as appropriate): the undisturbed space, pre-entry preparation, pre-work inspection work activities (McManus, manuscript) and emergency response. Fatal accidents have occurred during each of these segments. The undisturbed space refers to the status quo established between closure following one entry and the start of preparation for the next. Pre-entry preparations are actions taken to render the space safe for entry and work. Pre-work inspection is the initial entry and examination of the space to ensure that it is safe for the start of work. (This practice is required in some jurisdictions.) Work activities are the individual tasks to be performed by entrants. Emergency response is the activity in the event rescue of workers is required, or other emergency occurs. Hazards that remain at the start of work activity or are generated by it dictate the nature of possible accidents for which emergency preparedness and response are required.

Performing the hazard assessment for each segment is essential because the focus changes continuously. For example, the level of concern about a specific condition could disappear following pre-entry preparation; however, the condition could reappear or a new one could develop as a result of an activity which occurs either inside or outside the confined space. For this reason, assessing a level of concern to a hazardous condition for all time based only on an appraisal of pre-opening or even opening conditions would be inappropriate.

Instrumental and other monitoring methods are used for determining the status of some of the physical, chemical and biological agents present in and around the confined space. Monitoring could be required prior to entry, during entry or during work activity. Lockout/tagout and other procedural techniques are used to deactivate energy sources. Isolation using blanks, plugs and caps, and double block and bleed or other valve configurations prevents entry of substances through piping. Ventilation, using fans and eductors, is often necessary to provide a safe environment for working both with and without approved respiratory protection. Assessment and control of other conditions relies on the judgement of the Qualified Person.

The last part of the process is the critical one. The Qualified Person must decide whether the risks associated with entry and work are acceptable. Safety can best be assured through control. If hazardous and potentially hazardous conditions can be controlled, the decision is not difficult to make. The less the level of perceived control, the greater the need for contingencies. The only other alternative is to prohibit the entry.

Entry Control

The traditional methods for managing on-site confined space activity are the entry permit and the on-site Qualified Person. Clear lines of authority, responsibility and accountability between the Qualified Person and entrants, standby personnel, emergency responders and on-site management are required under either system.

The function of an entry document is to inform and to document. Table 58.14 (above) provides a formal basis for performing the hazard assessment and documenting the results. When edited to include only information relevant to a particular circumstance, this becomes the basis for the entry permit or entry certificate. The entry permit is most effective as a summary that documents actions performed and indicates by exception, the need for further precautionary measures. The entry permit should be issued by a Qualified Person who also has the authority to cancel the permit should conditions change. The issuer of the permit should be independent of the supervisory hierarchy in order to avoid potential pressure to speed the performance of work. The permit specifies procedures to be followed as well as conditions under which entry and work can proceed, and records test results and other information. The signed permit is posted at the entry or portal to the space or as specified by the company or regulatory authority. It remains posted until it is either cancelled, replaced by a new permit or the work is completed. The entry permit becomes a record upon completion of the work and must be retained for recordkeeping according to requirements of the regulatory authority.

The permit system works best where hazardous conditions are known from previous experience and control measures have been tried and proven effective. The permit system enables expert resources to be apportioned in an efficient manner. The limitations of the permit arise where previously unrecognized hazards are present. If the Qualified Person is not readily available, these can remain unaddressed.

The entry certificate provides an alternative mechanism for entry control. This requires an onsite Qualified Person who provides hands-on expertise in the recognition, assessment and evaluation, and control of hazards. An added advantage is the ability to respond to concerns on short notice and to address unanticipated hazards. Some jurisdictions require the Qualified Person to perform a personal visual inspection of the space prior to the start of work. Following evaluation of the space and implementation of control measures, the Qualified Person issues a certificate describing the status of the space and conditions under which the work can proceed (NFPA 1993). This approach is ideally suited to operations that have numerous confined spaces or where conditions or the configuration of spaces can undergo rapid change.

PRINCIPLES OF PREVENTION: MATERIALS HANDLING AND INTERNAL TRAFFIC

Kari Häkkinen

Materials handling and internal traffic are contributing factors in a major portion of accidents in many industries. Depending on the type of industry, the share of work accidents attributed to materials handling varies from 20 to 50%. The control of materials-handling risks is the foremost safety problem in dock work, the construction industry, warehousing, sawmills, shipbuilding and other similar heavy industries. In many process-type industries, such as the chemical products industry, the pulp and paper industry and the steel and foundry industries, many accidents still tend to occur during the handling of final products either manually or by fork-lift trucks and cranes.

This high accident potential in materials-handling activities is due to at least three basic characteristics:

- High amounts of potential and kinetic energies, which have the propensity for causing injury and damage, are found in transport and handling.
- The number of people required at transport and handling workplaces is still relatively high, and they are often exposed to the risks associated with such sites.
- Whenever several dynamic operations have to be carried out simultaneously and require cooperation in varying environments, there is an especially urgent need of clear and timely communication and information. The consequently high liability of many types of human errors and omissions may create hazardous situations.

Materials-Handling Accidents

Every time people or machines move loads, an accident risk is present. The magnitude of risk is determined by the technological and organizational characteristics of the system, the environment and the accident prevention measures implemented. For safety purposes, it is useful to depict materials handling as a system in which the various elements are interrelated (figure 58.103). When changes are introduced in any element of the system—equipment, goods, procedures, environment, people, management and organization—the risk of injuries is likely to change as well.

The most common materials-handling and internal traffic types involved in accidents are associated with manual handling, trans-

Figure 58.103 • A materials-handling system.

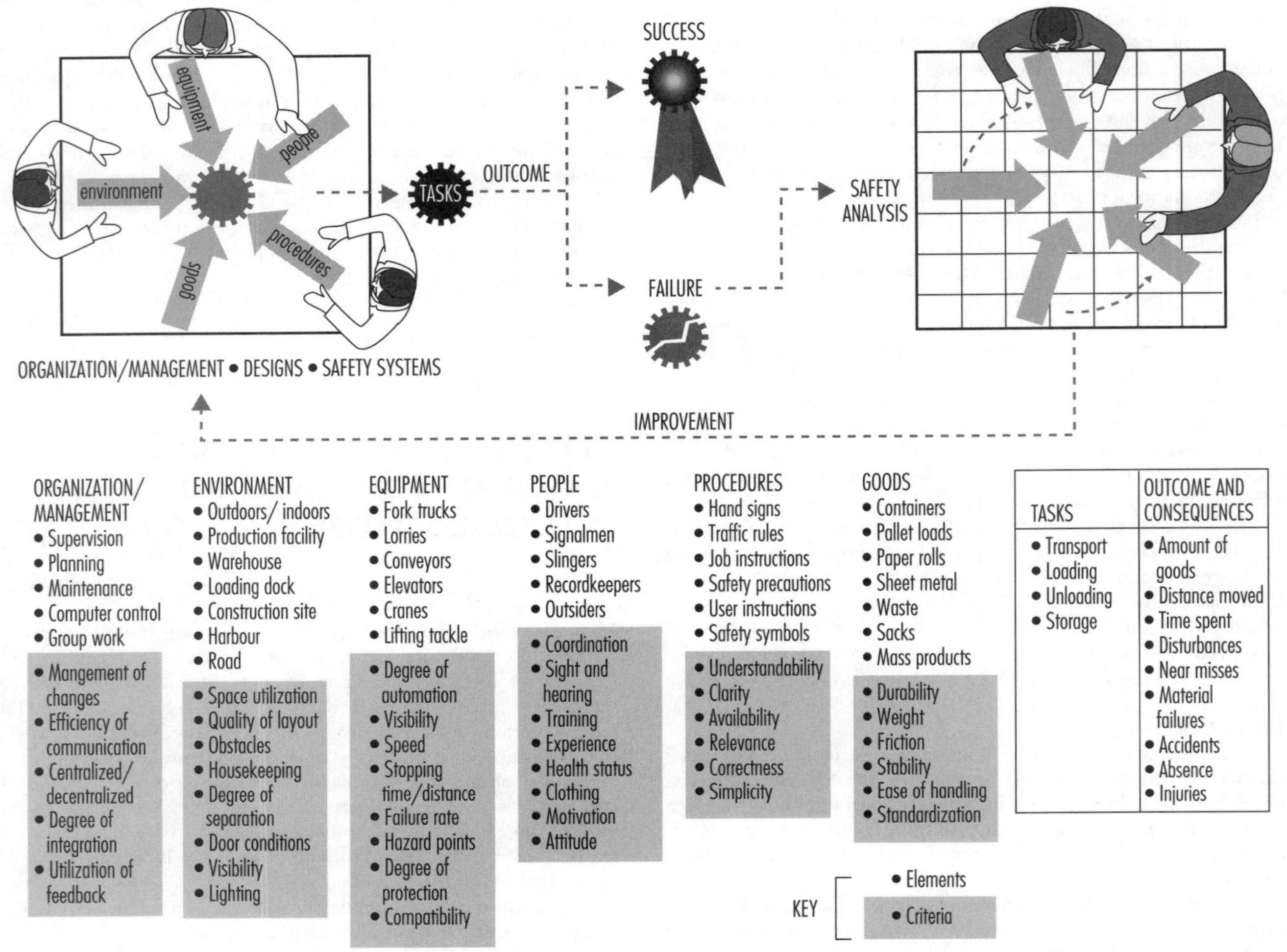
equipment
people
environment
TASKS
OUTCOME
procedures
goods
SUCCESS
FAILURE
SAFETY ANALYSIS
ORGANIZATION/MANAGEMENT • DESIGNS • SAFETY SYSTEMS
IMPROVEMENT
ORGANIZATION/ MANAGEMENT
• Supervision
• Planning
• Maintenance
• Computer control
• Group work
• Mangement of changes
• Efficiency of communication
• Centralized/ decentralized
• Degree of integration
• Utilization of feedback
ENVIRONMENT
• Outdoors/ indoors
• Production facility
• Warehouse
• Loading dock
• Construction site
• Harbour
• Road
• Space utilization
• Quality of layout
• Obstacles
• Housekeeping
• Degree of separation
• Door conditions
• Visibility
• Lighting
EQUIPMENT
• Fork trucks
• Lorries
• Conveyors
• Elevators
• Cranes
• Lifting tackle
• Degree of automation
• Visibility
• Speed
• Stopping time/distance
• Failure rate
• Hazard points
• Degree of protection
• Compatibility
PEOPLE
• Drivers
• Signalmen
• Slingers
• Recordkeepers
• Outsiders
• Coordination
• Sight and hearing
• Training
• Experience
• Health status
• Clothing
• Motivation
• Attitude
PROCEDURES
• Hand signs
• Traffic rules
• Job instructions
• Safety precautions
• User instructions
• Safety symbols
• Understandability
• Clarity
• Availability
• Relevance
• Correctness
• Simplicity
GOODS
• Containers
• Pallet loads
• Paper rolls
• Sheet metal
• Waste
• Sacks
• Mass products
• Durability
• Weight
• Friction
• Stability
• Ease of handling
• Standardization
TASKS
• Transport
• Loading
• Unloading
• Storage
OUTCOME AND CONSEQUENCES
• Amount of goods
• Distance moved
• Time spent
• Disturbances
• Near misses
• Material failures
• Accidents
• Absence
• Injuries
KEY
• Elements
• Criteria

port and moving by hand (carts, bicycles, etc.), lorries, fork-lift trucks, cranes and hoists, conveyors and rail transport.

Several types of accidents are commonly found in materials transport and handling at workplaces. The following list outlines the most frequent types:

- physical strain in manual handling
- loads falling onto people
- people trapped between objects
- collisions between equipment
- people falling
- hits, blows and cuts to people from equipment or loads.

Elements of Materials-Handling Systems

For each element in a materials-handling system, several design options are available, and the risk of accidents is affected accordingly. Several safety criteria must be considered for each element. It is important that the systems approach is used throughout the lifetime of the system—during the design of the new system, during the normal operation of the system and in following up on past accidents and disturbances in order to introduce improvements into the system.

General Principles of Prevention

Certain practical principles of prevention are generally regarded as applicable to safety in materials handling. These principles can be applied to both manual and mechanical materials-handling systems in a general sense and whenever a factory, warehouse or construction site is under consideration. Many different principles must be applied to the same project to achieve optimum safety results. Usually, no single measure can totally prevent accidents. Conversely, not all of these general principles are needed, and some of them may not work in a specific situation. Safety professionals and materials-handling specialists should consider the most relevant items to guide their work in each specific case. The most important issue is to manage the principles optimally to create safe and practicable materials-handling systems, rather than to settle upon any single technical principle to the exclusion of others.

The following 22 principles can be used for safety purposes in the development and assessment of materials-handling systems in their planned, present or historical stage. All of the principles are applicable in both pro-active and aftermath safety activities. No strict priority order is implied in the list that follows, but a rough division can be made: the first principles are more valid in the initial design of new plant layouts and materials-handling processes, whereas the last principles listed are more directed to the operation of existing materials-handling systems.

Twenty-two Principles of Prevention of Materials-Handling Accidents

1. *Eliminate all unnecessary transport and handling operations.* Because many transport and handling processes are inherently dangerous, it is useful to consider whether some materials handling might be eliminated. Many modern manufacturing processes can be arranged in a continuous flow without any separate handling and transport phases. Many assembly and construction operations can be planned and designed to eliminate strenuous and complex movements of loads. Options for more effective and rational transport can also be found by analysing logistics and material flow in the manufacturing and transport processes.

2. *Remove human beings from the transport and handling space.* When workers are not physically located under or in the vicinity of loads to be moved, safety conditions are *ipso facto* improved because of reduced exposure to hazards. People are not allowed to work in the scrap-handling area of steelworks because pieces of scrap may drop from the magnetic grippers that are used to move the scrap, presenting a continuous hazard of falling loads. Materials handling in harsh environments can often be automated by using robots and automatic trucks, an arrangement that reduces the accident risks posed to workers by moving loads. Moreover, by forbidding people to go unnecessarily through loading and unloading yards, exposure to several types of materials-handling hazards is basically eliminated.

3. *Segregate transport operations from each other as much as possible to minimize encounters.* The more frequently vehicles encounter one another, other equipment and people, the greater is the probability of collisions. Segregation of transport operations is important when planning for safe in-plant transport. There are many segregations to be considered, such as pedestrians/vehicles; heavy traffic/light traffic; internal traffic/traffic to and from outside; transport between workplaces/materials handling within a workplace; transport/storage; transport/production line; receiving/shipping; hazardous materials transportation/normal transport.

    When spatial segregation is not practicable, specific times can be allocated when transport and pedestrians respectively are allowed to enter a work area (e.g., in a warehouse open to the public). If separate pathways cannot be arranged for pedestrians, their routes can be designated by markings and signs. When entering a factory building, employees should be able to use separate pedestrian doors. If pedestrian traffic and fork-lift truck traffic are mixed in doorways, they also tend to be mixed beyond the doorways, thus presenting a hazard. During plant modifications, it is often necessary to limit transport and human motion through the areas which are under repair or construction. In overhead crane transport, collisions can be avoided by seeing to it that the tracks of the cranes do not overlap and by installing limit switches and mechanical barriers.

4. *Provide enough space for materials-handling and transport operations.* Too narrow a space for materials handling is often a cause of accidents. For example, workers' hands can be caught between a load and a wall in manual handling, or a person may be pinned between a moving pillar of a transport crane and a stack of materials when the minimum safety distance of 0.5 m is not available. The space needed for transport and handling operations should be carefully considered in plant design and planning of modifications. It is advisable to reserve some

"safety margin" of space in order to accommodate future changes in load dimensions and types of equipment. Often, the volume of the products being manufactured tends to grow as time goes on, but the space in which to handle them becomes smaller and smaller. Although the demand for cost-effective space utilization may be a reason for minimizing production space, it should be borne in mind that the manoeuvring space needed for counterbalanced fork-lift trucks to turn and to backtrack is larger than it seems to be at first sight.

5. *Aim at continuous transport processes, avoiding points of discontinuity in materials handling.* Continuous material flows reduce the potential for accidents. The basic arrangement of a plant layout is of crucial importance in carrying out this safety principle. Accidents concentrate in places where the material flow is interrupted because the moving and handling equipment is changed, or for production reasons. Human intervention is often required to unload and reload, to fasten, package, lift and drag, and so forth. Depending on the materials handled, conveyors generally give more continuous material flows than cranes or fork-lift trucks. It is good planning to arrange transport operations in such a way that motor vehicles can move in factory premises in a one-way circle, without any zigzag motion or backtracking. Because points of discontinuity tend to develop in boundary lines between departments or between working cells, production and transport should be planned to avoid such "no-man's lands" with uncontrolled materials movement.

6. *Use standard elements in materials-handling systems.* For safety purposes it is generally better to use standard items of loads, equipment and tools in materials handling. The concept of unit load is well-known to most transport professionals. Materials packed in containers and on pallets are easier to attach and move when the other elements in the transport chain (e.g., storage racks, fork-lift trucks, motor vehicles and fastening devices of cranes) are designed for these unit loads. The use of standard types of fork-lift trucks with similar controls decreases the probability of driver error, as accidents have occurred when a driver has changed from one sort of equipment to another with different controls.

7. *Know the materials to be handled.* Knowledge of the characteristics of the materials to be transported is a precondition for safe transfer. In order to select appropriate lifting or load restraints, one must take into account the weight, centre of gravity and dimensions of goods that are to be fastened for lifting and transport. When hazardous materials are handled, it is necessary that information be available as to their reactivity, flammability and health hazards. Special hazards are presented in the case of items which are fragile, sharp, dusty, slippery, loose, or when handling explosive materials and living animals, for example. The packages often provide important information for workers as to proper handling methods, but sometimes labels are removed or protective packaging conceals important information. For example, it may not be possible to view the distribution of the contents within a package, with the result that one cannot properly assess the load's centre of gravity.

8. *Keep the loading below the safe working-load capacity.* Overloading is a common cause of damage in materials-handling systems. Loss of balance and material breakage are typical results of overloading handling equipment. The safe working load of slings and other lifting tackle should be clearly marked, and proper configurations of slings must be selected. Overloading can take place when the weight or the centre of gravity of the load is misjudged, leading to improper fastening and manoeuvring of loads. When slings are used to handle loads, the

equipment operator should be aware that an inclined pathway may exert forces sufficient to cause the load to drop off or over-balance the equipment. The loading capacity of fork-lift trucks should be marked on the equipment; this varies according to the lifting height and the size of the load. Overloading due to fatigue failure may occur under repeated loadings well below the ultimate breaking load if the component is not correctly designed against this type of failure.

9. *Set the speed limits low enough to maintain safe movement.* Speed limits for vehicles moving in workplaces vary from 10 km/h to 40 km/h (about 5 to 25 mph). Lower speeds are required in inside corridors, in doorways, at crossings and in narrow aisles. A competent driver can adapt a vehicle's speed according to the demands of each situation, but signs notifying drivers of speed limitations are advisable at critical places. The maximum speed of a remote-controlled mobile crane, for example, must be determined first by fixing a vehicle speed comparable to a reasonable walking speed for a human, and then allowing for the time needed for simultaneous observations and control of loads so as not to exceed the response time of the human operator.

10. *Avoid overhead lifting in areas where people are working underneath.* Overhead lifting of materials always poses a risk of falling loads. Although people are ordinarily not allowed to work under hanging loads, the routine transportation of loads over people in production can expose them to danger. Fork-lift transport to high storage racks and lifting between floors are further examples of overhead lifting tasks. Overhead conveyors transporting stones, coke or casts may also constitute a risk of falling loads for those walking underneath if protective covers are not installed. In considering a new overhead transport system, the potential greater risks should be compared with the lesser risks associated with a floor-level transport system.

11. *Avoid materials-handling methods that require climbing and working at high levels.* When people have to climb up—for example, to unfasten sling hooks, to adjust a vehicle's canopy or to make markings on loads—they risk falling. This hazard can often be averted by better planning, by changing the sequence of work, by using various lifting accessories and remote-controlled tools, or by mechanization and automation.

12. *Attach guards at danger points.* Guards should be installed on danger points in materials-handling equipment such as the chains of fork-lift trucks, the rope drives of cranes and the trapping points of conveyors. Out-of-reach protection is often not enough, because the hazard point may be reached by using ladders and other means. Guards are also used to protect against technical failures that could lead to injuries (e.g., of wire rope retainers on crane sheaves, safety latches in lifting hooks and the protection pads of textile slings that shield against sharp edges). Guardrails and toeboards installed against the edges of loading platforms and overhead storage racks, and around floor openings, can protect both people and things from falling. This sort of protection is often needed when fork-lift trucks and cranes lift materials from one floor to another. People can be protected from falling objects in materials-handling operations by safety nets and permanent guards such as wire mesh or metal plate covers on conveyors.

13. *Transport and lift people only by the equipment designed for the purpose.* Cranes, fork-lift trucks, excavators and conveyors are machines for moving materials, not human beings, from one place to another. Special lifting platforms are available to lift persons, for example, to change lamps on ceilings. If a crane or a fork-lift truck is equipped with a special cage which can be securely attached to the equipment and which meets proper safety requirements, persons can be lifted without an excessive risk of severe injury.

14. *Keep equipment and loads stable.* Accidents happen when equipment, goods or storage racks lose their stability, especially in the case of fork-lift trucks or mobile cranes. The selection of actively stable equipment is a first step to reduce hazards. Further, it is advisable to use equipment that emits a warning signal before the limit of collapse is reached. Good working practices and qualified operators are the next stops of prevention. Experienced and trained employees are able to estimate centres of gravity and recognize unstable conditions where materials are piled and stacked, and to make the necessary adjustments.

15. *Provide good visibility.* Visibility is always limited when handling materials with fork-lift trucks. When new equipment is purchased, it is important to assess how much the driver can see through the mast structures (and, for high-lifting trucks, the visibility through the overhead frame). In any case, the materials handled cause some loss of visibility, and this effect should be considered. Whenever possible, a clear line of sight should be provided—for example, by removing piles of goods or by arranging openings or empty sections at critical points in racks. Mirrors can be applied to the equipment and at suitable locations in factories and warehouses to make blind corners safer. However, mirrors are a secondary means of prevention compared to the actual elimination of blind corners in order to allow direct vision. In crane transport it is often necessary to assign a special signal person to check that the area where the load will be lowered is unoccupied by people. A good safety practice is to paint or otherwise mark danger points and obstructions in the working environment—for example, pillars, edges of doors and of loading docks, protruding machine elements and moving parts of equipment. Appropriate illumination can often improve visibility considerably—for example, on stairs, in corridors and at exit doors.

16. *Eliminate manual lifting and carrying of loads by mechanical and automated handling.* About 15% of all work-related injuries involve the manual lifting and carrying of loads. Most of the injuries are due to over-exertion; the rest are slips and falls and hand injuries inflicted by sharp edges. Cumulative trauma disorders and back disorders are typical health problems due to manual-handling work. Although mechanization and automation have eliminated manual-handling tasks to a large extent in industry, there still exist a number of workplaces where people are physically overloaded by lifting and carrying heavy loads. Consideration should be given to providing appropriate handling equipment—for example, hoists, lifting platforms, elevators, fork-lift trucks, cranes, conveyors, palletizers, robots and mechanical manipulators.

17. *Provide and maintain effective communication.* A common factor in serious accidents is a failure in communication. A crane driver must communicate with a slinger, who fastens the load, and if the hand signs between the driver and the loader are incorrect or radio phones have a low audibility, critical errors may result. Communication links are important between materials-handling operators, production people, loaders, dock workers, equipment drivers and maintenance people. For instance, a fork-lift truck driver has to pass along information about any safety problems encountered—for example, aisles with blind corners due to stacks of material—when turning over the truck to the next driver during shift change. Drivers of motor vehicles and mobile cranes working as contractors in a workplace are often unfamiliar with the particular risks they may encounter, and should therefore receive special guidance or training. This may include providing a map of the factory

premises at the access gate together with the essential safe work and driving instructions. Traffic signs for workplace traffic are not as highly developed as the those for public roads. However, many of the risks encountered in road traffic are common within factory premises, too. It is therefore important to provide appropriate traffic signs for internal traffic in order to facilitate the communication of hazard warnings and to alert drivers to whatever precautions may be required.

18. *Arrange the human interfaces and the manual handling according to ergonomic principles.* Materials-handling work should be accommodated to the capacity and skills of people by applying ergonomics so as to obviate errors and improper straining. The controls and displays of cranes and fork-lift trucks should be compatible with the natural expectations and habits of people. In manual handling it is important to make sure that there is enough space for the human motions necessary to carry out the tasks. Furthermore, excessively strenuous working postures should be avoided—for example, manually lifting loads over one's head, and not exceeding the maximum permissible weights for manual lifting. Individual variations in age, strength, health status, experience and anthropometric considerations may require modification of the workspace and tasks accordingly. Order picking in storage facilities is an example of a task in which ergonomics is of utmost importance for safety and productivity.

19. *Provide adequate training and advice.* Materials-handling tasks are often regarded as too low-status to warrant any special training for the workforce. The number of specialized crane operators and fork-lift drivers is decreasing at workplaces; and there is a growing tendency to make crane and fork-lift truck driving a job that almost anybody in a workplace should be prepared to do. Although hazards can be reduced by technical and ergonomic measures, it is the skill of the operator that is ultimately decisive in averting hazardous situations in dynamic work settings. Accident surveys have indicated that many of the victims in materials-handling accidents are people not involved in materials-handling tasks themselves. Therefore, training should also be provided to some extent for bystanders in the materials-handling areas.

20. *Supply the people working in transport and handling with appropriate personal outfits.* Several types of injuries can be prevented by using appropriate personal protective equipment. Safety shoes which do not cause slips and falls, heavy gloves, safety glasses or goggles, and hard hats are typical personal protectors worn for materials-handling tasks. When special hazards demand it, fall protection, respirators and special safety garments are used. Appropriate working gear for materials handling should provide good visibility and should not include parts that may easily be caught on equipment or gripped by moving parts.

21. *Carry out proper maintenance and inspection duties.* When accidents happen because of failures in equipment, the reasons are often to be found in poor maintenance and inspection procedures. Instructions for maintenance and inspections are given in safety standards and in manufacturers' manuals. Deviations from the given procedures can lead to dangerous situations. Material-handling equipment users are responsible for daily maintenance and inspection routines involving such tasks as checking batteries, rope and chain drives, lifting tackle, brakes and controls; cleaning windows; and adding oil when needed. More thorough, less frequent, inspections are carried out regularly, such as weekly, monthly, semi-annually or once a year, depending on the conditions of use. Housekeeping, including adequate cleaning of floors and workplaces, is also important for safe materials handling. Oily and wet floors cause people and trucks to slip. Broken pallets and storage racks should be discarded whenever observed. In operations involving the transporting of bulk materials by conveyors it is important to remove accumulations of dust and grain in order to prevent dust explosions and fires.

22. *Plan for changes in the environmental conditions.* The capacity to adapt to varying environmental conditions is limited among equipment and people alike. Fork-lift truck operators need several seconds to adapt themselves when driving from a gloomy hall through doorways to a sunlit yard outside, and when moving inside from outdoors. To make these operations safer, special lighting arrangements can be set up at doorways. In the outdoors, cranes are often subjected to high wind loads, which have to be taken into account during lifting operations. In extreme wind conditions, lifting with cranes must be interrupted entirely. Ice and snow may cause considerable extra work for workers who have to clean the surfaces of loads. Sometimes, this also means taking extra risks; for instance, when the work is done upon the load or even under the load during lifting. Planning should cover safe procedures for these tasks, too. An icy load may glide away from a pallet fork during a forklift transport. Corrosive atmospheres, heat, frost conditions and seawater can cause degradation of materials and subsequent failures if the materials are not designed to withstand such conditions.

References

Arteau, J, A Lan, and J-F Corveil. 1994. *Use of Horizontal Lifelines in Structural Steel Erection.* Proceedings of the International Fall Protection Symposium, San Diego, California (October 27–28, 1994). Toronto: International Society for Fall Protection.

Backström, T. 1996. Accident risk and safety protection in automated production. Doctoral thesis. *Arbete och Hälsa* 1996:7. Solna: National Institute for Working Life.

Backström, T and L Harms-Ringdahl. 1984. A statistical study of control systems and accidents at work. *J Occup Acc.* 6:201–210.

Backström, T and M Döös. 1994. Technical defects behind accidents in automated production. In *Advances in Agile Manufacturing,* edited by PT Kidd and W Karwowski. Amsterdam: IOS Press.

—. 1995. A comparison of occupational accidents in industries with of advanced manufacturing technology. *Int J Hum Factors Manufac.* 5(3). 267–282.

—. In press. The technical genesis of machine failures leading to occupational accidents. *Int J Ind Ergonomics.*

—. Accepted for publication. Absolute and relative frequencies of automation accidents at different kinds of equipment and for different occupational groups. *J Saf Res.*

Bainbridge, L. 1983. Ironies of automation. *Automatica* 19:775–779.

Bell, R and D Reinert. 1992. Risk and system integrity concepts for safety related control systems. *Saf Sci* 15:283–308.

Bouchard, P. 1991. *Échafaudages.* Guide série 4. Montreal: CSST.

Bureau of National Affairs. 1975. *Occupational Safety and Health Standards. Roll-over Protective Structures for Material Handling Equipment and Tractors, Sections 1926, 1928.* Washington, DC: Bureau of National Affairs.

Corbett, JM. 1988. Ergonomics in the development of human-centred AMT. *Applied Ergonomics* 19:35–39.

Culver, C and C Connolly. 1994. Prevent fatal falls in construction. *Saf Health* September 1994:72–75.

Deutsche Industrie Normen (DIN). 1990. *Grundsätze für Rechner in Systemen mit Sicherheitsaufgaben.* DIN V VDE 0801. Berlin: Beuth Verlag.

—. 1994. *Grundsätze für Rechner in Systemen mit Sicherheitsaufgaben Änderung A 1.* DIN V VDE 0801/A1. Berlin: Beuth Verlag.

—. 1995a. *Sicherheit von Maschinen—Druckempfindliche Schutzeinrichtungen* [Machine safety—Pressure-sensitive protective equipment]. DIN prEN 1760. Berlin: Beuth Verlag.

—. 1995b. *Rangier-Warneinrichtungen—Anforderungen und Prüfung* [Commercial vehicles—obstacle detection during reversing—requirements and tests]. DIN-Norm 75031. February 1995.

Döös, M and T Backström. 1993. Description of accidents in automated materials handling. In *Ergonomics of Materials Handling and Information Processing at Work,* edited by WS Marras, W Karwowski, JL Smith, and L Pacholski. Warsaw: Taylor and Francis.

—. 1994. Production disturbances as an accident risk. In *Advances in Agile Manufacturing*, edited by PT Kidd and W Karwowski. Amsterdam: IOS Press.

European Economic Community (EEC). 1974, 1977, 1979, 1982, 1987. *Council Directives on Rollover Protection Structures of Wheeled Agricultural and Forestry Tractors.* Brussels: EEC.

—. 1991. *Council Directive on the Approximation of the Laws of the Member States relating to Machinery.* (91/368/EEC) Luxembourg: EEC.

Etherton, JR and ML Myers. 1990. Machine safety research at NIOSH and future directions. *Int J Ind Erg* 6:163–174.

Freund, E, F Dierks and J Roßmann. 1993. *Unterschungen zum Arbeitsschutz bei Mobilen Rototern und Mehrrobotersystemen [Occupational safety tests of mobile robots and multiple robot systems].* Dortmund: Schriftenreihe der Bundesanstalt für Arbeitsschutz.

Goble, W. 1992. *Evaluating Control System Reliability.* New York: Instrument Society of America.

Goodstein, LP, HB Anderson and SE Olsen (eds.). 1988. *Tasks, Errors and Mental Models.* London: Taylor and Francis.

Gryfe, CI. 1988. Causes and prevention of falling. In *International Fall Protection Symposium.* Orlando: International Society for Fall Protection.

Health and Safety Executive. 1989. Health and safety statistics 1986–87. *Employ Gaz* 97(2).

Heinrich, HW, D Peterson and N Roos. 1980. *Industrial Accident Prevention.* 5th edn. New York: McGraw-Hill.

Hollnagel, E, and D Woods. 1983. Cognitive systems engineering: New wine in new bottles. *Int J Man Machine Stud* 18:583–600.

Hölscher, H and J Rader. 1984. *Mikrocomputer in der Sicherheitstechnik.* Rheinland: Verlag TgV-Reinland.

Hörte, S-Å and P Lindberg. 1989. *Diffusion and Implementation of Advanced Manufacturing Technologies in Sweden.* Working paper No. 198:16. Institute of Innovation and Technology.

International Electrotechnical Commission (IEC). 1992. *122 Draft Standard: Software for Computers in the Application of Industrial Safety-related Systems.* IEC 65 (Sec). Geneva: IEC.

—. 1993. *123 Draft Standard: Functional Safety of Electrical/Electronic/Programmable Electronic Systems; Generic Aspects.* Part 1, General requirements Geneva: IEC.

International Labour Organization (ILO). 1965. *Safety & Health in Agricultural Work.* Geneva: ILO.

—. 1969. *Safety and Health in Forestry Work.* Geneva: ILO.

—. 1976. *Safe Construction and Operation of Tractors. An ILO Code of Practice.* Geneva: ILO.

International Organization for Standardization (ISO). 1981. *Agricultural and Forestry Wheeled Tractors. Protective Structures. Static Test Method and Acceptance Conditions.* ISO 5700. Geneva: ISO.

—. 1990. *Quality Management and Quality Assurance Standards: Guidelines for the Application of ISO 9001 to the Development, Supply and Maintenance of Software.* ISO 9000-3. Geneva: ISO.

—. 1991. *Industrial Automation Systems—Safety of Integrated Manufacturing Systems—Basic Requirements* (CD 11161). TC 184/WG 4. Geneva: ISO.

—. 1994. *Commercial Vehicles—Obstacle Detection Device during Reversing—Requirements and Tests.* Technical Report TR 12155. Geneva: ISO.

Johnson, B. 1989. *Design and Analysis of Fault Tolerant Digital Systems.* New York: Addison Wesley.

Kidd, P. 1994. Skill-based automated manufacturing. In *Organization and Management of Advanced Manufacturing*, edited by W Karwowski and G Salvendy. New York: Wiley.

Knowlton, RE. 1986. *An Introduction to Hazard and Operability Studies: The Guide Word Approach.* Vancouver, BC: Chemetics.

Kuivanen, R. 1990. The impact on safety of disturbances in flexible manufacturing systems. In *Ergonomics of Hybrid Automated Systems II*, edited by W Karwowski and M Rahimi. Amsterdam: Elsevier.

Laeser, RP, WI McLaughlin and DM Wolff. 1987. Fernsteuerung und Fehlerkontrolle von Voyager 2. *Spektrum der Wissenschaft* (1):S. 60–70.

Lan, A, J Arteau and J-F Corbeil. 1994. *Protection Against Falls from Above-ground Billboards.* International Fall Protection Symposium, San Diego, California, October 27–28, 1994. Proceedings International Society for Fall Protection.

Langer, HJ and W Kurfürst. 1985. *Einsatz von Sensoren zur Absicherung des Rückraumes von Großfahrzeugen [Using sensors to secure the area behind large vehicles].* FB 605. Dortmund: Schriftenreihe der bundesanstalt für Arbeitsschutz.

Levenson, NG. 1986. Software safety: Why, what, and how. *ACM Computer Surveys* (2):S. 129–163.

McManus, TN. N.d. *Confined Spaces.* Manuscript.

Microsonic GmbH. 1996. Company communication. Dortmund, Germany: Microsonic.

Mester, U, T Herwig, G Dönges, B Brodbeck, HD Bredow, M Behrens and U Ahrens. 1980. *Gefahrenschutz durch passive Infrarot-Sensoren (II) [Protection against hazards by infrared sensors].* FB 243. Dortmund: Schriftenreihe der bundesanstalt für Arbeitsschutz.

Mohan, D and R Patel. 1992. Design of safer agricultural equipment: Application of ergonomics and epidemiology. *Int J Ind Erg* 10:301–310.

National Fire Protection Association (NFPA). 1993. *NFPA 306: Control of Gas Hazards on Vessels.* Quincy, MA: NFPA.

National Institute for Occupational Safety and Health (NIOSH). 1994. *Worker Deaths in Confined Spaces.* Cincinnati, OH, US: DHHS/PHS/CDCP/NIOSH Pub. No. 94-103. NIOSH.

Neumann, PG. 1987. The N best (or worst) computer-related risk cases. *IEEE T Syst Man Cyb.* New York: S.11–13.

—. 1994. Illustrative risks to the public in the use of computer systems and related technologies. *Software Engin Notes SIGSOFT* 19, No. 1:16–29.

Occupational Safety and Health Administration (OSHA). 1988. *Selected Occupational Fatalities Related to Welding and Cutting as Found in Reports of OSHA Fatality/Catastrophe Investigations.* Washington, DC: OSHA.

Organization for Economic Cooperation and Development (OECD). 1987. *Standard Codes for the Official Testing of Agricultural Tractors.* Paris: OECD.

Organisme professionel de prévention du bâtiment et des travaux publics (OPPBTP). 1984. *Les équipements individuels de protection contre les chutes de hauteur.* Boulogne-Bilancourt, France: OPPBTP.

Rasmussen, J. 1983. Skills, rules and knowledge: Agenda, signs and symbols, and other distinctions in human performance models. *IEEE Transactions on Systems, Man and Cybernetics.* SMC13(3): 257–266.

Reason, J. 1990. *Human Error.* New York: Cambridge University Press.

Reese, CD and GR Mills. 1986. Trauma epidemiology of confined space fatalities and its application to intervention/prevention now. In *The Changing Nature of Work and Workforce.* Cincinnati, OH: NIOSH.

Reinert, D and G Reuss. 1991. Sicherheitstechnische Beurteilung und Prüfung mikroprozessorgesteuerter Sicherheitseinrichtungen. In *BIA-Handbuch.* Sicherheitstechnisches Informations-und Arbeitsblatt 310222. Bielefeld: Erich Schmidt Verlag.

Society of Automotive Engineers (SAE). 1974. *Operator Protection for Industrial Equipment.* SAE Standard j1042. Warrendale, USA: SAE.

—. 1975. *Performance Criteria for Rollover Protection. SAE Recommended Practice.* SAE standard j1040a. Warrendale, USA: SAE.

Schreiber, P. 1990. Entwicklungsstand bei Rückraumwarneinrichtungen [State of developments for rear area warning devices]. *Technische Überwachung*, Nr. 4, April, S. 161.

Schreiber, P and K Kuhn. 1995. *Informationstechnologie in der Fertigungstechnik* [Information technology in production technique, series of the Federal Institute for Occupational Safety and Health]. FB 717. Dortmund: Schriftenreihe der bundesanstalt für Arbeitsschutz.

Sheridan, T. 1987. Supervisory control. In *Handbook of Human Factors*, edited by G. Salvendy. New York: Wiley.

Springfeldt, B. 1993. *Effects of Occupational Safety Rules and Measures with Special Regard to Injuries. Advantages of Automatically Working Solutions.* Stockholm: The Royal Institute of Technology, Department of Work Science.

Sugimoto, N. 1987. Subjects and problems of robot safety technology. In *Occupational Safety and Health in Automation and Robotics*, edited by K Noto. London: Taylor & Francis. 175.

Sulowski, AC (ed.). 1991. *Fundamentals of Fall Protection.* Toronto, Canada: International Society for Fall Protection.

Wehner, T. 1992. *Sicherheit als Fehlerfreundlichkeit.* Opladen: Westdeutscher Verlag.

Zimolong, B, and L Duda. 1992. Human error reduction strategies in advanced manufacturing systems. In *Human-robot Interaction*, edited by M Rahimi and W Karwowski. London: Taylor & Francis.

Other relevant readings

Börner, F and F Kreutzkampf. 1994. Infälle und Störfälle, verursacht durch das Versagen von Steuerungen. In *BIA-Handbuch.* Sicherheitstechnisches Informations-und Arbeitsblatt 330250. Bielefeld: Erich Schmidt.

Emery, FE. 1969. *Systems Thinking.* Harmondsworth, UK: Penguin.

Grams, T. 1990. *Denkfallen und Programmierfehler.* Berlin: Springer.

Meffert, K and J Germer. 1985. Einsatz von Rechnern für Sicherheitsaufgaben—Standortbestimmung. *Die BG* 5:S. 246–253.

Schreibwer, P, G Becker, and W Dicke. 1985. *Gefahrenschutz durch Kontaktmatten und-böden [Danger protection using contact mats and floors].* FB 414. Dortmund: Schriftenreihe der bundesanstalt für Arbeitsschutz.

System Safety Society. 1993. *System Safety Analysis Handbook.* Albuquerque, NM, US: New Mexico Chapter, System Safety Society.

Thomas, M. 1988. Should we trust computers? In *SHARE.* Nijwegen, Netherlands: Eur. Assoc.

US Nuclear Regulatory Commission. 1975. *Reactor Safety Study. Wash 1400.* Washington, DC: Nuclear Regulatory Commission. (Also published in French: Projet Rasmussen. *Etude de la sûreté des réacteurs*, Paris 1975, Documentation française.)

Villemeur, A. 1988. *Sûreté de fonctionnement des systèmes industriels. Fiabilité. Facteurs humains. Informatisation [Operational safety of industrial systems. Reliability. Human factors. Computerization].* Paris: Editions Eyrolles.

Yoshinobu, Sato. 1985. *Safety Assessment of Automated Production Systems using Microelectronics. The Comprehensive Logic Models for the Analysis of Accidents Caused by Robots.* (Research reports of the Research Institute of Industrial Safety, March 1985 (21–31), in Japanese with summary and illustration captions in English.) Tokyo: Research Institute of Industrial Safety.

Chapter Editor
Jorma Saari

Contents

SAFETY POLICY, LEADERSHIP AND CULTURE

Dan Petersen

The subjects of leadership and culture are the two most important considerations among the conditions necessary to achieve excellence in safety. Safety policy may or may not be regarded as being important, depending upon the worker's perception as to whether management commitment to and support of the policy is in fact carried out every day. Management often writes the safety policy and then fails to ensure that it is enforced by managers and supervisors on the job, every day.

Safety Culture and Safety Results

We used to believe that there were certain "essential elements" of a "safety programme". In the United States, regulatory agencies provide guidelines as to what those elements are (policy, procedures, training, inspections, investigations, etc.). Some provinces in Canada state that there are 20 essential elements, while some organizations in the United Kingdom suggest that 30 essential elements should be considered in safety programmes. Upon close examination of the rationale behind the different lists of essential elements, it becomes obvious that the lists of each reflect merely the opinion of some writer from the past (Heinrich, say, or Bird). Similarly, regulations on safety programming often reflect the opinion of some early writer. There is seldom any research behind these opinions, resulting in situations where the essential elements may work in one organization and not in another. When we do actually look at the research on safety system effectiveness, we begin to understand that although there are many essential elements which are applicable to safety results, it is the worker's perception of the culture that determines whether or not any single element will be effective. There are a number of studies cited in the references which lead to the conclusion that there are no "must haves" and no "essential" elements in a safety system.

This poses some serious problems since safety regulations tend to instruct organizations simply to "have a safety programme" that consists of five, seven, or any number of elements, when it is obvious that many of the prescribed activities will not work and will waste time, effort and resources which could be used to undertake the pro-active activities that will prevent loss. It is not which elements are used that determines the safety results; rather it is the culture in which these elements are used that determines success. In a positive safety culture, almost any elements will work; in a negative culture, probably none of the elements will get results.

Building Culture

If the culture of the organization is so important, efforts in safety management ought to be aimed first and foremost at building culture in order that those safety activities which are instituted will get results. *Culture* can be loosely defined as "the way it is around here". Safety culture is positive when the workers honestly believe that safety is a key value of the organization and can perceive that it is high on the list of organization priorities. This perception by the workforce can be attained only when they see management as credible; when the *words* of safety policy are lived on a daily basis; when management's decisions on financial expenditures show that money is spent for people (as well as to make more money); when the measures and rewards provided by management force midmanager and supervisory performance to satisfactory levels; when workers have a role in problem solving and decision making; when there is a high degree of confidence and trust between management and the workers; when there is openness of communications; and when workers receive positive recognition for their work.

In a positive safety culture like that described above, almost any element of the safety system will be effective. In fact, with the right culture, an organization hardly even needs a "safety programme", for safety is dealt with as a normal part of the management process. To achieve a positive safety culture, certain criteria must be met:

1. A system must be in place that ensures regular daily pro-active supervisory (or team) activities.
2. The system must actively ensure that middle-management tasks and activities are carried out in these areas:
   - ensuring subordinate (supervisory or team) regular performance
   - ensuring the quality of that performance
   - engaging in certain well-defined activities to show that safety is so important that even upper managers are doing something about it.
3. Top management must visibly demonstrate and support that safety has a high priority in the organization.
4. Any worker who chooses to should be able to be actively engaged in meaningful safety-related activities.
5. The safety system must be flexible, allowing choices to be made at all levels.
6. The safety effort must be seen as positive by the workforce.

These six criteria can be met regardless of the style of management of the organization, whether authoritarian or participative, and with completely different approaches to safety.

Culture and Safety Policy

Having a policy on safety seldom achieves anything unless it is followed up with systems that make the policy live. For example, if the policy states that supervisors are responsible for safety, it means nothing unless the following is in place:

- Management has a system where there is a clear definition of role and of what activities must be carried out to satisfy the safety responsibility.
- The supervisors know how to fulfil that role, are supported by management, believe the tasks are achievable and carry out their tasks as a result of proper planning and training.
- They are regularly measured to ensure they have completed the defined tasks (but not measured by an accident record) and to obtain feedback to determine whether or not tasks should be changed.
- There is a reward contingent upon task completion in the performance appraisal system or in whatever is the driving mechanism of the organization.

These criteria are true at each level of the organization; tasks must be defined, there must be a valid measure of performance (task completion) and a reward contingent upon performance. Thus, safety policy does not drive performance of safety; accountability does. Accountability is the key to building culture. It is only when the workers see supervisors and management fulfilling their safety tasks on a daily basis that they believe that management is credible and that top management really meant it when they signed the safety policy documents.

Leadership and Safety

It is obvious from the above that leadership is crucial to safety results, as leadership forms the culture that determines what will and will not work in the organization's safety efforts. A good leader makes it clear what is wanted in terms of results, and also makes it clear exactly what will be done in the organization to achieve the results. Leadership is infinitely more important than policy, for leaders, through their actions and decisions, send clear messages throughout the organization as to which policies are important and which are not. Organizations sometimes state via policy that health and safety are key values, and then construct measures and reward structures that promote the opposite.

Leadership, through its actions, systems, measures and rewards, clearly determines whether or not safety will be achieved in the organization. This has never been more apparent to every worker in industry than during the 1990s. There has never been more stated allegiance to health and safety than in the last ten years. At the same time, there has never been more down-sizing or "right-sizing" and more pressure for production increases and cost reduction, creating more stress, more forced overtime, more work for fewer workers, more fear for the future and less job security than ever before. Right-sizing has decimated middle managers and supervisors and put more work on fewer workers (the key persons in safety). There is a general perception of overload at all levels of the organization. Overload causes more accidents, more physical fatigue, more psychological fatigue, more stress claims, more repetitive motion conditions and more cumulative trauma disorder. There has also been deterioration in many organizations of the relationship between the company and the worker, where there used to be mutual feelings of trust and security. In the former environment, a worker may have continued to "work hurt". However, when workers fear for their jobs and they see that management ranks are so thin, they are non-supervised, they begin to feel as though the organization does not care for them any more, with the resultant deterioration in safety culture.

Gap Analysis

Many organizations are going through a simple process known as gap analysis consisting of three steps: (1) determining where you want to be; (2) determining where you are now and (3) determining how to get from where you are to where you want to be, or how to "bridge the gap".

Determining where you want to be. What do you want your organization's safety system to look like? Six criteria have been suggested against which to assess an organization's safety system. If these are rejected, you must measure your organization's safety system against some other criteria. For example, you might want to look at the seven climate variables of organizational effectiveness as established by Dr. Rensis Likert (1967), who showed that the better an organization is in certain things, the more likely it will be successful in economic success, and thus in safety. These climate variables are as follows:

- increasing the amount of worker confidence and managers' general interest in the understanding of safety problems
- giving training and help where and as needed
- offering needed teaching as to how to solve problems
- providing the available required trust, enabling information sharing between management and their subordinates
- soliciting the ideas and opinions of the worker
- providing for approachability of top management
- recognizing the worker for doing a good job rather than for merely giving answers.

There are other criteria against which to assess oneself such as the criterion established to determine the likelihood of catastrophic events suggested by Zembroski (1991).

Determining where you are now. This is perhaps the most difficult. It was originally thought that safety system effectiveness could be determined by measuring the number of injuries or some subset of injuries (recordable injuries, lost time injuries, frequency rates, etc.). Due to the low numbers of these data, they usually have little or no statistical validity. Recognizing this in the 1950s and 1960s, investigators tended away from incident measures and attempted to judge safety system effectiveness through audits. The attempt was made to predetermine what must be done in an organization to get results, and then to determine by measurement whether or not those things were done.

For years it was assumed that audit scores predicted safety results; the better the audit score this year, the lower the accident record next year. We now know (from a variety of research) that audit scores do not correlate very well (if at all) with the safety record. The research suggests that most audits (external and sometimes internally constructed) tend to correlate much better with regulatory compliance than they do with the safety record. This is documented in a number of studies and publications.

A number of studies correlating audit scores and the injury record in large companies over periods of time (seeking to determine whether the injury record does have statistical validity) have found a zero correlation, and in some cases a negative correlation, between audit results and the injury record. Audits in these studies do tend to correlate positively with regulatory compliance.

Bridging the Gap

There appear to be only a few measures of safety performance that are valid (that is, they truly correlate with the actual accident record in large companies over long periods of time) which can be used to "bridge the gap":

- behaviour sampling
- in-depth worker interviews
- perception surveys.

Perhaps the most important measure to look at is the perception survey, which is used to assess the current status of any organization's safety culture. Critical safety issues are identified and any differences in management and employee views on the effectiveness of company safety programmes are clearly demonstrated.

The survey begins with a short set of demographic questions which can be used to organize graphs and tables to show the results (see figure 59.1). Typically participants are asked about their employee level, their general work location, and perhaps their trade group. At no point are the employees asked questions which would enable them to be identified by the people who are scoring the results.

The second part of the survey consists of a number of questions. The questions are designed to uncover employee

---

Figure 59.1 • Example of perception survey results.

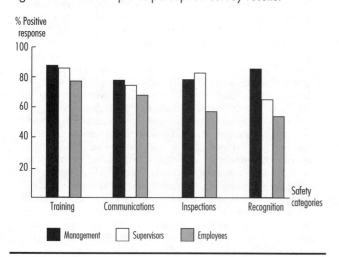

% Positive response

Safety categories

■ Management ☐ Supervisors ▨ Employees

perceptions about various safety categories. Each question may affect the score of more than one category. A cumulative per cent positive response is computed for each category. The percentages for the categories are graphed (see figure 59.1) to display the results in descending order of positive perception by the line workers. Those categories on the right-hand side of the graph are the ones that are perceived by employees as being the least positive and are therefore the most in need of improvement.

Summary

Much has been learned about what determines the effectiveness of a safety system in recent years. It is recognized that culture is the key. The employees' perception of the culture of the organization dictates their behaviour, and thus the culture determines whether or not any element of the safety programme will be effective.

Culture is established not by written policy, but rather by leadership; by day-to-day actions and decisions; and by the systems in place that ensure whether safety activities (performance) of managers, supervisors and work teams are carried out. Culture can be built positively through accountability systems that ensure performance and through systems that allow, encourage and get worker involvement. Moreover, culture can be validly assessed through perception surveys, and improved once the organization determines where it is they would like to be.

● SAFETY CULTURE AND MANAGEMENT

Marcel Simard

Safety culture is a new concept among safety professionals and academic researchers. Safety culture may be considered to include various other concepts referring to cultural aspects of occupational safety, such as safety attitudes and behaviours as well as a workplace's safety climate, which are more commonly referred to and are fairly well documented.

A question arises whether safety culture is just a new word used to replace old notions, or does it bring new substantive content that may enlarge our understanding of the safety dynamics in organizations? The first section of this article answers this question by defining the concept of safety culture and exploring its potential dimensions.

Another question that may be raised about safety culture concerns its relationship to the safety performance of firms. It is accepted that similar firms classified in a given risk category frequently differ as to their actual safety performance. Is safety culture a factor of safety effectiveness, and, if so, what kind of safety culture will succeed in contributing to a desirable impact? This question is addressed in the second section of the article by reviewing some relevant empirical evidence concerning the impact of safety culture on safety performance.

The third section addresses the practical question of the management of the safety culture, in order to help managers and other organizational leaders to build a safety culture that contributes to the reduction of occupational accidents.

Safety Culture: Concept and Realities

The concept of safety culture is not yet very well defined, and refers to a wide range of phenomena. Some of these have already been partially documented, such as the attitudes and the behaviours of managers or workers towards risk and safety (Andriessen 1978; Cru and Dejours 1983; Dejours 1992; Dodier 1985; Eakin 1992; Eyssen, Eakin-Hoffman and Spengler 1980; Haas 1977). These studies are important for presenting evidence about the

social and organizational nature of individuals' safety attitudes and behaviours (Simard 1988). However, by focusing on particular organizational actors like managers or workers, they do not address the larger question of the safety culture concept, which characterizes organizations.

A trend of research which is closer to the comprehensive approach emphasized by the safety culture concept is represented by studies on the safety climate that developed in the 1980s. The safety climate concept refers to the perceptions workers have of their work environment, particularly the level of management's safety concern and activities and their own involvement in the control of risks at work (Brown and Holmes 1986; Dedobbeleer and Béland 1991; Zohar 1980). Theoretically, it is believed that workers develop and use such sets of perceptions to ascertain what they believe is expected of them within the organizational environment, and behave accordingly. Though conceptualized as an *individual* attribute from a psychological perspective, the perceptions which form the safety climate give a valuable assessment of the common reaction of workers to an *organizational* attribute that is socially and culturally constructed, in this case by the management of occupational safety in the workplace. Consequently, although the safety climate does not completely capture the safety culture, it may be viewed as a source of information about the safety culture of a workplace.

Safety culture is a concept that (1) includes the values, beliefs and principles that serve as a foundation for the safety management system and (2) also includes the set of practices and behaviours that exemplify and reinforce those basic principles. These beliefs and practices are *meanings* produced by organizational members in their search for strategies addressing issues such as occupational hazards, accidents and safety at work. These meanings (beliefs and practices) are not only shared to a certain extent by members of the workplace but also act as a primary source of motivated and coordinated activity regarding the question of safety at work. It can be deduced that culture should be differentiated from both concrete occupational safety structures (the presence of a safety department, of a joint safety and health committee and so on) and existent occupational safety programmes (made up of hazards identification and control activities such as workplace inspections, accident investigation, job safety analysis and so on).

Petersen (1993) argues that safety culture "is at the heart of how safety systems elements or tools … are used" by giving the following example:

Two companies had a similar policy of investigating accidents and incidents as part of their safety programmes. Similar incidents occurred in both companies and investigations were launched. In the first company, the supervisor found that the workers involved behaved unsafely, immediately warned them of the safety infraction and updated their personal safety records. The senior manager in charge acknowledged this supervisor for enforcing workplace safety. In the second company, the supervisor considered the circumstances of the incident, namely that it occurred while the operator was under severe pressure to meet production deadlines after a period of mechanical maintenance problems that had slowed production, and in a context where the attention of employees was drawn from safety practices because recent company cutbacks had workers concerned about their job security. Company officials acknowledged the preventive maintenance problem and held a meeting with all employees where they discussed the current financial situation and asked workers to maintain safety while working together to improve production in view of helping the corporation's viability.

"Why", asked Petersen, "did one company blame the employee, fill out the incident investigation forms and get back to work while the other company found that it must deal with fault at all levels of the organization?" The difference lies in the safety cultures, not the safety programmes themselves, although the cultural way this programme is put into practice, and the values and beliefs that give meaning to actual practices, largely determine whether the programme has sufficient real content and impact.

From this example, it appears that senior management is a key actor whose principles and actions in occupational safety largely contribute to establish the corporate safety culture. In both cases, supervisors responded according to what they perceived to be "the right way of doing things", a perception that had been reinforced by the consequent actions of top management. Obviously, in the first case, top management favoured a "by-the-book", or a bureaucratic and hierarchical safety control approach, while in the second case, the approach was more comprehensive and conducive to managers' commitment to, and workers' involvement in, safety at work. Other cultural approaches are also possible. For example, Eakin (1992) has shown that in very small businesses, it is common that the top manager completely delegates responsibility for safety to the workers.

These examples raise the important question of the dynamics of a safety culture and the processes involved in the building, the maintenance and the change of organizational culture regarding safety at work. One of these processes is the leadership demonstrated by top managers and other organizational leaders, like union officers. The organizational culture approach has contributed to renewed studies of leadership in organizations by showing the importance of the personal role of both natural and organizational leaders in demonstrating commitment to values and creating shared meanings among organizational members (Nadler and Tushman 1990; Schein 1985). Petersen's example of the first company illustrates a situation where top management's leadership was strictly structural, a matter merely of establishing and reinforcing compliance to the safety programme and to rules. In the second company, top managers demonstrated a broader approach to leadership, combining a structural role in deciding to allow time to perform necessary preventive maintenance with a personal role in meeting with employees to discuss safety and production in a difficult financial situation. Finally, in Eakin's study, senior managers of some small businesses seem to play no leadership role at all.

Other organizational actors who play a very important role in the cultural dynamics of occupational safety are middle managers and supervisors. In their study of more than one thousand first-line supervisors, Simard and Marchand (1994) show that a strong majority of supervisors are involved in occupational safety, though the cultural patterns of their involvement may differ. In some workplaces, the dominant pattern is what they call "hierarchical involvement" and is more control-oriented; in other organizations the pattern is "participatory involvement", because supervisors both encourage and allow their employees to participate in accident-prevention activities; and in a small minority of organizations, supervisors withdraw and leave safety up to the workers. It is easy to see the correspondence between these styles of supervisory safety management and what has been previously said about the patterns of upper-level managers' leadership in occupational safety. Empirically, though, the Simard and Marchand study shows that the correlation is not a perfect one, a circumstance that lends support to Petersen's hypothesis that a major problem of many executives is how to build a strong, people-oriented safety culture among the middle and supervisory management. Part of this problem may be due to the fact that most of the lower-level managers are still predominantly production-minded and prone to blame workers for workplace accidents and other safety mishaps (DeJoy 1987 and 1994; Taylor 1981).

This emphasis on management should not be viewed as disregarding the importance of workers in the safety culture dynamics of workplaces. Workers' motivation and behaviours regarding safety at work are influenced by the perceptions they have of the priority given to occupational safety by their supervisors and top managers (Andriessen 1978). This top-down pattern of influence has been proven in numerous behavioural experiments, using managers' positive feedback to reinforce compliance to formal safety rules (McAfee and Winn 1989; Näsänen and Saari 1987). Workers also spontaneously form work groups when the organization of work offers appropriate conditions that allow them to get involved in the formal or informal safety management and regulation of the workplace (Cru and Dejours 1983; Dejours 1992; Dwyer 1992). This latter pattern of workers' behaviours, more oriented towards the safety initiatives of work groups and their capacity for self-regulation, may be used positively by management to develop workforce involvement and safety in the building of a workplace's safety culture.

Safety Culture and Safety Performance

There is a growing body of empirical evidence concerning the impact of safety culture on safety performance. Numerous studies have investigated characteristics of companies having low accident rates, while generally comparing them with similar companies having higher-than-average accident rates. A fairly consistent result of these studies, conducted in industrialized as well as in developing countries, emphasizes the importance of senior managers' safety commitment and leadership for safety performance (Chew 1988; Hunt and Habeck 1993; Shannon et al. 1992; Smith et al. 1978). Moreover, most studies show that in companies with lower accident rates, the personal involvement of top managers in occupational safety is at least as important as their decisions in the structuring of the safety management system (functions that would include the use of financial and professional resources and the creation of policies and programmes, etc.). According to Smith et al. (1978) active involvement of senior managers acts as a motivator for all levels of management by keeping up their interest through participation, and for employees by demonstrating management's commitment to their well-being. Results of many studies suggest that one of the best ways of demonstrating and promoting its humanistic values and people-oriented philosophy is for senior management to participate in highly visible activities, such as workplace safety inspections and meetings with employees.

Numerous studies regarding the relationship between safety culture and safety performance pinpoint the safety behaviours of first-line supervisors by showing that supervisors' involvement in a participative approach to safety management is generally associated with lower accident rates (Chew 1988; Mattila, Hyttinen and Rantanen 1994; Simard and Marchand 1994; Smith et al. 1978). Such a pattern of supervisors' behaviour is exemplified by frequent formal and informal interactions and communications with workers about work and safety, paying attention to monitoring workers' safety performance and giving positive feedback, as well as developing the involvement of workers in accident-prevention activities. Moreover, the characteristics of effective safety supervision are the same as those for generally efficient supervision of operations and production, thereby supporting the hypothesis that there is a close connection between efficient safety management and good general management.

There is evidence that a safety-oriented workforce is a positive factor for the firm's safety performance. However, perception and conception of workers' safety behaviours should not be reduced to just carefulness and compliance with management safety rules, though numerous behavioural experiments have shown that a higher level of workers' conformity to safety practices reduces accident rates (Saari 1990). Indeed, workforce empowerment and active involvement are also documented as factors of successful occupational safety programmes. At the workplace level, some studies offer evidence that effectively functioning joint health and safety committees (consisting of members who are well trained in occupational safety, cooperate in the pursuit of their mandate and are supported by their constituencies) significantly contribute to the firm's safety performance (Chew 1988; Rees 1988; Tuohy and Simard 1992). Similarly, at the shop-floor level, work groups that are encouraged by management to develop team safety and self-regulation generally have a better safety performance than work groups subject to authoritarianism and social disintegration (Dwyer 1992; Lanier 1992).

It can be concluded from the above-mentioned scientific evidence that a particular type of safety culture is more conducive to safety performance. In brief, this safety culture combines top management's leadership and support, lower management's commitment and employees' involvement in occupational safety. Actually, such a safety culture is one that scores high on what could be conceptualized as the two major dimensions of the safety culture concept, namely *safety mission* and *safety involvement*, as shown in figure 59.2.

Safety mission refers to the priority given to occupational safety in the firm's mission. Literature on organizational culture stresses the importance of an explicit and shared definition of a mission that grows out of and supports the key values of the organization (Denison 1990). Consequently, the safety mission dimension reflects the degree to which occupational safety and health are acknowledged by top management as a key value of the firm, and the degree to which upper-level managers use their leadership to promote the internalization of this value in management systems and practices. It can then be hypothesized that a strong sense of safety mission (+) impacts positively on safety performance because it motivates individual members of the workplace to adopt goal-directed behaviour regarding safety at work, and facilitates

coordination by defining a common goal as well as an external criterion for orienting behaviour.

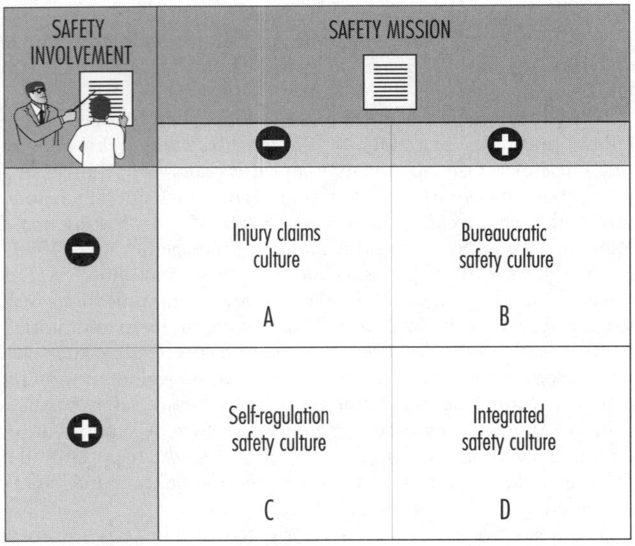

Safety involvement is where supervisors and employees join together to develop team safety at the shop-floor level. Literature on organizational culture supports the argument that high levels of involvement and participation contribute to performance because they create among organizational members a sense of ownership and responsibility leading to a greater voluntary commitment that facilitates the coordination of behaviour and reduces the necessity of explicit bureaucratic control systems (Denison 1990). Moreover, some studies show that involvement can be a managers' strategy for effective performance as well as a workers' strategy for a better work environment (Lawler 1986; Walton 1986).

According to figure 59.2, workplaces combining a high level of these two dimensions should be characterized by what we call an *integrated safety culture*, which means that occupational safety is integrated into the organizational culture as a key value, and into the behaviours of all organizational members, thereby reinforcing involvement from top managers down to the rank-and-file employees. The empirical evidence mentioned above supports the hypothesis that this type of safety culture should lead workplaces to the best safety performance when compared to other types of safety cultures.

The Management of an Integrated Safety Culture

Managing an integrated safety culture first requires the senior management's will to build it into the organizational culture of the firm. This is no simple task. It goes far beyond adopting an official corporate policy emphasizing the key value and priority given to occupational safety and to the philosophy of its management, although indeed the integration of safety at work in the organization's core values is a cornerstone in the building of an integrated safety culture. Indeed, top management should be conscious that such a policy is the starting point of a major organizational change process, since most organizations are not yet functioning according to an integrated safety culture. Of course, the details of the change strategy will vary depending on what the workplace's existing safety culture already is (see cells A, B and C of figure 59.2). In any case, one of the key issues is for the top management to behave congruently with such a policy (in other words to practice what it preaches). This is part of the personal leadership top managers should demonstrate in implementing and enforcing such a policy. Another key issue is for senior management to facilitate the structuring or restructuring of various formal management systems so as to support the building of an integrated safety culture. For example, if the existing safety culture is a bureaucratic one, the role of the safety staff and joint health and safety committee should be reoriented in such a way as to support the development of supervisors' and work teams' safety involvement. In the same way, the performance evaluation system should be adapted so as to acknowledge lower-level managers' accountability and the performance of work groups in occupational safety.

Lower-level managers, and particularly supervisors, also play a critical role in the management of an integrated safety culture. More specifically, they should be accountable for the safety performance of their work teams and they should encourage workers to get actively involved in occupational safety. According to Petersen (1993), most lower-level managers tend to be cynical about safety because they are confronted with the reality of upper management's mixed messages as well as the promotion of various programmes that come and go with little lasting impact. Therefore, building an integrated safety culture often may require a change in the supervisors' pattern of safety behaviour.

Figure 59.2 • Typology of safety cultures.

According to a recent study by Simard and Marchand (1995), a systematic approach to supervisors' behaviour change is the most efficient strategy to effect change. Such an approach consists of coherent, active steps aimed at solving three major problems of the change process: (1) the resistance of individuals to change, (2) the adaptation of existing management formal systems so as to support the change process and (3) the shaping of the informal political and cultural dynamics of the organization. The latter two problems may be addressed by upper managers' personal and structural leadership, as mentioned in the preceding paragraph. However, in unionized workplaces, this leadership should shape the organization's political dynamics so as to create a consensus with union leaders regarding the development of participative safety management at the shop-floor level. As for the problem of supervisors' resistance to change, it should not be managed by a command-and-control approach, but by a consultative approach which helps supervisors participate in the change process and develop a sense of ownership. Techniques such as the focus group and ad hoc committee, which allow supervisors and work teams to express their concerns about safety management and to engage in a problem-solving process, are frequently used, combined with appropriate training of supervisors in participative and effective supervisory management.

It is not easy to conceive a truly integrated safety culture in a workplace that has no joint health and safety committee or worker safety delegate. However, many industrialized and some developing countries now have laws and regulations that encourage or mandate workplaces to establish such committees and delegates. The risk is that these committees and delegates may become mere substitutes for real employee involvement and empowerment in occupational safety at the shop-floor level, thereby serving to reinforce a bureaucratic safety culture. In order to support the development of an integrated safety culture, joint committees and delegates should foster a decentralized and participative safety management approach, for example by (1) organizing activities that raise employees' consciousness of workplace hazards and risk-taking behaviours, (2) designing procedures and training programmes that empower supervisors and work teams to solve many safety problems at the shop-floor level, (3) participating in the workplace's safety performance appraisal and (4) giving reinforcing feedback to supervisors and workers.

Another powerful means of promoting an integrated safety culture among employees is to conduct a perception survey. Workers generally know where many of the safety problems are, but since no one asks them their opinion, they resist getting involved in the safety programme. An anonymous perception survey is a means to break this stalemate and promote employees' safety involvement while providing senior management with feedback that can be used to improve the safety programme's management. Such a survey can be done using an interview method combined with a questionnaire administered to all or to a statistically valid sample of employees (Bailey 1993; Petersen 1993). The survey follow-up is crucial for building an integrated safety culture. Once the data are available, top management should proceed with the change process by creating ad hoc work groups with participation from every echelon of the organization, including workers. This will provide for more in-depth diagnoses of problems identified in the survey and will recommend ways of improving aspects of the safety management that need it. Such a perception survey may be repeated every year or two, in order to periodically assess the improvement of their safety management system and culture.

ORGANIZATIONAL CLIMATE AND SAFETY

Nicole Dedobbeleer and François Béland

We live in an era of new technology and more complex production systems, where fluctuations in global economics, customer requirements and trade agreements affect a work organization's relationships (Moravec 1994). Industries are facing new challenges in the establishment and maintenance of a healthy and safe work environment. In several studies, management's safety efforts, management's commitment and involvement in safety as well as quality of management have been stressed as key elements of the safety system (Mattila, Hyttinen and Rantanen 1994; Dedobbeleer and Béland 1989; Smith 1989; Heinrich, Petersen and Roos 1980; Simonds and Shafai-Sahrai 1977; Komaki 1986; Smith et al. 1978).

According to Hansen (1993a), management's commitment to safety is not enough if it is a passive state; only active, visible leadership which creates a climate for performance can successfully guide a corporation to a safe workplace. Rogers (1961) indicated that "if the administrator, or military or industrial leader, creates such a climate within the organization, then staff will become more self-responsive, more creative, better able to adapt to new problems, more basically cooperative." Safety leadership is thus seen as fostering a climate where working safely is esteemed—a safety climate.

Very little research has been done on the safety climate concept (Zohar 1980; Brown and Holmes 1986; Dedobbeleer and Béland 1991; Oliver, Tomas and Melia 1993; Melia, Tomas and Oliver 1992). People in organizations encounter thousands of events, practices and procedures, and they perceive these events in related sets. What this implies is that work settings have numerous climates and that safety climate is seen as one of them. As the concept of climate is a complex and multilevel phenomenon, organizational climate research has been plagued by theoretical, conceptual and measurement problems. It thus seems crucial to examine these issues in safety climate research if safety climate is to remain a viable research topic and a worthwhile managerial tool.

Safety climate has been considered a meaningful concept which has considerable implications for understanding employee performance (Brown and Holmes 1986) and for assuring success in injury control (Matttila, Hyttinen and Rantanen 1994). If safety climate dimensions can be accurately assessed, management may use them to both recognize and evaluate potential problem areas. Moreover, research results obtained with a standardized safety climate score can yield useful comparisons across industries, independent of differences in technology and risk levels. A safety climate score may thus serve as a guideline in the establishment of a work organization's safety policy. This article examines the safety climate concept in the context of the organizational climate literature, discusses the relationship between safety policy and safety climate and examines the implications of the safety climate concept for leadership in the development and enforcement of a safety policy in an industrial organization.

The Concept of Safety Climate in Organizational Climate Research

Organizational climate research

Organizational climate has been a popular concept for some time. Multiple reviews of organizational climate have appeared since the mid-1960s (Schneider 1975a; Jones and James 1979; Naylor, Pritchard and Ilgen 1980; Schneider and Reichers 1983; Glick

1985; Koys and DeCotiis 1991). There are several definitions of the concept. *Organizational climate* has been loosely used to refer to a broad class of organizational and perceptual variables that reflect individual-organizational interactions (Glick 1985; Field and Abelson 1982; Jones and James 1979). According to Schneider (1975a), it should refer to an area of research rather than a specific unit of analysis or a particular set of dimensions. The term *organizational climate* should be supplanted by the word *climate* to refer to a climate for something.

The study of climates in organizations has been difficult because it is a complex and multi-level phenomenon (Glick 1985; Koys and DeCotiis 1991). Nevertheless, progress has been made in conceptualizing the climate construct (Schneider and Reichers 1983; Koys and DeCotiis 1991). A distinction proposed by James and Jones (1974) between psychological climates and organizational climates has gained general acceptance. The differentiation is made in terms of level of analysis. The psychological climate is studied at the individual level of analysis, and the organizational climate is studied at the organizational level of analysis. When regarded as an individual attribute, the term *psychological climate* is recommended. When regarded as an organizational attribute, the term *organizational climate* is seen as appropriate. Both aspects of climate are considered to be multi-dimensional phenomena, descriptive of the nature of employees perceptions of their experiences within a work organization.

Although the distinction between psychological and organizational climate is generally accepted, it has not extricated organizational climate research from its conceptual and methodological problems (Glick 1985). One of the unresolved problems is the aggregation problem. Organizational climate is often defined as a simple aggregation of psychological climate in an organization (James 1982; Joyce and Slocum 1984). The question is: How can we aggregate individuals' descriptions of their work setting so as to represent a larger social unit, the organization? Schneider and Reichers (1983) noted that "hard conceptual work is required prior to data collection so that (a) the clusters of events assessed sample the relevant domain of issues and (b) the survey is relatively descriptive in focus and refers to the unit (i.e., individual, subsystem, total organization) of interest for analytical purposes." Glick (1985) added that organizational climate should be conceptualized as an organizational phenomenon, not as a simple aggregation of psychological climate. He also acknowledged the existence of multiple units of theory and analysis (i.e., individual, subunit and organizational). Organizational climate connotes an organizational unit of theory; it does not refer to the climate of an individual, workgroup, occupation, department or job. Other labels and units of theory and analysis should be used for the climate of an individual and the climate of a workgroup.

Perceptual agreement among employees in an organization has received considerable attention (Abbey and Dickson 1983; James 1982). Low perceptual agreement on psychological climate measures are attributed to both random error and substantive factors. As employees are asked to report on the organization's climate and not their psychological or work group climate, many of the individual-level random errors and sources of bias are considered to cancel each other when the perceptual measures are aggregated to the organizational level (Glick 1985). To disentangle psychological and organizational climates and to estimate the relative contributions of organizational and psychological processes as determinants of the organizational and psychological climates, use of multi-level models appears to be crucial (Hox and Kreft 1994; Rabash and Woodhouse 1995). These models take into account psychological and organizational levels without using averaged measures of organizational climates that are usually taken on a representative sample of individuals in a number of organizations. It can be shown (Manson, Wong and Entwisle

1983) that biased estimates of organizational climate averages and of effects of organizational characteristics on climates result from aggregating at the organizational level, measurements taken at the individual level. The belief that individual-level measurement errors are cancelled out when averaged over an organization is unfounded.

Another persistent problem with the concept of climate is the specification of appropriate dimensions of organizational and/or psychological climate. Jones and James (1979) and Schneider (1975a) suggested using climate dimensions that are likely to influence or be associated with the study's criteria of interest. Schneider and Reichers (1983) extended this idea by arguing that work organizations have different climates for specific things such as safety, service (Schneider, Parkington and Buxton 1980), in-company industrial relations (Bluen and Donald 1991), production, security and quality. Although criterion referencing provides some focus in the choice of climate dimensions, climate remains a broad generic term. The level of sophistication required to be able to identify which dimensions of practices and procedures are relevant for understanding particular criteria in specific collectivities (e.g., groups, positions, functions) has not been reached (Schneider 1975a). However, the call for criterion-oriented studies does not per se rule out the possibility that a relatively small set of dimensions may still describe multiple environments while any particular dimension may be positively related to some criteria, unrelated to others and negatively related to a third set of outcomes.

The safety climate concept

The safety climate concept has been developed in the context of the generally accepted definitions of the organizational and psychological climate. No specific definition of the concept has yet been offered to provide clear guidelines for measurement and theory building. Very few studies have measured the concept, including a stratified sample of 20 industrial organizations in Israel (Zohar 1980), 10 manufacturing and produce companies in the states of Wisconsin and Illinois (Brown and Holmes 1986), 9 construction sites in the state of Maryland (Dedobbeleer and Béland 1991), 16 construction sites in Finland (Mattila, Hyttinen and Rantanen 1994, Mattila, Rantanen and Hyttinen 1994), and among Valencia workers (Oliver, Tomas and Melia 1993; Melia, Tomas and Oliver 1992).

Climate was viewed as a summary of perceptions workers share about their work settings. Climate perceptions summarize an individual's description of his or her organizational experiences rather than his or her affective evaluative reaction to what has been experienced (Koys and DeCotiis 1991). Following Schneider and Reichers (1983) and Dieterly and Schneider (1974), safety climate models assumed that these perceptions are developed because they are necessary as a frame of reference for gauging the appropriateness of behaviour. Based on a variety of cues present in their work environment, employees were believed to develop coherent sets of perceptions and expectations regarding behaviour-outcome contingencies, and to behave accordingly (Frederiksen, Jensen and Beaton 1972; Schneider 1975a, 1975b).

Table 59.1 demonstrates some diversity in the type and number of safety climate dimensions presented in validation studies on safety climate. In the general organizational climate literature, there is very little agreement on the dimensions of organizational climate. However, researchers are encouraged to use climate dimensions that are likely to influence or be associated with the study's criteria of interest. This approach has been successfully adopted in the studies on safety climate. Zohar (1980) developed seven sets of items that were descriptive of organizational events, practices and procedures and which were found to differentiate high- from low-accident factories (Cohen 1977).

Table 59.1 • Safety climate measures.

Author(s)	Dimensions	Items
Zohar (1980)	Perceived importance of safety training Perceived effects of required work pace on safety Perceived status of safety committee Perceived status of safety officer Perceived effects of safe conduct on promotion Perceived level of risk at workplace Perceived management attitudes toward safety Perceived effect of safe conduct on social status	40
Brown and Holmes (1986)	Employee perception of how concerned management is with their well-being Employee perception of how active management is in responding to this concern Employee physical risk perception	10
Dedobbeleer and Béland (1991)	Management's commitment and involvement in safety Workers' involvement in safety	9
Melia, Tomas and Oliver (1992)	Dedobbeleer and Béland two-factor model	9
Oliver, Tomas and Melia (1993)	Dedobbeleer and Béland two-factor model	9

Brown and Holmes (1986) used Zohar's 40-item questionnaire, and found a three-factor model instead of the Zohar eight-factor model. Dedobbeleer and Béland used nine variables to measure the three-factor model of Brown and Holmes. The variables were chosen to represent safety concerns in the construction industry and were not all identical to those included in Zohar's questionnaire. A two-factor model was found. We are left debating whether differences between the Brown and Holmes results and the Dedobbeleer and Béland results are attributable to the use of a more adequate statistical procedure (LISREL weighted least squares procedure with tetrachoric correlations coefficients). A replication was done by Oliver, Tomas and Melia (1993) and Melia, Tomas and Oliver (1992) with nine similar but not identical variables measuring climate perceptions among post-traumatic and pre-traumatic workers from different types of industries. Similar results to those of the Dedobbeleer and Béland study were found.

Several strategies have been used for improving the validity of safety climate measures. There are different types of validity (e.g., content, concurrent and construct) and several ways to evaluate the validity of an instrument. *Content validity* is the sampling adequacy of the content of a measuring instrument (Nunnally 1978). In safety climate research, the items are those shown by previous research to be meaningful measures of occupational safety. Other "competent" judges usually judge the content of the items, and then some method for pooling these independent judgements is used. There is no mention of such a procedure in the articles on safety climate.

Construct validity is the extent to which an instrument measures the theoretical construct the researcher wishes to measure. It requires a demonstration that the construct exists, that it is distinct from other constructs, and that the particular instrument measures that particular construct and no others (Nunnally 1978). Zohar's study followed several suggestions for improving validity. Representative samples of factories were chosen. A stratified random sample of 20 production workers was taken in each plant. All

questions focused on organizational climate for safety. To study the construct validity of his safety climate instrument, he used Spearman rank correlation coefficients to test the agreement between safety climate scores of factories and safety inspectors' ranking of the selected factories in each production category according to safety practices and accident-prevention programmes. The level of safety climate was correlated with safety programme effectiveness as judged by safety inspectors. Using LISREL confirmatory factor analyses, Brown and Holmes (1986) checked the factorial validity of the Zohar measurement model with a sample of US workers. They wanted to validate Zohar's model by the recommended replication of factor structures (Rummel 1970). The model was not supported by the data. A three-factor model provided a better fit. Results also indicated that the climate structures showed stability across different populations. They did not differ between employees who had accidents and those who had none, subsequently providing a valid and reliable climate measure across the groups. Groups were then compared on climate scores, and differences in climate perception were detected between the groups. As the model has the ability of distinguishing individuals who are known to differ, *concurrent validity* has been shown.

In order to test the stability of the Brown and Holmes three-factor model (1986), Dedobbeleer and Béland (1991) used two LISREL procedures (the maximum likelihood method chosen by Brown and Holmes and the weighted least squares method) with construction workers. Results revealed that a two-factor model provided an overall better fit. Construct validation was also tested by investigating the relationship between a perceptual safety climate measure and objective measures (i.e., structural and process characteristics of the construction sites). Positive relationships were found between the two measures. Evidence was gathered from different sources (i.e., workers and superintendents) and in different ways (i.e., written questionnaire and interviews). Mattila, Rantanen and Hyttinen (1994) replicated this study by showing that similar results were obtained from the objective measurements of the work environment, resulting in a safety index, and the perceptual safety climate measures.

A systematic replication of the Dedobbeleer and Béland (1991) bifactorial structure was done in two different samples of workers in different occupations by Oliver, Tomas and Melia (1993) and Melia, Tomas and Oliver (1992). The two-factor model provided the best global fit. The climate structures did not differ between US construction workers and Spanish workers from different types of industries, subsequently providing a valid climate measure across different populations and different types of occupations.

Reliability is an important issue in the use of a measurement instrument. It refers to the accuracy (consistency and stability) of measurement by an instrument (Nunnally 1978). Zohar (1980) assessed organizational climate for safety in samples of organizations with diverse technologies. The reliability of his aggregated perceptual measures of organizational climate was estimated by Glick (1985). He calculated the aggregate level mean rater reliability by using the Spearman-Brown formula based on the intraclass correlation from a one-way analysis of variance, and found an $ICC_{(1,k)}$ of 0.981. Glick concluded that Zohar's aggregated measures were consistent measures of organizational climate for safety. The LISREL confirmatory factor analyses conducted by Brown and Holmes (1986), Dedobbeleer and Béland (1991), Oliver, Tomas and Melia (1993) and Melia, Tomas and Oliver (1992) also showed evidence of the reliability of the safety climate measures. In the Brown and Holmes study, the factor structures remained the same for no accident versus accident groups. Oliver et al. and Melia et al. demonstrated the stability of the Dedobbeleer and Béland factor structures in two different samples.

Safety Policy and Safety Climate

The concept of safety climate has important implications for industrial organizations. It implies that workers have a unified set of cognitions regarding the safety aspects of their work settings. As these cognitions are seen as a necessary frame of reference for gauging the appropriateness of behaviour (Schneider 1975a), they have a direct influence on workers' safety performance (Dedobbeleer, Béland and German 1990). There are thus basic applied implications of the safety climate concept in industrial organizations. Safety climate measurement is a practical tool that can be used by management at low cost to evaluate as well as recognize potential problem areas. It should thus be recommended to include it as one element of an organization's safety information system. The information provided may serve as guidelines in the establishment of a safety policy.

As workers' safety climate perceptions are largely related to management's attitudes about safety and management's commitment to safety, it can therefore be concluded that a change in management's attitudes and behaviours are prerequisites for any successful attempt at improving the safety level in industrial organizations. Excellent management becomes safety policy. Zohar (1980) concluded that safety should be integrated in the production system in a manner which is closely related to the overall degree of control that management has over the production processes. This point has been stressed in the literature regarding safety policy. Management involvement is seen as critical to safety improvement (Minter 1991). Traditional approaches show limited effectiveness (Sarkis 1990). They are based on elements such as safety committees, safety meetings, safety rules, slogans, poster campaigns and safety incentives or contests. According to Hansen (1993b), these traditional strategies place safety responsibility with a staff coordinator who is detached from the line mission and whose task is almost exclusively to inspect the hazards. The main problem is that this approach fails to integrate safety into the production system, thereby limiting its ability to identify and resolve management oversights and insufficiencies that contribute to accident causation (Hansen 1993b; Cohen 1977).

Contrary to production workers in the Zohar and Brown and Holmes studies, construction workers perceived management's safety attitudes and actions as one single dimension (Dedobbeleer and Béland 1991). Construction workers also perceived safety as a joint responsibility between individuals and management. These results have important implications for the development of safety policies. They suggest that management's support and commitment to safety should be highly visible. Moreover, they indicate that safety policies should address the safety concerns of both management and workers. Safety meetings as the "cultural circles" of Freire (1988) can be a proper means for involving workers in the identification of safety problems and solutions to these problems. Safety climate dimensions are thus in close relationship with the partnership mentality to improve job safety, contrasting with the police enforcement mentality that was present in the construction industry (Smith 1993). In the context of expanding costs of health care and workers' compensation, a non-adversarial labour-management approach to health and safety has emerged (Smith 1993). This partnership approach thus calls for a safety-management revolution, moving away from traditional safety programmes and safety policies.

In Canada, Sass (1989) indicated the strong resistance by management and government to extension of workers' rights in occupational health and safety. This resistance is based upon economic considerations. Sass therefore argued for "the development of an ethics of the work environment based upon egalitarian principles, and the transformation of the primary work group into a community of workers who can shape the character of their work environment." He also suggested that the appropriate relationship in industry to reflect a democratic work environment is "partnership", the coming together of the primary work groups as equals. In Quebec, this progressive philosophy has been operationalized in the establishment of "parity committees" (Gouvernement du Québec 1978). According to law, each organization having more than ten employees had to create a parity committee, which includes employer's and workers' representatives. This committee has decisive power in the following issues related to the prevention programme: determination of a health services programme, choice of the company physician, ascertainment of imminent dangers and the development of training and information programmes. The committee is also responsible for preventive monitoring in the organization; responding to workers' and employer's complaints; analysing and commenting on accident reports; establishing a registry of accidents, injuries, diseases and workers' complaints; studying statistics and reports; and communicating information on the committee's activities.

Leadership and Safety Climate

To make things happen that enable the company to evolve toward new cultural assumptions, management has to be willing to go beyond "commitment" to participatory leadership (Hansen 1993a). The workplace thus needs leaders with vision, empowerment skills and a willingness to cause change.

Safety climate is created by the actions of leaders. This means fostering a climate where working safely is esteemed, inviting all employees to think beyond their own particular jobs, to take care of themselves and their co-workers, propagating and cultivating leadership in safety (Lark 1991). To induce this climate, leaders need perception and insight, motivation and skill to communicate dedication or commitment to the group beyond self-interest, emotional strength, ability to induce "cognition redefinition" by articulating and selling new visions and concepts, ability to create involvement and participation, and depth of vision (Schein 1989). To change any elements of the organization, leaders must be willing to "unfreeze" (Lewin 1951) their own organization.

According to Lark (1991), leadership in safety means at the executive level, creating an overall climate in which safety is a value and in which supervisors and non-supervisors conscientiously and in turn take the lead in hazard control. These executive leaders publish a safety policy in which they: affirm the value of each employee and of the group, and their own commitment to safety; relate safety to the continuance of the company and the achievement of its objectives; express their expectations that each individual will be responsible for safety and take an active part in keeping the workplace healthy and safe; appoint a safety representative in writing and empower this individual to execute corporate safety policy.

Supervisor leaders expect safe behaviour from subordinates and directly involve them in the identification of problems and their solutions. Leadership in safety for the non-supervisor means reporting deficiencies, seeing corrective actions as a challenge, and working to correct these deficiencies.

Leadership challenges and empowers people to lead in their own right. At the core of this notion of empowerment is the concept of power, defined as the ability to control the factors that determine one's life. The new health promotion movement, however, attempts to reframe power not as "power over" but rather as "power to" or as "power with" (Robertson and Minkler 1994).

Conclusions

Only some of the conceptual and methodological problems plaguing organizational climate scientists are being addressed in safety climate research. No specific definition of the safety climate concept has yet been given. Nevertheless, some of the research results are very encouraging. Most of the research efforts have been directed toward validation of a safety climate model. Attention has been given to the specification of appropriate dimensions of safety climate. Dimensions suggested by the literature on organizational characteristics found to discriminate high versus low accident rate companies served as a useful starting point for the dimension identification process. Eight-, three- and two-factor models are proposed. As Occam's razor demands some parsimony, the limitation of the dimensions seems pertinent. The two-factor model is thus most appropriate, in particular in a work context where short questionnaires need to be administered. The factor analytic results for the scales based on the two dimensions are very satisfactory. Moreover, a valid climate measure is provided across different populations and different occupations. Further studies should, however, be conducted if the replication and generalization rules of theory testing are to be met. The challenge is to specify a theoretically meaningful and analytically practical universe of possible climate dimensions. Future research should also focus on organizational units of analysis in assessing and improving the validity and reliability of the organizational climate for safety measures. Several studies are being conducted at this moment in different countries, and the future looks promising.

As the safety climate concept has important implications for safety policy, it becomes particularly crucial to resolve the conceptual and methodological problems. The concept clearly calls for a safety-management revolution. A process of change in management attitudes and behaviours becomes a prerequisite to attaining safety performance. "Partnership leadership" has to emerge from this period where restructuring and layoffs are a sign of the times. Leadership challenges and empowers. In this empowerment process, employers and employees will increase their capacity to work together in a participatory manner. They will also develop skills of listening and speaking up, problem analysis and consensus building. A sense of community should develop as well as self-efficacy. Employers and employees will be able to build on this knowledge and these skills.

PARTICIPATORY WORKPLACE IMPROVEMENT PROCESS

Jorma Saari

Behaviour Modification: A Safety Management Technique

Safety management has two main tasks. It is incumbent on the safety organization (1) to maintain the company's safety performance on the current level and (2) to implement measures and programmes which improve the safety performance. The tasks are different and require different approaches. This article describes a method for the second task which has been used in numerous companies with excellent results. The background of this method is behaviour modification, which is a technique for improving safety which has many applications in business and industry. Two independently conducted experiments of the first scientific applications of behaviour modification were published by Americans in 1978. The applications were in quite different locations. Komaki, Barwick and Scott (1978) did their study in a bakery. Sulzer-Azaroff (1978) did her study in laboratories at a university.

Consequences of Behaviour

Behaviour modification puts the focus on the consequences of a behaviour. When workers have several behaviours to opt for, they choose the one which will be expected to bring about more

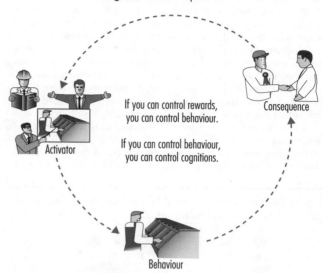

Figure 59.3 • Behaviour modification: a safety management technique.

If you can control rewards, you can control behaviour.

If you can control behaviour, you can control cognitions.

Activator

Consequence

Behaviour

In behaviour modification, one assumes that the expected consequences of behaviour determine the choice between behavioural options.

positive consequences. Before action, the worker has a set of attitudes, skills, equipment and facility conditions. These have an influence on the choice of action. However, it is primarily what follows the action as foreseeable consequences that determines the choice of behaviour. Because the consequences have an effect on attitudes, skills and so on, they have the predominant role in inducing a change in behaviour, according to the theorists (figure 59.3).

The problem in the safety area is that many unsafe behaviours lead workers to choose more positive consequences (in the sense of apparently rewarding the worker) than safe behaviours. An unsafe work method may be more rewarding if it is quicker, perhaps easier, and induces appreciation from the supervisor. The negative consequence—for instance, an injury—does not follow each unsafe behaviour, as injuries require other adverse conditions to exist before they can take place. Therefore positive consequences are overwhelming in their number and frequency.

As an example, a workshop was conducted in which the participants analysed videos of various jobs at a production plant. These participants, engineers and machine operators from the plant, noticed that a machine was operated with the guard open. "You cannot keep the guard closed", claimed an operator. "If the automatic operation ceases, I press the limit switch and force the last part to come out of the machine", he said. "Otherwise I have to take the unfinished part out, carry it several metres and put it back to the conveyor. The part is heavy; it is easier and faster to use the limit switch."

This little incident illustrates well how the expected consequences affect our decisions. The operator wants to do the job fast and avoid lifting a part that is heavy and difficult to handle. Even if this is more risky, the operator rejects the safer method. The same mechanism applies to all levels in organizations. A plant manager, for example, likes to maximize the profit of the operation and be rewarded for good economic results. If top management does not pay attention to safety, the plant manager can expect more positive consequences from investments which maximize production than those which improve safety.

Positive and Negative Consequences

Governments give rules to economic decision makers through laws, and enforce the laws with penalties. The mechanism is direct: any decision maker can expect negative consequences for breach of law. The difference between the legal approach and the approach advocated here is in the type of consequences. Law enforcement uses negative consequences for unsafe behaviour, while behaviour modification techniques use positive consequences for safe behaviour. Negative consequences have their drawbacks even if they are effective. In the area of safety, the use of negative consequences has been common, extending from government penalties to supervisor's reprimand. People try to avoid penalties. By doing it, they easily associate safety with penalties, as something less desirable.

Positive consequences reinforcing safe behaviour are more desirable, as they associate positive feelings with safety. If operators can expect more positive consequences from safe work methods, they choose this more as a likely role of behaviour. If plant managers are appraised and rewarded on the basis of safety, they will most likely give a higher value to safety aspects in their decisions.

The array of possible positive consequences is wide. They extend from social attention to various privileges and tokens. Some of the consequences can easily be attached to behaviour; some others demand administrative actions which may be overwhelming. Fortunately, just the chance of being rewarded can change performance.

Changing Unsafe Behaviour to Safe Behaviour

What was especially interesting in the original work of Komaki, Barwick and Scott (1978) and of Sulzer-Azaroff (1978) was the use of performance information as the consequence. Rather than using social consequences or tangible rewards, which may be difficult to administer, they developed a method to measure the safety performance of a group of workers, and used the performance index as the consequence. The index was constructed so that it was just a single figure that varied between 0 and 100. Being simple, it effectively communicated the message about current performance to those concerned. The original application of this technique aimed just at getting employees to change their behaviour. It did not address any other aspects of workplace improvement, such as eliminating problems by engineering, or introducing procedural changes. The programme was implemented by researchers without the active involvement of workers.

The users of the behaviour modification (BM) technique assume unsafe behaviour to be an essential factor in accident causation, and a factor which can change in isolation without subsequent effects. Therefore, the natural starting point of a BM programme is the investigation of accidents for the identification of unsafe behaviours (Sulzer-Azaroff and Fellner 1984). A typical application of safety-related behaviour modification consists of the steps given in figure 59.4. The safe acts have to be specified precisely, according to the developers of the technique. The first step is to define which are the correct acts in an area such as a department, a supervisory area and so on. Wearing safety glasses appropriately in certain areas would be an example of a safe act. Usually, a small number of specific safe acts—for example, ten—are defined for a behaviour modification programme.

A few other examples of typical safe behaviours are:

1. In working on a ladder, it should be tied off.
2. In working on a catwalk, one should not lean over the railing.
3. Lockouts should be used during electrical maintenance.
4. Protective equipment should be worn.
5. A fork-lift should be driven up or down a ramp with the boom in its proper position (Krause, Hidley and Hodgson 1990; McSween 1995).

If a sufficient number of people, typically from 5 to 30, work in a given area, it is possible to generate an observation checklist based on unsafe behaviours. The main principle is to choose checklist items which have only two values, correct or incorrect. If wearing safety glasses is one of the specified safe acts, it would be appropriate to observe every person separately and determine whether or not they are wearing safety glasses. This way the observations provide objective and clear data about the prevalence of safe behaviour. Other specified safe behaviours provide other items for inclusion in the observation checklist. If the list consists, for example, of one hundred items, it is easy to calculate a safety performance index of the percentage of those items which are marked correct, after the observation is completed. The performance index usually varies from time to time.

Figure 59.4 • Behaviour modification for safety consists of the following steps.

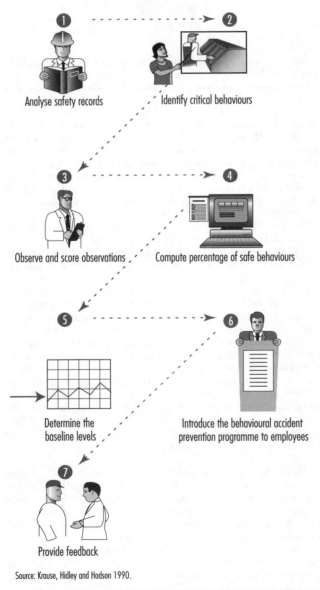

① Analyse safety records

② Identify critical behaviours

③ Observe and score observations

④ Compute percentage of safe behaviours

⑤ Determine the baseline levels

⑥ Introduce the behavioural accident prevention programme to employees

⑦ Provide feedback

Source: Krause, Hidley and Hodson 1990.

Table 59.2 • Differences between Tuttava and other programme/techniques.

Aspect	Behaviour modification for safety	Participatory workplace improvement process, Tuttava
Basis	Accidents, incidents, risk perceptions	Work analysis, work flow
Focus	People and their behaviour	Conditions
Implementation	Experts, consultants	Joint employee-management team
Effect	Temporary	Sustainable
Goal	Behavioural change	Fundamental and cultural change

When the measurement technique is ready, the users determine the baseline. Observation rounds are done at random times weekly (or for several weeks). When a sufficient number of observation rounds are done there is a reasonable picture of the variations of the baseline performance. This is necessary for the positive mechanisms to work. The baseline should be around 50 to 60% to give a positive starting point for improvement and to acknowledge previous performance. The technique has proven its effectiveness in changing safety behaviour. Sulzer-Azaroff, Harris and McCann (1994) list in their review 44 published studies showing a definite effect on behaviour. The technique seems to work almost always, with a few exceptions, as mentioned in Cooper et al. 1994.

Practical Application of Behavioural Theory

Because of several drawbacks in behaviour modification, we developed another technique which aims at rectifying some of the drawbacks. The new programme is called *Tuttava*, which is an acronym for the Finnish words *safely productive*. The major differences are shown in the table 59.2.

The underlying safety theory in behavioural safety programmes is very simple. It assumes that there is a clear line between *safe* and *unsafe*. Wearing safety glasses represents safe behaviour. It does not matter that the optical quality of the glasses may be poor or that the field of vision may be reduced. More generally, the dichotomy between *safe* and *unsafe* may be a dangerous simplification.

The receptionist at a plant asked me to remove my ring for a plant tour. She committed a safe act by asking me to remove my ring, and I, by doing so. The wedding ring has, however, a high emotional value to me. Therefore I was worried about losing my ring during the tour. This took part of my perceptual and mental energy away from observing the surrounding area. I was less observant and therefore my risk of being hit by a passing fork-lift truck was higher than usual.

The "no rings" policy originated probably from a past accident. Similar to the wearing of safety glasses, it is far from clear that it itself represents safety. Accident investigations, and people concerned, are the most natural source for the identification of unsafe acts. But this may be very misleading. The investigator may not really understand how an act contributed to the injury under investigation. Therefore, an act labelled "unsafe" may not really be generally speaking unsafe. For this reason, the application developed herein (Saari and Näsänen 1989) defines the behavioural targets from a work analysis point of view. The focus is on tools and materials, because the workers handle those every day and it is easy for them to start talking about familiar objects.

Observing people by direct methods leads easily to blame. Blame leads to organizational tension and antagonism between management and labour, and it is not beneficial for continuous safety improvements. It is therefore better to focus on physical conditions rather than try to coerce behaviour directly. Targeting the application to behaviours related to handling materials and tools, will make any relevant change highly visible. The behaviour itself may last only a second, but it has to leave a visible mark. For example, putting a tool back in its designated place after use takes a very short time. The tool itself remains visible and observable, and there is no need to observe the behaviour itself.

The visible change provides two benefits: (1) it becomes obvious to everybody that improvements happen and (2) people learn to read their performance level directly from their environment. They do not need the results of observation rounds in order to know their current performance. This way, the improvements start acting as positive consequences with respect to correct behaviour, and the artificial performance index becomes unnecessary.

The researchers and external consultants are the main actors in the application described previously. The workers need not think about their work; it is enough if they change their behaviour. However, for obtaining deeper and more lasting results, it would be better if they were involved in the process. Therefore, the application should integrate both workers and management, so that the implementation team consists of representatives from both sides. It also would be nice to have an application which gives lasting results without continuous measurements. Unfortunately, the normal behaviour modification programme does not create highly visible changes, and many critical behaviours last only a second or fractions of a second.

The technique does have some drawbacks in the form described. In theory, relapse to baseline should occur when the observation rounds are terminated. The resources for developing the programme and carrying out observation may be too extensive in comparison with the temporary change gained.

Tools and materials provide a sort of window into the quality of the functions of an organization. For example, if too many components or parts clutter a workstation it may be an indication about problems in the firm's purchasing process or in the suppliers' procedures. The physical presence of excessive parts is a concrete way of initiating discussion about organizational functions. The workers who are especially not used to abstract discussions about organizations, can participate and bring their observations into the analysis. Tools and materials often provide an avenue to the underlying, more hidden factors contributing to accident risks. These factors are typically organizational and procedural by nature and, therefore, difficult to address without concrete and substantive informational matter.

Organizational malfunctions may also cause safety problems. For example, in a recent plant visit, workers were observed lifting products manually onto pallets weighing several tons all together. This happened because the purchasing system and the supplier's system did not function well and, consequently, the product labels were not available at the right time. The products had to be set aside for days on pallets, obstructing an aisle. When the labels arrived, the products were lifted, again manually, to the line. All this was extra work, work which contributes to the risk of back or other injury.

Four Conditions Have to Be Satisfied in a Successful Improvement Programme

To be successful, one must possess correct theoretical and practical understanding about the problem and the mechanisms behind it. This is the foundation for setting the goals for improvement, following which (1) people have to know the new goals, (2) they

Figure 59.5 • The four steps of a successful safety programme.

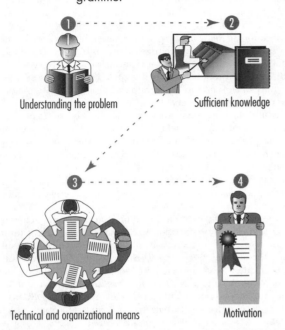

Understanding the problem

Sufficient knowledge

Technical and organizational means

Motivation

ble 59.3). The targets should be (1) positive and make work easier, (2) generally acceptable, (3) simple and briefly stated, (4) expressed at the start with action verbs to emphasize the important items to be done and (5) easy to observe and measure.

The key words for specifying the targets are *tools* and *materials*. Usually the targets refer to goals such as the proper placement of materials and tools, keeping the aisles open, correcting leaks and other process disturbances right away, and keeping free access to fire extinguishers, emergency exits, electric substations, safety

Figure 59.6 • The Tuttava programme consists of four stages and eight steps.

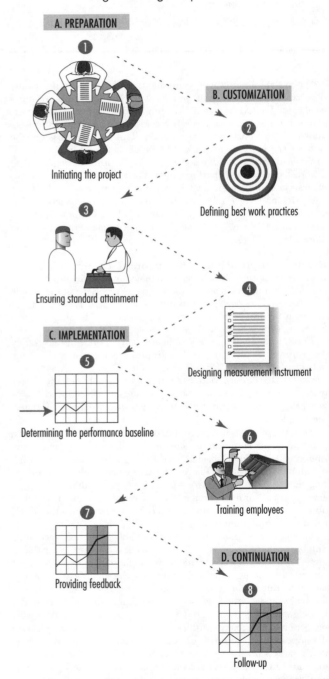

A. PREPARATION

Initiating the project

B. CUSTOMIZATION

Defining best work practices

Ensuring standard attainment

Designing measurement instrument

C. IMPLEMENTATION

Determining the performance baseline

Training employees

Providing feedback

D. CONTINUATION

Follow-up

have to have the technical and organizational means for acting accordingly and (3) they have to be motivated (figure 59.5). This scheme applies to any change programme.

A safety campaign may be a good instrument for efficiently spreading information about a goal. However, it has an effect on people's behaviour only if the other criteria are satisfied. Requiring the wearing of hard hats has no effect on a person who does not have a hard hat, or if a hard hat is terribly uncomfortable, for example, because of a cold climate. A safety campaign may also aim at increasing motivation, but it will fail if it just sends an abstract message, such as "safety first", unless the recipients have the skills to translate the message into specific behaviours. Plant managers who are told to reduce injuries in the area by 50% are in a similar situation if they do not understand anything about accident mechanisms.

The four criteria set out in figure 59.5 have to be met. For example, an experiment was conducted in which people were supposed to use stand-alone screens to prevent welding light from reaching other workers' areas. The experiment failed because it was not realized that no adequate organizational agreements were made. Who should put the screen up, the welder or the other nearby worker exposed to the light? Because both worked on a piece-rate basis and did not want to waste time, an organizational agreement about compensation should have been made before the experiment. A successful safety programme has to address all these four areas simultaneously. Otherwise, progress will be limited.

Tuttava Programme

The Tuttava programme (figure 59.6) lasts from 4 to 6 months and covers the working area of 5 to 30 people at a time. It is done by a team consisting of the representatives of management, supervisors and workers.

Performance targets

The first step is to prepare a list of performance targets, or best work practices, consisting of about ten well-specified targets (ta-

Table 59.3 • An example of best work practices.

- Keep gangways, aisles clear.
- Keep tools stored in proper places when not in use.
- Use proper containers and disposal methods for chemicals.
- Store all manuals at right place after use.
- Make sure of the right calibration on measuring instruments.
- Return trolleys, buggies, pallets at proper location after use.
- Take only right quantity of parts (bolts, nuts, etc.) from bins and return any un-used items back in proper place.
- Remove from pockets any loose objects that may fall without notice.

switches and so on. The performance targets at a printing ink factory are given in table 59.4.

These targets are comparable to the safe behaviours defined in the behaviour modification programmes. The difference is that Tuttava behaviours leave visible marks. Closing bottles after use may be a behaviour which takes less than a minute. However, it is possible to see if this was done or not by observing the bottles not in use. There is no need to observe people, a fact which is important for avoiding fingerpointing and blame.

The targets define the behavioural change that the team expects from the employees. In this sense, they compare with the safe behaviours in behaviour modification. However, most of the targets refer to things which are not only workers' behaviours but which have a much wider meaning. For example, the target may be to store only immediately needed materials in the work area. This requires an analysis of the work process and an understanding of it, and may reveal problems in the technical and organizational arrangements. Sometimes, the materials are not stored conveniently for daily use. Sometimes, the delivery systems work so slowly or are so vulnerable to disturbances that employees stockpile too much material in the work area.

Observation checklist

When the performance targets are sufficiently well defined, the team designs an observation checklist to measure to what extent the targets are met. About 100 measurement points are chosen from the area. For example, the number of measurement points was 126 in the printing ink factory. In each point, the team observes one or several specific items. For example, as regards a waste container, the items could be (1) is the container not too full,

Table 59.4 • Performance targets at a printing ink factory.

- Keep aisles open.
- Always put covers on containers when possible.
- Close bottles after use.
- Clean and return tools after use.
- Ground containers when moving flammable substances.
- Use personal protection as specified.
- Use local exhaust ventilation.
- Store in working areas only materials and substances needed immediately.
- Use only the designated fork-lift truck in the department making flexographic printing inks.
- Label all containers.

(2) is the right kind of waste put into it or (3) is the cover on, if needed? Each item can only be either correct or incorrect. Dichotomized observations make the measurement system objective and reliable. This allows one to calculate a performance index after an observation round covering all measurement points. The index is simply the percentage of items assessed correct. The index can, quite obviously, range from 0 to 100, and it indicates directly to what degree the standards are met. When the first draft of the observation checklist is available, the team conducts a test round. If the result is around 50 to 60%, and if each member of the team gets about the same result, the team can move on to the next phase of Tuttava. If the result of the first observation round is too low—say, 20%—then the team revises the list of performance targets. This is because the programme should be positive in every aspect. Too low a baseline would not adequately assess previous performance; it would rather merely set the blame for poor performance. A good baseline is around 50%.

Technical, organizational and procedural improvements

A very important step in the programme is ensuring the attainment of the performance targets. For example, waste may be lying on floors simply because the number of waste containers is insufficient. There may be excessive materials and parts because the supply system does not work. The system has to become better before it is correct to demand a behavioural change from the workers. By examining each of the targets for attainability, the team usually identifies many opportunities for technical, organizational and procedural improvements. In this way, the worker members bring their practical experience into the development process.

Because the workers spend the entire day at their workplace, they have much more knowledge about the work processes than management. Analysing the attainment of the performance targets, the workers get the opportunity to communicate their ideas to management. As improvements then take place, the employees are much more receptive to the request to meet the performance targets. Usually, this step leads to easily manageable corrective actions. For example, products were removed from the line for adjustments. Some of the products were good, some were bad. The production workers wanted to have designated areas marked for good and bad products so as to know which products to put back on the line and which ones to send for recycling. This step may also call for major technical modifications, such as a new ventilation system in the area where the rejected products are stored. Sometimes, the number of modifications is very high. For example, over 300 technical improvements were made in a plant producing oil-based chemicals which employs only 60 workers. It is important to manage the implementation of improvements well to avoid frustration and the overloading of the respective departments.

Baseline measurements

Baseline observations are started when the attainment of performance targets is sufficiently ensured and when the observation checklist is reliable enough. Sometimes, the targets need revisions, as improvements take a longer time. The team conducts weekly observation rounds for a few weeks to determine the prevailing standard. This phase is important, because it makes it possible to compare the performance at any later time to the initial performance. People forget easily how things were just a couple of months in the past. It is important to have the feeling of progress to reinforce continuous improvements.

Feedback

As the next step, the team trains all people in the area. It is usually done in a one-hour seminar. This is the first time when the results

Figure 59.7 • The results from a department at a shipyard.

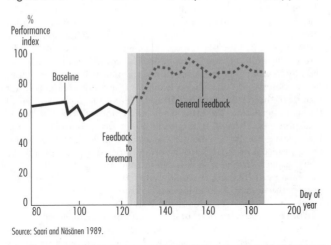

Source: Saari and Näsänen 1989.

of the baseline measurements are made generally known. The feedback phase starts immediately after the seminar. The observation rounds continue weekly. Now, the result of the round is immediately made known to everybody by posting the index on a chart placed in a visible location. All critical remarks, blame or other negative comments are strictly forbidden. Although the team will identify individuals not behaving as specified in the targets, the team is instructed to keep the information to themselves. Sometimes, all employees are integrated into the process from the very beginning, especially if the number of people working in the area is small. This is better than having representative implementation teams. However, it may not be feasible everywhere.

Effects on performance

Change happens within a couple of weeks after the feedback starts (figure 59.7). People start to keep the worksite in visibly better order. The performance index jumps typically from 50 to 60% and then even to 80 or 90%. This may not sound big in absolute terms, but it *is* a big change on the shop floor.

As the performance targets refer on purpose not only to safety issues, the benefits extend from better safety to productivity, saving of materials and floor footage, better physical appearance and so on. To make the improvements attractive to all, there are targets which integrate safety with other goals, such as productivity and quality. This is necessary to make safety more attractive for the management, who in this way will also provide funding more willingly for the less important safety improvements

Sustainable results

When the programme was first developed, 12 experiments were conducted to test the various components. Follow-up observations were made at a shipyard for 2 years. The new level of performance was well kept up during the 2-year follow-up. The sustainable results separate this process from normal behaviour modification. The visible changes in the location of materials, tools and so on, and the technical improvements deter the already secured improvement from fading away. When 3 years had gone by, an evaluation of the effect on accidents at the shipyard was made. The result was dramatic. Accidents had gone down by from 70 to 80%. This was much more than could be expected on the basis of the behavioural change. The number of accidents totally unrelated to performance targets went down as well.

The major effect on accidents is not attributable to the direct changes the process achieves. Rather, this is a starting point for other processes to follow. As Tuttava is very positive and as it brings noticeable improvements, the relations between management and labour get better and the teams get encouragement for other improvements.

Cultural change

A large steel mill was one of the numerous users of Tuttava, the primary purpose of which is to change safety culture. When they started in 1987 there were 57 accidents per million hours worked. Prior to this, safety management relied heavily on commands from the top. Unfortunately, the president retired and everybody forgot safety, as the new management could not create a similar demand for safety culture. Among middle management, safety was considered negatively as something extra to be done because of the president's demand. They organized ten Tuttava teams in 1987, and new teams were added every year after that. Now, they have less than 35 accidents per million hours worked, and production has steadily increased during these years. The process caused the safety culture to improve as the middle managers saw in their respective departments improvements which were simultaneously good for safety and production. They became more receptive to other safety programmes and initiatives.

The practical benefits were big. For example, the maintenance service department of the steel mill, employing 300 people, reported a reduction of 400 days in the number of days lost due to occupational injuries—in other words, from 600 days to 200 days. The absenteeism rate fell also by one percentage point. The supervisors said that "it is nicer to come to a workplace which is well organized, both materially and mentally". The investment was just a fraction of the economic benefit.

Another company employing 1,500 people reported the release of 15,000 m² of production area, since materials, equipment and so forth, are stored in a better order. The company paid US$1.5 million less in rent. A Canadian company saves about 1 million Canadian dollars per year because of reduced material damages resulting from the implementation of Tuttava.

These are results which are possible only through a cultural change. The most important element in the new culture is shared positive experiences. A manager said, "You can buy people's time, you can buy their physical presence at a given place, you can even buy a measured number of their skilled muscular motions per hour. But you cannot buy loyalty, you cannot buy the devotion of hearts, minds, or souls. You must earn them." The positive approach of Tuttava helps managers to earn the loyalty and the devotion of their working teams. Thereby the programme helps involve employees in subsequent improvement projects.

METHODS OF SAFETY DECISION MAKING

Terje Sten

A company is a complex system where decision making takes place in many connections and under various circumstances. Safety is only one of a number of requirements managers must consider when choosing among actions. Decisions relating to safety issues vary considerably in scope and character depending on the attributes of the risk problems to be managed and the decision maker's position in the organization.

Much research has been undertaken on how people actually make decisions, both individually and in an organizational context: see, for instance, Janis and Mann (1977); Kahnemann, Slovic and Tversky (1982); Montgomery and Svenson (1989). This article will examine selected research experience in this area as a basis for decision-making methods used in management of safety. In principle, decision making concerning safety is not much different from decision making in other areas of management. There is no simple method or set of rules for making good decisions in all situations, since the activities involved in safety management are too complex and varied in scope and character.

The main focus of this article will not be on presenting simple prescriptions or solutions but rather to provide more insight into some of the important challenges and principles for good decision making concerning safety. An overview of the scope, levels and steps in problem solving concerning safety issues will be given, mainly based on the work by Hale et al. (1994). Problem solving is a way of identifying the problem and eliciting viable remedies. This is an important first step in any decision process to be examined. In order to put the challenges of real-life decisions concerning safety into perspective, the principles of *rational choice theory* will be discussed. The last part of the article covers decision making in an organizational context and introduces the sociological perspective on decision making. Also included are some of the main problems and methods of decision making in the context of safety management, so as to provide more insight into the main dimensions, challenges and pitfalls of making decisions on safety issues as an important activity and challenge in management of safety.

The Context of Safety Decision Making

A general presentation of the methods of safety decision making is complicated because both safety issues and the character of the decision problems vary considerably over the lifetime of an enterprise. From concept and establishment to closure, the life cycle of a company may be divided into six main stages:

1. design
2. construction
3. commissioning
4. operation
5. maintenance and modification
6. decomposition and demolition.

Each of the life-cycle elements involves decisions concerning safety which are not only specific to that phase alone but which also impact on some or all of the other phases. During design, construction and commissioning, the main challenges concern the choice, development and realization of the safety standards and specifications that have been decided upon. During operation, maintenance and demolition, the main objectives of safety management will be to maintain and possibly improve the determined level of safety. The construction phase also represents a "production phase" to some extent, because at the same time that construction safety principles must be adhered to, the safety specifications for what is being built must be realized.

Safety Management Decision Levels

Decisions about safety also differ in character depending on organizational level. Hale et al. (1994) distinguish among three main decision levels of safety management in the organization:

The level of *execution* is the level at which the actions of those involved (workers) directly influence the occurrence and control of hazards in the workplace. This level is concerned with the recognition of the hazards and the choice and implementation of actions to eliminate, reduce and control them. The degrees of freedom present at this level are limited; therefore, feedback and correction loops are concerned essentially with correcting deviations from established procedures and returning practice to a norm. As soon as a situation is identified where the norm agreed

upon is no longer thought to be appropriate, the next higher level is activated.

The level of *planning, organization and procedures* is concerned with devising and formalizing the actions to be taken at the execution level in respect to the entire range of expected hazards. The planning and organization level, which sets out responsibilities, procedures, reporting lines and so on, is typically found in safety manuals. It is this level which develops new procedures for hazards new to the organization, and modifies existing procedures to keep up either with new insights about hazards or with standards for solutions relating to hazards. This level involves the translation of abstract principles into concrete task allocation and implementation, and corresponds to the improvement loop required in many quality systems.

The level of *structure and management* is concerned with the overall principles of safety management. This level is activated when the organization considers that the current planning and organizing levels are failing in fundamental ways to achieve accepted performance. It is the level at which the "normal" functioning of the safety management system is critically monitored and through which it is continually improved or maintained in face of changes in the external environment of the organization.

Hale et al. (1994) emphasize that the three levels are *abstractions* corresponding to three different kinds of feedback. They should not be seen as contiguous with the hierarchical levels of shop floor, first line and higher management, as the activities specified at each abstract level can be applied in many different ways. The way task allocations are made reflects the culture and methods of working of the individual company.

Safety Decision-Making Process

Safety problems must be managed through some kind of problem-solving or decision-making process. According to Hale et al. (1994) this process, which is designated the *problem-solving cycle*, is common to the three levels of safety management described above. The problem-solving cycle is a model of an idealized stepwise procedure for analysing and making decisions on safety problems caused by potential or actual deviations from desired, expected or planned achievements (figure 59.8).

Although the steps are the same in principle at all three safety management levels, the application in practice may differ somewhat depending on the nature of problems treated. The model shows that decisions which concern safety management span many types of problems. In practice, each of the following six basic decision problems in safety management will have to be broken down into several subdecisions which will form the basis for choices on each of the main problem areas.

1. What is an acceptable safety level or standard of the activity/department/company, etc.?
2. What criteria shall be used to assess the safety level?
3. What is the current safety level?
4. What are the causes of identified deviations between acceptable and observed level of safety?
5. What means should be chosen to correct the deviations and keep up the safety level?
6. How should corrective actions be implemented and followed up?

Rational Choice Theory

Managers' methods for making decisions must be based on some principle of rationality in order to gain acceptance among members of the organization. In practical situations what is rational may not always be easy to define, and the logical requirements of what may be defined as rational decisions may be difficult to fulfil. *Rational choice theory* (RCT), the conception of rational decision

Figure 59.8 • The problem-solving cycle.

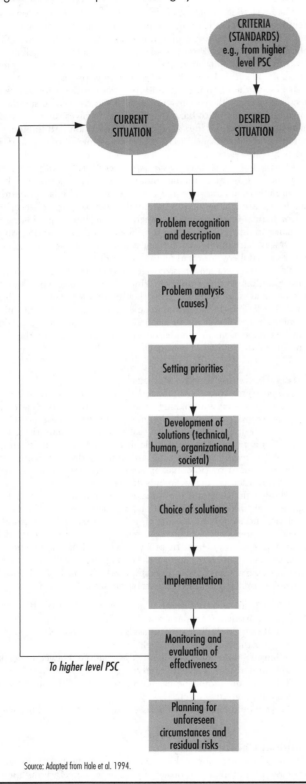

CRITERIA (STANDARDS) e.g., from higher level PSC

CURRENT SITUATION

DESIRED SITUATION

Problem recognition and description

Problem analysis (causes)

Setting priorities

Development of solutions (technical, human, organizational, societal)

Choice of solutions

Implementation

Monitoring and evaluation of effectiveness

To higher level PSC

Planning for unforeseen circumstances and residual risks

Source: Adapted from Hale et al. 1994.

economic behaviour but also the behaviour studied by nearly all social science disciplines, from political philosophy to psychology.

The psychological study of optimal human decision making is called *subjective expected utility theory* (SEU). RCT and SEU are basically the same; only the applications differ. SEU focuses on the thinking of individual decision making, while RCT has a wider application in explaining behaviour within whole organizations or institutions—see, for example, Neumann and Politser (1992). Most of the tools of modern operations research use the assumptions of SEU. They assume that what is desired is to maximize the achievement of some goal, under specific constraints, and assuming that all alternatives and consequences (or their probability distribution) are known (Simon and associates 1992). The essence of RCT and SEU can be summarized as follows (March and Simon 1993):

Decision makers, when encountering a decision-making situation, acquire and see the whole set of alternatives from which they will choose their action. This set is simply given; the theory does not tell how it is obtained.

To each alternative is attached a set of consequences—the events that will ensue if that particular alternative is chosen. Here the existing theories fall into three categories:

- *Certainty theories* assume the decision maker has complete and accurate knowledge of the consequences that will follow on each alternative. In the case of *certainty*, the choice is unambiguous.
- *Risk theories* assume accurate knowledge of a probability distribution of the consequences of each alternative. In the case of *risk*, rationality is usually defined as the choice of that alternative for which expected utility is greatest.
- *Uncertainty theories* assume that the consequences of each alternative belong to some subset of all possible consequences, but that the decision maker cannot assign definite probabilities to the occurrence of particular consequences. In the case of *uncertainty*, the definition of rationality becomes problematic.

At the outset, the decision maker makes use of a "utility function" or a "preference ordering" that ranks all sets of consequences from the most preferred to the least preferred. It should be noted that another proposal is the rule of "minimax risk", by which one considers the "worst set of consequences" that may follow from each alternative, then selects the alternative whose worst set of consequences is preferred to the worst sets attached to other alternatives.

The decision maker elects the alternative closest to the preferred set of consequences.

One difficulty of RCT is that the term *rationality* is in itself problematic. What is rational depends upon the social context in which the decision takes place. As pointed out by Flanagan (1991), it is important to distinguish between the two terms *rationality* and *logicality*. Rationality is tied up with issues related to the meaning and quality of life for some individual or individuals, while logicality is not. The problem of the benefactor is precisely the issue which rational choice models fail to clarify, in that they assume value neutrality, which is seldom present in real-life decision making (Zey 1992). Although the value of RCT and SEU as explanatory theory is somewhat limited, it has been useful as a theoretical model for "rational" decision making. Evidence that behaviour often deviates from outcomes predicted by expected utility theory does not necessarily mean that the theory inappropriately prescribes how people *should* make decisions. As a normative model the theory has proven useful in generating research concerning how and why people make decisions which violate the optimal utility axiom.

Applying the ideas of RCT and SEU to safety decision making may provide a basis for evaluating the "rationality" of choices

making, was originally developed to explain economic behaviour in the marketplace, and later generalized to explain not only made with respect to safety—for instance, in the selection of preventive measures given a safety problem one wants to alleviate. Quite often it will not be possible to comply with the principles of rational choice because of lack of reliable data. Either one may not have a complete picture of available or possible actions, or else the uncertainty of the effects of different actions, for instance, implementation of different preventive measures, may be large. Thus, RCT may be helpful in pointing out some weaknesses in a decision process, but it provides little guidance in improving the quality of choices to be made. Another limitation in the applicability of rational choice models is that most decisions in organizations do not necessarily search for optimal solutions.

Problem Solving

Rational choice models describe the process of *evaluating and choosing between alternatives*. However, deciding on a course of action also requires what Simon and associates (1992) describe as *problem solving*. This is the work of choosing issues that require attention, setting goals, and finding or deciding on suitable courses of action. (While managers may know they have problems, they may not understand the situation well enough to direct their attention to any plausible course of action.) As mentioned earlier, the theory of *rational choice* has its roots mainly in economics, statistics and operations research, and only recently has it received attention from psychologists. The theory and methods of problem solving has a very different history. Problem solving was initially studied principally by psychologists, and more recently by researchers in artificial intelligence.

Empirical research has shown that the process of problem solving takes place more or less in the same way for a wide range of activities. First, problem solving generally proceeds by selective search through large sets of possibilities, using rules of thumb (heuristics) to guide the search. Because the possibilities in realistic problem situations are virtually endless, a trial-and-error search would simply not work. The search must be highly selective. One of the procedures often used to guide the search is described as *hill climbing*—using some measure of approach to the goal to determine where it is most profitable to look next. Another and more powerful common procedure is *means-ends analysis*. When using this method, the problem solver compares the present situation with the goal, detects differences between them, and then searches memory for actions that are likely to reduce the difference. Another thing that has been learned about problem solving, especially when the solver is an expert, is that the solver's thought process relies on large amounts of information that is stored in memory and that is retrievable whenever the solver recognizes cues signalling its relevance.

One of the accomplishments of contemporary problem-solving theory has been to provide an explanation for the phenomena of intuition and judgement frequently seen in experts' behaviour. The store of expert knowledge seems to be in some way *indexed* by the recognition cues that make it accessible. Combined with some basic inferential capabilities (perhaps in the form of means-ends analysis), this indexing function is applied by the expert to find satisfactory solutions to difficult problems.

Most of the challenges which managers of safety face will be of a kind that require some kind of problem solving—for example, detecting what the underlying causes of an accident or a safety problem really are, in order to figure out some preventive measure. The problem-solving cycle developed by Hale et al. (1994)—see figure 59.8—gives a good description of what is involved in the stages of safety problem solving. What seems evident is that at present it is not possible and may not even be desirable to develop a strictly logical or mathematical model for what is an ideal problem-solving process in the same manner as has been followed for rational choice theories. This view is supported by the

knowledge of other difficulties in the real-life instances of problem solving and decision making which are discussed below.

Ill-Structured Problems, Agenda Setting and Framing

In real life, situations frequently occur when the problem-solving process becomes obscure because the goals themselves are complex and sometimes ill-defined. What often happens is that the very nature of the problem is successively transformed in the course of exploration. To the extent that the problem has these characteristics, it may be called *ill-structured*. Typical examples of problem-solving processes with such characteristics are (1) the development of new designs and (2) scientific discovery.

The solving of ill-defined problems has only recently become a subject of scientific study. When problems are ill-defined, the problem-solving process requires substantial knowledge about solution criteria as well as knowledge about the means for satisfying those criteria. Both kinds of knowledge must be evoked in the course of the process, and the evocation of the criteria and constraint continually modifies and remoulds the solution which the problem-solving process is addressing. Some research concerning problem structuring and analysis within risk and safety issues has been published, and may be profitably studied; see, for example, Rosenhead 1989 and Chicken and Haynes 1989.

Setting the agenda, which is the very first step of the problem-solving process, is also the least understood. What brings a problem to the head of the agenda is the identification of a problem and the consequent challenge to determine how it can be represented in a way that facilitates its solution; these are subjects that only recently have been focused upon in studies of decision processes. The task of setting an agenda is of utmost importance because both individual human beings and human institutions have limited capacities in dealing with many tasks simultaneously. While some problems are receiving full attention, others are neglected. When new problems emerge suddenly and unexpectedly (e.g., firefighting), they may replace orderly planning and deliberation.

The way in which problems are represented has much to do with the quality of the solutions that are found. At present the representation or *framing of problems* is even less well understood than agenda setting. A characteristic of many advances in science and technology is that a change in framing will bring about a whole new approach to solving a problem. One example of such change in the framing of problem definition in safety science in recent years, is the shift of focus away from the details of the work operations to the organizational decisions and conditions which create the whole work situation—see, for example, Wagenaar et al. (1994).

Decision Making in Organizations

Models of organizational decision making view the question of choice as a logical process in which decision makers try to maximize their objectives in an orderly series of steps (figure 59.9). This process is in principle the same for safety as for decisions on other issues that the organization has to manage.

These models may serve as a general framework for "rational decision making" in organizations; however, such ideal models have several limitations and they leave out important aspects of processes which actually may take place. Some of the significant characteristics of organizational decision-making processes are discussed below.

Criteria applied in organizational choice

While rational choice models are preoccupied with finding the optimal alternative, other criteria may be even more relevant in organizational decisions. As observed by March and Simon (1993), organizations for various reasons search for *satisfactory* rather than *optimal* solutions.

Figure 59.9 • The decision-making process in organizations.

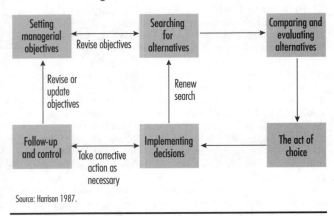

Source: Harrison 1987.

- *Optimal alternatives*. An alternative can be defined as optimal if (1) there exists a set of criteria that permits all alternatives to be compared and (2) the alternative in question is preferred, by these criteria, to all other alternatives (see also the discussion of rational choice, above).
- *Satisfactory alternatives*. An alternative is satisfactory if (1) there exists a set of criteria that describes minimally satisfactory alternatives and (2) the alternative in question meets or exceeds these criteria.

According to March and Simon (1993) most human decision making, whether individual or organizational, is concerned with the discovery and selection of *satisfactory* alternatives. Only in exceptional cases is it concerned with discovery and selection of *optimal* alternatives. In safety management, satisfactory alternatives with respect to safety will usually suffice, so that a given solution to a safety problem must meet specified standards. The typical constraints which often apply to optimal choice safety decisions are economic considerations such as: "Good enough, but as cheap as possible".

Programmed decision making

Exploring the parallels between human decision making and organizational decision making, March and Simon (1993) argued that organizations can never be perfectly rational, because their members have limited information-processing capabilities. It is claimed that decision makers at best can achieve only limited forms of rationality because they (1) usually have to act on the basis of incomplete information, (2) are able to explore only a limited number of alternatives relating to any given decision, and (3) are unable to attach accurate values to outcomes. March and Simon maintain that the limits on human rationality are institutionalized in the structure and modes of functioning of our organizations. In order to make the decision-making process manageable, organizations fragment, routinize and limit the decision process in several ways. Departments and work units have the effect of segmenting the organization's environment, of compartmentalizing responsibilities, and thus of simplifying the domains of interest and decision making of managers, supervisors and workers. Organizational hierarchies perform a similar function, providing channels of problem solving in order to make life more manageable. This creates a structure of attention, interpretation and operation that exerts a crucial influence on what is appreciated as "rational" choices of the individual decision maker in the

organizational context. March and Simon named these organized sets of responses *performance programmes*, or simply *programmes*. The term *programme* is not intended to connote complete rigidity. The content of the programme may be adaptive to a large number of characteristics that initiate it. The programme may also be conditional on data that are independent of the initiating stimuli. It is then more properly called a *performance strategy*.

A set of activities is regarded as routinized to the degree that choice has been simplified by the development of fixed response to defined stimuli. If searches have been eliminated, but choice remains in the form of clearly defined systematic computing routines, the activity is designated as *routinized*. Activities are regarded as unroutinized to the extent that they have to be preceded by programme-developing activities of a problem-solving kind. The distinction made by Hale et al. (1994) (discussed above) between the levels of execution, planning and system structure/management carry similar implications concerning the structuring of the decision-making process.

Programming influences decision making in two ways: (1) by defining how a decision process should be run, who should participate, and so on, and (2) by prescribing choices to be made based on the information and alternatives at hand. The effects of programming are on the one hand positive in the sense that they may increase the efficiency of the decision process and assure that problems are not left unresolved, but are treated in a way that is well structured. On the other hand, rigid programming may hamper the flexibility that is needed especially in the problem-solving phase of a decision process in order to generate new solutions. For example, many airlines have established fixed procedures for treatment of reported deviations, so-called flight reports or maintenance reports, which require that each case be examined by an appointed person and that a decision be made concerning preventive actions to be taken based on the incident. Sometimes the decision may be that no action shall be taken, but the procedures assure that such a decision is deliberate, and not a result of negligence, and that there is a responsible decision maker involved in the decisions.

The degree to which activities are programmed influences risk taking. Wagenaar (1990) maintained that most accidents are consequences of routine behaviour without any consideration of risk. The real problem of risk occurs at higher levels in organizations, where the unprogrammed decisions are made. But risks are most often not taken consciously. They tend to be results of decisions made on issues which are not directly related to safety, but where preconditions for safe operation were inadvertently affected. Managers and other high-level decision makers are thus more often *permitting opportunities for risks* than *taking risks*.

Decision Making, Power and Conflict of Interests

The ability to influence the outcomes of decision-making processes is a well-recognized source of power, and one that has attracted considerable attention in organization-theory literature. Since organizations are in large measure decision-making systems, an individual or group can exert major influence on the decision processes of the organization. According to Morgan (1986) the kinds of power used in decision making can be classified into the following three interrelated elements:

1. *The decision premises*. Influence on the decision *premises* may be exerted in several ways. One of the most effective ways of "making" a decision is to allow it to be made by default. Hence much of the political activity within an organization depends on the control of agendas and other decision premises that influence how particular decisions will be approached, perhaps in ways that prevent certain core issues from surfacing at all. In addition, decision premises are

manipulated by the unobtrusive control embedded in choice of those vocabularies, structures of communications, attitudes, beliefs, rules and procedures which are accepted without questioning. These factors shape decisions by the way we think and act. According to Morgan (1986), visions of what the problems and issues are and how they can be tackled, often act as mental straitjackets that prevent us from seeing other ways of formulating our basic concerns and the alternative courses of action that are available.

2. *The decision processes.* Control of decision *processes* is usually more visible than the control of decision premises. How to treat an issue involves questions such as who should be involved, when the decision should be made, how the issue should be handled at meetings, and how it should be reported. The ground rules that are to guide decision making are important variables that organization members can manipulate in order to influence the outcome.

3. *The decision issues and objectives.* A final way of controlling decision making is to influence the *issues and objectives* to be addressed and the evaluative criteria to be employed. An individual can shape the issues and objectives most directly through preparing reports and contributing to the discussion on which the decision will be based. By emphasizing the importance of particular constraints, selecting and evaluating the alternatives on which a decision will be made, and highlighting the importance of certain values or outcomes, decision makers can exert considerable influence on the decision that emerges from discussion.

Some decision problems may carry a conflict of interest—for example, between management and employees. Disagreement may occur on the definition of what is really the problem—what Rittel and Webber (1973) characterized as "wicked" problems, to be distinguished from problems that are "tame" with respect to securing consent. In other cases, parties may agree on problem definition but not on how the problem should be solved, or what are acceptable solutions or criteria for solutions. The attitudes or strategies of conflicting parties will define not only their problem-solving behaviour, but also the prospects of reaching an acceptable solution through negotiations. Important variables are how parties attempt to satisfy their own versus the other party's concerns (figure 59.10). Successful collaboration requires that both parties are assertive concerning their own needs, but are simultaneously willing to take the needs of the other party equally into consideration.

Another interesting typology based on the amount of agreement between goals and means, was developed by Thompson and Tuden (1959) (cited in Koopman and Pool 1991). The authors suggested what was a "best-fitting strategy" based on knowledge about the parties' perceptions of the causation of the problem and about preferences of outcomes (figure 59.11).

If there is agreement on goals and means, the decision can be calculated—for example, developed by some experts. If the means to the desired ends are unclear, these experts will have to reach a solution through consultation (majority judgement). If there is any conflict about the goals, consultation between the parties involved is necessary. However, if agreement is lacking both on goals and means, the organization is really endangered. Such a situation requires charismatic leadership which can "inspire" a solution acceptable to the conflicting parties.

Decision making within an organizational framework thus opens up perspectives far beyond those of rational choice or individual problem-solving models. Decision processes must be seen within the framework of organizational and management processes, where the concept of rationality may take on new and different meanings from those defined by the logicality of rational

Figure 59.10 • Five styles of negotiating behaviour.

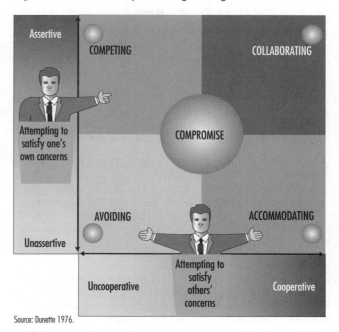

Source: Dunette 1976.

choice approaches embedded in, for example, operations research models. Decision making carried out within safety management must be regarded in light of such a perspective as will allow a full understanding of all aspects of the decision problems at hand.

Summary and Conclusions

Decision making can generally be described as a process starting with an initial situation (initial state) which decision makers perceive to be deviating from a desired goal situation (goal state), although they do not know in advance how to alter the initial state

Figure 59.11 • A typology of problem-solving strategy.

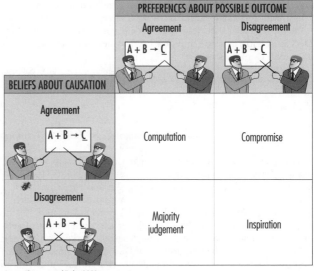

Source: Thompson and Tuden 1959.

into the goal state (Huber 1989). The problem solver transforms the initial state into the goal state by applying one or more *operators*, or activities to alter states. Often a sequence of operators is required to bring about the desired change.

The research literature on the subject provides no simple answers to how to make decisions on safety issues; therefore, the methods of decision making must be rational and logical. Rational choice theory represents an elegant conception of how optimal decisions are made. However, within safety management, rational choice theory cannot be easily applied. The most obvious limitation is the lack of valid and reliable data on potential choices with respect to both completeness and to knowledge of consequences. Another difficulty is that the concept *rational* assumes a benefactor, which may differ depending on which perspective is chosen in a decision situation. However, the rational choice approach may still be helpful in pointing out some of the difficulties and shortcomings of the decisions to be made.

Often the challenge is not to make a wise choice between alternative actions, but rather to analyse a situation in order to find out what the problem really is. In analysing safety management problems, structuring is often the most important task. Understanding the problem is a prerequisite for finding an acceptable solution. The most important issue concerning problem solving is not to identify a single superior method, which probably does not exist on account of the wide range of problems within the areas of risk assessment and safety management. The main point is rather to take a structured approach and document the analysis and decisions made in such a way that the procedures and evaluations are traceable.

Organizations will manage some of their decision making through programmed actions. Programming or fixed procedures for decision-making routines may be very useful in safety management. An example is how some companies treat reported deviations and near accidents. Programming can be an efficient way to control decision-making processes in the organization, provided that the safety issues and decision rules are clear.

In real life, decisions take place within an organizational and social context where conflicts of interest sometimes emerge. The decision processes may be hindered by different perceptions of what the problems are, of criteria, or of the acceptability of proposed solutions. Being aware of the presence and possible effects of vested interests is helpful in making decisions which are acceptable to all parties involved. Safety management includes a large variety of problems depending on which life cycle, organizational level and stage of problem solving or hazard alleviation a problem concerns. In that sense, decision making concerning safety is as wide in scope and character as decision making on any other management issues.

● RISK PERCEPTION

Bernhard Zimolong and Rüdiger Trimpop

In risk perception, two psychological processes may be distinguished: hazard perception and risk assessment. Saari (1976) defines the information processed during the accomplishment of a task in terms of the following two components: (1) the information required to execute a task (hazard perception) and (2) the information required to keep existing risks under control (risk assessment). For instance, when construction workers on the top of ladders who are drilling holes in a wall have to simultaneously keep their balance and automatically coordinate their body-hand movements, hazard perception is crucial to coordinate body movement to keep dangers under control, whereas conscious risk

assessment plays only a minor role, if any. Human activities generally seem to be driven by automatic recognition of signals which trigger a flexible, yet stored hierarchy of action schemata. (The more deliberate process leading to the acceptance or rejection of risk is discussed in another article.)

Risk Perception

From a technical point of view, a *hazard* represents a source of energy with the *potential* of causing immediate injury to personnel and damage to equipment, environment or structure. Workers may also be exposed to diverse toxic substances, such as chemicals, gases or radioactivity, some of which cause health problems. Unlike hazardous energies, which have an immediate effect on the body, toxic substances have quite different temporal characteristics, ranging from immediate effects to delays over months and years. Often there is an accumulating effect of small doses of toxic substances which are imperceptible to the exposed workers.

Conversely, there may be no harm to persons from hazardous energy or toxic substances provided that no danger exists. *Danger* expresses the relative exposure to hazard. In fact there may be little danger in the presence of some hazards as a result of the provision of adequate precautions. There is voluminous literature pertaining to factors people use in the final assessment of whether a situation is determined hazardous, and, if so, how hazardous. This has become known as *risk perception*. (The word *risk* is being used in the same sense that *danger* is used in occupational safety literature; see Hoyos and Zimolong 1988.)

Risk perception deals with the understanding of perceptual realities and indicators of hazards and toxic substances—that is, the perception of objects, sounds, odorous or tactile sensations. Fire, heights, moving objects, loud noise and acid smells are some examples of the more obvious hazards which do not need to be interpreted. In some instances, people are similarly reactive in their responses to the sudden presence of imminent danger. The sudden occurrence of loud noise, loss of balance, and objects rapidly increasing in size (and so appearing about to strike one's body), are fear stimuli, prompting automatic responses such as jumping, dodging, blinking and clutching. Other reflex reactions include rapidly withdrawing a hand which has touched a hot surface. Rachman (1974) concludes that the prepotent fear stimuli are those which have the attributes of novelty, abruptness and high intensity.

Probably most hazards and toxic substances are not directly perceptible to the human senses, but are inferred from indicators. Examples are electricity; colourless, odourless gases such as methane and carbon monoxide; x rays and radioactive subs-tances; and oxygen-deficient atmospheres. Their presence must be signalled by devices which translate the presence of the hazard into something which is recognizable. Electrical currents can be perceived with the help of a current checking device, such as may be used for signals on the gauges and meters in a control-room register that indicate normal and abnormal levels of temperature and pressure at a particular state of a chemical process. There are also situations where hazards exist which are not perceivable at all or cannot be made perceivable at a given time. One example is the danger of infection when one opens blood probes for medical tests. The knowledge that hazards exist must be deduced from one's knowledge of the common principles of causality or acquired by experience.

Risk Assessment

The next step in information-processing is *risk assessment*, which refers to the decision process as it is applied to such issues as whether and to what extent a person will be exposed to danger. Consider, for instance, driving a car at high speed. From the perspective of the individual, such decisions have to be made only in unexpected circumstances such as emergencies. Most of the required driving behaviour is automatic and runs smoothly without continuous attentional control and conscious risk assessment.

Hacker (1987) and Rasmussen (1983) distinguished three levels of behaviour: (1) skill-based behaviour, which is almost entirely automatic; (2) rule-based behaviour, which operates through the application of consciously chosen but fully pre-programmed rules; and (3) knowledge-based behaviour, under which all sorts of conscious planning and problem solving are grouped. At the skill-based level, an incoming piece of information is connected directly to a stored response that is executed automatically and carried out without conscious deliberation or control. If there is no automatic response available or any extraordinary event occurring, the risk assessment process moves to the rule-based level, where the appropriate action is selected from a sample of procedures taken out of storage and then executed. Each of the steps involves a finely tuned perceptual-motor programme, and usually, no step in this organizational hierarchy involves any decisions based on risk considerations. Only at the transitions is a conditional check applied, just to verify whether the progress is according to plan. If not, automatic control is halted and the ensuing problem solved at a higher level.

Reason's GEMS (1990) model describes how the transition from automatic control to conscious problem solving takes place when exceptional circumstances arise or novel situations are encountered. Risk assessment is absent at the bottom level, but may be fully present at the top level. At the middle level one can assume some sort of "quick-and-dirty" risk assessment, while Rasmussen excludes any type of assessment that is not incorporated in fixed rules. Much of the time there will be no conscious perception or consideration of hazards as such. "The lack of safety consciousness is both a normal and a healthy state of affairs, despite what has been said in countless books, articles and speeches. Being constantly conscious of danger is a reasonable definition of paranoia" (Hale and Glendon 1987). People doing their jobs on a routine basis rarely consider these hazards or accidents in advance: they *run* risks, but they do not *take* them.

Hazard Perception

Perception of hazards and toxic substances, in the sense of direct perception of shape and colour, loudness and pitch, odours and vibrations, is restricted by the capacity limitations of the perceptual senses, which can be temporarily impaired due to fatigue, illness, alcohol or drugs. Factors such as glare, brightness or fog can put heavy stress on perception, and dangers can fail to be detected because of distractions or insufficient alertness.

As has already been mentioned, not all hazards are directly perceptible to the human senses. Most toxic substances are not even visible. Ruppert (1987) found in his investigation of an iron and steel factory, of municipal garbage collecting and of medical laboratories, that from 2,230 hazard indicators named by 138 workers, only 42% were perceptible by the human senses. Twenty-two per cent of the indicators have to be inferred from comparisons with standards (e.g., noise levels). Hazard perception is based in 23% of cases on clearly perceptible events which have to be interpreted with respect to knowledge about hazardousness (e.g., a glossy surface of a wet floor indicates *slippery*). In 13% of reports, hazard indicators can be retrieved only from memory of proper steps to be taken (e.g., current in a wall socket can be made perceivable only by the proper checking device). These results demonstrate that the requirements of hazard perception range from pure detection and perception to elaborate cognitive inference processes of anticipation and assessment. Cause-and-effect relationships are sometimes unclear, scarcely detectable, or misinterpreted, and delayed or accumulating effects of hazards and

toxic substances are likely to impose additional burdens on individuals.

Hoyos et al. (1991) have listed a comprehensive picture of hazard indicators, behavioural requirements and safety-relevant conditions in industry and public services. A Safety Diagnosis Questionnaire (SDQ) has been developed to provide a practical instrument to analyse hazards and dangers through observation (Hoyos and Ruppert 1993). More than 390 workplaces, and working and environmental conditions in 69 companies concerned with agriculture, industry, manual work and the service industries, have been assessed. Because the companies had accident rates greater than 30 accidents per 1,000 employees with a minimum of 3 lost working days per accident, there appears to be a bias in these studies towards dangerous worksites. Altogether 2,373 hazards have been reported by the observers using SDQ, indicating a detection rate of 6.1 hazards per workplace and between 7 and 18 hazards have been detected at approximately 40% of all workplaces surveyed. The surprisingly low mean rate of 6.1 hazards per workplace has to be interpreted with consideration toward the safety measures broadly introduced in industry and agriculture during the last 20 years. Hazards reported do not include those attributable to toxic substances, nor hazards controlled by technical safety devices and measures, and thus reflect the distribution of "residual hazards".

In figure 59.12 an overview of requirements for perceptual processes of hazard detection and perception is presented. Observers had to assess all hazards at a particular workplace with respect to 13 requirements, as indicated in the figure. On the average, 5 requirements per hazard were identified, including visual recognition, selective attention, auditory recognition and vigilance. As expected, visual recognition dominates by comparison with auditory recognition (77.3% of the hazards were detected visually and only 21.2% by auditory detection). In 57% of all hazards observed, workers had to divide their attention between tasks and hazard control, and divided attention is a very strenuous mental achievement likely to contribute to errors. Accidents have frequently been traced back to failures in attention while performing dual tasks. Even more alarming is the finding that in 56% of all hazards, workers had to cope with rapid activities and responsiveness to avoid being hit and injured. Only 15.9% and 7.3% of all hazards were indicated by acoustical or optical warnings, respectively: consequently, hazard detection and perception was self-initiated.

In some cases (16.1%) perception of hazards is supported by signs and warnings, but usually, workers rely on knowledge, training and work experience. Figure 59.13 shows the requirements of anticipation and assessment required to control hazards at the worksite. The core characteristic of all activities summarized in this figure is the need for knowledge and experience gained in the work process, including: technical knowledge about weight, forces and energies; training to identify defects and inadequacies of work tools and machinery; and experience to predict structural weaknesses of equipment, buildings and material. As Hoyos et al. (1991) have demonstrated, workers have little knowledge relating to hazards, safety rules and proper personal preventive behaviour. Only 60% of the construction workers and 61% of the auto-mechanics questioned knew the right solutions to the safety-related problems generally encountered at their workplaces.

The analysis of hazard perception indicates that different cognitive processes are involved, such as visual recognition; selective and divided attention; rapid identification and responsiveness; estimates of technical parameters; and predictions of non-observable hazards and dangers. In fact, hazards and dangers are frequently unknown to job incumbents: they impose a heavy burden on people who have to cope sequentially with dozens of visual- and auditory-based requirements and are a source of proneness

Figure 59.12 • Detection and perception of hazard indicators in industry.

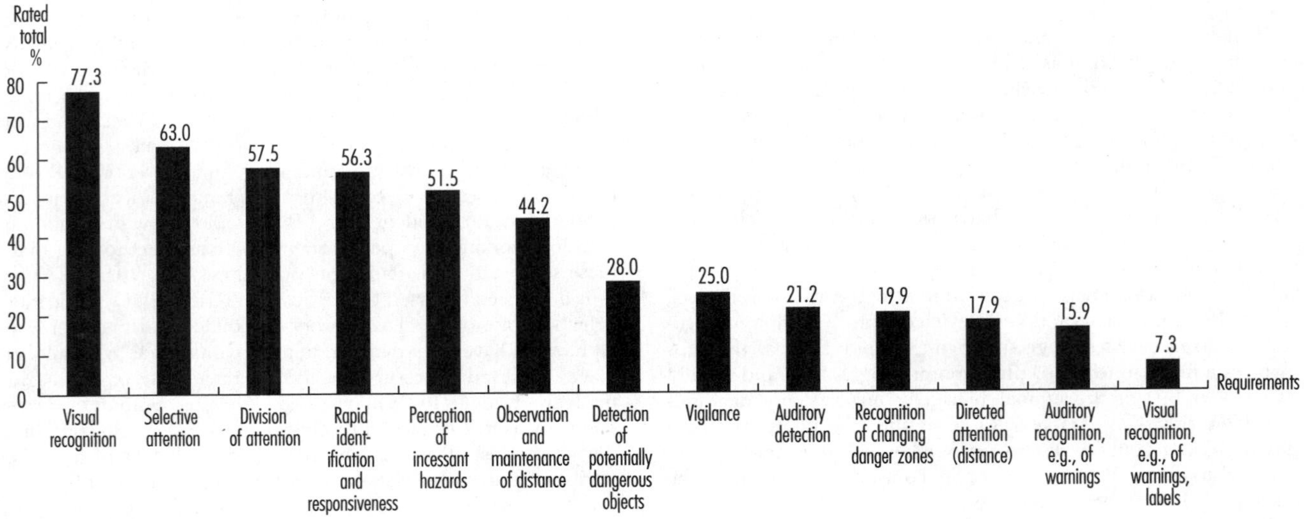

Source: Hoyos and Ruppert 1993.

to error when work and hazard control is performed simultaneously. This requires much more emphasis to be placed on regular analysis and identification of hazards and dangers at the workplace. In several countries, formal risk assessments of workplaces are mandatory: for example, the health and safety Directives of the EEC require risk assessment of computer workplaces prior to commencing work in them, or when major alterations at work have been introduced; and the US Occupational Safety and Health Administration (OSHA) requires regular hazard risk analyses of process units.

Coordination of Work and Hazard Control
As Hoyos and Ruppert (1993) point out, (1) work and hazard control may require attention simultaneously; (2) they may be managed alternatively in sequential steps; or (3) prior to the commencement of work, precautionary measures may be taken (e.g., putting on a safety helmet).

In the case of simultaneously occurring requirements, hazard control is based on visual, auditory and tactile recognition. In fact, it is difficult to separate work and hazard control in routine tasks. For example, a source of constant danger is present when performing the task of cutting off threads from yarns in a cotton-mill factory—a task requiring a sharp knife. The only two types of protection against cuts are skill in wielding the knife and use of protective equipment. If either or both are to succeed, they must be totally incorporated into the worker's action sequences. Habits such as cutting in a direction away from the hand which is holding the thread must be ingrained into the worker's skills from the outset. In this example hazard control is fully integrated into task control; no separate process of hazard detection is required. Probably there is a continuum of integration into work, the degree depending on the skill of the worker and the requirements of the task. On the one hand, hazard perception and control is inherently integrated into work skills; on the other hand, task execution and hazard control are distinctly separate activities. Work and hazard control may be carried out alternatively, in sequential steps, when *during* the task, danger potential steadily increases or there is an abrupt, alerting danger signal. As a consequence, workers interrupt the task or process and take preventive measures. For example, the checking of a gauge is a typical

example of a simple diagnostic test. A control room operator detects a deviation from standard level on a gauge which at first glance does not constitute a dramatic sign of danger, but which prompts the operator to search further on other gauges and meters. If there are other deviations present, a rapid series of scanning activities will be carried out at the rule-based level. If deviations on other meters do not fit into a familiar pattern, the diagnosis process shifts to the knowledge-based level. In most cases, guided by some strategies, signals and symptoms are actively looked for to locate causes of the deviations (Konradt 1994). The allocation of resources of the attentional control system is set to general monitoring. A sudden signal, such as a warning tone or, as in the case above, various deviations of pointers from a standard, shifts the attentional control system onto the specific topic of hazard control. It initiates an activity which seeks to identify the causes of the deviations on the rule-based level, or in case of misfortune, on the knowledge-based level (Reason 1990).

Preventive behaviour is the third type of coordination. It occurs prior to work, and the most prominent example is the use of personal protective equipment (PPE).

The Meanings of Risk
Definitions of risks and methods to assess risks in industry and society have been developed in economics, engineering, chemistry, safety sciences and ergonomics (Hoyos and Zimolong 1988). There is a wide variety of interpretations of the term *risk*. On the one hand, it is interpreted to mean "probability of an undesired event". It is an expression of the likelihood that something unpleasant will happen. A more neutral definition of risk is used by Yates (1992a), who argues that risk should be perceived as a multidimensional concept that as a whole refers to the prospect of loss. Important contributions to our current understanding of risk assessment in society have come from geography, sociology, political science, anthropology and psychology. Research focused originally on understanding human behaviour in the face of natural hazards, but it has since broadened to incorporate technological hazards as well. Sociological research and anthropological studies have shown that assessment and acceptance of risks have their roots in social and cultural factors. Short (1984) argues that responses to hazards are mediated by social influences transmitted

by friends, family, co-workers and respected public officials. Psychological research on risk assessment originated in empirical studies of probability assessment, utility assessment and decision-making processes (Edwards 1961).

Technical risk assessment usually focuses on the potential for loss, which includes the probability of the loss's occurring and the magnitude of the given loss in terms of death, injury or damages. Risk is the probability that damage of a specified type will occur in a given system over a defined time period. Different assessment techniques are applied to meet the various requirements of industry and society. Formal analysis methods to estimate degrees of risk are derived from different kinds of fault tree analyses; by use of data banks comprising error probabilities such as THERP (Swain and Guttmann 1983); or on decomposition methods based on subjective ratings such as SLIM-Maud (Embrey et al. 1984). These techniques differ considerably in their potential to predict future events such as mishaps, errors or accidents. In terms of error prediction in industrial systems, experts attained the best results with THERP. In a simulation study, Zimolong (1992) found a close match between objectively derived error probabilities and their estimates derived with THERP. Zimolong and Trimpop (1994) argued that such formal analyses have the highest "objectivity" if conducted properly, as they separated facts from beliefs and took many of the judgemental biases into account.

The public's sense of risk depends on more than the probability and magnitude of loss. It may depend on factors such as potential degree of damage, unfamiliarity with possible consequences, the involuntary nature of exposure to risk, the uncontrollability of damage, and possible biased media coverage. The feeling of control in a situation may be a particularly important factor. For many, flying seems very unsafe because one has no control over one's fate once in the air. Rumar (1988) found that the perceived risk in driving a car is typically low, since in most situations the drivers believe in their own ability to achieve control and are accustomed to the risk. Other research has addressed emotional reactions to risky situations. The potential for serious loss generates a variety of emotional reactions, not all of which are necessarily unpleasant. There is a fine line between fear and excitement. Again, a major determinant of perceived risk and of affective reactions to risky situations seems to be a person's feeling of control or lack thereof. As a consequence, for many people, risk may be nothing more than a feeling.

Decision Making under Risk

Risk taking may be the result of a deliberate decision process entailing several activities: identification of possible courses of action; identification of consequences; evaluation of the attractiveness and chances of the consequences; or deciding according to a combination of all the previous assessments. The overwhelming evidence that people often make poor choices in risky situations implies the potential to make better decisions. In 1738, Bernoulli defined the notion of a "best bet" as one which maximizes the expected utility (EU) of the decision. The EU concept of rationality asserts that people ought to make decisions by evaluating uncertainties and considering their choices, the possible consequences, and one's preferences for them (von Neumann and Morgenstern 1947). Savage (1954) later generalized the theory to allow probability values to represent subjective or personal probabilities.

Subjective expected utility (SEU) is a normative theory which describes how people should proceed when making decisions. Slovic, Kunreuther and White (1974) stated, "Maximization of expected utility commands respect as a guideline for wise behaviour because it is deduced from axiomatic principles that presumably would be accepted by any rational man." A good deal of debate and empirical research has centred around the question of whether this theory could also describe both the goals that motivate actual decision makers and the processes they employ when reaching their decisions. Simon (1959) criticized it as a theory of a person selecting among fixed and known alternatives, to each of which known consequences are attached. Some researchers have even questioned whether people should obey the principles of

59. SAFETY POLICY AND LEADERSHIP

Figure 59.13 • Anticipation and assessment of hazard indicators.

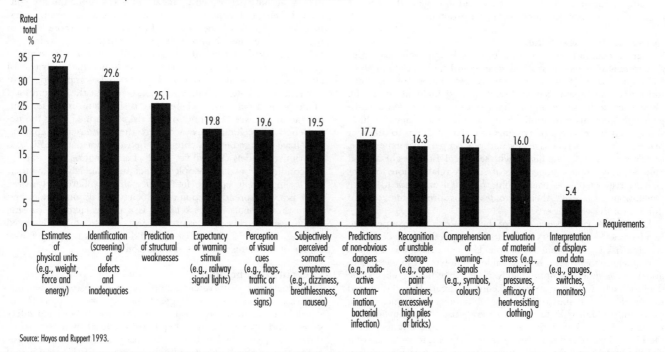

Source: Hoyos and Ruppert 1993.

expected utility theory, and after decades of research, SEU applications remain controversial. Research has revealed that psychological factors play an important role in decision making and that many of these factors are not adequately captured by SEU models.

In particular, research on judgement and choice has shown that people have methodological deficiencies such as understanding probabilities, negligence of the effect of sample sizes, reliance on misleading personal experiences, holding judgements of fact with unwarranted confidence, and misjudging risks. People are more likely to underestimate risks if they have been voluntarily exposed to risks over a longer period, such as living in areas subject to floods or earthquakes. Similar results have been reported from industry (Zimolong 1985). Shunters, miners, and forest and construction workers all dramatically underestimate the riskiness of their most common work activities as compared to objective accident statistics; however, they tend to overestimate any obvious dangerous activities of fellow workers when required to rate them.

Unfortunately, experts' judgements appear to be prone to many of the same biases as those of the public, particularly when experts are forced to go beyond the limits of available data and rely upon their intuitions (Kahneman, Slovic and Tversky 1982). Research further indicates that disagreements about risk should not disappear completely even when sufficient evidence is available. Strong initial views are resistant to change because they influence the way that subsequent information is interpreted. New evidence appears reliable and informative if it is consistent with one's initial beliefs; contrary evidence tends to be dismissed as unreliable, erroneous or unrepresentative (Nisbett and Ross 1980). When people lack strong prior opinions, the opposite situation prevails—they are at the mercy of the formulation of the problem. Presenting the same information about risk in different ways (e.g., mortality rates as opposed to survival rates) alters their perspectives and their actions (Tversky and Kahneman 1981). The discovery of this set of mental strategies, or heuristics, that people implement in order to structure their world and predict their future courses of action, has led to a deeper understanding of decision making in risky situations. Although these rules are valid in many circumstances, in others they lead to large and persistent biases with serious implications for risk assessment.

Personal Risk Assessment

The most common approach in studying how people make risk assessments uses psychophysical scaling and multivariate analysis techniques to produce quantitative representations of risk attitudes and assessment (Slovic, Fischhoff and Lichtenstein 1980). Numerous studies have shown that risk assessment based on subjective judgements is quantifiable and predictable. They also have shown that the concept of risk means different things to different people. When experts judge risk and rely on personal experience, their responses correlate highly with technical estimates of annual fatalities. Laypeople's judgements of risk are related more to other characteristics, such as catastrophic potential or threat to future generations; as a result, their estimates of loss probabilities tend to differ from those of experts.

Laypeople's risk assessments of hazards can be grouped into two factors (Slovic 1987). One of the factors reflects the degree to which a risk is understood by people. Understanding a risk relates to the degree to which it is observable, is known to those exposed, and can be detected immediately. The other factor reflects the degree to which the risk evokes a feeling of dread. Dread is related to the degree of uncontrollability, of serious consequences, of exposure of high risks to future generations, and of involuntary increase of risk. The higher a hazard's score on the latter factor, the higher its assessed risk, the more people want to see its current risks reduced, and the more they want to see strict regulation

employed to achieve the desired reduction in risk. Consequently, many conflicts about risk may result from experts' and laypeople's views originating from different definitions of the concept. In such cases, expert citations of risk statistics or of the outcome of technical risk assessments will do little to change people's attitudes and assessments (Slovic 1993).

The characterization of hazards in terms of "knowledge" and "threat" leads back to the previous discussion of hazard and danger signals in industry in this section, which were discussed in terms of "perceptibility". Forty-two per cent of the hazard indicators in industry are directly perceptible by human senses, 45% of cases have to be inferred from comparisons with standards, and 3% from memory. Perceptibility, knowledge and the threats and thrills of hazards are dimensions which are closely related to people's experience of hazards and perceived control; however, to understand and predict individual behaviour in the face of danger we have to gain a deeper understanding of their relationships with personality, requirements of tasks, and societal variables.

Psychometric techniques seem well-suited to identify similarities and differences among groups with regard to both personal habits of risk assessment and to attitudes. However, other psychometric methods such as multidimensional analysis of hazard similarity judgements, applied to quite different sets of hazards, produce different representations. The factor-analytical approach, while informative, by no means provides a universal representation of hazards. Another weakness of psychometric studies is that people face risk only in written statements, and divorce the assessment of risk from behaviour in actual risky situations. Factors that affect a person's considered assessment of risk in a psychometric experiment may be trivial when confronted with an actual risk. Howarth (1988) suggests that such conscious verbal knowledge usually reflects social stereotypes. By contrast, risk-taking responses in traffic or work situations are controlled by the tacit knowledge that underlies skilled or routine behaviour.

Most of the personal risk decisions in everyday life are not conscious decisions at all. People are, by and large, not even aware of risk. In contrast, the underlying notion of psychometric experiments is presented as a theory of deliberate choice. Assessments of risks usually performed by means of a questionnaire are conducted deliberately in an "armchair" fashion. In many ways, however, a person's responses to risky situations are more likely to result from learned habits that are automatic, and which are below the general level of awareness. People do not normally evaluate risks, and therefore it cannot be argued that their way of evaluating risk is inaccurate and needs to be improved. Most risk-related activities are necessarily executed at the bottom level of automated behaviour, where there is simply no room for consideration of risks. The notion that risks, identified after the occurrence of accidents, are accepted after a conscious analysis, may have emerged from a confusion between normative SEU and descriptive models (Wagenaar 1992). Less attention was paid to the conditions in which people will act automatically, follow their gut feeling, or accept the first choice that is offered. However, there is a widespread acceptance in society and among health and safety professionals that risk taking is a prime factor in causing mishaps and errors. In a representative sample of Swedes aged between 18 and 70 years, 90% agreed that risk taking is the major source of accidents (Hovden and Larsson 1987).

Preventive Behaviour

Individuals may deliberately take preventive measures to exclude hazards, to attenuate the energy of hazards or to protect themselves by precautionary measures (for instance, by wearing safety glasses and helmets). Often people are required by a company's directives or even by law to comply with protective measures. For example, a roofer builds a scaffolding prior to working on a roof to prevent the eventuality of suffering a fall. This choice might be the result of a conscious risk assessment process of hazards and of one's own coping skills, or, more simply, it may be the outcome of a habituation process, or it may be a requirement which is enforced by law. Often warnings are used to indicate mandatory preventive actions.

Several forms of preventive activities in industry have been analysed by Hoyos and Ruppert (1993). Some of them are shown in figure 59.14, together with their frequency of requirement. As indicated, preventive behaviour is partly self-controlled and partly enforced by the legal standards and requirements of the company. Preventive activities comprise some of the following measures: planning work procedures and steps ahead; use of PPE; application of safety work technique; selection of safe work procedures by means of proper material and tools; setting an appropriate work pace; and inspection of facilities, equipment, machinery and tools.

Personal Protective Equipment

The most frequent preventive measure required is the use of PPE. Together with correct handling and maintenance, it is by far the most common requirement in industry. There exist major differences in the usage of PPE between companies. In some of the best companies, mainly in chemical plants and petroleum refineries, the usage of PPE approaches 100%. In contrast, in the construction industry, safety officials have problems even in attempts to introduce particular PPE on a regular basis. It is doubtful that risk perception is the major factor which makes the difference. Some of the companies have successfully enforced the use of PPE which then becomes habitualized (e.g., the wearing of safety helmets) by establishing the "right safety culture" and subsequently altered

personal risk assessment. Slovic (1987) in his short discussion on the usage of seat-belts shows that about 20% of road users wear seat-belts voluntarily, 50% would use them only if it were made mandatory by law, and beyond this number, only control and punishment will serve to improve automatic use. Thus, it is important to understand what factors govern risk perception. However, it is equally important to know how to change behaviour and subsequently how to alter risk perception. It seems that many more precautionary measures need to be undertaken at the level of the organization, among the planners, designers, managers and those authorities that make decisions which have implications for many thousands of people. Up to now, there is little understanding at these levels as to which factors risk perception and assessment depend upon. If companies are seen as open systems, where different levels of organizations mutually influence each other and are in steady exchange with society, a systems approach may reveal those factors which constitute and influence risk perception and assessment.

Warning Labels

The use of labels and warnings to combat potential hazards is a controversial procedure for managing risks. Too often they are seen as a way for manufacturers to avoid responsibility for unreasonably risky products. Obviously, labels will be successful only if the information they contain is read and understood by members of the intended audience. Frantz and Rhoades (1993) found that 40% of clerical personnel filling a file cabinet noticed a warning label placed on the top drawer of the cabinet, 33% read part of it, and no one read the entire label. Contrary to expectation, 20% complied completely by not placing any material in the top

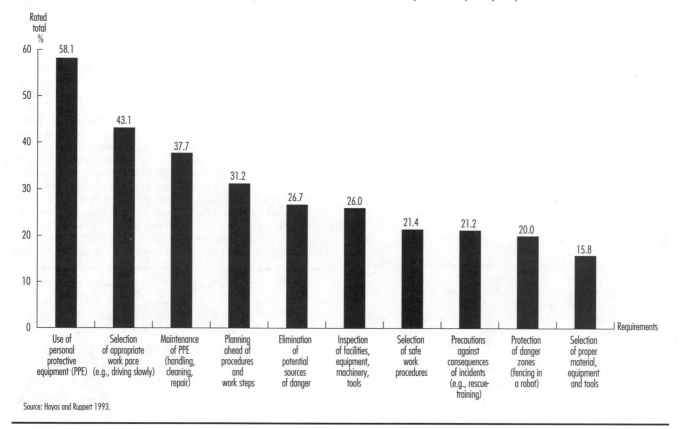

Figure 59.14 • Typical examples of personal preventive behaviour in industry and frequency of preventive measure.

Source: Hoyos and Ruppert 1993.

drawer first. Obviously it is insufficient to scan the most important elements of the notice. Lehto and Papastavrou (1993) provided a thorough analysis of findings pertaining to warning signs and labels by examining receiver-, task-, product- and message-related factors. Furthermore, they provided a significant contribution to understanding the effectiveness of warnings by considering different levels of behaviour.

The discussion of skilled behaviour suggests that a warning notice will have little impact on the way people perform a familiar task, as it simply will not be read. Lehto and Papastavrou (1993) concluded from research findings that interrupting familiar task performance may effectively increase workers' noticing warning signs or labels. In the experiment by Frantz and Rhoades (1993), noticing the warning labels on filing cabinets increased to 93% when the top drawer was sealed shut with a warning indicating that a label could be found within the drawer. The authors concluded, however, that ways of interrupting skill-based behaviour are not always available and that their effectiveness after initial use can diminish considerably.

At a rule-based level of performance, warning information should be integrated into the task (Lehto 1992) so that it can be easily mapped to immediate relevant actions. In other words, people should try to get the task executed following the directions of the warning label. Frantz (1992) found that 85% of subjects expressed the need for a requirement on the directions of use of a wood preservative or drain cleaner. On the negative side, studies of comprehension have revealed that people may poorly comprehend the symbols and text used in warning signs and labels. In particular, Koslowski and Zimolong (1992) found that chemical workers understood the meaning of only approximately 60% of the most important warning signs used in the chemical industry.

At a knowledge-based level of behaviour, people seem likely to notice warnings when they are actively looking for them. They expect to find warnings close to the product. Frantz (1992) found that subjects in unfamiliar settings complied with instructions 73% of the time if they read them, compared to only 9% when they did not read them. Once read, the label must be understood and recalled. Several studies of comprehension and memory also imply that people may have trouble remembering the information they read from either instruction or warning labels. In the United States, the National Research Council (1989) provides some assistance in designing warnings. They emphasize the importance of two-way communication in enhancing understanding. The communicator should facilitate information feedback and questions on the part of the recipient. The conclusions of the report are summarized in two checklists, one for use by managers, the other serving as a guide for the recipient of the information.

● RISK ACCEPTANCE

Rüdiger Trimpop and Bernhard Zimolong

The concept of risk acceptance asks the question, "How safe is safe enough?" or, in more precise terms, "The conditional nature of risk assessment raises the question of which standard of risk we should accept against which to calibrate human biases" (Pidgeon 1991). This question takes importance in issues such as: (1) Should there be an additional containment shell around nuclear power plants? (2) Should schools containing asbestos be closed? or (3) Should one avoid all possible trouble, at least in the short run? Some of these questions are aimed at government or other regulatory bodies; others are aimed at the individual who must decide between certain actions and possible uncertain dangers.

The question whether to accept or reject risks is the result of decisions made to determine the optimal level of risk for a given situation. In many instances, these decisions will follow as an almost automatic result of the exercise of perceptions and habits acquired from experience and training. However, whenever a new situation arises or changes in seemingly familiar tasks occur, such as in performing non-routine or semi-routine tasks, decision making becomes more complex. To understand more about why people accept certain risks and reject others we shall need to define first what risk acceptance is. Next, the psychological processes that lead to either acceptance or rejection have to be explained, including influencing factors. Finally, methods to change too high or too low levels of risk acceptance will be addressed.

Understanding Risk

Generally speaking, whenever risk is not rejected, people have either voluntarily, thoughtlessly or habitually accepted it. Thus, for example, when people participate in traffic, they accept the danger of damage, injury, death and pollution for the opportunity of benefits resulting from increased mobility; when they decide to undergo surgery or not to undergo it, they decide that the costs and/or benefits of either decision are greater; and when they are investing money in the financial market or deciding to change business products, all decisions accepting certain financial dangers and opportunities are made with some degree of uncertainty. Finally, the decision to work in any job also has varying probabilities of suffering an injury or fatality, based on statistical accident history.

Defining risk acceptance by referring only to what has not been rejected leaves two important issues open; (1) what exactly is meant by the term *risk*, and (2) the often made assumption that risks are merely potential losses that have to be avoided, while in reality there is a difference between merely tolerating risks, fully accepting them, or even wishing for them to occur to enjoy thrill and excitement. These facets might all be expressed through the same behaviour (such as participating in traffic) but have different underlying cognitive, emotional and physiological processes. It seems obvious that a merely tolerated risk relates to a different level of commitment than if one even has the desire for a certain thrill, or "risky" sensation. Figure 59.15 summarizes facets of risk acceptance.

If one looks up the term *risk* in the dictionaries of several languages, it often has the double meaning of "chance, opportunity" on one hand and "danger, loss" (e.g., *wej-ji* in Chinese, *Risiko* in German, *risico* in Dutch and Italian, *risque* in French, etc.) on the other. The word *risk* was created and became popular in the sixteenth century as a consequence of a change in people's perceptions, from being totally manipulated by "good and evil spirits," towards the concept of the chance and danger of every free individual to influence his or her own future. (Probable origins of *risk* lie in the Greek word *rhiza*, meaning "root and/or cliff", or the Arabic word *rizq* meaning "what God and fate provide for your

Figure 59.15 • Facets of risk acceptance and risk rejection.

life".) Similarly, in our everyday language we use proverbs such as "Nothing ventured, nothing gained" or "God helps the brave", thereby promoting risk taking and risk acceptance. The concept always related to risk is that of uncertainty. As there is almost always some uncertainty about success or failure, or about the probability and quantity of consequences, accepting risks always means accepting uncertainties (Schäfer 1978).

Safety research has largely reduced the meaning of risk to its dangerous aspects (Yates 1992b). Only lately have positive consequences of risk re-emerged with the increase in adventurous leisure time activities (bungee jumping, motorcycling, adventure travels, etc.) and with a deeper understanding of how people are motivated to accept and take risks (Trimpop 1994). It is argued that we can understand and influence risk acceptance and risk taking behaviour only if we take the positive aspects of risks into account as well as the negative.

Risk acceptance therefore refers to the behaviour of a person in a situation of uncertainty that results from the decision to engage in that behaviour (or not to engage in it), after weighing the estimated benefits as greater (or lesser) than the costs under the given circumstances. This process can be extremely quick and not even enter the conscious decision-making level in automatic or habitual behaviour, such as shifting gears when the noise of the engine rises. At the other extreme, it may take very long and involve deliberate thinking and debates among several people, such as when planning a hazardous operation such as a space flight.

One important aspect of this definition is that of perception. Because perception and subsequent evaluation is based on a person's individual experiences, values and personality, the behavioural acceptance of risks is based more on subjective risk than on objective risk. Furthermore, as long as a risk is not perceived or considered, a person cannot respond to it, no matter how grave the hazard. Thus, the cognitive process leading to the acceptance of risk is an information-processing and evaluation procedure residing within each person that can be extremely quick.

A model describing the identification of risks as a cognitive process of identification, storage and retrieval was discussed by Yates and Stone (1992). Problems can arise at each stage of the process. For example, accuracy in the identification of risks is rather unreliable, especially in complex situations or for dangers such as radiation, poison or other not easily perceptible stimuli. Furthermore, the identification, storage and retrieval mechanisms underlie common psychological phenomena, such as primacy and recency effects, as well as familiarity habituation. That means that people familiar with a certain risk, such as driving at high speed, will get used to it, accept it as a given "normal" situation and estimate the risk at a far lower value than people not familiar with the activity. A simple formalization of the process is a model with the components of:

Stimulus ⇒ Perception ⇒ Evaluation ⇒ Decision ⇒ Behaviour
⇒ Feedback loop

For example, a slowly moving vehicle in front of a driver may be the stimulus to pass. Checking the road for traffic is perception. Estimating the time needed to pass, given the acceleration capabilities of one's car, is evaluation. The value of saving time leads to the decision and following behaviour to pass the car or not. The degree of success or failure is noticed immediately and this feedback influences subsequent decisions about passing behaviour. At each step of this process, the final decision whether to accept or reject risks can be influenced. Costs and benefits are evaluated based on individual-, context- and object-related factors that have been identified in scientific research to be of importance for risk acceptance.

Which Factors Influence Risk Acceptance?

Fischhoff et al. (1981) identified the factors (1) individual perception, (2) time, (3) space and (4) context of behaviour, as important dimensions of risk taking that should be considered in studying risks. Other authors have used different categories and different labels for the factors and contexts influencing risk acceptance. The categories of properties of the task or risk object, individual factors and context factors have been used to structure this large number of influential factors, as summarized in figure 59.16.

In normal models of risk acceptance, consequences of new technological risks (e.g., genetic research) were often described by quantitative summary measures (e.g., deaths, damage, injuries), and probability distributions over consequences were arrived at through estimation or simulation (Starr 1969). Results were compared to risks already "accepted" by the public, and thus offered a measure of acceptability of the new risk. Sometimes data were presented in a risk index to compare the different types of risk. The methods used most often were summarized by Fischhoff et al. (1981) as professional judgement by experts, statistical and historical information and formal analyses, such as fault tree analyses. The authors argued that properly conducted formal analyses have the highest "objectivity" as they separate facts from beliefs and take many influences into account. However, safety experts stated that the public and individual acceptance of risks may be based on biased value judgements and on opinions publicized by the media, and not on logical analyses.

It has been suggested that the general public is often misinformed by the media and political groups that produce statistics in favour of their arguments. Instead of relying on individual biases, only professional judgements based on expert knowledge should be used as a basis for accepting risks, and the general public should be excluded from such important decisions. This has drawn substantial criticism as it is viewed as a question of both democratic values (people should have a chance to decide issues that may have catastrophic consequences for their health and safety) and social values (does the technology or risky decision benefit receivers more than those who pay the costs). Fischhoff,

Figure 59.16 • Factors influencing risk acceptance.

59. SAFETY POLICY AND LEADERSHIP

Furby and Gregory (1987) suggested the use of either expressed preferences (interviews, questionnaires) or revealed preferences (observations) of the "relevant" public to determine the acceptability of risks. Jungermann and Rohrmann have pointed out the problems of identifying who is the "relevant public" for technologies such as nuclear power plants or genetic manipulations, as several nations or the world population may suffer or benefit from the consequences.

Problems with solely relying on expert judgements have also been discussed. Expert judgements based on normal models approach statistical estimations more closely than those of the public (Otway and von Winterfeldt 1982). However, when asked specifically to judge the probability or frequency of death or injuries related to a new technology, the public's views are much more similar to the expert judgements and to the risk indices. Research also showed that although people do not change their first quick estimate when provided with data, they do change when realistic benefits or dangers are raised and discussed by experts. Furthermore, Haight (1986) pointed out that because expert judgements are subjective, and experts often disagree about risk estimates, that the public is sometimes more accurate in its estimate of riskiness, if judged after the accident has occurred (e.g., the catastrophe at Chernobyl). Thus, it is concluded that the public uses other dimensions of risk when making judgements than statistical number of deaths or injuries.

Another aspect that plays a role in accepting risks is whether the perceived effects of taking risks are judged positive, such as adrenaline high, "flow" experience or social praise as a hero. Machlis and Rosa (1990) discussed the concept of desired risk in contrast to tolerated or dreaded risk and concluded that in many situations increased risks function as an incentive, rather than as a deterrent. They found that people may behave not at all averse to risk in spite of media coverage stressing the dangers. For example, amusement park operators reported a ride becoming more popular when it reopened after a fatality. Also, after a Norwegian ferry sank and the passengers were set afloat on icebergs for 36 hours, the operating company experienced the greatest demand it had ever had for passage on its vessels. Researchers concluded that the concept of desired risk changes the perception and acceptance of risks, and demands different conceptual models to explain risk-taking behaviour. These assumptions were supported by research showing that for police officers on patrol the physical danger of being attacked or killed was ironically perceived as job enrichment, while for police officers engaged in administrative duties, the same risk was perceived as dreadful. Vlek and Stallen (1980) suggested the inclusion of more personal and intrinsic reward aspects in cost/benefit analyses to explain the processes of risk assessment and risk acceptance more completely.

Individual factors influencing risk acceptance

Jungermann and Slovic (1987) reported data showing individual differences in perception, evaluation and acceptance of "objectively" identical risks between students, technicians and environmental activists. Age, sex and level of education have been found to influence risk acceptance, with young, poorly educated males taking the highest risks (e.g., wars, traffic accidents). Zuckerman (1979) provided a number of examples for individual differences in risk acceptance and stated that they are most likely influenced by personality factors, such as sensation seeking, extroversion, overconfidence or experience seeking. Costs and benefits of risks also contribute to individual evaluation and decision processes. In judging the riskiness of a situation or action, different people reach a wide variety of verdicts. The variety can manifest itself in terms of calibration—for example, due to value-induced biases which let the preferred decision appear less risky so that overconfident people choose a different anchor value. Personality aspects,

however, account for only 10 to 20% of the decision to accept a risk or to reject it. Other factors have to be identified to explain the remaining 80 to 90%.

Slovic, Fischhoff and Lichtenstein (1980) concluded from factor-analytical studies and interviews that non-experts assess risks qualitatively differently by including the dimensions of controllability, voluntariness, dreadfulness and whether the risk has been previously known. Voluntariness and perceived controllability were discussed in great detail by Fischhoff et al. (1981). It is estimated that voluntarily chosen risks (motorcycling, mountain climbing) have a level of acceptance which is about 1,000 times as high as that of involuntarily chosen, societal risks. Supporting the difference between societal and individual risks, the importance of voluntariness and controllability has been posited in a study by von Winterfeldt, John and Borcherding (1981). These authors reported lower perceived riskiness for motorcycling, stunt work and auto racing than for nuclear power and air traffic accidents. Renn (1981) reported a study on voluntariness and perceived negative effects. One group of subjects was allowed to choose between three types of pills, while the other group was administered these pills. Although all pills were identical, the voluntary group reported significantly fewer "side-effects" than the administered group.

When risks are individually perceived as having more dreadful consequences for many people, or even catastrophic consequences with a near zero probability of occurrence, these risks are often judged as unacceptable in spite of the knowledge that there have not been any or many fatal accidents. This holds even more true for risks previously unknown to the person judging. Research also shows that people use their personal knowledge and experience with the particular risk as the key anchor of judgement for accepting well-defined risks while previously unknown risks are judged more by levels of dread and severity. People are more likely to underestimate even high risks if they have been exposed for an extended period of time, such as people living below a power dam or in earthquake zones, or having jobs with a "habitually" high risk, such as in underground mining, logging or construction (Zimolong 1985). Furthermore, people seem to judge human-made risks very differently from natural risks, accepting natural ones more readily than self-constructed, human-made risks. The approach used by experts to base risks for new technologies within the low-end and high-end "objective risks" of already accepted or natural risks seems not to be perceived as adequate by the public. It can be argued that already "accepted risks" are merely tolerated, that new risks add on to the existing ones and that new dangers have not been experienced and coped with yet. Thus, expert statements are essentially viewed as promises. Finally, it is very hard to determine what has been truly accepted, as many people are seemingly unaware of many risks surrounding them.

Even if people are aware of the risks surrounding them, the problem of behavioural adaptation occurs. This process is well described in risk compensation and risk homeostasis theory (Wilde 1986), which states that people adjust their risk acceptance decision and their risk-taking behaviour towards their target level of perceived risk. That means that people will behave more cautiously and accept fewer risks when they feel threatened, and, conversely, they will behave more daringly and accept higher levels of risk when they feel safe and secure. Thus, it is very difficult for safety experts to design safety equipment, such as seat-belts, ski boots, helmets, wide roads, fully enclosed machinery and so on, without the user's offsetting the possible safety benefit by some personal benefit, such as increased speed, comfort, decreased attention or other more "risky" behaviour.

Changing the accepted level of risk by increasing the value of safe behaviour may increase the motivation to accept the less dangerous alternative. This approach aims at changing individual values, norms and beliefs to motivate alternative risk acceptance and risk-taking behaviour. Among the factors that increase or decrease the likelihood of risk acceptance, are those such as whether the technology provides a benefit corresponding to present needs, increases the standard of living, creates new jobs, facilitates economic growth, enhances national prestige and independence, requires strict security measures, increases the power of big business, or leads to centralization of political and economic systems (Otway and von Winterfeldt 1982). Similar influences of situational frames on risk evaluations were reported by Kahneman and Tversky (1979 and 1984). They reported that if they phrased the outcome of a surgical or radiation therapy as 68% probability of survival, 44% of the subjects chose it. This can be compared to only 18% who chose the same surgical or radiation therapy, if the outcome was phrased as 32% probability of death, which is mathematically equivalent. Often subjects choose a personal anchor value (Lopes and Ekberg 1980) to judge the acceptability of risks, especially when dealing with cumulative risks over time.

The influence of "emotional frames" (affective context with induced emotions) on risk assessment and acceptance was shown by Johnson and Tversky (1983). In their frames, positive and negative emotions were induced through descriptions of events such as personal success or the death of a young man. They found that subjects with induced negative feelings judged the risks of accidental and violent fatality rates as significantly higher, regardless of other context variables, than subjects of the positive emotional group. Other factors influencing individual risk acceptance include group values, individual beliefs, societal norms, cultural values, the economic and political situation, and recent experiences, such as seeing an accident. Dake (1992) argued that

Figure 59.17 • Individual biases that influence risk evaluation and risk acceptance.

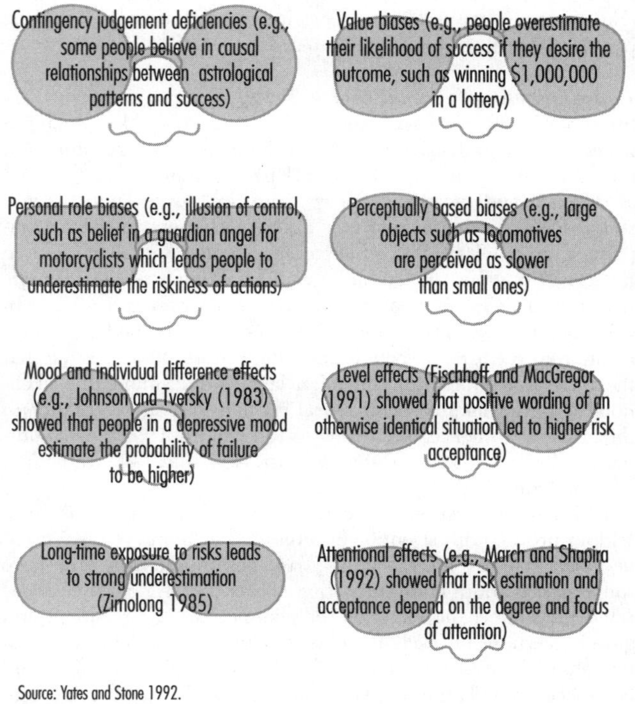

Source: Yates and Stone 1992.

risk is—apart from its physical component—a concept very much dependent on the respective system of beliefs and myths within a cultural frame. Yates and Stone (1992) listed the individual biases (figure 59.17) that have been found to influence the judgement and acceptance of risks.

Cultural factors influencing risk acceptance

Pidgeon (1991) defined culture as the collection of beliefs, norms, attitudes, roles and practices shared within a given social group or population. Differences in cultures lead to different levels of risk perception and acceptance, for example in comparing the work safety standards and accident rates in industrialized countries with those in developing countries. In spite of the differences, one of the most consistent findings across cultures and within cultures is that usually the same concepts of dreadfulness and unknown risks, and those of voluntariness and controllability emerge, but they receive different priorities (Kasperson 1986). Whether these priorities are solely culture dependent remains a question of debate. For example, in estimating the hazards of toxic and radioactive waste disposal, British people focus more on transportation risks; Hungarians more on operating risks; and Americans more on environmental risks. These differences are attributed to cultural differences, but may just as well be the consequence of a perceived population density in Britain, operating reliability in Hungary and the environmental concerns in the United States, which are situational factors. In another study, Kleinhesselink and Rosa (1991) found that Japanese perceive atomic power as a dreadful but not unknown risk, while for Americans atomic power is a predominantly unknown source of risk. The authors attributed these differences to different exposure, such as to the atomic bombs dropped on Hiroshima and Nagasaki in 1945. However, similar differences were reported between Hispanic and White American residents of the San Francisco area. Thus, local cultural, knowledge and individual differences may play an equally important role in risk perception as general cultural biases do (Rohrmann 1992a).

These and similar discrepancies in conclusions and interpretations derived from identical facts led Johnson (1991) to formulate cautious warnings about the causal attribution of cultural differences to risk perception and risk acceptance. He worried about the widely spread differences in the definition of culture, which make it almost an all-encompassing label. Moreover, differences in opinions and behaviours of subpopulations or individual business organizations within a country add further problems to a clear-cut measurement of culture or its effects on risk perception and risk acceptance. Also, the samples studied are usually small and not representative of the cultures as a whole, and often causes and effects are not separated properly (Rohrmann 1995). Other cultural aspects examined were world views, such as individualism versus egalitarianism versus belief in hierarchies, and social, political, religious or economic factors.

Wilde (1994) reported, for example, that the number of accidents is inversely related to a country's economic situation. In times of recession the number of traffic accidents drops, while in times of growth the number of accidents rises. Wilde attributed these findings to a number of factors, such as that in times of recession since more people are unemployed and gasoline and spare parts are more costly, people will consequently take more care to avoid accidents. On the other hand, Fischhoff et al. (1981) argued that in times of recession people are more willing to accept dangers and uncomfortable working conditions in order to keep a job or to get one.

The role of language and its use in mass media were discussed by Dake (1991), who cited a number of examples in which the same "facts" were worded such that they supported the political goals of specific groups, organizations or governments. For

Figure 59.18 • Six steps for choosing, deciding upon and accepting optimal risks.

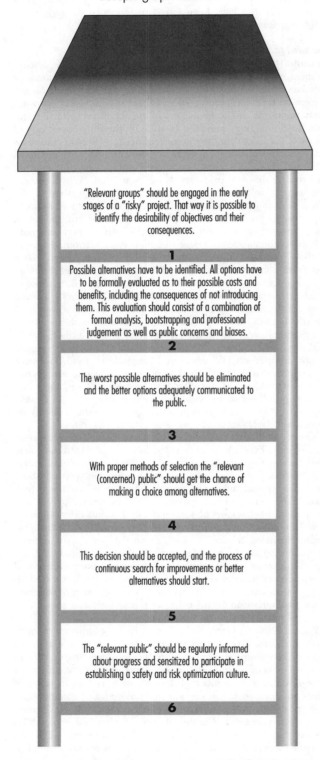

"Relevant groups" should be engaged in the early stages of a "risky" project. That way it is possible to identify the desirability of objectives and their consequences.

1

Possible alternatives have to be identified. All options have to be formally evaluated as to their possible costs and benefits, including the consequences of not introducing them. This evaluation should consist of a combination of formal analysis, bootstrapping and professional judgement as well as public concerns and biases.

2

The worst possible alternatives should be eliminated and the better options adequately communicated to the public.

3

With proper methods of selection the "relevant (concerned) public" should get the chance of making a choice among alternatives.

4

This decision should be accepted, and the process of continuous search for improvements or better alternatives should start.

5

The "relevant public" should be regularly informed about progress and sensitized to participate in establishing a safety and risk optimization culture.

6

evidence" or "scientific flotsam"? Do we face ecological "nightmares" or simply "incidences" or "challenges"? Risk acceptance thus depends on the perceived situation and context of the risk to be judged, as well as on the perceived situation and context of the judges themselves (von Winterfeldt and Edwards 1984). As the previous examples show, risk perception and acceptance strongly depend on the way the basic "facts" are presented. The credibility of the source, the amount and type of media coverage—in short, risk communication—is a factor determining risk acceptance more often than the results of formal analyses or expert judgements would suggest. Risk communication is thus a context factor that is specifically used to change risk acceptance.

Changing Risk Acceptance

To best achieve a high degree of acceptance for a change, it has proven very successful to include those who are supposed to accept the change in the planning, decision and control process to bind them to support the decision. Based on successful project reports, figure 59.18 lists six steps that should be considered when dealing with risks.

Determining "optimal risks"

In steps 1 and 2, major problems occur in identifying the desirability and the "objective risk" of the objective. while in step 3, it seems to be difficult to eliminate the worst options. For individuals and organizations alike, large-scale societal, catastrophic or lethal dangers seem to be the most dreaded and least acceptable options. Perrow (1984) argued that most societal risks, such as DNA research, power plants, or the nuclear arms race, possess many closely coupled subsystems, meaning that if one error occurs in a subsystem, it can trigger many other errors. These consecutive errors may remain undetected, due to the nature of the initial error, such as a nonfunctioning warning sign. The risks of accidents happening due to interactive failures increases in complex technical systems. Thus, Perrow (1984) suggested that it would be advisable to leave societal risks loosely coupled (i.e., independently controllable) and to allow for independent assessment of and protection against risks and to consider very carefully the necessity for technologies with the potential for catastrophic consequences.

Communicating "optimal choices"

Steps 3 to 6 deal with accurate communication of risks, which is a necessary tool to develop adequate risk perception, risk estimation and optimal risk-taking behaviour. Risk communication is aimed at different audiences, such as residents, employees, patients and so on. Risk communication uses different channels such as newspapers, radio, television, verbal communication and all of these in different situations or "arenas", such as training sessions, public hearings, articles, campaigns and personal communications. In spite of little research on the effectiveness of mass media communication in the area of health and safety, most authors agree that the quality of the communication largely determines the likelihood of attitudinal or behavioural changes in risk acceptance of the targeted audience. According to Rohrmann (1992a), risk communication also serves different purposes, some of which are listed in figure 59.19.

Risk communication is a complex issue, with its effectiveness seldom proven with scientific exactness. Rohrmann (1992a) listed necessary factors for evaluating risk communication and gave some advice about communicating effectively. Wilde (1993) separated the source, the message, the channel and the recipient and gave suggestions for each aspect of communication. He cited data that show, for example, that the likelihood of effective safety and health communication depends on issues such as those listed in figure 59.20.

example, are worker complaints about suspected occupational hazards "legitimate concerns" or "narcissistic phobias"? Is hazard information available to the courts in personal injury cases "sound

Figure 59.19 • Purposes of risk communication.

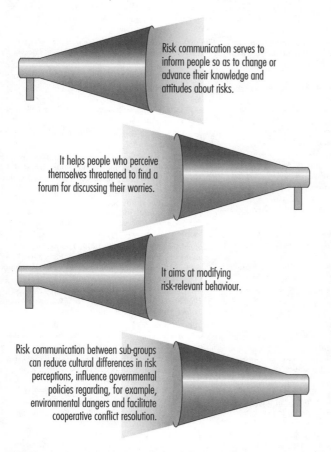

Risk communication serves to inform people so as to change or advance their knowledge and attitudes about risks.

It helps people who perceive themselves threatened to find a forum for discussing their worries.

It aims at modifying risk-relevant behaviour.

Risk communication between sub-groups can reduce cultural differences in risk perceptions, influence governmental policies regarding, for example, environmental dangers and facilitate cooperative conflict resolution.

Figure 59.20 • Factors influencing the effectiveness of risk communication.

Perceived credibility, expertise and similarity of the source relative to the recipient

Perceived distance and magnitude of required change through the content of the message

Primacy and recency effects (first and last message)

Paternalistic versus emotional/motivational style (telling people which safe behaviour to perform or merely sensitizing them, leaving the behavioural consequences open)

Personal relevance of the message

Exposure rate, number of recipients and message content determine the choice of channel

Personality traits and situational context of the recipient

59. SAFETY POLICY AND LEADERSHIP

Establishing a risk optimization culture

Pidgeon (1991) defined safety culture as a constructed system of meanings through which a given people or group understands the hazards of the world. This system specifies what is important and legitimate, and explains relationships to matters of life and death, work and danger. A safety culture is created and recreated as members of it repeatedly behave in ways that seem to be natural, obvious and unquestionable and as such will construct a particular version of risk, danger and safety. Such versions of the perils of the world also will embody explanatory schemata to describe the causation of accidents. Within an organization, such as a company or a country, the tacit and explicit rules and norms governing safety are at the heart of a safety culture. Major components are rules for handling hazards, attitudes toward safety, and reflexivity on safety practice.

Industrial organizations that already *live* an elaborate safety culture emphasize the importance of common visions, goals, standards and behaviours in risk taking and risk acceptance. As uncertainties are unavoidable within the context of work, an optimal balance of taking chances and control of hazards has to be stricken. Vlek and Cvetkovitch (1989) stated:

> Adequate risk management is a matter of organizing and maintaining a sufficient degree of (dynamic) control over a technological activity, rather than continually, or just once, measuring accident probabilities and distributing the message that these are, and will be, "negligibly low". Thus more often than not, "acceptable risk" means "sufficient control".

Summary

When people perceive themselves to possess sufficient control over possible hazards, they are willing to accept the dangers to gain the benefits. Sufficient control, however, has to be based on sound information, assessment, perception, evaluation and finally an optimal decision in favour of or against the "risky objective".

References

Abbey, A and JW Dickson. 1983. R&D work climate and innovation in semiconductors. *Acad Manage J* 26:362–368.

Andriessen, JHTH. 1978. Safe behavior and safety motivation. *J Occup Acc* 1:363–376.

Bailey, C. 1993. Improve safety program effectiveness with perception surveys. *Prof Saf* October:28–32.

Bluen, SD and C Donald. 1991. The nature and measurement of in-company industrial relations climate. *S Afr J Psychol* 21(1):12–20.

Brown, RL and H Holmes. 1986. The use of a factor-analytic procedure for assessing the validity of an employee safety climate model. *Accident Anal Prev* 18(6):445–470.

CCPS (Center for Chemical Process Safety). N.d. *Guidelines for Safe Automation of Chemical Processes*. New York: Center for Chemical Process Safety of the American Institution of Chemical Engineers.

Chew, DCE. 1988. Quelles sont les mesures qui assurent le mieux la sécurité du travail? Etude menée dans trois pays en développement d'Asie. *Rev Int Travail* 127:129–145.

Chicken, JC and MR Haynes. 1989. *The Risk Ranking Method in Decision Making*. Oxford: Pergamon.

Cohen, A. 1977. Factors in successful occupational safety programs. *J Saf Res* 9:168–178.

Cooper, MD, RA Phillips, VF Sutherland and PJ Makin. 1994. Reducing accidents using goal setting and feedback: A field study. *J Occup Organ Psychol* 67:219–240.

Cru, D and Dejours C. 1983. Les savoir-faire de prudence dans les métiers du bâtiment. *Cahiers médico-sociaux* 3:239–247.

Dake, K. 1991. Orienting dispositions in the perception of risk: An analysis of contemporary worldviews and cultural biases. *J Cross Cult Psychol* 22:61–82.

—. 1992. Myths of nature: Culture and the social construction of risk. *J Soc Issues* 48:21–37.

Dedobbeleer, N and F Béland. 1989. The interrelationship of attributes of the work setting and workers' safety climate perceptions in the construction industry. In *Proceedings of the 22nd Annual Conference of the Human Factors Association of Canada*. Toronto.

—. 1991. A safety climate measure for construction sites. *J Saf Res* 22:97–103.

Dedobbeleer, N, F Béland and P German. 1990. Is there a relationship between attributes of construction sites and workers' safety practices and climate perceptions? In *Advances in Industrial Ergonomics and Safety II*, edited by D Biman. London: Taylor & Francis.

Dejours, C. 1992. *Intelligence ouvrière et organisation du travail*. Paris: Harmattan.

DeJoy, DM. 1987. Supervisor attributions and responses for multicausal workplace accidents. *J Occup Acc* 9:213–223.

—. 1994. Managing safety in the workplace: An attribution theory analysis and model. *J Saf Res* 25:3–17.

Denison, DR. 1990. *Corporate Culture and Organizational Effectiveness*. New York: Wiley.

Dieterly, D and B Schneider. 1974. The effect of organizational environment on perceived power and climate: A laboratory study. *Organ Behav Hum Perform* 11:316–337.

Dodier, N. 1985. La construction pratique des conditions de travail: Préservation de la santé et vie quotidienne des ouvriers dans les ateliers. *Sci Soc Santé* 3:5–39.

Dunette, MD. 1976. *Handbook of Industrial and Organizational Psychology*. Chicago: Rand McNally.

Dwyer, T. 1992. *Life and Death at Work. Industrial Accidents as a Case of Socially Produced Error*. New York: Plenum Press.

Eakin, JM. 1992. Leaving it up to the workers: Sociological perspective on the management of health and safety in small workplaces. *Int J Health Serv* 22:689–704.

Edwards, W. 1961. Behavioural decision theory. *Annu Rev Psychol* 12:473–498.

Embrey, DE, P Humphreys, EA Rosa, B Kirwan and K Rea. 1984. An approach to assessing human error probabilities using structured expert judgement. In Nuclear Regulatory Commission NUREG/CR-3518, Washington, DC: NUREG.

Eyssen, G, J Eakin-Hoffman and R Spengler. 1980. Manager's attitudes and the occurrence of accidents in a telephone company. *J Occup Acc* 2:291–304.

Field, RHG and MA Abelson. 1982. Climate: A reconceptualization and proposed model. *Hum Relat* 35:181–201.

Fischhoff, B and D MacGregor. 1991. Judged lethality: How much people seem to know depends on how they are asked. *Risk Anal* 3:229–236.

Fischhoff, B, L Furby and R Gregory. 1987. Evaluating voluntary risks of injury. *Accident Anal Prev* 19:51–62.

Fischhoff, B, S Lichtenstein, P Slovic, S Derby and RL Keeney. 1981. *Acceptable risk*. Cambridge: CUP.

Flanagan, O. 1991. *The Science of the Mind*. Cambridge: MIT Press.

Frantz, JP. 1992. Effect of location, procedural explicitness, and presentation format on user processing of and compliance with product warnings and instructions. Ph.D. Dissertation, University of Michigan, Ann Arbor.

Frantz, JP and TP Rhoades.1993. Human factors. A task analytic approach to the temporal and spatial placement of product warnings. *Human Factors* 35:713–730.

Frederiksen, M, O Jensen and AE Beaton. 1972. *Prediction of Organizational Behavior*. Elmsford, NY: Pergamon.

Freire, P. 1988. *Pedagogy of the Oppressed*. New York: Continuum.

Glick, WH. 1985. Conceptualizing and measuring organizational and psychological climate: Pitfalls in multi-level research. *Acad Manage Rev* 10(3):601–616.

Gouvernement du Québec. 1978. *Santé et sécurité au travail: Politique québecoise de la santé et de la sécurité des travailleurs*. Québec: Editeur officiel du Québec.

Haas, J. 1977. Learning real feelings: A study of high steel ironworkers' reactions to fear and danger. *Sociol Work Occup* 4:147–170.

Hacker, W. 1987. *Arbeitspsychologie*. Stuttgart: Hans Huber.

Haight, FA. 1986. Risk, especially risk of traffic accident. *Accident Anal Prev* 18:359–366.

Hale, AR and AI Glendon. 1987. *Individual Behaviour in the Control of Danger*. Vol. 2. Industrial Safety Series. Amsterdam: Elsevier.

Hale, AR, B Hemning, J Carthey and B Kirwan. 1994. *Extension of the Model of Behaviour in the Control of Danger*. Volume 3—Extended model description. Delft University of Technology, Safety Science Group (Report for HSE). Birmingham, UK: Birmingham University, Industrial Ergonomics Group.

Hansen, L. 1993a. Beyond commitment. *Occup Hazards* 55(9):250.

—. 1993b. Safety management: A call for revolution. *Prof Saf* 38(30):16–21.

Harrison, EF. 1987. *The Managerial Decision-making Process*. Boston: Houghton Mifflin.

Heinrich, H, D Petersen and N Roos. 1980. *Industrial Accident Prevention*. New York: McGraw-Hill.

Hovden, J and TJ Larsson. 1987. Risk: Culture and concepts. In *Risk and Decisions*, edited by WT Singleton and J Hovden. New York: Wiley.

Howarth, CI. 1988. The relationship between objective risk, subjective risk, behaviour. *Ergonomics* 31:657–661.

Hox, JJ and IGG Kreft. 1994. Multilevel analysis methods. *Sociol Methods Res* 22(3):283–300.

Hoyos, CG and B Zimolong. 1988. *Occupational Safety and Accident Prevention. Behavioural Strategies and Methods*. Amsterdam: Elsevier.

Hoyos, CG and E Ruppert. 1993. *Der Fragebogen zur Sicherheitsdiagnose (FSD)*. Bern: Huber.

Hoyos, CT, U Bernhardt, G Hirsch and T Arnhold. 1991. Vorhandenes und erwünschtes sicherheitsrelevantes Wissen in Industriebetrieben. *Zeitschrift für Arbeits-und Organisationspsychologie* 35:68–76.

Huber, O. 1989. Information-procesing operators in decision making. In *Process and Structure of Human Decision Making*, edited by H Montgomery and O Svenson. Chichester: Wiley.

Hunt, HA and RV Habeck. 1993. The Michigan disability prevention study: Research highlights. Unpublished report. Kalamazoo, MI: E.E. Upjohn Institute for Employment Research.

International Electrotechnical Commission (IEC). N.d. *Draft Standard IEC 1508; Functional Safety: Safety-related Systems*. Geneva: IEC.

Instrument Society of America (ISA). N.d. *Draft Standard: Application of Safety Instrumented Systems for the Process Industries*. North Carolina, USA: ISA.

International Organization for Standardization (ISO). 1990. *ISO 9000-3: Quality Management and Quality Assurance Standards: Guidelines for the Application of ISO 9001 to the Development, Supply and Maintenance of Software*. Geneva: ISO.

James, LR. 1982. Aggregation bias in estimates of perceptual agreement. *J Appl Psychol* 67:219–229.

James, LR and AP Jones. 1974. Organizational climate: A review of theory and research. *Psychol Bull* 81(12):1096–1112.

Janis, IL and L Mann. 1977. *Decision-making: A Psychological Analysis of Conflict, Choice and Commitment*. New York: Free Press.

Johnson, BB. 1991. Risk and culture research: Some caution. *J Cross Cult Psychol* 22:141–149.

Johnson, EJ and A Tversky. 1983. Affect, generalization, and the perception of risk. *J Personal Soc Psychol* 45:20–31.

Jones, AP and LR James. 1979. Psychological climate: Dimensions and relationships of individual and aggregated work environment perceptions. *Organ Behav Hum Perform* 23:201–250.

Joyce, WF and JWJ Slocum. 1984. Collective climate: Agreement as a basis for defining aggregate climates in organizations. *Acad Manage J* 27:721–742.

Jungermann, H and P Slovic. 1987. Die Psychologie der Kognition und Evaluation von Risiko. Unpublished manuscript. Technische Universität Berlin.

Kahneman, D and A Tversky. 1979. Prospect theory: An analysis of decision under risk. *Econometrica* 47:263–291.

—. 1984. Choices, values, and frames. *Am Psychol* 39:341–350.

Kahnemann, D, P Slovic and A Tversky. 1982. *Judgement under Uncertainty: Heuristics and Biases*. New York: Cambridge University Press.

Kasperson, RE. 1986. Six propositions on public participation and their relevance for risk communication. *Risk Anal* 6:275–281.

Kleinhesselink, RR and EA Rosa. 1991. Cognitive representation of risk perception. *J Cross Cult Psychol* 22:11–28.

Komaki, J, KD Barwick and LR Scott. 1978. A behavioral approach to occupational safety: Pinpointing and reinforcing safe performance in a food manufacturing plant. *J Appl Psychol* 4:434–445.

Komaki, JL. 1986. Promoting job safety and accident precention. In *Health and Industry: A Behavioral Medicine Perspective*, edited by MF Cataldo and TJ Coats. New York: Wiley.

Konradt, U. 1994. Handlungsstrategien bei der Störungsdiagnose an flexiblen Fertigungs-einrichtungen. *Zeitschrift für Arbeits-und Organisations-pychologie* 38:54–61.

Koopman, P and J Pool. 1991. Organizational decision making: Models, contingencies and strategies. In *Distributed Decision Making. Cognitive Models for Cooperative Work*, edited by J Rasmussen, B Brehmer and J Leplat. Chichester: Wiley.

Koslowski, M and B Zimolong. 1992. Gefahrstoffe am Arbeitsplatz: Organisatorische Einflüsse auf Gefahrenbewußtsein und Risikokompetenz. In *Workshop Psychologie der Arbeitssicherheit*, edited by B Zimolong and R Trimpop. Heidelberg: Asanger.

Koys, DJ and TA DeCotiis. 1991. Inductive measures of psychological climate. *Hum Relat* 44(3):265–285.

Krause, TH, JH Hidley and SJ Hodson. 1990. *The Behavior-based Safety Process*. New York: Van Norstrand Reinhold.

Lanier, EB. 1992. Reducing injuries and costs through team safety. *ASSE J* July:21–25.

Lark, J. 1991. Leadership in safety. *Prof Saf* 36(3):33–35.

Lawler, EE. 1986. *High-involvement Management*. San Francisco: Jossey Bass.

Lehto, MR. 1992. Designing warning signs and warnings labels: Scientific basis for initial guideline. *Int J Ind Erg* 10:115–119.

Lehto, MR and JD Papastavrou. 1993. Models of the warning process: Important implications towards effectiveness. *Safety Science* 16:569–595.

Lewin, K. 1951. *Field Theory in Social Science*. New York: Harper and Row.

Likert, R. 1967. *The Human Organization*. New York: McGraw Hill.

Lopes, LL and P-HS Ekberg. 1980. Test of an ordering hypothesis in risky decision making. *Acta Physiol* 45:161–167.

Machlis, GE and EA Rosa. 1990. Desired risk: Broadening the social amplification of risk framework. *Risk Anal* 10:161–168.

March, J and H Simon. 1993. *Organizations*. Cambridge: Blackwell.

March, JG and Z Shapira. 1992. Variable risk preferences and the focus of attention. *Psychol Rev* 99:172–183.

Manson, WM, GY Wong and B Entwisle. 1983. Contextual analysis through the multilevel linear model. In *Sociologic Methodology, 1983–1984*. San Francisco: Jossey-Bass.

Mattila, M, M Hyttinen and E Rantanen. 1994. Effective supervisory behavior and safety at the building site. *Int J Ind Erg* 13:85–93.

Mattila, M, E Rantanen and M Hyttinen. 1994. The quality of work environment, supervision and safety in building construction. *Saf Sci* 17:257–268.

McAfee, RB and AR Winn. 1989. The use of incentives/feedback to enhance work place safety: A critique of the literature. *J Saf Res* 20(1):7–19.

McSween, TE. 1995. *The Values-based Safety Process*. New York: Van Norstrand Reinhold.

Melia, JL, JM Tomas and A Oliver. 1992. Concepciones del clima organizacional hacia la seguridad laboral: Replication del modelo confirmatorio de Dedobbeleer y Béland. *Revista de Psicologia del Trabajo y de las Organizaciones* 9(22).

Minter, SG. 1991. Creating the safety culture. *Occup Hazards* August:17–21.

Montgomery, H and O Svenson. 1989. *Process and Structure of Human Decision Making*. Chichester: Wiley.

Moravec, M. 1994. The 21st century employer-employee partnership. *HR Mag* January:125–126.

Morgan, G. 1986. *Images of Organizations*. Beverly Hills: Sage.

Nadler, D and ML Tushman. 1990. Beyond the charismatic leader. Leadership and organizational change. *Calif Manage Rev* 32:77–97.

Näsänen, M and J Saari. 1987. The effects of positive feedback on housekeeping and accidents at a shipyard. *J Occup Acc* 8:237–250.

National Research Council. 1989. *Improving Risk Communication*. Washington, DC: National Academy Press.

Naylor, JD, RD Pritchard and DR Ilgen. 1980. *A Theory of Behavior in Organizations*. New York: Academic Press.

Neumann, PJ and PE Politser. 1992. Risk and optimality. In *Risk-taking Behaviour*, edited by FJ Yates. Chichester: Wiley.

Nisbett, R and L Ross. 1980. *Human Inference: Strategies and Shortcomings of Social Judgement*. Englewood Cliffs: Prentice-Hall.

Nunnally, JC. 1978. *Psychometric Theory*. New York: McGraw-Hill.

Oliver, A, JM Tomas and JL Melia. 1993. Una segunda validacion cruzada de la escala de clima organizacional de seguridad de Dedobbeleer y Béland. Ajuste confirmatorio de los modelos unofactorial, bifactorial y trifactorial. *Psicologica* 14:59–73.

Otway, HJ and D von Winterfeldt. 1982. Beyond acceptable risk: On the social acceptability of technologies. *Policy Sci* 14:247–256.

Perrow, C. 1984. *Normal Accidents: Living with High-risk Technologies*. New York: Basic Books.

Petersen, D. 1993. Establishing good "safety culture" helps mitigate workplace dangers. *Occup Health Saf* 62(7):20–24.

Pidgeon, NF. 1991. Safety culture and risk management in organizations. *J Cross Cult Psychol* 22:129–140.

Rabash, J and G Woodhouse. 1995. MLn command reference. Version 1.0 March 1995, ESRC.

Rachman, SJ. 1974. *The Meanings of Fear*. Harmondsworth: Penguin.

Rasmussen, J. 1983. Skills, rules, knowledge, signals, signs and symbols and other distinctions. *IEEE T Syst Man Cyb* 3:266–275.

Reason, JT. 1990. *Human Error*. Cambridge: CUP.

Rees, JV. 1988. Self-regulation: An effective alternative to direct regulation by OSHA? *Stud J* 16:603–614.

Renn, O. 1981. Man, technology and risk: A study on intuitive risk assessment and attitudes towards nuclear energy. *Spezielle Berichte der Kernforschungsanlage Jülich*.

Rittel, HWJ and MM Webber. 1973. Dilemmas in a general theory of planning. *Pol Sci* 4:155-169.

Robertson, A and M Minkler. 1994. New health promotion movement: A critical examination. *Health Educ Q* 21(3):295–312.

Rogers, CR. 1961. *On Becoming a Person*. Boston: Houghton Mifflin.

Rohrmann, B. 1992a. The evaluation of risk communication effectiveness. *Acta Physiol* 81:169–192.

—. 1992b. Risiko Kommunikation, Aufgaben-Konzepte-Evaluation. In *Psychologie der Arbeitssicherheit*, edited by B Zimolong and R Trimpop. Heidelberg: Asanger.

—. 1995. Risk perception research: Review and documentation. In *Arbeiten zur Risikokommunikation*. Heft 48. Jülich: Forschungszentrum Jülich.

—. 1996. Perception and evaluation of risks: A cross cultural comparison. In *Arbeiten zur Risikokommunikation* Heft 50. Jülich: Forschungszentrum Jülich.

Rosenhead, J. 1989. *Rational Analysis for a Problematic World*. Chichester: Wiley.

Rumar, K. 1988. Collective risk but individual safety. *Ergonomics* 31:507–518.

Rummel, RJ. 1970. *Applied Factor Analysis*. Evanston, IL: Northwestern University Press.

Ruppert, E. 1987. Gefahrenwahrnehmung—ein Modell zur Anforderungsanalyse für die verhaltensabhängige Kontrolle von Arbeitsplatzgefahren. *Zeitschrift für Arbeitswissenschaft* 2:84–87.

Saari, J. 1976. Characteristics of tasks associated with the occurrence of accidents. *J Occup Acc* 1:273–279.

Saari, J. 1990. On strategies and methods in company safety work: From informational to motivational strategies. *J Occup Acc* 12:107–117.

Saari, J and M Näsänen. 1989. The effect of positive feedback on industrial housekeeping and accidents: A long-term study at a shipyard. *Int J Ind Erg* 4:3:201–211.

Sarkis, H. 1990. What really causes accidents. Presentation at Wausau Insurance Safety Excellence Seminar. Canandaigua, NY, US, June 1990.

Sass, R. 1989. The implications of work organization for occupational health policy: The case of Canada. *Int J Health Serv* 19(1):157–173.

Savage, LJ. 1954. *The Foundations of Statistics*. New York: Wiley.

Schäfer, RE. 1978. *What Are We Talking About When We Talk About "Risk"? A Critical Survey of Risk and Risk Preferences Theories*. R.M.-78-69. Laxenber, Austria: International Institute for Applied System Analysis.

Schein, EH. 1989. *Organizational Culture and Leadership*. San Francisco: Jossey-Bass.

Schneider, B. 1975a. Organizational climates: An essay. *Pers Psychol* 28:447–479.

—. 1975b. Organizational climate: Individual preferences and organizational realities revisited. *J Appl Psychol* 60:459–465.

Schneider, B and AE Reichers. 1983. On the etiology of climates. *Pers Psychol* 36:19–39.

Schneider, B, JJ Parkington and VM Buxton. 1980. Employee and customer perception of service in banks. *Adm Sci Q* 25:252–267.

Shannon, HS, V Walters, W Lewchuk, J Richardson, D Verma, T Haines and LA Moran. 1992. Health and safety approaches in the workplace. Unpublished report. Toronto: McMaster University.

Short, JF. 1984. The social fabric at risk: Toward the social transformation of risk analysis. *Amer Social R* 49:711–725.

Simard, M. 1988. La prise de risque dans le travail: un phénomène organisationnel. In *La prise de risque dans le travail*, edited by P Goguelin and X Cuny. Marseille: Editions Octares.

Simard, M and A Marchand. 1994. The behaviour of first-line supervisors in accident prevention and effectiveness in occupational safety. *Saf Sci* 19:169–184.

Simard, M et A Marchand. 1995. L'adaptation des superviseurs à la gestion participative de la prévention des accidents. *Relations Industrielles* 50: 567-589.

Simon, HA. 1959. Theories of decision making in economics and behavioural science. *Am Econ Rev* 49:253–283.

Simon, HA et al. 1992. Decision making and problem solving. In *Decision Making: Alternatives to Rational Choice Models*, edited by M Zev. London: Sage.

Simonds, RH and Y Shafai-Sahrai. 1977. Factors apparently affecting the injury frequency in eleven matched pairs of companies. *J Saf Res* 9(3):120–127.

Slovic, P. 1987. Perception of risk. *Science* 236:280–285.

—. 1993. Perceptions of environmental hazards: Psychological perspectives. In *Behaviour and Environment*, edited by GE Stelmach and PA Vroon. Amsterdam: North Holland.

59. SAFETY POLICY AND LEADERSHIP

Slovic, P, B Fischhoff and S Lichtenstein. 1980. Perceived risk. In *Societal Risk Assessment: How Safe Is Safe Enough?*, edited by RC Schwing and WA Albers Jr. New York: Plenum Press.

—. 1984. Behavioural decision theory perspectives on risk and safety. *Acta Physiol* 56:183–203.

Slovic, P, H Kunreuther and GF White. 1974. Decision processes, rationality, and adjustment to natural hazards. In *Natural Hazards, Local, National and Global*, edited by GF White. New York: Oxford University Press.

Smith, MJ, HH Cohen, A Cohen and RJ Cleveland. 1978. Characteristics of successful safety programs. *J Saf Res* 10:5–15.

Smith, RB. 1993. Construction industry profile: Getting to the bottom of high accident rates. *Occup Health Saf* June:35–39.

Smith, TA. 1989. Why you should put your safety program under statistical control. *Prof Saf* 34(4):31–36.

Starr, C. 1969. Social benefit vs. technological risk. *Science* 165:1232–1238.

Sulzer-Azaroff, B. 1978. Behavioral ecology and accident prevention. *J Organ Behav Manage* 2:11–44.

Sulzer-Azaroff, B and D Fellner. 1984. Searching for performance targets in the behavioral analysis of occupational health and safety: An assessment strategy. *J Organ Behav Manage* 6:2:53–65.

Sulzer-Azaroff, B, TC Harris and KB McCann. 1994. Beyond training: Organizational performance management techniques. *Occup Med: State Art Rev* 9:2:321–339.

Swain, AD and HE Guttmann. 1983. *Handbook of Human Reliability Analysis with Emphasis on Nuclear Power Plant Applications.* Sandia National Labora-tories, NUREG/CR-1278, Washington, DC: US Nuclear Regulatory Commission.

Taylor, DH. 1981. The hermeneutics of accidents and safety. *Ergonomics* 24:48–495.

Thompson, JD and A Tuden. 1959. Strategies, structures and processes of organizational decisions. In *Comparative Studies in Administration*, edited by JD Thompson, PB Hammond, RW Hawkes, BH Junker, and A Tuden. Pittsburgh: Pittsburgh University Press.

Trimpop, RM. 1994. *The Psychology of Risk Taking Behavior.* Amsterdam: Elsevier.

Tuohy, C and M Simard. 1992. The impact of joint health and safety committees in Ontario and Quebec. Unpublished report, Canadian Association of Administrators of Labour Laws, Ottawa.

Tversky, A and D Kahneman. 1981. The framing of decisions and the psychology of choice. *Science* 211:453–458.

Vlek, C and G Cvetkovich. 1989. *Social Decision Methodology for Technological Projects.* Dordrecht, Holland: Kluwer.

Vlek, CAJ and PJ Stallen. 1980. Rational and personal aspects of risk. *Acta Physiol* 45:273–300.

von Neumann, J and O Morgenstern. 1947. *Theory of Games and Ergonomic Behaviour.* Princeton, NJ: Princeton University Press.

von Winterfeldt, D and W Edwards. 1984. Patterns of conflict about risky technologies. *Risk Anal* 4:55–68.

von Winterfeldt, D, RS John and K Borcherding. 1981. Cognitive components of risk ratings. *Risk Anal* 1:277–287.

Wagenaar, W. 1990. Risk evaluation and causes of accidents. *Ergonomics* 33, Nos. 10/11.

Wagenaar, WA. 1992. Risk taking and accident causation. In *Risk-taking Behaviour*, edited by JF Yates. Chichester: Wiley.

Wagenaar, W, J Groeneweg, PTW Hudson and JT Reason. 1994. Promoting safety in the oil industry. *Ergonomics* 37, No. 12:1,999–2,013.

Walton, RE. 1986. From control to commitment in the workplace. *Harvard Bus Rev* 63:76–84.

Wilde, GJS. 1986. Beyond the concept of risk homeostasis: Suggestions for research and application towards the prevention of accidents and lifestyle-related disease. *Accident Anal Prev* 18:377–401.

—. 1993. Effects of mass media communications on health and safety habits: An overview of issues and evidence. *Addiction* 88:983–996.

—. 1994. Risk homeostatasis theory and its promise for improved safety. In *Challenges to Accident Prevention: The Issue of Risk Compensation Behaviour*, edited by R Trimpop and GJS Wilde. Groningen, The Netherlands: STYX Publications.

Yates, JF. 1992a. The risk construct. In *Risk Taking Behaviour*, edited by JF Yates. Chichester: Wiley.

—. 1992b. *Risk Taking Behaviour.* Chichester: Wiley.

Yates, JF and ER Stone. 1992. The risk construct. In *Risk Taking Behaviour*, edited by JF Yates. Chichester: Wiley.

Zembroski, EL. 1991. Lessons learned from man-made catastrophes. In *Risk Management*. New York: Hemisphere.

Zey, M. 1992. *Decision Making: Alternatives to Rational Choice Models.* London: Sage.

Zimolong, B. 1985. Hazard perception and risk estimation in accident causation. In *Trends in Ergonomics/Human Factors II*, edited by RB Eberts and CG Eberts. Amsterdam: Elsevier.

Zimolong, B. 1992. Empirical evaluation of THERP, SLIM and ranking to estimate HEPs. *Reliab Eng Sys Saf* 35:1–11.

Zimolong, B and R Trimpop. 1994. Managing human reliability in advanced manufacturing systems. In *Design of Work and Development of Personnel in Advanced Manufacturing Systems*, edited by G Salvendy and W Karwowski. New York: Wiley.

Zohar, D. 1980. Safety climate in industrial organizations: Theoretical and applied implications. *J Appl Psychol* 65, No.1:96–102.

Zuckerman, M. 1979. *Sensation Seeking: Beyond the Optimal Level of Arousal.* Hillsdale: Lawrence Erlbaum.

Other relevant readings

Baily, CW. 1988. *Using Behavioral Techniques to Improve Safety Programme Effectiveness.* Washington, DC: Association of American Railroads.

Deutsche Industrie Normen (DIN). 1990. *Grundsatze für Rechner in System mit Sicherheitsaufgaben [Principles for computers in safety-related systems].* DIN V VDE 0801. Berlin: Beuth Verlag.

Grandjean, E. 1988. *Fitting the Task to the Man.* London: Taylor and Francis.

Heller, FA, PJD Drenth, PL Koopman and V Rus. 1988. *Decisions in Organizations: A Three-country Comparative Study.* London: Sage.

HSE. N.d. *Out of Control: Control Systems—Why They Go Wrong, and How to Prevent Failure.* Sudbury UK: HSE Books.

—. N.d. *Programmable Electronic Systems in Safety-related Applications: 1. An Introductory Guide.* Sudbury, UK: HSE Books.

—. N.d. *Programmable Electronic Systems in Safety-related Applications: 2. General Technical Guidelines.* Sudbury, UK: HSE Books.

Johnson, B. 1989. *Design and Analysis of Fault Tolerant Digital Systems.* New York: Addison Wesley.

Jones, PG. N.d. Computers in chemical plant: A need for safety awareness. In *Hazards XI*, edited by PG Jones. Rugby, UK: Davis Building.

Jungermann, H, B Rohrmann and P Wiedemann. 1991. *Risikokontroversen-Konzepte, Konflikte, Kommuni-kation.* Berlin: Springer.

Larprie, JC. 1991. *Dependability: Basic Concepts and Terminology.* Berlin: Springer.

Levy, S and S Greene. 1988. The effectiveness of safety education materials. In *Safety Management, A Human Approach*, edited by DC Petersen. Goshen, NY: Aloray.

Petersen, DC. 1988. *Safety Management, A Human Approach.* Goshen, NY: Aloray.

—. 1989. *Techniques of Safety Management.* Goshen, NY: Aloray.

tions, or environmental controls. To prevent or reduce the risk of occupational injuries, safety practitioners may recommend or use engineering controls, such as equipment guards, interlocks, and ergonomically designed tools and machines; or administrative controls, such as work practices, schedules and training; or personal protective equipment, such as respirators, hard hats or fall protective devices. This means that in injury prevention, epidemiologists, biostatisticians and health educators are joined by engineers, physicists, industrial hygienists and ergonomists. The problem-solving process is the same; some of the intervention approaches, and therefore the disciplines involved in identifying, developing and testing interventions, may be different.

The mechanism of occupational safety and health research is the public health approach, an integrated, multidisciplinary approach to identification through (1) surveillance and investigation, (2) epidemiological and safety analysis, (3) research and development leading to preventive technologies and strategies, (4) evaluation and demonstration to ensure that these technologies and strategies are effective, and (5) communication of risk information, research methods and findings, and effective technologies and strategies. The public health approach and the safety analysis approach are merging in the study of occupational safety. The principal disciplines of epidemiology and engineering are collaborating to bring new insight into injury causation and prevention. New and advancing technologies, particularly digital electronic computer technology, are being adapted to solve workplace safety problems.

● GOVERNMENT SERVICES

Anthony Linehan

The establishment and control of acceptable standards of safety and health at work is universally regarded as a function of government, even though the legal responsibility for compliance rests with the employer. (It should be noted that in many countries, safety standards are established by consensus between manufactures, users, insurers, public and government and then adopted or referenced by government into regulations.) Government provides a range of safety services in order to discharge its function. In this context, government includes both national, regional and provincial authorities.

Legislative Framework
One of the most important services supporting safety in the workplace is the legislative framework within which it must operate, and the task of providing this framework is a vital function of government. Such legislation should be comprehensive in its scope and application, reflect international standards as well as national needs, give consideration to established, proven industry safe practices and provide for the means to carry its intentions into practical effect. Safety and health legislation which is based on extensive consultation with the social partners, industry and the community stands a much greater chance of being properly observed and respected, and therefore contributes significantly to sound standards of protection.

Compliance
The legislative framework, although important, must be effectively translated into practical action at the level of the enterprise. A vital government service is the creation of an effective inspectorate to carry the law into effect. Government must therefore establish an inspectorate, supply it with adequate resources in

terms of finance and personnel, and provide it with sufficient powers to do its work.

Safety and Health Information
A key service is that of publicity for safety and health. This function is not of course exclusive to government; safety associations, employers' groups, trade unions and consultants can all play a part in ensuring a greater awareness of legal requirements, of standards, of technical solutions and of new hazards and risk. Government may take a leading role in offering guidance on compliance with legislation and on compliance with standards governing safety practices, ranging from acceptable methods of machinery guarding to publicizing tables of exposure limits to hazardous substances.

Government should also provide the stimulus in identifying suitable topics for specific campaigns and initiatives. Such activities are usually carried out in cooperation with employers' associations and trade unions, and are often derived from analysis of government, industry and association statistics relating to accidents and ill health. In considering its publicity and information strategy, government must ensure that it reaches not only the more sophisticated and developed industries but also those with very limited knowledge and awareness of safety and health matters. This is particularly important in developing countries and those with economies heavily dependent upon agriculture and upon the family as the unit of employment.

The collection, analysis and publication of statistics on safety and health is an important service. Statistics provide the inspectorates and their social partners with the raw material that enables them to identify emerging trends or shifting patterns in accident and ill-health causation and to assess, in measurable terms, the effectiveness of national policies, of specific campaigns and of standards of compliance. Statistics can also provide some degree of comparative standards and of achievement on an international basis.

The accuracy of the statistical information on accidents is clearly of prime importance. Some countries have an accident reporting system which is wholly separate from the social benefit or injury compensation system. Reliance is placed on a legal requirement that accidents be reported to the enforcing authority. Statistical studies have shown that there can be a significant shortfall in the reporting of accidents (other than fatalities) under this system. Up to 60% of accidents in some industries are not reported to the enforcing authorities. This shortfall can only devalue the statistics which are produced. The integrity and accuracy of accident and ill-health statistics must be a priority for government.

Safety Training
Safety training is another area in which service may be provided by government. Most safety and health legislation features requirements for adequate training. The extent to which government is directly involved in organizing and providing training varies considerably. At the highest levels of training—that is, for the safety professionals—the work is usually undertaken at universities and colleges of technology. Direct government input at this level is relatively uncommon although government scientists, lawyers and technologists from inspectorates often do contribute as lecturers and by providing funding and training materials.

A similar pattern exists at the lower level of skills training for safety. Educational courses for workers are often conducted by industry, trade or training associations with an input and funding from the inspectorates, as are courses which are designed to increase the safety awareness of workers. The function of government is less to conduct and direct training services, than to stimulate and encourage non-governmental organizations to do this work, and to contribute directly wherever appropriate. More direct assistance can be provided through government subsidies to assist in defraying the costs of training to companies. Much of the material on which safety training is based is provided by official government publications, notes of guidance and formally published standards.

Services for Small Businesses

The problem of furnishing service to small businesses is singularly complex. There is the very real need to provide sympathetic help and encouragement to an important element of the national and local economy. At the same time there is a need to ensure that this be done effectively without lowering the standards of protection for employees and possibly endangering their safety and their health. In attempting to address this complexity, the service provided by government plays a key role.

Many governments provide a particular service to small enterprises which includes the management of safety and health. This service is provided in a variety of ways, including, for example, special "start-up" packs of information which provide (1) details on means of complying in practical terms with legal requirements, (2) facts as to where to find sources of information and (3) a contact point with the inspectorates. Some inspectorates have staff dedicated to dealing with the particular needs of small businesses and, in conjunction with trade associations, provide seminars and meetings where safety and health issues can be constructively discussed in a nonconfrontational atmosphere.

Safety Research

Research is another service provided by government, either directly through supporting its own laboratories and research programmes on safety and health problems, or indirectly by providing grants to independent research organizations for specific projects. Health and safety research may be divided into two broad categories, as follows:

- *forensic research*, exemplified by the research that follows major accidents in order to determine their causes
- *longer-term research* which investigates, for example, exposure levels for potentially hazardous substances.

There is also *laboratory service* which provides facilities for such tests as the analysis of samples counts, and for approvals systems for protective equipment. This service is important both for the inspectorates and for the social partners concerned in validating health standards in enterprises. There is debate whether government should maintain laboratory and research facilities, or whether these functions might more properly be the responsibility of universities and independent research units. But these arguments are about means rather than about basic purpose. Few would dispute that the research function in its broadest sense is a vital government service to safety and health, whether the government acts through its own facilities or stimulates and provides resources to non-governmental organizations to do the work.

Safety Representation

Finally, the government provides a service via its representational role within the international community. Many safety and health problems are international in character and cannot be confined within national boundaries. Cooperation between governments, the establishment of internationally accepted standards for hazardous substances, the exchange of information between governments, support for international organizations dealing with safety and health—all these are the functions of government, and the effective discharge of these duties can only serve to enhance both the standing and the standards of safety and health nationally and internationally.

SAFETY SERVICES: CONSULTANTS

Dan Petersen

Occasionally, those responsible for safety in an organization—whether they be concerned with the behavioural system, the safety system or the physical environment—call upon external resources such as professional safety consultants for help. When this occurs, it is important to bear in mind that the responsibility for the successful completion of the task (as distinguished from the performance of the task itself) of analysing a given system and making improvements to it cannot be delegated to outside agencies. Internal analysts (as opposed to external consultants) studying a system can usually obtain more reliable data because of their close familiarity with the organization. Nevertheless, the help of an outside consultant who has a wide range of experience with analysing safety problems and suggesting appropriate remedies, can be invaluable.

Seeking Outside Help

If there is no one in an organization who is familiar with safety laws and standards on the national level, it might be helpful to call in a safety regulations expert for assistance. Often there is no one in the organizational structure who may be able to analyse the behavioural system, and in such an eventuality it would be advisable to obtain help from someone who can do so. Kenneth Albert (1978) suggests that there are six specific occasions when outside help should be obtained:

- when special expertise is essential
- for a politically sensitive issue
- when impartiality is necessary
- if time is critical and the internal resources are not immediately available
- if anonymity must be maintained
- when the prestige of an outsider would be helpful.

Although Albert's remarks were not made in connection with safety, the above points seem valid in determining the need for an outside safety consultant. Often a safety problem is intertwined with managerial personalities and is extremely difficult to solve internally. In such a situation a solution may be acceptable to all parties involved just because it came from an outsider. If an organization needs an analysis in a hurry it often can be done faster by an outside consultant, and often the outsider's recommendation will carry more weight than the insider's. In the field of safety, it appears that outside help is needed by many organizations with behavioural system analysis, some with safety system analysis and a few with physical condition analysis. However, with regard to the availability of safety consultants, supply and demand are inversely related, as there seems to be an ample supply of physical condition consultants, whereas there are fewer safety system analysts, and safety behavioural analysis experts are almost non-existent.

Safety Consultants

While the types of external safety consultant help will vary by country, they might generally be classified into these categories:

- insurance company field safety engineers or consultants
- government safety consultants (national, state, provincial and local)
- private consulting firms and full-time professional safety consultants
- part-time private consultants
- safety council or safety association consultants
- industry association consultants.

Insurance consultants. Most of the safety consultants and safety engineers in the United States who do not work for government or industry are employed by insurance firms. Many other safety professionals started their careers working for insurance companies. Almost all companies, except the very large and self-insured, are helped routinely by insurance loss-control representatives.

Government consultants. The providers of government consulting services vary from country to country and as to their affiliation (national, state, provincial or local) and the sorts of tasks they are permitted and qualified to perform. In the United States, the stated goal of the onsite consultation programme offered by the Occupational Safety and Health Administration (OSHA) is to obtain "safe and healthful workplaces for employees". Thus by stipulation, the consultations will pertain only to physical conditions. An organization seeking this kind of help should consider OSHA's offering. If, however, consulting help is needed with the safety system or the behavioural system, OSHA is the wrong place to go.

The defined onsite responsibilities of OSHA consultants are as follows:

- to identify and properly classify hazards
- to recommend corrective measures (short of engineering assistance)
- to arrange abatement dates for serious hazards
- to report to their supervisors any serious hazards which the employer has not acted upon
- to follow up on employer actions.

It is obvious that there are some aspects of receiving OSHA consulting service by this route that are unusual. The purpose of the consultants is to help improve physical conditions, but in two instances the consultants have additional duties:

- In the case of serious violations of OSHA standards, they must set abatement dates and follow up on them.
- In the case of imminent violations of the OSHA standards, they must refer them to either their supervisors (and thence to the Department of Labor hierarchy) or to the organization's compliance staff for their immediate action.

In other words, OSHA consulting is true consulting only when nothing seriously wrong is found. If anything serious or imminently hazardous is found, the "customer" loses control of the decision process as to how and when to correct it.

Private consulting firms. A third source of external help is the (full-time) private consultant or the private consulting firms, who can provide help in any area—behavioural systems, safety systems or physical conditions—with none of the special limitations mentioned above. The only difficulty is ensuring that a consultant has been selected who has the necessary skills and knowledge to provide the desired work product.

Part-time private consultation and others. The fourth place to locate a private consultant is among those individuals who consult on a part-time basis to supplement their incomes. These consultants are either retired safety professionals who remain active, or college or university professors who supplement their income and stay knowledgeable about the world outside the academy. Here again the problem is to locate these people and ensure that the person hired has the competencies needed. Additional sources include consultants who make themselves available through national or local safety councils, and consultants with trade associations.

Locating a Consultant

In the first two categories of external help listed above, government and insurance, finding a consultant is easy. For example, in the United States, one can contact the appropriate workers' compensation insurance carrier or the local OSHA grant office and ask them to visit the organization. Many other countries provide similar governmental and insurance resources.

Finding a consultant in the second two categories, private individual consultants and consulting firms, is more difficult. In the United States, for instance, several organizations publish directories of consultants. As an example, the American Society of Safety Engineers (ASSE) publishes a national directory, which includes some 260 names of consultants. However, there seem to be considerable problems using this directory. An analysis of the 260 people on the list shows that 56% are individuals who indicate that they are for hire but who have not stated whether they work for companies and seek additional income or are full-time consultants or part-time retired safety consultants. An additional 32% were identified as being connected with consulting firms, 5% were connected with universities, 3% were insurance brokers, 3% were connected with manufacturing companies and 1% were associated with state governments. Actually, this directory, while advertised as a document which tells the reader "where the occupational safety/health experts are", is really a roster of those people who have paid their dues and are members of the consultants division of the ASSE.

There is no easy way to find a consultant who has the expertise needed. Probably the best approaches other than insurance or government are to (1) network with other organizations with similar problems to see who they have used and whether they were satisfied with the results, (2) contact a professional organization at the national level, or (3) make use of professional directories such as the one above, keeping in mind the qualifications made concerning it.

Insurance Consulting

The most readily available of the outside consultants are insurance consultants. Since the beginning of the industrial safety movement, the insurance industry has been involved with safety. For many years. the only possible external help for most companies had been that available from the company's insurance carrier. While this is no longer true, the insurance consultant is most often sought out.

The safety services departments of typical large insurance companies are charged with three specific functions:

- a sales assistance function
- an underwriting assistance function
- a customer service function.

Only the third of these is of value to the customer needing safety assistance. The underwriting assistance function is carried out by a field representative who is the "eyes and ears" of the insurance company, observing what is going on at the policyholder's place of business and reporting back to the desk-bound underwriter. The third function consists of assisting customers to improve their loss prevention and safety programmes and reducing the likelihood of those customers having accidents and suffering financial loss. The assistance offered varies considerably from company to company.

Over the years, different philosophies have emerged which dictate the value of the service that the insurance company is able to provide. In some companies the safety services department is still very much a part of the underwriting function and their duties are to observe and report, while in others, the engineering department reports to the underwriting department. In some insurance companies, the loss-control department is independent, existing primarily to serve the customer and only secondarily to assist the sales and underwriting functions. When the primary mission of the service is to assist sales, customer service will suffer. If the loss-control department is part of underwriting, it may be difficult

Figure 60.1 • Additional services of consultants.

Safety engineers service
- Inspection
- Engineering
- Consultant

Industrial hygiene services
- Dust
- Fumes
- Gases
- Vapours
- Noise

Nursing services
- Occupational health
- Rehabilitation

Specialists
- Fleet
- Construction
- Products
- Radiation
- Electricity
- Elevator
- Fire • Press
- Medical

Materials
- Forms
- Literature
- Posters
- Periodicals
- Films
- Awards

Training
- Safety management
- Supervisory training
- Speciality courses
- Fleet safety
- Products safety
- Construction
- Driver training
  - Classroom
  - In plant
  - Behind the wheel
  - Programmed instruction
- Symposia

Ergonomics services

Stress management

to get safety service from them, as they simply may not be staffed with trained, qualified people to provide that sort of service. If the loss-control department is not part of underwriting, then it may be able to provide good service to a customer. Conversely, it may also be quite ineffective, because numerous factors can intervene that can frustrate the effective provision of safety service.

When the service is an inspection-only service, as is very prevalent, the safety system and the behavioural system will be totally overlooked. When the service consists of the delivery of safety aids and materials, and nothing else, it is a virtually meaningless service. When the service consists primarily or totally of holding safety meetings for a customer, such as delivering the "canned" safety programme that the carrier's home office has devised for use at all insured companies, or merely ensuring that physical conditions are up to code, it is also a weak service.

Depending upon the sort of philosophy that underlies the service of the carrier, additional services may be available over and beyond that provided by the representative that calls on the customer. Figure 60.1 outlines some typical additional services that can be particularly useful to customers, such as industrial hygiene, nursing and specialist (engineering and fire protection) services, depending upon the organization's current needs. Training services are somewhat less common but are also valuable.

Government Consultants

As with the insurance consultants, certain considerations, such as the following, must be weighed by a company before deciding whether or not to request the assistance of government consultants.

- whether the terms under which government assistance is offered are acceptable
- the competence of the people
- the limited scope of the consulting
- the inability to direct the consulting focus

Probably the first consideration is whether or not a company wishes to become involved with a government at all. When using other kinds of consultants (either private or those provided by an insurance firm), whatever findings are obtained are strictly between the organization and the consultant. Whatever the company de-

cides to do is a decision reserved to the company alone, which retains control over the disposition of the information. With government consultants this is not totally true. For example, if the consultants find one or both of two kinds of hazards—violations of the law and those immediately dangerous to life or health—the organization may not be able to retain the power of decision as to what to do about the hazard and when to do it.

Government consultants can provide assistance with determining whether or not an organization is in compliance with regulations and standards. This is an extremely narrow focus and has many weaknesses, as pointed out by Peters (1978) in his article "Why only a fool relies on safety standards": "For those who know little about safety, it seems quite plausible and reasonable to expect that the existence of good safety standards and a sufficient conformance to those standards should be an adequate measure of safety assurance." Peters suggests that not only is such an expectation in error, but also that reliance on standards will subvert professional activities that are needed to reduce loss.

Private Consulting

With the private consultant, whether an independent individual or an employee of a consulting firm, full or part time, there are no mandatory reporting requirements. The private consultant does not have to abide by the mandates of a required referral system; the relationship is strictly between the organization and the individual consultant. The scope of the consultation is limited, as the "customer" can very directly control the focus of the consultant's activities. Thus the only thing the client has to worry about is whether or not the consultant is competent in the areas where help is needed and whether or not the fee is judged to be a fair one. Figure 60.2 lists some of the most basic functions of the management consultant.

G. Lippit (1969), who has written extensively on the consulting process, has identified eight specific consultant activities:

Figure 60.2 • Basic functions of the management consultant.

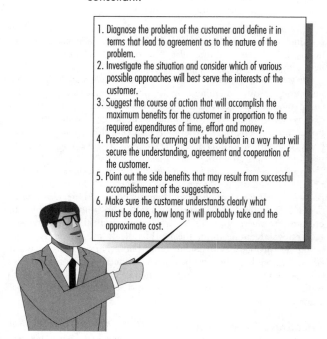

1. Diagnose the problem of the customer and define it in terms that lead to agreement as to the nature of the problem.
2. Investigate the situation and consider which of various possible approaches will best serve the interests of the customer.
3. Suggest the course of action that will accomplish the maximum benefits for the customer in proportion to the required expenditures of time, effort and money.
4. Present plans for carrying out the solution in a way that will secure the understanding, agreement and cooperation of the customer.
5. Point out the side benefits that may result from successful accomplishment of the suggestions.
6. Make sure the customer understands clearly what must be done, how long it will probably take and the approximate cost.

Source: Association of Consulting Management Engineers 1966.

Figure 60.3 • Five consultant approaches.

Source: Lippit 1969.

1. helps management examine organizational problems (e.g., organizes a management meeting for problem identification in the problem relationships between home and field personnel)
2. helps management examine the contribution of the proper dialogue to these problems (e.g., in relation to home and field office problems, explores with management how a conference on communication blocks might lead to problem solving)
3. helps examine the long- and short-range objectives of the renewal action (e.g., involves management in refining objectives and in setting goals)
4. explores, with management, alternatives to renewal plans
5. develops, with management, the renewal plans (e.g., based on the objectives, works with a task force to develop a process with built-in evaluation rather than simply submitting an independently developed plan to management for approval)
6. explores appropriate resources to implement renewal plans (e.g., provides management with a variety of resources both inside and outside the organization; the renewal stimulator must help management to understand what each resource can contribute to effective problem solving)
7. provides consultation for management on evaluation and review of renewal process (e.g., evaluation must be in terms of problem solving; working with management; the renewal stimulator must assess the current status of the problem, rather than check whether or not certain activities have been conducted)
8. explores with management the follow-up steps necessary to reinforce problem solving and outputs from the renewal process (e.g., encourages management to look at implications of the steps taken so far, and to assess the current status of the organization in terms of other actions that might be necessary to follow up on implementation of the renewal process).

Lippit (1969) has also identified five different positions which the consultants can adopt vis-à-vis their clients' needs (Figure 60.3).

Choosing a Consultant

When choosing a consultant, a process such as that given by figure 60.4 is suggested.

Whether or not to use a consultant, and which one to use, ought to be determined by the user's defined needs and by what kinds of skills and knowledge the consultant must have to be of real help. Then, it would seem logical to look for individuals or groups that have those sorts of skills and knowledge. It may be determined that as a result of this process, the job can be done without external help; for example, to locate the needed skills internally and apply those skills to the defined safety problems. Conversely, it may be decided to go to the outside for the skills needed.

Evaluating the Consultant's Performance

After having worked with consultants for a period of time, a company can judge their individual performance and worth to the organization much more accurately (figure 60.5). As a result of the analysis provided by the consultant, the conclusion may be made that perhaps the remainder of the job, or a similar job, can be done as well using internal resources. Many companies do this now, and more are turning to it, in both safety and nonsafety areas.

Problem-Solving Approaches

K. Albert, in his book, *How to Be Your Own Management Consultant* (1978), suggests that there are four different types of internal management problem-solving approaches:

Figure 60.4 • Choosing a consultant.

Figure 60.5 • Evaluating the consultant's performance.

DID HE?

- Diagnose the problem and define it?
- Consider possible alternatives for solution?
- Suggest the best of these?
- Present his proposed solution in a way you could understand?
- Point out the side benefits to the proposed solution?
- Make sure you understood, including what it would cost?

WHICH APPROACH DID HEOR SHE USE?

- Advocate
- Expert
- Alternative identifier
- Process specialist
- Reflector
- Was his approach the correct one for your situation?

ANSWER THESE QUESTIONS

- Did he identify the aim and scope of his study?
- Did he perform as he had outlined?
- Did he submit progress reports?
- Were they/he professional in approach?
- Did they/he work well with your people?

- Did your people work well with him?
- Did he teach you and your people?
- Are you/your people more competent as a result?
- Did he achieve his objectives?
- Did his proposed programme include you/your people's ideas?
- Were you satisfied in how he presented his suggestions?
- Was close contact maintained with you throughout?
- Was it accomplished in reasonable time and cost?
- How do your executives rate him?
- Would you retain him again?
- Did he get results? Explain the indicators.

- to hire a full-time internal consultant
- to put someone on a special assignment on a temporary basis
- to create a task force to work on a problem
- collaboration between an outside consultant and an internal consultant.

Furthermore, Albert suggests that no matter which approach is chosen, these ground rules must be followed for success:

- Get total support of top management.
- Establish confidentiality.
- Earn the acceptance of operation units.
- Avoid company politics.
- Report to a high level.
- Start slowly and maintain objectivity.

IMPLEMENTATION OF A SAFETY PROGRAMME

Tom B. Leamon

The implementation of a safety programme should reflect its nature as a normal, day-to-day concern of general management. The need for information for decision making at all stages and for communication between all levels of the enterprise form the basis for successful implementation of such a programme.

Executive Level
Initially, the introduction of a new or modified safety programme will require the agreement of senior management, who may regard it as a cost/benefit decision to be made in light of competition for resources from elsewhere in the enterprise. The desire to reduce damages, pain and suffering in the workplace through the implementation of a safety programme will be tempered by the organization's ability to sustain such an effort. Informed management decisions will require three elements:

1. an explicit description of the programme, which fully defines the proposed approach
2. an assessment of the impact of the programme on the company operations
3. an estimate of the costs of implementation with a prediction of the benefits that are likely to be produced.

The only exception to this will be when a safety programme is mandated by regulation and must be instituted in order to remain in business.

In the latter endeavour, it is useful to add an estimate of the *true* costs of the current safety record of the enterprise, as well as those costs covered by direct insurance or direct out-of-pocket expenses. The indirect costs are likely to be significant in all cases; estimates for serious incidents in the United Kingdom suggest that the real costs (borne by an enterprise as indirect costs) range from a factor of two to three up to a factor of ten times the actual, direct insurance costs. In those countries requiring compulsory insurance, the cost, and hence the savings, will vary widely depending on the social environment of each particular nation. Insurance costs in countries where the insurance carriers are required to cover full medical and rehabilitation costs, such as the United States, are likely to be higher than those in countries in which the treatment of the injured worker is part of the social contract. An ideal way to emphasize the significance of such losses is to identify the annual production required to generate revenue *lost* in paying for these losses. This is highly compatible with the concept that, while a business must necessarily assume the risk of doing business, it should be *managing* that risk in order to reduce the losses and improve its financial performance.

Management Level
Following acceptance at the senior management level, an implementation team should be formed to develop the strategy and the plan to introduce the programme of the roll-out plan. Such an approach is more likely to be effective than one that shifts the responsibility for safety to an individual designated as the safety engineer. The size and level of the involvement of this implementation team will vary widely, depending on the enterprise and the social environment. Nevertheless, input is essential from at least those with responsibility for operations, personnel, risk management and training, as well as key representatives of employee groups who will be affected by the programme. It is likely that a team of this composition will detect possible conflicts (for example, between production and safety) early on in the process, before attitudes and

positions, as well as procedures, hardware and equipment, have become fixed. It is at this point that collaboration, rather than confrontation, is likely to provide a better opportunity for problem solving. The output of this team should be a document that identifies the corporate view of the programme, the key elements of the programme, the schedule for implementation and the responsibilities of those involved.

Care should be taken to ensure that the executive commitment is particularly evident to managers at the operational level at which the safety programme can be effected. Perhaps the most significant way of achieving this is to establish a form of charge-back, or allocation of the true costs of an accident directly to this level of management. The assumption of medical and indemnity costs (or their associated insurance costs) as a corporate overhead should be avoided by management. The unit manager, concerned with day-to-day financial control of the organization, should have the real costs of inadequate safety programmes appearing on the same balance sheet as the production and development costs. For example, a unit manager of an organization in which all the workers' compensation costs are carried as a corporate overhead will be unable to justify expenditure of resources to remove a very serious hazard affecting a low number of workers. This difficulty can occur at the local level, despite the fact that such expenditures could produce major savings at the corporate level. It is essential that managers who are responsible for workplace design and operations bear the brunt, or reap the benefits, of the safety programme for which they are responsible.

Supervisor Level

The supervisor is responsible for understanding, transmitting and ensuring compliance with the managerial objectives of the safety programme. Successful safety programmes will address the question of educating and training supervisors in this responsibility. Although special safety trainers are sometimes used in educating workers, the supervisor should be responsible both for this training and for the attitudes of workers. In particular, informed supervisors see their responsibility as including the prevention of unsafe acts and exhibiting a high level of intolerance of unsafe conditions in the workplace. The control of the manufacturing process is accepted as the mainstream responsibility for supervisors; the application of such control will also produce benefits in the reduction of damages and unintentional injuries. Regardless of whether the safety function is staffed by safety officers, joint worker-management committees or consultants, the day-to-day responsibility for safe, error-free operation of the process should be a written component in the job description of supervisors.

Worker Level

At the beginning of the century, the primary emphasis for workers to perform safely was placed on negative reinforcement. Rules were set, workers were expected to follow those rules without question, and a transgression from the rules subjected the worker to disciplinary action. With increasingly complicated workplaces, flexible management systems and the rising social expectations of the workforce, the inadequacies and liabilities of such an approach have been revealed. It is not only in the military arena that flexibility and responsibility at the local level appears to be a vital component of high-performance units. This approach has led to an increasing reliance upon positive reinforcement and empowerment of the workforce, with the concomitant requirements for education and understanding. This thrust in safety mirrors the worldwide trend of labour to seek improvements in the quality of working life and the development of self-directed working groups.

Roll-out Plan

The key elements of the safety programme will identify the requirements for familiarization with the conceptual basis of the programme, the development of specific safety skills and the implementation of measurement tools. Responsibilities will be assigned to specific people within a phased programme at the point of introduction. The end of the roll-out process will be the establishment of a measurement system, or safety programme audit, in order to assess the continuing performance of the programme. Appropriate communication must be explicitly specified in the plan. In many cultures, multiple dialects and languages coexist in the workplace; and in certain cultures, a "managerial" dialect or language may normally not be used by the workforce. This problem includes the use of jargon and acronyms in communication between groups. Worker participation in the roll-out design may avert such shortcomings, and lead to solutions such as multilingual instructions and guidelines, a wider use of symbols and pictograms, and the selection of simple language. The wider approach to worker participation in the plan will produce benefits in terms of "buy-in" and acceptance of the plan's goals and approaches.

The review process, or safety programme audit, should be repeated on a regular (annual) basis and will form the basis for 3-year rolling (or cyclical) plans. These plans will establish the future direction of the programme and provide the impetus for continual improvement, even in the face of changing production and process systems.

Continuous Improvement

Successful safety programmes do not remain static, but change to reflect changes in both corporate and social environments. Equally, successful programmes avoid dramatic but unachievable goals. Instead, a philosophy of continuous improvement and of continually rising standards is a key approach. The annual 3-year rolling plan is a good way to achieve that. Each year, the plan identifies broad goals and estimates with respect to likely costs and benefits that will develop over the next 3-year period. This will automatically provide for adaptation and continued improvement. As such plans are to be reviewed by management each year, an additional benefit will be that the objectives of the safety function are continuously aligned with corporate objectives.

Conclusion

The implementation of the safety programme must reflect its being an integral component of the management of the enterprise. Success would depend on clearly identifying the responsibilities of the various levels of management. The participation of workers in the implementation programme, and particularly the roll-out plan, is likely to produce benefits in the widespread adoption of the plan. The roll-out plan is a document which identifies the necessary activities, the timing of those activities and the responsibility for implementing each activity. The components of each activity—whether training, development of a working procedure or education—must be described in a way that is unambiguous to all levels of the enterprise. The final stage in the roll-out plan is to ensure that a continuous improvement cycle can occur by the installation of a safety programme audit on at least an annual basis.

SUCCESSFUL SAFETY PROGRAMMES

Tom B. Leamon

The moral imperative of an enterprise to actively seek to reduce damages, pain and suffering in the workplace will be tempered by

Figure 60.6 • The management process and occupational safety.

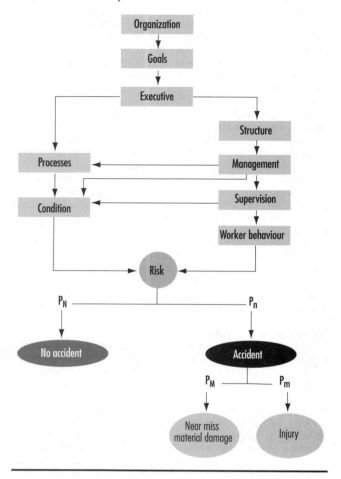

the ability of the organization to sustain such an effort. Most human activities have risk attached to them, and risks in the workplace vary widely, from those much lower than those associated with normal, non-occupational activities, to very significantly more hazardous ones. An essential part of an organization is its willingness to accept the risks of business which have the potential for producing financial losses and are based on the pain and suffering of employees that result from accidents. A successful safety programme is intended to control a portion of these losses by reducing the risks, particularly where such risks arise from unsafe conditions or unsafe acts. The safety programme, therefore, is simply another subsystem of management. Like other management programmes, the safety programme consists of complementary strategies, procedures and standards. Similarly, the measure of a safety programme is performance—that is, how well it reduces accidents and the consequent losses.

A safe workplace depends on the control of hazards and unsafe behaviours, and control such as this is the primary function of management. A safety programme should produce complementary benefits: a reduction in damages and pain and suffering in the workforce (from both acute and chronic injuries and illnesses) and a resultant reduction in the financial burden to the organization due to such accidents. To achieve such benefits, a successful safety programme will follow the general approach of all management tools by establishing goals, monitoring performance and

correcting deviations. This approach will be applied to a rather wide range of organizational activities, including organizational design, the production processes and the behaviour of the workers.

Safety in the Enterprise

A safe workplace is the end product of a complex and interactive process, and each process is a characteristic of an individual organization. A typical process is described in figure 60.6. The successful programme will need to address the various aspects of such a system.

Safety is often seen as a worker/workplace issue, but figure 60.6 indicates the pivotal role of management in safety as it responds to the overall goals of the organization. This can be seen from management's clear responsibility for the selection of the industrial processes utilized, the control of supervision, working conditions, and the attitudes and procedures of the worker, all of which are factors that establish the extent of a risk in a particular workplace. Usually there is a large probability that no accident will occur, and a small probability that there will be an accident leading to either material damage or injury to a worker. A safety programme is concerned with reducing that risk and also minimizing injuries that occur.

Understanding the Accident Process

There are several competing theories of accident causation, but the model first proposed by Frank Bird (1974) is particularly valuable, as it provides a ready analogy which is compatible with many management practices. Bird likened the process that leads to injury or damage to a row of dominoes, standing on edge (see figure 60.7). When any domino falls, it can disturb the others and a sequence is actuated which eventually leads to the fall of the final piece, corresponding to the occurrence of an injury. This analogy implies that if any one of the dominoes is removed from the sequence, or is robust enough to withstand the previous impact, then the chain of events will be broken and the ultimate event of injury or damage will not occur.

Despite more recent models, this approach is still valuable, for it clearly identifies the concept of *interventions* in the accident process and the role of the effective safety programme in introducing them to inhibit the process and prevent injury.

Organizational Goals

There is little disagreement among authors that the single most significant aspect of any safety programme is the visible continuous commitment of senior management. This commitment must be recognized and reflected by succeeding levels of management down through the supervisory ranks. Although executive management often believes its concern with safety is apparent to all in the enterprise, such clarity can be lost at the successive layers of management and supervision. In successful safety programmes, the executive management must demonstrate a clearly identified commitment to the concept that safety is a responsibility of all employees, from senior management to the temporary worker. Such a commitment should take the form of a brief written document, provided for everyone in the enterprise and utilized at the earliest possible stage for inducting new workers into the organization. Some organizations have recently extended this by introducing the concept that the commitment to a safe and healthy workplace for all its employees and customers is an explicit corporate value. Such corporations frequently express this point of view in written documents, together with more traditional corporate values, such as profitability, reliability, customer service and community commitment.

Clarity of communication is particularly important in large organizations, where the direct link between the owners of the

Figure 60.7 • The Bird domino theory as modified by E. Adams.

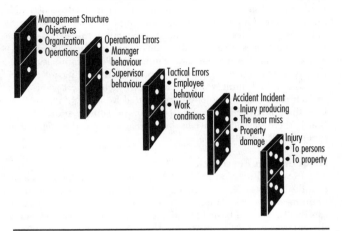

enterprise and the workforce can easily be broken. One of the clearest ways to achieve this is by the development of a series of written policies and procedures, starting with senior management's establishing objectives for the safety programme. These should be clear, concise, achievable, supportable and, above all, unambiguous. It is not sufficient for a manager to assume that everyone down the chain of command shares a similar background, understanding and perception of the safety programme. These aspects must be made perfectly explicit. Equally, in spelling out the terms of this written procedure, it is essential to have realistic goals.

Management Control

Developing effective safety programmes from this original commitment requires that the measurement of safety performance be an integral part of the annual performance review of all management and supervisory staff. In keeping with the philosophy that safety is only one measure, among many, of the manager's control of the process, safety performance must be included along with output, cost per unit, and profitability of the department. Such a philosophy, insofar as accidents occur from a lack of control of the process, appears to be highly compatible with the contemporary emphasis on total quality management (TQM). Both procedures adopt the position that deviations from normal are minimized in order to provide more control in achieving the corporate objectives. Additionally, the TQM concept of year-by-year, incremental improvement, is particularly significant in the long-term management of safety programmes.

Training and Education

Training and education are major components of any safety programme. This begins with the dissemination from senior management not only of the programme's objectives and goals, but also information on progress towards those goals, measured through record keeping and cost accounting. Education, by which is meant a more general understanding of the nature of a hazard and of approaches to risk reduction, appears to work well, particularly in circumstances where there is still doubt about individual risk factors. One example is the epidemic of upper extremity cumulative disorders in Australia, Europe and North America. These disorders have become more significant, especially given that broad agreement does not exist on criteria for control of these disorders. The cumulative nature of such disorders, however, makes control of this problem particularly amenable to education.

An increased awareness of risks allows individual workers to avoid such conditions by recognizing their exposures and modifying them by changes to procedures. Similarly, an understanding of the mechanics of low-back stresses can prepare workers to avoid some potentially dangerous work practices and substitute safer methods of accomplishing tasks.

Training is as necessary for management and supervisors as it is for the workers, so that they develop an understanding of their responsibilities and duties and increase their awareness levels of hazard potential. Individual workers need to be provided with clear and unambiguous process-relevant procedures for safe working. They should have an understanding of the hazards involved in the particular operations, and the likely effects of exposures to both toxic and physical agents. Additionally, managers, supervisors and workers should be familiar with the procedures for minimizing losses once an accident has occurred.

Safe Behaviour

Philosophically, the twentieth century has seen several swings in which safety programmes have allocated varying amounts of responsibility for the behaviour of workers to the individual, the employer and society. However, it is clear that safe behaviour is an absolutely crucial part of the safety process. An example of the significance of such behaviour is the development of group ethics, or team norms, in which the assumption of a risk by an individual might be perceived negatively by other members of the group. The converse is true: the acceptance of dangerous practices can become accepted as "normal". Such behaviours can be modified by specific procedures of training and reinforcement, as shown by the highly successful programmes that combated the spread of AIDS from careless needle use in the health care industry. The heightened emphasis by management, coupled with training and educational materials, fundamentally changed the procedures involved and reduced the incidence of this hazard.

Participation

Increasingly, societies are mandating worker participation in safety programmes. Although the validation of such participation tends to be somewhat variable, worker involvement can be valuable at several stages in the safety process. Undoubtedly the people who are exposed to the hazards are extremely valuable resources for identifying hazards, and frequently are aware of potential solutions for reducing them. When problems have been identified and solutions have been developed, implementation will be greatly facilitated if the workforce has been a partner in record keeping, identifying, developing and validating the proposed interventions. Finally, in terms of understanding management's commitment and resource constraints, participation embodied in a safety programme is beneficial.

Incentives

Incentives have been widely promulgated in some countries for increasing safe behaviours. The evidence that these incentives work is far from convincing, although, as part of a comprehensive safety programme, they can be used to demonstrate management's continuing concern with safety, and they can form a significant feedback of performance. Thus, those safety programmes in which a small financial award is mailed to a recipient are likely to be ineffective. The same award, made in public by senior management, and based on specific performance measures—for example, 2,500 hours of work without any accidents—is likely to form positive reinforcement. In practice, in many industries the reverse is true—there are considerable incentives that reward poor safety behaviours. For example, piece-rate payment systems clearly reward workers for cutting out any time-consuming elements in a work cycle, including any which may be related to

60. SAFETY PROGRAMMES

safe working procedures. Enterprises using incentives are more likely to need engineering controls and active surveillance techniques if they are truly committed to protecting the health and safety of the workforce.

Measurement and Control

Information is the lifeblood of management, and record keeping is an essential part of management information. Without a good source of data, progress toward accident reduction will be unreliable, and management's willingness to expend resources to reduce risks is likely to be impaired. In some countries, collection of such data is a legislative requirement, and clearly a successful safety programme must facilitate the gathering and collation of such data. Satisfaction of regulatory requirements may be necessary, but frequently is not sufficient for a successful safety programme. Local variations in such data requirements may occur—for example, between jurisdictions—with the result that the value of such data is obscured; this development is a particular problem in organizations with multiple locations located in different regional or national jurisdictions. Consequently, the standardization of, and approach to, data collection must be specifically established as part of the safety programme. Thus, each programme must first identify the information needed for compliance with regulations, but then determine the need for further collection and analysis necessary for accident reduction.

Costs of Accidents

An essential management aspect of the data system is the identification of the cost of losses. Loss source analysis—that is, the determination of the actual sources of losses—will include the measurement of the number of incidents, the severity of incidents and the direct costs of damages, injuries and illnesses. Such information is essential if management is to maintain its focus on the true problems in the workplace. In many countries, the compensation costs—whether borne directly by the employer, by a federation, or by a state organization—can be assumed to be proportional to the pain and suffering in the workplace. Thus, in identifying the source of loss, management is discharging its responsibility for providing safe working conditions for the workforce in a way that is highly compatible with the cost/benefit analysis approach used in other activities.

Direct costs are not the true financial costs from accidents and injuries borne by an enterprise. In many countries around the world, and with various degrees of rigour, attempts have been made to estimate indirect costs associated with accidents. These indirect costs include loss in supervisory time, loss of productive time during the accident investigation and cleanup, retraining of replacement workers, and the amount of overtime required to meet production schedules. These indirect costs have been found to exceed the direct costs substantially, often by factors estimated to be in a range of three to ten times those of the direct insurance losses.

Determining Costs

The measurement of losses normally involves *passive* surveillance, which requires that the preceding history be examined in terms of frequency and severity of accidents. Passive surveillance is not sufficient for certain situations, particularly those with very low probabilities of errors occurring, but large, uncontrolled potential damage in the case that they do occur. In such circumstances, particularly in complex process industries, it is necessary to perform an assessment of *potential* losses. It is clearly unacceptable that, simply because no process has yet claimed a victim, processes involving large amounts of energy or of toxic materials should not be analysed prior to such an accident. Thus, in some industries, it is wise to institute *active* surveillance, particularly

where similar processes elsewhere have led to losses. Information from trade associations and from national and international labour and safety organizations is a valuable source that can be used to establish pre-incident estimates which are likely to be valid and valuable. Other techniques, including fault tree analysis and failure mode analysis, are discussed elsewhere in this *Encyclopaedia*. In circumstances such as those involving chemical exposures, active surveillance may include routine medical examinations of the worker. Such an approach is particularly significant where well-established limit values have been determined. This approach of estimating potential and actual losses highlights a feature that the successful safety programme should address, and that is the difference between day-to-day risk and the effect of a potential catastrophe.

Information Feedback

The use of information feedback has been shown to be crucial in a wide range of organizational activities, including safety programmes. The calculation of both incidence rates and severity rates will form the basis for rational deployment of resources by the enterprise and for measuring the success of the programme. This information is as valuable to management for evaluating the safety function as it is to workers in the execution of the programme. However, the presentation of such data should reflect the end user: aggregated data will allow management comparison of operating units; department-specific data and visual aids (such as thermometer charts indicating the number of safe work days at the shop-floor level) can enhance understanding of, and buy-in from, the whole spectrum of employees.

Field Observation

The information system is an off-line component of a successful safety programme, which must be complemented by a hands-on approach to safety in the workplace. Such an approach would involve the *walk-through*, in which an informed and trained observer subjectively identifies hazards in the workplace. In addition to identifying hazards, the walk-through is particularly suitable for detecting issues of non-compliance with both corporate and legislative requirements. For example, the reduction of hazards by machine guarding is ineffective if many of the machines have had the guards removed—a typical finding of a walk-through. As the walk-through is an open-ended and adaptive procedure, it is also the easiest way to detect deficiencies in the training of the worker, and possibly those of the supervisor.

Effective safety programmes should utilize this technique on a regular but random basis. The walk-through, however, is not the only way of identifying hazards. The workers themselves can provide essential information. In many cases, they have experience of "near misses" that have never been reported, and are consequently in a good position to discuss these with the safety officer during the walk-through. Workers in general should be encouraged by supervision to report safety defects both actual and potential.

Accident Investigation

All accidents must be investigated by the responsible supervisor. Accidents such as those in the process industry often require investigation by a team of knowledgeable persons representing diverse interests, possibly including an outside expert. Successful programmes frequently involve workers in such accident investigations. This involvement brings benefits in terms of better understanding of the incident and of rapid dissemination of recommendations throughout the workforce. From figure 60.6, it is clear that, in this context, accidents are not only those events that conclude in an injury to a worker, but rather, events that encompass damage to equipment or materials or even significant events that result in neither (known as "near accidents"). The figure indicates that such incidents should be subject to management investigation and control even if, fortuitously, no worker is injured. Avoidance of similar incidents in the future will reduce the risk that they will result in injury. Accident investigations that seek to lay blame appear to be less successful than those seeking methods to determine cause. In an investigation that is seen to be an attempt to blame a worker, peer pressure and other psychosocial behaviours can severely degrade the quality of information collected.

The essentials of an accident report will include a formalized process, involving written descriptions of the events that occurred before, during and after the accident as well as an assessment of the factors that led to the accident. The report should end with a clear recommendation for action. The recommendation could range from immediate modification of the work process or, in the case of complex situations, to the need for further, professional investigation. Such reports should be signed by the responsible supervisor or the leader of the investigation team, and forwarded to an appropriate level of management. Management review and acceptance of the recommendations is an essential part of the accident reporting process. The signature of the manager should indicate his or her endorsement or rejection of the proposed changes to prevent future accidents, and rejections should be accompanied by an explanation. Accident investigations that do not lead to an individual responsibility for action for the recommendations are likely to be ineffective, and rapidly become viewed by all involved as irrelevant. A successful safety programme seeks to ensure that lessons learned from a particular incident are shared elsewhere within the organization.

Hazard Control

The best intervention as regards hazard control will always be the removal of the hazard by engineering design, substitution or modification. If the hazard is removed (or, at second best, shielded or guarded), then irrespective of the human variability arising from training, individual differences of strength, attention, fatigue or diurnal rhythm, the operator will be protected.

Unfortunately, in some cases, the costs of achieving this engineering design can reach or exceed the limits of economic liability. Certain processes are inherently much riskier than others, and feasible engineering designs are only partial solutions. Construction projects carried out at elevated sites, deep coal mining, steel production and over-the-road driving all require exposure of employees to higher than "normal" risks. In such cases, administrative control and personal protective devices may be necessary. Administrative control may involve specific training and procedures to reduce risks: consider, for example, the prohibition against individual workers entering confined spaces, or the provision of lockout systems designed to isolate dangerous equipment and processes from the operator during the work cycle. These procedures can be effective, but require continual maintenance. In particular, work practices tend to move away from compliance with the necessary administrative procedures. This trend must be halted by the implementation of procedures for training, and refresher training as well, for all workers and supervisors involved in the system.

The final component in hazard control is the use of personal protective devices, which include respirators, protective gloves, whole-body harnesses and hard hats, to mention just a few. In general, it can be seen that such devices are valuable when the hazards have not been entirely removed from the workplace, nor controlled by administrative procedures. They are intended to reduce the effect of such hazards on the worker, and typically are subject to concerns of improper use, design limitations, inadequate supervisor oversight, and failure of maintenance.

First Aid

Despite the best attempts to reduce hazards, the successful safety programme must address the post-accident scenario. The development of first aid and emergency medical treatment capabilities can provide major benefits for the safety programme. A protocol must be established for medical treatment following an accident. Selected workers must be familiarized with the written instructions for summoning medical assistance to the worksite. Such assistance should be prearranged, for a delay can seriously affect the condition of an injured worker. For accidents producing minor injuries, the inherent losses can be reduced by the provision of point-of-incident medical treatment. In-plant treatment for minor cuts and bruises, contusions and so on, can reduce operators' time away from their tasks.

The first aid capability must include acceptable levels of supplies, but more important, adequate medical/first aid training. Such training can directly affect the probability of survival in case of a potentially mortal injury, and can reduce the actual severity of a range of less serious accidents. First aid action such as cardiopulmonary resuscitation, or the stabilization of haemorrhaging, can make the difference between life and death to patients in need of major emergency treatment. Frequently, the provision of immediate first aid at the accident site provides the opportunity for subsequent major surgical interventions. Such a capability is even more significant in nonurban enterprises, where medical treatment may be delayed by a matter of hours.

First aid can also facilitate the efficient *return to work* of a worker involved in a minor injury. Such in-house intervention has been shown to reduce the need for lengthy medical visits outside the enterprise, and thus prevents a loss of productivity. Perhaps even more significant is the reduced chance of the medicalization of the injury, which is seen as an emerging problem in several countries.

Catastrophe Planning

Routinely, at least annually, a safety programme should identify potential causes of catastrophe. In some circumstances—for example, with the storage of large amounts of flammable or hazardous materials—the focus of attention is not too difficult. In other circumstances, great ingenuity may be required to make meaningful suggestions to plan for such catastrophes. By definition, catastrophes are rare, and it is unlikely that a particular enterprise would have suffered a similar catastrophe earlier. Definition of medical management, communication flows and managerial control of the catastrophe situation should form part of the safety programme. It is clear that in many enterprises such annual plans would be rather minimal, but the very exercise of developing them can be valuable in increasing the management's awareness of some of the risks that the business assumes.

Conclusion

The successful safety programme is not a book, or a binder of notes, but a conceptual plan to reduce the risks of injury as measured on the basis of both incidents and severity. Like all other processes in an enterprise, the safety process is the responsibility of management rather than that of a safety engineer or an individual worker. Management is responsible for setting the goals, providing resources, establishing means of measuring progress towards those goals and taking corrective action when this progress is unsatisfactory. In order to do this, information is the key requirement, followed in importance by communication of the objectives at all levels within the enterprise. At each level, from executive through management supervisor to the individual worker, contributions to safe working conditions can be made. But at the same time, organizational, procedural and behavioural inadequacies may regrettably prevent such contributions from occurring. The successful safety programme is one which recognizes and utilizes such factors in developing an integrated approach to reducing the pain and suffering in the workplace which arises from injuries and disease.

SAFETY INCENTIVE PROGRAMMES

Gerald J.S. Wilde

Safety incentive programmes have their intended effect: a reduction in the loss due to accidents. They also have positive side-effects. For one thing, they are a profitable proposition in industry, as the savings usually exceed the costs. For another, they may lead to better company morale. Incentive programmes can help improve the general organizational climate and, therefore, make a positive contribution to productivity over and above the gain due to accident reduction. Group-based safety incentive programmes give workers a common cause with each other as well as with management. Reinforcing safe acts "removes the unwanted side effects with discipline and the use of penalties; it increases the employees' job satisfaction; it enhances the relationship between the supervisor and employees" (McAfee and Winn 1989).

Cost-Effectiveness of Incentive Programmes

There have been many cases, in manufacturing, construction and other industries, in which the accident rate per employee was reduced by 50 to 80%. Sometimes the results are better still, as was the case in two mining companies in which the total lost days dropped by 89 and 98% respectively (Fox, Hopkins and Anger 1987). Sometimes the results are more modest. A cable plant reduced the accident costs per employee by 35%; a manufacturer of tobacco products by 31% (Stratton 1988); a grain processing and transportation company by 30%; a Pacific resort complex by 39%, and a manufacturer of food products by 10% (Bruening 1989).

These favourable effects continue to last over long periods of time. Incentive plans in two American mines were studied over periods of 11 and 12 years. In one mine the number of days lost due to accidents was reduced to about 11% of baseline and in another to about 2%. Benefit/cost ratios varied from year to year between 18 and 28 at one mine and between 13 and 21 at the other. There was no sign that the effectiveness of the incentive plans diminished over time at either mine (Fox et al. 1987). A high benefit/cost ratio—about 23 to 1—has also been observed for incentives for safety in the resort hotel business.

The ratios between benefits (savings due to accidents prevented) and programme costs (bonuses and administration) are usually greater than 2 to 1, meaning that companies can make money on such accident-prevention efforts. This is largely due to reduced fees to workers' compensation boards and other insurance, as well as to increased production, reduced downtime and a lesser need for replacement workers.

Requirements for Effective Incentive Programming

Incentive programmes, when properly designed, carry the approval of the people to whom they are addressed, and in this respect they compare favourably with the other forms of safety motivation such as laws, rule books and policing, which are much less popular. To put it plainly: a small carrot is not only much better liked than a big stick, it is also much more effective. Only one negative side-effect has been noticed so far, and that is the tendency of people to under-report accidents when incentive pro-

grammes are in effect. Fortunately, such under-reporting has been found to occur with respect to minor accidents only (McAfee and Winn 1989).

Past experience with incentive programmes also shows that some programmes have had much greater effect than others. For instance, a German incentive plan which promised professional truck and van drivers a bonus of DM 350 for each half-year of driving without being at fault in an accident, produced a reduction in direct accident cost to less than one-third in the first year of application and remained at that level for over three decades (Gros 1989). In the California "good driver" experiment, where drivers in the general population were offered free extension of their driver's licence by one year in return for each year of accident-free driving, the accident rate dropped by 22% in the first year of the programme (Harano and Hubert 1974).

An attempt has been made here to cull the ingredients of the most effective incentive plans from published reports. This has by necessity largely been based on inference, because to date there are no well-controlled experiments in which one particular incentive characteristic is being varied and all other factors are kept constant. For obvious reasons, such experiments are not likely to be forthcoming; industry is not in the business of running such experiments. Never the less, the items that appear in the checklist below would seem to make very good sense (Wilde 1988; McAfee and Winn 1989; Peters 1991).

Managerial vigour

The introduction and long-term maintenance of incentive programmes should be conducted with managerial vigour, commitment and coherence. Workers or drivers should not only be informed of the programme in existence, but they should also frequently be reminded of it in attention-catching ways. In order to motivate and to inform the relevant audience, those in charge of incentive programmes should provide clear and frequent knowledge of results to the audience (Komaki, Barwick and Scott 1978).

Rewarding the "bottom line"

Incentive programmes should reward the outcome variable (the fact of not having caused an accident), *not* some process variable like wearing safety glasses or seat-belts, being sober or obeying shop-floor safety rules. This is because rewarding specific behaviours does not necessarily strengthen the motivation towards safety. A potential safety benefit due to an increased frequency of one specific form of "safe" behaviour may simply be offset by road users less frequently displaying other forms of "safe" acting. "The risk is here that while the rewarded behaviour may improve, other related safe behaviours may deteriorate" (McAfee and Winn 1989).

Attractiveness of the reward

Incentive programmes can be expected to be more successful to the extent that they widen the difference between the perceived benefit of not having an accident and the perceived disadvantage of having an accident. Rewards for accident-free operation in industry have taken many different forms, ranging from cash to public commendation. They include trading stamps, lottery tickets, gift certificates, shares of company stock, extra holidays, promotions and other privileges. While the flexible use of money prevents satiation from occurring, merchandise, especially customized merchandise, may constitute a lasting reminder of the value of safety. Merchandise items also have a "value-added" component in the sense that they can be obtained at a lower price than the recipients would likely have to pay if they bought the items at retail. In the United States, a substantial industry has sprung up to provide the merchandise for safety prizes. Gift certificates hold a middle ground between cash and merchandise; they can be put to flexible use and yet be personalized and imprinted with a commemorative message. Drivers have been rewarded with cash, automobile insurance rebates and free licence renewal.

Awards do not have to be large to be effective. In fact, a case can be made for relatively small recognition awards, such as 1- and 5-year safe driving pins, these being preferable in some cases. Small awards make it possible to hand out awards more frequently, they are probably less conducive to under-reporting of accidents, and they may foster the internalization of pro-safety attitudes through the process of cognitive dissonance reduction (Geller 1990). When a small reward changes a person's behaviour, that person may justify the change by reasoning that the change was for safety's sake rather than due to the insignificant inducement. No such internalization of pro-safety attitudes is necessary when the external inducement is large, because in that case it fully justifies the behaviour change.

It should be noted, however, that the attitude-shaping effect of modest awards can take place only *after* the operators have changed their behaviour for whatever minor external inducement. So, the award should be desirable enough to achieve some behaviour change to begin with. Rewards should have "perceived value" in the minds of the recipients. In some cases, a small material reward might imply a major social reward because of its "symbolic function". Safe behaviour may thus become the "right thing to do". This might help explain why a modest incentive such as free licence renewal for one year produced a major reduction in the accident rate of California drivers. Moreover, analogous to earlier studies that found that accident rates in dangerous tasks (such as piece-work) were exponentially related (to the power of three) to higher wages, it may be suggested that relatively small increments in wages for having no accidents should reduce the accident rate by a larger amount (Starr 1969).

Progressive safety credits
The amount of the incentive should continue to grow progressively as the individual operator accumulates a larger number of uninterrupted accident-free periods; for example, the bonus for ten uninterrupted years of accident-free operation should be greater than ten times the bonus for one year of accident-free performance.

Programme rules
The operational rules of the programme should be kept simple, so that they are easily understood by all persons to whom the programme applies. It is of paramount importance that the incentive programme should be developed in cooperation and consultation with those people to whom it will be applied. People are more likely to actually strive for goals they have helped define themselves (Latham and Baldes 1975).

Perceived equity
The incentive programme should be perceived as equitable by those to whom it is addressed. The bonus should be such that it is viewed as a just reward for not causing an accident in a given time period. Similarly, incentive systems should be designed such that those workers who are not eligible for the (top) award do not resent the system, and that those who are rewarded will be seen by others as justly receiving the award. As chance plays a part in having or not having an accident, the actual receipt of the award may be made dependent on the additional requirement that the accident-free worker in question also maintains cleanliness and safety in his or her workstation. In the event that disincentives are used as well, it is necessary that the public view the penalty imposed as justified.

Perceived attainability
Programmes should be designed such that the bonus is viewed as within potential reach. This is of particular importance if the bonus is awarded in a lottery system. Lotteries make it possible to hand out greater awards, and this may enhance the attention-getting appeal of an incentive programme, but fewer among the people who have accumulated the safety credit will receive the bonus. This, in turn, may discourage some people from making an active attempt to accumulate the safety credit to begin with.

Short incubation period
The specified time period in which the individual has to remain accident-free in order to be eligible for the bonus should be kept relatively short. Delayed rewards and penalties tend to be discounted and are thus less effective in shaping behaviour than more immediate consequences. Periods as short as one month have been used. If longer periods apply, then monthly reminders, status reports and similar materials should be used. In the California experiment cited above, those drivers whose licenses were coming up for renewal within 1 year after being informed of the incentive programme showed a greater reduction in accident rate than was true for people whose licenses were not to be renewed until two or three years later.

Rewarding group as well as individual performance
Incentive programmes should be designed to strengthen peer pressure towards having no accident. Thus, the plan should not only stimulate each individual operator's concern for his or her own safety, but also motivate them to influence peers so that their accident likelihood is also reduced. In industrial settings this is achieved by extending a bonus for accident-free performance of the particular work team in addition to the bonus for individual freedom of accidents. Team bonuses increase the competitive motivation towards winning the team award. They also have been found effective in isolation—that is, in the absence of awards for individual performance. A dual bonus plan (individual *cum* team) can be further strengthened by informing families of the safety award programme, the safety goals and the potential rewards.

Prevention of accident under-reporting
Thought should be given to the question of how to counteract operators' tendency not to report the accidents they have. The possibility that incentive programmes may stimulate this tendency seems to be the only currently identified negative side-effect of such programmes (while occasionally moral objections have been raised against rewarding people for obtaining a goal they should aspire to on their own, without being "bribed into safety"). Some incentive programmes have clauses providing for deduction of safety credits in case accidents are not reported (Fox et al. 1987). Fortunately, only those accidents that are minor remain unreported at times, but the greater the safety bonus, the more frequent this phenomenon may become.

Reward all levels of the organization
Not only are shop-floor workers to be rewarded for safe performance, but their supervisors and middle management as well. This creates a more cohesive and pervasive safety orientation within a company (thus shaping a "safety culture").

Whether or not to supplement rewards with safety training
Although educating towards safety is different from motivating towards safety, and a person's *ability* to be safe should be clearly distinguished from that person's *willingness* to be safe, some authors in the field of incentives in industrial settings feel that it may be helpful to safety if workers are told through what specific behaviours accidents can be avoided (e.g., Peters 1991).

Maximizing net savings versus maximizing benefit/cost

In the planning of an incentive programme, thought should be given to the question of what actually constitutes its primary goal: the greatest possible accident reduction, or a maximal benefit/cost ratio. Some programmes may reduce the accident frequency only slightly, but achieve this at a very low cost. The benefit/cost ratio may thus be higher than is true for another programme where the ratio between benefits and costs is lower, but which is capable of reducing the accident rate by a much greater degree. As distinct from the issue of the size of the benefit/cost ratio, the total amount of money saved may well be much greater in the latter case. Consider the following example: Safety programme A can save $700,000 at an implementation cost of $200,000. Programme B can save $900,000 at a cost of $300,000. In terms of benefit/cost, A's ratio is 3.5, while B's ratio equals 3.0. Thus, judged by the benefit/cost criterion, A is superior, but if net savings are considered, the picture is different. While programme A saves $700,000 minus $200,000, or $500,000, programme B saves $900,000 minus $300,000, or $600,000. In terms of net savings, the larger programme is to be preferred.

Concluding Comment

Like any other accident countermeasure, an incentive plan should not be introduced without evaluating its short-term and long-term feasibility and its best possible form, nor without provision for scientifically adequate evaluation of its implementation costs and its observed effectiveness in reducing the accident rate. Without such research the surprising effect of one particular reward programme would never have come to light. Although there seems little chance for a safety incentive to actually have a negative effect, there is one variation of a series of California reward/incentive programmes for the general driving public that did produce *worse* driving records. In this particular programme component, a benefit was given to drivers with no accidents on their records without their prior knowledge of that benefit. It took the form of an unexpected reward rather than an incentive, and this highlights the importance of the distinction for safety promotion. The term *incentive* refers to a *pre-announced* gratification or bonus extended to workers or drivers on the specific condition that they do not have an accident of their own fault within a specified future time period.

● SAFETY PROMOTION

Thomas W. Planek

The aim of safety promotion is to induce employees to improve their own protective behaviour and that of their co-workers, and to support an organization's stated safety goals. Safety promotion objectives include increasing safety awareness at all organizational levels and confirming the furtherance of employee safety as a top management priority.

The ultimate effectiveness of any promotion programme or activity depends directly on how well an organization manages its safety programme. Safety promotion can play an important contributory role in improving workplace safety when sound hazard management practice exists at all operational phases, including facilities planning, machine design, employee training and supervision, personal protective equipment, environmental maintenance, housekeeping, emergency response and rehabilitation.

No matter how intrinsically effective and efficient a safety promotion scheme is in changing employee attitudes and behaviour, it requires management support in the form of visible leadership and commitment. This condition is a prerequisite for a successful promotion, be it focused on production, product quality or employee safety and health. It is also the consistent characteristic that marks all successful safety programmes, no matter how much their specifics differ.

Employee Motivation

Safety promotion relates directly to the concept of motivation, which has been the subject of a great deal of research. There is controversy about how and why people are "motivated" either to adopt new behaviours or change old ones. A central issue concerns the relation between attitudes and behaviour. Must attitude change come before behaviour change? Can behaviour change exist without attitude change? Does attitude change predict behaviour change? Does behaviour change cause attitude change?

Answers to these questions are uncertain. There are those who insist that motivation is best achieved by changing external behaviour alone, while others feel that internal attitude or cognitive change must be part of the behaviour change process. Both of these viewpoints have influenced the conduct of safety promotion.

Although not directly observable, motivation can be inferred from changes in behaviour and attitudes. Three variables that define motivation are as follows:

- *Direction of behaviour* requires the specification of objectives and the provision of the necessary training or education to achieve them.
- *Intensity of action* involves the realization and strengthening of behaviour and attitude change primarily through reinforcement and feedback.
- *Persistence of effort* involves making the desired behaviour and attitude changes permanent in all facets of employee performance.

Safety Promotion Models

The safety literature describes a variety of safety promotion theories and methods that address each of the motivational variables; among these, two models have shown the capacity to improve safety performance. One, *organization behaviour management* (OBM), focuses on behaviour modification and the application of behaviour control methods developed by B.F. Skinner. The other, *total quality management* (TQM), focuses on process modification and the application of quality control principles developed by W.E. Demming.

Behaviour modification is founded on the premise that the causes of behaviour are environmental in nature. Accordingly, one can predict and control behaviour by studying the interaction between individuals and their environments. This knowledge requires the specification of three conditions:

1. the antecedents of behaviour—that is, the occasion on which a response occurs
2. the behaviour or action that occurs
3. the consequences that reinforce the behaviour or action.

Quality improvement requires a "constancy of purpose" or commitment by both employees and management to make improved product and service quality a corporate priority. This attitude adjustment rests on a conscious management decision to do whatever it takes to make the quality improvement vision a reality. Quality improvement objectives are broader in scope and the methods for their achievement are less uniform than those of behaviour modification. They are more concerned with changing or even eliminating total processes than with modifying individual behaviours.

As shown in table 60.1, both models are responsive to the variables and supporting actions that motivation requires. The models differ, however, on the safety emphases used to motivate

Table 60.1 • OBM vs. TQM models of employee motivation.

Motivational variable	Supporting action	Safety emphasis	
		OBM	TQM
Direction of behaviour	Specify objectives.	Behaviour	Attitudes/behaviour
	Provide training.	Behaviour training	Process education
Intensity of action	Give reinforcement.	Behaviour occurrence	Process improvement
	Maintain feedback.	Behaviour data	Operating indicators
Persistence of effort	Commit employee.	Behaviour change	Continuous improvement

employees. As a result, they differ in terms of their efficiency in satisfying the requirements of the three motivational variables.

OBM Model

Direction of behaviour
OBM safety objectives are usually narrow in scope and focus on increasing the occurrence of specific safe behaviours, thereby decreasing the incidence of unsafe acts. The following sources can be used to select unsafe acts or behaviours as targets for observation and eventual reduction:

- analysis of incident investigations and related safety records
- interviews with employees at all levels to obtain data on unreported events, hazards and so forth
- observation of in-house safety inspections.

Based on information from these sources, employees are asked to assist in establishing a list of priority behaviours judged to be critical to improved safety performance. An observation system to track the occurrence of these critical behaviours is established, observers are trained and an observation schedule is set. The incidence of priority behaviours is then observed during a pre-intervention period. This phase of the problem definition process provides baseline data against which to measure the success of the behaviour modification process. These data also alert employees to the presence of unsafe behaviour in the workplace.

Employees are then exposed to training that covers the behaviours to be practised, offers safe behaviour performance guidelines, and allows for behavioural feedback. For example, workers are sometimes shown slides or videotapes of safe and unsafe practices, followed by discussion. At this time they are also shown baseline data and encouraged to improve their performance of critical safe behaviours. The data, often in chart form, are posted in the plant to prepare for the subsequent phases of the OBM programme. The activities of observation and recognition are performed on a continuing basis by supervisors or trained co-workers. As appropriate, new job safety performance elements are added to the training and become part of the programme.

Intensity of action
OBM uses both individual reinforcement and group feedback to modify behaviour. Reinforcement occurs at the individual employee level in the form of verbal praise or other sorts of recognition when a display of safety behaviour is seen in the workplace. Feedback about the level of safety behaviour exhibited by the group is also communicated throughout the programme.

Various types of rewards can be used to reinforce behaviour, such as the following:

- individual monetary incentives (e.g., cash awards and tokens for the purchase of consumer goods)
- praise and feedback (e.g., knowledge of results, congratulatory notes and positive comments)
- team competitions, which may involve the use of cash awards.

Rewards are often used in combination, so it is very difficult to isolate the impact of any individual type of reinforcement. Nevertheless, it is clear that positive responses to safe behaviour do increase its occurrence.

Reinforcement also includes group feedback about safety performance, which frequently takes the form of learning curves or bar charts tracking the percentage of safe behaviours that are observed during the intervention period. This information is displayed prominently so that the work group is aware of progress. This knowledge tends to maintain safe work group performance and stimulate future efforts at improvement.

In the OBM paradigm, reinforcement and feedback require a continuing programme of behavioural observation. This condition enables positive communication to occur on the spot when safe behaviours are seen or when unsafe practices require correction. Although behaviour modification emphasizes positive reinforcement rather than discipline, its proponents recognize that reprimands or other aversive actions may be necessary in certain situations. Whenever possible, however, these steps should be avoided because their effects are usually short-lived and may diminish employee commitment to the total programme.

Persistence of effort
OBM effectiveness in sustaining behaviour change depends on continuous observation and reinforcement of specific safe behaviours until they become self-reinforcing and a habitual part of an employee's job activity. The strength of OBM rests in the creation of a measurement system that allows a company to continually monitor and control critical behaviours. To achieve long-term success, use of this measurement system must become part of an organization's management style.

There is little doubt that the OBM approach produces positive results and does so relatively quickly. Most studies show that the use of positive reinforcement, in the form of incentives or feedback, enhances safety and/or reduces accidents in the workplace, at least over the short term. In contrast, longevity of behaviour change as produced by OBM procedures has not been fully demonstrated by research. In fact, most of the studies conducted are short-term in duration (less than one year). This situation has raised questions about the permanence of OBM treatment effects, although two studies of OBM techniques, one conducted in the United States and the other in Finland, have reported some long-term positive effects.

In the United States, the use of a trading stamp award system improved safety performance in two coal mines for more than ten years. In this study, employees earned stamps for working without lost-time injuries, for being in no lost-time injury work groups, for not being involved in equipment-damaging incidents, for making safety suggestions that were adopted, and for unusual incident or injury prevention behaviour. Besides the token award system, workers received extensive training during the baseline period, intended to prompt safe behaviour and to maintain safe work conditions. This training activity was regarded as very important to the improvements obtained.

In Finland, significant housekeeping improvements in a shipyard were achieved during a three-phase programme featuring feedback to foremen and workers following baseline measurement and employee training. These improvements, expressed as higher housekeeping indices, continued to be observed at the new high level throughout a two-year follow-up period during which no feedback was given. Significant accident reductions were also noted throughout the project's duration. The long-term effects of this programme were attributed to reinforcement that concentrates on the outcome of behaviour and persists in the environment (as housekeeping changes do), rather than simply on a behaviour, which influences workers for only seconds.

These studies notwithstanding, it is difficult to determine the long-term efficacy of OBM approaches in maintaining safety performance improvements. In the US study, the use of tokens evidently became an accepted part of the mines' management style, but there was also a strong emphasis on training. Learned feedback from environmental changes that are an outcome of behaviour, as reported in the Finnish study, looks promising. Here too, however, there is some indication that other factors may have been operative to influence shipyard employees during the follow-up "no feedback" period.

With these observations in mind, the bulk of research suggests that feedback must be maintained if OBM programmes are to achieve lasting success, and that this process must be accompanied by a management style that permits it. When these conditions are absent, positive behaviour change effects diminish rapidly and revert to previous levels. Where housekeeping improvements are involved, there is some evidence that the higher performance levels continue for a relatively long period, but the reasons for this remain to be determined.

TQM Model

Direction of behaviour

TQM goals are broad in scope and centre on creating improved processes. There is an emphasis on discovering and eliminating the conditions that cause or support the existence of unsafe behaviours, as opposed to a concentration on unsafe acts as the cause of injuries.

The TQM approach uses many of the same methods as OBM to uncover safety performance deficiencies that are to become targets for improvement. Additionally, it concentrates on the management systems and practices that contribute to these problems. These conditions may appear in all functions, from planning, through organizing and decision making, to evaluating cost-effectiveness. They also include the presence or absence of practices that incorporate employee safety considerations into everyday business processes such as the application of ergonomic principles to workplace and equipment design, review of purchasing specifications by safety and health professionals, and timely correction of reported hazards. Operational indicators such as the lattermost, combined with injury, downtime and employee absence records, provide baseline information on how well the management system supports the safety function.

Employee safety programme perception surveys have also become a popular tool for assessing the safety management system. Employees give their opinions about the effectiveness of the management practices and safety support activities that are present in their company. These data are gathered anonymously according to standard administrative procedures. Survey results help to set improvement priorities and provide another baseline against which to measure progress.

Just as TQM defines its performance objectives more broadly than OBM, it also makes a broader spectrum of training available to employees. TQM-based instruction teaches employees not only how to be safe but educates them about self-improvement and team-building methods that make possible ongoing contributions intended to increase safety throughout the organization.

The importance cannot be overstated of task planning at the systems level and providing sufficient safety training for employees whose jobs are expanded or enriched through process changes. There is some evidence indicating that as the number and variety of nonrepetitive tasks to which workers are exposed increases, so too does the frequency of accidents. It is not clear that this unwanted potential outcome has been recognized in the TQM literature.

Intensity of action

TQM uses various methods for reinforcing improved processes. These aim at creating an organizational culture that supports concerted employee effort to make process improvements. The mechanisms for behaviour change also incorporate reinforcement and feedback techniques to both recognize and reward performance improvement.

Several key conditions that support the development of improved processes are as follows:

- an open corporate climate with increased information sharing and removal of formal departmental barriers
- a focus on employee involvement, teamwork and training at all levels
- the removal of informal barriers to pride of workmanship
- a corporate culture that involves all employees in contributing to improvements
- follow-up to act upon or more fully develop new ideas for process improvement.

Adoption of these measures leads to higher employee morale and satisfaction that can increase the willingness to improve safety performance.

It should be noted that reinforcement at the employee level is regularly used in the TQM model. Rather than responding to specific critical behaviours, however, individuals receive praise for safe work at any phase of a process, with the goal being to encourage employees to internalize a process that incorporates improved safety performance.

Feedback about observed safety and health improvement results is also provided periodically through such media as meetings and newsletters, as well as through the conduct of follow-up surveys. These results are presented in the form of operating indicators. They may include such indices as lost workdays due to occupational injury and illness, number of safety and health improvement suggestions submitted, attendance levels, workers' compensation costs and employee attitudes toward safety.

Persistence of behaviour

The long-term effectiveness of the TQM approach resides in its capacity to create or continuously improve processes that support safe job performance. These improvements require both attitude and behaviour change. They also must be endorsed at the deepest levels of management practice and philosophy if they are to last. That is, they must become part of an organization's culture. For these reasons, positive results are not realized immediately. For example, successful users of TQM report an average of three years to achieve improved quality performance.

Evidence about the relationship between TQM and improved safety performance comes from two sources: the safety records of companies that have used TQM to successfully improve product and service quality, and the safety support processes used by companies with excellent safety records. Of 14 US companies receiving national recognition for excellence in quality management and achievement in the form of the Malcolm Baldrige National Quality Award, 12 had better lost-workday injury and illness rates than their industry average. Eleven of these companies also reported improved rates associated with the introduction of TQM practices, while only three companies had worse rates.

The efficacy of TQM techniques as applied to occupational safety is also exemplified by National Safety Council member companies with the most outstanding safety performance records in the United States. These successful programmes emphasize a "humanistic" approach to employee management, featuring less discipline, more active worker participation and better communication between workers and management.

Because TQM emphasizes employee involvement and empowerment in implementing system and process safety and health improvements, the potential for permanent change is maximized. Its emphasis on educating employees so that they are able to better contribute to future safety performance improvement also lays the groundwork for long-term effectiveness. Finally, TQM approaches visualize employees as active decision makers who are *responsible for* rather than simply *responsive to* the environment. These features make it highly likely that both employees and management will be committed to change produced through TQM on a long-term basis.

Comparison of OBM and TQM

OBM seeks to decrease specific unsafe practices and increase safe performance through a structured approach that defines critical behaviours, trains employees in safe/unsafe practices, establishes a system of behaviour observation, and uses a schedule of reinforcement and feedback to control employee behaviour. Its strengths are its emphasis on behaviour observation and results measurement, and the rapid production of positive results when the programme is present. Its weaknesses rest in its focus on specific behaviours that may not have been integrated with the need for management system changes, the use of an external control programme to maintain employee behaviour, and lack of demonstrated staying power.

TQM seeks to improve processes within the management system that affect employee safety and health. It stresses both attitude and behaviour changes and relies on a broad range of employee involvement and training programmes to define both safety and health improvement objectives and the means to achieve them. It uses reinforcement and feedback aimed at recognizing process improvements and employees' contribution to them. Its strengths are in its emphasis on employee participation and internal control (facilitating and reinforcing both attitude and behaviour change), its capacity to sustain safety and health improvements, and its integration within an organization's total management effort. Its weaknesses rest in its dependence on: (1) high levels of management/employee involvement that take time to develop and show improved results, (2) new process measurement systems, and (3) management's willingness to allot the time and resources it takes to produce positive results.

Safety Promotion Programmes and Practices

In what follows, the interaction between wage systems and safety will first be considered. Wage systems have a critical effect on employee motivation in general and have the potential to influence worker safety attitudes and behaviour in the context of job performance. Incentives, including both monetary and nonmonetary rewards, will be examined in light of their debated value as a safety promotion tactic. Finally, the role of communications and campaigns in safety promotions will be described.

Wage systems and safety

Wage systems can affect safety indirectly when incentive compensation, gain-sharing or bonuses are established to increase production, or when piece-work pay structures are in effect. Each of these arrangements may motivate workers to sidestep safe work procedures in an effort to increase earnings. Also, wage systems can be directly tied to safety considerations in the form of compensating wages that are paid for work that involves above-average risk.

Incentive wages

Incentive compensation or gain-sharing programmes can be established for productivity; for safety records; for scrap, rework and return rates; and for a variety of other performance criteria, alone or in combination. Such programmes have the potential to communicate management strategy and priorities to employees. For this reason, the performance criteria that an organization includes in its incentive wage system are critical. If safety performance and related factors are part of the package, than employees are likely to perceive them as being important to management. If they are not, then an opposite message is sent.

There are situations where work performance is introduced as a wage incentive criterion to induce workers to put up with dangerous conditions, or to fail to report accidents. Some commentators have noted the increased occurrence of this abuse, particularly in enterprise bargaining agreements and in efforts to reduce workers' compensation premiums. Obviously, this practice not only sends employees the wrong message but is counterproductive and will ultimately increase employer costs.

Although the theory behind incentive compensation appears to be strong, in practice its influence on worker productivity is far from certain. Research on the effects of financial incentive schemes on productivity shows extreme variability of results, indicating that naive approaches to the planning and implementation of incentive compensation programmes can lead to problems. However, when applied correctly, these programmes can have very positive effects on productivity, especially output.

A US investigation of the effects of bonus plans on accidents and productivity in 72 mines yielded little evidence that they had any significant impact either on improving safety or increasing production. Some 39% of these plans included safety in bonus calculations, while the rest did not. Within the study sample there was wide variability in the bonus payout frequency. Although the modal payout period was monthly, in many cases miners earned productivity bonuses only once or twice a year, or even less often. In such cases, the effect on production was negligible and, as might be expected, safety performance was not affected. Even among mines that paid production bonuses more than 80% of the time, no significant negative effects upon miner safety (i.e., increased lost-time accident frequency rates) were found. Mines that had monetary bonus plans directed solely at safety also failed to produce accident rate reductions. Most of these used lost-time accidents and violations as performance criteria, and experienced the same low payout problem that plagued many of the productivity-based plans.

The failure to find a clear-cut relationship between incentive compensation and productivity or safety in this study highlights the complexity of trying to conduct successful wage incentive programmes. Although increased wages are important, the perceived value of money varies among workers. There are also many other factors that can influence whether monetary incentives will have the desired motivational effect. Incentive or gain-sharing programmes often fail to produce expected results when employees think the programme is unfair. Actions that can be taken to help prevent this from happening and reinforce the motivational properties of an incentive programme include the following:

- Set a performance standard that employees perceive to be reasonable.
- Make bonus earning intervals short.

- Use multiple performance criteria.
- Include only performance objectives that employees can control.

Controversy also surrounds the use of piece-rate pay. It is, perhaps, the most direct way to relate pay to performance. Even so, the literature is full of studies that describe adverse behaviour that piece-rate plans produce. Piece-rate plans often create adversarial relationships between employees and employers in matters that are inherent to productivity. These involve the determination of production rates, the establishment of informal limits on production, and the negotiation of off-standard piece-rate plans. In some situations, performance may decline in spite of higher rates of payment.

Unfortunately, the very existence of piece-rate plans, whether or not they have their intended effect in the form of increased productivity, creates an atmosphere that can be detrimental to safe job performance. For example, a study investigating the transition from piece-rate to time-based wages in the Swedish forestry industry found reduced accident frequency and severity. Following the wage system change, several hundred forestry workers were questioned about its effect on their job performance. They indicated three major reasons for the reduction, including:

- reduced pressure to work fast, take risks and ignore specific safety guidelines
- reduced stress, leading to fewer errors in judgement
- more time to consider safety matters, try new methods, and benefit from interactions with peers.

The Swedish experience was only partially corroborated by earlier research conducted in British Columbia in Canada. In this case, there were no differences in accident frequency between piece-work versus salaried "fallers" in the logging industry, although more severe accidents among piece-work fallers as compared with their salaried counterparts were reported.

In the final analysis, opinion remains divided as regards the potential uses and abuses of incentive wage systems, their contribution to increased productivity, and their effect on safety. Nevertheless, research supporting any of them is scarce, and what evidence exists certainly is not conclusive. Clearly, the effect of incentive compensation programmes on safety depends on their content, their mode of conduct, and the circumstances surrounding them.

Compensating wages

Economists have been studying the subject of extra pay for high-risk work in an effort to place an economic value on human life and to determine whether the marketplace already compensates for high-risk exposures. If so, it may be argued that government interventions to reduce risk in these areas are not cost-effective because workers are already being compensated for their exposure to increased hazards. Attempts to validate the compensatory wage theory have been made in the United States and England using available mortality estimates. At this time, it would appear that the compensatory wage theory has been supported to a degree in England but not in the United States.

Another problem that besets the compensatory wage theory is the fact that many workers are unaware of the true risks associated with their jobs, particularly occupational disease exposures. Surveys done in the United States suggest that large percentages of workers are not aware of their exposures to hazardous working conditions. Also, psychologically speaking, individuals have a tendency to minimize the importance of very low probabilities associated with their own death. As a result, even if workers were aware of the actual risks associated with their work, they would be willing to take those risks.

Although the issue of compensatory wages poses some intriguing theoretical questions which remain currently unresolved, the true danger of a compensatory wage structure relates to its underlying causes. When employers use extra pay in any form as an excuse for continuing a substandard safety and health programme, the practice is harmful and totally unacceptable.

Safety incentives

The term *incentive* can be defined as a reason for undertaking action with extra zeal in an effort to receive a reward. The use of incentives to motivate employees is a common practice throughout the world. Nevertheless, the value of incentive programmes is a subject of controversy among scientists and practitioners alike. Opinions range from the denial of any link between incentives and motivation to the contention that incentives are primary factors in the behaviour change process. Between these two extremes, there are those who see incentive programmes as a useful stimulus to improve productivity and those who see them as promoting the wrong sort of employee behaviour with results that are exactly the opposite of what is intended.

In the area of safety and health, opinions about the utility of incentive programmes are no less diverse. In some organizations, for example, management is reluctant to offer extra incentives for safety because it is already an integral part of job performance and needn't be singled out for special emphasis. Another opinion suggests that offering incentives for improved safety performance diminishes the perceived intrinsic value of worker well-being on the job, which is, after all, the most important reason for emphasizing safety in the first place.

Along with the philosophical reasons for questioning the value of incentive programmes there are other issues that must be considered when discussing their merits or potential contributions as a safety promotion practice. These are problems related to the criteria upon which incentive programmes are based, the possibility for abuse of the programme by both employers and employees, and the maintenance of employee participation.

The criteria for awarding incentives are critical to the success of the programme. There are shortcomings attached to incentive programmes that are tied solely (1) to accumulating a certain number of safe days, (2) to lost-time injury rate (to workers' compensation premium reduction), and (3) to some other accident-related measures. Accident criteria are not very sensitive. Success is measured negatively, by the reduction or non-occurrence of events. Because accidents are rare events, it can take a relatively long time for significant improvements to occur. Such indices do not assess an organization's safety record but its reported accident record, which can be influenced by numerous factors not under the control of incentive programme participants.

Both employers and workers can abuse safety incentive programmes. Employers sometimes use incentive programmes as a substitute for the establishment of a legitimate safety and health management system or as a short-term cure for long-standing safety and health deficiencies that require much different and more fundamental treatment than can be rendered by a promotion effort. At the employee level, the principal form of abuse appears to be the failure to report an injury or incident for fear that either an individual or work group will not receive an award. The chance of this problem occurring appears to be increased when monetary incentives are at stake or financial incentive plans for improved safety performance are written into labour contracts or agreements.

The success of an incentive programme is heavily influenced by the nature of employee participation and their perceptions about its fairness. If goals are set too high or if employees cannot perceive how their personal efforts can affect reaching the goals, then the programme is not going to be effective. Also, the longer the distance between safe job performance and reward reception, the less influence the incentive system is likely to have. It is difficult to maintain worker motivation with an incentive programme that won't pay off for several months or longer, and even then only if things go well for the entire period.

Clearly the pitfalls that have been described help to explain why many organizations hesitate to use incentive programmes as a safety promotion device. It is easy to design an incentive programme that doesn't work. But, there is a good deal of evidence, both quasi-experimental and anecdotal, that documents the contributions of incentives to the successful operation of safety and health programmes. The use of incentives, awards and recognitions to motivate employees to perform safely is an accepted feature of both the OBM and the TQM models. In the OBM model, use of incentives to reinforce employee behaviour is critical to programme success. With TQM, rewards, promotions and other incentives are used to recognize individuals for contributions to process improvement. Also, at the group, team or company level, special days or other functions are used to celebrate achievement.

Broadly speaking, the use of incentives may be viewed to have a positive influence on employee attitudes and behaviour. When evaluation of safety and health performance is made part of the decisions to increase an employee's pay, these factors take on added significance as important job-related requirements. As indicated above, accident rate and related measures present significant problems when they are established as the sole incentive criteria. In contrast, the use of positive safety performance measures in the form of behavioural or process improvements provide specificity for employee action and create an opportunity for frequent feedback and incentive distribution. The characteristics of successful incentive programmes appear to remedy some of the problems associated with performance criteria, programme abuse and the nature of employee participation. Although the research into these areas is far from complete, sufficient data are available to provide guidance for organizations that want to make incentive programmes part of their safety and health management system.

Employer and employee abuses are largely circumstantial in nature. The reasons that incentive programmes are used to remedy safety management deficiencies largely determine whether the abuse can be corrected. If management sees employee safety and health as a low-priority concern, then such abuse is likely to continue until circumstances force a change in policy. In contrast, if management is committed to making safety and health improvements, then the need for a comprehensive approach to solving problems will be understood and accepted, and the support role played by incentive programmes will be recognized and valued. Similarly, the problem of employees not reporting accidents can be substantially reduced by changing the criteria that govern how incentives are awarded.

Research has shown that, to be effective in holding employee interest, rewards must be both frequent and tied to improved performance. If possible, to stimulate the feeling of participation in an incentive programme, employees should be involved in the selection of safety performance priorities. In this regard, it is necessary to insure that attention to priority behaviours does not lead employees to neglect other important job functions. Specific criteria and means for successful job performance should be clearly communicated and frequent progress reports given to programme participants.

There is also some evidence that distinguishes between the effects of rewards that are perceived as "controlling" and those that are viewed as "informational". Studies of these differences have found that rewards for achievement that recognize personal competence are stronger than those that simply provide positive performance feedback. One explanation for this finding is that employees perceive informational rewards, which recognize achievement and personal competence, to be under their own control, rather than in the hands of another person who gives or withholds rewards based on the performance being observed. Accordingly, the focus for control of informational rewards is within the employee, or intrinsic, as opposed to being outside the employee, or extrinsic, as is the case of controlling rewards.

In summary, the appropriate use of incentives can play an important helping role for organizations that use them wisely. They can increase employee interest in safety and can stimulate enhanced self-protective actions by workers.

Communication in safety promotions

Communications of various kinds are used to enhance the effectiveness of any safety promotion effort. The communication process can be summed up by the following question: "Who says what in which channel, to whom, with what effect?" Accordingly, communication programmes usually involve a source, message, medium, target and objectives.

Communications vary in terms of their coverage and impact. Safety posters, banners and other mass media are high in *coverage,* because they are easily exposed to large number of people over time. They are generally considered to be low in *impact,* because it is unlikely that every exposure will produce the desired effect. Mass media or one-way communications are most effective in increasing general awareness about safety and health topics, and giving directives or safety reminders. They can also be a useful vehicle for making employees aware of management's general interest in their welfare. In contrast, person-to-person or two-way communication, either through group discussions or individual contacts, though low in coverage value, can be high in impact and lead to decisions to change behaviour.

Credibility of source is very important in safety and health communications. In the workplace, for example, knowledge of a task and its hazards and the setting of a good example are important to making supervisors credible sources of safety and health information.

With regard to communication content, the use of fear has been a topic of research and controversy for years. Fear messages are used to change attitudes about the risks involved in hazardous behaviours by frightening the target audience. The message goes on to reduce the fear it has instilled by providing methods to prevent the danger or lower the risk. Workplace examples include campaigns to promote the use of personal protective equipment, while non-workplace examples include anti-smoking campaigns and auto seat-belt programmes. The main argument against using fear messages is the contention that receivers block out or suppress the message. Reactions such as these are likely to occur when the highly threatening communications fail to reduce the fear and individuals feel personally or situationally unable to handle the danger.

If fear messages are used, the following precautions should be taken:

- The message should attempt to evoke a high level of concern, and stress the positive benefits of the action to be taken.
- The suggested preventive actions should be concrete, relatively detailed, and specific.
- The guidelines for risk reduction should be presented, at one time, immediately after the fear response is evoked.
- The suggested preventive actions must be understandable and perceived by the target audience to be effective in preventing danger.
- The source of the communication should have high credibility.
- Use of statistics or risk data should be specific to the workplace or situation.

Finally, safety and health communications should consider the target groups at which messages are aimed. For example, research has shown that fear messages are more effective with new employees than with seasoned employees, who can use their experiences to discount the message. Additionally, fear messages have been found to be especially effective in influencing employees who are not under direct supervision and are thus expected to comply with safety regulations on their own.

As an aid both to defining targets and establishing objectives, the use of employee surveys is recommended to assess prevailing levels of safety and health knowledge, attitudes toward safety management programmes and practices, and compliance with rules and procedures. Such measurements assist in pinpointing education and persuasion priorities, and set a baseline for later evaluations of the effectiveness of communication efforts.

Safety campaigns

Safety campaigns usually are conducted to focus employee attention on a specific accident problem and are frequently associated with a particular slogan or theme to maintain interest and visibility. They use mass media such as posters, banners, videotapes, booklets and a variety of written or oral communications. Campaigns may be aimed at increasing awareness, conveying information, and changing attitudes in an effort to produce behaviour change.

The intended effect of safety campaigns is the same as that of behaviour modification and other programmes that attempt to get employees, supervisors and managers to make safety an integral feature of proficient job performance. Compared with behaviour modification programmes, however, safety campaigns are much less precise in defining target behaviours and outcomes, and less rigorous in the reinforcement of these behaviours. Even so, the major objective of both approaches is to emphasize the importance of safe work practices with the expectation that they will become habitual in nature.

Unfortunately, few studies have examined the effectiveness of safety campaigns in occupational settings. Case histories of successful efforts are frequently described in occupational safety publications, but these reports are seldom accompanied by convincing empirical evidence. Research has been done on the behavioural effects of specific media, such as posters, which indicates some positive results and provides a basis for guiding campaign communications, but meaningful research on safety campaign effectiveness in industry is simply not available. Rather, most of the useful information on the effectiveness of safety campaigns comes from the field of highway safety, particularly as reported in the United States and Australia.

Among the general recommendations that flow from anecdotal reports, the study of media effectiveness, and experience with highway safety promotion, the following can increase the power of any safety campaign and deserve special emphasis:

- Conduct needs studies to select campaign targets, using employee feedback to supplement data gathered from other sources.
- Assure employee involvement in campaign planning and materials selection.
- Pilot test the campaign theme and materials on the intended target groups.
- Involve all levels of management in the campaign from the top person to the lowest line supervisor.
- Use emotional/persuasive themes more than rational/informative ones.

Safety campaigns are intended to support an organization's total safety programme. For this reason, it is usually preferable to judge their effectiveness by how well they attain defined support objectives. These include maintaining interest in safety, expressing management's concern for employee safety, generating employee participation in safety activities, increasing morale and reminding employees to take special precautions.

Attempts to use accident reduction criteria to measure the effectiveness of campaigns, though seemingly appropriate, are usually confounded by the effects of the existing safety programme. Also, because accidents and injuries occur rarely, they are relatively insensitive criteria for evaluating the effects of specific safety programme changes that deal with the human or behavioural components of the safety system.

CASE STUDY: OCCUPATIONAL HEALTH AND SAFETY CAMPAIGNS AT THE NATIONAL LEVEL IN INDIA

K. C. Gupta

Background

This case study, which presents an example of a successful national safety campaign, is based on 24 years of experience organizing the annual National Safety Day (NSD) Campaign in India. The Campaign celebrates the foundation by the Government of India of the National Safety Council (NSC) in the Ministry of Labour on 4 March 1966 as an autonomous, non-political and non-profit-making organization at the national level to generate, develop and sustain a voluntary movement with respect to occupational safety and health (OSH). The NSC's Board of Governors is broad-based, with representation from all the central organizations of employers and trade unions. Total membership was approximately 4,000 in April 1995, drawn predominantly from the industrial sector, although there also is some membership from non-industrial sectors. In 1966, industrial workplaces in India experienced a rising trend of accidents, and enforcement of safety and health statutes by government agencies alone was not sufficient to reverse this trend. The birth of the NSC as a voluntary body in such a national perspective therefore constituted an important milestone. For many years, the NSC mainly concerned itself with industrial safety; however, with the coverage of some non-industrial sectors in recent years, its scope has been expanded from industrial to occupational safety. The coverage of occupational health, however, is still in its infancy in India. As the idea found favour of commemorating the foundation day of the NSC in the form of a national awareness campaign, the first NSD Campaign was launched in 1972. NSD became an annual event, and even though the duration of the Campaign has been increased to a week, it continues to be known as the National Safety Day Campaign due to the popularity that the title has gained.

Objectives

The objectives of the NSD Campaign, which have been kept broad, general and flexible, include the following:

- to increase OSH standards throughout India
- to enlist the support and participation of all major participants in different sectors at different levels, such as the central and state governments and their regulatory agencies and institutions; district and local administrations; non-governmental organizations (NGOs); employers' organizations; public, private and joint-sector undertakings; trade unions
- to promote the active participation of employers in the education of their employees to achieve OSH goals in their workplace through the use of local knowledge, experience and talent
- to foster development of need-based programmes and activities, self-compliance with statutory requirements, and strength-

Text of National Safety Day Pledge

On this day, I solemnly affirm that I will rededicate myself to the cause of safety, health and protection of environment and will do my best to observe rules, regulations and procedures and develop attitudes and habits conducive for achieving these objectives.

I fully realize that accidents and diseases are a drain on the national economy and may lead to disablement, death, damage to health and property, social suffering and general degradation of environment.

I will do everything possible for prevention of accidents and occupational diseases and protection of environment in the interest of self, my family, community and the nation at large.

(In some states, the above pledge has been administered by the Governor of State to state ministers, other government officials, executives and workers from industries, and the public participating in NSD functions. In private enterprise, it is usual for the chief executive or some other top executive to administer the pledge to all employees.)

ening of professional OSH management systems in undertakings

- to bring into the fold of the voluntary OSH movement certain sectors not so far covered by safety and health legislation in the country—for instance, the construction sector, the research and development sector, and small shops and establishments using hazardous machines, equipment and materials.

The above objectives are part of an overall goal of creating and strengthening OSH culture in workplaces and integrating it with the work culture. In a developing country, achievement of this goal continues to be a highly challenging task.

Methodology and Approach

The methodology and approach used to introduce and promote the Campaign initially comprised two elements: (1) issuing of letters of appeal to NSC member organizations to organize the Campaign; and (2) providing them with professionally designed promotional materials such as badges, copies of the NSD pledge (see box), cloth banners, posters, stickers and so on, and promotional-cum-utility items such as key chains, ball-point pens, and paperweights with OSH messages printed on them. These materials are centrally designed, produced and distributed by the NSC with the following three aims.

1. to make it convenient for the participants to organize the Campaign without having to go through the time-consuming and costly process of designing and producing such materials in small quantities themselves
2. to ensure that the Campaign materials are of professional quality with appealing messages reflecting national OSH issues
3. to generate income to contribute to NSC's financial self-reliance with respect to the fulfilment of the wider objective of strengthening the voluntary OSH movement in India.

In its initial years, the Campaign was confined to NSC members and grew gradually. After about a decade, the methodology and approach were widened in the following strategic ways:

1. The Union Ministry of Labour, responsible for OSH in the workplace, was asked to extend support to the NSC's efforts to approach the State Governments for aid in the organization of celebrations. Since then, the Union Labour Minister has requested that the State Labour Ministers organize celebrations by constituting Campaign Committees at the state and district levels; these committees would be comprised of

representatives of industries, workers and officials of the concerned government departments, and would send reports to the Central Government. Such support has given the Campaign national stature.

2. The electronic media (television and radio) under state control has been advised by the Government to cover the Campaign. Such coverage has made the Campaign highly visible.
3. The NSC's own journals, as well as newspapers and magazines published by employers and trade unions and the national and local press, have been involved more effectively.
4. The duration of the Campaign has been increased to a week, and flexibility has been provided to participants to start or conclude the Campaign on any convenient date, taking care to include 4 March (NSC foundation day) in the week. This has increased the span of visible impact of the Campaign.
5. The state chapters and district action centres of the NSC have actively involved the state governments and district administrations in the Campaign at the grass roots.
6. The Campaign has grown over the years. Figures 60.8, 60.9 and 60.10 show this growth in terms of the persons reached for the pinning of the badge and the financial receipts from the sale of Campaign materials.

Participation at Different Levels

Participation by all stakeholders at the national, state, district and individual enterprise levels has been of vital importance to the success and effectiveness of the Campaign. However, the degree of involvement by various stakeholders has not been uniform. In the first instance, different stakeholders started participating in the Campaign in different years. Furthermore, their perceptions regarding their roles and needs vary greatly. For example, some governments, particularly those of industrialized states, have been organizing elaborate and purposeful activities, but in some other less industrialized states, they have been low-key. Similarly, while some industry associations have lent great support to the Campaign, others have yet to start participating. While activities at the national, state and district levels have dealt with broad issues, those at the individual enterprise/undertaking level have been more detailed and need-based.

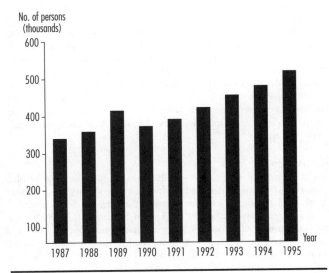

Figure 60.8 • Growth of NSD campaign in terms of persons reached for pinning badge.

Figure 60.9 • Growth in terms of financial receipts from sale of NSD campaign materials (1972–1982).

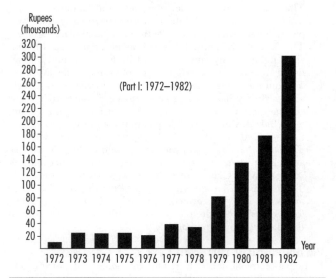

Campaign Materials

The national OSH issues and messages to be projected through a particular year's campaign materials produced by the NSC are identified by a core group of professionals from the NSC, industry and trade unions. The visuals for communicating them in a simple, humorous and effective way are designed by eminent cartoonists. In this way it is ensured that the campaign materials are original, attractive, appealing and rooted in Indian culture.

These materials fall into two broad categories: (1) purely promotional materials used for display and educational purposes; and (2) promotional-cum-utility materials which, besides promoting the OSH messages, are also good for day-to-day use. In the second category, most items are for the daily use of workers and are relatively inexpensive and affordable by managements of various enterprises for free distribution to all their employees. Some items appropriate for use of executives are also produced to give them a sense of involvement. To prevent the items from becoming monotonous, they are changed either completely or in style and appearance in different years.

As the Campaign has grown over the years and the demand for Campaign materials substantially increased, a number of private producers and suppliers have emerged who produce materials as per their own market research. This has been a welcome development. Individual enterprises also produce materials relevant to specific themes of their need-based campaigns. Many of these organize contests among their employees to generate ideas and then publicize the prize winners through their campaign materials.

Activities

At the national level, activities have taken the form of public functions, seminars, discussions and debates, the issuance of appeals and messages and the release of special films on national OSH issues. Participation of the Union Minister and top officials of the Ministry of Labour, Chairman and senior officials of NSC, senior executives from industry, national trade union leaders and eminent persons from institutions, NGOs and the public has imparted to these activities the desired level of impact. The na-

tional television and radio networks, the press and other print media have been involved in propagating these activities widely.

At the state level, activities vary from state to state but are generally of the same type as at the national level. The emphasis of these activities is on the projection of specific state issues through the medium of regional language. A welcome trend observed in state activities in recent years has been that an important government function, namely, distribution of state safety awards, is combined with the Campaign celebrations.

The activities at the individual enterprise level are more practical and varied. Generally, such activities are designed by the safety committee (if existing as per statutory requirements applicable to enterprises employing a certain minimum number of employees) or by a specially constituted task force set up by management. Some typical activities are contests among employees or among different departments for good housekeeping, lowest accident frequency rate, and accident-free work, safety posters, safety slogans, safety suggestions and so on, exhibitions, skits, dramas, one-act plays, songs, training programmes and seminars, lectures, screening of films, practical demonstrations, organizing of emergency drills, holding of functions, and so on. Experts from outside the enterprise are also invited as guest speakers.

Some of the most common and important approaches which have contributed to the effectiveness of activities at the enterprise level may be summarized as follows:

- The dramatizations and plays staged by employees of some enterprises have been of good professional quality and offer effective entertainment, communicating accident case histories with lessons to be learnt. Such plays have been video recorded for telecasting on state and national television networks, thereby increasing their impact.
- Qwaali, a popular form of song on the Indian subcontinent, has also been commonly used for communicating OSH messages while providing entertainment consistent with Indian cultural traditions.
- A number of large companies, in both the public and private sectors, have their own residential colonies and schools for the benefit of their employees. Many of these companies have designed activities including contests to involve families and

Figure 60.10 • Growth in terms of financial receipts from sale of NSD campaign materials (1983–1995).

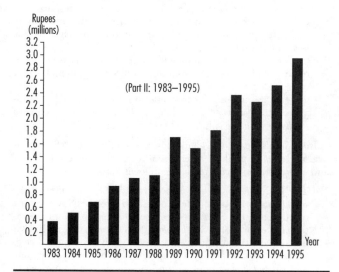

Table 60.2 • Number of Indian working factories, estimated average daily employment, reportable injuries and their incidence rates.

Year	No. of working factories	Estimated average daily employment (in thousands)	Industrial injuries		Rate of injuries per thousand employees in factories submitting returns	
			Fatal	Total	Fatal	Total
1971	81,078	5,085	635	325,180	0.15	75.67
1972	86,297	5,349	655	285,912	0.15	63.63
1973	91,055	5,500	666	286,010	0.15	62.58
1974	97,065	5,670	650	249,110	0.14	53.77
1975	104,374	5,771	660	242,352	0.14	50.86
1976	113,216	6,127	831	300,319	0.17	61.54
1977	119,715	6,311	690	316,273	0.14	63.95
1978	126,241	6,540	792	332,195	0.15	68.62
1979	135,173	6,802	829	318,380	0.16	62.19
1980	141,317	7,017	657	316,532	0.14	66.92
1981	149,285	7,240	687	333,572	0.16	76.73
1982(P)	157,598	7,388	549	296,027	0.13	69.10
1983(P)	163,040	7,444	456	213,160	0.13	55.63
1984(P)*	167,541	7,603	824	302,726	0.10	36.72
1985(P)*	175,316	7,691	807	279,126	0.23	58.70
1986(P)	178,749	7,795	924	276,416	0.14	49.31
1987(P)	183,586	7,835	895	236,596	0.14	41.54
1988(P)	188,136	8,153	694	200,258	0.15	41.68
1989(P)	193,258	8,330	706	162,037	0.16	35.11
1990(P)	199,826	8,431	663	128,117	0.21	33.11
1991(P)*	207,980	8,547	486	60,599	0.21	26.20
1992(P)*	207,156	8,618	573	74,195	0.20	26.54

Key to Symbols: P = provisional; * = incomplete data.
Source: Labour Bureau.

students in safety and health; this has had a positive impact on the motivation of the employees. Even undertakings not having their own residential colony or school have used this approach to involve the families and school-age children of their employees with similar success.

- In the wake of the Bhopal disaster, many enterprises engaged in manufacture, storage or use of hazardous chemicals and having potential for major accidents have developed activities to create awareness of OSH in nearby communities. They invite members of these communities to visit their plants for exhibitions or functions during the Campaign. They also invite government authorities as guests of honour. This approach has been useful in building cooperation among industry, government and community, so important to ensure quick and effective response to chemical emergencies at the local level.

- Activities involving practical demonstrations of important safety-oriented resources such as the use of firefighting methods and personal protective equipment, the holding of emergency drills and the conducting of tailor-made in-plant training courses and seminars on specific needs have proved successful in creating enthusiasm and a supportive environment within enterprises.

The approaches listed are particularly suitable for OSH campaigns at the unit level.

Impact Achieved

The NSD Campaign has shown a positive impact on the trend of industrial injuries (reportable under the Factories Act) in India. As shown in table 60.2, the incidence rate of industrial injuries (injuries per 1,000 workers) decreased from 75.67 in 1971 to 26.54 in 1992 (the latest year for which published statistics are available), a reduction of about 65%. It should be noted that this reduction is due to the combined impact on OSH of government policy and legislation, enforcement, education and training, promotion, modernization of industrial processes and operations, and so on, as well as of NSD Campaign activities.

The research and development sector under the Central Government, comprising 40 national laboratories located all over India and employing over 26,000 employees, including over 9,000 scientists, does not fall under the purview of any OSH legislation. For the last 3 years, the corporate level and the individual laboratories have started organizing NSD celebrations, have set up safety cells and are proceeding in a systematic way towards establishing a sound system of OSH management. This is

60. SAFETY PROGRAMMES

a concrete example of the impact of the NSD Campaign in strengthening the voluntary OSH movement in India.

The organizations in charge of nuclear power stations, heavy water plants and research reactors, as well as other divisions in the Department of Atomic Energy (DAE) of the Government, have been organizing celebrations during the NSD Campaign. They have instituted interdepartmental contests and awards for achievements in the fields of safety, health and environmental protection. The enforcement of safety and health statutes in the above establishments is carried out by an independent agency under the control of DAE, but these units are not open to inspection by state regulating agencies covering other workplaces. Activities under the Campaign have served to create interaction between departmental and external regulatory agencies and between the NSC and other institutions, and have furthermore facilitated the dissemination of OSH information to the public.

Located on the west coast, Gujarat is one of the most industrialized states in India. The state has 525 medium and large factories manufacturing, storing or using one or more of 38 hazardous chemicals. All these factories have prepared and rehearsed emergency plans. As a part of the last NSD Campaign, each of these larger entities was requested by the Chief Inspector of Factories to impart practical training in the use of breathing apparatus and fire extinguishers to emergency-response workers from 10 small factories located in its neighbourhood. Six workers (two from each shift) were selected from each small unit, for a total of 31,500 workers from 5,250 units. This case is illustrative of the impact of the Campaign in making available practical emergency training to small units engaged in hazardous processes.

In conclusion, the most important contribution of the NSD Campaign may be summed up as creating awareness in business and industrial circles and the public that safety, health and environmental protection constitute a vital and integral part of the strategy for sustainable development. However, there is a long way to go before this strategy is translated into a greater reality. The NSD Campaign will no doubt have an increasing role to play in achieving this reality.

References

Albert, K. 1978. *How to Be Your Own Management Consultant.* New York: McGraw-Hill.

American Society of Safety Engineers (ASSE). 1974. *Directory of Safety Consultants.* Oakton, IL, US: ASSE.

Association of Consulting Management Engineers. 1966. *Professional Practices in Management Consulting.* New York: Association of Consulting Management Engineers.

Bird, FE. 1974. *Management Guide to Loss Control.* Atlanta: Institute Press.

Bruening, JC. 1989. Incentives strengthen safety awareness. *Occup Haz* 51:49-52.

Centers for Disease Control and Prevention (CDC). 1988. *Guidelines for Evaluating Surveillance Systems.* MMWR 37 (suppl. No. S-5). Atlanta: CDC.

Fox, DK, BL Hopkins and WK Anger. 1987. The long-term effects of a token economy on safety performance in open pit mining. *J App Behav Anal* 20:215-224.

Geller, ES. 1990. In Bruening, JC. Shaping workers' attitudes toward safety. *Occup Haz* 52:49-51.

Gibson, JJ. 1961. The contribution of experimental psychology to the formulation of the problem of safety: A brief for basic research. In *Behavioral Approaches to Accident Research.* New York: Association for the Aid of Crippled Children.

Gordon, JE. 1949. The epidemiology of accidents. *Am J Public Health* 39, April:504–515.

Gros J. 1989. Das Kraft-Fahr-Sicherheitsprogramm. *Personalführung* 3:246-249.

Haddon, W, Jr. 1973. Energy damage and the ten countermeasure strategies. *J Trauma* 13:321–331.

Haddon, W, EA Suchman and D Klein. 1964. *Accident Research: Methods and Approaches.* New York: Harper and Row.

Harano, RM and DE Hubert. 1974. *An Evaluation of California's Good Driver Incentive Program.* Report No. 6. Sacramento: California Division of Highways.

Komaki, J. KD Barwick and LR Scott. 1978. A behavioural approach to occupational safety: pinpointing and reinforcing safe performance in a food manufacturing plant. *J App Psy* 63:434-445.

Latham, GP and JJ Baldes. 1975. The practical significance of Locke's theory of goal setting. *J App Psy* 60: 122-124.

Lippit, G. 1969. *Organization Renewal.* New York: Meredith Corp.

McAfee, RB and AR Winn. 1989. The use of incentives/feedback to enhance work place safety: a critique of the literature. *J Saf Res* 20:7-19.

Peters, G. 1978. Why only a fool relies on safety standards. *Prof Saf* May 1978.

Peters, RH. 1991. Strategies for encouraging self-protective employee behaviour. *J Saf Res* 22:53-70.

Robertson, LS. 1983. *Injuries: Causes, Control Strategies, and Public Policy.* Lexington, MA, US: Lexington Books.

Starr, C. 1969. Social benefits versus technological risk. What is our society willing to pay for safety? *Science* 165:1232-1238.

Stratton, J. 1988. Low-cost incentive raises safety consciousness of employees. *Occup Health Saf* March:12-15.

Suokas, J. 1988. The role of safety analysis in accident prevention. *Accident Anal Prev* 20(1):67–85.

Veazie, MA, DD Landen, TR Bender and HE Amandus. 1994. Epidemiologic research on the etiology of injuries at work. *Annu Rev Publ Health* 15:203–221.

Wilde, GJS. 1988. Incentives for safe driving and insurance management. In CA Osborne (ed.), *Report of Inquiry into Motor Vehicle Accident Compensation in Ontario.* Vol. II. Toronto: Queen's Printer for Ontario.

Other relevant readings

Baker, SP. 1991. *Injury Fact Book.* New York: Oxford University Press.

Haddon, WJ. 1980. Advances in the epidemiology of injuries as a basis for public policy. *Publ Health Rep* 95(5):411–421.

National Injury Control Conference. 1992. *Occupational Injury Prevention. Position Papers from the Third National Injury Control Conference: Setting the National Agenda for Injury Control in the 1990s, April 22–25, 1991, Denver, Colorado.* Washington, DC: US Government Printing Office.

National Research Council/Institute of Medicine. 1985. *Injury in America: A Continuing Public Health Problem.* Washington, DC: National Academy Press.

National Institute for Occupational Safety and Health (NIOSH). 1984. *Request for Assistance in Preventing the Injury of Workers by Robots.* DHHS (NIOSH) Publication No. 85-103. Cincinnati, OH: NIOSH.

—.1993. *Fatal Injuries to Workers in the United States. 1980–1989: A Decade of Surveillance (National Profile).* DHHS (NIOSH) Publication No. 93-108. Cincinnati, OH: NIOSH.